ALASKA

RULES OF COURT

2007 — 2008

MAIN EDITION

With amendments through August 1, 2007

TOWER

PUBLISHING

Tower Publishing

Tower Publishing specializes in providing legal and business information in the form of books, data bases, and CD-Roms. Tower welcomes manuscript solicitations within the legal market.

Tower Publishing has created this publication to provide the reader with accurate information concerning the subject at hand. This publication, however, was not prepared by individuals licensed to practice law. Tower is not engaged in providing legal or other professional advice; if legal advice or other expert assistance is required, the service of a competent professional should be sought. This publication is not a substitute for legal or other professional advice.

ISBN 978-1-932056-62-4

Tower Publishing
Standish, ME 04084

Published 2007
Printed in the United States of America

www.TowerPub.com

PREFACE

We are pleased to work with the Alaska Court System under an exclusive contract to publish the ***Official Alaska Rules of Court***.

The **2007–2008 Main Volume Edition** of the Official Rules is the edition used by Alaska Courts.

This edition has been completely updated and includes amendments effective October 2007. We have also included 124 new annotations and 7 Law Review Commentaries, as well as an updated Index. The tab bleeds at the beginning of each chapter should improve usability as well as the quick index on the back cover.

The **Main Volume** will be republished in its entirety each October; with a **Supplement Volume** to be issued each April with interim changes as issued by the Court System. This schedule has been selected by the Alaska Court System to coincide with the effective dates of future Supreme Court Orders.

We welcome any and all questions or suggestions concerning the ***Alaska Rules of Court***. You may contact us at:

Tower Publishing
588 Saco Rd.
Standish, ME 04084-6239
Tel: 1-800-969-8693
Fax: 1-800-264-3870
info@towerpub.com

We may be found on-line at: **www.TowerPub.com.**

RULES CHANGED IN THIS EDITION

Listed below are rules affected since the prior Main Edition of the Alaska Rules of Court 2006–2007 was published in October 2006. Rules included in the April 2007 supplement are marked with an asterisk (*). This new edition and listing reflect rule changes effective through October 2007.

Rules of Civil Procedure			**Effective Date**
6	(Amended)	SCO 1639	October 15, 2007
16	(Amended)	SCO 1647	October 15, 2007
26	(Note added)	SCO 1647	October 15, 2007
27*	(Amended)	SCO 1610	April 16, 2007
28*	(Amended)	SCO 1610	April 16, 2007
79 *	(Amended)	SCO 1631	April 16, 2007
81	(Amended)	SCO 1627-Amended	October 15, 2007
95	(Amended)	SCO 1643	October 15, 2007

Rules of Criminal Procedure

6	(Amended)	SCO 1646-Amended	October 15, 2007
18	(Amended & Note added)	SCO 1644	October 15, 2007
35.1*	(Amended)	SCO 1625	April 16, 2007
37*	(Amended)	SCO 1626	April 16, 2007
40	(Amended)	SCO 1639	October 15, 2007
43	(Amended)	SCO 1648	October 15, 2007

Rules of Appellate Procedure

403*	(Amended)	SCO 1628	April 16, 2007
404*	(Amended)	SCO 1628	April 16, 2007
502	(Amended)	SCO 1639	October 15, 2007
503*	(Amended)	SCO 1628	April 16, 2007
505	(Amended)	SCO 1638	October 15, 2007
513.5*	(Amended)	SCO 1628	April 16, 2007

Adoption Rules

6	(Amended)	SCO 1650	October 15, 2007

Child in Need of Aid Rules of Procedure

17.1	(Amended)	SCO 1651	October 15, 2007
18	(Amended/Note amended)	SCO 1651	October 15, 2007

Rules of Probate Procedure

14	(Amended)	SCO 1635	October 15, 2007

Alaska Bar Rules

3	(Amended)	SCO 1652	October 15, 2007
5	(Amended)	SCO 1652	October 15, 2007
8*	(Amended)	SCO 1601	April 16, 2007
22*	(Amended)	SCO 1601	April 16, 2007
43.2	(Added)	SCO 1641	October 15, 2007
61	(Amended)	SCO 1652	October 15, 2007

Code of Judicial Conduct

4*	(Amended)	SCO 1629	December 31, 2006

Rules of Administration

9*	(Amended)	SCO 1630	April 16, 2007
9	(Amended)	SCO 1650	October 15, 2007
12	(Amended)	SCO 1649	July 1, 2007
23*	(Amended)	SCO 1629	December 31, 2006
28	(Amended)	SCO 1642	October 15, 2007
37.6	(Note amended)	SCO 1633	May 15, 2007
37.8	(Amended)	SCO 1633	May 15, 2007
40	(Amended)	SCO 1633	May 15, 2007
43.1*	(Amended)	SCO 1934	December 20, 2006
43.2*	(Amended)	SCO 1632	October 1, 2006
43.6*	(Amended)	SCO 1636	December 31, 2006
44*	(Amended)	SCO 1624	April 16, 2007

MEMBERSHIP OF ALASKA SUPREME COURT ADVISORY COMMITTEES
Court Rules and Pattern Jury Instructions

Adoption Rules Committee

Master John E. Duggan, Chairperson

Mary Ellen Ashton
Daniel L. Callahan
Master Alicemary L. Rasley
Robert B. Flint
Judge Michael I. Jeffery

Nancy Meade, Court Rules Attorney
Beth Adams, Court Rules Analyst

Appellate Rules Committee

Marilyn May, Chairperson

Ruth Botstein
Chancy Croft
Justice Robert L. Eastaugh
Joanne M. Grace
Andrew R. Harrington
Kenneth C. Kirk
Douglas H. Kossler
Jahna Lindemuth
Paul E. Malin
Judge William F. Morse
William B. Rozell
Judge David C. Stewart

Nancy Meade, Court Rules Attorney
Beth Adams, Court Rules Analyst

CINA/Delinquency Rules Committee

Judge Peter A. Michalski, Co-Chairperson
Judge Morgan B. Christen, Co-Chairperson

Anita Alves
Linda R. Beecher
Elizabeth Brennan
Rosemary Haffner
Master Bethany Spalding Harbison
Judge Michael I. Jeffery
Natalie Landreth
Judge Anna M. Moran
Christopher Provost
Master Colleen A. Ray
Carla Raymond
Nancy R. Simel

Nancy Meade, Court Rules Attorney
Beth Adams, Court Rules Analyst

Civil Rules Committee

Justice Alexander O. Bryner, Chairperson

Judge Douglas Blankenship
Dani Crosby
Jeffrey Feldman
Ann G. Gifford
Judge Sharon L. Gleason
Nancy R. Gordon
Matthew D. Jamin
Marc W. June
Stacey Marz
Judge Sigurd E. Murphy
Daniel T. Quinn
Judge John E. Reese
Susan E. Reeves
Alyce M. Roberts
John J. Tiemessen
Thomas V. Van Flein

Nancy Meade, Court Rules Attorney
Beth Adams, Court Rules Analyst

Criminal Rules Committee

Philip Volland, Chairperson

Judge Elaine M. Andrews
Judge Marvin Hamilton III
Robert Herz
Victor Kester
Judge David Mannheimer
John E. McConnaughy
Marjorie A. Mock
John M. Murtagh
Judge Nancy J. Nolan
Greggory M. Olson
Quinlan Steiner
Richard Svobodny

Nancy Meade, Court Rules Attorney
Beth Adams, Court Rules Analyst

Family Rules Committee

Judge Sharon L. Gleason, Chairperson

Katherine R. Alteneder
Judge Joel H. Bolger
Bruce Bookman
Master Andrew M. Brown
Daniel L. Callahan
Maryann E. Foley
Deborah A. Holbrook
Jennifer L. Holland
Christine Pate
Judge Trevor Stephens
Master Jennifer K. Wells
Judge Mark Wood

Nancy Meade, Court Rules Attorney
Beth Adams, Court Rules Analyst

Mediation Rules Committee

Judge Elaine M. Andrews, Chairperson

Robert P. Blasco
Glenn E. Cravez
Susanne D. DiPietro
Michael P. Hostina
Arden E. Page
Drew Peterson
Judge Herbert Ross
Larry D. Wood

Nancy Meade, Court Rules Attorney
Beth Adams, Court Rules Analyst

Probate Rules Committee

Trigg T. Davis, Chairperson

Master Alicemary L. Rasley
Master John E. Duggan
Susan B. Foley
Richard W. Hompesch
Ame W. Ivanov
Robert L. Manley

Nancy Meade, Court Rules Attorney
Beth Adams, Court Rules Analyst

Civil Pattern Jury Instructions Committee

Judge Sen K. Tan, Chairperson

Thomas P. Amodio
James N. Leik
Peter J. Maassen
Antonia Morris
Ann W. Resch
Judge John Suddock
Richard J. Todd

Christine Johnson, Reporter

Criminal Pattern Jury Instructions Committee

Judge Beverly W. Cutler, Chairperson

Adrienne Bachman
Susan Carney
Judge Brian C. Clark
Judge Robert Coats
George B. Davenport
Judge Raymond M. Funk
Bonnie Lembo
Blair McCune
Kenneth M. Rosenstein
Judge Fred Torrisi

Beth Adams, Court Rules Analyst

TABLE OF CONTENTS

RULES OF CIVIL PROCEDURE

Table of Contents

PART I. SCOPE OF RULES—CONSTRUCTION—ONE FORM OF ACTION

PART II. COMMENCEMENT OF ACTION—SERVICE OF PROCESS, PLEADINGS, MOTIONS AND ORDERS

PART III. PLEADINGS AND MOTIONS

PART IV. PARTIES

PART V. DEPOSITIONS AND DISCOVERY

PART VII. EVIDENCE AND CONDUCT OF TRIAL

PART VIII. MASTERS

PART IX. JUDGMENT

PART X. PROVISIONAL AND FINAL REMEDIES AND SPECIAL PROCEEDINGS

PART XIII. GENERAL PROVISIONS

PART I. SCOPE OF RULES—CONSTRUCTION—ONE FORM OF ACTION

Rule 1. Scope of Rules—Construction.

The procedure in the superior court and, so far as applicable, in the district court shall be governed by these rules in all actions or proceedings of a civil nature—legal, equitable, or otherwise. These rules shall be construed to secure the just, speedy and inexpensive determination of every action and proceeding.

(Adopted by SCO 5 October 9, 1959; amended by SCO 993 effective January 15, 1990)

Annotations

Cases

In the one form of action procedure under the [federal] Rules of Civil Procedure, the parties should be granted the relief to which they are entitled irrespective of the theory of their pleadings and a court is not justified in depriving a party of his rights because he mistakes the nature of his remedy. **Mitchell v. Land,** Op. No. 19, 355 P2d 682 (Alaska 1960).

Where evidence supported finding that defendant had committed a trespass and that plaintiff was entitled to relief, proper construction of the rules of procedure supported recovery by plaintiff regardless of the fact that his claim for relief was based on a theory of contract. **Brayton v. City of Anchorage,** Op. No. 171, 386 P2d 832 (Alaska 1963).

Where nearly four years had elapsed between the date appellant's default was entered as a result of a belated entry of appearance in propria persona within one or two days after the 20-day period for answering had expired and the entry of default judgment and the extraordinary long delay were not attributable to appellant's fault, the speedy determination of actions within the purview of this rule was in no way promoted by insisting that appellants permanently lost their standing in court and the entry of default and default judgment were set aside so that the case may be disposed on the merits. **Sanuita v. Hedberg,** Op. No. 296, 404 P2d 647 (Alaska 1965).

In a civil action for assault and battery the trial court's ruling which allowed the defendant to amend his answer so as to enable him to plead self-defense and to test his defense on the merits was consistent with the overall purpose of the civil rules. **Merrill v. Faltin,** Op. No. 425, 430 P2d 913 (Alaska 1967).

When an appellant wishes to seek relief from judgment in the superior court under Civil Rule 60(b) while an appeal from the judgment is pending in the Supreme Court, the most satisfactory resolution consonant with the objective of these rules is for the appellant to file his motion in the superior court and for the Supreme Court to stay appellate proceedings until the superior court would indicate that the motion should be granted and then, upon application to remand the case to the superior court for the stated purpose of granting the motion. **Duriron Company, Inc. v. Bakke,** Op. No. 432, 431 P2d 499 (Alaska 1967).

Presiding judge in a small claims action was not authorized, sua sponte, to deny defendant's right to elect formal rules or to reverse the determination of the district court judge sitting on the case that formal rules shall apply. **Jimmie v. Alaska Village Electric Co-Op, Inc.,** Op. No. 2310, 624 P2d 1258 (Alaska 1981).

Rule 2. One Form of Action.

There shall be one form of action to be known as a "civil action."

(Adopted by SCO 5 October 9, 1959)

Annotations

Cases

In the one form of action procedure under the [federal] Rules of Civil Procedure the parties should be granted relief to which they are entitled irrespective of the theory of their pleadings; and a court is not justified in depriving a party of his rights because he mistakes the nature of his remedy. **Mitchell v. Land,** Op. No. 19, 355 P2d 682 (Alaska 1960).

Under the one form of action one may, and in fact should join in a single action a demand for lien foreclosure and a demand for consequential damages when both grow out of the same transaction. **Miller v. Johnson,** Op. No. 70, 370 P2d 171 (Alaska 1962).

Although plaintiff had brought his action to recover possession under the forcible entry and detainer statute, the one-form of-action procedure permitted to extend the inquiry at the trial to the question of existence of an alleged lease under which defendants had claimed a right of possession where defendants did not object to testimony regarding existence or nonexistence of a lease. **Thrift Shop, Inc. v. Alaska Mutual Savings Bank,** Op. No. 277, 398 P2d 657 (Alaska 1965).

Broad meaning ascribed to civil action in Fed. R. Civ. P. 2 would seem to encompass probate actions and no good reason was advanced to interpret Alaska R. Civ. P. 2 more narrowly than its federal counterpart. **Crittell v. Bingo,** Op. No. 5737 (Alaska 2004).

PART II. COMMENCEMENT OF ACTION—SERVICE OF PROCESS, PLEADINGS, MOTIONS AND ORDERS

Rule 3. Commencement of Action and Venue.

(a) A civil action is commenced by filing a complaint with the court. The complaint, in order to be accepted for filing, must be accompanied by a completed case description on a form provided by the clerk of court. The complaint shall also be accompanied by an envelope addressed to the plaintiff with sufficient postage to mail the envelope and all summonses that will be issued in the case.

(b) All actions in ejectment, for recovery of possession, for quieting title, for partition, or for the enforcement of liens upon real property shall be commenced in the superior court in the judicial district in which the real property, or any part of it affected by the action, is situated. Such actions may also be commenced in the venue district in which the real property is located if the superior court in the district accepts such cases for filing.

(c) If, in a civil action other than one specified in (b) of this rule, a defendant can be personally served within a judicial district of the State of Alaska, the action may be commenced either in: (1) the judicial district in which the claim arose; or (2) a judicial district where the defendant may be personally served; or (3) a venue district where the claim arose if the superior court in the district accepts such cases for filing.

(d) Subject to a change of venue motion under AS 22.10.040, a trial and any hearings in an action shall be conducted in a venue district within the judicial district at a location which would best serve the convenience of the parties and witnesses. However, if there is any part of more than one venue district within the boundaries of a borough, the trial and related hearings shall be conducted within the borough's boundaries at a location which would best serve the convenience of the parties and witnesses.

(e) Actions in cases not otherwise covered under this rule may be commenced in any judicial district of the state.

(f) Failure to make timely objection to improper venue waives the venue requirements of this rule.

(g) Venue districts as used in this rule refer to the districts referenced in the Venue District Map attached to Criminal Rule 18.

(h) A petition or request for a protective order on domestic violence under AS 18.66 may be filed in the judicial district

(1) where the petitioner currently or temporarily resides;

(2) where the respondent resides; or

(3) where the domestic violence occurred.

(Adopted by SCO 5 October 9, 1959; amended by SCO 554 effective April 4, 1983; by SCO 683 effective May 15, 1986; by SCO 697 effective September 15, 1986; by SCO 714 effective September 15, 1986; by SCO 744 effective December 15, 1986; by SCO 760 effective December 15, 1986; by SCO 811 effective August 1, 1987; by SCO 1097 effective January 15, 1993; by SCO 1128 effective July 15, 1993; by SCO 1269 effective July 15, 1997; by SCO 1397 effective October 15, 2000; by SCO 1402 effective October 15, 2000; and by SCO 1450 effective October 15, 2001)

Note to SCO 1269: Civil Rule 3(h) was added by § 68 ch. 64 SLA 1996. Section 8 of this order is adopted for the sole reason that the legislature has mandated the amendment.

Note: In 1996, the legislature enacted AS 37.15.583(b), which requires that certain actions pertaining to Alaska clean water fund revenue bonds be commenced and conducted in the superior court at Juneau. According to § 13 ch. 141 SLA 1996, this statute has the effect of amending Civil Rule 3.

Note: In 2000, the legislature amended AS 37.15.583(a) to allow the owners of Alaska drinking water fund revenue bonds to file suit to enforce their rights. An action brought under AS 37.15.583(a) must be commenced and conducted in the superior court at Juneau. According to § 24 ch. 61 SLA 2000, the amendment to AS 37.15.583(a) has the effect of amending Civil Rule 3.

Note: Ch. 79 SLA 2002 (HB 182), Section 9, adds a new Chapter 25 to Title 45 of the Alaska Statutes, concerning motor vehicle sales and dealers. According to Section 14 of the Act, AS 45.25.020(b) has the effect of amending Civil Rule 3 by establishing a different rule for determining where a legal dispute described in AS 45.25.020(a) may be brought.

Cross References

CROSS REFERENCE: AS 09.10.010

Annotations

Cases

Rule 3, Rules of Civil Procedure, is a procedural rule the regulation of which has been committed to the Supreme Court, and the provision of AS 09.10.020 providing how a civil action shall be commenced is ineffective. **Silverton v. Marler,** Op. No. 186, 389 P2d 3 (Alaska 1964).

The time when an action is commenced is exclusively covered by Rule 3 of Rules of Civil Procedure. **Silverton v. Marler,** Op. No. 186, 389 P2d 3 (Alaska 1964).

Since, in the absence of compelling other considerations, an action in which the complaint was filed first has priority over an independently filed second action between the same parties and involving identical issues, the party filing later in time should be enjoined from pursuing the action. **Coughlan v. Coughlan,** Op. No. 395, 423 P2d 1010 (Alaska 1967).

Petition to perpetuate testimony, filed before complaint, does not commence on action. **Chiei v. Stern,** Op. No. 1400, 561 P2d 1216 (Alaska 1977).

Where plaintiff sought to take deposition before end of limitation period but filed complaint after end of limitation period, action was barred. **Chiei v. Stern,** Op. No. 1400, 561 P2d 1216 (Alaska 1977).

Filing of complaint tolls the applicable statute of limitations and has the legal effect of commencing an action. **Hamilton v. Seattle Marine & Fishing Supply Co.,** Op. No. 1401,562 P2d 333 (Alaska 1977).

When complaint was filed in action to enforce foreign judgment before applicable statutes of limitation of either Alaska or other state had run, claim was not barred. **Hamilton v. Seattle Marine & Fishing Supply Co.,** Op. No. 1401, 562 P2d 333 (Alaska 1977).

The superior court in the location where an action is begun does not have the discretion to relax the venue requirements of this rule when the complaint is filed in the wrong judicial district; the complaint must be filed in the proper judicial district, and then, if that forum is inconvenient, the plaintiff can move for a change of venue, thereby ensuring that the superior court in the proper venue, rather than one in the venue of plaintiff's choosing, makes the initial determination as to which forum is inconvenient. **Ketchikan General Hosp. v. Dunnagan,** Op. No. 3357, 757 P2d 57, 380 P2d 591 (Alaska 1988).

Rule 4. Process.

(a) **Summons—Issuance.** Upon the filing of the complaint the clerk shall forthwith issue a summons and deliver it to the plaintiff or the plaintiff's attorney, who shall cause the summons and a copy of the complaint to be served in accordance with this rule. Upon request of the plaintiff separate or additional summonses shall issue against any defendants.

(b) **Summons—Form.**

(1) The summons shall be signed by the clerk, bear the seal of the court, identify the court and the parties, be directed to the defendant, and state the name and address of the plaintiff's attorney or the plaintiff's name and address if the plaintiff is unrepresented. It shall also state the time within which the defendant must appear and defend, and notify the defendant that failure to do so will result in judgment by default against the defendant for the relief demanded in the complaint. The summons must also notify the defendant that the defendant has a duty to inform the court and all other parties, in writing, of the defendant's or defendant's attorney's current mailing address and telephone number, and to inform

the court and all other parties of any changes, as set out in Civil Rule 5(i).

(2) The summons must be on the current version of the summons form developed by the administrative director or a duplicate of the court form. A party or attorney who lodges a duplicate certifies by lodging the duplicate that it conforms to the current version of the court form.

(c) **Methods of Service—Appointments to Serve Process—Definition of Peace Officer.**

(1) Service of all process shall be made by a peace officer, by a person specially appointed by the Commissioner of Public Safety for that purpose or, where a rule so provides, by registered or certified mail.

(2) A subpoena may be served as provided in Rule 45 without special appointment.

(3) Special appointments for the service of all process relating to remedies for the seizure of persons or property pursuant to Rule 64 or for the service of process to enforce a judgment by writ of execution shall only be made by the Commissioner of Public Safety after a thorough investigation of each applicant, and such appointment may be made subject to such conditions as appear proper in the discretion of the Commissioner for the protection of the public. A person so appointed must secure the assistance of a peace officer for the completion of process in each case in which the person may encounter physical resistance or obstruction to the service of process.

(4) Special appointments for the service of all process other than the process as provided under paragraph (3) of this subdivision shall be made freely when substantial savings in travel fees and costs will result.

(5) The term "peace officer" as used in these rules shall include any officer of the state police, members of the police force of any incorporated city, village or borough, United States Marshals and their deputies, other officers whose duty is to enforce and preserve the public peace, and within the authority conferred upon them, persons specially appointed pursuant to paragraph (3) of this subdivision.

(d) **Summons—Personal Service.** The summons and complaint shall be served together. The plaintiff shall furnish the person making service with such copies as are necessary. Service shall be made as follows:

(1) *Individuals.* Upon an individual other than an infant or an incompetent person, by delivering a copy of the summons and of the complaint to the individual personally, or by leaving copies thereof at the individual's dwelling house or usual place of abode with some person of suitable age and discretion then residing therein, or by delivering a copy of the summons and of the complaint to an agent authorized by appointment or by law to receive service of process.

(2) *Infants.* Upon an infant, by delivering a copy of the summons and complaint to such infant personally, and also to the infant's father, mother or guardian, or if there be none within the state, then to any person having the care or control of such infant, or with whom the infant resides, or in whose service the infant is employed; or if any service cannot be made upon any of them, then as provided by order of the court.

(3) *Incompetent Persons.* Upon an incompetent person, by delivering a copy of the summons and complaint personally—

(A) To the guardian of the person or a competent adult member of the person's family with whom the person resides, or if the person is living in an institution, then to the director or chief executive officer of the institution, or if service cannot be made upon any of them, then as provided by order of the court; and

(B) Unless the court otherwise orders, also to the incompetent person.

(4) *Corporations or Limited Liability Companies.* Upon a domestic or foreign corporation or limited liability company, by delivering a copy of the summons and of the complaint to a managing member, an officer, a managing or general agent, or to any other agent authorized by appointment or by law to receive service of process.

(5) *Partnerships.* Upon a partnership, by delivering a copy of the summons and of the complaint personally to a general partner of such partnership, or to a managing or general agent of the partnership, or to any other agent authorized by appointment or by law to receive service of process, or to a person having control of the business of the partnership; or if service cannot be made upon any of them, then as provided by order of the court.

(6) *Unincorporated Associations.* Upon an unincorporated association, by delivering a copy of the summons and the complaint personally to an officer, a managing or general agent, or to any other person authorized by appointment or by law to receive service of process; or if service cannot be made upon any of them, then as provided by order of the court.

(7) *State of Alaska.* Upon the state, by sending a copy of the summons and the complaint by registered or certified mail to the Attorney General of Alaska, Juneau, Alaska, and

[a] to the chief of the attorney general's office in Anchorage, Alaska, when the matter is filed in the Third Judicial District; or

[b] to the chief of the attorney general's office in Fairbanks, Alaska, when the matter is filed in the Fourth Judicial District.

(8) *Officer or Agency of State.* Upon an officer or agency of the state, by serving the State of Alaska as provided in the preceding paragraph of this rule, and by delivering a copy of the summons and of the complaint to such officer or agency. If the agency is a corporation, the copies shall be delivered as provided in paragraph (4) of this subdivision of this rule.

(9) *Public Corporations.* Upon a borough or

incorporated city, town, school district, public utility district, or other public corporation in the state, by delivering a copy of the summons and of the complaint to the chief executive officer or chief clerk or secretary thereof.

(10) *Unknown Parties.* Upon unknown persons who may be made parties in accordance with statute and these rules, by publication as provided in subdivision (e) of this rule.

(11) *Officer or Agency of State as Agent for Non-governmental Defendant.* Whenever, pursuant to statute, an officer or an agency of the State of Alaska has been appointed as agent to receive service for a non-governmental defendant, or whenever, pursuant to statute, an officer or agency of the State of Alaska, has been deemed, considered or construed to be appointed as agent for a non-governmental defendant by virtue of some act, conduct or transaction of such defendant, service of process shall be made in the manner provided by statute.

(12) *Personal Service Outside State.* Upon a party outside the state in the same manner as if service were made within the state, except that service shall be made by a sheriff, constable, bailiff, peace officer or other officer having like authority in the jurisdiction where service is made, or by a person specifically appointed by the court to make service, or by service as provided in subsection (h) of this rule. In an action to enforce any lien upon or claim to, or to remove any encumbrance or lien or cloud upon the title to, real or personal property within the state, such service shall also be made upon the person or persons in possession or in charge of such property, if any. Proof of service shall be in accordance with (f) of this rule.

(13) *Personal Service in a Foreign Country.* Upon an individual in a foreign country—

(A) by any internationally agreed means reasonably calculated to give notice, such as those means authorized by the Hague Convention on the Service Abroad of Judicial and Extrajudicial Documents;

(B) if there is no internationally agreed means of service or the applicable international agreement allows other means of service, provided that service is reasonably calculated to give notice:

(i) in the manner prescribed by the law of the foreign country for service in that country in an action in any of its courts of general jurisdiction;

(ii) as directed by the foreign authority in response to a letter rogatory or letter of request; or

(iii) unless prohibited by the law of the foreign country, by delivery to the individual personally of a copy of the summons and the complaint, or by any form of mail requiring a signed receipt by the party to be served, so long as the return receipt is filed with the court; or

(C) by other means not prohibited by international agreement as may be directed by the court.

Regardless of which method of service is followed for personal service in a foreign country, before entry of judgment, the court must be satisfied that the method used was a method reasonably likely to effect actual notice.

(e) **Other Service.** When it shall appear by affidavit of a person having knowledge of the facts filed with the clerk that after diligent inquiry a party cannot be served with process under (d) of this rule, service may be made by publication or as otherwise directed by the court as provided in this subdivision. Service by publication will be allowed in adoption cases only if ordered by the court for compelling reasons.

(1) *Diligent Inquiry.* Inquiry as to the absent party's whereabouts shall be made by the party who seeks to have service made, or by the party's attorney actually entrusted with the conduct of the action, or by the agent of the attorney. It shall be made of any person who the inquirer has reason to believe possesses knowledge or information as to the absent party's residence or address or the matter inquired of. The inquiry shall be undertaken in person or by letter, and the inquirer shall state that an action has been or is about to be commenced against the party inquired for, that the object of the inquiry is to give such party notice of the action in order that such party may appear and defend it. When the inquiry is made by letter, postage shall be enclosed sufficient for the return of an answer. The affidavit of inquiry shall be made by the inquirer. It shall fully specify the inquiry made and of what persons and in what manner so that by the facts stated therein it may appear that diligent inquiry has been made for the purpose of effecting actual notice.

(2) *Service by Publication.* A notice shall be published four times during four consecutive calendar weeks, once in each week, in a newspaper published in the district in which the action is pending, or if none be published therein, then in a newspaper published in this state circulating in such district. Prior to the last publication a copy of the notice and the complaint or the pleading shall be sent by registered or certified mail, with return receipt requested, with postage prepaid, to the absent party, addressed in care of such party's residence or the place where such party usually receives mail, unless it shall appear by affidavit that such residence or place is unknown or cannot be ascertained after inquiry.

(3) *Other Service.* In its discretion the court may allow service of process to be made upon an absent party in any other manner which is reasonably calculated to give the party actual notice of the proceedings and an opportunity to be heard, if an order permitting such service is entered before service of process is made.

(4) *Form and Contents of Notice—Time.* The notice referred to in paragraph (2) of this subdivision shall be in the form of a summons. It shall state briefly the nature of the action, the relief demanded, and why the party to whom it is addressed is made a party to the action. Where the action concerns real property or where real property of a party has been attached, the notice shall set forth a legal description of the property, shall state the municipality or district in which it is located, and the street or road on which the property is situated, and if the property is improved, it shall state the street

number of the same. Where personal property of a party has been attached, the notice shall generally describe the property. If a mortgage is to be foreclosed, the notice shall state the names of all parties thereto and the dates that the mortgage was executed. The notice shall specify the time within which the absent party has to appear or answer or plead, which shall not be less than 20 days after personal service or, if service is made by publication, not less than 30 days after the last date of publication, and shall state the effect of a failure to appear or answer or plead. If the absent party does not appear or answer or plead within the time specified within the notice, the court may proceed as if such party had been served with process within the state.

(5) *Proof of Service.* If service is made by publication, proof of publication shall be made by the affidavit of the newspaper's publisher, printer, manager, foreman, or principal clerk, or by the certificate of the attorney for the party at whose instance the service was made. A printed copy of the published notice with the name of the newspaper and dates of publication marked therein shall be attached to the affidavit or certificate. Proof of mailing shall be made by affidavit of a deposit in a post office of the copies of the notice and the complaint or other pleadings.

(f) **Return.** The person serving the process shall give proof of service thereof to the party requesting issuance of the process or to the party's attorney promptly and in any event within the time during which the person served must respond to the process. Within 120 days after filing of the complaint, the party shall file and serve an affidavit identifying the parties who have been served, the date service was made and the parties who remain unserved. If service is made by a person other than a peace officer, the person shall make affidavit thereof, proof of service shall be in writing and shall set forth the manner, place, date of service, and all pleadings or other papers served with the process. Failure to make proof of service does not affect the validity of the service.

(g) **Amendment.** At any time in its discretion and upon such terms as it deems just, the court may allow any process or proof of service thereof to be amended, unless it clearly appears that material prejudice would result to the substantial rights of the parties against whom the process issued.

(h) **Service of Process by Mail.** In addition to other methods of service provided for by this rule, process may also be served within this state or the United States or any of its possessions by registered or certified mail, with return receipt requested, upon an individual other than an infant or an incompetent person and upon a corporation, partnership, unincorporated association, or public corporation. In such case, copies of the summons and complaint or other process shall be mailed for restricted delivery only to the party to whom the summons or other process is directed or to the person authorized under federal regulation to receive the party's restricted delivery mail. All receipts shall be so addressed that they are returned to the party serving the summons or process or the party's attorney. Service of process by mail under this paragraph is complete when the return receipt is signed.

(i) RESERVED

(j) **Summons—Time Limit for Service.** The clerk shall review each pending case 120 days after filing of the complaint to determine whether all defendants have been served. If any defendant has not been served, the clerk shall send notice to the plaintiff to show good cause in writing why service on that defendant is not complete. If good cause is not shown within 30 days after distribution of the notice, the court shall dismiss without prejudice the action as to that defendant. The clerk may enter the dismissal if the plaintiff has not opposed dismissal. If the court finds good cause why service has not been made, the court shall establish a new deadline by which plaintiff must file proof of service or proof that plaintiff has made diligent efforts to serve.

(Adopted by SCO 5 October 9, 1959; amended by SCO 49 effective January 1, 1963; by SCO 66 effective July 1, 1964; by SCO 90 effective July 24, 1967; by SCO 168 dated June 25, 1973; by SCO 215 effective May 23, 1975; by SCO 266 effective March 31, 1977; by SCO 282 effective November 15, 1977; by SCO 306 effective April 11, 1978; by SCO 357 effective June 30, 1978; by SCO 373 effective August 15, 1979; by SCO 465 effective June 1, 1981; by SCO 591 effective July 1, 1984; by SCO 679 effective June 15, 1986; by SCO 697 effective September 15, 1986; by SCO 714 effective September 15, 1986; by SCO 788 effective March 15, 1987; by SCO 815 effective August 1, 1987; by SCO 836 effective August 1, 1987; by SCO 1025 effective July 15, 1990; by SCO 1128 effective July 15, 1993; by SCO 1153 effective July 15, 1994; by SCO 1269 effective July 15, 1997; by SCO 1295 effective January 15, 1998; by SCO 1445 effective October 15, 2001; by SCO 1482 effective October 15, 2002; by SCO 1522 effective October 15, 2003; by SCO 1570 effective October 15, 2005; and by SCO 1607 effective October 15, 2006)

Note: In, 1996, the legislature enacted AS 18.66.160, which relates to service of process in a proceeding to obtain a domestic violence protective order. According to § 77 ch. 64 SLA 1996, this statute has the effect of amending Civil Rule 4.

Note: AS 10.06.580(b), as enacted by ch. 166, § 1, SLA 1988, amended Civil Rule 4 by allowing a corporation in an action brought under AS 10.06.580 to serve non-resident dissenting shareholders by certified mail and publication without satisfying the conditions under which certified mail and publication can be used under Civil Rule 4. AS 10.06.638, as enacted by ch. 166, § 1, SLA 1988, amended Civil Rule 4 by changing (1) the requirements for service by publication, and (2) how long a corporation has to respond to a complaint in an involuntary dissolution proceeding before the Commissioner of Commerce and Economic Development may take a default judgment against the corporation.

Note: Section 132 of ch. 87 SLA 1997 adds AS 25.27.265(c) which authorizes the court to allow CSED to serve a party by mailing documents to the last known address on file with the agency. This is permitted only if the court finds that CSED has made diligent efforts to serve documents in the appropriate manner. According to § 153 of the Act, § 132 has the effect of amending Civil Rules 4 and 5 by allowing service at the opposing party's last known address on file with the child support enforcement agency in certain circumstances.

Note: Ch. 61 SLA 2002 (HB 52), Section 2, repeals and reenacts AS 33.36.110 to authorize the governor to execute the Interstate Compact for Adult Offender Supervision. According to Section 6 of the Act, Article VIII(a)(2) of the Compact, contained in the new AS 33.36.110, would have the effect of amending Civil Rule 4 by entitling the Interstate Commission for Adult Offender Supervision to receive service of process of a judicial proceeding in this state that pertains to the Interstate Compact for Adult Offender Supervision and that may affect the powers, responsibilities or actions of that commission.

Note: Ch. 128 SLA 2002 (HB 393), Section 3, adds a new Chapter 66 to Title 45 of the Alaska Statutes, concerning the sale of business opportunities. According to Section 4 of the Act, AS 45.66.120(b) has the effect of amending Civil Rule 4 by requiring that the clerk of the court mail a copy of the complaint to the attorney general when an action is filed under AS 45.66.120.

Note: Chapter 87 SLA 03 (HB 1) enacted AS 18.65.865, which addresses service of process of protective orders issued under AS 18.65.850-860 for persons who are victims of stalking not involving domestic violence. According to Section 8(a) of the Act, the new AS 18.65.865 has the effect of amending Civil Rule 4 relating to service of process by requiring that service be made in accordance with AS 18.66.160, which governs service of domestic violence protective orders.

Note to SCO 1570: Civil Rule 4(d)(13), concerning service on individuals in a foreign country, parallels the language in Federal Rule of Civil Procedure 4(f).The Hague Convention on the Service Abroad of Judicial and Extrajudicial Documents, referred to in Civil Rule 4(d)(13), generally provides for service of process by a central authority (usually the Ministry of Justice) in the Convention countries pursuant to a request submitted on a form USM-94 available at the office of any United States Marshall or at http:www.usmarshals.gov/ forms/usm94.pdf. The Convention also permits service of process by international registered mail subject to the option of individual countries to object to such service. Many countries have objected, including Argentina, China, the Czech Republic, Egypt, Germany, Greece, the Republic of South Korea, Latvia, Lithuania, Luxembourg, Norway, Poland, the Slovak Republic, Sri Lanka, Switzerland, Turkey, Ukraine, and Venezuela; service by registered mail is therefore not appropriate in those countries. The full text of the Convention may by found at http://hcch.e-vision.nl/index_en.php?act= conventions.text&cid=17. Current information on the Convention may be found in the United States Department of State's Circular on Service of Process Abroad, available at http://travel.state.gov/law/info/ judicial/judicial_ 686.html.

Note: Chapter 54 SLA 2005 (HB 95) enacted extensive amendments and new provisions related to public health, including public health emergencies and disasters. According to Section 13(a) of the Act, AS 18.15.375(c)(3), (d), and (e), and 18.15.385(d) –(k), enacted in Section 8, have the effect of amending Civil Rule 4 by adding special proceedings, timing, and pleading requirements for matters involving public health.

Cross References

(d) **CROSS REFERENCE:** AS 09.05.010

(e)(5) **CROSS REFERENCE:** AS 09.05.070

Annotations

Cases

The court did not acquire jurisdiction over an infant where copies of the summons and complaint were merely delivered to the infant's father, as copies must also be delivered to the infant personally. The requirement for delivering copies of the summons and complaint is not contingent upon the infant's age. **Hartwell v. Cooper,** Op. No. 140, 380 P2d 591 (Alaska 1962).

Where a foreign corporation has no officer or agent in Alaska, service made by delivering copies to the State Commissioner of Commerce is in accordance with rule and statute, but to resolve whether such service is effective to give jurisdiction over the foreign corporation depends on the issue (1) whether state law provides for assertion of jurisdiction under the facts of the case and (2) whether such assertion is consistent with due process. **Northern Supply, Inc. v. Curtiss-Wright Corporation,** Op. No. 271, 397 P2d 1013 (Alaska 1965).

Service of order requiring appearance of insurance company as garnishee was properly made upon the State Department of Commerce under this rule as made available by Civil Rule 89(f)(1) and under statute (AS 21.10.155). **Liberty National Insurance Co. v. Eberhart,** Op. No. 281, 398 P2d 997 (Alaska 1965).

Once service of process had been achieved upon a party, the service related back to the date of the complaint. **Coughlan v. Coughlan,** Op. No. 395, 423 P2d 1010 (Alaska 1967).

Where suits between the same parties and for the same relief were commenced in two different courts of competent jurisdiction, the court in which the complaint was filed first was the first to obtain jurisdiction although service of summons had been achieved at an earlier date in the second action than it was obtained in the first action. **Coughlan v. Coughlan,** Op. No. 395, 423 P2d 1010 (Alaska 1967).

Process in a juvenile proceeding must be delivered to the child himself. Jurisdiction over the child cannot be obtained by delivering the summons and petition to his parents. **RLR v. State,** Op. No. 706, 487 P2d 27 (Alaska 1971).

Infancy does not render all waivers void. **RLR v. State,** Op. No. 706, 487 P2d 27 (Alaska 1971).

Appearance by a child in a juvenile proceeding and failure to object to the failure to serve him with a copy of the petition waives any defect in process where the infant is represented by counsel. **RLR v. State,** Op. No. 706,487 P2d 27 (Alaska 1971).

The State-Operated School System is a state agency for purposes of service and process. **Alaska State-Operated School System v. Mueller,** Op. No. 1157, 536 P2d 99 (Alaska 1975).

Civil Rule 5(b), not this rule, applies to proceedings which seek to enforce the terms of a prior divorce decree relating to child support payments. **Balchen v. Balchen,** Op. No. 1469, 566 P2d 1324 (Alaska 1977).

A local or the agent of a local is not the agent for an international union for purposes of service unless the facts of an individual case reveal the opposite to be true. **Intern. Bro. of Team., Local 959 v. King,** Op. No. 1532, 572 P2d 1168 (Alaska 1977).

Jurisdiction is obtained over a partnership when service is perfected on any member or agent, and the court acquires jurisdiction over all partners therein. **Coleman v. Lofgren,** Op. No. 1839, 593 P2d 632 (Alaska 1979).

Court did not abuse its discretion in revoking process server's license for improper conduct in attempting a levy of execution. **Cowles v. Wolfe,** Op. No.

2512, 645 P2d 201 (Alaska 1982).

Where service of process is by certified mail, a return receipt is generally not adequate as proof of service in the absence of an affidavit attesting to the fact that the mail which was delivered contained the required documents. **D.A. v. D.R.L.,** Op. No. 3138, 727 P2d 768 (Alaska 1986).

In mortgage foreclosure action, service of process on the husband and wife at their mortgaged residence, service having been personally received only by the wife, was insufficient for the court to obtain personal jurisdiction over the husband, where the couple had previously obtained a divorce, the residence had been awarded to the wife, the husband had moved out six months prior to service of process, and the husband had not expressly or impliedly made his ex-wife an agent for service of process. **Beam v. Adams,** Op. No. 3269, 749 P2d 366 (Alaska 1988).

Service of process on state was defective, thus default judgment against state was set aside; summons and complaint were mailed to assistant attorney general in Juneau and to attorney general's office in Fairbanks, but this rule required summons and complaint to be mailed to attorney general in Juneau and chief of attorney general's office in Fairbanks. **State, Dept. of Corrections v. Kila, Inc.,** Op. No. 4141, 884 P2d 661 (Alaska 1994).

Civil Rule 65, rather than Civil Rule 4, determines when person becomes bound by domestic violence protective order. **MacDonald v. State,** Op. No. 1665, 997 P2d 1187 (Alaska 2000).

Defendant, who had actual knowledge of domestic violence protective order, was bound by order even though he was not formally served with written copy of order. **MacDonald v. State,** Op. No. 1665, 997 P2d 1187 (Alaska 2000).

Conviction of defendant for violation of ex parte domestic violence protective order did not violate constitutional right to due process where defendant had not been served with written copy of order but did have actual knowledge that order had been issued against him. **MacDonald v. State,** Op. No. 1665, 997 P2d 1187 (Alaska 2000).

Where a pro se litigant established that she effectuated service of process by sending the summons and complaint to defendants by certified mail, a superior court should have granted a motion to reopen a previously dismissed case because she remedied any prior defect in service of process. **Gilbert v. Nina Plaza Condo Ass'n,** Op. No. 5666, 64 P.3d 126, 366 P2d 714, 717 (Alaska 2003).

Rule 5. Service and Filing of Pleadings and Other Papers.

(a) **Service—When Required.** Every order required by its terms to be served, every pleading subsequent to the original complaint unless the court otherwise orders because of numerous defendants, every paper relating to discovery required to be served upon a party unless the court otherwise orders, every written motion other than one which may be heard ex parte, and every written notice, appearance, demand, offer of judgment, and similar paper shall be served upon each of the parties but no service need be made on parties in default for failure to appear except that pleadings asserting new or additional claims for relief against them shall be served upon them in the manner provided for service of summons in Rule 4.

In an action begun by seizure of property, whether through arrest, attachment, garnishment or similar process, in which no person need be or is named as defendant, any service required to be made prior to the filing of an answer, claim, or appearance shall be made upon the person having custody or possession of the property at the time of its seizure.

(b) **Service—How Made.** Whenever under these rules service is required or permitted to be made upon a party represented by an attorney the service shall be made upon the attorney unless service upon the party is ordered by the court. Service upon the attorney or upon a party shall be made by delivering a copy to the attorney or party, by mailing it to the attorney's or party's last known address, by transmitting it to the attorney's or party's facsimile machine telephone number as provided in Civil Rule 5.1(b), or, if no address is known, by leaving it with the clerk of the court. Delivery of a copy within this rule means: handing it to the attorney or to the party; or leaving it at the attorney's or party's office with a clerk or other person in charge thereof; or, if there is no one in charge, leaving it in a conspicuous place therein; or, if the office is closed or the person to be served has no office, leaving it at the attorney's or party's dwelling house or usual place of abode with some person of suitable age and discretion then residing therein. Mailing of a copy means mailing it by first class United States mail. Service by mail is complete upon mailing. Service by a commercial delivery company constitutes service by delivery and is complete upon delivery.

(c) **Service—Numerous Defendants.** In any action in which there are unusually large numbers of defendants, the court, upon motion or of its own initiative, may order that service of the pleadings of the defendants and replies thereto need not be made as between the defendants and that any cross-claim, counterclaim, or matter constituting an avoidance or affirmative defense contained therein shall be deemed to be denied or avoided by all other parties and that the filing of any such pleading and service thereof upon the plaintiff constitutes due notice of it to the parties. A copy of every such order shall be served upon the parties in such manner and form as the court directs.

(d) **Filing.**

(1) Except as provided in (2) of this paragraph, all papers after the complaint required to be served upon a party shall be filed with the court either before service or within a reasonable time thereafter.

(2) Unless filing is ordered by the court on motion of a party or on its own motion, the following may not be filed unless and until they are used in the proceedings:

(i) disclosures under Rule 26(a);

(ii) notices of taking depositions and transcripts of depositions;

(iii) interrogatories and requests for admissions and answers thereto;

(iv) requests for production and responses thereto;

(v) subpoenas, including subpoenas duces tecum;

(vi) offers of judgment;

(vii) proof of service of any of the above;

(viii) copies of correspondence between counsel;

(ix) exhibits.

(e) **Filing With the Court Defined.** The filing of pleadings and other papers with the court as required by these rules shall be made by filing them with the clerk of the court at the court location where the case is filed unless otherwise directed by the court, except that the judge may permit the papers to be filed with the judge, in which event the judge shall note thereon the filing date and forthwith transmit them to the office of the clerk. Papers may be filed by facsimile transmission only as permitted by Civil Rule 5.1(a).

(f) **Proof of Service.** Proof of service of all papers required or permitted to be served, other than those for which a particular method of proof is prescribed in these rules, must state the name of each person who has been served, must show the day and manner of service and may be by written acknowledgment of service, by certificate of an attorney, an authorized agent of the attorney, or a pro se litigant, by affidavit of the person who served the papers, or by any other proof satisfactory to the court. Proof of service must be made promptly and in any event before action is to be taken on the paper served by the court or the parties. Failure to make the proof of service required by this subdivision does not affect the validity of service; and the court may at any time allow the proof of service to be amended or supplied unless it clearly appears that to do so would result in material prejudice to the substantial rights of any party.

(g) **Service After Final Judgment.**

(1) Notwithstanding the provisions of paragraph (b) of this rule requiring service upon an attorney, a party who has been represented by an attorney in an action or proceeding shall be served rather than the attorney in accordance with the provisions of paragraph (b) with a motion or other request for relief filed in the action or proceeding where a period of one year has elapsed since the filing of any paper or the issuance of any process in the action or proceeding, and

(i) The final judgment or decree has been entered and the time for filing an appeal has expired, or

(ii) If an appeal has been taken, the final judgment or decree upon remand has been entered or the mandate has been issued affirming the judgment or decree, and

(iii) The party's attorney has not filed a notice of continued representation under Rule 81(d)(2).

(2) If a party is served under circumstances described in Section (1) of this paragraph, or if a party appeared in his or her own behalf in the prior action or proceeding, the paper served shall include notice to the party of the party's right to file written opposition or response, the time within which such opposition or response must be filed, and the place where it must be filed.

(h) **Service on Custody Investigator and Guardian Ad Litem.** In all cases involving the custody or visitation of a minor in which a custody investigator or a guardian ad litem has been appointed, the parties shall serve the custody investigator and the guardian ad litem with all pleadings involving the care, custody, or control of the minor.

(i) **Changes in Mailing Address and Telephone Number.** While a case is pending, the parties must immediately inform the court and all other parties, in writing, of any changes in their mailing addresses and telephone numbers, except as provided in Civil Rule 65.1.

(Adopted by SCO 5 October 9, 1959; amended by SCO 258 effective November 15, 1976; by SCO 354 effective April 1, 1979; by SCO 372 effective August 15, 1979; by SCO 375 effective August 15, 1979; by SCO 410 effective May 15, 1980; by SCO 471 effective June 1, 1981; by SCO 522 effective October 1, 1982; by SCO 695 effective September 15, 1986; by SCO 731 effective December 15, 1986; by SCO 817 effective August 1, 1987; by SCO 1153 effective July 15, 1994; by SCO 1172 effective July 15, 1995; by SCO 1295 effective January 15, 1998; by SCO 1307 effective January 15, 1998; by SCO 1414 effective October 15, 2000; by SCO 1424 effective April 15, 2001; by SCO 1482 effective October 15, 2002; and by SCO 1570 effective October 15, 2005)

Note: Section 132 of ch. 87 SLA 1997 adds AS 25.27.265(c) which authorizes the court to allow CSED to serve a party by mailing documents to the last known address on file with the agency. This is permitted only if the court finds that CSED has made diligent efforts to serve documents in the appropriate manner. According to § 153 of the Act, § 132 has the effect of amending Civil Rules 4 and 5 by allowing service at the opposing party's last known address on file with the child support enforcement agency in certain circumstances.

Annotations

Cases

Service by mail is complete upon mailing regardless of whether the service is timely received. **Jefferson v. Spenard Builder's Supply, Inc.,** Op. No. 51, 366 P2d 714 (Alaska 1961).

Notice made by the clerk to all counsels of the entry of judgment constituted timely notice to parties. **Whitney Bros. Plumbing & Heating v. Industrial & Commercial Constr., Inc.,** Op. No. 438, 432 P2d 533 (Alaska 1967).

A motion to confirm an execution sale cannot be heard ex parte; service upon the opposing party is necessary. **Mallonee v. Grow,** Op. No. 841, 502 P2d 432 (Alaska 1972).

A motion for confirmation of an execution sale need not be served on a judgment debtor who defaults on an underlying claim. **Lunsford v. Kaiser Gypsum Company, Inc.,** Op. No. 961, 516 P2d 151 (Alaska 1973).

A plaintiff's attorney's secretary's affidavit that she personally served a copy of a notice for taking deposition on the office of the attorney for defendants creates a rebuttable presumption that there has been compliance with this rule. A burden is then placed upon the defendant of proving that the nonexistence of the presumed fact was more probable than its existence. The defendant does not meet this burden by merely producing evidence which the trial court evaluates as "stand off" testimony. **Martens v. Metzgar,** Op. No. 1059, 524 P2d 666 (Alaska 1974).

Paragraph (b) of this rule, not Civil Rule 4, applies to proceedings which seek to enforce the terms of a prior divorce decree relating to child support payments. **Balchen v. Balchen,** Op. No. 1469, 566 P2d 1324 (Alaska 1977).

While it is preferred procedure to obtain court's permission before serving complaint on defendant in action to enforce child support provisions of divorce decree, rather than on attorney, failure to do so does not require vacation of judgment. **Balchen v. Balchen,** Op. No. 1469, 566 P2d 1324 (Alaska 1977).

Personal notice of execution sale is not required under Civil Rule 5(a). **Queen of the North, Inc. v. LeGrue,** Op. No. 1670, 582 P2d 144 (Alaska 1978).

Failure of default judgment creditor to serve motion for issuance of deed on property subject to execution sale was error, since although no service need be made on parties in default for failure to appear, the judgment debtor was not such a part because he had appeared prior to the motion in an unsuccessful effort to have the default judgment set aside. **Law Offices of Murphy L. Clark v. Altman,** Op. No. 2811, 680 P2d 1125 (Alaska 1984).

Although a default judgment had been entered against defendant on November 23, 1982 with respect to a new action by ex-wife seeking unpaid support payments, once the new action was consolidated with the earlier divorce action by court order entered December 14, 1982, defendant was entitled to be served with all pleadings and papers filed with the court pertaining to subsequent proceedings involving the new action, including written notice of a hearing on damages held on January 10, 1983. **Case v. Winters,** Op. No. 2876, 689 P2d 467 (Alaska 1984).

Since the information was neither personally delivered nor delivered by certified or registered mail, the information was never served on defendant in a manner which would trigger running of the speedy-trial period. **Hayes v. State,** Op. No. 1031, 790 P2d 713 (Alaska App. 1990).

Default judgment against corporation was upheld notwithstanding that plaintiff violated this rule by serving the corporate officers directly rather than serving the attorney of record for the corporation. **Murat v. F/V Shelikof Strait,** Op. No. 3607, 793 P2d 69 (Alaska 1990).

Service of notice of motion for entry of default judgment on corporation's officers rather than corporation's counsel did not violate the corporation's due process rights. **Murat v. F/V Shelikof Strait,** Op. No. 3607, 793 P2d 69 (Alaska 1990).

Trial court did not violate the father's procedural due process rights by retroactively modifying his child support obligation to the date he was served with notice of the Child Support Enforcement Division's (CSED) petition for modification as provided in Alaska R. Civ. P. 90.3(h)(2) because there was adequate evidence that the father actually received the CSED's notice, where the record showed, among other things, that the CSED mailed the notice to the father's last known address, in compliance with Alaska R. Civ. P. 5. The formal complaint-summons service requirements of Alaska R. Civ. P. 4 are inappropriate in proceedings which seek to enforce the terms of a prior divorce decree relating to child support payments. **Crumpler v. State ex rel. Armstrong,** Op. No. 5927, 117 P.3d 730 (Alaska 2005).

Rule 5.1. Filing and Service by Facsimile Transmission.

(a) **Filing by Facsimile Transmission.** A party may file documents by fax as permitted by administrative order of the presiding judge or with prior written consent of the judge assigned to the case. Unless the court orders that the original document be filed, a party filing a document by fax shall retain the original and shall produce it for inspection upon request of another party to the action or as ordered by the court.

(b) **Service by Facsimile Transmission.**

(1) *Application of this Rule.* This rule governs the service of documents by fax. It applies only to documents that may be served under Civil Rule 5(b). It does not apply to documents that must be served under Civil Rule 4. It applies to service by parties and by the court.

(2) *Method of Service.* Service by fax is made by transmitting the paper to the facsimile machine telephone number of a person who has consented to be served in this manner. Additional service by mail is not required; however, a copy of the paper must be mailed to the person upon request.

(3) *Consent to Service.* A person who is willing to accept service by fax in an action shall so indicate beneath the signature in the person's initial filing or by serving and filing a separate notice of consent. A party may revoke consent by serving and filing a separate notice that consent has been revoked.

(4) *Page Limit.* A person may serve by fax a total of 25 pages per recipient per day unless the parties have agreed to a different page limit. Cover sheets and separators do not count toward the page limit.

(5) *When Service is Complete.* Service by fax is complete upon receipt of the entire document by the receiving party's facsimile machine. Service that occurs in whole or in part after 4:30 p.m. shall be deemed to have occurred at the opening of business on the next day that is not a Saturday, a Sunday or a judicial holiday listed in Administrative Rule 16.

(6) *Proof of Service.* If service is made by fax, proof of service must be made by affidavit of the person making service, or by certificate of an attorney, an authorized agent of the attorney, or a pro se litigant. The affidavit or certificate must include the following information:

(A) the date and time of the transmission;

(B) the telephone number of the transmitting facsimile machine;

(C) the recipient's name and facsimile machine telephone number;

(D) the number of pages transmitted; and

(E) a statement that the document was transmitted by facsimile transmission and the person signing the affidavit or certificate believes the transmission to have been complete and without error.

In lieu of including this information, the person signing the affidavit or certificate may attach a copy of the transmission report issued by the transmitting facsimile machine if the report is an accurate record of the transmission.

(Adopted by SCO 1307 effective January 15, 1998)

Note: Presiding judges' fax filing orders are available on the court system's website at: http://www.state.ak.us/courts/judord.htm. Copies may also be obtained from the office of the court rules attorney, 820 W. 4th Ave., Anchorage, AK 99501, (907) 264-8264.

Rule 6. Time.

(a) **Computation.** In computing any period of time prescribed or allowed by these rules, by order of court, or by any applicable statute, the day of the act, event, or default from which the designated period of time begins to run is not to be included. The last day of the period is to be included, unless it is a Saturday, a Sunday, or a legal holiday, in which event the period runs until the end of the next day which is not a Saturday, Sunday, or legal holiday. When the period of time prescribed or allowed is less than seven days, intermediate Saturdays, Sundays, and legal holidays shall be excluded in the computation. A half holiday shall be considered as other days and not as a holiday.

(b) **Enlargement.** When by these rules or by a notice given thereunder or by order of the court an act is required or allowed to be done at or within a specified time, the court for cause shown may at any time in its discretion (1) with or without motion or notice order the period enlarged if request therefor is made before the expiration of the period originally prescribed or as extended by a previous order or (2) upon motion made after the expiration of the specified period permit the act to be done where the failure to act was the result of excusable neglect; but it may not extend the time for taking any action under Rules 50(b), 52(b), 59(b), and (e) and (f), and 60(b), except to the extent and under the conditions stated in them.

(c) **Additional Time After Service or Distribution by Mail.** Whenever a party has the right or is required to act within a prescribed period after the service or distribution of a document, other than documents served under Civil Rule 4(h), and the document is served or distributed by mail, three calendar days shall be added to the prescribed period. However, no additional time shall be added if a court order specifies a particular calendar date by which an act must occur.

(Adopted by SCO 5 October 9, 1959; amended by SCO 49 effective January 1, 1963; by SCO 98 effective September 16, 1968; by SCO 258 effective November 15, 1976; by SCO 274 effective June 15, 1977; by SCO 704 effective September 15, 1986; by SCO 836 effective August 1, 1987; by SCO 878 effective July 15, 1988; by SCO 1007 effective January 15, 1990; and by SCO 1639 effective October 15, 2007)

Note: Ch. 77 SLA 2002 (HB 157), Section 2, adds new Chapter 26 to Title 6 of the Alaska Statutes, concerning providers of fiduciary services. According to Section 9 of the Act, AS 06.26.760(b)(2) has the effect of amending Civil Rule 6 by postponing the deadlines for the filing of pleadings and other documents by a trust company in a civil action when the Department of Community and Economic Development has taken possession of the trust company.

Annotations

Cases

Under Rule 8(c) of the [Federal] Rules of Civil Procedure affirmative defenses must be pleaded, but the court may grant a motion for judgment on the pleadings and if matters outside the pleadings are presented the motion shall be treated as one for summary judgment under [Federal] R. Civ. P. 56 and all parties must be given reasonable opportunity to present all matters pertinent to such motion, and the party against whom the motion is made may apply to the court for further time to prepare his resistance to the motion under Rule 6(b). **Mitchell v. Land,** Op. No. 19, 355 P2d 682 (Alaska 1960).

Computation under this rule relates only to matters of procedure and has no effect on substantive rights. **Wade v. Dworkin,** Op. No. 306, 407 P2d 587 (Alaska 1965).

A condemnor which fails to file a timely notice of appeal from a master's report can be granted an enlargement of time under this rule. **State v. Chuckwm, Inc.,** Op. No. 522, 449 P2d 776 (Alaska 1968).

A condemnor's request for relief from its failure to file timely notice of appeal from a master's report and for relief from an oppressive proceeding is addressed to the sound discretion of the trial court, and its ruling will not be disturbed on appeal in the absence of a showing of abuse of discretion. **State v. Chuckwm, Inc.,** Op. No. 522, 449 P2d 776 (Alaska 1968).

The trial court has jurisdiction under this rule to enlarge the period of time for appealing from a master's report in a condemnation action, even though such motion was made after the expiration of the specified time for appeal. **Collart et al. (6,656 Square Feet) v. State,** Op. No. 565, 456 P2d 480 (Alaska 1969).

The Supreme Court will not pass on the sufficiency of a landowner's showing that he is entitled for an enlargement of time for appealing from the report of a master in condemnation until the trial court's discretionary powers have been exercised. **Collart et al. (6,656 Square Feet) v. State,** Op. No. 565, 456 P2d 480 (Alaska 1969).

Orders to show cause are barred by this rule where not provided for by other rules. **Dimmick v. O'Neill,** Op. No. 734, 490 P2d 483 (Alaska 1971).

A Saturday when court is closed is a holiday for purposes of computation of time. **David v. Sturm, Ruger & Co., Inc.,** Op. No. 1356, 557 P2d 1133 (Alaska 1976).

Argument that offer of judgment was untimely because it was presented five calendar days rather than five court days after the close of discovery was rejected. **Fairbanks North Star Borough v. Tundra Tours,** Op. No. 3052, 719 P2d 1020 (Alaska 1986).

The court's authority to enlarge the time for an act pursuant to Rule 6(b) is a function addressed to the sound discretion of the trial court. **Estate of Lampert v. Estate of Lampert,** Op. No. 4203, 896 P2d 214 (Alaska 1995).

Trial court did not abuse its discretion in enlarging time for decedent's estate to substitute in as plaintiff for decedent. **Estate of Lampert v. Estate of Lampert,** Op. No. 4203, 896 P2d 214 (Alaska 1995).

Trial court did not abuse its discretion in allowing the attorney to file a late post-trial brief pursuant to Alaska R. Civ. P. 6(b) and ordering the attorney to pay the opposing party's reasonable attorney fees and costs associated with its reply to the attorney's late-filed brief pursuant to Alaska R. Civ. P. 95(a) because the attorney had violated multiple rules that granted the trial court the authority to impose reasonable deadlines. The Supreme Courtof Alaska has held that the failure to comply with a briefing schedule is a reason for imposing sanctions under Alaska R. Civ. P. 95(a). **Schmidt v. Koivisto,** Op. No. 5914, 114 P.3d 816 (Alaska 2005).

PART III. PLEADINGS AND MOTIONS

Rule 7. Pleadings Allowed—Form of Motions.

(a) **Pleadings.** There shall be a complaint and an answer; a reply to a counterclaim denominated as such; an answer to a cross-claim, if the answer contains a cross-claim; a third-party complaint, if leave is given under Rule 14 to summon a person who was not an original party; and a third-party answer, if a third-party complaint is served. No other pleading shall be allowed, except that the court may order a reply to an answer or a third-party answer.

(b) **Motions and Other Papers.**

(1) An application to the court for an order shall be by motion which, unless made during a hearing or trial, shall be made in writing, shall state with particularity the grounds therefor, and shall set forth the relief or order sought. The requirement of writing is fulfilled if the motion is stated in a written notice of the hearing of the motion.

(2) The rules applicable to captions, signing, and other matters of form of pleadings apply to all motions and other papers provided for by these rules.

(3) The procedure for the submission and hearing of motions shall be as provided in Rule 77.

(c) **Demurrers, Pleas, etc., Abolished.** Demurrers, pleas and exceptions for insufficiency of a pleading shall not be used.

(Adopted by SCO 5 October 9, 1959; amended by SCO 57 effective November 8, 1963; by SCO 258 effective November 15, 1976)

Note: Chapter 54 SLA 2005 (HB 95) enacted extensive amendments and new provisions related to public health, including public health emergencies and disasters. According to Section 13(a) of the Act, AS 18.15.375(c)(3),(d), and (e), and 18.15.385(d) –(k), enacted in Section 8, have the effect of amending Civil Rule 7 by adding special proceedings, timing, and pleading requirements for matters involving public health.

Annotations

Cases

The fact that an insurer's motion to amend and answer to include a setoff against the insured was made orally at hearing on the insured's motion for a summary judgment is not a proper ground for the trial court's refusal to consider the motion or for denying it. **United States Fire Insurance Co. v. Schnabel,** Op. No. 852, 504 P2d 847 (Alaska 1972).

Where defendant in suit on a contract raised issue of inadequate performance, plaintiff had no obligation to reply by raising issue of waiver. **City of Palmer v. Anderson,** Op. No. 1978, 603 P2d 495 (Alaska 1979).

Where defendant had access to grand jury testimony of witnesses who later testified to police reports, witness interviews and test results, defendant had adequate knowledge of the charge and a motion for a bill of particulars requesting the state to reveal the "overt acts" the state would rely on to prove criminal negligence was properly denied. **Lupro v. State,** Op. No. 1960, 603 P2d 468 (Alaska 1979).

A motion for a bill of particulars requesting detailed information regarding all facets of the state's case, including every fact to be proved at trial, the names, addresses, telephone numbers and occupations of every witness to be called to prove those facts, and every item of physical evidence to be presented, went far beyond the proper scope of a bill of particulars. **Lupro v. State,** Op. No. 1960, 603 P2d 468 (Alaska 1979).

Where plaintiff's counsel requested exclusion of certain testimony at a hearing on motions in limine made by defendant, a written motion was not required for exclusion of the testimony. **Loof v. Sanders,** Op. No. 2859, 686 P2d 1205 (Alaska 1984).

Motion for declaratory judgment was unnecessary where declaratory judgment was sought in pleadings. **State Dept. of Nat. Res. v. Transamerica,** Op. No. 3979, 856 P2d 766 (Alaska 1993).

Rule 8. General Rules of Pleading.

(a) **Claims for Relief.** A pleading which sets forth a claim for relief, whether an original claim, counterclaim, cross-claim or third-party claim, shall contain (1) a short and plain statement of the claim showing that the pleader is entitled to relief, and (2) a demand for judgment for the relief the pleader seeks. Relief in the alternative or of several different types may be demanded.

(b) **Defenses—Form of Denials.** A party shall state in short and plain terms the party's defenses to each claim asserted and shall admit or deny the averments upon which the adverse party relies. If a party is without knowledge or information sufficient to form a belief as to the truth of an averment, the party shall so state and this has the effect of a denial. Denial shall fairly meet the substance of the averments denied. When a pleader intends in good faith to deny only a part or a qualification of an averment, the pleader shall specify so much of it as is true and material and shall deny only the remainder. Unless the pleader intends in good faith to controvert all the averments of the preceding pleading, the pleader may make denials as specific denials of designated averments or paragraphs, or may generally deny all the averments except such designated averments or paragraphs as the pleader expressly admits; but when the pleader does so intend to controvert all its averments, the pleader may do so by general denial subject to the obligations set forth in Rule 11.

(c) **Affirmative Defenses.** In pleading to a preceding pleading, a party shall set forth affirmatively accord and satisfaction, arbitration and award, assumption of risk, contributory negligence, discharge in bankruptcy, duress, estoppel, failure of consideration, fraud, illegality, injury by fellow servant, laches, license, payment, release, res judicata, statute of frauds, statute of limitations, waiver, and any other matter constituting an avoidance or affirmative defense. When a party has mistakenly designated a defense as a counterclaim, or a counterclaim as a defense, the court on terms, if justice so requires, shall treat the pleading as if there had been a proper designation.

(d) **Effect of Failure to Deny.** Averments in a pleading to which a responsive pleading is required, other than those as to the amount of damage, are admitted when not denied in the responsive pleading. Averments in a pleading to which no responsive pleading is required or permitted shall be taken as denied or avoided.

(e) **Pleading to Be Concise and Direct—Consistency.**

(1) Each averment of a pleading shall be simple, concise and direct. No technical forms of pleading or motions are required.

(2) A party may set forth two or more statements of a claim or defense alternatively or hypothetically, either in one count or defense or in separate counts or defenses. When two or more statements are made in the alternative and one of them if made independently would be sufficient, the pleading is not made insufficient by the insufficiency of one or more of the alternative statements. A party may also state as many separate claims or defenses as the party regardless of consistency and whether based on legal or on equitable grounds or on both. All

statements shall be made subject to the obligations set forth in Rule 11.

(f) **Construction of Pleading.** All pleadings shall be so construed as to do substantial justice.

(Adopted by SCO 5 October 9, 1959; amended by SCO 1153 effective July 15, 1994; and by SCO 1269 effective July 15, 1997)

Note: In 1996, the legislature enacted AS 45.08.114, which establishes special pleading requirements in an action on a certificated security against the issuer. According to § 70 ch. 17 SLA 1996, this statute has the effect of amending Civil Rule 8 by requiring that a denial of a signature on a certificated security be specific or the signature is admitted, and by requiring a denial even if a responsive pleading is not required.

Note: Chapter 54 SLA 2005 (HB 95) enacted extensive amendments and new provisions related to public health, including public health emergencies and disasters. According to Section 13(a) of the Act, AS 18.15.375(c)(3),(d), and (e), and 18.15.385(d)–(k), enacted in Section 8, have the effect of amending Civil Rule 8 by adding special proceedings, timing, and pleading requirements formatters involving public health.

Cross References

CROSS REFERENCE: AS 09.68.020

Annotations

Cases

I. In General.
II. Claims for Relief.
III. Defenses.
  A. In General.
  B. Affirmative Defenses.
IV. Counterclaims.

I. In General.

Pleadings are intended to serve as a means of arriving at fair and just settlements of controversy between litigants. They should not raise barriers which prevent the achievement of that end. **Mitchell v. Land,** Op. No. 19, 355 P2d 682 (Alaska 1960).

The fact that an insurer's motion to amend an answer to include a setoff against the insured was made orally at a hearing on the insured's motion for a summary judgment is not a proper ground for the trial court's refusal to consider the motion or for denying it. **United States Fire Insurance Co. v. Schnabel,** Op. No. 852, 504 P2d 847 (Alaska 1972).

A trial court has "inherent discretionary authority" to decide a case on a legal theory not presented in the pleadings. **Alaska Protection Service v. Frontier Colorcable,** Op. No. 2800, 680 P2d 1119 (Alaska 1984).

The adequacy of pleadings is reviewed **de novo. Gamble v. Northstore Partnership,** Op. No. 4291, 907 P2d 477 (Alaska 1995).

Trial court erred in not granting plaintiffs additional time under Rule 56 to respond to affirmative defenses raised in defendant's summary judgment motion. **Gamble v. Northstore Partnership,** Op. No. 4291, 907 P2d 477 (Alaska 1995).

Cause of action is sufficiently pled if it provides defendant with fair notice of nature of claim. **Sykes v. Melba Creek Min., Inc.,** Op. No. 4938, 952 P2d 1164 (Alaska 1998).

II. Claims for Relief.

A complaint to quiet title sufficiently states a claim if it (1) sets forth in general terms the title of the plaintiff, (2) declares generally that the defendant claims some interest in the property without defining it, (3) avers that the claim is without foundation and, (4) alleges that plaintiff is in possession. **Davis v. Tant,** Op. No. 35, 361 P2d 763, 766 (Alaska 1961).

Where giving notice of an employee's claim is, by agreement of the parties, a condition precedent to recovery on the claim, the employee-plaintiff must plead performance of the condition and the defendant employer is not required to plead lack of notice as an affirmative defense, failure of defendant to plead lack of notice is not a waiver of the defense. **Inman v. Clyde Hall Drilling,** Op. No. 73, 369 P2d 498 (Alaska 1962).

Where a claim is stated by a complaint, even though it does not demand the relief to which the plaintiffs are entitled, the complaint should not be dismissed, but plaintiffs should be denied relief only when, under the facts proved, they are entitled to none. **Miller v. Johnson,** Op. No. 70, 370 P2d 171 (Alaska 1962).

When in an alleged wrongful death case the complaint and two amended complaints did not clearly show if the case should not be brought under a workmen's compensation act rather than under the wrongful death statute, but the trial court had permitted plaintiff to file a third amended complaint which set forth that this was an action brought under the wrongful death statute and that the decedents were guest passengers on the defendant's airplane, and the defendant never filed an answer to this third amended complaint nor did he ever produce any evidence in opposition thereto, it did not appear with certainty that plaintiff was not entitled to any relief which could be proved in support of his claim and it was error for the court to dismiss the action on the basis of failure to state a claim for which relief can be granted. **Lieb v. Interior Enterprises, Inc.,** Op. No. 244, 395 P2d 32 (Alaska 1964).

The dismissal of a complaint in which the plaintiff requests that the mortgage lien be adjudged paramount and be foreclosed is proper for failure to state a claim upon which relief can be granted where the complaint does not disclose adequate information as to the basis for the claim. **Dworkin v. First National Bank of Fairbanks,** Op. No. 499, 444 P2d 777 (Alaska 1968).

A litigant may plead in the alternative and advance inconsistent claims or defenses, but such a right does not relieve him of his obligation to set forth the alternative or inconsistent claims in his pleadings in order to give notice to the opposite side of what it must meet at trial. **Golden Valley Electric Association, Inc. v. College Enterprises, Inc.,** Op. No. 556, 455 P2d 215 (Alaska 1969).

Though the court's statement, in a suit by an electric cooperative to recover reimbursement for the cost of relocating its power lines, that the cooperative was bound by its pleadings and could not be permitted to change its theory of recovery and rely on an easement by prescription instead of an easement by grant is erroneous since the defendant, by failing to object to the cooperative's introduction of evidence tending to prove an easement by prescription, waived its right to confine the issues, the error is harmless in view of the fact that the cooperative's proof of an easement by prescription was fatally deficient. **Golden Valley Electric Association, Inc. v. College Enterprises, Inc.,** Op. No. 556, 455 P2d 215 (Alaska 1969).

Where an issue is not pleaded and it does not appear that the issue was tried by the consent of the party not raising the issue, the trial court is not required to give an instruction concerning the issue when requested by the party raising the issue. **Transamerica Title Insurance Co. v. Ramsey,** Op. No. 869, 507 P2d 492 (Alaska 1973).

Where title or complaint contained reference to Title 42 U.S.C. § 1983, and body of complaint specifically mentioned other statutes but did not specifically plead or refer to § 1983, the complaint stated a cause of action under § 1983 entitling plaintiffs to attorney fees. **Fairbanks Correctional Center v. Williamson,** Op. No. 1937, 600 P2d 743 (Alaska 1979).

Complaint alleging that defendant had a contractual obligation to make direct payments to plaintiff and breached the contract causing damage sufficiently put defendant on notice of the claims against it and of the grounds upon which they rested; there was no need to allege consideration. **Great Western Sav. v. George W. Easley,** Op. No. 3471, 778 P2d 569 (Alaska 1989).

Corporation officer's argument that plaintiff's pleadings were inadequate to inform him that personal liability was sought on the corporate debt was rejected. **Murat v. F/V Shelikof Strait,** Op. No. 3607, 793 P2d 69 (Alaska 1990).

III. Defenses.

A. In General.

Where plaintiff brought an action for declaratory judgment that it was not a bank, evidence could be introduced by defendants to show that plaintiff did the business of banking, after alleging such acts as a "third defense," and defendants were not required to make this "third defense" a "counterclaim." **American Building & Loan v. State,** Op. No. 112, 376 P2d 370 (Alaska 1962).

Where defendant's answer complied with Civ. R. 8(b), and the answer was not attacked by motion to strike, the issues were properly joined by the matter set forth in the complaint and answer and all that remained was for the trial court to hear the evidence and render its decision. **American Building & Loan v. State,** Op. No. 112, 376 P2d 370 (Alaska 1962).

Where defendant did not plead estoppel as an affirmative defense, nor request an amendment of the pleadings to include estoppel, court did not err in refusing to permit defendant to present evidence of estoppel. **Stanton v. Fuchs,** Op. No. 2646, 660 P2d 1197 (Alaska 1983).

B. Affirmative Defenses.

Under Rule 8(c) of the [Federal] Rules of Civil Procedure affirmative defenses must be pleaded, but the court may grant a motion for judgment on the pleadings and if matters outside the pleadings are presented the motion shall be treated as one for summary judgment under [Federal] R. Civ. P. 56 and all parties must be given reasonable opportunity to present all matters pertinent to such motion, and the party against whom the motion is made may apply to the court for further time to prepare his resistance to the motion under Rule 6(b). **Mitchell v. Land,** Op. No. 19, 355 P2d 682 (Alaska 1960).

Instruction on assumption of risk was error, where it had been pleaded as affirmative defense but no evidence was introduced in support of the defense. **Evans v. Buchner,** Op. No. 174, 386 P2d 836 (Alaska 1963).

Estoppel must be pleaded as an affirmative defense, but failure to conform pleadings to proof submitted in support of estoppel was not fatal, where the issue of estoppel was not controlling since pleadings could be amended at any time to conform to proof. **Gilbert v. Sexton,** Op. No. 276,401 P2d 300 (Alaska 1965).

In a civil action for assault and battery self-defense was an affirmative defense which was waived by failure to plead it in accordance with this rule. **Merrill v. Faltin,** Op. No. 425, 430 P2d 913 (Alaska 1967).

Pleading of failure of consideration mistakenly styled as a counterclaim was treated as affirmative defense. **Nordin Construction Co. v. Whitney Bros. Plumbing & Heat., Inc.,** Op. No. 482, 441 P2d 122 (Alaska 1968).

Since the real party in interest objection is dilatory in nature, it should be raised with reasonable promptness. **Burns v. Anchorage Funeral Chapel,** Op. No. 773, 495 P2d 70 (Alaska 1972).

An affirmative defense can generally be defined as a new matter not set forth in the complaint which constitutes a defense or a new matter which, assuming the complaint to be true, is a defense to it. **Rollins v. Leibold,** Op. No. 910, 512 P2d 937 (Alaska 1973).

An affirmative defense can consist of matter which avoids an action, and which the plaintiff does not have to prove at the outset in support of an action. **Rollins v. Leibold,** Op. No. 910, 512 P2d 937 (Alaska 1973).

A statutory presumption of fraud is an affirmative defense which must be specially pleaded. **Rollins v. Leibold,** Op. No. 910, 512 P2d 937 (Alaska 1973).

Where a novation is not properly pleaded as an affirmative defense, it will be considered waived. **Kupka v. Morey,** Op. No. 1197, 541 P2d 740 (Alaska 1975).

Party raising an affirmative defense generally bears the burden of the proof on that issue. **Morrow v. New Moon Homes, Inc.,** Op. No. 1253, 548 P2d 279 (Alaska 1976).

That want of personal jurisdiction was raised as an affirmative defense rather than merely by denial does not shift burden of proof to defendant. **Morrow v. New Moon Homes, Inc.,** Op. No. 1253, 548 P2d 279 (Alaska 1976).

When defense of statute of limitations is not pled as required by Civil Rule 8(c), it is waived by operation of Civil Rule 12(h). **Barrett v. Byrnes,** Op. No. 1340, 556 P2d 1254 (Alaska 1976).

Plaintiff in contract action need not plead his responses to possible defense of inadequate performance. **City of Palmer v. Anderson,** Op. No. 1978, 603 P2d 495 (Alaska 1979).

Reliance on a statute of limitations is ordinarily an affirmative defense which must be pleaded and proved by the defendant. **Hitt v. J.B. Coghill, Inc.,** Op. No. 2474, 641 P2d 211 (Alaska 1982).

Estoppel is an affirmative defense which must be properly pleaded or it is considered waived. **Stanton v. Fuchs,** Op. No. 2646, 660 P2d 1197 (Alaska 1983).

Defense of failure of consideration was not adequately raised in responsive pleading. **Alaska Protection Service v. Frontier Colorcable,** Op. No. 2800, 680 P2d 1119 (Alaska 1984).

Where defendant sought damages for lack of full performance in its counterclaim, but did not seek to avoid its obligation altogether, it could not point to its counterclaim or to its pretrial memorandum as adequately raising the issue of substantial performance. **Alaska Protection Service v. Frontier Colorcable,** Op. No. 2800, 680 P2d 1119 (Alaska 1984).

Because negligence is a complete bar to indemnification, it is an affirmative defense under this rule and must be affirmatively pled. **Koehring Mfg. v. Earthmovers of Fairbanks,** Op. No. 3390, 763 P2d 499 (Alaska 1988).

Given the pleadings and memoranda submitted in a strict product liability action, trial court did not err in concluding that one of the two defendants failed to affirmatively plead the other defendant's negligence as a bar to indemnification even though some ambiguity as to the nature of the pleadings arose during an oral colloquy between the defendant and the trial court. **Koehring Mfg. v. Earthmovers of Fairbanks,** Op. No. 3390, 763 P2d 499 (Alaska 1988).

Where both the manufacturer and lessor of a crane were held strictly liable for injuries to workers caused by a defect in the design of the crane, trial court did not err in holding the lessor entitled to indemnification from the manufacturer where the manufacturer did not affirmatively plead the lessor's independent negligence, proof of which would have been necessary for the manufacturer to escape its indemnity obligation; furthermore, the trial court did not abuse its discretion in refusing to allow the manufacturer belatedly to amend its pleadings to allege negligence on the part of the lessor. **Koehring Mfg. v. Earthmovers of Fairbanks,** Op. No. 3390, 763 P2d 499 (Alaska 1988).

As the defense of bona fide purchaser was closely related to the facts presented in the complaint, it was not waived by the failure to affirmatively plead it in the answer. **Gamble v. Northstore Partnership,** Op. No. 4291, 907 P2d 477 (Alaska 1995).

A Rule 8(b) denial of lack of knowledge is not the sort of affirmative pleading which Rule 8(c) minimally demands. **Gamble v. Northstore Partnership,** Op. No. 4291, 907 P2d 477 (Alaska 1995).

The purpose of the pleading requirements of Rule 8(c) is to give the plaintiff sufficient notice of her opponent's defenses to allow adequate trial preparation. Failure to adequately plead a defense can result in waiver of the defense. **Gamble v. Northstore Partnership,** Op. No. 4291, 907 P2d 477 (Alaska 1995).

The defenses of bona fide purchaser and affirmance in a case for reformation of a recorded grant of easement were affirmative defenses to which Rule 8(c) applied. **Gamble v. Northstore Partnership,** Op. No. 4291, 907 P2d 477 (Alaska 1995).

The standards governing the pleading of affirmative defenses under Rule 8(c) are no different than the liberal approach taken for all pleadings. **Gamble v. Northstore Partnership,** Op. No. 4291, 907 P2d 477 (Alaska 1995).

An affirmative defense is adequately pleaded if it provides the opponent with fair notice of the nature of the defenses. **Gamble v. Northstore Partnership,** Op. No. 4291, 907 P2d 477 (Alaska 1995).

The defense of affirmance was adequately pled where the defendant specifically pled defenses which, although not synonymous with "affirmance," invoked some of the same concerns in more general terms. **Gamble v. Northstore Partnership,** Op. No. 4291, 907 P2d 477 (Alaska 1995).

Assertion by easement holder in pleadings that it was "without knowledge or information sufficient to form a belief as to the truth" of whether easement was unilaterally altered was insufficient to give opposing party notice of easement holder's intent to rely upon defense of bona fide purchaser. **Gamble v. Northstore Partnership,** Op. No. 4291, 907 P2d 477 (Alaska 1995).

IV. Counterclaims.

Where counterclaim was based on a mistaken theory, counterclaimants were entitled to whatever relief the evidence indicated. **Litton v. Hiltz,** Op. No. 190, 389 P2d 433 (Alaska 1964).

The taking of private property by the state for a public purpose was an exercise of eminent domain and the fact that the state mistakenly relied on an asserted but invalid patent reservation could not alter the nature of this taking so that property owner's claim for relief in damages albeit incorrectly framed as a trespass action, was treated as a demand for just compensation and the entire action had to be treated as an "inverse condemnation action," utilizing so far as practicable procedure relating to a condemnation action, and dismissal below of the state's counterclaim for "inverse condemnation" was error. **State, Department of Highways v. Crosby,** Op. No. 322, 410 P2d 724 (Alaska 1966).

Motion by defendant, the obligor on a promissory note, to join credit union as a third party defendant, was improper, since the credit union had no obligation to indemnify the defendant for any liability to plaintiffs, rather, the motion was essentially a counterclaim against plaintiffs as assignees of defendant's promissory note to the credit union; accordingly, the trial court had discretionary authority to join the credit union as a defendant to the counterclaim but failure to do so was harmless error, since the joinder motion was untimely and since relief was granted on the counterclaim despite absence of the credit union as a party. **Jackson v. Nangle,** Op. No. 2773, 677 P2d 242 (Alaska 1984).

Where defendant sought damages for lack of full performance in its counterclaim, but did not seek to avoid its obligation altogether, it could not point to its counterclaim or to its pretrial memorandum as adequately raising the issue of substantial performance. **Alaska Protection Service v. Frontier Colorcable,** Op. No. 2800, 680 P2d 1119 (Alaska 1984).

Insured's failure to plead arbitration in his complaint against an insurance company and an insurance agent in which the insured sought a declaration of coverage did not waive the insured's right to arbitration, and the trial court erred in finding that the insured waived the arbitration remedy. **Blood v. Kenneth Murray Ins., Inc.,** 68 P.3d 1251 (Alaska 2003).

Rule 9. Pleading Special Matters.

(a) **Capacity.** It is not necessary to aver the capacity of a party to sue or be sued or the authority of a party to sue or be sued in a representative capacity or the legal existence of and organized association of persons that is made a party, except to the extent required to show the jurisdiction of the court. When a party desires to raise an issue as to the legal existence of any party or the capacity of any party to sue or be sued or the authority of a party to sue or be sued in a representative capacity, the party desiring to raise the issue shall do so by specific negative averment, which shall include such supporting particulars as are peculiarly within the pleader's knowledge.

(b) **Fraud, Mistake, Condition of the Mind.** In all averments of fraud or mistake, the circumstances constituting fraud or mistake shall be stated with particularity. Malice, intent, knowledge, and other condition of mind of a person may be averred generally.

(c) **Conditions Precedent.** In pleading the performance or occurrence of conditions precedent, it is sufficient to aver generally that all conditions precedent have been performed or have occurred. A denial of performance or occurrence shall be made specifically and with particularity.

(d) **Official Document or Act.** In pleading an official document or official act it is sufficient to aver that the document was issued or the act done in compliance with law.

(e) **Judgment.** In pleading a judgment or decision of a domestic or foreign court, judicial or quasi-judicial tribunal, or of a board or officer, it is sufficient to aver the judgment or decision without setting forth matter showing jurisdiction to render it.

(f) **Statutes and Ordinances.** In pleading any statute or ordinance or other enactment of the state or a subdivision thereof, it is sufficient to identify the statute, ordinance or enactment without setting forth the matter contained therein.

(g) **Time and Place.** For the purpose of testing the sufficiency of a pleading, averments of time and place are material and shall be considered like all other averments of material matter.

(h) **Special Damage.** When items of special damage are claimed, they shall be specifically stated.

(Adopted by SCO 5 October 9, 1959; amended by SCO 1153 effective July 15, 1994)

Annotations

Cases

An answer to a complaint by a corporate plaintiff which denies the allegation of compliance with statute for "want of knowledge or information" is not sufficient to raise the issue as to capacity. **Brown v. Music, Inc.,** Op. No. 25, 359 P2d 295 (Alaska 1961).

Where giving notice of an employee's claim is, by agreement of the parties, a condition precedent to recovery on the claim, the employee-plaintiff must plead performance of the condition and the defendant employer is not required to plead lack of notice as an affirmative defense;

failure of defendant to plead lack of notice is not a waiver of the defense. **Inman v. Clyde Hall Drilling,** Op. No. 73, 369 P2d 498 (Alaska 1962).

A general denial is not enough to raise the issue of capacity to sue. **Smith v. Sellar,** Op. No. 88, 371 P2d 809 (Alaska 1962).

Where defendant contended on appeal that plaintiff could not bring an action for a debt defendant owed to a partnership without joining all partners or alleging an assignment of the debt to plaintiff, defendant was required to point that out specifically in his answer and, by failing to do so, waived the objection. **Smith v. Sellar,** Op. No. 88, 371 P2d 809 (Alaska 1962).

Authority of Secretary-Treasurer of plaintiff labor union to act for the union was sufficiently alleged by his signature of the complaint in his capacity as an officer of the union which was not contradicted by defendants. **Sanuita v. Common Laborer's and Hod Carriers Union,** Op. No. 290, 402 P2d 199 (Alaska 1965).

The testimony of the vice-president and secretary of a Colorado automobile dealer, which had repossessed trucks in Alaska, sold them, and then sued the buyer for a deficiency judgment, that the dealer had an interest in trucks because it had obtained a reassignment is sufficient to justify the trial court's denial of a buyer's motion for directed verdict on the grounds that the dealer was not the real party in interest. **Weaver v. O'Meara Motor Company,** Op. No. 535, 452 P2d 87 (Alaska 1969).

AS 13.20.330, providing for the survivorship of those claims which the decedent held before death, cannot be used by the administrator to qualify as the real party in interest in a suit against a funeral home for wrongful interference with the right of a next of kin to preserve the body of a deceased. **Burns v. Anchorage Funeral Chapel,** Op. No. 773, 495 P2d 70 (Alaska 1972).

The trial court has the discretion to determine whether in the particular factual context of the litigation a waiver of a real party in interest issue has occurred. **Burns v. Anchorage Funeral Chapel,** Op. No. 773, 495 P2d 70 (Alaska 1972).

Failure to aver properly superior court's jurisdiction was procedural and harmless in nature and complaint would be deemed amended accordingly. **A.R.C. Industries, Inc. v. State,** Op. No. 1283, 551 P2d 951 (Alaska 1976).

Where plaintiff's claim would not have been barred if state had been required to file answer within time set by court rule, state was prohibited by equitable estoppel from asserting plaintiffs incapacity to sue when answer was filed at end of extended period allowed by stipulation. **State v. Reefer King Co., Inc.,** Op. No. 1344, 559 P2d 56 (Alaska 1976).

Where defendant sought damages for lack of full performance in its counterclaim, but did not seek to avoid its obligation altogether, it could not point to its counterclaim or to its pretrial memorandum as adequately raising the issue of substantial performance. **Alaska Protection Service v. Frontier Colorcable,** Op. No. 2800, 680 P2d 1119 (Alaska 1984).

Although defendant properly pleaded issue of plaintiff's capacity to sue in its answer, defendant waived issue for appeal by failing to bring the issue to trial court's attention by motion. **Von Stauffenberg v. Committee for Honest and Ethical School Board,** Op. No. 4269, 903 P2d 1055 (Alaska 1995).

Fraud, even in an initial pleading, must be averred with particularity. **Law Off. of Vincent Vitale v. Tabbytite,** Op. No. 4852, 942 P2d 1141 (Alaska 1997).

Confirmation of attorney fee arbitration award may not be resisted merely by reciting without specificity that fraud occurred; evidentiary support for particular fraud claims must be presented in opposition to award. **Law Off. of Vincent Vitale v. Tabbytite,** Op. No. 4852, 942 P2d 1141 (Alaska 1997).

Rule 10. Form of Pleadings.

(a) **Caption—Names of Parties.** Every pleading shall contain a caption setting forth the title of the court, the judicial district in which the action is filed, the city in which the court is located, the title of the action (i.e., the names of the parties), the case number, and a designation as in Rule 7(a). In the complaint the title of the action shall include the names of all the parties, but in other pleadings it is sufficient to state the name of the first party on each side with appropriate indication of other parties. When identifying parties in the complaint, the plaintiff shall include as much of each party's full legal name as is known to the plaintiff.

(b) **Paragraphs—Separate Statements.** All averments of claim or defense shall be made in numbered paragraphs, the contents of each of which shall be limited as far as practicable to a statement of a single set of circumstances; and a paragraph may be referred to by number in all succeeding pleadings. Each claim founded upon a separate transaction or occurrence and each defense other than denials shall be stated in a separate count or defense whenever a separation facilitates the clear presentation of the matters set forth.

(c) **Adoption by Reference—Exhibits.** Statements in a pleading may be adopted by reference in a different part of the same pleading or in another pleading or in any motion. A copy of any written instrument which is an exhibit to a pleading is a part thereof for all purposes.

(d) **Title of Pleading—Citation of Statute.** A party filing a complaint, counterclaim, or cross-claim seeking relief under any specific statute is required to cite the statute relied upon in parentheses following the title of the pleading or in the heading for the section asserting the statutory claim.

(e) **Conformity With Rule 76.** All pleadings shall be prepared and filed in conformity with the provisions of Rule 76 as well as this rule.

(Adopted by SCO 5 October 9, 1959; amended by SCO 1415 effective October 15, 2000)

Note: AS 10.06.915, as enacted by ch. 166, § 1, SLA 1988, amended Civil Rule 10 by requiring that certain documents be attached to a complaint that appeals the disapproval of a writing under AS 10.06.915 by the commissioner of commerce and economic development.

Annotations

Cases

A complaint for additional payment of work done under a construction contract was skillfully and artfully drawn where plaintiff pleaded the contract, its own performance, acceptance by defendant of what it claimed to be tender of part payment, and then in separate paragraphs for each item for which additional compensation was claimed set out (a) that a certain amount of work was performed under pertinent terms of contract each pertinent item pleaded as separate exhibit, (b) that defendant had received payment for specific portion of the work performed, (c) that plaintiff's claim for payment of the balance had been rejected. **Stock & Grove, Inc. v. City of Juneau,** Op. No. 292, 403 P2d 171 (Alaska 1965).

Rule 11. Signing of Pleadings, Motions, and Other Papers; Sanctions.

Every pleading, motion and other paper of a party represented by an attorney shall be signed by at least one attorney of record in the attorney's individual name, whose address shall be stated. A party who is not represented by an attorney shall sign the party's pleading, motion, or other paper and state the party's address. Except when otherwise specifically provided by rule or statute, pleadings need not be verified or accompanied by affidavit. The rule in equity that the averments of an answer under oath must be overcome by the testimony of two witnesses or of one witness sustained by corroborating circumstances is abolished. The signature of an attorney or party constitutes a certificate by the signer that the signer has read the pleading, motion, or other paper; that to the best of the signer's knowledge, information, and belief formed after reasonable inquiry it is well grounded in fact and is warranted by existing law or a good faith argument for the extension, modification, or reversal of existing law, and that it is not interposed for any improper purpose, such as to harass or to cause unnecessary delay or needless expense in the cost of litigation. If a pleading, motion, or other paper is not signed, it shall be stricken unless it is signed promptly after the omission is called to the attention of the pleader or movant.

(Adopted by SCO 5 October 9, 1959; amended by SCO 743 effective December 15, 1986; by SCO 1009 effective January 15, 1990; and by SCO 1153 effective July 15, 1994)

Note: AS 10.06.628, as enacted by ch. 166, § 1, SLA 1988, amended Civil Rule 11 by requiring that a complaint for an involuntary dissolution of a corporation under AS 10.06.628 be verified.

Annotations

Cases

Sanctions for failure to sign a pleading are a matter in the discretion of the trial court. **Sanuita v. Common Laborer's and Hod Carriers Union,** Op. No. 290, 402 P2d 199 (Alaska 1965).

Where appellants did not draw the trial court's attention to the failure of counsel to sign the complaint and made no motion to strike under this rule, and it was not contended that counsel's failure to sign was anything other than an oversight, the trial court had no opportunity to pass on the matter and failure to comply with this rule was not considered the first time on appeal. **Sanuita v. Common Laborer's and Hod Carriers Union,** Op. No. 290, 402 P2d 199 (Alaska 1965).

The purpose of this rule requiring signature of counsel as plainly set out in its present wording has been to insure the good faith of counsel by holding them strictly accountable for all the allegations contained in the complaint. **Sanuita v. Common Laborer's and Hod Carriers Union,** Op. No. 290, 402 P2d 199 (Alaska 1965).

Imposition of attorney fees and monetary sanctions against defense attorney in criminal case for filing frivolous, unnecessary and legally deficient pleadings was error requiring remand where attorney was not given notice of the charges against him nor a hearing on the issue of sanctions. **Weidner v. Superior Court, Third Judicial Dist.**, Op. No. 589, 715 P2d 264 (Alaska App. 1986).

Attorney had no right to jury trial on issue of whether sanctions should be imposed against him for filing frivolous, unnecessary and legally deficient pleadings in a criminal case. **Weidner v. Superior Court, Third Judicial Dist.,** Op. No. 589, 715 P2d 264 (Alaska App. 1986).

Attorney was not entitled to discovery at hearing on sanctions for filing frivolous, unnecessary and legally deficient pleadings in a criminal case, since notice requirements, in conjunction with any affidavits filed by the prosecution, would alert him to the issues. **Weidner v. Superior Court, Third Judicial Dist.,** Op. No. 589, 715 P2d 264 (Alaska App. 1986).

Attorney was not entitled to a change of judge as a matter of right at hearing on sanctions for filing frivolous, unnecessary and legally deficient pleadings in a criminal case. **Weidner v. Superior Court, Third Judicial Dist.,** Op. No. 589, 715 P2d 264 (Alaska App. 1986).

Where the complaint mentioned this rule only in the context of an abuse of process claim and the plaintiffs did not motion the superior court to impose sanctions under the rule, the issue of whether sanction should have been imposed pursuant to the rule was not properly raised below and would not be heard on appeal. **Kollodge v. State,** Op. No. 3355, 757 P2d 1028 (Alaska 1988).

On review of a lower court's decision to impose sanctions under this rule, all factors relevant to the issue of whether the attorney's inquiry into facts and law was reasonable are reviewed under an abuse of discretion standard. **Keen v. Ruddy,** Op. No. 3538, 784 P2d 653 (Alaska 1989).

This rule creates an objective standard of "reasonableness under the circumstances" and is intended to be more stringent than a mere "good faith" formula. **Keen v. Ruddy,** Op. No. 3538, 784 P2d 653 (Alaska 1989).

Where plaintiff's legal theories were frivolous and the suit was brought in bad faith, plaintiff's attorney could not have signed the pleadings with a reasonable belief that the pleadings were supported by existing law or that there was a good faith argument for extending the law; accordingly, imposition of sanction against attorney was appropriate. **Keen v. Ruddy,** Op. No. 3538, 784 P2d 653 (Alaska 1989).

Argument that $100 sanction against attorney under this rule was too low was rejected; although $100 was a small sum compared to the attorney's fees imposed against the attorney's client, it nevertheless carried with it a stigma and a message of disapproval. **Keen v. Ruddy,** Op. No. 3538, 784 P2d 653 (Alaska 1989).

A trial court's imposition or nonimposition of sanctions remains subject to review only for abuse of discretion. **Alaska Federal S & L v. Bernhardt,** Op. No. 3562, 794 P2d 579 (Alaska 1990).

This rule no longer strictly requires willful conduct or subjective bad faith to impose sanctions; the determining factor is whether there was a reasonable basis for the attorney's signature. **Alaska Federal S & Lv. Bernhardt,** Op. No. 3562, 794 P2d 579 (Alaska 1990).

This rule concerns the veracity and propriety of purpose of affirmative representations by counsel; it does not reach omissions. **Alaska Federal S & L v. Bernhardt,** Op. No. 3562, 794 P2d 579 (Alaska 1990).

Under this rule, a court cannot impose sanctions on a party simply for losing; instead, a court imposes sanctions on an attorney or party when it finds that the pleading signed by him: (1) is not well grounded in fact, or (2) is not warranted by existing law or a reasonable argument for its extension, modification or reversal, or (3) was interposed for an improper purpose. **State Employees Ass'n v. Pub. Emp. Ass'n,** Op. No. 3711, 813 P2d 669 (Alaska 1991).

Sanctions under this rule against new bargaining representative, that filed suit against the previous bargaining representative seeking injunctive and monetary relief from attempts by the old representative to collect back dues, were an abuse of discretion; the new representative's legal arguments and theories of relief were not so devoid of merit as to justify the imposition of sanctions. **State Employees Ass'n v. Pub. Emp. Ass'n,** Op. No. 3711, 813 P2d 669 (Alaska 1991).

Sanctions against plaintiff's attorney for filing a disqualification motion against opposing counsel were improper where the affidavit by plaintiff's attorney demonstrated that the motion was well granted in fact and the trial court allowed only one day in which to decide whether to file the motion. **Matter of Benson,** Op. No. 3749, 816 P2d 200 (Alaska 1991).

Claims by employee, who was suspended and then terminated from his employment for marijuana use, that he was entitled to reinstatement and back pay as remedy for his suspension and that the employer's discriminatory treatment of him constituted a violation of the covenant of good faith and fair dealing were not frivolous. **Luedtke v. Nabors Alaska**

Drilling, Inc., Op. No. 3844, 834 P2d 1220 (Alaska 1992).

Where trial court's sanction order was improperly entered without factual findings and without hearing, normal procedure would have been to remand the award of sanctions to the trial court for entry of findings, but appellate court instead reversed the award because it found no evidence in the record that could possibly support it. **Luedtke v. Nabors Alaska Drilling, Inc.**, Op. No. 3844, 834 P2d 1220 (Alaska 1992).

Rule 12. Defenses and Objections—When and How Presented—By Pleading or Motion—Motion for Judgment on Pleadings.

(a) **When Presented.** A defendant shall serve an answer within 20 days after the service of the summons and complaint upon that defendant, unless otherwise directed when service of process is made pursuant to Rule 4(e). A party served with a pleading stating a cross-claim against that party shall serve an answer thereto within 20 days after the service upon that party. The plaintiff shall serve a reply to a counterclaim in the answer within 20 days after service of the answer or, if a reply is ordered by the court, within 20 days after service of the order, unless the order otherwise directs. The state or an officer or agency thereof shall serve an answer to the complaint or to a cross-claim, or a reply to a counterclaim, within 40 days after the service upon the attorney general of the pleading in which the claim is asserted. A non-governmental party shall serve an answer to the complaint or to a cross-claim, or a reply to a counterclaim within 40 days after service upon an officer or agency of the state appointed, authorized, or designated as agent to receive service for such party pursuant to statute. An individual in a foreign country who is served with a summons and complaint under subsection (d)(13) of Rule 4 shall serve an answer to the complaint or to a cross-claim, or a reply to a counterclaim, within 40 days after service upon that individual. The service of a motion permitted under this rule alters these periods of time as follows, unless a different time is fixed by order of the court: (1) if the court denies the motion or postpones its disposition until the trial on the merits, the responsive pleading shall be served within 10 days after notice of the court's action; (2) if the court grants a motion for a more definite statement the responsive pleading shall be served within 10 days after the service of the more definite statement.

(b) **How Presented.** Every defense, in law or fact, to a claim for relief in any pleading, whether a claim, counterclaim, cross-claim, or third-party claim, shall be asserted in the responsive pleading thereto if one is required, except that the following defenses may at the option of the pleader be made by motion: (1) lack of jurisdiction over the subject matter, (2) lack of jurisdiction over the person, (3) improper venue, (4) insufficiency of process, (5) insufficiency of service of process, (6) failure to state a claim upon which relief can be granted, (7) failure to join a party under Rule 19. A motion making any of these defenses shall be made before pleading if a further pleading is permitted. No defense or objection is waived by being joined with one or more other defenses or objections in a responsive pleading or motion. If a pleading sets forth a claim for relief to which the adverse party is not required to serve a responsive pleading, the adverse party may assert at the trial any defense in law or fact to that claim for relief. If, on a motion asserting the defense numbered (6) to dismiss for failure of the pleading to state a claim upon which relief can be granted, matters outside the pleading are presented to and not excluded by the court, the motion shall be treated as one for summary judgment and disposed of as provided in Rule 56, and all parties shall be given reasonable opportunity to present all material made pertinent to such a motion by Rule 56. A decision granting a motion to dismiss is not a final judgment under Civil Rule 58. When the decision adjudicates all unresolved claims as to all parties, the judge shall direct the appropriate party to file a proposed final judgment. The proposed judgment must be filed within 20 days of service of the decision, on a separate document distinct from any opinion, memorandum or order that the court may issue.

(c) **Motion for Judgment on the Pleadings.** After the pleadings are closed but within such time as not to delay the trial, any party may move for judgment on the pleadings. If, on a motion for judgment on the pleadings, matters outside the pleadings are presented to and not excluded by the court, the motion shall be treated as one for summary judgment and disposed as provided in Rule 56, and all parties shall be given reasonable opportunity to present all material made pertinent to such a motion by Rule 56. A decision granting a motion for judgment on the pleadings is not a final judgment under Civil Rule 58. When the decision adjudicates all unresolved claims as to all parties, the judge shall direct the appropriate party to file a proposed final judgment. The proposed judgment must be filed within 20 days of service of the decision, on a separate document distinct from any opinion, memorandum or order that the court may issue.

(d) **Preliminary Hearings.** The defenses specifically enumerated (1)-(7) in subdivision (b) of this rule, whether made in a pleading or by motion, and the motion for judgment mentioned in subdivision (c) of this rule shall be heard and determined before trial on application of any party, unless the court orders that the hearing and determination thereof be deferred until the trial.

(e) **Motion for More Definite Statement.** If a pleading to which a responsive pleading is permitted is so vague or ambiguous that a party cannot reasonably be required to frame a responsive pleading, the party may move for a more definite statement before interposing a responsive pleading. The motion shall point out the defects complained of and the details desired. If the motion is granted and the order of the court is not obeyed within 10 days after notice of the order or within such other times as the court may fix, the court may strike the pleading to which the motion was directed or make such order as it deems just.

(f) **Motion to Strike.** Upon motion made by a party before responding to a pleading, or, if no responsive pleading is permitted by these rules, upon motion by a party within 20 days after the service of the pleading upon the party or upon the court's own initiative at any time, the court may order stricken from any pleading any insufficient defense or any redundant, immaterial, impertinent, or scandalous matter.

(g) **Consolidation of Defenses in Motion.** A party who

makes a motion under the rule may join with it any other motions herein provided for and then available to the party. If a party makes a motion under this rule, but omits therefrom any defense or objection then available to the party which this rule permits to be raised by motion, the party shall not thereafter make a motion based on the defense or objection so omitted, except as provided in subdivision (h) (2) hereof on any of the grounds there stated.

(h) **Waiver or Preservation of Certain Defenses.**

(1) A defense of lack of jurisdiction over the person, improper venue, insufficiency of process, or insufficiency of service of process is waived (A) if omitted from a motion in the circumstances described in subdivision (g), or (B) if it is neither made by motion under this rule nor included in a responsive pleading or an amendment thereof permitted by Rule 15 (a) to be made as a matter of course.

(2) A defense of failure to state a claim upon which relief can be granted, a defense of failure to join a party indispensable under Rule 19, and an objection of failure to state a legal defense to a claim may be made in any pleading permitted or ordered under Rule 7(a), or by motion for judgment on the pleadings, or at the trial on the merits.

(3) Whenever it appears by suggestion of the parties or otherwise that the court lacks jurisdiction of the subject matter the court shall dismiss the action.

(Adopted by SCO 5 October 9, 1959; amended by SCO 258 effective November 15, 1976; by SCO 1153 effective July 15, 1994; by SCO 1430 effective April 15, 2002; and by SCO 1570 effective October 15, 2005)

Note: Ch. 77 SLA 2002 (HB 157), Section 2, adds new Chapter 26 to Title 6 of the Alaska Statutes, concerning providers of fiduciary services. According to Section 9 of the Act, AS 06.26.760(b)(2) has the effect of amending Civil Rule 12 by postponing the deadlines for serving an answer to a complaint, a third-party answer, a reply to a counterclaim, a cross-claim, and an answer to a cross-claim by a trust company in a civil action when the Department of Community and Economic Development has taken possession of the trust company.

Annotations

Cases

I. In General.
II. Presentation of Defenses.
  A. Waiver.
  B. Non-waiver.
III. Failure to State a Claim.
  A. Considerations by Court.
  B. Decisions.
IV. Indispensable Party.
V. Motions for Summary Judgment.
VI. Service.

I. In General.

Federal authorities supporting the practice to hear and determine the affirmative defense of lack of jurisdiction on pleadings, affidavit counter-affidavits and similar documents prior to the trial of the merits are persuasive for Alaska. **Fenner v. Bassett,** Op. No. 331, 412 P2d 318 (Alaska 1966).

Where complaint stated a claim for relief, defendant who needed more facts to frame a responsive pleading could have called for them under this rule or could have obtained them by utilizing discovery proceedings and summary dismissal for failure to set out evidentiary facts was error. **Shannon v. City of Anchorage,** Op. No. 416, 429 P2d 17 (Alaska 1967).

Party raising an affirmative defense generally bears the burden of proof on that issue. **Morrow v. New Moon Homes, Inc.,** Op. No. 1253, 548 P2d 279 (Alaska 1976).

That want of personal jurisdiction was raised as an affirmative defense rather than merely by denial does not shift burden of proof to defendant. **Morrow v. New Moon Homes, Inc.,** Op. No. 1253, 548 P2d 279 (Alaska 1976).

Where plaintiff's claim would not have been barred if state had been required to file answer within time set by court rule, state was prohibited by equitable estoppel from asserting plaintiff's incapacity to sue when answer was filed at end of extended period allowed by stipulation. **State v. Reefer King Co., Inc.,** Op. No. 1344, 559 P2d 56 (Alaska 1976).

A complaint is subject to dismissal under Civil Rule 12(b)(6) when its allegations indicate the existence of an affirmative defense, but the defense must clearly appear on the face of the pleading. The pleading must clearly allege the fact upon which the motion to dismiss is based. **Martin v. Mears,** Op. No. 1958, 602 P2d 421 (Alaska 1979).

When material outside the pleadings is presented to the trial court a motion to dismiss is automatically converted into one for summary judgment unless the court "affirmatively" and "expressly" rules that it is not considering evidence outside of the pleadings. **Adkins v. Nabors Alaska Drilling, Inc.,** Op. No. 2056, 609 P2d 15 (Alaska 1980).

Plaintiff's demand for jury trial on issues raised in defendant's counterclaim was untimely where plaintiff's reply to the counterclaim was filed more than a year and a half after the counterclaim and only 18 days before trial. **Pankratz v. State, Depart. of Highways,** Op. No. 2564, 652 P2d 68 (Alaska 1982).

Given the narrow scope of the materials outside of the pleadings which were consulted by the superior court and appellants' failure to show any prejudice occurring to them as a result of the court's unarticulated conversion of a Rule 12(b)(6) motion to a motion for summary judgment court's error in not expressly indicating whether it had considered or excluded matters submitted outside the pleadings was harmless. **Brice v. State, Div. of Forest, Land & Water,** Op. No. 2731, 669 P2d 1311 (Alaska 1983).

Where trial court considered matters outside the pleadings in deciding to dismiss a suit upon the court's own motion for failure to state a claim upon which relief could be granted, the motion should have been treated as one for summary judgment, the reviewing court chose to treat the dismissal as a judgment on the pleadings and confined review to the issue of whether plaintiff did fail to state a claim upon which relief could be granted since treating the trial court's sua sponte dismissal as a motion for summary judgment would have denied plaintiff certain procedural safeguards relevant to summary judgments. **Shooshanian v. Wagner,** Op. No. 2747, 672 P2d 455 (Alaska 1983).

Trial judge did not abuse his discretion in granting defendant's oral motion to amend the answer to add a statute of limitations defense where the only claim of prejudice by plaintiff was $4,000 spent litigating the two million dollar lawsuit before defendant raised the limitation defense. **Blake v. Gilbert,** Op. No. 2947, 702 P2d 631 (Alaska 1985).

Motions to dismiss are viewed with disfavor and should rarely be granted. **Kollodge v. State,** Op. No. 3342, 757 P2d 1024 (Alaska 1988).

If a trial court considers matters outside the pleadings, it must treat a motion to dismiss for failure to state a claim as a motion for summary judgment; if the trial court does not state whether or not it excluded evidence outside the pleadings, the appellate court may remand for proper consideration, review the decision as if the motion for failure to state a claim was granted after exclusion of the outside materials, or review the decision as if the trial court granted a motion for summary judgment. **Homeward Bound v. Anchorage**

School Dist., Op. No. 3589, 791 P2d 610 (Alaska 1990).

If matters outside pleadings are presented in motion to dismiss for failure to state claim upon which relief may be granted, and trial court fails to state expressly what materials it considered, appellate court may remand for proper consideration, review decision as if motion was granted after exclusion of outside materials, or review decision as if trial court granted motion for summary judgment. **Andrews v. Wade & DeYoung, Inc., P.C.,** Op. No. 4088, 875 P2d 89 (Alaska 1994).

Client's malpractice claim was not compulsory counterclaim in attorney's fee recovery action, although both arose from same litigation, because trial court in fee recovery action converted motion to dismiss to motion for summary judgment without notice, thereby depriving client of reasonable opportunity to present all material pertinent to such motion. **Andrews v. Wade & DeYoung, Inc., P.C.,** Op. No. 4088, 875 P2d 89 (Alaska 1994).

Where a proposed amendment to the pleadings challenges the trial court's subject matter jurisdiction, it is an abuse of discretion to deny the amendment. **Rodriquez v. Rodriquez,** Op. No. 4302, 908 P2d 1007 (Alaska 1995).

Where trial court did not explicitly exclude outside materials in granting motion to dismiss for failure to state claim upon which relief could be granted, reviewing court could review dismissal order as if trial court had excluded the outside materials or it could review dismissal order as if trial court had converted the motion to dismiss into one for summary judgment. **Alaska Nat. Ins. Co. v. Jones,** Op. No. 5215, 993 P2d 424 (Alaska 1999).

Any error by trial court in converting motion for judgment on the pleadings into motion for summary judgment without giving non-moving party additional time to marshal evidence and submit affidavits was harmless. **White v. State Dept. of Natural Resources,** Op. No. 5343, 14 P3d 956 (Alaska 2000).

When a defendant on a motion for judgment on the pleadings asserts a statute of limitations defense and the opposition to the motion raises questions regarding the applicability of the relation back doctrine, unless the applicability or non-applicability of relation back is clear on the face of the pleadings judgment on the pleadings is not appropriate because of the necessity of looking outside the pleadings to resolve the issue. **Herbert v. Honest Bingo,** Op. No. 5365, 18 P3d 43 (Alaska 2001).

Trial court did not err in dismissing mother's suit against school board regarding its awarding of a school transportation contract where the court found that the mother did not have citizen-taxpayer standing. **Ruckle v. Anchorage Sch. Dist.,** Op. No. 5784, 85 P.3d 1030.

Insured's motion for judgment on the pleadings was properly granted where an insurance policy clearly did not exclude the mother, who was insured under the policy, from uninsured/ underinsured motorist coverage; she could recover for negligent infliction of emotional distress resulting from the death of her son, an occupant of the insured vehicle. **Allstate Ins. Co. v. Teel,** Op. No. 5832, 100 P.3d 2 (Alaska 2004).

In a landlord-tenant dispute, tenant argued that the superior court's findings were not sufficiently clear to meet standards under Alaska R. Civ. P. 52, but findings of fact and conclusions of law were unnecessary on decisions of motions under this rule or Rule 52, or any other motion except as provided in Rule 41(b). **Fyffe v. Wright,** Op. No. 5819 (Alaska 2004).

II. Presentation of Defenses.

A. Waiver.

The defense of non-payment of corporate taxes and filing of corporate records is waived if not raised sufficiently. **Brown v. Music, Inc.,** Op. No. 25, 359 P2d 295 (Alaska 1961).

Where defendant contended on appeal that plaintiff could not bring an action for a debt defendant owed to a partnership without joining all partners or alleging an assignment of the debt to plaintiff, defendant was held to be required to point that out specifically in his answer and, by failing to do so, he waived the objection. **Smith v. Sellar,** Op. No. 88, 371 P2d 809 (Alaska 1962).

Ordinarily, defects in venue are waived by the failure of a defendant to make a timely motion for change of venue. No inquiry into reasons for failure to make such a motion is normally entertained. **Aguchak v. Montgomery Ward Co., Inc.,** Op. No. 1026, 520 P2d 1352 (Alaska 1974).

Where a novation is not properly pleaded as an affirmative defense, it will be considered waived. **Kupka v. Morey,** Op. No. 1197, 541 P2d 740 (Alaska 1975).

The defense of lack of personal jurisdiction must be pleaded either on the answer or by motion or be waived. **Morrow v. New Moon Homes, Inc.,** Op. No. 1253, 548 P2d 279 (Alaska 1976).

When defense of statute of limitations is not pled as required by Civil Rule 8(c), it is waived by operation of Civil Rule 12(h). **Barrett v. Byrnes,** Op. No. 1340, 556 P2d 1254 (Alaska 1976).

Trial court properly rejected defendant's argument that since he did not protest the insufficiency of process or its service, the defect was waived, triggering the running of the speedy-trial period; since defendant was not asserting insufficiency of process as a defense to prosecution, the rule authorizing waiver of any defect in service of process did not apply. **Hayes v. State,** Op. No. 1031, 790 P2d 713 (Alaska App. 1990).

B. Non-waiver.

Where giving notice of an employee's claim is, by agreement of the parties a condition precedent to recovery on the claim, the employee-plaintiff must plead performance of the conditions and the defendant employer is not required to plead lack of notice as an affirmative defense; failure of defendant to plead lack of notice is not a waiver of the defense. **Inman v. Clyde Hall Drilling,** Op. No. 73, 369 P2d 498 (Alaska 1962).

The defenses of failure to state a claim for relief and failure to join an indispensable party may be raised at any time and are not waived by a delay in making the objection. **Burns v. Anchorage Funeral Chapel,** Op. No. 773, 495 P2d 70 (Alaska 1972).

A statute of limitation's defense is not waived if made by way of motion in lieu of pleadings. **Blake v. Gilbert,** Op. No. 2947, 702 P2d 631 (Alaska 1985).

III. Failure to State a Claim.

A. Considerations by Court.

A motion to dismiss for failure to state a claim upon which relief can be granted tests the legal sufficiency of the complaint's allegations, and well-pleaded allegations, are deemed admitted for purposes of the motion, but unwarranted factual inferences and conclusions of law are not considered admitted in resolving the merits of such motion. **Dworkin v. First National Bank of Fairbanks,** Op. No. 499, 444 P2d 777 (Alaska 1968).

In reviewing a lower court's dismissal of a complaint for failure to state a claim upon which relief can be granted the Supreme Court will not consider matters extraneous to the complaint. **Dworkin v. First National Bank of Fairbanks,** Op. No. 499, 444 P2d 777 (Alaska 1968).

An order dismissing a complaint for the failure to state a claim for which relief can be granted is appealable where it is clear that the trial court determined that the complaint could not be amended so as to prevent future dismissals, thereby preventing the claimant from proceeding. **Nizinski v. Currington,** Op. No. 982, 517 P2d 754 (Alaska 1973).

Normally, the defense of privilege must be asserted as an affirmative defense to a libel claim. However, privilege is properly before the court on a motion to dismiss for failure to state a claim for which relief can be granted, where the complaint itself clearly alleges or shows the existence of circumstances creating the privilege. **Nizinski v. Currington,** Op. No. 982, 517 P2d 754 (Alaska 1973).

Although normally a motion to dismiss for failure to state a claim for which relief can be granted is determined solely on the basis of the pleadings, the court may also consider public record. **Nizinski v. Currington,** Op. No. 982, 517 P2d 754 (Alaska 1973).

Statutes which require a party to plead and prove the existence of an occupational license make the existence of such a license a necessary element of a cause of action. The general defense of failing to state a claim sufficiently raises the issue. **Sumner Development Corp. v. Shivers,** Op. No. 984, 517 P2d 757 (Alaska 1974).

The court has complete discretion to determine whether or not to accept any material beyond the pleadings that is offered in conjunction with a Rule 12(b)(6) motion. **Martin v. Mears,** Op. No. 1958, 602 P2d 421 (Alaska 1979).

Where court dismissed complaint for failure to state a claim upon which relief could be granted without entering a final judgment dismissing the action and without specifying that the complaint could be amended, and where the complaint could not be amended so as to satisfy either of the possible grounds under which is was dismissed, the dismissal was final and appealable under Appellate Rule 5. **Clary v. Stack Steel and Supply Co.,** Op. No. 2093, 611 P2d 80 (Alaska 1980).

In determining the sufficiency of a stated claim, it is enough that the complaint set forth allegations of fact consistent with and appropriate to some enforceable cause of action, and well pleaded allegations of the complaint are deemed admitted for purposes of a motion to dismiss for failure to state a claim upon which relief can be granted. **Linck v. Barokas & Martin,** Op. No. 2701, 667 P2d 171 (Alaska 1983).

If, within the framework of the complaint, evidence may be introduced which will sustain a grant of relief to the plaintiff, the complaint is sufficient. **Linck v. Barokas & Martin,** Op. No. 2701, 667 P2d 171 (Alaska 1983).

Trial court's error in granting a Rule 12(b)(6) motion to dismiss without expressly indicating whether it had considered or excluded matters submitted outside the pleadings did not require a remand. **Brice v. State, Div. of Forest, Land & Water,** Op. No. 2731, 669 P2d 1311 (Alaska 1983).

A complaint should not be dismissed unless it appears beyond doubt that the plaintiff can prove no set of facts in support of his claim which would entitle him to relief. **Shooshanian v. Wagner,** Op. No. 2747, 672 P2d 455 (Alaska 1983).

Where trial court considered matters outside the pleadings in deciding to dismiss a suit upon the court's own motion for failure to state a claim upon which relief could be granted, the motion should have been treated as one for summary judgment; the reviewing court chose to treat the dismissal as a judgment on the pleadings and confined review to the issue of whether plaintiff did fail to state a claim upon which relief could be granted, since treating the trial court's sua sponte dismissal as a motion for summary judgment would have denied plaintiff certain procedural safeguards relevant to summary judgments. **Shooshanian v. Wagner,** Op. No. 2747, 672 P2d 455 (Alaska 1983).

The appellate court will accept as true all well-pleaded material allegations of a nonmoving party in its review of a dismissal on the pleadings. **J & L Diversified Ent. v. Anchorage,** Op. No. 3173, 736 P2d 349 (Alaska 1987).

Plaintiff's allegations must be viewed as true in reviewing dismissal of claim for failure to state a claim upon which relief could be granted. **Croft v. Wicker,** Op. No. 3183, 737 P2d 789 (Alaska 1987).

A complaint is subject to dismissal under this rule if an affirmative defense appears clearly on the face of the pleading. **Aspen Exploration Corp. v. Sheffield,** Op. No. 3189, 739 P2d 150 (Alaska 1987).

If, as a matter of law, the trial court determines in a tort action against a public official that the immunity of the public official from suit should be absolute, then allegations of improper motive become irrelevant and the case should be dismissed for insufficiency of the complaint; if, on the other hand, the court determines that only qualified immunity is appropriate, injury into motive becomes relevant, in which case properly pled allegations of malice or corruption should generally withstand a motion to dismiss for failure to state a claim. **Aspen Exploration Corp. v. Sheffield,** Op. No. 3189, 739 P2d 150 (Alaska 1987).

If the trial court fails to treat a motion to dismiss for failure to state a claim on which relief can be granted as a motion for summary judgment when matters outside the pleadings have been presented and not excluded, the appellate court may reverse and remand for proper consideration, or may review the trial court's decision as if the motion for dismissal had been granted after exclusion of outside materials, or as if summary judgment had been granted after conversion of the motion to dismiss into one for summary judgment. **Reed v. Municipality of Anchorage,** Op. No. 3218, 741 P2d 1181 (Alaska 1987).

Where trial court on a motion to dismiss for failure to state a claim upon which relief can be granted did not exclude materials presented outside the pleadings, it was under a mandatory duty to treat the motion as one for summary judgment and to dispose of it after giving the parties a reasonable opportunity to present all materials pertinent to a summary judgment motion. **Reed v. Municipality of Anchorage,** Op. No. 3218, 741 P2d 1181 (Alaska 1987).

Supreme Court reviews de novo an order dismissing a complaint for failure to state a claim. **Kollodge v. State,** Op. No. 3342, 757 P2d 1024 (Alaska 1988).

If a trial court considers matters outside the pleadings, it must treat a motion to dismiss for failure to state a claim as a motion for summary judgment; if the trial court does not state whether or not it excluded evidence outside the pleadings, the appellate court may remand for proper consideration, review the decision as if the motion for failure to state a claim was granted after exclusion of the outside materials, or review the decision as if the trial court granted a motion for summary judgment. **Homeward Bound v. Anchorage School Dist.,** Op. No. 3589, 791 P2d 610 (Alaska 1990).

In a claim for intentional infliction of emotional distress, the trial court must make a threshold determination whether the severity of the emotional distress and the conduct of the offending party warrant such a claim; to be legally viable, the claim must meet this standard rather than the lower standard for stating a claim usually applicable under this rule. **Beard v. Baum,** Op. No. 3620, 796 P2d 1344 (Alaska 1990).

Where trial court did not explicitly exclude outside materials in granting motion to dismiss for failure to state claim upon which relief could be granted, reviewing court could review dismissal order as if trial court had excluded the outside materials or it could review dismissal order as if trial court had converted the motion to dismiss into one for summary judgment. **Alaska Nat. Ins. Co. v. Jones,** Op. No. 5215, 993 P2d 424 (Alaska 1999).

Motion to dismiss for failure to state a claim upon which relief can be granted is viewed with disfavor and should rarely be granted. **Guerrero v. Alaska Housing Finance Corp.,** Op. No. 5301, 6 P3d 250 (Alaska 2000).

A complaint survives a motion to dismiss for failure to state a claim upon which relief can be granted if it alleges even a single set of facts consistent with and appropriate to some enforceable cause of action. **Guerrero v. Alaska Housing Finance Corp.,** Op. No. 5301, 6 P3d 250 (Alaska 2000).

Failure to file a complaint within the statute of limitations is grounds for a motion to dismiss for failure to state a claim upon which relief can be granted. **Hutton v. Realty Executives, Inc.,** Op. No. 5351, 14 P3d 977 (Alaska 2000).

A complaint should not be dismissed for failure to state a claim upon which relief can be granted unless it appears beyond doubt that the plaintiff can prove no set of facts in support of the claims that would entitle the plaintiff to relief. **Angnabooguk v. State,** Op. No. 5431, 26 P3d 447 (Alaska 2001).

In considering an appeal from a dismissal under Rule 12(b)(6), the Supreme Court applies de novo review, presuming all factual allegations of the complaint to be true and making all reasonable inferences in favor of the non-moving party. **J & S Services, Inc. v. Tomter**, Op. No. 11375, 139 P.3d 544 (Alaska 2006).

Civ 12(b)(6)

To survive a motion for dismissal under Rule 12(b)(6), it is enough that the complaint set forth allegations of fact consistent with and appropriate to some enforceable cause of action. **J & S Services, Inc. v. Tomter**, Op. No. 11375, 139 P.3d 544 (Alaska 2006).

Motions to dismiss under Rule 12(b)(6) are viewed with disfavor and, unless it appears beyond doubt that the plaintiff can prove no set of facts in support of his claim which would entitle him to relief, the motion should be denied. **Division of Family and Youth Serv. v. Native Village of Curyung,** Op. No. 11355, 151 P.3d 388 (Alaska 2006).

In determining the sufficiency of the stated claim in a 12(b)(6) motion, it is enough that the complaint set forth allegations of fact consistent with some enforceable cause of action on any possible theory. **State, Dept. of Health and Social Services, Div. of Family and Youth Services v. Native Village of Curyung,** Op. No. 11355, 151 P.3d 388 (Alaska 2006).

B. Decisions.

Motion to dismiss a complaint for failure to state a claim upon which relief can be granted should be denied if a complaint states a claim upon which some relief may be granted, even though the relief demanded may not be the kind to which the party is in fact entitled to obtain. **Miller v. Johnson,** Op. No. 70, 370 P2d 171 (Alaska 1962).

Where in an alleged wrongful death case the complaint and two amended complaints did not clearly show if the case should not be brought under a workmen's compensation act rather than under the wrongful death statute, but the trial court had permitted plaintiff to file a third amended complaint which set forth that this was an action brought under the wrongful death statute and the decedents were guest passengers on the defendant's airplane, the defendant never filed an answer to this third amended complaint nor did he ever produce any evidence in opposition thereto. It did not appear with certainty that plaintiff was not entitled to any relief which could be proved in support of his claim and it was error for the court to dismiss the action on the basis of failure to state a claim under which relief can be granted. **Lieb v. Interior Enterprises, Inc.,** Op. No. 244, 395 P2d 32 (Alaska 1964).

Where injured crew member of vessel moored to the defendant's dock alleged that defendant was negligent in failing to fulfill its duty of furnishing Jacob's ladders for use of plaintiff, the complaint stated a claim for relief and dismissal of the action was error. **Shannon v. City of Anchorage,** Op. No. 416, 429 P2d 17 (Alaska 1967).

The dismissal of a complaint in which the plaintiff requests that the mortgage lien be adjudged paramount and be foreclosed is proper for failure to state a claim upon which relief can be granted where the complaint does not disclose adequate information as to the basis for the claim. **Dworkin v. First National Bank of Fairbanks,** Op. No. 499, 444 P2d 777 (Alaska 1968).

A change in teachers' salaries brought about by contract renegotiation did not abuse any vested rights entitled to judicial protection; accordingly, the trial court's dismissal of a complaint by two teachers against the school district for denial of a salary increase allegedly due them was proper. **Rouse v. Anchorage School Dist.,** Op. No. 2106, 613 P2d 263 (Alaska 1980).

Allegations in building owners' complaint against manufacturer and installer of formaldehyde foam insulation that they relied upon express representations by the manufacturer and installer as to the properties and characteristics of insulation which turned out to be false, reducing the value of the building and the number of customers to the building, stated a claim upon which relief could be granted. **Shooshanian v. Wagner,** Op. No. 2747, 672 P2d 455 (Alaska 1983).

Where complaint made clear that defendants were a municipality and its employees, and that the claim was one for damages based upon the defendant's appeal of a platting board decision and the delay thereby caused, the complaint was properly dismissed for failure to state a claim for relief, since statutory immunity provided an affirmative defense for municipalities against such damage actions. **J & L Diversified Ent. v. Anchorage,** Op. No. 3173, 736 P2d 349 (Alaska 1987).

Claim against governor of Alaska for defamation was improperly dismissed for failure to state a claim upon which relief could be granted, since public officials have only a qualified immunity from defamation actions. **Aspen Exploration Corp. v. Sheffield,** Op. No. 3189, 739 P2d 150 (Alaska 1987).

Absence of findings of fact and conclusions of law did not prevent a dismissal under Alaska R. Civ. P. 12(b)(6) from having res judicata effect where the reviewing court could infer the trial court's reasons for the ruling on the merits from its subsequent opinion denying attorney's fees. **Alaska Wildlife Alliance v. State,** Op. No. 5771, 74 P.3d 201 (Alaska 2003).

Dismissal of parents' tort actions against a Native village association for injuries their children sustained was improper as the association, a nonprofit corporation, was not entitled to the protection of the villages' tribal sovereign immunity. **Runyon v. Ass'n of Vill. Council Presidents,** Op. No. 5776, 84 P.3d 437 (Alaska 2003).

To survive a motion to dismiss under Rule 12(b)(6), a complaint need only allege a set of facts consistent with and appropriate to some cause of action. **Catholic Bishop of Northern Alaska v. Does 1-6**, Op. No. 11295, 141 P.3d 719 (Alaska 2006).

Prisoner's constitutional complaint against state corrections contractor could not be dismissed for failure to state a claim under Rule 12(b)(6) where prisoner's brief argued that contractor's actions "violated Alaska inmate's constitutional rights." Where the essence of a pro se litigant's argument is easily discerned from his briefs, the trial court should consider the pro se litigant's argument, provided that the applicable law is well established and the opposing party would not be prejudiced by the court's consideration of the issue. **Rathke v. Corrections Corp. of America, Inc.**, Op. No. 11885, 153 P.3d 303 (Alaska 2007).

IV. Indispensable Party.

Where as part of an agreement in which landowners were to convey land to a corporation in return for stock and a loan, and in which the defendant and a third party to the agreement were each to receive one third of the corporation's stock, the third party is an "indispensable party" to the landowners' action for recision and reconveyance. However, since the corporation and the defendant were foreclosed because of their failure to raise the indispensable party issue at trial from asking the court to weight the dangers of their being subjected to inconsistent decisions, and in view of the third party's failure to intervene despite his knowledge of the scope of relief sought in the litigation, defendant and the corporation are estopped, by the virtue of the third party's interest required that the judgment be set aside. **Padgett v. Theus,** Op. No. 692, 484 P2d 697 (Alaska 1971).

The court reviewing a judgment entered in an action in which an indispensable party was not joined will consider the ramifications of its failure to raise the indispensable party issue at the trial, the significance of the fact that a binding judgment has been entered, and the justice and feasibility of fashioning appropriate relief at the appellate level in order to lessen or avoid any substantial prejudice to the indispensable party flowing from the trial court's judgment. **Padgett v. Theus,** Op. No. 692, 484 P2d 697 (Alaska 1971).

While, in general, only those parties to a contract whose interests might be affected need be joined in an action based on the contract, in actions for recision all parties are indispensable unless the interest of those present are completely separable from the interests of those absent. **Padgett v. Theus,** Op. No. 692, 484 P2d 697 (Alaska 1971).

V. Motions for Summary Judgment.

Under Rule 8(c) of the [Federal] Rules of Civil Procedure affirmative defenses must be pleaded, but the court may grant a motion for judgment on the pleadings and if matters outside the pleadings are presented the motion shall be treated as one for summary judgment under [Federal] R. Civ. P. 56

and all parties must be given reasonable opportunity to present all matters pertinent to such motion, and the party against whom the motion is made may apply to the court for further time to prepare his resistance to the motion under Rule 6(b). **Mitchell v. Land,** Op. No. 19, 355 P2d 682 (Alaska 1960).

When matters outside pleadings are presented to trial court and not excluded, motion for judgment on the pleadings will be treated as a motion for summary judgment. **Adams v. State,** Op. No. 1318, 555 P2d 235 (Alaska 1976).

The terms of Rule 12(b) make conversion into a motion for summary judgment mandatory whenever matters outside the pleadings are presented to and not affirmatively excluded by the court. **Marlin v. Mears,** Op. No. 1958, 602 P2d 421 (Alaska 1979).

When material outside the pleadings is presented to the trial court, a motion to dismiss is automatically converted into one for summary judgment unless the court "affirmatively" and "expressly" rules that it is not considering evidence outside the pleadings. **Adkins v. Nabors Alaska Drilling, Inc.,** Op. No. 2056, 609 P2d 15 (Alaska 1980).

Given the narrow scope of the materials outside of the pleadings which were consulted by the superior court and appellants' failure to show any prejudice occurring to them as a result of the court's unarticulated conversion of a Rule 12(b)(6) motion to a motion for summary judgment, court's error in not expressly indicating whether it had considered or excluded matters submitted outside the pleadings was harmless. **Brice v. State, Div. of Forest, Land & Water,** Op. No. 2731, 669 P2d 1311 (Alaska 1983).

Where trial court considered matters outside the pleadings in deciding to dismiss a suit upon the court's own motion for failure to state a claim upon which relief could be granted, the motion should have been treated as one for summary judgment; the reviewing court chose to treat the dismissal as a judgment on the pleadings and confined review to the issue of whether plaintiff did fail to state a claim upon which relief could be granted, since treating the trial court's sua sponte dismissal as a motion for summary judgment would have denied plaintiff certain procedural safeguards relevant to summary judgments. **Shooshanian v. Wagner,** Op. No. 2747, 672 P2d 455 (Alaska 1983).

If a trial court considers matters outside the pleadings, it must treat a motion to dismiss for failure to state a claim as a motion for summary judgment; if the trial court does not state whether or not it excluded evidence outside the pleadings, the appellate court may remand for proper consideration, review the decision as if the motion for failure to state a claim was granted after exclusion of the outside materials, or review the decision as if the trial court granted a motion for summary judgment. **Homeward Bound v. Anchorage School Dist.,** Op. No. 3589, 791 P2d 610 (Alaska 1990).

If matters outside pleadings are presented in motion to dismiss for failure to state claim upon which relief may be granted, and trial court fails to state expressly what materials it considered, appellate court may remand for proper consideration, review decision as if motion was granted after exclusion of outside materials, or review decision as if trial court granted motion for summary judgment. **Andrews v. Wade & DeYoung, Inc., P.C.,** Op. No. 4088, 875 P2d 89 (Alaska 1994).

Client's malpractice claim was not compulsory counterclaim in attorney's fee recovery action, although both arose from same litigation, because trial court in fee recovery action converted motion to dismiss to motion for summary judgment without notice, thereby depriving client of reasonable opportunity to present all material pertinent to such motion. **Andrews v. Wade & DeYoung, Inc., P.C.,** Op. No. 4088, 875 P2d 89 (Alaska 1994).

Trial court committed reversible error by converting defendant's motion for judgment on the pleadings to motion for summary judgment without giving plaintiff's notice and opportunity to oppose the motion as a motion for summary judgment; on remand, trial court had option to treat motion as motion for summary judgment, as long as it complied with requirements of Civil Rule 56, or to treat motion as motion for judgment on the pleadings, excluding all matters outside the pleadings. **Demmert v. Kootznoowoo, Inc.,** Op. No. 5006, 960 P2d 606 (Alaska 1998).

Party's Rule 12(b)(6) motion to dismiss due to the running of the applicable statute of limitations was denied because under the discovery rule, the date on which the statute of limitations begins to run is a question of fact and the possibility could not be ruled out that evidence may be introduced that would show that the statute of limitations had not run. **Catholic Bishop of Northern Alaska v. Does 1-6,** Op. No. 11295, 141 P.3d 719 (Alaska 2006).

VI. Service.

Service by mail is complete upon mailing regardless of whether the service is timely received. **Jefferson v. Spenard Builder's Supply, Inc.,** Op. No. 51, 366 P2d 714 (Alaska 1961).

The State-Operated School System is a state agency for purposes of service of process. **Alaska State-Operated School System v. Mueller,** Op. No. 1157, 536 P2d 99 (Alaska 1975).

Rule 13. Counterclaim and Cross—Claim.

(a) **Compulsory Counterclaims.** A pleading shall state as a counterclaim any claim which at the time of serving the pleading the pleader has against any opposing party, if it arises out of the transaction or occurrence that is the subject matter of the opposing party's claim and does not require for its adjudication the presence of third parties of whom the court cannot acquire jurisdiction. But the pleader need not state the claim if (1) at the time the action was commenced the claim was the subject of another pending action, or (2) the opposing party brought suit upon the claim by attachment or other process by which the court did not acquire jurisdiction to render a personal judgment on that claim, and the pleader is not stating any counterclaim under this Rule 13.

(b) **Permissive Counterclaims.** A pleading may state as a counterclaim any claim against an opposing party not arising out of the transaction or occurrence that is the subject matter of the opposing party's claim.

(c) **Counterclaim Exceeding Opposing Claim.** A counterclaim may or may not diminish or defeat the recovery sought by the opposing party. It may claim relief exceeding in amount or different in kind from that sought in the pleading of the opposing party.

(d) **Counterclaim Against the State.** These rules shall not be construed to enlarge beyond the limits now fixed by law the right to counterclaims or to claim credits against the state or an officer or agency thereof.

(e) **Counterclaim Maturing or Acquired After Pleading.** A claim which either matured or was acquired by the pleader after serving a pleading may, with the permission of the court, be presented as a counterclaim by supplemental pleading.

(f) **Omitted Counterclaim.** When a pleader fails to set up a counterclaim through oversight, inadvertence or excusable neglect or when justice requires, the pleader may by leave of court set up the counterclaim by amendment.

(g) **Cross—Claim Against Co-Party.** A pleading may state as a cross-claim any claim by one party against a co-party arising out of the transaction or occurrence that is the subject matter either of the original action or of a counterclaim therein or relating to any property that is the subject matter of the original action. Such cross-claim may include a claim that the party against whom it is aimed is or may be liable to the cross-claimant for all or part of a claim asserted in the action against the cross-claimant.

(h) **Joinder of Additional Parties.** Persons other than those made parties to the original action may be made parties to a counterclaim or cross-claim in accordance with the provisions of Rules 19 and 20.

(i) **Separate Trials—Separate Judgment.** If the court orders separate trials as provided in Rule 42(b), judgment on a counterclaim or cross-claim may be rendered in accordance with the terms of Rule 54(b) when the court has jurisdiction so to do, even if the claims of the opposing party have been dismissed or otherwise disposed of.

(Adopted by SCO 5 October 9, 1959; amended by SCO 258 effective November 15, 1976; and by SCO 1153 effective July 15, 1994)

Cross References

(d) **CROSS REFERENCE:** AS 09.60.050; AS 09.50.250

(e) **CROSS REFERENCE:** AS 09.68.020

Annotations

Cases

A compulsory counterclaim is required to be pleaded and proved in the first action between the parties and cannot be made the subject of another action against the former plaintiff. **Wells v. Noey,** Op. No. 286, 399 P2d 217 (Alaska 1965).

Fact that prayers for relief as to counterclaim in a previous action and for relief in the complaint in a subsequent action between the same parties were not the same, was not the criterion to determine whether the claims for relief were the same. **Wells v. Noey,** Op. No. 286, 399 P2d 217 (Alaska 1965).

If in a previous action between the same parties to quiet title to the same real property plaintiff had proceeded on a theory of adverse possession for seven years and the defendant in the previous action had claimed in a counterclaim that the tax deed alleged to be "color of title," was "illegal, erroneous and void," but no evidence was introduced pro and con regarding the counterclaim in the first action this was a compulsory counterclaim abandoned at the trial, and regardless of the fact that plaintiff's possession as proved in the first action fell short of being adverse for a sufficient period of time, the defendant in the previous action could not sue the former plaintiff in a second action to remove a cloud on the title on grounds of invalidity of the tax deed. **Wells v. Noey,** Op. No. 286, 399 P2d 217 (Alaska 1965).

Res judicata and collateral estoppel do not bar a claim that might have been asserted against impleaded party in a prior action. **Drickersen v. Drickersen,** Op. No. 1228, 546 P2d 162 (Alaska 1976).

Appellate review of a court order of attorney's fees to the prevailing party in a dismissed third-party action was warranted where the court departed from the accepted and usual course of proceedings in dismissing the claim rather than either severing it from the main action or ordering the pleadings amended and the purported third-party defendants joined as additional counterclaim defendants. **Aleut Corp. v. Rogers,** Op. No. 2212, 619 P2d 472 (Alaska 1980).

Court erred in not allowing as untimely appellant's cross-claim for indemnity against a co-party where appellant's indemnity claims were derivative of claims made against it by plaintiff, since appellant was in no position to allege its new indemnity theories until plaintiff filed a long-delayed amendment to the complaint. **Vertecs Corp. v. Reichhold Chemicals, Inc.,** Op. No. 2730, 671 P2d 1273 (Alaska 1983).

Motion by defendant, the obligor on a promissory note, to join credit union as a third party defendant, was improper, since the credit union had no obligation to indemnify the defendant for any liability to plaintiffs; rather, the motion was essentially a counterclaim against plaintiffs as assignees of defendant's promissory note to the credit union; accordingly, the trial court had discretionary authority to join the credit union as a defendant to the counterclaim, but failure to do so was harmless error, since the joinder motion was untimely and since relief was granted on the counterclaim despite absence of the credit union as a party. **Jackson v. Nangle,** Op. No. 2773, 677 P2d 242 (Alaska 1984).

A claim for contribution is substantively separate from the underlying tort and does not arise until the contribution claimant has paid more than his or her proportionate share of the total claim. **Providence Washington Ins. C. v. McGee,** Op. No. 3397, 764 P2d 712 (Alaska 1988).

In negligence action arising out of automobile accident, contribution claim against joint tortfeasor was not a compulsory counterclaim because it did not accrue until after the last pleading was filed in that action, when one of the claimants settled her claim. **Providence Washington Ins. C. v. McGee,** Op. No. 3397, 764 P2d 712 (Alaska 1988).

This rule does not require tort actions between married persons to be litigated in a divorce proceeding. **Nelson v. Jones,** Op. No. 3561, 787 P2d 1031 (Alaska 1990).

When State sued borrower to collect on defaulted loans, and borrower responded by filing Chapter 11 bankruptcy proceeding, borrower, but for that petition, would have been required to file his lender liability claims against the State as compulsory counterclaims in the state court proceeding; because he failed to disclose his claims during the bankruptcy proceeding, the claims were barred by the doctrines of equitable and quasi estoppel. **Wright v. State,** Op. No. 3802, 824 P2d 718 (Alaska 1992).

Client's malpractice claim was not compulsory counterclaim in attorney's fee recovery action, although both arose from same litigation, because trial court in fee recovery action converted motion to dismiss to motion for summary judgment without notice, thereby depriving client of reasonable opportunity to present all material pertinent to such motion. **Andrews v. Wade & DeYoung, Inc., P.C.,** Op. No. 4088, 875 P2d 89 (Alaska 1994).

Claim is not compulsory if it is not mature at time party serves its pleading. **Andrews v. Wade & DeYoung, Inc., P.C.,** Op. No. 4923, 950 P2d 574 (Alaska 1997).

Although claim which either matures or is acquired by pleader after pleading is served may with court's permission be presented as counterclaim by supplemental pleading, claim is permissive, not mandatory. **Andrews v. Wade & DeYoung, Inc., P.C.,** Op. No. 4923, 950 P2d 574 (Alaska 1997).

Action against State by purchaser under Alaska land lottery sales program for breach of contract because she received quitclaim deed rather than patent from State's assignee was not sufficiently related to subsequent quite title action brought by assignee against purchaser following missed installment payments on contract to make quiet title action a compulsory counterclaim in contract suit. **Ellingstad v. State Dept. of Nat. Res.,** Op. No. 5120, 979 P2d 1000, 498 P2d 702 (Alaska 1999).

Rule 14. Third-Party Practice.

(a) **When Defendant May Bring in Third Party.** At any time after commencement of the action a defending party, as a third-party plaintiff, may cause a summons and complaint to be served upon a person not a party to the action who is or maybe liable to the third-party plaintiff for all or part of the plaintiff's claim against the third-party plaintiff. The third-party plaintiff need not obtain leave to make the service if the third-party plaintiff files the third-party complaint not later than 10 days after serving the original answer. Otherwise the third-party plaintiff must obtain leave on motion upon notice to all parties to the action. The person served with the summons and third-party complaint, hereinafter called the third-party defendant, shall make any defenses to the third-party plaintiff's claim as provided in Rule 12 and any counterclaims against the third-party plaintiff and cross-claims against other third-party defendants as provided in Rule 13. The third-party defendant may assert against the plaintiff any defenses which the third-party plaintiff has to the plaintiff's claim. The third-party defendant may also assert any claim against the plaintiff arising out of the transaction or occurrence that is the subject matter of the plaintiff's claim against the third-party plaintiff. The plaintiff may assert any claim against the third-party defendant arising out of the transaction or occurrence that is the subject matter of the plaintiff's claim against the third-party plaintiff, and the third-party defendant thereupon shall assert any defenses as provided in Rule 12 and any counterclaims and cross-claims as provided in Rule 13. Any party may move to strike the third-party claim or for its severance or separate trial. A third-party defendant may proceed under this rule against any person not a party to the action who is or maybe liable to the third-party defendant for all or part of the claim made in the action against the third-party defendant.

(b) **When Plaintiff May Bring in Third Party.** When a counterclaim is asserted against the plaintiff, the plaintiff may cause a third party to be brought in under circumstances which under this rule would entitle a defendant to do so.

(c) **Equitable Apportionment.** For purposes of apportioning damages under AS 09.17.080, a defendant, as a third-party plaintiff, may follow the procedure of paragraph (a) to add as a third-party defendant any person whose fault may have been a cause of the damages claimed by the plaintiff. Judgment may be entered against a third-party defendant in favor of the plaintiff in accordance with the third-party defendant's respective percentage of fault, regardless of whether the plaintiff has asserted a direct claim against the third-party defendant.

(Adopted by SCO 5 October 9, 1959; amended by SCO 258 effective November 15, 1976; by SCO 1153 effective July 15, 1994; and by SCO 1200 effective July 15, 1995)

Annotations

Cases

The fact that an insurance company's agent is a party to an action brought by the insured against the agent and insurer does not preclude the insurer from impleading the agent when the agent, who has obtained a summary judgment against the insured, is no longer a party to action. **Austin v. Fulton Insurance Co.,** Op. No. 808, 498 P2d 702 (Alaska 1972).

Res judicata and collateral estoppel do not bar a claim that might have been asserted against impleaded party in a prior action. **Drickersen v. Drickersen,** Op. No. 1228, 546 P2d 162 (Alaska 1976).

Appellate review of a court order of attorney's fees to the prevailing party in a dismissed third-party action was warranted where the court departed from the accepted and usual course of proceedings in dismissing the claim rather than either severing it from the main action or ordering the pleadings amended and the purported third-party defendants joined as additional counterclaim defendants. **Aleut Corp. v. Rogers,** Op. No. 2212, 619 P2d 472 (Alaska 1980).

Motion by defendant, the obligor on a promissory note, to join a third-party defendant was meritorious, but any error in the trial court's denial of the motion was harmless, since the third party had already confessed liability to the obligor. **Jackson v. Nangle,** Op. No. 2773, 677 P2d 242 (Alaska 1984).

Trial court's decision denying leave to permit the filing of a third-party complaint more than ten days after service of the original answer was not an abuse of discretion. **Ross Laboratories v. Thies,** Op. No. 3125, 725 P2d 1076 (Alaska 1986).

Because AS 09.17.080 allows allocation of fault to a co-plaintiff as a party to the action without requiring defendant to implead the co-plaintiff as a third-party defendant and because defendant provided adequate notice of its intent to allocate fault to co-plaintiff, trial court did not err in reducing plaintiffs' recovery by co-plaintiff's allocation of fault despite defendant's failure to implead co-plaintiff as third-party defendant under this rule. **Fancyboy v. Alaska Village Elec. Co-Op.,** Op. No. 5153, 984 P2d 1128 (Alaska 1999).

Statute of limitations for tort actions does not apply to claims for equitable apportionment, thus third-party defendant who was sued for apportionment of fault under AS 09.17.080 after statute of limitations on plaintiff's underlying personal injury claim had run could nonetheless be liable to plaintiff for money damages. **Alaska General Alarm, Inc. v. Grinnell,** Op. No. 5263, 1 P3d 98 (Alaska 2000).

Where a seller allegedly installed dry-cleaning equipment and a water and percholoroethylene (PCE) separator system that facilitated spillage, leakage, and direction of PCE into the city sewer system, the purchasers' claim for equitable apportionment against the seller's successor failed because they were not attempting to add the successor as a third-party defendant in an existing lawsuit. **Berg v. Popham,** 412 F.3d 1122 (9th Cir. 2005).

Rule 15. Amended and Supplemental Pleadings.

(a) **Amendments.** A party may amend the party's pleading once as a matter of course at any time before a responsive pleading is served or, if the pleading is one to which no responsive pleading is permitted and the action has not been placed upon the trial calendar, the party may so amend it at any time within 20 days after it is served. Otherwise a party may amend the party's pleading only by leave of court or by written consent of the adverse party; and leave shall be freely given when justice so requires. A party shall plead in response to an amended pleading within the time remaining for response to the original pleading or within 10 days after service of the amended pleading, whichever period may be the longer, unless the court otherwise orders.

(b) **Amendments to Conform to the Evidence.** When issues not raised by the pleadings are tried by express or implied consent of the parties, they shall be treated in all respects as if they had been raised in the pleadings. Such amendment of the pleadings as may be necessary to cause them to conform to the evidence and to raise these issues may be made upon motion of any party at any time, even after judgment; but failure so to amend does not affect the result of the trial of these issues. If evidence is objected to at the trial on the ground that it is not within the issues made by the pleadings, the court may allow the pleadings to be amended and shall do so freely when the presentation of the merits of the action will be subserved thereby and the objecting party fails to satisfy the court that the admission of such evidence would prejudice the party in maintaining the party's action or defense upon the merits. The court may grant a continuance to enable the objecting party to meet such evidence.

(c) **Relation Back of Amendments.** Whenever the claim or defense asserted in the amended pleading arose out of the conduct, transaction or occurrence set forth or attempted to be set forth in the original pleading, the amendment relates back to the date of the original pleading. An amendment changing the party against whom a claim is asserted relates back if the foregoing provision is satisfied and, within the period provided by Rule 4(j) for service of the summons and complaint, that party (1) has received such notice of the institution of the action that the party will not be prejudiced in maintaining a defense on the merits, and (2) knew or should have known that, but for a mistake concerning the identity of the proper party, the action would have been brought against the party.

(d) **Supplemental Pleadings.** Upon motion of a party the court may, upon reasonable notice and upon such terms as are just, permit the party to serve a supplemental pleading setting forth transactions or occurrences or events which have happened since the date of the pleading sought to be supplemented. Permission may be granted even though the original pleading is defective in its statement of a claim for relief or defense. If the court deems it advisable that the adverse party plead to the supplemental pleading, it shall so order, specifying the time therefor.

(e) **Form.** Unless otherwise permitted by the court, every pleading to which an amendment is permitted as a matter of right or has been allowed by order of the court, must be retyped or reprinted and filed so that it will be complete in itself, including the exhibits, without reference to the superseded pleading. No pleading will be deemed to be amended until this subdivision of this rule has been complied with. All amended pleadings shall contain copies of all exhibits referred to in such amended pleadings. Permission may be obtained from the court, if desired, for the removal of any exhibit or exhibits attached to prior pleadings, in order that the same may be attached to the amended pleading.

(Adopted by SCO 5 October 9, 1959; amended by SCO 258 effective November 15, 1976; by SCO 1153 effective July 15, 1994; and by SCO 1571 effective October 15, 2005)

Annotations

Cases

I. In General.
II. Amendments — Court Discretion.
III. Issue of Consent.
IV. Relation Back.

I. In General.

Failure to amend pleading to conform to proof of estoppel submitted during trial was not fatal where the issue of estoppel was not controlling, since pleadings could be amended at any time to conform to proof. **Gilbert v. Sexton,** Op. No. 276, 401 P2d 300 (Alaska 1965).

A party should be granted leave to amend where there is no showing that the amendment will result in an injustice. **Estate of Thompson v. Mercedes-Benz, Inc.,** Op. No. 952, 514 P2d 1269 (Alaska 1973).

An amendment must arise from the same transaction as the original pleading. **Estate of Thompson v. Mercedes-Benz, Inc.,** Op. No. 952, 514 P2d 1269 (Alaska 1973).

Cross-claims will be allowed in the absence of a showing of injustice to someone or a delay of the court. **Estate of Thompson v. Mercedes-Benz, Inc.,** Op. No. 952, 514 P2d 1269 (Alaska 1973).

Prejudice to the opposing party, the most frequent reason for denying leave to amend, can result from the opposing party being put to an added expense, a more burdensome and lengthy trial, or if the issues being raised in the amendment are remote from the scope of the original case. **Estate of Thompson v. Mercedes-Benz, Inc.,** Op. No. 952, 514 P2d 1269 (Alaska 1973).

Amendment to a counterclaim was allowed during trial where omission of claim was oversight, opponent knew of claim, no continuance was sought by opponent to prepare, and amendment was necessary in order to have a presentation of the real issues in the case. **Van Horn Lodge, Inc. v. Ahearn,** Op. No. 1873, 596 P2d 1159 (Alaska 1979).

A party is not prejudiced simply because the opponent is more likely to succeed under the amended complaint. **Wright v. Vickaryous,** Op. No. 1886, 598 P2d 490 (Alaska 1979).

Amendment of complaint to change lease for years to month-to-month lease was change in theory only and did not prejudice defendant by placing new facts in issue. **Wright v. Vickaryous,** Op. No. 1886, 598 P2d 490 (Alaska 1979).

Where plaintiff filed suit on July 20 and the statute of limitations period expired on August 9, plaintiff's attempt to amend the complaint after August 9 to add a party defendant was denied where the latter did not learn of the lawsuit until after the statute of limitations period had expired. **Adkins v. Nabors Alaska Drilling, Inc.,** Op. No. 2056, 609 P2d 15 (Alaska 1980).

Appellate review of a court order of attorney's fees to the prevailing party in a dismissed third-party action was warranted where the court departed from the accepted and usual course of proceedings in dismissing the claim rather than either severing it from the main action or ordering the pleadings amended and the purported third-party defendants joined as additional counterclaim defendant. **Aleut Corp. v. Rogers,** Op. No. 2212, 619 P2d 472 (Alaska 1980).

An allowance of an amended pleading was in error where the adverse party was not accorded an appropriate opportunity to dispute the amendments concerning interest payments on a note. **Coleman v. Lofgren,** Op. No. 2418, 633 P2d 1365 (Alaska 1981).

Trial court erred in dismissing complaint for lack of subject matter jurisdiction due to failure of the complaint to allege that corporate defendant was "doing business" in Alaska; leave to amend the complaint should have been granted to allow plaintiff to cure the technical pleading deficiency. **Shooshanian v. Wagner,** Op. No. 2747, 672 P2d 455 (Alaska 1983).

Plaintiffs' motion to add a party defendant, filed 32 months after plaintiffs' first opportunity to amend the pleadings, was properly denied, where joinder would have required additional delays and substantial expense on the part of the additional defendant. **Shooshanian v. Wagner,** Op. No. 2747, 672 P2d 455 (Alaska 1983).

Where issue of liquidated damages was actually litigated at trial, the issue would be heard on appeal despite the failure to plead the defense. **Industrial Indemnity Co. v. Wick Const. Co.,** Op. No. 2791, 680 P2d 1100 (Alaska 1984).

Injured passenger whose claim against aircraft manufacturer was untimely could not intervene as a plaintiff in a consolidated case, the court refusing to allow a total stranger to the original plaintiff to avoid the statute of limitations by intervening in a suit timely filed. **Atkins v. DeHavilland Aircraft Co. of Canada,** Op. No. 2938, 699 P2d 352 (Alaska 1985).

Defendant's argument that civil judgment was improper because it contained a claim for lost profits and earnings not raised in the pleadings was rejected. Although plaintiff did fail to specifically allege loss of income in her complaint, she did allude to it in the papers supporting her motion for summary judgment on the issue of damages. Since the issue was never raised before the trial court, neither party moved to amend the pleadings, but the failure to amend did not affect the result of the trial. **Pletnikoff v. Johnson,** Op. No. 3399, 765 P2d 973 (Alaska 1988).

When a party requests leave to amend a pleading, the court is not required to make findings as to asserted claims of prejudice from the other side. **Revelle v. Marston,** Op. No. 4224, 898 P2d 917 (Alaska 1995).

Alaska follows the widely-used approach which, if undue prejudice would not be visited upon the opposing party, allows a litigant to raise new affirmative defenses at any time through a motion for summary judgment. **Gamble v. Northstore Partnership,** Op. No. 4291, 907 P2d 477 (Alaska 1995).

Defendants were prejudiced by the inability to present evidence as to the amount of rent due plaintiff, where the trial court allowed plaintiff to amend its pleadings after the close of evidence. **Alderman v. Iditarod Props., Inc.,** Op. No. 5486,32 P3d 373 (Alaska 2001).

Trial court must apply a balancing test to decide whether amendment of a pleading should be granted under Alaska R. Civ. P. 15(a), weighing the degree of prejudice to the opposing party against the hardship to the movant if the amendment is denied; trial court may also deny amendment when it is unduly delayed, offered in bad faith, or futile. **Alderman v. Iditarod Props., Inc.,** Op. No. 5486, 32 P3d 373 (Alaska 2001).

Application of Alaska R. Civ. P. 15(b) is appropriate in two general situations: when evidence supporting the amendment was offered at trial (1) with the opposing party's express or implied consent, or (2) over the opposing party's objection that the evidence is not within the issues raised by the pleadings. **Alderman v. Iditarod Props., Inc.,** Op. No. 5486, 32 P3d 373 (Alaska 2001).

II. Amendments — Court Discretion.

In a civil action for assault and battery the trial court's ruling to allow an amendment of defendant's answer so as to enable him to plead the affirmative defense of self-defense and to test his defense on the merits was consistent with the overall purpose of the civil rules. **Merrill v. Faltin,** Op. No. 425, 430 P2d 913 (Alaska 1967).

A trial court does not abuse its discretion in refusing to grant a defendant's motion to amend his answer where, after the plaintiff's motion for summary judgment had been noted for hearing on September 28, defendant files a motion to amend his answer to include defenses of duress, lack of consideration and unclean hands, noting it for hearing on October 5, which amended answer states proposed defenses in one-sentence conclusions containing no facts. **Barber v. Northern Heating Oil, Inc.,** Op. No. 512, 447 P2d 72 (Alaska 1968).

A trial court has discretion to grant or deny leave to amend, and the reviewing court will interfere with an exercise of that discretion only where it has been abused. **United States Fire Insurance Co. v. Schnabel,** Op. No. 852, 504 P2d 847 (Alaska 1972).

A trial court may allow whatever amendment may be necessary to rectify any deficiency in the pleadings. **Copper Valley Trading Co. v. Kratz,** Op. No. 927, 513 P2d 1113 (Alaska 1973).

Leave to amend should be liberally granted, but the trial judge has discretion whether to allow leave to amend. His ruling will be overturned only when there is an abuse of discretion. **Estate of Thompson v. Mercedes-Benz, Inc.,** Op. No. 952, 514 P2d 1269 (Alaska 1973).

In considering a motion for leave to amend, it is improper for a trial judge to consider only the statute of limitations. **Estate of Thompson v. Mercedes-Benz, Inc.,** Op. No. 952, 514 P2d 1269 (Alaska 1973).

Denial of relief from judgment based on trial court's conclusion that this rule does not allow complaint to be amended to add defendant after limitation period has run was not abuse of discretion such as to leave Supreme Court with definite and firm conclusion that a mistake had been made. **McCraken v. Davis,** Op. No. 1389, 560 P2d 771 (Alaska 1977).

An amended complaint need not be based on the identical conduct, transaction or occurrence set forth in the original pleading, but it must be sufficiently related to the conduct, transaction or occurrence originally set forth so as to avoid prejudice to the opposing party and to insure that the opposing party has notice of the nature of the claim from the beginning. **Norman v. Nichiro Gyogyo Kaisha, Ltd.,** Op. No. 2511, 645 P2d 191 (Alaska 1982).

Where the "conduct, transaction or occurrence" underlying the original complaint involved circumstances surrounding purchase and sale of company stock and the subsequent failure to pay for it, trial court did not err in refusing to allow complaint to be amended to include tort claims related to mismanagement or abandonment of the company. **Norman v. Nichiro Gyogyo Kaisha, Ltd.,** Op. No. 2511, 645 P2d 191 (Alaska 1982).

Where defendant did not plead estoppel as an affirmative defense, nor request an amendment of the pleadings to include estoppel, court did not err in refusing to permit defendant to present evidence of estoppel. **Stanton v. Fuchs,** Op. No. 2646, 660 P2d 1197 (Alaska 1983).

Even if defendant's reference to estoppel before trial amounted to a motion to amend the pleadings, the denial of that motion was within the trial court's discretion. **Stanton v. Fuchs,** Op. No. 2646, 660 P2d 1197 (Alaska 1983).

Trial court did not abuse its discretion by denying plaintiffs' motion to supplement their dismissed complaint with additional allegations of personal injury where granting the motion would have prejudiced the defendant due to an unreasonable delay by plaintiffs in filing the motion. **Shooshanian v. Wagner,** Op. No. 2747, 672 P2d 455 (Alaska 1983).

Dismissal of complaint for failure to state a claim upon which relief could be granted did not necessarily bar supplementing the complaint with additional allegations of personal injury. **Shooshanian v. Wagner,** Op. No. 2747, 672 P2d 455 (Alaska 1983).

Trial court has broad discretion in allowing or denying proposed amendments after the initial time limit has passed under either Civil Rule 15(a) or Civil Rule 15(d). **Rutledge v. Alyeska Pipeline Service Co.,** Op. No. 3141, 727 P2d 1050 (Alaska 1986).

Plaintiff's motion to amend wrongful discharge complaint to include a cause of action for interference with prospective employment was properly denied where the probability of a more lengthy trial involving different factual and legal issues and the necessity for more extensive discovery outweighed plaintiff's need to try the claims together. **Rutledge v. Alyeska Pipeline Service Co.,** Op. No. 3141, 727 P2d 1050 (Alaska 1986).

Superior court discretion to allow or refuse a party's request to amend the complaint after a responsive pleading has been filed will be overturned only when the reviewing court is left with a definite and firm conviction that the trial court erred. **Betz v. Chena Hot Springs Group,** Op. No. 3227, 742 P2d 1346 (Alaska 1987).

Trial court abused its discretion in not allowing plaintiffs to amend their antitrust claim to allege violation of AS 45.50.564 as well as 45.50.562 and in not allowing the amendment to relate back to the date of the original pleading. **Betz v. Chena Hot Springs Group,** Op. No. 3227, 742 P2d 1346 (Alaska 1987).

Where both the manufacturer and lessor of a crane were held strictly liable for injuries to workers caused by a defect in the design of the crane, trial court did not err in holding the lessor entitled to indemnification from the manufacturer where the manufacturer did not affirmatively plead the lessor's independent negligence, proof of which would have been necessary for the manufacturer to escape its indemnity obligation; furthermore, the trial court did not abuse its discretion in refusing to allow the manufacturer belatedly to amend its pleadings to allege negligence on the part of the lessor. **Koehring Mfg. v. Earthmovers of Fairbanks,** Op. No. 3390, 763 P2d 499 (Alaska 1988).

Mere mention in counterclaimant's answers to plaintiff's interrogatories of misrepresentation by the plaintiff did not require the trial court to allow the counterclaimant to amend its pleadings to claim misrepresentation. **Superior Fire Protection Company v. Du Alaska Company, Inc.,** Op. No. 3435, 772 P2d 1089 (Alaska 1989).

Denial of plaintiff's motion to amend its complaint to allege a new theory of legal liability, based on the same factual occurrence set out in the original complaint, was error; furthermore, defendant's contention that the amended complaint should not relate back to the date of the original complaint, thereby bringing the amended complaint within the statute of limitations, because it failed to give defendant timely notice of a change of legal theories, was rejected, since the original complaint, by notifying defendant of the occurrence giving rise to the action, gave the defendant all the notice that statutes of limitation are intended to afford. **Mogestra v. State,** Op. No. 3555, 785 P2d 1211 (Alaska 1990).

Given the substantial amount of time remaining before trial, superior court did not abuse its discretion either by granting plaintiff leave to amend his complaint or by implicitly rejecting defendant's claim of prejudice and request for attorney's fees and costs. **Revelle v. Marston,** Op. No. 4224, 898 P2d 917 (Alaska 1995).

Whether a litigant is unduly prejudiced by an opponent's post-answer attempt to obtain summary judgment on the basis of an affirmative defense not set forth in the pleadings invokes the same concerns as a motion to amend the pleadings with leave of the court. Several factors may bear upon a finding of prejudice, including added expense, a more burdensome and lengthy trial, or if the issues being raised are remote from the scope of the original case. **Gamble v. Northstore Partnership,** Op. No. 4291, 907 P2d 477 (Alaska 1995).

Where a proposed amendment to the pleadings challenges the trial court's subject matter jurisdiction, it is an abuse of discretion to deny the amendment. **Rodriquez v. Rodriquez,** Op. No. 4302, 908 P2d 1007 (Alaska 1995).

In an election contest, where the record showed that appellee candidate failed to disclose all of his assets under AS 39.50.030(b), judgment for the candidate was affirmed because denial of the voters' motion for leave to amend under Alaska R. Civ. P. 15(a) was proper because of prejudice to the opposing party, the late stage of the litigation, and the expedited trial schedule. **Grimm v. Wagoner,** Op. No. 5737, 77 P.3d 423 (Alaska 2003).

Supreme Court of Alaska adopts the rule that where a plaintiff demonstrates valid reasons for amending a pleading, he will be permitted to do so with leave of the court after an order of dismissal. **Ruckle v. Anchorage Sch. Dist.,** Op. No. 5784, 85 P.3d 1030 (Alaska 2004).

Trial court erred in denying a mother leave to amend her suit against a school board because of its award of a school transportation contract where she wished to assert that she had interest-injury standing because she had school-age children who would be riding the buses of the transportation provider selected by the district, was not futile. **Ruckle v. Anchorage Sch. Dist.,** Op. No. 5784, 85 P.3d 1030 (Alaska 2004).

Where employee, who was terminated by a grocery store after he refused to cut his hair, sued on the basis of race, religion, and gender discrimination, and the violation of his right to privacy, court abused its discretion by denying his motion to amend his complaint to allege claims for breach of the implied covenant of good faith and fair dealing, wrongful discharge, and common law privacy. **Miller v. Safeway, Inc.,** Op. No. 5849, 102 P.3d 282 (Alaska 2004).

When a clear mistake in the designation of a party is made, and insurer has knowledge of the mistake, there is a presumption under this rule that the insured had imputed knowledge that he was the correct party; the insured can rebut that presumption by showing that his interests conflict with the insurer, but absent such evidence an amended complaint substituting him as defendant relates back to the original filing date. **Phillips v. Gieringer,** Op. No. 5878, 108 P.3d 889 (Alaska 2005).

In an eviction action, a lessor was not allowed to amend its complaint to conform to the evidence because no modification issue was addressed at trial. **Tufco, Inc. v. Pac. Envtl. Corp.,** Op. No. 5904, 113 P.3d 668 (Alaska 2005).

The trial court has broad discretion to determine whether to allow a party to amend a pleading. **Larson v. Benediktsson**, Op. No. 11674, 152 P.3d 1159 (Alaska 2007).

An appellate court will reverse an order allowing amendment only when a review of the entire record leaves a firm and definite conviction that the trial court erred in its ruling. **Larson v. Benediktsson**, Op. No. 11674, 152 P.3d 1159 (Alaska 2007).

Where a party sought leave to include counterclaims in an amended answer and opposing party argued denial of amendment in part because the motion was untimely, the amendment was allowed where party's attorney had prepared and submitted the motion soon after being retained and the motion was filed shortly after the sixty-day deadline for amending as a matter of right had expired. **Larson v. Benediktsson**, Op. No. 11674, 152 P.3d 1159 (Alaska 2007).

III. Issue of Consent.

Where in an action brought for damages for breach of a contract of sale an issue of negligence was not raised in the pleadings, but such issue was tried with the implied consent of the parties, failure to amend pleadings to conform to evidence did not, under Civil Rule 15(b) affect the result of the trial of such issues and the court did not err in awarding damages to plaintiff on proof of negligence. **Harris v. Deveau,** Op. No. 164, 385 P2d 283 (Alaska 1963).

Though the court's statement, in a suit by an electric cooperative to recover reimbursement for the cost of relocating its power lines, that the cooperative was bound by its pleadings and could not be permitted to change its theory of recovery and rely on an easement by prescription instead of an easement by grant is erroneous since the defendant, by failing to object to the cooperative's introduction of evidence tending to prove an easement by prescription, waived its right to confine the issues, the error is harmless in view of the fact that the cooperative's proof of an easement by prescription was fatally deficient. **Golden Valley Electric Association, Inc. v. College Enterprises, Inc.,** Op. No. 556, 455 P2d 215 (Alaska 1969).

After the entry of a pretrial order stating that the issue to be tried was whether an electric cooperative, which sued for the reimbursement of the cost of relocating its power lines, had an easement by grant from a prior record owner, the plaintiff has no rights to introduce evidence of an easement by prescription in reply to the defendant's claim of trespass. Nonetheless, the plaintiff has no complaint since it was accorded, by reason of the defendant's failure to object to the plaintiff's introduction of evidence tending to prove an easement by prescription, an unrestricted right to introduce evidence of a prescriptive right. **Golden Valley Electric Association, Inc. v. College Enterprises, Inc.,** Op. No. 556, 455 P2d 215 (Alaska 1969).

Where an issue is not pleaded and it does not appear that the issue was tried by the consent of the party not raising the issue, the trial court is not required to give an instruction concerning the issue when requested by the party raising the issue. **Transamerica Title Insurance Co. v. Ramsey,** Op. No. 869, 507 P2d 492 (Alaska 1973).

When evidence is relevant to an issue already in a case and there is no indication that the party introducing evidence is seeking to introduce a new issue, it will not be considered as creating an implied consent to try the issue and does not justify amending the pleadings. **Transamerica Title Insurance Co. v. Ramsey,** Op. No. 869, 507 P2d 492 (Alaska 1973).

Even if the issue of fraud has not been raised in the pleadings, defendant will still be entitled to a review of the issue on appeal if the issue was tried by the express or implied consent of the parties. **Rollins v. Leibold,** Op. No. 910, 512 P2d 937 (Alaska 1973).

Where the plaintiff's counsel makes no objections to the defendant's motion for a directed verdict, based on a statutory presumption of fraud, on the ground that the issue had not been pleaded, but instead argues the issue, plaintiff will be deemed to have consented by implication to the trial of the issue. **Rollins v. Leibold,** Op. No. 910, 512 P2d 937 (Alaska 1973).

Where issue of statute of limitations was only introduced after plaintiff rested her case, it was not tried by implied consent. **Barrett v. Byrnes,** Op. No. 1340, 556 P2d 1254 (Alaska 1976).

Where issue of liquidated damages was actually litigated at trial, the issue would be heard on appeal despite the failure to plead the defense. **Industrial Indemnity Co. v. Wick Const. Co.,** Op. No. 2791, 680 P2d 1100 (Alaska 1984).

The failure to plead a theory of recovery is immaterial where that theory is tried with the express or implied consent of the appellants. **Sparks v. Gustafson,** Op. No. 3271, 750 P2d 338 (Alaska 1988).

Where defense counsel indicated at the beginning of trial that he viewed plaintiffs' claims as one for unjust enrichment and was prepared to try the case as such, and where testimony was then taken without objection on the elements necessary to prove unjust enrichment, the trial court did not err in deciding the case on an unjust enrichment theory even though that theory was not set forth in the complaint. **Sparks v. Gustafson,** Op. No. 3271, 750 P2d 338 (Alaska 1988).

Mere mention in counterclaimant's answers to plaintiff's interrogatories of misrepresentation by the plaintiff did not require the trial court to allow the counterclaimant to amend its pleadings to claim misrepresentation. **Superior Fire Protection Company v. Du Alaska Company, Inc.,** Op. No. 3435, 772 P2d 1089 (Alaska 1989).

Where a party raised the statute of limitations defense in its pretrial memorandum and in its opening remarks, and where the trial judge inquired into the issue before closing arguments and each party addressed substantive arguments on the merits of the defense to the court, the issue should have been considered tried by the implied consent of the parties and, therefore, considered part of the pleadings. **Oaksmith v. Brusich,** Op. No. 3434, 774 P2d 191 (Alaska 1989).

Party's failure to object to an opponent's passing mention of a potential new claim does not amount to implied consent to amend complaint to include that issue. **Belluomini v. Fred Meyer of Alaska, Inc.,** Op. No. 5218, 993 P2d 1009 (Alaska 1999).

In wrongful termination of employment action, employer's failure to object to employee's testimony that his at-will employment had been converted to contract employment did not imply that employer consented to trial on that issue, thus trial court did not err in denying employee's motion to amend his complaint to reflect contract theory of employment. **Belluomini v. Fred Meyer of Alaska, Inc.,** Op. No. 5218, 993 P2d 1009 (Alaska 1999).

IV. Relation Back.

The amendment of an administrator's complaint against a funeral home for wrongful interference with the right of a next of kin to preserve the body of a deceased, to add the next of kin as parties plaintiff, relates back to the date of the original complaint. In such situation, the two-year tort statute of limitations will not bar prosecution of the claim. **Burns v. Anchorage Funeral Chapel,** Op. No. 773, 495 P2d 70 (Alaska 1972).

A counterclaim should relate back under this rule if the counterclaim arises from the same transaction. The same test should be applied to an omitted cross-claim. **Estate of Thompson v. Mercedes-Benz, Inc.,** Op. No. 952, 514 P2d 1269 (Alaska 1973).

An amendment which changes the capacity in which a party brings an action will relate back. **Estate of Thompson v. Mercedes-Benz, Inc.,** Op. No. 952, 514 P2d 1269 (Alaska 1973).

Where plaintiff filed suit on July 20 and the statute of limitations period expired on August 9, plaintiff's attempt to amend the complaint after August 9 to add a party defendant was denied where the latter did not learn of the lawsuit until after the statute of limitations period had expired. **Adkins v. Nabors Alaska Drilling, Inc.,** Op. No. 2056, 609 P2d 15 (Alaska 1980).

Unfair Trade Practices claim in amended complaint arose out of the same transaction set forth in the original pleading; it therefore related back to the original claim, barring dismissal on statute of limitation grounds. **Shooshanian v. Wagner,** Op. No. 2747, 672 P2d 455 (Alaska 1983).

Injured aircraft passenger's amended complaint adding the name of the aircraft manufacturer did not relate back to the date of the filing of the original complaint because there was no mistake as to the true identity of the manufacturer. **Atkins v. DeHavilland Aircraft Co. of Canada,** Op. No. 2938, 699 P2d 352 (Alaska 1985).

Denial of plaintiff's motion to amend its complaint to allege a new theory of legal liability, based on the same factual occurrence set out in the original complaint, was error; further more, defendant's contention that the amended complaint should not relate back to the date of the original complaint, thereby bringing the amended complaint within the statute of limitations, because it failed to give defendant timely notice of a change of legal theories, was rejected, since the original complaint, by notifying defendant of the occurrence giving rise to the action, gave the defendant all the notice that statutes of limitation are intended to afford. **Mogestra v. State,** Op. No. 3555, 785 P2d 1211 (Alaska 1990).

The touchstone of whether amendment of a complaint to substitute or add a party relates back to the original complaint is fairness: does the substituted or additional party have fair notice of the cause of action, within the prescribed statutory period, such that the party's rights will not be prejudiced? **Farmer v. State,** Op. No. 3567, 788 P2d 43 (Alaska 1990).

Where a new party defendant has constructive notice of an action, imputed through the same attorney retained by existing parties to the action, and through no fault of the plaintiff the new party defendant's identity was unknown at the time of pleading, amendment of the complaint to add the new party defendant relates back to the date of the original complaint so long as the new party defendant is not prejudiced thereby. **Farmer v. State,** Op. No. 3567, 788 P2d 43 (Alaska 1990).

Constructive notice of suit was imputed to police officer through his counsel, the state attorney general's office, which represented all of the defendants in the action; accordingly, amendment of the complaint to name the police officer as a defendant related back to the date of the original complaint. **Farmer v. State,** Op. No. 3567, 788 P2d 43 (Alaska 1990).

Where complaint in personal injury action arising out of vehicle accident named as the sole defendant the father of the minor driver of the vehicle, plaintiffs' motion, filed after the running of the statute of limitations, to add the defendant's wife and son as defendants and to have the amendment relate back to the date of the original complaint, was properly rejected, since plaintiffs failed to demonstrate that they were mistaken as to the identity of the proper parties and that defendant's wife and son knew or should have known that, but for such mistake, claims would have been brought against them. **Siemion v. Rumfelt,** Op. No. 3812, 825 P2d 896 (Alaska 1992).

In foreclosure action, junior lien holder's amended counterclaim sounding in tort related back to date of original pleading, thus statute of limitations did not bar counterclaim. **Mogg v. National Bank of Alaska,** Op. No. 3929, 846 P2d 806 (Alaska 1993).

Amendments adding representatives of estates of deceased persons as defendants may relate back to date of original proceeding even if original pleading erroneously named only decedent as defendant. **Hamilton v. Blackman,** Op. No. 4352, 915 P2d 1210 (Alaska 1996).

Relation back may be permitted even where substitution of new defendant first requires that personal representative of defendant be appointed. **Hamilton v. Blackman,** Op. No. 4352, 915 P2d 1210 (Alaska 1996).

Where husband filed complaint to disestablish paternity, then filed amended complaint to establish paternity, and later again amended complaint to seek disestablishment, termination date for husband's duty of support once paternity was disestablished was date first complaint was filed. **T.P.D. v. A.C.D.,** Op. No. 5127, 981 P2d 116 (Alaska 1999).

In the part of this rule pertaining to relation back of amendments, the phrase "within the period provided by law for commencing the action" must be interpreted to encompass, when the complaint is timely filed, the reasonable time for service of process on a named defendant permitted by Civil Rule 4. **West v. Buchanan,** Op. No. 5134, 981 P2d 1065 (Alaska

1999).

In personal injury action arising out of traffic accident where plaintiff sued the owner of the car rather than the driver on the last day available under the statute of limitations, then substituted the driver as the named defendant within the period allowed by court rule for service of the complaint, the amended complaint substituting the driver as named defendant related back to the time of the initial filing; driver received notice of the institution of the action and knew or should have known before expiration of the period for commencement of the action that she was the proper party in the suit. **West v. Buchanan,** Op. No. 5134, 981 P2d 1065 (Alaska 1999).

Where homeowner's original complaint alleged that search of his home for marijuana was unconstitutional, trial court erred in denying homeowner's motion to amend complaint to add claim of malicious prosecution against city police chief; proposed amendment related back to original complaint, and was therefore not untimely, since both complaints arose out of criminal citation for misconduct involving marijuana and its subsequent dismissal; homeowner's failure to allege malice with specificity in original complaint did not mean that city police chief was not on notice of general facts that gave rise to the malicious prosecution claim. **Brown v. Ely,** Op. No. 5347, 14 P3d 257 (Alaska 2000).

Rule 16. Pretrial Conferences; Scheduling; Management.

(a) **Pretrial Conferences; Objectives.** In any action, the court may in its discretion direct the attorneys for the parties and any unrepresented parties to appear before it for a conference or conferences before trial for such purposes as:

(1) expediting the disposition of the action;

(2) establishing early and continuing control so that the case will not be protracted because of lack of management;

(3) discouraging wasteful pretrial activities;

(4) improving the quality of the trial through more thorough preparation; and

(5) facilitating the settlement of the case, including use of alternative dispute resolution procedures such as mediation, early neutral evaluation, arbitration, and settlement conferences.

(b) **Scheduling Order.**

(1) Except in categories of actions exempted under Rule 16(g), the judge shall enter a scheduling order that limits or establishes the time:

(A) to join other parties and to amend the pleadings;

(B) under AS 09.17.080,

(i) to specifically identify potentially responsible persons;

(ii) to move to join specifically identified potentially responsible persons; and

(iii) to move to determine whether a sufficient opportunity to join a potentially responsible person is lacking;

(C) to file motions;

(D) to disclose expert witnesses and reports required under Rule 26(a)(2);

(E) to supplement disclosures required under Rule 26(a);

(F) to identify witnesses and exhibits;

(G) to complete discovery; and

(H) for trial or the trial setting conference.

The scheduling order may also address:

(I) modification of the discovery limitations contained in these rules, including the length of depositions in light of the factors listed in Rule 30(d)(2), and the extent of discovery to be permitted;

(J) the date or dates for conferences before trial;

(K) the use and timing of an alternative dispute resolution procedure;

(L) the time to file any challenges to the reliability of scientific evidence;

(M) any issues related to proceedings to determine the amount of punitive damages; and

(N) any other matters appropriate in the circumstances of the case.

The order shall issue as soon as practicable but in any event within 90 days after the appearance of the defendants or pursuant to a local uniform pretrial order issued and adopted according to the provisions of Administrative Rule 46. A schedule shall not be modified except upon a showing of good cause and by leave of court.

(2) The judge shall meet with the attorneys for the parties and any unrepresented parties prior to entering the scheduling order unless the judge determines that a conference is unnecessary or a local uniform pretrial order issued and adopted under Administrative Rule 46 establishes a different procedure. The court shall distribute notice of the conference date as soon as practicable after the appearance of the defendants. The conference may be held on or off the record.

(c) **Subjects for Consideration at Pretrial Conferences.** At any conference under this rule consideration may be given, and the court may take appropriate action, with respect to:

(1) the formulation and simplification of the issues, including the elimination of frivolous claims or defenses;

(2) the necessity or desirability of amendments to the pleadings;

(3) the possibility of obtaining admissions of fact and of documents which will avoid unnecessary proof, stipulations regarding the authenticity of documents, and advance rulings from the court on the admissibility of evidence;

(4) the avoidance of unnecessary proof and of cumulative evidence, and limitations or restrictions on the use of testimony under Evidence Rule 702;

(5) the appropriateness and timing of summary adjudication under Rule 56;

(6) the control and scheduling of discovery, including orders affecting disclosures and discovery pursuant to Rule 26 and Rules 29 through 37;

(7) the identification of witnesses and documents, the need and schedule for filing and exchanging pretrial briefs, and the date or dates for further conferences and for trial;

(8) the advisability of referring matters to a master;

(9) settlement and the use of special procedures to assist in resolving the dispute when authorized by statute or local rule;

(10) the form and substance of the pretrial order;

(11) the disposition of pending motions;

(12) the need for adopting special procedures for managing potentially difficult or protracted actions that may involve complex issues, multiple parties, difficult legal questions, or unusual proof problems;

(13) an order for a separate trial pursuant to Rule 42(b) with respect to a claim, counterclaim, cross-claim, or third-party claim, or with respect to any particular issue in the case;

(14) an order directing a party or parties to present evidence early in the trial with respect to a manageable issue that could, on the evidence, be the basis for a judgment as a matter of law under Rule 50(a);

(15) an order establishing a reasonable limit on the time allowed for presenting evidence; and

(16) such other matters as may facilitate the just, speedy, and inexpensive disposition of the action.

At least one of the attorneys for each party participating in any conference before trial shall have authority to enter into stipulations and to make admissions regarding all matters that the participants may reasonably anticipate may be discussed. If appropriate, the court may require that a party or its representative be present or reasonably available by telephone in order to consider possible settlement of the dispute.

(d) **Final Pretrial Conference.** Any final pretrial conference shall be held as close to the time of trial as reasonable under the circumstances. The participants at any such conference shall formulate a plan for trial, including a program for facilitating the admission of evidence. The conference shall be attended by at least one of the attorneys who will conduct the trial for each of the parties and by any unrepresented parties.

(e) **Pretrial Orders.** After any conference held pursuant to this rule, an order shall be entered reciting the action taken. This order shall control the subsequent course of the action unless modified by a subsequent order. The order following a final pretrial conference shall be modified only to prevent manifest injustice.

(f) **Sanctions.** If a party or party's attorney fails to obey a scheduling or pretrial order, or if no appearance is made on behalf of a party at a scheduling or pretrial conference, or if a party or party's attorney is substantially unprepared to participate in the conference, or if a party or party's attorney fails to participate in good faith, the judge, upon motion or the judge's own initiative, may make such orders with regard thereto as are just, and among others any of the orders provided in Rule 37(b)(2)(B), (C), (D). In lieu of or in addition to any other sanction, the judge shall require the party or the attorney representing the party or both to pay the reasonable expenses incurred because of any noncompliance with this rule, including attorney's fees, unless the judge finds that the noncompliance was substantially justified or that other circumstances make an award of expenses unjust.

(g) **Actions Exempted from Rule 16(b).** The following categories of cases are exempted from the requirement of scheduling conferences and scheduling orders under Rule 16(b):

(1) special proceedings listed in Part XII of these rules, including habeas corpus petitions, forcible entry and detainer claims, and dissolution of marriage and divorce actions;

(2) paternity cases;

(3) custody cases;

(4) small claims cases;

(5) actions to enforce out-of-state judgments;

(6) eminent domain cases;

(7) proceedings for post-conviction relief under Criminal Rule 35.1; and

(8) proceedings to obtain a domestic violence protective order under AS 18.66.100 and AS 18.66.110 or a stalking protective order under AS 18.65.850 and AS 18.65.855.

(Adopted by SCO 5 October 9, 1959; amended by SCO 29 effective December 27, 1960; by SCO 49 effective January 1, 1963; by SCO 413 effective August 1, 1980; by SCO 865 effective July 15, 1988; by SCO 1153 effective July 15, 1994; by SCO 1172 effective July 15, 1995; by SCO 1266 effective July 15, 1997; by SCO 1318 effective July 15, 1998; by SCO 1403 effective October 15, 2000; by SCO 1425 effective April 15, 2001; by SCO 1437 effective October 15, 2001; by SCO 1529 effective November 5, 2003; by SCO 1569 effective October 15, 2005; and by SCO 1647 effective October 15, 2007)

Note: Civil Rule 16(b)(1)(K) is intended specifically to govern challenges to scientific evidence brought under the standard set forth in *State v. Coon,* 974 P.2d 386 (Alaska 1999) *(discussing Daubert v. Merrell Dow Pharmaceuticals,*

Inc., 509 U.S. 579 (1993))

Note to SCO 1647: The supreme court has approved pretrial procedures for Anchorage cases that vary from those specified in this rule. Civil Rule 16(b)(1) sets out the normal timing for issuance of a scheduling order and allows a validly-adopted local uniform pretrial order to set a different time. Civil Rule 16(b)(2) provides that a validly-adopted local uniform pretrial order may set a different procedure. As permitted under Civil Rule 16(b)(1), the superior court in Anchorage issues its scheduling order, Administrative Order 3AO-03-04 (Amended) at a different time. That Order also sets a different procedure under Civil Rule 16(b)(2). Administrative Order 3AO-03-04 (Amended), commonly referred to as the Anchorage Uniform Pretrial order, was issued and adopted according to the provisions of Administrative Rule 46, and is available on the court system's website at htt://www.state.ak.us/courts/orders-cr16-26.htm.

Annotations

Cases

Pre-trial procedure is intended to clearly define the issues to be tried before the trial judge. **Lumbermens Mut. Cas. Co. v. Continental Cas. Co.,** Op. No. 160, 387 P2d 104 (Alaska 1963).

Counsel have a particular responsibility to assist the court that a pretrial order in final form defines all issues to be tried. **Lumbermens Mut. Cas. Co. v. Continental Cas. Co.,** Op. No. 160, 387 P2d 104 (Alaska 1963).

This rule must not be so construed as to deprive the court of authority to order prior to entry of the pre-trial order that the parties exchange the names of witnesses to be called at the trial. **Bertram v. Harris,** Op. No. 393, 423 P2d 909 (Alaska 1967).

The pre-trial order is controlling only as to matters mentioned in the order in accordance with this rule. **Bertram v. Harris,** Op. No. 393, 423 P2d 909 (Alaska 1967).

The discretion which the trial judge reserved to himself under his order for a pretrial conference by requiring the exchange of lists of witnesses and by providing that noncompliance may result in the exclusion of witnesses, was not disturbed on appeal and refusal to allow one of the witnesses to testify was sustained in light of the record indicating no abuse of discretion and no justification for failure to furnish the witness' name. **Bertram v. Harris,** Op. No. 393, 423 P2d 909 (Alaska 1967).

Parties were bound by pre-trial order providing for a non-jury trial even though the order was not signed by counsel. **Pankratz v. State, Depart. of Highways,** Op. No. 2564, 652 P2d 68 (Alaska 1982).

Where defendant sought damages for lack of full performance in its counterclaim, but did not seek to avoid its obligation altogether, it could not point to its counterclaim or to its pretrial memorandum as adequately raising the issue of substantial performance. **Alaska Protection Service v. Frontier Colorcable,** Op. No. 2800, 680 P2d 1119 (Alaska 1984).

Fact that trial court allowed a deposition to be taken on October 27, 1981, without explicitly amending a pretrial order requiring discovery to be completed by September11, 1981, did not constitute abuse of discretion. **City of Kotzebue v. McLean,** Op. No. 2949, 702 P2d 1309 (Alaska 1985).

While plaintiff's initial demand for a jury trial may have been timely even though it accompanied an untimely responsive pleading, his post-demand conduct, including acquiescence to pretrial order specifying a non-jury trial, constituted a waiver of his right to a jury trial; the trial judge did not abuse his discretion by not modifying the pretrial order to allow a jury trial, since to do so would have prejudiced the opposing party. **Howard S. Lease Const. Co. v. Holly,** Op. No. 3123, 725 P2d 712 (Alaska 1986).

District court's practice of proceeding to trial on merits after granting motion to set aside default judgment constituted reversible error for failing to conform to 15-day trial notice requirement of this rule. **Romero v. Alaska Financial Services,** Op. No. 4080, 873 P2d 1278 (Alaska 1994).

The sanctions of Civil Rule 16.1(g) and Civil Rule 4 1(d) afford courts the tools necessary to deter litigants from judge shopping through voluntary or involuntary dismissals. **Staso v. State, Department of Transportation,** Op. No. 4214, 895 P2d 988 (Alaska 1995).

Trial court order rejecting defendant's untimely witness list in its entirety and precluding defendant from calling witnesses at trial amounted to sanction for defendant's violation of pretrial order to submit witness lists by certain date, thus preclusion order had to be considered under rules governing sanctions. **Sykes v. Melba Creek Min., Inc.,** Op. No. 4938, 952 P2d 1164 (Alaska 1998).

Trial court committed reversible error in precluding all expert defense witnesses for defendant's failure to timely submit witness list since harsh effect on defense rendered sanction disproportionate to severity of violation. **Sykes v. Melba Creek Min., Inc.,** Op. No. 4938, 952 P2d 1164 (Alaska 1998).

Rule 16.1. Special Procedures for Reducing Litigation Delay. (Rescinded)

(SCO 669 effective February 24, 1986; amended by SCO 709 effective September 15, 1986; by SCO 742 effective December 15, 1986; by SCO 879 effective July 15, 1988; by SCO 954 effective July 15, 1989; by SCO 1032 effective nunc pro tunc January 15, 1990; and by SCO 1172 effective July 15, 1995; and rescinded by SCO 1266 effective July 15, 1997)

PART IV. PARTIES

Rule 17. Parties Plaintiff and Defendant—Capacity.

(a) **Real Party in Interest.** Every action shall be prosecuted in the name of the real party in interest. An executor, administrator, guardian, trustee of an express trust, a party with whom or in whose name a contract has been made for the benefit of another, or a party authorized by statute may sue in that person's own name without joining the party for whose benefit the action is brought; and when a statute of the state so provides, an action for the use or benefit of another shall be brought in the name of the state. No action shall be dismissed on the ground that it is not prosecuted in the name of the real party in interest until a reasonable time has been allowed after objection for ratification of commencement of the action by, or joinder or substitution of, the real party in interest; and such ratification, joinder, or substitution shall have the same effect as if the action had been commenced in the name of the real party in interest.

(b) **Capacity to Sue or be Sued.** The capacity of an individual, other than one acting in a representative capacity, to sue or be sued shall be determined by the law of the individual's domicile. The capacity of a corporation to sue or be sued shall be determined by the law under which it was organized. A partnership or other unincorporated association may sue or be sued in its common name.

(c) **Infants or Incompetent Persons.** Whenever an infant or incompetent person has a representative, such as a general guardian, committee, conservator, or other like fiduciary, the representative may sue or defend on behalf of the infant or incompetent person. An infant or incompetent person who does not have a duly appointed representative may sue by a next friend or by a guardian ad litem. The court shall appoint a guardian ad litem for an infant or incompetent person not otherwise represented in an action or shall make such other order as it deems proper for the protection of the infant or incompetent person.

(d) **Unknown Parties.** All persons who are or may be interested in the subject matter of an action relating to real property in the state whose names cannot be ascertained after diligent inquiry may be made parties by being named and described as unknown claimants or unknown owners, or as unknown heirs, devisees, legatees, or assigns of any deceased person who may have been interested in the subject matter of the action. If it cannot be ascertained after diligent inquiry whether a person who is or may be interested in the subject matter of the action is alive or dead, or what disposition may have been made of the person's interests, or where the person resides if alive, the person and everyone claiming under the person may be made a party by naming the person and adding to such name "or the unknown heirs, devisees, legatees, or assigns of [the person's name]."

(Adopted by SCO 5 October 9, 1959; amended by SCO 49 effective January 1, 1963, by SCO 258 effective November 15, 1976; by SCO 465 effective June 1, 1981; and by SCO 1277 effective July 15, 1997)

Editor's Note: Ch. 63, § 30, SLA 1977 provides that "Section 3 of this Act has the effect of limiting the discretionary authority of the court to appoint a guardian ad litem under Rule 17(b), Alaska Rules of Civil Procedure, and Rules 11(a) and 15, Alaska Rules of Children's Procedure, by requiring as a condition of appointment that the court find that the best interests of the child need articulation. Further, this Act requires limitation of the duration of the appointment, limits the scope of the guardian ad litem's authority, and establishes the geographical area from which the guardian ad litem may be selected."

Section 3 added a subsection (c) to AS 09.65.130.

Note: Chapter 84 SLA 04 (HB 427) enacted extensive changes to the guardianship and conservatorship statutes. According to Section 32 of the Act, AS 08.26.100, enacted in Section 2, has the effect of changing Civil Rule 17(c) by restricting the persons that can be appointed as guardians or conservators and thereby limiting the orders the court is authorized to make with regard to the protection of infants and incompetent persons.

Cross References

CROSS REFERENCE: AS 09.15.010; AS 09.15.020; AS 09.15.030

Annotations

Cases

Where defendant contended on appeal that plaintiff could not bring an action for a debt defendant owed to a partnership without joining all partners or alleging an assignment of the debt to plaintiff, defendant was required to point out that specifically in his answer and, by failing to do so, waived the objection. **Smith v. Sellar,** Op. No. 88, 371 P2d 809 (Alaska 1962).

An administrator must have a right which is to be judicially enforced to be considered a real party interest. **Burns v. Anchorage Funeral Chapel,** Op. No. 773, 495 P2d 70 (Alaska 1972).

A claim for relief for the wrongful interference with the right to preserve a dead body belongs exclusively to the surviving spouse or to the next of kin of the decedent, and an administrator is not the real party in interest to the litigation. **Burns v. Anchorage Funeral Chapel,** Op. No. 773, 495 P2d 70 (Alaska 1972).

AS 13.20.330, providing for the survivorship of those claims which the decedent held before death, cannot be used by the administrator to qualify as the real party in interest in a suit against a funeral home for wrongful interference with the right of a next of kin to preserve the body of a deceased. **Burns v. Anchorage Funeral Chapel,** Op. No. 773, 495 P2d 70 (Alaska 1972).

The defenses of failure to state a claim for relief and failure to join an indispensable party may be raised at any time and are not waived by a delay in making the objection. **Burns v. Anchorage Funeral Chapel,** Op. No. 773, 495 P2d 70 (Alaska 1972).

The trial court has the discretion to determine whether in the particular factual context of the litigation a waiver of a real party in interest issue has occurred. **Burns v. Anchorage Funeral Chapel,** Op. No. 773, 495 P2d 70 (Alaska 1972).

Since the real party in interest objection is dilatory in nature, it should be raised with reasonable promptness. **Burns v. Anchorage Funeral Chapel,** Op. No. 773, 495 P2d 70 (Alaska 1972).

A judgment debtor is a real party in interest regarding an order confirming an execution sale to satisfy a judgment, even though he has conveyed the property to another, where the judgment debtor reacquires a one-half interest in the property prior to seeking a vacation of the order confirming the sale. **Mallonee v. Grow,** Op. No. 841, 502 P2d 432 (Alaska 1972).

In contested custody cases, the trial court is empowered to appoint a guardian ad litem to represent the interest of the minor child. **Carle v. Carle,** Op. No. 847, 503 P2d 1050 (Alaska 1972).

A partnership which is reduced from four to two members and whose name is changed may yet remain the real party in interest as to an interest originally held by the partnership under its former name. **Kos v. Williams,** Op. No. 2167, 616 P2d 868 (Alaska 1980).

In interpreting the real party in interest rule, the court must identify the real party who must ratify the action or join it within a reasonable time before the court can then dismiss the action after the reasonable time passes without ratification or joinder. **Kos v. Williams,** Op. No. 2167, 616 P2d 868 (Alaska 1980).

Since ratification is the functional equivalent of joinder with respect to assessment of attorney's fees and costs, any request for ratification is subject to the same requirement of timeliness as a joinder motion. **Truckweld Equipment Co. v. Swenson Trucking,** Op. No. 2545, 649 P2d 234 (Alaska 1982).

Motion to join partially subrogated insurance company as a real party in interest, which was made five months after the insurance company's interest in the litigation became evident, and only a month before trial, was untimely, since pleading amendments were closed 60 days before the motion was made. **Truckweld Equipment Co. v. Swenson Trucking,** Op. No. 2545, 649 P2d 234 (Alaska 1982).

Where plaintiff sued to recover the entire amount of damages even though its insurer had already paid part of the amount, insurer should have been joined as a real party in interest whether or not lack of joinder would have created a substantial risk of multiple litigation. **Truckweld Equipment Co. v. Swenson Trucking,** Op. No. 2545, 649 P2d 234 (Alaska 1982).

Ratification under this rule requires explicit adoption of the court proceedings in question; it does not occur by silence or acquiescence.

Truckweld Equipment Co. v. Swenson Trucking, Op. No. 2545, 649 P2d 234 (Alaska 1982).

Where employee of independent contractor sued oil company for injuries sustained at job site, and oil company brought third-party claim against the independent contractor for indemnification, fact that employee received workers' compensation benefits for his injuries did not require that he join the employer as a party plaintiff, since the ordinary rules of joinder regarding subrogees do not apply in a workers' compensation context. **Exxon Corp. v. Alvey,** Op. No. 2883, 690 P2d 733 (Alaska 1984).

Where a claimant sued a third party for negligence after receiving worker's compensation benefits from his employer's insurer, joinder of the insurer as a party plaintiff and admission of the fact that claimant received worker's compensation benefits violated the collateral source rule and constituted reversible error. **Tolan v. ERA Helicopters, Inc.,** Op. No. 2924, 699 P2d 1265 (Alaska 1985).

Absent unusual circumstances, a partially subrogated insurer should have the option of ratifying an action brought by its insured. **Anchorage v. Baugh Constr. & Eng'g Co.,** Op. No. 3083, 722 P2d 919 (Alaska 1986).

In a suit for damages by municipality against construction company, the trial court erred in joining the municipality's insurer as a party plaintiff after the insurer had formally ratified the action brought by the municipality, but the erroneous joinder was not sufficiently prejudicial to require reversal. **Anchorage v. Baugh Constr. & Eng'g Co.,** Op. No. 3083, 722 P2d 919 (Alaska 1986).

Conditions of "Loan Receipt and Agreement" under which municipality's insurer "loaned" money to the municipality for damages caused by an explosion and fire put the insurer in a situation identical to that of a partially subrogated insurer who had made payment to the insured under the policy, thus the insurer was a "real party in interest" to action by the municipality to recover the damages from a third party, but joinder of the insurer as a party plaintiff was not required under this rule because the insurer had formally ratified the municipality's bringing the action. **Anchorage v. Baugh Constr. & Eng'g Co.,** Op. No. 3083, 722 P2d 919 (Alaska 1986).

A real party in interest need not expressly agree to be bound to an adverse judgment regarding costs and attorney fees when ratifying an action; it is sufficient if the ratifying party simply agrees to adopt the court proceedings. **Smith v. Lee,** Op. No. 3420, 770 P2d 754 (Alaska 1989).

In a suit for judgment on a note and for foreclosure of a deed of trust, a bank, an assignee of the note and deed of trust as collateral security for a loan, was a real party in interest who adequately ratified the suit brought by the assignor by explicitly agreeing to be bound by the outcome of the litigation and acknowledging that the conduct of its borrower, the other plaintiffs, and their attorneys, in the action would affect, with binding consequences, its interest in the collateral and that it assented to the consequences. **Smith v. Lee,** Op. No. 3420, 770 P2d 754 (Alaska 1989).

Where plaintiff-employer in action against defendant- employee for breach of employment contract and violation of fiduciary duties did not disclose that it had assigned all of its claims against defendant to another corporation, trial court erred in setting aside the judgment against defendant on the grounds of newly discovered evidence and fraud, misrepresentation, or other misconduct of the plaintiff; the appropriate sanction for plaintiff's concealment of the assignment was to vacate the trial court's award of costs and attorney fees against defendant. **McCall v. Coats,** Op. No. 3464, 777 P2d 655 (Alaska 1989).

In suit arising out of a road construction contact awarded by borough to Kandik Construction, Inc. & Associates, a joint venture composed of Kandik Construction, Inc. and another company, wherein Kandik & Associated asserted a claim for "business destruction" damages resulting from Kandik Construction's loss of bonding capacity, joinder of Kandik Construction on the eve of trial as the real party in interest was not an abuse of discretion since the borough knew that the business purportedly destroyed was that of Kandik Construction and not Kandik & Associates. **Fairbanks North Star Borough v. Kandik Const.,** Op. No. 3571, 795 P2d 793 (Alaska 1990).

Where suit against corporation was dismissed for lack of capacity to be sued because corporation had been involuntarily dissolved by the State for failure to pay taxes, trial court erred in refusing to vacate the dismissal after the State reinstated the corporation. **Gerik-Jones, Inc. v. Timberline Industries, Inc.,** Op. No. 3897, 840 P2d 999 (Alaska 1992).

Although defendant properly pleaded issue of plaintiff's capacity to sue in its answer, defendant waived issue for appeal by failing to bring the issue to trial court's attention by motion. **Von Stauffenberg v. Committee for Honest and Ethical School Board,** Op. No. 4269, 903 P2d 1055 (Alaska 1995).

Under this rule, Washington law applied to determine whether a suit against a dissolved Washington corporation could properly be filed. **University of Alaska v. Thomas Architectural Products, Inc.,** Op. No. 4288, 907 P2d 448 (Alaska 1995).

Award of attorney fees to property claimant in civil forfeiture proceeding had to be reversed if property claimant used fictitious name. **State v. Johnson,** Op. No. 4991, 958 P2d 440 (Alaska 1998).

Where insured ignored insurer's request not to include insurer's subrogated claim for medical expenses in her tort action against defendant, insured's lack of authority to pursue medical expenses was legitimate partial defense to tort claim. **Ruggles ex rel. Estate of Mayor v. Grow,** Op. No. 5161, 984 P2d 509 (Alaska 1999).

It was error not to substitute rifle distributor's fully subrogated insurers as real party in interest in indemnity claim brought by rifle distributor against successor corporation in products liability action. **Savage Arms, Inc. v. Western Auto Supply,** Op. No. 5370, 18 P3d 49 (Alaska 2000).

While a "next friend" may sue on behalf of a minor, she may not defend a suit against a minor. Further, a next friend cannot generally represent a minor, even as a plaintiff, without counsel **Shields v. Cape Fox Corp.,** Op. No. 5547, 42 P3d 1083 (Alaska 2002).

Real party in interest objections under subsection (a) of this rule must be brought with reasonable promptness and waiting over four years was not a reasonable time period to claim that named party was not the appropriate party to bring the lawsuit. **Bethel Family Clinic v. Bethel Wellness Assoc.,** Op. No. 12233, 160 P.3d 142 (Alaska 2007).

Rule 18. Joinder of Claims and Remedies.

(a) **Joinder of Claims.** A party asserting a claim to relief as an original claim, counterclaim, cross-claim, or third-party claim, may join, either as independent or as alternate claims, as many claims either legal or equitable or both as the party has against an opposing party.

(b) **Joinder of Remedies—Fraudulent Conveyances.** Whenever a claim is one heretofore cognizable only after another claim has been prosecuted to a conclusion, the two claims may be joined in a single action; but the court shall grant relief in that action only in accordance with the relative substantive rights of the parties. In particular, a plaintiff may state a claim for money and a claim to have set aside a conveyance fraudulent as to that plaintiff, without first having obtained a judgment establishing the claim for money.

(Adopted by SCO 5 October 9, 1959; amended by SCO 258 effective November 15, 1976; and by SCO 1153 effective July 15, 1994)

Annotations

Cases

Under this rule plaintiff may join as many claims as he may have against defendant and a provision of the forcible entry and detainer statute, AS 09.45.070 (b), purporting to limit recovery to arrears and damage to property is without significance as attempting to regulate procedure. **Thrift Shop, Inc. v. Alaska Mutual Savings Bank,** Op. No. 277, 398 P2d 657 (Alaska 1965).

When a custodial parent seeks both a modification of the divorce decree and reimbursement for past child support expenditures, he or she may join the claims, and bring both by motion in the original divorce action. **Matthews v. Matthews,** Op. No. 3206, 739 P2d 1298 (Alaska 1987).

In prosecution of car dealership for several violations of Unfair Trade Practices and Consumer Protection Act, trial court did not abuse its discretion in denying defendant's motion for severance of the charges since (1) evidence of any given transaction was not offered for sole purpose of showing that defendant acted in conformity with some bad character trait, (2) any prejudice to defendant was limited by jury instruction, and (3) primary relief sought by state was permanent injunction, not damages. **Anchorage Nissan, Inc. v. State,** Op. No. 4850, 941 P2d 1229 (Alaska 1997).

Rule 19. Joinder of Persons Needed for Just Adjudication.

(a) **Persons to Be Joined if Feasible.** A person who is subject to service of process and whose joinder will not deprive the court of jurisdiction over the subject matter of the action shall be joined as a party in the action if (1) in the person's absence complete relief cannot be accorded among those already parties, or (2) the person claims an interest relating to the subject of the action and is so situated that the disposition of the action in the person's absence may (i) as a practical matter impair or impede the person's ability to protect that interest or (ii) leave any of the persons already parties subject to a substantial risk of incurring double, multiple, or otherwise inconsistent obligations by reason of the claimed interest. If the person has not been joined, the court shall order that the person be made a party. If the person should join as a plaintiff but refuses to do so, the person may be made a defendant, or, in a proper case, an involuntary plaintiff. If the joined party objects to venue and joinder of that party would render the venue of the action improper, that party shall be dismissed from the action.

(b) **Determination by Court Whenever Joinder Not Feasible.** If a person as described in subsection (a)(1)–(2) hereof cannot be made a party, the court shall determine whether in equity and good conscience the action should proceed among the parties before it, or should be dismissed, the absent person being thus regarded as indispensable. The factors to be considered by the court include: first, to what extent a judgment rendered in the person's absence might be prejudicial to the person or those already parties; second, the extent to which, by protective provisions in the judgment, by the shaping of relief, or other measures, the prejudice can be lessened or avoided; third, whether a judgment rendered in the person's absence will be adequate; fourth, whether the plaintiff will have an adequate remedy if the action is dismissed for nonjoinder.

(c) **Pleading Reasons for Nonjoinder.** A pleading asserting a claim for relief shall state the names, if known to the pleader, of any persons as described in subdivision (a) (1)–(2) hereof who are not joined, and the reasons why they are not joined.

(d) **Exception of Class Actions.** This rule is subject to the provisions of Rule 23.

(Adopted by SCO 5 October 9, 1959; rescinded and promulgated by SCO 258 effective November 15, 1976; amended by SCO 1153 effective July 15, 1994)

Note: AS 10.06.015(a)(1), as enacted by ch. 166, § 1, SLA 1988, amended Civil Rule 19 by making parties to a contract covered by AS 10.06.015(a)(1), indispensable parties to an action under AS 10.06.015(a)(1). AS 10.06.378(c) as enacted by ch. 166, § 1, SLA 1988, amended Civil Rule 19 by allowing a shareholder sued under the section to join certain parties in a lawsuit against the shareholder without using the criteria of Civil Rule 19. AS 10.06.463, as enacted by ch. 166, § 1, SLA 1988, amended Civil Rule 19 by requiring that a corporation be made a party to an action to remove a director of the corporation. AS 10.06.580(b), as enacted by ch. 166, § 1, SLA 1988, amended Civil Rule 19 by making qualified dissenting shareholders indispensable parties to an action covered by AS 10.06.580.

Annotations

Cases

I. In General.

This rule deals with the compulsory joinder of parties and recognizes the classes of indispensable, necessary and proper parties that were first developed in the equity courts. **State, Department of Highways v. Crosby,** Op. No. 322, 410 P2d 724 (Alaska 1966).

The court's determination of indispensability or lack of it of a party not under its jurisdiction involves a consideration of the adverse effect of a judgment on persons not before the court, the danger of inconsistent decisions and of multiplicity of actions as balanced against the desirability of a meaningful determination of the dispute rather than leaving parties before the court without remedy. **State, Department of Highways v. Crosby,** Op. No. 322, 410 P2d 724 (Alaska 1966).

While Civ. R. 72(c)(2) states a requirement that all persons having or claiming an interest in the property to be condemned be added as defendants in an eminent domain action, the question whether such a person is indispensable so that the action may not proceed to a conclusion unless such person is made a party is to be determined under Civil Rule 19(b). **City of Fairbanks v. Electric Distribution Sys.,** Op. No. 339, 413 P2d 165 (Alaska 1966).

Where as part of an agreement in which landowners were to convey land to a corporation in return for stock and a loan, and in which the defendant and a third party to the agreement were each to receive one third of the corporation's stock, the third party is an "indispensable party" to the landowner's action for rescission and reconveyance. However, since the corporation and the defendant were foreclosed because of their failure to raise the indispensable party issue at trial from asking the court to weigh the dangers of their being subjected to inconsistent decisions, and in view of third party's failure to intervene despite his knowledge of the scope of relief sought in the litigation, defendant and the corporation are estopped, by the virtue of the third party's inaction, from asserting that the third party's interest required that the judgment be set aside. **Padgett v. Theus,** Op. No. 692, 484 P2d 697 (Alaska 1971).

The court reviewing a judgment entered in an action in which an indispensable party was not joined will consider the ramifications of its failure to raise the indispensable party issue at the trial, the significance of the fact that a binding judgment has been entered, and the justice and feasibility of fashioning appropriate relief at the appellate level in order to lessen or avoid any substantial prejudice to the indispensable party flowing from the trial court's judgment. **Padgett v. Theus,** Op. No. 692, 484 P2d 697 (Alaska 1971).

Individual shareholders in arrears in child support payments were required by this rule to be made parties to action against native corporation to obtain cash distribution to mothers to whom child support was owed. **Calista Corp. v. DeYoung,** Op. No. 1403, 562 P2d 338 (Alaska 1977).

Where a process server in possession of personal property by reason of a writ of attachment is subject to an action brought by a third party claiming an interest superior to the attachment levy, courts should insure that the real contestants in interest are before it. **First National Bank of Anchorage v. Zawodny,** Op. No. 1976, 602 P2d 1254 (Alaska 1979).

As a general proposition, a partially subrogated insurer who is clearly bound by the result of the lawsuit should not be joined under this rule. **Anchorage v. Baugh Constr. & Eng'g Co.,** Op. No. 3083, 722 P2d 919 (Alaska 1986).

Tenants in common are not always indispensable parties to litigation involving the property, particularly where the judgment will not directly affect the interests of the co-tenant; however, co-tenants should be joined where the right of any one tenant is not distinct and the relief sought is interwoven with the rights of the other tenants. **B.B.P. Corp. v. Carroll,** Op. No. 3377, 760 P2d 519 (Alaska 1988).

Rule 19 expressly pertains only to joinder of parties, not to dismissal of parties through a Rule 54(b) judgment. **Williams v. Mammoth of Alaska, Inc.,** Op. No. 4174,890 P2d 581 (Alaska 1995).

Where party fails to join necessary party, appropriate remedy is not dismissal, but rather joinder of the necessary party. **Silvers v. Silvers,** Op. No. 5258, 999 P2d 786 (Alaska 2000).

II. Court Determination.

A. Indispensable Parties.

The mandatory duty under Civ. R. 19(a) to order other parties brought in is shown only when the trial court finds or the record indisputably discloses that such parties are indispensable. **Nordin v. Zimmer,** Op. No. 96, 373 P2d 738 (Alaska 1962).

Joint obligees are indispensable parties to an action to enforce contract rights between themselves and the obligors. **Nordin v. Zimmer,** Op. No. 96, 373 P2d 738 (Alaska 1962).

Where electric distribution facilities were mortgaged to the United States pursuant to the Rural Electrification Act of 1936, the interest of the United States as mortgagee under loans administered within the provisions of this act was not merely that of a money lender, but was an interest in the continued ability of the cooperative borrower to provide its service within the rural areas served at reasonable rates and since such interest would be adversely affected by a judgment of condemnation in an eminent domain action, the United States was an indispensable party to such action within the meaning of this rule and where it had not consented to be sued, the action was subject to dismissal. **City of Fairbanks v. Electric Distribution Sys.,** Op. No. 339, 413 P2d 165 (Alaska 1966).

While, in general, only those parties to a contract whose interest might be affected need to be joined in an action based on the contract, in actions for rescission all parties are indispensable unless the interests of those present are completely separable from the interests of those absent. **Padgett v. Theus,** Op. No. 692, 484 P2d 697 (Alaska 1971).

In an action by real estate brokers against alleged sellers for specific performance of a contract, the alleged purchasers of the real property are the real parties in interest and are indispensable parties to the action. **Sowash v. Garrett,** Op. No. 2377, 630 P2d 8 (Alaska 1981).

Where plaintiff sued to recover the entire amount of damages even though its insurer had already paid part of the amount, insurer should have been joined as a real party in interest whether or not lack of joinder would have created a substantial risk of multiple litigation. **Truckweld Equipment Co. v. Swenson Trucking,** Op. No. 2545, 649 P2d 234 (Alaska 1982).

A grantee of an alleged fraudulent conveyance is indispensable to a proceeding to strike the transfer, and must therefore be joined as a party to the action if subject to service of process. **Sylvester v. Sylvester,** Op. No. 3097, 723 P2d 1253 (Alaska 1986).

Where bank filed a complaint seeking a personal judgment on a promissory note secured by a deed of trust, but chose not to foreclose on the security, only the maker of the note was an indispensable party; the fact that the maker executed the note to guarantee the debts of a third person or that other persons had interests of record in the security did not make them indispensable parties to the bank's suit on the note. **Moening v. Alaska Mut. Bank,** Op. No. 3274, 751 P2d 5 (Alaska 1988).

Co-tenants were indispensable parties to a lawsuit raising the issue of abandonment of subdivision covenants. **B.B.P. Corp. v. Carroll,** Op. No. 3377, 760 P2d 519 (Alaska 1988).

If city was indispensable party in action against city clerk challenging city charter's three-year durational residency requirement for city council candidates, failure to join city would not warrant dismissal, since appropriate remedy would be order joining city as party. **Peloza v. Freas,** Op. No. 4067, 871 P2d 687 (Alaska 1994).

Where party fails to join necessary party, appropriate remedy is not dismissal, but rather joinder of the necessary party. **Silvers v. Silvers,** Op. No. 5258, 999 P2d 786 (Alaska 2000).

B. Not Indispensable Parties.

Parties will not be considered indispensable if they are beneficiaries of a trust whose interest their trustee may adequately represent. **Hardy v. Island Homes, Inc.,** Op. No. 48, 363 P2d 637, 643 (Alaska 1961).

Finding that a third person was not a party to an agreement entered into between the parties, and therefore not an indispensable party to this suit was amply supported by the evidence. **Nordin v. Zimmer,** Op. No. 96, 373 P2d 738 (Alaska 1962).

The United States was not an indispensable party to an action involving taking of appellee's land by the state for highway purposes without payment of just compensation where the state and not the United States was seeking to utilize an asserted reservation in the United States patent to appellee's land, although the United States, as grantor of the land, could have an interest effectuating this asserted reservation for the benefit of the state and future litigation by the United States to determine the validity of the reservation could conceivably arise. **State v. Crosby,** Op. No. 322, 410 P2d 724 (Alaska 1966).

Where an issue was presented whether the state may take appellee's land without the payment of just compensation and the determination of this issue depended on the validity of a right-of-way reservation across appellee's land in the United States patent for highways constructed by the "United States or by any State created out of the Territory of Alaska," a holding that the United States was an indispensable party to such proceeding would mean that the issue could not be decided at all and appellees be deprived of constitutional safeguards against taking of property without compensation since the United States could not be made a party without its consent. **State v. Crosby,** Op. No. 322, 410 P2d 724 (Alaska 1966).

United States was not an indispensable party to action challenging decision by State of Alaska to lease offshore tracts for oil and gas exploration and development even though relief given covered tracts whose ownership was disputed by the State of Alaska and the United States. **Hammond v. North Slope Borough,** Op. No. 2499, 645 P2d 750 (Alaska 1982).

In a suit for damages by municipality against construction company, the trial court erred in joining the municipality's insurer as a party plaintiff after the insurer had formally ratified the action brought by the municipality, but the erroneous joinder was not sufficiently prejudicial to require reversal. **Anchorage v. Baugh Constr. & Eng'g Co.,** Op. No. 3083, 722 P2d 919 (Alaska 1986).

All residents of the subdivision were not indispensable parties to a lawsuit raising the issue of abandonment of a subdivision covenant. **B.B.P. Corp. v. Carroll,** Op. No. 3377, 760 P2d 519 (Alaska 1988).

Where plaintiff became involved in a dispute with the president of a corporation over ownership of certain logs harvested by plaintiff, and two policemen summoned to the dispute confiscated the logs, the corporation was not an indispensable party to plaintiff's suit against the policemen for depriving him of property without due process of law and for unreasonable seizure without a warrant, since the corporation could be subpoenaed as a witness on the issue of ownership of the logs. **Farmer v. State,** Op. No. 3567, 788 P2d 43 (Alaska 1990).

Although the State was a party to agreement which created one of three funds involved in suit by successor state employees association against former state employees association to obtain possession of pro-rated portions of the funds, the State was not a necessary party to the suit. **ASEA v. APEA,** Op. No. 3779, 825 P2d 451 (Alaska 1991).

In breach of contract action between two subcontractors, trial court did not abuse its discretion in vacating joinder of prime contractor as third party defendant where plaintiff, who did not seek joinder, would obtain complete relief if defendant were found liable; prime contractor and defendant could not be joint obligors due to settlement agreement between them, thus prim contractor's presence was unnecessary for just adjudication. **Martech Const. v. Ogden Env. Services,** Op. No. 3957, 852 P2d 1146 (Alaska 1993).

In action against city clerk challenging city charter's three-year durational residency requirement for city council candidates, city was not indispensable party, since city's interests were identical to those of city clerk. **Peloza v. Freas,** Op. No. 4067, 871 P2d 687 (Alaska 1994).

If beneficiary's interest will not as practical matter be impaired by trustee's absence, then neither trustee nor beneficiary are necessary parties. **Matter of Pacific Marine Ins. Co.,** Op. No. 4100, 877 P2d 264 (Alaska 1994).

In liquidation proceeding, neither trustee nor beneficiary was indispensable party to adjudication of motion seeking determination of proper ownership of trust annuity. **Matter of Pacific Marine Ins. Co.,** Op. No. 4100, 877 P2d 264 (Alaska 1994).

Rural Utility Service, which provided federal financial incentives to utilities serving rural areas, was not indispensable party to action by Alaska Public Utility Commission eliminating overlapping service territory between two utility companies. **Tlingit-Haida Regional Electrical Authority v. State,** Op. No. 5357, 15 P3d 754 (Alaska 2001).

Where state attorney general filed suit on behalf of various charitable organizations, alleging that defendants had violated state's gaming laws by charging the charities unreasonably high expenses, and the charities had already dismissed or compromised their claims against the defendants, joinder of charities was not compelled by this rule. **Botelho v. Griffin,** Op. No. 5424, 25 P3d 689 (Alaska 2001).

Rule 20. Permissive Joinder of Parties.

(a) **Permissive Joinder.** All persons may join in one action as plaintiffs if they assert any right to relief jointly, severally, or in the alternative in respect of or arising out of the same transaction, occurrence, or series of transactions or occurrences and if any question of law or fact common to all these persons will arise in the action. All persons may be joined in one action as defendants if there is asserted against them jointly, severally, or in the alternative, any right to relief in respect of or arising out of the same transaction, occurrence, or series of transactions or occurrences and if any question of law or fact common to all of them will arise in the action. A plaintiff or defendant need not be interested in obtaining or defending against all the relief demanded. Judgment may be given for one or more of the plaintiffs according to their respective rights to relief, and against one or more defendants according to their respective liabilities.

(b) **Separate Trials.** The court may make such orders as will prevent a party from being embarrassed, delayed or put to expense by the inclusion of a party against whom the party asserts no claim and who asserts no claim against the party, and may order separate trials or make other orders to prevent delay or prejudice.

(Adopted by SCO 5 October 9, 1959; amended by SCO 258 effective November 15, 1976; and by SCO 1153 effective July 15, 1994)

Note: AS 10.06.675, as enacted by ch. 166, § 1, SLA 1988, amended Civil Rule 20 by allowing a corporation to join a member who received an improper distribution in an action under AS 10.06.675 without regard to the criteria for joinder in Civil Rule 20.

Annotations

Cases

Appellate review of a court order of attorney's fees to the prevailing party in a dismissed third-party action was warranted where the court departed from the accepted and usual course of proceedings in dismissing the claim rather than either severing it from the main action or ordering the pleadings amended and the purported third-party defendants joined as additional counterclaim defendants. **Aleut Corp. v. Rogers,** Op. No. 2212, 619 P2d 472 (Alaska 1980).

Motion by defendant, the obligor on a promissory note, to join credit union as a third party defendant, was improper, since the credit union had no obligation to indemnify the defendant for any liability to plaintiffs; rather, the motion was essentially a counterclaim against plaintiffs as assignees of defendant's promissory note to the credit union; accordingly, the trial court had discretionary authority to join the credit union as a defendant to the counterclaim, but failure to do so was harmless error, since the joinder motion was untimely and since relief was granted on the counterclaim despite absence of the credit union as a party. **Jackson v. Nangle,** Op. No. 2773, 677 P2d 242 (Alaska 1984).

Trial court did not err in joining real estate licensee as party to action arising out of surety fund claim under the Real Estate Surety Fund Act. **Warner v. State,** Op. No. 3764, 819 P2d 28 (Alaska 1991).

Rule 21. Misjoinder and Non-Joinder of Parties.

Misjoinder of parties is not ground for dismissal of an action. Parties may be dropped or added by order of the court on motion of any party or of its own initiative at any stage of the action and on such terms as are just. Any claim against a party may be severed and proceeded with separately.

(Adopted by SCO 5 October 9, 1959)

Annotations

Cases

Where a process server in possession of personal property by reason of writ of attachment is subject to an action brought by a third party claiming an interest superior to the attachment levy, courts should insure that the real contestants in interest are before it. **First National Bank of Anchorage v. Zawodny,** Op. No. 1976, 602 P2d 1254 (Alaska 1979).

Where a property owner sued the borough and the city claiming that their enforcement of certain land use ordinances violated the property owner's constitutional rights, while there was no indication in the record that the city moved for dismissal in response to the property owner's civil suit, the Alaska Supreme Court found that dismissal was appropriate given that the cases were consolidated and the city had no interest or stake in the action. **Varilek v. City of Houston,** Op. No. 5822, 104 P.3d 849 (Alaska 2004).

Rule 22. Interpleader.

Persons having claims against the plaintiff may be joined as defendants and required to interplead when their claims are such that the plaintiff is or may be exposed to double or multiple liability. It is not ground for objection to the joinder that the claims of the several claimants or the titles on which their claims depend do not have a common origin or are not identical but are adverse to and independent of one another, or that the plaintiff avers that the plaintiff is not liable in whole or in part to any or all of the claimants. A defendant exposed to similar liability may obtain such interpleader by way of cross-claim or counterclaim. The provisions of this rule supplement and do not in any way limit the joinder of parties permitted in Rule 20.

(Adopted by SCO 5 October 9, 1959; amended by SCO 1153 effective July 15, 1994)

Annotations

Cases

This rule is to be liberally construed. **Johnston v. All State Roofing & Paving Co., Inc.,** Op. No. 1351, 557 P2d 770 (Alaska 1976).

When stakeholder does not waive contention that he is not liable to any of the claimants, interpleader relief is still available. **Johnston v. All State Roofing & Paving Co., Inc.,** Op. No. 1351, 557 P2d 770 (Alaska 1976).

Where partial summary judgment has been granted in favor of one claimant in interpleader action, it would be deemed to have been satisfied to the extent of the amount previously paid into court, to obviate multiple claims. **Johnston v. All State Roofing & Paving Co., Inc.,** Op. No. 1351, 557 P2d 770 (Alaska 1976).

Garnishee was required to satisfy writ of execution served on it by judgment creditor-garnishor after garnishee failed to prove its affirmative defense that payments by it to an assignee of the judgment debtor were made under a good faith belief that a valid assignment existed. **Steenmeyher Corp. v. Mortenson Neal,** Op. No. 3154, 731 P2d 1221 (Alaska 1987).

This rule eliminates requirement that stakeholder not be independently liable to any claimant. **Nome Commercial Co. v. Nat. Bank of Alaska,** Op. No. 4892, 948 P2d 443 (Alaska 1997).

Claimant may not recover from innocent stakeholder damages caused by stakeholder's filing of interpleader. **Nome Commercial Co. v. Nat. Bank of Alaska,** Op. No. 4892, 948 P2d 443 (Alaska 1997).

Stakeholder does not become immune to suit for damages occurring after filing of interpleader action if damages were caused by stakeholder's independent, pre-interpleader activities. **Nome Commercial Co. v. Nat. Bank of Alaska,** Op. No. 4892, 948 P2d 443 (Alaska 1997).

Rule 23. Class Actions.

(a) **Prerequisites to a Class Action.** One or more members of a class may sue or be sued as representative parties on behalf of all only if (1) the class is so numerous that joinder of all members is impracticable, (2) there are questions of law or fact common to the class, (3) the claims or defenses of the representative parties are typical of the claims or defenses of the class, and (4) the representative parties will fairly and adequately protect the interests of the class.

(b) **Class Actions Maintainable.** An action may be maintained as a class action if the prerequisites of subdivision (a) are satisfied, and in addition:

(1) The prosecution of separate actions by or against individual members of the class would create a risk of

(A) Inconsistent or varying adjudications with respect to individual members of the class which would establish incompatible standards of conduct for the party opposing the class, or

(B) Adjudications with respect to individual members of the class which would as a practical matter be dispositive of the interests of the other members not parties to the adjudications or substantially impair or impede their ability to protect their interests; or

(2) The party opposing the class has acted or refuses to act on grounds generally applicable to the class, thereby making appropriate final injunctive relief or corresponding declaratory relief with respect to the class as a whole; or

(3) The court finds that the questions of law or fact common to the members of the class predominate over any questions affecting only individual members, and that a class action is superior to other available methods for the fair and efficient adjudication of the controversy. The matters pertinent to the finding include: (A) the interest of members of the class in individually controlling the prosecution or defense of separate actions; (B) the extent and nature of any litigation concerning the controversy already commenced by or against members of the class; (C) the desirability or undesirability of concentrating the litigation of the claims in the particular forum; (D) the difficulties likely to be encountered in the management of a class action.

(c) **Determination by Order Whether Class Action to Be Maintained—Notice—Judgment—Actions Conducted Partially as Class Actions.**

(1) As soon as practicable after the commencement of an action brought as a class action, the court shall determine by order whether it is to be so maintained. An order under this subdivision may be conditional, and may be altered or amended before the decision on the merits.

(2) In any class action maintained under subdivision (b)(3), the court shall direct to the members of the class the best notice practicable under the circumstances, including individual notice to all members who can be identified through reasonable effort. The notice shall advise each member that (A) the court will exclude the member from the class if the member so requests by a specified date; (B) the judgment, whether favorable or not, will include all members who do not request exclusion; and (C) any member who does not request exclusion may, if the member desires, enter an appearance through his counsel.

(3) The judgment in an action maintained as a class action under subdivision (b) (1) or (b) (2), whether or not favorable to the class, shall include and describe those whom the court finds to be members of the class. The judgment in the

action maintained as a class action under subdivision (b) (3), whether or not favorable to the class, shall include and specify or describe those to whom the notice provided in subdivision (c) (2) was directed, and who have not requested exclusion, and whom the court finds to be members of the class.

(4) When appropriate (A) an action may be brought or maintained as a class action with respect to particular issues, or (B) a class may be divided into subclasses and each subclass treated as a class, and the provisions of this rule shall then be construed and applied accordingly.

(d) **Orders in Conduct of Actions.** In the conduct of actions to which this rule applies, the court may make appropriate orders: (1) determining the course of proceedings or prescribing measures to prevent undue repetition or complication in the presentation of evidence or argument; (2) requiring, for the protection of the members of the class or otherwise for the fair conduct of the action, that notice be given in such manner as the court may direct to some or all of the members of any step in the action, or of the proposed extent of the judgment, or of the opportunity of members to signify whether they consider the representation fair and adequate, to intervene and present claims or defenses, or otherwise to come into the action; (3) imposing conditions on the representative parties or on intervenors; (4) requiring that the pleadings be amended to eliminate therefrom allegations as to representation of absent persons, and that the action proceed accordingly; (5) dealing with similar procedural matters. The orders may be combined with an order under Rule 16, and may be altered or amended as may be desirable from time to time.

(e) **Dismissal or Compromise.** A class action shall not be dismissed or compromised without the approval of the court, and notice of the proposed dismissal or compromise shall be given to all members of the class in such manner as the court directs.

(Adopted by SCO 5 October 9, 1959; rescinded and promulgated by SCO 258 effective November 15, 1976; amended by SCO 1153 effective July 15, 1994; by SCO 1163 effective July 15, 1994; and by SCO 1361 effective October 15, 1999)

Note: Chapter 79 § 2 SLA 1999 enacts AS 09.65.260(c), which relates to class actions for damages arising from the year 2000 date change and caused directly or indirectly by a failure of an electronic computing device. According to § 4 of the act, the enactment of AS 09.65.260(c) has the effect of amending Civil Rule 23, by requiring, in a class action relating to the year 2000 date change, that the aggregate claim of all members of the class for economic loss exceeds $150,000.

Annotations

Cases

Designation as class action excuses requirement of actual notice to members of defendant class, where all members had either been served with complaint or service had been attempted. **Calista Corp. v. DeYoung,** Op. No. 1403, 562 P2d 338 (Alaska 1977).

This rule, allowing the filing of a class action complaint to toll the statute of limitations as to all members of the class, supersedes AS 23.10.130(b) which requires that class members be specifically named as a party in order to toll the statute of limitations for such members. **Nolan v. Sea Airmotive, Inc.,** Op. No. 2337, 627 P2d 1035 (Alaska 1981).

Determination of the adequacy of representation in a class action is a question of fact which will not be reversed on appeal unless clearly erroneous. **State. v. Alex,** Op. No. 2488, 646 P2d 203 (Alaska 1982).

Defendants, by initiating summary judgment proceedings while plaintiffs' second motion for certification of class action was pending, waived objection to court deciding the merits of the case prior to certifying the class action. **State v. Alex,** Op. No. 2488, 646 P2d 203 (Alaska 1982).

Where purpose of class action suit was to have statute declared unconstitutional, defendant's contention that plaintiffs should not be permitted to represent the class because of interests antagonistic to other class members was rejected, since the interests of antagonistic class members would nevertheless be adequately represented by defendants seeking to have the statute declared constitutional. **State v. Alex,** Op. No. 2488,646 P2d 203 (Alaska 1982).

For reasons of judicial economy, a court must be allowed some latitude in deciding what issues may be determined before class action question is confronted. **Gold Bondholders v. Atchison, Topeka,** Op. No. 2551, 649 P2d 947 (Alaska 1982).

In case involving the enforceability of certain "gold clauses" in bonds issued in nineteenth century by a private corporation, superior court had discretion to rule on motion to dismiss the complaint before ruling on the question of class certification. **Gold Bondholders v. Atchison, Topeka,** Op. No. 2551, 649 P2d 947 (Alaska 1982).

Although notice to members of class of lot owners being represented by State against land developer did not state that those electing to participate would be bound by the final judgment, under the circumstances of the case, the error could be substantially corrected by requiring each lot owner, prior to receiving money under a judgment ordering restitution, to consent in writing to be bound by the judgment. **State v. First Nat'l Bank of Anchorage,** Op. No. 2591, 660 P2d 406 (Alaska 1982).

Absence of notice and court approval in violation of this rule, which appellants alleged affected their class eligibility determination, was harmless error, since there were independent grounds for excluding appellants from the class. **Riley v. Simon,** Op. No. 3583, 790 P2d 1339 (Alaska 1990).

Pro se plaintiff could not properly represent a class. **Hertz v. Cleary,** Op. No. 3846, 835 P2d 438 (Alaska 1992).

Trial court did not err in failing to grant prisoner's motion to intervene as pro se plaintiff in class action litigation challenging prison conditions since his application to intervene was untimely filed and his interests were adequately represented by the class members. **Hertz v. Cleary,** Op. No. 3846, 835 P2d 438 (Alaska 1992).

In class action suit where class certification was initially denied but subsequently granted, statute of limitations period remained tolled from date of complaint. **Fred Meyer of Alaska, Inc. v. Adams,** Op. No. 5027, 963 P2d 1025 (Alaska 1998).

In class action suit by legal aliens residing in Alaska seeking declaratory judgment as to constitutionality of statute restricting permanent fund dividend eligibility to persons lawfully admitted for permanent residence in the United States, trial court did not err in concluding that class members were not required to exhaust administrative remedies, since to do so would have been futile, or in concluding that class certification was proper. **State Dept. of Revenue v. Andrade,** Op. No. 5414, 23 P3d 58 (Alaska 2001).

Evidentiary hearing or discovery is not always required before class certification; it is within the discretion of the trial court to determine whether to hold an evidentiary hearing or permit discovery before granting class certification. **Bartek v. State,** Op. No. 5473, 31 P3d 100 (Alaska 2001).

Federal decisions are especially persuasive in interpreting Alaska R. Civ. P. 23. **Bartek v. State,** Op. No.5473,31 P3d 100 (Alaska 2001).

Trial court erred, and remand was necessary, when it decertified a class and failed to mention Alaska R. Civ. P. 23, or any of its requirements, and instead gave merit-related grounds for its order. **Shook v. Alyeska Pipeline Serv. Co.,** Op. No. 5600, 51 P.3d 935 (Alaska 2002).

Class actions suits are necessary to avoid a multiplicity of duplicative lawsuits; thus, in a lawsuit centering on whether Alaska could charge nonresidents more for commercial fishing licenses than it charged resident commercial fishers, requiring each nonresident commercial fisherman to file suit on the fisherman's own behalf would produce exactly that result; therefore, the trial judge's decision that named class members could sue on behalf of unnamed class members was proper. **State v. Carlson,** Op. No. 5673, 65 P.3d 851 (Alaska 2003).

Court of appeals rejected language in a class action notification stating that defendants' attorney's fees could be imposed on absent class members; absent class members have no obligation to pay attorneys' fees and litigation costs, except when they elect to accept the benefit of the litigation. **Turner v. Alaska Communs. Sys. Long Distance,** Op. No. 5742, 78 P.3d 264 (Alaska 2003).

A court's decision to certify a class will be overturned only if the court abused its discretion, which requires a definite and firm conviction that the trial court erred in its ruling, after reviewing the record as a whole. **International Seafoods of Alaska, Inc. v. Bissonette,** Op. No. 11568, 146 P.3d 561 (Alaska 2006).

The superior court did not err in ruling that class satisfied each of the prerequisites for a class action where the class of 110 plaintiffs met the numerosity requirement and it would have been impracticable to join class members who are dispersed in several states; the commonality and typicality requirements were met because the plaintiffs shared a single legal issue arising out of the same sequence of events; the class representatives had the same interests as the rest of the class and class counsel was competent. Moreover, because questions of law and fact common to the class predominate over questions affecting individual members, it would be more fair and efficient to adjudicate these questions as a class. **International Seafoods of Alaska, Inc. v. Bissonette,** Op. No. 11568, 146 P.3d 561 (Alaska 2006).

While there is no "magic number" satisfying the numerosity requirement of a class action claim, a proposed class containing more than forty members has been presumed to meet the requirement. **International Seafoods of Alaska, Inc. v. Bissonette,** Op. No. 11568, 146 P.3d 561 (Alaska 2006).

The typicality requirement of a class action claim is satisfied when each class member's claim arises from the same course of events, and each class member makes similar legal arguments to prove the defendant's liability. **International Seafoods of Alaska, Inc. v. Bissonette,** Op. No. 11568, 146 P.3d 561 (Alaska 2006).

The commonality requirement of a class action claim is satisfied if the named plaintiffs share at least one question of fact or law with the grievances of the prospective class. **International Seafoods of Alaska, Inc. v. Bissonette,** Op. No. 11568, 146 P.3d 561 (Alaska 2006).

For representation to be adequate in a class action claim, the plaintiff's attorney must be qualified, and there must be no conflict of interest between the named plaintiff and the other members of the class. **International Seafoods of Alaska, Inc. v. Bissonette,** Op. No. 11568, 146 P.3d 561 (Alaska 2006).

Class certification was necessary where the plaintiffs otherwise faced a risk of inconsistent adjudications and many of them may have elected not to litigate. **International Seafoods of Alaska, Inc. v. Bissonette,** Op. No. 11568, 146 P.3d 561 (Alaska 2006).

Rule 23.1. Derivative Actions By Shareholders.

(a) An action may be brought in the right of a domestic or foreign corporation to procure a judgment in its favor by a holder of shares of the corporation of voting trust certificates of the corporation, or of a beneficial interest in shares or certificates of the corporation.

(b) In a derivative action, the complaint shall be verified and shall allege that the plaintiff was a shareholder, of record or beneficially, or the holder of voting trust certificates at the time or during any part of the transaction of which the plaintiff complains or that the plaintiff's shares or voting trust certificates devolved upon the plaintiff by operation of law from a holder who was a holder at the time or during any part of the transaction complained of. A shareholder who does not meet the requirements of this section may be allowed in the discretion of the court to maintain the action on a preliminary showing to and determination by the court, by motion and after a hearing at which the court considers evidence, by affidavit or testimony, as it considers material, that

(1) there is a strong prima facie case in favor of the claim asserted on behalf of the corporation;

(2) no other similar action has been or is likely to be instituted;

(3) the plaintiff acquired the shares before there was disclosure to the public or to the plaintiff of the wrongdoing of which the plaintiff complains;

(4) unless the action can be maintained the defendant may retain a gain derived from the defendant's willful breach of a fiduciary duty; and

(5) the requested relief will not result in unjust enrichment of the corporation or a shareholder of the corporation.

(c) Unless excused on grounds that a majority of the directors is implicated in or under the direct or indirect control of a person who is implicated in the injury to the corporation, before an action in the right of a domestic or foreign corporation is instituted a plaintiff who has standing under (b) of this section shall make a formal demand upon the board to secure the action the plaintiff desires.

(d) If a shareholder fails to make a formal demand under (c) of this section the complaint shall state with particularity the facts establishing excuse under (c) of this section. In a motion to dismiss for failure to make demand on the board the shareholder shall have the burden to establish excuse.

(e) In a case in which demand on the board is made under (c) of this section, a decision by the board that, in its business judgment, the litigation would not be in the best interest of the corporation terminates the right created by (a) of this section.

(f) In a case in which demand on the board is excused under (c) of this section or the decision of the board under (e) of this section is rejected by the court as inconsistent with the directors' duties of care and loyalty to the corporation, a plaintiff who has standing under (b) of this section shall have the right to commence or continue the action created by (a) of this section. Notwithstanding (c) or (e) of this section, disinterested, noninvolved directors acting as the board or a duly charged board committee may petition the court to dismiss the plaintiff's action on grounds that in their independent, informed business judgment the action is not in the best interests of the corporation. The petitioners shall have the burden of establishing to the satisfaction of the court their disinterest, independence from any direct or indirect control of defendants in the action, and the informed basis on which they have exercised their asserted business judgment. If the court is satisfied that the petitions are disinterested, independent, and informed it shall then exercise an independent appraisal of the plaintiff's action to determine whether, considering the welfare of the corporation and relevant issues of public policy, it should dismiss the action.

(g) A shareholder action otherwise in conformity with this section shall not be dismissed because the alleged injury or wrong to the corporation has been ratified by the outstanding shares. A court may consider the fact of ratification in framing any order for relief to which it considers the corporation entitled.

(h) In an action instituted or maintained in the right of a corporation by the holder or holders of record of less than five percent of the outstanding shares of any class of the corporation or of voting trust certificates for these shares, the corporation in whose right the action is brought or the defendants may at any time before final judgment move the court to require the plaintiff to give security for the reasonable expense, including attorney fees, that may be incurred by the moving party. The amount of the security may be increased or decreased from time to time in this discretion of the court upon a showing that the security has become inadequate or excessive. The corporation or other defendants may have recourse to the security in an amount as the court may determine upon the termination of the derivative action, whether or not the court finds the action was brought without reasonable cause.

(i) A derivative action may not be discontinued, abandoned, compromised or settled without the approval of the court having jurisdiction of the action. If the court determines that the interests of the shareholders or any class or classes of shareholders will be substantially affected by a discontinuance, abandonment, compromise, or settlement, the court in its discretion may direct that notice, by publication or otherwise, shall be given to the shareholders or class or classes of shareholders whose interests will be affected. If the court directs notice to be given, it shall determine which of the parties to the action shall bear the expense of giving the notice in an amount the court determines to be reasonable in the circumstances. The amount shall be awarded as special costs of the action.

(j) If the derivative action is successful, in whole or in part, or if anything is received as a result of the judgment, compromise, or settlement of that action, the court may award to the plaintiff or plaintiffs reasonable expenses, including reasonable attorney fees, and shall direct an accounting to the corporation for the remainder of the proceeds. This subsection does not apply to a judgment rendered only for the benefit of injured shareholders and limited to a recovery of the loss or damage sustained by them.

(Added by SCO 258 effective November 15, 1976; amended by Chief Justice Special Order No. 2052a effective July 1, 1989)

Note: Civil Rule 23.1 in its entirety was adopted by the Alaska Legislature in ch. 166, §§ 1, 17, SLA 1988, rather than by the Alaska Supreme Court.

Annotations

Cases

Shareholders who filed a derivative suit against the directors of a village corporation were not prevailing parties because the trial court found that the shareholders' failure to make a pre-suit demand was not excused; the trial court did not err in denying the shareholders' request for attorney fees. **Jerue v. Millett,** Op. No. 5676, 66 P.3d 736 (Alaska 2003).

Where a village corporation did not become a party plaintiff until after the events occurred that mooted a derivative suit, the village was not a prevailing party for purposes of recovering attorney fees. **Jerue v. Millett,** Op. No. 5676, 66 P.3d 736 (Alaska 2003).

Rule 23.2. Actions Relating to Unincorporated Associations.

An action brought by or against the members of an unincorporated association as a class by naming certain members as representative parties may be maintained only if it appears that the representative parties will fairly and adequately protect the interest of the association and its members. In the conduct of the action the court may make appropriate orders corresponding with those described in Rule 23 (d), and the procedure for dismissal or compromise of the action shall correspond with that provided in Rule 23(e).

(Added by SCO 258 effective November 15, 1976)

Rule 24. Intervention.

(a) **Intervention of Right.** Upon timely application anyone shall be permitted to intervene in an action when the applicant claims an interest relating to the property or transaction which is the subject of the action and the applicant is so situated that the disposition of the action may as a practical matter impair or impede the applicant's ability to protect that interest, unless the applicant's interest is adequately represented by existing parties.

(b) **Permissive Intervention.** Upon timely application anyone may be permitted to intervene in an action when an applicant's claim or defense and the main action have a question of law or fact in common. When a party to an action relies for ground of claim or defense upon any statute or executive order administered by a federal or state governmental officer or agency or upon any regulation, order, requirement, or agreement issued or made pursuant to the statute or executive order, the officer or agency upon timely application may be permitted to intervene in the action. In exercising its discretion the court shall consider whether the intervention will unduly delay or prejudice the adjudication of the rights of the original parties.

(c) **Procedure.** A person desiring to intervene shall serve a motion to intervene upon the parties as provided in Rule 5. The motion shall state the ground therefor and shall be accompanied by a pleading setting forth the claim or defense for which intervention is sought. When the constitutionality of a state statute affecting the public interest is drawn in question in any action to which the state or an officer, agency, or employee thereof is not a party, the court shall notify the Attorney General of Alaska of such fact, and the state shall be permitted to intervene in the action.

(Adopted by SCO 5 October 9, 1959; amended by SCO 258 effective November 15, 1976; corrected January, 1993; amended by SCO 1153 effective July 15, 1994; and by SCO 1342 effective September 15 1998)

Note: AS 10.06.628, as enacted by ch. 166, § 1, SLA 1988, amended Civil Rule 24 by allowing a shareholder or creditor of a corporation to intervene in an action for involuntary dissolution of the corporation under AS 10.06.628.

Note: Chapter 105 SLA 1998 adopts AS 13.36.175 pertaining to contract actions against a trustee. According to section 23 of the act, subsection (c) of this statute amends Civil Rule 24 by allowing a beneficiary, or the attorney general and certain corporations under certain circumstances, to intervene in a contract action against a trustee without satisfying the criteria in the court rule. The act also adopts AS 13.36.185 pertaining to the tort liability of a trust. According to section 23 of the act, subsection (d) of this statute also amends Civil Rule 24 by allowing a beneficiary to intervene in a tort action against a trust without satisfying the criteria in the court rule.

Note: Ch. 61 SLA 2002 (HB 52), Section 2, repeals and reenacts AS 33.36.110 to authorize the governor to execute the Interstate Compact for Adult Offender Supervision. According to Section 7 of the Act, Article VIII(a)(2) of the Compact, contained in the new AS 33.36.110, would have the effect of amending Civil Rule 24 by entitling the Interstate Commission for Adult Offender Supervision to have standing to intervene in a judicial proceeding in this state that pertains to the Interstate Compact for Adult Offender Supervision and that may affect the powers, responsibilities, or actions of that commission.

Annotations

Cases

Intervention in action over disputed proxies must be allowed to directors who would be displaced if disputed proxies were found valid. **Brown v. Cook Inlet Region, Inc.,** Op. No. 1507, 569 P2d 1321 (Alaska 1977).

A four-part test is imposed to determine if the court is required to grant intervention as a matter of right: (1) the motion must be timely; (2) the applicant must show an interest in the subject matter of the action; (3) it must be shown that this interest may be impaired as a consequence of the action; and (4) it must be shown that the interest is not adequately represented by an existing party. **State v. Weidner,** Op. No. 2788, 684 P2d 103 (Alaska 1984).

A requisite interest for intervention as a matter of right must be direct, substantial, and significantly protectable; a contingent interest is insufficient. **State v. Weidner,** Op. No. 2788, 684 P2d 103 (Alaska 1984).

A party seeking intervention as a matter of right must show that its interest is inadequately represented by the existing party to the suit; inadequacy is proven by a showing of collusion, adversity of interest, possible nonfeasance, or incompetence. **State v. Weidner,** Op. No. 2788, 684 P2d 103 (Alaska 1984).

In a case challenging the legality of an agricultural land lottery which was allowed to proceed without transfer of title to lottery winners pending a court decision on the merits, the lottery winners could not intervene as a matter of right and the court did not abuse its discretion in denying permissive intervention. **State v. Weidner,** Op. No. 2788, 684 P2d 103 (Alaska 1984).

In deciding whether or not a litigant is entitled to intervene in an action as of right, the court looks to the "interest" he claims, the extent to which "disposition of the action may as a practical matter impair or impede his ability to protect that interest," and the possibility that the interest is "adequately represented by existing parties." **Matter of J.R.S.,** Op. No. 2869, 690 P2d 10 (Alaska 1984).

Superior court's decision to set aside the placement preferences of the Indian Child Welfare Act in adoption proceeding was reversible error due to court's denial of Indian village's motion to intervene in the proceeding. **Matter of J.R.S.,** Op. No. 2869, 690 P2d 10 (Alaska 1984).

Where foster parents filed an adoption petition with the consent of the children's biological parents and the children's maternal grandparents filed an adoption petition without the consent of the biological parents, trial court committed reversible error in excluding the grandparents from participating as parties in the hearing on the foster parents' petition. **Matter of W.E.G.,** Op. No. 2998, 710 P2d 410 (Alaska 1985).

Where buyer contracted with the State to purchase oil which the State received as royalty payments from lessees of oil rights at a price to be determined by the results of a pending case between the State and certain of the lessees, and the buyer contractually agreed not to intervene in the pending case absent the State's consent, the trial court properly upheld the nonintervention clause, rejecting buyer's contention that the State had misrepresented the position it intended to take in the pending case and that the State did not exercise good faith when it withheld its consent to intervene. **Tesoro Alaska Petroleum Co. v. State,** Op. No. 3352, 757 P2d 1045 (Alaska 1988).

Any error in trial court's refusal to permit a person to intervene as a party plaintiff was harmless since his interests were adequately protected by court order allowing him to participate as an amicus curiae. **Alaska Christian Bible Inst. v. State,** Op. No. 3426, 772 P2d 1079 (Alaska 1989).

The grant or denial of a motion for permissive intervention is subject to review for abuse of discretion. **State v. Enserch Alaska Const. Inc.,** Op. No. 3539, 787 P2d 624 (Alaska 1989).

Where intervenors did not raise any issues not already raised by plaintiff and the defendant was able to depose the intervenors before argument or motion for summary judgment began, defendant was not unduly prejudiced by late intervention. **State v. Enserch Alaska Const. Inc.,** Op. No. 3539, 787 P2d 624 (Alaska 1989).

City's decision against appealing trial court's order enjoining it from pursuing a recall petition against certain school board members, although perhaps adequate for purposes of representing the general public interest, inadequately represented the particular interests of appellants (a school board member not subject to the recall petition, a sponsor of the petition, and a signer of the petition), thus appellants were entitled to intervene as of right in the case given that their motion to intervene was timely, they had sufficient interest in the subject matter of the action, and their interests could be impaired as a result of the case. **McCormick v. Smith,** Op. No. 3605, 793 P2d 1042 (Alaska 1990).

Once Child Support Enforcement Division (CSED) sought to modify prior child support order, partly to insure that State would be reimbursed before any arrearages were paid, interests of mother, who had assigned her support rights to CSED, diverged from interests of agency, since mother had interest in arrearages as well as in obtaining highest level of on-going support for child, thus mother met requirements for intervention of right. **Keating v. Traynor,** Op. No. 3862, 833 P2d 695 (Alaska 1992).

Pro se plaintiff could not properly represent a class. **Hertz v. Cleary,** Op. No. 3846, 835 P2d 438 (Alaska 1992).

Trial court did not err in failing to grant prisoner's motion to intervene as pro se plaintiff in class action litigation challenging prison conditions since his application to intervene was untimely filed and his interests were adequately represented by the class members. **Hertz v. Cleary,** Op. No. 3846, 835 P2d 438 (Alaska 1992).

Permissive intervention was proper where intervenors' claims shared common issues of law and fact with the defendants'. **Keane v. Local Boundary Commission,** Op. No. 4187, 893 P2d 1239 (Alaska 1995).

Mere assertion that there are increased complications in tripartite litigation is not sufficient to establish that superior court abused its discretion in allowing intervention. **Keane v. Local Boundary Commission,** Op. No. 4187, 893 P2d 1293 (Alaska 1995).

Superior court did not abuse its discretion in allowing intervention where intervenors raised additional arguments and interests not raised by original defendants and intervention did not appear to have unduly delayed or prejudiced the original parties. **Keane v. Local Boundary Commission,** Op. No. 4187, 893 P2d 1239 (Alaska 1995).

Although grantee under deeds did not seek to intervene until within ten days after trial court entered final judgment granting landowner's motion to quiet title to parcels it had received under settlement agreement with grantor and to invalidate all deeds conveying those parcels from grantor to other parties, grantee's application to intervene was timely, since it was unclear whether grantee knew that her parcels would be affected by motion until after trial court entered its judgment. **Mundt v. Northwest Explorations, Inc.,** Op. No. 4901, 947 P2d 827 (Alaska 1997).

Grantee under deeds should have been permitted to intervene in litigation arising from landowner's post-judgment motion to quiet title to parcels it had received under settlement agreement with grantor and to invalidate all deeds conveying those parcels from grantor to other parties since grantee's interests were not coextensive with those of grantor and were therefore not adequately represented by grantor. **Mundt v. Northwest Explorations, Inc.,** Op. No. 4901, 947 P2d 827 (Alaska 1997).

In declaratory judgment action brought by group of nonunion employees, taxpayers and employers challenging validity of borough's decision to require successful bidders on construction project to enter into labor agreement with local labor unions, trial court abused its discretion in denying unions' motion to intervene as of right. **Laborers Local No. 942 v. Lampkin,** Op. No. 4958, 956 P2d 422 (Alaska 1998).

Speed at which trial court conducted litigation, moving from complaint to trial in two weeks, could not be basis for holding motion to intervene untimely. **Laborers Local No. 942 v. Lampkin,** Op. No. 4958, 956 P2d 422 (Alaska 1998).

Mining claim grantor's motion to intervene as matter of right eight months after end of quiet title action on claim was untimely; argument that because one of grantor's shareholders lacked notice of transfer of mining claim same lack of notice should be imputed to entire company was rejected because several of grantor's shareholders did know of transfer. **Red Top Mining, Inc. v. Anthony,** Op. No. 5143, 983 P2d 743 (Alaska 1999).

In CINA proceeding, child's adult sister, who never moved to intervene but instead moved for placement of child with her under statute giving relatives preference in placement, was entitled to intervene as of right on remand, since state conceded that she was effectively a party by virtue of the appeal and neither state nor guardian ad litem opposed her motion on ground that she was not entitled to intervene. **S.S.M. v. State Dept. of Health,** Op. No. 5285, 3 P3d 342 (Alaska 2000).

Supreme Court of Alaska reviews denial of intervention as a matter of right for abuse of discretion if timeliness is at issue, but applies its independent judgment if timeliness is not at issue and if facts relevant to intervention are not in dispute. **Alaskans for a Common Language v. Kritz,** Op. No. 5284, 3 P3d 906 (Alaska 2000).

Generally when the government exercises its sovereign power to enforce and defend duly enacted laws, no other entity can have an interest sufficient to satisfy the requirements for intervention as of right under this rule; however, when the people of a state have reserved the power of direct legislation, those who take responsibility for that direct legislation may have a sufficient interest. **Alaskans for a Common Language v. Kritz,** Op. No. 5284, 3 P3d 906 (Alaska 2000).

In lawsuit to determine the constitutionality of a successful ballot initiative requiring the government to use English, incorporated organization which supported the initiative had sufficient interest to intervene as of right because the incorporators of the organization were also the sponsors on the initiative committee and because the executive branch publicly opposed the initiative before the election. **Alaskans for a Common Language v. Kritz,** Op. No. 5284,3 P3d 906 (Alaska 2000).

Where an employer was first informed of a hearing to allocate fault to it on January 17, that was the date upon which the employer's duty to intervene arose. Measured from January 17, only 12 days elapsed before the employer submitted its motion to intervene; that was a relatively short delay, and the trial court erred in denying the motion. **Scammon Bay Ass'n v. Ulak,** Op. No. 5971, 126 P.3d 138 (Alaska 2005).

In determining whether a motion to intervene meets Rule 24's timeliness standard, Alaska courts have adopted a four-part analysis widely used by federal courts; this test requires consideration of: (1) the length of time the applicant knew or reasonably should have known that its interest was imperiled before it moved to intervene; (2) the foreseeable prejudice to existing parties if intervention is granted; (3) the foreseeable prejudice to the applicant if intervention is denied; and (4) idiocratic circumstances which, fairly viewed, militate for or against intervention. **Kirk v. Demientieff,** Op. No. 11760, 145 P.3d 512 (Alaska 2006).

Rule 25. Substitution of Parties.

(a) **Death.**

(1) If a party dies and the claim is not thereby extinguished, the court may order substitution of the proper parties. The motion for substitution may be made by the successors or representatives of the deceased party or by any party and, together with the notice of hearing, shall be served on the parties as provided in Rule 5 and upon persons not parties in the manner provided in Rule 4 for the service of a summons. Unless the motion for substitution is made not later than 90 days after the death is suggested upon the record by service of a statement of the fact of the death as provided herein for the service of the motion, the action shall be dismissed as to the deceased party.

(b) **Incompetency.** If a party becomes incompetent, the court upon motion served as provided in subdivision (a) of this rule may allow the action to be continued by or against the party's representative.

(c) **Transfer of Interest.** In case of any transfer of interest, the action may be continued by or against the original party, unless the court upon motion directs the person to whom the interest is transferred to be substituted in the action or joined with the original party. Service of the motion shall be made as provided in subdivision (a) of this rule.

(d) **Public Officers—Death or Separation From Office.**

(1) When a public officer is a party to an action in an official capacity and during its pendency dies, resigns, or otherwise ceases to hold office, the action does not abate and the officer's successor is automatically substituted as a party.

Proceedings following the substitution shall be in the name of the substituted party, but any misnomer not affecting the substantial rights of the parties shall be disregarded. An order of substitution may be entered at any time, but the omission to enter such an order shall not affect the substitution.

(2) When a public officer sues or is sued in an official capacity, the officer may be described as a party by official title rather than by name; but the court may require the officer's name to be added.

(Adopted by SCO 5 October 9, 1959; amended by SCO 258 effective November 15, 1976; by SCO 633 effective September 15, 1985; by SCO 1153 effective July 15, 1994; and by SCO 1396 effective October 15, 2000)

Note: Chapter 115 SLA 00 adopts AS 32.06.906 relating to the merger of partnerships. This section is effective January 1, 2001. Under AS 32.06.906(a)(4), an action or proceeding pending against a partnership or limited partnership that is a party to a merger may be continued as if the merger had not occurred, or the surviving entity may be substituted as a party to the action or proceeding. According to section 9 of the act, this provision has the effect of amending Civil Rule 25(c) by allowing certain substitutions of parties as a matter of right.

Annotations

Cases

Where judgment was entered against originally named defendant state officers, trial court would be directed to substitute successor incumbent or parties on remand. **McGinnis v. Stevens,** Op. No. 3094, 570 P.2d 735 (Alaska 1977).

This rule applies to post-judgment proceedings to enforce a judgment. **State v. 18,018 Square Feet,** Op. No. 2232, 621 P2d 887 (Alaska 1981).

Whether or not a party should be substituted for another rests in the sound discretion of the trial court. **State v. 18,018 Square Feet,** Op. No. 2232, 621 P2d 887 (Alaska 1981).

Mechanic's lien claimant was entitled to amend his complaint to add as a defendant to the action the subsequent purchaser of the burdened real property. **First National Bank of Anchorage v. Dent,** Op. No. 2839, 683 P2d 722 (Alaska 1984).

Where bank went into receivership during the pendency of a suit against the bank in state court, the receiver did not become a party to the action until the court exercised its discretion to substitute the receiver as a party defendant. **Interior Glass Services, Inc. v. FDIC,** 691 FS 1255 (D. Alaska 1988).

Trial court did not abuse its discretion in enlarging time for decedant's estate to substitute in as plaintiff for decedant. **Estate of Lampert v. Estate of Lampert,** Op. No. 4203, 896 P2d 214 (Alaska 1995).

PART V. DEPOSITIONS AND DISCOVERY

Rule 26. General Provisions Governing Discovery; Duty of Disclosure.

(a) **Required Disclosures; Methods to Discover Additional Matter.** Disclosure under subparagraphs (a)(1), (2), and (3) of this rule is required in all civil actions, except those categories of cases exempted from the requirement of scheduling conferences and scheduling orders under Civil Rule 16(g), adoption proceedings, and prisoner litigation against the state under AS 09.19.

(1) *Initial Disclosures.* Except to the extent otherwise directed by order or rule, a party shall, without awaiting a discovery request, provide to other parties:

(A) the factual basis of each of its claims or defenses;

(B) the name and, if known, the address and telephone number of each individual likely to have discoverable information relevant to disputed facts alleged with particularity in the pleadings, identifying the subjects of the information and whether the attorney-client privilege applies;

(C) the name and, if known, the address and telephone number of each individual who has made a written or recorded statement and, unless the statement is privileged or otherwise protected from disclosure, either a copy of the statement or the name and, if known, the address and telephone number of the custodian;

(D) subject to the provisions of Civil Rule 26(b)(3), a copy of, or a description by category and location of, all documents, data compilations, and tangible things that are relevant to disputed facts alleged with particularity in the pleadings;

(E) subject to the provisions of Civil Rule 26(b)(3), all photographs, diagrams, and videotapes of persons, objects, scenes and occurrences that are relevant to disputed facts alleged with particularity in the pleadings;

(F) each insurance agreement under which any person carrying on an insurance business may be liable to satisfy part or all of a judgment which may be entered in the action or to indemnify or reimburse for payments made to satisfy the judgment;

(G) all categories of damages claimed by the disclosing party, and a computation of each category of special damages, making available for inspection and copying as under Rule 34 the documents or other evidentiary material, not privileged or protected from disclosure, on which such claims are based, including materials bearing on the nature and extent of injuries suffered; and

(H) the identity, with as much specificity as may be known at the time, of all potentially responsible persons within the meaning of AS 09.17.080, and whether the party will choose to seek to allocate fault against each identified potentially responsible person.

Unless otherwise directed by the court, these disclosures shall be made at or within 10 days after the meeting of the parties under subsection (f). A party shall make its initial disclosures based on the information then reasonably available to it and is not excused from making its disclosures because it has not fully completed its investigation of the case or because it challenges the sufficiency of another party's disclosures or because another party has not made its disclosures.

(2) *Disclosure of Expert Testimony.*

(A) In addition to the disclosures required by subparagraph (a)(1), a party shall disclose to other parties the identity of any person who may be used at trial to present evidence under Evidence Rules 702, 703, or 705.

(B) Except as otherwise stipulated or directed by the court, this disclosure shall, with respect to a witness who is retained or specially employed to provide expert testimony in the case or whose duties as an employee of the party regularly involve giving expert testimony, be accompanied by a written report prepared and signed by the witness. The report shall contain a complete statement of all opinions to be expressed and the basis and reasons therefor; the data or other information considered by the witness in forming the opinions; any exhibits to be used as a summary of or support for the opinions; the qualifications of the witness, including a list of all publications authored by the witness within the preceding ten years; the compensation to be paid for the study and testimony; and a listing of any other cases in which the witness has testified as an expert at trial or by deposition within the preceding four years.

(C) These disclosures shall be made at the times and in the sequence directed by the court. The parties shall supplement these disclosures when required under subparagraph (e)(1).

(D) No more than three independent expert witness may testify for each side as to the same issue in any given case. For purposes of this rule, an independent expert is an expert from whom a report is required under section (a)(2)(B). The court, upon the showing of good cause, may increase or decrease the number of independent experts to be called.

(3) *Pretrial Disclosures.* In addition to the disclosures required in the preceding paragraphs, a party shall provide to other parties the following information regarding the evidence that it may present at trial other than solely for impeachment purposes:

(A) the name and, if not previously provided, the address and telephone number of each witness, separately identifying those whom the party expects to present and those whom the party may call if the need arises;

(B) the designation of those witnesses whose testimony is expected to be presented by means of a deposition and, if not taken stenographically, a transcript of the pertinent portions of the deposition testimony; and

(C) an appropriate identification of each document or other exhibit, including summaries of other evidence, separately identifying those which the party expects to offer and those which the party may offer if the need arises.

These disclosures shall be made at the times and in the sequence directed by the court. Within 14 days thereafter, unless a different time is specified by the court, a party may serve and file a list disclosing (i) any objections to the use under Rule 32(a) of a deposition designated by another party under subparagraph (B), and (ii) any objection, together with the grounds therefor, that may be made to the admissibility of materials identified under subparagraph (C). Objections not so disclosed, other than objections under Rules 402 and 403 of the Rules of Evidence, shall be deemed waived unless excused by the court for good cause shown.

(4) *Form of Disclosures.* Unless otherwise directed by the court, all disclosures under subparagraphs (a)(1) and (2) shall be made in writing, signed, and served in accordance with Rule 5.

(5) *Methods to Discover Additional Matter.* Parties may obtain discovery by one or more of the following methods: depositions upon oral examination or written questions; written interrogatories; production of documents or things or permission to enter upon land or other property, for inspection and other purposes; physical and mental examinations; and requests for admission.

(b) **Discovery Scope and Limits.** Unless otherwise limited by order of the court in accordance with these rules, the scope of discovery is as follows:

(1) *In General.* Parties may obtain discovery regarding any matter, not privileged which is relevant to the subject matter involved in the pending action, whether it relates to the claim or defense of the party seeking discovery or to the claim or defense of any other party, including the existence, description, nature, custody, condition and location of any books, documents, or other tangible things and the identity and location of persons having knowledge of any discoverable matter. The information sought need not be admissible at the trial if the information sought appears reasonably calculated to lead to the discovery of admissible evidence.

(2) *Limitations.* The court may alter the limits in these rules on the number of depositions and interrogatories, the length of depositions under Rule 30, and the number of requests under Rule 36. The frequency or extent of use of the discovery methods otherwise permitted under these rules shall be limited by the court if it determines that: (i) the discovery sought is unreasonably cumulative or duplicative, or is obtainable from some other source that is more convenient, less burdensome, or less expensive; (ii) the party seeking discovery has had ample opportunity by discovery in the action to obtain the information sought; or (iii) the burden or expense of the proposed discovery outweighs its likely benefit, taking into account the needs of the case, the amount in controversy, the parties' resources, the importance of the issues at stake in the litigation, and the importance of the proposed discovery in resolving the issues. The court may act upon its own initiative after reasonable notice or pursuant to a motion under paragraph (c).

(3) *Trial Preparation: Materials.* Subject to the provisions of subparagraph (b)(4) of this rule, a party may obtain discovery of documents and tangible things otherwise discoverable under subparagraph (b)(1) of this rule and prepared in anticipation of litigation or for trial by or for another party or by or for that other party's representative (including the other party's attorney, consultant, surety, indemnitor, insurer, or agent) only upon a showing that the party seeking discovery has substantial need of the materials in the preparation of the party's case and that the party is unable

without undue hardship to obtain the substantial equivalent of the materials by other means. In ordering discovery of such materials when the required showing has been made, the court shall protect against disclosure of the mental impressions, conclusions, opinions or legal theories of an attorney or other representative of a party concerning the litigation.

A party may obtain without the required showing a statement concerning the action or its subject matter previously made by that party. Upon request, a person not a party may obtain without the required showing a statement concerning the action or its subject matter previously made by that person. If the request is refused, the person may move for a court order. The provisions of Rule 37(a) (4) apply to the award of expenses incurred in relation to the motion. For purposes of this paragraph, a statement previously made is (A) a written statement signed or otherwise adopted or approved by the person making it, or (B) a stenographic, mechanical, electrical, or other recording, or a transcription thereof, which is a substantially verbatim recital of an oral statement by the person making it and contemporaneously recorded.

(4) *Trial Preparation: Experts.*

(A) A party may depose any person who has been identified as an expert whose opinions may be presented at trial. If a report from the expert is required under section (a)(2)(B), the deposition shall not be conducted until after the report is provided.

(B) A party may, through interrogatories or by deposition, discover facts known or opinions held by an expert who has been retained or specially employed by another party in anticipation of litigation or preparation for trial and who is not expected to be called as a witness at trial, only as provided in Rule 35(b) or upon a showing of exceptional circumstances under which it is impracticable for the party seeking discovery to obtain facts or opinions on the same subject by other means.

(C) Unless manifest injustice would result, (i) the court shall require that the party seeking discovery pay the expert a reasonable fee for time spent in responding to discovery under this subparagraph; and (ii) with respect to discovery obtained under section (b)(4)(B) of this rule the court shall require the party seeking discovery to pay the other party a fair portion of the fees and expenses reasonably incurred by the latter party in obtaining facts and opinions from the expert.

(5) *Claims of Privilege or Protection of Trial Preparation Materials.* When a party withholds information otherwise discoverable under these rules by claiming that it is privileged or subject to protection as trial preparation material, the party shall make the claim expressly and shall describe the nature of the documents, communications, or things not produced or disclosed in a manner that, without revealing information itself privileged or protected, will enable other parties to assess the applicability of the privilege or protection.

(c) **Protective Orders.** Upon motion by a party or by the person from whom discovery is sought, accompanied by a certification that the movant has in good faith conferred or attempted to confer with other affected parties in an effort to resolve the dispute without court action, and for good cause shown, the court in which the action is pending or alternatively, on matters relating to a deposition, the court in the judicial district where the deposition is to be taken may make any order which justice requires to protect a party or person from annoyance, embarrassment, oppression, or undue burden or expense, including one or more of the following: (1) that the disclosure or discovery not be had; (2) that the disclosure or discovery may be had only on specified terms and conditions, including a designation of the time or place; (3) that the discovery may be had only by a method of discovery other than that selected by the party seeking discovery; (4) that certain matters not be inquired into, or that the scope of the disclosure or discovery be limited to certain matters; (5) that discovery be conducted with no one present except persons designated by the court; (6) that a deposition, after being sealed, be opened only by order of the court; (7) that a trade secret or other confidential research, development, or commercial information not be revealed or be revealed only in a designated way; and (8) that the parties simultaneously file specified documents or information enclosed in sealed envelopes to be opened as directed by the court.

If the motion for a protective order is denied in whole or in part, the court may, on such terms and conditions as are just, order that any party or other person provide or permit discovery. The provisions of Rule 37(a)(4) apply to the award of expenses incurred in relation to the motion.

(d) **Timing and Sequence of Discovery.**

(1) *Timing of Discovery—Non-Exempted Actions.* In an action in which disclosure is required under Rule 26(a), a party may serve up to ten of the thirty interrogatories allowed under Rule 33(a) at the times allowed by section (d)(2)(C) of this rule. Otherwise, except by order of the court or agreement of the parties, a party may not seek discovery from any source before the parties have met and conferred as required by paragraph (f).

(2) *Timing of Discovery—Exempted Actions.* In actions exempted from disclosure under Rule 26(a), discovery may take place as follows:

(A) For depositions upon oral examination under Civil Rule 30, a defendant may take depositions at any time after commencement of the action. The plaintiff must obtain leave of court if the plaintiff seeks to take a deposition prior to the expiration of 30 days after service of the summons and complaint upon any defendant or service by publication if authorized, except that leave is not required (i) if a defendant has served a notice of taking deposition or otherwise sought discovery, or (ii) the plaintiff seeks to take the deposition under Civil Rule 30(a)(2)(C).

(B) For depositions upon written questions under Civil Rule 31, a party may serve questions at any time after commencement of the action.

(C) For interrogatories, requests for production, and requests for admission under Civil Rules 33, 34, and 36, discovery requests may be served upon the plaintiff at any time after the commencement of the action, and upon any other party with or after service of the summons and complaint upon that party.

(3) *Sequence of Discovery.* Unless the court upon motion, for the convenience of parties and witnesses and in the interests of justice, orders otherwise, methods of discovery may be used in any sequence, and the fact that a party is conducting discovery, whether by deposition or otherwise, shall not operate to delay any other party's discovery.

(e) **Supplementation of Disclosures and Responses.** A party who has made a disclosure under paragraph (a) or Civil Rule 26.1(b) or responded to a request for discovery with a disclosure or response is under a duty to supplement or correct the disclosure or response to include information thereafter acquired if ordered by the court or in the following circumstances:

(1) A party is under a duty to supplement at appropriate intervals its disclosures under paragraph (a) if the party learns that in some material respect the information disclosed is incomplete or incorrect and if the additional or corrective information has not otherwise been made known to the other parties during the discovery process or in writing. With respect to testimony of an expert from whom a report is required under subdivision (a)(2)(B) the duty extends both to information contained in the report and to information provided through a deposition of the expert.

(2) A party is under a duty seasonably to amend a prior response to an interrogatory, request for production, or request for admission if the party learns that the response is in some material respect incomplete or incorrect and if the additional or corrective information has not otherwise been made known to the other parties during the discovery process or in writing.

(f) **Meeting of Parties; Planning for Discovery and Alternative Dispute Resolution.** Except when otherwise ordered and except in actions exempted from disclosure under Rule 26(a), the parties shall, as soon as practicable and in any event at least 14 days before a scheduling conference is held or a scheduling order is due under Rule 16(b), meet to discuss the nature and basis of their claims and defenses and the possibilities for a prompt settlement or resolution of the case, including whether an alternative dispute resolution procedure is appropriate, to make or arrange for the disclosures required by subparagraph (a)(1), and to develop a proposed discovery plan and a proposed alternative dispute resolution plan. The plan shall indicate the parties' views and proposals concerning:

(1) what changes should be made in the timing or form of disclosures under paragraph (a), including a statement as to when the disclosures under subparagraph (a)(1) were made or will be made and what are appropriate intervals for supplementation of disclosure under Rule 26(e)(1);

(2) the subjects on which discovery may be needed, when discovery should be completed, and whether discovery should be conducted in phases or be limited to or focused upon particular issues;

(3) what changes should be made in the limitations on discovery imposed under these rules and what other limitations should be imposed;

(4) the plan for alternative dispute resolution, including its timing, the method of selecting a mediator, early neutral evaluator, or arbitrator, or an explanation of why alternative dispute resolution is inappropriate;

(5) whether a scheduling conference is unnecessary; and

(6) any other orders that should be entered by the court under paragraph (c) or under Rule 16(b) and (c).

The attorneys of record and all unrepresented parties that have appeared in the case are jointly responsible for arranging and being present or represented at the meeting, for attempting in good faith to agree on the proposed discovery plan, and for submitting to the court within 10 days after the meeting a written report outlining the plan.

(g) **[Applicable to cases filed on or after August 7, 1997.] Limited Discovery; Expedited Calendaring.** In a civil action for personal injury or property damage involving less than $100,000 in claims, the parties shall limit discovery to that allowed under District Court Civil Rule 1(a)(1) and shall avail themselves of the expedited calendaring procedures allowed under District Court Civil Rule 4.

(Adopted by SCO 5 October 9, 1959; amended by SCO 49 effective January 1, 1963; by SCO 149 dated December 27, 1971; by SCO 158 effective February 15, 1973; by Amendment No. 2 to SCO 158 dated July 30, 1973; by SCO 336 effective January 1, 1979; by SCO 1026 effective July 15, 1990; by SCO 1153 effective July 15, 1994; by SCO 1172 effective July 15, 1995; by SCO 1266 effective July 15, 1997; by SCO 1281 effective August 7, 1997; by SCO 1318 effective July 15, 1998; by SCO 1325 effective July 15, 1998; by SCO 1341 effective September 10, 1998; and by SCO 1569 effective October 15, 2005)

Note to SCO 1281: Paragraph (g) of this rule was added by ch. 26, sec. 40, SLA 1997. According to sec. 55 of the Act, the amendment to Civil Rule 26 applies "to all causes of action accruing on or after the effective date of this Act." The amendment to Rule 26 adopted by paragraph 1 of this order applies to all cases filed on or after August 7, 1997. See paragraph 17 of this order. The change is adopted for the sole reason that the legislature has mandated the amendment.

Note: Ch. 26, sec. 10, SLA 1997 repeals and reenacts AS 09.17.020 concerning punitive damages. New AS 09.17.020(e) prohibits parties from conducting discovery relevant to the amount of punitive damages until after the fact finder has determined that an award of punitive damages is allowed. This provision applies to causes of action accruing on or after August 7, 1997. See ch. 26, sec. 55, SLA 1997. According to sec. 48 of the Act, new AS 09.17.020(e) has the effect of amending Civil Rule 26 by limiting discovery in certain actions.

Note: Section 2 of chapter 95 SLA 1998 amends AS 09.19.050 to state that the automatic disclosure provisions of Civil Rule 26 do not apply in prisoner litigation against the state. According to section 13 of the act, this amendment has the effect of changing Civil Rule 26 "by providing that the automatic disclosure provisions of the rule do not apply to litigation against the state brought by prisoners."

Note to SCO 1647: The supreme court has approved certain procedures for Anchorage cases that vary from those specified in this rule. Civil Rule 26(a)(1) sets out a procedure to be used "[e]xcept to the extent otherwise directed by order or rule," and sets a timeline for disclosures "[u]nless otherwise directed by the court." Civil Rule 26(f) also sets out a procedure to be sued "except when otherwise ordered." In Anchorage, Administrative Order 3AO-03-04 (Amended) applies to modify the procedures set out in subdivisions (a)(1) and (f). That Order, commonly referred to as the Anchorage Uniform Pretrial Order, was issued and adopted according to the provisions of Administrative Rule 46, and is available on the court system's website at http://www.state.ak.us/courts/orders-cr16-26.htm.

Annotations

Cases

In a personal injury case, it was error to deny motion to require attending physician to testify at a deposition regarding the injuries sustained by plaintiff where waiver of privilege during trial appeared to be almost inevitable. **Mathis v. Hilderbrand,** Op. No. 349, 416 P2d 8 (Alaska 1966).

The nature of the condemnation action, standing alone, constituted "exceptional circumstances" within the meaning of this rule, justifying trial court order directing the State to furnish the condemnee appraisal reports on the condemned property made by experts whom the State had retained but did not intend to call as witnesses. **State v. Leach,** Op. No. 980, 516 P2d 1383 (Alaska 1973).

In view of the commitment to liberal pretrial discovery, the scope of the attorney-client privilege should be strictly construed in accordance with its purpose. **United Services Automobile Association v. Werley,** Op. No. 1079, 526 P2d 28 (Alaska 1974).

The attorney-client privilege cannot be used to protect a client in perpetration of a crime or other evil enterprise in concert with an attorney. **United Services Automobile Association v. Werley,** Op. No. 1079, 526 P2d 28 (Alaska 1974).

The exception to the attorney-client privilege that it cannot be used to protect a client in perpetration of a crime or other evil enterprise in concert with the attorney comes into play only when the communications between the advisor and client pertain to ongoing or future, rather than prior, wrongdoing and when advice sought is for a knowingly unlawful end. There is generally also the restriction of the exception to cases involving crime or civil fraud or tort. **United Services Automobile Association v. Werley,** Op. No. 1079, 526 P2d 28 (Alaska 1974).

Once a litigant has presented prima facie evidence of perpetration of fraud or crime in the attorney-client relationship, the other party may not then claim privilege as bar to discovery of relevant communications and documents. **United Services Automobile Association v. Werley,** Op. No. 1079, 526 P2d 28 (Alaska 1974).

Discovery rules should be given a liberal interpretation in order to effectuate the underlying purpose of such rules. **Van Alen v. Anchorage Ski Club, Inc.,** Op. No. 1164, 536 P2d 784 (Alaska 1975).

Absent a showing of "exceptional circumstances," a plaintiff could not be required in a products liability case to disclose the names of and submit to deposition all experts consulted before plaintiff indicates whether such experts will be called as witness for trial. **Manns v. Volkswagenwerk,** Op. No. 1186, 539 P2d 1180 (Alaska 1975).

Filing of a personal injury action waives physician-patient privilege as to information relevant to matters which the plaintiff has put in issue. **Trans-World Investments v. Drobny,** Op. No. 1317, 554 P2d 1148 (Alaska 1976).

Trial court was well within its discretion in ordering plaintiffs to turn over to defendants a film made of the hill on which the accident in issue occurred, even though defendants could have made a similar film. **Beaumaster v. Crandall,** Op. No. 1589, 576 P2d 988 (Alaska 1978).

This rule does not create any new privileges; it only provides that matters already protected by a recognized privilege cannot be discovered. **Pharr v. Fairbanks North Star Borough,** Op. No. 2455, 638 P2d 666 (Alaska 1981).

Trial court has broad discretion in imposing sanctions respecting this rule, and its decision will only be overturned upon an abuse of discretion. **Grimes v. Haslett,** Op. No. 2476, 641 P2d 813 (Alaska 1982).

Where plaintiff breached her duty to supplement discovery of expert medical witness, trial court's decision to allow defendant additional time to develop rebutting testimony, rather than excluding the testimony of the expert witness altogether, was appropriate sanction. **Grimes v. Haslett,** Op. No. 2476, 641 P2d 813 (Alaska 1982).

Although expert witness for plaintiff did not change his overall diagnosis that plaintiff suffered from a mechanical compression of the spine, his changed recommendation as to treatment, which related directly to ascertaining plaintiff's chances of recovery, should have been communicated to defendant, and failure to do so was a breach of plaintiff's duty to supplement discovery. **Grimes v. Haslett,** Op. No. 2476, 641 P2d 813 (Alaska 1982).

Since pleadings only give notice generally of the issues involved in the case, permitting the discovery of factually oriented opinions and contentions serves to further the purposes of discovery, which are to narrow the issues, obtain evidence for use at trial, and secure information about where and how such evidence can be obtained. **McKibben v. Mohawk Oil Co., Ltd.,** Op. No. 2706, 667 P2d 1223 (Alaska 1983).

During discovery, a party is not required to state what evidence will be relevant, set out his conception of the law as applied to the particular facts, indicate on what legal principles he will rely, or reveal his conception of the strong and weak points of his case. **McKibben v. Mohawk Oil Co., Ltd.,** Op. No. 2706, 667 P2d 1223 (Alaska 1983).

Although a specification of facts necessarily requires a party to make opinions and draw conclusions, such opinions and conclusions are factually oriented within the meaning of the civil rules, and are therefore not privileged under the work product rule; accordingly, trial court erred in not ordering defendants to answer an interrogatory requiring them to provide factual information supporting each affirmative defense. **McKibben v. Mohawk Oil Co., Ltd.,** Op. No. 2706, 667 P2d 1223 (Alaska 1983).

Plaintiffs' interrogatory, which required defendants to state the legal theory along with citations to statutes and cases which supported their affirmative defenses, clearly requested information protected under the work product doctrine; accordingly, the trial court properly refused to compel defendants to answer it. **McKibben v. Mohawk Oil Co., Ltd.,** Op. No. 2706, 667 P2d 1223 (Alaska 1983).

Failure of plaintiffs to supplement their answers to defendant's interrogatories after plaintiffs' expert witnesses revised their valuation of the property in question did not require exclusion of the expert testimony, since the trial court offered defendant a recess to study the revised figures. **Advanced, Inc. v. Wilks,** Op. No. 3004, 711 P2d 524 (Alaska 1985).

Dismissal of plaintiff's claims for false arrest and malicious prosecution together with issuance of an establishment order that the police had probable cause when they arrested plaintiff for prostitution, all imposed as discovery sanctions for plaintiff's failure to turn over the customer lists of her massage parlor, constituted an abuse of discretion requiring a new trial, since the customer lists had no bearing on probable cause and were therefore not discoverable in the action. **Hazen v. Municipality of Anchorage,** Op. No. 3043, 718 P2d 456 (Alaska 1986).

Requiring an attorney to give a detailed summary of his nonexpert witnesses' testimony violated the work-product rule. **Hayes v. Xerox Corp.,**

Op. No. 3045, 718 P2d 929 (Alaska 1986).

The relevancy standard of this rule is not controlling if discovery is expressly prohibited by statute. **Doe v. Alaska Sup. Ct., Third Jud. Dist.,** Op. No. 3073, 721 P2d 617 (Alaska 1986).

Governor's appointment file containing inter alia internal staff memoranda and letters from concerned citizens was relevant for discovery purposes to action by doctor against an anti-abortion organization for defamation of character in which the doctor alleged that defamatory statements by defendant intimidated the Governor and caused him to withdraw the doctor's appointment to the State Medical Board. **Doe v. Alaska Sup. Ct., Third Jud. Dist.,** Op. No. 3073, 721 P2d 617 (Alaska 1986).

Trial court did not err in awarding personal injury action defendant $1,000.00 in costs in redeposing a physician after plaintiff, who originally hired the physician to render a second opinion, argued that defendant could not retain the physician as an expert witness due to the fiduciary nature of the physician's relationship to the plaintiff; the award was well justified in view of the fact that defendant would foreseeably either have been deprived of the physician's testimony or forced to assume the cost because of plaintiff's spurious claim. **Norris v. Gatts,** Op. No. 3187, 738 P2d 344 (Alaska 1987).

In order for materials to qualify for "work product" protection, three requirements must be met: the material involved must be (1) a document or other tangible thing, (2) prepared in anticipation of litigation or for trial, and (3) prepared by or for the opposing party's attorney or representative. **Langdon v. Champion,** Op. No. 3291, 752 P2d 999 (Alaska 1988).

Statements made by an insured to an insurer are not protected by the attorney-client privilege unless it can be shown that the insurer, in receiving such communications, was acting at the express direction of counsel for the insured. **Langdon v. Champion,** Op. No. 3291, 752 P2d 999 (Alaska 1988).

Materials contained in an insurer's files shall be presumed to have been compiled in the ordinary course of business, and, thus, outside the scope of the work product doctrine, absent a showing that the materials were prepared at the request or under the supervision of the insured's attorney. **Langdon v. Champion,** Op. No. 3291, 752 P2d 999 (Alaska 1988).

A governmental agency was not entitled to use depositions to delay access to public documents requested pursuant to the Public Records Act and the Open Meetings Act where it had presented no prima facie defense to release of the documents. **Municipality of Anchorage v. Daily News,** Op. No. 3597, 794 P2d 584 (Alaska 1990).

In action for injuries caused by the collapse of a step in an apartment stairway, trial court could reasonably have concluded that plaintiff had no duty under this rule to supplement discovery responses to disclose that she had been struck by a bicycle three weeks before trial. **Babinec v. Yabuki,** Op. No. 3644, 799 P2d 1325 (Alaska 1990).

This rule's thirty question limitation on written interrogations means that no more than thirty separate answers may be required without court approval. **Otis Elevator Co., Inc. v. Garber,** Op. No. 3770, 820 P2d 1072 (Alaska 1991).

In divorce trial court's refusal to permit discovery of husband's 1984 mental health records on relevancy grounds was error. **Carstens v. Carstens,** Op. No. 4052, 867 P2d 805 (Alaska 1994).

A superior court order to produce an attorney's billing records in their entirety violated Civil Rule 26(b)(3) by compelling production of attorney work product without adopting measures to assure that protected information was not disclosed. **Matter of Mendel,** Op. No. 4223, 897 P2d 68 (Alaska 1995).

Convictions of contempt for attorney's failure to answer deposition questions were set aside where questions were not relevant to any inquiry that might be pursued in the pending litigation. **Matter of Mendel,** Op. No. 4223, 897 P2d 68 (Alaska 1995).

Where contempt citation arose out of attorney's failure to comply with a discovery request, the appellate court's determination of whether the information sought was relevant was necessarily guided by Alaska Civil Rule 26(b)(1). **Matter of Mendel,** Op. No. 4223, 897 P2d 68 (Alaska 1995).

In conducting an *in camera* review of attorney work product, the trial judge should redact the attorney's mental impressions, conclusions, opinions or legal theories as well as any privileged attorney-client communications which are unrelated to the subject matter of the litigation. The court should then give the attorney the opportunity to examine the redacted records and make any arguments as to why any of the unredacted material is subject to the absolute privilege discussed in Rule 26(b)(3). Only at that point should the relevant, unprivileged information be produced. **Matter of Mendel,** Op. No. 4223, 897 P2d 68 (Alaska 1995).

In light of very short notice that defendant was given regarding deposition and fact that defendant had filed motion for stay of discovery, it was not abuse of discretion for trial court to deny motion for sanctions against defendant for failing to produce witnesses for deposition. **Stone v. International Marine Carriers,** Op. No. 4358, 918 P2d 551 (Alaska 1996).

In suit by police chief against city for wrongful termination, documents showing bias of persons who removed him from office were irrelevant and therefore not discoverable, since employment contract gave city right to fire him for any reason at all. **Ramsey v. City of Sand Point,** Op. No. 4802, 936 P2d 126 (Alaska 1997).

Doctor, who testified that his earlier expert opinion would not have been different had he been supplied with unedited videotape rather than edited version upon which his opinion was based, was fact witness, not expert witness. **Nelson v. Progressive Corp.,** Op. No. 5099, 976 P2d 859 (Alaska 1999).

Trial court did not abuse its discretion in child custody modification case by requiring that mother pay $1,200 fee before deposing custody investigator; mother neither argued nor demonstrated that the $1,200 fee constituted a manifest injustice under this rule. **R.M. v. S.G.,** Op. No. 5340, 13 P3d 747 (Alaska 2000).

Where all parties were on notice of punitive damage claim in the complaint, appellate court declined to treat any later failure to mention punitive damages as waiver or abandonment of the punitive damage claim. **Mapco Express, Inc. v. Faulk,** Op. No. 5422, 24 P3d 531 (Alaska 2001).

In a medical malpractice suit, the trial court erred by refusing to relax the requirements in Alaska. R. Civ. P. 26(a)(2)(B) that experts must produce an expert report and a curriculum vitae. Rule 26 did not apply because the expert witness was plaintiffs' treating physician, not a specially retained expert. **Fletcher v. S. Peninsula Hosp.,** Op. No. 5701, 71 P.3d 833 (Alaska 2003).

Trial court did not abuse its discretion by awarding costs and attorney's fees in a medical malpractice case because several healthcare providers did not violate this rule or Alaska R. Civ. P. 37, where the answers given in response to a patient's discovery requests were appropriate, and there was no evidence that the providers interfered with an attorney-client relationship when defense counsel merely inquired as to whether an attorney was representing the patient. **Parker v. Tomera,** Op. No. 5801 (Alaska 2004).

In an insurance bad faith case, a court properly admitted an expert's opinion where, although the expert did not disclose a basis for his ultimate conclusion in his expert report, if there was any dissatisfaction with the report, plaintiffs should have filed a motion to compel further disclosures, or should have taken the expert's deposition to discover how he arrived at his ultimate opinion; the expert's opinion was only part of the insurer's evidence, and the report and subsequent trial testimony of another expert witness echoed the conclusion that the insurer's refusal to settle was reasonable, and that it was not obligated to give the insured written assurances. **Jackson v. Am. Equity Ins. Co.,** Op. No. 5791 (Alaska 2004).

Trial court's order to compel a contractor to disclose his father's address in a breach of contract action concerning the renovation and selling of a boat was appropriate under this rule, and within its discretion where the boat's owner stated that the contractor had discussed the contract with his father; the parties' understanding of the contract at the time of its execution was central to many of the contractor's claims at trial, and the father might have been able to provide relevant and admissible evidence. **Peterson v. Ek,** Op. No. 5818, 93 P.3d 458 (Alaska 2004).

Trial court properly relied on the employer's expert's report to demonstrate that the employer was notified of, but failed to act on, the fact that the employee's position should not be classified as exempt. **Fred Meyer of Alaska, Inc. v. Bailey,** Op. No. 5840, 100 P.3d 881 (Alaska 2004).

In a case alleging sexual harassment liability, an award of attorney's fees under Alaska R. Civ. P. 68 was proper because it applied to settlement offers made prior to Alaska R. Civ. P. 26 initial disclosures; the offers were timely because they were served no later than 60 days after both parties made the disclosures required by Rule 26. **Ellison v. Plumbers & Steam Fitters Union Local 375,** Op. No. 5934, 118 P.3d 1070 (Alaska 2005).

Offer of judgment is not premature or invalid even if it was made before the parties made Alaska R. Civ. P. 26 disclosures; therefore, attorney's fees were properly awarded to the holder of a first deed of trust in an action concerning a dispute over a foreclosure sale where the offer was made prior to discovery disclosures. **Cook Schuhmann & Groseclose, Inc. v. Brown & Root, Inc.,** Op. No. 5291, 116 P.3d 592 (Alaska 2005).

In a case involving a dispute over the production of certain public documents, the same documents were not discoverable under this rule because their production was the subject of the suit. **Fuller v. City of Homer,** Op. No. 5902, 113 P.3d 659 (Alaska 2005).

Court did not err by denying plaintiff's motion to discover defendant's experts' tax returns, where plaintiff sought to compel discovery of their income tax returns to prove what she believed to be a strong financial motivation on the part of both experts to provide testimony that favored the defense; court's ruling that opposing witness bias could be exposed by plaintiff on cross-examination, and that plaintiff's right of discovery must be balanced with expert's right of privacy, was not an abuse of discretion. **Marron v. Stromstad,** Op. No. 5955, 123 P.3d 992 (Alaska 2005).

In a plaintiff's suit against defendant involving and automobile accident, the superior court was not required to consider a doctor, as plaintiff's treating physician, to be an expert witness, and was thus within its discretion to admit his testimony without an Alaska R. Civ. P. 26(a)(2)(B) expert report. **Marron v. Stromstad,** Op. No. 5955, 123 P.3d 992 (Alaska 2005).

When a treating physician testifies regarding a course of treatment, the physician's testimony need not be subjected to a Daubert analysis. **Marron v. Stromstad,** Op. No. 5955, 123 P.3d 992 (Alaska 2005).

Although subsection (g) does not incorporate language expressly requiring amendments to be "freely given," the policies underlying subsection (g) favor the same lenient approach counseled by Alaska R. Civ. P. 15(a); trial court erred in a premises liability case when it denied a tenant's motion to withdraw an election to proceed under subsection (g) where there was no evidence of dilatory conduct or bad faith. **Kay v. Danbar, Inc.,** Op. No. 5999, 132 P.3d 262 (Alaska 2006).

Discovery rules are to be broadly construed and relevance for purposes of discovery is broader than for purposes of trial, so trial court properly rejected assertion that discovery should be limited to information directly related to the pleadings. **Lee v. State**, Op. No. 11396, 141 P.3d 342 (Alaska 2006).

In consumer protection litigation, the superior court reasonably concluded that the party did not attempt to comply with the discovery requests, despite the party's offers to demonstrate the product of the litigation to the state in a private show, to prove that the products worked as claimed. The civil rules do not allow for this kind of response to interrogatories and requests for production. **Lee v. State**, Op. No. 11396, 141 P.3d 342 (Alaska 2006).

The superior court has broad discretion to determine the scope and extent of discovery and to craft protective orders. **DeNardo v. Bax,** Op. No. 11508, 147 P.3d 672 (Alaska 2006).

A court's protective order restricting discovery will not be overruled absent abuse of discretion. **DeNardo v. Bax,** Op. No. 11508, 147 P.3d 672 (Alaska 2006).

The superior court did not abuse its discretion when it crafted a protective order designed to balance one party's right to the discovery of relevant information against the other party's right to privacy and her fears for the personal safety of herself and her daughter. **DeNardo v. Bax,** Op. No. 11508, 147 P.3d 672 (Alaska 2006).

Where the only issue of material fact to be litigated at trial was the extent of damages plaintiff sustained in car wreck, testimony of insurance investigators was not relevant to plaintiff's damages and therefore not within the scope of discovery where investigators had no personal knowledge about the extent of plaintiff's injuries and insurer bad faith was not an issue. **Gibson v. GEICO General Ins. Co.,** Op. No. 12109, 153 P.3d 312 (Alaska 2007).

Rule 26.1. Discovery and Disclosure in Divorce and Legal Separation Actions.

(a) **Generally.** This rule governs the information that must be disclosed by the parties in a divorce or legal separation case and the time when other discovery methods may be used. Discovery and disclosure in divorce and legal separation actions are otherwise governed by Civil Rule 26(a)(4) through (e), Civil Rules 27 through 37, and Civil Rule 90.1.

(b) **Initial Disclosures.**

(1) In all divorce and legal separation actions, a party shall, without awaiting a discovery request, provide to the other party:

(A) the legal description and street address of all real property, wherever located, in which either party has an interest, together with all appraisals, tax assessments, and broker's opinions regarding each such property obtained within the last two years;

(B) a signed and dated release, valid for six months from the date of signature, authorizing the other party to obtain all earnings and employee benefit information (including but not limited to health insurance, cashable leave, stock options, and perquisites or in-kind compensation such as employer provided housing or transportation benefits) from the party's current employer;

(C) a signed and dated release, valid for six months from the date of signature, authorizing the other party to obtain all pension, retirement, deferred compensation, and profit sharing information from any plan in which the party is a participant or has accrued benefits;

(D) a listing of all accounts in banks, credit unions, brokerages, and other financial institutions on which the party has been a signatory within the past two years and in which the party has a personal or business interest, together with a signed and dated release, valid for six months from the date of signature, authorizing the other party to obtain all information regarding such accounts;

(E) copies of account statements for the past three months for all accounts listed in subparagraph (D);

(F) a listing of all outstanding debts together with written documentation or an account statement from each creditor indicating the principal balance currently owed and the payment terms;

(G) a listing by description and location of all personal property with a current fair market value over $100 in which either party has an interest, together with all appraisals, tax assessments, and broker's opinions regarding each such property obtained within the last two years;

(H) the most recent statements and reports from financial institutions or other sources pertaining to investments in which the party has an interest (including but not limited to stocks, bonds, certificates of deposit, IRAs, life insurance, and annuities);

(I) federal tax returns filed by the party or on the party's behalf, including all schedules and attachments (W-2 forms, 1099 forms, etc.) for the past three years, together with all year-end tax documentation (W-2 forms, 1098 forms, 1099 forms, extension requests, etc.) for the most recent tax year in the event that return has not yet been filed;

(J) pay stubs, vouchers, or other similar proof of income from all sources for the past two months, including but not limited to salaries and wages, overtime and tips, commissions, interest and dividends, income derived from self-employment and from businesses and partnerships, social security, veterans benefits, worker's compensation, unemployment compensation, Alaska Temporary Assistance Program (ATAP), Supplemental Security Income (SSI), disability benefits, Veteran Administration benefits, income from trusts or from an interest in an estate (direct or through a trust), and net rental income;

(K) an itemized list by description and location of all assets and debts listed above in (A) through (H) which the party considers non-marital and the basis for the non-marital designation;

(L) a description of the party's current medical coverage, including but not limited to the name of the provider, the policy or group number, the monthly cost of the policy, the names of family members currently covered by the policy, and whether any family members are eligible for other medical coverage, such as Medicare, Medicaid, Indian Health Service, or military medical benefits; and

(M) any other information or documentation required by local order.

(2) Unless otherwise permitted by the court, these disclosures shall be made within forty-five days after the filing of the answer. A party shall make its initial disclosures based on the information then reasonably available to it and is not excused from making its disclosures because it has not fully completed its investigation of the case or because it challenges the sufficiency of another party's disclosures or because another party has not made its disclosures.

(c) **Scope and Timing of Discovery.**

(1) *Scope.* The disclosures mandated by subsection (b) are intended to provide minimum base information. Subsection (b) does not limit the scope or amount of discovery parties may properly request in a divorce or legal separation action.

(2) *Timing.* Discovery in a divorce or legal separation case may take place at the times allowed by Civil Rule 26(d)(2).

(Adopted by SCO 1325 effective July 15, 1998 and amended by SCO 1596, effective October 15, 2006)

Rule 27. Depositions Before Action or Pending Appeal.

(a) **Before Action.**

(1) *Petition.* A person who desires to perpetuate testimony regarding any matter that may properly be the subject of an action or proceeding in any court of the state, may file a verified petition in the superior court. The petition shall be entitled in the name of the petitioner and shall show: (1) that the petitioner expects to be a party to an action in a court of the state but is presently unable to bring it or cause it to be brought, (2) the subject matter of the expected action and the petitioner's interest therein, (3) the facts which the petitioner desires to establish by the proposed testimony and the reasons for desiring to perpetuate it, (4) the names or description of the persons the petitioner expects will be adverse parties and their addresses so far as known, and (5) the names and addresses of the persons to be examined and the substance of the testimony which the petitioner expects to elicit from each, and shall ask for an order authorizing the petitioner to take the depositions of the persons to be examined named in the petition, for the purpose of perpetuating their testimony.

(2) *Notice and Service.* The petitioner shall thereafter serve a notice upon each person named in the petition as an expected adverse party, together with a copy of the petition stating that the petitioner will apply to the court, at a time and place named therein, for the order described in the petition. At least 20 days before the date of hearing the notice shall be served either within or without the state in the manner provided in Rule 4(d) for service of summons; but if such service cannot with due diligence be made upon any expected adverse party named in the petition, the court may make such order as is just for service by publication or otherwise, and shall appoint, for persons not served in the manner provided in Rule 4(d), an attorney who shall represent them, and, in case they are not otherwise represented, shall cross-examine the deponent. The compensation of the attorney may be fixed by the court and charged to the petitioner. If any expected adverse party is a minor or incompetent the provisions of Rule 17(c) apply. Upon a person other than an infant or an incompetent person, the notice may also be served in the manner provided by Civil Rule 4(h).

(3) *Order and Examination.* If the court is satisfied that the perpetuation of the testimony may prevent a failure or delay of justice, it shall make an order designating or

describing the persons whose depositions may be taken and specifying the subject matter of the examination and whether the deposition shall be taken upon oral examination or written interrogatories. The depositions may then be taken in accordance with these rules; and the court may make orders of the character provided for by Rules 34 and 35. For the purpose of applying these rules to depositions for perpetuating testimony, each reference therein to the court in which the action is pending shall be deemed to refer to the court in which the petition for such decision was filed.

(4) *Use of Deposition.* If a deposition to perpetuate testimony is taken under these rules or if, although not so taken, it would be admissible in evidence in the courts of the United States or of the state in which it is taken, it may be used in any action involving the same subject matter subsequently brought in a court of this state, in accordance with the provisions of Rule 32(a).

(b) **Pending Appeal and Review.** The court in which a judgment, order or decision has been rendered may allow the taking of the depositions of witnesses to perpetuate their testimony for use in the event of further proceedings in the court, as follows:

(1) If an appeal has been taken from a judgment.

(2) If a petition for review of an order or decision of the court has been filed with the supreme court.

(3) If before the taking of an appeal or filing a petition for review, the time therefor has not expired.

In any case the party who desires to perpetuate the testimony may make a motion in the court for leave to take the depositions, upon the same notice and service thereof as if the action was pending in the court. The motion shall show (1) the names and addresses of persons to be examined and the substance of the testimony which the party expects to elicit from each; (2) the reasons for perpetuating their testimony. If the court finds that the perpetuation of the testimony is proper to avoid a failure or delay of justice, it may make an order allowing the depositions to be taken and may make orders of the character provided for by Rules 34 and 35, and thereupon the depositions may be taken and used in the same manner and under the same conditions as are prescribed in these rules for depositions taken in actions pending in the court.

(Adopted by SCO 5 October 9, 1959; amended by SCO 90 effective July 24, 1967, by SCO 158 effective February 15, 1973; by SCO 888 effective July 15, 1988; by SCO 1153 effective July 15, 1994; and by SCO 1610 effective April 16, 2007)

Annotations

Cases

Petition to perpetuate testimony, filed before complaint, does not commence an action. **Chiei v. Stern,** Op. No. 1400, 561 P2d 1216 (Alaska 1977).

Where plaintiff sought to take deposition before end of limitation period but filed complaint after end of limitation period, action was barred. **Chiei v. Stern,** Op. No. 1400, 561 P2d 1216 (Alaska 1977).

Appropriate standard of review for granting or denial of petition to preserve pre-litigation testimony is abuse of discretion. **McNett v. Alyeska Pipeline Service Co.,** Op. No. 3992, 856 P2d 1165 (Alaska 1993).

Mere fact that petitioner had relocated to another state did not establish that she was presently unable to bring action, thus trial court did not abuse its discretion in denying her petition to perpetuate testimony prior to filing of action. **McNett v. Alyeska Pipeline Service Co.,** Op. No. 3992, 856 P2d 1165 (Alaska 1993).

Alaska R. Civ. P. 27's "failure or delay of justice" phrase appears in a sentence dealing with perpetuating evidence allowing court-ordered production only if a court was satisfied that the perpetuation of the testimony might prevent a failure or delay of justice; that singular focus on perpetuating evidence strongly suggests that courts should generally refrain from applying the rule unless the petitioner demonstrates a need to prevent a failure or delay of justice specifically arising from a risk of losing evidence. **Williams v. Engen,** Op. No. 5757, 80 P.3d 745 (Alaska 2003).

Where, prior to his filling suit in a real estate transaction, a real estate broker, relying on Alaska R. Civ. P. 27, petitioned the trial court to compel a mortgage company to produce an engineering report regarding a home's foundation, the trial court did not err in applying the rule's conventional meaning and not ordering production of the letter because there was no evidence that the letter might have been lost. **Williams v. Engen,** Op. No. 5757, 80 P.3d 745 (Alaska 2003).

Rule 28. Persons Before Whom Depositions May be Taken; Foreign Commissions and Letters Rogatory.

(a) **Within the State.** Within the state, depositions shall be taken before an officer authorized by the laws of this state to administer oaths, or before a person appointed by the court in which the action is pending. A person appointed has power to administer oaths and take testimony.

(b) **In Foreign Jurisdictions.** In all jurisdictions outside Alaska, depositions may be taken (1) on notice before a person authorized to administer oaths in the place in which the examination is held, either by the law thereof or by the law of the United States, or (2) before a person commissioned by the court, and a person so commissioned shall have the power by virtue of the commission to administer any necessary oath and take testimony, or (3) pursuant to a letter rogatory. A commission or letter rogatory shall be issued on application and notice and on terms that are just and appropriate. It is not requisite to the issuance of a commission or a letter rogatory that the taking of the deposition in any other manner is impracticable or inconvenient; and both a commission and a letter rogatory may be issued in proper cases. A notice or commission may designate the person before whom the deposition is to be taken either by name or descriptive title. A letter rogatory may be addressed "To the Appropriate Authority in [here name the jurisdiction]." Evidence obtained in a foreign country in response to a letter rogatory need not be excluded merely for the reason that it is not a verbatim transcript or that the testimony was not taken under oath or for any similar departure from the requirements for depositions taken within the United States under these rules.

(c) **Testimony for Use in Foreign Jurisdictions.** When the deposition of any person is to be taken in this state pursuant to the laws of another jurisdiction outside Alaska for use in proceedings in that other jurisdiction, the court upon motion may order issuance of a subpoena in aid of taking such deposition, as provided in Rule 45(d).

(d) **Disqualification for Interest.** No deposition shall be taken before a person who is a relative or employee or attorney or counsel of any of the parties, or is a relative or employee of such attorney or counsel, or is financially interested in the action, except that in the case of an audio or audio-visual deposition, an attorney involved in the case may also operate or direct the operation of the recording machinery.

(Adopted by SCO 5 October 9, 1959; amended by SCO 158 effective February 15, 1973; by SCO 733 effective December 15, 1986; by SCO 1153 effective July 15, 1994; and by SCO 1610 effective April 16, 2007)

Rule 29. Stipulations Regarding Discovery Practice.

Unless otherwise directed by the court, the parties may by written stipulation (1) provide that depositions may be taken before any person, at any time or place, upon any notice, and in any manner and that when so taken may be used like other depositions, and (2) modify other procedures governing or limitations placed upon discovery, except that stipulations extending the time provided in Rules 33, 34, and 36 for responses to discovery may, if they would interfere with any time set for filing of motions, for hearing of a motion, or for trial, be made only with the approval of the court.

(Adopted by SCO 5 October 9, 1959; amended by SCO 158 effective February 15, 1973; by SCO 411 effective June 15, 1980; and by SCO 1172 effective July 15, 1995)

Rule 30. Depositions Upon Oral Examination.

(a) **When Depositions May Be Taken; When Leave is Required.**

(1) A party may take the testimony of any person, including a party, by deposition upon oral examination without leave of court except as provided in paragraph (2). The attendance of witnesses may be compelled by subpoena as provided in Rule 45.

(2) A party must obtain leave of court, which shall be granted to the extent consistent with the principles stated in Rule 26(b)(2), if the person to be examined is confined in prison or if, without the written stipulation of the parties,

(A) a proposed deposition would result in more than three depositions being taken under this rule or Rule 31 by the plaintiffs, or by the defendants, or by third-party defendants, of witnesses other than:

(i) parties, which means any individual identified as a party in the pleadings and any individual whom a party claims in its disclosure statements is covered by the attorney-client privilege;

(ii) independent expert witnesses expected to be called at trial;

(iii) treating physicians; and

(iv) document custodians whose depositions are necessary to secure the production of documents or to establish an evidentiary foundation for the admissibility of documents;

(B) the person to be examined already has been deposed in the case; or

(C) a party seeks to take a deposition before the time specified in Rule 26(d) unless the notice contains a certification, with supporting facts, that the person to be examined is expected to leave Alaska and be unavailable for examination in this state unless deposed before that time.

(b) **Notice of Examination: General Requirements; Method of Recording; Production of Documents and Things; Deposition of Organization; Deposition by Telephone.**

(1) A party desiring to take the deposition of any person upon oral examination shall give reasonable notice in writing to every other party to the action. The notice shall state the time and place for taking the deposition and the name and address of each person to be examined, if known, and, if the name is not known, a general description sufficient to identify the person or the particular class or group to which the person belongs. If a subpoena duces tecum is to be served on the person to be examined, the designation of the materials to be produced as set forth in the subpoena shall be attached to, or included in, the notice.

(2) *Reserved.*

(3) *Reserved.*

(4) *Reserved.*

(5) The notice to a party deponent may be accompanied by a request made in compliance with Rule 34 for the production of documents and tangible things at the taking of the deposition. The procedure of Rule 34 shall apply to the request.

(6) A party may in the party's notice and in a subpoena name as the deponent a public or private corporation or a partnership or association or governmental agency and describe with reasonable particularity the matters on which examination is requested. In that event, the organization so named shall designate one or more officers, directors, or managing agents, or other persons who consent to testify on its behalf, and may set forth, for each person designated, the matters on which the person will testify. A subpoena shall advise a nonparty organization of its duty to make such a designation. The persons so designated shall testify as to matters known or reasonably available to the organization. This subparagraph (b)(6) does not preclude taking a deposition by any other procedure authorized in these rules.

(7) The parties may stipulate in writing or the court may upon motion order that a deposition be taken by telephone or other remote electronic means. For purposes of this rule and Rules 28(a), 37(a)(1), and 37(b)(1), a deposition taken by such means is taken in the judicial district and at the place where the deponent is to answer questions.

(c) **Examination and Cross-Examination; Record of Examination; Oath; Objections.** Examination and cross-examination of witnesses may proceed as permitted at the trial under provisions of the Rules of Evidence. The officer before whom the deposition is to be taken shall put the witness on oath or affirmation and shall personally, or by someone acting under the officer's direction and in the officer's presence, record the testimony of the witness. For an audio or audio-visual deposition, any officer authorized by the laws of this state to administer oaths shall swear the witness. The recording machinery may be operated by such officer, or someone acting under the officer's direction and in the officer's presence, even where such officer is also an attorney in the case. The testimony shall be taken stenographically or recorded by audio or audiovisual means. A party may arrange at the party's own expense to have any portion of the record typewritten.

All objections made at the time of the examination to the qualifications of the officer taking the deposition, to the manner of taking it, to the evidence presented, to the conduct of any party, or to any other aspect of the proceedings, shall be noted by the officer upon the record of the deposition; but the examination shall proceed, with the testimony being taken subject to the objections. In lieu of participating in the oral examination, parties may serve written questions in a sealed envelope on the party taking the deposition and the party taking the deposition shall transmit them to the officer, who shall propound them to the witness and record the answers verbatim.

(d) **Schedule and Duration; Motion to Terminate or Limit Examination.**

(1) Any objection to evidence during a deposition shall be stated concisely and in a non-argumentative and non-suggestive manner. No specification of the defect in the form of the question or the answer shall be stated unless requested by the party propounding the question. A party may instruct a deponent not to answer only when necessary to preserve a privilege, to enforce a limitation on evidence directed by the court, or to present a motion under paragraph (3). Continual and unwarranted off the record conferences between the deponent and counsel following the propounding of questions and prior to the answer or at any time during the deposition are prohibited.

(2) Depositions shall be of reasonable length. Oral depositions shall not, except pursuant to stipulation of the parties or order of the court, exceed six hours in length for parties, independent expert witnesses, and treating physicians and three hours in length for other deponents. The court shall allow additional time consistent with Rule 26(b)(2) if needed for a fair examination of the deponent or if the deponent or another party impedes or delays the examination. In deciding whether to allow additional time for fair examination of a deponent or class of deponents, the court may take into account, among other factors, the complexity of the case, the number of parties likely to examine a deponent, and the extent of relevant information possessed by the deponent. If the court finds that there has been an impediment, delay, or other conduct that has frustrated the fair examination of the deponent, it may impose upon the persons responsible an appropriate sanction, including the reasonable costs and attorney's fees incurred by any parties as a result thereof.

(3) At any time during a deposition, on motion of a party or of the deponent and upon a showing that the examination is being conducted in bad faith or in such manner as unreasonably to annoy, embarrass, or oppress the deponent or party, the court in which the action is pending or the court in the judicial district where the deposition is being taken may order the officer conducting the examination to cease forthwith from taking the deposition, or may limit the scope and manner of the taking of the deposition as provided in Rule 26(c). If the order made terminates the examination, it shall be resumed thereafter only upon the order of the court in which the action is pending. Upon demand of the objecting party or deponent, the taking of the deposition shall be suspended for the time necessary to make a motion for an order. The provisions of Rule 37(a)(4) apply to the award of expenses incurred in relation to the motion.

(e) **Review by Witness; Changes; Signing.** If requested by the deponent or a party before completion of the deposition, the deponent shall have 30 days in which to review the transcript or recording after being notified by the officer that the transcript or recording is available and, if there are changes in form or substance, to sign a statement reciting such changes and the reasons given by the deponent for making them. The officer shall indicate in the certificate prescribed by subparagraph (f)(1) whether any review was requested and, if so, shall append any changes made by the deponent during the period allowed.

(f) **Certification and Filing by Officer; Exhibits; Copies; Notice of Filing.**

(1) The officer shall certify that the witness was duly sworn by the officer and that the deposition is a true record of the testimony given by the witness. This certificate shall be in writing and accompany the record of the deposition. The officer shall securely seal the deposition in an envelope or package indorsed with the title of the action and marked "Deposition of [here insert name of witness]" and shall promptly send it to the attorney who arranged for the transcript or recording, who shall store it under conditions that will protect it against loss, destruction, tampering, or deterioration.

Documents and things produced for inspection during the examination of the witness, shall, upon the request of a party, be marked for identification and annexed to the deposition, and may be inspected and copied by any party, except that if the person producing the materials desires to retain them the person may (A) offer copies to be marked for identification and annexed to the deposition and to serve thereafter as originals if the person affords to all parties fair opportunity to verify the copies by comparison with the originals, or (B) offer the originals to be marked for identification, after giving to each party an opportunity to inspect and copy them, in which event the materials may then be used in the same manner as if annexed to the deposition. Any party may move for an order that the original be annexed to and returned with the deposition to the court, pending final disposition of the case.

(2) Unless otherwise ordered by the court or agreed by the parties, the officer shall retain stenographic notes of any deposition taken stenographically or a copy of the recording of any deposition taken by another method. Upon payment of reasonable charges therefor, the officer shall furnish a copy of the transcript or other recording of the deposition to any party or to the deponent.

(3) The party taking the deposition shall give prompt notice of its filing to all other parties.

(4) A party dismissed from an action shall deliver original depositions in the party's possession to the plaintiff or another party remaining in the action and shall promptly certify to the court that all depositions have been delivered and identify the party now responsible for their safekeeping. Unless otherwise ordered by the court or agreed to by the parties, a party who has custody of an original deposition at the conclusion of a case must retain the deposition for one year after expiration of the time for filing an appeal, or, if an appeal is filed, for one year after conclusion of the appeal and any proceedings after remand. The deposition must be stored under conditions that will protect it against loss, destruction, tampering, or deterioration.

(g) **Failure to Attend or to Serve Subpoena; Expenses.**

(1) If the party giving the notice of the taking of a deposition fails to attend and proceed therewith and another party attends in person or by attorney pursuant to the notice, the court may order the party giving the notice to pay to such other party the reasonable expenses incurred by that party and that party's attorney in attending, including reasonable attorney's fees.

(2) If the party giving the notice of the taking of a deposition of a witness fails to serve a subpoena upon the witness and the witness because of such failure does not attend, and if another party attends in person or by attorney because that party expects the deposition of that witness to be taken, the court may order the party giving the notice to pay to such other party the reasonable expenses incurred by that party and that party's attorney in attending, including reasonable attorney's fees.

(Adopted by SCO 5 October 9, 1959; amended by SCO 158 effective February 15, 1973; by SCO 634 effective September 15, 1985: by SCO 731 effective December 15, 1986; by SCO 732 effective December 15, 1986; by SCO 773 effective December 15, 1986; by SCO 1085 effective January 15, 1992; by SCO 1124 effective July 15, 1993; by SCO 1153 effective July 15, 1994; by SCO 1172 effective July 15, 1995; and by SCO 1446 effective October 15, 2001)

Note to Rule 30(a)(2)(A): Evidence Rule 702(b) limits the number of expert witness who may be called to testify at trial.

Annotations

Cases

The provision of this rule permitting a motion by a party during the taking of a deposition for a court to order a deposition terminated covers those situations where the deponent, after showing bad faith or a course of conduct that unreasonably annoys, embarrasses or oppresses deponent, to receive appropriate relief by court order. Such suspension has no application to a motion for relief made prior to the commencement of the deposition. **Jefferson v. Greater Anchorage Area Borough,** Op. No. 536, 451 P2d 730 (Alaska 1969).

The person filing a motion to set aside subpoenas to appear and depose is not automatically excused from appearing and deposing. The motion must be noticed for hearing and ruled on favorably by the court before the movant is excused from obeying the subpoena. **Jefferson v. Greater Anchorage Area Borough,** Op. No. 536, 451 P2d 730 (Alaska 1969).

Rule 30.1. Audio and Audio-Visual Depositions.

(a) **Authorization of Audio-Visual Depositions.**

(1) Any deposition upon oral examination may be recorded by audio or audio-visual means without a stenographic record. Any party may make at the party's own expense a simultaneous stenographic or audio record of the deposition. Upon request and at the expense of the requesting party, any party is entitled to an audio or audio-visual copy of the audio-visual recording.

(2) The audio or audio-visual recording is an official record of the deposition. A transcript prepared in accordance with Rule 30(c) is also an official record of the deposition.

(3) On motion for good cause the court may order the party taking, or who took, a deposition by audio or audio-visual recording to furnish at that party's expense a transcript of the deposition.

(b) **Use.** An audio or audio-visual deposition may be used for any purpose and under any circumstances in which a stenographic deposition may be used.

(c) **Notice.** The notice for taking an audio or audio-visual deposition and the subpoena for attendance at that deposition must state that the deposition will be recorded by audio or audio-visual means. If a court reporter will not be used to record the deposition, the notice must also state this fact.

(d) **Procedure.** The following procedure must be observed in recording an audio or audio-visual deposition:

(1) The deposition must begin with an oral statement which includes:

(A) the operator's name and business address;

(B) the name and business address of the operator's employer;

(C) the date, time, and place of the deposition;

(D) the caption of the case;

(E) the name of the witness;

(F) the party on whose behalf the deposition is being taken; and

(G) any stipulations by the parties.

(2) Counsel shall identify themselves on the recording.

(3) The oath must be administered to a witness on the recording.

(4) The videotaped deposition shall depict the witness in a waist-up shot, seated at a table. The camera and lens shall not be varied except as may be necessary to follow natural body movements of the witness or to present exhibits or describe evidence that is being used during the deposition.

(5) If the length of the deposition requires the use of more than one recording unit, the end of each unit and the beginning of each succeeding unit must be announced on the recording.

(6) At the conclusion of the deposition, a statement must be made on the recording that the deposition is concluded. A statement may be made on the recording setting forth any stipulations made by counsel concerning the custody of the recording and exhibits or other pertinent matters.

(7) Audio depositions must be indexed by a brief written log notation of the recorder counter number at the beginning of each examination whether direct, cross, redirect, etc. The log must be attached to the tape.

(8) Audio-visual depositions may be indexed by a time generator or similar method.

(9) An objection must be made as in the case of stenographic depositions.

(10) Unless otherwise stipulated by the parties, the original audio or audio-visual recording of a deposition shall be held by the party noticing the deposition.

(11) If the court issues an editing order, the original audio or audio-visual recording must not be altered.

(e) **Costs.** The reasonable expense of recording, editing, and using an audio or audio-visual deposition may be taxed as costs.

(f) **Standards.** The Administrative Director may establish standards for audio or audio-visual equipment and guidelines for taking and using audio or audio-visual depositions. Incompatible audio or audio-visual recordings must be conformed to the standards at the expense of the proponent. Conformed recordings may be used as originals.

(SCO 734 effective December 15, 1986; amended by SCO 990 effective January 15, 1990; and by SCO 1153 effective July 15, 1994)

Note to Civil Rule 30.1(f): The Administrative Director has not established standards for audio or audio-visual equipment or guidelines for taking and using audio or audio-visual depositions.

Rule 31. Depositions Upon Written Questions.

(a) **Serving Questions; Notice.**

(1) A party may take the testimony of any person, including a party, by deposition upon written questions without leave of court except as provided in paragraph (2). The attendance of witnesses may be compelled by the use of subpoena as provided in Rule 45.

(2) A party must obtain leave of court, which shall be granted to the extent consistent with the principles stated in Rule 26(b)(2), if the person to be examined is confined in prison or if, without the written stipulation of the parties,

(A) a proposed deposition would result in more than three depositions being taken under this rule or Rule 30 by the plaintiffs, or by the defendants, or by third-party defendants, of witnesses other than:

(i) parties, which means any individual identified as a party in the pleadings and any individual whom a party claims in its disclosure statements is covered by the attorney-client privilege;

(ii) independent expert witnesses expected to be called at trial;

(iii) treating physicians; and

(iv) document custodians whose depositions are necessary to secure the production of documents or to establish an evidentiary foundation for the admissibility of documents;

(B) the person to be examined already has been deposed in the case; or

(C) a party seeks to take a deposition before the time specified in Rule 26(d).

(3) A party desiring to take a deposition upon written questions shall serve them upon every other party with a notice stating (1) the name and address of the person who is to answer them, if known, and if the name is not known, a general description sufficient to identify the person or the particular class or group to which the person belongs, and (2) the name or descriptive title and address of the officer before whom the deposition is to be taken. A deposition upon written questions may be taken of a public or private corporation or a partnership or association or governmental agency in accordance with the provisions of Rule 30(b)(6).

(4) Within 30 days after the notice and written questions are served, a party may serve cross questions upon all other parties. Within 10 days after being served with cross questions, a party may serve redirect questions upon all other parties. Within 10 days after being served with redirect questions, a party may serve recross questions upon all other parties. The court may for cause shown enlarge or shorten the time.

(b) **Officer to Take Responses and Prepare Record.** A copy of the notice and copies of all questions served shall be delivered by the party taking the deposition to the officer designated in the notice, who shall proceed promptly, in the manner provided by Rule 30(c), (e), and (f), to take the testimony of the witness in response to the questions and to prepare, certify, and file or mail the deposition, attaching thereto the copy of the notice and the questions received by the officer.

(c) **Notice of Filing.** When the deposition is filed the party taking it shall promptly give notice thereof to all other parties.

(Adopted by SCO 5 October 9, 1959; amended by SCO 158 effective February 15, 1973; by SCO 888 effective July 15, 1988; by SCO 1153 effective July 15, 1994; and by SCO 1172 effective July 15, 1995)

Rule 32. Use of Depositions in Court Proceedings.

(a) **Use of Depositions.** At the trial or upon the hearing of a motion or an interlocutory proceeding, any part or all of a deposition, so far as admissible under the rules of evidence applied as though the witness were then present and testifying, may be used against any party who was present or represented at the taking of the deposition or who had reasonable notice thereof, in accordance with any of the following provisions:

(1) Any deposition may be used by any party for the purpose of contradicting or impeaching the testimony of deponent as a witness, or for any other purpose permitted by the Alaska Rules of Evidence.

(2) The deposition of a party or of any one who at the time of taking the deposition was an officer, director, or managing agent, or a person designated under Rule 30(b)(6) or 31(a) to testify on behalf of a public or private corporation, partnership or association or governmental agency which is a party may be used by an adverse party for any purpose.

(3) The deposition of a witness, whether or not a party, may be used by any party for any purpose if the court finds:

(A) that the witness is dead; or

(B) that the witness is at a greater distance than 100 miles from the place of trial or hearing, or is out of the state, unless it appears that the absence of the witness was procured by the party offering the deposition; or

(C) that the witness is unable to attend or testify because of age, illness, infirmity, or imprisonment; or

(D) that the party offering the deposition has been unable to procure the attendance of the witness by subpoena; or

(E) upon application and notice, that such exceptional circumstances exist as to make it desirable, in the interest of justice and with due regard to the importance of presenting the testimony of witnesses orally in open court, to allow the deposition to be used; or

(F) that the witness' testimony has been recorded on video tape.

A deposition taken without leave of court pursuant to a notice under Rule 30(a)(2)(C) shall not be used against a party who demonstrates that, when served with the notice, the party was unable through the exercise of diligence to obtain counsel to represent the party at the taking of the deposition; nor shall a deposition be used against a party who, having received less than 11 days notice of a deposition, has promptly upon receiving such notice filed a motion for a protective order under Rule 26(c)(2) requesting that the deposition not be held or be held at a different time or place and such motion is pending at the time the deposition is held.

(4) If only part of a deposition is offered in evidence by a party, an adverse party may require the offeror to introduce any other part which ought in fairness to be considered with the part introduced, and any party may introduce any other parts.

Substitution of parties pursuant to Rule 25 does not affect the right to use depositions previously taken; and, when an action has been brought in any court of the United States or of any State and another action involving the same subject matter is afterward brought between the same parties or their representatives or successors in interest, all depositions lawfully taken and duly filed in the former action may be used in the latter as if originally taken therefor. A deposition previously taken may also be used as permitted by the Alaska Rules of Evidence.

(b) **Objections to Admissibility.** Subject to the provisions of Rule 28(c) and subdivision (d)(3) of this rule, objection may be made at the trial or hearing to receiving in evidence any deposition or part thereof for any reason which would require the exclusion of the evidence if the witness were then present and testifying.

(c) **Effect of Taking or Using Depositions.** A party does not make a person the party's witness for any purpose by taking the person's deposition. The introduction in evidence of the deposition or any part thereof for any purpose other than that of contradicting or impeaching the deponent makes the deponent the witness of the party introducing the deposition, but this shall not apply to the use by an adverse party of a deposition under subdivision (a)(2) of this rule. At the trial or hearing any party may rebut any relevant evidence contained in a deposition whether introduced by that party or by any other party.

(d) **Effect of Errors and Irregularities in Depositions.**

(1) *As to Notice.* All errors and irregularities in the notice for taking a deposition are waived unless written objection is promptly served upon the party giving the notice.

(2) *As to Disqualification of Officer.* Objection to taking a deposition because of disqualification of the officer before whom it is to be taken is waived unless made before the taking of the deposition begins or as soon thereafter as the disqualification becomes known or could be discovered with reasonable diligence.

(3) *As to Taking of Deposition.*

(A) Objections to the competency of a witness or to the competency, relevancy, or materiality of testimony are not waived by failure to make them before or during the taking of the deposition, unless the ground of the objection is one which might have been obviated or removed if presented at that time.

(B) Errors and irregularities occurring at the oral examination in the manner of taking the deposition, in the form of the questions or answers, in the oath or affirmation, or in the conduct of parties, and errors of any kind which might be obviated, removed, or cured if promptly presented, are waived unless seasonable objection thereto is made at the taking of the deposition.

(C) Objections to the form of written questions submitted under Rule 31 are waived unless served in writing upon the party propounding them within the time allowed for serving the succeeding cross or other questions and within five days after service of the last questions authorized.

(4) *As to Completion and Return of Deposition.* Errors and irregularities in the manner in which the testimony is transcribed or the deposition is prepared, signed, certified, sealed, endorsed, transmitted, filed, or otherwise dealt with by the officer under Rules 30 and 31 are waived unless a motion to suppress the deposition or some part thereof is made with reasonable promptness after such defect is, or with due diligence might have been, ascertained.

(Adopted by SCO 5 October 9, 1959; amended by SCO 158 effective February 15, 1973 and by Amendment No. 1 to SCO 158 effective February 15, 1973; by SCO 888 effective July 15, 1988; by SCO 1026 effective July 15, 1990; by SCO 1153 effective July 15, 1994; by SCO 1172 effective July 15, 1995; by SCO 1203 effective July 15, 1995; and by SCO 1482 effective October 15, 2002)

Annotations

Cases

Return of subpoena stating that the server was informed the witness was "working north of Willow, Alaska" and that he was unable to find him in the third district, was not a record showing that the witness was more than 100 miles from the place of trial. **Otis Elevator Co. v. McLaney,** Op. No. 300, 406 P2d 7 (Alaska 1965).

The trial court's discretion to allow a deposition to be read under Rule 32(a) was not disturbed on appeal, where the return of the subpoena had set forth that the server was unable to locate the witness in the district and was informed that the witness was "working north of Willow, Alaska" because any error which may have been committed thereby, was harmless error. **Otis Elevator Co. v. McLaney,** Op. No. 300, 406 P2d 7 (Alaska 1965).

Return of subpoena stating the server was unable to find the witness after due search and diligent inquiry in the third district, but was informed the witness was "working north of Willow, Alaska," was not an "exceptional" circumstance in the meaning of subsection. **Otis Elevator Co. v. McLaney,** Op. No. 300, 406 P2d 7 (Alaska 1965).

"Exceptional circumstances" permitting use of a deposition do not exist where the party seeking to introduce the deposition is given an opportunity to contact the deponent, but neither makes a showing of what efforts were made to locate the deponent nor attempts to subpoena him. **Palfy v. Rice,** Op. No. 634, 473 P2d 606 (Alaska 1970).

Where there is no showing of due diligence in attempting to secure the testimony contained in the deposition is merely cumulative, the deposition may be excluded. **Palfy v. Rice,** Op. No. 634, 473 P2d 606 (Alaska 1970).

Denial of leave to proceed on deposition was improper in adoption proceedings where petitioners resided more than 100 miles from place of trial or hearing on petitions and there was no showing of intent to avoid personal appearance. **In re Adoption of I.J.W.,** Op. No. 1439, 565 P2d 842 (Alaska 1977).

Telephonic depositions are admissible when they comply with the requirements of this rule. **City of Kotzebue v. McLean,** Op. No. 2949, 702 P2d 1309 (Alaska 1985).

Regarding admission of telephonic depositions, jurors should be instructed that they may consider the credibility of such testimony in light of the fact that they have not seen the witness testify. **City of Kotzebue v. McLean,** Op. No. 2949, 702 P2d 1309 (Alaska 1985).

In contract action against school district, deposition testimony taken from person who was an employee of the school district at the time the pertinent events occurred, but was not an employee at the time the deposition was taken, was inadmissible under this rule. **Fairbanks North Star Borough v. Tundra Tours,** Op. No. 3052, 719 P2d 1020 (Alaska 1986).

Evidence that witness who resided in London was in London or North Africa shortly before trial established unavailability even though witness was deposed in Anchorage and stated in deposition that he could be in Anchorage for trial. **Buster v. Gale,** Op. No. 4044, 866 P2d 837 (Alaska 1994).

This rule does not create an unrestricted right to use deposition testimony in cross-examination. **Sweet v. Sisters of Providence in Washington,** Op. No. 4200, 895 P2d 484 (Alaska 1995).

Plaintiffs did not have an unrestricted right to use deposition testimony of defense experts not called for trial in cross-examination of defense witnesses who did testify. **Sweet v. Sisters of Providence in Washington,** Op. No. 4200, 895 P2d 484 (Alaska 1995).

Where plaintiffs' proposed use of limited deposition testimony from defense experts who would not appear at trial presented substantial dangers of unfair prejudice to the defendants, as well as jury confusion, undue delay and waste of time, trial court properly refused to allow plaintiffs unlimited use of certain depositions for cross-examination, and instead required a hearing to assess the specific facts of each situation. **Sweet v. Sisters of Providence in Washington,** Op. No. 4200, 895 P2d 484 (Alaska 1995).

Where proposed use of limited deposition testimony from defense experts who would not appear at trial presented substantial dangers of unfair prejudice, jury confusion, undue delay and waste of time, and there was no indication of whether plaintiffs could lay a proper foundation for the testimony, trial court properly refused to allow unlimited use of the deposition for cross-examination, and instead required a hearing to assess the specific facts of each situation. **Sweet v. Sisters of Providence in Washington,** Op. No. 4200, 895 P2d 484 (Alaska 1995).

Rule 33. Interrogatories to Parties.

(a) **Availability.** Any party may serve upon any other party written interrogatories to be answered by the party served or, if the party served is a public or private corporation, a partnership, an association, or governmental agency, by any officer or agent, who shall furnish such information as is available to the party. Without leave of court or written stipulation, a party may serve only thirty interrogatories upon another party, including all discrete subparts. This limit includes interrogatories served under Rule 26(d)(1). Leave to serve additional interrogatories shall be granted to the extent consistent with the principles of Rule 26(b)(2). Without leave of court or written stipulation, interrogatories may not be served before the time specified in Rule 26(d). There shall be sufficient space provided so that answers to the interrogatories propounded may be inserted thereon.

(b) **Answers and Objections.**

(1) Each interrogatory shall be answered separately and fully in writing under oath, unless it is objected to, in which event the objecting party shall state the reasons for objection and shall answer to the extent the interrogatory is not objectionable.

(2) The answers are to be signed by the person making them, and the objections signed by the attorney making them.

(3) The party upon whom the interrogatories have been served shall serve a copy of the answers, and objections if any, within 30 days after the service of the interrogatories. A shorter or longer time may be directed by the court or, in the absence of such an order, agreed to in writing by the parties subject to Rule 29.

(4) All grounds for an objection to an interrogatory shall be stated with specificity. Any ground not stated in a timely objection is waived unless the party's failure to object is excused by the court for good cause shown.

(5) The party submitting the interrogatories may move for an order under Rule 37(a) with respect to any objection to or other failure to answer an interrogatory.

(c) **Scope; Use at Trial.** Interrogatories may relate to any matters which can be inquired into under Rule 26(b)(1), and the answers may be used to the extent permitted by the rules of evidence.

An interrogatory otherwise proper is not necessarily objectionable merely because an answer to the interrogatory involves an opinion or contention that relates to fact or the application of law to fact, but the court may order that such an interrogatory need not be answered until after designated discovery has been completed or until a pretrial conference or other later time.

(d) **Option to Produce Business Records.** Where the answer to an interrogatory may be derived or ascertained from the business records of the party upon whom the interrogatory has been served or from an examination, audit or inspection of such business records, or from a compilation, abstract or summary based thereon, and the burden of deriving or ascertaining the answer is substantially the same for the party serving the interrogatory as for the party served, it is a sufficient answer to such interrogatory to specify the records from which the answer may be derived or ascertained and to afford to the party serving the interrogatory reasonable opportunity to examine, audit or inspect such records and to make copies, compilations, abstracts or summaries.

(Adopted by SCO 5 October 9, 1959; amended by SCO 158 effective February 15, 1973; amended by SCO 337 effective January 1, 1979; by SCO 465 effective June 1, 1981; by SCO 1172 effective July 15, 1995; by SCO 1266 effective July 15, 1997; and by SCO 1305 effective January 15, 1998)

Annotations

Cases

Excluding the testimony of defendant's mechanic pertaining to his inspection of allegedly defective crane was of proper sanction for defendant's failure to disclose the same evidence in response to relevant interrogatory by plaintiff. **Yukon Equipment v. Gordon,** Op. No. 2630, 660 P2d 428 (Alaska 1983).

Since pleadings only give notice generally of the issues involved in the case, permitting the discovery of factually oriented opinions and contentions serves to further the purposes of discovery, which are to narrow the issues, obtain evidence for use at trial, and secure information about where and how such evidence can be obtained. **McKibben v. Mohawk Oil Co., Ltd.,** Op. No. 2706, 667 P2d 1223 (Alaska 1983).

During discovery, a party is not required to state what evidence will be relevant, set out his conception of the law as applied to the particular facts, indicate on what legal principles he will rely, or reveal his conception of the strong and weak points of his case. **McKibben v. Mohawk Oil Co., Ltd.,** Op. No. 2706, 667 P2d 1223 (Alaska 1983).

Plaintiffs' interrogatory, which required defendants to state the legal theory along with citations to statutes and cases which supported their affirmative defenses, clearly requested information protected under the work product doctrine; accordingly, the trial court properly refused to compel defendants to answer it. **McKibben v. Mohawk Oil Co., Ltd.,** Op. No. 2706, 667 P2d 1223 (Alaska 1983).

Although a specification of facts necessarily requires a party to make opinions and draw conclusions, such opinions and conclusions are factually oriented within the meaning of the civil rules, and are therefore not privileged under the work product rule; accordingly, trial court erred in not ordering defendants to answer an interrogatory requiring them to provide factual information supporting each affirmative defense. **McKibben v. Mohawk Oil Co., Ltd.,** Op. No. 2706, 667 P2d 1223 (Alaska 1983).

Requiring an attorney to give a detailed summary of his nonexpert witnesses' testimony violated the work product rule. **Hayes v. Xerox Corp.,** Op. No. 3045, 718 P2d 929 (Alaska 1986).

In negligence action against hospital, defendant's answer to interrogatory bore directly upon hospital's duty of care and should have been admitted for that purpose. **D.P. v. Wrangell Gen. Hosp.,** Op. No. 5274, 5 P.3d 225 (Alaska 2000).

Rule 34. Production of Documents and Things and Entry Upon Land for Inspection and Other Purposes.

(a) **Scope.** Any party may serve on any other party a request (1) to produce and permit the party making the request, or someone acting on the requestor's behalf, to inspect and copy, any designated documents (including writings, drawings, graphs, charts, photographs, phono-records, and other data compilations from which information can be obtained, translated, if necessary, by the respondent through detection devices into reasonably usable form), or to inspect and copy, test, or sample any tangible things which constitute or contain matters within the scope of Rule 26(b) and which are in the possession, custody or control of the party upon whom the request is served; or (2) to permit entry upon designated land or other property in the possession or control of the party upon whom the request is served for the purpose of inspection and measuring, surveying, photographing, testing, or sampling the property or any designated object or operation thereon, within the scope of Rule 26(b).

(b) **Procedure.** The request shall set forth, either by individual item or by category, the items to be inspected, and describe each with reasonable particularity. The request shall specify a reasonable time, place, and manner of making the inspection and performing the related acts. Without leave of court or written stipulation, a request may not be served before the time specified in Rule 26(d).

The party upon whom the request is served shall serve a written response within 30 days after the service of the request. A shorter or longer time may be directed by the court or, in the absence of such an order, agreed to in writing by the parties, subject to Rule 29. The response shall state, with respect to each item or category, that inspection and related activities will be permitted as requested, unless the request is objected to, in which event the reasons for the objection shall be stated. If objection is made to part of an item or category, the part shall be specified and inspection permitted of the remaining parts. The party submitting the request may move for an order under Rule 37(a) with respect to any objection to or other failure to respond to the request or any part thereof, or any failure to permit inspection as requested.

A party who produces documents for inspection shall produce them as they are kept in the usual course of business or shall organize and label them to correspond with the categories in the request.

(c) **Persons Not Parties.** This rule does not preclude an independent action against a person not a party for production of documents and things and permission to enter upon land.

(Adopted by SCO 5 October 9, 1959; amended by SCO 158 effective February 15, 1973; by SCO 1026 effective July 15, 1990; by SCO 1153 effective July 15, 1994; and by SCO 1172 effective July 15, 1995)

Annotations

Cases

An extended showing of relevancy to produce written statements was not required where reasons for discovery and production were obvious from the subject matter of litigation. **Miller v. Harpster,** Op. No. 217, 392 P2d 21 (Alaska 1964).

Ends of justice as served by liberal rules on discovery require that written statements recording early impressions of an accident as gathered from witnesses by diligent counsel, be made available to opposing counsel. **Miller v. Harpster,** Op. No. 217, 392 P2d 21 (Alaska 1964).

Order requiring defendant in injury action to produce public liability and property damage insurance policy covering the operation of his vehicle at the time of collision, was sustained. **Miller v. Harpster,** Op. No. 217, 392 P2d 21 (Alaska 1964).

The attorney's "work-product" rule was not extended so as to shelter reports, conclusions and opinions of experts from discovery. **Security Industries, Inc. v. Fickus,** Op. No. 466, 439 P2d 172 (Alaska 1968).

In a wrongful death action where expert testimony will be required to establish liability issues with regard to alleged defects of camper unit, denial of discovery of conclusions and opinions of experts was error. **Security Industries, Inc. v. Fickus,** Op. No. 466, 439 P2d 172 (Alaska 1968).

The discovery rule is sufficiently flexible to allow the trial judge to minimize or eliminate any possible unfairness by an imaginative administration of this rule. **Security Industries, Inc. v. Fickus,** Op. No. 466, 439 P2d 172 (Alaska 1968).

A defendant who seeks to inspect corporate records makes a prima facie showing that the plaintiff has sufficient control over the records to justify the court's order to produce such records where the plaintiff was employed by the corporation in a position of trust and authority and was also employed during the same time by a controlling shareholder in the corporation to handle the controlling shareholder's business affairs in the area, even though the plaintiff is no longer an officer of the corporation at the time the motions to produce corporate records are made. **Hart v. Wolff,** Op. No. 724, 489 P2d 114 (Alaska 1971).

Review of a trial court's order of dismissal for refusal to comply with an order to produce corporate records is limited to an inquiry as to whether the trial court abused its discretion in finding that the plaintiff willfully refused to comply with the court's discovery order. **Hart v. Wolff,** Op. No. 724, 489 P2d 114 (Alaska 1971).

The dismissal of a complaint for refusal to comply with an order to produce corporate records is not an abuse of discretion where there is support in the record for the finding that the plaintiff willfully refused to obey the discovery order, in that he himself testified that he had made no efforts to produce corporate records during the 30 days following that order, and where he did not make any satisfactory explanation to the court as to the reason that such records had not been produced. **Hart v. Wolff,** Op. No. 724, 489 P2d 114 (Alaska 1971).

A prima facie case of control of requested records is all that need be established to justify an order to produce such records. **Hart v. Wolff,** Op. No. 724, 489 P2d 114 (Alaska 1971).

Liberal construction should be given the civil rules governing discovery. **Hart v. Wolff,** Op. No. 724, 489 P2d 114 (Alaska 1971).

Erroneous admission of deposition testimony was harmless error since the evidence contained in the depositions was cumulative. **Fairbanks North Star Borough v. Tundra Tours,** Op. No. 3052, 719 P2d 1020 (Alaska 1986).

Rule 35. Physical and Mental Examination of Persons.

(a) **Order for Examination.** When the mental or physical condition (including the blood group) of a party, or of a person in the custody or under the legal control of a party, is in controversy, the court in which the action is pending may order the party to submit to a physical or mental examination by a suitably licensed or certified examiner or to produce for examination the person in the party's custody or legal control. The order may be made only on motion for good cause shown and upon notice to the person to be examined and to all parties and shall specify the time, place, manner, conditions, and scope of the examination and the person or persons by whom it is to be made.

(b) **Report of Examiner.**

(1) If requested by the party against whom an order is made under Rule 35(a) or the person examined, the party causing the examination to be made shall deliver to the requesting party a copy of a detailed written report of the examiner setting out the examiner's findings, including results of all tests made, diagnoses and conclusions, together with like reports of all earlier examinations of the same condition. After delivery the party causing the examination shall be entitled upon request to receive from the party against whom the order is made a like report of any examination, previously or thereafter made, of the same condition, unless, in the case of a report of examination of a person not a party, the party shows that the party is unable to obtain it. The court on motion may make an order against a party requiring delivery of a report on such terms as are just, and if an examiner fails or refuses to make a report the court may exclude the examiner's testimony if offered at trial.

(2) By requesting and obtaining a report of the examination so ordered or by taking the deposition of the examiner, the party examined waives any privilege the party may have in that action or any other involving the same controversy, regarding the testimony of every other person who has examined or may thereafter examine the party in

respect of the same mental or physical condition.

(3) This subdivision applies to examinations made by agreement of the parties, unless the agreement expressly provides otherwise. This subdivision does not preclude discovery of a report of an examiner or the taking of a deposition of the examiner in accordance with the provisions of any other rule.

(Adopted by SCO 5 October 9, 1959; amended by SCO 158 effective February 15, 1973; by SCO 1122 effective July 15, 1993; and by SCO 1295 effective January 15, 1998)

Note: Ch. 69, § 3, SLA 1989 provided that AS 25.20.050(e), enacted by ch. 69, § 1, SLA 1989, amended Civil Rule 35 by requiring the court, in action in which paternity is contested and to which the state is a party, to order certain genetic tests on the request of a party.

Note: Sections 38 and 41 of ch. 87 SLA 1997 amend AS 25.20.050 relating to paternity actions. According to § 149 of the Act, §§ 38 and 41 have the effect of amending Civil Rule 35 by requiring the court to order genetic testing in contested paternity actions in certain circumstances and preventing the court from ordering such testing if good cause is shown.

Annotations

Cases

A party in a civil action has the right to have his attorney present during an examination by a physician hired by his opponent. **Langfeldt-Haaland v. Saupe Enterprises,** Op. No. 3415, 768 P2d 1144 (Alaska 1989).

Two prerequisites must be met before psychological examination may be ordered under this rule: (1) mental condition must be in controversy and (2) good cause must exist for examination. **Dingeman v. Dingeman,** Op. No. 4038, 865 P2d 94 (Alaska 1993).

In child custody hearing, husband's conclusory allegations about mother's mental health were insufficient to support order requiring mother to undergo psychological testing. **Dingeman v. Dingeman,** Op. No. 4038, 865 P2d 94 (Alaska 1993).

Standing order requiring putative fathers to submit to blood tests in any action where state was party and putative father denied paternity was unconstitutional, although reliance on standing order in instant case was harmless. **Grober v. State, Dept. of Revenue,** Op. No.4981,956 P2d 1230 (Alaska 1998).

Where counsel for prisoner in lawsuit against state for injuries suffered in correctional center agreed after close of discovery to permit independent medical evaluation of prisoner pursuant to Civil Rule 35 but did not waive prisoner's right to have counsel present during examination, examination of prisoner without presence of counsel and without reasonable notice to counsel violated prisoner's right to counsel, and exclusion of examining doctor's testimony and exam report was appropriate sanction for state's wrongful conduct. **State Dept. of Corrections v. Johnson,** Op. No. 5269, 2 P3d 56 (Alaska 2000).

In the context of child-in-need-of-aid proceedings, Alaska R. Civ. P.35(a), should be invoked cautiously, only after the movant has demonstrated sufficient justification for a mental or physical examination. This ensures that trial courts can guard against misuse of Rule 35(a) as an unwarranted mechanism for discovering mental or physical issues absent good reason to believe that such issues actually exist. **Alyssa B. v. Dep't of Health & Social Servs.,** Op. No. 5930, 123 P.3d 646 (Alaska 2005).

In a child-in-need-of-aid proceeding, as the mother's mental state was in controversy because her mental or emotional condition allegedly placed her child at risk, AS 47.10.011(11), and there was sufficient evidence to establish good cause for a psychological evaluation, the trial court did not abuse its discretion in ordering her to undergo such an evaluation under Alaska R. Civ. P. 35(a). **Alyssa B. v. Dep't of Health & Social Servs.,** Op. No. 5930, 123 P.3d 646 (Alaska 2005).

That Alaska CINA R. 16(b) allows a court to order mental and physical examinations of a child's parents at the predisposition phase of a child-in-need-of-aid proceeding does not limit the court's authority under Alaska R. Civ. P. 35(a) to order a mental examination at the adjudication stage. **Alyssa B. v. Dep't of Health & Social Servs.,** Op. No. 5930, 123 P.3d 646 (Alaska 2005).

Rule 36. Requests for Admission.

(a) **Request for Admission.** A party may serve upon any other party a written request for the admission, for purposes of the pending action only, of the truth of any matters within the scope of Rule 26(b)(1) set forth in the request that relate to statements or opinions of fact or of the application of law to fact, including the genuineness of any documents described in the request. Copies of documents shall be served with the request unless they have been or are otherwise furnished or made available for inspection and copying. Without leave of court or written stipulation, requests for admission may not be served before the time specified in Rule 26(d).

Each matter of which an admission is requested shall be separately set forth. The matter is admitted unless, within 30 days after service of the request, or within such shorter or longer time as the court may allow or as the parties may agree to in writing, subject to Rule 29, the party to whom the request is directed serves upon the party requesting the admission a written answer or objection addressed to the matter, signed by the party or by the party's attorney. If objection is made, the reasons therefor shall be stated. The answer shall specifically deny the matter or set forth in detail the reasons why the answering party cannot truthfully admit or deny the matter. A denial shall fairly meet the substance of the requested admission, and when good faith requires that a party qualify an answer or deny only a part of the matter of which an admission is requested, the party shall specify so much of it as is true and qualify or deny the remainder. An answering party may not give lack of information or knowledge as a reason for failure to admit or deny unless the party states that the party has made reasonable inquiry and that the information known or readily obtainable by the party is insufficient to enable the party to admit or deny. A party who considers that a matter of which an admission has been requested presents a genuine issue for trial may not, on that ground alone, object to the request; the party may, subject to the provisions of Rule 37(c), deny the matter or set forth reasons why the party cannot admit or deny it.

The party who has requested the admissions may move to determine the sufficiency of the answers or objections. Unless the court determines that an objection is justified, it shall order that an answer be served. If the court determines that an answer does not comply with the requirements of this rule, it may order either that the matter is admitted or that an amended answer be served. The court may, in lieu of these orders, determine that final disposition of the request be made at a pretrial conference or at a designated time prior to trial. The provisions of Rule 37(a)(4) apply to the award of expenses incurred in relation to the motion.

(b) **Effect of Admission.** Any matter admitted under this rule is conclusively established unless the court on motion permits withdrawal or amendment of the admission. Subject to the provisions of Rule 16 governing amendment of a pretrial order, the court may permit withdrawal or amendment when the presentation of the merits of the action will be subserved thereby and the party who obtained the admission fails to satisfy the court that withdrawal or amendment will prejudice the party in maintaining the action or defense on the merits. Any admission made by a party under this rule is for the purpose of the pending action only and is not an admission for any other purpose nor may it be used against the party in any other proceeding.

(Adopted by SCO 5 October 9, 1959; amended by SCO 98 effective September 16, 1968; amended by SCO 158 effective February 15, 1973; by SCO 1153 effective July 15, 1994; and by SCO 1172 effective July 15, 1995)

Annotations

Cases

A request for admissions as to alleged purchases and costs of goods and materials by a concessionaire of the State of Alaska in the performance of work and services under his concessionaire contract in an action by creditors of the concessionaire to recover for goods and materials was directed to the important and central issues of the case and was within the proper scope of requests under this rule. **Palzer v. Serv-U-Meat Co.,** Op. No. 367, 419 P2d 201 (Alaska 1966).

Where amount owed is admitted by reason of failure to respond to request for admissions, party is foreclosed from attempting to prove that amount admitted included usurious rates and charges. **Molitor v. ATZ Travel, Inc.,** Op. No. 1271, 550 P2d 810 (Alaska 1976).

A summary judgment granted to the plaintiff for a defendant's failure to make timely responses for a request for admissions may be reversed when the plaintiff on appeal disclaims reliance upon defendant's failure to respond and the defendant had no opportunity to reply to an alternative basis for the summary judgment contained in plaintiff's reply memorandum. **Bittner v. State,** Op. No. 2340, 627 P2d 648 (Alaska 1981).

Summary judgment may be based on deemed admissions if such facts are dispositive. **Riley v. Northern Commercial Co.,** Op. No. 2534, 648 P2d 961 (Alaska 1982).

Summary judgment was proper in action to collect amounts due on promissory note where the effect of admissions was to acknowledge that all amounts were in fact owed. **Riley v. Northern Commercial Co.,** Op. No. 2534, 648 P2d 961 (Alaska 1982).

Trial court did not err in deeming plaintiff's requests for admissions admitted and not allowing defendant to file a late response to the requests where the response was tendered nearly two months after a deadline already extended by the parties and where the response was quite perfunctory. **Riley v. Northern Commercial Co.,** Op. No. 2534, 648 P2d 961 (Alaska 1982).

A party can demonstrate that withdrawal of an admission subserves the merits of an action by showing that the admission concerns a key factual issue. **City of Kenai v. Ferguson,** Op. No. 3155, 732 P2d 184 (Alaska 1987).

Award to plaintiff of $700 in interim attorney's fees for its cost in litigating defendant's successful motion to have defendant's deemed admissions withdrawn was proper. **City of Kenai v. Ferguson,** Op. No. 3155, 732 P2d 184 (Alaska 1987).

Service of requests for admissions mailed to the defendant's last known address was complete when mailed even if defendant did not receive it, thus defendant, who never served a written answer or objection to any of the requests, and who never moved either to withdraw the admissions or to file a late answer to the requests, was deemed to have admitted the requests. **Pletnikoff v. Johnson,** Op. No. 3399, 765 P2d 973 (Alaska 1988).

General rule is that admissions made in pleadings are conclusively established. **Darnall Kemna & Co., Inc. v. Heppinstall,** Op. No. 3951, 851 P2d 73 (Alaska 1993).

Trial court abused its discretion in refusing to allow party to withdraw admission that resulted from party's failure to formally respond to request for admission since admission concerned key factual issue, party had informally responded to request, and withdrawal would not have resulted in actual prejudice to opposing party. **Hughes v. Bobich,** Op. No. 4092, 875 P2d 749 (Alaska 1994).

In plaintiff's defamation action, where plaintiff failed to admit that he was a public figure, pursuant to Alaska R. Civ. P. 37(c)(2) the trial court properly awarded defendants sanctions because plaintiff clearly failed to abide by the procedural requirements of Alaska R. Civ. P. 36(a) in that the requested admission was not objectionable. **Lowell v. Hayes,** Op. No. 5924, 117 P.3d 745 (Alaska 2005).

Rule 37. Failure to Make Disclosure or Cooperate in Discovery: Sanctions.

(a) **Motion for Order Compelling Disclosure or Discovery.** A party, upon reasonable notice to other parties and all persons affected thereby, may apply for an order compelling disclosure or discovery as follows:

(1) *Appropriate Court.* An application for an order to a party may be made to the court in which the action is pending, or, on matters relating to a deposition, to the court in the judicial district where the deposition is being taken. An application for an order to a deponent who is not a party shall be made to the court in the judicial district where the deposition is being taken.

(2) *Motion.*

(A) If a party fails to make a disclosure required by Rule 26(a) or Rule 26.1(b), any other party may move to compel disclosure and for appropriate sanctions. The motion must include a certification that the movant has in good faith conferred or attempted to confer with the party not making the disclosure in an effort to secure the disclosure without court action.

(B) If a deponent fails to answer a question propounded or submitted under Rules 30 or 31, or a corporation or other entity fails to make a designation under Rule 30(b)(6) or 31(a), or a party fails to answer an interrogatory submitted under Rule 33, or if a party, in response to a request for inspection submitted under Rule 34, fails to respond that inspection will be permitted as requested or fails to permit inspection as requested, the discovering party may move for an order compelling an answer, or a designation, or an order compelling inspection in accordance with the request. The motion must include a certification that the movant has in good faith conferred or attempted to confer with the person or party failing to make the discovery in an effort to secure the information or material without court action. When taking a deposition on oral examination, the proponent of the question may complete or adjourn the examination before applying for an order.

(3) *Evasive or Incomplete Disclosure, Answer, or Response.* For purposes of this subdivision an evasive or incomplete disclosure, answer, or response is to be treated as a failure to disclose, answer, or respond.

(4) *Expenses and Sanctions.*

(A) If the motion is granted or if the disclosure or requested discovery is provided after the motion was filed, the court shall, after affording an opportunity to be heard, require the party or deponent whose conduct necessitated the motion or the party or attorney advising such conduct or both of them to pay to the moving party the reasonable expenses incurred in making the motion, including attorney's fees, unless the court finds that the motion was filed without the movant's first making a good faith effort to obtain the disclosure or discovery without court action, or that the opposing party's nondisclosure, response or objection was substantially justified, or that other circumstances make an award of expenses unjust.

(B) If the motion is denied, the court may enter any protective order authorized under Rule 26(c) and shall, after affording an opportunity to be heard, require the moving party or the attorney filing the motion or both of them to pay to the party or deponent who opposed the motion the reasonable expenses incurred in opposing the motion, including attorney's fees, unless the court finds that the making of the motion was substantially justified or that other circumstances make an award of expenses unjust.

(C) If the motion is granted in part and denied in part, the court may enter any protective order authorized under Rule 26(c) and may, after affording an opportunity to be heard, apportion the reasonable expenses incurred in relation to the motion among the parties and persons in a just manner.

(b) **Failure to Comply With Order.**

(1) *Sanctions by Court in Judicial District Where Deposition is Taken.* If a deponent fails to be sworn or to answer a question after being directed to do so by the court in the judicial district in which the deposition is being taken, the failure may be considered a contempt of that court.

(2) *Sanctions By Court in Which Action is Pending.* If a party or an officer, director, or managing agent of a party or a person designated under Rule 30(b)(6) or 31(a) to testify on behalf of a party fails to obey an order to provide or permit discovery, including an order made under subdivision (a) of this rule or Rule 35, or if a party fails to obey an order entered under Rule 16(e) or 26(b), the court in which the action is pending may make such orders in regard to the failure as are just, and among others the following:

(A) An order that the matters regarding which the order was made or any other designated facts shall be taken to be established for the purposes of the action in accordance with the claim of the party obtaining the order;

(B) An order refusing to allow the disobedient party to support or oppose designated claims or defenses, or prohibiting that party from introducing designated matters in evidence;

(C) An order striking out pleadings or parts thereof, or staying further proceedings until the order is obeyed, or dismissing the action or proceeding or any part thereof, or rendering a judgment by default against the disobedient party;

(D) In lieu of any of the foregoing orders or in addition thereto, an order treating as a contempt of court the failure to obey any orders except an order to submit to physical or mental examination;

(E) Where a party has failed to comply with an order under Rule 35(a) requiring that party to produce another for examination, such orders as are listed in paragraphs (A), (B), and (C) of this subdivision, unless the party failing to comply shows that that party is unable to produce such person for examination.

In lieu of any of the foregoing orders or in addition thereto, the court shall require the party failing to obey the order or the attorney advising that party or both to pay the reasonable expenses, including attorney's fees, caused by the failure, unless the court finds that the failure was substantially justified or that other circumstances make an award of expenses unjust.

(3) *Standard for Imposition of Sanctions.* Prior to making an order under sections (A), (B), or (C) of subparagraph (b)(2) the court shall consider

(A) the nature of the violation, including the willfulness of the conduct and the materiality of the information that the party failed to disclose;

(B) the prejudice to the opposing party;

(C) the relationship between the information the party failed to disclose and the proposed sanction;

(D) whether a lesser sanction would adequately protect the opposing party and deter other discovery violations; and

(E) other factors deemed appropriate by the court or required by law.

The court shall not make an order that has the effect of establishing or dismissing a claim or defense or determining a central issue in the litigation unless the court finds that the party acted willfully.

(c) **Failure to Disclose; False or Misleading Disclosure; Refusal to Admit.**

(1) A party that without substantial justification fails to disclose information required by Rules 26(a), 26(e)(1), or 26.1(b) shall not, unless such failure is harmless, be permitted to use as evidence at a trial, at a hearing, or on a motion any witness or information not so disclosed. In addition to or in lieu of this sanction, the court, on motion and after affording an opportunity to be heard, may impose other appropriate sanctions. In addition to requiring payment of reasonable expenses, including attorney's fees, caused by the failure, these sanctions may include any of the actions authorized under sections (A), (B), and (C) of subparagraph (b)(2) of this rule

and may include informing the jury of the failure to make the disclosure.

(2) If a party fails to admit the genuineness of any document or the truth of any matter as requested under Rule 36, and if the party requesting the admissions thereafter proves the genuineness of the document or the truth of the matter, the requesting party may apply to the court for an order requiring the other party to pay the reasonable expenses incurred in making that proof, including reasonable attorney's fees. The court shall make the order unless it finds that (A) the request was held objectionable pursuant to Rule 36(a), or (B) the admission sought was of no substantial importance, or (C) the party failing to admit had reasonable ground to believe that the party might prevail on the matter, or (D) there was other good reason for the failure to admit.

(d) **Failure of Party to Attend at Own Deposition or Serve Answers to Interrogatories or Respond to Request for Inspection.** If a party or an officer, director, or managing agent of a party or a person designated under Rule 30(b)(6) or 31(a) to testify on behalf of a party fails (1) to appear before the officer who is to take the deposition, after being served with a proper notice, or (2) to serve answers or objections to interrogatories submitted under Rule 33, after proper service of the interrogatories, or (3) to serve a written response to a request for inspection submitted under Rule 34, after proper service of the request, the court in which the action is pending on motion may make such orders in regard to the failure as are just, and among others it may take any action authorized under sections (A), (B), and (C) of subparagraph (b)(2) of this rule. Any motion specifying a failure under clause (2) or (3) of this subdivision shall include a certification that the movant has in good faith conferred or attempted to confer with the party failing to answer or respond in an effort to obtain such answer or response without court action. In lieu of any order or in addition thereto, the court shall require the party failing to act or the attorney advising that party or both to pay the reasonable expenses, including attorney's fees, caused by the failure, unless the court finds that the failure was substantially justified or that other circumstances make an award of expenses unjust.

The failure to act described in this paragraph may not be excused on the ground that the discovery sought is objectionable unless the party failing to act has a pending motion for a protective order as provided by Rule 26(c).

(e) **Reserved.**

(f) **Reserved.**

(g) **Failure to Cooperate in Discovery or to Participate in the Framing of a Discovery Plan.** If a party or a party's attorney engages in unreasonable, groundless, abusive, or obstructionist conduct during the course of discovery or fails to participate in good faith in the development and submission of a proposed discovery plan as required by Rule 26(f), the court may, after opportunity for hearing, require such party or attorney to pay to any other party the reasonable expenses, including attorney's fees, caused by the conduct.

(Adopted by SCO 5 October 9, 1959; amended by SCO 158 effective February 15, 1973; by SCO 888 effective July 15, 1988; by SCO 1026 effective July 15, 1990; by SCO 1153 effective July 15, 1994; by SCO 1172 effective July 15, 1995; and by SCO 1325 effective July 15, 1998)

Cross References

(b)(1) **CROSS REFERNCE:** AS 09.50.010

Annotations

Cases

This rule makes various sanctions available to the trial judge for enforcing discovery orders in his discretion, but appellate courts will not hesitate to set any order imposed hereunder aside if they are convinced that the trial court exceeded this discretion by imposing a sanction either too drastic or unnecessary under the circumstances. **Oaks v. Rojcewicz,** Op. No. 318, 409 P2d 839 (Alaska 1966).

In construing this provision the court adheres to the views expressed by the Supreme Court of the United States on Fed. R. Civ. P. 37(b)(2)(iii) which was the source of our rule, that the dismissal of claims or proceedings as sanction for non-compliance with a discovery order is authorized only where the non-compliance was willful. **Oaks v. Rojcewicz,** Op. No. 318, 409 P2d 839 (Alaska 1966).

The record failed to establish a willful refusal to comply with a production order pursuant to Civ. R. 34 to produce all tax returns from 1955 to 1963, where appellant's failure to produce some of these returns within 30 days was explained through plaintiff's counsel by a fire appellant had suffered and order of the trial court striking all of appellant's pleadings and dismissing his complaint was reversed. **Oaks v. Rojcewicz,** Op. No. 318, 409 P2d 839 (Alaska 1966).

Where under the record the court below could well have concluded that petitioner was recalcitrant and was not in good faith attempting to produce the designated item for inspection, the reviewing court could not hold that an establishment-preclusion order under this rule was unjustified. **Bachner v. Pearson,** Op. No. 437, 432 P2d 525 (Alaska 1967).

A court's power to punish evasion of discovery orders by establishing facts in favor of a party is broad. **Bachner v. Pearson,** Op. No. 665, 479 P2d 319 (Alaska 1970).

When facts established pursuant to an order entered for non-compliance with a discovery order are dispositive of the issue, summary judgment may be granted to the opposing party. **Bachner v. Pearson,** Op. No. 665, 479 P2d 319 (Alaska 1970).

The power of a court to punish a litigant who fails to comply with a discovery order by ruling in favor of the opposing party has limits and any such attempt at punishment must remain within the confines of due process of law. **Bachner v. Pearson,** Op. No. 665, 479 P2d 319 (Alaska 1970).

Application of sanctions against a party who has failed to make discovery is not proper unless the court finds that there has been a willful refusal on the part of a party ordered to make discovery. **Hart v. Wolff,** Op. No. 724, 489 P2d 114 (Alaska 1971).

Review of a trial court's order of dismissal for refusal to comply with an order to produce corporate records is limited to an inquiry as to whether the trial court abused its discretion in finding that the plaintiff willfully refused to comply with the court's discovery order. **Hart v. Wolff,** Op. No. 724, 489 P2d 114 (Alaska 1971).

The dismissal of a complaint for refusal to comply with an order to produce corporate records is not an abuse of discretion where there is support in the record for the finding that the plaintiff willfully refused to obey the discovery order, in that he himself testified that he had made no efforts to produce corporate records during the 30 days following that order, and where he did not make any satisfactory explanation to the court as to the reason that such records had not been produced. **Hart v. Wolff,** Op. No. 724, 489 P2d 114 (Alaska 1971).

The major purpose of this rule is to insure that an individual has a just determination of his case on the merits. **Ketchikan Cold Storage Co. v. State,** Op. No. 751, 491 P2d 143 (Alaska 1971).

Absent a showing of a willful failure to comply with a discovery order, entry of an establishment-preclusion order is improper. **Ketchikan Cold Storage Co. v. State,** Op. No. 751, 491 P2d 143 (Alaska 1971).

The failure of the plaintiff's son, the only witness to the occurrence giving rise to a suit, to appear for deposition is not an appropriate basis for a motion to dismiss the suit. **Schandelmeier v. Winchester Western,** Op. No. 1013, 520 P2d 70 (Alaska 1974).

The father-son relationship does not make the son the equivalent of an officer or managing agent of his father for purpose of this rule as formerly written. **Schandelmeier v. Winchester Western,** Op. No. 1013, 520 P2d 70 (Alaska 1974).

When noncompliance with a discovery order is in issue, this rule, rather than Rule 41, is the source of the court's authority to impose sanctions. **Schandelmeier v. Winchester Western,** Op. No. 1013, 520 P2d 70 (Alaska 1974).

Proof that the sanction of preclusion under Civil Rule 37(b)(2) is warranted involves the same elements that would warrant a finding of criminal contempt. **Continental Ins. Cos. v. Bayless & Roberts, Inc.,** Op. No. 1251, 548 P2d 398 (Alaska 1976).

Order striking testimony of former state trooper because of state's failure to produce trooper's notebook was neither too strict nor unnecessary. **State v. Guinn,** Op. No. 1315, 555 P2d 530 (Alaska 1976).

Where defendant's expert had not formed final opinion at time plaintiff deposed him, and where such opinion was not disclosed to plaintiff prior to defendant's offer of evidence at trial, trial judge did not abuse discretion by excluding expert's testimony. **Drickerson v. Drickerson,** Op. No. 1992, 604 P2d 1082 (Alaska 1979).

Willfulness, in the sense of a conscious intent to impede discovery, and not mere delay, inability or good faith resistance, must be demonstrated before sanctions may be imposed under Civil Rule 37(b)(2). **Hawes Firearms Co. v. Edwards,** Op. No. 2424, 634 P2d 377 (Alaska 1981).

Non-compliance with Civil Rule 37(b)(2) cannot be found to be willful where the information sought is not within the party's possession, custody or control. **Hawes Firearms Co. v. Edwards,** Op. No. 2424, 634 P2d 377 (Alaska 1981).

It was error for court to dismiss shareholder's complaint seeking production of corporate documents pursuant to statutory shareholder inspection right on the ground that the same could be accomplished through discovery in shareholder's pending case involving the corporation. **Knaebel v. Heiner,** Op. No. 2513, 645 P2d 201 (Alaska 1982).

An order requiring a party who fails to admit the genuineness of any document or the truth of any matter requested under this rule to pay the other party the reasonable expense of proving the document genuine or the matter true is appropriate only where the party willfully intended to impede the discovery process. **Riley v. Northern Commercial Co.,** Op. No. 2534, 648 P2d 961 (Alaska 1982).

Excluding the testimony of defendant's mechanic pertaining to his inspection of allegedly defective crane was of proper sanction for defendant's failure to disclose the same evidence in response to relevant interrogatory by plaintiff. **Yukon Equipment v. Gordon,** Op. No. 2630, 660 P2d 428 (Alaska 1983).

Failure of court to impose harsher sanctions against defendants for willful obstruction of discovery, i.e., an order establishing liability against defendants and precluding defenses or an order striking a certain witness from defendants' witness list, was not an abuse of discretion. **Gloper v. Sager,** Op. No. 2703, 667 P2d 1198 (Alaska 1983).

The test for validity of a discovery sanction that dismisses claims or orders facts or issues to be taken as established is whether those claims or issues are elements of a dispute which cannot be determined on the merits without disclosure of the evidence the court has ordered the party to produce; if the issues established or claims dismissed are not related to the information that the party has refused to supply, then the discovery sanction is mere punishment and is impermissible. **Hazen v. Municipality of Anchorage,** Op. No. 3043, 718 P2d 456 (Alaska 1986).

Dismissal of plaintiff's claims for false arrest and malicious prosecution together with issuance of an establishment order that police had probable cause when they arrested plaintiff for prostitution, all imposed as discovery sanctions for plaintiff's failure to turn over the customer lists of her massage parlor, constituted an abuse of discretion requiring a new trial, since the customer lists had no bearing on probable cause and were therefore not discoverable in the action. **Hazen v. Municipality of Anchorage,** Op. No. 3043, 718 P2d 456 (Alaska 1986).

This rule does not authorize sanctions when one party contests another's compliance with a production request; it only permits sanctions where a party fails to serve a written response to a request for inspections. **Wien Air Alaska v. Bubbel,** Op. No. 3098, 723 P2d 627 (Alaska 1986).

Although defendant corporation failed to answer interrogatories until after the time limit of this rule expired, defendant should have been excused from doing so because it filed for bankruptcy prior to expiration of the time limit, thus discovery sanctions imposed by the trial court for violation of this rule were improper. **Wien Air Alaska v. Bubbel,** Op. No. 3098, 723 P2d 627 (Alaska 1986).

Where defendant in paternity action arranged for a friend to submit blood for testing in his stead, trial court's entry of an establishment-preclusion order conclusive of paternity was a proper sanction for defendant's failure to comply with the discovery order. **Dade v. State, Child Support Enforcement Div.,** Op. No. 3126, 725 P2d 706 (Alaska 1986).

Award to plaintiff of $700 in interim attorney's fees for its cost in litigating defendant's successful motion to have defendant's deemed admissions withdrawn was proper. **City of Kenai v. Ferguson,** Op. No. 3155, 732 P2d 184 (Alaska 1987).

Although sanctions which end litigation are generally disfavored and may even constitute a denial of due process, the imposition of such sanctions is justified if the failure to comply with a discovery order is willful; once noncompliance is shown, the burden is upon the noncomplying party to prove that its failure to provide discovery was not willful. **Alaska Trams v. Alaska Elec. L. & Power,** Op. No. 3229, 743 P2d 350 (Alaska 1987).

Dismissal of party's action with prejudice as a sanction for an unexcused and willful refusal to comply with discovery orders by a stated deadline was not an abuse of discretion; the fact that the party ultimately produced the requested materials did not remove the taint of its willful disregard of the discovery orders. **Alaska Trams v. Alaska Elec. L. & Power,** Op. No. 3229, 743 P2d 350 (Alaska 1987).

Argument that dismissal of entire action with prejudice for willful violation of discovery orders was excessive because the materials withheld related primarily to damages issues on only certain of plaintiff's tort claims was rejected. **Alaska Trams v. Alaska Elec. L. & Power,** Op. No. 3229, 743 P2d 350 (Alaska 1987).

Party's repeated failure to provide requested documents constituted willful violation of the court's order, justifying sanctions, but the court did not err in awarding only costs as sanctions rather than imposing more extreme sanctions. **Koehring Mfg. v. Earthmovers of Fairbanks,** Op. No. 3390, 763 P2d 499 (Alaska 1988).

Before sanctions under this rule are appropriate, willfulness, in the sense of a conscious intent to impede discovery, and not mere delay, inability or good faith resistance, must be demonstrated. **Rohweder v. Fleetwood Homes of Oregon,** Op. No. 3405, 767 P2d 187 (Alaska 1989).

Where discoverable documents are withheld, the burden of showing that noncompliance was not willful shifts to the party from whom discovery was sought. **Rohweder v. Fleetwood Homes of Oregon,** Op. No. 3405, 767 P2d 187 (Alaska 1989).

Trial court did not abuse its discretion in concluding that plaintiff had a conscious intent to impede discovery, thus order precluding plaintiff from using the documents he was ordered to produce but did not produce was appropriate. **Rohweder v. Fleetwood Homes of Oregon,** Op. No. 3405, 767 P2d 187 (Alaska 1989).

Trial court did not abuse its discretion in finding that plaintiff's change of counsel did not mitigate his noncompliance with discovery. **Rohweder v. Fleetwood Homes of Oregon,** Op. No. 3405, 767 P2d 187 (Alaska 1989).

An order that imposes liability on a defendant is an extreme sanction which should be used only in extreme cases. **Otis Elevator Co., Inc. v. Garber,** Op. No. 3770, 820 P2d 1072 (Alaska 1991).

Evidence did not demonstrate willful noncompliance with discovery order, which, as distinct from delay, inability, or good faith resistance, is necessary to justify litigation-ending sanctions; to the extent that defendant elevator company fell short of compliance by too narrowly interpreting what was meant by "similar" elevator, its noncompliance was trivial, and the trial court's statement that the company failed to make discovery from the outset of the litigation was too general to serve as basis for affirming sanctions for failure to comply with a specific discovery order. **Otis Elevator Co., Inc. v. Garber,** Op. No. 3770, 820 P2d 1072 (Alaska 1991).

Dismissal of suit with prejudice as sanction for plaintiff's willful noncompliance with court orders was improper absent evidence that court considered alternative sanctions. **Sandstrom & Sons, Inc. v. State,** Op. No. 3909, 843 P2d 645 (Alaska 1992).

In action by insured against insurer for breach of contract and bad-faith refusal to pay claim, court order striking insurer's answer, resolving all liability in insured's favor, as sanction for insurer's production of only the complaints, answers and judgments in its "bad faith" files rather than the files themselves, was abuse of discretion, since court did not review the documents produced to determine if they were an adequate response to the discovery order and since court failed to explore possibility of less drastic sanctions. **Underwriters v. The Narrows,** Op. No. 3923, 846 P2d 118 (Alaska 1993).

In action by insured against insurer for breach of contract and bad-faith refusal to pay claim, court order striking insurer's answer, resolving all liability in insured's favor, as sanction for not producing financial information, was mere punishment and was therefore vacated, since financial information was only relevant to punitive damages, not liability on the contract and tort claims. **Underwriters v. The Narrows,** Op. No. 3923, 846 P2d 118 (Alaska 1993).

Superior court had jurisdiction to order judgment debtor to comply with judgment creditor's post-judgment discovery requests pending appeal and to enforce order with sanctions, where judgment debtor did not obtain stay pending appeal on file security bond. **Heppinstall v. Darnall Kemna & Co., Inc.,** Op. No. 3952, 851 P2d 78 (Alaska 1993).

The appellate court applies its independent judgment to decide the legal issue of whether Civil Rule 37(b)(2) applies to a given fact situation. **McGilvary v. Hansen,** Op. No. 4227, 897 P2d 605 (Alaska 1995).

It was an abuse of discretion to impose the sanction of liability where the trial court failed to consider any lesser sanction or remedy. **McGilvary v. Hansen,** Op. No. 4227, 897 P2d 605 (Alaska 1995).

Issue establishment under Rule 37(b) is an extreme sanction which should be used only in extreme cases. For this reason, the trial court must find that the non-complying party "willfully" violated the discovery order in question. Before a court may impose litigation ending sanctions for discovery violations the record must clearly indicate a reasonable exploration of possible and meaningful alternatives to dismissal. Finally, the sanction must be sufficiently related to the discovery violation. The established issue must be an element of the dispute which cannot be determined on the merits without disclosure of the evidence the court has ordered the party to produce. **McGilvary v. Hansen,** Op. No. 4227, 897 P2d 605 (Alaska 1995).

Before conclusive resolution of issue against party as sanction for discovery violation, trial court must (1) find willfulness on part of non-complying party; (2) undertake reasonable exploration of possible and meaningful alternatives to litigation-ending sanctions; and (3) determine that the information is not available by other means. **SAC v. Lot 3, Block 1, Evergreen,** Op. No. 4245, 902 P2d 766 (Alaska 1995).

A finding of willfulness is not required for sanction of attorney's fees and expenses under this rule. **SAC v. Lot 3, Block 1, Evergreen,** Op. No. 4245, 902 P2d 766 (Alaska 1995).

Trial court erred in failing to make findings in support of award of $12,000 in costs and attorney's fees as sanction. **SAC v. Lot 3, Block 1, Evergreen,** Op. No. 4245, 902 P2d 766 (Alaska 1995).

In light of very short notice that defendant was given regarding deposition and fact that defendant had filed motion for stay of discovery, it was not abuse of discretion for trial court to deny motion for sanctions against defendant for failing to produce witnesses for deposition. **Stone v. International Marine Carriers,** Op. No. 4358, 918 P2d 551 (Alaska 1996).

If meaningful alternative sanctions are available, trial court must ordinarily impose those sanctions rather than dismissal with prejudice. **Arbelovsky v. Ebasco Services, Inc.,** Op. No. 4382, 922 P2d 225 (Alaska 1996).

Trial court erred in excluding testimony of plaintiff's witness as sanction for her refusal to answer questions at deposition, particularly since witness was not a party and defendants did not seek order to compel deposition testimony. **Wasserman v. Bartholomew,** Op. No. 4404, 923 P2d 806 (Alaska 1996).

Trial court committed reversible error in precluding all expert defense witnesses for defendant's failure to timely submit witness list since harsh effect on defense rendered sanction disproportionate to severity of violation. **Sykes v. Melba Creek Min., Inc.,** Op. No. 4938, 952 P2d 1164 (Alaska 1998).

Trial court order rejecting defendant's untimely witness list in its entirety and precluding defendant from calling witnesses at trial amounted to sanction for defendant's violation of pretrial order to submit witness lists by certain date, thus preclusion order had to be considered under rules governing sanctions. **Sykes v. Melba Creek Min., Inc.,** Op. No. 4938, 952 P2d 1164 (Alaska 1998).

Appointment of special discovery master as a discovery sanction potentially runs afoul of the procedural requirements of Civil Rule 37. **Peter v. Progressive Corp.,** Op. No. 5168, 986 P2d 865 (Alaska 1999).

Where counsel for prisoner in lawsuit against state for injuries suffered in correctional center agreed after close of discovery to permit independent medical evaluation of prisoner pursuant to Civil Rule 35 but did not waive prisoner's right to have counsel present during examination, examination of prisoner without presence of counsel and without reasonable notice to counsel violated prisoner's right to counsel, and exclusion of examining doctor's testimony and exam report was appropriate sanction for state's wrongful conduct. **State Dept. of Corrections v. Johnson,** Op. No. 5269, 2 P3d 56 (Alaska 2000).

Husband's repeated failure in divorce case to respond to discovery requests by wife justified discovery sanction limiting the evidence that husband could present at trial to his own testimony and any documentation previously disclosed to wife, which sanction prevented husband from presenting evidence that certain promissory notes existed and were marital debts. **Coffland v. Coffland,** Op. No. 5295, 4 P3d 317 (Alaska 2000).

In negligence action brought by pedestrian who was struck by taxicab, taxicab driver had no reason to believe that medical records of injuries suffered by pedestrian were not authentic, thus failure of taxicab driver to concede the admissibility of the medical records entitled pedestrian to fees under this rule. **Dobos v. Ingersoll,** Op. No. 5318, 9 P3d 1020 (Alaska

2000).

In negligence action brought by pedestrian who was struck by taxicab, the "reasonable grounds" exception of this rule excused taxicab driver's failure to admit negligence or causation, thus trial court did not err in denying pedestrian's claim for fees under this rule; if taxicab driver acted reasonably in believing that he might prevail at trial, fact that negligence or causation was ultimately proven does not mean that it was unreasonable not to concede it. **Dobos v. Ingersoll,** Op. No. 5318, 9 P3d 1020 (Alaska 2000).

Exceptions to Civil Rule 37(c)(2) that raise legal questions are reviewed de novo, while exceptions that rely on factual findings are reviewed for clear error; the exception for "other good reason for the failure to admit" is reviewed for abuse of discretion. **Dobos v. Ingersoll,** Op. No. 5318, 9 P3d 1020 (Alaska 2000).

Once trial court has determined that failure to admit is not subject to any exception, sanctions under this rule are mandatory. **Dobos v. Ingersoll,** Op. No. 5318, 9 P3d 1020 (Alaska 2000).

Trial court was not required to first issue an order compelling compliance before imposing sanctions for discovery violations. **Hikita v. Nichiro Gyogyo Kaisha, Ldt.,** Op. No. 5330, 12 P3d 1169 (Alaska 2000).

A party cannot satisfy a discovery request by claiming that it is attempting to ascertain the answers and putting off the answers to a later date. **Hikita v. Nichiro Gyogyo Kaisha, Ldt.,** Op. No. 5330, 12 P3d 1169 (Alaska 2000).

Trial court's discretion in sanctioning discovery violations is limited when effect of sanction is to impose liability on offending party, establish outcome of or preclude evidence on a central issue, or end the litigation entirely. **Hikita v. Nichiro Gyogyo Kaisha, Ldt.,** Op. No. 5330, 12 P3d 1169 (Alaska 2000).

Trial court may not issue litigation-ending sanctions without first exploring possible and meaningful alternatives to dismissal, and if meaningful alternative sanctions are available, the trial court must ordinarily impose the lesser sanctions rather than a dismissal with prejudice. **Hikita v. Nichiro Gyogyo Kaisha, Ldt.,** Op. No. 5330, 12 P3d 1169 (Alaska 2000).

Trial court in child custody modification case properly denied mother's motion to exclude from evidence custody investigator's entire testimony and report as a sanction for father's refusal to authorize access to raw data from custody investigator's psychological testing of father; this rule precludes extreme remedies for relatively minor discovery violations, and trial court could not be held responsible for mother's failure to seek more reasonable relief. **R.M. v. S.G.,** Op. No. 5340, 13 P3d 747 (Alaska 2000).

Where a party had moved to compel discovery and asked for sanctions, and the trial court granted their motions to compel but did not address their request for sanctions, the party waived their right on appeal regarding the issue of sanctions because they failed to request a ruling from the trial court on the unresolved matters of the sanctions before final judgment. **Cizek v. Concerned Citizens of Eagle River Valley, Inc.,** Op. No. 5584, 49 P3d 228 (Alaska 2002).

In an employment matter, the court did not abuse its discretion in imposing the sanction of involuntary dismissal as a sanction for a party's failure to provide discovery of tax returns as ordered by the court. **DeNardo v. ABC Inc. RVs Motorhomes,** Op. No. 5599, 51 P.3d 919 (Alaska 2002).

Trial court did not err in declining to reduce attorney's fees awarded to plaintiff citizens group, which sued defendant property owners who were seeking to have their land rezoned to permit its use as a private airstrip, by imposing discovery sanctions against the group under Alaska R. Civ. P. 37(c)(2); based on conflicting testimony presented to the trial court, the group did not unreasonably persist in its denial that the airstrip was capable of being used and was actually used at least once each year between 1984 and 1995 **Cizek v. Concerned Citizens of Eagle River Valley, Inc.,** 71 P.3d 845 (Alaska 2003).

Where a corporation and its owner had for years failed to pay a sizeable judgment awarded to companies on their counterclaims and failed to provide discovery and the owner had been held in contempt for failing to appear for a judgment debtor examination, the trial court showed that neither an order compelling compliance with discovery requests nor the imposition of another sanction less severe than dismissal would have been effective in compelling the production of the requested discovery; hence, on appeal the court affirmed the dismissal of the corporation and its owner's claims as a discovery sanction. **Hikita v. Nichiro Gyogyo Kaisha, Ltd.,** Op. No.5780,85 P.3d 458 (Alaska 2004).

Where a corporation and its owner appealed from a reimposed discovery sanction, dismissing their claims against two companies, the judgment was reviewed for an abuse of discretion. **Hikita v. Nichiro Gyogyo Kaisha, Ltd.,** Op. No.5780,85 P.3d 458 (Alaska 2004).

Trial court did not abuse its discretion by awarding costs and attorney's fees in a medical malpractice case because several healthcare providers did not violate Alaska R. Civ. P. 26 or this rule, where the answers given in response to a patient's discovery requests were appropriate, and there was no evidence that the providers interfered with an attorney-client relationship when defense counsel merely inquired as to whether an attorney was representing the patient. **Parker v. Tomera,** Op. No. 5801 (Alaska 2004).

In a landlord-tenant dispute, where landlord failed to disclose a document she relied upon to show the amount of back rent she was allegedly owed; but tenant failed to move to compel disclosure, tenant waived her objection. **Fyffe v. Wright,** Op. No. 5819 (Alaska 2004).

In plaintiff's defamation action, where plaintiff failed to admit that he was a public figure, pursuant to Alaska R. Civ. P. 37(c)(2) the trial court properly awarded defendants sanctions because plaintiff clearly failed to abide by the procedural requirements of Alaska R. Civ. P. 36(a) in that the requested admission was not objectionable. **Lowell v. Hayes,** Op. No. 5924, 117 P.3d 745 (Alaska 2005).

On appeal, a superior court's imposition of sanctions for a party's failure to comply with a discovery order under subsection (b) of this rule is reviewed for abuse of discretion, but the appellate court uses its independent judgment to decide the legal issue whether Civil Rule 37(b)(2) applies to a given fact situation. **Lee v. State**, Op. No. 11396, 141 P.3d 342 (Alaska 2006).

A superior court's discretion to impose liability-establishing sanctions under this rule is limited. **Lee v. State**, Op. No. 11396, 141 P.3d 342 (Alaska 2006).

PART VI. TRIAL

Rule 38. Jury Trial.

(a) **Right Preserved.** The right of trial by jury as declared by section 16 of article I of the constitution, or as given by a statute of the state, shall be preserved to the parties inviolate.

(b) **Demand.** Any party may demand a trial by jury of any issue triable of right by a jury by serving upon the other parties a demand therefor in writing at any time after the commencement of the action and not later than 10 days after the service of the last pleading directed to such issue. Such demand shall be made in a separate written document signed by the party making the demand or by the party's attorney.

(c) **Demand—Specification of Issues.** In the demand a party may specify the issues which the party wishes so tried; otherwise the party shall be deemed to have demanded trial by jury for all the issues so triable. If the party has demanded trial by jury for only some of the issues, any other party within 10 days after service of the demand or such lesser time as the court may order, may serve a demand for trial by jury of any other or all of the issues of fact in the action.

(d) **Waiver.** The failure of a party to serve a demand as required by this rule and to file it as required by Rule 5(d) constitutes a waiver by the party of trial by jury. A demand for trial by jury made as herein provided may not be withdrawn without the consent of the parties. A party's consent to withdraw the jury trial demand may be implied by a failure to appear at trial.

(Adopted by SCO 5 October 9, 1959; amended by SCO 66 effective July 1, 1964; by SCO 74 effective January 25, 1965; by SCO 465 effective June 1, 1981; by SCO 620 effective June 15, 1985; and by SCO 1153 effective July 15, 1994)

Note: Chapter 54 SLA 2005 (HB 95) enacted extensive amendments and new provisions related to public health, including public health emergencies and disasters. According to Section 13(b) of the Act, AS 18.15.375(c)(3), (d), and (e), and 18.15.385(d)–(k), enacted in Section 8, have the effect of amending Civil Rule 38 by requiring a court trial in matters involving public health.

Annotations

Cases

Provisions requiring written demand for trial by jury are not an unreasonable regulation of exercising the right to trial by jury in civil cases and are constitutional. **Patrick v. Sedwick,** Op. No. 206, 391 P2d 453 (Alaska 1964).

A defendant waives jury trial by failing to make a demand within ten days following the filing of his answer. **Hollembaek v. Alaska Rural Rehabilitation Corp.,** Op. No. 511, 447 P2d 67 (Alaska 1968).

The effect of signing by defendant's counsel of a pretrial order, in which it is stipulated that trial will be without jury, is to officially establish, as the rule governing a trial of the case, that the trial is to be without jury. **Hollembaek v. Alaska Rural Rehabilitation Corp.,** Op. No. 511, 447 P2d 67 (Alaska 1968).

A defendant is bound by the act of his counsel in signing a pretrial order, in which it is stipulated that trial is to be without jury. **Hollembaek v. Alaska Rural Rehabilitation Corp.,** Op. No. 511, 447 P2d 67 (Alaska 1968).

The undisclosed mental state of the attorney who signs a pretrial order, in which it is stipulated that trial will be without jury, can be given no controlling effect in interpreting the effect of the pretrial order. **Hollembaek v. Alaska Rural Rehabilitation Corp.,** Op. No. 511, 447 P2d 67 (Alaska 1968).

An attorney is presumed to be aware of the provisions of a pretrial order, in which it is stipulated that trial will be without jury. **Hollembaek v. Alaska Rural Rehabilitation Corp.,** Op. No. 511, 447 P2d 67 (Alaska 1968).

Children are constitutionally entitled to a jury trial in the adjudicative stage of a delinquency proceeding, but the child should first consult with his counsel and his parents, or guardian when appropriate, and then affirmatively assert his right to trial by jury before it is finally granted. **RLR v. State,** Op. No. 706, 487 P2d 27 (Alaska 1971).

If a child waives a jury trial in a juvenile proceeding, the state may not require it, but a jury trial shall be provided only on demand. **RLR v. State,** Op. No.706,487 P2d 27 (Alaska 1971).

Under certain circumstances, an interlocutory order striking a demand for jury will be reviewed to avoid delay until an appeal could normally be perfected. **University of Alaska v. National Aircraft Leasing, Ltd.,** Op. No. 1158, 536 P2d 121 (Alaska 1975).

One party may rely on a demand for jury trial made by the other. **Webb v. City and Borough of Sitka,** Op. No. 1395, 561 P2d 731 (Alaska 1977).

Defendant's request for a jury trial in an employment discrimination case was timely when filed simultaneously with his "last pleading," namely, his formal answer to the complaint. **Hall v. Morozewych,** Op. No. 2849, 686 P2d 708 (Alaska 1984).

Where defendant defaulted after properly demanding a jury trial, trial court committed reversible error in conducting a non jury trial. **Hall v. Morozewych,** Op. No. 2849, 686 P2d 708 (Alaska 1984).

Although third party claimants in a proceeding adjudicating ownership of personal property were entitled to a jury trial upon proper demand, mere inquiry by counsel at preliminary hearing concerning the need for a jury trial did not constitute a demand for one, since the inquiry was not definite and was not in writing; accordingly, claimants waived their right to a jury trial. **Keltner v. Curtis,** Op. No. 2913, 695 P2d 1076 (Alaska 1985).

Worker who claimed that the Worker's Compensation Act did not apply to his injury because he was an independent contractor was not entitled to a jury trial on the issue. **Benson v. City of Nenana,** Op. No. 3118, 725 P2d 490 (Alaska 1986).

While plaintiff's initial demand for a jury trial may have been timely even though it accompanied an untimely responsive pleading, his post demand conduct, including acquiescence to pretrial order specifying a non jury trial, constituted a waiver of his right to a jury trial; the trial judge did not abuse his discretion by not modifying the pretrial order to allow a jury trial, since to do so would have prejudiced the opposing party. **Howard S. Lease Const. Co. v. Holly,** Op. No. 3123, 725 P2d 712 (Alaska 1986).

Failure to file jury instructions within the time mandated by the pretrial order did not amount to a waiver of the right to trial by jury. **Frank v. Golden Valley Elec. Ass'n, Inc.,** Op. No. 3264, 748 P2d 752 (Alaska 1988).

Jury trial demand, once made, may not be withdrawn without consent of other parties to action. **Denali Federal Credit Union v. Lange,** Op. No. 4413, 924 P2d 429 (Alaska 1996).

Counterclaims for damages by tenant in forcible entry and detainer action brought by landlord did not collaterally estop tenant from litigating her damages claims anew in a separate action before a jury. **Chilton-Wren v. Olds,** Op. No. 5268, 1 P.3d 693 (Alaska 2000).

Tenant did not receive adequate notice that by raising affirmative defenses in forcible entry and detainer action brought by landlord she would waive jury trial on merits of her damages claims against landlord, therefore tenant did not waive her constitutional right to jury trial. **Chilton-Wren v. Olds,** Op. No. 5268, 1 P.3d 693 (Alaska 2000).

Rule 39. Trial by Jury or by the Court.

(a) **By Jury.** When trial by jury has been demanded and not waived as provided in Rule 38, the trial of all issues so demanded shall be by jury, unless (1) the parties or their attorneys of record, by written stipulation filed with the court or by an oral stipulation made in open court, consent to trial by the court sitting without a jury or (2) the court upon motion by a party or upon its own motion finds that a right of trial by jury of some or all of those issues does not exist under the state constitution or statutes of the state.

(b) **By the Court.** Issues not demanded for trial by jury as provided in Rule 38 shall be tried by the court; but notwithstanding the failure of a party to demand a jury in an action in which such a demand might have been made of right, the court in its discretion upon motion may order a trial by a jury of any or all issues.

(c) **Advisory Jury and Trial by Consent.** In all actions not triable of right by a jury the court upon motion by a party or upon its own motion may try an issue with an advisory jury or, with the consent of both parties, may order a trial with a jury whose verdict has the same effect as if trial by jury had been a matter of right.

(Adopted by SCO 5 October 9, 1959; amended by SCO 554 effective April 4, 1983; and by SCO 621 effective June 15, 1985)

Annotations

Cases

Denial of demand to order a trial by jury under Civil Rule 39(b) made orally by counsel at the day set for the trial to commence was no abuse of discretion. **Patrick v. Sedwick,** Op. No. 206, 391 P2d 453 (Alaska 1964).

Where appellant could have obtained representation by substitute counsel for the date set for trial and, moreover, counsel of his first choice rather than insisting on a full 30-day continuance could and should have met his trial obligations by requesting a day to day continuance, appellant could not urge on appeal that his own refusal to participate in the selection of a jury was based on lack of representation by counsel for reasons beyond his control and that his right to a trial by jury had been infringed or denied. **Gregoire v. National Bank of Alaska,** Op. No. 336, 413 P2d 27 (Alaska 1966).

Where defendant's attorney signs pretrial order, in which it is stipulated that trial will be without jury, and which permits the defendant to file an amended answer and counterclaim, and where the answer and counterclaim are subsequently filed along with a demand for jury trial, the refusal eight months later, just prior to trial, to grant defendant a jury trial on new issues raised in the counterclaim is improper. **Hollembaek v. Alaska Rural Rehabilitation Corp.,** Op. No. 511, 447 P2d 67 (Alaska 1968).

A motion to withdraw a jury demand presented only by the plaintiff and not consented to by the defendant and not accompanied by any supporting papers or memoranda cannot properly be granted. **Hill v. Vetter,** Op. No. 1067, 525 P2d 529 (Alaska 1974).

Where the court, upon the defendant's failure to appear, does not give three days' notice prior to entering default, but rather allows the trial to commence in the defendant's absence, the defendant does not lose his right to a jury trial by waiver through default or by failing to appear. **Hill v. Vetter,** Op. No. 1067, 525 P2d 529 (Alaska 1974).

The trial court has discretion whether to use an advisory jury. In the event an advisory jury is used, it is entirely within the trial court's discretion to accept or reject, in whole or in part, the verdict of the advisory jury. On appeal from a trial conducted with an advisory jury, review is limited to findings of fact and conclusions of law of the trial court as if there had been no verdict from the advisory jury. **State v. I'Anson,** Op. No. 1102, 529 P2d 188 (Alaska 1974).

Where defendant defaulted after properly demanding a jury trial, trial court committed reversible error in conducting a non-jury trial. **Hall v. Morozewych,** Op. No. 2849, 686 P2d 708 (Alaska 1984).

Failure to file jury instructions within the time mandated by the pretrial order did not amount to a waiver of the right to trial by jury. **Frank v. Golden Valley Elec. Ass'n, Inc.,** Op. No. 3264, 748 P2d 752 (Alaska 1988).

Where a jury found that a former corporate director should be barred from service on the board for fifteen years, and such a bar from service under AS 10.06.463 is an equitable remedy, the superior court properly treated this portion of the jury's special verdict as advisory under section (c) of this rule. **Martinez v. Cape Fox Corp.,** Op. No. 5909, 113 P.3d 1226 (Alaska 2005).

Rule 40. Assignment and Hearing of Cases—Calendars—Continuances.

(a) **Master Calendar.** At the commencement of each regular or special term of the court, or at such other time as the presiding judge shall direct, the clerk shall prepare a calendar of all cases on the docket which are not on the trial calendar or motion calendar or in which neither party has requested setting for trial. The clerk shall list the cases in numerical order and show the number, title and names of counsel of record in each case, together with such information as will enable the court to readily determine the type and status of the case. At such times as the court shall direct, the calendar shall be called, at which time the court (1) may order cases placed on the trial calendar if desired, or (2) may order that cases be dismissed for want of prosecution under the provisions of Rule 41, or (3) may make such other disposition of cases as the court may consider appropriate.

(b) **Trial Calendar—Memorandum to Set Civil Case for Trial.**

(1) Unless otherwise ordered, a civil case shall be set for a pretrial conference, a trial setting conference, or a trial when it is at issue and when a party thereto has served and filed therein a memorandum to set civil case for trial, stating:

(a) The title and number of the case;

(b) The nature of the case;

(c) That all essential parties have been served with process or appeared herein and that the case is at issue as to all such parties;

(d) Whether the case is entitled to legal preference and, if so, the citation of the section number of the statute or other authority granting such preference;

(e) Whether or not a jury trial has been demanded;

(f) The time estimated for trial;

(g) The names, addresses and telephone numbers of the attorneys for the parties or of the parties appearing in person.

(2) Any party not in agreement with the information or estimates given in the memorandum to set civil case for trial shall within ten days after the service thereof serve and file a memorandum on his behalf.

(c) **Visiting Judges.** Whenever a visiting judge may be present, assisting the judge of any judicial district, the presiding judge of that district shall be solely responsible for the assignment of cases and proceedings to the visiting judge. The judge to whom any particular action or proceeding is assigned will thereupon have charge of such action or proceeding so long as such assignment continues.

(d) **Application for Orders.** Except as provided in Rule 63, application for any order in an action or proceeding, including appellate proceedings, shall be made to, and ruled upon, by the judge to whom the action or proceeding is assigned. However, application may be made to and signed by another judge if the judge who is assigned the case is not available and the application concerns a stipulation or uncontested motion; a petition for emergency domestic violence injunction; a motion for temporary restraining order or other emergency motion; findings, judgments and orders based upon decisions previously announced by the judge assigned to the case; or other matters when the application is presented to the presiding judge, or in the presiding judge's absence, to any other available judge within the state, upon good cause shown.

(e) **Continuances.** *

(1) All cases set for trial shall be heard on the date set unless the same are continued by order of the court for cause shown. The presiding judge of a judicial district may require that a visiting or pro tem judge obtain approval from the presiding judge before granting any continuance of trial.

(2) Unless otherwise permitted by the court, application for the continuance of the trial of the case shall be made to the court at least five days before the date set for trial. The application must be supported by the affidavit of the applicant setting forth all reasons for the continuance. If such case is not tried upon the day set, the court in its discretion may impose such terms as it sees fit, and in addition may require the payment of jury fees and other costs by the party at whose request the continuance has been made.

(3) When parties are present in court and ready for trial on the day set for trial, but their case is not reached on that day, they will retain their relative position on the calendar and on the next open trial day they will be entitled to precedence over cases set for trial on the last-mentioned day.

(Adopted by SCO 5 October 9, 1959; amended by SCO 36 effective May 8, 1961; by SCO 44 effective February 26, 1962; by SCO 193 effective November 1, 1974; by SCO 229 effective January 1, 1976; by SCO 393 effective January 2, 1980; by SCO 710 effective September 15, 1986; by SCO 717 effective September 15, 1986; by SCO 766 effective March 15, 1987; by SCO 894 effective July 15, 1988; by SCO 1153 effective July 15, 1994; by SCO 1172 effective July 15, 1995; and by SCO 1279 effective July 31, 1997)

***EDITOR'S NOTE:** Subsection (e)(3) of Alaska Civil Rule 40 is hereby suspended for the Anchorage trial courts until further notice. The presiding judge shall determine appropriate alternative calendaring procedures.

Note: In 1997 the legislature enacted AS 18.16.030(c), which required the court to hold a hearing in a proceeding to bypass parental consent to an abortion within five days after the petition is filed. According to ch. 14, sec. 7 SLA 1997, this provision has the effect of amending Civil Rule 40 by setting a specific timetable for hearing certain cases. Instead of amending individual rules to implement AS 18.16.030, the supreme court has adopted a separate rule on judicial bypass proceedings. See Probate Rule 20.

Note: Chapter 54 SLA 2005 (HB 95) enacted extensive amendments and new provisions related to public health, including public health emergencies and disasters. According to Section 13(c) of the Act, AS 18.15.375(c)(3), (d), and (e), and 18.15.385(d) –(k), enacted in Section 8, have the effect of amending Civil Rule 40 by requiring expedited hearings and specific standards for and timing of granting of continuances in matters involving public health.

Annotations

Cases

Refusal to grant a continuance will generally not be disturbed on appeal unless an abuse of discretion is demonstrated. **Gregoire v. National Bank of Alaska,** Op. No. 336, 413 P2d 27 (Alaska 1966).

Counsel's insistence on a full 30-day continuance in order to attempt to honor all conflicting trial commitments except the case for which this continuance was sought, was unwarranted and denial of the continuance by trial judge no abuse of discretion where the trial setting of the instant case was senior to all of counsel's other commitments and counsel might have asked for day-to-day continuances or for a definite short term continuance. **Gregoire v. National Bank of Alaska,** Op. No. 336, 413 P2d 27 (Alaska 1966).

Where appellant had been granted previous continuances and 5 1/2 months' notice had been accorded for his eventual trial setting, counsel was not entitled to insist on a further full 30-day continuance which he had sought on the ground that he had committed himself to the trial of three criminal matters in the month of the trial in another state in which counsel was also admitted to the practice of law. **Gregoire v. National Bank of Alaska,** Op. No. 336, 413 P2d 27 (Alaska 1966).

The "with prejudice" aspect of a judgment of dismissal was set aside and trial judge directed to allow appellants their day in court upon terms and conditions appropriate under this rule, where continuance had been properly denied because of appellant's failure to make a timely attempt to obtain substitute counsel, but the supreme court entertained some doubt that the failure was such that dismissal with prejudice of appellant's counterclaim and third party complaint should stand. **Gregoire v. National Bank of Alaska,** Op. No. 336, 413 P2d 27 (Alaska 1966).

Attorney's understanding that the calendar clerk would call him on September 7 if the trial was to take place as scheduled on September 8 did not justify his failure to call the clerk before instructing his client not to appear, and the trial court's refusal to grant the attorney's request for a continuance on the ground that his client was not present was not an abuse of discretion. **W.E.W. v. D.A.M.,** Op. No. 2222, 619 P2d 1023 (Alaska 1980).

A judge may not be appointed to sign orders in place of the absent judge originally assigned to the case unless good cause specifically is shown. **Fairbanks North Star Borough v. Nolan,** Op. No. 2351, 628 P2d 36 (Alaska 1981).

Successor judge's vacation of orders and judgment was not abuse of discretion since she erred in signing them when judge who heard case on merits was still available. **Gallagher v. Gallagher,** Op. No. 4041, 866 P2d 123 (Alaska 1994).

Speedy trial time period begins to run one day following remand for new trial. **Mustafoski v. State,** Op. No. 1576, 954 P2d 1042, 370 P2d 171, 173 (Alaska App. 1998).

Trial court did not violate the father's procedural due process rights by retroactively modifying his child support obligation to the date he was served with notice of the Child Support Enforcement Division's (CSED) petition for modification as provided in Alaska R. Civ. P. 90.3(h)(2) because there was adequate evidence that the father actually received the CSED's notice, where the record showed, among other things, that the CSED mailed the notice to the father's last known address, in compliance with Alaska R. Civ. P. 5. The formal complaint-summons service requirements of Alaska R. Civ. P. 4 are inappropriate in proceedings which seek to enforce the terms of a prior divorce decree relating to child support payments. **Crumpler v. State ex rel. Armstrong,** Op. No. 5927, 117 P.3d 730 (Alaska 2005).

Rule 41. Dismissal of Actions.

(a) **Voluntary Dismissal—Effect Thereof.**

(1) *By Plaintiff—By Stipulation.* Subject to the provisions of Rule 23(c), of Rule 66 and of any statute of the state, an action may be dismissed by the plaintiff without an order of the court: [a] by filing a notice of dismissal at any time before service by the adverse party of an answer or of a motion for summary judgment, whichever first occurs; or [b] by filing a

stipulation of dismissal signed by all parties who have appeared in the action. A notice of dismissal must include a certification signed by or on behalf of the plaintiff that the plaintiff has submitted the information required under AS 09.68.130 and (a)(3) of this rule to the Alaska Judicial Council or that the case is exempt from this requirement. A stipulation of dismissal must include a certification signed by or on behalf of all parties who have appeared in the action. Unless otherwise stated in the notice of dismissal or stipulation, the dismissal is without prejudice, except that a notice of dismissal operates as an adjudication upon the merits when filed by a plaintiff who has once dismissed in any court of this state, or of any other state, or in any court of the United States, an action based on or including the same claim.

(2) *By Order of Court.* Except as provided in paragraph (1) of this subdivision of this rule, an action shall not be dismissed at the plaintiff's instance save upon order of the court and upon such terms and conditions as the court deems proper. If a counterclaim has been pleaded by a defendant prior to the service upon the defendant of the plaintiff's motion to dismiss, the action shall not be dismissed against the defendant's objection unless the counterclaim can remain pending for independent adjudication by the court. Unless otherwise specified in the order, a dismissal under this paragraph is without prejudice.

(3) *Information about the Resolution of Civil Cases.* If an action is voluntarily dismissed under paragraph (a) of this rule, each party or, if a party is represented by an attorney, the party's attorney must submit the information described in AS 09.68.130(a) to the Alaska Judicial Council. The information must be submitted within 30 days after the case is finally resolved as to that party and on a form specified by the Alaska Judicial Council. The following types of cases are exempt from this requirement:

(A) divorce and dissolution;

(B) adoption, custody, support, visitation, and emancipation of children;

(C) children-in-need-of-aid cases under AS 47.10 or delinquent minors cases under 47.12;

(D) domestic violence protective orders under AS 18.66.100–18.66.180;

(E) estate, guardianship, and trust cases filed under AS 13;

(F) small claims under AS 22.15.040;

(G) forcible entry and detainer cases;

(H) administrative appeals; and

(I) motor vehicle impound or forfeiture actions under municipal ordinance.

(b) **Involuntary Dismissal—Effect Thereof.** For failure of the plaintiff to prosecute or to comply with these rules or any order of court, a defendant may move for dismissal of an action or of any claim against the defendant. After the plaintiff, in an action tried by the court without a jury, has completed the presentation of the plaintiff's evidence, the defendant, without waiving the right to offer evidence in the event that a motion is not granted, may move for a dismissal on the ground that upon the facts and the law the plaintiff has shown no right to relief. The court as trier of the facts may then weigh the evidence, evaluate the credibility of witnesses and render judgment against the plaintiff even if the plaintiff has made out a prima facie case. Alternately, the court may decline to render any judgment until the close of all the evidence. If the court renders judgment on the merits against the plaintiff, the court shall make findings as provided in Rule 52(a). Unless the court in its order for dismissal otherwise specifies, a dismissal under this subdivision and any dismissal not provided for in this rule, other than a dismissal for lack of jurisdiction, for improper venue, or for failure to join a party under Rule 19, operates as an adjudication upon the merits.

(c) **Dismissal of Counterclaim, Cross-Claim, or Third-Party Claim.** The provisions of this rule apply to the dismissal of any counterclaim, cross-claim, or third-party claim. A voluntary dismissal by the claimant alone pursuant to paragraph (1) of subdivision (a) of this rule shall be made before a responsive pleading is served or, if there is none, before the introduction of evidence at the trial or hearing.

(d) **Costs of Previously Dismissed Action.** If a plaintiff who has once dismissed an action in any court commences an action based upon or including the same claim against the same defendant, the court may make such order for the payment of costs of the action previously dismissed as it may deem proper and may stay the proceedings in the action until the plaintiff has complied with the order.

(e) **Dismissal for Want of Prosecution.**

(1) The court on its own motion or on motion of a party to the action may dismiss a case for want of prosecution if

(A) the case has been pending for more than one year without any proceedings having been taken, or

(B) the case has been pending for more than one year, and no trial or mandatory pretrial scheduling conference has been scheduled or held.

(2) The clerk shall review all pending cases semi-annually and in all cases that are subject to dismissal under (e)(1), the court shall hold a call of the calendar or the clerk shall send notice to the parties to show cause in writing why the action should not be dismissed.

(3) If good cause to the contrary is not shown at a call of the calendar or within sixty days after distribution of the notice, the court shall dismiss the action. The clerk may dismiss actions under this paragraph if a party has not opposed dismissal.

(4) A dismissal for want of prosecution is without prejudice unless the court states in the order that the case is dismissed with prejudice.

(5) If a case dismissed under this paragraph is filed

again, the court may make such order for the payment of costs of the case previously dismissed as it may deem proper, and may stay the proceedings in the case until the party has complied with the order.

(Adopted by SCO 5 October 9, 1959; amended by SCO 239 effective March 1, 1976; by SCO 258 effective November 15, 1976; by SCO 465 effective June 1, 1981; by SCO 798 effective March 15, 1987; by SCO 834 effective August 1, 1987; by SCO 1153 effective July 15, 1994; by SCO 1266 effective July 15, 1997; by SCO 1283 effective September 2, 1997; and by SCO 1361 effective October 15, 1999)

Annotations

Cases

I. In General.

An order of dismissal "with prejudice" operates as an adjudication on the merits. **Miller v. Johnson,** Op. No. 70, 370 P2d 171 (Alaska 1962).

One and one-half page memorandum devoid of authorities was not statement required by Civil Rule 77(b) (2), so that motion to dismiss was frivolous and issue was not joined, precluding award of attorney's fees. **State v. Alaska International Air, Inc.,** Op. No. 1409, 562 P2d 1064 (Alaska 1977).

Party seeking relief from judgment of dismissal must show the existence of a meritorious claim. **Corso v. Commissioner of Education,** Op. No. 1412, 563 P2d 246 (Alaska 1977).

To show the existence of meritorious claim, party must show facts which if established, might reasonably be said to meet affirmative defenses of adversary. **Corso v. Commissioner of Education,** Op. No. 1412, 563 P2d 246 (Alaska 1977).

Proper test for granting motion to dismiss without prejudice involves balancing the interests of both plaintiff and defendant to obtain a result which will be fair and equitable under the circumstances of each case. **Dome Laboratories v. Farrell,** Op. No. 1917, 599 P2d 152 (Alaska 1979).

A judgment of dismissal without prejudice is considered a final judgment for purposes of appeal. **Farrell v. Dome Laboratories,** Op. No. 2556, 650 P2d 380 (Alaska 1982).

Trial court had jurisdiction under rule allowing relief from judgment to amend a voluntary dismissal entered without prejudice under this rule. **Farrell v. Dome Laboratories,** Op. No. 2556, 650 P2d 380 (Alaska 1982).

Where defendant does not object to plaintiff's notice of dismissal under this rule, the validity of the dismissal will not be questioned on review. **Sisters of Providence v. Van Linder,** Op. No. 2678, 663 P2d 956 (Alaska 1983).

Once an action has been dismissed as of right by a plaintiff pursuant to this rule, the trial court lacks jurisdiction to enforce an interlocutory order entered prior to the dismissal. **Sisters of Providence v. Van Linder,** Op. No. 2678, 663 P2d 956 (Alaska 1983).

The "lack of jurisdiction" exception to the rule that an involuntary dismissal operates as an adjudication on the merits includes dismissals due to a corporation's statutory incapacity to sue. **Blake v. Gilbert,** Op. No. 2947, 702 P2d 631 (Alaska 1985).

A stipulation to dismiss claims with prejudice operates as an adjudication on the merits; it is just as valid as a final judgment resulting from a trial on the merits, and is res judicata as to all issues that were raised or could have been determined under the pleadings. **Tolstrup v. Miller,** Op. No. 3129, 726 P2d 1304 (Alaska 1986).

Order No. 798, adopting an amendment to Civil Rule 41(b), effective March 15, 1987, was signed by three justices. Two justices filed a dissent to the order, expressing doubt that the amendment would result in an overall saving of judicial time and their belief that it creates a distinct risk of premature and inaccurate decisions. **Supreme Court Order 798, dissenting statement of Chief Justice Rabinowitz and Justice Matthews, dated January 14, 1987.**

Where liability and damages issues are tried by the court, prejudgment motion for dismissal rather than for a directed verdict is appropriate. **Frank v. Golden Valley Elec. Ass'n, Inc.,** Op. No. 3264, 748 P2d 752 (Alaska 1988).

A court need not make explicit findings concerning alternatives to dismissal; the record need only clearly indicate a reasonable exploration of possible and meaningful alternatives. **Power Constructors v. Acres American,** Op. No. 3689, 811 P2d 1052 (Alaska 1991).

Civil Rule 16.1 provides the exclusive procedure for dismissing "fast-track" cases and supersedes this and other civil rules in conflict therewith. **Ford v. Municipality of Anchorage,** Op. No. 3703, 813 P2d 654 (Alaska 1991).

In liquidation proceeding, trial court's denial, for lack of jurisdiction, of motion to set aside and terminate irrevocable trust did not constitute dismissal upon which collateral estoppel could be based. **Matter of Pacific Marine Ins. Co.,** Op. No. 4100, 877 P2d 264 (Alaska 1994).

The sanctions of Civil Rule 16.1(g) and Civil Rule 41(d) afford courts the tools necessary to deter litigants from judge shopping through voluntary or involuntary dismissals. **Staso v. State, Department of Transportation,** Op. No. 4214, 895 P2d 988 (Alaska 1995).

Consolidated Rule 16.1 cases retain their "fast-track" status and can be dismissed only by following Rule 16.1 dismissal procedures, not Rule 41 dismissal procedures. **Prazak v. Alaska Local No. 1,** Op. No. 4277, 904 P2d 428 (Alaska 1995).

If meaningful alternative sanctions are available, trial court must ordinarily impose those sanctions rather than dismissal with prejudice. **Arbelovsky v. Ebasco Services, Inc.,** Op. No. 4382, 922 P2d 225 (Alaska 1996).

Absence of findings of fact and conclusions of law did not prevent a dismissal under Alaska R. Civ. P. 12(b)(6) from having res judicata effect where the reviewing court could infer the trial court's reasons for the ruling on the merits from its subsequent opinion denying attorney's fees. **Alaska Wildlife Alliance v. State,** Op. No. 5771, 74 P.3d 201 (Alaska 2003).

Political question as to the composition of the Gaming Board was an issue of justiciability, not jurisdiction, and therefore dismissal of a complaint raising that question was a dismissal on the merits and had a preclusive effect. **Alaska Wildlife Alliance v. State,** Op. No. 5771, 74 P.3d 201 (Alaska 2003).

In a second action challenging the composition of the Gaming Board, public interest plaintiffs did not defeat res judicata by replacing lesser state entities with the State of Alaska as defendant because the claim was based on the same conduct and because the same defense of non-justiciability applied regardless of which specific state entity was named. **Alaska Wildlife Alliance v. State,** Op. No. 5771, 74 P.3d 201 (Alaska 2003).

Amendment of this rule in 1987 eliminated the former Alaska R. Civ. P. 41(b) requirement that the trial judge deny a motion to dismiss when the plaintiff has made an unimpeached prima facie case; the change in the text of the rule brought it into compliance with the analogous federal rule, Fed. R. Civ. P. 52(c), that the trial judge is not to draw any special inferences in the nonmovant's favor nor concern itself with whether the nonmovant has made out a prima facie case **Fletcher v. Trademark Constr., Inc.,** Op. No. 5760 (Alaska 2003).

II. Voluntary Dismissal.

A. Conditions.

Voluntary dismissal of plaintiff's causes of action was with prejudice pursuant to terms stated in the stipulation. **Albritton v. Estate of Larson,** Op. No. 413, 428 P2d 379 (Alaska 1967).

This rule does not authorize court to regard the condemnor's dismissals of its appeals from a master's awards as matters to be determined within the condemnor's discretion and to be granted on such terms as it might think proper. **Inglima v. Alaska State HousingAuthority,** Op. No. 594,462 P2d 1002 (Alaska 1970).

Under AS 09.55.320, which provides that an interested party may appeal a master's award in which case there shall be a trial by jury on the question of the amount of damages and the value of property, unless the jury is waived by the consent of all parties, a condemnee against whom an appeal is taken is entitled to a jury trial as a matter of right. A condemnor cannot, after the jury has rendered verdicts higher than the master's awards, obtain a dismissal of its appeal without the consent of the condemnees. **Inglima v. Alaska State Housing Authority,** Op. No. 594, 462 P2d 1002 (Alaska 1970).

The primary purpose of this rule is to allow the plaintiff to dismiss as a matter of right before an issue has been joined. **Miller v. Wilkes,** Op. No. 788, 496 P2d 176 (Alaska 1972).

Where defendant is dismissed under Civil Rule 41(a)(1)[a] before service of any pleading or motion by defendant that would have required trial court to consider merits of controversy, there is no joinder of issue, or prevailing party, and an award of attorney's fees is precluded. **State v. Alaska International Air, Inc.,** Op. No. 1409, 562 P2d 1064 (Alaska 1977).

No findings of fact should be made in conjunction with a voluntary dismissal when the court has no evidentiary basis for such findings. **Sherry v. Sherry,** Op. No. 2271, 622 P2d 960 (Alaska 1981).

Where plaintiff moved for a voluntary dismissal without prejudice of her motion to modify a child custody agreement, it was abuse of discretion for the court to condition the grant of dismissal on plaintiff not attempting to modify the decree for two years and on a prohibition on psychological or psychiatric examination without the consent of both parents. **Sherry v. Sherry,** Op. No. 2271, 622 P2d 960 (Alaska 1981).

Superior court abused its discretion in amending a prior judgment of voluntary dismissal without prejudice in order to require the plaintiff to refile his suit against defendant by a certain date. **Farrell v. Dome Laboratories,** Op. No. 2556, 650 P2d 380 (Alaska 1982).

Since responses filed by defendants to plaintiff's petition seeking to perpetuate testimony before filling of action required trial court to consider merits of petition, voluntary dismissal without order of court was no longer possible, and condition imposed by court on dismissal, that plaintiff bring no further action on matter until he paid defendants' fees and costs, was not abuse of discretion. **Stahlman v. State,** Op. No. 3987, 856 P2d 1162 (Alaska 1993).

It was abuse of discretion for trial court to condition voluntary dismissal on payment of attorney fees by public interest litigant. **Eyak Elders Council v. Sherstone, Inc.,** Op. No. 4273, 904 P2d 420 (Alaska 1995).

B. Termination of Right to Dismiss.

Where an affidavit which is filed by the defendant denies several factual allegations of the plaintiff and a memorandum filed by the defendant raises four defenses, such documents are tantamount to an answer and the plaintiff's right to dismiss the suit is terminated. Thus, although the plaintiff files a voluntary dismissal of the suit the trial court has the authority to award to defendant attorney fees. **Miller v. Wilkes,** Op. No. 788, 496 P2d 176 (Alaska 1972).

If an issue has been joined by means other than those specified in this rule, the plaintiff's right to dismiss by notice is nonetheless terminated. **Miller v. Wilkes,** Op. No. 788, 496 P2d 176 (Alaska 1972).

Not every action by the defendant cuts off the right of the plaintiff to dismiss under this rule, but only those actions which would require the court to consider on the merits of the controversy or which involve considerable expense and effort on the part of the defendant. **Miller v. Wilkes,** Op. No. 788, 496 P2d 176 (Alaska 1972).

Since responses filed by defendants to plaintiff's petition seeking to perpetuate testimony before filling of action required trial court to consider merits of petition, voluntary dismissal without order of court was no longer possible, and condition imposed by court on dismissal, that plaintiff bring no further action on matter until he paid defendants' fees and costs, was not abuse of discretion. **Stahlman v. State,** Op. No. 3987, 856 P2d 1162 (Alaska 1993).

III. Involuntary Dismissal.

A. Conditions.

The "lack of jurisdiction" exception to the rule that an involuntary dismissal operates as an adjudication on the merits includes dismissals due to a corporation's statutory incapacity to sue. **Blake v. Gilbert,** Op. No. 2947, 702 P2d 631 (Alaska 1985).

Where plaintiff's evidence does not establish a prima facie case, a motion to dismiss made at the close of plaintiff's case should be granted. **Pope v. Anderson,** Op. No. 72, 370 P2d 185, 187 (Alaska 1962); **Correa v. Stephens,** Op. No. 730, 429 P.2d 254 (Alaska 1967).

The trial court's dismissal of a previous complaint brought by another on the behalf of all electors contesting a bond election, on the grounds that plaintiff had not delivered on the borough as sensible a written notice of contest of the election as required by a borough ordinance, operates as an adjudication on the merits in the absence of a specification by the trial court to the contrary and is res judicata to a suit brought by the plaintiff challenging the same bond election. **Jefferson v. Greater Anchorage Area Borough,** Op. No. 536, 451 P2d 730 (Alaska 1969).

Even though a complaint alleges basis for a claimed illegality of a bond election not mentioned in a previous complaint brought by another on behalf of all electors, the doctrine of res judicata is applicable and dismissal of the complaint is not error. **Jefferson v. Greater Anchorage Area Borough,** Op. No. 536, 451 P2d 730 (Alaska 1969).

Where the general doctrine of res judicata is inapplicable and supports the dismissal of a complaint, the contention that the trial court should have permitted ten of the plaintiffs to belatedly sign the complaint is as rendered moot. **Jefferson v. Greater Anchorage Area Borough,** Op. No. 536, 451 P2d 730 (Alaska 1969).

Where plaintiff had received ample notice from opinion on earlier appeal that it was incumbent upon him to promptly take steps to prosecute claim upon his release from prison, and during seven-month period had taken no such steps, denial of motion to reconsider dismissal for lack of prosecution was not abuse of discretion. **Brown v. State,** Op. No. 1418, 563 P2d 275 (Alaska 1977).

On appeal from grant of a Civil Rule 41(a)(2) motion, appellant must show that trial court failed to exercise or abused its discretion, or exercised an unpermitted discretion. **Dome Laboratories v. Farrell,** Op. No. 1917, 599 P2d 152 (Alaska 1979).

Where defendants had not incurred extensive expenses in preparation for trial or pecuniary judgment hearing was not abuse of discretion for trial judge to deny award of attorney fees to defendant. **Dome Laboratories v. Farrell,** Op. No. 1917, 599 P2d 152 (Alaska 1979).

Where plaintiff established a prima facie case of breach of contract, superior court was precluded from granting an involuntary dismissal under this rule. **Glover v. Sager,** Op. No. 2703, 667 P2d 1198 (Alaska 1983).

When the trial court dismisses a complaint on the ground that the plaintiff has shown no right to relief, it must enter findings of fact and conclusions of law. **Winn v. Mannhalter,** Op. No. 2988, 708 P2d 444 (Alaska 1985).

In order to withstand a motion for involuntary dismissal under this rule, plaintiff must have presented evidence that the defendant breached a duty, thereby causing injury to the plaintiff. **Winn v. Mannhalter,** Op. No. 2988, 708 P2d 444 (Alaska 1985).

If a trial court refuses to delay ruling on an Alaska R. Civ. P. 41(b) motion, it is because the plaintiff has failed to prove its case for the reasons set out in the court's findings under Alaska R. Civ. P. 52(a); nothing would be gained from an additional requirement that the trial court explain why it did not delay its ruling. **Fletcher v. Trademark Constr., Inc.,** Op. No. 5760 (Alaska 2003).

Trial court did not err in granting a general contractor's motion to dismiss a subcontractor's suit against it where the court's findings of fact were sufficient to show the legal and factual bases for its ruling so as to allow for appellate review, and its interpretation of Alaska R. Civ. P. 41(b) was proper where: (1) The subcontractor's witness was unable to testify as to the cost of materials relating to the change orders; (2) the documents presented did not provide a basis for distinguishing between base and revised materials costs; (3) the classification of hours worked on the project as "base" or "extra" was arbitrary; and (4) no evidence supported the assumption that all hours not budgeted for in the base contract bid must have been expended as the result of additions and revisions to the contract. **Fletcher v. Trademark Constr., Inc.,** Op. No. 5760 (Alaska 2003).

B. Denial of Motion to Dismiss.

The function of the trial court is to deny a motion to dismiss at the close of plaintiff's evidence, if the evidence would be, in a jury case, sufficient to take the case to the jury although the court as trier of the facts would find against the plaintiff on the evidence. Thus where plaintiff has presented a prima facie case based upon unimpeached evidence the trial judge should not grant the motion even though he is the trier of the facts and may not himself feel at that point of the trial that the plaintiff has sustained his burden of proof. **Rogge v. Weaver,** Op. No. 63, 368 P2d 810 (Alaska 1962).

Where plaintiff at the close of his evidence presents a prima facie case based on unimpeached evidence, the trial judge should not grant a motion for involuntary dismissal, but should follow the alternative provided by Civil Rule 41(b) and decline to render any judgment until the close of all the evidence. **Trusty v. Jones,** Op. No. 71, 369 P2d 420 (Alaska 1962).

Where an action by a prisoner against the state for injuries allegedly sustained while being transported in a truck after a hip operation is dismissed on the merits without any findings of fact being made, the case will be remanded for purposes of making adequate findings of fact and conclusions of law, including findings as to the court's judgment of credibility of the plaintiff and his witnesses. **Bohm v. State,** Op. No. 543, 453 P2d 410 (Alaska 1969).

Motions under this rule should not invariably be resolved by weighing the evidence. Where the plaintiff has presented a prima facie case based on unimpeached evidence, the trial judge should not grant the motion even though he is the trier of facts and may not himself feel at that point that the plaintiff has sustained the burden of proof. **King v. Alaska State Housing Authority,** Op. No. 917, 512 P2d 887 (Alaska 1973).

The failure of the plaintiff's son, the only witness to the occurrence giving rise to a suit, to appear for deposition is not an appropriate basis for motion to dismiss the suit. **Schandelmeier v. Winchester Western,** Op. No. 1013, 520 P2d 70 (Alaska 1974).

When noncompliance with a discovery order is in issue, this rule, rather than Rule 37, is the source of the court's authority to impose sanctions. **Schandelmeier v. Winchester Western,** Op. No. 1013, 520 P2d 70 (Alaska 1974).

Where plaintiff has been in prison for most of the period since filing his action, is unavailable for deposition and unable to obtain another attorney when his original counsel withdraws, and otherwise attempts to prosecute his complaint, the dismissal for failure to prosecute is an abuse of discretion. **Brown v. State,** Op. No. 1089, 526 P2d 1365 (Alaska 1974).

This rule calls for the exercise of sound discretion by the trial court, and should not be permitted to work an injustice where there are special circumstances impeding the plaintiff's efforts to prosecute his complaint. **Brown v. State,** Op. No. 1089, 526 P2d 1365 (Alaska 1974).

IV. Dismissal for Want of Prosecution.

This rule applies only where a motion to dismiss is filed before the period of lapse is terminated by some affirmative action. Where the last act in the record occurred more than one year prior to a motion to dismiss and where the plaintiff's motion terminates the lapse, and a motion for summary judgment and a motion to set for trial are filed subsequent to the lapse and prior to the defendant's motion to dismiss, the lapse is insufficient to allow dismissal. **First National Bank of Fairbanks v. Taylor,** Op. No. 723, 488 P2d 1026 (Alaska 1971).

Unless there is another indication by judge dismissal sua sponte for want of prosecution for one year is without prejudice. **Champion Oil Co. v. Herbert,** Op. No. 1293, 552 P2d 670 (Alaska 1976).

Case that had been reinstated and set for trial should not have been dismissed for want of prosecution. **Atlas Enterprises, Inc. v. Consolidated Construction Co .,** Op. No. 1526, 572 P2d 68 (Alaska 1977).

Where letter from plaintiffs requesting trial date was sent prior to filing of defendant's motion to dismiss, dismissal under Civil Rule 41(e) was improper. **Zeller v. Poor,** Op. No. 1610, 577 P2d 695 (Alaska 1978).

Although a case may be dismissed with prejudice under Civil Rule 4 1(e), this sanction should be reserved only for gross violations of the rule; alternative remedies which do not bar a litigant from his day in court are favored. **Zeller v. Poor,** Op. No. 1610, 577 P2d 695 (Alaska 1978).

A "proceeding" as the term is used in this rule is a step, act or measure of record, by the plaintiff, which reflects the serious determination by the plaintiff to bring the suit to a resolution; or a step, act or measure of record, by either party, which reflects that the suit is not stagnant. **Shiffman v. "K," Inc.,** Op. No. 2603, 657 P2d 401 (Alaska 1983).

The filing of an answer by the defendant was a "proceeding" within the meaning of this rule which indicated that the suit was not stagnant. **Shiffman v. "K," Inc.,** Op. No. 2603, 657 P2d 401 (Alaska 1983).

A case stands stagnant and may be dismissed when to the court it appears that for lack of activity of record neither party has taken the steps, acts or measures to be reasonably expected in pursuit or defense of the particular cause of action. **Shiffman v. "K," Inc.,** Op. No. 2603, 657 P2d 401 (Alaska 1983).

Plaintiffs' note asking the court not to dismiss their action for want of prosecution because they had not been able to find an attorney was not a "proceeding" within the meaning of this rule. **Cleary Diving Service v. Thomas, Head and Greisen,** Op. No. 2873, 688 P2d 940 (Alaska 1984).

Appellate court could not dismiss complaint for failure of timely prosecution where the trial court did not hold a call of calendar or send a show cause notice to the parties. **Reed v. Municipality of Anchorage,** Op. No. 3218, 741 P2d 1181 (Alaska 1987).

A pretrial memorandum filed after the court issues a notice of dismissal does not constitute a "proceeding" under this rule. **Power Constructors v. Acres American,** Op. No. 3689, 811 P2d 1052 (Alaska 1991).

Substitution of counsel and the consequent need for more time to review the case did not, standing alone, constitute good cause for plaintiff's 16-month delay prosecuting the case. **Power Constructors v. Acres American,** Op. No. 3689, 811 P2d 1052 (Alaska 1991).

Plaintiff's unexcused failure to proceed with its case for three years justified dismissal with prejudice. **Power Constructors v. Acres American,** Op. No. 3689, 811 P2d 1052 (Alaska 1991).

Where order gave plaintiff 180 days to take action to prepare malpractice case for trial, here filing of amended complaint and request for appearance of nonresident attorney satisfied the order, thus trial court erred in dismissing case for want of prosecution even though original complaint was not filed until two days before expiration of limitations period and defendant was not served with complaint until 20 months later. **Johnson v. Siegfried,** Op. No. 3890, 838 P2d 1252 (Alaska 1992).

Trial court is not under duty to explore meaningful alternatives before entering dismissal without prejudice for want of prosecution. **Willis v. Wetco, Inc.,** Op. No. 3963, 853 P2d 533 (Alaska 1993).

Pretrial memorandum filed after court issued notice of dismissal did not constitute "proceeding" under rule authorizing dismissal for want of prosecution. **Willis v. Wetco, Inc.,** Op. No. 3963, 853 P2d 533 (Alaska 1993).

Counterclaimant's statement that his injuries at hand of plaintiff were continuing to accumulate did not constitute good cause for failure to prosecute counterclaim. **Willis v. Wetco, Inc.,** Op. No. 3963, 853 P2d 533 (Alaska 1993).

A "proceeding" occurs for purposes of this rule when step is taken by either party which reflects that suit is not stagnant. **Novak v. Orca Oil Co., Inc.,** Op. No. 4091, 875 P2d 756 (Alaska 1994).

Plaintiff's motion to disqualify defendant's attorney was proceeding within meaning of this rule that prevented dismissal of defendant's counterclaim, notwithstanding trial judge's ruling that proceeding did not relate to counterclaim. **Novak v. Orca Oil Co., Inc.,** Op. No. 4091, 875 P2d 756 (Alaska 1994).

Rule 42. Consolidation—Separate Trials—Change of Judge.

(a) **Consolidation.** When actions involving a common question of law or fact are pending before the court, it may order a joint hearing or trial of any or all the matters in issue in the actions; it may order all the actions consolidated; and it may make such orders concerning proceedings therein as may tend to avoid unnecessary costs or delay.

A motion requesting consolidation shall be filed in the court where the case is sought to be consolidated. The motion shall contain the name of every case sought to be consolidated. A notice of filing together with a copy of the motion shall be filed in all courts and served on all parties who would be affected by consolidation.

(b) **Separate Trials.** The court, in furtherance of convenience or to avoid prejudice, or when separate trials will be conducive to expedition and economy, may order a separate trial of any claim, cross-claim, counterclaim, or third-party claim, or of any separate issue or of any number of claims, cross-claims, counterclaims, third-party claims, or issues, always preserving inviolate the right of trial by jury as declared by the Alaska Constitution and Statutes of Alaska.

(c) **Change of Judge as a Matter of Right.** In all courts of the state, a judge or master may be peremptorily challenged as follows:

(1) *Nature of Proceedings.* In an action pending in the Superior or District Courts, each side is entitled as a matter of right to a change of one judge and of one master. Two or more parties aligned on the same side of an action, whether or not consolidated, shall be treated as one side for purposes of the right to a change of judge, but the presiding judge may allow an additional change of judge to a party whose interests in the action are hostile or adverse to the interests of another party on the same side. A party wishing to exercise the right to change of judge shall file a pleading entitled "Notice of Change of Judge." The notice may be signed by an attorney, it shall state the name of the judge to be changed, and it shall neither specify grounds nor be accompanied by an affidavit.

(2) *Filing and Service.* The notice of change of judge shall be filed and copies served on the parties in accordance with Rule 5, Alaska Rules of Civil Procedure.

(3) *Timeliness.* Failure to file a timely notice precludes change of judge as a matter of right. Notice of change of judge is timely if filed before the commencement of trial and within five days after notice that the case has been assigned to a specific judge. Where a party has been served or enters an action after the case has been assigned to a specific judge, a notice of change of judge shall also be timely if filed by the party before the commencement of trial and within five days after a party appears or files a pleading in the action.

(4) *Waiver.* A party waives the right to change as a matter of right a judge who has been permanently assigned to the case by knowingly participating before that judge in:

(i) Any judicial proceeding which concerns the merits of the action and involves the consideration of evidence or of affidavits; or

(ii) A pretrial conference; or

(iii) The commencement of trial; or

(iv) If the parties agree upon a judge to whom the case is to be assigned. Such waiver is to apply only to the agreed upon judge.

(5) *Assignment of Action.* After a notice of change of judge is timely filed, the presiding judge shall immediately assign the matter to a new judge within that judicial district. Should that judge be challenged, the presiding judge shall continue to assign the case to new judges within the judicial district until all parties have exercised or waived their right to change of judge or until all superior court judges, or all district court judges, within the judicial district have been challenged peremptorily or for cause. Should all such judges in the district be disqualified, the presiding judge shall immediately notify the administrative director in writing and request that the administrative director obtain from the Chief Justice an order assigning the case to another judge.

If a judge to whom an action has been assigned later becomes unavailable because of death, illness, or other physical or legal incapacity, the parties shall be restored to their several positions and rights under this rule as they existed immediately before the assignment of the action to such judge.

(Adopted by SCO 5 October 9, 1959; amended by SCO 186 effective July 1, 1974; by SCO 258 effective November 15, 1976; by SCO 262 effective December 31, 1976; by SCO 465 effective June 1, 1981; by SCO 705 effective September 15, 1986; by SCO 716 effective September 15, 1986; by SCO 741 effective December 15, 1986; by SCO 877 effective July 15, 1988; by SCO 1153 effective July 15, 1994 and by SCO 1196 effective July 15, 1995)

Note: Ch. 80 SLA 2002 (HB 196), Section 1, adds new sections to AS 25.24 concerning the right of action for legal separation. According to Section 3 of the Act, AS 25.24.430 has the effect of amending Civil Rule 42(a) by requiring consolidation of subsequent divorce and annulment actions with legal separation actions filed by the same parties.

Annotations

Cases

Consolidation is a matter within the trial court's discretion. **Brown v. Hawkins,** Op. No. 362, 418 P2d 28 (Alaska 1966).

In a negligence action for personal injuries where defendants alleged the bar of the two-year statute of limitations as affirmative defense and plaintiff alleged estoppel from reliance on the statute of limitations, motion for separate trial of the estoppel-statute of limitations issue was granted under this rule. **Groseth v. Ness,** Op. No. 370, 421 P2d 624 (Alaska 1966).

Motion for change of judge as matter of right was timely when filed by guardian ad litem within five days of his appointment. **Veazey v. Veazey,** Op. No. 1381, 560 P2d 382 (Alaska 1977).

Where other party on same side had filed affidavit of disqualification which was denied, side had not obtained change of judge to which it was entitled. **Veazey v. Veazey,** Op. No. 1381, 560 P2d 382 (Alaska 1977).

In cases where the determination to be made is whether sanctions should be imposed under Civil Rule 95(b), the automatic change of judge authorized by Civil Rule 42 is inapplicable, and a judge will not be disqualified from presiding over such a proceeding unless his actions indicate feelings of personal rancor against the attorney involved. **Esch v. Superior Court of Third Jud. Dist.,** Op. No. 1601, 577 P2d 1039 (Alaska 1978).

On remand for new trial, presided over by same judge that presided over first trial, party is not entitled to a peremptory challenge under C.R. 42(c)(3). **Priest v. Lindig,** Op. No. 1812, 591 P2d 1299 (Alaska 1979).

A party which appears before a judge in pretrial proceedings without knowing whether that particular judge will be assigned as the trial judge in the case does not waive the right to a peremptory challenge under this rule. **Smith v. State,** Op. No. 2161, 616 P2d 863 (Alaska 1980).

While AS 22.20.022 creates a substantive right to a peremptory challenge, this rule controls the procedure and scope of such challenges in civil proceedings. **Tunley v. Municipality of Anchorage School Dist.,** Op. No. 2160, 617 P2d 490 (Alaska 1980), as amended, 631 P2d 67 (Alaska 1981).

A waiver of a party's right to peremptorily challenge a judge exists only where the requisite participation before the judge occurs after the party is informed that the judge before whom the party is appearing is the judge permanently assigned to the trial or to hear the case. **Tunley v. Municipality of Anchorage School Dist.,** Op. No. 2160, 617 P2d 490 (Alaska 1980), as amended, 631 P2d 67 (Alaska 1981).

A case is not at issue on the facts as the result of a temporary restraining order if the court requests a stipulation and does not consider evidence or affidavits. **Schmid v. Miller,** Op. No. 2210, 619 P2d 1 (Alaska 1980).

Where the only judicial proceeding prior to notice of change of judge was a hearing on a request for a temporary restraining order at which the judge did not consider evidence or affidavits, the petitioner did not waive her right to a peremptory challenge of that judge by participating in the hearing. **Schmid v. Miller,** Op. No. 2210, 619 P2d 1 (Alaska 1980).

In a single judge district, a party waives its right to peremptorily challenge the judge when it makes a Civil Rule 12(b)(6) motion before him. **Kodiak Island Borough v. Large,** Op. No. 2270, 622 P2d 440 (Alaska 1981).

A right to peremptorily challenge a judge exists in an appeal to the superior court from a final administrative determination of the Alaska Commercial Fisheries Entry Commission. **Commercial Fisheries Entry Commission v. Polushkin,** Op. No. 2300, 628 P2d 6 (Alaska 1981).

This rule does not give a litigant the right to challenge without cause the retrial of a case before the same judge who presided over the original trial and who granted the opposing party's motion for the new trial. **Sebring v. Colver,** Op. No. 2549, 649 P2d 932 (Alaska 1982).

Since the Alaska Supreme Court has by rule endorsed the concept of peremptory challenges of judges without cause, the contention that a statute authorizing such challenges violates the separation of powers doctrine was rejected. **Hornaday v. Rowland,** Op. No. 2761, 674 P2d 1333 (Alaska 1983).

Court did not err in consolidating dissolution and fraudulent conveyance actions. **Dean v. Firor,** Op. No. 2819, 681 P2d 321 (Alaska 1984).

Superior court erred in denying a peremptory challenge by defendant of the master assigned to her case, since although defendant had appeared before the same master in a related hearing for a preliminary injunction, she was not made a party to the lawsuit until over a month after her appearance at the hearing and could not reasonably have foreseen that the same master would be assigned to the lawsuit. **Dean v. Firor,** Op. No. 2819, 681 P2d 321 (Alaska 1984).

When an action to enforce an order of the Alaska State Commission for Human Rights was filed while an appeal of the order was pending in another court, it was error not to consolidate the two actions. **Pipeliners Union v. Alaska State Commission,** Op. No. 2820, 681 P2d 330 (Alaska 1984).

Court rule providing that judgment on one issue in a multi-issue case is not a final judgment unless expressly designated as such by the trial court applies to cases which contain multiple issues only because of consolidation. **Currington v. Johnson,** Op. No. 2828, 685 P2d 73 (Alaska 1984).

Defendant in criminal contempt proceeding was not entitled to peremptorily challenge the trial court judge who had presided over the civil matter out of which the contempt charge arose; having waived his right to challenge the judge in the civil proceeding, he waived the right to peremptorily challenge the judge in the ancillary criminal action. **Webber v. Webber,** Op. No. 509, 706 P2d 329 (Alaska App. 1985).

Attorney was not entitled to a change of judge as a matter of right at hearing on sanctions against him for filing frivolous, unnecessary and legally deficient pleadings in a criminal case. **Weidner v. Superior Court, Third Judicial Dist.,** Op. No. 589, 715 P2d 264 (Alaska App. 1986).

Where new claim involved the same parties but raised entirely new issues, trial judge did not abuse his discretion when he gave plaintiff the choice of either amending his complaint or bringing an entirely separate action at a later date. **Wien Air Alaska v. Bubbel,** Op. No. 3098, 723 P2d 627 (Alaska 1986).

It is unclear whether a peremptory challenge of a judge in a post-conviction relief proceeding must be made under the criminal rules or the civil rules and whether an appeal from a denial of such a motion must be made on an expedited basis under the appellate rules. **Hastings v. State,** Op. No. 706, 736 P2d 1157 (Alaska App. 1987).

The right to peremptorily challenge judge in probation revocation proceeding arises under this rule, not the criminal rules. **Wallace v. State,** Op. No. 1221, 829 P2d 1208 (Alaska App. 1992).

Trial court did not abuse its discretion in ordering separate trial of third-party claims where first-party defendant did not seek to join third-party defendants until three months before scheduled trial date; given need for additional discovery, strong possibility existed that ordering single trial would have caused significant delay. **Borg-Warner v. Avco Corp.,** Op. No. 3938, 850 P2d 628 (Alaska 1993).

A refiled suit, even if identical to a case dismissed under Civil Rule 16.1(g), is a new "action" for civil Rule 42 purposes. **Staso v. State, Department of Transportation,** Op. No. 4214, 895 P2d 988 (Alaska 1995).

The sanctions of Civil Rule 16.1(g) and Civil Rule 4 1(d) afford courts the tools necessary to deter litigants from judge shopping through voluntary or involuntary dismissals. **Staso v. State, Department of Transportation,** Op. No. 4214, 895 P2d 988 (Alaska 1995).

The trial court's interpretation and application of Alaska Civil Rule 42(c) is a question of law which the appellate court must review **Staso v. State, Department of Transportation,** Op. No. 4214, 895 P2d 988 (Alaska 1995).

Although AS 22.20.022 creates a substantive right of peremptory disqualification, Civil Rule 42(c) controls the procedure and scope of such disqualifications in civil proceedings. **Staso v. State, Department of Transportation,** Op. No. 4214, 895 P2d 988 (Alaska 1995).

A party is not entitled to a second peremptory disqualification of a judge, or to relief from the waiver or timeliness requirements of this rule, where the proceeding in which the disqualification is sought is ancillary to and a continuation of the underlying action. **Staso v. State, Department of Transportation,** Op. No. 4214, 895 P2d 988 (Alaska 1995).

None of the plaintiff's actions in a dismissed case before a certain judge waived his right to peremptorily disqualify that judge in a refiled suit. **Staso v. State, Department of Transportation,** Op. No. 4214, 895 P2d 988 (Alaska 1995).

A litigant cannot waive his or her right to peremptorily disqualify a judge until the judge has been permanently assigned to the case. **Staso v. State, Department of Transportation,** Op. No. 4214, 895 P2d 988 (Alaska 1995).

A party's repeated appearances before a judge before his motion to disqualify the judge was ruled on did not waive his right to peremptorily disqualify the judge. **Staso v. State, Department of Transportation,** Op. No. 4214, 895 P2d 988 (Alaska 1995).

Where party was notified in domestic relations pre-trial order that judge had been assigned to case, his failure to move to recuse judge within 15 days of such notice precluded change of judge as matter of right. **Musser v. Johnson,** Op. No. 4325, 914 P2d 1241 (Alaska 1996).

In case involving settlement agreement which resulted in termination of trust, contingent beneficiary of trust, despite his nominal non-party status, should not have been denied right to peremptorily challenge judge. **Barberv. Barber,** Op. No.4345, 915 P2d 1204 (Alaska 1996).

Contingent beneficiary of trust who was not served notice of settlement proceeding concerning sale of trust property did not waive right to peremptorily challenge judge by discovering existence of that proceedings and expressing dissatisfaction to one of lawyers to the proceedings who, acting on contingent beneficiary's behalf, withdrew his approval of settlement agreement, since contingent beneficiary did not knowingly participate before judge. **Barber v. Barber,** Op. No. 4345, 915 P2d 1204 (Alaska 1996).

In prosecution of car dealership for several violations of Unfair Trade Practices and Consumer Protection Act, trial court did not abuse its discretion in denying defendant's motion for severance of the charges since (1) evidence of any given transaction was not offered for sole purpose of showing that defendant acted in conformity with some bad character trait, (2) any prejudice to defendant was limited by jury instruction, and (3) primary relief sought by state was permanent injunction, not damages. **Anchorage Nissan, Inc. v. State,** Op. No. 4850, 941 P2d 1229 (Alaska 1997).

State's peremptory challenge of judge was timely where trial had not commenced and challenge was filed on same day state defendants entered appearance. **Karen L. v. Dept. of Health & Soc. Services,** Op. No. 4943, 953 P2d 871 (Alaska 1998).

Intervenor who entered case after initial judgment and appeal had right to peremptorily change judge. **Mundt v. Northwest Explorations, Inc.,** Op. No. 5022, 963 P2d 265 (Alaska 1998).

Substituted defendant and originally-named defendant were not single party for purposes of right to change of judge, thus time limitation for notice of change of judge which would have applied to originally-named defendant did not apply to substituted defendant. **West v. Buchanan,** Op. No. 5134, 981 P2d 1065 (Alaska 1999).

Defendant who files application for post-conviction relief challenging criminal conviction does not have right to peremptory challenge of judge who presided over trial that led to conviction. **Plyler v. State,** Op. No. 1695, 10 P3d 1173 (Alaska App. 2000).

Pro se Litigant's document challenging assigned judge that was incorrectly entitled "Plaintiff's Challenge to the Assignment of Judge" sufficiently conformed to the requirements of this rule even though it was not entitled "Notice of Change of Judge," as subsection (c)(1) of this rule requires because Alaska courts are lenient to filings by pro se litigants. **Sengupta v. University of Alaska,** Op. No. 11805, 139 P.3d 572 (Alaska 2006).

A separate trial on a defendant's counterclaims is unnecessary when the counterclaims share the same issues of fact as the defendant's affirmative defenses, as the plaintiff suffers no prejudice other than the unavoidable prejudice caused by the defendant's assertion of the factual basis of the affirmative defenses, so trying the counterclaims with the plaintiff's case in chief is "conducive to expedition and economy" as stated in this rule. **Domke v. Alyeska Pipeline Serv. Co., Inc.**, Op. No. 10885, 137 P.3d 295 (Alaska 2006).

A trial court's decision to deny a severance motion is reviewed by appellate courts only for abuse of discretion. **Domke v. Alyeska Pipeline Serv. Co., Inc.**, Op. No. 10885, 137 P.3d 295 (Alaska 2006).

PART VII. EVIDENCE AND CONDUCT OF TRIAL

Rule 43. Evidence.

(Rescinded by Supreme Court Order 366 effective August 1, 1979)

Rule 43.1. Exhibits.

(a) **Parties Mark Exhibits.** All intended exhibits shall be marked by the parties for identification prior to trial. At the beginning of trial an original and one copy of an exhibit list shall be filed with the in-court clerk.

(b) **Procedure.** Exhibits shall be marked for identification in the manner prescribed by the administrative director in the bulletin required by paragraph (h) of this rule. All exhibits marked for identification shall be listed on an exhibit list provided by the court. The form of the exhibit list shall be prescribed by the administrative director.

(c) **Admission.** Exhibits properly marked for identification may be admitted into evidence upon the motion of any party or upon the court's own motion. After an identified exhibit is admitted by the court, the clerk shall mark the exhibit "admitted" in a manner prescribed by the administrative director. When an exhibit is admitted into evidence, the fact of its admission shall be noted immediately on the exhibit list.

(d) **Custody of Exhibits.** At the time an exhibit is offered into evidence, the exhibit shall be placed in and remain in the clerk's custody until released as provided in paragraph (g) of this rule or as set forth in the administrative bulletin required by paragraph (h) of this rule. Exhibits which have not been offered into evidence shall not be placed in the custody of the clerk unless otherwise ordered by the court.

(e) **Final Check.** Prior to submission of the case to the jury or to the court sitting without a jury, the court shall require counsel and those parties not represented by counsel to (1) examine all intended, identified, offered, or admitted exhibits and the in-court clerk's exhibit list, (2) confirm to the court that the list accurately reflects the status of the exhibits, and (3) confirm that any modifications to the exhibits ordered by the court have been made. Upon proper motion or the court's own motion, the court may order additional exhibits marked for identification and/or admitted into evidence. At the time of the final check, identified exhibits which have not been offered for admission but which the court has previously ordered placed in the clerk's custody shall be returned to the appropriate party, unless otherwise ordered by the court.

(f) **Submission to the Jury.** Unless otherwise ordered by the court, all exhibits admitted into evidence shall be given to the jury for deliberation, except the following exhibits will not be given to the jury without a specific court order:

(1) live ammunition;

(2) firearms;

(3) drugs and alcoholic beverages;

(4) perishable, flammable or hazardous materials; and

(5) money, jewelry or other valuable items.

The court may allow a photograph to be submitted to the jury in place of the physical exhibit.

(g) **Return of Some Exhibits After Hearing or Trial.** At the conclusion of a hearing or trial, the court shall inquire whether counsel stipulate to the return of any exhibits to counsel for safekeeping pending appeal and to the substitution of photographs for any of the physical (i.e., nondocumentary) exhibits. Whether or not counsel stipulate, the court may also order counsel to take custody of the following exhibits, store said exhibits in a safe location and maintain the chain of custody pending appeal:

(1) live ammunition;

(2) firearms;

(3) drugs and alcoholic beverages;

(4) perishable, flammable or hazardous materials;

(5) money, jewelry or other valuable items; and

(6) items which are unwieldy due to bulk and/or weight.

Whenever exhibits are returned to counsel for safekeeping pending appeal, the court may require counsel to submit an affidavit setting forth the specific measures taken to insure safekeeping of the exhibits.

(h) **Administrative Bulletin.** The administrative director shall establish standards and procedures by appropriate bulletin consistent with these rules governing the marking, handling, storage, safekeeping, and disposal of all exhibits coming into the court's custody. Unless otherwise ordered by the court, such standards and procedures are controlling.

(Added by SCO 598 effective September 1, 1984; amended by SCO 948 effective January 15, 1989)

Informational Note: Administrative Bulletin No. 9, relating to Civil Rule 43.1 can be found on the following page.

ALASKA COURT SYSTEM
OFFICE OF THE ADMINISTRATIVE DIRECTOR
ADMINISTRATIVE BULLETIN NO. 9
AMENDED EFFECTIVE OCTOBER 15, 2005

TO ALL HOLDERS OF ADMINISTRATIVE BULLETIN SETS:

Presiding Judges
Area Court Administrators
Clerk of the Appellate Courts
Rural Training Assistants
Full-Time Clerks of Court
Magistrates at locations with no full-time clerk
Law Libraries at Anchorage, Fairbanks, Juneau, & Ketchikan

Senior Staff
Administrative Associate
Rural Court Analyst
General Services Manager

OTHERS:
In-Court Clerk Supervisors, Anchorage and Fairbanks
Records Division Supervisor, Anchorage

SUBJECT: Exhibit Procedures

This policy is being issued under the authority granted to the administrative director by Civil Rule 43.1 and Criminal Rule 26.1. The procedures described below must be followed in all trials, pretrial hearings and other court hearings in the Alaska trial courts.

Contents **Page**

I. DEFINITIONS

A. Marked for Identification: means an exhibit has received an exhibit sticker and exhibit number and has been listed on the exhibit list.

B. Offered into Evidence: means counsel or a party not represented by counsel has asked the court to admit the exhibit into evidence

C. Admitted: means the court has determined that the exhibit should be considered as evidence by the trier-of-fact (i.e., the judge or jury).

D. Withdrawn: means the court has allowed the exhibit to be removed from custody of the court either during or after trial.

II. MARKING EXHIBITS

A. When to Mark

1. Civil Cases

a. Formal Civil Trials

In all trials under the formal rules of civil procedure, the parties shall, prior to trial, mark for identification all intended exhibits in the manner prescribed by this bulletin. Parties must obtain standard exhibit stickers and exhibit list forms (forms TF-200 and TF-201) from the in-court clerk or other designated clerk. The parties must type a brief description of the identified exhibits on the exhibit list and must list the exhibits in the order that the party intends to use them at trial. At the beginning of trial the original and one copy of the exhibit list shall be filed with the in-court clerk. (Civil Rule 43.1) Prior to trial, the parties must serve all other parties with a copy of the exhibit list.

b. Other Civil Hearings and Small Claims Trials

In all other hearings and in all trials under the Small Claims rules, exhibits will be marked for identification by the in-court clerk at the time of trial or hearing unless the judge orders pre-marking of the exhibits.

2. Criminal Cases

The procedure described in paragraph 1.a. above may be required in criminal cases at the discretion of the trial judge. If the procedure described in paragraph 1.a. is not required, the in-court clerk shall mark all exhibits at the time of trial or hearing.

B. Exhibit Numbering

The following examples show how exhibits should be numbered:

Single Parties:

Plaintiff State of Alaska:	Exhibits start with 1
Defendant Tom Johnson:	Exhibits start with A

Multiple Parties:

Plaintiff Tom Jones:	Exhibits start with J-1
Plaintiff John Miller:	Exhibits start with M-1
Defendant Sam Smith:	Exhibits start with S-A
Defendant James Orange:	Exhibits start with JO-A
Defendant Mary Orange:	Exhibits start with MO-A

Plaintiff's exhibits must be marked in numerical order starting with 1. Defendant's exhibits must be marked in alphabetical order starting with A.

If there is more than one plaintiff or more than one defendant, the first letter of the party's last name must precede the number or letter as shown above.

If there is more than one plaintiff or defendant with the same last initial, the initials of both the first and last names must be added to the exhibit number as shown above.

Defendant's exhibits will be marked A through Z in order, then AA, AB, AC, etc., through AZ, then BA, BB, BC, etc. through BZ, and so forth.

In cases with multiple parties and large volumes of exhibits, the court may require alternative exhibit numbering procedures to be used. For example, the court may want to assign each party a block of one thousand numbers.

C. Exhibit Stickers

1. Exhibits must be marked for identification with an exhibit sticker provided by the court before being referred to in court.

2. Exhibit stickers will only be placed on those exhibits intended to be submitted into evidence at a trial or hearing. Exhibit stickers shall not be placed on any other copies of exhibits.

3. Exhibit stickers in all cases must be marked with the full case number and exhibit number or letter and must show whether the exhibit was admitted.

4. Exhibit stickers are color coded as follows:

a. Yellow stickers will be used for plaintiffs or petitioners.
b. Blue stickers will be used for defendants or respondents.
c. Red stickers will be used for grand jury proceedings.
d. Red stickers will be used for coroner proceedings.
e. Green stickers will be used for miscellaneous parties or proceedings.

5. Placement of Exhibit Stickers:

a. Stickers will be placed on the exhibits in a manner which will not interfere with the viewing of the exhibit. If at all possible, exhibit stickers should be placed in the lower right corner of the front side of the first page of documents. If the sticker is placed on the back of a document or photograph, then the sticker should be placed in the lower right corner. Caution: Exhibit stickers will not adhere well to some surfaces, e.g. smooth metal or plastic. In such cases, the sticker must also be securely taped to the exhibit.

b. If an exhibit sticker cannot be attached directly to the exhibit, the sticker will be attached to a wired or stringed tag which will then be attached to the exhibit.

c. To aid in locating exhibits, exhibit stickers should be visible at all times. However, if this is not possible because the exhibit is stored in a non-transparent container, the container must be labeled with a plain white sticker marked with the following information:

Contains:
Exhibit No. ____________

d. If an exhibit was marked for a prior court hearing, see section VI.

6. When the court orders an exhibit admitted into evidence, the clerk shall note on the exhibit sticker and the exhibit list that the exhibit has been admitted.

D. Marking Photographs Substituted for Exhibits

1. If an exhibit is ordered returned to a party and a photograph of the exhibit substituted in its place, an exhibit sticker will be placed on the photograph showing the same exhibit number assigned to the substituted exhibit. A notation will be made on the exhibit list that the exhibit was returned and a photograph substituted in its place.

2. For marking of photographs when a photograph is sent to the jury in place of a physical exhibit but the physical exhibit remains in court custody, see section V.B.

III. EXHIBIT LIST

A. All exhibits marked for identification must be listed on the standard exhibit list, forms TF-200 and TF-201, provided by the court.

Exception: Small Claims and Forcible Entry and Detainer (FED) Cases

The procedure described below may be used in small claims and FED cases if all exhibits in the case are documentary and can be stored in the case file. This procedure is optional and may be used at the discretion of the clerk of court for each court.

1. List exhibits in the log notes

2. Exhibits need not be listed on an exhibit list.

3. After trial or hearing, place exhibits in an envelope. Note case title, case number and exhibit numbers on outside of envelope.

4. Store envelope of exhibits in the case file.

5. Return of exhibits is governed by Section VIII of this Bulletin.

The above procedure may not be used if any exhibit is stored outside the case file. In that event, all exhibits must be listed on an exhibit list and all exhibits must be stored outside the case file.

B. The case title, case number, attorney's name and a brief description of each exhibit will be noted on the exhibit list. The in-court clerk will indicate on the exhibit list whether exhibits were offered for admission, admitted or the date they were withdrawn.

C. See section VI for additional information the in-court clerk must write on the exhibit list if the exhibit was previously marked for a prior court hearing and if the exhibit is still in the court's custody.

D. At the conclusion of each hearing, the original exhibit lists will be filed in the appropriate case file. If the exhibit lists apply to more than one case, photocopies of the exhibit lists must be placed in each case file to which the exhibit lists apply.

IV. PREPARING EXHIBITS FOR COURT

Trial counsel must comply with the following requirements when submitting exhibits.

A. All ammunition will be submitted in sealable containers.

B. All clothing, shoes, boots, hats, gloves, jackets or other wearing apparel must be dried to prevent molding and submitted in either clear plastic bags or paper sacks.

C. Any firearm will have all ammunition removed prior to submission to the court. When submitted, the firearm must be in a condition that will not allow the trigger to be pulled thereby detonating any live ammunition which may be placed in the weapon. For example: firearms must have bolts removed and taped securely to the side or locked to the rear, cylinders swung out, loading gates open, or slides or breeches locked open.

D. Breakable exhibits must be submitted in protective containers strong enough to prevent breakage and contain spillage.

E. All perishable exhibits (e.g., food) and those emanating odors (e.g., untanned animal hides) must be submitted in transparent plastic bags or other types of transparent airtight containers. During trial, such exhibits will be stored in a manner and in a place approved by the trial judge. The judge may allow a photograph of such an exhibit to be substituted in place of the physical exhibit.

F. All drugs must be submitted in clear heavy-duty plastic bags or other types of transparent nonbreakable containers. The opening of the bag or other container must be completely sealed with exhibit tape.

G. Hazardous substances (such as acid, gasoline, explosives, etc.) must be submitted in containers approved for storage of the hazardous substance strong enough to prevent breakage and contain spillage. The outside of the container must clearly a) identify the contents, b) be marked hazardous and c) be labeled as required by city, state and federal regulations.

H. Multipage documents not securely fastened may be placed in transparent plastic bags to ensure that pages are not lost.

I. In cases in which counsel anticipate that there will be more than 50 documentary exhibits, the documentary exhibits must be submitted in an organized system which will help in handling and locating the exhibits. For example: documentary exhibits may be placed in 3-ring binders with tab dividers or in file folders marked with the exhibit numbers.

V. SUBMISSION OF CERTAIN EXHIBITS TO JURY

A. Unless otherwise ordered by the court, all exhibits admitted into evidence shall be given to the jury for deliberation, except the following exhibits will not be given to the jury without a specific court order:

1. live ammunition;
2. firearms;
3. drugs and alcoholic beverages;
4. perishable, flammable or hazardous materials; and
5. money, jewelry or other valuable items.

B. The court may allow a photograph of an exhibit to be submitted to the jury in place of the physical exhibit. If this is done, an exhibit sticker will be placed on the photograph showing the same exhibit number assigned to the physical exhibit with the words "photo of" noted above the exhibit number. A notation will be made on the exhibit list that a photograph of the exhibit was submitted to the jury. The physical exhibit will remain in court custody, unless otherwise ordered by the court.

VI. EXHIBITS MARKED IN PRIOR HEARINGS OR PRIOR CASES

If counsel wish to use an exhibit which is in court custody because it was offered in a prior court proceeding, the following procedures must be used.

A. Obtaining Exhibit

The in-court clerk, upon request of counsel, shall arrange to have exhibits from prior court hearings available for further hearings in the same case or hearings in a different case.

B. Record of Transfer

1. New Exhibit List

The prior exhibit number and case number must be noted in the exhibit description on the new exhibit list.

2. Prior Exhibit List

The transfer of an exhibit to a new case must also be noted on the exhibit list in the prior case or otherwise documented in the file of the prior case.

C. Exhibit Sticker Placement

A new exhibit sticker will be placed next to the previous sticker. An "X" will be drawn through the previous sticker. The previous exhibit sticker must remain legible. If, however, the court orders the prior exhibit sticker covered or removed, that fact must be noted on the new exhibit list.

VII. SAFEKEEPING EXHIBITS

A. When Clerk Takes Custody of Exhibits

Each exhibit will be placed in the custody of the clerk at the time the exhibit is offered into evidence at a hearing or trial. Counsel/parties will not be allowed to keep exhibits that have been offered into evidence at counsel table during recesses or any other time the exhibits are not in immediate use.

B. Use of Exhibit Tape to Seal Sensitive Exhibits

1. Certain sensitive exhibits as described below must be sealed. Sealing means the in-court clerk must place the exhibit in a transparent plastic bag and completely seal the opening of the bag with exhibit tape in such a manner that the bag cannot be opened without destroying the tape or tearing the bag. The in-court clerk must then write on the tape the date of sealing and the clerk's full signature. Taped bags may not be opened without an order from the court.

2. Drugs

At the time of the final check, the in-court clerk shall place any bag or other container holding drugs inside a new transparent bag and seal it.

3. Rolls of Coins

The in-court clerk does not need to open and count the coins contained in a roll of coins offered as an exhibit. However, when a roll of coins is offered into evidence, the in-court clerk shall place the roll of coins in a transparent plastic bag and seal it.

4. All Other Cash

The in-court clerk, in the presence of the party offering the cash as an exhibit, must, at the first available recess, count the cash, place it in a transparent plastic bag and seal it. Both the in-court clerk and the party offering the cash must date and sign the tape sealing the bag. The in-court clerk must note on the exhibit list that the amount of cash was verified and the date. The in-court clerk and submitting party must then initial this note on the exhibit list.

If the bag is opened during trial, the party who opened it and the in-court clerk must recount the cash, reseal it with exhibit tape, note the reverification on the exhibit list, sign and date the tape and exhibit list.

It is not necessary for the clerk in charge of exhibit storage to open a sealed bag to count money when it is turned over to that clerk. However, cash that comes to the exhibit storage clerk unsealed or in a torn bag must be recounted by the exhibit storage clerk in the presence of a witness. After resealing the cash in a new bag, the reverification must be noted on the exhibit list and both the clerk and witness must sign and date the tape and exhibit list. If any money is missing, the procedures for missing exhibits (section VII. G.) must be followed.

5. Jewelry, Loose Gems, Gold Dust, Gold Nuggets, etc.

When jewelry, loose gems, gold dust, gold nuggets and other such valuable exhibits are offered into evidence, the in-court clerk shall place the exhibit in a transparent plastic bag and seal it.

C. When Accounting of Exhibits Is Required

1. After the court has recessed each day, the in-court clerk must check to be sure that offered or admitted exhibits are in the court's possession. A written inventory is not required.

2. The in-court clerk must complete a final check in accordance with Civil Rule 43.1 and Criminal Rule 26.1 before the case is submitted to the jury or to the court sitting without a jury. The parties are required to participate in the final check. At the time of the final check, identified exhibits which have not been offered for admission but which the court has previously ordered placed in the clerk's custody shall be returned to the appropriate party, unless otherwise ordered by the court.

3. The exhibits must be delivered to the jury room by the in-court clerk or another court employee. The in-court clerk will then date and sign the Exhibit List certifying which exhibits were delivered to the jury.

4. After a verdict has been returned and accepted, the in-court clerk, in the presence of the bailiff and jury foreperson, must complete an inventory of the exhibits being returned by the jury. After the accounting is completed, the in-court clerk will date and sign the Exhibit List certifying which exhibits were returned from the jury. Upon a showing of good cause in specific case, the trial judge may relax this requirement. Such a finding must be on the record.

5. Before placing the exhibits in storage, the clerk responsible for exhibit storage (who may be the in-court clerk or a designated exhibits clerk) is required to complete an inventory of the exhibits being received before placing them in storage. After the accounting is complete the clerk responsible for exhibit storage must date and sign the Exhibit List certifying which exhibits have been placed in storage.

D. Safekeeping of Exhibits During Trial or Hearing

1. During Recesses

During court recesses, sensitive exhibits must be placed in a secure place unless the in-court clerk or another court employee is guarding the exhibits or the courtroom is empty and the exhibits are locked in the courtroom. For the purposes of this paragraph, "sensitive exhibits" includes money, drugs, firearms, jewelry and other valuable items.

2. Overnight

Storage of exhibits overnight during a trial must be in either the designated exhibit storage area (described in section VII. F.) or a locked exhibit cabinet in the courtroom. If there are no lockable exhibit storage cabinets in the courtroom, exhibits may be stored in the courtroom overnight only if authorized by the judge. Overnight storage of sensitive exhibits (drugs, firearms, money, etc.) must be in the designated exhibit storage area described in section VII. F.

E. Safekeeping of Exhibits During Deliberation

1. Jury Deliberation Room

The following requirements apply to any room used as a jury deliberation room, including courtrooms.

a. For any room which may be used as a jury deliberation room, each court must provide a lock system which will allow only the bailiff and clerk of court to have access to the room when exhibits are stored in the room. This separately keyed lock system should be in addition to the lock system ordinarily used to lock such rooms.

b. During jury deliberation, no one may enter the jury deliberating room unless authorized by the trial judge while there are jurors, jurors' notes or exhibits in the jury deliberation room. This prohibition includes entry for such housekeeping purposes as cleaning the room, making coffee, etc.

2. Delivery of Exhibits to Jury

Only court employees may assist in the delivery of exhibits to the jury. During delivery of exhibits to the jury deliberation room, other exhibits left in the courtroom must be placed in a locked exhibit cabinet in the courtroom unless a court employee is guarding the exhibits or the courtroom is emptied and the exhibits are locked in the courtroom. Unless otherwise ordered by the court, exhibits delivered to the jury must remain with the jury until deliberations are concluded.

3. Exhibits Not Given to Jury

Exhibits in the clerk's custody which are not submitted to the jury must be properly secured in either the designated exhibit storage area (described in section F below) or a locked exhibit cabinet. If the courtroom is used as a jury deliberation room, all exhibits which are not to be submitted to the jury must be removed from the courtroom or locked in exhibit storage cabinets in the courtroom.

4. Safekeeping While Jury Is Absent

Whenever the jury leaves the jury deliberation room during deliberations, the bailiff must lock the exhibits in the room with a lock which may be opened only by the bailiff and clerk of court or otherwise secure the exhibits in an area authorized by the court.

F. Required Exhibit Storage

Each court must establish a permanent storage area (cabinet, vault, safe or room) specifically designated for the storage of exhibits. The designated exhibit storage area must have a lock system independent of other locks used in the court. Access to the designated exhibit storage area must be limited to the clerk of court or a small number of court personnel designated by the clerk of court.

1. Except during court proceedings or upon order of the court, all exhibits will be stored in the designated exhibit storage area. Exception: In small claims cases and forcible entry and detainer cases if all exhibits in the case are documentary, exhibits may be stored in an envelope in the case file. The case title, case number, and exhibit numbers must be noted on the outside of the envelope.

2. The designated exhibit storage area will be accessible only to court personnel and will be kept locked at all times except when in use.

3. All exhibits stored in the designated exhibit storage area, except for bulky exhibits, must be stored in envelopes or suitable boxes. The case number and case name shall be noted on the outside of the envelope or box. A list of the exhibit numbers contained in the envelope or box will be noted on or in the envelope or box.

4. Perishable exhibits (e.g. food) or exhibits too large for the court's designated exhibit storage area will be stored in a manner and in a place approved by the trial judge.

5. Before placing in storage, the clerk will insure that exhibits needing special storage containers as required by section IV, are adequately packaged to prevent odor, breakage and spillage.

6. Before a firearm is placed in storage, it must be checked to be sure that there is no ammunition in it.

G. Missing Exhibits

If an exhibit cannot be located after a thorough search, and in no event longer than 24 hours after an exhibit is found to be missing, the Administrative Staff Counsel must be notified of the loss of the exhibit. All courts will establish in writing a procedure for the systematic and immediate notification of supervisors and the Administrative Staff Counsel if an exhibit is lost.

VIII. RETURN OF EXHIBITS (Civil Rule 74(g))

A. When Exhibits May Be Returned

1. An exhibit which is in the clerk's custody because it has been offered into evidence will be released to the party who submitted the exhibit only when one or more of the following circumstances occur:

a. Counsel withdraws the exhibit on the record with the consent of the court.

b. The court orders the exhibit returned either on the record or in writing.

c. Parties stipulate to the return of exhibits either on the record or in writing.

d. Defendant is acquitted in a criminal case. The exhibits will be returned to counsel promptly after the court recesses. Counsel must sign the exhibit list to indicate receipt of the exhibits.

e. Final judgment has been entered and the time for appeal has elapsed or the appeal decided and the time for further appeal has elapsed.

2. Exhibits which have not been offered into evidence but which the judge has directed taken into court custody during trial will be returned to counsel at the time of final check, unless the judge orders otherwise.

3. Any exhibit, whether or not it has been offered into evidence, which is in the possession of the clerk following the conclusion of a trial or hearing will be released only under the circumstances set out in paragraph 1. (a - e) above.

4. Return of Some Exhibits at Conclusion of Hearing/Trial.

At the conclusion of a hearing or trial, the court shall inquire whether counsel stipulate to the return of any exhibits to counsel for safekeeping pending appeal and to the substitution of photographs for any of the physical (i.e., non-documentary) exhibits. Whether or not counsel stipulate, the court may also order counsel to take custody of the following exhibits, store said exhibits in a safe location and maintain the chain of custody pending appeal:

a. live ammunition;
b. firearms;
c. drugs and alcoholic beverages:
d. perishable, flammable or hazardous materials;
e. money, jewelry or other valuable items; and
f. items which are unwieldy due to bulk and/or weight.

Whenever exhibits are returned to counsel for safekeeping pending appeal, the court may require counsel to submit an affidavit setting forth the specific measures taken to insure safekeeping of the exhibits. (Civil Rule 43.1 and Criminal Rule 26.1)

B. To Whom Exhibits May Be Returned

Exhibits may be returned only to the submitting party unless otherwise ordered by the court. State, municipal, city or borough exhibits in criminal cases may be returned to the appropriate police agency if there is no resident prosecuting attorney in the court location or the resident prosecuting attorney has directed that exhibits be returned to the appropriate police agency. The party submitting the exhibit is responsible for returning the exhibit to the rightful owner.

C. Grand Jury Exhibits

All exhibits used at grand jury proceedings will be returned to the District Attorney following the conclusion of the grand jury proceeding in which the exhibits were used unless the exhibit is currently in the custody of the clerk on another matter. The District Attorney shall state on the record that he has received the exhibits from the clerk and/or sign the exhibit list and note that the exhibits have been withdrawn.

D. Procedure for Return of Exhibits

1. After the final verdict has been returned and the time for appeal has elapsed or the appeal has been decided and the time for further appeal has elapsed, exhibits still in the court's custody will be returned by one of the methods described in paragraph 2 below. If an exhibit was used in more than one case, the exhibit can only be returned after the time for appeal has elapsed in all cases in which the exhibit was offered into evidence.

2. The clerk shall return all exhibits by one of the following methods:

a. Delivery: The clerk may return exhibits together with a copy of the "Inventory and Receipt" form, TF-206, by:

(1) Certified mail; or

(2) Personal delivery at the courthouse to the attorney, an employee of the attorney's firm or the attorney's courier service. The person receiving the exhibits must complete and sign the court's copy of the "Inventory and Receipt" form, TF-206.

b. Notice to Pick Up: The clerk may either telephone the attorney or party or send an "Exhibit Notice Card", form TF-205, by first class mail to the attorney or party indicating that the attorney or party must pick up the exhibits within 33 days from the date the "Exhibit Notice Card" is sent.

If the "Exhibit Notice Card" is returned to the court undelivered, the clerk shall make reasonable attempts to locate the attorney or party through such means as telephoning, contacting the Alaska Bar Association, etc. Upon locating a current address for the attorney or party, the clerk shall then send a supplemental "Exhibit Notice Card" to the attorney or party.

c. Judgment Stamp: In lieu of the notice to pick up, the final judgment or order may be stamped or printed with a notice notifying counsel that if no appeal is filed they must pick up the exhibits between 31 and 60 days from the date of distribution of the final judgment or order.

If this judgment/order is returned undelivered, the clerk shall follow the procedures in subparagraph b. above to attempt to locate counsel.

E. Procedures for Destruction of Exhibits

1. Prosecution exhibits in criminal cases will not be destroyed unless specifically ordered by the court. If destruction is ordered, notice will be given to the prosecuting attorney and police prior to the destruction of the prosecution's exhibits.

2. If the notice to counsel to pick up exhibits is returned to the court undelivered, and the clerk has not been able to otherwise locate the attorney or party, and 33 days have elapsed since the notice was sent, the clerk shall complete the "Affidavit and Order for Disposal of Exhibits", form TF-209, and submit it to the presiding or trial judge. Upon order of the court, the clerk shall dispose of the exhibits as set forth in subparagraph 3 below.

3. If the attorney or party does not pick up the exhibits after receiving the notice described in paragraph VIII. D. above, the clerk shall dispose of the items as follows:

a. For items of value, the clerk shall arrange for the sale of such items at public auction. The proceeds will be deposited into the General Fund Revenue Account for the State of Alaska.

b. For items of value that cannot be sold, the clerk shall attempt to locate a charitable institution or other public service organization to which such items can be donated.

c. For all other items, the clerk shall arrange to have the items appropriately destroyed.

d. If exhibits are sold, donated, or destroyed, the clerk must fill out form TF-210, "Affidavit Following Disposal of Exhibits".

IX. EXHIBIT FORMS AND DOCUMENTS

All exhibit forms, certified mail receipts and other documents regarding exhibit control will be filed in the case file.

Dated: ___________________ ___________________________

Effective Date: ___________ Stephanie Cole Administrative Director

This bulletin was originally issued as No. 84-1 Amended, effective September 1, 1984; amended October 18, 988, effective January 15, 1989; amended August 8, 2005, effective October 15, 2005

Rule 44. Proof of Official Record.

(Rescinded by Supreme Court Order 366 effective August 1, 1979)

Rule 44.1. Determination of Foreign Law.

(Rescinded by Supreme Court Order 366 effective August 1, 1979)

Rule 45. Subpoena.

(a) **For Attendance of Witnesses—Form—Issuance.** Every subpoena shall be issued by the clerk under the seal of the court, shall state the name of the court and title of the action, and shall command each person to whom it is directed to attend and give testimony or to produce documents at a time and place therein specified. The clerk shall issue a subpoena for the attendance of a witness, signed and sealed but otherwise in blank, to a party requesting it, who shall fill it in before service. The clerk shall issue a subpoena for the production of documentary evidence signed and sealed and indicating the date, time and place of the deposition or court proceeding at which the documentary evidence is to be produced.

(b) **For Production of Documentary Evidence.** A subpoena may also command the person to whom it is directed to produce the books, papers, documents, or tangible things designated therein; but the court, upon motion made promptly and in any event at or before the time specified in the subpoena for compliance therewith, may (1) void or modify the subpoena if it is unreasonable and oppressive or (2) condition denial of the motion upon the advancement by the person in whose behalf the subpoena is issued of the reasonable cost of producing the books, papers, documents or tangible things.

(c) **Service.** A subpoena may be served by a peace officer, or any other person who is not a party and is not less than 18 years of age. Service of a subpoena upon a person named therein shall be made by delivering a copy thereof to such person and by tendering to the person the fees for one day's attendance and the mileage prescribed by rule. When the subpoena is issued on behalf of the state, a municipality, a borough, a city, or an officer or agency thereof, fees and mileage need not be tendered. A subpoena may also be served by registered or certified mail. In such case the clerk shall mail the subpoena for delivery only to the person subpoenaed and, unless not required under this rule, shall enclose a warrant or postal money order in the amount of the fees for one day's attendance and of the mileage prescribed by rule. The returned delivery receipt shall be so addressed that it is returned to the party requesting the subpoena or that party's attorney. Proof of service shall be made by affidavit.

(d) **Subpoena for Taking Depositions—Place of Examination.**

(1) Proof of service of a notice to take a deposition as provided in Rules 30(b) and 31(a) constitutes a sufficient authorization for the issuance by the clerk of the court for any judicial district of subpoenas for the persons named or described therein. The subpoena may command the person to whom it is directed to produce and permit inspection and copying of designated books, papers, documents, or tangible things which constitute or contain matters within the scope of the examination permitted by Rule 26(b), but in that event the subpoena will be subject to the provisions of Rule 26(c) and subparagraph (b) of this rule.

The person to whom the subpoena is directed may, within 10 days after the service thereof or on or before the time specified in the subpoena for compliance if such time is less than 10 days after service, serve upon the attorney designated in the subpoena written objection to inspection or copying of any or all of the designated materials. If objection is made, the party serving the subpoena shall not be entitled to inspect and copy the material except pursuant to an order of the court from which the subpoena was issued. The party serving the subpoena may, if objection has been made, move upon notice to the deponent for an order at any time before or during the taking of the deposition.

(2) A resident of the judicial district in which the deposition is to be taken may be required to attend an examination at any place within the district, unless otherwise ordered by the court. A nonresident of the judicial district in which the deposition is to be taken, and a nonresident of the state subpoenaed within the state, may be required to attend at any place within the district wherein the nonresident is served with a subpoena, unless otherwise ordered by the court.

(e) **Subpoena for a Hearing or Trial.** At the request of any party subpoenas for attendance at a hearing or trial shall be issued by the clerk of the court for the judicial district in which the hearing or trial is held. A subpoena requiring the attendance of a witness at a hearing or trial may be served at any place within the state.

(f) **Contempt.** Failure by any person without adequate excuse to obey a subpoena served upon that person may be deemed a contempt of the court from which the subpoena issued.

(g) **Enforcement of Administrative Subpoenas.** When any officer or agency of the state has the authority to issue subpoenas, enforcement of such subpoenas to compel the giving of testimony or the production of documents may be secured by proceedings brought in the court in the manner provided by the Administrative Procedures Act of the state.

(Adopted by SCO 5 October 9, 1959; amended by SCO 90 effective July 24, 1967; by SCO 167 dated June 25, 1973; by SCO 258 effective November 15, 1976; by SCO 374 effective August 15, 1979; by SCO 465 effective June 1, 1981; by SCO 558 effective May 2, 1983; by SCO 934 effective January 15, 1989; and by SCO 1153 effective July 15, 1994)

Cross References

CROSS REFERENCE: AS 09.20.110; AS 09.20.120; AS 09.20.130; AS 09.20.140; AS 09.20.150; AS 09.20.160; AS 09.50.010

(c) **CROSS REFERENCE:** AS 09.20.110

(f) **CROSS REFERENCE:** AS 09.20.120; AS 09.50.010

Note: Ch. 75 SLA 2002 (HB 106), Section 4, adds a new section to AS 06.01 relating to the confidentiality of depositor and customer records at banking and other financial institutions. According to Section 56 of the Act, AS 06.01.028(b) has the effect of changing Civil Rule 45, Criminal Rules 17 and 37, and Alaska Bar Rule 24 by requiring certain court orders compelling disclosure of records to provide for reimbursement of a financial institution's reasonable costs of complying with the order.

Note: Chapter 10 FSSLA 2005 (SB 130) enacted changes relating to workers' compensation. According to section 76 of the Act, AS 23.30.280(i), as enacted by section 65 of the Act, has the effect of changing Civil Rule 45 by changing the procedure relating to subpoenas.

Annotations

Cases

The appropriate sanction for the lower court to utilize when a witness is subpoenaed to appear for a deposition and fails to appear is the contempt power as set forth in this rule. **Schandelmeier v. Winchester Western,** Op. No. 1013, 520 P2d 70 (Alaska 1974).

Rule 46. Conduct of Trials.

(a) **Statement of Case.** Before the introduction of any evidence, the plaintiff shall state briefly the claim for relief and the issues to be tried. The defendant shall then state the defense or counterclaim.

(b) **Introduction of Evidence.** Unless otherwise ordered by the court, which may regulate the order of proof in the exercise of sound discretion, the plaintiff shall then introduce evidence, and when the plaintiff has concluded the defendant shall do the same.

(c) **Rebutting Evidence.** The parties may then respectively introduce rebutting evidence only, unless the court, for good reason and in the furtherance of justice, permits them to introduce other evidence.

(d) **Examination of Witnesses.** Unless otherwise ordered by the court no more than one attorney on each side may examine or cross-examine a witness.

(e) **Attorney as Witness.** If counsel for either party is a witness on behalf of that counsel's client and gives evidence on the merits of the case, that counsel shall not argue the case to the jury unless by permission of the court.

(f) **Exceptions Unnecessary.** Formal exceptions to rulings or orders of the court are unnecessary; but for all purposes for which an exception has heretofore been necessary it is sufficient that a party, at the time the ruling or order of the court is made or sought, makes known to the court the action which the party desires the court to take or the party's objection to the action of the court and the grounds therefor; and, if a party has no opportunity to object to a ruling or order at the time it is made, the absence of an objection does not thereafter prejudice the party.

(g) **Argument of Counsel.** When the evidence is concluded, and unless the case is submitted to the jury by mutual agreement of both sides without argument, the plaintiff shall open with the plaintiff's argument; the defendant shall follow with the defendant's argument and the plaintiff may conclude the argument. Not more than two counsel shall be allowed to address the jury on behalf of either party, unless otherwise allowed by the court. If the plaintiff waives the opening argument and the defendant then argues the case to the jury, the plaintiff shall not be permitted to reply to the defendant's argument.

(h) **Time for Opening Statements and Argument.** The court may fix the time allowed each party for opening statements and final argument. The parties shall be given adequate time for argument having due regard to the complexity of the case and may make separate time allowances for co-parties whose interests are adverse.

(i) **Regulation of Conduct in the Courtroom.** The taking of photographs in the courtroom during the progress of judicial proceedings, or radio or television broadcasting of judicial proceedings from the courtroom shall not be permitted except in accordance with Administrative Rule 50.

(Adopted by SCO 5 October 9, 1959; amended by SCO 49 effective January 1, 1963; by SCO 321 effective September 15, 1978; by SCO 994 effective January 15, 1990; and by SCO 1153 effective July 15, 1994)

Annotations

Cases

Incompetent testimony which is otherwise relevant, when admitted without objection, has the force and effect of competent evidence. **Gregory v. Padilla,** Op. No. 139, 379 P2d 951 (Alaska 1963).

A statement in counsel's argument in an automobile accident case: "Would you want a judgment against you based on evidence such as that—a small bump on the head?" bordered on the improper "golden rule" type of argument, but in the circumstances disclosed by the record, the trial court's refusal to grant a motion to strike was not held to be prejudicial error. **Mallonee v. Finch,** Op. No. 337, 413 P2d 159 (Alaska 1966).

In the absence of abuse of discretion, the trial court's refusal to relax or dispense with the provision that the plaintiff who waived the opening argument shall not be permitted to reply to defendant's argument was not disturbed on appeal. **Merrill v. Faltin,** Op. No. 425, 430 P2d 913 (Alaska 1967).

Trial court did not abuse its discretion in allowing plaintiff to present, during rebuttal, a friendly witness to impeach a hostile witness who had been called by plaintiff in her case-in-chief. **Amer. Nat. Watermattress Corp. v. Manville,** Op. No. 2477, 642 P2d 1330 (Alaska 1982).

Although rules of civil procedure do not require parties to make formal exceptions to rulings by judges, parties are required to communicate how they want judge to rule or explain their reason for disagreeing with him. **Tompkins v. Tompkins,** Op. No. 5010, 961 P2d 419 (Alaska 1998).

Rule 47. Jurors.

(a) **Examination of Jurors.** The court shall require the jury to be selected in a prompt manner. The court may permit the parties or their attorneys to conduct the examination of prospective jurors or may itself conduct the examination. In the latter event the court shall permit the parties or their attorneys to supplement the examination by such further inquiry as it deems proper or shall itself submit to the prospective jurors such additional questions of the parties or their attorneys as it deems proper. The court may also require the parties to question the panel as a whole rather than individually and impose reasonable time limits on the examination of prospective jurors.

(b) **Alternate Jurors.**

(1) *Generally.* A court may impanel alternate jurors using one of the procedures set out in subparagraph (b)(2) below. If alternate jurors are called,

(A) they shall be drawn in the same manner, shall have the same qualification, shall be subject to the same examination and challenges, shall take the same oath, and shall have the same functions, powers, facilities and privileges as the principal jurors; and

(B) each party is entitled to one peremptory challenge in addition to those otherwise allowed by paragraph (d) of this rule.

(2) *Procedures.*

(A) The court may direct that one or two jurors in addition to the regular jury be called and impaneled to sit as alternate jurors. Alternate jurors in the order in which they are called shall replace jurors who, prior to the time the jury retires to consider its verdict, become unable or disqualified to perform their duties. An alternate juror who does not replace a principal juror shall be discharged after the jury retires to consider its verdict.

The additional peremptory challenge allowed by section (b)(1)(B) may be used only against an alternate juror, and the other peremptory challenges allowed by paragraph (d) of this rule, shall not be used against the alternates.

(B) The court may direct that one or two jurors be called and impaneled in addition to the number of jurors required by law to comprise the jury. The court may excuse jurors who, prior to the time the jury retires to consider its verdict, become unable or disqualified to perform their duties. If more than the required number are left on the jury when the jury is ready to retire, the clerk in open court shall select at random the names of a sufficient number of jurors to reduce the jury to the number required by law. The jurors selected for elimination shall be discharged after the jury retires to consider its verdict.

(c) **Challenges for Cause.** After the examination of prospective jurors is completed and before any juror is sworn, the parties may challenge any juror for cause. A juror challenged for cause may be directed to answer every question pertinent to the inquiry. Every challenge for cause shall be determined by the court. The following are grounds for challenge for cause:

(1) That the person is not qualified by law to be a juror.

(2) That the person is biased for or against a party or attorney.

(3) That the person shows a state of mind which will prevent the person from rendering a just verdict, or has formed a positive opinion on the facts of the case or as to what the outcome should be, and cannot disregard such opinion and try the issue impartially.

(4) That the person has opinions or conscientious scruples which would improperly influence the person's verdict.

(5) That the person has been subpoenaed as a witness in the case.

(6) That the person has already sat upon a trial of the same issue.

(7) That the person has served as a grand or petit juror in a criminal case based on the same transaction.

(8) That the person was called as a juror and excused either for cause or peremptorily on a previous trial of the same action, or in another action by the same parties for the same cause of action.

(9) That the person is related within the fourth degree (civil law) of consanguinity or affinity to one of the parties or attorneys.

(10) That the person is the guardian, ward, landlord, tenant, employer, employee, partner, client, principal, agent, debtor, creditor, or member of the family of a party or attorney; provided, however, that challenge for cause may not be taken because of the employer-employee relationship when the State of Alaska or a municipal corporation is the employer and the person challenged is not employed by an agency, department, division, commission, or other unit of the State or municipal corporation which is directly involved in the case to be tried.

(11) That the person is or has been a party adverse to the challenging party or attorney in a civil action, or has been a complaining witness against the challenging party or attorney in a criminal prosecution.

(12) That the person has, within the previous two years, been accused by the challenging party or attorney in a criminal prosecution.

(13) That the person has a financial interest, other than that of a taxpayer or a permanent fund dividend recipient in the outcome of the case.

(14) That the person was a member of the grand jury returning an indictment in the case.

(d) **Peremptory Challenges.** A party who waives peremptory challenge as to the jurors in the box does not thereby lose the challenge but may exercise it as to new jurors who may be called. A juror peremptorily challenged is excused without cause. Each party may challenge peremptorily three jurors. Two or more parties on the same side are considered a single party for purposes of peremptory challenge, but where multiple parties having adverse interests are aligned on the same side, three peremptory challenges shall be allowed to each such party represented by a different attorney.

(e) **Procedure for Using Challenges.** The court has discretion to set procedures for the exercise of challenges and for the replacement of challenged jurors, except that the entire trial panel will be asked general questions concerning the for cause challenges listed in Civil Rule 47(c)(5)–(13) before proceeding to other questioning.

(f) **Juries of Less Than Twelve—Majority Verdict.** The parties may stipulate that the jury shall consist of any number less than twelve or that a verdict or a finding of a stated majority of the jurors shall be taken as the verdict or finding of the jury.

(g) **Oath of Jurors.** The jury shall be sworn by the clerk substantially as follows:

"Do each of you solemnly swear or affirm that you will well and truly try the issues in the matter now before the court solely on the evidence introduced and in accordance with the instructions of the court?"

(Adopted by SCO 5 October 9, 1959; amended by SCO 49 effective January 1, 1963; by SCO 277 effective June 30, 1977; by SCO 465 effective June 1, 1981; by SCO 808 effective August 1, 1987; by SCO 969 effective July 15, 1989; by SCO 1013 effective January 15, 1990; by SCO 1095 effective January 15, 1993; by SCO 1153 effective July 15, 1994; by SCO 1448 effective October 15, 2001; by SCO 1447 effective October 15, 2002; and by SCO 1593 effective April 15, 2006)

Cross References

CROSS REFERENCE: AS 09.20.010; AS 09.20.100

(c) **CROSS REFERENCE:** AS 09.20.010; AS 09.20.020

Annotations

Cases

Supreme Court shall interfere with the exercise of trial judge's discretion in the determination of challenges for cause only in exceptional cases and to prevent a miscarriage of justice. **Mitchell v. Knight,** Op. No. 241, 394 P2d 892 (Alaska 1964).

When challenged juror stated that he would be more conservative than the average juror, but also that he felt he could be fair and impartial, that he would allow a justifiable award and that he would follow the instructions of the court, it could not be said that the judge was wrong in concluding that the juror's state of mind was such that he was able to render a just verdict. **Mitchell v. Knight,** Op. No. 241, 394 P2d 892 (Alaska 1964).

Challenge was properly denied because sale of an insurance policy to counsel's law partnership from which the juror received commissions did not create debtor-creditor relationship within the purview of this rule. **Mitchell v. Knight,** Op. No. 241, 394 P2d 892 (Alaska 1964).

The denial of a defendant's challenge for cause of a juror who, defendant claims, has impaired hearing is not an abuse of discretion, especially when the defendant does not exhaust his peremptory challenges. **City of Kotzebue v. Ipalook,** Op. No. 588, 462 P2d 75 (Alaska 1969).

A relationship to a witness is not a ground for challenge for cause. **City of Kotzebue v. Ipalook,** Op. No. 588, 462 P2d 75 (Alaska 1969).

The Supreme Court is reluctant to overturn the trial court's grant or denial of a challenge for cause, since such grant or denial is largely discretionary. **Malvo v. J. C. Penney Co., Inc.,** Op. No. 901, 512 P2d 575 (Alaska 1973).

Once a factual circumstance or relationship exists for granting a challenge for cause, the court has no discretion in the matter. **Malvo v. J. C. Penney Co., Inc.,** Op. No. 901, 512 P2d 575 (Alaska 1973).

In an action against a department store for false imprisonment and slander, the failure to grant plaintiff's challenge of those jurors who have outstanding balances on their charge accounts with the department store is a prejudicial error as to a plaintiff who has used all her peremptory challenges. **Malvo v. J. C. Penney Co., Inc.,** Op. No. 901, 512 P2d 575 (Alaska 1973).

Mere membership in an organization which adheres to a membership policy excluding those of a race to which a party to the action belongs is not per se a ground for challenge for cause but is an indication that the juror may be incapable of discharging his duties free from improper influences or bias. **Malvo v. J. C. Penney Co., Inc.,** Op. No. 901, 512 P2d 575 (Alaska 1973).

Where a prospective juror is challenged for cause because of his membership in an organization which excludes from membership the race of which one of the parties is a member, it is incumbent on the trial judge to satisfy himself by appropriate questions and by observing the juror's demeanor that the prospective juror is in fact capable of rendering an impartial and just verdict. **Malvo v. J. C. Penney Co., Inc.,** Op. No. 901,512 P2d 575 (Alaska 1973).

Where there is sufficient evidence in the record to show that the trial judge adequately performed his duty of inquiring as to whether a juror, who is a member of an organization which excludes from membership members of the race of which one of the parties is a member, was capable of rendering an impartial and just verdict, the Supreme Court will not interfere. **Malvo v. J. C. Penney Co., Inc.,** Op. No. 901, 512 P2d 575 (Alaska 1973).

In a black plaintiff's action against a department store for false imprisonment and slander, the refusal to disqualify for cause a juror who is a member of an organization adhering to a white-only admission policy, who testifies that he would be concerned if he were a black plaintiff and who is evasive as to racial nature of the membership oath he has taken is an abuse of discretion. **Malvo v. J. C. Penney Co., Inc.,** Op. No. 901, 512 P2d 575 (Alaska 1973).

A trial court does not abuse its discretion in refusing to declare a mistrial because of the answer of a prospective juror regarding honesty of the State's chief witness, where immediately after the exchange the trial judge asks the prospective juror, as well as the entire jury panel, whether they understand that any verdict they reach must be based on evidence produced in the courtroom and that they may not take into account evidence or things that they may have heard outside the room. **Darling v. State,** Op. No. 1027, 520 P2d 793 (Alaska 1974).

In personal injury action by child against mother, plaintiff's attorney properly inquired whether any prospective juror had interest in or connection with, the insurance company, and whether they would be prejudiced by fact lawsuit was between family members. **Drickerson v. Drickerson,** Op. No. 1992,604 P2d 1082 (Alaska 1979).

Where council accepted the trial court's erroneous belief that plaintiff had exhausted her peremptory challenges, attempt to exercise the challenge the next day, after the jury had been sworn, was untimely, and it was therefore properly denied by the court. **Grimes v. Haslett,** Op. No. 2476, 641 P2d 813 (Alaska 1982).

Plaintiff did not waive her peremptory challenge to a second alternate juror by not challenging the first alternate interviewed. **Grimes v. Haslett,** Op. No. 2476, 641 P2d 813 (Alaska 1982).

A stockholder's interest in an ANCSA-created village corporation can be the basis of a challenge for cause under this rule when the corporation is involved in the litigation. **Noey v. Ukpeagvik Inupiat Corp.,** Op. No. 2836, 683 P2d 260 (Alaska 1984).

A juror's personal knowledge of facts of the case gives rise to a challenge for cause committed to the trial court's discretion. **Dalkovski v. Glad,** Op. No. 3436, 774 P2d 202 (Alaska 1989).

Abuse of discretion standard of review is used to review method of jury selection utilized by trial court. **Van Huff v. Sohio Alaska Petroleum Co.,** Op. No. 3857, 835 P2d 1181 (Alaska 1992).

This rule does not prohibit "struck jury" method of jury selection. **Van Huff v. Sohio Alaska Petroleum Co.,** Op. No. 3857, 835 P2d 1181 (Alaska (1992).

Because juror did not state in good faith that she would be fair, impartial and follow court's instructions, and because she exhibited substantial inclination to be governed by her own opinions rather than the evidence and the court's instructions, trial court committed reversible error in denying challenge for cause. **Beck v. Dept. of Transp. & P. Facilities,** Op. No. 3871, 837 P2d 105 (Alaska 1992).

The text of this rule makes no provision for preemptive exclusion of prospective jurors; a challenge for cause may be granted only after the prospective juror has been examined. **Joseph v. State,** Op. No. 5432, 26 P3d 459 (Alaska 2001).

After state indicated it would invoke this rule and challenge any prospective juror who had ever been charged criminally by the state, trial court's decision to remove from the jury list all persons who had been charged with criminal offenses without examining them individually was error since court's exclusive reliance on criminal records potentially caused errors that only individual examinations could have avoided, but the error was harmless because it did not alter the random nature or objectivity of the selection process. **Joseph v. State,** Op. No. 5432, 26 P3d 459 (Alaska 2001).

The record failed to show that potential selection errors resulting from use of computer records to remove individuals with criminal history from the jury pool altered the random nature or objectivity of the selection process; thus a wrongful death case was not reversed on this point. **Joseph v. State,** Op. No. 5432, 26 P3d 459 (Alaska 2001).

Rule permitted, and trial court properly held, the exclusion of shareholders of a corporation which was not a party to the lawsuit but which had a financial interest in the lawsuit's outcome; the per se rule that excluded as jurors stockholders in a company which was party to the litigation also applied to stockholders in a corporation which was not a party but which was nonetheless financially interested in the outcome. **Reich v. Cominco Alaska, Inc.,** Op. No. 5637, 56 P.3d 18 (Alaska 2002).

Rule 48. Order of Trial Proceedings—Management of Juries.

(a) **Conduct of Trial.** Conduct of a jury trial shall be governed by Rule 46 and this rule.

(b) **Instructions—Argument—Retirement of Jury.** When argument of counsel is concluded or waived, the court shall then charge the jury. Such charge shall be reduced to writing and read to the jury. The jury must take the written charge with it to the jury room.

(c) **View of Premises by Jury.** When the court deems proper, it may order a proper officer to conduct the jury in a body to view the property which is the subject of the litigation or the place where a material fact occurred and to show such property or place to it. While the jury is making its inspection no one shall speak to it on any subject connected with the trial. The court may order the person applying for a jury view to pay the expenses connected therewith.

(d) **Separation of Jury—Admonition—Manner of Keeping Jury Before Submission of Case.** If any juror is permitted to separate from the jury during the trial the juror must be admonished by the court that it is the juror's duty not to converse with any person, including another juror, on any subject connected with the trial, nor to form or express any opinion thereon until the case is finally submitted to the jury. If any juror is permitted to separate from the jury after the case is submitted the juror must be admonished by the court that it is the juror's duty not to converse with any person on any subject connected with the trial, and that the juror is to discuss the case only with other jurors in the jury room.

(e) **Juror Unable to Continue.** If, prior to the time the jury retires to consider its verdict, a juror is unable or disqualified to perform the juror's duty, the court may order the juror to be discharged. If an alternate juror has not been impaneled as provided in the rules, the trial may proceed with the other jurors with the consent of the parties, or another juror may be sworn and the trial may begin anew; or the jury may be discharged and a new jury then or afterwards formed.

(f) **Jury—Deliberation—Communications.** After hearing the charge the jury shall retire for deliberation. No persons other than the jurors and any interpreter necessary to assist a juror who is hearing or speech impaired shall be present while the jury is deliberating or voting. The jury shall be and remain under the charge of an officer until it agrees upon its verdict or is discharged by the court. Unless otherwise ordered by the court, the officer having charge of the jury must keep the jury together, separate from other persons; and the officer must not suffer any communication to be made to it, nor make any except to ask it if it has agreed upon its verdict, and the officer must not, before the verdict is rendered, communicate to any person the state of its deliberations or the verdict agreed upon. Such officer shall be sworn to act according to the provisions of this section.

(g) **Items Which May Be Taken Into the Jury Room.** Upon retiring for deliberation the jury shall take with it any exhibits, except depositions, that have been introduced into evidence which the court deems proper.

(h) **Discharge of Jury Before Verdict.** Except as may be provided in these rules or as the interest of justice may require, the jury shall not be discharged after the cause is submitted to them until they have agreed upon a verdict and given it in open court, except:

(1) By the consent of all parties entered in the record.

(2) At the expiration of such period as the court deems proper if it appears that there is no probability of an agreement being arrived at among the jurors necessary to return a verdict.

(i) **Retrial in the Event of Discharge Without Verdict.** In all cases where the jury is discharged without having given a verdict, or is prevented from giving a verdict by reason of accident or other cause during the progress of the trial, or after the cause is submitted to it, the action may be again tried immediately, or at a future time, as the court directs.

(j) **Adjournment During Absence of Jury.** While the jury is absent the court may adjourn from time to time, in respect to other business, but it is nevertheless open for every purpose connected with the cause submitted to the jury until a verdict is rendered or the jury discharged.

(Adopted by SCO 5 October 9, 1959; amended by SCO 49 effective January 1, 1963; by SCO 1153 effective July 15, 1994; and by SCO 1439 effective October 15, 2001)

Cross References

CROSS REFERENCE: AS 09.50.010

Annotations

Cases

The trial court did not err in denying the requested jury view of the premises under Alaska R. Civ. P. 48(c) because, in his order denying the request, the judge wrote that his decision was based on his belief that a view of the scene would not assist the jury in resolving the disputes before it, adequate pictures were available, and the testimony had been extensive to illustrate the neighborhood. **Fernandes v. Portwine,** Op. No. 5632, 56 P.3d 1 (Alaska 2002).

Rule 49. Special Verdicts and Interrogatories.

(a) **Returning a Verdict—Polling a Jury—Filing and Entering Verdict.** When the jury, or such a majority of it as may be required by the law or stipulation of the parties, have agreed upon a verdict, they shall be conducted into court, their names called, and the verdict shall be given by the foreperson. The verdict shall be in writing and signed by the foreperson. The court may permit the foreperson of the jury to date, sign and seal in an envelope a verdict reached after the usual business hours. The jury may then separate, but all must be in the jury box to deliver the verdict when the court next convenes or as instructed by the court. When the court authorizes a sealed verdict, it shall admonish the jurors not to make any disclosure concerning it nor speak with other persons concerning the case until the verdict has been returned and the jury discharged. Any party may require the jury to be polled as to any verdict, which is done by asking each juror if it is the juror's verdict. If upon such polling it appears that a verdict has not been agreed upon, the jury shall be sent out for further deliberation. After a verdict has been agreed upon, the jury shall be discharged from the case. The verdict shall be filed and an entry thereof made in the minutes of the court. The word "verdict" shall include, where applicable, answers to questions or interrogatories.

(b) **Special Verdicts.** The court may require a jury to return only a special verdict in the form of a special written finding upon each issue of fact. In that event the court may submit to the jury written questions susceptible of categorical or other brief answer or may submit written forms of the several special findings which might properly be made under the pleadings and evidence; or it may use such other method of submitting the issues and requiring the written findings thereon as it deems most appropriate. The court shall give to the jury such explanation and instruction concerning the matter thus submitted as may be necessary to enable the jury to make its findings upon each issue. If in so doing the court omits any issue of fact raised by the pleadings or by the evidence, each party waives the right to a trial by jury of the issue so omitted unless before the jury retires the party demands its submission to the jury. As to an issue omitted without such demand the court may make a finding; or, if it fails to do so, it shall be deemed to have made a finding in accord with the judgment on the special verdict.

(c) **General Verdict Accompanied by Answer to Interrogatories.** The court may submit to the jury, together with appropriate forms for a general verdict, written interrogatories upon one or more issues of fact the decision of which is necessary to a verdict. The court shall give such explanation or instruction as may be necessary to enable the jury both to make answers to the interrogatories and to render a general verdict, and the court shall direct the jury both to make written answers and to render a general verdict. When the general verdict and the answers are harmonious, the appropriate judgment upon the verdict and answers shall be entered pursuant to Rule 58. When the answers are consistent with each other but one or more is inconsistent with the general verdict, judgment may be entered pursuant to Rule 58 in accordance with the answers, notwithstanding the general verdict, or the court may return the jury for further consideration of its answers and verdict or may order a new trial. When the answers are inconsistent with each other and one or more is likewise inconsistent with the general verdict, judgment shall not be entered, but the court shall return the jury for further consideration of its answers and verdict or shall order a new trial.

(Adopted by SCO 5 October 9, 1959; amended by SCO 258 effective November 15, 1976; by SCO 715 effective September 15, 1976; by SCO 1153 effective July 15, 1994; and by SCO 1281 effective August 7, 1997))

Note: Ch. 139, § 5, SLA 1986, provided that AS 09.17.040 and 09.17.080, enacted by ch. 139, § 1, SLA 1986, amended Civil Rule 49 by requiring the jury to answer special interrogatories listed in AS 09.17.090 regarding the amount of damages and the percentage of fault to be allocated among the parties and to itemize the verdict regarding economic, noneconomic and punitive damages as specified in AS 09.17.040.

Sec. 09.17.040. Award of damages.

(a) In every case where damages for personal injury are awarded by the court or jury, the verdict shall be itemized between economic loss and noneconomic loss, if any, as follows:

(1) past economic loss;

(2) past noneconomic loss;

(3) future economic loss;

(4) future noneconomic loss; and

(5) punitive damages.

(b) The fact finder shall reduce future economic damages to present value. In computing the portion of a lump sum award that is attributable to future economic loss, the fact finder shall determine the present amount that, if invested at long term future interest rates in the best and safest investments, will produce over the life expectancy of the injured party the amount necessary to compensate the injured party for(1)the amount of wages the injured party could have been expected to earn during future years, taking into account future anticipated inflation and reasonably anticipated increases in the injured party's earnings; and

(1) the amount of wages the injured party could have

been expected to earn during future years, taking into account future anticipated inflation and reasonably anticipated increases in the injured party's earnings; and

(2) the amount of money necessary during future years to provide for all additional economic losses related to the injury, taking into account future anticipated inflation.

(c) Subsection (b) of this section does not apply to future economic damages if the parties agree that the award of future damages may be computed under the rule adopted in the case of Beaulieu v. Elliott, 434 P.2d 655 (Alaska 1967).

(d) In an action to recover damages, the court shall, at the request of an injured party, enter judgment ordering that amounts awarded a judgment creditor for future damages be paid to the maximum extent feasible by periodic payments rather than by a lump sum payment.

(e) The court may require security be posted, in order to ensure that funds are available as periodic payments become due. The court may not require security to be posted if an authorized insurer, as defined in AS 21.90.900, acknowledges to the court its obligation to discharge the judgment.

(f) A judgment ordering payment of future damages by periodic payment shall specify the recipient, the dollar amount of the payments, the interval between payments, and the number of payments in the period of time over which payments shall be made. Payments may be modified only in the event of the death of the judgment creditor, in which case payments may not be reduced or terminated, but shall be paid to persons to whom the judgment creditor owed a duty of support, as provided by law, immediately before death. In the event the judgment creditor owed no duty of support to dependents at the time of the judgment creditor's death, the money remaining shall be distributed in accordance with a will of the deceased judgment creditor accepted into probate or under the intestate laws of the state if the deceased had no will.

(g) If the court finds that the judgment debtor has exhibited a continuing pattern of failing to make payments required under (c) of this section, the court shall, in addition to the required periodic payments, order the judgment debtor to pay the judgment creditor any damages caused by the failure to make periodic payments, including costs and attorney fees. (§ 1 ch. 139 SLA 1986)

Sec. 09.17.080. Apportionment of damages.

(a) In all actions involving fault of more than one party to the action, including third party defendants and persons who have been released under AS 09.17.090, the court, unless otherwise agreed by all parties, shall instruct the jury to answer special interrogatories or, if there is no jury, shall make findings, indicating

(1) the amount of damages each claimant would be entitled to recover if contributory fault is disregarded; and

(2) the percentage of the total fault of all of the parties to each claim that is allocated to each claimant, defendant, third party defendant, and person who has been released from liability under AS 09.17.090.

(b) In determining the percentages of fault, the trier of fact shall consider both the nature of the conduct of each party at fault, and the extent of the causal relation between the conduct and the damages claimed. The trier of fact may determine that two or more persons are to be treated as a single party if their conduct was a cause of the damages claimed and the separate act or omission of each person cannot be distinguished.

(c) The court shall determine the award of damages to each claimant in accordance with the findings, subject to a reduction under AS 09.17.090, and enter judgment against each party liable. The court also shall determine and state in the judgment each party's equitable share of the obligation to each claimant in accordance with the respective percentages of fault.

(d) The court shall enter judgment against each party liable on the basis of joint and several liability, except that a party who is allocated less than 50 percent of the total fault allocated to all the parties may not be jointly liable for more than twice the percentage of fault allocated to that party. (§ 1 ch. 139 SLA 1986)

Note: Ch. 26, § 11, SLA 1997 amends AS 09.17.080(a) concerning allocation of fault. This provision applies to causes of action accruing on or after August 7, 1997. See ch. 26, § 55, SLA 1997. According to § 50 of the Act, the amendments to AS 09.17.080(a) have the effect of amending Civil Rule 49 by requiring the jury to answer the special interrogatory listed in AS 09.17.080(a)(2) regarding the percentages of fault to be allocated among the claimants, defendants, third-party defendants, persons who have been released from liability, or other persons who are potentially responsible for the damages.

Annotations

Cases

It is incumbent on a party requesting a special verdict to see that the court gives the instruction required by Rule 49(b), and failure of a jury to answer special interrogatories is not error where no instruction or explanation was requested and none given. **Gregory v. Padilla,** Op. No. 139, 379 P2d 951 (Alaska 1963).

Uncontradicted testimony of two witnesses sustained jury's finding in answer to written interrogatories that area was overcut and supported verdict and judgment entered below. **United Geophysical Corporation v. Culver,** Op. No. 230, 394 P2d 393 (Alaska 1964).

Number and form of interrogatories rested in the sound discretion of the trial judge which was not abused where issue was fairly presented to the jury by the interrogatories he elected to submit. **Patterson v. Cushman,** Op. No. 233, 394 P2d 657 (Alaska 1964).

Where counsel for the defendant is given an opportunity prior to discharge of the jury to object to plaintiff's verdict and the defense counsel expresses his satisfaction with the verdict, the right to challenge the consistency of answers to jury interrogatories and the verdict is waived. **City of Homer v. Land's End Marine,** Op. No. 583, 459 P2d 475 (Alaska 1969).

An error in submitting compound interrogatories to a jury does not necessarily constitute plain error. **Holiday Inns of America, Inc. v. Peck,** Op. No. 1024, 520 P2d 87 (Alaska 1974).

Although one interrogatory of the special verdict was erroneous, other interrogatories plainly instructed the jury to do that which the erroneous one did not, and so rendered the error harmless. **Loof v. Sanders,** Op. No.

2859, 686 P2d 1205 (Alaska 1984).

Where jury returned a verdict based on answers to special interrogatories which was internally inconsistent and inconsistent with the general verdict concerning just compensation in an eminent domain proceeding, the state was entitled to a new trial; the jury's conclusion that the remaining property was worth more after the taking than the entire parcel was worth before the taking was irreconcilable with its conclusion that the remainder received no special benefit from the project. **State v. Lewis,** Op. No. 3544, 785 P2d 24, 400 P2d 454 (Alaska 1990).

Rule 50. Motion for a Directed Verdict and for Judgment.

(a) **Motion for Directed Verdict—When Made—Effect.** A party who moves for a directed verdict at the close of the evidence offered by an opponent may offer evidence in the event that the motion is not granted, without having reserved the right so to do and to the same extent as if the motion had not been made. A motion for a directed verdict which is not granted is not a waiver of trial by jury even though all parties to the action have moved for directed verdicts. A motion for a directed verdict shall state the specific grounds therefor. The order of the court granting a motion for a directed verdict is effective without any assent of the jury.

(b) **Motion for Judgment Notwithstanding the Verdict.** Whenever a motion for a directed verdict made at the close of all the evidence is denied or for any reason is not granted, the court is deemed to have submitted the action to the jury subject to a later determination of the legal questions raised by the motion. Not later than 10 days after the date shown in the clerk's certificate of distribution on the judgment, a party who has moved for a directed verdict may move to have the verdict and any judgment entered thereon set aside and to have judgment entered in accordance with the party's motion for a directed verdict; or if a verdict was not returned such party, within 10 days after the jury has been discharged, may move for judgment in accordance with the party's motion for a directed verdict. A motion for a new trial may be joined with this motion, or a new trial may be prayed for in the alternative. If a verdict was returned the court may allow the judgment to stand or may set aside the judgment and either order a new trial or direct the entry of judgment as if the requested verdict had been directed. If no verdict was returned the court may direct the entry of judgment as if the requested verdict had been directed or may order a new trial.

(c) **Same—Conditional Rulings on Grant of Motion.**

(1) If the motion for judgment notwithstanding the verdict, provided for in subdivision (b) of this rule, is granted, the court shall also rule on the motion for a new trial, if any, by determining whether it should be granted if the judgment is thereafter vacated or reversed, and shall specify the grounds for granting or denying the motion for the new trial. If the motion for a new trial is thus conditionally granted, the order thereon does not affect the finality of the judgment. In case the motion for a new trial has been conditionally granted and the judgment is reversed on appeal, the new trial shall proceed unless the appellate court has otherwise ordered. In case the motion for a new trial has been conditionally denied, the appellee on appeal may assert error in that denial; and if the judgment is reversed on appeal, subsequent proceedings shall be in accordance with the order of the appellate court.

(2) The party whose verdict has been set aside on motion for judgment notwithstanding the verdict may serve a motion for a new trial pursuant to Rule 59 not later than 10 days after entry of the judgment notwithstanding the verdict.

(d) **Same—Denial of Motion.** If the motion for judgment notwithstanding the verdict is denied, the party who prevailed on that motion may, as appellee, assert grounds entitling the party to a new trial in the event the appellate court concludes that the trial court erred in denying the motion for judgment notwithstanding the verdict. If the appellate court reverses the judgment, nothing in this rule precludes it from determining that the appellee is entitled to a new trial, or from directing the trial court to determine whether a new trial shall be granted.

(Adopted by SCO 5 October 9, 1959; amended by SCO 258 effective November 15, 1976; by SCO 554 effective April 4, 1983; and by SCO 1153 effective July 15, 1994)

Annotations

Cases

I. Standard of Review.
- A. In General.
- B. Tests.

II. Motion for Directed Verdict.
III. Motion for Judgment Notwithstanding the Verdict.
IV. Motion for a New Trial.

I. Standard of Review.

A. In General.

Granting motion for judgment notwithstanding the verdict did not mean automatic denial of an alternative motion for a new trial based on grounds which were not appropriate for consideration on motion for judgment n.o.v. **Alaska Brick Co. v. McCoy,** Op. No. 287, 400 P2d 454 (Alaska 1965).

While a distinction between handling of motions for a judgment notwithstanding the verdict and for a new trial is recognized, the distinction had no application where in a case of alternative motions the judge had granted a judgment notwithstanding the verdict, whereupon the judgment was reversed in the Supreme Court on applying a test of reasonableness to the verdict of the jury, and on remand, the judge properly concluded that the decision of the jury was not contrary to the weight of evidence and denied motion for new trial. **Alaska Brick Co. v. McCoy,** Op. No. 287, 400 P2d 454 (Alaska 1965).

In determining whether error was committed below in denying motions for directed verdict and for judgment notwithstanding verdict, the Supreme Court views the evidence in its strongest light in favor of the party against whom the motion was made. **Otis Elevator Company v. McLaney,** Op. No. 300, 406 P2d 7 (Alaska 1965).

A defendant does not waive the right to question the consistency of verdicts by failing to move for acquittal at the close of evidence. **DeSacia v. State,** Op. No. 608, 469 P2d 369 (Alaska 1970).

Although claims of fraud and breach of fiduciary duty were pled separately, they were effectively merged throughout trial, thus trial court's denial of party's motion for judgment notwithstanding verdict on issue of breach of fiduciary duty was reviewable even though party moved at close of evidence at trial for directed verdict on issue of fraud but not on issue of breach of fiduciary duty. **Ben Lamond, Inc. v. Schwartz,** Op. No. 4349, 915 P2d 632 (Alaska 1996).

B. Tests.

Different tests apply in ruling on motion for judgment notwithstanding the verdict (n.o.v.) and for a new trial. Judgment n.o.v. shall be sustained by the Supreme Court only if the evidence was such that there was no room for diversity among reasonable men, but only in the most exceptional circumstances to prevent a miscarriage of justice shall the Supreme Court interfere with the discretion of a trial court in granting or denying motion for a new trial. **Alaska State Housing Authority v. Vincent,** Op. No. 261, 396 P2d 531 (Alaska 1964); **Bolden v. City of Kodiak,** Op. No. 475, 439 P2d 796 (Alaska 1968).

Court's denial of motion for directed verdict and judgment notwithstanding the verdict was sustained on appeal where in an accident case review of record indicated that fair-minded jurors could differ as to conclusions from the evidence presented as to the issues of negligence and of proximate cause. **Otis Elevator Co. v. McLaney,** Op. No. 300, 406 P2d 7 (Alaska 1965); **Merrill v. Faltin,** Op. No. 425, 430 P2d 913 (Alaska 1967).

Alternative motions for judgment notwithstanding the verdict and for new trial were properly denied in an accident case in which the value of expert testimony on the cause of an airplane crash was not so diminished by a courtroom demonstration that the judge was required to disregard it and reasonable men could justifiably have different views as to the proximate cause of the crash. **Crawford v. Rogers,** Op. No. 303, 406 P2d 189 (Alaska 1965).

The trial court correctly as a matter of law denied motions for a directed verdict and for judgment n.o.v. where in an automobile accident case the evidence adduced was such that fair-minded jurors could differ on the question whether or not appellee was negligent as to when he should have first observed that the vehicle in which appellant was riding was stopped in his lane of traffic and whether he operated his vehicle negligently immediately prior to collision. **Mallonee v. Finch,** Op. No. 337, 413 P2d 159 (Alaska 1966); **Bertram v. Harris,** Op. No. 393, 423 P2d 909 (Alaska 1967).

Although sufficiency of evidence is not reviewable on appeal unless raised below by motions for directed verdict or judgment n.o.v., the record was reviewed on appeal with regard to legal sufficiency to support the verdict in order to ascertain whether or not there has been a miscarriage of justice. **Bolden v. City of Kodiak,** Op. No. 475, 439 P2d 796 (Alaska 1968).

The proper role of the Supreme Court in reviewing motions for a directed verdict or for judgment notwithstanding the verdict is not to weigh conflicting evidence or judge the credibility of witnesses, but rather to determine whether evidence when viewed in a light most favorable to the nonmoving party, is such that reasonable men could not differ in their judgment. **Holiday Inns of America, Inc. v. Peck,** Op. No. 1024, 520 P2d 87 (Alaska 1974).

In reviewing denial of motions for a directed verdict or judgment notwithstanding the verdict, the court is not to weigh conflicting evidence or judge the credibility of witnesses; rather, it is to determine whether the evidence, when viewed in the light most favorable to the nonmoving party, is such that reasonable persons could not differ in their judgment as to the facts. **Mullen v. Christiansen,** Op. No. 2482, 642 P2d 1345 (Alaska 1982).

II. Motion for Directed Verdict.

Evidence was sufficient to preclude the granting of a directed verdict on the question of damages. **Gregory v. Padilla,** Op. No. 139, 379 P2d 951 (Alaska 1963).

Denial of motion for directed verdict was error where plaintiff's evidence did not warrant submission to jury. **Groseth v. Ness,** Op. No. 370, 421 P2d 624 (Alaska 1966).

Trial court correctly directed a verdict in favor of defendant as to a claim for relief on an alleged breach of contract where in viewing the evidence in a light most favorable to plaintiff fair-minded jurors could have only reached the one conclusion that no such contract was entered. **Howarth v. Pfeifer,** Op. No. 386, 423 P2d 680 (Alaska 1967).

Where it appears from the record that there is evidence from which fair-minded jurors can reach differing conclusions, a motion for directed verdict is properly denied. **Mertz v. J. M. Covington Corp.,** Op. No. 620, 470 P2d 532 (Alaska 1970).

In determining whether the trial court erred in denying a motion for a directed verdict, the evidence must be viewed in a light most favorable to the party against whom the motion was made. **Mertz v. J. M. Covington Corp.,** Op. No. 620, 470 P2d 532 (Alaska 1970).

The purpose of a directed verdict is to allow the judge to resolve factual issues where, viewing evidence in light most favorable to the nonmoving party, fair-minded jurors could not reach different conclusions on the issues. **Martinez v. Bullock,** Op. No. 1152, 535 P2d 1200 (Alaska 1975).

When ruling on a motion for a directed verdict, the judge must view the evidence in the light most favorable to the nonmoving party and may grant such a motion only if fair-minded jurors in the exercise of reasonable judgment could reach but one conclusion on the issue in controversy. **Beaumaster v. Crandall,** Op. No. 1589, 576 P2d 988 (Alaska 1978).

Where estimate of plaintiff's contract damages was based on profits of previous years, and where evidence that contract existed was already sufficient, court did not err in denying motion for directed verdict. **City of Palmer v. Anderson,** Op. No. 1978, 603 P2d 495 (Alaska 1979).

Where plaintiff failed to move for a directed verdict at the close of the evidence and none of the plaintiff's proposed jury instructions could fairly be read as amounting to a request for a directed verdict, the superior court's refusal to grant a judgment notwithstanding the verdict could not be considered on appeal. **Metcalf v. Wilbur,** Op. No. 2506, 645 P2d 163 (Alaska 1982).

Where liability and damages issues are tried by the court, prejudgment motion for dismissal rather than for a directed verdict is appropriate. **Frank v. Golden Valley Elec. Ass'n, Inc.,** Op. No. 3264, 748 P2d 752 (Alaska 1988).

Car accident plaintiff's motion for a directed verdict was interpreted as pertaining only to defendant's negligence, this plaintiff was precluded from moving for a judgment notwithstanding the verdict on the causation and damages issues ultimately resolved by the jury. **Richey v. Oen,** Op. No. 3801, 824 P2d 1371 (Alaska 1992).

While a party does not preserve for appeal a denial of a motion for judgment notwithstanding the verdict (JNOV) unless the party moved for a directed verdict at the close of evidence, a party is not required to move for a JNOV to preserve a denial of a directed verdict; in fact, a motion for a directed verdict merely provides a moving party with the option of moving for a JNOV. **Sherbahn v. Kerkove,** Op. No. 5178, 987 P2d 195 (Alaska 1999).

III. Motion for Judgment Notwithstanding the Verdict.

Where defendant moved for judgment notwithstanding the verdict or new trial, the judge who entered judgment for defendant should have ruled on the motion for a new trial. **Snipes v. March,** Op. No. 132, 378 P2d 827 (Alaska 1962).

Under this rule the 10-day period for moving for judgment notwithstanding the verdict did not start until the clerk made notation in the docket "Filed Judgment." **McCoy v. Alaska Brick Co.,** Op. No. 192, 389 P2d 1009 (Alaska 1964).

Judgment for a defendant in negligence action notwithstanding the verdict would have been justified only if the evidence was such that fair-minded men in the exercise of reasonable judgment could not differ on the question of defendant's negligence, but could only come to the conclusion that he was not negligent. **Snipes v. March,** Op. No. 132, 378 P2d 827 (Alaska 1962); **Bertram v. Harris,** Op. No. 393, 423 P2d 909 (Alaska 1967); **National Bank of Alaska v. McHugh,** Op. No. 352, 416 P2d 239 (Alaska 1966).

Where plaintiff failed to move for a direct verdict at the close of the evidence and none of the plaintiff's proposed jury instructions could fairly be read as amounting to a request for a directed verdict, the superior court's refusal to grant a judgment notwithstanding the verdict could not be considered on appeal. **Metcalf v. Wilbur,** Op. No. 2506, 645 P2d 163 (Alaska 1982).

Affirmance of trial court's denial of appellant's motion for judgment N.O.V. was required due to appellant's failure to move for a directed verdict at the close of the evidence. **Clark v. City of Seward,** Op. No. 2628, 659 P2d 1227 (Alaska 1983).

A motion to alter or amend a judgment suspends the time for filing an appeal; similarly, it suspends the time for filing a motion for judgment N.O.V. or new trial. **Blackford v. Taggart,** Op. No. 2749, 672 P2d 888 (Alaska 1983).

Where judgment was entered March 26, defendant filed an "Objection to Notice of Entry of Judgment" on March 30, and a corrected judgment was filed April 5, defendant's motion for judgment notwithstanding the verdict and new trial filed April 13 was timely. **Blackford v. Taggart,** Op. No. 2749, 672 P2d 888 (Alaska 1983).

If a party fails to move for a directed verdict at the close of the evidence, trial court's refusal to grant a judgment notwithstanding the verdict cannot be considered on appeal. **Richey v. Oen,** Op. No. 3801, 824 P2d 1371 (Alaska 1992).

Car accident plaintiff's motion for a directed verdict was interpreted as pertaining only to defendant's negligence, thus plaintiff was precluded from moving for a judgment notwithstanding the verdict on the causation and damages issues ultimately resolved by the jury. **Richey v. Oen,** Op. No. 3801, 824 P2d 1371 (Alaska 1992).

Although claims of fraud and breach of fiduciary duty were pled separately, they were effectively merged throughout trial, thus trial court's denial of party's motion for judgment notwithstanding verdict on issue of breach of fiduciary duty was reviewable even though party moved at close of evidence at trial for directed verdict on issue of fraud but not on issue of breach of fiduciary duty. **Ben Lamond, Inc. v. Schwartz,** Op. No. 4349, 915 P2d 632 (Alaska 1996).

While a party does not preserve for appeal a denial of a motion for judgment notwithstanding the verdict (JNOV) unless the party moved for a directed verdict at the close of evidence, a party is not required to move for a JNOV to preserve a denial of a directed verdict; in fact, a motion for a directed verdict merely provides a moving party with the option of moving for a JNOV. **Sherbahn v. Kerkove,** Op. No. 5178, 987 P2d 195 (Alaska 1999).

In a doctor's suit against a hospital, acting through his professional corporation, court erred by granting a judgment notwithstanding the verdict to the hospital on the issue of damages; just as a professional corporation could recover as damages for lost profits lost compensation to its principals, it was entitled to recover as damages earnings losses suffered by its principals, and, therefore, the corporation had the right to sue for the breach of the doctor's hospital privileges. **Sisters of Providence in Wash. v. A.A. Pain Clinic, Inc.,** Op. No.5764, 81 P3d 989 (Alaska 2003).

In a doctor's suit against a hospital, court erred by granting a judgment notwithstanding the verdict to the hospital on the issue of damages where the cancellation and rescheduling of the procedure led to a disruption in the doctor's professional schedule apart from litigation preparation; although not specifically quantified, the loss of professional time was without question a compensable injury, entitling the doctor to at least nominal damages. **Sisters of Providence in Wash. v. A.A. Pain Clinic, Inc.,** Op. No. 5764, 81 P3d 989 (Alaska 2003).

In a doctor's suit against a hospital, court properly granted a judgment notwithstanding the verdict to the hospital on the issue of attorney's fees as part of the damages where attorney's fees for the work in the case were not recoverable as damages; thus, the attorney's fees could not be considered a part of a damage award, and neither should the court have considered the doctor's time spent actually preparing the litigation. **Sisters of Providence in Wash. v. A.A. Pain Clinic, Inc.,** Op. No.5764, 81 P3d 989 (Alaska 2003).

IV. Motion for a New Trial.

Where there was an evidentiary basis for the jury's decision, trial court did not abuse its discretion in refusing a new trial. **Olson v. McRae,** Op. No. 188, 389 P2d 576 (Alaska 1964); **West v. Administratrix of Estate of Nershak,** Op. No. 880, 440 P2d 119 (Alaska 1968).

A motion to alter or amend a judgment suspends the time for filing on appeal; similarly, it suspends the time for filing a motion for judgment N.O.V. or new trial. **Blackford v. Taggart,** Op. No. 2749, 672 P2d 888 (Alaska 1983).

Where judgment was entered March 26, defendant filed an "Objection to Notice of Entry of Judgment" on March 30, and a corrected judgment was filed April 5, defendant's motion for judgment notwithstanding the verdict and new trial filed April 13 was timely **Blackford v. Taggart,** Op. No. 2749, 672 P2d 888 (Alaska 1983).

Rule 51. Instructions to Jury.

(a) **Requested Instructions—Objections.** At the close of the evidence or at such earlier time as the court reasonably directs, any party may file written requests that the court give the jury specific instructions. The court shall inform counsel of the final form of jury instructions prior to their arguments to the jury. Following the close of the evidence, before or after the arguments of counsel, the court shall instruct the jury. Additionally, the court may give the jury such instructions as it deems necessary at any stage of the trial. No party may assign as error the giving or the failure to give an instruction unless the party objects thereto before the jury retires to consider its verdict, stating distinctly the matter to which the party objects and the grounds of the objection. Opportunity must be given to make the objection out of the hearing of the jury, by excusing the jury or hearing objections in chambers.

(b) **Instructions to Be Given.** The court shall instruct the jury that they are the exclusive judges of all questions of fact and of the effect and value of evidence presented in the action. The court shall instruct the jury on all matters of law that it considers necessary for their information in giving their verdict.

(Adopted by SCO 5 October 9, 1959; amended by SCO 49 effective January 1, 1963; by SCO 79 effective February 1, 1966; by SCO 920 effective January 15, 1989; by SCO 1153 effective July 15, 1994; and by SCO 1436 effective October 15, 2001)

Annotations

Cases

I. Requested Instructions—Objections.
II. Jury Instructions.

I. Requested Instructions—Objections.

The last sentence of Civil Rule 5 1(a) was designed to avoid softly spoken conferences at the bench, inaudible to the clerk transcribing from the electronic recorder. Trial judges should voluntarily comply with the rule and counsel should not be hesitant in insisting upon such compliance. **Goss v. State,** Op. No. 76, 369 P2d 884 (Alaska 1962).

In the absence of proper objection taken below, instructions and verdict forms will not be reviewed by the Supreme Court unless it appears after a reading of all the instructions that a miscarriage of justice may occur. **Reiten v. Hendricks,** Op. No. 68, 370 P2d 166 (Alaska 1962).

In the absence of a proper objection taken below, an instruction will not be reviewed by the Supreme Court unless it appears that a miscarriage of justice may occur. **Gregory v. Padilla,** Op. No. 139, 379 P2d 951 (Alaska 1963).

Failure of trial court to give proposed instructions was considered on appeal where specifications of error did not point out any place in the trial record where appellant objected to the court's refusal to give these instructions. **Higgins v. Lantz,** Op. No. 239, 394 P2d 776 (Alaska 1964).

For an appellate consideration of failure to give instruction, trial court must have been distinctly informed of matter to which counsel objected and of grounds of objection. **Mitchell v. Knight,** Op. No. 241, 394 P2d 892 (Alaska 1964).

Where a party objects at trial to certain instructions only on the basis of insufficiency of the evidence he waives any objections based on other theories. **Nordin Construction Co. v. City of Nome,** Op. No. 730, 489 P2d 455 (Alaska 1971).

An error which is likely to result in a miscarriage of justice will be considered by the reviewing court even though not raised in the trial court. **Holiday Inns of America, Inc. v. Peck,** Op. No. 1024, 520 P2d 87 (Alaska 1974).

This rule is intended to insure that the trial court is clearly made aware of precise nature of alleged error. **Girves v. Kenai Peninsula Borough,** Op. No. 1168, 536 P2d 1221 (Alaska 1975).

A party who fails to object is not entitled to review of instruction unless a miscarriage of justice would occur if the instruction were not reviewed. **Haskins v. Shelden,** Op. No. 1357, 558 P2d 487 (Alaska 1976).

If a jury instruction is plainly erroneous, it can be reviewed despite lack of objection to it at trial. **Brown v. Estate of Jonz,** Op. No. 1808, 591 P2d 532 (Alaska 1979).

In order to satisfy the requirements of Civil Rule 5 1(a), counsel should make a specific objection to a given instruction, even if it is clear that the court understands his position on the issue. **Brown v. Estate of Jonz,** Op. No. 1808, 591 P2d 532 (Alaska 1979).

Where the only explicit objection to the instructions given to the jury occurred at a hearing on a motion for a new trial, which did not take place until a month after the end of the trial, such objection did not satisfy the requirements of Civil Rule 5 1(a). **Brown v. Estate of Jonz,** Op. No. 1808, 591 P2d 532 (Alaska 1979).

Where, objecting to an instruction defining term "supervisor" as one who does not regularly perform duties of any type regularly performed by employees supervised except for periods not exceeding 8 hours per week, attorney specifically referred to the propriety of the "eight hour limitation," there was sufficient notice to the court of the nature of the objection to preserve it for appeal. **Alaska International Industries v. Musana,** Op. No. 1966, 602 P2d 1240 (Alaska 1979).

Where court expressly stated that sufficient objection to jury instructions had been made, failure of record to show specific grounds did not prevent review on appeal. **Drickerson v. Drickerson,** Op. No. 1992, 604 P2d 1082 (Alaska 1979).

Where defendant objected on one ground to an instruction on "recklessness," he could not rely on a different ground for the objection on appeal. **Clary Insurance Agency v. Doyle,** Op. No. 2225, 620 P2d 194 (Alaska 1980).

Allowing a party only forty-five minutes to argue a requested jury instruction was not error. **Godfrey v. Hemenway,** Op. No. 2176, 617 P2d 3 (Alaska 1980).

Appellant's challenge to jury instruction in employment discrimination case was not preserved on appeal because she did not distinctly state the grounds of her objection or suggest corrective language consistent with McDonnell Douglas Principles. **Hout v. NANA Commercial Catering,** Op. No. 2457, 638 P2d 186 (Alaska 1981).

Even if trial court's instructions as to punitive damages had been in error, appellant approved the instructions at trial, thus his appeal on the point would be rejected. **Ben Lomond, Inc. v. Campbell,** Op. No. 2887, 691 P2d 1042 (Alaska 1984).

Objection to jury instruction would not be heard on appeal where objection on appeal was entirely different from objection at trial. **Van Huff v. Sohio Alaska Petroleum Co.,** Op. No. 3857, 835 P2d 1181 (Alaska 1992).

Jury instruction not objected to at trial will not be reviewed unless giving of instruction was plain error; plain error means an obvious mistake creating high likelihood of miscarriage of justice. **Conam Alaska v. Bell Lavalin, Inc.,** Op. No. 3900, 842 P2d 148 (Alaska 1992).

The exception set forth in **Zeman v. Lufthansa German Airlines,**699 P2d 1274 (Alaska 1985), to general policy against reviewing issues and objected to at trial does not apply to reviewing jury instructions. **Conam Alaska v. Bell Lavalin, Inc.,** Op. No. 3900, 842 P2d 148 (Alaska 1992).

Plaintiff did not lose right to challenge on appeal adverse ruling on motion in limine by not subsequently objecting to jury instruction which reflected adverse ruling. **Landers v. Municipality of Anchorage,** Op. No. 4343, 915 P2d 614 (Alaska 1996).

This rule requires specific objection if party is to claim error for giving or failing to give jury instruction; court's knowledge of party's position with respect to instruction is not sufficient. **Jaso v. McCarthy,** Op. No. 4407, 923 P2d 795 (Alaska 1996).

Jury instruction for calculating lost future wage and benefit award was not plain error where jury used reasonable basis for calculation. **Alaska Housing Finance Corp. v. Salvucci,** Op. No. 4917, 950 P2d 1116 (Alaska 1997).

Where party objected to instruction by asserting that it could not be held vicariously liable for sexual harassment, issue of vicarious liability for punitive damages for sexual harassment was subsumed within objection, thus preserving issue on appeal. **Veco, Inc. v. Rosebrock,** Op. No. 5084, 970 P2d 906 (Alaska 1999).

In a driver's false confinement suit against a city, the city's counsel's remark did not clearly lodge an objection to a jury instruction, where, while the city might have intended to raise the issue to challenge the court's refusal to give the instruction, its response of "Right" to the trial court's denial of the proposed instruction did not distinctly state an objection or the grounds. **City of Kodiak v. Samaniego,** Op. No. 5772, 83 P.3d 1077 (Alaska 2004).

II. Jury Instructions.

Where in action for damages sustained in an automobile accident, there was no evidence from which the jury could have inferred that it was dangerous for plaintiff to ride with defendant and that she was aware of these facts and comprehended the danger, it was error to give an instruction on assumption of risk. **Evans v. Buchner,** Op. No. 174, 386 P2d 836 (Alaska 1963).

Failure to instruct jury that the burden of establishing the defense of assumption of risk by preponderance of evidence rested upon defendant was error. **Evans v. Buchner,** Op. No. 174, 386 P2d 836 (Alaska 1963).

This rule was not violated by an instruction that a deposition is entitled to the same consideration, the same rebuttal presumption that the witness speaks the truth, and the same judgment on the part of the jury with reference to its weight, as is oral testimony by a witness in open court. **Patterson v. Cushman,** Op. No. 233, 394 P2d 657 (Alaska 1964).

It is difficult to conceive of any situation in any ordinary negligence action where an instruction on "unavoidable accident" would be appropriate and the use by trial courts of such an instruction as a standard instruction in negligence cases is disapproved. **Alaska Brick Co. v. McCoy,** Op. No. 287, 400 P2d 454 (Alaska 1965).

If a requested instruction is defective, the court is under no duty to give it or to supply a correct instruction. **Pepsi Cola Bottling Co. v. Superior Burner Service Co., Inc.,** Op. No. 411, 427 P2d 833 (Alaska 1967).

Where a defective requested instruction directed the court's attention to an issue of differentiation between maintenance and acts and omissions of plaintiff which the jury had not been instructed upon but which was necessary to enable the jury to intelligently determine the issue of contributory negligence, the court's failure to charge the jury in an appropriate manner was not excused by the technical defects in the request to charge. **Pepsi Cola Bottling Co. v. Superior Burner Service Co., Inc.,** Op. No. 411, 427 P2d 833 (Alaska 1967).

Rejection of proposed instruction was not error where the substance of the requested instruction was adequately covered by the instructions which were given by the court. **City of Fairbanks v. Nesbett,** Op. No. 439, 432 P2d 607 (Alaska 1967).

It was not error for the court to give requested instructions defining the duty of one in a sudden emergency where the circumstances of the sudden emergency were covered by instructions defining negligence generally. **Ferrell v. Baxter,** Op. No. 688, 484 P2d 250 (Alaska 1971).

Splitting jury instructions concerning loss of consortium into one instruction defining consortium damages and another informing the jury how to evaluate such damages is error. **Grasle Electric Co. v. Clark,** Op. No. 2073, 525 P2d 1081 (Alaska 1974).

In "slip and fall" tort case, jury need not be instructed as to how a reasonable person performs the activity of walking. **Hatfield v. Universal Services, Inc.,** Op. No. 2288, 622 P2d 984 (Alaska 1981).

Appellant who did not object to jury instruction at trial did not meet his burden on appeal of proving that erroneous instruction, which pertained to law of piercing corporate veil, was highly likely to have altered the result. **Conam Alaska v. Bell Lavalin, Inc.,** Op. No. 3900, 842 P2d 148 (Alaska 1992).

Appellant who did not object to jury instruction at trial did not meet his burden on appeal of proving that erroneous instruction, which pertained to law of undue influence in will contests, was highly likely to have altered the result. **Matter of Estate of McCoy,** Op. No. 3919, 844P2d 1131 (Alaska 1993).

Employer's objection to incompleteness of mixed-motive instruction was held not distinctly raised at trial under section (a) of this rule, where employer failed to offer proposed language that would have correctly allocated the burden of proof, thus failing to provide the superior court an identifiable opportunity to rule on the issue. **Reust v. Alaska Petroleum Contrs., Inc.,** Op. No. 5951, 127 P.3d 807 (Alaska 2005).

Rule 52. Findings by the Court.

(a) **Effect.** In all actions tried upon the facts without a jury or with an advisory jury, the court shall find the facts specially and state separately its conclusions of law thereon and judgment shall be entered pursuant to Rule 58; and in granting or refusing interlocutory injunctions the court shall similarly set forth the findings of fact and conclusions of law which constitute the grounds of its action. Requests for findings are not necessary for purposes of review. Findings of fact shall not be set aside unless clearly erroneous, and due regard shall be given to the opportunity of the trial court to judge the credibility of the witnesses. The findings of a master, to the extent that the court adopts them, shall be considered as the findings of the court. If an opinion or memorandum of decision is filed, it will be sufficient if the findings of fact and conclusions of law appear therein. Findings of fact and conclusions of law are unnecessary on decisions of motions under Rules 12 or 56 or any other motion except as provided in Rule 41(b).

(b) **Amendment.** Upon motion of a party made not later than 10 days after the date shown in the clerk's certificate of distribution on the judgment the court may amend its findings or make additional findings and may amend the judgment accordingly. The motion may be made with a motion for new trial pursuant to Rule 59. When findings of fact are made in actions tried by the court without a jury, the question of the sufficiency of the evidence to support the findings may thereafter be raised whether or not the party raising the question has made in the court an objection to such findings or has made a motion to amend them or a motion for judgment.

(c) **Preparation and Submission.** The preparation and submission of findings of fact and conclusions of law shall be governed by Rule 78.

(Adopted by SCO 5 October 9, 1959; amended by SCO 258 effective November 15, 1976; by SCO 554 effective April 4, 1983; and by SCO 1295 effective January 15, 1998)

Note: Ch. 139, § 6, SLA 1986, provided that AS 09.17.080, enacted by ch. 139, § 1, SLA 1986, amended Civil Rule 52 by requiring the court to make specific findings regarding the amount of damages and the percentages of fault to be allocated among the parties.

Sec. 09.17.080. Apportionment of damages.

(a) In all actions involving fault of more than one party to the action, including third party defendants and persons who have been released under AS 09.17.090, the court, unless otherwise agreed by all parties, shall instruct the jury to answer special interrogatories or, if there is no jury, shall make findings, indicating

(1) the amount of damages each claimant would be entitled to recover if contributory fault is disregarded; and

(2) the percentage of the total fault of all of the parties to each claim that is allocated to each claimant, defendant, third party defendant, and person who has been released from liability under AS 09.17.090.

(b) In determining the percentages of fault, the trier of fact shall consider both the nature of the conduct of each party at fault, and the extent of the causal relation between the conduct and the damages claimed. The trier of fact may determine that two or more persons are to be treated as a single party if their conduct was a cause of the damages claimed and the separate act or omission of each person cannot be distinguished.

(c) The court shall determine the award of damages to each claimant in accordance with the findings, subject to a reduction under AS 09.17.090, and enter judgment against each party liable. The court also shall determine and state in the judgment each party's equitable share of the obligation to each claimant in accordance with the respective percentages of fault.

(d) The court shall enter judgment against each party liable on the basis of joint and several liability, except that a party who is allocated less than 50 percent of the total fault allocated to all the parties may not be jointly liable for more than twice the percentage of fault allocated to that party. (§ 1 ch. 139 SLA 1986)

Note: Sections 41, 43, 45, and 46 of chapter 87 SLA 1997 amend AS 25.20.050(n), AS 25.24.160(d), AS 25.24.210(e), and AS 25.24.230(i), respectively, to require that an order or acknowledgement of paternity, a divorce decree, a petition for dissolution of marriage, and a dissolution decree include the social security number of each party to the action and each child whose rights are being addressed. According to § 151 of the Act, these provisions have the effect of amending Civil Rules 52, 58, 78, and 90.1 by requiring the court to include social security numbers, if ascertainable, of parties and children in certain petitions, pleadings, and judgments.

Annotations

Cases

A. Requirements.
B. Construction.
III. Unsupported Findings — Clearly Erroneous Rule.

I. In General.

Finding which has the indirect effect of finding that proceedings of a tax sale up to and including the issuance of the tax deed were not erroneous, illegal or void, was set aside where this was not an issue in the case. **Wells v. Noey,** Op. No. 142, 380 P2d 876 (Alaska 1963).

Civil Rule 52(a) was disregarded by trial judge's failure to direct entry of judgment in the civil docket in the manner provided by Civil Rule 74. **Lowe v. Senior,** Op. No. 168, 385 P2d 942 (Alaska 1963).

Objections to the findings of fact, conclusions of law or judgment below are not a prerequisite to challenge the insufficiency of evidence on appeal. **Isaacs v. Hickey,** Op. No. 210, 391 P2d 449 (Alaska 1964).

This rule which requires findings of fact was not applicable to appellate review by the superior court on an administrative agency's decision where the superior court did not conduct a trial de novo and was not the finder of fact. **Employers' Liability Assurance Corp. v. Bradshaw,** Op. No. 360, 417 P2d 600 (Alaska 1966).

In disposing of motions for summary judgment it is unnecessary for the trial court to make findings of fact. **Palzer v. Serv-U-Meat Co.,** Op. No. 367, 419 P2d 201 (Alaska 1966); **Alaska State Hous. Auth. v. Contento,** Op. No. 435, 432 P2d 117 (Alaska 1967).

Judging the credibility of witnesses and weighing conflicting evidence was the trial court's function. **Associated Engineers & Contractors, Inc. v. H. & W. Const. Co., Inc.,** Op. No. 462, 438 P2d 224 (Alaska 1968).

It is not the intent of Rule 78, requiring counsel for the successful party to prepare findings of fact, to delegate to counsel the trial judge's primary duty of personally finding the facts under this rule. **Fairbanks Builders, Inc. v. Morton DeLima, Inc.,** Op. No. 682, 483 P2d 194 (Alaska 1971).

An appellate court in reviewing a decision must take the view of the evidence most favorable to the prevailing party in the lower court. **Graham v. Rockman,** Op. No. 854, 504 P2d 1351 (Alaska 1972).

Where there is a variance between the court's oral ruling on a motion for summary judgment and the written findings prepared by the prevailing party, the oral ruling controls. **Concerned Citizens of South Kenai Peninsula v. Kenai Peninsula Borough,** Op. No. 1093, 527 P2d 447 (Alaska 1974).

Credibility choices are for the trier of facts to make and his selection will generally be accepted by a reviewing court. **B.B. & S. Construction Co., Inc. v. Stone,** Op. No. 1143, 535 P2d 271 (Alaska 1975).

Failure to object to finding of fact in action tried by court without jury does not waive any objection to such finding on appeal. **Casperson v. Meech,** Op. No. 1700, 583 P2d 218 (Alaska 1978).

In reviewing superior court's assumed conclusion that petitioner's activity was abnormally dangerous, leading to imposition of absolute liability, the Supreme Court was free to reach an independent conclusion based on the same nontestimonial record of undisputed facts presented below. **Yukon Equipment v. Fireman's Fund Ins. Co.,** Op. No. 1754, 585 P2d 1206 (Alaska 1978).

In contract action where extrinsic evidence was in dispute, the trial court's factual findings based upon the extrinsic evidence could not be reversed unless clearly erroneous. **Jackson v. Nangle,** Op. No. 2773, 677 P2d 242 (Alaska 1984).

In guardianship proceeding, incorporation of probate master's report in superior court's order appointing guardian was proper. **Matter of O.S.D.,** Op. No. 2744, 672 P2d 1304 (Alaska 1983).

Issuance of a temporary restraining order pending determination of a motion for preliminary injunction did not have the effect of a preliminary injunction, thus the temporary restraining order expired within 10 days of its issuance. **Ostrow v. Higgins,** Op. No. 3085, 722 P2d 936 (Alaska 1986).

A party who initially obtains a temporary restraining order is not entitled to receive its benefits indefinitely by not proceeding to request a preliminary injunction hearing. **Ostrow v. Higgins,** Op. No. 3085, 722 P2d 936 (Alaska 1986).

On appeal of trial court child support modification order, court's failure to make factual findings was defect requiring remand. **Keating v. Traynor,** Op. No. 3862, 833 P2d 695 (Alaska 1992).

Questions for trier of fact are normally reviewed only for clear error; however, appellate court may review application of legal doctrine to undisputed facts without usual deference to trial court. **Luedtke v. Nabors Alaska Drilling, Inc.,** Op. No. 3844, 834 P2d 1220 (Alaska 1992).

Trial court did not err in not making findings of fact when it denied husband's motion to dismiss wife's action for alimony arrearages. **Lawns v. Lawns,** Op. No. 3922, 845 P2d 429 (Alaska 1993).

Findings of fact are reviewed under a clearly erroneous standard. **Matter of Estate of Brandon,** Op. No. 4216, 902 P2d 1299 (Alaska 1995).

In reviewing the factual findings of a trial court, the appellate court must view the evidence in the light most favorable to the prevailing party. Due regard must be given to the trial court's opportunity to judge the credibility of the witnesses. **Voss v. Brooks,** Op. No. 4294, 907 P2d 465 (Alaska 1995).

Trial court's determination that a modification of child support was not warranted because the father, an attorney, was voluntarily and unreasonably underemployed where he decided to quit practicing law and become a teacher was not clearly erroneous because father's earning capacity had not changed and the mother and child were not required to finance his choice to change careers. **Olmstead v. Ziegler,** Op. No. 5543, 42 P3d 1102 (Alaska 2002).

Amendment in 1987, which eliminated the former requirement in Alaska R. Civ. P. 41(b) that the trial judge deny a motion to dismiss when the plaintiff has made an unimpeached prima facie case, brought that rule into compliance with the analogous federal rule, Fed. R. Civ. P. 52(c), that the trial judge is not to draw any special inferences in the nonmovant's favor nor concern itself with whether the nonmovant has made out a prima facie case. **Fletcher v. Trademark Constr., Inc.,** Op. No. 5760 (Alaska 2003).

If a trial court refuses to delay ruling on an Alaska R. Civ. P. 41(b) motion, it is because the plaintiff has failed to prove its case for the reasons set out in the court's findings under Alaska R. Civ. P. 52(a); nothing would be gained from an additional requirement that the trial court explain why it did not delay its ruling. The Supreme Court of Alaska declines to hold that such an explanation is required under Alaska R. Civ. P. 41(b). **Fletcher v. Trademark Constr., Inc.,** Op. No. 5760 (Alaska 2003).

In a landlord-tenant dispute, where tenant argued that the superior court's findings were not sufficiently clear to meet standards under Alaska R.Civ P. 56, but findings of fact and conclusions of law by the superior court on decisions of motions under Rule 12 or Rule 56, or any other motions except as provided in Rule 41(b). **Fyffe v. Wright,** Op. No. 5819 (Alaska 2004).

Where no evidence was presented to the superior court regarding a former director's unclean hands defense, the superior court was not required to make a specific finding on that defense. **Martinez v. Cape Fox Corp.,** Op. No. 5909, 113 P.3d 1226 (Alaska 2005).

II. Support for Findings.

A. Requirements.

The trial court cannot make a temporary restraining order into a preliminary injunction unless it sets forth the findings of fact and conclusions of law in support of its action. **Miller v. Atkinson,** Op. No. 49, 365 P2d 550 (Alaska 1961).

It is the duty of a trial court to deal adequately with and state with clarity what it finds as facts and what it holds as conclusions of law. The findings and conclusions should be so clear and explicit as to give the Supreme Court a clear understanding of the basis for the decision made. **Dickerson v. Geiermann,** Op. No. 60, 368 P2d 217 (Alaska 1962).

Rule 52(a) is mandatory and must be complied with. **Merrill v. Merrill,** Op. No. 62, 368 P2d 546 (Alaska 1962).

The purposes of Rule 52(a) are threefold: as an aid in the trial judge's process of adjudication; for the purposes of res adjudicate and estoppel by judgment; and as an aid to the appellate court on review. **Merrill v. Merrill,** Op. No. 62, 368 P2d 546 (Alaska 1962).

Under Rule 52(a) it is the duty of the trial court, by sufficiently detailed and explicit findings "to give the appellate court a clear understanding of the basis of the trial court's decision, and to enable it to determine the grounds on which the trial court reached its decision." **Merrill v. Merrill,** Op. No. 62, 368 P2d 546 (Alaska 1962).

Findings need only be sufficient to indicate the factual basis for the ultimate conclusion. **Spenard Plumbing & Heating v. Wright,** Op. No. 81, 370 P2d 519 (Alaska 1962).

Where the trial court, as trier of the facts, with every opportunity to judge the credibility of all the witnesses, found the existence of an oral contract and the terms of that contract, the Supreme Court is bound by those findings unless they are clearly erroneous. **Nordin v. Zimmer,** Op. No. 96, 373 P2d 738 (Alaska 1962).

Trial court committed no error in failing to make findings of fact and conclusions of law where it granted defendant's motion for summary judgment. **Lowe v. Boggess,** Op. No. 110, 375 P2d 199 (Alaska 1962).

The Supreme Court's scope of review in judge-tried cases is limited to the determination of whether the court's findings are clearly erroneous. **State v. Phillips,** Op. No. 619, 470 P2d 266 (Alaska 1970).

The findings of a trial court sitting in admiralty will not be disturbed unless they are clearly erroneous. **State v. Stanley,** Op. No. 865, 506 P2d 1284 (Alaska 1973).

The Supreme Court in reviewing a criminal conviction in which there is a challenge to the sufficiency of the evidence cannot add to a finding of fact but will take notice of facts appearing in evidence which are undisputed. **Hughes v. State,** Op. No. 926, 513 P2d 1115 (Alaska 1973).

In reviewing findings of fact of a trial judge sitting without a jury, the Supreme Court is bound by the "clearly erroneous" standard. **Larman v. Kodiak Electric Association,** Op. No. 950, 514 P2d 1275 (Alaska 1973).

This rule does not require that findings and conclusions be properly labeled or even that express findings be made on all questions, so long as the record clearly indicates that the court considered the matter and resolved each critical and actual dispute. **Urban Development Co. v. Dekreon,** Op. No. 1083, 526 P2d 325 (Alaska 1974).

It is the trial court's duty under this rule to make findings sufficient to give a clear understanding of the basis of its decision in order to enable an intelligent review on appeal. **State v. I'Anson,** Op. No. 1102, 529 P2d 188 (Alaska 1974).

It is the duty of a trial court by sufficiently detailed and explicit findings to give the appellate court a clear understanding of the basis of the trial court's decision and to enable it to determine the ground on which the trial court breached its decision. **Wigger v. Olson,** Op. No. 1125, 533 P2d 6 (Alaska 1975).

In making a written statement of reasons for denying a motion to appeal at public expense, a judge should take care to state with particularity and in detail preliminary and basic facts upon which he relied. Only if the judge makes such findings will the Supreme Court be able to have a clear understanding of the basis for the judge's decision. **Johnson v. Johnson,** Op. No. 1229, 544 P2d 1028 (Alaska 1976).

As a general rule, findings of fact must include as much of the subsidiary facts as are necessary to disclose to the reviewing court the steps by which the trial court reached its ultimate conclusion on each factual issue. **State v. Kaatz,** Op. No. 1536, 572 P2d 775 (Alaska 1977).

Court's decision to increase child support payments pursuant to a motion to modify original divorce decree was deficient because it contained no findings of fact. **Headlough v. Headlough,** Op. No. 2463, 639 P2d 1010 (Alaska 1982).

Findings are sufficient if they provide the reviewing court with a clear understanding of the basis for the trial court's decision. **Uchitel v. Telephone Co.,** Op. No. 2519, 646 P2d 229 (Alaska 1982).

When the trial court dismisses a complaint on the ground that the plaintiff has shown no right to relief, it must enter findings of fact and conclusions of law. **Winn v. Mannhalter,** Op. No. 2988, 708 P2d 444 (Alaska 1985).

Findings by court that condominium association's rule was validly promulgated, was not invalid on its face or as might be applied, and was being violated by defendant, were sufficient to warrant injunctive relief where a statute, the Horizontal Property Regimes Act, specifically authorized injunctive relief under such circumstances. **Dunlap v. Bavarian Village Condominium Ass'n,** Op. No. 3511, 780 P2d 1012 (Alaska 1989).

Written findings of fact and conclusions of law by trial court in interpleader action were unnecessary; oral findings of fact and conclusions of law were sufficient to permit appellate review. **Noey v. Bledsoe,** Op. No. 5107, 978 P2d 1264 (Alaska 1999).

Where trial court clearly accepted plaintiff's methodology for computation of damages as laid out in plaintiff's motion for reconsideration and based on specific testimony presented at trial, remand for clear and explicit findings on damages was unnecessary. **Mapco Express, Inc. v. Faulk,** Op. No. 5422, 24 P3d 531 (Alaska 2001).

Trial court's findings are sufficiently "clear and explicit" as required by this rule if they allow for meaningful appellate review and resolve all critical issues and disputes between the parties; trial court is not required to explain its determination of each witness's credibility or to explain why it finds one witness more credible than another. **Mapco Express, Inc. v. Faulk,** Op. No. 5422, 24 P3d 531 (Alaska 2001).

Absence of findings of fact and conclusions of law did not prevent a dismissal under Alaska R. Civ. P. 12(b)(6) from having res judicata effect where the reviewing court could infer the trial court's reasons for the ruling on the merits from its subsequent opinion denying attorney's fees. **Alaska Wildlife Alliance v. State,** Op. No. 5771, 74 P.3d 201 (Alaska 2003).

Trial court did not err in granting a general contractor's motion to dismiss a subcontractor's suit against it where the court's findings of fact were sufficient to show the legal and factual bases for its ruling so as to allow for appellate review, and its interpretation of Alaska R. Civ. P. 41(b) was proper where: (1) The subcontractor's witness was unable to testify as to the cost of materials relating to the change orders; (2) the documents presented did not provide a basis for distinguishing between base and revised materials costs; (3) the classification of hours worked on the project as "base" or "extra" was arbitrary; and (4) no evidence supported the assumption that all hours not budgeted for in the base contract bid must have been expended as the result of additions and revisions to the contract. **Fletcher v. Trademark Constr., Inc.,** Op. No. 5760 (Alaska 2003).

Where no evidence was presented to the superior court regarding a former director's unclean hands defense, the superior court was not required to make a specific finding on that defense. **Martinez v. Cape Fox Corp.,** Op. No. 5909, 113 P.3d 1226 (Alaska 2005).

While the trial court's findings in a custody and division of marital property dispute could have been clearer, and its reasoning more explicit, the record was sufficiently detailed to permit meaningful review. **Chase v. Chase,** Op. No. 5881, 109 P.3d 942 (Alaska 2005).

In determining the scope of the public prescriptive easement on the landowner's property, the trial court failed to make specific factual findings as to the scope, and the matter was remanded. **Price v. Eastham,** Op. No. 5983, 128 P.3d 725 (Alaska 2006).

B. Construction.

In an action involving an attorney's claim for legal services rendered, the trial court ought to have determined whether an attorney-client relationship was created by contract, express or implied, and should have made findings of fact and conclusions of law to disclose the basis for its decision. **Dickerson v. Geiermann,** Op. No. 60, 368 P2d 217 (Alaska 1962).

If one of the questions presented at trial is controlled by equitable principles which underlie the common law action in assumpsit for money had and received, the superior court ought to have decided whether the evidence disclosed a state of facts which, measured by equitable standards, would have entitled appellant to the recovery which she sought. **Dickerson v. Geiermann,** Op. No. 60, 368 P2d 217 (Alaska 1962).

Evidence held sufficient to support finding of adequate consideration in action to set aside land contract. **Hitz v. Property Investments, Inc.,** Op. No. 65, 368 P2d 929 (Alaska 1962).

Finding of trial court that enforceable oral contract was formed held justified. **Elliot et al. v. Sandal,** Op. No. 74, 369 P2d 890 (Alaska 1962).

Finding of trial court that an agency by estoppel existed was supported by adequate evidence. **Elliot et al. v. Sandal,** Op. No. 74, 369 P2d 890 (Alaska 1962).

Finding that a third person was not a party to an agreement entered into between the parties, and therefore not an indispensable party, was amply supported by the evidence. **Nordin v. Zimmer,** Op. No. 96, 373 P2d 738 (Alaska 1962).

Evidence supported finding of gross or wanton negligence where defendant left a truck parked on a bush airfield causing plaintiff's airplane to collide with it. **McLemore v. Harris,** Op. No. 102, 374 P2d 410 (Alaska 1962).

Evidence supported finding that testator was competent to execute will. **Waft v. Kraft,** Op. No. 103, 374 P2d 413 (Alaska 1962).

Evidence supported finding that changes made by a lessee in leased premises were alterations instead of redecorations. **Anderson v. Jacobs,** Op. No. 105, 374 P2d 489 (Alaska 1962).

Findings that fire department was negligent were not clearly erroneous and would not be set aside. **Fairbanks & Lathrop Co. v. Schaible,** Op. No. 97, 375 P2d 201 (Alaska 1962).

Evidence supported finding that a fire was caused by loose fuel fittings. **George v. Willman,** Op. No. 134, 379 P2d 103 (Alaska 1962).

Evidence supported findings that plaintiff was negligent. **Van Reenan v. Golden Valley Electric,** Op. No. 127, 379 P2d 958 (Alaska 1962).

Trial court was correct in finding that defendant had failed to prove the allegations of their counterclaim. **Wells v. Noey,** Op. No. 142, 380 P2d 876 (Alaska 1963).

In a case heavy with demeanor evidence and tried without a jury, it was the task of the trial court to resolve apparent conflict between the evidence of the plaintiff and of the defendant. **Monsma v. Williams,** Op. No. 161, 385 P2d 107 (Alaska 1963).

In action for damages for an alleged assault which was tried without a jury, trial court committed no error in finding defendant's plea of guilty in prior criminal action arising out of the same events persuasive but not conclusive against the defendant. **Monsma v. Williams,** Op. No. 161, 385 P2d 107 (Alaska 1963).

Oral decision of trial judge indicated a sufficient factual basis for entry of a formal judgment by a successor judge. **Hale v. City of Anchorage,** Op. No. 189, 389 P2d 434 (Alaska 1964).

For setting aside findings of fact of the trial court as "clearly erroneous," there must exist a stronger basis than a mere difference in personal judgment. **Isaacs v. Hickey,** Op. No. 210, 391 P2d 449 (Alaska 1964).

Findings of trial court approving a receiver's report and failing to find him guilty of negligence or bad faith could not be set aside under Civil Rule 52(a) although the Supreme Court may have viewed the facts differently as initial trier of fact, where no clear error and no failure to make a sound survey of or to accord the proper effect to cogent facts appeared from the examination of the records. **First National Bank of Fairbanks v. Dual,** Op. No. 223, 392 P2d 463 (Alaska 1964).

The trial court's specific finding that defendant had orally promised to be solely responsible for the payment of a promissory note, sufficiently negatived the contention that plaintiff who was co-signer of the note was entitled at the most to sue for contribution and it was not necessary for the trial court to make findings asserting the negative of the issue presented. **Herning v. Wigger,** Op. No. 284, 398 P2d 1002 (Alaska 1965).

Where the trial judge had a rational basis for concluding that the mother was a fit person to have custody of the child such finding shall not be disturbed on appeal. **Wilson v. Mitchell,** Op. No. 301, 406 P2d 4 (Alaska 1965).

Findings of trial court which under the record were supported by substantial evidence could not be disturbed on appeal because of some inconsistencies in the testimony. **Kenai Power Corp. v. Strandberg,** Op. No. 350, 415 P2d 659 (Alaska 1966).

The rule that a trial judge has the duty to make sufficiently detailed and explicit findings of fact in order to afford the reviewing court a clear understanding of the basis for his decision applies to mechanics' and materialmen's foreclosure actions. **Moores v. Alaska Metal Buildings, Inc.,** Op. No. 515, 448 P2d 581 (Alaska 1968).

Strict compliance with provisions of this rule requiring findings of fact and conclusions of law and setting out reasons for the issuance of a preliminary injunction is required particularly in circumstances where the trial court is enjoining enforcement of an administrative regulation or statute. **Department of Fish & Game v. Pinnell,** Op. No. 586, 461 P2d 429 (Alaska 1969).

Where an order of final judgment incorporates language of an earlier interlocutory order which is supported with necessary findings of fact and conclusions of law, no prejudice results from a lack of findings and conclusions to support the entry of partial judgment. **Moran v. Kenai Towing and Salvage, Inc.,** Op. No. 1056, 523 P2d 1237 (Alaska 1974).

Finding of oral contract for sale of homestead would not be reversed because not clearly erroneous. **Jackson v. White,** Op. No. 1334, 556 P2d 530 (Alaska 1976).

Findings of fact and conclusions of law were sufficiently detailed to meet the requirements of paragraph (a) of this rule. **City of Kenai v. Filler,** Op. No. 1463, 566 P2d 670 (Alaska 1977).

The court's findings of fact concerning its apportionment of percentages in a comparative negligence case were adequate to meet the requirements of this rule. **State v. Kaatz,** Op. No. 1536, 572 P2d 775 (Alaska 1977).

The determination of whether the doctrine of quasi-estoppel is applicable is essentially a factual one and, as such, will not be disturbed on appeal unless the findings on which it is based are clearly erroneous. **Jamison v. Consolidated Utilities, Inc.,** Op. No. 1576, 576 P2d 97 (Alaska 1978).

In an action on an open account, trial court's implicit factual finding that certain insurance payments were paid was not clearly erroneous. **Eagle Air v. Corroon, Etc.,** Op. No. 2538, 648 P2d 1000 (Alaska 1982).

Where court held that a purported lease agreement created a security interest by giving the lessee the option of owning the property for a nominal consideration, the nominality of the option price was a factual determination which could not be set aside unless clearly erroneous. **Western Enterprises v. Artic Office Machines,** Op. No. 2707, 667 P2d 1232 (Alaska 1983).

Trial court's factual findings did not support its conclusion on the proximate cause of the property damage at issue, requiring remand. **Bakke v. State,** Op. No. 3238, 744 P2d 655 (Alaska 1987).

Where father filed motion for reduction in child support obligation alleging that his income fell significantly because he lost valuable housing allowances when he began living free of charge in barracks on United States Coast Guard base, trial court's denial of motion because free housing was worth $700 per month required remand where court neither described method it used to value the housing nor provided explanation that would permit appellate court to glean from record basis for the calculation. **Beard v. Morris,** Op. No. 4956, 956 P2d 418 (Alaska 1998).

Alaska Supreme Court has long read the language in Alaska R. Civ. P. 52(a) to require that a trial court give the supreme court a clear understanding of the basis for the decision made, but the rule does not require that the trial court's findings and conclusions be properly labeled, or even that express findings be made on all questions, so long as the record clearly indicates that the trial court considered the matter and resolved each critical factual dispute. **Crittell v. Bingo,** Op. No. 5496, 36 P3d 634 (Alaska 2001).

Trial court's challenged findings of fact regarding a father's visitation were not clearly erroneous, where they were supported by the mother's testimony. **Potter v. Potter,** Op. No. 5636, 55 P.3d 726 (Alaska 2002).

While the trial court's findings in a custody and division of marital property dispute could have been clearer, and its reasoning more explicit, the record was sufficiently detailed to permit meaningful review. **Chase v. Chase,** Op.

No. 5881, 109 P.3d 942 (Alaska 2005).

III. Unsupported Findings — Clearly Erroneous Rule.

The findings of the trial court were not supported by the evidence and were "clearly erroneous" as to whether there had been a mistake in payment of partnership salaries. **Durkee v. Busk,** Op. No. 17, 355 P2d 588, 593 (Alaska 1960).

While regard must be given to the opportunity of the trial court to judge the credibility of witnesses, the findings of that court are not conclusive when the entire evidence convinces the reviewing court that a mistake has been committed. **Link v. Patrick,** Op. No. 52, 367 P2d 157, 159 (Alaska 1961).

Where the trial court has failed to comply with Civil Rule 52(a), the normal practice is for the appellate court to remand the case for appropriate findings of fact and conclusions of law, but where the judgment itself cannot be understood, the court may vacate the judgment and return the case to the superior court for a new trial. **Dickerson v. Geiermann,** Op. No. 60, 368 P2d 217 (Alaska 1962).

Where the basis for the trial court's decision cannot be determined from the finding of facts, the Supreme Court will remand the case to the superior court for the purpose of making appropriate findings of fact, and if this cannot be done, the superior court shall, in lieu of making further findings of fact, grant a new trial. **Merrill v. Merrill,** Op. No. 62, 368 P2d 546 (Alaska 1962).

Evidence held insufficient to support finding that real estate broker had failed to produce a purchaser who was ready, willing and able to purchase in accordance with terms of the earnest money receipt and agreement. **Pasley v. Barber,** Op. No. 64, 368 P2d 549 (Alaska 1962).

Where findings of fact are clearly erroneous, they will be set aside. **Rogge v. Weaver,** Op. No. 63, 368 P2d 810 (Alaska 1962).

Finding of trial court that promissory note had been paid held not supported by evidence. **Awes, Adm. v. Walker,** Op. No. 67, 370 P2d 187 (Alaska 1962).

Where defendant's automobile skidded out of its lane of traffic on an icy street and struck plaintiff, trial court's finding that defendant was not negligent was not supported by the evidence, as the burden of proving excuse or justification for violation fell on defendant and he failed to discharge this burden. **Rogers v. Dubiel,** Op. No. 94, 373 P2d 295 (Alaska 1962).

Where findings of the trial court were not sufficiently detailed and explicit to give the appellate court a clear understanding of the basis of the decision, case was remanded for the purpose of making sufficient findings of fact. **Hamilton v. Lotto,** Op. No. 211, 391 P2d 948 (Alaska 1964).

Findings of fact were not adequate to determine with certainty what facts were found by the court, and as a result the conclusions of law served no helpful purpose. **Stock & Grove, Inc. v. City of Juneau,** Op. No. 292, 403 P2d 171 (Alaska 1965).

Medical malpractice case tried without a jury was remanded for the purpose of making more specific and detailed findings in regard to past and future damages for physical impairment and past and future damages by loss of time and impairment of earning capacity. **Patrick v. Sedwick,** Op. No. 338, 413 P2d 169 (Alaska 1966).

Where in a case arising under a mechanic's lien statute the findings of fact did not indicate whether a determination of "knowledge" of construction by the owner as required under the applicable statute for the creation of such lien was made by the court, and the conclusions of law were insufficiently articulate as to the rules of law relied on by the court, the case was remanded and the trial judge was empowered, if he so determines, to hear additional evidence or order a new trial. **Vaara v. Ketchikan Spruce Mills,** Op. No. 441, 432 P2d 618 (Alaska 1967).

Where an action by a prisoner against the state for injuries allegedly sustained while being transported in a truck after a hip operation is dismissed on the merits without any findings of fact being made, the case will be remanded for purposes of making adequate findings of fact and conclusions of law, including findings as to the court's judgment of credibility of the plaintiff and his witnesses. **Bohm v. State,** Op. No. 543, 453 P2d 410 (Alaska 1969).

Clear error will not be found unless the reviewing court is convinced on the whole record that a mistake has been committed. **Paskvan v. Mesich,** Op. No. 557, 455 P2d 229 (Alaska 1969).

A preliminary injunction which is granted without setting forth the reasons for the issuance of the injunction and without findings of fact and conclusions of law which articulate grounds for the issuance of the preliminary injunction as required by this rule is procedurally defective and will be vacated. **Department of Fish & Game v. Pinnell,** Op. No. 586, 461 P2d 429 (Alaska 1969).

The Supreme Court will vacate rather than remand where a preliminary injunction is procedurally defective and where a hearing has been held on a motion for permanent injunction and where a decision on the merits of the permanent injunction is anticipated in the near future. **Department of Fish & Game v. Pinnell,** Op. No. 586, 461 P2d 429 (Alaska 1969).

A finding is not clearly erroneous, unless, from a review of the entire record, the Supreme Court is left with definite and firm conviction that a mistake has been made. **State v. Phillips,** Op. No. 619, 470 P2d 266 (Alaska 1970).

The clearly erroneous standard of review applies to all factual findings, including findings in cases tried entirely on the basis of written depositions, documentary evidence and statements of undisputed facts, as well as cases involving demeanor evidence. **Alaska Foods, Inc. v. American Mfr.'s Mut. Ins Co.,** Op. No. 678, 482 P2d 842 (Alaska 1971).

The clearly erroneous standard of review of findings of fact means something more than merely showing that it is more probable than not that the trial judge was mistaken. The reviewing court must be convinced, in a definite and firm way, that a mistake has been committed and must be well persuaded by the party seeking to have the trial judge's finding set aside. **Alaska Foods, Inc. v. American Mfr.'s Mut. Ins Co.,** Op. No. 678, 482 P2d 842 (Alaska 1971).

A finding is "clearly erroneous" when, although there may be evidence to support it, the reviewing court is left with the definite and firm conviction on the entire record that a mistake has been committed. **State v. Abbott,** Op. No. 804,498 P2d 712 (Alaska 1972).

Before the supreme court will reverse a finding of fact as clearly erroneous, the court must be convinced, in a definite firm way, that a mistake has been committed. **Moran v. Holman,** Op. No. 945, 514 P2d 817 (Alaska 1973).

A finding is clearly erroneous and may be set aside on review when, although there may be evidence to support it, the court is left with the definite and firm conviction on the entire record that a mistake has been made. **Peters v. Juneau-Douglas Girl Scout Council,** Op. No. 1018, 519 P2d 826 (Alaska 1974).

A "clearly erroneous" finding which may be set aside in review, is one which leaves the Supreme Court with a definite and firm conviction in the entire record that a mistake has been made, although there may be evidence to support the finding. **Frontier Saloon, Inc. v. Short,** Op. No. 1345, 557 P2d 779 (Alaska 1976).

A finding of fact by a judge in a trial without a jury will be disturbed by a reviewing court only if clearly erroneous; a finding is clearly erroneous only when the court is left with the definite and firm conviction on the entire record that a mistake has been committed. **Hausam v. Wodrich,** Op. No. 1558, 574 P2d 805 (Alaska 1978).

Finding by trial court that the Alaska Gay Coalition was deleted from City's Blue Book on municipal services because of its political focus was clearly erroneous where it was apparent that the deletion occurred because the coalition was a homosexual organization. **Alaska Gay Coalition v. Sullivan,** Op. No. 1616, 578 P2d 951 (Alaska 1978).

It was clearly erroneous for trial court to conclude that certain facts were so generally known that judicial notice could be taken of them while at the same time deciding that a company, whose work routinely involved those same facts, was not chargeable with at least the same degree of knowledge. **Lewis v. Anchorage Asphalt Pav. Co.,** Op. No. 1639, 579 P2d 532 (Alaska 1978).

The supreme court will only disturb trial court findings when it is convinced that they are clearly erroneous, that is, when it is left with a definite and firm conviction on the entire record that a mistake has been made, even though there may be evidence to support the finding. **Martens v. Metzgar,** Op. No. 1806, 591 P2d 541 (Alaska 1979).

Under the "clearly erroneous" standard of appellate review, the amount of deference that must be given to factual determinations of the sentencing supporting the court will vary, depending upon the extent to which the sentencing court relied upon testimony in which the demeanor and credibility of witnesses played an important role. **Juneby v. State,** Op. No. 72, 641 P2d 823 (Alaska App. 1982).

The "clearly erroneous" standard is still to be applied when the trial court's findings are adopted from those submitted by the prevailing party. **Stack v. Miller,** Op. No. 2508, 645 P2d 184 (Alaska App. 1982).

Although breach of contract claim was dismissed by summary judgment, review of trial court's finding that the contract partially integrated would be based upon the "clearly erroneous" standard, since during subsequent trial on reformation of the contract, the court reviewed and reaffirmed its summary judgment findings on the integration issue. **Alaska Northern Development, Inc. v. Alyeska Pipeline Service Co.,** Op. No. 2689, 666 P2d 33 (Alaska 1983).

Although a reviewing court will exercise its independent judgment in reviewing a trial court's interpretation of a written contract when such findings are based exclusively upon documentary evidence, a "clearly erroneous" standard should be applied where extrinsic testimonial evidence has been presented and relied upon by the trial court in formulating its findings. **Kennedy Associates, Inc. v. Fischer,** Op. No. 2700, 667 P2d 174 (Alaska 1983).

Where trial court heard and relied upon extensive oral testimony in interpreting inspection clause in a disputed real estate loan commitment agreement application of "clearly erroneous" standard was appropriate in reviewing the court's resolution of the dispute. **Kennedy Associates, Inc. v. Fischer,** Op. No. 2700, 667 P2d 174 (Alaska 1983).

Since arbitrator's exclusion of witness did not lead to the complete omission of critical evidence, party was afforded his right to a fair hearing, at most, one form of argument was closed off by the arbitrator, the argument itself was not; accordingly, trial court's conclusion that it was gross error for the arbitrator to exclude the witness was clearly erroneous. **City of Fairbanks Mun. Util. System v. Lees,** Op. No. 2977, 705 P2d 457 (Alaska 1985).

Findings of fact by trial court will not be overturned unless clearly erroneous. **Weason v. Harville,** Op. No. 2980, 706 P2d 306 (Alaska 1985).

Whether the parties to an informal agreement became bound prior to the drafting and execution of contemplated formal writings was a question of intent reviewable under the clearly erroneous standard. **Juliano v. Angelini,** Op. No. 2994,708 P2d 1289 (Alaska 1985).

On appeal the Alaska supreme court will intervene only when convinced that the trial court's findings of fact are "clearly erroneous." **State v. Northwestern Const., Inc.,** Op. No. 3204, 741 P2d 235 (Alaska 1987).

Factual findings are reversed only if clearly erroneous; to find a trial court's factual findings clearly erroneous, the court must have a definite and firm conviction that a mistake has been made. **Donnybrook Bldg. Supply v. Interior City,** Op. No. 3637, 798 P2d 1263 (Alaska 1990).

In a property division case, the trial court's valuation of available property is usually a factual determination to be upset on appeal only if there is clear error. **Doyle v. Doyle,** Op. No. 3723, 815 P2d 366 (Alaska 1991).

In divorce action, trial court's decision to place a value of zero on certain business realty, rather than taking into account the negative equity in the property, was not error. **Mack v. Mack,** Op. No. 3746, 816 P2d 197 (Alaska 1991).

Failure of trial court to issue findings of fact when it denied motion to modify divorce decree did not require remand. **Olson v. Olson,** Op. No. 3975, 856 P2d 482 (Alaska 1993).

Fact-specific determination was needed on issue of attorney fees to determine whether senior citizens, who brought suit against the state and its officials, had an economic interest in bringing suit, or if the suit only involved narrow issues lacking general importance. **Simpson v. Murkowski,** Op. No. 5984, 129 P.3d 435 (Alaska 2006).

PART VIII. MASTERS

Rule 53. Masters.

(a) **Appointment and Compensation.** The presiding judge of the superior court for each judicial district with the approval of the chief justice of the Supreme Court may appoint one or more standing masters for such district, and the court in which any action is pending may appoint a special master therein. As used in these rules the word "master" includes a referee, an auditor and an examiner, and a magistrate or a deputy magistrate. The compensation, if any, to be allowed to a master shall be fixed by the court, and shall be charged upon such of the parties or paid out of any fund or subject matter of the action which is in the custody and control of the court, as the court may direct. The master shall not retain the master's report as security for compensation; but when the party ordered to pay the compensation allowed by the court does not pay it after notice and within the time prescribed by the court, the master is entitled to a writ of execution against the delinquent party.

(b) **Powers.** The order of reference to the master may specify or limit the master's powers and may direct the master to report only upon particular issues or to do or perform particular acts or to receive and report evidence only and may fix the time and place for beginning and closing the hearings and for the filing of the master's report. Subject to the specifications and limitations stated in the order, the master has and shall exercise the power to regulate all proceedings in every hearing before the master and to do all acts and take all measures necessary or proper for the efficient performance of the master's duties under the order. The master may require the production of evidence upon all matters embraced in the reference, including the production of all books, papers, vouchers, documents, and writings applicable thereto. The master may rule upon the admissibility of evidence unless otherwise directed by the order of reference and has the authority to put witnesses on oath and may examine them and may call the parties to the action and examine them upon oath. When a party so requests, the master shall make a record of the evidence offered and excluded in the same manner and subject to the same limitations as provided in Evidence Rule 103(b) for a court sitting without a jury.

(c) **Proceedings.**

(1) *Meetings.* When a reference is made, the clerk shall forthwith furnish the master with a copy of the order of reference. Upon receipt thereof unless the order of reference otherwise provides, the master shall forthwith set a time and place for the first meeting of the parties or their attorneys to be held within 20 days after the date of the order of reference and shall notify the parties or their attorneys. It is the duty of the master to proceed with all reasonable diligence. Either party, on notice to the parties and master, may apply to the court for an order requiring the master to speed the proceedings and to make the report. If a party fails to appear at the time and place

appointed, the master may proceed ex parte or, in the master's discretion, adjourn the proceedings to a future day, giving notice to the absent party of the adjournment.

(2) *Witnesses.* The parties may procure the attendance of witnesses before the master by the issuance and service of subpoenas as provided in Rule 45. If without adequate excuse a witness fails to appear or give evidence, the witness may be punished for a contempt and be subjected to the consequences, penalties and remedies provided in Rules 37 and 45.

(3) *Statement of Accounts.* When matters of accounting are in issue before the master, the master may prescribe the form in which the accounts shall be submitted and in any proper case may require or receive in evidence a statement by a certified public accountant who is called as a witness. Upon objection of a party to any of the items thus submitted or upon a showing that the form of statement is insufficient, the master may require a different form of statement to be furnished, or the accounts or specific items thereof to be proved by oral examination of the accounting parties or upon written interrogatories or in such other manner as the master directs.

(d) **Report.**

(1) *Contents and Filing.* The master shall prepare a report upon the matters submitted to the master by the order of reference and, if required to make findings of fact and conclusions of law, the master shall set them forth in the report. The master shall file the report with the clerk of the court and in an action to be tried without a jury, unless otherwise directed by the order of reference, shall file with it a transcript of the proceedings and of the evidence and the original exhibits. The clerk shall forthwith mail to all parties notice of the filing.

(2) *In Non-Jury Actions.* In an action to be tried without a jury the court shall accept the master's findings unless clearly erroneous. Within 10 days after being served with notice of the filing of the report any party may serve written objections thereto upon the other parties. Application to the court for an action upon the report and upon objections thereto shall be by motion and upon notice as prescribed in Rule 77. The court may adopt the report or may modify it or may reject it in whole or in part or may receive further evidence or may recommit it with instructions.

(3) *In Jury Actions.* In an action to be tried by a jury the master shall not be directed to report the evidence. The master's findings upon the issues submitted to the master are admissible as evidence of the matters found and may be read to the jury, subject to the ruling of the court upon any objections in point of law which may be made to the report.

(4) *Stipulation as to Findings.* The effect of a master's report is the same whether or not the parties have consented to the reference; but, when the parties stipulate that a master's findings of fact shall be final, only questions of law arising upon the report shall thereafter be considered.

(5) *Draft Report.* Before filing the master's report a master may submit a draft thereof to counsel for all parties for the purpose of receiving their suggestions.

(6) *Report of Magistrate or Deputy Magistrate.* Where a magistrate or a deputy magistrate has been appointed a standing or special master for any purpose, the master's report shall include such findings of fact, transcript of evidence or proceedings and recommendations as may have been requested by the superior court in its order of reference.

(Adopted by SCO 5 October 9, 1959; amended by SCO 358 effective March 22, 1979; by SCO 888 effective July 15, 1988, by SCO 1096 effective January 15, 1993; and by SCO 1153 effective July 15, 1994)

Annotations

Cases

It is within the proper scope of a master's functions and powers to determine the assets and liabilities of a public utility district annexed by a city, when he is authorized only to make investigations, find facts, and make reports to the court. **Fairview PUD v. City of Anchorage and Hawk v. Fairview PUD,** Op. No. 61, 368 P2d 540 (Alaska 1962).

Where neither party applied to the court for action upon the master's report and upon the objections filed, both were equally at fault for the failure of the judge to act promptly on the report. **Hickey v. Bell,** Op. No. 209, 391 P2d 447 (Alaska 1964).

This rule was inapplicable to eminent domain proceedings. **State v. 7.536 Acres and Evenson,** Op. No. 434, 431 P2d 897 (Alaska 1967).

Where husband in divorce proceeding did not file a motion for a hearing on his objections to the master's report, the "lack of hearing" issue would not be heard on appeal. **Hinchey v. Hinchey,** Op. No. 2312, 625 P2d 297 (Alaska 1981).

While a master can, within the limits set by the clearly erroneous standard determine facts, his recommendation on the proper course of action to be taken in light of those facts is not controlling, and the superior court is free to disregard it. **Headlough v. Headlough,** Op. No. 2463, 639 P2d 1010 (Alaska 1982).

In order to raise on appeal the qualifications of an appointed master, the objecting party should object at the time the appointment is made; if this is unfeasible, the objection should be made to the appointing judge at the earliest possible opportunity. **Dean v. Firor,** Op. No. 2819, 681 P2d 321 (Alaska 1984).

In action to void certain property conveyances as fraudulent and therefore void, it was error for the trial court to allow a master to decide that a fraudulent conveyance took place. **Dean v. Firor,** Op. No. 2819, 681 P2d 321 (Alaska 1984).

Trial court, in establishing a minimum bid or "upset price" for the sale of real property at a judicial foreclosure sale, did not abuse its discretion by failing to appoint a master to hear evidence on a fair and adequate upset price. **Hayes v. Alaska USA Federal Credit Union,** Op. No. 3406, 767 P2d 1158 (Alaska 1989).

Appointment of a discovery master should generally be reserved for cases (1) where the issues are unusually complex or specialized; (2) where discovery is particularly document intensive; (3) where resolving discovery disputes will be especially time consuming; (4) where the parties are particularly contentious or obstructionist; or (5) where a master will facilitate a more speedy and economical determination of the case. **Peter v. Progressive Corp.,** Op. No. 5168, 986 P2d 865 (Alaska 1999).

Trial courts have an implied obligation under both the Civil Rules and the Alaska Constitution to consider the parties' financial status before ordering appointment of a discovery master and to choose a method of compensation that does not restrict litigants' meaningful access to discovery or, more generally, to the justice system. **Peter v. Progressive Corp.,** Op. No. 5168, 986 P2d 865 (Alaska 1999).

Appointment of a discovery master as a discovery sanction potentially runs afoul of the procedural requirements of Civil Rule 37. **Peter v. Progressive**

Corp., Op. No. 5168, 986 P2d 865 (Alaska 1999).

While the inmate's case involved claims of medical negligence, which was a specialized area, there was no indication that the trial court was unduly burdened by the specialized issues; there was no indication that any of the other factors applied, as such, the superior court's denial of the inmate's request to appoint a master was not in error. **Willoya v. State,** Op. No. 5622, 53 P.3d 1115 (Alaska 2002).

In post-divorce proceedings to establish a father's child support obligation, under Alaska R. Civ. P. 53(d)(2) the mother's failure to object to a special master's recommendation as to the amount of the father's retroactive obligation resulted in her failure to preserve for review on appeal her claim that the ordered amount was erroneous. **Duffus v. Duffus,** Op. No. 10206 72 P.3d 313 (Alaska 2003).

In a divorce action, the master erred in its calculation of the husband's annual income, where his testimony did not support finding that his 1997 income was $ 192,827; error required remand to the superior court for correction and for a modification of husband's child support obligation. **Keturi v. Keturi,** Op. No. 5774, 84 P.3d 408 (Alaska 2003).

Superior court did not err in rejecting the custody investigator's report because the custody investigator was not a standing master, whose findings were binding upon the court. **Chase v. Chase,** Op. No. 5881, 109 P.3d 942 (Alaska 2005).

PART IX. JUDGMENT

Rule 54. Judgments—Costs.

(a) **Definition—Form—Preparation and Submission.** "Judgment" as used in these rules includes a decree. A judgment shall not contain a recital of pleadings, the report of a master, or the record of prior proceedings. Judgments for the payment of money must be in the form required by Civil Rule 58.2. The procedure for the preparation and submission of proposed judgments and orders is governed by Rule 78.

(b) **Judgment Upon Multiple Claims or Involving Multiple Parties.** When more than one claim for relief is presented in an action, whether as a claim, counterclaim, cross-claim, or third-party claim, or when multiple parties are involved, the court may direct the entry of a final judgment as to one or more but fewer than all of the claims or parties only upon an express determination that there is no just reason for delay and upon an express direction for the entry of judgment. In the absence of such determination and direction, any order or other form of decision, however designated, which adjudicates fewer than all of the claims or the rights and liabilities of fewer than all the parties shall not terminate the action as to any of the claims or parties, and the order or other form of decision is subject to revision at any time before the entry of judgment adjudicating all the claims and the rights and liabilities of all the parties.

(c) **Demand for Judgment.** A default judgment shall not be different in kind from or exceed in amount that prayed for in the demand for judgment. Except as to a party against whom a default judgment is entered, every final judgment shall grant the relief to which the party in whose favor it is rendered is entitled, even if the party has not demanded such relief in the pleadings.

(d) **Costs.** Except when express provision therefor is made either in a statute of the state or in these rules, costs shall be allowed as of course to the prevailing party unless the court otherwise directs. The procedure for the taxing of costs by the clerk and review of the clerk's action by the court shall be governed by Rule 79.

(Adopted by SCO 5 October 9, 1959; amended by SCO 258 effective November 15, 1976; by SCO 554 effective April 4, 1983; by SCO 1153 effective July 15, 1994; and by SCO 1415 effective October 15, 2000)

Note: AS 25.24.150(f), 25.24.155, and 25.24.160(c), added by ch. 76. §§ 1–3, SLA 1991, amended Civil Rule 54(b) by prohibiting the separation of claims in an action for divorce or an action declaring a marriage void without compliance with AS 25.24.155, as added by ch. 76, § 2, SLA 1991.

Cross References

(d) **CROSS REFERENCE:** AS 09.60.050

Annotations

Cases

I. In General.
II. Multiple Claims or Parties.
III. Demand for Judgment.
  A. Default.
  B. Pleadings.
IV. Costs.

I. In General.

Judgment on the pleadings or summary judgment should be given only when there is no genuine issue as to any material fact and when the merits can be determined in that way. **Mitchell v. Land,** Op. No. 19, 355 P2d 682 (Alaska 1960).

Under the definition in Civil Rule 54(a), a memorandum opinion will be regarded as a judgment, though not formally a judgment or so labeled, where it clearly evidences the trial judge's intent to presently and finally dispose of the matter at issue. **Patrick v. Sedwick,** Op. No. 154, 387 P2d 294 (Alaska 1963).

The denial of a motion to vacate the judgment of dismissal of appellant's complaint was a judgment from which an appeal lies. **Gravel v. Alaskan Village, Inc.,** Op. No. 321, 409 P2d 983 (Alaska 1966).

Order of superior court acting pursuant to stipulation, the effect of which was to dismiss with prejudice plaintiff's causes of action, was a "judgment" as that term has been defined in these rules. **Albritton v. Estate of Larson,** Op. No. 413, 428 P2d 379 (Alaska 1967).

The purpose of this rule is to encourage settlement of civil litigation as well as to avoid protracted litigation. **Miklautsch v. Dominick,** Op. No. 538, 452 P2d 438 (Alaska 1969).

A partial summary judgment entered in favor of the plaintiff on a conversion count, in an action by a seller of property to a bank against the buyer from the bank for conversion of property allegedly not included in plaintiff's sale to the bank, and for breach of contract, is appealable in light of an unusual fact situation together with the fact that a money judgment was entered against the defendant with execution being stayed pending determination of the case on appeal, even though neither party raised the issue of finality before the lower court or on review, and the judgment did not note that there was no reason for delay. **Braund, Inc. v. White,** Op. No. 693, 486 P2d 50 (Alaska 1971).

In ascertaining the intention of the court all parts of the judgment must be examined; the judgment is to be read in its entirety, construed as a whole, and are to be given that interpretation which will render them reasonable, effective, conclusive and in harmony with the facts and law of the case. **Pennington v. Employer's Liability Assurance Corporation,** Op. No. 1023, 520 P2d 96 (Alaska 1974).

Although a trial court has not complied with this rule, the Supreme Court may take jurisdiction of the case if the interests of justice so require.

Domer v. Sleeper, Op. No. 1128, 533 P2d 9 (Alaska 1975).

Judgments entered under this rule are final for res judicata purposes. **Vertecs Corp. v. Reichhold Chemicals, Inc.,** Op. No. 2730, 671 P2d 1273 (Alaska 1983).

In case involving state adverse possession claim under color of title, factual issue was present as to whether the state had an honest and reasonable belief in the validity of the title, thus precluding summary judgment. **Ault v. State,** Op. No. 2878, 688 P2d 951 (Alaska 1984).

Trial judge correctly used the power of the trial court to revise or reverse interlocutory rulings deemed erroneous, despite contention that he was bound by the doctrine of law of the case. **C.J.M. Const. v. Chandler Plumbing,** Op. No. 2963, 708 P2d 60 (Alaska 1985).

Failure to immediately appeal interlocutory order awarding interim maintenance to spouse did not waive right to raise propriety of that award on appeal of final decree of divorce. **Johnson v. Johnson,** Op. No. 3867, 836 P2d 930 (Alaska 1992).

No orders in liquidation or receivership are applicable as of right until receivership action is terminated, unless trial court certifies issue under this rule. **Matter of Pacific Marine Ins. Co.,** Op. No. 4100, 877 P2d 264 (Alaska 1994).

A party taking an early appeal in circumstances where there is uncertainty as to whether a final judgment exists does not thereby lose the right to appeal, thus father, who appealed April 17, 1998 judgment for child support arrearages when in fact the final appealable judgment in the matter was an October 27, 1998 judgment ordering him to pay prospective child support, was treated as if his appeal had been taken after the October 27, 1998 judgment. **Spott v. Spott,** Op. No. 5361, 17 P3d 52 (Alaska 2001).

Argument that final judgment under this rule against claimants in their individual capacity was procedurally flawed for lack of express factual finding was rendered moot by true final judgment entered three months later against claimants in their corporate capacity. **Garrison v. Dixon,** Op. No. 5378, 19 P3d 1229 (Alaska 2001).

Trial court's order permitting writs of execution to issue on a partial money judgment was vacated; because the court permitted execution without first certifying that there was no just reason for delay, the judgment was not final. **Bradley v. Bradley,** Op. No. 5476, 32 P3d 372 (Alaska 2001).

Alaska Supreme Court requests the Alaska Appellate Rules Committee to recommend amendments to the Alaska Appellate Rules that will ensure early identification of appeals from judgments entered under Alaska R. Civ. P. 54(b) and enable the supreme court to require preliminary briefing and resolution of questions concerning the appropriateness of the partial judgments at issue in such cases. To prevent uncontested but arguably improvident partial final judgments from continuing to evade appellate review, the Alasaka Supreme Court requests the Appellate Rules Committee to recommend amendments to the Appellate Rules that would ensure early identification of appeals from judgments entered under section (b) of this rule and enable the court to require preliminary briefing and resolution of questions concerning the appropriateness of the partial judgments at issue in such cases. **Cole v. State Farm Ins. Co.,** Op. No. 5978, 128 P.3d 171 (Alaska 2006).

II. Multiple Claims or Parties.

A judgment under Rule 54(b) should contain an express determination that there is no just reason for delay and an express direction for the entry of judgment, both of which are requisites for finality of judgment from which an appeal can be taken. But when in the exercise of a sound discretion the Supreme Court finds the policy permitting appeals only from final decisions to be outweighed by the need for early consideration of a non-appealable order, the court has the authority to review such order or decision of the superior court, regardless of the concept of finality. **Jefferson v. Spenard Builder's Supply, Inc.,** Op. No. 51, 366 P2d 714 (Alaska 1961).

In determining the time within which an appeal may be taken, the term "entry of judgment" as it applies to trials by jury, is set forth in Civ. R. 58. **Vogt v. Winbauer,** Op. No. 117, 376 P2d 1007 (Alaska 1962).

Fact that prayers for relief as to counterclaim in a previous action and for relief in the complaint in subsequent action between parties were not the same could not be a criterion in determining whether the claims for relief were the same. **Wells v. Noey,** Op. No. 286, 399 P2d 217 (Alaska 1965).

Statutory language giving a declaratory judgment the force of a final judgment and making it reviewable as such does not change the effect of this rule's provision that when multiple claims for relief are involved in an action, partial summary judgment may be entered as to one or more, but fewer than all of the claims or parties only upon the express determination that there is no just reason for delay, and upon express direction by the court for the entry of judgment. **Alaska Airlines, Inc. v. Red Dodge Aviation, Inc.,** Op. No. 640, 475 P2d 229 (Alaska 1970).

Where an order of final judgment incorporates language of an earlier interlocutory order which is supported with necessary findings of fact and conclusions of law, no prejudice results from a lack of findings and conclusions to support the entry of partial judgment. **Moran v. Kenai Towing and Salvage, Inc.,** Op. No. 1056, 523 P2d 1237 (Alaska 1974).

In order to activate Civil Rule 54(b), the trial court must find "no just reason for delay," and such finding should be premised on considerations similar to those governing the Supreme Court's exercise of discretion in considering petitions for review from interlocutory orders under Appellate Rules 23 and 24. **Johnson v. State,** Op. No. 1609, 577 P2d 706 (Alaska 1978).

Use of Civil Rule 54(b) was not appropriate where neither party would suffer any appreciable hardship if review awaited the final determination of the case. **Johnson v. State,** Op. No. 1609, 577 P2d 706 (Alaska 1978).

Although an order adjudicating liability but leaving damages to be subsequently determined generally lacks finality, an exception to this rule arises when it appears that one of the parties would otherwise be subjected to irreparable injury. **Aleutian Region R.E.A.A. v. Wolansky,** Op. No. 2380, 630 P2d 529 (Alaska 1981).

Trial court did not abuse its discretion under this rule in finding no just reason for delay and in directing a final judgment against convicted intentional killer on his action for negligence and breach of warranty against the manufacturer and distributor of the firearm used in the killing. **Adkinson v. Rossi Arms Co.,** Op. No. 2631, 659 P2d 1236 (Alaska 1983).

Summary judgment order dismissing plaintiff's cause of action as to the Borough, but not as to the state of Alaska, could not have been appealed until plaintiff's motion for entry of final judgment was granted, at which time the 30-day appeal period began to run. **Kanayurak v. North Slope Borough,** Op. No. 2782, 677 P2d 893 (Alaska 1984).

Court rule providing that judgment on one issue in a multi-issue case is not a final judgment unless expressly designated as such by the trial court applies to cases which contain multiple issues only because of consolidation. **Currington v. Johnson,** Op. No. 2828, 685 P2d 73 (Alaska 1984).

Although summary judgment was granted in favor of only two of four defendants, and the trial court's order with respect to the other two was not appealable, appellate court decided sua sponte to treat plaintiff's appeal from the order as a petition for review and to grant the same in order to prevent unnecessary delay. **Kendall v. State, Div. of Corrections,** Op. No. 2890, 692 P2d 953 (Alaska 1984).

A partial summary judgment that decides only some of the issues pertinent to a single claim is interlocutory and therefore not within the scope of the trial court's authority under this rule to direct the entry of final judgment as to one or more but fewer than all of the claims for relief in actions involving more than one claim for relief. **Zeilinger v. Standard Alaska Petroleum Company (Mem.),** 769 P2d 436 (Alaska 1989).

Trial court did not abuse its discretion in entering a final judgment against mining company and individual partner even though action against corporate partner's principal and joint venture was still pending. **S & B Min. Co. v. Northern Commercial Co.,** Op. No. 3697, 813 P2d 264 (Alaska 1991).

If action involves multiple claims or multiple parties, and some claims are adjudicated before others, no appeal may be taken until court has disposed of entire case on all substantive issues, except as provided under this rule. **Patterson v. State, Dept. of Agriculture,** Op. No. 4108, 880 P2d 1038 (Alaska 1994).

In action involving multiple claims and multiple parties, grant of permission to file late appeal of final judgment as to one claim constituted permission to file late appeal of all claims. **Patterson v. State, Dept. of Agriculture,** Op. No. 4108, 880 P2d 1038 (Alaska 1994).

An entry of judgment under Rule 54(b) is reviewed for an abuse of discretion. **Williams v. Mammoth of Alaska, Inc.,** Op. No. 4174, 890 P2d 581 (Alaska 1995).

Rule 19 expressly pertains only to joinder of parties, not to dismissal of parties through a Rule 54(b) judgment. **Williams v. Mammoth of Alaska, Inc.,** Op. No. 4174,890 P2d 581 (Alaska 1995).

The superior court should not grant a Rule 54(b) judgment merely because a party requests one. Typically, use of Rule 54(b) is appropriate only if the party seeking judgment is likely to suffer actual hardship otherwise. **Williams v. Mammoth of Alaska, Inc.,** Op. No. 4174, 890 P2d 581 (Alaska 1995).

Trial court did not err in entering a Rule 54(b) judgment as to two defendants when proceedings against third defendant had to be stayed pending that defendant's bankruptcy proceedings. **Williams v. Mammoth of Alaska, Inc.,** Op. No. 4174, 890 P2d 581 (Alaska 1995).

Potential delay in collecting judgment because proceedings against primary obligors were stayed by bankruptcy proceedings was properly considered by court in entering final judgment against only one party in multiple party case. **Bradford v. First National Bank of Anchorage,** Op. No. 4786, 932 P2d 256 (Alaska 1997).

Where a corporation and its owner had appealed from a judgment in favor of two companies on the corporation and its owner's claims but there was no appeal from the judgment in favor of the companies on their counterclaims, the partial reversal of the judgment appealed from did not render the judgment on the counterclaim non-final; hence, the companies were not obligated to obtain a judgment under Alaska R. Civ. P. 54(b) before attempting to enforce the judgment on the counterclaims. **Hikita v. Nichiro Gyogyo Kaisha, Ltd.,** Op. No. 5780, 85 P.3d 458 (Alaska 2004).

III. Demand for Judgment.

A. Default.

Rule 54(c) is an absolute ban against the entry of any judgment by default which is different in kind from that prayed for, and a judgment entered in violation of the rule is clearly erroneous and invalid. **Oaks v. Grocers Wholesale,** Op. No. 123, 377 P2d 1001 (Alaska 1963).

The purpose of Civ. R. 54(c) is to limit the relief granted in a default judgment, and that purpose can be effected only if the prayer for relief is sufficiently specific. **Oaks v. Grocers Wholesale,** Op. No. 123, 377 P2d 1001 (Alaska 1963).

Relief which may be granted in judgment by default is determined by the demand for judgment and not by the complaint as a whole. **Oaks v. Grocers Wholesale,** Op. No. 123, 377 P2d 1001 (Alaska 1963).

The entry of a default judgment and the refusal to set aside a default judgment are reviewed for abuse of discretion. An abuse of discretion is found only where we are left with "a definite and firm conviction, after reviewing the whole record, that the trial court erred in its ruling. **Hicks v. Pleasants**, Op. No. 12110, 158 P.3d 817 (Alaska 2007).

In order for a default judgment to comply with subsection (c) of this rule, a complaint must give a defendant adequate notice upon which to make an informed judgment on whether to default or actively defend. **Hicks v. Pleasants**, Op. No. 12110, 158 P.3d 817 (Alaska 2007).

In order for a default judgment to comply with Alaska R. Civ P. 54(c), a complaint must give a defendant adequate notice upon which to make an informed judgment on whether to default or actively defend. **Hicks v. Pleasants**, Op. No. 12110, 158 P.3d 817 (Alaska 2007).

B. Pleadings.

In the one form of action procedure under the [Federal] Rules of Civil Procedure, the parties should be granted the relief to which they are entitled irrespective of the theory of their pleadings, and a court is not justified in depriving a party of his rights because he mistakes the nature of his remedy. **Mitchell v. Land,** Op. No. 19, 355 P2d 682 (Alaska 1960).

Where a claim is stated by a complaint, even though it does not demand the relief to which the plaintiffs are entitled, the complaint should not be dismissed, but plaintiffs should be denied relief only when, under the facts proved, they are entitled to none. **Miller v. Johnson,** Op. No. 70, 370 P2d 171 (Alaska 1962).

Trial court was justified in affording complete relief to plaintiff in divorce action, even though plaintiff had not specifically prayed for such relief. **Rhodes v. Rhodes,** Op. No. 83, 370 P2d 902 (Alaska 1962).

Where the demand for judgment in a complaint did not ask for a money judgment against defendant, but only a foreclosure and sale of mortgaged property, a money judgment against him could not properly be entered under Civ. R. 54(c). **Oaks v. Grocers Wholesale,** Op. No. 123, 377 P2d 1001 (Alaska 1962).

Where complaint demanded only a foreclosure and sale of mortgaged property, the addition of the words "such other relief as may seem meet and just" does not meet the requirements of Rule 54(c) and a money judgment could not properly be entered. **Oaks v. Grocers Wholesale,** Op. No. 123, 377 P2d 1001 (Alaska 1962).

Under Civil Rule 54(c) the court was required to enter judgment for the relief to which the prevailing party was entitled, and it was error to limit the judgment to the amount of damages demanded in the complaint. **Wilson v. Interior Airways, Inc.,** Op. No. 151, 384 P2d 956 (Alaska 1963).

Where plaintiffs' complaint in quiet title action asked to be declared owners of property free of any payment obligation, but their default judgment request was to be declared owners of property upon payment to defendant of $28,231, trial court's exclusion of payment provision in default judgment on ground that payment to defendant has not been pleaded was error; default judgment providing less extensive relief than requested in complaint does not violate this rule. **Melendrez v. Bode,** Op. No. 4856, 941 P2d 1254 (Alaska 1997).

Party to a divorce could make a general claim that the court "adjudicate the assets and liabilities in a fair and equitable manner" without listing individual items and the court could equitably divide the assets and debts of the parties in a default context where the parties were both aware of the property subject to division, the responding party knew that the petitioner sought a division of that property. **Hicks v. Pleasants**, Op. No. 12110, 158 P.3d 817 (Alaska 2007).

IV. Costs.

Prevailing party within the meaning of this rule is the one in whose favor the decision or verdict is rendered and judgment entered even though not to the extent of the original contention. **Buza v. Columbia Lumber Company,** Op. No. 254, 395 P2d 511 (Alaska 1964).

Allowance of costs for attorney's fees is a matter governed by Rules of Civil Procedure promulgated by the Supreme Court pursuant to constitutional rulemaking authority. **McDonough v. Lee,** Op. No. 378, 420 P2d 459 (Alaska 1966).

Even if it may be assumed that appellants were "prevailing party" within the meaning of Civil Rules 54(d) and 82(a)(1), the trial court's determination as to denial of attorney's costs where the action was settled pursuant to Civil Rule 68 was not disturbed on appeal in the absence of a showing of clear abuse of the wide discretion allowed under this rule. **Albritton v. Estate of Larson,** Op. No. 413, 428 P2d 379 (Alaska 1967).

Even though there has not been a final determination on the merits in the case, where the complaint has been dismissed for failure to comply with an order to produce corporate records, the defendant is the "prevailing party," and as such is entitled to attorney fees and costs. **Hart v. Wolff,** Op. No. 724,489 P2d 114 (Alaska 1971).

Where defendant defeated plaintiff's claim for $119,663 in damages, incidental recovery by plaintiff of $7,363 did not bar defendant from being considered the prevailing party. **Owen Jones & Sons, Inc. v. C.R. Lewis Co.,** Op. No. 795, 497 P2d 312 (Alaska 1972).

The determination of which party prevails and is entitled to costs is within the discretion of the trial judge. **Owen Jones & Sons, Inc. v. C. R. Lewis Co., Inc.,** Op. No. 795, 497 P2d 312 (Alaska 1972).

The determination of which party prevails and is entitled to costs is within the discretion of the trial judge. **DeWitt v. Liberty Leasing Co. of Alaska,** Op. No. 818, 499 P2d 599 (Alaska 1972).

Where a defendant receives a judgment of over seventeen thousand dollars on a counterclaim and suffers an offset of under one hundred dollars, the trial court's ruling that neither party prevailed is manifestly unreasonable. **DeWitt v. Liberty Leasing Co. of Alaska,** Op. No. 818, 499 P2d 599 (Alaska 1972).

A party is not barred from appealing from the disallowance of costs and attorney's fees by his acceptance of payment of the judgment and by signing a document entitled "Satisfaction of Judgment." **DeWitt v. Liberty Leasing Co. of Alaska,** Op. No. 818, 499 P2d 599 (Alaska 1972).

A party may be the "prevailing party" within this rule if he is successful with regard to the main issues in the action. **Cooperv. Carlson,** Op. No. 907, 511 P2d 1305 (Alaska 1973).

A successful defendant may be a "prevailing party" within the meaning of this rule. **Malvo v. J. C. Penney Co., Inc.,** Op. No. 901, 512 P2d 575 (Alaska 1973).

A party does not have to prevail on all of the issues in a case to be a "prevailing party" within this rule. **Malvo v. J. C. Penney Co., Inc.,** Op. No. 901, 512 P2d 575 (Alaska 1973).

The prevailing party in each case should not automatically be awarded the full amount of attorney fees incurred. **Malvo v. J. C. Penney Co., Inc.,** Op. No. 901, 512 P2d 575 (Alaska 1973).

Plaintiffs are entitled to an award for attorney's fees incurred to the date of offer of judgment, even though the judgment awarded is less than the offer. **Jakoski v. Holland,** Op. No. 1015, 520 P2d 569 (Alaska 1974).

In ascertaining the amount of attorney's fees to be allowed a defendant successful in holding a verdict to less than his offer, the judge should use the same general criteria used in cases where the defendant is the prevailing party. **Jakoski v. Holland,** Op. No. 1015, 520 P2d 569 (Alaska 1974).

The trial court does not abuse its discretion in awarding $6,250 as attorney's fees to a defendant for services rendered after the date of an offer of judgment of $25,000, despite the fact that plaintiffs first asked for a verdict of $545,000, where the verdict rendered is less than the offer. **Jakoski v. Holland,** Op. No. 1015, 520 P2d 569 (Alaska 1974).

Where the defendants in litigation stemming from a contested gubernatorial election were the state and the primary winners, it was proper to award costs against the state as a co-prevailing party since the litigation was caused by the irregularities of state election officials in the conduct of the election. **Thomas v. Croft,** Op. No. 2135, 614 P2d 795 (Alaska 1980).

Where a judgment on offer and acceptance was signed January 18, but the action was not dismissed by court order until July 24, a request by counsel filed August 1 for a hearing on the amount of attorney fees was timely, July 24 being the proper date from which the request period should have been calculated. **Salmine v. Knagin,** Op. No. 2501, 645 P2d 148 (Alaska 1982).

Absent the discretionary imposition by the trial court of a time limit for the filing of attorney's fees, the appropriate time within which a request for attorney's fees may be filed is a reasonable time after the entry of a judgment from which an appeal may be taken. **Brunet v. Dresser Olympic,** Op. No. 2641, 660 P2d 846 (Alaska 1983).

The Civil Rules do not preclude a party from requesting attorney's fees following the entry of an interlocutory judgment. **Brunet v. Dresser Olympic,** Op. No. 2641, 660 P2d 846 (Alaska 1983).

Trial court did not abuse its discretion by awarding attorney fees to the prevailing party without first requesting an itemization. **Knight v. Amer. Guard & Alert, Inc.,** Op. No. 3021,714 P2d 788 (Alaska 1986).

Expert witness fees in excess of state limits were proper where awarded pursuant to a federal act, 15 U.S.C. § 2310, rather than state law. **Universal Motors, Inc., v. Waldock,** Op. No. 3060, 719 P2d 254 (Alaska 1986).

Rule 55. Default.

(a) **Entry.**

(1) *Application for Default.* When a party against whom a judgment for affirmative relief is sought has failed to appear and answer or otherwise defend as provided by these rules, and that fact is shown by affidavit or otherwise, the clerk shall enter a default. Service of the application is not required if the party has failed to appear.

(2) *When Service Required.* A party who appears but fails to answer or otherwise defend may be defaulted by the clerk not less than three days following service of the application for default.

(b) **Judgment by the Clerk.**

(1) *Failure to Appear.* If the defendant has been defaulted for failure to appear and the plaintiff's claim(s) is for a sum certain or for a sum that can by computation be made certain, upon the filing of an application for default judgment including an affidavit of the amount due which also states that the person against whom judgment is sought is: (i) not an infant or an incompetent person; and (ii) not a member of the Armed Forces of the United States protected by the Service members Civil Relief Act (50 App. U.S.C. § 521), as amended, the clerk shall enter default judgment for the amount due and costs and attorney's fees against the defendant.

(2) *Multiple Parties or Claims.* The clerk may not enter a default judgment in a case involving multiple defendants unless all defendants have been defaulted.

(c) **Judgment by the Court.**

(1) In all other cases the party entitled to a default judgment shall apply to the court therefor; but no default judgment shall be entered against an infant or incompetent person unless represented in the action by a general guardian, committee, conservator, or other such representative who has appeared therein. If the party against whom default judgment is sought has appeared in the action, that party (or, if appearing by representative, the party's representative) shall be served with written notice of the application for judgment at least three days prior to a decision on the application. This written notice requirement and the memorandum requirement of (c)(2) do not apply if the party fails to appear for trial in which case the court may proceed ex parte upon any motion for default or default judgment. If, in order to enable the court to enter judgment or to carry it into effect, it is necessary to take an account or to determine the amount of damages or to establish the truth of any averment by evidence or to make an investigation of any other matter, the court may conduct such hearings or order such references as it deems necessary and proper.

(2) When application is made to the court for a default judgment, counsel shall file a memorandum of the default, showing when and against what parties it was entered and the

pleadings to which no defense has been made. If any party against whom default judgment is sought is shown by the record to be an infant or incompetent person, or in the military service of the United States, counsel shall also file a memorandum stating whether or not that person is represented in the action by a general guardian, committee, conservator, attorney or such other representative who has appeared therein. If the party against whom default judgment is sought has appeared in the action or proceeding, the memorandum shall also indicate whether or not the record shows that notice has been served as required by paragraph (1) of this subdivision.

(3) If the amount of damages claimed in an application to the court for default judgment is unliquidated, the applicant may submit evidence by affidavit showing the amount of damages and if, under the provisions of paragraph (1) of this subdivision, notice of the application is necessary, the parties against whom judgment is sought may submit affidavits in opposition.

(4) If the case involves multiple defendants and all defendants have not been defaulted, the court may not enter a default judgment unless the nondefaulting defendant's defenses would not be available to the defaulting defendant. A default judgment issued under such circumstances is nevertheless subject to Civil Rule 54(b).

(d) **Response to Pleading.** A party may respond to any pleading at any time before a default is entered.

(e) **Setting Aside Default.** For good cause shown the court may set aside an entry of default and, if a default judgment has been entered, may likewise set it aside in accordance with Rule 60(b).

(f) **Plaintiffs, Counterclaimants, Cross-Claimants.** The provisions of this rule apply whether the party entitled to the default judgment is a plaintiff, a third-party plaintiff, or a party who has pleaded a cross-claim or counterclaim. In all cases a default judgment is subject to the limitations of Rule 54(c).

(g) **Judgment Against the State.** No default judgment shall be entered against the state or an officer or agency thereof unless the claimant establishes the claim or right to relief by evidence satisfactory to the court.

(h) **Costs and Attorney Fees.** To recover costs and attorney fees, a party entitled to entry of default judgment without the need for further hearing under (c)(1) must include in the application for default judgment (1) an itemized statement of costs incurred in the action and allowable under Civil Rule 79(f), and (2) the party's actual attorney's fees. In such case, no cost bill or motion for attorney's fees is required. Civil Rule 82(b)(4) governs the amount of attorney's fees that may be awarded in a default case.

(i) **Proposed Judgment.** An application for default judgment must be accompanied by a proposed judgment in the form required by Civil Rule 58.2.

(Adopted by SCO 5 October 9, 1959; amended by SCO 30 effective February 1, 1961; by SCO 498 effective January 18, 1982; by SCO 554 effective April 4, 1983; by SCO 787 effective March 1, 1987; by SCO 1415 effective October 15, 2000; and by SCO 1584 effective October 15, 2005)

Annotations

Cases

Where a party has appeared in an action, he is entitled to notice of an application for default judgment against him, and its absence is ground for setting aside a default judgment. **Jefferson v. Spenard Builder's Supply, Inc.,** Op. No. 51, 366 P2d 714 (Alaska 1961).

Even if an answer is not timely mailed, the court may set aside a default in its discretion, if it appears that the delay was due to excusable neglect and that the answer raises a meritorious defense, or if the court finds that the equities of the case warrant such relief. **Jefferson v. Spenard Builder's Supply, Inc.,** Op. No. 51, 366 P2d 714 (Alaska 1961).

Relief which may be granted in judgment by default is determined by the demand for judgment, and not by the complaint as a whole. **Oaks v. Grocers Wholesale,** Op. No. 123, 377 P2d 1001 (Alaska 1962).

Where the demand for judgment in a complaint did not ask for a money judgment against defendant, but only a foreclosure and sale of mortgaged property, a money judgment against him could not properly be entered under Civ. R. 54(c). **Oaks v. Grocers Wholesale,** Op. No. 123, 377 P2d 1001 (Alaska 1962).

Where complaint demanded only a foreclosure and sale of mortgaged property, the addition of the words "such other relief as may seem meet and just" does not meet the requirements of Rule 54(c) and a money judgment could not properly be entered. **Oaks v. Grocers Wholesale,** Op. No. 123, 377 P2d 1001 (Alaska 1962).

The courts as a general rule will require that a meritorious defense be shown before setting aside a default judgment, but that rule has no application where there is no authority to enter a default judgment which is different in kind from that prayed for. **Oaks v. Grocers Wholesale,** Op. No. 123, 377 P2d 1001 (Alaska 1962).

Where affiant had shown that he had requested his case to be heard on the 19th or 20th of the month and the calendar clerk advised "this could probably be arranged," but affiant could show no effort to follow through on the request, and the case was heard on the 16th of the month, the trial judge did not abuse his discretion in refusing to set aside the default. **Alaska Truck Transport v. Inter-Alaska Credit Service,** Op. No. 266, 397 P2d 618 (Alaska 1965).

Where party against whom judgment for default is sought, has appeared in the action, notice of application for default must be given in accordance with this rule. **Sanuita v. Hedberg,** Op. No. 296, 404 P2d 647 (Alaska 1965).

This rule must be construed to mean that the court may set aside a default only if good cause is shown, but may not set aside a default in an absence of such showing. **Sanuita v. Hedberg,** Op. No. 296, 404 P2d 647 (Alaska 1965).

On appellate review of an order denying a motion to set aside an appeal, the test as to abuse of discretion is if the judge could have justifiably concluded that good cause was not shown or if the Supreme Court was left with the definite and firm conviction on the whole of the record that the judge had made a mistake in concluding that there was no showing of good cause and in the latter case it would be required to reverse and order the default set aside. **Sanuita v. Hedberg,** Op. No. 296, 404 P2d 647 (Alaska 1965).

Justice was best served by setting aside the default and the default judgment, where appellants had filed entry of appearance and a demand for jury trial in propria persona within a day or two after the 20-day period for answering had expired, and this technical default was due to lack of familiarity with rules of procedure and not to gross negligence or lack of good faith, and nearly four years had elapsed between the date the default was entered and the date the default judgment was entered. **Sanuita v. Hedberg,** Op. No. 296, 404 P2d 647 (Alaska 1965).

Where uncontroverted affidavit in support of motion under this rule suggested that the wrong person had been billed for certain work, case was remanded for vacating default and default judgment and for disposition on the merits. **Guard v. Benson,** Op. No. 460, 438 P2d 219 (Alaska 1968).

The affidavit of the amount due contemplated by this rule may be executed by the plaintiff or by plaintiff's attorney as illustrated by forms 98 and 99 provided for use with these rules. **Guard v. Benson,** Op. No. 460, 438 P2d 219 (Alaska 1968).

Where the court, upon the defendant's failure to appear, does not give three days' notice prior to entering a default, but rather allows the trial to commence in the defendant's absence, the defendant does not lose his right to a jury trial by waiver through default or by failing to appear. **Hill v. Vetter,** Op. No. 1067, 525 P2d 529 (Alaska 1974).

Entry of default judgment without hearing does not deny due process. **Allen v. Bussell,** Op. No. 1353, 558 P2d 496 (Alaska 1976).

Refusal of trial court to vacate default judgment against defendant was error where defendant alleged a meritorious defense and made a showing of excusable neglect due to illness and difficulty in obtaining counsel for her failure to answer the summons on time. **Gregor v. Hodges,** Op. No. 2110, 612 P2d 1008 (Alaska 1980).

Where adequacy of creditor's case against debtor was debatable, and where debtor's response to the complaint, although technically inadequate to prevent entry of default, was prompt, trial court's refusal to set aside default judgment was abuse of discretion. **Kennedy v. First Nat. Bank of Fairbanks,** Op. No. 2448, 637 P2d 297 (Alaska 1981).

Where plaintiff's attorney did not reply to defendant's attorney as requested prior to applying for default, trial court abused its discretion in not setting aside default judgment. **City of Valdez v. Salomon,** Op. No. 2450, 637 P2d 298 (Alaska 1981).

In quiet title action, trial court erred in refusing to enter default judgment against defendant where circumstances indicated that the chances of defendant ever coming forward to claim an ownership interest in the subject property were minimal. **Peter Pan Seafoods, Inc. v. Stepanoff,** Op. No. 2555, 650 P2d 375 (Alaska 1982).

Although a party has no absolute right to a default judgment following entry of a technical default, the court may not arbitrarily deny entry of judgment against the defaulting party. **Peter Pan Seafoods, Inc. v. Stepanoff,** Op. No. 2555, 650 P2d 375 (Alaska 1982).

A defendant against whom a default has been entered may disprove a material allegation of the plaintiff's complaint at the trial on damages and thereby avoid liability, but the evidence disproving the allegation must be such that it could not possibly be rebutted if the non-defaulting party were permitted a trial. **Syndoulos Lutheran Church v. A.R.C. Industries,** Op. No. 2649, 662 P2d 109 (Alaska 1983).

A default, as distinguished from a default judgment, is an interlocutory matter not governed by the strict time limits imposed by the civil rules on motions for relief from judgments or orders. **Syndoulos Lutheran Church v. A.R.C. Industries,** Op. No. 2649, 662 P2d 109 (Alaska 1983).

The notice provision of this rule is intended to give the defendant an opportunity to argue to the judge that a default judgment should not be entered, notwithstanding the fact of the default, and the same reasoning applies to the requirement of notice of the hearing on damages, if there is to be one. **Case v. Winters,** Op. No. 2876, 689 P2d 467 (Alaska 1984).

Although a default judgment had been entered against defendant on November 23, 1982 with respect to a new action by ex-wife seeking unpaid support payments, once the new action was consolidated with the earlier divorce case by court order entered December 14, 1982, defendant was entitled to be served with all pleadings and papers filed with the court pertaining to subsequent proceedings involving the new action, including written notice of a hearing on damages held on January 10, 1983. **Case v. Winters,** Op. No. 2876, 689 P2d 467 (Alaska 1984).

The meritorious defense required to set aside an entry of default demands something more than a perfunctory statement that a meritorious defense exists; it demands a showing that if relief is granted the outcome of the suit may be different than if the entry of default or the default judgment is allowed to stand; and "different outcome" does not necessarily mean a different prevailing party, but could mean a reduction in the amount of the plaintiffs award. **Hertz v. Berzanske,** Op. No. 2967, 704 P2d 767 (Alaska 1985).

In exercising its discretion to set aside an entry of default, a court should consider the following factors: whether defendant has established the required meritorious defense, prejudice to plaintiffs, the culpability of defendant's conduct, the length of the period of default, the size of any potential award to plaintiffs, alternative sanctions against defendant, and whether the parties had prior contact such that the plaintiff should have given defendant notice that a default would be sought. **Hertz v. Berzanske,** Op. No. 2967, 704 P2d 767 (Alaska 1985).

Whether "good cause" exists to set aside an entry of default does not depend on a showing of "excusable neglect" or some other excuse or justification, as is required to set aside a default judgment; instead, "good cause" is a question of equity, left to the discretion of the trial court upon the showing of a meritorious defense. **Hertz v. Berzanske,** Op. No. 2967, 704 P2d 767 (Alaska 1985).

Although party may have been untruthful regarding the reasons for a default, as long as he did not act in bad faith or intentionally in allowing the default to occur, his conduct by itself would not prevent a finding of good cause for setting aside the entry of default. **Hertz v. Berzanske,** Op. No. 2967, 704 P2d 767 (Alaska 1985).

Default judgments in personal injury suits should be entered by the court, not by the clerk. **Davis v. Criterion Ins. Co.,** Op. No. 3334, 754 P2d 1331 (Alaska 1988).

Default judgment against corporation was upheld notwithstanding that plaintiff violated civil rule by serving the corporation officers directly rather than serving the attorney of record for the corporation. **Murat v. F/V Shelikof Strait,** Op. No. 3607, 793 P2d 69 (Alaska 1990).

Although default judgment was erroneous, trial court did not err in refusing to set aside entry of default where defendant attempted to avoid service, failed to respond to summons and complaint, and two-month delay occurred between his entry of appearance and motion to set aside entry of default. **Melendrez v. Bode,** Op. No. 4856, 941 P2d 1254 (Alaska 1997).

Trial court decree quieting title to mining claim in favor of claimant did not constitute default judgment against mining claim grantor who was not a named defendant in the action since trial court expressly reserved grantor's claims against claimant; accordingly, trial court did not abuse its discretion by refusing to set aside the non-existent default judgment. **Red Top Mining, Inc. v. Anthony,** Op. No. 5143, 983 P2d 743 (Alaska 1999).

Despite the willful failure of a custodial parent to follow court procedures or orders, custody cannot be changed without an evidenciary hearing addressing fully the question whether the change is in the child's best interests. **Platz v. Aramburo,** Op. No. 5362, 17 P3d 65 (Alaska 2001).

Defendant's telephone call to plaintiff's attorney in which he left a message asking "when he was going to court" did not constitute an "appearance" within the meaning of this rule. **Brown v. Lange,** Op. No. 5400, 21 P3d 822 (Alaska 2001).

Because defendant did not "appear" within the meaning of this rule, he was not entitled to notice of either the entry of default or the default judgment. **Brown v. Lange,** Op. No. 5400, 21 P3d 822 (Alaska 2001).

Trial court erred when it did not set aside default judgment where appellant's failure to respond to complaint in a timely fashion was excusable; inter alia, he was served with lawsuit within two weeks of suffering multiple serious gunshot wounds. **Cook v. Rowland,** Op. No. 5586, 49 P3d 5586, 375 P2d 139 (Alaska 2002).

In suit against former finance officer, which alleged that finance officer had misappropriated funds by writing unauthorized check to himself, where finance officer failed to appear for trial, and subsequently moved to set aside the summary judgment entered against him, the trial court did not abuse its discretion in denying the motion, because failure to appear for trial supported assumption that the finance officer was forfeiting the right to defend himself. **Snyder v. Am. Legion Spenard Post No. 28,** Op. No. 5940, 119 P.3d 996 (Alaska 2005).

Offer of judgment is not premature or invalid even if it was made before the parties made Alaska R. Civ. P. 26 disclosures; therefore, attorney's fees were properly awarded to the holder of a first deed of trust in an action concerning a dispute over a foreclosure sale where the offer was made prior to discovery disclosures. **Cook Schuhmann & Groseclose, Inc. v. Brown & Root, Inc.,** Op. No. 5291, 116 P.3d 592 (Alaska 2005).

In a dispute over foreclosure proceedings, an offer of judgment made by a first deed of trust holder was valid and unambiguous, even though it did not specify a definite sum; nonmonetary offers of judgment were valid as long as they were unambiguous and unconditional. **Cook Schuhmann & Groseclose, Inc. v. Brown & Root, Inc.,** Op. No. 5291, 116 P.3d 592 (Alaska 2005).

Party to a divorce could make a general claim that the court "adjudicate the assets and liabilities in a fair and equitable manner" without listing individual items and the court could equitably divide the assets and debts of the parties in a default context where the parties were both aware of the property subject to division, the responding party knew that the petitioner sought a division of that property. **Hicks v. Pleasants**, Op. No. 12110, 158 P.3d 817 (Alaska 2007).

"Good cause" under subsection (e) of this rule is a question of equity left to the discretion of the trial court upon showing of a meritorious defense. **Hicks v. Pleasants**, Op. No. 12110, 158 P.3d 817 (Alaska 2007).

Where pro se divorce litigant arrived at the hearing a few minutes late and promptly informed the court that while he had agreed to be defaulted to the divorce, he did not intend to stipulate to the values of any of the property and debts at issue, the court could have construed litigant's statements as a request to set aside the default. **Hicks v. Pleasants**, Op. No. 12110, 158 P.3d 817 (Alaska 2007).

Rule 56. Summary Judgment.

(a) **For Claimant.** A party seeking to recover upon a claim, counterclaim or cross-claim or to obtain a declaratory judgment may, at any time after the expiration of 20 days from the commencement of the action or after service of a motion for summary judgment by the adverse party, move for a summary judgment in the party's favor upon all or any part thereof.

(b) **For Defending Party.** A party against whom a claim, counterclaim or cross-claim is asserted or a declaratory judgment is sought may, at any time, move for a summary judgment in the party's favor as to all or any part thereof.

(c) **Motion and Proceedings Thereon.** The motion shall be made pursuant to Rule 77, and may be supported by affidavits setting forth concise statements of material facts made upon personal knowledge. There must also be served and filed with each motion a memorandum showing that there is no genuine issue as to any material fact and that the moving party is entitled to judgment as a matter of law. The adverse party in accordance with Rule 77 may serve opposing affidavits, a concise "statement of genuine issues" setting forth all material facts as to which it is contended there exists a genuine issue necessary to be litigated, and any other memorandum in opposition to the motion. Judgment shall be rendered forthwith if the pleadings, depositions, answers to interrogatories, and admissions on file, together with the affidavits, show that there is no genuine issue as to any material fact and that any party is entitled to a judgment as a matter of law. A summary judgment, interlocutory in character, may be rendered on the issue of liability alone although there is a genuine issue as to the amount of damages. Summary judgment, when appropriate, may be rendered against the moving party. A decision granting a motion for summary judgment is not a final judgment under Civil Rule 58. When the decision adjudicates all unresolved claims as to all parties, the judge shall direct the appropriate party to file a proposed final judgment. The proposed judgment must be filed within 20 days of service of the decision, on a separate document distinct from any opinion, memorandum or order that the court may issue.

(d) **Case Not Fully Adjudicated on Motion.** If on motion under this rule judgment is not rendered upon the whole case or for all the relief asked and a trial is necessary, the court at the hearing of the motion, by examining the pleadings and the evidence before it and by interrogating counsel, shall if practicable ascertain what material facts exist without substantial controversy and what material facts are actually and in good faith controverted. It shall thereupon make an order specifying the facts that appear without substantial controversy, including the extent to which the amount of damages or other relief is not in controversy, and directing such further proceedings in the action as are just. Upon the trial of the action the facts so specified shall be deemed established, and the trial shall be conducted accordingly.

(e) **Form of Affidavits—Further Testimony—Defense Required.** Supporting and opposing affidavits shall be made on personal knowledge, shall set forth such facts as would be admissible in evidence, and shall show affirmatively that the affiant is competent to testify to the matters stated therein. Sworn or certified copies of all papers or parts thereof referred to in an affidavit shall be attached thereto or served therewith. The court may permit affidavits to be supplemented or opposed by depositions or by further affidavits. When a motion for summary judgment is made and supported as provided in this rule, an adverse party may not rest upon the mere allegations or denials of the adverse party's pleading, but the adverse party's response, by affidavits or as otherwise provided in this rule, must set forth specific facts showing that there is a genuine issue for trial. If the adverse party does not so respond, summary judgment, if appropriate, shall be entered against the adverse party.

(f) **When Affidavits Are Unavailable.** Should it appear from the affidavits of a party opposing the motion that the party cannot for reasons stated present by affidavit facts essential to justify the party's opposition, the court may refuse the application for judgment or may order a continuance to permit affidavits to be obtained or depositions to be taken or discovery to be had or may make such other order as is just.

(g) **Affidavits Made in Bad Faith.** Should it appear to the satisfaction of the court at any time that any of the affidavits presented pursuant to this rule are presented in bad faith or solely for the purpose of delay, the court shall forthwith order the party employing them to pay to the other party the amount of the reasonable expenses which the filing of the affidavits caused the other party to incur, including reasonable attorney's fees, and any offending party or attorney may be adjudged guilty of contempt.

(Adopted by SCO 5 October 9, 1959; amended by SCO 258 effective November 15, 1976; by SCO 1153 effective July 15, 1994; and by SCO 1430 effective April 15, 2002)

Annotations

Cases

I. Motion and Proceedings.

A. In General.

Issues of negligence are ordinarily not susceptible of summary adjudication, but should be resolved by a trial in the ordinary manner. **Lillegraven v. Tengs,** Op. No. 109, 375 P2d 139 (Alaska 1962).

Plaintiff's contention "that the affidavits submitted by either party cannot be used as a basis for terminating an action" is contrary to the authorities and the plain provisions of Civ. R. 56(c). **Lowe v. Boggess,** Op. No. 110, 375 P2d 199 (Alaska 1962).

On a motion for summary judgment trial court properly considered unauthenticated copies of a telegram and of letters attached to and identified by an affidavit made upon information and belief rather than personal knowledge, where the record did not show that the affidavit was objected to nor the authenticity of the correspondence disputed by appellee. **Kvasnikoff v. Weaver Bros., Inc.,** Op. No. 229, 405 P2d 781 (Alaska 1965).

Failure on the part of defendants to respond to requests for admissions within the ten day period provided by rule, the denial of a motion for relief from a summary judgment granted on the basis of failure to respond did not advance the objectives of the rules of procedure where the court was aware of an extension of the ten day period given by opposing counsel, where no discovery was had and where defendants' counsel had offered at the hearing of the motion for relief to retype the responses and to have them sworn to within half an hour, and under these circumstances the denial of relief was an abuse of discretion. **Palzer v. Serv-U-Meat Co.,** Op. No. 367, 419 P2d 201 (Alaska 1966).

Admissions on file may be used in support of a motion for summary judgment. **Palzer v. Serv-U-Meat Co.,** Op. No. 367, 419 P2d 201 (Alaska 1966).

A summary judgment may be based upon facts which are deemed admitted through a party's failure to serve sworn responses or objections to matters of which admission is requested. **Palzer v. Serv-U-Meat Co.,** Op. No. 367, 419 P2d 201 (Alaska 1966).

In order to justify summary judgment not only must it be shown that there is no genuine issue of fact to be litigated, but also that the moving party is entitled to judgment as a matter of law. **Whaley v. State,** Op. No. 465,438 P2d 718 (Alaska 1968).

A factual question between the parties will be considered material so as to prevent entry of summary judgment only if as a matter of law, assuming the factual situation to be as contended such fact would be basis for relief as against the opponent. **Whaley v. State,** Op. No. 465, 438 P2d 718 (Alaska 1968).

The party opposing a summary judgment motion need not establish that he will ultimately prevail at trial. **Gablick v. Wolfe,** Op. No. 613, 469 P2d 391 (Alaska 1970).

Inferences of fact from proffered proofs are drawn in favor of the party opposing a motion for summary judgment and against the movant. **Nizinski v. Golden Valley Electric Association,** Op. No. 878, 509 P2d 280 (Alaska 1973).

Statements not made under oath do not meet the requirements of this rule. **Miller v. City of Fairbanks,** Op. No. 881, 509 P2d 826 (Alaska 1973).

Statements which are not made under oath may not be considered as evidence on a summary judgment motion. **Alaska Rent-A-Car, Inc. v. Ford Motor Co.,** Op. No. 1086, 526 P2d 1136 (Alaska 1974).

The party opposing a motion for summary judgment need not establish that it will ultimately prevail at trial but only that there exists a genuine issue of fact to be litigated. **Alaska Rent-A-Car , Inc. v. Ford Motor Co.,** Op. No. 1086, 526 P2d 1136 (Alaska 1974).

All inferences of fact from proffered proofs are to be drawn in favor of the party opposing summary judgment and against the movant. **Alaska Rent-A-Car, Inc. v. Ford Motor Co.,** Op. No. 1086, 526 P2d 1136 (Alaska 1974).

Any assertions of fact in pleadings and memoranda, unauthenticated and unsworn documents and uncertified copies of public records are not admissible in evidence and cannot be relied upon for purposes of summary judgment. **Concerned Citizens of South Kenai Peninsula v. Kenai Peninsula Borough,** Op. No. 1093, 527 P2d 447 (Alaska 1974).

Generally, where a party intends to rely upon answers to interrogatories as the basis for summary judgment, he should notify the court and opposing counsel to permit opportunity to challenge factual basis for the answers. **Concerned Citizens of South Kenai Peninsula v. Kenai Peninsula Borough,** Op. No. 1093, 527 P2d 447 (Alaska 1974).

Assertions of fact in pleadings and memoranda are not admissible in evidence and cannot be relied upon for purposes of summary judgment. **Brock v. Rogers & Babler, Inc.,** Op. No. 1166, 536 P2d 778 (Alaska 1975).

An oral contract is capable of being resolved by means of summary judgment, absent any factual dispute. **Howarth v. First National Bank of Anchorage,** Op. No. 1188, 540 P2d 486 (Alaska 1975).

In ruling on motion for summary judgment the court is required to draw all reasonable inferences in favor of the nonmoving party and against the movant. **Clabaugh v. Bottcher,** Op. No. 1235, 545 P2d 172 (Alaska 1976).

In review of summary judgment, Supreme Court must determine whether there were any genuine issues of material fact, and whether the moving parties were entitled to judgment as a matter of law. **Moore v. State,** Op. No. 1284, 553 P2d 8 (Alaska 1976).

Records produced by state in course of discovery proceedings were admissible in summary judgment proceeding against state. **Moore v. State,** Op. No. 1284, 553 P2d 8 (Alaska 1976).

When matters outside pleadings are presented to trial court and not excluded, motion for judgment on the pleadings will be treated as motion for summary judgment. **Adams v. State,** Op. No. 1318, 555 P2d 235 (Alaska 1976).

Assertions of fact in unverified pleadings and memoranda or in oral argument do not satisfy Civil Rule 56(e), and cannot be relied on in ruling on a motion for summary judgment. **Jennings v. State,** Op. No. 1467, 566 P2d 1304 (Alaska 1977).

There is no right to amend pleadings after opposing party has been granted summary judgment. **Jennings v. State,** Op. No. 1467, 566 P2d 1304 (Alaska 1977).

Under circumstances of case, dismissal with prejudice after summary judgment and before hearing motion to amend pleadings was an abuse of discretion. **Jennings v. State,** Op. No. 1467, 566 P2d 1304 (Alaska 1977).

Motion to compel discovery and statements in opposition to summary were not sufficient to be considered a Rule 56(f) motion for additional time. **Jennings v. State,** Op. No. 1467, 566 P2d 1304 (Alaska 1977).

In ruling on appeal from grant of summary judgment, the superior court was obliged to consider, on its own motion, at least those portions of a deposition to which reference was made in the memoranda and arguments of the parties, even though the deposition had not been formally opened and presented to the trial court. **Totem Marine T. & B. v. Alyeska Pipeline, Etc.,** Op. No. 1698, 584 P2d 15 (Alaska 1978).

Mere assertions of fact in pleadings and memoranda are insufficient for denial of a motion for summary judgment. **State, Dept. of Highways v. Green,** Op. No. 1706, 586 P2d 595 (Alaska 1978).

Trial court retains some discretion in deciding whether to grant summary judgment in cases where there is no response to filing of summary judgment motion. **Dome Laboratories v. Farrell,** Op. No. 1917, 599 P2d 152 (Alaska 1979).

Where record presented issue of whether summary judgment should be entered, and parties had opportunity to present affidavits and other evidence, and appellate court viewed the Civil Rule 12(b)(6) motion as having been converted into a summary judgment motion by the admission of matters outside the pleadings, the appellate court decided the issue of whether summary judgment was proper, in the interests of judicial economy. **Martin v. Mears,** Op. No. 1958, 602 P2d 421 (Alaska 1979).

Where questions which appellant denominates as "triable issues of fact" were not presented to trial court at summary judgment hearing, appellate review is precluded. **Williams v. City of Valdez,** Op. No. 1969, 603 P2d 483 (Alaska 1979).

Where hydraulic ram collapsed after rebuilt by defendant due to defect in original manufacture, triable issue was established as to whether defendant's failure to detect the defect resulted from defendant's failure to exercise ordinary care in inspection. **Swenson Trucking, Etc. v. Truckweld Equip.,** Op. No. 2008, 604 P2d 1113 (Alaska 1980).

When material outside the pleadings is presented to the trial court, a motion to dismiss is automatically converted into one for summary judgment unless the court "affirmatively" and "expressly" rules that it is not considering evidence outside of the pleadings. **Adkins v. Nabors Alaska Drilling, Inc.,** Op. No. 2056, 609 P2d 15 (Alaska 1980).

Summary judgment may be based on deemed admissions if such facts are dispositive. **Riley v. Northern Commercial Co.,** Op. No. 2534, 648 P2d 961 (Alaska 1982).

At oral argument on summary judgment motion, movant's request that trial transcript from prior proceeding be considered in ruling on the motion was correctly denied as untimely. **Pankratz v. State, Dept. of Highways,** Op. No. 2564, 652 P2d 68 (Alaska 1982).

Where the scope of an earlier decision is unclear, a court should not grant summary judgment on res judicata grounds. **Pankratz v. State, Dept. of Highways,** Op. No. 2564, 652 P2d 68 (Alaska 1982).

Given the narrow scope of the materials outside of the pleadings which were consulted by the superior court and appellant's failure to show any prejudice occurring to them as a result of the court's unarticulated conversion of a Rule 12(b)(6) motion to a motion for summary judgment, court's error in not expressly indicating whether it had considered or excluded matters submitted outside the pleadings was harmless. **Brice v. State, Div. of Forest, Land & Water,** Op. No. 2731, 669 P2d 1311 (Alaska 1983).

Borough's motion for amendment of judgment against defendant for sales tax liability, which motion was made pursuant to a stipulation under which the borough agreed to conduct an audit and then move for a new judgment in the amount determined by the audit to be due, reserving to the taxpayer the right to contest the amount, was in actuality a motion for summary judgment and should have been granted only if there was no genuine issue as to any material fact. **Underwood v. Fairbanks North Star Borough,** Op. No. 2768, 674 P2d 785 (Alaska 1983).

In wrongful death action against a Borough arising out of a prisoner's suicide, statements made by Borough employees to police investigators were admissions of a party opponent which should have been considered by the trial court in ruling on a summary judgment motion, and the fact that the statements were unsworn was immaterial. **Kanayurak v. North Slope Borough,** Op. No. 2782, 677 P2d 893 (Alaska 1984).

Motion to amend the complaint to allege that plaintiff was a registered contractor should have been granted despite the pendency of a summary judgment motion. **Fomby v. Whisenhunt,** Op. No. 2801, 680 P2d 787 (Alaska 1984).

Where there is conflicting evidence sufficient to establish a genuine issue of material fact, summary judgment is not authorized unless it can be said that a party is otherwise entitled to judgment as a matter of law. **State v. Weidner,** Op. No. 2788, 684 P2d 103 (Alaska 1984).

Trial judge correctly used the power of the trial court to revise or reverse interlocutory rulings deemed erroneous, despite contention that he was bound by the doctrine of law of the case. **C.J.M. Const. v. Chandler Plumbing,** Op. No. 2963, 708 P2d 60 (Alaska 1985).

The filing of a statement of "genuine issues of material fact" under this rule is merely permissive; it remains the duty of the trial court to determine whether the record presents any factual issues which would preclude the entry of summary judgment as a matter of law. **Drake v. Hosley,** Op. No. 3016, 713 P2d 1203 (Alaska 1986).

Where trial court on a motion to dismiss for failure to state a claim upon which relief can be granted did not exclude materials presented outside the pleadings, it was under a mandatory duty to treat the motion as one for summary judgment and to dispose of it after giving the parties a reasonable opportunity to present all materials pertinent to a summary judgment motion. **Reed v. Municipality of Anchorage,** Op. No. 3218, 741 P2d 1181 (Alaska 1987).

The summary judgment standard for libel cases enunciated in **Anderson v. Liberty Lobby, Inc.,** 477 U.S. 242, 106 S.Ct. 2505, 91 L.Ed.2d 202 (1986), is not binding on state courts which follow their own state summary judgment procedures. **Moffatt v. Brown,** Op. No. 3283, 751 P2d 939 (Alaska 1988).

Rather than the substantive evidentiary standards used in federal courts, the standard in Alaska for ruling on summary judgment motions in libel actions is the traditional summary judgment text: the motion shall be granted when there is no genuine issue as to any material fact and the moving party is entitled to judgment as a matter of law. **Moffatt v. Brown,** Op. No. 3283, 751 P2d 939 (Alaska 1988).

The proponent of a summary judgment motion has no absolute right to summary judgment merely because the opponent fails to respond. **Bauman v. State, Div. of Family & Youth Services,** Op. No. 3408, 768 P2d 1097 (Alaska 1989).

Where non-moving party had not been dilatory, trial court abused its discretion in not granting his request for a Rule 56(f) continuance to depose certain out-of-state witnesses. **Munn v. Bristol Bay Housing Authority,** Op. No. 3458, 777 P2d 188 (Alaska 1989).

If a trial court considers matters outside the pleadings, it must treat a motion to dismiss for failure to state a claim as a motion for summary judgment; if the trial court does not state whether or not it excluded evidence outside the pleadings, the appellate court may remand for proper consideration, review the decision as if the motion for failure to state a claim was granted after exclusion of the outside materials, or review the decision as if the trial court granted a motion for summary judgment. **Homeward Bound v. Anchorage School Dist.,** Op. No. 3589, 791 P2d 610 (Alaska 1990).

Timely objection by party opposing summary judgment to consideration of unauthenticated documents is in itself sufficient, there being no requirement that the party also raise some doubt as to whether the documentary evidence is in fact authentic. **Murat v. F/V Shelikof Strait,** Op. No. 3607, 793 P2d 69 (Alaska 1990).

This rule allows an expert to base an opinion on hearsay evidence, which is by definition unverified testimony; accordingly, affidavit by expert was properly considered by trial court in ruling on summary judgment motion even if the data relied upon by the expert was unverified. **Broderick v. King's Way Assembly of God,** Op. No. 3677, 808 P2d 1211 (Alaska 1991).

Opinion testimony and hearsay statements that would be inadmissible at trial are inadmissible in a motion for summary judgment. **Broderick v. King's Way Assembly of God,** Op. No. 3677, 808 P2d 1211 (Alaska 1991).

Expert testimony that a child had been sexually molested and was suffering from post-traumatic stress would be admissible at trial and could therefore be considered by trial court in ruling on a motion for summary judgment. **Broderick v. King's Way Assembly of God,** Op. No. 3677, 808 P2d 1211 (Alaska 1991).

Inadmissible hearsay assertions in an affidavit cannot be used either to oppose or support a motion for summary judgment. **Broderick v. King's Way Assembly of God,** Op. No. 3677, 808 P2d 1211 (Alaska 1991).

Hearsay accounts of child's identification of her abuser were admissible under the residential exceptions to the hearsay rule. **Broderick v. King's Way Assembly of God,** Op. No. 3677, 808 P2d 1211 (Alaska 1991).

In its determination of summary judgment motion in wrongful termination case in which the employer argued that the termination stemmed from a reduction in force, the trial court did not abuse its discretion in denying the plaintiff a continuance to conduct additional discovery relevant to the employer's excuse; plaintiff knew of the defense 13 months before the employer filed its summary judgment motion, yet plaintiff had conducted no discovery on the issue at all, thus plaintiff was dilatory. **Braun v. Alaska Com. Fishing & Agr. Bank,** Op. No. 3727, 816 P2d 140 (Alaska 1991).

Lack of opposition to motion for summary judgment does not reduce usual standard of review for such motions. **Newton v. Magill,** Op. No. 4075, 872 P2d 1213 (Alaska 1994).

Deposition testimony should be considered in determining whether a genuine issue of material fact exists. **American Restaurant Group v. Clark,** Op. No. 4163, 889 P2d 595 (Alaska 1995).

Even if appellant failed to bring relevant deposition testimony to superior court's particular attention in deciding summary judgment motion, superior court was not relieved of its obligation to examine the record before determining that no genuine issue of material fact existed. **American Restaurant Group v. Clark,** Op. No. 4163, 889 P2d 595 (Alaska 1995).

In cases partially adjudicated on a summary judgment motion, Civil Rule 56(d) provides that the facts that pertained to the entry of partial summary judgment "shall be deemed established." Although the trial court retains the option to hear additional evidence on the matter, it is not required to do so. The decision to preclude further evidence is reserved for the discretion of the trial court. **Neal & Company, Inc. v. Association of Village Council Presidents Regional Housing Authority,** Op. No. 4206, 895 P2d 497 (Alaska 1995).

When reviewing a grant of summary judgment, the appellate court must determine whether any genuine issue of material fact exists and whether the moving party is entitled to judgment on the law applicable to the established facts. The matter is reviewed **de novo** and the facts are viewed in the light most favorable to the non-moving party. **Beilgard v. State,** Op. No. 4215, 896 P2d 230 (Alaska 1995).

Question of whether **de novo** judicial review of a school board action affecting a tenured teacher was required was irrelevant as a superior court decided the case on summary judgment on the agency record in favor of the party to be protected by **de novo** review. **Nenana City School District v. Coghill,** Op. No. 4229, 898 P2d 929 (Alaska 1995).

On motion for summary judgment, moving party bears initial burden of proving through admissible evidence absence of genuine factual disputes and its entitlement to judgment. **Shade v. Co. & Anglo Alaska Service Corp.,** Op. No. 4253, 901 P2d 434 (Alaska 1995).

On motion for summary judgment, non-moving party is not obligated to demonstrate genuine issue for trial until moving party makes prima facie showing of its entitlement to judgment on established facts. **Shade v. Co. & Anglo Alaska Service Corp.,** Op. No. 4253, 901 P2d 434 (Alaska 1995).

Trial court erred in not granting plaintiffs additional time under Rule 56 to respond to affirmative defenses raised in defendant's summary judgment motion. **Gamble v. Northstore Partnership,** Op. No. 4291, 907 P2d 477 (Alaska 1995).

Because appellate review is **de novo,** appellant's assertion that the superior court misconstrued this rule in granting summary judgment was moot. **Taranto v. North Slope Borough,** Op. No. 4310, 909 P2d 354 (Alaska 1996).

Trial court's decision on whether to permit further discovery under this rule was reviewed for abuse of discretion. **Mt. Juneau Enterprises v. City of Juneau,** Op. No. 4396, 923 P2d 768 (Alaska 1996).

Trial court committed reversible error by converting defendant's motion for judgment on the pleadings to motion for summary judgment without giving plaintiffs notice and opportunity to oppose the motion as a motion for summary judgment; on remand, trial court had option to treat motion as motion for summary judgment, as long as it complied with requirements of Civil Rule 56, or to treat motion as motion for judgment on the pleadings, excluding all matters outside the pleadings. **Demmert v. Kootznoowoo, Inc.,** Op. No. 5006, 960 P2d 606 (Alaska 1998).

Party need not specifically identify Rule 56(f) when seeking a continuance; rather, party need only provide adequate reasons explaining why party cannot produce facts necessary to oppose summary judgment within original time frame. **Parson v. Marathon Oil Co.,** Op. No. 5007, 960 P2d 615 (Alaska 1998).

Assertions of fact in unverified pleadings and memoranda cannot be relied on in denying motion for summary judgment. **Bennett v. Weimar,** Op. No. 5104, 975 P2d 691 (Alaska 1999).

This rule does not preclude successive motions for summary judgment. **Taranto v. North Slope Borough,** Op. No. 5217, 992 P2d 1111 (Alaska 1999).

Assertions of fact in unverified pleadings and memoranda cannot be relied on in denying motion for summary judgment. **Martinez v. Ha,** Op. No. 5332, 12 P3d 1159 (Alaska 2000).

Any error by trial court in converting motion for judgment on the pleadings into motion for summary judgment without giving non-moving party additional time to marshal evidence and submit affidavits was harmless. **White v. State Dept. of Natural Resources,** Op. No. 5343, 14 P3d 956 (Alaska 2000).

Where party has not been dilatory in seeking discovery and identifies the people whom it intends to depose, party should be granted extra time for discovery under this rule. **Sopko v. Dowell Schlumberger, Inc.,** Op. No. 5396, 21 P3d 1265 (Alaska 2001).

Alaska R. Civ. P. 56, which lays out the procedures for summary judgment hearings, allows for affidavits, depositions, interrogatories, pleadings, and admissions, but does not allow for live witnesses. **Jourdan v. Nationsbanc Mtg. Corp.,** Op. No. 5545, 42 P3d 1072 (Alaska 2002).

In a former buyer's action to set aside a strict foreclosure, the former buyer need not have been able to perform financially on the real estate contract at all times during the litigation in order to avoid the seller's motion for summary judgment. **Yates v. Halford,** Op. No. 5712, 73 P.3d 1236 (Alaska 2003).

Trial court erred in granting summary judgment upholding a liability policy endorsement that purported to limit coverage for attorney fees in an airplane crash case; the endorsement lacked regulatory approval and contained language more complex than the model form. **Therchik v. Grant Aviation, Inc.,** Op. No. 5715, 74 P.3d 191 (Alaska 2003).

Summary judgment was improperly granted in favor of employer university in retiree's suit for breach of contract, negligent record keeping, and promissory estoppel; assuming that an agreement that the university would credit the retiree with 20 years of actual service, a release could not have immunized the university from a suit to enforce such an agreement, and the university's promise was to be performed after the date of the release such that the contract would have been illusory if it had been governed by the release. **Barry v. Univ. of Alaska,** Op. No. 5785, 85 P.3d 1022 (Alaska 2004).

An insurer offering to pay policy limits to an unrepresented claimant under the terms of a motor vehicle insurance policy has no duty to include attorney fees as part of the settlement offer. **Maloney v. Progressive Specialty Ins. Co,** Op. No. 1183, 99 P.3d 565 (Alaska 2004).

In a landlord-tenant dispute, tenant argued that the superior court's findings were not sufficiently clear to meet standards under this rule, but findings of fact and conclusions of law were unnecessary on decisions of motions under Rule 12 or this rule, or any other motions except as provided in Rule 41(b).when the court denied the motion brought under this section. **Fyffe v. Wright,** Op. No. 5819 (Alaska 2004).

Where the husband did not assert the defenses of mistake or misrepresentation in the execution of a guaranty, those defenses were waived and could not be asserted on appeal. **Still v. Cunningham,** Op. No. 5825 (Alaska 2004).

A movant does not have a right to summary judgment merely because the non-moving party fails to respond: The provision in section (e) of this Rule that, where the non-moving party fails to offer an affidavit setting forth specific facts showing a genuine issue for trial, a court shall enter summary judgment against that party "if appropriate," indicates that the court retains some degree of discretion in deciding whether to grant summary judgment in cases where there is no response to the filing of the motion; the court is not required to grant summary judgment even where the motion is unopposed. **Rockstad v. Erikson,** Op. No. 5908, 113 P.3d 1215 (Alaska 2005).

Summary judgment is appropriate where there is no genuine issue as to any material fact and any party is entitled to judgment as a matter of law. **Interior Cabaret, Hotel, Restaurant & Retailers Ass'n v. Fairbanks North Star Borough**, Op. No. 11481, 135 P.3d 1000 (Alaska 2006).

The appellate courts review grants of summary judgment de novo and draw all factual inferences in favor of, and view the facts in the light most favorable to, the party against whom summary judgment was granted. **Interior Cabaret, Hotel, Restaurant & Retailers Ass'n v. Fairbanks North Star Borough**, Op. No. 11481, 135 P.3d 1000 (Alaska 2006).

A complete failure of proof concerning an essential element of the nonmoving party's case necessarily renders all other facts immaterial. **Greywolf v. Carroll,** Op. No. 11830, 151 P.3d 1234 (Alaska 2007).

B. Burden of Proof.

Where plaintiff demonstrated that there was no genuine issue of fact to be litigated, it was incumbent upon the defendants, in order to prevent the entry of a summary judgment, to set forth facts showing that they could produce admissible evidence which reasonably would tend to dispute or contradict plaintiff's evidence, and thus demonstrate to the court that a triable issue of fact existed. **Isler v. Jensen,** Op. No. 149, 382 P2d 901 (Alaska 1963).

Where a clear showing in support of a motion for summary judgment has been made, it is incumbent on the party opposing the motion clearly to state its position or defense and show the court how it plans to support its position or defense with facts which would be admissible in evidence at the trial. **McKean v. Hammond,** Op. No. 504, 445 P2d 679 (Alaska 1968).

On a motion for summary judgment, the moving party has the burden of proving that the allegations he makes are true and that any defenses alleged are inapplicable under the facts of the case. **Braund, Inc. v. White,** Op. No. 693, 486 P2d 50 (Alaska 1971).

In attempting to satisfy their burdens, the party moving for summary judgment and the party opposing summary judgment may utilize pleadings, affidavits and any other materials otherwise admissible in evidence. **Miller v. City of Fairbanks,** Op. No. 881, 509 P2d 826 (Alaska 1973).

The burden is on the party moving for summary judgment to establish the absence of a material issue of fact. **Alaska Rent-A-Car, Inc. v. Ford Motor Co.,** Op. No. 1086, 526 P2d 1136 (Alaska 1974).

The party seeking summary judgment has the burden of showing both that the case presents no material issue of fact requiring the taking of testimony and that the applicable law requires judgment in its favor, which burden must be met by the submission of material admissible as evidence. **Concerned Citizens of South Kenai Peninsula v. Kenai Peninsula Borough,** Op. No. 1093, 527 P2d 447 (Alaska 1974).

Once a party moving for summary judgment has shown that the case presents no material issue of fact and that the law requires judgment in its favor, the opposing party can avoid summary judgment only by producing competent evidence to show that there are issues of material fact to be tried. **Brock v. Rogers & Babler, Inc.,** Op. No. 1166, 536 P2d 778 (Alaska 1975).

Party seeking summary judgment has the burden of showing an absence of material issues of fact. **Clabaugh v. Bottcher,** Op. No. 1235, 545 P2d 172 (Alaska 1976).

The burden is on the party requesting summary judgment to show, by evidence which would be admissible if presented at trial, that there exists no genuine issue of material fact and that he is entitled to judgment as a matter of law. **Wickwire v. McFadden,** Op. No. 1597, 576 P2d 986 (Alaska 1978).

A party opposing summary judgment need not produce all of the evidence it may have at its disposal but need only show that issues of material fact exist. **Totem Marine T. & B. v. Alyeska Pipeline, Etc.,** Op. No. 1698, 584 P2d 15 (Alaska 1978).

Once the movant has satisfied his burden of establishing an absence of genuine issues of material fact and its right, on the basis of the undisputed facts, to judgment as a matter of law, the nonmovant is required, in order to prevent summary judgment, to set forth specific facts showing that he could produce evidence reasonably tending to dispute or contradict the movant's evidence and thus demonstrate that a material issue of facts exists. **State, Dept. of Highways v. Green,** Op. No. 1706, 586 P2d 595 (Alaska 1978).

In action by borrower against lender alleging racial discrimination in credit transactions, trial court erred in granting lender's motion for summary judgment, since failure of lender to deny discriminating against the borrower released the borrower from the obligation to support his assertions of fact with competent evidence under this rule. **Ratcliff v. Security Nat. Bank,** Op. No. 2738, 670 P2d 1139 (Alaska 1983).

Where arguments offered by plaintiff in support of its claim that the defendants abused their monopoly power by conspiring to fix prices consisted only of unsupported allegations, summary judgment for defendants was proper. **KOS v. Alyeska Pipeline Service Co.,** Op. No. 2733, 676 P2d 1069 (Alaska 1983).

Assertion by plaintiff, seeking payment for excavating services performed for defendant, that the "services were performed under the name of Shamrock Excavating" was, in the context of the record, an unsupported conclusionary allegation, not a statement of specific fact sufficient to prevent summary judgment for defendant on the ground that plaintiff was not a registered contractor. **Fomby v. Whisenhunt,** Op. No. 2801, 680 P2d 787 (Alaska 1984).

Since insurer did not meet its initial burden of showing that there were no genuine issues of material fact the summary judgment motion should have been denied regardless of whether the other party failed to respond to the motion with affidavits or other evidence. **Weaver Bros., Inc. v. Chappel,** Op. No. 2838, 684 P2d 123 (Alaska 1984).

Where defendant's motion was sufficient, based upon a properly admitted report by an expert panel, to establish the absence of a genuine issue of negligence in a medical malpractice action, summary judgment was proper where plaintiff presented no expert affidavits and did not show, based on the evidence presented, that a reasonably arguable case of medical negligence existed. **Kendall v. State, Div. of Corrections,** Op. No. 2890, 692 P2d 953 (Alaska 1984).

The proponent of a summary judgment motion has no absolute right to summary judgment merely because the opponent fails to respond. **Bauman v. State, Div. of Family & Youth Services,** Op. No. 3408, 768 P2d 1097 (Alaska 1989).

There is no compelling reason to interpret Rule 56(f) on requests for stays or continuances to require that non-moving opposing parties state what specific facts discovery will produce; it is sufficient that a party state in the affidavit adequate reasons why he cannot within the original time frame present facts essential to justify his opposition to the motion for summary judgment. **Munn v. Bristol Bay Housing Authority,** Op. No. 3458, 777 P2d 188 (Alaska 1989).

While federal courts grant summary judgment in libel cases only where the plaintiff has shown actual malice by clear and convincing evidence or where no reasonable jury could find such actual malice was present, Alaska courts continue to apply the standard of review for summary judgment motions under Alaska Civil Rule 56(c). It is somewhat harder for a libel defendant to win summary judgment in Alaska State courts using the "no genuine issue of material fact" standard than it is in federal court. **Mt. Juneau Enterprises, Inc. v. Juneau Empire,** Op. No. 4180, 891 P2d 829 (Alaska 1995).

In a libel suit, an evidentiary hearing may sometimes be required in order to determine whether an individual is a public figure, but such a determination may be resolved on summary judgment if the facts relating to public figure status are uncontroverted. **Mt. Juneau Enterprises, Inc. v. Juneau Empire,** Op. No. 4180, 891 P2d 829 (Alaska 1995).

Presumption, rebuttable by clear and convincing evidence, that putative father was biological father was overcome by blood evidence that putative father could not be biological father, thus no genuine issue of material fact on question of paternity existed for summary judgment purposes. **Matter of J.B.,** Op. No. 4383, 922 P2d 878 (Alaska 1996).

Granting of summary judgment in favor of the fishing association was error where the alleged renewal policy was not inconsistent with the charter agreements, such that the parole evidence rule did not bar extrinsic evidence tending to prove the policy's adopting and continued existence; reasonable jurors viewing the evidence in the light most favorable to the fisherman could find that the association adopted and breached a policy of this kind. **Froines v. Valdez Fisheries Dev. Ass'n.,** Op. No. 5714, 75 P.3d 83 (Alaska 2003).

The movant has the burden of showing that there is an absence of a factual dispute on a material fact and that this absence of a dispute constitutes a failure of proof on an essential element. **Greywolf v. Carroll,** Op. No. 11830, 151 P.3d 1234 (Alaska 2007).

If a prima facie case is established by the moving party, then the nonmoving party must set forth specific facts showing that admissible evidence could be produced that reasonably tends to dispute or contradict the moving party's evidence in order to demonstrate the existence of a dispute of material fact and prevent entry of summary judgment. **Greywolf v. Carroll,** Op. No. 11830, 151 P.3d 1234 (Alaska 2007).

Any admissible evidence in favor of the nonmoving party concerning a material fact is sufficient to render summary judgment inappropriate. **Greywolf v. Carroll,** Op. No. 11830, 151 P.3d 1234 (Alaska 2007).

C. Affidavits.

Regardless of a textual difference between the Alaska Rule 56(c) and subdivision (c) of the federal rule, a party moving for summary judgment is not required under this rule to use affidavits in support of his motion, affidavits being but one of the materials and combinations of materials which may be used as potential bases for the granting of summary judgments. **Palzer v. Serv-U-Meat Co.,** Op. No. 367, 419 P2d 201 (Alaska 1966).

Affidavits in support of or in opposition to a motion of summary judgment are permissive, not mandatory. **Jennings v. State,** Op. No. 1467, 566 P2d 1304 (Alaska 1977).

Where no affidavits were presented on motion for summary judgment, court should go outside the pleadings and consider other material on file and brought to its attention by parties. **Jennings v. State,** Op. No. 1467, 566 P2d 1304 (Alaska 1977).

Party who claims to be unable to oppose motion for summary judgment because opponent has not complied with discovery must state so by affidavit. **Jennings v. State,** Op. No. 1467, 566 P2d 1304 (Alaska 1977).

Three letters which were filed with the court only seventeen hours before oral argument on a motion for summary judgment were properly before the court and had to be considered in determining whether to grant the motion. **Walker v. White,** Op. No. 2196, 618 P2d 561 (Alaska 1980).

In contract dispute, affidavit presented in response to a motion for summary judgment containing mere allegations as to what the other party knew, did not set forth specific facts as required by this rule to defeat a summary judgment motion. **Husky Oil v. Sea Airmotive,** 724 P2d 531 (Alaska 1986).

Requests under Rule 56(f) should be fully granted. However, the litigant seeking relief must make it clear to the trial court and opposing party that he opposes summary judgment on this ground. **Gamble v. Northstore Partnership,** Op. No. 4291, 907 P2d 477 (Alaska 1995).

A Rule 56(f) decision will be reversed only for an abuse of discretion. **Gamble v. Northstore Partnership,** Op. No. 4291, 907 P2d 477 (Alaska 1995).

A party requesting a continuance for the purpose of opposing summary judgment is not required to specifically mention Rule 56(f) or to file a separate motion. **Gamble v. Northstore Partnership,** Op. No. 4291, 907 P2d 477 (Alaska 1995).

A request for Rule 56(f) relief need not state what specific facts further discovery will produce. The request will generally be granted if the party provides adequate reasons why the party cannot produce facts necessary to oppose summary judgment within the original time frame, and if the party has not been dilatory in his use of discovery. **Gamble v. Northstore Partnership,** Op. No. 4291, 907 P2d 477 (Alaska 1995).

Plaintiffs satisfied Rule 56(f)'s requirement of making an unambiguous request by submitting an affidavit stating that if the court were to reject their waiver argument, they would require additional discovery; explaining that the need for additional time to oppose summary judgment was their surprise when defendants raised an unanticipated affirmative defense; and identifying specific people they hoped to depose. **Gamble v. Northstore Partnership,** Op. No. 4291, 907 P2d 477 (Alaska 1995).

Declaration by non-moving party in opposition to summary judgment motion which was not notarized and did not assert that notary was unavailable was inadmissible even if declaration was made under penalty of perjury. **Bennett v. Weimar,** Op. No. 5104, 975 P2d 691 (Alaska 1999).

Summary judgment affidavit of a state labor relations analyst did not contain hearsay to the extent that it recited the testimony of a director as to the reason for terminating a public employee. That testimony did not go to the truth of the matter asserted, i.e. that the employee's position was one of public trust, but rather to the director's own belief why she thought the termination was for just cause. **Alaska State Emples. Association/ AFSCME Local 52 v. State,** Op. No. 5713, 74 P.3d 881 (Alaska 2003).

Superior court did not abuse its discretion in excluding an unsigned and unsworn declaration from its consideration of summary judgment, as assertions of fact in unverified pleadings and memoranda cannot be relied on in denying a motion for summary judgment. **Maines v. Kenworth Alaska, Inc.,** Op. No. 11255, 155 P.3d 318 (Alaska 2007).

II. Grant of Motion.

Under Rule 8(c) of the [Federal] R. Civ. P. affirmative defenses must be pleaded, but the court may grant a motion for judgment on the pleadings and if matters outside the pleadings are presented the motion shall be treated as one for summary judgment under [Federal] R. Civ. P. 56 and all parties must be given reasonable opportunity to present all matters pertinent to such motion, and the party against whom the motion is made may apply to the court for further time to prepare his resistance to the motion under Rule 6(b). **Mitchell v. Land,** Op. No. 19, 355 P2d 682 (Alaska 1960).

The granting of a motion for summary judgment in an action for the recovery for sums owed for utility services furnished was affirmed. **Gilbertson v. City of Fairbanks,** Op. No. 58, 368 P2d 214 (Alaska 1962).

Where defendant moved for summary judgment, it was incumbent upon plaintiff to produce facts of her own in controversion to the facts and circumstances set forth in defendant's affidavit, and the trial court did not err in granting a summary judgment in favor of the defendant. **Lowe v. Boggess,** Op. No. 110, 375 P2d 199 (Alaska 1962).

Where alleged factual issues were not material to a proper disposition of the controversy under applicable rules of law, summary judgment was properly granted. **Century Insurance Agency, Inc. v. City Commerce Corporation,** Op. No. 260, 396 P2d 80 (Alaska 1964).

Where opponents to motion for summary judgment failed to file a statement of material facts as required under this rule, they did not sustain their burden of demonstrating to the court by admissible evidence that a triable issue of fact existed. **Hickel v. Stevenson,** Op. No. 351, 416 P2d 236 (Alaska 1966).

In granting summary judgment it is unnecessary for the trial court to make findings in regard to the lack of any genuine issues of material facts. **Palzer v. Serv-U-Meat Co.,** Op. No. 367, 419 P2d 201 (Alaska 1966).

Plaintiff's assertion of "Jones Act" status could not preclude grant of defendant's motion for summary judgment where there was no evidentiary basis which could support a jury's finding that the plaintiff was a seaman and a member of a crew at the time he was injured. **Bowers v. Kaiser Steel Corp.,** Op. No. 384, 422 P2d 848 (Alaska 1967).

No genuine issue as to the effective date of a restrictive endorsement of an insurance policy was raised where the party opposing a cross-motion for summary judgment offered no evidence to dispute the fact that the restrictive endorsement was effective as of June 3, 1964, nor produced any evidence contradicting the fact that the date of June 3, 1965, which appeared on a copy filed with movant's complaint was the result of a typographical error. **Hart v. National Indemnity Co.,** Op. No. 387, 422 P2d 1015 (Alaska 1967).

A vague allegation in an affidavit in response to motion for summary judgment that a compromise and settlement between the parties was not properly authorized, which did not inform the court what admissible evidence would be produced at trial to support such an allegation, could not create a real issue of fact in the face of a specific showing of authority and compromise and of final settlement made by the motion for summary judgment. **Alaska-Canadian Corp. v. Ancow Corp.,** Op. No. 445, 434 P2d 534 (Alaska 1967).

Where by affidavit in support of motion for summary judgment the moving party had specifically set forth the making of an agreement as a final settlement of the dispute between the parties, a response affidavit which failed to come to grips with this allegation and instead, set forth the existence of a subsequent, rejected counter proposal to modify the existing contracts was not material to the determination of the basic issue, so that summary judgment was affirmed on appeal. **Alaska-Canadian Corp. v. Ancow Corp.,** Op. No. 445, 434 P2d 534 (Alaska 1967).

Where written agreement between the parties clearly and unambiguously superseded prior agreements between the parties so that basis for admissibility of parole evidence with regard to prior agreement was lacking, summary judgment was affirmed. **The Port Valdez Company, Inc. v. City of Valdez,** Op. No. 458, 437 P2d 768 (Alaska 1968).

An issue of the understanding of a fact raised by one party only by means of hearsay evidence which at a trial would be inadmissible over objection. While the other party's understanding of the fact was based on direct, non-hearsay evidence, was not a genuine triable issue of fact so as to prevent entry of summary judgment. **1200 "L" Street Corp. v. Inlet Co., Inc., Earl S. Kin g, and R. J. Cherrier,** Op. No. 464, 438 P2d 708 (Alaska 1968).

A showing in support of a preliminary injunction is sufficient to support a preliminary injunction for the buyer where the buyer of a seller's interest in a fuel oil business establishes the right to preliminary injunction against the seller's violation of a covenant not to compete, and the only matter before the court in opposition to a motion for summary judgment is that presented in opposition to the preliminary injunction plus a memorandum stating that there are genuine issues of fact without setting forth facts showing issues of material fact. **Barber v. Northern Heating Oil, Inc.,** Op. No. 512, 447 P2d 72 (Alaska 1968).

Summary judgment is proper where the pleadings, affidavits, depositions, and admissions on file show that there are no genuine issues as to any material fact. **Semlek v. National Bank of Alaska,** Op. No. 580, 458 P2d 1003 (Alaska 1969).

Where partial summary judgment had been granted in favor of one claimant in interpleader action, it would be deemed to have been satisfied to the extent of the amount previously paid into court, to obviate multiple claims. **Johnston v. All State Roofing & Paving Co., Inc.,** Op. No. 1351, 557 P2d 770 (Alaska 1976).

Summary judgment was proper where facts in affidavit of moving party were not controverted and adequately established claim. **Alaska National Bank v. Linck,** Op. No. 1372, 559 P2d 1049 (Alaska 1977).

Where nothing in record indicated a material dispute on issue of whether plaintiff passenger was a passenger of defendant airline at time of crash, trial court did not err in granting summary judgment on that issue. **Alaska Airlines, Inc. v. Sweat,** Op. No. 1464, 568 P2d 916 (Alaska 1977).

Trial court's grant of summary judgment, although incorrect as a matter of law, will be upheld if there is any other grant which as a matter of law, will support the result reached by the trial court. **Carlson v. State,** Op. No. 1903, 598 P2d 969 (Alaska 1978).

Where court decided that inverse condemnation had occurred, without deciding the amount of damages or to whom damages would be payable, it made an interlocutory summary judgment. **Williams v. City of Valdez,** Op. No. 1969, 603 P2d 483 (Alaska 1979).

Where moving party had presented affidavits in support of motion for summary judgment, adverse party could not rely on allegation in moving party's pleading as presenting an issue of material fact, and failure to present competent evidence on the issue justified granting of summary judgment. **Williams v. City of Valdez,** Op. No. 1969, 603 P2d 483 (Alaska 1979).

Where admissible evidence submitted by plaintiff was sufficient to raise a genuine issue of fact as to his incompetency, summary judgment based upon expiration of the statute of limitations period was improperly granted. **Adkins v. Nabors Alaska Drilling, Inc.,** Op. No. 2056, 609 P2d 15 (Alaska 1980).

Court erred in granting defendant's motion for summary judgment in an insurance company's suit for indemnification where there existed material questions of fact concerning whether statements made by defendant were the proximate cause of the loss suffered by the company. **Ambassador Insurance Co. v. Tobey, Inc.,** Op. No. 2197, 618 P2d 572 (Alaska 1980).

Summary judgment was proper in action to collect amounts due on promissory note where the effect of admissions was to acknowledge that all amounts were in fact owed. **Riley v. Northern Commercial Co.,** Op. No. 2534, 648 P2d 961 (Alaska 1982).

Where second deed of trust holder to apartment complex which was sold at a foreclosure sale offered no opposing affidavit to support his allegation that third deed of trust holder had been paid off by other sources, summary judgment in favor of the third deed of trust holder was proper, particularly when the second deed of trust holder made no attempt at discovery during the ten months between filing of the complaint and the granting of summary judgment. **Bevins v. Peoples Bank and Trust Co.,** Op. No. 2746, 671 P2d 875 (Alaska 1983).

State's refusal to close highway due to icy conditions falls within ambit of the discretionary function exception provided for in AS 09. 50.250(1). Accordingly, the State is immune from liability for its failure to close highway and summary judgment on that question was appropriate. **Estate of Arrowwood v. State,** Op. No. 4196, 894 P2d 642 (Alaska 1995).

Arbitrator committed gross error in finding that there was not just cause to terminate an administrative clerk from the Child Support Enforcement Division where the clerk was convicted for theft of public funds, had access to confidential information, and was in a position of public trust: therefore, summary judgment vacating the arbitration award was appropriate. **Alaska State Emples. Association/AFSCME Local 52 v. State,** Op. No. 5713, 74 P.3d 881 (Alaska 2003).

Summary judgment was properly granted to the State of Alaska where a probationary public employee failed to raise genuine issues of material fact on claims that despite the employee's probationary at-will status the employee could only be dismissed for good cause, that the State breached the covenant of good faith and fair dealing, or that the State breached a collective bargaining agreement by engaging in impermissible contracting. **Witt v. State,** Op. No. 5723, 75 P.3d 1030 (Alaska 2003).

Summary judgment was properly granted in favor of the patients where the health care provider liens the Alaska Native Tribal Health Consortium recorded on the settlements that two patients obtained from their respective tortfeasors were valid and had to be paid in full, less a pro rata share of the patient's attorney's fees and costs incurred in obtaining the recovery. **Alaska Native Tribal Health Consortium v. Settlement Funds Held for E.R.,** Op. No. 5775, 84 P.3d 418 (Alaska 2004).

In an action seeking to compel a corporation to seat a candidate on its board of directors, summary judgment was properly granted in favor of a member where the business judgment rule did not apply; the corporation had no discretion to disqualify an otherwise successful candidate based on campaign violations where the evidence showed that the candidate complied with the corrective procedures set forth in the bylaws within 30 days after receiving notice of the violations. **Matanuska Elec. Ass'n v. Waterman,** Op. No. 5790, 87 P.3d 820 (Alaska 2004).

In a case involving informed consent, summary judgment was improperly granted in favor of several healthcare providers where no evidence was presented regarding whether the risks associated with a catheterization were discussed with a patient prior to the performance of the procedure. **Parker v. Tomera,** Op. No. 5801, 89 P.3d 761 (Alaska 2004).

In a medical malpractice case, summary judgment was properly granted in favor of several healthcare providers because a patient failed to offer expert testimony to rebut the providers' expert, who opined that a procedure performed to ascertain whether or not the patient had interstitial cystitis was appropriate based on the symptoms described and that the procedure could not have caused sexual dysfunction. **Parker v. Tomera,** Op. No. 5801, 89 P.3d 761 (Alaska 2004).

Family recovery center owed a duty of care to protect a patient who was raped by another participant in her continuing care substance abuse treatment group, where the center knew that the rapist had a criminal history of sexual assaults; in the patient's lawsuit against the family recovery center, summary judgment was properly granted in favor of the patient on the issue of duty. **Bryson v. Banner Health Sys.,** Op. No. 5799, 89 P.3d 800 (Alaska 2004).

Grant of summary judgment against a corporation and in favor of the Department of Public Safety (DPS) and the Department of Community and Economic Development (DCED) was proper where the adoption of the International Mechanical Code complied with the requirements of AS 44.62.190; the DPS not only was permitted to issue regulations, but was required to issue them pursuant to AS 18.70.080(a)(2), and the DCED likewise had express statutory authority and responsibility to issue regulations in accordance with AS 08.40.240. **Mech. Contrs. of Alaska, Inc. v. State,** Op. No. 5805, 91 P.3d 240 (Alaska 2004).

Summary judgment for a contractor working with a laborer's employer, for intentional interference with a contract, was not proper where evidence of emails by the contractor implying that plaintiff laborer had possibly sabotaged the workplace made the contractor susceptible to a defamation claim; through other emails, the contractor demonstrated a pattern of attempts at undermining the laborer's desirability as an employee. **Kinzel v. Discovery Drilling, Inc.,** Op. No. 5820, 93 P.3d 427 (Alaska 2004).

Where the parties' prudent utility practice agreement applied to the electricity seller's debt management practices, the superior court's grant of summary judgment on this issue was reversed. **Matanuska Elec. Ass'n v. Chugach Elec. Ass'n,** Op. No. 5838, 99 P.3d 553, 2004 (Alaska 2004).

Summary judgment was improperly granted in a case alleging breach of contract and breach of fiduciary duty because there was a genuine issue of material fact as to whether releases in a settlement agreement were invalid due to misrepresentation. **Indus. Commer. Elec., Inc. v. McLees,** Op. No. 5843, 101 P.3d 593 (Alaska 2004).

In a customer's suit against an airline, arising from a series of customer service encounters, the superior court properly granted the airline summary judgment on some of the customer's defamation claims, based on statute of limitations and privilege grounds, and on the customer's failure to present evidence that one of the allegedly defamatory statements was published. **Hallam v. Alaska Airlines, Inc.,** Op. No. 1173, 91 P.3d 279 (Alaska 2004).

Where a trustee conducted a foreclosure sale for a first deed of trust beneficiary, complying with the terms of the deed of trust, postponing the sale to allow bidders to collect more money, and the ultimate acceptance of the highest bid from the first deed of trust beneficiary when the sale resumed did not violate Alaska law; summary judgment was properly granted to the first deed of trust beneficiary in a suit filed by a second deed of trust beneficiary arising from the foreclosure sale. **Cook Schuhmann & Groseclose, Inc. v. Brown & Root, Inc.,** Op. No. 5291, 116 P.3d 592 (Alaska 2005).

III. Denial of Motion.

The burden of showing the absence of a genuine issue of fact is upon the party who moves for summary judgment, and where there are genuine issues of fact, it is error to enter a summary judgment. **Ransom v. Haner,** Op. No. 37, 362 P2d 282, 289-90 (Alaska 1961).

Plaintiff's claim that justice required that her case not be subject to summary disposition inasmuch as she appeared in propria persona while the opposition consisted of three trained attorneys was without basis in law or reason. **Lowe v. Boggess,** Op. No. 110, 375 P2d 199 (Alaska 1962).

Evidence consisting only of an ex parte sworn statement was entirely insufficient to support summary judgment in a case involving important public issues. **Ault v. Alaska State Mortgage Association,** Op. No. 179, 387 P2d 698 (Alaska 1964).

Where an explanation of unanswered questions of intent of parties and of the interpretation of insurance contracts might be furnished by a trial of the case and appellant requested the opportunity to supplement evidence of intent, summary judgment was premature and the case was remanded for trial of the issues. **Pepsi Cola Bottling Co. v. New Hampshire Ins. Co.,** Op. No. 308, 407 P2d 1009 (Alaska 1965).

Denial of summary judgment to appellants was affirmed and summary judgment granted to appellee was reversed where study of record and of the applicable law disclosed the existence of a genuine issue as to a material fact. **Hartsfield v. Carolina Casualty Insurance Co.,** Op. No. 328, 411 P2d 396 (Alaska 1966).

The denial by the insured of receiving notice of cancellation of insurance policy rebuts a prima facie case of mailing and where under the applicable law, mailing of cancellation rather than receiving of the notice was the prerequisite for effective termination of the policy, a material issue of fact was raised which called for its resolution by the trier of fact, and granting of summary judgment to the insurer was error. **Hartsfield v. Carolina Casualty Insurance Co.,** Op. No. 328, 411 P2d 396 (Alaska 1966).

It was error to grant summary judgment on the basis of affidavits from a witness who admitted therein that she had previously made a material false statement to police officers in an automobile accident case because such admission raised an issue of credibility and thereby presented genuine issues of material facts. **Wilson v. Pollet,** Op. No. 354, 416 P2d 381 (Alaska 1966).

In an ejectment action in which plaintiff must recover on the strength of his own title and not upon the weakness of his adversary's title, evidence in support of plaintiff's motion for summary judgment which revealed the existence of questions as to plaintiff's claim of title and right to possession failed to meet the burden of showing the absence of any genuine issue as to any material facts. **Wright v. Prior,** Op. No. 358, 417 P2d 602 (Alaska 1966).

Where testimony at the time of plaintiff's motion for summary judgment had raised a factual issue in regard to plaintiff's contributory negligence, motion was properly denied. **Bertram v. Harris,** Op. No. 393, 423 P2d 909 (Alaska 1967).

Questions of existence of an oral contract to sell real property and of admission of its existence in pleadings in another action so as to take the contract out of the statute of frauds, were genuine issues of material facts, and entry of summary judgment of dismissal of action for specific performance of the alleged oral contract was error. **Gray v. Fields,** Op. No.

480, 440 P2d 855 (Alaska 1968).

An affidavit filed by counsel in a declaratory judgment action is insufficient to support a summary judgment where it is not demonstrably made upon personal knowledge, fails to set forth facts that are admissible in evidence, and does not show affirmatively that affiant would be competent to testify as to matters stated. **National Indemnity Co. v. Flesher,** Op. No. 612, 469 P2d 360 (Alaska 1970).

Where the defendant alleges that the out of state court which rendered judgment against him lacked personal jurisdiction, it is error for a court of this state to grant summary judgment to the plaintiff, seeking to enforce the extraterritorial judgment, since such action prevents the defendant from being heard on his defenses. **Belon v. Belon,** Op. No. 811, 498 P2d 711 (Alaska 1972).

Where facts were not material, argument that existence of factual issues made summary judgment inappropriate was without merit. **Alaska Airlines, Inc. v. Sweat,** Op. No. 1464, 568 P2d 916 (Alaska 1977).

Motion for summary judgment ordering specific performance of a contract to sell real estate denied where moving party could not demonstrate that it was entitled to judgment as a matter of law. **Alaska Laborers Tr. Fund v.P & R Enterprises,** Op. No. 1705, 583 P2d 825 (Alaska 1978).

Grant of a motion for summary judgment is in error where a genuine issue of fact exists in determining whether a municipality which gratuitously rendered a service exercised reasonable care in its undertaking. **Williams v. Municipality of Anchorage,** Op. No. 2408, 633 P2d 248 (Alaska 1981).

Superior court did not abuse its discretion in denying plaintiffs request for additional time for discovery under this rule where plaintiff had not initiated discovery during the three year period which had elapsed since the accident which gave rise to the suit. **Brock v. Weaver Bros., Inc.,** Op. No. 2470, 640 P2d 833 (Alaska 1982).

Where city did not establish as a matter of law that city employee did not have a contractual right not to be dismissed under the city's personnel ordinance, the granting of summary judgment in favor of the city was error. **Stanfill v. City of Fairbanks,** Op. No. 2624, 659 P2d 579 (Alaska 1983).

In action to establish priority of claims to fire insurance proceeds, summary judgment in favor of claim by law firm was error, where disputed fact existed as to whether law firm had notice of court ordered assignment of proceeds to tort claimants prior to time when the firm obtained a written assignment from one of the insureds. **McKnight v. Rice, Hoppner, Brown & Brunner,** Op. No. 2798, 678 P2d 1330 (Alaska 1984).

In action by pipeline company against contractor pursuant to indemnity provision in contract, an issue of material fact existed as to whether the pipeline company breached its implied contractual duty of good faith and fair dealing, precluding summary judgment. **Alyeska Pipeline Service v. H. C. Price Co.,** Op. No. 2897, 694 P2d 782 (Alaska 1985).

Grantor's intent was an unresolved issue of material fact in an easement controversy, thus trial court erred in entering summary judgment. **Aszmus v. Nelson,** Op. No. 3236, 743 P2d 377 (Alaska 1987).

In a claim by a crane operator against a company for intentional interference with contractual rights, arising out of the company's refusal to allow him to work on its oil platform, the trial court erred in granting summary judgment, since a genuine issue of material fact existed as to whether the company's predominant motivation in requesting another crane operator was work safety or personal ill will. **Hatten v. Union Oil Co. of California,** Op. No. 3494, 778 P2d 1150 (Alaska 1989).

Summary judgment was improper where a genuine issue of material fact existed as to whether appellees, as bona fide executives, were exempt from the overtime pay provisions of the Alaska Wage and Hour Act. **American Restaurant Group v. Clark,** Op. No. 4163, 889 P2d 595 (Alaska 1995).

Question of whether appellees were "professional employees" as defined in 8AAC 15.910(a)(11) was a genuine issue of material fact which precluded entry of pretrial summary judgment. **American Restaurant Group v. Clark,** Op. No. 4163, 889 P2d 595 (Alaska 1995).

Trial court did not err in denying a motion for summary judgment filed by a representative and an estate on the issue of permission in a wrongful death action after treating the issue as disputed under Alaska R. Civ. P. 15(b) because a driver's statement regarding permission was not a judicial admission; it was susceptible of more than one meaning, only one of which would have established a violation of AS 28.15.281(b). **Crosby v. Hummell,** Op. No. 5664, 63 P.3d 1022 (Alaska 2003).

In an insurance coverage lawsuit, the trial court properly denied the insured's motion for partial summary judgment against an insurance company and an insurance agent on the issue of coverage; although the insured alleged that the agent was negligent in failing to use reasonable efforts to obtain the insured's "last known address," and that the insurance company's attempts to cancel his policy for non-payment of the renewal premium were ineffective, there was a genuine dispute as to whether the insured gave the agent his new address. **Blood v. Kenneth Murray Ins., Inc.,** 68 P.3d 1251 (Alaska 2003).

In a medical malpractice suit where plaintiffs argued the hospital was liable for the negligence of an independent contractor surgeon, the trial court erred in granting partial summary judgment to the hospital; plaintiffs were permitted to proceed under a theory of direct liability based on corporate negligence. **Fletcher v. S. Peninsula Hosp.,** Op. No. 5701, 71 P.3d 833 (Alaska 2003).

Summary judgment motion filed by a creditor of an insolvent life insurer was properly denied as the creditor was not entitled to have its claim allowed under the automatic approval rule of AS 21.78.293(b) based on the trial court's failure to disapprove the claim within 120 days of the filing of the receiver's report; AS 21.78.293(b) pertained to claims allowed by the receiver, while AS 21.78.170(d) pertained to claims such as the creditor's, which had been disallowed by the receiver. **In re Life Ins. Co.,** Op. No. 5729, 76 P.3d 366 (Alaska 2003).

In a dispute regarding a contract to purchase a dredge, which did not specify the items included in the sale, material factual issues existed as to which items were dredge equipment and related facilities; because the parties' expectations could not be ascertained from the words of the contract or from extrinsic evidence, and a settlement agreement regarding certain items was not an accord and satisfaction, the trial court erred in granting summary judgment with respect to personal property. **K & K Recycling, Inc. v. Alaska Gold Co.,** Op. No. 5752, 80 P.3d 702 (Alaska 2003).

Denial of summary judgment as to repudiation, in a contract dispute involving the purchase of a dredge, was proper because factual issues existed as to whether alleged acts of interference by an assignee clearly manifested an intention to prevent performance under the contract. **K & K Recycling, Inc. v. Alaska Gold Co.,** Op. No. 5752, 80 P.3d 702 (Alaska 2003).

Assignee's known motive to interfere with performance of a contract to purchase and remove a dredge gave rise to a material factual issue precluding summary judgment as to whether the assignment was a breach of contract under AS 45.02.210(b). **K & K Recycling, Inc. v. Alaska Gold Co.,** Op. No. 5752, 80 P.3d 702 (Alaska 2003).

Court properly denied a city's motion for summary judgment in a false confinement suit where an officer did not have a reasonable belief that a driver had information to aid his investigation, and therefore, exigent circumstances were lacking. **City of Kodiak v. Samaniego,** Op. No. 5772, 83 P.3d 1077 (Alaska 2004).

In a commercial sublease dispute, a court erred by granting summary judgment to a tenant where whether the landlord's refusal to consent to a sublease was unreasonable was a question of fact that should not have been resolved by summary judgment; the landlord's reasons for refusing consent—concerns about competition with a primary tenant and about the fact that the subleased space would not be contributing to gross sales for purposes of percentage rent calculations—were plausible, and whether they were genuine and reasonable under the circumstances of the case were questions of fact. **Norville v. Carr Gottstein Foods Co.,** Op. No. 5778, 84 P.3d 996 (Alaska 2004).

Curfew ordinance at former Anchorage, Ala., Mun. Ordinance 8.05.440, renumbered at Anchorage, Ala., Mun. Ordinance 8.75.060, was facially constitutional because it was the least restrictive means for achieving the municipality's compelling interests in protecting minors from crime and curbing juvenile crime; summary judgment was improperly denied to a municipality in a declaratory action challenging the constitutionality of the ordinance. **Treacy v. Municipality of Anchorage,** Op. No. 5807, 91 P.3d 252 (Alaska 2004).

In a customer's suit against an airline arising from a series of customer service encounters, the superior court properly denied the customer's motion for further time under section (f) of this rule; the customer only identified two missing documents, neither of which made a case for reopening discovery. **Hallam v. Alaska Airlines, Inc.,** Op. No. 1173, 91 P.3d 279 (Alaska 2004).

Summary judgment was properly denied to the gym where the gym patron's claim that the gym failed to meet basic standards of maintenance and safety by failing to correct known hazards, thereby causing her knee injury, was not conspicuously and unequivocally precluded by a release she had signed, read as a whole; the patron was not barred by the release from bringing her claim, and the gym was not entitled to summary judgment on the issue of liability. **Ledgends, Inc. v. Kerr,** Op. No. 5810, 91 P.3d 960 (Alaska 2004).

Inmate and his wife, who brought a suit alleging malpractice and other things, against prison medical personnel, properly met the three requirements for a continuance to obtain an expert's affidavit pursuant to Alaska R. Civ. P. 56(f). The inmate and his wife showed that they had made an unambiguous request for relief, they were not dilatory about discovery, and they provided reasons why additional time was needed. **Hymes v. Deramus,** Op. No. 5936, 119 P.3d 963 (Alaska 2005).

Where case is a single action against two defendants, dismissal as to only one of the two defendants cannot support entry of a final judgment for the other in the absence of an express finding of good cause for a partial judgment under Alaska Civil Rule 54(b). **J&S Serv., Inc. v. Tomter,** Op. No. 11375, 139 P.3d 544 (Alaska 2006).

Rule 57. Declaratory Judgments—Judgments by Confession.

(a) **Declaratory Judgments.** The procedure for obtaining a declaratory judgment pursuant to statute shall be in accordance with these rules, and the right to trial by jury may be demanded under the circumstances and in the manner provided in Rules 38 and 39. The existence of another adequate remedy does not preclude a judgment for declaratory relief in cases where it is appropriate. The court may order a speedy hearing of an action for a declaratory judgment and may advance it on the calendar.

(b) **Confession Judgments—After Commencement of Action.**

(1) On the confession of the defendant, with the assent of the plaintiff or the plaintiff's attorney, a judgment may be given against the defendant in any action, for any amount not exceeding or relief different from that demanded in the complaint.

(2) The confession shall be in writing and signed by the defendant. The assent shall be in writing and signed by the parties or their attorneys. The confession and assents shall each be acknowledged before an officer authorized by law to administer oaths unless the parties or their attorneys appear in court when the judgment is given. The confession, assent and acknowledgment, if any, shall be filed with the clerk.

(c) **Confession Judgments—Without Action.**

(1) On the confession of any person capable of being made a defendant to an action, judgment may be given against such person without action, in favor of anyone, either for money due or to become due, or to secure any person against contingent liability on behalf of the defendant in such judgment, or both, if it be in favor of the same person.

(2) The confession shall be made, assented to and acknowledged and judgment given in the same manner as a confession in an action pending, but in addition, the confession shall be verified by the oath of the person making it, and shall authorize a judgment to be given for a particular sum. If it be for money due or to become due it shall state plainly and concisely the facts out of which such indebtedness arose, and shall show that the sum confessed therefor is justly due or to become due. If it be for the purpose of securing the plaintiff in the judgment against a contingent liability, it shall state plainly and concisely the facts constituting such liability and shall show that the sum confessed therefor does not exceed the same. When judgment is given so as to be payable in installments, executions may issue to enforce the payment of such installments as they become due.

(Adopted by SCO 5 October 9, 1959; amended by SCO 49 effective January 1, 1963; and by SCO 1153 effective July 15, 1994)

Cross References

(b)(1) **CROSS REFERENCE:** AS 09.30.050; AS 09.30.060
(b)(2) **CROSS REFERENCE:** AS 09.30.050; AS 09.30.060
(c)(1) **CROSS REFERENCE:** AS 09.30.050; AS 09.30.060

Annotations

Cases

Where plaintiff brought an action for declaratory judgment that it was not a bank, evidence could be introduced by defendants to show that plaintiff did the business of banking after alleging such acts as a "third defense," and defendants were not required to make this "third defense" a "counterclaim." **American Building & Loan v. State,** Op. No. 112, 376 P2d 370 (Alaska 1962).

In declaratory judgment action it was not error for the trial court to grant relief for the defendants where defendants had not prayed for any relief whatsoever. Where upon the merits of the controversy the plaintiff is not entitled to a favorable declaration, the court should render a judgment embodying such determination and should not merely dismiss the action. **American Building & Loan v. State,** Op. No. 112, 376 P2d 370 (Alaska 1962).

A payment document which was filed by the defendant in a personal injury case in the superior court stating in substance that the full policy amount plus $1,000 as "costs to date" were paid into the registry of the court and requesting that the court notify the plaintiff of such tender and relieve the defendant of liability for costs and attorney's fees, was not a confession of judgment in the meaning of this rule. **Albritton v. Estate of Larson,** Op. No. 413, 428 P2d 379 (Alaska 1967).

The general rules of pleading and of civil procedure apply to actions of declaratory relief. **Jefferson v. Asplund,** Op. No. 579, 458 P2d 995 (Alaska 1969).

All that is required of a complaint seeking declaratory relief is a simple statement of the facts demonstrating that the superior court had jurisdiction and that an actual justiciable case or controversy is presented. **Jefferson v. Asplund,** Op. No. 579, 458 P2d 995 (Alaska 1969).

Statutory language giving a declaratory judgment the force of a final judgment and making it reviewable as such does not change the effect of this rule's provision that when multiple claims for relief are involved in an action, partial summary judgment may be entered as to one or more, but fewer than all, of the claims or parties only upon the express determination that there is no just reason for delay, and upon express direction by the court for the entry of judgment. **Alaska Airlines, Inc. v. Red Dodge Aviation, Inc.,** Op. No. 640, 475 P2d 229 (Alaska 1970).

This rule does not independently give a court jurisdiction to hear declaratory judgment actions, but only governs such actions when they are otherwise properly before the court. **Standard Prod. v. Dept. of Revenue,** Op. No. 3425, 773 P2d 201 (Alaska 1989).

Motion for declaratory judgment was unnecessary where declaratory judgment was sought in pleadings. **State Dept. of Nat. Res. v. Transamerica,** Op. No. 3979, 856 P2d 766 (Alaska 1993).

In class action suit by legal aliens residing in Alaska seeking declaratory judgment as to constitutionality of statute restricting permanent fund dividend eligibility to persons lawfully admitted for permanent residence in the United States, trial court did not err in concluding that class members were not required to exhaust administrative remedies, since to do so would have been futile, or in concluding that class certification was proper. **State Dept. of Revenue v. Andrade,** Op. No. 5414, 23 P3d 58 (Alaska 2001).

Declaratory action under Alaska R. Civ. P. 57(a) and AS 22.10.020(g) was properly dismissed because by the time a former assemblyman had brought his defamation action, the dispute at issue had already "ripened" into an alleged actual violation of law, and the superior court therefore did not abuse its discretion in determining that the coercive remedies available to the assemblyman would be more effective, or "final and conclusive." **Lowell v. Hayes,** Op. No. 5924, 117 P.3d 745 (Alaska 2005).

Rule 58. Entry of Judgment.

Subject to the provisions of Rule 54(b): (1) upon a general verdict of a jury, or upon a decision by the court that a party shall recover only a sum certain or costs or that all relief shall be denied, the court or the clerk, upon direction of the court, shall forthwith enter the judgment; (2) upon a decision by the court granting other relief, or upon a special verdict or a general verdict accompanied by answers to interrogatories, the court shall promptly enter judgment. Every judgment must be set forth on a separate document distinct from any findings of fact, conclusions of law, opinion, or memorandum. Entry of the judgment shall not be delayed, nor the time for appeal extended, for the taxing of costs or the award of fees. Judgments for the payment of money must be in the form required by Civil Rule 58.2.

(Adopted by SCO 5 October 9, 1959; amended by SCO 258 effective November 15, 1976; by SCO 554 effective April 4, 1983; by SCO 1281 effective August 7, 1997; by SCO 1295 effective January 15, 1998; by SCO 1415 effective October 15, 2000; and by SCO 1482 effective October 15, 2002)

Note: Ch. 139, Sec. 1. SLA 1986, enacted AS 09.17.040 and AS 09.17.080 regarding awards of damages for personal injury and the apportionment of damages. According to Section 7 of the Act, AS 09.17.040 and AS 09.17.080 have the effect of amending Civil Rule 58. AS 09.17.040 requires verdicts to include an itemization between economic and non-economic losses, and allows for periodic payment in certain circumstances. AS 09.17.080, as amended, requires special interrogatories or finding on the amount to damages and percentages of fault, and requires that judgment be entered against each liable party on the basis of several liability.

Note: Ch. 26, sec. 10, SLA 1997 repeals and reenacts AS 09.17.020 concerning punitive damages. New AS 09.17.020(j) requires that 50 percent of an award of punitive damages be deposited in the state general fund. This provision applies to causes of action accruing on or after August 7, 1997. See ch. 26, sec. 55, SLA 1997. According to sec. 49 of the Act, new AS 09.17.020(j) has the effect of amending Civil Rule 58 by requiring the court to order that a certain percentage of an award of punitive damages be deposited into the general fund.

Note: Ch. 26, sec. 19, SLA 1997 amends AS 09.30.070 by adding subsection (c) concerning prejudgment interest on awards of future economic damages, future noneconomic damages, and punitive damages. This provision applies to causes of action accruing on or after August 7, 1997. See ch. 26, sec. 55, SLA 1997. According to sec. 53 of the Act, new AS 09.30.070(c) has the effect of amending Civil Rule 58 by providing that prejudgment interest may not be awarded for future economic or noneconomic damages or punitive damages.

Note: Sections 41, 43, 45, and 46 of chapter 87 SLA 1997 amend AS 25.20.050(n), AS 25.24.160(d), AS 25.24.210(e), and AS 25.24.230(i), respectively, to require that an order or acknowledgement of paternity, a divorce decree, a petition for dissolution of marriage, and a dissolution decree include the social security number of each party to the action and each child whose rights are being addressed. According to § 151 of the Act, these provisions have the effect of amending Civil Rules 52, 58, 78, and 90.1 by requiring the court to include social security numbers, if ascertainable, of parties and children in certain petitions, pleadings, and judgments.

Cross References

CROSS REFERENCE: AS 09.30.010; AS 09.30.020; AS 09.17.020(j)

Annotations

Cases

In determining the time within which an appeal may be taken the term "entry of judgment," as it applies to trials by jury is set forth in Civ. R. 58. **Vogt v. Winbauer,** Op. No. 117, 376 P2d 1007 (Alaska 1962).

The 30-day period within which notice of appeal had to be given by the appellant commenced to run on the date upon which judgment was noted by the clerk in the civil docket. **Vogt v. Winbauer,** Op. No. 117, 376 P2d 1007 (Alaska 1962).

Where the court directs that all relief be denied, the clerk shall enter judgment forthwith upon receipt by him of the directions. **Patrick v. Sedwick,** Op. No. 154, 387 P2d 294 (Alaska 1963).

It is contrary to the letter and purpose of Rule 58 to postpone entry of judgment until after a formal written judgment has been signed by the judge and filed. **McCoy v. Alaska Brick Co.,** Op. No. 192, 389 P2d 1009 (Alaska 1964).

Where on February 1st, the jury returned a general verdict accompanied by answers to interrogatories, but the court waited until February 8 to direct the entry of a formal judgment, the ten-day period for service and filing of a cost bill commenced at the latter date. **Patterson v. Cushman,** Op. No. 233, 394 P2d 657 (Alaska 1964).

Where the parties had stipulated that their agreement for settlement of a dispute constituted a final disposition of the litigation and a docket entry was made on January 12, clearly indicating the final settlement and dismissal by the court of the claim and counterclaim by M.O. and on April 6 following a transcript of the proceedings was filed in accordance with the settlement and dismissal and a docket entry of the same date clearly so stated, a final judgment dismissing the complaint and counterclaim with prejudice was entered either on January 12 or at the latest on April 6, and an erroneous docket entry by the clerk dated July 28 of "judgment of dismissal of complaint and counterclaim" which did not correctly reflect what occurred on that date, was not the entry of a judgment from which an appeal could be taken.

Gravel v. Alaskan Village, Inc., Op. No. 321, 409 P2d 983 (Alaska 1966).

The Supreme Court will not indulge in literalism in reading the rule that the notation of a judgment in the civil docket as provided by Civil R. 74 constitutes the entry of the judgment where the parties with concurrence of the court below had clearly stipulated that a transcript of proceedings wherein they had agreed to a dismissal with prejudice of their respective complaint and counterclaim constituted a final and complete settlement of their dispute and the docket entries without stating in so many words that a "judgment was entered," nevertheless clearly expressed the intent of the parties and the concurrence of the court. **Gravel v. Alaskan Village, Inc.,** Op. No. 321, 409 P2d 983 (Alaska 1966).

Prejudgment interest is in the nature of damages and is necessary to compensate the plaintiff, not only for the amount by which he has suffered damage in the usual sense but also for the loss of use of the money to which he is entitled. **Davis v. Chism,** Op. No. 919, 513 P2d 475 (Alaska 1973).

Where relief was obtained by summary judgment but final judgment was entered at a later time, the date of entry of the final judgment triggered the 30-day appeal period. **Schneider v. Pay'n Save Corp.,** Op. No. 3095, 723 P2d 619 (Alaska 1986).

This rule mandates that the entry of judgment not be delayed while the court determined fees and costs, making it appropriate for the court to enter the judgment on the merits without waiting for a final determination of fees and costs. **Kozevnikoff v. Tanana Village Council,** Op. No. 5800, 89 P.3d 757 (Alaska 2004).

Rule 58.1. Judgments and Orders— Effective Dates and Commencement of Time for Appeal, Review and Reconsideration.

(a) **Effective Dates of Orders and Judgments.** Orders and judgments become effective the date they are entered.

(1) *Oral Orders.* The date of entry of an oral order is the date the order is put on the official electronic record by the judge unless otherwise specified by the judge. At the time the judge announces an oral order, the judge shall also announce on the record whether the order shall be reduced to writing. If the oral order is reduced to writing, the effective date shall be included in the written order.

(2) *Written Orders Not Preceded by Oral Orders.* The date of entry of a written order not preceded by an oral order is the date the written order is signed unless otherwise specified in the order.

(3) *Judgments.* The date of entry of a civil judgment is the date it is signed unless otherwise specified in the judgment. All judgments shall be reduced to writing.

(b) **Commencement of Time for Appeal, Review and Reconsideration.** The time within which a notice of appeal may be filed and reconsideration or review of orders and judgments may be requested begins running on the date of notice as defined below.

(c) **Date of Notice.**

(1) *Oral Orders.*

(i) As to the parties present when an oral order is announced, the date of notice is the date the judge announces the order on the official electronic record, unless at that time the judge announces that the order will be reduced to writing in which case the date of notice is the date shown in the clerk's certificate of distribution on the written order.

(ii) As to parties not present at the announcement of an oral order, the date of notice is the date shown in the clerk's certificate of distribution of notice of the order. If, however, at the time the judge announces the oral order the judge announces that the order will be reduced to writing, the date of notice is the date shown in the clerk's certificate of distribution on the written order.

(2) *Written Orders.* The date of notice of a written order is the date shown in the clerk's certificate of distribution on the written order.

(3) *Judgments.* All judgments must be reduced to writing. The date of notice of a judgment is the date shown in the clerk's certificate of distribution on the written judgment.

(4) *Other Service Requirements.* The notice provisions apply to the notice of orders and judgments under Rule 73(d) and do not affect the service requirements of any other rule of civil procedure.

(d) **Clerk's Certificate of Distribution.** Every written notice of an oral order and every written order and judgment shall include a clerk's certificate of distribution showing the date copies of the notice, order or judgment were distributed, the name of each person to whom a copy was distributed, and the name or initials of the court employee who distributed the copies.

(Added by SCO 554 effective April 4, 1983; amended by SCO 900 effective January 15, 1989; by SCO 1153 effective July 15, 1994; and by SCO 1414 effective October 15, 2000)

Cross References

CROSS REFERENCE: App. R. 204

Annotations

Cases

Where defendant executed a confession of judgment without action which was entered as a judgment on September 18, 1986, but was not sent a copy of the judgment and did not learn of it until September 26, 1988, his motion to set aside the confession of judgment filed October 18, 1988 was deemed timely. **Princiotta v. Municipality of Anchorage,** Op. No. 3548, 785 P2d 559 (Alaska 1990).

Written orders are considered effective on the date they are entered, that is, the date on which the order is signed **Johnson v. Siegfried,** Op. No. 3890, 838 P2d 1252 (Alaska 1992).

Rule 58.2. Judgments for the Payment of Money.

(a) **Form Generally.** In addition to identifying each judgment creditor and each judgment debtor, a judgment for the payment of money must include the following information, if applicable, in the form shown in the sample judgment published at the end of this rule:

(A) the principal amount of the judgment;

(B) the portion of the principal that accrues prejudgment interest and the prejudgment interest rate, except as provided in (b);

(C) the date from which prejudgment interest should be

calculated, except as provided in (b);

(D) a blank space for the court to fill in the amount of prejudgment interest;

(E) a blank space for the court to fill in the amount of attorney's fees awarded;

(F) a blank space for the court to fill in the amount of costs awarded;

(G) a blank space for the total judgment amount; and

(H) the post-judgment interest rate.

(b) **Prejudgment Interest.** The total amount of prejudgment interest will be calculated by the court. If more than one interest rate applies or interest is calculated from more than one date, the interest rate and date should not be listed in the judgment as provided in (a). Instead, the party preparing the judgment must submit a separate computation sheet showing the interest calculations, including all applicable interest rates and dates, any payments, and how payments were applied to interest, costs, and principal.

(c) **Identification of Judgment Creditors and Judgment Debtors.** When identifying judgment creditors and judgment debtors, the party preparing the judgment must include as much of each person's full legal name as is known to that party and each person's date of birth, if known to that party.

(d) **Name of Judge.** In a proposed judgment, the name of the judge, if known, must be typed under the judge's signature line.

(e) **Child Support Orders.** This rule does not apply to child support orders. The form of child support orders is governed by Civil Rule 90.3(j).

(f) **Rejection for Noncompliance.** The clerk may reject proposed judgments that do not comply with this rule and Civil Rule 76.

(Adopted by SCO 1415 effective October 15, 2000)

CIVIL

SAMPLE JUDGMENT

(not to scale)

IN THE SUPERIOR COURT FOR THE STATE OF ALASKA

THIRD JUDICIAL DISTRICT AT ANCHORAGE

BARBARA A. JONES,	)	
Plaintiff,	)	
vs.	)	
	)	
MARY JANE SMITH and	)	
FRED R. SMITH,	)	Case No. 3AN-00-1234CI
	)	
Defendants.	)	FINAL JUDGMENT
	)	

IT IS ORDERED that judgment is entered as follows:

1. Plaintiff Barbara Ann Jones, d.o.b. 1/24/57, shall recover from and have judgment against defendants Mary Jane Smith, d.o.b. 1/26/56, and Frederick Ronald Smith, d.o.b. 3/24/56, jointly and severally, as follows:

   a. Principal Amount $________

   b. Prejudgment Interest on $_________________ $________

   (computed at the annual rate of________ %

   from ________ to date of judgment)

   c. Sub-Total: $________

   d. Attorney's Fees $________

   Date Awarded: _________

   Judge: ___________

   e. Costs ___________

   Date Awarded: _________

   Clerk: ___________

   f. TOTAL JUDGMENT: $________

   g. Post-Judgment Interest Rate: _________ %

2. (non-monetary provision)

______________ ________________________________

Date George W. Black

Superior Court Judge

Judgments longer than one page must have footer setting out the document title (e.g., "Final Judgment"), case name, case number, and page numbering (page x of y). See Civil Rule 76(a)(5).

Rule 59. New Trials—Amendment of Judgments.

(a) **Grounds.** A new trial may be granted to all or any of the parties and on all or part of the issues in an action in which there has been a trial by jury or in an action tried without a jury, if required in the interest of justice. On a motion for a new trial in an action tried without a jury, the court may take additional testimony, amend findings of fact and conclusions of law or make new findings and conclusions, and direct the entry of a new judgment.

(b) **Motion: Time for Serving—Statement of Grounds.** A motion for a new trial shall be served not later than 10 days after the date shown in the clerk's certificate of distribution on the judgment. The motion shall state the grounds upon which the moving party relies and shall refer to the papers on which the motion is to be based.

(c) **Time for Serving Affidavits.** When a motion for a new trial is based upon affidavits they shall be served with the motion. The opposing party has 10 days after such service within which to serve opposing affidavits, which period may be extended for an additional period not exceeding 20 days either by the court for good cause shown or by the parties by written stipulation. The court may permit reply affidavits.

(d) **Contents of Affidavit.** If a ground of the motion is newly discovered evidence, the motion shall be supported by the affidavit of the party, or of the party's agent or any officer within whose charge or knowledge the facts are, and also by the affidavit of the party's attorney, showing that the evidence was in fact newly discovered and why it could not with reasonable diligence have been produced at the trial. If the newly discovered evidence consists of oral testimony, the motion shall be supported by the affidavit of the witness or witnesses to the effect that the witness or witnesses would give the testimony proposed. If the newly discovered evidence is documentary, the motion shall be supported by the documents themselves or by duly authenticated copies thereof, or if that is impracticable, by satisfactory evidence of their contents.

(e) **On Initiative of Court.** Not later than 10 days after entry of judgment the court of its own initiative may order a new trial for any reason for which it might have granted a new trial on motion of a party. After giving the parties notice and an opportunity to be heard on the matter, the court may grant a motion for a new trial, timely served, for a reason not stated in the motion. In either case, the court shall specify the grounds therefor.

(f) **Motion to Alter or Amend a Judgment.** A motion to alter or amend the judgment shall be served not later than 10 days after the entry of the judgment.

(Adopted by SCO 5 October 9, 1959; amended by SCO 258 effective November 15, 1976; by SCO 554 effective April 4, 1983; by SCO 1153 effective July 15, 1994; and by SCO 1361 effective October 15, 1999)

Note: Chapter 42 § 2 SLA 1999 enacts AS 09.19.200 which governs the remedies available in civil litigation involving conditions in correctional facilities. According to § 3 of the act, the enactment of AS 09.19.200 has the effect of amending Civil Rules 59(f), 60(b), 62, and 65 by altering the remedies available and the procedure to be used in litigation involving correctional facilities.

Annotations

Cases

I. Grounds.
- A. In General.
- B. Newly Discovered Evidence.
- C. Damages.
- D. Jury Action.

II. Time for Motion.

I. Grounds.

A. In General.

The granting or refusal of a request for a new trial rests in the sound discretion of the trial judge which shall be disturbed on appeal only in exceptional circumstances and to prevent a miscarriage of justice. **Montgomery Ward v. Thomas,** Op. No. 236, 394 P2d 774 (Alaska 1964).

Denial of a new trial was sustained where evidence of the value of property on which jury based its verdict in a condemnation case, was not so slight and unconvincing as to make the verdict plainly unreasonable and unjust. **Alaska State Housing Authority v. Vincent,** Op. No. 261, 396 P2d 531 (Alaska 1964).

Granting motion for judgment notwithstanding the verdict did not amount to automatic denial of an alternative motion for a new trial based on grounds which were not appropriate for consideration in connection with motion for judgment n.o.v., and reversal by the Supreme Court of the judgment n.o.v. and trial court's subsequent decision to deny a new trial resulted for the first time in a judgment appealable by appellant for alleged errors of law committed at the trial. **Alaska Brick Co. v. McCoy,** Op. No. 287, 400 P2d 454 (Alaska 1965).

Where motion for a new trial asserted misconduct of opposing counsel by intentional and repeated propounding of questions framed to elicit inadmissible testimony, the trial judge was best able to determine in his discretion whether there was intentional misconduct and to evaluate possible impact of the questioning upon the jury, and the trial judge's ruling denying the motion was sustained on appeal. **Otis Elevator Co. v. McLaney,** Op. No. 300, 406 P2d 7 (Alaska 1965).

Where reasonable men could differ on a question whether appellee's conduct measured up to that of a reasonably prudent man under the circumstances, denial of motion for new trial was sustained. **National Bank of Alaska v. McHugh,** Op. No. 352, 416 P2d 239 (Alaska 1966).

In order to hold that a trial judge's refusal to order a remittitur or grant a new trial was an abuse of discretion, the Supreme Court would have to be left with a definite and firm conviction on the whole record that the refusal was a mistake. **National Bank of Alaska v. McHugh,** Op. No. 352,416 P2d 239 (Alaska 1966).

Where appellant did not move for a new trial, the discretion of the court below to grant a new trial was never invoked so that it could be held that there was nothing to review in regard to failure to grant a new trial. **Heacock v. Town,** Op. No. 368, 419 P2d 622 (Alaska 1966).

This rule was intended to limit any new trial to issues incorrectly decided or not decided at all. **City of Fairbanks v. Nesbett,** Op. No. 439, 432 P2d 607 (Alaska 1967).

A trial court may deny a new trial on the condition that the plaintiff accept a remittitur. **City of Kotzebue v. Ipalook,** Op. No. 588, 462 P2d 75 (Alaska 1969).

Where a motion for post judgment relief is made within ten days after the entry of judgment, it should ordinarily be treated as having been made under section (f) of this rule. **United States Fire Insurance Co. v. Schnabel,** Op. No. 852, 504 P2d 847 (Alaska 1972).

In reviewing the trial court's exercise of discretion on motion for a new trial, the Supreme Court must examine the record and determine whether evidence to support the verdict was completely lacking or was so slight and unconvincing as to make the verdict plainly unreasonable and unjust. **Sloan v. Atlantic Richfield Co.,** Op. No. 2047, 541 P2d 717 (Alaska 1975).

Order granting motion for new trial may be vacated although Supreme Court had denied petition for review. **Wolff v. Arctic Bowl, Inc.,** Op. No. 1380, 560 P2d 758 (Alaska 1977).

Defendant's "Objection to Notice of Entry of Judgment" was treated by the Supreme Court as a motion to alter or amend the judgment. **Blackford v. Taggart,** Op. No. 2749, 672 P2d 888 (Alaska 1983).

Trial court did not abuse its discretion in denying father's motion to reopen evidence or set aside judgment which conditioned the father's right to supervised visitation with his daughter on treatment by a psychologist; the father's assertion that he entered into stipulations under duress were directly contradicted by his own attorney and the father's new evidence on the issue of whether he had sexually abused his daughter would probably not change the result of a new trial. **Nelson v. Jones,** Op. No. 3522, 781 P2d 964 (Alaska 1989).

This rule allows the court to limit any new trial to issues incorrectly decided or not decided at all. **State v. Municipality of Anchorage,** Op. No. 3664, 805 P2d 971 (Alaska 1991).

Whether the issues of liability and damages are sufficiently separable to warrant a partial new trial depends upon the facts and circumstances in each case. **State v. Municipality of Anchorage,** Op. No. 3664, 805 P2d 971 (Alaska 1991).

Order denying plaintiff's motion for a new trial as to the municipality of Anchorage, the state's codefendant in a tort action, but granting it as to the state, was proper. **State v. Municipality of Anchorage,** Op. No. 3664, 805 P2d 971 (Alaska 1991).

An appellate court will reject a jury's award of damages and order a new trial only when the evidence supporting the jury's conclusion is so completely lacking or slight and unconvincing as to make the verdict plainly unreasonable and unjust. **Domke v. Alyeska Pipeline Serv. Co., Inc.,** Op. No. 10885, 137 P.3d 295 (Alaska 2006).

B. Newly Discovered Evidence.

Trial judge did not abuse discretion in denying new trial on grounds of newly discovered evidence in a civil case where the new evidence tendered in support of motion did not meet the requirements that (1) it must be such as would probably change the result on a new trial; (2) must have been discovered since the trial; (3) must be of such a nature that it could not have been discovered before trial by thorough diligence; (4) must be material; (5) must not be merely cumulative or impeaching. **Montgomery Ward v. Thomas,** Op. No. 236, 394 P2d 774 (Alaska 1964).

Trial judge is in better position than the appellate court to determine the possible effect and merit of the newly discovered evidence. **Montgomery Ward v. Thomas,** Op. No. 236, 394 P2d 774 (Alaska 1964).

In order to come within the category of "newly discovered evidence" as grounds for motion for a new trial or for relief from judgment, such evidence must relate to facts which were in existence at the time of the trial. **Patrick v. Sedwick,** Op. No. 338, 413 P2d 169 (Alaska 1966).

In order to justify the granting of a new trial, newly discovered evidence must be such as would probably change the result of a new trial. **National Bank of Alaska v. McHugh,** Op. No. 352, 416 P2d 239 (Alaska 1966).

Where new evidence was of such a nature that it could have been discovered before trial by due diligence, it did not constitute grounds for granting new trial. **State, Palmer Supply Co. v. Walsh & Co., Inc.,** Op. No. 1583, 575 P2d 1213 (Alaska 1978).

Although appellant filed a motion for relief from judgment rather than a motion for new trial, since the underlying ground was "new evidence," the analysis was similar. **Grothe v. Olafson,** Op. No. 2619, 659 P2d 602 (Alaska 1983).

Motions based upon newly discovered evidence under either Civil Rule 59 or Civil Rule 60(b)(2), challenging not only judgments entered after trial but also summary judgments, warrant relief only if the newly discovered evidence is likely to change the result at a new trial, was discovered after trial, was not discoverable with due diligence before trial, is material, and is not cumulative or impeaching. **Sengupta v. University of Alaska,** Op. No. 5397, 21 P3d 1240 (Alaska 2001).

C. Damages.

Damages assessed by a jury were not so clearly excessive as to call for a new trial. **Gregory v. Padilla,** Op. No. 139, 379 P2d 951 (Alaska 1963).

Although no motion for new trial was made and no alleged abuse of discretion in denying a new trial could be reviewed on appeal, the record was reviewed to ascertain that damages were not so grossly inadequate as to amount to a miscarriage of justice. **Heacock v. Town,** Op. No. 368, 419 P2d 622 (Alaska 1966).

In the light of evidence of past and future pain, suffering and physical impairment, a verdict of $34,626 was not so excessive that refusal of trial court to grant a new trial or a remittitur was an abuse of discretion. **Peters v. Benson,** Op. No. 397, 425 P2d 149 (Alaska 1967).

In a false arrest, false imprisonment, and assault and battery action against police officers, the trial court's action in ordering a remittitur or new trial on the issue of punitive damages which have been awarded the plaintiff is not error. **Hash v. Hogan,** Op. No. 547, 453 P2d 468 (Alaska 1969).

Motions for remittitur or new trial on the grounds that a verdict is excessive are addressed to the sound discretion of the trial court. **Hash v. Hogan,** Op. No. 547, 453 P2d 468 (Alaska 1969).

Remittiturs are not proper where the verdict is the result of passion and prejudice. **Hash v. Hogan,** Op. No. 547, 453 P2d 468 (Alaska 1969).

Where defendant raised issue of excessive punitive damages in motion for new trial and for judgment notwithstanding the verdict, separate motion for remittitur was not required. **Sturm, Ruger & Co. v. Day,** Op. No. 1834, 594 P2d 38 (Alaska 1979).

Trial court did not abuse its discretion in granting a new trial on the limited issue of damages where contractor improperly inquired at trial into value which purchaser placed on house during settlement discussions and where, once liability was established, there was no reasonable evidentiary basis for the low damage award. **Sebring v. Colver,** Op. No. 2549, 649 P2d 932 (Alaska 1982).

In personal injury action against helicopter company, the trial court acted within its discretion in concluding that the inadequacy of the damages warranted the grant of a new trial; contrary to defendant's arguments, the trial court did not base its order granting a new trial solely on the jury's failure to award damages for pain and suffering or because the jury's damage findings were inconsistent, objections to which should have been made prior to the discharge of the jury. **Buoy v. ERA Helicopters, Inc.,** Op. No. 3423, 771 P2d 439 (Alaska 1989).

In tort action against electric cooperative for fire to family home which killed one child and injured father and second child, jury verdict, which awarded damages for property loss and medical expenses but not non-economic damages for painful burns and loss of consortium, was inconsistent as a matter of law, requiring new trial. **Fancyboy v. Alaska Village Elec. Co-Op.,** Op. No. 5153, 984 P2d 1128 (Alaska 1999).

Evidence supporting complete denial of damages was so slight and unconvincing as to make jury's verdict denying damages unreasonable and unjust, thus new trial was required. **Pugliese v. Perdue,** Op. No. 5169, 988 P2d 577 (Alaska 1999).

D. Jury Action.

Unlike a motion for directed verdict or judgment n.o.v., a motion for new trial on the ground that the jury's verdict was contrary to the clear weight of the evidence involves the trial judge's discretion. **Mallonee v. Finch,** Op. No. 337, 413 P2d 159 (Alaska 1966).

Denial of motion for a new trial was no abuse of discretion if there was an evidentiary basis for the jury's decisions. **Mallonee v. Finch,** Op. No. 337, 413 P2d 159 (Alaska 1966); **Bolden v. City of Kodiak,** Op. No. 475, 439 P2d 796 (Alaska 1968).

Where there is a possibility that a jury has rendered a compromise verdict and it is not clear whether the jury clearly separated the issues of liability and damages, the court's declining to exercise its power to grant restricted retrial is not an abuse of discretion. **Dowling Supply & Equipment, Inc. v. City of Anchorage,** Op. No. 739, 490 P2d 907 (Alaska 1971).

In tort action against electric cooperative for fire to family home which killed one child and injured father and second child, jury verdict, which awarded damages for property loss and medical expenses but not non-economic damages for painful burns and loss of consortium, was inconsistent as a matter of law, requiring new trial. **Fancyboy v. Alaska Village Elec. Co-Op.,** Op. No. 5153, 984 P2d 1128 (Alaska 1999).

Evidence supporting complete denial of damages was so slight and unconvincing as to make jury's verdict denying damages unreasonable and unjust, thus new trial was required. **Pugliese v. Perdue,** Op. No. 5169, 988 P2d 577 (Alaska 1999).

II. Time for Motion.

Failure of opposing counsel to object when a motion for new trial was not timely served, and the fact that the court inferentially exercised its power under Civ. R. 94 (formerly Civ. R. 88) to relax the strict requirement as to timeliness, does not waive untimeliness in filing the motion, and the filing of an untimely motion for a new trial did not toll the running of the thirty-day appeal time. **Vogt v. Winbauer,** Op. No. 117, 376 P2d 1007 (Alaska 1962).

A motion to alter a supplemental judgment which was served 12 days after the entry of said judgment, was not timely under the provisions of this rule so to terminate the time for giving notice of appeal. **City of Anchorage v. Mugach Electric Association,** Op. No. 231, 394 P2d 673 (Alaska 1964).

Defendant did not waive right to challenge judgment where it did not object under Civil Rule 78(b) but filed timely Rule 59(f) motion to amend judgment. **Beech Aircraft Corp. v. Harvey,** Op. No. 1338, 558 P2d 879 (Alaska 1976).

Where issue of remittitur was brought to trial judge's attention following the jury verdict, but prior to entry of judgment, it was timely under Civil Rule 59(f). **Sturm, Ruger & Co. v. Day,** Op. No. 1834, 594 P2d 38 (Alaska 1979).

A motion to alter or amend a judgment suspends the time for filing an appeal; similarly, it suspends the time for filing a motion for judgment N.O.V. or new trial. **Blackford v. Taggart,** Op. No. 2749, 672 P2d 888 (Alaska 1983).

Husband's motion, entitled Motion for Reconsideration, filed 10 days after entry of divorce decree, was in effect a motion to alter or amend the judgment; consequently, the trial court did not lack jurisdiction 37 days later to modify the property division in the decree, notwithstanding contention that the trial court's failure to grant reconsideration within 20 days deprived it of jurisdiction. **Julsen v. Julsen,** Op. No. 3211, 741 P2d 642 (Alaska 1987).

Where an employee was not tested before a workers' compensation hearing to determine if she was allergic to dust mites, but the technology existed to do so, the fact that she was later determined to be allergic to dust mites did not constitute newly-discovered evidence under section (d) of this rule, and as it was applied to AS 23.30.130(a), and denial of her petition for modification and rehearing was proper. **Lindhag v. Dep't of Natural Res.,** Op. No. 5946, 123 P.3d 948 (Alaska 2005).

Rule 60. Relief From Judgment or Order.

(a) **Clerical Mistakes.** Clerical mistakes in judgments, orders or other parts of the record and errors therein arising from oversight or omission may be corrected by the court at any time of its own initiative or on the motion of any party and after such notice, if any, as the court orders. During the pendency of an appeal or petition for review to the Supreme Court, such mistakes may be so corrected before the record is filed in the Supreme Court, and thereafter may be so corrected with leave of the Supreme Court. For purposes of this rule, the record includes electronic information maintained about the case.

(b) **Mistakes—Inadvertence—Excusable Neglect—Newly Discovered Evidence—Fraud—Etc.** On motion and upon such terms as are just, the court may relieve a party or a party's legal representative from a final judgment, order, or proceeding for the following reasons:

(1) mistake, inadvertence, surprise or excusable neglect;

(2) newly discovered evidence which by due diligence could not have been discovered in time to move for a new trial under Rule 59(b);

(3) fraud (whether heretofore denominated intrinsic or extrinsic), misrepresentation, or other misconduct of an adverse party;

(4) the judgment is void;

(5) the judgment has been satisfied, released, or discharged, or a prior judgment upon which it is based has been reversed or otherwise vacated, or it is no longer equitable that the judgment should have prospective application; or

(6) any other reason justifying relief from the operation of the judgment.

The motion shall be made within a reasonable time, and for reasons (1), (2) and (3) not more than one year after the date of notice of the judgment or orders as defined in Civil Rule 58.1(c). A motion under this subdivision (b) does not affect the finality of a judgment or suspend its operation. This rule does not limit the power of a court to entertain an independent action to relieve a party from a judgment, order or proceeding, or to grant relief to a defendant not personally served, or to set aside a judgment for fraud upon the court. Writs of coram nobis, coram vobis and audita querela are abolished, and the procedure for obtaining any relief from a judgment shall be by motion as prescribed in these rules or by an independent action.

(c) **Form of Amended or Corrected Judgments.** A motion to amend or correct a judgment must be accompanied by a proposed amended or corrected judgment and a separate proposed order. The new judgment must include the word "amended" or "corrected" in the title.

(Adopted by SCO 5 October 9, 1959; amended by SCO 554 effective April 4, 1983; by SCO 1153 effective July 15, 1994; by SCO 1361 effective October 15, 1999; by SCO 1415 effective October 15, 2000; and by SCO 1622 effective October 15, 2006)

Note: Chapter 42 § 2 SLA 1999 enacts AS 09.19.200 which governs the remedies available in civil litigation involving conditions in correctional facilities. According to § 3 of the act, the enactment of AS 09.19.200 has the effect of amending Civil Rules 59(f), 60(b), 62, and 65 by altering the remedies available and the procedure to be used in litigation involving correctional facilities.

Annotations

Cases

I. In General.
II. Clerical Mistakes.
III. Relief from Final Judgment, Order or Proceeding.
  A. Grounds.
  B. Standard for Appellate Review.
  C. Procedure.

I. In General.

The purpose of this rule is to provide relief from judgments which are unjust. **Wellman, Inc. v. City of Anchorage,** Op. No. 623, 471 P2d 408 (Alaska 1970).

Rule 60(b)(6) is not intended as a substitute for proper litigation of a case. **Allen v. Bussell,** Op. No. 1353, 558 P2d 496 (Alaska 1976).

Rule 60(b)(6) may not be used to contest validity of a default judgment. **Allen v. Bussell,** Op. No. 1353, 558 P2d 496 (Alaska 1976).

The provisions of a decree adjudicating property rights, unlike provisions for child support, child custody and alimony, constitute a final judgment not subject to modification, except by another final judgment. **Allen v. Allen,** Op. No. 2514, 645 P2d 774 (Alaska 1982).

A judgment of dismissal without prejudice is considered a final judgment for purposes of appeal. **Farrell v. Dome Laboratories,** Op. No. 2556, 650 P2d 380 (Alaska 1982).

Clause of this rule allowing relief when it is no longer equitable that a judgment have prospective application is applicable to any judgment having prospective effect. **Farrell v. Dome Laboratories,** Op. No. 2556, 650 P2d 380 (Alaska 1982).

As a general rule, the clause permitting relief when it is no longer equitable that a judgment have prospective application provides no basis for relief from an unconditional dismissal without prejudice. **Farrell v. Dome Laboratories,** Op. No. 2556, 650 P2d 380 (Alaska 1982).

The general requirement that a meritorious defense to the matter on which the judgment or order rests must be presented to justify relief under this rule does not apply where the basis for the motion for relief is a due process violation. **Pew v. Foster,** Op. No. 2637, 660 P2d 447 (Alaska 1983).

Rules governing relief from final judgments on such grounds as mistake or fraud apply to support awards and to property settlements incorporated in divorce decrees. **Larson v. Larson,** Op. No. 2648, 661 P2d 626 (Alaska 1983).

An attorney's failure to act responsibly toward his or her clients when the attorney reasonably could be expected to do so constitutes inexcusable neglect. **Rill v. State, Dept. of Hwys.,** Op. No. 2725, 669 P2d 573 (Alaska 1983).

Execution sale of real property pursuant to default judgment for legal fees was properly set aside under this rule. **Law Offices of Murphy L. Clark v. Altman,** Op. No. 2811, 680 P2d 1125 (Alaska 1984).

There is no time limit on a motion attacking a judgment as void. **Kennecorp Mortgage v. First Nat. Bank,** Op. No. 2837, 685 P2d 1232 (Alaska 1984).

Mere fact that superior court order terminating parental rights could be attacked under this rule did not change the fact that it was a final order for purposes of the Indian Child Welfare Act. **Matter of J.R.S.,** Op. No. 2869, 690 P2d 10 (Alaska 1984).

This rule is not a substitute for a party failing to file a timely appeal, nor does it allow relitigation of issues that have been resolved by the judgment. **Burrell v. Burrell,** Op. No. 2795, 696 P2d 157 (Alaska 1984).

There is no time limit for an attack on a judgment as void. **Burrell v. Burrell,** Op. No. 2795, 696 P2d 157 (Alaska 1984).

Judge had authority to sua sponte vacate orders and judgment that she signed in error. **Gallagher v. Gallagher,** Op. No. 4041, 866 P2d 123 (Alaska 1994).

This rule is not a substitute for a party filing a timely appeal; nor does it allow relitigation of issues that have been resolved by the judgment. **Morris v. Morris,** Op. No. 4298, 908 P2d 425 (Alaska 1995).

Rules governing relief from final judgments on grounds such as mistake or fraud are applicable to property settlements in divorce decrees. **Hatten v. Hatten,** Op. No. 4354, 917 P2d 667 (Alaska 1996).

Former wife's 1989 motion for relief from 1984 dissolution decree did not constitute unreasonable delay since she reasonably relied on husband's assurances at time of dissolution that he would sell house and split proceeds, which he failed to do, and since there still existed an unresolved custody dispute. **Lowe v. Lowe,** Op. No. 4865, 944 P2d 29 (Alaska 1997).

Since child support orders are treated like judgments, trial courts may look to this rule for guidance in determining when relief is available. **State Dept. of Revenue, CSED v. Maxwell,** Op. No. 5306, 6 P3d 733 (Alaska 2000).

Because Alaska statutes treat child support orders as judgments for certain purposes, trial court may grant relief from support orders by analogy to this rule upon a showing of grounds that would justify relief under this rule. **Atcherian v. State Dept. of Revenue, CSED,** Op. No. 5350, 14 P3d 970 (Alaska 2000).

Where a party sought relief from judgment under Alaska R. Civ. P. 60(b), rather than attorney's fees under Alaska R. Civ. P. 82(c), the limitations period for requesting attorney's fees did not apply, and the party did not waive her request for attorney's fees. **Fleegel v. Estate of Boyles,** Op. No. 5641, 61 P.3d 1267 (Alaska 2002).

Clause (b)(3) of this rule gives the court authority to remedy misconduct by a party to a contract or an attorney; in fact, the court has a duty to rectify a wrong to protect the integrity of the judicial process. **Adams v. Adams,** Op. No. 5798, 89 P.3d 743 (Alaska 2004).

II. Clerical Mistakes.

Where record of eminent domain proceeding indicated that the land was never surveyed and acreages stated therein were modified by the term "more or less," a slight variance in acreage between the master's original and his clarified report was the probable result of clerical error which was not fatal to the judgment and the case was remanded to the trial court for correction of judgment based on correct computation. **State v. 7.536 Acres and Evenson,** Op. No. 434, 431 P2d 897 (Alaska 1967).

Trial courts have the inherent power to correct their records so that they shall conform to the facts and reflect the truth. **Titus v. State,** Op. No. 529, 451 P2d 342 (Alaska 1969).

The inherent power of trial courts to correct their records to conform to facts and reflect the truth is not suspended once an appeal has been taken. **Titus v. State,** Op. No. 529, 451 P2d 342 (Alaska 1969).

Clerical error, for purposes of this rule, may be made by other than a clerk. **Allen v. Bussell,** Op. No. 1353, 558 P2d 496 (Alaska 1976).

Errors in prejudgment interest and cost award were clerical, therefore trial court did not err in amending its judgment to change those amounts. **Alaskan Village, Inc. v. Smalley,** Op. No. 3069, 720 P2d 945 (Alaska 1986).

As a clerical mistake may include those made by a party, trial court did not abuse its discretion in amending prevailing party's attorney fee award when the party, instead of applying the formula for determining the award to the actual judgment, mistakenly computed it using only the jury verdict. **Babinec v. Yabuki,** Op. No. 3644, 799 P2d 1325 (Alaska 1990).

Whether error in properly classified as "clerical error" involves interpretation of this rule and therefore is question of law. **De Vaney v.**

State Dept. of Revenue, Op. No. 4447, 928 P2d 1198 (Alaska 1996).

Mistake by court in 1984 dissolution decree in ordering child support of $175 per month rather than $175 per month per child was properly characterized as clerical error under this rule, thus 1991 court order correcting error without first notifying parties was valid; obligor-parent's argument that error was judicial in character rather than clerical, requiring notice and hearing prior to correction, was rejected. **De Vaney v. State Dept. of Revenue,** Op. No. 4447, 928 P2d 1198 (Alaska 1996).

In 1995, trial court awarded plaintiff a judgment of $3,194 against defendant for debt that court originally ordered defendant to pay in March 1989 and the judgment provided on its face for interest of 10.5 percent but failed to specify when the interest began to accrue; acting on plaintiff's request, the trial court in 1997 changed the judgment to specify that interest accrued from March 1989, which change was proper under this rule permitting courts to correct judgments for clerical errors, mistakes and omissions since the court actually awarded the disputed interest and merely neglected to incorporate the award into its judgment. **Jensen v. Froissart,** Op. No. 5136, 982 P2d 263 (Alaska 1999).

Because the trial court had the power to correct clerical errors or ambiguities in a motion for attorney's fees and because 10 days was a reasonable amount of time, supplementation of a motion for fees within that period was allowed. **Kozevnikoff v. Tanana Village Council,** Op. No. 5800, 89 P.3d 757 (Alaska 2004).

III. Relief from Final Judgment, Order or Proceeding. A. Grounds.

Relief for inadvertent errors is provided by the rule. **Patterson v. Cushman,** Op. No. 233, 394 P2d 657 (Alaska 1964).

In order to come within the category of "newly discovered evidence" as grounds for motion for a new trial or for relief from judgment, such evidence must relate to facts which were in existence at the time of the trial. **Patrick v. Sedwick,** Op. No. 338, 413 P2d 169 (Alaska 1966).

Denial of motion for relief under this rule was sustained because appellant did not show how the claimed surprise affected his substantial rights. **National Bank of Alaska v. McHugh,** Op. No. 352, 416 P2d 239 (Alaska 1966).

Where in an action to enforce the sale of real estate the trial court by oral decision on May 12 ordered specific performance in favor of purchasers and stipulated that all payments be brought current within ten days of this decision, and plaintiffs were able to demonstrate that a delay beyond the ten day period of an $800 installment was engendered by the trial court's confusing remarks as to the meaning of the oral decision, and it further appeared that entry of judgment requiring compliance with the time schedule calling for payment on May 23 was made only on July 30, a modification of the payment provisions of the judgment was in the interest of justice although technically no final judgment had been entered. **Brown v. Hawkins,** Op. No. 362, 418 P2d 28 (Alaska 1966).

In spite of a failure on the part of defendants to respond to requests for admission within the ten day period provided by rule, the denial of a motion for relief from a summary judgment granted on the basis of failure to respond did not advance the objectives of the rules of procedure where the court was aware of an extension of the ten day period given by opposing counsel, where no discovery was had and where defendants' counsel had offered at the hearing of the motion for relief to retype the responses and to have them sworn to within half an hour, and under those circumstances the denial of relief was an abuse of discretion. **Palzer v. Serv-U-Meat Co.,** Op. No. 367, 419 P2d 201 (Alaska 1966).

Denial of motion to vacate compromise judgment pursuant to agreement of parties was not disturbed on appeal where appellant's contention that he was induced to settle the case under coercion and duress was not supported by the record. **Gravel v. Alaskan Village, Inc.,** Op. No. 388, 423 P2d 273 (Alaska 1967).

In a proper case this clause would give relief from a judgment on grounds of duress and coercion. **Gravel v. Alaskan Village, Inc.,** Op. No. 388, 423 P2d 273 (Alaska 1967).

A condemnor which fails to file a timely notice of appeal from a master's report can be granted relief on grounds of excusable neglect under this rule. **State v. Chuckwm, Inc.,** Op. No. 522, 449 P2d 776 (Alaska 1968).

Where the failure of a condemnor to enter a timely appeal from a master's report is due to the failure of counsel handling litigation to receive actual notice that the report had been filed because of a breakdown in established office routine, the condemnor is not entitled to extension of time since such failure cannot be considered excusable neglect. **State v. Chuckwm, Inc.,** Op. No. 522, 449 P2d 776 (Alaska 1968).

An error of law made by counsel or the court through mistake, inadvertence, or excusable neglect can constitute grounds for granting a party relief from a final judgment. **Alaska Truck Transport, Inc. v. Berman Packing Co.,** Op. No. 610, 469 P2d 697 (Alaska 1970).

A motion in opposition to an order of dismissal, filed after such order was entered, does not require setting aside the order to correct an injustice, where the motion is nothing more than a belated attempt to present to the trial court reasons for opposing the dismissal, without a showing of mistake, inadvertence, surprise or excusable neglect. **Wellman, Inc. v. City of Anchorage,** Op. No. 623, 471 P2d 408 (Alaska 1970).

An order, entered in probate authorizing an executor to sell stock in a corporation, which leaves pending the rights of the widow, is not a "final order." **Briggs v. Estate of Briggs,** Op. No. 824, 500 P2d 550 (Alaska 1972).

Where a trial court's order grants the defendant's motion for relief from judgment by deletion of a paragraph from the judgment but the rest of the judgment is left in force, such order is final and is subject to full review. **Alaska Placer Co. v. Lee,** Op. No. 840, 502 P2d 128 (Alaska 1972).

Where the trial court finds that the plaintiff has neither pled nor proven issues relevant to the relief provisions of a paragraph struck from the judgment, and where the plaintiff is not precluded from seeking that relief, the trial court does not abuse its discretion in deleting the paragraph from the judgment. **Alaska Placer Co. v. Lee,** Op. No. 840, 502 P2d 128 (Alaska 1972).

A motion for relief from a judgment where a mistake of law has been committed by counsel or by the court is not a substitute for appeal. **Pearson v. Bachner,** Op. No. 850, 503 P2d 1401 (Alaska 1972).

A motion for relief from a judgment based on a subsequent change in law should be made within the time for appeal from the judgment. **Pearson v. Bachner,** Op. No. 850, 503 P2d 1401 (Alaska 1972).

The grant or denial of a motion to vacate a default judgment is a matter involving the sound discretion of the trial court. **Markland v. City of Fairbanks,** Op. No. 923, 513 P2d 658 (Alaska 1973).

The party who moves to vacate default has the burden of establishing his entitlement to relief. **Markland v. City of Fairbanks,** Op. No. 923, 513 P2d 658 (Alaska 1973).

A judgment is void and subject to attack if the court that rendered it lacked personal jurisdiction over the defendant or if it acted in a manner inconsistent with due process. **Aguchak v. Montgomery Ward Co., Inc.,** Op. No. 1026, 520 P2d 1352 (Alaska 1974).

Movant seeking relief from a judgment does not have to show that he could present a meritorious defense in a subsequent proceeding. **Aguchak v. Montgomery Ward Co., Inc.,** Op. No. 1026, 520 P2d 1352 (Alaska 1974).

A motion to set aside a judgment is a final, appealable order. **Aguchak v. Montgomery Ward Co., Inc.,** Op. No. 1026, 520 P2d 1352 (Alaska 1974).

An entry of judgment of $150,000 against a defendant upon his failure to appear for trial is an excessive sanction where the failure to appear is due to confusion over whether the court had, at the request of the plaintiff, set trial for October 30 or merely set October 30 as the date for hearing plaintiff's motion for a continuance, which motion the defendant did not oppose. **Hill v. Vetter,** Op. No. 1067, 525 P2d 529 (Alaska 1974).

Intent to defraud is not an element of fraud upon the court. **Allen v. Bussell,** Op. No. 1353, 558 P2d 496 (Alaska 1976).

To constitute fraud upon the court, conduct must be egregious and involve a corruption of the judicial process. **Allen v. Bussell,** Op. No. 1353, 558 P2d 496 (Alaska 1976).

Motion to reconsider denial of attorney's fees made before Civil Rule 77(m) was effective would be treated as motion for relief from judgment. **Miller v. McManus,** Op. No. 1361, 558 P2d 891 (Alaska 1977).

Appeal from denial of motion to reconsider denial of attorney's fees presents only question of merits of reconsideration; not merits of underlying order. **Miller v. McManus,** Op. No. 1361, 558 P2d 891 (Alaska 1977).

Motion to reconsider denial of attorney's fees is addressed to discretion of trial court and decision will be reversed only if discretion was abused. **Miller v. McManus,** Op. No. 1361, 558 P2d 891 (Alaska 1977).

Order denying reconsideration of denial of attorney's fees, which was entered without explanation could not be reviewed and would be remanded so that trial court could again pass upon motion, stating reasons for its decision. **Miller v. McManus,** Op. No. 1361, 558 P2d 891 (Alaska 1977).

Denial of relief from judgment based on conclusion that Civil Rule 15 does not allow complaint to be amended to add defendant after limitation period has run was not abuse of discretion. **McCraken v. Davis,** Op. No. 1389, 560 P2d 771 (Alaska 1977).

Party seeking relief from judgment of dismissal must show the existence of a meritorious claim. **Corso v. Commissioner of Education,** Op. No. 1412, 563 P2d 246 (Alaska 1977).

To show the existence of meritorious claim, party must show facts which, if established, might reasonably be said to meet affirmative defenses of adversary. **Corso v. Commissioner of Education,** Op. No. 1412, 563 P2d 246 (Alaska 1977).

A judgment rendered without jurisdiction is void and is vulnerable to attack pursuant to a Rule 60(b)(4) motion. **Balchen v. Balchen,** Op. No. 1469, 566 P2d 1324 (Alaska 1977).

Except in very unusual instances, the Supreme Court will not reverse the denial of a Rule 60(b) motion where the moving party has not made a showing of a meritorious defense should the judgment be reopened. **Balchen v. Balchen,** Op. No. 1469, 566 P2d 1324 (Alaska 1977).

After judgment has been entered, question of trial court's jurisdiction should be raised by motion for relief from judgment on the ground that the judgment is void. **Livingston v. Livingston,** Op. No. 1528, 572 P2d 79 (Alaska 1977).

Where trial court had not been informed of physical location of child subject of custody dispute, decree would be vacated under paragraph (b)(6) of this rule. **Livingston v. Livingston,** Op. No. 1528, 572 P2d 79 (Alaska 1977).

Trial court did not abuse its discretion in denying motion to set aside default judgment where movant had adequate opportunity to answer the complaint but did not. **Miracle v. Thompson,** Op. No. 1677, 581 P2d 666 (Alaska 1978).

A Rule 60(b) motion is not a substitute for the usual appellate mechanism and Rule 60(b) motions based upon errors of law must be brought within the time for taking the appeal. **Anderson v. State Dept. of Highways,** Op. No. 1718, 584 P2d 537 (Alaska 1978).

Refusal of trial court to vacate default judgment against defendant was error where defendant alleged a meritorious defense and made a showing of excusable neglect due to illness and difficulty in obtaining counsel for her failure to answer the summons on time. **Gregor v. Hodges,** Op. No. 2110, 612 P2d 1008 (Alaska 1980).

Evidence which could have been discovered by effective cross-examination at trial which merely serves to impeach a witness's testimony and which is unlikely to change the result of the trial is not basis for a new trial under the rule of newly discovered evidence. **State v. Alaska Continental Dev. Corp.,** Op. No. 2254, 630 P2d 977 (Alaska 1981).

Even if the conduct of a witness falls within the guidelines of statutory perjury, where perjury by a witness is unassisted by the party in interest or by counsel, the general rule is that the misconduct does not amount to fraud upon the court. **State v. Alaska Continental Dev. Corp.,** Op. No. 2254, 630 P2d 977 (Alaska 1981).

Relief under Civil Rule 60(b)(5), concerning judgments which no longer have equitable application, is appropriate from a money judgment awarded in association with an order of specific performance which is subsequently set aside. **Guard v. P & R Enterprises, Inc.,** Op. No. 2385, 631 P2d 1068 (Alaska 1981).

Relief under Civil Rule 60(b)(6), concerning other reasons justifying relief from a judgment, is reserved for extraordinary circumstances not covered by the preceding five clauses of Civil Rule 60(b). **O'Link v. O'Link,** Op. No. 2394, 632 P2d 225 (Alaska 1981).

Civil Rule 60(b) is not applicable when the moving party seeks adjudication of undecided issues that had been withdrawn from consideration of the court in a divorce decree under the court's belief that the issues had been settled. **Van Brocklin v. Van Brocklin,** Op. No. 2437, 635 P2d 1186 (Alaska 1981).

Where adequacy of creditor's case against debtor was debatable, and where debtor's response to the complaint, although technically inadequate to prevent entry of default, was prompt, trial court's refusal to set aside default judgment was abuse of discretion. **Kennedy v. First Nat. Bank of Fairbanks,** Op. No. 2448, 637 P2d 297 (Alaska 1981).

Wife's motion for relief from terms of a property division in a divorce decree should have been granted on grounds of excusable neglect given the wife's past history of mental instability, the self-defeating course of conduct she engaged in with respect to the divorce proceedings, and her inability to appear at the hearing on the property division because of lack of air fare. **Lovell v. Lovell,** Op. No. 2504, 645 P2d 151 (Alaska 1982).

Granting plaintiff's motion to amend judgment to include an order of sale for attached property in the judgment was proper. **Eagle Air v. Corroon, Etc.,** Op. No. 2538, 648 P2d 1000 (Alaska 1982).

Where record indicated no good reason for husband's 9-month delay in moving to set aside default divorce decree, trial court's finding of no excusable neglect was not abuse of discretion requiring vacation of decree. **Allen v. Allen,** Op. No. 2514, 645 P2d 774 (Alaska 1982).

Where appellant did not present evidence suggesting that case involved something more than one of the grounds stated in the first five clauses of this rule, mutual exclusivity barred relief under clause (6). **Farrell v. Dome Laboratories,** Op. No. 2556, 650 P2d 380 (Alaska 1982).

Superior court abused its discretion in amending a prior judgment of voluntary dismissal without prejudice in order to require the plaintiff to refile her suit against defendant by a certain date. **Farrell v. Dome Laboratories,** Op. No. 2556, 650 P2d 380 (Alaska 1982).

Denial of motion for relief from order directing entry of judgment by default, which order was entered as a sanction against appellant for failure to comply with court order to answer two interrogatories, was improper, where court did not address appellant's claim that her attorney had not been served notice of the motion for sanctions. **Pew v. Foster,** Op. No. 2637, 660 P2d 447 (Alaska 1983).

Failure of attorney to appear for trial because he was undergoing treatment for a back injury was not excusable neglect for which relief could be obtained under Civil Rule 60(b)(1), where the attorney clearly had the time and ability to contact either the court or his client and make adequate arrangements for the trial but did not do so. **Rill v. State, Dept. of Hwys.,**

Op. No. 2725, 669 P2d 573 (Alaska 1983).

Offset bid of $2000 on a judgment of $388.13 was a substantial irregularity having a natural tendency to deter the right to redeem and was therefore a proper consideration in trial judge's decision to set aside execution sale. **Law Offices of Murphy L. Clark v. Altman,** Op. No. 2811, 680 P2d 1125 (Alaska 1984).

Filing of a motion for extension of time did not constitute an answer sufficient to preclude default judgment since the motion was denied and was itself late, having been received after the default judgment was entered. **Kennecorp Mortgage v. First Nat. Bank,** Op. No. 2837, 685 P2d 1232 (Alaska 1984).

Trial court did not abuse its discretion under this rule in modifying the property disposition provisions of a dissolution decree, which essentially gave the husband sole discretion to decide whether and when the property would be sold, to require the husband to either buy the wife's share of the property or sell the property and divide the net proceeds, where the underlying assumption upon which the property settlement agreement was based, i.e., that the husband and wife would continue to live together after the dissolution and would eventually remarry, had become unworkable. **Foster v. Foster,** Op. No. 2850, 684 P2d 869 (Alaska 1984).

In order to prevail on a motion for relief from judgment or order, a movant must generally show the existence of a meritorious claim as well as one of the grounds stated in this rule, such as excusable neglect or mistake. **Cleary Diving Service v. Thomas, Head and Greisen,** Op. No. 2873, 688 P2d 940 (Alaska 1984).

Plaintiffs' argument that the judgment dismissing their case for want of prosecution should be vacated due to excusable neglect for their failure to contest the dismissal, which occurred because a court clerk told them that a note left in the file would guarantee them a hearing, was rejected, where plaintiffs were sent notice of the defendants' motion to dismiss and in fact received notice of the motion before it was granted. **Cleary Diving Service v. Thomas, Head and Greisen,** Op. No. 2873, 688 P2d 940 (Alaska 1984).

That former husband chose to marry again and incur additional personal and legal obligations was not sufficient reason to relieve him from terms of property division entered upon his divorce from previous spouse. **Burrell v. Burrell,** Op. No. 2795, 696 P2d 157 (Alaska 1984).

Possible inheritance by former wife was speculative and therefore did not represent a changed circumstance justifying former husband's relief from terms of property division judgment. **Burrell v. Burrell,** Op. No. 2795, 696 P2d 157 (Alaska 1984).

Former husband's contention that prior support judgment was unconstitutional was not an attack on the judgment as void within the meaning of this rule. **Burrell v. Burrell,** Op. No. 2795, 696 P2d 157 (Alaska 1984).

Where former husband waited two and one-half years after entry of final property division order to raise issue of potential adverse tax consequences from division of his separate property interest in a trust, during which time there was no change in his potential tax liability, the issue provided no basis for modifying the original property division because of changed circumstances. **Burrell v. Burrell,** Op. No. 2795, 696 P2d 157 (Alaska 1984).

In any circumstance where the judgment in question has prospective application, relief under Civil Rule 60 (b)(5) may be granted from the judgment's prospective features when subsequent events make it no longer equitable that the judgment have prospective application; a change in law accomplished by judicial decision may furnish such cause for relief. **Lawrence v. Lawrence,** Op. No. 3044, 718 P2d 142 (Alaska 1986).

Relief under clause (6) of this rule, covering any other reason justifying relief from a judgment, is not available unless the circumstances justifying relief are extraordinary and do not come within the reasons listed in clauses (1) through (5) of this rule. **Village of Chefornak v. Hooper Bay Const.,** Op. No. 3360, 758 P2d 1266 (Alaska 1988).

Village's allegation that it did not understand or become aware of a judgment against it because its officers do not speak English amounted to a claim of mistake or excusable neglect covered by clause (1) of this rule, thus the village was not entitled to claim relief under clause (6) covering any other reason justifying relief from a judgment. **Village of Chefornak v. Hooper Bay Const.,** Op. No. 3360, 758 P2d 1266 (Alaska 1988).

To constitute fraud on the court under this rule, conduct must be so egregious that it involves a corruption of the judicial process; fraud may be found even in the absence of intent to defraud. **Village of Chefornak v. Hooper Bay Const.,** Op. No. 3360, 758 P2d 1266 (Alaska 1988).

Allegation by village that it was entitled to relief from a judgment because its attorney committed a fraud upon the court by signing a stipulation for entry of judgment against the village without securing the village's knowing consent and failing to adequately explain the consequences of the judgment was rejected. **Village of Chefornak v. Hooper Bay Const.,** Op. No. 3360, 758 P2d 1266 (Alaska 1988).

In considering motions for relief from a final judgment under Civil Rule 60(b)(6), pertaining to relief for reasons not listed in the rule, the court must balance the interest in the finality of judgments against the interest in granting relief from judgment when justice so requires; additionally, the following factors are to be considered: the prejudice, if any, to the nonmoving party if relief from judgment is granted, whether any intervening equities make the granting of relief inappropriate, and any other circumstances relevant to consideration of the equities of the case. **Norman v. Nichiro Gyogyo Kaisha, Ltd.,** Op. No. 3383, 761 P2d 713 (Alaska 1988).

A change in law after a final judgment has been rendered will not ordinarily justify relief under this rule unless there are other extraordinary circumstances. **Norman v. Nichiro Gyogyo Kaisha, Ltd.,** Op. No. 3383, 761 P2d 713 (Alaska 1988).

Where two plaintiffs have suffered similar injuries as a result of the same acts committed by the same defendants, but have been treated differently because of an intervening change in the law, it is an abuse of discretion to deny relief under this rule. **Norman v. Nichiro Gyogyo Kaisha, Ltd.,** Op. No. 3383, 761 P2d 713 (Alaska 1988).

Where the Supreme Court of Alaska in 1982 affirmed a judgment entered against appellant on the ground that a shareholder could not maintain an action for loss of value of stock for breach of a shareholders agreement, but four years later reversed itself and allowed a different shareholder to pursue identical claims against the same defendants arising from the same transactions and shareholders agreement, justice required that appellant be given relief from the judgment. **Norman v. Nichiro Gyogyo Kaisha, Ltd.,** Op. No. 3383, 761 P2d 713 (Alaska 1988).

Where trial court order in divorce case required the husband and wife to file a joint tax return to maximize their tax deductions, the trial court did not abuse its discretion in amending the order after the trial under this rule to permit the wife to file a separate return when the husband refused to sign the return her accountant prepared. **Streb v. Streb,** Op. No. 3443, 774 P2d 798 (Alaska 1989).

Enforcement of a 1981 post-majority child support award was held no longer equitable following 1984 Alaska Supreme Court decision overruling previous decision that superior courts had statutory authority to enter post-majority child support awards. **Propst v. Propst,** Op. No. 3451, 776 P2d 780 (Alaska 1989).

It was not an abuse of discretion for the superior court to modify a dissolution decree to award the wife a one-half interest in the marital residence where the following factors were present: (1) the fundamental, underlying assumption of the dissolution agreement had been destroyed; (2) the parties' property division was poorly thought out; (3) the property division was reached without benefit of counsel; and (4) the marital residence was the parties' principal asset. **Schofield v. Schofield,** Op. No. 3461, 777 P2d 197 (Alaska 1989).

Where plaintiff-employer in action against defendant-employee for breach of employment contract and violation of fiduciary duties did not disclose that it had assigned all of its claims against defendant to another corporation, trial court erred in setting aside the judgment against defendant pursuant to this rule on the grounds of newly discovered evidence and fraud, misrepresentation, or other misconduct of the plaintiff; the appropriate sanction for plaintiff's concealment of the assignment was to vacate the trial court's award of costs and attorney fees against defendant. **McCall v. Coats,** Op. No. 3464, 777 P2d 655 (Alaska 1989).

Relief under the catch-all provision of subsection (b)(6) of this rule is inappropriate when a party takes a deliberate action they later regret as a mistake, thus defendant's allegation that his attorney's negligence led him into accepting an unfair child custody agreement was not a ground for relief under subsection (b)(6). **Hartland v. Hartland,** Op. No. 3459, 777 P2d 636 (Alaska 1989).

Where both parties forcefully contested the issues in the case and it was highly questionable whether defendant's attorney's alleged malpractice appreciably affected the result, relief from judgment under the catch-all provision of subsection (b)(6) of this rule would have been inappropriate. **Hartland v. Hartland,** Op. No. 3459, 777 P2d 636 (Alaska 1989).

Defendant's motion for relief from judgment on the grounds that his attorney failed to act responsibly towards him by not conducting needed discovery and failing to recognize a prejudicial conflict of interest when he reasonably could have been expected to do so presented allegations to inexcusable neglect not entitling him to relief under subsection (b)(1) of this rule. **Hartland v. Hartland,** Op. No. 3459, 777 P2d 636 (Alaska 1989).

Award of just over fifty percent of the prevailing party's actual attorney fees was not an abuse of discretion. **Kenai Peninsula Borough v. English Bay Village Corp.,** Op. No. 3517, 781 P2d 6 (Alaska 1989).

Trial court did not abuse its discretion in denying father's motion to reopen evidence or set aside judgment which conditioned the father's right to supervised visitation with his daughter on treatment by a psychologist; the father's assertion that he entered into stipulations under duress were directly contradicted by his own attorney and the father's new evidence on the issue of whether he had sexually abused his daughter would probably not change the result of a new trial. **Nelson v. Jones,** Op. No. 3522, 781 P2d 964 (Alaska 1989).

In denying a motion to set aside a judgment, the trial court committed a per se abuse of discretion by ignoring uncontradicted affidavits that the moving party's obligation under the contract giving rise to the judgment had been released or satisfied. **Princiotta v. Municipality of Anchorage,** Op. No. 3548, 785 P2d 559 (Alaska 1990).

Genuine and severe medical disability generally suffices as excusable neglect for purposes of setting outside a default judgment. **Rapoport v. Tesoro Alaska Petroleum Co.,** Op. No. 3595, 790 P2d 1374 (Alaska 1990).

Trial court did not abuse its discretion in denying defendant's motion to vacate default judgment on grounds of excusable neglect; defendant's claim that disorientation and depression following a car accident caused his neglect was inconsistent with his knowing receipt of certified mail and his numerous complex business dealings during the period of alleged incapacity. **Rapoport v. Tesoro Alaska Petroleum Co.,** Op. No. 3595, 790 P2d 1374 (Alaska 1990).

A judgment can be set aside for newly discovered evidence only if the evidence (1) would probably change the result of the trial; (2) has been discovered since the trial; (3) could not have been discovered before trial by due diligence; (4) be material; and (5) not be merely cumulative or impeaching. **Babinec v. Yabuki,** Op. No. 3644, 799 P2d 1325 (Alaska 1990).

A misrepresentation or misconduct need not be accompanied by an intent to deceive in order to justify relief under this rule. **Babinec v. Yabuki,** Op. No. 3644, 799 P2d 1325 (Alaska 1990).

Where misconduct as a ground for relief under this rule relates to falsehoods conveyed in the course of discovery, the information withheld need not be of such nature as would necessarily alter the result in the case; misconduct as a ground for relief is aimed at judgments which were unfairly obtained, not at those that are factually incorrect. **Babinec v. Yabuki,** Op. No. 3644, 799 P2d 1325 (Alaska 1990).

Where intent to deceive exists, the burden may shift to the nonmoving party to prove that the misconduct did not interfere with full and fair presentation of the case; where, however, there was no intent to deceive, the burden remains on the movant to show that he was prevented by the misconduct from a full and fair presentation of his case or defense. **Babinec v. Yabuki,** Op. No. 3644, 799 P2d 1325 (Alaska 1990).

Where counsel for defendant made a tactical decision to demonstrate plaintiff's discovery misconduct to the jury rather than to take further steps during discovery to obtain the information he knew he did not have, his motion for relief on misconduct grounds was properly denied. **Babinec v. Yabuki,** Op. No. 3644, 799 P2d 1325 (Alaska 1990).

In wrongful job reclassification action against municipality which turned on whether filing for arbitration would have been futile, the judgment for the municipality was set aside for fraud on the court because the municipality was at least reckless in misrepresenting its policy on arbitration and clearly violated its duty of honest dealing with the court. **Higgins v. Municipality of Anchorage,** Op. No. 3684, 810 P2d 149 (Alaska 1991).

Actual intent to defraud is not required for fraud on the court to be present; reckless disregard of procedural safeguards is enough. **Higgins v. Municipality of Anchorage,** Op. No. 3684, 810 P2d 149 (Alaska 1991).

Where, four years after parties stipulated to a marital property settlement in which wife was awarded a portion of husband's military pension, husband elected to waive his military pension in order to collect veterans disability benefits, resulting in termination of payments to wife, wife was entitled to relief from the final property settlement judgment under Civil Rule 60(b)(6). **Clauson v. Clauson,** Op. No. 3836, 831 P2d 1257 (Alaska 1992).

Where suit for wrongful death against manufacturer of airplane carburetor was dismissed as barred by statute of limitations, trial court's subsequent denial of plaintiff's motion for relief from judgment was abuse of discretion where court failed to consider whether evidence of fraudulent concealment by the manufacturer and the doctrine of equitable estoppel would have probably changed the result in a new proceeding. **Palmer v. Borg-Warner Corp.,** Op. No. 3887, 838 P2d 1243 (Alaska 1992).

Where suit against corporation was dismissed for lack of capacity to be sued because the corporation had been involuntarily dissolved by the State for failure to pay taxes, trial court erred in refusing to vacate the dismissal after the State reinstated the corporation. **Gerik-Jones, Inc. v. Timberline Industries, Inc.,** Op. No. 3897, 840 P2d 999 (Alaska 1992).

Trial court's refusal to take into account husband's post-trial injuries when it reconsidered on remand equitable division of parties' marital estate was error. **Murray v. Murray,** Op. No. 3978, 856 P2d 463 (Alaska 1993).

Ex-husband's loss of employment did not constitute sufficient grounds for modifying divorce decree. **Olson v. Olson,** Op. No. 3975, 856 P2d 482 (Alaska 1993).

Statutorily unauthorized decree terminating parental rights and obligations was beyond subject matter jurisdiction of court and therefore subject to attack as void under this rule without regard to time limits. **Perry v. Newkirk,** Op. No.4072,871 P2d 1150 (Alaska 1994).

Where basis for stepfather's motion for relief from divorce decree obligation to support stepdaughter was essentially that he had been mistaken as to his legal obligation to support her when he consented to decree, motion was subject to one-year time limitation for motions based upon mistake, not reasonable time limitation for motions based upon other reasons. **Dewey v. Dewey,** Op. No. 4149, 886 P2d 623 (Alaska 1995).

Stepfather's possible mistake as to his legal obligation when he entered into contractual obligation to support stepdaughter, which was incorporated into divorce decree, did not warrant relief from support obligation. **Dewey v. Dewey,** Op. No. 4149, 886 P2d 623 (Alaska 1995).

Relief under Rule 60(b)(6) is available only in extraordinary circumstances, and only when clauses (1) through(5) of the rule do not apply. **Bauman v. Day,** Op. No. 4182, 892 P2d 817 (Alaska 1995).

While Rule 60(b)(5) can apply to any final judgment with prospective effect, by definition it cannot apply to a judgment that simply offers a present remedy for a past wrong. **Bauman v. Day,** Op. No. 4182, 892 P2d 817 (Alaska 1995).

The preclusive effect of a dismissal with prejudice is not a prospective effect for the purposes of Rule 60(b)(5). **Bauman v. Day,** Op. No. 4182, 892 P2d 817 (Alaska 1995).

Where appellants failed to offer a reason for relief under Rule 60(b)(6), their claim for relief was denied as groundless. **Bauman v. Day,** Op. No. 4182, 892 P2d 817 (Alaska 1995).

Relief from a judgment adjudicating property rights, as opposed to child custody, child support or alimony, is available only under Rule 60(b). **Morris v. Morris,** Op. No. 4298, 908 P2d 425 (Alaska 1995).

Personal factors such as bankruptcy, poverty, medical conditions and attorney neglect did not support claim for relief under Civil Rule 60(b)(6) since those factors come within scope of Civil Rule 60(b)(1), and relief was not available under Civil Rule 60(b)(1) because motion for relief was filed more than one year after order was entered. **Neilson v. Neilson,** Op. No. 4337, 914 P2d 1268 (Alaska 1996).

Given that California URESA child support order did not explicitly modify, nullify, or supersede pre-existing Alaska support order, Alaska order was not void, thus obligor-father was not entitled to relief from it under this rule. **Neilson v. Neilson,** Op. No. 4337, 914 P2d 1268 (Alaska 1996).

Letter of 1989 from mother to father stating that she would accept whatever California courts decided regarding child support amounts did not preclude further modifications, thus letter did not constitute release, satisfaction, or discharge of 1990 Alaska child support order, therefore obligor-father was not entitled to relief from 1990 order under this rule. **Neilson v. Neilson,** Op. No. 4337, 914 P2d 1268 (Alaska 1996).

Trial court did not abuse its discretion in ruling that husband's failure to challenge judgment until almost one year after judgment was entered did not constitute excusable neglect under this rule; husband, who was initially unable to afford attorney, neither filed motion pro se, nor south pro bono legal assistance, nor communicated with court in any way. **Sandoval v. Sandoval,** Op. No. 4351, 915 P2d 1222 (Alaska 1996).

Father was not entitled to relief from $830 child support judgment on basis of secret waiver agreement in which mother waived father's obligation to pay any child support over $300. **Richmond v. Pluid,** Op. No. 4418, 925 P2d 251 (Alaska 1996).

Where decedent's son alleged after probate order was entered that excessive professional fees and costs were incurred during administration of estate, trial court erred in not granting him relief from probate order based upon excusable neglect; appellate court rejected trial court's conclusion that son's involvement in administration of estate and representation by counsel were reasons to deny relief. **Johnson v. Doris,** Op. No. 4793, 933 P2d 1139 (Alaska 1997).

Where husband's attorney inserted child support credit in child custody and support order that parties had not agreed to during divorce settlement negotiations, wife was entitled to relief from order due to misconduct of husband's attorney in not bringing change to attentions of wife's attorney. **Pierce v. Pierce,** Op. No. 4914, 949 P2d 498 (Alaska 1997).

Divorced mother's miscalculation of filing period for motion to set aside order modifying custody was excusable neglect, thus trial court abused its discretion in not granting her motion under this rule to accept late-filed opposition and to set aside motion modifying custody. **Conger v. Conger,** Op. No. 4920, 950 P2d 119 (Alaska 1997).

To gain relief for excusable neglect, part must show not only "neglect," but valid "excuse" therefore. **Dickerson v. Williams,** Op. No. 4968, 956 P2d 458 (Alaska 1998).

When party makes deliberate, strategic choice to settle case, he cannot be relieved of such choice merely because his assessment of consequences was incorrect. **Dickerson v. Williams,** Op. No. 4968, 956 P2d 458 (Alaska 1998).

In case involving road easement where plaintiff agreed to settle after defendants promised to pay $6,500 within seven days and to widen easement so that plaintiff could build new road, trial court properly refused to relieve plaintiff from judgment enforcing settlement agreement notwithstanding that defendants had missed seven-day deadline and that plaintiff had learned that land for new road included federal wetlands which would complicate building or road. **Dickerson v. Williams,** Op. No. 4968, 956 P2d 458 (Alaska 1998).

Misidentification of parcel of real property identified as Lot 3 in ejectment action was not clerical error within meaning of this rule where discovery of plat following judgment revealed that Lot 3 no longer existed, that defendant's house never sat on Lot 3, and that defendant's house did not sit on property owned by plaintiff at time plaintiff brought ejectment action; accordingly, it was error for court to amend judgment to substitute Lot 3B, upon which the house in fact sat, for Lot 3, notwithstanding that Lot 3B was deeded to plaintiff shortly after judgment, and it was error for court to deny defendant's motion for relief from judgment based upon newly discovered evidence. **Frost v. Ayojiak,** Op. No. 4984, 957 P2d 1353 (Alaska 1998).

In motion to set aside default judgment in paternity action, defendant's statement of non-paternity was meritorious defense. **Wright v. Shorten,** Op. No. 5033, 964 P2d 441 (Alaska 1998).

Where defendant, upon receipt of filing of paternity action against him, wrote trail court denying paternity, letter should have been treated as answer to complaint, thus motion to set aside default judgment should have been granted on basis that any deficiencies in answer were result of mistake or excusable neglect. **Wright v. Shorten,** Op. No. 5033, 964 P2d 441 (Alaska 1998).

Trial court did not lack jurisdiction in 1985 dissolution proceeding to enter child support order conforming to stepfather's express agreement to pay support for stepdaughter, notwithstanding that literal reading of dissolution statute gave court jurisdiction only over children born of marriage or adopted during marriage. **Dewey v. Dewey,** Op. No. 5065, 969 P2d 1154 (Alaska 1999).

Creation of governmental fishing quota program shortly after issuance of dissolution decree constituted "extraordinary circumstances" justifying CR 60(b)(6) relief from property settlement portion of decree which did not address or anticipate fishing quota program which significantly increased value of fishing vessel awarded to husband. **McGee v. McGee,** Op. No. 5092, 974 P2d 983 (Alaska 1999).

DNA test results revealing that husband was not biological father of child constituted change in conditions that could make continued enforcement of support order in divorce decree inequitable under Rule 60(b)(5) if motion for relief from judgment was brought within reasonable time. **Dixon v. Pouncy,** Op. No. 5116, 979 P2d 520 (Alaska 1999).

Equity demanded modification of property settlement agreement under Civil Rule 60(b)(6) where provision of agreement which obligated ex-husband to name ex-wife as recipient of his civil service pension's survivorship benefits was unenforceable because of federal regulations which both parties were unaware of when they entered into the agreement. **Williams v. Crawford,** Op. No. 5135, 982 P2d 250 (Alaska 1999).

In 1995, trial court awarded plaintiff a judgment of $3,194 against defendant for debt that court originally ordered defendant to pay in March 1989 and the judgment provided on its face for interest of 10.5 percent but failed to specify when the interest began to accrue; acting on plaintiff's request, the trial court in 1997 changed the judgment to specify that interest accrued from March 1989, which change was proper under this rule permitting courts to correct judgments for clerical errors, mistakes and omissions since the court actually awarded the disputed interest and merely neglected to incorporate the award into its judgment. **Jensen v. Froissart,** Op. No. 5136, 982 P2d 263 (Alaska 1999).

A judgment is void if the court that rendered it lacked personal jurisdiction over the defendant. **Cramer v. Wade,** Op. No. 5155, 985 P2d 467 (Alaska 1999).

Pursuant to authority given to courts under this rule to relieve a party from a final judgment for "any other reason justifying relief from the operation of the judgment," trial court properly granted motion to modify original dissolution decree's property distribution where decree failed to dispose of substantial items of marital property. **Lacher v. Lacher,** Op. No. 5214, 993

P2d 413 (Alaska 1999).

Where real estate agent, who did not attend trial at which he was found by jury to have breached his fiduciary duty to buyers of home and was held liable for damages, moved under this rule for relief from the resulting judgment, making prima facie showing that he had been incompetent at time of trial, it was abuse of discretion for trial court to deny his motion without determining the issue of competence. **Stinson v. Holder,** Op. No. 5252, 996 P2d 1238 (Alaska 2000).

Where buyers of home filed lawsuit for negligence against engineer who inspected home two months after obtaining verdict in separate lawsuit for breach of fiduciary duty against real estate agent who sold the home, real estate agent's claim that buyers' complaint against the engineer was newly discovered evidence that required relief from judgment under this rule was rejected. **Stinson v. Holder,** Op. No. 5252, 996 P2d 1238 (Alaska 2000).

Where state child support enforcement division took formal action to enforce presumption that husband was legal father of child born during marriage by issuing administrative child support order against him without providing him a meaningful opportunity to rebut the presumption, husband was entitled to relief from child support order pursuant to this rule because he was not accorded due process of law. **State Dept. of Revenue CSED v. Maxwell,** Op. No. 5306, 6 P3d 733 (Alaska 2000).

Where state child support enforcement division took formal action to enforce presumption that husband was legal father of child born during marriage by issuing administrative child support order against him without providing him a meaningful opportunity to rebut the presumption, husband was entitled to relief from child support order pursuant to this rule because he was not accorded due process of law. **State Dept. of Revenue, CSED v. Maxwell,** Op. No. 5306, 6 P3d 733 (Alaska 2000).

Motions based upon newly discovered evidence under either Civil Rule 59 or Civil Rule 60(b)(2), challenging not only judgments entered after trial but also summary judgments, warrant relief only if the newly discovered evidence is likely to change the result at a new trial, was discovered after trial, was not discoverable with due diligence before trial, is material, and is not cumulative or impeaching. **Sengupta v. University of Alaska,** Op. No. 5397, 21 P3d 1240 (Alaska 2001).

Superior court abused its discretion in denying the ex-wife's post remand motion to vacate the awards of attorney fees and costs because that order was reversed and the fees and costs awards should have been vacated as a matter of course under the provisions of Alaska R. Civ. P. 60(b)(5). **Williams v. Crawford,** Op. No. 5532, 47 P3d 1077 (Alaska 2001).

On the question of whether, under any possible evidence that the State might present, the superior court had the statutory authority to order forfeiture of bail for a defendant's violation of the conditions of release (other than the obligation to appear in court), although the legislature has since granted this power to the superior court, the answer at the time the case was litigated was "no." The superior court had no statutory authority to forfeit a defendant's bail for this type of misconduct. Accordingly, the court's judgment was "void" for purposes of Alaska R. Civ. P. 60(b)(4), and person who paid bond was entitled to seek relief under the rule. **State v. Superior Court,** Op. No. 2235, 40 P3d 1239 (Alaska Ct. App. 2002).

Alaska R. Civ. P. 60(b)(6) is a catch-all provision and should be liberally construed to enable courts to vacate judgments whenever such action is necessary to accomplish justice. **Juelfs v. Gough,** Op. No. 5535, 41 P3d 593 (Alaska 2002).

Trial court erred when it did not set aside default judgment where appellant's failure to respond to complaint in a timely fashion was excusable; inter alia, he was served with lawsuit within two weeks of suffering multiple serious gunshot wounds. **Cook v. Rowland,** Op. No. 5586, 49 P3d 262 (Alaska 2002).

Where the sentencing court issued a supplemental order barring the department of corrections from housing defendant in the same facility as another named inmate and the prosecutor stated that the State had no opposition to defendant's request, the supplemental order was reversed because (1) the superior court lacked jurisdiction to order the department of corrections to hold defendant and the other inmate in separate facilities and that provision of the judgment was void for purposes of Alaska R. Civ. P. 60(b)(4), and (2) the department of corrections was not collaterally estopped by the State's failure to oppose the challenged provision of the judgment because the concerns of the department of corrections were not aired in the superior court in that the prosecutor failed to question the sentencing court's authority to restrict the department of corrections' actions under the provisions of AS 33.30.061(a). **State v. Combs,** Op. No. 1857, 64 P.3d 135 (Alaska Ct. App. 2003).

Order dividing a husband and wife's property was void because the court that issued the order did so without having personal jurisdiction over the wife, and the state supreme court affirmed the trial court's judgment vacating the order even though it was 17 years old, and also affirmed the trial court's subsequent judgment awarding the wife half of the marital portion of her ex-husband's pension, but only from the date she filed an action seeking an interest in the pension, not from the date the husband began receiving it. **Inman v. Inman,** Op. No. 5679, 67 P.3d 655 (Alaska 2003).

The parental rights of a father were properly terminated following his conviction and sentence for sexually assaulting and attempting to assault his minor children, where the length of his sentence made efforts to reunite the family unnecessary. **Frank E. v. State,** Op. No. 5741, 77 P.3d 715 (Alaska 2003).

Trial court which heard a wife's action seeking a divorce and ancillary relief erred when it failed to make findings on a husband's request for credits he allegedly discovered after the court divided the parties' marital estate. **Beal v. Beal,** Op. No. 5782, 88 P.3d 104 (Alaska 2004).

Trial court did not abuse its discretion when it denied a motion for relief from judgment because, to the extent that a motion relied on the grounds of mistake under Civil Rule 60(b)(1), it was unpersuasive and untimely; insofar as it sought to introduce new evidence, the motion made no showing that the evidence was newly discovered or that the standards of Civil Rule 60(b)(2) had been met. **Evans v. McTaggart,** Op. No. 5794, 88 P.3d 1078 (Alaska 2004).

Party's act of adding a term to an agreement without notifying the opposing party was misconduct within the meaning of clause (b)(3) of this rule. **Adams v. Adams,** Op. No. 5798, 89 P.3d 743 (Alaska 2004).

Judgment ordering specific performance of an option to purchase in a lease was properly vacated, where the lessee's conduct in changing a right of first refusal provision in a lease to an option to purchase without notice to the lessor was a constructive fraud. **Adams v. Adams,** Op. No. 5798, 89 P.3d 743 (Alaska 2004).

Ten years after decree of divorce was entered, husband was entitled to an amendment of the decree, which ordered him to pay more than 50 percent of his military retirement benefits to the wife in contravention of the Uniformed Services Former Spouses' Protection Act, 10 U.S.C.S. §1408(c) and (e). **Cline v. Cline,** Op. No. 5803, 90 P.3d 147 (Alaska 2004).

Denial of the mother's motion for reconsideration under clause (b)(1) of this rule was properly vacated where the mother had established that her failure to file objections to the father's request for support was an inadvertent mistake caused in part by her attorney's support staff's deliberate attempts to sabotage certain cases by failing to file documents with the court and by failing to provide the attorney with court orders for a number of months. **Harris v. Westfall,** 90 P.3d 167 (Alaska 2004).

Lower court's order that denied the mother's motion for reconsideration under clause (b)(3) of this rule was properly vacated where the mother had pointed to several areas in the father's motion for child support in which the father had made material misrepresentations about the custody arrangements and the need for support. **Harris v. Westfall,** 90 P.3d 167 (Alaska 2004).

A judgment or order is void where the state in which the judgment was rendered had no jurisdiction to subject the parties or the subject matter to its control, or where the defendant was not given proper notice of the action and opportunity to be heard, or where the judgment was not rendered by a duly constituted court with competency to render it, or where there was a failure to comply with such requirements as are necessary for the valid exercise of power by the court. **Rowland v. Monsen,** Op. No. 11603, 135 P.3d 1036 (Alaska 2006).

The untimeliness of a motion or the inadequacy of findings are not fundamental flaws that would make an order void. **Rowland v. Monsen,** Op. No. 11603, 135 P.3d 1036 (Alaska 2006).

What constitutes reasonable time under Rule 60(b)(6) necessarily depends on the facts in each case. Courts consider whether the party opposing the motion has been prejudiced by the delay in seeking relief and whether the moving party had some good reason for failing to act sooner. **Rowland v. Monsen**, Op. No. 11603, 135 P.3d 1036 (Alaska 2006).

A party must move for relief under Rule 60(b)(6) within a reasonable time, and what constitutes reasonable time necessarily depends on the facts in each case. **Morgan v. Morgan**, Op. No. 11728, 143 P.3d 975 (Alaska 2006).

A judgment is void under subsection (b) of this rule where the defendant was not given proper notice of the action and opportunity to be heard or where there was a failure to comply with such requirements as are necessary for the valid exercise of power by the court. **Hicks v. Pleasants**, Op. No. 12110, 158 P.3d 817 (Alaska 2007).

B. Standard for Appellate Review.

Relief from a judgment is addressed to the sound discretion of the trial court and the court's ruling will not be disturbed except upon a showing of abuse of discretion. **Alaska Truck Transport v. Inter-Alaska Credit Service,** Op. No. 266, 397 P2d 618 (Alaska 1965); **Gravel v. Alaskan Village, Inc.,** Op. No. 388, 423 P2d 273 (Alaska 1967).

The standard for reviewing a denial of a motion for relief from final judgment on grounds of a mistake, newly rediscovered evidence, fraud, equity, or for other reasons is whether the trial court abused its discretion in denying the motion. **Nordin Construction Co. v. City of Nome,** Op. No. 730, 489 P2d 455 (Alaska 1971).

The standard for reviewing an order entered pursuant to a motion for relief from a judgment is one of abuse of discretion. An order will be reversed only if the reviewing court is left with definite and firm conviction on the whole record that the trial judge has made a mistake. **Alaska Placer Co. v. Lee,** Op. No. 840, 502 P2d 128 (Alaska 1972).

The determination of a trial court as to the grant or denial of a motion to vacate a default judgment will not be disturbed on appeal except for an abuse of discretion. **Markland v. City of Fairbanks,** Op. No. 923, 513 P2d 658 (Alaska 1973).

The standard of review of claims based on fraud upon the court is abuse of discretion. **Allen v. Bussell,** Op. No. 1353, 558 P2d 496 (Alaska 1976).

Standard for appellate review of order denying relief from judgment is whether superior court abused its discretion, which would be the case only when Supreme Court were left with definite and firm conviction that trial judge had made a mistake. **McCraken v. Davis,** Op. No. 1389, 560 P2d 771 (Alaska 1977).

Denial of relief pursuant to this rule will be overturned if the trial court abuses its discretion, i.e., if the reviewing court is left with the definite and firm conviction on the whole record that the trial judge has made a mistake. **Gregor v. Hodges,** Op. No. 2110, 612 P2d 1008 (Alaska 1980).

Although appellant filed a motion for relief from judgment rather than a motion for new trial, since the underlying ground was "new evidence," the analysis was similar. **Grothe v. Olafson,** Op. No. 2619, 659 P2d 602 (Alaska 1983).

In reviewing denial of a motion to set aside a judgment on the ground that the judgment is void, the reviewing court does not defer to the discretion of the trial court. **Kennecorp Mortgage v. First Nat. Bank,** Op. No. 2837, 685 P2d 1232 (Alaska 1984).

A party on appeal who alleges that oral argument was improperly denied must show both that the denial was in error and that the error caused substantial prejudice. **Cleary Diving Service v. Thomas, Head and Greisen,** Op. No. 2873, 688 P2d 940 (Alaska 1984).

Validity of judgment is strictly question of law, thus motion attacking judgment does not involve question of whether lower court abused its discretion. **De Vaney v. State Dept. of Revenue,** Op. No. 4447, 928 P2d 1198 (Alaska 1996).

The Supreme Court reviews orders denying Rule 60(b)(6) relief under the abuse of discretion standard. **Morgan v. Morgan**, Op. No. 11728, 143 P.3d 975 (Alaska 2006).

C. Procedure.

Relief under this rule did not require leave of the Supreme Court where notice of appeal was filed but the record on appeal was not yet filed in the Supreme Court. **Patterson v. Cushman,** Op. No. 233, 394 P2d 657 (Alaska 1964).

Under this rule an aggrieved party may seek relief in the trial court from a consent judgment from which no appeal may be taken, and if such relief is denied, an appeal lies from the denial of the motion. **Gravel v. Alaskan Village, Inc.,** Op. No. 321, 409 P2d 983 (Alaska 1966).

A motion for rehearing on a grant of summary judgment was, technically, a motion for relief from judgment. **Palzer v. Serv-U-Meat Co.,** Op. No. 367, 419 P2d 201 (Alaska 1966).

In order to have authority to enter an order determining that a motion for relief from judgment should be granted while a civil appeal is pending in the Supreme Court, the superior court must first apply for and obtain a remand of the case from the Supreme Court for the stated purpose of granting such order. **Duriron Company, Inc. v. Bakke,** Op. No. 432, 431 P2d 499 (Alaska 1967).

The superior court has jurisdiction to deny a motion made under this rule for relief from judgment while a civil appeal is being perfected and pending in the Supreme Court. **Duriron Company, Inc. v. Bakke,** Op. No. 432, 431 P2d 499 (Alaska 1967).

Upon application to the Supreme Court by a movant for relief from judgment in the superior court under Civil Rule 60(b), all appellate proceedings pending in Supreme Court in the case will be stayed pending the superior court's resolution of the motion. **Duriron Company, Inc. v. Bakke,** Op. No. 432, 431 P2d 499 (Alaska 1967).

The Supreme Court will not pass on the sufficiency of a landowner's showing that he is entitled to an enlargement of time for appealing from the report of a master in condemnation until the trial court's discretionary powers have been exercised. **Collart et al. (6,656 Square Feet) v. State,** Op. No. 565, 456 P2d 480 (Alaska 1969).

A motion to set aside a judgment based on errors of law should be made within thirty days from the entry of the judgment; however, this rule may be relaxed or dispensed with where justice requires it. **Alaska Truck Transport, Inc. v. Berman Packing Co.,** Op. No. 610, 469 P2d 697 (Alaska 1970).

A motion to set aside judgment, filed eleven months after the entry of judgment, cannot be considered filed within a reasonable time, where the motion is based on an error of law arising from the counsel's inadvertence in not being aware of and making known to the trial court the correct principle of law bearing on the outcome of the litigation. **Alaska Truck Transport, Inc. v. Berman Packing Co.,** Op. No. 610, 469 P2d 697 (Alaska 1970).

The filing of a motion for relief from a final judgment does not terminate the running of the time for appeal from the judgment. **Wellman, Inc. v. City of Anchorage,** Op. No. 623, 471 P2d 408 (Alaska 1970).

The appeal from a denial of a motion for relief from the final judgment does not bring up the final judgment for review. **Wellman, Inc. v. City of Anchorage,** Op. No. 623, 471 P2d 408 (Alaska 1970).

A state court has the general power to grant equitable relief against the effects of a judgment rendered by a federal court or a sister state court to the extent that such relief would be available in the rendering forum. Such principle does not violate the requirement that full faith and credit be given to a judgment of a court of a sister state or a federal court, as the judgment is given the same effect as it would be entitled to under the laws and usage of the forum of its rendition. **Moran v. Poland,** Op. No. 771, 494 P2d 814 (Alaska 1972).

Res judicata prevents the relitigation, in a second suit for relief from a judgment, of matters which have been adjudged or could fairly have been judged in a prior proceeding between the same parties raising the same claim for relief. **Moran v. Poland,** Op. No. 771, 494 P2d 814 (Alaska 1972).

A federal district court decision denying a motion for relief from that court's prior judgment on the ground that the motion was not supported by facts sufficient to establish any of the reasons set forth in Federal Rule 60 is an adjudication on the merits. The movant is barred by res judicata from seeking relief in a state court from the federal judgment on the identical grounds urged in federal court. **Moran v. Poland,** Op. No. 771, 494 P2d 814 (Alaska 1972).

Where a defendant's motion for relief from judgment alleges they were denied the opportunity to object to the judgment, such motion is not based on an error of law. It therefore need not be brought within 30 days from entry of the judgment. **Alaska Placer Co. v. Lee,** Op. No. 840, 502 P2d 128 (Alaska 1972).

The one-year limitation of this rule does not apply to proceedings to correct orders obtained by fraud upon the court. **Mallonee v. Grow,** Op. No. 841, 502 P2d 432 (Alaska 1972).

A motion to set aside an order for fraud upon the court should be made reasonably in regard for all the circumstances and interest involved. **Mallonee v. Grow,** Op. No. 841, 502 P2d 432 (Alaska 1972).

In determining whether a motion to set aside an order because of a fraud upon the court has been made reasonably, the interests of the parties and of the courts must be considered.

Though the parties have an interest in the finality of judgments, the interests of the parties are not the only factors to be considered. **Mallonee v. Grow,** Op. No. 841, 502 P2d 432 (Alaska 1972).

A party seeking relief from a judgment on the basis of a subsequent change in the law would proceed under this rule. **Pearson v. Bachner,** Op. No. 850, 503 P2d 1401 (Alaska 1972).

A motion for relief from a judgment based on a subsequent change in law should be made within the time for appeal from the judgment. **Pearson v. Bachner,** Op. No. 850, 503 P2d 1401 (Alaska 1972).

Motions not subject to one-year limitation must be filed within a reasonable time. **Allen v. Bussell,** Op. No. 1353, 558 P2d 496 (Alaska 1976).

Appeal from order denying relief from judgment does not bring up the underlying judgment for review. **McCraken v. Davis,** Op. No. 1389, 560 P2d 771 (Alaska 1977).

A court may impose attorney's fees as a condition granting a motion to set aside a default judgment. **Nichiro Gyogyo Kaisha, Ltd. v. Norman,** Op. No. 2025, 606 P2d 401 (Alaska 1980).

Although a default order was properly entered against the first of two allegedly jointly liable parties, a judgment based on the default was improperly entered before the second party had had an opportunity to defend on the merits. Under these circumstances, the superior court abused its discretion in awarding attorney's fees to plaintiff as a condition of the setting aside of the default judgment. **Nichiro Gyogyo Kaisha, Ltd. v. Norman,** Op. No. 2025, 606 P2d 401 (Alaska 1980).

The denial of a motion to set aside judgment under this rule is to be treated as a final judgment for res judicata purposes. **Calhoun v. Greening,** Op. No. 2435, 636 P2d 69 (Alaska 1981).

Factors which a court may use to determine if motion was made within a reasonable time under this rule are whether there was prejudice to the other party caused by the delay and whether the moving party had good reason for failing to take action sooner. **Allen v. Allen,** Op. No. 2514, 645 P2d 774 (Alaska 1982).

Superior court lacked jurisdiction to grant wife relief from property settlement agreement in divorce decree where wife's motion for modifications, which alleged, in essence, fraud, misrepresentation or other misconduct by husband, was not filed until 15 months after the divorce decree was entered. **Stone v. Stone,** Op. No. 2522, 647 P2d 582 (Alaska 1982).

Where motion could have been brought under one of the reasons listed in this rule for which a one-year time limit is imposed, relief could not be obtained after the one-year period under clause allowing relief for "any other reason justifying relief from the operation of the judgment," since relief available under that clause is exclusive of the other remedies offered by the rule. **Stone v. Stone,** Op. No. 2522, 647 P2d 582 (Alaska 1982).

Although court did not state its reasons for finding that the failure to request the inclusion of an order of sale in the original judgment was inadvertent or excusable neglect, the finding was not an abuse of discretion under this rule, especially in light of statutory language which makes it appear as though no request is necessary. **Eagle Air v. Corroon, Etc.,** Op. No. 2538, 648 P2d 1000 (Alaska 1982).

Trial court had jurisdiction under this rule to amend a voluntary dismissal without prejudice entered pursuant to rule on dismissal of actions. **Farrell v. Dome Laboratories,** Op. No. 2556, 650 P2d 380 (Alaska 1982).

Trial court had jurisdiction under this rule to amend its prior judgment of voluntary dismissal without prejudice notwithstanding that the order of dismissal was previously affirmed on appeal. **Farrell v. Dome Laboratories,** Op. No. 2556, 650 P2d 380 (Alaska 1982).

Courts do not have the power to extend the one year time limit of this rule. **Farrell v. Dome Laboratories,** Op. No. 2556, 650 P2d 380 (Alaska 1982).

The pendency of an appeal does not extend the one year time limit for a motion for relief based upon mistake, inadvertence, surprise or excusable neglect. **Farrell v. Dome Laboratories,** Op. No. 2556, 650 P2d 380 (Alaska 1982).

Where new evidence in personal injury case consisted of physician's testimony which would have been similar to the testimony given by other physicians, trial court did not err in refusing to grant defendant's motion for relief from judgment, rejecting defendant's contention that the evidence would not be cumulative because the physician was a recognized expert in the area. **Grothe v. Olafson,** Op. No. 2619, 659 P2d 602 (Alaska 1983).

The general requirement that a meritorious defense to the matter on which the judgment or order rests must be presented to justify relief under this rule does not apply where the basis for the motion for relief is a due process violation. **Pew v. Foster,** Op. No. 2637, 660 P2d 447 (Alaska 1983).

Denial of motion for relief from order directing entry of judgment by default, which order was entered as a sanction against appellant for failure to comply with court order to answer two interrogatories, was improper, where court did not address appellant's claim that her attorney had not been served notice of the motion for sanctions. **Pew v. Foster,** Op. No. 2637, 660 P2d 447 (Alaska 1983).

Wife's mistake as to amount of time and money necessary to complete her education did not entitle her to modification of terms of support payments from husband where modification was sought more than three years after the divorce decree. **Larson v. Larson,** Op. No. 2648, 661 P2d 626 (Alaska 1983).

A default, as distinguished from a default judgment, is an interlocutory matter not governed by the strict time limits imposed by the civil rules on motions for relief from judgments or orders. **Syndoulos Lutheran Church v. A.R.C. Industries,** Op. No. 2649, 662 P2d 109 (Alaska 1983).

Motion for relief under this rule from a final decree of dissolution on the ground that duress was used to obtain consent to the decree was filed more than one year after the decree and therefore could not be considered. **J.C. v. M.L.C.,** Op. No. 2724, 668 P2d 1351 (Alaska 1983).

An independent collateral action for relief from a final judgment on grounds of duress filed more than one year after the judgment would not be barred by this rule, but such action would have to be maintained independently and could not be brought as a Rule 60(b) proceeding. **J.C. v. M.L.C.,** Op. No. 2724, 668 P2d 1351 (Alaska 1983).

There is no time limit on a motion attacking a judgment as void. **Kennecorp Mortgage v. First Nat. Bank,** Op. No. 2837, 685 P2d 1232 (Alaska 1984).

Trial court's dismissal as untimely of motion to set aside default judgment for "any other reason justifying relief from the operation of the judgment" was Proper where the motion was filed well over a year after entry of the judgment. **Kennecorp Mortgage v. First Nat. Bank,** Op. No. 2837, 685 P2d 1232 (Alaska 1984).

Appellants were not improperly denied a hearing on their motion attacking the dismissal of their case because, although they filed a timely notice of hearing, that notice did not include a certificate by appellants' counsel that he had attempted to resolve the matter with opposing counsel. **Cleary Diving Service v. Thomas, Head and Greisen,** Op. No. 2873, 688 P2d 940 (Alaska 1984).

Former husband's motion for retrospective modification of divorce decree on the ground that the support order was unconstitutional was treated as a request for relief from the prior judgment rather than a request for modification. **Burrell v. Burrell,** Op. No. 2795, 696 P2d 157 (Alaska 1984).

Appeal by former husband of dismissal of his claim for relief from judgment dividing up couple's property did not bring the merits of the underlying judgment before the appellate court. **Burrell v. Burrell,** Op. No. 2795, 696 P2d 157 (Alaska 1984).

Failure of former husband to appeal court order, which required him to maintain insurance on his life for the benefit of his wife, within the period required by the Appellate Rules, or to request relief from the order under this rule within a reasonable time, barred him as a matter of law from requesting relief from the order. **Burrell v. Burrell,** Op. No. 2795, 696 P2d 157 (Alaska 1984).

As a matter of law, a period of almost seven and one-half years is not a reasonable time within which to file a motion for relief under subsections b(5) or b(6) of this rule. **Burrell v. Burrell,** Op. No. 2795, 696 P2d 157 (Alaska 1984).

There is no time limit for an attack on a judgment as void. **Burrell v. Burrell,** Op. No. 2795, 696 P2d 157 (Alaska 1984).

This rule is not a substitute for a party failing to file a timely appeal, nor does it allow relitigation of issues that have been resolved by the judgment. **Burrell v. Burrell,** Op. No. 2795, 696 P2d 157 (Alaska 1984).

A Rule 60(b)(1) motion made on the basis of a subsequent change in the law must be made within the same time period allowed for an appeal. **Lawrence v. Lawrence,** Op. No. 3044, 718 P2d 142 (Alaska 1986).

When a party seeks relief from a judgment, which does not have prospective application, because of a subsequent change in the law, a Civil Rule 60(b)(1) motion should be used. **Lawrence v. Lawrence,** Op. No. 3044, 718 P2d 142 (Alaska 1986).

Superior court properly refused to grant relief pursuant to Civil Rule 60(b)(1) from that portion of divorce decree which required husband to pay post-majority child support, since his 60(b)(1) motion was not filed within the 30 days allowed for appeals from divorce decrees. **Lawrence v. Lawrence,** Op. No. 3044, 718 P2d 142 (Alaska 1986).

Failure of the judgment to grant attorney's fees on punitive damage award was a legal error, but trial judge had discretion to waive the thirty-day rule for correcting such errors so as to grant a late request for modification of the judgment. **Alaskan Village, Inc. v. Smalley,** Op. No. 3069, 720 P2d 945 (Alaska 1986).

Clause (6) of this rule, covering any other reason justifying relief from a judgment, cannot be relied on to circumvent the time limit for claims for relief under clause (1) of this rule if the circumstances actually amount to a clause (1) claim. **Village of Chefornak v. Hooper Bay Const.,** Op. No. 3360, 758 P2d 1266 (Alaska 1988).

Father's delay in filing motion for relief from post-majority educational child support award on the ground that it was no longer equitable to give the judgment prospective application did not preclude consideration of the merits of his claim where the mother had agreed not to raise the passage of time to defeat a motion to modify the award, the state falsely represented that it would not enforce the post-majority support order, and his family acquiesced in the state's determination. **Propst v. Propst,** Op. No. 3451, 776 P2d 780 (Alaska 1989).

Wife's motion to modify dissolution decree eight years after the decree was entered was made within a reasonable time. **Schofield v. Schofield,** Op. No. 3461, 777 P2d 197 (Alaska 1989).

A motion to set aside a judgment under this rule is not a substitute for appeal. **Kenai Peninsula Borough v. English Bay Village Corp.,** Op. No. 3517, 781 P2d 6 (Alaska 1989).

Contentions based on facts which are known to a party at a time when a direct appeal is possible must either be raised on direct appeal or in a motion for relief from judgment under this rule made during the time for taking the appeal. **Kenai Peninsula Borough v. English Bay Village Corp.,** Op. No. 3517, 781 P2d 6 (Alaska 1989).

Where defendant executed a confession of judgment without action which was entered as a judgment on September 18, 1986, but was not sent a copy of the judgment and did not learn of it until September 26, 1988, his motion to set aside the confession of judgment, filed October 18, 1988, was deemed timely. **Princiotta v. Municipality of Anchorage,** Op. No. 3548, 785 P2d 559 (Alaska 1990).

Supreme Court can sua sponte set aside a judgment for fraud on the court. **Higgins v. Municipality of Anchorage,** Op. No. 3684, 810 P2d 149 (Alaska 1991).

Trial court had jurisdiction to amend its judgment pursuant to a motion filed within six weeks of the order of judgment. **Wood v. Collins,** Op. No. 3698, 812 P2d 951 (Alaska 1991).

A motion under this rule to set aside a judgment for "any other reason justifying relief from the operation of the judgment" is not subject to a one year time limit, but still must be brought within a reasonable time. **Lowe v. Lowe,** Op. No. 3726, 817 P2d 453 (Alaska 1991).

Fact that dissolution petition provided that husband would have primary custody of the children, when in fact the wife had primary custody after the dissolution, was a valid basis for modifying the property division of the dissolution decree pursuant to the subsection of this rule authorizing judgments to be set aside for "any other reason justifying relief from the operation of the judgment." **Lowe v. Lowe,** Op. No. 3726, 817 P2d 453 (Alaska 1991).

Factors which constitute extraordinary circumstances justifying relief under this rule from a marriage dissolution property division of military retirement benefits were: (1) the fundamental, underlying assumption of the dissolution agreement had been destroyed; (2) the parties' property division was poorly thought out; (3) the property division was reached without the benefit of counsel; and (4) the military retirement benefits were a major asset of the parties' marriage. **Lowe v. Lowe,** Op. No. 3726, 817 P2d 453 (Alaska 1991).

Trial court erred in refusing to consider CR 60(b) motion in a case on appeal unless a remand for that specific purpose had first been obtained; a remand is only required if the trial court considers the motion and decides to grant it. **Barnes v. Barnes,** Op. No. 3724, 820 P2d 294 (Alaska 1991).

Appellate court remand order was sufficiently explicit to empower the trial court to grant motion for CR 60(b) relief, even though the order did not specifically mention a CR 60(b) motion; the order explicitly remanded "to allow for resolution of the issue of distribution of certain deferred compensation funds," the same issue resolved by the trial court on remand. **Barnes v. Barnes,** Op. No. 3724, 820 P2d 294 (Alaska 1991).

Superior court did not err in granting CR 60(b) motion in a case on appeal without first applying for and obtaining a remand from the appellate court, where the appellate court had already ordered a remand for the purpose of considering the issue that later became the substance of the CR 60(b) motion.

Barnes v. Barnes, Op. No. 3724, 820 P2d 294 (Alaska 1991).

Where property rights have been purportedly adjudicated and incorporated into a final judgment, relief may only be granted within the parameters of Civil Rule 60(b). **Johnson v. Johnson,** Op. No. 3798, 824 P2d 1381 (Alaska 1992).

Ex-husband's motion to modify divorce decree did not toll or affect deadline for appealing judgment awarding attorney fees to ex-wife. **Olson v. Olson,** Op. No. 3975, 856 P2d 482 (Alaska 1993).

Failure of trial court to issue findings of fact when it denied motion to modify divorce decree did not require remand. **Olson v. Olson,** Op. No. 3975, 856 P2d 482 (Alaska 1993).

Rule that contentions based upon facts known toparty at time when direct appeal is possible must be raised on direct appeal or by Rule 60(b) motion brought within time for appeal applies only to Rule 60(b) motions that claim mistake of law. **Sandoval v. Sandoval,** Op. No. 4351, 915 P2d 1222 (Alaska 1996).

Failure of lender to give prior notice of intent to seek default judgment against borrower was inappropriate but did not render ensuing judgment void or justify borrower's one-year delay in filing motion for relief from judgment. **Benedict v. Key Bank of Alaska,** Op. No. 4353, 916 P2d 489 (Alaska 1996).

Only Rule 60(b) motions alleging mistake of law need be filed within time frame applicable to an appeal. **Hatten v. Hatten,** Op. No. 4354, 917 P2d 667 (Alaska 1996).

Trial court's failure in divorce decree property settlement to account for husband's pending tort suit even though subject was raised at trial was inadvertent factual mistake, not mistake of law, thus wife's motion for relief from judgment, filed 47 days after trial court decision, was properly granted, notwithstanding that time limit for filing notice of appeal was 30 days. **Hatten v. Hatten,** Op. No. 4354, 917 P2d 667 (Alaska 1996).

One-year limitation in this rule for motion for relief because of fraud did not apply to petition asking Workers' Compensation Board to set aside compromise and release settlement allegedly obtained by fraud. **Blanas v. Brower Co.,** Op. No. 4833, 938 P2d 1056 (Alaska 1997).

Pro se litigant could not use Civil Rule 60(b) motion to cure failure to raise issue in trial court and to present that issue on direct appeal. **Ghete v. Anchorage,** Op. No. 4912, 948 P2d 973 (Alaska 1997).

Wife's motion for relief from dissolution decrees filed within nine months after court entered decree was timely notwithstanding husband's argument that she could have filed earlier. **Song v. Song,** Op. No. 5061, 972 P2d 589 (Alaska 1999).

Trial court properly exercised its discretion in vacating stipulated property settlement portion of dissolution decree on ground of fraud by husband but erred in redividing marital property without giving husband advance notice or opportunity for hearing on property division issues. **Song v. Song,** Op. No. 5061, 972 P2d 589 (Alaska 1999).

Wife's motion for relief from property settlement portion of dissolution decree on ground that decree did not address or anticipate subsequently-enacted governmental fishing quota program which significantly increased value of fishing vessel awarded to husband was timely; husband's argument that CR 60(b)(1) or (2) applied to motion, requiring motion to be filed within one year of dissolution decree, was rejected, trial court concluding that CR 60(b)(6) applied. **McGee v. McGee,** Op. No. 5092, 974 P2d 983 (Alaska 1999).

Relief under Civil Rule 60(b)(5) is available against only prospective or executory aspects of judgments. **Ferguson v. State ex rel. P.G.,** Op. No. 5110, 977 P2d 95 (Alaska 1999).

Vacation of paternity judgment under Court Rule 60(b)(5) eliminated only its prospective effect and did not preclude collection of amounts past due under the judgment. **Ferguson v. State ex rel. P.G.,** Op. No. 5110, 977 P2d 95 (Alaska 1999).

Rule that res judicata cannot bar direct attack upon judgment applied to husband's Rule 60(b) motion to set aside portion of divorce decree attributing paternity to husband following DNA test which excluded him as father; trial court erred in concluding that res judicata can bar Rule 60(b) motions generally. **Dixon v. Pouncy,** Op. No. 5116, 979 P2d 520 (Alaska 1999).

Where language of motion for relief from judgment placed motion squarely under categories of "mistake or inadvertence" or "newly discovered evidence," which require motion to be made within one year of notice of judgment, argument that motion fell under category of "any other reason justifying relief," which requires motion to be made within "reasonable time" after notice of judgment, was rejected; latter category is to be employed only when grounds for relief do not fall within other categories specified in this rule. **Snook v. Bowers,** Op. No. 5329, 12 P3d 771 (Alaska 2000).

Where alleged father moved in 1996 to vacate 1991 default judgment of paternity based on mother's misrepresentation that he was the father and genetic test results definitively excluding him as the father, alleged father was not entitled to full restitution of child support payments but only to refund of child support payments made on or after the date he filed his motion to vacate. **Atcherian v. State Dept. of Revenue, CSED,** Op. No. 5350, 14 P3d 970 (Alaska 2000).

A party can invoke Alaska R. Civ. P. 60(b)(6) only if none of the other five clauses apply and extraordinary circumstances exist. **Juelfs v. Gough,** Op. No. 5535, 41 P3d 593 (Alaska 2002).

In deciding Alaska R. Civ. P. 60(b)(6) motions, courts give consideration to the following factors: the prejudice, if any, to the non-moving party if relief from judgment is granted, whether any intervening equities make the granting of relief inappropriate, and any other circumstances relevant to consideration of the equities of the case. The court thus balances the interest in the finality of judgments against the interest in granting relief from judgment when justice so requires. **Juelfs v. Gough,** Op. No. 5535, 41 P3d 593 (Alaska 2002).

Where an employee was not tested before a workers' compensation hearing to determine if she was allergic to dust mites, but the technology existed to do so, the fact that she was later determined to be allergic to dust mites did not constitute newly-discovered evidence under section (d) of this rule, and as it was applied to AS 23.30.130(a), and denial of her petition for modification and rehearing was proper. **Lindhag v. Dep't of Natural Res.,** Op. No. 5946, 123 P.3d 948 (Alaska 2005).

Where appellant filed her Rule 60(b)(6) motion for relief approximately three years and nine months after the original court order and the facts did not indicate that either party was hurt by the delay, the court determined that the facts failed to show good reason for appellant's delay, and the court's ruling was upheld. **Rowland v. Monsen**, Op. No. 11603, 135 P.3d 1036 (Alaska 2006).

Party to a divorce did not move for relief within a reasonable time under Rule 60(b) to add ex-husband's pension to the divorce calculation where the party learned of the pension's existence twenty-six years after the divorce, and waited an additional three years to file for relief. Party offered no explanation why fear of her ex-husband prevented her from moving for relief when she discovered the pension and there is no evidence of circumstances beyond the party's control which prevented her from asking for relief sooner. **Morgan v. Morgan**, Op. No. 11728, 143 P.3d 975 (Alaska 2006).

Rule 61. Harmless Error.

No error in either the admission or the exclusion of evidence and no error or defect in any ruling or order or in anything done or omitted by the court or by any of the parties is ground for granting a new trial or for setting aside a verdict or for vacating, modifying or otherwise disturbing a judgment or order, unless refusal to take such action appears to the court inconsistent with substantial justice. The court at every stage of the proceeding must disregard any error or defect in the proceeding which does not affect the substantial rights of the parties.

(Adopted by SCO 5 October 9, 1959)

Annotations

Cases

I. In General.
II. Jury Instruction.
III. Burden of Proof.

I. In General.

Where a trial court commits error in denying a motion for judgment on the pleadings or to dismiss, such error will be disregarded if it is harmless. **Reiten v. Hendricks,** Op. No. 68, 370 P2d 166 (Alaska 1962).

Noncompliance with subdivisions (a) and (b) of Rule 78 does not in itself require a reversal of the judgment, and an appellant claiming noncompliance was required to show that she had been prejudiced in some way, which she failed to do. **Briggs v. Kelly,** Op. No. 115, 376 P2d 715 (Alaska 1962).

If the jury could have relied upon inadmissible hearsay evidence to draw an inference of negligence in an accident case, the error was prejudicial and required that cause be remanded for a new trial. **Otis Elevator Co. v. McLaney,** Op. No. 300, 406 P2d 7 (Alaska 1965).

Deposition admitted into evidence was merely cumulative of other evidence that the plaintiff had introduced, and if any error was committed in permitting such deposition to be read, such error was harmless. **Otis Elevator Co. v. McLaney,** Op. No. 300, 406 P2d 7 (Alaska 1965).

Trial court's failure to declare a mistrial in the absence of motion for a mistrial and in the absence of request for admonition of jurors to disregard the remark was not prejudicial where there was no basis for content that failure to object could have resulted in injustice. **Heacock v. Town,** Op. No. 368, 419 P2d 622 (Alaska 1966).

Error in jury instructions concerning estoppel questions was harmless where there was no evidence from which the jury could have found an estoppel. **Groseth v. Ness,** Op. No. 370, 421 P2d 624 (Alaska 1966).

Erroneous instruction deemed prejudicial where it could not be said that verdict may not have been different without such erroneous instruction. **Howarth v. Pfeifer,** Op. No. 386, 423 P2d 680 (Alaska 1967).

Only in exceptional circumstances and to prevent a miscarriage of justice would the supreme court interfere with the exercise of wide discretionary authority of the trial court in its determination whether a mistrial should be declared. **Peters v. Benson,** Op. No. 397, 425 P2d 149 (Alaska 1967).

Permitting reference to insurance in the trial of a negligence case if error at all was not reversible error where no prejudicial effect on the result of the trial was perceived. **Peters v. Benson,** Op. No. 397, 425 P2d 149 (Alaska 1967).

Plain errors which are so substantial as to result in injustice, will be considered on appeal even though not objected to below. **Merrill v. Faltin,** Op. No. 425, 430 P2d 913 (Alaska 1967).

The standard of Criminal Rule 47(b) under which questions raised for the first time on appeal will be considered if necessary to effect substantial justice or prevent the denial of fundamental rights, is apart from rule applied by the supreme court in civil cases. **Goreson v. State,** Op. No. 436, 432 P2d 326 (Alaska 1967).

Record indicated that inclusion of an incompetent sale in testimony on value of land to be condemned in an eminent domain proceeding did not mislead the jury and did not call for reversal. **Alaska State Housing Authority v. DuPont,** Op. No. 469, 439 P2d 427 (Alaska 1968).

The exclusion of expert testimony sought to be elicited by a hypothetical question, as to whether the defendant's physical and mental abilities were impaired by the consumption of alcoholic beverages, on the ground that the amount of alcohol in the beverages consumed has never been established, is erroneous. The testimony should be admitted based on the assumption that the drinks were of ordinary alcoholic content. **Haisley v. Grant,** Op. No. 701, 486 P2d 367 (Alaska 1971).

Where opponents do not argue that photocopies of public records are inaccurate or that the original public records have been altered, the failure of the superior court to notify the parties and identify the documents to be relied upon before taking judicial notice of documents is harmless error. **Concerned Citizens of South Kenai Peninsula v. Kenai Peninsula Borough,** Op. No. 1093, 527 P2d 447 (Alaska 1974).

Exclusion of cumulative evidence is not prejudicial. **Sloan v. Atlantic Richfield Co.,** Op. No. 2047, 541 P2d 717 (Alaska 1975).

Harmless error does not mean that, elided from the record, there would be enough evidence to support a verdict. **Poulin v. Zartman,** Op. No. 1204, 542 P2d 251 (Alaska 1975).

In determining whether an erroneous evidentiary ruling was harmless, proof of harm beyond a reasonable doubt is not required, but the members of the supreme court will necessarily put themselves, as nearly as possible, in the position of the jury to determine whether, as reasonable men, any error committed probably affected their verdict. **Poulin v. Zartman,** Op. No. 1204, 542 P2d 251 (Alaska 1975).

That a juror may develop a like or dislike for one side during trial and that such in turn may affect the way that the juror votes in the jury room is a fact which inheres in the verdict and is not a reason to reverse the verdict. **Poulin v. Zartman,** Op. No. 1204, 542 P2d 251 (Alaska 1975).

Failure to afford opportunity for oral argument was harmless error. **McCraken v. Davis,** Op. No. 1389, 560 P2d 771 (Alaska 1977).

Where defendant had testified on speed and relative positions of vehicles, and issue was thoroughly covered, exclusion of further evidence on the issue was harmless error if it was error at all. **Drickerson v. Drickerson,** Op. No. 1992, 604 P2d 1082 (Alaska 1979).

Where breathalyzer and other evidence clearly established that defendant was intoxicated, failure to exclude defendant's admission that he had drunk5 or 6 beers, prior to being advised of Miranda rights, was harmless error. **Palmer v. State,** Op. No. 2002, 604 P2d 1106 (Alaska 1979).

Inadvertent inclusion in the jury room of an exhibit excluded from evidence is harmless error when the individual jurors did not recall or rely upon the exhibit and the exhibit did not contain new or damaging evidence. **Renfroe v. Green,** Op. No. 2233, 626 P2d 1068 (Alaska 1980).

Although the presentation of irrelevant evidence as to the scope of burglaries is error, it is harmless error if the presentation produces little or no prejudicial effect. **Nelson v. State,** Op. No. 2350, 628 P2d 884 (Alaska 1981).

Among factors to be considered in determining if erroneously admitted during the trial, both during questioning and in the closing arguments. **Alyeska Pipeline Service Co. v. O'Kelley,** Op. No. 2510, 645 P2d 767 (Alaska 1982).

In contract dispute, admission of irrelevant testimony by one of plaintiff's witnesses that defendant refused to aid a sick baby was harmless error. **Alyeska Pipeline Service Co. v. O'Kelley,** Op. No. 2510, 645 P2d 767 (Alaska 1982).

In action against snow machine manufacturer for negligence and strict products liability, exclusion of evidence regarding defects found in similar machines and foreseeable use on the ground of undue prejudice was harmless error because the same evidence was presented to the jury in a different form. **Hiller v. Kawasaki Motors Corp.,** Op. No. 2711, 671 P2d 369 (Alaska 1983).

Although one interrogatory of the special verdict was erroneous, other interrogatories plainly instructed the jury to do that which the erroneous one did not, and so rendered the error harmless. **Loof v. Sanders,** Op. No. 2859, 686 P2d 1205 (Alaska 1984).

Erroneous admission of deposition testimony was harmless error since the evidence contained in the depositions was cumulative. **Fairbanks North Star Borough v. Tundra Tours,** Op. No. 3052, 719 P2d 1020 (Alaska 1986).

Where motion for reconsideration was granted during the pendency of an appeal, movant's failure to obtain a stay of the appellate proceedings and a remand was harmless error, since the opposing party did not dispute the substance of the trial court's action on reconsideration or otherwise show that his rights were affected. **Howard S. Lease Const. Co. v. Holly,** Op. No. 3123, 725 P2d 712 (Alaska 1986).

Absence of notice and court approval in violation of this rule, which appellants alleged affected their class eligibility determination, was harmless error, since there were independent grounds for excluding appellant from the class. **Riley v. Simon,** Op. No. 3583, 790 P2d 1339 (Alaska 1990).

II. Jury Instruction.

Error in giving an instruction must be disregarded if it does not interfere with substantial justice. **Davidsen v. Kirkland,** Op. No. 38, 362 P2d 1068 (Alaska 1961).

An erroneous jury instruction which could not have confused or misled the jury to appellant's prejudice, did not call for reversal. **Mitchell v. Knight,** Op. No. 241, 394 P2d 892 (Alaska 1964).

Where jury returned a verdict for plaintiff in a typical accident case, the jury must have found that there was negligence on defendant's part and an instruction given by the judge on the concept of "unavoidable accident," albeit improper in that type of case was harmless error. **Alaska Brick Co. v. McCoy,** Op. No. 287, 400 P2d 454 (Alaska 1965).

Prejudice that may have existed by court's initial ruling allowing prejudicial testimony to be admitted was waived by appellant's acquiescence in court's instruction to the jury to disregard the testimony. **National Bank of Alaska v. McHugh,** Op. No. 352, 416 P2d 239 (Alaska 1966).

Jury instruction which placed on the plaintiff a greater burden than was required by erroneously making it necessary for him to prove malice of the defendant in a civil action for assault and battery, was reversible error. **Merrill v. Faltin,** Op. No. 425, 430 P2d 913 (Alaska 1967).

Where the appellant does not prevail and her requested instructions as to strict liability are not given, the reviewing court cannot infer that the facts of her case were viewed as favorably by the jury under warranty instructions which were given as they might have been under strict liability instructions. **Clary v. Fifth Avenue Chrysler Center, Inc.,** Op. No. 552,454 P2d 244 (Alaska 1969).

Mere uncertainty regarding the effect of an erroneous instruction on verdict does not, of itself, require a new trial. **Martinez v. Bullock,** Op. No. 1152, 535 P2d 1200 (Alaska 1975).

In "slip and fall" tort case, jury need not be instructed as to how a reasonable person performs the activity of walking. **Hatfield v. Universal Services, Inc.,** Op. No. 2288, 622 P2d 984 (Alaska 1981).

Even if comparative negligence instruction was improper, error was harmless where jury found neither defendant negligent. **Baker v. Werner,** Op. No. 2541, 654 P.2d 263 (Alaska 1982).

In malpractice action, instruction which provided that a physician is not negligent merely because he makes a mistake or errs in judgment was erroneous, but since other jury instructions plainly instructed the jury to evaluate the physician's conduct, error was harmless. **Baker v. Werner,** Op. No. 2541, 654 P.2d 263 (Alaska 1982).

Applying the harmless error doctrine to failure of trial court to give a proposed instruction requires the reviewing court to determine whether the error had a substantial influence on the original judgment; the reviewing court must consider the circumstances of the refusal to give the instruction as well as determine the likelihood that a contrary decision would have resulted in a different verdict. **Loof v. Sanders,** Op. No. 2859, 686 P2d 1205 (Alaska 1984).

In action for injuries arising out of crewman's fall from dock ladder while boarding boat, any error committed by trial court in refusing plaintiff's instruction on a master's duty to his crew was harmless, since the jury found that the crewman's intoxication was the sole cause of the fall. **Loof v. Sanders,** Op. No. 2859, 686 P2d 1205 (Alaska 1984).

An erroneous instruction is prejudicial unless it can be said that the jury's verdict would not have been different had it not been so instructed. **Hazen v. Municipality of Anchorage,** Op. No. 3043, 718 P2d 456 (Alaska 1986).

III. Burden of Proof.

This rule requires appellant on appeal to bear the burden of proving prejudice as well as error and where a specification of error asserts that hospital records excluded in error would have substantiated appellant's own testimony but did not explain why his testimony needed to be substantiated and did not make the hospital records part of the record on appeal, he did not meet the burden of showing that the error was prejudicial and reversible. **Zerbinos v. Lewis,** Op. No. 242, 394 P2d 886 (Alaska 1964).

An appellant has the burden of proving prejudice as well as error. **Sloan v. Atlantic Richfield Co.,** Op. No. 2047, 541 P2d 717 (Alaska 1975).

The appellant has the burden of proving both error in admission of testimony and prejudice resulting there from. **Poulin v. Zartman,** Op. No. 1204, 542 P2d 251 (Alaska 1975).

A party appealing the exclusion of evidence must show not only that such exclusion was improper, but also that it resulted in prejudice to that party. **Estate of Arrowwood v. State,** Op. No. 4196, 894 P2d 642 (Alaska 1995).

Failure to admit transcript of recorded interview, if error, would not require reversal of jury's special verdict where appellant failed to show prejudice. **Estate of Arrowwood v. State,** Op. No. 4196, 894 P2d 642 (Alaska 1995).

The party alleging that a failure to admit evidence was prejudicial must designate those portions of the record, including the trial transcript, which are necessary for proper appellate review. Where appellants failed to designate trial transcripts as part of record on appeal, appellate court was unable to conclude that they had been prejudiced and therefore had to uphold jury's verdict. **Estate of Arrowwood v. State,** Op. No. 4196, 894 P2d 642 (Alaska 1995).

In a personal injury case, court did not err by denying plaintiff's motion for a new trial where it had properly denied plaintiff's motion to cross-examine defendant regarding his liability insurance; although the court excluded explicit testimony that Allstate was defendant's insurer, the implication that defendant was insured was at least as apparent as any contrary implication from defendant's opening statement. **Marron v. Stromstad,** Op. No. 5955, 123 P.3d 992 (Alaska 2005).

Rule 62. Stay of Proceedings to Enforce a Judgment.

(a) **Automatic Stay—Exceptions.** Except as to judgments entered on default or by consent or on confession, and except as stated herein, no execution shall issue upon a judgment nor shall proceedings be taken for its enforcement until the expiration of 10 days after the date shown in the clerk's certificate of distribution on the judgment. Unless otherwise ordered by the court, an interlocutory or final judgment in an action for an injunction or in a receivership action shall not be stayed during the period after its entry and until an appeal is taken or during the pendency of an appeal. The provisions of subdivision (c) of this rule govern the suspending, modifying, restoring, or granting of an injunction during the pendency of an appeal or proceedings for review.

(b) **Stay on Motion for New Trial or for Judgment.** In

its discretion and on such conditions for the security of the adverse party as are proper, the court may stay the execution of or any proceedings to enforce a judgment pending the disposition of a motion for a new trial or to alter or amend a judgment made pursuant to Rule 59, or of a motion for relief from a judgment or order made pursuant to Rule 60, or of a motion for judgment in accordance with a motion for a directed verdict made pursuant to Rule 50, or of a motion for amendment to the findings or for additional findings made pursuant to Rule 52(b).

(c) **Injunction Pending Appeal or Review.** When an appeal is taken or review sought from an interlocutory or final judgment or order or decision granting, dissolving or denying an injunction, the court in its discretion may suspend, modify, restore or grant an injunction during the pendency of the appeal or the proceedings for review upon such terms as to bond or otherwise as it considers proper for the security of the rights of the adverse party.

(d) **Stay Upon Appeal or Proceedings for Review.** When an appeal is taken or review sought the appellant or petitioner by giving a supersedeas bond may obtain a stay subject to the exceptions contained in subdivision (a) of this rule. The bond may be given at or after the time of filing the notice of appeal or of filing the petition for review, as the case may be. The stay is effective when the supersedeas bond is approved by the court.

(e) **Stay in Favor of the State or Agency Thereof.** When an appeal is taken or review sought by the state or an officer or agency thereof, and the operation or enforcement of the judgment, order or decision is stayed, no bond, obligation or other security shall be required from the appellant or the petitioner, as the case may be.

(f) **Power of Supreme Court Not Limited.** The provisions in this rule do not limit any power of the supreme court or of a justice thereof to stay proceedings during the pendency of an appeal or proceedings for review, or to suspend, modify, restore or grant an injunction during the pendency of an appeal or proceedings for review, or to make any order appropriate to preserve the status quo or the effectiveness of the judgment subsequently to be entered.

(g) **Stay of Judgment Upon Multiple Claims or Multiple Parties.** When a court has ordered a final judgment under the conditions stated in Rule 54(b), the court may stay enforcement of that judgment until the entering of a subsequent judgment or judgments and may prescribe such conditions as are necessary to secure the benefit thereof to the party in whose favor the judgment is entered.

(Adopted by SCO 5 October 9, 1959; amended by SCO 30 effective February 1, 1961; by SCO 44 effective February 26, 1962; by SCO 258 effective November 15, 1976; by SCO 554 effective April 4, 1983; and by SCO 1361 effective October 15, 1999)

Note: Chapter 42 § 2 SLA 1999 enacts AS 09.19.200 which governs the remedies available in civil litigation involving conditions in correctional facilities. According to § 3 of the act, the enactment of AS 09.19.200 has the effect of amending Civil Rules 59(f), 60(b), 62, and 65 by altering the remedies available and the procedure to be used in litigation involving correctional facilities.

Annotations

Cases

The supreme court has the power to modify an injunction during the pendency of proceedings for review. **State v. Norene,** Op. No. 572, 457 P2d 926 (Alaska 1969).

Judgments in an action for injunction are not stayable as of right. Whether a stay pending appeal on an order granting or dissolving an injunction will be granted is a question directed to the sound discretion of the court. **Powell v. Anchorage,** Op. No. 1167, 536 P2d 1228 (Alaska 1975).

In considering whether to grant a stay pending appeal, the lower court must consider criteria much the same as it would in determining whether to grant a preliminary injunction. **Powell v. Anchorage,** Op. No. 1167, 536 P2d 1228 (Alaska 1975).

In the usual case, the trial court should be given the first opportunity to consider an application for a stay of judgment granting or denying an injunction. Exceptions should be made where the applicant makes a showing that relief in the superior court is unavailable, or that relief to be effective must be immediate and that it is improbable that the superior court can afford such immediate relief. **Powell v. Anchorage,** Op. No. 1167, 536 P2d 1228 (Alaska 1975).

Alaska State Housing Authority is a "state agency" and need not post bond to stay enforcement of judgment on appeal. **Alaska State Housing Authority v. Riley Pleas, Inc.,** Op. No. 1382, 560 P2d 25 (Alaska 1977).

To the extent that this rule conflicts with Alaska Appellate Rule 204(d), the appellate rule governs. **City of Nome v. Catholic Bishop of Northern Alaska,** Op. No. 2986, 707 P2d 870 (Alaska 1985).

If appellant seeks to stay enforcement of judgment pending appeal, he must present bond as security to trial court; failure to file bond or obtain stay leaves judgment debtor open to trial court's enforcement of judgment against him. **Heppinstall v. Darnall Kemna & Co., Inc.,** Op. No. 3952, 851 P2d 78 (Alaska 1993).

Superior court had jurisdiction to order judgment debtor to comply with judgment creditor's post-judgment discovery requests pending appeal and to enforce order with sanctions, where judgment debtor did not obtain stay pending appeal or file security bond. **Heppinstall v. Darnall Kemna & Co., Inc.,** Op. No. 3952, 851 P2d 78 (Alaska 1993).

Rule 63. Disability of a Judge

(a) **Before Trial.** If by reason of death, sickness or other disability, a judge before whom an action is pending is unable to perform the duties to be performed by the court under these rules prior to the beginning of the trial or hearing, then any other judge of the court assigned by the presiding judge of the judicial district where the action is pending or by the chief justice of the supreme court may perform those duties.

(b) **During Trial.** If by reason of death, sickness or other disability, a judge before whom an action is pending is unable to perform the duties to be performed by the court under these rules after the trial or hearing of the action has commenced, then any other judge of the court, assigned by the presiding judge of the judicial district where the action is pending or by the chief justice of the supreme court, may perform those duties, as if such other judge had been present and presiding from the commencement of such trial or hearing; provided, however, that from the beginning of the taking of testimony at such trial or hearing a stenographic or electronic recording of the proceedings shall have been made so that the judge so continuing may become familiar with the previous proceedings.

(c) **After Verdict, etc.** If by reason of death, sickness or other disability, a judge before whom an action has been tried is unable to perform the duties to be performed by the court under these rules after a verdict is returned or findings of fact and conclusions of law are filed, then any other judge of the court, assigned by the presiding judge of the judicial district where the action has been tried or by the chief justice of the supreme court, may perform those duties; but if that judge is satisfied that that judge cannot perform those duties because the judge did not preside at the trial or for any other reason, that judge may grant a new trial.

(Adopted by SCO 5 October 9, 1959; amended by SCO 1153 effective July 15, 1994)

Annotations

Cases

The termination of an interim U.S. District Court for the District (Territory) of Alaska and the trial judge's office there under is a "disability." **Pollastrine v. Severance,** Op. No. 108, 375 P2d 528 (Alaska 1962).

A successor judge held not to have authority to file findings of fact. **Pollastrine v. Severance,** Op. No. 108, 375 P2d 528 (Alaska 1962).

Filing of transcript of the trial judge's oral opinion satisfied the requirements of filed findings of fact and conclusions of law under Civ. R. 63(c), and a successor judge had authority to enter a final decree. **Pollastrine v. Severance,** Op. No. 108, 375 P2d 528 (Alaska 1962).

Record did not disclose that trial judge who had disqualified himself, notified his presiding superior court judge of his disability to hear the cause. **Nelson v. Fitzgerald,** Op. No. 293, 403 P2d 677 (Alaska 1965).

Although a judge should do so only for the most compelling reasons, a superior court judge may sua sponte disqualify himself from hearing any matter that may come before him. **Nelson v. Fitzgerald,** Op. No. 293, 403 P2d 677 (Alaska 1965).

Unless the trial judge becomes disabled, he should be the person who makes all fact based rulings concerning the case that he tried. **United Bank Alaska v. Dischner,** Op. No. 2835, 685 P2d 90 (Alaska 1984).

Absent compelling circumstances, a case should normally be assigned on remand to the same judge who conducted the original trial. **United Bank Alaska v. Dischner,** Op. No. 2835, 685 P2d 90 (Alaska 1984).

If a party acquiesces to the authority of a successor judge by failing to make a timely objection to that judge's authority, the party has waived any objection he or she may have to challenge that authority. **Moffitt v. Moffitt,** Op. No. 3261, 749 P2d 343 (Alaska 1988).

The record clearly established that husband in divorce action waived any objection to successor judge's authority to enter new findings of fact and conclusions of law which differed from those initially entered but not finalized by the preceding judge. **Moffitt v. Moffitt,** Op. No. 3261, 749 P2d 343 (Alaska 1988).

Successor judge's vacation of orders and judgment that had been signed by her was not abuse of discretion since she erred in signing them when judge who heard case on merits was still available. **Gallagher v. Gallagher,** Op. No. 4041, 866 P2d 123 (Alaska 1994).

PART X. PROVISIONAL AND FINAL REMEDIES AND SPECIAL PROCEEDINGS

Rule 64. Seizure of Person or Property.

At the commencement of and during the course of an action, all remedies providing for seizure of person or property for the purpose of securing satisfaction of the judgment ultimately to be entered in the action are available under the circumstances and in the manner provided by law existing at the time the remedy is sought. The remedies thus available include arrest, attachment, garnishment, replevin, sequestration, and other corresponding or equivalent remedies, however designated and regardless of whether by law the remedy is ancillary to an action or must be obtained by an independent action.

(Adopted by SCO 5 October 9, 1959)

Annotations

Cases

This rule does not create any remedy. **Aleut Corp. v. Arctic Slope Regional Corp.,** 424 FS 397 (USDC Alaska 1976).

Rule 65. Injunctions.

(a) **Preliminary Injunction.**

(1) *Notice.* No preliminary injunction shall be issued without notice to the adverse party.

(2) *Consolidation of Hearing with Trial on Merits.* Before or after the commencement of the hearing of an application for a preliminary injunction, the court may order the trial of the action on the merits to be advanced and consolidated with the hearing of the application. Even when this consolidation is not ordered, any evidence received upon an application for a preliminary injunction which would be admissible upon the trial on the merits becomes part of the record on the trial and need not be repeated upon the trial. This subdivision (a) (2) shall be so construed and applied as to save the parties any rights they may have to trial by jury.

(b) **Temporary Restraining Order—Notice—Hearing—Duration.** A temporary restraining order may be granted without written or oral notice to the adverse party or that party's attorney only if (1) it clearly appears from specific facts shown by affidavit or by the verified complaint that immediate and irreparable injury, loss, or damage will result to the applicant before the adverse party or that party's attorney can be heard in opposition, and (2) the applicant's attorney certifies to the court in writing the efforts, if any, which have been made to give the notice and the reasons supporting the claim that notice should not be required. Every temporary restraining order granted without notice shall be endorsed with the date and hour of issuance; shall be filed forthwith in the clerk's office and entered of record; shall define the injury and state why it is irreparable and why the order was granted without notice; and shall expire by its terms within such time after entry, not to exceed 10 days, as the court fixes, unless within the time so fixed the order, for good cause shown, is extended for a like period or unless the party against whom the order is directed consents that it may be extended for a longer period. The reasons for the extension shall be entered of record. In case a temporary restraining order is granted without notice, the motion for a preliminary injunction shall be set down for hearing at the earliest possible time and takes precedence of all matters except older matters of the same character; and when the motion comes on for hearing the party who obtained the temporary restraining order shall proceed with the application for a preliminary injunction and, if the party does not do so, the court shall dissolve the temporary restraining order. On two days' notice to the party who obtained the temporary restraining order without notice or on such shorter notice to that party as the court may prescribe, the adverse party may appear and move its dissolution or modification and in that event the court shall proceed to hear and determine such motion as expeditiously as the ends of justice require.

(c) **Security.** No restraining order or preliminary injunction shall issue except upon the giving of security by the applicant, in such sum as the court deems proper, for the payment of such costs and damages as may be incurred or suffered by any party who is found to have been wrongfully enjoined or restrained. No such security shall be required of the state or a municipality or of an officer or agency thereof, or unless otherwise ordered by the court, in domestic relations actions or proceedings.

A surety upon a bond or undertaking under this rule submits to the jurisdiction of the court and irrevocably appoints the clerk of the court as the surety's agent upon whom any papers affecting the surety's liability on the bond or undertaking may be served. The surety's liability may be enforced on motion without the necessity of an independent action. The motion and such notice of the motion as the court prescribes may be served on the clerk of the court who shall forthwith mail copies to the persons giving the security if their addresses are known.

(d) **Form and Scope of Injunction or Restraining Order.** Every order granting an injunction and every restraining order shall set forth the reasons for its issuance; shall be specific in terms; shall describe in reasonable detail, and not by reference to the complaint or other document, the act or acts sought to be restrained; and is binding only upon the parties to the action, their officers, agents, servants, employees, and attorneys, and upon those persons in active concert or participation with them who receive actual notice of the order by personal service or otherwise.

(e) **Standing Preliminary Injunctions in Domestic Relations Actions.** The presiding judge of each judicial district may issue a standing injunction which restrains the parties in all domestic relations actions, except dissolutions, domestic violence actions and uniform reciprocal enforcement actions, from:

(1) removing any child who is the subject of the action from the State of Alaska without the written consent of the other party;

(2) disposing of, encumbering or transferring any marital property without the written consent of the other party, except reasonably using funds for the parties or the parties' children's personal and necessary expenses; and

(3) threatening, harassing, or harming the other party.

Such a standing injunction shall be effective against a party upon receipt of a copy of the standing injunction by the party or the party's attorney.

(Adopted by SCO 5 October 9, 1959; amended by SCO 30 effective February 1, 1961; by SCO 223 effective January 1, 1976; by SCO 258 effective November 15, 1976; by Section 2, Chapter 82, Session Laws of Alaska 1977 effective September 1, 1977; by SCO 708 effective July 15, 1986; by SCO 1153 effective July 15, 1994; by SCO 1269 effective July 15, 1997; and by SCO 1361 effective October 15, 1999)

Note: AS 10.06.630, as enacted by ch. 166, § 1, SLA 1988, amended Civil Rule 65 by changing the procedure for enjoining dissolution proceedings under AS 10.06.630.

Note: In 1996, the legislature enacted AS 18.66.110–18.66.130 relating to domestic violence protective orders. According to § 78 ch. 64 SLA 1996, these statutes have the effect of amending Civil Rule 65 relating to temporary restraining orders, the method of obtaining those orders, and the timing of those orders.

Note: Chapter 42 § 2 SLA 1999 enacts AS 09.19.200 which governs the remedies available in civil litigation involving conditions in correctional facilities. According to § 3 of the act, the enactment of AS 09.19.200 has the effect of amending Civil Rules 59(f), 60(b), 62, and 65 by altering the remedies available and the procedure to be used in litigation involving correctional facilities.

Note: Chapter 87 SLA 03 (HB 1) enacted AS 18.65.850-860, which addresses protective orders for persons who are victims of stalking not involving domestic violence. According to Section 8(b) of the Act, these provisions have the effect of amending Civil Rule 65 relating to temporary restraining orders, the method of obtaining those orders, and the timing of those orders.

Note: Chapter 54 SLA 2005 (HB 95) enacted extensive amendments and new provisions related to public health, including public health emergencies and disasters. According to Section 13(d) of the Act, AS 18.15.375(c)(3), (d), and (e), and 18.15.385(d) –(k), enacted in Section 8, have the effect of amending Civil Rule 65 by allowing temporary and ex parte injunctions to be issued and by expediting the procedures related to injunctive relief in matters involving public health.

Note: Chapter 36 SLA 2006 (SB 54) enacted changes to the protective order statutes for crimes involving stalking to include crimes involving sexual assault and sexual abuse. According to section 12 of the Act, the amendments to AS 18.65.850 and AS 18.65.855 made in sections 4 through 8 of the Act have the effect of changing Civil Rule 65 by changing the method for obtaining, and the timing of, temporary restraining orders.

Cross References

CROSS REFERENCE: AS 09.40.230

Annotations

Cases

Consent of a party to an extension of a temporary restraining order does not deprive the consenting party of his right to seek review of the issuance of the restraining order in the first instance. **Miller v. Atkinson,** Op. No. 49, 365 P2d 550 (Alaska 1961).

Where the state had already appropriated private property for a public purpose in mistaken reliance on an invalid patent reservation and property owner had brought an action inaccurately framed as "trespass action" for damages whereupon the state counterclaimed on the ground of "inverse condemnation," the issue then remaining before the court was the award of a just compensation, and a permanent injunction prohibiting the state from entering upon or appropriating the property, meaning that the state must first initiate a condemnation before utilizing the property, was unrealistic and unnecessary and was dissolved. **State v. Crosby,** Op. No. 322, 410 P2d 724 (Alaska 1966).

This rule, dealing with injunctions, is inapplicable to proceedings before the district judge court, but where in connection with a garnishee proceeding the district judge restrained an employer from applying wages to other obligations, the district judge did not proceed under Rule 65 but exercised an authority conferred to him by Civil Rule 89 (f)(6). **Anchorage Helicop. Serv., Inc. v. Anchorage W. Hotel,** Op. No. 361, 417 P2d 903 (Alaska 1966).

The requirement of this rule that an order granting an injunction set forth reasons for its issuance applies to every type of preliminary injunction. **Department of Fish & Game v. Pinnell,** Op. No. 586, 461 P2d 429 (Alaska 1969).

A preliminary injunction which is granted without setting forth the reasons for the issuance of the injunction and without findings of fact and conclusions of law which articulate grounds for the issuance of the preliminary injunction as required by this rule is procedurally defective and will be vacated. **Department of Fish & Game v. Pinnell,** Op. No. 586, 461 P2d 429 (Alaska 1969).

Strict compliance with provisions of this rule requiring findings of fact and conclusions of law and setting out reasons for the issuance of a preliminary injunction is required particularly in circumstances where the trial court is enjoining enforcement of an administrative regulation or statute. **Department of Fish & Game v. Pinnell,** Op. No. 586, 461 P2d 429 (Alaska 1969).

The supreme court will vacate rather than remand where a preliminary injunction is procedurally defective and where a hearing has been held in a motion for permanent injunction and where a decision on the merits of the permanent injunction is anticipated in the near future. **Department of Fish & Game v. Pinnell,** Op. No. 586, 461 P2d 429 (Alaska 1969).

In considering whether to grant a stay pending appeal, the lower court must consider criteria much the same as it would in determining whether to grant a preliminary injunction. **Powell v. Anchorage,** Op. No. 1167, 536 P2d 1228 (Alaska 1975).

Where precise information as to time and courtroom for hearing on motion for restraining order was unavailable, notice to opposing counsel that the motion would be made in Fairbanks Superior Court at "approximately 3:00" on November 3rd complied with this rule when the motion was actually filed at 3:17 p.m. on November 3rd. **Knaebel v. Heiner,** Op. No. 2513, 645 P2d 201 (Alaska 1982).

A party who initially obtains a temporary restraining order is not entitled to receive its benefits indefinitely by not proceeding to request a preliminary injunction hearing. **Ostrow v. Higgins,** Op. No. 3085, 722 P2d 936 (Alaska 1986).

Issuance of a temporary restraining order pending determination of a motion for preliminary injunction did not have the effect of a preliminary injunction, thus the temporary restraining order expired within 10 days of its issuance. **Ostrow v. Higgins,** Op. No. 3085, 722 P2d 936 (Alaska 1986).

Any extension of a temporary restraining order must be approved by the court. **Ostrow v. Higgins,** Op. No. 3085, 722 P2d 936 (Alaska 1986).

A temporary restraining order automatically expires within 10 days under this rule and the party against whom it is served is under no obligation to take any further legal action to verify its expiration. **Ostrow v. Higgins,** Op. No. 3085, 722 P2d 936 (Alaska 1986).

Where a court intends to supplant a temporary restraining order with a preliminary injunction of unlimited duration pending a final decision on the merits or further order of the court, it should issue an order clearly saying so; and where it has not done so, a party against whom a temporary restraining order has issued may reasonably assume that the order has expired within the time limits imposed by this rule. **Ostrow v. Higgins,** Op. No. 3085, 722 P2d 936 (Alaska 1986).

Where deed of trust issued to secure promissory note for purchase of property required the purchaser to maintain fire insurance on the property, the sellers were the sole beneficiaries of all insurance proceeds payable under the deed of trust and automatically deserved those proceeds, thus continued acceptance of the insurance payments, by the sellers after issuance of a temporary restraining order against foreclosure did not constitute an implied agreement on the part of the sellers to an extension of the temporary restraining order. **Ostrow v. Higgins,** Op. No. 3085, 722 P2d 936 (Alaska 1986).

As a general rule, when the court's findings of fact and conclusions of law are sufficient to warrant injunctive relief under CR 52(a), they, almost of necessity, also state reasons for the injunction's issuance that are sufficient to satisfy this rule. **Dunlap v. Bavarian Village Condominium Ass'n,** Op. No. 3511, 780 P2d 1012 (Alaska 1989).

Civil Rule 65, rather than Civil Rule 4, determines when person becomes bound by domestic violence protective order. **MacDonald v. State,** Op. No. 1665, 997 P2d 1187 (Alaska 2000).

Defendant, who had actual knowledge of domestic violence protective order, was bound by order even though he was not formally served with written copy of order. **MacDonald v. State,** Op. No. 1665, 997 P2d 1187 (Alaska 2000).

Conviction of defendant for violation of ex parte domestic violence protective order did not violate his constitutional right to due process where defendant had not been served with written copy of order but did have actual knowledge that order had been issued against him. **MacDonald v. State,** Op. No. 1665, 997 P2d 1187 (Alaska 2000).

Rule 65.1. Domestic Violence and Stalking Protective Orders—Access to Information.

A petitioner who is appearing pro se in a proceeding to obtain a domestic violence protective order under AS 18.66.100 or 18.66.110 or a stalking protective order under AS 18.65.850 or 18.65.855 may submit the petitioner's mailing address and telephone number on a separate form and omit this information from other pleadings and papers filed with the court. Access to the form containing the petitioner's mailing address and telephone number is limited to the court, authorized court system personnel, and the petitioner. If a child support order is entered in a domestic violence proceeding, court system personnel may also provide a copy of the address information form to the Child Support Enforcement Division. Further disclosure of this form by the Child Support Enforcement Division is prohibited. If the petitioner submits an information sheet containing the petitioner's address and telephone number for use by law enforcement agencies, the court may retain a copy of this document. Access to the copy is limited to the court, authorized court system personnel, and the petitioner.

(Adopted by SCO 1345 effective August 13, 1998; amended

by SCO 1527 effective September 11, 2003)

Rule 66. Receivers.

An action wherein a receiver has been appointed shall not be dismissed except by order of the court. The practice in the administration of estates by receivers or by the other similar officers appointed by the court shall be in accordance with the practice set forth by statute. In all other respects the action in which the appointment of a receiver is sought or which is brought by or against a receiver is governed by law and these rules.

(Adopted by SCO 5 October 9, 1959)

Cross References

CROSS REFERENCE: AS 09.40.240; AS 09.40.250

Annotations

Cases

Where Rule 66, [Federal] R. Civ. P., which governs the practice in the territorial district court does not expressly provide for the verification of the petition for appointment of a receiver, the rule does provide that the practice in the administration of estates by receiver shall be in accordance with the practice theretofore filed in the federal courts, and that practice required the complaint to be verified. **Wood v. Gray,** Op. No. 29, 359 P2d 951 (Alaska 1961).

In suit against former finance officer, which alleged that finance officer had misappropriated funds by writing unauthorized check to himself, where finance officer failed to appear for trial, and subsequently moved to set aside the summary judgment entered against him, the trial court did not abuse its discretion in denying the motion, because failure to appear for trial supported assumption that the finance officer was forfeiting the right to defend himself. **Snyder v. Am. Legion Spenard Post No. 28,** Op. No. 5940, 119 P.3d 996 (Alaska 2005).

Rule 67. Deposit in Court.

Upon notice to every other party and upon leave of court, a party may deposit with the court all or any part of any sum of money or any other thing capable of physical delivery which is the subject of the action or due under a judgment. Money deposited with the court under this rule shall be managed in accordance with the provisions of Rule 5, Rules Governing the Administration of All Courts. The court shall release the deposit to the party entitled to it when that party becomes entitled to it. No interest shall accrue against a party making a deposit, to the extent of that deposit, after it is made.

(Adopted by SCO 5 October 9, 1959; amended by SCO 251 effective July 1, 1976; by SCO 465 effective June 1, 1981; by SCO 474 effective July 1, 1981; by SCO 1085 effective January 15, 1992; by SCO 1093 effective July 15, 1992; and by SCO 1192 effective July 15, 1995)

Annotations

Cases

Isolated in itself a payment document filed by defendant in a personal injury case in the superior court which was not served upon the plaintiff's and which stated in substance that the full policy amount plus $1,000 as costs to date were paid into registry of court with a request that the court notify plaintiff's of such tender and relieve the defendant of liability for costs and attorney's fees, was neither a confession of judgment under Civil Rule 57(b) nor an offer of judgment under Civil Rule 68 but could at most, be considered a deposit in court under Civil Rule 67(a). **Albritton v. Estate of Larson,** Op. No. 413, 428 P2d 379 (Alaska 1967).

Rule 68. [Applicable to cases filed before August 7, 1997.] Offer of Judgment.

(a) At any time more than 10 days before the trial begins, either the party making a claim or the party defending against a claim may serve upon the adverse party an offer to allow judgment to be entered in complete satisfaction of the claim for the money or property or to the effect specified in the offer, with costs then accrued. The offer may not be revoked in the 10 day period following service of the offer. If within 10 days after service of the offer the adverse party serves written notice that the offer is accepted, either party may then file the offer and notice of acceptance together with proof of service, and the clerk shall enter judgment. An offer not accepted within 10 days is considered withdrawn and evidence of the offer is not admissible except in a proceeding to determine costs. The fact that an offer is made but not accepted does not preclude a subsequent offer.

(b) If the judgment finally rendered by the court is not more favorable to the offeree than the offer, the prejudgment interest accrued up to the date judgment is entered shall be adjusted as follows:

(1) if the offeree is the party making the claim, the interest rate will be reduced by the amount specified in AS 09.30.065 and the offeree must pay the costs and attorney's fees incurred after the making of the offer (as would be calculated under Civil Rules 79 and 82 if the offeror were the prevailing party). The offeree may not be awarded costs or attorney's fees incurred after the making of the offer.

(2) if the offeree is the party defending against the claim, the interest rate will be increased by the amount specified in AS 09.30.065.

(c) When the liability of one party to another has been determined by verdict or order or judgment, but the amount or extent of the liability remains to be determined by further proceedings, the party adjudged liable may make an offer of judgment, which shall have the same effect as an offer made before trial if it is served within a reasonable time not less than 10 days prior to the commencement of hearings to determine the amount or extent of liability.

(Adopted by SCO 5 October 9, 1959; amended by SCO 818 effective August 1, 1987)

EDITOR'S NOTE: See Note to SCO 1281 following text of Rule 68 applicable after August 7, 1997.

Rule 68. [Applicable to cases filed on or after August 7, 1997.] Offer of Judgment.

(a) At any time more than 10 days before the trial begins, either the party making a claim or the party defending against a claim may serve upon the adverse party an offer to allow judgment to be entered in complete satisfaction of the claim for the money or property or to the effect specified in the offer, with costs then accrued. The offer may not be revoked in the

10 day period following service of the offer. If within 10 days after service of the offer the adverse party serves written notice that the offer is accepted, either party may then file the offer and notice of acceptance together with proof of service, and the clerk shall enter judgment. An offer not accepted within 10 days is considered withdrawn and evidence of the offer is not admissible except in a proceeding to determine costs. The fact that an offer is made but not accepted does not preclude a subsequent offer.

(b) If the judgment finally rendered by the court is at least 5 percent less favorable to the offeree than the offer, or, if there are multiple defendants, at least 10 percent less favorable to the offeree than the offer, the offeree, whether the party making the claim or defending against the claim, shall pay all costs as allowed under the Civil Rules and shall pay reasonable actual attorney's fees incurred by the offeror from the date the offer was made as follows:

(1) if the offer was served no later than 60 days after the date established in the pretrial order for initial disclosures required by Civil Rule 26, the offeree shall pay 75 percent of the offeror's reasonable actual attorney's fees;

(2) if the offer was served more than 60 days after the date established in the pretrial order for initial disclosures required by Civil Rule 26 but more than 90 days before the trial began, the offeree shall pay 50 percent of the offeror's reasonable actual attorney's fees;

(3) if the offer was served 90 days or less but more than 10 days before the trial began, the offeree shall pay 30 percent of the offeror's reasonable actual attorney's fees.

(c) If an offeror would be entitled to receive costs and reasonable actual attorney's fees under paragraph (b), that offeror shall be considered the prevailing party for purposes of an award of attorney's fees under Civil Rule 82. Notwithstanding paragraph (b), if the amount awarded an offeror for attorney's fees under Civil Rule 82 is greater than a party would receive under paragraph (b), the offeree shall pay to the offeror attorney's fees specified under Civil Rule 82 and is not required to pay reasonable actual attorney's fees under paragraph (b). A party who receives attorney's fees under this rule may not also receive attorney's fees under Civil Rule 82.

(Adopted by SCO 5 October 9, 1959; amended by SCO 818 effective August 1, 1987; by SCO 1281 effective August 7, 1997; and by SCO 1565 effective April 15, 2005)

Note to SCO 1281: In 1997 the legislature amended AS 09.30.065 concerning offers of judgment. According to ch. 26, sec 52, SLA 1997, the amendment to AS 09.30.065 has the effect of amending Civil Rules 68 and 82 by requiring the offeree to pay costs and reasonable actual attorney fees on a sliding scale of percentages in certain cases, by eliminating provisions relating to interest, and by changing provisions relating to attorney fee awards. According to sec. 55 of the session law, the amendment to AS 09.30.065 applies "to all causes of action accruing on or after the effective date of this Act." However, the amendments to Civil Rule 68 adopted by paragraph 5 of this order are applicable to all cases filed on or after August 7, 1997. See paragraph 17 of this order.

Annotations

Cases

I. In General.
II. Payment of Costs.
  A. Construction.
  B. Prejudgment Interest.

I. In General.

A payment document which, in itself, did not have the criterion of an offer of judgment and could, at most, be considered as a deposit in the superior court, made under the provisions of Civil Rule 67(a), was by virtue a stipulation of the parties as reasonably construed converted into an offer of judgment which plaintiff's accepted under the stipulation. **Albritton v. Estate of Larson,** Op. No. 413, 428 P2d 379 (Alaska 1967).

The purpose of this rule is to encourage settlement of civil litigation as well as to avoid protracted litigation. **Miklautsch v. Dominick,** Op. No. 538, 452 P2d 438 (Alaska 1969).

An offer of judgment and acceptance thereof is a contract and the amount of the offer of judgment must be definite so that it is clear there is a meeting of the minds on an essential term of the contract. **Davis v. Chism,** Op. No. 919, 513 P2d 475 (Alaska 1973).

This rule does not apply to eminent domain proceedings. **Anchorage v. Schavenius,** Op. No. 1183, 539 P2d 1169 (Alaska 1975).

The purpose of this rule is to encourage settlement and to avoid protracted litigation. **Continental Ins. Co. v. U.S. Fid. & Guar. Co.,** Op. No. 1298, 552 P2d 1122 (Alaska 1976).

Offer of judgment that paralleled Form 128, Forms for Rules of Civil Procedure, differing only in that it supplied defendant's identity and filled in blank spaces, was valid compliance with Civil Rule 68. **Farnsworth v. Steiner,** Op. No. 1955, 601 P2d 266 (Alaska 1979).

This rule applies not only when the offeree obtains judgment in his favor but also when the offeree does not prevail at all. **Wright v. Vickaryous,** Op. No. 2075, 611 P2d 20 (Alaska 1980).

A contract for an entry of judgment is not formed if the written notice of acceptance of an offer under this rule is not served within the ten day limit. **Gumear v. Interior Credit Bureau,** Op. No. 2339, 627 P2d 647 (Alaska 1981).

A defendant is not bound under this rule to make an offer of judgment commensurate with any degree of compensation. **Rules v. Sturn,** Op. No. 2640, 661 P2d 615 (Alaska 1983).

An offer of judgment under this rule must be in writing to be valid. **Rules v. Sturn,** Op. No. 2640, 661 P2d 615 (Alaska 1983).

An offer of judgment made pursuant to this rule is irrevocable for 10 days after it is served on the adverse party. **Rules v. Sturn,** Op. No. 2640, 661 P2d 615 (Alaska 1983).

Where written offer of judgment by defendant was silent as to an offset for sums which had been advanced to plaintiff for medical treatment, defendant was required to pay the full amount of the offer without the offset. **Rules v. Sturn,** Op. No. 2640, 661 P2d 615 (Alaska 1983).

Joint offers are excluded from the penal cost provisions of this rule. **Brinkerhoff v. Swearingen Aviation Corp.,** Op. No. 2666, 663 P2d 937 (Alaska 1983).

The cost provision of this rule refers to those costs permitted by the Civil Rules and the Administrative Rules. **Hayes v. Xerox Corp.,** Op. No. 3045, 718 P2d 929 (Alaska 1986).

This rule awards actual costs although it does not award actual attorney's fees. **Hayes v. Xerox Corp.,** Op. No. 3045, 718 P2d 929 (Alaska 1986).

Where settlement offer to plaintiffs specifically designated the amount offered to each plaintiff individually, did not contain a proviso mandating joint acceptance, and could be construed as permitting one plaintiff to accept and the other to go to trial, the settlement offer came within the penal cost provisions of this rule. **Hayes v. Xerox Corp.,** Op. No. 3045, 718 P2d 929 (Alaska 1986).

Joint offers of settlement are generally excluded from the penal cost provisions of this rule. **Hayes v. Xerox Corp.,** Op. No. 3045, 718 P2d 929 (Alaska 1986).

Because an offer of a lump sum presents problems of apportionment between offerees, it is treated as a joint offer and excluded from the penal cost provisions of this rule. **Hayes v. Xerox Corp.,** Op. No. 3045, 718 P2d 929 (Alaska 1986).

Failure of court, which made an award of attorney fees at variance with the schedule in the Civil Rules, to state its specific reasons for the amount awarded, required reversal. **Hayes v. Xerox Corp.,** Op. No. 3045, 718 P2d 929 (Alaska 1986).

Offer of judgment was not invalid as indefinite regarding the amount for attorney's fees. **Hayes v. Xerox Corp.,** Op. No. 3045, 718 P2d 929 (Alaska 1986).

Trial court did not err in refusing to deduct the amount of worker's compensation benefits received by plaintiff from his judgment against defendant in computing the "judgment finally obtained" for purpose of comparing plaintiff's judgment with the prejudgment offer made by defendant. **Alyeska Pipeline Service Co. v. Beadles,** Op. No. 3151, 731 P2d 572 (Alaska 1987).

To the extent that the trial court concluded that defendant prevailed because much of his attorney fees were incurred after his offer of judgment was made, the trial court considered an impermissible factor; while consideration of that factor is relevant in determining the amount of attorney fees to be awarded under this rule, it is irrelevant to the determination of which party prevailed in the action. **Mitchell v. Smith,** Op. No. 3220, 742 P2d 220 (Alaska 1987).

Offer of settlement made by multiple defendants, one of which was counterclaiming against the plaintiff, was sufficient to trigger the penal cost sanctions of this rule where the settlement offer clearly indicated that all claims between the parties would be resolved if the offer were accepted. **Taylor Const. Services, Inc. v. URS Co.,** Op. No. 3364, 758 P2d 99 (Alaska 1988).

Judgment of $162,000 for plaintiff, offset by an award of $223,700 to a counterclaiming defendant, was clearly less favorable than a joint and several settlement offer by all of the defendants of $70,000 which included dismissal of the counterclaim; thus award of costs to defendants pursuant to this rule was proper. **Taylor Const. Services, Inc. v. URS Co.,** Op. No. 3364, 758 P2d 99 (Alaska 1988).

This rule expresses the exclusive way by which settlement offers can be taken into account in determining costs and attorney fees. **Myers v. Snow White Cleaners & L. Supply,** Op. No. 3419, 770 P2d 750 (Alaska 1989).

This rule does not preclude the making of an offer of judgment while a motion to amend the pleading is pending. **Farr v. Stepp,** Op. No. 3570, 788 P2d 35 (Alaska 1990).

Superior court erred in considering defendant's recovery on a counterclaim in determining whether penal sanctions were to be imposed under this rule since defendant's offer of judgment was silent regarding the counterclaim, which was pending when the offer was made. **Farr v. Stepp,** Op. No. 3570, 788 P2d 35 (Alaska 1990).

This rule does not preclude multiple offers of judgment. **Pratt & Whitney Canada, Inc. v. Sheehan,** Op. No. 3959, 852 P2d 1173 (Alaska 1993).

Given the amendments to Civil Rule 82 effective July 15, 1993, pre-amendment case law discussing the impact of successful Rule 68 offers on attorney fee awards have limited application. **Fairbanks North Star Borough v. Lakeview Enterprises, Inc.,** Op. No. 4218, 897 P2d 47 (Alaska 1995).

Judgment offer of $20,000 by defendant was more favorable than jury award of $3,000 in medical expenses and $1,000 in non-medical expenses notwithstanding that offer was subject to $24,620 medical lien asserted by plaintiff's insurer. **Jaso v. McCarthy,** Op. No. 4407, 923 P2d 795 (Alaska 1996).

Offer of judgment by defendant which stated that plaintiff would be required to satisfy from the judgment all liens and subrogated interests was neither conditional nor joint and was therefore valid. **Jaso v. McCarthy,** Op. No. 4407, 923 P2d 795 (Alaska 1996).

Nothing in this rule implies that mandatory awards of liquidated damages should be automatically added to an offer of judgment. **Bobich v. Hughes,** Op. No. 5032, 965 P2d 1196 (Alaska 1998).

Actual award of liquidated damages had to be added to award for overtime wages in determining whether final judgment was more favorable that rejected earlier offer of judgment. **Bobich v. Hughes,** Op. No. 5032, 965 P2d 1196 (Alaska 1998).

Offers of judgment generally remain valid despite appeal and remand. **Mackie v. Chizmar,** Op. No. 5035, 965 P2d 1202 (Alaska 1998).

Penalties of this rule for rejecting judgment offer more favorable than final judgment did not apply were recovery was obtained through alternative dispute resolution procedure absent stipulation by parties that offer of judgment would apply to results of alternative procedure. **Mackie v. Chizmer,** Op. No. 5035, 965 P2d 1202 (Alaska 1998).

Trial court erred in concluding that plaintiff's offer of judgment was more favorable to defendant than final judgment: when prejudgment interest was properly applied to entire $38,000 offer but only to past damages portion of jury award, value of offer was $49,970 and value of judgment was $44,165. **Andrus v. Lena,** Op. No. 5098, 975 P2d 54 (Alaska 1999).

Once offer of judgment is served, offeror cannot modify terms of offer. **White v. Harvey,** Op. No. 5117, 979 P2d 1012 (Alaska 1999).

Where offer of judgment accepted by plaintiff was silent on issue of subrogated claim of plaintiff's insurer for $4,000 paid to plaintiff for past medical expenses and where plaintiff had made binding admission that she did not seek those damages, defendant's insurer was not entitled to deduct the $4,000 from the judgment amount. **White v. Harvey,** Op. No. 5117,979 P2d 1012 (Alaska 1999).

The formula in **Farnsworth,** 601 P2d 266 (Alaska 1979), for comparing the value of an offer and the final judgment under this rule, is not limited to offers made by defendants. **Lloyd's & Inst. of London v. Fulton,** Op. No. 5271, 2 P3d 1199 (Alaska 2000).

This rule applies to offers of judgment made more than ten days before trail begins; accordingly, plaintiff's offer of judgment, made more than ten days prior to scheduled start of trial but not more than ten days before trial actually began, did not come within rule, thus trial court properly refused to affirm defendant's acceptance of the offer, particularly since defendant did not accept the offer until after the verdict was rendered. **Mapco Express, Inc. v. Faulk,** Op. No. 5422, 24 P3d 531 (Alaska 2001).

In a second deed of trust beneficiary's suit against a first deed of trust beneficiary, alleging improprieties in a foreclosure sale of property secured by both deeds of trust, this rule did not preclude the first deed of trust beneficiary from making a pre-disclosure offer of judgment. **Cook Schuhmann & Groseclose, Inc. v. Brown & Root, Inc.,** Op. No. 5291, 116 P.3d 592 (Alaska 2005).

II. Payment of Costs.

A. Construction.

The provision of this rule that a party who made an offer of judgment which was not accepted, is not responsible for costs incurred after the making of the offer, did not apply to a case where judgment finally obtained was more favorable than the offer and where the offeror was an insurance company which had offered the insurance policy limit, and was not a party to the main cause, but had appealed from a garnishment proceeding. **Liberty National Insurance Co. v. Eberhart,** Op. No. 281, 398 P2d 997 (Alaska 1965).

Even if it may be assumed that appellants were "pevailing party" within the meaning of Civil Rules 54(d) and 82(a) (1), the trial court's determination as to denial of attorney's costs where the action was settled pursuant to Civil Rule 68 was not disturbed on appeal in the absence of a showing of clear abuse of the wide discretion allowed under this rule. **Albritton v. Estate of Larson,** Op. No. 413, 428 P2d 379 (Alaska 1967).

Where in a personal injury action the defendant had filed a payment document which, in itself, could be considered at best a deposit in court under Civil Rule 67(a) but by stipulation between the parties was converted into an offer of judgment, and by virtue of such stipulation and the court's order appended thereto, plaintiff's causes of action were dismissed with prejudice, the action had been settled pursuant to Civil Rule 68 and under the "with costs then accrued" portion of said rule the trial court was vested with wide discretion in determining award of attorney's fees. **Albritton v. Estate of Larson,** Op. No. 413, 428 P2d 379 (Alaska 1967).

If the judgment recovered at trial is less than an offer of judgment, the offeree is liable for the costs incurred by the offeror subsequent to the time the offer was made. **Miklautsch v. Dominick,** Op. No. 538, 452 P2d 438 (Alaska 1969).

For purposes of this rule, an offer of judgment that specifies only a total sum must be construed as including the defendant's assessment of all the damages that the plaintiff is entitled to, including that occasioned by the loss of the use of the money. **Davis v. Chism,** Op. No. 919, 513 P2d 475 (Alaska 1973).

An offer of judgment will be construed as including the defendant's assessment of all the damages that plaintiff is entitled to, including costs and attorney's fees. **Bayly, Martin & Fay, Inc. v. Arctic Auto Rental, Inc.,** Op. No. 993, 517 P2d 1406 (Alaska 1974).

An award of costs and attorney's fees to both the plaintiff and the defendant are properly computed as of the date the offer of judgment is made and not at a later time when accepted. **Bayly, Martin & Fay, Inc. v. Arctic Auto Rental, Inc.,** Op. No. 993, 517 P2d 1406 (Alaska 1974).

Where radically different standards of partial compensation are applied in awarding attorney's fees to the parties, the award will be considered an abuse of discretion unless there are findings or an explanation by the trial court supporting such disparate treatment. **Irving v. Bullock,** Op. No. 1261, 549 P2d 1184 (Alaska 1976).

This rule does not require that costs incurred prior to an offer of judgment be awarded; such awards are within the trial court's discretion. **Continental Ins. Co. v. U.S. Fid. & Guar. Co.,** Op. No. 1298, 552 P2d 1122 (Alaska 1976).

An award of $5,000.00 for attorney's fees to defendant, a "limited prevailing party" under Civil Rule 68, was not manifestly unreasonable when actual attorney's fees were $14,053.12, considering that Rule 68 is designed to encourage reasonable settlement after a lawsuit is filed. **Scott v. Robertson,** Op. No. 1674, 583 P2d 188 (Alaska 1978).

An award of attorney's fees under Civil Rule 68 is designed to "partially" compensate the prevailing party. **Scott v. Robertson,** Op. No. 1674, 583 P2d 188 (Alaska 1978).

Court should make factual determination of offeror's actual expenses incurred after offer of judgment, then take into account the partial recovery principles of Civil Rule 82 in awarding offeror reasonable partial attorney's fees and costs based on such factual determination. **Farnsworth v. Steiner,** Op. No. 1955, 601 P2d 266 (Alaska 1979).

Where a judgment on offer and acceptance was signed January 18, but the action was not dismissed by court order until July 24, a request by counsel filed August 1 for a hearing on the amount of attorney fees was timely, July 24 being the proper date from which the request period should have been calculated. **Salmine v. Knagin,** Op. No. 2501, 645 P2d 148 (Alaska 1982).

Partial attorney's fees, not actual attorney's fees, are to be awarded to a prevailing party after an offer of judgment. **Truckweld Equipment Co. v. Swenson Trucking,** Op. No. 2545, 649 P2d 234 (Alaska 1982).

When counsel requests attorney's fees, other than based on the schedule in the Civil Rules, accurate records of the hours expended and a brief description of the services reflected by those hours would be submitted. **Hayes v. Xerox Corp.,** Op. No. 3045, 718 P2d 929 (Alaska 1986).

Prevailing defendant was entitled to costs incurred after date of his offer of judgment. **Hutchins v. Schwartz,** Op. No. 3110, 724 P2d 1194 (Alaska 1986).

As the prevailing party at trial, defendant could receive the maximum amount of attorney fees under Civil Rule 82; the fact that defendant had made an offer of judgment under Civil Rule 68 would not increase or diminish the award of attorney fees. **Hutchins v. Schwartz,** Op. No. 3110, 724 P2d 1194 (Alaska 1986).

A defendant who ultimately fares better than his offer of judgment is entitled only to partial compensation for post-offer attorney's fees. **Wickwire v. State,** Op. No. 3116, 725 P2d 695 (Alaska 1986).

In an action against the State for wrongful termination of an assistant attorney general, trial court, in awarding attorney's fees, improperly considered additional expenses incurred by the State resulting from plaintiff's decision to sue several individual defendants as well as the State, where a stipulation dismissing the individual defendants provided that each side would pay its own attorney's fees. **Wickwire v. State,** Op. No. 3116, 725 P2d 695 (Alaska 1986).

Pretrial offers not in compliance with Civil Rule 68 should not be considered in determining questions of costs and attorney fees; accordingly, trial court erred when it used past settlement negotiations, which did not result in an offer of judgment in compliance with Civil Rule 68, to justify a reduction in the amount of attorney's fees that it would have awarded. **Myers v. Snow White Cleaners & L. Supply,** Op. No. 3419, 770 P2d 750 (Alaska 1989).

The argument that trial courts should never be permitted to award fees in excess of those established under the "noncontested" or "without trial" schedules of Civil Rule 82 following acceptance of an offer of judgment under Civil Rule 68 was rejected. **Van Dort v. Culliton,** Op. No. 3630, 797 P2d 642 (Alaska 1990).

Where an offer of judgment specifies only a lump sum figure without any provision for attorney's fees, attorney's fees may be awarded by the trial court in accordance with standard Civil Rule 82 principles; where extraordinary circumstances would otherwise justify deviation from the Civil Rule 82 schedule, such deviation is appropriate following acceptance of the offer of judgment under Civil Rule 68. **Van Dort v. Culliton,** Op. No. 3630, 797 P2d 642 (Alaska 1990).

A trial court may not use past settlement negotiations as a reason to justify a reduction or increase in the amount that it would otherwise have awarded; accordingly, where trial court considered, among other things, the fact that party made ridiculously low settlement offers, reversal of the attorney fee award was required. **Van Dort v. Culliton,** Op. No. 3630, 797 P2d 642 (Alaska 1990).

Offer by defendant stating that plaintiff would be "responsible for" any liens that insurer might have for advances already made to plaintiff did not require concessions beyond money judgment necessary to settle case; accordingly, since offer was $35,000 over plaintiff's medical expenses and jury awarded only $14,760 over medical expenses, defendant, pursuant to this rule, was entitled to attorney fees from date of offer. **Grow v. Ruggles,** Op. No. 4014, 860 P2d 1225 (Alaska 1993).

When a trial court awards attorney's fees, it may, but need not, take into account the existence of an unaccepted Rule 68 offer if the claimant-offeree fails to better the offer. **Fairbanks North Star Borough v. Lakeview Enterprises, Inc.,** Op. No. 4218, 897 P2d 47 (Alaska 1995).

This rule applies only from the date when an offer of judgment is made, thus trial courts may not award attorney's fees under this rule for services performed prior to that date. **Kellis v. Crites,** Op. No. 5380, 20 P3d 1112 (Alaska 2001).

Where there is no dispute about the reasonableness of attorney's fees awarded under this rule, the factors listed in Civil Rule 82 cannot be applied to reduce the award. **Kellis v. Crites,** Op. No. 5380, 20 P3d 1112 (Alaska 2001).

Although breach of contract case by fishers against a packing company was worth $200,000, attorney's fee award over $172,970 was not unreasonable under Alaska R. Civ. P. 68(b)(1); the trial court found there were not a lot of unnecessary filings, the packing company's actions were not dilatory or in bad faith, and some responsibility for the large amount of fees lay with the fishermen who vigorously pushed the case and insisted on a forum choice that was more expensive for the parties. **Magill v. Nelbro Packing Co.,** Op. No. 5459, 43 P3d 140 (Alaska 2001).

Where the trial court's order awarding the interested parties in a will contest case 50 percent of their total fees conflicted with the plain language of Alaska R. Civ. P. 68(b)(2), the order constituted plain error and required the reviewing court to vacate the order awarding attorney's fees and to remand the issue of fees for reconsideration. **Crittell v. Bingo,** Op. No. 5496, 36 P3d 634 (Alaska 2001).

Two factors should be analyzed in deciding whether a joint offer should trigger Alaska R. Civ. P. Rule 68 penalties in the context of an offer made by joint offerors to a single offeree. First, if the offer was inclusive of all the relationships among the parties and their conflicting claims, and second, if no apportionment difficulty existed, the unaccepted offer could trigger Rule 68 penalties. **John's Heating Serv. v. Lamb,** Op. No. 5572, 46 P3d 1024 (Alaska 2002).

Because a stipulation to dismiss plaintiffs' remaining claims clearly contemplated an award of attorney's fees, did not specify that fees could only be recovered under Alaska R. Civ. P. 82, and did not preclude recovery under Alaska R. Civ. P. 68, the trial court erred in not considering defendants' Rule 68 request for fees. **Van Deusen v. Seavey,** Op. No. 5613, 53 P.3d 596 (Alaska 2002).

Because both the legal and equitable claims were based on the same set of facts, and settling only the legal claims would not have avoided litigation, the trial court properly denied Rule 68 attorney's fees to both parties. **Fernandes v. Portwine,** Op. No. 5632, 56 P.3d 1 (Alaska 2002).

In a personal injury case, a court properly awarded attorneys' fees to the insurer, as the prevailing party, where plaintiff wife expressly indicated that she did not oppose an order requiring the insurer to retain an independent attorney to represent defendant husband's interests, and without citation to any persuasive authority, the wife reasoned that, because she sued the husband rather than the insurer, she should only have been held accountable for fees incurred by the husband's independent attorney. **Doxsee v. Doxsee,** Op. No. 5754, 80 P.3d 225 (Alaska 2003)

It is error for a superior court to consider past settlement negotiations when awarding enhanced fees under Alaska R. Civ. P. 82; the only method by which fees may be enhanced for failure to accept an offer of judgment is found in this rule, and if an offer of judgment fails due to a procedural defect, the superior court may not then penalize the offeree by awarding enhanced fees under Rule 82. **Alderman v. Iditarod Props.,** Op. No. 5856, 104 P.3d 136 (Alaska 2004).

Trial court's award of attorney fees pursuant to this section in a breach of contract action concerning the renovation and selling of a boat was proper where the owner made an offer of settlement to her contractor, which was not accepted, and ultimately recovered an amount that was more than five percent less favorable to the contractor than the amount offered in settlement. **Peterson v. Ek,** Op. No. 5818, 93 P.3d 458 (Alaska 2004).

Where a driver's offer of judgment was indefinite in its proposed disposition of the individual's medical claims, the offer failed to meet the requirements of this rule and the trial court erred in awarding the driver attorney's fees and costs **Thomann v. Fouse,** Op. No. 5824,93 P.3d 1048 (Alaska 2004).

This rule, concerning offer of judgment, applied to buyers' breach of warranty action against a seller of a sailboat, as it was not preempted by the Magnuson-Moss Warranty Act, 15 U.S.C.S. § 2312; seller was entitled to seek post-offer attorney fees and costs where the total amount awarded to the buyers in the action was less than the settlement amount offered to the buyers. **Catalina Yachts v. Pierce,** Op. No. 5860, 105 P.3d 125 (Alaska 2005).

Where this rule authorizes reasonable actual fees, a court may not award attorney's fees to a party who has not itemized his or her requested fees, when the opposing party has requested such itemization. **Marron v. Stromstad,** Op. No. 5955, 123 P.3d 992 (Alaska 2005).

In a state employee's wrongful termination case, court properly awarded attorney fees to the state under this rule because the employee declined the state's pretrial offer of judgment for $12,000 and the jury awarded the employee $3,900. **Jones v. Dep't of Corrections,** Op. No. 5969 125 P.3d 343 (Alaska 2005).

B. Prejudgment Interest.

The phrase "judgment finally obtained by the offeree" within this rule includes the amount assessed as prejudgment interest but does not require the prejudgment interest to be tacked onto the offer of judgment if the offer is accepted and does not require the trial court to compare the jury's verdict plus prejudgment interest with the defendant's offer of judgment plus prejudgment interest. **Davis v. Chism,** Op. No. 919, 513 P2d 475 (Alaska 1973).

Prejudgment interest is in the nature of compensatory damages. It is reasonable for the trial court to include that figure in the "judgment finally obtained by the offeree" and to compare that total to the amount of the offer of judgment in order to determine whether the offeree should pay the costs. **Davis v. Chism,** Op. No. 919, 513 P2d 475 (Alaska 1973).

The date of the offer, not the date of the ultimate judgment, is the critical time in determining whether the offer, including prejudgment interest, is sufficient to avoid the operation of this rule. **Davis v. Chism,** Op. No. 919, 513 P2d 475 (Alaska 1973).

Trial judge may properly, as an exercise of discretion, refuse to award offeree interest on a judgment from the date of the offer through date of judgment when offeree ultimately recovers less than amount offered. **Continental Ins. Co. v. U.S. Fid. & Guar. Co.,** Op. No. 1298, 552 P2d 1122 (Alaska 1976).

A party who succeeds at trial but who rejected an offer of judgment which exceeded his trial recovery, is permitted to recover expenses and fees—including prejudgment interest, only from the date the cause of action accrues to the date of the rejected offer of judgment. **Farnsworth v. Steiner,** Op. No. 1955, 601 P2d 266 (Alaska 1979).

Since interest is not "costs," a successful offer of judgment does not terminate the running of prejudgment interest. **Farnsworth v. Steiner,** Op. No. 1955, 601 P2d 266 (Alaska 1979).

Trial court erred in concluding that plaintiff's offer of judgment was more favorable to defendant than final judgment: when prejudgment interest was properly applied to entire $38,000 offer but only to past damages portion of jury award, value of offer was $49,970 and value of judgment was $44,165. **Andrus v. Lena,** Op. No. 5098, 975 P2d 54 (Alaska 1999).

In a case alleging sexual harassment liability, an award of attorney's fees under both Alaska R. Civ. P. 68 and Alaska R. Civ. P. 82 was improper because such an award was clearly prohibited under Alaska R. Civ. P. 68(c). **Ellison v. Plumbers & Steam Fitters Union Local 375,** Op. No. 5934, 118

P.3d 1070 (Alaska 2005).

In a case alleging sexual harassment liability, an award of attorney's fees under Alaska R. Civ. P. 68 was proper because it applied to settlement offers made prior to Alaska R. Civ. P. 26 initial disclosures; the offers were timely because they were served no later than 60 days after both parties made the disclosures required by Rule 26. **Ellison v. Plumbers & Steam Fitters Union Local 375,** Op. No. 5934, 118 P.3d 1070 (Alaska 2005).

In a case alleging sexual harassment, a joint offer triggered Alaska R. Civ. P. 68 for purposes of a fee award to one party because the offer was made to settle all of the claims, and there were no apportionment problems since there was only one offeree. **Ellison v. Plumbers & Steam Fitters Union Local 375,** Op. No. 5934, 118 P.3d 1070 (Alaska 2005).

LAW REVIEW COMMENTARIES

"Erie Similarities: Alaska Civil Rule 68, 'Direct Collisions' and the Problem of Non-Aligning Background Assumptions," 23 Alaska L. Rev. 81 (2006).

Rule 69. Execution—Examination of Judgment Debtor—Restraining Disposition of Property—Execution After Five Years.

(a) **Execution—Discovery.** Process to enforce a judgment shall be by a writ of execution, unless the court directs otherwise. The procedure on execution, in proceedings supplementary to and in aid of a judgment, and in proceedings on and in aid of execution shall be in accordance with these rules and applicable statutes. In aid of the judgment or execution, the judgment creditor or a successor in interest, when that interest appears of record, may obtain discovery from any person, including the judgment debtor, in the manner provided in these rules.

(b) **Examination of Judgment Debtor in Court.**

(1) Before or after the issuing of an execution against property, the judgment debtor may be made to appear before the court, or before a master appointed by such court, at a time and place specified by an order, and to answer under oath all questions concerning property the judgment debtor has which may be subject to execution. The court may also order the debtor to bring to the examination documents concerning property which may be subject to execution.

(2) The examination may be reduced to writing and filed with the clerk by whom the execution was issued. Either party may examine witnesses in that party's behalf. If by such examination it appears that the judgment debtor has any property liable to execution the court shall make an order requiring the judgment debtor to apply the same in satisfaction of the judgment, or that such property be levied on by execution, or both, as may seem most likely to effect the object of the proceeding.

(c) **Order Restraining Disposition of Property.** At the time of allowing the order prescribed in subdivision (b)(1) of this rule or at any time thereafter pending the proceeding, the court may make an order restraining the judgment debtor from selling, transferring, or in any manner disposing of any property liable to execution pending the proceeding. For disobeying any order or requirement authorized by this rule the judgment debtor may be punished as for a contempt.

(d) **Execution After Five Years.** Whenever a period of five years shall elapse without an execution being issued on a judgment, no execution shall issue except on order of the court in the following manner:

(1) The judgment creditor shall file a motion supported by affidavit with the court where the judgment is entered for leave to issue an execution. The motion and affidavit shall state the names of the parties to the judgment, the date of its entry, the reasons for failure to obtain a writ for a period of five years and the amount claimed to be due thereon or the particular property of which possession was adjudged to the judgment creditor remaining undelivered.

(2) Upon filing such motion and affidavit the judgment creditor shall cause a summons to be served on the judgment debtor in accordance with the provisions of Rule 4. In the event the judgment debtor is deceased, the summons may be served upon the judgment debtor's representative. The summons shall state the amount claimed or the property sought to be recovered under the judgment.

(3) The judgment debtor, or, in the event of his death, the judgment debtor's representative, may file and serve a verified answer to such motion within the time allowed to answer a complaint, alleging any defense to such motion which may exist. The judgment creditor may file and serve a verified reply to such answer. The judgment debtor waives all defenses and objections which the judgment debtor does not present by answer as herein provided.

(4) The order shall specify the amount for which execution is to issue, or the particular property possession of which is to be delivered.

(5) At the time of filing the motion for leave to issue execution or at any time thereafter before the final order is entered, the judgment creditor may cause the property of the judgment debtor to be attached and held during the time said motion is pending and until the final order is entered. Such attachment shall be made in accordance with these rules and applicable statutes, and for the purpose of such attachment the judgment shall be deemed an implied contract for the direct payment of money. In the event that the court shall order that execution be issued, it shall further order that any property of the judgment debtor attached hereunder shall be sold for the satisfaction of such execution and the peace officer shall apply the property attached by the peace officer or the proceeds thereof upon the execution.

(e) **Multiple Executions.**

(1) Only one original writ of execution and one original writ of execution for garnishment of earnings may be issued and outstanding at any one time except:

(a) An additional writ of execution may be issued while another is outstanding if either of the writs is to be served on the Department of Revenue to seize the debtor's Alaska Permanent Fund Dividend; or

(b) Additional writs may be issued if the creditor alleges facts by affidavit which show there is property which cannot be served by the process server holding an outstanding writ because the property is outside the community in which the process server is authorized to operate and there is good cause to believe the debtor may remove or dispose of the property unless immediate action is taken.

(2) A process server to whom a writ of execution is issued may make copies of the writ as necessary. However, no writ or copies may be transferred to another process server except within the same firm. If the creditor discovers property which could be seized under the writ in another community in which the original process server does not serve, the outstanding writ must be returned to the court so that the clerk of court can cancel the first writ and issue a new writ to a process server serving the other community.

(f) **Service of Writ of Execution and Other Paper.**

(1) If personal service is used, the clerk shall deliver the papers for service to a process server or to a person specially appointed to serve them. Papers allowed to be served by registered or certified mail shall be mailed by the clerk as provided in Civil Rule 4(h). Postal delivery receipts for writs of execution served on the Permanent Fund Division of the Department of Revenue shall be made returnable to the judgment creditor. All other postal delivery receipts shall be made returnable to the court.

(2) A process server who receives money as a result of a levy must deliver the money and a return of service to the court on the next day of business after receipt. The process server must file the original writ unless the money received by the server will satisfy only part of the judgment and the server expects to seize more money or property with the writ. In this situation, the process server may make a partial return by delivery to the court of all money received, a return of service and a copy of the writ. The original writ must be returned to the court when the process server no longer expects to seize more money or property with the writ.

(g) **Confirmation of Sale of Real Property on Execution—Objections—Disposition of Proceeds.**

(1) *Confirmation.* Where real property has been sold on execution the plaintiff in the writ of execution, on motion, is entitled to have an order confirming the sale, after the expiration of 10 days after the filing of the return of sale, unless the judgment debtor has filed objections to the sale within 10 days after the filing of the return of sale.

(2) *Objections.* If objections are filed the court shall determine at a hearing whether there were substantial irregularities in the proceedings of sale which caused probable loss or injury to the judgment debtor. If not, the order confirming the sale shall be granted. If so, the court shall deny the motion and direct that the property be resold, in whole or in part as upon an execution received of that date.

(3) *Disposition of Proceeds of Sale.* After entry of an order confirming the sale of real property, the clerk shall apply the proceeds of the sale, or so much thereof as may be necessary, in satisfaction of the judgment and costs. Any proceeds remaining shall be paid to the judgment debtor. Such payments shall be made prior to the entry of the order of confirmation if the judgment debtor files with the clerk a waiver of all objections made or to be made to the proceedings concerning the sale.

(h) **Execution on Alaska Permanent Fund Dividends.**

(1) When an Alaska Permanent Fund Dividend is levied upon to satisfy a judgment, the Department of Revenue may deliver the seized funds directly to the court instead of turning them over to the process server who served the writ. Upon receipt of the funds, the court shall promptly notify the process server of the amount seized. Based on this information, the process server shall prepare and file a return of service. The court shall disburse the funds as provided by law.

(2) The administrative director may adopt procedures for executing upon Alaska Permanent Fund dividends by electronic means to satisfy judgments in criminal and minor offense cases and judgments in other cases in favor of the state. The procedures shall be established by administrative bulletin and may include procedures for issuance of writs of execution in electronic format, service of writs and notices of levy by electronic means, return of service, deposit of funds seized and other execution procedures.

(Adopted by SCO 5 October 9, 1959; amended by SCO 56 effective November 1, 1963; by SCO 258 effective November 15, 1976; by SCO 465 effective June 1, 1981; by SCO 675 effective June 15, 1986; by SCO 721 effective December 15, 1986; by SCO 1094 effective January 15, 1993; by SCO 1125 effective July 15, 1993; by SCO 1135 effective July 15, 1993; by SCO 1138 effective July 15, 1994; by SCO 1153 effective July 15, 1994; and by SCO 1290 effective October 1, 1997)

Note to Civil Rule 69(h): See Administrative Bulletins 43, 43.1, and 43.2.

Cross References

CROSS REFERENCE: AS 09.30.030; AS 09.35.010—AS 09.35.330

(a) **CROSS REFERENCE:** AS 09.35.010

(b)(1) **CROSS REFERENCE:** AS 09.35.070—AS 09.38

(d)(1) **CROSS REFERENCE:** AS 09.35.020

(d)(2) **CROSS REFERENCE:** AS 09.35.060

(e)(1) **CROSS REFERENCE:** AS 09.35.180

(e)(2) **CROSS REFERENCE:** AS 09.35.180

Annotations

Cases

Offset bid of $2000 on a judgment of $388.13 was a substantial irregularity having a natural tendency to deter the right to redeem and was therefore a proper consideration in trial judge's decision to set aside execution sale. **Law Offices of Murphy L. Clark v. Altman,** Op. No. 2811, 680 P2d 1125 (Alaska 1984).

In divorce case, husband's attempt to quash wife's writ of execution on the grounds of financial hardship and to offer to satisfy the obligation with alternative assets was frivolous, thus award to wife for costs involved in defending against the motion to quash was proper. **Hartland v. Hartland,** Op. No. 3459, 777 P2d 636 (Alaska 1989).

Superior court had jurisdiction to order judgment debtor to comply with judgment creditor's post-judgment discovery requests pending appeal and to enforce order with sanctions, where judgment debtor did not obtain stay pending appeal or file security bond. **Heppinstall v. Darnall Kemna & Co., Inc.,** Op. No. 3952, 851 P2d 78 (Alaska 1993).

If a judgment creditor seeks to execute upon a valid judgment after a lapse of five years, good cause must be demonstrated for the delay. **State ex rel. Inman v. Dean,** Op. No. 4244, 902 P2d 1321 (Alaska 1995).

Evidence of previous attempts to execute upon past due child support payments tends to support a finding of "good cause" under AS 09.35.020 and Civil Rule 69(d). **State ex rel. Inman v. Dean,** Op. No. 4244, 902 P2d 1321 (Alaska 1995).

Collections of past due child support payments were executions upon valid judgments and subject to the time limitations set forth in AS 09.35.020 and Civil Rule 69(d) rather than the time limitation of former AS 09.10.040, which applied only to an "action upon ajudgment." **State ex rel. Inman v. Dean,** Op. No. 4244, 902 P2d 1321 (Alaska 1995).

Where objections by property owner were not to irregularity in method of sale but rather to very right of creditors to sell property, time limit of this rule for objecting to confirmation of sale of real property on execution did not apply. **Hydaburg Co-Op. Ass'n v. Hydaburg Fisheries,** Op. No. 4415, 925 P2d 246 (Alaska 1996).

Judgment creditor was permitted to maintain supplementary fraudulent conveyance proceedings against nonparties to underlying action. **Thomas, Head and Greisen Employees Trust v. Buster,** 95 F.3d 1449 (9th Cir. 1996).

Civil Rule 69(d), pertaining to procedures for execution of judgments after five years have elapsed without execution, does not apply to administrative, non-judicial collection proceedings. **State, Dept. of Revenue v. Gerke,** Op. No. 4857, 942 P2d 423 (Alaska 1997).

Credit union showed just and sufficient reason for executing on a debtor's permanent fund dividend more than five years after a judgment was entered where, before that time, the debtor had no assets which were not exempt from execution. **Magden v. Alaska USA Fed. Credit Union,** Op. No. 5506, 36 P3d 659, 590 P2d 906 (Alaska 2001).

A superior court's decision to allow execution on a judgment more than five years old is a mixed question of law and fact and the appeals court reviews such a question de novo. **Brotherton v. Brotherton**, Op. No. 11852, 142 P.3d 1187 (Alaska 2006).

In a divorce proceeding to resolve a debt arising out of the marital property division first made in 1995, the superior court found two reasons for party's delay that it considered just and sufficient: (1) "the high level of animosity in this case"; and (2) "the fact that the case was appealed and was not affirmed until 2000." The first reason is a factual determination well within the superior court's discretion and the second is a just and sufficient reason as a matter of law. **Brotherton v. Brotherton**, Op. No. 11852, 142 P.3d 1187 (Alaska 2006).

If a judgment creditor seeks execution upon a valid judgment after five years, just and sufficient reasons must be demonstrated for the delay. **Brotherton v. Brotherton**, Op. No. 11852, 142 P.3d 1187 (Alaska 2006).

Rule 70. Judgment for Specific Acts—Vesting Title.

If a judgment directs a party to execute a conveyance of land or to deliver deeds or other documents or to perform any other specific act and the party fails to comply within the time specified, the court may direct the act to be done at the cost of the disobedient party by some other person appointed by the court and the act when so done has like effect as if done by the party. On application of the party entitled to performance, the clerk shall issue a writ of attachment or sequestration against the property of the disobedient party to compel obedience to the judgment. The court may also in proper cases adjudge the party in contempt. If real or personal property is within the state, the court in lieu of directing a conveyance thereof may enter a judgment divesting the title of any party and vesting it in others and such judgment has the effect of a conveyance executed in due form of law. When any order or judgment is for the delivery of possession, the party in whose favor it is entered is entitled to a writ of execution or assistance upon application to the clerk.

(Adopted by SCO 5 October 9, 1959)

Annotations

Cases

An order pursuant to Civil Rule 70 compelling a vendor to comply with a purchaser's request was erroneous to the extent that it required more of the vendor than was required by the underlying judgment and agreement. **Byrnes v. Mercier,** Op. No. 1804, 590 P2d 906 (Alaska 1979).

Trial judge had the authority to hold husband in contempt for his failure to comply with divorce decree directing him to transfer stocks to his wife. The judge was not acting to enforce a money judgment; rather, he was acting to effect the transfer to specific property awarded by the decree. **Hartland v. Hartland,** Op. No. 3459, 777 P2d 636 (Alaska 1989).

Rule 71. Process in Behalf of and Against Persons Not Parties.

When an order is made in favor of a person who is not a party to the action, the person may enforce obedience to the order by the same process as a party; and, when obedience to an order may be lawfully enforced against a person who is not a party, that person is liable to the same process for enforcing obedience to the order as a party.

(Adopted by SCO 5 October 9, 1959; amended by SCO 1153 effective July 15, 1994)

Rule 72. Eminent Domain.

(a) **Applicability of Other Rules.** The procedure for the condemnation of property under the power of eminent domain is governed by the Civil Rules, except as otherwise provided in this rule.

(b) **Joinder of Properties.** The plaintiff may join in the same action one or more separate pieces of property, whether in the same or different ownership and whether or not sought for the same use. Severance shall be freely granted in furtherance of convenience or to avoid prejudice, or when separate trials will be conducive to expedition and economy.

(c) **Commencement of Action.**

(1) *Complaint.* An action for the condemnation of property under the power of eminent domain is commenced by filing a complaint and, if used, a declaration of taking. The complaint, in order to be accepted for filing, must be accompanied by a completed case description on a form provided by the clerk of court.

(2) *Contents of Complaint.*

(A) The complaint must contain:

(i) a caption naming as defendants the persons described in subsection (c)(2)(A)(vii), commencing with the apparent owners of the fee simple interest in the property to be taken, and the property designated generally by kind, quantity, and location;

(ii) a statement of the authority and necessity for the taking;

(iii) a statement of the use for which the property is to be taken;

(iv) a description of the property to be taken sufficient to identify and locate it;

(v) a statement of the interests to be acquired, including the terms and conditions of any easements;

(vi) a statement of the amount of money the plaintiff estimates to be just compensation for the taking;

(vii) the name and apparent interest of all persons having or claiming an interest in the property who can be ascertained by a reasonably diligent search of the records or otherwise known to the plaintiff to claim an interest in the property.

(B) The statement of just compensation required under subsection (c)(2)(A)(vi) constitutes a judicial admission by the plaintiff. The names and apparent interests required under subsection (c)(2)(A)(vii) do not constitute admissions by the plaintiff.

(3) *Exhibits to Complaint.* The decisional document for the taking and a map or plat of the property to be taken must be attached as exhibits to the complaint.

(d) **Process.**

(1) *Summons.* Upon filing of the complaint, the clerk shall forthwith issue a summons in condemnation and deliver it to the plaintiff, who shall cause the summons and a copy of the complaint to be served in accordance with Civil Rule 4. Upon request of the plaintiff, separate or additional summonses shall issue against any defendants.

(2) *Contents of Summons.* (A) A summons in condemnation must state:

(i) the court where the action was filed;

(ii) the caption of the action;

(iii) the name of the defendant to whom the summons is directed;

(iv) the name, address and telephone number of plaintiff's counsel; and

(v) the name of the judge to whom the case is assigned.

(B) The summons must also state:

(i) that if the defendant disputes the authority and necessity for the taking or objects to the declaration of taking, the defendant must file within twenty days after service of the summons upon the defendant an answer stating all of the defendant's objections and defenses;

(ii) that failure to file an answer within such time constitutes a waiver by the defendant of all objections and defenses to the authority and necessity for the taking and to the validity of the declaration of taking;

(iii) that if the action is not dismissed, the time when plaintiff may take possession, the amount of compensation to be paid for the taking, and the distribution of compensation will be determined by further proceedings in the action;

(iv) that if the defendant disputes the amount of just compensation, or claims any part of the compensation to be paid in the action, or desires notice of further proceedings in the action, the defendant must file within twenty days after service of the summons upon the defendant a notice of appearance, stating the name and address of the person to whom notice should be sent, or the court will proceed to a final determination of just compensation without further notice to the defendant; and

(v) that a defendant who fails to appear within the time specified may file a notice of appearance at any time before a final determination of just compensation is made and may present evidence as to the amount of just compensation to be paid or its distribution; however, the filing of an untimely notice of appearance, absent a showing of good cause that would justify setting aside a default under Civil Rule 55(e), does not relieve a defendant of the effect of prior orders entered by the court or a final determination of just compensation;

(vi) that ten days following a final determination of just compensation the court will enter judgment by default for the relief demanded in the complaint against any defendant who has failed to appear.

(3) *Service.* The summons, a copy of the complaint and, if used, a copy of the declaration of taking must be served on the defendants and return of service made in conformity with Civil Rule 4.

(e) **Answer or Appearance.**

(1) *Answer.* If the defendant objects to the authority and necessity for the taking or to the validity of the declaration of taking, the defendant must file an answer stating all of the defendant's objections and defenses. The answer must be filed within twenty days after service of the summons upon the defendant.

(2) *Notice of Appearance.* If the defendant disputes the amount of just compensation, or claims any part of the compensation to be paid in the action, or desires to receive notice of further proceedings in the action, the defendant must file a notice of appearance, stating the name and address of the person to whom notice should be sent. The notice of appearance must be filed within twenty days after service of the summons upon the defendant. A notice of appearance preserves all claims concerning the amount of compensation to be paid and its distribution. A notice of appearance may be filed with an answer.

(3) *Disclaimer.* If a defendant has no objection to the

taking or to loss of possession of the property, or no claim to any part of the compensation deposited or to be paid in the action, the defendant may file a disclaimer of interest in the proceedings. A disclaimer may be filed after an answer or appearance. The parties and the court are not required to provide notice of proceedings to a defendant who has filed a disclaimer.

(4) *Failure to Respond.* Failure to file an answer within the time specified in subparagraph (e)(1) constitutes a waiver by the defendant of all objections and defenses to the authority and necessity for the taking and to the validity of the declaration of taking. The filing of an untimely notice of appearance, absent a showing of good cause that would justify setting aside a default under Civil Rule 55(e), does not relieve a defendant of the effect of prior orders entered by the court or a final determination of just compensation. Ten days following a final determination of just compensation, the court upon motion, may enter judgment by default for the relief demanded in the complaint against a defendant who has not filed a notice of appearance.

(5) *Other Pleadings or Motions.* All objections and defenses to the taking must be set forth in the answer. No counterclaims, cross-claims, or third party claims are allowed, unless the court determines that such claims should be consolidated with the condemnation action under Civil Rule 42(a).

(f) **Amendment of Pleadings.** The plaintiff may amend the complaint without leave of court at any time before trial of the issue of compensation and as many times as desired; however, no amendment may be made which would result in a dismissal prohibited under paragraph (i) of this rule. Service of the amended complaint upon a party who has appeared must be made as provided in Civil Rule 5(b). Service upon a party who has not appeared must be made as provided in paragraph (d) of this rule. A defendant who is served with an amended complaint may file and serve a response within the time allowed by paragraph (e) of this rule.

(g) **Substitution of Parties.** If a defendant dies or becomes incompetent or transfers its interest in the litigation, the court shall order substitution of the proper party upon motion. The provisions of Civil Rule 25(a) do not apply to actions proceeding under this rule. Service of the motion upon a person not already a party to the action must be made as provided in Civil Rule 4.

(h) **Hearing and Trial.**

(1) *Special Discovery Rules.*

(A) *Expedited Discovery on Authority, Necessity and Possession.* Any time after service of the summons, any party may conduct discovery, including depositions, regarding matters to be decided at the hearing provided for under subparagraph (h)(2). Responses to interrogatories, requests for production or inspection, and requests for admissions must be served within fifteen days after service of the interrogatories or requests; however, a defendant need not respond earlier than ten days after the time allowed for filing an answer.

(B) *Appraisals and Expert Reports.* Each party, within forty-five days after filing its complaint, answer, or appearance, must exchange with every other party who has answered or appeared all appraisals of property within the scope of the taking completed within the five years preceding the date of taking. Forty-five days before the master's hearing and again thirty days before the close of discovery, the parties must simultaneously exchange all appraisals of the property and expert reports relating to just compensation completed since the summons was issued.

(2) *Authority/Necessity/Possession.*

(A) *Declaration of Taking.* If no objection to authority and necessity for the taking is contained within the answer, filed within the time period provided by subparagraph (e)(1) of this rule, the court shall enter an order confirming authority and necessity. If timely objection is made, the objecting party must, within thirty days after service of the summons, file a motion to dismiss setting forth the objections with specificity. The plaintiff may file an opposition to the motion within ten days after service of the motion upon the plaintiff. The objecting party may file a reply within three days after service of the opposition upon the objecting party. Either party may request a hearing. The court shall hold a hearing within twenty days after a request for hearing is filed. The hearing will be based on the record unless a request for evidentiary hearing and statement of genuine issues of material fact is filed by the objecting party with the motion or by the plaintiff with the opposition and the court determines that there are genuine issues of material fact. In the event the objections are found to be valid, the court may dismiss the action, remand to the condemning entity for further findings, or order such other relief as allowed by law.

(B) *Motions for Possession under AS 09.55.390 and .400.* Upon the filing of a motion pursuant to AS 09.55.390 or 09.55.400, the court shall schedule and conduct a hearing on the motion. The motion, any opposition to the motion, and any reply by the moving party must be in the form and filed within the time limits prescribed by Civil Rule 77 for dispositive motions, except that no opposition shall be due earlier than thirty days after service of the summons upon that defendant.

(C) *Other Condemnation Actions.* In an action in which neither a declaration of taking nor the procedures set forth in AS 09.55.390–.400 have been utilized, a party may move, no earlier than sixty days after service of the summons upon all defendants, for an order determining whether there is authority and necessity for the taking. The motion, any opposition to the motion, and any reply by the moving party must be in the form and filed within the time limits prescribed by Civil Rule 77 for dispositive motions.

(D) *Possession.* In an action in which a declaration of taking has been filed, a party may move, either contemporaneously with proceedings on authority and necessity or after authority and necessity has been determined, for an order setting the date and terms under which possession of the property will vest in the plaintiff. In an action subject to AS 09.55.380, any party may move to have the questions of possession decided after a final determination of compensation is made or after the plaintiff has deposited sufficient funds or security to satisfy the court that the parties are protected.

(E) *Finality.* An order entered under section (h)(2)(A), (B), or (C) is a final judgment for purposes of appeal under Appellate Rule 202.

(3) *Master's Hearing.*

(A) *Procedure.* A master will be appointed to hear evidence and to ascertain the amount to be paid by the plaintiff to each owner or other person interested in the property, unless the master's hearing is waived under section (h)(3)(B) of this rule. Any interested party may move the court for an order appointing the master. The motion must set forth the name, address and phone number of any individual proposed as master, proposed instructions to the master, a written oath, and a form of report for use by the master. The form of report must incorporate a cover sheet in a form prescribed by the Administrative Director of the Courts. The court may appoint a master from the nominees of the parties or of its own nomination, subject to the provisions of Civil Rule 42(c). The order of reference to the master must set forth the master's duties and powers and must be accompanied by instructions on the law that the master must apply. Civil Rule 53 does not apply to master's proceedings under this rule.

(B) *Waiver.* If all parties agree, the master's hearing may be waived and the matter set for trial. In that event, A Notice of Waiver of Master's Hearing shall be filed, along with proof of service under Civil Rule 5 upon all parties to the action.

(4) *Filing of Master's Report.* The master shall file the master's report with the cover sheet prescribed by the Administrative Director of the Courts. The clerk of court shall promptly serve the report on all parties who have answered or appeared.

(5) *Appeal From Master's Report.*

(A) Appeal in the form of a trial de novo may be taken from the master's report by filing a memorandum to set trial within the following time limits:

(i) the plaintiff may appeal within ten days after service of the master's report; and

(ii) a defendant may appeal within fifteen days after service of the master's report.

(B) The memorandum to set trial must contain the information required by Rule 40(b)(1)(a)–(d), (f), and (g).

(6) *Demand for Jury Trial.*

(A) If all parties to the action have waived appointment of a master under subparagraph (h)(3), a jury trial may be had if demand is made by any party within twenty days after service of the Notice of Waiver of Master's Hearing upon that party. Otherwise, trial will be by the court.

(B) Upon filing of an appeal under subparagraph (h)(5), a jury trial may be had if demand is made by any party within twenty days after filing of the appeal from the master's report. Otherwise, trial will be by the court.

(i) **Dismissal of Action.**

(1) *As of Right.* If no hearing has commenced to determine the compensation to be paid for the property and the plaintiff has not acquired title or a lesser interest in or taken possession of the property, the plaintiff may dismiss the action as to that property, without an order of the court, by filing a notice of dismissal describing the property as to which the action is dismissed.

(2) *By Stipulation.* Before entry of judgment vesting the plaintiff with title or a lesser interest in or possession of the property, the action may be dismissed in whole or in part, without an order of the court, as to any property by stipulation of the plaintiff and the defendant affected thereby; and, if the parties so stipulate, the court may vacate any judgment that has been entered.

(3) *By Order of the Court.* Any time before compensation for property has been determined and paid, the court may dismiss the action as to that property after motion and hearing, except that the court may not dismiss the action as to any part of the property of which the plaintiff has taken possession or in which the plaintiff has taken title or a lesser interest, but shall award just compensation for the possession, title or lesser interest taken. The court may dismiss at any time a defendant unnecessarily or improperly joined.

(4) *Want of Prosecution.* The court shall not enter an order dismissing a case for want of prosecution. On its own motion or upon motion of a party, the court may schedule a pretrial conference to expedite resolution of a case.

(5) *Effect.* A dismissal under this paragraph is without prejudice except as otherwise provided in the notice, stipulation, or order.

(j) **Deposit and Its Distribution.** The plaintiff shall deposit with the court any money required by law as a condition to the exercise of the power of eminent domain, and may make such deposit even when not required to do so by law. The notice of deposit must disclose the extent to which the deposit represents principal, interest, costs and fees, if any. The court and attorneys shall expedite the proceedings for distribution of the deposit and for ascertainment and payment of just compensation. The court may order distribution of the deposit at any time. Such order is effective only as to parties whose time to appear has expired. Upon entry of an order distributing funds on deposit, the clerk of court shall disburse the funds expeditiously. If the compensation finally awarded to a defendant exceeds the amount that has been paid to the defendant on distribution of the deposit, the court shall enter judgment against the plaintiff and in favor of the defendant for the deficiency. If the compensation finally awarded to a defendant is less than the amount that has been paid to the defendant, the court shall enter judgment against the defendant and in favor of the plaintiff for the overpayment.

(k) **Costs.** Costs and attorney's fees incurred by a

defendant must be assessed against the plaintiff if:

(1) the taking of the property is denied;

(2) the plaintiff appeals from the master's award and the defendant does not appeal;

(3) the award of the court was at least ten (10) percent larger than the amount deposited by the condemning authority or the allowance of the master from which an appeal was taken by the defendant;

(4) the action was dismissed under the provisions of paragraph (i) of this rule; or

(5) allowance of costs and attorney's fees appears necessary to achieve a just and adequate compensation of the defendant.

Attorney's fees allowed under this paragraph must be commensurate with the time expended by the attorney throughout the proceedings.

(*l*) **Offer of Judgment.** A party may make an offer of judgment to another party under the provisions of Civil Rule 68, which shall apply to eminent domain actions in all respects except as set forth below.

(1) If the plaintiff makes a successful offer of judgment against a defendant, the defendant may not recover costs and fees incurred after the making of the offer of judgment except as reasonable and necessary to evaluate the offer of judgment. This shall not preclude the award of costs and fees as allowed under Civil Rule 72(k)(1)–(5) incurred prior to the making of the offer of judgment. In no event shall a defendant be required to pay the costs and fees of the plaintiff.

(2) If a defendant makes a successful offer of judgment against the plaintiff, the defendant is entitled to recover full reasonable and necessary costs and attorney's fees without regard to Civil Rule 72(k).

(3) For purposes of applying Civil Rule 68, the defendant is the party making the claim and the plaintiff is the party defending against the claim. Any adjustment in interest rates shall operate only from the date the offer of judgment was made. When two defendants use Civil Rule 68 as against the other, the adjustment in prejudgment interest provisions do not apply.

(m) **Definitions.** For purposes of this rule, a final determination of just compensation is not made until all issues of the amount of just compensation to be paid and its distribution to the parties entitled to just compensation are resolved by the entry of judgment on a jury verdict, the court's confirmation of an award of the master, a final order of the court accepting a settlement agreement of the parties, or the last such order or judgment that resolves any part of these issues.

(Adopted by SCO 5 October 9, 1959; amended by SCO 49 effective January 1, 1963; by SCO 56 effective November 1, 1963; by SCO 57 effective November 8, 1963; by SCO 90 effective July 24, 1967; by SCO 98 effective September 16, 1968; by SCO 414 effective August 1, 1980; by SCO 468 effective June 1, 1981; and by SCO 1153 effective July 15, 1994; rescinded and reenacted by SCO 1216 effective January 1, 1996)

Note to (c)(3): For an explanation of the decisional document requirement in cases under AS 09.55.420–.460, see Ship Creek Hydraulic Syndicate v. State, 685 P.2d 715, 715–20 (Alaska 1984).

Note to (*l*)(1): The limitation on a defendant's right to recover costs and fees incurred after the making of an offer of judgment is subject to any constitutional right the defendant may have to receive compensation for these expenses.

Notes: Chapter 54 SLA 2005 (HB 95) enacted extensive amendments and new provisions related to public health, including public health emergencies and disasters. According to Section 13(e) of the Act, AS 18.15.390, enacted in Section 8, has the effect of amending Civil Rule72 by authorizing the Department of Health and Social Services to take immediate control over certain businesses and property in cases of public health disasters.

Cross References

CROSS REFERENCE: AS 09.55.240—AS 09.55.460

(c) **CROSS REFERENCE:** AS 09.55.240— AS 09.55.270

(e)(3) **CROSS REFERENCE:** AS 09.55.420— AS 09.55.460

(e)(4) **CROSS REFERENCE:** AS 09.55.310

(h)(4) **CROSS REFERENCE:** AS 09.55.310

Annotations

Cases

I. In General.
II. Appeals.
  A. Procedure.
  B. Timeliness.
III. Attorney's Fees.

I. In General.

The question whether a party joining as a defendant in a condemnation action pursuant to this rule is an indispensable party so that the action may not proceed to a conclusion unless such person is made a party, must be determined under Civil Rule 19(b). **City of Fairbanks v. Electric Distribution Sys.,** Op. No. 339, 413 P2d 165 (Alaska 1966).

Eminent domain proceedings are unique and are governed by comprehensive rules of procedure applicable to condemnation actions alone. **Stewart & Grindle, Inc. v. State,** Op. No. 1052, 524 P2d 1242 (Alaska 1974).

The phrase "these rules" as used in this rule, refers to all other rules of civil procedure and administration. **Stewart & Grindle, Inc. v. State,** Op. No. 1052, 524 P2d 1242 (Alaska 1974).

The phrase "throughout the entire proceedings" in Civil Rule 72(k) refers to all phases of the proceedings before the superior court. It does not mean proceedings before the supreme court. **State Dept. of Highways v. Salzwedel,** Op. No. 1961, 596 P2d 17 (Alaska 1979).

In condemnation action, state was not entitled to an offset against condemnee's claimed costs and attorney's fees despite state's contention that certain motions by condemnee were unnecessary; the state's request was not authorized by this rule, and the motions referred to as unnecessary by the state were in fact germane to condemnee's attempt to secure just compensation rather than part of a separate claim on his behalf. **Vezey v. State,** Op. No. 3575, 798 P2d 327 (Alaska 1990).

Under this rule, either State or trial court had right to dismiss eminent domain complaint initiated by State against holder of mining claim on property owned by State on which State built power line towers; mining claim was by statute subject to reasonable concurrent surface uses, thus State, by acquiring right of way and construction power line, did not acquire title or lesser interest in, or take possession of, any property interest held by holder of mining claim, making eminent domain action unnecessary and subject to dismissal. **Parker v. Alaska Power Authority,** Op. No. 4331, 913 P2d 1089 (Alaska 1996).

II. Appeals.

A. Procedure.

The lower court's order dismissing a declaration of taking in eminent domain of a first class city was affirmed on review, because a declaration of taking is not a matter of procedure and AS 29.55 .030 cannot be read to authorize a first class city to use a declaration of taking. **City of Anchorage v. Lot 1 in Block 68 of Orig. Town.,** Op. No. 316, 409 P2d 609 (Alaska 1966).

The proper and only method of attacking a master's report in an eminent domain proceeding is by way of appeal and trial de novo before a jury unless a jury trial is waived. **State v. 7.536 Acres and Evenson,** Op. No. 434, 431 P2d 897 (Alaska 1967).

Entry of judgment based on the master's report in an eminent domain proceeding foreclosed the owner's right of appeal from that report. **State v. 7.536 Acres and Evenson,** Op. No. 434, 431 P2d 897 (Alaska 1967).

Federal authorities construing F.R.C.P. 71 A are not applicable to Alaska's counterpart Civil Rule 72(h), because under the federal rules a jury trial on the question of just compensation is not an absolute right, whereas in Alaska the appellant from a master's report under this rule may receive a trial de novo under AS 09. 55.320. **State v.7.536 Acres and Evenson,** Op. No. 434, 431 P2d 897 (Alaska 1967).

Under AS 09.55.320, which provides that an interested party may appeal a master's award in which case there shall be a trial by jury on the question of the amount of damages and on the value of property, unless the jury is waived by the consent of all parties, a condemnee against whom an appeal is taken is entitled to a jury trial as a matter of right. A condemnor cannot, after the jury has rendered verdicts higher than the master's awards, obtain a dismissal of its appeal without the consent of the condemnees. **Inglima v. Alaska State Housing Authority,** Op. No. 594, 462 P2d 1002 (Alaska 1970).

In condemnation action, an appeal from a master's award preserves a full jury trial on all issues; the appeal may not raise only a portion of the issues on which damages are grounded. **Rebischke v. State,** Op. No. 1541, 572 P2d 432 (Alaska 1977).

B. Timeliness.

Where appellant's objections to the master's report were not filed within 10 days, trial court did not err in granting judgment based on the report of the master. **State v. 7.536 Acres and Evenson,** Op. No. 434, 431 P2d 897 (Alaska 1967).

A condemnor which fails to file a timely notice of appeal from a master's report can be granted an enlargement of time under Civil Rule 6 or relief for excusable neglect under Civil Rule 60. **State v. Chuckwm, Inc.,** Op. No. 522, 449 P2d 776 (Alaska 1968).

A condemnor's request for relief from failure to file timely notice of appeal from a master's report and for relief from an oppressive proceeding is addressed to the sound discretion of the trial court, and its ruling will not be disturbed on appeal in the absence of a showing of abuse of discretion. **State v. Chuckwm, Inc.,** Op. No. 522, 449 P2d 776 (Alaska 1968).

Where the failure of a condemnor to enter a timely appeal from a master's report is due to the failure of the counsel handling the litigation to receive actual notice that the report had been filed because of a breakdown in established office routine, the condemnor is not entitled to an extension of time since such failure cannot be considered excusable neglect. **State v. Chuckwm, Inc.,** Op. No. 522, 449 P2d 776 (Alaska 1968).

The trial court has jurisdiction under Rule 6, pertaining to the enlargement of time, Rule 60, pertaining to grounds for obtaining relief from a judgment or order, or Rule 94, pertaining to relaxation of these rules, to enlarge the period for appealing from the report of a master in condemnation, even though the period for appeal has run. **Collart etal. (6,656 Square Feet) v. State,** Op. No. 565, 456 P2d 480 (Alaska 1969).

The Supreme Court will not pass on the sufficiency of a landowner's showing that he is entitled to an enlargement of time for appealing from the report of a master in condemnation until the trial court's discretionary powers have been exercised. **Collart et al. (6,656 Square Feet) v. State,** Op. No. 565, 456 P2d 480 (Alaska 1969).

III. Attorney's Fees.

A condemnee is entitled to an attorney fee where the amount awarded is at least 10% larger than the amount which the state stipulated could be withdrawn by the condemnee, and where the allowance of costs and attorney fees appears necessary to achieve a just and adequate compensation to the condemnee. **Russian Orthodox Greek Catholic Church of North America v. State Housing Authority,** Op. No. 809, 408 P2d 737 (Alaska 1972).

The fact that a stipulated settlement is at least ten percent greater than the State's initial offer does not entitle landowners to recover attorney fees and appraisers' fees from the State. **Stewart & Grindle, Inc. v. State,** Op. No. 1052, 524 P2d 1242 (Alaska 1974).

Where property to be taken has a readily ascertainable market value or is worth too little to warrant a professional appraisal, a landowner is not entitled to compensation for such an appraiser's fee. Where property has a readily ascertainable market value and the State has offered at least that amount, any attorney fee subsequently incurred is not necessary and is not recoverable under this rule. **Stewart & Grindle, Inc. v. State,** Op. No. 1052, 524 P2d 1242 (Alaska 1974).

Party was properly awarded attorney's fees where award of court was more than ten percent higher than the amount awarded by the master. **State v. Hammer,** Op. No. 1268, 550 P2d 820 (Alaska 1976).

State should not be charged attorney's fees resulting from portion of litigation relating to dispute between owners of different interests in condemned property. **State v. Hammer,** Op. No. 1268, 550 P2d 820 (Alaska 1976).

Where jury in eminent domain action awarded compensation less than master's award but higher than initial tender, condemnee appealing master's award would be allowed attorney's fees incurred before date of master's award; condemnee not appealing master's award would be allowed attorney's fees incurred in appeal. **Greater Anchorage Area Borough v. 10 Acres,** Op. No. 1417, 563 P2d 269 (Alaska 1977).

When condemnee is eligible for attorney's fees in eminent domain action, he must receive full compensation under Civil Rule 72, not partial compensation under Civil Rule 82. **Greater Anchorage Area Borough v. 10 Acres,** Op. No. 1417, 563 P2d 269 (Alaska 1977).

Scope of Civil Rule 72 is not limited to statutory condemnation proceedings and while all of the special procedures of Civil Rule 72 cannot be followed in inverse condemnation proceedings, the policy concerns underlying Civil Rule 72(k)'s implicit disallowance of condemnor attorney's fees are still implicated. **Williams v. City of Valdez,** Op. No. 1969, 603 P2d 483 (Alaska 1979).

The test for whether costs and attorney's fees are to be awarded is whether they were necessarily incurred in connection with the condemnation of the property, and they are "necessarily incurred" if the condemnee must undertake them to insure that he gets a fair price for his land. **Martens v. State Dept. of Highways,** Op. No. 2287, 623 P2d 331 (Alaska 1981).

Costs and attorney's fees incurred prior to commencement of condemnation action may be awarded to condemnee. **Martens v. State Dept. of Highways,** Op. No. 2287, 623 P2d 331 (Alaska 1981).

The 10 percent limit of this rule applies only when a landowner appeals a master's award, not when the state appeals. **Martens v. State Dept. of Highways,** Op. No. 2287, 623 P2d 331 (Alaska 1981).

When second trial in condemnation proceeding was ordered by Alaska supreme court, and the award in the second trial was less than ten percent larger than the award in the first trial, landowner was still entitled to costs and attorney's fees incurred because of the second trial. **Martens v. State Dept. of Highways,** Op. No. 2287, 623 P2d 331 (Alaska 1981).

When state appeals a master's award, award of attorney's fees in connection with the trial to the landowner are not contingent on the landowner acknowledging on the record his acceptance of the master's award. **Martens v. State Dept. of Highways,** Op. No. 2287, 623 P2d 331 (Alaska 1981).

Where jury verdict greatly exceeded any pretrial offer by the state, attorney's fees in connection with the trial were necessary to achieve a just and adequate compensation of the landowner in condemnation proceeding. **Martens v. State Dept. of Highways,** Op. No. 2287, 623 P2d 331 (Alaska 1981).

Costs incurred by the owner in a defense to a condemnation proceeding are compensable under this rule only to the extent they are reasonable, i.e. necessarily incurred. **Badger Construction Co. v. State,** Op. No. 2365, 628 P2d 921 (Alaska 1981).

Only costs which are necessarily incurred should be awarded under the "10 percent" rule of Civil Rule 72(k)(2), although only Civil Rule 72(k)(4) expressly requires that the award appear necessary for just compensation. **State v. Alaska Continental Dev. Corp.,** Op. No. 2254, 630 P2d 977 (Alaska 1981).

While full attorney's fees are the norm under Civil Rule 72(k), fees awarded under Civil Rule 72(k)(2) must be reasonable as well as necessary. **Triangle, Inc. v. State,** Op. No. 2405, 632 P2d 965 (Alaska 1981).

If there is a reduction from actual attorney's fees in the amount awarded under this rule, it is incumbent upon the court to state the reasons for the reduction. **Triangle, Inc. v. State,** Op. No. 2405, 632 P2d 965 (Alaska 1981).

Trial court did not abuse its discretion in awarding attorney's fees under this rule which were less than the property owner's actual fees, **Resource Investments v. State, Dept. of Transportation,** Op. No. 2853, 687 P2d 280 (Alaska 1984).

Civil rule authorizing attorney's fees and costs in condemnation actions is limited to situations in which the defendant prevails. **Stewart v. State, Dept. of Transportation,** Op. No. 2895, 693 P2d 827 (Alaska 1984).

Although property owners were entitled to fees and costs incurred prior to State's agreement to dismiss condemnation action, they were not entitled to attorney fees and costs incurred thereafter with respect to their unsuccessful attempt to prevent the State from removing trees and from building a retaining wall on the State's own property, since those fees and costs were not incurred in seeking dismissal of the condemnation action. **Stewart v. State, Dept. of Transportation,** Op. No. 2895, 693 P2d 827 (Alaska 1984).

Although full attorney's fees are the norm under this rule, those fees must be both reasonable and necessarily incurred to obtain just compensation; thus the trial court may award less than the full amount of the charges when it finds the amount unreasonable in view of the nature and extent of the services rendered. **State v. Doyle,** Op. No. 3167, 735 P2d 733 (Alaska 1987).

Considering the issues involved and the length of trial, as well as the fact that the compensation awarded to plaintiffs in their inverse condemnation action was $715,000.22, the trial court did not abuse its discretion in awarding plaintiffs less than the actual $357,500.10 in attorney's fees owed under a negotiated fee agreement, awarding instead an amount commensurate with the time committed by counsel. **State v. Doyle,** Op. No. 3167, 735 P2d 733 (Alaska 1987).

Attorney's fees are awarded in condemnation actions to compensate the landowner for expenses incurred in connection with the condemnation of his property, since the landowner, without compensation, would pay an unfairly large portion of the costs of a public project; attorney's fees are not compensation for lost future earning capacity. **Bocek Bros. v. Anchorage,** Op. No. 3270, 750 P2d 335 (Alaska 1988).

Trial court was not required to award prejudgment interest on award of attorney's fees in condemnation action. **Bocek Bros. v. Anchorage,** Op. No. 3270, 750 P2d 335 (Alaska 1988).

In determining whether attorney's fees were necessarily incurred by the landowner in an eminent domain action, the trial court should have taken into consideration the landowner's rejection of the state's offer of settlement. **State, Dept. of Transp. v. 4.085 Acres,** Op. No. 3292, 752 P2d 1008 (Alaska 1988).

In an eminent domain proceeding, if the condemning authority appeals and the landowner does not, then, ordinarily, the landowner's reasonable expenses are necessarily incurred and therefore are awardable. **State, Dept. of Transp. v. 4.085 Acres,** Op. No. 3292, 752 P2d 1008 (Alaska 1988).

This rule contemplates an award of costs at the conclusion of the proceeding, and does not contemplate an interim award. **Vezey v. State,** Op. No. 3575, 798 P2d 327 (Alaska 1990).

Although full attorney's fees are the norm under this rule, trial court did not err in denying full attorney's fees to condemnee where the court adequately explained its reasons for deeming the claimed fees excessive. **Vezey v. State,** Op. No. 3575, 798 P2d 327 (Alaska 1990).

In condemnation action, state was not entitled to an offset against condemnee's claimed costs and attorney's fees despite state's contention that certain motions by condemnee were unnecessary; the state's request was not authorized by this rule, and the motions referred to as unnecessary by the state were in fact germane to condemnee's attempt to secure just compensation rather than part of a separate claim on his behalf. **Vezey v. State,** Op. No. 3575, 798 P2d 327 (Alaska 1990).

This rule contemplates that the condemnee must risk out-of-pocket expenses, such as drilling costs, in challenging the state's estimate of just compensation; the condemnee will be able to recover those expenses if he or she receives an award which is 10 percent higher than the state's estimate; accordingly, trial court did not err in denying condemnee's request for an interim award of costs under this rule for the expenses of drilling in order to ascertain whether the condemned parcel contained gold. **Vezey v. State,** Op. No. 3575, 798 P2d 327 (Alaska 1990).

In condemnation action, property owner was not entitled to recover costs for his own time. **Vezey v. State,** Op. No. 3575, 798 P2d 327 (Alaska 1990).

Trial court erred in basing part of its award for attorney fees in condemnation proceeding upon the contingent fee agreement between the property owners and their lawyer. **Anchorage v. Babinec,** Op. No. 3811, 823 P2d 1248 (Alaska 1992).

Full attorney's fees and costs are not the "norm" in eminent domain actions if final award is substantially same as amount deposited by condemning authority. **Four Separate Parcels v. City of Kodiak,** Op. No. 4785, 938 P2d 448 (Alaska 1997).

Where city prevailed on an inverse condemnation action filed against it, it was entitled to collect attorney's fees and Alaska R. Civ. P. 79 and Rule 82 did not prohibit that recovery. **R & Y, Inc. v. Municipality of Anchorage,** Op. No. 5466, 34 P3d 289 (Alaska 2001).

Rule 72.1. Expert Advisory Panels in Health Care Provider Malpractice Actions.

(a) **Identification of Action.** Either party in a health care malpractice action subject to AS 09.55.536 may request that the court appoint an expert advisory panel to evaluate the claim. The request should identify the specialty of the health care provider named as defendant. Either party may recommend that the court appoint specific professions or specialties to the expert advisory panel.

(b) **Appointment of Panel.**

(1) After the case is at issue and a party has requested the appointment of an expert advisory panel (or the court has raised the issue), the court shall nominate a three person panel and notify the parties of the names, professions and specialties of the persons so nominated. The court may initially nominate alternate panel members if it believes nominees may be disqualified. Within 10 days after service of this notice, either party may move to disqualify a nominee, citing the reasons for the motion. The other party may submit an opposition within

five days after service of the motion for disqualification. No reply may be filed.

(2) The nominated panel members must inform the court within 10 days of the notice of appointment of any financial relationship with a party or party's attorney, of any other reason which would cause the nominee to be biased in the case or present an appearance of bias, and of any other reason why the nominee cannot serve on the panel. The court shall disqualify a nominee if the nominee is biased for or against a party or if a conflict of interest raises a substantial appearance of bias.

(3) If additional nominees are required, the parties must be given the opportunity to recommend nominees' professions or specialties and move to disqualify as provided above.

(c) **Submission of Medical Records.**

(1) Within 30 days after service of the court's initial panel nominations, the plaintiff and each health care provider defendant shall serve on other parties one legible copy of all discoverable medical records in such party's possession, custody, or control. Original exhibits which are impractical or impossible to copy must be made available to all parties for review. Medical reports of consultants retained by a party for the advancement or defense of the case and medical literature must also be served on other parties if such literature or reports is to be submitted to the panel.

(2) Each party shall file with the Clerk and serve on each other party a list of all medical records, medical reports and medical literature which the party will transmit or make available to the panel.

(3) Medical records include medical records of hospitals, physicians, or other health care providers, addressing an issue of health relevant to the plaintiffs' complaint, whether generated before or subsequent to the event giving rise to the claim and whether generated by the health care provider named in the complaint or by other health care providers. Medical records also include autopsy reports and exhibits such as x-rays and slides.

(4) Upon agreement of the parties or order of the court, and after a reasonable time for inspection, each party shall submit to each member of the panel one legible copy of such party's medical records, medical reports and medical literature, and notify the panel members of the availability and location of original exhibits for which submission to the panel is impractical or impossible. If the plaintiff serves the defendant with medical reports of consultants, the defendant has 30 days to serve medical reports of its consultants on the plaintiff. Thereafter, the reports may be submitted to the panel. Any additional reports may be submitted only with leave of the court.

(5) A party may file and serve on each member of the panel a notice advising the panel of further relevant medical records of which the noticing party does not have possession, custody or control.

(6) In the event a party fails or is unable to submit relevant medical records to the panel, and the panel is unable to obtain access to such records by reason thereof, any party or the panel may apply to the court for leave to obtain such records by court order. The court may delay further proceedings until the panel is provided with the additional medical records.

(7) Within 30 days after service of the court's initial panel nominations, each party shall serve upon the panel and all other parties the information and materials required to be disclosed under Rule 26(a)(1)(A), (B), (C), and 26(a)(2).

(d) **Preliminary Findings of Fact and Conclusions of Law.** A party may move the court to resolve issues of fact or law prior to submission of the case to the panel, or to furnish instructions of fact or law to the panel. Submission of the case to the panel will be deferred pending determination of the motion by the court.

(e) **Instructions to Panel.** The court shall provide the panel with a written order which states:

(1) The questions listed in AS 09.55.536, clarified or changed as the court deems appropriate to the case.

(2) That the panel is to prepare and submit to the court a list of all persons interviewed, a list of treatises or medical literature used by the panel in its deliberations, and a list of exhibits it examined (such as X-rays, slides, and other items which are not reproducible on paper).

(3) The general nature of the allegations made against each health care provider and of the answer to those allegations. Alternately, the court may submit a copy of the complaint and the answer and advise the panel that they are to address only the medical issues.

(4) That the panel or the Alaska State Medical Association is to retain copies of medical records submitted to them until further notice from the court. The court may make special provision for the safekeeping or retention by the Clerk of Court of X-rays or other original exhibits.

(5) That the panel must maintain a recording of any testimony or oral statements of witnesses and shall keep copies of all written statements the panel may receive or take, whether from witnesses, consultants, or other sources.

(6) That the panel is to review the case of each health care provider individually and render an individual, separate opinion with regard to the allegations against each health care provider.

(7) The name and location of the court personnel who might assist the panel, and that the panel may communicate with the court concerning any questions it may have, or make any requests for assistance.

(8) Any matters of fact or law on which the court has ruled, and that the panel is to review the matter in light of the court's finding and instructions on the law.

(9) That in the event parties are named as defendants who are not health care providers, the panel's consideration is to be directed to the health care providers only.

(10) That the panel is not to communicate with the parties or their attorneys, except to arrange to obtain or review an original exhibit in the possession of one of the parties, or to arrange an examination of the plaintiff, or to arrange an interview with the plaintiff or health care provider, or to arrange the scheduling of the testimony of a panel member at a deposition or at trial.

(f) **Interviews by the Panel.**

(1) If an attorney desires to be present at an interview of his or her client by the panel, the attorney must give reasonable notice of an intent to do so to the other parties so they may also appear at the interview. If the attorney for the person being interviewed does not appear, no other attorney or party may appear. An attorney appearing before the panel may not question his or her client or any other persons appearing before the panel, nor may an attorney or party cross-examine witnesses or ask questions of the panel. A person being interviewed by the panel may not be accompanied by any representative other than the person's attorney.

(2) Any party may request the panel to interview any person or party.

(g) **[Applicable to cases filed before August 7, 1997] Discovery.** Except by leave of court, no discovery may be conducted until the report of the panel has been filed or until 80 days have elapsed from the date the case is at issue, whichever is first to occur, unless discovery is further stayed for good cause by order of the court.

(g) **[Applicable to cases filed on or after August 7, 1997.] Discovery.** Except by leave of court, no discovery may be conducted until the report of the panel has been filed or until 60 days after selection of the panel, whichever is first to occur, unless discovery is further stayed for good cause by order of the court.

(Added by SCO 837 effective August 1, 1987; amended by SCO 1172 effective July 15, 1995; and by SCO 1281 effective August 7, 1997)

Note to SCO 1281: Paragraph (g) of this rule was amended by ch. 26, sec. 42, SLA 1997. According to sec. 55 of the Act, the amendment to Civil Rule 72.1 applies "to all causes of action accruing on or after the effective date of this Act." The amendment to Rule 72.1 adopted by paragraph 7 of this order applies to all cases filed on or after August 7, 1997. See paragraph 17 of this order. The change is adopted for the sole reason that the legislature has mandated the amendment.

Annotations

Cases

Under this rule, advisory panel interviews are not mandatory but merely optional. **Gerber v. Juneau Bartlett Mem. Hosp.,** Op. No. 5276, 2 P3d 74 (Alaska 2000).

PART XI. SUPERIOR COURT AND CLERKS

Rule 73. The Clerk.

(a) **When Clerk's Office Is Open.** The clerk's office with the clerk or a deputy in attendance shall be open during business hours on all days except judicial holidays and Saturdays.

(b) **Orders by Clerk.** The clerk is authorized to enter the following orders of the superior or district court without further direction by the court:

(1) Orders on consent for the substitution of attorneys.

(2) Orders on consent satisfying a judgment or an order for the payment of money, withdrawing stipulations, annulling bonds and exonerating sureties.

(3) Orders entering default for failure to plead or otherwise defend as provided in Rule 55(a).

(4) Orders upon motions and applications for issuing mesne process and issuing final process to enforce and execute judgments.

(5) Any other orders which do not require allowance or order of the court.

The clerk must forthwith notify the judge before whom the action is pending of the clerk's action in entering any such order. Any order so entered may be suspended, altered or rescinded by the court for cause shown.

(c) **Judgments by Clerk.** The clerk is authorized to enter the following judgments of the superior or district court forthwith without further direction from the court:

(1) Default judgments under Rule 55(b) upon the following proof: an affidavit that the person against whom judgment is sought is not an infant or an incompetent person, and an affidavit under the Soldiers' and Sailors' Civil Relief Act of 1940, as amended, that defendant is not in the armed forces of the United States.

(2) Judgments on offers of judgment in the circumstances set forth in Rule 68.

(d) **Notice of Orders or Judgments.** Immediately upon the entry of an order or judgment, the clerk shall give notice by distributing a copy to each party who is not in default for failure to appear.

(Adopted by SCO 5 October 9, 1959; amended by SCO 77 effective July 30, 1965; by SCO 258 effective November 15, 1976; by SCO 289 effective January 15, 1978; by SCO 447 effective November 24, 1980; by SCO 499 effective January 18, 1982; by SCO 500 effective January 18, 1982; by SCO 554 effective April 4, 1983; and by SCO 1153 effective July 15, 1994)

Note: AS 10.06.658, as enacted by ch. 166, § 1, SLA 1988, amended Civil Rule 73 by requiring the clerk of the superior court to send a copy of an order dissolving a corporation to the commissioner of commerce and economic development.

Note: Ch. 128 SLA 2002 (HB 393), Section 3, adds a new Chapter 66 to Title 45 of the Alaska Statutes, concerning the sale of business opportunities. According to Section 4 of the Act, AS 45.66.120(b) has the effect of amending Civil Rule 73 by requiring the clerk of the court to mail a copy of an order or judgment in an action under AS 45.66.120 to the attorney general.

Annotations

Cases

Notice mailed by the clerk to all counsel of the entry of judgment constituted timely notice to parties. **Whitney Bros. Plumbing & Heating v. Industrial & Commercial Constr., Inc.,** Op. No. 438, 432 P2d 533 (Alaska 1967).

Where defendant executed a confession of judgment without action which was entered as a judgment on September 18, 1986, but was not sent a copy of the judgment and did not learn of it until September 26, 1988, his motion to set aside the confession of judgment, filed October 18, 1988, was deemed timely. **Princiotta v. Municipality of Anchorage,** Op. No. 3548, 785 P2d 559 (Alaska 1990).

Rule 74. Books and Records Kept by Clerk and Entries Therein.

(a) **Civil Case File and Index.** All papers filed with the clerk shall be marked with the case number and the date of filing and shall be placed in the case file in chronological order. The clerk shall maintain an alphabetical index of every civil case filed. All parties in each case shall be included in the index.

(b) **Civil Judgments and Orders.** The clerk shall keep, in such form and manner as the administrative director of courts may prescribe, a record of every final judgment or order.

(c) **Civil Calendar.** The clerk shall prepare a calendar listing all cases scheduled for hearings and trials. The calendar shall indicate the type of proceeding and shall distinguish jury actions from nonjury actions. A copy of the calendar shall be posted in a public place within the court building.

(d) **Other Books and Records of the Clerk.** The clerk shall also keep such other books and records as may be required from time to time by the administrative director of the courts.

(e) **Records to Remain in Custody of Clerk.** Except as otherwise provided by these rules or by order of the court, no record or paper belonging to the files of the court may be taken from the office or custody of the clerk.

(f) **Use of Records by Court Officers.** If it is necessary for a judge, master, examiner, magistrate or court reporter to use pleadings or other papers for purposes of the action or proceeding, at places other than the clerk's office, courtroom or judge's chambers, the same may be taken from the office of the clerk upon the delivery to the clerk of a receipt signed by the officer who desires the use of said papers.

(g) **Records After Final Determination.**

(1) After final judgment and after the time has passed for taking an appeal or filing a petition for review, all models, diagrams, exhibits and depositions heretofore or hereafter filed in any action, shall be returned to the submitting party, without the necessity of filing any copies thereof.

(2) After final judgment, and upon the filing of a stipulation waiving and abandoning the right to appeal, to petition for review, or to move for a new trial, all such models, diagrams, exhibits and depositions may be withdrawn from the clerk's office by the submitting party, without the necessity of filing any copies thereof.

(3) If such models, diagrams, exhibits, and depositions are not so returned or withdrawn as above indicated, the clerk shall destroy the same or make such other disposition of them as the court may approve.

(4) Nothing contained in this subdivision (g) of this rule shall prevent the court, for special reasons and after notice, from making such other order with respect to any files, models, exhibits and depositions as it may deem advisable.

(h) **Documents Presented Ex Parte.** Every document presented by counsel to the court ex parte in support of an order, when signed by the court, will be deemed to be in the custody of the court. Each such document shall forthwith be delivered by counsel presenting the same to the clerk for filing, unless the judge or the judge's secretary desires to retain any such document in chambers for delivery by such judge or the judge's secretary to the clerk.

(Adopted by SCO 5 October 9, 1959; amended by SCO 152 effective April 20, 1972; by SCO 163 effective May 30, 1973; by SCO 554 effective April 4, 1983; by SCO 1098 effective January 15, 1993; by SCO 1153 effective July 15, 1994; and by SCO 1210 effective July 15, 1994)

Rule 75. Record of Proceedings—Transcript as Evidence.

(a) **Record of Proceedings.** In all actions and proceedings in the superior court there shall be kept a stenographic or electronic record of the following:

(1) All proceedings had in open court unless the parties with the approval of the judge shall specifically agree to the contrary; and

(2) Such other proceedings as may be required by court rule or order of the court.

(b) **Transcript as Evidence.** Whenever the testimony of a witness at a trial or a hearing which was stenographically reported or electronically recorded is admissible in evidence at a later trial, it may be proved by the transcripts thereof duly certified by the person who reported the testimony or by an officer of the court.

(Adopted by SCO 5 October 9, 1959; amended by SCO 465 effective June 1, 1981)

Annotations

Cases

Where one hour of testimony of each party was lost because of malfunction of recording equipment in child custody action, and evidence was opaque as to relative parental fitness, matter would be remanded for further proceedings. **Horutz v. Horutz,** Op. No. 1390, 560 P2d 397 (Alaska 1977).

Rule 76. Form of Papers.

(a) **Form in General.** All pleadings, motions, affidavits, memoranda, instructions and other papers and documents presented for filing with the clerk or intended for use by the judge, must conform to the following requirements:

(1) *Paper Size and Quality:* Documents must be 8-1/2 x 11 inches. The paper must be opaque, unglazed white paper of good quality and at least sixteen pound weight.

(2) *Typed or Hand Printed in Ink:* Text must be typed in clear and legible black typeface or hand printed in black ink.

(3) *Typeface and Size:* If typed, the text of a document, including headings and footnotes, must be at least 12 point Courier or another typeface allowed under Appellate Rule 513.5(c) if its size meets the requirements of that rule. Footers required under (a)(5) of this rule and certificates of distribution or service may be typed in a smaller font, but not smaller than 10 point.

(4) *Line Spacing:* Unless otherwise provided in these rules, text must be double-spaced or one-and-one-half spaced, except that headings and footnotes must be single-spaced, and longer quotations must be single-spaced and indented at least one-half inch on each side. Other parts of a document, including the case caption, headers and footers, signature blocks, certificates, and notarizations, should be single-spaced.

(5) *Footer:* Documents longer than one page must contain a footer that sets out the title of the document, case name, case number, and page numbering (page x of y). The title of the document and the case name may be abbreviated.

(6) *Single-Sided:* Text may only be typed or printed on one side of the paper.

(7) *Two-Hole Punched:* Documents must be two-hole punched at the top center of each page.

(8) *Stapled:* If a document is longer than one page, all pages must be stapled together at the upper left corner. Documents that are too thick to be stapled must be bound together at the top with a metal fastener (e.g., an Acco fastener).

(b) **Interlineations.** Interlineations are not permitted unless made by the court.

(c) **Exhibits.**

(1) Each page of an exhibit must be marked with the number or letter of the exhibit, the page number, and the total number of pages in the exhibit. Example: Ex. A, p. 1 of 10

(2) Exhibits must be attached to the principal document unless they are confidential. Confidential exhibits must be submitted in a sealed envelope marked with the case name, case number, number or letter of the exhibit, and name of the document to which they relate.

(d) **Information To Be Placed on First Page.**

(1) *Attorney Information.* The name, address and telephone number of the attorney appearing for a party to an action or proceeding, or of a person appearing in propria personal, should be typewritten or printed in the left-margin of the first page of the document. However, this information may be printed in the space to the left of center of the paper beginning one inch below the top edge. The typeface must be no smaller than 10 point and no larger than 12 point.

(2) *Caption.* Every document must contain a caption setting forth the title of the court, the city in which the court is located, the title of the action (i.e., the names of the parties), the case number, and the document name. This information must be formatted as follows:

(A) The title of the court and the city in which the court is located must be centered at the top of the page, beginning 1 inch below the top edge or 1/2 inch below the name, address and telephone number of the attorney or pro se party, if this information appears at the top of the page.

(B) The title of the action (i.e., the names of the parties) must be inserted below the title of the court and to the left of center of the page.

(C) A space must be reserved for the clerk's file stamp to the right of the title of the action. The case number must be inserted below this space.

(D) The document name may be centered on the page below the title of the action and the case number or placed to the right of the title of the action beneath the case number.

(3) *Title of the Action.* The complaint must include the names of all the parties in the title of the action, but in other documents it is sufficient to state the name of the first party on each side with appropriate indication of other parties ("et al" or "and others"). *Note: See Civil Rule 10(a) for other requirements related to the names of parties in complaints.*

(e) **Name and Bar Number Typed Beneath Signature Line.** The name of the person signing a pleading or paper must be typed under the signature line. If the person is an attorney, the person's Alaska Bar Association membership number must be entered following the person's name. Documents must be dated and signed in blue or black ink.

(f) **Judge's Name Typed on Orders and Judgments.** The name of the judge signing an order or judgment must be typed under the judge's signature line.

(g) **Replacing Papers Lost or Withheld.** If an original paper or pleading is lost or withheld by any person, the court may order a verified copy of the document to be filed and used in lieu of the original.

(h) **Compliance With Rule.** The clerk may refuse to accept for filing any document that does not comply with the requirements of this rule. The judge to whom the case is assigned may, in cases of emergency or necessity, permit departure from the requirements of this rule.

(Adopted by SCO 5 October 9, 1959; amended by SCO 258 effective November 15, 1976; by SCO 441 effective November 15, 1980; by SCO 567 effective July 1, 1983; by SCO 568 effective September 1, 1983; by SCO 687 effective May 1, 1986; by SCO 907 effective August 1, 1988; by SCO 931 effective January 15, 1989; by SCO 1153 effective July 15, 1994; by SCO 1210 effective July 15, 1995; by SCO 1287 effective July 15, 1998; by SCO 1344 effective August 13, 1998; by SCO 1386 effective April 15, 2000; rescinded and readopted by SCO 1415 effective October 15, 2000)

Rule 77. Motions.

(a) **Service.** All motions, orders to show cause, petitions, applications and every other such matter shall be served upon the adverse party, or, after the adverse party has appeared by counsel, upon counsel for the adverse party.

(b) **Requirements.** There shall be served and filed with the motion:

(1) legible copies of all photographs, affidavits and other documentary evidence which the moving party intends to submit in support of the motion;

(2) a brief, complete written statement of the reasons in support of the motion, which shall include a memorandum of the points and authorities upon which the moving party will rely; and

(3) an appropriate order for the court's signature in the event that the motion is granted.

(4) In addition, if a motion is filed and served on a defendant before an answer to the complaint is due under the rules, the motion must be accompanied by a notice advising the defendant of the right to file a written opposition to the motion, the time within which the opposition must be filed under Civil Rule 77(c)(2)(i), and the place where it must be filed.

(c) **Opposition.** Unless otherwise ordered by the court or otherwise stipulated by the parties with court approval, opposition to the motion or other application shall be made as follows:

(1) *Form.* Each party opposing the motion or other application shall serve and file either:

(i) legible copies of all photographs, affidavits and other documentary evidence upon which the party intends to rely; and

(ii) a brief, complete written statement of the reasons in opposition to the motion, which shall include an adequate answering brief of points and authorities; and

(iii) an appropriate order for the court's signature in the event that the motion is denied; or

(iv) a written statement that the party does not oppose the motion.

(2) *Time.* The time for filing opposition to the motion or other application shall be 10 days from the date of service of the motion or application, except as follows:

(i) for motions or other applications filed and served on defendant before an answer to the complaint is due under the rules, the time for filing opposition shall be either 10 days from the date of service, or the date the defendant's answer is due under the rules, whichever is later;

(ii) for motions to dismiss, motions for summary judgment and motions for judgment on the pleadings, the time for filing opposition shall be either 15 days from the date of service or, if the plaintiff is the movant, the date the defendant's answer is due under the rules, whichever is later; and

(iii) for motions filed under Civil Rules that prescribe their own response times (for example, Civil Rule 88 and Civil Rule 89) or that authorize expedited relief (for example, Civil Rule 77(g) or Civil Rule 65), the time for filing opposition shall be governed by the specific rule under which the motion is filed.

(d) **Reply.** Reply and supplemental materials and memoranda, if any, may be served and filed by the moving party within five days of the date of the service of the opposition to the motion.

(e) **Oral Argument.**

(1) If either party desires oral argument on the motion, that party shall request a hearing within five days after service of a responsive pleading or the time limit for filing such a responsive pleading, whichever is earlier.

(2) Except on motions to dismiss; motions for summary judgment; motions for judgment on the pleadings; other dispositive motions; motions for delivery and motions for attachment, oral argument shall be held only in the discretion of the judge. The amount of time to be allowed for oral argument shall be set by the judge.

(3) If oral argument is to be held, the argument shall be set for a date no more than 45 days from the date the request is filed or the motion is ripe for decision, whichever is later.

(f) **Disposition Without Oral Argument.** If oral argument is not heard, the court shall promptly rule on the motion and comply with Administrative Rule 3.

(g) **Expedited Consideration.** A party may move for expedited consideration of its principal motion by filing a second motion requesting relief in less time than would normally be required for the court to issue a decision.

(1) The motion must be captioned "Motion for Expedited Consideration" and must have an appropriate order on the issue of expedited consideration attached.

(2) The motion for expedited relief must comply with

other provisions of this rule, including paragraph (e) concerning any request for oral argument except as the provisions of this paragraph specify otherwise.

(3) The motion for expedited consideration must include an affidavit or other evidence showing the facts which justify expedited consideration, and the date before which a decision on the principal motion is needed.

(4) If the parties are represented by counsel, the motion for expedited consideration shall include a certification of counsel that a good faith effort has been made to resolve the issues raised with opposing counsel, but that these efforts were not successful; or, in the alternative, that it was not possible to attempt to resolve the issues with opposing counsel beforehand. The certification shall include a description of what efforts were made to resolve the issues for which expedited consideration is sought, or an explanation of why no efforts were made.

(5) The motion for expedited consideration must include proof of service; and, if the motion requests a decision before the usual time for response to the motion, must include a certificate indicating when and how the opposing party was notified of the motion, or, if the opposing party was not notified, what efforts were made to notify the opposing party and why it was not practical to notify the opposing party in a manner and at a time that a response could be made.

(6) The court may not grant the motion for expedited consideration prior to allowing the opposing party a reasonable opportunity to respond, either in person, by telephone or in writing, absent compelling reasons for a prompt decision and a showing that reasonable efforts were made to notify the opposing party of the motion for expedited consideration in time to allow a reasonable opportunity to respond.

(7) The court may not grant the principal motion prior to allowing the opposing party a reasonable opportunity to respond, either in person, by telephone or in writing, unless it clearly appears from the specific facts in the motion papers or court records that immediate and irreparable injury, loss or damage would result to the moving party before any reasonable opportunity to respond could be given. In no event will a decision be rendered on the principal motion without a response until at least 24 hours after the date of service of the principal motion or the date actual notice is given, whichever is sooner. However, this limitation does not preclude a decision in less than 24 hours on an application for relief made pursuant to Civil Rule 65(b) or any other rule or statute authorizing such action.

(h) **Stipulations.** Stipulations between counsel may be submitted in support of motions, but are not binding on the court unless otherwise specifically provided by rule.

(i) **Evidence.** When a motion is based on facts not appearing of record, the court may hear the matter on affidavits or other documentary evidence presented by the respective parties, but the court may direct that the matter be heard wholly or partly on testimony or deposition.

(j) **Frivolous Motions or Oppositions.** The presentation to the court of frivolous or unnecessary motions or frivolous or unnecessary opposition to motions, which unduly delay the course of the action proceeding, or the filing of any motion to dismiss or motion to strike for the purpose of delay where no reasonable ground appears therefor subjects counsel presenting or filing such, at the discretion of the court, to imposition of costs and attorney's fees to the opposing party, to be fixed by the court and paid to the clerk of court, and any other sanctions, which may be authorized by rule or law.

(k) **Motions for Reconsideration.** A motion to reconsider the ruling must be made within ten days after the date of notice of the ruling as defined in Civil Rule 58.1(c) unless good cause is shown why a later filing should be accepted. In no event shall a motion to reconsider a ruling be made more than ten days after the date of notice of the final judgment in the case.

(1) A party may move the court to reconsider a ruling previously decided if, in reaching its decision:

(i) The court has overlooked, misapplied or failed to consider a statute, decision or principle directly controlling; or

(ii) The court has overlooked or misconceived some material fact or proposition of law; or

(iii) The court has overlooked or misconceived a material question in the case; or

(iv) The law applied in the ruling has been subsequently changed by court decision or statute.

(2) The motion for reconsideration shall specifically state which of the grounds for reconsideration specified in the prior subparagraph exists, and shall specifically designate that portion of the ruling, the memorandum, or the record, or that particular authority, which the movant wishes the court to consider. The motion for reconsideration and supporting memorandum shall not exceed five pages.

(3) No response shall be made to a motion for reconsideration unless requested by the court, but a motion for reconsideration will ordinarily not be granted in the absence of such a request.

(4) The motion for reconsideration shall be decided by the court without oral argument. If the motion for reconsideration has not been ruled upon by the court within 30 days from the date of the filing of the motion, or within 30 days of the date of filing of a response requested by the court, whichever is later, the motion shall be taken as denied.

(5) The court, on its own motion, may reconsider a ruling at any time not later than 10 days from the date of notice of the final judgment in the case.

(*l*) **Citation of Supplemental Authorities.** When pertinent authorities come to the attention of a party after the party's memorandum has been filed, or after oral argument but before decision, the party may promptly advise the court, by letter, with a copy to adversary counsel, setting forth the citations. There must be a reference either to the page of the memorandum or to a point argued orally to which the citations pertain, but the letter may not contain argument or explanations. Any response must be made promptly and must be similarly limited.

(m) **Filings in Microfilmed Cases.** If a motion, petition or request is filed in a case that has been microfilmed and destroyed pursuant to the Records Retention Schedule, the attorney or party must attach (1) a copy of any relevant orders, judgments and other documents necessary for the court's ruling, and (2) either proof of notice pursuant to Civil Rule 5(g) or an affidavit that Rule 5(g) is not applicable. If such documents are not attached, the clerk will notify counsel that such documents must be submitted before the court will consider the motion, petition or request.

(Adopted by SCO 5 October 9, 1959; amended by SCO 49 effective January 1, 1963; by SCO 158 effective February 15, 1973; by SCO 236 effective March 1, 1976; by SCO 359 effective October 1, 1979; by SCO 367 effective August 1, 1979; by SCO 415 effective August 1, 1980; by SCO 434 effective November 1, 1980; by SCO 447 effective November 24, 1980; by SCO 554 effective April 4, 1983; by SCO 720 effective December 15, 1986; by SCO 819 effective August 1, 1987; by SCO 953 effective July 15, 1989; by SCO 1027 effective July 15, 1990; by SCO 1050 effective January 15, 1991; by SCO 1121 effective July 15, 1993; by SCO 1153 effective July 15, 1994; by SCO 1159 effective July 15, 1994; by SCO 1423 effective April 15, 2001; and by SCO 1564 effective April 15, 2005)

Editor's Note: Section 1 of Chapter 96 of the Session Laws of Alaska 1981 has the effect of changing Civil Rule 77 by establishing a procedure and time limits for court review of an income assignment order which differ from those generally applicable in civil actions.

Notes: Chapter 54 SLA 2005 (HB 95) enacted extensive amendments and new provisions related to public health, including public health emergencies and disasters. According to Section 13(a) of the Act, AS 18.15.375(c)(3), (d), and (e), and 18.15.385(d) –(k), enacted in Section 8, have the effect of amending Civil Rule 77 by adding special proceedings, timing, and pleading requirements for matters involving public health.

Annotations

Cases

I. In General.
II. Presentation and Review.
III. Opposition to Motion.

I. In General.

Under this rule a notice of hearing to set aside a default shall be served upon the adverse party. **Sanuita v. Hedberg,** Op. No. 296, 404 P2d 647 (Alaska 1965).

Where the court, upon a defendant's failure to appear, does not give three days' notice prior to entering a default, but rather allows the trial to commence in the defendant's absence, the defendant does not lose his right to a jury trial by waiver through default or by failing to appear. **Hill v. Vetter,** Op. No. 1067, 525 P2d 529 (Alaska 1974).

Failure to afford opportunity for oral argument was harmless error. **McCraken v. Davis,** Op. No. 1389, 560 P2d 771 (Alaska 1977).

This rule may not be used to circumvent rule limiting the time within which appeals may be taken. **Lowe v. Severance,** Op. No. 1442, 564 P2d 1222 (Alaska 1977).

Paragraph (k) of this rule applies to Criminal Rule 25(d)(5), so that a stipulation there under is not binding on the court. **Padie v. State,** Op. No. 1465, 566 P2d 1024 (Alaska 1977).

Stipulation for extension of time for filing memorandum in opposition to motion to dismiss is not effective when not approved by court. **Jerrel v. Kenai Peninsula Borough School District,** Op. No. 1458, 567 P2d 760 (Alaska 1977).

Failure of default judgment creditor to serve motion for issuance of deed on property subject to execution sale was error, since although no service need be made on parties in default for failure to appear, the judgment debtor was not such a party because he had appeared prior to the motion in an unsuccessful effort to have the default judgment set aside. **Law Offices of Murphy L. Clark v. Altman,** Op. No. 2811, 680 P2d 1125 (Alaska 1984).

Appellants were not improperly denied a hearing on their motion attacking the dismissal of their case because, although they filed a timely notice of hearing, that notice did not include a certificate by appellants' counsel that he had attempted to resolve the matter with opposing counsel. **Cleary Diving Service v. Thomas, Head and Greisen,** Op. No. 2873, 688 P2d 940 (Alaska 1984).

Civil Rule 77 was intended to provide a uniform procedure for handling the many and diverse types of general procedural motions that arise in the course of litigation, both civil and criminal. **Adams v. State,** Op. No. 497, 704 P2d 794 (Alaska App. 1985).

In the absence of a conflict in the evidence the trial court may rely on Civil Rule 77(k) in making fact findings based upon affidavits or other documentary evidence regarding suppression motions; where, however, the defendant testifies under oath and is subject to cross-examination, the trial court may abuse its discretion if it does not require oral testimony from the state's witnesses. **Adams v. State,** Op. No. 497, 704 P2d 794 (Alaska App. 1985).

Civil Rule 77(k), authorizing motions to be heard on affidavits, was not intended to substitute affidavits for the vital oral testimony of necessary witnesses essential in the determination of whether an accuser's constitutional right to remain silent when questioned by the police has been scrupulously honored. **Adams v. State,** Op. No. 497,704 P2d 794 (Alaska App. 1985).

Attorney had no right to jury trial on issue of whether sanctions should be imposed against him for filing frivolous, unnecessary and legally deficient pleadings in a criminal case. **Weidner v. Superior Court, Third Judicial Dist.,** Op. No. 589, 715 P2d 264 (Alaska App. 1986).

Attorney had no right to jury trial on issue of whether sanctions should be imposed against him for filing frivolous, unnecessary and legally deficient pleadings in a criminal case. **Weidner v. Superior Court, Third Judicial Dist.,** Op. No. 589, 715 P2d 284 (Alaska App. 1986).

Imposition of attorney fees and monetary sanctions against defense attorney in criminal case for filing frivolous, unnecessary and legally deficient pleadings was error requiring remand where attorney was not given notice of the charges against him nor a hearing on the issue of sanctions. **Weidner v. Superior Court, Third Judicial Dist.,** Op. No. 589, 715 P2d 264 (Alaska App. 1986).

Attorney was not entitled to a change of judge as a matter of right at hearing on sanctions against him for filing frivolous, unnecessary and legally deficient pleadings in a criminal case. **Weidner v. Superior Court, Third Judicial Dist.,** Op. No. 589, 715 P2d 264 (Alaska App. 1986).

Attorney was not entitled to discovery at hearing on sanctions against him for filing frivolous, unnecessary and legally deficient pleadings in a criminal case, since notice requirements, in conjunction with any affidavits filed by the prosecution, would alert him to the issues. **Weidner v. Superior Court, Third Judicial Dist.,** Op. No. 589, 715 P2d 264 (Alaska App. 1986).

While an appeal is pending, the trial court has jurisdiction to consider and deny a motion for reconsideration involving substantive legal error; if the court determines that the motion should be granted, the movant should obtain a stay of the appellate proceedings and a remand for the stated purpose of granting the motion. **Howard S. Lease Const. Co. v. Holly,** Op. No. 3123, 725 P2d 712 (Alaska 1986).

Where motion for reconsideration was granted during the pendency of an appeal, movant's failure to obtain a stay of the appellate proceedings and a remand was harmless error, since the stance of the trial court's action on reconsideration or otherwise show that his rights were affected. **Howard S. Lease Const. Co. v. Holly,** Op. No. 3123, 725 P2d 712 (Alaska 1986).

Where trial court in a divorce proceeding heard on shortened time a motion by the wife to accept her valuation of the couple's four mobile homes, the court did not abuse its discretion in refusing to allow the husband 10 days to respond to the motion, since only 24-hour notice of the hearing on the motion was required; moreover, the husband's attorney in fact had at least six consecutive days to respond, even if only two "working days" were included. **Brooks v. Brooks,** Op. No. 3164,733 P2d 1044 (Alaska 1987).

Defendant, under the rules of evidence, could have filed affidavits setting out his version of the facts at a suppression hearing without forfeiting his fifth amendment right to remain silent at trial. **Selig v. State,** Op. No. 785, 750 P2d 834 (Alaska App. 1988).

Requiring a criminal defendant to comply with this rule and to support his motion to suppress with affidavits of fact and memoranda of law did not impermissibly put the burden of proof on the defendant to show that evidence was illegally obtained. **Selig v. State,** Op. No. 785, 750 P2d 834 (Alaska App. 1988).

Where a defendant makes a timely pretrial suppression motion but does not substantially comply with applicable procedural rules so that the matter cannot be resolved prior to trial without disruption to the trial date or other significant prejudice to the prosecution, the defendant may be held to have forfeited his right to object to the evidence. **Selig v. State,** Op. No. 785, 750 P2d 834 (Alaska App. 1988).

When pretrial motions are not timely but are made sufficiently in advance of trial to permit their resolution without disrupting the trial or prejudicing the prosecution, it is an abuse of discretion not to resolve them and, if necessary, impose other sanctions to enforce the rules. **Selig v. State,** Op. No. 785, 750 P2d 834 (Alaska App. 1988).

In divorce case, husband's attempt to quash wife's writ of execution on the grounds of financial hardship and to offer to satisfy the obligation with alternative assets was frivolous, thus award to wife for costs involved in defending against the motion to quash was proper. **Hartland v. Hartland,** Op. No. 3459, 777 P2d 636 (Alaska 1989).

If a party desires oral argument on a motion, that party must file a timely notice of hearing. **Hermosillo v. Hermosillo,** Op. No. 3634, 797 P2d 1206 (Alaska 1990).

Motion for declaratory judgment was unnecessary where declaratory judgment was sought in pleadings. **State Dept. of Nat. Res. v. Transamerica,** Op. No. 3979, 856 P2d 766 (Alaska 1993).

Running of appellate clock terminates upon timely filing of motion for reconsideration and begins all over again after court's disposition of motion; consequently, litigants had thirty days following denial of their motion for reconsideration to appeal judgment. **Newton v. Magill,** Op. No. 4075, 872 P2d 1213 (Alaska 1994).

Superior court is obligated to carefully examine motion and any supporting materials to determine if granting motion is warranted, even if opposing party failed to respond to motion. **S.L. v. J.H.,** Op. No. 4139, 883 P2d 984 (Alaska 1994).

The limited purpose of Rule 77(k) is to remedy mistakes in judicial decision making where grounds exist, while recognizing the need for a fair and efficient administration of justice. **Neal & Company, Inc. v. Association of Village Council Presidents Regional Housing Authority,** Op. No. 4206, 895 P2d 497 (Alaska 1995).

Claim that divorced parent should not have to pay child support because he was not child's biological parent could not be raised for first time in motion for reconsideration. **Miller v. Miller,** Op. No. 4172, 890 P2d 574 (Alaska 1995).

Failure of the defendant to follow this rule's specific requirements did not relieve the superior court of its duty to exercise its independent judgment to determine if the plaintiff's motion to modify child custody support should be granted. **Howlett v. Howlett,** Op. No. 4179, 890 P2d 1125 (Alaska 1995).

A trial court's decision on a motion to reconsider will not be reversed on appeal absent an abuse of discretion. **Neal & Company, Inc. v. Association of Village Council Presidents Regional Housing Authority,** Op. No. 4206, 895 P2d 497 (Alaska 1995).

Because appellant neither alleged nor demonstrated any prejudice from trial court's error in denying oral argument prior to granting summary judgment, the denial did not constitute reversible error. **Bennett v. Hedglin,** Op. No. 5239, 995 P2d 668 (Alaska 2000).

Trial court's acceptance of arbitrator's affidavit under Civil Rule 77(l) was error because that rule only provides for submission of citations to legal authorities that come to the attention of a party after that party's memorandum has been filed; arbitrator's affidavit was not a legal authority. **Wing v. Geico Ins. Co.,** Op. No. 5366, 17 P3d 783 (Alaska 2001).

Former husband was entitled to relief under section (k) of this rule through amendment of his divorce decree, which ordered him to pay more than 50 percent of his military retirement benefits to wife, where, after entry of the decree, part of the husband's retirement benefits were reduced to the extent of payment of military disability benefits; under the Uniformed Services Former Spouses' Protection Act, 10 U.S.C.S. § 1408, the court did not have jurisdiction to award any of the disability benefits to the wife. **Cline v. Cline,** Op. No. 5803, 90 P.3d 147(Alaska 2004).

II. Presentation and Review.

A motion to withdraw a jury demand presented only by the plaintiff and not consented to by the defendant and not accompanied by any supporting papers or memoranda cannot properly be granted. **Hill v. Vetter,** Op. No. 1067, 525 P2d 529 (Alaska 1974).

Motion to reconsider denial of attorney's fees made before Civil Rule 77(m) was effective would be treated as motion for relief from judgment. **Miller v. McManus,** Op. No. 1361, 558 P2d 891 (Alaska 1977).

Appeal from denial of motion to reconsider denial of attorney's fees presents only question of merits of reconsideration; not merits of underlying order. **Miller v. McManus,** Op. No. 1361, 558 P2d 891 (Alaska 1977).

Motion to reconsider denial of attorney's fees is addressed to discretion of trial court and decision will be reversed only if discretion was abused. **Miller v. McManus,** Op. No. 1361, 558 P2d 891 (Alaska 1977).

Order denying reconsideration of denial of attorneys' fees, which was entered without explanation could not be reviewed and would be remanded so that trial court could again pass upon motion, stating reasons for its decision. **Miller v. McManus,** Op. No. 1361, 558 P2d 891 (Alaska 1977).

One and one-half page memorandum devoid of authorities was not statement required by Civil Rule 77(b)(2), so that motion to dismiss was frivolous and issue was not joined, precluding award of attorney's fees. **State v. Alaska International Air, Inc.,** Op. No. 1409, 562 P2d 1064 (Alaska 1977).

Motion to reconsider does not extend the time for taking an appeal. **Corso v. Commissioner of Education,** Op. No. 1412, 563 P2d 246 (Alaska 1977).

Motion to reconsider does not terminate the running of the time for filing an appeal from the judgment or order sought to be reconsidered. **Brown v. State,** Op. No. 1418, 563 P2d 275 (Alaska 1977).

Appeal of motion to reconsider does not bring merits of judgment sought to be reconsidered before Supreme Court. **Brown v. State,** Op. No. 1418, 563 P2d 275 (Alaska 1977).

Denial of motion to reconsider will be reversed only for abuse of discretion, which exists when Supreme Court is left with definite and firm conviction on the whole record that the trial judge has made a mistake. **Brown v. State,** Op. No. 1418, 563 P2d 275 (Alaska 1977).

Where plaintiff had received ample notice from opinion on earlier appeal but it was incumbent upon him to promptly take steps to prosecute claim upon his release from prison, and during seven-month period had taken no such steps, denial of motion to reconsider dismissal for lack of prosecution was not abuse of discretion. **Brown v. State,** Op. No. 1418, 563 P2d 275 (Alaska 1977).

Fact that administrative agency was close to time limit for completing investigation did not justify proceeding under accelerated motion practice procedures where court would have been justified in extending such time limit. **Allstate Ins. Co. v. Municipality of Anchorage,** Op. No. 1913, 599 P2d 140 (Alaska 1979).

Where partial summary judgment was granted on March 21, and proposed findings of fact and conclusions of law were lodged with the court and served on other party on March 29, but not signed by the court until September 16, a motion for reconsideration filed on September 26 was timely. **Fairbanks Correctional Center v. Williamson,** Op. No. 1937, 600 P2d 743 (Alaska 1979).

Husband's motion entitled Motion for Reconsideration, filed 10 days after entry of divorce decree, was in effect a motion to alter or amend the judgment; consequently, the trial court did not lack jurisdiction 37 days later to modify the property division in the decree, notwithstanding contention that the trial court's failure to grant reconsideration within 20 days deprived it of jurisdiction. **Julsen v. Julsen,** Op. No. 3211, 741 P2d 642 (Alaska 1987).

Husband's claims that wife's motion for entry of judgment for unpaid health care expenses due under divorce decree failed to state its asserted grounds for relief with particularity and lacked a sufficient supporting memorandum was rejected. The motion set forth the amount prayed for as well as the relevant provisions in the divorce decree entitling her to that amount; moreover, her memorandum in support of the motion, filed the same day as the motion, as well as her affidavit, provided information sufficient to satisfy this rule requiring a supporting memorandum. **Cedergreen v. Cedergreen,** Op. No. 3687, 811 P2d 784 (Alaska 1991).

A motion for reconsideration cannot be used as a means to seek an extension of time for the presentation of additional evidence on the merits of the claim. **Neal & Company, Inc. v. Association of Village Council Presidents Regional Housing Authority,** Op. No. 4206, 895 P2d 497 (Alaska 1995).

Denial of motion to reconsider was not clear error. The motion did not contain any legal proposition that differs from those presented in opposition to the original motion for summary judgment. Furthermore, the court could not reconsider its ruling based on evidence that was not before it at the time it made its original decision. **Neal & Company, Inc. v. Association of Village Council Presidents Regional Housing Authority,** Op. No. 4206, 895 P2d 497 (Alaska 1995).

Where defenses of mistake or misrepresentation in the execution of a guaranty were not asserted, those defenses were waived and could not be asserted on appeal. **Still v. Cunningham,** Op. No. 5825 (Alaska 2004).

III. Opposition to Motion.

Dismissal of his client's case with prejudice was held too drastic a sanction for attorney's failure to file affidavit or statement in opposition to motion for dismissal with prejudice nor a written statement that he would not oppose the motion until the day of hearing. **Mely v. Morris,** Op. No. 320, 409 P2d 979 (Alaska 1966).

When an objection is made to the late filing of papers in opposition to a motion for a preliminary injunction, the trial judge must decide whether he will enforce this rule or grant the moving party additional time to meet any new matter contained in the late filed papers. He should consider whether the late filing will be an injustice to the moving party. **Channel Flying, Inc. v. Bernhardt,** Op. No. 530, 451 P2d 570 (Alaska 1969).

Where late filed papers in opposition to a motion for a preliminary injunction raise factual matters which the moving parties must meet if they are to succeed in their efforts to obtain a preliminary injunction, the trial judge, in lieu of enforcing the sanction for late filing or refusing to consider late filed papers, should continue the hearing and allow the moving parties reasonable opportunity to meet these matters and any failure to do so is a mistake, and an abuse of discretion. In such a situation, the case will be remanded for appropriate action prior to a hearing and decision on the motion. **Channel Flying, Inc. v. Bernhardt,** Op. No. 530, 451 P2d 570 (Alaska 1969).

Notwithstanding the former rule which authorized the court to assume that a party who did not resist a motion to dismiss consented to such notion, the court should scrutinize the motion and supporting memorandum in order to determine whether the granting of the motion would be proper. **Schandelmeier v. Winchester Western,** Op. No. 1013, 520 P2d 70 (Alaska 1974).

Where a reviewing court reverses the trial court's dismissal of action, the trial court on remand is empowered to assess costs or attorney fees on plaintiff's trial counsel for failure to oppose the initial motion to dismiss. **Schandelmeier v. Winchester Western,** Op. No. 1013, 520 P2d 70 (Alaska 1974).

On a motion to dismiss, it is not the duty of the trial court to supply points and authorities for either side, but the court may not accept one party's law simply because opposing party fails to adequately respond. **State v. Johnson,** Op. No. 1069, 525 P2d 532 (Alaska 1974).

The effect of this rule that a party failing to serve items in opposition to a motion will be deemed as having consented to the granting of the motion imposes a very severe sanction which should be imposed with great caution by the trial court. In no case should the court replace or in any way minimize its duty to exercise its independent judgment. **State v. Johnson,** Op. No. 1069, 525 P2d 532 (Alaska 1974).

Failure to respond to motion for summary judgment within 15 days does not create absolute right to summary judgment in favor of the moving party. **Dome Laboratories v. Farrell,** Op. No. 1917, 599 P2d 152 (Alaska 1979).

Whether an error in ruling on a motion for attorney's fees before the opposing party has an opportunity to respond is prejudicial or harmless depends on whether, as a matter of law, the party denied the opportunity to respond could not have prevailed on the issue of attorney's fees. **Bowman v. Blair,** Op. No. 4169, 889 P2d 1069 (Alaska 1995).

It is error for the court to rule on a motion for an award of attorney's fees before the opposing party is given an opportunity to respond. **Bowman v. Blair,** Op. No. 4169, 889 P2d 1069 (Alaska 1995).

In absence of compelling reason, trial court abused its discretion in granting motion for reconsideration without affording nonmoving party opportunity to respond. **Boone v. Gipson,** Op. No. 4364, 920 P2d 746 (Alaska 1996).

Where the superior court's order granting the wife's motion to reconsider its earlier order expressly invited the husband to respond, the order substantially tracked the requirements of subsection (k)(3) of this rule. **Mattfield v. Mattfield,** Op. No. 6003, 133 P.3d 667 (Alaska 2006).

Rule 78. Findings, Conclusions, Judgments and Orders—Preparation and Submission.

(a) **Preparation and Submission—Service.** Unless otherwise ordered by the court, counsel for the successful party to an action or proceeding shall prepare in writing and file and serve on each of the other parties proposed findings of fact, conclusions of law, judgments and orders. In a case in which the custody of children is at issue, a party required to prepare findings of fact, conclusions of law, or a judgment or order pertaining to that issue shall serve and file them within 10 days after the day on which the judge announces on the record that the party is to prepare them, pursuant to Rule 58.1(a)(1). Proof of service on the other parties must be on a separate document.

(b) **Objections.** Within 5 days after service of any of the documents mentioned in paragraph (a), a party may file and serve a written detailed statement of objections to any such document and the reasons therefor. If objections are filed and served within the time specified herein, the court may thereafter require the attorneys interested to appear before it, or it may sign the document as prepared by counsel for the successful party or as modified by the court.

(c) **Punitive Damages Award.** When punitive damages are awarded, the party preparing the proposed judgment shall serve on the Attorney General in Juneau a notice entitled "Notice of Award of Punitive Damages" and a copy of the proposed judgment.

(d) **Order Upon Stipulation.** When a party desires an order of court pursuant to stipulation, the party shall title the document "Stipulation and Order" and shall endorse at the end of the instrument the words "It is so ordered" with the date and a blank line for the signature of the judge. The word "Judge" shall appear at the end of the blank line. The name of the judge, if known, shall be typed immediately under the signature line prior to presentation for signature. A stipulation extending time or providing for a continuance shall state the grounds therefor.

(e) **Instruments on Which Judgment Entered.** In all cases in which a judgment upon a written instrument is entered, such instrument shall be filed with the court, and unless the court otherwise orders, it shall be canceled by marks and writing upon its face. The clerk shall retain the same in the files unless otherwise directed by the court.

(f) **Form of Judgments.** Judgments for the payment of money must be in the form required by Civil Rule 58.2.

(Adopted by SCO 5 October 9, 1959; amended by SCO 554 effective April 4, 1983; by SCO 580 effective February 1, 1984; by SCO 616 effective May 15, 1985; by SCO 1153 effective July 15, 1994; and by SCO 1415 effective October 15, 2000)

Note: Sections 41, 43, 45, and 46 of chapter 87 SLA 1997 amend AS 25.20.050(n), AS 25.24.160(d), AS 25.24.210(e), and AS 25.24.230(i), respectively, to require that an order or acknowledgement of paternity, a divorce decree, a petition for dissolution of marriage, and a dissolution decree include the social security number of each party to the action and each child whose rights are being addressed. According to § 151 of the Act, these provisions have the effect of amending Civil Rules 52, 58, 78, and 90.1 by requiring the court to include social security numbers, if ascertainable, of parties and children in certain petitions, pleadings, and judgments.

Cross References

CROSS REFERENCE: AS 09.17.020(j)

Annotations

Cases

Noncompliance with subdivisions (a) and (b) of Rule 78 does not in itself require a reversal of the judgment, and an appellant claiming non-compliance was required to show that she had been prejudiced in some way, which she failed to do. **Briggs v. Kelly,** Op. No. 115, 376 P2d 715 (Alaska 1962).

Under Civil Rule 78(b) the trial judge should have waited five days before acting upon the supplemental opinion submitted to him. **City of Anchorage v. Chugach Electric Association,** Op. No. 231, 394 P2d 673 (Alaska 1964).

Where there was no claim or showing by appellant that he had a mind to serve and file a statement of written objections to supplemental judgment within the five days specified by Civil Rule 78(b), judge's failure to wait out the five days before signing supplemental judgment was not prejudicial. **City of Anchorage v. Chugach Electric Association,** Op. No. 231, 394 P2d 673 (Alaska 1964).

Noncompliance with Civil Rule 78(a) and (b) did not require reversal where appellants did not make a showing that they had been prejudiced by the terms of the judgment and how they would have moved to modify it if they had been served in compliance with the rule. **Sanuita v. Common Laborer's and Hod Carriers Union,** Op. No. 290,402 P2d 199 (Alaska 1965).

Under this rule the court entered an order on the basis of a stipulation converting an instrument filed in the superior court in a personal injury case and captioned as "payment into court of policy limits and costs to date" into an offer of judgment in the meaning of Civil Rule 68. **Albritton v. Estate of Larson,** Op. No. 413, 428 P2d 379 (Alaska 1967).

Absent a showing of prejudice or in what respect plaintiff would have objected to a proposed judgment dismissing a complaint contesting a bond election, the signing of a judgment four days after the hearing rather than providing a five-day period for filing of objections after service of the proposed judgment, is harmless error. **Jefferson v. Greater Anchorage Area Borough,** Op. No. 536, 451 P2d 730 (Alaska 1969).

It is not the intent of this rule to delegate to counsel for the successful party the trial judge's primary duty of finding the facts under Rule 52. **Fairbanks Builders, Inc. v. Morton DeLima, Inc.,** Op. No. 682, 483 P2d 194 (Alaska 1971).

Where a defendant's motion for relief from judgment alleges they were denied the opportunity to object to the judgment, such motion is not based on an error of law. It therefore need not be brought within 30 days from entry of the judgment. **Alaska Placer Co. v. Lee,** Op. No. 840, 502 P2d 128 (Alaska 1972).

A judgment is not illegal if it is signed in chambers rather than rendered in open court. **Jefferson v. City of Anchorage,** Op. No. 930, 513 P2d 1099 (Alaska 1973).

Where the court announces its decision regarding the main issue in a case on June 8th, where the plaintiff submits on June 27th proposed findings, which the defendant objects to where the proposed partial judgment is entered on August 1st, and where findings of fact, conclusions of law, and final judgment are entered on January 12th, the defendant is not denied the five-day period within which to object to the proposed findings, even though he receives the findings of fact and conclusions of law with respect to the final judgment on January 9th. The court is merely acting within its authority to modify documents which had earlier been submitted to it. **Moran v. Kenai Towing and Salvage, Inc.,** Op. No. 1056, 523 P2d 1237 (Alaska 1974).

The trial court's failure to hold a hearing on appellant's objections to appellee's proposed findings and conclusions is not error; such a hearing is discretionary. **Urban Development Co. v. Dekreon,** Op. No. 1083, 526 P2d 325 (Alaska 1974).

Provision in this rule for written objections to findings of fact is discretionary. **Frontier Saloon, Inc. v. Short,** Op. No. 1345, 557 P2d 779 (Alaska 1976).

Defendant did not waive right to challenge judgment where it did not object under Civil Rule 78(b) but filed timely Rule 59(f) motion to amend judgment. **Beech Aircraft Corp. v. Harvey,** Op. No. 1338, 558 P2d 879 (Alaska 1976).

A trial court is entitled to adopt findings and conclusions prepared by counsel so long as they reflect the court's independent view of the weight of the evidence. **Industrial Indemnity Co. v. Wick Const. Co.,** Op. No.

2791, 680 P2d 1100 (Alaska 1984).

When judgment is entered on a secured note, the note merges with judgment, and any further proceedings will be to enforce the judgment rather than the note. **Moening v. Alaska Mut. Bank,** Op. No. 3274, 751 P2d 5 (Alaska 1988).

A judgment recovered upon a promissory note secured by a deed of trust did not merge the deed of trust nor operate as a discharge, abandonment, or release of the deed of trust; in essence, the judgment creditor ended up with a secured judgment. **Moening v. Alaska Mut. Bank,** Op. No. 3274, 751 P2d 5 (Alaska 1988).

Although trial court could have canceled promissory note after entering judgment on the note, conditionally canceling the note was not an abuse of discretion. **Moening v. Alaska Mut. Bank,** Op. No. 3274, 751 P2d 5 (Alaska 1988).

Rule 79. Costs—Taxation and Review.

(a) **Allowance to Prevailing Party.** Unless the court otherwise directs, the prevailing party is entitled to recover costs allowable under paragraph (f) that were necessarily incurred in the action. The amount awarded for each item will be the amount specified in this rule or, if no amount is specified, the cost actually incurred by the party to the extent this cost is reasonable.

(b) **Cost Bill.** To recover costs, the prevailing party must file and serve an itemized and verified cost bill, showing the date costs were incurred, within 10 days after the date shown in the clerk's certificate of distribution on the judgment. Failure of a party to file and serve a cost bill within 10 days, or such additional time as the court may allow, will be construed as a waiver of the party's right to recover costs. The prevailing party must have receipts, invoices, or other supporting documentation for each item claimed. This documentation must be available to other parties for inspection and copying upon request and must be presented to the clerk upon request. Documentation may be filed only if requested by the clerk or in response to an objection.

(c) **Objection and Reply.** A party may object to a cost bill by filing and serving an objection within 7 days after service of the cost bill. The prevailing party may respond to an objection by filing and serving a reply within 5 days after service of the objection.

(d) **Taxing of Costs by Clerk.** Promptly upon expiration of the time for filing objections, or if an objection is filed, the time for filing a reply, the clerk shall issue an itemized award of costs allowable under this rule. No cost bill hearing will be held unless requested by the clerk. If a hearing is held, it will be limited to issues identified by the clerk in the notice of hearing. The clerk may deny costs requested by the prevailing party on grounds that

(1) the cost is not allowed under paragraph (f);

(2) the party failed to provide an adequate description or adequate supporting documentation following a request by the clerk or another party; or

(3) the amount claimed by the prevailing party is unreasonable.

The clerk may not deny costs on grounds that the costs were not necessarily incurred in the action. If a party objects on this basis, the party must seek review under paragraph (e) of the clerk's action in awarding the cost.

(e) **Review by Court.** A party aggrieved by the clerk's action in awarding costs may file a motion for review of the clerk's award. The motion must be filed and served within five days after the date shown on the clerk's certificate of distribution on the award. The motion must particularly designate each ruling of the clerk to which objection is made. Matters not so designated will not be considered by the court. Costs awarded by the clerk are presumed to be reasonable.

(f) **Allowable Costs.** The following items are the only items that will be allowed as costs:

(1) the filing fee;

(2) fees for service of process allowable under Administrative Rule 11 or postage when process is served by mail;

(3) other process server fees allowable under Administrative Rule 11;

(4) the cost of publishing notices required by law or by these rules;

(5) premiums paid on undertakings, bonds, or security stipulations where required by law, ordered by the court, or necessary to secure some right accorded in the action;

(6) the cost of taking and transcribing a deposition allowed by Civil Rule 30(a) or 31(a) (including a deposition that is ordered by the court or agreed to by the parties under those rules), as follows:

(A) the court reporter's fee and travel expenses to communities where a local court reporter is not available;

(B) expenses allowed by Civil Rule 30.1(e) for recording, editing, or using an audio or audio-visual deposition; and

(C) the cost of the original plus one copy of the transcript;

(7) witness fees allowed under Administrative Rule 7;

(8) the fee of an interpreter or translator for a witness when that witness is entitled to a fee under Administrative Rule 7;

(9) travel costs allowed under paragraph (g) of this rule;

(10) long distance telephone charges for telephonic participation by an attorney or party at court proceedings, depositions, the meeting of the parties required by Civil Rule 26(f), and interviews of witnesses other than the party;

(11) charges paid by the prevailing party's attorney for computerized legal research;

(12) copying costs for paper copies, photographs, and

microfilm, the cost of scanning, imaging, coding, and creating electronic media files, such as computer diskettes or tapes, and the cost of duplicating text files or otherwise copying documents or data in an electronic medium, as follows:

(A) for copies from the court, a copy center, or a person or entity other than the prevailing party's attorney, the amount charged for the copies; and

(B) for copies from the prevailing party's attorney, the amount charged by the attorney or $.15 per copy, whichever is less;

(13) exhibit preparation costs;

(14) the cost of transcripts ordered by the court;

(15) other costs allowed by statute; and

(16) any sales or other taxes necessarily incurred by the party in connection with a cost allowed in this subsection.

(g) **Travel Costs.**

(1) Travel costs will be allowed for

(A) one attorney to attend trial, hearings on dispositive motions, settlement conferences, and the meeting of the parties required by Civil Rule 26(f), but only if no local attorney is present; if more than one out-of-town attorney attends a proceeding at which no local attorney is present, travel costs will be allowed for the attorney who traveled the shortest distance to the trial site;

(B) one attorney to attend depositions, interviews of witnesses who are not deposed, and meetings to review documents produced in the course of discovery;

(C) one legal assistant or investigator to interview witnesses who are not deposed or to review documents produced in the course of discovery; and

(D) witnesses to the extent permitted by Administrative Rule 7.

(2) Travel costs are subject to the following limitations:

(A) air fare is allowed at the coach class fare or the actual fare, whichever is less;

(B) ground transportation, including car rental, is allowed outside the traveler's home city; and

(C) food and lodging is allowed at the same per diem rate allowed for court employees.

(3) In unusually complex cases, the court may allow a prevailing party to recover travel costs for more than one attorney to participate in the activities described in section (g)(1)(A) of this rule. To request travel costs for more than one attorney, the prevailing party must file a motion for court review of the clerk's award as provided in paragraph (e) and must include supporting documentation for each item claimed. These costs should not be included in the cost bill filed with the clerk.

(4) To recover travel costs, the prevailing party must include the following information for each trip: the name of the traveler, whether the traveler is an attorney, legal assistant, or investigator, the reasons for the travel, and the travel dates.

(h) **Equitable Apportionment Under AS 09.17.080.** In a case in which damages are apportioned among the parties under AS 09.17.080, costs must be apportioned and awarded according to the provisions of Civil Rule 82(e).

(Adopted by SCO 5 October 9, 1959; amended by SCO 56 effective November 1, 1963; by SCO 258 effective November 15, 1976; by SCO 554 effective April 4, 1983; by SCO 1085 effective January 15, 1992; by SCO 1118 effective July 15, 1993; by SCO 1153 effective July 15, 1994; by SCO 1200 effective July 15, 1995; by SCO 1246 effective July 15, 1996; and by SCO 1279 effective July 31, 1997; rescinded and readopted by SCO 1306 effective January 15, 1998; amended by SCO 1340 effective January 15, 1999; and by SCO 1631 effective April 16, 2007)

Note: AS 25.25.313(c), added by § 6 of ch. 57 SLA 1995 (the Uniform Interstate Family Support Act), has the effect of amending Civil Rule 79 by requiring the court to award costs and fees against a party who requests a hearing primarily for delay in a support proceeding listed in AS 25.25.301.

Note: In 1997 the legislature enacted AS 18.16.030(m), which provides that a filing fee may not be required of, and court costs may not be assessed against, a minor in a proceeding to bypass parental consent to an abortion. According to ch. 14, § 10 SLA 1997, AS 18.16.030(m) has the effect of amending Administrative Rule 9, Civil Rule 79, and Appellate Rule 508 by prohibiting filing fees and assessment of court costs in certain actions. Instead of amending individual rules to implement AS 18.16.030, the supreme court has adopted a separate rule on judicial bypass proceedings in the superior court and a separate rule on judicial bypass appeals. See Probate Rule 20 & Appellate Rule 220.

Note: Chapter 94 SLA 1998 adopts AS 46.03.761, which allows the Department of Environmental Conservation to impose administrative penalties against an entity that fails to construct or operate a public water supply system in compliance with state law or a term or condition imposed by the department. According to section 5 of the act, subsection (j) of this statute has the effect of amending Civil Rules 79 and 82 by allowing the recovery of full reasonable attorney fees and costs in an action to collect administrative penalties assessed under AS 46.03.761.

Note: Chapter 136 SLA 03 (HB 151) amends Chapters 10 and 45 of Title 9 of the Alaska Statutes relating to claims and court actions for defects in the design, construction, and remodeling of certain dwellings and limits on when certain court actions may be brought. According to Section 4(2) of the Act, AS 09.45.889(b) has the effect of amending Civil Rule 79 by allowing the court to deny costs to a claimant in the situation described in AS 09.45.889(b), even if the claimant is the prevailing party.

Annotations

Cases

Ten-day period for service and filing of a cost bill commenced only at the date of docketing of the formal judgment and not at the date of docketing of the verdict without any direction by the court as to the entry of judgment. **Patterson v. Cushman,** Op. No. 233, 394 P2d 657 (Alaska 1964).

Appellant who did not serve cost bill and notice waived its right to recover costs. **M-B Contracting Company v. Davis,** Op. No. 275, 399 P2d 433 (Alaska 1965).

Taxing of costs rests in the sound discretion of the trial court. **Beaulieu v. Elliott,** Op. No. 443, 434 P2d 665 (Alaska 1968).

Refusal to allow as costs expenses incident to the taking of depositions was no abuse of discretion where in a personal injury case the prevailing plaintiff had failed to point out what depositions were involved, when they were taken, or when the concession of liability was made by the defendant. **Beaulieu v. Elliott,** Op. No. 443, 434 P2d 665 (Alaska 1968).

Failure to contest costs within the time limit of this rule bars raising the issue on appeal. **A.R.C. Industries, Inc. v. State,** Op. No. 1283, 551 P2d 951 (Alaska 1976).

Trial courts award of costs will be affirmed unless there has been a clear abuse of discretion. **Kaps Transport, Inc. v. Henry,** Op. No. 1527, 572 P2d 72 (Alaska 1977).

Where defendant could properly defend in main suit by prosecuting cross-claim, costs for expert witness fees were properly charged to cross-claim defendant. **Kaps Transport, Inc. v. Henry,** Op. No. 1527, 572 P2d 72 (Alaska 1977).

Allowance of costs for unused depositions of key witness who testified at trial was not abuse of discretion. **Kaps Transport, Inc. v. Henry,** Op. No. 1527, 572 P2d 72 (Alaska 1977).

An award of costs to the prevailing parties which included expenses incurred by their attorney for travel, food and lodging was not an abuse of discretion where the attorney had to travel from his office in Juneau to Nome for the proceedings. **Davis v. Hallett,** Op. No. 1772, 587 P2d 1170 (Alaska 1978).

Alaska does not include prejudgment interest among the items allowed as costs. **Guin v. Ha,** Op. No. 1810, 591 P2d 1281 (Alaska 1979).

While attorney's fees are costs, they are not covered by the literal requirements of Civil Rule 79(b). **State v. University of Alaska,** Op. No. 2303, 624 P2d 807 (Alaska 1981).

Trial court did not abuse its discretion in permitting a request for attorney's fees thirteen days after judgment. **State v. University of Alaska,** Op. No. 2303, 624 P2d 807 (Alaska 198 1).

The taxing of costs for witness fees is governed by Civil Rule 83 and Administrative Rule 7(c) rather than the general provisions of Civil Rule 79(b). **Miller v. Sears,** Op. No. 2447, 636 P2d 1183 (Alaska 1981).

The premium on a supersedeas bond was properly included in an award of costs. **Isaacson Steel v. Armco Steel,** Op. No. 2466, 640 P2d 812 (Alaska 1982).

Filing of bill of costs prior to entry of judgment violated this rule, but did not constitute a waiver of the right to recover costs. **Isaacson Steel v. Armco Steel,** Op. No. 2466, 640 P2d 812 (Alaska 1982).

Superior court erred in awarding costs at the time judgment was entered because it prevented the losing party from objecting at a hearing on costs before the clerk of the court to the inclusion of specific expenditures in the award, which in turn prevented these objections from being considered on appeal. **Isaacson Steel v. Armco Steel,** Op. No. 2466, 640 P2d 812 (Alaska 1982).

Award of air travel costs incurred by prevailing party to bring its Seattle-based attorneys to Alaska for trial was not abuse of discretion. **Eagle Air v. Corroon, Etc.,** Op. No. 2538, 648 P2d 1000 (Alaska 1982).

Given previous conduct of defendant in removing assets from the state, trial court was justified in appointing an individual to supervise and prevent the removal or destruction of defendant's assets, which were the subject of a prejudgment attachment, and ordering defendant to pay the reasonable cost of the individual's employment. **Eagle Air v. Corroon, Etc.,** Op. No. 2538, 648 P2d 1000 (Alaska 1982).

Refusal to award food costs incurred in the taking of depositions was not abuse of discretion. **Truckweld Equipment Co. v. Swenson Trucking,** Op. No. 2545, 649 P2d 234 (Alaska 1982).

Where the depositions in question were not used solely for discovery purposes, but were used to prepare for and to assert a motion to dismiss, trial court did not abuse its discretion in requiring the losing party to pay for the cost of the depositions. **Gold Bondholders, Etc. v. Atchison, Topeka and Santa Fe Ry. Co.,** Op. No. 2608, 658 P2d 776 (Alaska 1983).

It was within the superior court's discretion to affirm an award of travel expenses necessarily incurred in taking deposition used to prepare for and to assert a pre-trial motion to dismiss. **Gold Bondholders, Etc. v. Atchison, Topeka and Santa Fe Ry. Co.,** Op. No. 2608, 658 P2d 776 (Alaska 1983).

The Civil Rules do not preclude a party from requesting attorney's fees following the entry of an interlocutory judgment. **Brunet v. Dresser Olympic,** Op. No. 2641, 660 P2d 846 (Alaska 1983).

Absent the discretionary imposition by the trial court of a time limit for the filing of attorney's fees, the appropriate time within which a request for attorney's fees may be filed is a reasonable time after the entry of a judgment from which an appeal may be taken. **Brunet v. Dresser Olympic,** Op. No. 2641, 660 P2d 846 (Alaska 1983).

Although attorney for wife in divorce action failed to meet trial court's deadline for motion and affidavit on attorney's fee, trial court did not abuse its discretion in awarding attorney's fees on the late motion. **Gabaig v. Gabaig,** Op. No. 3032, 717 P2d 835 (Alaska 1986).

Where allegedly premature submission of cost bill did not deprive the losing party of a timely hearing on the costs, it would have been "senseless formalism" to hold that the cost bill was untimely. **Fairbanks North Star Borough v. Tundra Tours,** Op. No. 3052, 719 P2d 1020 (Alaska 1986).

Where notice of cost hearing was not served on the losing party, trial court judgment granting the prevailing party's request for costs was error requiring remand. **Matanuska Elec. Association, Inc. v. Weissler,** Op. No. 3089, 723 P2d 600 (Alaska 1986).

Trial court could not award the State as the prevailing party expenses for travel, paralegal assistance, and computer research time without first determining what portion of those expenses were necessarily incurred. **Atlantic Richfield Co. v. State,** Op. No. 3096, 723 P2d 1249 (Alaska 1986).

A contribution-claim defendant is not a prevailing party entitled to costs and attorney's fees when it secures summary judgment against the contribution-claimant by settling with the injured plaintiff. **Foss Alaska Line, Inc. v. Northland Services,** Op. No. 3112, 724 P2d 523 (Alaska 1986).

Attendance at trial by corporate plaintiff's representative, who did not function as an attorney or expert witness, was not a compensable cost. **Dahle v. Atlantic Richfield Co.,** Op. No. 3120, 725 P2d 1069 (Alaska 1986).

This rule did not make an award of expert witness fees in excess of the $25.00 per hour authorized by the Alaska Administrative Rules permissible. **Norris v. Gatts,** Op. No. 3187, 738 P2d 344 (Alaska 1987).

Party could not on appeal contest the cost award after failing to contest the cost award at the superior court level as required by this rule. **Ursin Seafoods v. Keener Packing Co.,** Op. No. 3217, 741 P2d 1175 (Alaska 1987).

Expert fees in preparing exhibits may not be recovered as costs under this rule's "producing exhibits" provision. **CTA Architects v. Active Erectors,** Op. No. 3527, 781 P2d 1364 (Alaska 1989).

Computer research and paralegal expenses are correctly characterized as costs recoverable under this rule and may be awarded in full. **CTA Architects v. Active Erectors,** Op. No. 3527, 781 P2d 1364 (Alaska 1989).

Attorney fees are not recoverable under this rule. **Alaska Federal S & L v. Bernhardt,** Op. No. 3562, 794 P2d 579 (Alaska 1990).

Paralegal services and document production expenses were properly characterized as costs under this rule. **Alaska Federal S & L v. Bernhardt,** Op. No. 3562, 794 P2d 579 (Alaska 1990).

Paralegal expenses which are necessarily incurred are recoverable under this rule. **Yurioff v. American Honda Motor Co.,** Op. No. 3648, 803 P2d 386 (Alaska 1990).

For award of attorney fees to the State, trial court could order State's counsel to itemize the hours and nature of the work spent on the case. **Lyman v. State,** Op. No. 3797, 824 P2d 703 (Alaska 1992).

In a multi-claim, multi-defendant case where the moving party won on some claims and lost on others, argument that request for costs had to be appropriately apportioned so that only those costs incurred as part of the moving party's winning claims would be the subject of the cost award was rejected. **Anchorage v. Frank Coluccio Const. Co.,** Op. No. 3808, 826 P2d 316 (Alaska 1992).

Argument that deposition costs may be awarded only where depositions are actually used at trial, or where depositions are actually relied upon in ruling on a pre-trial motion, was rejected. **Bozarth v. Atlantic Richfield Oil Co.,** Op. No. 3843, 833 P2d 2 (Alaska 1992).

Where defendant prevailed in wrongful death action, trial court erred in imposing liability for costs and fees against decedent's estate, since action was brought on behalf of surviving statutory beneficiaries, not on behalf of estate. **In re Soldotna Air Crash Litigation,** Op. No. 3859, 835 P2d 1215 (Alaska 1992).

Trial court did not abuse its discretion in refusing to impose costs and fees upon nonprevailing plaintiffs in wrongful death action since, although captions in several of the complaints listed plaintiffs as individuals, in substance plaintiffs brought suit as decedents' personal representatives. **In re Soldotna Air Crash Litigation,** Op. No. 3859, 835 P2d 1215 (Alaska 1992).

Post-judgment attorney's fees in civil actions may not be awarded under this rule; rule is limited to costs other than attorney's fees and only relates to costs expended up to time of judgment. **Torrey v. Hamilton,** Op. No. 4073, 872 P2d 186 (Alaska 1994).

Trial court did not abuse its discretion in awarding $18,323 for computerized research to prevailing party. **Sever v. Alaska Pulp Corp.,** Op. No. 4420, 931 P2d 354 (Alaska 1996).

Award of expert costs incurred in preparation of necessary exhibits was proper even though expert did not testify. **Matanuska-Susitna Borough School v. State,** Op. No. 4470, 931 P2d 391 (Alaska 1997).

Alaska Wage and Hour Act, prior to its amendment in August 1995, did not permit award of attorney fees and costs to prevailing employer. **Grimes v. Kinney Shoe Corp.,** Op. No. 4815, 938 P2d 997 (Alaska 1997).

Final findings of fact and conclusions of law in which trial court denied grandparents' petition for adoption and awarded physical custody of child to father was final judgment triggering 10-day period for filing of motion for attorney fees and costs; petition for review of interim custody order had no effect on finality of trial court's entry of findings and conclusions, and stay of trial court's order did not affect trial court's jurisdiction to entertain motions for costs and attorney fees. **D.L.M. v. M.W.,** Op. No. 4840, 941 P2d 900 (Alaska 1997).

Argument that losing plaintiff in civil rights action should be shielded from liability for fees and costs under this rule unless plaintiff's lawsuit is frivolous, unreasonable or without foundation was rejected. **Moody-Herrera v. State Dept. of Natural Resources,** Op. No. 5050, 967 P2d 79 (Alaska 1998).

It was error to award actual paralegal fees to prevailing party who received money judgment. **Andrus v. Lena,** Op. No. 5098, 975 P2d 54 (Alaska 1999).

Catch-all provision of former version of Civil Rule 79(b) did not authorize award to prevailing plaintiff of $5,146 for cost of accountant where cost exceeded limits of Administrative Rule 7(c) for expert witnesses even though Administrative Rule 7(c) would have barred recovery because accountant did not testify; plaintiff's argument that Administrative Rule 7(c) should not apply because accountant was a consulting expert rather than a testifying expert was rejected. **Strong Enterprises, Inc. v. Seaward,** Op. No. 5118, 980 P2d 456 (Alaska 1999).

Civil Rules 79(h) and 82(e), which address the allocation of costs and attorney's fees respectively between third-party plaintiffs and third-party defendants joined in an action under Alaska's equitable apportionment statute, do not apply where the original plaintiff has made a direct claim against the third-party defendant; in such cases, the usual Alaska practice of awarding costs and attorney's fees to the prevailing party applies. **City of Kodiak v. Parish,** Op. No. 5170, 986 P2d 201 (Alaska 1999).

Award of full expert witness fees to prevailing party was vacated and remanded where cost bill was ambiguous and did not permit trial court to distinguish between what appeared to be excessive fees and unknown travel expenses. **Kellis v. Crites,** Op. No. 5380, 20 P3d 1112 (Alaska 2001).

Where defendant prevails on state law claims brought in state court that are integrally related to federal civil rights claims, defendant is entitled to award of attorney's fees without showing that plaintiff's claims were frivolous, unreasonable or without foundation. **Sengupta v. University of Alaska,** Op. No. 5397, 21 P3d 1240 (Alaska 2001).

Alaska R. Civ. P. 82(a) provides for an award of attorney's fees to the prevailing party "except as otherwise provided by law." If a specific statutory scheme for attorney's fees or costs exists, Alaska R. Civ. P. 79 and 82 do not apply. **Enders v. Parker,** Op. No. 5446, 28 P3d 280 (Alaska 2001).

Court can award costs and attorney's fees even after it concludes that it lacks subject matter jurisdiction over a party's claims. **Foster v. State,** Op. No. 5504, 34 P3d 1288 (Alaska 2001).

Denial of the personal representative's motion seeking attorney's fees and costs under Alaska R. Civ. P. 82(b) and 79(b) was proper where the legislature provided in AS 13.16.435 that a designated personal representative, the stepdaughter, could recover necessary expenses and disbursements, including reasonable attorney fees incurred; if a specific statutory scheme for attorney's fees existed, then Alaska R. Civ. P. 82 did not apply and because AS 13.16.435 also clearly covered costs incurred in the litigation, Alaska R. Civ. P. 79 likewise was inapplicable. **Enders v. Parker,** Op. No. 5675, 66 P.3d 11 (Alaska 2003).

This rule allows a prevailing party to recover costs; however, where the plaintiff did not file a cost bill, the superior court did not err in denying the costs. **Fyffe v. Wright,** Op. No. 5819 (Alaska 2004).

Prevailing party is not limited to the fees recoverable under this rule where a provision in a contract allows for a full recovery of costs; a lessee was awarded the full amount of costs incurred in defending an eviction action where there was no such limitation in the lease. **Tufco, Inc. v. Pac. Envtl. Corp.,** Op. No. 5904, 113 P.3d 668 (Alaska 2005).

For purposes of Civ. R. 82(a), and subsection (a), plaintiff lessor was the prevailing party because the lessee received far less on its counterclaim than it requested, and the lessor had the larger monetary award. **Alaska Constr. & Eng'g, Inc. v. Balzer Pac. Equip. Co.,** Op. No. 5981, 130 P.3d 932 (Alaska 2006).

Court costs were not waived where cost request was made in a motion presented to the superior court rather than in the form of a cost bill presented to the clerk of court as required by subsection (b) of this rule. Party's motion requesting costs was timely and was sufficiently detailed to meet the requirements of this rule. **Vazquez v. Campbell**, Op. No. 11316, 146 P.3d 1 (Alaska 2006).

Travel expenses for child's father in custody litigation were authorized under this rule's the allowance of other costs allowed by statute because such expenses are authorized under AS 25.30.500(a). **Vazquez v.**

Campbell, Op. No. 11316, 146 P.3d 1 (Alaska 2006).

Clerk properly denied certain costs related to insurance litigation even though the clerk did not specifically request receipts as opposing party specifically requested additional supporting documentation that was not provided. **Gibson v. GEICO General Ins. Co.**, Op. No. 12109, 153 P.3d 312 (Alaska 2007).

Rule 80. Bonds and Undertakings.

(a) **Approval by Clerk.** Except where approval by a judge is required by law, the clerk is authorized to approve all undertakings, bonds, and stipulations of security given in the form and amount prescribed by statute or order of the court, where the same are executed by approved surety companies.

(b) **Qualifications of Sureties.**

(1) *Individuals.* Each individual surety must be a resident of the state. Each must be worth the sum specified in the undertaking, exclusive of property exempt from execution, and over and above all just debts and liabilities, except that where there are more than two sureties, each may be worth a lesser amount if the total net worth of all of them is equal to twice the sum specified in the undertaking. No attorney at law, peace officer, clerk of any court, or other officer of any court is qualified to be surety on the undertaking.

(2) *Corporations.* A corporate surety must be in compliance with applicable laws of the state, and must be qualified by law to act as surety in furnishing bail.

(c) **Affidavits of Sureties.**

(1) *Individuals.* The undertaking must contain an affidavit of each surety which shall state that the surety possesses the qualifications prescribed by subdivision (b) of this rule.

(2) *Corporations.* The undertaking of a corporate surety must contain affidavits showing the authority of the agent to act for the corporation and compliance by the corporation with all statutory requirements.

(d) **Justification of Sureties.**

(1) *Information to Be Furnished.* Sureties on any bond or undertaking shall furnish such information as may be required by the judge or magistrate approving the same, upon forms provided by the clerk of court for such purpose.

(2) *Examination as to Sureties' Qualifications.* Upon three days' notice to a party, an adverse party may require an individual surety or the agent of a corporate surety to be examined under oath concerning the surety's qualifications. Evidence as to such qualifications shall be taken before any judge or magistrate who shall have the authority to approve or reject the bond or undertaking.

(3) *Where Not Applicable.* The requirements set forth in paragraphs (1) and (2) of this subdivision shall not apply to individual sureties for a national banking association or for a state bank or other financial institution regulated under Title 6 Alaska Statutes.

(e) **Approval by Attorneys.** Every recognizance, bond, stipulation or undertaking hereinafter presented to the clerk or a judge for approval shall have appended thereto a certificate of an attorney, if a party is represented by an attorney, substantially in the following form:

> "Examined and recommended for approval as provided in Rule 80.
> Attorney"

Such endorsement by an attorney will signify to the court that the attorney has carefully examined the recognizance, bond, stipulation or undertaking, and that the attorney knows the contents thereof; that the attorney knows the purposes for which it is executed; and that in the attorney's opinion the same is in due form. The recognizance, bond, stipulation or undertaking shall further have appended thereto a form substantially as follows:

"I hereby approve the foregoing. Dated this _ day of __________, 19____.

____
Judge (or Clerk)"

(f) **Enforcement Against Sureties.** By entering into a bond or undertaking, the surety submits to the jurisdiction of the court and irrevocably appoints the clerk of court as the surety's agent upon whom any papers affecting the surety's liability on the bond may be served. The surety's liability may be enforced on motion without the necessity of an independent action. The motion and such notice of the motion as the court prescribes may be served on the clerk who shall forthwith mail copies to the surety if the surety's address is known. Every bond or undertaking shall contain the consent and agreement of the surety to the provisions of this subdivision of this rule.

(g) **Cash Deposit in Lieu of Bond.** A cash deposit of the required amount may be made with the clerk in lieu of furnishing a surety bond. At the time of such cash deposit, there shall be filed a written instrument properly executed and acknowledged by the owner of the cash, or by the owner's attorney or authorized agent, setting forth the conditions under which the deposit is being made, the ownership of the fund, and the consent and agreement to the provisions of subdivision (f) of this rule.

(Adopted by SCO 5 October 9, 1959; amended by SCO 49 effective January 1, 1963; by SCO 90 effective July 24, 1967; by SCO 258 effective November 15, 1976; and by SCO 1153 effective July 15, 1994)

Cross References

(a) **CROSS REFERENCE:** AS 09.68.030

Annotations

Cases

Individual surety's affidavit stating that he was worth more than $750 after exemptions and liabilities satisfied the qualification requirements of this rule and provided adequate security for a cost bond on appeal. **Acevedo v. City of North Pole,** Op. No. 2748, 672 P2d 130 (Alaska 1983).

Attorney appellant may not use his or her professional corporation as surety for attorney's personal appeal. **Breck v. Moore,** Op. No. 4318, 910 P2d 599 (Alaska 1996).

Rule 81. Attorneys.

(a) **Who May Practice.**

(1) *Members of the Alaska Bar Association.* Subject to the provisions of paragraph (2) of this subdivision, only attorneys who are members of the Alaska Bar Association shall be entitled to practice in the courts of this state.

(2) *Other Attorneys.* A member in good standing of the bar of a court of the United States, or of the highest court of any state or any territory or insular possession of the United States, who is not a member of the Alaska Bar Association and not otherwise disqualified from engaging in the practice of law in this state, may be permitted, upon motion and payment of the required fee to the Alaska Bar Association, to appear and participate in a particular action or proceeding in a court of this state. The motion, and the notice of hearing, if any, shall be served on the executive director of the Alaska Bar Association and, unless the court directs otherwise by an order pursuant to Rule 5(c) of these Rules, on each of the parties to the action or proceeding. With the motion, the applicant must file with the court the following:

(A) The name, address and telephone number of a member of the Alaska Bar Association with whom the applicant will be associated, who is authorized to practice in the courts of this state.

(B) A written consent to the motion, signed by such member of the Alaska Bar Association.

(C) A certificate from the presiding judge, clerk of the court, or bar association where the applicant has been admitted to practice, executed not earlier than 60 days prior to the filing of the motion, showing that the applicant has been so admitted in such court, that he is in good standing therein and that the applicant's professional character appears to be good.

(D) Proof of payment of the required fee to the Alaska Bar Association.

An attorney thus permitted to appear may participate in a particular action or proceeding in all respects, except that all documents requiring signature of counsel for a party may not be signed solely by such attorney, but must bear the signature also of local counsel with whom the attorney is associated.

(3) *Authority and Duties of Attorneys.* Local counsel shall be primarily responsible to the court for the conduct of all stages of the proceedings, and their authority shall be superior to that of attorneys permitted to appear under paragraph (2) of this subdivision.

(b) **Ex Parte Applications.** All motions for ex parte orders must be made by an attorney or in propria persona.

(c) **General Appearance by Counsel.**

(1) An attorney who files a pleading or appears in a court proceeding on behalf of a party shall be deemed to have entered an appearance for all purposes in that case unless the attorney has filed and served a limited entry of appearance under (d) of this rule.

(2) Except as otherwise ordered by the court, or except as provided in Rule 81(d) and 81(e)(1)(D), a party who has appeared by an attorney may not thereafter appear or act in the party's own behalf in any action or proceeding, unless order of substitution shall have been made by the court after notice to such attorney.

(d) **Limited Appearance By Counsel.** A party in a non-criminal case may appear through an attorney for limited purposes during the course of an action, including, but not limited to, depositions, hearings, discovery, and motion practice, if the following conditions are satisfied:

(1) The attorney files and serves an entry of appearance with the court before or during the initial action or proceeding that expressly states that the appearance is limited, and all parties of record are served with the limited entry of appearance; and

(2) The entry of appearance identifies the limitation by date, time period, or subject matter.

(e) **Withdrawal of Attorney.**

(1) An attorney who has appeared for a party in an action or proceeding may be permitted to withdraw as counsel for such party only as follows:

(A) For good cause shown, upon motion and notice of hearing served upon the party in accordance with Rule 77 and after the withdrawing attorney provides

(i) to the client a list of pending pretrial or post-trial deadlines, appellate deadlines, motion deadlines, and hearing dates and times; and

(ii) to the court the last known address and telephone number of the attorney's client and a certification that the attorney has complied with (e)(1)(A)(i) of this rule; or

(B) Where the party has other counsel ready to be substituted for the attorney who wishes to withdraw; or

(C) Where the party expressly consents in open court or in writing to the withdrawal of the party's attorney, the party has provided in writing or on the record a current service address and telephone number, and the attorney who wishes to withdraw has provided to the client a list of pending pretrial or post-trial deadlines, appellate deadlines, motion deadlines, and hearing dates and times; or

(D) In accordance with the limitations set forth in any limited entry of appearance filed pursuant to Civil Rule 81(d). An attorney may withdraw under this subparagraph by filing a notice with the court, served on all parties of record, stating that the attorney's limited representation has concluded; certifying that the attorney has taken all actions necessitated by the limited representation; and providing to the court a current service address and telephone number and to the client a list of pending pretrial or post-trial deadlines, appellate deadlines, motion deadlines, and hearing dates and times. Upon the filing of such notice, the withdrawal shall be effective, without court action or approval.

(2) An attorney shall be considered to have properly withdrawn as counsel for a party in an action or proceeding in which a period of one year has elapsed since the filing of any paper or the issuance of any process in the action or proceeding, and

(A) The final judgment or decree has been entered and the time for filing an appeal has expired, or

(B) If an appeal has been taken, the final judgment or decree upon remand has been entered or the mandate has issued affirming the judgment or decree.

This subparagraph (2) shall not apply to an attorney who files and serves a notice of continued representation.

(f) **Stipulations.** Stipulations between parties or their attorneys will be recognized only when made in open court, or when made in writing and filed with the clerk.

(g) **Time for Argument.** Unless otherwise specially ordered no longer than one quarter hour shall be allowed each party for argument upon any motion, or on any hearing other than a final hearing on the merits. The time for opening statements and arguments at the trial of an action shall be determined in accordance with Civil Rule 46(h).

(h) **Disbarment and Discipline.** Whenever it appears to the court that any member of the bar has been disbarred or suspended from practice or convicted of a felony, that member shall not be permitted to practice before the court until the member is thereafter reinstated according to existing statutes and rules.

(Adopted by SCO 5 October 9, 1959; amended by SCO 98 effective September 16, 1968; by SCO 258 effective November 15, 1976; by SCO 355 effective April 1, 1979; by SCO 390 effective November 7, 1979; by SCO 604 effective September 14, 1984; by SCO 612 effective January 1, 1985; by SCO 696 effective September 15, 1986; by SCO 876 effective July 15, 1988; by SCO 1153 effective July 15, 1994; by SCO 1450 effective October 15, 2001; by SCO 1544 effective October 15, 2004; by SCO 1627 effective October 15, 2007; and by SCO 1627-Amended issued on April 10, 2007, effective October 15, 2007)

Note: An entry of appearance filed under (d) of this rule must identify the limitation of representation. For example, a limitation by date may state "representation is provided through December 31, 2004;" a limitation by time period may state "representation is provided through the end of discovery;" or a limitation by subject matter may state "representation is provided only for the purpose of drafting an opposition to summary judgment and appearing at oral argument on summary judgment."

Annotations

Cases

Trial court did not abuse discretion but acted appropriately and with high regard to propriety and to the public image of the legal profession in granting motion of counsel for his voluntary disqualification where a conflict of interest was not yet actually indicated but it could not be determined that such a conflict might not develop by testimony to be offered during the trial. **Gregoire v. National Bank of Alaska,** Op. No. 336, 413 P2d 27 (Alaska 1966).

Where a client states by affidavit that he has discharged his attorney by means of letter, it is not error to allow that attorney to withdraw, even though the attorney does not serve the client with notice of hearing on a motion to be allowed to withdraw. **Moran v. Kenai Towing and Salvage, Inc.,** Op. No. 1056, 523 P2d 1237 (Alaska 1974).

Where there is no dispute as to the material terms of a settlement, the provisions of paragraph (e) of this rule are met if both parties admit either in a writing filed with the clerk or orally in open court that a settlement had been reached. **Interior Credit Bureau, Inc., v. Bussing,** Op. No. 1366, 559 P2d 104 (Alaska 1977).

Trial court did not err in holding that plaintiff, who was both a doctor and a lawyer, could either represent himself or be represented by counsel, but not both, in his action against hospital for its failure to renew his staff privileges. **Eufemio v. Kodiak Island Hosp.,** Op. No. 3868, 837 P2d 95 (Alaska 1992).

Trial court abused its discretion in denying attorney's properly presented motion to withdraw as counsel. **Devincenzi v. Wright,** Op. No. 4136, 882 P2d 1263 (Alaska 1994).

Rule 82. Attorney's Fees.

(a) **Allowance to Prevailing Party.** Except as otherwise provided by law or agreed to by the parties, the prevailing party in a civil case shall be awarded attorney's fees calculated under this rule.

(b) **Amount of Award.**

(1) The court shall adhere to the following schedule in fixing the award of attorney's fees to a party recovering a money judgment in a case:

Judgment and, If Awarded, Prejudgment Interest		Contested With Trial	Contested Without Trial	Non-Contested
First	$25,000	20%	18%	10%
Next	$75,000	10%	8%	3%
Next	$400,000	10%	6%	2%
Next	$500,000	10%	2%	1%

(2) In cases in which the prevailing party recovers no money judgment, the court shall award the prevailing party in a case which goes to trial 30 percent of the prevailing party's reasonable actual attorney's fees which were necessarily incurred, and shall award the prevailing party in a case resolved without trial 20 percent of its actual attorney's fees which were necessarily incurred. The actual fees shall include fees for legal work customarily performed by an attorney but which was delegated to and performed by an investigator, paralegal or law clerk.

(3) The court may vary an attorney's fee award calculated under subparagraph (b)(1) or (2) of this rule if, upon consideration of the factors listed below, the court determines a variation is warranted:

(A) the complexity of the litigation;

(B) the length of trial;

(C) the reasonableness of the attorneys' hourly rates and the number of hours expended;

(D) the reasonableness of the number of attorneys used;

(E) the attorneys' efforts to minimize fees;

(F) the reasonableness of the claims and defenses pursued by each side;

(G) vexatious or bad faith conduct;

(H) the relationship between the amount of work performed and the significance of the matters at stake;

(I) the extent to which a given fee award may be so onerous to the non-prevailing party that it would deter similarly situated litigants from the voluntary use of the courts;

(J) the extent to which the fees incurred by the prevailing party suggest that they had been influenced by considerations apart from the case at bar, such as a desire to discourage claims by others against the prevailing party or its insurer; and

(K) other equitable factors deemed relevant.

If the court varies an award, the court shall explain the reasons for the variation.

(4) Upon entry of judgment by default, the plaintiff may recover an award calculated under subparagraph (b)(1) or its reasonable actual fees which were necessarily incurred, whichever is less. Actual fees include fees for legal work performed by an investigator, paralegal, or law clerk, as provided in subparagraph (b)(2).

(c) **Motions for Attorney's Fees.** A motion is required for an award of attorney's fees under this rule or pursuant to contract, statute, regulation, or law. The motion must be filed within 10 days after the date shown in the clerk's certificate of distribution on the judgment as defined by Civil Rule 58.1. Failure to move for attorney's fees within 10 days, or such additional time as the court may allow, shall be construed as a waiver of the party's right to recover attorney's fees. A motion for attorney's fees in a default case must specify actual fees.

(d) **Determination of Award.** Attorney's fees upon entry of judgment by default may be determined by the clerk. In all other matters the court shall determine attorney's fees.

(e) **Equitable Apportionment Under AS 09.17.080.** In a case in which damages are apportioned among the parties under AS 09.17.080, the fees awarded to the plaintiff under (b)(1) of this rule must also be apportioned among the parties according to their respective percentages of fault. If the plaintiff did not assert a direct claim against a third-party defendant brought into the action under Civil Rule 14(c), then

(1) the plaintiff is not entitled to recover the portion of the fee award apportioned to that party; and

(2) the court shall award attorney's fees between the third-party plaintiff and the third-party defendant as follows:

(A) if no fault was apportioned to the third-party defendant, the third-party defendant is entitled to recover attorney's fees calculated under (b)(2) of this rule;

(B) if fault was apportioned to the third-party defendant, the third-party plaintiff is entitled to recover under (b)(2) of this rule 30 or 20 percent of that party's actual attorney's fees incurred in asserting the claim against the third- party defendant.

(f) **Effect of Rule.** The allowance of attorney's fees by the court in conformance with this rule shall not be construed as fixing the fees between attorney and client.

(Adopted by SCO 5 October 9, 1959; amended by SCO 497 effective January 18, 1982; by SCO 712 effective September 15, 1986; by SCO 921 effective January 15, 1989; by SCO 1006 effective January 15, 1990; by SCO 1066 effective July 15, 1991; repealed and reenacted by SCO 1118am effective July 15, 1993; amended by SCO 1195 effective July 15, 1995; by SCO 1200 effective July 15, 1995; by SCO 1241 effective July 15, 1996; by SCO 1246 effective July 15, 1996; by SCO 1281 effective August 7, 1997; by SCO 1340 effective January 15, 1999; and by SCO 1455 effective July 15, 1993)

Note to SCO 1118am: By adopting these amendments to Civil Rule 82, the court intends no change in existing Alaska law regarding the award of attorney's fees for or against a public interest litigant, **see, e.g., Anchorage Daily News v. Anchorage School Dist.**, 803 P.2d 402, 404 (Alaska 1990); **City of Anchorage v. McCabe**, 568 P.2d 986, 993-94 (Alaska 1977); **Gilbert v. State**, 526 P.2d 1131, 1136 (Alaska 1974), or in the law that an award of full attorney's fees is manifestly unreasonable in the absence of bad faith or vexatious conduct by the non-prevailing party. **See, e.g., Malvo v. J.C. Penney Co.**, 512 P.2d 575, 588 (Alaska 1973); **Demoski v. New**, 737 P.2d 780, 788 (Alaska 1987).

Note: AS 25.25.313(c), added by § 6 of ch. 57 SLA 1995 (the Uniform Interstate Family Support Act), has the effect of amending Civil Rule 82 by requiring the court to award costs and fees against a party who requests a hearing primarily for delay in a support proceeding listed in AS 25.25.301.

RABINOWITZ, Justice dissenting.

I dissent from the court's adoption of the amendments to Civil Rule 82 called for in [SCO 1118am.] In my view no compelling case has been made demonstrating the need for these changes. *1* Further, my judicial hunch is that these amendments to Civil Rule 82, in particular the new provisions reflected in (b)(3)(A) through (K), will unnecessarily and dramatically increase litigation over attorney's fees awards both in our trial courts as well as in this court. *2*

[1] In this regard I note that the Alaska Judicial Council is scheduled to conduct an in depth empirical study of the workings of Civil Rule 82. My preference is to await the results of the Council's study before deciding whether any of the current provisions of Rule 82 should be amended. Such a study should position this court to make a more informed

assessment as to whether the current rule operates in a fashion which unjustly denies access to our courts. I further note that our Civil Rules Committee recently surveyed the Alaska Bar membership on discrete aspects of Civil Rule 82. A clear majority of those responding to the committee's questionnaire indicated: that Civil Rule 82 does not deter people of moderate means from filing valid claims; that the rule does not put excessive pressure on moderate income people to settle valid claims; and that the rule is needed to discourage frivolous litigation.

[2] Any attorney worth his or her salt will, pursuant to the expansive provisions of (b)(3)(A) through (K), request variations from the attorney's fees awards called for under either the monetary recovery schedule provisions of (b)(1), or the provisions of (b)(2) which apply where no money judgment is recovered by the prevailing party.

Note to SCO 1281: In 1997 the legislature amended AS 09.30.065 concerning offers of judgment. According to ch. 26, sec. 52, SLA 1997, the amendment to AS 09.30.065 has the effect of amending Civil Rules 68 and 82 by requiring the offeree to pay costs and reasonable actual attorney fees on a sliding scale of percentages in certain cases, by eliminating provisions relating to interest, and by changing provisions relating to attorney fee awards. According to sec. 55 of the session law, the amendment to AS 09.30.065 applies "to all causes of action accruing on or after the effective date of this Act." However, the amendments to Civil Rule 68 adopted by paragraph 5 of this order are applicable to all cases filed on or after August 7, 1997. See paragraph 17 of this order.

Note: Chapter 94 SLA 1998 adopts AS 46.03.761, which allows the Department of Environmental Conservation to impose administrative penalties against an entity that fails to construct or operate a public water supply system in compliance with state law or a term or condition imposed by the department. According to section 5 of the act, subsection (j) of this statute has the effect of amending Civil Rules 79 and 82 by allowing the recovery of full reasonable attorney fees and costs in an action to collect administrative penalties assessed under AS 46.03.761.

Note: Chapter 136 SLA 03 (HB 151) amends Chapters 10 and 45 of Title 9 of the Alaska Statutes relating to claims and court actions for defects in the design, construction, and remodeling of certain dwellings and limits on when certain court actions may be brought. According to Section 4(1) of the Act, AS 09.45.889(b) has the effect of amending Civil Rule 82 by allowing the court to deny attorney fees to a claimant in the situation described in AS 09.45.889(b), even if the claimant is the prevailing party.

Annotations

Cases

I. In General.
II. Prevailing Party.
III. Review.
  A. Standard.
  B. Abuse of Discretion or Error.
IV. Fee Schedule.

I. In General.

The common law did not permit allowance of attorney's fees as costs to the prevailing party, but in Alaska such allowance is of relatively ancient origin and prior to attainment of statehood the matter was regulated by statute. **McDonough v. Lee,** Op. No. 378, 420 P2d 459 (Alaska 1966).

The purpose of this rule is to encourage settlement of civil litigation as well as to avoid protracted litigation. **Miklautsch v. Dominick,** Op. No. 538, 452 P2d 438 (Alaska 1969).

Where a mechanics' lienor files a four-count complaint against the beneficiary of a deed of trust to foreclose the mechanics' liens but prevails on only one count, the trial court may properly refuse to award either party costs or attorney's fees. **Brand v. First Federal Savings & Loan Association of Fairbanks,** Op. No. 658, 478 P2d 829 (Alaska 1970).

This rule does not apply where plaintiffs seek an injunction and are awarded an injunction which is to be void if the defendant pays certain damages, since the rule in such case is not an accurate criterion for determining a fee. **Stauber v. Granger,** Op. No. 777, 495 P2d 67 (Alaska 1972).

The purpose of this rule is only to partially compensate a client for the productive work done by his attorney. It is irrelevant that actual attorney's fees are several times the amount awarded. **State v. Abbott,** Op. No. 804, 498 P2d 712 (Alaska 1972).

The determination of which party prevails and is entitled to costs is within the discretion of the trial judge. **DeWitt v. Liberty Leasing Co. of Alaska,** Op. No. 818, 499 P2d 599 (Alaska 1972).

A party is not barred from appealing from the disallowance of costs and attorney's fees by his acceptance of payment of the judgment and by signing a document entitled "Satisfaction of Judgment." **DeWitt v. Liberty Leasing Co. of Alaska,** Op. No. 818, 499 P2d 599 (Alaska 1972).

Under this rule, an award of prejudgment interest is to be included in the amount of the "money judgment." **Era Helicopters, Inc. v. Digicon Alaska, Inc.,** Op. No. 999, 518 P2d 1057 (Alaska 1974).

Under this rule, a trial judge may award attorney fees without a formal motion and without a hearing, especially in a situation where the parties seeking to be heard did not file a formal request for fees. **Urban Development Co. v. Dekreon,** Op. No. 1083, 526 P2d 325 (Alaska 1974).

This rule does not apply in a divorce action. **Burrell v. Burrell,** Op. No. 1169, 537 P2d 1 (Alaska 1975).

A trial judge may award attorney's fees without a formal motion and without a hearing. **National Bank of Alaska v. J.B.L. & K. of Alaska, Inc.,** Op. No. 1239, 546 P2d 579 (Alaska 1976).

A "hold harmless" indemnity clause includes the cost of recovery in the clause itself. **Manson-Osberg Co. v. State,** Op. No. 1292, 552 P2d 654 (Alaska 1976).

Where parties' potential liability for payment of actual recovery greatly exceeded potential liability for cost of defense, the main issue could not be said to be the cost of defense. **Continental Ins. Co. v. U.S. Fid. & Guar. Co.,** Op. No. 1298, 552 P2d 1122 (Alaska 1976).

The cost of in-house counsel is not an attorney's fee within the meaning of this rule. **Continental Ins. Co. v. U.S. Fid. & Guar. Co.,** Op. No. 1298, 552 P2d 1122 (Alaska 1976).

Attorney's fees should be computed on basis of net, not gross, recovery. **Fairbanks Builders, Inc. v. Sandstrom Plumbing & Heating, Inc.,** Op. No. 1324, 555 P2d 964 (Alaska 1976).

Attorney's fees are not recoverable under this rule in an action in federal court grounded on both admiralty and diversity jurisdiction. **Kalanback, Inc. v. Insurance Co. of the State of Pennsylvania, Inc.,** 422 FS 44 (USDC Alaska 1976).

Where defendant is dismissed under Civil Rule 41(a)(1)[a] before service of any pleading or motion by defendant but would have required trial court to consider merits of controversy, there is no joinder of issue, no prevailing party, and an award of attorney's fees is precluded. **State v. Alaska**

International Air, Inc., Op. No. 1409, 562 P2d 1064 (Alaska 1977).

One and one-half page memorandum devoid of authorities was not statement required by Civil Rule 77(b)(2), so that motion to dismiss was frivolous and issue was not joined, precluding award of attorney's fees. **State v. Alaska International Air, Inc.**, Op. No. 1409, 562 P2d 1064 (Alaska 1977).

When condemnee is eligible for attorney's fees in eminent domain action, he must receive full compensation under Civil Rule 72, not partial compensation under Civil Rule 82. **Greater Anchorage Area Borough v. 10 Acres,** Op. No. 1417, 563 P2d 269 (Alaska 1977).

It was proper to allow party attorney's fees for defending against one party, and separate fee for prevailing on cross-claim against third party. **Kaps Transport, Inc. v. Henry,** Op. No. 1527, 572 P2d 72 (Alaska 1977).

When a public corporation's active representation in litigation is by in-house counsel rather than retained counsel, award of attorney's fees pursuant to Rule 82 is proper. **Greater Anchorage Area Borough v. Sisters, Etc.,** Op. No. 1550, 573 P2d 862 (Alaska 1978).

An oral explanation on the record by the trial judge is adequate to justify decision denying attorney's fees. **Larry v. Dupree,** Op. No. 1652, 580 P2d 326 (Alaska 1978).

Civil Rule 82 applies only to "costs of the action," and not to attorney's fees incurred in the conduct of a prior arbitration. **Alaska State Housing v. Riley Pleas, Inc.,** Op. No. 1765, 586 P2d 1244 (Alaska 1978).

Attorney's fees could not be assessed against a public school teacher whose dismissal from employment was upheld by the superior court where the teacher had a statutorily guaranteed right to contest his dismissal in the courts. **Crisp v. Kenai Peninsula Borough Sch. Dist.,** Op. No. 1771, 587 P2d 1168 (Alaska 1978).

Civil Rule 82 had no application to claim for attorney fees by defendant retailer in suit based on strict tort liability against retailer and manufacturer, but retailer could recover costs based on indemnification obligation of manufacturer. **Heritage v. Pioneer Brokerage & Sales,** Op. No. 1855, 604 P2d 1059 (Alaska 1979).

Plaintiffs were jointly and severally liable for costs and attorney's fees although they filed separate complaints, where cases were consolidated for trial. **Stepanov v. Gavrilovich,** Op. No. 1823, 594 P2d 30 (Alaska 1979).

Civil Rule 82 does not govern appeals to Superior Court from administrative agency decision. **Kodiak Western Alaska v. Bob Harris Flying Service,** Op. No. 1820, 592 P2d 1200 (Alaska 1979).

A client's absence of obligation to pay for legal services rendered does not preclude an award of attorney's fees. **Arctic Slope Native Assoc. v. Paul,** Op. No. 2058, 609 P2d 32 (Alaska 1980).

Where prevailing party's attorneys, apparently motivated by considerations of professional courtesy, charged him for their services at the rate of $30.00 per hour rather than the customary rate of $75.00 per hour, the court would be justified in valuing those services using the customary rate. **Arctic Slope Native Assoc. v. Paul,** Op. No. 2058, 609 P2d 32 (Alaska 1980).

In determining the amounts of attorney's fees on appeal in public interest litigation, the same considerations are applicable as at the trial level, and it is therefore appropriate to award full attorney's fees on appeal to a successful public interest litigant. **Thomas v. Bailey,** Op. No. 2094, 611 P2d 536 (Alaska 1980).

It was not unreasonable for the superior court to find that plaintiffs exercising their rights under the election contest statute, were public interest litigants against whom an assessment of attorney's fees would be improper. **Thomas v. Croft,** Op. No. 2135, 614 P2d 795 (Alaska 1980).

Where the defendants in litigation stemming from a contested gubernatorial election were the state and the primary winners, it was proper to award attorney's fees against the state as a co-prevailing party since the litigation was caused by the irregularities of state election officials in the conduct of the election. **Thomas v. Croft,** Op. No. 2135, 614 P2d 795 (Alaska 1980).

Under this rule, trial court could in its discretion order one co-defendant to pay all of the fees awarded to the prevailing party, especially where the court believed that particular codefendant to be the wrongdoer. **Moses v. McGarvey,** Op. No. 2139, 614 P2d 1363 (Alaska 1980).

This rule does not require the court to limit its award to the amount requested. **State v. Fairbanks North Star Borough School Dist.,** Op. No. 2257, 621 P2d 1329 (Alaska 1981).

To the extent that work performed is duplicative and unnecessary, it should not be considered in determining the proper award under this rule. **State v. Fairbanks North Star Borough School Dist.,** Op. No. 2257, 621 P2d 1329 (Alaska 1981).

An attorney-litigant who defends an action through retained counsel should not be reimbursed for his own participation unless the court clearly segregates his compensable time, expended as an attorney active in the litigation, and his noncompensable time, expended as client. **Sherry v. Sherry,** Op. No. 2271, 622 P2d 960 (Alaska 1981).

The decision in **Crisp v. Kenai Peninsula Borough School District,** 587 P2d 1168 (Alaska 1978) does not apply to appeals of administrative decisions if the consequences thereof are for less significant than in the **Crisp** case, and courts may continue to assess reasonable attorney's fees against the losing party in such cases. **Sjong v. State,** Op. No. 2269, 622 P2d 967 (Alaska 1981).

While attorney's fees are costs, they are not covered by the literal requirements of Civil Rule 79(b). **State v. University of Alaska,** Op. No. 2303, 624 P2d 807 (Alaska 1981).

Under this rule an attorney is entitled to attorney's fees on a punitive damage award unless the court in its discretion specifically states otherwise. **Sturm, Ruger & Co. v. Day,** Op. No. 2330, 627 P2d 204 (Alaska 1981).

Superior court does not have authority to award costs and fees in a child in need of aid proceeding. **Cooper v. State,** Op. No. 2453, 638 P2d 174 (Alaska 1981).

Award of costs and fees in child custody action may not include costs or fees incurred in any other action, such as a child in need of aid proceeding, no matter how closely related the issues might be. **Cooper v. State,** Op. No. 2453, 638 P2d 174 (Alaska 1981).

On appeal to superior court of a municipal zoning decision, it was error for the court to award attorney's fees to the prevailing parties based upon the civil rules rather than the appellate rules. **Royal Krest Const. v. Anchorage,** Op. No. 2400, 640 P2d 133 (Alaska 1981).

Award of attorney's fees under this rule to prevailing party in state action arising out of the admiralty jurisdiction of the United States was proper. **Williams v. Eckert,** Op. No. 2489, 643 P2d 991 (Alaska 1982).

Where natural parent consented to adoption of her child and then unsuccessfully sought to withdraw such consent, an award of substantial attorney's fees to the prevailing party was manifestly unreasonable. **S.O. v. W.S.,** Op. No. 2491, 643 P2d 997 (Alaska 1982).

Where it was unclear what the parties intended in a judgment on offer and acceptance which provided that attorney's fees be provided under the terms of "an Alaska Civil Rule 82 endorsement" contained in an insurance policy of defendant, remittal was appropriate to determine whether there was a meeting of the minds of the parties on the issue of attorney fees. **Salmine v. Knagin,** Op. No. 2501, 645 P2d 148 (Alaska 1982).

Where a judgment on offer and acceptance was signed January 18, but the action was not dismissed by court order until July 24, a request by counsel filed August 1 for a hearing on the amount of attorney fees was timely, July 24 being the proper date from which the request period should have been calculated. **Salmine v. Knagin,** Op. No. 2501, 645 P2d 148 (Alaska 1982).

In a proceeding to modify the terms of a property settlement incorporated into a divorce decree, an award of attorney's fees and costs is properly made pursuant to this rule. **Stone v. Stone,** Op. No. 2522, 647 P2d 582 (Alaska

1982).

Trial court's award of twenty percent of prevailing party's costs and fees in case where no recovery was had was not abuse of discretion. **Alvey v. Pioneer Oilfield Services,** Op. No. 2532, 648 P2d 599 (Alaska 1982).

When assessing attorney's fees in litigation under the Truthin-Lending Act, the standards set out in **Johnson v. Georgia Highway Express, Inc.,**488 F2d 714 (5th Cir. 1974) should be applied. **Hayer v. National Bank of Alaska,** Op. No. 2658, 663 P2d 547 (Alaska 1983).

Given the dissimilar underlying policies between awards of attorney's fees under this rule and 15 U.S.C. § 1640(a)(3) of the Truth-in-Lending Act, it was error for the trial court to resort to the guidelines of this rule in determining its fee award under the federal act. **Hayer v. National Bank of Alaska,** Op. No. 2658, 663 P2d 547 (Alaska 1983).

Where the right to the conveyance of certain real property was the "main issue" in litigation involving a demand for specific performance and a claim of unlawful detainer, the party prevailing on the "main issue" was entitled to attorney's fees notwithstanding that the final accounting between the parties showed that on balance the prevailing party owed damages to the other party. **Currington v. Johnson,** Op. No. 2828, 685 P2d 73 (Alaska 1984).

Where State's motion for attorney's fees cited Appellate Rule 508 as authority for its request for fees, the court's order granting the State's motion, which appeared on the very same document, could not reasonably be construed as based on any other authority. **Rosen v. State Bd. of Public Accountancy,** Op. No. 2880, 689 P2d 478 (Alaska 1984).

Unsuccessful challenger to a rezoning decision on ground that open meetings act was violated qualified as a public interest litigant under this rule. **Brookwood Area Homeowners v. Anchorage,** Op. No. 2953, 702 P2d 1317 (Alaska 1984).

In a divorce action, the "prevailing party" standard of this rule does not apply. **H.P.A. v. S.C.A.,** Op. No. 2961, 704 P2d 205 (Alaska 1985).

Although award of attorney fees was not unreasonable, the judgment for attorney's fee had to be vacated since part of the judgment on which it was based was reversed. **Dilingham Comm. Co. v. City of Dillingham,** Op. No. 2966, 705 P2d 410 (Alaska 1985).

In unsuccessful negligence action by sawmill employee against state for alleged failure of state to properly inspect the sawmill for safety violations, it was not manifestly unreasonable to award $65,000 to the state for attorney fees even though the employer insisted on full satisfaction of its compensation lien, making settlement impossible. **Smith v. State,** Op. No. 2984, 706 P2d 1160 (Alaska 1985).

An explanation is required in all cases where the trial court refuses to award attorney fees to the prevailing party. **Pratt v. Kirkpatrick,** Op. No. 3054, 718 P2d 962 (Alaska 1986).

When counsel requests attorney's fees, other than based on the schedule in the Civil Rules, accurate records of the hours expended and a brief description of the services reflected by those hours should be submitted. **Hayes v. Xerox Corp.,** Op. No. 3045, 718 P2d 929 (Alaska 1986).

Failure of the judgment to grant attorney's fees on punitive damage award was a legal error, but trial judge had discretion to waive the thirty-day rule for correcting such errors so as to grant a late request for modification of the judgment. **Alaskan Village, Inc. v. Smalley,** Op. No. 3069, 720 P2d 945 (Alaska 1986).

As the prevailing party at trial, defendant could receive the maximum amount of attorney fees under Civil Rule 82; the fact that defendant had made an offer of judgment under Civil Rule 68 would not increase or diminish the award of attorney fees. **Hutchins v. Schwartz,** Op. No. 3110, 724 P2d 1194 (Alaska 1986).

A defendant who ultimately fares better than his offer of judgment is entitled only to partial compensation for post-offer attorney's fees. **Wickwire v. State,** Op. No. 3116, 725 P2d 695 (Alaska 1986).

In an action against the State for wrongful termination of an assistant attorney general, trial court, in awarding attorney's fees, improperly considered additional expenses incurred by the State resulting from plaintiff's decision to sue several individual defendants as well as the State, where a stipulation dismissing the individual defendants provided that each side would pay its own attorney's fees. **Wickwire v. State,** Op. No. 3116, 725 P2d 695 (Alaska 1986).

Superior court's award of $55,000 in attorney's fees, which amounted to approximately 60 percent of the requested amount and 45 percent of the actual fees incurred, was sustained on appeal. **Dahle v. Atlantic Richfield Co.,** Op. No. 3120,725 P2d 1069 (Alaska 1986).

Where party successfully enjoined nonjudicial foreclosure of deed of trust, award of $5000 in attorney fees, based upon the party's potential liability of $57,000, the amount by which he was alleged to be in default, was not manifestly unreasonable. **Tolstrup v. Miller,** Op. No. 3129, 726 P2d 1304 (Alaska 1986).

Award of 80 percent of prevailing party's attorney fees was not manifestly unreasonable where trial court characterized the losing party's defense as bordering on bad faith. **Crook v. Mortenson-Neal,** Op. No. 3128, 727 P2d 297 (Alaska 1986).

In computing prejudgment interest on negligence action award to plaintiff, trial court correctly computed the interest on the entire judgment amount rather than computing the interest on the judgment amount less worker's compensation benefits paid to plaintiff. **Alyeska Pipeline Service Co. v. Beadles,** Op. No. 3151, 731 P2d 572 (Alaska 1987).

Trial court's award of 75 percent of the prevailing party's actual attorney's fees was not manifestly unreasonable. **Steenmeyer Corp. v. Mortenson-Neal,** Op. No. 3154, 731 P2d 1221 (Alaska 1987).

Trial court's award of 75 percent of the prevailing party's actual attorney's fees was not manifestly unreasonable. **Steenmeyher Corp. v. Mortenson-Neal,** Op. No. 3154, 731 P2d 1221 (Alaska 1987).

Award to plaintiff of $700 in interim attorney's fees for its cost in litigating defendant's successful motion to have defendant's own admissions withdrawn was proper. **City of Kenai v. Ferguson,** Op. No. 3155, 732 P2d 184 (Alaska 1987).

The purpose of this rule is to compensate a prevailing party partially, not fully, for attorney's fees; an award of full attorney's fees is "manifestly unreasonable" in the absence of bad faith or vexatious conduct by the losing party. **Demoski v. New,** Op. No. 3184, 737 P2d 780 (Alaska 1987).

Contract provision allowing the prevailing party "reasonable" attorney fees justified trial court's award of full instead of partial attorney fees since the plain meaning of a contract provision prevails over any limitation otherwise imposed by this rule. **Ursin Seafoods v. Keener Packing Co.,** Op. No. 3217, 741 P2d 1175 (Alaska 1987).

Trial court had no authority to require the state to pay costs or attorney's fees as a sanction in a juvenile case. **State v. Superior Court, Third Jud. Dist.,** Op. No. 744, 743 P2d 381 (Alaska App. 1987).

Although workers' compensation claim by employees against an adjustor was not made in bad faith, it was frivolous, justifying an award of full attorneys' fees. **Crawford and Co. v. Vienna,** Op. No. 3243, 744 P2d 1175 (Alaska 1987).

This rule does not apply to judgments in divorce cases. **L.L.M. v. P.M.,** Op. No. 3323, 754 P2d 262 (Alaska 1988).

The "prevailing party" standard and the divorce action judgment exception to this rule are inappropriate standards for determining the question of attorney's fees in connection with motions to amend or enforce child custody orders. **L.L.M. v. P.M.,** Op. No. 3323, 754 P2d 262 (Alaska 1988).

The statutory standard of "willfully and without just excuse" is appropriate for determining the question of attorney's fees after a motion to amend or enforce a custody or visitation order is adjudicated; in this way any unsuccessful party who reasonably, and in good faith, believes that his or her action was justified by the best interests of the children will not be deterred from action by the possibility of an award of fees and costs. **L.L.M. v. P.M.,** Op. No. 3323, 754 P2d 262 (Alaska 1988).

Projected attorney's fees under this rule based on a stipulated projected verdict were a part of a wrongful death defendant's liability insurance policy limits. **Schultz v. Travelers Indem. Co.,** Op. No. 3325, 754 P2d 265 (Alaska 1988).

Whether an entity is a public interest litigant cannot depend on the interests of a single member; rather, it must depend on the interests of typical members; accordingly, where only a few out of more than 100 members of a nonprofit corporation bringing suit had sufficient personal economic incentive to bring such a suit, the nonprofit corporation could qualify as a public interest litigant. **Citizens for the Preservation v. Sheffield,** Op. No. 3368, 758 P2d 624 (Alaska 1988).

In child support modification action, trial court did not err in awarding attorney's fees to the Child Support Enforcement Division under this rule. **Patch v. Patch,** Op. No. 3379, 760 P2d 526 (Alaska 1988).

The prevailing party rule for determining attorney fee awards under this rule does not apply to fee awards in divorce cases. **Mann v. Mann,** Op. No. 3491, 778 P2d 590 (Alaska 1989).

The divorce judgment exception to this rule does not extend to post-judgment modifications and enforcement motions. **Hartland v. Hartland,** Op. No. 3459, 777 P2d 636 (Alaska 1989).

Clause in lease/option agreement providing for full reasonable attorney's fees to prevailing party in any legal action relating to the demised premises was not superseded by subsequent earnest money agreement which did not mention attorney's fees. **Jackson v. Barbero,** Op. No. 3456, 776 P2d 786 (Alaska 1989).

The "prevailing party" rule used for determining attorney fees under this rule does not apply to divorce cases; instead, relevant considerations are the relative economic situation and earning power of each party. Also, the court may award attorney fees where there is bad faith. **Streb v. Streb,** Op. No. 3443,774 P2d 798 (Alaska 1989).

Trial court erred in awarding attorney fees to the prevailing party in a post-judgment child custody and support case absent a finding that the other party acted in bad faith. **House v. House,** Op. No. 3498, 779 P2d 1204 (Alaska 1989).

Award of attorney fees in a child custody and support case between unmarried individuals is to be governed by the standard used in divorce actions rather than the prevailing party standard. **Bergstrom v. Lindback,** Op. No. 3516, 779 P2d 1235 (Alaska 1989).

Superior court did not err in allowing the prevailing party to file a supplemental memorandum five months after the party's initial motion for attorney fees was made, where the supplemental memorandum itemized fees requested for work done after the initial motion was filed in opposing the losing party's motion for relief from judgment. **Kenai Peninsula Borough v. English Bay Village Corp.,** Op. No. 3517, 781 P2d 6 (Alaska 1989).

Trial court erred in taking past settlement negotiations into account in making an award of attorney fees under this rule. **Doyle v. Peabody,** Op. No. 3519, 781 P2d 957 (Alaska 1989).

Trial court did not abuse its discretion in ruling that request for attorney fees, filed 70 days after entry of judgment, was filed within a reasonable time, absent any substantial prejudice resulting from the delay. **T & G Aviation, Inc. v. Footh,** Op. No. 3609, 792 P2d 671 (Alaska 1990).

In suit by insured against insurer for violating insurance agreement, trial court erred in permitting jury to award the insured attorney fees beyond those authorized by this rule. **Alaska Pacific Assurance Co. v. Collins,** Op. No. 3614, 794 P2d 936 (Alaska 1990).

A non-attorney pro se litigant is not entitled to attorney fees under this rule. **Alaska Federal S & Lv. Bernhardt,** Op. No. 3562, 794 P2d 579 (Alaska 1990).

The argument that trial courts should never be permitted to award fees in excess of those established under the "noncontested" or "without trial" schedules of Civil Rule 82 following acceptance of an offer of judgment under Civil Rule 68 was rejected. **Van Dort v. Culliton,** Op. No. 3630, 797 P2d 642 (Alaska 1990).

In arbitration proceeding by borough against brokerage firm in which the brokerage firm sued certain borough officials for contribution, ascertain by brokerage firm that law firm had a conflict of interest in representing both the borough in the arbitration proceeding and the individual defendants in the contribution case, and should therefore be barred on public policy grounds from receiving an award of attorney fees, was rejected. **Integrated Res. Equity v. Fairbanks Boro.,** Op. No. 3633, 799 P2d 295 (Alaska 1990).

Where nationwide class action law suit was not first submitted to Alaska attorney general as required by Alaska statute, the action was deemed frivolous as to Alaska claimants; accordingly, the defendant, as prevailing party vis-a-vis the Alaska claimants, was entitled to recover for its attorney fees spent in Alaska. **Deadwyler v. Volkswagen of America, Inc.,** 748 F. Supp. 1146 (W.D.N.C. 1990).

In property dispute case, award of attorney fees to an adverse possessor was appropriate notwithstanding argument that the award amounted to an unjustified "windfall." **Nome 2000 v. Fagerstorm,** Op. No. 3638, 799 P2d 304 (Alaska 1990).

The appellate rules rather than the civil rules control an award of attorney fees when the superior court determines an administrative appeal. **Diedrich v. City of Ketchikan,** Op. No. 3661, 805 P2d 362 (Alaska 1991).

The divorce judgment exception to this rule does not apply to post-judgment modification and enforcement motions; accordingly, fees in such cases are awarded under the prevailing party standard of this rule for post-judgment money and property issues, under which the parties' relative economic positions are irrelevant. **Lowe v. Lowe,** Op. No. 3726, 817 P2d 453 (Alaska 1991).

Any award of attorney fees for legal services incurred subsequent to a judgment for past due child support is a cost of the action to the extent the fees are attributable to reasonable and necessarily incurred legal efforts to collect the judgment. **Cameron v. Hughes,** Op. No. 3805, 825 P2d 882 (Alaska 1992).

The four criteria for determining whether a particular lawsuit involves the public interest are: (1) Is the case designed to effectuate strong public policies? (2) If the plaintiff succeeds will numerous people receive benefits from the lawsuit? (3) Can only a private party have been expected to bring the suit? (4) Would the purported public interest litigant have sufficient economic incentive to file suit even if the action involved only narrow issues lacking general importance? **Anchorage Daily News v. Anchorage School Dist.,** Op. No. 3652, 803 P2d 402 (Alaska 1990); **Citizens Coalition for Tort Reform v. McAlpine,** Op. No. 3686, 810 P2d 162 (Alaska 1991); **Loeb v. Rasmussen,** Op. No. 3786, 822 P2d 914 (Alaska 1991).

Any award of attorney fees for legal services incurred subsequent to a judgment for past due child support is a cost of the action to the extent the fees are attributable to reasonable and necessarily incurred legal efforts to collect the judgment. **Cameron v. Hughes,** Op. No. 3805, 825 P2d 882 (Alaska 1992).

Award of attorney fees in divorce cases is not governed by this rule. **Hilliker v. Hilliker,** Op. No. 3831, 828 P2d 1205 (Alaska 1992).

The "prevailing party" standard of this rule does not apply in divorce actions; instead, court must base award of fees on parties' relative economic situations and earning power. **Jones v. Jones,** Op. No. 3856, 835 P2d 1173 (Alaska 1992).

Argument that this rule violates due process clauses of state and federal constitutions because risk of incurring large attorney fee award deters many plaintiffs from bringing suit was rejected. **Van Huff v. Sohio Alaska Petroleum Co.,** Op. No. 3857, 835 P2d 1181 (Alaska (1992).

Opposing party should have been allowed ten days to file motion opposing award of attorney's fees. **McGill v. Wahl,** Op. No. 3886, 839 P2d 393 (Alaska 1992).

Where a statute expressly calls for an award of reasonable attorney's fees to successful plaintiffs, full fees should be awarded as long as those fees are reasonable. **Bobich v. Stewart,** Op. No. 3913, 843 P2d 1232 (Alaska 1992).

In awarding attorney fees and costs to plaintiffs who successfully challenged state legislative redistricting plan, trial court did not err by (1) failing to apportion awards by issue, (2) awarding fees for post-trial litigation in which plaintiffs did not prevail, and (3) awarding fees and costs for work attributable to both state case and noncompensable Department of Justice proceedings. **Hickel v. Southeast Conference,** Op. No. 4055, 868 P2d 919 (Alaska 1994).

Award of attorney's fees under this rule must relate solely to attorney's services performed in case in which judgment is entered and must only provide compensation for services performed up to time of judgment. **Torrey v. Hamilton,** Op. No. 4073, 872 P2d 186 (Alaska 1994).

Attorney's fees incurred in adversary proceeding in bankruptcy were not recoverable as costs of collection for original state court judgment. **Torrey v. Hamilton,** Op. No. 4073, 872 P2d 186 (Alaska 1994).

It is within the trial court's discretion to consider a party's pre-litigation fees in determining an award of attorney's fees. **Bowman v. Blair,** Op. No. 4169, 889 P2d 1069 (Alaska 1995).

It is error for the court to rule on a motion for an award of attorney's fees before the opposing party in given an opportunity to respond. **Bowman v. Blair,** Op. No. 4169, 889 P2d 1069 (Alaska 1995).

Attorney's fees award was vacated in light of ruling requiring remand of case for further evidencing hearing. **Sweet v. Sisters of Providence in Washington,** Op. No. 4200, 893 P2d 1252 (Alaska 1995).

An award of only approximately thirty percent of the prevailing party's attorney's fees was within the court's discretion since the case was the first Alaska case dealing with arbitral immunity. **Feichtinger v. Conant,** Op. No. 4189, 893 P2d 1266 (Alaska 1995).

When a trial court awards attorney's fees, it may, but need not, take into account the existence of an unaccepted Rule 68 offer if the claimant-offeree fails to better the offer. **Fairbanks North Star Borough v. Lakeview Enterprises, Inc.,** Op. No. 4218, 897 P2d 47 (Alaska 1995).

Given the amendments to Civil Rule 82 effective July 15, 1993, pre-amendment case law discussing the impact of successful Rule 68 offers on attorney's fees awards have limited application. **Fairbanks North Star Borough v. Lakeview Enterprises, Inc.,** Op. No. 4218, 897 P2d 47 (Alaska 1995).

Where case was in process when new Rule 82 went into effect, new rule was to be applied of attorney's fees. **Bishop v. Municipality of Anchorage,** Op. No. 392, 685 P2d 103 (Alaska App. 1984).

Non-profit corporation organized for purpose of discouraging prostitution which brought action to abate house of prostitution qualified as public interest litigant. **SAC v. Lot 3, Block 1, Evergreen,** Op. No. 4245, 902 P2d 766 (Alaska 1995).

Amendment to this rule effective July 15, 1993, should have been applied to case where summary judgment was entered on June 7, 1993, defendants were declared prevailing parties on August 16, 1993; and attorney's fees were award on November 1, 1993. **Nielson v. Benton,** Op. No.4978, 957 P2d 971 (Alaska 1998).

The rule of **Cameron v. Hughes,** 825 P2d 882 (Alaska 1992), that legal costs reasonably and necessarily incurred in collecting a judgment for past-due child support should be treated as "costs of the action" and awarded to the collecting party, applies only to post-judgment fees incurred after a support obligation has been reduced to a unitary, fixed-sum judgment and only in child support cases. It does not apply in an action to reduce a spousal support obligation to judgment. **Saltz v. Saltz,** Op. No. 4272, 903 P2d 1070 (Alaska 1995).

While this rule does not generally apply to divorce cases, it does apply to post-judgment enforcement and modification motions. **Saltz v. Saltz,** Op. No. 4272, 903 P2d 1070 (Alaska 1995).

Native Alaskan Council of elders which filed suit to prevent clearcut harvesting of tract of timber believed to be location of historic Eyak village and burial ground qualified as public interest litigant. **Eyak Elders Council v. Sherstone, Inc.,** Op. No. 4273, 904 P2d 420 (Alaska 1995).

This rule does not preempt applicability of common fund doctrine, wholly or in part. **Edwards v. Alaska Pulp Corp.,** Op. No. 4362, 920 P2d 751 (Alaska 1996).

This rule, a fee-shifting tool which provides partial reimbursement of prevailing party's legal fees, was not intended to cap recovery of attorney fees under common fund doctrine, a fee-spreading mechanism which prevents unjust enrichment of those who derive benefit from efforts of others. **Edwards v. Alaska Pulp Corp.,** Op. No. 4362, 920 P2d 751 (Alaska 1996).

Where class representatives agreed to pay their lawyers whatever fees the court awarded, determination by court of "actual" fees was not necessarily limited to hourly fees. **Municipality of Anchorage v. Gallion,** Op. No. 4869, 944 P2d 436 (Alaska 1997).

Where police officers and fire fighters prevailed in class action against municipality to prevent reduction of post-retirement medical benefits, and class representatives had agreed to pay their attorneys whatever attorney fees were awarded by trial court, trial court had discretion to use risk enhancement and common fund doctrine as factors in calculating fee award and to require class members to contribute to attorney fees from benefits created or protected by class action. **Municipality of Anchorage v. Gallion,** Op. No. 4869, 944 P2d 436 (Alaska 1997).

All motions for attorney fees, including motions grounded on statutes, made after July 15, 1996, must be made within 10-day time frame of this rule. **Jones v. Jones,** Op. No. 4430, 925 P2d 1339 (Alaska 1996).

Excess insurer was not responsible for part of attorney's fees paid by primary insurer. **Safety Nat. Cas. v. Pacific Employees,** Op. No. 4440, 927 P2d 748 (Alaska 1996).

Trial court's ruling that labor organization representing city firefighters in litigation against city was not entitled to full, reasonable attorney fees under bad faith exception to this rule was not clearly erroneous. **Fairbanks Fire Fight. Ass'n v. Fairbanks,** Op. No. 4801, 934 P2d 759 (Alaska 1997).

Final findings of fact and conclusions of law in which trial court denied grandparents' petition for adoption and awarded physical custody of child to father was final judgment triggering 10-day period for filing of motion for attorney fees and costs; petition for review of interim custody order had no effect on finality of trial court's entry of findings and conclusions, and stay of trial court's order did not affect trial court's jurisdiction to entertain motions for costs and attorney fees. **D.L.M. v. M.W.,** Op. No. 4840, 941 P2d 900 (Alaska 1997).

Contractors who filed declaratory judgment action asserting that amendments to Little Davis-Bacon Act should apply to their pre-existing contracts failed to qualify as public interest litigants since each had substantial economic incentive to bring suit. **Eastwind, Inc. v. State,** Op. No. 4927, 951 P2d 844 (Alaska 1997).

Court does not abuse its discretion if it fails to treat non-prevailing party's victory on subsidiary issue as "equitable factor" mandating reduction of award to prevailing party. **Nielson v. Benton,** Op. No. 4978, 957 P2d 971 (Alaska 1998).

Award of attorney fees to property claimant in civil forfeiture proceeding had to be reversed if property claimant used fictitious name. **State v. Johnson,** Op. No. 4991, 958 P2d 440 (Alaska (1998).

Where trial court unquestionably possessed personal jurisdiction over state in civil forfeiture proceeding, it had power to award attorney's fees against state notwithstanding that court released jurisdiction over res prior to award. **State v. Johnson,** Op. No. 4991, 958 P2d 440 (Alaska (1998).

Superior court hearing appeal form administrative agency awards attorney's fees under Appellate Rule 508, not Civil Rule 82. **Stalnaker v. Williams,** Op. No. 5003, 960 P2d 590 (Alaska 1998).

Argument that losing plaintiff in civil rights action should be shielded form liability for fees and costs under this rule unless plaintiff's lawsuit is frivolous, unreasonable or without foundation was rejected. **Moody-Herrera v. State Dept. of Natural Resources,** Op. No. 5050, 967 P2d 79 (Alaska 1998).

Divorce exception to this rule did not apply to paternity action. **Rubright v. Arnold,** Op. No. 5083, 973 P2d 580 (Alaska 1999).

Where trial ended after three days when directed verdict motion was granted, case did in fact go "to trial" for purposes of this rule. **Martin v.**

State, Op. No. 1622, 973 P2d 1151 (Alaska App. 1999).

This rule is not authority for assessing attorney's fee award against counsel. **Wilson v. Municipality of Anchorage,** Op. No. 5111, 977 P2d 713 (Alaska 1999).

Civil Rules 79(h) and 82(e), which address the allocation of costs and attorney's fees respectively between third-party plaintiffs and third-party defendants joined in an action under Alaska's equitable apportionment statute, do not apply where the original plaintiff has made a direct claim against the third-party defendant; in such cases, the usual Alaska practice of awarding costs and attorney's fees to the prevailing party applies. **City of Kodiak v. Parish,** Op. No. 5170, 986 P2d 201 (Alaska 1999).

Award of attorney's fees in any proceeding arising out of Alaska's Uniform Landlord and Tenant Act should be made under AS 34.03.350 rather than Civil Rule 82. **Sullivan v. Subramanion,** Op. No. 5270, 2 P3d 66 (Alaska 2000).

Because child support case was settled without any reference to attorney's fees and because alleged prevailing party failed to notify other party of her intent to pursue Rule 82 attorney's fees in addition to terms negotiated in settlement agreement, any award of Rule 82 attorney's fees was barred. **Sanders v. Barth,** Op. No. 5328, 12 P3d 766 (Alaska 2000).

Award of attorney fees under this rule may not include fees incurred in defending against 42 U.S.C. § 1988 claims. **Brown v. Ely,** Op. No. 5347, 14 P3d 257 (Alaska 2000).

Where plaintiffs' claims were based upon common law and the Unfair Trade Practices Act, trial court had discretion to look to both this rule and the statute in deciding attorney's fees. **Garrison v. Dixon,** Op. No. 5378, 19 P3d 1229 (Alaska 2001).

This rule does not allow for awards of "several" attorney's fees against multiple non-prevailing parties; an award is based on the amount of the prevailing party's actual reasonable attorney's fees, and the number of non-prevailing parties is inconsequential. **Garrison v. Dixon,** Op. No. 5378, 19 P3d 1229 (Alaska 2001).

Where there is no dispute about the reasonableness of attorney's fees awarded under Civil Rights 68, the factors listed in this rule cannot be applied to reduce the award. **Kellis v. Crites,** Op. No. 5380, 20 P3d 1112 (Alaska 2001).

Where defendant prevails on state law claims brought in state court that are integrally related to federal civil rights claims, defendant is entitled to award of attorney's fees without showing that plaintiff's claims were frivolous, unreasonable or without foundation. **Sengupta v. University of Alaska,** Op. No. 5397, 21 P3d 1240 (Alaska 2001).

In action for reformation of recorded easement, this rule, which provides for award of partial attorney's fees to prevailing party, was overridden by provision in easement agreement calling for "reasonable attorney's fees," which was interpreted as meaning full reasonable attorney's fees. **Gamble v. Northstore Partnership,** Op. No. 5445, 22 P3d 457 (Alaska 2001).

This rules only applies to "costs of action," not attorney's fees incurred in conduct of prior arbitration. **Holderness v. State Farm Fire and Casualty Co.,** Op. No. 5425, 24 P3d 1235 (Alaska 2001).

Alaska R. Civ. P. 82(a) provides for an award of attorney's fees to the prevailing party 'except as otherwise provided by law.' If a specific statutory scheme for attorney's fees or costs exists, Alaska R. Civ. P. 79 and 82 do not apply. **Enders v. Parker,** Op. No. 5446, 28 P3d 280 (Alaska 2001).

Court can award costs and attorney's fees even after it concludes that it lacks subject matter jurisdiction over a party's claims. **Foster v. State,** Op. No. 5504, 34 P3d 1288 (Alaska 2001).

Accepting a motion for attorney's fees despite the fact that it was one day past the Alaska R. Civ. P. 82(c) deadline was well within the superior court's discretion. **Kaiser v. Sakata,** Op. No. 5526, 40 P3d 800 (Alaska 2002).

In the context of an award of attorney fees, Alaska R. Civ. P. 82 applies to claims for breach of contract and for violation of AS 23.05.140(b). **Diaz v. Silver Bay Logging, Inc.,** Op. No. 5635, 55 P.3d 732 (Alaska 2002).

Where a party sought relief from judgment under Alaska R. Civ. P. 60(b), rather than attorney's fees under Alaska R. Civ. P. 82(c), the limitations period for requesting attorney's fees did not apply, and the party did not waive her request for attorney's fees. **Fleegel v. Estate of Boyles,** Op. No. 5641, 61 P.3d 1267 (Alaska 2002).

Trial court did not abuse its discretion in applying the divorce exception to Alaska R. Civ. P. 82 and denying a former wife's motion for attorney's fees and costs after the property division because the economic situation of her bankrupt former husband was not significantly better than that of the former wife, who had interim support, the marital home, and a potential additional recovery for a 50 percent share of the former husband's claims in oil spill litigation. **Edelman v. Edelman,** Op. No. 5652, 61 P.3d 1 (Alaska 2002).

Denial of the personal representative's motion seeking attorney's fees and costs under Alaska R. Civ. P. 82(b) and 79(b) was proper where the legislature provided in AS 13.16.435 that a designated personal representative, the stepdaughter, could recover necessary expenses and disbursements, including reasonable attorney fees incurred; if a specific statutory scheme for attorney's fees existed, then Alaska R. Civ. P. 82 did not apply and because AS 13.16.435 also clearly covered costs incurred in the litigation, Alaska R. Civ. P. 79 likewise was inapplicable. **Enders v. Parker,** Op. No. 5675, 66 P.3d 11 (Alaska 2003).

Trial court did not abuse its discretion in denying the father attorney's fees after he prevailed on the issue of his child support obligation, because both sides had prevailed on significant issues in the revisiting of the parties' divorce decree, the father's income was greater than the mother's, and the father's past dishonesty and sharp litigation practices which increased the effort that the mother needed to exert to defend herself. **Hixson v. Sarkesian,** Op. No. 5677,66 P.3d 753 (Alaska 2003).

Trial court did not err in awarding attorney's fees to plaintiff citizens group, which sued defendant property owners who were seeking to have their land rezoned to permit its use as a private airstrip, even though the group had no obligation to pay its attorney, and had not erred in granting the group additional time to establish its claim for fees. **Cizek v. Concerned Citizens of Eagle River Valley, Inc.,** 71 P.3d 845 (Alaska 2003).

Trial court did not err in awarding plaintiff citizens group, which sued defendant property owners who were seeking to have their land rezoned to permit its use as a private airstrip, enhanced prevailing party fees under Alaska R. Civ. P. 82. **Cizek v. Concerned Citizens of Eagle River Valley, Inc.,** 71 P.3d 845 (Alaska 2003).

Trial court did not err in ordering the father to pay the mother's attorneys' fees even though they had never married and never lived together, because due to the fact the parties were litigating custody of their child, the divorce exception applied such that the father, who had a significantly higher earnings potential was obligated to pay the mother's fees. **Koller v. Reft,** 71 P.3d 800 (Alaska 2003).

Liability policy endorsement, lacking regulatory approval and containing language more complex than the model form, was ineffective to limit coverage for attorney fees in an airplane crash case. **Therchik v. Grant Aviation, Inc.,** Op. No. 5715,74 P.3d 191.

Where public interest plaintiffs immediately filed a second complaint following the dismissal of their first complaint, it was an abuse of discretion to award fees because the complaint was neither frivolous nor brought in bad faith. **Alaska Wildlife Alliance v. State,** Op. No. 5771, 74 P.3d 201.

Alaska R. Civ. P. 82's possible reach is limited to named parties. **Turner v. Alaska Communs. Sys. Long Distance,** Op. No. 5742, 78 P.3d 264 (Alaska 2003).

Alaska R. Civ. P. 82 does not require the court to impose attorney's fees on absent class members in the event of an adverse judgment. **Turner v. Alaska Communs. Sys. Long Distance,** Op. No. 5742, 78 P.3d 264 (Alaska 2003).

Language in a class action notification stating that defendants' attorney's fees could be imposed on absent class members was rejected, as absent class members have no obligation to pay attorneys' fees and litigation costs, except when they elect to accept the benefit of the litigation. **Turner v. Alaska Communs. Sys. Long Distance,** Op. No. 5742, 78 P.3d 264 (Alaska 2003).

In a probate proceeding, pursuant to Alaska R. Prob. P. 1(e), Alaska R. Civ. P. 82 governs the award of attorney's fees unless a specific provision of the Alaska Probate Rules apply. **Crittell v. Bingo,** Op. No. 5737 (Alaska 2004).

Alaska R. Civ. P. 82 governed award of fees where AS 13.16.435 did not apply to the interested parties' request for fees, since they did not bring their case as personal representatives and did not claim to be persons nominated as personal representatives under either of the decedent's wills; while one of the beneficiaries did claim to be the personal representative under the decedent's 1995 will, the trial court ruled that he had acted fraudulently in claiming to represent the estate under that will and that the will was fraudulent. **Crittell v. Bingo,** Op. No. 5737 (Alaska 2004).

Notations made by a court clerk and not signed by the judge reflecting fact that no attorney's fees would be awarded were not judicial orders. **Kozevnikoff v. Tanana Village Council,** Op. No. 5800, 89 P.3d 757.

Award of attorney fees was governed by AS 34.03.350, not this rule; where tenant had proceeded, at least in part, pro se; the award of attorney fees was unavailable, and the superior court's error in applying the wrong provision was harmless. **Fyffe v. Wright,** Op. No. 5819 (Alaska 2004).

By undertaking to pay coverage up to $50,000, plus limited attorney fees, as assessed under this rule, insurer did not obligate itself to extend an offer to pay attorney fees to the driver, who appeared to be unrepresented at the time of an insurer's initial offer. **Maloney v. Progressive Specialty Ins. Co,** Op. No. 1183, 99 P.3d 565 (Alaska 2004)

It was error for a superior court to consider past settlement negotiations when awarding enhanced fees under this rule because the only method by which fees may be enhanced for failure to accept an offer of judgment is found in Alaska R. Civ. P. 68; if an offer of judgment fails due to a procedural defect, the superior court may not then penalize the offeree by awarding enhanced fees under this rule. **Alderman v. Iditarod Props.,** Op. No. 5856, 104 P.3d 136 (Alaska 2004).

When state law, and not federal bankruptcy law, provides the rule of decision in a contested matter, the bankruptcy court will award attorney's fees to the same extent allowed under the governing state law. **Barstow v. Giordano (In re Giordano),** —Bankr. —(Bankr. D. Alaska Jan. 7,2004).

In a suit against an airline arising from changes to the airline's frequent flyer program, the class representative could not be held liable for attorney fees arising from litigation on issues related solely to class certification and notice; that litigation was for the benefit of putative class members, and offered no monetary benefit to the named plaintiff. **Monzingo v. Alaska Air Group, Inc.,** Op. No. 5894, 112 P.3d 655 (Alaska 2005).

Act of the 2003 Legislature (HB 145) that modifies the public interest litigant exception to Alaska Civil Rule 82 was valid even though the legislature did not change the rule by a two-thirds vote of the members of each house. The act did not change either the text or a judicial interpretation of the court rule, but instead it modified a policy-based nontextual exception that is an appropriate subject for legislative action. **State v. Native Village of Nunapitchuk**, Op. Nos. 11525, 11745, 156 P.3d 389 (Alaska 2007).

Act of the 2003 Legislature (HB 145) does not preclude consideration of any factors under subsection (b)(3) of this rule that may justify varying attorney's fee awards calculated under subsections (b)(1) and (2). **State v. Native Village of Nunapitchuk**, Op. Nos. 11525, 11745, 156 P.3d 389 (Alaska 2007).

II. Prevailing Party.

Even though there has not been a final determination on the merits in the case, where the complaint has been dismissed for failure to comply with an order to produce corporate records, the defendant is the "prevailing party," and as such is entitled to attorney fees as costs. **Hart v. Wolff,** Op. No. 724, 489 P2d 114 (Alaska 1971).

A party may be the "prevailing party" within this rule if he is successful with regard to the main issues in the action. **Cooper v. Carlson,** Op. No. 907, 511 P2d 1305 (Alaska 1973).

The prevailing party in each case should not automatically be awarded the full amount of attorney fees incurred. **Malvo v. J. C. Penney Co., Inc.,** Op. No. 901, 512 P2d 575 (Alaska 1973).

The purpose of this rule is to partially compensate the prevailing party for the costs and fees incurred where such compensation is justified, not to penalize a party for litigating a goodfaith claim. **Malvo v. J. C. Penney Co., Inc.,** Op. No. 901, 512 P2d 575 (Alaska 1973).

The purpose of this rule is to compensate partially a prevailing party for costs which he has incurred in litigation. **City of Valdez v. Valdez Development Company,** Op. No. 1051, 523 P2d 177 (Alaska 1974).

It is not the purpose of this rule to penalize a party for litigating goodfaith claim but rather partially to compensate the prevailing party where such compensation is justified. **Gilbert v. State,** Op. No. 1085, 526 P2d 1131 (Alaska 1974).

Generally, for purposes of awarding costs and attorney fees to the prevailing party, the 'prevailing party' is considered to be the party who has successfully prosecuted or defended against the action—the one who is successful on the main issue of the action and in whose favor the decision or verdict is rendered and the judgment entered. **Adoption of V.M.C.,** Op. No. 1103, 528 P2d 788 (Alaska 1974).

Determination of prevailing party does not automatically follow if party receives an affirmative recovery, but is grounded in which party prevails on the main issues. **Continental Ins. Co. v. U.S. Fid. & Guar. Co.,** Op. No. 1298, 552 P2d 1122 (Alaska 1976).

Litigant may be prevailing party if he is successful with regard to the main issue in the action, even if other side receives some affirmative recovery. **Alaska Placer Co. v. Lee,** Op. No. 1294, 553 P2d 54 (Alaska 1976).

When trial court does not award attorney's fees to a prevailing party who was not awarded a money judgment, it must state the basis for its decision. **Stordahl v. Government Employees Insurance Co.,** Op. No. 1422, 564 P2d 63 (Alaska 1977).

Attorney's fees are to be awarded to plaintiff who prevails in public interest case, although they would not be assessed against him if he did not prevail. **Anchorage v. McCabe,** Op. No. 1490, 568 P2d 986 (Alaska 1977).

The trial court retains discretion to refrain from characterizing either party as "prevailing" for purposes of awarding attorney's fees. **Tobeluk v. Lind,** Op. No. 1781, 589 P2d 873 (Alaska 1979).

The purpose of Civil Rule 82 is to compensate a prevailing party partially, not fully, for costs and attorney's fees incurred. **Stepanov v. Gavrilovich,** Op. No. 1823, 594 P2d 30 (Alaska 1979).

Where jury assessed damages against principal, failure to assess damages against agent did not convert agent into prevailing party entitled to attorney's fees in discretion of court. **Dowling Supply & Equipment v. Gardner,** Op. No. 1974, 602 P2d 1250 (Alaska 1979).

Two teachers who brought suit against their school district for a salary increase allegedly due them did not meet the "public interest" exception to the normal rule permitting a discretionary award of attorney's fees to the prevailing party. **Rouse v. Anchorage School Dist.,** Op. No. 2106, 613 P2d 263 (Alaska 1980).

If a debtor raises a claim under the Truth in Lending Act as a partial defense, the debtor may be awarded a reasonable attorney's fee pursuant to the provisions of that act for successful assertion of his claim; however, success on one claim does not necessarily make the debtor the prevailing party in the entire action, and need not preclude the court from awarding offsetting attorney's fees to the prevailing party under this rule. **Hayer v. National Bank**

of Alaska, Op. No. 2211, 619 P2d 474 (Alaska 1980).

The party who obtains an affirmative recovery is not necessarily the prevailing party within the meaning of this rule, and it is error for a court to rely solely on that factor in awarding attorney's fees. **Hayer v. National Bank of Alaska,** Op. No. 2211, 619 P2d 474 (Alaska 1980).

A dispute between the state and three individuals concerning valuable private property seized for violating state laws regulating a commercial enterprise does not fall within the "public interest" exception to the normal award of attorney's fees to the prevailing party. **F/V American Eagle v. State,** Op. No. 2227, 620 P2d 657 (Alaska 1980).

Where disposition of issues presented on appeal clearly established husband as the prevailing party, award of attorney's fees to wife, who initiated action seeking modification of terms of property settlement incorporated into divorce decree, was properly vacated and remanded to afford husband an opportunity to seek award of attorney's fees. **Stone v. Stone,** Op. No. 2522, 647 P2d 582 (Alaska 1982).

Class action against state and borough asserting that service area provisions of statute violated constitutional rights of all borough residents was public interest litigation, thus court's failure to award attorney's fees to the borough as prevailing party was not error. **Falke v. Fairbanks North Star Borough,** Op. No. 2530, 648 P2d 597 (Alaska 1982).

Plaintiff had sufficient private economic reasons to litigate decision by Alaska Department of Health and Social Services, which allowed a "certificate of need" for a hospital facility to remain in effect indefinitely, to justify superior court's award of attorney's fees to defendant as the prevailing party, against plaintiff's contention that the case came within the public interest litigation exception to this rule. **Sisters of Providence v. Dept. of Health, Etc.,** Op. No. 2536, 648 P2d 970 (Alaska 1982).

In applying the public interest exception to this rule, it makes no difference whether the defendant is a private rather than a public entity. **Southeast Alaska Conservation Council v. State,** Op. No. 2662, 665 P2d 544 (Alaska 1983).

In action by a private conservation council against the state challenging on constitutional and statutory grounds a timber sales contract entered into between the state and a timber company, it was a violation of the public interest exception to this rule for the court to award attorney's fees against the conservation council. **Southeast Alaska Conservation Council v. State,** Op. No. 2662, 665 P2d 544 (Alaska 1983).

Where grant of summary judgment against corporations for violating implied duty of good faith and fair dealing in employment contract was reversed, award of attorneys' fees to the corporations was vacated even though the corporations prevailed with respect to other related issues. **Mitford v. de Lasala,** Op. No. 2679, 666 P2d 1000 (Alaska 1983).

If a condemnee asserts counterclaims that are basically common law actions, such as negligence, the condemnor can be awarded costs and attorney's fees if it is the prevailing party on those issues. **Stewart v. State, Dept. of Transportation,** Op. No. 2895, 693 P2d 827 (Alaska 1984).

Once the State agreed to dismissal of condemnation action, condemnation was no longer an issue, thus State was entitled to attorney's fees thereafter incurred in successfully defending against condemnee's counterclaims seeking to prevent the State from removing trees and building a retaining wall on the State's own property. **Stewart v. State, Dept. of Transportation,** Op. No. 2895, 693 P2d 827 (Alaska 1984).

Unsuccessful challenger to a rezoning decision on ground that open meetings act was violated qualified as a public interest litigant under this rule. **Brookwood Area Homeowners v. Anchorage,** Op. No. 2953, 702 P2d 1317 (Alaska 1984).

In a divorce action, the "prevailing party" standard of this rule does not apply. **H.P.A. v. S.C.A.,** Op. No. 2961, 704 P2d 205 (Alaska 1985).

Unsuccessful suit by Labor Federation to enforce the wage requirements of the Little Davis Bacon Act was motivated principally by private rather than public concerns, hence the Federation was not a public interest litigant; therefore, trial court's award of attorney fees to the prevailing party was not an abuse of discretion. **Alaska State Federation of Labor v. State,** Op. No. 3014, 713 P2d 1208 (Alaska 1986).

In contested marriage and partnership dissolution proceeding, trial court did not abuse its discretion in awarding the prevailing party actual attorney's fees of $21,932 due to vexatious conduct by the losing party. **Horton v. Hansen,** Op. No. 3072, 722 P2d 211 (Alaska 1986).

Generally, since a dismissal with prejudice is an adjudication on the merits, a "prevailing party" determination is possible for purposes of this rule. **Anchorage v. Baugh Constr. & Eng'g Co.,** Op. No. 3083, 722 P2d 919 (Alaska 1986).

Defendant was clearly the prevailing party even if two of its affirmative defenses were rejected. **Anchorage v. Baugh Constr. & Eng'g Co.,** Op. No. 3083, 722 P2d 919 (Alaska 1986).

Trial court did not abuse its discretion in awarding the prevailing party $12,000 for attorney fees instead of the $22,594 actually incurred, since although the losing party's case was weak, it was not vexatious or brought in bad faith. **Wickwire v. Arctic Circle Air Services,** Op. No. 3084, 722 P2d 930 (Alaska 1986).

Where taxpayer paid the challenged tax under protest, then sued for a refund on constitutional grounds and lost, the judgment merely upheld the constitutionality of the tax statute and did not result in a money judgment, thus the state as the prevailing party was only entitled to attorney fees "in a reasonable amount" rather than attorney fees "commensurate with the amount and value of legal services rendered." **Atlantic Richfield Co. v. State,** Op. No. 3096, 723 P2d 1249 (Alaska 1986).

A contribution-claim defendant is not a prevailing party entitled to costs and attorney's fees when it secures summary judgment against the contribution claimant by settling with the injured plaintiff. **Foss Alaska Line, Inc. v. Northland Services,** Op. No. 3112, 724 P2d 523 (Alaska 1986).

A party who successfully defeats a claim of great potential liability may be the prevailing party even if the other side is successful in receiving an affirmative recovery. **Hutchins v. Schwartz,** Op. No. 3110, 724 P2d 1194 (Alaska 1986).

Defendant, who faced a potential liability of $275,000 but was required to pay only $1,937 less 40 percent, was the prevailing party. **Hutchins v. Schwartz,** Op. No. 3110, 724 P2d 1194 (Alaska 1986).

The "prevailing party" standard and the divorce action judgment exception to this rule are inappropriate standards for determining the question of attorney's fees in connection with motions to amend or enforce child custody orders. **L.L.M. v. P.M.,** Op. No. 3323, 754 P2d 262 (Alaska 1988).

The statutory standard of "willfully and without just excuse" is appropriate for determining the question of attorney's fees after a motion to amend or enforce a custody or visitation order is adjudicated; in this way any unsuccessful party who reasonably, and in good faith, believes that his or her action was justified by the best interests of the children will not be deterred from action by the possibility of an award of fees and costs. **L.L.M. v. P.M.,** Op. No. 3323, 754 P2d 262 (Alaska 1988).

The prevailing party rule used for determining attorney's fees awards under this rule does not apply to fee awards in divorces. **Rhodes v. Rhodes,** Op. No. 3339, 754 P2d 1333 (Alaska 1988).

As long as defense costs are reasonable, a successful defendant may recover whatever portion the trial court in its sound discretion sees fit to award; attorney's fees which prevailing defendants may recover are not limited as a matter of law by the amount of damages the unsuccessful plaintiff sought. **Stevens By Park View Corp. v. Richardson,** Op. No. 3313, 755 P2d 389 (Alaska 1988).

Plaintiff, who successfully prosecuted his action against defendant for moneys owed from the 1984 fishing season and defeated defendant's counterclaim for damages, was the prevailing party despite failing on his claim for moneys owed from the 1982 season and on his claim that he was defendant's employee rather than an independent contractor. **Day v. Moore,** Op. No. 3422, 771 P2d 436 (Alaska 1989).

For purposes of awarding fees pursuant to this rule, the general rule is that the prevailing party is the one who has successfully prosecuted or defended against the action, the one who is successful on the main issue of the action and in whose favor the decision or verdict is rendered and the judgment entered. **Day v. Moore,** Op. No. 3422, 771 P2d 436 (Alaska 1989).

A party does not have to prevail on all the issues in the case to be a "prevailing party"; one who defeats a claim of great potential liability may be the prevailing party even though the other side receives an affirmative recovery. **Day v. Moore,** Op. No. 3422, 771 P2d 436 (Alaska 1989).

In personal injury action by plaintiffs against helicopter owner following plaintiff's settlement with the helicopter component manufacturers, where defendant ultimately did not have to pay plaintiffs anything after the verdict in the plaintiff's favor was reduced by the amount of their previous settlements, the trial court did not abuse its discretion in holding that the defendant was the prevailing party. **Buoy v. ERA Helicopters, Inc.,** Op. No. 3423, 771 P2d 439 (Alaska 1989).

Trial court did not abuse its discretion in concluding that each side should bear its own costs and attorney fees since each side prevailed in substantial areas of the litigation. **Oaksmith v. Brusich,** Op. No. 3434, 774 P2d 191 (Alaska 1989).

The divorce judgment exception to this rule does not apply to post-judgment modification and enforcement motions; accordingly, fees in such cases are awarded under the prevailing party standard of this rule for post-judgment money and property issues, under which the parties' relative economic positions are irrelevant. **Lowe v. Lowe,** Op. No. 3726, 817 P2d 453 (Alaska 1991).

Estate of deceased minor, which prevailed in action for damages against store that illegally sold alcohol to the minor, did not satisfy the "public interest" litigant criteria, thus was not entitled to actual attorney fees. **Loeb v. Rasmussen,** Op. No. 3786, 822 P2d 914 (Alaska 1991).

The four criteria for determining whether a particular lawsuit involves the public interest are: (1) Is the case designed to effectuate strong public policies? (2) If the plaintiff succeeds will numerous people receive benefits from the lawsuit? (3) Can only a private party have been expected to bring the suit? (4) Would the purported public interest litigant have sufficient economic incentive to file suit even if the action involved only narrow issues lacking general importance? **Anchorage Daily News v. Anchorage School Dist.,** Op. No. 3652, 803 P2d 402 (Alaska 1990); **Citizens Coalition for Tort Reform v. McAlpine,** Op. No. 3686, 810 P2d 162 (Alaska 1991); **Loeb v. Rasmussen,** Op. No. 3786, 822 P2d 914 (Alaska 1991).

Where insureds prevailed on their claim of policy coverage and received $50,000 on that claim, but failed on their claim of bad faith against insurance company, trial court erred in designating insurance company rather than insureds as prevailing party. **Hillman v. Nationwide Mut. Fire Ins. Co.,** Op. No. 3971, 855 P2d 1321 (Alaska 1993).

Public interest litigant's general prevailing party status did not mean litigant should recover fees incurred in bringing or defending petitions for review on which it did not prevail. **Hickel v. Southeast Conference,** Op. No. 4055, 868 P2d 919 (Alaska 1994).

Plaintiff, whose recovery was slight compared to $700,000 in damages requested, but who succeeded in obtaining full damages requested for past medical expenses and $16,000 for past and future physical impairment and pain and suffering, was prevailing party. **Blumenshine v. Baptiste,** Op. No. 4060, 869 P2d 470 (Alaska 1994).

The "prevailing party" is the party who is successful with regard to the main issues in the action, even if the other party receives some affirmative recovery. **Bowman v. Blair,** Op. No. 4169, 889 P2d 1069 (Alaska 1995).

Party who retained ownership of the majority of the disputed items in a probate case was the prevailing party for purposes of awarding attorney's fees. **Bowman v. Blair,** Op. No. 4169, 889 P2d 1069 (Alaska 1995).

Trustee bank was neutral party in action concerning whether sale of trust property would be in best interest of all trust beneficiaries; as such, beneficiary input regarding proposed course of action could not be contrary to trustee's interests, thus award of fees against beneficiary and to trustee was unjustified. **Barber v. Barber,** Op. No. 4345, 915 P2d 1204 (Alaska 1996).

In state court action by merchant mariners against ship owners and asbestos manufacturers for injuries and wrongful deaths caused by exposure to asbestos which was dismissed on forum non conveniens grounds, court did not err in awarding attorney fees and costs to defendants as prevailing parties, nor did such award conflict with admiralty law. **Hughes v. Foster,** Op. No. 4790, 932 P2d 784 (Alaska 1997).

Alaska Wage and Hour Act, prior to its amendment in August 1995, did not permit award of attorney fees and costs to prevailing employer. **Grimes v. Kinney Shoe Corp.,** Op. No. 4815, 938 P2d 997 (Alaska 1997).

Where main issue in action for reformation of public trust was approval or rejection of settlement agreement, intervenor who prevailed on that issue was entitled to attorney's fees even if intervenor's legal arguments did not directly, primarily or necessarily cause court's favorable decision. **Alaska Center for the Environment v. State,** Op. No. 4830, 940 P2d 916 (Alaska 1997).

Prevailing defendants in actions to recover wages under Alaska Wage and Hour Act are not entitled to award of attorney's fees pursuant to this rule. **Schorr v. Frontier Transp. Co.,** Op. No. 4847, 942 P2d 418 (Alaska 1997).

In an in rem civil forfeiture proceeding in which trial court dismissed state's forfeiture complaint because of state's delay and ordered res released to claimant, claimant was prevailing party for purposes of attorney fee award even though res was seized by federal government when claimant did not show to take receipt of res. **State v. Johnson,** Op. No. 4991, 958 P2d 440 (Alaska 1998).

Trial court did not abuse its discretion by splitting prevailing party status for divergent claims. **Bliss v. Bobich,** Op. No. 5043, 971 P2d 141 (Alaska 1998).

In cases involving mixed causes of action, some governed by attorney fee provisions of this rule and some governed by attorney fee provisions of Alaska Wage and Hour Act, determination of prevailing party status remains matter of trial court discretion. **Bliss v. Bobich,** Op. No. 5043,971 P2d 141 (Alaska 1998).

Prevailing plaintiff did not waive its claim to an enhanced attorney's fee award, even though it did not request an enhanced award in its original motion for fees. **Alderman v. Iditarod Props., Inc.,** Op. No. 5486, 32 P3d 373 (Alaska 2001).

Viewing the matter as a whole, the court concluded that neither party could be considered the prevailing party for purposes of Rule 82; therefore, justice required that each party bear its own costs and fees. **Fernandes v. Portwine,** Op. No. 5632, 56 P.3d 1 (Alaska 2002).

Shareholders who filed a derivative suit against the directors of a village corporation were not prevailing parties because the trial court found that the shareholders' failure to make a pre-suit demand was not excused; the trial court did not err in denying the shareholders' request for attorney fees. **Jerue v. Millett,** Op. No. 5676, 66 P.3d 736 (Alaska 2003).

Where a village corporation did not become a party plaintiff until after the events occurred that mooted a derivative suit, the village was not a prevailing party for purposes of recovering attorney fees. **Jerue v. Millett,** Op. No. 5676, 66 P.3d 736 (Alaska 2003).

In a derivative suit filed on behalf of a village corporation by plaintiff shareholders, defendant directors were not prevailing parties and were not entitled to Alaska R. Civ. P. 82 attorney fees, where the directors did not prove that the lawsuit was not a cause of the remedial action the directors took, or that if a demand had been made the directors would have taken the remedial action. **Jerue v. Millett,** Op. No. 5676, 66 P.3d 736 (Alaska 2003).

In a doctor's suit against a pain management clinic, a court properly awarded the clinic attorney's fees, as the prevailing party, even though the clinic was able to afford to pay its own attorney's fees. **Sisters of Providence in Wash. v. A.A. Pain Clinic, Inc.,** Op. No. 5764, 81 P3d 989 (Alaska 2003).

In a doctor's antitrust case against a hospital, because he only prevailed on common law claims, he was not entitled to recovery under the full reasonable fees standard of AS 45.50.576(a)(1): rather, under Alaska R. Civ. P. 82, he was only entitled to an award of partial fees, and the superior court exceeded its bounds of broad discretion in awarding the doctor fees that could only be justified by a claim on which he did not prevail, and against a defendant against whom he did not prevail. **Sisters of Providence in Wash. v. A.A. Pain Clinic, Inc.,** Op. No. 5764, 81 P3d 989 (Alaska 2003).

Named plaintiff should not ordinarily be held liable for attorney's fees that fall beyond the scope of litigating the merits of his claim. This rule does not eliminate the award of attorney fees against unsuccessful named plaintiffs in class action lawsuits; it simply limits this rule's reach to the substantive merits of their claims. **Monzingo v. Alaska Air Group, Inc.,** Op. No. 5894, 112 P.3d 655 (Alaska 2005).

In an eviction action, full attorney's fees were awarded to the prevailing party where a provision in the lease allowed for such; the amount awarded was not limited by this rule. **Tufco, Inc. v. Pac. Envtl. Corp.,** Op. No. 5904, 113 P.3d 668 (Alaska 2005).

Prevailing party's request for full attorney's fees was affirmed despite the non-prevailing party's arguments that the underlying lease was contrary to public policy, unconscionable, and a contract of adhesion. **OK Lumber Co. v. Alaska R.R. Corp.,** Op. No. 5960, 123 P.3d 1076 (Alaska 2005).

In a state employee's wrongful termination case, court properly awarded the state attorney's fees under Civ. R. 68 where the employee declined the state's pretrial offer of judgment for $12,000 and the jury awarded the employee $3,900. **Jones v. Dep't of Corrections,** Op. No. 5969 125 P.3d 343 (Alaska 2005).

For purposes of subsection (a) of this rule, and Civ. R. 79(a), plaintiff lessor was the prevailing party because the lessee received far less on its counterclaim than it requested, and the lessor had the larger monetary award. **Alaska Constr. & Eng'g, Inc. v. Balzer Pac. Equip. Co.,** Op. No. 5981, 130 P.3d 932 (Alaska 2006).

The prevailing party is not entitled to an award of attorney's fees under Civil Rule 82 where the other party is a public interest litigant. There are four criteria for determining public interest litigant status: (1) Is the case designed to effectuate strong public policies? (2) If the plaintiff succeeds will numerous people receive benefits from the lawsuit? (3) Can only a private party have been expected to bring the suit? (4) Would the purported public interest litigant have sufficient economic incentive to file suit even if the action involved only narrow issues lacking general importance? **Fairbanks North Star Borough v. Interior Cabaret, Hotel, Restaurant & Retailers Ass'n**, Op. No. 11612, 137 P.3d 289 (Alaska 2006).

An automobile insurer is not required to pay unlimited attorney's fees under this rule to settle an underinsured motorist insurance claim if it has already paid unlimited fees on the same underlying projected jury verdict to settle a liability insurance claim and the policyholder was not underinsured with respect to court-awarded attorney's fees. **State Farm Mut. Auto. Ins. Co. v. Lestenkof**, Op. No. 11754, 155 P.3d 313 (Alaska 2007).

III. Review.

A. Standard.

The trial judge has large discretion in allowing attorney's fees for the prevailing party, but the supreme court will reduce the allowance where the amount awarded is unduly high. **Davidsen v. Kirkland,** Op. No. 38, 362 P2d 1068 (Alaska 1961).

Court-initiated amendment as to attorney's fees awarded as costs under this rule, did not affect the running of the time for appeal as provided under Supreme Court Rule 7(a). **Radich v. Fairbanks Builders, Inc.,** Op. No. 285, 399 P2d 215 (Alaska 1965).

Where appellant employer, albeit rightly so, prosecuted an appeal in a workmen's compensation case and thereby imposed upon employee the necessity to engage counsel to represent him in the superior court, trial judge did not abuse his discretion under this rule in denying an attorney's fee to appellant. **M-B Contracting Company v. Davis,** Op. No. 275, 399 P2d 433 (Alaska 1965).

Even if it may be assumed that appellant were "prevailing party" within the meaning of Civil Rule 54(d) and 82(a)(1), the trial court's determination as to denial of attorney's costs where the action was settled pursuant to Civil Rule 68 was not disturbed on appeal in the absence of a showing of clear abuse of the wide discretion allowed under this rule. **Albritton v. Estate of Larson,** Op. No. 413, 428 P2d 379 (Alaska 1967).

Awarding attorney's fees to the prevailing party is committed to the broad discretion of the trial. **Da v. Greater Anchorage Area Borough,** Op. No. 476, 439 P2d 790 (Alaska 1968); **Froelicher v. Hadley,** Op. No. 486, 442 P2d 51 (Alaska 1968).

The award of $1,300 as attorney's fees rather than $4,465, requested on the basis of hourly charges of $30 and $40 per hour and $350 per day for trial, is not an abuse of discretion. **Connelly v. Peede,** Op. No. 577, 459 P2d 362 (Alaska 1969).

The supreme court will interfere with the trial court's exercise of discretion in awarding attorney's fees as costs only where such discretion has been abused. An abuse of discretion is established where it appears that the trial court's determination is manifestly unreasonable. **Palfy v. Rice,** Op. No. 634,473 P2d 606 (Alaska 1970).

The award of $7,100 attorney's fees in an action arising out of a collision of an automobile and a tractor trailer combination on an ice and snow-covered curve of a highway is not an abuse of discretion, in view of the complexity of the factual issues, the length of the trial and the potentially large liability of the parties. **Ferrell v. Baxter,** Op. No. 688, 484 P2d 250 (Alaska 1971).

Where an affidavit which is filed by the defendant denies several factual allegations of the plaintiff and a memorandum filed by the defendant raises four defenses, such documents are tantamount to an answer and the plaintiff's right to dismiss suit is terminated. Thus, although the plaintiff files a voluntary dismissal of the suit, the trial court has the authority to award to defendant attorney fees. **Miller v. Wilkes,** Op. No. 788, 496 P2d 176 (Alaska 1972).

Where a subcontractor is the prevailing party in an action by a contractor against a subcontractor for recovery of progress payments, an award of $10,000 as attorney's fees to the subcontractor is not an abuse of discretion in view of the potentially large liability of the subcontractor. **Owen Jones & Sons, Inc. v. C.R. Lewis Co., Inc.,** Op. No. 795, 497 P2d 312 (Alaska 1972).

A trial court does not necessarily abuse its discretion by refusing to award attorney's fees to a property owner who successfully defends a suit for specific performance of a contract to sell property. **Hollaus v. Arend,** Op. No. 896, 511 P2d 1074 (Alaska 1973).

The award of attorney's fees is discretionary with the trial judge and is reviewable on appeal only for an abuse of discretion. **Cooper v. Carlson,** Op. No. 907, 511 P2d 1305 (Alaska 1973).

Although an award of attorney's fees to a prevailing party is not mandatory, the denial of a motion for such fees may not be arbitrary or capricious or result from improper motive. **Cooper v. Carlson,** Op. No. 907, 511 P2d 1305 (Alaska 1973).

In an action against the state to recover additional compensation arising out of a contract, an award to the state of attorney fees of $22,633.91 is not an abuse of discretion, where the case was pending for over four years, the case involved potential liability of over $500,000 and culminated in a five-day trial, as against the contention that the state should receive costs no greater than the equivalent to the hourly salary of the highest paid assistant attorney general who worked on the case, multiplied by the number of hours allowed by the trial court. **Morrison-Knudson Co., Inc., v. State,** Op. No. 1012, 519 P2d 834 (Alaska 1974).

The amount award as attorney fees is within the sound discretion of the trial court. Review is limited to question of whether the court exceeded that discretion. **City of Valdez v. Valdez Development Company,** Op. No. 1051, 523 P2d 177 (Alaska 1974).

The refusal to award attorney's fees in a case where each party prevails in part, and in which each award is of approximately equal value, it is not an abuse of discretion. **City of Valdez v. Valdez Development Company,** Op. No. 1051, 523 P2d 177 (Alaska 1974).

The award of attorney's fees is vested in the sound discretion of the trial court, and will be interfered with on appeal only when that discretion is manifestly abused. **Grasle Electric Co. v. Clark,** Op. No. 2073, 525 P2d 1081 (Alaska 1974).

Where the trial in a personal injury action lasts over four days and involves complicated medical and psychiatric issues, an award of attorney's fees of over $15,000, based entirely on the schedule set out in this rule, is not an abuse of discretion. **Grasle Electric Co. v. Clark,** Op. No. 2073, 525 P2d 1081 (Alaska 1974).

Both the award of costs and attorney fees to a prevailing party and the actual determination of who the "prevailing" party is are within broad discretion of the trial court. Only on a clear abuse of discretion will the supreme court interfere with its exercise, such abuse being established only where it appears that the trial court's determination is manifestly unreasonable. **Adoption of V.M.C.,** Op. No. 1103, 528 P2d 788 (Alaska 1974).

In reviewing a trial court's settlement of attorneys' fees granted at its discretion, the supreme court will disturb such a finding only upon a showing that a warrant was manifestly unreasonable. **Western Airlines, Inc., v. Lathrop Co.,** Op. No. 1146, 535 P2d 1209 (Alaska 1975).

Determination of which party prevails and is entitled to costs is within discretion of the trial judge. **First National Bank of Fairbanks v. Enzler,** Op. No. 1170, 537 P2d 517 (Alaska 1975).

Moot issues will not be reviewed solely to provide a means of contesting trial court's award of attorney's fees. **Munroe v. City Council for City of Anchorage,** Op. No. 1236, 545 P2d 165 (Alaska 1976).

To require widow to pay $10,750 in attorney's fees to defendant in wrongful death action whose counsel was provided by insurance carrier was not improper. **Sloan v. Atlantic Richfield Co.,** Op. No, 2047, 552 P2d 157 (Alaska 1976).

Determination of which party is the prevailing party is in the trial judge's discretion and is reviewable only for abuse. **Continental Ins. Co. v. U.S. Fid. & Guar. Co.,** Op. No. 1298, 552 P2d 1122 (Alaska 1976).

Trial court's discretion in awarding attorney's fees will be interfered with only when manifestly unreasonable. **Alaska Placer Co. v. Lee,** Op. No. 1294, 553 P2d 54 (Alaska 1976).

An award of attorney's fees under this rule will not be reversed unless manifestly unreasonable, arbitrary or designed for a purpose other than justly deserved compensation. **Fairbanks Builders, Inc. v. Sandstrom Plumbing & Heating, Inc.,** Op. No. 1324, 555 P2d 964 (Alaska 1976).

It was not abuse of discretion to award additional attorney's fees as compensation for efforts to force opposing party to answer interrogatories and appear at depositions. **Fairbanks Builders, Inc. v. Sandstrom Plumbing & Heating, Inc.,** Op. No. 1324, 555 P2d 964 (Alaska 1976).

Trial court's discretion under this rule is broad enough to warrant the denial of attorney's fees altogether. **Haskins v. Shelden,** Op. No. 1357, 558 P2d 487 (Alaska 1976).

Trial court's discretion under this rule will be interfered with only when abuse is established by a "manifestly unreasonable" award. **Haskins v. Shelden,** Op. No. 1357, 558 P2d 487 (Alaska 1976).

In view of complexity of issues, time during which case was pending before trial, amount of potential liability, and amount of trial preparation and presentation, trial court was not manifestly unreasonable in awarding $192,111 attorney's fees. **Beech Aircraft Corp. v. Harvey,** Op. No. 1338, 558 P2d 879 (Alaska 1976).

Award of $14,000 in attorney's fees where $1,750 would have been awarded under this rule was not abuse of discretion in six-day trial with extensive pre- and post-trial briefing and with a significant number of difficult and complex legal issues. **Chugach Electric Association v. Northern Corp.,** Op. No. 1408, 562 P2d 1053 (Alaska 1977).

An award of attorney's fees which represented 86 percent of the total bill submitted by plaintiffs' counsel was somewhat high but not manifestly unreasonable under the circumstances of the case. **Hausam v. Wodrich,** Op. No. 1558, 574 P2d 805 (Alaska 1978).

It was not manifestly unreasonable in determining attorney's fees and costs for the court to take into account that it ruled against the prevailing party on one of the contested issues. **Alaska State Bank v. Gen. Ins. Co.,** Op. No. 1564, 579 P2d 1362 (Alaska 1978).

Court did not abuse its discretion in denying attorney's fees to defendant who prevailed in paternity suit brought in good faith even though denial was based in part on fact that defendant admitted to having sexual relations with a minor. **Larry v. Dupree,** Op. No. 1652, 580 P2d 326 (Alaska 1978).

Where plaintiffs' status as a prevailing party could not be inferred from the settlement agreement because of the political nature of the case, the trial court did not err in denying plaintiffs' claim for attorney fees. **Tobeluk v. Lind,** Op. No. 1781, 589 P2d 873 (Alaska 1979).

Attorney fee award of $9,861 was not abuse of discretion where party had agreed to accept legal services in partial consideration of claim against attorney and the value of the attorney services was well in excess of $10,000. **Puritan Life Ins. Co. v. Guess,** Op. No. 1881, 598 P2d 900 (Alaska 1979).

Complexity of a case may be considered in determining the amount of attorney's fees, but that factor alone does not justify an award of full fees. **Moses v. McGarvey,** Op. No. 2139, 614 P2d 1363 (Alaska 1980).

Award of $55,000 in attorney's fees was not manifestly unreasonable for complex litigation which extended for over two years. **F/V American Eagle v. State,** Op. No. 2227, 620 P2d 657 (Alaska 1980).

Award of $15,000 for attorney's fees to successful public interest plaintiff was not abuse of discretion where the award did not cover actual attorney's fees but did constitute full "reasonable" attorney's fees. **City of Yakutat v. Ryman,** Op. No. 2581, 654 P2d 785 (Alaska 1982).

Prevailing plaintiff in action brought pursuant to the Uniform Reciprocal Enforcement of Support Act was entitled to attorney's fees under this rule, the fees to be based on the amount and value of the legal services rendered rather than upon the amount of the judgment. **Bailey v. Haas,** Op. No. 2593, 655 P2d 764 (Alaska 1982).

Although plaintiff's suit raised an issue of important public interest, attorney's fees were properly awarded to the prevailing defendant because the one-half million dollars involved would have prompted the suit regardless of the public interest. **Gold Bondholders, Etc. v. Atchison, Topeka and Santa Fe Ry. Co.,** Op. No. 2608, 658 P2d 776 (Alaska 1983).

Award of over one-half of the attorneys' fees actually incurred was not per se unreasonable. **Gold Bondholders, Etc. v. Atchison, Topeka and Santa Fe Ry. Co.,** Op. No. 2608, 658 P2d 776 (Alaska 1983).

Trial court did not err in awarding attorneys' fees to the prevailing party for time spent on issues on which it did not prevail. **Gold Bondholders, Etc. v. Atchison, Topeka and Santa Fe Ry. Co.,** Op. No. 2608, 658 P2d 776 (Alaska 1983).

Where the money judgment was not an accurate criterion for determining award of attorney's fees, trial court did not err in determining that only 250 of the 611.5 hours claimed by the State were necessary to develop and try the State's case and in further determining that the State's award should be based on 20 percent of those hours at the average private billing rate of $75.00 per hour. **AMFAC Hotels v. State Dept. of Transportation,** Op. No. 2620, 659 P2d 1189 (Alaska 1983).

Where no recovery was had, an award of $6,000.00 in attorney's fees from a total of $9,818.50 incurred was not an abuse of discretion. **Brunet v. Dresser Olympic,** Op. No. 2641, 660 P2d 846 (Alaska 1983).

Where prevailing party's attorney spent over a year in preparation, the prevailing party's potential liability was in excess of $50,000, numerous depositions were taken, and the trial lasted three days, award of $6,000 in attorney's fees and $1,641.74 in costs was not manifestly unreasonable. **Blackford v. Taggart,** Op. No. 2749, 672 P2d 888 (Alaska 1983).

Pretrial offers not in compliance with Civil Rule 68 should not be considered in determining questions of costs and attorney fees; accordingly, trial court erred when it used past settlement negotiations, which did not result in an offer of judgment in compliance with Civil Rule 68, to justify a reduction in the amount of attorney's fees that it would have awarded. **Myers v. Snow White Cleaners & L. Supply,** Op. No. 3419, 770 P2d 750 (Alaska 1989).

In a multiparty lawsuit, trial court's order requiring the plaintiff to pay 20 percent of a defendant's actual attorney fees and costs was a reasonable allocation between defendant's actual attorney fees and costs necessarily incurred in prevailing against the plaintiff's direct claim, as opposed to fees spent defending against the cross-claims of other defendants. **Myers v. Snow White Cleaners & L. Supply,** Op. No. 3419, 770 P2d 750 (Alaska 1989).

Each request for attorney fees or costs to a prevailing party in a multiparty lawsuit should be considered objectively on its own merits. The trial court is not required to compare the attorney fees awarded to each of the prevailing parties so as to provide for a particular net award of fees, although the trial court cannot apply radically different standards of awarding partial compensation to the parties without findings or an explanation supporting such disparate treatment. **Myers v. Snow White Cleaners & L. Supply,** Op. No. 3419, 770 P2d 750 (Alaska 1989).

The trial court impermissibly considered defendant's pretrial settlement posture, which the court characterized as unwarranted and unreasonable, when it made its attorney's fee award determination under this rule. **Day v. Moore,** Op. No. 3422,771 P2d 436 (Alaska 1989).

Because the husband in a divorce action engaged in unwarranted delay and had imposed unnecessary costs in the course of the action, it was not an abuse of discretion to award the wife attorney fees and 25 percent of her costs. **Hartland v. Hartland,** Op. No. 3459, 777 P2d 636 (Alaska 1989).

The argument that trial courts should never be permitted to award fees in excess of those established under the "noncontested" or "without trial" schedules of Civil Rule 82 following acceptance of any offer of judgment under Civil Rule 68 was rejected. **Van Dort v. Culliton,** Op. No. 3630, 797 P2d 642 (Alaska 1990).

Where an offer of judgment specifies only a lump sum figure without any provision for attorney's fees, attorney's fees may be awarded by the trial in accordance with standard Civil Rule 82 principles; where extraordinary circumstances would otherwise justify deviation from the Civil Rule schedule, such deviation is appropriate following acceptance of the offer of judgment under Civil Rule 68. **Van Dort v. Culliton,** Op. No. 3630, 797 P2d 642 (Alaska 1990).

It is for the trial judge to determine whether too much time was spent by attorneys for the prevailing party or whether too many attorneys were employed. **Integrated Res. Equity v. Fairbanks Boro.,** Op. No. 3633, 799 P2d 295 (Alaska 1990).

Whether an error in ruling on a motion for attorney's fees before the opposing party has an opportunity to respond is prejudicial or harmless depends on whether, as a matter of law, the party denied the opportunity to respond could not have prevailed on the issue of attorney's fees. **Bowman v. Blair,** Op. No. 4169, 889 P2d 1069 (Alaska 1995).

An award of attorneys' fees under this rule will be reversed only for an abuse of discretion. **Mt. Juneau Enterprises, Inc. v. Juneau Empire,** Op. No. 4180, 891 P2d 829 (Alaska 1995).

Attorney's fees awards are reviewed for an abuse of discretion. **Sweet v. Sisters of Providence in Washington,** Op. No. 4200, 893 P2d 1252 (Alaska 1995).

An award of attorney's fees will be overturned only upon a showing of abuse of discretion or a showing that the award is manifestly unreasonable. **Feichtinger v. Conant,** Op. No.4189, 893 P2d 1266 (Alaska 1995).

Attorney fee awards made pursuant to the schedule contained in this rule are presumptively correct. **McGlothin v. Municipality of Anchorage,** Op. No. 5205, 991 P2d 1273 (Alaska 1999).

There was ample evidence to support the trial court's findings that the will advocated by the beneficiaries was both conceived in fraud and advanced at trial through the beneficiaries' fraudulent actions; thus, the trial court properly applied the concept of vexatious and bad faith conduct in enhancing the attorney's fee award and properly granted the interested parties' motion for enhanced attorney's fees pursuant to Alaska R. Civ. P. 82(b)(3). **Crittell v. Bingo,** Op. No. 5737 (Alaska 2004).

When a party has taken a legitimate position, it has not acted unreasonably for the purposes of variation of attorney's fees under this rule. **Alderman v. Iditarod Props.,** Op. No. 5856, 104 P.3d 136 (Alaska 2004).

Conduct undertaken in "bad faith" for the purposes of section (b)(3)(G) of this rule must relate to conduct during the litigation, and not to actions taken during the underlying transaction or other litigation between the parties **Alderman v. Iditarod Props.,** Op. No. 5856, 104 P.3d 136 (Alaska 2004).

Upon a finding that attorney's fees were appropriate for a defendant under the Equal Credit Opportunity Act, the wife, who was exonerated from her personal guaranty, should have been awarded reasonable actual attorney's fees, instead of the partial attorney's fees. **Still v. Cunningham,** Op. No. 5825 (Alaska 2004).

Where public interest litigants brought a meritorious claim against the city and obtained a preliminary injunction, they did not lose their prevailing party status under AS 09.60.010 for purposes of attorney's fees recovery under this rule where, through the political process, the city later mooted the lawsuit and accomplished the claimants' goals. **City of Kenai v. Friends of the Rec. Ctr.,** Op. No. 5989, 129 P.3d 452 (Alaska 2006).

Act of the 2003 Legislature (HB 145) that modifies the public interest litigant exception to Alaska Civil Rule 82 was valid even though the legislature did not change the rule by a two-thirds vote of the members of each house. The act did not change either the text or a judicial interpretation of the court rule, but instead it modified a policy-based nontextual exception that is an appropriate subject for legislative action. **State v. Native Village of Nunapitchuk,** Op. Nos. 11525, 11745, 156 P.3d 389 (Alaska 2007).

Act of the 2003 Legislature (HB 145) does not preclude consideration of any factors under subsection (b)(3) of this rule that may justify varying attorney's fee awards calculated under subsections (b)(1) and (2). **State v. Native Village of Nunapitchuk,** Op. Nos. 11525, 11745, 156 P.3d 389 (Alaska 2007).

B. Abuse of Discretion or Error.

In a factually complex case requiring extensive preparation, in which counsel has been engaged in preparation for over three and one-half years, in which the potential liability of the prevailing party is considerable, in which numerous depositions are taken, and in which trial takes three weeks, and in respect to which the prevailing party is obliged to commence and litigate a separate action in federal court in order to discover certain records, the award of $3,700 attorney's fees as costs to the prevailing party is unreasonably low and an abuse of discretion. **Palfy v. Rice,** Op. No. 634, 473 P2d 606 (Alaska 1970).

Where a defendant receives a judgment of over seventeen thousand dollars on a counterclaim and suffers an offset of under one hundred dollars, the trial court's finding that neither party prevailed is manifestly unreasonable. **DeWitt v. Liberty Leasing Co. of Alaska,** Op. No. 818, 499 P2d 599 (Alaska 1972).

It is an abuse of discretion to award attorney's fees to the state against a potential candidate for the state legislature who in good faith challenges the constitutionality of the residency requirements. **Gilbert v. State,** Op. No. 1085, 526 P2d 1131 (Alaska 1974).

It is an abuse of discretion to award attorney fees against a losing party who has in good faith brought a genuine public issue before the court. **Gilbert v. State,** Op. No. 1085, 526 P2d 1131 (Alaska 1974).

Where radically different standards of partial compensation are applied in awarding attorney's fees to the parties the award will be considered an abuse of discretion unless there are findings or an explanation by the trial court supporting such disparate treatment. **Irving v. Bullock,** Op. No. 1261, 549 P2d 1184 (Alaska 1976).

Award of full attorney's fees was an abuse of discretion. **Continental Ins. Co. v. U.S. Fid. & Guar. Co.,** Op. No. 1298, 552 P2d 1122 (Alaska 1976).

It was abuse of discretion to award extra sum for defense of counterclaim where defense did not prevail. **Fairbanks Builders, Inc. v. Sandstrom Plumbing & Heating, Inc.,** Op. No. 1324, 555 P2d 964 (Alaska 1976).

Award to plaintiff of $15,337 in attorney fees, which represented 80 percent of actual attorney fees, was not abuse of discretion where defendants insisted on litigating weak and incredible defense that bordered on bad faith and where defendants' intransigence required plaintiff to expend considerable effort on motions and trial practice. **Crook v. Mortenson-Neal,** Op. No. 3128, 727 P2d 297 (Alaska 1986).

Superior court's denial of prevailing party's motion for attorney's fees on the basis that the party had no obligation to pay his attorney for legal services rendered was error. **Gregory v. Sauser,** Op. No. 1560, 574 P2d 445 (Alaska 1978).

Statement by superior court that "under the circumstances, justice will best be served if each party bears [its] own costs and attorney's fees" was not a sufficient explanation of its failure to award attorney's fees to the prevailing party. **Cunan v. Hastreiter,** Op. No. 1632, 579 P2d 524 (Alaska 1978).

In the absence of a bad faith defense or vexatious conduct by the losing party, it is manifestly unreasonable to award full attorney's fees to the prevailing party. **Davis v. Hallett,** Op. No. 1772, 587 P2d 1170 (Alaska 1978).

An enhanced award of attorney's fees for a successful public interest litigant computed by applying a multiple of the reasonable fee was not deemed appropriate in this case where the successful litigant was a nonprofit corporation represented by in-house counsel, where the prospect of such fees was not a factor used by the corporation in determining which cases to accept, and where counsel's major argument was not relied on in the court's opinion. **Thomas v. Bailey,** Op. No. 2094, 611 P2d 536 (Alaska 1980).

In a suit brought by shareholders against a corporation and its president it was error for the court to award full attorney's fees against the president since to do so saddles the unsuccessful party with the expenses, and does not impose the costs on the class that has benefited from the litigation. **Moses v. McGarvey,** Op. No. 2139, 614 P2d 1363 (Alaska 1980).

Where two attorneys hired by shareholders to file suit against a corporation were subsequently prevented by the court from representing the shareholders due to a conflict of interest, it was error for the trial court to award any attorney's fees for their services. **Moses v. McGarvey,** Op. No. 2139, 614 P2d 1363 (Alaska 1980).

Assessment of attorney's fees against plaintiffs in a class action suit concerning the constitutionality of applying a local sales tax to long-distance phone calls was error because it would deter other legitimate suits protecting citizens' rights against abusive taxation. **Douglas v. Glacier State Telephone Co.,** Op. No. 2144, 615 P2d 580 (Alaska 1980).

Superior court abused its discretion in awarding attorney's fees to the state as the prevailing party on a motion made pursuant to AS 45.52.210(f) to set aside an investigative demand. **Matanuska Maid, Inc. v. State,** Op. No. 2223, 620 P2d 182 (Alaska 1980).

Where there was no evidence that the losing party's claim was frivolous, vexatious, or devoid of good faith, an award of attorney's fees which was over 90 percent of the amount requested by the prevailing party was excessive. **State v. University of Alaska,** Op. No. 2303, 624 P2d 807 (Alaska 1981).

Trial court did not abuse its discretion in permitting a request for attorney's fees thirteen days after judgment. **State v. University of Alaska,** Op. No. 2303, 624 P2d 807 (Alaska 1981).

Court abused its discretion in a divorce action by awarding costs and attorney's fees on the prevailing party concept rather than on the economic situations and earning powers of the parties. **Cooke v. Cooke,** Op. No. 2275, 625 P2d 291 (Alaska 1981).

Assertion by losing party that work done by prevailing party's attorneys was duplicative and excessive was unsupported by evidence. **Alaska State Federation of Labor v. State,** Op. No. 3014, 713 P2d 1208 (Alaska 1986).

Failure of court, which made an award of attorney fees at variance with the schedule in the Civil Rules, to state its specific reasons for the amount awarded, required reversal. **Hayes v. Xerox Corp.,** Op. No. 3045, 718 P2d 929 (Alaska 1986).

Where both parties to a divorce had adequate incomes and where the wife was more favorably situated than the husband in terms of assets awarded by the court, the court abused its discretion in awarding attorney's fees to the wife. **Rhodes v. Rhodes,** Op. No. 3339, 754 P2d 1333 (Alaska 1988).

Attorney's fees award of more than half the actual fee was not an abuse of discretion. **Stevens By Park View Corp. v. Richardson,** Op. No. 3313, 755 P2d 389 (Alaska 1988).

Where prevailing party submitted 653.7 hours of attorney time spent on the case, opposing party's contention that $25,000 award for attorney's fees was excessive because 230.6 hours of the time submitted should have been excluded was rejected; assuming that 423.1 hours should have been billed, the award still represented only $60 per hour to attorneys who billed at the rate of $90 to $125 per hour. **O.K. Lumber v. Providence Washington Ins.,** Op. No. 3367, 759 P2d 523 (Alaska 1988).

A trial court may not use past settlement negotiations as a reason to justify a reduction or increase in the amount that it would otherwise have awarded; accordingly, where trial court considered, among other things, the fact that party made ridiculously low settlement offers, reversal of the attorney fee award was required. **Van Dort v. Culliton,** Op. No. 3630, 797 P2d 642 (Alaska 1990).

Trial court's award of attorney fees predicated on the amount awarded at arbitration was error. **Integrated Res. Equity v. Fairbanks Boro.,** Op. No. 3633, 799 P2d 295 (Alaska 1990).

Award of $30,000 in attorney's fees to prevailing bank in an action arising out of a mortgage foreclosure did not violate equal protection despite losing party's contention that, had he prevailed, his recovery for attorney's fees would have been limited to $6,000 under this rule. **Barber v. National Bank of Alaska,** Op. No. 3721, 815 P2d 857 (Alaska 1991).

Where attorney's fee award was based upon the total amount of the judgment for plaintiff, trial court erred in ordering the two defendants, who were jointly liable for the judgment amount, to each pay the attorney's fees award. **Frontier Companies v. Jack White Co.,** Op. No. 3759, 818 P2d 645 (Alaska 1991).

Claimed actual attorney fees of $200,000 in wrongful discharge case appeared clearly excessive, requiring remand for new attorney fee award based upon reasonable expenditures. **Zeilinger v. Sohie Alaska Petroleum Co.,** Op. No. 3794, 823 P2d 653 (Alaska 1992).

Where Borough successfully sued to enjoin property owners from violating zoning regulations, trial court did not abuse its discretion in awarding Borough seventy-four percent of its legal expenses. **LeDoux v. Kodiak Island Borough,** Op. No. 3822, 827 P2d 1211 (Alaska 1992).

Where defendant prevailed in wrongful death action, trial court erred in imposing liability for costs and fees against decedent's estate, since action was brought on behalf of surviving statutory beneficiaries, not on behalf of estate. **In re Soldotna Air Crash Litigation,** Op. No. 3859, 835 P2d 1215 (Alaska 1992).

Trial court did not abuse its discretion in refusing to impose costs and fees upon nonprevailing plaintiffs in wrongful death action since, although captions in several of the complaints listed plaintiffs as individuals, in substance plaintiffs brought suit as decendants' personal representatives. **In re Soldotna Air Crash Litigation,** Op. No. 3859, 835 P2d 1215 (Alaska 1992).

It did not constitute bad faith or vexatious conduct for municipality to challenge constitutionality of its own ordinance, thus award of full attorney fees to prevailing opposing party without explanation was error. **Municipality of Anchorage v. Police Dept.,** Op. No. 3893, 839 P2d 1080 (Alaska 1992).

When two parties who are aligned together are awarded differing percentages of attorney's fees, it constitutes an abuse of discretion unless fully explained, **Municipality of Anchorage v. Police Dept.,** Op. No. 3893, 839 P2d 1080 (Alaska 1992).

Attorney fee award of $531,563, which constituted eighty percent of total fees, was abuse of discretion, absent serious allegations of bad faith or vexatious conduct. **Exxon Corp. v. Burglin,** 42 F.3d 948 (5th Cir. 1995).

Superior court's use of the factor of "measure of success" in awarding attorney's fees in an administrative appeal did not on its face constitute an abuse of discretion. **North Slope Borough v. Barraza,** Op. No. 4285, 906 P2d 1377 (Alaska 1995).

Trial court's award of attorney's fees to prevailing party as prescribed by this rule without fact findings was not error and did not prevent appellate review of award. **Reid v. Williams,** Op. No. 5034, 964 P2d 453 (Alaska 1998).

Trial court did not abuse its discretion by allowing the plaintiff 70 days to file a corrected motion for attorney's fees, where plaintiff filed a timely original motion for fees and defendants were not prejudiced by the allegedly tardy motion. **Alderman v. Iditarod Props., Inc.,** Op. No. 5486, 32 P3d 373 (Alaska 2001).

Where a passenger sued the driver of the car in which he was riding for injuries stemming from a car accident, and the trial court ultimately granted the passenger attorney's fees and costs, the trial court erred when it failed to explain why it had deviated from the Alaska R. Civ. P. 82(b)(1) fee schedule with respect to fees for the arbitration of the case. **United Servs. Auto. Ass'n v. Pruitt,** Op. No. 5521, 38 P3d 528 (Alaska 2001).

Amount of attorney's fees awarded to a doctor was improper where his billings appeared to include specific amounts attributable to appellate work and lobbying efforts before the legislature. The superior court failed to address those parts of the billings or to explain why it found them to be compensable. **Marsingill v. O'Malley,** Op. No. 5977, 128 P.3d 151 (Alaska 2006).

Where the district court dismissed some of a business owner's claims as untimely but granted the business owner partial summary judgment on the remaining claims for payment for services rendered to a limited partnership, the district court did not abuse its discretion by declining to award the limited partnership attorney fees. **Johnson v. Columbia Props. Anchorage, LP,** 437 F.3d 894 (9th Cir. 2006).

Superior court's award of attorney's fees was not an abuse of discretion where appellant did not allege bad faith or that denial of the upward variance was an abuse of discretion. Appellant's reasoning that insurance company refused to arbitrate to force an expensive forum upon its insured may have some merit, but this argument was only hinted at by Appellant, and it was countered by the insurance company, which noted that it made an offer of judgment that was only slightly below the jury verdict. **Gibson v. GEICO General Ins. Co.,** Op. No. 12109, 153 P.3d 312 (Alaska 2007).

IV. Fee Schedule.

If the trial court departs from the schedule of fees fixed by this rule, the reasons of such non-adherence should appear in the record. **Patrick v. Sedwick,** Op. No. 338, 413 P2d 169 (Alaska 1966).

Although trial before court was concluded in one day an award of attorney's fees according to the schedule in this rule based on average contested cases was no abuse of discretion where extensive preparatory work and study was required over a two-year period to process the matter to a judgment. **Kenai Power Corp. v. Strandberg,** Op. No. 350, 415 P2d 659 (Alaska 1966).

On appeal from an award of about $32,000 in attorney's fees as part of the costs to the prevailing party calculated in adherence to the schedule provided under Civil Rule 82(a)(1), the supreme court did not interfere with the discretion of the trial judge where no abuse of such discretion appeared from the record. **McDonough v. Lee,** Op. No. 378, 420 P2d 459 (Alaska 1966).

A $2,500 fee to counsel of the plaintiff who recovers a $6,000 judgment is justified, even though in excess of the usual fee schedule, where counsel is forced to litigate all matters of liability and damage against stiff opposition, where matters of fact and law presented are complicated and difficult, where the jury might have found substantially in excess of the verdict, where counsel has been engaged in preparation for 2½ years, where many attempts for adjustment and settlement are made, where several pretrial hearings were attended and where the trial lasted 4½ days. **Froelicher v. Hadley,** Op. No. 486, 442 P2d 51 (Alaska 1968).

For there to be an abuse of discretion in setting attorney's fees in excess of fee schedule contained in this rule, it is necessary to show that a judge's action is manifestly unreasonable. **Froelicher v. Hadley,** Op. No. 486, 442 P2d 51 (Alaska 1968).

When trial court departs from the fee schedule of this rule, the reasons for nonadherence should appear in the record. **Haskins v. Shelden,** Op. No. 1357, 558 P2d 487 (Alaska 1976).

Reasons for departure from fee schedule of this rule should be set forth. **Alaska Airlines, Inc. v. Sweat,** Op. No. 1464, 568 P2d 916 (Alaska 1977).

Where the only money judgment was awarded on a counterclaim, and not on the main issue, the court correctly ruled that attorney's fees were to be awarded in a reasonable amount rather than according to the schedule in Civil Rule 81. **Alaska State Bank v. Gen. Ins. Co.,** Op. No. 1564, 579 P2d 1362 (Alaska 1978).

It was unnecessary for the court to state its reasons for initial non-adherence to the fee schedule contained in Civil Rule 82(a) when, on remand, it decided to comply with that schedule. **Alaska Airlines, Inc. v. Sweat,** Op. No. 1722, 584 P2d 544 (Alaska 1978).

Where no reasons appear in record to justify departure from schedule in Civil Rule 82(a), judgment as to that part must be vacated. **Farnsworth v. Steiner,** Op. No. 1955, 601 P2d 266 (Alaska 1979).

The policy favoring arbitration dictated that appellees be awarded attorney's fees exceeding the schedule of this rule to adequately compensate them for the cost involved in defending an appeal by the other party following arbitration, where that party had specifically agreed to regard the arbitrator's decisions as binding. **Board of Education v. Ewig,** Op. No. 2048, 609 P2d 10 (Alaska 1980).

Although it may be manifestly unreasonable for a court to automatically award the full amount of attorney's fees incurred, adherence by a court to the schedule of attorney's fees set out in this rule is not manifestly unreasonable. **Municipality of Anchorage v. Sisters of Providence in Washington, Inc.,** Op. No. 2343, 628 P2d 22 (Alaska 1981).

A deviation from the schedule of attorney's fees contained in this rule is justified when adherence to the schedule would produce fees which are disproportionately large in view of the time counsel devoted in the case. **Alyeska Pipeline Service Co. v. Anderson,** Op. No. 2364, 629 P2d 512

(Alaska 1981).

Courtroom time for numerous motions and the accumulation of documentation justified an award of attorney's fees in excess of the amount established by this rule. **Safeco Ins. Co. v. Honeywell,** Op. No. 2460, 639 P2d 996 (Alaska 1981).

Where actual attorney's fees were $15,486.33, award of $8,000 in attorney's fees to prevailing party was not manifestly unreasonable, even though that party received a money judgment of only $5,000. **Joseph v. Jones,** Op. No. 2464, 639 P2d 1014 (Alaska 1982).

Award to plaintiff of attorney's fees in excess of amount authorized by the schedule contained in this rule and which totaled 68 percent of his actual attorney's fees was not manifestly unreasonable in light of fact that his legitimate claim became the battleground for disputes between the codefendants. **Joseph v. Jones,** Op. No. 2464, 639 P2d 1014 (Alaska 1982).

Where prevailing party won a decree of specific performance rather than a money judgment, resort to the schedule of attorney's fees set forth in this rule was inappropriate, but award was nevertheless reasonable and would not be disturbed on appeal. **Dillingham Commercial Co. v. Spears,** Op. No. 2468, 641 P2d 1 (Alaska 1982).

Trial court must state its reasons when it makes an award of attorney's fees that varies from the schedule in this rule. **Mullen v. Christiansen,** Op. No. 2482, 642 P2d 1345 (Alaska 1982).

A prevailing pro se attorney is entitled to receive fees under this rule. **Burrell v. Hanger,** Op. No. 2557, 650 P2d 386 (Alaska 1982).

Where award of attorney's fees to pro se attorney was based upon the fee schedule of this rule and not upon the number of hours the attorney worked on the case, it was not necessary for the court to segregate the hours expended in the attorney role from the hours expended in the client role. **Burrell v. Hanger,** Op. No. 2557, 650 P2d 386 (Alaska 1982).

Where contract action was brought in good faith but going to trial on issue of contract reformation after summary judgment on breach of contract issue was frivolous, award to prevailing party of 53 percent of actual attorney's fees was not manifestly unreasonable. **Alaska Northern Development, Inc. v. Alyeska Pipeline Service Co.,** Op. No. 2689, 666 P2d 33 (Alaska 1983).

In the context of a post-judgment motion for attorney's fees, award of $27,433 pursuant to the fee schedule of this rule on a judgment of $356,117 was not abuse of discretion. **Gratrix v. Pine Tree, Inc.,** Op. No. 2790, 677 P2d 1264 (Alaska 1984).

Where prevailing party had pursued his personal injury claim through two extensive and complicated trials and one appeal, trial court's adherence to this rule's schedule in awarding $384,264 in attorney's fees was not manifestly unreasonable. **Dura Corp. v. Harned,** Op. No. 2952, 703 P2d 396 (Alaska 1985).

Trial court erred in awarding attorney's fees without explaining why it deviated from the schedule of fees set forth in this rule. **Stefano v. Coppock,** Op. No. 2968, 705 P2d 443 (Alaska 1985).

Where contribution award was made in favor of an aircraft manufacturer against the employer of a pilot killed in a plane crash, trial court did not err in disregarding the fee schedule of this rule and awarding reasonable attorney fees instead. **Ehredt v. DeHavilland Aircraft Co.,** Op. No. 2974, 705 P2d 913 (Alaska 1985).

In light of the complex nature of the case and in deference to the trial judge's observations of the performance of counsel, trial court's award of attorney's fees in the amount of $172,414.89 to the prevailing party pursuant to the schedule of this rule was affirmed, despite prevailing party's refusal to disclose what its actual fees were and how many hours its counsel spent on the case. **Fairbanks North Star Borough v. Tundra Tours,** Op. No. 3052, 719 P2d 1020 (Alaska 1986).

Where there is no money judgment, the fee schedule of this rule does not apply, therefore the court need not explain why it is departing from the schedule. **Wickwire v. Arctic Circle Air Services,** Op. No. 3084, 722 P2d 930 (Alaska 1986).

In a case where the fee schedule of this rule does apply, the trial court need not set forth its reasons for deviating from the schedule if the reasons are obvious. **Wickwire v. Arctic Circle Air Services,** Op. No. 3084, 722 P2d 930 (Alaska 1986).

Trial court has broad discretion to award attorney's fees in amounts greater than would be allowed under the schedule of this rule so long as the court specifies in the record its reasons for the departing from the schedule. **Taylor Const. Services, Inc. v. URS Co.,** Op. No. 3364, 758 P2d 99 (Alaska 1988).

Where the city prevailed in an action against it for which there was potentially a significant amount of money at stake in regard to punitive damages, partial award of $3500 in attorney fees for over $5000 in actual attorney time spent on the case was not unreasonable even though the compensatory damages at stake were quite small. **Murphy v. City of Wrangell,** Op. No. 3393, 763 P2d 229 (Alaska 1988).

Award of $305,358 in attorney fees pursuant to the schedule of this rule was affirmed notwithstanding the absence of an affidavit setting forth the number of hours expended for legal services. **Korean Air Lines, Co., Ltd. v. State,** Op. No. 3492, 779 P2d 333 (Alaska 1989).

Award of just over fifty percent of the prevailing party's actual attorney fees was not an abuse of discretion. **Kenai Peninsula Borough v. English Bay Village Corp.,** Op. No. 3517, 781 P2d 6 (Alaska 1989).

In suit by insured against insurer for violating insurance agreement, trial court erred in permitting jury to award the insured attorney fees beyond those authorized by this rule. **Alaska Pacific Assurance Co. v. Collins,** Op. No. 3614, 794 P2d 936 (Alaska 1990).

Attorney fee awards made pursuant to the schedule of this rule are presumptively correct; the prevailing party bears no burden to justify such awards, thus time itemization of counsel's services is not required. **Babinec v. Yabuki,** Op. No. 3644, 799 P2d 1325 (Alaska 1990).

Trial court could have awarded a larger attorney fee, but adhering to this rule's schedule was not an abuse of discretion; nevertheless, the award was vacated because part of the money judgment on which the scheduled fee was based had been vacated. **Hancock v. Northcutt,** Op. No. 3658, 808 P2d 251 (Alaska 1991).

Attorney fees of $165 to $175 per hour were not unreasonable. **Bozarth v. Atlantic Richfield Oil Co.,** Op. No. 3843, 833 P2d 2 (Alaska 1992).

In action for wrongful job termination, attorney fee award of $117,251 to prevailing defendant, which was 30 percent of defendant's actual fee, was not excessive. **Van Huff v. Sohio Alaska Petroleum Co.,** Op. No. 3857, 835 P2d 1181 (Alaska 1992).

An award of full attorney's fees must generally be explained. **Municipality of Anchorage v. Police Dept.,** Op. No. 3893, 839 P2d 1080 (Alaska 1992).

While deviation from the schedule of fees must be explained, if fee schedule does not apply, trial court need not set forth its reasons for award. **Municipality of Anchorage v. Police Dept.,** Op. No. 3893, 839 P2d 1080 (Alaska 1992).

In case involving sale of fishing vessel, trial court properly calculated attorney fees pursuant to terms of sales agreement, which specifically provided for reasonable attorney fees, rather than pursuant to this rule. **Gudenau v. Bierria,** Op. No. 4045, 868 P2d 907 (Alaska 1994).

Trail court did not abuse its discretion in not varying from the presumptive Rule 82 formula despite claims that an enhanced award was warranted by the complexity of the facts and issues, the extremely high monetary stakes involved and the underlying need to indicate the public policy announced in AS 45.45.900. **Aetna Casualty & Surety Co. v. Marion Equipment Co.,** Op. No. 4205, 894 P2d 664 (Alaska 1995).

Where a party appeals an administrative decision, but receives no money judgment, the guidelines in Civil Rule 82(b)(2) may be applied by analogy to Appellate Rule 508(e) to determine a reasonable award of attorney's fees. **CarrGottstein Properties v. State,** Op. No. 4230, 899 P2d 136 (Alaska 1995).

Where superior court did not state its reasons for deviating from the Rule 82 schedule, the attorney's fees award was vacated and the case remanded. **Saltz v. Saltz,** Op. No. 4272, 903 P2d 1070 (Alaska 1995).

In award of attorney fees to prevailing employer in suit brought by former employee, trial court's award of 7.5 percent of actual fees rather than 30 percent authorized by civil rules was justified by combination of very large number of attorneys defending the case, fact that employer had not treated employee fairly in past, and fact that large fee award might have deterrent effect on future employer/employee litigation. **Sever v. Alaska Pulp Corp.,** Op. No. 4420, 931 P2d 354 (Alaska 1996).

In class action lawsuit, attorney fees that class agreed to pay did not necessarily measure fair value of services provided. **Municipality of Anchorage v. Gallion,** Op. No. 4869, 944 P2d 436 (Alaska 1997).

In calculating attorneys fees to be awarded prevailing party in class action, trial court must determine compensable value of services attorneys rendered to class and then apply this rule to that amount. **Municipality of Anchorage v. Gallion,** Op. No. 4869, 944 P2d 436 (Alaska 1997).

Separate awards of attorney fees under this rule to plaintiffs based on their separate judgments against defendant did not constitute abuse of discretion even if combining judgment awards to calculate fee would have resulted in lesser attorney fee award. **St. Paul Fire & Marine Ins. Co. v. F.H.,** 117 F3d 435 (9th Cir. 1997).

An attorney's fees provision in a contract controls an award of attorney's fees, prevailing over any limitation otherwise imposed by this rule. **Johnson v. Olympic Liquidating Trust,** Op. No. 4939, 953 P2d 494 (Alaska 1998).

Where public interest litigants prevailed on one of three issues, trial court did not err in denying some expert witness fees and in reducing attorney fees to reasonable amount, but did err in apportioning fees by issue. **Dansereau v. Ulmer,** Op. No. 4962, 955 P2d 916 (Alaska 1998).

Trial court judgment awarding purchasers fifty percent of their actual reasonable attorney and paralegal fees for litigating dispute concerning failed home sale was not abuse of discretion notwithstanding that award of twenty percent is benchmark under this rule. **Nielson v. Benton,** Op. No. 4978, 957 P2d 971 (Alaska 1998).

Argument by prevailing plaintiff in medical malpractice case that he should be awarded enhanced attorney's fees so that in the future non-wealthy individuals will not be discouraged from litigating good faith claims was rejected. **Reid v. Williams,** Op. No. 5034, 964 P2d 453 (Alaska 1998).

Asymmetry inherent in two different methods for calculating presumptive attorney fee awards under this rule (percentage of damage award for prevailing parties who recover money judgment and percentage of incurred attorney's fees for prevailing parties who do not) did not justify enhanced attorney fee award to prevailing plaintiff. **Reid v. Williams,** Op. No. 5034, 964 P2d 453 (Alaska 1998).

Trial court did not err in declining to award enhanced attorney's fees under this rule to prevailing defendant in civil rights lawsuit. **Moody-Herrera v. State Dept. of Natural Resources,** Op. No. 5050, 967 P2d 79 (Alaska 1998).

"With trial" fee schedule rather than "without trial" fee schedule should have been used to award attorney fees to prevailing defendants where plaintiffs' claims against them were dismissed by directed verdict entered after plaintiffs presented their evidence at trial. **Bliss v. Bobich,** Op. No. 5043, 971 P2d 141 (Alaska 1998).

Award of substantially full attorney fees was manifestly unreasonable in absence of bad faith or vexatious conduct. **Marathon Oil Co. v. Arco Alaska, Inc.,** Op. No. 5068, 972 P2d 595 (Alaska 1999).

In support of request for enhanced attorney fees under this rule, party is required to submit records within brief description of services provided, hours worker, and hourly rates. **Andrus v. Lena,** Op. No. 5098, 975 P2d 54 (Alaska 1999).

It was error to award actual paralegal fees to prevailing party who received money judgment. **Andrus v. Lena,** Op. No. 5098, 975 P2d 54 (Alaska 1999).

Where final judgment required plaintiff's former partners to perform accountings and to pay plaintiff for his interest in partnership, but did not specify amounts payable nor how parties should calculate those amounts and did not require parties to return to court for approval of the accountings or amounts to be paid as determined by the accountings, trial court correctly treated final judgment as non-money judgment in awarding attorney's fees under this rule. **Strong Enterprises, Inc. v. Seaward,** Op. No. 5118, 980 P2d 456 (Alaska 1999).

Civil Rules 79(h) and 82(e), which address the allocation of costs and attorney's fees respectively between third-party plaintiffs and third-party defendants joined in an action under Alaska's equitable apportionment statute, do not apply where the original plaintiff has made a direct claim against the third-party defendant; in such cases, the usual Alaska practice of awarding costs and attorney's fees to the prevailing party applies. **City of Kodiak v. Parish,** Op. No. 5170, 986 P2d 201 (Alaska 1999).

Attorney fee awards made pursuant to the schedule contained in this rule are presumptively correct. **McGlothin v. Municipality of Anchorage,** Op. No. 5205, 991 P2d 1273 (Alaska 1999).

Trial court did not abuse its discretion in awarding fees for work that was duplicative if work was not shown to be unnecessary. **Tenala, Ltd. v. Fowler,** Op. No. 5219, 993 P2d 447 (Alaska 1999).

Even if none of the allegations in one count of plaintiff's complaint formed basis for her successful action against defendant, trial court could still award attorney's fees for work which included that claim; this rule does not require that attorneys fees be calculated with reference to the disposition of individual issues. **Tenala, Ltd. v. Fowler,** Op. No. 5219, 993 P2d 447 (Alaska 1999).

Fact that prevailing party's motions for summary judgment were unsuccessful did not prevent award of attorney's fees for those motions. **Belluomini v. Fred Meyer of Alaska, Inc.,** Op. No. 5218, 993 P2d 1009 (Alaska 1999).

Award of fees under this rule to party for its participation in administrative proceedings in addition to fees for its participation in superior court lawsuit was proper where lawsuit forced party to incur substantial fees to monitor administrative proceedings closely related to lawsuit. **Aloha Lumber Corp. v. University of Alaska,** Op. No. 5225, 994 P2d 991 (Alaska 1999).

If one or more Rule 82(b)(2) factors justify departure from the schedule for fee awards, trial court may base its decision on those factors, without specifically explaining why the other factors are not relevant. **Tenala, Ltd. v. Fowler,** Op. No. 5219, 993 P2d 447 (Alaska 1999).

Trial court's enhancement of attorney fee award to plaintiff to seventy-five percent because defendant increased the complexity of the case and because defendant's claims and defenses were not reasonable was not abuse of discretion; moreover, a seventy-five percent fee award does not constitute a "substantially full award" and thus does not require vexatious or bad faith conduct. **Cole v. Bartels,** Op. No. 5296,4 P3d 956 (Alaska 2000).

Trial court is under no obligation to give reasons for an award that complies with the percentages expressed in this rule, **Nichols v. State Farm Fire and Casualty Co.,** Op. No. 5304, 6 P3d 300 (Alaska 2000).

Divorce exception to this rule remains an exception rather than a rule and should be limited to cases that closely resemble divorce actions; accordingly, it was error for trial court to apply divorce exception to award of attorney's fees in child support action brought more than ten years after relationship broke up. **Sanders v. Barth,** Op. No. 5328, 12 P3d 766 (Alaska 2000).

Trial court did not err in failing to apply a risk enhancement or lodestar multiplier to attorney fees awarded to prevailing party in employment sex discrimination case. **Era Aviation v. Lindfors,** Op. No. 5335, 17 P3d 40 (Alaska 2000).

Even if adoptive mother who prevailed in adoption proceeding against child's grandparents could apply $2,000 federal adoption subsidy to attorney's fees, her remaining actual attorney's fees would still equal $4,150, thus $1,000 fee award made by the trial court was still well below the thirty percent of actual fees contemplated by this rule and therefore not an abuse of discretion. **C.L. v. P.C.S.,** Op. No. 5360, 17 P3d 769 (Alaska 2001).

Trial court did not abuse its discretion in awarding full, actual attorney's fees under this rule on grounds of vexatious and bad faith litigation. **Garrison v. Dixon,** Op. No. 5378, 19 P3d 1229 (Alaska 2001).

Insured's failure to plead arbitration in his complaint against an insurance company and an insurance agent in which the insured sought a declaration of coverage did not waive the insured's right to arbitration, and the trial court erred in finding that the insured waived the arbitration remedy. **Blood v. Kenneth Murray Ins., Inc.,** 68 P.3d 1251 (Alaska 2003).

In awarding attorney fees to plaintiff citizens group, which sued defendant property owners who were seeking to have their land rezoned to permit its use as a private airstrip, the trial court did not err in calculating the base amount of the group's reasonable, actual attorney's fees by using the owners' fees as a reasonable estimation of what the group's attorney could have claimed. **Cizek v. Concerned Citizens of Eagle River Valley, Inc.,** 71 P.3d 845 (Alaska 2003).

Trial court's award of attorney fees in a breach of contract action concerning the renovation and selling of a boat was proper where the owner made an offer of settlement to her contractor, which was not accepted, and ultimately recovered an amount that was more than five percent less favorable to the contractor than the amount offered in settlement. **Peterson v. Ek,** Op. No. 5818, 93 P.3d 458 (Alaska 2004).

In a case alleging sexual harassment liability, an award of attorney's fees under both Alaska R. Civ. P. 68 and Alaska R. Civ. P. 82 was improper because such an award was clearly prohibited under Alaska R. Civ. P. 68(c). **Ellison v. Plumbers & Steam Fitters Union Local 375,** Op. No. 5934, 118 P.3d 1070 (Alaska 2005).

When counsel requests attorney's fees other than based on the schedule in subparagraph (b)(1) of this rule, accurate records of the hours expended and a brief description of the services reflected by those hours should be submitted. **Valley Hosp. Ass'n, Inc. v. Brauneis**, Op. No. 11902, 141 P.3d 726 (Alaska 2006).

Documentation of actual fees is necessary in a default case under Rule 82(c) because Rule 82(b)(4) requires the court to award the lesser of actual reasonable fees or the scheduled amount under Rule 82(b)(1). In a simple default case in which little substantive legal work was necessary, an itemization of work performed and an affidavit certifying its veracity are essential for determining whether fees based on the Rule 82(b)(1) schedule are proper. **Valley Hosp. Ass'n, Inc. v. Brauneis**, Op. No. 11902, 141 P.3d 726 (Alaska 2006).

When counsel requests attorney's fees other than based on the schedule in subparagraph (b)(1) of this rule, accurate records of the hours expended and a brief description of the services reflected by those hours should be submitted. **Valley Hosp. Ass'n, Inc. v. Brauneis**, Op. No. 11902, 141 P.3d 726 (Alaska 2006).

Documentation of actual fees is necessary in a default case under Rule 82(c) because Rule 82(b)(4) requires the court to award the lesser of actual reasonable fees or the scheduled amount under Rule 82(b)(1). In a simple default case in which little substantive legal work was necessary, an itemization of work performed and an affidavit certifying its veracity are essential for determining whether fees based on the Rule 82(b)(1) schedule are proper. **Valley Hosp. Ass'n, Inc. v. Brauneis**, Op. No. 11902, 141 P.3d 726 (Alaska 2006).

LAW REVIEW COMMENTARIES

"Erie Similarities: Alaska Civil Rule 68, 'Direct Collisions' and the Problem of Non-Aligning Background Assumptions," 23 Alaska L. Rev. 81 (2006).

Rule 83. Fees: Witnesses—Physicians—Interpreters and Translators.

The payment of fees and mileage for witnesses, and for physicians and interpreters and translators, shall be governed by the rules for the administration of the courts.

(Adopted by SCO 5 October 9, 1959)

Annotations

Cases

The taxing of costs for witness fees is governed by Civil Rule 83 and Administrative Rule 7(c) rather than the general provisions of Civil Rule 79(b). **Miller v. Sears,** Op. No. 2447, 636 P2d 1183 (Alaska 1981).

Where expert witness for prevailing public interest litigant was not paid for his work and had no binding agreement to be paid for his work and did not testify, trial court did not err in failing to award costs for his expert services. **Dansereau v. Ulmer,** Op. No. 4962, 955 P2d 916 (Alaska 1998).

PART XII. SPECIAL PROCEEDINGS

Rule 84. Change of Name.

(a) **Petition.** Every action for change of name shall be commenced by filing a verified petition entitled in the name of petitioner, showing the name which petitioner desires to adopt and setting forth the reasons for requesting a change of name.

(b) **Notice of Application.** The court by order shall set a date for hearing not less than 40 days after the date of the order. Notice of the filing of the petition with a statement of the relief sought therein and the date of hearing thereon shall be published in a newspaper designated by the court as being the publication most likely to give appropriate notice under the circumstances. Publication of the notice shall be made once each week for 4 consecutive calendar weeks prior to the date of the hearing. In its discretion, the court by order may also require the posting of the notice at such place or places, in designated communities as may be appropriate. Proof of publication shall be made as prescribed in Rule 4(e)(5). Proof of posting shall be made by affidavit.

(c) **Judgment—Notice—Filing.** If satisfied that there is no reasonable objection to the assumption of another name by petitioner, the court shall by judgment authorize petitioner to assume such other name after a time to be fixed in the judgment, which shall not be less than 30 days after the date shown in the clerk's certificate of distribution on the judgment. Within 10 days after the date shown in the clerk's certificate of distribution on the judgment, a copy thereof shall be published once in the newspaper designated by the court under the provisions of subdivision (b). The court may also require the posting of a copy of the judgment as provided in subdivision (b). Within 20 days after the date shown in the clerk's certificate of distribution on the judgment, proof of publication and of any posting shall be filed with the clerk. The petitioner may then submit a certificate to be issued by the clerk stating that the judgment has been entered and that all requirements for posting a copy of the judgment have been met.

(d) **Applicability.** This rule shall not apply to restoration of a prior name sought in a complaint for divorce or in a petition for dissolution of marriage.

(e) **Change of Name for Minor Child.** An action for change of name for a minor child will be commenced by the filing of a verified petition in the name of a parent or guardian on behalf of the minor child, showing the name which the petitioner desires the child to assume and setting forth the reasons for requesting the change of name. No petition will be heard unless written consent to the petition is filed by both the child's legal parents and the child's legal guardian (if any), or unless proof of service is filed with the court showing that the child's parent(s) and legal guardian(s) have been served with a summons and a copy of the petition at least 30 days prior to the date set for hearing. Service of the petition and summons will be in accord with the provisions of these rules applicable to the service of a complaint and summons. The summons must advise the recipient of the date set for hearing on the petition.

If the court receives an objection to the proposed name change presented by a parent and/or legal guardian of the child prior to or at the time of the hearing on the proposed name change, the court shall consider the objection and shall only grant the name change if the court finds the name change to be in the best interest of the child. The court shall also consider the desires of a child old enough to express the same in determining whether a requested name change will be granted.

The requirements of (b) and (c) of this rule apply to a change of name proceeding brought under this section.

(Amended by SCO 49 effective January 1, 1963; by SCO 56 effective November 1, 1963; by SCO 252(2) effective September 22, 1976; by SCO 542 effective October 1, 1982; by SCO 554 effective April 4, 1983; by SCO 624 effective June 15, 1985; by SCO 671 effective June 15, 1986; and by SCO 999 effective January 15, 1990)

Cross References

(a) **CROSS REFERENCE:** AS 09.55.010

Rule 85. Forcible Entry and Detainer.

(a) **Practice and Procedure.** In an action for the possession of any land, tenement or other real property brought under the forcible entry and detainer provisions of law, the practice and procedure shall be as in other civil actions, subject to the following:

(1) *Description of Premises.* The premises claimed shall be described in the complaint with such certainty that the defendant will be distinctly advised of their location so that possession thereof may be delivered according to that description.

(2) *Summons.* Summons shall be served not less than two days before the day of the eviction hearing. The date set for the eviction hearing shall be not more than 15 days from the date of filing of the complaint unless otherwise ordered by the court.

(3) *Continuances.* No continuance shall be granted for a longer period than 2 days, unless the defendant applying therefor shall give an undertaking to the adverse party, with sureties approved by the court, conditioned to the payment of the rent that may accrue if judgment is rendered against defendant.

(4) *Appearance by Defendant.* An appearance by a defendant at the eviction hearing is an appearance in the entire matter for purposes of Civil Rule 55(a).

(5) *Service—How Made.* A defendant cannot be served under Civil Rule 5 by mailing a copy of the document to the address from which the defendant was evicted unless the defendant's current mailing address and whereabouts are not readily ascertainable.

(6) *Dismissal of Action for Want of Prosecution.*

(A) *By Clerk.* A forcible entry and detainer case may be dismissed by the clerk for want of prosecution under the procedures set out in Civil Rule 41(e)(2) and (3) if

(i) the case has been pending for more than 180 days from the date the complaint was filed;

(ii) no trial or hearing is scheduled; and

(iii) no application for default judgment has been filed.

(B) *By Order of Court.* The court on its own motion or on motion of a party to the action may enter a judgment of dismissal if the plaintiff fails to appear for a scheduled trial or hearing.

(C) *Dismissal Without Prejudice.* A case dismissed for want of prosecution under this rule is dismissed without prejudice unless otherwise ordered by the court.

(b) **Referral to District Courts for Trial.** Any such action filed in the superior court may be referred by the court to a district court for trial when the amount does not exceed the jurisdiction of district court.

(Amended by SCO 49 effective January 1, 1963; amended by SCO 678 effective June 15, 1986; by SCO 739 effective August 28, 1986; and by SCO 1461 effective April 15, 2002)

Cross References

(a) (generally) **CROSS REFERENCE:** AS 09.45.070

Annotations

Cases

Although appellants were brought to trial under the summary procedure provided for a forcible entry and detainer action, it would have been contrary to the one form of action principle to have forced appellees to resort to a separate ejectment action where proof showed that the appellants were not entitled to the possession of the premises because of nonexistence of an alleged lease and where appellants had not objected to an extension of the scope of testimony beyond the narrow issues of a forcible entry and detainer action at the trial and did not contend that they were prejudiced thereby. **Thrift Shop, Inc. v. Alaska Mutual Savings Bank,** Op. No. 277, 398 P2d 657 (Alaska 1965).

The provision in the forcible entry and detainer statute, AS 09.45.070 (b) purporting to limit recovery in such an action to arrears of rent and damage to property is without significance as attempting to regulate a matter of practice and procedure regulated by court rule. **Thrift Shop, Inc. v. Alaska Mutual Savings Bank,** Op. No. 277, 398 P2d 657 (Alaska 1965).

Where superior court twice continued the trial to allow tenant in a forcible entry and detainer action to obtain substitute counsel after his first attorney withdrew, and specifically informed tenant that no further continuance would be granted, the superior court did not abuse its discretion in denying tenant's request for a third continuance to allow his substitute counsel to return from vacation. **Taylor v. Gill Street Investments,** Op. No. 3228, 743 P2d 345 (Alaska 1987).

A forcible entry and detainer action is summary in nature, and traditionally the court will recognize almost no affirmative defense or counterclaim. **Vinson v. Hamilton,** Op. No. 3967, 854 P.2d 733 (Alaska 1993).

Where motion for a continuance stated two valid defenses to an action for possession, retaliatory eviction and the existence of an oral one-year lease, and there was no indication that the movant did not act diligently in his efforts to obtain the assistance of counsel and prepare himself for trial, movant was held to have shown good cause for a continuance. **Vinson v. Hamilton,** Op. No. 3967, 854 P.2d 733 (Alaska 1993).

A mutual help and occupancy agreement was held to be a "hybrid" lease/option contract, based upon several of its provisions, including its listing of homebuyer obligations similar to those under the Landlord Tenant Act, such as the housing authority's ability to change variable monthly payments at its discretion, required counseling and inspection, mandated income reports, restrictions upon who could reside in the home, prohibition of subletting and assignment, controlled insurance, and detailed termination procedures. **Kopanuk v. AVCP Regional Hous. Auth.,** Op. No. 4257, 902 P.2d 813 (Alaska 1995).

Housing authority could not maintain a forcible entry and detainer action against a homebuyer under a mutual help and occupancy agreement, because the agreement created equitable interests in the homebuyer under state law; the homebuyer under the mutual help occupancy program should be treated as a homeowner with equitable title. **Kopanuk v. AVCP Regional Hous. Auth.,** Op. No. 4257, 902 P.2d 813 (Alaska 1995).

The Indian Housing Act of 1988,(former 42 U.S.C. § 1437aa et seq. and its imposition of the duty of maintenance on a homebuyer, directly conflicts with the Landlord Tenant Act's imposition of that duty on the landlord; accordingly, the Landlord Tenant Act cannot control this aspect of a mutual help and occupancy agreement because federal law preempts it, and a ruling that the Landlord Tenant Act imposed a duty of maintenance on the housing authority, rather than on the homeowner, was error.. **Interior Regional Hous. Auth. v. James,** Op. No. 5186, 989 P.2d 145 (Alaska 1999).

Where the initial extent of a housing authority's duty may have been to use reasonable care in repairing the defective furnace in a home occupied under a mutual help and occupancy agreement, the housing authority may have voluntarily broadened its duty by engaging in ongoing maintenance and repair, and may be liable for negligent failure to discover and remedy hazardous problems with the furnace. **Interior Regional Hous. Auth. v. James,** Op. No. 5186, 989 P.2d 145 (Alaska 1999).

Rule 86. Habeas Corpus.

(a) **Scope of Civil Rules.** The procedure in an action for habeas corpus shall be governed by the rules governing the procedure in civil actions in the superior court to the extent that such rules are applicable.

(b) **Complaint.** The complaint shall be verified by the prisoner or by someone on the prisoner's behalf who shall be known as the plaintiff and shall state in substance as follows:

(1) That the person in whose behalf the writ is applied for (the prisoner) is restrained of liberty.

(2) The name of the prisoner, if known, or the prisoner's description.

(3) The name of the officer or person by whom the prisoner is so restrained, if known, or the officer's or person's description.

(4) The place of restraint, if known.

(5) That the action for habeas corpus by or on behalf of the prisoner is not prohibited by law.

(6) The cause or pretense of such restraint, according to the best of the knowledge and belief of the plaintiff.

(7) The reasons why the restraint is illegal.

(8) If the restraint is by virtue of any warrant, judgment, order or process, a copy thereof shall be attached as an exhibit, or an explanation of its absence shall be made in the complaint.

(9) That the legality of the restraint has not been already adjudged upon a prior writ of habeas corpus to the knowledge or belief of the plaintiff.

(c) **Writ—Order to Show Cause—Warrant.**

(1) *Issuance Upon Application.* Upon the presentation or filing of a complaint, the court (or judge) shall, unless it appears that the plaintiff is not entitled to that relief:

[a] Issue a writ of habeas corpus directed to the person having custody of the prisoner, or the person's superior, ordering the person or superior to answer the writ stating the authority for restraining the prisoner and to bring the person alleged to be restrained before the court (or judge) forthwith, or at a designated time and place; or

[b] Issue an order to show cause why the writ should not be issued, returnable as in [a] above; or

[c] Issue a warrant in lieu of habeas corpus.

(2) *Issuance Without Application.* Any judicial officer may issue a writ of habeas corpus, or an order to show cause, sua sponte whenever it appears that any person is illegally restrained. A writ issued by a district court judge or magistrate is returnable before a judge of the superior court.

(3) *Duplicate Original Writs.* Duplicate original writs or orders to show cause may be issued in any number required.

(d) **Sufficiency of Writ.** The writ or order to show cause shall not be disobeyed for any defect of form. It is sufficient (1) if the person having custody of the prisoner is designated simply as the person having custody of the prisoner, and (2) if the person restrained, or who is directed to be produced, is designated by name; or if that person's name is uncertain or unknown, if that person is described in any other way, so as to designate the person intended. Anyone served with the writ is deemed the person to whom it is directed.

(e) **Service of Writ.**

(1) *Person to Be Served.* The writ or order to show cause shall be served on the person having custody of the prisoner, who shall be known and designated as the defendant, in the manner prescribed in Rule 4. If the defendant cannot be found, or if the defendant does not have the prisoner in custody, the

writ or order to show cause may be served upon anyone having the prisoner in custody, or that person's superior, in the manner and with the same effect as if that person or the superior had been made defendant in the action.

(2) *Tender of Fees.* To make the service of a writ of habeas corpus effective as to the production of the prisoner, the person making service shall tender to the person having custody of the prisoner, or that person's superior, the fees as follows:

[a] No fees need be tendered if the action is brought by the Attorney General or a prosecuting attorney, nor if the writ is issued by the judge on the judge's own motion.

[b] If the prisoner is in the custody of a public officer, the fees tendered shall be in a sum adequate to cover the cost of producing the prisoner and of returning the prisoner if remanded, said sum to be established by the judge upon the issuance of the writ and endorsed thereon by the judge.

[c] If the prisoner is in the custody of any other person, and if the judge allowing the writ so orders, the fees tendered shall be those established by the judge and endorsed on the writ, not to exceed the cost of producing and returning the prisoner.

[d] If the prisoner is not returned, the amount of the fee tendered to cover the cost of return shall be refunded to the owner.

(f) **Return.** Every person who serves or attempts to serve a writ or order to show cause shall make a return in accordance with the provisions of Rule 4(f). The execution or service and return of a warrant shall be governed by the provisions of Criminal Rule 4(c).

(g) **Answer.**

(1) *Contents.* The answer shall state plainly and unequivocally:

[a] Whether the defendant or person served then has, or at any time has had, the prisoner in custody, and if so, the authority and cause therefor; and

[b] If the prisoner has been transferred, to whom, when the transfer was made, and the reason and authority therefor.

[c] If the prisoner has been admitted to bail, the time of such admission to bail and the amount thereof.

[d] That the prisoner has not been produced as ordered for the reason that the tender of fees was not made or the amount tendered was inadequate, if such be the case.

(2) *Exhibits.* If the prisoner is detained by virtue of any judgment, order, warrant, or other written authority, a copy thereof shall be attached to the answer as an exhibit, and the original shall be produced and exhibited at the hearing.

(3) *Verification.* The answer shall be signed by the person answering and, except when the person is a sworn public officer and answers in the person's official capacity, it shall be verified by oath.

(h) **Contempt.** Neglect to produce the prisoner or to answer the writ or order to show cause in compliance with its terms shall constitute contempt.

(i) **Controverting Answer.** The plaintiff or the prisoner may, in a reply or at the hearing, controvert the answer under oath, to show either that the restraint of the prisoner was unlawful, or that the prisoner is entitled to discharge or other appropriate remedy.

(j) **Hearing and Judgment.** The court shall proceed in a summary manner to hear the matter and render judgment accordingly.

(k) **Notice of Hearing Before Discharge.** When the answer indicates that the prisoner is in custody on any process under which any other person has an interest in continuing the prisoner's restraint, no order may be made for the prisoner's discharge unless the person so interested, or that person's attorney, has had reasonable notice of the time and place of the hearing. When the answer indicates that the prisoner is detained upon a criminal accusation, the prisoner shall not be discharged until reasonable notice of the time and place of the hearing is given to the prosecuting attorney of the district within which the prisoner is detained or, if there is no prosecuting attorney within the district, to the Attorney General.

(*l*) **Custody of Child.** An order to show cause, and not a writ of habeas corpus, shall be issued initially if the action is brought by a parent, foster parent, or other relative of the child, to obtain custody of the child under the age of sixteen years from a parent, foster parent, or other relative of the child, the Commissioner of Health and Social Services, or any other person.

(m) **Superseded By Post-Conviction Relief Procedure Under Criminal Rule 35.1.** This rule does not apply to any post-conviction proceeding that could be brought under Criminal Rule 35.1. The court shall treat such a complaint as an application for post-conviction relief under Criminal Rule 35.1 and, if necessary, transfer the application to the court of appropriate jurisdiction for proceedings under that rule.

(n) **Not a Substitute for Remedies in Trial Court or Direct Review.** This remedy is not a substitute for nor does it affect any remedy incident to the proceedings in the trial court, or direct review of a sentence or conviction.

(Amended by SCO 49 effective January 1, 1963; by SCO 107 effective July 1, 1970; by SCO 457 effective March 15, 1981; by SCO 880 effective July 15, 1988; by SCO 1153 effective July 15, 1994; and by SCO 1186 effective July 15, 1995)

Cross References

(b) **CROSS REFERENCE:** AS 12.75.010; AS 12.75.020; AS 12.75.030

(c)(1) **CROSS REFERENCE:** AS 12.75.180; AS 12.75.190; AS 12.75.200

(e)(1) **CROSS REFERENCE:** AS 12.75.040

(g)(1) **CROSS REFERENCE:** AS 12.75.110

Annotations

Cases

Because petitioner's application for writ of habeas corpus for ineffective assistance of counsel did not claim that the underlying judgment of conviction was void, trial court order directing him to refile his complaint as an application for postconviction relief under Criminal Rule 35.1 was not an impermissible suspension of the writ of habeas corpus. **Hertz v. State,** Op. No. 1686, 8 P3d 1144 (Alaska App. 2000).

Claim that Civil Rule 86(m), which provides that habeas corpus procedure does not apply to any postconviction proceeding that could be brought under Criminal Rule 35.1, did not apply to an action that could be brought pursuant to Criminal Rule 35.1 but that might later be dismissed because of substantive or procedural shortcomings, was rejected. **Hertz v. State,** Op. No. 1686, 8 P3d 1144 (Alaska App. 2000).

Rule 87. Civil Arrest.

A motion for an order of arrest in a civil action shall be accompanied by affidavit setting out the facts supporting the ground for arrest. The order of arrest shall state the amount of bail. The arresting officer, at the time of arrest, shall deliver to the defendant copies of the order of arrest and all affidavits supporting the motion.

(Amended by SCO 49 effective January 1, 1963)

Cross References

CROSS REFERENCE: AS 09.40.120—AS 09.40.180

Rule 88. Procedure for Claiming Delivery of Personal Property.

(a) **Prejudgment Delivery of Personal Property to Plaintiff; Availability.** When the plaintiff has commenced a civil action to recover possession of personal property, the plaintiff may make application to the court to have the property delivered to the plaintiff. The court may order the prejudgment seizure of the property in accordance with the provisions of this rule.

(b) **Motion and Affidavit for Delivery.** The plaintiff shall file a motion with the court requesting the delivery of personal property, together with an affidavit showing:

(1) A particular description of the property claimed, and if the property claimed is a portion of divisible property of uniform kind, quality and value, that such is the case, and the amount thereof which the plaintiff claims; and

(2) That the plaintiff is the owner of the property or lawfully entitled to its possession, and the facts and circumstances relating thereto; and

(3) The value of the property claimed; and if more than one article is claimed, the current value of each article; and

(4) That the property is in the possession of the defendant, and the facts and circumstances relating to such possession according to the plaintiff's best knowledge or belief; and

(5) That the prejudgment seizure is not sought and the action is not prosecuted to hinder, delay or defraud any other creditor of the defendant; and

(6) That the plaintiff has no information or belief that the defendant has filed any proceeding under the National Bankruptcy Act or has made a general assignment for the benefit of creditors, or, if any such proceeding has been terminated, that the claim of the plaintiff was not discharged in such proceeding.

The plaintiff or the plaintiff's attorney shall endorse in writing upon the motion attached to the affidavit a request that the property claimed be taken by a peace officer from the defendant and be delivered to the plaintiff.

(c) **Notice of Motion; Pre-Seizure Hearing.** Except as section (j) provides, the court may order prejudgment delivery of personal property to the plaintiff only after:

(1) The defendant is served with notice of the motion and a copy of the affidavit; and

(2) The defendant is given an opportunity for a judicial hearing to determine the necessity of and justification for the prejudgment seizure of the property. The hearing shall be held not less than three (3), nor more than seven (7) business days (exclusive of Saturdays, Sundays, and legal holidays) after the service of the notice of motion upon the defendant.

(3) The hearing shall be held before the court on the day specified and shall take precedence over all other matters not of a similar nature pending on that day. If the defendant does not appear at the hearing, in person or by counsel, the court, without taking further evidence, shall immediately order the prejudgment seizure of the property. The hearing shall be conducted in conformity with Civil Rule 77, except where the provisions of Rule 77 conflict with the specific requirements of the instant rule, in which case, the requirements of the instant rule shall control.

(d) **Hearing; Burden of Proof.** At the hearing the court shall require the plaintiff to establish by a preponderance of the evidence the probable validity of the plaintiff's claim to the property and the absence of any reasonable probability that a successful defense can be asserted by the defendant.

(e) **Issuance of Order; Seizure.** If at the hearing the court finds that the plaintiff has met the burden of proof as set forth in paragraph (d) of this rule, the court shall issue an order prescribing the written undertaking, with sufficient sureties, to be provided by the plaintiff and directing a peace officer to seize and take into custody the property described in the affidavit upon the furnishing of the undertaking by the plaintiff.

(f) **New or Additional Undertaking.** The court at any time may require the giving of a new or additional undertaking to protect the interest of the defendant, the peace officer, or any party who intervenes, if good reason is shown that a new or additional bond is necessary.

(g) **Sureties on Undertaking.** The qualifications of sureties and their justification shall be as prescribed by these rules.

(h) **Return by Peace Officer.** The peace officer shall file a return with the court promptly and in any event within 20 days after the taking of the property from the defendant. Such return shall contain an inventory of the property taken, a statement of the claims, if any, by persons other than the plaintiff, and the name of the person to whom the property has been delivered. If the property is not taken, the peace officer shall promptly make a return to the court stating the fact and giving the reasons therefor.

(i) **Defendant's Security.** No order for prejudgment seizure of personal property may issue, or the peace officer shall redeliver to the defendant any property seized pursuant to the hearing, when the defendant provides a written undertaking with sufficient sureties as ordered by the court. The court may take into account a defendant's indigency, and may, in its discretion, permit the defendant to establish security by means other than the posting of bonds or the provision of a written undertaking. Such alternative means may include an installment payment arrangement or any other mechanism which the court deems just.

(j) **Ex Parte Prejudgment Delivery of Personal Property.** The court may issue a prejudgment order for delivery of personal property in an ex parte proceeding upon the plaintiff's motion, affidavit, and undertaking only in the following extraordinary situations:

(1) *Imminence of Defendant Concealing, Destroying or Conveying the Property.* The court may issue an ex parte order for delivery if the plaintiff establishes the probable validity of the plaintiff's claim for possession of the property, and if the plaintiff states in the affidavit specific facts sufficient to support a judicial finding of one of the following circumstances:

(i) The defendant is concealing, or about to conceal, the property; or

(ii) The defendant is about to destroy the property; or

(iii) The defendant is causing, or about to cause, the property to be removed beyond the limits of the state; or

(iv) The defendant is about to convey or encumber the property; or

(v) The defendant is otherwise disposing, or about to dispose, of the property in a manner so as to defraud the defendant's creditors, including the plaintiff.

(2) *Defendant's Waiver of Right to Pre-Seizure Hearing.* The court may issue an ex parte order for delivery if the plaintiff establishes the probable validity of the plaintiff's claim for possession of the property, and if the plaintiff accompanies the affidavit and motion with a document signed by the defendant voluntarily, knowingly and intelligently waiving the defendant's constitutional right to a hearing before prejudgment seizure of the property.

(3) *The Government as Plaintiff.* The court may issue an ex parte order for delivery when the possessory action and claim for delivery is brought by a government agency (state or federal), provided the government-plaintiff demonstrates that an ex parte seizure is necessary to protect an important governmental or general public interest.

(k) **Execution, Duration, and Vacation of Ex Parte Orders.** When the peace officer executes an ex parte delivery order, the peace officer shall at the same time serve on the defendant copies of the plaintiff's affidavit, motion and undertaking, and the order. No ex parte order shall be valid for more than seven (7) business days (exclusive of Saturdays, Sundays, and legal holidays), unless the defendant waives the right to a pre-seizure hearing in accordance with subsection (j)(2) of this rule, or unless the defendant consents in writing to an additional extension of time for the duration of the ex parte order. The defendant may at any time after service of the order request an emergency hearing at which the defendant may refute the special need for the seizure and the validity of the plaintiff's claim for possession of the property.

(*l*) **Duration and Vacation of Prejudgment Seizure Orders Issued Pursuant to Hearing.** A prejudgment seizure order issued pursuant to a hearing provided for in section (c) of this rule shall unless sooner released or discharged, cease to be of any force or effect and the property seized shall be released from the operation of the order at the expiration of six (6) months from the date of the issuance of the order, unless a notice of readiness for trial is filed or a judgment is entered against the defendant in the action in which the order was issued, in which case the order shall continue in effect until released or vacated after judgment as provided in these rules. However, upon motion of the plaintiff, made not less than ten (10) nor more than sixty (60) days before the expiration of such period of six (6) months, and upon notice of not less than five (5) days to the defendant, the court in which the action is pending may, by order filed prior to the expiration of the period, extend the duration of the order for an additional period or periods as the court may direct, if the court is satisfied that the failure to file the notice of readiness is due to the dilatoriness of the defendant and was not caused by any action of the plaintiff. The order may be extended from time to time in the manner herein prescribed.

(Amended by SCO 49 effective January 1, 1963; by SCO 156 effective December 8, 1972; by SCO 416 effective August 1, 1980; by SCO 1153 effective July 15, 1994; and by SCO 1435, effective October 15, 2001)

Cross References

(b) **CROSS REFERENCE:** AS 09.40.260

(e) **CROSS REFERENCE:** AS 09.40.270 — AS 09.40.300

Annotations

Cases

This rule provides procedure to obtain possession of personal property after an action to recover personal property has been commenced so that a seller of an automobile under a conditional sales contract who had a security interest in the chattel in the meaning of the Uniform Commercial Code would have to proceed under subdivisions (a) and (b) against a party withholding possession from him rather than by writ of attachment. **Decker v. Aurora Motors, Inc.,** Op. No. 314, 409 P2d 603 (Alaska 1966).

The summary prejudgment attachment procedure provided for by this rule does not meet the due process requirements of the State and Federal

Constitutions. **Etheredge v. Bradley,** Op. No. 842, 502 P2d 146 (Alaska 1972)

Where a process server in possession of personal property by reason of a writ of attachment is subject to an action brought by a third party claiming an interest superior to the lien of attachment levy, court should ensure that a process server who has acted properly suffers no loss. **First National Bank of Anchorage v. Zawodny,** Op. No. 1976, 602 P2d 1254 (Alaska 1979).

Rule 89. Attachment.

(a) **Prejudgment Attachment; Availability.** After a civil action is commenced, the plaintiff may apply to the court to have the property of the defendant attached under AS 09.40.010–.110 as security for satisfaction of a judgment that may be recovered. The court may issue the writ of attachment in accordance with the provisions of this rule. However, no writ may be issued unless the plaintiff has provided a written undertaking with sufficient sureties as ordered by the court.

Any party bringing a claim against another party may utilize prejudgment attachment procedures and is considered a plaintiff for purposes of this rule.

(b) **Motion and Affidavit for Attachment.** The plaintiff shall file a motion with the court requesting the writ of attachment, together with an affidavit showing:

(1) That the action is one upon an express or implied contract for the payment of money, and the facts and circumstances relating thereto; and

(2) That the sum for which the attachment is asked is an existing debt due and owing from the defendant to the plaintiff, over and above all legal setoffs and counterclaims, and the facts and circumstances relating thereto; and

(3) That the payment of such debt has not been secured by any mortgage, lien or pledge upon real or personal property, or if so secured, that the value of the security (specifying its value) is insufficient to satisfy any judgment that may be recovered by the plaintiff in the action; and

(4) That the attachment is not sought nor the action prosecuted to hinder, delay, or defraud any other creditor of the defendant; and

(5) That the plaintiff has no information or belief that the defendant has filed any proceeding under the National Bankruptcy Act or has made a general assignment for the benefit of creditors, or, if any such proceeding has been terminated, that the claim of the plaintiff was not discharged in such proceeding.

(c) **Notice of Motion; Pre-Attachment Hearing.** Except as section (m) provides, the court may issue the writ of attachment only after:

(1) The defendant is served with notice of the motion and a copy of the affidavit; and

(2) The defendant is given an opportunity for a judicial hearing to determine the necessity of and justification for the prejudgment attachment of the property. The hearing shall be held not less than three (3), nor more than seven (7) business days (exclusive of Saturdays, Sundays and legal holidays) after the service of the notice of motion upon the defendant.

(3) The hearing shall be held before the court on the days specified and shall take precedence over all other matters not of a similar nature pending on that day. If the defendant does not appear at the hearing, in person or by counsel, the court, without taking further evidence, shall immediately order the prejudgment attachment of the property. The hearing shall be conducted in conformity with Civil Rule 77, except where the provisions of Rule 77 conflict with the specific requirements of the instant rule, in which case, the requirements of the instant rule shall control.

(d) **Hearing; Burden of Proof.** At the hearing the court shall require the plaintiff to establish by a preponderance of the evidence the probable validity of the plaintiff's claim for relief in the action and the absence of any reasonable probability that a successful defense can be asserted by the defendant.

(e) **Issuance of Writ.** If at the hearing the court finds that the plaintiff has met his burden of proof set forth in section (d) of this rule, the court shall order that a writ of attachment be issued unless the defendant posts security as provided in section (j). The writ shall be directed to a peace officer and shall require the peace officer to attach and safely keep property of the defendant not exempt from execution sufficient to satisfy the plaintiff's demand (the amount of which shall be stated in conformity with the complaint), together with costs and expenses. Several writs may be issued at the same time and delivered to different peace officers, provided the total amount of the several writs does not exceed the plaintiff's claim. Additional writs may be issued where previous writs have been returned unexecuted, or executed in an amount insufficient to satisfy the full amount of the plaintiff's claim.

(f) **Execution of Writ.** The peace officer shall execute the writ without delay, as follows:

(1) Real property shall be attached by leaving a certified copy of the writ with the occupant of such property, or if there be no occupant, then in a conspicuous place on such property.

(2) Personal property capable of manual delivery to the peace officer, and not in the possession of a third party, shall be attached by the peace officer by taking it into custody.

(3) Other personal property shall be attached by leaving a certified copy of the writ, and a notice specifying the property attached, with the person having possession of same, or if it be a debt, then with the debtor.

(g) **New or Additional Undertaking.** The court at any time may require the giving of a new or additional undertaking to protect the interests of the defendant, the peace officer, or any party who intervenes, if good reason is shown that a new or additional bond is necessary.

(h) **Sureties on Undertaking.** The qualifications of sureties and their justification shall be as prescribed by these rules.

(i) **Return by Peace Officer.** The peace officer shall note upon the writ of attachment the date of its receipt. When the writ has been executed, the peace officer shall promptly return it to the clerk with the officer's proceedings endorsed thereon, including a full inventory of any property attached. If the writ cannot be executed, the peace officer shall promptly return it to the clerk stating thereon the reasons why it could not be executed.

(j) **Defendant's Security.** No writ of attachment may issue, or the peace officer shall redeliver to the defendant any property seized pursuant to the hearing, when the defendant provides a written undertaking with sufficient sureties as ordered by the court. The court may take into account a defendant's indigency, and may, in its discretion, permit the defendant to establish security by means other than the posting of bonds or the provision of a written undertaking. Such alternative means may include an installment payment arrangement or any other mechanism which the court deems just.

(k) **Wages of Defendant.** No part of the defendant's wages shall be attached prior to entry of final judgment except as permitted under 15 U.S.C. § 1673, AS 09.38.030–09.38.050, AS 09.38.065 and AS 09.40.030.

(*l*) **Garnishee Proceedings.**

(1) *Order of Appearance—Service.* When a person is ordered to appear before the court to be examined as to any property or debt held by the person belonging to a defendant, such person shall be known as the garnishee. The order shall state the time and place where the garnishee is to appear, shall be served upon the garnishee and return of service made in the manner provided for service of summons and return thereof in Rule 4.

(2) *Failure to Appear—Default.* When a garnishee fails to appear in compliance with the order, the court on motion may compel the garnishee to do so.

(3) *Discovery.* After entry of the order mentioned in subsection (1), plaintiff may utilize the rules of discovery under the supervision of the court with respect to all matters relating to property of the defendant believed to be in the possession of the garnishee. The consequences of the garnishee's failure or refusal to make discovery shall be governed by these rules.

(4) *Trial of Issues of Fact.* Issues of fact arising between the plaintiff and the garnishee shall be resolved and disposed of in accordance with these rules as in the case of issues of fact arising between plaintiff and defendant. Witnesses, including the defendant and garnishee, may be required to appear and testify as upon the trial of an action.

(5) *Judgment Against Garnishee.* If it shall be found that the garnishee, at the time of service of the writ of attachment and notice, had any property of the defendant liable to attachment beyond the amount admitted in the garnishee's statement, or in any amount if a statement is not furnished, judgment may be entered against the garnishee for the value of such property in money. At any time before judgment, the garnishee may be discharged from liability by delivering, paying or transferring the property to the peace officer.

(6) *Order Restraining Garnishee.* At the time of the application by plaintiff for the order provided for in subsection (1), and at any time thereafter and prior to the entry of judgment against the garnishee, the court may enter an order restraining the garnishee from paying, transferring, or in any manner disposing of or injuring any of the property of the defendant alleged by the plaintiff to be in the garnishee's possession or control, or owing by the garnishee to the defendant. Disobedience of such order may be punished as a contempt.

(7) *Execution.* Execution may issue upon a judgment against a garnishee as upon a judgment between plaintiff and defendant, and costs and disbursements shall be allowed and recovered in like manner.

(m) **Ex Parte Attachments.** The court may issue a writ of attachment in an ex parte proceeding based upon the plaintiff's motion, affidavit, and undertaking only in the following extraordinary situations:

(1) *When Defendant Non-Resident.* In an action upon an express or implied contract against a defendant not residing in the state, the court may issue an ex parte writ of attachment only when necessary to establish jurisdiction in the court. To establish necessity, the plaintiff must demonstrate that personal jurisdiction over the defendant is not readily obtainable under AS 09.05.015.

(2) *Imminence of Defendant Avoiding Legal Obligations.* The court may issue an ex parte writ of attachment if the plaintiff establishes the probable validity of the plaintiff's claim for relief in the main action, and if the plaintiff states in the affidavit specific facts sufficient to support a judicial finding of one of the following circumstances:

(i) The defendant is fleeing, or about to flee, the jurisdiction of the court; or

(ii) The defendant is concealing the defendant's whereabouts; or

(iii) The defendant is causing, or about to cause, the defendant's property to be removed beyond the limits of the state; or

(iv) The defendant is concealing, or about to conceal, convey or encumber property in order to escape the defendant's legal obligations; or

(v) The defendant is otherwise disposing, or about to dispose, of property in a manner so as to defraud the defendant's creditors, including the plaintiff.

(3) *Defendant's Waiver of Right to Pre-Attachment Hearing.* The court may issue an ex parte writ of attachment if the plaintiff establishes the probable validity of the plaintiff's claim for relief in the main action, and if the plaintiff accompanies the affidavit and motion with a document signed

by the defendant voluntarily, knowingly and intelligently waiving the constitutional right to a hearing before prejudgment attachment of the property.

(4) *The Government as Plaintiff.* The court may issue an ex parte writ of attachment when the motion for such writ is made by a government agency (state or federal), provided the government-plaintiff demonstrates that such ex parte writ is necessary to protect an important governmental or general public interest.

(n) **Execution, Duration, and Vacation of Ex Parte Writs of Attachment.** When the peace officer executes an ex parte writ of attachment, the peace officer shall at the same time serve on the defendant copies of the plaintiff's affidavit, motion and undertaking, and the order. No ex parte attachment shall be valid for more than seven (7) business days (exclusive of Saturdays, Sundays, and legal holidays), unless the defendant waives the right to a pre-attachment hearing in accordance with subsection (m) (3) of this rule, or unless the defendant consents in writing to an additional extension of time for the duration of the ex parte attachment, or the attachment is extended, after hearing, pursuant to section (e) of this rule. The defendant may at any time after service of the writ request an emergency hearing at which the defendant may refute the special need for the attachment and validity of the plaintiff's claim for relief in the main action.

(o) **Discharge of Attachment Where Perishable Goods Have Been Sold.** Whenever the defendant shall have appeared in the action, the defendant may apply to the court for an order to discharge the attachment on perishable goods which have been sold. If the order be granted, the peace officer shall deliver to the defendant all proceeds of sales of perishable goods, upon the giving by the defendant of the undertaking provided for in section (j).

(p) **Duration and Vacation of Writs of Attachment Issued Pursuant to Hearing.** A writ of attachment issued pursuant to a hearing provided for in section (c) of this rule shall unless sooner released or discharged, cease to be of any force or effect and the property attached shall be released from the operation of the writ at the expiration of six (6) months from the date of the issuance of the writ unless a notice of readiness for trial is filed or a judgment is entered against the defendant in the action in which the writ was issued, in which case the writ shall continue in effect until released or vacated after judgment as provided in these rules. However, upon motion of the plaintiff, made not less than ten (10) nor more than sixty (60) days before the expiration of such period of six (6) months, and upon notice of not less than five (5) days to the defendant, the court in which the action is pending may, by order filed prior to the expiration of the period, extend the duration of the writ for an additional period or periods as the court may direct, if the court is satisfied that the failure to file the notice of readiness is due to the dilatoriness of the defendant and was not caused by any action of the plaintiff. The order may be extended from time to time in the manner herein prescribed.

(q) The administrative director may adopt alternative procedures from those set out in this rule in order to allow electronic executions pursuant to Civil Rule 69(h).

(Amended by SCO 49 effective January 1, 1963; by SCO 156 effective December 8, 1972; by SCO 417 effective August 1, 1980; by SCOs 635, 636 and 637 effective September 15, 1985; by SCO 820 effective August 1, 1987; by SCO 853 effective January 15, 1988; by SCO 1135 effective July 15, 1993; and by SCO 1153 effective July 15, 1994)

Cross References

(b) **CROSS REFERENCE:** AS 09.40.010

(k) **CROSS REFERENCE:** AS 09.40.010

(m)(1) **CROSS REFERENCE:** AS 09.40.060

(n)(1) **CROSS REFERENCE:** AS 09.40.010

(p) **CROSS REFERENCE:** AS 09.40.070

Annotations

Cases

Service of order of the court requiring appearance of insurance company as garnishee was made upon the State Department of Commerce in accordance with rule and statute (AS 21.10.155(a)). **Liberty National Insurance Co. v. Eberhart,** Op. No. 281, 398 P2d 997 (Alaska 1965).

The time within which a garnishee must appear in court in response to an order requiring his appearance is a matter of court practice and procedure, the regulation of which has been committed to the Supreme Court by the constitution and the statutory provision, AS 21.10.160 attempting to regulate this matter of procedure is ineffective. **Liberty National Insurance Co. v. Eberhart,** Op. No. 281, 398 P2d 997 (Alaska 1965).

Issuance of the writ was in order where plaintiff had delivered machinery in the manner provided by law and could properly allege in the affidavit that the indebtedness was not secured by any lien or pledge upon the personal property. **Herning v. Wigger,** Op. No. 284, 398 P2d 1002 (Alaska 1965).

Failure of trial court to vacate a writ of attachment improperly obtained for a debt secured by a perfected security interest albeit strongly disapproving of appellee's actions in obtaining it, not held reversible error where no prejudice to appellant was shown. **Decker v. Aurora Motors, Inc.,** Op. No. 314, 409 P2d 603 (Alaska 1966).

Seller under a "Retail Installment Contract" who had a perfected security interest in the chattel under the Uniform Commercial Code, improperly obtained a writ of attachment instead of proceeding under Rule 88 and the costs of attachment previously granted below were disallowed on appeal. **Decker v. Aurora Motors, Inc.,** Op. No. 314, 409 P2d 603 (Alaska 1966).

Garnishee proceedings are not proceedings of an equitable nature to which the jurisdiction of the district judge does not extend, and the provisions of this rule are applicable to proceedings before the district judge court. **Anchorage Helicop. Serv., Inc. v. Anchorage W. Hotel,** Op. No. 361, 417 P2d 903 (Alaska 1966).

The plaintiff had the burden of establishing that at the time of service of the garnishment process the garnishee owed wages to the defendant, and garnishee had the burden to establish as an affirmative defense an asserted right of offset to wages due by reason of salary advances. **Anchorage Helicop. Serv., Inc. v. Anchorage W. Hotel,** Op. No. 361, 417 P2d 903 (Alaska 1966).

Although not payable until the regular salary payment date fixed by the employer's schedule, wages already earned by employee were money owing and were subject to garnishment prior to pay-day. **Anchorage Helicop. Serv., Inc. v. Anchorage W. Hotel,** Op. No. 361, 417 P2d 903 (Alaska 1966).

The restraint authorized under this provision could be imposed only as to wages earned and owing at the time of the order of restraint, and so far as an order purported to regulate the disposition of future wages, such order was unauthorized and invalid. **Anchorage Helicop. Serv., Inc. v. Anchorage W. Hotel,** Op. No. 361, 417 P2d 903 (Alaska 1966).

The summary prejudgment attachment procedure provided for by this rule does not meet the due process requirements of the State and Federal Constitutions. **Etheredge v. Bradley,** Op. No. 842, 502 P2d 146 (Alaska 1972).

Rule requiring a garnishor to serve upon the garnishee a notice specifying the property garnished requires service of a written notice of garnishment, not just a specification garnishable property. **Beery v. Browning,** Op. No. 3037, 717 P2d 365 (Alaska 1986).

Real estate escrow account was property subject to execution. **Von Gemmingen v. First Nat. Bank,** Op. No. 3579, 789 P2d 353 (Alaska 1990).

Trial court did not abuse its discretion in granting landlord's request for ex parte writ of attachment on ground that guarantors of lease agreement were about to dispose of property to defraud creditors. **Klosterman v. Hickel Inv. Co.,** Op. No. 3716, 821 P2d 118 (Alaska 1991).

Landlord improperly executed on lease agreement guarantor's airplane, which was in the possession of a third party, by removing its engines, propellers, radio and cowlings, since landlord could have secured the airplane by posting it with a copy of the writ of attachment and then chaining the propeller; landlord was therefore liable for damage caused by dismantling of the airplane. **Klosterman v. Hickel Inv. Co.,** Op. No. 3716, 821 P2d 118 (Alaska 1991).

Rule 90. Contempts.

(a) **Contempt in Presence of Court.** A contempt may be punished summarily if the judge certifies that the judge saw or heard the conduct constituting the contempt and that it was committed in the actual presence of the court. The order of contempt shall recite the facts and shall be signed by the judge and entered of record.

(b) **Other Contempts—Proceedings—Parties.** For every contempt other than that specified in subdivision (a) of this rule, upon a proper showing on ex parte motion supported by affidavits, the court shall either order the accused party to show cause at some reasonable time, to be therein specified, why the accused party should not be punished for the alleged contempt, or shall issue a bench warrant for the arrest of such party. Such proceeding may be commenced and prosecuted in the same action or in an independent proceeding either by the state, or by the aggrieved party whose right or remedy in an action has been defeated or prejudiced or who has suffered a loss or injury by the act constituting a contempt.

(c) **Party in Custody.** If the party charged with contempt is imprisoned or otherwise in custody under any judicial order or process, the court may require such party to be brought before it, and may make such provision as is appropriate for the disposition and custody of the party.

(d) **Bond for Appearance.** The court may permit the giving of a bond in lieu of arrest. In such case the court shall state in the bench warrant the amount of the bond and the time when the party charged with contempt must appear before the court. Such party shall be discharged from arrest upon delivering to the officer serving the warrant a bond in the amount stated in the warrant, executed by sufficient surety, and conditioned upon such party appearing before the court at the time stated and abiding the orders of the court. The amount recovered in a proceeding to enforce liability on the bond shall be applied first as compensation to the aggrieved party for damages resulting from the act constituting the contempt, with costs of the proceeding, and the residue, if any, shall become the property of the state and be deposited with the court.

(e) **Return.** Proof of service of an order to show cause or execution of a bench warrant shall be governed by Rule 4(f). Any bond delivered to an officer making service shall be filed by the officer with the court.

(f) **Hearing and Determination.** When the defendant has been brought before the court or has appeared, the court or judicial officer shall proceed to investigate the charge by examining the defendant and witnesses for or against the defendant. Upon the evidence so taken, the court or judicial officer shall determine the defendant's guilt or innocence of the contempt charged.

(Amended by SCO 49 effective January 1, 1963; amended by SCO 1153 effective July 15, 1994)

Cross References

CROSS REFERENCE: AS 09.50.010—AS 09.50.060

(b) **CROSS REFERENCE:** AS 09.50.030

(d) **CROSS REFERENCE:** AS 09.50.040; AS 09.50.060

(f) **CROSS REFERENCE:** AS 09.50.030

Annotations

Cases

Subdivision (a) of this rule deals with direct contempt and is not applicable to counsel's failure to appear in court at the time required. **Taylor v. District Court for the 4th Judicial District,** Op. No. 446, 434 P2d 679 (Alaska 1967).

Counsel's failure to appear in court at the time specified by the order of the court, may amount to an indirect contempt as contemplated under subdivision (b) of this rule. **Taylor v. District Court for the 4th Judicial District,** Op. No. 446, 434 P2d 679 (Alaska 1967).

A judgment of contempt was not fatally defective by absence of the affidavit required under this rule in a case where contempt proceedings were grounded on counsel's failure to appear as required by court order, because the due process requirement was satisfied by notice under the order to show cause and an affidavit by the judge would have added nothing to the requirement of informing the defendant of the charge against him. **Taylor v. District Court for the 4th Judicial District,** Op. No. 446, 434 P2d 679 (Alaska 1967).

Careless and neglectful conduct of counsel in not appearing at the required dates which did not manifest willful disregard or disobedience to the court's order, did not justify holding counsel in contempt. **Taylor v. District Court for the 4th Judicial District,** Op. No. 446, 434 P2d 679 (Alaska 1967).

Counsel's actions in agreeing to a trial setting in the superior court close to a date previously set for trial of a case in the district court resulting in failure of counsel to appear in district court at the time required by court's order, signified exercise of poor judgment and carelessness but did not give rise to an inference of willful disregard or disobedience of the district court's order. **Taylor v. District Court for the 4th Judicial District,** Op. No. 446, 434 P2d 679 (Alaska 1967).

Proof that the sanction of preclusion under Civil Rule 37(b)(2) is warranted involves the same elements that would warrant a finding of criminal contempt. **Continental Ins. Cos. v. Bayless & Roberts, Inc.,** Op. No. 1251, 548 P2d 398 (Alaska 1976).

It may not be necessary to furnish any notice for a direct contempt committed in the presence of the court, but a notice and hearing is required for indirect contempts. **Continental Ins. Cos. v. Bayless & Roberts, Inc.,** Op. No. 1251, 548 P2d 398 (Alaska 1976).

Failure to comply with order of court was indirect contempt if any and prior notice was required. **Continental Ins. Cos. v. Bayless & Roberts, Inc.,** Op. No. 1251, 548 P2d 398 (Alaska 1976).

Where it was unclear from the transcript which of appellant's remarks were considered contemptuous, and where neither the judge's remarks at the time the contempt citation was given nor the contempt order itself gave a clue as to the basis for the citation, the court's failure to make findings of fact as required by Rule 90 was reversible error. **Weaver v. Superior Court, Third Judicial Dist.,** Op. No. 1539, 572 P2d 425 (Alaska 1977).

The purpose of Rule 90(a)'s requirement that the judge recite the facts upon which the contempt citation is based is to aid the appellate court's review of the record, as well as apprise the contemnor of the conduct for which he is being sanctioned. **Weaver v. Superior Court, Third Judicial Dist.,** Op. No. 1539, 572 P2d 425 (Alaska 1977).

Where the court characterized $50.00 fine imposed upon attorney as a sanction, rather than "costs," sanction was reversed on ground that court failed completely to meet notice requirements of Rule 90(b). **West v. District Court, Third Judicial Dist.,** Op. No. 1582, 575 P2d 797 (Alaska 1978).

Direct criminal contempt committed in the presence of the trial judge may be dealt with summarily without a jury trial in exceptional cases. **Wood v. Superior Court,** Op. No. 2884, 690 P2d 1225 (Alaska 1984).

A post-trial hearing on contempt charge was not required where the sanction, a fine, was imposed for actions constituting direct contempt committed in court in the trial judge's presence. **Weidner v. State,** Op. No. 871, 764 P2d 717 (Alaska App. 1988).

A jury panelist who left the courthouse during a recess and failed to return was entitled to the procedural safeguards of this rule; the conduct constituted indirect contempt, not contempt occurring in the presence of the court. **Stadler v. State,** Op. No. 3702, 813 P2d 270 (Alaska 1991).

Evidentiary hearing was required to determine whether good cause existed to deviate from child support formula of this rule. **Perry v. Newkirk,** Op. No. 4072, 871 P2d 1150 (Alaska 1994).

Rule 90.1. Dissolution of Marriage, Divorce, and Legal Separation Actions.

(a) **Dissolution of Marriage.**

(1) *Commencement of Action.* An action for dissolution of marriage under AS 25.24.200–.260 shall be commenced by the filing of a petition in superior court containing the recitations required by statute. The petition may not be filed more than 60 days after the date of the signature of the first person signing the petition.

(2) *Verification.* The petition shall be signed and verified by both petitioners if the petition is filed by husband and wife together or by the petitioner filing the action if filed separately.

(3) *Form of Petition.* The petition may be filed on forms approved by the supreme court. Information may be inserted on the form in legible handwriting.

(b) **Divorce Actions—Corroborating Witnesses Not Required.** No corroborating witnesses as to legal residence shall be required in any divorce action unless ordered by the court; provided however, that the evidence of such residence shall be specific as to time, place, and manner of residence, and to the pertinent facts in the knowledge of the party attending to corroborate such residence.

(c) **Hearing of Divorce and Dissolution Cases.** Unless otherwise ordered upon good cause shown, no divorce or dissolution action shall be tried or heard on the merits within thirty days of the filing of the complaint.

(d) **Divorce Actions—Discovery and Disclosure.** Discovery and disclosure in divorce actions is governed by Civil Rule 26.1.

(e) **Divorce Actions—Property Division Table.** In divorce cases involving property division disputes, and unless otherwise ordered by the court, the parties shall file and serve the information required by this paragraph 5 days before trial is scheduled to begin. The required information consists of:

(1) a list, including a brief description of all assets and liabilities of the parties, whether owned jointly or individually;

(2) whether the party asserts each asset or liability is marital property, separate property of the husband, or separate property of the wife;

(3) the value of each asset and liability; and

(4) the proposed disposition, if any, of each asset or liability.

(f) **Confidential Information.**

(1) *Social Security Numbers.* Social security numbers, when required, shall not become part of the public record and shall be provided to the court confidentially as follows:

(A) A petition for dissolution or a complaint and answer for divorce, custody, legal separation, or annulment must be accompanied by an information sheet stating the name, date of birth, and social security number of each party to the action and each child who is or may be subject to a child support order in the action, to the extent known. The information sheet is confidential and shall not be considered part of the public record. The clerk of court shall provide a copy of the confidential information sheet to the Child Support Services Division upon request or whenever the court provides a child support order to a child support agency as required by state law. The clerk of court may also disclose the social security numbers on the confidential information sheet to the Bureau of Vital Statistics upon entry of a decree of divorce, dissolution, legal separation, or annulment of marriage, as required by state law. Further disclosure shall be authorized by court order only upon a showing of good cause.

(B) Once a complete confidential information sheet has been submitted to the court listing names, dates of birth, and social security numbers as required, the parties shall omit or redact social security numbers from documents subsequently filed in the action unless otherwise ordered by the court.

(C) A person whose interest in confidentiality may be adversely affected by disclosure of a social security number on a document filed in an action may move for an order requiring (i) the social security number to be redacted or the document to be treated as confidential, if the document has already been filed with the social security number included, or (ii) the document to be filed with the social security number redacted, if the document has not yet been filed.

(2) *Financial Account Numbers.* Unless otherwise ordered by the court, financial account numbers, when required under subsection (e) of this rule or when submitted in support of a motion, need not be provided in full. To protect against public disclosure of sensitive financial information, partial account numbers may be provided, as follows:

(A) a party may identify any credit card, bank card, or debit card account by using only the last four digits of the account number and the name of the issuing institution;

(B) a party may identify any bank, credit union, or other financial institution account by using only the last three digits of the account number and the name of the financial institution; and

(C) a person whose interest in confidentiality may be adversely affected by disclosure of a financial account number on a document filed in an action may move for an order requiring (i) the financial account number to be redacted or the document to be treated as confidential, if the document has already been filed with the financial account number included, or (ii) the document to be filed with the financial account number redacted, if the document has not yet been filed.

(g) **Qualified Domestic Relations Orders.** The party submitting a proposed Qualified Domestic Relations Order, or any similar order requiring the social security number of the beneficiary and alternate payee, shall submit a duplicate of the original proposed order with the social security number of the beneficiary and alternate payee redacted. The original proposed order is confidential and shall not be considered part of the public record. Only the redacted duplicate shall become part of the public case file.

(h) **Applicability.** Subsections (f) and (g) of this rule apply to documents filed with the court on or after October 15, 2006.

(i) **Action for Divorce, Dissolution, or Annulment Filed After Action for Legal Separation.**

(1) *Notice of Legal Separation Action.* A divorce, dissolution, or annulment action that is filed after the filing of an action for legal separation must include notice of the prior action.

(2) *Consolidation of Cases.* The consolidation of a divorce, dissolution, or annulment action with a legal separation action previously filed in Alaska is governed by AS 25.24.430 and Civil Rule 42(a).

(j) **Action for Legal Separation—Commencement.** An action for legal separation under AS 25.24.400-.460 is commenced by the filing of a complaint in the superior court.

(Adopted by SCO 252(1) effective September 22, 1976; amended by SCO 265 effective January 1, 1977; by SCO 370 effective August 1, 1979; by SCO 717 effective September 15, 1986; by SCO 805 effective August 1, 1987; by SCO 975 effective July 15, 1989; by SCO 1172 effective July 15, 1995; by SCO 1266 effective July 15, 1997; by SCO 1295 effective January 15, 1998; by SCO 1325 effective July 15, 1998; by SCO 1595 effective October 15, 2006, and by SCO 1596 effective October 15, 2006)

Note: Sections 41, 43, 45, and 46 of chapter 87 SLA 1997 amend AS 25.20.050(n), AS 25.24.160(d), AS 25.24.210(e), and AS 25.24.230(i), respectively, to require that an order or acknowledgement of paternity, a divorce decree, a petition for dissolution of marriage, and a dissolution decree include the social security number of each party to the action and each child whose rights are being addressed. According to § 151 of the Act, these provisions have the effect of amending Civil Rules 52, 58, 78, and 90.1 by requiring the court to include social security numbers, if ascertainable, of parties and children in certain petitions, pleadings, and judgments.

Rule 90.2. Settlement and Judgments in Favor of a Minor.

(a) **Approval of Settlement of Claims on Behalf of Minors.**

(1) *Approval.* A parent or guardian of a minor who has a claim against another person has the power to execute a full release or a covenant not to sue, or to execute a stipulation for entry of judgment on such claim. However, before such a document is effective, it must be approved by the court upon the filing of a petition or motion.

(2) *Petition or Motion.* A petition or motion for court approval of a minor's settlement under this rule must state the date of birth of the minor, the relationship between the moving party and the minor, the circumstances giving rise to the claim, the amount of any applicable liability insurance, and the basis for determining that the settlement is fair and reasonable. If the settlement arises from personal injuries to the minor, the petition or motion must describe the extent of the injuries, the medical treatment provided and the probable future course of treatment. If the settlement arises from the wrongful death or injury of another person, the petition or motion must describe the relationship between the other person and the minor and state whether the amount of the settlement is consistent with applicable state law.

(3) *Attorneys' Fees and Costs.* The court shall approve any attorneys' fees and costs that are to be paid from the settlement proceeds when the minor claimant is represented by counsel.

(4) *Hearing.* The court may approve the minor's settlement without a hearing if the settlement proceeds, after attorney's fees and costs are deducted, do not exceed $25,000. When a hearing on the petition or motion is held, the court may require the presence of any person that has information concerning the minor's claim, the fairness of the settlement or any related matter.

(5) *Termination of Minor's Rights.* No instrument executed under this rule is effective to terminate a minor's interests until such funds are paid as directed by the court.

(b) **Disbursement of Proceeds.**

(1) *Order Directing Payment of Expenses, Costs and Fees.* The court shall order that reasonable expenses (medical or otherwise, including reimbursement to a parent, guardian or conservator), costs and attorney's fees be paid from the settlement.

(2) *Disposition of Remaining Balance.* The court shall order that the remaining balance of the settlement, including any future payments, be disposed of in a manner which benefits the best interests of the minor. Dispositions which may be allowed include:

(A) ordering the settlement to be held by a parent or guardian for the benefit of the minor if the remaining balance of the settlement does not exceed $10,000;

(B) ordering that a formal trust be established for the benefit of the minor;

(C) ordering the appointment of a conservator to hold the proceeds of the settlement for the benefit of the minor;

(D) ordering that the proceeds of the settlement be deposited in a federally insured financial institution in an account from which withdrawal is not permitted without authority of the court; or

(E) ordering that the proceeds of the settlement be transferred to a custodian for the benefit of the minor under the Alaska Uniform Transfers to Minors Act (commencing with AS 13.46.010).

(3) *Standards for Disbursement of Proceeds.* The person or institution with authority under subparagraph (b) (2) may authorize disbursement of the settlement proceeds:

(A) for the support and education of the minor if the settlement proceeds are the result of the death or disability of another person;

(B) for the medical bills, special education or other costs related to the minor's injuries if the settlement proceeds are the result of injuries to the minor; or

(C) for any payment in the best interests of the minor after consideration of the benefit to the minor, the resources of the parents or guardian, and the amount of remaining settlement proceeds.

(c) **Probate Master.**

A master appointed to hear probate proceedings has the authority under this rule to:

(1) conduct the hearing set forth in paragraph (a) (4) and recommend to the court that the settlement be approved; (2) receive proof that the proceeds have been disposed of as set forth in subparagraph (b) (2); and (3) issue orders approving the withdrawal of funds pursuant to subparagraph (b) (2) (D).

(d) **Disbursement of Proceeds Resulting from Judgment.**

Proceeds resulting from a judgment in favor of a minor must be disbursed as set forth in paragraph (b).

(Adopted by SCO 835 effective August 1, 1987; amended by SCO 1106 effective January 15, 1993)

Annotations

Cases

Allocation of the proceeds of a wrongful death lawsuit was reversed because superior court failed to satisfy the requirements of this rule. **Matter of Estate of Brandon,** Op. No. 4216, 902 P2d 1299 (Alaska 1995).

The appellate court exercises its independent judgment in deciding whether this rule applies to particular aspects of a settlement affecting a minor's interests, and if so, whether the proceedings satisfy that rule. **Matter of Estate of Brandon,** Op. No. 4216, 902 P2d 1299 (Alaska 1995).

Attorney's fees equaling 89% of net amount minor was to receive in wrongful death settlement were potentially excessive. **Matter of Estate of Brandon,** Op. No. 4216, 902 P2d 1299 (Alaska 1995).

Total fee award was potentially excessive given several attorneys, each operating under a separate contingent fee agreement, asked the court to order the minor to pay attorneys' fees based on those agreements. **Matter of Estate of Brandon,** Op. No. 4216, 902 P2d 1299 (Alaska 1995).

If settlement of a paternity claim was the result of duress, the settlement did not satisfy this rule. **Matter of Estate of Brandon,** Op. No. 4216, 902 P2d 1299 (Alaska 1995).

Where allegations raising possible ethical and fiduciary violations, fee splitting and duress, relative to an allocation of wrongful death proceeds were not patently insufficient, the trial court should have considered them when allocating settlement proceeds. **Matter of Estate of Brandon,** Op. No. 4216, 902 P2d 1299 (Alaska 1995).

Court, in determining whether to approve a 1992 wrongful death settlement, could only determine whether the settlement's allocations were fair and reasonable by considering the substance and effects of all aspects of a 1990 paternity agreement which potentially disadvantaged the minor. Because the 1990 agreement never received the scrutiny required by this rule, the court erred in relying on that agreement to calculate the final distribution of wrongful death proceeds in 1992. **Matter of Estate of Brandon,** Op. No. 4216, 902 P2d 1299 (Alaska 1995).

Active involvement of minor's mother and attorney retained by mother to represent minor's interests in settlement of paternity suit which could determine whether minor would receive any proceeds from a wrongful death action did not excuse failure to follow Rule 90.2 regarding the paternity settlement or to consider the terms of the paternity settlement in ultimately considering settlement of the wrongful death case. **Matter of Estate of Brandon,** Op. No. 4216, 902 P2d 1299 (Alaska 1995).

When a minor's paternity is in dispute, and that dispute may determine whether the minor receives anything from wrongful death proceeds, the court, before approving a complete or partial relinquishment of the minor's claims to those proceeds, must meaningfully assess the minor's chances of prevailing on the paternity issue. If paternity is virtually certain, the court should not normally permit any distribution that compromises the minor's interests. **Matter of Estate of Brandon,** Op. No. 4216, 902 P2d 1299 (Alaska 1995).

In determining whether a settlement is fair and reasonable, the court must determine whether the benefit the minor receives is commensurate with what the minor gives up, and must take into account all consideration to be given or received by the minor. This necessarily requires the court to evaluate the risks and benefits of prosecuting the claim to completion. **Matter of Estate of Brandon,** Op. No. 4216, 902 P2d 1299 (Alaska 1995).

The trial court cannot approve a proposed minor settlement without first determining that it is fair and reasonable. The court may conduct its own investigation of the facts in making that determination and must exercise its independent judgment. **Matter of Estate of Brandon,** Op. No. 4216, 902 P2d 1299 (Alaska 1995).

By giving the court authority to require **sua sponte**the presence of persons whose knowledge may bear on the "fairness" of the settlement, Rule 90.2(a)(4) allows the court to take an active and independent role in the approved process and adduce facts the parties themselves may fail or choose not to produce. **Matter of Estate of Brandon,** Op. No. 4216, 902 P2d 1299 (Alaska 1995).

The court must approve any attorneys' fees and costs to be paid from the settlement proceeds and must conduct a hearing before approving a settlement if the net proceeds exceeding $25,000. **Matter of Estate of Brandon,** Op. No. 4216, 902 P2d 1299 (Alaska 1995).

A person claiming on behalf of a minor against another person has the power to execute a full release or covenant not to sue or a stipulation for entry of judgment on such claim. Before that document is effective, however, it must be approved by the court. **Matter of Estate of Brandon,** Op. No. 4216, 902 P2d 1299 (Alaska 1995).

An abuse of discretion standard applies in reviewing a trial court's order approving a settlement of a minor's claims and distributing proceeds of a minor's settlement under this rule. **Matter of Estate of Brandon,** Op. No. 4216, 902 P2d 1299 (Alaska 1995).

This rule gave probate court jurisdiction over a fee dispute where one attorney claimed he had a separate contract to work on a wrongful death case with a second attorney even though first attorney had no agreement with wrongful death plaintiffs because over 90% of any fees owed to the first attorney would have come from proceeds to be paid to minor wrongful death plaintiffs. **Matter of Estate of Katchatag,** Op. No. 4295, 907 P2d 458 (Alaska 1995).

Although Rule 90.2(a)(3) refers to a "settlement" and not a "judgment," it applies to proceeds recovered as a result of a judgment in favor of a minor. Attorney's fees and costs may not be paid from the proceeds of a judgment without court approval. **Matter of Estate of Katchatag,** Op. No. 4295, 907 P2d 458 (Alaska 1995).

Rule 90.3. Child Support Awards.

(a) **Guidelines—Primary Physical Custody.** A child support award in a case in which one parent is awarded primary physical custody as defined by paragraph (f) will be calculated as an amount equal to the adjusted annual income of the non-custodial parent multiplied by a percentage specified in subparagraph (a)(2).

(1) Adjusted annual income as used in this rule means the parent's total income from all sources minus:

(A) mandatory deductions such as:

(i) federal, state, and local income tax,

(ii) Social Security tax or the equivalent contribution to an alternate plan established by a public employer, and self-employment tax,

(iii) medicare tax,

(iv) mandatory union dues,

(v) mandatory contributions to a retirement or pension plan;

(B) voluntary contributions to a retirement or pension plan or account in which the earnings are tax-free or tax-deferred, except that the total amount of these voluntary contributions plus any mandatory contributions under item (a)(1)(A)(v) above may not exceed 7.5% of the parent's gross wages and self-employment income;

(C) child support and alimony payments arising from prior relationships which are required by other court or administrative proceedings and actually paid;

(D) child support for children from prior relationships living with the parent, calculated by using the formula provided by this rule; and

(E) work-related child care expenses for the children who are the subject of the child support order.

(2) The percentage by which the non-custodial parent's adjusted income must be multiplied in order to calculate the child support award is:

(A) 20% (.20) for one child;

(B) 27% (.27) for two children;

(C) 33% (.33) for three children; and

(D) an extra 3% (.03) for each additional child.

(3) The court may allow the obligor parent to reduce child support payments by up to 75% for any period in which the obligor parent has extended visitation of over 27 consecutive days. The order must specify the amount of the reduction which is allowable if the extended visitation is exercised.

(4) Potential Income. The court may calculate child support based on a determination of the potential income of a parent who voluntarily and unreasonably is unemployed or underemployed. A determination of potential income may not be made for a parent who is physically or mentally incapacitated, or who is caring for a child under two years of age to whom the parents owe a joint legal responsibility. Potential income will be based upon the parent's work history, qualifications, and job opportunities. The court also may impute potential income for non-income or low income producing assets.

(b) **Shared, Divided, and Hybrid Physical Custody.**

(1) *Shared Physical Custody.* A child support award in a case in which the parents are awarded shared physical custody as defined by paragraph (f) will be calculated by:

(A) Calculating the annual amount each parent would pay to the other parent under paragraph (a) assuming the other parent had primary custody. In this calculation the income limit in subparagraph (c)(2) and the minimum support amount in subparagraph (c)(3) apply.

(B) Multiplying this amount for each parent by the percentage of time the other parent will have physical custody of the children. However, if the court finds that the percentage of time each parent will have physical custody will not accurately reflect the ratio of funds each parent will directly spend on supporting the children, the court shall vary this percentage to reflect its findings.

(C) The parent with the larger figure calculated in the preceding subparagraph is the obligor parent and the annual award is equal to the difference between the two figures multiplied by 1.5. However, if this figure is higher than the amount of support which would be calculated under paragraph (a) assuming primary custody, the annual support is the amount calculated under paragraph (a).

(D) The child support award is to be paid in 12 equal monthly installments except as follows:

(i) if shared custody is based on the obligor parent having physical custody for periods of 30 consecutive days or more, the total annual award may be paid in equal installments over those months in which the obligor parent does not have physical custody; or

(ii) if the obligor parent's income is seasonal, the court may order unequal monthly support payments as provided in subparagraph (c)(5).

(E) The child support order must state that failure to exercise sufficient physical custody to qualify for shared physical custody under this rule is grounds for modification of the child support order. Denial of visitation by the custodial parent is not cause to increase child support.

(2) *Divided Physical Custody.* A child support award in a case in which the parents have divided custody is calculated, first, by determining what each parent would owe the other for children in that parent's primary physical custody under paragraph (a), taking into account the income limit in subparagraph (c)(2) and the minimum support amount in subparagraph (c)(3), and offsetting those amounts. Second, because divided custody is an "unusual circumstance," the court must consider whether this support amount should be varied under subparagraph (c)(1).

(3) *Hybrid Physical Custody.* A child support award in a case in which the parents have hybrid custody is calculated by applying paragraph (a), taking into account the income limit in subparagraph (c)(2) and the minimum support amount in subparagraph (c)(3), to determine support for children in the primary physical custody of each parent and applying subparagraph (b)(1) to determine support for children in the shared physical custody of the parents. In these calculations, the sub-paragraph (a)(2) percentages must be adjusted pro rata based on the number of children in each type of custody. These results are then combined to determine the net obligation. Finally, because hybrid custody is an "unusual circumstance," the court must consider whether this support amount should be varied under subparagraph (c)(1).

(c) **Exceptions.**

(1) The court may vary the child support award as calculated under the other provisions of this rule for good cause upon proof by clear and convincing evidence that manifest injustice would result if the support award were not varied. The court must specify in writing the reason for the variation, the amount of support which would have been required but for the variation, and the estimated value of any property conveyed instead of support calculated under the other provisions of this rule. Good cause may include a finding that unusual circumstances exist which require variation of the award in order to award an amount of support which is just and proper for the parties to contribute toward the nurture and education of their children. The court shall consider the custodial parent's income in this determination.

(2) Paragraph (a) does not apply to the extent that the parent has an adjusted annual income of over $100,000. In such a case, the court may make an additional award only if it is just and proper, taking into account the needs of the children, the standard of living of the children and the extent to which that standard should reflect the supporting parent's ability to pay.

(3) The minimum child support amount that may be ordered is $50 per month ($600 per year) except as provided in subparagraph (a)(3) and paragraph (b).

(4) In addition to ordering a parent to pay child support as calculated under this rule, the court may, in appropriate circumstances, order one or more grandparents of a child to pay child support to an appropriate person in an amount determined by the court to serve the best interests of the child. However, the amount may not exceed the smaller of (A) a proportionate share of the amount required to provide care in a supervised setting to the grandchild, as determined by the court, or (B) the amount that would have been awarded if the child's parents had the incomes of the child's grandparents and paragraphs (a) and (b) were applied. An order under this paragraph may be issued only with respect to a child whose parents are both minors, and the order terminates when either parent becomes 18 years of age. The court must specify in writing the reasons why it considers it to be appropriate to order a grandparent to pay child support under this paragraph and the factors considered in setting the amount of the child support award. In this paragraph, "grandparent" means the natural or adoptive parent of the minor parent.

(5) If the non-custodial parent's income is seasonal, the court may order that the annual support amount be paid in unequal monthly payments, with higher payments during the months the parent expects to receive higher income and lower payments in other months. The court should not make such an order unless (a) it finds that the burden of budgeting for periods of unequal income should be placed on the obligee rather than the obligor and (b) the obligee agrees. The court's order must specify the annual support amount, the average monthly support amount, and the amount due month by month. The order must provide that variations from the average

monthly amount begin with monthly payments in excess of the average monthly amount such that a deficit situation cannot occur. Until the excess payments begin, the average monthly amount must be ordered.

(d) **Health Care Coverage.**

(1) *Health Insurance.* The court shall address coverage of the children's health care needs and require health insurance for the children if insurance is available to either parent at a reasonable cost. The court shall consider whether the children are eligible for services through the Indian Health Service (or any other entity) or other insurance coverage before ordering the obligor to provide health care coverage through insurance or other means. The court shall allocate equally the cost of this insurance between the parties unless the court orders otherwise for good cause. An obligor's child support obligation will be decreased by the amount of the obligee's portion of health insurance payments ordered by the court and actually paid by the obligor. A child support award will be increased by the obligor's portion of health insurance if the obligee is ordered to, and actually does obtain and pay for insurance. . The cost of insurance is the cost attributable to the children for whom support is paid. If the cost to the employee of covering the employee alone is the same as the cost to the employee of covering the employee and dependents, then there is no additional cost to the employee for adding the children and no portion of the cost of coverage may be allocated to the children. If dependent coverage can be added for a single cost, rather than per dependent, and the dependent coverage covers dependents in addition to the children subject to the order, the cost of the dependent coverage will be allocated equally among the dependents covered. If there is reason to believe that there is an incremental cost to the employee for insuring dependents but evidence of that incremental cost is unavailable, the cost of insurance is determined by dividing the total cost of coverage by the number of family members covered and multiplying that amount by the number of children subject to the order.

(2) *Uncovered Health Care Expenses.* The court shall allocate equally between the parties the cost of reasonable health care expenses not covered by insurance unless the court orders otherwise for good cause. A party shall reimburse the other party for his or her share of the uncovered expenses within 30 days of receipt of the bill for the health care, payment verification, and, if applicable, a health insurance statement indicating what portion of the cost is uncovered. Reasonable, uncovered expenses exceeding $5,000 in a calendar year will be allocated based on the parties' relative financial circumstances when the expenses occur.

(e) **Child Support Affidavit and Documentation.**

(1) Subject to the confidentiality requirements of Civil Rule 90.1(f), each parent in a court proceeding at which child support is involved must file a statement under oath which states the parent's adjusted annual income and the components of this income as provided in subparagraph (a)(1). This statement must be filed with a party's initial pleading (such as the dissolution petition, divorce complaint or answer, etc.), motion to modify, and any response to a motion to modify. The statement must be accompanied by documentation verifying the income. The documents must be redacted to delete social security numbers and to provide only partial financial account information as provided in Civil Rule 90.1(f). The statement must state whether the parent has access to health insurance for the children and, if so, the additional cost to the parent of the children's health insurance. For any infraction of these rules, the court may withhold or assess costs or attorney's fees as the circumstances of the case and discouragement of like conduct in the future may require; and such costs and attorney's fees may be imposed upon offending attorneys or parties.

(2) While there is an ongoing monthly support obligation, either party must provide to the other party, within 30 days of a written request, documents such as tax returns and pay stubs showing the party's income for the prior calendar year. The party making the request must provide documentation of his or her annual income for the same period at the time the request is made. A request under this section may not be made more than once per year. This section does not preclude discovery under other civil rules.

(3) Unless the information has already been provided to the court under Civil Rule 90.1(f), a statement under subsection (e)(1) of this rule must be accompanied by a confidential information sheet as described in Civil Rule 90.1(f). Once a complete confidential information sheet has been submitted to the court listing names, dates of birth, and social security numbers as required, the parties shall omit or redact social security numbers from documents subsequently filed in the action unless otherwise ordered by the court. This paragraph applies to documents filed with the court on or after October 15, 2006.

(f) **Definitions.**

(1) *Shared Physical Custody.* A parent has shared physical custody (or shared custody) of children for purposes of this rule if the children reside with that parent for a period specified in writing in the custody order of at least 30, but no more than 70, percent of the year, regardless of the status of legal custody.

(2) *Primary Physical Custody.* A parent has primary physical custody (or primary custody) of children for purposes of this rule if the children reside with the other parent for a period specified in the custody order of less than 30 percent of the year.

(3) *Divided Custody.* Parents have divided custody under this rule if one parent has primary physical custody of one or more children of the relationship and the other parent has primary custody of one or more other children of the relationship, and the parents do not share physical custody of any of their children.

(4) *Hybrid Custody.* Parents have hybrid custody under this rule if at least one parent has primary physical custody of one or more children of the relationship, and the parents have shared physical custody of at least one child of the relationship.

(5) *Health Care Expenses.* Health care expenses include medical, dental, vision, and mental health counseling expenses.

(g) **Travel Expenses.** After determining an award of child support under this rule, the court shall allocate reasonable travel expenses which are necessary to exercise visitation between the parties as may be just and proper for them to contribute.

(h) **Modification.**

(1) *Material Change of Circumstances.* A final child support award may be modified upon a showing of a material change of circumstances as provided by state law. A material change of circumstances will be presumed if support as calculated under this rule is more than 15 percent greater or less than the outstanding support order. For purposes of this paragraph, support includes health insurance payments made pursuant to (d)(1) of this rule.

(2) *No Retroactive Modification.* Child support arrearage may not be modified retroactively, except as allowed by AS 25.27.166(d). A modification which is effective on or after the date that a motion for modification, or a notice of petition for modification by the Child Support Services Division, is served on the opposing party is not considered a retroactive modification.

(3) *Preclusion.* The court may find that a parent and a parent's assignee are precluded from collecting arrearages for support of a child that accumulated during a time period exceeding nine months for which the parent agreed or acquiesced to the obligor exercising primary custody of the child. A finding that preclusion is a defense must be based on clear and convincing evidence.

(i) **Third Party Custody.**

(1) When the state, or another third party entitled to child support, has custody of all children of a parent, the parent's support obligation to the third party is an amount equal to the adjusted annual income of the parent multiplied by the percentage specified in subparagraph (a)(2). If the third party has custody of some but not all children, the parent's support obligation to the third party is an amount equal to the adjusted annual income of the parent, multiplied by the percentage specified in subparagraph (a)(2) for the total number of the parent's children, multiplied by the number of the parent's children in third party custody, divided by the total number of the parent's children. For purposes of this paragraph, the number of the parent's children only includes children of the parent who live with the parent, are substantially supported by the parent or who are in custody of the third party entitled to support.

(2) If, in addition to a support obligation to a third party, one or both parents retain primary or shared physical custody of at least one of their children, the support obligation between the parents is calculated pursuant to the other paragraphs of this rule, without consideration of the third party custodian or any children in the custody of the third party custodian, except that the percentage in 90.3(a)(2) must be adjusted pro rata for the number of children in the primary custody of a parent, or shared custody of the parents, compared to the total number of children. After that calculation is completed, any support owed may be offset with support owed to a third party custodian under the preceding subparagraph in order to minimize transactions.

(j) **Support Order Forms.** All orders for payment or modification of child support shall be entered on a form developed by the administrative director. A party may lodge a duplicate of the court form produced by a laser printer or similar device. A device may also print, in a contrasting typestyle equivalent to that produced by a typewriter, text that otherwise would have been entered by a typewriter or word processor. A party or attorney who lodges a duplicate certifies by lodging the duplicate that it is identical to the current version of the court form.

(k) **Dependent Tax Deduction.** The court may allocate the dependent tax deduction for each child between the parties as is just and proper and in the child's best interests. The allocation must be consistent with AS 25.24.152 and federal law.

(Adopted by SCO 833 effective August 1, 1987; amended by SCO 935 effective January 15, 1989; by SCO 1008 effective January 15, 1990; by SCO 1192 effective July 15, 1995; by SCO 1246 effective July 15, 1996; by SCO 1269 effective July 15, 1997; by SCO 1295 effective January 15, 1998; by SCO 1362 effective October 15, 1999; by SCO 1399, effective October 15, 2000; by SCO 1417 effective April 15, 2001; by SCO 1526 effective April 15, 2005; and by SCO 1595 effective October 15, 2006)

Note: This rule is adopted under the supreme court's interpretive authority pursuant to Article IV, Section I of the Alaska Constitution. Thus, it may be superseded by legislation even if the legislation does not meet the procedural requirements for changing rules promulgated under Article IV, Section 15.

Note to Civil Rule 90.3(c)(1)(B): The Federal Poverty Guidelines are usually revised each February. The new poverty income guideline for one person in Alaska in 1999 is $10,320 (Federal Register, Vol. 64, No. 52, 13428–13430, March 18, 1999). The Alaska Supreme Court has indicated that the poverty guideline that should be used is the guideline for the state in which the obligor resides. See **Carstens v. Carstens**, 867 P.2d 805, 810 (Alaska 1994).

Note to Civil Rule 90.3(h)(1): Section 44 of ch. 87 SLA 1997 amended AS 25.24.170(b) to allow support to be modified without a showing of a material change in circumstances as necessary to comply with federal law. Federal law eliminates the need for a showing only in cases being enforced by CSED that are being reviewed under CSED's periodic review and modification program. According to § 152 of ch. 87 SLA 1997, the amendment to AS 25.24.170(b) has the effect of amending Civil Rule 90.3 by changing the standard for certain modifications of a support order.

Note to Civil Rule 90.3(h)(2): AS 25.27.166(d), enacted by § 14 of ch. 57 SLA 1995, has the effect of amending Civil Rule 90.3(h)(2) by allowing retroactive modification of child support arrearage under circumstances involving disestablishment of paternity, to the extent such modification is not prohibited by federal law.

Note: Civil Rule 90.3(c)(3) was added by § 44 ch, 107 SLA 1996. Section 22 of ch. 107 SLA 1996 enacts 25.27.195(b), which allows CSED to vacate an administrative support order that was based on a default amount rather than the obligor's actual ability to pay. If an order is vacated on this basis, AS 25.27.195(d) allows the agency to modify the obligor's arrearages under the original order. According to § 50 ch. 107 SLA 1996, AS 25.27.195(d) has the effect of amending Rule 90.3(h)(2), which prohibits retroactive modification of child support arrearages.

Note: Section 41 of ch. 87 SLA 1997 amends AS 25.20.050 relating to paternity actions. According to § 150 of the Act, § 41 has the effect of amending Civil Rule 90.3 by requiring the court in a paternity action to issue a temporary child support order upon a showing by clear and convincing evidence of paternity.

Note: Chapter 106 SLA 2000 amends various laws relating to medical support orders. According to section 24 of the act, the act amends Civil Rule 90.3 "by specifying that a medical support order may be issued even when a support order for periodic monetary payments is not issued and by setting the requirements for medical support orders."

Note: Chapter 108 SLA 04 (HB 514) enacted several amendments to the child support statutes, including a provision that permits periodic modifications of a child support order without a showing of materially changed circumstances. According to Section 17 of the Act, statutory modifications to AS 25.27.190(e) have the effect of amending Civil Rule 90.3 by changing the grounds for modifying a support order.

Civil Rule 90.3

COMMENTARY

I. INTRODUCTION

A. Committee Commentary. This commentary to Civil Rule 90.3 was prepared by the Child Support Guidelines Committee. The commentary has not been adopted or approved by the Supreme Court, but is published by the court for informational purposes and to assist users of Rule 90.3.

B. Purpose. The primary purpose of Rule 90.3 is to ensure that child support orders are adequate to meet the needs of children, subject to the ability of parents to pay.

The second purpose of 90.3 is to promote consistent child support awards among families with similar circumstances. Third, the rule is intended to simplify and make more predictable the process of determining child support, both for the courts and the parties. Predictable and consistent child support awards will encourage the parties to settle disputes amicably and, if resolution by the court is required, will make this process simpler and less expensive.

The final purpose of 90.3 is to ensure that Alaska courts comply with state and federal law. AS 25.24.160(a)(1) requires that child support be set in an amount which is "just and proper...."The Child Support Enforcement Amendments of 1984 (P.L. 98–378) and its implementing regulations (45 CFR 302.56) require states to adopt statewide guidelines for establishing child support. The Family Support Act of 1988 (P.L. 100–485) requires that the guidelines presumptively apply to all child support awards and that the guidelines be reviewed every four years.

The Nature of Child Support. Child support is the contribution to a child's maintenance required of both parents. The amount of support a child is entitled to receive from a particular parent is determined by that parent's ability to provide for the child.

C. Scope of Application. Rule 90.3 applies to all proceedings involving child support, whether temporary or permanent, contested or non-contested, including without limitation actions involving separation, divorce, dissolution, support modification, domestic violence, paternity, Child in Need of Aid and Delinquency. The support guidelines in the rule may be varied only as provided by paragraph (c) of the rule. Rule 90.3 applies to support of children aged 18 authorized by Chapter 117, SLA 1992, but otherwise does not apply to set support which may be required for adult children.

II. PERCENTAGE OF INCOME APPROACH

Rule 90.3 employs the percentage of income approach. This approach is based on economic analyses which show the proportion of income parents devote to their children in intact families is relatively constant across income levels up to a certain upper limit. Applications of the rule should result in a non-custodial parent paying approximately what the parent would have spent on the children if the family was intact.

Integral to the rule is the expectation that the custodial parent will contribute at least the same percentage of income to support the children. The rule operates on the principle that as the income available to both parents increases, the amount available to support the children also will increase. Thus, at least in the primary custodial situation, the contribution of one parent does not affect the obligation of the other parent.

III. DEFINING INCOME

A. Generally. The first step in determination of child support is calculating a "parent's total income from all sources" Rule 90.3(a)(1). This phrase should be interpreted broadly to include benefits which would have been available for support if the family had remained intact. Income includes, but is not limited to:

1. salaries and wages (including overtime and tips);
2. commissions;
3. severance pay;

4. royalties;

5. bonuses and profit sharing;

6. interest and dividends, including permanent fund dividends;

7. income derived from self-employment and from businesses or partnerships;

8. social security;

9. veterans benefits;

10. insurance benefits in place of earned income such as workers' compensation or periodic disability payments;

11. workers' compensation;

12. unemployment compensation;

13. pensions;

14. annuities;

15. income from trusts;

16. capital gains in real and personal property transactions to the extent that they represent a regular source of income;

17. spousal support received from a person not a party to the order;

18. contractual agreements;

19. perquisites or in-kind compensation to the extent that they are significant and reduce living expenses, including but not limited to employer provided housing and transportation benefits (but excluding employer provided health insurance benefits);

20. income from life insurance or endowment contracts;

21. income from interest in an estate (direct or through a trust);

22. lottery or gambling winnings received either in a lump sum or an annuity;

23. prizes and awards;

24. net rental income;

25. disability benefits;

26. Veteran Administration benefits;

27. G.I. benefits (excluding education allotments);

28. National Guard and Reserves drill pay; and

29. Armed Service Members base pay plus the obligor's allowances for quarters, rations, COLA and specialty pay.

Lump sum withdrawals from pension or profit sharing plans or other funds will not be counted as income to the extent that the proceeds have already been counted as income for the purposes of calculating child support under this rule (i.e., contributions to a voluntary pension plan).

Means based sources of income such as Alaska Temporary Assistance Program (ATAP), formerly Aid to Families with Dependent Children (AFDC), Food Stamps and Supplemental Security Income (SSI) should not be considered as income. The principal amount of one-time gifts and inheritances should not be considered as income, but interest from the principal amount should be considered as income and the principal amount may be considered as to whether unusual circumstances exist as provided by 90.3(c). Tax deferred dividends and interest earned on pension or retirement accounts, including individual retirement accounts, which are not distributed to the parent are not income. Child support is not income.

B. Self Employment Income. Income from self-employment, rent, royalties, or joint ownership of a partnership or closely held corporation includes the gross receipts minus the ordinary and necessary expenses required to produce the income. Ordinary and necessary expenses do not include amounts allowable by the IRS for the accelerated component of depreciation expenses, investment tax credits, or any other business expenses determined by the court to be inappropriate. Expense reimbursements and in-kind payments such as use of a company car, free housing or reimbursed meals should be included as income if the amount is significant and reduces living expenses.

C. Potential Income. The court may calculate child support based on a determination of the potential income of a parent who voluntarily and unreasonably is unemployed or underemployed. A determination of potential income may not be made for a parent who is physically or mentally incapacitated, or who is caring for a child under two years of age to whom the parents owe a joint legal responsibility. Potential income will be based upon the parent's work history, qualifications and job opportunities. The court shall consider the totality of the circumstances in deciding whether to impute income. When a parent makes a career change, this consideration should include the extent to which the children will ultimately benefit from the change. The court also may impute potential income for non-income or low income producing assets.

D. Deductions. A very limited number of expenses may be deducted from income. Mandatory deductions such as taxes and mandatory union dues are allowable.

Mandatory retirement contributions are a deduction. Voluntary contributions, up to the limit stated in the rule, are also a deduction if the earnings on the retirement account or plan are tax-free or tax-deferred. If a parent is not a participant in a mandatory plan, the limit on voluntary contributions is 7.5 % of gross wages and self-employment income. If a parent is a participant in a mandatory plan, the limit on voluntary contributions is 7.5 % of gross wages and self-employment income minus the amount of the mandatory contribution. Some examples of plans and accounts that qualify for the voluntary contribution are: those qualified under the Internal Revenue Code, 26 USC §§ 401, 403, 408 or 457 (such as a traditional IRA, Roth IRA, SEP-IRA, SIMPLE IRA, Keogh Plan, 401(k) Plan, etc.); Thrift Savings Plans under 5 USC § 8440, 37 USC § 211, etc.; and any other pension plan as defined by § 3 (2) of ERISA (P.L. 93–406; 29 USC § 1002(2)).

Child support and alimony payments paid to another person arising out of different cases are deductible if three conditions are met. First, the child support or alimony actually must be paid. Second, it must be required by a court or administrative order. (Support which is paid voluntarily without a court or administrative order may be considered under Rule 90.3(c).) Third, it must relate to a prior relationship. A child support order for children of a second marriage should take into account an order to pay support to children of a first marriage, but not vice-versa. But see commentary VI.B.2.

A deduction also is allowed for the support of the children of prior relationships even if the party is the custodial parent of the "prior" children and does not make child support payments to the other parent of the children. In this situation support provided directly to the children is calculated by Rule 90.3 as if the children from the prior relationship were the only children.

Also, reasonable child care expenses that are necessary to enable a parent to work, or to be enrolled in an educational program which will improve employment opportunities, are deductible. However, the expense must be for the children who are the subject of the support order.

E. Time Period for Calculating Income. Child support is calculated as a certain percentage of the income which will be earned when the support is to be paid. This determination will necessarily be somewhat speculative because the relevant income figure is expected future income. The court must examine all available evidence to make the best possible calculation.

The determination of future income may be especially difficult when the obligor has had very erratic income in the past. In such a situation, the court may choose to average the obligor's past income over several years.

Despite the difficulty in estimating future income, a child support order should award a specific amount of support, rather than a percentage of whatever future income might be. The latter approach has been rejected because of enforcement and oversight difficulties.

IV. PRIMARY CUSTODY

A. Generally. "Primary custody" as this term is used in Rule 90.3 covers the usual custodial situation in which one parent will have physical custody of the child—in other words, the child will be living with that parent—for over seventy percent of the year. The shared custody calculation in paragraph (b) applies only if the other parent will have physical custody of the child at least thirty percent of the year (110 overnights per year). The visitation schedule must be specified in the decree or in the agreement of the parties which has been ratified by the court. **See also** commentary V.A.

The calculation of child support for the primary custodial case under 90.3(a) simply involves multiplying the obligor's adjusted income times the relevant percentage given in subparagraph (a)(2). (Normally, the portion of an adjusted annual income over $100,000 per year will not be counted. **See** Commentary VI.D.) As discussed above, the rule assumes that the custodial parent also will support the children with at least the same percentage of his or her income.

B. Visitation Credit. An obligor who exercises extended visitation, even if the visitation does not reach the thirty percent level of shared custody, probably will spend significant funds directly for the children during visitation. The parent with primary custody conversely will have somewhat lower expenses during the extended visitation even though that parent's fixed costs such as housing will not decrease. Consequently, 90.3(a)(3) authorizes the trial court, in its discretion, to allow a partial credit (up to 75% of total support for the period of extended visitation) against a child support obligation. In considering a visitation credit, the court may consider the financial consequences to the parties of the visitation arrangement and a credit. The court shall insure that support for the child, including contributions from both parents, is adequate to meet the child's needs while the child resides with the custodial parent. A visitation credit may be taken only if the extended visitation actually exercised exceeds 27 consecutive days and the court has authorized the specific amount of the credit. Nominal time with the custodial parent during the visitation period, including occasional overnights, does not defeat the visitation credit.

V. SHARED DIVIDED, AND HYBRID PHYSICAL CUSTODY

A. Shared Custody—Generally.

"Shared custody" as this term is used in Rule 90.3 means that each parent has physical custody of the children at least thirty percent of the year according to a specified visitation schedule in the decree. "Shared custody" as used in 90.3 has no relation to whether a court has awarded sole or joint legal custody. "Shared custody" is solely dependent on the time that the decree or agreement of the parties which has been ratified by the court specifies the children will spend with each parent.

In order for a day of visitation to count towards the required thirty percent, the children normally must remain overnight with that parent. (Thirty percent of the overnights in a year total 110 overnights.) Thus, a day or an evening of visitation by itself will not count towards the total of time necessary for shared custody. Visitation from Saturday morning until Sunday evening would count as one overnight. However, the court may use another method of calculating the percentages of custody when counting overnights does not accurately reflect the ratio of expenditures by the parents.

B. Calculation of Shared Custody Support. The calculation of support in shared custody cases is based on two premises. First, the fact that the obligor is spending a substantial amount of the time with the children probably means the obligor also is paying directly for a substantial amount of the expenses of the children. Thus, the first step in calculating shared custody support is to calculate reciprocal support amounts for the time each parent will have custody based on the income of the other parent. The "high income" limit of paragraph (c)(2) ($100,000) applies to the determination of adjusted income at the first stage of this process. A parent's annual support amount for purposes of this calculation will be no less than $600. The support amounts then are offset.

This calculation assumes that the parents are sharing expenses in roughly the same proportion as they are sharing custody. If this assumption is not true, the court should make an appropriate adjustment in the calculation.

The second premise is that the total funds necessary to support children will be substantially greater when custody is shared. For example, each parent will have to provide housing for the children. Thus, the amount calculated in the first step is increased by 50% to reflect these increased shared custody costs. However, the obligor's support obligation never will exceed the amount which would be calculated for primary custody under 90.3(a). The amount which would be calculated under 90.3(a) should include any appropriate visitation credit as provided by (a)(3).

C. Failure to Exercise Shared Custody. An inequity may arise under the shared custody calculation of support if the obligor does not actually exercise the custody necessary to make shared custody applicable (i.e., at least 30% of the time). If the obligor parent does not actually exercise sufficient physical custody to qualify for the shared custody calculation in the rule (at least 110 overnights per year—See Commentary, Section V.A), then (a)(2) of this rule will apply to the child support calculation. Failure to exercise custody in this regard is grounds for modification of support, even if the custody order is not modified. However, this provision may not be interpreted to allow the custodial parent to profit by denying visitation.

D. Divided Custody. Rule 90.3(f)(3) defines divided custody as when both parents have primary physical custody of at least one of the parent's children and the parents do not share custody of any of their children. The calculation of support for divided custody is a two-part process.

The first step is to offset the amounts of support each parent would pay the other for the children in that parent's primary custody calculated under 90.3(a). For example, if the father has primary custody of one child and the mother primary custody of three children (four children total), the father would owe support to the mother of 33% (three children) of his adjusted annual income. This amount would be offset by 20% (one child) of the mother's adjusted annual income. This method was implicitly approved in *Bunn v. House,* 934 P.2d 753, 755–58 (Alaska 1997). Note that this method of calculation supercedes the method used in *Rowen v. Rowen,* 963 P.2d 249, 254 (Alaska 1998).

The second step in determining divided custody support is for the court to carefully consider whether the support amount should be varied under paragraph (c)(1). A divided custody case should be treated as an unusual circumstance under which support will be varied if such a variation is "just and proper..."

E. Hybrid Custody. Rule 90.3(f)(4) defines hybrid custody as when at least one parent has primary physical custody of at least one child of the relationship, and the parents share physical custody of at least one child of the relationship.

The method for calculating child support in a hybrid custody situation in Rule 90.3(b)(3) comes from *Turinsky v. Long*, 910 P.2d 590, 596–97 n.13 (Alaska 1996).

Step One. Determine the percentage of income to use in both the "primary" and "shared" calculations as follows: divide the Rule 90.3(a)(2) percentage for the total number of children by the total number of children to determine a per-child percentage. For example, if there are four children, divide 36% by 4 to get a per child percent of 9%.

Step Two. Use Rule 90.3(a) to calculate the amount each parent owes for any children in the primary physical custody of the other parent. However, instead of using the percentages in (a)(2), use the per-child percent from Step One multiplied by the number of children in the other parent's primary physical custody. For example, if two of the four children are in the mother's primary physical custody, the father would owe 18% (2 x 9%) of his adjusted annual income for the support of those children.

Step Three. Use Rule 90.3(b) to determine the amount owed for the children in shared physical custody and which parent owes it. Use the per-child percentage from Step One multiplied by the number of children in shared physical custody instead of the percentage in (a)(2). For example, if two of the four children are in shared physical custody, each parent's adjusted annual income will be multiplied by 18% (2 x 9%).

Step Four. Add the amounts calculated in Steps Two and Three if they are owed by the same parent. Offset the amounts calculated in Steps Two and Three if they are owed by different parents. The result is the total amount owed each year.

Step Five. Consider whether the support amount should be varied under paragraph (c)(1) of the rule. Hybrid custody is an unusual circumstance in which support must be varied if such a variation is "just and proper."

Sample hybrid custody calculation: In the following sample calculation, there are four children in the family. Mother has primary custody of two, and the parents share custody of the other two. The shared two children will be in mother's physical custody 70 percent of the time and in father's 30 percent of the time. Father's adjusted annual income is $50,000. Mother's is $40,000. *Step One.* The percentage of income from (a)(2) of the rule for four children is 36 percent. Therefore, the percentage per child is 9 percent [36 divided by 4]. *Step Two.* Father owes mother $9000 per year for the two children in mother's primary custody [$50,000 x 18%]. *Step Three.* Father owes mother $6210 per year for the two children in shared custody [(father owes $50,000 x 18% = $9000 x 70% = $6300)—(mother owes $40,000 x 18%

= $7200 x 30% = $2160). $6300 - $2160 = $4140 x 1.5 = $6210]. *Step Four.* Thus, for all four children, father owes mother $15,210 [$9000 + $6210].

VI. EXCEPTIONS

A. Generally. Child support in the great majority of cases should be awarded under 90.3(a) or (b) in order to promote consistency and to avoid a tendency to underestimate the needs of the children. Nevertheless, the circumstances in which support issues arise may authorize courts to vary support awards for good cause.

The court may apply this good cause exception only if the parent requesting that support be varied presents clear and convincing evidence that manifest injustice would result if the support award were not varied. In addition, a prerequisite of any variation under 90.3(c) is that the reasons for it must be specified in writing by the court.

What constitutes "good cause" will depend on the circumstances of each cause. Three situations constituting "good cause" are discussed below in sections VI.B D. These three specific exceptions are not exclusive; however, the general exception for good cause may not be interpreted to replace the specific exceptions. Absent the (c)(1) exception (unusual circumstances), the (c)(2) exception (high income), or the (c)(3) exception (low income), the rule presumes that support calculated under 90.3(a) or (b) does not result in manifest injustice.

B. Unusual Circumstances. 90.3(c)(1) provides that a court shall vary support if it finds, first, that unusual circumstances exist and, second, that these unusual circumstances make application of the usual formula unjust. Examples might include especially large family size, significant income of a child, health or other extraordinary expenses, or unusually low expenses. This determination should be made considering the custodial parent's income because the percentage of income approach used in Alaska tends to slightly understate support relative to the national average for cases in which the custodial spouse does not earn a significant income. This understatement relative to the national average becomes substantial if the custodial parent has child care expenses. The application of the unusual circumstances exception to particular types of factual situations is considered below.

1. Agreement of the Parents. The fact that the parties, whether or not represented by counsel, agree on an amount of support is not reason in itself to vary the guidelines. The children have an interest in adequate support independent of either parent's interest. Thus, approval of any agreement which varies the guidelines, whether in a dissolution, by stipulation or otherwise, must be based upon an explanation by the parties of what unusual factual circumstances justify the variation.

2. Subsequent Children. A parent with a support obligation may have other children living with him or her who were born or adopted after the support obligation arose. The existence of such "subsequent" children, even if the obligor has a legal obligation to support these children, will not generally constitute good cause to vary the guidelines. However, the circumstances of a particular case involving subsequent children might constitute unusual circumstances justifying variation of support. The court should reduce child support if the failure to do so would cause substantial hardship to the "subsequent" children.

In addition, the interests of the subsequent family may be taken into account as a defense to a modification action where an obligor proves he or she has taken a second job or otherwise increased his or her income specifically to better provide for a subsequent family. This defense to an upward modification action should not be allowed to the extent that the prior support was set at a lower amount prior to the adoption of this rule, or to the extent that the obligor's increase in income is limited to ordinary salary increases.

In considering whether substantial hardship to "subsequent" children exists, or whether the existence of a subsequent family should defeat a motion to increase child support, the court should consider the income, including the potential income, of both parents of the "subsequent" children.

3. Relocation of Custodial Parent. The relocation of the custodial parent to a state with a lower cost of living normally will not justify a reduction in support. The level of Alaska's guidelines is comparable to the national average. The fact that the obligor parent's income has in effect marginally increased relative to the children's living expenses simply enables the children to be supported at a slightly higher level.

4. Prior and Subsequent Debts. Prior or subsequent debts of the obligor, even if substantial, normally will not justify a reduction in support. The obligation to provide child support is more important than the obligation to fulfill most other obligations. However an obligor parent may attempt to present evidence which shows the existence of exceptional circumstances in an individual case.

5. Income of New Spouse (or other person in the household). The income of a new spouse of either the custodial or obligor parent normally will not justify a variation in support. Either party may attempt to show that exceptional circumstances exist in a particular case. A parent who does not work because of the income of a new spouse (or other person in the household) may be assigned a potential income.

6. Age of Children. While the costs of raising children who are very young or who are over about ten years old are generally greater than raising other children, this in itself does not justify an increase in support. However, it should be considered in concert with other circumstances, and a parent always may seek to establish exceptional expenses in a particular case.

7. Denial of Visitation. A denial of visitation may not be countered with a reduction in support. See AS 25.27.080(c). Neither may non-payment of support be countered by a denial of visitation. Courts should use their powers to strictly enforce the visitation and custody rights of obligor parents.

8. Property Settlement. A parent may justify variation

of the guidelines by proving that a property settlement in a divorce or dissolution between the parents provided one of the parents with substantially more assets than the parent otherwise would have been entitled to, that this inequity was intended to justify increasing or decreasing child support, and that this intent specifically was stated on the record. Any such change in monthly child support may not exceed the actual excess of the property settlement apportioned over the minority of the child.

However, courts should not approve in the first instance unequal property settlements which are meant to increase or decrease child support payments. "Property divisions are final judgments which can be modified only under limited circumstances, whereas child support awards can be changed periodically under much more liberal standards. One should not be a trade-off for the other." *Arndt v. Arndt,* 777 P.2d 668, (Alaska 1989)

9. Overtime Income. In most cases income from overtime or a second job will be counted as adjusted annual income under Rule 90.3(a). However, the court has discretion not to include this income when, for example, the extra work is undertaken to pay off back child support.

C. Low Income of Obligor. Paragraphs (a) and (b) of the rule must be applied even in low-income situations. However, in a paragraph (a) [primary custody] calculation and in the first stage of a paragraph (b) [shared, divided or hybrid custody] calculation, if the calculations result in a support amount below $50.00 per month, a minimum support amount of $50.00 per month ($600 per year) must be set. This $50.00 minimum support applies for all children, not to each child separately. The minimum level may be reduced if an extended visitation credit is granted under Rule 90.3(a)(3). This minimum support amount does not apply to final support amounts for shared, divided, or hybrid custody entered under Rule 90.3(b).

D. High Income of a Parent. Rule 90.3 provides that the percentages for child support will not be applied to a parent's adjusted annual income of over $100,000, unless the other parent is able to present evidence which justifies departure from this general rule. The factors which the court should consider in such a determination are specified in the rule.

E. Retroactive Establishment.

1. Retroactive Establishment of Child Support. It will sometimes be necessary for the court to establish support for a time when no complaint or petition for support had yet been served, and there was no other court or administrative order in effect. The court has determined that Civil Rule 90.3 applies to such calculations. *Vachon v. Pugliese*, 931 P.2d 371, 381–2 (Alaska 1996). However, in some circumstances unfairness may result from rigid application of the rule. The court should consider all relevant factors in such a situation, including whether the obligor was aware of the support obligation, especially if the obligor had children subsequent to that child. See also Commentary VI.B.2.

2. Retroactive Application of Amendments. When establishing support for a period of time before a complaint or petition was served, the court should apply the most current version of the rule, except for portions of the rule that state dollar amounts. This is because Civil Rule 90.3, unlike most other court rules, is interpretive. The most current version of the rule is presumably the most refined interpretation to date of the statute calling for fair and equitable child support awards. For example, the credit for prior children living with the obligor was not found in early versions of the rule, but nonetheless should be applied when support is being established. However, the dollar amounts in the rule, such as the minimum support amount (increased from $40 to $50) and the income cap (increased from $60,000 to $100,000), have been revised over time to reflect inflation or for other reasons. With regard to these amounts, the court should apply the version of the rule that was in effect in the month for which support is being calculated.

F. Seasonal Income. In Alaska, seasonal employment is common. Obligors employed in such seasonal industries as commercial fishing, tourism, and construction often earn a large percentage of their income during only a few months of the year. It might be easier for some seasonally-employed obligors to meet their child support obligations if their child support orders required the bulk of their annual child support amount to be paid during the months they are employed. Thus, the rule allows courts the flexibility of ordering unequal monthly payments, as long as the total annual amount equals the amount calculated in paragraph (a) or (b) of the rule. The court should not make such an order unless it finds that the burden of budgeting for periods of unequal income should be placed on the obligee rather than the obligor.

The court's order must specify the annual support amount, the average monthly support amount, and the amount due for each month. For example, if the annual child support amount is $3600, the average monthly amount is $300. Instead of requiring 12 equal monthly payments of $300, the order could require payments of $500 per month from April through September and $100 per month from October through March.

Payments under the order must be set up so that a deficit situation will not occur. This means that, at any point in time, the total amount owed under the order (for the entire period the order has been in effect) must not be less than the amount that would have been owed for that entire period if no seasonal adjustment had been made. Therefore, in the above example, if the order is entered in April through September, it can order $500 monthly payments for the April–September period, followed by $100 monthly payments for October–March. However, if the order is entered anytime in October through March, the order must require $300 payments through March, then $500 payments from April through October, and then $100 payments the following October–March.

VII. HEALTH CARE COVERAGE

A. Health Insurance. Rule 90.3(d) requires that the court address coverage of the children's health care needs including expenses not covered by insurance. The court must require health insurance if the insurance is available to either party at a reasonable cost. The health insurance will be paid by the party to whom it is available. However, the court must allocate the cost of insurance between the parties. Note that the cost to be allocated is limited to that portion of the total cost necessary to insure the children involved—not the parent, the parent's new spouse or children of another relationship. If the insurance for the children also covers other members of the purchaser's family, and evidence is unavailable on the specific cost of insuring only the children subject to the order, the cost of covering the children must be determined by allocating the total cost of coverage pro rata among all covered family members. See *Rusenstrom v. Rusenstrom,* 981 P.2d 558 (Alaska 1999). If there is no additional cost to the employee for adding children to the coverage—that is, the cost of coverage is the same whether there are no dependents or several dependents—no portion of the cost of coverage may be allocated to the children. In such cases, no adjustment may be made to the child support obligation because none of the cost of coverage can be allocated to the children.

The allocation of the cost of the children's insurance between the parents should be 50/50 unless the court finds good cause to change that percentage. A substantial difference in the parties' relative financial circumstances may constitute good cause. The rule requires the court to adjust child support either upward or downward to reflect the allocation. Paragraph (h)(1) provides that payments for health care insurance are included in deciding whether there has been a 15% change in support which constitutes a material change of circumstances.

B. Uncovered Health Care Expenses. Rule 90.3(d)(2) provides that the court also allocate reasonable health expenses not covered by insurance. The rule requires the party who did not obtain the health care to reimburse the other party within 30 days of receiving the necessary paperwork. The paperwork should include the medical bill, payment verification, and, if medical insurance applies, an insurance statement indicating any uncovered health care expenses. These materials should be sent to the other party within a reasonable time. The rule should be read to require prepayment of allowable uncovered medical cost when prepayment is required by the health care provider.

The rule provides that the usual 50/50 presumption does not apply for any amount in excess of $5,000 per calendar year. In such a situation, the excess expenses should be allocated based on the parties' relative financial circumstances during the approximate time period when the expenses occurred.

C. Definition of Health Care Expenses. Paragraph (f) defines health care expenses to include medical, dental, vision and mental health counseling expenses.

VIII. CHILD SUPPORT AFFIDAVIT AND DOCUMENTATION

A. Affidavit and Documentation Each parent in a proceeding involving a determination of child support must provide the court with an income statement under oath. The rule also requires that the income statement of a parent be verified with documentation of current and past income. Suitable documentation of earnings might include paystubs, employer statements, or copies of federal tax returns. The income statement, with documentation, must be filed with the party's first pleading in the action. This first pleading is the dissolution petition in a dissolution, the complaint or answer in a divorce, the custody petition or response in a child custody case under AS 25.20.060, or the motion or opposition in a motion to modify child support or motion to change custody. The court may impose sanctions on a party who does not timely file the income statement with appropriate documentation. The rule repeats language set out in Civil Rule 95(a). In a default case the court must decide support on the best available information, but should require the present party to make reasonable efforts to obtain reasonably accurate information.

Income affidavits must be filed even by a parent whose income is not presently being used to calculate child support. That parent's income may be relevant if there is a request by either parent for a variation under subsection (c), or it may be needed to determine what percentage of uncovered health care expenses each parent will pay under subsection (d)(2) or how much of travel expenses each parent will pay under subsection (g). In addition, the court may wish to enter an order which automatically shifts the child support obligation if a child changes his or her primary residence, as permitted under *Karpuleon v. Karpuleon*, 881 P.2d 318 (Alaska 1994).

B. Request for Income Information Paragraph (h) of the rule allows child support orders to be modified if a material change of circumstances is shown. A change in a parent's income qualifies as a 'material change' if it would increase or decrease the support amount by 15 percent. Paragraph (e)(2) of the rule provides an informal method either parent can use, while a support order is in effect, to learn whether there has been a large enough change in the other parent's income to justify a change in the amount of child support. This paragraph allows a parent to send the other parent a written request for documents such as tax returns and pay stubs showing the other parent's income for the prior calendar year (January through December). However, the parent making this request must attach to the request a copy of the same type of documents showing his or her own income for the prior calendar year. This request can only be made once each year. The parent who receives the request must provide the requested information within 30 days after the request is made. The parents can then do the necessary calculations to determine whether a motion to modify child support should be filed. In addition, a parent may always use the formal discovery procedures provided in the other civil rules to obtain income information from the other parent.

IX. TRAVEL EXPENSES

The court shall allocate any travel expenses that are necessary to exercise visitation. This allocation should generally be done on a percentage basis because the actual costs may not be known or may change. The court should take care that its allocation of these expenses does not interfere with a parent's ability to provide the basic necessities for the children.

X. MODIFICATION

A. Material Change in Circumstances.

Alaska law allows the modification of support orders upon a material change in circumstances. A significant amendment to Rule 90.3 constitutes a material change in circumstances pursuant to AS 25.24.170(b). Rule 90.3(h) states that a material change in circumstances will be presumed whenever the change would result in an increase or decrease of support under the rule of at least 15%. However, a support order can provide that the support obligation will be adjusted without further order of the court upon a change of health insurance costs and notice of the change to the other parent (and CSSD if CSSD is handling collections).

See *Flannery v. Flannery, 950 P.2d 126 (Alaska 1997)* , concerning what constitutes a material change of circumstances when the parties by agreement originally set support at a level higher than would have normally been required under Rule 90.3.

A temporary reduction in income normally will not justify an ongoing modification reducing child support. However, a temporary, unforeseen, and involuntary reduction in income may justify a temporary reduction in support subject to the retroactivity provisions in Rule 90.3(h)(2). In considering such a reduction, the court should consider the needs of the children, the ability of the other parent to provide support, liquid assets available to provide support, and the future earning capability of the obligor parent. See *Flannery v. Flannery,* 950 P.2d 126, 133 (Alaska 1997); *Patch v. Patch,* 760 P.2d 526, 530 (Alaska 1988).

Federal law, recognized in AS 25.24.170(b) and AS 25.27.193, appears on its face to require allowing modifications every three years without a showing of a material change in circumstances. See 42 U.S.C. 666(a)(10)(A)(iii). However, in response to questions from states, the federal Office of Child Support Enforcement has stated (in Action Transmittal OCSE-97-10, pages 28–31) that existing regulations which allow reasonable quantitative standards for modifications (such as Alaska's 15% standard) continue to apply.

B. No Retroactive Modification.

The Omnibus Budget Reconciliation Act of 1986, P.L. 99–509, Section 9103(a) (the Bradley Amendment), prohibits retroactive modification of child support arrearages. Rule 90.3(h)(2) is intended to restate this prohibition, including the exception allowed by federal law for modification during the pendency of a modification motion. Pursuant to this rule, the notice of petition for modification sent by the Child Support Services Division triggers the legal process for modification of child support awards and thus an increase or decrease of support back to the date of this notice does not constitute retroactive modification.

The prohibition against retroactive modification limits both requested decreases and increases in child support. See Prohibition of Retroactive Modification of Child Support Arrearages, 54 Fed. Reg. 15,763 (1989). Thus, either the custodial or the obligor parent should promptly apply for a modification of child support when a material change in circumstances occurs.

See Section VI.(B).(2) of the commentary as to the extent support of a "subsequent" family may be used as a defense to a modification action to increase child support.

C. Preclusion.

The sometimes harsh effect of the rule against retroactive modification may be mitigated by the preclusion provision of Rule 90.3, which limits collection of a support arrearage in limited and appropriate cases. Preclusion may be applied to limit collection by a parent's assignee, such as the child support services agency of this or another state. Clear and convincing evidence is required to support a finding of preclusion.

Preclusion may apply only in cases in which the obligor assumed primary physical custody of a child for the time period for which the obligee now attempts to collect support. The time period must be more than nine months. Preclusion does not apply in cases in which the proportion of shared custody changed or when there is a shift from primary physical custody to shared custody. Preclusion may apply when the obligor assumes primary physical custody of any number of the children on which the support obligation in arrearage is based. *Murphy v. Newlynn*, 34 P.3d 331 (Alaska 2001).

As an alternative to preclusion, AS 25.27.020(b) may allow a reduction of support owed to the other parent when the obligor assumes custody of one or more of the children. See *State v. Gause,* 967 P.2d 599 (Alaska 1998).

XI. THIRD PARTY CUSTODY

A. Support Owed to the Third Party

If the state or another third party entitled to child support has custody of all of a parent's children, child support is calculated in the same way as it would be calculated in other cases. In other words, support is equal to the parent's adjusted annual income multiplied by the relevant percentage in paragraph (a)(2) based on the number of children.

However, this basic calculation does not work when the state or other third party has custody of only some of a parent's children. In this case, the rule provides that the total support calculation (as calculated for the total number of the parent's children) be reduced to only the proportion of the parent's children of whom the third party has custody. For example, the third party might have custody of two of a parent's three children. Support would be calculated as the parent's adjusted annual income, multiplied by .33 (the relevant percentage for three children), multiplied by 2/3 (the third party has custody of two of the parent's three children). Note that the calculation only takes into account children which are either in third party custody, substantially supported by the parent or living with the parent. A child of the parent, for example, living with a relative without substantial support would not be counted in the above calculation.

The deduction for prior children in (a)(1)(B) and (C) would not apply because these children are already taken into account as children living with or supported by the parent.

B. Support Owed Between the Parents

There will be instances when a third party is entitled to support for some of the parent's children, but one or both parents retain primary or shared custody of their remaining children. In this case, child support between the parents should be calculated using Rule 90.3 based on the pro rata support percentages for the children not in third party custody. After that calculation, any support owed may be offset with amounts owed under 90.3(i)(1) to minimize transactions.

For example, a father might have custody of two children and the mother's sister might have custody of, and be entitled to support for, the parents' third child. Both parents in this example have a $45,000 adjusted annual income. Under Rule 90.3(i)(1), the sister is entitled to $4,950 per year from the father [$45,000 (annual income) x 33% (percentage for three children) x 1/3 (custodian has one of three children)]. The sister also is entitled to the same amount from the mother. (The parents' incomes are the same and the mother supports the children living with the father.)

The pro rata percentage for each child under 90.3 (a)(2) would be 33% (three children), 3 or 11% per child. Under 90.3(i)(2), the mother owes the father $9,900 per year in support ($45,000 x 22%). If the support amounts are offset, the mother will owe her sister $9,900 per year and the father $4,950 per year. The court could decide, however, that it was preferable not to offset the support amounts because one of the parents might not pay the third party.

XII. SUPPORT ORDER FORMS

Paragraph (j) was formerly Civil Rule 67(b).

XII. DEPENDENT TAX DEDUCTION

Waggoner v. Foster, 904 P.2d 1234 (Alaska 1995), provides that tax deductions for the children should be allocated based on the child's best interests. AS 25.24.152 places some limits on giving the deduction to the parent with less physical custody. Federal income tax law also may limit who can take the deduction.

(Amended by SCO 1417, effective April 15, 2001; and by SCO 1526 effective April 15, 2005)

Annotations

Cases

I. In General.
II. Primary Physical Custody/Guidelines.
III. Shared Physical Custody.
IV. Exceptions.
V. Health Care Coverage.
VI. Child Support Affidavit and Documentation.
VII. Definitions.
VIII. Travel Expenses.
IX. Modification.
X. Third Party Custody.

I. In General.

Child support awards made prior to the effective date of this rule are subject to redetermination under this rule. **Richmond v. Richmond,** Op. No. 3500, 779 P2d 1211 (Alaska 1989).

When tortious sexual conduct results in the birth of a child, the victim is not entitled to recover as damages the cost of raising the child, but is entitled to partial reimbursement for actual, reasonable child care expenditures, and an award of prospective child support pursuant to this rule. **Poor v. Moore,** Op. No. 3580, 791 P2d 1005 (Alaska 1990).

Trial court did not abuse its discretion in calculating the earning capacity of a voluntarily unemployed obligor parent based upon his premarriage income. **Kowalski v. Kowalski,** Op. No. 3669, 806 P2d 1368 (Alaska 1991).

Trial court's finding that obligor parent was voluntarily unemployed was upheld on appeal. **Kowalski v. Kowalski,** Op. No. 3669, 806 P2d 1368 (Alaska 1991).

This rule applies to all awards of child support, whether agreed to by the parties or contested. **Keating v. Traynor,** Op. No. 3862, 833 P2d 695 (Alaska 1992).

Where father failed to establish that there was any genuine issue of material fact before the court, trial court properly determined his child support obligation under this rule without an evidentiary hearing. **Epperson v. Epperson,** Op. No. 3873, 835 P2d 451 (Alaska 1992).

Father's past voluntary contributions in excess of child support obligation did not constitute good cause for reducing future child support obligation. **Epperson v. Epperson,** Op. No. 3873, 835 P2d 451 (Alaska 1992).

Child support formula imposed by this rule held constitutional. **Coghill v. Coghill,** Op. No. 3865, 836 P2d 921 (Alaska 1992).

Superior court presumptively does not abuse its discretion when it awards child support based upon child support formula of this rule. **Coghill v. Coghill,** Op. No. 3865, 836 P2d 921 (Alaska 1992).

Child support waiver is not valid and enforceable until court has reviewed and approved waiver's substantive adequacy under this rule. **Nix v. Nix,** Op. No. 3984, 855 P2d 1332 (Alaska 1993).

Child support waiver presented after initial dissolution proceeding will be given only prospective effect from date of judicial approval. **Nix v. Nix,** Op. No. 3984, 855 P2d 1332 (Alaska 1993).

Where child support award has been established through initial dissolution proceeding, any subsequent proposed waiver must be presented to court for review under modification procedures of this rule. **Nix V. Nix,** Op. No. 3984, 855 P2d 1332 (Alaska 1993).

Trial court is required to make specific findings to support determination of adjusted income under this rule, thus remand was required where trial court simply set adjusted income without explaining its calculation of gross income or amounts and types of deductions. **Gallant v. Gallant,** Op. No. 4122, 882 P2d 1252 (Alaska 1994).

Department of Revenue, which adopted this rule as its child support guidelines, could assess $50 monthly support obligation against incarcerated parent who had no assets and earned less than $50 per month. **Douglas v. State, Dept. of Revenue,** Op. No. 4109, 880 P2d 113 (Alaska 1994).

Child support awards are reviewed for an abuse of discretion and will not be set aside unless a review of the record as a whole leaves the appellate court with a definite and firm conviction that a mistake has been made. **Moore v. Moore,** Op. No. 4190, 893 P2d 1268 (Alaska 1995).

This rule governed determination of support mandated by statute extending support obligation to dependent unmarried 18-year-old children actively pursuing high-school diplomas. **Sanders v. Sanders,** Op. No. 4254, 902 P2d 310 (Alaska1995).

Original orders of child support are considered judgments which under certain conditions are prospectively modifiable. **State ex rel. Inman v. Dean,** Op. No. 4244, 902 P2d 1321 (Alaska 1995).

Where no material factual dispute regarding child support existed, trial court did not err in deciding child support without hearing. **Thriusky v. Long,** Op. No. 4319, 910 P2d 590 (Alaska 1996).

Retroactive to date of adoption of the rule, child support waivers are not valid or enforceable until and unless court has reviewed and approved their substantive adequacy under this rule. **Richmond v. Pluid,** Op. No. 4418, 925 P2d 251 (Alaska 1996).

Absent extraordinary circumstances, courts should apply calculation methodology of this rule to determine amounts to be reimbursed to custodial parents for support of children during periods not covered by support orders. **Vachon v. Pugliese,** Op. No. 4428, 931 P2d 371 (Alaska 1996).

Monthly statements by Child Support Enforcement Division indicating that father owed $100 per month in child support were not equivalent of child support orders. **Benson v. Benson,** Op. No. 5109, 977 P2d 88 (Alaska 1999).

Trial court abused its discretion in granting retroactive child support award to father for year he had de jure physical custody of child but mother had de facto physical custody. **Bennett v. Bennett,** Op. No. 5300, 6 P3d 724 (Alaska 2000).

The proper method of calculating child support, which is a question of law, is reviewed de novo. **Spott v. Spott,** Op. No. 5361, 17 P3d 52 (Alaska 2001).

Child support obligation may not be based solely on the father's seasonal income where he chooses not to seek year-round employment. **Nunley v. State,** Op. No. 5837, 99 P.3d 7 (Alaska 2004).

Percentage of income approach in determining child support has a fair and substantial relationship to the goals of this rule. **Lawson v. Lawson,** Op. No. 5876, 108 P.3d 883 (Alaska 2005).

Alaska's legislature has ratified the Supreme Court of Alaska's child support enforcement powers on multiple occasions; the legislature has the ability to alter or supersede provisions of this rule via legislation, but at no point has the legislature questioned the court's ability to order child support. **Lawson v. Lawson,** Op. No. 5876, 108 P.3d 883 (Alaska 2005).

Submission of child support financial affidavits does not violate the Fifth Amendment right against self-incrimination. **Lawson v. Lawson,** Op. No. 5876, 108 P.3d 883 (Alaska 2005).

Court properly ordered the father to be responsible for seventy-five percent of the costs of visitation and the children's uncovered medical expenses while the mother was actively pursuing her master's degree; mother's financial resources were limited while she was enrolled as a student, which constituted good cause for ordering the father to pay a greater share of the expenses. **Veselsky v. Veselsky,** Op. No. 5901, 113 P.3d 629 (Alaska 2005).

Where the parties' child ran away, did not live with either parent, and the mother was not financially supporting the child, the trial court erred by reinstating the father's child support obligation under this rule absent a showing that the mother incurred expenses in an effort to find the child and secure custody of her, and to maintain a suitable place for her pending her return. **Killary v. Killary,** Op. No. 5956, 123 P.3d 1039 (Alaska 2005).

II. Primary Physical Custody/Guidelines.

Absent sufficient evidence to the contrary presented by the non-custodial parent, trial court did not err in concluding that a $1,000 per month support obligation for his son, arrived at by applying the formula of this rule, was fair. **Coats v. Finn,** Op. No. 3441, 779 P2d 775 (Alaska 1989).

In determining father's child support requirement, trial court did not err in including his investment income in the calculation despite father's claim that such income was too speculative to be considered. **Coats v. Finn,** Op. No. 3441, 779 P2d 775 (Alaska 1989).

In determining father's child support requirement, trial court erred in not including in the mother's income her income from a past, part-time teaching position. **Bergstrom v. Lindback,** Op. No. 3516, 779 P2d 1235 (Alaska 1989).

In determining father's support requirement, trial court did not err in refusing to include in the mother's income a portion of their joint federal tax refund. **Bergstrom v. Lindback,** Op. No. 3516, 779 P2d 1235 (Alaska 1989).

In determining father's child support requirement, the trial court erred in failing to credit the father's premium payments for a life insurance policy on behalf of the children. **Bergstrom v. Lindback,** Op. No. 3516, 779 P2d 1235 (Alaska 1989).

In determining father's child support requirement, the trial court erred in including the father's income deferred compensation funds without considering the tax liability he would incur should he draw upon those funds. **Bergstrom v. Lindback,** Op. No. 3516, 779 P2d 1235 (Alaska 1989).

In determining father's child support requirement, trial court erred in reducing the father's total income by the amount of tax withheld from his paycheck rather than his actual federal income tax liability. **Bergstrom v. Lindback,** Op. No. 3516, 779 P2d 1235 (Alaska 1989).

In calculating husband's child support obligation, a single pay statement showing that his pension contribution was deducted from his gross pay did not mean that the total wage figure reported on his W-2 form was also a pre-deduction figure. **Bays v. Bays,** Op. No. 3676, 807 P2d 482 (Alaska 1991).

Where husband was in business for himself and the trial court used gross receipts rather than tax records to calculate his adjusted annual income, trial court was required to factor in straight-line depreciation of business equipment unless the equipment was acquired to avoid or reduce his child support obligation. **Ogard v. Ogard,** Op. No. 3679, 808 P2d 815 (Alaska 1991).

Where father had earned his living as a fisherman but testified that he was changing careers to work as a welder, the trial court did not err in calculating his income for child support purposes based upon his potential income as a fisher-man rather than his lower prospective earnings as a welder. **Pugil v. Cogar,** Op. No. 3694, 811 P2d 1062 (Alaska 1991).

Where noncustodial parent's reduction in income was voluntary and temporary in nature, trial court, upon consideration of all the evidence, properly determined that the equities did not justify placing a greater burden of support on the custodial parent. **Pugil v. Cogar,** Op. No. 3694, 811 P2d 1062 (Alaska 1991).

Bad faith on the part of plaintiff's attorney was a totally inappropriate factor to consider in determining a child support order. **Murphy v. Murphy,** Op. No. 3700,812 P2d 960 (Alaska 1991).

Trial court's findings in child support award did not demonstrate consideration of the special needs of the children; on remand, the trial court was advised to specifically identify the reasonable needs of the children and the ability of the parents to meet those needs. **Murphy v. Murphy,** Op. No. 3700, 812 P2d 960 (Alaska 1991).

Father's child support obligation under this rule would have to be recalculated if order modifying dissolution decree to award a portion of his military retirement benefits to his former wife were upheld; a child support obligation under this rule must be based on the parent's adjusted annual income. **Lowe v. Lowe,** Op. No. 3726, 817 P2d 453 (Alaska 1991).

Trial court improperly coordinated, or failed to coordinate, child visitation and support awards, requiring remand for a calculation conforming to this rule. **Long v. Long,** Op. No. 3734, 816 P2d 145 (Alaska 1991).

In calculating self-employed person's income for child support purposes, trial court properly disallowed deduction for imputed taxes based on income available as result of adding back a deduction for accelerated depreciation. **Coghill v. Coghill,** Op. No. 3865, 836 P2d 921 (Alaska 1992).

In calculating self-employed person's income for child support purposes, trial court did not err in disallowing deductions for meals, work clothes, automobile use, etc., even if they were legitimate business expenses. **Coghill**

v. Coghill, Op. No. 3865, 836 P2d 921 (Alaska 1992).

Trial court did not err in including as part of obligation parent's adjusted gross income money deposited in capital construction fund which, under IRS regulations, was deductible from income. **Zimin v. Zimin,** Op. No. 3872, 837 P2d 118 (Alaska 1992).

Trial court did not err in calculating obligor-parent's income based upon his 1990 projected earnings rather than on his average income over ten years even though he was a fisherman whose income fluctuated from year to year. **Zimin v. Zimin,** Op. No. 3872, 837 P2d 118 (Alaska 1992).

Lack of clear factual findings and lack of substantial evidence of parent's income required vacation of child support award. **Adrian v. Adrian,** Op. No. 3892, 838 P2d 808 (Alaska 1992).

In determining earning capacity of father whose annual income had changed from $36,000 per year as sales manager to $24,000 as owner of his own business, trial court did not err in averaging past and present income figures. **Renfro v. Renfro,** Op. No. 3939, 848 P2d 830 (Alaska 1993).

Father was not entitled to mandatory credit against child support award for expenses of raising son from prior marriage, where son lived with him and received support directly from him. **Renfro v. Renfro,** Op. No. 3939, 848 P2d 830 (Alaska 1993).

Because trial court's findings of fact neither indicated that child support adjustment for extended visitation period was considered nor, if considered, expressed court's rationale for declining to make adjustment, award of child support was remanded for findings on issue. **Renfro v. Renfro,** Op. No. 3939, 848 P2d 830 (Alaska 1993).

Having decided to disallow deduction for accrued but unpaid mortgage interest payments in calculating income for child support purposes, superior court had to reduce resulting annual income by income taxes which would have been paid had that portion of mortgage interest deduction been disallowed for that year's income for tax purposes. **Eagley v. Eagley,** Op. No. 3928, 849 P2d 777 (Alaska 1993).

Where wife in divorce action had moved from Alaska to Iowa, determination of whether wife was below poverty level had to be based upon poverty level in Iowa, not Alaska, **Carstens v. Carstens,** Op. No. 4052, 867 P2d 805 (Alaska 1994).

This rule does not preclude social security benefits from offsetting the full amount of the child support obligation. **Miller v. Miller,** Op. No. 4172, 890 P2d 574 (Alaska 1995).

Social security benefits the child receives through the parent should be included as income in calculating the parent's child support obligation. **Miller v. Miller,** Op. No. 4172, 890 P2d 574 (Alaska 1995).

A divorced parent who is required to pay support to a child under Alaska Civil Rule 90.3 is entitled to child support credit for social security payments the child receives on the parent's behalf. **Miller v. Miller,** Op. No. 4172, 890 P2d 574 (Alaska 1995).

Monthly mortgage expenses were properly treated as a constituent part of the standard of living of the children where the property division did not require the non-custodial parent to make the custodial parent's mortgage payments. **Moore v. Moore,** Op. No. 4190, 893 P2d 1268 (Alaska 1995).

Trial court abused its discretion in reaffirming a child support obligation of $300 per month without fully taking into account the parent's present mental disability and the impact it had on her earning capacity. **A.H. v. W.P.,** Op. No. 4222, 896 P2d 240 (Alaska 1995).

Gifts are not to be included as income in determining child support obligations. **Nass v. Seaton,** Op. No. 4275, 904 P2d 412 (Alaska 1995).

Business accounts receivable were properly included as income in determining child support obligation. **Nass v. Seaton,** Op. No. 4275, 904 P2d 412 (Alaska 1995).

Portion of obligor father's residence used for business could be depreciated straightline in calculating his adjusted income for support purposes. **Nass v. Seaton,** Op. No. 4275, 904 P2d 412 (Alaska 1995).

Imputed potential income could be used to determine child support obligation of voluntarily underemployed parent. **Nass v. Seaton,** Op. No. 4275, 904 P2d 412 (Alaska 1995).

Trial court's findings that obligor-parent was voluntarily underemployed were not clearly erroneous. **Nass v. Seaton,** Op. No. 4275, 904 P2d 412 (Alaska 1995).

Trial court erroneously based child support arrearages on amount of visitation actually exercised rather than amount of visitation awarded. **Turinsky v. Long,** Op. No. 4319, 910 P2d 590 (Alaska 1996).

Child support award was remanded for specific findings following allegation that court did not take into account obligor parent's permanent fund dividend or his employer-provided transportation in calculating adjusted income. **Brown v. Brown,** Op. No. 4328, 914 P2d 206 (Alaska 1996).

Trial court decision to allow obligor parent to reduce child support payments for period in which that parent had extended visitation of over 27 consecutive days had to be supported by specific findings. **Brown v. Brown,** Op. No. 4328, 914 P2d 206 (Alaska 1996).

In calculating self-employment income, there is no bright line test that all expenses recognized by the IRS are similarly recognized under this rule; instead, determinative factor as to whether claimed expense is deductible under this rule is whether it is ordinary and necessary expense required to produce income and whether allowance of expense would defeat goals of this rule. **Neilson v. Neilson,** Op. No. 4337, 914 P2d 1268 (Alaska 1996).

In calculating self-employment income, deductions for home office expenses should be subject to scrutiny but should not be categorically disallowed; accordingly, disallowing all deductions for rent, utilities and repairs, when record clearly indicated that such expenses occurred and were necessary, was error. **Neilson v. Neilson,** Op. No. 4337, 914 P2d 1268 (Alaska 1996).

In calculating father's self-employment income under this rule, it was error to compute social security tax at 7.65 percent rather than 15.3 percent rate for self-employed persons and error to fail to consider California state income taxes. **Neilson v. Neilson,** Op. No. 4337, 914 P2d 1268 (Alaska 1996).

Non-custodial parent's "fair share" of child support is presumed to be amount fixed under guidelines of this rule; to rebut presumption, non-custodial parent must show that his expenses are extraordinary. **Berkbigler v. Berkbigler,** Op. No. 4377, 921 P2d 628 (Alaska 1996).

Prior or subsequent debts of obligor parent, even if substantial, normally will not justify reduction in child support. **Berkbigler v. Berkbigler,** Op. No. 4377, 921 P2d 628 (Alaska 1996).

Obligor parent who experiences increase in income cannot avoid paying additional support merely by showing that children's needs are being met by existing support award. **Berkbigler v. Berkbigler,** Op. No. 4377, 921 P2d 628 (Alaska 1996).

Obligor parent's argument that cost of living allowance and overseas housing allowance should not be included in his adjusted annual income because they were temporary increases in income was rejected. **Berkbigler v. Berkbigler,** Op. No. 4377, 921 P2d 628 (Alaska 1996).

Ongoing support obligations of obligor parents are offset by children's insurance benefit payments made to their children because of obligor parents' eligibility for social security benefits. **State Dept. of Revenue v. Fry,** Op. No. 4437, 926 P2d 1170 (Alaska 1996).

Trial court erred in not granting father credit against his child support obligations for Social Security disability benefits paid on his behalf to his children, and credit should have been allowed automatically without necessity of prior modification motion. **Pacana v. State,** Op. No. 4854, 941 P2d 1263 (Alaska 1997).

Gift of money received by mother was to be included in calculating her income for specific period for purpose of determining her obligation to reimburse father for expenses made by him during same period when children were temporarily in his custody. **Crayton v. Crayton,** Op. No. 4885, 944 P2d 487 (Alaska 1997).

For period when no child support order was in effect and children were with father, father was entitled to reimbursement for child support expenditures he made during period as offset against child support payments he was required to make to mother once she had primary physical custody of children. **Crayton v. Crayton,** Op. No. 4885, 944 P2d 487 (Alaska 1997).

Trial court properly refused to permit parent to deduct expenses of his closely held corporation from his net income for purpose of calculating child support obligation. **Gallant v. Gallant,** Op. No. 4884, 945 P2d 795 (Alaska 1997).

Trial court erred in reducing obligor parent's child support obligation by 100 percent for periods in which child resided in medical facilities. **Gallant v. Gallant,** Op. No. 4884, 945 P2d 795 (Alaska 1997).

Trial court's reduction without explanation of obligor parent's child support payments by 100 percent during children's visitation periods with obligor parent of over 27 consecutive days was error, requiring payments for such periods to be reduced by 50 percent rather than 100 percent. **Gallant v. Gallant,** Op. No. 4884, 945 P2d 795 (Alaska 1997).

This rule leaves to court's discretion whether obligor is entitled to child support credit and actual amount of credit; obligor is not automatically entitled to credit, which must be negotiated for as part of divorce settlement. **Pierce v. Pierce,** Op. No. 4914, 949 P2d 498 (Alaska 1997).

Trial court does not have independent obligation to consider appropriateness of child support credit during times of extended visitation if credit is not requested by one of parties. **Pierce v. Pierce,** Op. No. 4914, 949 P2d 498 (Alaska 1997).

Where husband's attorney inserted child support credit in child custody and support order that parties had not agreed to during divorce settlement negotiations, wife was entitled to relief from order due to misconduct of husband's attorney in not bringing change to attention of wife's attorney. **Pierce v. Pierce,** Op. No. 4914, 949 P2d 498 (Alaska 1997).

Trial court erred when it relied exclusively on 1992 through 1994 average of child support obligor's income to determine that he had not experienced reduction in income, ignoring evidence that his income declined during first six months of 1995. **Flannery v. Flannery,** Op. No. 4922, 950 P2d 126 (Alaska 1997).

Trial court did not err in including dividends earned in noncustodial parent's IRA as income for purpose of calculating child support. **Dunn v. Dunn,** Op. No. 4933, 952 P2d 268 (Alaska 1998).

Contention that stock dividends should not be considered income under this rule if they go directly to state to pay child support arrearages was rejected. **Robinson v. Robinson,** Op. No. 5011, 961 P2d 1000 (Alaska 1998).

Contention that proceeds from property sale should not be considered income under this rule if used to pay child support arrearages was rejected. **Robinson v. Robinson,** Op. No. 5011, 961 P2d 1000 (Alaska 1998).

Child support obligation may be based on potential rather than actual earnings if obligor voluntarily fails to realize his income potential. **Robinson v. Robinson,** Op. No. 5011, 961 P2d 1000 (Alaska 1998).

Whether item qualifies as income under this rule is question of law to be reviewed de novo, adopting the rule that is most persuasive in light of precedent, reason and policy. **Robinson v. Robinson,** Op. No. 5011, 961 P2d 1000 (Alaska 1998).

In calculating father's income for child support purposes, trial court erred in imputing as income the rental value of an apartment that he owned and lived in. **Hilderbrand v. Hilderbrand,** Op. No. 5023, 962 P2d 887 (Alaska 1998).

In calculating father's income for child support purposes, father was not allowed to deduct from adjusted income depreciation on triplex that he owned; husband did not show that same deduction could be made for income tax purposes and provided no authority to support his proposed method of depreciation. **Hilderbrand v. Hilderbrand,** Op. No. 5023, 962 P2d 887 (Alaska 1998).

Trial court was not required by First Amendment to hold hearing on sincerity of father's religious beliefs before choosing to disbelieve his affidavit and imputing to him for purpose of child support calculation an annual income of $39,181 based on the average Alaska wage for a man of his age; father refused to submit tax returns to document his affidavit, claiming that he was self-employed on cash-only basis and that his religious beliefs prevented him from paying federal taxes. **Elsberry v. Elsberry,** Op. No. 5047, 967 P2d 1004 (Alaska 1998).

Voluntary retirement from military was not voluntary underemployment by father where evidence indicated that he might have been passed over for promotion due to disabilities and that person who retires voluntarily has better chance of securing civilian employment at comparable or higher wage than person who has been passed over for promotion. **Maloney v. Maloney,** Op. No. 5056, 969 P2d 1148 (Alaska 1998).

Trial court did not lack jurisdiction in 1985 dissolution proceeding to enter child support order conforming to stepfather's express agreement to pay support for stepdaughter, notwithstanding that literal reading of dissolution statute gave court jurisdiction only over children born of marriage or adopted during marriage. **Dewey v. Dewey,** Op. No. 5065, 969 P2d 1154 (Alaska 1999).

The rule's preclusion provision was applied where the obligor parent assumed primary custody of only one of the parties' children; because requiring him to pay child support for the child living with him would have provided the mother with an undeserved windfall. **Murphy v. Newlynn,** Op. No. 5494, 34 P3d 331 (Alaska 2001).

Trial court erred in using predicted income rather than actual income to determine retrospective interim child support award. **Spott v. Spott,** Op. No. 5361, 17 P3d 52 (Alaska 2001).

This rule gives courts broad discretion to impute income based on realistic estimates of earning potential in cases of voluntary and unreasonable unemployment or underemployment, but it does not rigorously require obligor parent to pursue maximum earnings. **Beaudoin v. Beaudoin,** Op. No. 5420, 24 P3d 523 (Alaska 2001).

Where father moved for order establishing mother's support obligation following new custody agreement under which shared custody of two of the children and sole custody by father of the other child replaced old custody agreement under which mother had sole custody of all three children, trial court erred in refusing without an evidentiary hearing father's request that income be imputed to mother based upon her earning capacity; because father offered evidence that mother was employable but chose not to work, his claim that she was voluntarily underemployed required an evidentiary hearing. **Beaudoin v. Beaudoin,** Op. No. 5420, 24 P3d 523 (Alaska 2001).

A child support award was vacated and remanded for recalculation of the mother's child support obligation, allowing her a deduction for the straight line depreciation of her rental properties. **Faulkner v. Goldfuss,** Op. No. 5565, 46 P3d 993 (Alaska 2002).

In calculating a child support award, it was error to include as gross income child support a mother received from the biological father of her child. **Faulkner v. Goldfuss,** Op. No. 5565,46 P3d 993 (Alaska 2002).

Although it was settled that Alaska Civ. R. 90.3(h)(2) allowed an automatic credit against child support arrearages for Children's Insurance Benefit payments, and although the parties' minor child received such payments, because the trial court did not properly consider the ex-wife's argument that the ex-husband waived the claim, the matter was remanded for further proceedings. **Whah v. Whah,** Op. No. 5612, 53 P.3d 604 (Alaska 2002).

Where the trial court found reason to allocate four-fifths of all future unreimbursed medical expenses for the parties' minor children to the father, namely that the father's income was four times greater than that of the mother, the trial court did not abuse its discretion in its allocation. **Hixson v. Sarkesian,** Op. No. 5677, 66 P.3d 753 (Alaska 2003).

Trial court erred in basing father's prospective child support obligation on the amount he had made in a prior job when there was no evidence that the father could currently make the same amount in the local job market. **Koller v. Reft,** Op. No. 10088 , 71 P.3d 800 (Alaska 2003).

Special master's reliance on the child and dependent care tax credit in determining a father's retroactive child support obligation was plain error because under Alaska R. Civ. P. 90.3(a)(1)(D) the special master should have determined whether the amounts of actual child care expenses both parents claimed on their tax returns were in fact reasonable and necessary to enable them to work. **Duffus v. Duffus,** Op. No. 10088, 72 P.3d 313 (Alaska 2003).

Civil Rule 90.3(b) relates only to cases in which parents were awarded are awarded shared physical custody; third-party custody is provided for under Rule 90.3(i), which relies on the percentages set out in Rule 90.3(a)(2). **Evans v. McTaggart,** Op. No. 5794, 88 P.3d 1078 (Alaska 2004).

The preclusion provisions of this rule apply only when child lives with a child-support obligor, and were inapplicable to obligor father's claim that he did not owe child support for the time his children lived with their grandmothers. **Webb v. Dept. of Revenue ex rel. Webb,** Op. No. 5941, 120 P.3d 197 (Alaska 2005).

In a child support dispute, the superior court was not required to impute income to the mother because she took maternity leave to have a new child with her current spouse. Subsection (a)(4) of this rule allows income to be imputed only when a parent voluntarily and unreasonably is unemployed or underemployed. **Mattfield v. Mattfield,** Op. No. 6003, 133 P.3d 667 (Alaska 2006).

III. Shared Physical Custody.

According to visitation schedule, children spent enough time with their father to require a finding of shared custody. **Ogard v. Ogard,** Op. No., 3679, 808 P2d 815 (Alaska 1991).

In calculating husband's child support obligation, trial court erred in including as income the imputed benefit of living in a four-plex which he owned. **Ogard v. Ogard,** Op. No. 3679, 808 P2d 815 (Alaska 1991).

Regardless of status of legal custody, if child resides with one parent at least 30 percent of year court must calculate child support using shared physical custody formula rather than sole custody formula. **Wright v. Gregorlo,** Op. No. 3973, 855 P2d 772 (Alaska 1993).

In hybrid situation where for interim period one parent had sole or primary physical custody of one child and parents shared physical custody of other children, trial court should have relied on both Civil Rule 90.3(a) and Civil Rule 90.3(b) to calculate child support. **Turinsky v. Long,** Op. No. 4319, 910 P2d 590 (Alaska 1996).

Civil Rule 90.3(b)(2) permits trial court to vary percentages used in calculating award of child support upon finding that percentage of time each parent will have physical custody will not correspond to percentage of children's total expenses that each parent will directly pay. **Marine v. Marine,** Op. No. 4976, 957 P2d 314 (Alaska 1998).

Percentage of time each parent has custody must be determined by reference to child custody order, not parties' actual conduct. **Rowen v. Rowen,** Op. No. 5014, 963 P2d 249 (Alaska 1998).

Trial court erred in calculating the divided custody child support award under former Alaska R. Civ. P. 90.3(b) without accurately accounting for each parent's period of physical custody. **Kelly v. Joseph,** Op. No. 5570, 46 P3d 1014 (Alaska 2002).

Even though the divided custody rule reflected in Alaska R. Civ. P. 90.3(b)(6) had an effective date of April 15, 2001, the formula on which the rule is based was earlier approved in the case of Bunn v. House. Therefore, it was not error to use the Bunn v. House formula prior to the effective date of its codification. **Corbin v. Corbin,** 68 P.3d 1269 (Alaska 2003).

Where neither parent had physical custody of two of the parents' three children for five months, with custody of two placed with the maternal grandparents and the third child with the mother, the parents owed support to the maternal grandparents and the trial court erred in basing the parent's support on a 50/50 shared custody arrangement for all three boys **Corbin v. Corbin,** 68 P.3d 1269 (Alaska 2003).

Where father had custody of one child for a month, the trial court erred in using a shared physical custody formula in determining the child support obligation for that child. **Corbin v. Corbin,** 68 P.3d 1269 (Alaska 2003).

IV. Exceptions.

Parents may not make a child support agreement which is not subject to this rule. **Cox v. Cox,** Op. No. 3455, 776 P2d 1045 (Alaska 1989).

An agreement between the parties as to child support is not an exceptional circumstance justifying deviation from the guidelines of this rule where the agreement requires support less than called for by the guidelines. **Cox v. Cox,** Op. No. 3455, 776 P2d 1045 (Alaska 1989).

Trial court did not abuse its discretion in setting father's child support obligation as a specific monthly amount rather than as a percentage of his income. **Cox v. Cox,** Op. No. 3455, 776 P2d 1045 (Alaska 1989).

This rule does not abrogate the general rule that a noncustodial parent is obligated to contribute only a fair share of the amount required to meet the reasonable needs of the parties' minor children. **Coats v. Finn,** Op. No. 3441, 779 P2d 775 (Alaska 1989).

The "good cause" exceptions enumerated in this rule for departing from the rule's formula are not exclusive. **Coats v. Finn,** Op. No. 3441, 779 P2d 775 (Alaska 1989).

An unfair result justifying departure from the formula of this rule is an award which substantially exceeds or falls short of the amount needed to provide for the child's reasonable needs or which requires the non-custodial parent, unreasonably, to contribute substantially more or less than his or her fair share of the amount needed to satisfy the child's reasonable needs. **Coats v. Finn,** Op. No. 3441, 779 P2d 775 (Alaska 1989).

When a party objects to application of the formula in this rule, a departure therefrom must be based on clear and convincing evidence that manifest injustice would result if the formula were applied; moreover, the reasons for the departure must be supported by specific findings, and the burden of persuasion is on the objecting party. **Coats v. Finn,** Op. No. 3441, 779 P2d 775 (Alaska 1989).

Child support award beyond the upper limit of this rule would require justification by the court. **Richmond v. Richmond,** Op. No. 3500, 779 P2d 1211 (Alaska 1989).

A parent may not waive the requirements of this rule by contract; therefore, trial court did not err in refusing to consider evidence of a purported settlement agreement in which mother waived her right to child support. **Bergstrom v. Lindback,** Op. No. 3516, 779 P2d 1235 (Alaska 1989).

In determining whether "good cause" exists for varying a child support award calculated pursuant to this rule, the court must focus first and foremost on the needs of the children. **Doyle v. Doyle,** Op. No. 3723, 815 P2d 366 (Alaska 1991).

Award to father of child support for his teenage son that was lower than the amount this rule should normally require was vacated where the trial court's purpose for the low award was to punish the father and son, a reason not justifying a variance under this rule. **Doyle v. Doyle,** Op. No. 3723, 815 P2d 366 (Alaska 1991).

Good cause supported by clear and convincing evidence of potential manifest injustice is not required to waive the $60,000 cap and award additional child support under this rule. **Farrell v. Farrell,** Op. No. 3767, 819 P2d 896 (Alaska 1991).

A parent may not waive requirements of this rule by private agreement.

Keating v. Traynor, Op. No. 3862, 833 P2d 695 (Alaska 1992).

Low level of mother's household costs did not constitute good cause for variance from child support formula of this rule. **Coghill v. Coghill,** Op. No. 3865, 836 P2d 921 (Alaska 1992).

The availability of social security benefits may be considered as a factor in determining whether variance from the Rule 90.3 formula is necessary to avoid manifest injustice. **Miller v. Miller,** Op. No. 4172, 890 P2d 574 (Alaska 1995).

Parents may not make child support agreement which is not subject to this rule, and no such agreement is valid until ii receives judicial scrutiny under this rule. **Agen v. State, CSED,** Op. No. 4874, 945 P2d 1215 (Alaska 1997).

In agreeing to entry of order for support exceeding that required by this rule, parties may reach bargained-for result based on their understanding of circumstances at time of agreement and anticipation of contingent future events. **Robinson v. Robinson,** Op. No. 4944, 953 P2d 880 (Alaska 1998).

Parties who agree upon support exceeding that required by this rule should express their understanding of relevant material circumstances; likewise, trial court should determine basis for contract when first approving agreement or when considering modification motion that asserts changed circumstances. **Robinson v. Robinson,** Op. No. 4944, 953 P2d 880 (Alaska 1998).

If trial court determines there is good cause to excuse parent from paying child support arrearages calculated pursuant to this rule, it must explain in writing its reason for the variation. **Boone v. Boone,** Op. No. 5000, 960 P2d 579 (Alaska 1998).

Where obligor parent failed to appeal 1993 decision of Child Support Enforcement Division (CSED) establishing his child support obligation in excess of amount permitted by statute, trial court erred in using the excess amount paid as justification for downward departure from the child support award guidelines of this rule in its 1996 decision modifying the support amount. **State CSED v. Bromley,** Op. No. 5180, 987 P2d 183 (Alaska 1999).

Cost of living in Pennsylvania, where custodial parent lived, even if lower than cost of living in Alaska, where non-custodial parent lived, was not the kind of unusual circumstance justifying downward departure from child support guidelines of this rule. **State CSED v. Bromley,** Op. No. 5180, 987 P2d 183 (Alaska 1999).\Fact that obligor parent had never been in arrears is support payments was not type of unusual circumstance justifying downward departure from child support aware guidelines under this rule. **State CSED v. Bromley,** Op. No. 5180, 987 P2d 183 (Alaska 1999).

Absence of evidence to show that child's reasonable needs were not being met at current level of obligor parent's support obligation was not type of unusual circumstance justifying downward departure from child support award guidelines under this rule. **State CSED v. Bromley,** Op. No. 5180, 987 P2d 183 (Alaska 1999).

Fact that custodial parent and child had never lived in Alaska did not justify downward departure from child support award guidelines of this rule in calculating obligor parent's support obligation. **State CSED v. Bromley,** Op. No. 5180, 987 P2d 183 (Alaska 1999).

Trial court's conclusion, based upon father's $95,000-plus gross income, that his adjusted income would exceed this rule's $72,000 (now $84,000) income cap for establishing child support payments, was error, since rule expressly requires courts to calculate adjusted annual income; error was not harmless because potential cumulative impact of father's allowable deductions could have reduced his adjusted annual income to less than $72,000. **Hammer v. Hammer,** Op. No. 5199, 991 P2d 195 (Alaska 1999).

By requiring courts to fully explain only those decisions finding good cause to depart from child support guidelines of this rule, this rule implicitly recognizes that the guidelines are presumptively appropriate and that decisions applying them ordinarily need no justification. **Willis v. State Dept. of Revenue,** Op. No. 5208, 992 P2d 581 (Alaska 1999).

Where a wife divorced her husband, and because the husband worked in a well-paying career in medicine while the wife stayed home to care for the children, the trial court awarded the wife increased child support under Alaska R. Civ. P. 90.3(c), the trial court's orders were upheld because unusual circumstances existed to justify varying the child support award under Alaska R. Civ. P. 90.3(c). **Fernau v. Rowdon,** Op. No. 5540, 42 P3d 1047 (Alaska 2002).

Trial court erred in treating proceeds of the sale of husband's video business as a five-year stream of income in determining the husband's duty to pay support; continued availability of the sale proceeds could be an exceptional factor warranting some increase in the husband's support obligation, but only if the trial court considered the totality of the circumstances, including the need for support and the wife's income, and then made express findings under subsection (c) of this rule. **Caldwell v. State,** Op. No. 5861, 105 P.3d 570 (Alaska 2005).

V. Health Care Coverage.

This rule, which allows child support to be reduced by half the cost "actually paid" for health insurance for the child, does not require that the cost be paid directly or out of present take-home income; the "actually paid" requirement includes a situation where non-custodial parent opts for employer-funded insurance coverage over payments into retirement plan. **Rusenstrom v. Rusenstrom,** Op. No. 5130, 981 P2d 558 (Alaska 1999).

Change in this rule relating to credit for providing children with health insurance was irrelevant to issue of tax exemptions, hence change in rule could not be deemed material change in circumstances for purposes of non-custodial parent's motion seeking modification of child support award to allocate to him a dependency tax exemption. **Rusenstrom v. Rusenstrom,** Op. No. 5130, 981 P2d 558 (Alaska 1999).

VI. Child Support Affidavit and Documentation.

This rule does not authorize child support trials by affidavit; trial courts must obtain all evidence necessary for an accurate determination of each parent's adjusted annual income. **Adrian v. Adrian,** Op. No. 3892, 838 P2d 808 (Alaska 1992).

Determination of future income may be especially difficult when the obligor has had very erratic income in the past. In a divorce matter where the husband's income varied from year to year, the superior court did not err in using an average of his income over a four-year period to achieve a base figure from which to calculate his child support obligation. **Keturi v. Keturi,** Op. No. 5774, 84 P.3d 408 (Alaska 2004).

Letters from the Alaska Child Support Enforcement Division to the father did not meet the requirements of Appellate Procedure Rule 602(a)(2), meaning the division's review of the father's financial circumstances file was not closed properly; failure to send the father a closure letter had the consequence of keeping the review file open, and the modification was not retroactive. **Paxton v. Gavlak,** Op. No. 5839, 100 P.3d 7 (Alaska 2004).

Submission of child support financial affidavits and income disclosure does not violate privacy rights because the state has a compelling interest in supporting children; non-custodial parents are required to supply financial information so the courts can calculate appropriate and adequate child support. **Lawson v. Lawson,** Op. No. 5876, 108 P.3d 883 (Alaska 2005).

Where appellant claimed that the youngest child born during his marriage was not his biological son, but had voluntarily filed documents with the superior court listing the son as his child after paternity was disestablished, the court did not err by including the son in its calculation of his monthly child support obligation. **Ray v. Ray,** Op. No. 5918, 115 P.3d 573 (Alaska 2005).

VII. Definitions.

For purposes of calculating child support obligations under this rule, whether or not a parent has "sole or primary" custody or only "shared or joint" custody is to be determined by the divorce decree rather than the actual situation. **Charlesworth v. Child Support Enf. Div.,** Op. No. 3503, 779 P2d 792 (Alaska 1989).

Order requiring financial information is designed to assist the court in establishing a non-custodial parent's adjusted income in order to calculate the appropriate amount of child support under this rule; this does not constitute a "search," but rather requires compliance with a court order. **Lawson v. Lawson,** Op. No. 5876, 108 P.3d 883 (Alaska 2005).

VIII. Travel Expenses.

Abuse of discretion was standard for appellate review of allocation of visitation travel expenses under this rule absent-persuasive argument to contrary. **C.R.B. v. C.C.,** Op. No. 4993, 959 P2d 375 (Alaska 1998).

In order denying father's motion to modify award of custody to maternal grandparents, court did not abuse its discretion in ordering grandparents to pay half of airfare for children's twice-yearly visits to father. **C.R.B. v. C.C.,** Op. No. 4993, 959 P2d 375 (Alaska 1998).

IX. Modification.

The adoption of this rule constituted a material change in circumstances for purposes of a motion to modify child support. **Charlesworth v. Child Support Enf. Div.,** Op. No. 3503, 779 P2d 792 (Alaska 1989).

Self-executing agreement for future shifting of child support payments, incorporated by reference into decree of dissolution, was legally effective, despite prohibition in this rule on retroactive modifications of child support arrearages. **Karpuleon V. Karpuleon,** Op. No. 4123, 881 P2d 318 (Alaska 1994).

Self-executing increase in child support per terms of dissolution agreement did not violate rule prohibiting retroactive modification of child support. **Van Alfen v. Van Alfen,** Op. No. 4313, 909 P2d 1075 (Alaska 1996).

Trial court could not retroactively modify child support agreement even though agreement had never been subject to judicial oversight or approval. **Taylor v. McGlothlin,** Op. No. 4366, 919 P2d 1349 (Alaska 1996).

Trial court, in modifying child support prospectively, did not err by ordering amount less than required by this rule's formula; deviation from formula was justified to prevent substantial hardship to subsequent children of obligor. **Taylor v. McGlothlin,** Op. No. 4366, 919 P2d 1349 (Alaska 1996).

Former Civil Rule 90.3(h)(2) prohibited both retroactive decreases and retroactive increases in child support awards. **Boone v. Gipson,** Op. No. 4364, 920 P2d 746 (Alaska 1996).

Under former Civil Rule 90.3(h)(92), exception to general prohibition on modifying child support payments retroactively could be triggered only by motion or petition for modification, not "functional equivalents" thereof. **Boone v. Gipson,** Op. No. 4364, 920 P2d 746 (Alaska 1996).

This rule prohibits both retroactive decreases and increases in child support awards prior to date modification motion is served on opposing party. **Yerrington v. Yerrington,** Op. No. 4791, 933 P2d 555 (Alaska 1997).

Retrospective averaging of obligor parent's income to calculate child support could not include 1993 income because that income had already been basis for child support payable under presumptive schedule of this rule. **Yerrington v. Yerrington,** Op. No. 4791, 933 P2d 555 (Alaska 1997).

Trial court erred in refusing to modify obligor parent's child support in 1995 after she demonstrated that her 1994 income was less than one-sixth her 1993 income which was basis for setting her child support obligation under this rule. **Yerrington v. Yerrington,** Op. No. 4791, 933 P2d 555 (Alaska 1997).

Fact that one method of child support calculation yields result more than 15 percent different from another method used in extant order is not material change of circumstances justifying modification of child support; accordingly, it was reversible error for judge to increase child support obligation from $154 per month to $399 per month by using different formula where parties' incomes had not significantly changed. **Bairn v. House,** Op. No. 4804, 934 P2d 753 (Alaska 1997).

Trial court erred in failing to consider father's motion to modify child support under guidelines of this rule notwithstanding that settlement agreement set fixed level of child support irrespective of this rule and provided father with greater share of marital property. **Aga V. Aga,** Op. No. 4855, 941 P2d 1260 (Alaska 1997).

Private agreement that based child support on income exceeding income cap of this rule was subject to modification under this rule based on material change of circumstances. **Flannery v. Flannery,** Op. No. 4922, 950 P2d 126 (Alaska 1997).

An agreement for child support cannot prevent modification because parties may not waive application of this rule; nonetheless, final order incorporating agreement should not be modified just because one party decides agreement was improvident. **Robinson v. Robinson,** Op. No. 4944, 953 P2d 880 (Alaska 1998).

To determine whether motion for reduction of child support due to changed circumstances should have been granted, remand was required for fact finding regarding parties' expectations and assumptions when father agreed to pay child support exceeding amount required by this rule; at time of agreement, father was unemployed, had no income, had been charged with six felonies, and had filed for bankruptcy, but following conviction and again after incarceration, he moved for reduction of child support alleging material changes of circumstances. **Robinson v. Robinson,** Op. No. 4944, 953 P2d 880 (Alaska 1998).

The presumption in this rule that change of circumstances will be presumed if support as calculated under this rule is more than 15 percent greater or less than outstanding support order is a rule of materiality, not a definition of what constitutes change of circumstances; court cannot compare amount obligor agreed to pay to what rule minimally requires; instead, it must compare amount obligor agreed to pay and amount agreement would require after change in circumstances in light of parties' contracting intentions and expectations. **Robinson v. Robinson,** Op. No. 4944, 953 P2d 880 (Alaska 1998).

Where father filed motion for reduction in child support obligation alleging that his income fell significantly because he lost valuable housing allowances when he began living free of charge in barracks on United States Coast Guard base, trial court's denial of motion because free housing was worth $700 per month required remand where court neither described method it used to value the housing nor provided explanation that would permit appellate court to glean from record basis for the calculation. **Beard v. Morris,** Op. No. 4956, 956 P2d 418 (Alaska 1998).

Absent good cause for different effective date, father was entitled to modification of child support effective on date his modification motion was served. **Boone v. Boone,** Op. No. 5000, 960 P2d 579 (Alaska 1998).

Children's change of residence to father's home, although not ordered by court, was sufficiently permanent to constitute material change in circumstances, thus father was entitled to recover child support arrearages for period during which he had custody. **Boone v. Boone,** Op. No. 5000, 960 P2d 579 (Alaska 1998).

Trial court's failure to enter findings supporting decision to decrease father's child support obligation required remand. **Robinson v. Robinson,** Op. No. 5011, 961 P2d 1000 (Alaska 1998).

In modifying child support obligation, trial court should have considered obligor's initial promise to make payments in excess of requirements of this rule to reflect high cost of living in area where obligee resided. **Robinson v. Robinson,** Op. No. 5011, 961 P2d 1000 (Alaska 1998).

Trial court erred in refusing to modify father's child support payments on sole ground that criminal incarceration amounted to voluntary unemployment; this rule imposes same payment requirement on all parents who cannot afford support, even parents whose indigence stems from incarceration. **Bendixen v. Bendixen,** Op. No. 5016, 962 P2d 170 (Alaska 1998).

Where father voluntarily retired from military and then moved to reduce his child support obligation, trial court did not clearly err in finding that father was not voluntarily underemployed and that mother's income and father's reduced support were sufficient to meet their child's needs; trial court therefore did not abuse its discretion in reducing father's child support obligation. **Maloney v. Maloney,** Op. No. 5056, 969 P2d 1148 (Alaska 1998).

Stepfather's argument that conventional child support modification principles under this rule did not apply to his purely contractual child support obligation because contract was entered into prior to adoption of this rule was rejected. **Dewey v. Dewey,** Op. No. 5065, 969 P2d 1154 (Alaska 1999).

If no child support order is in effect during a relevant period, amount of obligation must be calculated under this rule, and application of rule under such circumstance does not constitute modification of existing arrearages. **Benson v. Benson,** Op. No. 5109, 977 P2d 88 (Alaska 1999).

Under this rule, revised child support order presumptively relates back to date obligor received Child Support Enforcement Division's notice of petition for modification; absent good cause for later effective date, presumptive date must govern. **CSED v. Dillon,** Op. No. 5129, 977 P2d 118 (Alaska 1999).

Because neither Child Support Enforcement Division nor obligor father filed or served a motion for modification of child support, their agreement in 1992 that the proper amount of monthly support should be reduced from $385.52 to $286.00 did not meet the requirements of this rule for a modification of child support; thus 1997 court order reducing obligor father's arrears to judgment which was based upon a monthly obligation of $286.00 rather than $385.52, constituted retroactive modification of child support obligation prohibited by this rule. **CSED, Ex Rel. Husa v. Schofield,** Op. No. 5212, 993 P2d 405 (Alaska 1999).

Where father, who was required by 1997 divorce decree to pay child support, remarried in 1998 to woman with three children, trial court erred in not considering father's efforts to provide for his new family as a defense to an increase in his child support obligation; father argued that he was entitled to a variance from the child support calculation under this rule because his increase in income was directly attributable to extra overtime worked for the sole purpose of providing for his stepchildren's special medical and education needs. **Schuyler v. Briner,** Op. No. 5341, 13 P3d 738 (Alaska 2000).

Fact that court had already awarded interim child support for one brother did not make award of interim child support for other brother invalid as a retroactive modification of child support; fact that latter award was combined with the award already ordered for the first brother was a matter of form rather than substance, and did not violate the prohibition on retroactivity. **Spott v. Spott,** Op. No. 5361, 17 P3d 52 (Alaska 2001).

This rule prohibits retroactive modification of child support obligation without a valid pending motion or petition for modification that establishes the date from which modification can be made. **Wright v. Wright,** Op. No. 5405, 22 P3d 875 (Alaska 2001).

Trial court's determination that a modification of child support was not warranted because the father, an attorney, was voluntarily and unreasonably underemployed where he decided to quit practicing law and become a teacher was not clearly erroneous because father's earning capacity had not changed and the mother and child were not required to finance his choice to change careers. **Olmstead v. Ziegler,** Op. No. 5543, 42 P3d 1102 (Alaska 2002).

Father's child support obligation was properly modified based on the parties' actual visitation practices. **Potter v. Potter,** Op. No. 5636, 55 P.3d 726 (Alaska 2002).

Where parties' settlement agreed that father's child support would exceed the income cap of Alaska R. Civ. P. 90.3(h)(1) and father's reduction in income, while exceeding 15 percent, did not reduce his income to the level of the income cap, applying the income cap to the father was improper. **Hixson v. Sarkesian,** Op. No. 5677, 66 P.3d 753 (Alaska 2003).

Although the difference between applying the income cap of Alaska R. Civ. P. 90.3(h)(1) and the parties agreement to exceed the income cap resulted in only a $22.84 a month difference in the father's child support obligation, the amount was not de minimus or in itself justified application of Rule 90.3's income cap. **Hixson v. Sarkesian,** Op. No. 5677, 66 P.3d 753 (Alaska 2003).

The mere fact that the father had a 15 percent decrease in his income, but the father's income still exceed the income cap of Alaska R. Civ. P. 90.3(h)(1), was not grounds to waive the parties' agreement to exceed the cap and impose the cap in modifying the father's child support obligation. **Hixson v. Sarkesian,** Op. No. 5677, 66 P.3d 753 (Alaska 2003).

Where a mother waited nearly ten years after entry of a divorce judgment to seek the establishment of the father's child support obligation, under Alaska R. Civ. P. 90.3(h) the retroactive obligation established as of the year of the divorce was subject to modification in the ensuing years up to the time the obligation order was entered if the mother could show a substantial change in circumstances since the retroactive first post-divorce year child support obligation. **Duffus v. Duffus,** 72 P.3d 313 (Alaska 2003).

Trial court abused its discretion by increasing a husband's child support without going through the Alaska R. Civ. P. 90.3 calculations using the wife's income and allowing deductions such as the child support the husband paid for his children from a prior marriage as provided in Alaska R. Civ. P. 90.3(a)(1)(B). **Teseniar v. Teseniar,** Op. No. 5720,74 P.3d 910 (Alaska 2003).

Trial court abused its discretion by increasing a husband's child support obligation without going through the Alaska R. Civ. P. 90.3 calculations and by applying the increase retroactively to a date preceding the date the wife filed her motion to modify in violation of Alaska R. Civ. P. 90.3(h)(2). **Teseniar v. Teseniar,** Op. No. 5720, 74 P.3d 910 (Alaska 2003).

Superior court erred in modifying a father's child support obligation by imputing income to him without making findings of his physical abilities and qualifications, the employment opportunities available to him, and what he should earn from them. **O'Connell v. Christenson,** Op. No. 5724, 75 P.3d 1037 (Alaska 2003).

Because a child support waiver was not valid and enforceable until a court had reviewed and approved the waiver's substantive adequacy under this rule, neither the mother's letter to the father nor her withdrawal from the Alaska Child Support Enforcement Division's services modified the father's court-ordered child support obligation. **Paxton v. Gavlak,** Op. No. 5839, 100 P.3d 7 (Alaska 2004).

Retroactive modification of child support arrearages is allowed in certain circumstances under AS 25.27.166, which serves to amend this rule. **Lawson v. Lawson,** Op. No. 5876, 108 P.3d 883 (Alaska 2005).

Standard for certain modifications of support orders was altered by AS 25.24.170, amending this rule; support may be modified without a showing of changed circumstances when necessary to comply with federal law. **Lawson v. Lawson,** Op. No. 5876, 108 P.3d 883 (Alaska 2005).

Trial court did not err in retroactively modifying the father's child support obligation to the December 2002 date he was served with notice of the Child Support Enforcement Division's (CSED) petition for modification because the father failed to establish good cause for deviating from the Dillon rule, which provided that absent good cause, Alaska R. Civ. P. 90.3(h)(2) required a trial court to make its modification order effective as of the filing date of the modification petition. **Crumpler v. State ex rel. Armstrong,** Op. No. 5927, 117 P.3d 730 (Alaska 2005).

Where Child Support Services Division sought to have an increase in child support applied retroactively to the date of the father's release from prison, section (h)(2) of this rule did not prevent the superior court from applying a modified child support order retroactively because, in this case, the original order had terminated upon the father's release. **State v. Wallace,** Op. No. 5938, 119 P.3d 992 (Alaska 2005).

Superior court erred by making an order modifying child support effective on the date the State filed its motion to modify, rather than from the date that it served the parents with notice of the petition; an administrative delay was not a sufficient reason to diverge from the presumptive effective date under section (h)(2) of this rule. **State v. Wise,** Op. No. 5948, 122 P.3d 212 (Alaska 2005).

In determining whether and how fluctuations in the exchange rate from Swiss francs and U.S. dollars should have been assessed in deciding whether to modify child support, the trial court erred by not following the methodology specified in Alaska R. Civ. P. 90.3(h)(1) or the same methodology it previously used to calculate support. **Hixson v. Sarkesian,** Op. No. 5958, 123 P.3d 1072 (Alaska 2005).

Trial court did not err in modifying a father's child support obligation, allowing discovery on the mother's motion to modify, and imputed income to the father based on his expenses, but the trial court erred in failing to deduct the father's federal taxes and a portion of his voluntary retirement contributions from the income available for child support as required by subsection (a)(1)(B) of this rule. **Byers v. Ovitt,** Op. No. 6004, 133 P.3d 676 (Alaska 2006).

X. Third Party Custody.

In third-party custody arrangements, trial courts should set parents' child support payments and allocate support between children based on equities of case. **Gallant v. Gallant,** Op. No. 4122, 882 P2d 1252 (Alaska 1994).

The word "obligor" in Alaska R. Civ. P. 90.3 does not refer to the parent who must pay the other parent child support, because under Rule 90.3(i) both parents have a duty to pay support to third-party custodians. **Corbin v. Corbin,** 68 P.3d 1269 (Alaska 2003).

Where trial court set father's child support based on a 50/50 shared custody formula, even though one child was residing with a third-party, the trial court erred when it calculated child support as if the one child was in a shared custody status. The trial court should have calculated child support without considering the children in the custody of third parties. **Corbin v. Corbin,** 68 P.3d 1269 (Alaska 2003).

Civil Rule 90.3 follows an intact family model, based on economic analyses showing that the proportion of income that parents devote to their children in intact families is relatively constant across income levels up to a certain upper limit; third-party custodians were never part of the intact family and could not be treated as parents. **Evans v. McTaggart,** Op. No. 5794, 88 P.3d 1078 (Alaska 2004).

Rule 90.4. Proceedings to Establish Parentage.

When genetic testing is ordered under AS 25.20.050, test results must be served on all parties to the action at least 20 days prior to any hearing or trial at which such results may be introduced into evidence. The test results must be accompanied by an affidavit, prepared by a qualified person, which addresses the qualifications of the affiant and the validity of the testing procedures and results. Any objection to the test results must be filed and served no later than 10 days before the hearing or trial. If no timely objection is filed, the test results are admissible as evidence of paternity at the hearing or trial without the need for foundation testimony or other proof of authenticity or accuracy.

(Adopted by SCO 1221 effective September 1, 1995)

Rule 90.5. Expedited Judicial Relief from Action Against Occupational or Driver's License for Unpaid Child Support.

(a) **Scope.** This rule sets out the procedure for requesting expedited judicial relief from a decision by the Child Support Enforcement Division (CSED) under AS 25.27.244 (adverse action against delinquent obligor's occupational license) or AS 25.27.246 (adverse action against delinquent obligor's driver's license).

(b) **Petition.**

(1) *Requirements.* To request expedited judicial relief under AS 25.27.244 or 25.27.246, a person must file a petition in the superior court. The petition must be on a form published by the Alaska Court System and must specify which of the statutory grounds for relief the petitioner is relying on. The petition should be accompanied by:

(A) a written explanation of why the petitioner is entitled to judicial relief (not to exceed five pages);

(B) any documents that the petitioner intends to present to the court;

(C) a list of the witnesses whom the petitioner intends to present at the court hearing;

(D) a copy of CSED's decision (titled "Notice of Occupational License Review Decision" or "Notice of Driver's License Review Decision"); and

(E) a copy of the child support order or payment schedule that CSED seeks to enforce.

(2) *Number of Copies.* The petitioner must file the original plus one copy of the petition and any attachments.

(3) *Deadline for Filing.* The petition must be filed within 30 days after the date that the petitioner receives CSED's decision (titled "Notice of Occupational License Review Decision" or "Notice of Driver's License Review Decision"). The petition may be filed either by delivering or mailing it to the clerk of court. A petition is deemed to be filed on the date it is received by the clerk.

(4) *Service on CSED.* Upon receipt of the petition, the court shall promptly serve CSED by mailing or delivering the extra copy to the appropriate office of the Department of Law.

(5) *Grounds for Rejecting Petition.* The clerk shall refuse to accept the petition for filing if the petitioner has failed to specify which of the statutory grounds for relief the petitioner is relying on and has provided no other written explanation of why the petitioner is entitled to judicial relief.

(c) **Response.** CSED's response to the petition must be filed and served within fifteen days after service of the petition under (b)(4). The response must include a written explanation of CSED's position (not to exceed five pages) and must be accompanied by any documents that CSED intends to present at the hearing and a list of the witnesses whom CSED intends to present.

(d) **Hearing.** Upon receipt of the petition, the court shall schedule a hearing. The hearing must be held not less than 20 nor more than 30 days after the petition is served under (b)(4). Telephonic participation at the hearing is governed by Civil Rule 99.

(e) **Peremptory Challenge.** A party may file a notice of change of judge under Civil Rule 42(c). A party's notice is timely if filed within five days after notice that the case has been assigned to a specific judge.

(f) **Relief Available in Expedited Proceeding.** The court's decision is limited to a determination of the following issues, which the court shall determine de novo:

(1) whether a support order or payment schedule is in effect;

(2) whether the petitioner is the obligor under the support order that CSED is seeking to enforce; and

(3) whether the petitioner is in substantial compliance with the support order or payment schedule. A petitioner is in substantial compliance if: (A) the petitioner owes less than four times the monthly obligation; or (B) the petitioner is making the best possible efforts under the circumstances to pay the arrearages.

(g) **Other Judicial Relief.** To obtain other judicial relief, the petitioner must file an appeal from an administrative agency decision under Appellate Rule 602.

(Adopted by SCO 1375 effective October 15, 1999)

Note: The petition forms (DR-335 for occupational licenses and DR-336 for driver's licenses) are available at all superior court locations and from the Child Support Enforcement Division.

Rule 90.6. Appointment of Child Custody Investigator.

(a) **Appointment.** In an action under AS 25.20, AS 25.24, or AS 18.66, the court may appoint an expert under Evidence Rule 706 to investigate custody, access, and visitation issues and provide an independent opinion concerning the child's best interests. If the parties cannot afford a private custody investigator, the court may appoint the court custody investigator to conduct the investigation and provide an expert opinion.

(b) **Qualifications.**

(1) A custody investigator should possess knowledge, skill, experience, training, or education that allows the custody investigator to conduct a thorough and impartial investigation and offer an informed opinion to the court regarding custody and visitation issues. Specifically, the custody investigator should have an understanding of the following as appropriate to the case:

(A) child development from infancy through adolescence;

(B) impact of divorce and parental separation on a child;

(C) unique issues related to families involved in custody disputes;

(D) domestic violence and substance abuse and their impact on children;

(E) Alaska statutes and rules relating to custody determinations;

(F) the ability to communicate effectively with children and adults;

(G) the ability to communicate recommendations orally and in writing; and

(H) other qualifications appropriate to the particular case.

(2) Upon request of a party, a custody investigator or prospective custody investigator shall provide to the parties a written summary of relevant education and experience.

(c) **Disclosure of Conflicts.** The custody investigator shall disclose any relationships or associations between the investigator and any party which might reasonably cause the investigator's impartiality to be questioned. This disclosure must be made no later than 10 days after appointment.

(d) **Report.**

(1) *Deadline for Filing and Contents.* The court shall specify the date by which the custody investigator must file and serve a written report. The report must describe the investigation, including who was interviewed and what records were reviewed, summarize the information obtained, and explain the custody investigator's conclusions and recommendations utilizing the applicable statutory factors.

(2) *Admission of Report into Evidence.* Unless otherwise ordered, the custody investigator's report is deemed to be admitted into evidence upon filing and may be reviewed by the court before the hearing or trial. A party may require the custody investigator to appear at a hearing or trial to testify about the report. To preserve this right, the party must include the custody investigator on the party's final witness list. The party must also take appropriate steps to ensure the custody investigator's presence at the hearing or trial, which may include requesting the issuance of a subpoena.

(3) *Confidentiality.* The custody investigator's report is confidential unless otherwise ordered by the court. However, it may be disclosed to a party's expert for the purpose of consultation for trial.

(4) *Meeting with Parties.* The custody investigator may meet with the parties jointly or separately at any time to discuss the investigation and the investigator's conclusions in order to facilitate a voluntary resolution of the issues.

(e) **Investigation.** Unless the court has limited the scope of the investigation, a custody investigation should usually include:

(1) individual interviews with each parent;

(2) individual interviews with new spouses, live-in partners, or significant others of each parent;

(3) individual interviews with or observations of each child in the family;

(4) observation of parent-child interactions;

(5) review of the court file and other documents provided by the parties;

(6) criminal and child protection record checks on the parents, new spouses, and other people living in the household;

(7) review of relevant records pertaining to the child and household members, subject to applicable privileges;

(8) review of personal references provided by friends or family members of the parents;

(9) in-person or telephone interviews with other individuals who have information about the family, as the investigator believes is necessary.

(f) **Release of Records.** Unless otherwise specified in the appointment order, the custody investigator may request a party to execute a release authorizing the investigator to inspect and copy confidential records pertaining to the child or to the party. Within ten days after receiving a request for a release, a party must either execute the release or file a motion for a protective order under Civil Rule 26(c). A motion for a protective order must be accompanied by a certification that the party has conferred or attempted to confer with the custody investigator in an effort to resolve the dispute without court action. If the party fails to respond, the custody investigator may notify the court and the court shall enter an order directing that the records be released.

(g) **Contact with Parties and the Court.**

(1) *Contact with Parties.* Unless otherwise ordered, a custody investigator may communicate with a party who is represented by an attorney without prior notice to the attorney.

(2) *Contact with Court.* Unless all parties consent, a custody investigator shall not engage in ex parte communications with the court concerning a pending case except for scheduling and other administrative purposes when circumstances require.

(h) **Discovery.** A party may depose a custody investigator appointed under this rule after completion of a report. Documents and records in the possession of the custody investigator are discoverable under Civil Rule 30(b)(5) and Civil Rule 34 as though the custody investigator were a party to the action subject to any limitations set by the court as to the use and dissemination of confidential records.

(i) **Compensation.** Fees and costs for a private custody investigator will be divided equally between the parties unless the court finds good cause to change this allocation.

Commentary.—*Evidence Rule 706 authorizes the court to appoint independent experts in civil or criminal litigation. An expert appointed under Rule 706 must advise the parties of the expert's findings, may be deposed by either party, and may be called to testify by either party or the court.*

When a private custody investigator is being appointed, the court may ask the parties to suggest individuals for appointment.

A full custody investigation should usually include all of the elements listed in paragraph (e). Some of these elements may be dispensed with if the court has limited the scope of the investigation, either by narrowing the issues that the custody investigator should address or by limiting the tasks that the investigator should perform. If the court has appointed a private custody investigator, for example, the court may agree to dispense with some of the elements of a full investigation in order to reduce the cost to the parties. In addition, for budget reasons, the presiding judge of the judicial district may enter an administrative order limiting the tasks that court custody investigators will routinely perform. Even when the court has requested a full investigation, the custody investigator has discretion to dispense with interviews or record checks that are clearly unwarranted in a particular case.

Paragraph (e) also indicates that the custody investigator should review relevant records of the child and other household members. Relevant records may include school records, medical records, alcohol or drug abuse treatment records, and records regarding incidents of domestic violence.

(Adopted by SCO 1377 effective April 15, 2000 and amended by SCO 1591 effective January 15, 2006)

Note to SCO 1591: "Confidential" in Civil Rule 90.6(d)(3) has the meaning set out in Administrative Bulletin No. 48, Standard 6.F.2., and in Administrative Rule 37.5(c)(4).

Annotations

Cases

Superior court did not err when it granted custody of a child to its care givers rather than allowing her grandparents to adopt her where the issue was not merely primary caregiving, but whether removing the child from the primary custody of the people with whom she had spent 21 of her 24 months would be unnecessarily traumatic for her, especially since she had already lost one set of parents; the superior court carefully questioned in voir dire each expert who testified on child psychology about the possible effects on the child of being separated from the caregivers and overruled objections to such questions when asked. **In re Adoption of L.E.K.M.,** Op. No. 5695, 70 P.3d 1097 (Alaska 2003).

Superior court did not err when it allowed the evidence of an investigator that recommended that an orphaned child be placed with her care givers because she did not want the child to suffer yet another loss of attachment with a primary caregiver; the record showed that the court shared the custody investigator's concern that a third family placement for a two-year-old could be damaging to her emotional health, and consulted all the experts available to him at trial while deciding not to take that risk. **In re Adoption of L.E.K.M.,** Op. No. 5695,70 P.3d 1097 (Alaska 2003).

Trial court did not abuse its discretion in ordering the father to pay all of the costs associated the custody investigator as the father had a significantly higher income potential than the mother. **Koller v. Reft,** 71

P.3d 800 (Alaska 2003).

Rule 90.7. Appointment of Guardian Ad Litem in Child Custody Proceedings.

(a) **When Guardian Ad Litem May Be Appointed.** In an action under AS 25.20, 25.24, or 18.66 involving custody, support, or visitation of a child, the court may appoint a guardian ad litem for the child only when the court finds separate representation of the child's best interests is necessary, such as when the guardian ad litem may be expected to present evidence not otherwise likely to be available or presented, or the proceeding is unusually complex.

Commentary.*—AS 25.24.310 authorizes the court to appoint a guardian ad litem in any action involving custody, support, or visitation of a child. AS 25.24.310(c) states in part:*

> *"Instead of, or in addition to, appointment of an attorney under (a) of this section, the court may, upon motion of either party or upon its own motion, appoint an attorney or other person or the office of public advocacy to provide guardian ad litem services to a child in any legal proceeding involving the child's welfare. The court shall require a guardian ad litem when, in the opinion of the court, representation of the child's best interests, to be distinguished from preferences, would serve the welfare of the child."*

Courts should not routinely appoint guardians ad litem in custody, support, and visitation proceedings. In most instances, the child's best interests are adequately protected and presented by the parties. In most contested proceedings in which professional input is warranted, a child custody investigator (whether public or private) should be appointed instead of a guardian ad litem. The child custody investigator can provide the court and the parties with an independent analysis of the dispute and may serve as a catalyst to settlement without adding another party to the proceeding.

(b) **Qualifications.**

(1) A guardian ad litem should possess knowledge, skill, experience, training, or education that allows the guardian ad litem to conduct a thorough and impartial investigation and effectively advocate for the best interests of the child. Specifically, the guardian ad litem should have an understanding of the following as appropriate to the case:

(A) child development from infancy through adolescence;

(B) impact of divorce and parental separation on a child;

(C) unique issues related to families involved in custody disputes;

(D) domestic violence and substance abuse and their impact on children;

(E) Alaska statutes, rules, and supreme court decisions relating to custody, support, and visitation;

(F) the ability to communicate effectively with children and adults; and

(G) other qualifications appropriate to the particular case.

Further, the guardian ad litem should possess the knowledge and skills to effectively negotiate settlements on behalf of the child and to effectively advocate the child's best interests in contested litigation.

(2) Upon request of a party, a guardian ad litem or prospective guardian ad litem shall provide to the parties a written summary of relevant education and experience.

(c) **Appointment Order.** An order appointing a guardian ad litem must include findings why the appointment is necessary and must set forth the role of the guardian ad litem, the duties to be performed by the guardian ad litem in the case, deadlines for completion of these duties to the extent appropriate, the duration of the appointment, and compensation as provided in paragraph (m). If the court denies a motion for appointment of a guardian ad litem, the court must make findings to explain the denial. An order appointing a guardian ad litem should authorize the guardian ad litem access, without further release, to all confidential and privileged records of the child, including but not limited to psychiatric records, psychological treatment records, drug and alcohol treatment records, medical records, evaluations, law enforcement records, and school records.

Commentary. *—If the court determines that the appointment of a guardian ad litem is appropriate in a particular case, the court may ask the parties to suggest individuals for appointment.*

There is no right to a peremptory change of a guardian ad litem. Allegations that a guardian ad litem appointment is unnecessary, that a particular appointee is unqualified or otherwise unsuitable, or that an appointee is or has become biased should be addressed by trial courts through motion practice.

The appointment order should authorize the guardian ad litem to review confidential and privileged records pertaining to the child. To review records pertaining to a parent, the guardian ad litem must file a motion requesting access to those records unless the parent agrees to sign a release.

(d) **Disclosure of Conflicts.** The guardian ad litem shall disclose any relationships or associations between the guardian ad litem and any party which might reasonably cause the guardian ad litem's impartiality to be questioned. This disclosure must be made no later than 10 days after appointment.

(e) **Role of Guardian Ad Litem.** The guardian ad litem shall represent and advocate the best interests of the child. The court may appoint an attorney to advise or represent a non-attorney guardian ad litem if the court finds that legal advice or legal representation of the guardian ad litem is necessary to represent the child's best interests. The guardian ad litem shall be treated as a party to the proceeding for all purposes, except as otherwise provided in this rule.

Commentary.—When custody is contested, the court has discretion to appoint a custody investigator, a guardian ad litem, and/or an attorney for the child. See AS 25.24.310(a), (c). The roles of a custody investigator, a guardian ad litem, and an attorney for the child are different and must be clearly distinguished:

■ ***custody investigator:*** *A custody investigator is an expert witness appointed by the court. The custody investigator's duty is to conduct a thorough investigation and give an expert opinion on the custody arrangement that is in the best interests of the child. A custody investigator does not participate in court proceedings, other than to testify as an expert witness.*

■ ***guardian ad litem:*** *A guardian ad litem has the duty to conduct a thorough factual investigation. Based on this investigation, the guardian ad litem must decide what course of action is in the child's best interests. The guardian ad litem must then advocate this course of action, regardless of whether the child agrees with the guardian ad litem's position. The guardian ad litem participates as a party in court proceedings that affect the child, but only testifies in exceptional circumstances and then only as to factual matters. The guardian ad litem never testifies as an expert witness.*

The guardian ad litem must be served with copies of all pleadings and papers relating to the child, see Civil Rule 4(i), and must be given notice of all court appearances and conferences involving issues that affect the child. The guardian ad litem's rights include the right to appear and participate at hearings, engage in motion practice, conduct discovery, introduce evidence, examine and cross-examine witnesses, make objections, and make opening statements and closing arguments.

The guardian ad litem's advocacy need not be confined to custody and visitation issues. If included within the scope of the appointment, the guardian ad litem should be prepared to participate in decisions about any special education or psychological needs of the child (such as counseling) and child support and other financial issues related to the child.

■ ***attorney for child:*** *A child's attorney represents the child, and it is the child who ultimately decides what position will be advocated in court. The attorney's duty is to conduct a thorough investigation, advise and consult the client, and zealously advocate the client's position in court. See Wagstaff v. Superior Court, 535 P.2d 1220 (Alaska 1975) (concerning child's right to select attorney when child's interests are hostile to parents' interests).*

The court may appoint an attorney to advise or represent a non-attorney guardian ad litem. If the court takes this action, the court should take care to specify the scope and duration of the appointment and the attorney's compensation.

(f) **Duty to Investigate.** The guardian ad litem shall investigate the pertinent facts of the case.

(1) The guardian ad litem shall review and consider any child custody investigation already conducted in the case and confer with the investigator. The guardian ad litem shall promptly conduct any further investigation necessary to carry out the order of appointment.

(2) If no child custody investigation has been done, the guardian ad litem shall either conduct an appropriate investigation or arrange for a custody investigation under Civil Rule 90.6. The investigation shall be conducted as soon as reasonably possible after the appointment.

Commentary.—In developing a position, the guardian ad litem should usually solicit and receive input from professionals and other persons with experience or evidence related to the family, such as mental health professionals, teachers, day care providers, medical providers, close relatives of the child, and other adults residing in the home of either parent.

The guardian ad litem may move for an order requiring the child or one or both parents to undergo evaluation or assessment related to psychological, substance abuse, or other issues raised in the investigation.

Paragraph (m) requires a guardian ad litem to seek court approval before hiring a private custody investigator to conduct an investigation. If the parties cannot afford a private custody investigator, the court may appoint the court custody investigator to conduct the investigation. See Civil Rule 90.6(a).

(g) **Contact with Child, Other Parties, and the Court.**

(1) *Contact with Child.* The guardian ad litem may meet with the child as often as necessary to ascertain and represent the child's best interests. An attorney for a party shall not have independent contact with the child without the consent of the guardian ad litem or a court order. A party or attorney shall not arrange for mental health evaluations or assessments of the child without the consent of the guardian ad litem or a court order.

(2) *Contact with Other Parties.* A guardian ad litem may communicate with a party who is represented by an attorney unless the party's attorney has notified the guardian ad litem in writing that such communication should not occur outside the attorney's presence.

(3) *Contact with Court.* Unless all parties consent, a guardian ad litem shall not engage in ex parte communications with the court concerning a pending case except for scheduling and other administrative purposes when circumstances require.

(h) **Trial or Hearing Brief.** The court shall set a deadline for the guardian ad litem to file a trial or hearing brief. The brief must describe the guardian ad litem's investigation, including who was interviewed and what records were reviewed, analyze the facts that the guardian ad litem believes will be presented, explain the position taken by the guardian ad litem utilizing the applicable statutory factors, and address other matters the guardian ad litem believes to be appropriate. If there is a conflict between the guardian ad litem's position and the child's preference, that conflict must be disclosed in the brief.

Commentary.*—The guardian ad litem's brief cannot be treated as testimony or as evidence of any fact unless agreed to by the parties. Absent a stipulation, facts discussed in the guardian ad litem's brief must be proved at trial.*

In many cases, the parties will not know the guardian ad litem's position or what facts the guardian ad litem has relied on until they receive the guardian ad litem's brief. Ideally, that brief should be due at least 30 days before the trial or hearing date so that the parties have sufficient time to prepare evidence in order to respond at trial. An early due date is also desirable because the guardian ad litem's brief often serves as a catalyst for settlement. At a minimum, the brief should be filed before the parties' briefs are due so that the parties can address the guardian ad litem's position in their briefs.

If there is a conflict between the guardian ad litem's position and the child's preference, the court may appoint a separate attorney to represent the child. The court should take this action only if the child's preference cannot be presented adequately by one of the parties. If the court appoints a separate attorney for the child, the court may either discharge the guardian ad litem or continue the guardian ad litem appointment to represent what the guardian ad litem believes to be in the child's best interests.

(i) **Testimony.**

(1) The guardian ad litem shall not testify at the trial or hearing unless:

(A) the testimony relates to an uncontested issue;

(B) the testimony relates to the nature and value of services rendered by the guardian ad litem in the case; or

(C) the testimony is necessary to present factual evidence on a material issue that is not available from another source.

(2) If the guardian ad litem intends to testify, the guardian ad litem shall file and serve notice of this intent with the trial or hearing brief. The notice must identify the subject of the guardian ad litem's testimony.

(3) Upon receiving notice that the guardian ad litem intends to testify, the court should consider whether the guardian ad litem can still effectively represent the best interests of the child. If not, the court may discharge the guardian ad litem, appoint another guardian ad litem, or appoint an attorney for the guardian ad litem or the child.

(4) If the guardian ad litem testifies, the guardian ad litem may be cross-examined as any other witness.

Commentary.*—Subparagraph (i)(1) reflects the principles of Alaska Rule of Professional Conduct 3.7(a), which under most circumstances prohibits an attorney from acting as an advocate in a proceeding in which the attorney is likely to be a witness.*

In opening statements and closing arguments, a guardian ad litem is free to comment on the evidence and to suggest conclusions that the court should draw from the evidence. But the statements themselves are not and cannot be treated as testimony or evidence.

(j) **Discovery.**

(1) *Discovery of Documents in Guardian Ad Litem's Possession.* A party may obtain discovery of documents in the possession, custody, or control of the guardian ad litem, subject to the following limitations:

(A) the documents must be discoverable under Civil Rule 26(b)(1); and

(B) trial preparation materials as defined in Civil Rule 26(b)(3) are discoverable only as permitted by that rule.

(2) *Discovery Regarding Guardian Ad Litem's Testimony.* If the guardian ad litem has served notice that the guardian ad litem intends to testify, a party may obtain discovery from the guardian ad litem about the substance of this testimony.

(3) *Other Inquiry.* A party may obtain other discovery from a guardian ad litem only as permitted by the court upon a showing of good cause. The court may permit a party to question a guardian ad litem about the guardian ad litem's professional qualifications and experience or the guardian ad litem's actions in the case. But this inquiry must be conducted in the presence of the court.

(k) **Duty to Maintain Confidentiality.** The guardian ad litem shall not disclose communications made by the child or reveal information relating to the child, except as necessary to carry out the representation, unless:

(1) the guardian ad litem determines that disclosure is in the best interests of the child;

(2) disclosure would be permitted under Alaska Rule of Professional Conduct 1.6(b) as if the guardian ad litem were the child's lawyer;

(3) disclosure is required under paragraph (h) (duty to tell the court that child's preference differs from guardian ad litem's position); or

(4) disclosure is permitted by court order or by law.

Commentary.*—A guardian ad litem should the child that statements made by the child will ordinarily be kept confidential but may be disclosed if the guardian ad litem determines that disclosure is in the child's best interests and in the other circumstances described in this rule.*

(*l*) **Privileges.**

(1) The guardian ad litem has a privilege to refuse to disclose and to prevent anyone other than the child from disclosing confidential communications made by the child. This privilege does not apply if disclosure of the communication is required by law or if the court finds there are compelling reasons to reveal the communication.

(2) The attorney-client privilege does not apply to

confidential communications between the child and an attorney guardian ad litem.

Commentary.*—An attorney serving as a guardian ad litem does not act as legal counsel for the child but rather as a party to the proceeding. Therefore, the attorney-client privilege does not apply. But the policy behind the attorney-client privilege is equally compelling in the guardian ad litem-child relationship: to encourage the child to talk openly and candidly to the guardian ad litem so that the guardian ad litem can make the best possible determination about what is in the child's best interests. Therefore, this rule adopts a limited privilege for confidential communications between an attorney or non-attorney guardian ad litem and the child. It also allows the guardian ad litem to protect confidential communications made by the child to other persons.*

(m) **Compensation.** The guardian ad litem, an attorney for a guardian ad litem, and expert witnesses used by the guardian ad litem will be compensated at a rate that the court determines is reasonable. Fees and costs for a private guardian ad litem will be divided equally between the parties unless the court finds good cause to change this allocation. The guardian ad litem must seek court approval before incurring extraordinary expenses, such as expert witness fees. The appointment order, or order authorizing the guardian ad litem to hire expert witnesses, must specify the hourly rate to be paid to the guardian ad litem, attorney, or expert witness, the maximum fee that may be incurred without further authorization of the court, how the fee will be allocated between the parties, and when payment is due. Unless otherwise ordered, bills must be submitted on a monthly basis and must state the total amount billed to date.

(Adopted by SCO 1377 effective April 15, 2000)

Annotations

Cases

In an adoption case, the court erred in failing to make findings on the record explaining the court's decision not to appoint a guardian ad litem. **Faulkner v. Goldfuss,** Op. No. 5565, 46 P3d 993 (Alaska 2002).

Rule 90.8. Expedited Applications to Compel Correction of Any Error in Redistricting Plan.

(a) **Scope.** This rule applies to applications to the superior court under art. VI, sec. 11, Constitution of the State of Alaska, to compel the Redistricting Board to correct any error in its redistricting plan. This rule supersedes the other civil rules to the extent that they may be inconsistent with this rule.

(b) **Application.**

(1) Application to compel the Redistricting Board to correct any error in redistricting must be made within 30 days following the adoption of the final redistricting plan and proclamation by the Redistricting board.

(2) Service of the application shall be made on the Redistricting Board, the Office of the Attorney General, and the Office of the Lieutenant Governor.

(c) **Expedited Proceeding.** Applications under this rule shall be expedited, and shall have priority over all other matters pending before the court. The date for the court's decision shall be no later than 120 days prior to the statutory filing deadline for the first statewide election in which the challenged redistricting plan is scheduled to take effect.

(d) **Record.** The record in the superior court proceeding consists of the record from the Redistricting Board (original papers and exhibits filed before the board and the electronic record or transcript, if any, of the board's proceedings), as supplemented by such additional evidence as the court, in its discretion, may permit. If the court permits the record to be supplemented by the testimony of one or more witnesses, such testimony may be presented by deposition without regard to the limitations contained in Civil Rule 32(a)(3)(B). A paginated copy of the record from the Redistricting Board shall be filed in the supreme court at the same time it is filed in the superior court.

(e) **Scheduling Conference.** Within ten days of the application, the assigned judge shall hold a scheduling conference, which all parties must attend. Telephonic participation may be permitted at the judge's discretion. At the conference, the judge shall enter a scheduling order that addresses all matters appropriate in the circumstances of the case.

(f) **Assignment.** Cases shall be assigned by presiding judges and may be assigned across judicial district lines in coordination with other presiding judges and the administrative director.

(Adopted by SCO 1457 effective November 15, 2001)

PART XIII. GENERAL PROVISIONS

Rule 91. Applicability of Civil Rules In General.

(a) **Scire Facias—Quo Warranto.** The writs of scire facias and quo warranto, and proceedings by information in the nature of quo warranto, are abolished. Relief available under those forms or under the provisions of statutes may be obtained by appropriate action or by appropriate motion under the practice prescribed in these rules.

(b) **Mandamus.** The writ of mandamus is abolished. Relief heretofore available by mandamus as prescribed by statutes may be obtained by appropriate action or by appropriate motion under the practice prescribed in these rules.

(c) **Administrative Subpoenas.** These rules are applicable to proceedings in court to compel the giving of testimony or production of documents in accordance with subpoena issued or other authority exercised by an officer or agency of the state, except as otherwise provided by order of the court in the proceedings.

(Adopted by SCO 5 October 9, 1959; amended by SCO 49 effective January 1, 1963)

Annotations

Cases

Relief seeking to require the Secretary of State to order a recount of votes was available in the lower court in an action in the nature of mandamus. **Wade v. Dworkin,** Op. No. 306, 407 P2d 587 (Alaska 1965).

Where the hearing in question was not a proceeding in court to compel production, but was rather a hearing to modify or set aside an investigative demand, use of the procedure authorized in AS 45.52.210(f) for the enforcement of an administrative subpoena did not conflict with this rule. **Matanuska Maid, Inc. v. State,** Op. No. 2223, 620 P2d 182 (Alaska 1980).

Since the rules of procedure allow other claims for relief to be joined with a mandamus claim, a judgment granting mandamus should preclude subsequent litigation of other claims which could have been joined. **State v. Smith,** Op. No. 3067, 720 P2d 40 (Alaska 1986).

Rule 92. Construction of Rules.

These rules are designed to provide for the efficient operation of the courts of the State of Alaska. If no specific procedure is prescribed by rule, the court may proceed in any lawful manner not inconsistent with these rules, the constitution, and the common law.

(Adopted by SCO 5 October 9, 1959; amended by SCO 49 effective January 1, 1963)

Annotations

Cases

Where nearly four years had elapsed between the date appellant's default was entered as a result of a belated entry of appearance in propria persona within one or two days after the 20-day period for answering had expired, and the entry of default judgment and the extraordinary long delay was not attributable to appellant's fault, the speedy determination of actions within the purview of this rule was in no way promoted by insisting that appellants permanently lost their standing in court and the entry of default and default judgment were set aside so that the case may be disposed on the merits. **Sanuita v. Hedberg,** Op. No. 296, 404 P2d 647 (Alaska 1965).

Rule 93. Legal Effect of Rules—Statutes Superseded.

These rules are promulgated pursuant to constitutional authority granting rule making power to the supreme court, and to the extent that they are inconsistent with any procedural provisions of any statute not enacted for the specific purpose of changing a rule, shall supersede such statute to the extent of such inconsistency.

(Adopted by SCO 5 October 9, 1959; amended by SCO 49 effective January 1, 1963)

Annotations

Cases

A legislative enactment will not be effective to change court rules of practice and procedure under Section 15 of Article IV of the constitution, unless the bill specifically states that its purpose is to effect such a change. Thus a portion of a statute which purported to forbid the granting of stays pending appeal, which statute did not contain such a statement of purpose, is ineffective and does not change rules of practice and procedure made and promulgated by the supreme court. **Leege v. Martin,** Op. No. 131, 379 P2d 447 (Alaska 1962).

The allowance of attorney's fees as costs which was not permitted under the common law and was governed by statute prior to the attainment of statehood is now a matter of regulation under the Rules of Civil Procedure promulgated by the supreme court pursuant to its constitutional rulemaking authority. **McDonough v. Lee,** Op. No. 378, 420 P2d 459 (Alaska 1966).

A statute [AS 09.60.060] under which a resident defendant may require that a non-resident plaintiff post an undertaking to secure the payment of costs and attorney's fees, creates substantial rights and liabilities and is therefore substantive in nature and not within the purview of the constitutional rule-making power of the supreme court. **Ware v. City of Anchorage,** Op. No. 477, 439 P2d 793 (Alaska 1968).

Rule 94. Relaxation of Rules.

These rules are designed to facilitate business and advance justice. They may be relaxed or dispensed with by the court in any case where it shall be manifest to the court that a strict adherence to them will work injustice.

(Adopted by SCO 5 October 9, 1959; amended by SCO 49 effective January 1, 1963)

Annotations

Cases

I. Application of Rule.

Failure of opposing counsel to object when a motion for new trial was not timely served, and the fact that the court, inferentially exercised its power under Civ. R. 94 (formerly Civ. R. 88) to relax the strict requirement as to timeliness does not waive untimeiness in filing the motion, and the filing of untimely motion for a new trial did not toll the running of the thirty-day appeal time. **Vogt v. Winbauer,** Op. No. 117, 376 P2d 1007 (Alaska 1962).

Counsel cannot waive the strict requirements of the rules. **Vogt v. Winbauer,** Op. No. 117, 376 P2d 1007 (Alaska 1962).

The Supreme Court will not indulge in literalism in reading the rule that the notation of a judgment in the civil docket as provided by Civil Rule 74 constitutes the entry of the judgment where the parties with concurrence of the court below had clearly stipulated that a transcript of proceedings wherein they had agreed to a dismissal with prejudice of their respective complaint and counterclaim constituted a final and complete settlement of their dispute and the docket entries without stating in so many words that a "judgment was entered," nevertheless clearly expressed the intent of the parties and the concurrence of the court. **Gravel v. Alaskan Village, Inc.,** Op. No. 321, 409 P2d 983 (Alaska 1966).

In the absence of abuse of discretion, the trial court's refusal to relax or dispense with the provision that the plaintiff who waived the opening argument shall not be permitted to replay to defendant's argument was not disturbed on appeal. **Merrill v. Faltin,** Op. No. 425, 430 P2d 913 (Alaska 1967).

The trial court has jurisdiction under this rule to enlarge the period for appealing from the report of a master in condemnation even though the period of appeal has run. **Collart et al. (6,656 Square Feet) v. State,** Op. No. 565, 456 P2d 480 (Alaska 1969).

Compliance with this rule's requirement that a notice of appeal contain a statement of grounds for appeal is not jurisdictional. **Cook v. Aurora Motors, Inc.,** Op. No. 848, 503 P2d 1046 (Alaska 1972).

In deciding whether the requirements of district court rules requiring a concise statement of the grounds for appeal should be relaxed or dispensed with, a lower court should examine the standards applied by the Supreme Court in enforcing analogous rules. **Cook v. Aurora Motors, Inc.,** Op. No. 848, 503 P2d 1046 (Alaska 1972).

Where the appellees move to dismiss an appeal for failure to give a concise statement of the grounds for appeal, but make no contention of surprise, the lower court hearing the appeal should require a showing by appellant that he would suffer an injustice if the rule was strictly construed against him. **Cook v. Aurora Motors, Inc.,** Op. No. 848, 503 P2d 1046 (Alaska 1972).

In examining the circumstances of a case where the appellant has failed to set forth in his appeal, a concise statement of the grounds for appeal, the superior court hearing an appeal from a district court decision should balance the right to appellate review, the willfulness and extent of the rules violations, and the possible injustice that might result from dismissal. Depending on its findings, the court may then either relax the rules and allow the appeal, dismiss the appeal for noncompliance with the rules, or allow an appeal but assess costs or attorney's fees as a penalty for the rules infraction in order to discourage similar future conduct. **Cook v. Aurora Motors, Inc.,** Op. No. 848, 503 P2d 1046 (Alaska 1972).

Defendant did not waive right to challenge judgment where it did not object under Civil Rule 78(b) but filed timely Rule 59(f) motion to amend judgment. **Beech Aircraft Corp. v. Harvey,** Op. No. 1338, 558 P2d 879 (Alaska 1976).

Where dismissed tenured teacher first knew of need to appeal in April was served with decision in June, and did not attempt to appeal until August, it was not abuse of discretion to refuse to relax rules to permit appeal. **Jerrel v. Kenai Peninsula Borough School District,** Op. No. 1458, 567 P2d 760 (Alaska 1977).

Where party timely filed a bill of costs, but failed to file a notice of taxation of costs until 15 days after judgment, it was not abuse of discretion for trial court to suspend application of the rule and award costs to such party. **City and Borough of Juneau v. Commercial Ins. Co.,** Op. No. 1906, 598 P2d 957 (Alaska 1979).

Failure of judgment to grant attorney's fees on punitive damage award was a legal error, but trial judge had discretion to waive the thirty-day rule for correcting such errors so as to grant a late request for modification of the judgment. **Alaskan Village, Inc. v. Smalley,** Op. No. 3069, 720 P2d 945 (Alaska 1986).

At telephonic hearing on father's opposition to mother's motion seeking child support arrears, judge's ruling limiting hearing to oral arguments, which preventing father from testifying and his counsel from cross-examining the mother, was error, even though father did not file motion to participate telephonically in the hearing. **Carvalho v. Carvalho,** Op. No. 3881, 838 P2d 259 (Alaska 1992).

Where only one of several defendants filed brief in opposition to summary judgment motion, failure of other defendants to file in opposition did not constitute waiver of their opposition where filing defendant's interests were almost exactly the same as interests of other defendants and same law firm represented all dependents. **Foster v. Hanni,** Op. No. 3894, 841 P2d 164 (Alaska 1992).

Where expert witness for prevailing public interest litigant was not paid for his work and had no binding agreement to be paid for his work and did not testify, trial court did not err in failing to award costs for his expert services. **Dansereau v. Ulmer,** Op. No. 4962, 955 P2d 916 (Alaska 1998).

II. Failure to Apply Rule.

A more flexible attitude on the part of the trial court would have been appropriate where appellants' failure to meet a ten day time limit for payment of an installment on a real estate contract was largely engendered by a confusing oral decision whereby counsel and plaintiffs were misled and a modification of the payment provisions was ordered on appeal in the interest of justice. **Brown v. Hawkins,** Op. No. 362, 418 P2d 28 (Alaska 1966).

In spite of a failure on the part of defendants to respond to requests for admissions within the ten day period provided by rule, the denial of a motion for relief from a summary judgment granted on the basis of failure to respond did not advance the objectives of the rules of procedure but was abuse of discretion where the court was aware of an extension of the ten day period given by opposing counsel, where no discovery was had and where defendants' counsel had offered at the hearing of the motion for relief to retype the responses and to have them sworn to within half an hour. **Palzer v. Serv-U-Meat Co.,** Op. No. 367, 419 P2d 201 (Alaska 1966).

Rule 95. Penalties.

(a) For any infraction of these rules, the court, after providing reasonable notice and an opportunity to be heard, may withhold or assess costs or attorney's fees as the circumstances of the case and discouragement of like conduct in the future may require; and such costs and attorney's fees may be imposed upon offending attorneys or parties.

(b) **[Applicable to cases filed before August 7, 1997].** In addition to its authority under (a) of this rule and its power to punish for contempt, a court may, after reasonable notice and an opportunity to show cause to the contrary, and after hearing by the court, if requested, impose a fine not to exceed $1,000.00 against any attorney who practices before it for failure to comply with these rules or any rules promulgated by the supreme court.

(b) **[Applicable to cases filed on or after August 7, 1997].** In addition to its authority under (a) of this rule and its power to punish for contempt, a court may, after reasonable notice and an opportunity to show cause to the contrary, and after hearing by the court, if requested, impose a fine not to exceed $50,000.00 against any attorney who practices before it for failure to comply with these rules or any rules promulgated by the supreme court.

(Adopted by SCO 5 October 9, 1959; amended by SCO 49 effective January 1, 1963; by SCO 246 effective May 1, 1976; by SCO 1099 effective January 15, 1993; by SCO 1281 effective August 7, 1997; and by SCO 1643 effective October 15, 2007)

Note to SCO 1281: Paragraph (b) of this rule was amended by ch. 26, sec. 43, SLA 1997. According to sec. 55 of the Act, the amendment to Civil Rule 95 applies "to all causes of action accruing on or after the effective date of this Act." The amendment to Rule 95 adopted by paragraph 9 of this order applies to all cases filed on or after August 7, 1997. See paragraph 17 of this order. The change is adopted for the sole reason that the legislature has mandated the amendment.

Annotations

Cases

In examining the circumstances of a case where the appellant has failed to set forth in his appeal a concise statement of the grounds for appeal, the superior court hearing an appeal from a district court decision should balance the right to appellate review, the willfulness and extent of the rules violations, and the possible injustice that might result from dismissal. Depending on its findings, the court may then either relax the rules and allow the appeal, dismiss the appeal for noncompliance with the rules, or allow an appeal but assess costs or attorney's fees as a penalty for the rules infraction in order to discourage similar future conduct. **Cook v. Aurora Motors, Inc.,** Op. No. 848, 503 P2d 1046 (Alaska 1972).

Where a reviewing court reverses the trial court's dismissal of action, the trial court on remand is empowered to assess costs or attorney fees on plaintiff's trial counsel for failure to oppose the initial motion to dismiss. **Schandelmeier v. Winchester Western,** Op. No. 1013, 520 P2d 70 (Alaska 1974).

Court had no "inherent power" to impose Rule 95 sanction prior to the effective date of that rule. **Esch v. Superior Court of Third Jud. Dist.,** Op. No. 1601, 577 P2d 1039 (Alaska 1978).

A Rule 95 sanction may not be imposed without notice and opportunity to show cause why it should not be imposed. **Esch v. Superior Court of Third Jud. Dist.,** Op. No. 1601, 577 P2d 1039 (Alaska 1978).

Courts should make a clear record concerning the reason for imposing a particular sanction and the authority relied on to do so. **Esch v. Superior Court of Third Jud. Dist.,** Op. No. 1601, 577 P2d 1039 (Alaska 1978).

In cases where the determination to be made is whether sanctions should be imposed under Civil Rule 95(b), the automatic change of judge authorized by Civil Rule 42 is inapplicable, and a judge will not be disqualified from presiding over such a proceeding unless his actions indicate feelings of personal rancor against the attorney involved. **Esch v. Superior Court of Third Jud. Dist.,** Op. No. 1601, 577 P2d 1039 (Alaska 1978).

Trial court has power to impose fines under Civil Rule 95(b) against attorneys for violation of court rules when necessary for the orderly and efficient operation of the courtroom. **Davis v. Superior Court,** Op. No. 1657, 580 P2d 1176 (Alaska 1978).

The notice required by Civil Rule 95(b) need only be sufficient to acquaint counsel with the nature of the alleged infraction; the particular rules alleged to have been violated need not be specified. **Davis v. Superior Court,** Op. No. 1657, 580 P2d 1176 (Alaska 1978).

Sanctions imposed under this rule differ from those imposed for contempt in that a showing of willfulness is not required. **Tobey v. Superior Court,** Op. No. 2806, 680 P2d 782 (Alaska 1983).

Trial court had authority to fine attorney for failure to comply with the terms of a pretrial order, but failure of the trial court to explicitly notify the attorney that sanctions were being considered and to afford him a reasonable time in which to show cause why the sanctions were not warranted required a remand. **Tobey v. Superior Court,** Op. No. 2806, 680 P2d 782 (Alaska 1983).

An order to show cause why attorney should not be held in contempt or sanctioned, delivered to the attorney only minutes prior to the hearing on the matter, was adequate notice where there was no reason to believe that additional time would have allowed the attorney to present a better defense. **Stephenson v. Superior Court, Fourth Jud. Dist.,** Op. No. 2922, 697 P2d 653 (Alaska 1985).

Imposition of attorney fees and monetary sanctions against defense attorney in criminal case for filing frivolous, unnecessary and legally deficient pleadings was error requiring remand where attorney was not given notice of the charges against him nor a hearing on the issue of sanctions. **Weidner v. Superior Court, Third Judicial Dist.,** Op. No. 589, 715 P2d 264 (Alaska App. 1986).

Attorney had no right to jury trial on issue of whether sanctions should be imposed against him for filing frivolous, unnecessary and legally deficient pleadings in a criminal case. **Weidner v. Superior Court, Third Judicial Dist.,** Op. No. 589, 715 P2d 264 (Alaska App. 1986).

Attorney was not entitled to a change of judge as a matter of right at hearing on sanctions against him for filing frivolous, unnecessary and legally deficient pleadings in a criminal case. **Weidner v. Superior Court, Third Judicial Dist.,** Op. No. 589, 715 P2d 264 (Alaska App. 1986).

Attorney was not entitled to discovery at hearing on sanctions against him for filing frivolous, unnecessary and legally deficient pleadings in a criminal case, since notice requirements, in conjunction with any affidavits filed by the prosecution, would alert him to the issues. **Weidner v. Superior Court, Third Judicial Dist.,** Op. No. 589, 715 P2d 264 (Alaska App. 1986).

Trial court had no authority to require the state to pay costs or attorney's fees as a sanction in a juvenile case. **State v. Superior Court, Third Jud. Dist.,** Op. No. 744, 743 P2d 381 (Alaska App. 1987).

This rule, authorizing courts to impose fines against attorneys, applies in criminal matters. **Weidner v. State,** Op. No. 871, 764 P2d 717 (Alaska App. 1988).

The validity of a court's order is not at issue in reviewing criminal contempt or sanctions under this rule; a person is not entitled to disobey the court's orders because he believes them invalid. **Weidner v. State,** Op. No. 871, 764 P2d 717 (Alaska App. 1988).

Although the rule requires that a sanctioned attorney receive a hearing, the amount of notice, the amount of time for the attorney to prepare, and the extensiveness of the hearing required depend on the facts of the case; where the facts are straightforward and there is no showing that a more extensive hearing is necessary to present other evidence, a brief hearing on short notice may be sufficient. **Weidner v. State,** Op. No. 871, 764 P2d 717 (Alaska App. 1988).

The trial court has considerable discretion in determining the time of the hearing required by this rule. **Weidner v. State,** Op. No. 871, 764 P2d 717 (Alaska App. 1988).

Trial court did not abuse its discretion in requiring immediate hearings on fines imposed against an attorney for in-court violations of the judge's orders; separate post-trial hearings were unnecessary. **Weidner v. State,** Op. No. 871, 764 P2d 717 (Alaska App. 1988).

Attorney was not entitled to a jury trial prior to the imposition of sanctions under this rule. **Weidner v. State,** Op. No. 871,764 P2d 717 (Alaska App. 1988).

An individual facing imposition of sanctions under this rule is not entitled to a change of judge as a matter of right, but where the totality of circumstances indicates that the judge is prejudiced against counsel, counsel has the right to challenge the judge for cause. **Weidner v. State,** Op. No. 871, 764 P2d 717 (Alaska App. 1988).

Imposition of monetary sanctions against district attorney for failing to appear at calendaring proceedings in criminal case was proper. **Matter of McNally,** Op. No. 4241, 901 P2d 415 (Alaska 1995).

Initial warning was not required prior to imposing monetary sanctions against supervising attorney. **Matter of McNally,** Op. No. 4241, 901 P2d 415 (Alaska 1995).

Where this rule was not cited as authority for award of attorney's fees against counsel, nor were rules which counsel violated identified, award of attorney's fees against counsel was reversed. **Wilson v. Municipality of Anchorage,** Op. No. 5111, 977 P2d 713 (Alaska 1999).

Trial court did not abuse its discretion in ordering an attorney to pay the opposing party's reasonable attorney fees and costs associated with its reply to the attorney's late-filed brief pursuant to Alaska R. Civ. P. 95(a) because the attorney had violated multiple rules that granted the trial court the authority to impose reasonable deadlines. The Supreme Court of Alaska has held that the failure to comply with a briefing schedule is a reason for imposing sanctions under Alaska R. Civ. P. 95(a). **Schmidt v. Koivisto,** Op. No. 5914, 114 P.3d 816 (Alaska 2005).

Rule 97. Title.

These rules may be known and cited as the Rules of Civil Procedure.

Rule 98. Effective Date.

These rules become effective on the date to be established by order of the supreme court. They shall govern all civil actions and proceedings thereafter commenced and so far as just and practicable all proceedings then pending.

Annotations

Cases

Where case was in process when new Rule 82 went into effect, new rule was to be applied in determining award of attorney's fees. **Bishop v. Municipality of Anchorage,** Op. No. 4233, 899 P2d 149 (Alaska 1995).

Rule amended effective July 15, 1993, should have been applied to case where summary judgment was entered on June 7, 1993, defendants were declared prevailing parties on August 16, 1993, and attorney's fees were awarded on November 1, 1993. **Nielson v. Benton,** Op. No. 4258, 903 P2d 1049 (Alaska 1995).

Rule 99. Telephonic Participation in Civil Cases.

(a) **Authorization for Telephonic Participation.** The court may allow one or more parties, counsel, witnesses or the judge to participate telephonically in any hearing or deposition for good cause and in the absence of substantial prejudice to opposing parties. Authorization for a witness to telephonically participate in a deposition does not bar the witnesses' testimony from being videotaped under Civil Rule 30.1; nor does it bar a party or attorney from being present at the site at which the witness is physically present.

(b) **Procedure.** The following procedure must be observed concerning telephonic participation in court hearings:

(1) Hearings involving telephonic participation must be scheduled in the same manner as other hearings.

(2) When telephonic participation is requested, the court, before the hearing, shall designate the party responsible for arranging the call and the party or parties responsible for payment of the call pursuant to Administrative Rule 48.

(3) Upon convening a telephonic proceeding, the judge shall:

(i) Recite the date, time, case name, case number, names and locations of parties and counsel, and the type of hearing;

(ii) Ascertain that all statements of all parties are audible to all participants;

(iii) Give instructions on how the hearing is to be conducted, including notice that in order to preserve the record speakers must identify themselves each time they speak.

(4) A verbatim record must be made in accord with Administrative Rule 35.

(c) The right of public access to court proceedings must be preserved in accordance with law.

(Added by SCO 623 effective June 15, 1985; amended by SCO 790 effective March 15, 1987; and by SCO 922 effective January 15, 1989)

Annotations

Cases

Where father participated telephonically in parental rights termination action, his due process right to confront and cross-examine witnesses was not violated, since his attorney was present in the courtroom and did effectively cross-examine witnesses and since the transcript of the hearing indicated that the father could hear well enough to follow the proceedings. **E.J.S. v. Dept. of Health & Social Serv.,** Op. No. 3318, 754 P2d 749 (Alaska 1988).

Trial judge did not err in accepting telephonic testimony over the objection of a party. **Gregg v. Gregg,** Op. No. 3454, 776 P2d 1041 (Alaska 1989).

Trial judge could administer oath to witness appearing by telephone. **Gregg v. Gregg,** Op. No. 3454, 776 P2d 1041 (Alaska 1989).

Oath administered to witness appearing by telephone was valid even though the witness was not physically present in the state. **Gregg v. Gregg,** Op. No. 3454, 776 P2d 1041 (Alaska 1989).

At telephonic hearing on father's opposition to mother's motion seeking child support arrears, judge's ruling limiting hearing to oral arguments, which preventing father from testifying and his counsel from cross-examining the mother, was error, even though father did not file motion to participate telephonically in the hearing. **Carvalho v. Carvalho,** Op. No. 3881, 838 P2d 259 (Alaska 1992).

Entry of civil judgment against defendant who did not appear personally at trial was reversed because trial court erred in rejecting defendant's request to appear at trial telephonically where defendant was residing in Washington State at time of trial, where plaintiff agreed to defendant's request, and where, pursuant to Civil Rule 32, defendant could have presented his testimony by deposition, thereby depriving trial court of the same opportunity to view his demeanor in person as would telephonic testimony. **Silvers v. Silvers,** Op. No. 5258, 999 P2d 786 (Alaska 2000).

Rule 100. Mediation and Other Forms of Alternative Dispute Resolution.

(a) **Application.** At any time after a complaint is filed, a party may file a motion with the court requesting mediation for the purpose of achieving a mutually agreeable settlement. The motion must address how the mediation should be conducted as specified in paragraph (b), including the names of any acceptable mediators. If domestic violence has occurred between the parties and mediation is requested in a matter covered by AS 25, mediation may only be ordered when permitted under AS 25.20.080, AS 25.24.060, or 25.24.140. In matters not covered by AS 25, the court may order mediation in response to such a motion, or on its own motion, whenever it determines that mediation may result in an equitable settlement. In making this determination, the court shall consider whether there is a history of domestic violence between the parties which could be expected to affect the fairness of the mediation process or the physical safety of the domestic violence victim. Mediation may not be ordered between the parties to, or in, a case filed under AS 18.66.100–18.66.180.

(b) **Order.** An order of mediation must state:

(1) the name of the mediator, or how the mediator will be decided upon;

(2) any changes in the procedures specified in paragraphs (d) and (e), or any additional procedures;

(3) that the costs of mediation are to be borne equally by the parties unless the court apportions the costs differently between the parties; and

(4) a date by which the initial mediation conference must commence.

(c) **Challenge of Mediator.** Each party has the right once to challenge peremptorily any mediator appointed by the court if the "Notice of Challenge of Mediator" is timely filed pursuant to Civil Rule 42(c).

(d) **Mediation Briefs.** Any party may provide a confidential brief to the mediator explaining its view of the dispute. If a party elects to provide a brief, the brief may not exceed five pages in length and must be provided to the mediator not less than three days prior to the mediation. A party's mediation brief may not be disclosed to anyone without the party's consent and is not admissible in evidence.

(e) **Conferences.** Mediation will be conducted in informal conferences at a location agreed to by the parties or, if they do not agree, at a location designated by the mediator. All parties shall attend the initial conference at which the mediator shall first meet with all parties. Thereafter the mediator may meet with the parties separately. Counsel for a party may attend all conferences attended by that party.

(f) **Termination.** After the initial joint conference and the first round of separate conferences if separate conferences are required by the mediator, a party may withdraw from mediation, or the mediator may terminate the process if the mediator determines that mediation efforts are likely to be unsuccessful. Upon withdrawal by a party or termination by the mediator, the mediator shall notify the court that mediation efforts have been terminated.

(g) **Confidentiality.** Mediation proceedings shall be held in private and are confidential. The mediator shall not testify as to any aspect of the mediation proceedings. Evidence of conduct or statements made in the course of court-ordered mediation is inadmissible to the same extent that conduct and statements are inadmissible under Alaska Rule of Evidence 408. This rule does not *relieve any person of a duty imposed by statute.*

(h) **Dismissal.** If the mediation is successful, the party requesting mediation shall prepare a stipulation for dismissal which dismisses all or such portions of the action as have been concluded by mediation as agreed upon at the mediation.

(i) Other Forms of Alternative Dispute Resolution.

(1) *Early Neutral Evaluation.* Parties or the court may use the procedure set out in this rule to refer a case to early neutral evaluation instead of mediation. All provisions of this rule apply to a case in which early neutral evaluation has been ordered under paragraph (a).

(2) *Arbitration.* Parties may stipulate to arbitration without further order of the court.

(3) *Settlement Conference.* At any time after a complaint is filed, a party may file a motion with the court requesting a settlement conference with a judge for the purpose of achieving a mutually agreeable settlement. The court may order a settlement conference in response to such a motion or on its own motion.

(4) *Local Dispute Resolution.* Parties may agree to resolve disputes, subject to court approval, by referring them to tribal courts, tribal councils, elders' courts, or ethnic organizations.

(Added by SCO 1116 effective July 15, 1993; amended by SCO 1130 effective July 15, 1993; by SCO 1269 effective July 15, 1997; by SCO 1318 effective July 15, 1998; and by SCO 1469 effective October 15, 2002)

Note to SCO 1269: Civil Rule 100(a) was amended by § 69 ch. 64 SLA 1996.

DISTRICT COURT RULES OF CIVIL PROCEDURE

Table of Contents

PART I. PROCEEDINGS BEFORE DISTRICT JUDGES AND MAGISTRATES

PART I. PROCEEDINGS BEFORE DISTRICT JUDGES AND MAGISTRATES.

Rule 1. Scope of Rules—Construction.

(a) **Scope of Rules.**

(1) **[Applicable to cases filed before August 7, 1997.]** The procedure in civil actions and proceedings before district judges and magistrates shall be governed by the rules governing the procedure in the superior court to the extent that such rules are applicable.

(1) **[Applicable to cases filed on or after August 7, 1997.]** The procedure in civil actions and proceedings before district judges and magistrates shall be governed by the rules governing the procedure in the superior court to the extent that such rules are applicable. However, in a civil action for personal injury or property damage, unless otherwise agreed by all parties or permitted by order of the court in exceptional cases and for good cause shown, discovery shall be limited to the disclosures required under Civil Rule 26(a) and to the taking by each party of the deposition of one or more opposing parties and of one additional person who is not a party.

(2) If in any action or proceeding a magistrate finds it impracticable to proceed or is at a disadvantage because of the application of any of such rules, the magistrate may hold the action or proceeding in abeyance, without prejudice to the rights of the parties, for further action by a district judge.

(3) The following rules are inapplicable in their entirety to proceedings before district judges and magistrates:

CIVIL RULE	TITLE
Rule 18(b)	Joinder of Remedies— Fraudulent Conveyances.
Rule 27	Deposition Before Actions or Pending Appeal.
Rule 40(c)	Visiting Judges.
Rule 40(d)	Applications for Orders.
Rule 48(b)	Instructions; Argument; Retirement of Jury.
Rule 57(a)	Declaratory Judgments.
Rule 65	Injunctions.
Rule 66	Receivers.
Rule 70	Judgment for Specific Acts—Vesting Title.
Rule 72	Eminent Domain.
Rule 84	Change of Name.

(4) To the extent authorized by law, the provisions of Civil Rule 100 apply to any civil matter brought in district court.

(b) **Construction.** Where the words "court" or "judge" are used in these rules, they shall be construed to include a district judge or a magistrate, and where functions and duties are prescribed for the clerk, they shall be performed by a magistrate or a clerk.

(Amended by SCO 540 effective October 1, 1982; by SCO 1153 effective July 15, 1994; by SCO 1281 effective August 7, 1997; by SCO 1469 effective October 15, 2002; and by SCO 1522 effective October 15, 2003)

Note to SCO 1281: Subparagraph (a)(1) of this rule was amended by ch. 26, sec. 44, SLA 1997. According to sec. 55 of the Act, the amendment to District Court Civil Rule 1 applies "to all causes of action accruing on or after the effective date of this Act." The amendment to District Court Civil Rule 1 adopted by paragraph 11 of this order applies to all cases filed on or after August 7, 1997. See paragraph 17 of this order. The change is adopted for the sole reason that the legislature has mandated the amendment.

Note: The maximum amount of a district court civil claim under AS 22.15.030 is $100,000.

Cross References

CROSS REFERENCE: AS 22.15.030

Annotations

Cases

Compliance with this rule's requirement that a notice of appeal contain a statement of the grounds for appeal is not jurisdictional. **Cook v. Aurora Motors, Inc.**, Op. No. 848, 503 P2d 1046 (Alaska 1972).

In deciding whether the requirements of district court rules requiring a concise statement of the grounds for appeal should be relaxed or dispensed with, a lower court should examine the standards applied by the Supreme Court in enforcing analogous rules. **Cook v. Aurora Motors, Inc.**, Op. No. 848, 503 P2d 1046 (Alaska 1972).

Presiding judge in a small claims action was not authorized, sua sponte to deny defendant's right to elect formal rules or to reverse the determination of the district court judge sitting on the case that that formal rules shall apply. **Jimmie v. Alaska Village Electric Co-Op, Inc.**, Op. No. 2310, 624 P2d 1258 (Alaska 1981).

Rule 2. Record of Proceedings—Transcript as Evidence.

There shall be kept an electronic record of the following:

(1) All contested actions and proceedings had in open court unless the parties with the approval of the judge shall specifically agree to the contrary; and

(2) Such other proceedings as the judge may direct or as may be required by order of the court or as may be requested by any party to the action or proceeding.

Rule 3. Notice of Orders or Judgments.

Notice of the entry of an order or judgment shall be given as provided by Civil Rule 73(d). Every order and judgment shall include a clerk's certificate of distribution as defined in Civil Rule 58.1(d).

(Amended by SCO 554 effective April 4, 1983)

Rule 4. Assignment and Hearing of Cases—Calendars.

(a) The assignment and calendaring of cases in the district court shall be as set forth in Civil Rule 40(a), or by such procedures established by the presiding judge as will cause all cases to be regularly reviewed for placement on the trial calendar for dismissal for want of prosecution, or other appropriate disposition.

(b) **[Applicable to cases filed on or after August 7,**

1997.] In a civil action for personal injury or property damage, unless otherwise permitted by order of the court in exceptional cases and for good cause shown, all parties shall file a memorandum to set the case for trial, as set out in Civil Rule 40(b), no later than 180 days after service of the complaint on all parties to the case. The memorandum shall contain a certification that each party has exchanged the information described in Civil Rule 26(a) and may state their separate positions if they do not agree concerning information or estimates to be provided in the memorandum. After the court satisfies itself that the information described in Civil Rule 26(a) has been disclosed, the court shall set the case for trial as soon as practicable, but no sooner than 30 days after the court makes the determination regarding disclosure.

(Amended by SCO 838 effective August 1, 1987; and by SCO 1281 effective August 7, 1997)

Note to SCO 1281: Paragraph (b) of District Court Civil Rule 4 was added by ch. 26, § 45, SLA 1997. According to § 55 of the Act, the amendment to District Court Civil Rule 4 applies 'to all causes of action accruing on or after the effective date of this Act." The amendment to District Court Civil Rule 4 adopted by paragraph 13 of this order applies to all cases filed on or after August 7, 1997. See paragraph 17 of this order. The change is adopted for the sole reason that the legislature has mandated the amendment.

Rule 5. Jurors.

The procedure for the selection, summoning and impaneling of jurors shall be as provided by statute. The procedure for the examination of jurors shall be governed by Civil Rule 47.

Cross References

CROSS REFERENCE: AS 09.20.010— AS 09.20.090

Rule 6. Instructions to the Jury.

If an action is tried by a jury, the district judge is not required to instruct the jury other than to define the nature of the action and the issues of fact to be determined by the jury.

Rule 7. Appointment and Authority of Clerk.

In court locations where there is no superior court judge regularly sitting, a district judge may by order appoint a clerk authorized to issue process and to enter the orders and judgments set forth in Civil Rule 73 (b) and (c). In the absence of an order appointing a clerk, process shall be issued and orders and judgments shall be entered by the district judge or by a magistrate.

(Amended by SCO 290 effective January 15, 1978; and by SCO 554 effective April 4, 1983)

PART II. SMALL CLAIMS RULES*

Rule 8. Scope and Applicability.

(a) Procedure in small claim actions, as defined by AS 22.15.040, is governed by these rules and other rules specifically incorporated herein by reference, when all parties to the action elect to be governed by them. Part I of the District Court Rules of Civil Procedure governs small claim actions when the parties do not elect small claim procedure.

(b) A party having a claim or claims exceeding the maximum amount of a small claim as defined by AS 22.15.040 may waive the right to recover the excess amount and elect to proceed under this Part II, by filing a written waiver of the excess amount.

(c) Actions to foreclose or enforce statutory, common law or possessory liens and actions for recovery of real property may not be brought as small claims actions. The court may, on its own motion, order the rules in Part I to apply in any other action when important or difficult questions of fact or law are involved.

(SCO 225 effective May 1, 1976*; amended by SCO 854 effective January 15, 1988; and by SCO 1153 effective July 15, 1994)

Note: The maximum amount of a small claim under AS 22.15.040 is $10,000. (Amended by SCO 1556, effective September 14, 2004)

***Editor's Note:** The effective date of Supreme Court Order 225, amending all of the small claims rules, was postponed by Supreme Court Orders 235, 237 and 242. The small claims rules were finally effective on May 1, 1976.

Annotations

Cases

Presiding judge in a small claims action was not authorized, sua sponte, to deny defendant's right to elect formal rules or to reverse the determination of the district court judge sitting on the case that formal rules shall apply. **Jimmie v. Alaska Village Electric Co-Op, Inc.,** Op. No. 2310, 624 P2d 1258 (Alaska 1981).

Cross References

CROSS REFERENCE: AS 22.15.040

Rule 9. Informality.

Formality in pleadings, motions, and the introduction of evidence is not required. A writing filed as a complaint, answer, or application shall be legible and brief.

(SCO 225 effective May 1, 1976)

Annotations

Cases

In a small claims case, a party may file a written statement showing the nature of any defense he might have. **Aguchak v. Montgomery Ward Co., Inc.,** Op. No. 1026, 520 P2d 1352 (Alaska 1974).

Rule 10. Pleadings.

(a) A small claim action is commenced by filing a complaint on the form provided by the Alaska court system. The complaint is a short, plain written statement showing the nature of the claim for relief, signed by the plaintiff. The complaint shall contain a statement that the plaintiff elects to have the claim treated as a small claim and waives the right to jury trial and the right to proceed formally. A complaint which does not contain a waiver of the right to jury trial and formal proceedings is governed by Part I of the District Court Rules of Civil Procedure. The plaintiff's mailing address shall be shown on the complaint. When the complaint is based upon a written document, the document or a copy of it shall be attached to the complaint.

(b) A party defending against a claim shall file an answer on the form provided by the Alaska court system. The answer is a short, plain statement showing the nature of the defense and any claim that the defendant has against the plaintiff arising from the same transaction or occurrence and shall conform with Rule 12 of these rules. The answer must be filed with or mailed to the court where the action was commenced and be signed by the defendant. When the answer or counterclaim is based upon a written document, the document or a copy of it shall be attached to the answer. The defendant's mailing address shall be shown on the answer. The clerk or magistrate shall mail a copy of the answer to the plaintiff, and shall maintain a record of the mailing.

(c) An answer form shall be served with the complaint and shall advise the defendant of the right to proceed informally under this Part II or formally under Part I of these rules. The form shall contain a statement that when the defendant requests informal proceedings, the defendant waives the right to trial by jury and to proceed formally. A plaintiff against whom a counterclaim is filed shall have ten days after such claim is mailed to the plaintiff to withdraw the plaintiff's election to proceed under Part II, and failure to withdraw the election waives the plaintiff's right to trial by jury and formal procedure as to the counterclaim.

(d) A defendant who does not wish to contest the claim may default by failing to file an answer or may file an answer agreeing with the complaint. The latter shall be sufficient basis for entry of judgment on the pleadings by the court or clerk when the claim is for a specific amount of damages.

(SCO 225 effective May 1, 1976; amended by SCO 713 effective September 15, 1986; by SCO 740 effective August 28, 1986; and by SCO 1153 effective July 15, 1994)

Rule 11. Process.

(a) The summons shall be issued and the summons and complaint served, according to the procedures of Civil Rule 4, except that:

(1) If personal service is used, the clerk shall deliver the summons for service to a peace officer or to a person specially appointed to serve it.

(2) If service is by registered or certified mail, the clerk shall mail the summons and a copy of the complaint as provided in Civil Rule 4(h).

(3) Service by publication or posting shall not be allowed.

(4) Service on a defendant who is outside the state shall be allowed

(A) in accordance with the Landlord-Tenant Act, AS 34.03.340;

(B) in accordance with AS 09.05.020, entitled Service of Process on Nonresident Owner or Operator of Motor Vehicle; or

(C) as otherwise permitted under Civil Rule 4.

(5) The affidavit required by Civil Rule 4(f) is not required in small claims cases and Civil Rule 4(j) shall not apply.

(b) A copy of the Alaska Small Claims Handbook and a blank answer form shall be served with the summons and complaint.

(c) If the summons and complaint are served by registered or certified mail, a delivery receipt returnable to the district court shall be required. All returned delivery receipts shall be attached to the copy of the summons retained by the court.

(d) All parties shall inform the court and other parties of any change in mailing address during the pendency of the action. The parties are deemed to have received all documents mailed to them at the addresses furnished by them.

(e) Service of any pleading or process, including the summons and complaint, shall be valid even though refused by the recipient and returned after such refusal. Upon receiving a returned refused mailing, the clerk shall mail to the refusing party by first class mail a copy of the mailing refused and a notice that service of the original was valid upon refusal and that the case will proceed as if the recipient had accepted the original mailing.

(f) Civil Rule 45(a), (b), (c), (e), and (f), concerning subpoenas is incorporated in these rules for the purpose of securing the attendance of witnesses at trial, except that the fee tendered with a subpoena need only cover the fees for mileage and for one-half day's attendance if the person's attendance, including travel time, requires no more than three consecutive hours.

(SCO 225 effective May 1, 1976; amended by SCO 264 effective February 15, 1977; by SCO 381 effective October 1, 1979; by SCO 713 effective September 15, 1986; by SCO 754 effective December 15, 1986; by SCO 1075 effective January 15, 1992; and by SCO 1138 effective July 15, 1993; and by SCO 1556 effective September 14, 2004)

Note: Chapter 65 § 6 SLA 2004 amended District Court Civil Rule 11(a)(4)(C) to allow service of process on out-of-state defendants in small claims actions to the extent permitted by Civil Rule 4. Section 1 of this order is adopted for the sole reason that the legislature has mandated the amendments.

Rule 12. Venue.

(a) The action shall be filed and the complaint shall contain a statement that it is filed:

(1) At the nearest place to the residence or place of employment of an individual defendant; or

(2) At the place where the defendant's alleged wrongful conduct caused personal injury or damage to the plaintiff's property; or

(3) At a place where the defendant does or solicits business; and

(4) At a place which will not cause unnecessary expense or inconvenience to the defendant.

(b) The answer shall contain any application of the defendant for change of place of trial. The change shall be granted if the action is not filed in accordance with Rule 12(a). An effective waiver of Rule 12(a) can be made only after the commencement of the action.

(c) The plaintiff shall have twenty days from the date of mailing receipt of the answer by the clerk or magistrate to file a statement opposing an application for change of place of trial. The court shall consider the application upon the statements of the parties, and shall issue an order granting or denying the application. A copy of the order shall be sent to the parties by first class mail at the addresses shown on their pleadings. When the application is granted, the file shall be transferred. When the application is denied, the court shall set the action for trial.

(SCO 225 effective May 1, 1976)

Rule 13. Defenses and Objections—When and How Presented.

(a) A defendant shall file or state an answer within 20 days after service of the summons and complaint upon the defendant. A counterclaim shall be deemed denied by the plaintiff.

(b) When an answer is plainly insufficient to state a defense, the court may on its own motion enter judgment on the pleadings without trial. A judgment on the pleadings shall state the reasons for its entry.

(SCO 225 effective May 1, 1976; amended by SCO 1153 effective July 15, 1994)

Rule 14. Joinder of Parties and Claims.

(a) Minors and other persons under legal disability may appear only through guardians, guardians ad litem, or conservators.

(b) Any person having a claim or against whom a claim is made arising from the same transaction or occurrence which gave rise to the complaint may be joined as a party to the action.

(c) Persons having a joint interest in the subject matter of the action and other persons whose participation is necessary for the court to give complete relief to those already parties shall be joined in the action if the court can obtain jurisdiction over them.

(d) Parties may be added or dropped by order of the court on application of any party or on its own motion at any stage of the action and on such terms as are just. A person not already a party to the action added by the court shall be served copies of all pleadings and a summons in the manner provided by these rules unless such service is waived.

(e) A party may join any number of claims arising from any number of transactions and occurrences against an opposing party, so long as the total amount of the claims does not exceed the small claim jurisdictional limitation.

(f) The court may order any claim against any party to be severed and proceed to try it separately.

(SCO 225 effective May 1, 1976)

Rule 15. Attorneys—Interns.

(a) A corporation or other public or private organization may be represented in any stage of a small claims proceeding including an appeal by any officer or employee authorized in writing to represent it, AS 22.20.040 notwithstanding.

(b) Any party to a small claims action may be represented at any stage of the proceedings by an attorney at law or a legal intern.

(c) Any party, except an attorney at law, asserting a claim as an assignee thereof, whether for collection, fee, or value, shall be represented at all stages of an action upon the claim by an attorney at law, or a legal intern. On application of a party or on its own motion, the court shall dismiss without prejudice any action filed or proceeded with in violation of this rule.

(d) Representation of a party by a legal intern at any stage of an action shall be governed by Part IV of the Alaska Bar Rules.

(SCO 225 effective May 1, 1976; amended by SCO 952 effective July 15, 1989; and by SCO 1085 effective January 15, 1992)

Rule 16. Trial.

(a) Every small claims action shall be tried by the court without a jury. A judge may not be peremptorily challenged either under Civil Rule 42(c) or AS 22.20.022.

(b) The court shall admit any evidence which is relevant and material, despite the fact that such evidence might be inadmissible under formal rules of evidence.

(c) The court may investigate the controversy between the parties either in or out of court. The investigation must be made in the presence of the parties and the findings of fact resulting from the investigation must be stated on the record or reduced to writing and placed in the case file by the court.

(d) Testimony shall be given under oath and may be given in narrative fashion, and the examination of witnesses shall be informal. An adverse party has the right to cross-examine a party or witness. The court may take an active role in the examination of witnesses.

(e) The court may, at any time, consult with the parties on the record for the purpose of reaching a compromise or conciliation.

(f) The date set for trial shall be not less than 15 days from the date the court mails notice of the trial date to the parties.

(SCO 225 effective May 1, 1976; amended by SCO 674 effective June 15, 1986; and by SCO 759 effective December 15, 1986)

Rule 17. Judgment.

(a) If the defendant fails to answer the complaint within 20 days after service of process or fails to attend trial, the defendant is in default. Default judgment shall be entered only upon proof under oath made upon personal knowledge that the defendant is not an infant or otherwise incompetent, and that the defendant is not in the active military service of the United States. The court shall also require proof under oath, made upon personal knowledge or based on business records, of the truth of every essential element of the claim for relief. The clerk may enter a default judgment if the damages alleged are liquidated and no default hearing is required. If the defendant answers but fails to appear at trial, the court may nevertheless consider any relevant and material evidence filed with the answer. The court may allow an answer to be filed after the defendant is in default, but before judgment is entered, upon a showing of good cause. The plaintiff may move the court to enter a default judgment if the defendant is in default. Affidavits or exhibits necessary to the entry of default judgment under this rule shall accompany the motion.

(b) Judgment on the pleadings may be entered pursuant to Rules 13(b) and 10(d).

(c) If the plaintiff fails to attend the trial, the plaintiff is in default. When neither party appears, the court may dismiss the action with prejudice. When the defendant appears and the plaintiff does not, the court shall inquire of the defendant concerning the validity of the defendant's defense and the defendant's knowledge, if any, of the reasons for the plaintiff's absence. The court may then, in its discretion, enter judgment dismissing the claim with prejudice. If the defendant has asserted a counterclaim, it shall be disposed of according to paragraph (a) of this rule.

(d) When more than one claim for relief is presented in an action, whether as a claim, counterclaim, cross-claim, or third-party claim, or when multiple parties are involved, the court may direct the entry of a final judgment as to one or more but fewer than all of the claims or parties only upon an express determination that there is no just reason for delay and upon an express direction for the entry of judgment. In the absence of such determination and direction, any order or other form of decision, however designated, which adjudicates fewer than all of the claims or the rights and liabilities of fewer than all the parties shall not terminate the action as to any of the claims or parties, and the order or other form of decision is subject to revision at any time before the entry of judgment adjudicating all the claims and the rights and liabilities of all the parties.

(e) A default judgment shall not be different in kind from or exceed in amount that prayed for in the demand for judgment. Except as to a party against whom a default judgment is entered, every final judgment shall grant the relief to which the party in whose favor it is rendered is entitled, even if the party has not demanded such relief in the pleadings.

(f) **Dismissal for Want of Prosecution.** Actions which have been pending in a court for more than six months without any proceedings having been taken may be dismissed as a matter of course for want of prosecution by the court on its own motion or on motion of a party to the action. The clerk shall review all pending cases semi-annually, and in all cases in which no proceedings have been taken for more than six months, shall send notice to the parties to show cause in writing why the action should not be dismissed. If good cause to the contrary is not shown within 30 days of distribution of the notice, the court shall dismiss the action. The clerk may dismiss actions under this paragraph if a party has not opposed dismissal. A dismissal for want of prosecution is without prejudice unless the court states in the order that the case is dismissed with prejudice.

(g) A claim may be dismissed with or without prejudice and without court order at any time by agreement of the parties, or upon written notice by the plaintiff at any time before the defendant has filed an answer. A dismissal with prejudice bars action in any court based on the claim dismissed.

(h) Judgment by confession may be entered pursuant to Civil Rule 57. Judgment pursuant to a compromise may be entered by written agreement of the parties or by oral declarations on the record at trial.

(i) After trial, the court shall enter judgment. The judgment need not be supported by findings of fact or conclusions of law. The judgment shall specify the exact relief given.

(j) If the judgment is entered upon a written instrument, the instrument shall be filed with the court and canceled by marks or writing across its face, unless the court orders otherwise.

(k) The court or the clerk may order a money judgment payable in installments and stay levy of execution upon stipulation of the parties. In the event the judgment is ordered payable in installments, it shall bear interest as provided by law. If the terms of a judgment made payable in installments are violated, execution may issue for the balance of the judgment remaining unpaid.

(l) The clerk shall distribute a copy of every order or

judgment entered to all parties to the action. Every order and judgment shall include a clerk's certificate of distribution as defined in Civil Rule 58.1(d).

(SCO 225 effective May 1, 1976; amended by SCO 554 effective April 4, 1983; by SCO 745 effective December 15, 1986; by SCO 753 effective December 15, 1986; by SCO 799 effective February 17, 1987; by SCO 839 effective August 1, 1987; and by SCO 1153 effective July 15, 1994)

Rule 18. Appeal.

Either party may appeal a judgment or an order refusing to relieve any party from a default. The procedure on appeal shall be governed by the rules for appeal of judgments of the district court to the superior court, except that the superior court shall grant trial de novo if the proceedings in the district court were not of record.

(SCO 225 effective February 2, 1976; amended by SCO 440 effective November 15, 1980)

Rule 19. Relief from Judgment.

Civil Rule 60 applies to motions for relief from judgment in small claim actions.

(SCO 225 effective May 1, 1976)

Rule 20. Remedies.

(a) A small claims judgment may be enforced in the same manner as other judgments. No execution shall issue for two days after the date shown in the clerk's certificate of distribution on the judgment.

(b) No attachment or garnishment shall issue before judgment in a small claim action.

(c) Costs shall be allowed as of course to a prevailing party. A party entitled to costs may be allowed the filing fee and other charges made by the court, the expense of service of process, witness fees, and reasonable attorney's fees.

(d) A party may deposit with the court all or any part of any sum of money or any other thing capable of manual delivery which is sought in the action or due under a judgment. The party making the deposit shall inform all other parties to the action of the deposit. The court shall be governed by Rule 5, Alaska Rules Governing the Administration of All Courts, and shall release the deposit to the party entitled to it when the party becomes entitled to it. No interest shall accrue against a party making a deposit, to the extent of the deposit, after it is made.

(e) When the judgment has been satisfied, the judgment creditor shall file an acknowledgment of satisfaction with the court. The court may issue a satisfaction of judgment if the judgment debtor, by motion served on the judgment creditor, establishes that the judgment has been satisfied. The clerk may issue the satisfaction if the motion is unopposed.

(SCO 225 effective May 1, 1976; amended by SCO 449 effective November 24, 1980; by SCO 554 effective April 4, 1983; and by SCO 755 effective December 15, 1986)

Cross References

(e) **CROSS REFERENCE:** AS 09.30.300 and AS 09.30.310

Rule 21. Assistance to Litigants—Handbook.

Magistrates and clerks of any district court are authorized, where necessary, to assist litigants in the preparation of complaints and answers. First recourse should be had to the Alaska Small Claim Handbook, which shall be available for distribution to prospective litigants at all locations of any court empowered to handle small claims actions, and shall be served upon the defendant with the summons and complaint. When a party is illiterate or otherwise unable to write his pleading, and is unable to obtain assistance from a friend or relative, the clerk or magistrate shall write it on the appropriate form. A form written by the clerk or magistrate shall be signed by the party or bear the party's witnessed mark. The clerk shall note upon its face the method of preparing the pleading under this rule.

(SCO 225 effective May 1, 1976; amended by SCO 748 effective December 15, 1986; and by SCO 1153 effective July 15, 1994)

Rule 22. Legal Effect of Rules.

(a) The forms published by the Alaska Court System to accompany these rules are legally sufficient and are intended to indicate the simplicity and brevity which the rules contemplate.

(b) The Alaska Small Claims Handbook published by the Alaska Court System to accompany these rules is not a rule of court.

(c) The forms for the complaint, the summons and the answer published by the Alaska Court System shall be used by the parties. All other forms are illustrative and not mandatory.

(SCO 225 effective May 1, 1976; amended by SCO 333 effective January 1, 1979; and by SCO 713 effective September 15, 1986)

PART III. PROCEEDINGS AFTER TRIAL AND APPEALS

Rule 24. Stay of Proceedings to Enforce Judgment.

(a) **Automatic Stay.** Except as to judgments entered on default or by consent or on confession, no execution shall issue upon a judgment of the district court nor shall proceedings be taken for the enforcement of such judgment until the expiration of two days after the date shown in the clerk's certificate of distribution on the judgment.

(b) **Stay Upon Appeal.** When an appeal is taken, the appellant may obtain a stay of proceedings to enforce the judgment by following the procedure set forth in Appellate Rule 603(a).

(Rescinded by SCO 440 effective November 15, 1980; added by SCO 554, effective April 4, 1983)

Note: Rules 23 and 25 through 31 were rescinded by Supreme Court Order 440 effective Nov. 15, 1980.

PART V. SPECIAL PROCEEDINGS

Rule 32. Presumption of Death.

(a) **Petition.** Any interested person desiring to establish the presumption of death of a missing person in cases authorized by statute may file a verified petition in a district court in the district where it is believed the missing person has suffered death or in the district where such person last resided prior to the person's disappearance. The petition shall show the following:

(1) The name of the person believed to have suffered death.

(2) The circumstances leading to such belief.

(3) That after due and diligent search such person cannot be found.

(b) **Jury.** If the court is satisfied that the circumstances surrounding the disappearance of the missing person afford reasonable grounds for believing that such person has suffered death, the court shall summon and impanel a jury of qualified persons. The members of the jury, before beginning their duties, shall be sworn to diligently inquire into and justly consider all the facts and circumstances concerning the disappearance of the missing person, and from a fair consideration thereof to determine whether the court is justified in entering an order declaring that such person is presumed to be dead.

(c) **Hearing.** The jury shall inquire into the facts set forth in the petition. The testimony of witnesses under oath shall be heard and other evidence presented as upon the trial of an action. Depositions may be accepted where the magistrate believes that travel time and costs do not warrant a personal appearance.

(d) **Verdict—Approval by Court—Order.** After having heard all of the evidence presented, the jury shall retire for deliberation. If by its unanimous verdict in writing the jury finds that it may be fairly presumed that the missing person has suffered death, the court must endorse upon the verdict its approval or disapproval of such findings. If approval is given, the court shall enter an order declaring that the missing person is presumed to be dead. The order shall take effect at the expiration of six months from the date that the jury's findings and verdict are approved, except that in cases where there is clear and convincing evidence of the presumed death the order will take effect at such earlier time as the court shall specify therein.

(e) **Presumptive Death Certificate.** After the order of approval referred to in subdivision (d) has become effective or upon receiving a copy of an order or decree of the superior court that a person has not been heard of for a period of five continuous years and is presumed to be dead, the magistrate shall make out, sign, and file with the Bureau of Vital Statistics a presumptive death certificate containing such information as may be required by the bureau. On the effective date of the order of presumptive death, the missing person shall be presumed to be dead, and the person's estate may be administered in accordance with the then existing provisions of law applicable to the administration of the estates of deceased persons.

(f) **Correction of Presumptive Death Order and Certificate.** If the body of the missing person is found, or such person is discovered to be alive after an order of presumptive death has been entered, the court shall conduct a hearing, with or without a jury, to determine the facts, and shall enter an appropriate order for the correction, substitution or removal by the Bureau of Vital Statistics of the presumptive death certificate in accordance with the findings made if additional facts are brought to light.
(Renumbered by SCO 225 effective February 2, 1976; amended by SCO 554 effective April 4, 1983; by SCO 899 effective January 15, 1989; by SCO 1153 effective July 15, 1994; and by SCO 1605 effective October 15, 2006)

Cross References

CROSS REFERENCE: AS 09.55.020

(d) **CROSS REFERENCE:** AS 09.55.030

(e) **CROSS REFERENCE:** AS 09.55.050

(f) **CROSS REFERENCE:** AS 09.55.060

PART VI. TITLE—EFFECTIVE DATE

Rule 33. Title.

These rules shall be known and cited as the District Court Rules of Civil Procedure.

(Renumbered by SCO 225 effective February 2, 1976)

Rule 34. Effective Date.

These rules shall become effective on a date to be established by order of the supreme court.

(Renumbered by SCO 225 effective February 2, 1976)

Rule 35. Legal Effect of Rules—Procedural Portions of Statutes Superseded

These rules are promulgated pursuant to constitutional authority granting rule making power to the supreme court, and to the extent that they are inconsistent with any procedural provisions of any statute not enacted for the specific purpose of changing a rule, shall supersede such statute to the extent of such inconsistency.

(Renumbered by SCO 225 effective February 2, 1976)

RULES OF CRIMINAL PROCEDURE

Table of Contents

CrR

PART I. SCOPE, PURPOSE AND CONSTRUCTION

PART II. PRELIMINARY PROCEEDINGS

PART III. INDICTMENT AND INFORMATION

PART V. VENUE — PRETRIAL

PART VI. TRIAL

PART I. SCOPE, PURPOSE AND CONSTRUCTION

Rule 1. Scope.

These rules govern the practice and procedure in the superior court in all criminal proceedings and, insofar as they are applicable, the practice and procedure in all other courts in criminal proceedings.

(Adopted by SCO 4 October 4, 1959; amended by SCO 427 effective August 1, 1980)

Cross References

CROSS REFERENCE: Alaska Const. Art. IV § 15; AS 12.85.010

Annotations

Cases

Probation and parole revocation hearings are not criminal proceedings within the meaning of the Rules of Criminal Procedure. **State v. Sears,** Op. No. 1306, 553 P2d 907, 553 P2d 907, 423 P2d 686 (Alaska 1976).

Rule 2. Purpose and Construction.

These rules are intended to provide for the just determination of every criminal proceeding. They shall be construed to secure simplicity in procedure, fairness in administration and the elimination of unjustifiable expenses and delay.

(Adopted by SCO 4 October 4, 1959)

Annotations

Cases

Probation and parole revocation hearings are not criminal proceedings within the meaning of the Rules of Criminal Procedure. **State v. Sears,** Op. No. 1306, 553 P2d 907, 553 P2d 907, 423 P2d 686 (Alaska 1976).

PART II. PRELIMINARY PROCEEDINGS

Rule 3. The Complaint.

(a) The complaint is a written statement of the essential facts constituting the offense charged. A citation issued for the commission of a misdemeanor or a violation shall have the same force and effect as a complaint and shall be filed as a complaint; provided, that the citation satisfies the requirements of a valid complaint as provided by these rules. A complaint or citation shall be made upon oath or affirmation before any judge or magistrate, except that the following complaints and citations may be signed before any person authorized by law to administer oaths or affirmations, or signed with a certification under penalty of perjury that the complaint or citation is true:

(1) A citation for a minor offense as defined in District Court Criminal Rule 8(b).

(2) A complaint or citation for a misdemeanor where arrest has been made without a warrant.

(3) A citation which the defendant has signed thereby promising to appear.

(b) A copy of the complaint shall be served upon the defendant at the time of service of the summons, and whenever practicable, upon execution of the warrant.

(c) **Defendant and Offense Information To Be Included in Complaint.** The complaint must include the following information in the form shown in the sample published at the end of this rule:

(1) the defendant's full name, including middle name or initial, if known;

(2) the defendant's date of birth, if known;

(3) the defendant's Alaska Public Safety Information Network (APSIN) identification number, if known;

(4) the defendant's driver's license number or state identification number, if known, including the issuing state and whether the license is a commercial driver's license;

(5) the arrest tracking number (ATN) on the Criminal Case Intake and Disposition (CCID) form for the incident;

(6) the three-digit charge tracking number assigned on the CCID form to each offense; and

(7) the statute, regulation, or ordinance that the defendant is alleged to have violated, as identified in the Uniform Offense Citation Table.** Regulations not listed in the Uniform Offense Citation Table must be cited by the regulation number.

(d) **Crimes Involving Domestic Violence.** If a defendant is charged with an offense listed in AS 18.66.990, the complaint must indicate whether the prosecuting authority intends to claim that the alleged offense is a crime involving domestic violence as defined in AS 18.66.990(3) and (5).

(e) **Search Warrant Information.** A complaint must include a listing of the numbers of any search warrants issued in relation to the case, as required by Criminal Rule 37(e)(2).

(f) **Information Not To Be Included in Complaint.** The defendant's social security number may not appear on a complaint. This subsection applies to complaints filed on or after October 15, 2006.

** The Uniform Offense Citation table was developed by the Department of Public Safety. Changes to the table must be approved by either the Department of Law or the appropriate municipal prosecuting authority. It is available at http://www.dps.state.ak.us/uoct/.

(Adopted by SCO 4 October 4, 1959; amended by SCO 85 effective September 1, 1966; by SCO 157 effective February 15, 1973; by SCO 188 effective July 18, 1974; by SCO 317 effective September 1, 1978; by SCO 427 effective August 1, 1980; by SCO 886 effective July 15, 1988; by SCO 902 effective July 15, 1988; by SCO 936 effective January 15, 1989; by SCO 1289 effective January 15, 1998; by SCO 1587 effective December 15, 2005; and by SCO 1614 effective October 15, 2006)

Annotations

Cases

Where police officers could lawfully arrest defendants without a warrant pursuant to AS 12.25.030 (3), the arrests could he validated without reliance on the validity of warrants issued for their arrest and it was unnecessary to pass upon the constitutional sufficiency of the complaints for determining the existence of probable cause. **Merrill v. State,** Op. No. 392, 423 P2d 686 (Alaska 1967).

When valid arrest was made without a warrant, a complaint showing only the essential elements of the offense was sufficient. **Drahosh v. State,** Op. No. 485, 442 P2d 42 (Alaska 1968).

Where arrest is valid, it is not required that probable cause be shown on the face of the complaint as a prerequisite to issuance of a summons. **Kristich v. State,** Op. No. 1264, 550 P2d 796 (Alaska 1976).

A Uniform Summons and Complaint that was served on defendant but was never sworn to nor filed with the court never became a lawful complaint. **Ahmaogak v. State,** Op. No. 4171, 595 P2d 985 (Alaska 1979).

SAMPLE FIRST PAGE OF CRIMINAL COMPLAINT

IN THE DISTRICT COURT FOR THE STATE OF ALASKA
AT ANCHORAGE

STATE OF ALASKA,	)
Plaintiff,	)
	)
vs.	)
	)
JOHN CLIFFORD DOE,	) Case Number:* _________
DOB: 05-17-72	)
APSIN: 1231231	)
DL: 0630722 [state/CDL]	)
ATN: 123456789	)
	)
JAMES B. SMITH,	) Case Number:* _________
DOB: 02-15-79	)
APSIN: 2342342	)
DL: 7783432 [state/CDL]	)
ATN: 987654321	)
Defendants.	)
________________________________	)

Related Search Warrants: ___________

COMPLAINT

[Insert Victim Information pursuant to Criminal Rule 44(f)]

Count I - AS 11.41.500(a)(1)
Robbery I - Armed w/Deadly Weapon
John Doe - 001
James Smith - 005

Count II - AS 11.61.195(a)(1)
Misconduct w/Weapons 2 - Re Drug Crime
James Smith - 004

THE DISTRICT ATTORNEY CHARGES: [text]

* *NOTE: Alternatively, the Case Number may be printed directly below the case caption on the left side of the page*

Rule 4. Warrant or Summons Upon Complaint.

(a) **Issuance.**

(1) *Probable Cause.* A warrant or summons shall be issued by a judge or magistrate only if it appears from the complaint, or from an affidavit or affidavits filed with the complaint, that there is probable cause to believe that an offense has been committed and that the defendant has committed it.

(2) *Summons.* A summons shall be issued in all cases unless the judge or magistrate has reason to believe that the defendant will not appear in response to a summons or that the defendant poses a danger to other persons and the community.

No warrant shall issue where bail has previously been established in that case except upon a showing that conditions of release have been violated, that a warrant is necessary to assure the presence of the defendant in court, or that the defendant poses a danger to other persons and the community. In any case in which it is lawful for an officer to arrest a person without a warrant, the officer may give the person a summons instead of arresting the person.

(3) *Failure of Defendant to Appear After Summons.* If a defendant who has been duly summoned fails to appear or if there is reasonable cause to believe that the defendant will fail to appear, a warrant of arrest shall issue; provided that in the case of a defendant charged with a minor offense as defined in Rule 8, District Court Rules of Criminal Procedure, additional summons may issue in lieu of a warrant of arrest. If a defendant corporation fails to appear after having been duly summoned, a plea of not guilty shall be entered by the court if the court is empowered to try the offense for which the summons was issued and the court may proceed to trial and judgment without further process. If the court is not so empowered it shall proceed as though the defendant has appeared.

(4) *Additional Warrants or Summonses.* More than one warrant or summons may issue on the same complaint.

(b) **Form and Contents.**

(1) *Warrant.* The warrant shall be signed by the judge or magistrate, or by a clerk directed to do so on the record. The warrant shall contain the name of the defendant or, if the defendant's name is unknown, any name or description by which the defendant can be identified with reasonable certainty, and shall describe the offense charged in the complaint. The warrant shall be directed to any peace officer or other person authorized by law to execute the warrant and shall command that the defendant be arrested and brought before the nearest available judge or magistrate without unnecessary delay. The judge or magistrate shall endorse the amount of bail upon the warrant.

(2) *Summons.* The summons shall be signed by the judge or magistrate or by a clerk directed to do so on the record. The summons shall be in the same form as the warrant, except that it shall summon the defendant to appear before a judge or magistrate at the time and place stated therein, and shall inform the defendant that if the defendant fails to appear a warrant will issue for the defendant's arrest.

(c) **Execution or Service and Return.**

(1) *By Whom.* The warrant shall be executed by any peace officer or other officer authorized by law. The summons may be served by any peace officer or by any other person authorized to serve a summons in a civil action.

(2) *Territorial Limits.* The warrant may be executed or the summons may be served at any place within the jurisdiction of the State of Alaska.

(3) *Manner.* The warrant shall be executed by the arrest of the defendant. The officer need not possess the warrant at the time of the arrest, but upon request shall show the warrant to the defendant as soon as possible. If the officer does not possess the warrant at the time of the arrest, the officer shall then inform the defendant of the offense charged and of the fact that a warrant has been issued. The summons shall be served upon the defendant by delivering a copy to the defendant personally, or by leaving it at the defendant's dwelling house or usual place of abode with some person of suitable age and discretion then residing therein or in any other manner provided for service of process in civil actions.

(4) *Return.* The officer executing the warrant shall make return thereof to the judge or magistrate before whom the defendant is brought pursuant to Rule 5. At the request of the prosecuting attorney any unexecuted warrant shall be returned to the judge or magistrate by whom it was issued and shall be canceled by the judge or magistrate. On or before the return day, the person who served the summons shall make return thereof to the judge or magistrate before whom the summons is returnable. At any time while the complaint is pending and upon the request of the prosecuting attorney, any unexecuted and uncancelled warrant or unserved original or duplicate summons shall be re-executed or re-served.

(Adopted by SCO 4 October 4, 1959; amended by SCO 98 effective September 16, 1968; by SCO 127 effective April 29, 1971; by SCO 157 effective February 15, 1973; by SCO 224 effective December 15, 1975; by SCO 517 effective October 1, 1982; by SCO 650 effective July 1, 1985; by SCO 904 effective January 15, 1989; by SCO 1100 effective January 15, 1993; and by SCO 1153 effective July 15, 1994)

Annotations

Cases

Where police officers could lawfully arrest defendants without a warrant pursuant to AS 12.25.030(3), the arrests could be validated without reliance on the validity of warrants issued for their arrest and it was unnecessary to pass upon the constitutional sufficiency of the complaints for determining the existence of probable cause. **Merrill v. State,** Op. No. 392, 423 P2d 686 (Alaska 1967).

Complaint must set forth a basis for probable cause so as to support a legal warrant for arrest. **Merrill v. State,** Op. No. 392, 423 P2d 686 (Alaska 1967).

The prosecution of traffic violations or infractions are quasi-criminal proceedings to which the rules of criminal procedure, including Criminal Rule 4(a) (3), apply. **State v. Clayton,** Op. No. 1734, 584 P2d 1111 (Alaska

1978).

The context of Alaska R. Crim. P. 4(c)(1) indicates that the rule's purpose is to define authority—not to impose a duty—to execute warrants and to serve civil summons. Rule 4 allows any peace officer or any other authorized person to serve a summons but allows only the police or other authorized officers to execute a warrant. Thus, Alaska R. Crim. P. 4 does not impose a duty to arrest on the police. **Wongittilin v. State,** Op. No. 5509,36 P3d 678 (Alaska 2001).

Rule 5. Proceedings Before the Judge or Magistrate.

(a) **Appearance Before Judge or Magistrate.**

(1) Except when the person arrested is issued a citation for a misdemeanor or a violation and immediately thereafter released, the arrested person shall be taken before the nearest available judge or magistrate without unnecessary delay. This appearance may be accomplished by the use of telephonic or television equipment pursuant to Criminal Rules 38.1 and 38.2. Unnecessary delay within the meaning of this paragraph (a) is defined as a period not to exceed twenty-four hours after arrest, including Sundays and holidays.

(2) If

(i) The judge or magistrate commits the arrested person to jail for a purpose other than to serve a sentence, and

(ii) The jail is situated in a different community from the place where the judge or magistrate committed the arrested person to jail, and

(iii) The arrested person is not represented by counsel, and

(iv) The arrested person has not previously had a bail review, and

(v) The arrested person has no date, time and place established for his or her next court appearance,

then the arrested person shall be taken before a judge or magistrate in the community where the jail is located within twenty-four hours of the person's detention in that jail

(aa) in order for bail to be reviewed, and

(bb) in order to determine if the person is represented by counsel, and

(cc) in order for the counsel to be appointed, if appropriate.

(3) The responsibility for ensuring that the arrested person is taken before a judge or magistrate as specified in subsections (1) and (2) of this section (a) shall be borne equally by

(i) municipal police officers and municipal jail personnel, and by

(ii) state troopers, state jail personnel, and all other peace officers.

No distinction shall be drawn between cases in which arrest was made pursuant to a warrant and cases in which arrest was made without a warrant.

(4) Whenever the person arrested is taken for examination before a judge or magistrate other than the one who issued the warrant, the complaint and any other statement or deposition on which the warrant was granted must be furnished to the defendant and must be communicated to the judge or magistrate before whom the person arrested appears.

(5) Whenever a person arrested without a warrant is brought before a judge or magistrate, a complaint shall be filed forthwith.

(6) Judges and magistrates shall be available at all times to receive bail, and each judge and magistrate individually shall have authority to delegate this duty to the person admitting the defendant to jail, or to such other person as shall in the determination of a judge or magistrate be qualified for this purpose.

(b) **Rights of Prisoner to Communicate with Attorney or Other Person.** Immediately after arrest, the prisoner shall have the right forthwith to telephone or otherwise to communicate with both an attorney and any relative or friend. Any attorney at law entitled to practice in the courts of Alaska, at the request of either the prisoner or any relative or friend of the prisoner, shall have the right forthwith to visit the prisoner in private. This paragraph does not provide a prisoner with the right to initiate communication or attempt to initiate communication under circumstances proscribed under AS 11.56.755.

(c) **Statement by Judge or Magistrate—Right to Counsel—Bail.** The judge or magistrate

(1) shall inform the defendant of the complaint and of any affidavit filed therewith, and

(2) shall require that a copy of the complaint and of any affidavit filed therewith be delivered to the defendant if this has not already been done, and

(3) shall inform the defendant

(i) of the right to retain counsel, and

(ii) of the right to request the assignment of counsel if the defendant is unable to obtain counsel, and

(iii) of the right to have a preliminary examination, and

(4) shall inform the defendant that the defendant is not required to make a statement and that any statement may be used against the defendant. The judge or magistrate shall allow the defendant reasonable time and opportunity to consult counsel and shall admit the defendant to bail as provided by law and by these rules.

(d) **Initial Determination of Probable Cause.**

(1) If the defendant was arrested without a warrant, the

judicial officer at the first appearance shall determine whether the arrest was made with probable cause to believe that an offense had been committed and that the defendant had committed it. This determination shall be made from the complaint, from an affidavit or affidavits filed with the complaint, or from an oral statement under oath of the arresting officer or other person which is recorded by the judicial officer. The determination shall be noted in the file.

(2) If the defendant was arrested on a warrant for a failure to appear at a prior proceeding, the court shall determine from the file whether the defendant's initial arrest was pursuant to a warrant and, if not, whether at a prior proceeding the court made an initial determination of probable cause as required by subparagraph (d)(1). If there has been no judicial determination of probable cause, the court shall proceed as under subparagraph (d)(1).

(3) If probable cause is not shown, the judicial officer shall discharge the defendant.

(e) **Felonies.**

(1) If the charge against the defendant is a felony, the defendant shall not be called upon to plead.

(2) The judicial officer shall inform the defendant of the right to a preliminary examination. A defendant is entitled to a preliminary examination if the defendant is charged with a felony for which the defendant has not been indicted, unless

(A) the defendant waives the preliminary examination, or

(B) an information has been filed against the defendant with the defendant's consent in the superior court.

(3) If the defendant after having had the opportunity to consult with counsel waives preliminary examination, the judicial officer shall forthwith hold the defendant to answer in the superior court.

(4) If the defendant does not waive preliminary examination, the judicial officer shall schedule a preliminary examination. Such examination shall be held within a reasonable time, but in no event later than

(A) 10 days following the initial appearance, if the defendant is in custody, or

(B) 20 days following the initial appearance, if the defendant is not in custody.

With the consent of the defendant and upon a showing of good cause, taking into account the public interest in prompt disposition of criminal cases, the judicial officer may extend the time limits specified in this subsection one or more times. In the absence of consent by the defendant, the judicial officer may extend these time limits only upon a showing that extraordinary circumstances exist and that delay is indispensable to the interest of justice.

(f) **Misdemeanors.**

(1) The judicial officer shall ask the defendant to enter a plea pursuant to Criminal Rule 11.

(2) If the defendant pleads not guilty, the court shall fix a date for trial at such time as will afford the defendant a reasonable opportunity to prepare.

(Adopted by SCO 4 October 4, 1959; amended by SCO 98 effective September 16, 1968; by SCO 157 effective February 15, 1973, by SCO 165 dated June 25, 1973 and by directive from the Clerk of the Court dated June 28, 1973; renumbered by Amendment No. 3 to SCO 157 effective February 15, 1973; by SCO 427 effective August 1, 1980; by SCO 458 effective May 1, 1981; and by SCO 719 effective August 1, 1986; by SCO 723 effective December 15, 1986; by SCO 1153 effective July 15, 1994; by SCO 1189 effective July 15, 1995; and by SCO 1339, effective June 13, 1998)

Note to SCO 1339: Criminal Rule 5(b) was amended by § 17 ch. 86 SLA 1998 to make it clear that the rule does not give a prisoner the right to contact a victim or witness in violation of AS 11.56.755. Section 1 of this order is adopted for the sole reason that the legislature has mandated the amendment.

Cross References

(a) **CROSS REFERENCE:** AS 12.25.150

(b) **CROSS REFERENCE:** AS 12.25.150

(c) **CROSS REFERENCE: AS 12.30.010**

Annotations

Cases

I. In General.
II. Initial Appearance.
III. Preliminary Examination.

I. In General.

When a person is arrested for operating a motor vehicle in violation of state or local drunken driving ordinances and requests to contact an attorney, he must be afforded a reasonable opportunity to do so before being required to decide whether or not to submit to a breathalyzer test, and if that opportunity is denied, subsequent evidence, whether in the form of the test results or the refusal to submit to it, are inadmissible at trial. **Copelin v. State,** Op. No. 2617, 659 P2d 1206 (Alaska 1983).

The holding in **Copelin v. State,** 659 P2d 1206 (Alaska 1983), that drunk driving arrestees must be afforded a reasonable opportunity to contact an attorney before taking or refusing to take a breathalyzer test, is applicable to all cases pending in the trial court or on direct review at the time it was decided, February 18, 1983. **Yerrington v. Anchorage,** Op. No. 326, 675 P2d 649 (Alaska App. 1983).

Defendant, charged with drunk driving, was deprived of his right to a reasonable opportunity to speak privately with counsel when, during defendant's telephone conversation with an attorney, a police officer stood next to defendant and took notes on the conversation despite objections by both defendant and the attorney; accordingly, all evidence subsequently obtained by police from defendant, including his refusal to take a breathalyzer test and a videotape of his conduct, was suppressed. **Farrell v. Municipality of Anchorage,** Op. No. 386, 682 P2d 1128 (Alaska App. 1984).

Where defendant upon being arrested for drunk driving was given the opportunity to consult on the telephone with his attorney, the police were under no duty to delay administration of the breathalyzer examination until the attorney could be present, regardless of how short a period that might be. **Municipality of Anchorage v. Marrs,** Op. No. 440, 694 P2d 1163 (Alaska App. 1985).

Although police officers did not guarantee arrestee complete privacy in telephone conversation with his attorney, his right to contact and consult with an attorney was not violated. **Municipality of Anchorage v. Marrs,** Op. No. 440, 694 P2d 1163 (Alaska App. 1985).

Where drunk-driving defendant had been given a reasonable opportunity to contact an attorney and had spoken with one, the prosecution was under no burden to show that the police acted reasonably in denying defendant's request to make a second call to an attorney prior to making a decision whether to take the breathalyzer test. **Romo v. Municipality of Anchorage,** Op. No. 457, 697 P2d 1065 (Alaska App. 1985).

Drunk driving defendant's argument that after he became dissatisfied with the public defender he had agreed to speak with, he should have been permitted another opportunity to contact counsel prior to deciding whether to take the breathalyzer test was foreclosed on the record because defendant never requested a specific attorney or even asked to see a phone book. **Pappas v. Municipality of Anchorage,** Op. No. 470, 698 P2d 1236 (Alaska App. 1985).

It is only when the totality of the arrestee's words constitute a request, express or implied, to contact counsel for the purpose of discussing a breathalyzer examination that an opportunity to consult counsel must be provided prior to administration of the breathalyzer. **Van Wormer v. State,** Op. No. 473, 699 P2d 895 (Alaska App. 1985).

Defendant's statements regarding having someone present during administration of breathalyzer examination were properly construed as not being a request to consult with an attorney, but rather as relating to having someone present to observe the test to insure its validity. **Van Wormer v. State,** Op. No. 473, 699 P2d 895 (Alaska App. 1985).

Since troopers had no duty to inform DWI arrestee of a right to consult counsel prior to taking field sobriety tests, they also had no duty to inform her of the availability of the public defender agency or the number at which a public defender could be reached. **Anderson v. State,** Op. No. 585, 713 P2d 1220 (Alaska App. 1986).

Defendant's waiver of his right to counsel prior to pleading guilty to a DWI charge was valid where the magistrate advised him of the maximum and minimum penalties for the offense and after he responded affirmatively to the question: "Do you know what a lawyer is?." **Tobuk v. State,** Op. No. 683, 732 P2d 1099 (Alaska App. 1987).

Where no reason is given by a DWI arrestee for a request to contact a friend or a relative, the police may defer the request until the process of administering the Intoximeter test has been completed. **Zsupnik v. State,** Op. No. 934, 772 P2d 1098 (Alaska App. 1989).

Where DWI arrestee was given an opportunity to talk by phone with his attorney, after which he took an intoximeter test, he had no right to again call his attorney prior to deciding whether to have an independent blood test done. **Babb v. Municipality of Anchorage,** Op. No. 1138, 813 P2d 312 (Alaska App. 1991).

Unsolicited, voluntary statement made by defendant to magistrate at bail hearing was admissible against him at trial even though magistrate did not fully advise defendant of his rights as set out in this rule. **Brandon v. State,** Op. No. 1251, 839 P2d 400 (Alaska App. 1992).

Reasonable post-arrest interrogation of an arrestee does not constitute "unnecessary delay" for purposes of this rule which requires arrested person to the taken before nearest available magistrate without unnecessary delay. **Riney v. State,** Op. No. 1523, 935 P2d 828 (Alaska App. 1997).

State trooper's failure to read "attorneys" section of Yellow Pages to drunk driving arrestee who did not have his reading glasses did not violate arrestee's right to reasonable opportunity to consult with counsel before deciding whether to submit to breathalyzer test. **Saltz v. State, Dept. of Public Safety,** Op. No. 4860, 942 P2d 1151 (Alaska 1997).

The provisions of this rule and Criminal Rule 5.1 that a defendant must be advised of the right to counsel at arraignment and has the right to counsel at a preliminary examination, implement the constitutional right to counsel and do not supersede it. **Gladden v. State,** Op. No. 9429, 153 P.3d 1028 (Alaska App. 2007).

II. Initial Appearance.

A defendant's confession to having set a fatal fire is not inadmissible as having been given during a period of unlawful detention where the defendant has been arrested for and convicted of driving while intoxicated and is interrogated during his detention for that offense, although he is not arraigned on arson and homicide charges within 24 hours after his arrest. **Thessen v. State,** Op. No. 555, 454 P2d 341 (Alaska 1969).

If a defendant is legally detained on conviction of crime, and the police would not have had probable cause to arrest him for a second crime had he been free, he may be questioned while in custody and his statement may be obtained as to the second crime, although he is not brought before a magistrate on the charge of the second crime within 24 hours of the arrest. **Thessen v. State,** Op. No. 555, 454 P2d 341 (Alaska 1969).

Although he may not deny bail to an accused prior to conviction, the trial judge can consider the danger to the community as a factor in assessing the amount of bail or fixing the terms of a conditional release. **Gilbert v. State,** Op. No. 1190, 540 P2d 485 (Alaska 1975).

That defendant's statement might have been product of prearraignment delay did not require mistrial in trial to court where admission was harmless error and issue was not raised until guilt had been found. **Scharver v. State,** Op. No. 1397, 561 P2d 300 (Alaska 1977).

Initial appearance required by Rule 5(a) is not a "critical stage" requiring the assistance of counsel. **Padgett v. State,** Op. No. 1801, 590 P2d 432 (Alaska 1979).

III. Preliminary Examination.

There is no constitutional requirement for holding of a preliminary hearing after an indictment has been returned on the same charges. **Martinez v. State,** Op. No. 389, 423 P2d 700 (Alaska 1967).

Sixteen days was not an unreasonable delay under this rule as formerly written where the charge was first degree murder and the defendant was without counsel and desired to procure counsel and the state needed time to prepare its case. **Martinez v. State,** Op. No. 389, 423 P2d 700 (Alaska 1967).

It must be determined by considering the facts in each case in the light of legitimate needs of the accused and of the state and of the nature of the charge whether the preliminary hearing was set within a "reasonable time." **Martinez v. State,** Op. No. 389, 423 P2d 700 (Alaska 1967).

After return of an indictment on his case, the accused was not deprived of a constitutional right by denial of demand for a preliminary hearing. **Maze v. State,** Op. No. 400, 425 P2d 235 (Alaska 1967).

Inasmuch as Criminal Rule 6(k) [now Criminal Rule 6(q)] subjects the grand jury to a more strict standard of finding an indictment than the standard of "sufficient cause" required under Criminal Rule 5(d)(5) [now Criminal Rule 5.1] for the district judge to hold the accused to answer, appellant's rights under article I of the Alaska Constitution were not violated by denial of a demand for preliminary hearing after return of indictment. **Maze v. State,** Op. No. 400, 425 P2d 235 (Alaska 1967).

Rule 5.1. Preliminary Examination.

(a) **Representation by Counsel.** The defendant is entitled to be represented by counsel. If the defendant cannot secure counsel, counsel shall be appointed for the defendant.

(b) **Order of Proof—Witnesses Called by the State.** The state shall first present the evidence in support of its case. All witnesses called by the state shall be examined in the presence of the defendant and may be cross-examined by the defendant's or by the defendant's counsel.

(c) **Witnesses Called by the Defendant.** The defendant may produce and examine witnesses on the defendant's behalf. All witnesses, including the defendant should the defendant choose to testify, may be cross-examined. The production of witnesses shall be governed by Rule 17, so far as it is applicable.

(d) **Evidence.** At the preliminary examination, the admissibility of evidence other than written reports of experts shall be governed by the Alaska Rules of Evidence. Rulings pertaining to the admissibility of evidence shall not be binding upon any subsequent judicial proceeding.

(e) **Telephonic Testimony.**

(1) A witness may participate telephonically if the witness:

(A) would be required to travel more than 50 miles to court; or

(B) lives in a place from which people customarily travel by air to the court.

(2) A witness who is not entitled to participate telephonically under subparagraph (1) may participate telephonically with approval of the court.

(f) **Record.** The proceedings shall be electronically recorded.

(g) **Exclusion of Witnesses.** At the request of either party, the judge or magistrate shall exclude from the courtroom any witness of an adverse party, if at the time of the request the witness is not under examination.

(h) **Discharge of the Defendant.** If from the evidence, it appears that

(1) there is no probable cause to believe that an offense has been committed, or

(2) if there is probable cause to believe that an offense has been committed, but no probable cause to believe that defendant committed the offense, then the judge or magistrate shall dismiss the complaint and discharge the defendant. The discharge of the defendant shall not preclude the state from instituting a subsequent prosecution for the same offense.

(i) **Commitment of Defendant.** If from the evidence it appears that there is probable cause to believe that an offense has been committed and that the defendant committed it, the judge or magistrate shall enter an order holding the defendant to answer to the charge and committing the defendant to proper custody. The judge or magistrate shall admit the defendant to bail as provided by law and by these rules.

(j) **Records.** When a judge or magistrate has held a defendant to answer, the judge or magistrate shall transmit to the clerk of the superior court of the judicial district in which the offense is triable all papers in the proceedings, any bail taken by the judge or magistrate, and all exhibits introduced at the examination.

(k) **Counsel for Complaining Witness—Counsel for Prosecution.** A complaining witness may be represented by counsel at every stage of the preliminary hearing. The attorney general or some attorney authorized to act for the attorney general may appear on behalf of the State of Alaska and control the conduct of the prosecution.

(Added by SCO 157 effective February 15, 1973; amended by SCO 368 effective August 1, 1979; by SCO 1153 effective July 15, 1994; and by SCO 1460 effective October 15, 2003)

Annotations

Cases

The main purpose of a preliminary hearing is to determine whether there is a sufficient basis for holding the accused until the grand jury has reviewed the facts and after an indictment has been returned no further reason for conducting a hearing for the purpose of determining probable cause exists. **Martinez v. State,** Op. No. 389, 423 P2d 700 (Alaska 1967).

The fact that an error of the district judge in a preliminary hearing which error had not affected the character of the trial the defendants were accorded and which did not, on the record, prejudice or disadvantage defendants, did not result in a reversal of convictions must not be taken to indicate that violations of the requirements of this rule will be readily condoned. **Merrill v. State,** Op. No. 392, 423 P2d 686 (Alaska 1967).

In the light of the character of proceedings provided under Criminal Rule 5(d) as formerly written a preliminary hearing under this provision was not a "critical stage" of the criminal proceedings and failure to appoint counsel for defendants at this hearing was no error. **Merrill v. State,** Op. No. 392, 423 P2d 686 (Alaska 1967).

The constitutional right of an accused to be confronted with the witnesses against him was not denied to defendants in a criminal case where they had requested that two police officers be summoned for examination at the preliminary hearing which request was denied by the district judge but where subsequent to indictment the superior court pursuant to a motion for stay and to agreement by counsel ordered a further preliminary hearing wherein defendants may be represented by their appointed counsel and may examine the officers and where no transcript of any testimony of either of the two officers was introduced into evidence at the trial. **Merrill v. State,** Op. No. 392, 423 P2d 686 (Alaska 1967).

District judge's ruling which denied request of defendants to subpoena police officers who were complainants against the defendants was error but on the record demonstrating that the defendants were subsequently afforded an opportunity to examine these officers at a second hearing held pursuant to order of the superior court and that no transcript of the depositions of these officers was introduced in the trial, defendants were not significantly prejudiced and reversal was not warranted. **Merrill v. State,** Op. No. 392, 423 P2d 686 (Alaska 1967).

Where after return of indictment the superior court pursuant to an agreement by respective counsel had ordered that a second preliminary hearing be held "as if prior to return of indictment," no error was committed when defendants were denied the opportunity to examine witnesses as to their testimony before the grand jury. **Merrill v. State,** Op. No. 392, 423 P2d 686 (Alaska 1967).

It is not a principal function of a preliminary hearing to provide pretrial discovery. **Martinez v. State,** Op. No. 389, 423 P2d 700 (Alaska 1967).

Defendant has no right to demand that prosecution present its case at scheduled preliminary hearing when state elects to take matter to grand jury hearing. **Buchanan v. State,** Op. No. 2553, 554 P2d 1153 (Alaska 1976).

State is under no obligation to present any evidence at a preliminary hearing when an indictment is being sought but has not been returned. **Buchanan v. State,** Op. No. 2553, 554 P2d 1153 (Alaska 1976).

The right to counsel set forth in Criminal Rule 5.1(a) is also guaranteed by the United States Constitution, hence violation of that right is reversible error unless it was harmless beyond a reasonable doubt. **Gipson v. State,** 575 P.2d 782 (Alaska 1978).

The provisions of this rule and Criminal Rule 5 that a defendant must be advised of the right to counsel at arraignment and has the right to counsel at a preliminary examination, implement the constitutional right to counsel and do not supersede it. **Gladden v. State**, Op. No. 9429, 153 P.3d 1028 (Alaska App. 2007).

PART III. INDICTMENT AND INFORMATION

Rule 6. The Grand Jury.

(a) **By Whom Convened.** The presiding superior court judge of the judicial district encompassing the grand jury location specified in section (b) shall convene the grand jury.

(b) **Where Grand Juries Shall Be Convened.** The grand jury shall be convened at the superior court location shown in the following table, based on the superior court venue district in which the matter under investigation occurred. The superior court venue districts are defined in the Criminal Rule 18 venue map.

Superior Court Venue District in which the matter under investigation occurred	Location at which the grand jury will be convened
Anchorage	Anchorage
Barrow	Barrow
Bethel	Bethel
Cordova	Anchorage or Palmer
Craig	Juneau, Ketchikan, or Sitka
Delta Junction	Fairbanks
Dillingham	Dillingham or Anchorage
Fairbanks	Fairbanks
Glennallen	Anchorage or Palmer
Homer	Kenai
Juneau	Juneau, Sitka, or Ketchikan
Kenai	Kenai
Ketchikan	Ketchikan, Sitka, or Juneau
Kodiak	Kodiak
Kotzebue	Kotzebue
Naknek	Anchorage
Nome	Nome
Palmer	Palmer
Petersburg	Juneau, Ketchikan, or Sitka
Seward	Kenai
Sitka	Sitka, Juneau, or Ketchikan
Tok	Fairbanks
Unalaska	Anchorage
Valdez	Anchorage or Palmer
Wrangell	Juneau, Ketchikan, or Sitka

The presiding judge of a judicial district shall be empowered to call a special jury to be convened at a site other than the site designated in this subsection if the presiding judge determines that the designation of a special site is necessary in the interest of justice.

(c) **Selection of Prospective Grand Jurors.** Prospective grand jurors shall have the qualifications and shall be drawn and selected as set forth by law, with the additional provisions:

(1) prospective grand jurors shall be selected from the population within a fifty-mile radius of the place where the grand jury is convened, and

(2) the presiding judge of the superior court may with the approval of the administrative director select prospective grand jurors at large from the judicial district in which the matter under investigation occurred.

(d) **Summoning Grand Jurors.** At least once each year the presiding judge of the superior court in each judicial district shall order one or more grand juries to be convened at such times as the public interest requires. The grand jury shall consist of not less than 12 nor more than 18 members. The court shall direct that a sufficient number of legally qualified persons be summoned to meet this requirement. Any qualified member of the grand jury panel not designated to serve as a member of the grand jury may be placed on the petit jury panel. An otherwise qualified person called for petit jury service may be placed on the grand jury panel. A grand jury shall serve until discharged by the presiding judge but no grand jury may serve more than 4 months, unless this period is extended for good cause.

(e) **Swearing and Instructing Jurors.**

(1) The following oath shall be administered by the clerk of the superior court to the persons selected for grand jury duty:

"You and each of you as members of this grand jury for the State of Alaska, do solemnly swear that you will diligently inquire and true presentment make of all such matters as shall be given to you for consideration, or shall otherwise come to your knowledge in connection with your present service; that you will preserve the secrecy required by law as to all proceedings had before you; that you will present no one through envy, hatred or malice, or leave any one unpresented through fear, affection, gain, reward, or hope thereof; but that you will present all things truly and impartially as they shall come to your knowledge according to the best of your understanding, so help you God."

(2) When the grand jury is sworn, the court shall charge the jury with written instructions, which the court deems proper, concerning the powers and duties of the grand jury.

(f) **Alternate Jurors.** The presiding judge may direct that alternate jurors be designated at the time a grand jury is selected. Alternate jurors in the order in which they were designated may thereafter be impaneled as provided in paragraph (s) of this rule. Alternate jurors shall be drawn in the same manner and shall have the same qualifications as the regular jurors, and if impaneled shall be subject to the same challenges, shall take the same oath and shall have the same functions, powers, facilities and privileges as the regular jurors.

(g) **Objections to Grand Jury and to Grand Jurors.** A motion to dismiss the indictment or to expunge a report of the grand jury may be based upon objections to the array or the lack of legal qualification of an individual juror, if not previously determined upon challenge. An indictment shall not be dismissed nor a report expunged upon the ground that one or more members of the grand jury were not legally qualified if it appears from the record kept pursuant to paragraph (h) of this rule that a majority of the total number of grand jurors comprising the grand jury when the grand jury is sworn and charged with instructions, after deducting the number not legally qualified, concurred in finding the indictment or making the report.

(h) **Foreperson and Deputy Foreperson.** The presiding judge shall appoint one of the jurors to be foreperson and another to be deputy foreperson. The foreperson shall have power to administer oaths and affirmations and shall sign all indictments and reports. The foreperson or another juror designated by the foreperson shall keep a record of the number of jurors concurring in the finding of every indictment and the issuance of every report and shall file the record with the clerk of the court, but the record shall not be made public except on order of the presiding judge. During the absence of the foreperson, the deputy foreperson shall act as foreperson.

(i) **Preparing Indictments and Presentments.** The prosecuting attorney shall prepare all indictments and presentments for the grand jury, and shall attend their sittings to advise them of their duties and to examine witnesses in their presence.

(j) **Record of Proceedings.** All proceedings before the grand jury, including the testimony of witnesses and any statements made by the prosecuting attorney or by any of the jurors, shall be electronically recorded.

(k) **Who May Be Present.** The prosecuting attorney, the witness under examination, interpreters when needed, and a deputy clerk of the court for the purpose of recording the proceedings may be present while the grand jury is in session. No persons other than the jurors and any interpreter necessary to assist a juror who is hearing or speech impaired shall be present while the grand jury is deliberating or voting.

(*l*) **Secrecy of Proceedings and Disclosure.**

(1) The selection, swearing, and charging of grand jurors and all matters occurring before the grand jury are secret, except as otherwise provided by this rule. Disclosure of matters, other than the grand jury's deliberations and the vote of any juror, may be made to the prosecuting attorney for use in the performance of the prosecuting attorneys' duties. Otherwise a judge, juror, attorney, interpreter, court clerk or stenographer, or a typist who transcribes recorded testimony may disclose matters only when so directed by the court preliminary to or in connection with a judicial or administrative proceeding.

(2) The returns of indictments to the superior court are public proceedings, unless the court directs that the proceedings be closed to the public and the indictment kept secret until the defendant is in custody or has given bail. In that event, the clerk shall seal the indictment and no person shall disclose the finding of the indictment except when necessary for the issuance and execution of a warrant or summons.

(3) No obligation of secrecy may be imposed upon any person except in accordance with this rule.

(m) **Availability of Grand Jury Record to Defendant.** Upon request, a defendant shall be entitled to listen to the electronic recording of the grand jury proceedings and inspect all exhibits presented to the grand jury. Upon further request the defendant may obtain a transcript of such proceedings and copies of such exhibits. The trial of the case shall not be delayed because of the failure of a defendant to request the transcript. The availability of a grand jury report is governed by Criminal Rule 6.1.

(n) **Finding and Return of Indictment.**

(1) An indictment may be found only upon the concurrence of a majority of the total number of jurors comprising the grand jury when the grand jury is sworn and charged with instructions, after deducting the number not legally qualified.

(2) If an indictment is not found, the indictment shall be endorsed "not a true bill" and signed by the foreperson. If an indictment is found, the indictment shall be endorsed "a true bill" and signed by the foreperson.

(3) (i) If an indictment is endorsed "a true bill," the indictment shall be presented in open court and filed with the clerk where it shall be open to public inspection.

(ii) If an indictment is endorsed "not a true bill" and a complaint or information was previously filed in a district court, the indictment shall be presented in open court and filed with the clerk where it shall be open to public inspection.

(iii) If an indictment is endorsed "not a true bill" and no complaint or information was previously filed in district court, the indictment shall be filed with the clerk and held under seal.

(iv) The foreperson or deputy foreperson may present an indictment in open court without the presence of other grand jury members.

(4) If no indictment is found, the court shall hold the minutes, notes and record of the grand jury proceeding under seal.

(5) The return of exhibits used during the grand jury proceedings is governed by Criminal Rule 26.1(h).

(o) **Presentment.**

(1) Whenever there is doubt from the evidence presented

(i) whether the facts constitute a crime, or

(ii) whether a defendant is subject to prosecution by reason of either a lapse of time or a former acquittal or conviction, then the grand jury by a concurrence of at least five members may make a presentment of the facts of the case to the court with a request for instructions on the law.

(2) The presentment shall be made by the foreperson in the presence of the grand jury.

(3) The presentment shall not mention the names of individuals. The presentment shall not be filed with the court, nor shall it be kept by the court beyond the time that the grand jury is discharged.

(4) When the presentment is made the court shall give such instructions on the law as it considers necessary.

(p) **Defense Witnesses.** Although the grand jury has no duty to hear evidence on the behalf of the defendant, it may do so.

(q) **Sufficiency of Evidence.** When the grand jury has reason to believe that other available evidence will explain away the charge, it shall order such evidence to be produced and for that purpose may require the prosecuting attorney to subpoena witnesses. An indictment shall not be found nor a presentment made upon the statement of a grand juror unless such grand juror is sworn and examined as a witness. The grand jury shall find an indictment when all the evidence taken together, if unexplained or uncontradicted, would warrant a conviction of the defendant.

(r) **Admissibility of Evidence.**

(1) Evidence which would be legally admissible at trial shall be admissible before the grand jury. In appropriate cases, however, witnesses may be presented to summarize admissible evidence if the admissible evidence will be available at trial. Except as stated in subparagraphs (2), (3), and (6), hearsay evidence shall not be presented to the grand jury absent compelling justification for its introduction. If hearsay evidence is presented to the grand jury, the reasons for its use shall be stated on the record.

(2) In a prosecution for an offense under AS 11.41.410—11.41.458, hearsay evidence of a statement related to the offense, not otherwise admissible, made by a child who is the victim of the offense may be admitted into evidence before the grand jury if

(i) the circumstances of the statement indicate its reliability;

(ii) the child is under 10 years of age when the hearsay evidence is sought to be admitted;

(iii) additional evidence is introduced to corroborate the statement; and

(iv) the child testifies at the grand jury proceeding or the child will be available to testify at trial.

(3) Hearsay evidence related to the offense, not otherwise admissible, may be admitted into evidence before the grand jury if

(i) the individual presenting the hearsay evidence is a peace officer involved in the investigation; and

(ii) the hearsay evidence consists of the statement and observations made by another peace officer in the course of an investigation; and

(iii) additional evidence is introduced to corroborate the statement.

(4) If the testimony presented by a peace officer under paragraph (3) of this section is inaccurate because of intentional, grossly negligent, or negligent misstatements or omissions, then the court shall dismiss an indictment resulting from the testimony if the defendant shows that the inaccuracy prejudices substantial rights of the defendant.

(5) In this section "statement" means an oral or written assertion or nonverbal conduct if the nonverbal conduct is intended as an assertion.

(6) In a prosecution for driving while intoxicated under AS 28.35.030(n) or for refusal to submit to a chemical test under AS 28.35.032(p), hearsay evidence received through the Alaska Public Safety Information Network or from other government agencies of prior convictions of driving while intoxicated or refusal to submit to a chemical test may be presented to the grand jury.

(s) **Excusing Grand Jurors.** A seated juror may be excused for a particular case, permanently excused, or temporarily excused under the following circumstances:

(1) The prosecutor shall excuse a juror for a particular case when the juror informs the prosecutor that the juror cannot be fair or impartial in deciding that case. The prosecutor may ask the presiding judge to impanel an alternate.

(2) If the prosecutor is made aware of a grand juror's potential prejudice or bias that could affect the grand jury's impartial deliberations, or if the prosecutor seeks to challenge a juror for cause, the prosecutor shall present the information as to prejudice or bias or the challenge to the presiding judge. The judge shall provide the juror with notice of the prosecutor's action and shall question the juror concerning the potential bias or challenge. After hearing from the juror, the judge may request additional information from the prosecutor, other jurors, or other sources. If potential bias or cause is shown, the judge may excuse the juror permanently or for a particular case. The judge may impanel an alternate juror in place of the juror excused. If no potential bias or cause is shown, the judge shall allow the juror to remain and may take other appropriate action.

(3) The presiding judge may excuse a juror temporarily because of illness or a personal or business matter that requires the juror's attention. The presiding judge may delegate this authority to another judicial officer.

(4) An alternate juror must be present during the presentation of all evidence related to that case in order to vote on the proposed bill.

(t) **Delegation of Duties.** Whenever a superior court is sitting other than where the presiding judge is sitting, or the presiding judge is unavailable, the presiding judge may delegate duties under this rule to another judicial officer. However, the presiding judge may delegate duties under Criminal Rule 6.1 only to another superior court judge.

(u) **Telephonic Testimony.**

(1) A witness may participate telephonically in grand jury proceedings if the witness:

(A) would be required to travel more than 50 miles to the situs of the grand jury; or

(B) lives in a place from which people customarily travel by air to the situs of the grand jury.

(2) A witness who is not entitled to participate telephonically under subparagraph (1) may participate telephonically with approval of the presiding judge of the judicial district, or the presiding judge's designee. A motion to allow telephonic testimony under this subparagraph may be ex parte and shall be accompanied by an affidavit of the prosecuting attorney that states the reason telephonic testimony is requested.

(3) If a witness participates telephonically in grand jury proceedings, after the witness is sworn, the prosecuting attorney shall require the witness to:

(A) state the location from which the witness is testifying; and

(B) verify

(i) that the witness' conversation cannot be overheard;

(ii) that no extension for the telephone from which the witness is testifying is in use; and

(iii) that the witness will notify the grand jury immediately if any person can overhear the witness' testimony or if the witness becomes aware that an extension for the telephone enters use during the testimony.

(Adopted by SCO 4 October 4, 1959; amended by SCO 30 effective February 1, 1961; by SCO 49 effective January 1, 1963; by SCO 136 dated August 27, 1971; by SCO 136A dated September 13, 1971; by Amendment No. 1 to SCO 136 dated October 17, 1972; by SCO 146 effective October 31, 1971; by Amendment No. 1 to SCO 146 effective October 31, 1971; by SCO 157 effective February 15, 1973; by SCO 216 effective October 1, 1975; by SCO 261 effective December 30, 1976; by SCO 539 effective October 1, 1982; by SCO 706 effective May 21, 1986; by SCO 711 effective September 15, 1986; by SCO 881 effective July 15, 1988; by SCO 937 effective January 15, 1989; by SCO 945 effective January 15, 1989; by SCO 956 effective July 15, 1989; by SCO 967 effective July 15, 1989; by SCO 969 effective July 15, 1989; by SCO 973 effective July 15, 1989; by SCO 991 effective January 15, 1990; by SCO 997 effective January 15, 1990; by SCO 1012 effective January 15, 1990; by SCO 1039 effective January 15, 1991; by SCO 1046 effective January 15, 1991; by SCO 1061 effective July 15, 1991; by SCO 1115 effective November 12, 1992; by SCO 1171 effective July 15, 1995; by SCO 1181 effective July 15, 1995; by SCO 1204 effective July 15, 1995; by SCO 1269 effective July 15, 1997; by SCO 1293 effective January 15, 1998; by SCO 1338 effective June 11, 1998; by SCO 1381 effective April 15, 2000; by SCO 1439 effective October 15, 2001; by SCO 1482 effective October 15, 2002; by SCO 1490 effective October 15, 2002; by SCO 1618 effective October 15, 2006; and by SCO 1646-Amended effective October 15, 2007)

Note to SCO 1269: Criminal Rule 6(r) was amended by §§ 18 & 19 ch. 143 SLA 1996 to allow certain hearsay evidence to be presented to the grand jury in a prosecution for felony DWI or felony refusal to submit to a chemical test. Section 21 of this order is adopted for the sole reason that the legislature has mandated the amendments.

Note: Subparagraphs (r)(2) and (3) of Criminal Rule 6 were added by ch. 41, §§ 1-2, SLA 1985, adopting AS 12.40.110.

Note to SCO 1204: Criminal Rules 6(r)(3) & (4) were added by ch. 114 § 2 SLA 1994. Section 4 of this order is adopted for the sole reason that the legislature has mandated the amendments.

Note to SCO 1293: Criminal Rule 6(u) was amended by §§ 20 & 25 ch. 63 SLA 1997 to eliminate the requirement that the prosecution must obtain permission from the court before a victim can testify by telephone. Section 1 of this order is adopted for the sole reason that the legislature has mandated the amendment.

Note to SCO 1338: Criminal Rule 6(r)(2) was amended by § 21 ch. 81 SLA 1998 to allow hearsay evidence of a statement made by a child to be admitted before the grand jury in a prosecution for first degree indecent exposure as well as the other sex offenses defined in AS 11.41. Section 1 of this order is adopted for the sole reason that the legislature has mandated the amendment.

Cross References

(b) **CROSS REFERENCE:** AS 12.40.030; AS 12.40.040; AS 12.40.050; AS 12.40.060

Annotations

Cases

I. Grand Jury Proceedings.
- A. In General.
- B. Selecting and Convening Grand Jury.
- C. Sufficiency of Evidence.
- D. Hearsay Testimony.
- E. Record of Proceedings.

I. Grand Jury Proceedings.

A. In General.

Indictment was not subject to dismissal where record showed that after deducting the one juror not qualified to serve as grand juror, a majority of the grand jurors had concurred in finding the indictment. **Crawford v. State,** Op. No. 312, 408 P2d 1002 (Alaska 1965).

An indictment is not defective where a grand jury foreman serves for a few months, is temporarily excused, and then resumes service a few months later. **Miller v. State,** Op. No. 589, 462 P2d 421 (Alaska 1969).

District attorney's statements to grand jury did not constitute an improper attempt to influence grand jury. **Coleman v. State,** Op. No. 1288, 553 P2d 40 (Alaska 1976).

This rule does not prohibit admission before grand jury of evidence of defendant's silence after arrest. **Coleman v. State,** Op. No. 1288, 553 P2d 40 (Alaska 1976).

Indictment need not state every element of crime since records of grand jury proceedings are available to defendant. **Peterson v. State,** Op. No. 1411, 562 P2d 1350 (Alaska 1977).

Grand jury's determination that it would not hear defendant did not invalidate the indictment. **Webb v. State,** Op. No. 1638, 580 P2d 295 (Alaska 1978).

This rule imposes on the prosecutor a duty to disclose exculpatory evidence to the grand jury. **Frink v. State,** Op. No. 1870, 597 P2d 154 (Alaska 1979).

A peace officer testifying before a grand jury may present autopsy report of doctor and ballistics report of lab technician, and may answer questions about such reports. but the officer may not offer far-ranging opinions about how she thinks an expert would answer hypothetical questions. **Frink v. State,** Op. No. 1870, 597 P2d 154 (Alaska 1979).

A peace officer may not testify before a grand jury concerning the contents of an autopsy or lab report unless the reports are presented to the grand jury. **Frink v. State,** Op. No. 1870, 597 P2d 154 (Alaska 1979).

Prosecutor did not breach the duty imposed by this rule by not informing the grand jury in a rape case of defendant's .31 breathalyzer reading. **Mallott v. State,** Op. No. 2027, 608 P2d 737 (Alaska 1980).

An unintentional misstatement of fact to a grand jury by a police officer which was nonmaterial and which did not substantially affect the grand jury's decision to indict the defendant was not reversible error. **Keith v. State,** Op. No. 2099, 612 P2d 977 (Alaska 1980).

Fact that indictment charged defendant with theft of ripper teeth but did not allege a specific theory of theft did not deny defendant due process since liberal discovery rules permit an accused to obtain adequate discovery of the state's case and to get adequate notice of the state's theory or theories of prosecution. **Williams v. State,** Op. No. 106, 648 P2d 603 (Alaska App. 1982).

Even if taped interview of defendant in which he denied guilt would have been admissible before the grand jury as an exculpatory statement, the prosecutor's failure to present the taped interview to the jury was not error, since the interview was not substantially favorable to the defendant. **Lipscomb v. State,** Op. No. 477, 700 P2d 1298 (Alaska App. 1985).

Where the indictment read together with the grand jury transcript gave specific notice of every element of the crime charged, defendant's claim that the indictment was facially defective for failing to allege one element of the crime charged was properly rejected. **Azzarella v. State,** Op. No.490,703 P2d 1182 (Alaska App. 1985).

The duty of the state to present exculpatory evidence to the grand jury imposes only an obligation to present evidence known to the prosecutor which tends to negate guilt. **Wilkie v. State,** Op. No. 599, 715 P2d 1199 (Alaska App. 1986).

In the absence of any basis for concluding that the presence of a legal intern during the presentation of defendant's case to the grand jury determined the policy of grand jury secrecy or unduly influenced either a witness appearing before the grand jury or the grand jury itself, the indictment would not be dismissed. **Soper v. State,** Op. No. 675, 731 P2d 587 (Alaska App. 1987).

Police officer's testimony to grand jury disparaging the credibility of a statement by a potential witness was improper but harmless in light of the subsequent trial record. **Esmailka v. State,** Op. No. 721, 740 P2d 466 (Alaska App. 1987).

Where grand jury voted unanimously to indict defendant and defendant at most established bias on the part of only one member of the panel, no deprivation of his right to a fair and unbiased grand jury had been established. **Patterson v. State,** Op. No. 761, 747 P2d 535 (Alaska App. 1987).

Even if the grand jury understood the prosecutor to say that they could not issue a no true bill without asking about lesser included offenses, which seems to conflict with this rule, defendant was not prejudiced because the grand jury issued a true bill, thus trial court properly denied defendant's motion to dismiss the indictment. **Ciervo v. State,** Op. No. 813, 756 P2d 907 (Alaska App. 1988).

Presence of prosecutor's two-year-old child in grand jury room during a portion of the grand jury proceedings violated this rule but did not require dismissal of the indictment. **Boggess v. State,** Op. No. 988, 783 P2d 1173 (Alaska App. 1989).

Allowing alleged victim to testify by telephone in grand jury proceeding was not error although it would have been preferable for the prosecution to have established for the record that no one was present with the victim during her testimony in violation of the criminal rules for grand jury proceedings. **Boggess v. State,** Op. No. 988, 783 P2d 1173 (Alaska App. 1989).

Where defendant was ultimately convicted of sexual abuse of a minor in the second degree, the prosecutor's failure in the grand jury proceeding to answer the jury's question as to whether the victim had been given a physical examination, when in fact there had been a physical examination showing no evidence of sexual assault or fondling, was error, but the error was harmless, since the examination was taken several months after the alleged crime and would therefore probably not have uncovered signs of any sexual contact which did occur. **Sheldon v. State,** Op. No. 1059, 796 P2d 831 (Alaska App. 1990).

Indictment will not be dismissed for violation of rule prohibiting presence of persons other than jurors during grand jury deliberations absent showing that violation prejudiced fairness of proceedings. **Hurn v. State,** Op. No. 1340, 872 P2d 189 (Alaska App. 1994).

Trial court did not abuse its discretion in refusing to dismiss indictment because of prosecutor's alleged violation of this rule; prosecutor interrupted grand jury's deliberations to inform jurors that their voices could be heard outside jury room and then answered unsolicited request for clarification of law of self-defense. **Hurn v. State,** Op. No. 1340, 872 P2d 189 (Alaska App. 1994).

Irregularity in taking of telephonic testimony at grand jury will not invalidate ensuing indictment unless defendant shows that irregularity affected testimony heard by grand jury or affected grand jury's deliberations. **State v. Aloysius,** Op. No. 1621, 975 P2d 1096 (Alaska App. 1999).

Prosecution's failure to comply with rules governing presentation of telephonic testimony to grand jury and prosecutor's error in excusing wrong two alternate grand jurors when reducing grand jury panel to eighteen were not legally sufficient reasons for dismissing indictment. **State v. Aloysius,** Op. No. 1621, 975 P2d 1096 (Alaska App. 1999).

Rule requiring the concurrence of a majority of the grand jurors sworn in, rather than a majority of the grand jurors deliberating on the case, to indict a defendant for a crime was constitutional. **Sanford v. State,** Op. No. 1748, 24 P3d 1263 (Alaska App. 2001).

Subsection (p) of this rule imposes no additional duty on a prosecutor to apprise the grand jury of evidence favoring the defendant, even if the evidence consists of defendant's own proposed testimony. **State v. Cameron,** Op. No. 1986, 113 P.3d 687 (Alaska App. 2005).

Defendant's proposed grand jury testimony, regarding his state of mind when he threatened the victims with his rifle while they were trying to repossess his vehicle, did not, in and of itself, tend to negate defendant's guilt where he admitted to facts that constituted an assault; the question of defendant's state of mind is an issue to be left to the trial jury. **State v. Cameron,** Op. No. 1986, 113 P.3d 687 (Alaska App. 2005).

B. Selecting and Convening Grand Jury.

A member of the petit jury panel is not qualified to serve on a grand jury. **Crawford v. State,** Op. No. 312, 408 P2d 1002 (Alaska 1965).

Where grand jury was improperly constituted, but no group of citizens was systematically excluded from selection process, correction on indictment would be upheld. **Peterson v. State,** Op. No. 1411, 562 P2d 1350 (Alaska 1977).

Presiding judge's order that grand jury be convened at a place other than that specified by this rule was invalid and grand jury was improperly constituted. **Peterson v. State,** Op. No. 1411, 562 P2d 1350 (Alaska 1977).

The authority to convene a grand jury can be delegated to a judge of the district court. **Oxereok v. State,** Op. No. 2076, 611 P2d 913 (Alaska 1980).

A valid order convening a grand jury at a special site must address a specific case or specific subject for investigation and establish that factors differentiating that case or subject from typical cases warrants a special grand jury. **Nicholson v. State,** Op. No. 193, 656 P2d 1209 (Alaska App. 1982).

Fact that convening the grand jury in Anchorage rather than Kodiak cost the court system less and was more convenient for the district attorney's office did not justify the Anchorage site. **Nicholson v. State,** Op. No. 193, 656 P2d 1209 (Alaska App. 1982).

Merely showing that a cognizable group of citizens exists and that such group is underrepresented on the grand jury which returns the indictment does not warrant dismissal of the indictment. **Nicholson v. State,** Op. No. 193, 656 P2d 1209 (Alaska App. 1982).

Although grand jury which indicted defendant was improperly convened in Anchorage rather than Kodiak, dismissal of indictment was not warranted, the court rejecting defendant's argument that non-urban residents were systematically excluded from the Anchorage grand jury and that non-urban residents are a legally cognizable group. **Depp v. State,** Op. No. 390, 686 P2d 712 (Alaska App. 1984).

Even if three grand jurors were selected from beyond a 50-mile radius of the place where the grand jury was convened, the error would not require dismissal of the verdict. **Harris v. State,** Op. No. 346, 678 P2d 397 (Alaska App. 1984).

Under the circumstances of the case, individuals serving on the grand jury who had not taken the oath of office were nonetheless de facto members of the jury; therefore, their participation in the grand jury proceedings was not improper. **State v. Roark,** Op. No. 507, 705 P2d 1274 (Alaska App. 1985).

Error in excusing grand juror, which reduced number of jurors from 18 to 17, was harmless to defendant, since 10 votes were still needed to return indictment. **Gustafson v. State,** Op. No. 1298, 854 P2d 751 (Alaska App. 1993).

Where presiding judge was unavailable, another superior court judge had authority to excuse grand juror for cause. **Gustafson v. State,** Op. No. 1298, 854 P2d 751 (Alaska App. 1993).

Prosecution's failure to comply with rules governing presentation of telephonic testimony to grand jury and prosecutor's error in excusing wrong two alternate grand jurors when reducing grand jury panel to eighteen were not legally sufficient reasons for dismissing indictment. **State v. Aloysius,** Op. No. 1621, 975 P2d 1096 (Alaska App. 1999).

C. Sufficiency of Evidence.

The requirement under AS 12.45.020 of corroboration of the testimony of an accomplice is one of sufficiency rather than competency of the evidence and is inapplicable to grand jury proceedings. **Merrill v. State,** Op. No. 392, 423 P2d 686 (Alaska 1967).

Denial of motion to dismiss indictment for alleged lack of evidence was no abuse of discretion where the record showed that the victim of the robbery, an accomplice and a police officer had testified before the grand jury. **Merrill v. State,** Op. No. 392, 423 P2d 686 (Alaska 1967).

Where record indicated that sufficient competent evidence was presented to the grand jury, mere presence of same illegally seized evidence would not invalidate indictment. **Merrill v. State,** Op. No. 392, 423 P2d 686 (Alaska 1967).

The test for the sufficiency of an indictment adopted for Alaska is whether the evidence presented to the grand jury is adequate to persuade reasonable minded persons that if unexplained or uncontradicted it would warrant conviction, and this test does not require that the evidence would be admissible at the trial even though objected to by the defendant. **State v. Parks,** Op. No. 456, 437 P2d 642 (Alaska 1968).

Where peace officer's hearsay testimony was only evidence before grand jury on essential element of offense, the state offered no justification for admission of part of it and inadequate justification of prohibitive cost for other part, the indictment was invalid. **Adams v. State,** Op. No. 1865, 598 P2d 503 (Alaska 1979).

Evidence that victim had been hit by vehicle going relatively fast, that others were driving 10-15 miles per hour, that defendant either ran a stop sign or made very fast start, and that visibility was limited, coupled with substantial evidence of defendant's negligent driving before and after the accident, presented a sufficiently detailed account of defendant's activity that, if uncontroverted, would warrant his conviction. **Lupro v. State,** Op. No. 1960, 603 P2d 468 (Alaska 1979).

Evidence that property was stolen, that defendants possessed the property, and that they knew it was stolen is sufficient under this rule to support a charge of receiving and concealing stolen property. **Nelson v. State,** Op. No. 2350, 628 P2d 884 (Alaska 1981).

Prosecutor need not "develop" evidence for the defendant or present leads "possibly favorable" to defendant. He does have the duty of presenting evidence which will tend to negate guilt. **Tookak v. State,** Op. No. 108, 648 P2d 1018 (Alaska App. 1982).

The prosecutor need only present evidence material to the charge upon which the defendant is accused. Only material substantially favorable to the defendant need be presented. **Tookak v. State,** Op. No. 108, 648 P2d 1018 (Alaska App. 1982).

Prosecutor did not violate his duty to present exculpatory evidence by failing to introduce evidence that alleged witnesses to the crime failed to identify defendant as the perpetrator. **Tookak v. State,** Op. No. 108, 648 P2d 1018 (Alaska App. 1982).

Prosecutor's failure to mention that victim was unable to identify gun found in defendant's home as the weapon used in the crime was not a breach of his duty to present exculpatory evidence nor adequate ground to reconvene the grand jury where prosecutor was not aware during the grand jury proceeding that victim could not identify the weapon, the weapon was similar to the weapon previously described by the victim, and other evidence presented pointed overwhelmingly to defendant's guilt. **Tookak v. State,** Op. No. 108, 648 P2d 1018 (Alaska App. 1982).

Prosecutor's duty to present exculpatory evidence to the grand jury does not require him to develop evidence for the defendant or present every lead possibly favorable to the defendant. **Dyer v. State,** Op. No. 268, 666 P2d 438 (Alaska App. 1983).

Although the grand jury was told that they were to determine whether there was probable cause to believe that the accused was guilty of the offense charged, the instruction was not improper, since probable cause was defined in the instruction itself by the language set forth in this rule requiring the grand jury to return an indictment when all the evidence taken together, if unexplained or uncontradicted, would warrant a conviction. **Hohman v. State,** Op. No. 290, 669 P2d 1316 (Alaska App. 1983).

Technical specificity argument advanced by defendant to have indictment dismissed was rejected where the indictment read together with the grand jury transcript gave specific notice of every element of the crime charged. **Azzarella v. State,** Op. No. 490, 703 P2d 1182 (Alaska App. 1985).

Failure of the prosecution to produce exculpatory evidence was rendered harmless where the strength of the evidence presented to the grand jury would have been enough to allow the grand jury to return a true bill even if the exculpatory evidence had also been presented. **Clifton v. State,** Op. No. 657, 728 P2d 649 (Alaska App. 1986).

Where the grand jury was informed of the existence of certain exculpatory testimony by the suspect's father but chose not to subpoena the father to testify, apparently because it did not view his testimony as particularly important, the prosecutor did not violate his obligation to present exculpatory evidence to the grand jury. **Esmailka v. State,** Op. No. 721, 740 P2d 466 (Alaska App. 1987).

Although the evidence against defendant presented to the grand jury was mostly circumstantial, it was clearly sufficient to persuade reasonable grand jurors that a conviction would be warranted. **Gorz v. State,** Op. No. 776, 749 P2d 1349 (Alaska App. 1988).

Although evidence before grant jury would have supported indictment of defendant as a principal for her delivery of cocaine to the purchaser, it did not support her indictment as an accomplice to the purchaser's resale of the cocaine, thus reversal of her conviction was required even though sufficient evidence for conviction was presented at trial. **Murray v. State,** Op. No. 955, 778 P2d 237 (Alaska App. 1989).

A grand jury proceeding is not intended to be a mini trial in which the state presents all of the evidence necessary to establish guilt beyond a reasonable doubt; the prosecutor's burden is to introduce sufficient evidence to establish a probability of guilt. **Sheldon v. State,** Op. No. 1059, 796 P2d 831 (Alaska App. 1990).

A physical examination is of sufficient significance in a case of sexual assault or sexual abuse that the prosecutor charged with the responsibility of presenting a case to the grand jury should undertake to determine whether such an examination had taken place so that he or she will be in position to adequately advise the grand jury. **Sheldon v. State,** Op. No. 1059, 796 P2d 831 (Alaska App. 1990).

In the context of the case, the instructions to the grand jury, which did not define the quantum of evidence that would warrant a conviction by a trial jury, did not violate due process or equal protection; considering the entirety of the charge, the grand jury was left with the understanding that it should not return an indictment unless it was satisfied that the evidence presented, if unexplained or uncontradicted, established a probability of the accused's guilt and would therefore justify holding the accused for trial. **Sheldon v. State,** Op. No. 1059, 796 P2d 831 (Alaska App. 1990).

Where defendant was ultimately convicted of sexual abuse of a minor in the second degree, the prosecutor's failure in the grand jury proceeding to answer the jury's question as to whether the victim had been given a physical examination, when in fact there had been a physical examination showing no evidence of sexual assault or fondling, was error, but the error was harmless, since the examination was taken several months after the alleged crime and would therefore probably not have uncovered signs of any sexual contact which did occur. **Sheldon v. State,** Op. No. 1059, 796 P2d 831 (Alaska App. 1990).

Absent inadmissible hearsay testimony regarding furtive movements by defendant, the only evidence that the defendant possessed illegal drugs was his mere presence as passenger in a car containing the drugs; such evidence was insufficient to establish a prima facie case of possession, thus indictment had to be dismissed. **Marion v. State,** Op. No. 1109, 806 P2d 857 (Alaska App. 1991).

Although State introduced inadmissible evidence to grand jury, trial court properly refused to dismiss the indictment, since the admissible evidence presented to the grand jury made a strong case against defendant. **Bright v. State,** Op. No. 1195, 826 P2d 765 (Alaska App. 1992).

This rule does not require prosecutor to present any and all potentially exculpatory evidence to grand jury; rather, prosecutor is required only to present evidence substantially favorable to defendant. **Hurn v. State,** Op. No. 1340, 872 P2d 189 (Alaska App. 1994).

Prosecutor's duty to present exculpatory evidence is satisfied if omitted evidence would be cumulative. **Hurn v. State,** Op. No. 1340, 872 P2d 189 (Alaska App. 1994).

Exculpatory evidence will not be deemed substantially favorable, and its production by prosecution to grand jury will not be required, unless it is evidence that tends, in and of itself, to negate defendant's guilt. **State v. McDonald,** Op. No. 1342, 872 P2d 627 (Alaska App. 1994).

The appellate court must review the evidence presented to the grand jury to determine whether it presented a sufficiently detailed account of criminal activity and the defendant's participation in this activity to meet the necessary standard. In making this determination, the appellant court must view the evidence in the light most favorable to the state. However, the appellate court may not consider evidence that was improperly presented to the grand jury. **Fox v. State,** Op. No. 1449, 908 P2d 1053 (Alaska App. 1995).

Evidence before grand jury was sufficient to establish defendants' identities as the persons who sold cocaine to an undercover investigator. The investigator unequivocally identified defendants as the people who sold him cocaine. **Fox v. State,** Op. No. 1449, 908 P2d 1053 (Alaska App. 1995).

D. Hearsay Testimony.

While it is the proper function of a grand jury to determine whether certain evidence, if unexplained or uncontradicted, would rationally warrant conviction of the defendant at the trial, it is not the province of the grand jury to determine questions of admissibility or inadmissibility of evidence at the trial and hearsay evidence may rationally establish facts and therefore may be sufficient evidence to justify the finding of an indictment. **State v. Parks,** Op. No. 456, 437 P2d 642 (Alaska 1968).

Dismissal of indictment on the ground that it was founded solely upon hearsay was error. **State v. Parks,** Op. No. 456,437 P2d 642 (Alaska 1968).

Credibility of a hearsay declarant who testifies before a grand jury must be established on the record so that the grand jury may know how much weight to give the hearsay testimony. **McKinnon v. State,** Op. No. 1075, 526 P2d 18 (Alaska 1974).

Evidence of a hearsay declarant's professional status may justify the introduction of declarant's hearsay statements in a grand jury proceeding under appropriate circumstances. **McKinnon v. State,** Op. No. 1075, 526 P2d 18 (Alaska 1974).

A professional laboratory technician is presumptively qualified to perform chemical analysis in a competent manner, and the admission of his laboratory report in his absence before the grand jury is justified. **McKinnon v. State,** Op. No. 1075, 526 P2d 18 (Alaska 1974).

A record which indicates that any hearsay testimony produced before a grand jury is either peripheral or cumulative to direct testimony and that direct testimony is adequate to justify indictment does not require dismissal of indictment against the accused. **Webb v. State,** Op. No. 1091, 527 P2d 35 (Alaska 1974).

In circumstances involving hearsay evidence which would be inadmissible at trial, there must be a compelling justification for its introduction to a grand jury. **Galauska v. State,** Op. No. 1094, 527 P2d 459 (Alaska 1974).

Where a hearsay admission of the defendant's companion in crime is properly admitted before a grand jury, and the statement is corroborated by other evidence, the evidence is sufficient to support an indictment. **Galauska v. State,** Op. No. 1094, 527 P2d 459 (Alaska 1974).

The mere expense of transportation of out of state witnesses is not a compelling reason for the use of hearsay under this rule. **State v. Gieffels,** Op. No. 1309, 554 P2d 460 (Alaska 1976).

Where hearsay testimony before grand jury was either peripheral or cumulative to direct testimony, it did not invalidate the indictment. **Webb v. State,** Op. No. 1638, 580 P2d 295 (Alaska 1978).

Neither the cost of compensating an expert witness for his time nor the mere expense of transportation are sufficient reasons for the admission of hearsay evidence in a grand jury proceeding. **Metler v. State,** Op. No. 1678, 581 P2d 669 (Alaska).

Admission made by a defendant is admissible against him but not against co-defendant and should not be presented to grand jury as such, absent compelling justification. **State v. Taylor,** Op. No. 1457, 566 P2d 1016 (Alaska 1977).

The use of inadmissible hearsay evidence before a grand jury will not vitiate the indictment if other evidence was presented which justified the indictment. **Gieffels v. State,** Op. No. 1787, 590 P2d 55 (Alaska 1979); **Giacomazzi v. State,** Op. No. 2404, 633 P2d 218 (Alaska 1981).

Where there was sufficient admissible evidence presented to grand jury to justify a conviction if uncontradicted or unexplained, the admission of hearsay was not critical to the return of a true bill. **Frink v. State,** Op. No. 1870, 597 P2d 154 (Alaska 1979).

When hearsay evidence has been presented to a grand jury, character evidence concerning the hearsay declarant's credibility is permissible to the same extent to which it would be permissible at trial had the declarant's character been challenged. **Putnam v. State,** Op. No. 2251, 629 P2d 35 (Alaska 1980).

When testimony is offered merely to establish the fact that a statement was made and not to prove the truth of the matter stated, the hearsay rule does not apply. **Putnam v. State,** Op. No. 2251, 629 P2d 35 (Alaska 1980).

Mere fact that declarant was participating in a residential drug treatment program did not establish the compelling need necessary to admit his declaration as hearsay testimony before the grand jury. **Lofquist v. State,** Op. No. 203, 656 P2d 1222 (Alaska App. 1983).

Prosecutor did not err in not allowing police officer to respond to grand juror's question concerning the whereabouts of another possible suspect at the time of the incident in question on the basis that the response would be hearsay. **Wilkie v. State,** Op. No. 599, 715 P2d 1199 (Alaska App. 1986).

Failure to state on the record the reason for using hearsay evidence in the form of a written laboratory analysis rather than live testimony was not error. **Gibson v. State,** Op. No. 621,719 P2d 687 (Alaska App. 1986).

Hearsay evidence in the form of a written laboratory analysis was admissible at grand jury proceeding. **Gibson v. State,** Op. No. 621, 719 P2d 687 (Alaska App. 1986).

Testimony of statements made by alleged child abuse victim was hearsay admitted in violation of this rule; however, the other evidence which the state presented, excluding the hearsay evidence, was clearly sufficient to support the indictment. **Sluka v. State,** Op. No. 606, 717 P2d 394 (Alaska App. 1986).

Rule that hearsay can be presented to the grand jury only if it comes within an exception to the hearsay rule or is otherwise necessary applies only to testimony upon which the State relies for the return of an indictment; it has no application to allegedly exculpatory evidence which the State is under a duty to present in order to enable the grand jury to fulfill its obligations under this rule. **Esmailka v. State,** Op. No. 721, 740 P2d 466 (Alaska App. 1987).

Three-year-old victim's hearsay statements identifying defendant as the person who sexually abused her, made during her medical treatment, presented sufficient evidence for the grand jury to indict, since even if the testimony identifying the defendant did not fall within the medical diagnosis exception to the hearsay rule, it was arguable that the child's inability to testify before the grand jury constituted "compelling justification" for presenting hearsay evidence. **State v. Nollner,** Op. No. 780, 749 P2d 905 (Alaska App. 1988).

The likelihood of codefendant's invocation of fifth amendment rights provided the compelling necessity required to admit the hearsay statements of the codefendant for grand jury consideration. **Arnold v. State,** Op. No. 779, 751 P2d 494 (Alaska App. 1988).

Where hearsay is improperly presented to the grand jury, the reviewing court determines whether sufficient admissible evidence was presented to justify the indictment and, if so, whether the improper evidence appreciably affected the outcome of the proceedings. **Arnold v. State,** Op. No. 779, 751 P2d 494 (Alaska App. 1988).

Because calling codefendant before the grand jury would have led to direct evidence only if the codefendant incriminated himself, concern for codefendant's right not to incriminate himself constituted a compelling reason to use his hearsay statement before the grand jury even if the statement would not be admissible at trial. **Mudge v. State,** Op. No. 847, 760 P2d 1046 (Alaska App. 1988).

Statutory classification which permitted hearsay from child declarants to be presented to grand juries in sexual abuse cases, but implicitly rejected the use of hearsay in other cases involving crimes against children, did not violate equal protection. **Murray v. State,** Op. No. 919,770 P2d 1131 (Alaska App. 1989).

Statute permitting hearsay before a grand jury in cases of sexual assault on children did not deprive defendant of due process or of his constitutional right to a grand jury review of the prosecution's evidence before the return of an indictment. **Murray v. State,** Op. No. 919, 770 P2d 1131 (Alaska App. 1989).

Testimony relating to defendant's failure to make exculpatory statements would have been inadmissible at trial for lack of foundation for application of the adoptive admissions theory, and was therefore improperly admitted in grand jury proceeding; the State's argument that admissibility of the evidence at trial would have turned on a balancing of probative value against prejudicial impact was rejected. **State v. Green,** Op. No. 1131, 810 P2d 1023 (Alaska App. 1991).

E. Record of Proceedings.

Order of presiding judge to make the record of the number of grand jurors concurring with findings of the indictment public, was in accordance with this rule. **Crawford v. State,** Op. No. 312, 408 P2d 1002 (Alaska 1965).

Where, pursuant to stipulation of counsel and order of the trial court, defendants were afforded the right to cross-examine the prosecution witnesses before the grand jury at a "second preliminary hearing" and where, at their trial, no effort was made by the defendants to obtain a transcript of the grand jury testimony of any of these witnesses for impeachment or to test their credibility, a particularized need requiring this disclosure of the grand jury minutes was not demonstrated. **Merrill v. State,** Op. No. 392, 423 P2d 686 (Alaska 1967).

Disclosure of grand jury minutes is a matter committed to the discretion of the trial judge. **Merrill v. State,** Op. No. 392, 423 P2d 686 (Alaska 1967).

Inspection of grand jury minutes to determine whether any illegal seized evidence was presented to that body was denied in proper exercise of trial judge's discretion where sufficient competent testimony to return indictment had been before the grand jury. **Merrill v. State,** Op. No. 392, 423 P2d 686 (Alaska 1967).

Where counsel for the defendant vigorously cross-examines the trial witnesses who were the same witnesses who appeared before the grand jury and no reason, other than the use of the transcript as a possible instrument of impeachment, is suggested as to how the transcript will strengthen the defendant's attack on the indictment or his cross-examination of such witnesses, the failure to record such proceedings does not require setting aside the conviction. **Robinson v. State,** Op. No. 735, 489 P2d 1271 (Alaska 1971).

The justification for maintaining the secrecy of grand jury proceedings no longer exists when deliberations have been completed, an indictment has been returned, and the defendant has been arrested and is ready for trial. **Burkholder v. State,** Op. No. 753, 491 P2d 754 (Alaska 1971).

A defendant is entitled to a transcript of grand jury minutes to enable him to determine the sufficiency of the indictment. **Burkholder v. State,** Op. No. 753, 491 P2d 754 (Alaska 1971).

Defendants can listen to recordings of and acquire transcripts of grand jury proceedings and can inspect exhibits presented to the grand jury. **Azzarella v. State,** Op. No. 490, 703 P2d 1182 (Alaska App. 1985).

Grand jury's failure to keep an accurate record of its votes did not result in prejudice to any substantial right of the defendants, and therefore did not warrant dismissal of the indictment. **State v. Roark,** Op. No. 507, 705 P2d 1274 (Alaska App. 1985).

Rule 6.1. Grand Jury Reports.

(a) **Authority to Issue Reports.**

(1) A grand jury may investigate and make reports and recommendations concerning the public safety or welfare. An indictment is not a "report" as used in this rule and Criminal Rule 6.

(2) A grand jury report may be made only upon the concurrence of a majority of the total number of grand jurors on the panel at the commencement of the proceedings resulting in the report. The report must be signed by the foreperson. A grand jury report may include allegations of criminal conduct.

(b) **Initial Judicial Review.** The grand jury shall present any proposed report to the presiding judge of the judicial district. The judge shall examine the report and the grand jury record before the grand jury is discharged. The judge may order production of audio copies or transcripts of the grand jury proceeding and may request the prosecuting attorney to submit a summary of the evidence presented to the grand jury. The judge shall make specific findings on the record as required by the following subparagraphs.

(1) The judge shall determine first whether the report satisfies the requirements of subparagraphs (a)(1) & (2). If it does not, the judge shall proceed under subparagraph (b)(3).

(2) The judge shall then determine if publication of the report would improperly infringe upon a constitutional right of any person, including but not limited to improper interference with a person's right to privacy or right to a fair trial in a pending or planned criminal proceeding. The judge shall make an ex parte on the record inquiry of the prosecuting attorney about any planned or pending criminal prosecutions related to the subject of the grand jury report.

(3) If the judge determines that the report does not meet the standards of subparagraphs (a)(1), (a)(2) or (b)(2) the judge shall return the report to the grand jury with an explanation of the reasons for returning the report. The grand jury may conduct further proceedings, revise the report, or seek appellate review of the judge's decision not to release the report.

(c) **Judicial Review If Report Adversely Reflects on Identifiable Person.** If the judge determines that the standards of paragraph (b) are satisfied, the judge shall determine whether any part of the report may reflect adversely on any person who is named or otherwise identified in the report. "Person" includes a natural person or an organization, but does not include a governmental subdivision or agency. If the report may adversely reflect on any identifiable person, the judge shall proceed under the following subparagraphs (c)(1)–(5).

(1) The judge shall order that notice of the report be provided to the person. The notice must advise the person of his or her rights as provided in this paragraph.

(2) The person may move, within ten days of notice of the report, for a hearing. The hearing will be held in camera and on the record.

(3) The person must be given a reasonable period of time prior to the hearing to examine the grand jury report and the record of the grand jury proceedings. A person receiving notice or a copy of the report and record may not disclose any matter occurring before the grand jury except as permitted by the court. Each person receiving these materials must be advised of this obligation.

(4) The person named or otherwise identified in the report may be represented by counsel at the hearing and may present argument as to whether the standards stated in subparagraph (c)(5) are satisfied. The prosecuting attorney may be present at this hearing and may also present argument. Neither side may present evidence nor examine witnesses, except that the named or otherwise identifiable person may submit a written response to the grand jury report which the person may request that the court issue with the report under paragraph (d).

(5) The judge shall determine at the close of the hearing whether that part of the report which may adversely reflect upon a named or otherwise identified person is supported by substantial evidence or, if raised at the hearing, whether the report satisfies the requirements of paragraph (b) of this rule and paragraph (1) of Criminal Rule 6. If the judge finds that these requirements are not satisfied, the judge shall return the report to the grand jury with an explanation of why the report has not been released. The court may request that the grand jury consider further evidence as to the named or otherwise identifiable person. The grand jury may conduct further proceedings, revise the report, or seek appellate review of the decision not to release the report.

(d) **Release of Report.**

(1) The court shall withhold publication of the report until the expiration of the time for making a motion for a hearing under paragraph (c). If such a motion is made, publication must be withheld pending a ruling on the motion or pending any review under paragraph (e). All proceedings under this rule are confidential until the presiding judge orders the report released.

(2) If the judge finds that the standards of paragraphs (b) and (c) are met, the judge shall order the report released. The judge may order that a response to the report by a person

named or otherwise identified, or other additional materials, be attached to the report as an appendix. The report and any appendices will be filed with the clerk of the court and made available for public inspection. The court shall also direct that copies of the report and any appendices be sent to other persons as reasonably requested by the grand jury.

(e) **Appeal.**

(1) A judicial determination under paragraph (d) of this rule is a final order for purposes of appeal. Such an appeal is governed by Appellate Rule 216 except that the appeal is to the Supreme Court. Any named or otherwise identifiable person, the state, or the grand jury by majority vote may seek review of the presiding judge's decision.

(2) The grand jury will be permitted access to the record of the in camera hearing to assist it in determining whether to pursue appellate review. The grand jury shall maintain the confidentiality of this record.

(Added by SCO 938 effective January 15, 1989)

Annotations

Cases

This rule, which provides for judicial review of grand jury reports before they are published, does not violate Article 1, Section 8 or Article 1, Section 5 of the Alaska Constitution, or the first amendment of the United States Constitution. **O'Leary v. Superior Court,** Op. No. 3736, 816 P2d 163 (Alaska 1991).

This rule, which provides for judicial review of the grand jury reports before they are published, is not an improper exercise of the court's rule-making power, is not contrary to the state's public records acts, and does not unconstitutionally expand the superior court's jurisdiction. **O'Leary v. Superior Court,** Op. No. 3736, 816 P2d 163 (Alaska 1991).

Where grand jury report reflected adversely on individuals in a manner unsupported by substantial evidence, the names of the interested parties whose reputations would otherwise unjustly be damaged were ordered withheld by the state supreme court. **O'Leary v. Superior Court,** Op. No. 3736, 816 P2d 163 (Alaska 1991).

Details in grand jury report relating to a previously confidential investigation of allegations of sexual misconduct on the part of the two teachers were ordered expunged from the report by the state supreme court because the allegations would improperly infringe the constitutionally protected reputational interests of the teachers, and because publication of the allegations were unnecessary to an understanding of the recommendations made by the grand jury **O'Leary v. Superior Court,** Op. No. 3736, 816 P2d 163 (Alaska 1991).

Rule 7. Indictment and Information.

(a) **Use of Indictment and Information.** An offense which may be punished by imprisonment for a term exceeding one year shall be prosecuted by indictment, unless indictment is waived. Any other offense may be prosecuted by indictment or information. Any information may be filed without leave of court.

(b) **Waiver of Indictment.** An offense which may be punished by imprisonment for a term exceeding one year may be prosecuted by information if the defendant, after having been advised of the nature of the charge and of the defendant's rights, waives in open court prosecution by indictment.

(c) **Nature and Contents—Defects of Form Do Not Invalidate.**

(1) The indictment or the information shall be a plain, concise and definite written statement of the essential facts constituting the offense charged. It shall be signed by the prosecuting attorney. It need not contain a formal commencement, a formal conclusion or any other matter not necessary to such statement. Allegations made in one count may be incorporated by reference in another count. It may be alleged in a single count that the means by which the defendant committed the offense are unknown or that the defendant committed it by one or more specified means.

(2) An indictment or information must include:

(A) the defendant and offense information required by Criminal Rule 3(c);

(B) search warrant information as required by Criminal Rule 37(e)(2);

(C) the victim information certificate required by Criminal Rule 44(f); and

(D) if the defendant is charged with an offense listed in AS 18.66.990, whether the prosecution claims that the alleged offense is a crime involving domestic violence as defined in AS 18.66.990(3) and (5).

(3) The defendant's social security number may not appear on an indictment or information. This subsection applies to an indictment or information filed on or after October 15, 2006.

(4) Error in a citation or omission of a citation to the statute, regulation, or ordinance that the defendant is alleged to have violated shall not be ground for dismissal of the indictment or information or for reversal of a conviction if the error or omission did not mislead the defendant to the defendant's prejudice. No indictment is insufficient nor can the trial, judgment or other proceedings thereon be affected, by reason of a defect or imperfection in matter of form in the indictment which does not tend to prejudice the substantial rights of the defendant.

(5) When an indictment is found, the names of all witnesses examined before the grand jury must be inserted at the foot of the indictment, or endorsed thereon, before it is presented to the court.

(d) **Surplusage.** The court, on motion of the defendant, may strike surplusage from the indictment or information.

(e) **Amendment of Indictment or Information.** The court may permit an indictment or information to be amended at any time before verdict or finding if no additional or different offense is charged and the substantial rights of the defendant are not prejudiced.

(f) **Bill of Particulars.** The court may direct the filing of a bill of particulars. A motion for a bill of particulars may be made before arraignment or within ten days after arraignment or at such later time as the court may permit. A bill of particulars may be amended at any time subject to such conditions as justice requires.

(Adopted by SCO 4 October 4, 1959; amended by SCO 98 effective September 16, 1968; amended by SCO 483 effective November 2, 1981; by SCO 1153 effective July 15, 1994; by SCO 1289 effective January 15, 1998; by SCO 1304 effective January 15, 1998; by SCO 1587 effective December 15, 2005; and by SCO 1614 effective October 15, 2006)

Note: SCO 906 incorporated changes in Criminal Rule 8(a) made by the legislature in ch. 66, §§ 8 and 9. SLA 1988. The legislation added the language in subparagraph (a)(1), "and it can be determined before trial that it is likely that evidence of one charged offense would be admissible to prove another charged offense."

Note: SCO 906 is amended by adding a new paragraph 3 which provides: "3. This order is made for the sole reason that the legislature has mandated the above amendments. If the act mandating these amendments is invalidated by a court of competent jurisdiction, this order shall be considered automatically rescinded." This amendment is effective retroactively to May 28, 1988.

Note: Paragraph (b) was amended by ch. 79, § 2, SLA 1991.

Cross References

(a) **CROSS REFERENCE:** AS 12.80.020

(b) **CROSS REFERENCE:** AS 12.80.020

(c) **CROSS REFERENCE:** AS 12.40.100

Annotations

Cases

I. Information.
II. Indictment.
  A. In General.
  B. Sufficiency.
  C. Amendment.
III. Bill of Particulars.

I. Information.

On appeal it was assumed that no prejudice resulted from a claimed error in the citation of a statute in the information, where appellant made no attempt to show wherein he was prejudiced. **Theodore v. State,** Op. No. 305, 407 P2d 182 (Alaska 1965).

It cannot be said as a matter of law that the application of this rule as to information would in no case be practicable in a magistrate (district) court. **State v. Smith,** Op. No. 356, 417 P2d 252 (Alaska 1966).

II. Indictment.

A. In General.

While requirement of endorsement of the names of witnesses before the grand jury at the foot of the indictment is a substantial right of the accused, it is nevertheless a personal right which was waived by not pressing the claim of surprise and by his failure to accept the court's suggestions or to follow through his later motion for judgment of acquittal in the trial court. **Thomas v. State,** Op. No. 200, 391 P2d 18 (Alaska 1964).

In the absence of a statute or court rule requiring the state to furnish a defendant with the names of witnesses to be called at the trial who were not examined before the grand jury, the matter of excluding witnesses not known to the defendant until the time of the trial or granting a continuance for preparation as to such witnesses is within the discretion of the trial court and the exercise of such discretion will be disturbed on appeal only in case of abuse. **Battese v. State,** Op. No. 402, 425 P2d 606 (Alaska 1967).

Where no testimony is recorded at either session of a grand jury which returns an indictment, even if a proper motion has been made for production of grand jury minutes, no error is committed by failing to produce such a transcript, where the only specific information available was the name of each testifying witness whose names were endorsed on the indictment as required by this rule. **Robinson v. State,** Op. No. 712, 487 P2d 681 (Alaska 1971).

Where count I of an indictment charges robbery and count II charges the use of a firearm in the commission of a felony. No error results from the trial court's submission of both counts to the jury for their consideration even though only one sentence might constitutionally be imposed on the two counts charged. **Robinson v. State,** Op. No. 712, 487 P2d 681 (Alaska 1971).

A motion to dismiss is not an appropriate method to remedy duplicity in an indictment. **Trounce v. State,** Op. No. 801, 498 P2d 106 (Alaska 1972).

The rule against duplicity is a pleading rule rather than a rule of substance. Duplicity is not necessarily a fatal defect, and charges improperly joined in a single count can be segregated into separate counts in the same indictment. **Trounce v. State,** Op. No. 801, 498 P2d 106 (Alaska 1972).

Trial judge did not abuse his discretion in reinstating by court order a dismissed rape charge without reindictment. **Morgan v. State,** Op. No. 320, 673 P2d 897 (Alaska App. 1983).

Grand jury's failure to keep an accurate record of its votes did not result in prejudice to any substantial right of the defendants, and therefore did not warrant dismissal of the indictment. **State v. Roark,** Op. No. 507, 705 P2d 1274 (Alaska App. 1985).

Indictment by a grand jury is required for felony prosecutions in Alaska. **Michael v. State,** Op. No. 3663, 805 P2d 371 (Alaska 1991).

B. Sufficiency.

An indictment charging murder in the first degree is sufficient if its allegations leave no doubt in the mind of a person of common understanding that the element of purpose was intended to be, and is reflected in the words used in the indictment to describe the nature of the killing. **Marrone v. State,** 359 P2d 969, 979 (Alaska 1961).

Where indictment for contributing to delinquency of a minor alleged that the defendant committed the crime "on or about the 29th, 30th, and 31st day of May, 1961" and the state at the trial produced proof that the defendant had actually engaged in sexual intercourse with the prosecutrix at least twice on each of the dates alleged in the indictment, defendant was not prejudiced by denial of request to require the state to elect on what day he was alleged to have committed the crime. **Anderson v. State,** Op. No. 156, 384 P2d 669 (Alaska 1963).

Indictment for burglary which failed to specify by name the ulterior crime which it is alleged the accused intended to commit, was fatally defective. **Adkins v. State,** Op. No. 191, 389 P2d 915 (Alaska 1964).

An indictment for uttering and publishing forged instruments and for offering for recordation forged instruments which described the instruments as deeds of real property, indicated the date of execution, the names of grantors and grantees, and the dates where offered for recordation, but did not set forth the descriptions of the real property, sufficiently identified the instruments so to preclude the possibility that defendant could ever be retried for the same offense and was a sufficient indictment. **Chambers v. State,** Op. No. 237, 394 P2d 778 (Alaska 1964).

Since statutory language "record, writing, instrument or matter" plainly included a deed, indictment under such statute for uttering and publishing a forged deed was not defective. **Chambers v. State,** Op. No. 237, 394 P2d 778 (Alaska 1964).

One of the separate acts denounced under AS 11.40.4 10 was plainly and concisely stated in an indictment charging that defendant violated the statute by living with a prostitute. **Dunn v. State,** Op. No. 409, 426 P2d 993 (Alaska 1967).

In the absence of a showing that a claimed deficiency or imperfection in an indictment prejudiced substantial rights of the defendant, the indictment could not be held fatally defective. **Price v. State,** Op. No. 454, 437 P2d 333 (Alaska 1968).

Indictment for forgery of payee's name on a check which did not specify the date, amount or maker of the check or of the drawee bank was not insufficient for lack of particularity necessary to plead the judgment in bar of further prosecution for the same offense, because in determining whether a plea of double jeopardy may be made the whole record of a former trial may be examined and the fact that the check in question was introduced into evidence eliminated possible use of this check by the state for further prosecution. **Price v. State,** Op. No. 454, 437 P2d 333 (Alaska 1968).

Failure of original indictment for forgery of payee's name on a check to name, date, amount, maker and drawee bank was in imperfection "in matter of form" only where the check referred to in the indictment was introduced into evidence without defendant's objection, the defendant knew prior to putting on his defense the precise nature of the charge, and the court upon granting a motion to amend the indictments, offered a reasonable continuance to defendant if he claimed surprise but the defendant made no such claim and did not request a continuance. **Price v. State,** Op. No. 454,437 P2d 333 (Alaska 1968).

Erroneous citation of statute was not fatal to an indictment a fair reading of which was sufficient to enable the defendant to understand the nature of the offense charged in order to prepare his defense, and to plead former jeopardy in the case of subsequent prosecution for the same offense. **Stewart v. State,** Op. No. 457, 438 P2d 387 (Alaska 1968).

An indictment charging a defendant with the first-degree killing of a victim "by a method and means unknown" is sufficient. **Flores v. State,** Op. No. 491, 443 P2d 73 (Alaska 1968).

An indictment alleging an offense in the form approved by statute and rule is sufficient. **Spight v. State,** Op. No. 524, 450 P2d 157 (Alaska 1969).

The unnecessary detailed description of a material allegation in an indictment is to be treated as analogous to an "imperfection in a matter of form" of an indictment. Any failure to prove, or failure to submit instructions requiring the jury to find an existence of fact which corresponds to an unnecessary description of the necessary element of the indictment will constitute reversible error only if the substantial rights of the accused are prejudiced. **Roberts v. State,** Op. No. 574, 458 P2d 340 (Alaska 1969).

An indictment which charges that the defendants "did unlawfully and feloniously sell and transfer a narcotic drug, to wit, heroin" is sufficient to alert defendants to the elements of the offense charged, notwithstanding their claim that the indictment fails to meet the scienter requirement. **Thomas v. State,** Op. No. 1040, 522 P2d 528 (Alaska 1974).

An indictment charging attempted rape and citing only the rape statute is sufficient. **State v. Thomas,** Op. No. 1077, 525 P2d 1092 (Alaska 1974).

An indictment need not precisely cite the statute allegedly violated when it is clear from its language that a crime has been charged. **State v. Thomas,** Op. No. 1077,525 P2d 1092 (Alaska 1974).

Indictment for embezzlement by bailee which alleged but refused to account or deliver funds was knowing, willful, unlawful and felonious charged specific intent to deprive owner of money in question with sufficient specificity. **Amidon v. State,** Op. No. 1434, 565 P2d 1248 (Alaska 1977).

Where the indictment charged defendant with intent to "kill and wound" but the jury instruction followed the statutory language of "kill or wound," the variance between the two did not prejudice the substantial rights of the defendant. **Christie v. State,** Op. No. 1644, 580 P2d 310 (Alaska 1978).

The indictment need not state every element of the charge necessary to be proved at trial. **Lupro v. State,** Op. No. 1960, 603 P2d 468 (Alaska 1979).

Where indictments were insufficient for burglary convictions, it was proper to reverse the burglary convictions and remand for entry of judgment on the misdemeanor offenses of unlawful entry and simple assault, since the indictments adequately charged those offenses and the jury's guilty verdicts justified entry of judgment on them. **Nix v. State,** Op. No.2264,624 P2d 823 (Alaska 1981).

A defendant may bring a post-trial motion to contest the sufficiency of a felony indictment which failed to give clear and unequivocal notice that the charge against the defendant was technically a felony. **Post v. State,** Op. No. 56, 635 P2d 1194 (Alaska App. 1981).

Fact that indictment charged defendant with theft of ripper teeth but did not allege a specific theory of theft did not deny defendant due process since liberal discovery rules permit an accused to obtain adequate discovery of the state's case and to get adequate notice of the state's theory or theories of prosecution. **Williams v. State,** Op. No. 106, 648 P2d 603 (Alaska App. 1982).

Where the indictment read together with the grand jury transcript gave specific notice of every element of the crime charged, defendant's claim that the indictment was facially defective for failing to allege one element of the crime charged was properly rejected. **Azzarella v. State,** Op. No.490,703 P2d 1182 (Alaska App. 1985).

Where the record clearly disclosed two distinct incidents of sexual touching of the victim, the first on June 1 and the second on August 2, and defendant was indicted for the first incident, reversal was required where defendant was convicted of the second incident. **Simpson v. State,** Op. No. 512, 705 P2d 1328 (Alaska App. 1985).

In trial for attempted murder, the failure of the indictment to include "substantial step" language was a defect only as to the form which did not make the indictment insufficient since the indictment included a concise description of defendant's actions that constituted the offense, including the proper language regarding defendant's state of mind, and since the caption of the indictment made clear that defendant was charged with attempted murder in the first degree; accordingly, amendment of the indictment to correct the defect was properly allowed. **Ciervo v. State,** Op. No. 813, 756 P2d 907 (Alaska App. 1988).

Conviction of a defendant for second degree assault, when he was charged by the grand jury only with first degree assault, violated his right to be tried only on the charges presented by the grand jury, requiring reversal of his conviction. **Michael v. State,** Op. No. 3663, 805 P2d 371 (Alaska 1991).

Date on which an offense was committed is normally not an element of that offense; thus, a variance between the date specified in the indictment and the date shown by the evidence at trial will normally be deemed a defect of form (rather than a material defect) for purposes of section (c) of this rule, unless the defendant can show that the variance prejudiced their ability to prepare or present their defense at trial. **Larkin v. State,** Op. No. 1922, 88 P.3d 153.

Adkins v. State, 389 P.2d 915 (Alaska 1964), is overruled to the extent that it holds that failure to include the intended offense in a burglary indictment is a defect of substance that can be raised at any time; state is required to identify the intended offense in a burglary indictment and failure to do so is a defect of form that must be raised before trial. **State v. Semancik,** Op. No. 5833, 99 P.3d 538.

Court of appeals erred by reversing defendant's conviction for attempted burglary upon his challenge to the sufficiency of his attempted burglary indictment, raised for the first time on appeal, on the basis that it failed to specify what crime he intended to commit when he entered the dwelling. **State v. Semancik,** Op. No. 5833, 99 P.3d 538.

C. Amendment.

Amendment of indictment to correct "error in form" was properly allowed where the amended indictment did not charge an additional or different offense and no substantial rights of the defendant were prejudiced. **Price v. State,** Op. No. 454, 437 P2d 333 (Alaska 1968).

Since materiality is not an essential element of the crime of perjury, it is proper for the trial court under this rule to amend indictments by striking as surplusage any allegations that matters respecting which the accused perjured himself are material to the criminal trial in which the accused was a witness. **Beckley v. State,** Op. No. 490, 443 P2d 51 (Alaska 1968).

Where defendant was charged with attempting to destroy evidence, it was error for the court to allow the state to amend the charge to attempted destruction and concealment of evidence on the day of the trial and to deny a requested continuance by the defense to study the new charge. **McGahan v. State,** Op. No. 2021, 606 P2d 396 (Alaska 1980).

Amendment of indictment, which charged defendant with a May 5 assault, to charge defendant with a second assault against the same victim on May 1, was reversible error, particularly since the error was compounded by allowing the jury to render a single verdict on the indictment without an instruction requiring the jury to unanimously agree that defendant committed one of the offenses. **Bell v. State,** Op. No. 607, 716 P2d 1004 (Alaska App. 1986).

In trial for attempted murder, the failure of the indictment to include "substantial step" language was a defect only as to the form which did not make the indictment insufficient since the indictment included a concise description of defendant's actions that constituted the offense, including the proper language regarding defendant's state of mind, and since the caption of the indictment made clear that defendant was charged with attempted murder in the first degree; accordingly, amendment of the indictment to correct the defect was properly allowed. **Ciervo v. State,** Op. No. 813, 756 P2d 907 (Alaska App. 1988).

Court did not err in allowing the state to amend the indictment at the close of defendant's stalking trial where defendant did not suggest, nor was there any indication in the record, that he would have pursued a different defense to the stalking charge even if the trial court had accepted the defense attorney's argument as to the relevant time period. **Kenison v. State,** Op. No. 1970, 107 P.3d 335 (Alaska App. 2005).

III. Bill of Particulars.

A bill of particulars filed by the state to specify some of the counts of an indictment for the offense of transporting females for immoral purposes and for the offense of procuring a female for prostitution could not be looked to test the sufficiency of the indictment challenged by a motion in arrest of judgment. **State v. Adkerson,** Op. No. 294, 403 P2d 673 (Alaska 1965).

The purpose of a bill of particulars is to inform the defendant of the charges against him so that he may prepare a defense to avoid prejudicial surprise at trial and to protect against a second prosecution for the same offense. **Lupro v. State,** Op. No. 1960, 603 P2d 468 (Alaska 1979).

Rule 8. Joinder of Offenses and of Defendants.

(a) **Joinder of Offenses.** Two or more offenses may be charged in the same indictment or information in a separate count for each offense if the offenses charged, whether felonies, misdemeanors or both,

(1) are of the same or similar character and it can be determined before trial that it is likely that evidence of one charged offense would be admissible to prove another charged offense,

(2) are based on the same act or transaction, or

(3) are based on two or more acts or transactions connected together or constituting parts of a common scheme or plan.

(b) **Joinder of Defendants.** Two or more defendants may be charged in the same indictment or information if they are alleged to have participated in the same act or transaction or in the same series of acts or transactions constituting an offense or offenses, or if the defendants are parties to an express or tacit agreement to aid each other to commit an act or transaction constituting a criminal offense or offenses. Such defendants may be charged in one or more counts together or separately and all of the defendants need not be charged in each count. The disposition of the indictment or information as to one of several defendants joined in the same indictment or information shall not affect the right of the state to proceed against the other defendants.

(Adopted by SCO 4 October 4, 1959; amended by SCO 906 effective nunc pro tunc May 28, 1988; by SCO 1092 effective July 15, 1992; corrected January, 1993)

Note: SCO 906 incorporated changes in Criminal Rule 8(a) made by the legislature in ch. 66, §§ 8 and 9. SLA 1988. The legislation added the language in subparagraph (a)(1), "and it can be determined before trial that it is likely that evidence of one charged offense would be admissible to prove another charged offense."

Note: SCO 906 is amended by adding a new paragraph 3 which provides: "3. This order is made for the sole reason that the legislature has mandated the above amendments. If the act mandating these amendments is invalidated by a court of competent jurisdiction, this order shall be considered automatically rescinded." This amendment is effective retroactively to May 28, 1988.

Note: Paragraph (b) was amended by ch. 79, § 2, SLA 1991.

Annotations

Cases

Crime of uttering or publishing a forged instrument and crime of procuring of offering forged instruments for recordation were properly charged in the same indictment in several counts. **Chambers v. State,** Op. No. 237, 394 P2d 778 (Alaska 1964).

A complaint which charged defendant in one and the same count with the separate crimes of failure to remain at the scene of an accident [AS 28.35.050(a)] and failure to render assistance to passenger [AS 28.35.060(a)] was duplicitous. **Drahosh v. State,** Op. No. 485, 442 P2d 44 (Alaska 1968).

Prejudice must be shown before the Supreme Court will reverse on grounds that a trial judge erred or abused his discretion in failing to order separate trials for different counts of an indictment. **Richards v. State,** Op. No. 527, 451 P2d 359 (Alaska 1969).

An allegation that the joint trial of two counts for escape created in the jurors' minds the image of defendant as criminally disposed toward escaping from jail is insufficient to raise the question whether the joint trial of the offenses prejudiced the defendant. **Richards v. State,** Op. No. 527, 451 P2d 359 (Alaska 1969).

The rationale underlying the prohibition of duplicitous indictments is to give notice to the defendant of exactly what charges he must defend against and to avoid the consequences of the inability of the jury to indicate which way they are voting on each of the charges. **Kimble v. State,** Op. No. 1184, 539

P2d 73 (Alaska 1975).

Propriety of joinder in cases where there are multiple defendants must be tested by Criminal Rule 8(b) alone. **Amidon v. State,** Op. No. 1434, 565 P2d 1248 (Alaska 1977).

Where one defendant shot at gas station shortly after he and his brother had attacked gas station attendant, their actions were "the same series of acts or transactions," and it was proper to consolidate their trials. **Larson v. State,** Op. No. 1459, 566 P2d 1019 (Alaska 1977).

Assault by firing a shot towards two people is a single offense and may be included in a single count. **Larson v. State,** Op. No. 1502, 569 P2d 783 (Alaska 1977).

Offense of robbery in the first degree for theft of taxi and offense of theft in the second degree for theft of apartment were closely connected and constituted parts of a common scheme or plan, so as to justify charging both offenses in the same indictment. **Nell v. State,** Op. No. 77, 642 P2d 1361 (Alaska App. 1982).

Where each larceny count against defendant involved airplane theft accomplished through his role as partner in aircraft company and all of the thefts occurred within a five-week period, there was a common scheme or plan within the meaning of this rule justifying joinder of the offenses. **Montes v. State,** Op. No. 289, 669 P2d 961 (Alaska App. 1983).

Antagonistic defenses do not ordinarily require severance; however, where the defenses are irreconcilable, that is, mutually exclusive to the extent that one must be disbelieved if the other is to be believed, severance should be granted. **Abdulbaqui v. State,** Op. No. 659, 728 P2d 1211 (Alaska App. 1986).

Where codefendants presented defenses which were different but not irreconcilable, trial court did not abuse its discretion in refusing to grant severance. **Abdulbaqui v. State,** Op. No. 659, 728 P2d 1211 (Alaska App. 1986).

Trial court erred in denying severance of two similar sexual assault charges involving the same defendant where the evidence did not establish a common scheme or plan, whether or not the evidence of the assault on each victim would have been admissible in a trial for assault on the other victim. **Johnson v. State,** Op. No. 668, 730 P2d 175 (Alaska App. 1986).

Where the weapons that were the subject of theft by receiving charges against defendant were also the subject of felon in possession charges against him, the charges stemmed from the same act or transaction, thus initial joinder of the offenses was proper. **Elerson v. State,** Op. No. 679, 732 P2d 192 (Alaska App. 1987).

Where prior conviction, admissible as an element of felon in possession of firearm charges, would have been inadmissible in a separate trial on theft by receiving charges, trial court erred in denying defendant's severance motion without pursuing the alternative of bifurcation, requiring reversal of the theft by receiving conviction but not the felon in possession conviction. **Elerson v. State,** Op. No. 679, 732 P2d 192 (Alaska App. 1987).

Unless joinder is permitted under this rule, codefendants may not be tried together. **Greiner v. State,** Op. No. 736, 741 P2d 662 (Alaska App. 1987).

Trial court committed reversible error in denying defendant's motion to sever his trial on Counts I and IV from that of this codefendants on Counts II and III, in which he was not charged, since although each count involved drug offenses and there was evidence that all defendants were willing to sell drugs and were well-acquainted and cooperated with each in individual drug sales, there was no real evidence of a conspiracy, joint venture, or common scheme or plan justifying joinder. **Greiner v. State,** Op. No. 736, 741 P2d 662 (Alaska App. 1987).

Since the charges against defendant could properly have been joined in a single indictment, contemporaneous preservation of the same charges in separate indictments to the same grand jury did not violate defendant's due process right to an unbiased grand jury. **Massey v. State,** Op. No. 915, 771 P2d 448 (Alaska App. 1989).

Wherever there is more than one defendant, the joinder of both defendants and issues is governed by the subsection of this rule pertaining to joinder of defendants; the subsection of this rule pertaining to joinder of offenses has no bearing on situations were multiple counts involve multiple defendants. **Mathis v. State,** Op. No. 951, 778 P2d 1161 (Alaska App. 1989).

Trial court did not err in joining cocaine charges with murder, kidnapping, and robbery charges against two defendants, but did err in denying their timely motion to sever based upon prejudice. **Mathis v. State,** Op. No. 951, 778 P2d 1161 (Alaska App. 1989).

Where defendant was charged with a murder which occurred on August 5 and several murders which occurred on August 6, joinder of the offenses was proper, since the August 6 murders resulted from defendant's belief that he was going to be killed because of his role in the August 5 murder; furthermore, the trial court did not err in denying defendant's motion for severance given the relevance of the August 5 murder to the August 6 murders and the absence of any specific and convincing showing prejudice from joinder. **Collins v. State,** Op. No. 962, 778 P2d 1171 (Alaska App. 1989).

Joinder before grand jury is not impermissible merely because joinder at trial would be improper. **Clossen v. State,** Op. No. 992, 784 P2d 661 (Alaska App. 1989).

Grand jury's decision to charge defendant with theft was not appreciably affected by his joinder in the proceedings with murder suspects where a sufficient nexus existed between the theft and the murder and abundant evidence was presented to support the theft charge, thus defendant's motion to dismiss the charge was properly denied. **Clossen v. State,** Op. No. 992,784 P2d 661 (Alaska App. 1989).

Where defendant escaped from a correctional facility and was subsequently charged with escape, assault and attempted murder, the latter charges resulting from his attempt to resist capture, the obvious nexus between the escape charge and the charges arising from subsequent efforts to apprehend him was sufficient to warrant joinder of the charges as being "connected together." **Newcomb v. State,** Op. No. 1088, 800 P2d 935 (Alaska App. 1990).

Automatic severance pursuant to **Stevens v. State,** 582 P2d 621 (Alaska 1978) applies only when the sole basis for joinder is the similar nature of the charges; accordingly, where charges were properly subject to joinder as "connected acts" under this rules. **Stevens** was inapplicable. **Newcomb v. State,** Op. No. 1088, 800 P2d 935 (Alaska App. 1990).

Perjury charges against defendant and the substantive charges against him relating to a car bombing were based on the same act on transaction and therefore were properly joined initially. **Machado v. State,** Op. No. 1067, 797 P2d 677 (Alaska App. 1990).

The nexus between two sexual assault incidents was sufficient to permit their joinder as charges "connected together" within the meaning of this rule; defendant's contention that he was entitled to automatic severance under **Johnson v. State,** Op. No. 668, 730 P2d 175 (Alaska App. 1986), was rejected. **Yearty v. State,** Op. No. 1106, 805 P2d 987 (Alaska App. 1991).

Charges against defendant of selling cocaine from his home on August 5 and of processing with intent to deliver cocaine found in his home on August 6 were properly joined because of their similarity. **McLaughlin v. State,** Op. No. 1159, 818 P2d 683 (Alaska App. 1991).

Evidence relating to Count 1, selling cocaine, was relevant to prove Count 2, possession with intent to deliver cocaine, regardless of its technical sufficiency to support a finding of guilt beyond a reasonable doubt on Count 1, thus trial court did not err in failing to sever the two charges or to order a mistrial as to Count 2 after granting a judgment of acquittal on Count 1. **McLaughlin v. State,** Op. No. 1159, 818 P2d 683 (Alaska App. 1991).

To be charged in a single indictment, it is not necessary that each defendant participate in each act; however, the defendant's offenses will only constitute a series of acts or transactions under this rule if there is a significant connection between the different acts charged. **Erickson v. State,** Op. No. 1179, 824 P2d 725 (Alaska App. 1991).

Where defendant was charged with second degree assault for initiating murder plan, and codefendant was charged with attempted first degree murder, arson, criminal possession of explosives and perjury, all of which charges related to the murder plan, joinder of the two cases was proper. **Erickson v. State,** Op. No. 1179, 824 P2d 725 (Alaska App. 1991).

Defendant's abuse of several young children at his mother's day-care center could reasonably be viewed as separate instances of a common scheme or plan. **Sharp v. State,** Op. No. 1233, 837 P2d 718 (Alaska App. 1992).

Pursuant to 1988 amendment to this rule, defendant's are no longer entitled to automatic severance upon request when similar offenses are joined if the government can demonstrate before trial that evidence of each offense will likely be cross-admissible. **Sharp v. State,** Op. No. 1233, 837 P2d 718 (Alaska App. 1992).

Where defendant committed arson as police attempted to arrest him for unlawful evasion, arson and unlawful evasion charges were properly joined. **West v. State,** Op. No. 1482, 923 P2d 110 (Alaska App. 1996).

A motion to sever joined offenses encompasses two separate inquiries: (1) whether the two offenses charged are so related as to make joinder proper and (2) whether joinder would unduly prejudice the defendant. **Ashley v. State,** Op. No. 1683, 6 P3d 738 (Alaska App. 2000).

Trial court did not abuse its discretion in denying motion to sever charges of reckless driving and failure to report a motor vehicle accident that arose out of the same accident; trial court properly rejected defendant's claim that alcohol evidence at accident scene was not admissible on the reckless driving charge. **Ashley v. State,** Op. No. 1683, 6 P3d 738 (Alaska App. 2000).

Trial court did not err by joining charges imposed against defendant by two grand juries located in Anchorage and Palmer under Alaska R. Crim. P. 13 because joinder was proper under Alaska R. Crim. P. 8(a)(3) - the trial court could properly conclude that the Anchorage robbery and assault, the Palmer vehicle theft, and the Glennallen escape and murder constituted acts that were connected together; defendant committed the armed robbery and assault shortly after being released, he had no intention of paying for the cab ride between Anchorage and Palmer, and defendant's commission of the Anchorage offenses was relevant to explain his decision to assault the officer and escape from custody. Defendant was not prejudiced by the joinder under Alaska R. Crim. P. 14. **Phillips v. State,** Op. No. 1880, 70 P.3d 1128 (Alaska 2003).

Rule 9. Warrant or Summons Upon Indictment or Information.

(a) **Issuance.** Upon the return of the indictment or filing of the information the court shall issue a warrant of arrest for each defendant named in the information, if it is supported by oath, or in the indictment, except that no warrant should be issued for any defendant who has theretofore been held to answer for the offense or offenses charged or who is on bail or recognizance for that offense or offenses, and in other cases no warrant should be issued unless the court has reason to believe that the defendant will not appear in response to a summons. The clerk shall issue a summons instead of a warrant upon the request of the prosecuting attorney, or by direction of the court. Upon like request or direction the clerk shall issue more than one warrant or summons for the same defendant. The clerk shall deliver the warrant or summons to a peace officer or other person authorized by law to execute or serve it. If a defendant fails to appear in response to the summons, a warrant shall issue.

(b) **Form.**

(1) *Warrant.* The form of the warrant shall be as provided in Rule 4 (b) (1) except that it shall be signed by the clerk, it shall describe the offense charged in the indictment or information and it shall command that the defendant be arrested and brought before the court. The amount of bail shall be fixed by the court and endorsed on the warrant.

(2) *Summons.* The summons shall be in the same form as the warrant except that it shall summon the defendant to appear before the court at a stated time and place.

(c) **Execution or Service and Return.**

(1) *Execution or Service.* The warrant shall be executed or the summons served as provided in Rule 4(c) (1), (2), and (3). A summons to a corporation shall be served by delivering a copy to an officer or to a managing or general agent or to any other agent authorized by appointment or by law to receive service of process and, if the agent is one authorized by statute to receive service, by also mailing a copy to the corporation's last known address within the state or at its principal place of business elsewhere in the United States. The officer executing the warrant shall bring the arrested person promptly before the court or, for the purpose of admission to bail, before a magistrate.

(2) *Return.* The officer executing a warrant shall make return thereof to the court. At the request of the prosecuting attorney any unexecuted warrant shall be returned and canceled. On or before the return day the person to whom a summons was delivered for service shall make return thereof. At the request of the prosecuting attorney made at any time while the indictment or information is pending, a warrant returned unexecuted and not canceled or a summons returned unserved or a duplicate thereof may be delivered by the clerk to a peace officer or other person authorized for execution or service.

(3) *Service of Summons by Mail.* In addition to other methods of service provided by this rule, summons instead of a warrant as issued under the provisions of subdivision (a) of this rule may also be served upon a defendant of known residence within the jurisdiction of the State of Alaska by registered or certified mail. In such case a copy or copies of the summons shall be mailed by the clerk to each defendant named in the indictment or the information for delivery only to each such named defendant. The returned delivery receipts shall be attached to the copies of summons retained by the clerk. If a delivery receipt is returned unsigned by the defendant named in the indictment or information to whom the summons was addressed, at the request of the prosecuting attorney made at any time while the indictment or information is pending the summons or duplicate thereof may be delivered by the clerk to a peace officer or other authorized person for service.

(Adopted by SCO 4 October 4, 1959; amended by SCO 90 effective July 24, 1967; amended by SCO 127 effective April 29, 1971; and by SCO 1153 effective July 15, 1994)

Annotations

Cases

Criminal Rule 9(a) does not require that the trial court articulate a reason for the issuance of a bench warrant. **Moreau v. State,** Op. No. 1770, 588 P2d 275 (Alaska 1978).

A bench warrant signed by a deputy clerk, and not by a magistrate or a clerk, was valid. **Moreau v. State,** Op. No. 1770, 588 P2d 275 (Alaska 1978).

PART IV. ARRAIGNMENT AND PREPARATION FOR TRIAL

Rule 10. Arraignment.

(a) **Generally.** Arraignment shall be conducted in open court and shall consist of reading the indictment or information to the defendant or stating to the defendant the substance of the charge and calling on the defendant to plead thereto. The defendant may appear by use of telephonic or television equipment pursuant to Criminal Rules 38.1 and 38.2.

(b) **Defendant's Name.**

(1) When arraigned, the defendant shall be informed of the name which appears in the indictment or information.

(2) The defendant shall then be given the opportunity to declare the defendant's true name.

(i) If the defendant states that another name is the defendant's true name, the court shall direct entry thereof to be made in the record. Subsequent proceedings on the indictment or information shall be had against the defendant by both the declared true name and the name which appears on the indictment or information.

(ii) If the defendant declares no other name to be the defendant's true name, the case against the defendant shall proceed under the name which appears in the indictment or information.

(c) **Peremptory Disqualification of the Judge.** At the arraignment any defendant who has waived counsel shall be advised that the defendant may peremptorily disqualify the judge to whom the defendant's case has been assigned on the grounds that the defendant believes the defendant cannot obtain a fair and impartial trial before that judge. In any court in the state where a master calendar system has been adopted, a defendant who has waived counsel shall be advised at the arraignment that the defendant may give notice of change of judge under Rule 25 (d).

(Adopted by SCO 4 October 4, 1959; amended by SCO 49 effective January 1, 1963; amended by SCO 157 effective February 15, 1973; by SCO 255 effective December 30, 1976; by SCO 589 effective January 1, 1984; by SCO 606 effective October 4, 1984; by SCO 660 effective November 7, 1985; by SCO 719 effective August 1, 1986; and by SCO 1153 effective July 15, 1994)

Annotations

Cases

In arraignment proceeding before disqualified judge, defendant should be advised of his right to have bail heard by another judge and setting of bail should be immediately referred to another judicial officer if it becomes a disputed issue. **Gieffels v. State,** Op. No. 2787, 552 P2d 661 (Alaska 1976).

Judge at arraignment has no discretion before plea is taken so that disqualified judge may act. **Gieffels v. State,** Op. No. 1295, 552 P2d 661 (Alaska 1976).

Since plea of guilty or nolo contendere require judicial determination of voluntary nature and reasonable basis of plea, disqualified arraignment judge should immediately assign case to another judge. **Gieffels v. State,** Op. No. 1295, 552 P2d 661 (Alaska 1976).

If defendant pleads not guilty, disqualified arraignment judge need only refer case to another judge if calendaring becomes a disputed issue. **Gieffels v. State,** Op. No. 1295, 552 P2d 661 (Alaska 1976).

Defendant may not be punished for standing mute when asked his true name since he is not required to respond. **Gieffels v. State,** Op. No. 1295, 552 P2d 661 (Alaska 1976).

Rule 11. Pleas.

(a) **Alternatives.** A defendant may plead not guilty, guilty or nolo contendere. If a defendant refuses to plead, stands mute, or if a defendant corporation fails to appear, the court shall enter a plea of not guilty. The defendant may appear by use of telephonic or television equipment pursuant to Criminal Rules 38.1 and 38.2.

(b) **Extension of Time for Pleading.** If the defendant requests an extension of time for entering a plea, then the court shall allow the defendant until the next day following the arraignment, or until such further time as the court considers reasonable, to plead to the indictment or information.

(c) **Pleas of Guilty or Nolo Contendere.** The court shall not accept a plea of guilty or nolo contendere from a defendant without first addressing the defendant personally and

(1) determining that the defendant understands the nature of the charge; and

(2) informing the defendant that by a plea of guilty or nolo contendere the defendant waives the right to trial by jury or trial by a judge and the right to confront adverse witnesses; and

(3) informing the defendant:

(A) of the mandatory minimum punishment, if any, and the maximum possible punishment provided by the statute defining the offense to which the plea is offered, and

(B) that the defendant has the right to plead not guilty or to persist in that plea if it has already been made, or to plead guilty, and

(C) that if the defendant is not a citizen of the United States, a conviction of a crime may have the consequences of deportation, exclusion from admission to the United States, or denial of naturalization pursuant to federal law; and

(4) if the defendant is charged with a sex offense as defined in AS 12.63.100 or child kidnapping as defined in AS 12.63.100, informing the defendant in writing of the requirements of AS 12.63.010 and, if it can be determined by the court, the period of registration required under AS 12.63; and

(5) in cases when a plea agreement has been accepted by a court, informing the defendant:

(A) that the defendant waives the right to appeal a sentence as excessive and waives the right to seek reduction of a sentence under Criminal Rule 35 if a plea agreement between the defendant and the prosecuting attorney provides for a specific sentence or a sentence equal to or less than a specified maximum; and

(B) that the defendant waives the right to appeal as excessive that portion of a sentence that is less than or equal to a minimum sentence specified in a plea agreement between the defendant and the prosecuting attorney and waives the right to seek reduction of a sentence under Criminal Rule 35 to a length less than the length of the minimum sentence.

(d) **Insuring That the Plea is Voluntary.** The court shall not accept a plea of guilty or nolo contendere without first, by addressing the defendant personally in open court, determining that the plea is voluntary and not the result of force or threats or of promises apart from a plea agreement. The court shall also inquire of the prosecuting attorney, defense counsel and the defendant to determine whether the defendant's willingness to plead guilty or nolo contendere results from prior discussions between the attorney for the state and the defendant or the defendant's attorney.

(e) **Plea Agreement Procedure.**

(1) *Disclosure of Sentencing Agreement.* If the parties reach a sentencing agreement, the court shall require disclosure of the agreement in open court at the time the plea is offered. Once the agreement has been disclosed, the court may accept or reject the agreement, or may defer that decision until receipt of a presentence report. If the court accepts the agreement, the court may impose sentence without a presentence investigation.

(2) *Acceptance of Agreement.* If the court accepts the agreement, the court shall impose sentence in accordance with the terms of that agreement.

(3) *Rejection of Agreement.* If the court rejects the agreement, the court shall inform the parties of this fact and advise the prosecuting attorney and the defendant personally in open court that the court is not bound by the agreement. If the court rejects the agreement as too lenient, the court shall then afford the defendant the opportunity to withdraw the plea. If the court rejects the agreement as too severe, the court shall then afford the prosecuting attorney the opportunity to withdraw from the agreement.

(f) **Determining the Accuracy of Plea.** The court shall not enter a judgment upon a plea of guilty without first being satisfied that there is a reasonable basis for the plea.

(g) **Record.** An electronic recording shall be made of the entire proceeding or proceedings.

(h) **Plea Withdrawal.**

(1) A defendant may not withdraw a plea of guilty or nolo contendere as a matter of right. A defendant may move for withdrawal of the plea without alleging innocence of the charge to which the plea has been entered.

(2) Before sentencing, the trial court shall allow a defendant to withdraw a plea whenever the defendant, upon timely motion, proves that withdrawal is necessary to correct manifest injustice. Absent a showing that withdrawal is necessary to correct manifest injustice, the trial court may in its discretion allow the defendant to withdraw a plea for any fair and just reason unless the prosecution has been substantially prejudiced by reliance upon the defendant's plea.

(3) After imposition of sentence, the withdrawal of a plea may be sought only under AS 12.72. A defendant requesting post-sentence plea withdrawal must prove that withdrawal is necessary to correct a manifest injustice.

(4) Withdrawal is necessary to correct a manifest injustice whenever it is demonstrated that:

(A) The defendant was denied the effective assistance of counsel guaranteed by constitution, statute or rule, or

(B) The plea was not entered or ratified by the defendant or a person authorized to act in the defendant's behalf, or

(C) The plea was involuntary, or was entered without knowledge of the charge or that the sentence actually imposed could be imposed, or

(D) The defendant did not receive the charge or sentence concessions contemplated by the plea agreement, and

(i) the prosecuting attorney failed to seek or opposed the concessions promised in the plea agreement, or

(ii) after being advised that the court no longer concurred and after being called upon to affirm or withdraw the plea, the defendant did not affirm the plea.

(5) A plea of guilty or nolo contendere which is not accepted or has been withdrawn shall not be received against the defendant in any criminal proceeding.

(Adopted by SCO 4 October 4, 1959; amended by SCO 98 effective September 16, 1968; amended by SCO 157 effective February 15, 1973; by SCO 427 effective August 1, 1980; by SCO 589 effective January 1, 1984; by SCO 606 effective October 4, 1984; SCO 660 effective November 7, 1985; by SCO 662 effective March 15, 1986; and by SCO 719 effective August 1, 1986; by SCO 750 effective December 15, 1986; by SCO 1153 effective July 15, 1994; by SCO 1194 effective July 15, 1995; by SCO 1204 effective July 15, 1995; by SCO 1222 effective August 8, 1995; by SCO 1242 effective July 15, 1996; by SCO 1343 effective January 1, 1999; by SCO 1382 (as revised by SCO 1413) effective April 15, 2000; and by SCO 1590 effective April 15, 2006)

Note to SCO 1204: Criminal Rule 11(c)(4) was added by ch. 41 § 10 SLA 1994. Section 5 of this order is adopted for the sole reason that the legislature has mandated the amendments.

Note to SCO 1242: Criminal Rules 11(c) and (h) were amended by ch. 79 §§ 24 & 26 SLA 1995. Sections 1 and 2 of this order are adopted for the sole reason that the legislature has mandated the amendments.

Annotations

Cases

I. Pleas.
- A. In General.
- B. Voluntariness and Understanding.
- C. Withdrawal.
- D. Plea Agreements.

I. Pleas.

A. In General.

Where record failed to show that the defendant was ever called upon to enter a plea but record showed that the trial was conducted as though he had entered a plea of not guilty and that the defendant's situation would not have been altered in any respect if such a plea had been entered, failure to enter a plea did not render the conviction void. **State v. Pete,** Op. No. 372, 420 P2d 338 (Alaska 1966).

A defendant who was adequately represented by counsel and who voluntarily and knowingly entered a plea of guilty, waived all non-jurisdictional defenses. **Thompson v. State,** Op. No. 408, 426 P2d 995 (Alaska 1967).

A plea of nolo contendere, like a guilty plea, is both an admission of guilt and a waiver of all non-jurisdictional defects. **Cooksey v. State,** Op. No. 1063, 524 P2d 1251 (Alaska 1974).

A plea of guilty is generally regarded as a waiver of all nonjurisdictional defects; such plea provides a means by which a defendant may acknowledge his guilt and manifest a willingness to assume responsibility for his actions. **Cooksey v. State,** Op. No. 1063, 524 P2d 1251 (Alaska 1974).

When defendant pleads guilty without the assistance of counsel, the plea is invalid unless defendant waived his right to counsel. **Gregory v. State,** Op. No. 1269, 550 P2d 374 (Alaska 1976).

Since plea of guilty or nolo contendere requires judicial determination of voluntary nature and reasonable basis of plea, disqualified arraignment judge should immediately assign case to another judge. **Gieffels v. State,** Op. No. 2787, 552 P2d 661 (Alaska 1976).

If defendant pleads not guilty, disqualified arraignment judge need only refer case to another judge if calendaring becomes a disputed issue. **Gieffels v. State,** Op. No. 1295, 552 P2d 661 (Alaska 1976).

It was proper to conduct hearing to determine if defendant's nolo contendere plea has been obtained in accordance with the rules when electronic recording system had failed. **Joe v. State,** Op. No. 1448, 565 P2d 508 (Alaska 1977).

In absence of record which affirmatively demonstrates compliance with this rule by sentencing court, the burden is on the state to prove substantial compliance by a preponderance of the evidence. **Joe v. State,** Op. No. 1448, 565 P2d 508 (Alaska 1977).

Defendant's plea of nolo contendere conditioned on his right to appeal did not waive his right to appeal where defendant was not told by the court that the conditional nature of his plea was a nullity and would preserve no appellate rights. **Deacon v. State,** Op. No. 1586, 575 P2d 1225 (Alaska 1978).

Trial courts shall not accept confessions in return for deferred prosecution, but shall instead proceed by means of the established suspended imposition of sentence procedure. **Stobaugh v. State,** Op. No. 2127, 614 P2d 767 (Alaska 1980).

In a case involving a simple offense and a quite specific charge, i.e. operating a motor vehicle while intoxicated, the requirement that the court establish a factual basis for the plea was satisfied by the reading of the charge and defendant's subsequent plea. **Swensen v. Municipality of Anchorage,** Op. No. 2179, 616 P2d 874 (Alaska 1980).

This rule does not permit the court to inquire as to whether there is a reasonable basis for a plea of nolo contendere. **Miller v. State,** Op. No. 2186, 617 P2d 516 (Alaska 1980).

Where a defendant pleads guilty to a lesser offense and a review of the facts establishes that he, in fact, committed a greater offense, the court may legitimately find that he is a worst offender for purposes of sentencing him for the lesser offense. **Schnecker v. State,** Op. No. 732, 739 P2d 1310 (Alaska App. 1987).

If a defendant establishes that there has been a violation of this rule, the state must bear the burden of showing, by a preponderance of the evidence, that the court substantially complied with the rule. **Walsh v. State,** Op. No. 829, 758 P2d 124 (Alaska App. 1988).

The list of circumstances that constitute "manifest injustice" in this rule are not exhaustive; other circumstances may constitute manifest injustice and thus permit withdrawal of a plea. **Peterson v. State,** Op. No. 1640, 988 P2d 109 (Alaska App. 1999).

Alleged violations of the rule at defendant's plea hearing at the time of his earlier convictions could not be raised in an attempted collateral attack on those convictions, in a challenge to sentencing as a second offender; defendant could still raise his challenge via post-conviction relief petition. **Brockway v. State,** Op. No. 1777, 37 P3d 427 (Alaska App. 2001).

B. Voluntariness and Understanding.

Plea of guilty made in 1952 under the similar federal rule was voluntarily made when the defendant had discussed the plea of guilty with counsel of his choice who advised him of the effect thereof and was present at plea, and the trial judge had determined at a conference with counsel though not in open court that the plea was not improvidently made, and the judge had asked appellant if he had anything to say why sentence should not be imposed. **Oughton v. State,** Op. No. 377, 420 P2d 452 (Alaska 1966).

The fact that a plea of guilty was entered because of the possibility of obtaining a more lenient sentence did not, standing alone, vitiate the plea, when it was established on the record that appellant was fully aware of the consequences of his plea. **Thompson v. State,** Op. No. 408, 426 P2d 995 (Alaska 1967).

Record of post-conviction hearing on remand disclosed sufficient basis for superior court's finding that appellant's change of plea to guilty was made voluntarily and with understanding of the nature of the charge. **Thompson v. State,** Op. No. 408, 426 P2d 995 (Alaska 1967).

Where a guilty plea is in fact entered voluntarily and with an understanding of the nature of the charge, the failure of the trial court to determine, prior to accepting the guilty plea, that the plea is made voluntarily with an understanding of the nature of the charge is harmless, and there is no reason to vacate defendant's sentence in order to allow him to withdraw his guilty plea; however, in such a situation, the burden is on the state to demonstrate that the plea was in fact made voluntarily and with an understanding of the nature of the charge. **Ingram v. State,** Op. No. 523, 450 P2d 161 (Alaska 1969).

Where a defendant suffers from mental deficiencies, it is incumbent upon either his counsel or the court, before acceptance of a guilty plea to a charge of second-degree murder, to explain to the defendant as clearly as possible the difference between first and second-degree murder and the consequences of entering a plea of guilty to second-degree murder. **Ingram v. State,** Op. No. 523, 450 P2d 161 (Alaska 1969).

The phrase "understanding of the nature of the charge" encompasses an awareness of the consequences of a guilty plea, including a knowledge of both the maximum sentence and the mandatory minimum sentence in the defendant's particular situation. **Ingram v. State,** Op. No. 523, 450 P2d 161 (Alaska 1969).

Before accepting a guilty plea, the court must investigate the circumstances under which the plea is made with sufficient thoroughness so that it can objectively be concluded that the defendant entered his plea voluntarily and with the understanding of the nature of the charge against him. **Ingram v. State,** Op. No. 523, 450 P2d 161 (Alaska 1969).

The entering of a plea by an accused is a critical stage in the criminal proceeding; hence, courts have been very concerned that a plea of guilty or nolo contendere, which pleas act as a waiver of many constitutionally guaranteed rights, be both voluntary and intelligently entered. If the plea does not possess both attributes then it is generally not regarded as valid and binding. **Cooksey v. State,** Op. No. 1063, 524 P2d 1251 (Alaska 1974).

A court must personally address defendant before accepting a plea of guilty or nolo contendere to determine the defendant's understanding of the consequences of his plea. **McKinnon v. State,** Op. No. 1075, 526 P2d 18 (Alaska 1974).

An accused need not be informed of every conceivable collateral effect a conviction might have prior to the trial court's acceptance of a plea of guilty. The trial judge is not required to recite to the accused all his rights nor is he required to obtain a specific waiver or statement by the defendant that he understands each one of them. The record, taken as a whole, must show an understanding of the nature of the offense charged and that the plea was made voluntarily and intelligently. **Barrett v. State,** Op. No. 1225, 544 P2d 830 (Alaska 1975).

Court improperly accepted plea of guilty of assault with a dangerous weapon from defendant appearing pro se who did not know that unloaded weapon was not dangerous under statute. **Else v. State,** Op. No. 1332, 555 P2d 1210 (Alaska 1976).

Single response from pro se defendant that he understands a charge is inadequate basis for believing that he does. **Else v. State,** Op. No. 1332, 555 P2d 1210 (Alaska 1976).

To adequately assure defendant's understanding of the nature of the charge, trial judge should have informed him that an unloaded gun not used as a bludgeon is not a dangerous weapon under Alaska Statute. **Else v. State,** Op. No. 1332, 555 P2d 1210 (Alaska 1976).

Where the court was informed by the district attorney of the plea bargain and neither the defendant or his attorney objected to the district attorney's description, the court substantially complied with the requirements of Criminal Rule 11(d), although the preferred procedure would have been for the court to ask the defendant to detail his understanding of the bargain. **Winkler v. State,** Op. No. 1653, 580 P2d 1167 (Alaska 1978).

Trial court's failure to comply with requirements of Criminal Rule 11(c) did not affect defendant's substantial rights and was, therefore, harmless error. **Morgan v. State,** Op. No. 1663, 582 P2d 1017 (Alaska 1978).

Criminal Rule 11(c)(3)(i) does not require that defendant be advised of the mandatory period he would have to serve before being eligible for parole. **Morgan v. State,** Op. No. 1663, 582 P2d 1017 (Alaska 1978).

Where defendant's waiver of statute of limitations on lesser included offense was knowingly, intelligently and voluntarily made, and was for defendant's benefit and was made after consultation with counsel, and did not contravene any of the policy reasons underlying criminal statutes of limitations, that trial court had jurisdiction to accept defendant's plea of nolo contendere to the lesser included offense. **Padie v. State,** Op. No. 1843, 594 P2d 50 (Alaska 1979).

In accepting defendant's plea of guilty to the crime of shooting with intent to wound, the judge's failure to explain that shooting with intent to wound is a specific intent crime did not prevent defendant from understanding the charge well enough to realize that he had a possible diminished capacity defense due to intoxication. **Larson v. State,** Op. No. 2128, 614 P2d 776 (Alaska 1980).

Among the factors which may be considered in determining whether a defendant understands the nature of a charge are his age, intelligence, prior history of involvement in legal proceedings, the complexity of the statute, possible language barriers, and whether the defendant is represented by counsel. **Larson v. State,** Op. No. 2128, 614 P2d 776 (Alaska 1980).

It is the duty of defendant's lawyer, not the trial judge, to suggest affirmative defenses. **Larson v. State,** Op. No. 2128, 614 P2d 776 (Alaska 1980).

Where defendant was arraigned en masse along with a number of other misdemeanor defendants, the recitation of rights to the group, followed by the questioning as to each defendant concerning whether he or she understood those rights, was an acceptable procedure. **Swensen v. Municipality of Anchorage,** Op. No. 2179, 616 P2d 874 (Alaska 1980).

In a group arraignment each defendant with a right to a jury trial must be individually apprised of that right unless the entire group is unconditionally advised of their right to jury trials. **Swensen v. Municipality of Anchorage,** Op. No. 2179, 616 P2d 874 (Alaska 1980).

Defendant charged with operating a motor vehicle while intoxicated was adequately informed of the "nature of the charge" when the court read the charge to him and gave him an opportunity to ask any questions he might have. **Swensen v. Municipality of Anchorage,** Op. No. 2179, 616 P2d 874 (Alaska 1980).

Where prior to his plea defendant was informed by the court that action "may" be taken on his driver's license, when in fact temporary revocation was mandated by statute, the court was in error but the error, considered alone, was harmless. **Swensen v. Municipality of Anchorage,** Op. No. 2179, 616 P2d 874 (Alaska 1980).

When the court determines that a plea of nolo contendere is knowing and voluntary, it is bound to accept the plea and, once accepted, the plea cannot then be rejected. **Miller v. State,** Op. No. 2186, 617 P2d 516 (Alaska 1980).

Where evidence indicated that defendant understood that a verdict of not guilty by reason of insanity would not be guaranteed in return for his waiver of a jury trial, but that its likelihood would be enhanced as a result of the waiver, the waiver was valid. **Dolchok v. State,** Op. No. 2458, 639 P2d 277 (Alaska 1982).

A person pleading guilty to criminal mischief in the third degree, a crime involving property damage of less than $500, can be required to pay an amount of restitution in excess of $500 so long as the payment is made to "an aggrieved party" and the amount does not exceed the actual damage or loss caused by the crime. **Fee v. State,** Op. No. 187, 656 P2d 1202 (Alaska App. 1982).

Failure of trial judge to address defendant personally to determine his understanding of the nature of the offense required that defendant be permitted to withdraw his plea of nolo contendere and reinstate his original plea of not guilty. **Bratcher v. State,** Op. No. 368, 681 P2d 358 (Alaska App. 1984).

It is not necessary to inform a person entering a guilty or nolo contendere plea of his privilege against self-incrimination as long as it can be determined that the plea was voluntarily and intelligently made. **Travelstead v. State,** Op. No. 407, 689 P2d 494 (Alaska App. 1984).

Trial judge committed reversible error in not allowing defendant, charged with drunk driving in 1984, to have a 1975 drunk driving conviction set aside on the ground that, although informed by the magistrate taking his guilty plea in 1975 of his right to an attorney, he was not informed of what an attorney could do for him. **Petranovich v. State,** Op. No. 547, 709 P2d 867 (Alaska App. 1985).

A trial judge, accepting a plea of no contest or guilty, must address the defendant personally and inform him of any mandatory minimum punishment: failure to substantially comply with this requirement invalidates any subsequent plea. **State v. Price,** Op. No. 595, 715 P2d 1183 (Alaska App. 1986).

Failure of court to advise defendant that he had a right to persist in his plea of not guilty was error, but the error did not affect defendant's substantial rights. **Aiken v. State,** Op. No. 672, 730 P2d 821 (Alaska App. 1987).

Where court asked DWI defendant if he understood the maximum and mandatory minimum penalties for the offense and the defendant responded affirmatively, the court substantially complied with the requirement of this rule that defendant be informed of the possible penalties for the crime. **Aiken v. State,** Op. No. 672, 730 P2d 821 (Alaska App. 1987).

Defendant's waiver of his right to counsel prior to pleading guilty to a DWI charge was valid where the magistrate advised him of the maximum and minimum penalties for the offense and after he responded affirmatively to the question: "Do you know what a lawyer is?" **Tobuk v. State,** Op. No. 683, 732 P2d 1099 (Alaska App. 1987).

When a defendant who has pled no contest, particularly one who is not represented by counsel, offers an explanation at allocation consistent with innocence, the trial court is obligated to ascertain that the defendant understands the elements of the offense but wishes to plea no contest despite the knowledge that if a jury accepts his explanation he could be exonerated; accordingly, failure of the judge to address such a defendant personally to determine his understanding of the nature of the offense, in light of his claim of innocence, requires that defendant be permitted to withdraw his plea of nolo contendere and reinstate a plea of not guilty. **Walsh v. State,** Op. No. 829, 758 P2d 124 (Alaska App. 1988).

This rule requires the court, before it accepts a plea of guilty or no contest, to advise the defendant of any mandatory minimum or statutory maximum term applicable to the case, but it does not require specific information concerning the applicable presumptive term. **Wiley v. State,** Op. No. 1181, 822 P2d 940 (Alaska App. 1991).

In absence of valid, on-the-record election by defendant to persist in his original no contest plea and to refrain from exercising his right of withdrawal following trial court's rejection of original plea agreement, trial court erred in holding defendant to terms of amended plea bargain and in entering judgment on no contest plea entered in anticipation of original plea agreement; actions by defendant's counsel were no substitute for defendant's personal affirmation of original plea, nor was defendant's ambiguous response at sentencing hearing to court's inquiry as to whether he wanted to be sentenced under newly offered agreement. **Kolkman v. State,** Op. No. 1310, 857 P2d 1202 (Alaska App. 1993).

If defendant prevailed on claims of ineffective assistance of counsel which implicated his original counsel's handling of the case at the change-of-plea stage, he would have been entitled as a matter of right to reinstatement of his original not guilty pleas. **DeJesus v. State,** Op. No. 1415, 897 P2d 608 (Alaska App. 1995).

C. Withdrawal.

Defendant whose confession was obtained without fraud and coercion, and who waived prosecution by indictment and pled guilty, could not after sentencing withdraw his plea under this rule. **Rivett v. State,** Op. No. 249, 395 P2d 264 (Alaska 1964).

Motions for withdrawal of guilty pleas are addressed to the sound discretion of the court and upon direct review any rulings will be set aside only for abuses of discretion. **Knaub v. State,** Op. No. 489, 443 P2d 44 (Alaska 1968).

Where the judge who presided over a petitioner's mental competency hearing and who adjudged the petitioner competent to stand trial and who was assigned to preside over the trial and to accept the petitioner's changes of pleas from not guilty to guilty is absent from the district at the time of the petitioner's making a motion to withdraw his guilty pleas, the presiding judge has jurisdiction to hear the motion. **Knaub v. State,** Op. No. 489, 443 P2d 44 (Alaska 1968).

Findings of fact and conclusions of law are not required to be filed by a judge in determining a motion for the withdrawal of a plea of guilty. **Knaub v. State,** Op. No. 489, 443 P2d 44 (Alaska 1968).

A defendant is entitled to the vacation of his sentence to allow him to withdraw his plea of guilty where the trial court, prior to accepting the guilty plea, fails to determine that the plea was made voluntarily with an understanding of the nature of the charge and where the state fails to demonstrate that the plea was in fact made voluntarily and with an understanding of the nature of the charge. **Ingram v. State,** Op. No. 523, 450 P2d 161 (Alaska 1969).

Where the plea of guilty was made without assistance of counsel or valid waiver of right to counsel, plea may be withdrawn under this rule. **Gregory v. State,** Op. No. 1269, 550 P2d 374 (Alaska 1976).

Withdrawal of guilty plea or vacation of conviction for failure to comply with Criminal Rule 11 will only be granted when noncompliance affected substantial rights of defendant. **Lewis v. State,** Op. No. 1447, 565 P2d 846 (Alaska 1977).

Where court only inquired if defendant understood he could be sentenced on a no contest plea as on a guilty plea, defendant would be allowed to withdraw no contest plea. **Solberg v. State,** Op. No. 1478, 568 P2d 1 (Alaska 1977).

Defendant's failure to withdraw guilty plea when prosecutor offered to allow him to do so when violation of plea bargain was claimed, was a waiver of argument that he had a right to withdraw plea under this rule. **Salazar v. State,** Op. No. 1404, 562 P2d 694 (Alaska 1977).

A defendant cannot challenge the voluntariness of his plea on direct appeal from the judgment entered upon his plea; a motion to withdraw the plea must first be made in superior court. **Gordon v. State,** Op. No. 1608, 577 P2d 701 (Alaska 1978).

Defendant's subjective impression from the tone of pre-plea discussions that he would receive probation was not sufficient to support his claim that manifest injustice would result from a denial of post-sentencing opportunity to withdraw his guilty plea where neither the district attorney or defendant's own counsel promised probation. **Winkler v. State,** Op. No. 1653, 580 P2d 1167 (Alaska 1978).

Defendant must prove manifest injustice before withdrawal of plea will be permitted. **Morgan v. State,** Op. No. 1663, 582 P2d 1017 (Alaska 1978).

A person moving to withdraw a guilty plea and moving for post-conviction relief need not show that the former motion has been made with "due diligence." **Swensen v. Municipality of Anchorage,** Op. No. 2179, 616 P2d 874 (Alaska 1980).

A defendant must move to withdraw his plea pursuant to this rule before he will be allowed to challenge its validity on appeal. **Osborne v. State,** Op. No. 2291, 623 P2d 784 (Alaska 1981).

The withdrawal of a guilty plea prior to sentencing should be allowed when the defendant shows a breakdown in the attorney-client relationship at the time of the plea and was able to consult with his attorney for only a short time before entering the plea, and the prosecution has not alleged prejudice from a withdrawal. **Love v. State,** Op. No. 28, 630 P2d 21 (Alaska App. 1981).

When there is a violation of the requirements of this rule in taking a defendant's plea, the defendant, in withdrawing his plea, does not have the burden to show that his plea was not voluntary or that there was manifest injustice. **Fulton v. State,** Op. No. 34, 630 P2d 1004 (Alaska App. 1981).

Where defendant did not attempt to withdraw his plea of nolo contendere until seven months after it was entered, and did not support his contention that he was pressured into the plea with an affidavit from his former attorney, trial court did not abuse its discretion in denying defendant's request to withdraw the plea even though the request was made prior to sentencing. **Travelstead v. State,** Op. No. 407, 689 P2d 494 (Alaska App. 1984).

While permitting withdrawal of a plea is within the sound discretion of the trial court, presentence requests for withdrawal of pleas should be granted liberally. **Wahl v. State,** Op. No. 425, 691 P2d 1048 (Alaska App. 1984).

Absent unfair prejudice to the state or unfair advantage to the accused, the arguments against permitting withdrawal of a plea prior to sentencing weaken considerably; and the test of what constitutes a fair and just reason for withdrawal should be commensurately less demanding. **Wahl v. State,** Op. No. 425, 691 P2d 1048 (Alaska App. 1984).

Where defendant filed a motion to withdraw his plea prior to sentencing no prejudice was claimed by the prosecution, and there was no indication that defendant was attempting to manipulate the criminal justice system, defendant's good faith, unilateral mistake about the existence of a sentencing agreement constituted a fair and just reason to permit withdrawal of the plea, and trial court abused its discretion in denying the motion. **Wahl v. State,** Op. No. 425, 691 P2d 1048 (Alaska App. 1984).

Trial court did not abuse its discretion in refusing to allow defendant to withdraw his guilty plea after reasonably concluding that defendant entered his plea to manipulate the system to obtain a continuance and that the State would be potentially prejudiced if the plea were withdrawn. **Ningealook v. State,** Op. No. 426, 691 P2d 1053 (Alaska App. 1984).

Trial judge properly denied defendant's motion to withdraw his no contest plea prior to sentencing on the ground that defendant was attempting to manipulate the system. **Resek v. State,** Op. No. 597, 715 P2d 1188 (Alaska App. 1986).

A showing that a plea resulted from ineffective assistance of counsel is equivalent to a showing of manifest injustice, entitling the defendant to withdraw his plea without further inquiry into the issue of manifest injustice. **Smith v. State,** Op. No. 610, 717 P2d 402 (Alaska App. 1986).

The decision of whether to grant the withdrawal of a plea is within the trial court's discretion, but presentence requests for withdrawal should be liberally granted. **McClain v. State,** Op. No. 741, 742 P2d 269 (Alaska App. 1987).

In seeking to withdraw a plea, the burden is on the defendant to establish a fair and just reason for withdrawal. **McClain v. State,** Op. No. 741, 742 P2d 269 (Alaska App. 1987).

Defendant's reasons for seeking withdrawal of a plea must be evaluated against the delay preceding the request, the extent of prejudice to the prosecution, and the likelihood that the defendant is attempting to manipulate the system to obtain an unfair advantage. **McClain v. State,** Op. No. 741, 742 P2d 269 (Alaska App. 1987).

Trial court in sexual abuse case involving a young girl, after considering the psychological effect on the victim of allowing defendant to withdraw his no contest plea and to proceed to a trial at which the victim would have to testify, did not abuse its discretion in denying defendant's request to withdraw his plea, which request was apparently triggered by defendant's reconciliation with his wife and the resultant prospect of favorable testimony from her. **McClain v. State,** Op. No. 741, 742 P2d 269 (Alaska App. 1987).

Defendant's request to withdraw his plea, based upon allegations unsupported by the record that he was surprised that he would be subjected to presumptive sentencing and that there was a manifest breakdown in the attorney-client relationship, was properly rejected by the trial court. **Shetters v. State,** Op. No. 790, 751 P2d 31 (Alaska App. 1988).

A defendant's mere change of mind or reevaluation of his chances for a favorable verdict is not sufficient reason for a plea withdrawal even if the withdrawal request comes before sentencing and the state would suffer no prejudice if trial were held. **Shetters v. State,** Op. No.790,751 P2d 31 (Alaska App. 1988).

Where a person enters a plea on the advice of counsel and is sentenced pursuant to a plea and sentence agreement, he may not withdraw his plea merely because the trial court failed to give the warnings and inquiries specified in this rule. **Severson v. Municipality of Anchorage,** Op. No. 1061, 794 P2d 1351 (Alaska App. 1990).

Trial court had no authority to impose a due diligence requirement on a motion to withdraw plea, where the motion was predicated on the contention that the trial court did not comply with the provisions of this rule. **Severson v. Municipality of Anchorage,** Op. No. 1061, 794 P2d 1351 (Alaska App. 1990).

This rule requires the court, before it accepts a plea of guilty or no contest, to advise the defendant of any mandatory minimum or statutory maximum term applicable to the case, but it does not require specific information concerning the applicable presumptive term. **Wiley v. State,** Op. No. 1181, 822 P2d 940 (Alaska App. 1991).

Fact that judge at plea hearing mistakenly indicated that the applicable presumptive sentence in the case would be eight years instead of ten years did not entitle defendant to withdraw his no contest plea. **Wiley v. State,** Op. No. 1181, 822 P2d 940 (Alaska App. 1991).

Defendant's attorney misinformed him when she told him that he did not have a defense to the charge of being a felon in possession of a concealable firearm, thus trial court erred in refusing to let him withdraw his guilty plea. **Hansen v. State,** Op. No. 1196, 824 P2d 1384 (Alaska App. 1992).

In motion under this rule to withdraw plea because of ineffective assistance of counsel, defendant bears same burden of proving ineffective assistance as he would bear if issue arose on application for post-conviction relief or on direct appeal. **Lott v. State,** Op. No. 1228, 836 P2d 371 (Alaska App. 1992).

Allegations of incompetence contained in affidavits filed by defendant in support of motion to withdraw guilty plea because of ineffective assistance of counsel, coupled with sketchy and abbreviated testimony presented by defendant at evidentiary hearing, fell far short of providing evidentiary context necessary to overcome strong presumption that trial counsel performed competently and that his actions were motivated by sound tactical considerations. **Lott v. State,** Op. No. 1228, 836 P2d 371 (Alaska App. 1992).

Defendants bore the burden of proving, by clear and convincing evidence that they were entitled to withdraw their no contest pleas to assault; nevertheless, the trial court's findings that defendants understood the collateral consequences of their pleas were not clearly erroneous, and the finding was also not clearly erroneous that the possibility that they could be sued in a civil suit did not affect their decision to plead. The trial court did not err in denying defendants' request to withdraw the plea. **Register v. State,** Op. No. 1882, 71 P.3d 337 (Alaska 2003).

Defendants bore the burden of proving, by clear and convincing evidence that they were entitled to withdraw their no contest pleas to assault; nevertheless, the trial court's findings that defendants understood the collateral consequences of their pleas were not clearly erroneous, and the finding was also not clearly erroneous that the possibility that they could be sued in a civil suit did not affect their decision to plead. The trial court did not err in denying defendants' request to withdraw the plea. **Register v. State,** Op. No. 1882, 71 P.3d 337 (Alaska 2003).

D. Plea Agreements.

Since terms of any agreement must be disclosed on the record before the superior court may accept a nolo contendere plea, and failure to abide by a condition of the plea renders it invalid, defendant is guaranteed the benefit of his bargain with the state as long as Criminal Rule 11(e) is substantially complied with. **Padie v. State,** Op. No. 1843, 594 P2d 50 (Alaska 1979).

Failure of court to expressly inform defendant that court accepted the terms of the plea agreement, and that the sentence would be at least as favorable to him as that contemplated in the plea agreement, did not violate substantial compliance standards where defendant in fact received the benefit of his bargain with the state. **Padie v. State,** Op. No. 1843, 594 P2d 50 (Alaska 1979).

Plea bargain pursuant to which defendant pled no contest to attempted assault in the first degree, for which his presumptive sentence was 4 years, did not preclude the trial court from sentencing him to a longer sentence based on a finding that defendant's conduct was among the most serious contemplated within the definitions of the offense of attempted assault in the first degree. **Schnecker v. State,** Op. No. 732, 739 P2d 1310 (Alaska App. 1987).

Inmate alleged that he was not aware that after two years of imprisonment he would be released and would serve the remainder of his six year sentence on mandatory parole; the inmate established a prima facie case that he received ineffective assistance of counsel about the nature of the sentence he would receive if he entered into the plea bargain, and that he would not have entered into the plea bargain had he received accurate advice regarding mandatory parole. **Knox v. State,** Op. No. 2035, 130 P.3d 971 (Alaska App. 2006).

Rule 12. Pleadings and Motions Before Trial—Defenses and Objections.

(a) **Pleadings and Motions.** Pleadings in criminal proceedings shall be the complaint, the indictment and the information, and the pleas of not guilty, guilty and nolo contendere. All other pleas, demurrers and motions to quash are abolished, and defenses and objections raised before trial which heretofore could have been raised by one or more of them shall be raised only by motion to dismiss or to grant appropriate relief, as provided in these rules.

(b) **Pretrial Motions*.** Any defense, objection, or request which is capable of determination without the trial of the general issue may be raised before trial by motion. Any or all of the following shall be raised prior to trial:

(1) Defenses and objections based on defects in the institution of the prosecution;

(2) Defenses and objections based on defects in the indictment or information (other than a failure to show jurisdiction in the court or to charge an offense, which objections shall be noticed by the court at any time during pendency of the proceeding);

(3) Motions to suppress evidence on the ground that it was illegally obtained;

(4) Requests for a severance of charges or defendants under Rule 14.

(c) **Pretrial Motion Date.** All pretrial motions listed in Rule 12(b) must be filed within 45 days after the defendant's arraignment. The court may vary the time for good cause shown.

(d) **Ruling on Motion.** A motion made before trial shall be determined before trial unless the court orders that it be deferred for determination at the trial of the general issue. Where factual issues are involved in determining a motion to suppress evidence, the court shall state its essential findings on the record.

(e) **Effect of Failure to Raise Defenses or Objections.** Failure by the defendant to raise defenses or objections or to make requests which must be made prior to trial, at the time set by the court pursuant to section (c), or prior to any extension thereof made by the court, shall constitute waiver thereof, but the court for cause shown may grant relief from the waiver.

(f) **Record.** An electronic recording shall be made of all judicial proceedings under this rule.

(g) **Effect of Determination.** If the court grants a motion based on a defect in the institution of the prosecution or in the indictment or information, it may also order that the defendant be held in custody or that bail be continued for a specified time pending the filing of a new indictment or information.

(h) **Continuance of Trial.** A motion for continuance of a trial date will be granted by the court only for cause shown. The presiding judge of a judicial district may require that a visiting or pro tem judge obtain approval from the presiding judge before granting any continuance of trial.

(Adopted by SCO 4 October 4, 1959; amended by SCO 157 effective February 15, 1973; by SCO 557 effective April 4, 1983; by SCO 894 effective July 15, 1988; by SCO 1126 effective July 15, 1993; by SCO 1153 effective July 15, 1994; and by SCO 1592 effective April 15, 2006)

*See Chapter 119 SLA 1972 effective September 10, 1972.

Annotations

Cases

The trial court's unequivocal ruling upon a motion for acquittal on grounds of insufficiency of evidence that it dismissed the count only for a defect in the indictment, was considered as the equivalent of the granting of a motion to dismiss pursuant to Crim. R. 12(b)(2). **State v. Selman,** Op. No. 302, 406 P2d 181 (Alaska 1965).

If dismissal is based upon what the court considered a defect in the indictment, the state has a right to appeal to test the sufficiency of the indictment. **State v. Selman,** Op. No. 302, 406 P2d 181 (Alaska 1965).

In the absence of showing sufficient cause to grant relief from waiver, improper joinder of counts of an indictment was waived by failure to request severance before trial. **State v. Selman,** Op. No. 302, 406 P2d 181 (Alaska 1965).

The defense that an indictment fails to charge an offense cannot be tested by a motion for judgment of acquittal, but must be raised by motion under this rule. **Stewart v. State,** Op. No. 457, 438 P2d 387 (Alaska 1968).

A defense motion to dismiss an indictment on the basis that it had been issued by a grand jury composed entirely of Juneau, rather than Ketchikan, residents can properly be denied, where it is presented after the jury has been selected and sworn, it does not charge that the indictment fails to show jurisdiction in the court, and the defense counsel offers no explanation for failure to raise the motion between the defendant's arraignment and trial. **Wright v. State,** Op. No. 833, 501 P2d 1360 (Alaska 1972).

A mere formal defect does not require dismissal of an indictment after the defendant's guilt has been established at a fair trial. However, a conviction must be overturned when an indictment is invalid and the error is properly preserved by timely objection prior to trial. **Taggard v. State,** Op. No. 821, 500 P2d 238 (Alaska 1972).

If a motion for peremptory disqualification of the trial judge is timely filed, then the trial judge errs in not automatically excluding himself from sitting on the case. **McCracken v. State,** Op. No. 1028, 521 P2d 499 (Alaska 1974).

A defendant's failure to raise a constitutional challenge to the statute which he is charged with violating prior to trial or at the pretrial omnibus hearing does not constitute a waiver of the constitutional challenge. **Gray v. State,** Op. No. 1068, 525 P2d 524 (Alaska 1974).

A motion to dismiss an indictment must be made before trial to allow the trial court to rule on any defects in the indictment prior to trial so that the prosecution may reindict a defendant. **Gaona v. State,** Op. No. 31, 630 P2d 534 (Alaska App. 1981).

A defendant may bring a post-trial motion to contest the sufficiency of a felony indictment which failed to give clear and unequivocal notice that the charge against the defendant was technically a felony. **Post v. State,** Op. No. 56, 635 P2d 1194 (Alaska App. 1981).

In the absence of a timely pretrial objection, hearsay testimony presented to and considered by a grand jury should be regarded on appeal as constituting admissible and fully competent evidence. **Cassell v. State,** Op. No. 91, 645 P2d 219 (Alaska App. 1982).

Failure of defendant at his first trial to request disclosure of evidence taken from the victim, which evidence was destroyed after the trial, waived any right he may have had to the evidence at his second trial on the same charge, reversal of his first conviction not having revived discovery rights which had already lapsed; consequently, the prosecution had no duty to preserve the evidence in question unless it was so clearly exculpatory that the prosecutor was obligated to preserve it absent a request. **Carman v. State,** Op. No. 206, 658 P2d 131 (Alaska App. 1983).

Motion to dismiss grand jury indictment on the ground that improper information was presented to the grand jury was properly denied as untimely, since the motion was not raised until during or after jury selection, and because the other evidence presented was so strong that the grand jury's decision to indict was clearly not affected by the allegedly improper information. **Pritchard v. State,** Op. No. 319, 673 P2d 291 (Alaska App. 1983).

Where motion to suppress evidence was filed late but prior to trial, it was abuse of discretion for the trial court to deny the motion as untimely where defendant was not personally responsible for the late filing and his attorney did not act in bad faith for the purpose of delay. **Fox v. State,** Op. No. 394, 685 P2d 1267 (Alaska App. 1984).

Where charge of being a felon in possession of a firearm was properly joined to kidnapping and other charges, thereby allowing the jury to be informed of defendant's prior felony conviction, which would not have been the case had the firearm possession charge been severed, trial judge did not abuse his discretion in refusing as untimely defendant's severance motion made on the morning of trial. **Wortham v. State,** Op. No. 414, 689 P2d 1133 (Alaska App. 1984).

A party intending to rely upon a subsistence defense to charges of violating hunting laws must make a preliminary showing at a reasonable time before trial; failure to give notice of the defense before trial or in the manner prescribed in a pretrial order may, unless excuse for good cause, result in the forfeiture of the defense. **State v. Eluska,** Op. No. 456, 698 P2d 174 (Alaska App. 1985).

Argument that search warrants were improperly broad and premature was not made to trial court and would not therefore be considered on appeal. **Stuart v. State,** Op. No. 464, 698 P2d 1218 (Alaska App. 1985).

Where the trial court permits an untimely pretrial challenge to the indictment and rules on the merits of that challenge, the challenge will not be deemed forfeited on appeal. **Abruska v. State,** Op. No. 502, 705 P2d 1261 (Alaska App. 1985).

Where there is a direct conflict in testimony, it is crucial that the trial court summarize the evidence, identify factual conflicts, and resolve them on the record. **Burks v. State,** Op. No. 522, 706 P2d 1190 (Alaska App. 1985).

Because trial court denied without explanation a pretrial motion to suppress defendant's confession, conviction was vacated and remanded. **Burks v. State,** Op. No. 522, 706 P2d 1190 (Alaska App. 1985).

Defendant's claim that the state failed to present exculpatory evidence to the grand jury did not relate to the sufficiency of the indictment on its face nor call into question the trial court's jurisdiction to hear the case; therefore, defendant's failure to make a timely pretrial motion challenging the indictment constituted forfeiture of the issue. **Buffington v. State,** Op. No. 755, 745 P2d 78 (Alaska App. 1987).

When pretrial motions are not timely but are made sufficiently in advance of trial to permit their resolution without disrupting the trial or prejudicing the prosecution, it is an abuse of discretion not to resolve them and, if necessary, impose other sanctions to enforce the rules. **Selig v. State,** Op. No. 785, 750 P2d 834 (Alaska App. 1988).

When a defendant fails to seek pretrial resolution of suppression issues in time to avoid disrupting the trial date or otherwise prejudicing the prosecution, he may be held to have forfeited the right to object to the evidence. **Selig v. State,** Op. No. 785, 750 P2d 834 (Alaska App. 1988).

Where a defendant makes a timely pretrial suppression motion but does not substantially comply with applicable procedural rules so that the matter cannot be resolved prior to trial without disruption to the trial date or other significant prejudice to the prosecution, the defendant may be held to have forfeited his right to object to the evidence. **Selig v. State,** Op. No. 785, 750 P2d 834 (Alaska App. 1988).

State's argument that criminal defendant could not challenge the constitutionality of the fishing regulation he allegedly violated as a defense to the charge against him was rejected; if the charging regulation was invalid, then the criminal complaint failed to state an offense and the defendant was entitled to a dismissal. **State v. Hebert,** Op. No. 3651, 803 P2d 863 (Alaska 1990).

Constitutional challenge to statute under which defendant is indicted need not be raised before trial. **Gudmundson v. State,** Op. No. 3780, 822 P2d 1328 (Alaska 1991).

When the ruling of judge, whatever its label, actually represents a resolution, correct or not, of some or all of factual elements of offense charged, ruling is judgment of acquittal, precluding appellate review. **State v. Martushev,** Op. No. 1280, 846 P2d 144 (Alaska App. 1993).

When court orders dismissal on legal grounds that do not require resolution of factual elements of offense, order does not amount to judgment of acquittal, regardless of timing or label attached thereto. **State v. Martushev,** Op. No. 1280, 846 P2d 144 (Alaska App. 1993).

Defendant who did not challenge admissibility of his statements to police in original trial proceeding could not raise a suppression argument in his petition for post-conviction relief. **Beltz v. State,** Op. No. 1409, 895 P2d 513 (Alaska App. 1995).

Failure to move to suppress evidence results in waiver of that issue regardless of the lack of defendant's personal assent to attorney's tactical decision to not seek suppression. **Beltz v. State,** Op. No. 1409, 895 P2d 513 (Alaska App. 1995).

Failure to raise before trial the argument that evidence was improperly introduced during the grand jury proceedings resulted in waiver of the argument. **Harmon v. State,** Op. No. 1450, 908 P2d 434 (Alaska App. 1995).

Failure to preserve arguments in trial court forfeited them. **Cornwall v. State,** Op. No. 1460, 909 P2d 360 (Alaska App. 1996).

In fishing violations case, Ketchikan trial court did not err in refusing to take judicial notice of documents filed by defendant in two Juneau cases in which he had previously been charged with fishing violations since defendant did not submit copies of the Juneau pleadings to the Ketchikan court, did not state good cause for taking judicial notice, and did not explain the untimeliness of his request. **Scudero v. State,** Op. No. 1469, 917 P2d 683 (Alaska App. 1996).

Term "omnibus hearings" in Criminal Rule 38.1 includes additional evidentiary hearings needed to resolve pretrial motions, thus trial court erred in allowing witness to testify by telephone at pretrial evidentiary hearing over objection of defendant. **Kailukiak v. State,** Op. No. 1588, 959 P2d 771 (Alaska App. 1998).

Court of appeals erred by reversing defendant's conviction for attempted burglary upon his challenge to the sufficiency of his attempted burglary indictment; claim that the indictment failed to specify what crime defendant intended to commit when he entered the dwelling was raised for the first time on appeal. **State v. Semancik,** Op. No. 5833, 99 P.3d 538 (Alaska 2004).

Adkins v. State, 389 P.2d 915 (Alaska 1964), is overruled to the extent that it holds that failure to include the intended offense in a burglary indictment is a defect of substance that can be raised at any time; state is required to identify the intended offense in a burglary indictment, but failure to do so is a defect of form that must be raised before trial. **State v. Semancik,** Op. No. 5833, 99 P.3d 538 (Alaska 2004).

Rule 13. Trial of Indictments or Informations Together.

The court may order two or more indictments or informations or both to be tried together if the offenses, and the defendants, if there is more than one, could have been joined in a single indictment or information. The procedure shall be the same as if the prosecution were under such single indictment or information.

(Adopted by SCO 4 October 4, 1959)

Annotations

Cases

Propriety of joinder in cases where there are multiple defendants must be tested by Criminal Rule 8(b) alone. **Amidon v. State,** Op. No. 1434, 565 P2d 1248 (Alaska 1977).

Where one defendant shot at gas station shortly after he and his brother had attacked station attendant, their actions were "the same series of acts or transactions," and it was proper to consolidate their trials. **Larson v. State,** Op. No. 1459, 566 P2d 1019 (Alaska 1977).

Trial court did not err by joining charges imposed against defendant by two grand juries located in Anchorage and Palmer under Alaska R. Crim. P. 13 because joinder was proper under Alaska R. Crim. P. 8(a)(3) - the trial court could properly conclude that the Anchorage robbery and assault, the Palmer vehicle theft, and the Glennallen escape and murder constituted acts that were connected together; defendant committed the armed robbery and assault shortly after being released, he had no intention of paying for the cab ride between Anchorage and Palmer, and defendant's commission of the Anchorage offenses was relevant to explain his decision to assault the officer and escape from custody. Defendant was not prejudiced by the joinder under Alaska R. Crim. P. 14. **Phillips v. State,** Op. No. 1880, 70 P.3d 1128 (Alaska 2003).

Rule 14. Relief From Prejudicial Joinder.

If it appears that a defendant or the state is unfairly prejudiced by a joinder of offenses or of defendants in an indictment or information or by such joinder for trial together, the court may order an election or separate trials of counts, grant a severance of defendants, or provide whatever other relief justice requires. A showing that evidence of one offense would not be admissible during a separate trial of a joined offense or a codefendant does not constitute prejudice that warrants relief under this rule. In ruling on a motion by a defendant for severance the court may order the attorney for the state to deliver to the court for inspection in camera any statements or confessions made by the defendants which the state intends to introduce at trial.

(Adopted by SCO 4 October 4, 1959; amended by SCO 98 effective September 16, 1968; and by SCO 1092 effective July 15, 1992)

Note: The rule was amended by ch. 79 § 3, SLA 1991.

Annotations

Cases

This rule permits the trial court to order election or separate trial of counts if a defendant is prejudiced by the joinder, but a motion to sever counts not made until after the jury had been selected and sworn, was properly denied in absence of a showing of sufficient cause and prejudice. **State v. Selman,** Op. No. 302, 406 P2d 181 (Alaska 1965).

Prejudice must be shown before the Supreme Court will reverse on grounds that a trial judge erred or abused his discretion in failing to order separate trials for different counts of an indictment. **Richards v. State,** Op. No. 527, 451 P2d 359 (Alaska 1969).

An allegation that the joint trial of two counts for escape created in the jurors' minds the image of defendant as criminally disposed toward escaping from jail is insufficient to raise the question whether the joint trial of the offenses prejudiced the defendant. **Richards v. State,** Op. No. 527, 451 P2d 359 (Alaska 1969).

That defendant's trial was consolidated with that of his brother, who had shot at gas station after the assault on attendant with which defendant was charged was not prejudicial in view of instructions. **Larson v. State,** Op. No. 1459, 566 P2d 1019 (Alaska 1977).

Trial court did not abuse its discretion in denying defendant's request for separate trials on two offenses charged to him where the charges arose out of the same incident, where much of the evidence pertaining to one charge would be relevant to the other, and where the public interest in avoiding duplicative trials might reasonably have been thought to outweigh any possible prejudice which might inhere in a combined trial. **Catlett v. State,** Op. No. 1752, 585 P2d 553 (Alaska 1978).

Where co-defendant refused to take the stand, but by affidavit indicated that if she were called in a court proceeding in which she was not a defendant she would testify in favor of one of the other co-defendants, refusal to grant the latter co-defendant's motion for severance was not error where the proposed testimony was only marginally relevant. **Hawley v. State,** Op. No. 2137, 614 P2d 1349 (Alaska 1980).

Where defendant, charged with both theft and robbery, had a good possibility of being able to testify on the robbery charge without being cross-examined on the theft charge, his generalized fifth amendment argument for establishing his need to refrain from testifying on the theft charge was not sufficient to support a severance motion. **Nell v. State,** Op. No. 77, 642 P2d 1361 (Alaska App. 1982).

It was not error to deny severance on charges of misdemeanor assault, felony assault and felony escape, where second assault occurred while police officers were arresting defendant for the first assault and the escape occurred shortly after defendant had been arrested. **Maynard v. State,** Op. No. 136, 652 P2d 489 (Alaska App. 1982).

Where trial court has made a decision to deny severance under this rule, it can be overturned only for abuse of discretion. **Maynard v. State,** Op. No. 136, 652 P2d 489 (Alaska App. 1982).

Defendant's generalized fifth amendment argument, standing alone, did not suffice to show that joinder was prejudicial; a defendant must make a convincing showing that he has both important testimony to give concerning one count and strong need to refrain from testifying on the other. **Montes v. State,** Op. No. 289, 669 P2d 961 (Alaska App. 1983).

Contention that severance should be routinely granted whenever an accused moves to sever similar offenses was rejected; on appeal, denial of a motion for severance will be reversed only when the court has abused its discretion and a showing of prejudice to the defendant has been made. **Montes v. State,** Op. No. 289, 669 P2d 961 (Alaska App. 1983).

Trial court erred in denying severance of two similar sexual assault charges involving the same defendant where the evidence did not establish a common scheme or plan, whether or not the evidence of the assault on each victim would have been admissible in a trial for assault on the other victim. **Johnson v. State,** Op. No. 668, 730 P2d 175 (Alaska App. 1986).

Where prior conviction, admissible as an element of felon in possession of firearm charges, would have been inadmissible in a separate trial on theft by receiving charges, trial court erred in denying defendant's severance motion without pursuing the alternative of bifurcation, requiring reversal of the theft by receiving conviction but not the felon in possession conviction. **Elerson v. State,** Op. No. 679, 732 P2d 192 (Alaska App. 1987).

By waiting until the date of trial to move for severance, defendant waived his ability to do so. **Knutson v. State,** Op. No. 702, 736 P2d 775 (Alaska App. 1987).

Trial court erred in not granting defendants' motion to sever cocaine and murder charges where substantial risk existed that their defense on the cocaine charges was severely prejudiced by the evidence of murder; accordingly, the appellate court vacated the cocaine convictions but affirmed the murder convictions. **Mathis v. State,** Op. No. 951, 778 P2d 1161 (Alaska App. 1989).

Where defendant was charged with a murder which occurred on August 5 and several murders which occurred on August 6, joinder of the offenses was proper, since the August 6 murders resulted from defendant's belief that he was going to be killed because of his role in the August 5 murder; furthermore, the trial court did not err in denying defendant's motion for severance given the relevance of the August 5 murder to the August 6 murders and the absence of any specific and convincing showing of prejudice resulting from joinder. **Collins v. State,** Op. No. 962, 778 P2d 1171 (Alaska App. 1989).

There was a close nexus between the drug charges against defendant and drug charges against his codefendants, thus defendant's argument that he was prejudiced by the trial court's failure to sever his trial from that of the codefendants because there was little evidence linking him to their activities was rejected. **Badoino v. State,** Op. No. 1002, 785 P2d 39 (Alaska App. 1990).

Where a perjury charge is joined with a closely related substantive offense, the evidence pertaining to the perjury charge is admissible in the prosecution for the substantive offense and vice versa. **Machado v. State,** Op. No. 1067, 797 P2d 677 (Alaska App. 1990).

Evidence of defendant's perjury and evidence relating to charges against him arising out of a car bombing would have been cross-admissible, thus trial court did not err in refusing to grant defendant's motion to sever the perjury and car bombing charges. **Machado v. State,** Op. No. 1067,797 P2d 677 (Alaska App. 1990).

To be entitled to severance under this rule, defendant must show actual prejudice from joinder. **Newcomb v. State,** Op. No. 1088, 800 P2d 935 (Alaska App. 1990).

Evidence relating to Count 1, selling cocaine, was relevant to prove Count 2, possession with intent to deliver cocaine, regardless of its technical sufficiency to support a finding of guilt beyond a reasonable doubt on Count 1, thus trial court did not err in failing to sever the two charges or to order a mistrial as to Count 2 after granting a judgment of acquittal on Count 1. **McLaughlin v. State,** Op. No. 1159, 818 P2d 683 (Alaska App. 1991).

Trial court decision to deny severance is to be overturned only for abuse of discretion; abuse of discretion is to be found only where defendant shows prejudice from joinder. **Erickson v. State,** Op. No. 1179, 824 P2d 725 (Alaska App. 1991).

Evidence did not establish that defendant, charged with initiating murder plan, was prejudiced by joinder of codefendant, charged with attempting the murder; defendant's inability to call codefendant as a witness was not prejudiced since there was no showing that codefendant was willing to testify or that his testimony would have been significantly exculpatory, and admission of codefendant's statements into evidence was not prejudicial since in the statements codefendant denied knowing anything about defendant's involvement. **Erickson v. State,** Op. No. 1179, 824 P2d 725 (Alaska App. 1991).

Trial court did not err by joining charges imposed against defendant by two grand juries located in Anchorage and Palmer under Alaska R. Crim. P. 13 because joinder was proper under Alaska R. Crim. P. 8(a)(3)—the trial court could properly conclude that the Anchorage robbery and assault, the Palmer vehicle theft, and the Glennallen escape and murder constituted acts that were connected together; defendant committed the armed robbery and assault shortly after being released, he had no intention of paying for the cab ride between Anchorage and Palmer, and defendant's commission of the Anchorage offenses was relevant to explain his decision to assault the officer and escape from custody. Defendant was not prejudiced by the joinder under Alaska R. Crim. P. 14. **Phillips v. State,** Op. No. 1880, 70 P.3d 1128 (Alaska 2003).

Rule 15. Depositions.

(a) **When Taken.** The deposition of a prospective witness may be taken by either party, upon notice as provided in (b) of this rule and upon motion filed with the court if the court finds by clear and convincing evidence that (1) the witness will not be present to testify at trial; or (2) due to exceptional circumstances, the deposition is necessary to prevent a failure of justice. Any designated book, paper, document, record, recording, or other material not privileged may be subpoenaed at the same time and place of the taking of the deposition. If a witness is committed for failure to give bail or appear to testify at a trial or hearing, the court on written motion of the witness and upon notice to the parties may direct that the witness' deposition be taken. After the deposition has been subscribed the court may discharge the witness. In considering a request for the taking of depositions, the court shall grant such motion only if the taking of such deposition will not cause unreasonable delay in the trial of the action and shall apply a presumption against granting a deposition under (a)(2) of this rule if, in regard to that action, the witness has testified before the grand jury or in a prior court proceeding, or has given a recorded statement to a law enforcement agency and the moving party had the opportunity to obtain such a recorded statement.

(b) **Notice of Taking.** The party at whose instance a deposition is to be taken shall give to every other party reasonable written notice of the time and place for taking the deposition. The notice shall state the name and address of each person to be examined. On motion of a party upon whom the notice is served, the court for cause shown may extend or shorten the time.

(c) **How Taken.** The court shall preside over a deposition it orders under (a) of this rule. The deposition shall be conducted in a closed proceeding and recorded in the same manner as other closed court proceedings. This rule does not preclude a party from also recording the deposition by other means approved by the court. In no event shall a deposition be taken of a party defendant without that defendant's consent.

(d) **Use.** At the trial or upon any hearing, a part or all of a deposition, so far as otherwise admissible under the rules of evidence, may be used by stipulation of the parties or if the witness is unavailable, as defined in section (e) of this rule, or if the witness gives testimony at the trial or hearing inconsistent with the witness' deposition. If only a part of a deposition is offered in evidence by a party, an adverse party may require the offering of all of it which is relevant to the part offered and any party may offer other parts.

(e) **Unavailability.** A witness is "unavailable" when the witness is:

(1) Exempted by ruling of the judge on the ground of privilege from testifying concerning the subject matter of the witness' statement; or

(2) Persistent in refusing to testify despite an order of the judge to do so; or

(3) Unable to be present or testify at the hearing because of death or then existing physical or mental illness or infirmity; or

(4) Absent from the hearing and beyond the jurisdiction of the court to compel appearance and the proponent of the witness' statement has exercised reasonable diligence but has been unable to procure the witness' attendance.

(f) **Objections to Admissibility.** Objections to receiving in evidence a deposition or part thereof, may be made as provided in civil actions.

(g) **Deposition by Agreement Not Precluded.** Nothing in this rule shall preclude the taking of a deposition, orally or upon written questions, or the use of a deposition, by agreement of the parties with the consent of the court.

(h) **Joint Defendants.** Where persons are jointly tried, the court for good cause shown may refuse to permit the use at the trial of a deposition taken at the instance of a defendant over the objection of any other defendant.

(Adopted by SCO 4 October 4, 1959; amended by SCO 157 effective February 15, 1973; by SCO 639 effective May 30, 1985; by SCO 1153 effective July 15, 1994; and by SCO 1239 effective July 15, 1996)

Note to SCO 1239: Criminal Rule 15(a) and (c) were amended by ch. 12 SLA 1995. Sections 1 and 2 of this order are adopted for the sole reason that the legislature has mandated the amendments.

Annotations

Cases

Denial of motion to take depositions of witnesses who had testified before the grand jury was no error where appellants had not made a showing sufficient under this rule. **Merrill v. State,** Op. No. 392, 423 P2d 686 (Alaska 1967).

Where the direct penalty for conviction of an offense may be incarceration, loss of a valuable license, or a fine heavy enough to indicate criminality, such offense is a "serious crime" within the public defender statute. A defendant who is charged with any such misdemeanor and who cannot afford to hire his own lawyer is eligible for representation by a public defender. **Alexander v. City of Anchorage,** Op. No. 738, 490 P2d 910 (Alaska 1971).

Expansion of discovery beyond provisions contained in court rules is most appropriately done though amendment of existing rules after thorough study. **Buchanan v. State,** Op. No. 2553, 561 P2d 1197 (Alaska 1977).

Where statements of juvenile codefendants were taken in juvenile proceedings, but juveniles testified at trial and statements were not introduced, no violation of the right to notice of a deposition occurred. **Linden v. State,** Op. No. 1905, 598 P2d 960 (Alaska 1979).

The admission of a witness' pretrial videotaped deposition at trial was reversible error where the state failed to subpoena the witness despite advance knowledge of her plan to be out of the state during the trial. **Stores v. Seattle,** Op. No. 2252, 625 P2d 820 (Alaska 1981).

Trial court did not err in denying defense motion to admit video deposition of expert witness where defendant failed to demonstrate either that the witness was beyond the jurisdiction of the court or that due diligence was exercised in attempting to secure her appearance. **Dunbar v. State,** Op. No. 347, 677 P2d 1275 (Alaska App. 1984).

In sexual abuse case, trial court did not abuse its discretion in refusing to allow defendant to depose his sons, who had given statements to the police and testified before the grand jury, but did not wish to be interviewed further, where on appeal the defense did not argue surprise at the children's trial testimony but instead argued, without further amplification, that the denial of discovery impaired its ability to adequately prepare for trial. **State v. Covington,** Op. No. 557, 711 P2d 1183 (Alaska App. 1985).

Trial court erred in denying motion by purchasers of land to amend their complaint for breach of contract to include request for damages; purchasers' previous attempt to amend complaint, which was unsuccessful because trial court had erroneously ruled that contract claim was barred by statute of limitations, could not be characterized as repeated failure to cure deficiencies. **Bauman v. Day,** Op. No. 4853, 942 P2d 1130 (Alaska 1997).

Where defendant's attorney sought to question foster families caring for abused animals, unless and until the court ordered a deposition and the foster families were properly subpoenaed to attend that deposition, the families were under no legal obligation to respond to the attorney's questionnaire; thus, the defense attorney was not entitled to a writ of assistance to have the police intimidate the families to answer her questionnaires. **Mahan v. State,** 51 P.3d 962 (Alaska App. 2002).

Rule 16. Discovery.

(a) **Scope of Discovery.** In order to provide adequate information for informed pleas, expedite trial, minimize surprise, afford opportunity for effective cross-examination, and meet the requirements of due process, discovery prior to trial should be as full and free as possible consistent with protection of persons, effective law enforcement, and the adversary system.

(b) **Disclosure to the Accused.**

(1) *Information within Possession or Control of Prosecuting Attorney.*

(A) Except as is otherwise provided as to matters not subject to disclosure and protective orders, the prosecuting attorney shall disclose the following information within the prosecuting attorney's possession or control to defense counsel and make available for inspection and copying:

(i) The names and addresses of persons known by the government to have knowledge of relevant facts and their written or recorded statements or summaries of statements;

(ii) Any written or recorded statements and summaries of statements and the substance of any oral statements made by the accused;

(iii) Any written or recorded statements and summaries of statements and the substance of any oral statements made by a co-defendant;

(iv) Any books, papers, documents, photographs or tangible objects, which the prosecuting attorney intends to use in the hearing or trial or which were obtained from or belong to the accused; and

(v) Any record of prior criminal convictions of the defendant and of persons whom the prosecuting attorney intends to call as witnesses at the hearing or trial.

(B) *Expert Witnesses.* Unless a different date is set by the court, as soon as known and no later than 45 days prior to trial, the prosecutor shall inform the defendant of the names and addresses of any expert witnesses performing work in connection with the case or whom the prosecutor is likely to call at trial. The prosecutor shall also make available for inspection and copying any reports or written statements of these experts. With respect to each expert whom the prosecution is likely to call at trial, the prosecutor shall also furnish to the defendant a curriculum vitae and a written description of the substance of the proposed testimony of the expert, the expert's opinion, and the underlying basis of that opinion. Failure to provide timely disclosure under this rule shall entitle the defendant to a continuance. If the court finds that a continuance is not an adequate remedy under the circumstances of the case, the court may impose other sanctions, including prohibiting the prosecutor from calling the expert at trial or declaring a mistrial.

(2) *Information Provided by Informant—Electronic Surveillance.* The prosecuting attorneys shall inform defense counsel:

(i) of any relevant material or information relating to the guilt or innocence of the defendant which has been provided by an informant, and

(ii) of any electronic surveillance, including wiretapping, of

(aa) conversations to which the accused or the accused's attorney was a party,

(bb) premises of the accused or the accused's attorney.

(3) *Information Tending to Negate Guilt or Reduce Punishment.* The prosecuting attorney shall disclose to defense counsel any material or information within the prosecuting attorney's possession or control which tends to negate the guilt of the accused as to the offense or would tend to reduce the accused's punishment therefor.

(4) *Information Within Possession or Control of Other Members of Prosecuting Attorney's Staff.* The prosecuting attorney's obligations extend to material and information in the possession or control of

(i) members of the prosecuting attorney's staff, and

(ii) any others who have participated in the investigation or evaluation of the case and who either regularly report or with reference to the particular case have reported to the prosecuting attorney's office.

(5) *Availability of Information to Defense Counsel.* Whenever defense counsel designates and requests production of material or information which is not in the possession or control of the prosecuting attorney but would be discoverable if in the possession or control of the prosecuting attorney, the court shall issue suitable subpoenas or orders to cause such material to be made available to defense counsel.

(6) *Information Regarding Searches and Seizures—Statements From the Accused—Relationship of Witnesses to Prosecuting Attorney.* Except as otherwise provided the prosecuting attorney shall, upon request of defense counsel, disclose and permit inspection, testing, copying and photographing of any relevant material and information regarding:

(i) Specified searches and seizures;

(ii) The acquisition of specified statements from the accused; and

(iii) The relationship, if any, of specified witnesses to the prosecuting authority.

(7) *Other Information.* Upon a reasonable request showing materiality to the preparation of the defense, the court in its discretion may require disclosure to defense counsel of relevant material and information not covered by subsections (b) (1), (b) (2), (b) (3), and (b) (6).

(8) *Legal Research and Records of Prosecuting Attorney.* Disclosure shall not be required of legal research or of records, correspondence, reports or memoranda to the extent that they contain the opinions, theories or conclusions of the prosecuting attorney or members of the prosecuting attorney's legal staff.

(c) **Disclosure to the Prosecuting Attorney.**

(1) *Non-Testimonial Identification Procedures—Authority.* Upon application of the prosecuting attorney, the court by order may direct any person to participate in one or more of the procedures specified in subsection (c) (2) of this rule if affidavit or testimony shows probable cause to believe that:

(i) An offense has been committed by one of several persons comprising a narrow focal group that includes the subject person;

(ii) The evidence sought may be of material aid in identifying who committed the offense; and

(iii) The evidence sought cannot practicably be obtained from other sources.

(2) *Non-Testimonial Identification Procedures—Scope.* An order issued under subsection (c) (1) of this rule may direct the person to do or submit to any and all of the following:

(i) Appear in a line-up;

(ii) Speak words, phrases or sentences relevant to the

case for identification by witnesses;

(iii) Be fingerprinted;

(iv) Pose for photographs not involving reenactment of a scene;

(v) Try on articles of clothing;

(vi) Permit the taking of specimens of material under the person's fingernails;

(vii) Permit the taking of samples of blood, hair and other materials of the person's body which involve no unreasonable intrusion thereof;

(viii) Provide specimens of the person's handwriting;

(ix) Submit to a reasonable physical or medical inspection of the person's body.

(3) *Right to Counsel.* When issuing an order under subsection (c) (1) of this rule, the court shall also order that the person be represented by counsel or waive the right to be represented by counsel before being required to appear in a lineup, give a specimen of handwriting, or speak for identification by witnesses to an offense.

(4) *Expert Witnesses.* Unless a different date is set by the court, no later than 30 days prior to trial, the defendant shall inform the prosecutor of the names and addresses of any expert witnesses the defendant is likely to call at trial. The defendant shall also make available for inspection and copying any reports or written statements of these experts. For each such expert witness, the defendant shall also furnish to the prosecutor a curriculum vitae and a written description of the substance of the proposed testimony of the expert, the expert's opinion, and the underlying basis of that opinion. Failure to provide timely disclosure under this rule shall entitle the prosecutor to a continuance. If the court finds that a continuance is not an adequate remedy under the circumstances of the case, the court may impose other sanctions, including prohibiting the defendant from calling the expert at trial. Information obtained by the prosecutor under this rule may be used only for cross-examination or rebuttal of defense testimony.

(5) *Notice of Defenses.* Unless a different date is set by the court, no later than 10 days prior to trial, the defendant shall inform the prosecutor of the defendant's intention to rely upon a defense of alibi, justification, duress, entrapment, or other statutory or affirmative defense. Failure to provide timely notice under this rule shall entitle the prosecutor to a continuance. If the court finds that a continuance is not an adequate remedy under the circumstances of the case, the court may impose other sanctions, including prohibiting the defendant from asserting the designated defense. The defendant shall give notice of an insanity defense or a defense of diminished capacity due to mental disease or defect in compliance with AS 12.47.

(6) *Physical Evidence.* If defense counsel or defense counsel's agent acquires physical evidence of the offense, defense counsel must immediately notify the prosecutor and must make arrangements to turn over the evidence to the prosecutor within a reasonable time. Differences concerning what amount of time is "reasonable" shall be resolved by the court. Defense counsel must not test or substantively alter the evidence, unless defense counsel has first notified the prosecutor and given the prosecutor a reasonable opportunity to seek court action. Defense counsel must reveal all information concerning the manner in which the evidence was obtained and handled unless that information is privileged. When physical evidence is disclosed by the defense, the prosecutor cannot reveal to the jury that the evidence was obtained from the defense.

(d) **Regulation of Discovery.**

(1) *Advice to Refrain From Discussing Case.* Except as is otherwise provided as to matters not subject to disclosure and protective orders, neither counsel for the parties nor other prosecution or defense personnel shall advise persons (except the accused) having relevant material or information to refrain from discussing the case with opposing counsel or showing opposing counsel any relevant material, nor shall they otherwise impede opposing counsel's investigation of the case.

(2) *Additional or Newly Discovered Information.* If, subsequent to compliance with these rules or orders issued pursuant thereto, a party discovers additional material or information which is subject to disclosure, that party shall promptly notify the other party or the other party's counsel of its existence. If the additional material or information is discovered during trial, the court shall also be notified.

(3) *Materials to Remain in Exclusive Custody of Attorney.*

(A) Materials furnished to an attorney pursuant to these rules shall remain in the attorney's exclusive custody, shall be used only for the purposes of conducting the case, and shall be subject to other terms and conditions that the court may provide if the information is

(i) a criminal history record of a victim or witness;

(ii) a medical, psychiatric, psychological, or counseling record of a victim or witness;

(iii) an adoption record;

(iv) a record that is confidential under AS 47.12.300 or a similar law in another jurisdiction;

(v) a report of a presentence investigation of a victim or witness prepared pursuant to Criminal Rule 32 or a similar law in another jurisdiction;

(vi) a record of the Department of Corrections other than an incident report relating to the crime with which the defendant is charged; or

(vii) any other record that the court orders be kept in the exclusive custody of the attorney.

(B) An attorney shall not disclose to a defendant the residence or business address or telephone number of a victim or witness, obtained from information provided under this rule, even if the defendant is acting as co-counsel. If the address and telephone numbers of all victims and witnesses have been obliterated, materials that had contained the address or telephone number of a victim or witness may be provided to a defendant proceeding without counsel only as allowed by AS 12.61.120.

(C) Notwithstanding a defendant's status as co-counsel, materials covered by subsection (d)(3)(A) shall remain in the exclusive custody of the defendant's attorney.

(D) If a defendant is proceeding without counsel, materials covered by subsection (d)(3)(A) may be provided to the defendant. If materials are provided to an unrepresented defendant under this paragraph, the court shall order that the materials remain in the defendant's exclusive custody, be used only for purposes of conducting the case, and be subject to other terms, conditions, and restrictions that the court may provide. The court shall also inform the defendant that violation of an order issued under this paragraph is punishable as a contempt of court.

(4) *Restriction or Deferral of Disclosure of Information.* Upon a showing of cause, the court may at any time order that specified disclosure be restricted or deferred, or make such other order as is appropriate, provided that all material and information to which a party is entitled shall be disclosed in time to permit the party's counsel to make beneficial use thereof.

(5) *Material Partially Discoverable.* When some parts of certain material are discoverable under these rules, and other parts are not discoverable, as much of the material shall be disclosed as is consistent with this rule. Excision of certain material and disclosure of the balance shall be preferred to withholding of the whole. Material excised pursuant to court order shall be sealed and preserved in the records of the court, and shall be made available to the court of appeals and the supreme court in the event of an appeal.

(6) *Denial or Regulation of Disclosure— Disclosure to Court in Camera—Record of Proceedings.*

Upon request of any party, the court may permit:

(i) any showing of cause for denial or regulation of disclosure, or

(ii) any portion of any showing of cause for denial or regulation of disclosure

to be made to the court in camera ex parte. A record shall be made of such proceedings. If the court enters an order granting relief following such a showing, the entire record of the proceedings shall be sealed and preserved in the records of the court, to be made available to the court of appeals and the supreme court in the event of an appeal.

(e) **Sanctions.**

(1) *Failure to Comply with Discovery Rule or Order.* If at any time during the course of the proceedings it is brought to the attention of the court that a party has failed to comply with an applicable discovery rule or an order issued pursuant thereto, the court shall order such party to permit the discovery of material and information not previously disclosed or enter such other order as it deems just under the circumstances.

(2) *Willful Violations.* Willful violation by counsel of an applicable discovery rule or an order issued pursuant thereto may subject counsel to appropriate sanctions by the court.

(f) **Omnibus Hearing.**

(1) *Time for Hearing—When Set.* If the defendant is charged with a felony, the court shall set a time for an omnibus hearing when a plea of not guilty is entered. The omnibus hearing shall be scheduled for a time when the briefing of pretrial motions should be complete.

The omnibus hearing may be cancelled by the court only upon the stipulation of counsel that there are no motions which require hearing and that discovery is complete. Counsel shall also provide the information outlined in section (f)(2)(D).

The court may set an omnibus hearing in a misdemeanor case.

(2) *Duties of Trial Court at Hearing.* At the omnibus hearing the court shall:

(A) ensure that discovery under this rule is complete;

(B) rule on any pending motions which are ripe for decision;

(C) schedule any necessary evidentiary hearings; and

(D) obtain case management information from the parties, including the expected length of trial, the likelihood of trial, and any anticipated scheduling difficulties.

(Adopted by SCO 4 October 4, 1959; amended by SCO 157 effective February 15, 1973; by SCO 211 effective July 15, 1975; by SCO 212 effective July 15, 1975; by SCO 329 effective January 1, 1979; by SCO 331 effective January 1, 1979; by SCO's 640 and 641 effective September 15, 1985; by SCO 1086 effective July 15, 1992; by SCO 1092 effective July 15, 1992; by SCO 1126 effective July 15, 1993; by SCO 1153 effective July 15, 1994; by SCO 1191 effective July 15, 1995; amended by SCO 1269 and 1274 effective July 15, 1997; and by SCO 1444 effective October 15, 2001)

Note: AS 12.61.120, added by ch. 57, § 13, SLA 1991, amended Criminal Rule 16 by restricting discovery available to criminal defendants.

Note: Criminal Rule 16 was repealed and reenacted by chapter 95 SLA 1996. In **State v. Summerville,** 926 P.2d 465 (Alaska App. 1996), the Alaska Court of Appeals found that the legislature's version of the rule was unconstitutional. This decision was affirmed by the Alaska Supreme Court in **State v. Summerville,** 948 P.2d 469 (Alaska 1997). Thus, the pre-existing version of the rule remains in effect.

Annotations

Cases

I. In General.
II. Disclosure to Accused.
III. Disclosure to Prosecution.

I. In General.

This rule affords limited discovery in criminal cases. **Martinez v. State,** Op. No. 389, 423 P2d 700 (Alaska 1967).

Where a defendant's substantive rights are not affected by the introduction into evidence of a reference to physical evidence which had been negligently destroyed by the police, the admission of the testimony is not "plain error." **Torres v. State,** Op. No. 1017, 519 P2d 788 (Alaska 1974).

Existence of this rule gives notice to state that evidence might be the object of discovery and should be preserved. **Lauderdale v. State,** Op. No. 1254, 548 P2d 376 (Alaska 1976).

This rule is designed to further discovery in order to eliminate jockeying for tactical advantage and trial by surprise. **Des Jardins v. State,** Op. No. 1245, 551 P2d 181 (Alaska 1976).

Where there is a violation of this rule not of constitutional dimensions the "harmless error" test will be applied. **Des Jardins v. State,** Op. No. 1245, 551 P2d 181 (Alaska 1976).

Even where violations of this rule did not prejudice defendant, matter would be remanded to trial court for hearing on sanctions that might be imposed on prosecutor under Rule 16(e)(2). **Des Jardins v. State,** Op. No. 1245, 551 P2d 181 (Alaska 1976).

Expansion of discovery beyond provisions contained in court rules is most appropriately done through amendment of existing rules after thorough study. **Buchanan v. State,** Op. No. 2553, 561 P2d 1197 (Alaska 1977).

Paragraph (d) of this rule, does not justify conducting an ex parte in camera hearing to consider evidence in conjunction with a bail reduction proceeding. **Carman v. State,** Op. No. 1428, 564 P2d 361 (Alaska 1977).

Order denying motion for discovery is a final order and may be appealed even if motion is not renewed. **Batson v. State,** Op. No. 1486, 568 P2d 973 (Alaska 1977).

Failure to order discovery of relevant material was not reversible error where the material sought to be discovered would have been merely cumulative. **Braham v. State,** Op. No. 1522, 571 P2d 631 (Alaska 1977).

Superior court's in camera examination of kidnap victim's journal did not deprive defendant of "effective confrontation" or of access to evidence which was potentially helpful to his defense where that portion of journal pertaining to defendant was turned over to defense and where defense could reasonably have assumed that the remainder of the journal contained no references to the defendant or the alleged crime. **Morrell v. State,** Op. No. 1577, 575 P2d 1200 (Alaska 1978).

Where confession of co-defendant was disclosed by prosecution for the first time after the trial began, but out of the presence of the jury, the trial court acted properly in denying a motion by the other defendants for a mistrial, in granting a continuance, and in refusing to allow the prosecution to use the confession at trial. **Hawley v. State,** Op. No. 2137, 614 P2d 1349 (Alaska 1980).

The remedy of exclusion of significant evidence for a violation of the discovery rules should be imposed only in rare situations, and absent substantial prejudice to the nonoffending party, the appropriate remedies are the granting of continuances, imposition of monetary sanctions, or the exercise of contempt powers by the court. **State v. Lewis,** Op. No. 35, 632 P2d 547 (Alaska App. 1981).

In the absence of a timely pretrial objection, hearsay testimony presented to and considered by a grand jury should be regarded on appeal as constituting admissible and fully competent evidence. **Cassell v. State,** Op. No. 91, 645 P2d 219 (Alaska App. 1982).

Fact that indictment charged defendant with theft of ripper teeth but did not allege a specific theory of theft did not deny defendant due process since liberal discovery rules permit an accused to obtain adequate discovery of the state's case and to get adequate notice of the state's theory or theories of prosecution. **Williams v. State,** Op. No. 106, 648 P2d 603 (Alaska App. 1982).

Defendant's motion to strike telephone record evidence based upon his constitutional right of privacy after the state had already introduced much of the evidence was properly denied on the ground that defendant had waived the objection by not making the motion at the omnibus hearing prior to trial. **Hohman v. State,** Op. No. 290, 669 P2d 1316 (Alaska App. 1983).

Motion to dismiss grand jury indictment on the ground that improper information was presented to the grand jury was properly denied as untimely, since the motion was not raised until during or after jury selection, and because the other evidence presented was so strong that the grand jury's decision to indict was clearly not affected by the allegedly improper information. **Pritchard v. State,** Op. No. 319, 673 P2d 291 (Alaska App. 1983).

Where motion to suppress evidence was filed late but prior to trial, it was abuse of discretion for the trial court to deny the motion as untimely where defendant was not personally responsible for the late filing and his attorney did not act in bad faith for the purpose of delay. **Fox v. State,** Op. No. 394, 685 P2d 1267 (Alaska App. 1984).

Where charge of being a felon in possession of a firearm was properly joined to kidnapping and other charges, thereby allowing the jury to be informed of defendant's prior felony conviction, which would not have been the case had the firearm possession charge been severed, trial judge did not abuse his discretion in refusing as untimely defendant's severance motion made on the morning of trial. **Wortham v. State,** Op. No. 414, 689 P2d 1133 (Alaska App. 1984).

A party intending to rely upon a subsistence defense to charges of violating hunting laws must make a preliminary showing at a reasonable time before trial; failure to give notice of the defense before trial or in the manner prescribed in a pretrial order may, unless excused for good cause, result in the forfeiture of the defense. **State v. Eluska,** Op. No. 456, 698 P2d 174 (Alaska App. 1985).

Argument that search warrants were improperly broad and premature was not made to trial court and would not therefore be considered on appeal. **Stuart v. State,** Op. No. 464, 698 P2d 1218 (Alaska App. 1985).

The broad rights to discovery granted a criminal defendant under the Alaska rules will render a bill of particulars unnecessary in most cases. **Covington v. State,** Op. No. 491, 703 P2d 436 (Alaska App. 1985).

Where the trial court permits an untimely pretrial challenge to the indictment and rules on the merits of that challenge, the challenge will not be deemed forfeited on appeal. **Abruska v. State,** Op. No. 502, 705 P2d 1261 (Alaska App. 1985).

An in camera examination of material submitted by the prosecutor must involve more than a cursory determination that the material is not discoverable; where there is a suggestion that the prosecutor has not submitted all the requested material, the court should inquire further. **Braaten v. State,** Op. No. 504,705 P2d 1311 (Alaska App. 1985).

Where defendant's discovery request was for evidence which the state was under obligation to provide and defendant did not request action of the court regarding the request and no court action was taken, defendant's discovery request was not a discovery motion; accordingly, trial court erred in excluding the period during which the request was pending from the speedy trial computation. **Miller v. State,** Op. No. 511, 706 P2d 336 (Alaska App. 1985).

Violation of the affirmative duty to collect and preserve material evidence requires reversal on appeal only where the defendant is denied due process as a result of the violation; due process is violated only if the evidence, if collected and/or preserved, could possibly affect the outcome. **Klumb v. State,** Op. No. 575, 712 P2d 909 (Alaska App. 1986).

Failure to preserve tissue samples from the area of the victim's wounds did not violate defendant's due process rights where photographs of the wounds and the pathologist's reports provided the necessary evidence. **Klumb v. State,** Op. No. 575, 712 P2d 909 (Alaska App. 1986).

Although defendant had a right to be present at his omnibus hearing, his absence from the hearing was held harmless beyond a reasonable doubt despite his claim that attendance would have alerted him to the need to peremptorily challenge the trial judge and to affirmatively protect his speedy trial rights. **Trudeau v. State,** Op. No. 581, 714 P2d 362 (Alaska App. 1986).

Failure to raise an objection at trial to the state's reliance on testimony of a sexual assault victim's physician resulted in forfeiture of the objection. **Hilburn v. State,** Op. No. 800, 765 P2d 1382 (Alaska App. 1988).

Defendant forfeited his argument that the prosecutor, who had participated in a videotaped interrogation of defendant, should be recused, by failing to make a motion to that effect at the omnibus hearing prior to trial. **Kanulie v. State,** Op. No. 1070, 796 P2d 844 (Alaska App. 1990).

This rule requires disclosure of "rebuttal" witnesses. **Bostic v. State,** Op. No. 3659, 805 P2d 344 (Alaska 1991).

Constitutional challenge to statute under which defendant is indicted need not be raised before trial. **Gudmundson v. State,** Op. No. 3780, 822 P2d 1328 (Alaska 1991).

Argument that this rule precludes trial judge from ordering defendant to submit to independent psychiatric examination unless defendant intends to raise insanity defense was rejected. **Nelson v. State,** Op. No. 1346, 874 P2d 298 (Alaska App. 1994).

Criminal discovery in federal cases differs significantly from discovery as prescribed by this rule. Therefore, federal case law is not necessarily to be followed in construing the state rule. **Johnson v. State,** Op. No. 1390, 889 P2d 1076 (Alaska App. 1995).

There is no basis for categorically exempting pre-sentence reports from discovery under this rule. **Johnson v. State,** Op. No. 1390, 889 P2d 1076 (Alaska App. 1995).

This rule permits the state to withhold disclosure of records whose contents are potentially discoverable only if a two-step procedure has been met: first the state must make a threshold showing of good cause to maintain the records' confidentiality; second, but only if such showing is made, the trial judge must review the records **in camera** and determine that the material therein is not relevant. **Johnson v. State,** Op. No. 1390, 889 P2d 1076 (Alaska App. 1995).

Disclosure of presentence reports is expressly restricted by Criminal Rule 32(d)(2). However, before a presentence report of a complaining witness could be withheld from the defendant, the trial court would have to determine in an **in camera** review that the material in the report was not relevant to the case at bar. **Johnson v. State,** Op. No. 1390, 889 P2d 1076 (Alaska App. 1995).

Criminal Rule 16(c) as amended by chapter 95 of 1996 Session Laws was unconstitutional and invalid in its entirety, thus pre-existing version of rule remained in effect. **State v. Summerville,** Op. No. 1496, 926 P2d 465 (Alaska App. 1996).

In trial of defendant for robbing sandwich shop of eighty dollars and meatball sandwich, trial court committed reversible error in denying defense motion to compel production of palm print of employee who handed money and sandwich bag to robber, since print did not match defendant and evidence of third person's print on bag might have altered jury's decision; appellate court rejected state's argument that trial court had no authority to compel employee to submit to fingerprinting or, alternatively, that trial court's failure to exercise authority was not abuse of discretion. **Fathke v. State,** Op. No. 1549, 945 P2d 1243 (Alaska App. 1997).

Amendment to this rule in 1996 allowing reciprocal discovery was invalid, thus pre-existing version of rule remained in effect. **State v. Summerville,** Op. No. 4904, 948 P2d 469 (Alaska 1997).

In trial of defendant charged with sexually abusing his sons, defense motion to use defendant's body as a demonstrative aid during cross-examination of prosecution witness was properly barred by trial judge unless defendant took the stand; the purpose of defendant's request was to demonstrate that he was too obese to touch his groin as the prosecution witness testified he did. **Schumacher v. State,** Op. No. 1697, 11 P3d 397 (Alaska App. 2000).

In a criminal trial where defendant was charged with prostitution for soliciting an undercover policewoman to have oral sex with him, the defendant waived his entrapment claim by failing to raise it in a pretrial motion. **Parrott v. Municipality of Anchorage,** 69 P.3d 1 (Alaska App. 2003).

II. Disclosure to Accused.

The trial court should require the state to produce for in camera examination police reports of oral statements made to them by a witness called by the state who has testified, as well as any reports or summaries that may exist of pretrial statements made by such witness, when demand is made by the defendant. **Mahle v. State,** Op. No. 84, 371 P2d 21 (Alaska 1962).

The prosecution has an affirmative duty to disclose to an accused any information within its control which tends to negate the defendant's guilt. **Scott v. State,** Op. No. 1004, 519 P2d 774 (Alaska 1974).

Generally, rebuttal witnesses do not come within the requirement that the prosecution furnish a list of witnesses to the defense, so long as the rebuttal is true rebuttal and not an attempt to present the state's case-in-chief in the rebuttal. **McCurry v. State,** Op. No. 1173, 538 P2d 100 (Alaska 1975).

Where the state produces a rebuttal witness whose name has not been included on witness list, the court is bound on motion to grant a continuance to allow the defense to investigate the witness' background. **McCurry v. State,** Op. No. 1173, 538 P2d 100 (Alaska 1975).

District court properly exercised discretion in requiring production of ampules used in breathalyzer test. **Lauderdale v. State,** Op. No. 1254, 548 P2d 376 (Alaska 1976).

Where failure to disclose oral statements of defendant was harmless and introduction of statement was not objected to by defense, conviction would not be reversed nor would hearing be had on sanctions under Rule 16(e)(2). **Kristich v. State,** Op. No. 1264, 550 P2d 796 (Alaska 1976).

This rule imposes a duty on the prosecutor to disclose the information listed in subsection (b) and other information as the court may order. **Des Jardins v. State,** Op. No. 1245, 551 P2d 181 (Alaska 1976).

Prosecutor has an obligation to disclose evidence which tends to negate guilt, mitigate the degree of the offense or reduce punishment. **Des Jardins v. State,** Op. No. 1245, 551 P2d 181 (Alaska 1976).

Witness testifying in rebuttal need not be placed on prosecution's witness list. **Des Jardins v. State,** Op. No. 1245, 551 P2d 181 (Alaska 1976).

When prosecution fails to disclose evidence it is required to provide until just before it plans to use it, trial court should grant a continuance to allow defense adequate time to prepare. **Des Jardins v. State,** Op. No. 1245, 551 P2d 181 (Alaska 1976).

Prosecutor is obliged to use diligent good faith efforts to make discoverable material available to defense counsel. **Des Jardins v. State,** Op. No. 1245, 551 P2d 181 (Alaska 1976).

Where defense counsel was not furnished discoverable police reports until six days before testimony was taken, but after proceedings had commenced, defense was not entitled to dismissal. **Scharver v. State,** Op. No. 1397, 561 P2d 300 (Alaska 1977).

This rule requires only disclosure of information in prosecution's possession. **State v. Clark,** Op. No. 1497, 568 P2d 406 (Alaska 1977).

Expense logs showing amounts of money and gifts given to defendants by undercover officers were relevant to defense of entrapment and denial of discovery was improper. **Batson v. State,** Op. No. 1486, 568 P2d 973 (Alaska 1977).

If material of which discovery is sought is relevant to defense, it must be disclosed even if disclosure would be inconsistent with law enforcement or protection of persons, unless prosecution is abandoned. **Braham v. State,** Op. No. 1522, 571 P2d 631 (Alaska 1977).

If claim that disclosure of material sought to be discovered would be inconsistent with law enforcement or protection of persons fails, material must be disclosed to defense counsel and issue of relevance decided in adversary context. **Braham v. State,** Op. No. 1522, 571 P2d 631 (Alaska 1977).

Defense motion to prevent essential prosecution witness from testifying because of prosecution's failure to comply with court order to turn the witness' personal file over to defense was properly denied in the absence of a showing of prejudice to defendant of such a nature as likely to have a substantial effect on the outcome of the case, since failure of counsel to comply with discovery order should not be utilized as a basis for ultimate disposition of litigation. **Johnson v. State,** Op. No. 1596, 577 P2d 230 (Alaska 1978).

State's failure to preserve and produce the position and direction of fingerprints found on lamp at scene of crime did not violate Criminal Rule 16(b)(7) where the materiality of the evidence was marginal at best and there was no hint or suggestion of bad faith on the government's part. **White v. State,** Op. No. 1605, 577 P2d 1056 (Alaska 1978).

Trial court did not err in not dismissing the charge when the state failed to provide immediate discovery, since substantial rights of defendant were not impinged. **Christie v. State,** Op. No. 1644, 580 P2d 310 (Alaska 1978).

Failure of prosecution to disclose police report which contained information used on cross-examination by prosecution to impeach defendant's alibi witnesses clearly contravened the policies which underlie Criminal Rule 16. **Stevens v. State,** Op. No. 1658, 582 P2d 621 (Alaska 1978).

Failure of prosecution to disclose police report which it used on cross-examination constituted prejudicial error since it could not fairly be said that the error did not appreciably affect the jury's verdict. **Stevens v. State,** Op. No. 1658, 582 P2d 621 (Alaska 1978).

If a rebuttal witness is a person known by the prosecution to have knowledge of relevant facts, then his name, address and any statement he has given must be disclosed to defense counsel. **Howe v. State,** Op. No. 1780, 589 P2d 421 (Alaska 1979).

Non-disclosure of the names of rebuttal witnesses whose knowledge is reasonably not thought to be germane to the case, until a position taken by the defense during trial makes it so, is justified. **Howe v. State,** Op. No. 1780, 589 P2d 421 (Alaska 1979).

The state's failure to preserve and make available to the defendant the physical items from which fingerprint evidence was taken did not violate the defendant's statutory right of discovery. **Wyrick v. State,** Op. No. 1790, 590 P2d 46 (Alaska 1979).

Where prosecution failed to produce documents pursuant to request for discovery, but violation was in good faith, and where defendant did not request a continuance, it was not error to admit documents. **Williams v. State,** Op. No. 1939, 600 P2d 741 (Alaska 1979).

State had a responsibility to disclose to defense the fact that reward for witness existed, that state's witness had been told early on that he was potential recipient, that witness had requested money when he first approached the police, and the fact that witness was paid money after he gave the initial statement. **Carman v. State,** Op. No. 1994, 604 P2d 1076 (Alaska 1979).

Pretrial request for a psychiatric report to which the state had access concerning the state's key witness was properly denied where the report would not have contributed in a meaningful way to a more effective cross-examination of the witness. **Gunnerud v. State,** Op. No. 2091, 611 P2d 69 (Alaska 1980).

Prosecution's failure to disclose oral statement of defendant which destroyed defense theory did not require new trial where the theory was not reasonably credible. **Hampton v. State,** Op. No. 2283, 623 P2d 318 (Alaska 1981).

Where, on the morning of trial, the prosecutor presented defendant's attorney for the first time with a newly discovered police report containing the name and address of an apparent witness to the alleged crime, it was error for the court to deny a defense motion for continuance, but the error was harmless. **Russell v. Municipality of Anchorage,** Op. No. 14, 626 P2d 586 (Alaska App. 1981).

The imposition of sanctions for the state's failure to make evidentiary material available to the defendant depends upon the degree of culpability as to the state weighed against the prejudice to the defendant. **Putnam v. State,** Op. No. 2251, 629 P2d 35 (Alaska 1980).

A tape which the prosecution inadvertently failed to disclose to the defendant prior to trial is admissible if the defendant does not suffer substantial prejudice from its admission. **Fields v. State,** Op. No. 2360, 629 P2d 46 (Alaska 1981).

Destruction of taped evidence which should be preserved under this rule does not deny defendant due process when the evidence merely would have been cumulative of other evidence on trial. **Williams v. State,** Op. No. 2366, 629 P2d 54 (Alaska 1981).

Trial court's failure to insure that prosecution witness, rather than the state, opposed disclosure of the witness' medical and psychiatric records was error, but the error was harmless where there was nothing in those records bearing on her credibility and competency that was not cumulative to her trial testimony and where those records were not inconsistent with her testimony. **Spencer v. State,** Op. No. 80, 642 P2d 1371 (Alaska App. 1982).

Failure of defendant at his first trial to request disclosure of evidence taken from the victim, which evidence was destroyed after the trial, waived any right he may have had to the evidence at his second trial on the same charge, reversal of his first conviction not having revived discovery rights which had already lapsed; consequently, the prosecution had no duty to preserve the evidence in question unless it was so clearly exculpatory that the prosecutor was obligated to preserve it absent a request. **Carman v. State,** Op. No. 206, 658 P2d 131 (Alaska App. 1983).

Where defendant was charged with obtaining or attempting to obtain money by deception from an elderly male friend, trial court's order that the State disclose all financial records upon which it intended to rely, rather than ordering production of all bank records of the victim from May 1980 through March 1981 as requested by defendant, was proper. **Linne v. State,** Op. No. 324, 674 P2d 1345 (Alaska App. 1983).

Although trial court should have allowed discovery of a police report concerning rape victim's activities during the period the defendant claimed he met her, the error was harmless, since the police report itself did not contain any exculpatory material, nor was there any reason to believe that any other statements taken by the police in connection with the report disclosed exculpatory information. **Braaten v. State,** Op. No. 504, 705 P2d 1311 (Alaska App. 1985).

Although the prosecution should have given drunk driving defendant pretrial notice of its intent to call an expert witness to testify concerning an analysis of defendant's blood taken following his arrest, it was not an abuse of discretion for trial court to permit the witness to testify. **Russell v. Municipality of Anchorage,** Op. No. 514, 706 P2d 687 (Alaska App. 1985).

Trial court's decision not to compel disclosure of information relating to the case obtained by police through calls to the "crime stoppers" program, a program which solicits information from the public concerning crimes under investigation, did not substantially impair the fairness of defendant's trial, or otherwise impermissibly infringe upon his constitutionally protected trial rights. **Balentine v. State,** Op. No. 538, 707 P2d 922 (Alaska App. 1985).

Assuming without deciding that the State had a duty to preserve police dispatch tape, the State met its burden of establishing that the destruction of the tape was done in good faith and that the defendant was not prejudiced by the destruction, thus trial court did not abuse its discretion in refusing to sanction the State by dismissing the indictment against defendant. **Abdulbaqui v. State,** Op. No. 659, 728 P2d 1211 (Alaska App. 1986).

Failure of the prosecution to provide appropriate pretrial discovery did not require preclusion of disputed testimony since the continuance offered by the trial court would have cured any prejudice stemming from the discovery violation; however, the lack of prejudice was purely fortuitous; in future cases appellate courts will continue to scrutinize prosecutorial conduct in this area, and will not hesitate to reverse where it appears that the defendant has been prejudiced by such action. **Bostic v. State,** Op. No 932, 772 P2d 1089 (Alaska App. 1989).

Where defendant made no showing that he was significantly disadvantaged by the introduction without prior notice of testimony regarding a statement he made to the police, the trial court's offer of a continuance was the proper remedy for the violation of this rule. **Longley v. State,** Op. No. 940, 776 P2d 339 (Alaska App. 1989).

Where prosecution violates this rule by not disclosing to defense counsel a witness it intends to call, the prosecution has the burden of showing that the defendant has not been prejudiced in the manner he specifically claims; if this burden is not met in regard to a violation of this rule which surfaces during trial, and the prosecution deems the evidence too important to proceed without it, the proper remedy is a mistrial rather than a continuance. **Bostic v. State,** Op. No. 3659, 805 P2d 344 (Alaska 1991).

A prosecutor should disclose to the defense, upon request, criminal records of jurors, at least in cases where the prosecution intends to rely on them. **Tagala v. State,** Op. No. 1134, 812 P2d 604 (Alaska App. 1991).

In drug case where an issue was whether the police investigation was the product of an illegal search by police informants, and the state asserted its privilege not to identify the informants, upon which the judge conducted an in camera hearing in which he questioned the informants using questions submitted by the defendant and the state and concluded that the identity of informants did not have to be revealed, the defendant was entitled to see the transcript of the in camera hearing with all information deleted that might identify the informants. **Peterson v. State,** Op. No. 1139, 813 P2d 685 (Alaska App. 1991).

In prosecution of defendant for burglary, prosecutor was not required to disclose unrecorded oral statement of witness made during pretrial preparation shortly before trial that hammer and putty knife found on defendant came from burglarized building. **Sivertsen v. State,** Op. No. 1600, 963 P2d 1069 (Alaska App. 1998).

In trial for speeding, Magistrate did not abuse her discretion in refusing to order additional discovery under Criminal Rule 16 where defendant sought irrelevant information on the creation of the courts, the chartering of Anchorage, the true name of the government accuser, IRS documents, and police operating procedures. **Collier v. Municipality of Anchorage**, Op. No. 9404, 138 P.3d 719 (Alaska App. 2006).

Defendant's right to discovery under Criminal Rule 16 was not violated where the State did not give him documents demonstrating that the judicial officers and prosecutors involved in his case were public officers of the State where defendant did not elaborate on the precise documents he was seeking and trial court determined that defendant was seeking bar rules, rules of professional conduct and legal opinions and not police reports, criminal records, or other documents that the State must disclose under this rule. **Gladden v. State**, Op. No. 9429, 153 P.3d 1028 (Alaska App. 2007).

III. Disclosure to Prosecution.

The mere fact that a court orders an accused to submit pretrial information which is not specifically included in this rule does not establish that the court has abused its discretion. **Scott v. State,** Op. No. 1004, 519 P2d 774 (Alaska 1974).

An order requiring an accused to produce information not expressly provided for in these rules for criminal procedure does not constitute an improper promulgation of a new rule of criminal procedure. **Scott v. State,** Op. No. 1004, 519 P2d 774 (Alaska 1974).

The privilege against compelled self-incrimination under the Alaska Constitution prohibits extensive pretrial prosecutorial discovery in criminal proceedings. **Scott v. State,** Op. No. 1004, 519 P2d 774 (Alaska 1974).

The fundamental right not to incriminate one's self applies at every stage of a criminal inquiry or proceedings regardless of any judge-made exclusionary or evidentiary rules. **Scott v. State,** Op. No. 1004, 519 P2d 774 (Alaska 1974).

A pretrial order requiring an accused to disclose the names and addresses of witnesses, to produce for inspection and copying all written or recorded statements of prospective defense or government witnesses which the accused possesses, and to produce advance notice of the alibi defense together with information indicating any place or places he claims to have been, violates the accused's privilege against self-incrimination under the state Constitution. **Scott v. State,** Op. No. 1004, 519 P2d 774 (Alaska 1974).

A pretrial discovery order requiring an accused to furnish notice of the alibi defense does not violate an accused's privilege against self-incrimination under the state Constitution. **Scott v. State,** Op. No. 1004, 519 P2d 774 (Alaska 1974).

Where there was no indication that defendant ever intended to use the report of a firearms expert at trial, it was error for the court to compel its disclosure to the state. **Gipson v. State,** Op. No. 2066, 609 P2d 1038 (Alaska 1980).

Criminal Rule 16(c)(1) has no relevance when a person whose fingerprints are sought consents to give them. **Henry v. State,** Op. No. 2188, 621 P2d 1 (Alaska 1980).

This rule, as it pertains to obtaining identification evidence such as fingerprints, does not apply to persons lawfully in custody. **Liston v. State,** Op. No. 219, 658 P2d 1346 (Alaska App. 1983).

Trial court did not err in failing to suppress evidence of palm print taken from defendant without a warrant while defendant was lawfully in custody. **Liston v. State,** Op. No. 219, 658 P2d 1346 (Alaska App. 1983).

In a criminal trial where defendant was charged with prostitution for soliciting an undercover policewoman to have oral sex with him, the defendant waived his entrapment claim by failing to raise it in a pretrial motion. **Parrott v. Municipality of Anchorage,** 69 P.3d 1 (Alaska App. 2003).

LAW REVIEW COMMENTARIES

"If you knew him like I did, you'd have shot him too…A survey of Alaska's Law of Self Defense," 23 Alaska L. Rev. 171 (2006).

Rule 17. Subpoena.

(a) For Attendance of Witnesses—Form—Issuance.

(1) Subpoenas shall be issued by the clerk under the seal of the court, and shall be signed and sealed but otherwise in blank. The party requesting a subpoena shall fill in the blanks before the subpoena is served.

(2) A subpoena shall

(i) state the name of the court and the title, if any, of the proceeding, and

(ii) state whether the witness is to testify on behalf of the state, a municipality, city or borough, and order any witness testifying on behalf of the state, a municipality, city or borough, to appear without the prepayment of any witness fee, and

(iii) command each person to whom the subpoena is directed to attend and give testimony at the time and place specified therein.

(3) Magistrates may issue subpoenas in any proceeding before them.

(b) **Defendants Unable to Pay.** A subpoena shall be issued by the clerk as provided in section (a) for a defendant financially unable to pay the fees of the witness. The determination of financial inability shall be made in accordance with the criteria provided under Rule 39 (b) of these rules, and if the defendant is represented by court appointed counsel no further showing of financial inability shall be required. Subpoenas issued under this section (b) shall contain an order to appear without the prepayment of any witness fee. The cost incurred by the process and the fees of the witness so subpoenaed, shall be paid by the public agency providing representation.

(c) **For Production of Documentary Evidence and of Objects.** A subpoena may also command the person to whom it is directed to produce the books, papers, documents or other objects designated therein. The court on motion made promptly may suppress or modify the subpoena if compliance would be unreasonable or oppressive. The court may direct that books, papers, documents or objects designated in the subpoena be produced before the court at a time prior to the trial or prior to the time when they are to be offered in evidence and may, upon their production permit the books, papers, documents or objects or portions thereof to be inspected by the parties and their attorneys.

(d) **Service.**

(1) A subpoena may be served by any peace officer or any other person who is not a party and who is not less than 18 years of age. Service of a subpoena shall be made by delivering a copy thereof to the person named and subject to the provisions of sections (a) and (b) of this rule, by tendering to that person the fee for one day's attendance and the mileage allowed by law or by rule.

(2) A subpoena may also be served upon a person of known residence within the state by registered or certified mail. In such case the clerk shall mail the subpoena for delivery only to the person subpoenaed and, unless not required under section (a) or (b) of this rule, shall enclose a warrant or postal money order in the amount of the fees for one day's attendance and for the mileage allowed by law or rule. The return address on the envelope and the address on the returned delivery receipt shall be that of the party requesting the subpoena or the party's attorney.

(3) Unless filing is ordered by the court on motion of a party or on its own motion, subpoenas and proofs of service thereto shall be returned to the party requesting issuance and may not be filed unless and until they are used in the proceedings.

(e) **Place of Service.** A subpoena requiring the attendance of a witness at a hearing or trial may be served at any place within the State of Alaska.

(f) **For Taking Deposition—Place of Examination.**

(1) *Issuance.* An order to take a deposition authorizes the issuance by the clerk of the court or by a magistrate of subpoenas for the persons named or described therein.

(2) *Place.* The witness whose deposition is to be taken may be required by subpoena to attend at any place designated by the trial court within the state.

(g) **Contempt.** Failure by any person without adequate excuse to obey a subpoena served upon that person may be deemed a contempt of the court from which the subpoena issued.

(Adopted by SCO 4 October 4, 1959; amended by SCO 90 effective July 24, 1967; by SCO 98 effective September 16, 1968; amended by SCO 157 effective February 15, 1973; by SCO 456 effective March 15, 1981; by SCO 518 effective October 1, 1982; by SCO 519 effective October 1, 1982; by SCO 939 effective January 15, 1989; and by SCO 1153 effective July 15, 1994)

Note: Ch. 75 SLA 2002 (HB 106), Section 4, adds a new section to AS 06.01 relating to the confidentiality of depositor and customer records at banking and other financial institutions. According to Section 56 of the Act, AS 06.01.028(b) has the effect of changing Civil Rule 45, Criminal Rules 17 and 37, and Alaska Bar Rule 24 by requiring certain court orders compelling disclosure of records to provide for reimbursement of a financial institution's reasonable costs of complying with the order.

Cross References

(b) **CROSS REFERENCE:** AS 12.50.050

(g) **CROSS REFERENCE:** AS 12.80.010

Annotations

Cases

Under this rule denial of subpoena at state expense of a possible eyewitness on the speculative ground that such witness if called might exercise his privilege against self-incrimination, was error. **Smiloff v. State,** Op. No. 474, 439 P2d 772 (Alaska 1968).

Under a charge of attempted rape testimony of potential witnesses expected to impeach the credibility of the prosecutrix, to testify as to previous consensual intercourse between prosecutrix and defendant and to offer character evidence on behalf of the defendant, was relevant and material testimony and denial of subpoena of these witnesses upon a motion under this rule was reversible error. **Smiloff v. State,** Op. No. 474, 439 P2d 772 (Alaska 1968).

Where under an indictment for attempted rape character evidence and evidence of prior consensual intercourse between the prosecutrix and the defendant were relevant and material, and the trial judge nowhere precisely articulated what criterion he employed in deciding to allow or not to allow subpoenas at state expense, but stated that he would issue a subpoena only if the witness could show that he was with the defendant during the entire time in question, the trial judge applied too rigid a standard in administering this rule. **Smiloff v. State,** Op. No. 474, 439 P2d 772 (Alaska 1968).

The right to have a witness subpoenaed at state expense is not absolute and the trial court is vested with discretion in order to prevent abuses. **Smiloff v. State,** Op. No. 474, 439 P2d 772 (Alaska 1968).

Trial judge correctly dispensed with a requirement of this rule as formerly written that the showing in support of a motion must be made by affidavit in a case where it appeared that the defendant was illiterate, that linguistic and cultural barriers existed between defendant and his counsel and where the prosecution did not object to oral and written statements of defendant's counsel as to what testimony the witness would give. **Smiloffv. State,** Op. No. 474,439 P2d 772 (Alaska 1968).

Where the state had acquiesced in the court's suggestion that in regard to a motion under this rule as formerly written oral and written statements from defense counsel as to what testimony the witness would give be furnished, state was not permitted to argue on appeal that the court's ruling denying the motion should be tested only on the basis of averments made by appellant in his sworn affidavit. **Smiloff v. State,** Op. No. 474, 439 P2d 772 (Alaska 1968).

Under this rule as formerly written, the right to have a witness subpoenaed at state expense is not absolute, and the trial court is vested with discretion in order to prevent abuses. **McCracken v. State,** Op. No. 1028, 521 P2d 499 (Alaska 1974).

In trial of defendant for robbing sandwich shop of eighty dollars and meatball sandwich, trial court committed reversible error in denying defense motion to compel production of palm print of employee who handed money and sandwich bag to robber, since print did not match defendant and evidence of third person's print on bag might have altered jury's decision; appellate court rejected state's argument that trial court had no authority to compel employee to submit to fingerprinting or, alternatively, failure to exercise authority was not abuse of discretion. **Fathke v. State,** Op. No. 1549, 945 P2d 1243 (Alaska App. 1997).

Trial court had authority under this rule to compel witness to produce palm and fingerprints. **Fathke v. State,** Op. No. 1571, 951 P2d 1226 (Alaska App. 1998).

PART V. VENUE—PRETRIAL

Rule 18. Venue: Place of Trial.

(a) **Venue Districts.** The venue map promulgated by the supreme court establishes the district and superior court venue districts and the presumptive trial site for each district. The venue map includes a chart listing each community that appears on the map along with each community's presumptive district court trial site and presumptive superior court trial site.

(b) **Determination of Trial Location.**

(1) *Initial Assignment.* A Criminal case must be initially assigned for trial at the presumptive trial site for the district or superior court venue district, as determined by reference to the venue map and community chart described in (a) of this rule, in which the crime is alleged to have occurred.

(2) *Transfer to Approved Additional Trial Site.* As provided in (e) of this rule, the defendant may cause venue to be transferred to a trial site on the list of approved additional trial sites described in (d) of this rule.

(3) *Change of Venue.* Either party may move to change venue as provided in (g) of this rule.

(c) **Additional Trial Site Standards.** Subject to supreme court approval, the administrative director shall devise and promulgate an administrative bulletin establishing minimum standards for additional trial sites, including standards for courtroom needs and standards for transportation, housing, and feeding of all trial participants.

(d) **List of Approved Additional Trial Sites.** The administrative director shall promulgate an administrative bulletin listing approved additional trial sites for six- and twelve-person juries meeting the standards established under (c) of this rule. Changes in the list may be made as follows:

(1) A presiding judge, area court administrator, town council, or similar public representative group, or the attorney general, the public defender, or the public advocate may ask the administrative director for an investigation to determine whether a community should be added to or deleted from the list.

(2) The administrative director will distribute the list of approved additional trial sites to the attorney general, the public defender, and the public advocate.

(e) **Motion to Transfer by Right.** After assignment to the presumptive trial site, a defendant may move by right for the setting of venue in an approved additional trial site within the venue district where the crime charged is alleged to have occurred if such site is the trial site nearest the place where the crime charged is alleged to have occurred. This right is waived unless the defendant requests the transfer within ten days after the defendant enters a plea, absent good cause for an extension of this time limit.

(f) **Fair Cross-Section.** If the trial location assignment under the above subsections will not provide a petit jury which is a representative cross-section of the appropriate community, the trial court on its own motion or that of a party may change the jury selection area as provided in Administrative Rule 15(c).

(g) **Change of Venue.** Any other motion for a change of venue shall be determined under the standards listed in AS 22.10.040.

(h) **Limitations of Rule.** The presumptive trial sites established by this rule do not determine the court location where a criminal case must be filed or the court location where pretrial proceedings take place.

(Adopted by SCO 4 effective October 4, 1959; amended by SCO 136 effective September 2, 1971; by SCO 157 effective February 15, 1973; by SCO 666 effective January 1, 1986; by SCO 670 effective March 15, 1986; by SCO 682 effective May 15, 1986; by SCO 1334 effective July 15, 1998; by SCO 1348 effective October 1, 1998; by SCO 1644 effective October 15, 2007; and by SCO 1645 effective July 1, 2007)

Note: A map of venue districts for the Alaska Court System is available from the office of the court rules attorney, 820 W. 4th Ave., Anchorage, AK 99501. Administrative Bulletin 28 establishes the minimum standards for additional trial site locations and is available on the court system's website [http://www.state.ak.us/courts], in law libraries, and from the office of the court rules attorney. Administrative Bulletin 27 lists approved additional trial site locations, and is included at the end of this rule.

Note: The boundaries of the Anchorage venue district, the Seward venue district, and the Kenai venue district were changed by SCO 1348 effective October 1, 1998. A copy of this order is available in law libraries and from the court rules attorney.

Note: The venue map promulgated by the supreme court and the community chart referenced in subsection (a) of this rule are available on the Alaska Court System website at: http://www.state.ak.us/courts/venuemapinfo.htm

Annotations

Cases

When the trial court complies with AS 22.10.030 and this rule, a party requesting a change of venue because of alleged cultural and social differences between place where offense allegedly occurred and the site set for trial has the affirmative burden of establishing that systematic exclusion from the jury of a distinct group or class of persons will occur unless venue is changed. **Dana v. State,** Op. No. 3, 623 P2d 348 (Alaska App. 1982).

In order to be entitled to an evidentiary hearing on a claim that change of venue is necessary because of social and cultural differences between place set for trial and place where offense allegedly occurred, the moving party should at a minimum be prepared to make a clear and nonconclusory showing, by affidavit or other reliable offer of proof, that the party is capable of producing evidence which, if true, would require venue to be changed. **Dana v. State,** Op. No. 3, 623 P2d 348 (Alaska App. 1982).

Failure of trial court to exercise due care in summoning for trial in a remote village a jury panel sufficiently numerous to ensure that a jury of twelve persons would be selected invalidated the subsequent trial where defendant waived a jury of twelve and proceeded to trial with a jury of seven persons chosen from the area in which the crime occurred. **Erick v. State,** Op. No. 75, 642 P2d 821 (Alaska App. 1982).

Defendant's contention that application of this rule violated his constitutional rights by effectively excluding all members of a cognizable group, i.e. Caucasian members of the Russian Orthodox church, was properly rejected where defendant offered no evidence regarding the attitudes, ideas, experiences, or beliefs of members of the group. **Sundberg v. State,** Op. No. 188, 652 P2d 113 (Alaska App. 1982).

Filing fish and game violation charges and holding the trial in Anchorage, rather than in Naknek, which was the closest urban center to the place where the violations occurred, did not violate this rule, where defendants were not residents of the senate district in which the offenses occurred, but were merely present on a temporary basis for the duration of their hunt. **Graybill v. State,** Op. No. 300, 672 P2d 138 (Alaska App. 1983).

In trial in Ketchikan at which defendant was convicted of assault for an incident that occurred in the village of Metlakatla, exclusion of Metlakatla citizens from the jury pool because of the expense and the inconvenience of housing them for the duration of the trial did not violate defendant's constitutional right to an impartial jury absent a showing by defendant that Metlakatlans comprise a distinctive group in the community. **Wyatt v. State,** Op. No. 961,778 P2d 1169 (Alaska App. 1989).

Given the strong presumption that motions for change of venue should not be decided until voir dire has at least been attempted, judge did not abuse her discretion in denying without prejudice defendant's pretrial motion for change of venue and leaving the issue to be reconsidered after voir dire examination. **Wylie v. State,** Op. No. 1063,797 P2d 651 (Alaska App. 1990).

Judge did not abuse her discretion in denying pretrial motion for change of venue prior to voir dire despite defendant's arguments regarding the small size of the relevant community and the nature of the pretrial publicity. **Wylie v. State,** Op. No. 1063, 797 P2d 651 (Alaska App. 1990).

To effectuate the high court's intention in promulgating a rule that would assure that villagers would not be denied trial by a cross-section of their community, instead of being tried in urban areas, the court interpreted the rule as requiring that felonies be tried in court within the venue area in which the crime occurred, even though in some cases, this would mean trial in a place that lacked a permanent superior court judge. **John v. State,** Op. No. 1772, 35 P3d 53 (Alaska App. 2001).

When all of the judges who reside in the place of venue specified by Alaska R. Crim. P. 18 are disqualified, thus requiring the assignment of a judge from another community, this situation constitutes "good cause" for a delay of a criminal trial under Alaska R. Crim. P. 45(d)(7). **Keller v. State,** Op. No. 1916, 84 P.3d 1010.

Venues available for criminal jury trials are limited, and defendant's trial was held in a venue he had suggested; on appeal, his allegation that the jury pool did not adequately reflect the jury he would have received had it been possible to hold the trial in the venue where the crime occurred was dismissed for failure to raise the objection at trial. **Wholecheese v. State,** Op. No. 1950, 100 P.3d 14 (Alaska App. 2004).

When subsection (e) of this rule speaks of the locating a trial venue "nearest the place where the alleged crime was committed," the rule is referring to geographic proximity rather than ease of transportation and logistics. Geographic proximity best serves the aim of obtaining jurors who are more likely to share the culture and life experience of the community where the crime occurred, while ease of transportation and logistics will almost always favor holding the trial in an urban center. Holding the trial in the urban center goes against the policy of obtaining similar jurors for crimes that occurred outside of urban areas. **Stickman-Sam v. State**, Op. No. 9307, 135 P.3d 1036 (Alaska App. 2006).

Community Appearing on Venue Map	Presumptive District Court Trial Site	Presumptive Superior Court Trial Site
Adak	Unalaska	Unalaska
Afognak	Kodiak	Kodiak
Akhiok	Kodiak	Kodiak
Akiachak	Bethel	Bethel
Akiak	Bethel	Bethel
Akutan	Unalaska	Unalaska
Alakanuk	Emmonak	Bethel
Alatna	Nenana	Fairbanks
Alcan	Tok	Tok
Aleknagik	Dillingham	Dillingham
Allakaket	Nenana	Fairbanks
Ambler	Kotzebue	Kotzebue
Anaktuvuk Pass	Barrow	Barrow
Anchor Point	Homer	Homer
Anchorage	Anchorage	Anchorage
Anderson	Nenana	Fairbanks
Angoon	Angoon	Sitka
Aniak	Aniak	Bethel
Anvik	Aniak	Bethel
Arctic Village	Fort Yukon	Fairbanks
Atka	Unalaska	Unalaska
Atmautluak	Bethel	Bethel
Atqasuk	Barrow	Barrow
Attu	Unalaska	Unalaska
Auke Bay	Juneau	Juneau
Ayakulik	Kodiak	Kodiak
Barrow	Barrow	Barrow
Beaver	Fort Yukon	Fairbanks
Belkofski	Sand Point	Anchorage
Beluga	Kenai	Kenai
Bethel	Bethel	Bethel
Bettles	Nenana	Fairbanks
Big Delta	Delta Junction	Delta Junction
Big Lake	Palmer	Palmer
Bill Moores	Emmonak	Bethel
Birch Creek	Fort Yukon	Fairbanks
Boundary	Tok	Tok
Brevig Mission	Nome	Nome
Buckland	Kotzebue	Kotzebue
Candle	Kotzebue	Kotzebue
Cantwell	Healy	Fairbanks
Central	Fairbanks	Fairbanks
Chalkyitsik	Fort Yukon	Fairbanks
Chase	Palmer	Palmer
Chefornak	Bethel	Bethel
Chena Hot Springs	Fairbanks	Fairbanks
Chenega	Seward	Seward
Chevak	Bethel	Bethel
Chickaloon	Palmer	Palmer
Chicken	Tok	Tok
Chignik	Naknek	Naknek

Community Appearing on Venue Map	Presumptive District Court Trial Site	Presumptive Superior Court Trial Site
Chignik Lagoon	Naknek	Naknek
Chignik Lake	Naknek	Naknek
Chiniak	Kodiak	Kodiak
Chisana	Tok	Tok
Chistochina	Glennallen	Glennallen
Chitina	Glennallen	Glennallen
Chuathbaluk	Aniak	Bethel
Chugiak	Anchorage	Anchorage
Chuloonawick	Emmonak	Bethel
Circle	Fairbanks	Fairbanks
Circle Hot Springs	Fairbanks	Fairbanks
Clam Gulch	Kenai	Kenai
Clarks Point	Dillingham	Dillingham
Coffman Cove	Craig	Craig
Cohoe	Kenai	Kenai
Cold Bay	Sand Point	Anchorage
Coldfoot	Nenana	Fairbanks
Cooper Landing	Seward	Seward
Copper Center	Glennallen	Glennallen
Cordova	Cordova	Cordova
Council	Nome	Nome
Craig	Craig	Craig
Crooked Creek	Aniak	Bethel
Deadhorse	Barrow	Barrow
Deering	Kotzebue	Kotzebue
Delta Junction	Delta Junction	Delta Junction
Dillingham	Dillingham	Dillingham
Diomede	Nome	Nome
Dot Lake	Tok	Tok
Douglas	Juneau	Juneau
Dry Creek	Delta Junction	Delta Junction
Dutch Harbor	Unalaska	Unalaska
Eagle	Tok	Tok
Eagle River	Anchorage	Anchorage
Eagle Village	Tok	Tok
Edna Bay	Craig	Craig
Eek	Bethel	Bethel
Egegik	Naknek	Naknek
Eklutna	Anchorage	Anchorage
Ekuk	Dillingham	Dillingham
Ekwok	Dillingham	Dillingham
Elfin Cove	Sitka	Sitka
Elim	Nome	Nome
Emmonak	Emmonak	Bethel
Ester	Fairbanks	Fairbanks
Evansville	Nenana	Fairbanks
Excursion Inlet	Juneau	Juneau
Eyak	Cordova	Cordova
Fairbanks	Fairbanks	Fairbanks
False Pass	Sand Point	Anchorage
Ferry	Healy	Fairbanks

Community Appearing on Venue Map	Presumptive District Court Trial Site	Presumptive Superior Court Trial Site
Flat	Aniak	Bethel
Fort Yukon	Fort Yukon	Fairbanks
Fox	Fairbanks	Fairbanks
Gakona	Glennallen	Glennallen
Galena	Galena	Fairbanks
Gambell	Nome	Nome
Georgetown	Aniak	Bethel
Girdwood	Anchorage	Anchorage
Glennallen	Glennallen	Glennallen
Golovin	Nome	Nome
Goodnews Bay	Bethel	Bethel
Grayling	Aniak	Bethel
Gulkana	Glennallen	Glennallen
Gustavus	Juneau	Juneau
Haines	Haines	Juneau
Halibut Cove	Homer	Homer
Hamilton	Emmonak	Bethel
Happy Valley	Homer	Homer
Harding-Birch Lakes	Fairbanks	Fairbanks
Healy	Healy	Fairbanks
Healy Lake	Delta Junction	Delta Junction
Hobart Bay	Petersburg	Petersburg
Hollis	Craig	Craig
Holy Cross	Aniak	Bethel
Homer	Homer	Homer
Hoonah	Hoonah	Juneau
Hooper Bay	Bethel	Bethel
Hope	Anchorage	Anchorage
Houston	Palmer	Palmer
Hughes	Nenana	Fairbanks
Huslia	Galena	Fairbanks
Hydaburg	Craig	Craig
Hyder	Ketchikan	Ketchikan
Iditarod	Aniak	Bethel
Igiugig	Naknek	Naknek
Iliamna	Naknek	Naknek
Ivanof Bay	Naknek	Naknek
Juneau	Juneau	Juneau
Kachemak	Homer	Homer
Kaguyak	Kodiak	Kodiak
Kake	Kake	Petersburg
Kaktovik	Barrow	Barrow
Kalifornsky	Kenai	Kenai
Kaltag	Galena	Fairbanks
Karluk	Kodiak	Kodiak
Kasaan	Craig	Craig
Kasigluk	Bethel	Bethel
Kasilof	Kenai	Kenai
Kenai	Kenai	Kenai
Kenny Lake	Glennallen	Glennallen
Ketchikan	Ketchikan	Ketchikan

Community Appearing on Venue Map	Presumptive District Court Trial Site	Presumptive Superior Court Trial Site
Kiana	Kotzebue	Kotzebue
King Cove	Sand Point	Anchorage
King Island	Nome	Nome
King Salmon	Naknek	Naknek
Kipnuk	Bethel	Bethel
Kivalina	Kotzebue	Kotzebue
Klawock	Craig	Craig
Klukwan	Haines	Juneau
Knik	Palmer	Palmer
Kobuk	Kotzebue	Kotzebue
Kodiak	Kodiak	Kodiak
Kokhanok	Naknek	Naknek
Koliganek	Dillingham	Dillingham
Kongiganak	Bethel	Bethel
Kotlik	Emmonak	Bethel
Kotzebue	Kotzebue	Kotzebue
Koyuk	Nome	Nome
Koyukuk	Galena	Fairbanks
Kupreanof	Petersburg	Petersburg
Kwethluk	Bethel	Bethel
Kwigillingok	Bethel	Bethel
Lake Louise	Palmer	Palmer
Lake Minchumina	McGrath	Bethel
Larsen Bay	Kodiak	Kodiak
Levelock	Naknek	Naknek
Lignite	Healy	Fairbanks
Lime Village	Aniak	Bethel
Livengood	Nenana	Fairbanks
Lower Kalskag	Aniak	Bethel
Lower Tonsina	Glennallen	Glennallen
Manokotak	Dillingham	Dillingham
Manley Hot Springs	Nenana	Fairbanks
Marshall	Bethel	Bethel
Marys Igloo	Nome	Nome
McCarthy	Glennallen	Glennallen
McGrath	McGrath	Bethel
McKinley Park	Healy	Fairbanks
Medfra	McGrath	Bethel
Mekoryuk	Bethel	Bethel
Mendeltna	Glennallen	Glennallen
Mentasta Lake	Glennallen	Glennallen
Metlakatla	Ketchikan	Ketchikan
Meyers Chuck	Ketchikan	Ketchikan
Minto	Nenana	Fairbanks
Moose Creek	Fairbanks	Fairbanks
Moose Pass	Seward	Seward
Mountain Village	Bethel	Bethel
Nabesna	Glennallen	Glennallen
Naknek	Naknek	Naknek
Nanwalek	Homer	Homer
Napaimiut	Aniak	Bethel

Community Appearing on Venue Map	Presumptive District Court Trial Site	Presumptive Superior Court Trial Site
Napakiak	Bethel	Bethel
Napaskiak	Bethel	Bethel
Naukati Bay	Craig	Craig
Nelchina	Glennallen	Glennallen
Nelson Lagoon	Sand Point	Anchorage
Nenana	Nenana	Fairbanks
Newhalen	Naknek	Naknek
New Stuyahok	Dillingham	Dillingham
Newtok	Bethel	Bethel
Nightmute	Bethel	Bethel
Nikiski	Kenai	Kenai
Nikolaevsk	Homer	Homer
Nikolai	McGrath	Bethel
Nikolski	Unalaska	Unalaska
Ninilchik	Homer	Homer
Noatak	Kotzebue	Kotzebue
Nome	Nome	Nome
Nondalton	Naknek	Naknek
Noorvik	Kotzebue	Kotzebue
North Pole	Fairbanks	Fairbanks
Northway	Tok	Tok
Northway Junction	Tok	Tok
Nuiqsut	Barrow	Barrow
Nulato	Galena	Fairbanks
Nunam Iqua	Emmonak	Bethel
Nunapitchuk	Bethel	Bethel
Ohogamiut	Bethel	Bethel
Old Harbor	Kodiak	Kodiak
Ophir	McGrath	Bethel
Oscarville	Bethel	Bethel
Ouzinkie	Kodiak	Kodiak
Paimiut	Bethel	Bethel
Palmer	Palmer	Palmer
Pauloff Harbor	Sand Point	Anchorage
Paxson	Glennallen	Glennallen
Pedro Bay	Naknek	Naknek
Pelican	Sitka	Sitka
Perryville	Naknek	Naknek
Petersburg	Petersburg	Petersburg
Petersville	Palmer	Palmer
Pilot Point	Naknek	Naknek
Pilot Station	Bethel	Bethel
Pitkas Point	Bethel	Bethel
Platinum	Bethel	Bethel
Pleasant Valley	Fairbanks	Fairbanks
Point Baker	Petersburg	Petersburg
Point Hope	Kotzebue	Kotzebue
Point Lay	Barrow	Barrow
Port Alexander	Sitka	Sitka
Port Alsworth	Naknek	Naknek
Port Clarence	Nome	Nome

Community Appearing on Venue Map	Presumptive District Court Trial Site	Presumptive Superior Court Trial Site
Port Graham	Homer	Homer
Port Heiden	Naknek	Naknek
Port Lions	Kodiak	Kodiak
Port Moller	Sand Point	Anchorage
Port Protection	Petersburg	Petersburg
Portage Creek	Dillingham	Dillingham
Primrose	Seward	Seward
Prudhoe Bay	Barrow	Barrow
Quinhaguk	Bethel	Bethel
Rampart	Nenana	Fairbanks
Red Devil	Aniak	Bethel
Red Dog Mine	Kotzebue	Kotzebue
Ruby	Galena	Fairbanks
Russian Mission	Bethel	Bethel
Saint George	Saint Paul	Anchorage
Saint Marys	Bethel	Bethel
Saint Michael	Nome	Nome
Saint Paul	Saint Paul	Anchorage
Salamatof	Kenai	Kenai
Salcha	Fairbanks	Fairbanks
Sand Point	Sand Point	Anchorage
Savoonga	Nome	Nome
Saxman	Ketchikan	Ketchikan
Scammon Bay	Bethel	Bethel
Selawik	Kotzebue	Kotzebue
Seldovia	Homer	Homer
Seward	Seward	Seward
Shageluk	Aniak	Bethel
Shaktoolik	Nome	Nome
Shemya Station	Unalaska	Unalaska
Shishmaref	Nome	Nome
Shungnak	Kotzebue	Kotzebue
Sitka	Sitka	Sitka
Skagway	Skagway	Juneau
Skwentna	Palmer	Palmer
Slana	Glennallen	Glennallen
Sleetmute	Aniak	Bethel
Soldotna	Kenai	Kenai
Solomon	Nome	Nome
South Naknek	Naknek	Naknek
Stebbins	Nome	Nome
Sterling	Kenai	Kenai
Stevens Village	Fort Yukon	Fairbanks
Stony River	Aniak	Bethel
Summit Lake	Glennallen	Glennallen
Susitna	Palmer	Palmer
Sutton	Palmer	Palmer
Takotna	McGrath	Bethel
Talkeetna	Palmer	Palmer
Tanacross	Tok	Tok
Tanana	Tanana	Fairbanks

Community Appearing on Venue Map	Presumptive District Court Trial Site	Presumptive Superior Court Trial Site
Tatitlek	Valdez	Valdez
Tazlina	Glennallen	Glennallen
Telida	McGrath	Bethel
Teller	Nome	Nome
Tenakee Springs	Juneau	Juneau
Tetlin	Tok	Tok
Tetlin Junction	Tok	Tok
Thorne Bay	Craig	Craig
Tin City	Nome	Nome
Togiak	Dillingham	Dillingham
Tok	Tok	Tok
Tonsina	Glennallen	Glennallen
Toksook Bay	Bethel	Bethel
Tuluksak	Bethel	Bethel
Tuntutuliak	Bethel	Bethel
Tununak	Bethel	Bethel
Twin Hills	Dillingham	Dillingham
Two Rivers	Fairbanks	Fairbanks
Tyonek	Kenai	Kenai
Uganik	Kodiak	Kodiak
Ugashik	Naknek	Naknek
Umkumiut	Bethel	Bethel
Unalakleet	Nome	Nome
Unalaska	Unalaska	Unalaska
Unga	Sand Point	Anchorage
Upper Kalskag	Aniak	Bethel
Uyak	Kodiak	Kodiak
Valdez	Valdez	Valdez
Venetie	Fort Yukon	Fairbanks
Wainwright	Barrow	Barrow
Wales	Nome	Nome
Wasilla	Palmer	Palmer
Waterfall	Craig	Craig
Whale Pass	Craig	Craig
White Mountain	Nome	Nome
Whittier	Anchorage	Anchorage
Willow	Palmer	Palmer
Willow Creek	Glennallen	Glennallen
Wiseman	Nenana	Fairbanks
Womens Bay	Kodiak	Kodiak
Woody Island	Kodiak	Kodiak
Wrangell	Wrangell	Wrangell
Yakutat	Yakutat	Juneau

ALASKA COURT SYSTEM
OFFICE OF THE ADMINISTRATIVE DIRECTOR
ADMINISTRATIVE BULLETIN NO. 27
(AMENDED EFFECTIVE JULY 1, 2007)

TO: ALL HOLDERS OF ADMINISTRATIVE BULLETIN SETS:

All Justices
All Judges
Area Court Administrators
Clerk of the Appellate Courts
Rural Court Training Assistants
All Clerks of Court
All Magistrates
Law Libraries at Anchorage, Fairbanks, Juneau & Ketchikan
Senior Staff
Court Analysts
General Services Manager
Judicial Services
APD Warrants

SUBJECT: LIST OF APPROVED ADDITIONAL TRIAL SITE LOCATIONS

The following sites are approved additional trial site locations under Criminal Rule 18(d):

	Add'l Trial Sites for Six-Person Juries	Add'l Trial Sites for Twelve-Person Juries
First District		
Angoon		X
Second District		
Wainwright	X	
Kiana	X	
Pt. Hope	X	
Selawick	X	
Shungnak	X	
Unalakleet	X	X
Third District		
St. Paul		X
Sand Point		X
Fourth District		
Nenana		X

Date: June 29, 2007
Effective: July 1, 2007

Stephanie J. Cole, Administrative Director

This bulletin applies to motions filed under Criminal Rule 18(e) on or after July 1, 2007

Original order in effect since July 23, 1986; amended August 17, 1987, effective January 15, 1988; amended January 19, 1988, effective July 15, 1988; amended June 6, 1988, effective January 15, 1989; amended October 18, 1988, effective January 15, 1989; amended December 13, 1993, effective December 13, 1993; amended October 15, 2002, effective October 15, 2002; amended February 19, 2004, effective April 15, 2004 amended November 8, 2004, effective November 8, 2004; amended August 17, 2005, effective October 15, 2005; amended March 8, 2007, effective March 8, 2007; amended June 29, 2007, effective July 1, 2007.

cc: Attorney General
Public Defender
Public Advocate
Alaska Bar Association

Rule 19. Change of Venue—Application to Court.

All applications for change of place of trial in the cases provided by AS 22.10.040 shall be made by motion, supported by affidavit, upon five days' notice to the other party. In the event that a change of place of trial shall be ordered, the clerk of the court in which the case is pending shall transmit to the clerk of the court to which the proceeding is transferred all papers in the proceeding, or duplicates thereof, and the prosecution shall continue in that court.

(Adopted by SCO 4 October 4, 1959; amended by SCO 49 effective January 1, 1963; by SCO 56 effective November 1, 1963)

Annotations

Cases

A motion for change of venue under [federal] Rule 2 1(a) is addressed to the sound discretion of the trial court, and in the absence of abuse of discretion denial of the motion is not error. **Marrone v. State,** Op. No. 5, 359 P2d 969 (Alaska 1961).

Rule 20. Temporary Transfer of Case File.

(a) A defendant may request a temporary transfer of a case pending against the defendant to another court location in the state if (1) the defendant is arrested in a court location other than that in which the action is pending or (2) the defendant has been notified that a charge is pending against the defendant in a court location other than that nearest to where the defendant is residing.

(b) A defendant requesting a temporary transfer of a case shall state in writing or in open court that the defendant wishes to be arraigned and enter a plea in the court location where the defendant was arrested or nearest to where the defendant resides. Transfer of a case is contingent upon approval by the prosecuting attorney for the court location in which the action is pending. Approval may be given in writing, in open court, or by telephonic authorization to the clerk of the court who shall note the prosecuting attorney's approval in the file.

(c) Upon notification of the request and approval by the prosecuting attorney, the clerk of the court in which the action is pending shall transmit the papers in the action or certified copies thereof to the clerk of court for the court location requested by the defendant.

(d) If a defendant enters a plea of guilty or nolo contendere, the defendant may be sentenced in the court in which the defendant enters the plea. If a defendant enters a plea of not guilty, the court in which the defendant enters the plea shall at the time of the plea set the case for trial in the originating court.

(e) After the plea has been entered, the court to which the action is transferred shall return all papers to the originating court.

(Adopted by SCO 4 October 4, 1959; amended by SCO 520 effective October 1, 1982; and by SCO 642 effective May 30, 1985)

Rule 21. Time of Motion to Transfer.

A motion to transfer under these rules may be made at or before arraignment or at such other time as the court or these rules may prescribe.

(Adopted by SCO 4 October 4, 1959)

Rule 22. Pretrial Procedure.

(a) At any time after the return of the indictment or the filing of the information the court upon motion of any party or upon its own motion may invite the attorneys to appear before it for a conference in open court, at which the defendant shall have the right to be present, to consider:

(1) The simplification of the issues;

(2) The possibility of obtaining admissions of fact and documents which will avoid unnecessary proof;

(3) The number of expert witnesses or character witnesses or other witnesses who are to give testimony of a cumulative nature;

(4) Such other matters as may aid in the disposition of the proceeding.

(b) The court shall make an order reciting the agreements made by the parties as to any of the matters considered, which shall be signed by the court and the attorneys for the parties, and when entered shall control the subsequent course of the proceedings, unless modified at the trial to prevent manifest injustice.

(c) This rule shall not be invoked in the case of any defendant who is not represented by counsel.

(Adopted by SCO 4 October 4, 1959; amended by SCO 90 effective July 24, 1967)

Annotations

Cases

Absence of defendant from pretrial in chambers conference which was limited to purely legal and procedural questions was error, but the error was harmless since there was no indication that defendant's presence would have aided his defense. **Dolchok v. State,** Op. No. 2458, 639 P2d 277 (Alaska 1982).

PART VI. TRIAL

Rule 23. Trial by Jury or by the Court.

(a) **Trial by Jury*.** Cases required to be tried by jury shall be so tried unless the defendant waives a jury trial in writing with the approval of the court and the consent of the state.

(b) **Jury of Less Than Twelve.** Juries shall be of 12 persons but at any time before verdict the parties may stipulate in writing with the approval of the court that the jury shall consist of any number less than 12.

(c) **Trial Without a Jury.** In a case tried without a jury the court shall make a general finding and shall, in addition, on request, find the facts specially. If an opinion or memorandum of decision is filed, it will be sufficient if the findings of fact appear therein.

(Adopted by SCO 4 October 4, 1959; amended by SCO 98 effective September 16, 1968)

*See Chapter 119 SLA 1972 effective September 10, 1972.

Annotations

Cases

Criminal Rule 29 on motions for judgment of acquittal does not pertain to cases tried by the court without a jury under this rule. **Beck v. State,** Op. No. 310, 408 P2d 996 (Alaska 1965).

Although the right to jury of twelve persons may be waived orally, the court must personally address the defendant to inquire whether the waiver is voluntary and knowing, and failure to do so is error per se. **Walker v. State,** Op. No. 1635, 578 P2d 1388 (Alaska 1978).

Even if a lesser-included offense is a violation for which a person is not entitled to a jury trial or a public defender, there is no statutory or constitutional prohibition against submission of the lesser violation to the jury when a jury trial on the greater offense is required. **Kuzmin v. State,** Op. No. 642,725 P2d 721 (Alaska 1986).

Where the state refused to consent to a court trial, trial court did not err in denying defendant's request to waive a jury trial where defendant did not present any reason for his request other than that he preferred a court trial. **Horton v. State,** Op. No. 825, 758 P2d 628 (Alaska App. 1988).

Even though this rule requires written waiver of right to jury trial, otherwise valid waiver will not be nullified simply because it was oral. **McGlauflin v. State,** Op. No. 1309, 857 P2d 366 (Alaska App. 1993).

Trial court committed reversible error in not establishing that defendant's oral waiver of jury trial right was knowing and voluntary. **McGlauflin v. State,** Op. No. 1309, 857 P2d 366 (Alaska App. 1993).

Rule 24. Jurors.

(a) **Examination.** The court shall require the jury to be selected in a prompt manner. The court may permit the defendant or the defendant's attorney and the prosecuting attorney to conduct the examination of prospective jurors or may itself conduct the examination. In the latter event the court shall permit the defendant or the defendant's attorney and the prosecuting attorney to supplement the examination by such further inquiry as it deems proper or shall itself submit to the prospective jurors such additional questions by the parties or their attorneys as it deems proper. The court may also require the parties to question the panel as a whole rather than individually and impose reasonable time limits on the examination of prospective jurors.

(b) **Alternate Jurors.**

(1) *Generally.* A court may impanel alternate jurors using one of the procedures set out in subparagraph (b)(2) below. If alternate jurors are called,

(A) they shall be drawn in the same manner, shall have the same qualifications, shall be subject to the same examination and challenges, shall take the same oath, and shall have the same functions, powers, facilities and privileges as the regular jurors; and

(B) each side is entitled to one peremptory challenge in addition to those otherwise allowed by law if one or two alternate jurors are to be impaneled, and two peremptory challenges if three or four alternate jurors are to be impaneled.

(2) *Procedures.*

(A) The court may direct that not more than four jurors in addition to the regular panel be called and impaneled to sit as alternate jurors. Alternate jurors in the order in which they are called shall replace jurors who, prior to the time the jury retires to consider its verdict, become unable or disqualified to perform their duties. An alternate juror who does not replace a regular juror shall be discharged after the jury retires to consider its verdict. The additional peremptory challenges allowed by section (b)(1)(B) may be used against an alternate jury only, and the other peremptory challenges allowed by these rules may not be used against an alternate juror.

(B) The court may direct that one or two jurors be called and impaneled in addition to the number of jurors required by law to comprise the jury. The court may excuse jurors who, prior to the time the jury retires to consider its verdict, become unable or disqualified to perform their duties. If more than the required number are left on the jury when the jury is ready to retire, the clerk in open court shall select at random the names of a sufficient number of jurors to reduce the jury to the number required by law. The jurors selected for elimination shall be discharged after the jury retires to consider its verdict.

(c) **Challenges for Cause.** After the examination of prospective jurors is completed and before any juror is sworn, the parties may challenge any juror for cause. A juror challenged for cause may be directed to answer every question pertinent to the inquiry. Every challenge for cause shall be determined by the court. The following are grounds for challenges for cause:

(1) That the person is not qualified by law to be a juror.

(2) That the person is biased for or against a party or attorney.

(3) That the person shows a state of mind which will prevent the person from rendering a just verdict, or has formed a positive opinion on the facts of the case or as to what the outcome should be, and cannot disregard such opinion and try the issue impartially.

(4) That the person has opinions or conscientious scruples which would improperly influence the person's verdict.

(5) That the person has been subpoenaed as a witness in the case.

(6) That the person has already sat upon a trial of the same issue.

(7) That the person has served as a petit juror in a civil case based on the same transaction.

(8) That the person was called as a juror and excused either for cause or peremptorily on a previous trial of the same action, or in another action by the same parties for the same cause of action.

(9) That the person is related within the fourth degree (civil law) of consanguinity or affinity to one of the parties or attorneys.

(10) That the person is the guardian, ward, landlord, tenant, employer, employee, partner, client, principal, agent, debtor, creditor, or a member of the family of the defendant, of the person alleged to be injured by the crime charged in the indictment, complaint, or information, of the person on whose complaint the prosecution was instituted, or of one of the attorneys.

(11) That the person within the previous two years:

(i) has been a party adverse to the challenging party or attorney in a civil action; or

(ii) has complained against or been accused by the challenging party or attorney in a criminal prosecution.

(12) That the person has a financial interest other than that of a taxpayer or a permanent fund dividend recipient in the outcome of the case.

(13) That the person was a member of the grand jury returning an indictment in the cause.

(14) That the person is employed by an agency, department, division, commission, or other unit of the State of Alaska, including a municipal corporation, which is directly involved in the case to be tried.

(d) **Peremptory Challenges.** A party who waives peremptory challenge as to the jurors in the box does not thereby lose the challenge but may exercise it as to new jurors who may be called. A juror peremptorily challenged is excused without cause. If the offense is punishable by imprisonment for more than one year, each side is entitled to 10 peremptory challenges. If the offense charged is punishable by imprisonment for not more than one year, or by a fine or both, each side is entitled to 3 peremptory challenges. If there is more than one defendant, the court may allow the defendants additional peremptory challenges and permit them to be exercised separately or jointly.

(e) **Procedure for Using Challenges.** The court has discretion to set procedures for the exercise of challenges and for the replacement of challenged jurors except that the entire trial panel will be asked general questions concerning the for cause challenges listed in Criminal Rule 24(c)(5)-(14) before proceeding to other questioning.

(f) **Oath of Jurors.** The jury shall be sworn by the clerk substantially as follows:

"Do each of you solemnly swear or affirm that you will well and truly try the issues in the matter now before the court solely on the evidence introduced and in accordance with the instructions of the court?"

(Adopted by SCO 4 October 4, 1959; amended by SCO 49 effective January 1, 1963; amended by SCO 276 effective June 30, 1977; and by SCO 428 effective September 1, 1980; by SCO 807 effective August 1, 1987; by SCO 969 effective July 15, 1989; by SCO 1013 effective January 15, 1990; by SCO 1095 effective January 15, 1993; by SCO 1153 effective July 15, 1994; by SCO 1204 effective July 15, 1995; by SCO 1448 effective October 15, 2001; and by SCO 1593 effective April 15, 2006)

Note to SCO 1204: The provision granting ten peremptory challenges to each side was added by ch. 117 § 1 SLA 1994. Section 6 of this order is adopted for the sole reason that the legislature has mandated the amendment.

Annotations

Cases

Trial judge's question propounded during voir dire of the prospective jurors whether any of the panel ever sat on a jury in which the defendant was involved, as viewed in connection with questions asked at the outset of the examination and immediately thereafter could not indicate to the jury that the defendant had been tried previously and convicted and was no error. **McCracken v. State,** Op. No. 430, 431 P2d 513 (Alaska 1967).

Assuming, arguendo, that Criminal Rule 24(d) concerns substantive rights, it was not unconstitutional as being beyond the power of the Supreme Court to promulgate. **Smiloff v. State,** Op. No. 1637, 579 P2d 28 (Alaska 1978).

Technical violations of the jury selection methods constitute substantial failure to comply only when they affect the random nature or objectivity of the selection process. **Calantas v. State,** Op. No. 1914, 599 P2d 147 (Alaska 1979).

Where potential juror had been charged with or convicted of crime was entitled to challenge for cause. **Lupro v. State,** Op. No. 1960, 603 P2d 468 (Alaska 1979).

A prospective juror's adverse contact with a law enforcement agency is a reasonable ground for assuming that he would be hostile to the state's interest in prosecution. **Mallott v. State,** Op. No. 2027, 608 P2d 737 (Alaska 1980).

Although this rule does not contemplate a challenge for cause on the basis of mere exposure to prejudicial information, trial judge used a proper degree of caution in allowing defendant as many additional peremptory challenges as necessary for selection of an impartial jury. **Mallott v. State,** Op. No. 2027, 608 P2d 737 (Alaska 1980).

The requirements of Criminal Rule 24(d) and (3) concerning peremptory challenges and juror replacements may be relaxed by the trial court if good cause exists to streamline the jury selection procedure. **Ketzler v. State,** Op. No. 47, 634 P2d 561 (Alaska App. 1981).

In drug prosecution, trial court committed reversible error by failing to excuse for cause the same jurors used in the drug prosecution of defendant's companion the previous week where they heard testimony that defendant sold marijuana and "speed" to a police officer. **Zartman v. State,** Op. No. 274, 667 P2d 1256 (Alaska App. 1983).

Trial judges who wish to take over voir dire should adhere to the written question requirement or permit counsel an opportunity to substitute an oral offer of proof. **Bolhouse v. State,** Op. No. 402, 687 P2d 1166 (Alaska App. 1984).

Requirement that trial judge permit council to submit questions in writing for the court's consideration during judge-conducted voir dire does not require the judge to ask the questions but only requires that he consider them. **Bolhouse v. State,** Op. No. 402, 687 P2d 1166 (Alaska App. 1984).

Trial judge's refusal during judge-conducted voir dire to accept written questions from defense counsel or to permit defense counsel an opportunity to substitute an oral offer of proof was error, but the error was harmless under the circumstances. **Bolhouse v. State,** Op. No. 402, 687 P2d 1166 (Alaska App. 1984).

Trial judge properly exercised his discretion to conduct voir dire examination of jurors where questioning was sufficient to allow counsel to intelligently exercise challenges for cause and peremptory challenges and where judge allowed counsel to submit written questions to the court to be asked of the jurors. **Nylund v. State,** Op. No. 604, 716 P2d 387 (Alaska App. 1986).

Where defendant used only nine of his ten peremptory challenges and then requested additional peremptory challenges after the jury was sworn and seated, the trial judge did not abuse his discretion in rejecting the request as untimely. **Arnold v. State,** Op. No. 779, 751 P2d 494 (Alaska App. 1988).

A trial court may decline to grant challenges for cause in a liberal manner so long as the court offers the defendant extra peremptory challenges; where, after defendant had exhausted his peremptory challenges, the trial court failed to grant defendant's challenge of a juror for cause despite the juror's equivocal description of her impartiality, the court's failure to allow defendant's request for an extra peremptory challenge violated defendant's right to an impartial jury and therefore constituted reversible error. **Jerrel v. State,** Op. No. 815, 756 P2d 301 (Alaska App. 1988).

Since the criminal record of a prospective juror is relevant to the use of challenges for cause, a prosecutor may use criminal justice information systems to run criminal record checks on prospective jurors. **Tagala v. State,** Op. No. 1134, 812 P2d 604 (Alaska App. 1991).

If defendant does not use all peremptory challenges during jury selection, he cannot be prejudiced by trial court's denial of one challenge for cause. **Sharp v. State,** Op. No. 1233, 837 P2d 718 (Alaska App. 1992).

This rule does not permit trial judge to substitute alternate juror for regular juror once jury deliberations have begun. **Plate v. State,** Op. No. 1493, 925 P2d 1057 (Alaska App. 1996).

Provisions of this rule which permits challenge for cause of prospective juror who is guardian of victim applies only if prospective juror is currently guardian of victim, not if prospective juror was past guardian of victim. **Adams v. State,** Op. No. 1497, 927 P2d 751 (Alaska App. 1996).

Where prospective juror was police officer who admitted during voir dire that he would weigh testimony of police officers more heavily than testimony of other people, trial court erred in not granting defense challenge of juror for cause, but error was not prejudicial because defense used peremptory challenge to remove him from jury panel. **Minch v. State,** Op. No. 1518, 934 P2d 764 (Alaska App. 1997).

Where parties had waived remaining peremptory challenges and had accepted panel of twelve jurors, but court adjourned for evening without requiring jurors to take their trial oath, trial judge abused his discretion in denying defense attorney's request to exercise belated peremptory challenge to juror about whom defense attorney had received new information during evening adjournment. **Pearce v. State,** Op. No. 1569, 951 P2d 445 (Alaska App. 1998).

Defendant's argument that he should have been given the opportunity to exercise a late peremptory challenge against a juror after the juror revealed that his mother had been the victim of domestic violence was rejected; the law requires attorneys to assiduously employ the voir dire process to elicit facts necessary to proper evaluation of the suitability of prospective jurors. **Soundara v. State,** Op. No. 1971, 107 P.3d 290 (Alaska App. 2005).

Rule 25. Judge—Disqualification or Disability.

(a) **Before Trial.** Where a judge of the superior court is disqualified or for any other reason is unable to sit in the trial or hearing of any pending matter, the presiding judge or the chief justice of the supreme court shall designate another judge of the judicial district in which the matter is pending, or a judge temporarily assigned thereto, to hear the matter.

(b) **During Trial.** If a judge holding superior court be prevented during a trial from continuing to preside therein, the presiding judge or the chief justice of the supreme court shall designate another judge of the superior court to sit in such court to complete such trial, as if such other judge had been present and presiding from the commencement of such trial, provided, however, that from the beginning of the taking of testimony at such trial a stenographic or electronic record of such trial shall have been made so that the judge so continuing may become familiar with the previous proceedings at such trial.

(c) **After Verdict.** If by reason of absence from the district, death, sickness or other disability, the judge before whom the action has been tried is unable to perform the duties to be performed by the court after a verdict or finding of guilt, any other judge regularly sitting in or assigned to the court may perform those duties; but if the other judge is satisfied that a judge who did not preside at the trial cannot perform those duties or that it is appropriate for any other reason, that judge may grant a new trial.

(d) **Change of Judge as a Matter of Right.** In all courts of the state, a judge may be peremptorily challenged as follows:

(1) *Entitlement.* In any criminal case in superior or district court, the prosecution and the defense shall each be entitled as a matter of right to one change of judge. When multiple defendants are unable to agree upon the judge to hear the case, the trial judge may, in the interest of justice, give them more than one change as a matter of right; the prosecutor shall be entitled to the same number of changes as all the defendants combined.

(2) *Procedure.* A party may exercise the party's right to a change of judge by filing a "Notice of Change of Judge" signed by counsel, if any, stating the name of the judge to be changed. The notice shall neither specify grounds nor be accompanied by an affidavit. The notice of change of judge is timely if filed within five days after notice that the case has been assigned to a specific judge.

(3) *Re-Assignment.* When a request for change of judge is timely filed under this rule, the judge shall proceed no further in the action, except to make such temporary orders as may be absolutely necessary to prevent immediate and irreparable injury before the action can be transferred to another judge. However, if the named judge is the presiding judge, the judge shall continue to perform the functions of the presiding judge.

(4) *Timeliness.* Failure to file a timely request precludes a change of judge under this rule as a matter of right.

(5) *Waiver.* A party loses the right under this rule to change a judge when the party, after reasonable opportunity to consult with counsel, agrees to the assignment of the case to a judge or knowing that the judge has been permanently assigned to the case, participates before the judge in an omnibus hearing, any subsequent pretrial hearing, a hearing under Rule 11, or the commencement of trial. No provision of this rule shall bar a stipulation as to the judge before whom a plea of guilty or of nolo contendere shall be taken under Rule 11.

(Adopted by SCO 4 October 4, 1959; amended by SCO 185 effective July 1, 1974; by SCO 292 effective February 21, 1978; by SCO 832 effective August 1, 1987; by SCO 875 effective July 15, 1988; by SCO 1011 effective January 15, 1990; by SCO 1070 effective July 15, 1991; and by SCO 1153 effective July 15, 1994)

Annotations

Cases

Where the judge who presided over a Petitioner's mental competency hearing and who adjudged the petitioner competent to stand trial and who was assigned to preside over the trial and to accept the petitioner's changes of pleas from not guilty to guilty is absent from the district at the time of the petitioner's making a motion to withdraw his guilty pleas, the presiding judge has jurisdiction to hear the motion. **Knaub v. State,** Op. No. 489, 443 P2d 44 (Alaska 1968).

If a motion for peremptory disqualification of the trial judge is timely filed, then the trial judge errs in not automatically excluding himself from sitting on case. **McCracken v. State,** Op. No. 1028, 521 P2d 499 (Alaska 1974).

Where a petitioner fails to challenge a judge until prior to a revocation hearing, a peremptory challenge at that point is not timely. **Kvasnikoff v. State,** Op. No. 1153, 535 P2d 464 (Alaska 1975).

When a judge has entered an order placing a defendant on probation, any subsequent hearing held to determine whether probation should be revoked is a supplemental proceeding. **Kvasnikoffv. State,** Op. No. 1153, 535 P2d 464 (Alaska 1975).

In arraignment proceeding before disqualified judge, defendant should be advised of his right to have bail heard by another judge and setting of bail should be immediately referred to another judicial officer if it becomes a disputed issue. **Gieffels v. State,** Op. No. 1295, 552 P2d 661 (Alaska 1976).

Judge at arraignment has no discretion before plea is taken so that disqualified judge may act. **Gieffels v. State,** Op. No. 1295, 552 P2d 661 (Alaska 1976).

Since plea of guilty or nolo contendere requires judicial determination of voluntary nature and reasonable basis of plea, disqualified arraignment judge should immediately assign case to another judge. **Gieffels v. State,** Op. No. 1295, 552 P2d 661 (Alaska 1976).

If defendant pleads not guilty, disqualified arraignment judge need only refer case to another judge if calendaring becomes a disputed issue. **Gieffels v. State,** Op. No. 1295, 552 P2d 661 (Alaska 1976).

Where two proceedings involve the same defendant and the necessity of proving the same facts and issues, a judge preempted in first proceeding is automatically preempted in the second. **Gieffels v. State,** Op. No. 1295, 552 P2d 661 (Alaska 1976).

Preempted judge may act at arraignment so long as substantive rights conferred by AS 22.20.022 are not interfered with. **Gieffels v. State,** Op. No. 1295, 552 P2d 661 (Alaska 1976).

Defense and state are each entitled to only one peremptory challenge of a judge. **Peterson v. State,** Op. No. 1411, 562 P2d 1350 (Alaska 1977).

Paragraph (d)(5) of this rule does not give parties the power to determine by stipulation the judge who is to hear defendant's plea. **Padie v. State,** Op. No. 1465, 566 P2d 1024 (Alaska 1977).

A stipulation under paragraph (d)(5) of this rule is not binding on the court. **Padie v. State,** Op. No. 1465, 566 P2d 1024 (Alaska 1977).

Judge disqualified by peremptory challenge may rule on defendant's case in capacity as presiding judge. **Padie v. State,** Op. No. 1465, 566 P2d 1024 (Alaska 1977).

The trial court did not err in denying defendant's motion for peremptory challenge of the judge on the ground that since the time period for a challenge under Criminal Rule 25 is not tolled during the time required for consideration of a challenge for cause under AS 22.20.020. **Wamser v. State,** Op. No. 1768, 587 P2d 232 (Alaska 1978).

If a challenge for cause is granted, parties who have not previously exercised a peremptory challenge have the right to challenge the newly-appointed judge. **Wamser v. State,** Op. No. 1768, 587 P2d 232 (Alaska 1978).

Where defendants did not have the opportunity to consult counsel prior to expiration of the time limit for peremptorily challenging the judge, the court abused its discretion in failing to waive the time limit. **Riley v. State,** Op. No. 2038, 608 P2d 27 (Alaska 1980).

Where there are several defendants in a criminal trial, each individual defendant is not entitled to one peremptory challenge; rather, the defense as a whole is entitled as a matter of right to but one peremptory challenge. **Hawley v. State,** Op. No. 2137, 614 P2d 1349 (Alaska 1980).

A party which appears before a judge in pretrial proceedings without knowing whether that particular judge will be assigned as the trial judge in the case does not waive the right to a peremptory challenge under this rule. **Smith v. State,** Op. No. 2161, 616 P2d 863 (Alaska 1980).

The right to peremptorily challenge a judge exists by virtue of AS 22.20.022. Criminal Rule 25(d) merely regulates the exercise of that right. **Halligan v. State,** Op. No. 2299, 624 P2d 281 (Alaska 1981).

A superior court judge assigned to review of a district court ruling is not subject to peremptory disqualification. **Halligan v. State,** Op. No. 2299, 624 P2d 281 (Alaska 1981).

A defendant may appeal the denial of a change of judge motion, and such appeal on the limited issue of peremptory disqualification will be processed pursuant to Appellate Rule 216 governing expedited appeals. **Morgan v. State,** Op. No. 2429, 635 P2d 472 (Alaska 1981).

The proper interpretation of Criminal Rule 25(d)(2) in conjunction with AS 22.20.022 is that the later of the two dates listed in the rule should control. **Morgan v. State,** Op. No. 2429, 635 P2d 472 (Alaska 1981).

Although the preferable procedure is to have multiple defendants confer in reaching a decision to exercise a peremptory challenge, it is not required; accordingly, peremptory challenge of judge by one defendant prevented codefendant from peremptorily challenging the succeeding judge. **Murdock v. State,** Op. No. 256, 664 P2d 589 (Alaska App. 1983).

To the extent that the waiver provisions of this rule conflict with the five-day period allowed by statute for peremptorily challenging a judge, the provisions of this rule prevail. **Main v. State,** Op. No. 287, 668 P2d 868 (Alaska App. 1983).

Attempt to remove judge after commencement of trial pursuant to statute authorizing a party to exercise a peremptory challenge of a judge within five days after the judge is appointed was denied for noncompliance with this rule requiring peremptory challenges to be exercised prior to commencement of trial. **Main v. State,** Op. No. 287, 668 P2d 868 (Alaska App. 1983).

Since the Alaska Supreme Court has by rule endorsed the concept of peremptory challenges of judges without cause, the contention that a statute authorizing such challenges violates the separation of powers doctrine was rejected. **Hornaday v. Rowland,** Op. No. 2761, 674 P2d 1333 (Alaska 1983).

Participation by defendant in a contested bail hearing before a judge, held shortly after arraignment and well in advance of the omnibus hearing date, did not waive defendant's right to a peremptory challenge of that judge. **Gardner v. State,** Op. No. 485, 702 P2d 250 (Alaska App. 1985).

Defendant in criminal contempt proceeding was not entitled to peremptorily challenge the trial court judge who had presided over the civil matter out of which the contempt charge arose; having waived his right to challenge the judge in the civil proceeding, he waived the right to peremptorily challenge the judge in the ancillary criminal action. **Webber v. Webber,** Op. No. 509, 706 P2d 329 (Alaska App. 1985).

When a defendant who is represented by counsel fails to interpose a peremptory challenge to the trial judge prior to the selection of the jury, he forfeits the right to do so. **Trudeau v. State,** Op. No. 581, 714 P2d 362 (Alaska App. 1986).

The defendant must show actual prejudice in order to establish that the trial court abused its discretion in failing to excuse defendant's forfeiture of his right to speedy trial and his right to a change of judge. **Trudeau v. State,** Op. No. 581, 714 P2d 362 (Alaska App. 1986).

Attorney was not entitled to a change of judge as a matter of right at hearing on sanctions against him for filing frivolous, unnecessary and legally deficient pleadings in a criminal case. **Weidner v. Superior Court, Third Judicial Dist.,** Op. No. 589, 715 P2d 264 (Alaska App. 1986).

It is unclear whether a peremptory challenge of a judge in a post-conviction relief proceeding must be made under the criminal rules or the civil rules and whether an appeal from a denial of such a motion must be made on an expedited basis under the appellate rules. **Hastings v. State,** Op. No. 706, 736 P2d 1157 (Alaska App. 1987).

Failure of defendant to file a peremptory challenge within five days after the judge was assigned to the case amounted to a waiver of his peremptory challenge right; the trial judge did not abuse his discretion in refusing to relax the five-day limitation. **Washington v. State,** Op. No. 804, 755 P2d 401 (Alaska App. 1988).

Motion for new trial on the ground that defendant's sentencing hearing was conducted by a different judge than the one who conducted the trial was properly denied. **Konrad v. State,** Op. No. 869, 763 P2d 1369 (Alaska App. 1988).

Under ordinary circumstances the judge who imposes sentence should be assigned any subsequent petitions to revoke probation. **Trenton v. State,** Op. No. 1024, 789 P2d 178 (Alaska App. 1990).

It was an abuse of discretion to assign a petition to revoke probation to a visiting judge rather than the judge who imposed the sentence, absent evidence that the sentencing judge was not available or could not have become available within a reasonable time. **Trenton v. State,** Op. No. 1024,789 P2d 178 (Alaska App. 1990).

In considering a post-verdict motion for a new trial based upon newly discovered evidence, where the judge who presided over the trial had retired and a new judge had therefore been assigned to the case, the new judge abused his discretion in declining defendant's request that the judge review the trial transcript before ruling on the motion. **Shapiro v. State,** Op. No. 1046, 793 P2d 535 (Alaska App. 1990).

Although this rule contemplates that the court system will give prompt notice of the assignment of a judge to a case, the time for peremptorily challenging the judge begins to run when the assignment is made rather than when the defendant learns of the assignment. **Martin v. State,** Op. No. 1065, 797 P2d 1209 (Alaska App. 1990).

Probation revocation proceeding is not criminal proceeding for purposes of applying peremptory challenge provisions of this rule. **Wallace v. State,** Op. No. 1221, 829 P2d 1208 (Alaska App. 1992).

Peremptory challenge to judge at defendant's initial appearance should have been honored even though case had not yet been formally assigned to specific judge, thus judge's pretrial discovery orders were invalid. **Smith v. State,** Op. No. 1385, 887 P2d 979 (Alaska App. 1994).

A litigant has no right to insist that a matter be heard by any particular judge. **Moore v. State,** Op. No. 1411, 895 P2d 507 (Alaska App. 1995).

This rule was not designed to allow a party to obtain strategic advantage by forum shopping for an ideal judge. **Moore v. State,** Op. No. 1411, 895 P2d 507 (Alaska App. 1995).

A trial court has considerable discretion in determining whether to grant multiple defendants additional peremptory challenges. **Moore v. State,** Op. No. 1411,895 P2d 507 (Alaska App. 1995).

It is not unfair to allow a single defendant in a multi-party case to unilaterally exercise a peremptory challenge. This rule does not give the remaining defendants veto power over another party's peremptory challenge. **Moore v. State,** Op. No. 1411, 895 P2d 507 (Alaska App. 1995).

Because a motion for additional peremptory challenges in a multiple defendant case will implicitly declare that the moving defendants wish to challenge the currently assigned judge, the better practice is to have such motions heard by a judge other than the currently assigned judge. **Moore v. State,** Op. No. 1411, 895 P2d 507 (Alaska App. 1995).

The trial court can reject a request for additional peremptory challenges. When it appears that a party's request is based on considerations of prospective strategic advantage rather than the party's fear of the second judge's potential bias or partiality. **Moore v. State,** Op. No. 1411, 895 P2d 507 (Alaska App. 1995).

Where defendants failed to even suggest that the second judge could not be fair and impartial, trial court did not err in denying motion for additional peremptory challenges. **Moore v. State,** Op. No. 1411, 895 P2d 507 (Alaska App. 1995).

Superior court did not err in precluding three defendants from vetoing a fourth defendant's unilateral exercise of their single shared peremptory challenge in multiple defendant case. **Moore v. State,** Op. No. 1411, 895 P2d 507 (Alaska App. 1995).

Appeal of superior court's refusal to grant multiple defendants additional peremptory challenges and refusal to allow three of the defendants to object to the fourth's use of their single shared peremptory challenge should be allowed by Appellate Rule 216(a)(2) and 216(b)(2). To the extent there was any doubt that the appeal was a peremptory challenge appeal as defined by Appellate Rule 216(b)(2), the appellate court treated the appeal as a petition for review and granted it. **Moore v. State,** Op. No. 1411, 895 P2d 507 (Alaska App. 1995).

Criminal Rule 25 is the criminal analog to Civil Rule 42. **Staso v. State, Department of Transportation,** Op. No. 4214, 895 P2d 988 (Alaska 1995).

Defendant in probation revocation proceeding was not entitled to exercise a peremptory challenge against a new judge who was assigned to conduct the adjudicative phase of the revocation proceedings because the probation revocation hearing was a continuation of the original criminal proceedings and defendant had exercised his only preemptory challenge when he challenged a judge assigned to the case when criminal charges were first initiated. **McRae v. State,** Op. No. 1452, 909 P2d 1079 (Alaska App. 1996).

A defendant's "Request For Calendar Setting" did not meet the requirements of the rules for exercising a right of peremptory challenge. The rules require filing of a "Notice of Change of Judge" which specifies "the name of the judge to be changed." **Tan v. State,** Op. No. 1423, 900 P2d 759 (Alaska App. 1995).

If defendant's attorney was told that a particular judge had not been permanently assigned to defendant's case, then she may not have waived her challenge to the judge when she appeared in front of him for the change-of-plea hearing. Alternatively, defendant might be entitled to a relaxation of Criminal Rule 25(d)(5) under the provisions of Criminal Rule 53 if the clerk had assured defense counsel that even though the judge had been permanently assigned to the case, defendant could appear in a change-of-plea hearing in front of him and still have five days to file a peremptory challenge of him. **Tan v. State,** Op. No. 1423, 900 P2d 759 (Alaska App. 1995).

Litigation of challenge for cause is not "subsequent pretrial proceeding" within meaning of this rule, thus party who challenges assigned trial judge for cause is not thereafter barred form exercising peremptory challenge against same judge. **DeNardo v. Municipality of Anchorage,** Op. No. 1533,

938 P2d 1099 (Alaska App. 1997).

Superior court judge's assignment of defendant's case to himself for trial in the superior court while case was still in district court could not extinguish defendant's right to a peremptory challenge upon the entry of a plea in superior court. **Watt v. State,** Op. No. 1848, 61 P.3d 446 (Alaska App. 2003).

Peremptory challenge to assigned trial judge was filed when received, not when mailed, since an exception to the common law rule in the appellate rules applied only to appellate filings; furthermore, the movant failed to provide any evidence in support of an argument that a discretionary relaxation of the rules would be appropriate in the interests of justice. **Black v. State,** Op. No. 1896, 76 P.3d 417 (Alaska App 2003).

Subsection (b) of this rule does not explicitly limit the mid-trial substitution of judges to jury trials; the rule refers to the substitution of judges "during a trial." **Morgan v. State**, Op. No. 8639, 139 P.3d 1272 (Alaska App. 2006).

Defendant convicted of second-degree sexual assault was entitled to new trial where trial was remanded to superior court and original judge had retired and was no longer able to hear continued proceedings. New trial judge could not determine witness's credibility from a reading of the trial transcript, so a pre-verdict substitution of judges under subsection (b) of this rule is permitted only when the substitution does not violate the parties' due process rights. **Morgan v. State**, Op. No. 8639, 139 P.3d 1272 (Alaska App. 2006).

Rule 26.1. Exhibits.

(a) **Mark for Identification.** All exhibits shall be marked for identification at the time of trial or hearing unless the judge orders pre-marking of the exhibits.

(b) **Procedure.** Exhibits shall be marked for identification in the manner prescribed by the administrative director in the bulletin required by paragraph (h) of this rule. All exhibits marked for identification shall be listed on an exhibit list provided by the court. The form of the exhibit list shall be prescribed by the administrative director.

(c) **Admission.** Exhibits properly marked for identification may be admitted into evidence upon the motion of any party or upon the court's own motion. After an identified exhibit is admitted by the court, the clerk shall mark the exhibit "admitted" in a manner prescribed by the administrative director. When an exhibit is admitted into evidence, the fact of its admission shall be noted immediately on the exhibit list.

(d) **Custody of Exhibits.** At the time an exhibit is offered into evidence, the exhibit shall be placed in and remain in the clerk's custody until released as provided in paragraph (g) of this rule or as set forth in the administrative bulletin required by paragraph (h) of this rule. Exhibits which have not been offered into evidence shall not be placed in the custody of the clerk unless otherwise ordered by the court.

(e) **Final Check.** Prior to submission of the case to the jury or to the court sitting without a jury, the court shall require counsel and those parties not represented by counsel to (1) examine all intended, identified, offered, or admitted exhibits and the in-court clerk's exhibit list, (2) confirm to the court that the list accurately reflects the status of the exhibits, and (3) confirm that any modifications to the exhibits ordered by the court have been made. Upon proper motion or the court's own motion, the court may order additional exhibits marked for identification and/or admitted into evidence. At the time of the final check, identified exhibits which have not been offered for admission but which the court has previously ordered placed in the clerk's custody shall be returned to the appropriate party, unless otherwise ordered by the court.

(f) **Submission to the Jury.** Unless otherwise ordered by the court, all exhibits admitted into evidence shall be given to the jury for deliberation, except the following exhibits will not be given to the jury without a specific court order:

(1) live ammunition;

(2) firearms;

(3) drugs and alcoholic beverages;

(4) perishable, flammable or hazardous materials; and

(5) money, jewelry or other valuable items.

The court may allow a photograph of an exhibit to be submitted to the jury in place of the physical exhibit.

(g) **Return of Some Exhibits After Hearing or Trial.** At the conclusion of a hearing or trial, the court shall inquire whether counsel stipulate to the return of any exhibits to counsel for safekeeping pending appeal and to the substitution of photographs for any of the physical (i.e., non-documentary) exhibits. Whether or not counsel stipulate, the court may also order counsel to take custody of the following exhibits, store said exhibits in a safe location and maintain the chain of custody pending appeal:

(1) live ammunition;

(2) firearms;

(3) drugs and alcoholic beverages;

(4) perishable, flammable or hazardous materials;

(5) money, jewelry or other valuable items; and

(6) items which are unwieldy due to bulk and/or weight.

Whenever exhibits are returned to counsel for safekeeping pending appeal, the court may require counsel to submit an affidavit setting forth the specific measures taken to insure safekeeping of the exhibits.

(h) **Administrative Bulletin.** The administrative director shall establish standards and procedures by appropriate bulletin consistent with these rules governing the marking, handling, storage, safekeeping, and disposal of all exhibits coming into the court's custody. Unless otherwise ordered by the court, such standards and procedures are controlling.

(Added by SCO 599 effective September 1, 1984; amended by SCO 949 effective January 15, 1989)

Informational Note: Administrative Bulletin No. 9 governing the standards and procedures concerning exhibits is included in the Rules of Court following Civil Rule 43.1.

Rule 27. Proceedings Upon Trial—Management of Juries.

(a) **Order of Proceedings.** After a jury is impanelled and sworn, the trial shall proceed in the following order:

(1) The prosecuting attorney shall state the case of the prosecution, and may briefly state the evidence by which the prosecuting attorney expects to sustain it.

(2) (i) The defendant, or the defendant's counsel, may then state the defense, and may briefly state the evidence the defendant expects to offer in support of it.

(ii) If no statement of the defendant's case is made after the statement of the prosecution's case, then after the state has produced its evidence and presented its case in chief, the defendant, or the defendant's counsel, if the defendant intends to produce evidence, shall state the defense, and may briefly state the evidence the defendant expects to offer in support of it.

(3) The state shall first produce its evidence, and the defendant may then produce the defendant's evidence. The state will then be confined to rebutting evidence unless the court, for good reason and in furtherance of justice, permits it to offer evidence in chief.

(4) Unless the case be submitted without argument, counsel for the state shall commence, the defendant or the defendant's counsel shall follow and counsel for the state shall conclude the arguments to the jury. Unless good cause is shown, the state shall present in its concluding argument no theory of law or fact which was not presented in one or both of the prior arguments. The court may, in its discretion, limit the time of such arguments.

(5) At the conclusion of the arguments the court shall charge the jury. Either party may offer requested instructions; objections shall be heard and considered by the court in accordance with Rule 30.

(b) **View of Premises by Jury.**

(1) The court may, on application of a party or on its own motion, order the jury in a body to view the property which is the subject of the litigation or the place where a material fact occurred. The court may order the applying party to pay the expenses connected with fulfilling the order.

(2) An officer of the court shall accompany the jury at such times and shall ensure that no one speaks to the jury on any subject connected with the trial while the jury makes its inspection.

(c) **Admonition to Juror Upon Separation From Jury.**

(1) If any juror is permitted to separate from the jury during the trial, the court shall admonish the juror that it is the juror's duty

(i) not to converse with any person, including other jurors, on any subject connected with the trial, and

(ii) not to form or express any opinion thereon until the case is finally submitted to the jury.

(2) If any juror is permitted to separate from the jury after the case is submitted to the jury, the court shall admonish the juror that it is the juror's duty

(i) to discuss the case only with other jurors in the jury room, and

(ii) not to converse with any other person on any subject connected with the trial.

(d) **Juror Unable to Continue.** If, prior to the time the jury retires to consider its verdict, a juror is unable to perform or is disqualified from performing the juror duty, the court may order the juror to be discharged. If an alternate juror has not been impanelled as provided in the rules,

(1) the trial may proceed with the other jurors with the consent of the parties, or

(2) another juror may be sworn and the trial may begin anew, or

(3) the jury may be discharged and a new jury then or afterwards formed.

(e) **Selection of Foreperson—Deliberations of Jury—Communications.**

(1) When the jury has retired to consider their verdict, they shall elect one of their number foreperson. The foreperson shall preside over their deliberations, sign the verdict unanimously agreed upon, and speak for them on the return of their verdict in open court.

(2) No persons other than the jurors and any interpreter necessary to assist a juror who is hearing or speech impaired shall be present while the jury is deliberating or voting. The jury shall be and remain under the charge of an officer of the court until they agree upon their verdict or are discharged by the court; except that the court may permit the jurors to adjourn their deliberations and return to their homes for reasonable periods of rest. Such periods of adjournment for rest shall be ordered only after hearing from all parties outside the presence of the jury; however, a request for overnight sequestration shall be made by the parties before the jury is sworn unless good cause is shown for a later request. The admonition set forth in section (c) shall be given before any adjournment for rest, and the court shall specifically state that no deliberations are to take place unless all jurors are present in the jury room.

(3) Unless otherwise ordered by the court, the officer of the court having charge of the jury shall keep the jurors together, and separate from other persons. The officer shall not suffer any communication to be made to the jury nor shall the officer make any communication except to ask the jury if they have agreed upon their verdict. The officer shall not, before the

verdict is rendered, communicate to any person the state of their deliberations or the verdict agreed upon. The officer shall be sworn to act according to the provisions of this section (e).

(Adopted by SCO 4 October 4, 1959; amended by SCO 49 effective January 1, 1963; amended by SCO 157 effective February 15, 1973; by Supreme Court Order 735 effective December 15, 1986; by SCO 1153 effective July 15, 1994; and by SCO 1439 effective October 15, 2001)

Note: Chapter 65, section 3, SLA 2005 (HB 54) enacted new AS 12.45.015 relating to the introduction of the victim and the defendant to the jury. According to section 7 of the Act, section 3 of the Act has the effect of amending Criminal Rule 27 by changing the order of proceedings of a trial before a jury.

Annotations

Cases

Trial court properly allowed a view of the premises before evidence was taken so that the jury may more readily understand evidence relating to burglarized premises. **Battese v. State,** Op. No. 402, 425 P2d 606 (Alaska 1967).

Absent circumstances requiring a denial of a jury request to rehear the electronic recording of specific testimony, justice is more likely to be promoted than obstructed by allowing such a rehearing in the discretion of the trial judge. **Price v. State,** Op. No. 454, 437 P2d 333 (Alaska 1968).

Trial judge did not abuse discretion in a murder trial in permitting rebuttal evidence that state witness was a police informant, where the state witness had been subjected to intensive cross-examination for the purpose of destroying his credibility and for suggesting that the witness rather than the defendant was the slayer, and where the testimony had a tendency to rehabilitate the credibility of the witness and the defendant was afforded opportunity to present surrebuttal evidence and was not limited to any manner from delving into this subject. **Gafford v. State,** Op. No. 478, 440 P2d 405 (Alaska 1968).

Absent abuse, the trial judge has wide discretion as to the order of proof and as to the permissible scope of evidence offered in rebuttal. **Gafford v. State,** Op. No. 478, 440 P2d 405 (Alaska 1968).

The alleged misconduct of three jurors who are experienced fishermen in stating during jury deliberations that one of the pieces of metal placed in evidence in a prosecution for assault with intent to kill arising out of a bomb explosion closely resembles a homemade trolling spoon does not entitle the defendant to a new trial even though the defendant testifies that he sometimes made homemade trolling spoons. **Jordan v. State,** Op. No. 674, 481 P2d 383 (Alaska 1971).

Application of Criminal Rule 27 to district court trial was not impracticable where trial court had rooms available for jury sequestration and where judge had authority to obtain accommodation for that purpose in a private hotel. **Kimoktoak v. State,** Op. No. 1624, 578 P2d 594 (Alaska 1978).

Where the court without defendant's consent allows the jury to separate during deliberations, it is per se reversible error. **Kimoktoak v. State,** Op. No. 1624, 578 P2d 594 (Alaska 1978).

In prosecution for resisting arrest where the issue of defendant's intoxication was not part of the prosecution's case-in-chief and was first raised during defendant's own testimony, the trial court did not abuse its discretion in allowing a videotape of defendant made at the police station following his arrest to be used by the prosecution to rebut defendant's testimony that he had consumed liquor but was not influenced by it. **Carson v. State,** Op. No. 700, 736 P2d 356 (Alaska App. 1987).

Defense counsel's failure to make an opening statement did not violate this rule. **Gorz v. State,** Op. No. 776, 749 P2d 1349 (Alaska App. 1988).

Even if this rule did require defense counsel to make an opening statement, failure of defense counsel to do so did not automatically amount to ineffective assistance of counsel. **Gorz v. State,** Op. No. 776, 749 P2d 1349 (Alaska App. 1988).

Rule 27.1. Defendant's Right to Testify.

(a) **Advice of Right.** Prior to the prosecutor's opening statement, the court shall advise the defendant on the record outside the presence of the jury that it is the defendant's right to choose whether to testify or remain silent.

(b) **Inquiry of Nontestifying Defendant.** Before the defense rests, the defense shall notify the court outside the presence of the jury that the defense intends to rest. If the defendant has not testified, the court shall ask the defendant to confirm that the decision not to testify is voluntary. This inquiry must be directed to the defendant personally and must be made on the record outside the presence of the jury.

(Adopted by SCO 1206 effective July 15, 1995; amended by SCO 1222 effective August 8, 1995)

Annotations

Cases

Failure of trial court to determine through inquiry required by this rule that defendant's waiver of this right to testify was knowing and voluntary was not reversible error absent prejudice. **Weist v. Municipality of Anchorage,** Op. No. 1508, 929 P2d 669 (Alaska App. 1997).

Motion for new trial on ground that trial judge did not inform defendant of his right to testify was properly denied where defendant's affidavit did not allege that he would have testified. **Pitka v. State,** Op. No. 1659, 995 P2d 677 (Alaska 2000).

Rule 28. Expert Witnesses.

The court may order the defendant or the state or both to show cause why expert witnesses should not be appointed, and may request the parties to submit nominations. The court may appoint any expert witnesses agreed upon by the parties, and may appoint witnesses of its own selection. An expert witness shall not be appointed by the court unless the witness consents to act. A witness so appointed shall be informed of the witness' duties by the court in writing, a copy of which shall be filed with the clerk, or at a conference in which the parties shall have opportunity to participate. A witness so appointed shall advise the parties of the witness' findings, if any, and may thereafter be called to testify by the court or by any party. The witness shall be subject to cross-examination by each party. The court may, unless otherwise provided for by rule, determine the reasonable compensation of such witness and direct its payment out of such funds as may be provided by law. The parties also may call expert witnesses of their own selection.

(Adopted by SCO 4 October 4, 1959; amended by SCO 98 effective September 16, 1968; and by SCO 1153 effective July 15, 1994)

Rule 29. Motion for Acquittal.

(a) **Motions for Judgment of Acquittal.** Motions for directed verdict shall not be used and motions for judgment of acquittal shall be used in their place. The court, on motion of a defendant or on its own motion, shall enter judgment of acquittal of one or more offenses charged in the indictment or information after the evidence on either side is closed if the evidence is insufficient to sustain a conviction of such offense or offenses. If a defendant's motion for judgment of acquittal at the close of the state's case is not granted, the defendant may offer evidence without having reserved the right.

(b) **Reservation of Decision on Motion —Renewal of Motion.** If a motion for judgment of acquittal is made at the close of all the evidence, the court may reserve decision on the motion, submit the case to the jury and decide the motion either before the jury returns a verdict or after it returns a verdict of guilty or is discharged without having returned a verdict. If the motion is denied and the case is submitted to the jury, the motion may be renewed within 5 days after the jury is discharged and may include in the alternative a motion for a new trial. If a verdict of guilty is returned the court may on motion set aside the verdict and order a new trial or enter judgment of acquittal. If no verdict is returned the court may order a new trial or enter judgment of acquittal.

(Adopted by SCO 4 October 4, 1959; amended by SCO 554 effective April 4, 1983)

Annotations

Cases

I. Procedural Considerations.
II. Weighing the Evidence.
  A. In General.
  B. Particular Judgments.

I. Procedural Considerations.

The change over to the provision for a motion for judgment of acquittal rather than motion for directed verdict is purely one of nomenclature. **Hallback v. State,** Op. No. 34, 361 P2d 336 (Alaska 1961).

Indictments in the district courts for the territory of Alaska need only conform with the requirements of Rule 7(c) of the Federal Rules of Criminal Procedure, and the names of witnesses are not required to be endorsed thereon. **Oxenberg v. State,** Op. No. 36, 362 P2d 893, 898 (Alaska 1961).

Where upon motion for acquittal court weighed the evidence in the light of what it determined to be the governing law and granted acquittal, the state has no right of appeal. **State v. Selman,** Op. No. 302, 406 P2d 181 (Alaska 1965).

This rule pertains only to jury tried cases. **Beck v. State,** Op. No. 310, 408 P2d 996 (Alaska 1965).

Denial of a motion for acquittal under this rule where a new trial has been ordered is not a final appealable decision within the criteria of Appellate Rule 5. **Stewart v. State,** Op. No. 457, 438 P2d 387 (Alaska 1968).

In every case whether or not the defendant moved for acquittal, the Supreme Court on appeal will determine whether the evidence is sufficient to support the verdict. **Shafer v. State,** Op. No. 563, 456 P2d 466 (Alaska 1969).

A defendant does not waive his right to question the sufficiency of the evidence by failing to move for an acquittal. **Shafer v. State,** Op. No. 563, 456 P2d 466 (Alaska 1969).

The issue of entrapment is to be determined by the trial judge, not the jury. Where that issue has been determined by the jury, the case must be remanded for determination by the trial judge. **Grossman v. State,** Op. No. 566, 457 P2d 226 (Alaska 1969).

If, at the close of the prosecution's case-in-chief, the prosecution has failed to establish the defendant's guilt, the trial judge sitting without a jury should, sua sponte, order judgment of acquittal. **Martin v. City of Fairbanks,** Op. No. 562, 456 P2d 462 (Alaska 1969).

A trial judge sitting without a jury may permit the defendant's counsel at the close of the prosecution's case-in-chief to argue a motion for acquittal, if the trial judge feels that argument of the defendant's counsel would be helpful in deciding the adequacy of the prosecution's case-in-chief. **Martin v. City of Fairbanks,** Op. No. 562, 456 P2d 462 (Alaska 1969).

A motion for acquittal at the close of the prosecution's case-in-chief is not a prerequisite to any subsequent proceedings in a judge-tried case. **Martin v. City of Fairbanks,** Op. No. 562, 456 P2d 462 (Alaska 1969).

With regard to viewing the record on appeal, a motion for acquittal at the close of the prosecution's case-in-chief has no more effect in a judge-tried case than a case tried before a court with a jury. **Martin v. City of Fairbanks,** Op. No.562,456 P2d 462 (Alaska 1969).

If a trial judge refuses to order an acquittal on the defendant's motion after the prosecution's case-in-chief, the defendant may test that refusal by introducing no evidence and resting his case directly. **Martin v. City of Fairbanks,** Op. No. 562, 456 P2d 462 (Alaska 1969).

A motion for judgment of acquittal puts into issue the sufficiency of the evidence. **Beavers v. State,** Op. No. 765, 492 P2d 88 (Alaska 1971).

Motions for a directed verdict of acquittal and for judgment notwithstanding the verdict are regarded as motions for a judgment of acquittal on appeal from a conviction. **Gray v. State,** Op. No. 1068, 525 P2d 524 (Alaska 1974).

Motion for acquittal under this rule puts into issue the sufficiency of the state's evidence. **Ladd v. State,** Op. No. 1480, 568 P2d 960 (Alaska 1977).

Where felony charges of lewd or lascivious conduct toward a child were dismissed at the close of the state's case because the child was unable to testify, the dismissal was the equivalent of a judgment of acquittal for insufficient evidence, thus trial court erred in subsequently accepting a plea of nolo contendere to a count of the information which was necessarily included in the felony charges, since doing so constituted a violation of double jeopardy. **Miller v. State,** Op. No. 2540, 648 P2d 1015 (Alaska 1982).

II. Weighing the Evidence.

A. In General.

Trial judge's determination in submitting a case to the jury will not be set aside unless there has been an abuse of direction. **Braham v. State,** Op. No. 119, 376 P2d 714 (Alaska 1962).

On a motion for a judgment of acquittal the judge must take the view of the evidence and the inferences there from most favorable to the state. **Bush v. State,** Op. No. 265, 397 P2d 616 (Alaska 1964).

Evidence which is all circumstantial must be of sufficient weight to exclude every reasonable hypothesis except that of guilty, but when the sufficiency of the evidence is challenged on appeal, only those facts which are favorable to the State shall be considered along with such reasonable inferences as the jury may have drawn from them. **State v. Selman,** Op. No. 302,406 P2d 181 (Alaska 1965).

Motion for judgment of acquittal should be granted only if fair-minded men in the exercise of reasonable judgment could not differ on the question of whether guilt had been established by the evidence beyond a reasonable doubt, but must necessarily have such a doubt. **Jennings v. State,** Op. No. 295, 404 P2d 652 (Alaska 1965); **Martinez v. State,** Op. No. 389, 423 P2d 700 (Alaska 1967); **Pedersen v. State,** Op. No. 369, 420 P2d 327 (Alaska 1966).

On appeal a record as a whole is viewed, not just the prosecution's case-in-chief, regardless of when the defendant moves for acquittal. **Martin v. City**

of Fairbanks, Op. No. 562, 456 P2d 462 (Alaska 1969).

Where a defendant alleges that the trial court sitting without a jury erred in failing to grant the defendant's motion for acquittal, the Supreme Court will consider only those facts in the record most favorable to the prosecution and such reasonable inferences as the jury may have drawn from them. **Martin v. City of Fairbanks,** Op. No. 562, 456 P2d 462 (Alaska 1969).

In passing on motions for the judgment of acquittal, a trial judge must view the evidence and any reasonable inferences there from in the light most favorable to the State and must deny the motion if reasonable men could differ on the question of whether guilty has been established beyond a reasonable doubt. **Gray v. State,** Op. No. 1068, 525 P2d 524 (Alaska 1974).

On appeal from denial of motion for acquittal, Supreme Court must view evidence and inferences drawn there from in light most favorable to state. **Ladd v. State,** Op. No. 1480, 568 P2d 960 (Alaska 1977).

B. Particular Judgments.

Where wholly circumstantial evidence did not establish guilt of defendants charged with burglary, motion for judgment of acquittal should have been granted. **Davis & Widermyre v. State,** Op. No. 75, 369 P2d 879 (Alaska 1962); **Stewart v. State,** Op. No. 457, 438 P2d 387 (Alaska 1968).

Where all the circumstances, taken together and unexplained, are sufficient to support a verdict against defendant charged with burglary, the trial court properly denied motion for judgment of acquittal. **Goss v. State,** Op. No. 76, 369 P2d 884 (Alaska 1962).

Where in a homicide case a fair-minded person could conclude beyond a reasonable doubt that defendant's account of his altercation with the victim was fabricated, there was no error in denying motions for acquittal. **Bush v. State,** Op. No. 265, 397 P2d 616 (Alaska 1964).

Evidence albeit circumstantial from which fair-minded persons could conclude beyond a reasonable doubt that defendant's account of the altercation was unrealistic in view of extensive injuries causing death of victim and that defendant had purposely and maliciously and without justification caused the death of victim, warranted denial of a motion for acquittal and submission of the case to the jury on the charge of second degree murder. **Jennings v. State,** Op. No. 295, 404 P2d 652 (Alaska 1965).

Judgment of acquittal at the conclusion of the state's case and motion for judgment n.o.v. or with alternative for a new trial were properly refused where in a homicide case there was sufficient factual basis for the conclusion of medical experts that the blows inflicted upon the victim were capable of and did produce trauma inducing a state of shock and causing victim's death and these pertinent facts were embodied in hypothetical questions asked of the medical experts. **West v. State,** Op. No. 319, 409 P2d 847 (Alaska 1965).

A juror's affidavit and testimony that his vote was "coerced" by fatigue and exhaustion did not clearly establish a serious violation of the juror's duty and a deprivation of the defendant of a fair trial and where the juror was polled, had answered that the verdict just read was his verdict, and the exhaustion was not shown any greater than experienced by other jurors, trial judge's refusal to set aside the verdict and order a new trial was sustained. **West v. State,** Op. No. 319, 409 P2d 847 (Alaska 1965).

As one of the exceptions to the general rule prohibiting jurors to impeach their verdicts, the verdict must not be allowed to stand where a party was deprived of a fair trial and since affidavits of jurors that they were exposed to a newspaper article containing information previously held so prejudicial as to require a new trial established that the appellant was deprived of such a fair trial, that the trial court erred in denying motion for new trial. **Watson v. State,** Op. No. 335, 413 P2d 22 (Alaska 1966).

Trial court did not err in refusing to grant appellant's motion for judgment of acquittal in a perjury case on the ground that state failed to prove willfulness or criminal intent where record showed that appellant's explanations along with all other evidence bearing on willfulness or criminal intent were before the jury. **Risher v. State,** Op. No. 363, 418 P2d 983 (Alaska 1966).

Evidence of larceny albeit entirely circumstantial was sufficient to take the case to the jury where it appeared that complaining witness had entered his hotel room accompanied by appellant, that appellant accepted $20 from witness to engage in sexual intercourse with him, that witness took this money out of a suitcase and the balance of $340 was visible to appellant, that immediately after engaging in sexual intercourse the witness fell asleep to awake about five hours later, that the appellant and the balance of the money had gone, and that the door of the hotel room was self-locking and was locked. **Allen v. State,** Op. No. 374, 420 P2d 465 (Alaska 1966).

Motion for judgment of acquittal based on lack of evidence of specific intent was properly denied where, viewing the evidence in light most favorable to state, fair-minded people exercising reasonable judgment could differ on the question. **Calantas v. State,** Op. No. 1914, 599 P2d 147 (Alaska 1979).

Where defendant admitted that he had been driving his automobile, and defendant failed field sobriety test and blood test, more than sufficient evidence existed to support a conviction of driving under the influence of intoxicants. **Anchorage v. Cook,** Op. No. 1899, 598 P2d 939 (Alaska 1979).

Rule 30. Instructions.

(a) **Requested Instructions—Objections.** At the close of the evidence or at such earlier time as the court reasonably directs, any party may file written requests that the court give the jury specific instructions. Such requests must be furnished to adverse parties. The court shall inform counsel of the final form of jury instructions prior to their arguments to the jury. Following the close of the evidence, before or after the arguments of counsel, the court shall instruct the jury. Additionally, the court may give the jury such instructions as it deems necessary at any stage of the trial. The instructions must be reduced to writing and read to the jury and must be taken to the jury room by the jury. No party may assign as error any portion of the charge or omission therefrom unless the party objects thereto before the jury retires to consider its verdict, stating distinctly the matter to which the party objects and the grounds of the objections. Opportunity must be given to make the objection out of the hearing of the jury by excusing the jury or hearing objections in chambers.

(b) **Instructions to Be Given.** The court shall instruct the jury on all matters of law which it considers necessary for the jury's information in giving their verdict.

(Adopted by SCO 4 October 4, 1959; amended by SCO 49 effective January 1, 1963; by SCO 79 effective February 1, 1966; by SCO 222 effective December 15, 1975; and by SCO 923 effective January 15, 1989)

Annotations

Cases

I. In General.

II. Duty to Instruct.

III. Content.

IV. On Review.

I. In General.

A supplemental jury instruction on the elements of the crime of burglary, which was ambiguous and could have led the jury to find the defendant guilty without having found that he had the requisite statutory intent to steal, affected a substantial right of the defendant and giving this instruction outside the presence of the defendant was reversible error. **Noffke v. State,**

Op. No. 383, 422 P2d 102 (Alaska 1967).

In a criminal trial, it was error for the trial court to have sent requested additional instructions to the jury during its deliberation outside the defendant's presence. **Noffke v. State,** Op. No. 383, 422 P2d 102 (Alaska 1967).

The main purpose of this rule's provision that no party may assign as error any portion of any charge or omission therefrom unless he objects before the jury retires to consider its verdict is to require errors to be drawn to the attention of the trial court in time for their correction to avoid the inconvenience and expense of a new trial. **Dimmick v. State,** Op. No. 521, 449 P2d 774 (Alaska 1969).

While an oral request for an instruction may suffice in some cases to alert the court to the necessity of a mandatory instruction, requested instructions are required to be in written form, and the practice of making oral requests is frowned upon. **Hawthorn v. State,** Op. No. 828, 501 P2d 155 (Alaska 1972).

The purpose of the portion of this rule regarding accomplice instructions is to emphasize the suspect motivations of an accomplice witness. **Gordon v. State,** Op. No. 1126, 533 P2d 25 (Alaska 1975).

This rule was designed to grant discretion to trial judges whether to give general instructions at the outset of a trial, at its close, or at both times. **Grant v. State,** Op. No. 2261, 621 P2d 1338 (Alaska 1981).

The trial court is under a duty to instruct the jury on the essential elements of the crime charged; however, whether or not a particular instruction should be given is left to the discretion of the trial judge. **Sears v. State,** Op. No. 584, 713 P2d 1218 (Alaska App. 1986).

Where the State did not object to defendant's withdrawal of a proposed lesser-included offense instruction, and the instructions that were given to the jury, which were approved prior to final argument in accordance with this rule, omitted reference to the lesser-included offense of fourth-degree assault, the trial court committed reversible error when, in response to the jury's inquiry, it instructed the jury on fourth-degree assault for the first time during jury deliberations. **Rollins v. State,** Op. No. 822, 757 P2d 601 (Alaska App. 1988).

II. Duty to Instruct.

This rule required an instruction to be given by the trial court that the jury was to consider with caution and weigh with great care all evidence relating to any admissions or incriminatory statements made by the defendant outside of court. **Daniels v. State,** Op. No. 185, 388 P2d 813 (Alaska 1964).

Failure to give an instruction which was never requested by appellants and which was not a basic mandatory instruction required under the rules, was not assignable as error. **Daniels v. State,** Op. No. 185, 388 P2d 813 (Alaska 1964).

In trial for larceny in a building, it was not error for the trial court to refuse instruction on shoplifting as the lesser offense, because the crime as described in the shoplifting statute is not an offense necessarily included in the crime of larceny in a building. **Mahle v. State,** Op. No. 218, 392 P2d 19 (Alaska 1964).

A requested instruction, suggesting police officers are not as likely to tell the truth as other witnesses, was properly refused. **Battese v. State,** Op. No. 402, 425 P2d 606 (Alaska 1967).

Defendant charged with murder was not entitled to instruction on the testimony of accomplices required under this rule, when there was no evidence in the case that the prosecution witnesses assisted the defendant to shoot the victim and no evidence of a prearranged plan between the witnesses and defendant with respect to the shooting; and knowledge that a crime was being committed at the time of the fatal shooting and concealment of such knowledge would make them accessories after the fact and not accomplices. **Gafford v. State,** Op. No. 478, 440 P2d 405 (Alaska 1968).

The instruction that the jury should determine, in connection with a confession, whether the defendant had been warned of his rights and waived those rights, is not a basic, mandatory, instruction. **Thessen v. State,** Op. No. 555, 454 P2d 341 (Alaska 1969).

An alleged error in failing to inform the jury that the state must prove each element of the crime of robbery beyond a reasonable doubt is not so serious and manifest as to constitute "plain error," where the trial court properly defines reasonable doubt for the jury and defines all elements of the crime of armed robbery. **Avery v. State,** Op. No. 942, 514 P2d 637 (Alaska 1973).

Failure to give the instruction that oral admissions ought to be viewed with caution does not constitute reversible error where there are no oral admissions of the defendants in evidence. **Avery v. State,** Op. No. 942, 514 P2d 637 (Alaska 1973).

Where the only evidence which places the defendant at the scene of the murder or which demonstrates motive or guilty knowledge is the testimony of the victim's widow, an accomplice, and the conviction is substantially procured by the accomplice's testimony, the failure to give the cautionary instruction that the testimony of an accomplice ought to be viewed with distrust constitutes reversible error. **Anthony v. State,** Op. No. 1025, 521 P2d 486 (Alaska 1974).

A trial court is under a duty to instruct the jury on essential elements of an offense. **Thomas v. State,** Op. No. 1040, 522 P2d 528 (Alaska 1974).

In a prosecution for the illegal sale of heroin, a trial court's failure, not objected to by defendant, to instruct the jury that knowledge of the nature of the drug is a necessary element of the offense does not constitute plain error, where knowledge of the nature of the substance is not an issue and where there is no possibility of prejudice to the defendants arising from the instructional omission. **Thomas v. State,** Op. No. 1040, 522 P2d 528 (Alaska 1974).

Trial court's refusal to give an accomplice instruction was not error where defendant accused another party of the crime who in turn accused defendant. Under the circumstances, neither was the accomplice of the other. **Galuska v. State,** Op. No. 1094, 532 P2d 1017 (Alaska 1975).

Whenever a reasonable doubt exists on the issue of complicity of a witness, such doubt should be resolved in favor of the defendant, and the accomplice instruction should be given. **Gordon v. State,** Op. No. 1126, 533 P2d 25 (Alaska 1975).

Instruction that the oral admissions of a party ought to be viewed with caution is mandatory and must be given even if not requested. **Kristich v. State,** Op. No. 1264, 550 P2d 796 (Alaska 1976).

Failure to give mandatory instruction on admissions of a party was harmless error. **Kristich v. State,** Op. No. 1264, 550 P2d 796 (Alaska 1976).

Whether or not a particular instruction should be given is in the discretion of the trial court. **Buchanan v. State,** Op. No. 2553, 554 P2d 1153 (Alaska 1976).

Defendant charged with murder is not entitled to instruction on manslaughter as a lesser included offense when manslaughter prosecution is barred by statute of limitations. **Padie v. State,** Op. No. 1359, 557 P2d 1138 (Alaska 1976).

Whether or not a particular instruction should be given is in the discretion of the trial court. **Buchanan v. State,** Op. No. 2553, 561 P2d 1197 (Alaska 1977).

Failure to give requested instruction on identification was not error, where instruction given embodied correct statements of controlling law. **Buchanan v. State,** Op. No. 2553, 561 P2d 1197 (Alaska 1977).

Failure of trial court to give an accomplice instruction to jury was not plain error where the evidence against both defendants was strong and the jury was instructed that in weighing testimony it could consider the witness' relation to the case, his interest in the outcome, and could distrust the testimony of any person who appeared to make a misstatement with the design to deceive. **Middleton v. State,** Op. No. 1604, 577 P2d 1050 (Alaska 1978).

Defendant charged with assault with a dangerous weapon was

entitled to a jury instruction on the lesser-included offense of assault and battery, and failure of the court to so instruct was reversible error. **Rivett v. State,** Op. No. 1611, 578 P2d 946 (Alaska 1978).

Where the time set by the trial court for submission of jury instruction was not unreasonable, the court did not err in refusing to give an instruction submitted at a later date just prior to submission of the case to the jury. **Smiloff v. State,** Op. No. 1637, 579 P2d 28 (Alaska 1978).

Where there was some evidence tending to show that the killing was neither premeditated nor committed in perpetration of a robbery, defendant charged with first degree murder was entitled to requested instruction on second degree murder, but failure of court to do so was not reversible error when the special interrogatory returned by the jury indicated that all jurors believed the killing was committed in perpetration of the robbery. **Bendle v. State,** Op. No. 1710, 583 P2d 840 (Alaska 1978).

District court's refusal to give a requested jury instruction relating to the bias of the primary witnesses for the prosecution was not an abuse of its discretion where the potential bias of the witness was illuminated during defense counsel's cross-examination and final argument and where the jury was properly instructed concerning the criteria they should consider in determining the credibility of witnesses. **Huske v. Municipality of Anchorage,** Op. No. 1675, 585 P2d 504 (Alaska 1978).

Defendant charged with assault with a dangerous weapon was entitled to an instruction on careless use of a firearm, where facts stated in the indictment were sufficient to notice the crime of careless use of a firearm and defendant presented evidence negating intent element of assault. **Elisorsky v. State,** Op. No. 1816, 592 P2d 1221 (Alaska 1979).

Failure to give a cautionary instruction regarding admissions of a codefendant, where witnesses used such phrases as "they said" and "they asked," was not abuse of discretion in context of the entire testimony of each witness and the objections and corrections made during trial. **Carman v. State,** Op. No. 1979, 602 P2d 1255 (Alaska 1979).

It was not error for the trial court to refuse to give a cautionary instruction concerning oral admissions by the defendant where the defendant testified and explained exactly what he had said and why and where the court carefully instructed the jury as to its duty to determine the credibility of witnesses and weigh the evidence. **Alexander v. State,** Op. No. 2077, 611 P2d 469 (Alaska 1980).

Trial court did not abuse its discretion in choosing not to repeat the jury instructions it had given at the beginning of the trial where the defendant made only a blanket objection to this and did not specify any of the instructions which particularly needed repeating. **Grant v. State,** Op. No. 2261, 621 P2d 1338 (Alaska 1981).

Absence of an accomplice-as-a-matter-of-law instruction is not erroneous where such instruction might infer that the accused was one of the accomplices and therefore guilty. **Mossberg v. State,** Op. No. 2305, 624 P2d 796 (Alaska 1981).

The decision as to whether the jury should be given an accomplice-as-a-matter-of-law instruction is generally a tactical one, as to which defense counsel's preferences should be given great weight. **Mossberg v. State,** Op. No. 2305, 624 P2d 796 (Alaska 1981).

Failure to comply with form rule requiring trial court to instruct jury that testimony of accomplice is to be viewed with distrust was reversible error. **Price v. State,** Op. No. 100, 647 P2d 611 (Alaska App. 1982).

Failure of trial court to instruct the jury to distrust the state's evidence because it was within the state's power to produce stronger and more satisfactory evidence was not plain error. **Walker v. State,** Op. No. 2570, 652 P2d 88 (Alaska 1982).

Failure to give an instruction is plain error if reasonable judges could not differ in concluding that the instruction was necessary to adequately inform the jury of the offense or of defenses to the offense clearly established in the evidence and the failure to give the instruction substantially prejudiced the defendant. **Bidwell v. State,** Op. No. 199, 656 P2d 592 (Alaska App. 1982).

The trial court is under a duty to instruct the jury on the essential elements of the crime charged; however, whether or not a particular instruction should be given is left to the discretion of the trial judge. **Sears v. State,** Op. No. 584, 713 P2d 1218 (Alaska App. 1986).

Failure to instruct the jury that oral administrations of the defendant should be viewed with caution was not abuse of discretion, particularly where defendant did not request the instruction. **Longley v. State,** Op. No. 940, 776 P2d 339 (Alaska App. 1989).

The jury must be instructed on the elements of the charge and on any defense that finds support in the evidence; beyond that, however, the court's discretion to decide what instructions to give to the jury is broad. **Stoneking v. State,** Op. No. 1091, 800 P2d 949 (Alaska App. 1990).

When a standard instruction correctly sets out the elements of an offense or a defense, the court is under no obligation to give an instruction tailor-made to the facts of a specific case unless unique circumstances exist that would render the special instruction especially helpful to the jury. **Stoneking v. State,** Op. No. 1091, 800 P2d 949 (Alaska App. 1990).

Despite prosecutor's announcement that he felt accomplice instruction to jury was unnecessary, it was not error for trial judge to give the instruction nor error for prosecutor to argue accomplice liability to jury where State's theory of crime required judge to give the instruction and defendant was not surprised or prejudiced by the instruction. **Baker v. State,** Op. No. 1444, 905 P2d 479 (Alaska 1995).

III. Content.

Instructions to the jury which spelled out the elements of the crime of robbery but did not specifically include a definition of "steal," fulfilled the requirements of Criminal Rule 30(b). **Thomas v. State,** Op. No. 200, 391 P2d 18 (Alaska 1964).

In trial for second degree murder it was not error for the trial court to instruct the jury on involuntary manslaughter as necessarily included lesser offense. **Jennings v. State,** Op. No. 295, 404 P2d 652 (Alaska 1965).

An instruction that in order to establish guilt by circumstantial evidence in a criminal case the evidence must be of such nature as reasonably to lead to the inference of the defendant's guilt and be inconsistent with any other reasonable theory than that of guilt was proper. **Allen v. State,** Op. No. 374, 420 P2d 465 (Alaska 1966).

Where in a robbery case a strong showing as to the flight of the defendants from the place of the crime had been made and the only testimony adduced by the defendants at the trial was in rebuttal of the evidence of flight, an instruction that flight though not creating a presumption of guilt may tend to prove consciousness of guilt and should be weighed by the jury in connection with all other evidence could have been clarified so as to more clearly indicate that the jury must first find that the evidence does in fact show the flight of the accused but was not erroneous on the record. **Merrill v. State,** Op. No. 392, 423 P2d 686 (Alaska 1967).

Where an alleged accomplice gives testimony exonerating the defendant but the state impeaches the witness by introducing prior inconsistent statements, the defendant's counsel elicits from the alleged accomplice circumstances surrounding the taking of the statements which, if believed, demonstrates the statements' unreliability, and the court's instructions limit the use of the statements to their potential impact upon the witness' credibility, any error in failing to give a cautionary instruction that the testimony of an accomplice ought to be viewed with distrust was harmless. **Johnson v. State,** Op. No. 726, 489 P2d 134 (Alaska 1971).

Taken as a whole, an instruction which attempts to define "reasonable doubt" in terms of proof to a "moral certainty" defines "reasonable doubt" in a permissible fashion where the instruction is not of the type to mislead the jury in finding no reasonable doubt when in fact there is some. However, the better practice is to avoid such an instruction since it is likely to raise more questions that it puts to rest in the minds of jurors. **Avery v. State,** Op. No. 942, 514 P2d 637 (Alaska 1973).

An instruction which uses the phrase "moral certainty" in the context of defining the reasonable doubt standard is not fatally defective, although the preferable form of instruction is to define reasonable doubt as "a doubt that would cause prudent men to hesitate before acting in matters of importance to themselves." **Davenport v. State,** Op. No. 1007, 519 P2d 452 (Alaska 1974).

The use of a jury instruction which states that witnesses are presumed to speak the truth is condemned since it interferes with the province of the jury to determine the credibility of witnesses, conflicts with the presumption of innocence, and serves to raise doubt in the minds of jurors as to their role and adds a confusing factor to their deliberations. **Galuska v. State,** Op. No. 1094, 532 P2d 1017 (Alaska 1975).

Instruction that required mere negligence rather than culpable negligence to convict for manslaughter was plain error. **Stork v. State,** Op. No. 1365, 559 P2d 99 (Alaska 1977).

Where defendant was convicted of a specific intent charge, giving of the Mann instruction to the jury was reversible error. **Howard v. State,** Op. No. 1707, 583 P2d 827 (Alaska 1978).

An instruction which omitted the requirement that some physical gesture of force or an actual attempted battery occur to constitute assault with a deadly weapon was not deficient. **Coleman v. State,** Op. No. 2190, 621 P2d 869 (Alaska 1980).Instructions to jury that defendant must be found not guilty if the evidence "points equally to the defendant's innocence as well as to his guilt" was not sufficiently misleading as to constitute plain error. **Dorman v. State,** Op. No. 2272, 622 P2d 448 (Alaska 1981).

Failure of court to instruct the jury that a subjective belief that the victim consented to restraint was a defense to kidnapping was not plain error. **Bidwell v. State,** Op. No. 199, 656 P2d 592 (Alaska App. 1982).

Instruction which informed the jury that it could infer an actor's intent from his words and conduct, and further informed the jury that it might infer that an actor intends the natural and probable consequences of acts he knowingly does or knowingly omits, did not shift the burden of proof to defendant on the issue of intent and was therefore not plain error. **Bidwell v. State,** Op. No. 199, 656 P2d 592 (Alaska App. 1982).

Failure of trial court to give intent instruction utilizing the phrase "specific intent" was not plain error. **Bidwell v. State,** Op. No. 199, 656 P2d 592 (Alaska App. 1982).

Failure of the trial court to instruct the jury on the element of premeditation and to define the element of intent needed for first-degree murder was not plain error. **Weston v. State,** Op. No. 183, 656 P2d 1186 (Alaska App. 1982).

The jury must be instructed on the elements of the charge and on any defense that finds support in the evidence; beyond that, however, the court's discretion to decide what instructions to give to the jury is broad. **Stoneking v. State,** Op. No. 1091, 800 P2d 949 (Alaska App. 1990).

When a standard instruction correctly sets out the elements of an offense or a defense, the court is under no obligation to give an instruction tailor-made to the facts of a specific case unless unique circumstances exist that would render the special instruction especially helpful to the jury. **Stoneking v. State,** Op. No. 1091, 800 P2d 949 (Alaska App. 1990).

IV. On Review.

An instruction that an accomplice's testimony should be viewed with caution and weighed with great care is not reversible error, although the required instruction is that such testimony ought to be viewed with distrust where there is no objection or request for the proper instruction, there is a further instruction on accomplice testimony, and there is extensive corroborating evidence. **Flores v. State,** Op. No. 491, 443 P2d 73 (Alaska 1968).

The power of the Supreme Court to consider a question presented for the first time on appeal under Criminal Rule 47, allowing a plain error or defect affecting substantial rights to be noted for the first time on appeal, is an exception to this rule and will be exercised only where necessary to prevent a miscarriage of justice. **Dimmick v. State,** Op. No. 521, 449 P2d 774 (Alaska 1969).

The allegation that it is error to give an instruction that it is sufficient for the jury to find that a robbery was committed on or about a certain date will not be considered on appeal where the defendant fails to object prior to the giving of the instruction. **Spight v. State,** Op. No. 524, 450 P2d 157 (Alaska 1969).

The reviewing court will not consider a defendant's objection to an instruction on admissibility of his confession, which fails to require the jury to determine whether the defendant had been given the proper warnings and had waived his rights, where this was not an objection raised in the trial court. **Thessen v. State,** Op. No. 555, 454 P2d 341 (Alaska 1969).

Where a defendant requests two separate instructions concerning burden of proof and insanity, but focuses his entire presentation and argument on the burden of proof issue, the issue of insanity is not presented with sufficient clarity to be reviewed on appeal. **Pope v. State,** Op. No. 660, 480 P2d 697 (Alaska 1971).

The provisions of this rule precluding any party from assigning as error any portion of a charge or omission unless he objects before the jury retires does not prevent the application of the plain error rule where the court's charge has resulted in a miscarriage of justice. **Bakken v. State,** Op. No. 728, 489 P2d 120 (Alaska 1971).

Where a defendant does not request at trial an instruction informing the jury of the deposition of the defendant that would be made if the jury returns a verdict of not guilty by reason of insanity, the defendant is precluded from assigning error on appeal. **Kinsman v. State,** Op. No. 914, 512 P2d 901 (Alaska 1973).

Ordinarily, the supreme court will not notice errors in jury instructions unless a timely request is made for an omitted instruction or a timely objection made to an erroneous one. **Anthony v. State,** Op. No. 1025, 521 P2d 486 (Alaska 1974).

Failure to give the cautionary instruction that the testimony of an accomplice ought to be viewed with distrust is plain error which the supreme court will consider on appeal even though the defendant does not request the instruction or object to its omission. **Anthony v. State,** Op. No. 1025, 521 P2d 486 (Alaska 1974).

Supreme Court will consider faulty instruction on appeal where it constituted plain error, even though no objection was made at trial. **Stork v. State,** Op. No. 1365, 559 P2d 99 (Alaska 1977).

Where testimony as to defendant's three conflicting versions of shooting was a substantial factor leading to his conviction, failure to give instruction on admissions required by this rule before 1975 amendment was prejudicial error. **Stork v. State,** Op. No. 1365, 559 P2d 99 (Alaska 1977).

Failure to give mandatory instruction is error that must be noticed on appeal, even though it was not requested at trial. **Stork v. State,** Op. No. 1365, 559 P2d 99 (Alaska 1977).

Motion for acquittal for insufficiency of proof is not a specific objection to instruction sufficient to preserve instruction issue for appeal. **Larson v. State,** Op. No. 2433, 564 P2d 365 (Alaska 1977).

This rule requires a party to specifically object to instructions in order to assign them as error on appeal. **Larson v. State,** Op. No. 1502, 569 P2d 783 (Alaska 1977).

When defendant failed to request instruction limiting charge to assault by firing pistol and not just pointing it, question would not be considered on appeal as substance of state's case related to shooting and failure to instruct was therefore not plain error. **Larson v. State,** Op. No. 1502, 569 P2d 783 (Alaska 1977).

The standards for reversible error with respect to jury instruction differs depending on whether timely objection is made; unless a defendant challenges a jury instruction "before the jury retires to consider its verdict," the point cannot be given consideration on appeal unless there exists plain error. **Howard v. State,** Op. No. 1707, 583 P2d 827 (Alaska 1978).

Where there was some evidence tending to show that the killing was neither premeditated nor committed in perpetration of a robbery, defendant charged with first degree murder was entitled to requested instruction on second degree murder, but failure of court to do so was not reversible error when the special interrogatory returned by the jury indicated that all jurors believed the killing was committed in perpetration of the robbery. **Bendle v. State,** Op. No. 1710, 583 P2d 840 (Alaska 1978).

Where appellant did not object to trial to the court's instructions to the jury concerning accomplices, the issue was not properly reserved for review. **Mossberg v. State,** Op. No. 2305, 624 P2d 796 (Alaska 1981).

Although defense counsel stated at trial that an alternative instruction would be preferable, he failed to comply with this rule by not distinctly informing the trial court as to the specific wording of the instruction he deemed objectionable. **Burke v. State,** Op. No. 2194, 624 P2d 1240 (Alaska 1981).

When defendant objected to "theft by receiving" instruction on the ground that the evidence was insufficient to support it, he did not preserve on appeal objection to the same instruction on the ground that the term "recklessly" as used in the instruction was not defined. **Williams v. State,** Op. No. 106, 648 P2d 603 (Alaska App. 1982).

Where defendant's attorney expressed concern about the jury instruction defining the elements of second-degree assault, he never articulated the problem that he subsequently raised on appeal, and where attorney told judge that he had no problem with the instruction, on appeal, defendant had to demonstrate that the instruction constituted plain error. **Willis v. State,** Op. No. 1839, 57 P.3d 688, 404 P2d 652 (Alaska App. 2002).

LAW REVIEW COMMENTARIES

"If you knew him like I did, you'd have shot him too…A survey of Alaska's Law of Self Defense," 23 Alaska L. Rev. 171 (2006).

Rule 31. Verdict.

(a) **Return.** The verdict shall be unanimous. It shall be returned by the jury to the judge in open court.

(b) **Several Defendants.** If there are two or more defendants, the jury at any time during its deliberations may return a verdict or verdicts with respect to a defendant or defendants as to whom it has agreed; if the jury cannot agree with respect to all, the defendant or defendants as to whom it does not agree may be tried again.

(c) **Conviction of Lesser Offense.** The defendant may be found guilty of an offense necessarily included in the offense charged, or of an attempt to commit either the offense charged or the offense necessarily included therein if the attempt is an offense. When it appears that the defendant has committed a crime, and there is reasonable ground of doubt in which of two or more degrees the defendant is guilty, the defendant can be convicted of the lowest of those degrees only.

(d) **Poll of Jury.** When the verdict is returned and before it is recorded the jury shall be polled at the request of any party or upon the court's own motion. If, upon the poll, there is not unanimous concurrence, the jury may be directed to retire for further deliberations or may be discharged.

(e) **Special Verdicts—Insanity.** Where a defendant interposes the defense of insanity and evidence thereof is given at the trial, the jury, if it finds the defendant not guilty on that ground, shall declare that fact in their verdict.

(f) **Sealed Verdict.** The court may permit the foreman of the jury to date, sign and seal in an envelope a verdict reached after the usual business hours. The jury may then separate, but all must be in the jury box to deliver the verdict when the court next convenes or as instructed by the court.

When the court authorizes a sealed verdict, it shall admonish the jurors not to make any disclosure concerning it nor speak with other persons concerning the case until the verdict has been returned and the jury discharged.

(Adopted by SCO 4 October 4, 1959; amended by SCO 49 effective January 1, 1963; amended by SCO 316 effective September 1, 1978; by SCO 427 effective August 1, 1980; by SCO 1114 effective January 15, 1993; and by SCO 1153 effective July 15, 1994)

Annotations

Cases

Where in a trial for second degree murder, the jury was instructed that if they found the killing excusable or accidental, the defendant must be found not guilty of second degree murder and not guilty of both voluntary and involuntary manslaughter and forms of verdict for such findings were furnished, the court did not err in not providing a form of verdict: "not guilty by reason of excusable homicide." **Jennings v. State,** Op. No. 295, 404 P2d 652 (Alaska 1965).

When the jury foreman informs the judge, without being asked, of an eleven to one split in the panel, it is not error for the court to deliver the supplemental "Allen charge," stating that a dissenting juror should consider whether a doubt in his mind is a reasonable one which makes no impression upon the minds of so many men, equally honest, equally intelligent with himself, who have heard the same evidence with the same attention. **Gafford v. State,** Op. No. 478, 440 P2d 405 (Alaska 1968).

Trial court's use of sealed verdict over objection of counsel is reversible error. **Johnson v. State,** Op. No. 1612, 577 P2d 1063 (Alaska 1978).

Defendant charged with the offense of shooting with intent to kill, wound or maim and assault with a dangerous weapon was entitled to a jury instruction on the lesser-included offense of careless use of firearms; however, failure to give such instruction was harmless error where a jury's verdict under the circumstances necessarily contained a rejection of defendant's contention that he committed only the lesser-included offense. **Christie v. State,** Op. No. 1644, 580 P2d 310 (Alaska 1978).

Conviction for joyriding reversed where court permitted a sealed verdict over defense objection. **Komoktoak v. State,** Op. No. 1704, 584 P2d 25 (Alaska 1978).

The failure to poll the jury as to each defendant, when such poll was not requested and the record suggests no jury confusion or failure to consider each defendant, is not reversible error. **Moreau v. State,** Op. No. 1770, 588 P2d 275 (Alaska 1978).

Trial court's instruction on first degree assault, which combined the alternative definitions of the offense, thus permitting individual jurors to render a general verdict convicting on either theory, was reversible error. **James v. State,** Op. No. 304, 671 P2d 885 (Alaska App. 1983).

Where on the evidence presented it would realistically have been impossible for the jury to find defendant guilty of robbery without also finding him guilty of assault, a lesser-included offense instruction on assault was required. **Marker v. State,** Op. No. 432, 692 P2d 977 (Alaska App. 1984).

A lesser-included offense instruction is not necessarily inappropriate even if there is a reasonable theory under which the jury could find defendant guilty of the crime charged without also finding him guilty of the lesser offense. **Marker v. State,** Op. No. 432, 692 P2d 977 (Alaska App. 1984).

This rule does not preclude a mistrial in a case in which the jurors cannot agree on a greater offense but can agree on a lesser offense. **Desnek v. State,** Op. No. 455, 697 P2d 1059 (Alaska App. 1985).

Juries need not unanimously agree upon a particular statutory theory of the crime charged if there is sufficient evidence in the record to support either theory. **State v. James,** Op. No. 2925, 698 P2d 1161 (Alaska 1985).

Under this rule, a jury may not convict a defendant of offenses which are related to the crime charged but which are not necessarily included therein. **State v. Minano,** Op. No. 3006, 710 P2d 1013 (Alaska 1985).

An indictment charging a greater offense necessarily also charges all lesser-included offenses as well as attempts; consequently, where a trial court finds that there was insufficient evidence to permit an indictment charging the greater offense, but sufficient evidence to charge the lesser offense including an attempt, the indictment should not be dismissed, but the charges should be reduced to charge the lesser offense. **State v. Ison,** Op. No. 754, 744 P2d 416 (Alaska App. 1987).

Although the crime of robbery based upon accomplice liability and the crime of hindering prosecution may have been related offenses, the latter offense was not necessarily included in the former; consequently, trial court did not err in refusing to give a lesser-included offense instruction on hindering prosecution at defendant's trial for robbery. **Thiel v. State,** Op. No. 855, 762 P2d 478 (Alaska App. 1988).

A defense is "necessarily" included in the offense "charged" when it is impossible to commit the charged offense without also committing the included offense; before one offense may be deemed a lesser-included offense of the other, there must exist a disputed fact which distinguishes the two offenses and there must be an inherent relationship between the two offenses. **Kennedy v. State,** Op. No. 1013, 786 P2d 928 (Alaska App. 1990).

Driving without a license (DWOL) was deemed to be a lesser-included offense of driving while license suspended (DWLS). **Kennedy v. State,** Op. No. 1013, 786 P2d 928 (Alaska App. 1990).

In second degree theft prosecution, failure of the jury to ascertain and declare in the verdict the value of the property that was the subject of the crime, as required by this rule, was not plain error, defendant was not substantially prejudiced by the failure to receive a special verdict, thus his motion for a new trial was denied. **Salvato v. State,** Op. No. 1145, 814 P2d 741 (Alaska App. 1991).

A lesser offense is "necessarily included" in the offense charged when it would be impossible in the context of the case to convict of the charged offense without also convicting of the lesser. **Willett v. State,** Op. No. 1240, 836 P2d 955 (Alaska App. 1992).

Lesser-included offense instruction is required when factual dispute exists as to element of greater offense so that jury could rationally acquit on greater offense and convict on lesser offense; whether factual dispute exists is determined by whether there is some evidence from which reasonable juror could entertain reasonable doubt as to element in question. **Willett v. State,** Op. No. 1240, 836 P2d 955 (Alaska App. 1992).

Where defendant was charged with second-degree assault for repeatedly kicking victim in face with his shod foot, trial court committed reversible error in refusing to instruct on lesser-included offense of fourth-degree assault. **Willett v. State,** Op. No. 1240, 836 P2d 955 (Alaska App. 1992).

Felony murder is not lesser included offense of first-degree murder. **Hansen v. State,** Op. No. 1279, 845 P2d 449 (Alaska App. 1993).

Where defendant was indicted for first-degree murder, first-degree robbery, and first-degree arson, trial court erred in instructing jury on second-degree felony murder, even if facts would have supported felony murder charge based upon combination of murder and robbery charges, since it would be unwarranted expansion of doctrine of lesser included offenses to allow elements of lesser included crime to be stitched together from elements of two or more charged crimes. **Hansen v. State,** Op. No. 1279, 845 P2d 449 (Alaska App. 1993).

After a poll of the jury indicated to the court that there was not unanimous concurrence, and in fact that verdict forms had been switched, the judge had discretion under Alaska R. Crim. P. 31 to send the jury back into deliberations with the jury instructions and the correct verdict forms. **Crouse v. Municipality of Anchorage,** Op. No. 1905, 79 P.3d 660 (Alaska App. 2003).

PART VII. JUDGMENT

Rule 32. Sentence and Judgment.

(a) **Sentence.** Sentence shall be imposed without unreasonable delay. Sentencing in felony cases shall follow the procedures established in this rule and Rules 32.1 through 32.6. Sentencing in misdemeanor cases shall follow the procedures established in this rule and Rules 32.2, 32.3, 32.5, and 32.6. When imposing sentence, the judge or magistrate shall explain on the record the reasons for the sentence.

(b) **Other Counts.** At sentencing, the prosecuting attorney must announce the disposition of all counts brought under the same case number that are not addressed in the judgment or in a written notice of dismissal or deferred prosecution. The court will notify the Department of Public Safety of any counts dismissed on the record.

(c) **Judgment.**

(1) *Conviction.* A judgment of conviction must, for each count, set forth the offense, including the statute or regulation violated, the defendant's plea, the verdicts or findings, and the sentence imposed. The judge or magistrate must sign the judgment.

(A) *Incarceration.* When the sentence includes a term of incarceration, the clerk promptly shall deliver a copy of the judgment to a peace officer or correctional facility. If the defendant does not appear at the correctional facility at the time specified, the peace officer or a representative of the correctional facility promptly shall notify the court by sworn statement on the record or by affidavit.

(B) *Restitution.* When the sentence includes a requirement that the defendant pay restitution, the judge shall order restitution as described in Rule 32.6. The judgment for restitution is enforceable in the same manner as a judgment in a civil action. If the defendant is placed on probation, the judgment of conviction shall include the payment of restitution as a condition of probation.

(C) *Conviction of a Corporation.* If a corporation is convicted of any criminal offense, the judge shall enter judgment against the corporation and the judgment shall be enforced in the same manner as a judgment in a civil action, or as otherwise provided by law.

(2) *Discharge.* If the defendant is found not guilty or for any other reason is entitled to be discharged, judgment shall be entered accordingly.

(d) **Judgment for Sex Offenses or Child Kidnapping.** When a defendant is convicted of a sex offense defined in AS 12.63.100 or child kidnapping as defined in AS 12.63.100, the written judgment must state the requirements of AS 12.63.010 and the period of registration required under AS 12.63 if the required period can be determined by the court.

(e) **Judgment for Crimes Involving Domestic Violence.** In a case in which the defendant is convicted of an offense listed in AS 18.66.990(3) and the prosecution claims at sentencing that the offense is a crime involving domestic violence, the written judgment must set forth whether the offense is a crime involving domestic violence as defined in AS 18.66.990(3) and (5). A factual and legal determination supporting this finding must be made on the record.

(f) **Judgment for Crime Against a Person.** In a case in which the defendant is convicted of a crime against a person as defined in AS 44.41.035(j), the written judgment must set out the requirements of AS 12.55.015(i).

(g) **Information To Be Included in Judgment.** If provided by the prosecuting authority in the charging document, the judgment must include the following information:

(1) the defendant's full name, including middle name or initial;

(2) the defendant's date of birth;

(3) the defendant's Alaska Public Safety Information Network (APSIN) identification number;

(4) the defendant's driver's license number or state identification number, including the issuing state and whether the license is a commercial driver's license;

(5) the arrest tracking number (ATN) on the Criminal Case Intake and Disposition (CCID) form for each offense being addressed in the judgment;

(6) the three-digit charge tracking number assigned on the CCID form for each offense being addressed in the judgment; and

(7) the statute, regulation, or ordinance, as identified in the Uniform Offense Citation Table,** corresponding to each offense being addressed in the judgment. Regulations not listed in the Uniform Offense Citation Table must be cited by the regulation number.

**The Uniform Offense Citation table was developed by the Department of Public Safety. Changes to the table must be approved by the Department of Law or the appropriate municipal prosecuting authority. It is available at: http://www.dps.state.ak.us/uoct/.

(Adopted by SCO 4 October 4, 1959; amended by SCO 157 effective February 15, 1973; by Amendment No. 5 to SCO 157 effective July 1, 1974; by SCO 330 effective January 1, 1979; by SCO 418 effective August 1, 1980; by SCO 436 effective October 21, 1980; by SCO 437 effective October 21, 1980; by SCO 550 effective February 1, 1983; by SCO 554 effective April 4, 1983; by SCO 603 effective September 14, 1984; by SCO 976 effective January 15, 1990; by SCO 979 effective August 28, 1989; by SCO 1028 effective July 15, 1990; by SCO 1049 effective January 15, 1991; by SCO 1092 effective July 15, 1992; repealed and reenacted by SCO 1136 effective July 15, 1993; amended by SCO 1204 effective July 15, 1995; by SCO 1289 effective January 15, 1998; by SCO 1341 effective September 10, 1998; by SCO 1343 effective January 1, 1999; by SCO 1464 effective March 5, 2002; and by SCO 1614 effective October 15, 2006)

Note to SCO 1204: The requirement that a judgment for conviction of a sex offense must set out the requirements of AS 12.63.010 was added by ch. 41 § 3 SLA 1994. Section 7 of this order is adopted for the sole reason that the legislature has mandated the amendments.

Note to SCO 1341: Paragraph (e) of Criminal Rule 32 was added by § 11 ch. 95 SLA 1998. Section 3 of this order is adopted for the sole reason that the legislature has mandated the amendment.

Cross References

(a) **CROSS REFERENCE:** AS 12.55.010

(b) **CROSS REFERENCE:** Administrative Bulletin No. 17.

Annotations

Cases

I. In General.
II. Pre Sentence Report.
III. Sentencing.

I. In General.

Defendant who speaks only Eskimo has a right of allocution. **State v. Abraham,** Op. No. 1438, 566 P2d 267 (Alaska 1977).

Criminal Rule 32(a) creates no rights not contained in the speedy trial clause of Article I, Section 11 of the Alaska Constitution. **Gonzales v. State,** Op. No. 1666, 582 P2d 630 (Alaska 1978).

II. Pre-Sentence Report.

On his first application to vacate or set aside sentence and to withdraw plea of guilty on ground of coercion, an indigent prisoner had a constitutional right to have counsel appointed by the court to represent him at such hearing. **Nichols v. State,** Op. No. 398, 425 P2d 247 (Alaska 1967).

Where trial counsel was given the opportunity to read the pre-sentence report prior to sentencing and no objection to its factual contents was raised, it was no denial of due process that the pre-sentence investigation and the pre-sentence report contained references to admissions of appellant concerning his involvement in two charges which had been dismissed. **Thompson v. State,** Op. No. 408, 426 P2d 995 (Alaska 1967).

Pre-sentence reports assist the judge in considering both the possibility of the defendant's reformation and the need for protection of the public. **Egelak v. State,** Op. No. 463, 438 P2d 712 (Alaska 1968).

No error arose from inclusion in a pre-sentence report in a manslaughter case of reference to defendant's previous indictment for, and acquittal of, the crime of manslaughter, because it cannot be assumed that a sentencing judge would be prejudiced by such reference in his task of tailoring an appropriate sentence in the light of the fullest information possible concerning the defendant's life and characteristics. **Egelak v. State,** Op. No. 463, 438 P2d 712 (Alaska 1968).

An accused has a right to be present at a pre-sentence conference. Such a right is a substantial right. **Speidel v. State,** Op. No. 584, 460 P2d 77 (Alaska 1969).

Whenever a probation report contains information on police contacts, the trial judge shall state in the record that he is not relying on that information upon request by defense. **Thurkill v. State,** Op. No. 1279, 551 P2d 541 (Alaska 1976).

Where pre-sentence report contained inaccurate derogatory statements, sentence would be upheld where defendant was allowed to rebut them. **Thurkill v. State,** Op. No. 1279, 551 P2d 541 (Alaska 1976).

Pre-sentence report may contain psychiatric report based in part on police contacts. **Buchanan v. State,** Op. No. 2553, 554 P2d 1153 (Alaska 1976).

Verified reports of anti-social behavior having a bearing on the crime are not unexplained police contacts and may be included in pre-sentence report. **Nukapigak v. State,** Op. No. 1410, 562 P2d 697 (Alaska 1977).

Pre-sentence report should contain basic information pertaining to the victim of the crime. **Sandvik v. State,** Op. No. 1419, 564 P2d 20 (Alaska 1977).

An unsolicited letter received by the court concerning the sentencing of defendant became, in effect, part of the pre-sentence report, and failure of the court to disclose the letter to the attorneys for the state and defendant was error, requiring vacation of the sentence in the absence of any affirmative statement in the record assuring that the court disregarded the letter in imposing sentence. **Bowlin v. State,** Op. No. 81, 643 P2d 1 (Alaska App. 1982).

This rule requires an updated pre-sentence report prior to revocation of probation and the imposition of sentence. **Dodd v. State,** Op. No. 398, 686 P2d 737 (Alaska App. 1984).

Disclosure of pre-sentence reports is expressly restricted by this rule; however, before a pre-sentence report of a complaining witness could be withheld from the defendant, the trial court would have to determine in an **in camera** review that the material in the report was not relevant to the case at bar. **Johnson v. State,** Op. No. 1390, 889 P2d 1076 (Alaska App. 1995).

III. Sentencing.

On his first application to vacate or set aside sentence and to withdraw plea of guilty on ground of coercion, an indigent prisoner had a constitutional right to have counsel appointed by the court to represent him at such hearing. **Nichols v. State,** Op. No. 398, 425 P2d 247 (Alaska 1967).

It was not prejudicial error for the sentencing judge to have examined photographs of the victim's body in a homicide case prior to sentencing where the pictures were pertinent with regard to details of the defendant's criminal conduct, shed light on his behavior and character, and review of the record failed to disclose that the judge in fact became prejudiced against the defendant subsequent to his viewing the pictures. **Egelak v. State,** Op. No. 463, 438 P2d 712 (Alaska 1968).

Prosecutor's remarks at sentencing proceedings of a defendant convicted of manslaughter which referred to the fact that the defendant had been previously indicted for the crime of manslaughter and had been acquitted thereof, was not model advocacy but did not require the setting aside of the judgment. **Egelak v. State,** Op. No. 463, 438 P2d 712 (Alaska 1968).

Where the sentencing judge has knowledge of the defendant's prior record, his psychological background, his drug addiction and his previous rehabilitative failures, the absence of a presentence report and psychiatric evaluation does not require the vacation of sentences, the imposition of which has previously been deferred. **Adams v. State,** Op. No. 1032, 521 P2d 516 (Alaska 1974).

Where the defendant admits to the lower court that he had committed felonies while on probation, and where the prosecutor informed the court that he is ready and willing to support allegations of additional offenses with witnesses in the courtroom, and neither the defendant nor his counsel objects to the prosecutor's references to such other offenses, such reference is not error justifying vacation of sentence. **Adams v. State,** Op. No. 1032, 521 P2d 516 (Alaska 1974).

Consecutive sentences totaling 11 years' imprisonment with eligibility for parole to be determined by the parole board in its discretion are not excessive for an admitted heroin addict who has been unable to overcome his addiction and was convicted of various burglary and larceny charges. **Adams v. State,** Op. No. 1032, 521 P2d 516 (Alaska 1974).

Consideration of an accused's cooperation with law enforcement officials in revealing evidence leading to conviction of another is not improper in determining a sentence to be imposed against the accused. **Burleson v. State,** Op. No. 1222, 543 P2d 1195 (Alaska 1975).

The supreme court's function, in a sentence appeal, is to ascertain whether the trial court was clearly mistaken in imposing the particular sanction. **Burleson v. State,** Op. No. 1222, 543 P2d 1195 (Alaska 1975).

Sentencing court must unequivocally bring home to defendant that he has right to make a statement in his own behalf and to present any information in mitigation of punishment. **Nattrass v. State,** Op. No. 1314, 554 P2d 399 (Alaska 1976).

Actual consideration of police contacts will not invalidate sentence if from the record or by witnesses' testimony the judge is aware of the circumstances and outcome of the contacts. **Buchanan v. State,** Op. No. 2553, 561 P2d 1197 (Alaska 1977).

Sentencing court may rely on psychiatric report which considers explained police contacts in reaching a diagnosis. **Buchanan v. State,** Op. No. 2553, 561 P2d 1197 (Alaska 1977).

Mere awareness by sentencing court of other police contacts will not serve to invalidate an otherwise valid sentence. **Buchanan v. State,** Op. No. 2553, 561 P2d 1197 (Alaska 1977).

Sentencing judge may consider instances of past anti-social behavior, substantiated by supporting information, even though defendant was not charged or convicted. **Nukapigak v. State,** Op. No. 1410, 562 P2d 697 (Alaska 1977).

Question, "Do you have anything you want to say before I impose sentence?" was minimal compliance with allocution requirement of this rule, where defendant was sentenced four days before Supreme Court imposed more stringent Nattrass standard. **Capwell v. State,** Op. No. 1482, 568 P2d 10 (Alaska 1978).

Trial court's failure to afford defendant the opportunity to make a statement on his own behalf at sentencing hearing was not harmless error. **Mohn v. State,** Op. No. 1719, 584 P2d 40 (Alaska 1978).

Under Rule 32(a) the obligation is on the court to afford the defendant the opportunity to speak and not on the defendant to request such an opportunity, hence defendant's failure to assert actively his right of allocution did not constitute waiver. **Mohn v. State,** Op. No. 1719, 584 P2d 40 (Alaska 1978).

Defendant's contention that consideration of his juvenile record by the court imposing sentence violated his right to privacy was rejected. **Penn v. State,** Op. No. 1774,588 P2d 288 (Alaska 1978).

Despite the fact that defendant spoke at some length under direct examination by his counsel at the sentencing hearing, the court's failure to inform him of his right of allocution required resentencing. **Law v. State,** Op. No. 2301, 624 P2d 284 (Alaska 1981).

In order to establish a claim of racial bias in sentencing defendant must show that the sentence was probably higher than that which would have been imposed upon a defendant of a different race with a like criminal history who committed a similar offense. **Coleman v. State,** Op. No. 2190, 621 P2d 869 (Alaska 1980).

Trial court, in conducting a hearing pursuant to this rule to determine whether mitigating and aggravating factors have been established, may consider evidence previously introduced at the trial. **Wolf v. State,** Op.

No. 99, 647 P2d 609 (Alaska App. 1982).

Where defendant was given a chance to exercise his right of allocution just prior to sentencing and did not exercise that right on the ground that he needed more time to prepare, failure of the trial judge to give the defendant more time was not error. **Hastings v. State,** Op. No. 706, 736 P2d 1157 (Alaska App. 1987).

Denial of allocution may be harmless where the defendant is subject to presumptive sentencing, no aggravating or mitigating factors are established, and the totality of the circumstances would not warrant referral to a three-judge panel for sentencing. **Johnson v. State,** Op. No. 858, 762 P2d 493 (Alaska App. 1988).

Trial judge's oversight in denying defendant allocution was harmless beyond a reasonable doubt where the judge had already rejected proposed mitigating factors and possible referral to a three judge panel for sentencing. **Johnson v. State,** Op. No. 858, 762 P2d 493 (Alaska App. 1988).

Rule 32.1. Presentence Procedure for Felony Sentencings.

(a) **Scheduling & Preliminary Filings.**

(1) At the time guilt in a felony case is established by verdict or plea, the judge shall establish the date for a sentencing hearing and a presentencing hearing, if appropriate, and, except as provided in paragraph (g) of this rule, shall order a presentence investigation by the Department of Corrections. The judge may order a presentence investigation in a case in which an investigation is not required under paragraph (g). If the judge elects to schedule a single hearing, all of the procedures for the presentencing and sentencing hearings shall be applicable at the single hearing.

(2) At the time guilt is established as described in (a)(1) above, the parties shall be directed to make the following preliminary filings within ten days, unless otherwise ordered by the court:

(A) *Presumptive Sentencing.* The state shall file a notice indicating whether the defendant's sentence is governed by presumptive sentencing and, if so, listing the defendant's prior convictions that qualify as prior felony convictions under AS 12.45.145, as well as any other factor that triggers a specific presumptive term; and

(B) *Financial Statement.* In cases where restitution may be ordered, the defendant shall submit a financial statement on a form designated by the Administrative Director to the probation office.

(b) **Presentence Investigation and Report.**

(1) *Contents and Filing.* The Department of Corrections shall prepare a presentence report. The report shall be filed with the court and served on counsel at least 30 days before the sentencing hearing, or 30 days before the presentencing hearing, if one is scheduled. The report shall contain all of the defendant's prior criminal convictions and findings of delinquency and any other information about the defendant's characteristics, financial condition, and the circumstances affecting the defendant's behavior that may be helpful in fashioning the defendant's sentence, a victim impact statement, and any other information required by the judge. The presentence report shall comply with the Victims' Rights Act, AS 12.61.100 — 12.61.150 and AS 12.55.022.

(2) *Restitution Information.* In cases where the court may order the defendant to pay restitution, the presentence report must include:

(A) defendant's financial statement completed under subparagraph (a)(2)(B) of this rule; and

(B) information concerning the identity of any victims or other persons seeking restitution and, if known, whether any victim or other person expressly declines restitution, the nature and amount of any damages together with any supporting documentation, a restitution amount recommendation, and the names of any co-defendants and their case numbers.

(3) *Disclosure.* Unless the judge finds that providing specific portions of the report to the defendant would prove detrimental to the rehabilitation of the defendant or the safety of the public, the defense attorney may give a full copy of the report to the defendant. Unless otherwise ordered, or except as specifically allowed by other provisions of law, further disclosure of the report shall be limited to agents of the state's attorney or the defendant's attorney, any reviewing courts, and the agencies having charge of the defendant's rehabilitation.

(4) *Plea Agreements.*

(A) If the parties request preparation of a presentence report to aid them in reaching a plea agreement, the judge may order the department to prepare such a report prior to the time stated in this rule. If a report is prepared prior to entry of a verdict or plea of guilty or no contest, the report shall be submitted only to the parties and not to the judge.

(B) Notwithstanding subparagraph (b)(4)(A), the judge may use the presentence report to determine whether to accept a plea agreement under Criminal Rule 11.

(5) *Service.* The parties must serve the Department of Corrections with all filings relating to sentencing, and the court must distribute all orders related to sentencing to the department.

(c) **Notice of Aggravating Factors, Extraordinary Circumstances, and Restitution.** Within seven days after service of the presentence report on the parties:

(1) The state shall list the aggravating factors and describe the nature of any extraordinary circumstances on which the state intends to rely at sentencing. This notice shall include a written summary of the evidence that the state will rely on to establish each aggravating factor or extraordinary circumstance.

(2) The state shall give notice if it will seek restitution from the defendant in an amount different from the recommendation in the presentence report. The notice shall specify the amount of restitution sought and shall set forth the facts establishing the basis for this amount, and shall include information concerning the identity of any victims or other persons seeking restitution and, if known, whether any victim

or other person expressly declines restitution, the nature and amount of any damages together with any supporting documentation, and the names of any co-defendants and their case numbers.

(3) The state shall give notice of any evidence on which it intends to rely at sentencing that is not contained in the presentence report. If the state intends to present any witness, the notice shall contain a brief summary of the witness's anticipated testimony. The notice need not include any information to be presented by a victim's oral or written statement.

(4) Notices under this rule shall be served by delivery to parties in the same community as the party making service, and by facsimile transmission ("fax") to parties in outlying communities. When service is made by fax, a paper copy of the notices shall also be mailed to the intended recipient.

(d) **Notice of Mitigating Factors, Extraordinary Circumstances, and Responses to State's Notices.** Within seven days after service of the notices required by paragraph (c):

(1) The defendant shall file a notice responding to each notice filed by the state under paragraphs (a)(2)(A) and (c)(1). The notice shall indicate whether the defendant concedes or disputes each felony conviction, aggravating factor and extraordinary circumstance and, if so, shall include a description of the basis for the opposition.

(2) The defendant shall list the mitigating factors and describe the nature of any extraordinary circumstances on which the defense intends to rely at sentencing. This notice shall include a written summary of the evidence that the defendant will rely on to establish each mitigating factor or extraordinary circumstance.

(3) If the defendant objects to any recommendation for restitution included in the presentence report or in a notice filed by the state under paragraph (c)(2), the defendant shall file a notice disputing the legal basis for restitution, the factual basis for restitution, or the amount sought. The notice shall set out the specific grounds for contesting the restitution or provide information that the victim or other person entitled to the restitution expressly declines restitution.

(4) The defendant shall give notice of any evidence on which the defendant intends to rely at sentencing that is not contained in the presentence report. If the defendant intends to present any witness, the notice shall contain a brief summary of the witness's anticipated testimony. The notice need not include any information to be presented in the defendant's allocution.

(5) The defendant shall give notice of any objection to any information contained in the presentence report or to any other material the judge or the state has identified as a source of information to be relied upon at sentencing. The notice shall state the basis for the defendant's objection. If the defendant objects to information as inaccurate, the notice shall include any information upon which the defendant intends to rely to refute the objected-to information.

(6) Notices under this rule shall be served by delivery to parties in the same community as the party making service, and by fax to parties in outlying communities. When service is made by fax, a paper copy of the notices shall also be mailed to the intended recipient.

(e) **Disputing Mitigating Factors, Extraordinary Circumstances, and Objections to Restitution.** Within seven days after service of the notices required by paragraph (d):

(1) The state shall file a notice responding to each notice filed by the defendant under paragraph (d)(2). The notice shall indicate whether the state concedes or disputes each mitigating factor and extraordinary circumstance, and shall include a description of the basis for the opposition.

(2) The state shall file a notice responding to each notice filed by the defendant under paragraph (d)(3). The notice shall indicate whether the state disagrees with the contention of the defendant concerning restitution and shall include a brief summary of the basis for its position.

(3) Notices under this rule shall be served by delivery to parties in the same community as the party making service, and by fax to parties in outlying communities. When service is made by fax, a paper copy of the notices shall also be mailed to the intended recipient.

(f) **Adjudicating Disputed Factual and Legal Issues.** The court shall give the parties the opportunity to present evidence and argument on the disputed factual and legal issues related to sentencing at the sentencing hearing or at any presentencing hearing or other supplemental evidentiary hearings that the court may order.

(1) The court shall enter findings regarding whether the defendant's sentence is governed by presumptive sentencing, the number of the defendant's prior felonies as defined in AS 12.55.145, and the existence of any other factor that triggers a specific presumptive term.

(2) The court shall enter findings regarding the aggravating factors, mitigating factors, and extraordinary circumstances raised by the parties. However, no finding is necessary if the court affirmatively determines that resolution of a disputed factor or extraordinary circumstance is immaterial to the imposition of a just sentence.

(3) If the sentencing judge believes that the parties have overlooked a prior felony conviction or any other factor triggering a specific presumptive term, or have overlooked an applicable aggravating or mitigating factor or extraordinary circumstance, the judge shall notify the parties of the court's belief. The judge shall inform the parties of the specific facts which the judge believes establish the prior felony or presumptive sentencing factor, and the judge must allow the parties an opportunity to respond to the judge's information.

(4) The court shall resolve any factual disputes related to restitution.

(5) The court shall enter findings regarding any disputed assertion in the presentence report. Any assertion that has not been proved shall be deleted from the report; any assertion that has been proved only in part shall be modified in the report. Alternatively, if the court determines that the disputed assertion is not relevant to its sentencing decision so that resolution of the dispute is not warranted, the court shall delete the assertion from the report without making any finding. After the court has made the necessary deletions and modifications, the court's corrected copy shall be labeled the "approved version" of the presentence report. A copy of the approved version must be delivered to the Department of Corrections within seven days after sentencing.

(g) **When Presentence Investigation Not Required.** Unless the defendant may be sentenced to a presumptive term of imprisonment under AS 12.55.125(e)(1) or (2), or the court otherwise orders, a presentence investigation by the Department of Corrections is not required if the defendant is convicted of the following offenses:

(1) vehicle theft in the first degree in violation of AS 11.46.360;

(2) driving while intoxicated under AS 28.35.030(n); or

(3) refusal to submit to a chemical test under AS 28.35.032(p).

(h) **Restitution Procedures When No Presentence Investigation.**

(1) In cases where the court may order the defendant to pay restitution but no presentence investigation report is submitted, the prosecuting authority must file a notice concerning restitution at least ten days before the sentencing hearing, unless otherwise ordered by the court. The notice shall include information concerning the identity of any victims or other persons seeking restitution and, if known, whether any victim or other person expressly declines restitution, the nature and amount of any damages together with any supporting documentation, a restitution amount recommendation, and the names of any co-defendants and their case numbers.

(2) Unless otherwise ordered by the court, the defendant shall file any objections to the information submitted under paragraph (h)(1), or provide information that the victim or other person expressly declines restitution, at least five days before the sentencing hearing, together with defendant's financial statement on a form designated by the Administrative Director.

(Added by SCO 157 effective February 15, 1973; amended by SCO 218 effective January 15, 1976; by SCO 536 effective October 1, 1982; by SCO 643 effective September 15, 1985; repealed and reenacted by SCO 1136 effective July 15, 1993; amended by SCO 1269 effective July 15, 1997; by SCO 1464 effective March 5, 2002; and by SCO 1554 effective April 15, 2006)

Note to SCO 1269: In 1996, the legislature amended Criminal Rule 32.1 to eliminate presentence investigations for certain defendants convicted of joyriding (§§ 9 & 10 ch. 71 SLA 1996) or felony DWI or refusal (§§ 20 & 21 ch. 143 SLA 1996). Section 15 of this order is adopted for the sole reason that the legislature has mandated the amendments.

Annotations

Cases

Sentence of five years' imprisonment for burglary, two of which were suspended, was not clearly mistaken, even though the defendant was 19 years old and it was his first felony offense. **Zurfluh v. State,** Op. No. 2238, 620 P2d 690 (Alaska 1980).

Where defendant was convicted of assault with a dangerous weapon for striking another person in the face with a beer bottle, sentencing court was not clearly mistaken in imposing a five-year sentence. **Wire v. State,** Op. No. 2, 621 P2d 18 (Alaska 1980).

Thirty-year sentence for third rape conviction and ten-year sentence for assault with a dangerous weapon, the sentences to run consecutively, were not excessive. **Coleman v. State,** Op. No. 2190, 621 P2d 869 (Alaska 1980).

Four month jail term for selling marijuana on school premises was appropriate notwithstanding sentencing guideline which suggested not more than thirty days for the quantity of marijuana involved. **Anderson v. State,** Op. No. 2263, 621 P2d 1345 (Alaska 1981).

Sentence of ten years with five suspended for sale of cocaine was excessive for a youthful first offender. **Kelly v. State,** Op. No. 2268, 622 P2d 432 (Alaska 1981).

A total sentence of 55 years was not excessive for second degree murder and two counts of shooting with intent to kill where defendant had a lengthy criminal record and a propensity for violent crime. **Nielsen v. State,** Op. No. 2279, 623 P2d 304 (Alaska 1981).

Sentence of 35 years for murder was not excessive even though defendant had no prior criminal record. **Bryant v. State,** Op. No. 2280, 623 P2d 310 (Alaska 1981).

Fifteen-year sentence was not inappropriate for shooting with intent to wound. **Kagak v. State,** Op. No. 2311, 624 P2d 818 (Alaska 1981).

Ten-year sentence for manslaughter was not excessive for defendant, an alcoholic, 67 years of age, with extensive criminal record and one prior homicide conviction. **Phillips v. State,** Op. No. 2229, 625 P2d 816 (Alaska 1981).

Where assertions that defendant had violated his probation by possessing alcohol and drugs had already been litigated and resolved in defendant's favor at probation revocation hearing, sentencing judge was required to strike the unproven assertions from pre-sentence report even if judge had concluded that he should or would disregard them when he sentenced defendant for other probation violations. **Cragg v. State,** Op. No. 1589, 957 P2d 1365 (Alaska App. 1998).

Remedy for late-filed notice of aggravating factor was continuance of sentencing hearing rather than prohibiting state from pursuing the proposed aggravator, even if state did not have good excuse for missing filing deadline. **Brown v. State,** Op. No. 1706, 12 P3d 201 (Alaska App. 2000).

Although a presentence report can include information regarding an informal disposition of a juvenile case, defendant can challenge the accuracy of this information under this section. **State v, Short,** Op. No. 1944,96 P3d 526 (Alaska App. 2004).

Rule 32.2. Sentencing Hearing.

(a) **Consideration of Victim's Statement.** If a victim as defined in AS 12.55.185 prepares and submits a written statement, gives sworn testimony or makes an unsworn oral presentation under AS 12.55.023, the court shall take the content of the statement, testimony, or presentation into consideration when preparing those elements of the sentencing report required by AS 12.55.025 that relate to the effect of the offense on the victim, and when considering the need for restitution under AS 12.55.045. The court also may take the content of the statement, testimony, or presentation into consideration for any other appropriate purpose.

(b) **Defendant's Allocution.** Before imposing sentence the court shall afford the defendant an opportunity to make a statement in the defendant's own behalf and to present any information in mitigation of punishment.

(c) **The Sentence.**

(1) At the sentencing hearing, the judge shall state clearly the precise terms of the sentence, the reasons for selecting the particular sentence, and the purposes the sentence is intended to serve.

(2) If the defendant is sentenced to a term of imprisonment for a felony offense, to a term of imprisonment exceeding 90 days for a misdemeanor offense, or to a term of imprisonment for a violation of AS 04, a regulation adopted under AS 04, or an ordinance adopted in conformity with AS 04.21.010, the judge shall identify

(A) the approximate term of imprisonment the defendant must serve if the defendant is eligible for and does not forfeit good conduct deductions under AS 33.20.010; and

(B) if applicable, the approximate minimum term of imprisonment the defendant must serve before becoming eligible for release on discretionary parole.

These approximate terms of imprisonment are not part of the sentence imposed and do not form a basis for review or appeal of the sentence imposed.

(3) The court shall order that the defendant be fingerprinted at the conclusion of the sentencing hearing.

(d) **Transcript of Sentencing Proceeding.** A transcript or electronic recording of any sentencing proceeding at which the defendant is committed to serve a term of incarceration in excess of six months on one or more charges shall be prepared and furnished to the Department of Law, the defendant, the Department of Corrections, the State Board of Parole, if the defendant will be eligible for parole, and to the Alcohol Beverage Control Board if the defendant was convicted of a violation of AS 04, a regulation adopted under AS 04, or an ordinance adopted under AS 04.21.010.

(Added by SCO 1136 effective July 15, 1993; amended by SCO 1288 effective nunc pro tunc to August 13, 1997; by SCO 1464 effective March 5, 2002; and by SCO 1555 effective October 15, 2004)

Annotations

Cases

Where assertions that defendant had violated his probation by possessing alcohol and drugs had already been litigated and resolved in defendant's favor at probation revocation hearing, sentencing judge was required to strike the unproven assertions from pre-sentence report even if judge had concluded that he should or would disregard them when he sentenced defendant for other probation violations. **Cragg v. State,** Op. No. 1589, 957 P2d 1365 (Alaska App. 1998).

Where defendant pleaded no contest to one count of first-degree sexual abuse and the State dismissed the other ten counts of sexually abusing a minor, and defendant took the stand at the sentencing hearing and denied every allegation of sexual misconduct contained in the pre-sentence report, sentencing judge was obligated under this rule to either resolve the disputed allegations or expressly declare that he did not need to resolve them and then order them removed from the pre-sentence report; sentencing judge's act of adding handwritten comments to the pre-sentence report noting that the allegations were contested and that there was evidence supporting defendant's attack on some of the allegations did not comply with this rule. **Evans v. State,** Op. No. 1726, 23 P3d 650 (Alaska App. 2001).

Rule 32.3. Judgments and Orders.

(a) **Effective Dates of Orders and Judgments.** Orders and judgments become effective the date they are entered.

(1) *Oral Orders.* The date of entry of an oral order is the date the order is put on the official electronic record by the judge unless otherwise specified by the judge. At the time the judge announces an oral order, the judge also shall announce on the record whether the order shall be reduced to writing. If the oral order is reduced to writing, the effective date shall be included in the written order.

(2) *Written Orders Not Preceded by Oral Orders.* The date of entry of a written order not preceded by an oral order is the date the written order is signed unless otherwise specified in the order.

(3) *Judgments.* The date of entry of a criminal judgment is the date the judgment is put on the official electronic record by the judge unless otherwise specified by the judge. All judgments shall be reduced to writing and the effective date shall be included in the written judgment.

(b) **Commencement of Time for Appeal, Review and Reconsideration.** The time within which a notice of appeal may be filed and reconsideration or review of orders and judgments may be requested begins running on the date of notice as defined below.

(c) **Date of Notice.**

(1) *Oral Orders.*

(i) As to the parties present when an oral order is announced, the date of notice is the date the judge announces the order on the official electronic record, unless at that time the judge announces that the order will be reduced to writing in which case the date of notice is the date shown in the clerk's certificate of distribution on the written order.

(ii) As to parties not present at the announcement of an oral order the date of notice is the date shown in the clerk's certificate of distribution of notice of the order. If, however, at the time the judge announces the oral order the judge announces that the order will be reduced to writing, the date of notice is the date shown in the clerk's certificate of distribution on the written order.

(2) *Written Orders.* The date of notice of a written order is the date shown in the clerk's certificate of distribution on the written order.

(3) *Judgments.* All judgments must be reduced to writing. The date of notice of a judgment is the date shown in the clerk's certificate of distribution on the written judgment.

(4) *Other Service Requirements.* These notice provisions apply to the notice of orders and judgments under Rule 44(c) and do not affect the service requirements of any other rule of criminal procedure.

(d) **Clerk's Certificate of Distribution.** Every written notice of an oral order and every written order and judgment shall include a clerk's certificate of distribution showing the date copies of the notice, order or judgment were distributed, to whom they were distributed, and the name or initials of the court employee who distributed them.

(Added by SCO 554 effective April 4, 1983; amended by SCO 905 effective January 15, 1989; by SCO 1153 effective July 15, 1994; and by SCO 1464 effective March 5, 2002)

Cross References

CROSS REFERENCE: App. R. 204

Rule 32.4. Sentencing Referrals to Three-Judge Panel.

(a) **Referral to Panel.** If the trial judge finds that extraordinary circumstances exist under AS 12.55.165, the case shall be transferred forthwith to a three-judge sentencing panel of the superior court. All pertinent files, records and transcripts shall be transmitted to the sentencing panel by the clerk of the court within 30 days of the date of the order transferring the case.

(b) **Appointment of Panel.** Three judges of the superior court shall be appointed by the chief justice to be the regular members of the sentencing panel. Two other judges of the superior court shall be appointed by the chief justice as first and second alternate members of the sentencing panel. At least one of the three regular members and one of the two alternate members of the sentencing panel shall reside outside of Anchorage. The term of appointment of the regular and alternate members of the sentencing panel shall be two years, except that the first three regular members appointed shall serve staggered terms of one, two, and three years. The chief justice may appoint additional alternate members of the sentencing panel to serve on a case-by-case basis in the event of the disability or disqualification of more than two judges.

(c) **Repository of Documents.** The chief justice shall appoint one of the three regular members to be administrative head of the sentencing panel and his or her office shall serve as the administrative repository for all papers and documents pertaining to cases submitted to the sentencing panel.

(d) **Challenge of Panel Member.** Both the prosecuting attorney and the defendant may exercise in a timely fashion a challenge for cause, or a peremptory challenge if not previously exercised, to one judge on the sentencing panel in accordance with AS 22.20.022 and Criminal Rule 25(d)(1). In the event that a judge on the sentencing panel is the same judge who made the finding under paragraph (a) of this rule, that judge shall be automatically disqualified.

(e) **Time for Decision.** Within 60 days from the date that the case was transmitted to the sentencing panel, the sentencing panel shall either sentence the defendant or remand the case to the judge who referred the case to the sentencing panel. The sentencing panel shall provide a written statement of its findings and conclusions in support of any order remanding a case to the referring judge.

(f) **Hearing.** If the sentencing panel elects to take testimony or sentence the defendant under AS 12.55.175(b) or (c), both the prosecution and the defendant shall have the right to be present in court during the proceedings. The defendant shall have the right to address the sentencing panel personally before sentence is imposed. The proceedings shall be held in a location best suited to the convenience of the parties and the court as determined by the sentencing panel.

(g) **Further Sentencing Proceedings.** If the sentencing panel imposes sentence on the defendant, proceedings relating to sentence modification under Criminal Rule 35(a) shall be assigned to the sentencing panel sitting at the time such action is ready for decision. All other post-sentencing proceedings shall be assigned to the judge who referred the matter to the sentencing panel for consideration. The referring judge may impose any sentence which the sentencing panel would be empowered to impose, except that the referring judge may not reduce a sentence imposed by the sentencing panel.

(h) **Right to Bail.** The right to bail of a convicted defendant is neither conferred nor enlarged by this rule.

(Added by SCO 1136 effective July 15, 1993)

Rule 32.5. Appeal From Conviction or Sentence—Notification of Right to Appeal.

A person convicted of a crime after trial shall be advised by the judge or magistrate:

(a) that the person has the right to appeal from the judgment of conviction within 30 days (or 15 days in appeals from the district court made under Appellate Rule 217) from the date shown in the clerk's certificate of distribution on the judgment appealed from by filing a notice of appeal with the clerk of the appellate courts; and

(b) that if the defendant wants counsel and is unable to pay for the services of an attorney, the court will appoint an attorney to represent the defendant on the appeal.

In addition, at the time of imposition of any sentence of imprisonment, the judge or magistrate shall advise the defendant as required by Appellate Rule 215(b).

(Added by SCO 1136 effective July 15, 1993; amended by SCO 1184 effective July 15, 1995; and by SCO 1226 effective January 22, 1996)

Rule 32.6. Judgment for Restitution

(a) **Definition.** When a sentence includes a requirement that the defendant pay restitution, the judge shall either enter a separate judgment for restitution or shall include the order of restitution as a separate section of the criminal judgment. For the purpose of these rules, either of these constitutes a "judgment for restitution."

(b) **Content.** The judgment for restitution must:

(1) Identify each victim or other person entitled to restitution and the amount of restitution owed to each.

(2) State the date restitution is due or, if the court schedules installment payments, the amount and due date of each payment. If no due date is stated, the restitution amount is due immediately.

(3) State whether payment must be made through the clerk of court or the Collections Unit of the Department of Law. Ordinarily, the restitution payment will be made through the Collections Unit of the Department of Law unless (A) the victim or other person elects to pursue collection without the assistance of the Collections Unit; (B) the order requires restitution to be made in a form other than payment of a specific dollar amount; or (C) the case is being prosecuted by a municipality. When payment is to be made through the Collections Unit, the judgment must state that the court will also accept payments and prepayments of restitution.

(4) Identify by name and case number any defendants who are jointly and severally liable for the restitution owed to each victim or other person.

(5) State whether post-judgment interest is owed on the judgment and, if so, when it begins to accrue.

(c) **Entering the Judgment for Restitution.**

(1) *At Sentencing.* If the amount of restitution and the names of the victims are known at the time of sentencing, the court shall enter the judgment of restitution at the time of sentencing.

(2) *After Sentencing.* If the amount of restitution and the names of the victims or other persons seeking restitution are not known at the time of sentencing, the prosecutor shall file and serve within 90 days after sentencing a proposed judgment for restitution on a form designated by the Administrative Director, and a notice that includes information concerning the identity of any victims or other persons seeking restitution, whether any victim or other person expressly declines restitution, the nature and amount of any damages together with any supporting documentation, a restitution amount recommendation, and the names of any co-defendants and their case numbers. Within 30 days after receipt of the proposed judgment for restitution, the defense shall file any objection to the proposed judgment, a statement of grounds for the objection, and a financial statement on a form designated by the Administrative Director under AS 12.55.045(j). If the defendant does not file an objection, the court may enter the judgment for restitution without further proceedings. If the defendant files an objection and either party requests a hearing, the court shall schedule a hearing.

(3) *Municipal Cases.* In addition to the requirements of (c)(1) and (2) above, a municipal prosecutor shall file an *ex parte* victim information statement on a form provided by the Administrative Director, which includes information concerning the identity and addresses of the victims. The victim information statement shall be filed within 15 days after entry of the restitution judgment under (c)(1) above or at the time the municipal prosecutor submits a proposed judgment to the court under (c)(2) above.

(d) **Hearing Regarding Payment Schedule.** A defendant who is unable to pay restitution because of financial circumstances may request a hearing to ask the court to modify the restitution payment schedule. If the court holds a hearing and the defendant proves by a preponderance of the evidence that the defendant is unable through good faith efforts to satisfy the payment schedule in the judgment for restitution, the court may modify the payment schedule, but may not reduce the amount of restitution.

(e) **Execution.** Civil execution to enforce the judgment may issue if restitution is ordered to be paid by a specified date and defendant fails to make full payment by that date. If restitution is ordered to be paid in specified installments and defendant fails to make one or more installment payments, civil execution to collect the entire remaining balance may issue. The automatic stays on enforcement provided in Civil Rule 62(a) and District Court Civil Rule 24(a) do not apply to the enforcement of restitution judgments.

(f) **Transfer of State Restitution Judgments and Payments to the Collections Unit of the Department of Law.**

(1) Upon issuance of a judgment for restitution in cases prosecuted by the state, the court will send, either on paper or electronically, a copy of the judgment to the Collections Unit of the Department of Law. The court will also send the name, address, birth date, and social security number of each victim or other person entitled to restitution and each defendant, to the extent the court has the information.

(2) If payment for restitution is tendered to the court, the court shall accept the tendered payment. If the victim or other person entitled to restitution has elected to proceed through the Collections Unit, the court shall forward the payment to the Collections Unit within five days after clearance of the payment tendered to the court.

(g) **Priority of Payments.** Unless the court finds good cause to order a different priority, payments received from or on behalf of a defendant will be allocated as follows:

(1) If a defendant makes a voluntary payment and designates how or to what criminal or civil judgments the payment should be applied, the payment will be applied as designated by the defendant.

(2) Payments received as the result of execution on the

defendant's permanent fund dividend will be applied to judgments according to the priorities stated in AS 43.23.065.

(3) If a defendant makes a voluntary payment but does not designate how the payment is to be applied or if a payment is received as a result of execution by the Collections Unit of the Department of Law or a comparable unit of a municipality, the payment will be applied using the following rules:

(A) Judgments for restitution will be paid in full before any amounts collected from the defendant will be applied to criminal or civil judgments owed to the state or a municipality.

(B) If restitution is owed to the state or a municipality, amounts collected from the defendant will be applied first to judgments for restitution owed to victims other than the state or a municipality.

(C) When restitution is ordered to be paid by a defendant to victims in the same criminal case, amounts collected from the defendant will be allocated among the victims based on the percentage of the amount of restitution owed to each victim to the total amount of restitution owed by the defendant to all of the victims; except that if a payment is less than $100, the payment may be paid to a single victim if such payments are paid to all victims on an alternating basis.

(D) When restitution is ordered to be paid by a defendant to victims in different criminal cases, amounts collected from the defendant will be applied to the judgment that is first in time.

(4) If a payment is received as a result of execution by a victim, the payment will be applied to the judgment for restitution owed to that victim.

(h) **Financial Statement.**

(1) If restitution has been ordered and has not been paid, and no financial statement has been required under Rule 32.1(a)(2)(B) or Rule 32.6(c)(2), the court shall order the defendant to complete and submit such statement within 30 days of the restitution judgment. The statement shall be on a form designated by the administrative director and shall be submitted to the Collections Unit of the Department of Law in state cases or the prosecuting authority in municipal cases.

(2) If the defendant fails to submit a completed financial statement as ordered, the probation officer or prosecuting authority (including the Collections Unit of the Department of Law) may notify the court by affidavit. Upon receipt of an affidavit under this paragraph, the court shall schedule a hearing for the defendant to show cause why the defendant should not be held in contempt for failure to comply with the order to submit the financial statement.

(3) At any time after sentencing, the probation officer or prosecuting authority (including the Collections Unit of the Department of Law) may request that the defendant be ordered to provide a financial statement pursuant to AS 12.55.045(k).

(i) **Victim Election.** If, after the judgment for restitution has been transferred to the Collections Unit of the Department of Law, the victim elects to pursue collections without the assistance of the Collections Unit, the Collections Unit shall notify the court of the victim's election. The Collections Unit shall include with the notice copies of

(1) the judgment for restitution;

(2) the signed election form received from the victim;

(3) a statement of all payments received from the defendant and applied to the restitution judgment; and

(4) any relevant victim and defendant identifying information needed by the court system to properly identify and distribute restitution payments.

(j) **Suspended Imposition of Sentence.** The judgment for restitution remains civilly enforceable after the expiration of the period of probation or the set-aside of conviction in a case where imposition of sentence is suspended.

(Adopted by SCO 1464 effective March 5, 2002; amended by SCO 1482 effective October 15, 2002; and by SCO 1554 effective April 15, 2006)

Rule 33. New Trial.

(a) **Grounds.** The court may grant a new trial to a defendant if required in the interest of justice.

(b) **Subsequent Proceedings.** If trial was by the court without a jury, the court may vacate the judgment if entered, take additional testimony and enter a new judgment.

(c) **Time for Motion.** A motion for a new trial based on the ground of newly discovered evidence may be made only before or within 180 days after final judgment, but if an appeal is pending the court may grant the motion only on remand of the case. A motion for a new trial based on any other grounds shall be made within 5 days after verdict or finding of guilt, or within such further time as the court may fix during the 5-day period.

(Adopted by SCO 4 October 4, 1959; amended by SCO 554 effective April 4, 1983; and SCO 1242 effective July 15, 1996)

Note to SCO 1242: Criminal Rule 33 was amended by ch. 79 § 28 SLA 1995. Section 3 of this order is adopted for the sole reason that the legislature has mandated the amendment.

Annotations

Cases

Where a case has been appealed, a trial court cannot grant a motion for new trial based on newly discovered evidence without first applying for and obtaining a remand of the case from the supreme court to the trial court for the stated purpose of granting a new trial. **State v. Salinas,** Op. No. 39, 362 P2d 298 (Alaska 1961).

A motion for new trial based on the grounds of newly discovered evidence must meet the following requirements: (1) It must appear from the motion that the evidence relied on is, in fact, newly discovered, i.e., discovered after the trial; (2) the motion must allege facts from which the court may infer diligence on the part of the movant; (3) the evidence relied on must not be merely cumulative or impeaching; (4) must be material to the issues involved; and (5) must be such as, on a new trial, would probably produce an acquittal. **Rank v. State,** Op. No. 144, 382 P2d 760 (Alaska 1963).

Where newly discovered evidence was not such as would probably produce an acquittal on a new trial, and motion failed to satisfy the requirement that there be a showing of diligence in attempting to locate a witness before or at the time of trial, the trial judge properly exercised his discretion in denying a motion for new trial based on newly discovered evidence. **Rank v. State,** Op. No. 144, 382 P2d 760 (Alaska 1963).

Where in a criminal case erroneous and prejudicial admission of hearsay evidence had resulted in reversal and in retrial of appellant, it was reversible error for the trial court at his retrial to deny a motion for a new trial which was supported by six affidavits of jurors showing that prejudicial evidence received in the first trial was actually before the jury at the retrial by virtue of the jury's knowledge of the contents of a local newspaper article printed at the last day of the retrial quoting the statement erroneously received at the first trial. **Watson v. State,** Op. No. 335, 413 P2d 22 (Alaska 1966).

As one of the exceptions to the general rule prohibiting jurors to impeach their verdicts, the verdict must not be allowed to stand where a party was deprived of a fair trial and since affidavit of jurors that they were exposed to a newspaper article containing information previously held so prejudicial as to require a new trial established that the appellant was deprived of such a fair trial, the trial court erred in denying motion for new trial. **Watson v. State,** Op. No. 335, 413 P2d 22 (Alaska 1966).

Denial of motion for new trial sustained on appeal where movant had contended that his right of cross-examination had been unduly curtailed but failed to give the trial judge the benefit of any authority or citation from the record in support of his contention and where trial judge exercised sound discretion in finding that the verdict was not against the weight of the evidence. **Pedersen v. State,** Op. No. 369, 420 P2d 327 (Alaska 1966).

Denial of motion for new trial grounded on one juror's affidavit asserting exhaustion and mental intimidation of the affiant and alleging that jurors attempted to inquire beyond evidence as to certain aspects of the case, was no abuse of discretion in the absence of a clear showing of serious violations of the juror's duties and of a concomitant deprivation of a fair trial. **Gafford v. State,** Op. No. 478, 440 P2d 405 (Alaska 1968).

Where the defendant does not move for an evidentiary hearing or base his motion for a new trial on misconduct by the bailiff, the issue of whether the trial court erred in failing to grant him an evidentiary hearing concerning an allegedly improper statement made by the bailiff to the jury during the course of their deliberations is not properly before the supreme court. The defendant is not precluded from raising the issue in a future proceeding on a motion for a new trial or through other means seeking post-conviction relief. **Howard v. State,** Op. No. 754, 491 P2d 154 (Alaska 1971).

Where prosecutrix and principal corroborating witness who had recanted testimony in incest prosecution did not testify at hearing on new trial motion on grounds of self-incrimination, trial court properly concluded that no evidence was produced which would probably produce an acquittal at a new trial. **Dunbar v. State,** Op. No. 1329, 555 P2d 548 (Alaska 1976).

Where prejudicial effect of prosecutor's remark "I think that's true, that's exactly what happened" was corrected by his subsequent explanation, denial of motion for new trial was not error. **Amidon v. State,** Op. No. 1434, 565 P2d 1248 (Alaska 1977).

A defense motion for new trial predicated on allegedly newly discovered evidence, which consisted of the reports of a polygraph expert and a voice stress analysis expert, was properly denied on ground that it was not newly discovered evidence under this rule. **Adkinson v. State,** Op. No. 2090, 611 P2d 528 (Alaska 1980).

Motions under this rule are within the sound discretion of the trial court and its decision will not be disturbed unless abuse of discretion is shown. **Nygren v. State,** Op. No. 2164, 616 P2d 20 (Alaska 1980).

Where there was no evidence of bad faith in the investigation or purposeful hindrance of defendant's own ability to pursue investigative leads, failure of the police to investigate other suspects did not require new trial. **Dorman v. State,** Op. No. 2272, 622 P2d 448 (Alaska 1981).

Testimony of witness subsequent to a trial could not be basis for new trial on the ground of newly discovered evidence where defense counsel was aware of the witness and could have subpoenaed his testimony prior to the end of the trial. **Dorman v. State,** Op. No. 2272, 622 P2d 448 (Alaska 1981).

The time limits of the rule governing new trial motions are not jurisdictional. **Davidson v. State,** Op. No. 78, 642 P2d 1383 (Alaska App. 1982).

Claims of ineffective assistance of counsel will not be entertained on appeal unless defendant has first moved for a new trial or sought post-conviction relief, supporting the claim with affidavits alleging facts which would establish a basis for relief; to the extent that the criminal rule on motions for new trials places unreasonable time limitations on the presentation of this issue, the trial court should exercise its discretion to provide reasonable time. **Barry v. State,** Op. No. 334, 675 P2d 1292 (Alaska App. 1984).

Defendant's new evidence did not require a new trial since it was cumulative of information which he could have presented at trial and since there was no reasonable possibility that the new evidence would produce an acquittal in a new trial. **Charles v. State,** Op. No. 963, 780 P2d 377 (Alaska App. 1989).

Even though jury's verdicts may not be logically inconsistent, trial judge may grant new trial if verdicts demonstrate such skewed or inconsistent view of evidence as to indicate that jury failed to understand evidence, failed to understand court's instructions, or simply returned compromise verdict when case proved too difficult. **State v. Walker,** Op. No. 1384, 887 P2d 971 (Alaska App. 1994).

Before trial judge negates jury's decision by ordering new trial, jury's verdicts must clearly manifest jury's failure to engage in valid fact-finding process and, in cases where allegation of flawed jury deliberations is premised on inconsistency of jury's verdicts, it must be clear that flaw affected jury's decision to convict rather than merely jury's concurrent decision to acquit. **State v. Walker,** Op. No. 1384, 887 P2d 971 (Alaska App. 1994).

A motion for a new trial based on newly discovered evidence must meet the following requirements: (1) It must appear from the motion that the evidence relied on is, in fact, newly discovered, i.e., discovered after the trial; (2) the motion must allege facts from which the court may infer diligence on the part of the defendant; (3) the evidence relied on must not be merely cumulative or impeaching; (4) the evidence must be material to the issues involved; and (5) the evidence must be such as, on a new trial, would probably produce an acquittal. **Lampley v. Municipality of Anchorage**, Op. No. 8994, 159 P.3d 515 (Alaska 2007).

Defendant could not move for a new trial based on newly discovered evidence where defendant asserted that his attorney-client communications were monitored by corrections officers and the trial record showed that the trial court granted defendant's request for an order directing jail personnel to stop monitoring his attorney-client conversations instead of asking the court to declare a mistrial. **Lampley v. Municipality of Anchorage**, Op. No. 8994, 159 P.3d 515 (Alaska 2007).

Rule 34. Arrest of Judgment.

(a) **Grounds.** A motion in arrest of judgment following a plea or verdict of guilty may be founded on one or more of the following grounds, and not otherwise:

(1) That the grand jury by which the indictment was found had no legal authority to inquire into the crime charged, or that the court was without jurisdiction of the offense charged.

(2) That the facts stated in the indictment or information do not constitute a crime.

(b) **Time for Making Motion.** The motion shall be made within 5 days after verdict or finding of guilt, or within such further time as the court may fix during the 5-day period.

(c) **Effect of Order Arresting Judgment.** The effect of allowing a motion in arrest of judgment is to place the defendant in the same situation the defendant was in before the indictment was found.

(d) **Recommitting Defendant or Admission to Bail.** If from the evidence given on the trial, there is reasonable ground to believe the defendant guilty, and a new indictment or information can be framed upon which the defendant may be convicted, the court shall order the defendant to be recommitted to custody or admitted to bail, to answer the new indictment or information, if one be found or filed. If the evidence shows the defendant to be guilty of another crime than that charged in the indictment or information, the defendant must in like manner be committed or held thereon, and in neither case is the verdict a bar to another action for the same crime.

(e) **Discharge of Defendant.** If no evidence appears sufficient to charge the defendant with any crime, the defendant must, if in custody, be discharged, or, if the defendant has given bail or deposited money in lieu thereof, the bail is exonerated or the money must be refunded to the defendant, and in such case the arrest of judgment operates as an acquittal of the charge upon which the indictment or information was founded.

(Adopted by SCO 4 October 4, 1959; amended by SCO 49 effective January 1, 1963; and by SCO 1153 effective July 15, 1994)

Annotations

Cases

A motion in arrest of judgment raises only objections which appear on the face of the record. **State v. Adkerson,** Op. No. 294, 403 P2d 673 (Alaska 1965).

A motion to dismiss an indictment on the grounds that it did not charge an offense which was filed after the verdict was returned, was treated as a motion in arrest of judgment. **State v. Adkerson,** Op. No. 294, 403 P2d 673 (Alaska 1965).

Trial court was correct in granting motions in arrest of judgment where appellees had been charged in the indictment and were found guilty of the offenses of procuring a female for an immoral purpose "to appear in a lewd show" and of transporting a female for an immoral purpose "to appear in a lewd show" and an analysis of AS 11.40.330 and of AS 11.40. 350 impelled the conclusion that a "lewd show" was not within the prohibitions of this statute. **State v. Adkerson,** Op. No. 294, 403 P2d 673 (Alaska 1965).

Rule 35. Reduction, Correction or Suspension of Sentence.

(a) **Correction of Sentence.** The court may correct an illegal sentence at any time.

(b) **Modification or Reduction of Sentence.** The court

(1) may modify or reduce a sentence within 180 days of the distribution of the written judgment upon a motion made in the original criminal case;

(2) may not entertain a second or successive motion for similar relief brought under this paragraph on behalf of the same defendant;

(3) may not reduce or modify a sentence so as to impose a term of imprisonment that is less than the minimum required by law;

(4) may not reduce a sentence imposed in accordance with a plea agreement between the defendant and the prosecuting attorney that provided for imposition of a specific sentence or a sentence equal to or less than a specified maximum; and

(5) may not reduce a sentence below the minimum specified in a plea agreement between the defendant and the prosecuting attorney.

(c) **Victim's Rights.** The victim may comment on motions made under this rule as follows:

(1) When an individual convicted of a crime against a person or arson in the first degree files a motion to modify or reduce a sentence, the court shall, if feasible, send a copy of the motion to the Department of Corrections sufficiently in advance of any scheduled hearing or briefing deadline to enable the department to notify the victim, as directed by AS 12.55.088(e).

(2) The court shall provide copies of the victim's comments to the prosecuting attorney and to the person filing the motion to reduce or modify a sentence, or the person's attorney.

(3) The court shall consider the comments of the victim when relevant, and any response offered by the prosecuting attorney or the person filing the motion, in deciding whether to reduce or modify a sentence.

(4) If more than one person who qualifies as a victim under paragraph (d)(2) of this rule requests the opportunity to exercise rights under this paragraph, the court shall allow the person designated under AS 12.55.172 to exercise those rights, or if a person has not been designated under AS 12.55.172, the court shall designate one person for purposes of exercising rights under this paragraph.

(d) **Definitions.** In this rule,

(1) "crime against a person" has the meaning given in AS 33.30.901; and

(2) "victim" has the meaning given in AS 12.55.185.

(e) **Appointed Counsel.** An indigent defendant not already represented by counsel may request the court to appoint counsel for purposes of filing a motion under this rule. If the defendant is represented by appointed counsel, counsel may file with the court and serve on the prosecuting attorney a certificate that counsel

(1) does not have a conflict of interest;

(2) has completed a review of the facts and law related to sentence;

(3) has consulted with the applicant and, if appropriate, with trial and appellate counsel; and

(4) has determined that a motion under this subsection would not warrant relief by the court.

(f) **Withdrawal of Appointed Counsel and Dismissal.** If appointed counsel has filed a certificate under (e) of this rule, and it appears to the court that the applicant is not entitled to relief, the court shall indicate its intention to permit counsel to withdraw and, if appropriate, to dismiss the motion. The applicant and the prosecuting attorney shall be given an opportunity to reply to the proposed withdrawal or dismissal. If the applicant files a response and the court finds that a motion under this rule would not warrant relief, the court shall permit counsel to withdraw and, if appropriate, dismiss the motion. If the court finds that a motion under this rule may warrant relief, the court may direct that the proceedings continue or take other appropriate action.

(g) **Relaxing the Time Period for Request.** A court may not relax by more than 10 days the time period in which a request to modify or reduce a sentence under (b) of this rule must be filed.

(Adopted by SCO 4 October 4, 1959; amended by SCO 30 effective February 1, 1961; amended by SCO 49 effective January 1, 1963; by SCO 98 effective September 16, 1968; by SCO 319 effective August 16, 1978; by SCO 426 effective August 1, 1980; by SCO 477 effective August 17, 1981; by SCO 554 effective April 4, 1983; and by SCO 644 effective September 15, 1985; by SCO 822 effective August 1, 1987; by SCO 974 effective January 15, 1990; SCO 979 effective August 28, 1989; by SCO 1240 effective July 15, 1996; and by SCO 1341, effective September 10, 1998)

Note: Paragraphs (c) and (d) of Criminal Rule 35 were added by ch. 59, § 28, SLA 1989.

Note: Ch. 79 § 25 SLA 1992, effective September 14, 1992, has the effect of amending Criminal Rule 35(b)(2). This legislation added AS 12.55.125(j) which allows a defendant sentenced to a mandatory 99-year term of imprisonment under AS 12.55.125(a) to apply for a modification or reduction of sentence after serving one-half of the mandatory term without consideration of good time earned under AS 33.20.010.

Note to SCO 1240: Ch. 79 §§ 29-31 SLA 1995, effective July 1, 1995, repealed and reenacted paragraphs (a) and (b) of Criminal Rule 35 and added paragraphs (e) and (f). Sections 1, 2, and 5 of this supreme court order are adopted for the sole reason that the legislature has mandated the amendments.

Sec. 42 of ch. 79 SLA 1995 includes the following statement regarding the applicability of the changes to Criminal Rule 35: "Notwithstanding Rule 35, Alaska Rules of Criminal Procedure, as amended in secs. 29–31 of this Act, the trial court, under Rule 35(b), as amended by the Act, may reduce the sentence of a defendant sentenced before the effective date of this section if the defendant took an appeal and the sentence reduction occurs within 120 days of the day that jurisdiction is returned to the trial court under Rule 507(b), Alaska Rules of Appellate Procedure, unless the defendant petitions the United States Supreme Court for certiori, in which case the 120 days commences on the day that the Supreme Court denies relief."

Ch. 7 § 6 SLA 1996, effective June 27, 1996, has the effect of amending Criminal Rule 35(b) as revised by the legislature in 1995. Ch. 7 § 6 SLA 1996 amends AS 12.55.125(j) to allow a defendant sentenced to a mandatory 99-year term of imprisonment under AS 12.55.125(a) to apply once for a modification or reduction of sentence after serving one-half of the mandatory term without consideration of good time earned under AS 33.20.010. It also amends AS 12.55.125(j) to allow a defendant sentenced to a definite term of imprisonment under AS 12.55.125(l) to apply once for a modification or reduction of sentence after serving the greater of one-half the definite term or 30 years.

Note to SCO 1341: Paragraph (g) of Criminal Rule 35 was added by § 12 ch. 95 SLA 1998. Section 5 of this order is adopted for the sole reason that the legislature has mandated the amendment.

Note: Ch. 64 SLA 2001, adds a new section to the uncodified laws of the State of Alaska concerning therapeutic courts for alcohol- and drug-addicted offenders. According to §4 of the Act, §1(h) of the Act has the effect of amending Criminal Rule 35 by allowing a court to consider and reduce a criminal sentence outside of the time periods currently provided in the rule.

Note: Chapter 56 SLA 2006 (HB 441) enacted changes relating to criminal sentencing and court-ordered treatment programs for certain offenses. According to section 8 of the Act, AS 28.35.028(b), added by section 3 of the Act, has the effect of amending Criminal Rule 35 by allowing a court to consider and reduce a criminal sentence outside of the time periods currently provided by that rule.

Cross References

(b) **CROSS REFERENCE:** AS 12.75.010

(c) **CROSS REFERENCE:** AS 12.55.080; AS 12.55.090

Annotations

Cases

I. In General.

Criminal Rule 53, on relaxation of rules applies to this rule. **Thomas v. State,** Op. No. 1445, 566 P2d 630 (Alaska 1977).

Criminal Rule 35(a) is not the appropriate procedural vehicle to seek relief as to conditions within custodial institutions or the civil rights of inmates.

Rust v. State, Op. No. 1668, 584 P2d 38 (Alaska 1978).

Where defendant received the presentence report on the same day sentence was pronounced, it was error for the court, which apparently relied on its power to alter or reduce a sentence within 120 days of its pronouncement, to deny defendant's request for a continuance to study the report, but the error was harmless. **Page v. State,** Op. No. 205, 657 P2d 850 (Alaska App. 1983).

Prisoner's claims that he was not receiving constitutionally mandated rehabilitation treatment from the Division of Corrections was not appropriate for consideration in a proceeding brought pursuant to this rule. **Mitchell v. State,** Op. No. 894, 767 P2d 203 (Alaska App. 1988).

Trial court abused its discretion in using this rule, which allows sentencing courts to modify or reduce sentence within 180 days of distribution of written judgment, to grant furlough to prisoner; furloughs are within authority of Department of Corrections, not the courts. **State v. Couch,** Op. No. 1654, 991 P2d 1286 (Alaska App. 1999).

Sentencing panel's decision denying defendant's request to grant him a limited license so he could drive for work-related purposes was vacated; decision to grant a limited license would not have constituted a modification of defendant's sentence for manslaughter. **Hill v. State,** Op. No. 1766, 32 P3d 10 (Alaska App. 2001).

A motion for a new trial based on newly discovered evidence must meet the following requirements: (1) It must appear from the motion that the evidence relied on is, in fact, newly discovered, i.e., discovered after the trial; (2) the motion must allege facts from which the court may infer diligence on the part of the defendant; (3) the evidence relied on must not be merely cumulative or impeaching; (4) the evidence must be material to the issues involved; and (5) the evidence must be such as, on a new trial, would probably produce an acquittal. **Lampley v. Municipality of Anchorage**, Op. No. 8994, 159 P.3d 515 (Alaska 2007).

Defendant could not move for a new trial based on newly discovered evidence where defendant asserted that his attorney-client communications were monitored by corrections officers and the trial record showed that the trial court granted defendant's request for an order directing jail personnel to stop monitoring his attorney-client conversations instead of asking the court to declare a mistrial. **Lampley v. Municipality of Anchorage**, Op. No. 8994, 159 P.3d 515 (Alaska 2007).

The purpose of procedural rules like Rule 35(a) is to confer continuing jurisdiction on a sentencing court to correct an illegal sentence, even if the claimed error was not raised at the time of sentencing or in the defendant's direct appeal. But these procedural rules are not intended to allow defendants to litigate claims of sentence illegality on a clean slate, as if no procedural default had occurred previously. **Lockuk v. State**, Op. No. 9534, 153 P.3d 1012 (Alaska App. 2007).

II. Correction of Illegal Sentence.

Where a defendant convicted of contempt had already served half of an illegal jail sentence, the court would not remand the case for imposition of a fine which was the maximum punishment the court had power to impose. **Jefferson v. City of Anchorage,** Op. No. 101, 374 P2d 241 (Alaska 1962).

A sentence is illegal within the meaning of Criminal Rule 35(a) if it is rendered in excess of an applicable statute. **Shagloak v. State,** Op. No. 1688, 582 P2d 1034 (Alaska 1978).

The term "illegal sentence" in this rule applies only to sentences which the judgment of conviction did not authorize, not to sentences illegally imposed; the rule does not permit consideration of matters outside the sentencing record, nor does it authorize a collateral attack on the proceedings which resulted in the sentence imposed. **Bishop v. Municipality of Anchorage,** Op. No. 392, 685 P2d 103 (Alaska App. 1984).

Defendant's inability to obtain a parole hearing subsequent to being sentenced for violation of a municipal ordinance did not render his original sentence "illegal" within the meaning of this rule. **Bishop v. Municipality of Anchorage,** Op. No. 392, 685 P2d 103 (Alaska App. 1984).

District court did not have jurisdiction over defendant's application for post conviction relief which alleged that his sentence for violation of municipal ordinance on drunk driving was either illegal or unconstitutional due to parole board's interpretation of statute rendering defendant ineligible for parole. **Bishop v. Municipality of Anchorage,** Op. No. 392, 685 P2d 103 (Alaska App. 1984).

State's challenge to trial court's refusal to correct an illegal sentence was not within the appellate jurisdiction of the Court of Appeals, but the court, due to the importance of the issue, treated the appeal as a petition for review and granted the petition. **State v. Price,** Op. No. 595, 715 P2d 1183 (Alaska App. 1986).

Trial court lacked jurisdiction to impose a fine in excess of $300 for a strict liability violation of fishing regulations, thus imposition of a $1000 fine for such violation was illegal, and could be attached as illegal under this rule regardless of whether the point could have been raised on an earlier direct appeal. **Stein v. State,** Op. No. 836, 758 P2d 132 (Alaska App. 1988).

An illegal sentence is one that contravenes an applicable statute. **Dunham v. City and Borough of Juneau,** Op. No. 1033, 790 P2d 239 (Alaska App. 1990).

Where defendant was sentenced as a first DWI offender but was in fact a second DWI offender, the first sentence was illegal to the extent it fell short of the mandatory minimum sentence for a second DWI offender and was therefore subject to correction under this rule, but the original sentence could not be increased beyond the mandatory minimum for second offenders. **Dunham v. City and Borough of Juneau,** Op. No. 1033, 790 P2d 239 (Alaska App. 1990).

Defendant's motion to correct an illegal sentence, requesting return of a fine illegally imposed by the State, was not barred by sovereign immunity, because it was not an action against the State. **State v. Danielson,** Op. No. 1128, 809 P2d 937 (Alaska App. 1991).

District court had jurisdiction to hear defendant's motion to correct an illegal sentence; the authority to correct the illegality of the sentence included the authority to put the parties in the position they would have been in had a legal sentence been imposed, thus court's order requiring the State to refund excess fine imposed against defendant was valid. **State v. Danielson,** Op. No. 1128, 809 P2d 937 (Alaska App. 1991).

Where defendant's conviction was valid but the fine imposed by the court was greater than could legally be imposed, defendant was entitled to restitution of the excess fine paid. **State v. Stein,** Op. No. 1110, 806 P2d 346 (Alaska App. 1991).

Appellate court found that, to constitute an illegal sentence under subsection (a), the sentence itself had to be illegal, not the just manner in which it was imposed. **Tyler v. State,** Op. No. 2039, 133 P.3d 686 (Alaska App. 2006).

When a defendant raises a Blakely claim for the first time in a motion to correct an illegal sentence under Criminal Rule 35(a), the defendant must demonstrate plain error. **Lockuk v. State,** Op. No. 9534, 153 P.3d 1012 (Alaska App. 2007).

A motion for correction of an illegal sentence under subsection (a) of this rule is treated as part of the defendant's original criminal case, unlike a petition for post-conviction relief, which is litigated as a separate civil case. **Lockuk v. State**, Op. No. 9534, 153 P.3d 1012 (Alaska App. 2007).

III. Reduction or Vacation of Sentence. A. In General.

The rule contemplates that the sentencing court should be initially called upon to review the sentence. **State v. Pete,** Op. No. 372, 420 P2d 338 (Alaska 1966).

Where a sentence has been imposed, the judge cannot in connection with a motion for reduction of the sentence amend the judgment by providing that the board of parole should not consider parole until the defendant has served a certain number of years. **Faulkner v. State,** Op. No. 506, 445 P2d 815 (Alaska 1968).

When a sentence is reduced under Criminal Rule 35 (a), it amounts to the imposition of a new sentence which the state may appeal. **State v. Trunnel,** Op. No. 1260, 549 P2d 550 (Alaska 1976).

Power to reduce a sentence is an inherent judicial power of sentencing court. **Thomas v. State,** Op. No. 1445, 566 P2d 630 (Alaska 1977).

Court rule authorizing reduction of sentences is not unconstitutional. **Thomas v. State,** Op. No. 1445, 566 P2d 630 (Alaska 1977).

Denial of motion to reduce sentence is not the imposition of a sentence for the purposes of Criminal Rule 2 1(b). **Davis v. State,** Op. No. 1453, 566 P2d 640 (Alaska 1977).

In considering whether to reduce a sentence, trial court may consider whether and to what extent defendant has rehabilitated himself since original sentence was imposed. **Davis v. State,** Op. No. 1453, 566 P2d 640 (Alaska 1977).

Whether to grant a reduction of sentence on the ground of rehabilitation is in the sound discretion of the trial court. **Davis v. State,** Op. No. 1453, 566 P2d 640 (Alaska 1977).

Given the number and severity of the crimes for which defendant was sentenced, it was not an abuse of discretion for court to deny his motion for a reduction of sentence, notwithstanding that his stated reason for the motion was to secure the continuation of psychological counseling rather than to reduce the period of incarceration. **Brandon v. State,** Op. No. 1684, 581 P2d 1116 (Alaska 1978).

A Rule 35(a) motion for reduction of sentence presupposes a valid sentence and conviction and is essentially a plea for leniency. **Thomas v. State,** Op. No. 1445, 566 P2d 630 (Alaska 1977).

Where the defendant appeared as the sole witness in his own behalf at a hearing on his initial motion to reduce sentence, and where documents supporting a motion to reconsider emphasized the differences between defendant's inability to articulate his attitudes in a courtroom setting as contrasted to his ability to communicate with his counsel in private, it was not abuse of discretion for the court to deny the motion. **Cossey v. State,** Op. No. 2078, 611 P2d 68 (Alaska 1980).

This rule authorizes the trial court to modify a sentence without regard to the date of its original imposition. **Fermoyle v. State,** Op. No. 64, 638 P2d 1320 (Alaska App. 1982).

Appellant's motion for modification of sentence should have been considered on the merits notwithstanding that the motion was filed prior to August 1, 1980, the effective date of the relevant revision to this rule. **Fermoyle v. State,** Op. No. 64, 638 P2d 1320 (Alaska App. 1982).

It was not error to impose sentence without a psychological or psychiatric evaluation where defendant did not request such evaluation prior to sentencing and where there was no showing of how it would have benefited him. **Spencer v. State,** Op. No. 80, 642 P2d 1371 (Alaska App. 1982).

Defendant's request that he be given credit for time spent in jail for parole violation arising out of same conduct for which he was convicted of crime in question should have been considered a request for discretionary relief under this rule, and while trial court was not obligated to provide credit for that period of incarceration, it clearly had discretion to do so. **Hawley v. State,** Op. No. 112, 648 P2d 1035 (Alaska App. 1982).

Parole eligibility is not a proper consideration in deciding an application under this rule for reduction of a lawful sentence. **Bishop v. Municipality of Anchorage,** Op. No. 392, 685 P2d 103 (Alaska App. 1984).

Because the trial court's power to initially sentence is subject to presumptive sentencing, it necessarily follows that in the absence of mitigating factors, or a basis for a referral to the three-judge panel, the court is obligated to imposed the presumptive term, and such a sentence is not subject to modification thereafter pursuant to this rule. **Gabrieloffv. State,** Op. No. 833, 758 P2d 128 (Alaska App. 1988).

Superior court did not have authority under this rule, which allows the court to modify a sentence in light of changed circumstances, to order the release of a sentenced prisoner to attend a ceremonial potlatch for a period of four days, absent evidence that the potlatch directly related to any basic sentencing goal or that the sentencing goal of rehabilitation would be defeated if the prisoner did not attend the potlatch. **State v. Ambrose,** Op. No. 840, 758 P2d 639 (Alaska App. 1988).

The trial court has discretion to consider a person's rehabilitation while incarcerated in evaluating an application for reduction of sentence pursuant to Criminal Rule 35(a). **Fowler v. Alaska,** Op. No. 891, 766 P2d 588 (Alaska App. 1988).

The prerequisites to relief under Criminal Rule 35(b) are: (1) some change in conditions or circumstances affecting the defendant must occur after the original sentence is imposed; (2) the change must relate to the purposes of the original sentence; and (3) the effect of the subsequent change in conditions or circumstances must be so significant as to defeat or substantially frustrate implementation of the sentencing goal or objective. **Mitchell v. State,** Op. No. 894,767 P2d 203 (Alaska App. 1988).

A trial court has no power to impose a sentence, pursuant to Criminal Rule 35(b), which it would not have been permitted to impose at initial sentencing. **Mitchell v. State,** Op. No. 894, 767 P2d 203 (Alaska App. 1988).

Prisoner's contention that his original sentence was excessive and that he had been rehabilitated during his period of imprisonment were factors properly addressed in a sentence appeal or in an application under Criminal Rule 35(a), but not a motion under Criminal Rule 35(b). **Mitchell v. State,** Op. No. 894,767 P2d 203 (Alaska App. 1988).

Since prisoner's motion for modification of sentence under Criminal Rule 35(b) did not state a prima facie case, for modification under the standards adopted in **State v. Ambrose,** Op. No. 840, 758 P2d 639 (Alaska App. 1988), the trial court did not abuse its discretion in denying the motion without a hearing. **Mitchell v. State,** Op. No. 894, 767 P2d 203 (Alaska App. 1988).

Where defendant was convicted of two driving offenses and his sentence for each offense included revocation of his driver's license for 10 years, the sentences to run concurrently, modification of the sentence to make the revocations concurrent if defendant were to have no jailable traffic violations during the first 10 years was error, since its effect would be to defer modification of the originally imposed sentence for 20 years; deferring modification for a 10-year period is plainly violative of the 120-day time limit for sentence reductions imposed under this rule. **Rollefson v. Municipality of Anchorage,** Op. No. 983, 782 P2d 305 (Alaska App. 1989).

On motion for post-conviction relief, trial court did not have to take sex offender's progress toward rehabilitation into account and refer his case to a three-judge panel for sentencing. **S.B. v. State,** Op. No. 997, 785 P2d 900 (Alaska App. 1989).

If a defendant intends to bring a motion within the 120-day period but negligently calculates the time, or if defense counsel refuses to bring the motion or discourages defendant from bringing the motion, it might be an abuse of discretion to refuse to relax the 120-day time limit of this rule. **Cook v. State,** Op. No. 1052, 792 P2d 682 (Alaska App. 1990).

Although convicted sex offender's motion to reduce sentence would have failed if made within the 120-day time limit of this rule because his completion of an institutional sex-offender program, upon which the motion was based, did not occur until after the time limit, the trial court did not err in refusing to relax the time limit. **Cook v. State,** Op. No. 1052, 792 P2d 682 (Alaska App. 1990).

Trial court abused its discretion in using this rule, which allows sentencing courts to modify or reduce sentence within 180 days of distribution of written judgment, to grant furlough to prisoner; furloughs are within authority of Department of Corrections, not the courts. **State v. Couch,** Op. No. 1654, 991 P2d 1286 (Alaska App. 1999).

Alaska R. Crim. P. 35(b) did not permit the district court to interrupt a criminal sentence to address a prisoner's short-term needs. **State v. Felix,** Op. No. 1808, 50 P.3d 807 (Alaska App. 2002).

B. Specific Grounds.

Where change in defendant's testimony would be considered newly discovered evidence only by concluding that he had lied at original hearing, it did not provide grounds for reducing sentence. **Davis v. State,** Op. No. 1453, 566 P2d 640 (Alaska 1977).

The imposition by the superior court of a ten-year sentence with five years suspended upon an eighteen-year-old who committed a series of burglaries was not clearly mistaken. **Winslow v. State,** Op. No. 1767, 587 P2d 738 (Alaska 1978).

Prisoner's contention that his original sentence was excessive and that he had been rehabilitated during his period of imprisonment were factors properly addressed in a sentence appeal or in an application under Criminal Rule 35(a), but not a motion under Criminal Rule 35(b). **Mitchell v. State,** Op. No. 894,767 P2d 203 (Alaska App. 1988).

Prisoner's claims that he was not receiving constitutionally mandated rehabilitation treatment from the Division of Corrections was not appropriate for consideration in a proceeding brought pursuant to this rule. **Mitchell v. State,** Op. No. 894, 767 P2d 203 (Alaska App. 1988).

Even if exceptionally good progress toward rehabilitation qualifies as a changed circumstance under this rule, evidence that prisoner's progress toward rehabilitation would be disrupted by his reclassification from work release status back to the general inmate population, which would occur unless his sentence was changed to a non-presumptive sentence, did not justify a sentence modification; the record fell short of supporting a conclusion that the disruption (Amounting to a year or more) would prevent the goal of rehabilitation from eventually being accomplished. **Bartholomew v. State,** Op. No. 970, 779 P2d 1253 (Alaska App. 1989).

IV. Procedure.

Where a magistrate revoked a suspended sentence without authority the supreme court remanded the case in order that a reduction of sentence could be considered in accordance with Cr. R. 35(a). **Pete v. State,** Op. No. 137, 379 P2d 625 (Alaska 1962).

A sentence is imposed at the time it is first announced upon the record by the court. **State v. Trunnel,** Op. No. 1260, 549 P2d 550 (Alaska 1976).

Rule 35(b) proceeding is separate from original criminal proceeding, is governed by civil procedure, results in a final judgment and may be appealed by either state or applicant. **State v. Hannagan,** Op. No. 1374, 559 P2d 1059 (Alaska 1977).

When a criminal appeal has been dismissed, though no mandate has been issued, the appellant may seek relief in superior court under Criminal Rule 35(a). **Singletary v. State,** Op. No. 1711, 583 P2d 847 (Alaska 1978).

Criminal Rule 35(a) is not the appropriate procedural vehicle to seek relief as to conditions within custodial institutions or the civil rights of inmates. **Rust v. State,** Op. No. 1668, 584 P2d 38 (Alaska 1978).

Defendant's request that he be given credit for time spent in jail for parole violation arising out of same conduct for which he was convicted of crime in question should have been considered a request for discretionary relief under this rule, and while trial court was not obligated to provide credit for that period of incarceration, it clearly had discretion to do so. **Hawley v. State,** Op. No. 112, 648 P2d 1035 (Alaska App. 1982).

Presence of defendant at a hearing attacking the sentence was not mandatory where there were no substantial issues of fact as to the events in which the petitioner participated. **Rivett v. State,** Op. No. 249, 395 P2d 264 (Alaska 1964).

It is discretionary with the trial court whether to hold an evidentiary hearing, hear oral argument, or require the defendant's presentence in connection with decision on a Rule 35(a) application. **Fowler v. Alaska,** Op. No. 891, 766 P2d 588 (Alaska App. 1988).

Criminal Rule 35(b) does not permit the trial court to refer a case to a three-judge sentencing panel based upon a nonstatutory mitigating factor (institutional rehabilitation) arising after the defendant has served a significant part of his sentence. **Fowler v. Alaska,** Op. No. 891, 766 P2d 588 (Alaska App. 1988).

Since prisoner's motion for modification of sentence under Criminal Rule 35(b) did not state a prima facie case, for modification under the standards adopted in **State v. Ambrose,** Op. No. 840, 758 P2d 639 (Alaska App. 1988), the trial court did not abuse its discretion in denying the motion without a hearing. **Mitchell v. State,** Op. No. 894, 767 P2d 203 (Alaska App. 1988).

A motion to modify a sentence which is not brought within the 120-day time limitation prescribed in Criminal Rule 35(a) is governed by the narrower prerequisites of Criminal Rule 35(b). **Mitchell v. State,** Op. No. 894, 767 P2d 203 (Alaska App. 1988).

When a defendant asserts that his or her trial attorney failed to present important evidence, either because of incompetent trial tactics or because the attorney failed to competently investigate the case, the defendant must furnish the court with affidavits, depositions, or reports of the witnesses who stand ready to provide this evidence. Failing this, the defendant must explain to the court why the witnesses' statements are unobtainable. **Allen v. State,** Op. No. 9343, 153 P.3d 1019 (Alaska App. 2007).

V. Time Limits.

Where motion to modify sentence was filed two years after sentence was imposed, trial court did not abuse discretion in refusing to relax rule imposing 60-day limitation on such motions. **Taylor v. State,** Op. No. 1436, 564 P2d 1219 (Alaska 1977).

Where defendant's counsel had a bona fide belief that a motion for reduction or modification of sentence had been timely filed, defendant had requested such a motion and tried to learn if it had been filed, within prescribed period, and defendant was imprisoned in institution that could not afford him treatment for alcoholism, to fail to relax the 60-day limit of Criminal Rule 35(a) pursuant to Rule 53 would work an injustice. **Wheeles v. State,** Op. No. 3046, 566 P2d 1013 (Alaska 1977).

Superior Court is without authority to modify sentence absent a timely motion under this rule. **Szeratics v. State,** Op. No. 1525, 572 P2d 63 (Alaska 1977).

The filing of a supplemental application for correction of sentence did not terminate the running of the time for filing an appeal from the denial of the original application for correction of sentence. **Abraham v. State,** Op. No. 1747, 585 P2d 526 (Alaska 1978).

By relaxing the rules to permit a late sentence appeal because it was unclear whether counsel for defendant had failed him in not making a timely appeal, the court did not relax Rule 35(a) so as to allow defendant to take advantage of that rule in a manner which would not be available to an ordinary criminal defendant who appeals in a timely fashion. **Davis v. State,** Op. No. 2101, 612 P2d 49 (Alaska 1980).

The time limitations in this rule are subject to the trial court's power to relax rules in the interest of justice. **Mitchell v. State,** Op. No. 894, 767 P2d 203 (Alaska App. 1988).

A motion to modify a sentence which is not brought within the 120-day time limitation prescribed in Criminal Rule 35(a) is governed by the narrower prerequisites of Criminal Rule 35(b). **Mitchell v. State,** Op. No. 894, 767 P2d 203 (Alaska App. 1988).

Where defendant was convicted of two driving offenses and his sentence for each offense included revocation of his driver's license for 10 years, the sentences to run concurrently, modification of the sentence to make the revocations concurrent if defendant were to have no jailable traffic violations during the first 10 years was error, since its effect would be to defer modification of the originally imposed sentence for 20 years; deferring modification for a 10-year period is plainly violative of the 120-day time limit for sentence reductions imposed under this rule. **Rollefson v. Municipality of Anchorage,** Op. No. 983, 782 P2d 305 (Alaska App. 1989).

Where request for reduction of sentence came almost three years after defendant's conviction was affirmed on appeal, and there was nothing in the record to suggest that he intended to make the request within 120-days permitted by the rule or was somehow frustrated by his attorney or the court system in taking action, the trial court did not err in refusing to relax the 120-day time limit. **S.B. v. State,** Op. No. 997, 785 P2d 900 (Alaska App. 1989).

If a defendant intends to bring a motion within the 120-day period but negligently calculates the time, or if defense counsel refuses to bring the motion or discourages defendant from bringing the motion, it might be an abuse of discretion to refuse to relax the 120-day time limit of this rule. **Cook v. State,** Op. No. 1052, 792 P2d 682 (Alaska App. 1990).

Although convicted sex offender's motion to reduce sentence would have failed if made within the 120-day time limit of this rule because his completion of an institutional sex-offender program, upon which the motion was based, did not occur until after the time limit, the trial court did not err in refusing to relax the time limit. **Cook v. State,** Op. No. 1052, 792 P2d 682 (Alaska App. 1990).

Trial judge abused his discretion in relaxing former Criminal Rule 35(a), which required motion for reduction of sentence to be filed within 120 days of imposition of sentence, to allow defendant to file such motion seven years after imposition of sentence. **State v. Tinsley,** Op. No. 1500, 928 P2d 1220 (Alaska App. 1996).

Exception to this rule, which under certain conditions authorizes motion to reduce sentence to be made within 120 days after United States Supreme Court denies petition for certiori, applies only to appeals from original case in which defendant was convicted, not to collateral attacks on conviction. **Thompson v. State,** Op. No. 1707, 13 P3d 276 (Alaska App. 2000).

Rule 35.1. Post-Conviction Procedure.

(a) **Scope.** A person who has been convicted of or sentenced for a crime may institute a proceeding for post-conviction relief under AS 12.72.010–12.72.040 if the person claims:

(1) that the conviction or the sentence was in violation of the constitution of the United States or the constitution or laws of Alaska;

(2) that the court was without jurisdiction to impose sentence;

(3) that a prior conviction has been set aside and the prior conviction was used as a statutorily required enhancement of the sentence imposed;

(4) that there exists evidence of material facts, not previously presented and heard, that requires vacation of the conviction or sentence in the interest of justice;

(5) that the applicant's sentence has expired, that the applicant's probation, parole or conditional release has been unlawfully revoked, or that the applicant is otherwise unlawfully held in custody or other restraint;

(6) that the conviction or sentence is otherwise subject to collateral attack upon any ground or alleged error heretofore available under any common law, statutory or other writ, motion, petition, proceeding, or remedy;

(7) that

(A) there has been a significant change in law, whether substantive or procedural, applied in the process leading to the applicant's conviction or sentence;

(B) the change in law was not reasonably foreseeable by a judge or a competent attorney;

(C) it is appropriate to retroactively apply the change in law because the change in law requires observance of procedures without which the likelihood of an accurate and fair conviction is seriously diminished; and

(D) the failure to retroactively apply the change in law would result in a fundamental miscarriage of justice, which is established by demonstrating that, had the change in law been in effect at the time of the applicant's trial, a reasonable trier of fact would have a reasonable doubt as to the guilt of the applicant;

(8) that the applicant should be allowed to withdraw a plea of guilty or nolo contendere in order to correct manifest injustice as set out in Criminal Rule 11(h); or

(9) that the applicant was not afforded effective assistance of counsel at trial or on direct appeal.

(b) **Not a Substitute for Remedies in Trial Court—Replaces All Other Remedies for Challenging the Validity of a Sentence.** This remedy is not a substitute for nor does it affect any remedy incident to the proceedings in the trial court, or direct review of the sentence or conviction. It is intended to provide a standard procedure for accomplishing the objectives of all of the constitutional, statutory or common law writs.

(c) **Commencement of Proceedings— Filing—Service.** A proceeding is commenced by filing an application with the clerk at the court location where the underlying conviction is filed. Application forms will be furnished by the clerk of court. An application must be filed within the time limitations set out in AS 12.72.020. The clerk shall open a new file for the application, promptly bring it to the attention of the court and give a copy to the prosecuting attorney.

(d) **Application—Contents.** The application shall (1) identify the proceedings in which the applicant was convicted, (2) state the date shown in the clerk's certificate of distribution on the judgment complained of, (3) state the sentence complained of and the date of sentencing, (4) specifically set forth the grounds upon which the application is based, and (5) clearly state the relief desired. If the application challenges a Department of Corrections or Board of Parole decision, the application shall (1) identify the specific nature of the proceedings or challenged decision, (2) state the date of the proceedings or decision, (3) specifically set forth the facts and legal grounds upon which the application is based, and (4) clearly state the relief desired. Facts within the personal knowledge of the applicant shall be set out separately from other allegations of facts and shall be under oath. Affidavits, records, or other evidence supporting its allegations shall be attached to the application or the application shall recite why they are not attached. The application shall identify all previous proceedings, together with the grounds therein asserted, taken by the applicant to secure relief from the conviction or sentence including any previous applications for post-conviction relief. Argument, citations and discussion of authorities are unnecessary. Applications which are incomplete shall be returned to the applicant for completion.

(e) **Indigent Applicant.**

(1) If the applicant is indigent, filing fees shall be paid under the provisions of AS 09.19 and counsel shall be appointed consistent with AS 18.85.100 to assist the applicant.

(2) Within 60 days of an attorney's appointment on behalf of an indigent applicant, the attorney shall file with the court and serve on the prosecuting attorney

(A) a statement that the litigation will proceed on the claims alleged in the application filed by the applicant; or

(B) an amended application for post-conviction relief; or

(C) a certificate that the attorney

(i) does not have a conflict of interest;

(ii) has reviewed the facts of the underlying proceeding or action challenged in the application, and the pertinent law;

(iii) has consulted with the applicant and, if appropriate, with trial counsel; and

(iv) has determined that the claims presented in the application have no arguable merit and that the applicant has no other colorable claims for post-conviction relief.

(3) The certificate described in subparagraph (e)(2)(C) shall include a full description of

(A) the claims the attorney has considered;

(B) the materials the attorney has reviewed;

(C) the investigations the attorney has conducted; and

(D) the reasons why the attorney has concluded that all of the applicant's potential claims have no arguable merit.

(f) **Pleadings and Judgment on Pleadings.**

(1) The state shall file an answer or a motion within 45 days of service of an original, amended, or supplemental application filed by counsel or by an applicant who elects to proceed without counsel, or of a notice of intent to proceed on the original application under (e)(2)(A) of this rule. The applicant shall have 30 days to file an opposition, and the state shall have 15 days to file a reply. The motion, opposition, and reply may be supported by affidavit. At any time prior to entry of judgment the court may grant leave to withdraw the application. The court may make appropriate orders for amendment of the application or any pleading or motion, for pleading over, for filing further pleadings or motions, or for extending the time of the filing of any pleading. In considering a pro se application the court shall consider substance and disregard defects of form, but a pro se applicant will be held to the same burden of proof and persuasion as an applicant proceeding with counsel. If the application is not accompanied by the record of the proceedings challenged therein, the respondent may file with its answer the record or portions thereof that are material to the questions raised in the application.

(2) If appointed counsel has filed a certificate under (e)(2)(C) of this rule, and it appears to the court that the applicant is not entitled to relief, the court shall indicate to the parties its intention to permit counsel to withdraw and dismiss the application and its reasons for so doing. The applicant and the prosecuting attorney shall be given an opportunity to reply to the proposed withdrawal and dismissal. If the applicant files a response and the court finds that the application does not present a colorable claim, or if the applicant does not file a response, the court shall permit counsel to withdraw and order the application dismissed. If the court finds that the application presents a colorable claim, the court may grant leave to file an amended application or direct that the proceedings otherwise continue.

(3) The court may grant a motion by either party for summary disposition of the application when it appears from the pleadings, depositions, answers to interrogatories, and admissions and agreements of fact, together with any affidavits submitted, that there is no genuine issue of material fact and the moving party is entitled to judgment as a matter of law.

(g) **Hearing—Evidence—Order.** The application shall be heard in, and before any judge of, the court in which the underlying criminal case is filed. An electronic recording of the proceeding shall be made. All rules and statutes applicable in civil proceedings, including pretrial and discovery procedures are available to the parties except that Alaska Rule of Civil Procedure Rule 26(a)(1)-(4) does not apply to post-conviction relief proceedings. The court may receive proof by affidavits, depositions, oral testimony, or other evidence. Unless otherwise required by statute or constitution, the applicant bears the burden of proving all factual assertions by clear and convincing evidence. The court may order the applicant brought before it for the hearing or allow the applicant to participate telephonically or by video conferencing. If the court finds in favor of the applicant, it shall enter an appropriate order with respect to the conviction or sentence in the former proceedings, and any supplementary orders as to rearraignment, retrial, custody, bail, discharge, correction of sentence, or other matters that may be necessary and proper. The court shall make specific findings of fact, and state expressly its conclusions of law, relating to each issue presented. The order made by the court is a final judgment.

(h) **Expedited Consideration.** An applicant may move for expedited consideration of the application for post-conviction relief. The motion must comply with Civil Rule 77(g).

(Added by SCO 822, effective August 1, 1987; amended by SCO 1153 effective July 15, 1994; by SCO 1186 effective July 15, 1995; by SCO 1242 effective July 15, 1996; by SCO 1273 effective July 15, 1997; by SCO 1303 effective January 15, 1998; and by SCO 1625 effective April 16, 2007)

Note to SCO 1242: Criminal Rule 35.1 was amended by

ch. 79 §§ 32-39 SLA 1995. Sections 4 through 10 of this order are adopted for the sole reason that the legislature has mandated the amendments.

Annotations

Cases

I. In General.

Appellate Rule 46 was invoked where strict adherence to the 40-day time limit for appeal under Criminal Rule 35 would have prevented consideration of appellant's contentions that his conditions of imprisonment deprived him of his right to rehabilitation and reformation and to be free of cruel and unusual punishment. **Abraham v. State,** Op. No. 1747, 585 P2d 526 (Alaska 1978).

Post-conviction relief proceeding is not another trial; it is separate from the original criminal proceeding and is governed primarily by rules of civil procedure. **Hensel v. State,** Op. No. 1983, 604 P2d 222 (Alaska 1979).

The Criminal Rules promulgated by the Alaska Supreme Court are part of the general "laws" of Alaska as the term is used in this rule. **Price v. State,** Op. No. 100, 647 P2d 611 (Alaska App. 1982).

An attorney, appointed to represent an indigent in bringing his first application for post-conviction relief based on alleged ineffective assistance of counsel, was not permitted to withdraw on the basis that there were no nonfrivolous issuance to be presented to the court where the indigent was unwilling to forego the application; the court, rather than counsel, had to determine the merits of petitioner's contention. **Hertz v. State,** Op. No. 806, 755 P2d 406 (Alaska App. 1988).

Res judicata applies in post-conviction relief proceedings; accordingly where a party thoroughly litigates an issue and has his appeal resolved on the merits, the trial court can dismiss a claim for post-conviction relief on that issue. **Brown v. State,** Op. No. 1099, 803 P2d 887 (Alaska App. 1990).

District court did not have jurisdiction to entertain applications for post-conviction relief made under this rule. **State v. Danielson,** Op. No. 1128, 809 P2d 937 (Alaska App. 1991).

Applicant for post-conviction relief who brings forth new evidence and seeks relief pursuant to this rule must meet same burden as defendant who files timely motion under Criminal Rule 33 for new trial based on newly discovered evidence; in either procedural setting, new trial is warranted only upon showing that proposed new evidence is newly discovered and would probably produce acquittal. **Lewis v. State,** Op. No. 4253, 901 P2d 448 (Alaska App. 1995).

Claim that Civil Rule 86(m), which provides that habeas corpus procedure does not apply to any postconviction proceeding that could be brought under Criminal Rule 35.1, did not apply to an action that could be brought pursuant to Criminal Rule 35.1 but that might later be dismissed because of substantive or procedural shortcomings, was rejected. **Hertz v. State,** Op. No. 1686, 8 P3d 1144 (Alaska App. 2000).

Because petitioner's application for writ of habeas corpus for ineffective assistance of counsel did not claim that the underlying judgment of conviction was void, trial court order directing him to refile his complaint as an application for postconviction relief under Criminal Rule 35.1 was not an impermissible suspension of the writ of habeas corpus. **Hertz v. State,** Op. No. 1686, 8 P3d 1144 (Alaska App. 2000).

Rule announced in **Hertz v. State,** Op. No. 806,755 P2d 406 (Alaska App. 1988), that an attorney representing an indigent petitioner for post-conviction relief should never be allowed to withdraw and should be required to pursue the petition even if the attorney has concluded that it is frivolous, has been superseded by amendments to this court rule. **Griffin v. State,** Op. No. 1720, 18 P3d 71 (Alaska App. 2001).

An attorney who is appointed to represent an indigent petitioner for post-conviction relief and who seeks to withdraw from the case on the ground that there is no arguable merit to the litigation must provide the court with a full explanation of why he believes that the petitioner has no colorable claim to post-conviction relief; the attorney must certify both that the petitioner's existing application does not allege a colorable claim for relief and that the application cannot be amended to assert one or more colorable claims for relief. **Griffin v. State,** Op. No. 1720, 18 P3d 71 (Alaska App. 2001).

There are five requirements that a defendant must meet before the court may grant a new trial based upon new evidence: (1) It must appear from the motion that the evidence relied on is, in fact, newly discovered, i.e., discovered after the trial; (2) the motion must allege facts from which the court may infer diligence on the part of the movant; (3) the evidence relied on must not be merely cumulative or impeaching; (4) must be material to the issues involved; and (5) must be such as, on a new trial, would probably produce an acquittal. **James v. State,** Op. No. 5773, 4 P.3d 404 (Alaska 2004).

Attorney's certificate must contain sufficient detail to allow the superior court to fulfill its duty to independently assess whether the defendant has any potentially arguable claims for post-conviction relief. **Goldsbury v. State,** Op. No. 1937, 93 P.3d 468 (Alaska App. 2004).

In order for the court to perform its role under this section, and thereby fulfill its duty to make sure that indigent litigants do in fact receive zealous investigation and presentation of any colorable claims for postconviction relief, an attorney seeking to withdraw from a case must provide the court with a full explanation of all the claims the attorney has considered and why the attorney has concluded that these claims are frivolous. **Goldsbury v. State,** Op. No. 1937, 93 P.3d 468 (Alaska App. 2004).

II. Vacation of Conviction.

A. In General.

At a fact hearing upon a post-conviction petition which alleged that petitioner was coerced by appointed trial counsel to enter a guilty plea and also alleged that trial counsel had given the petitioner false assurance regarding probation, specific findings must be made in the record as to as many of the following matters that may be applicable in addition to others possibly raised, namely the court's jurisdiction, the adequacy of petitioner's representation, intelligent waiver of counsel if there was such, questions of suppression of evidence or knowing use of perjured testimony, use of involuntary confessions, competency of petitioner to understand the proceedings and statutory range of sentence. **Thompson v. State,** Op. No. 334, 412 P2d 628 (Alaska 1966).

Order denying petition to vacate on ground that plea of guilty was coerced by threats and promises of probation officer was reversed and remanded directing the court below to place the probation officer under oath, to afford full opportunity for cross-examination at a full fact hearing on petitioner's charges, to weigh the testimony and to file written findings and decision. **Nichols v. State,** Op. No. 398, 425 P2d 247 (Alaska 1967).

If the record of a post-conviction hearing is silent with regard to an issue and the witnesses are unable to remember, the State has not failed to substantiate its case. Instead, the prisoner has failed in his collateral attack on the judgment of conviction. **Merrill v. State,** Op. No. 568, 457 P2d 231 (Alaska 1969).

To secure relief in a habeas corpus proceeding, the petitioner has the burden of alleging and proving by a preponderance of the evidence all facts necessary to overturn the prior judgment of conviction. **Merrill v.**

State, Op. No. 568, 457 P2d 231 (Alaska 1969).

Where the counsel for a prisoner seeking post-conviction relief is unable to find witnesses having information to substantiate a jury-tampering claim, the trial court may dismiss the claim. **Flores v. State,** Op. No. 642, 475 P2d 37 (Alaska 1970).

A defendant is precluded from raising on application for post-conviction relief the contention that the jury was improperly constituted where no challenge to the composition of the jury panel was made at the trial. **Fajeriak v. State,** Op. No. 1761, 520 P2d 795 (Alaska 1974).

A genuine issue of material fact, precluding summary disposition of an application for post-conviction relief, is presented where it is alleged that the district attorney, by resort to threats and intimidation, prevented potential defense witnesses from testifying. **Fajeriak v. State,** Op. No. 1761, 520 P2d 795 (Alaska 1974).

Vacation of conviction for failure to comply with Criminal Rule 11 will only be granted when noncompliance affected substantial rights of defendant. **Lewis v. State,** Op. No. 1447, 565 P2d 846 (Alaska 1977).

A defendant seeking to set aside a conviction on grounds of newly discovered evidence must prove by a preponderance of the evidence those facts which entitle him to have the conviction set aside. **Hensel v. State,** Op. No. 1983, 604 P2d 222 (Alaska 1979).

Defendant has the burden of proving by a preponderance of the evidence that newly discovered evidence would be likely to change the result of the trial, that is, that the evidence would be sufficient to create a reasonable doubt as to his guilt. **Hensel v. State,** Op. No. 1983, 604 P2d 222 (Alaska 1979).

Defendant had burden of proving by a preponderance of the evidence that newly discovered evidence of diminished capacity would be sufficient to create a reasonable doubt in a new trial. **Hensel v. State,** Op. No. 1983, 604 P2d 222 (Alaska 1979).

Defendant's new evidence did not require a new trial since it was cumulative of information which he could have presented trial and since there was not reasonable possibility that the new evidence would produce an acquittal in a new trial. **Charles v. State,** Op. No. 963, 780 P2d 377 (Alaska App. 1989).

B. Specific Grounds.

Conviction set aside under this rule and case remanded for new trial, because trial court's exclusion from evidence of tape recorded inconsistent statements of state witness had resulted in keeping from jury relevant and important facts on the trustworthiness of crucial testimony even though witness had admitted making the statements. **Bentley v. State,** Op. No. 270, 397 P2d 976 (Alaska 1965).

Motion to vacate judgment of conviction under this provision based on the ground that plea of guilty made in 1952 was not voluntary in the meaning of federal criminal rule 11, was properly denied where records showed that the petitioner had discussed the plea with counsel of his own choice and that the judge had made a determination that the plea was not improvidently made. **Oughton v. State,** Op. No. 377, 420 P2d 452 (Alaska 1966).

Record of post-conviction hearing on remand disclosed sufficient basis for superior court's finding that appellant's change of plea to guilty was made voluntarily and with understanding of the nature of the charge. **Thompson v. State,** Op. No. 408, 426 P2d 995 (Alaska 1967).

The allegations of a petitioner for post-conviction relief that he had taken drugs some 12 hours prior to time he changed his plea to guilty and that at the time he appeared in court to enter his change of plea he was under the influence of drugs, and thus rendered incompetent, were sufficient to require an evidentiary hearing. Despite the apparent regularity of the competency hearing, the change of plea and the sentencing proceedings, the possibility still exists that the petitioner did not knowingly and understandingly plead to the offense as charged. **Widermyre v. State,** Op. No. 540, 452 P2d 885 (Alaska 1969).

Where a prisoner seeking post-conviction relief refuses to waive the attorney-client privilege so that his trial counsel can testify on the question of the adequacy of representation, and the prisoner thus forestalls further inquiry into such ground for relief, the claim of inadequate representation by trial counsel is deemed to have been abandoned. **Flores v. State,** Op. No. 642, 475 P2d 37 (Alaska 1970).

A defendant is not deprived of a public trial merely because a newspaper reporter is unable to enter the building in which the courtroom is located, where such exclusion is unintentional, is for less than one hour and takes place at a time after submission of the case to the jury, while the jury is listening to a replay of certain recorded testimony. **Flores v. State,** Op. No. 642, 475 P2d 37 (Alaska 1970).

Proof that the State intimidated potential material defense witnesses and prevented them from testifying requires the granting of a new trial. A defendant, seeking post-conviction relief, will not have to demonstrate prejudice. **Fajeriak v. State,** Op. No. 1761, 520 P2d 795 (Alaska 1974).

Where a defendant successfully proves on application for post-conviction relief that his confidential communications with his attorney were electronically monitored, he ordinarily must be granted a new trial, even without demonstrating that he was prejudiced by such action. **Fajeriak v. State,** Op. No. 1761, 520 P2d 795 (Alaska 1974).

After conviction as accomplice to burglary not in a dwelling and malicious destruction of property, evidence of diminished capacity was admissible to negate showing by state that defendant had knowledge of the criminal enterprise and that defendant specifically intended, by his conduct, to aid, abet, assist or participate in the criminal enterprise. **Hensel v. State,** Op. No. 1983, 604 P2d 222 (Alaska 1979).

Where attorney did not inform his client of the possibility of a diminished capacity defense, but did himself consider it in preparing for trial, his failure to explain the possible defense did not render his legal assistance ineffective when the chances of acquittal or conviction on a lesser offense due to the use of the diminished capacity defense were improbable. **Larson v. State,** Op. No. 2128, 614 P2d 776 (Alaska 1980).

In order to obtain post-conviction relief for ineffective assistance of counsel, defendant must first show that his lawyer's skill fell below that of a lawyer with ordinary training and skill in the criminal law, and second, that the lawyer's defective performance contributed in some way to defendant's conviction. **Larson v. State,** Op. No. 2128, 614 P2d 776 (Alaska 1980).

In attempting to eliminate consideration of the nature of the offense from its consideration of relevant factors at sentencing, the superior court committed reversible error. **Kelly v. State,** Op. No. 2268, 622 P2d 432 (Alaska 1981).

Post-conviction relief litigation allows defendant to delve into basis for his attorney's decisions in order to show that decisions fell below range of competency expected of criminal law practitioners, but burden of proving incompetence rests on defendant. **Steffensen v. State,** Op. No. 1246, 837 P2d 1123 (Alaska App. 1992).

Defendant was not entitled to post-conviction relief on ground that his attorney failed to file potentially dispositive suppression motion; defendant did not meet burden of showing reasonable possibility that attorney's reasons for not filing motion were completely invalid. **Steffensen v. State,** Op. No. 1246, 837 P2d 1123 (Alaska App. 1992).

Where an inmate attacked his guilty verdict in a petition for post-conviction relief, claiming that jurors formed and announced opinions and discussed the merits of the case before jury deliberations, relied on personal knowledge in the deliberations, and viewed the inmate's decision not to testify and his wife's absence as evidence of his guilt, under Alaska R. Evid. 606(b) the juror affidavits could not be relied on to support the petition because they described matters that inhered in the jury's decision-making process and because the use of the affidavits was incompatible with the policies underlying R. 606(b) of protecting jurors from harassment, encouraging free jury deliberation, and promoting the finality of verdicts; therefore, the trial court properly dismissed the inmate's petition for post-conviction relief. **Larson v. State,** Op. No. 1904, 79 P.3d 650 (Alaska App.

2003).

III. Procedure.

A. In General.

A petitioner seeking post-conviction relief on the grounds that she was transported out of the state for purposes of out-of-state incarceration prior to the expiration of the ten-day period within which she is required to file a notice of appeal, should attempt to show what impact her physical removal from the state has had on her ability to file a timely notice of appeal. She should further show what attempt she has made during the period between the imposition of sentence and the alleged removal from the state to engage services of trial counsel. **Pore v. State,** Op. No. 437, 452 P2d 433 (Alaska 1969).

An appeal from the denial of a petition for writ of habeas corpus is characterized as one from the denial of a motion for post-conviction relief. **Knaub v. State,** Op. No. 489, 443 P2d 44 (Alaska 1968).

If the trial court determines conclusively that a petitioner is entitled to no post-conviction relief after an examination of the files and records of a case, it may properly deny the petition without hearing. **Knaub v. State,** Op. No. 489, 443 P2d 44 (Alaska 1968).

A trial judge in acting upon a motion for post-conviction relief is entitled to rely upon his recollection of the proceedings during the trial. **Knaub v. State,** Op. No. 489, 443 P2d 44 (Alaska 1968).

It is not necessary to hold an evidentiary hearing concerning an alleged deprivation of the right to appeal where petitioner alleges she requested her trial defense counsel to file an appeal from her conviction, but fails to indicate time, location, manner and circumstances under which she had requested her counsel to make such appeal. **Pore v. State,** Op. No. 437, 452 P2d 433 (Alaska 1969).

The determination that a petition for post-conviction relief alleging the deprivation of the right to appeal does not require the holding of an evidentiary hearing does not preclude the petitioner from making a second application for post-conviction relief and presenting evidence supporting the assertion, first presented on appeal from a denial of the first post-conviction motion, that she was transported out of the state for purposes of out-of-state incarceration prior to the expiration of the ten-day period within which she was required to file her notice of appeal. **Pore v. State,** Op. No. 437,452 P2d 433 (Alaska 1969).

If the trial court can determine conclusively that the petitioner is not entitled to post-conviction relief after examining the files and records of the case, it may properly deny the petition without hearing. **Widermyre v. State,** Op. No. 540, 452 P2d 885 (Alaska 1969).

Post-conviction relief is an appropriate vehicle for the effectuation of the right of appeal where counsel has failed to file a timely notice of appeal. **McCracken v. State,** Op. No 677, 482 P2d 269 (Alaska 1971).

Where a convicted defendant presents important questions of substantive criminal law never before decided in the state, the court will consider the merits of the issues, even though the petitioner had not asserted his claims in prior motions. **Mead v. State,** Op. No. 731, 489 P2d 738 (Alaska 1971).

If an applicant for post-conviction relief is represented by counsel in the first application, there will be no presumption in his favor in a second application, and he will incur the burden of showing sufficient reason for any failure to raise grounds for relief in the first application. **Thompson v. State,** Op. No. 792, 496 P2d 651 (Alaska 1972).

Indigent prisoners seeking relief under this rule must be provided with counsel at the time their application is filed. **Donnelly v. State,** Op. No. 965, 516 P2d 396 (Alaska 1973).

Generally, a petitioner for post-conviction relief has a right to represent himself without counsel in criminal proceedings. **McCracken v. State,** Op. No. 986, 518 P2d 85 (Alaska 1974).

The right to self-representation on a petition for post-conviction relief is not absolute. In order to prevent a perversion of the judicial process, the trial judge should first ascertain whether a prisoner is capable of presenting his allegations in a rational and coherent manner before allowing him to proceed pro se, and the trial judge should satisfy himself that the prisoner understands precisely what he is giving up by declining assistance of counsel. The advantages of legal representation should be explained to the prisoner in some detail, and in the event of an evidentiary hearing at which the prisoner is present he should be given the option of having legal counsel available for consultation. **McCracken v. State,** Op. No. 986, 518 P2d 85 (Alaska 1974).

Where a petitioner for post-conviction relief desires to represent himself, the trial judge should determine whether the prisoner is willing to conduct himself with at least a modicum of courtroom decorum, but the hearing judge must bear in mind that prisoners are not experienced trial lawyers, and are not practiced in the formalities of courtroom etiquette. **McCracken v. State,** Op. No. 986, 518 P2d 85 (Alaska 1974).

Where pleadings filed by a petitioner seeking post-conviction relief demonstrate a certain knowledge of the merits of his allegations, and indicate at least to some extent that he might have the ability to represent himself, his rights might best be vindicated by an order permitting him to represent himself with the assistance of counsel from the public defender's office appointed by the court. If it should be determined that the prisoner's presence would be necessary at a hearing, a more thorough inquiry into the propriety of permitting him to represent himself could be undertaken at that time. **McCracken v. State,** Op. No. 986, 518 P2d 85 (Alaska 1974).

Even though post-conviction applications are assigned to the original trial judge, he is not chargeable with knowledge of the entire original trial record, where the transcript and record is extremely lengthy and the trial took place several years earlier. Portions of the record relied on for post-conviction relief should be specifically indicated to the judge. **Fajeriak v. State,** Op. No. 1761, 520 P2d 795 (Alaska 1974).

All post-conviction challenges other than by direct appeal or motion after trial must be initiated in the trial court in which the conviction occurred. **McKinnon v. State,** Op. No. 1075, 526 P2d 18 (Alaska 1974).

A sentence is imposed at the time it is first announced upon the record by the court. **State v. Trunnel,** Op. No. 1260, 549 P2d 550 (Alaska 1976).

Rule 35(b) proceeding is separate from original criminal proceeding, is governed by civil procedure, results in a final judgment and may be appealed by either state or applicant. **State v. Hannagan,** Op. No. 1374, 559 P2d 1059 (Alaska 1977).

When a criminal appeal has been dismissed, though no mandate has been issued, the appellant may seek relief in superior court under Criminal Rule 35(a). **Singletary v. State,** Op. No. 1711, 583 P2d 847 (Alaska 1978).

Criminal Rule 35(a) is not the appropriate procedural vehicle to seek relief as to conditions within custodial institutions or the civil rights of inmates. **Rust v. State,** Op. No. 1668, 584 P2d 38 (Alaska 1978).

An appeal from denial of a supplemental application for correction of sentence presents only the question of whether the denial of reconsideration of the original application was proper and does not bring up for review the decision denying the original application for correction of sentence. **Abraham v. State,** Op. No. 1747, 585 P2d 526 (Alaska 1978).

The provisions of Criminal Rule 35(g)(2) [now 35(h)(2)] are applicable only to post-conviction proceedings under Criminal Rule 35(b) and are not applicable to requests for relief under Criminal Rule 35(a). **Winslow v. State,** Op. No. 1767, 587 P2d 738 (Alaska 1978).

Where defendant in probation revocation proceeding did not file motion for post-conviction relief on form provided by court, or file the motion in the court where the original conviction occurred, he did substantially comply with requirements of Criminal Rule 35 by filing separate "Motion to Dismiss Probation Revocation Proceeding, or in the Alternative, to Strike Felony Conviction" and by sending copy of the motion to judge who presided in the original case, where judge by special arrangement ruled on the motion while in the jurisdiction where probation revocation hearing was held. **Holton v. State,** Op. No. 1967, 602 P2d 1228 (Alaska 1979).

Post-conviction relief proceeding is not another trial; it is separate from the original criminal proceeding and is governed primarily by rules of civil procedure. **Hensel v. State,** Op. No. 1983, 604 P2d 222 (Alaska 1979).

An error need not be of constitutional magnitude in order to be attacked under this rule. **Price v. State,** Op. No. 100, 647 P2d 611 (Alaska App. 1982).

Errors in jury instructions which render a criminal trial fundamentally unfair warrant relief under this rule. **Price v. State,** Op. No. 100, 647 P2d 611 (Alaska App. 1982).

Defendant's failure to object at trial to jury instruction forfeited his right to challenge the instruction in a post-conviction proceeding where the instruction did not significantly change the law so as to excuse a timely failure to object, and defendant did not show either good cause for failing to object or substantial prejudice. **Marrone v. State,** Op. No. 156, 653 P2d 672 (Alaska App. 1982).

Trial court is not obligated to dismiss an application for post-conviction relief sua sponte even if it is convinced it has no merit. **Hampton v. Huston,** Op. No. 155, 653 P2d 1058 (Alaska App. 1982).

Trial court erred in ruling on pro se appellant's motion for post-conviction relief without a knowing, intelligent and voluntary waiver of counsel by appellant and without determining whether or not appellant was competent to represent himself. **Hampton v. Huston,** Op. No. 155, 653 P2d 1058 (Alaska App. 1982).

Summarily dismissing defendant's motion for post-conviction relief which alleged ineffective assistance of counsel, without advance notice to defendant indicating the court's intention to dismiss the motion or its reasons for the proposed dismissal, was reversible error, even though the motion itself did not establish a prima facie case of ineffective assistance of counsel. **Wood v. Endell,** Op. No. 488, 702 P2d 248 (Alaska App. 1985).

In post-conviction relief actions, particularly in cases involving pro se applicants who are incarcerated and do not have ready access to court documents, the court's discretion to relax technical pleading requirements should be liberally exercised. **State v. Jones,** Op. No. 832, 759 P2d 558 (Alaska App. 1988).

Sentenced prisoners may avail themselves of the rule recognizing extraordinary potential for rehabilitation as a nonstatutory mitigating factor permitting referral to a three-judge panel to avoid manifest injustice if they can make a prima facie case for referral based upon the original sentencing record. **S.B. v. State,** Op. No. 997, 785 P2d 900 (Alaska App. 1989).

Defendant did not waive claim that his confession should have been suppressed by not raising the issue in his original application for post-conviction relief where his court-appointed counsel had been appointed only to investigate ineffective assistance of counsel claims. **Billingsley v. State,** Op. No. 1117, 807 P2d 1102 (Alaska App. 1991).

Indigent applicant for post-conviction relief was entitled to court-appointed counsel at time application was filed even though application did not comply with procedural requirements of this rule. **Millerv. State,** Op. No. 1311, 857 P2d 1210 (Alaska App. 1993).

Administrative appeal, not petition for writ of habeas corpus or petition for post-conviction relief, was sole method for prisoner to challenge Department of Corrections' revocation of his good time credit. **Higgins v. Briggs,** Op. No. 1354, 876 P2d 539 (Alaska App. 1994).

Rejection of claim on grounds of credibility is premature at first phase of post-conviction relief process since in that phase trial court must accept as true all allegations in application and inquire whether those facts, if proven, would entitle applicant to relief sought. **Hampel v. State,** Op. No. 1457, 911 P2d 517 (Alaska App. 1996).

On issue of what constitutes sufficient reason under this rule to excuse failure to raise claim in prior post-conviction relief application, sufficient reason will almost always, if not always, be established by showing that failure to assert claim resulted from ineffective assistance of counsel, which includes broad spectrum of possible reasons short of actual incompetence of counsel; however, applicant's showing of sufficient reason for late claim must at least negate possibility of prior tactical bypass of claim by either applicant or applicant's counsel, and showing must also at minimum rule out inexcusable neglect or bad faith on applicant's part. **Bangs v. State,** Op. No. 1459, 911 P2d 1067 (Alaska App. 1996).

In a second petition for post-conviction relief based on allegations that a defendant received ineffective assistance of counsel during first post-conviction relief action, defendant's petition will be insufficient unless supported by the affidavits and other documentation specified in this rule and by evidence that affirmatively rebuts the presumption that the prior post-conviction relief attorney was competent and, with respect to layered claims of ineffective assistance, the further presumption that the trial attorney was competent. **Grinols v. State,** Op. No. 1694, 10 P3d 600 (Alaska App. 2000).

Advance notice by the court of its intent to dismiss a post-conviction relief application is not required by this rule when the court grants a dismissal in response to a motion by the state and for the reasons advanced in the motion. **Tall v. State,** Op. No. 1739, 25 P3d 704 (Alaska App. 2001).

Court erred by granting defendant's postconviction relief motion where the court failed to make specific findings regarding the ineffectiveness of defendant's counsel. **State v. Zeciri,** Op. No. A-7712, 43 P3d 169 (Alaska App. 2002).

Appellate court remanded trial court's judgment dismissing petition for post-conviction relief because the record did not show that counsel who was appointed to represent an indigent petitioner investigated the petitioner's claims, sought to adduce support for them through discovery, or sought to reformulate them so that they might survive the State's motion to dismiss. **Tazruk v. State,** Op. No. 1865, 67 P.3d 687 (Alaska App. 2003).

Superior court erred in denying defendant's post-conviction motion for a new trial without considering whether the recantation of an eyewitness' testimony would produce an acquittal. **James v. State,** Op. No. 5773, 4 P.3d 404 (Alaska 2004).

Defendant has the burden of proving by a preponderance of the evidence that newly discovered evidence would be likely to change the result of the trial, that is, that the evidence would be sufficient to create a reasonable doubt as to his guilt. **James v. State,** Op. No. 5773, 4 P.3d 404.

B. Hearing on Motion.

On his first application to vacate or set aside sentence and to withdraw plea of guilty on ground of coercion, an indigent prisoner had a constitutional right to have counsel appointed by the court to represent him at such hearing. **Nichols v. State,** Op. No. 398, 425 P2d 247 (Alaska 1967).

The allegations of a petitioner for post-conviction relief that he had taken drugs some 12 hours prior to time he changed his plea to guilty and that at the time he appeared in court to enter his change of plea he was under the influence of drugs, and thus rendered incompetent, were sufficient to require an evidentiary hearing. Despite the apparent regularity of the competency hearing, the change of plea and the sentencing proceedings, the possibility still exists that the petitioner did not knowingly and understandingly plead to the offense as charged. **Widermyre v. State,** Op. No. 540, 452 P2d 885 (Alaska 1969).

A prisoner seeking post-conviction relief is not denied a fair determination of his motion merely because he is not present in person at hearings on the motion. **Flores v. State,** Op. No. 642, 475 P2d 37 (Alaska 1970).

In a post-conviction proceeding, the attorney who has served as trial counsel for the defendant properly refuses to testify on the question of the adequacy of his representation, in the absence of a waiver of the attorney-client privilege. **Flores v. State,** Op. No. 642, 475 P2d 37 (Alaska 1970).

Normally, whether to produce the prisoner is a decision left to the discretion of the court, but where the defendant's own testimony would be an essential prerequisite to proper adjudication of an issue raised on application for post-conviction relief, the defendant should be permitted to testify. **Fajeriak v. State,** Op. No. 1761, 520 P2d 795 (Alaska 1974).

Where the court elects to consider a petition for post-conviction relief summarily, it must give advance warning of its decision to the parties in a written order spelling out in some detail its reasons for concluding that the petition warrants summary disposition. **Hampton v. Huston,** Op. No. 155, 653 P2d 1058 (Alaska App. 1982).

Reversal of the denial of an applicant's request for post-conviction relief was required when the superior court failed to give the applicant notice that it would treat the state's answer and opposition as a motion to dismiss; further, the superior court did not have the power to dismiss the application sua sponte. **Serradell v. State,** Op. No. 2032, 129 P.3d 461 (Alaska App. 2006).

C. On Review.

Where appellant claimed that he was coerced into a plea of guilty by court appointed counsel who had also given him alleged false assurances of probation, and upon a post-conviction petition under this rule the trial court had found that these charges were unsubstantiated basing its finding upon matter not contained in the record, the case was remanded to the trial court for further proceedings to create a record upon appropriate and specific findings. **Thompson v. State,** Op. No. 334, 412 P2d 628 (Alaska 1966).

The rule contemplates that the sentencing court should be initially called upon to review the sentence. **State v. Pete,** Op. No. 372, 420 P2d 338 (Alaska 1966).

The sole question before a reviewing court when confronted with an order denying, without hearing, a motion for post-conviction relief is whether the petitioner in his application for relief made such a showing as to require a hearing. **Widermyre v. State,** Op. No. 540, 452 P2d 885 (Alaska 1969).

On an appeal from a motion attacking a sentence, the factual findings of the lower court are judged by the same criterion as findings made in a judge-tried civil case. **Merrill v. State,** Op. No. 568, 457 P2d 231 (Alaska 1969).

Where the defendant does not move for an evidentiary hearing or base his motion for a new trial on misconduct by the bailiff, the issue of whether the trial court erred in failing to grant him an evidentiary hearing concerning an allegedly improper statement made by the bailiff to the jury during the course of their deliberations is not properly before the Supreme Court. The defendant is not precluded from raising the issue in a future proceeding on a motion for a new trial or through other means seeking post-conviction relief. **Howard v. State,** Op. No. 754, 491 P2d 154 (Alaska 1971).

Trial court's finding that new evidence, if presented at a new trial, would probably not create a reasonable doubt as to defendant's guilt will be upheld unless such finding constitutes an abuse of discretion. **Hensel v. State,** Op. No. 1983, 604 P2d 222 (Alaska 1979).

Standard for review of trial court's denial of motion for post-conviction relief is one of abuse of discretion. **Hensel v. State,** Op. No. 1983, 604 P2d 222 (Alaska 1979).

An appellant should not be able to raise issues on appeal from the denial of an application for post-conviction relief that he would have been barred from raising on direct appeal from his original conviction. **Marrone v. State,** Op. No. 156, 653 P2d 672 (Alaska App. 1982).

Ad hoc procedural course followed by the trial court departed markedly from the orderly procedure for the expeditious disposition of non-meritorious applications for post-conviction relief contemplated by this rule, depriving the state of a fair opportunity to contest defendant's application for post-conviction relief and requiring reversal of the trial court order setting aside defendant's convictions. **State v. Jones,** Op. No. 832, 759 P2d 558 (Alaska App. 1988).

Given clear indications of attorney neglect, trial court abused its discretion in dismissing petition for post-conviction relief without investigating and resolving issue of whether defendant received effective assistance of counsel; defendant's attorney allowed deadline for filing amended petition to correct deficiencies in original petition to expire without taking action and court received several pleadings and letters from defendant personally, complaining that attorney was neglecting his case. **Howarth v. State,** Op. No. 1708, 13 P3d 754 (Alaska App. 2000).

IV. Time Limits.

Appellate Rule 46 was invoked where strict adherence to the 40-day time limit for appeal under Criminal Rule 35 would have prevented consideration of appellant's contentions that his conditions of imprisonment deprived him of his right to rehabilitation and reformation and to be free of cruel and unusual punishment. **Abraham v. State,** Op. No. 1747, 585 P2d 526 (Alaska 1978).

A person moving to withdraw a guilty plea under Criminal Rule 32(d) and moving for post-conviction relief under Criminal Rule 35(b) need not show that the former motion was made with "due diligence." **Swensen v. Municipality of Anchorage,** Op. No. 2179, 616 P2d 874 (Alaska 1980).

Filing of technically deficient petition for post-conviction relief within time allowed by statute of limitations satisfied statute. **Mullin v. State,** Op. No. 1663, 996 P2d 737 (Alaska App. 2000).

Statutory time limits on petitions for post-conviction relief do not violate the habeas corpus clauses of the federal and state constitutions. **Flanigan v. State,** Op. No. 1677, 3 P3d 372 (Alaska App. 2000).

Where an attorney's certificate pursuant to this rule failed to state why the inmate did not have an arguable defense to the two-year limitations period codified in AS 12.72.020(a)(3)(A), the certificate should not have been accepted, and the post-conviction petition should not have been dismissed. **One v. State,** Op. No. 2025, 127 P.3d 853 (Alaska App. 2006).

Rule 35.2. Discharge and Set-Aside of Conviction.

(a) Where the court has suspended imposition of sentence, the defendant has completed the probationary term without imposition of sentence and no petition to revoke probation is pending, the court shall discharge the defendant from probation. At the time discharge is entered, which shall occur 30 days after defendant's probationary term has expired, or at such later time as the court for cause may direct, the court shall consider whether the conviction should be set-aside. If the court determines that the conviction should be set-aside, it shall issue a certificate to that effect to the defendant. If the court determines that the conviction should not be set-aside, it shall set forth with specificity its reasons for that decision.

(b) The court shall notify the state at least 20 days prior to the expiration of defendant's probationary term that the court will consider whether to discharge the defendant from probation and to set aside the defendant's conviction. In the event any party opposes discharge or set-aside of the conviction, that party shall file a motion with appropriate support not less than 20 days prior to the time discharge is to be entered pursuant to paragraph (a). The defendant must be served with a copy of any such motion and have an opportunity to respond. A copy of the motion also must be mailed to defendant's last attorney of record. Any party, or the court on its own motion, may set the matter for hearing.

(c) In the event that no party has filed a motion opposing set-aside of the conviction, the court may refuse to set-aside the conviction only after affording the defendant notice and an opportunity to be heard. Notice must be served on the defendant and a copy mailed to defendant's last attorney of record.

(Added by SCO 901 effective January 15, 1989)

Annotations

Cases

AS 12.55.085(e), implemented by this rule, does not authorize a court to expunge a defendant's criminal record relating to the underlying conviction which is to be set aside. **Journey v. State,** Op. No. 4197, 895 P2d 955 (Alaska 1995).

Rule 36. Clerical Mistakes.

Clerical mistakes in judgments, orders or other parts of the record, and errors in the record arising from oversight or omission, may be corrected by the court at any time and after such notice, if any, as the court orders. For purposes of this rule, the record includes electronic information maintained about the case.

(Adopted by SCO 4 October 4, 1959; amended by SCO 1622 effective October 15, 2006)

Annotations

Cases

The issue whether a superior court has power to forfeit an aircraft as condition of probation for unlawful possession and transportation of contraband by an airplane is not timely raised by appeal taken after a February 1973 order which amends an August 1972 judgment of conviction by identifying the airplane ordered forfeited. Such issue will not be considered, absent a showing of surprise or injustice or a showing of reason for an accused's failure to appeal the forfeiture within the required ten days. **Graybill v. State,** Op. No. 1045, 522 P2d 539 (Alaska 1974).

Post-conviction proceedings, such as a motion for new trial or for an arrest of judgment, extend the period for taking an appeal. **Graybill v. State,** Op. No. 1045, 522 P2d 539 (Alaska 1974).

A motion to correct a clerical error in a criminal judgment can be made at any time to conform the judgment to the court's original intent insofar as that intent is clearly ascertainable from the record. **Graybill v. State,** Op. No. 1045, 522 P2d 539 (Alaska 1974).

An order entered to correct a clerical error in a criminal judgment may be appealed, but some prejudice such as surprise, must be shown. **Graybill v. State,** Op. No. 1045, 522 P2d 539 (Alaska 1974).

The identification of an airplane ordered forfeited, as a condition of probation, of an accused, who was convicted of unlawfully possessing and transporting contraband by airplane, is a proper modification of a clerical mistake. **Graybill v. State,** Op. No. 1045, 522 P2d 539 (Alaska 1974).

Where the effect of a judgment amendment is to increase the severity of a sentence, Criminal Rule 36 must be interpreted to be applicable only to sentencing errors which obviously conflict with the intention of the court. **Shagloak v. State,** Op. No. 1688, 582 P2d 1034 (Alaska 1978).

Under Criminal Rule 36, only an objectively ascertainable mistake—a mistake which can be determined by contemporaneous record evidence - will justify increasing a sentence. **Shagloak v. State,** Op. No. 1688, 582 P2d 1034 (Alaska 1978).

Contemporaneous record of original probation revocation hearing showed that magistrate intended to revoke defendant's suspended jail time but that 227-day sentence imposed by magistrate reflected miscalculation of defendant's then-suspended incarceration; since this was unquestionably an objectively ascertainable mistake, sentence was subject to subsequent correction under this rule without violating double jeopardy prohibition. **DeMario v. State,** Op. No. 1515, 933 P2d 558 (Alaska App. 1997).

PART VIII. SPECIAL PROCEEDINGS

Rule 37. Search and Seizure.

(a) **Search Warrant Issuance and Contents.**

(1) A search warrant authorized by law shall issue only on affidavit sworn to before a judge or magistrate or any person authorized to take oaths under the law of the state, or sworn testimony taken on the record and establishing the grounds for issuing the warrant.

(2) If the judge or magistrate is satisfied that grounds for the application exist or that there is probable cause to believe that they exist, the judge or magistrate shall issue a warrant identifying the property and naming or describing the person or place to be searched.

(3) The warrant shall be directed to a peace officer of the state authorized to enforce or assist in enforcing any law thereof; and

(A) shall state the ground or probable cause for its issuance and the names of the persons whose affidavits have been taken in support thereof; and

(B) shall command the officer to search the person or place named for the property specified within a reasonable period not to exceed 10 days of the issuance of the warrant; and

(C) shall direct that it be served between 7:00 a.m. and 10:00 p.m., unless the issuing authority by appropriate provision in the warrant, and for reasonable cause shown, authorizes its execution at other than this time; and

(D) shall designate the court, judge, or magistrate to whom it shall be returned.

(b) **Execution and Return with Inventory.** The warrant shall be executed and returned within 10 days after its date. However, upon sworn application made before the expiration of the initial 10 day period or any subsequent extension, the court may for good cause extend the execution period for a reasonable time not to exceed 10 days. The officer taking property under the warrant

(1) shall give to the person from whom or from whose premises the property was taken a copy of the warrant, a copy of the supporting affidavits, and receipt for the property taken, or

(2) shall leave the copies and the receipt at the place from which the property was taken.

The return shall be made promptly and shall be accompanied by a written inventory of any property taken as a result of the search pursuant to or in conjunction with the warrant. The inventory shall be made in the presence of the applicant for the warrant and the person from whose possession or premises the property was taken, if they are present, or in the presence of at least one credible person other than the applicant for the warrant or the person from whose possession or premises the property was taken, and shall be signed by the officer under the penalty of perjury pursuant to

AS 09.63.020 or sworn to in front of a magistrate or judge, or a notary public. The magistrate or judge or the court to which the return is made shall upon request deliver a copy of the inventory to the person from whom or from whose premises the property was taken and to the applicant for the warrant.

(c) **Motion for Return of Property and to Suppress Evidence.** A person aggrieved by an unlawful search and seizure may move the court in the judicial district in which the property was seized or the court in which the property may be used for the return of the property and to suppress for use as evidence anything so obtained on the ground that the property was illegally seized.

(d) **In Camera Hearing.** A person who challenges the validity of a search and seizure predicated on information gained from an informant used either in

(1) support of an application for a warrant, or

(2) as the basis of a search without warrant may move the court for disclosure of the identity of the informant pursuant to Rule 16. In the event the court determines that disclosure of the identity of the informant is not required under Rule 16, the court shall conduct an in camera recorded hearing in which it shall investigate and take evidence so as to determine whether or not a search based on the informant's information was justified. Following the in camera hearing, the court shall grant or deny the motion to suppress on the record, and shall make written findings concerning the validity of the search based on the informer's information. The written findings, together with the record of the hearing, shall be sealed, and if the validity of the search is upheld the sealed testimony and findings shall, on appeal of a conviction in which evidence of the search was admitted, be transmitted to the court of appeals and the supreme court for automatic review of the motion to suppress.

(e) **Confidentiality of Warrant Information.**

(1) The record of proceedings under this rule and all documents related to those proceedings, including search warrants, affidavits, receipts and inventories, must be kept sealed until charges related to the warrant have been filed or four years have elapsed since the issuance of the warrant. However, the court may order prior release of these documents for good cause shown.

(2) After charges related to the warrant are filed, the record of proceedings and all related documents shall be open to public inspection unless the court, for good cause shown, orders that the documents remain sealed for a further period. The initial charging document in all prosecutions must be accompanied by a listing of the numbers of all warrants issued in relation to the case unless the court waives this requirement for good cause shown.

(3) If four years have elapsed since the issuance of the warrant and no charges related to the warrant have been filed, the record of proceedings and all related documents shall be unsealed and shall thereafter be deemed "confidential" as defined in the Administrative Rules and Bulletins. For good cause shown, the court may delay the unsealing.

(Adopted by SCO 4 October 4, 1959; amended by SCO 49 effective January 1, 1963: by Chapter 17 SLA 1969 effective June 25, 1969; by SCO 157 effective February 15, 1973; by SCO 505 effective April 16, 1982; by SCO 645 effective September 15, 1985; by SCO 784 effective March 15, 1987; by SCO 882 effective July 15, 1988; by SCO 968 effective July 15, 1989; by SCO 1149 effective July 15, 1994; by SCO 1153 effective July 15, 1994; by SCO 1389 effective April 15, 2000; by SCO 1553 effective October 15, 2004; and by SCO 1626 effective April 16, 2007)

Note: The Administrative Bulletin defining "confidential" and "sealed" is Administrative Bulletin No. 48, Standard 6. The definitions are also set out in Administrative Rule 37.5(c)(4) and (5). Administrative Bulletin 53, Section IV, discusses sanitizing search warrants in accordance with the Victims' Rights Act after the search warrants are no longer confidential under this rule.

Note: Ch. 75 SLA 2002 (HB 106), Section 4, adds a new section to AS 06.01 relating to the confidentiality of depositor and customer records at banking and other financial institutions. According to Section 56 of the Act, AS 06.01.028(b) has the effect of changing Civil Rule 45, Criminal Rules 17 and 37, and Alaska Bar Rule 24 by requiring certain court orders compelling disclosure of records to provide for reimbursement of a financial institution's reasonable costs of complying with the order.

Editor's Note: Section 43, Chapter 143, Session Laws of Alaska 1982, provides that "AS 12.35.015, added by sec. 18 of this Act [Chapter 143, Session Laws of Alaska 1982], has the effect of changing Rule 37, Rules of Criminal Procedure, by allowing search warrants to be issued upon sworn oral testimony communicated by telephone or other appropriate means."

Cross References

(a) **CROSS REFERENCE:** AS 12.35.010; AS 12.35.020

(b) **CROSS REFERENCE:** AS 12.36

Annotations

Cases

Where defendant failed to move for return of property under Criminal Rule 37(c), the admission of such property taken from defendant was not error. **Goss v. State,** Op. No. 76, 368 P2d 884 (Alaska 1962).

Right to attack search of suitcase and seizure of gun as illegal was waived by pleading guilty to a charge of illegal possession of firearm. **Rivett v. State,** Op. No. 249, 395 P2d 264 (Alaska 1964).

Denial of motion to suppress evidence sustained where probable cause existed for arresting appellant without warrant and evidence was taken from him as an incident to such arrest. **Maze v. State,** Op. No. 400, 425 P2d 235 (Alaska 1967); **Merrill v. State,** Op. No. 392, 423 P2d 686 (Alaska 1967).

Where in the investigation of a rape case the accused, his father and an accused accomplice were voluntarily present in the police station, and the police officer learned through a statement of the accomplice that a note written by victim was in the accused's possession, constitutional provisions proscribing unreasonable searches and seizures did not prohibit seizure of the note to prevent its destruction or removal and motion to suppress the note as illegally obtained evidence was properly defined. **Woltz, et al. v. State,** Op. No. 433, 431 P2d 502 (Alaska 1967).

Since order of trial court suppressing evidence obtained by search would likely result in terminating the prosecution and involved a controlling question of law, review was appropriate. **State v. Stump,** Op. No. 1250, 547 P2d 305 (Alaska 1976).

Search warrant need not set out contents of the affidavit on which it is issued. **Kirstich v. State,** Op. No. 1264, 550 P2d 796 (Alaska 1976).

Valid service of a search warrant between the hours of 10:00 p.m. and 7:00 a.m. requires a determination by issuing judge that the warrant may be served at any time. **State v. Shelton,** Op. No. 1311, 554 P2d 404 (Alaska 1976).

That warrant was presented to judge in the middle of the night, with affidavit containing requisite showing for nighttime service under this rule and requesting an immediate search, clearly indicates that nighttime service was contemplated and authorized. **State v. Shelton,** Op. No. 1311, 554 P2d 404 (Alaska 1976).

A showing of probable credibility of a confidential informant is adequate where the affidavit alleges "that the informant has given accurate information in the past." **Johnson v. State,** Op. No. 2169, 617 P2d 1117 (Alaska 1980).

Fact that judge met police at a parking lot and then issued a search warrant within just a few minutes after an affidavit was presented to him did not mean that he failed to act in a neutral and detached manner. **Johnson v. State,** Op. No. 2169, 617 P2d 1117 (Alaska 1980).

A description of the property to be searched is sufficient if there is no reasonable probability that the wrong premises will be searched. **Johnson v. State,** Op. No. 2169, 617 P2d 1117 (Alaska 1980).

A warrant for a nighttime search may be issued pursuant to an affidavit showing probable cause that at some future time certain evidence will be at the location set forth in the warrant. **Johnson v. State,** Op. No. 2169, 617 P2d 1117 (Alaska 1980).

An explicit statement by the affiant that he is positive that the property sought is at the place to be searched is not required to validate a nighttime search warrant. **Johnson v. State,** Op. No. 2169, 617 P2d 1117 (Alaska 1980).

The word "positive" as used in this rule means "reasonably certain." **Johnson v. State,** Op. No. 2169, 617 P2d 1117 (Alaska 1980).

Written log notes suffice as a record of the search warrant hearing in the absence of an electronic record due to equipment failure. **Nelson v. State,** Op. No. 2350, 628 P2d 884 (Alaska 1981).

An in camera hearing is mandatory if the court determines that the identity of an informant upon whose information a search warrant was issued need not be disclosed. **Schmid v. State,** Op. No. 2126, 615 P2d 565 (Alaska 1980).

This rule requires service of an inventory upon an individual who has been the subject of a warrant for participant electronic monitoring of conversations, but service may be postponed for a reasonable period of time, such period to be governed by the exigencies established in each case by the affidavit accompanying the state's application for the warrant. **Jones v. State,** Op. No. 93, 646 P2d 243 (Alaska App. 1982).

Where, through the course of indictment and pretrial discovery, defendant, who had been the subject of a warrant for participant electronic monitoring of conversations, was given information equivalent to that which he would have been entitled to under this rule, trial court's error in failing to make provision for eventual service of inventory as required by this rule was harmless. **Jones v. State,** Op. No. 93, 646 P2d 243 (Alaska App. 1982).

Validity of nighttime warrant was upheld where the articles described in the warrant were reasonably certain to be present on the premises to be searched. **Garibay v. State,** Op. No. 221, 658 P2d 1350 (Alaska App. 1983).

The positivity requirement of this rule does not restrict nighttime searches only to those cases where a daytime search would be ineffective. **Garibay v. State,** Op. No. 221, 655 P2d 1350 (Alaska App. 1983).

Untimely notification of execution of warrant authorizing defendant's telephone conversation to be recorded did not justify suppression of the recording where no prejudice to defendant was shown and the late notification was not the result of bad faith on the part of investigating officers. **Bell v. State,** Op. No. 288, 668 P2d 829 (Alaska App. 1983).

To the extent that Section 18 of Chapter 143, SLA 1982, enacted as AS 12.35.015, conflicts with this rule, this rule controls. **Galbraith v. State,** Op. No. 437, 693 P2d 880 (Alaska App. 1985).

Suppression of evidence is an extreme sanction that should only be utilized in the most egregious cases of violation of this rule. **State v. White,** Op. No. 519, 707 P2d 271 (Alaska App. 1985).

The determination of whether to apply a suppression sanction for improper execution of a warrant is to be made on the particular facts of each case; no per se rule of suppression should be adopted, even in cases of intentional or bad faith failure to comply with the requirements. **State v. White,** Op. No. 519, 707 P2d 271 (Alaska App. 1985).

Police officer's off-the-record statement to the magistrate who issued the search warrant could not be considered as part of the affidavit in support of the search warrant. **State v. White,** Op. No. 519, 707 P2d 271 (Alaska App. 1985).

Where affidavit in support of warrant to search defendant's residence contained no express connection between defendant and the residence, the warrant was invalid. **State v. White,** Op. No. 519, 707 P2d 271 (Alaska App. 1985).

Misstatements on warrants were material and intentional, justifying suppression of evidence obtained through use of the warrants. **State v. White,** Op. No. 519, 707 P2d 271 (Alaska App. 1985).

When notice of a wiretap is not given, suppression of the intercepted evidence is a remedy only when officers intentionally violate the notice requirement or the defendant can show actual prejudice; prejudice is not found when a defendant receives notice from another source, nor is there prejudice when notice is not so late as to undermine a defendant's ability to challenge the evidence intercepted. **Brannen v. State,** Op. No. 1076, 798 P2d 337 (Alaska App. 1990).

Evidence did not support defendant's assertion that police officer intentionally failed to notify him of a wiretap. **Brannen v. State,** Op. No. 1076, 798 P2d 337 (Alaska App. 1990).

Prejudice resulting from lack of notice under this rule could not be established by mere claim by defendant that had he been notified he would have been able to take evasive action to thwart future investigation efforts. **Brannen v. State,** Op. No. 1076, 798 P2d 337 (Alaska App. 1990).

In drug case where an issue was whether the police investigation was the product of an illegal search by police informants, and the state asserted its privilege not to identify the informants, upon which the judge conducted an in camera hearing at which he questioned the informants using the questions submitted by the defendant and the state and concluded that the identity of the informants did not have to be revealed, the defendant was entitled to see the transcript of the in camera hearing with all information deleted that might identify the informants. **Peter son v. State,** Op. No. 1139, 813 P2d 685 (Alaska App. 1991).

Cases where the police deliberately violate the notification requirement of Criminal Rule 37(b) are treated differently than those where the violation was not deliberate. **Steffensen v. State,** Op. No. 1420, 900 P2d 735 (Alaska App. 1995).

The notification requirement of Rule 37(b) is aimed at protecting the person who has suffered a trespass to land and/or chattels, but is not intended to notify targets of a criminal investigation that the government has commenced an inquiry into their activities. **Steffensen v. State,** Op. No. 1420, 900 P2d 735 (Alaska App. 1995).

Claim for post-conviction relief was based upon defendant's loss of evidence, stemming from the government's delay in notifying him of the planned criminal charges. This claim was cognizable under the doctrine of pre-accusation delay. The government's failure to provide the notice required by Criminal Rule 37(b) did not alter the proof required under the doctrine of pre-accusation delay. **Steffensen v. State,** Op. No. 1420, 900 P2d 735 (Alaska App. 1995).

Violation of the notification requirement of Criminal Rule 37(b) should result in suppression of the fruits of a validly issued **Glass**warrant only when the violation is intentional or when the delay in notification results in actual prejudice to the accused. **Steffensen v. State,** Op. No. 1420, 900 P2d 735 (Alaska App. 1995).

In the context of **Glass**warrants, tardy notification of the execution of a warrant "prejudices" a defendant when the lateness of the notice impairs the defendant's ability to challenge the intercepted conversion. However, "prejudice" does not include the delay in the defendant's finding out that he or she is under investigation. This second type of delay is directly addressed by the doctrine of pre-accusation delay. **Steffensen v. State,** Op. No. 1420, 900 P2d 735 (Alaska App. 1995).

Assuming that officer was authorized to commit a second trespass upon defendant's property because he had forgotten to leave defendant an inventory of the property seized during a warrant-authorized search of defendant's land, the second trespass was necessarily of limited scope and did not include an additional search of defendant's land for evidence of marijuana cultivation. **Braund v. State,** Op. No. 1703, 12 P3d 187 (Alaska App. 2000).

Where trial court was able to judge the credibility of the police who obtained the search warrant against the defendant, and found that the police had not sought to deliberately mislead the magistrate, the defendant's claim that the police recklessly omitted information that was material to the issuance of the warrant failed. **Stavenjord v. State,** Op. No. 1863, 66 P.3d 762 (Alaska App. 2003).

State troopers' failure to inform the magistrate that they had not seen evidence of a 22 caliber weapon when visiting the defendant's residence might have been reckless, but not material to the issuance of a warrant because lack of evidence of the weapon did not undercut the other evidence supporting probable cause. **Stavenjord v. State,** Op. No. 1863, 66 P.3d 762 (Alaska App. 2003).

PART IX. GENERAL PROVISIONS

Rule 38. Presence of the Defendant.

(a) **Presence: Required.** The defendant shall be present at the arraignment, at the preliminary hearing, at the time of plea, at the omnibus hearing, and at every stage of the trial, including the impaneling of the jury and return of the verdict, and at the imposition of sentence, except as otherwise provided in this rule.

(b) **Continued Presence Not Required.** The further progress of the trial to and including the return of the verdict shall not be prevented whenever a defendant, initially present:

(1) Is absent voluntarily after the trial has commenced; or

(2) Engages in conduct which is such as to justify exclusion from the courtroom.

(c) **Presence Not Required.** A defendant need not be present in the following situations:

(1) A corporation may appear by counsel for all purposes;

(2) In prosecutions for offenses punishable by fine or by imprisonment for not more than one year or both, the court, with the written consent of the defendant, may permit arraignment, plea, trial, and imposition of sentence in the defendant's absence;

(3) The defendant's presence is not required at a hearing on reduction of sentence under Rule 35(a).

(Adopted by SCO 4 October 4, 1959; amended by SCO 157 effective February 15, 1973; and by SCO 1153 effective July 15, 1994)

Annotations

Cases

I. In General.
II. Communication Between Judge and Jury.

I. In General.

In a prosecution for a felony, Rule 38 required defendant's presence at a hearing held before trial to determine whether defendant's wife would testify and whether she should be held as a material witness. **Brown v. State,** Op. No. 89, 372 P2d 785 (Alaska 1962).

While a prisoner cannot be prevented from testifying on his own behalf in support of a substantial claim where his testimony would be material, the presence of a petitioner at a fact hearing under a post-conviction petition is not automatically required and having due regard to costs of transporting state prisoners the sentencing court has discretion to ascertain whether the claim is substantial before requiring such presence. **Thompson v. State,** Op. No. 334, 412 P2d 628 (Alaska 1966).

The first sentence of this rule which is identical to the first sentence of Fed. R. Crim. P. 43 represents a restatement of existing law that, after indictment found, nothing shall be done in the absence of the prisoner. **Noffke v. State,** Op. No. 383, 422 P2d 102 (Alaska 1967).

While conferences held between court and counsel during a trial for the purpose of hearing arguments of law on evidentiary ruling and similar matters are not "stages of a trial" within this rule and the requirement of presence of the defendant at such conferences is a matter for the sound discretion of the trial judge, the better practice is to require such presence and to grant readily requests from counsel or the defendant himself to be present. **Kugzruk v. State,** Op. No. 451, 436 P2d 962 (Alaska 1968).

Absence of defendant from anteroom conferences did not constitute reversible error where trial counsel had not objected to the defendant's absence and no substantial rights of the defendant were affected by anything which transpired at these conferences. **Kugzruk v. State,** Op. No. 451, 436 P2d 962 (Alaska 1968).

Defendant was not denied his constitutionally protected rights at the critical stage of the actual sentencing where the prosecutor was exhibiting to the trial judge photographs of the deceased victim, at the time defendant's counsel entered the chambers but record affirmatively showed that within minutes of the ex parte incident sentencing procedures in open court were held in the presence of defendant and his counsel. **Egelak v. State,** Op. No. 463, 438 P2d 712 (Alaska 1968).

Sentencing is a critical stage in the proceeding at which the criminal defendant has a constitutional right to be present and to be assisted by counsel. **Egelak v. State,** Op. No. 463, 438 P2d 712 (Alaska 1968).

Defendant's presence was required when court heard arguments by counsel on (1) whether jury could hear replay of certain testimony and (2) whether jury would be allowed to separate once deliberations had begun. **Kimoktoak v. State,** Op. No. 1624, 578 P2d 594 (Alaska 1978).

Trial court did not err in failing to require defendant's presence at a deposition concerning a contempt charge brought against one of his attorneys where his absence could not have prejudiced his defense. **Osborne v. State,** Op. No. 2291, 623 P2d 784 (Alaska 1981).

Absence of defendant from pretrial in-chambers conference which was limited to purely legal and procedural questions was error, but the error was harmless since there was no indication that defendant's presence would have aided his defense. **Dolchok v. State,** Op. No. 2458, 639 P2d 277 (Alaska 1982).

Trial court erred in excusing juror in the absence of defendant, but the error was harmless. **Coney v. State,** Op. No. 471, 699 P2d 899 (Alaska App. 1985).

Although defendant had a right to be present at his omnibus hearing, his absence from the hearing was held harmless beyond a reasonable doubt despite his claim that attendance would have alerted him to the need to peremptorily challenge the trial judge and to affirmatively protect his speedy trial rights. **Trudeau v. State,** Op. No. 581, 714 P2d 362 (Alaska App. 1986).

Even when a hearsay exception applies to a nontestifying victim's statement, the confrontation clause requires a high degree of reliability and trustworthiness and a demonstrated need for admission. **Drumbarger v. State,** Op. No. 601, 716 P2d 6 (Alaska App. 1986).

Right of confrontation was not violated by admission of child's out-of court statement even though child was not called to testify. **Drumbarger v. State,** Op. No. 601, 716 P2d 6 (Alaska App. 1986).

Trial court did not have the authority to assess costs against defendant as a sanction for defendant's non-willful failure to appear on time for his jury trial. **Jerrel v. State,** Op. No. 885, 765 P2d 982 (Alaska App. 1988).

Unless defendant consents to communicate with sentencing judge by telephone, judge must be physically present when defendant exercises his right of allocution and when judge initially pronounces defendant's sentence. **Henry v. State,** Op. No. 1321, 861 P2d 582 (Alaska App. 1993).

When witness in criminal trial asserts privilege not to testify, trial judge has authority to hear witness's explanation ex parte. **Taylor v. State,** Op. No. 1625, 977 P2d 123 (Alaska App. 1999).

In assault and kidnapping trial, trial judge's incarceration of complaining witness following ex parte hearing at which prosecutor told judge that witness was likely to recant, was intoxicated, and should be incarcerated until she testified, was reversible error, since ex parte hearing violated defendant's right to be present at hearing under this rule. **Raphael v. State,** Op. No. 5229, 994 P2d 1004 (Alaska 2000).

While court agreed that defendant's federal and state constitutional right to be present throughout the trial was violated, and that Alaska R. Crim. P. 38(a) was violated, because the court staff erred in providing the jury with a verdict form without authorization from the court and notice to defendant, the error was harmless beyond a reasonable doubt. **Crouse v. Municipality of Anchorage,** Op. No. 1905, 79 P.3d 660 (Alaska App. 2003).

Even if a trial court violated this rule by conducting a portion of a telephone conference regarding sentence without defendant being present, the error was harmless beyond a reasonable doubt because defendant was aware of the nature of the conversation before it ended, and defendant could have objected to the action taken because the sentencing did not occur until several months later. **Hurd v. State,** Op. No. 1923, 107 P.3d 314 (Alaska App. 2005).

II. Communication Between Judge and Jury.

Unauthorized communication between judge and jury constitutes reversible error only if the violation of the rule affects a substantial right of the defendant. **Noffke v. State,** Op. No. 383, 422 P2d 102 (Alaska 1967).

In a criminal trial, it was error for the trial court to have sent requested additional instructions to the jury during its deliberations outside the defendant's presence. **Noffke v. State,** Op. No. 383, 422 P2d 102 (Alaska 1967).

A supplemental jury instruction on the elements of the crime of burglary, which was ambiguous and could have led the jury to find the defendant guilty without having found that he had the requisite statutory intent to steal, affected a substantial right of the defendant and giving this instruction outside the presence of the defendant was reversible error. **Noffke v. State,** Op. No. 383, 422 P2d 102 (Alaska 1967).

An exchange of notes between the trial judge and the jury foreman without the knowledge of defendant and his counsel violated the requirement of presence of defendant at all stages of criminal proceedings but did not constitute reversible error in a case where the communication had no direct bearing on the merits of the case and did not affect a substantial right of the defendant. **Gafford v. State,** Op. No. 478,440 P2d 405 (Alaska 1968).

Where the defendant has no knowledge that the jury returned a note stating that they felt they were deadlocked with no hope of reaching a unanimous decision, whereupon the trial judge discharges them from further deliberative duties, the defendant's absence from proceedings is not "voluntary" so as to constitute a waiver of his right to be present. **Koehler v. State,** Op. No. 1000, 519 P2d 442 (Alaska 1974).

When a jury indicates that it is deadlocked, the trial court's decision to proceed in the absence of both the accused and his counsel and to discharge the jury from further deliberative duties deprives the defendant of the important right to have his trial completed by that particular jury. Where a defendant has not voluntarily absented himself from the proceedings his substantial rights are affected and the error cannot be regarded as harmless, notwithstanding a trial judge's statement that on a motion to dismiss the indictment, he would have discharged the jury regardless of any suggestion the defendant might have made. **Koehler v. State,** Op. No. 1000, 519 P2d 442 (Alaska 1974).

This rule requires that defendant be present when recorded testimony is played back to jury. **State v. Hannagan,** Op. No. 1374, 559 P2d 1059 (Alaska 1977).

Defendant's right to be present while testimony is replayed may not be waived by counsel. **State v. Hannagan,** Op. No. 1374, 559 P2d 1059 (Alaska 1977).

A violation of this rule is reversible unless harmless beyond a reasonable doubt. **State v. Hannagan,** Op. No. 1374, 559 P2d 1059 (Alaska 1977).

Defendant's absence during playback of testimony was harmless error. **State v. Hannagan,** Op. No. 1374, 559 P2d 1059 (Alaska 1977).

Superior court's ex parte communication to the jury in the absence of defendant and his attorney in violation of Criminal Rule 38(a) was reversible error as it could not under the circumstances be considered harmless beyond a reasonable doubt. **Cox v. State,** Op. No. 1567, 575 P2d 297 (Alaska 1978).

Trial court committed reversible error in responding to a written communication from the jury during its deliberations concerning a playback of certain crucial testimony without notifying the defendant or either counsel of the communication and without allowing the parties to be present and to be heard on the matter. **Dixon v. State,** Op. No. 2010, 605 P2d 882 (Alaska 1980).

Defendant's right to be present at all stages of trial was not violated by allowing jurors to submit questions in writing to court after each witness testified, although questions deemed inadmissible by court were not shown to counsel, where counsel did not request to see such questions. **Linden v. State,** Op. No. 1905, 598 P2d 960 (Alaska 1979).

Where judge excused juror from further service on fifth day of trial, in absence of defendant and his counsel and over the objection of counsel, who wanted to voir dire juror regarding grounds for excuse and where replacement juror was approved by defendant, no violation of defendant's right to be present at all stages of trial occurred. **Huff v. State,** Op. No. 1895, 598 P2d 928 (Alaska 1979).

A post-verdict conference to determine whether the jury had misunderstood the expert witness instruction is a stage of trial which requires the presence of the defendant, but the defendant's absence during the conference may constitute harmless error. **Meyer v. State,** Op. No. 2333, 627 P2d 636 (Alaska 1981).

Bailiff's failure to deliver a jury deadlock note to the trial judge precluded an opportunity to conduct proceedings on the record in defendant's presence and thus constituted reversible error. **Wamser v. State,** Op. No. 2571, 652 P2d 98 (Alaska 1982).

Where either prior to or immediately following the jury's verdict the court received a communication from the jury that they felt threatened by the presence of defendant's boyfriend, the court's failure to notify the defense of the communication was reversible error. **Newman v. State,** Op. No. 174, 655 P2d 1302 (Alaska App. 1982).

Failure to notify the defendant of a jury communication is constitutional error that requires reversal on appeal unless the error is found harmless beyond a reasonable doubt. **Jones v. State,** Op. No. 622, 719 P2d 265 (Alaska App. 1986).

Rule 38.1. Telephonic Participation in Criminal Cases.

(a) In any proceeding at which the defendant's presence is required under Criminal Rule 38(a), as modified by Rule 38.2, the defendant may waive the right to be present and request to participate by telephone. The defendant's waiver of the right to be physically present may be obtained orally on the record or in writing. The court may allow telephonic participation of one or more parties, counsel or the judge at any proceeding in its discretion. The court may allow telephonic participation of witnesses at bail hearings, omnibus hearings, probation revocation hearings or at trial with the consent of the prosecution and the defendant. The court may allow telephonic participation of witnesses at other hearings in its discretion.

(b) The provisions of AS 12.35.015 shall govern the issuance of search warrants by telephone.

(c) The provisions of Criminal Rule 6(u) govern telephonic participation in grand jury proceedings.

(Amended by SCO 622 effective June 15, 1985; by SCO 897 effective July 15, 1988; by SCO 960 effective July 15, 1989; by SCO 1115 effective January 15, 1993; and by SCO 1161 effective July 15, 1994)

Annotations

Cases

Allowing alleged victim to testify by telephone in grand jury proceeding was not error although it would have been preferable for the prosecution to have established for the record that no one was present with the victim during her testimony in violation of criminal rules for grand jury proceedings. **Boggess v. State,** Op. No. 988, 783 P2d 1173 (Alaska App. 1989).

Trial judge did not err in admitting documents using telephonic testimony without the defendant's consent where the judge also directed the state to immediately send properly self-authenticated copies of the documents to the court; the fact that the court received the properly authenticated documents after the jury retired for its deliberations was of no consequence, since this was simply the court's means to ensure the propriety of its ruling, and it was not necessary for the new documents to be presented at trial. **Tuckfield v. State,** Op. No. 1103, 805 P2d 982 (Alaska App. 1991).

Unless defendant consents to communicate with sentencing judge by telephone, judge must be physically present when defendant exercises his right of allocution and when judge initially pronounces defendant's sentence. **Henry v. State,** Op. No. 1321, 861 P2d 582 (Alaska App. 1993).

Term "omnibus hearings" in this rule includes additional evidentiary hearings needed to resolve pretrial motions, thus trial court erred in allowing witness to testify by telephone at pre-trail evidentiary hearing over objection of defendant. **Kailukiak v. State,** Op. No. 1588, 959 P2d 771 (Alaska App. 1998).

Rule 38.2. Televised Appearance by Defendant.

(a) The Administrative Director of the Alaska Court System, after consultation with the presiding judge, Public Defender Agency, and Attorney General's Office, may enter into agreements with the Department of Public Safety and Department of Corrections which approve systems allowing judges to provide for the appearance by a defendant at certain criminal proceedings by way of television equipment in lieu of the physical presence of the defendant in the courtroom. Such an agreement must provide for a procedure by which the defendant may confer with the defendant's attorney in private.

(b) In those court locations in which a television system has been approved by the supreme court and has been installed, in custody defendants shall appear by way of television for arraignment, pleas, and non-evidentiary bail reviews in traffic and misdemeanor cases; and initial appearance hearings, non-evidentiary bail reviews, and not guilty plea arraignments in felony cases, unless otherwise ordered for cause stated by the presiding judge. With the defendant's consent, sentencings may be done by way of television in traffic and misdemeanor cases.

In any particular case, the trial court may order that the defendant be transported to court for court proceedings if the trial judge finds that the defendant's rights would be prejudiced by use of the system.

(c) Facsimile telecopy orders issued in proceedings conducted under this rule are acceptable as originals for the purposes of release or detention by correctional officers.

(d) Nothing in this rule diminishes any other existing right of a criminal defendant.

(Added by SCO 719 effective August 1, 1986; amended by SCO 863 effective July 15, 1988)

Rule 39. Appointment of Counsel.

(a) **Informing Defendant of Right to Counsel.** The court shall advise a defendant who appears without counsel for arraignment, change of plea, or trial of the right to be represented by counsel, and ask if the defendant desires the aid of counsel. The court shall not allow a defendant to proceed without an attorney unless the defendant understands the benefits of counsel and knowingly waives the right to counsel.

(b) **Appointment of Counsel for Persons Financially Unable to Employ Counsel.**

(1) If a defendant desires the aid of counsel but claims a financial inability to employ counsel, the court or its designee shall determine whether the defendant is eligible for court-

appointed counsel under Criminal Rule 39.1.

(2) Before the court appoints counsel for an indigent defendant at public expense, the court shall advise the defendant that the defendant will be ordered to repay the prosecuting authority for the cost of appointed counsel, in accordance with paragraph (d) of this rule, if the defendant is convicted of an offense. The court may enter such orders as appear reasonably necessary to prevent the defendant from dissipating assets to avoid payment of this cost.

(3) If the court or its designee determines that a defendant is eligible for court-appointed counsel under Criminal Rule 39.1, the court shall appoint counsel pursuant to Administrative Rule 12 and notify counsel of the appointment.

(4) In the absence of a request by a defendant otherwise entitled to appointment of counsel, the court shall appoint counsel unless the court finds that the defendant understands the benefits of counsel and knowingly waives the right to counsel.

(5) If the trial court denies a defendant's request for appointed counsel, the defendant may request review of this decision by the presiding judge of the judicial district by filing a motion with the trial court within three days after the date of notice, as defined in Criminal Rule 32.3(c), of the denial. The trial court shall forward the motion, relevant materials from the court file, and an electronic recording of any relevant proceedings to the presiding judge. The presiding judge or his or her designee shall issue a decision within three days of receipt of these materials.

(c) ***Costs of Appointed Counsel.***

(1) *Entry of Judgment.*

(A) At the time of sentencing, revocation of probation, denial of a motion to withdraw plea, and denial of an application brought under Criminal Rule 35.1, the court shall inquire whether there is good cause why the court should not enter judgment for the cost of appointed counsel in the amount set out in subsection (d) of this rule. If no one asserts good cause to reduce the amount called for in subsection (d), the court shall enter judgment against the defendant in that amount. If it is alleged that there is good cause to reduce the normal amount, the court may either decide the issue at that time and enter judgment accordingly or schedule another hearing to consider the issue.

(B) If the court finds that the actual cost of appointed counsel is less than the amount of payment called for in subsection (d), the court shall not enter judgment in an amount greater than the actual cost of counsel.

(C) The judgment must be in writing. A copy of the judgment must be served on the defendant. The judgment bears interest at the rate specified in AS 09.30.070(a) from the date judgment is entered. The court shall order the defendant to apply for permanent fund dividends every year in which the defendant qualifies for the dividend until the judgment is paid in full.

(2) *Collection.*

(A) The judgment has the same force and effect as a judgment in a civil action in favor of the prosecuting authority and is subject to execution.

(B) All proceedings to enforce the judgment shall be in accordance with the statutes and court rules applicable to civil judgments. The judgment is not enforceable by contempt. Payment of the judgment may not be made a condition of a defendant's probation. Default or failure to pay the judgment may not affect or reduce the rendering of services on appeal or any other phase of a defendant's case in any way. A defendant does not have a right to be represented by appointed counsel in connection with proceedings under paragraph 39(c) or any proceedings to collect the judgment.

(C) Upon showing of financial hardship, the court shall allow a defendant subject to a judgment under this rule to make payments under a repayment schedule. A defendant may petition the court at any time for remission, reduction or deferral of the unpaid portion of the judgment. The court may remit or reduce the balance owing on the judgment or change the method of payment if the payment would impose manifest hardship on the defendant or the defendant's immediate family.

(D) Notwithstanding section 39(c)(2)(B), a defendant may be held in contempt for failing to comply with an order under this rule to apply for a permanent fund dividend.

(3) *Appeal.*

(A) If the defendant appeals the conviction, enforcement of the judgment may be stayed by the trial court or the appellate court upon such terms as the court deems proper.

(B) If the defendant's conviction is reversed, the clerk shall vacate the judgment and order the prosecuting authority to repay all sums paid in satisfaction of the judgment, plus interest at the rate specified in AS 09.30.070(a).

(d) **Schedule of Costs.** Except for good cause shown as provided in paragraph (c)(1), the following schedules govern the assessment of costs of appointed counsel under subsection (c). If a defendant is convicted of more than one offense in a single dispositive court proceeding, costs shall be based on the most serious offense of which the defendant is convicted. If a defendant is otherwise convicted of more than one offense, costs shall be separately assessed for each conviction. For good cause shown, the court may waive the schedule of costs and assess fees up to the actual cost of appointed counsel, including actual expenses.

Misdemeanors

Trial	$500.00
Change of plea	200.00
Post-conviction relief or contested probation revocation proceedings in the trial court	250.00

Felonies

	Class B & C	Class A and Unclassified (Except Murder)	Murder in the 1st and 2nd Degrees
Trial	$1,500.00	$2,500.00	$5,000.00
Change of plea after substantive motion work and hearing and before trial commences	1,000.00	1,500.00	2,500.00
Change of plea post-indictment but prior to substantive motion work and hearing	500.00	1,000.00	2,000.00
Change of plea prior to indictment	250.00	500.00	750.00
Post-conviction relief or probation revocation proceeding in trial court	250.00	500.00	750.00

(e) **Review of Defendant's Financial Condition.**

(1) The court may review a defendant's financial status at any time after appointment of counsel to determine (A) whether the defendant continues to be eligible for court-appointed counsel under Criminal Rule 39.1; or (B) whether the defendant was eligible for court-appointed counsel when the appointment was made.

(2) If the court determines that a defendant is no longer eligible for court-appointed counsel under Criminal Rule 39.1, the court may

(A) terminate the appointment; or

(B) continue the appointment and, at the conclusion of the criminal proceedings against the defendant in the trial court, enter judgment against the defendant for the actual cost of appointed counsel, including actual expenses, from the date of the change in the defendant's financial status through the conclusion of the trial court proceedings.

(3) If the court determines that a defendant was not eligible for court-appointed counsel when the appointment was made, the court may

(A) terminate the appointment and enter judgment against the defendant for the actual costs of appointed counsel, including actual expenses, from the date of appointment through the date of termination; or

(B) continue the appointment and, at the conclusion of the criminal proceedings against the defendant in the trial court, enter judgment against the defendant for the actual cost of appointed counsel from the date of the appointment through the conclusion of the trial court proceedings.

(4) A defendant may request review of the court's decision to terminate the appointment according to the procedure set out in subparagraph 39(b)(5).

(5) Judgment may be entered against a defendant under this paragraph regardless of whether the defendant is convicted of an offense.

(Adopted by SCO 4 October 4, 1959; amended by SCO 90 effective July 24, 1967: by SCO 157 effective February 15, 1973; by Amendment No. 4 to SCO 157 dated March 12, 1973; by SCO 187 effective July 2, 1974; by SCO 328 effective January 1, 1979; by SCO 448 effective November 24 1980; by SCO 677 effective June 15, 1986; and by SCO 888 effective July 15, 1988; rescinded and re-promulgated by SCO 1088 effective July 1, 1992; amended by SCO 1139 effective July 1, 1993; by SCO 1145 effective October 1, 1993; by SCO 1351 effective May 15, 1999; by SCO 1555 effective October 15, 2004; and by SCO 1566 effective May 15, 2005)

Dissent to SCO 1088:

RABINOWITZ, Chief Justice, with whom COMPTON, Justice, joins, dissenting:

I am not persuaded that either existing Criminal Rule 39, or Appellate Rule 209, requires amendment. I think it can be safely predicted that these amendments will have a chilling effect on an indigent defendant's obtaining the services of appointed counsel as well as on an indigent defendant's decision whether or not to seek review or to appeal.

Annotations

Cases

I. Right to Counsel.

A. In General.

A defendant in a criminal proceeding has a constitutional right to court appointed counsel at a preliminary hearing only when the preliminary hearing is in the nature of a critical stage of the proceedings. **Merrill v. State,** Op. No. 392, 423 P2d 686 (Alaska 1967).

Where the court over defendant's explicit protest, dismisses counsel from a public defender agency on the belief that the agency has exhibited a lack of preparation and then appoints unwanted counsel to represent the defendant, the court deprives the defendant of his right to counsel of his choice. **McKinnon v. State,** Op. No. 1075, 526 P2d 18 (Alaska 1974).

Where a defendant has been denied the right to be represented by his chosen counsel, the subsequent entry of a plea of guilty or nolo contendere does not shield a conviction from challenge on appeal, since the voluntariness and reliability of such a plea is inherently suspect. **McKinnon v.**

State, Op. No. 1075, 526 P2d 18 (Alaska 1974).

The advice given to a nonindigent defendant concerning the right to counsel must include at least a brief explanation of the benefits of counsel. **Swensen v. Municipality of Anchorage,** Op. No. 2179, 616 P2d 874 (Alaska 1980).

It is within the court's discretion to allow both defendant and counsel to participate actively in the trial, so that a defendant may represent himself and also have the assistance of counsel. **Cano v. Municipality of Anchorage,** Op. No. 20, 627 P2d 660 (Alaska 1980).

This rule does not violate the equal protection guarantees of the Alaska or the federal constitutions. **State v. Albert,** Op. No. 4225, 899 P2d 103 (Alaska 1995).

Alaska's recoupment system for recovery of costs of appointed counsel does not violate the right to counsel guaranteed by the Sixth Amendment to the United States Constitution. **State v. Albert,** Op. No. 4225, 899 P2d 103 (Alaska 1995).

Alaska's recoupment system for recovery of costs of appointed counsel does not violate the right to counsel expressed in article 1, section 11 of the Alaska constitution. **State v. Albert,** Op. No. 4225, 899 P2d 103 (Alaska 1995).

Trial court had discretion to require Office of Public Advocacy to continue to represent the father of children alleged to be children in need of aid despite fact that trial court found that father was no longer eligible for appointed counsel; Administrative Rule 12 adopts Criminal Rule 39, and that rule permits the court to continue an appointment even if the client is ineligible. **Office of Public Advocacy v. Superior Court, Second Judicial Dist.,** Op. No. 5291, 3 P3d 932 (Alaska 2000).

Use of rule-making power to authorize courts to order a defendant to apply for a permanent fund dividend in some criminal cases does not imply that the superior court lacks discretion to enter such an order in a civil case when necessary to enforce a judgment. **State v. DeLeon,** Op. No. 5853, 103 P.3d 897 (Alaska 2004).

B. Indigents.

Even when read in relation to recent United States Supreme Court decisions, AS 12.25.150(b) does not require the appointment of counsel for an indigent immediately after his arrest. **Martinez v. State,** Op. No. 389, 423 P2d 700 (Alaska 1967).

Mere speculation as to what might have been done by a defense counsel during an interval between arrest and appearance for arraignment when counsel was assigned cannot be a basis for inferring that indigent defendant in a criminal case was deprived of counsel during a critical stage of the proceedings. **Martinez v. State,** Op. No. 389, 423 P2d 700 (Alaska 1967).

Where the direct penalty for conviction of an offense may be incarceration, loss of a valuable license, or a fine heavy enough to indicate criminality, such offense is a "serious crime" within the public defender statute. A defendant who is charged with any such misdemeanor and who cannot afford to hire his own lawyer is eligible for representation by a public defender. **Alexander v. City of Anchorage,** Op. No. 738, 490 P2d 910 (Alaska 1971).

A indigent defendant is not entitled to representation by any particular attorney. **McKinnon v. State,** Op. No. 1075, 526 P2d 18 (Alaska 1974).

Once counsel is appointed to represent an indigent defendant, the parties enter into an attorney-client relationship which is no less inviolable than if counsel had been retained. **McKinnon v. State,** Op. No. 1075, 526 P2d 18 (Alaska 1974).

Where defendant claimed that he did not have the financial resources to hire an attorney, the trial court had a duty under subsection (e) of this rule to put the defendant under oath and determine, based on the totality of the circumstances, whether or not the defendant is indigent, either by placing the defendant under oath and asking about the defendant's financial status, or by requiring the defendant to complete a signed sworn financial statement. **Benson v. State,** Op. No. 8765, 160 P.3d 161 (Alaska App. 2007).

II. Waiver of Right to Counsel.

To be valid, a waiver of the right to counsel must be made with an apprehension of the nature of the charges, the offenses included within them, the range of punishments, possible defenses, mitigating circumstances and all other facts essential to a broad understanding of the whole matter. **Gregory v. State,** Op. No. 1269, 550 P2d 374 (Alaska 1976).

Magistrate must ascertain whether defendant understands benefits of counsel by recorded colloquy with defendant before right to counsel may be waived. **Gregory v. State,** Op. No. 1269, 550 P2d 374 (Alaska 1976).

When defendant is unable to make an intelligent choice as to waiver of right to counsel it is the duty of the court to assign counsel. **Gregory v. State,** Op. No. 1269, 550 P2d 374 (Alaska 1976).

When defendant pleads guilty without the assistance of counsel, the plea is invalid unless defendant waived his right to counsel. **Gregory v. State,** Op. No. 1269, 550 P2d 374 (Alaska 1976).

Failure of arraignment or trial record to demonstrate that defendant understood what he was giving up by declining the assistance of counsel was cause for reversal even though record showed that defendant had been advised of his right to counsel. **O'Dell v. Municipality of Anchorage,** Op. No. 1588, 576 P2d 104 (Alaska 1978).

Failure of court to ask questions of defendant to assure that he understood precisely what rights he was giving up by declining legal representation at sentencing hearing required vacation of sentence. **Smith v. State,** Op. No. 134, 651 P2d 1191 (Alaska App. 1982).

Trial judge committed reversible error in not allowing defendant, charged with drunk driving in 1984, to have a 1975 drunk driving conviction set aside on the ground that, although informed by the magistrate taking his guilty plea in 1975 of his right to an attorney, he was not informed of what an attorney could do for him. **Petranovich v. State,** Op. No. 547, 709 P2d 867 (Alaska App. 1985).

Failure of the trial court to assure by an on-the-record inquiry that the accused understood the benefits of counsel and the dangers of self-representation prior to waiving his right to counsel was reversible error notwithstanding the accused's previous contacts with the criminal justice system. **James v. State,** Op. No. 669, 730 P2d 811 (Alaska App. 1987).

Defendant's waiver of his right to counsel prior to pleading guilty to a DWI charge was valid where the magistrate advised him of the maximum and minimum penalties for the offense and after he responded affirmatively to the question: "Do you know what a lawyer is?." **Tobuk v. State,** Op. No. 683, 732 P2d 1099 (Alaska App. 1987).

III. Effective Assistance of Counsel.

A defense counsel must perform at least as well as a lawyer with ordinary training and skill in the criminal law and must conscientiously protect his client's interest, undeflected by conflicting considerations. **Risher v. State,** Op. No. 1053, 523 P2d 421 (Alaska 1974).

All that is required of counsel in rendering effective assistance of counsel is that his decisions, when viewed in the framework of trial pressures, be within the range of reasonable actions which might have been taken by an attorney skilled in the criminal law, regardless of the outcome of such decisions. **Risher v. State,** Op. No. 1053, 523 P2d 421 (Alaska 1974).

A defendant does not suffer an unconstitutional deprivation of effective assistance of counsel because of an error committed by his attorney which in no manner contributes to the conviction. **Risher v. State,** Op. No. 1053, 523 P2d 421 (Alaska 1974).

A defendant who has not demonstrated that he understands the benefits of counsel cannot be said to have waived counsel. **Gregory v. State,** Op. No. 1269, 550 P2d 374 (Alaska 1976).

Rule 39.1. Determining Eligibility for Court-Appointed Counsel.

(a) **Scope of Application.** This rule specifies the procedure courts shall follow to assess whether a defendant is eligible for court-appointed counsel in a criminal case.

(b) **Eligibility for Appointment.**[1]

(1) *Standard.* A defendant is eligible for court-appointed counsel if the court finds that the total financial resources available to the defendant are not sufficient to pay allowable household expenses and the likely cost of private representation through trial.

(2) *Exception.* The court may determine that a defendant is ineligible for court-appointed counsel under AS 18.85.170(4) if the defendant has disposed of assets in order to qualify for appointed counsel.

(c) **Financial Resources Defined.**

(1) *Resources to be Considered.* In assessing the defendant's ability to pay the likely cost of private representation through trial, the court shall consider all resources available to the defendant, including all sources of expected income, cash, the value of assets readily convertible to cash, and credit or borrowing ability.

(2) *Parents' Resources.* If the defendant is a minor or an adult who cannot live independently, the court shall consider the resources of both the defendant and the defendant's parents, unless the parents were victims of the alleged offense or the court finds other good cause to treat their resources as being unavailable to the defendant.

(3) *Income.* Parents' Resources. Income includes all categories of income listed in Section II, Parts A and B of the Commentary to Civil Rule 90.3, including permanent fund dividends.

(4) *Cash.* Cash includes cash on hand and accounts in financial institutions. All savings should be considered, except where the use of the savings would deprive the defendant or the defendant's family of food, clothing, shelter, or necessary medical care.

(5) *Assets.* The court shall consider the value of all assets that are readily convertible to cash, other than health aids, clothing, and ordinary household furnishings. With the following exceptions, in valuing an asset, the court shall consider either the amount the defendant would realize if the asset were sold or the amount the defendant could borrow using the asset as collateral, whichever is greater.

(A) The court shall consider the loan value of tools and equipment essential to employment or to subsistence activity. Tools and equipment are essential only if the defendant could not earn a living or provide basic necessities without them. If the defendant cannot borrow against these assets while continuing to have use of them, the court shall disregard their value in calculating the defendant's available resources.

(B) In valuing the defendant's principal residence, the court shall consider the entire loan value or the amount of the sale value that exceeds the homestead exemption allowed under the Alaska Exemptions Act.[2] If the defendant cannot borrow against the residence and would realize less than the homestead exemption amount if the residence were sold, the court shall disregard the value of the residence in calculating the defendant's available resources.

(C) In assessing the loan value of essential tools and equipment and the principal residence, the court shall consider only the amount the defendant can realistically afford to repay.

(6) *Credit.* Available credit includes amounts available on credit cards and amounts that can be borrowed against life insurance policies or from pension or savings plans. In assessing available credit, the court shall consider only the amount the defendant can realistically afford to repay.

(d) **Likely Cost of Private Representation.**

(1) For purposes of this rule, the following amounts represent the likely cost of private representation through trial:

	Estimated Total Cost of Representation
Misdemeanor	$ 2,000
C Felony	5,000
B Felony	7,500
A or Unclassified Felony	20,000

(2) The court may adjust these amounts under the following circumstances:

(A) If the court finds that the scheduled amount differs from the amount charged by local attorneys, the court may use the amount charged locally.

(B) If the court finds that no local attorneys are available to handle the case, the court may adjust the scheduled amount to include the additional fees and travel costs that an out-of-town attorney would charge.

(C) If the court finds that the case has special characteristics that are likely to increase the cost of private representation, such as the need for expert witnesses, special investigations, or expensive tests, the court may adjust the scheduled amount to include this additional expense.

(3) In assessing a defendant's ability to pay the likely cost of private representation, the court should assume that at least 50 percent of the likely fee must be paid immediately and that the total fee must be paid within four months.

(e) **Determining Eligibility.** The court or its designee shall determine whether a defendant is eligible for court-appointed counsel by placing the defendant under oath and asking about the defendant's financial status, or by requiring the defendant to complete a signed sworn financial statement. A defendant who requests appointed counsel must execute a general waiver authorizing the release of financial information to the court as required by AS 18.85.120.

(f) **Presumptive Eligibility.** The court may appoint counsel without further inquiry if:

(1) the defendant currently receives public assistance benefits through a state or federal program for indigent persons, such as Aid to Families with Dependent Children, the Alaska Temporary Assistance Program, Adult Public Assistance, General Relief, Food Stamps, Medicaid, or Supplemental Security Income (SSI);

(2) counsel was appointed for the defendant within the past twelve months based on an examination of the defendant's financial circumstances, and the defendant's financial condition has not significantly improved; or

(3) the gross annual income available to the defendant is less than the adjusted federal poverty guidelines amount for the defendant's household size, and other financial resources (cash, assets, and credit) available to the defendant are worth less than 50 percent of the amount shown in (d)(1) (the likely cost of private representation through trial).

(g) **Other Eligibility.** If the court does not find that the defendant is presumptively eligible under paragraph (f), the court shall conduct an inquiry sufficient to determine whether the defendant is eligible for court-appointed counsel under the standard stated in paragraph (b). The court may make this determination based on the information then available to the court or, when appropriate, may

(1) require the defendant to submit a completed financial resources affidavit with supporting documentation of income;

(2) require the defendant to submit information or documentation concerning particular assets or expenses;

(3) require the defendant to appear at a representation hearing or a pretrial services interview; or

(4) require the defendant to make reasonable efforts to retain private counsel and to report these efforts to the court orally or in writing.

(h) **Allowable Household Expenses.**

(1) *Allowable Expenses.* The following household expenses are allowable to the extent they are reasonable:

(A) housing;

(B) utilities;

(C) food;

(D) health care;

(E) child care;

(F) insurance;

(G) transportation (for one vehicle for each person whose income is considered);

(H) minimum loan and credit card payments; and

(I) mandatory child support and other court-imposed obligations; and

(J) other expenses that the court deems essential.

(2) *Alternative to Calculating Actual Expenses.* As an alternative to calculating actual household expenses, the court may assume that these expenses are approximately equal to the adjusted federal poverty guidelines amount for the defendant's household size.

(3) *Expenses Paid by Other Persons.* The expenses described in (h)(1) and (h)(2) are allowable only to the extent they are paid (or were supposed to be paid) by the defendant. If another person, such as a spouse, relative, or roommate, pays some or all of the household expenses, the court shall disregard the portion of the expenses paid by that person. If the defendant is married, the court should assume, absent a showing of good cause, that each spouse pays an amount proportionate to that spouse's relative income.

(i) **Adjusted Federal Poverty Guidelines.** The "adjusted federal poverty guidelines amount" is the federal poverty guidelines amount for Alaska increased by the geographic cost-of-living adjustment established in AS 39.27.020 for the court location nearest the defendant's residence.

(j) **Responsibilities of Administrative Director.** The administrative director shall

(1) publish annually an administrative bulletin specifying the adjusted federal poverty guidelines amount for each court location;[3] and

(2) periodically review the efficacy of the appointment procedure established by this rule.

(Adopted by SCO 1351, effective May 15, 1999.)

Editor's notes.

Notes

[1] AS 18.85.170(4) defines "indigent person" for purposes of public defender appointments as "a person who, at the time need is determined, does not have sufficient assets, credit, or other means to provide for payment of an attorney and all other necessary expenses of representation without depriving the party or the party's dependents of food, clothing, or shelter and who has not disposed of any assets since the commission of the offense with the intent or for the purpose of establishing eligibility for assistance under this chapter."

[2] For the current homestead exemption amount, **See** 8 AAC 95.030. This Department of Labor regulation, rather than AS 09.38.010, establishes the amount of the homestead exemption. **See** AS 09.38.115.

[3] **See** Admin. Bulletin 65.1

Rule 40. Time.

(a) **Computation.** Except as otherwise specifically provided in these rules, in computing any period of time, the day of the act or event from which the designated period of time begins to run is not to be included. The last day of the period so computed is to be included, unless it is a Saturday, Sunday, or a legal holiday, in which event the period runs until the end of the next day which is not a Saturday, Sunday, or legal holiday. When a period of time prescribed or allowed is less than seven days, intermediate Saturdays, Sundays and legal holidays shall be excluded in the computation. A half holiday shall be considered as other days and not as a holiday.

(b) **Enlargement.** When an act is required or allowed to be done at or within a specified time, the court for cause shown may at any time in its discretion:

(1) With or without motion or notice, order the period enlarged if application therefor is made before the expiration of the period originally prescribed or as extended by a previous order; or

(2) Upon motion permit the act to be done after the expiration of the specified period if the failure to act was the result of excusable neglect; but the court may not enlarge the period for taking any action under Rules 33, 34 and 35 except as otherwise provided in those rules, or the period for taking an appeal.

(c) **Unaffected by Expiration of Term.** The period of time provided for the doing of any act or the taking of any proceeding is not affected or limited by the expiration of a term of court. The expiration of a term of court in no way affects the power of a court to do any act in a criminal proceeding.

(d) **Additional Time After Service or Distribution by Mail.** Whenever a party has the right or is required to act within a prescribed period after the service or distribution of a document, and the document is served or distributed by mail, three calendar days shall be added to the prescribed period. However, no additional time shall be added if a court order specifies a particular calendar date by which an act must occur.

(Adopted by SCO 4 October 4, 1959; amended by SCO 157 effective February 15, 1973; by SCO 273 effective June 15, 1977; by SCO 661 effective March 15, 1986; by SCO 1007 effective January 15, 1990; by SCO 1126 effective July 15, 1993; and by SCO 1639 effective October 15, 2007)

Note: Ch. 77 SLA 2002 (HB157), Section 2, adds new Chapter 26 to Title 6 of the Alaska Statutes, concerning providers of fiduciary services. According to Section 9 of the Act, AS 06.26.760(b)(2) has the effect of amending Criminal Rule 40 by postponing the deadlines set in the Alaska Rules of Criminal Procedure for the filing of documents by a trust company in a criminal action when the Department of Community and Economic Development has taken possession of the trust company.

Annotations

Cases

Computation under this rule relates only to matters of procedure and has no effect on substantive rights. **Wade v. Dworkin,** Op. No. 306, 407 P2d 487 (Alaska 1965).

Post-conviction relief is an appropriate vehicle for the effectuation of the right of appeal where counsel has failed to file a timely notice of appeal. **McCracken v. State,** Op. No. 677,482 P2d 269 (Alaska 1971).

The day of a defendant's arrest is not to be counted in determining whether defendant is brought to trial within 120 days. **Nickels v. State,** Op. No. 1238, 545 P2d 163 (Alaska 1976).

Paragraph (b)(2) of this rule does not supersede Criminal Rule 53 as applied to Rule 35(a). **Thompson v. State,** Op. No. 1445, 566 P2d 630 (Alaska 1977).

When motion is neither routine nor frivolous, and when assertions of fact and law contained in motion do not appear to justify requested relief, judge should call other party's attention to this rule, which requires opposing party to respond to the motion, before making his ruling on the motion. **Willie v. State,** Op. No. 1211, 829 P2d 310 (Alaska App. 1992).

In a DWI case, defendant was not denied his speedy trial rights by a delay due to the recusals of three judges because defendant's father was a bailiff where those recusals and the assignment of a judge from another area constituted "good cause." **Keller v. State,** Op. No. 1916, 84 P.3d 1010 (Alaska App. 2004).

Rule 41. Bail.

(a) **Admission to Bail.** The defendant in a criminal proceeding is entitled to be admitted to bail pursuant to AS 12.30.010–12.30.080.

(b) **Types of Bonds.** The court may require:

(1) the execution of an unsecured appearance bond in an amount specified, under the criteria set forth in AS 12.30.020(a);

(2) the execution of an appearance bond in a specified amount and the deposit in the registry of the court, in cash or other security, of a sum not to exceed 10 percent of the amount of the bond;

(3) the execution of a bail bond with sufficient solvent sureties or the deposit of cash; or

(4) the execution of a performance bond in a specified amount and the deposit in the registry of the court of cash or other security.

(c) **Separate Bonds.** If a performance bond is required, it must be enforced separately from any appearance or bail bond. Appearance in court may not be a condition of a performance bond.

(d) **Misdemeanor Bail Schedule.**

(1) The presiding judge of each judicial district may adopt, under Administrative Rule 46, a misdemeanor bail schedule for use in each community within that district. Before adopting a schedule for a community, the presiding judge shall consult with the judicial officers in that community who regularly set bail in misdemeanor cases.

(2) Any order adopting a misdemeanor bail schedule must provide that the arresting police agency may apply to a judicial officer for a different bail. The order must also provide

that a judicial officer must be contacted at the defendant's request if the defendant is immediately unable to post the scheduled amount in any case in which circumstances exist indicating that protection of the public and the defendant's appearance at subsequent proceedings can be reasonably assured by one of the following:

(A) release on personal recognizance;

(B) release on other appropriate conditions;

(C) the execution of an unsecured appearance bond in an amount equal to or less than the scheduled bail amount, and the deposit in cash or other security of not more than 10 percent of the amount of the bond; or

(D) the execution of a bail bond in an amount less than the scheduled bail amount, secured by cash or other solvent sureties; or

(E) the execution of a performance bond.

(3) A misdemeanor bail schedule may not be set for crimes involving domestic violence as defined in AS 18.66.990 or for the crime of stalking under AS 11.41.270.

(e) **Other Bail Schedules.** No bail schedule shall be established for felonies.

(f) **Prosecuting Attorney—Appearance and Notice.** The prosecuting attorney may appear and be heard in all proceedings relating to bail. The judge or magistrate may require that notice of such proceedings be given the prosecuting attorney.

(g) **Surrender of Defendant.** At any time before forfeiture of the undertaking or the cash deposit in lieu thereof, the sureties on the undertaking or the owner of the deposit may surrender the defendant to the custody of a peace officer or the defendant may surrender personally to the officer. There shall be delivered to the officer at the time of surrender a certified copy of the undertaking or a certificate as to the cash deposit executed by the clerk of court. The peace officer shall thereupon detain the defendant in custody as upon a commitment and acknowledge the surrender by a written certificate.

(h) **Appearance and Bail Bonds.**

(1) *Judgment of Forfeiture.* If the person released on bail on the giving or pledging of security fails to appear before a court or a judicial officer as required, the judge or magistrate before whom the person released was to appear shall forfeit the security. The clerk may sign the judgment of forfeiture if directed to do so on the record in the particular proceeding by the judge. However, the judgment of forfeiture may not be enforced until a hearing is held pursuant to subparagraph (h)(3) or, if no hearing is requested, until 30 days after the date of notice of the judgment of forfeiture. Nothing in this subparagraph shall interfere with the issuance of a summons or bench warrant for a person who fails to appear as required before a court or judicial officer.

(2) *Notice of Forfeiture.* The clerk shall send notice of the judgment of forfeiture to the defendant, defendant's attorney and the person giving or pledging the security at their last known addresses. The notice must state that a hearing will be held on the forfeiture if timely requested pursuant to subparagraph (h)(3).

(3) *Hearing.* If requested by the defendant or person giving or pledging the security within 30 days of the date of notice of the forfeiture, the court shall hold a hearing to determine whether the defendant's failure to appear was willful. The state, the defendant, the defense attorney, and the person giving or pledging the security have the right to be heard at this hearing. The court shall set aside the judgment of forfeiture if it is proven by a preponderance of the evidence that the failure to appear was not willful. The court may set aside the judgment of forfeiture if the court concludes that justice does not require the enforcement of the judgment. An appeal may be taken from the judgment of forfeiture in the manner of other appeals.

(4) *Remission.* Within one year after entry of judgment of forfeiture, a person who has given or pledged security may apply to the court for a remission, either in whole or in part, based on the return of the defendant with the assistance of the person who gave or pledged security or upon such other extraordinary circumstances as justice requires. The conditions of remission may include payment of expenses incurred for enforcement of the forfeiture and for securing the return of the defendant to custody.

(5) *Exoneration.* When the condition of the bond has been satisfied or the forfeiture thereof has been remitted, the court shall exonerate the obligors and release any bail. A surety may be exonerated by a deposit of cash in the amount of the bond or by a timely surrender of the defendant into custody.

(6) *Enforcement.* Execution shall issue on judgments of forfeiture in the same manner as on other judgments for the payment of money.

(i) **Performance Bonds.**

(1) *Exoneration.* When the defendant has met all of the conditions of the bond, the court shall exonerate the bond and release any security to the person giving or pledging the security.

(2) *Petition for Forfeiture.* At any time prior to exoneration, the prosecuting attorney may file a petition for forfeiture with the court alleging that the defendant violated one or more of the conditions of the performance bond. The petition shall set forth the allegations and shall be supported by an affidavit. The prosecuting attorney shall serve copies of the petition and affidavit on the defendant, defendant's attorney, and the person giving or pledging the security at their last known addresses.

(3) *Notice of Intent to Contest.* The defendant or any person giving or pledging the security shall have 30 days from the date of the petition for forfeiture in which to file a written

notice of an intent to contest the forfeiture. The notice shall be served on the prosecuting attorney. If the notice is filed by the defendant, it shall also be served on any person giving or pledging the security. If the notice is filed by a person giving or pledging security, it shall also be served on the defendant and the defendant's attorney. If no notice is filed, the court shall deem the allegations admitted and shall forfeit the security.

(4) *Hearing.* If the defendant or the person giving or pledging the security gives notice that the forfeiture is contested, the court shall schedule a hearing within 45 days of the filing of the notice. However, if the defendant has been charged with the offense of violation of a condition of release under state or municipal law, or has been charged with a new criminal offense, the court shall not hold a hearing on the petition for forfeiture until the criminal charges are resolved.

(5) *Disposition.* The prosecuting attorney has the burden of proving by a preponderance of the evidence that the defendant violated a condition of the performance bond knowingly or with reckless disregard for the fact that the conduct violated the condition. If the court finds that the defendant violated a condition of the performance bond, then the court may forfeit all or part of the security. If the defendant is found guilty or enters a plea of guilty to the crime of violation of a condition of release under state or municipal law, or to a new criminal offense, the court shall consider the finding or plea conclusive evidence that the defendant violated these conditions of the performance bond. An appeal may be taken from the judgment of forfeiture in the manner of other appeals.

(6) *No Effect on Bail.* Nothing in this rule is intended to affect procedures regarding bail release or remand.

(Adopted by SCO 4 October 4, 1959; amended by SCO 79 effective February 1, 1966; by SCO 90 effective July 24, 1967; amended by SCO 157 effective February 15, 1973; by SCO 821 effective August 1, 1987; by SCO 864 effective July 15, 1988; by SCO 1153 effective July 15, 1994; by SCO 1267 effective July 15, 1997; and by SCO 1419 effective February 8, 2001)

Cross References

(a) **CROSS REFERENCE:** AS 12.30.010—AS 12.30.080 (as amended by c. 20 SLA 1966)

(c) **CROSS REFERENCE:** AS 12.30.020

Annotations

Cases

Fixing of bail under this rule must be based upon the purpose of insuring the defendant's appearance at the trial. **Reeves v. State,** Op. No. 329, 411 P2d 212 (Alaska 1966).

Where record disclosed that the trial judge perceptively explored the possibilities of alternative deterrent to forfeiture of bail in the case of an indigent defendant, but found that the defendant had no ties whatever in the state which could be a reasonable alternative assurance of his presence at the time of trial, and motion for release on his own recognizance was grounded only on an alleged constitutional right to be so released under all circumstances, and not on the strength of an alternative deterrent, order denying such motion was affirmed. **Reeves v. State,** Op. No. 329, 411 P2d 212 (Alaska 1966).

Subsequent amendments to the bail statute, including the 1980 amendments, are adopted by reference in this rule; accordingly, there is no conflict between this rule and the bail statutes. **Stiegele v. State,** Op. No. 382, 685 P2d 1255 (Alaska App. 1984).

Trial court had no inherent authority to grant bail in derogation of statute to defendant pending appeal of defendant's conviction of an unclassified felony. **Stiegele v. State,** Op. No. 382, 685 P2d 1255 (Alaska App. 1984).

The Superior Court has discretion to order remission or partial remission of a forfeited bail bond after considering all relevant factors including: (1) cost, inconvenience, or prejudice to the government in regaining custody, (2) delay resulting from the nonappearance, (3) willfulness of the failure to appear, and (4) public interest in ensuring the appearance. **Adkerson v. State,** Op. No. 3153, 731 P2d 1218 (Alaska 1987).

This rule allows court to forfeit bail when defendant willfully fails to appear but does not allow court to forfeit bail when defendant fails to comply with other conditions of release. **Lonisv. State,** Op. No. 1661, 998 P2d 441 (Alaska App. 2000).

An order directing the forfeiture of bail is not treated as just another mid-litigation decision in the criminal prosecution. Instead, Alaska R. Crim. P. 41 refers to the order as a "judgment," and the court's decision is deemed a final order for purposes of appeal. The person who has suffered forfeiture of their money can appeal the forfeiture regardless of how or when the underlying criminal case ends, and the deadline for filing this appeal is calculated from the distribution date of the judgment of forfeiture. The appellate court concludes that bail forfeiture litigation is primarily civil in nature and holds that Alaska R. Civ. P. 60(b) applies to bail forfeiture litigation, giving the trial court the authority to grant relief from judgments of forfeiture. **State v. Superior Court,** Op. No. 2235, 40 P3d 1239 (Alaska App. 2002).

Rule 42. Motions.

(a) **Generally.** An application to the court for an order shall be by motion. A motion other than one made during a trial or hearing shall be in writing unless the court permits it to be made orally.

(b) **Supporting Evidence—Memorandum—Order.** There shall be served and filed with the motion:

(1) legible copies of all photographs and other documentary evidence which the moving party intends to submit in support of the motion;

(2) a brief, complete written statement of the reasons in support of the motion, which shall include a memorandum of the legal points and authorities upon which the moving party will rely and a detailed statement of material facts which can be proved by the party; and

(3) an appropriate order for the court's signature in the event that the motion is granted.

(c) **Response.** Each party responding to the motion shall either:

(1) serve and file a written statement that the party does not oppose the motion; or

(2) serve and file a brief but complete written statement of its reasons for opposing the motion, which shall include (A)

an answering memorandum of legal points and authorities, (B) a detailed statement of the material facts disputed by the responding party, as well as any additional material facts that can be provided by the party, (C) legible copies of all photographs and other documentary evidence upon which the party intends to rely, and (D) an appropriate order for the court's signature in the event that the motion is denied.

Unless a different time is specified by these rules or is ordered by the court, responses to motions shall be filed within 10 days after service of the motion.

(d) **Reply.** Reply and supplemental materials and memoranda, if any, may be served and filed by the moving party within five days of the date of service of the opposition to the motion.

(e) **Evidentiary Hearing.**

(1) If either party desires that an evidentiary hearing be held, that party shall request an evidentiary hearing on or before the date a reply is due. The party shall submit a proposed order with the request.

(2) The request for evidentiary hearing shall set forth an estimate of time needed for all parties to submit evidence.

(3) If material issues of fact are not presented in the pleadings, the court need not hold an evidentiary hearing. The amount of time to be allowed for evidentiary hearing shall be set by the court.

(4) Where appropriate, the court shall make factual findings in accordance with Rule 12(d).

(f) **Oral Argument.**

(1) If either party desires oral argument on the motion, that party shall request a hearing on or before the date a reply was due. The party shall submit a proposed order with the request.

(2) The request for hearing shall set forth an estimate of time needed of argument.

(3) Oral argument shall be held only in the discretion of the court. The amount of time to be allowed for oral argument shall be set by the court. If an evidentiary hearing is held, oral argument will be heard at the close of the evidence, unless otherwise ordered by the court.

(g) **Combined Request and Motion.** A party may combine a request for evidentiary hearing or a request for oral argument with the principal motion. The language "Request for Oral Argument" or "Request for Evidentiary Hearing" must appear in the title of the document.

(h) **Ruling.** The court shall rule promptly on all motions. If no opposition or statement of non-opposition has been filed, the court may determine whether the moving party has made a prima facie showing of entitlement to the relief requested without further notice to the parties. If a prima facie showing is made, the court may grant the motion. If the court denies a motion to which no opposition has been filed, the court must set forth the reasons for the denial with specificity.

(i) **Expedited Consideration.** A party may move for expedited consideration of its principal motion by filing a second motion requesting relief in less time than would normally be required for the court to issue a decision.

(1) The motion must be captioned "Motion for Expedited Consideration" and must have an appropriate order on the issue of expedited consideration attached.

(2) The motion for expedited relief must comply with other provisions of this rule.

(3) The motion for expedited consideration must include an affidavit or other evidence showing the facts which justify expedited consideration, and the date before which a decision on the principal motion is needed.

(4) The motion for expedited consideration must include proof of service; and, if the motion requests a decision before the usual time for response to the motion, must include a certificate of counsel indicating when and how the opposing party was notified of the motion, or, if the opposing party was not notified, what efforts were made to notify the opposing party and why it was not practical to notify the opposing party in a manner and at a time that a response could be made.

(5) The court may not grant the motion for expedited consideration prior to allowing the opposing party a reasonable opportunity to respond, either in person, by telephone or in writing, absent compelling reasons for a prompt decision and a showing that reasonable efforts were made to notify the opposing party of the motion for expedited consideration in time to allow a reasonable opportunity to respond.

(6) The court may not grant the principal motion prior to allowing the opposing party a reasonable opportunity to respond, either in person, by telephone or in writing, unless it clearly appears from the specific facts in the motion papers or court records that immediate and irreparable injury, loss or damage would result to the moving party before any reasonable opportunity to respond could be given.

(j) **Stipulations.** Stipulations between counsel may be submitted in support of motions, but are not binding on the court unless otherwise specifically provided by rule.

(k) **Reconsideration.** A motion to reconsider the ruling must be made within ten days after the date of notice of the ruling as defined in Criminal Rule 32.3(c). In no event shall a motion to reconsider a ruling be made more than ten days after the date of notice of the final judgment in the case.

(1) A party may move the court to reconsider a ruling previously decided if, in reaching its decision,

(A) the court has overlooked, misapplied or failed to consider a statute, decision, or principle directly controlling; or

(B) the court has overlooked or misconceived some material fact or proposition of law; or

(C) the court has overlooked or misconceived a material question in the case; or

(D) the law applied in the ruling has been subsequently changed by court decision or statute.

(2) The motion for reconsideration shall specifically state which of the grounds for reconsideration specified in the prior subparagraph exist, and shall specifically designate that portion of the ruling, the memorandum, or the record, or that particular authority, which the movant wishes the court to consider. The motion for reconsideration and supporting memorandum shall not exceed five pages.

(3) No response shall be made to a motion for reconsideration unless requested by the court, but a motion for reconsideration will ordinarily not be granted in the absence of such a request.

(4) If the motion for reconsideration has not been ruled upon by the court within 30 days from the date of the filing of the motion, or within 30 days of the date of filing of a response requested by the court, whichever is later, the motion shall be taken as denied.

(5) The court, on its own motion, may reconsider a ruling at any time not later than 10 days from the date of notice of the final judgment in the case.

(*l*) **Citation of Supplemental Authorities.** When pertinent authorities come to the attention of a party after the party's memorandum has been filed, or after oral argument but before decision, the party may promptly advise the court, by letter, with a copy to adversary counsel, setting forth the citations. There must be a reference either to the page of the memorandum or to a point argued orally to which the citations pertain, but the letter may not contain argument or explanations. Any response must be made promptly and must be similarly limited.

(m) **No Effect on Substantive Law.** Nothing in this rule should be construed as allocating the burden of pleading or production to any party.

(n) **Variations on Time Periods.** The court may vary any of the time periods established in this rule for good cause shown.

(Adopted by SCO 4, October 4, 1959; repealed and reenacted by SCO 1126 effective July 15, 1993; and amended by SCO 1576 effective December 15, 2005)

Annotations

Cases

Where defendant moved for reconsideration of a restitution order and the superior court failed to act, the motion was deemed denied by operation of law. **Dayton v. State,** Op. No. 1902, 78 P.3d 270 (Alaska App. 2003).

Rule 43. Dismissal and Deferred Prosecution.

(a) **By Prosecuting Attorney.** The prosecuting attorney may file a dismissal of an indictment, information or complaint and the prosecution shall thereupon terminate. Such a dismissal shall not be filed during the trial without the consent of the defendant.

(b) **By Court.** If there is unnecessary delay in presenting the charge to a grand jury or in filing an information against a defendant who has been held to answer to the superior court, or if there is unnecessary delay in bringing a defendant to trial pursuant to Criminal Rule 45, the court shall dismiss the indictment, information or complaint.

(c) **In Furtherance of Justice.** The court may, either on its own motion or upon the application of the prosecuting attorney, and in furtherance of justice, order an action, after indictment or waiver of indictment, to be dismissed. The reasons for the dismissal shall be set forth in the order.

(d) **Identity Error in Charging Document.** If the prosecution initiates or concurs with the dismissal of charges against a defendant because the named defendant was not the person whom the prosecution intended to charge with the offense, the court shall enter a written order of dismissal clearly stating that this is the reason for the dismissal.

(e) **Discharge from Custody—Exoneration of Bail.** Except as provided in AS 12.30.035, when dismissal is ordered pursuant to this rule the defendant shall be discharged from custody, or if admitted to bail, the bail exonerated, or money deposited in lieu thereof refunded to the depositors.

(f) **Information To Be Included in Notice or Order of Dismissal.** A notice or order of dismissal must include the following information:

(1) the defendant's full name, including middle name or initial, if known;

(2) the defendant's date of birth, if known;

(3) the defendant's Alaska Public Safety Information Network (APSIN) identification number, if known;

(4) the defendant's driver's license number or state identification number, if known, including the issuing state and whether the license is a commercial driver's license;

(5) the arrest tracking number (ATN) on the Criminal Case Intake and Disposition (CCID) form for each offense being addressed;

(6) the three-digit charge tracking number assigned on the CCID form for each offense being addressed; and

(7) the statute, regulation, or ordinance, as identified in the Uniform Offense Citation Table,** corresponding to each offense being addressed. Regulations not listed in the Uniform Offense Citation Table must be cited by the regulation number.

(g) **Information To Be Included in Notice of Deferred Prosecution.** A notice of deferred prosecution must include the defendant and offense information required by subsection (e) of this rule.

**The Uniform Offense Citation table was developed by the

Department of Public Safety. Changes to the table must be approved by the Department of Law or the appropriate municipal prosecuting authority. It is available at http://www.dps.state.ak.us/uoct/.

(Adopted by SCO 4 October 4, 1959; amended by SCO 49 effective January 1, 1963; amended by SCO 157 effective February 15, 1973; by SCO 1153 effective July 15, 1994; by SCO 1293 effective January 15, 1998; by SCO 1614 effective October 15, 2006; and by SCO 1648 effective October 15, 2007)

Cross References

(a) **CROSS REFERENCE:** AS 12.20.020; AS 12.20.050

Annotations

Cases

Right to speedy-trial was waived by failure to assert it. **Goss v. State,** Op. No. 193, 390 P2d 220 (Alaska 1964).

This rule does not authorize court to accept plea of guilty to lesser included offense without concurrence of district attorney. **State v. Carlson,** Op. No. 1327, 555 P2d 269 (Alaska 1976).

Trial judge did not abuse his discretion in reinstating by court order a dismissed rape charge without reindictment. **Morgan v. State,** Op. No. 320, 673 P2d 897 (Alaska App. 1983).

Trial judge did not abuse his discretion in ordering the State to give use immunity to a witness or, in the interest of justice, face dismissal of sexual abuse charges against defendant. **State v. Echols,** Op. No. 1045, 793 P2d 1066 (Alaska App. 1990).

Magistrate was not permitted to dismiss two hunting violations with prejudice based on a failure to prosecute because a delay of several days did not compromise defendants' ability to defend their case. **Schouten v. State,** Op. No. 1901, 77 P.3d 739 (Alaska App. 2003).

Trial court properly refused to dismiss a criminal prosecution under subsection (c) of this rule, despite the state's refusal to immunize a witness who had exculpatory evidence to offer; the witness's proposed testimony did not appear likely to affect the verdict. **Cogdill v. State,** Op. No. 1957, 101 P.3d 632 (Alaska App. 2004).

Rule 43.1. Clerk's Authority.

Unless otherwise ordered by the court, the clerk is authorized to quash or recall warrants, summonses, and orders to show cause where it is uncontroverted or clearly proven that:

(a) The defendant has paid the fine or restitution for which the warrant, summons, or order to show cause was issued;

(b) The defendant has posted the bail listed on the warrant; or

(c) The charging document for which the warrant, summons, or order to show cause was issued has been dismissed or withdrawn.

(Adopted by SCO 1079 effective January 15, 1992)

Rule 44. Service and Filing of Papers.

(a) **Service—When Required.** Written motions other than those which are heard ex parte, written notices, and similar papers shall be served upon the adverse parties.

(b) **Service—How Made.** Whenever under these rules or by an order of the court service is required or permitted to be made upon a party represented by an attorney, the service shall be made upon the attorney unless service upon the party is ordered by the court. Service upon the attorney or upon a party shall be made in the manner provided in civil actions.

(c) **Distribution of Orders and Judgments.** The clerk shall distribute to each party affected a copy of every order or judgment entered. Every order and judgment shall include a clerk's certificate of distribution as defined in Criminal Rule 32.3(d).

(d) **Filing.** Papers required to be served shall be filed with clerk at the court location where the case is filed unless otherwise directed by the court. Papers shall be filed in the manner provided in the Alaska Rules of Civil Procedure.

(e) **Proof of Service.** Proof of service of all papers required by law or these rules to be served shall be filed in the clerk's office promptly and in any event before action is to be taken therein by the court or the parties. The proof shall show the day and manner of service, and may be written acknowledgment of service, by certificate of an attorney, an authorized agent of the attorney, or a pro se defendant, by return of any peace officer, or by affidavit of any other person who served the papers.

(f) **Form.** Pleadings and other filings shall contain a certificate indicating whether the document contains information which is confidential under AS 12.61.100 through 12.61.150. The administrative director shall specify the form and content of the certificate and may exempt types of documents from the certificate requirement. In other respects, the form of pleadings and other filings shall be as provided in Alaska Rules of Civil Procedure 76.

(g) **Filings in Microfilmed Cases.** If a motion, petition or request is filed in a case that has been microfilmed and destroyed pursuant to the Records Retention Schedule, the attorney or party must attach (1) a copy of any relevant orders, judgments and other documents necessary for the court's ruling, and (2) either proof of notice pursuant to Civil Rule 5(g) or an affidavit that Rule 5(g) is not applicable. If such documents are not attached, the clerk will notify counsel that such documents must be submitted before the court will consider the motion, petition or request.

(Adopted by SCO 4 October 4, 1959; amended by SCO 471 effective June 1, 1981; by SCO 554 effective April 4, 1983; by SCO 685 effective May 1, 1986; by SCO 694 effective September 15, 1986; by SCO 1081 effective nunc pro tunc September 17, 1991; by SCO 1121 effective July 15, 1993; and by SCO 1153 effective July 15, 1994)

Note: The form of the certificate required by Criminal Rule 44(f) is specified in Administrative Bulletin 53. The certificate may be included in the document being filed or attached as a separate page. Parties may use Criminal Form CR-101 to satisfy the certificate requirement. It is available in clerk's offices.

Annotations

Cases

Failure of the clerk of the superior court to notify a defendant of entry of the order denying motion for rehearing in accordance with Criminal Rule 44(c), was not in itself considered a factor which would impel the supreme court to dispense with the time period for appeal provided under Supreme Ct. R. 19 [now Appellate Rule 19]. **Stephens v. City of Anchorage,** Op. No. 162, 384 P2d 959 (Alaska 1963).

Since the information was neither personally delivered nor delivered by certified or registered mail, the information was never served on defendant in a manner which would trigger running of the speedy trial period. **Hayes v. State,** Op. No. 1031, 790 P2d 713 (Alaska App. 1990).

Rule 45. Speedy Trial.

(a) **Priorities in Scheduling Criminal Cases.** The court shall provide for placing criminal proceedings upon appropriate calendars. Preference shall be given to criminal proceedings and the trial of defendants in custody shall be given preference over other criminal cases. Trial dates in criminal cases in the superior court shall be set at the time of arraignment, and if a trial date is thereafter vacated, the trial shall be immediately set for a date certain.

(b) **Speedy Trial Time Limits.** A defendant charged with a felony, a misdemeanor, or a violation shall be tried within 120 days from the time set forth in paragraph (c) of this rule.

(c) **When Time Commences to Run.**

(1) *Generally.* Except as provided in subparagraphs (2) through (5), the time for trial shall begin running, without demand by the defendant, from the date the charging document is served upon the defendant.

(2) *Refiling of Original Charge.* If a charge is dismissed by the prosecution, the refiling of the charge shall not extend the time. If the charge is dismissed upon motion of the defendant, the time for trial shall begin running from the date of service of the second charge.

(3) *New Charges.* The Rule 45 commencement date for a new charge arising out of the same criminal episode shall be the same as the commencement date for the original charge, unless the evidence on which the new charge is based was not available to the prosecution on the commencement date for the original charge. When the new charge is based on new evidence and the prosecution has acted with due diligence in investigating and bringing the new charge, the Rule 45 commencement date for the original charge shall be the same as the commencement date for the new charge.

(4) *Mistrial, New Trial or Remand.* If the defendant is to be tried again following a mistrial, an order for a new trial, or an appeal or collateral attack, the time for trial shall run from the date of mistrial, order granting a new trial, or remand.

(5) *Withdrawal of Plea, or Notice That Defendant No Longer Intends to Enter a Plea of Guilty or Nolo Contendere.* When a defendant withdraws a plea of guilty or nolo contendere, the time for trial shall run from the date of the order permitting the withdrawal. When a defendant who previously informed the court of an intention to plead guilty or nolo contendere notifies the court that the defendant now intends to proceed to trial, the time for trial shall run from the date of that notification.

(6) *Minor Offenses.* In cases involving minor offenses under District Court Criminal Rule 8, the defendant must be tried within 120 days from the date the defendant's request for trial is received by the court or the municipality, whichever occurs first.

(d) **Excluded Periods.** The following periods shall be excluded in computing the time for trial:

(1) The period of delay resulting from other proceedings concerning the defendant, including but not limited to motions to dismiss or suppress, examinations and hearings on competency, the period during which the defendant is incompetent to stand trial, interlocutory appeals, and trial of other charges. No pretrial motion shall be held under advisement for more than 30 days and any time longer than 30 days shall not be considered as an excluded period.

(2) The period of delay resulting from an adjournment or continuance granted at the timely request or with the consent of the defendant and the defendant's counsel. The court shall grant such a continuance only if it is satisfied that the postponement is in the interest of justice, taking into account the public interest in the prompt disposition of criminal offenses. A defendant without counsel shall not be deemed to have consented to a continuance unless the defendant has been advised by the court of the right to a speedy trial under this rule and of the effect of consent.

(3) The period of delay resulting from a continuance granted at the timely request of the prosecution, if:

(a) The continuance is granted because of the unavailability of evidence material to the state's case, when the prosecuting attorney has exercised due diligence to obtain such evidence and there are reasonable grounds to believe that such evidence will be available at the later date; or

(b) The continuance is granted to allow the prosecuting attorney in a felony case additional time to prepare the state's case and additional time is justified because of the exceptional complexity of the particular case.

(4) The period of delay resulting from the absence or unavailability of the defendant. A defendant should be considered absent whenever the defendant's whereabouts are unknown and in addition the defendant is attempting to avoid apprehension or prosecution or the defendant's whereabouts cannot be determined by due diligence. A defendant should be considered unavailable whenever the defendant's whereabouts are known but the defendant's presence for trial cannot be obtained or the defendant resists being returned to the state for trial.

(5) A reasonable period of delay when the defendant is joined for trial with a codefendant as to whom the time for trial has not run and there is good cause for not granting a severance. In all other cases, the defendant shall be granted a severance in order that the defendant may be tried within the time limits applicable to the defendant.

(6) The period of delay resulting from detention of the defendant in another jurisdiction provided the prosecuting attorney has been diligent and has made reasonable efforts to obtain the presence of the defendant for trial. When the prosecution is unable to obtain the presence of the defendant in detention, and seeks to exclude the period of detention, the prosecution shall cause a detainer to be filed with the official having custody of the defendant and request the official to advise the defendant of the detainer and to inform the defendant of the defendant's rights under this rule.

(7) Other periods of delay for good cause.

(e) **Rulings on Motions to Dismiss or Continue.** In the event the court decides any motion brought pursuant to this rule, either to continue the time for trial or to dismiss the case, the reasons underlying the decision of the court shall be set forth in full on the record.

(f) **Waiver.** Failure of a defendant represented by counsel to move for dismissal of the charges under these rules prior to plea of guilty or trial shall constitute waiver of the defendant's rights under this rule.

(g) **Absolute Discharge.** If a defendant is not brought to trial before the running of the time for trial, as extended by excluded periods, the court upon motion of the defendant shall dismiss the charge with prejudice. Such discharge bars prosecution for the offense charged and for any other lesser included offense within the offense charged.

(Adopted by SCO 4 October 4, 1959; amended by SCO 131 effective September 1, 1971; by SCO 151 on March 9, 1972, nunc pro tunc as of September 1, 1971; by SCO 227 effective January 1, 1976; by SCO 240 effective February 4, 1976; by SCO 427 effective August 1, 1980; by SCO 486 effective November 16, 1981; by SCO 746 effective December 15, 1986; by SCO 932 effective January 15, 1989; by SCO 1127 effective July 15, 1993; by SCO 1153 effective July 15, 1994; by SCO 1291 effective January 15, 1998; by SCO 1383 effective April 15, 2000; and by SCO 1422 effective April 15, 2001)

Annotations

Cases

Prior to 1993, Criminal Rule 45(c) provided that the time for bringing a defendant to trial began to run from the date the defendant was arrested, initially arraigned, or from the date the charge was served upon the defendant, whichever occurred first. The rule was amended in 1993 so that the time for trial would no longer begin running from the date of arrest, but would instead begin to run from the date the defendant was held to answer to a charge, that is, from "the date the charging document [was] served upon the defendant." Note that many of the following annotations relate to cases decided under the pre-1993 version of the rule.

I. In General.
II. Computation of Time.
III. Waiver.

I. In General.

The 120-day period after arrest within which the defendant is required to be brought to trial is only a basis datum. A considerably longer period may elapse prior to trial without unfairness or injustice to the accused. **Snyder v. State,** Op. No. 1061, 524 P2d 661 (Alaska 1974).

An appeal is permissible from a plea of nolo contendere where an integral part of the negotiated plea is the stipulation that the defendant retains the right to appeal the speedy trial issue and such issue has been fully argued at pretrial hearing. **Cooksey v. State,** Op. No. 1063, 524 P2d 1251 (Alaska 1974).

"Advisement," under this rule, is the act of the judge in taking time for consideration or deliberation, that is, in taking time to consider all of his judgment before rendering and signing judgment. **Dunbar v. State,** Op. No. 1212, 543 P2d 409 (Alaska 1975).

This rule does not apply to probation revocation proceedings. **Paul v. State,** Op. No. 1375, 560 P2d 754 (Alaska 1977).

Defendant has no duty to demand trial and failure to do so does not deprive him of right to speedy trial. **Peterson v. State,** Op. No. 1411, 562 P2d 1350 (Alaska 1977).

Only a very small number of cases are so unusual that relaxation of speedy trial rule would be justified. **Peterson v. State,** Op. No. 1411, 562 P2d 1350 (Alaska 1977).

Relaxation of speedy-trial rule in prosecution for quadruple murder was not abuse of discretion because of combination of (1) severity of crimes alleged, (2) lack of prejudice to defendant due to delay, (3) extremely short period of delay, and (4) unique difficulty of investigating crimes in bush areas. **Peterson v. State,** Op. No. 1411, 562 P2d 1350 (Alaska 1977).

This rule is not directly applicable to delinquency proceedings brought against a minor. **R.S.D.M. v. Intake Officer,** Op. No. 1449, 565 P2d 855 (Alaska 1977).

Defendant has no right to Rule 45 protection until he is arrested, initially arraigned or served with the complaint filed against him. **O'Dell v. Municipality of Anchorage,** Op. No. 1556, 573 P2d 1381 (Alaska 1978).

No trial date should be vacated without a new date then being established. **Deacon v. State,** Op. No. 1586, 575 P2d 1225 (Alaska 1978).

It is the responsibility of the trial court to develop "failsafe" procedure to avoid the dismissal of cases pursuant to Criminal Rule 45. **DeMille v. State,** Op. No. 1676, 581 P2d 675 (Alaska 1978).

The supreme court of Alaska has never ruled that a defendant must show prejudice in order to involve Criminal Rule 45. **DeMille v. State,** Op. No. 1676, 581 P2d 675 (Alaska 1978).

There are significant differences in the handling of trial court motions on appeal and petitions for review, and petitions for review are not subject to the thirty day limitation of Criminal Rule 45(d)(1). **Vail v. State,** Op. No. 1922, 599 P2d 1371 (Alaska 1979).

Defendant's speedy-trial right will not be suspended where only misdemeanor charged, even though delay was short and non-prejudicial. **Westdahl v. State,** Op. No. 1818, 592 P2d 1214 (Alaska 1979).

Failure to follow a particular path of investigation to locate a defendant will not necessarily result in a finding of lack of diligence under this rule, so long as reasonable steps have been taken. **Spencer v. State,** Op. No. 2071, 611 P2d 1 (Alaska 1980).

Argument that this is not a rule of procedure but only confers a substantive right to be tried within 120 days was rejected. **State v. Williams,** Op. No. 159, 653 P2d 1067 (Alaska App. 1982).

Rule requiring that a defendant charged with a violation be tried within 120 days had retrospective application to a traffic infraction. **Koch v. State,** Op. No. 162, 653 P2d 664 (Alaska App. 1982).

This rule held constitutional against contention that it is substantive rather than procedural and therefore beyond the court's rule-making authority. **State v. Williams,** Op. No. 2817, 681 P2d 313 (Alaska 1984).

Dismissal with prejudice sanction for non-compliance with this rule was appropriate. **State v. Williams,** Op. No. 2817, 681 P2d 313 (Alaska 1984).

This rule does not apply to juvenile proceedings. **Brower v. State,** Op. No. 380, 683 P2d 290 (Alaska App. 1984).

There are policy reasons for interpreting the word "arrest" differently for fourth amendment purposes than for the purposes of this rule. **Lindsay v. State,** Op. No. 458, 698 P2d 659 (Alaska App. 1985).

"Arrest" for purposes of this rule is the taking of a person into custody in order that the person may be held to answer for the commission of a crime; accordingly, although defendant was initially detained on February 20, 1983 for questioning, after which the police told him that he would be charged with a crime but that he was not under arrest and he was then released, the speedy trial time period did not begin to run until defendant's formal arrest in April of 1983. **Lindsay v. State,** Op. No. 458, 698 P2d 659 (Alaska App. 1985).

Trial judge's conclusion that the state exercised due diligence in attempting to get Washington authorities to return defendant to the state, thus satisfying the precondition to the filing of a detainer, was not clearly erroneous. **Conway v. State,** Op. No. 537, 707 P2d 930 (Alaska App. 1985).

State's awareness after arrest on one charge of other potential charges becomes relevant to determine whether delay will be excused only when subsequent charges are based on the same conduct for which the prior arrest occurred. **Kizzire v. State,** Op. No. 591, 715 P2d 272 (Alaska App. 1986).

The knowledge of attorneys not present at setting of trial date will not be imputed to the attorney who accepts a trial date beyond the speedy-trial period. **State v. Andrew,** Op. No. 3057, 718 P2d 471 (Alaska 1986).

A requirement that the State first seek extradition before filing a detainer would serve no useful purpose. **Miller v. State,** Op. No. 728, 739 P2d 1303 (Alaska App. 1987).

The rule requires the State to exercise diligence and to make reasonable efforts to obtain the presence of the defendant for trial in order to avoid dismissal; the rule does not preclude the State from initially relying on the interstate Agreement on Detainers as a means of exercising diligence and reasonable effort. **Miller v. State,** Op. No. 728, 739 P2d 1303 (Alaska App. 1987).

Once jury selection begins, the accused forfeits the right to assert a violation of the speedy-trial rule regardless of whether his failure to make a timely motion resulted from an informed decision. **Ray v. State,** Op. No. 1053, 792 P2d 685 (Alaska App. 1990).

This rule is not determinative of the constitutional right to speedy trial; defendant's constitutional right to speedy trial attached when he was formally and publicly charged by information with the crime, even though his rights under this rule did not attach until he was arrested. **State v. Mouser,** Op. No. 1105, 806 P2d 330 (Alaska App. 1991).

Defendant was timely brought to trial where the rule was properly applied to defendant after he entered a plea conditioned on future acceptance by court, and later withdrew that plea and requested a trial. **Cook v. State,** Op. No. 1770, 36 P3d 710 (Alaska App. 2001).

When all of the judges who reside in the place of venue specified by Alaska R. Crim. P. 18 are disqualified, thus requiring the assignment of a judge from another community, this situation constitutes "good cause" for a delay of a criminal trial under Alaska R. Crim. P. 45(d)(7). **Keller v. State,** Op. No. 1916, 84 P.3d 1010 (Alaska App. 2004).

In a DWI case, defendant was not denied his speedy trial rights by a delay due to the recusals of three judges because defendant's father was a bailiff where those recusals and the assignment of a judge from another area constituted "good cause." **Keller v. State,** Op. No. 1916, 84 P.3d 1010 (Alaska App. 2004).

Court's finding that defendant's motion for a continuance caused a nearly two month delay was supported by the record and was proper despite defendant's earlier objection to a continuance; the court was entitled to rely on defense counsel's later request for a continuance, and defendant did not show that he did anything subsequent to his counsel's filing for a continuance to bring his objection to the continuance to the court's attention. **Baker v. State,** Op. No. 1980, 110 P.3d 996 (Alaska App. 2005).

The purpose of this rule is to protect a defendant's right to have the criminal charges which the State has brought against him resolved within a reasonable period of time. **State v. Gottschalk**, Op. No. 8798, 138 P.3d 1170 (Alaska App. 2006).

II. Computation of Time.

The period between the filing of an accused's pretrial motions and the denial of the motions should be excluded in computing the time within which the accused is required to be brought to trial even though the motions do not cause postponement of the trial date. **State v. Clouatre,** Op. No. 975, 516 P2d 1189 (Alaska 1973).

An order dismissing an indictment for lack of speedy-trial, pursuant to a ruling that the time necessary for determination of motions filed by the state was not to be excluded from period for bringing the defendant to trial, is of sufficient substance and importance to merit review. **State v. Strelewicz,** Op. No. 1178, 538 P2d 1009 (Alaska 1975).

The day of a defendant's arrest is not to be counted in determining whether defendant is brought to trial within 120 days. **Nickels v. State,** Op. No. 1238, 545 P2d 163 (Alaska 1976).

Later filing of charges based on same criminal episode does not extend the speedy-trial period unless the evidence on which the new charges are based was not available at time of original filing. **Peterson v. State,** Op. No. 1411, 562 P2d 1350 (Alaska 1977).

Defendant's non-opposition to prosecution's motion for continuance was tantamount to consent, hence the period of the continuance was excluded from the 120 days computation under Rule 45(d)(2). **O'Dell v. Municipality of Anchorage,** Op. No. 1556, 573 P2d 1381 (Alaska 1978).

The entire period between a motion for psychiatric examination and the filing of the psychiatric report must be excluded from computation of the 120 day period in Rule 45. **Deacon v. State,** Op. No. 1586, 575 P2d 1225 (Alaska 1978).

The 120-day requirement of Rule 45 is not violated where delay is a direct result of a request for a continuance made by counsel on behalf of the defendant and with his consent. **Henson v. State,** Op. No. 1590, 576 P2d 1352 (Alaska 1978).

The 120-day period in Criminal Rule 45 does not run during postponements requested by defendant. **Miller v. State,** Op. No. 1620, 577 P2d 1077 (Alaska 1978).

Speedy-trial period began to run when defendant was arrested for possession of open alcoholic beverage containers in an automobile and state had information necessary to charge OMVI, even though OMVI charge not filed until over five weeks later. **Westdahl v. State,** Op. No. 1818, 592 P2d 1214 (Alaska 1979).

Speedy-trial period of Criminal Rule 45(b) began to run when defendant was served with Uniform Summons and Complaint, although that document was never filed with the court and defendant was prosecuted under a subsequent complaint properly served and filed. **Ahmoaqak v. State,** Op. No. 1857, 595 P2d 985 (Alaska 1979).

Where defendant's counsel withdrew and new counsel was appointed, the period of delay due to the motion to withdraw was excluded from the computation of the time of trial under Criminal Rule 45(d)(1). **Linden v. State,** Op. No. 1905, 598 P2d 960 (Alaska 1979).

Where at time of arrest extent of injury to victim could not be determined, delay in filing of charge for mayhem was for good cause and period of delay was properly excluded in computing time for that. **Adams v. State,** Op. No. 1864, 598 P2d 503 (Alaska 1979).

Defendant-prisoner's transfer from prison dormitory to maximum security, and search and interrogation by state trooper, did not constitute an "arrest" which would initiate speedy-trial period of Criminal Rule 45. **Aldridge v. State,** Op. No. 1971, 602 P2d 798 (Alaska 1979).

A three-month delay in appellant's trial was not an excludable period under this rule where the delay was occasioned by the state's decision to try appellant's co-defendant first so that he would be available to testify against appellant. **Mullins v. State,** Op. No. 2052, 608 P2d 764 (Alaska 1980).

Even if a period of lack of diligence chargeable against the state exists, the state's subsequent efforts showing due diligence to find the defendant will again toll the running of the 120-day period under this rule. **Spencer v. State,** Op. No. 2071, 611 P2d 1 (Alaska 1980).

Where defendant was arrested and charged on November 6 with assault with a dangerous weapon in the shooting of her fiance, which charge was dismissed on December 3 and replaced on December 10 with a charge of manslaughter following the fiance's death on December 7, the trial court was correct in concluding that the manslaughter complaint constituted a new charge based on new evidence not available at the time of the original arrest; accordingly, the commencement date for the running of time under this rule was December 10. **Spencer v. State,** Op. No. 2071, 611 P2d 1 (Alaska 1980).

Delays occasioned by the withdrawal of defendant's first counsel and a continuance required by defendant's new counsel to allow adequate time for preparation were properly excluded from the 120-day time limit for instituting a criminal prosecution. **Stobaugh v. State,** Op. No. 2127, 614 P2d 767 (Alaska 1980).

The speedy-trial period begins to run anew where: (1) the defendant intentionally fails to appear for court; (2) his disappearance is followed by a substantial period of absence; and (3) by virtue of defendant's inaction no progress is made in the normal pretrial process before the defendant's disappearance. **Russell v. Municipality of Anchorage,** Op. No. 14, 626 P2d 586 (Alaska App. 1981).

The period of delay "resulting from the absence of the defendant" includes not only the actual period of absence itself, but also all subsequent delay which is occasioned by and attributable to the absence. **Russell v. Municipality of Anchorage,** Op. No. 14, 626 P2d 586 (Alaska App. 1982).

The apparent violation of the provisions of District Court Rule of Criminal Procedure 1 requiring trial to be set by a judge or magistrate has no bearing on computation of excluded periods for purposes of this rule. **McKenzie v. Municipality of Anchorage,** Op. No. 26, 631 P2d 514 (Alaska App. 1982).

Where Fairbanks police had defendant's word that he would arrive at Ft. Huachuca on October 1, due diligence did not require them to pursue avenues for locating defendant other than to send arrest warrant copies to officials in Arizona; accordingly, the ten-day period between the day when the complaint and arrest warrant were issued and October 1, when defendant reported to Ft. Huachuca, constituted a delay resulting from the absence of defendant and could therefore be excluded in computing the speedy-trial time period. **Harker v. State,** Op. No. 60, 637 P2d 716 (Alaska App. 1981).

Trial court's finding that defendant was attempting to avoid apprehension during period in question, thus excluding that period in computing the time for trial, was clearly erroneous, since evidence presented did not justify conclusion that defendant fled the state knowing that charges were imminent, nor did fact that defendant's mother hesitated to provide her son's current address to a total stranger, a police officer, who contacted her by phone, permit an inference that defendant was hiding from the authorities. **Odekirk v. State,** Op. No. 133, 648 P2d 1039 (Alaska App. 1982).

For purpose of calculating speedy-trial period, period between March of 1979 and February of 1980 was charged to the state because of its lack of due diligence in searching for defendant, since, although defendant left no forwarding address, state did not act upon its knowledge of a Utah mailing address for defendant or its knowledge that defendant was from Nevada. **Odekirk v. State,** Op. No. 113, 648 P2d 1039 (Alaska App. 1982).

Where negligent homicide charge arose out of same conduct for which defendant was initially charged with the traffic infraction of following too close, the 120-day speedy-trial time limit on the negligent homicide charge began to run when defendant was charged with following too close. **Koch v. State,** Op. No. 161, 653 P2d 664 (Alaska App. 1982).

Court decision which clarified the legal relationship between intoxication and negligence did not constitute new evidence which would extend the 120 day time limit of this rule. **Koch v. State,** Op. No. 161, 653 P2d 664 (Alaska App. 1982).

Fact that testimony of witnesses at a hearing or trial may differ somewhat from their former statements does not constitute evidence not before available which would justify extension of the speedy-trial time limit. **Koch v. State,** Op. No. 161, 653 P2d 664 (Alaska App. 1982).

Coroner's inquest which yielded no new evidence did not extend the speedy-trial time limit. **Koch v. State,** Op. No. 161, 653 P2d 664 (Alaska App. 1982).

Where there was sufficient evidence to convict defendant of tampering with evidence when he was indicted for murder, defendant's admission at his murder trial that he tampered with evidence did not justify extension of the 120-day speedy-trial time limit on the charge of tampering with the evidence. **State v. Williams,** Op. No. 159, 653 P2d 1067 (Alaska App. 1982).

Arrest on murder charge started the running of the 120-day speedy-trial period on subsequent charge of tampering with evidence which arose from the same conduct as the murder charge. **State v. Williams,** Op. No. 159, 653 P2d 1067 (Alaska App. 1982).

Twenty-eight month delay between arrest and trial did not violate speedy-trial rule where tolling periods occasioned by change of counsel, time between issuance of arrest warrant and arraignment, and time for which defendant signed a formal waiver amounted to all but 116 days of the twenty-eight month period. **Springer v. State,** Op. No. 266, 666 P2d 431 (Alaska App. 1983).

The 120-day period allowed by this rule does not begin to run anew following a petition for review; nevertheless, a reasonable time should be allowed for the court and prosecution to get the case back on the calendar before the time period begins to run again after remand from an appellate court. **Sundberg v. State,** Op. No. 272, 667 P2d 1268 (Alaska App. 1983).

Where case was remanded twice following petitions for review, at least sixty days was a reasonable period of additional delay to attribute to the petitions for review for the purpose of setting the case for trial before the 120-day speedy-trial period began to run again. **Sundberg v. State,** Op. No. 272, 667 P2d 1268 (Alaska App. 1983).

Where the prosecution, relying on defendant's guilty pleas to three of the four charges against him, dismissed the fourth charge of rape, but defendant subsequently motioned for withdrawal of his pleas and the motion was granted on appeal, the time from entry of defendant's guilty pleas to reversal of his conviction on appeal was properly excluded in computing the speedy-trial time period for the reinstated rape charge. **Morgan v. State,** Op. No. 320, 673 P2d 897 (Alaska App. 1983).

This rule requires the 120-day speedy-trial period to begin running on all charges arising out of the same conduct when a defendant is arrested for any one offense; furthermore, an event which suspends the 120-day period for one charge suspends it for all charges arising out of the same conduct, whether or not the charges were filed when the event took place. **State v. Williams,** Op. No. 2817, 681 P2d 313 (Alaska 1984).

Where defendant appeared at a child in need of aid hearing concerning his daughter and was ordered to participate in psychological counseling and to move out of his home, but was not served with the information charging him with sexual assault of his daughter until four and one-half months later, the initial court order did not constitute a de facto arrest; accordingly, the 120-day speedy-trial period did not begin to run until the information was served. **G. D. v. State,** Op. No. 374, 681 P2d 366 (Alaska App. 1984).

When a juvenile is waived to adult court, the speedy-trial time limit of this rule begins to run on the day the waiver order is signed. **Brower v. State,** Op. No. 380, 683 P2d 290 (Alaska App. 1984).

A reindictment following dismissal of an indictment must be treated as a continuation of the original prosecution for purposes of the speedy-trial rule, thus periods of time excluded under the original indictment must also be deemed excluded under the superseding indictment. **State v. Nitz,** Op. No. 385, 684 P2d 134 (Alaska App. 1984).

Where the state elected to proceed with a third indictment of defendant after initially deciding to appeal the dismissal of the second indictment, the exclusion for interlocutory appeals under this rule applied to the period between the filing of the appeal and the date of the third indictment, and the period could not be included in computing the time for trial on the third indictment. **State. v. Nitz,** Op. No. 385, 684 P2d 134 (Alaska App. 1984).

Although defendant was in police custody at hospital as a drunk driving suspect following an automobile wreck, he was in custody for a limited duration and for the limited purpose of ascertaining his blood-alcohol level, after which he was released without having been handcuffed or moved from the hospital; accordingly, the custody never amounted to an arrest which would trigger the running of the speedy-trial time period. **Greenawalt v. Municipality of Anchorage,** Op. No. 434, 692 P2d 983 (Alaska App. 1985).

"Arrest" for purposes of this rule is the taking of a person into custody in order that the person may be held to answer for the commission of a crime; accordingly, although defendant was initially detained on February 20, 1983 for questioning, after which the police told him that he would be charged with a crime but that he was not under arrest and he was then released, the speedy-trial time period did not begin to run until defendant's formal arrest in April of 1983. **Lindsay v. State,** Op. No. 458, 698 P2d 659 (Alaska App. 1985).

In determining whether due diligence in attempting to locate the accused has been shown, the primary emphasis is on the reasonableness of the efforts actually made, not on the alternatives that might have been available. **Ingram v. State,** Op. No. 489, 703 P2d 415 (Alaska App. 1985).

In order to comply with the due diligence requirement for excluding the period of delay resulting from the absence or unavailability of the defendant, police must take reasonable steps to ascertain the whereabouts of the accused but need not follow up on every conceivable lead. **Ingram v. State,** Op. No. 489, 703 P2d 415 (Alaska App. 1985).

Due diligence of police in searching for absent defendant was supported by the record, thus the period of his absence was properly excluded in calculating speedy-trial time period, whether or not the defendant was attempting to avoid apprehension. **Ingram v. State,** Op. No. 489, 703 P2d 415 (Alaska App. 1985).

A 102-day delay granted to the prosecution over defendant's objection for the purpose of extraditing a codefendant for a joint trial was not a reasonable period of delay; the trial court therefore erred in treating the 102 days as excluded from computation of the speedy-trial time limit. **Miller v. State,** Op. No. 511, 706 P2d 336 (Alaska App. 1985).

Where defendant's discovery request was for evidence which the state was under obligation to provide and defendant did not request action of the court regarding the request and no court action was taken, defendant's discovery request was not a discovery motion; accordingly, trial court erred in excluding the period during which the request was pending from the speedy-trial computation. **Miller v. State,** Op. No. 511, 706 P2d 336 (Alaska App. 1985).

A continuance granted to one codefendant does not automatically extend the time for trying his codefendant, at least where the codefendant objects to the continuance. **Miller v. State,** Op. No. 511, 706 P2d 336 (Alaska App. 1985).

A trial court must, as a condition precedent to excluding any time against a defendant under the speedy-trial rule when a continuance has been granted to the state for the purpose of bringing a codefendant to trial at the same time, specifically consider the question of severance; the trial court may not simply rely upon having previously denied a severance. **Miller v. State,** Op. No. 511, 706 P2d 336 (Alaska App. 1985).

Where charges are pending against someone who is detained outside the jurisdiction, the prosecution must attempt to obtain that person's presence for trial, and only if those attempts fail may a detainer be filed, which will then justify exclusion from speedy-trial calculations of the detention period. **Conway v. State,** Op. No. 537, 707 P2d 930 (Alaska App. 1985).

Period between day defendant was sentenced on Washington charges and the day the Washington parole board set a minimum term for defendant was a period during which defendant was unavailable by reason of executive decisions by the Washington authorities, thus period was properly excluded from speedy-trial computation. **Conway v. State,** Op. No. 537, 707 P2d 930 (Alaska App. 1985).

Defendant's refusal while detained by authorities in another state to accept parole to an Alaska detainer and his subsequent action in filing a pro se writ of habeas corpus, supplemented by his attorney's formal application for writ of habeas corpus, constituted resistance under this rule, warranting exclusion of the delay caused by the resistance from speedy-trial calculations. **Conway v. State,** Op. No. 537, 707 P2d 930 (Alaska App. 1985).

Where defendant intentionally failed to appear for court, and his disappearance was followed by a substantial period of absence during which he was rearrested in another state, his speedy-trial right lapsed at the time he intentionally failed to appear for court and commenced anew when he was arrested in the other state. **Conway v. State,** Op. No. 537, 707 P2d 930 (Alaska App. 1985).

Period between good-time release date on defendant's Washington sentence and the day on which Washington authorities turned defendant over to Alaska authorities constituted "other proceedings concerning the defendant," warranting exclusion of the period from speedy-trial calculations. **Conway v. State,** Op. No. 537, 707 P2d 930 (Alaska App. 1985).

When appellate court grants a petition for interlocutory review, the time necessary to decide the petition is excludable from computation of the "speedy-trial" time period, whether or not a stay of proceedings is obtained. **State v. R.H.,** Op. No. 566, 711 P2d 558 (Alaska App. 1985).

Where sexual offender was arrested on August 21, 1984 for violating probation condition requiring him to refrain from being in the presence of children, and after the arrest admitted to sexual acts several months previously with two of the children he was seen with, the speedy-trial time period began to run when he was indicted on November 14, 1984 for sexual abuse of those children, not the August 21 arrest date. **Kizzire v. State,** Op. No. 591, 715 P2d 272 (Alaska App. 1986).

The running of defendant's speedy-trial time period commenced with his arrest on September 18, 1985 and ended on November 12, 1985 when his case was scheduled for trial and defendant notified the court of his intent to plead guilty; the period between November 12, 1985 and April 8, 1986, during which evidence of defendant's prior convictions in Texas was sought for purposes of sentence enhancement, was excluded from the speedy-trial time period because defendant never unequivocally canceled his offer to plead guilty to the charge until April 8, 1986. **Morris v. State,** Op. No. 694,734 P2d 1012 (Alaska App. 1987).

Trial court's finding that defendant was not in custody at the time he was initially interviewed by a state trooper was not clearly erroneous, thus defendant's contention that he was under arrest at that time for purposes of computing the time for trial was rejected. **Zaukar v. State,** Op. No. 692, 734 P2d 1005 (Alaska App. 1987).

Although appellate court opinion reversing defendant's conviction and remanding the case for a new trial was issued on June 6, 1986, the opinion did not become operative and had no force or validity as an order for a new trial until the date specified for return of the record, thus the date specified for return, not the issuance date, triggered commencement of the 120-day speedy-trial period. **Nitz v. State,** Op. No. 759, 745 P2d 1379 (Alaska App. 1987).

Whether the issue of defendant's competency was raised by his court-appointed counsel, by the court sua sponte, or by defendant's own effort to waive counsel and represent himself, the time necessary to determine his competency was properly excluded from calculation of the speedy-trial time period. **Burks v. State,** Op. No.774,748 P2d 1178 (Alaska App. 1988).

Delay necessitated by the last minute withdrawal of defendant's first attorney and the time necessary for his new attorney to adequately prepare was excludable from the speedy-trial time period even though defendant did not consent to the delay. **Bereskin v. State,** Op. No. 856, 762 P2d 486 (Alaska App. 1988).

Where bench warrant was served upon defendant on June 27, 1986 because of his failure to appear at a sentencing hearing relating to his conviction for possession of cocaine, service of the bench warrant did not begin the running of the 120-day speedy-trial time period for the offense of failing to appear at the sentencing hearing, since his arrest pursuant to the warrant acted only to secure his presence for the sentencing proceeding he had previously missed; accordingly, his October 13, 1986 arraignment on an October 9, 1986 indictment for failure to appear was the event triggering the running of the speedy-trial time period on the charge. **Cannizzaro v. State,** Op. No. 879, 765 P2d 110 (Alaska App. 1988).

Where delay in bringing defendant to trial was caused by interlocutory review of trial court's decision to suppress certain testimony, a period of 30 days could be excluded from the 120 speedy-trial time period following remand without a showing by the state that any particular time was needed to put the case on the trial calendar; accordingly, since defendant was brought to trial within 150 days following remand, the speedy-trial rule was not violated. **Contreras v. State,** Op. No. 897, 767 P2d 1169 (Alaska App. 1989).

When defendant was read the implied consent form informing him that he was under arrest for driving while intoxicated, the speedy-trial time period began to run; the state's contention that an arrest for implied consent purposes is not an arrest which triggers the running of the speedy-trial time period was rejected. **Longley v. State,** Op. No. 940, 776 P2d 339 (Alaska App. 1989).

Despite the temporal proximity of the charges against defendant for drunk driving and murder (she stopped the car and shot her passenger), the two offenses did not arise from the same criminal episode for purposes of the speeding trial rule, thus her arrest for DWI did not trigger the running of the speedy trial time limit on the murder charge. **State v. Dunten,** Op. No. 1009, 785 P2d 907 (Alaska App. 1990).

Since the information was neither personally delivered nor delivered by certified or registered mail, the information was never served on defendant in a manner which would trigger running of the speedy-trial period. **Hayes v. State,** Op. No. 1031, 790 P2d 713 (Alaska App. 1990).

Trial court properly rejected defendant's argument that since he did not protest the insufficiency of process or its service, the defect was waived, triggering the running of the speedy-trial period; since defendant was not asserting insufficiency of process as a defense to prosecution, the rule authorizing waiver of any defect in service of process did not apply. **Hayes v. State,** Op. No. 1031, 790 P2d 713 (Alaska App. 1990).

Where defendant was arrested based upon a bench warrant issued in response to his failure to appear for sentencing on a sexual abuse conviction, the warrant acted only to secure his presence for sentencing, and did not trigger the speedy-trial period for the offense of failing to appear. **Hayes v. State,** Op. No. 1031, 790 P2d 713 (Alaska App. 1990).

The time for trial begins to run from the date the defendant is arrested and held to answer for the commission of a specific crime as well as any subsequent charges arising out of the same conduct or same criminal episode. **Knowiton v. State,** Op. No. 1057, 795 P2d 1287 (Alaska App. 1990).

Arrest of parolee for conduct constituting a parole violation, which conduct was also an independent crime, did not trigger the 120-day period for prosecution of the underlying crime. **Knowiton v. State,** Op. No. 1057, 795 P2d 1287 (Alaska App. 1990).

Speedy trial time period for murder defendant began to run on December 24, 1987, when he was arraigned for murder, not on October 6, 1987, when he was arrested for violating the conditions of his probation, even if the murder charge arose from the same conduct as the probation violation. **Demientieff v. State,** Op. No. 1144, 814 P2d 745 (Alaska App. 1991).

When a defendant asserts that he or she never consented to a continuance obtained or stipulated to by defense counsel, the running of the speedy trial time period remains tolled until the judge makes an affirmative finding that the defendant did not consent to the continuance. **State v. Jeske,** Op. No. 1188, 823 P2d 6 (Alaska App. 1991).

Defendant's speedy-trial time period for criminal contempt began to run on date criminal information was served on defendant for willful noncompliance with court orders to pay child support, not on earlier date when he was charged with civil contempt for failure to pay child support. **Moss v. State,** Op. No. 1237, 834 P2d 1256 (Alaska App. 1992).

When defendant in a criminal case withdraws a plea of no contest or guilty, speedy trial time period does not commence running again until at least 30 days following date of withdrawal. **Petersen v. State,** Op. No. 1247, 838 P2d 812 (Alaska App. 1992).

Defense counsel's request for renewed calendar call/omnibus hearing tolled running of speedy trial period from date of request until October 3 when requested hearing was held, even though trial date had already been set for October 7 and additional hearing had no bearing on setting of trial date. **State v. Angalak,** Op. No. 1287, 847 P2d 1068 (Alaska App. 1993).

The running of the speedy-trial clock is tolled by any proceeding involving defendant, whether or not it leads to ascertainable delay. **Bright v. State,** Op. No. 1353, 875 P2d 100 (Alaska App. 1994).

A pretrial motion to compel the State to disclose information and records relating to its informant tolled the speedy trial period for the five days it was pending. **Drake v. State,** Op. No. 1421, 899 P2d 1385 (Alaska App. 1995).

Motions asking the court to affirmatively intervene in the discovery process toll the running of the speedy trial period. **Drake v. State,** Op. No. 1421, 899 P2d 1385 (Alaska App. 1995).

Defense requested continuances of the pre-indictment hearing toll the running of the speedy trial period during the continuances. **Rhames v. State,** Op. No. 1446, 907 P2d 21 (Alaska App. 1995).

A 28-day continuance of the trial date was properly excluded from the speedy trial period where the superior court was never apprised that the defendant no longer consented to the continuance. **Rhames v. State,** Op. No. 1446, 907 P2d 21 (Alaska App. 1995).

The speedy trial period began to run when defendant was arraigned on an indictment for sexual assault and murder, not when he was arrested by federal authorities for a federal firearms violation which was discovered as part of the investigation leading to the state charges. **Harmon v. State,** Op. No. 1450, 908 P2d 434 (Alaska App. 1995).

For purposes of this rule, no contest plea is same as agreement to be tried and found guilty on stipulated statement of facts, and each has same effect as plea of guilty. **Minch v. State,** Op. No. 1518, 934 P2d 764 (Alaska App. 1997).

Despite two-year delay in bringing defendant to trial, speedy trial rule was not violated: defendant waived time limit when he knowingly agreed to trial date outside limit and later terminated running of time limit by announcement that he intended to change his plea to guilty. **Minch v. State,** Op. No. 1518, 934 P2d 764 (Alaska App. 1997).

When defendant told court that his plea agreement with state had broken down and that he now intended to go to trial, speedy trial clock was extended by reasonable amount of time (a minimum of 30 days) to allow court to work his case back into trial calendar. **Minch v. State,** Op. No. 1518, 934 P2d 764 (Alaska App. 1997).

Where charges of driving while intoxicated were dismissed on double jeopardy grounds but reinstated several months later following remand by court of appeals of dismissal orders, beginning of speedy trial time period was reset to day jurisdiction over defendants' cases was returned to district court. **Garcia v. State,** Op. No. 1556, 947 P2d 1363 (Alaska App. 1997).

Defendant's argument that because his attorneys did not act with due diligence in filing plea-withdrawal motion, Rule 45 clock should have restarted when he instructed attorneys to file motion rather than when motion was actually filed was rejected; even if in fact attorneys failed to diligently act, Rule 45 clock would not have surreptitiously started to run before plea-withdrawal motion was filed. **Bobby v. State,** Op. No. 1563, 950 P2d 135 (Alaska App. 1997).

Speedy trial time period begins to run one day following remand for new trial. **Mustafoski v. State,** Op. No. 1576, 954 P2d 1042 (Alaska App. 1998).

Speedy trial calculation was terminated, not tolled, when defendant on remand informed court that he intended to change his plea to guilty; accordingly, when he subsequently decided not to change his plea, speedy trial period began anew. **Mustafoski v. State,** Op. No. 1576, 954 P2d 1042 (Alaska App. 1998).

For speedy trial purposes, a defendant's announcement that he or she intends to plead guilty or no contest is same as actual entry of such plea; in either situation, speedy trial calculation stops because speedy trial requirement is satisfied. **Mustafoski v. State,** Op. No. 1576, 954 P2d 1042 (Alaska App. 1998).

Where motion by defendants to dismiss DWI charges on double jeopardy was granted by trial court, and appeal of dismissal was held in abeyance by appellate court pending its decision in a group of consolidated cases involving same double jeopardy issue, effect of appellate court order remanding jurisdiction to trial court to give further consideration to double jeopardy motions was to place defendants' double jeopardy motions under advisement again, thus Rule 45 computation remained tolled until either (a) trial court ruled on motions or (b) held those motions under advisement, undecided, for longer than 30 days. **Billman v. Municipality of Anchorage,** Op. No. 1578, 954 P2d 1380 (Alaska App. 1998).

Where dismissal of DWI charges against defendants on double jeopardy grounds by trial court was appealed by municipality that brought charges, and appellate court held appeal in abeyance pending its decision in a group of consolidated cases involving same double jeopardy issue, appellate court order delivered January 15, 1996, holding that dismissal of DWI charges in such cases was improper and remanding such cases to trial courts, triggered beginning of speedy trial on January 16, 1996; statement in appellate court order that "any previously filed motion for stay that has not already been granted shall be deemed to have been granted nunc pro tunc" was not intended to retain jurisdiction of such cases in appellate court. **Billman v. Municipality of Anchorage,** Op. No. 1578, 954 P2d 1380 (Alaska App. 1998).

Issuance by magistrate of "Order and Conditions of Release" form following arrestee's initial appearance did not constitute "charging document" triggering time period for bringing arrestee to trial. **Bailey v. Municipality of Anchorage,** Op. No. 1583, 955 P2d 947 (Alaska App. 1998).

Speedy-trial period began to run when defendant was served with copy of charge, not when he was arrested. **Snider v. State,** Op. No. 1592, 958 P2d 1114 (Alaska App. 1998).

Argument that speedy-trial rule was not tolled by motion to dismiss because motion was never ruled on was rejected; time under rule was tolled until motion to dismiss was withdrawn. **Snider v. State,** Op. No. 1592, 958 P2d 1114 (Alaska App. 1998).

Defendant's assertion that his cocaine charge arose from the same criminal episode as his criminal trespass and criminal mischief charges was rejected; accordingly, the speedy-trial commencement date for the cocaine charge was the date on which that charge was served on defendant rather than the earlier date on which the criminal trespass and criminal mischief charges were served on defendant. **Pitka v. State,** Op. No. 1728, 19 P3d 604 (Alaska App. 2001).

Where defendant filed motion to delay his trial "until after May 14th," and did not object to rescheduled trial date of June 23rd, defendant's contention that for speedy-trial purposes the 40 days between May 14 and June 23 should be charged to the state, not to defendant, was rejected. **Wolfe v. State,** Op. No. 1740, 24 P3d 1252 (Alaska App. 2001).

In a dog bite case, defendant's statutory speedy-trial rights were not violated where defendant's case was remanded to the district court on December 20, 2002, and went to trial three months later, on March 17, 2003, well within the 120-day speedy trial period. **Alvarez v. Ketchikan Gateway Borough,** Op. No. 1929, 91 P.3d 289 (Alaska App. 2004).

For purposes of this rule's service requirement, defendant was not "served" when the State gave him a copy of the indictment in court on the petition to revoke his probation. Rather, he was served when he was formally served with the charge. **State v. Gottschalk,** Op. No. 8798, 138 P.3d 1170 (Alaska App. 2006).

The 120-day time for trial in this rule stops running on the date a defendant announces his intent to change his plea as at that point, the parties and court no longer anticipate a trial. However, if the defendant later changes his mind and demands a trial, the 120-day period restarts at day 1. **Bush v. State,** Op. No. 9535, 157 P.3d 1059 (Alaska App. 2007).

III. Waiver.

A waiver of the speedy-trial right for a specifically defined period is highly preferable to an open-ended waiver. A waiver until a specific date in the future, which waiver could be extended by further waivers, obviates many interpretive difficulties. **Cooksey v. State,** Op. No. 1063, 524 P2d 1251 (Alaska 1974).

A defendant's waiver of his speedy-trial right may extend a period of exclusion beyond that provided by statute but it cannot shorten such excluded period. **Cooksey v. State,** Op. No. 1063, 524 P2d 1251 (Alaska 1974).

When motion for dismissal is not made before jury selection is commenced, rights under this rule are waived. **James v. State,** Op. No. 1470, 567 P2d 298 (Alaska 1977).

The argument that affirmative steps to protect the right to a speedy-trial are not required is inapplicable to post-waiver situations, where affirmative steps to withdraw a waiver may reasonably be required. **Coffey v. State,** Op. No. 1732, 585 P2d 514 (Alaska 1978).

Defendant waived any objection to court's failure to comply with Criminal Rule 45 when counsel knew or should have known that the time set for trial fell outside the permissible 120-day period. **DeMille v. State,** Op. No. 1676, 581 P2d 675 (Alaska 1978).

Waiver of defendant's speedy-trial right by defendant's attorney occurred where attorney was present at setting of trial date and was aware that the trial date did not conform to the requirements of Criminal Rule 45. **Westdahl v. State,** Op. No. 1818, 592 P2d 1214 (Alaska 1979).

Defendant's waiver of speedy-trial rule on murder charge did not constitute waiver of speedy-trial rule on subsequent charge of tampering with evidence which arose from the same conduct as the murder charge. **State v. Williams,** Op. No. 159, 653 P2d 1067 (Alaska App. 1982).

Absent extraordinary circumstances, a defendant's right to a speedy-trial is relinquished only when it is knowingly waived by the defendant or the defendant's counsel. **Andrew v. State,** Op. No. 439, 694 P2d 168 (Alaska App. 1985).

An affirmative duty to object to a trial date arises only when defense counsel is actually aware that the court has set a date beyond the speedy-trial limit. **Andrew v. State,** Op. No. 439, 694 P2d 168 (Alaska App. 1985).

This rule does not, in and of itself, impose a general duty requiring defense counsel to affirmatively object to a trial date in order to preserve the defendant's speedy-trial rights, but defense counsel could be compelled by an express pretrial order to raise any speedy-trial objections either at the time a trial date is set or within a reasonable period of time thereafter. **Andrew v. State,** Op. No. 439, 694 P2d 168 (Alaska App. 1985).

The defendant must show actual prejudice in order to establish that the trial court abused its discretion in failing to excuse defendant's forfeiture of his right to speedy-trial and his right to a change of judge. **Trudeau v. State,** Op. No. 581, 714 P2d 362 (Alaska App. 1986).

Defendant forfeited his right to claim a violation of the speedy-trial rule by not complaining until after his trial had begun. **Trudeau v. State,** Op. No. 581, 714 P2d 362 (Alaska App. 1986).

When a defendant's attorney knows at the time the trial date is set of all the circumstances that make the trial date violate this rule, but fails to correctly calculate the relevant 120-day period, the court may imply a knowing waiver. **State v. Andrew,** Op. No. 3057, 718 P2d 471 (Alaska 1986).

Whether defense counsel waived defendant's right to a speedy-trial under this rule by failing to object when the trial date was set beyond the 120-day limit depended upon whether defense council was actually aware of all pertinent information concerning the commencement of the speedy-trial period; mere failure to calculate the 120-day deadline would not excuse the failure to object. **Buffington v. State,** Op. No. 755, 745 P2d 78 (Alaska App. 1987).

Generally, the court may rely upon the request of counsel for a continuance, without seeking a separate waiver from the defendant. **Machado v. State,** Op. No. 1067, 797 P2d 677 (Alaska App. 1990).

Attorney who appeared from defendant at calendar call was empowered to relinquish defendant's rights under this rule without defendant's personal waiver; absent an affirmative showing to the contrary, it had to be assumed that the attorney's request for a continuance beyond the speedy-trial date was with defendant's knowledge and consent. **Yearty v. State,** Op. No. 1106, 805 P2d 987 (Alaska App. 1991).

When a defendant asserts that he or she has never consented to a continuance obtained or stipulated to by defense counsel, the running of the speedy-trial time period remains tolled until the judge makes an affirmative finding that the defendant did not consent to the continuance. **State v. Jeske,** Op. No. 1188, 823 P2d 6 (Alaska App. 1991).

Substitute counsel's failure to object to announced trial date did not constitute waiver of defendant's speedy-trial right under this rule since counsel did not know enough about events that started and arguably tolled running of speedy-trial period to be aware that trial date violated the rule. **State v. Angaiak,** Op. No. 1287, 847 P2d 1068 (Alaska App. 1993).

If an attorney assents to a trial date knowing that the proposed date will violate this rule, the attorney thereby waives the potential Rule 45 objection to holding the trial on that date. **Drake v. State,** Op. No. 1421, 899 P2d 1385 (Alaska App. 1995).

Despite two-year delay in bringing defendant to trial, speedy-trial rule was not violated: defendant waived time limit when he knowingly agreed to trial date outside limit and later terminated running of time limit by announcement that he intended to change his plea to guilty. **Minch v. State,** Op. No. 1518, 934 P2d 764 (Alaska App. 1997).

When defendant's attorney consented to trial date of September 22nd, knowing that it fell outside the speedy-trial expiration date, she waived defendant's right to challenge that trial date. **Wardlow v. State,** Op. No. 1676, 2 P3d 1238 (Alaska App. 2000).

In a criminal prosecution for third-degree criminal mischief, defendant waived his speedy-trial claim, because he went to trial and never sought dismissal of the charges under Alaska R. Crim. P. 45. **McGee v. State,** Op. No. 1942, 95 P.3d 945 (Alaska App. 2004).

Rule 46. Exceptions Unnecessary.

Exceptions to rulings or orders of the court are unnecessary. It is sufficient that a party, at the time the ruling or order of the court is made or sought, makes known to the court the action which the party desires the court to take or the party's objection to the action of the court and the grounds therefor; but if a party has no opportunity to object to a ruling or order, the absence of an objection does not thereafter prejudice him.

(Adopted by SCO 4 October 4, 1959; amended by SCO 1153 effective July 15, 1994)

Annotations

Cases

While it is unnecessary for a party to take exception to rulings or orders of the court, a party should be specific in stating his grounds for objection when objection to actions taken by the trial court is made, and if he does not so state his grounds, he may not raise the point for the first time on appeal. **McBride v. State,** Op. No. 66, 368 P2d 925 (Alaska 1962).

The admission of a police officer's testimony that defendant refused to take the Harger test was not plain error; and since no objection was made in the trial court, the supreme court would not consider an objection on appeal. **Gilley v. City of Anchorage,** Op. No. 114, 376 P2d 454 (Alaska 1962).

The failure of defense counsel, in objecting to cross-examination, to specify that the cross-examination elicits character evidence tending to impeach the truth and veracity of the defendant prior to his having taken the stand in his defense, thereby putting pressure on him to take the stand to reconstruct his good character, and hence violates his right not to incriminate himself is a technical failure and does not preclude the assertion of the claim on appeal. **Newsom v. State,** Op. No. 909, 512 P2d 557 (Alaska 1973).

Under Alaska R. Crim. P. 46, an attorney does not preserve a claim of error unless, at the time of the ruling or order of the court is made or sought, the attorney makes known to the court the action which the party desires the court to take or the attorney's objection to the action and the grounds therefor. **Waters v. State,** Op. No. 1853, 64 P.3d 169 (Alaska App. 2003).

The minimum requirements for an objection under this rule were not met where the defense attorney announced an open-ended, unspecified objection to all aspects of the sentencing proceeding if later appellate decisions showed or indicated that one or more aspects of the proceeding were flawed. **Active v. State**, Op. No. 8984, 153 P.3d 355 (Alaska App. 2007).

Rule 47. Harmless Error and Plain Error.

(a) **Harmless Error.** Any error, defect, irregularity or variance which does not affect substantial rights shall be disregarded.

(b) **Plain Error.** Plain errors or defects affecting substantial rights may be noticed although they were not brought to the attention of the court.

(Adopted by SCO 4 October 4, 1959)

Annotations

Cases

I. In General.
II. Harmless Error.
III. Plain Error.

I. In General.

While it is unnecessary for a party to take exception to rulings or orders of the court, a party should be specific in stating his grounds for objection when objection to actions taken by the trial court is made, and if he does not so state his grounds, he may not raise the point for the first time on appeal. **McBride v. State,** Op. No. 66, 368 P2d 925 (Alaska 1962).

Where both counsel appointed to represent appellant came to the same conclusion that the trial record disclosed no meritorious grounds which they could urge on appeal and which they could argue in an appeal brief, supreme court made its own review of the record to determine that the evaluation was correct and that there was no reversible error below. **Selman v. State,** Op. No. 315, 409 P2d 602 (Alaska 1966).

The fact that an error of the district judge in a preliminary hearing which had not affected the character of the trial the defendants were accorded and which did not, on the record, prejudice or disadvantage defendants did not result in a reversal of convictions must not be taken to indicate that violations of the requirements of this rule will be readily condoned. **Merrill v. State,** Op. No. 392, 423 P2d 686 (Alaska 1967).

In the matter of deciding whether a mistrial should be declared, the trial court has wide discretion and commits error only if it abuses that discretion. **Maze v. State,** Op. No. 400, 425 P2d 235 (Alaska 1967).

Apart from rule the same standard has been applied by the supreme court in civil cases. **Goreson v. State,** Op. No. 436, 432 P2d 326 (Alaska 1967).

Where counsel for appellant had informed the trial court that they would not request an instruction in order not "to underline" a potentially prejudicial answer of a witness mentioning a lie detector test, appellant was precluded from asserting on appeal that failure to instruct jury with regard to the answer was error. **Gafford v. State,** Op. No. 478, 440 P2d 405 (Alaska 1968).

The failure of defense counsel, in objecting to cross-examination, to specify that the cross-examination elicits character evidence tending to impeach the truth and veracity of the defendant prior to his having taken the stand in his defense, thereby putting pressure on him to take the stand to reconstruct his good character, and hence violates his right not to incriminate himself is a technical failure and does not preclude the assertion of the claim on appeal. **Newsom v. State,** Op. No. 909, 512 P2d 557 (Alaska 1973).

Appellate court must consider the record and applicable law in deciding whether under circumstances of particular case, a pretrial identification was so unnecessarily suggestive that it amounted to a violation of due process; but where no glaring error appears court need not review evidence in depth. **Gilbert v. State,** Op. No. 3406, 598 P2d 87 (Alaska 1979).

If an error affects substantial rights and is obviously prejudicial, it may be noticed although not brought to the attention of the court. **Diggs v. Diggs,** Op. No. 2680, 663 P2d 950 (Alaska 1983).

Unless inconsistency between two verdicts is obvious and appellate review is necessary to prevent manifest injustice, claims of inconsistency will not be considered on appeal unless an objection to the verdicts is first made in the trial court, before the jury is discharged. **Roberts v. State,** Op. No. 355, 680 P2d 503 (Alaska App. 1984).

II. Harmless Error.

Refusal to strike irrelevant testimony did not constitute prejudicial error, where none of such testimony constituted evidence of another crime and where there was no reasonable probability that the jury would have arrived at a different verdict had the testimony objected to been stricken. **Daniels v. State,** Op. No. 185, 388 P2d 813 (Alaska 1964).

Unauthorized communication between judge and jury constitutes reversible error only if the violation of the rule affected a substantial right of the defendant. **Noffke v. State,** Op. No. 383, 422 P2d 102 (Alaska 1967).

A supplemental jury instruction on the elements of the crime of burglary which was ambiguous and could have led the jury to find the defendant guilty without having found that he had the requisite statutory intent to steal, affected a substantial right of the defendant and giving this instruction outside the presence of the defendant was reversible error. **Noffke v. State,** Op. No. 383, 422 P2d 102 (Alaska 1967).

Where defendant was charged in the indictment with the crime of "living with a prostitute" and an instruction was given to the jury that the state was required to prove in addition thereto that he had lived on her earnings, the error of instructing the jury to find elements of a separate crime denounced disjunctively under AS 11.40.410 was harmless and constituted no ground for reversal. **Dunn v. State,** Op. No. 409, 426 P2d 993 (Alaska 1967).

Under the "obviously prejudicial" test denial of defendant's rights to be present at every stage of the trial was not fatal where trial counsel had not objected to the defendant's absence at several anteroom conferences which concerned discussions regarding materiality of testimony concerning certain objects, the identification of photographs which eventually were not used by the prosecution, and an uncertainty about the import of a witness' testimony and where nothing which transpired at these conferences could have prejudiced substantial rights of the defendant. **Kugzruk v. State,** Op. No. 451, 436 P2d 962 (Alaska 1968).

In the absence of a showing that a claimed deficiency or imperfection in an indictment prejudiced substantial right of defendant, the indictment could not be held fatally defective. **Price v. State,** Op. No. 454, 437 P2d 330 (Alaska 1968).

Denial of motion for a mistrial was no abuse of the wide discretion resting in the trial judge, where prosecutor's incompetent but inadvertent remarks as to venereal disease of defendant charged with statutory rape was followed by the prompt instruction of the trial judge to the jury to disregard the remark and by prosecutor's simultaneous apology and there was sufficient competent evidence in the record from which the jury could have found defendant guilty of the crime charged. **Anderson v. State,** Op. No. 461, 438 P2d 228 (Alaska 1968).

Prosecutor's remarks at sentencing proceedings of a defendant convicted of manslaughter which referred to the fact that the defendant had been previously indicted for the crime of manslaughter and had been acquitted thereof, was not model advocacy but did not require the setting aside of the judgment. **Egelak v. State,** Op. No. 463, 438 P2d 712 (Alaska 1968).

Prosecutor's partial ex parte presentation of photographs of victim in homicide case prior to sentencing was improper and was not condoned, but in a setting where this incident was followed within minutes by a sentencing hearing in open court in the presence of defendant and counsel, prosecutor's conduct did not result in prejudicial error. **Egelak v. State,** Op. No. 463, 438 P2d 712 (Alaska 1968).

Although testimony of state witness at a murder trial that she as well as defendant's wife were arrested for vagrancy and that defendant paid the fine which resulted in an indebtedness owing from witness's husband (who was the murder victim) to the defendant, who may have placed before the jury the innuendo that defendant was engaged in the white slave trade, the evidence of the arrest and payment of fine of the witness was admissible for the purpose of establishing a possible motive for the slaying, and the reception of evidence as to the vagrancy arrest of appellant's wife was harmless error as measured against the entire record of the case. **Gafford v. State,** Op. No. 478, 440 P2d 405 (Alaska 1968).

An exchange of notes between the trial judge and the jury foreman without the knowledge of defendant and his counsel violated the requirement of presence of defendant at all stages of a criminal proceedings but did not constitute reversible error in a case where the communication had no direct bearing on the merits of the case and did not affect a substantial right of the defendant. **Gafford v. State,** Op. No. 478,440 P2d 405 (Alaska 1968).

As a general rule, the results of polygraph tests are not admissible in evidence, but denial of mistrial was not error where in a murder trial a statement was elicited from a prosecution witness during vigorous cross-examination that he took a lie detector test but no prejudicial inference was raised thereby against the defendant. **Gafford v. State,** Op. No. 478, 440 P2d 405 (Alaska 1968).

An instruction that an accomplice's testimony should be viewed with caution and weighed with great care is not reversible error. Although the required instruction is that such testimony ought to be viewed with distrust, where there is no objection or request for the proper instruction, there is a further instruction on accomplice testimony, and there is extensive corroborating evidence. **Flores v. State,** Op. No. 491, 443 P2d 73 (Alaska 1968).

This rule applies to constitutional errors. **Rubey v. City of Fairbanks,** Op. No. 561, 456 P2d 470 (Alaska 1969).

All trial error violating constitutional provisions do not automatically call for a reversal, but such errors cannot be declared harmless if there is a reasonable possibility that evidence admitted in violation of such constitutional rights might have contributed to a conviction. Before such constitutional error can be held to be harmless, the court must be able to declare beyond a reasonable doubt that the error did not contribute to the verdict. **Rubey v. City of Fairbanks,** Op. No. 561, 456 P2d 470 (Alaska 1969).

When an alleged accomplice gives testimony exonerating the defendant but the state impeaches the witness by introducing prior inconsistent statements, the defendant's counsel elicits from the alleged accomplice circumstances surrounding the taking of the statements which, if believed, demonstrates the statements' unreliability, the court's instructions limit the use of the statements to their potential impact upon the witness' credibility, any error in failing to give a cautionary instruction that the testimony of an accomplice ought to be viewed with distrust was harmless. **Johnston v. State,** Op. No. 726,489 P2d 134 (Alaska 1971).

Where a jury first returns two verdicts which find the defendant guilty of both the greater and the lesser included offenses and the court with the acquiescence of counsel informs the jury he will not accept the verdicts after which the jury deliberates again and signs only the first verdict form finding the defendant guilty of the greater offense, the trial court's action is a proper attempt to alleviate the confusion. So long as the judge applies no coercion on the jury to compel them to reach a verdict there is no prejudice to the defendant. **Gravel v. State,** Op. No. 819, 499 P2d 1022 (Alaska 1972).

In a rape prosecution, testimony that the defendant, in talking to his fellow workers on the jobsite, had expressed in coarse language, that he found the victim sexually attractive and that it would be nice if a person could get into her apartment by a trapdoor or other entrance is relevant and material. The probative value of such testimony is not outweighed by its prejudicial effect. **Gordon v. State,** Op. No. 831, 501 P2d 772 (Alaska 1972).

A denial of a constitutional right, in the normal case, will affect substantial rights and give rise to plain error. However, when an error, even of constitutional dimension, may be said to be harmless beyond a reasonable doubt, the rights of an accused are not prejudiced and the requirements of plain error have not been met. **Burford v. State,** Op. No. 954, 515 P2d 382 (Alaska 1973).

Where evidence wrongfully admitted is merely cumulative and the prosecutor's case apart from the alleged error is very strong, harmless error may still be found. **Burford v. State,** Op. No. 954, 515 P2d 382 (Alaska 1973).

Denial of a constitutional right affects substantial rights. Plain error requiring reversal will be deemed present unless the defect is harmless beyond a reasonable doubt. **Martin v. State,** Op. No. 991, 517 P2d 1399 (Alaska 1974).

Where one of two persons who could have identified the defendant as the purveyor of illicit drugs asserts that the defendant is not the man who sold the amphetamines, improper exclusion of evidence tending to impugn testimony of a witness who states that defendant had sold the drugs is not harmless error. **Hutchings v. State,** Op. No. 995, 518 P2d 767 (Alaska 1974).

Withdrawal of guilty plea or vacation of conviction for failure to comply with Criminal Rule 11 will only be granted when noncompliance affected substantial rights of defendant. **Lewis v. State,** Op. No. 1447, 565 P2d 846 (Alaska 1977).

Considering the speculative nature of testimony concerning possible negligence of deceased and that defense attorney was permitted to present arguments on that possibility to jury, failure of the court to give instruction that deceased's conduct could be considered as bearing on question of defendant's alleged negligence was harmless error. **Wren v. State,** Op. No. 1598, 577 P2d 235 (Alaska 1978).

Insufficient proof of a point which is not an element of the offense charged does not affect substantial rights and is therefore not adequate ground for reversal. H **Hayes v. State,** Op. No. 1662, 581 P2d 221 (Alaska 1978).

Where testimony of prosecution witnesses was corroborated and jury was apprised of possible sources of bias, excluding evidence of particular wrongful acts intended to impeach credibility, even if error, was harmless error. **Taylor v. State,** Op. No. 1932, 600 P2d 5 (Alaska 1979).

Where facts surrounding accident were stipulated, testimony of victim's husband regarding such facts was inadmissible, but admission was harmless error. **O'Leary v. State,** Op. No. 2003, 604 P2d 1099 (Alaska 1979).

Where state presented substantial evidence that defendant was a violent man, it was harmless error to admit further testimony where prejudicial impact outweighed probative value. **Frink v. State,** Op. No. 1870, 597 P2d 154 (Alaska 1979).

Where court erred in allowing prosecution to amend its complaint against defendant, the error was harmless considering that the amended complaint did not allege a change in the nature of the underlying criminal act and considering that the defendant did not specify how his trial tactics were altered by the amended complaint. **McGahan v. State,** Op. No. 2021, 606 P2d 396 (Alaska 1980).

Where defendant was charged with assault with a dangerous weapon and assault while armed, the admission into evidence over his objection of testimony relating to an arson investigation focusing on two of his close friends was prejudicial error and should have been excluded; however, it was harmless error since the case against defendant was strong despite the challenged evidence and since the prejudicial effect of the arson testimony was not extreme. **Sevier v. State,** Op. No. 2134, 614 P2d 791 (Alaska 1980).

It was harmless error for the trial court to admit hearsay testimony concerning statements made by a coconspirator which were not in furtherance of the conspiracy. **Crump v. State,** Op. No. 2309, 625 P2d 857 (Alaska 1981).

In prosecution for attempted sexual abuse of a minor, trial court erred in allowing testimony about statements defendant made one week after the incident concerning his sexual fantasies and orientation since the testimony was clearly character evidence and was not relevant to show proof of motive, opportunity, intent, preparation, plan, knowledge, identity or absence of mistake or accident; nevertheless, due to the strength of the other evidence against defendant, the error was deemed harmless. **Stevens v. State,** Op. No. 773, 748 P2d 771 (Alaska App. 1988).

In trial of defendant for murder where the only question at issue was intent, any error in allowing admission of defendant's prior felony conviction for possession of a concealable firearm despite defendant's offer to stipulate to a prior felony conviction in order to keep the exact nature of the felony from the jury was harmless; given the overwhelming evidence of intent, evidence of the prior felony conviction was not overly prejudicial. **Weitz v. State,** Op. No. 1058, 794 P2d 952 (Alaska App. 1990).

III. Plain Error.

The imposition of an unlawful sentence is plain error which may be noticed although not brought to the attention of the magistrate who heard the case. **Lapham v. City of Haines,** Op. No. 100, 374 P2d 239 (Alaska 1962).

The admission of a police officer's testimony that defendant refused to take the Harger test was not plain error; and since no objection was made in the trial court, the supreme court would not consider an objection on appeal.

Gilley v. City of Anchorage, Op. No. 114, 376 P2d 484 (Alaska 1962).

Where defendant contended on appeal that newspaper account of trial must have been read by jurors and prevented her from having a fair trial, but an article was never brought to attention of trial court, held it was not so obviously prejudicial as to be noticed as "plain error." **Bowker v. State,** Op. No. 91, 373 P2d 500 (Alaska 1962).

Admission of defendant's refusal to submit to polygraph test was not error so fundamental it would be noticed by Supreme Court where defendant's counsel clearly waived any error that might have occurred by bringing to the attention of the jury the defendant's refusal to take the examination. **Rank v. State,** Op. No. 92, 373 P2d 734 (Alaska 1962).

Under Criminal Rule 47(b) providing that only plain errors or defects affecting substantial rights may be noticed even though they were not brought to the attention of the court, failure of indictment to show the name of witness before the grand jury cannot be urged for the first time on appeal. **Thomas v. State,** Op. No. 200, 391 P2d 18 (Alaska 1964).

Since it is plain that the terms "record, writing, instrument, or matter" in the statute under which defendant was indicted for uttering and publishing a forged deed, included a deed, the indictment stated a crime and the alleged error in the language of the indictment could not for the first time be noticed on appeal. **Chambers v. State,** Op. No. 237, 394 P2d 778 (Alaska 1964).

The Supreme Court may consider questions raised for the first time on appeal if necessary to effect substantial justice or prevent the denial of fundamental rights, in both criminal and civil cases. **Hammond v. State,** Op. No. 483, 442 P2d 39 (Alaska 1968).

The admission of statements made by the defendant to an interrogating officer, who does not inform the defendant that he has the right to court-appointed counsel does not constitute plain error where the failure to object is an intelligent waiver of a known right. **Hammond v. State,** Op. No. 483, 442 P2d 39 (Alaska 1968).

Plain error, which affected substantial rights of defendant, may be noticed the first time on appeal. **Noffke v. State,** Op. No. 383, 422 P2d 102 (Alaska 1967); **Hammond v. State,** Op. No. 483, 442 P2d 39 (Alaska 1968); **Drahosh v. State,** Op. No. 485, 442 P2d 44 (Alaska 1968).

Under this rule, "plain error" means error which is both obvious and substantial. **Dimmick v. State,** Op. No. 521, 449 P2d 774 (Alaska 1969).

For purposes of this rule, an error is not plain where the record does not present the question in reasonable detail. **Dimmick v. State,** Op. No. 521, 449 P2d 774 (Alaska 1969).

The power of the Supreme Court to consider a question presented for the first time on appeal under this rule is an exception to Criminal Rule 30, forbidding a party from assigning as error any part of an objection unless proper objection had been taken at trial, and will be exercised only where necessary to prevent a miscarriage of justice. **Dimmick v. State,** Op. No. 521, 449 P2d 774 (Alaska 1969).

A defendant does not waive the right to question the consistency of verdicts by failing to move for acquittal at the close of evidence. **DeSacia v. State,** Op. No. 608, 469 P2d 369 (Alaska 1970).

The Supreme Court will consider objections to the inconsistency of a verdict, even if the defendant should have objected to instructions which permitted the inconsistency. **DeSacia v. State,** Op. No. 608, 469 P2d 369 (Alaska 1970).

In a case where the defendant is ultimately convicted of "selling or possessing" a narcotic drug, the fact that the indictment, jury instructions and verdict did not separate the offenses of selling and possessing does not constitute plain error where there is no possibility of confusion. **Nickerson v. State,** Op. No. 759, 492 P2d 118 (Alaska 1971).

Absent objection at trial, the Supreme Court will reverse for prosecutorial misconduct in a closing argument only on a showing that the misconduct constitutes plain error. **Garroutte v. State,** Op. No. 877, 508 P2d 1190 (Alaska 1973).

A defendant asserting for the first time on appeal that prosecutorial misconduct during trial constituted plain error requiring reversal must shoulder the heavy burden of demonstrating that the alleged conduct raises a substantial and important question. Where the misconduct fails to rise to the level of plain error, considerations of judicial economy dictate that reviewing court deal with the matter summarily. **Garroutte v. State,** Op. No. 877, 508 P2d 1190 (Alaska 1973).

If the statute under which a defendant is charged is unconstitutional, the resulting indictment and conviction constitutes "plain error" under this rule. Accordingly, the Supreme Court will consider the issue although it was not brought to the attention of the trial court. **Tarnef v. State,** Op. No. 911, 512 P2d 923 (Alaska 1973).

If a defendant is denied due process of law and deprived of his right to a speedy-trial because of a total delay exceeding 20 months from offense to trial, "plain error" is committed. The Supreme Court will consider the issue, although there is no indication in the record or transcript that the defendant had prior to trial moved to dismissal for alleged deprivation of due process and speedy-trial. **Tarnefv. State,** Op. No. 911, 512 P2d 923 (Alaska 1973).

The failure to raise a point at trial court level or include it in statements of points to be raised on appeal generally will foreclose the appeal of an alleged error, unless it reaches the level of plain error. **Burford v. State,** Op. No. 954, 515 P2d 382 (Alaska 1973).

In order for the supreme court to notice plain error, the alleged error must affect substantial rights and be obviously prejudicial. **Burford v. State,** Op. No. 954, 515 P2d 382 (Alaska 1973).

The general impeachment of a defendant with invalid misdemeanor convictions is an error of constitutional dimension. A criminal defendant who is so impeached is deprived of due process of law. **Burford v. State,** Op. No. 954, 515 P2d 382 (Alaska 1973).

A denial of a constitutional right, in the normal case, will affect substantial rights and give rise to plain error. However, when an error, even of constitutional dimension, may be said to be harmless beyond a reasonable doubt, the rights of an accused are not prejudiced and the requirements of plain error have not been met. **Burford v. State,** Op. No. 954, 515 P2d 382 (Alaska 1973).

Failure to object to an error during probation revocation proceedings precludes its consideration on appeal unless the defect may be said to constitute plain error which is obviously prejudicial. **Martin v. State,** Op. No. 991, 517 P2d 1399 (Alaska 1974).

Denial of a constitutional right affects substantial rights. Plain error requiring reversal will be deemed present unless the defect is harmless beyond a reasonable doubt. **Martin v. State,** Op. No. 991, 517 P2d 1399 (Alaska 1974).

In order to be plain error, the alleged error must affect substantive rights and be obviously prejudicial. **Torres v. State,** Op. No. 1017, 519 P2d 788 (Alaska 1974).

Where a defendant's substantive rights are not affected by the introduction into evidence of a reference to physical evidence which has been negligently destroyed by the police, the admission of the testimony is not "plain error." **Torres v. State,** Op. No. 1017, 519 P2d 788 (Alaska 1974).

A claim of error which is not raised at trial or in points on appeal will not be considered unless it constitutes plain error, i.e., it affects substantial rights and is obviously prejudicial. **Davenport v. State,** Op. No. 1218, 543 P2d 1204 (Alaska 1975).

To constitute "plain error," defect should be both obvious and substantial and have been obviously prejudicial. **Evans v. State,** Op. No. 1272, 550 P2d 830 (Alaska 1976).

Supreme Court will consider faulty instruction on appeal where it constituted plain error, even though no objection was made at trial. **Stork v.**

State, Op. No. 1365, 559 P2d 99 (Alaska 1977).

Instruction that required mere negligence rather than culpable negligence to convict for manslaughter was plain error. **Stork v. State,** Op. No. 1365, 559 P2d 99 (Alaska 1977).

Statement by prosecution during final argument that it is difficult to convict attorneys like defendant who specializes in criminal cases and that defendant recently represented a member of a criminal organization did not constitute plain error. **Webb v. State,** Op. No. 1638, 580 P2d 295 (Alaska 1978).

Where alleged improper cross-examination was not objected to at trial level, conviction could be reversed on that ground only if the alleged misconduct resulted in a substantial interference with defendant's right to a fair trial. **Randall v. State,** Op. No. 1691, 583 P2d 196 (Alaska 1978).

The exclusionary rule requiring suppression of illegally obtained evidence was not applied on appeal where the defendant had not objected to admission of the evidence at the trial. **Moreau v. State,** Op. No. 1770, 588 P2d 275 (Alaska 1978).

Defense counsel's failure to properly object to introduction of testimony concerning defendant's momentary refusal to consent to a search of his vehicle or to object to the prosecutor's comment on it during final arguments falls within the plain error doctrine reflected by Criminal Rule 47(b). **Padgett v. State,** Op. No. 1801, 590 P2d 432 (Alaska 1979).

Where defendant did not request instruction that informer's testimony be viewed with caution, failure of court to give such instruction was not plain error. **Robinson v. State,** Op. No. 1837, 593 P2d 621 (Alaska 1979).

Display of rape victim's bloodstained trousers to the jury during final argument may have been prejudicial but it did not affect defendant's rights to the extent that he was denied a fair trial, nor did the court's failure to order removal of the pants amount to plain error. **Alexander v. State,** Op. No. 2077, 611 P2d 469 (Alaska 1980).

Where defendant, charged with assault with a dangerous weapon did not request a jury instruction on the lesser included offenses of careless use of firearms and simple assault, failure of court to give such instruction was not plain error. **McGee v. State,** Op. No. 2136, 614 P2d 800 (Alaska 1980).

Prosecutor's comment during closing argument that guilt should be inferred from defendant's silence between the time he was advised of his Miranda rights was cognizable under the plain error rule and constituted reversible error. **Dorman v. State,** Op. No. 2272, 622 P2d 448 (Alaska 1981).

Instruction to jury that defendant must be found not guilty if the evidence "points equally to the defendant's innocence as well as to his guilt" was not sufficiently misleading as to constitute plain error. **Dorman v. State,** Op. No. 2272, 622 P2d 448 (Alaska 1981).

Jury instruction on weighing of conflicting evidence which was not particularly confusing or a misstatement of law did not constitute plain error. **Burke v. State,** Op. No. 2194, 624 P2d 1240 (Alaska 1981).

Giving of instruction that rape victim's testimony need not be corroborated was a mistake, but was not plain error. **Burke v. State,** Op. No. 2194, 624 P2d 1240 (Alaska 1981).

Failure to contest the constitutionality of an administrative regulation defining a criminal prohibition at trial is plain error and the constitutional challenge may be raised and considered for the first time on appeal. **Crutchfield v. State,** Op. No. 2207, 627 P2d 196 (Alaska 1980).

Double jeopardy violation met the standard of plain error because it affected a substantial right, was obvious, and was prejudicial. **Tookak v. State,** Op. No. 108, 648 P2d 1018 (Alaska App. 1982).

If reasonable judges, aware of applicable constitutional provisions, statutes, court rules, and binding appellate authority, would differ regarding the propriety of giving a particular instruction to the jury at the time given, its use is not plain error. **Marrone v. State,** Op. No. 156, 653 P2d 672 (Alaska App. 1982).

Failure of trial court to instruct the jury to distrust the state's evidence because it was within the state's power to produce stronger and more satisfactory evidence was not plain error. **Walker v. State,** Op. No. 2570, 652 P2d 88 (Alaska App. 1982).

Failure to give an instruction is plain error if reasonable judges could not differ in concluding that the instruction was necessary to adequately inform the jury of the offense or of defenses to the offense clearly established in the evidence and the failure to give the instruction substantially prejudiced the defendant. **Bidwell v. State,** Op. No. 199, 656 P2d 592 (Alaska App. 1982).

Failure of court to instruct the jury that a subjective belief that the victim consented to restraint was a defense to kidnapping was not plain error. **Bidwell v. State,** Op. No. 199, 656 P2d 592 (Alaska App. 1982).

Failure of trial court to give intent instruction utilizing the phrase "specific intent" was not plain error. **Bidwell v. State,** Op. No. 199, 656 P2d 592 (Alaska App. 1982).

Instruction which informed the jury that it could infer an actor's intent from his words and conduct, and further informed the jury that it might infer that an actor intends the natural and probable consequences of acts he knowingly does or knowingly omits, did not shift the burden of proof to defendant on the issue of intent and was therefore not plain error. **Bidwell v. State,** Op. No. 199, 656 P2d 592 (Alaska App. 1982).

Failure of the trial court to instruct the jury on the element of premeditation and to define the element of intent needed for first-degree murder was not plain error. **Weston v. State,** Op. No. 183, 656 P2d 1186 (Alaska App. 1982).

To establish plain error a litigant must do more than show that the rule of law he relies upon in the appellate court should have been obvious to the trial court; he must, in addition, establish that the application of that rule of law to the facts of his case was so obvious that it should have been noticed by the trial court sua sponte. **Carman v. State,** Op. No. 206, 658 P2d 131 (Alaska App. 1983).

In murder trial, instruction to jury that it should not consider punishment in determining the issue of guilt was not plain error, nor was it plain error not to inform the jury of the twenty-year minimum penalty for first-degree murder. **Martin v. State,** Op. No. 261, 664 P2d 612 (Alaska App. 1983).

A party relying on plain error must go beyond a mere showing that error was committed and that the error involved a constitutional right; he must also show that the error was obviously prejudicial. **Van Hatten v. State,** Op. No. 269, 666 P2d 1047 (Alaska App. 1983).

The correct measure of obvious prejudice under the plain error rule is whether it can be fairly said that the alleged error did not appreciably affect the jury's verdict. **Van Hatten v. State,** Op. No. 269, 666 P2d 1047 (Alaska App. 1983).

Police officer's reference at trial to defendant's decision to remain silent until he obtained an attorney was not plain error. **Van Hatten v. State,** Op. No. 269, 666 P2d 1047 (Alaska App. 1983).

Where defendant does not object to an instruction at trial, on appeal he must show that the instruction amounts to plain error, i.e., that the instruction is an obvious error that substantially affected his right to a fair trial. **Wilson v. State,** Op. No. 294, 670 P2d 1149 (Alaska App. 1983).

Defendant charged with sexual assault in the third degree did not meet the substantial burden necessary to show that instruction to jury was plain error which required defendant to know that the victim was incapacitated when it should have required only that the victim be incapacitated regardless of defendant's knowledge. **Dexter v. State,** Op. No. 302, 672 P2d 144 (Alaska App. 1983).

Although no prior evidentiary hearing is necessary when "plain error" appears in the record, ineffective assistance of counsel is rarely apparent in the record, since counsel may have had strategic reasons for engaging in the conduct in question. **Barry v. State,** Op. No. 334, 675 P2d 1292 (Alaska App. 1984).

Where charges against defendant grew out of a motor vehicle accident in which defendant's car collided with a truck, injuring the truck driver and killing a passenger in the truck, inconsistent verdicts reflecting a conclusion that defendant caused the passenger's death but not the driver's injuries were so obviously inconsistent that they satisfied the plain error test. **Davis v. State,** Op. No. 391, 684 P2d 147 (Alaska App. 1984).

Admission of defendant's statements in taped interview concerning his drug addiction and alcoholism was not plain error. **Lipscomb v. State,** Op. No. 477, 700 P2d 1298 (Alaska App. 1985).

There being no constitutional difference between stipulating to prior convictions, as defendant agreed to do, or presenting the uncontroverted convictions to the court without a jury, defendant's claim that it was plain error not to have the jury decide whether he had prior convictions was properly rejected. **Azzarella v. State,** 703 P2d 1182 (Alaska App. 1985).

Instruction to jury in drunk driving case as to the effect to be given intoximeter test results was not plain error. **Russell v. Municipality of Anchorage,** Op. No. 514, 706 P2d 687 (Alaska App. 1985).

Trial court's error in sexual abuse case in not requiring the state to elect a specific sexual incident applicable to each count relied upon for conviction, or alternatively, in failing to provide a curative instruction, was not plain error, where jury's verdict of guilty on all counts indicated that the jury accepted the victim's testimony that defendant committed all of the incidents charged. **State v. Covington,** Op. No. 557, 711 P2d 1183 (Alaska App. 1985).

Prosecutor's statements in child molestation case to the effect that defendant refused to receive psychological treatment and would receive help only if convicted were improper but did not constitute plain error requiring reversal. **Potts v. State,** Op. No. 553, 712 P2d 385 (Alaska App. 1985).

Amendment of indictment, which charged defendant with a May 5 assault, to charge defendant with a second assault against the same victim on May 1, was reversible error, particularly since the error was compounded by allowing the jury to render a single verdict on the indictment without an instruction requiring the jury to unanimously agree that defendant committed one of the offenses. **Bell v. State,** Op. No. 607, 716 P2d 1004 (Alaska App. 1986).

Whether lesser-included offense instruction should have been given was subject to plain error analysis on appeal where defense counsel at trial had conceded that the instruction was not appropriate. **Norbert v. State,** Op. No. 616, 718 P2d 160 (Alaska App. 1986).

Counselor's statements at sentencing hearing concerning her opinion as to child victim's credibility should not have been admitted, but the admission did not amount to plain error. **Dymenstein v. State,** Op. No. 624, 720 P2d 42 (Alaska App. 1986).

Where defendant, convicted of robbery in the first degree based on his role as an accomplice, had furnished gun used by the person who committed the robber, it was not plain error to subject defendant to the statutory seven-year presumptive term for persons who "possess a firearm" during commission of a felony. **Hale v. State,** Op. No. 872, 764 P2d 313 (Alaska App. 1988).

Unless the record precludes the possibility that defense counsel's actions may have been tactical, a finding of plain error based upon trial court rulings not objected to by counsel is rarely appropriate. **Massey v. State,** Op. No. 915, 771 P2d 448 (Alaska App. 1989).

When trial counsel's failure to object to inadmissible and substantially prejudicial evidence stems from reliance on a tactic that is patently unsound, the failure to object will not preclude a finding of plain error. **Massey v. State,** Op. No. 915, 771 P2d 448 (Alaska App. 1989).

Issues involving the applicability of the exclusionary rule are not appropriately raised for the first time on appeal. **Longley v. State,** Op. No. 940, 776 P2d 339 (Alaska App. 1989).

Error in allowing police officer to refer to her "police report" during testimony, which arguably constituted evidence of a prior bad act by defendant, was harmless in light of the overwhelming evidence of guilt and fell far short of plain error. **Collins v. State,** Op. No. 962, 778 P2d 1171 (Alaska App. 1989).

Failure of trial court to inform the foreperson of the jury in a criminal case that she would not be penalized by the airline if she missed her flight because of jury deliberations was not plain error. **Badoino v. State,** Op. No. 1002,785 P2d 39 (Alaska App. 1990).

Failure of trial court to properly instruct jury on the elements of criminal nonsupport, specifically by omitting to advise the jury of the need to find that defendant acted recklessly with regard to her children's need for medical attention, constituted plain error, requiring vacation of her conviction. **S.R.D. v. State,** Op. No. 1161, 820 P2d 1088 (Alaska App. 1991).

Error required remand where jury instruction shifted the burden of proving necessity to the defendant in a criminal mischief conviction while the jury acquitted defendant of a related charge. The split verdicts indicated that the instruction played a substantial part in defendant's conviction. **McGee v. State,** Op. No. 11611, 162 P3d 1251 (Alaska 2007).

Rule 48. Regulation of Conduct in the Court Room.

The taking of photographs in the court room during the progress of judicial proceedings, or radio or television broadcasting of judicial proceedings from the court room, shall not be permitted by the court except in accordance with applicable provisions of the Administrative Rule 50.

(Adopted by SCO 4 October 4, 1959; amended by SCO 322 effective September 15, 1978; and by SCO 1158 effective July 15, 1994)

Rule 49. Records.

The clerks of court shall keep such records in criminal proceedings as may be prescribed by rule or order of the supreme court or by the administrative director with the approval of the chief justice.

(Adopted by SCO 4 October 4, 1959; amended by SCO 1297 effective January 15, 1998)

Rule 50. Attorneys.

(a) **Appearance by Counsel—Withdrawal.** In all criminal actions, counsel retained to represent the accused shall, immediately after being retained as such, file with the clerk a formal written appearance upon a form to be provided by the court. The Rules of Civil Procedure relating to the withdrawal of an attorney for a party shall apply with equal force with respect to any attorney retained to represent the accused in criminal actions.

(b) **Civil Rules to Apply.** All other provisions of the Rules of Civil Procedure relating to attorneys, regarding examining witnesses, counsel as a witness, non-resident attorneys, and disbarment and discipline, shall apply to practice in criminal actions in the courts of the state.

(c) **Penalties.** After giving the attorney reasonable notice and an opportunity to be heard, the court may impose against any attorney a fine not to exceed $500.00 for failure to comply with these rules or any other rules of court.

(Adopted by SCO 4 October 4, 1959; amended by SCO 1055 effective July 15, 1991; and by SCO 1126 effective July 15, 1993)

Annotations

Cases

Civil Rule 77 governing motion practice is made applicable to criminal actions by this rule. **State v. Johnson,** Op. No. 1069, 525 P2d 532 (Alaska 1974).

This rule makes Civil Rule 77(k) applicable to Criminal Rule 25(d)(5), so that stipulations thereunder are not binding on the court. **Padie v. State,** Op. No. 1465, 566 P2d 1024 (Alaska 1977).

Civil Rule 77 was intended to provide a uniform procedure for handling the many and diverse types of general procedural motions that arise in the course of litigation, both civil and criminal. **Adams v. State,** Op. No. 497, 704 P2d 794 (Alaska App. 1985).

In the absence of a conflict in the evidence the trial court may rely on Civil Rule 77(k) in making fact findings based upon affidavits or other documentary evidence regarding suppression motions; where, however, the defendant testifies under oath and is subject to cross-examination, the trial court may abuse its discretion if it does not require oral testimony from the state's witnesses. **Adams v. State,** Op. No. 497, 704 P2d 794 (Alaska App. 1985).

Civil Rule 77(k), authorizing motions to be heard on affidavits, was not intended to substitute affidavits for the vital oral testimony of necessary witnesses essential in the determination of whether an accused's constitutional right to remain silent when questioned by the police has been scrupulously honored. **Adams v. State,** Op. No. 497,704 P2d 794 (Alaska App. 1985).

Imposition of attorney fees and monetary sanctions against defense attorney in criminal case for filing frivolous, unnecessary and legally deficient pleadings was error requiring remand where attorney was not given notice of the charges against him nor a hearing on the issue of sanctions. **Weidner v. Superior Court, Third Judicial Dist.,** Op. No. 589, 715 P2d 264 (Alaska App. 1986).

Trial court had no authority to require the state to pay costs or attorney's fees as a sanction in a juvenile case. **State v. Superior Court, Third Jud. Dist.,** Op. No. 744, 743 P2d 381 (Alaska App. 1987).

Trial court did not have the authority to assess costs against defendant as a sanction for his non-willful failure to appear on time for his jury trial. **Jerrel v. State,** Op. No. 885, 865 P2d 982 (Alaska App. 1988).

Trial judge did not err in requiring defense counsel to coordinate all defense motions and pleadings rather than allowing defendant to file his own pro se motions. **Martin v. State,** Op. No. 1065, 797 P2d 1209 (Alaska App. 1990).

Rule 51. Procedure Not Otherwise Specified—Construction of Statutes.

These rules are designated to provide for the efficient operation of the court of the State of Alaska. If no specific procedure is prescribed by rule or statute, the court may proceed in any lawful manner not inconsistent with these rules, the constitution, and the common law.

(Adopted by SCO 4 October 4, 1959)

Annotations

Cases

The request of a defendant, raising the insanity defense, for a bifurcated trial is within the trial court's discretion, and a ruling on such issue is reviewable if such discretion is abused. **Kinsman v. State,** Op. No. 914, 512 P2d 901 (Alaska 1973).

The supreme court in reviewing a criminal conviction in which there is a challenge to the sufficiency of the evidence cannot add to a finding of fact but will take notice of facts appearing in evidence which are undisputed. **Hughes v. State,** Op. No. 926, 513 P2d 1115 (Alaska 1973).

The Superior Court has discretion to order remission or partial remission of a forfeited bail bond after considering all relevant factors including: (1) costs, inconvenience, or prejudice to the government in regaining custody, (2) delay resulting from the nonappearance, (3) willfulness of the failure to appear, and (4) public interest in ensuring the appearance. **Adkerson v. State,** Op. No. 3153, 731 P2d 1218 (Alaska 1987).

Rule 52. Legal Effect of Rules—Statutes Superseded.

These rules are promulgated pursuant to constitutional authority granting rule making power to the supreme court, and to the extent that they are inconsistent with any procedural provisions of any statute not enacted for the specific purpose of changing a rule, shall supersede such statute to the extent of such inconsistency.

(Adopted by SCO 4 October 4, 1959)

Annotations

Cases

A legislative enactment will not be effective to change court rules of practice and procedure under Section 15 of Article IV of the Constitution, unless the bill specifically states that its purpose is to effect such a change. Thus a portion of a statute which purported to forbid the granting of stays pending appeal, which statute did not contain such a statement of purpose, is ineffective and does not change rules of practice and procedure made and promulgated by the supreme court. **Leege v. Martin,** Op. No. 131, 379 P2d 447 (Alaska 1962).

Rule 53. Relaxation of Rules.

These rules are designed to facilitate business and advance justice. They may be relaxed or dispensed with by the court in any case where it shall be manifest to the court that a strict adherence to them will work injustice.

(Adopted by SCO 4 October 4, 1959)

Annotations

Cases

Where in giving oral notice of appeal from a judgment of conviction of the district judge appellant had failed to state the grounds of appeal whereupon the state had moved for dismissal of appeal solely for failure to file an appeal brief, but the superior court had then provided for a time schedule for briefs and appellant had filed an appeal brief in compliance with such order stating grounds for appeal and only after such filing of brief the state had moved for dismissal for failure to state grounds for appeal, dismissal of appeal by the superior court resulted in an injustice in the meaning of Criminal Rule 53 which the supreme court corrected by reinstating the appeal. **Cowgill v. State,** Op. No. 709, 423 P2d 907 (Alaska 1967).

Requirement of Criminal Rule 17(b) as formerly written that showing in support of motion under that rule be made by affidavit, was correctly dispensed with by trial judge in a case where it appeared that defendant was illiterate and that linguistic and cultural barriers existed between defendant and his counsel. **Smiloff v. State,** Op. No. 474, 439 P2d 772 (Alaska 1968).

Where the defendant does not move for an evidentiary hearing or base his motion for a new trial on misconduct by the bailiff, the issue of whether the trial court erred in failing to grant him an evidentiary hearing concerning an allegedly improper statement made by the bailiff to the jury during the course of their deliberations is not properly before the supreme court. The defendant is not precluded from raising the issue in a future proceeding on a motion for a new trial or through other means seeking post-conviction relief. **Howard v. State,** Op. No. 754, 491 P2d 154 (Alaska 1971).

Fairness dictates that a post-conviction claimant who was sentenced prior to the enactment of a statute requiring that credit be given for any time served pending trial, sentencing, or appeal be granted credit against his sentence for any presentence time served. **Thompson v. State,** Op. No. 792, 496 P2d 651 (Alaska 1972).

Where there was no showing of manifest injustice in sentencing procedure or in sentences themselves, waiver of the time limitations of Rule 35(a) was not warranted. **Jones v. State,** Op. No. 1258, 548 P2d 958 (Alaska 1976).

Only a very small number of cases are so unusual that relaxation of speedy-trial rule would be justified. **Peterson v. State,** Op. No. 1411, 562 P2d 1350 (Alaska 1977).

Relaxation of speedy-trial rule in prosecution for quadruple murder was not abuse of discretion because of combination of (1) severity of crimes alleged, (2) lack of prejudice to defendant due to delay, (3) extremely short period of delay, and (4) unique difficulty of investigating crimes in bush area. **Peterson v. State,** Op. No. 1411, 562 P2d 1350 (Alaska 1977).

Where motion to modify sentence was filed two years after sentence was imposed, trial court did not abuse discretion in refusing to relax rule imposing 60-day limitation on such motions. **Taylor v. State,** Op. No. 1436, 564 P2d 1219 (Alaska 1977).

This rule applies to Criminal Rule 35(a), on modification of sentences. **Thomas v. State,** Op. No. 1445, 566 P2d 630 (Alaska 1977).

When defendant's counsel had a bona fide belief that a motion for reduction or modification of sentence had been timely filed, defendant had requested such a motion and tried to learn if it had been filed, within prescribed period, and defendant was imprisoned in institution that could not afford him treatment for alcoholism, to fail to relax the 60-day limit of Criminal Rule 35(a) pursuant to Rule 53 would work an injustice. **Wheeles v. State,** Op. No. 1454, 566 P2d 1013 (Alaska 1977).

Criminal Rule 45 should not be suspended for a misdemeanor, even though delay was short and nonprejudicial because a misdemeanor is not sufficiently serious to outweigh society's interest in the orderly administration of justice through adherence to the Rules of Criminal Procedure. **Westdahl v. State,** Op. No. 1818, 592 P2d 1214 (Alaska 1979).

Where neither defendant had the opportunity to consult counsel prior to expiration of the time limit for peremptorily challenging the judge, the court abused its discretion in failing to waive the time limit. **Riley v. State,** Op. No. 2038, 608 P2d 27 (Alaska 1980).

Trial court correctly dispensed with the spousal testimonial immunity privilege where defendant married on the eve of trial and had a strong motivation to prevent the testimony of the woman he married. **Osborne v. State,** Op. No. 2291, 623 P2d 784 (Alaska 1981).

The time limits of the rule governing new trial motions are not jurisdictional. **Davidson v. State,** Op. No. 78, 642 P2d 1383 (Alaska App. 1982).

Trial judge did not abuse his discretion in reinstating by court order a dismissed rape charge without reindictment. **Morgan v. State,** Op. No. 320, 673 P2d 897 (Alaska App. 1983).

Claims of ineffective assistance of counsel will not be entertained on appeal unless defendant has first moved for a new trial or sought post-conviction relief, supporting the claim with affidavits alleging facts which would establish a basis for relief; to the extent that the criminal rule on motions for new trials places unreasonable time limitations on the presentation of this issue, the trial court should exercise its discretion to provide reasonable time. **Barry v. State,** Op. No. 334, 675 P2d 1292 (Alaska App. 1984).

The defendant must show actual prejudice in order to establish that the trial court abused its discretion in failing to excuse defendant's forfeiture of his right to speedy-trial and his right to a change of judge. **Trudeau v. State,** Op. No. 581, 714 P2d 362 (Alaska App. 1986).

Where request for reduction of sentence came almost three years after defendant's conviction was affirmed on appeal, and there was nothing in the record to suggest that he intended to make the request within 120-days permitted by the rule or was somehow frustrated by his attorney or the court system in taking action, the trial court did not err in refusing to relax the 120-day time limit. **S.B. v. State,** Op. No. 997, 785 P2d 900 (Alaska App. 1989).

Superior court did not have authority to set aside valid delinquency adjudication after statutory time limit on court's jurisdiction over case had expired. **State v. T.M.,** Op. No. 1322, 860 P2d 1286 (Alaska App. 1993).

If defendant's attorney was told that a particular judge had not been permanently assigned to defendant's case, then she may not have waived her challenge to the judge when she appeared in front of him for the change-of-plea hearing. Alternatively, defendant might be entitled to a relaxation of Criminal Rule 25(d)(5) under the provisions of Criminal Rule 53 if the clerk had assured defense counsel that even though the judge had been permanently assigned to the case, defendant could appear in a change-of-plea hearing in front of him and still have five days to file a peremptory challenge of him. **Tan v. State,** Op. No. 1423, 900 P2d 759 (Alaska App. 1995).

This rule authorizes court to take remedial action in face of clear injustice, but this authority must be exercised with due regard for wording and policy of rule to be relaxed. **State v. Tinsley,** Op. No. 1500, 928 P2d 1220 (Alaska App. 1996).

Trial judge abused his discretion in relaxing former Criminal Rule 35(a), which required motion for reduction of sentence to be filed within 120 days of imposition of sentence, to allow defendant to file such motion seven years after imposition of sentence. **State v. Tinsley,** Op. No. 1500, 928 P2d 1220 (Alaska App. 1996).

Peremptory challenge to assigned trial judge was filed when received, not when mailed, since an exception to the common law rule in the appellate rules applied only to appellate filings; furthermore, the movant failed to provide any evidence in support of an argument that a discretionary relaxation of the rules would be appropriate in the interests of justice. **Black v. State,** Op. No. 1896, 76 P.3d 417 (Alaska App. 2003).

Rule 54. Process.

Process issued in all criminal actions in the superior court shall be issued, and return thereon made, in the manner prescribed by Rule 4, Rules of Civil Procedure.

(Adopted by SCO 4 October 4, 1959)

Rule 56. Definitions.

As used in these rules, unless the content otherwise requires:

(a) "Prosecuting Attorney" includes the attorney general, assistant attorneys general, deputy attorneys general and any other attorneys, legal officers and assistants charged by law with the duty of prosecuting the violation of any law, statute or ordinance.

(b) "Magistrate" includes magistrates, district judges,

superior court judges and any other judicial officer authorized by law to conduct a preliminary examination of a person accused of a crime.

(c) "Presiding Judge" includes the duly-designated presiding judge of the superior court in each judicial district or, in the presiding judge's absence, the person designated presiding judge pro tem.

(d) "Offense" means conduct for which a sentence of imprisonment or payment of a fine is authorized by law.

(e) "Misdemeanor" means an offense for which a sentence of imprisonment for not more than one year may be imposed.

(f) "Violation" means:

(1) an offense as defined in AS 11.81.900(b)(61);

(2) a traffic infraction as defined in Title 28 of the Alaska Statutes; or

(3) Any other offense under state or local law which is punishable only by a fine.

(Adopted by SCO 4 October 4, 1959; amended by SCO 157 effective February 15, 1973; by SCO 427 effective August 1, 1980; by SCO 888 effective July 15, 1988; by SCO 1153 effective July 15, 1994; and by SCO 1450 effective October 15, 2001)

Annotations

Cases

Although criminal contempt charge amounted to a continuation of the superior court civil case from which it arose, district court had jurisdiction over the charge pursuant to its jurisdiction over all misdemeanors. **Rollins v. State, Municip. of Anchorage,** Op. No. 769, 748 P2d 767 (Alaska App. 1988).

Rule 57. Effective Date.

These rules become effective on the date to be established by order of the supreme court. They shall govern all criminal proceedings thereafter commenced and so far as just and practicable all proceedings then pending.

(Adopted by SCO 4 October 4, 1959)

Rule 58. Title.

These rules shall be known and cited as the Rules of Criminal Procedure.

(Adopted by SCO 4 October 4, 1959)

DISTRICT COURT RULES OF CRIMINAL PROCEDURE

Table of Contents

Rule 1. Applicability of Rules—Special Provisions.

Wherever practicable the Rules of Criminal Procedure shall apply to criminal actions within the jurisdiction of the district courts.

(a) **Commencement of Actions.** A criminal action is commenced by the filing of a complaint. Rules 3 and 4, Rules of Criminal Procedure, apply to a complaint filed in the district court and to the issuance of a warrant or summons. When a complaint is made by any person other than a peace officer, no judgment of conviction may be given except upon a guilty plea unless the person making the complaint, or the person injured by the offense charged, appears at the trial as a witness.

(b) **Arraignment and Plea.** When the defendant is brought before the district judge or magistrate the complaint shall be read to the defendant, and the defendant shall be furnished a copy of the complaint. The defendant may appear by use of telephonic or television equipment pursuant to Criminal Rules 38.1 and 38.2.

The district judge or magistrate shall inform the defendant

(1) of the right to counsel;

(2) of the right to have counsel appointed at public expense if the defendant could

(i) be sentenced to jail, or

(ii) suffer the loss of a valuable license, or

(iii) suffer a heavy enough fine to indicate criminality;

(3) of the right to be admitted to bail;

(4) that the defendant is not required to make a statement;

(5) that any statement made by the defendant may be used against the defendant;

(6) that if the defendant is charged by the State of Alaska the defendant may demand to be tried before a district judge;

(7) that the defendant may peremptorily disqualify the district judge or magistrate to whom the case is assigned pursuant to AS 22.20.022.

(c) **Trial.** The date of the trial shall be fixed by the district judge or magistrate at such time as will afford the defendant a reasonable opportunity for preparation. The trial shall be conducted as are trials in criminal cases in the superior court.

(d) **Trial by Jury—Waiver.** The manner of drawing juries shall be as provided by AS 09.20.040–09.20.090. Waiver by the defendant of jury trial need not be in writing, but shall be made in open court, and the district judge or magistrate shall make a proper notation thereof in the record of the proceedings.

(e) **Change of Venue.** All applications for a change of place of trial in the cases provided by AS 22.15.080 shall be by motion, either orally or in writing, specifying the particular grounds therefor, made to the district judge or magistrate prior to the date of the trial, and upon such notice to the prosecuting attorney as the court finds necessary. In the event that a change of place of trial is ordered, the district judge or magistrate shall transmit to the district court in whose district the proceeding is transferred all papers in the proceeding, and the prosecution shall continue in that court.

(f) **Proceedings Before Magistrate.** A defendant charged with a misdemeanor as defined in paragraph (e), Rule 56, Alaska Rules of Criminal Procedure, must give written consent to have the case tried before a magistrate. If a defendant does not give such written consent, the magistrate shall hold the proceedings in abeyance until a district judge becomes available to try the case.

(g) **Process—Return.** Process shall be issued as provided by AS 22.15.140. A person serving any process of the district courts shall promptly make proof thereof to the court, and in any event at or within the time during which the person served must respond to the process. If service is made by other than a peace officer, the person serving such process shall make affidavit thereof. Failure to make proof of service shall not affect the validity of the service.

(h) **Record of Proceedings.** Whenever practicable there shall be kept an electronic record of all criminal actions and proceedings in the district court.

(i) **Rules Inapplicable in Misdemeanor Cases.** In the case of a misdemeanor or violation the provisions of the following Rules of Criminal Procedure shall not apply:

(1) Rules 5(e) and 5.1, relating to preliminary hearings; and

(2) Rule 32(d), relating to presentence investigation.

(Amended by SCO 111 effective November 5, 1970; by SCO 157 effective February 15, 1973; by Amendment No. 2 to SCO 157 effective February 15, 1973; by SCO 218 effective January 15, 1976; by SCO 320 effective August 16, 1978; by SCO 419 effective August 1, 1980; by SCO 425 effective August 1, 1980; by SCO 444 effective August 1, 1980 nunc pro tunc; by SCO 554 effective April 4, 1983; by SCO 719 effective August 1, 1986; by SCO 888 effective July 15, 1988; by SCO 1153 effective July 15, 1994; and by SCO 1450 effective October 15, 2001)

Cross References

CROSS REFERENCE: AS 12.30.010—AS 12.30.040

Annotations

Cases

While the provisions of Mag. Crim. R. 1(b) (formerly Crim. R. 59(b)) as to arraignment must be complied with by the magistrate and the record must show that there was an arraignment, it is not necessary that the details of the arraignment be set forth, and an entry showing "Date Arraigned: June 1, 1961" is sufficient to raise a presumption that the magistrate performed his duties properly with respect to arraignment. **Hanrahan v. City of Anchorage,** Op. No. 121, 377 P2d 381 (Alaska 1962).

Under Mag. Crim. R. 1 (formerly Crim. R. 59), Crim. R.32(d) providing in part that to correct manifest injustice the court, after sentence, may set aside the judgment of conviction and permit the defendant to withdraw his plea of guilty or of nolo contendere, was made applicable in magistrate courts, including deputy magistrate courts. **Leege v. Strand,** Op. No. 157, 384 P2d 665 (Alaska 1963).

The provisions of this rule clearly indicate that the complaint forms the base of the district magistrate (now district) court's jurisdiction over a criminal case and that it also constitutes the accusatory pleading. **State v. Smith,** Op. No. 356, 417 P2d 252 (Alaska 1966).

Where a complaint was filed in the magistrate court under this provision, jurisdiction thus obtained was not lost because thereafter the state dismissed the complaint and filed an information in the magistrate court as a substitute for the complaint. **State v. Smith,** Op. No. 356, 417 P2d 252 (Alaska 1966).

Under this subdivision it is not prohibited to make use of an information as substitute for a complaint in a magistrate (district) court where such use may be practicable. **State v. Smith,** Op. No. 356, 417 P2d 252 (Alaska 1966).

Prior to SLA 1966, Ch. 24, which effected a change in nomenclature, the district court was known as the district magistrate court. **State v. Pete,** Op. No. 372, 420 P2d 338 (Alaska 1966).

The requirements of this rule relate only to a complaint signed by some person other than a district attorney or a peace officer. **State v. Pete,** Op. No. 372, 420 P2d 338 (Alaska 1966).

Where an information was substituted for a complaint to prosecute a criminal action in the district court, it was not a condition of entering a judgment of conviction that the district attorney who signed the complaint, or the person injured by the offense charged, appear as a witness at the trial. **State v. Pete,** Op. No. 372, 420 P2d 338 (Alaska 1966).

Where record failed to show that the defendant was ever called upon to enter a plea but record showed that the trial was conducted as though he had entered a plea of not guilty and that the defendant's situation would not have been altered in any respect if such a plea had been entered, failure to enter a plea did not render the conviction void. **State v. Pete,** Op. No. 372, 420 P2d 338 (Alaska 1966).

This rule which specifically mentions the rules of criminal procedure not applicable in a district court does not refer to Criminal Rule 35(b). **State v. Pete,** Op. No. 372, 420 P2d 338 (Alaska 1966).

Where duplicity of the complaint was compounded by trial court's failure to define the nature of the offense as mandated by Rule 1(c) of the District Court Criminal Rules and by an inaccurate and possibly misleading verdict blank, the defects were noticed on appeal although not brought to the attention of the trial court and the case was remanded. **Drahosh v. State,** Op. No. 485, 442 P2d 44 (Alaska 1968).

Where the direct penalty for conviction of an offense may be incarceration, loss of a valuable license, or a fine heavy enough to indicate criminality, such offense is a "serious crime" within the public defender statute. A defendant who is charged with any such misdemeanor and who cannot afford to hire his own lawyer is eligible for representation by a public defender. **Alexander v. City of Anchorage,** Op. No. 738, 490 P2d 910 (Alaska 1971).

Application of Criminal Rule 27 to district court trial was not impracticable where trial court had rooms available for jury sequestration and where judge had authority to obtain accommodations for that purpose in a private hotel. **Kimoktoak v. State,** Op. No. 1624, 578 P2d 594 (Alaska 1978).

A District Court is not "a court of record" merely because it is in fact required to keep a record of its proceedings "whenever practicable." **Lopez v. Anchorage,** Op. No. 1863, 597 P2d 146 (Alaska 1979).

The apparent violation of the provisions of this rule requiring trial to be set by a judge or magistrate has no bearing on computation of excluded periods for purposes of Criminal Rule 45 concerning speedy trials. **McKenzie v. Municipality of Anchorage,** Op. No. 26, 631 P2d 514 (Alaska App. 1981).

This rule was violated by lack of an express waiver of trial by jury by defendant in open court and by the court's failure to make any notation as to waiver in the record of the proceedings. **O'Donnell v. Municipality of Anchorage**, Op. No. 5696, 642 P2d 835 (Alaska 1982).

Rule 4. Title.

These rules shall be known and cited as the District Court Rules of Criminal Procedure.

Rule 6. Legal Effect of Rules—Procedural Portions of Statutes Superseded.

These rules are promulgated pursuant to constitutional authority granting rule making power to the supreme court, and to the extent that they are inconsistent with any procedural provisions of any statute not enacted for the specific purpose of changing a rule, shall supersede such statute to the extent of such inconsistency.

Rule 8. Minor Offenses.

(a) **Scope, Purpose and Construction.** This rule governs the procedure in cases involving minor offenses. It is intended to provide for the just determination of these cases and to that effect shall be construed to secure simplicity and uniformity in procedure, fairness in administration and the elimination of unjustifiable expense and delay.

(b) **Minor Offenses.** As used in this rule, "minor offenses" means

(1) an offense classified by statute as an infraction or a violation; or

(2) any offense for which a bail forfeiture amount has been authorized by statute and established by supreme court order; or

(3) any municipal motor vehicle or traffic offense for which a fine amount has been established in a fine schedule adopted by municipal ordinance under AS 28.05.151; or

(4) any offense under a municipal ordinance for which a conviction cannot result in incarceration or the loss of a valuable license and for which a fine schedule has been established under AS 29.25.070(a); or

(5) any offense under statute or municipal ordinance for which a conviction cannot result in incarceration, a fine greater than $500, or the loss of a valuable license.

(c) **Complaint and Summons.**

(1) The charging document for a minor offense may be in the form of a citation. If a citation is used, it must state that the defendant is entitled to a trial, to engage counsel, to confront and question witnesses, to testify and to subpoena witnesses on the defendant's behalf. The citation must also indicate whether a court appearance is mandatory or can be

waived, any applicable bail forfeiture amount established by the supreme court or scheduled fine established by municipal ordinance, the procedure the defendant must follow in responding to the citation, and the consequences of a failure to respond. A citation for a fish and game offense must also state that all seized equipment will be forfeited if the appearance is waived. If the form of a citation has been approved by the administrative director, the citation is presumed to provide adequate notice of the defendant's rights, the procedure for responding to the citation, and the consequences of a failure to respond.

(2) An offense for which a bail forfeiture amount has been established by the supreme court or for which a scheduled fine has been established by municipal ordinance must be charged on a citation and must not be filed, numbered, or processed as a criminal case.

(d) **Disposition Without Court Appearance.**

(1) A person charged with a minor offense for which a bail forfeiture amount has been established by supreme court order or for which a scheduled fine amount has been established by ordinance must within the time period stated on the citation:

(A) appear for arraignment at the time and place indicated on the citation; or

(B) mail or deliver a copy of the citation signed by the person to the location listed on the citation, indicating the person's waiver of the right to appear for arraignment and either a plea of no contest or a plea of not guilty and request for trial. If the person enters a plea of no contest, the person must also mail or deliver the bail or fine indicated on the citation, plus any surcharge established by statute, and request that the payment be used to satisfy the offense.

(2) A person who mails or delivers an unsigned copy of the citation with the person's payment will be deemed to have entered a plea of no contest unless the person designates otherwise.

(3) When a no contest plea is entered under Rule 8(d)(1)(B) or (d)(2), a judgment of conviction will be entered. When trial is requested, the case will be set on the calendar and notice sent to the parties.

(4) When a person is charged with a minor offense, and the statute, regulation, or ordinance provides that the citation will be dismissed upon providing proof to a law enforcement agency of compliance with the requirements of the statute, regulation or ordinance, the court or municipality shall dismiss the citation upon notification from the agency.

(5) If a person fails to respond as provided in Rule 8(d)(1), the court may enter a judgment of conviction requiring the person to pay the scheduled bail or fine, any surcharge established by statute, court costs in the amount of $25, and collection costs required under Rule 8(h). At least 15 days before judgment is entered, a notice advising the person of the consequences of a failure to respond must be sent to the person at the address on record with the Division of Motor Vehicles or the address shown on the citation.

(6) The court may also enter a judgment of conviction against a person who requests a trial under Rule 8(d)(1)(B) if the person has been sent notice of a trial date and then fails to appear on the scheduled date. The notice must advise the person of the consequences if the person fails to appear. A judgment entered under this subparagraph must require the person to pay the scheduled bail or fine, any surcharge established by statute, court costs in the amount of $25, and collection costs required under Rule 8(h).

(e) **Mandatory Court Appearance.**

(1) A person charged with a minor offense must appear for arraignment at the time and place indicated on the citation if:

(A) the person is charged with an offense for which no bail forfeiture amount has been established in a bail forfeiture schedule or no scheduled fine has been established by municipal ordinance; or

(B) the person has failed to provide proof of compliance to a law enforcement agency under a statute, regulation or ordinance that permits dismissal of the citation upon a showing of compliance.

A person under 18 years of age at the time of the offense must be accompanied by a parent, guardian or legal custodian. Arraignment must be conducted in accordance with District Court Criminal Rule 1. The person must be admitted to bail in accordance with AS 12.30.020 without regard to the bail amounts established in the applicable bail forfeiture schedule and with preference to release on the person's own recognizance. A person may not be incarcerated solely for inability to post the bail amount.

(2) The court may enter a judgment of conviction against a person who fails to appear for arraignment under Rule 8(e)(1). At least 15 days before judgment is entered, a notice advising the person of the consequences of a failure to respond must be sent to the person at the address on record with the Division of Motor Vehicles or the address shown on the citation. The court may also enter a judgment of conviction and forfeit any bail of a person who appears for arraignment under Rule 8(e)(1) but fails to appear at trial, if the person has received notice that the court may follow this procedure. No further notice of the forfeiture is necessary. A judgment entered under this subparagraph must impose the maximum penalty for the offense and must require the person to pay any surcharge established by statute, court costs in the amount of $25, and collection costs required under Rule 8(h).

(f) **Disposition of Records of Conviction.** Notice of conviction will be transmitted to the following agencies:

(1) In the case of a motor vehicle offense, the conviction will be transmitted to the Department of Administration, Division of Motor Vehicles, to become a part of the defendant's driving record and for the department to assess points pursuant to statute and regulation.

(2) In the case of a fish and game violation, the conviction will be transmitted to the Department of Public Safety, Division of Fish and Wildlife Protection, for the department to determine whether it has a basis for petitioning for license revocation.

(3) In the case of a smoking violation under AS 18.35.300–.365, the conviction will be transmitted to the Department of Environmental Conservation, Division of Environmental Health.

(g) **Failure to Respond to Citation, Complaint or Summons.**

(1) A defendant who fails to respond to a citation within the time period stated is subject to arrest on a bench warrant, without issuance of a summons or other notice. If the defendant has failed to respond in a timely fashion to a citation charging a fine schedule offense initially filed with a municipality, the bench warrant must be requested by the municipality and must be based on an affidavit from a municipal employee stating that the defendant has failed to respond. The bench warrant shall be signed by a judicial officer, and shall state that the defendant has failed to respond to the citation. A defendant who is served with a bench warrant under this subsection and cannot post bail shall be brought before a judicial officer

(A) immediately, if the defendant will be taken to the court which issued the warrant;

(B) without unnecessary delay within a period not to exceed twenty-four hours after arrest on the warrant if the defendant will be taken before a court other than the court which issued the bench warrant.

(2) The court in its discretion may issue a summons or other notice to a defendant before issuing a bench warrant for the defendant's arrest. If the court has issued a summons or other notice to the defendant prior to issuance of the bench warrant, and the person has failed to respond to the summons or notice and is arrested on a subsequent bench warrant, the person shall be taken before a judicial officer without unnecessary delay within a period not to exceed twenty-four hours after arrest on the warrant.

(h) **Costs.** A judgment of conviction in a minor offense case must require the person to pay collection costs in the amount of $25 if a writ of execution is issued to satisfy the judgment. In addition, if a bench warrant is issued, the court shall require the person to pay a bench warrant fee in the amount of $75 regardless of whether the person is convicted. The court may waive collection costs and the bench warrant fee upon a showing of good cause.

(i) **Relief from Judgment.** Upon a showing of good cause, the court may vacate or modify a judgment of conviction entered under (d)(5), (d)(6), or (e)(2) of this rule. The court may act on motion filed within one year after entry of the judgment or on its own initiative after reasonable notice.

(j) **Longevity of Warrants.** After a period of two years, the presiding judge for a judicial district may, upon the request of a clerk of court and after notice to the agency which issued the citation, order that warrants for minor offenses which have been outstanding for two years or more shall be quashed and the cases closed statistically.

(k) A municipal corporation or the State of Alaska may be represented by an employee of the state, the municipality, or other political subdivision of the state for the prosecution of minor offenses under this rule, AS 22.20.040 notwithstanding. However, the representative is limited to giving testimony and may not examine witnesses, make opening and closing arguments, or otherwise act as an attorney. The representative need not be employed by the same government entity represented, but must be authorized by the entity to represent it.

(*l*) **Authority of Clerk.** The clerk is authorized to enter judgments of conviction under Rules 8(d)(3), (d)(5), (d)(6), and (e)(2).

(m) **Disposition of Costs and Fees.** Court costs and bench warrant fees imposed under this rule are to be deposited in the state general fund. Collection costs belong to the political entity that prosecuted the offense.

(n) **Temporary Transfer of Minor Offense Cases.**

(1) For purposes of this rule, the term "original court" means the court in which a minor offense case is pending. The term "second court" means the court to which the defendant requests that the case be temporarily transferred.

(2) A minor offense case may be temporarily transferred from the original court to a second court for purposes of arraignment under the circumstances described below:

(A) If there is a mandatory court appearance for the minor offense, the defendant may request a temporary transfer from the original court to the court nearest the place where the defendant resides or is employed; or

(B) If a warrant relating to the minor offense is outstanding, the defendant may request a temporary transfer from the original court to the nearest court; or

(C) If the defendant is arrested on a bench warrant relating to the minor offense, the defendant may request a temporary transfer from the original court to the court where the defendant was arrested.

(3) The request for temporary transfer may be made in writing or in person to the clerk of court in the original court or to the clerk of court in the second court.

(4) If the requirements of subparagraph (2) are satisfied, the clerk shall grant the request for temporary transfer. Approval of the prosecuting authority at the original court is not required.

(5) The clerk who grants the request shall immediately notify the other court of the temporary transfer. Following notification, the clerk in the original court shall quash any outstanding warrants relating to the minor offense. If the

request is granted by the second court and the original court cannot immediately be contacted, the clerk in the second court shall quash any outstanding warrants relating to the minor offense.

(6) The defendant may be arraigned in the second court on a copy or facsimile of the citation.

(7) If the defendant enters a plea of guilty or no contest in the second court, the defendant shall be sentenced in the second court. If the defendant enters a plea of not guilty, the second court shall return the case to the original court for trial setting.

(8) After the plea has been entered, the second court shall, within 10 working days, return all papers to the original court.

(o) **Change of Venue.**

Change of venue of minor offense cases is governed by Criminal Rule 19.

(p) **Speedy Trial—When Time Commences to Run.** The right to speedy trial on minor offenses is governed by Criminal Rule 45. A defendant charged with a minor offense must be tried within 120 days from the date the defendant's request for trial is received by the court or the municipality, whichever occurs first.

(Added by SCO 649 effective July 1, 1985; amended by SCO 671 effective June 15, 1986; by SCO 751 effective September 11, 1986; by SCO 896 effective July 15, 1988; by SCO 961 effective July 15, 1989; by SCO 1080 effective January 15, 1992; by SCO 1309 effective July 15, 1998; by SCO 1421 effective April 15, 2001; by SCO 1422 effective April 15, 2001; and by SCO 1482 effective October 15, 2002)

Annotations

Cases

Trial court erred in denying a motorist's request to set aside a default judgment under Alaska Dist. Ct. R. Crim. P. 8(d)(5) where there was nothing that showed that a notice was sent to the motorist that a default judgment would be entered if he did not respond to his traffic citation pursuant to Alaska Dist. Ct. R. Crim. P. 8(d)(5). **Zok v. Municipality of Anchorage,** Op. No. 1776, 41 P3d 154 (Alaska App. 2001).

"Meritorious defense" requirement to set aside a default judgment under subsection (i) appears not to infringe the privilege against self-incrimination, at least to the extent that the "meritorious defense" rule merely requires defendant to give advance notice of his general theory of defense to his speeding charge. **Case v. Municipality of Anchorage,** Op. No. 2028, 128 P.3d 193 (Alaska App. 2006).

Rule 8.1. Judgments in Minor Offenses.

(a) **Electronic Judgments.**

(1) In those courts with an electronic case management system, the official judgment in a minor offense case is the electronic record in the case management system. The clerk will provide a printout of the electronic judgment upon request.

(2) An electronic judgment must contain the following information:

(A) the case number,

(B) the date of the offense,

(C) the defendant's full name,

(D) the following information if it appears on the citation:

(i) the defendant's date of birth,

(ii) the defendant's address, and

(iii) the defendant's driver's license or ID number,

(E) the name of the offense and number of the statute, regulation or ordinance of which the defendant is charged or convicted,

(F) the DMV code of the offense if it appears on the citation,

(G) the defendant's plea, and

(H) the final disposition (including sentence).

(b) **Paper Judgments.** In those courts without an electronic case management system, the judgment must be entered on the back of or attached to the original citation.

(c) **Distribution and Time for Appeal.**

(1) *Judgment Based on No Contest Plea.* When a defendant mails or delivers a no contest plea, a copy of the judgment will not be distributed to the parties, except upon request. To appeal a judgment based on a no contest plea, other than an appeal of the penalty, the defendant must first move to withdraw the plea under Criminal Rule 11. Appeal may be taken from an order denying (or granting) the motion. The appeal must be filed within 30 days after the date shown in the clerk's certificate of distribution on the order.

(2) *Default Judgment.* When a judgment of conviction is entered under District Court Criminal Rule 8(d)(5), (d)(6), or (e)(2), a copy of the judgment will not be distributed to the parties, except upon request. To appeal a default judgment, the defendant must first move to vacate or modify the judgment under District Court Criminal Rule 8(i). Appeal may be taken from an order denying (or granting) the motion. The appeal must be filed within 30 days after the date shown in the clerk's certificate of distribution on the order.

(3) *Judgment Entered in Open Court.* When judgment of conviction is entered in open court, parties who are present will be given written notice of the terms of the judgment. Any appeal must be filed within 30 days from the date the judgment is announced in court. This rule also applies to an order of dismissal entered in open court.

(4) *Matters Taken Under Advisement.* When a court takes a matter under advisement, the court will reduce its decision to writing. A copy of the written order or judgment will be distributed to the parties. Any appeal must be filed

within 30 days from the date of distribution of the order or judgment.

(d) **Execution.** Writs of execution may be issued to enforce minor offense judgments, including electronic judgments, as provided in Civil Rule 69.

(Added by SCO 1453 effective April 15, 2002)

Rule 8.2. Electronic Citations in Minor Offense Cases.

(a) **Authorization for Filing Citations Electronically.** The administrative director may enter into an agreement with a law enforcement agency to allow the law enforcement agency to file citations charging minor offenses, as defined in District Court Criminal Rule 8(b), by transmitting data electronically rather than by filing paper citations. The administrative director may enter into an agreement if the law enforcement agency's systems and procedures assure that:

(1) the charging officer will issue a paper citation to the defendant in accordance with AS 12.25.190;

(2) a paper citation issued from an electronic device will contain the charging officer's electronic or digital signature as defined in AS 09.80.190;

(3) the court will have the ability to view an electronic version of the paper citation that the charging officer issued to the defendant, including the charging officer's electronic, digital, or handwritten signature;

(4) the agency has a written acknowledgement from each peace officer authorized to issue electronic citations certifying that the officer understands that affixing an electronic or digital signature to a citation is the legally binding equivalent of signing a citation by hand, and that by affixing an electronic or digital signature, the officer intends to be bound by the signature;

(5) the agency employs policies that hold individual officers accountable and responsible for actions initiated under their electronic or digital signatures; and

(6) the agency employs adequate security procedures to verify that an electronic signature, record, or performance is that of a specific person and to detect changes or errors in the electronic records related to the citation.

(b) **Electronic Signature.** A charging officer's electronic or digital signature on a citation is the legally binding equivalent of the officer's handwritten signature and satisfies the requirement of Criminal Rule 3(a) that a citation for a minor offense must be signed with a certification under penalty of perjury that the citation is true.

(Adopted by SCO 1587 effective December 15, 2005)

RULES OF EVIDENCE

Table of Contents

ARTICLE I. GENERAL PROVISIONS

ARTICLE II. JUDICIAL NOTICE

ARTICLE III. PRESUMPTIONS

ARTICLE IV. ADMISSIBILITY OF RELEVANT EVIDENCE

ARTICLE V. PRIVILEGES

ARTICLE VI. WITNESSES—IMPEACHMENT

ARTICLE IX. DOCUMENTARY EVIDENCE

ARTICLE X. WRITINGS

ARTICLE XI. TITLE

ARTICLE I. GENERAL PROVISIONS

Rule 101. Scope and Applicability.

(a) **General Applicability.** These rules apply in all proceedings in the courts of the State of Alaska except as otherwise required by the Constitution of the United States or this state or as otherwise provided for by enactment of the Alaska Legislature, by the provisions of this rule, or by other rules promulgated by the Alaska Supreme Court. The word "judge" in these rules includes magistrates and masters.

(b) **Rules of Privilege.** The rules with respect to privileges apply at all stages of all actions, cases, and proceedings.

(c) **Rules Inapplicable.** The rules, other than those with respect to privileges, do not apply in the following situations:

(1) *Preliminary Questions of Fact.* The determination of questions of fact preliminary to admissibility of evidence when the issue is to be determined by the judge under Rule 104(a).

(2) *Miscellaneous Proceedings.* Proceedings relating to extradition or rendition; sentencing, probation, or parole; issuance of criminal summonses, or of warrants for arrest or search; and summary contempt.

(Added by SCO 364 effective August 1, 1979)

Annotations

Cases

Illegally seized evidence may be considered in fashioning a sentence when the illegally seized evidence is reliable, when the police conduct involved in obtaining the evidence does not shock the conscience of the court, and when it is clear that the evidence was not obtained for purposes of influencing the sentencing judge. **Elson v. State,** Op. No. 40, 633 P2d 292 (Alaska App. 1982).

The rules of evidence are relaxed at sentencing, allowing the court to consider hearsay. **Evan v. State,** Op. No. 1418, 899 P2d 926 (Alaska App. 1995).

At sentencing a defendant has only a limited right of confrontation, and the normal rules against the admission of hearsay do not apply. **Evan v. State,** Op. No. 1418, 899 P2d 926 (Alaska App. 1995).

When a hearsay declarant is available to testify, the State cannot rely on hearsay evidence at sentencing against a defendant who denies the allegations under oath and submits to cross-examination. **Evan v. State,** Op. No. 1418, 899 P2d 926 (Alaska App. 1995).

Evidence Rule 101(c)(2), which provides that the evidence rules are not applicable to certain proceedings, applies to proceedings relating to probation revocation in misdemeanor cases in district courts, thus district court judge did not err in ruling that evidence rules prohibiting hearsay did not apply to defendant's probation revocation hearing. **Veeder v. Municipality of Anchorage,** Op. No. 1612, 969 P2d 642, 658 P2d 131 (Alaska App. 1998).

Rule 102. Purpose and Construction

These rules shall be construed to secure fairness in administration, elimination of unjustifiable expense and delay, and promotion of growth and development of the law of evidence to the end that truth may be ascertained and proceedings justly determined.

(Added by SCO 364 effective August 1, 1979)

Rule 103. Rulings on Evidence

(a) **Effect of Erroneous Ruling.** Error may not be predicated upon a ruling which admits or excludes evidence unless a substantial right of the party is affected; and

(1) *Objection.* In case the ruling is one admitting evidence, a timely objection or motion to strike appears of record, stating the specific ground of objection, if the specific ground was not apparent from the context; or

(2) *Offer of Proof.* In case the ruling is one excluding evidence, the substance of the evidence was made known to the court by offer or was apparent from the context within which questions were asked.

(b) **Record of Offer and Ruling.** The court may add any other or further statement which shows the character of the evidence, the form in which it was offered, the objection made, and the ruling thereon. It may direct the making of an offer in question and answer form.

(c) **Hearing of Jury.** In jury cases, proceedings shall be conducted, to the extent practicable, so as to prevent inadmissible evidence from being suggested to the jury by any means, such as making statements or offers of proof or asking questions in the hearing of the jury.

(d) **Plain Error.** Nothing in this rule precludes taking notice of plain errors affecting substantial rights although they were not brought to the attention of the court.

(Added by SCO 364 effective August 1, 1979)

Annotations

Cases

To establish plain error a litigant must do more than show that the rule of law he relies upon in the appellate court should have been obvious to the trial court; he must, in addition, establish that the application of that rule of law to the facts of his case was so obvious that it should have been noticed by the trial court sua sponte. **Carman v. State,** Op. No. 206, 658 P2d 131 (Alaska App. 1983).

Where evidence of tampering with a witness was brought out by the defense on cross-examination and was followed up on by the state without objection, the defendant failed to preserve the issue for argument on appeal. **Garibay v. State,** Op. No. 221, 658 P2d 1350 (Alaska App. 1983).

Defendant's contention that the state's failure to preserve physical evidence depicted in photographs which were admitted at trial violated his right to confront and examine the evidence against him was not properly preserved for appeal due to defendant's failure to object to admission of the photographs at trial and his failure to request that items depicted in the photographs be produced for use as evidence. **Maloney v. State,** Op. No. 273, 667 P2d 1258 (Alaska App. 1983).

Defendant's contention that the trial court's limitation on his examination of a witness violated his constitutional rights to confrontation and compulsory process was rejected on the ground that the alleged error had not been preserved as required by this rule. **Hohman v. State,** Op. No. 290, 669 P2d 1316 (Alaska App. 1983).

Where defendant sought to show that arresting officer was biased toward him by testimony of friends that the officer induced them to write letters against defendant in earlier cases, defendant's statement that the witnesses would not have written unfavorable letters against him unless pressured to do so was not a sufficient offer of proof, thus court did not err in rejecting the proffered evidence. **Wilson v. State,** Op. No. 356, 680 P2d 1173 (Alaska App. 1984).

Where there was no indication in the record that the trial court considered alternative sanctions or balanced the prejudice to the defendant from excluding the testimony of a defense witness against the prejudice to the state from allowing it, trial court order disqualifying the witness for an inadvertent violation of a witness exclusion order was error, but the error was harmless since the excluded testimony was merely cumulative. **Babcock v. State,** Op. No. 383, 685 P2d 721 (Alaska App. 1984).

While evidence of treatment of simple incidents by the employer might have been relevant to the employee's wrongful termination action, such evidence was offered at trial only to prove the employee's reverse discrimination claim, and could not therefore provide a basis on appeal for reversal of the trial court's decision on the wrongful termination action. **Rutledge v. Alyeska Pipeline Service Co.,** Op. No. 3141, 727 P2d 1050 (Alaska 1986).

Reviewing court looked to party's offer of proof at trial court hearing on protective order forbidding admission of evidence of remedial repairs to determine whether trial court properly excluded the evidence. **Agostino v. Fairbanks Clinic,** Op. No. 3718, 821 P2d 714 (Alaska 1991).

Defense attorney's motion for mistrial on ground that trial record demonstrated juror misconduct did not preserve for appeal issue of whether judge failed to inquire fully into juror's conduct. **Cheely v. State,** Op. No. 1317, 861 P2d 1168 (Alaska App. 1993).

Failure to call a witness or make an offer of proof waived any claim regarding the exclusion of testimony or subjects other than the one specifically excluded by the trial court. **Estate of Arrowwood v. State,** Op. No. 4196, 894 P2d 642 (Alaska 1995).

Failure to request a hearing on the admissibility of certain deposition testimony, despite repeated statements by the court that it could not exclude any deposition testimony without a hearing addressing the precise testimony under consideration, waived any argument on appeal that the testimony was improperly excluded. **Sweet v. Sisters of Providence in Washington,** Op. No. 4200, 895 P2d 484 (Alaska 1995).

Report submitted by estate beneficiary to show that personal representative sold estate assets at price that was too low was properly struck from record where beneficiary did not establish qualifications of author of report and did not object to motion to strike. **Carroll v. Carroll,** Op. No. 4267, 903 P2d 579 (Alaska 1995).

Plaintiff did not waive right to challenge trial court's ruling excluding evidence by failing to make offer of proof since evidence at issue was excluded pursuant to pre-trial ruling on motion in limine. **Landers v. Municipality of Anchorage,** Op. No. 4343, 915 P2d 614 (Alaska 1996).

Fact that informant involved in arrest of defendant for selling cocaine was later indicted for possession of cocaine was not relevant evidence at defendant's trial since informant was not a witness at the trial and the case against defendant turned on testimony of police investigator rather than informant. **Haynes v. State,** Op. No. 1714, 15 P3d 1088 (Alaska App. 2001).

Where an arrestee claimed that the trial court erred by admitting testimony from a psychiatrist that she was malingering in her suit against a city, a police officer, and an immigration officer alleging the use of excessive force during her arrest, under Alaska R. Evid. 103(a)(1) the part of the psychiatrist's testimony that exceeded the trial court's ruling precluding testimony about the arrestee's credibility with regard to the arrestee's claims regarding recovery from bruises from the arrest was not subject to review because the arrestee did not object to the testimony at trial. **Samaniego v. City of Kodiak,** Op. No. 5751, 80 P.3d 216 (Alaska 2003).

Where landlord improperly failed to disclose a document she relied upon to show the amount of back rent she was allegedly owed, but tenant failed to move to compel disclosure, tenant waived the objection. **Fyffe v. Wright,** Op. No. 5819 (Alaska 2004).

Subsection (a) of this rule gives a trial judge wide-ranging authority to determine questions of fact that underlie the judge's rulings on the qualification of a person to be a witness, the existence of a privilege, or the admission of evidence. This rule declares that, in these matters, a judge is not bound by the rules of evidence except for the rules of privilege. **Huntington v. State,** Op. No. 9227, 151 P.3d 523 (Alaska App. 2007).

Subsection (a) of this rule does not directly apply to the issue of whether the judge should declare a mistrial or what facts a judge may properly rely on when assessing the potential unfair prejudice of challenged evidence. **Huntington v. State,** Op. No. 9227, 151 P.3d 523 (Alaska App. 2007).

Rule 104. Preliminary Questions.

(a) **Questions of Admissibility Generally.** Preliminary questions concerning the qualification of a person to be a witness, the existence of a privilege, or the admissibility of evidence shall be determined by the court, subject to the provisions of subdivision (b). In making its determination it is not bound by the rules of evidence except those with respect to privileges.

(b) **Relevancy Conditioned on Fact.** When the relevancy of evidence depends upon the fulfillment of a condition of fact, the court shall admit it upon, or subject to, the introduction of evidence sufficient to support a finding of the fulfillment of the condition.

(c) **Hearing of Jury.** Hearings on the admissibility of confessions shall in all cases be conducted out of the hearing of the jury. Hearings on other preliminary matters shall be so conducted when the interest of justice require or, when an accused is a witness, if the accused so requests.

(d) **Testimony by Accused.** The accused does not, by testifying upon a preliminary matter, become subject to cross-examination as to other issues in the case. Testimony given by the accused at the hearing is not admissible against the accused unless inconsistent with the accused's testimony at trial.

(e) **Weight and Credibility.** This rule does not limit the right of a party to introduce before the jury evidence relevant to weight or credibility.

(Added by SCO 364 effective August 1, 1979; amended by SCO 1153 effective July 15, 1994)

Annotations

Cases

The preponderance of the evidence standard is to be followed in proving the existence of a joint undertaking. **Hawley v. State,** Op. No. 2137, 614 P2d 1349 (Alaska 1980).

Warnings required by city ordinance constituted a foundation for admission of evidence of defendant's refusal to take breathalyzer test but were not separate elements of the offense to be proved to the jury. **Svedlund v. Municipality of Anchorage,** Op. No. 301, 671 P2d 378 (Alaska App. 1983).

When a timely and appropriate challenge to admissibility of a breathalyzer test result is made, the prosecution must, at a minimum, demonstrate that the breathalyzer instrument in question was tested successfully for radio frequency interference at least once in a manner substantially complying with the manufacturer's recommendation and that none of the conditions listed by the manufacturer for retesting occurred between the time of the initial radio frequency test and the challenged breath test. **Thayer v. Municipality of Anchorage,** Op. No. 395, 686 P2d 721 (Alaska App. 1984).

Defendant, under the rules of evidence, could have filed affidavits setting out his version of the facts at a suppression hearing without forfeiting his fifth amendment right to remain silent at trial. **Selig v. State,** Op. No. 785, 750 P2d 834 (Alaska App. 1988).

Rule 105. Limited Admissibility.

When evidence which is admissible as to one party or for one purpose but not admissible as to another party or for another purpose is admitted, the court, upon request, shall restrict the evidence to its proper scope and instruct the jury accordingly. In cases tried to a jury, evidence inadmissible as to one party shall not be admitted as to other parties until the court has made all reasonable efforts to effectively delete all references to the parties as to whom it is inadmissible.

(Added by SCO 364 effective August 1, 1979)

Rule 106. Remainder of, or Related Writings or Recorded Statements.

When a writing or recorded statement or part thereof is introduced by a party, an adverse party may require the introduction at that time of any other part or any other writing or recorded statement which ought in fairness to be considered contemporaneously with it.

(Added by SCO 364 effective August 1, 1979; amended by SCO 1153 effective July 15, 1994)

Annotations

Cases

Whether to admit or exclude evidence under this rule is within the trial court's discretion, and the trial court's ruling will be reversed only for an abuse of discretion. **Stumpf v. State,** Op. No. 770, 749 P2d 880 (Alaska App. 1988).

Generally, defendants may not offer their own statements into evidence because they are hearsay; when the state, however, presents one part of a conversation or statement, or one conversation in a series, the defendant may be entitled to offer or require the state to offer the rest of the statement or conversation in order to set the context for statements already in evidence, but the omitted portions of the statement need not be admitted if they are not relevant to explain or clarify the previously admitted statement. **Stumpf v. State,** Op. No. 770, 749 P2d 880 (Alaska App. 1988).

The limited purpose of this rule is to allow a party to admit omitted portions of a partially admitted statement only when and only to the extent that the omitted portions are necessary to provide context to the admitted portions, or to explain or clarify them; the rule does not make admissible statements that would otherwise be admissible; it is meant only to allow contemporaneous admission of evidence that would ordinarily not be admissible until later stages of the trial. **Stoneking v. State,** Op. No. 1091, 800 P2d 949 (Alaska App. 1990).

Where omitted portion of recorded interview that defendant sought to present to the jury was a type of exculpatory out-of-court statement that would normally amount to inadmissible hearsay, trial judge did not err in excluding that portion of the interview even though the prosecution was allowed to admit the rest of the interview. **Stoneking v. State,** Op. No. 1091, 800 P2d 949 (Alaska App. 1990).

Limited purpose of this rule is to allow party to admit omitted portions of partially admitted statement only when and only to extent that omitted portions are necessary to provide context to admitted portions or to explain or clarify them; rule does not make admissible statements that would otherwise be inadmissible. **D'Antorio v. State,** Op. No. 1236, 837 P2d 727 (Alaska App. 1992).

Judge did not err in determining that defendant's out of court statement was severable and that first part of statement, which was an admission that he lived at a certain address, was admissible, but that second part of statement, which was hearsay that someone else also lived there, was not admissible. **D'Antorio v. State,** Op. No. 1236, 837 P2d 727 (Alaska App. 1992).

ARTICLE II. JUDICIAL NOTICE

Rule 201. Judicial Notice of Fact.

(a) **Scope of Rule.** This rule governs only judicial notice of facts. Judicial notice of a fact as used in this rule means a court's on-the-record declaration of the existence of a fact normally decided by the trier of fact, without requiring proof of that fact.

(b) **General Rule.** A judicially noticed fact must be one not subject to reasonable dispute in that it is either (1) generally known within this state or (2) capable of accurate and ready determination by resort to sources whose accuracy cannot reasonably be questioned.

(c) **When Discretionary.** A court may take judicial notice as specified in subdivision (b), whether requested or not.

(d) **When Mandatory.** Upon request of a party, the court shall take judicial notice of each matter specified in subdivision (b) if the requesting party furnishes sufficient information and has given each party notice adequate to enable the party to meet the request.

(Added by SCO 364 effective August 1, 1979)

Annotations

Cases

It is impermissible for the trial court to take judicial notice of whether or not a mechanic would give a set bill to repair an aircraft for an annual inspection. **State v. Grogan,** Op. No. 2356, 628 P2d 570 (Alaska 1981).

In prosecution for fishing in closed waters, it was not error for the court to take judicial notice of the general validity of the scientific principles underlying the Loran C navigational system and of the reliability and accuracy of the system. **Wamser v. State,** Op. No. 312, 672 P2d 163 (Alaska App. 1983).

An agency is not limited to the administrative record as a basis for administrative rule making. **State v. Hebert,** Op. No. 748, 743 P2d 392 (Alaska App. 1987).

Taking judicial notice will be affirmed on appeal only if, viewing evidence in light most favorable to party against whom judicial notice was taken, fair-minded jurors could not disagree about truth of proposition noticed. **F.T. v. State,** Op. No. 4021, 862 P2d 857 (Alaska 1993).

In child in need of aid adjudication, trial court erred in taking judicial notice of domestic violence restraining orders for purpose of establishing that father had committed acts of violence in past. **F.T. v. State,** Op. No. 4021, 862 P2d 857 (Alaska 1993).

In fishing violations case, Ketchikan trial court did not err in refusing to take judicial notice of documents filed by defendant in two Juneau cases in which he had previously been charged with fishing violations since defendant did not submit copies of the Juneau pleadings to the Ketchikan court, did not state good cause for taking judicial notice, and did not explain the untimeliness of his request. **Scudero v. State,** Op. No. 1469, 917 P2d 683 (Alaska App. 1996).

Trial court's failure to take judicial notice of mortality table was error, as was its resulting grant of directed verdict barring future damages. **Manes v. Coats,** Op. No. 4839, 941 P2d 120 (Alaska 1997).

Borough ordinances, many of which referred to or regulated a city, could be judicially noticed with or without the request of a party. **Varilek v. City of Houston,** Op. No. 5822, 104 P.3d 849 (Alaska 2004).

Although this rule places limitations on a judge's authority to take notice of facts, it applies only to issues of fact that would otherwise be submitted to the jury. The question of whether a particular occurrence requires a mistrial is not a question of fact to be decided by the jury. It is, instead, a mixed question of fact and law addressed to the discretion of the trial judge. **Huntington v. State,** Op. No. 9227, 151 P.3d 523 (Alaska App. 2007).

Rule 202. Judicial Notice of Law.

(a) **Scope of Rule.** This rule governs only judicial notice of law.

(b) **Without Request—Mandatory.** Without request by a party, the court shall take judicial notice of the common law, the Constitution of the United States and of this state, the public statutes of the United States and this state, the provisions of the Alaska Administrative Code, and all rules adopted by the Alaska Supreme Court.

(c) **Without Request—Optional.** Without request by a party, the court may take judicial notice of:

(1) All duly adopted federal rules of court, and the constitutions, public statutes and duly adopted regulations and rules of court of every state, territory and jurisdiction of the United States.

(2) Private acts and resolutions of the Congress of the United States and of the legislature of this state and duly published regulations of agencies of the United States.

(3) Duly enacted ordinances of municipalities or other governmental subdivisions, and emergency orders or unpublished regulations adopted by agencies of this state.

(4) The laws of foreign countries, international law and maritime law.

(5) Any matter of law which would fall within the scope of this subdivision or subdivision (b) of this rule but for the fact that it has been replaced, superseded or otherwise rendered no longer in force.

(d) **With Request—Mandatory.** Upon request of a party, the court shall take judicial notice of each matter specified in subdivision (c) if the requesting party furnishes sufficient information and has given each party notice adequate to enable the party to meet the request.

(Added by SCO 364 effective August 1, 1979)

Annotations

Cases

In fishing violations case, Ketchikan trial court did not err in refusing to take judicial notice of documents filed by defendant in two Juneau cases in which he had previously been charged with fishing violations since defendant did not submit copies of the Juneau pleadings to the Ketchikan court, did not state good cause for taking judicial notice, and did not explain the untimeliness of his request. **Scudero v. State,** Op. No. 1469, 917 P2d 683 (Alaska App. 1996).

In a bad faith insurance case, a court did not err in failing to take judicial notice and instruct the jury of the general rule that an injured person could recover more than 100 percent of his or her damages by separately suing two severally liable defendants where an offset was permissible for the settlement proceeds from another insurer because the proceeds were from a non-collateral source and paid by a joint tortfeasor; the trial court's ruling did not prevent plaintiffs from offering evidence that the insurer improperly evaluated the liability exposure. **Jackson v. Am. Equity Ins. Co.,** Op. No. 5791 (Alaska 2004).

Borough ordinances, many of which referred to or regulated a city, could be judicially noticed with or without the request of a party. **Varilek v. City of Houston,** Op. No. 5822, 104 P.3d 849 (Alaska 2004).

Rule 203. Procedure for Taking Judicial Notice.

(a) **Determining Propriety of Judicial Notice.** Upon timely request, a party is entitled to be heard as to the propriety of taking judicial notice and the tenor of the matter noticed. In the absence of proper notification, the request may be made after judicial notice has been taken. In determining the propriety of taking judicial notice on a matter or the tenor thereof, the judge may consult and use any source of pertinent information, whether or not furnished by a party.

(b) **Time of Taking Notice.** Judicial notice may be taken at any stage of the proceeding.

(c) **Instructing the Jury.** In a civil action or proceeding, the court shall instruct the jury to accept as conclusive any fact judicially noticed. In a criminal case, the court shall instruct the jury that it may, but it is not required to, accept as conclusive any fact judicially noticed. Judicial notice of any matter of law falling within the scope of Rule 202 shall be a matter for the court and not the jury.

(Added by SCO 364 effective August 1, 1979)

Annotations

Cases

In trial of defendant for driving while license suspended, in which an element of the offense is driving on a highway, trial court committed reversible error in taking judicial notice that road upon which defendant was driving was a highway without instructing jury that it need not accept as conclusive any fact judicially noticed. **Fielding v. State,** Op. No. 1264, 842 P2d 614 (Alaska App. 1992).

Taking conclusive judicial notice of element of criminal charge violates this rule and constitutes reversible error without regard to whether there was objection from defense or whether defendant suffered any prejudice other than having his guilt adjudged by judge rather than jury. **Rae v. State,** Op. No. 1375, 884 P2d 163 (Alaska App. 1994).

ARTICLE III. PRESUMPTIONS

Rule 301. Presumptions in General in Civil Actions and Proceedings.

(a) **Effect.** In all civil actions and proceedings when not otherwise provided for by statute, by judicial decision or by these rules, a presumption imposes on the party against whom it is directed the burden of going forward with evidence to rebut or meet the presumption, but does not shift to such party the burden of proof in the sense of the risk of nonpersuasion, which remains throughout the trial upon the party on whom it was originally cast. The burden of going forward is satisfied by the introduction of evidence sufficient to permit reasonable minds to conclude that the presumed fact does not exist. If the party against whom a presumption operates fails to meet the burden of producing evidence, the presumed fact shall be deemed proved, and the court shall instruct the jury accordingly. When the burden of producing evidence to meet a presumption is satisfied, the court must instruct the jury that it may, but is not required to, infer the existence of the presumed fact from the proved fact, but no mention of the word "presumption" may be made to the jury.

(b) **Prima Facie Evidence.** A statute providing that a fact or group of facts is prima facie evidence of another fact establishes a presumption within the meaning of this rule.

(c) **Inconsistent Presumption.** If two presumptions arise which conflict with each other, the court shall apply the presumption which is founded on the weightier considerations of policy and logic. If there is no such preponderance, both presumptions shall be disregarded.

(Added by SCO 364 effective August 1, 1979)

Note: Ch. 80, SLA 2001 enacted a new subsection (b)(8) to AS 34.77.120 concerning the sufficiency of spousal testimony to rebut presumptions established under AS 34.77.120(b)(5) or (7). According to section 7 of the Act, this new subsection has the effect of amending Evidence Rule 301 by changing the rule's general criteria for the evidence that must be introduced to satisfy the burden of proof to rebut the presumptions.

Annotations

Cases

In will contests the presumption of undue influence shifts only the burden of production, not the burden of persuasion, to the proponent of the will. **Matter of Estate of McCoy,** Op. No. 3919, 844 P2d 1131 (Alaska 1993).

Presumption, rebuttable by clear and convincing evidence, that putative father was biological father was overcome by blood evidence that putative father could not be biological father, thus no genuine issue of material fact on question of paternity existed for summary judgment purposes. **Matter of J.B.,** Op. No. 4383, 922 P2d 878 (Alaska 1996).

Rule 302. Applicability of Federal Law in Civil Actions and Proceedings.

In civil actions and proceedings, the effect of a presumption respecting a fact which is an element of a claim or defense as to which federal law supplies the rule of decision is determined in accordance with federal law.

(Added by SCO 364 effective August 1, 1979)

Rule 303. Presumptions in General in Criminal Cases.

(a) **Effect.**

(1) *Presumptions Directed Against an Accused.* In all criminal cases when not otherwise provided for by statute, by these rules or by judicial decision, a presumption directed against the accused imposes no burden of going forward with evidence to rebut or meet the presumption and does not shift to the accused the burden of proof in the sense of the risk of nonpersuasion, which remains throughout the trial upon the party on whom it was originally cast. However, if the accused fails to offer evidence to rebut or meet the presumption, the court must instruct the jury that it may, but is not required to, infer the existence of the presumed fact from the proved fact, but no mention of the word "presumption" shall be made to the jury. If the accused offers evidence to rebut or meet the presumption, the court may instruct the jury that it may, but is not required to, infer the existence of the presumed fact from the proved fact, but no mention of the word "presumption" shall be made to the jury.

(2) *Presumptions Directed Against the Government.* In all criminal cases when not otherwise provided for by statute, by these rules, or by judicial decision, a presumption directed against the government shall be treated in the same manner as a presumption in a civil case under Rule 301.

(b) **Prima Facie Evidence.** A statute providing that a fact or group of facts is prima facie evidence of another fact establishes a presumption within the meaning of this rule.

(c) **Inconsistent Presumptions.** If two presumptions arise which conflict with each other, the court shall apply the presumption which is founded on the weightier considerations of policy and logic. If there is no such preponderance, both presumptions shall be disregarded.

(Added by SCO 364 effective August 1, 1979)

Annotations

Cases

Breathalyzer result alone established a prima facie case, entitling the prosecution to go to the jury on the issue of defendant's blood alcohol level at the time of her driving. **Erickson v. Municipality of Anchorage,** Op. No. 238, 662 P2d 963 (Alaska App. 1983).

Expert evidence is not necessary to relate a person's blood-alcohol rate at the time a test is administered to the blood-alcohol rate at an earlier time when the person was driving. **Erickson v. Municipality of Anchorage,** Op. No. 238, 662 P2d 963 (Alaska App. 1983).

Although a blood-alcohol level in excess of the statutory presumption does not necessarily establish criminal recklessness or culpable negligence as a matter of law, it was not error for the judge in a vehicular manslaughter case to instruct the jury on the statutory presumptions concerning intoxication. **Dresnek v. State,** Op. No. 455, 697 P2d 1059 (Alaska App. 1985).

In trial of defendant for theft of services for failing to pay cab fare, inclusion in jury instructions of statutory language that proof of absconding without payment amounts to prima facie showing of deception was reversible error absent instruction that presumption of deception is permissible inference but not mandatory one. **Brackhan v. State,** Op. No. 1252, 839 P2d 414, 599 P2d 751 (Alaska App. 1992).

ARTICLE IV. ADMISSIBILITY OF RELEVANT EVIDENCE

Rule 401. Definition of Relevant Evidence.

Relevant evidence means evidence having any tendency to make the existence of any fact that is of consequence to the determination of the action more probable or less probable than it would be without the evidence.

(Added by SCO 364 effective August 1, 1979)

Annotations

Cases

Where defendant was charged with assault and battery, evidence that victim was 9 months pregnant was relevant to show defendant's present ability to inflict a violent injury, to establish apprehension on part of the victim and to establish criminal intent and use of unlawful force. **Rathbun v. Anchorage,** Op. No. 1928, 599 P2d 751 (Alaska 1979).

At trial for murder, it was reversible error for the trial court to exclude a journal written by the victim, parts of which reflected a sense of mental instability and a violent nature. **Keith v. State,** Op. No. 2099, 612 P2d 977 (Alaska 1980).

Evidence of drug use by the accused was admissible where it established direct contact between the victim and the accused possessed sufficient amounts of cocaine for him to have invested more than pocket cash in his purchase from the victim. **Dorman v. State,** Op. No. 2272, 622 P2d 448 (Alaska 1981).

Testimony and photographs concerning the physical condition of a child allegedly kidnapped by defendant from state custody were admissible to show motive for kidnapping. **Crump v. State,** Op. No. 2309, 625 P2d 857 (Alaska 1981).

Evidence of actual sobriety offered to rebut the accuracy of a breathalyzer result is admissible as relevant circumstantial evidence. **Denison v. Anchorage,** Op. No. 32, 630 P2d 1001 (Alaska App. 1982).

Defendant's contention that because his conviction for driving while intoxicated was predicated on his blood alcohol rate and not his driving it was error for the trial court to admit evidence that he drove erratically and appeared intoxicated to arresting officers was properly rejected. **Byrne v. State,** Op. No. 169, 654 P2d 795 (Alaska App. 1982).

Admissibility of breathalyzer refusals should be determined on a case-by-case basis by weighing probative value against potential for unfair prejudice. **Coleman v. State,** Op. No. 229, 658 P2d 1364 (Alaska App. 1983).

Defendant's resistance to "pat down" search was admissible as evidence that defendant was aware of the cocaine found in his pocket, although there were other possible explanations for his behavior. **Elson v. State,** Op. No. 2615, 659 P2d 1195 (Alaska 1983).

In prosecution for murder, admission into evidence of a .380 caliber automatic pistol owned by the defendant was not error even though expert testimony could not conclusively establish that the gun was the murder weapon. **Bangs v. State,** Op. No. 253, 663 P2d 981 (Alaska App. 1983).

In drunk driving prosecution of defendant who refused to submit to a breathalyzer examination, court erred in excluding expert testimony for the defense concerning defendant's blood alcohol level at the time of his arrest. **Quinto v. City and Borough of Juneau,** Op. No. 265, 664 P2d 630 (Alaska App. 1983).

In prosecution for driving with a suspended license, attempted use by prosecution for impeachment purposes of voluntary statements made by defendant at the arrest scene concerning the reason she was driving, but which statements did not include the reason she later cited for driving, presented a question of whether the evidence was relevant and whether its probative value outweighed its prejudicial effect. **Nelson v. State,** Op. No. 427, 691 P2d 1056 (Alaska App. 1984).

Where defendant in murder trial claimed that he was defending himself against a homosexual rape by the victim who lured him into a car by offering him Quaaludes, trial court erred in excluding the testimony of a witness who would have testified that he had had a similar encounter with the victim one year before, and the trial court also erred in excluding evidence that the police found Quaaludes in the victim's home during their investigation. **Williamson v. State,** Op. No. 430, 692 P2d 965 (Alaska App. 1984).

Where defense strategy was to show that an alcoholic blackout prevented defendant from formulating an intent to kill, court did not err in rejecting lay testimony which defendant offered to establish the existence of alcoholic blackouts, since it would not have shed any light on the dispute between the experts who testified on the subject, nor would it have made it more or less probable that defendant was unable to form an intent to kill at the time of the shooting in question. **Staael v. State,** Op. No. 454, 697 P2d 1050 (Alaska App. 1985).

In negligence action where defendant alleged that the accident was caused by a design defect in her automobile which caused it to accelerate spontaneously, consumer complaint reports to the National Highway Traffic Safety Agency of similar incidents involving the same type of automobile were relevant and admissible as hearsay exceptions. **Norris v. Gatts,** Op. No. 3187, 738 P2d 344 (Alaska 1987).

In prosecution of defendant for lewd and lascivious acts toward children in which it was alleged that defendant would invite them to his house, offer them drugs, show them pornographic materials, and then attempt sexual acts with them, trial court did not abuse its discretion in refusing to allow defendant to call as witnesses two police officers who had been in his home at different times and who would have testified that they had not seen drugs, pornography, or film-making equipment in his home. **Rodriquez v. State,** Op. No. 735, 741 P2d 1200 (Alaska App. 1987).

In trial of defendant for refusing to submit to a breath test, in which defendant testified that nose and chest injuries sustained by him during his arrest prevented him from blowing into the Intoximeter tube, the trial court committed reversible error in precluding a defense witness, who drove defendant to the hospital for an examination the day after the arrest, from testifying as to her observations of his injuries, since her testimony would have been relevant and a proper subject for lay opinion under the rules of evidence. **Callahan v. State,** Op. No. 910, 769 P2d 444 (Alaska App. 1989).

In trial of defendant for refusing to submit to a breath test, in which defendant testified that nose and chest injuries sustained by him during his arrest prevented him from blowing into the Intoximeter tube, the trial court committed reversible error in precluding admission of photographs of defendant's injuries taken by his friend one day after the arrest, since the photographs were relevant circumstantial evidence of defendant's claim that he was physically incapable of taking the breath test; furthermore, defendant's friend was the proper person to authenticate the photographs for admission. **Callahan v. State,** Op. No. 910, 769 P2d 444 (Alaska App. 1989).

In action against airline for property damage resulting from a runway collision at Anchorage International Airport where jury concluded that the airline's flight crew committed willful misconduct in taking off in fog without knowing where they were on the runway, trial judge did not err in excluding, on grounds of relevance and potential prejudice to plaintiff, evidence that ground navigation in foggy conditions was known by the FAA and the State to be a dangerous problem at the airport, since the difficulty of taxiing in the fog was not a contested issue in the case and exclusion of the evidence did not in fact prejudice the airline, which was allowed to introduce other evidence as to the confusion on the taxiways on the day of the crash. **Korean Air Lines, Co., Ltd. v. State,** Op. No. 3492,779 P2d 333 (Alaska 1989).

In loss of consortium claim by husband arising out of injury to wife, trial court did not err in allowing husband to testify about his painful experiences during and after World War II since it had a bearing on the closeness of his relationship with his wife. **Babinec v. Yabuki,** Op. No. 3644, 799 P2d 1325 (Alaska 1990).

Evidence relating to Count 1, selling cocaine, was relevant to prove Count 2, possession with intent to deliver cocaine, regardless of its technical sufficiency to support a finding of guilt beyond a reasonable doubt on Count 1, thus trial court did not err in failing to sever the two charges or to order a mistrial as to Count 2 after granting a judgment of acquittal on Count 1. **McLaughlin v. State,** Op. No. 1159, 818 P2d 683 (Alaska App. 1991).

In medical malpractice suit, admission of evidence that plaintiff's primary expert witness had misstated his credentials at a previous unrelated trial and that the judge at that trial had made findings of fact concerning the misstatements constituted reversible error; defendant's arguments that the evidence was admissible to impeach the expert's character or to show bias were rejected. **Snyder v. Foote,** Op. No. 3787, 822 P2d 1353 (Alaska 1991).

In trial of defendant for statutory rape of 15-year-old girl, trial court properly rejected as irrelevant defendant's proposed evidence that victim was virgin before first act of alleged intercourse with defendant; defendant intended to attack victim's credibility by arguing that it was improbable that 15-year-old virgin would consent to sex with man she had known for only a few hours. **Heath v. State,** Op. No. 1290, 849 P2d 786 (Alaska App. 1993).

In suit by corporation against its former attorney for professional negligence and fiduciary fraud, evidence pertaining to attorney's conflict of interest was relevant to show that corporation would not have suffered damages if it had been aware of conflict, and evidence pertaining to attorney's role in involving corporation in limited partnership was relevant to establish context of advice which attorney gave to corporation throughout attorney-client relationship. **Cummings v. Sea Lion Corp.,** Op. No. 4416, 924 P2d 1011 (Alaska 1996).

In a driver's false confinement case against a city, a court did not err in precluding evidence regarding the driver's knife. The court acted within its discretion in finding that evidence of the knife could lead the jury to make its decision on an emotional basis or could confuse the jury because of uncertainty as to whether possessing the knife was legal. **City of Kodiak v. Samaniego,** Op. No. 5772, 83 P.3d 1077 (Alaska 2004).

Under the Smithart-Marrone rule, governing a criminal defendant's ability to introduce evidence tending to show that the crime was committed by someone else, evidence of another person's motive to commit the crime, or evidence of another person's opportunity to commit the crime, standing alone, is not admissible when offered to prove that the other person may have committed the crime; the Smithart-Marrone rule can be thought of as an issue-specific application of Alaska R. Evid. 403, even though that evidence might meet the test for relevance codified in this rule. **Cleveland v. State,** Op. No. 1934, 91 P.3d 965 (Alaska App. 2004).

In a second-degree sexual assault and second-degree assault case, based on a doctor's testimony regarding the victim's injuries and the size of the object used to sexually assault the victim, the physical dimensions of a chair leg, and the fact that the chair leg was attached to a chair in the victim's house in May 2001 when the victim's brother assaulted her, the trial judge did not abuse his discretion when he ruled that no reasonable fact-finder could conclude that the chair leg was the instrument used to sexually penetrate the victim. **Cleveland v. State,** Op. No. 1934, 91 P.3d 965 (Alaska App. 2004).

Where defendant was charged with refusal to submit to a breath test under AS 28.35.032, court did not err in allowing the state to cross-examine defendant concerning a prior episode in which he took a breath test; it was relevant to show that defendant was familiar with the breath test and that he understood what the officer was asking him to do. **Yang v. State,** Op. No. 2004, 107 P.3d 302 (Alaska App. 2005).

In a medical malpractice case, defendant doctor's experts were properly allowed to testify where their testimony concerning the amount and kinds of information that patients generally wanted in late night phone calls was relevant to establish whether the doctor gave the patient as much information as a reasonable patient would want to know. **Marsingill v. O'Malley,** Op. No. 5977, 128 P.3d 151 (Alaska 2006).

Because Alaska's implied consent law gives drivers the right to decline further testing after failing the mandatory breath test and the law requires the state to honor a driver's choice, evidence of a driver's refusal of further testing, though relevant under Evidence Rule 401, creates a danger of unfair prejudice greatly outweighing the refusal's impeachment value and is inadmissible under Evidence Rule 403. **Bluel v. State,** Op. No. 11564, 153 P.3d 982 (Alaska 2007).

Rule 402. Relevant Evidence Admissible— Exceptions — Irrelevant Evidence Inadmissible.

All relevant evidence is admissible, except as otherwise provided by the Constitution of the United States or of this state, by enactments of the Alaska Legislature, by these rules, or by other rules adopted by the Alaska Supreme Court. Evidence which is not relevant is not admissible.

(Added by SCO 364 effective August 1, 1979)

Note: Chapter 110 SLA 04 (HB 285) adopts the Uniform Electronic Transactions Act. According to Section 3 of the Act, AS 09.80.100, enacted in Section 1, has the effect of amending Evidence Rule 402 by adding a provision that prevents electronic evidence of a record or signature from being inadmissible as evidence just because it is in electronic form.

Annotations

Cases

Admission of evidence which had some tendency to establish an ultimate issue was not error, even though relevance of such evidence was marginal. **Alyeska Pipeline Serv. Co. v. Aurora Air Serv.,** Op. No. 2004, 604 P2d 1090 (Alaska 1979).

The evidencing rule precluding admission of post-injury accidents or design changes toward proof of negligence is inapplicable in products liability cases based on strict liability. **Caterpillar Tractor Co. v. Beck,** Op. No. 2304, 624 P2d 790 (Alaska 1981).

Evidence offered by defendant to show reasonableness of defendant's apprehension of being in imminent danger from shooting victim is not relevant when defendant did not know of such evidence at the time of the shooting. **Byrd v. State,** Op. No. 2184, 626 P2d 1057 (Alaska 1980).

Although the presentation of irrelevant evidence as to the scope of burglaries is error, it is harmless error if the presentation produces little or no prejudicial effect. **Nelson v. State,** Op. No. 2350, 628 P2d 884 (Alaska 1981).

Admissibility of breathalyzer refusals should be determined on a case-by-case basis by weighing probative value against potential for unfair prejudice. **Coleman v. State,** Op. No. 229, 658 P2d 1364 (Alaska App. 1983).

In prosecution for murder, admission into evidence of a .380 caliber automatic pistol owned by the defendant was not error even though expert testimony could not conclusively establish that the gun was the murder weapon. **Bangs v. State,** Op. No. 253, 663 P2d 981 (Alaska App. 1983).

In drunk driving prosecution of defendant who refused to submit to a breathalyzer examination, court erred in excluding expert testimony for the defense concerning defendant's blood alcohol level at the time of his arrest. **Quinto v. City and Borough of Juneau,** Op. No. 265, 664 P2d 630 (Alaska App. 1983).

Defendant's conviction for sexual abuse of child was reversed because extensive evidence of prior consistent statements made by the victim was admitted at trial without any determination of its actual probative value and before any charge of recent fabrication or improper motive or influence was made against the victim. **Nitz v. State,** Op. No. 629, 720 P2d 55 (Alaska App. 1986).

Evidence of consistent statements made by a child abuse victim on prior occasions may be admitted to bolster the testimony of the victim in a case involving the sexual abuse of the child, provided that it is actually relevant to rebut an express or implied charge of recent fabrication or improper motive or influence, and provided that its probative value outweighs its potential for prejudicial impact; before such evidence is admitted, however, the victim must testify and be subjected to a charge of recent fabrication or improper motive or influence; furthermore when it appears that the alleged motive to testify falsely arose before the prior statement was made, the statement may be admitted only for the purpose of rehabilitating the victim's credibility and may not be considered as substantive evidence of guilt. **Nitz v. State,** Op. No. 629, 720 P2d 55 (Alaska App. 1986).

In suit by road contractor against borough for breach of contract, trial court did not abuse its discretion in excluding evidence suggesting that the contractor falsified payroll records; although the evidence was arguably relevant to impeach the general reliability of the contractor's business records, it was not an abuse of discretion for the trial court to conclude that the probative value of the evidence was outweighed by the danger of prejudice, confusion of the issues, and waste of time. **Fairbanks North Star Borough v. Kandik Const.,** Op. No. 3571, 795 P2d 793 (Alaska 1990).

In tort action against city for injuries suffered by plaintiff as she went over a ski bump-jump at city ski hill, trial court did not err in prohibiting the city from discovering or using evidence relating to plaintiff's prior DWI conviction and prior drinking experience; although marginally relevant, since plaintiff admitted to consuming one to three beers prior to the accident, the potential prejudice, that the jury would punish plaintiff for her prior conduct, outweighed the relevance, particularly since other evidence existed suggesting her consumption and impairment. **Hibschman v. City of Valdez,** Op. No. 3783, 821 P2d 1354 (Alaska 1991).

In medical malpractice suit, admission of evidence that plaintiff's primary expert witness had misstated his credentials at a previous unrelated trial and that the judge at that trial had made findings of fact concerning the misstatements constituted reversible error; defendant's arguments that the evidence was admissible to impeach the expert's character or to show bias were rejected. **Snyder v. Foote,** Op. No. 3787, 822 P2d 1353 (Alaska 1991).

State was immune from liability for budget decisions. Therefore, superior court could properly exclude evidence regarding budget cuts in case seeking recovery for death and injuries occurring in State highway. **Estate of Arrowwood v. State,** Op. No. 4196, 894 P2d 642 (Alaska 1995).

In suit by corporation against its former attorney for professional negligence and fiduciary fraud, evidence pertaining to attorney's conflict of interest was relevant to show that corporation would not have suffered damages if it had been aware of conflict, and evidence pertaining to attorney's role in involving corporation in limited partnership was relevant to establish context of advice which attorney gave to corporation throughout attorney-client relationship. **Cummings v. Sea Lion Corp.,** Op. No. 4416, 924 P2d 1011 (Alaska 1996).

Alaska R. Evid. 402 governs all evidence offered under Alaska R. Evid. 404(b)(4). **Bingaman v. State,** Op. No. 1895, 76 P.3d 398 (Alaska App. 2003).

In a criminal prosecution for assault and sexual assault, the trial judge violated Alaska R. Evid. 402 by allowing the State to present evidence of sixty prior instances of defendant's misconduct which had little or nothing to do with the offenses charged. **Bingaman v. State,** Op. No. 1895, 76 P.3d 398 (Alaska App. 2003).

In a tort suit brought by a senior citizen who fell in the shower area of a city-owned senior center, the superior court correctly admitted a redacted report indicating that the senior citizen suggested more safety bars; court properly weighed relevance against prejudice and determined that the report, redacted to exclude evidence of the remedial measures taken, was admissible. **City of Bethel v. Peters,** Op. No. 5829, 97 P.3d 822 (Alaska App. 2003).

Post-accident investigations and recommendations are often relevant to the issue of negligence and, by revealing facts about the causes of an accident and the defendant's concerns about it, may be particularly useful to factfinders. **City of Bethel v. Peters,** Op. No. 5829, 97 P.3d 822 (Alaska 2004).

In a medical malpractice case, defendant doctor's experts were properly allowed to testify where their testimony concerning the amount and kinds of information that patients generally wanted in late night phone calls was relevant to establish whether the doctor gave the patient as much information as a reasonable patient would want to know. **Marsingill v. O'Malley,** Op. No. 5977, 128 P.3d 151 (Alaska 2006).

The 2004 amendments to AS 28.35.033 do not conflict with Rule 402 by preventing DWI defendants from introducing evidence relevant to their alcohol level at the time of driving. This rule expressly permits the legislature to define the parameters of relevant evidence within constitutional limits, and the language of AS 28.35.033(c) makes clear that the legislature intended to restrict the evidence that could be admitted in DWI prosecutions. **Valentine v. State,** Op. No. 9491, 155 P.3d 331 (Alaska App. 2007).

Rule 403. Exclusion of Relevant Evidence on Grounds of Prejudice, Confusion, or Waste of Time.

Although relevant, evidence may be excluded if its probative value is outweighed by the danger of unfair prejudice, confusion of the issues, or misleading the jury, or by considerations of undue delay, waste of time, or needless presentation of cumulative evidence.

(Added by SCO 364 effective August 1, 1979)

Annotations

Cases

Where only prejudice was possibility that jury might misestimate probative value of certain real evidence for state's case, even slight probative value outweighed such prejudice. **Eben v. State,** Op. No. 1920, 599 P2d 700 (Alaska 1979).

Where informant's credibility was relatively unimportant because testimony was corroborated by police officer's evidence that informant had made written statement alleging informant's testimony before grand jury in unrelated case was product of police coercion was properly excluded on grounds whatever relevancy statement had to issue of informant's credibility was outweighed by likelihood it would confuse the issues, mislead jury and consume an undue amount of time. **Taylor v. State,** Op. No. 1932, 600 P2d 5 (Alaska 1979).

Where defendant was charged with assault and battery, evidence that victim was 9 months pregnant was relevant and not unfairly prejudicial to right of defendant. **Rathbun v. Anchorage,** Op. No. 1928, 599 P2d 751 (Alaska 1979).

Exclusion of relevant evidence concerning rape victim's poor grades and excessive school absenteeism was proper where other evidence had already made the jury aware of these factors. **Alexander v. State,** Op. No. 2077, 611 P2d 469 (Alaska 1980).

Evidence regarding prior confrontations between the defendant and trespassers was relevant and admissible to show that the defendant's pointing of a shotgun at the victim was not accidental or inadvertent. **Adkinson v. State,** Op. No. 2090,611 P2d 528 (Alaska 1980).

At trial for murder, it was reversible error for the trial court to exclude a journal written by the victim, parts of which reflected a sense of mental instability and a violent nature. **Keith v. State,** Op. No. 2099, 612 P2d 977 (Alaska 1980).

Evidence of the circumstances of a prior rape committed by the defendant was properly admitted for the purpose of providing the identity of the assailant by showing a distinctive modus operandi employed in both the prior rape and the rape of the current victim. **Coleman v. State,** Op. No. 2190, 621 P2d 869 (Alaska 1980).

Evidence of drug use by the accused was admissible where it established direct contact between the victim and the accused and indicated that the accused possessed sufficient amounts of cocaine for him to have invested more than pocket cash in his purchase from the victim. **Dorman v. State,** Op. No. 2272, 622 P2d 448 (Alaska 1981).

The evidentiary rule precluding admission of post-injury accidents or design changes toward proof of negligence is inapplicable in products liability cases based on strict liability. **Caterpillar Tractor Co. v. Beck,** Op. No. 2304, 624 P2d 790 (Alaska 1981).

In statutory rape case, evidence of defendant's prior sexual conduct with victim was admissible. **Burke v. State,** Op. No. 2194, 624 P2d 1240 (Alaska 1981).

Testimony and photographs concerning the physical condition of a child allegedly kidnapped by defendant from state custody were admissible to show motive for kidnapping. **Crump v. State,** Op. No. 2309, 625 P2d 857 (Alaska 1981).

It was not error for the court to allow a defendant charged with drunk driving to be cross-examined regarding a possible law suit against the City of Fairbanks arising out of the same incident upon which the drunk driving charge was based. **Roth v. State,** Op. No. 13, 626 P2d 583 (Alaska 1981).

The trial court has considerable discretion in determining whether the probative value of an admission by silence is outweighed by the danger of unfair prejudice. **Doisher v. State,** Op. No. 30, 632 P2d 242 (Alaska App. 1982).

Evidence that defendant, charged with driving while intoxicated, refused to take the breathalyzer examination had possible probative value, and trial court did not err in finding that the probative value outweighed the possibility of prejudice. **Williford v. State,** Op. No. 148, 653 P2d 339 (Alaska App. 1982).

Where the evidence in each of five rape and assault incidents was sufficiently similar and sufficiently unusual when viewed in its totality and in the common pattern it presented to constitute a modus operandi probative of defendant being the assailant in all instances, trial court did not err in denying defendant's request for severance of the various rape, burglary with intent to rape, and assault charges. **Nix v. State,** Op. No. 157, 653 P2d 1093 (Alaska App. 1982).

Defendant's contention that because his conviction for driving while intoxicated was predicated on his blood alcohol rate and not his driving it was error for the trial court to admit evidence that he drove erratically and appeared intoxicated to arresting officers was properly rejected. **Byrne v. State,** Op. No. 169, 654 P2d 795 (Alaska App. 1982).

This rule, when properly applied and which excludes evidence which is minimally relevant, does not violate a defendant's constitutional right to confront the witnesses against him and to present evidence in his own behalf. **Larson v. State,** Op. No. 177, 656 P2d 571 (Alaska App. 1982).

Evidence that victim had assisted defendant in forging a prescription and that defendant's friend had previously assaulted a pharmacist in attempting to pass the forged prescription was admissible to show defendant's motive for kidnapping. **Bidwell v. State,** Op. No. 199, 656 P2d 592 (Alaska App. 1982).

Admissibility of breathalyzer refusals should be determined on a case-by-case basis by weighing probative value against potential for unfair prejudice. **Coleman v. State,** Op. No. 229, 658 P2d 1364 (Alaska App. 1983).

Defendant's resistance to "pat down" search was admissible as evidence that defendant was aware of the cocaine found in his pocket, although there were other possible explanations for his behavior. **Elson v. State,** Op. No. 2615, 659 P2d 1195 (Alaska 1983).

In damage action involving allegedly defective crane, experiments by defendant on the brake system of the crane to demonstrate the capabilities of such cranes in general, and not to have the jury draw conclusions about the particular crane, were properly excluded due to the danger of unfair prejudice, because the testing procedure was slipshod, because the tests were performed on the particular crane involved in the accident, and because the evidence was cumulative. **Yukon Equipment v. Gordon,** Op. No. 2630, 660 P2d 428 (Alaska 1983).

In assault prosecution in which defendant claimed self-defense, trial judge did not err in granting protective orders which prevented defendant from questioning victim about charges for possession of a shotgun while intoxicated and assault with a dangerous weapon which were pending against the victim at the time of trial and from asking the victim about prior alcoholism and convictions for driving while intoxicated. **Dyer v. State,** Op. No. 268, 666 P2d 438 (Alaska App. 1983).

In prosecution for murder, admission into evidence of a .380 caliber automatic pistol owned by the defendant was not error even though expert testimony could not conclusively establish that the gun was the murder weapon. **Bangs v. State,** Op. No. 253, 663 P2d 981 (Alaska App. 1983).

Court did not abuse its discretion in limiting cross-examination of prosecution witness concerning the dismissal or lenient disposition of previous charges against the witness absent evidence that the lenient dispositions had been received in return for past cooperation, where the jury was already aware that the witness was being treated favorably by the prosecution in return for his testimony. **Murdock v. State,** Op. No. 256, 664 P2d 589 (Alaska App. 1983).

In drunk driving prosecution of defendant who refused to submit to a breathalyzer examination, court erred in excluding expert testimony for the defense concerning defendant's blood alcohol level at the time of his arrest. **Quinto v. City and Borough of Juneau,** Op. No. 265, 664 P2d 630 (Alaska App. 1983).

The standard for appellate review of a trial court's decision to exclude testimony is whether the court abused its discretion. **Alaska Northern Development, Inc. v. Alyeska Pipeline Service Co.,** Op. No. 2689, 666 P2d 33 (Alaska 1983).

In prosecution for assault with a dangerous weapon, trial court did not abuse its discretion in determining that the probative value of defendant's flight from the crime outweighed the danger of unfair prejudice. **Dyer v. State,** Op. No. 268, 666 P2d 438 (Alaska App. 1983).

In action against state concerning alleged negligent inspection, trial court did not err in allowing expert to state his opinion as to whether the inspection was negligent, where the opinion was helpful to the trier of fact, was based upon facts or data reasonably relied on by other experts, and was not unduly prejudicial or misleading, particularly where any possible confusion or prejudice was cured by predicating the expert's opinion on a standard of care and issuing a cautionary instruction. **Wilson v. State,** Op. No. 2720, 669 P2d 1292 (Alaska 1983).

Complaining witness to crime, who prior to trial had been hypnotized to refresh her recollection, was not incompetent to testify at trial as to her after-hypnosis identification of the assailant. **State v. Contreras,** Op. No. 318, 674 P2d 792 (Alaska App. 1983).

Trial judge in drunk driving prosecution did not abuse his discretion in refusing to admit transcript of expert testimony on breathalyzer machine's failure point to counter testimony by police officer on the same subject even if the evidence was within the former testimony exception to the hearsay rule. **Thayer v. Municipality of Anchorage,** Op. No. 395, 686 P2d 721 (Alaska App. 1984).

In tort action where issue was whether plaintiff's injuries were caused solely by his own intoxication, evidence that plaintiff had previously undergone alcohol treatment was admissible. **Loof v. Sanders,** Op. No. 2859, 686 P2d 1205 (Alaska 1984).

Trial judge did not abuse his discretion in refusing to admit expert testimony that pimps would rather settle disputes among themselves than go to the police since the jurors themselves would certainly have arrived at that conclusion. **Wortham v. State,** Op. No. 414, 689 P2d 1133 (Alaska App. 1984).

In prosecution for driving with a suspended driver's license, trial judge abused his discretion in allowing admission of defendant's two recent convictions for driving while intoxicated which led to the license suspension. **Nelson v. State,** Op. No. 427, 691 P2d 1056 (Alaska App. 1984).

In prosecution for driving with a suspended license, attempted use by prosecution for impeachment purposes of voluntary statements made by defendant at the arrest scene concerning the reason she was driving, but which statements did not include the reason she later cited for driving, presented a question of whether the evidence was relevant and whether its probative value outweighed its prejudicial effect. **Nelson v. State,** Op. No. 427, 691 P2d 1056 (Alaska App. 1984).

Where defendant in murder trial claimed that he was defending himself against a homosexual rape by the victim who lured him into a car by offering him Quaaludes, trial court erred in excluding the testimony of a witness who would have testified that he had had a similar encounter with the victim one year before, and the trial court also erred in excluding evidence that the police found Quaaludes in the victim's home during their investigation. **Williamson v. State,** Op. No. 430, 692 P2d 965 (Alaska App. 1984).

When a prior bad act is relevant to a material fact other than propensity, the court may admit the evidence if it is more probative than prejudicial. **Lerchenstein v. State,** Op. No. 453, 697 P2d 312 (Alaska App. 1985).

Trial court's limiting curative instruction was not sufficient to remove the prejudice presented by improperly admitted evidence. **Lerchenstein v. State,** Op. No. 453, 697 P2d 312 (Alaska App. 1985).

In murder trial where self-defense was the issue, admission of evidence of recent prior bad acts of the defendant toward persons other than the victim was error notwithstanding the state's contention that the evidence was relevant to the question of whether defendant carried a gun to the crime scene in anticipation of a confrontation or merely pulled it from its customary place under his car seat and also relevant to defendant's state of mind at the time of the offense, since the evidence was to some extent cumulative and its prejudicial impact outweighed its probative value. **Lerchenstein v. State,** Op. No. 453, 697 P2d 312 (Alaska App. 1985).

Where defense strategy was to show that an alcoholic blackout prevented defendant from formulating an intent to kill, court did not err in rejecting lay testimony which defendant offered to establish the existence of alcoholic blackouts, since it would not have shed any light on the dispute between the experts who testified on the subject, nor would it have made it more or less probable that defendant was unable to form an intent to kill at the time of the shooting in question. **Staael v. State,** Op. No. 454, 697 P2d 1050 (Alaska App. 1985).

Admission of evidence that defendant failed to appear for a hearing, fled the jurisdiction after being charged with robbery, and used an alias when subsequently arrested on a different charge was not error. **Lipscomb v. State,** Op. No. 477, 700 P2d 1298 (Alaska App. 1985).

Where defendant was charged with sexual offenses against his daughter, evidence of alleged sexual relations between defendant and his daughter before and after the dates specified in the indictment was admissible to establish the ongoing relationship between the defendant and his daughter, explaining in part the daughter's inability to specifically describe separate incidents. **Covington v. State,** Op. No. 491, 703 P2d 436 (Alaska App. 1985).

In a trial for possession of cocaine with intent to distribute, a detailed analysis of the many items available for sale at defendant's drug paraphernalia business was unduly prejudicial. **Adams v. State,** Op. No. 525, 706 P2d 1183 (Alaska App. 1985).

DWI defendant's testimony that as a truck driver he could not afford the penalty of having his license revoked should have been excluded under this rule. **Browning v. State,** Op. No. 520, 707 P2d 266 (Alaska App. 1985).

Trial court did not err in permitting the prosecution to cross-examine defense witness concerning earlier allegations that defendant had sexually molested her for the purpose of impeaching her testimony that she did not believe the victim's claim of molestation and to counter defendant's testimony of accident or mistake. **Moor v. State,** Op. No. 543, 709 P2d 498 (Alaska App. 1985).

Where defendant cross-examined the prosecution witness, his former girlfriend, concerning their bitter breakup in order to establish her bias, trial court had erred in then allowing the state on redirect to inquire into all of the circumstances of the breakup, since it exceeded the scope of redirect permissible under the doctrine of curative admissibility, which exists to permit introduction of otherwise inadmissible evidence only to the extent necessary to remove any unfair prejudice which might otherwise ensue from the original evidence. **Bentley v. State,** Op. No. 560, 711 P2d 544 (Alaska App. 1985).

In prosecution of defendant for manslaughter for causing the death of the 18-month-old son of his live-in girlfriend, trial judge did not abuse his discretion in admitting evidence which tended to indicate that defendant had abused the child on prior occasions. **Garnerv. State,** Op. No. 569, 711 P2d 1191 (Alaska App. 1986).

In prosecution of defendant for manslaughter in the death of the 18-month-old son of his live-in girlfriend, trial judge abused his discretion by precluding defendant from offering extrinsic evidence that a neighbor, who had also taken care of the child on the day the fatal injuries were inflicted, had abused her own child on prior occasions, since such evidence was critical to defendant's defense, which suggested that the neighbor had inflicted the fatal injuries. **Garner v. State,** Op. No. 569, 711 P2d 1191 (Alaska App. 1986).

Evidence that defendant in sexual assault case had made sexual propositions to several other young girls was admissible to show design, scheme or plan, but not to establish motive. **Oswald v. State,** Op. No. 594, 715 P2d 276 (Alaska App. 1986).

Although trial court allowed testimony by sexual assault victim as to her virginity prior to the assault, it did not err in precluding defendant from cross-examining the victim regarding a prior incident in which the victim had allegedly been digitally penetrated by a school friend, since the probative value of the earlier incident as an alternative explanation for the perforation of the victim's hymen was very weak while the possible prejudice from invading her privacy unnecessarily and confusing the issues was very high. **Oswald v. State,** Op. No. 594, 715 P2d 276 (Alaska App. 1986).

Where purpose of allowing police officer to testify concerning out-of-court statement by child victim in sexual assault case was not to prove the truth of the matter asserted in the statement, i.e. that the child had engaged in fellatio with her father, but rather to establish that the child knew what a penis was, the testimony was admissible. **Drumbarger v. State,** Op. No. 601, 716 P2d 6 (Alaska App. 1986).

Trial court did not abuse its discretion in finding that the probative value of admitting photographs of alleged child abuse victim's injuries outweighed the danger of unfair prejudice. **Sluka v. State,** Op. No. 606, 717 P2d 394 (Alaska App. 1986).

In prosecution for assault, trial court's order excluding inquiry into a prior false report by the complaining witness against the defendant for assault did not amount to reversible error, since such inquiry would have allowed the prosecution to elicit a full explanation of the circumstances underlying the prior report to defendant's disadvantage. **Richey v. State,** Op. No. 611, 717 P2d 407 (Alaska App. 1986).

Circumstances surrounding death of defendant's first child from a skull fracture while alone with defendant was admissible in trial of defendant for first degree assault against his second child, who also suffered a skull fracture while alone in defendant's care, to show that defendant's actions manifested an extreme indifference to human life. **Rhodes v. State,** Op. No. 613, 717 P2d 422 (Alaska App. 1986).

When a witness has been previously hypnotized, his subsequent testimony at trial, as to facts and recollections adduced during hypnosis, is inadmissible; he may testify only to facts which he related prior to hypnosis. **Contreras v. State,** Op. No. 3042, 718 P2d 129 (Alaska 1986).

Error in jury instruction together with error in admission of certain character evidence constituted plain error. **Pletnikoff v. State,** Op. No. 625, 719 P2d 1039 (Alaska App. 1986).

Defendant's conviction for sexual abuse of child was reversed because extensive evidence of prior consistent statements made by the victim was admitted at trial without any determination of its actual probative value and before any charge of recent fabrication or improper motive or influence was made against the victim. **Nitz v. State,** Op. No. 629, 720 P2d 55 (Alaska App. 1986).

Evidence of consistent statements made by a child abuse victim on prior occasions may be admitted to bolster the testimony of the victim in case involving the sexual abuse of the child, provided that it is actually relevant to rebut an express or implied charge of recent fabrication or improper motive or influence, and provided that its probative value outweighs its potential for prejudicial impact; before such evidence is admitted, however, the victim must testify and be subjected to a charge of recent fabrication or improper motive or influence; furthermore when it appears that the alleged motive to testify falsely arose before the prior statement was made, the statement may be admitted only for the purpose of rehabilitating the victim's credibility and may not be considered as substantive evidence of guilt. **Nitz v. State,** Op. No. 629, 720 P2d 55 (Alaska App. 1986).

Evidence of sexual acts which the defendant allegedly committed with victims other than those named in the indictment was not relevant to a material fact other than propensity, thus admission of the evidence constituted reversible error. **Bolden v. State,** Op. No. 632, 720 P2d 957 (Alaska App. 1986).

Where defendant was charged with sexually molesting his daughters, admission of evidence concerning his alleged sexual molestation of other young girls was reversible error, since neither intent nor identity were at issue and since the alleged acts were not admissible as evidence of a common scheme or plan. **Bolden v. State,** Op. No. 632, 720 P2d 957 (Alaska App. 1986).

In trial of defendant for sexual abuse of a six-year-old, trial court committed reversible error in allowing the State to present evidence of a prior uncharged sexual incident involving defendant and the same girl 18 months earlier. **Johnson v. State,** Op. No. 655, 727 P2d 1062 (Alaska App. 1986).

In sexual assault case where the defendant was the alleged victim's father, the "lewd disposition" exception to the exclusionary rule was properly extended to allow the testimony of the victim's sisters who were allegedly seduced under substantially similar circumstances and at roughly the same age. **Soper v. State,** Op. No. 675, 731 P2d 587 (Alaska App. 1987).

Evidence that defendant has been convicted of sexually assaulting the same girl two years prior to the incidents alleged in his current indictment for sexual abuse was properly admissible before the grand jury and at trial to establish that defendant had a significant sexual desire for that particular girl. **Patterson v. State,** Op. No. 681, 732 P2d 1102 (Alaska App. 1987).

Admission of racial statement made by defendant to police officer was error since the statement was more prejudicial than probative, but the error was harmless in light of the substantial evidence of defendant's guilt. **Ward v. State,** Op. No. 685, 733 P2d 625 (Alaska App. 1987).

In prosecution for resisting arrest where the issue of defendant's intoxication was not part of the prosecution's case-in-chief and was first raised during defendant's own testimony, the trial court did not abuse its discretion in allowing a videotape of defendant made at the police station following his arrest to be used by the prosecution to rebut defendant's testimony that he had consumed liquor but was not influenced by it. **Carson v. State,** Op. No. 700, 736 P2d 356 (Alaska App. 1987).

In sexual assault prosecution where the defense was consent, the trial judge did not abuse his discretion in excluding evidence that the victim had posed for Penthouse Magazine and had acted in x-rated movies and had willingly told same to the defendant, which the defense offered for the purpose of showing that the defendant and the victim in the months prior to the assault had been involved in a relationship that was sexual, rather than merely platonic as alleged by the victim. **Wood v. State,** Op. No. 701, 736 P2d 363 (Alaska App. 1987).

In prosecution of defendant for lewd and lascivious acts toward children in which it was alleged that defendant would invite them to his house, offer them drugs, show them pornographic materials, and then attempt sexual acts with them, trial court did not abuse its discretion in refusing to allow defendant to call as witnesses two police officers who had been in his home at different times and who would have testified that they had not seen drugs, pornography, or film-making equipment in his home. **Rodriquez v. State,** Op. No. 735, 741 P2d 1200 (Alaska App. 1987).

In prosecution for attempted sexual abuse of a minor, trial court erred in allowing testimony about statements defendant made one week after the incident concerning his sexual fantasies and orientation since the testimony was clearly character evidence and was not relevant to show proof of motive, opportunity, intent, preparation, plan, knowledge, identity or absence of mistake or accident; nevertheless, due to the strength of the other evidence against defendant, the error was deemed harmless. **Stevens v. State,** Op. No. 773, 748 P2d 771 (Alaska App. 1988).

In action by union worker against the union for intentional infliction of emotional distress during a strike, testimony by another worker concerning episodes of violence aimed at that worker during the strike was relevant not to prove the facts asserted but to prove defendant's resultant state of mind based on the incidents related to him by the other worker, and the trial court exercised proper discretion in admitting the testimony on the basis that its probative value outweighed the danger of unfair prejudice. **Teamsters Local 959 v. Wells,** Op. No. 3263, 749 P2d 349 (Alaska 1988).

When a complaining witness testifies that he or she has been the subject of sexual or physical abuse and the defense seeks to discredit this testimony by showing that the witness' conduct was inconsistent with the claimed abuse and therefore that the claim of abuse was false, the state should be permitted to offer expert testimony that other members of the relevant class (i.e., abused or battered women or sexually abused children) characteristically exhibit such conduct even though they are, in fact, abused. **Anderson v. State,** Op. No. 771, 749 P2d 369 (Alaska App. 1988).

Before expert testimony seeking to establish that a person is a member of a particular class or group, i.e., battered women or sexually abused children, by showing that they exhibit behavioral characteristics common to that group, the proponent should establish, in a hearing out of the presence of the jury, that the probative value of the testimony outweighs its possible prejudicial effect; the trial court should require the proponent of such evidence to identify in advance what he or she intends to prove and why that evidence would be relevant to the case; furthermore, the court should consider the extent to which the expert witnesses' assumptions are shared by a consensus of those mental health practitioners knowledgeable about the subject matter. **Anderson v. State,** Op. No. 771, 749 P2d 369 (Alaska App. 1988).

In trial for attempted murder, the trial court did not err in admitting evidence of defendant's altercation with another person five hours prior to the attempted murder, since the altercation bore some causal connection to the reason the defendant and the victim came together, since the evidence gave the jury a complete picture of the series of events preceding the shooting, and since any prejudice caused by the evidence was minimal. **Ciervo v. State,** Op. No. 813, 756 P2d 907 (Alaska App. 1988).

Although witness admitted to making prior inconsistent statements, trial court did not err in admitting extrinsic evidence of the prior statements where the exact statements made and the demeanor of the witness when he made them had probative value, where the witness did not admit to making all of the prior statement, and where admission of the statements was not unduly prejudicial. **Clifton v. State,** Op. No. 826, 758 P2d 1279 (Alaska App. 1988).

In prosecution for manslaughter arising out of a motor vehicle accident allegedly caused by defendant's drunk driving, evidence of defendant's prior drunk driving convictions was not automatically admissible to prove that defendant was subjectively aware of the risk posed by his drunk driving. **Jansen v. State,** Op. No. 863, 764 P2d 308 (Alaska App. 1988).

In sexual assault cases where identity is not an issue, proof of modus operandi is irrelevant. **Velez v. State,** Op. No. 852, 762 P2d 1297 (Alaska App. 1988).

In date rape cases, use of evidence of other sexual assaults by defendant against other victims to rebut a consent defense cannot be reconciled with Alaska Evidence Rules. **Velez v. State,** Op. No. 852, 762 P2d 1297 (Alaska App. 1988).

Where defendant was charged with one count of sexual assault in the first degree and one count of attempted sexual assault in the first degree, each count involving a different incident and a different victim, and defendant was acquainted with each victim and claimed consent as a defense to the sexual assault charge, the trial court committed reversible error in denying defendant's motion for severance, since the evidence regarding the two charges was not cross admissible. **Velez v. State,** Op. No. 852, 762 P2d 1297 (Alaska App. 1988).

In prosecution of defendant for assault after his car struck a pedestrian on the side of the road, trial court did not err in admitting a video tape in which the victim reenacted her actions prior to being hit by defendant's car even though the lighting, weather, and other conditions portrayed in the video were dissimilar to the conditions that existed at the time of the accident. **Lee v. State,** Op. No. 843, 760 P2d 1039 (Alaska App. 1988).

The prosecution may not introduce a profile to show that the defendant is more likely to have committed an offense because the defendant fits that profile. **Haakason v. State,** Op. No. 837, 760 P2d 1030 (Alaska App. 1988).

In trial of defendant for sex crimes against children, admission of policeman's testimony regarding a child sexual abuser profile was reversible error. **Haakason v. State,** Op. No. 837, 760 P2d 1030 (Alaska App. 1988).

In trial of defendant for sex crimes against children, admission of testimony by girls not named in the indictment concerning inappropriate physical behavior by defendant toward them was error. **Haakason v. State,** Op. No. 837, 760 P2d 1030 (Alaska App. 1988).

In trial of defendant for sex crimes against children, admission of sexually suggestive statement by defendant to a girl not named in the indictment, on the ground that it was relevant to show defendant's state of mind, was error, there being no nonpropensity relevance to such evidence. **Haakason v. State,** Op. No. 837, 760 P2d 1030 (Alaska App. 1988).

The probative value of polygraph evidence is insubstantial because the polygraph has not been proven reliable, thus the prejudicial impact it may have on a jury clearly outweighs its probative value; accordingly, trial court did not abuse its discretion in refusing to admit defendant's polygraph results at trial. **Haakason v. State,** Op. No. 837, 760 P2d 1030 (Alaska App. 1988).

The primary purpose of the Rape Shield Statute is to prevent the use of evidence of past sexual conduct as proof of the victim's current willingness to consent; it is not intended to exclude evidence of prior sexual conduct when such evidence is directly relevant to establish bias, prejudice, or motive to fabricate. **Daniels v. State,** Op. No. 900, 767 P2d 1163 (Alaska App. 1989).

Where the defense witness in a DWI prosecution testified that she in fact had been driving the vehicle but traded places with the defendant because there was a warrant out for her arrest, the trial court did not commit error in permitting the state to cross-examine the witness on her prior DWI arrest and license suspension, since the knowledge that her license was suspended was directly relevant to her willingness to drive and since any additional prejudice was slight considering that the defendant introduced the issue. **Alward v. State,** Op. No. 901, 767 P2d 1175 (Alaska App. 1989).

In trial of defendant for murder arising out of an altercation between the defendant, the victim and the victim's brothers, where defendant claimed self-defense, the trial court did not err in preventing defendant from cross-examining one of the brothers about a prior hindering prosecution charge (later dismissed) against that brother as evidence of bias under this rule, since although the evidence arguably demonstrated the brother's willingness to engage in illegal conduct to protect his brother, the trial judge's conclusion that the probative value of the evidence was outweighed by the danger of unfair prejudice was not unreasonable considering that the brother had admitted to burglary and theft convictions and that defendant was still fully able to develop the brother's bias and interest in the case. **Lerchenstein v. State,** Op. No. 921, 770 P2d 1150 (Alaska App. 1989).

Trial court committed plain error requiring reversal by permitting questions concerning defendant's prearrest silence in the presence of police officers, silence which was at least as consistent with innocence as with guilt, without first determining whether the probative value of the challenged line of inquiry was outweighed by its potential for prejudicial impact. **Silvernail v. State,** Op. No. 945, 777 P2d 1169 (Alaska App. 1989).

There is a presumption that the prejudicial effect of propensity evidence outweighs its probative value; when, however, a prior bad act is relevant to a material fact other than propensity, the court may admit evidence of the prior bad act if it is more probative than prejudicial. **Mathis v. State,** Op. No. 951, 778 P2d 1161 (Alaska App. 1989).

In action against airline for property damage resulting from a runway collision at Anchorage International Airport where jury concluded that the airline's flight crew committed willful misconduct in taking off in fog without knowing where they were on the runway, trial judge did not err in excluding, on grounds of relevance and potential prejudice to plaintiff, evidence that ground navigation in foggy conditions was known by the FAA and the State to be a dangerous problem at the airport, since the difficulty of taxiing in the fog was not a contested issue in the case and exclusion of the evidence did not in fact prejudice the airline, which was allowed to introduce other evidence as to the confusion on the taxiways on the day of the crash. **Korean Air Lines, Co., Ltd. v. State,** Op. No. 3492,779 P2d 333 (Alaska 1989).

In murder trial, trial court did not err in refusing to allow an Immigration Department investigator to testify for the defense regarding reports from unidentified informants of rumors that the victim's family had threatened to kill anyone who testified in favor of the defendant at trial; although the testimony of the informants themselves might not have been hearsay, the investigator's testimony would have been; furthermore, the probative value of the investigator's testimony would have been outweighed by possible confusion of issues and needless presentation of cumulative evidence, particularly since the prosecution's primary witness against defendant acknowledged her awareness of the rumors. **Zeciri v. State,** Op. No. 956, 779 P2d 795 (Alaska App. 1989).

The standard of this rule, that relevant evidence can be excluded if the probative value of the evidence is outweighed by confusion of the issues or by considerations of undue delay, is the proper standard to apply in determining whether cross-examination should be allowed in criminal cases; the case law dealing with the issue of cross-examination in criminal cases does not create standards to replace this rule, but rather augment it. **Brown v. State,** Op. No. 957, 779 P2d 801 (Alaska App. 1989).

In trial of a black defendant for misconduct involving a controlled substance, trial court did not err in prohibiting him from cross-examining the undercover officer involved in the case concerning racial bias; because the evidence which would have been developed through the cross-examination was so marginally probative, the judge's decision to exclude it due to possible confusion of the issues and delay was justified. **Brown v. State,** Op. No. 957, 779 P2d 801 (Alaska App. 1989).

Trial judge did not abuse his discretion in admitting evidence of defendant's flight from the scene of the crime as evidence of his consciousness of guilt. **Charles v. State,** Op. No. 963, 780 P2d 377 (Alaska App. 1989).

In prosecution of defendant for criminally negligent homicide in failing to timely seek medical treatment for her child, statement by policeman in taped interview of defendant that the police received several calls from people saying that defendant had abused her child would have been unfairly prejudicial and therefore had to be excised from the tape. **Pinkerton v. State,** Op. No. 996, 784 P2d 671 (Alaska App. 1989).

In drunk driving prosecution, trial court did not err in admitting an audio tape recording, which the police made when defendant was arrested and while he was being transported to the police station, despite the tape's poor quality; the jury could tell when the voices on the tape were obscured by background noise and static and would not conclude that the background noise and static was slurred or garbled speech by defendant. **Suiter v. State,** Op. No. 991, 785 P2d 28 (Alaska App. 1989).

In trial of defendant for murder where the only question at issue was intent, trial court did not err in allowing admission of defendant's prior felony conviction for possession of a concealable firearm despite defendant's offer to stipulate to a prior felony conviction in order to keep the exact nature of the felony from the jury; given the overwhelming evidence of intent, evidence of the prior felony conviction was not overly prejudicial. **Weitz v. State,** Op. No. 1058, 794 P2d 952 (Alaska App. 1990).

In trial of defendant for murder and assault in shooting of police officers, trial court did not err in allowing evidence of prior bad acts to be introduced before the jury, including evidence that defendant had been in prison before and would kill rather than go back; the evidence was relevant and highly probative to show defendant's motive and intent when he shot at the officers, thus trial court could find that the probative value of the evidence outweighed any prejudice. **Weitz v. State,** Op. No. 1058, 794 P2d 952 (Alaska App. 1990).

In suit by road contractor against borough for breach of contract, trial court did not abuse its discretion in excluding evidence suggesting that the contractor falsified payroll records; although the evidence was arguably relevant to impeach the general reliability of the contractor's business records, it was not an abuse of discretion for the trial court to conclude that the probative value of the evidence was outweighed by the danger of prejudice, confusion of the issues, and waste of time. **Fairbanks North Star Borough v. Kandik Const.,** Op. No. 3571, 795 P2d 793 (Alaska 1990).

In determining whether to admit evidence of a prior bad act, the trial court must first determine that the evidence to be admitted has relevance apart from propensity and, secondly, must determine that the nonpropensity evidence outweighs the presumed highly prejudicial impact of the evidence. **Martin v. State,** Op. No. 1065, 797 P2d 1209 (Alaska App. 1990).

Where defendant was charged only with property crimes, a witness's reference to his prior criminal record together with the prosecutor's improper argument suggesting that defendant contemplated killing the arresting officer required reversal. **Martin v. State,** Op. No. 1065, 797 P2d 1209 (Alaska App. 1990).

Even if statement of witness in civil case was an admission of a party-opponent, it was inadmissible because its prejudicial impact outweighed its probativeness. **Zoerb v. Church Elec. Association, Inc.,** Op. No. 3636, 798 P2d 1258 (Alaska 1990).

In loss of consortium claim by husband arising out of injury to wife, trial court did not err in allowing husband to testify about his painful experiences during and after World War II since it had a bearing on the closeness of his relationship with his wife. **Babinec v. Yabuki,** Op. No. 3644, 799 P2d 1325 (Alaska 1990).

Testimony relating to defendant's failure to make exculpatory statements would have been inadmissible at trial for lack of foundation for application of the adoptive admissions theory, and was therefore improperly admitted in grand jury proceeding; the State's argument that admissibility of the evidence at trial would have turned on a balancing of probative value against prejudicial impact was rejected. **State v. Green,** Op. No. 1131, 810 P2d 1023 (Alaska App. 1991).

Defense attempt to impeach prosecution witness with a prior inconsistent statement by having her examine on the stand her 172-page deposition testimony was properly denied because of the undue delay it would cause; defendant's right of confrontation was not abridged because alternative methods were available, such as recalling the witness later, after she had an opportunity to read the transcript, or by refreshing her recollection with selected portions of the transcript. **Jones v. State,** Op. No. 1135, 812 P2d 613 (Alaska App. 1991).

In cocaine prosecution, grand jury testimony by defendant's girlfriend concerning her receipt on prior occasions of packages of cocaine, allegedly sent by defendant, was more probative than prejudicial, thus admissible, despite contention that it was inadmissible prior bad act evidence. **Castillo v. State,** Op. No. 1175, 821 P2d 133 (Alaska App. 1991).

Upon determining that evidence of remedial repairs genuinely impeaches a witness, trial court must next determine whether the impeachment value outweighs the prejudicial implication of negligence. **Agostino v. Fairbanks Clinic,** Op. No. 3718, 821 P2d 714 (Alaska 1991).

In tort action against city for injuries suffered by plaintiff as she went over a ski bump-jump at a city ski hill, trial court did not err in prohibiting the city from discovering or using evidence relating to plaintiff's prior DWI conviction and prior drinking experience; although marginally relevant, since plaintiff admitted to consuming one to three beers prior to the accident, the potential prejudice, that the jury would punish plaintiff for her prior conduct, outweighed the relevance, particularly since other evidence existed suggesting her consumption and impairment. **Hibschman v. City of Valdez,** Op. No. 3783, 821 P2d 1354 (Alaska 1991).

In prosecution of defendant for possession and sale of cocaine, trial judge did not abuse his discretion in concluding that probative value of $72,000 cash found in defendant's possession at time of arrest outweighed its potential for unfair prejudice. **Toney v. State,** Op. No. 1223, 833 P2d 15 (Alaska App. 1992).

In wrongful death action arising out of one-car accident, trial court did not err in admitting still photographs taken of accident scene after cautioning jury that photographs were not taken at time of accident. **Beck v. Dept. of Transp. & P. Facilities,** Op. No. 3871, 837 P2d 105 (Alaska 1992).

Where defendant was charged with first degree assault on his wife which he claimed was committed by another man, evidence that wife was assaulted by the other man while defendant was in prison awaiting trial was properly excluded due to danger of misleading or confusing jury, particularly since defendant chose not to have wife testify for him as she was willing to do. **Brandon v. State,** Op. No. 1251, 839 P2d 400 (Alaska App. 1992).

Even if opinion of judge who presided over witness' prior forgery trial was admissible as opinion evidence of witness' dishonest character, trial judge properly excluded the evidence as more prejudicial than probative. **Carr v. State,** Op. No. 1256, 840 P2d 1000 (Alaska App. 1992).

In robbery trial judge did not err in admitting evidence that defendant and accomplices trafficked in and used cocaine since evidence was relevant to show that robbery was part of common scheme or plan to bankroll larger drug enterprise in which defendant participated. **Miller v. State,** Op. No. 1330, 866 P2d 130 (Alaska App. 1994).

A trial judge's ruling on the admissibility of evidence will be reversed only when a clear abuse of discretion has been shown. **Johnson v. State,** Op. No. 1390, 889 P2d 1076 (Alaska App. 1995).

When properly applied, this rule does not violate a defendant's constitutional right of confrontation. **Johnson v. State,** Op. No. 1390, 889 P2d 1076 (Alaska App. 1995).

This rule gives the trial court broad discretion to restrict the admission of relevant evidence if its probative value is outweighed by unfair prejudice or confusion of the issues. **Johnson v. State,** Op. No. 1390, 889 P2d 1076 (Alaska App. 1995).

Trial court did not err in allowing State to display murder victim's skull to the jury during trial to assist in understanding the location of gunshot wounds. **Hilbish v. State,** Op. No. 1398, 891 P2d 841 (Alaska App. 1995).

The Pennsylvania rule that evidence "likely to inflame the passions of the jury" should be admitted only if essential to the prosecution's case" is at odds with Evidence Rule 403 which specifies that evidence is admissible when its probative value outweighs its potential for prejudice. **Hilbish v. State,** Op. No. 1398, 891 P2d 841 (Alaska App. 1995).

Superior court did not abuse its discretion in determining that prejudicial effect of evidence of state trooper's statement that decedent died because of budget cuts outweighed its probative values. **Estate of Arrowwood v. State,** Op. No. 4196, 894 P2d 642 (Alaska 1995).

It is entirely appropriate to require a hearing out of the jury's presence to inquire into whether evidence is relevant and material and whether it merits exclusion under this rule. **Sweet v. Sisters of Providence in Washington,** Op. No. 4200, 895 P2d 484 (Alaska 1995).

Evidence of a passenger's prior joyriding conviction was not, standing alone, relevant to the question of the accused's identity as the driver in the current joyriding prosecution and was properly excluded. **Jordan v. State,** Op. No. 1412, 895 P2d 994 (Alaska App. 1995).

Prior misconduct evidence should be more liberally admitted when it is offered against a witness instead of the accused. **Jordan v. State,** Op. No. 1412, 895 P2d 994 (Alaska App. 1995).

Evidence that wife had previously committed armed assault on husband had little prejudicial impact and supported defense theory that wife had manufactured allegation of sexual abuse against husband to obtain custody of their children. Consequently the evidence should have been admitted at trial. **Beltz v. State,** Op. No. 1409, 895 P2d 513 (Alaska App. 1995).

Where evidence of wife's armed assault was uniquely probative of her motives in testifying against husband in case alleging sexual assault of their daughter, error in excluding the evidence was not harmless. **Beltz v. State,** Op. No. 1409, 895 P2d 513 (Alaska App. 1995).

To reach the relaxed Evidence Rule 403 balancing analyses with regard to a witness' prior misconduct, the accused must first establish, under Evidence Rule 404(b), that the proffered evidence relates to some issue other than propensity. **Jordan v. State,** Op. No. 1412, 895 P2d 994 (Alaska App. 1995).

Trial court did not abuse its discretion in admitting testimony that in 1990 defendant threatened a rebuttal witness with a pistol that had been delivered to defendant, at his request, by his friend. This testimony was offered to refute other testimony that defendant had sold his friend the pistol in 1990 and his friend had never given it back to him. **Simmons v. State,** Op. No. 1419, 899 P2d 931 (Alaska App. 1995).

Evidence of two prior sexual assault convictions was properly admissible in subsequent sexual assault and murder trial to show that the defendant murdered the victim by a distinctive **modus operandi** which he had also employed in the prior sexual assaults. **Harmon v. State,** Op. No. 1450, 908 P2d 434 (Alaska App. 1995).

Prior sexual assault convictions which were twelve years old by time of present sexual assault and murder were not so remote in time as not to be sufficiently probative of **modus operandi** because defendant had been incarcerated for eight of those twelve years and thus had not had an opportunity during those years to commit a similar assault. **Harmon v. State,** Op. No. 1450, 908 P2d 434 (Alaska App. 1995).

In murder case, trial court did not abuse its discretion in allowing jury to see autopsy photographs of victim; by graphically illustrating near-pinpoint accuracy of bullet wounds, photographs refuted defendant's claim that he had fired twice in quick succession, reflexively, without taking aim and with no intention of killing. **Howell v. State,** Op. No. 1470, 917 P2d 1202 (Alaska App. 1996).

Fact that arson defendant claimed responsibility for prior killing minutes before setting fire to cabin in which he was trapped was admissible to establish his state of mind, absence of accident, and motive on the arson charge. **West v. State,** Op. No. 1482, 923 P2d 110 (Alaska App. 1996).

Evidence properly excludable as cumulative falls into tow categories: one is evidence supporting an uncontested or established fact, the other is evidence repeating point made by previous evidence. **Wasserman v. Bartholomew,** Op. No. 4404, 923 P2d 806 (Alaska 1996).

Because witness's testimony went to central issue in case, it was not excludable for reasons of undue delay or waste of time. **Wasserman v. Bartholomew,** Op. No. 4404, 923 P2d 806 (Alaska 1996).

Witness's account of disputed facts cannot be considered cumulative on basis that court has heard several versions of facts that differ substantially from excluded witness's version. **Wasserman v. Bartholomew,** Op. No. 4404, 923 P2d 806 (Alaska 1996).

Trial judge committed reversible error in requiring foundational proof that witness had made inconsistent statements before allowing defendant to introduce evidence of witness's probation status as potential reason why witness might be biased in favor of government. **Kameroff v. State,** Op. No. 1488, 926 P2d 1174 (Alaska App. 1996).

In prosecution of defendant for assaulting his wife, trial court committed reversible error in not allowing defense to cross-examine prosecution's main witness, a female, as to whether she was romantically involved with defendant's wife, for purpose of demonstrating witness's bias. **McIntyre v. State,** Op. No. 1521, 934 P2d 770 (Alaska App. 1997).

In prosecution of defendant for murder of roommate, prior incident in which roommate called police to apartment out of fear of defendant was admissible. **Brodine v. State,** Op. No. 1526, 936 P2d 545 (Alaska App. 1997).

In prosecution of defendant for violent sexual assault, evidence of defendant's violent assault on another woman just hours before was admissible to show state of mind. **Hoffman v. State,** Op. No. 1562, 950 P2d 141 (Alaska App. 1997).

Murder defendant's false statements to friend following death of defendant's wife that wife had premonitions of death and had made funeral preparations were relevant to demonstrate defendant's consciousness of guilt, and probative value of statements outweighed potential prejudicial effect. **Sakeagak v. State,** Op. No. 1568, 952 P2d 278 (Alaska App. 1998).

Where major disputed issue in prosecution for second degree theft of jewelry was whether defendant recklessly disregarded fact that jewelry was stolen, admission of defendant's prior convictions for forgery and theft was reversible error; past criminal acts were not shown to bear relevant factual similarity to charged offense and proved little of relevance except defendant's proclivity to lie and steal. **Calapp v. State,** Op. No. 1590, 959 P2d 385 (Alaska App. 1998).

In prosecution of defendant for burglary and theft, evidence that Ketchikan police phoned Juneau police to alert them that defendant was suspected burglar was admissible, with limiting instruction, to explain officers' interest in defendant. **Silvertsen v. State,** Op. No. 1600, 963 P2d 1069 (Alaska App. 1998).

Evidence properly excludable as "cumulative" falls into two categories: evidence supporting an uncontested or established fact and evidence repeating a point made by previous evidence. **Wasserman v. Bartholomew,** Op. No. 5179, 987 P2d 748 (Alaska 1999).

In suit against city and three police officers claiming that officers used excessive force in making arrest, trial court committed reversible error by prohibiting plaintiff from calling two officers as corroborative witnesses; officers' testimony was highly material and not cumulative and plaintiff made a sufficient offer of proof with respect to their testimony. **Wasserman v. Bartholomew,** Op. No. 5179, 987 P2d 748 (Alaska 1999).

Drunk driving defendant's argument that evidence of his refusal to take two field sobriety tests should have been excluded under this rule because it was more prejudicial than probative was rejected. **McCormick v. Municipality of Anchorage,** Op. No. 1658, 999 P2d 155 (Alaska App. 2000).

When evidence of other sexual assaults is admissible under Evidence Rule 404(b)(3) to prove defendant's propensity to commit sexual assaults, trial judge must still consider whether evidence should be excluded or limited pursuant to Evidence Rule 403; tendency of such evidence to prove defendant's propensity to commit sexual assaults can no longer be deemed unfair prejudice, but other aspects of the evidence can be unfairly prejudicial or can be cumulative, misleading or confusing. **Wadlow v. State,** Op. No. 1676, 2 P3d 1238 (Alaska App. 2000).

In sexual assault prosecution where the defense was consent and the state was allowed to present evidence of a prior sexual assault by defendant against a different victim, trial court committed reversible error in denying defendant's request that jury be informed of his acquittal on the prior sexual assault charge, since the evidence of that acquittal was relevant and not hearsay, its potential for confusion did not outweigh its potential probative value, and its exclusion was prejudicial to defendant. **Hess v. State,** Op. No. 5386, 20 P3d 1121 (Alaska 2001).

In sexual assault case where defendant was convicted of engaging in sexual penetration with a woman who was so intoxicated that she was either incapacitated or unaware of the sexual penetration, trial court did not err in ruling that defendant's proposed expert witness on "alcoholic blackouts" lacked the expertise to offer an opinion on the subject or in ruling that such testimony, offered to support the defense theory that victim consented to sexual intercourse but could not remember giving consent due to alcoholic blackout, was more prejudicial than probative. **Ragsdale v. State,** Op. No. 1746, 23 P3d 653 (Alaska App. 2001).

In a prosecution for transporting game that had been taken in violation of Alaska's hunting regulations, where a video tape showed only selected portions of the hike to the kill site, was potentially misleading, and was made at a different season of the year than when the crime was allegedly committed, the trial judge properly declined to allow the video tape in evidence, even though he did not view the tape. **Brigman v. State,** Op. No. 1854, 64 P.3d 152 (Alaska App. 2003).

As the State's superseded charging documents contained a clerical error rather than an admission of fact, the trial judge properly refused to admit them under Alaska R. Evid. 403. **Brigman v. State,** Op. No. 1854, 64 P.3d 152 (Alaska App. 2003).

Trial court did not abuse its discretion in excluding evidence of defendant's subsequent compliance with the Alaska Sex Offender Registration Act at defendant's trial for failing to comply with the Act because the subsequent compliance was marginally relevant at best to show defendant's mental stated before being charged and moreover, a magistrate ruled that the marginal evidence was outweighed by the risk of confusing or misleading the jury. **Dailey v. State,** Op. No. 1861, 65 P.3d 891 (Alaska App. 2003).

In a criminal prosecution for assault and sexual assault, the trial judge violated Alaska R. Evid. 402 by allowing the State to present evidence of sixty prior instances of defendant's misconduct which had little or nothing to do with the offenses charged. **Bingaman v. State,** Op. No. 1895, 76 P.3d 398.

In an arrestee's suit against a city, a police officer, and an immigration officer alleging the use of excessive force during her arrest, the trial court did not abuse its discretion by prohibiting the arrestee from referencing the officer's involvement in an employment dispute with the city except as it related to the officer's counterclaim for intentional infliction of emotional distress where the officer's testimony in the arrestee's case had been taken numerous times before the officer filed his action against the city and where the trial court found that the officer's alleged wrongful conduct that was the subject of his suit against the city and the issues surrounding the allegations might have had some marginal relevance to whether the officer would have been biased in the city's favor but the very low probative value of the testimony would have been outweighed by a substantial degree of prejudice. **Samaniego v. City of Kodiak,** Op. No. 5751, 80 P.3d 216 (Alaska 2003).

In a driver's false confinement case against a city, a court did not err in precluding evidence regarding the driver's knife. The court acted within its discretion in finding that evidence of the knife could lead the jury to make its decision on an emotional basis or could confuse the jury because of uncertainty as to whether possessing the knife was legal. **City of Kodiak v. Samaniego,** Op. No. 5772, 83 P.3d 1077 (Alaska 2004).

Under the Smithart-Marrone rule, governing a criminal defendant's ability to introduce evidence tending to show that the crime was committed by someone else, evidence of another person's motive to commit the crime, or evidence of another person's opportunity to commit the crime, standing alone, will not be admissible when offered to prove that the other person may have committed the crime; the Smithart-Marrone rule can be thought of as an issue-specific application of this rule. **Cleveland v. State,** Op. No. 1934, 91 P.3d 965 (Alaska App. 2004).

Although the trial court did not err in admitting evidence of defendant's prior assaults on his girlfriend, it was an abuse of discretion to admit evidence of defendant's assaults on a prior girlfriend; that evidence did go to show defendant's tendency to become very angry in domestic situations, and to threaten violence, but the state had available much more relevant evidence to establish this character trait. **Riggins v. State,** Op. No. 1959, 101 P.3d 1060 (Alaska App. 2004).

In a tort suit brought by a senior citizen who fell in the shower area of a city-owned senior center, the superior court correctly admitted a redacted report indicating that the senior citizen suggested more safety bars; court properly weighed relevance against prejudice and determined that the report, redacted to exclude evidence of the remedial measures taken, was admissible. **City of Bethel v. Peters,** Op. No. 5829, 97 P.3d 822 (Alaska 2004).

Trial court did not err in allowing introduction of evidence of defendant's prior conviction for sexual assault during defendant's trial for sexual assault in the first degree; facts in the prior case were similar to the facts of the current charges against defendant, and the evidence was probative. **Mooney v. State,** Op. No. 1965, 105 P.3d 149 (Alaska App. 2005.

Court properly allowed evidence of defendant's entire course of non-consensual contact with the victim and her male friends where the evidence was relevant to the stalking charge against defendant; trial court repeatedly engaged in a balancing process in light of this rule before deciding whether to allow the state to introduce various portions of the evidence. **Kenison v. State,** Op. No. 1970, 107 P.3d 335 (Alaska App. 2005).

Trial court erred in refusing to allow defendant to introduce evidence of his interaction with the victim following the alleged sexual assault, where the evidence was important to allow the jury to evaluate the victim's credibility, and the probative value of the testimony was not outweighed by the danger of unfair prejudice **Snyder v. State,** Op. No. 1985, 113 P3d 683 (Alaska App. 2005).

In a medical malpractice case, defendant doctor's experts were properly allowed to testify where their testimony concerning the amount and kinds of information that patients generally wanted in late night phone calls was relevant to establish whether the doctor gave the patient as much information as a reasonable patient would want to know. **Marsingill v. O'Malley,** Op. No. 5977, 128 P.3d 151 (Alaska 2006).

Trial courts have broad discretion when applying the balancing test in this rule to determine the admissibility of disputed evidence, and their decisions are ordinarily subject to reversal on appeal only when a review of the record shows convincingly that an abuse of discretion occurred. **Bluel v. State**, Op. No. 11564, 153 P.3d 982 (Alaska 2007).

To decide the relative merits of conflicting claims regarding the admissibility of disputed evidence, a court will first examine the probative value of the evidence, then assess the potential prejudice of the refusal, and last, balance the danger of unfair prejudice against the evidence's probative value to determine whether the potential danger predominated so greatly as to show convincingly that admitting the challenged evidence amounted to a clear abuse of discretion under this rule. **Bluel v. State**, Op. No. 11564, 153 P.3d 982 (Alaska 2007).

Because Alaska's implied consent law gives drivers the right to decline further testing after failing the mandatory breath test and the law requires the state to honor a driver's choice, evidence of a driver's refusal of further testing, though relevant under Evidence Rule 401, creates a danger of unfair prejudice greatly outweighing the refusal's impeachment value and is inadmissible under Evidence Rule 403. **Bluel v. State**, Op. No. 11564, 153 P.3d 982 (Alaska 2007).

LAW REVIEW COMMENTARIES

"If you knew him like I did, you'd have shot him too…A survey of Alaska's Law of Self Defense," 23 Alaska L. Rev. 171 (2006).

Rule 404. Character Evidence Not Admissible to Prove Conduct—Exceptions—Other Crimes.

(a) **Character Evidence Generally.** Evidence of a person's character or a trait of character is not admissible for the purpose of proving that the person acted in conformity therewith on a particular occasion, except:

(1) *Character of Accused.* Evidence of a relevant trait of character offered by an accused, or by the prosecution to rebut the same;

(2) *Character of Victim.* Evidence of a relevant trait of character of a victim of crime offered by an accused, or by the prosecution to rebut the same, or evidence of a relevant character trait of an accused or of a character trait for peacefulness of the victim offered by the prosecution in a case to rebut evidence that the victim was the first aggressor, subject to the following procedure:

(i) When a party seeks to admit the evidence for any purpose, the party must apply for an order of the court at any time before or during the trial or preliminary hearing.

(ii) The court shall conduct a hearing outside the presence of the jury in order to determine whether the probative value of the evidence is outweighed by the danger of unfair prejudice, confusion of the issues, or unwarranted invasion of the privacy of the victim. The hearing may be conducted in camera where there is a danger of unwarranted invasion of the privacy of the victim.

(iii) The court shall order what evidence may be introduced and the nature of the questions which shall be permitted.

(iv) In prosecutions for the crime of sexual assault in any degree and attempt to commit sexual assault in any degree, evidence of the victim's conduct occurring more than one year before the date of the offense charged is presumed to be inadmissible under this rule, in the absence of a persuasive showing to the contrary.

(3) *Character of Witness.* Evidence of the character of a witness, as provided in Rules 607, 608, and 609.

(b) **Other Crimes, Wrongs, or Acts.**

(1) Evidence of other crimes, wrongs, or acts is not admissible if the sole purpose for offering the evidence is to prove the character of a person in order to show that the person acted in conformity therewith. It is, however, admissible for other purposes, including, but not limited to, proof of motive, opportunity, intent, preparation, plan, knowledge, identity, or absence of mistake or accident.

(2) In a prosecution for a crime involving a physical or sexual assault or abuse of a minor, evidence of other acts by the defendant toward the same or another child is admissible if admission of the evidence is not precluded by another rule of evidence and if the prior offenses

(i) occurred within the 10 years preceding the date of the offense charged;

(ii) are similar to the offense charged; and

(iii) were committed upon persons similar to the prosecuting witness.

(3) In a prosecution for a crime of sexual assault in any degree, evidence of other sexual assaults or attempted sexual assaults by the defendant against the same or another person is admissible if the defendant relies on a defense of consent. In a prosecution for a crime of attempt to commit sexual assault in any degree, evidence of other sexual assaults or attempted sexual assaults by the defendant against the same or another person is admissible.

(4) In a prosecution for a crime involving domestic violence or of interfering with a report of a crime involving domestic violence, evidence of other crimes involving domestic violence by the defendant against the same or another person or of interfering with a report of a crime involving domestic violence is admissible. In this paragraph, "domestic violence" and "crime involving domestic violence" have the meanings given in AS 18.66.990.

(Added and amended by SCO 364 effective August 1, 1979; amended by SCO 906 effective nunc pro tunc May 28, 1988; by SCO 1092 effective July 15, 1992; by SCO 1153 effective July 15, 1994; by SCO 1204 effective July 15, 1995; by SCO 1293 effective January 15, 1998; and by SCO 1339, effective June 13, 1998)

Note: SCO 906 incorporated changes in Evidence Rule 404 made by the legislature in ch. 66, §§ 8 and 9, SLA 1988. The legislation added subparagraph (b)(2).

Note: SCO 906 is amended by adding a new paragraph 3 which provides: "3. This order is made for the sole reason that the legislature has mandated the above amendments. If the act mandating these amendments is invalidated by a court of competent jurisdiction, this order shall be considered automatically rescinded." This amendment is effective retroactively to May 28, 1988. Paschall v. State, No. S-4277 (Alaska Dec. 20, 1990) (order granting original application for relief).

Note: Subparagraph (b)(1) was amended by ch. 79, § 4, SLA 1991.

Note to SCO 1204: Ch. 116 § 2 SLA 1994 amended Evidence Rules 404(a)(2) and 404(b) to allow circumstantial use of character evidence and evidence of other crimes in certain criminal cases. Section 8 of this order is adopted for the sole reason that the legislature has mandated the amendments.

Note to SCO 1293: Evidence Rule 404(b) (4) was added by § 22 ch. 63 SLA 1997. Section 5 of this order is adopted for the sole reason that the legislature has mandated the amendment.

Note to SCO 1339: Evidence Rule 404(b) (3) was amended by § 18 ch. 86 SLA 1998 to expand the circumstances when evidence of other sexual assaults or attempted sexual assaults by the defendant will be admitted. Section 3 of this order is adopted for the sole reason that the legislature has mandated the amendment.

Annotations

Cases

In prosecution for negligent homicide of 18-month-old child, where no defense of accident or mistake was raised, admission of evidence that defendant had on a prior occasion beaten another child to the point of leaving belt marks was reversible error. **Harvey v. State,** Op. No. 1996, 604 P2d 586 (Alaska 1979).

Evidence regarding prior confrontations between the defendant and trespassers was relevant and admissible to show that the defendant's pointing of a shotgun at the victim was not accidental or inadvertent. **Adkinson v. State,** Op. No. 2090,611 P2d 528 (Alaska 1980).

The giving of a jury instruction which drew attention to possible prejudicial inadmissible information regarding the accused was prejudicial error. **Keith v. State,** Op. No. 2099, 612 P2d 977 (Alaska 1980).

A defendant may offer evidence of a relevant character trait of a victim without its having the effect of granting to the prosecution the right to introduce evidence of defendant's character. **Keith v. State,** Op. No. 2099, 612 P2d 977 (Alaska 1980).

An unintentional reference at trial to defendant's probation did not violate this rule to the extent that a motion for mistrial should have been granted. **Preston v. State,** Op. No. 2146, 615 P2d 594 (Alaska 1980).

Trial court's refusal to permit defendant and others to testify concerning alleged prior instances of violent conduct committed by the victim toward third parties was not abuse of discretion where reputation and character evidence concerning the victim's propensity for violence had been admitted. **Loesch v. State,** Op. No. 2202, 620 P2d 646 (Alaska 1980).

Evidence of the circumstances of a prior rape committed by the defendant was properly admitted for the purpose of proving the identity of the assailant by showing a distinctive modus operandi employed in both the prior rape and the rape of the current victim. **Coleman v. State,** Op. No. 2190, 621 P2d 869 (Alaska 1980).

Evidence of drug use by the accused was admissible where it established direct contact between the victim and the accused and indicated that the accused possessed sufficient amounts of cocaine for him to have invested more than pocket cash in his purchase from the victim. **Dorman v. State,** Op. No. 2272, 622 P2d 448 (Alaska 1981).

Defendant's conduct at a store minutes after the armed robbery of another store for which he was accused was admissible to show that he was the same man who robbed the first store. **Vessel v. State,** Op. No. 2295, 624 P2d 275 (Alaska 1981).

In statutory rape case, evidence of defendant's prior sexual conduct with victim was admissible. **Burke v. State,** Op. No. 2194, 624 P2d 1240 (Alaska 1981).

Evidence that defendant had previously vandalized the aircraft of customers who refused to pay their bills is admissible to prove the motive and identity of defendant as the one who vandalized plaintiffs' aircraft for their refusal to pay their bill. **State v. Grogan,** Op. No. 2356, 628 P2d 570 (Alaska 1981).

The admission of evidence proscribed by this rule is harmless error if the evidence does not have a substantial influence on the jury's verdict. **Fields v. State,** Op. No. 2360, 629 P2d 46 (Alaska 1981).

When a defendant through testimony places his intent in issue, evidence of similar assaults previously committed against other women by defendant is admissible upon the issue of intent. **Davis v. State,** Op. No. 23, 635 P2d 481 (Alaska App. 1982).

In negligence action against waterbed manufacturer, it was error to allow testimony concerning post-accident conduct of manufacturer in not recalling the product or issuing a warning. **Amer. Nat. Watermattress Corp. v. Manville,** Op. No. 2477, 642 P2d 1330 (Alaska 1982).

Trial court did not err in refusing to sever assault charge, arising from an incident which took place on September 19, 1977, from murder charge based on an incident which occurred six days later, since defendant's actions could be viewed as a continuing course of conduct and since the assault charge would have been admissible in the murder trial to prove criminal intent or motive or to show a common scheme or plan even if the charges had been severed. **Davidson v. State,** Op. No. 78, 642 P2d 1383 (Alaska App. 1982).

Where the evidence in each of five rape and assault incidents was sufficiently similar and sufficiently unusual when viewed in its totality and in the common pattern it presented to constitute a modus operandi probative of defendant being the assailant in all instances, trial court did not err in denying defendant's request for severance of the various rape, burglary with intent to rape, and assault charges. **Nix v. State,** Op. No. 157, 653 P2d 1093 (Alaska App. 1982).

Evidence that victim had assisted defendant in forging a prescription and that defendant's friend had previously assaulted a pharmacist in attempting to pass the forged prescription was admissible to show defendant's motive for kidnapping. **Bidwell v. State,** Op. No. 199, 656 P2d 592 (Alaska App. 1982).

In murder case where defendant alleged that the victim attempted a homosexual rape, trial court did not err in excluding literature on aberrant sexual activity discovered in murder victim's safe. **Page v. State,** Op. No. 205, 657 P2d 850 (Alaska App. 1983).

While evidence of other misconduct by the accused is inadmissible under this rule when relevant only to establish a general propensity to commit the type of offense charged, presentation of such evidence may be permitted in the discretion of the trial court if it is relevant to establish facts specifically in issue and if its relevance outweighs the potential for prejudice that it might create. **Garibay v. State,** Op. No. 221, 658 P2d 1350 (Alaska App. 1983).

Proof of defendant's proprietary interest in and involvement with a massage parlor was relevant and admissible to establish that they knew of and were involved with off-premises prostitution activities conducted from the massage parlor. **Garibay v. State,** Op. No. 221, 658 P2d 1350 (Alaska App. 1983).

Bad checks written by defendant near the time when he wrote the bad check for which he was prosecuted were admissible to prove intent and absence of mistake. **Kelly v. State,** Op. No. 251, 663 P2d 967 (Alaska App. 1983).

In drunk driving prosecution, court erred in excluding evidence of defendant's reputation for sobriety. **Quinto v. City and Borough of Juneau,** Op. No. 265, 664 P2d 630 (Alaska App. 1983).

In assault prosecution in which defendant claims self-defense, trial judge did not err in granting protective orders which prevented defendant from questioning victim about charges for possession of a shotgun while intoxicated and assault with a dangerous weapon which were pending against the victim at the time of trial and from asking the victim about prior alcoholism and convictions for driving while intoxicated. **Dyer v. State,** Op. No. 268, 666 P2d 438 (Alaska App. 1983).

Evidence of specific instances of stabbing victim's violent conduct was necessary to enable the jury to determine how much force a reasonable person with defendant's knowledge of the victim's propensity for violence would have felt compelled to use in self-defense. **Amarok v. State,** Op. No. 303, 671 P2d 882 (Alaska App. 1983).

In homosexual rape case where the defense was based partly on consent, trial court did not abuse its discretion in excluding evidence that the complaining witness was homosexual. **Kvasnikoff v. State,** Op. No. 314, 674 P2d 302 (Alaska App. 1983).

Evidence showing that defendant and his alibi witness were incarcerated together had probative value on the issues of bias and opportunity for recent fabrication; accordingly, trial court did not err in denying defendant's motion for a protective order barring the prosecution from impeaching the witness with this evidence, particularly since the potential for prejudice was mitigated by the court's restriction against questions concerning the circumstances of the witnesses' offense or the issue of his guilt, together with a limiting instruction. **Dunbar v. State,** Op. No. 347, 677 P2d 1275 (Alaska App. 1984).

Where defendant in murder trial claimed that he was defending himself against a homosexual rape by the victim who lured him into a car by offering him Quaaludes, trial court erred in excluding the testimony of a witness who would have testified that he had had a similar encounter with the victim one year before, and the trial court also erred in excluding evidence that the police found Quaaludes in the victim's home during their investigation. **Williamson v. State,** Op. No. 430, 692 P2d 965 (Alaska App. 1984).

When a prior bad act is relevant to a material fact other than propensity, the court may admit the evidence if it is more probative than prejudicial. **Lerchenstein v. State,** Op. No. 453, 697 P2d 312 (Alaska App. 1985).

Trial court's limiting curative instruction was not sufficient to remove the prejudice presented by improperly admitted evidence. **Lerchenstein v. State,** Op. No. 453, 697 P2d 312 (Alaska App. 1985).

This rule is a rule of exclusion of evidence, not one of admission; when evidence of prior misconduct is involved, the trial court must begin with the assumption that the evidence should be excluded. **Lerchenstein v. State,** Op. No. 453, 697 P2d 312 (Alaska App. 1985).

In murder trial where self-defense was the issue, admission of evidence of recent prior bad acts of the defendant toward persons other than the victim was error notwithstanding the state's contention that the evidence was relevant to the question of whether defendant carried a gun to the crime scene in anticipation of a confrontation or merely pulled it from its customary place under his car seat and also relevant to defendant's state of mind at the time of the offense, since the evidence was to some extent cumulative and its prejudicial impact outweighed its probative value. **Lerchenstein v. State,** Op. No. 453, 697 P2d 312 (Alaska App. 1985).

Where defendant was charged with sexual offenses against his daughter, evidence of alleged sexual relations between defendant and his daughter before and after the dates specified in the indictment was admissible to establish the ongoing relationship between the defendant and his daughter, explaining in part the daughter's inability to specifically describe separate incidents. **Covington v. State,** Op. No. 491, 703 P2d 436 (Alaska App. 1985).

Where victim was hit on the head, had his hands and feet bound, his mouth stuffed with a sock, and had been shot in the head, trial judge properly denied admission of a prior "assault with intent to rob" conviction of a key prosecution witness which involved entering a hotel room with a club and hitting the victim on the head, since the two crimes were not sufficiently similar and unusual in their pattern to constitute a modus operandi probative of the witness being the assailant in both instances as alleged by the defense. **Adams v. State,** Op. No. 497, 704 P2d 794 (Alaska App. 1985).

The manner in which the state introduced a photo of defendant, taken in connection with an earlier investigation and used in a photographic lineup in which the victim identified the defendant, was prejudicial because it suggested prior bad acts, but the error was harmless. **Braaten v. State,** Op. No. 504, 705 P2d 1311 (Alaska App. 1985).

The prosecution should be required to give advance notice to the defendant and the court, out of the presence of the jury, of its intent to utilize any evidence of other crimes by defendant. **Moor v. State,** Op. No. 543, 709 P2d 498 (Alaska App. 1985).

Evidence of other crimes, in order to be admissible, need not be strictly necessary to the prosecution's case in the sense that failure to admit the evidence would leave the case subject to a motion for directed judgment of acquittal; however, the issue upon which the evidence is offered must be truly disputed in the case. **Moor v. State,** Op. No. 543, 709 P2d 498 (Alaska App. 1985).

Incidents of prior sexual abuse are not always admissible in sexual abuse cases to show a "lewd disposition." **Moor v. State,** Op. No. 543, 709 P2d 498 (Alaska App. 1985).

Trial court did not err in permitting the prosecution to cross-examine defense witness concerning earlier allegations that defendant had sexually molested her for the purpose of impeaching her testimony that she did not believe the victim's claim of molestation and to counter defendant's testimony of accident or mistake. **Moor v. State,** Op. No. 543, 709 P2d 498 (Alaska App. 1985).

Where defendant cross-examined the prosecution witness, his former girlfriend, concerning their bitter breakup in order to establish her bias, trial court erred in then allowing the state on redirect to inquire into all of the circumstances of the breakup, since it exceeded the doctrine of curative inadmissibility, which exists to permit introduction of otherwise inadmissible evidence only to the extent necessary to remove any unfair prejudice which might otherwise ensue from the original evidence. **Bentley v. State,** Op. No. 560, 711 P2d 544 (Alaska App. 1985).

In prosecution of defendant for manslaughter for causing the death of the 18-month-old son of his live-in girlfriend, trial judge did not abuse his discretion in admitting evidence which tended to indicate that defendant had abused the child on prior occasions. **Garnerv. State,** Op. No.569,711 P2d 1191 (Alaska App. 1986).

In prosecution of defendant for manslaughter in the death of the 18-month-old son of his live-in girlfriend, trial judge abused his discretion by precluding defendant from offering extrinsic evidence that a neighbor, who had also taken care of the child on the day the fatal injuries were inflicted, had abused her own child on prior occasions, since such evidence was critical to defendant's defense, which suggested that the neighbor had inflicted the fatal injuries. **Garner v. State,** Op. No. 569, 711 P2d 1191 (Alaska App. 1986).

Although trial court allowed testimony by sexual assault victim as to her virginity prior to the assault, it did not err in precluding defendant from cross-examining the victim regarding a prior incident in which the victim had allegedly been digitally penetrated by a school friend, since the probative value of the earlier incident as an alternative explanation for the perforation of the victim's hymen was very weak while the possible prejudice from invading her privacy unnecessarily and confusing the court issues was very high. **Oswald v. State,** Op. No. 594, 715 P2d 276 (Alaska App. 1986).

Evidence that defendant in sexual assault case had made sexual propositions to several other young girls was admissible to show design, scheme or plan, but not to establish motive. **Oswald v. State,** Op. No. 594, 715 P2d 276 (Alaska App. 1986).

The court did not abuse its discretion in finding that the probative value of admitting photographs of alleged child abuse victim's injuries outweighed the danger of unfair prejudice. **Sluka v. State,** Op. No. 606, 717 P2d 394 (Alaska App. 1986).

In prosecution for assault, court's order excluding inquiry into a prior false report by the complaining witness against the defendant for assault did not amount to reversible error, since such inquiry would have allowed the prosecution to elicit a full explanation of the circumstances underlying the prior report to the defendant's disadvantage. **Richey v. State,** Op. No. 611,717 P2d 407 (Alaska App. 1986).

Circumstances surrounding death of defendant's first child from a skull fracture while alone with defendant was admissible in trial of defendant for first degree assault against his second child, who also suffered a skull fracture while alone in defendant's care, to show that defendant's actions manifested an extreme indifference to human life. **Rhodes v. State,** Op. No. 613, 717 P2d 422 (Alaska App. 1986).

Error in jury instruction together with error in admission of certain character evidence constituted plain error. **Pletnikoff v. State,** Op. No. 625, 719 P2d 1039 (Alaska App. 1986).

In sexual assault case involving defendant who conceded having sexual intercourse with the alleged victim but denied using force, trial court erred in permitting the jury to consider the testimony of the victim's roommate regarding an unrelated sexual encounter she had with the defendant approximately one week before the incident in question, which was used to show that defendant had a character trait or propensity for forcibly seducing women by wining and dining them and falsely promising that he would advance their careers if they were nice to him. **Pletnikoffv. State,** Op. No. 625, 719 P2d 1039 (Alaska App. 1986).

Evidence of sexual acts which the defendant allegedly committed with victims other than those named in the indictment was not relevant to a material fact other than propensity, thus admission of the evidence constituted reversible error. **Bolden v. State,** Op. No. 632, 720 P2d 957 (Alaska App. 1986).

Where defendant was charged with sexually molesting his daughters, admission of evidence concerning his alleged sexual molestation of other young girls was reversible error, since neither intent nor identity were at issue and since the alleged acts were not admissible as evidence of a common scheme or plan. **Bolden v. State,** Op. No. 632, 720 P2d 957 (Alaska App. 1986).

Evidence of negligence in inspecting one plane is not admissible as proof of negligence in inspecting another plane, **Wickwire v. Arctic Circle Air Services,** Op. No. 3084, 722 P2d 930 (Alaska 1986).

In trial of defendant for sexual abuse of a six-year-old girl, trial court committed reversible error in allowing the State to present evidence of a prior uncharged sexual incident involving defendant and the same girl 18 months earlier. **Johnson v. State,** Op. No. 655, 727 P2d 1062 (Alaska App. 1986).

In sexual assault case where the defendant was the alleged victim's father, the "lewd disposition" exception to the exclusionary rule was properly extended to allow the testimony of the victim's sisters who were allegedly seduced under substantially similar circumstances and at roughly the same age. **Soper v. State,** Op. No. 675, 731 P2d 587 (Alaska App. 1987).

Evidence that defendant had been convicted of sexually assaulting the same girl two years prior to the incidents alleged in his current indictment for sexual abuse was properly admissible before the grand jury and at trial to establish the defendant had a significant sexual desire for that particular girl. **Patterson v. State,** Op. No. 681, 732 P2d 1102 (Alaska App. 1987).

In sexual assault prosecution where the defense was consent, the trial judge did not abuse his discretion in excluding evidence that the victim had posed for Penthouse Magazine and had acted in x-rated movies and had willingly told same to the defendant, which the defense offered for the purpose of showing that the defendant and the victim in the months prior to the assault had been involved in a relationship that was sexual, rather than merely platonic as alleged by the victim. **Wood v. State,** Op. No. 701, 736 P2d 363 (Alaska App. 1987).

In prosecution for attempted sexual abuse of a minor, trial court erred in allowing testimony about statements defendant made one week after the incident concerning his sexual fantasies and orientation since the testimony was clearly character evidence and was not relevant to show proof of motive, opportunity, intent, preparation, plan, knowledge, identity or absence of mistake or accident; nevertheless, due to the strength of the other evidence against defendant, the error was deemed harmless. **Stevens v. State,** Op. No. 773, 748 P2d 771 (Alaska App. 1988).

When a complaining witness testifies that he or she has been the subject of sexual or physical abuse and the defense seeks to discredit this testimony by showing that the witness' conduct was inconsistent with the claimed abuse and therefore that the claim of abuse was false, the state should be permitted to offer expert testimony that other members of the relevant class (i.e., abused or battered women or sexually abused children) characteristically exhibit such conduct even though they are, in fact, abused. **Anderson v. State,** Op. No. 771, 749 P2d 369 (Alaska App. 1988).

Before expert testimony seeking to establish that a person is a member of a particular class or group, i.e., battered women or sexually abused children, by showing that they exhibit behavioral characteristics common to that group, the proponent should establish, in a hearing out of the presence of the jury, that the probative value of the testimony outweighs its possible prejudicial effect; the trial court should require the proponent of such evidence to identify in advance what he or she intends to prove and why that evidence would be relevant to the case; furthermore, the court should consider the extent to which the expert witnesses' assumptions are shared by a consensus of those mental health practitioners knowledgeable about the subject matter. **Anderson v. State,** Op. No. 771, 749 P2d 369 (Alaska App. 1988).

In trial for attempted murder, the trial court did not err in admitting evidence of defendant's altercation with another person five hours prior to the attempted murder, since the altercation bore some causal connection to the reason the defendant and the victim came together, since the evidence gave the jury a complete picture of the series of events preceding the shooting, and since any prejudice caused by the evidence was minimal. **Ciervo v. State,** Op. No. 813, 756 P2d 907 (Alaska App. 1988).

In trial of defendant for the crime of terroristic threatening where the threats were made over the telephone a woman he read about in a newspaper story, trial court did not err in admitting evidence of defendant's involvement in a similar incident years before they establish that defendant acted knowingly. **Allen v. State,** Op. No. 830, 759 P2d 541 (Alaska App. 1988).

The prosecution may not introduce a profile to show that the defendant is more likely to have committed an offense because the defendant fits that profile. **Haakason v. State,** Op. No. 837, 760 P2d 1030 (Alaska App. 1988).

In trial of defendant for sex crimes against children, admission of policeman's testimony regarding a child sexual abuser profile was reversible error. **Haakason v. State,** Op. No. 837, 760 P2d 1030 (Alaska App. 1988).

In trial of defendant for sex crimes against children, admission of sexually suggestive statement by defendant to a girl not named in the indictment, on the ground that it was relevant to show defendant's state of mind, was error, there being no nonpropensity relevance to such evidence. **Haakason v. State,** Op. No. 837, 760 P2d 1030 (Alaska App. 1988).

In trial of defendant for sex crimes against children, admission of testimony by girls not named in the indictment concerning inappropriate physical behavior by defendant toward them was error. **Haakason v. State,** Op. No. 837, 760 P2d 1030 (Alaska App. 1988).

In sexual assault cases where identity is not an issue, proof of modus operandi is irrelevant. **Velez v. State,** Op. No. 852, 762 P2d 1297 (Alaska App. 1988).

In date rape cases, use of evidence of other sexual assaults by defendant against other victims to rebut a consent defense cannot be reconciled with Alaska Evidence Rules. **Velez v. State,** Op. No. 852, 762 P2d 1297 (Alaska App. 1988).

In prosecution for attempted sexual assault where the victim's testimony, if believed, made clear that the defendant's intentions were blatantly sexual, the use of evidence of other sexual assaults by defendant to corroborate the victim's testimony as to consent would have been pure propensity evidence prohibited by this rule. **Velez v. State,** Op. No. 852, 762 P2d 1297 (Alaska App. 1988).

Where defendant was charged with one count of sexual assault in the first degree and one count of attempted sexual assault in the first degree, each count involving a different incident and a different victim, and defendant was acquainted with each victim and claimed consent as a defense to the sexual assault charge, the trial court committed reversible error in denying defendant's motion for severance, since the evidence regarding the two charges was not cross admissible. **Velez v. State,** Op. No. 852, 762 P2d 1297 (Alaska App. 1988).

Where the defense witness in a DWI prosecution testified that she in fact had been driving the vehicle but traded places with the defendant because there was a warrant out for her arrest, the trial court did not commit error in permitting the state to cross-examine the witness on her prior DWI arrest and license suspension, since the knowledge that her license was suspended was directly relevant to her willingness to drive and since any additional prejudice was slight considering that the defendant introduced the issue. **Alward v. State,** Op. No. 901, 767 P2d 1175 (Alaska App. 1989).

In trial of defendant for refusing to submit to a breath test, trial court did not abuse its discretion in allowing the prosecution to present evidence of defendant's refusal to take a breath test on two other occasions for the purpose of discrediting defendant's assertion that he would have submitted to the breath test had he not been suffering from nose and chest injuries.

Callahan v. State, Op. No. 910, 769 P2d 444 (Alaska App. 1989).

This is a presumption that the prejudicial effect of propensity evidence outweighs its probative value; when, however, a prior bad act is relevant to a material fact other than propensity, the court may admit evidence of the prior bad act if it is more probative than prejudicial. **Mathis v. State,** Op. No. 951, 778 P2d 1161 (Alaska App. 1989).

In prosecution for murder, kidnapping, robbery and misconduct involving a controlled substance, any error in admitting testimony that the defendant sold cocaine on occasions unrelated to the criminal charges was harmless given the substantial evidence of the defendant's cocaine involvement properly admitted at the trial. **Mathis v. State,** Op. No. 951, 778 P2d 1161 (Alaska App. 1989).

Error in allowing police officer to refer to her "police report" during testimony, which arguably constituted evidence of a prior bad act by defendant, was harmless in light of the overwhelming evidence of guilt and fell far short of plain error. **Collins v. State,** Op. No. 962, 778 P2d 1171 (Alaska App. 1989).

In trial of defendant for sexual abuse of a minor, admission of testimony that defendant had been sexually abused by his father was prejudicial error requiring reversal of his conviction. **Nelson v. State,** Op. No. 981, 782 P2d 290 (Alaska App. 1989).

In trial of defendant for sexual abuse of a minor, a response by a prosecution witness which violated a protective order precluding evidence concerning defendant's interactions with other children was not a deliberate violation of the order nor was it so damaging as to compel a mistrial. **Nelson v. State,** Op. No. 981, 782 P2d 290 (Alaska App. 1989).

In trial of defendant for sexual abuse of a minor, a line of questioning by the prosecutor which made it clear that defendant was being investigated for similar crimes against other children was error; however, the error was deemed harmless because the challenged inquiry was relatively brief, defendant did not move for a mistrial, ask for a curative instruction, or suggest any other relief that was not granted. **Nelson v. State,** Op. No. 981, 782 P2d 290 (Alaska App. 1989).

In trial of defendant for sexual abuse of a minor, prosecutor's reference in this opening statement to pending charges against defendant for alleged abuse of the victim's brother was improper; however, because the brothers were permitted to testify, the impropriety, standing alone, did not justify a mistrial. **Nelson v. State,** Op. No. 981, 782 P2d 290 (Alaska App. 1989).

In trial of defendant for murder and assault in shooting of police officers, trial court did not err in allowing evidence of prior bad acts to be introduced before the jury, including evidence that defendant had been in prison before and would kill rather than go back; the evidence was relevant and highly probative to show defendant's motive and intent when he shot at the officers, thus trial court could find that the probative value of the evidence outweighed any prejudice. **Weitz v. State,** Op. No. 1058, 794 P2d 952 (Alaska App. 1990).

In determining whether to admit evidence of a prior bad act, the trial court must first determine that the evidence to be admitted has relevance apart from propensity and, secondly, must determine that the nonpropensity evidence outweighs the presumed highly prejudicial impact of the evidence. **Martin v. State,** Op. No. 1065, 797 P2d 1209 (Alaska App. 1990).

Where defendant was charged only with property crimes, a witness's reference to his prior criminal record together with the prosecutor's improper argument suggesting that defendant contemplated killing the arresting officer required reversal. **Martin v. State,** Op. No. 1065, 797 P2d 1209 (Alaska App. 1990).

In prosecution of defendant for selling drugs, trial court did not err in refusing to grant a mistrial motion after improper testimony by prosecution witness concerning prior drug sales by defendant; the question of whether to grant a mistrial as a result of improper evidence is committed to the sound discretion of the trial judge, and a cautionary instruction is often an appropriate remedy. **McPherson v. State,** Op. No. 1089, 800 P2d 928 (Alaska App. 1990).

In cocaine prosecution, grand jury testimony by defendant's girlfriend concerning her receipt on prior occasions of packages of cocaine, allegedly sent by defendant, was more probative than prejudicial, thus admissible, despite contention that it was inadmissible prior bad act evidence. **Castillo v. State,** Op. No. 1175, 821 P2d 133 (Alaska App. 1991).

Trial court in felon-in-possession prosecution could not, in reliance on defendant's willingness to concede existence of prior felony conviction, bar proof of prior-conviction element entirely and withdraw issue from jury. **State v. McLaughlin,** Op. No. 1316, 860 P2d 1270 (Alaska App. 1993).

Testimony that defendant was jealous of partner's more active role in shooting was not character evidence within scope of this rule; testimony tended to prove element of prosecution's case, i.e., that defendant acted with intent to promote or facilitate shooting. **Cheely v. State,** Op. No. 1317, 861 P2d 1168 (Alaska App. 1993).

In robbery trial judge did not err in admitting evidence that defendant and accomplices trafficked in and used cocaine since evidence was relevant to show that robbery was part of common scheme or plan to bankroll larger drug enterprise in which defendant participated. **Miller v. State,** Op. No. 1330, 866 P2d 130 (Alaska App. 1994).

In trial of defendant for violating fishing regulations, trial court committed reversible error in allowing arresting officer to testify that his presence at fishing site was prompted by report that defendant had fished illegally there the previous year. **Pavlik v. State,** Op. No. 1339, 869 P2d 496 (Alaska App. 1994).

Prosecutor's questions to defense psychiatrist in murder trial about his knowledge of another crime possibly committed by defendant were not barred by this rule since they were pertinent to jury's evaluation of psychiatrist's expert opinion and involved act that psychiatrist would reasonably rely on in reaching conclusion about defendant's capacity to act with intent to kill. **Nelson v. State,** Op. No. 1346, 874 P2d 298 (Alaska App. 1994).

In presentation of case to grand jury charging defendant with sexual abuse of minor, testimony that defendant gave victims marijuana was admissible as evidence of defendant's common scheme or plan to exchange drugs for sex. **Steve v. State,** Op. No. 1351, 875 P2d 110 (Alaska App. 1994).

In trial of defendant for first-degree assault where defense combined elements of self-defense and accident, judge erred in excluding evidence of victim's violent character, since evidence was relevant to show why defendant armed himself with knife prior to assault. **Gottschalk v. State,** Op. No. 1373, 881 P2d 1139 (Alaska App. 1994).

An **in camera** examination of a sexual assault victim to determine the admissibility of evidence reflecting on the victim's character should be deemed necessary only upon a threshold showing of good cause - that is, upon proof of a colorable ground to believe that character evidence favorable to the defense actually does exist and will be disclosed by the requested examination. **Johnson v. State,** Op. No. 1390, 889 P2d 1076 (Alaska App. 1995).

The mere existence of two generically similar reports of sexual assault made almost fourteen years before the complaining witness's current accusation does not amount to colorable grounds for believing that **in camera** examination of the witness was necessary under this rule. **Johnson v. State,** Op. No. 1390, 889 P2d 1076 (Alaska App. 1995).

Evidence of sexual assault complaining witness's previous false paternity claim had no bearing on her bias, prejudice, or motive to fabricate and did not establish a pattern or scheme of falsification on her part, It was classic propensity evidence and therefore inadmissible. **Johnson v. State,** Op. No. 1390, 889 P2d 1076 (Alaska App. 1995).

Evidence of a passenger's prior joyriding conviction was not, standing alone, relevant to the question of the accused's identity as the driver in the current joyriding prosecution and was properly excluded. **Jordan v. State,** Op. No. 1412, 895 P2d 994 (Alaska App. 1995).

Prior misconduct evidence should be more liberally admitted when it is offered against a witness instead of the accused. **Jordan v. State,** Op. No. 1412, 895 P2d 994 (Alaska App. 1995).

To reach the relaxed Evidence Rule 403 balancing analyses with regard to a witness's prior misconduct, the accused must first establish, under Evidence Rule 404(b), that the proffered evidence relates to some issue other than propensity. **Jordan v. State,** Op. No. 1412, 895 P2d 994 (Alaska App. 1995).

Evidence of sexual abuse of same girl two years before charged offense was admissible even under former Rule 404(b). **Peratrovich v. State,** Op. No. 1441, 903 P2d 1071 (Alaska App. 1995).

The current version of this rule exists because the legislature wished to make it easier for the prosecution to introduce evidence of a defendant's other acts of sexual or physical abuse. Evidence admissible under the former version of the rule is admissible under the current version. **Peratrovich v. State,** Op. No. 1441, 903 P2d 1071 (Alaska App. 1995).

Evidence that on the day of the assaults in question, defendant's estranged wife telephoned him to tell him she had a restraining order against him was properly admitted where the judge explained to the jury that restraining orders are generally entered **ex parte** and the verdicts in the case turned on the jury's evaluation of the defendant's intent, making the knowledge of and reaction to the restraining order relevant. **Rhames v. State,** Op. No. 1446, 907 P2d 21 (Alaska App. 1995).

Evidence of two prior sexual assault convictions was properly admissible in subsequent sexual assault and murder trial to show that the defendant murdered the victim by a distinctive **modus operandi** which he had also employed in the prior sexual assaults. **Harmon v. State,** Op. No. 1450, 908 P2d 434 (Alaska App. 1995).

Prior sexual assault convictions which were twelve years old by time of present sexual assault and murder were not so remote in time as not to be sufficiently probative of **modus operandi** because defendant had been incarcerated for eight of those twelve years and thus had not had an opportunity during those years to commit a similar assault. **Harmon v. State,** Op. No. 1450, 908 P2d 434 (Alaska App. 1995).

In trial of defendant charged with cruelty to animals for shooting dog, trial court did not err in admitting evidence of prior incident in which defendant shot another dog to establish motive and intent, **Brown v. Municipality of Anchorage,** Op. No. 1468, 915 P2d 654 (Alaska App. 1996).

Fact that arson defendant claimed responsibility for prior killing minutes before setting fire to cabin in which he was trapped was admissible to establish his state of mind, absence of accident, and motive on the arson charge. **West v. State,** Op. No. 1482, 923 P2d 110 (Alaska App. 1996).

In prosecution of defendant for violating stalking statute enacted in May of 1993, pre-May 1993 acts of defendant toward victim were admissible to show that victim did not consent to defendant's post-May 1993 contacts and that victim feared injury or death from defendant. **Petersen v. State,** Op. No. 1507, 930 P2d 414 (Alaska App. 1996).

Defendant's prior sexual assault on another woman was not admissible in sexual assault prosecution since it was not probative of opportunity, intent or absence of mistake or accident. **Lamont v. State,** Op. No. 1522, 934 P2d 774 (Alaska App. 1997).

Fact that 1994 amendment of this rule referred to evidence of a defendant's other sexual assaults did not mean that legislature intended to exclude evidence of a defendant's non-sexual assaults in sexual assault prosecutions. **Russell v. State,** Op. No. 1520, 934 P2d 1335 (Alaska App. 1997).

In prosecution of defendant for murder of roommate, prior incident in which roommate called police to apartment because he feared defendant was admissible. **Brodine v. State,** Op. No. 1526, 936 P2d 545 (Alaska App. 1997).

In prosecution of car dealership for several violations of Unfair Trade Practices and Consumer Protection Act, trial court did not abuse its discretion in denying defendant's motion for severance of the charges since (1) evidence of any given transaction was not offered for sole purpose of showing that defendant acted in conformity with some bad character trait, (2) any prejudice to defendant was limited by jury instruction, and (3) primary relief sought by state was permanent injunction, not damages. **Anchorage Nissan, Inc. v. State,** Op. No. 4850, 941 P2d 1229 (Alaska 1997).

In prosecution of car dealership for violation of Unfair Trade Practices and Consumer Protection Act, evidence that repurchased car was sold by dealership for salvage only was admissible as probative of credibility of dealership's witnesses who asserted throughout trial that car was safe even after the repurchase. **Anchorage Nissan, Inc. v. State,** Op. No. 4850, 941 P2d 1229 (Alaska 1997).

Trial judge correctly applied 1994 amendment to this rule at defendant's trial even though charged offense occurred prior to effective date of amendment. **Allen v. State,** Op. No. 1547, 945 P2d 1233 (Alaska App. 1997).

Amendment to this rule, allowing admission of evidence of relevant character traits of accused to rebut evidence that victim was first aggressor, did not violate due process guarantees. **Allen v. State,** Op. No. 1547, 945 P2d 1233 (Alaska App. 1997).

In murder case where defendant claimed self-defense, evidence rules limited state to proving defendant's character for violence by means of reputation or opinion evidence, and barred state from introducing evidence of specific instances of defendant's violence. **Allen v. State,** Op. No. 1547, 945 P2d 1233 (Alaska App. 1997).

In prosecution of defendant for sexual assault and murder of 11-year-old girl, defense evidence that parents had accused potential suspect of having sex with their 15-year-old daughter was inadmissible absent foundational showing of when sex occurred and how alleged act of consensual sex was similar to abduction, sexual assault and murder of victim. **Smithart v. State,** Op. No. 1553, 946 P2d 1264 (Alaska App. 1997).

Where evidence indicated that young female victim had entered vehicle prior to being sexually assaulted and murdered, evidence that defendant had offered rides to two young girls with strikingly similar facial features to murder victim in weeks prior to murder was admissible. **Smithart v. State,** Op. No. 1553, 946 P2d 1264 (Alaska App. 1997).

In prosecution of defendant of violent sexual assault, evidence of defendant's violent assault on another woman just hours before was admissible to show state of mind. **Hoffman v. State,** Op. No. 1562, 950 P2d 141 (Alaska App. 1997).

Murder defendant's false statements to friend following death of defendant's wife that wife had premonitions of death and had made funeral preparations were relevant to demonstrate defendant's consciousness of guilt, and probative value of statements outweighed potential prejudicial effect. **Sakeagak v. State,** Op. No. 1568, 952 P2d 278 (Alaska App. 1998).

Admission of marginally relevant prior bad acts of defendant to prove defendant's state of mind and to rebut defendant's claim of necessity to crimes charged was not abuse of discretion given limiting instruction to jury. **Clark v. State,** Op. No. 1572, 953 P2d 159 (Alaska App. 1998).

Admission of other misconduct on issue of intent is permitted only if intent is seriously disputed and if evidence of other misconduct is similar to act of misconduct with which accused is charged. **Clark v. State,** Op. No. 1572, 953 P2d 159 (Alaska App. 1998).

In prosecution of defendant for attempter kidnapping and attempted sexual assault of two teenage girls, admission, as relevant evidence of defendant's intent, that defendant had sexually assaulted three other women was reversible error; circumstances of earlier assaults, which involved adult women, were not similar enough to current charges to justify admission under this rule. **Clark v. State,** Op. No. 1572, 953 P2d 159 (Alaska App. 1998).

Where major disputed issue in prosecution for second degree theft of jewelry was whether defendant recklessly disregarded fact that jewelry was stolen, admission of defendant's prior convictions for forgery and theft was reversible error; past criminal acts were not shown to bear relevant factual similarity to charged offense and proved little of relevance except defendant's proclivity to lie and steal. **Calapp v. State,** Op. No. 1590, 959 P2d 385 (Alaska App. 1998).

In suit by parents of injured newborn baby against midwife claiming midwife negligently caused injury by panicking when shoulder dystocia occurred during delivery, parents' contention that trial court erred in admitting evidence of midwife's lack of panic during other deliveries was rejected; most of the allegedly inadmissible character evidence consisted of testimony directly describing midwife's experience, knowledge and competency in dealing with dystocia, which was not character evidence, and to extent character evidence was admitted, it was either justified by parents' suggestion that midwife panicked or was clearly harmless. **Miller v. Phillips,** Op. No. 4998, 959 P2d 1247 (Alaska 1998).

Testimony about city's negligence in fighting one fire was not admissible as proof of negligence in fighting another. **Adams v. City of Tenakee Springs,** Op. No. 5026, 963 P2d 1047 (Alaska 1998).

In prosecution of defendant for burglary and theft, evidence that Ketchikan police phoned Juneau police to alert them that defendant was suspected burglar was admissible, with limiting instruction, to explain officers' interest in defendant. **Silvertsen v. State,** Op. No. 1600, 963 P2d 1069 (Alaska App. 1998).

In trial of defendant for rape and murder of eleven-year-old girl, evidence that prosecution witness, whom defendant alleged committed the crime, had consensual affair with fifteen-year-old girl constituted impermissible prosperity evidence under this rule since it was not probative of any disputed issue in the case. **Smithart v. State,** Op. No. 5183, 988 P2d 583 (Alaska 1999).

In prosecution for crime of domestic violence, evidence of other crimes involving domestic violence by defendant did not require proof of conviction to be admissible. **State v. Bingaman,** Op. No. 1651, 991 P2d 227 (Alaska App. 1999).

Evidence Rule 404(b)(3) authorizes admission of evidence of defendant's other sexual assaults and attempted sexual assaults when, in trial for sexual assault, defendant raises defense of consent; evidence of other assaults is admissible to prove defendant's propensity to commit sexual assaults. **Wardlow v. State,** Op. No. 1676, 2 P3d 1238 (Alaska App. 2000).

When evidence of other sexual assaults is admissible under Evidence Rule 404(b)(3) to prove defendant's propensity to commit sexual assaults, trial judge must still consider whether evidence should be excluded or limited pursuant to Evidence Rule 403; tendency of evidence to prove defendant's propensity to commit sexual assaults can no longer be deemed unfair prejudice, but other aspects of the evidence can be unfairly prejudicial or can be cumulative, misleading or confusing. **Wadlow v. State,** Op. No. 1676, 2 P3d 1238 (Alaska App. 2000).

In prosecution of defendant for third-degree assault for threatening his former girlfriend, defendant's argument that Evidence Rule 404(b)(4), pursuant to which defendant's prior acts of domestic violence against girlfriend were admitted for "propensity" purposes, is unconstitutional on due process and equal protection grounds was rejected. **Fuzzard v. State,** Op. No. 1709, 13 P3d 1163 (Alaska App. 2000).

Traditional ban on propensity evidence is not rooted in the constitution; any potential for abuse of character evidence can be adequately addressed by the rules of evidence. **McGill v. State,** Op. No. 1718, 18 P3d 77 (Alaska App. 2001).

In sexual assault trial, defendant's arguments that admission under this rule of evidence of other sexual assaults committed by defendant violated due process by permitting jury to infer that defendant had a propensity to commit sexual assault and violated his constitutional right not to be held to answer for a crime unless it is charged by indictment or information were rejected. **McGill v. State,** Op. No. 1718, 18 P3d 77 (Alaska App. 2001).

In sexual assault prosecution where the defense was consent and the state was allowed to present evidence of a prior sexual assault by defendant against a different victim, trial court committed reversible error in denying defendant's request that jury be informed of his acquittal on the prior sexual assault charge, since the evidence of that acquittal was relevant and not hearsay, its potential for confusion did not outweigh its potential probative value, and its exclusion was prejudicial to defendant. **Hess v. State,** Op. No. 5386, 20 P3d 1121 (Alaska 2001).

Where the challenged evidence was offered under Alaska R. Evid. 404(b)(1), and the State's theory of admissibility rested on an implicit assertion concerning defendant's sexual propensities, the appellate court found that the State failed to show the primary foundational facts that defendant's conduct with the three-year-old was similar to the offense charged or that defendant's conduct with an 11 year-old boy was similar to his conduct with an 8 year-old girl, and the admission of the evidence was prejudicial to the defendant because the State's case was not overwhelming. **Carpentino v. State,** Op. No. 1781, 38 P3d 547 (Alaska App. 2002).

There were significant differences between defendant's 1990 assault on a previous victim and the facts of the current case; thus the trial court abused its discretion when it allowed the state to introduce evidence of the 1990 assault; the 1990 assault was relevant, but only because it tended to establish defendant's propensity to commit rape. The evidence was therefore barred by Alaska R. Evid. 404(b)(1). **Nicholia v. State,** Op. No. 1769, 34 P3d 344 (Alaska App. 2001).

Where defendants' crimes were committed within a close temporal and physical proximity to each other, apparently involved the same perpetrators, and consisted of similar attacks on the victims, the evidence of each crime was cross-admissible under Alaska R. Evid. 404(b)(1) to prove state of mind and sequence of events. **Pease v. State,** Op. No. 1830, 54 P.3d 316 (Alaska App. 2002).

Alaska R. Evid. 402 governs all evidence offered under Alaska R. Evid. 404(b)(4). **Bingaman v. State,** Op. No. 1895, 76 P.3d 398 (Alaska App. 2003).

In prosecutions for crimes involving domestic violence, Alaska R. Evid. 404(b)(4) authorizes the court to admit evidence of the defendant's other acts of domestic violence even though the sole relevance of those acts is to show that the defendant characteristically commits such acts, so that the defendant's character can be taken as circumstantial evidence that the defendant acted true to character during the episode being litigated. **Bingaman v. State,** Op. No. 1895, 76 P.3d 398 (Alaska App. 2003).

In a criminal prosecution for assault and sexual assault, the trial judge violated Alaska R. Evid. 402 by allowing the State to present evidence of sixty prior instances of defendant's misconduct which had little or nothing to do with the offenses charged. **Bingaman v. State,** Op. No. 1895, 76 P.3d 398 (Alaska App. 2003).

The Smithart-Marrone rule, governing a criminal defendant's ability to introduce evidence tending to show that the crime was committed by someone else, is similar to this rule in that it restricts the admission of certain evidence only when that evidence is offered for a particular purpose, including the purpose of trying to show that some identified other person may have committed the crime. **Cleveland v. State,** Op. No. 1934, 91 P.3d 965 (Alaska App. 2004).

Defense attorney's proposed inference concerning brother's character was not self-evident from a single incident of assaultive behavior against victim, his sister, in May 2001; defendant was required to offer some additional evidence of the relationship between the victim and her brother to show that the May 2001 assault was part of a pattern of domestic violence or abuse before the evidence of the May 2001 assault could be introduced into evidence. **Cleveland v. State,** Op. No. 1934, 91 P.3d 965 (Alaska App. 2004).

Ruling that defendant could not introduce character evidence unless he testified was error; where defendant chose to testify he could not appeal the error, which was harmless. **Gross v. State,** Op. No. 1945, 96 P.3d 525 (Alaska App. 2004).

Although the trial court did not err in admitting evidence of defendant's prior assaults on his girlfriend, it was an abuse of discretion to admit evidence of defendant's assaults on a prior girlfriend; that evidence did go to show defendant's tendency to become very angry in domestic situations, and to threaten violence, but the state had available much more relevant evidence to establish this character trait. **Riggins v. State,** Op. No. 1959, 101 P.3d 1060 (Alaska App. 2004).

Trial court did not err in allowing introduction of evidence of defendant's prior conviction for sexual assault during defendant's trial for sexual assault in the first degree; facts in the prior case were similar to the facts of the current charges against defendant, and the evidence was probative. **Mooney v. State,** Op. No. 1965, 105 P3d 149 (Alaska App. 2005).

Court properly allowed evidence of defendant's entire course of non-consensual contact with the victim and her male friends where the evidence was relevant to the stalking charge against defendant; trial court repeatedly engaged in a balancing process in light of this rule before deciding whether to allow the state to introduce various portions of the evidence. **Kenison v. State,** Op. No. 1970, 107 P.3d 335 (Alaska App. 2005).

Evidence of past incidents of child abuse should have been allowed into evidence in a domestic violence proceeding because it was relevant; the non-disclosure order seeking to bar its presentation was contrary to public policy and void. **Lana C. v. Cameron P.,** Op. No. 5875, 108 P3d 896 (Alaska 2005).

Although previous false charges made by an alleged victim were admissible, it was not error to deny defendant's request to offer evidence that the victim's mother had made previous false charges of sexual abuse against other parties. **Bryant v. State,** Op. No. 1990, 115 P.3d 1249 (Alaska App. 2005).

It was not error to allow the State to admit hearsay evidence that tended to show that defendant had a sexual interest in minor children when defendant had offered testimony on his own behalf to portray defendant as having a benign and benevolent, non-sexual relationship with children in his life, including the alleged victim. **Bryant v. State,** Op. No. 1990, 115 P.3d 1249 (Alaska App. 2005).

Trial court properly admitted evidence of prior domestic assault between the same parties under both this rule's subsection (b)(4) to prove defendant's propensity to commit domestic violence and subsection (b)(1) to prove the nature of parties' relationship. Where defendant did not ask the trial court to give a cautionary instruction that evidence of other acts of domestic violence, standing alone, is insufficient to support a defendant's conviction, he was not entitled to the instruction. This instruction is mandatory only if the defendant requests it, or when the amount and nature of other crimes evidence introduced against the defendant demonstrates that the failure to give this instruction would amount to plain error. **Douglas v. State,** Op. No. 8799, 151 P.3d 495 (Alaska App. 2006).

LAW REVIEW COMMENTARIES

"If you knew him like I did, you'd have shot him too…A survey of Alaska's Law of Self Defense," 23 Alaska L. Rev. 171 (2006).

Rule 405. Methods of Proving Character.

(a) **Reputation or Opinion.** In all cases in which evidence of character or a trait of character of a person is admissible, proof may be made by testimony as to reputation in any community or group in which the individual habitually associated or by testimony in the form of an opinion. On cross-examination, inquiry is allowable into relevant specific instances of conduct.

(b) **Specific Instances of Conduct.** In cases in which character or a trait of character of a person is an essential element of a charge, claim, or defense, proof may also be made of specific instances of conduct.

(Added by SCO 364 effective August 1, 1979; amended by SCO 1522 effective October 15, 2003)

Annotations

Cases

When hearsay evidence has been presented to a grand jury, character evidence concerning the hearsay declarant's credibility is permissible to the same extent to which it would be permissible at trial had the declarant's character been challenged. **Putnam v. State,** Op. No. 2251, 629 P2d 35 (Alaska 1980).

In negligence action against waterbed manufacturer, it was error to allow testimony concerning post-accident conduct of manufacturer in not recalling the product or issuing a warning. **Amer. Nat. Watermattress Corp. v. Manville,** Op. No. 2477, 642 P2d 1330 (Alaska 1982).

Evidence of specific instances of stabbing victim's violent conduct was necessary to enable the jury to determine how much force a reasonable person with defendant's knowledge of the victim's propensity for violence would have felt compelled to use in self-defense. **Amarok v. State,** Op. No. 303, 671 P2d 882 (Alaska App. 1983).

In trial of defendant for first-degree assault where defense combined elements of self-defense and accident, judge erred in excluding evidence of victim's violent character, since evidence was relevant to show why defendant armed himself with knife prior to assault. **Gottschalk v. State,** Op. No. 1373, 881 P2d 1139 (Alaska App. 1994).

In prosecution of car dealership for violation of Unfair Trade Practices and Consumer Protection Act, evidence that repurchased car was sold by dealership for salvage only was admissible as probative of credibility of dealership's witnesses who asserted throughout trial that car was safe even after the repurchase. **Anchorage Nissan, Inc. v. State,** Op. No. 4850, 941 P2d 1229 (Alaska 1997).

In murder case where defendant claimed self-defense, evidence rules limited State to proving defendant's character for violence by means of reputation or opinion evidence, and barred State from introducing evidence of specific instances of defendant's violence. **Allen v. State,** Op. No. 830, 759 P2d 541 (Alaska App. 1988).

LAW REVIEW COMMENTARIES

"If you knew him like I did, you'd have shot him too…A survey of Alaska's Law of Self Defense," 23 Alaska L. Rev. 171 (2006).

Rule 406. Habit—Routine Practice.

Evidence of the habit of a person or of the routine practice of an organization, whether corroborated or not and regardless of the presence of eyewitnesses, is relevant to prove that the conduct of the person or organization on a particular occasion was in conformity with the habit or routine practice.

(Added by SCO 364 effective August 1, 1979)

Annotations

Cases

In a case involving a liquor licensee's liability for an accident caused by an intoxicated customer, trial court did not err in allowing witnesses to testify that on other occasions the licensee had served liquor to drunken persons. **Tommy's Elbow Room, Inc. v. Kavorkian,** Op. No. 3132, 727 P2d 1038 (Alaska 1986).

Rule 407. Subsequent Remedial Measures.

When, after an event, measures are taken which, if taken previously, would have made the event less likely to occur, evidence of the subsequent measures is not admissible to prove negligence or culpable conduct in connection with the event. This rule does not require the exclusion of evidence of subsequent measures when offered for another purpose, such as impeachment or, if controverted, proving ownership, control, feasibility of precautionary measures, or defective condition in a products liability action.

(Added by SCO 364 effective August 1, 1979)

Annotations

Cases

The evidentiary rule precluding admission of post-injury accidents or design changes toward proof of negligence is inapplicable in products liability cases based on strict liability. **Caterpillar Tractor Co. v. Beck,** Op. No. 2304, 624 P2d 790 (Alaska 1981).

In a products liability action, evidence of subsequent remedial measures is admissible to prove the feasibility of alternative designs as well as to prove a defective condition. **Dura Corp. v. Harned,** Op. No. 2952, 703 P2d 396 (Alaska 1985).

In personal injury action brought against oil company for injuries suffered by plaintiff when he fell into a "seismic" hole at an oil drilling site, trial court properly denied defendant's motion in limine which sought to exclude evidence that defendant had erected barricades and flashing lights around the seismic hole following the accident, since such evidence was relevant to show who had control over the accident site. **Exxon Corp. v. Alvey,** Op. No. 2883, 690 P2d 733 (Alaska 1984).

Upon determining that evidence of remedial repairs genuinely impeaches a witness, trial court must next determine whether the impeachment value outweighs the prejudicial implication of negligence. **Agostino v. Fairbanks Clinic,** Op. No. 3718, 821 P2d 714 (Alaska 1991).

In action for injuries sustained in fall on allegedly icy sidewalk, in which evidence of remedial repairs by defendant's employee appeared to have genuine impeachment value, trial court abused its discretion in excluding the evidence absent pretrial evidentiary hearing to determine whether the prejudicial effect of the evidence outweighed its impeachment value. **Agostino v. Fairbanks Clinic,** Op. No. 3718, 821 P2d 714 (Alaska 1991).

This rule excludes "subsequent measures" that would have reduced the likelihood of the accident if they had been "taken previously," meaning before the accident; one cannot investigate an accident before it occurs, so an investigation and report cannot be a measure that is excluded. **City of Bethel v. Peters,** Op. No. 5829, 97 P.3d 822.

Rule 408. Compromise and Offers to Compromise.

Evidence of (1) furnishing or offering or promising to furnish or (2) accepting or offering or promising to accept, a valuable consideration in compromising or attempting to compromise a claim which was disputed as to either validity or amount, is not admissible to prove liability for or invalidity of the claim or its amount. Evidence of conduct or statements made in compromise negotiations is likewise not admissible. This rule does not require the exclusion of any evidence otherwise discoverable merely because it is presented in the course of compromise negotiations. This rule also does not require exclusion when the evidence is offered for another purpose, such as proving bias or prejudice of a witness, negativing a contention of undue delay, or proving an effort to obstruct a criminal investigation or prosecution, but exclusion is required where the sole purpose for offering the evidence is to impeach a party by showing a prior inconsistent statement.

(Added by SCO 364 effective August 1, 1979)

Annotations

Cases

Evidence of discussions and statements made at a time when the parties agreed on the validity and the amount of the claim, but were negotiating remedies, was not excludable under this rule. **Alaska Statebank v. Kirschbaum,** Op. No. 2654, 662 P2d 939 (Alaska 1983).

Because of settlement agreement between codefendants, representatives of one defendant might be motivated to slant their testimony in favor of the other defendant and vice-versa, thus trial court did not err in allowing use of the settlement agreement to show witness bias, notwithstanding that codefendant's status as parties would suggest that their representatives might be biased in favor of the party employing them. **Frontier Companies v. Jack White Co.,** Op. No. 3759, 818 P2d 645 (Alaska 1991).

At hearing before Public Employees' Retirement Board concerning claim for occupational disability benefits, Board did not abuse its discretion by excluding compromise and release agreement between claimant and state from evidence; although agreement contained admission by state that claimant's injury was work-related, reliability of admission was low since it could represent state's desire for peace rather than any concession of weakness of position. **Lopez v. Adm'r, Pub. Emples. Retirement Sys.,** Op. No. 5383, 20 P3d 568 (Alaska 2001).

Rule 409. Payment of Medical and Similar Expenses.

Evidence of furnishing or offering or promising to pay medical, hospital, or similar expenses occasioned by an injury is not admissible to prove liability for the injury.

(Added by SCO 364 effective August 1, 1979)

Rule 410. Inadmissibility of Plea Discussions in Other Proceedings.

(a) Evidence of a plea of guilty or nolo contendere, or of an offer to plead guilty or nolo contendere to the crime charged or any other crime, or of statements or agreements made in connection with any of the foregoing pleas or offers, is not admissible in any civil or criminal action, case or proceeding against the government or an accused person who made the plea or offer if:

(i) A plea discussion does not result in a plea of guilty or nolo contendere, or

(ii) A plea of guilty or nolo contendere is not accepted or is withdrawn, or

(iii) Judgment on a plea of guilty or nolo contendere is reversed on direct or collateral review.

(b) This rule shall not apply to (1) the introduction of voluntary and reliable statements made in court on the record in connection with any of the foregoing pleas when offered in subsequent proceedings as prior inconsistent statements, and (2) proceedings by a defendant to attack or enforce a plea agreement.

(Added by SCO 364 effective August 1, 1979)

Rule 411. Liability Insurance.

Evidence that a person was or was not insured against liability is not admissible upon the issue whether the person acted negligently or otherwise wrongfully. This rule does not require the exclusion of evidence of insurance against liability when offered for another purpose, such as proof of agency, ownership, or control, or bias or prejudice of a witness.

(Added by SCO 364 effective August 1, 1979; amended by SCO 1153 effective July 15, 1994)

Annotations

Cases

When examining a defendant's conduct to determine whether punitive damages are appropriate, it should make no difference that the defendant is insured or uninsured; accordingly, where jury responded "no" to question on special verdict form on whether plaintiff was entitled to punitive damages, exclusion of evidence of liability insurance was, if error, merely harmless error, even though defendant was allowed to present evidence to demonstrate his inability to absorb a punitive damage award. **Shane v. Rhines,** Op. No. 2750, 672 P2d 895 (Alaska 1983).

Where liability was not an issue in victim's suit against driver, evidence of driver's insurance coverage focused on the relevance of insurance to the driver's financial condition, a purpose not excluded by Alaska R. Evid. 411. **Fleegel v. Estate of Boyles,** Op. No. 5641, 61 P.3d 1267 (Alaska 2002).

Rule 412. Evidence Illegally Obtained.

Evidence illegally obtained shall not be used over proper objection by the defendant in a criminal prosecution for any purpose except:

(1) a statement illegally obtained in violation of the right to warnings under Miranda v. Arizona, 384 U.S. 436 (1966), may be used in

(A) a prosecution for perjury if the statement is relevant to the issue of guilt or innocence and if the prosecution shows that the statement was otherwise voluntary and not coerced; or

(B) any prosecution, to impeach the defendant, codefendant, or a former defendant in the case who made the statement if the prosecution shows that the statement was

(i) otherwise voluntary and not coerced; and

(ii) recorded, if required by law, or has been determined to be covered by one of the recognized exceptions to the recording requirement; and

(2) other evidence illegally obtained may be admitted in

(A) a prosecution for perjury if it is relevant to the issue of guilt or innocence and if the prosecution shows that the evidence was not obtained in substantial violation of rights of the defendant; or

(B) any criminal action, to impeach the defendant, codefendant, or a former defendant in the case, if the prosecution shows that the evidence

(i) was the product of a statement illegally obtained in violation of the right to warnings under Miranda v. Arizona, 384 U.S. 436 (1966); and

(ii) was not obtained in substantial violation of the rights of the defendant, codefendant, or a former defendant in the case, as appropriate.

(Added by SCO 364 effective August 1, 1979; amended by SCO 1556 effective July 22, 2004)

Note: Chapter 16 § 1 SLA 2004 amended Evidence Rule 412 to allow evidence illegally obtained to be used to impeach a defendant, codefendant, or former defendant in a case, under specified circumstances. Section IV of this order is adopted for the sole reason that the legislature has mandated the amendments.

Annotations

Cases

Where the arrest is lawful, fact that arresting officer uses excessive force does not make the evidence obtained as a result of the arrest the product of illegality. **Martin v. State,** Op. No. 2298, 623 P2d 1225 (Alaska 1981).

Illegally seized evidence may be considered in fashioning a sentence when the illegally seized evidence is reliable, when the police conduct involved in obtaining the evidence does not shock the conscience of the court, and when it is clear that the evidence was not obtained for purposes of influencing the sentencing judge. **Elson v. State,** Op. No. 40, 633 P2d 292 (Alaska App. 1982).

The traditional requirement of standing has not been abrogated in search and seizure cases by adoption of this rule. **G.R. v. State,** Op. No. 61, 638 P2d 191 (Alaska App. 1982).

Defendant did not have standing to argue that his confession should be suppressed on the ground that it was the product of an illegal arrest and detention of his companion. **G.R. v. State,** Op. No. 61, 638 P2d 191 (Alaska App. 1981).

Defendant had no standing to object to police officers' contact with his building manager and no right to seek suppression of the evidence derived from her even if the contact was the result of a trespassory entrance into the apartment building. **Hubert v. State,** Op. No. 62, 638 P2d 677 (Alaska App. 1981).

Defendant had standing to contest the illegal arrest of codefendant which led to defendant's confession. **Unger v. State,** Op. No. 65, 640 P2d 151 (Alaska App. 1982).

This rule, which permits evidence illegally obtained to be used under certain circumstances in perjury prosecutions, applies to such evidence regardless of the basis for determining that it was illegally obtained. **Wortham v. State,** Op. No. 69, 641 P2d 223 (Alaska Op. No. 1982).

Suppression of illegally obtained evidence in defendant's cocaine prosecution was not res judicata nor did it collaterally estop the state from using the evidence in defendant's subsequent perjury prosecution where there was no suggestion that this rule was considered at the first suppression hearing. **Wortham v. State,** Op. No. 69, 641 P2d 223 (Alaska App. 1982).

Illegally obtained tape recording of conversation between defendant and undercover police agent which was properly suppressed at defendant's drug trial was admissible at defendant's subsequent perjury trial where the recording was made in good faith and was not an intentional violation of the law. **Wortham v. State,** Op. No. 214, 657 P2d 856 (Alaska App. 1983).

Although this rule is not necessarily limited to violations of constitutional rights, it does not automatically apply to violations of all statutes. **Harker v. State,** Op. No. 2665, 663 P2d 932 (Alaska 1983).

Illegally obtained tape recording of conversation between defendant and undercover police agent was admissible at defendant's perjury trial. **Wortham**

v. State, Op. No. 2697, 666 P2d 1042 (Alaska 1983).

This rule contains a standing requirement for search and seizure violations, but under the Alaska Constitution there are exceptions to the requirement. **Waring v. State,** Op. No. 2719, 670 P2d 357 (Alaska 1983).

A defendant has standing to assert the violation of a codefendant's fourth amendment rights if he or she can show (1) that a police officer obtained the evidence as a result of gross or shocking misconduct, or (2) that the officer deliberately violated the co-defendant's rights. **Waring v. State,** Op. No. 2719, 670 P2d 357 (Alaska 1983).

Assuming, without deciding, that the warnings received by defendant regarding his testimony at a coroner's inquest were less than adequate to safeguard his right to remain silent, his testimony was nevertheless not involuntary or the product of coercion; therefore, his testimony at the coroner's inquest could be used against him in subsequent trial for perjury. **Esmailka v. State,** Op. No. 721, 740 P2d 466 (Alaska App. 1987).

Exclusionary rule did not apply to error by trial court in using telephonic testimony in support of search warrant without following statutory procedure since violation of statute was not in bad faith and since there was no claim that absent telephonic testimony warrant would have been invalid. **Burrece v. State,** Op. No. 1618, 976 P2d 241 (Alaska App. 1999).

ARTICLE V. PRIVILEGES

Rule 501. Privileges Recognized Only as Provided.

Except as otherwise provided by the Constitution of the United States or of this state, by enactments of the Alaska Legislature, or by these or other rules promulgated by the Alaska Supreme Court, no person, organization, or entity has a privilege to:

(1) refuse to be a witness; or

(2) refuse to disclose any matter; or

(3) refuse to produce any object or writing; or

(4) prevent another from being a witness or disclosing any matter or producing any object or writing.

(Added by SCO 364 effective August 1, 1979)

Rule 502. Required Reports Privileged by Statute.

A person, corporation, association, or other organization or entity, either public or private, making a return or report required by law to be made has a privilege to refuse to disclose and to prevent any other person from disclosing the return or report, if the law requiring it to be made so provides. A public officer of an agency to whom a return or report is required by law to be made has a privilege to refuse to disclose the return or report if the law requiring it to be made so provides. No privilege exists under this rule in actions involving perjury, false statements, fraud in the return or report, or other failure to comply with the law in question.

(Added by SCO 364 effective August 1, 1979)

Rule 503. Lawyer—Client Privilege.

(a) **Definitions.** As used in this rule:

(1) A client is a person, public officer, or corporation, association, or other organization or entity, either public or private, who is rendered professional legal services by a lawyer, or who consults a lawyer with a view to obtaining professional legal services.

(2) A representative of the client is one having authority to obtain professional legal services and to act on advice rendered pursuant thereto, on behalf of the client.

(3) A lawyer is a person authorized, or reasonably believed by the client to be authorized, to practice law in any state or nation.

(4) A representative of the lawyer is one employed to assist the lawyer in the rendition of professional legal services.

(5) A communication is confidential if not intended to be disclosed to third persons other than those to whom disclosure is in furtherance of the rendition of professional legal services to the client or those reasonably necessary for the transmission of the communication.

(b) **General Rule of Privilege.** A client has a privilege to refuse to disclose and to prevent any other person from disclosing confidential communications made for the purpose of facilitating the rendition of professional legal services to the client, (1) between the client or the client's representative and the client's lawyer or the lawyer's representative, or (2) between the client's lawyer and the lawyer's representative, or (3) by the client or the client's lawyer to a lawyer representing another in a matter of common interest, or (4) between representatives of the client or between the client and a representative of the client, or (5) between lawyers representing the client.

(c) **Who May Claim the Privilege.** The privilege may be claimed by the client, the client's guardian or conservator, the personal representative of a deceased client, or the successor, trustee, or similar representative of a corporation, association, or other organization, whether or not in existence. The person who was the lawyer at the time of the communication may claim the privilege but only on behalf of the client. The authority to do so is presumed in the absence of evidence to the contrary.

(d) **Exceptions.** There is no privilege under this rule:

(1) *Furtherance of Crime or Fraud.* If the services of the lawyer were sought, obtained or used to enable or aid anyone to commit or plan to commit what the client knew or reasonably should have known to be a crime or fraud; or

(2) *Claimants Through Same Deceased Client.* As to a communication relevant to an issue between parties who claim through the same deceased client, regardless of whether the claims are by testate or intestate succession or by inter vivos transaction; or

(3) *Breach of Duty by Lawyer or Client.* As to a communication relevant to an issue of breach of duty by the lawyer to the client or by the client to the lawyer; or

(4) *Document Attested by Lawyer.* As to a

communication relevant to an issue concerning an attested document to which the lawyer is an attesting witness; or

(5) *Joint Clients.* As to a communication relevant to a matter of common interest between two or more clients if the communication was made by any of them to a lawyer retained or consulted in common, when offered in an action between any of the clients.

(Added by SCO 364 effective August 1, 1979; amended by SCO 1153 effective July 15, 1994; and by SCO 1522 effective October 15, 2003)

Annotations

Cases

Defendant was a "client" within the meaning of the attorney-client privilege when she communicated with an employee of a law firm in order to obtain legal advice, notwithstanding that the law firm had not yet accepted her case and that only raw facts, not legal points, were discussed. **Amer. Nat. Watermattress Corp. v. Manville,** Op. No. 2477, 642 P2d 1330 (Alaska 1982).

In drunk driving prosecution in which the defendant had an independent blood test performed, by hospital personnel at his request to verify the accuracy of the police intoximeter examination, admission of expert testimony regarding the blood test did not violate the attorney-client privilege, since no lawyer participated in defendant's decision to take the blood test, nor did it violate the physician-patient privilege, since the physician-patient privilege does not apply in criminal cases. **Russell v. Municipality of Anchorage,** Op. No. 514, 706 P2d 687 (Alaska App. 1985).

Statements made by an insured to an insurer are not protected by the attorney-client privilege unless it can be shown that the insurer, in receiving such communications, was acting at the express direction of counsel for the insured. **Langdon v. Champion,** Op. No. 3291, 752 P2d 999 (Alaska 1988).

While the attorney-client privilege protects communications regarding acts which the client may have committed prior to seeking representation, it will not protect communications which pertain to ongoing or future wrongdoing. **Munn v. Bristol Bay Housing Authority,** Op. No. 3458, 777 P2d 188 (Alaska 1989).

An attorney for a party is no more entitled to withhold information than any other potential witness, and may be required to testify at a deposition or trial as to material, nonprivileged matters. **Munn v. Bristol Bay Housing Authority,** Op. No. 3458, 777 P2d 188 (Alaska 1989).

Plaintiff would be entitled to depose defendant's attorney if plaintiff could present a prima facie case that defendants consulted the attorney for the purpose of interfering with plaintiff's employment relationship, since such conduct comes within the civil fraud exception to the attorney-client privilege; accordingly, trial court erred in quashing plaintiff's notice and subpoena for the taking of the deposition without considering whether he had made a prima facie showing that the information sought was not protected by the attorney-client privilege. **Munn v. Bristol Bay Housing Authority,** Op. No. 3458, 777 P2d 188 (Alaska 1989).

Services sought by a client from an attorney in aid of any crime or a bad faith breach of a duty are not protected by the attorney-client privilege. **Central Const. Co. v. Home Indem. Co.,** Op. No. 3606, 794 P2d 595 (Alaska 1990).

Before engaging in an in camera review to determine the applicability of the "crime of fraud" exception to the attorney-client privilege, the judge should require a showing of a factual basis adequate to support a good faith belief by reasonable person that in camera review of the materials may review evidence to establish the claim that the crime-fraud exception applies. **Central Const. Co. v. Home Indem. Co.,** Op. No. 3606, 794 P2d 595 (Alaska 1990).

In action by tort claim obligee against insurance company for bad faith inaction by the insurance company as surety on performance and payment bonds, trial court erred in denying the obligee discovery of the existence and amount of any loss reserve the insurance company may have established regarding the claims; the existence and amount of a loss reserve is not a protected confidential communication made for the purpose of facilitating the rendition of professional legal services nor is it prepared in anticipation of litigation. **Loyal Order of Moose v. Intern. Fidelity,** Op. No. 3626, 797 P2d 622 (Alaska 1990).

Where the state had DWI defendant's blood tested by its own experts, thereby obtaining blood test results without relying on the work of anyone hired or consulted by the defense, the blood sample itself, although drawn on the advice of the defendant's attorney, was not covered by the attorney-client privilege. **Birch v. State,** Op. No. 1198, 825 P2d 901 (Alaska App. 1992).

Attorney-client privilege was applicable to executive session of borough board of equalization which was called to obtain advice from board's attorney on how board members could avoid legal liability in tax dispute. **Cool Homes v. Fairbanks North Star Bor.,** Op. No. 4016, 860 P2d 1248 (Alaska 1993).

The obligation of confidentiality imposed by Professional Conduct Rule 1.6(a) does not expand the attorney-client privilege codified in Evidence Rule 503. **Downie v. Superior Court,** Op. No. 1389, 888 P2d 1306 (Alaska App. 1995).

The fact of communication of public information from an attorney to a client is not protected by the attorney-client privilege. **Downie v. Superior Court,** Op. No. 1389, 888 P2d 1306 (Alaska App. 1995).

A defense attorney may be compelled to testify concerning whether she informed her client of his trial date. **Downie v. Superior Court,** Op. No. 1389, 888 P2d 1306 (Alaska App. 1995).

The attorney-client privilege only ceases to exist for ongoing and future wrongdoing, not past wrongdoing. **Matter of Mendel,** Op. No. 4223, 897 P2d 68 (Alaska 1995).

Deposition questions to attorney regarding attorney's authority to represent client would require disclosure of confidential communications made for the purpose of facilitating the rendition of professional services to the client, thus the answers to the questions fell within the scope of the attorney-client privilege. **Matter of Mendel,** Op. No. 4223, 897 P2d 68 (Alaska 1995).

In most circumstances attorney-client privilege does not shield attorney from disclosing fact that client had contacted attorney or attorney's firm. **Moudy v. Superior Court,** Op. No. 1605, 964 P2d 469 (Alaska App. 1998).

Attorney-client privilege does not protect attorney's act of communicating trial date to client; this is true whether trial date was communicated to client directly by attorney or, alternatively, by attorney's staff. **Moudy v. Superior Court,** Op. No. 1605, 964 P2d 469 (Alaska App. 1998).

Rule 504. Physician and Psycho-therapist—Patient Privilege.

(a) **Definitions.** As used in this rule:

(1) A patient is a person who consults or is examined or interviewed by a physician or psychotherapist.

(2) A physician is a person authorized to practice medicine in any state or nation, or reasonably believed by the patient so to be.

(3) A psychotherapist is (A) a person authorized to practice medicine in any state or nation, or reasonably believed by the patient to be so, while engaged in the diagnosis or treatment of a mental or emotional condition, including alcohol or drug addiction, (B) a person licensed or certified as a psychologist or psychological examiner under the laws of any state or nation or reasonably believed by the patient so to be, while similarly engaged, (C) a person licensed as a marital or family therapist under the laws of a state or nation or reasonably believed by the patient so to be, while similarly engaged, or (D) a person licensed as a professional counselor under the laws of a state or nation, or reasonably believed by the patient so to be, while similarly engaged.

(4) A communication is confidential if not intended to be disclosed to third persons other than those present to further the interest of the patient in the consultation, examination, or interview, or persons reasonably necessary for the transmission of the communication, or persons who are participating in the diagnosis and treatment under the direction of the physician or psychotherapist, including members of the patient's family.

(b) **General Rule of Privilege.** A patient has a privilege to refuse to disclose and to prevent any other person from disclosing confidential communications made for the purpose of diagnosis or treatment of the patient's physical, mental or emotional conditions, including alcohol or drug addiction, between or among the patient, the patient's physician or psychotherapist, or persons who are participating in the diagnosis or treatment under the direction of the physician or psychotherapist, including members of the patient's family.

(c) **Who May Claim the Privilege.** The privilege may be claimed by the patient, by the patient's guardian, guardian ad litem or conservator, or by the personal representative of a deceased patient. The person who was the physician or psychotherapist at the time of the communication is presumed to have authority to claim the privilege but only on behalf of the patient.

(d) **Exceptions.** There is no privilege under this rule:

(1) *Condition on Element of Claim or Defense.* As to communications relevant to the physical, mental or emotional condition of the patient in any proceeding in which the condition of the patient is an element of the claim or defense of the patient, of any party claiming through or under the patient, of any person raising the patient's condition as an element of that person's own case, or of any person claiming as a beneficiary of the patient through a contract to which the patient is or was a party; or after the patient's death, in any proceeding in which any party puts the condition in issue.

(2) *Crime or Fraud.* If the services of the physician or psychotherapist were sought, obtained or used to enable or aid anyone to commit or plan a crime or fraud or to escape detection or apprehension after the commission of a crime or a fraud.

(3) *Breach of Duty Arising Out of Physician-Patient Relationship.* As to a communication relevant to an issue of breach, by the physician, or by the psychotherapist, or by the patient, of a duty arising out of the physician-patient or psychotherapist-patient relationship.

(4) *Proceedings for Hospitalization.* For communications relevant to an issue in proceedings to hospitalize the patient for physical, mental or emotional illness, if the physician or psychotherapist, in the course of diagnosis or treatment, has determined that the patient is in need of hospitalization.

(5) *Required Report.* As to information that the physician or psychotherapist or the patient is required to report to a public employee, or as to information required to be recorded in a public office, if such report or record is open to public inspection, or as to information or matters contained in or reasonably raised by a report submitted under AS 08.64.336, other than information that would establish the identity of a patient, unless the court finds that it is necessary to admit the identifying information in order to serve the interests of justice.

(6) *Examination by Order of Judge.* As to communications made in the course of an examination ordered by the court of the physical, mental or emotional condition of the patient, with respect to the particular purpose for which the examination is ordered unless the judge orders otherwise. This exception does not apply where the examination is by order of the court upon the request of the lawyer for the defendant in a criminal proceeding in order to provide the lawyer with information needed so that the lawyer may advise the defendant whether to enter a plea based on insanity or to present a defense based on the defendant's mental or emotional condition.

(7) *Criminal Proceeding.* For physician-patient communications in a criminal proceeding. This exception does not apply to the psychotherapist-patient privilege.

(Added by SCO 364 effective August 1, 1979; amended by SCO 850 effective January 15, 1988; by SCO 1108 effective January 15, 1993; by SCO 1153 effective July 15, 1994; by SCO 1337 effective March 1, 1999; and by SCO 1522 effective October 15, 2003)

Note: SCO 1108 incorporated changes in Evidence Rule 504(a)(3) made by the legislature in ch. 129 § 12 SLA 1992. This legislation added the language in subparagraph (a)(3), "or (C) a person licensed as a marital or family therapist under the laws of a state or nation or reasonably believed by the patient so to be, while similarly engaged."

SCO 1108 was entered for the sole reason that the legislature has mandated the above amendment. If ch. 129 § 12 SLA 1992 is invalidated by a court of competent jurisdiction, SCO 1108 shall be considered automatically rescinded.

Note to SCO 1337: Evidence Rule 504(a)(3) was amended by § 5 ch. 75 SLA 1998 to expand the definition of "psychotherapist" to include licensed professional counselors. Section 1 of this order is adopted for the sole reason that the legislature has mandated the amendment.

Annotations

Cases

The state enactment of the child abuse reporting statute did not abrogate the psychotherapist/patient privilege in child abuse cases. **State v. R.H.,** Op. No. 375, 683 P2d 269 (Alaska App. 1984).

Child abuse reports are not open to the public and therefore are not within the exception to the psychotherapist/patient privilege for information required to be recorded in a public office and open to public inspection. **State v. R.H.,** Op. No. 375, 683 P2d 269 (Alaska App. 1984).

Where court-ordered psychiatric examination of defendant clearly pertained to a child protection proceeding, the exception to the psychotherapist/patient privilege for certain court-ordered examination did not apply to testimony before a grand jury investigating a criminal charge against defendant, since preparing evidence for the grand jury was not the purpose for which the psychiatric examination was ordered. **State v. R.H.,** Op. No. 375, 683 P2d 269 (Alaska App. 1984).

In drunk driving prosecution in which the defendant had an independent blood test performed by hospital personnel at his request to verify the accuracy of the police intoximeter examination, admission of expert testimony regarding the blood test did not violate the attorney-client privilege, since no lawyer participated in defendant's decision to the take the blood test, nor did it violate the physician-patient privilege, since the physician-patient privilege does not apply in criminal cases. **Russell v. Municipality of Anchorage,** Op. No. 514, 706 P2d 687 (Alaska App. 1985).

Defense counsel in a personal injury action may engage in informal ex parte interviews with a plaintiff 's treating physician, but the physician cannot be compelled to submit to such interviews. **Langdon v. Champion,** Op. No. 3249, 745 P2d 1371 (Alaska 1987).

The psychotherapist-patient privilege is waived unless someone acts at trial to exercise the privilege. **Clifton v. State,** Op. No. 826, 758 P2d 1279 (Alaska App. 1988).

Where defendant told his minister, who was also a certified counselor, that he had sexually abused a child, the minister's report of the crime to the police did not violate the psychotherapist-patient or communication with clergy privileges. **Walstad v. State,** Op. No. 1165, 818 P2d 695 (Alaska App. 1991).

Admission at children's court waiver hearing of expert testimony concerning psychological evaluation of defendant that had been submitted pursuant to court order in previous delinquency proceeding did not violate psychotherapist-patient privilege. **M.R.S. v. State,** Op. No. 1334, 867 P2d 836 (Alaska App. 1994).

Basic principles of statutory construction provide guidance in interpreting this Rule. **M.R.S. v. State,** Op. No. 4219, 897 P2d 63 (Alaska 1995).

Communications made in the source of a court-ordered examination do qualify as "confidential communications" for purpose of this rule. **M.R.S. v. State,** Op. No. 4219, 897 P2d 63 (Alaska 1995).

Admission of a 1990 court-ordered psychological examination of a juvenile at a 1992 waiver hearing violated the juvenile's psychotherapist-patient privilege. **M.R.S. v. State,** Op. No. 4219, 897 P2d 63 (Alaska 1995).

A doctor's excuse sent to the patient's employer is not shielded by the rule. **In re Exxon Valdez,** 270 F.3d 1215 (9th Cir. 2001).

Trial court did not err in denying the crime victim's request to seal part of the sentencing hearing because none of the challenged statements contained information protected by the psychotherapist-patient privilege, and she did not file a contemporaneous objection. Under Alaska R. Evid. 510, the holder of an evidentiary privilege waives the privilege if she voluntarily consents to disclosure of any significant part of the matter or the communication. **Cooper v. Dist. Court,** Op. No. 2043, 133 P.3d 692 (Alaska App. 2006).

Rule 505. Husband-Wife Privileges.

(a) **Spousal Immunity.**

(1) *General Rule.* A husband shall not be examined for or against his wife, without his consent, nor a wife for or against her husband, without her consent.

(2) *Exceptions.* There is no privilege under this subdivision:

(A) In a civil proceeding brought by or on behalf of one spouse against the other spouse; or

(B) In a proceeding to commit or otherwise place a spouse, the property of a spouse or both the spouse and the property of the spouse under the control of another because of the alleged mental or physical condition of the spouse; or

(C) In a proceeding brought by or on behalf of a spouse to establish the spouse's competence; or

(D) In a proceeding in which one spouse is charged with:

(i) A crime against the person or the property of the other spouse or of a child of either, whether such crime was committed before or during marriage.

(ii) Bigamy, incest, adultery, pimping, or prostitution.

(iii) A crime related to abandonment of a child or nonsupport of a spouse or child.

(iv) A crime prior to the marriage.

(v) A crime involving domestic violence as defined in AS 18.66.990.

(E) In a proceeding involving custody of a child.

(F) Evidence derived from or related to a business relationship involving the spouses.

(b) **Confidential Marital Communications.**

(1) *General Rule.* Neither during the marriage nor afterwards shall either spouse be examined as to any confidential communications made by one spouse to the other during the marriage, without the consent of the other spouse.

(2) *Exceptions.* There is no privilege under this subdivision:

(A) If any of the exceptions under subdivision (a) (2) of this rule apply; or

(B) If the communication was made, in whole or in part, to enable or aid anyone to commit or plan to commit a crime or a fraud; or

(C) In a proceeding between a surviving spouse and a person who claims through the deceased spouse, regardless of whether such claim is by testate or intestate succession or by inter vivos transaction; or

(D) In a criminal proceeding in which the communication is offered in evidence by a defendant who is one of the spouses between whom the communication was made; or

(E) In a proceeding under the Rules of Children's Procedure; or

(F) If the communication was primarily related to and made in the context of a business relationship involving both spouses or the spouses and third parties.

(Added by SCO 364 effective August 1, 1979; amended by SCO 823 effective August 1, 1987; by SCO 1269 effective July 15, 1997; and by SCO 1522 effective October 15, 2003)

Note to SCO 1269: Evidence Rule 505(a) was amended by § 70 ch. 64 SLA 1996. Section 13 of this order is adopted for the sole reason that the legislature has mandated the amendment.

Annotations

Cases

Where defendant forcibly entered his wife's residence without permission and shot her boyfriend in her presence, wife's testimony against defendant was permissible under the "necessity" or "crimes-against-the-other" exception to the privilege against adverse spousal testimony. **Loesch v. State,** Op. No. 2202, 620 P2d 646 (Alaska 1980).

When there is conclusive evidence that a marriage is in fact destroyed, the trial court may properly rule that the state's interest in a spouse's testimony outweighs the defendant spouse's interest in suppressing it. **Loesch v. State,** Op. No. 2202, 620 P2d 646 (Alaska 1980).

Trial court correctly dispensed with the spousal testimonial immunity privilege where defendant married on the eve of trial and had a strong motivation to prevent the testimony of the woman he married. **Osborne v. State,** Op. No. 2291, 623 P2d 784 (Alaska 1981).

Crimes against foster children are within the exception to the husband wife privilege under this rule. **Daniels v. State,** Op. No. 357, 681 P2d 341 (Alaska App. 1984).

Rule 506. Communications to Clergymen.

(a) **Definitions.** As used in this rule:

(1) A member of the clergy is a minister, priest, rabbi, or other similar functionary of a religious organization, or an individual reasonably believed so to be by the person consulting the individual.

(2) A communication is confidential if made privately and not intended for further disclosure except to other persons present in furtherance of the purpose of the communication.

(b) **General Rule of Privilege.** A person has a privilege to refuse to disclose and to prevent another from disclosing a confidential communication by the person to a member of the clergy in that individual's professional character as spiritual adviser.

(c) **Who May Claim the Privilege.** The privilege may be claimed by the person, by the person's guardian or conservator, or by the person's personal representative if the person is deceased. The member of the clergy may claim the privilege on behalf of the person. The authority so to do is presumed in the absence of evidence to the contrary.

(Added by SCO 364 effective August 1, 1979; amended by SCO 1153 effective July 15, 1994)

Annotations

Cases

Where defendant told his minister, who was also a certified counselor, that he had sexually abused a child, the minister's report of the crime to the police did not violate the psychotherapist-patient or communications with clergy privileges. **Walstad v. State,** Op. No. 1165, 818 P2d 695 (Alaska App. 1991).

Person claiming clergyman-communicant privilege is required to prove four things: (1) that he subjectively believed that conversation with clergyman was being held in private; (2) that this belief was reasonable under the circumstances; (3) that he intended that the communication not be disclosed to anyone except in furtherance of its purpose of obtaining spiritual guidance; and (4) that he reasonably believed that this intention was shared by the clergyman. **Plate v. State,** Op. No. 1493, 925 P2d 1057 (Alaska App. 1996).

Rule 507. Political Vote.

Every person has a privilege to refuse to disclose the tenor of the person's vote at a political election conducted by secret ballot unless the vote was cast illegally.

(Added by SCO 364 effective August 1, 1979; amended by SCO 1522 effective October 15, 2003)

Rule 508. Trade Secrets.

A person has a privilege, which may be claimed by the person or the person's agent or employee, to refuse to disclose and to prevent other persons from disclosing a trade secret owned by the person, if the allowance of the privilege will not tend to conceal fraud or otherwise work injustice. When disclosure is directed, the judge shall take such protective measures as the interests of the holder of the privilege and of the parties and the furtherance of justice may require.

(Added by SCO 364 effective August 1, 1979; amended by SCO 1153 effective July 15, 1994)

Rule 509. Identity of Informer.

(a) **Rule of Privilege.** The United States, the State of Alaska and sister states have a privilege to refuse to disclose the identity of a person who has furnished information relating to or assisting in an investigation of a possible violation of law to a law enforcement officer or member of a legislative committee or its staff conducting an investigation.

(b) **Who May Claim.** The privilege may be claimed by an appropriate representative of the public entity to which the information was furnished by the informer.

(c) **Exceptions.**

(1) *Voluntary Disclosure—Informer a Witness.* No privilege exists under this rule if the identity of the informer or the informer's interest in the subject matter of the communication has been disclosed to those who would have cause to resent the communication by a holder of the privilege or by the informer's own action, or if the informer appears as a witness for the prosecution.

(2) *Testimony on Merits.*

(i) If a party claims that a government informer may be able to give testimony necessary to a fair determination of the issue of guilt, innocence, credibility of a witness testifying on the merits, or punishment in a criminal case, or of a material issue on the merits in a civil case to which the state is a party, and if the government invokes the privilege, the party shall be given an opportunity to show that the party's claim is valid. The judge shall hear all evidence presented by the party and the government, and both sides shall be permitted to be present with counsel during the presentation of evidence, subject to subdivision (c) (2) (ii) of this rule.

(ii) If the government requests an opportunity to submit to the court, by affidavit or testimony or otherwise, evidence concerning the information possessed by an informant, which submission might tend to reveal the informant's identity, the judge shall permit the government to make its submission without disclosure to the other party. Neither the attorney for the government, nor the other party or the other party's attorney may be present when the judge is examining the in camera submission. Although the submission generally will consist of affidavits, the judge may direct that witnesses appear before the judge, without the government or the other party present, to give testimony.

(iii) If the judge finds that there is a reasonable possibility that the informant can give the testimony sought, and if the government elects not to disclose the informant's identity, the judge shall, either on motion of a party or sua sponte, dismiss criminal charges to which the testimony would relate if the informant's testimony is material to guilt or innocence. In criminal proceedings in which the informant's testimony is not material to guilt or innocence and in civil proceedings the judge may make any order that justice requires.

(iv) Evidence submitted to the judge shall be sealed and preserved to be made available to the appellate court in the event of an appeal, and the contents shall not otherwise be revealed without consent of the government.

(3) *Legality of Obtaining Evidence.*

(i) When a defendant challenges the legality of the means by which evidence was obtained by the prosecution and the prosecution relies upon information supplied by an informer to support its claim of legality, if the judge is not satisfied that the information was received from an informer reasonably believed to be reliable or credible the judge may require the identity of the informer to be disclosed. In determining whether or not to require disclosure, the judge shall hear any evidence offered by the parties and both the defendant and the government shall have the right to be represented by counsel.

(ii) If the judge determines that disclosure of the informant's identity is necessary, upon request by the prosecution the disclosure shall be made to the court alone, not to the defendant. The judge may, if necessary, examine the informant or other witnesses about the informant, but such examination will be in camera and neither the defendant nor the prosecution shall be present or represented.

(iii) If disclosure of the identity of the informer is made to the court and not to the defendant, the record thereof shall be sealed and preserved to be made available to the appellate court in the event of an appeal, and the contents shall not otherwise be revealed without consent of the prosecution.

(Added by SCO 364 effective August 1, 1979; amended by SCO 1153 effective July 15, 1994)

Annotations

Cases

This rule protects only the identity of an informant, and not the information he or she provides. **Balentine v. State,** Op. No. 538, 707 P2d 922 (Alaska App. 1985).

To the extent the privilege for informants' identities denies the constitutionally guaranteed trial rights of a defendant, it may not be applied. **Balentine v. State,** Op. No. 538, 707 P2d 922 (Alaska App. 1985).

Trial court's decision not to compel disclosure of information relating to the case obtained by police through calls to the "crime stoppers" program, a program which solicits information from the public concerning crimes under investigation, did not substantially impair the fairness of defendant's trial, or otherwise impermissibly infringe upon his constitutionally protected trial rights. **Balentine v. State,** Op. No.538,707 P2d 922 (Alaska App. 1985).

The informer's privilege of this rule applied to airline employees who found marijuana while searching a package and reported it to the police. **Peterson v. State,** Op. No. 1139, 813 P2d 685 (Alaska App. 1991).

In drug case where an issue was whether the police investigation was the product of an illegal search by police informants and the state asserted its privilege not to identify the informants, and the judge conducted an in camera hearing in which he questioned the informants using questions submitted by the defendant and the state and concluded that the identity of the informants did not have to be revealed, the defendant was entitled to see the transcript of the in camera hearing with all information deleted that might identify the informants. **Peterson v. State,** Op. No. 1139, 813 P2d 685 (Alaska App. 1991).

Only the informer's identity is privileged under this rule; communications to and from the informer are not privileged except to the extent that disclosure would operate also to disclose the informer's identity. **Wilson v. State,** Op. No. 1700, 12 P3d 210 (Alaska App. 2000).

This rule does not authorize the government or a court to keep a search warrant application secret after the search has been conducted and the defendant publicly charged with a crime; the government is privileged to conceal or redact only those portions of the application that identify an informant. **Wilson v. State,** Op. No. 1700, 12 P3d 210 (Alaska App. 2000).

Trial court abused its discretion in keeping search warrant affidavit sealed to prevent disclosure of governmental informant following the search and the indictment of the defendant; only a few passages of the affidavit contained information that would disclose the informant's identity, and those passages could easily be paraphrased or edited so that the gist of those passages could be made public without disclosing details that would identify the informant. **Wilson v. State,** Op. No. 1700, 12 P3d 210 (Alaska App. 2000).

Rule 510. Waiver of Privilege by Voluntary Disclosure.

A person upon whom these rules confer a privilege against disclosure of the confidential matter or communication waives the privilege if the person or the person's predecessor while holder of the privilege voluntarily discloses or consents to disclosure of any significant part of the matter or communication. This rule does not apply if the disclosure is itself a privileged communication.

(Added by SCO 364 effective August 1, 1979; amended by SCO 1153 effective July 15, 1994)

Annotations

Cases

Trial court did not err in denying the crime victim's request to seal part of the sentencing hearing because none of the challenged statements contained information protected by the psychotherapist-patient privilege pursuant to Alaska R. Evid. 504, and she did not file a contemporaneous objection. Under this rule, the holder of an evidentiary privilege waives the privilege if she voluntarily consents to disclosure of any significant part of the matter or the communication. **Cooper v. Dist. Court,** Op. No. 2043, 133 P.3d 692 (Alaska App. 2006).

Rule 511. Privileged Matter Disclosed Under Compulsion or Without Opportunity to Claim Privilege.

Evidence of a statement or other disclosure of privileged matter is not admissible against the holder of the privilege if the disclosure was (a) compelled erroneously or (b) made without opportunity to claim the privilege.

(Added by SCO 364 effective August 1, 1979)

Annotations

Cases

This rule deals only with disclosures that were impermissible when originally made—that is, disclosures as to which a contemporaneous claim of privilege would have succeeded but for an erroneous ruling or the lack of opportunity for objection. **Walstad v. State,** Op. No. 1165, 818 P2d 695 (Alaska App. 1991).

Where defendant told his minister, who was also a certified counselor, that he had sexually abused a child, the minister's report of the crime to the police did not contravene this rule, and this rule did not require suppression of evidence resulting from the report. **Walstad v. State,** Op. No. 1165, 818 P2d 695 (Alaska App. 1991).

Rule 512. Comment Upon or Inference From Claim of Privilege—Instruction.

(a) **Comment or Inference Not Permitted.** The claim of privilege, whether in the present proceeding or upon a prior occasion, is not a proper subject of comment by judge or counsel. No inference may be drawn therefrom.

(b) **Claiming Privilege Without Knowledge of Jury.** In jury cases, proceedings shall be conducted, to the extent practicable, so as to facilitate the making of claims of privilege without the knowledge of the jury.

(c) **Jury Instruction.** Upon request, any party against whom the jury might draw an adverse inference from a claim of privilege is entitled to an instruction that no inference may be drawn therefrom.

(d) **Application—Self-Incrimination.** The foregoing subsections do not apply in a civil case with respect to the privilege against self-incrimination.

(Added by SCO 364 effective August 1, 1979)

Annotations

Cases

Trial courts are not obliged, sua sponte, to give an instruction pertaining to the accused's failure to testify. **Tugatuk v. State,** Op. No. 2322, 626 P2d 95 (Alaska 1981).

In federal court diversity action, court properly applied this rule to bar defendant from raising negative inferences before jury based upon plaintiff's assertion of attorney-client privilege and to instruct jury not to draw such inferences. **Home Indem. Co. v. Lane Powell Moss and Miller,** 43 F.3d 1322 (9th Cir. 1995).

Defense was not prejudiced by trial court's late decision on ninth day of 13-day trial to apply this rule to prevent defense from raising negative inferences based upon plaintiff's assertion of attorney-client privilege. **Home Indem. Co. v. Lane Powell Moss and Miller,** 43 F.3d 1322 (9th Cir. 1995).

Although plaintiff may have waived its right to object to admission of witnesses' testimony claiming attorney-client privilege prior to ninth day of 13-day trial, plaintiff did not waive its right to object to defense's future questioning of subsequent witnesses which was designed to elicit claims of privilege. **Home Indem. Co. v. Lane Powell Moss and Miller,** 43 F.3d 1322 (9th Cir. 1995).

Alaska R. Evid. 512(b) obviously applies when a witness validly claims a privilege, but the rule also applies when a witness claims a privilege, the court rejects the claim of privilege and orders the witness to testify, and the witness then obeys the court and answers the disputed questions. **David v. State,** Op. No. 1752, 28 P3d 309 (Alaska App. 2001).

ARTICLE VI. WITNESSES—IMPEACHMENT

Rule 601. Competency of Witnesses.

A person is competent to be a witness unless the court finds that (1) the proposed witness is incapable of communicating concerning the matter so as to be understood by the court and jury either directly or through interpretation by one who can understand the proposed witness, or (2) the proposed witness is incapable of understanding the duty of a witness to tell the truth.

(Added by SCO 364 effective August 1, 1979; amended by SCO 1153 effective July 15, 1994)

Annotations

Cases

Once a child's competency to testify has been determined, any inconsistency should go to the weight of his testimony, and not its admissibility. **Sevier v. State,** Op. No. 2134, 614 P2d 791 (Alaska 1980).

Before permitting a young child to testify, the trial judge must ascertain that the child is capable of receiving just impressions of the facts of which he or she is to testify and of relating them truly, in addition to understanding the necessity of testifying truthfully. **Sevier v. State,** Op. No. 2134, 614 P2d 791 (Alaska 1980).

Complaining witness to crime, who prior to trial had been hypnotized to refresh her recollection, was not incompetent to testify at trial as to her after-hypnosis identification of the assailant. **State v. Contreras,** Op. No. 318, 674 P2d 792 (Alaska App. 1983).

There is no minimum age below which a child is presumed incompetent to testify. **Blume v. State,** Op. No. 1064, 797 P2d 664 (Alaska App. 1990).

Trial court did not abuse its discretion in concluding that 5 year old girl was competent to testify. **Blume v. State,** Op. No. 1064, 797 P2d 664 (Alaska App. 1990).

Rule 602. Lack of Personal Knowledge.

A witness may not testify to a matter unless evidence is introduced sufficient to support a finding that the witness has personal knowledge of the matter. Evidence to prove personal knowledge may, but need not, consist of the witness' own testimony. This rule is subject to the provisions of Rule 703, relating to opinion testimony by expert witnesses.

(Added by SCO 364 effective August 1, 1979; amended by SCO 1153 effective July 15, 1994)

Annotations

Cases

Police coercion and intimidation of witnesses may result in exclusion of testimony and may require reversal of conviction on due process grounds. **Tucker v. State,** Op. No. 633, 721 P2d 639 (Alaska App. 1986).

Defects in a witness' recollection are proper subjects for cross-examination and impeachment, but the defects do not generally render the witness' testimony inadmissible. **Tucker v. State,** Op. No. 633, 721 P2d 639 (Alaska App. 1986).

Where defendant was able to fully cross-examine prosecution witness concerning the witness' defective memory and to apprise the jury fully of the coercive tactics used by the police to obtain the witness' testimony, defendant was not harmed substantially by admission of the testimony, particularly since the testimony was merely cumulative of other evidence presented. **Tucker v. State,** Op. No. 633, 721 P2d 639 (Alaska App. 1986).

Testimony of a witness in an action to quiet title regarding a conversation between a property owner and a property claimant, wherein they agreed that the claimant would live on the owner's land and in exchange he would supply her with food, was not inadmissible under this rule where a foundation was laid to establish the witness's personal knowledge. **Glover v. Glover,** Op. No. 5812, 92 P.3d 387 (Alaska 2004).

Rule 603. Oath or Affirmation.

Before testifying, every witness shall be required to declare that the witness will testify truthfully, by oath or affirmation administered in a form calculated to awaken the witness' conscience and impress the witness' mind with the duty to do so.

(Added by SCO 364 effective August 1, 1979; amended by SCO 1153 effective July 15, 1994)

Annotations

Cases

The failure to swear in a witness when the witness returned to the stand did not constitute plain error where the court reminded the witness that he had been previously sworn and remained under oath and appellant made no argument that injustice resulted from this failure. The intent of this rule was met as the witness was sworn in a manner calculated to awaken the witness' conscience and impress the witness' mind with the duty to testify truthfully. **Wetherhorn v. Alaska Psychiatric Institute**, Op. No. 11939, 156 P.3d 371 (Alaska 2007).

Rule 604. Interpreters.

An interpreter is subject to the provisions of these rules relating to qualifications as an expert and to the administration of an oath or affirmation that the interpreter will make a true translation of all communications to and from the person for whom the interpretation is made. In determining whether an interpreter is qualified and impartial, the court shall inquire into and consider the interpreter's education, certification and experience in interpreting relevant languages; the interpreter's understanding of and experience in the proceedings in which the interpreter is to participate; and the interpreter's impartiality. Parties to the proceedings may also question the interpreter concerning the interpreter's qualifications and impartiality.

(Added by SCO 364 effective August 1, 1979; by SCO 959 effective July 15, 1989)

Rule 605. Competency of Judge as Witness.

The judge presiding at the trial may not testify in that trial as a witness. No objection need be made in order to preserve the point.

(Added by SCO 364 effective August 1, 1979)

Annotations

Cases

Where one arbitrator on a five person panel asked a question which indicated that he had made an ex parte inquiry into certain facts, the argument that his question constituted testimony in violation of this rule was not preserved for appeal absent objection to the question at the hearing. **Integrated Res. Equity v. Fairbanks Boro.,** Op. No. 3633, 799 P2d 295 (Alaska 1990).

Rule 606. Competency of Juror as Witness.

(a) **At the Trial.** A member of the jury may not testify as a witness before that jury in the trial of the case in which the juror is sitting. No objection need be made in order to preserve the point.

(b) **Inquiry Into Validity of Verdict or Indictment.** Upon an inquiry into the validity of a verdict or indictment, a juror may not be questioned as to any matter or statement occurring during the course of the jury's deliberations or to the effect of any matter or statement upon that or any other juror's mind or emotions as influencing the juror to assent to or dissent from the verdict or indictment or concerning the juror's mental processes in connection therewith, except that a juror may testify on the question whether extraneous prejudicial information was improperly brought to the jury's attention or whether any outside influence was improperly brought to bear upon any juror. Nor may a juror's affidavit or evidence of any statement by the juror concerning a matter about which the juror would be precluded from testifying be received for these purposes.

(Added by SCO 364 effective August 1, 1979; amended by SCO 1153 effective July 15, 1994)

Annotations

Cases

Where prosecutor's comments, while inappropriate, were not extraneous, the trial court properly refused to consider juror affidavits in determining whether defendant was prejudiced by the prosecutor's comments. **Graham v. State,** Op. No. 184, 656 P2d 1192 (Alaska App. 1982).

Where trial judge concluded that the jury broke sequestration and consumed alcohol, he should have presumed prejudice to the defendant unless the state could rebut the presumption. **Lowery v. State,** Op. No. 853, 762 P2d 457 (Alaska App. 1988).

Allegations that jury broke sequestration and consumed alcoholic beverages were sufficient to justify an evidentiary hearing concerning the jury deliberations. **Lowery v. State,** Op. No. 853, 762 P2d 457 (Alaska App. 1988).

Juror affidavits detailed the jurors mental processes but did not demonstrate that there was any outside influence improperly brought to bear on any juror or the extraneous prejudicial information was improperly brought to the jury's attention, thus court did not err in refusing to grant new trial on that basis. **Hancock v. Northcutt,** Op. No. 3658, 808 P2d 251 (Alaska 1991).

For purpose of determining the likelihood that a juror's vote has been influenced, a reviewing court must apply an objective test, and is precluded from considering evidence concerning the subjective impact of the extraneous matter on any juror. **Swain v. State,** Op. No. 1158, 817 P2d 927 (Alaska App. 1991).

"Extraneous" information for purposes of this rule refers to information that reaches the jury other than through the normal trial process; it does not refer to objectionable statements of counsel made during trial or objectionable testimony given at trial. **Turpin v. State,** Op. No. 1395, 890 P2d 1128 (Alaska App. 1995).

Defendant was not entitled to a new trial on the grounds that the jury may have used the prosecutor's proper remarks as fuel for improper speculation about his possible other crimes because this rule strictly prohibits post-trial inquiry into the mental operations and emotional reactions of jurors during the deliberative process. **Turpin v. State,** Op. No. 1395, 890 P2d 1128 (Alaska App. 1995).

This rule precludes trial courts from conducting after-trial voir dire of jurors concerning allegations of intimidation or verbal coercion by other jurors during deliberative process. **Kailukiak v. State,** Op. No. 1588, 959 P2d 771 (Alaska App. 1998).

Pre-existing juror knowledge about facts of alleged crime constitutes extraneous prejudicial information within meaning of this rule. **Titus v. State,** Op. No. 5021, 963 P2d 258 (Alaska 1998).

Where an inmate attacked his guilty verdict in a petition for post-conviction relief, claiming that jurors formed and announced opinions and discussed the merits of the case before jury deliberations, relied on personal knowledge in the deliberations, and viewed the inmate's decision not to testify and his wife's absence as evidence of his guilt, under Alaska R. Evid. 606(b) the juror affidavits could not be relied on to support the petition because they described matters that inhered in the jury's decision-making process and because the use of the affidavits was incompatible with the policies underlying R. 606(b) of protecting jurors from harassment, encouraging free jury deliberation, and promoting the finality of verdicts **Larson v. State,** Op. No. 1904, 79 P.3d 650 (Alaska App. 2003).

Although Alaska R. Evid. 606(b) prohibited courts from questioning jurors about their mental or emotional processes in reaching a verdict, the rule did not bar a court from asking jurors to clarify a verdict when their reasoning processes were not at issue, and where a trial judge knew immediately that a verdict was not the jury's unanimous decision and that the verdict forms were switched, the judge properly inquired into the jurors' intent and sent them back into deliberations with proper verdict forms. **Crouse v. Municipality of Anchorage,** Op. No. 1905, 79 P.3d 660 (Alaska App. 2003).

Rule 607. Who May Impeach or Support.

(a) Subject to the limitation imposed by these rules, the credibility of a witness may be attacked by any party, including the party calling the witness.

(b) Evidence proffered by any party to support the credibility of a witness may be admitted to meet an attack on the witness' credibility.

(Added by SCO 364 effective August 1, 1979; amended by SCO 1153 effective July 15, 1994)

Rule 608. Evidence of Character and Conduct of Witness.

(a) **Opinion and Reputation Evidence of Character.** The credibility of a witness may be attacked or supported by evidence in the form of opinion or reputation, but subject to these limitations: (1) the evidence may refer only to character for truthfulness or untruthfulness; and (2) evidence of truthful character is admissible only after the character of the witness for truthfulness has been attacked by opinion or reputation evidence or otherwise.

(b) **Specific Instances of Conduct.** If a witness testifies concerning the character for truthfulness or untruthfulness of a previous witness, the specific instances of conduct probative of the truthfulness or untruthfulness of the previous witness, may be inquired into on cross-examination. Evidence of other specific instances of the conduct of a witness offered for the purpose of attacking or supporting that witness' credibility is inadmissible unless such evidence is explicitly made admissible by these rules, by other rules promulgated by the Alaska Supreme Court or by enactment of the Alaska Legislature.

(c) **Admissibility.** Before a witness may be impeached by inquiry into specific instances of conduct pursuant to subdivision (b), the court shall be advised of the specific instances of conduct upon which inquiry is sought and shall rule if the witness may be impeached by such inquiry by weighing its probative value against its prejudicial effect.

(Added by SCO 364 effective August 1, 1979)

Annotations

Cases

When hearsay evidence has been presented to a grand jury, character evidence concerning the hearsay declarant's credibility is permissible to the same extent to which it would be permissible at trial had the declarant's character been challenged. **Putnam v. State,** Op. No. 2251, 629 P2d 35 (Alaska 1980).

Allowing cross-examination of defendant's witnesses concerning incidents arguably reflective of defendant's honesty, although potentially prejudicial, was not a clear abuse of discretion. **Hohman v. State,** Op. No. 290, 669 P2d 1316 (Alaska App. 1983).

When defendant called witnesses who testified to his character for truthfulness, the prosecution was entitled to examine those witnesses about specific instances of conduct relating to truthfulness and to cross-examine them about whether they had considered allegations of misconduct by defendant which related to his character for truth and veracity. **Hohman v. State,** Op. No. 290, 669 P2d 1316 (Alaska App. 1983).

Where the defendant in a prosecution for manslaughter arising out of a motor vehicle accident called a psychiatrist to testify and the psychiatrist, on direct examination, stated that there was nothing about the circumstances of the accident or defendant's background or history suggestive of recklessness, his testimony was direct evidence of defendant's mens rea which opened the door for the state to impeach the testimony by reference to defendant's two prior drunk driving convictions. **Jansen v. State,** Op. No. 863, 764 P2d 308 (Alaska App. 1988).

Specific instances of behavior to show truthfulness or untruthfulness are admissible only to show that the witness who testifies as to character does not have a solid basis for his opinion. **Lahmeyer v. State,** Op. No. 886, 765 P2d 985 (Alaska App. 1988).

A party cannot make a witness a character witness for truth and veracity for the purpose of later cross-examining that witness by bringing out specific acts; however, there may be exceptional circumstances where the trial court should allow specific acts of untruthfulness to be used for purposes other than merely cross-examining a character witness for truth and veracity. **Lahmeyer v. State,** Op. No. 886, 765 P2d 985 (Alaska App. 1988).

In defendant's trial for sexually abusing children, the trial court did not err in forbidding the defense counsel from calling the children's mother as a witness to testify about two alleged incidents of untruthfulness by her children, particularly since the incidents, pertaining to breaking into a neighbor's basement and setting fire to some trees, had minimal relevance. **Lahmeyer v. State,** Op. No. 886, 765 P2d 985 (Alaska App. 1988).

Testimony on direct examination by mother of children allegedly molested by defendant that she would have to trust what her children told her did not convert the mother into a character witness on the truthfulness of her children, thus defense counsel could not on cross-examination ask the mother about two specific situations where the children had lied to her. **Lahmeyer v. State,** Op. No. 886, 765 P2d 985 (Alaska App. 1988).

Trial court did not err in precluding defendant from inquiring into an allegedly false claim by the prosecution's main witness that the witness had once been awarded the medal of honor; the witness's general credibility was a collateral issue at trial, and a trial court had broad discretion to restrict the admission of extrinsic evidence on collateral matters. **Latham v. State,** Op. No. 1030, 790 P2d 717 (Alaska App. 1990).

In medical malpractice suit, admission of evidence that plaintiff's primary expert witness had misstated his credentials at a previous unrelated trial and that the judge at that trial had made findings of fact concerning the misstatements constituted reversible error; defendant's arguments that the evidence was admissible to impeach the expert's character or to show bias were rejected. **Snyder v. Foote,** Op. No. 3787, 822 P2d 1353 (Alaska 1991).

Testimony of judge, who had presided over forgery trial of witness, as to his opinion of witness' honesty, was properly excluded, since testimony, though offered as "opinion" evidence, was tantamount to evidence of a specific instance of dishonesty. **Carr v. State,** Op. No. 1256, 840 P2d 1000 (Alaska App. 1992).

Under this rule, defendants were free to ask a witness to state his opinion of a complaining witness's credibility, but they had no right to impeach the complaining witness's credibility by recourse to evidence of specific incidents of past misconduct. **Johnson v. State,** Op. No. 1390, 889 P2d 1076 (Alaska App. 1995).

Evidence of sexual assault complaining witness's previous false paternity claim had no bearing on her bias, prejudice, or motive to fabricate and did not establish a pattern or scheme of falsification on her part, It was classic propensity evidence and therefore inadmissible. **Johnson v. State,** Op. No. 1390, 889 P2d 1076 (Alaska App. 1995).

Under this rule, defendant could properly ask an alleged rape victim's ex-fiance for his opinion of the alleged victim's general credibility, but defendant was not entitled to elicit ex-fiance's opinion as to the credibility of any specific statement by the alleged victim. **Kitchens v. State,** Op. No. 1414, 898 P2d 443 (Alaska App. 1995).

This rule, which generally prohibits use of specific instances of conduct to support or attack witness credibility except on cross examination of a character witness, does not prevent use of evidence to refute specific factual assertions by witnesses, a use that has nothing to do with proof of character for untruthfulness. **Alaska Tae Woong Venture v. Westward Seafoods,** Op. No. 5029, 963 P2d 1055 (Alaska 1998).

Trial court did not err in refusing to allow defendant to elicit testimony from a witness that she had seen the victim steal tip money from tables in the bar where the witness worked as a bartender; the testimony violated this rule's prohibition against introducing evidence of specific instances of bad conduct. **Mooney v. State,** Op. No. 1965, 105 P3d 149 (Alaska App. 2005).

Rule 609. Impeachment by Evidence of Conviction of Crime.

(a) **General Rule.** For the purpose of attacking the credibility of a witness, evidence that the witness has been convicted of a crime is only admissible if the crime involved dishonesty or false statement.

(b) **Time Limit.** Evidence of a conviction under this rule is inadmissible if a period of more than five years has elapsed since the date of the conviction. The court may, however, allow evidence of the conviction of the witness other than the accused in a criminal case after more than five years have elapsed if the court is satisfied that admission in evidence is necessary for a fair determination of the case.

(c) **Admissibility.** Before a witness may be impeached by evidence of a prior conviction, the court shall be advised of the existence of the conviction and shall rule if the witness may be impeached by proof of the conviction by weighing its probative value against its prejudicial effect.

(d) **Effect of Pardon, Annulment, or Certificate of Rehabilitation.** Evidence of a conviction is inadmissible under this rule if:

(1) The conviction has been the subject of a pardon, annulment, certificate of rehabilitation, or other equivalent procedure, and

(2) The procedure under which the same was granted or issued required a substantial showing of rehabilitation or was based on innocence.

(e) **Juvenile Adjudications.** The court may allow evidence of the juvenile adjudication of a witness if conviction of the offense would be admissible to attack the credibility of an adult and the court is satisfied that admission in evidence would substantially assist in determining the credibility of the witness.

(f) **Pendency of Appeal.** The pendency of an appeal therefrom does not render evidence of a conviction inadmissible. Evidence of the pendency of an appeal is admissible.

(Added by SCO 364 effective August 1, 1979; amended by SCO 1153 effective July 15, 1994)

Annotations

Cases

Robbery is a crime of dishonesty within the terms of this rule. **Alexander v. State,** Op. No. 2077, 611 P2d 469 (Alaska 1980).

Robbery is a crime involving dishonesty within the meaning of this rule. **Alexander v. State,** Op. No. 2077, 611 P2d 469 (Alaska 1980); **Frankson**

v. State, Op. No. 92, 645 P2d 225 (Alaska App. 1982).

In prosecution for robbery, it was reversible error to allow prosecutor to impeach defendant by divulging a previous robbery conviction; prosecution should have been restricted to proving that defendant had been convicted of a crime involving dishonesty or else proving that defendant had been convicted of a larceny type crime. **Frankson v. State,** Op. No. 92, 645 P2d 225 (Alaska App. 1982).

For the purposes of this rule, "conviction" includes those situations in which a verdict of guilty has been accepted but sentencing has not yet occurred. **Kelly v. State,** Op. No. 251, 663 P2d 967 (Alaska App. 1983).

Where defendant admitted that he had been drinking prior to the automobile accident in question and that he was responsible for the accident, trial court properly excluded evidence of defendant's past conviction for drunk driving to impeach his statement that "I usually don't drive and drink" or to impeach his veracity generally. **Shane v. Rhines,** Op. No. 2750, 672 P2d 895 (Alaska 1983).

In sexual assault case, the court's inspection of juvenile victim's arrest records in camera and ex parte and its refusal to reveal them after concluding that they contained no adjudications of delinquency or any other information potentially relevant to cross-examination of the victim was not an abuse of discretion. **Fox v. State,** Op. No. 394, 685 P2d 1267 (Alaska App. 1984).

When a prosecution witness's juvenile record constitutes arguably admissible information, it should be turned over to the defendant so that its relevancy can be argued in an adversary setting. **Coney v. State,** Op. No.471,699 P2d 899 (Alaska App. 1985).

Trial judge did not abuse his discretion in refusing to reveal important prosecution witness's juvenile record to the defense, given that the record was more than five years old and that there is a state policy of limiting the use of juvenile records. **Coney v. State,** Op. No. 471, 699 P2d 899 (Alaska App. 1985).

Where defendant in prosecution for concealment of merchandise had a prior conviction for the same crime, trial court erred in allowing the prosecution to impeach defendant's credibility as a witness by establishing that defendant had formerly been convicted of "a crime of dishonesty" even though the specific case was not made known to the jury since whether or not concealment of merchandise is a crime involving dishonesty, the prejudicial effect of admitting the prior conviction outweighed its probative value. **Johnson v. City of Fairbanks,** Op. No. 492, 703 P2d 442 (Alaska App. 1985).

In prosecution for concealment of merchandise, trial court did not err in allowing the prosecutor to impeach defendant with evidence of defendant's prior conviction for the same offense by referring to the offense as a "crime involving dishonesty" rather than by specifically naming the crime. **City of Fairbanks v. Johnson,** Op. No. 3093, 723 P2d 79 (Alaska 1986).

Violation of city ordinance prohibiting the willful concealment of merchandise was a crime involving dishonesty and could therefore be used for impeachment purposes, notwithstanding that intent to permanently deprive another of property was not an element of the crime. **City of Fairbanks v. Johnson,** Op. No. 3093, 723 P2d 79 (Alaska 1986).

Trial court did not err in allowing the State to impeach the key defense witness with evidence of 11 prior convictions involving dishonesty, all of which occurred 8 to 14 years prior to the trial. **Clifton v. State,** Op. No. 657, 728 P2d 649 (Alaska App. 1986).

Where murder defendant had been convicted of burglary and larceny in 1978, more than 5 years prior to his murder trial, but the sentence had been reversed on appeal and he was resentenced in 1981, within the 5-year period preceding the murder trial, the trial court erred in allowing the 1978 conviction to be used for impeachment purposes, but the error was harmless. **LaPierre v. State,** Op. No. 690, 734 P2d 997 (Alaska App. 1987).

In determining whether prior convictions which are more than five years old are admissible for impeachment purposes, the court must (1) weigh the probative value of the evidence against its prejudicial effect and (2) determine whether or not admission of the evidence is necessary for a fair determination of the case. **Clifton v. State,** Op. No. 3280, 751 P2d 27 (Alaska 1988).

The trial court should relax the five year limitation and admit a stale conviction under this rule only in rare circumstances. **Clifton v. State,** Op. No. 3280, 751 P2d 27 (Alaska 1988).

Trial court committed reversible error in allowing the prosecution to impeach a defense witness with prior convictions ranging from eight to fourteen years in age since admission of the stale convictions was not necessary to a fair determination of the case. **Clifton v. State,** Op. No. 3280, 751 P2d 27 (Alaska 1988).

Where the defendant in a prosecution for manslaughter arising out of a motor vehicle accident called a psychiatrist to testify and the psychiatrist, on direct examination, stated that there was nothing about the circumstances of the accident or defendant's background or history suggestive of recklessness, his testimony was direct evidence of defendant's mens rea which opened the door for the state to impeach the testimony by reference to defendant's two prior drunk driving convictions. **Jansen v. State,** Op. No. 863, 764 P2d 308 (Alaska App. 1988).

In trial of defendant for assault and manslaughter, defendant's prior convictions for perjury for statements made four years previously were admissible for impeachment purposes under this rule. **Wickham v. State,** Op. No. 907, 770 P2d 757 (Alaska App. 1989).

Criminal defendants must testify to preserve for review a claim of improper impeachment by prior conviction. **State v. Wickham,** Op. No. 3622, 796 P2d 1354 (Alaska 1990).

The holding of this case that criminal defendants must testify to preserve for review a claim of improper impeachment by prior conviction has prospective application only. **State v. Wickham,** Op. No. 3622, 796 P2d 1354 (Alaska 1990).

Evidence of past convictions which would be otherwise inadmissible under this rule may be introduced to contradict a witness's specific testimony as to a material issue even though it may indirectly impeach the witness's credibility. **Gargan v. State,** Op. No. 1108, 805 P2d 998 (Alaska App. 1991).

In prosecution of defendant for tampering with physical evidence where the only issue was whether defendant had the requisite specific intent to mislead a public servant, defendant's FBI conviction record, which was not admissible under this rule as evidence of crimes affecting defendant's veracity, was admissible to contradict defendant's testimony that he did not understand the workings of the criminal justice system. **Gargan v. State,** Op. No. 1108, 805 P2d 998 (Alaska App. 1991).

Where prosecuting attorney, without seeking court permission, cross-examined defendant about criminal charge that had been dismissed, this rule was violated, substantially prejudicing defendant and requiring reversal of conviction despite curative instruction. **Pruitt v. State,** Op. No. 1217, 829 P2d 1197 (Alaska App. 1992).

Trial court committed reversible error in allowing defendant to be impeached by evidence of two prior convictions that should have been set aside under Alaska's suspended imposition of sentence statute due to his successful completion of probation after receiving suspended sentences for those convictions. **Wickham v. State,** Op. No. 1276, 844 P2d 1140 (Alaska App. 1993).

Appellant's conviction of second-degree burglary, second-degree theft, and second-degree criminal mischief in violation of AS 11.46.310(a), 11.46.130, 11.46.482(d) was affirmed because, among other things, the trial court's refusal to allow impeachment of the State's witness based on an unspecified crime that was committed over ten years ago was proper because appellant failed to comply with the admissibility prerequisites of this rule. **Waters v. State,** Op. No. 1853, 64 P.3d 169 (Alaska App. 2003).

Rule 610. Religious Beliefs or Opinions.

Evidence of the beliefs or opinions of a witness on matters of religion is not admissible for the purpose of showing that by reason of their nature the credibility of the witness is impaired or enhanced.

(Added by SCO 364 effective August 1, 1979; amended by SCO 1522 effective October 15, 2003)

Rule 611. Mode and Order of Interrogation and Presentation.

(a) **Control by Court.** The court shall exercise reasonable control over the mode and order of interrogating witnesses and presenting evidence so as to (1) make the interrogation and presentation effective for the ascertainment of the truth, (2) avoid needless consumption of time, and (3) protect witnesses from harassment or undue embarrassment.

(b) **Scope of Cross-Examination.** Cross-examination should be limited to the subject matter of the direct examination and matters affecting the credibility of the witness. The court may, in the exercise of discretion, permit inquiry into additional matters as if on direct examination.

(c) **Leading Questions.** On direct examination, leading questions should not be allowed except: (1) when they are merely formal or preliminary, (2) when they are necessary to develop the witness' testimony, (3) when the witness is hostile, an adverse party, or identified with an adverse party, or (4) when they are necessary for the purposes of impeachment of the witness' testimony. On cross-examination, leading questions should ordinarily be permitted.

(Added by SCO 364 effective August 1, 1979)

Annotations

Cases

Trial court did not abuse its discretion in allowing plaintiff to present during rebuttal, a friendly witness to impeach a hostile witness who had been called by plaintiff in her case-in-chief. **Amer. Nat. Watermattress Corp. v. Manville,** Op. No. 2477, 642 P2d 1330 (Alaska 1982).

Where medical expert testified on direct examination that in his opinion defendant doctor acted reasonably, superior court did not err in not allowing plaintiff, on cross-examination, to elicit the expert's opinion as to whether a nurse's conduct fell below the applicable standard of care. **Baker v. Werner,** Op. No. 2541, 654 P.2d 263 (Alaska 1982).

Where the defendant in a prosecution for manslaughter arising out of a motor vehicle accident called a psychiatrist to testify and the psychiatrist, on direct examination, stated that there was nothing about the circumstances of the accident or defendant's background or history suggestive of recklessness, his testimony was direct evidence of defendant's mens rea which opened the door for the state to impeach the testimony by reference to defendant's two prior drunk driving convictions. **Jansen v. State,** Op. No. 863, 764 P2d 308 (Alaska App. 1988).

As applied to defendants in criminal cases who take stand, this rule is generally construed to mean that defendant is subject to cross-examination only to extent necessary to fairly test statements made during direct examination and inferences that might be drawn from such statements. **Landon v. State,** Op. No. 1534, 936 P2d 169 (Alaska App. 1997).

Defendant's argument that he was subjected to improperly broad cross-examination when he took stand at his trial was rejected; prosecutor's questions were manifestly relevant to testing defendant's assertions that he did not occupy or use buildings on property where marijuana was found. **Landon v. State,** Op. No. 1534, 936 P2d 169 (Alaska App. 1997).

Rule 612. Writing Used to Refresh Memory.

(a) **While Testifying.** Any writing or object may be used by a witness to refresh the memory of the witness while testifying. If, while testifying, a witness uses a writing or object to refresh his memory, any party seeking to impeach the witness is entitled, subject to subdivision (c), to inspect the writing or object, to cross-examine the witness thereon, and to introduce those portions which relate to the testimony of the witness.

(b) **Before Testifying.** If, before testifying, a witness uses a writing or object to refresh the memory of the witness for the purpose of testifying, and the court in its discretion determines that the interests of justice so require, any party seeking to impeach the witness is entitled, subject to subdivision (c), to have the writing or object produced, if practicable, at the hearing, to inspect it, and to cross-examine the witness thereon, as to those portions which relate to the testimony of the witness. If production of the writing or object at the hearing is impracticable, the court may make any appropriate order, including one for inspection.

(c) **Claims of Privilege or Irrelevance.** If it is claimed that a writing or object contains matters privileged or not related to the subject matter of the testimony the court shall rule on any claim of privilege raised and examine the writing or object in camera, excise any portions not so related and deliver the remainder to the party entitled thereto. Any portion withheld over objections shall be preserved and made available to the appellate court in the event of an appeal.

(d) **Failure to Produce.** If a writing or object is not produced or delivered pursuant to an order under this rule, the court shall make any order justice requires, except that in criminal cases when the prosecution elects not to comply, the order shall be one striking the testimony or, if the court in its discretion determines that the interests of justice so require, declaring a mistrial or dismissing the prosecution.

(Added by SCO 364 effective August 1, 1979; amended by SCO 1522 effective October 15, 2003)

Annotations

Cases

Where defense counsel on cross-examination used a summary of the witness' interview with a defense investigator to refresh the witness' recollections, the work-product privilege was waived with respect to the summary. **Lowery v. State,** Op. No. 853, 762 P2d 457 (Alaska App. 1988).

A witness's memory need not be completely exhausted before the use of a memory-refreshing document is permissible; rather, it is a matter of discretion for the trial court. **Matomco Oil v. Arctic Mechanical,** Op. No. 3618, 796 P2d 1336 (Alaska 1990).

In negligence action, trial court did not err in allowing witness to refer to the list of items in his proof of loss while he testified, particularly where opposing counsel was permitted inspection and extensive cross examination. **Matomco Oil v. Arctic Mechanical,** Op. No. 3618, 796 P2d 1336 (Alaska 1990).

Rule 613. Prior Inconsistent Statements—Bias and Interest of Witnesses.

(a) **General Rule.** Prior statements of a witness inconsistent with the testimony of the witness at a trial, hearing or deposition, and evidence of bias or interest on the part of a witness are admissible for the purpose of impeaching the credibility of a witness.

(b) **Foundation Requirement.** Before extrinsic evidence of a prior contradictory statement or of bias or interest may be admitted, the examiner shall lay a foundation for impeachment by affording the witness the opportunity, while testifying, to explain or deny any prior statement, or to admit, deny, or explain any bias or interest, except as provided in subdivision (b) (1) of this rule.

(1) The court shall permit witnesses to be recalled for the purpose of laying a foundation for impeachment if satisfied that failure to lay a foundation earlier was not intentional, or if intentional was for good cause; even if no foundation is laid, an inconsistent statement may be admitted in the interests of justice.

(2) In examining a witness concerning a prior statement made by the witness, whether written or not, the statement need not be shown nor its contents disclosed to the witness at that time, but on request the same shall be shown or disclosed to opposing counsel.

(Added by SCO 364 effective August 1, 1979; amended by SCO 1153 effective July 15, 1994; by SCO 1269 effective July 15, 1997; and by SCO 1522 effective October 15, 2003)

Note: In 1996, the legislature enacted AS 12.61.127, which provides that statements obtained from victims or witnesses in violation of AS 12.61.120 or 12.61.125 are presumed inadmissible. According to § 79, ch. 64 SLA 1996, this statute had the effect of amending Evidence Rule 613 relating to impeachment of witnesses.

Annotations

Cases

Testimony of victim's husband which was offered to impeach the victim's trial testimony by demonstrating a prior inconsistent statement was properly excluded where the victim witness was not told of the prior statement or asked to admit or explain it. **Moss v. State,** Op. No. 2239, 620 P2d 674 (Alaska App. 1980).

While defendant can properly seek to question the victim's credibility, this may not be done by extrinsic evidence on a collateral matter. **Moss v. State,** Op. No. 2239, 620 P2d 674 (Alaska App. 1980).

Trial court did not abuse its discretion in concluding that admission of three specific past charges against prosecution witness was not mandated by defendant's theory that the witness desired immunity and was consequently biased toward the prosecution. **Murdock v. State,** Op. No. 256, 664 P2d 589 (Alaska App. 1983).

Where a witness deliberately seeks to avoid testifying by claiming loss of memory in response to specific questions, prior statements of the witness relating to the subject matter of the questions are inconsistent within the meaning of this rule. **Van Hatten v. State,** Op. No. 269, 666 P2d 1047 (Alaska App. 1983).

Whether a defendant's constitutional rights of confrontation will be violated by use of prior, extra-judicial statements of a witness as substantive evidence of guilt when the witness has been evasive or suffers from lack of memory is to be determined on a case-by-case basis, focusing on the extent to which the witness actually testifies and can be cross-examined, as well as the nature and reliability of his prior, out-of-court statements. **Van Hatten v. State,** Op. No. 269, 666 P2d 1047 (Alaska App. 1983).

Prior grand jury testimony of uncooperative prosecution witness was admissible as substantive evidence of defendant's guilt. **Van Hatten v. State,** Op. No. 269, 666 P2d 1047 (Alaska App. 1983).

Evidence showing that defendant and his alibi witness were incarcerated together had probative value on the issues of bias and opportunity for recent fabrication; accordingly, trial court did not err in denying defendant's motion for a protective order barring the prosecution from impeaching the witness with this evidence, particularly since the potential for prejudice was mitigated by the court's restriction against questions concerning the circumstances of the witnesses' offense or the issue of his guilt, together with a limiting instruction. **Dumbar v. State,** Op. No. 347, 677 P2d 1275 (Alaska App. 1984).

Where defendant cross-examined the prosecution witness, his former girl-friend, concerning their bitter breakup in order to establish her bias, trial court erred in then allowing the state on redirect to inquire into all of the circumstances of the breakup, since it exceeded the scope of redirect permissible under the doctrine of curative admissibility, which exists to permit introduction of otherwise inadmissible evidence only to the extent necessary to remove any unfair prejudice which might otherwise ensue from the original evidence. **Bentley v. State,** Op. No. 560, 711 P2d 544 (Alaska App. 1985).

Prior statements of a witness are generally admissible for purposes of impeachment. **Bodine v. State,** Op. No. 708, 737 P2d 1072 (Alaska App. 1987).

Work-product privilege with respect to statements made by a prosecution witness to an investigator hired by the defense was waived when defense counsel questioned the witness about those statements on cross-examination. **Lowery v. State,** Op. No. 853, 762 P2d 457 (Alaska App. 1988).

In trial of defendant for murder arising out of an altercation between the defendant, the victim and the victim's brothers, where defendant claimed self-defense, the trial court did not err in preventing defendant from cross-examining one of the brothers about a prior hindering prosecution charge (later dismissed) against that brother as evidence of bias under this rule, since although the evidence arguably demonstrated the brother's willingness to engage in illegal conduct to protect his brother, the trial judge's conclusion that the probative value of the evidence was outweighed by the danger of unfair prejudice was not unreasonable considering that the brother had admitted to burglary and theft convictions and that defendant was still fully able to develop the brother's bias and interest in the case. **Lerchenstein v. State,** Op. No. 921, 770 P2d 1150 (Alaska App. 1989).

In medical malpractice suit, admission of evidence that plaintiff's primary expert witness had misstated his credentials at previous unrelated trial and that the judge at that trial had made findings of fact concerning the misstatements constituted reversible error; defendant's arguments that the evidence was admissible to impeach the expert's character or to show bias were rejected. **Snyder v. Foote,** Op. No. 3787, 822 P2d 1353 (Alaska 1991).

Trial court did not err in allowing videotape of witness' prior inconsistent statements to be played since it revealed her demeanor when she made allegations of sexual abuse against defendant; defendant's argument that State failed to establish prior foundation for tape's admission because prosecutor did not ask witness about each and every inconsistent statement contained on the videotape was rejected. **Nunn v. State,** Op. No. 1278, 845 P2d 435 (Alaska App. 1993).

Defendant could not argue for the first time in an appellate reply brief that that this rule precludes testimony concerning a witness's prior inconsistent statement unless that testimony is corroborated by physical evidence.

Slwooko v. State, Op. No. 8747, 139 P.3d 593 (Alaska App. 2006).

When a party wishes to introduce a witness's prior inconsistent statements and those statements are recorded either in writing or on tape, the party need not show the witness the writing, or play the tape for the witness, before questioning the witness about the prior statements under subsection (b)(2) of this rule. **Active v. State**, Op. No. 8984, 153 P.3d 355 (Alaska App. 2007).

Rule 614. Calling and Examination of Witnesses by Court.

(a) **Calling by Court.** The court may call witnesses on its own motion or at the suggestion of a party, and all parties are entitled to cross-examine witnesses thus called.

(b) **Examination by Court.** The court may examine any witness.

(c) **Objections.** Objections to the calling or examination of witnesses by the court may be made at the time or at the next available opportunity when the jury is not present.

(Added by SCO 364 effective August 1, 1979)

Annotations

Cases

Where the reasonable cost of a process server's services was at issue, trial court did not err in calling the process server as its own witness where the judgment debtor raised no objection and was given the opportunity to cross examine. **Dahlby v. Guzzardi,** Op. No. 3391, 763 P2d 223 (Alaska 1998).

Rule 615. Exclusion of Witnesses.

At the request of a party the court may order witnesses excluded so that they cannot hear the testimony of other witnesses, and it may make the order on its own motion. This rule does not authorize exclusion of

(1) a party who is a natural person;

(2) an officer or employee of a party which is not a natural person designated as its representative by its attorney;

(3) a person whose presence is shown by a party to be important to the presentation of the party's cause; or

(4) the victim of the alleged crime or juvenile offense during criminal or juvenile proceedings when the accused has the right to be present; in this paragraph, "victim" has the meaning given in AS 12.55.185.

(Added by SCO 364 effective August 1, 1979; amended by SCO 1293 effective January 15, 1998)

Note to SCO 1293: Paragraph (4) of Evidence Rule 615 was added by § 23 ch. 63 SLA 1997. Section 6 of this order is adopted for the sole reason that the legislature has mandated the amendment.

Annotations

Cases

A witness who should have been excluded from court during the testimony of another witness under the exclusionary rule but who was present may still be allowed to testify in the discretion of the trial judge. **Schroff v. State,** Op. No. 16, 627 P2d 653 (Alaska App. 1981).

Where there was no indication in the record that the trial court considered alternative sanctions or balanced the prejudice to the defendant from excluding the testimony of a defense witness against the prejudice to the state from allowing it, trial court order disqualifying the witness for an inadvertent violation of a witness exclusion order was error, but the error was harmless since the excluded testimony was merely cumulative. **Babcock v. State,** Op. No. 383, 685 P2d 721 (Alaska App. 1984).

ARTICLE VII. OPINION TESTIMONY AND EXPERT WITNESSES

Rule 701. Opinion Testimony by Lay Witnesses.

If the witness is not testifying as an expert, the witness's testimony in the form of opinions or inferences is limited to those opinions or inferences which are (a) rationally based on the perception of the witness and (b) helpful to a clear understanding of the witness's testimony or the determination of a fact in issue.

(Added by SCO 364 effective August 1, 1979; amended by SCO 1522 effective October 15, 2003)

Annotations

Cases

Lay testimony offered by a landowner as to the value of his property is admissible because of the owner's presumed knowledge about the value of his own property. **Schymanski v. Conventz,** Op. No. 2742, 674 P2d 281 (Alaska 1983).

In action for dissolution of partnership, trial court did not abuse its discretion in admitting a third person's lay opinion as to the value of the partnership's hunting lodge. **Schymanski v. Conventz,** Op. No. 2742, 674 P2d 281 (Alaska 1983).

Testimony of police officer to the effect that it was his "impression" that defendant was intoxicated was admissible. **Loof v. Sanders,** Op. No. 2859, 686 P2d 1205 (Alaska 1984).

In trial of defendant for refusing to submit to a breath test, in which defendant testified that nose and chest injuries sustained by him during his arrest prevented him from blowing into the Intoximeter tube, the trial court committed reversible error in precluding a defense witness, who drove defendant to the hospital for an examination the day after the arrest, from testifying as to her observations of his injuries, since her testimony would have been relevant and a proper subject for lay opinion under the rules of evidence. **Callahan v. State,** Op. No. 910, 769 P2d 444 (Alaska App. 1989).

In trial of defendant for refusing to submit to a breath test, in which defendant testified that nose and chest injuries sustained by him during his arrest prevented him from blowing into the Intoximeter tube, the trial court committed reversible error in precluding admission of photographs of defendant's injuries taken by his friend one day after the arrest, since the photographs were relevant circumstantial evidence of defendant's claim that he was physically incapable of taking the breath test; furthermore, defendant's friend was the proper person to authenticate the photographs for admission. **Callahan v. State,** Op. No. 910, 769 P2d 444 (Alaska App. 1989).

In a case involving a petition for adoption opposed by the child's natural mother, social worker's testimony that there had been no significant improvement in the mother's mental condition over a period of time was arguably admissible as a lay opinion since it was rationally based upon his own experiences and was helpful to a clear understanding of his testimony; however, if admission of the testimony was error, it was harmless as cumulative of other properly admitted testimony. **In re D.J.A.,** Op. No.

3603, 793 P2d 1033 (Alaska 1990).

In trial of defendant for sexual abuse of his nine-year-old daughter, even if expertise of certain expert witnesses fell short of meeting standard established for experts, their opinions were properly admitted under more permissive standard governing opinion testimony by lay witnesses. **Reutter v. State,** Op. No. 1380, 886 P2d 1298 (Alaska App. 1994).

Mother of alleged sexual assault victim could give lay testimony as to her daughter's mental capacity. **Jackson v. State,** Op. No. 1392, 890 P2d 587 (Alaska App. 1995).

Superior court did not abuse its discretion in excluding lay opinion on evaluation of reasonableness of State's road maintenance efforts where witness had no firsthand knowledge of State's road maintenance procedures or resources available for this purpose. **Estate of Arrowwood v. State,** Op. No. 4196, 894 P2d 642 (Alaska 1995).

Where witness had no recollection of road conditions or state's maintenance efforts on date of accident, her opinion of the reasonableness of the State's maintenance efforts was not relevant. **Estate of Arrowwood v. State,** Op. No. 4196, 894 P2d 642 (Alaska 1995).

Defendant was not entitled to present alleged rape victim's ex-fiance's lay opinion as to the alleged victim's credibility as the ex-fiance repeatedly acknowledged that his skepticism of the alleged victim's story was not rationally based on his observations of her behavior, but that it arose instead from his own jealous and possessive nature and the ex-fiance's opinion of the alleged victim's story could not have materially assisted the jury in deciding any disputed fact. **Kitchens v. State,** Op. No. 1414, 898 P2d 443 (Alaska App. 1995).

Contract manager was qualified to express his opinion as lay witness concerning contract negotiations and meaning of resulting equipment lease in which he was personally involved. **Little Susitna Const. v. Soil Processing,** Op. No. 4845, 944 P2d 20 (Alaska 1997).

So long as a lay witness's conclusion is rationally based on his perception and is helpful to a clear understanding of his testimony, the witness may testify that another person seemed scared. **Markgraf v. State,** Op. No. 1705, 12 P3d 197 (Alaska App. 2000).

In a negligence suit, a court did not err by admitting the investigating officer's testimony where it was not error to permit the officer to base opinions on the officer's expertise because plaintiff was fully aware of the content of the officer's proposed testimony, and where plaintiff was able to depose the officer and thus suffered no prejudice from defendant's decision to list the officer as a fact witness. **Getchell v. Lodge,** Op. No. 5668, 65 P.3d 50 (Alaska 2003).

Rule 702. Testimony by Experts.

(a) If scientific, technical, or other specialized knowledge will assist the trier of fact to understand the evidence or to determine a fact in issue, a witness qualified as an expert by knowledge, skill, experience, training, or education, may testify thereto in the form of an opinion or otherwise.

(b) No more than three independent expert witnesses may testify for each side as to the same issue in any given case. For purposes of this rule, an independent expert is a witness who is retained or specially employed to provide expert testimony in the case or whose duties as an employee of the party regularly involve giving expert testimony. The court, upon the showing of good cause, may increase or decrease the number of independent experts to be called.

(c) **[Applicable to cases filed on or after August 7, 1997.]** Professional Negligence Cases. In an action based on professional negligence, a person may not testify as an expert witness on the issue of the appropriate standard of care except as provided in AS 09.20.185.

(Added by SCO 364 effective August 1, 1979; amended by SCO 793 effective March 15, 1987; by SCO 1172 effective July 15, 1995; by SCO 1269 effective July 15, 1997; and by SCO 1281 effective August 7, 1997)

Note: In 1996, the legislature enacted AS 12.45.037 relating to the admissibility of expert testimony about criminal street gang activity. According to § 11 ch. 60 SLA 1996, this statute has the effect of amending Evidence Rule 702 to allow expert testimony to be admitted in a criminal prosecution to show criminal gang characteristics, activity, and practices.

AS 09.20.185, enacted by sec. 15, ch. 26, SLA 1997, effective August 7, 1997, has the effect of amending this rule by requiring certain qualifications from a person testifying as an expert witness.

Note to SCO 1281: In 1997 the legislature enacted AS 09.20.185 which prohibits a person from testifying as an expert in a professional negligence action unless the person has the qualifications listed in AS 09.20.185(a). According to ch. 26, § 51, SLA 1997, this statute has the effect of amending Evidence Rule 702 by requiring certain qualifications for a person testifying as an expert witness. According to § 55 of the session law, AS 09.20.185 applies "to all causes of action accruing on or after the effective date of this Act." However, Rule 702(c), adopted by paragraph 15 of this order, is applicable to all cases filed on or after August 7, 1997. See paragraph 17 of this order.

Annotations

Cases

In action against state concerning alleged negligent inspection, trial court did not err in allowing expert to state his opinion as to whether the inspection was negligent, where the opinion was helpful to the trier of fact, was based upon facts or data reasonably relied on by other experts, and was not unduly prejudicial or misleading, particularly where any possible confusion or prejudice was cured by predicating the expert's opinion on a standard of care and issuing a cautionary instruction. **Wilson v. State,** Op. No. 2720, 669 P2d 1292 (Alaska 1983).

Trial judge did not abuse his discretion in refusing to admit expert testimony that pimps would rather settle disputes among themselves than go to the police since the jurors themselves would certainly have arrived at that conclusion. **Wortham v. State,** Op. No. 414, 689 P2d 1133 (Alaska App. 1984).

Trial court is vested with considerable latitude to decide whether an expert should be allowed to testify; the court's decision is reviewable only for an abuse of discretion. **New v. State,** Op. No. 587, 714 P2d 378 (Alaska App. 1986).

Trial court did not abuse its discretion in excluding expert testimony of former truck driver in support of defendant's "point of no return" defense to manslaughter charge arising out of defendant's failure to stop his truck at a red light, since the testimony would have been cumulative, could have confused the jury, and in any case concerned a common sense concept readily capable of being understood by lay persons. **New v. State,** Op. No. 587, 714 P2d 378 (Alaska App. 1986).

There is no requirement that a witness possess a particular license or academic degree in order to qualify as an expert; the criterion in determining whether a person qualifies as an expert is whether the fact finder can receive appreciable help from that person. **Dymenstein v. State,** Op. No. 624, 720 P2d 42 (Alaska App. 1986).

Trial court at sentencing hearing did not err in allowing police officer to testify as an expert on the subject of pedophilia, even though his expertise was based on police investigation rather than academic studies. **Dymenstein v. State,** Op. No. 624, 720 P2d 42 (Alaska App. 1986).

Witness with credentials in the area of electronic engineering and computer technology who had experience with vehicle operating systems was qualified to be an expert witness in a negligence action against a driver of an Audi 5000 automobile who contended that the automobile had spontaneously accelerated through no fault of her own. **Norris v. Gatts,** Op. No. 3187, 738 P2d 344 (Alaska 1987).

A physician with extensive experience in treating native women was qualified to give an opinion on whether a native sexual assault victim's behavior was inconsistent with that of other Nakues who have undergone trauma. **Hilburn v. State,** Op. No. 800, 765 P2d 1382 (Alaska App. 1988).

Fairness requires equal treatment by the court of opposing experts; accordingly, where jury was specifically informed that prosecution's witness was accepted as an expert, a similar instruction for defendant's expert witness should have been given. **Nelson v. State,** Op. No. 981, 782 P2d 290 (Alaska App. 1989).

Expert testimony in child sexual abuse case, the overall tenor of which was that a child who consistently gave detailed reports of sexual abuse was reporting actual abuse, was so obviously prejudicial as to approach plain error, thus trial court committed reversible error in not allowing defendant to contact an expert to combat the testimony. **Cox v. State,** Op. No. 1102, 805 P2d 374 (Alaska App. 1991).

Expert testimony that a child had been sexually molested and was suffering from post-traumatic stress would be admissible at trial and could therefore be considered by trial court in ruling on a motion for summary judgment. **Broderick v. King's Way Assembly of God,** Op. No. 3677, 808 P2d 1211 (Alaska 1991).

In murder trial in which the defense claimed that the victim shot himself, trial court committed reversible error in excluding testimony of a psychiatrist who concluded that defendant's initial statements to the police claiming responsibility for the shooting were a product of psychogenic amnesia, confabulations and fugue states, and who also concluded that the victim was more likely to commit suicide than the average person; the expert testimony was crucial to the defense, the expert was a qualified psychiatrist, and his opinion was based upon a standard diagnosis contained in books by reliable psychiatric authorities. **Beagel v. State,** Op. No. 1142, 813 P2d 699 (Alaska App. 1991).

Policeman who had worked in sexual assault unit for four years and had received 120 hours of specialized training in the area of child sexual abuse was properly permitted to answer questions on why a child sexual abuse victim might give inconsistent answers and whether it was unusual for a sexual abuse complaint to be uncorroborated by medical evidence. **Kosbruk v. State,** Op. No. 1172, 820 P2d 1082 (Alaska App. 1991).

This rule does not require expertise in precisely the area upon which the expert proposes to comment; accordingly, trial court erred in excluding the testimony of expert on compressors on the ground that the particular compressor part at issue was not in the area of his expertise. **Colt Ind. v. Frank W. Murphy Manufacturer,** Op. No. 3788, 822 P2d 925 (Alaska 1991).

Exclusion of testimony by plaintiff's expert was error even though his conclusion was the same as that of another plaintiff's expert who did testify; the mere fact that another witness has already testified does not foreclose a litigant's right to introduce substantiating testimony, since juries may find one witness more compelling than another, or may attribute greater weight to a finding if more than one expert reaches the same conclusion. **Colt Ind. v. Frank W. Murphy Manufacturer,** Op. No. 3788, 822 P2d 925 (Alaska 1991).

In murder trial of defendant claiming self-defense, trial court committed reversible error in excluding expert testimony that defendant's failure to report the homicide and his efforts to cover it up resulted not from his consciousness of guilt but rather from post traumatic stress disorder, a psychological condition defendant claimed to suffer as result of war in Viet Nam. **Shepherd v. State,** Op. No. 1283, 847 P2d 75 (Alaska App. 1993).

In trial of defendant for sexual abuse of his nine-year-old daughter, trial court did not err in allowing social worker, child advocate, and assistant attorney general to testify as experts, since all had professional experiences that made their opinions helpful to trial court and all had considerable contact with victim. **Reutter v. State,** Op. No. 1380, 886 P2d 1298 (Alaska App. 1994).

In trial of defendant for sexual abuse of his nine-year-old daughter, even if expertise of certain expert witnesses fell short of meeting standard established for experts, their opinions were properly admitted under more permissive standard governing opinion testimony by lay witnesses. **Reutter v. State,** Op. No. 1380, 886 P2d 1298 (Alaska App. 1994).

In medical malpractice action, trial court did not abuse its discretion in refusing to exclude certain defense experts who disagreed as to some theories of causation, despite plaintiffs' contention that it served more to confuse than to assist jury. **Sweet v. Sisters of Providence in Washington,** Op. No. 4200, 895 P2d 484 (Alaska 1995).

Trial court's decision in medical malpractice case to allow defendant hospital and defendant doctors to jointly call eleven expert witnesses regarding causation and standard of care while plaintiffs called only five experts on those issues was not abuse of discretion. **Sweet v. Sisters of Providence in Washington,** Op. No. 4200, 895 P2d 484 (Alaska 1995).

Trial court's decision in medical malpractice case to allow defendant hospital and defendant doctors to jointly call eleven expert witnesses on issues of causation and standard of care with warning that court would not tolerate repetitive testimony was proper despite plaintiffs' contention that court should not have allowed so many expert witnesses. **Sweet v. Sisters of Providence in Washington,** Op. No. 4200, 895 P2d 484 (Alaska 1995).

In action for abatement of public nuisance against massage parlor and escort service, police officers' specific opinions as to whether business was operating as house of prostitution did not meet criteria for scientific, technical, or other specialized knowledge which would assist trier of fact as required by this rule, thus trial court abused its discretion in admitting their opinions. **SAC v. Lot 3, Block 1, Evergreen,** Op. No. 4245, 902 P2d 766 (Alaska 1995).

The trial court's finding that the laboratories that tested DNA in this case followed standard, generally accepted procedures was supported by the record. This made it unnecessary for the appellate court to decide whether **People v. Castro,** 144 Misc. 2d 956, 545 N.Y.S. 2d 985 (N.Y. Sup. 1989), applied to this case. **Harmon v. State,** Op. No. 1450, 908 P2d 434 (Alaska App. 1995).

Statistical analysis of the DNA test satisfied the **Frye** test and therefore the results were admissible in a sexual assault and murder prosecution. **Harmon v. State,** Op. No. 1450, 908 P2d 434 (Alaska App. 1995).

In AS 12.45.035, the Alaska legislature apparently declared that DNA evidence is admissible despite the potential problem that the presence of population substructures would tend to overstate the significance of a DNA match. **Harmon v. State,** Op. No. 1450, 908 P2d 434 (Alaska App. 1995).

The population statistical analyses of the PCR typing and the RFLP matching are generally accepted within the scientific community. Therefore, the trial court did not err in admitting evidence of DNA typing and the statistical interpretation of this evidence. **Harmon v. State,** Op. No. 1450, 908 P2d 434 (Alaska App. 1995).

Thirty years' experience in construction industry in Alaska qualified witness to testify as expert on impact of cold weather on construction equipment. **Little Susitna Const. v. Soil Processing,** Op. No. 4845, 944

P2d 20 (Alaska 1997).

Police officer may testify to results of horizontal gaze nystagmus test for intoxication if it is established that officer has been adequately trained in administration and assessment of test. **Ballard v. State,** Op. No. 1584, 955 P2d 931 (Alaska App. 1998).

The **Daubert** standard, articulated in **Daubert v. Merrell Dow Pharmaceuticals, Inc.,** 509 U.S. 579 (1993), rather than the **Frye**standard, articulated in **Frye v. United States,** 293 F. 1013 (D.C. Cir. 1923), is the standard for determining admissibility of scientific evidence; overruling **Contreras v. State,** 718 P2d 129 (Alaska 1986). **State v. Coon,** Op. No. 5091, 974 P2d 386 (Alaska 1999).

In prosecution of defendant for making terroristic telephone calls, it was not error to admit opinion evidence, based on voice spectrographic analysis, that defendant made those calls. **State v. Coon,** Op. No. 5091, 974 P2d 386 (Alaska 1999).

In sexual assault case where defendant was convicted of engaging in sexual penetration with a woman who was so intoxicated that she was either incapacitated or unaware of the sexual penetration, trial court did not err in ruling that defendant's proposed expert witness on "alcoholic blackouts" lacked the expertise to offer an opinion on the subject or in ruling that such testimony, offered to support the defense theory that victim consented to sexual intercourse but could not remember giving consent due to alcoholic blackout, was more prejudicial than probative. **Ragsdale v. State,** Op. No. 1746, 23 P3d 653 (Alaska App. 2001).

Inmate made no showing that the State submitted more than three experts as to any issue, and because the case never went to trial, the experts listed never actually testified; as such, there was no error by the superior court. **Willoya v. State,** Op. No. 5622, 53 P.3d 1115 (Alaska 2002).

In a negligence suit, a court did not err by admitting the investigating officer's testimony as an expert witness where the officer served as a state trooper for 20 years, and the officer routinely determined whether there were any human factors contributing to accidents involving moose, such as speeding, or whether the accident was simply the result of a moose interfering with motor vehicle traffic. **Getchell v. Lodge,** Op. No. 5668, 65 P.3d 50 (Alaska 2003).

In a negligence suit, a court did not err by admitting the investigating officer's testimony where it was not error to permit the officer to base opinions on the officer's expertise because plaintiff was fully aware of the content of the officer's proposed testimony, and where plaintiff was able to depose the officer and thus suffered no prejudice from defendant's decision to list the officer as a fact witness. **Getchell v. Lodge,** Op. No. 5668, 65 P.3d 50 (Alaska 2003).

Expert testimony on the issues of police interrogation practices and the risk of false confessions was excluded where the trial court, in its discretion, determined that the expert's testimony would not have appreciably aided the jury in determining whether or not defendant had made a false confession. **Vent v. State,** Op. No. 1864, 67 P.3d 661 (Alaska App. 2003).

In an arrestee's suit against a city, a police officer, and an immigration officer alleging the use of excessive force during her arrest, application of Daubert standard was not a prerequisite to the admission of a psychiatrist's testimony regarding the arrestee's malingering where the testimony stemmed from a typical psychiatric exam of the arrestee such an evaluation was a long-recognized technique that had been empirically tested, subjected to extensive peer review and publication, and generally accepted in the psychological community. **Samaniego v. City of Kodiak,** Op. No. 5751, 80 P.3d 216 (Alaska 2003).

In a driver's false confinement case against a city, a court properly excluded the city's expert testimony regarding the "use of force" where the expert's report contained solely conclusory opinions that the officer's actions toward the driver were at all times objectively reasonable, and that the seizure of the driver was objectively reasonable under the totality of the circumstances. Additionally, the expert's legal conclusion that the officer properly seized the driver as a material witness conflicted with the trial court's correct conclusion that exigent circumstances did not exist. **City of Kodiak v. Samaniego,** Op. No. 5772, 83 P.3d 1077 (Alaska 2004).

Expert witness was permitted to give an opinion that defendant was not driving while intoxicated at the time of her arrest, but was not permitted to base the opinion on the results of a preliminary breath test because defendant declined to submit testimony as to the scientific validity of the preliminary test. **Guerre-Chaley v. State,** Op. No. 1924, 88 P.3d 539 (Alaska App. 2004).

Test for evaluating the validity of scientific evidence does not apply to shoeprint analysis, and criminologist's explanation of shoeprint comparison and analysis was not something that could only be understood and interpreted by experts; the analysis did not rest on arcane scientific principles, or on the results of tests, and defendant failed to cast doubt on the methodological validity of expert's shoeprint analysis **Ratliff v. State,** Op. No. 1977, 110 P.3d 982 (Alaska App. 2005).

Admissibility of experience-based testimony should be governed by the traditional standards and rules of evidence where the expert testimony is plainly derived from experience — not from the scientific method — and is not dependent on sophisticated scientific theory, Daubert does not apply. **Marron v. Stromstad,** Op. No. 5955, 123 P.3d 992 (Alaska 2005).

In a medical malpractice case, defendant doctor's experts were properly allowed to testify where their testimony concerning the amount and kinds of information that patients generally wanted in late night phone calls was relevant to establish whether the doctor gave the patient as much information as a reasonable patient would want to know. **Marsingill v. O'Malley,** Op. No. 5977, 128 P.3d 151 (Alaska 2006).

This rule's requirement that a witness be qualified as an expert before proceeding to provide expert opinion testimony was not violated even though the court failed to qualify the witness during the hearing where the witness already qualified as an expert in a similar case, the witness made no attempt to hide his limited knowledge of the present case, and it was unclear what injustice resulted from the failure to qualify the witness. **Wetherhorn v. Alaska Psychiatric Institute**, Op. No. 11939, 156 P.3d 371 (Alaska 2007).

Rule 703. Basis of Opinion Testimony by Experts.

The facts or data in the particular case upon which an expert bases an opinion or inference may be those perceived by or made known to the expert at or before the hearing. Facts or data need not be admissible in evidence, but must be of a type reasonably relied upon by experts in the particular field in forming opinions or inferences upon the subject.

(Added by SCO 364 effective August 1, 1979; amended by SCO 1153 effective July 15, 1994, and by SCO 1247 effective July 15, 1996)

Note: Sec. 3 of ch. 7 SLA 1995 states: "AS 09.25.051, added by sec. 1 of this Act, and AS 12.45.035, added by sec. 2 of this Act, have the effect of amending Rule 703, Alaska Rules of Evidence, to the extent that Rule 703 would limit the admissibility of DNA profile evidence as a result of the application of the standard previously adopted by the Alaska Supreme Court in Pulakis v. State, 476 P.2d 474 (Alaska 1970), that requires a finding of general acceptance of scientific evidence in the relevant scientific community as a precondition of admission of scientific evidence."

Annotations

Cases

Trial court did not commit error in excluding statements made by murder defendant to psychiatrist that he was unable to recall the murder and did not recall other violent incidents which had occurred when he was intoxicated. **Evans v. State,** Op. No. 2505, 645 P2d 155 (Alaska 1982).

In action against state concerning alleged negligent inspection, trial court did not err in allowing expert to state his opinion as to whether the inspection was negligent, where the opinion was helpful to the trier of fact, was based upon facts or data reasonably relied on by other experts, and was not unduly prejudicial or misleading, particularly where any possible confusion or prejudice was cured by predicating the expert's opinion on a standard of care and issuing a cautionary instruction. **Wilson v. State,** Op. No. 2720, 669 P2d 1292 (Alaska 1983).

Consumer complaint reports to the National Highway Traffic Safety Agency, relied upon by an expert witness in a negligence action involving alleged spontaneous acceleration of an Audi 5000 automobile, met the "reasonable reliance" criteria of this rule. **Norris v. Gatts,** Op. No. 3187, 738 P2d 344 (Alaska 1987).

Argument that expert could not properly testify as to child's alleged sexual abuse because he improperly based his opinion on an inadmissible report was rejected; this rule explicitly allows an expert to rely on otherwise inadmissible evidence, so long as the material is of a type reasonably relied upon by the experts in the field. **Broderick v. King's Way Assembly of God,** Op. No. 3677, 808 P2d 1211 (Alaska 1991).

Psychiatrist as expert witness could rely on hypnotically-induced testimony to the extent that psychiatrists generally rely on such information to arrive at a diagnosis. **Beagel v. State,** Op. No. 1142, 813 P2d 699 (Alaska App. 1991).

In murder trial in which the defense claimed that the victim shot himself, trial court committed reversible error in excluding the testimony of a psychiatrist who concluded that defendant's initial statements to the police claiming responsibility for the shooting were a product of psychogenic amnesia, confabulation and fugue states, and who also concluded that the victim was more likely to commit suicide than the average person; the expert testimony was crucial to the defense, the expert was a qualified psychiatrist, and his opinion was based upon a standard diagnosis contained in books by reliable psychiatric authorities. **Beagel v. State,** Op. No. 1142, 813 P2d 699 (Alaska App. 1991).

Reliance by compressor manufacturer's expert on supplier's product return documents to substantiate opinion that supplier's product was defective satisfied the reasonable reliance test of Norris v. Gatts, Op. No. 3187, 738 P2d 344 (Alaska 1987). **Colt Ind. v. Frank W. Murphy Manufacturer,** Op. No. 3788, 822 P2d 925 (Alaska 1991).

In interpreting Alaska Rule 703, the courts are guided by cases and commentary interpreting Federal Rule of Evidence 703. **Estate of Arrowwood v. State,** Op. No. 4196, 894 P2d 642 (Alaska 1995).

Although this rule is meant to expand the breadth of information upon which an expert witness may rely, it is not intended merely to provide a conduit for the admission of otherwise inadmissible evidence. **Estate of Arrowwood v. State,** Op. No. 4196, 894 P2d 642 (Alaska 1995).

Subject to ER 705 (c) balancing test, if experts should have been allowed to rely on hearsay in the form of a transcript of a recorded interview in forming their opinion, they should have also been permitted to introduce the transcript at trial. **Estate of Arrowwood v. State,** Op. No. 4196, 894 P2d 642 (Alaska 1995).

This rule accords experts a degree of deference in determining whether specific facts or data are "of a type reasonably relied upon by experts in the particular field." However, the degree of deference that is appropriate varies by subject matter and underlying basis. **Estate of Arrowwood v. State,** Op. No. 4196, 894 P2d 642 (Alaska 1995).

Failure to admit transcript of recorded interview, if error, would not require reversal of jury's special verdict where appellant failed to show prejudice. **Estate of Arrowwood v. State,** Op. No. 4196, 894 P2d 642 (Alaska 1995).

Superior court did not abuse its discretion in concluding that it was not reasonable for highway maintenance and accident reconstruction experts to rely on a transcript of a recorded interview with a citizen who monitored police radio transmissions on the date of the accident calling for sanding trucks, and who personally observed "glare ice" on road and later saw sanding trucks. **Estate of Arrowwood v. State,** Op. No. 4196, 894 P2d 642 (Alaska 1995).

In suit by corporation against its former attorney for professional negligence and fiduciary fraud, defendant's argument that testimony of expert witness should have been disallowed because it was based upon evidence not presented at trial was rejected; facts and data that expert relied upon were same as reasonable experts in field would normally rely upon and therefore did not have to be admitted into evidence. **Cummings v. Sea Lion Corp.,** Op. No. 4416, 924 P2d 1011 (Alaska 1996).

The **Daubert** standard, articulated in **Daubert v. Merrell Dow Pharmaceuticals, Inc.,** 509 U.S. 579 (1993), rather than the **Frye** standard, articulated in **Frye v. United States,** 293 F. 1013 (D.C. Cir. 1923), is the standard for determining admissibility of scientific evidence; overruling **Contreras v. State,** 718 P2d 129 (Alaska 1986), **State v. Coon,** Op. No. 5091, 974 P2d 386 (Alaska 1999).

In prosecution of defendant for making terroristic telephone calls, it was not error to admit opinion evidence, based on voice spectrographic analysis, that defendant made those calls. **State v. Coon,** Op. No. 5091, 974 P2d 386 (Alaska 1999).

Expert witness was permitted to give an opinion that defendant was not driving while intoxicated at the time of her arrest, but was not permitted to base the opinion on the results of a preliminary breath test because defendant declined to submit testimony as to the scientific validity of the preliminary test; while Alaska R. Evid. 703 did not require underlying data to be independently admissible, where that data was derived from scientific tests or methods, the tests or methods had to meet the Daubert-Coon test for admissibility. **Guerre-Chaley v. State,** Op. No. 1924, 88 P.3d 539 (Alaska App. 2004).

Although defendant argued that the trial court abused its discretion by allowing testimony on DNA profile frequencies using the Athabascan database, there was substantial evidence to support the finding that the database used for statistical analysis of DNA profile frequencies was the type of data that experts in the field would have reasonably relied upon; therefore, the trial court did not abuse its discretion by allowing testimony on DNA profile frequencies using that database. **Dayton v. State,** Op. No. 1927, 89 P.3d 806 (Alaska App. 2004).

Alaska R. Evid. 407 prohibits evidence of "measures" that have been "taken;" "measures" means concrete actions, and leaves outside the rule's prohibition preliminary investigations and recommendations pointing toward those actions. Even if post-accident investigations and reports were considered "measures," the rule would not reach them **City of Bethel v. Peters,** Op. No. 5829, 97 P.3d 822 (Alaska 2004).

Trial court did not commit error in excluding statements made by murder defendant to psychiatrist that he was unable to recall the murder and did not recall other violent incidents which had occurred when he was intoxicated. **Ratliff v. State,** Op. No. 1977, 110 P.3d 982 (Alaska App. 2005).

Admissibility of experience-based testimony should be governed by the traditional standards and rules of evidence. Where the expert testimony is plainly derived from experience—not from the scientific method—and is not dependent on sophisticated scientific theory, Daubert does not apply. **Marron v. Stromstad,** Op. No. 5955, 123 P.3d 992 (Alaska 2005).

Rule 704. Opinion on Ultimate Issue.

Testimony in the form of an opinion or inference

otherwise admissible is not objectionable because it embraces an ultimate issue to be decided by the trier of fact.

(Added by SCO 364 effective August 1, 1979)

Annotations

Cases

In action against state concerning alleged negligent inspection, trial court did not err in allowing expert to state his opinion as to whether the inspection was negligent, where the opinion was helpful to the trier of fact, was based upon facts or data reasonably relied on by other experts, and was not unduly prejudicial or misleading, particularly where any possible confusion or prejudice was cured by predicating the expert's opinion on a standard of care and issuing a cautionary instruction. **Wilson v. State,** Op. No. 2720, 669 P2d 1292 (Alaska 1983).

Rule 705. Disclosure of Facts or Data Underlying Expert Opinion.

(a) **Disclosure of Facts or Data.** The expert may testify in terms of opinion or inference and give reasons therefor without prior disclosure of the underlying facts or data, unless the court requires otherwise. The expert may in any event disclose on direct examination, or be required to disclose on cross-examination, the underlying facts or data, subject to subdivisions (b) and (c).

(b) **Admissibility.** An adverse party may request a determination of whether the requirements of Rule 703 are satisfied before an expert offers an opinion or discloses facts or data.

(c) **Balancing Test—Limiting Instructions.** When the underlying facts or data would be inadmissible in evidence for any purpose other than to explain or support the expert's opinion or inference, the court shall exclude the underlying facts or data if the danger that they will be used for an improper purpose outweighs their value as support for the expert's opinion. If the facts or data are disclosed before the jury, a limiting instruction by the court shall be given upon request.

(Added by SCO 364 effective August 1, 1979; amended by SCO 1522 effective October 15, 2003)

Annotations

Cases

Trial court did not commit error in excluding statements made by murder defendant to psychiatrist that he was unable to recall the murder and did not recall other violent incidents which had occurred when he was intoxicated. **Evans v. State,** Op. No. 2505, 645 P2d 155 (Alaska 1982).

In parental rights termination proceeding, testimony of social workers and counselors as to information received from other caseworkers would have been admissible hearsay if the testimony had been offered as expert opinion. **Matter of J.R.B.,** Op. No. 3029, 715 P2d 1170 (Alaska 1986).

Where evidence relied upon by expert witness met the "reasonable reliance" test, trial court's failure to hold a hearing on that issue as required by this rule was harmless error. **Norris v. Gatts,** Op. No. 3187, 738 P2d 344 (Alaska 1987).

Subject to ER 705 (c) balancing test, if experts should have been allowed to rely on hearsay in the form of a transcript of a recorded interview in forming their opinion, they should have also been permitted to introduce the transcript at trial. **Estate of Arrowwood v. State,** Op. No. 4196, 894 P2d 642 (Alaska 1995).

Superior court did not abuse its discretion in concluding that it was not reasonable for highway maintenance and accident reconstruction experts to rely on a transcript of a recorded interview with a citizen who monitored police radio transmissions on the date of the accident calling for sanding trucks, and who personally observed "glare ice" on road and later saw sanding trucks. **Estate of Arrowwood v. State,** Op. No. 4196, 894 P2d 642 (Alaska 1995).

Failure to admit transcript of recorded interview, if error, would not require reversal of jury's special verdict where appellant failed to show prejudice. **Estate of Arrowwood v. State,** Op. No. 4196, 894 P2d 642 (Alaska 1995).

In condemnation action trial court had discretion to exclude tax assessments as evidence of market value even though assessments were contained in report of appraiser who testified at trial. **Four Separate Parcels v. City of Kodiak,** Op. No. 4785, 938 P2d 448 (Alaska 1997).

Alaska R. Evid. 705(c) supported a conclusion that establishing scientific validity was a prerequisite to the admission of evidence under Alaska R. Evid. 703; thus, a trial court properly permitted an expert to give an opinion that defendant was not driving while intoxicated at the time of her arrest, but precluded the expert from basing the opinion on the results of a preliminary breath test because defendant declined to submit testimony as to the scientific validity of the preliminary test. **Guerre Chaley v. State,** Op. No. 1924, 88 P.3d 539.

Rule 706. Court Appointed Experts.

(a) **Appointment.** The court may on its own motion or on the motion of any party enter an order to show cause why expert witnesses should not be appointed, and may request the parties to submit nominations. The court may appoint expert witnesses. An expert witness shall not be appointed by the court unless the witness consents to act. A witness so appointed shall be informed of the witness' duties by the court in writing, a copy of which shall be filed with the clerk, or at a conference in which the parties shall have opportunity to participate. A witness so appointed shall advise the parties of the witness' findings, if any; the witness' deposition may be taken by any party; and the witness may be called to testify by the court or any party. If the court determines that the interests of justice so require, the party calling an expert appointed under this rule may cross-examine the witness.

(b) **Disclosure of Appointment.** In the exercise of its discretion, the court may disclose to the jury the fact that the court appointed the expert witness.

(c) **Parties' Experts of Own Selection.** Nothing in this rule limits the parties in calling expert witnesses of their own selection.

(Added by SCO 364 effective August 1, 1979; amended by SCO 1153 effective July 15, 1994)

Annotations

Cases

Inmate was properly denied his motion to have an expert appointed because the rule was not intended as a means for an indigent party to obtain expert testimony at public expense; the superior court had no funds from which to support private litigation. **Willoya v. State,** Op. No. 5622, 53 P.3d 1115 (Alaska 2002).

ARTICLE VIII. HEARSAY

Rule 801. Definitions.

The following definitions apply under this article:

(a) **Statement.** A statement is (1) an oral or written assertion or (2) nonverbal conduct of a person, if it is intended by the person as an assertion.

(b) **Declarant.** A declarant is a person who makes a statement.

(c) **Hearsay.** Hearsay is a statement, other than one made by the declarant while testifying at the trial or hearing, offered in evidence to prove the truth of the matter asserted.

(d) **Statements Which Are Not Hearsay.** A statement is not hearsay if

(1) *Prior Statement by Witness.* The declarant testifies at the trial or hearing and the statement is

(A) inconsistent with the declarant's testimony. Unless the interests of justice otherwise require, the prior statement shall be excluded unless

(i) the witness was so examined while testifying as to give the witness an opportunity to explain or to deny the statement or

(ii) the witness has not been excused from giving further testimony in the action; or

(B) consistent with the declarant's testimony and is offered to rebut an express or implied charge against the declarant of recent fabrication or improper influence or motive; or

(C) one of identification of a person made after perceiving the person; or

(2) *Admission by Party-Opponent.* The statement is offered against a party and is (A) the party's own statement, in either an individual or a representative capacity, or (B) a statement of which the party has manifested an adoption or belief in its truth, or (C) a statement by a person authorized by the party to make a statement concerning the subject, or (D) a statement by the party's agent or servant concerning a matter within the scope of the agency or employment, made during the existence of the relationship, or (E) a statement by a co-conspirator of a party during the course and in furtherance of the conspiracy; or

(3) *Recorded Statement by Child Victims of Crime.* The statement is a recorded statement by the victim of a crime who is less than 16 years of age and

(A) the recording was made before the proceeding;

(B) the victim is available for cross-examination;

(C) the prosecutor and any attorney representing the defendant were not present when the statement was taken;

(D) the recording is on videotape or other format that records both the visual and aural components of the statement;

(E) each person who participated in the taking of the statement is identified on the recording;

(F) the taking of the statement as a whole was conducted in a manner that would avoid undue influence of the victim;

(G) the defense has been provided a reasonable opportunity to view the recording before the proceeding; and

(H) the court has had an opportunity to view the recording and determine that it is sufficiently reliable and trustworthy and that the interests of justice are best served by admitting the recording into evidence.

(Added by SCO 364 effective August 1, 1979; amended by SCO 1153 effective July 15, 1994; and by SCO 1580 effective July 7, 2005)

Note: Chapter 64, section 59, SLA 2005 (HB 53) amended Evidence Rule 801 as reflected in section 13 of this Order. The change to Evidence Rule 801 is adopted for the sole reason that the legislature has mandated the amendment.

Annotations

Cases

In suit against State for personal injury arising from collision of plaintiff's car and police car, report by state trooper's supervisors concerning his involvement in accident was admissible as statement of party opponent made by agent acting within scope of employment. **Rutherford v. State,** Op. No. 2001, 605 P2d 16 (Alaska 1979).

In suit for damages for unjust enrichment and misrepresentation, letter from defendant's attorney to state agency to effect that plaintiff had expended $35,000 on property repairs was properly admitted to show whether defendant had fulfilled promise to help plaintiff get liquor license, and thus had independent legal significance apart from fact it also tended to support plaintiff's claim for $15,000. **Willinaw Lodge v. Locke,** Op. No. 1951, 601 P2d 236 (Alaska 1979).

An admission is not inadmissible because it is not based on first-hand knowledge or is made in the form of an otherwise inadmissible opinion. **Rutherford v. State,** Op. No. 2001, 605 P2d 16 (Alaska 1979).

Memoranda prepared by state troopers concerning a traffic accident which they investigated were held admissible under Section (d)(2)(D) of this rule against the contention that the memoranda could be admitted only if the troopers were authorized to speak for the state on the question of negligence. **Rutherford v. State,** Op. No. 2001, 605 P2d 16 (Alaska 1979).

Evidence admissible under the joint undertaking exception to the hearsay rule does not automatically satisfy the requirements of the confrontation clause. To satisfy the right to confrontation, a statement must have sufficient indicia of reliability such that the unavailability of the declarant for cross-examination does not deprive the jury of a satisfactory basis for evaluating the truth of the extrajudicial declarations. **Hawley v. State,** Op. No. 2137, 614 P2d 1349 (Alaska 1980).

When an eight-year-old witness testifies at trial that he has forgotten much of what he had seen on the night of the crime, a videotape of his recollection of the crime made soon after the crime is admissible as a prior inconsistent statement. **Richards v. State,** Op. No. 2173, 616 P2d 870 (Alaska 1980).

When testimony is offered merely to establish the fact that a statement was made and not to prove the truth of the matter stated, the hearsay rule does not apply. **Putnam v. State,** Op. No. 2251, 629 P2d 35 (Alaska 1980).

An internal company document known as a "Surplus Disposal Request," whereby surplus materials were inventoried and disposal authorized, was not hearsay when admitted solely as evidence of surrounding circumstances relevant to interpretation of disputed contract. **Alyeska Pipeline Service Co. v. O'Kelley,** Op. No. 2510, 645 P2d 767 (Alaska 1982).

Trial court's admission at prosecution's request of defendant's police interview which contained exculpatory remarks by defendant was not hearsay since it was evidently not offered to demonstrate the truth of the matter asserted, i.e., defendant's innocence. **Walker v. State,** Op. No. 2570, 652 P2d 88 (Alaska 1982).

Where drug addict claimed to have heard third person confess to crime for which defendant's codefendant was convicted, trial judge did not abuse his discretion in holding that the prejudicial effect of the confession outweighed any probative value it might have had in impeaching the eyewitnesses' identification of codefendant and thereby undermining his identification of defendant where: (1) the drug addict had withdrawn a large part of his statement regarding the confession; (2) the third person denied ever having made the confession or committing the crime; (3) neither the fact that the third person made the statement or committed the crime was corroborated; and (4) the third person allegedly looked like the codefendant rather than defendant. **Larson v. State,** Op. No. 177, 656 P2d 571 (Alaska App. 1982).

Murder defendant's apparent unwillingness to answer employer's question about why he had failed to report shooting to the police qualified as an adoptive admission by silence admissible under this rule. **Bloomstrand v. State,** Op. No. 191, 656 P2d 584 (Alaska App. 1982).

Where a witness deliberately seeks to avoid testifying by claiming loss of memory in response to specific questions, prior statements of the witness relating to the subject matter of the questions are inconsistent within the meaning of this rule. **Van Hatten v. State,** Op. No. 269, 666 P2d 1047 (Alaska App. 1983).

Whether a defendant's constitutional right of confrontation will be violated by use of prior, extra-judicial statements of a witness as substantive evidence of guilt when the witness has been evasive or suffers from lack of memory is to be determined on a case-by-case basis, focusing on the extent to which the witness actually testifies and can be cross-examined, as well as the nature and reliability of his prior, out-of-court statements. **Van Hatten v. State,** Op. No. 269, 666 P2d 1047 (Alaska App. 1983).

Prior grand jury testimony of uncooperative prosecution witness was admissible as substantive evidence of defendant's guilt. **Van Hatten v. State,** Op. No. 269, 666 P2d 1047 (Alaska App. 1983).

In negligence action resulting from an oil platform explosion, trial court erred in excluding on hearsay grounds a letter from a fire safety company to the platform owner which was offered to prove solely that the owner was aware of a pressurization problem and that certain expert testimony was wrong, since the letter was not offered to prove the truth of the matter asserted, i.e., that there was a pressurization problem and that the defendant was negligent in not noticing it. **Wilson v. State,** Op. No. 2720, 669 P2d 1292 (Alaska 1983).

Trial court erred in excluding police dispatcher's testimony concerning phone call on the ground that she could not positively identify the caller since this rule does not require that a declarant be positively identified. **James v. State,** Op. No. 304, 671 P2d 885 (Alaska App. 1983).

In wrongful death action against a Borough arising out of a prisoner's suicide, statements made by Borough employees to police investigators were admissions of a party opponent which should have been considered by the trial court in ruling on a summary judgment motion, and the fact that the statements were unsworn was immaterial. **Kanayurak v. North Slope Borough,** Op. No. 2782, 677 P2d 893 (Alaska 1984).

In action concerning aircraft hull insurance policy, testimony of employees of the lessee of the aircraft as to statements made by Federal Aviation Administration officials, offered not to prove the truth of the statements, i.e., that pilots of public use aircraft need not be type rated, but rather to prove that the statements were made and that the lessee's belief that its pilots could legally fly the aircraft was therefore reasonable, was admissible. **Stewart-Smith Haidinger v. Avi-Truck, Inc.,** Op. No. 2810, 682 P2d 1108 (Alaska 1984).

In murder trial, admission of hearsay statement of codefendant that defendant "went out to roll a queer who had lots of money" was error, since the statement was not made "in furtherance of" a conspiracy, and the error required reversal of defendant's conviction. **Williamson v. State,** Op. No. 430, 692 P2d 965 (Alaska App. 1984).

In order to take advantage of the rule that a statement by a coconspirator of a party made during the course and in furtherance of the conspiracy is not hearsay, the state must show by a preponderance of the evidence: (1) existence of a conspiracy; (2) that the statement was made while the conspiracy was continuing; and (3) that the statement was made in furtherance of the conspiracy. **Adams v. State,** Op. No. 525, 706 P2d 1183 (Alaska App. 1985).

Although there are occasions when evidence rules must give way to due process considerations, so that evidence properly excludable under the rules of evidence must nonetheless be admitted to protect the constitutionally granted trial rights of the defendant, exclusion of hearsay statement did not raise a constitutional issue where the exclusion did not substantially affect defendant's ability to present his defense. **Balentine v. State,** Op. No. 538, 707 P2d 922 (Alaska App. 1985).

In suit by employee against employer for unlawful termination of employment, employee's testimony that the personnel manager told him that the reason for his termination was that "Mr. Wellington just wanted you terminated" was admissible as a statement within the scope of the personnel manager's employment, and was admissible without any showing of the basis for the statement. **Knight v. Amer. Guard & Alert, Inc.,** Op. No. 3021, 714 P2d 788 (Alaska 1986).

Personnel manager for security company guarding the Trans-Alaska Pipeline was not acting as the pipeline company's "agent or servant" within the meaning of this rule. **Knight v. Amer. Guard & Alert, Inc.,** Op. No. 3021, 714 P2d 788 (Alaska 1986).

Where purpose of allowing police officer to testify concerning out-of-court statement by child victim in sexual assault case was not to prove the truth of the matter asserted in the statement, i.e. that the child had engaged in fellatio with her father, but rather to establish that the child knew what a penis was, the testimony was admissible. **Drumbarger v. State,** Op. No. 601, 716 P2d 6 (Alaska App. 1986).

This rule does not require automatic exclusion of prior consistent statements made after a motive to testify falsely has arisen, but the statements may be used only for the purpose of rehabilitating the declarant's credibility, not as substantive evidence of defendant's guilt. **Nitz v. State,** Op. No. 629, 720 P2d 55 (Alaska App. 1986).

Where evidence of prior consistent statements was offered before the declarant testified, it was not properly admissible under this rule. **Nitz v. State,** Op. No. 629, 720 P2d 55 (Alaska App. 1986).

Defendant's conviction for sexual abuse of child was reversed because extensive evidence of prior consistent statements made by the victim was admitted at trial without any determination of its actual probative value and before any charge of recent fabrication or improper motive or influence was made against the victim. **Nitz v. State,** Op. No. 629, 720 P2d 55 (Alaska App. 1986).

Evidence of consistent statements made by a child abuse victim on prior occasions may be admitted to bolster the testimony of the victim in a case involving the sexual abuse of the child, provided that it is actually relevant to rebut an express or implied charge of recent fabrication or improper motive or influence, and provided that its probative value outweighs its potential for prejudicial impact; before such evidence is admitted, however, the victim must testify and be subjected to a charge of recent fabrication or improper motive or influence; furthermore when it appears that the alleged motive to testify falsely arose before the prior statement was made, the statement may be admitted only for the purpose of rehabilitating the victim's credibility and may not be considered as substantive evidence of guilt. **Nitz v. State,** Op. No. 629, 720 P2d 55 (Alaska App. 1986).

In trial of defendant for sexually assaulting his minor daughter, trial court did not err in admitting prior consistent statements about the rape made by the victim to her cousin and aunt. **Nusunginya v. State,** Op. No. 660, 730 P2d 172 (Alaska App. 1986).

In prosecution for sexual abuse of a five-year-old child, trial court did not abuse its discretion in ruling that the child's prior statements were inconsistent with her testimony at trial and therefore admissible where the child was given sufficient opportunity at trial to explain or deny those statements. **Bodine v. State,** Op. No. 708, 737 P2d 1072 (Alaska App. 1987).

In trial court did not err in admitting videotaped statement made by child sexual assault victim to a psychologist two days after the assault as a prior consistent despite discrepancies between the videotaped statement and her trial testimony, since her basic description of the assault was not inconsistent; furthermore, defendant's implication that the child had been recently influenced by the prosecution to incriminate him satisfied the requirement that a prior consistent statement be made before a motive to fabricate arises, since the videotaped statement was made before the child's conversation with the prosecutor and police. **Van Meter v. State,** Op. No. 747, 743 P2d 385 (Alaska App. 1987).

Admission of coconspirator's statements did not violate defendant's confrontation rights under either the United States or Alaska Constitutions. **Stumpfv. State,** Op. No.770,749 P2d 880 (Alaska App. 1988).

If one of the main goals of a conspirator is to receive money the conspiracy does not end until the money is paid; accordingly, statements made to further the conspiracy after the central crime is committed, but before payment is received, are admissible. **Stumpf v. State,** Op. No. 770,749 P2d 880 (Alaska App. 1988).

The underlying rationale of the coconspirator exception to the hearsay rule is an agency theory; accordingly, a coconspirator's simple admission to another person of complicity in the crime, that does not aid the accomplishment of the conspiracy's aims, is not admissible under the coconspirator exception to the hearsay rule. **Stumpf v. State,** Op. No. 770, 749 P2d 880 (Alaska App. 1988).

Before statements can be admitted at trial as statements of a coconspirator in the course of and in furtherance of the conspiracy, the state must show that there was an agreement of intent to carry out a criminal plan, that the statement was made during the conspiracy's existence, and that the statement was made in furtherance of the conspiracy. **Stumpf v. State,** Op. No. 770, 749 P2d 880 (Alaska App. 1988).

Under this rule, a statement is made "in furtherance of the conspiracy" if it was made with the intent to promote the conspiracy and its objectives; accordingly, casual admissions of guilt to third persons are not intended to further the conspiracy and are therefore not admissible under the rule. **Arnold v. State,** Op. No. 779, 751 P2d 494 (Alaska App. 1988).

Admissions of guilt or explanations of the conspiracy's aims or actions are admissible under this rule if the conspirator confides in persons who are not members of the conspiracy in order to induce them to provide assistance to the conspirators. **Arnold v. State,** Op. No.779,751 P2d 494 (Alaska App. 1988).

Where one of murder conspiracy's goals was received money for the murder, the conspiracy did not end until the money was paid sometime after the murder. **Arnold v. State,** Op. No. 779, 751 P2d 494 (Alaska App. 1988).

The state demonstrated by a preponderance of the evidence that there was an agreement to carry out a criminal plan, that a coconspirator's statement was made during the conspiracy's existence, and that the statement was made to further the conspiracy, thus the statement was admissible against the defendant pursuant to this rule. **Arnold v. State,** Op. No. 779, 751 P2d 494 (Alaska App. 1988).

Trial court erred in not making a specific finding as to the existence of a conspiracy before admitting evidence under the coconspirator doctrine, but the error was harmless due to the overwhelming evidence that a conspiracy existed. **Arnold v. State,** Op. No. 779, 751 P2d 494 (Alaska App. 1988).

In determining whether there is independent evidence of a defendant's participation in a conspiracy, the court may use statements of coconspirators that are independently admissible under an exception to the hearsay rule. **Stewart v. State,** Op. No. 809, 756 P2d 900 (Alaska App. 1988).

Declarant's statement that he was going to the airport to pick up drugs was admissible under the "state of mind" exception to the hearsay rule to show declarant's purpose in going to the airport; that statement, along with independent evidence that defendant met the declarant at the airport and then accompanied him to the place where a heroin sale was made, demonstrated by a preponderance of the evidence defendant's participation in a conspiracy to distribute heroin, therefore statements of defendant's coconspirators were admissible against him. **Stewart v. State,** Op. No. 809, 756 P2d 900 (Alaska App. 1988).

Admission of policeman's written synopsis of a statement made by the victim to the policeman was properly admitted for testimonial completeness in connection with a question that arose concerning whether the victim had made prior inconsistent statements. **Lee v. State,** Op. No. 843, 760 P2d 1039 (Alaska App. 1988).

Although a prior consistent statement made after an improper influence or motive arises cannot be used as substantive evidence, it is admissible to rehabilitate the declarant's credibility when it is relevant to rebut an implied charge of recent fabrication or improper influence or motive and when the statement's probative value outweighs its potential prejudicial effect. **Jonas v. State,** Op. No. 936, 773 P2d 960 (Alaska App. 1989).

In action alleging equipment damage from the sale of defective fuel, trial court committed reversible error in excluding as inadmissible hearsay offered testimony concerning admissions by one of the buyer's employees, a mechanic, that the equipment failure was not caused by defective fuel. **Klawock Heenya Corp. v. Dawson Const.,** Op. No. 3489, 778 P2d 219 (Alaska 1989).

In action for lost profits allegedly caused by purchase of defective fuel, a written summary of the lost profits prepared before trial by an employee of the purchaser, who did not testify at trial, was inadmissible hearsay since it was offered to prove the truth of matter asserted, namely the extent of the purchaser's lost profits. **Klawock Heenya Corp. v. Dawson Const.,** Op. No. 3489, 778 P2d 219 (Alaska 1989).

The rule that a statement is not hearsay if the statement is offered against a party and is a statement by his agent or servant concerning a matter within the scope of his agency or employment, made during the existence of the relationship, includes statements which merely concern the employee's duties. **Klawock Heenya Corp. v. Dawson Const.,** Op. No. 3489, 778 P2d 219 (Alaska 1989).

In joint trial, out-of-court statement by defendant introduced as part of the prosecution's case-in-chief, which was favorable to the codefendant but prejudicial to defendant, did not require severance, since the statement would have been admissible in a separate trial of defendant as an admission by a party opponent. **Miller v. State,** Op. No. 954, 778 P2d 593 (Alaska App. 1989).

In murder trial, trial court did not err in refusing to allow an Immigration Department investigator to testify for the defense regarding reports from unidentified informants of rumors that the victim's family had threatened to kill anyone who testified in favor of the defendant at trial; although the testimony of the informants themselves might not have been hearsay, the investigator's testimony would have been; furthermore, the probative value of the investigator's testimony would have been outweighed by possible confusion of issues and needless presentation of cumulative evidence, particularly since the prosecution's primary witness against defendant acknowledged her awareness of the rumors. **Zeciri v. State,** Op. No. 956, 779 P2d 795 (Alaska App. 1989).

A written medical report on injured worker prepared at the request and expense of the employer, introduced into evidence before the Alaska Workers' Compensation Board by the worker, was not hearsay, and the Board erred in requiring the worker to bear the cost of the employer's cross-examination of the authors of the report. **Frazier v. H.C. Price/CIRI Const. JV.,** Op. No. 3613, 794 P2d 103 (Alaska 1990).

Statements which are admitted as prior inconsistent statements may be used as substantive evidence. **Sheldon v. State,** Op. No. 1059, 796 P2d 831 (Alaska App. 1990).

Even if statement of witness in civil case was an admission of a party-opponent, it was inadmissible because its prejudicial impact outweighed its probativeness. **Zoerb v. Church Elec. Association, Inc.,** Op. No. 3636, 798 P2d 1258 (Alaska 1990).

Inadmissible hearsay assertions in an affidavit cannot be used either to oppose or support a motion for summary judgment. **Broderick v. King's Way Assembly of God,** Op. No. 3677, 808 P2d 1211 (Alaska 1991).

Testimony relating to defendant's failure to make exculpatory statements would have been inadmissible at trial for lack of foundation for application of the adoptive admissions theory, and was therefore improperly admitted to grand jury proceeding; the State's argument that admissibility of the evidence at trial would have turned on a balancing of probative value against prejudicial impact was rejected. **State v. Green,** Op. No. 1131, 810 P2d 1023 (Alaska App. 1991).

In action for wrongful job termination, out-of-court statements by supervisors who terminated plaintiff about plaintiff's work performance were not hearsay because they were introduced as proof of supervisors' state of mind, not as proof of truth of matter asserted in the statements. **Van Huff v. Sohio Alaska Petroleum Co.,** Op. No. 3857, 835 P2d 1181 (Alaska 1992).

Prior inconsistent statements of six-year-old witness made three years earlier were admissible even if he did not remember making the statements. **Brandon v. State,** Op. No. 1251, 839 P2d 400 (Alaska App. 1992).

Trial court did not err in allowing videotape of witness' prior inconsistent statements to be played since it revealed her demeanor when she made allegations of sexual abuse against defendant; defendant's argument that State failed to establish prior foundation for tape's admission because prosecutor did not ask witness about each and every inconsistent statement contained on the videotape was rejected. **Nunn v. State,** Op. No. 1278, 845 P2d 435 (Alaska App. 1993).

Admissions and confessions by party-opponent are not hearsay when used against party-opponent; as to any other person, such statements are hearsay and inadmissible unless exception to hearsay rule independently applies. **State v. McDonald,** Op. No. 1342, 872 P2d 627 (Alaska App. 1994).

Transcript of recorded interview with local resident who had been monitoring police radio transmissions was hearsay. **Estate of Arrowwood v. State,** Op. No. 4196, 894 P2d 642 (Alaska 1995).

Failure to admit transcript of recorded interview, if error, would not require reversal of jury's special verdict where appellant failed to show prejudice. **Estate of Arrowwood v. State,** Op. No. 4196, 894 P2d 642 (Alaska 1995).

Superior court did not abuse its discretion in concluding that it was not reasonable for highway maintenance and accident reconstruction experts to rely on a transcript of a recorded interview with a citizen who monitored police radio transmissions on the date of the accident calling for sanding trucks, and who personally observed "glare ice" on road and later saw sanding trucks. **Estate of Arrowwood v. State,** Op. No. 4196, 894 P2d 642 (Alaska 1995).

The law distrusts hearsay, allowing it only when the circumstances of the utterance and/or the motivation of the speaker affirmatively demonstrate good reason to credit the out-of-court statement. **Ryan v. State,** Op. No. 1417, 899 P2d 1371 (Alaska App. 1995).

At trial of father for sexual abuse of daughter at which daughter testified that she did not remember being abused, prior statements of daughter detailing father's sexual abuse were admissible under this rule which permits use of hearsay statements for truth of the matter asserted if declarant testifies at trial and statements are inconsistent with declarant's testimony; father's argument that daughter did not meaningfully "testify" at trial, thereby making this rule inapplicable, was rejected. **Natkong v. State,** Op. No. 1485, 925 P2d 672 (Alaska App. 1996).

Statements by employees in company investigator's memorandum concerning sexual harassment by another employee were admissible in sexual harassment trial as non-hearsay admissions of party-opponent. **Norcon, Inc. v. Kotowski,** Op. No. 5085, 971 P2d 158 (Alaska 1999).

In action against city for negligence in connecting plaintiff's water line to water line of neighboring house, out-of-court statements by city employees that lines were interconnected were admissions by a party-opponent under this rule and therefore not inadmissible hearsay; statements did not have to be authorized by employer as long as they concerned employees' duties, nor did they have to be based on first-hand knowledge. **Lane v. City of Kotzebue,** Op. No. 5140, 982 P2d 1270 (Alaska 1999).

In action by insurance agent to equitably estop Alaska Division of Insurance from suspending his license, statements by former Director of the Division of Insurance to the agent that the "matter was over" and that "the Director had decided to impose no sanctions" were admissions of a party-opponent and therefore admissible non-hearsay. **State, Dept. of Commerce and Economic Development v. Schnell,** Op. No. 5314, 8 P3d 351 (Alaska 2000).

So long as a lay witness's conclusion is rationally based on his perception and is helpful to a clear understanding of his testimony, the witness may testify that another person seemed scared. **Markgraf v. State,** Op. No. 1705, 12 P3d 197 (Alaska App. 2000).

In sexual assault prosecution where the defense was consent and the state was allowed to present evidence of a prior sexual assault by defendant against a different victim, trial court committed reversible error in denying defendant's request that jury be informed of his acquittal on the prior sexual assault charge, since the evidence of that acquittal was relevant and not hearsay, its potential for confusion did not outweigh its potential probative value, and its exclusion was prejudicial to defendant. **Hess v. State,** Op. No. 5386, 20 P3d 1121 (Alaska 2001).

In a prosecution of defendant for assaulting defendant's mother and father, the trial court did not abuse its discretion when it: (1) admitted the father's prior inconsistent statement with minimal foundation presented, and (2) ruled that the father's prior statements were inconsistent with the father's genuine lack of memory at trial. **Wassiie v. State,** Op. No. 1836, 57 P.3d 719 (Alaska App. 2002).

If a witness claims not to remember the substance of a prior statement at trial, the witness's trial testimony is inconsistent with the prior statement for purposes of Alaska R. Evid. 801(d)(1)(A). It is irrelevant for purposes of the rule whether the claimed memory loss is genuine or feigned because the claimed lack of memory at trial (whether genuine or feigned) is inconsistent with the witness's earlier claim to remember. **Wassilie v. State,** Op. No. 1836, 57 P.3d 719 (Alaska App. 2002).

Any arguable hearsay error in allowing an investigating trooper to describe a translated interview with a Spanish-speaking criminal defendant was harmless because the translating trooper also testified, his account of the conversation was the same as the investigating trooper's, and the defense did not attack the accuracy of that account. The court noted that the weight of recent authority favored the rule that a translator—at least, a translator who was capable and fair—did not add another layer of hearsay. **Cruz-Reyes v. State,** Op. No. 1891, 74 P.3d 219 (Alaska App. 2003).

In a criminal prosecution for sexual abuse of a minor, the court was permitted to hear evidence of the child-victim's hearsay statements of the abuse made to her mother; because the child-victim had no memory of the statements, they were admissible as prior inconsistent statements. **Vaska v. State,** Op. No. 1890, 74 P.3d 225 (Alaska App. 2003).

Affidavit of a state labor relations analyst did not contain hearsay to the extent that it recited the testimony of a director as to the reason for terminating a public employee. That testimony did not go to the truth of the matter asserted, i.e. that the employee's position was one of public trust, but rather to the director's own belief why she thought the termination was for just cause. **Alaska State Emples. Association/AFSCME Local 52 v. State,** Op. No. 5713, 74 P.3d 881 (Alaska 2003).

Testimony of a witness in an action to quiet title regarding a conversation between a property owner and a property claimant, wherein they agreed that the claimant would live on the owner's land and in exchange he would supply her with food, was not hearsay under Alaska R. Evid. 802 and this rule because it was not offered to prove the truth of the matter; the testimony was relevant to prove that they said they would perform and therefore entered an agreement. **Glover v. Glover,** Op. No. 5812, 92 P.3d 387 (Alaska 2004).

In a retaliatory discharge case, the trial court properly struck the testimony by a manager that he had been told that morning that the employee's position had been eliminated due to a company reorganization, because such statement was inadmissible hearsay that did not fall into any hearsay exception. **Reust v. Alaska Petroleum Contrs., Inc.,** Op. No. 5951, 127 P.3d 807 (Alaska 2005).

The party offering a statement under the inconsistent statement exception to the hearsay rule must satisfy two foundational conditions. First, the offering party must show that the prior statement is indeed inconsistent with the declarant's testimony. Second, the witness who made the prior statement must be given an opportunity to explain or deny it. **Vaska v. State**, Op. No. 11171, 135 P.3d 1011 (Alaska 2006).

"Inconsistency" in the inconsistent statement exception to the hearsay rule does not necessarily require textual conflict; other circumstances, including lack of memory at trial, may suffice. **Vaska v. State**, Op. No. 11171, 135 P.3d 1011 (Alaska 2006).

A claim of inconsistency based on faulty memory normally must be raised by the offering party at the trial court level because the question whether a declarant's alleged lack of memory establishes inconsistency often becomes a disputed issue. The trial court is best situated to resolve testimonial disputes of this kind, and raising the issue in the trial court ensures that the party against whom the prior statement is offered will have ample notice that inconsistency has been asserted and a fair opportunity to contest this foundational point. **Vaska v. State**, Op. No. 11171, 135 P.3d 1011 (Alaska 2006).

Rule 802. Hearsay Rule.

Hearsay is not admissible except as provided by these rules, by other rules prescribed by the Alaska Supreme Court, or by enactment of the Alaska Legislature.

(Added by SCO 364 effective August 1, 1979)

Annotations

Cases

In action concerning aircraft hull insurance policy, testimony of employees of the lessee of the aircraft as to statements made by Federal Aviation Administration officials, offered not to prove the truth of the statements, i.e., that pilots of public use aircraft need not be type rated, but rather to prove that the statements were made and that the lessee's belief that its pilots could legally fly the aircraft was therefore reasonable, was admissible. **Stewart Smith Haidinger v. Avi-Truck, Inc.,** Op. No. 2810, 682 P2d 1108 (Alaska 1984).

Admission of allegedly hearsay statements in questions asked by police officers in taped interview of defendant, if error, was harmless. **Lipscomb v. State,** Op. No. 477, 700 P2d 1298 (Alaska App. 1985).

In action for lost profits allegedly caused by purchase of defective fuel, a written summary of the lost profits prepared before trial by an employee of the purchaser, who did not testify at trial, was inadmissible hearsay since it was offered to prove the truth of the matter asserted, namely the extent of the purchaser's lost profits. **Klawock Heenya Corp. v. Dawson Const.,** Op. No. 3489, 778 P2d 219 (Alaska 1989).

Transcript of recorded interview with local resident who had been monitoring police radio transmissions was hearsay. **Estate of Arrowwood v. State,** Op. No. 4196, 894 P2d 642 (Alaska 1995).

Failure to admit transcript of recorded interview, if error, would not require reversal of jury's special verdict where appellant failed to show prejudice. **Estate of Arrowwood v. State,** Op. No. 4196, 894 P2d 642 (Alaska 1995).

Superior court did not abuse its discretion in concluding that it was not reasonable for highway maintenance and accident reconstruction experts to rely on a transcript of a recorded interview with a citizen who monitored police radio transmissions on the date of the accident calling for sanding trucks, and who personally observed "glare ice" on road and later saw sanding trucks. **Estate of Arrowwood v. State,** Op. No. 4196, 894 P2d 642 (Alaska 1995).

The law distrusts hearsay, allowing it only when the circumstances of the utterance and/or the motivation of the speaker affirmatively demonstrate good reason to credit the out-of-court statement. **Ryan v. State,** Op. No. 1417, 899 P2d 1371 (Alaska App. 1995).

The "first complaint of rape" exception to the hearsay rule applies only when the victim testifies. **Ryan v. State,** Op. No. 1417, 899 P2d 1371 (Alaska App. 1995).

A police officer's testimony that a woman said she had been sexually assaulted by two men and later, in a line-up, identified these men as defendants was hearsay and could not be used over defendant's objection unless it fell within an exception to the hearsay rule. **Ryan v. State,** Op. No. 1417, 899 P2d 1371 (Alaska App. 1995).

Testimony of a witness in an action to quiet title regarding a conversation between a property owner and a property claimant, wherein they agreed that the claimant would live on the owner's land and in exchange he would supply her with food, was not hearsay under Alaska R. Evid. 801 and this rule because it was not offered to prove the truth of the matter; the testimony was relevant to prove that they said they would perform and therefore entered an agreement. **Glover v. Glover,** Op. No. 5812, 92 P.3d 387 (Alaska 2004).

Trial court properly relied on the employer's expert's report to demonstrate that the employer was notified that the employee's position should not be classified as exempt; the report was not offered to support the employee's contention that he was not an exempt manager but to demonstrate the employer's state of mind and to show the employer's lack of good faith and lack of reasonable efforts to comply with Alaska law. **Fred Meyer of Alaska, Inc. v. Bailey,** Op. No. 5840, 100 P.3d 881 (Alaska 2004).

Rule 803. Hearsay Exceptions—Availability of Declarant Immaterial.

The following are not excluded by the hearsay rule, even though the declarant is available as a witness:

(1) **Present Sense Impression.** A statement describing or explaining an event or condition made while the declarant was perceiving the event or condition, or immediately thereafter.

(2) **Excited Utterance.** A statement relating to a startling event or condition made while the declarant was under the

stress of excitement caused by the event or condition.

(3) **Then Existing Mental, Emotional, or Physical Condition.** A statement of the declarant's then existing state of mind, emotion, sensation, or physical condition (such as intent, plan, motive, design, mental feeling, pain, and bodily health) offered to prove the declarant's present condition or future action, but not including a statement of memory or belief to prove the fact remembered or believed unless it relates to the execution, revocation, identification, or terms of declarant's will.

(4) **Statements for Purposes of Medical Diagnosis or Treatment.** Statements made for purposes of medical diagnosis or treatment and describing medical history, or past or present symptoms, pain, or sensations, or the inception or general character of the cause or external source thereof insofar as reasonably pertinent to diagnosis or treatment.

(5) **Recorded Recollection.** A memorandum or record concerning a matter about which a witness once had knowledge but now has insufficient recollection to enable the witness to testify fully and accurately, shown to have been made or adopted by the witness when the matter was fresh in the witness' memory and to reflect that knowledge correctly. If admitted, the memorandum or record may be read into evidence but may not itself be received as an exhibit unless offered by an adverse party.

(6) **Business Records.** A memorandum, report, record, or data compilation, in any form, of acts, events, conditions, opinions, or diagnoses, made at or near the time by, or from information transmitted by, a person with knowledge acquired of a regularly conducted business activity, and if it was the regular practice of that business activity to make and keep the memorandum, report, record, or data compilation, all as shown by the testimony of the custodian or other qualified witness, unless the source of information or the method or circumstances of preparation indicate lack of trustworthiness. The term "business" as used in this paragraph includes business, institution, association, profession, occupation, and calling of every kind, whether or not conducted for profit.

(7) **Absence of Record.** Evidence that a matter is not included in the memoranda, reports, records, or data compilations, in any form, kept in accordance with the provisions of subdivision (6), to prove the nonoccurrence or nonexistence of the matter, if the matter was of a kind which a memorandum, report, record, or data compilation was regularly made and preserved, unless the sources of information or other circumstances indicate lack of trustworthiness.

(8) **Public Records and Reports.** (a) To the extent not otherwise provided in (b) of this subdivision, records, reports, statements, or data compilations in any form of a public office or agency setting forth its regularly conducted and regularly recorded activities, or matters observed pursuant to duty imposed by law and as to which there was a duty to report, or factual findings resulting from an investigation made pursuant to authority granted by law.

(b) The following are not within this exception to the hearsay rule: (i) investigative reports by police and other law enforcement personnel; (ii) investigative reports prepared by or for a government, a public office or an agency when offered by it in a case in which it is a party; (iii) factual findings offered by the state in criminal cases; (iv) factual findings resulting from special investigation of a particular complaint, case, or incident; (v) any matter as to which the sources of information or other circumstances indicate lack of trustworthiness. Any writing admissible under this subdivision shall be received only if the party offering such writing has delivered a copy of it or so much thereof as may relate to the controversy, to each adverse party a reasonable time before the trial, unless the court finds that such adverse party has not been unfairly surprised by the failure to deliver such copy.

(9) **Records of Vital Statistics.** Records or data compilations, in any form, of birth, fetal deaths, deaths, or marriages, if the report thereof was made to a public office pursuant to requirements of law.

(10) **Absence of Public Record or Entry.** To prove the absence of a record, report, statement, or data compilation, in any form, or the nonoccurrence or nonexistence of a matter of which a record, report, statement, or data compilation, in any form, was regularly made and preserved by a public office or agency, evidence in the form of a certification in accordance with Rule 902, or testimony, that diligent search failed to disclose the record, report, statement, or data compilation, or entry.

(11) **Records of Religious Organizations.** Statements of births, marriages, divorces, deaths, legitimacy, ancestry, relationship by blood or marriage, or other similar facts of personal or family history, contained in a regularly kept record of a religious organization.

(12) **Marriage, Baptismal, and Similar Certificates.** Statements of facts contained in a certificate that the maker performed a marriage or other ceremony or administered a sacrament, made by a clergyman, public official, or other person authorized by the rules or practices of a religious organization or by law to perform the act certified, and purporting to have been issued at the time of the act or within a reasonable time thereafter.

(13) **Family Records.** Statements of fact concerning personal or family history contained in family bibles, genealogies, charts, engravings on rings, inscriptions on family portraits, engravings and urns, crypts, or tombstones, or the like.

(14) **Records of Documents Affecting an Interest in Property.** The record of a document purporting to establish or affect an interest in property, as proof of the content of the original recorded document and its execution and delivery by each person by whom it purports to have been executed, if the record is a record of a public office and an applicable statute authorizes the recording of documents of that kind in that office.

(15) **Statements in Documents Affecting an Interest in Property.** A statement contained in a document purporting to establish or affect an interest in property if the matter stated was relevant to the purpose of the document, unless dealings with the property since the document was made have been inconsistent with the truth of the statement or the purport of the document.

(16) **Statements in Ancient Documents.** Statements in a document in existence twenty years or more the authenticity of which is established.

(17) **Market Reports, Commercial Publications.** Market quotations, tabulations, lists, directories, codes, standards, or other published compilations, generally used and relied upon by the public or by persons in particular occupations.

(18) **Learned Treatises.** To the extent called to the attention of an expert witness upon cross-examination or relied upon by the expert witness in direct examination, statements contained in published treatises, periodicals, or pamphlets on a subject of history, medicine, or other science or art, established as a reliable authority by the testimony or admission of the witness or by other expert testimony or by judicial notice. If admitted, the statements may be read into evidence but may not be received as exhibits.

(19) **Reputation Concerning Personal or Family History.** Reputation among members of a person's family by blood, adoption, or marriage, or among the person's associates, or in the community, concerning the person's birth, adoption, marriage, divorce, death, legitimacy, relationship by blood, adoption, or marriage, ancestry, or other similar fact of personal or family history.

(20) **Reputation Concerning Boundaries or General History.** Reputation in a community, arising before controversy, as to boundaries of or customs affecting lands in the community, and reputation as to events of general history important to the community or state or nation in which located.

(21) **Reputation as to Character.** Reputation of a person's character among associates or in the community.

(22) **Judgment as to Personal, Family, or General History, or Boundaries.** A judgment as proof of a matter of personal, family or general history, or boundaries, essential to the judgment, if the same would be provable by evidence of reputation.

(23) **Other Exceptions.** A statement not specifically covered by any of the foregoing exceptions but having equivalent circumstantial guarantees of trustworthiness, if the court determines that (a) the statement is offered as evidence of a material fact; (b) the statement is more probative on the point for which it is offered than any other evidence which the proponent can procure through reasonable efforts; and (c) the general purposes of these rules and the interest of justice will best be served by admission of the statement into evidence. However, a statement may not be admitted under this exception unless the proponent of it makes known to the adverse party sufficiently in advance of the trial or hearing to provide the adverse party with a fair opportunity to prepare to meet it, the proponent's intention to offer the statement and the particulars of it, including the name and address of the declarant.

(Added by SCO 364 effective August 1, 1979; amended by SCO 1153 effective July 15, 1994; and by SCO 1522 effective October 15, 2003)

Annotations

Cases

Where custodial interrogation of defendant occurred approximately one and one-half hours after the crime and after presentation of his Miranda rights, it was error for the court to rule that defendant's statements were admissible under the excited utterance exception to the hearsay rule. **State v. Agoney,** Op. No. 2051, 608 P2d 762 (Alaska 1980).

Although statement of plaintiff's supervisor in employment discrimination case should have been admitted under the state of mind exception to the hearsay rule, trial court's exclusion of the testimony was harmless, since plaintiff was permitted to testify as to conversations with her supervisor which contained substantially the same statement. **Hout v. NANA Commercial Catering,** Op. No. 2457, 638 P2d 186 (Alaska 1981).

Trial court did not commit error in excluding statements made by murder defendant to psychiatrist that he was unable to recall the murder and did not recall other violent incidents which had occurred when he was intoxicated. **Evans v. State,** Op. No. 2505, 645 P2d 155 (Alaska 1982).

Before a factual finding offered by the state in a criminal case can be excluded from the public records exception to the hearsay rule, it must be made under circumstances in which the person making the factual finding can foresee its use in litigation and use this knowledge to manipulate the ultimate decision in the litigation. **Byrne v. State,** Op. No. 169, 654 P2d 795 (Alaska App. 1982).

In prosecution for driving while intoxicated, trial court did not err in finding that the various documents within a breathalyzer packet were admissible under the public records exception to the hearsay rule. **Byrne v. State,** Op. No. 169, 654 P2d 795 (Alaska App. 1982).

A group of documents referred to collectively as a "breathalyzer packet" were hearsay but admissible under the public records exception to the hearsay rule. **State v. Huggins,** Op. No. 127, 659 P2d 613 (Alaska App. 1982).

In prosecution for leaving the scene of a non-injury accident, admission of police officer's hearsay testimony concerning the description of the vehicle by the only eyewitness to the accident was reversible error where the record failed to show that the prosecution made diligent efforts to obtain the testimony of the eyewitness or that the eyewitness was unavailable. **Miessner v. Municipality of Anchorage,** Op. No. 323, 673 P2d 285 (Alaska App. 1983).

The state established a sufficient foundation to admit bank officer's testimony about stamp marks on traveler's checks under the business record exception to the hearsay rule. **Harris v. State,** Op. No. 346, 678 P2d 397 (Alaska App. 1984).

Although the robbery in question did not involve unnecessary violence, hearsay statements of the robbery victim made to police approximately 10 minutes after the robbery were admissible as excited utterances. **Lipscomb v. State,** Op. No. 477, 700 P2d 1298 (Alaska App. 1985).

Statements of robbery victim about what was taken and the precise order of events which occurred during the robbery were not excited utterances due to their narrative nature, the fact that they were in response to police questioning, and their relative remoteness in time from the robbery itself. **Lipscomb v. State,** Op. No. 477, 700 P2d 1298 (Alaska App. 1985).

Public records are not excluded by the hearsay rule provided there are no circumstances indicating they are untrustworthy; the burden of proving untrustworthiness is on the party seeking to exclude the public record. **Ehredt v. DeHavilland Aircraft Co.,** Op. No. 2973, 705 P2d 446 (Alaska 1985).

In negligence action where the exclusivity provision of the Workers' Compensation Act was raised as an affirmative defense, trial court was within its discretion in excluding admission of a coverage card issued by the Workers' Compensation Board on the basis that conflicting testimony by Board employees as to the lack of signature and unclear source rendered the card untrustworthy. **Ehredt v. DeHavilland Aircraft Co.,** Op. No. 2973, 705 P2d 446 (Alaska 1985).

The unavailability of the declarant as a witness is immaterial to the applicability of the exceptions to the hearsay rule. **Balentine v. State,** Op. No. 538, 707 P2d 922 (Alaska App. 1985).

It was within trial court's discretion to conclude that the immediacy of declarant's statement, made 40 minutes after the event in question, was not sufficient to bring the statement within the "present sense impression" exception to the hearsay rule. **Balentine v. State,** Op. No. 538, 707 P2d 922 (Alaska App. 1985).

Although there are occasions when evidence rules must give way to due process considerations, so that evidence properly excludable under the rules of evidence must nonetheless be admitted to protect the constitutionally granted trial rights of the defendant, exclusion of hearsay statement did not raise a constitutional issue where the exclusion did not substantially affect defendant's ability to present his defense. **Balentine v. State,** Op. No. 538, 707 P2d 922 (Alaska App. 1985).

Testimony concerning statement made by child moments after she had been sexually assaulted by her father was admissible under the excited utterance exception to the hearsay rule. **Drumbarger v. State,** Op. No. 601, 716 P2d 6 (Alaska App. 1986).

The identity of the assailant of an assault victim does not fall within the medical treatment and diagnosis hearsay exception. **Bell v. State,** Op. No. 607, 716 P2d 1004 (Alaska App. 1986).

Because alleged child abuse victim, who was three years old, was not shown to be unavailable, and because the child's out-of-court statements did not contain sufficient guarantees of trustworthiness, admission of testimony concerning the child's out-of-court statements denied defendant his right of confrontation. **Sluka v. State,** Op. No. 606,717 P2d 394 (Alaska App. 1986).

Testimony of doctor who treated alleged child abuse victim as to out-of-court statements by the child identifying her assailant did not fall within the hearsay exception for statements made for purposes of medical diagnosis or treatment. **Sluka v. State,** Op. No. 606, 717 P2d 394 (Alaska App. 1986).

Testimony concerning out-of-court statements by alleged victim of child abuse did not fall within the excited utterance exception to the hearsay rule, where the statements were made 4 hours after the incident in response to questions and there was no showing that the child at that time was "emotionally engulfed" by the situation. **Sluka v. State,** Op. No. 606, 717 P2d 394 (Alaska App. 1986).

In negligence action where defendant alleged that the accident was caused by design defect in her automobile which caused it to accelerate spontaneously, consumer complaint reports to the National Highway Traffic Safety Agency of similar incidents involving the same type of automobile were relevant and admissible as hearsay exceptions. **Norris v. Gatts,** Op. No. 3187, 738 P2d 344 (Alaska 1987).

Reports about the contents of a telephone call made by the call's recipient to a third party, immediately after the call terminated, were admissible as present sense impressions. **Stumpf v. State,** Op. No. 770, 749 P2d 880 (Alaska App. 1988).

Three-year-old victim's hearsay statements identifying defendant as the person who sexually abused her, made during her medical treatment, presented sufficient evidence for the grand jury to indict, since even if the testimony identifying the defendant did not fall within the medical diagnosis exception to the hearsay rule, it was arguable that the child's inability to testify before the grand jury constituted "compelling justification" for presenting hearsay evidence. **State v. Nollner,** Op. No. 780, 749 P2d 905 (Alaska App. 1988).

Declarant's statement that he was going to the airport to pick up drugs was admissible under the "state of mind" exception to the hearsay rule to show declarant's purpose in going to the airport; that statement, along with independent evidence that defendant met the declarant at the airport and then accompanied him to the place where a heroin sale was made, demonstrated by a preponderance of the evidence defendant's participation in a conspiracy to distribute heroin, therefore statements of defendant's coconspirators were admissible against him. **Stewart v. State,** Op. No. 809, 756 P2d 900 (Alaska App. 1988).

In prosecution of husband for assaulting and kidnapping his wife, out-of-court statements by the wife and their 3-year-old son were too far removed in time from the event to constitute excited utterances. **Brandon v. State,** Op. No. 947, 778 P2d 221 (Alaska App. 1989).

Where wife did not testify at trial of husband who was convicted of assaulting and kidnapping her, the erroneous admission of several out-of-court statements by the wife implicating the husband was reversible error. **Brandon v. State,** Op. No. 947, 778 P2d 221 (Alaska App. 1989).

Out-of-court statements by 3-year old child which did not qualify as excited utterances were also not admissible under the residual or catch-all exception to the hearsay rule, since no reasons were given for finding the statements so trustworthy that they should be admitted under that exception except that they were similar to excited utterances. **Brandon v. State,** Op. No. 947, 778 P2d 221 (Alaska App. 1989).

In prosecution of husband for assaulting and kidnapping his wife, the state's argument that the proper admission of some of the wife's out-of-court statements implicating her husband made the erroneous admission of other out-of-court statements by the wife cumulative and therefore harmless was rejected. **Brandon v. State,** Op. No. 947, 778 P2d 221 (Alaska App. 1989).

Where deceased declarant's statement qualified as an excited utterance, admission of the statement did not violate defendant's constitutional right to confront the witness against him. **Charles v. State,** Op. No. 963, 780 P2d 377 (Alaska App. 1989).

Statement made in response to police officer's questions 37 minutes after declarant had witnessed an attempted murder qualified as an excited utterance where the declarant appeared quite shaken at the time of the interview, the attempted murder involved one of declarant's relations, and there was reason to believe that declarant was also an intended victim. **Charles v. State,** Op. No. 963, 780 P2d 377 (Alaska App. 1989).

Defendant's self-serving denials did not qualify as present sense impressions since he had time to reflect and a motive to fabricate before he made the statements. **Brannen v. State,** Op. No. 1076, 798 P2d 337 (Alaska App. 1990).

Hearsay accounts of child's identification of her abuser were admissible under the residential exceptions to the hearsay rule. **Broderick v. King's Way Assembly of God,** Op. No. 3677, 808 P2d 1211 (Alaska 1991).

In general, the public records exception to the hearsay rule does not allow admission of prior civil judgments. **Snyder v. Foote,** Op. No. 3787, 822 P2d 1353 (Alaska 1991).

Factual findings of judge in prior unrelated case concerning misstatements by expert witness concerning credentials were inadmissible hearsay in later case at which expert testified. **Snyder v. Foote,** Op. No. 3787, 822 P2d 1353 (Alaska 1991).

Statement by 2-year-old girl to her mother that she had been sexually assaulted was admissible as an excited utterance despite fact that statement was made 10 hours following the assault. **Dezarn v. State,** Op. No. 1226, 832 P2d 589 (Alaska App. 1992).

Police officer's exclamation, "I found some cocaine," made during pat-down search of defendant, was admissible as statement of present sense impression under this rule. **Toney v. State,** Op. No. 1223, 833 P2d 15 (Alaska App. 1992).

The out-of-court statements of a child in proceedings where abuse is alleged are often necessary to the administration of justice; therefore, if the child is unavailable to testify, the courts should admit the statements if the statements are sufficiently reliable. **Matter of A.S.W.,** Op. No. 3847, 834 P2d 801 (Alaska 1992).

The factors used in determining whether a child's out-of-court statement exhibits sufficient guarantees of trustworthiness are not inclusive nor should they be applied mechanically. **Matter of A.S.W.,** Op. No. 3847, 834 P2d 801 (Alaska 1992).

In action for wrongful job termination, out-of-court statements by supervisors who terminated plaintiff about plaintiff's work performance were not hearsay because they were introduced as proof of supervisors' state of mind, not as proof of truth of matter asserted in the statements. **Van Huff v. Sohio Alaska Petroleum Co.,** Op. No. 3857, 835 P2d 1181 (Alaska 1992).

In product liability action, plaintiff's statement to doctor that his back injury occurred when he fell from truck was admissible as statement made for purpose of medical diagnosis or treatment. **Williams v. Utility Equipment,** Op. No. 3875, 837 P2d 1112 (Alaska 1992).

Statements admitted pursuant to state-of-mind exception to hearsay rule do not violate confrontation clause. **State v. McDonald,** Op. No. 1342, 872 P2d 627 (Alaska App. 1994).

Murder defendant's inquiries prior to murder about airline fares to Thailand were admissible under state-of-mind exception to hearsay rule. **State v. McDonald,** Op. No. 1342, 872 P2d 627 (Alaska App. 1994).

Declarant's statement that she intended to meet defendant after work, while not admissible to prove she did meet him, was admissible under state-of-mind exception to hearsay rule to prove she intended to meet him. **State v. McDonald,** Op. No. 1342, 872 P2d 627 (Alaska App. 1994).

In trial of defendant murdering his wife, trial court did not abuse its discretion in allowing testimony of three witnesses describing wife's fear of husband as evidence of her state of mind. **Linton v. State,** Op. No. 1367, 880 P2d 123 (Alaska App. 1994).

The law distrusts hearsay, allowing it only when the circumstances of the utterance and/or the motivation of the speaker affirmatively demonstrate good reason to credit the out-of-court statement. **Ryan v. State,** Op. No. 1417, 899 P2d 1371 (Alaska App. 1995).

The residual exceptions to the hearsay rule are to be used only on rare occasions. **Ryan v. State,** Op. No. 1417, 899 P2d 1371 (Alaska App. 1995).

The residual hearsay exceptions are not firmly rooted hearsay exceptions. Thus, any hearsay admitted under these exceptions must demonstrate particularized guarantees of trustworthiness to satisfy the demands of the confrontation clause. **Ryan v. State,** Op. No. 1417, 899 P2d 1371 (Alaska App. 1995).

An abuse of discretion standard is applied in reviewing the admission of hearsay under the residual hearsay exception. **Ryan v. State,** Op. No. 1417, 899 P2d 1371 (Alaska App. 1995).

For Confrontation Clause purposes, the trustworthiness of the hearsay must be established solely from the circumstances of the statement and the mental state of the declarant. The required "guarantees of trustworthiness" may not be established by showing the hearsay statement is corroborated by other evidence. **Ryan v. State,** Op. No. 1417, 899 P2d 1371 (Alaska App. 1995).

The fact that the hearsay declarant has made inconsistent statements can be used to determine the trustworthiness of the hearsay statements proposed for admission. **Ryan v. State,** Op. No. 1417, 899 P2d 1371 (Alaska App. 1995).

The fact that the declarant may have been under stress is not sufficient by itself to establish hearsay statements admissible under the excited utterance exception. Where hearsay statements concededly contained several conscious fabrications, the trial court did not abuse its discretion in finding they were not excited utterances. **Ryan v. State,** Op. No. 1417, 899 P2d 1371 (Alaska App. 1995).

Criminal conviction of non-party following trial is not admissible as evidence in subsequent civil proceeding. **SAC v. Lot 3, Block 1, Evergreen,** Op. No. 4245, 902 P2d 766 (Alaska 1995).

Defendant's statements during police interrogation following accusation by police that he was guilty of murder did not constitute "excited utterances" under this rule. **Marino v. State,** Op. No. 1519, 934 P2d 1321 (Alaska App. 1997).Diary entries, not made by witness but verified by witness when made, could be admissible as record concerning matter about which witness once had knowledge but now had insufficient recollection to testify fully and accurately. **Harris v. Keys,** Op. No. 4903, 948 P2d 460 (Alaska 1997).

Where witness did not express difficulty recalling event, diary entries about event were not admissible under this rule as record concerning matter about which witness once had knowledge but now had insufficient recollection to testify fully and accurately. **Harris v. Keys,** Op. No. 4903, 948 P2d 460 (Alaska 1997).

In light of evidence that diaries were inaccurate and not regularly kept and considering conflict of opinion on significance of entries that were made, trial court's refusal to admit them under business records exception to hearsay rule was not error. **Harris v. Keys,** Op. No. 4903, 948 P2d 460 (Alaska 1997).

Statements by employees in company investigator's memorandum concerning sexual harassment by another employee were admissible in sexual harassment trial as non-hearsay admissions of party-opponent. **Norcon, Inc. v. Kotowski,** Op. No. 5085, 971 P2d 158 (Alaska 1999).

At trial of defendant for murdering his wife, testimony of women's shelter employee that wife called the shelter the day before her death and stated that she planned to divorce defendant and that there would be "a possible lethal situation" if he learned of her plan was admissible under state-of-mind exception to hearsay rule since wife's intent to divorce defendant was a disputed issue at trial and her statement demonstrated the seriousness of her purpose and intent. **Wyatt v. State,** Op. No. 5128, 981 P2d 109 (Alaska 1999).

Murdered wife's hearsay statement fell within state-of-mind exception to hearsay rule and therefore did not implicate defendant-husband's right to confrontation, thus harmless error standard rather than harmless beyond a reasonable doubt standard was properly used in determining whether any error in admission of the potentially inflammatory statement affected jury's verdict. **Wyatt v. State,** Op. No. 5128, 981 P2d 109 (Alaska 1999).

To fall within the present sense impression exception to the hearsay rule, a statement must meet three requirements: it must describe or explain the event or condition; it must be made during or immediately after the event; and it must be based on the perception of the declarant. **Dobos v. Ingersoll,** Op. No. 5318, 9 P3d 1020 (Alaska 2000).

Witness's testimony that another person told her "he was scared," testimony which was offered to prove the truth of the matter asserted and was therefore hearsay, was admissible as an out-of-court statement, offered to prove the declarant's then-existing state of mind or emotion. **Markgraf v. State,** Op. No. 1705, 12 P3d 197 (Alaska App. 2000).

Trial court properly concluded that, despite the passage often or fifteen minutes, defendant's wife was still under the stress of excitement engendered by the alleged assault when she blurted out a statement without conscious reflection that her husband had struck her as she watched her husband being escorted to the patrol car, and therefore, the statement was admissible as an excited utterance. **Blair v. State,** Op. No. 1793, 42 P3d 1152 (Alaska App. 2002).

In a criminal prosecution for sexual abuse of a minor, defendant failed to make a timely objection to a treating physician's testimony that the child identified defendant as her abuser; therefore, the appellate court would not review defendant's claim that the statement was not made for the purposes of medical diagnosis under Alaska R. Evid. 803(4). **Vaska v. State,** Op. No. 1890, 74 P.3d 225 (Alaska App. 2003).

In an assault case, defendant's statements did not qualify as excited utterances; even though he might have been under stress at the time he spoke with witnesses, he also had time to reflect, he had time to fabricate, and he was not in such a state of excitement that it stilled his capacity to fabricate. **Sipary v. State,** Op. No. 1933, 91 P.3d 296 (Alaska App. 2004).

In an assault case, defendant's statements to a co-defendant, made while the two were in jail together, were not excited utterances; the court found that the proposed testimony was exculpatory, self-serving hearsay **Sipary v. State,** Op. No. 1933, 91 P.3d 296 (Alaska App. 2004).

Victim's response to the officer's question of "what happened" was admissible as an excited utterance under this rule, and was not "testimonial" for purposes of the Confrontation Clause, because an excited answer by a crime victim to a police officer's question was not testimonial. **Anderson v. State,** Op. No. 1978, 111 P.3d 350 (Alaska App. 2005).

Under Alaska R. Evid. 803(3), in order for defendant's statement that he believed that the victim was 16 years old to be relevant, the statement had to show defendant's state of mind at the time that his sexual contact with the victim took place; the record showed that defendant's attorney represented to the court that the witness would testify that defendant told him, on the night in question, that defendant believed that the victim was 16 years old; therefore defendant represented that, had the witness been allowed to testify, he would have testified to defendant's contemporaneous statement concerning his belief as to the victim's age, the statement was offered to prove defendant's state of mind at the time the statement was made, and was offered to prove that he acted under a reasonable mistake of fact. **Kelly v. State,** Op. No. 1992, 116 P.3d 602 (Alaska App. 2005).

Rule 804. Hearsay Exceptions—Declarant Unavailable.

(a) **Definition of Unavailability.** Unavailability as a witness includes situations in which the declarant

(1) is exempted by ruling of the court on the ground of privilege from testifying concerning the subject matter of the declarant's statement; or

(2) persists in refusing to testify concerning the subject matter of the declarant's statement despite an order of the court to do so; or

(3) establishes a lack of memory of the subject matter of the declarant's statement; or

(4) is unable to be present or to testify at the hearing because of death or then existing physical or mental illness or infirmity; or

(5) is absent from the hearing and the proponent of the declarant's statement has been unable to procure the declarant's attendance (or in the case of a hearsay exception under subdivision (b) (2), (3), (4), or (5), of this rule, the declarant's attendance or testimony) by reasonable means including process.

A declarant is not unavailable as a witness if the declarant's exemption, refusal, claim of lack of memory, inability, or absence is due to the procurement or wrongdoing of the proponent of the statement for the purpose of preventing the witness from attending or testifying.

(b) **Hearsay Exceptions.** The following are not excluded by the hearsay rule if the declarant is unavailable as a witness:

(1) *Former Testimony.* Testimony given as a witness at another hearing of the same or a different proceeding, or in a deposition taken in compliance with law in the course of another proceeding, if the party against whom the testimony is now offered, or, in a civil action or proceeding a predecessor in interest, had an opportunity and similar motive to develop the testimony by direct, cross, or redirect examination.

(2) *Statement Under Belief of Impending Death.* A statement made by a declarant while believing that the declarant's death was imminent, concerning the cause or circumstances of what the declarant believed to be impending death.

(3) *Statement Against Interest.* A statement which was at the time of its making so far contrary to the declarant's pecuniary or proprietary interest, or so far tended to subject the declarant to civil or criminal liability, or to render invalid a claim by the declarant against another, that a reasonable person in the declarant's position would not have made the statement unless believing it to be true. A statement tending to expose the declarant to criminal liability and offered to exculpate the accused is not admissible unless corroborating circumstances clearly indicate the trustworthiness of the statement.

(4) *Statement of Personal or Family History.* (A) A statement concerning the declarant's own birth, adoption, marriage, ancestry, or other similar fact of personal or family history, even though declarant had no means of acquiring personal knowledge of the matter stated; or (B) a statement concerning the foregoing matters, and death also, of another person, if the declarant was related to the other by blood, adoption, or marriage or was so intimately associated with the other's family as to be likely to have accurate information concerning the matter declared.

(5) *Other Exceptions.* A statement not specifically covered by any of the foregoing exceptions but having equivalent circumstantial guarantees of trustworthiness, if the court determines that (A) the statement is offered as evidence of a material fact; (B) the statement is more probative on the point for which it is offered than any other evidence which the proponent can procure through reasonable efforts; and (C) the general purposes of these rules and the interests of justice will best be served by admission of the statement into evidence. However, a statement may not be admitted under this exception unless the proponent of it makes known to the adverse party sufficiently in advance of the trial or hearing to provide the adverse party with a fair opportunity to prepare to meet it, the proponent's intention to offer the statement and the particulars of it, including the name and address of the declarant.

(Added by SCO 364 effective August 1, 1979; amended by SCO 1153 effective July 15, 1994; and by SCO 1522 effective

October 15, 2003)

Annotations

Cases

In prosecution for possession of cocaine, statements made by defendant's partner, also charged with possession of the same cocaine, that the cocaine belonged only to him and not to the defendant, which statements were made at the time of arrest and again during the arresting officer's testimony in a preliminary hearing, should have been admitted as statements against interest under this rule, it being reasonable for the court to assume that the partner would exercise his fifth amendment right not to testify and was therefore not available. **Gutierrez v. State,** Op. No. 321, 673 P2d 287 (Alaska App. 1983).

Where codefendant in theft prosecution pleaded guilty to the charge and subsequently told his probation officer that the other defendant was not guilty, a statement which exposed the co-defendant to only a slight possibility of prosecution or punishment, the probation officer could not testify as to the codefendant's statement at defendant's trial even if the codefendant was unavailable, because the statement was not corroborated by circumstances clearly indicating its trustworthiness. **Garroute v. State,** Op. No. 372, 683 P2d 262 (Alaska App. 1984).

Because defendant did not seek the state's assistance in locating his brother, and because he did not make use of the Uniform Act to Secure Attendance in Criminal Proceedings, trial judge did not abuse his discretion in concluding that the defendant had not proved his brother's unavailability as a witness and therefore excluding hearsay testimony of statements made by the brother. **Morton v. State,** Op. No. 388, 684 P2d 144 (Alaska App. 1984).

Trial judge in drunk driving prosecution did not abuse his discretion in refusing to admit transcript of expert testimony on breathalyzer machine's failure point to counter testimony by police officer on the same subject even if the evidence was within the former testimony exception to the hearsay rule. **Thayer v. Municipality of Anchorage,** Op. No. 395, 686 P2d 721 (Alaska App. 1984).

Unavailable declarant's statement to police that she was a prostitute and that victim was her pimp was not a statement against interest since there was no indication she was under any danger of being prosecuted for being a prostitute at the time she made the statement and since she would have every motive to give the police a false name as to the identity of her pimp. **Wortham v. State,** Op. No. 414, 689 P2d 1133 (Alaska App. 1984).

Witnesses may be deemed unavailable when they cannot be found despite diligent efforts, or when they are located but beyond the means available to obtain their attendance, but absence from the jurisdiction alone does not satisfy the requirement. **Bentley v. State,** Op. No. 530, 706 P2d 1193 (Alaska App. 1985).

The state failed to show that key prosecution witness was "unavailable" to testify as that term must be interpreted in light of the constitutional right of confrontation, thus admission of the witnesses' prior recorded testimony was error requiring reversal. **Bentley v. State,** Op. No. 530, 706 P2d 1193 (Alaska App. 1985).

Trial court did not err in refusing to allow murder defendant to call a fellow inmate to testify regarding a conversation he overheard between defendant and defendant's codefendant in which the codefendant admitted that he rather than the defendant actually killed the victim, since the statements attributed to the codefendant did not bear sufficient indicia of trustworthiness to warrant admissibility and since the statements in the context in which they were made, i.e., by one codefendant to another, were not declarations against penal interest. **Lewis v. State,** Op. No. 673, 731 P2d 68 (Alaska App. 1987).

Out-of-court statements by 3-year old child which did not qualify as excited utterances were also not admissible under the residual or catch-all exception to the hearsay rule, since no reasons were given for finding the statements so trustworthy that they should be admitted under that exception except that they were similar to excited utterances. **Brandon v. State,** Op. No. 947, 778 P2d 221 (Alaska App. 1989).

To find declarant unavailable, this rule only requires that the declarant refuse to testify despite an order of the court; the rule does not expressly require that the court hold the witness in contempt. **Rychart v. State,** Op. No. 948, 778 P2d 229 (Alaska App. 1989).

Where declarant was already incarcerated, trial judge did not err in finding him unavailable without holding him in contempt, since contempt proceedings were unlikely to motivate declarant to testify. **Rychart v. State,** Op. No. 948, 778 P2d 229 (Alaska App. 1989).

For admission of a statement under the catch-all exception to the hearsay rule, the guarantees of trustworthiness must be equivalent to those supporting the specific hearsay exceptions; the presence or absence of corroborative evidence of trustworthiness is irrelevant. **Rychart v. State,** Op. No. 948, 778 P2d 229 (Alaska App. 1989).

Unavailable declarant's testimony at his own trial for driving while intoxicated was inadmissible under the catch-all exception to the hearsay rule to defendant's trial for driving with a revoked license since the declarant clearly had a motive to lie and the jury which convicted him apparently believed he was lying when he testified that defendant was doing the driving. **Rychart v. State,** Op. No. 948, 778 P2d 229 (Alaska App. 1989).

The requirements of the catch-all exception to the hearsay rule are conjunctive, not disjunctive, and a court must find that a hearsay statement is sufficiently trustworthy as well as material and probative before admitting it into evidence. **Rychart v. State,** Op. No. 948, 778 P2d 229 (Alaska App. 1989).

Nontestifying codefendant's declarations against interest to police implicating defendant did not have sufficient indicia of reliability to overcome the presumption that the statements were unreliable; admission of the statements was reversible error. **Newcomb v. State,** Op. No. 960, 779 P2d 1240 (Alaska App. 1989).

In prosecution of unrepresented defendant for negligent driving, trial court committed reversible error in declining to consider the tape-recorded testimony of an alibi witness who had formerly testified in court for defendant in a domestic violence dispute without granting a continuance to let defendant call the witness. **Davenport v. State,** Op. No. 1073, 795 P2d 817 (Alaska App. 1990).

Hearsay accounts of child's identification of her abuser were admissible under the residential exceptions to the hearsay rule. **Broderick v. King's Way Assembly of God,** Op. No. 3677, 808 P2d 1211 (Alaska 1991).

A statement inculpatory to the declarant and exculpatory to the accused is only admissible if the declarant is unavailable, the statement is against the declarant's penal interest, and there are corroborating circumstances that clearly indicate the trustworthiness of the statement. **Bright v. State,** Op. No. 1195, 826 P2d 765 (Alaska App. 1992).

Hearsay statements against interest by codefendants that they, not defendant, shot the victim were properly ruled inadmissible in defendant's murder trial because the circumstances surrounding the statements did not indicate that the statements were trustworthy. **Bright v. State,** Op. No. 1195, 826 P2d 765 (Alaska App. 1992).

Under the residual provision of this rule that allows admission of hearsay statements not otherwise admissible under an enumerated exception, an independent analysis must be undertaken to see if the case involves exceptional circumstances where guarantees of trustworthiness are equivalent to or exceed the guarantees reflected in the enumerated exceptions; the finding of trustworthiness upon which admission of the statement is predicated is a substantive requirement, not a procedural formality. **Shakespeare v. State,** Op. No. 1208, 827 P2d 454 (Alaska App. 1992).

Where statement was inadmissible under the statement against interest exception to the hearsay rule because it lacked circumstantial indicia of trustworthiness, the lack of trustworthiness necessarily precluded the statement's admission under the residual provision of this rule that allows admission of hearsay statements not otherwise admissible under an enumerated exception. **Shakespeare v. State,** Op. No. 1208, 827 P2d 454 (Alaska App. 1992).

Statements by defendant's wife to police officers implicating herself and defendant in cocaine purchases were not admissible against defendant under the statement against interest exception to the hearsay rule because a reasonable person would have construed the officers' assurances that her statements would not be held against her as a promise against prosecution and therefore would not have perceived the statements as being against penal interest. **Shakespeare v. State,** Op. No. 1208, 827 P2d 454 (Alaska App. 1992).

The factors used in determining whether a child's out-of court statement exhibits sufficient guarantees of trustworthiness are not inclusive nor should they be applied mechanically. **Matter of A.S.W.,** Op. No. 3847, 834 P2d 801 (Alaska 1992).

In adjudicatory phase of Child in Need of Aid proceeding, alleged abuser's due process right to cross-examine child is adequately protected by unavailability and reliability requirements of the Rules of Evidence; accordingly, where 4-year-old child was unavailable to testify, but child's videotaped statement describing sexual abuse by father was reliable, father's lack of opportunity to cross-examine or confront child did not deny him due process of law. **Matter of A.S.W.,** Op. No. 3847, 834 P2d 801 (Alaska 1992).

Out-of-court statements of child in proceedings where abuse is alleged are often necessary to the administration of justice; therefore, if child is unavailable to testify, courts should admit the statements if the statements are sufficiently reliable. **Matter of A.S.W.,** Op. No. 3847, 834 P2d 801 (Alaska 1992).

Videotaped interview with 4-year-old child, in which she described how father sexually abused her, was admissible in "child in need of aid" hearing under "catch-all" exception to hearsay rule, despite father's argument that videotape lacked necessary guarantees of trustworthiness. **Matter of A.S.W.,** Op. No. 3847, 834 P2d 801 (Alaska 1992).

Six-year-old girl's persistent refusal to testify despite prodding of judge, counsel and mother was sufficient to support finding of unavailability even though judge did not specifically order girl to respond. **Matter of T.P.,** Op. No. 3889, 838 P2d 1236 (Alaska 1992).

Trial court has discretion to rule that child's testimony indirectly reveals child's lack of memory when child's age and relative maturity makes it difficult for child to clearly articulate lack of memory of relevant events. **Matter of T.P.,** Op. No. 3889, 838 P2d 1236 (Alaska 1992).

Given six-year-old child's apparent lack of motive to fabricate, the spontaneity and timing of her statements, and fact that she located alleged sexual abuse as occurring on porch, trial judge properly admitted child's out-of-court statements. **Matter of T.P.,** Op. No. 3889, 838 P2d 1236 (Alaska 1992).

Out-of-court statement by murder defendant's father incriminating his son and admitting his own involvement in disposing of body was admissible as statement against penal interest even though statement was made to intimate companion and statute of limitations for father's crime, tampering with evidence, had possibly expired. **Linton v. State,** Op. No. 1367, 880 P2d 123 (Alaska App. 1994).

The residual exceptions to the hearsay rule are to be used only on rare occasions. **Ryan v. State,** Op. No. 1417, 899 P2d 1371 (Alaska App. 1995).

The residual hearsay exceptions are not firmly rooted hearsay exceptions. Thus, any hearsay admitted under these exceptions must demonstrate particularized guarantees of trustworthiness to satisfy the demands of the confrontation clause. **Ryan v. State,** Op. No. 1417, 899 P2d 1371 (Alaska App. 1995).

For Confrontation Clause purposes, the trustworthiness of the hearsay must be established solely from the circumstances of the statement and the mental state of the declarant. The required "guarantees of trustworthiness" may not be established by showing the hearsay statement is corroborated by other evidence. **Ryan v. State,** Op. No. 1417, 899 P2d 1371 (Alaska App. 1995).

An abuse of discretion standard is applied in reviewing the admission of hearsay under the residual hearsay exception. **Ryan v. State,** Op. No. 1417, 899 P2d 1371 (Alaska App. 1995).

The fact that the hearsay declarant has made inconsistent statements can be used to determine the trustworthiness of the hearsay statements proposed for admission. **Ryan v. State,** Op. No. 1417, 899 P2d 1371 (Alaska App. 1995).

The law distrusts hearsay, allowing it only when the circumstances of the utterance and/or the motivation of the speaker affirmatively demonstrate good reason to credit the out-of-court statement. **Ryan v. State,** Op. No. 1417, 899 P2d 1371 (Alaska App. 1995).

The primary factor used to evaluate the trustworthiness of hearsay is the potential motivation of the absent speaker to speak the truth or, conversely, to withhold or alter the truth. **Ryan v. State,** Op. No. 1417, 899 P2d 1371 (Alaska App. 1995).

The touchstone for determining the admissibility of hearsay under Rule 804(b)(5) is trustworthiness. The shortness of the elapsed time between an occurrence and a witness's account of it may indicate that the witness has an accurate memory of the occurrence. However, this does not prove trustworthiness as accurate memory will help ensure the trustworthiness of the witness's statements only if the witness is motivated to give an accurate account. **Ryan v. State,** Op. No. 1417, 899 P2d 1371 (Alaska App. 1995).

Where hearsay arises in the context of a criminal prosecution, the hearsay must satisfy not only the requirements of the Evidence Rules, but also the requirements of the Confrontation Clauses of the federal and Alaska constitutions. **Ryan v. State,** Op. No. 1417, 899 P2d 1371 (Alaska App. 1995).

Evidence is admissible under the residual exception if the proponent of the evidence proves (1) that the person who made the out-of-court statement is "unavailable as a witness," (2) that the proposed evidence manifests "circumstantial guarantees of trustworthiness" equivalent to the guarantees of trustworthiness possessed by the hearsay covered in the other listed exceptions, (3) that the evidence is relevant to a "material" fact, (4) that the evidence is more probative on that point than any other evidence which the proponent could procure through reasonable efforts, and (5) that the general purposes of the evidence rules and the interests of justice would best be served by admission of the hearsay. **Ryan v. State,** Op. No. 1417, 899 P2d 1371 (Alaska App. 1995).

Hearsay statements reporting a rape made to a police officer did not have circumstantial guarantees of trustworthiness sufficient to allow admission under the residual exception to the hearsay rule where evidence indicated that the declarant may have been motivated to say she has been raped by her fear of her boyfriend's reaction to her having been with two other men. **Ryan v. State,** Op. No. 1417, 899 P2d 1371 (Alaska App. 1995).

In defendant's murder-arson trial, hearsay statements of his wife and a third party implicating both defendant and his wife in the crimes were admissible as statements against interest. **Porterfield v. State,** 68 P.3d 1286 (Alaska App. 2003).

In a criminal prosecution for sexual abuse of a minor, defendant failed to make a timely objection to a treating physician's testimony that the child identified defendant as her abuser. The court admitted the statements under the "catchall exception" of Alaska R. Evid. 804(b)(5). **Vaska v. State,** Op. No. 1890, 74 P.3d 225 (Alaska App. 2003).

Trial judge did not abuse his discretion when he ruled that the victim's brother's statements to a trooper concerning his visits to defendant's house on the weekend of the sexual assault and assault on the victim did not carry the circumstantial guarantees of trustworthiness required by section (b)(5) of this rule; defendant's proposed hearsay testimony was not admissible under the residual hearsay exception. **Cleveland v. State,** Op. No. 1934, 91 P.3d 965 (Alaska App. 2004).

Because defendant's proposed hearsay testimony failed to meet the criteria for admission under the residual hearsay exception, under section (b)(5) of this rule, the evidence was inadmissible regardless of defendant's right to present a defense that someone else could have committed the crime; defendant's right did not make the hearsay rules irrelevant. **Cleveland v. State,** Op. No. 1934, 91 P.3d 965 (Alaska App. 2004).

The catchall exception to the hearsay rule applies only when (a) the declarant is "unavailable" as a witness; (b) no other hearsay exception specifically covers the proposed out-of-court statements; and (c) the statement's trustworthiness is so strong that adversarial testing through cross-examination would not benefit the defendant. **Vaska v. State**, Op. No. 11171, 135 P.3d 1011 (Alaska 2006).

Admissibility of witness's statements under Evidence Rule 804(b)(5)'s catchall exception was overruled where cross-examination was necessary, as the lower court was effectively determined that the witness had shown herself to be incapable of providing any useful testimony, that her prior statements were not "specifically covered" by any other exception, and that they were so reliable that defendant had no need to cross-examine her. **Vaska v. State**, Op. No. 11171, 135 P.3d 1011 (Alaska 2006).

Rule 805. Hearsay Within Hearsay.

Hearsay included within hearsay is not excluded under the hearsay rule if each part of the combined statement conforms with an exception to the hearsay rule provided in these rules.

(Added by SCO 364 effective August 1, 1979)

Rule 806. Attacking and Supporting Credibility of Declarant.

When a hearsay statement, or a statement defined in Rule 801 (d)(2) (C), (D), or (E), has been admitted in evidence, the credibility of the declarant may be attacked, and if attacked may be supported, by any evidence which would be admissible for those purposes if declarant had testified as a witness. Evidence of a statement or conduct by the declarant at any time, inconsistent with the declarant's hearsay statement, is not subject to any requirement that the declarant may have been afforded an opportunity to deny or explain. If the party against whom a hearsay statement or a statement defined in Rule 801(d)(2) (C), (D), or (E) has been admitted calls the declarant as a witness, the party is entitled to examine the declarant on the statement as if under cross-examination.

(Added by SCO 364 effective August 1, 1979; amended by SCO 1153 effective July 15, 1994)

Annotations

Cases

A hearsay declarant may be impeached and rehabilitated in the same ways a witness can be. **Jordan v. State,** Op. No. 1412, 895 P2d 994 (Alaska App. 1995).

If a declarant's statement is not being offered for its truth, then it is not hearsay, and impeachment of the declarant is not permitted under this rule. **Jordan v. State,** Op. No. 1412, 895 P2d 994 (Alaska App. 1995).

ARTICLE IX. DOCUMENTARY EVIDENCE

Rule 901. Requirement of Authentication or Identification.

The requirement of authentication or identification as a condition precedent to admissibility is satisfied by evidence sufficient to support a finding that the matter in question is what its proponent claims, except as provided in paragraphs (a) and (b) below:

(a) Whenever the prosecution in a criminal trial offers (1) real evidence which is of such a nature as not to be readily identifiable, or as to be susceptible to adulteration, contamination, modification, tampering, or other changes in form attributable to accident, carelessness, error or fraud, or (2) testimony describing real evidence of the type set forth in (1) if the information on which the description is based was acquired while the evidence was in the custody or control of the prosecution, the prosecution must first demonstrate as a matter of reasonable certainty that the evidence is at the time of trial or was at the time it was observed properly identified and free of the possible taints identified by this paragraph.

(b) In any case in which real evidence of the kind described in paragraph (a) of this rule is offered, the court may require additional proof before deciding whether to admit or exclude evidence under Rule 403.

(Added by SCO 364 effective August 1, 1979; amended by SCO 1295 effective January 15, 1998)

EDITOR'S NOTE: To the extent that this rule conflicts with AS 12.45.086 the rule controls, as sec. 44, ch. 143, SLA 1982 did not receive the required 2/3 vote in the legislature.

Note: Section 41 of ch. 87 SLA 1997 adds AS 25.20.050(j) which provides that invoices and other standard documents showing charges for medical and related costs of pregnancy, childbirth or genetic testing are admissible in an action to establish paternity without testimony or other foundational evidence from the medical provider or third party payor. According to § 154 of the Act, this provision has the effect of amending Evidence Rule 901 by limiting discretion of the court to exclude documentary evidence of specified costs in a paternity action.

Annotations

Cases

Where state showed as a matter of reasonable certainty that knives were same as those found in apartment, trial court did not abuse discretion in admitting them into evidence. **Eben v. State,** Op. No. 1920, 599 P2d 700 (Alaska 1979).

When a timely and appropriate challenge to admissibility of a breathalyzer test result is made, the prosecution must, at a minimum, demonstrate that the breathalyzer instrument in question was tested successfully for radio frequency interference at least once in a manner substantially complying with the manufacturer's recommendation and that none of the conditions listed by the manufacturer for retesting occurred between the time of the initial radio frequency test and the challenged breath test. **Thayer v. Municipality of Anchorage,** Op. No. 395, 686 P2d 721 (Alaska App. 1984).

To the extent that Section 40 of Chapter 143, SLA 1982, enacted as AS 12.80.050, conflicts with this rule, this rule controls. **Galbraith v. State,** Op.

No. 437, 693 P2d 880 (Alaska App. 1985).

In drunk driving prosecution, trial court did not abuse its discretion in requiring that defendant's intoximeter sample be retested before entertaining a challenge to the intoximeter based on alleged deficiencies in the sample retained, where the court expressly found that the system for preserving samples was functioning properly but left open the possibility that retained samples might be defective in individual cases. **Ansay v. State,** Op. No. 598, 715 P2d 1194 (Alaska App. 1986).

In prosecution for theft of meat and seafood from grocery store, photographs of the meat where admissible to illustrate the testimony of witnesses, even if the statutory requirement that photographic evidence of property wrongfully taken be accompanied by a written description of the property was not complied with. **Page v. State,** Op. No. 643, 725 P2d 1082 (Alaska App. 1986).

In trial of defendant for refusing to submit to a breath test, in which defendant testified that nose and chest injuries sustained by him during his arrest prevented him from blowing into the Intoximeter tube, the trial court committed reversible error in precluding admission of photographs of defendant's injuries taken by his friend one day after the arrest, since the photographs were relevant circumstantial evidence of defendant's claim that he was physically incapable of taking the breath test; furthermore, defendant's friend was the proper person to authenticate the photographs for admission. **Callahan v. State,** Op. No. 910, 769 P2d 444 (Alaska App. 1989).

Timely objection by party opposing summary judgment to consideration of unauthenticated documents is in itself sufficient, there being no requirement that the party also raise some doubt as to whether the documentary evidence is in fact authentic. **Murat v. F/V Shelikof Strait,** Op. No. 3607, 793 P2d 69 (Alaska 1990).

Where confidential informant purchased cocaine from defendant in a house and give police officers the slips of cocaine involved in the sale upon leaving the house, the state established a chain of custody as to those slips sufficient to meet the requirements of this rule; defendant's assertion that the evidence should not have been admitted without the testimony of the confidential informant was rejected. **McLaughlin v. State,** Op. No. 1159, 818 P2d 683 (Alaska App. 1991).

Defendant's contention that State did not present sufficient evidentiary foundation to support admission of cocaine found in his possession at time of arrest was rejected; although officer who actually seized cocaine from defendant was out of state at time of trial and did not testify, testimony of other officer who participated in arrest satisfied foundational requirement even though bag of cocaine taken from defendant was not in that officer's view at all times during the arrest. **Toney v. State,** Op. No. 1223, 833 P2d 15 (Alaska App. 1992).

This rule does not require the State, for purposes of establishing chain of custody, to call as witnesses all persons who exercised custody over evidence sought to be admitted, nor does it require State to rule out of possibility of tampering. **HoustonHult v. State,** Op. No. 1270, 843 P2d 1262 (Alaska (App. 1992).

Determination of paternity based upon DNA reports not accompanied by authenticating affidavits was reversible error. **Mattox v. State, Dept. of Revenue,** Op. No. 4094, 875 P2d 763 (Alaska 1994).

This rule requires the prosecution to demonstrate as a matter of reasonable certainty that the evidence was at the time it was observed properly identified and free of possible taints. The reasonable certainty requirement does not obligate the state to conclusively rule out the possibility of tampering or to produce as chain-of-custody witnesses all persons who had contact with the evidence. **Fox v. State,** Op. No. 1449, 908 P2d 1053 (Alaska App. 1995).

For purposes of a drug prosecution, the state's duty to prove proper identification and freedom from taint at the time the evidence was observed, must focus on the integrity of the evidence from the time of purchase to the time of testing; potential post-testing alteration is wholly immaterial. **Fox v. State,** Op. No. 1449, 908 P2d 1053 (Alaska App. 1995).

In prosecution for possession of drugs, government must prove to a reasonable certainty (1) that substance identified by laboratory testing as controlled substance is same substance that was earlier in defendant's possession and (2) that substance was not altered before it was tested; however, this does not mean that State must conclusively rule out all possibility of tampering, nor does it means that State must produce any and all persons who had contact with the evidence. **Patterson v. State,** Op. No. 1604, 966 P2d 553 (Alaska App. 1998).

Where State presented testimony describing procedures adopted by both police department and crime lab to ensure integrity of physical evidence, and State also presented testimony which viewed in light most favorable to State demonstrated to reasonable certainty that procedures were followed, trial court did not abuse its discretion in overruling defendant's objections to admission of physical evidence. **Patterson v. State,** Op. No. 1604, 966 P2d 553 (Alaska App. 1998).

Rule 902. Self-Authentication.

Extrinsic evidence of authenticity as a condition precedent to admissibility is not required with respect to the following:

(1) **Domestic Public Documents Under Seal.** A document bearing a seal purporting to be that of the United States, or of any state, district, commonwealth, territory, or insular possession thereof, or the Panama Canal Zone, or the Trust Territory of the Pacific Islands, or of a political subdivision, department, officer, or agency thereof, and a signature purporting to be an attestation or execution.

(2) **Domestic Public Documents Not Under Seal.** A document purporting to bear the signature in an official capacity of an officer or employee of any entity included in paragraph (1) hereof, having no seal, if a public officer having a seal and having official duties in the district or political subdivision of the officer or employee certifies under seal that the signer has the official capacity and the signature is genuine.

(3) **Foreign Public Documents.** A document purporting:

(a) To bear the seal of state of a nation recognized by the executive power of the United States; or

(b) To be executed or attested in an official capacity by a person authorized by the laws of a foreign country to make the execution or attestation, and accompanied by a final certification as to the genuineness of the signature and official position (i) of the executing or attesting person, or (ii) of any foreign official whose certificate of genuineness of signature and official position relates to the execution or attestation or is in a chain of certificates of genuineness of signature and official position relating to the execution or attestation.

(4) **Certified Copies of Public Records.** A copy of an official record or report or entry therein, or of a document authorized by law to be recorded or filed and actually recorded or filed in a public office, including data compilations in any form, certified as correct by the custodian or other person authorized to make the certification, by certificate complying with paragraph (1), (2), or (3) of this rule or complying with any enactment of the Alaska Legislature or other rule prescribed by the Alaska Supreme Court.

(5) **Official Publications.** Books, pamphlets, or other publications purporting to be issued by public authority.

(6) **Newspapers and Periodicals.** Printed materials purporting to be newspapers or periodicals.

(7) **Trade Inscriptions and the Like.** Inscriptions, signs, tags, or labels purporting to have been affixed in the course of business and indicating ownership, control or origin.

(8) **Acknowledged Documents.** Documents accompanied by a certificate of acknowledgment executed in the manner provided by law by a notary public or other officer authorized by law to take acknowledgments.

(9) **Commercial Paper and Related Documents.** Commercial paper, signatures therein, and documents relating thereto to the extent provided by general commercial law.

(10) **Presumptions Created by Law.** Any signature, document, or other matter declared by enactment of the Alaska Legislature or rule prescribed by the Alaska Supreme Court to be presumptively or prima facie genuine or authentic.

(11) **Certified Records of Regularly Conducted Activity.** The original or a duplicate of a record of regularly conducted activity, within the scope of Rule 803(6), which the custodian thereof or another qualified person certified under penalty of perjury (i) was made at or near the time of the occurrence of the matter set forth, by (or from information transmitted by) a person with knowledge of those matters, (ii) or kept in the course of regularly conducted activity and (iii) was made by the regularly conducted activity as a regular practice, unless the source of information or the method or circumstances of preparation indicate lack of trustworthiness. A party intending to rely on this paragraph must serve on other parties a notice of this intent and make available for copying relevant documents at least 20 days before the documents are to be introduced at a hearing unless the court shortens this time for good cause shown. The word "certifies" as used in this subsection means with respect to a domestic record, a written declaration under oath subject to the penalty of perjury and, with respect to a foreign record, a written declaration signed in a country which, if falsely made, would subject the maker to criminal penalty under the laws of the country. The certificate relating to a foreign record must be accompanied by a final certificate as to the genuineness of the signature and official position (i) of the person executing the certificate and (ii) of any foreign official who certifies the genuineness of signature and official position of the executing person, or is in a chain of certificates of genuineness of signature and official position of the executing person. A final certification may be made by a secretary of embassy or legation, consul general, consul, vice consul, or consular agent of the United States, or a diplomatic or consular official of the foreign country assigned or accredited to the United States.

(Added by SCO 364 effective August 1, 1979; amended by SCO 851 effective January 15, 1988; and by SCO 1522 effective October 15, 2003)

Annotations

Cases

Although breathalyzer calibration documents did not comply with this rule, admission of the documents did not preclude defendant from disputing the authenticity of the documents or of the breathalyzer test before the jury as a factual matter; accordingly, there was no reason to bar the prosecution from establishing the authenticity of the documents on remand. **Morgan v. Municipality of Anchorage,** Op. No. 86, 643 P2d 691 (Alaska App. 1982).

Superior court erred in not granting subcontractor's motion to reopen case to permit filing of certificate of compliance with statute requiring corporation, in order to maintain an action, to prove that it paid annual corporation tax, where the motion would not have required any additional testimony, the certificate was self-authenticating, and would have demonstrated peradventure that subcontractor had complied with statute; accordingly, reviewing court deemed the record on appeal to be augmented by the certificate. **A.C.E. Construction v. Chena Construction,** Op. No. 2526, 647 P2d 602 (Alaska 1982).

A group of documents referred to collectively as a "breathalyzer packet" were self-authenticating under this rule. **State v. Huggins,** Op. No. 127, 659 P2d 613 (Alaska App. 1982).

Absent evidence to the contrary, the trial court should presume that what purports to be a state official's signature, under seal, certifying a document, or a signature, or that a person is a public custodian, is in fact a valid signature even if the signature is a stamped or printed facsimile. **State v. Huggins,** Op. No. 127, 659 P2d 613 (Alaska App. 1982).

Separate certification as to individual documents in "breathalyzer packet" is not required unless the documents are certified by different custodians, so long as the certification as to the multiple documents makes clear, on its face, the documents to which it applies. **State v. Huggins,** Op. No. 127, 659 P2d 613 (Alaska App. 1982).

When a timely and appropriate challenge to admissibility of a breathalyzer test result is made the prosecution must, at a minimum, demonstrate that the breathalyzer instrument in question was tested successfully for radio frequency interference at least once in a manner substantially complying with the manufacturer's recommendation and that none of the conditions listed by the manufacturer for retesting occurred between the time of the initial radio frequency test and the challenged breath test. **Thayer v. Municipality of Anchorage,** Op. No. 395, 686 P2d 721 (Alaska App. 1984).

Trial judge did not err in admitting documents using telephonic testimony without the defendant's consent where the judge also directed the state to immediately send properly self-authenticated copies of the documents to the court; the fact that the court received the properly authenticated documents after the jury retired for its deliberations was of no consequence, since this was simply the court's means to ensure the propriety of its ruling, and it was not necessary for the new documents to be presented at trial. **Tuckfield v. State,** Op. No. 1103, 805 P2d 982 (Alaska App. 1991).

Copies of Division of Measurement Standards calibration certificates offered to establish that the radar unit used in a speeding case was properly calibrated, which were submitted in conjunction with a written attestation by a custodian of records for the Alaska State Troopers stating that the calibration reports where true and correct copies of the original certified record under seal on file in his office, were not self-authenticating because (1) the original calibration certificates did not bear an official state or department seal, (2) although the original calibration certificates were signed by the state metrologist, the record custodian's attestation vouched neither for the genuineness of the metrologists signature nor for his standing as a state metrologist, and (3) the record custodian's attestation was not itself under seal, nor was it accompanied by a sealed certificate from some other state official attesting to the custodian's official status and to the genuineness of his signature on the attestation. **Buening v. State,** Op. No. 1146, 814 P2d 1373 (Alaska App. 1991).

Rule 903. Subscribing Witness's Testimony Unnecessary.

When the execution of an attested writing is in issue, whether or not attestation is a statutory requisite of its effective execution, no attester is a necessary witness even though all attesters are available unless the statute requiring attestation specifically provides otherwise.

(Added by SCO 364 effective August 1, 1979)

ARTICLE X. WRITINGS

Rule 1001. Definitions.

For purposes of this article the following definitions are applicable:

(1) **Writings and Recordings.** Writings and recordings consist of letters, words, or numbers, or their equivalent, set down by handwriting, typewriting, printing, photo-stating, photographing, magnetic impulse, mechanical or electronic recording, or other form of data compilation.

(2) **Photographs.** Photographs include still photographs, x-ray films, video tapes, and motion pictures.

(3) **Original.** An original of a writing or recording is the writing or recording itself or any counterpart intended to have the same effect by a person executing or issuing it. An original of a photograph includes the negative or any print therefrom. If data are stored in a computer or similar device, any printout or other output readable by sight, shown to reflect that data accurately, is an original.

(4) **Duplicate.** A duplicate is a counterpart produced by the same impression as the original, or from the same matrix, or by means of photography, including enlargements and miniatures, or by mechanical or electronic rerecording, or by chemical reproduction, or by other equivalent techniques which accurately reproduce the original.

(Added by SCO 364 effective August 1, 1979)

Annotations

Cases

Where fishermen were charged with fishing in closed waters, the subject Loran C readings were not "set down" or otherwise stored as a magnetic impulse, a mechanical or electronic recording, or in some other form of data compilation, and the fishermen did not convinced the appellate court the best evidence rule required that it be so stored; the appellate court held the actual electronic readings displayed by the Loran C receivers were not subject to the best evidence rule. **State v. Andrews,** Op. 1915, 84 P.3d 441 (Alaska App. 2004).

Rule 1002. Requirement of Original.

To prove the content of a writing, recording, or photograph, the original writing, recording, or photograph is required, except as otherwise provided by an enactment of the Alaska Legislature or by these or other rules promulgated by the Alaska Supreme Court.

(Added by SCO 364 effective August 1, 1979)

Annotations

Cases

This rule was not violated when prosecutor related to the grand jury a summary of allegedly perjured trial testimony where the transcript of the trial was presented to the grand jury and the jurors were instructed to make their findings based upon the transcript rather than on the prosecutor's summary. **Newman v. State,** Op. No. 174, 655 P2d 1302 (Alaska App. 1982).

In prosecution for fishing in closed waters, best evidence rule did not require that arresting officer's Loran C receiver be equipped with a printout mechanism or that the original digital display on the receiver be preserved either photographically or mechanically. **Wamser v. State,** Op. No. 312, 672 P2d 163 (Alaska App. 1983).

Rule 1003. Admissibility of Duplicates.

A duplicate is admissible to the same extent as an original unless (1) a genuine question is raised as to the authenticity of the original or (2) in the circumstances it would be unfair to admit the duplicate in lieu of the original.

(Added by SCO 364 effective August 1, 1979)

Annotations

Cases

Photocopies of marked bills used in purchase of LSD were admissible as evidence against defendant where the original bills had been returned to the police department for use in other drug cases. **Ingram v. State,** Op. No. 489,703 P2d 415 (Alaska App. 1985).

Trial court erred in holding that burden of proof for admissibility of copy of lost promissory note was clear and convincing evidence that copy was authentic; proponent only had to establish foundation from which factfinder could legitimately infer that copy was authentic. **Buster v. Gale,** Op. No. 4044, 866 P2d 837 (Alaska 1994).

Rule 1004. Admissibility of Other Evidence of Contents.

The original is not required, and other evidence of the contents of a writing, recording, or photograph is admissible if

(a) **Originals Lost or Destroyed.** All originals are lost or have been destroyed, unless the proponent in bad faith lost or destroyed them; or

(b) **Original Not Obtainable.** No original can be obtained by any available judicial process or procedure; or

(c) **Original in Possession of Opponent.** At a time when an original was under the control of the party against whom offered, that party was put on notice, by the pleadings or otherwise, that the contents would be a subject of proof at the hearing, and that party does not produce the original at the hearing; or

(d) **Collateral Matters.** The writing, recording, or photograph is not closely related to a controlling issue.

(Added by SCO 364 effective August 1, 1979; amended by SCO 1153 effective July 15, 1994)

Annotations

Cases

Trial court erred in holding that burden of proof for admissibility of copy of lost promissory note was clear and convincing evidence that copy was authentic; proponent only had to establish foundation from which factfinder could legitimately infer that copy was authentic. **Buster v. Gale,** Op. No. 4044, 866 P2d 837 (Alaska 1994).

Rule 1005. Public Records.

The contents of an official record, or of a document authorized to be recorded or filed and actually recorded or filed, including data compilations in any form, if otherwise admissible, may be proved by copy, certified as correct in accordance with Rule 902 or testified to be correct by a witness who has compared it with the original. If a copy which complies with the foregoing cannot be obtained by the exercise of reasonable diligence, then other evidence of the contents may be given.

ER

(Added by SCO 364 effective August 1, 1979)

Rule 1006. Summaries.

The contents of voluminous writings, recordings, or photographs which cannot conveniently be examined in court may be presented in the form of a chart, summary, or calculation. The originals, or duplicates, shall be made available for examination or copying, or both, by other parties at a reasonable time and place. The court may order that they be produced in court.

(Added by SCO 364 effective August 1, 1979)

Rule 1007. Testimony or Written Admission of Party.

Without accounting for the nonproduction of the original, the contents of writings, recordings, or photographs may be proved by the testimony or deposition of the party against whom offered or by the party's written admission, including the testimony, deposition or writing of a declarant whose statements are attributable to a party under Rule 801(d)(2)(C), (D), or (E).

(Added by SCO 364 effective August 1, 1979; amended by SCO 1522 effective October 15, 2003)

Rule 1008. Functions of Court and Jury.

When the admissibility of other evidence of contents of writings, recordings, or photographs under these rules depends upon the fulfillment of a condition of fact, the question whether the condition has been fulfilled is ordinarily for the court to determine in accordance with the provisions of Rule 104. However, when an issue is raised (a) whether the asserted writing ever existed, or (b) whether another writing, recording, or photograph produced at the trial is the original, or (c) whether other evidence of contents correctly reflects the contents, the issue is for the trier of fact to determine as in the case of other issues of fact.

(Added by SCO 364 effective August 1, 1979)

ARTICLE XI. TITLE

Rule 1101. Title.

These rules may be cited as the Alaska Rules of Evidence.

(Added by SCO 364 effective August 1, 1979)

COMMENTARY TO ALASKA RULES OF EVIDENCE

Table of Contents

ARTICLE I. GENERAL PROVISIONS

ARTICLE II. JUDICIAL NOTICE

ARTICLE III. PRESUMPTIONS

ARTICLE IV. ADMISSIBILITY OF RELEVANT EVIDENCE

ARTICLE V. PRIVILEGES
INTRODUCTORY COMMENT

ARTICLE VI. WITNESSES

ARTICLE VII. OPINION TESTIMONY

EVIDENCE RULES COMMENTARY

Introduction

The Commentary to the Alaska Rules of Evidence was prepared by Professor Stephen A. Saltzburg, who served as Reporter for the Rules of Evidence. Some changes to the Commentary have been made by the staffs of the Administrative Office and the Supreme Court Clerk's Office to reflect the form of the rules as ultimately adopted by the Alaska Supreme Court. This Commentary has not been adopted or approved by the Supreme Court, but is being published for informational purposes and to assist the users of the Rules of Evidence.

The Alaska Supreme Court extends its thanks to Professor Saltzburg and to the members of the Advisory Committee on the Rules of Evidence for the considerable time and effort they have devoted to the preparation of the rules and of this Commentary. Serving on the Advisory Committee were Alexander O. Bryner, Chairman; Superior Court Judges James R. Blair, Victor D. Carlson, William H. Sanders, and Thomas B. Stewart; and attorneys Walter L. Carpeneti, Richard O. Gantz, Patrick Gullufsen, and Dick L. Madsen.

The Commentary to the Alaska Rules of Evidence which follows does not necessarily reflect amendments which have been made to the Alaska Rules of Evidence after the Evidence Rules were originally adopted. Any amendment after the Rules were added by SCO 364, effective August 1, 1979, would be reflected in the legislative history note following each Evidence Rule.

ARTICLE I. GENERAL PROVISIONS

Rule 101. Scope and Applicability.

(a) **General Applicability.** There are three courts in the Alaska judicial system—the Supreme Court, the Superior Court, and the District. Trials, both civil and criminal, are conducted at the Superior Court and District Court level. The judges who sit on these courts should find the new Rules of Evidence no more difficult to apply—and hopefully somewhat easier—than common law rules. But magistrates, whose authority is delimited under AS 22.15, are working on a part time basis and may find the New Rules difficult. Nevertheless, experience has shown that they exhibit a workable grasp of the existing rules of evidence. Thus, this subdivision states that the Rules of Evidence shall apply in cases tried before magistrates as well as judges.

These rules are not applicable in areas directly covered by other rules promulgated by the Alaska Supreme Court. For example, Criminal Rule 5.1(d) as amended (preliminary examinations in criminal cases) and Criminal Rule 6(r) (grand jury) govern the admission of evidence in their respective areas. *See, State v. Gieffels,* 554 P.2d 460 (Alaska 1976). Children's Rules specifying special rules of evidence for children's proceedings will remain in effect *(e.g.,* 13(a) (2)), unless they are superseded by these Rules (*e.g.,* 17(a)).

(b) **Rules of Privilege.** This subdivision implements the privilege article of the rules. "It recognizes that confidentiality once destroyed cannot be restored, and that a privilege is effective only if it bars all disclosure at all times." 5 Weinstein's *Evidence* Paragraph 1101 [1].

(c) **Rules Inapplicable.** It should be noted that this rule does not decide the reach of constitutional principles as applied to admission of illegally seized evidence. *See State v. Sears,* Reporter's Comment to that rule.

(1) *Preliminary Questions of Fact.* Paragraph (1) states for convenience, the provisions of Rule 104(a), *supra. See* Reporter's Comment to that rule.

(2) *Miscellaneous Proceedings.* Extradition and rendition proceedings are essentially administrative, and traditionally the rules of evidence have not applied. 1 Wigmore § 4(6).

The rules of evidence have not been regarded as applicable to sentencing or probation proceedings, where great reliance is placed upon the presentence investigation and report. This is in accord with previous law. *Cf. State v. Sears, supra.*

Warrants for arrest, criminal summonses, and search warrants are issued upon complaint or affidavit showing probable cause. The nature of the proceedings make application of the formal rules of evidence inappropriate and impractical.

Because summary contempt proceedings are not full adversary contests but immediate responses to special problems of misbehavior, the rules of evidence do not apply.

Habeas corpus hearings are treated like all other cases under subdivision (b), *supra,* and the rules apply in these hearings.

Rule 102. Purpose and Construction.

Alaska Rule 102 copies the text of Federal Rule 102.

While this Rule provides that all of the evidence rules shall be interpreted so as "to secure...promotion of growth and development of the law of evidence to the end that truth may be ascertained," this should not be read to encourage the search for truth at any cost. Another end is also sought: that "proceedings [may be] justly determined." Occasionally, situations will arise where justice requires that accuracy in fact-finding gives way to a more significant social goal.

Deciding when proceedings are "justly determined" requires an examination of federal and state constitutional protections (*see, e.g.,* U.S. Const., amends, IV and V; Alaska Const., art. I, § 22; *Ravin v. State,* 537 P.2d 494, 504 (Alaska 1975)) and legislative attempts to protect individuals from official intrusion, including judicial intrusion. *See, e.g.,* AS 47.10.080 (g). Evidence that is apparently probative may be excluded to create disincentives to governmental abuses (*see, e.g., Lauderdale v. State,* 548 P2d 376 (Alaska 1976 (Alaska 1976) to recognize and perhaps to foster socially desirable private conduct (*see, e.g.,* Rules 407 & 410, *infra*) to protect personal privacy (*see, e.g.,* Rule 505 *infra*) and to enable persons to maximize the effectiveness of professional counseling (*see, e.g.,* Rules 503 & 504).

In short, the search for truth is important in its practical impact and philosophical overtones. Sometimes the search for fact-finding precision itself may have constitutional roots. *See Davis v. Alaska,* 415 U.S. 308, 39 L.Ed. 2d 347 (1974). But it is not the end all of a system of justice; other values must be weighed.

"Insuring that 'proceedings [are] justly determined' as this Rule states is by no means a simple task." K. Redden & S. Saltzburg, Federal Rules of Evidence Manual 15 (2d ed. 1977).

Rule 103. Rulings on Evidence.

(a) **Effect of Erroneous Ruling.** Subdivision (a) is a codification of the basic rules of offering evidence and objecting to the admission of evidence. It corresponds closely with the substance of Rules 4 and 5 of the Uniform Rules of Evidence and Rules 6 and 7 of the Model Code of Evidence (1942). The Rule is designed to reject the Court of Exchequer's misguided view in *Crease v. Barrett,* 1 C.M.&R. 919 (1835), that any error might require reversal. In the case of a ruling admitting evidence, to constitute grounds for a reversal an error must affect a substantial right of the party and a timely objection stating the specific grounds of the objection must be made. If the ruling is to exclude evidence, the substance of the offered evidence must be made known to the court in order to ascertain on appeal whether a substantial right has been affected. While noting the existence of basic requirements in the form, timing, and specificity of objections, this rule does not attempt to set forth details or nuances which are better dealt with on a case by case basis. The common law tradition requiring prompt challenges to questions, to offers of evidence, and to qualifications of witnesses, and reasonable prompt motions to strike is continued in these general rules. No formal exceptions need be noted. See Morgan, Basic Problems of Evidence 53-54 (1962).

In rejecting the notion of automatic reversal on the basis of any error whatsoever, this rule does not prescribe any particular test for distinguishing reversible from harmless errors. The one certain rule is that a constitutional error requires reversal unless an appellate court can be certain beyond a reasonable doubt that the error did not influence the verdict. *Chapman v. California,* 386 U.S. 18, 17 L.Ed.2d 705 (1967). There is disagreement on the proper test for determining when non-constitutional errors are harmless. See generally, R. Traynor, The Riddle of Harmless Error (1970). Saltzburg, The Harm of Harmless Error, 59 Va. L. Rev. 988 (1973). Although harmless error rules can be found in Rule 47(a), Alaska R. Crim. P., and Rule 61, Alaska R. Civ. P., no formula is offered in either place for determining when an error affects substantial rights. There is some authority in existing case law for distinguishing the tests of harmlessness used in criminal and civil cases. *Compare Love v. State,* 457 P.2d 622 (Alaska 1969), *Daniels v. State,* 388 P2d 813 (Alaska 1964), and *Biele v. State,* 371 P.2d 811, 814 (Alaska 1962) *with Zerbinos v. Lewis,* 394 P.2d 886 (Alaska 1964). But there is also authority suggesting that the civil test closely resembles the criminal test. See *Howarth v. Pfeifer,* 423 P.2d 680 (Alaska 1967). This Rule does not attempt to set forth any test; that is left for adjudication, the approach preferred in *Love v. State,* and more recently in *McCracken v. Davis,* 560 P.2d 771 (Alaska 1977). For recent cases invoking the doctrine of harmless error, *see, Hayes v. State,* 581 P.2d 221 (Alaska 1978) and *Priest v. Lindig,* 583 P.2d 173 (Alaska 1978).

(b) **Record of Offer and Ruling.** Like its federal counterpart, this section borrows from the wording of a preexisting rule of civil procedure, rule 43(c). The obvious purpose of the rule is to provide an appellate tribunal with an accurate record of the trial proceedings—*i.e.,* to insure that the specific objections and proper offers of proof are accurately reflected in the record. "It is designed to resolve doubts as to what testimony the witness would have in fact given, and, in nonjury cases, to provide the appellate court with material for possible final disposition of the case in the event of reversal of a ruling which excluded evidence.... Application is made discretionary in view of the practical impossibility of formulating a satisfactory rule in mandatory terms." Fed. R. Evid. 103(b), Advisory Committee Note (citation omitted).

(c) **Hearing of Jury.** A ruling excluding evidence may be pointless if the jury hears the evidence as part of an offer of proof. Hence, this subdivision provides that proceedings surrounding rulings on evidence should be conducted as much as possible outside the presence of the jury. As reflected in the note accompanying subdivision (a), the Rule does not specify the form that an offer of proof will take. Subdivision (b) recognizes, however, that the trial judge may require a question and answer format. When this is the format, the questions and answers should be asked outside the jury's hearing. While this subdivision should have its principal impact on offers of proof, arguments on extended objections should also be outside the presence of the jury, if practicable, since rulings on preliminary questions, and law and argument relating thereto, are the province of the judges alone.

(d) **Plain Error.** This subdivision incorporates the doctrine of plain error found in Alaska case law, *Stork v. State,* 559 P2d 99 (Alaska 1977), *Merrill v. Faltin,* 430 P2d 913 (Alaska 1967); and Rule 47(b), Alaska R. Crim. P., [modeled after Fed. R. Crim. P. 52(b)]. Most codifications have included some provision resembling this one. The 1974 revision of the Uniform Rules of Evidence, for example, includes a similar provision but omits the word "plain." Maine Rules of Evidence, based on the Federal rules of Evidence, uses the word "obvious" instead of "plain." Maine Rule of Evidence 103(d). There is apparently some worry about the ambiguity of the plain error concept. The Report of the Committee on the Revision of the Law of Evidence to the Supreme Court of New Jersey (1955) stated the general view of plain error:

> Our courts have been loathe to apply this escape in the case of the failure to interpose timely objection to the introduction of evidence...The policy behind the necessity for timely objection is obvious; the escape apparently will only be applied where a shocking miscarriage of justice would result. It seems desirable that the "plain error" rule be retained to take care of extreme cases.

No precise formula for determining when the plain error doctrine should be invoked is offered in the Rule. This, like the harmless error test, is left for a case by case determination.

It is arguable that plain error is a principle that should be excluded from rules governing trial procedure, since it relates to the willingness of appellate courts to review claims not raised below. Subdivision (d) is included in these Rules for these reasons: 1) to promote uniformity with the Federal Rules; 2) to negate any implication that there is no such doctrine; 3) to alert the trial judge that intervention may be necessary when plain error would result in reversal on appeal; 4) to also remind the state appellate courts that invocation of the doctrine may remove the need for federal scrutiny of state judgments.

> If a federal court is going to review a criminal conviction and perhaps set it aside in a federal habeas corpus proceeding, the state may feel it would rather consider the error in the first instance itself, and may utilize the doctrine of plain error to do so.

Saltzburg, *Another Ground for Decision-Harmless Trial Court Errors*, 47 Temp. L. Q. 193, 200-01 n.25 (1974).

Applying the plain error concept has not been easy for most appellate courts, and it has not been easy for the Alaska Supreme Court. *See, e.g., Stork v. State,* 559 P2d 99 (Alaska 1977); *Bakken v. State,* 489 P2d 120 (Alaska 1971). The obvious tension is between the natural instinct of an appellate court to affirm a result that may only have been reached, or may have been reached in part, because of an error committed below and the understandable reluctance of appellate judges to create incentives for litigants to allow errors to go uncorrected at trial in order to preserve possible arguments for appeal. The dilemma is most apparent in cases where a clearly erroneous instruction on an important point is given to a jury. On the one hand, it would seem that the mistake cannot be permitted to support a verdict lest the "wrong" party win and subvert the goals of the legal rules at stake in the litigation. On the other hand, it may be argued that it is not likely that a lawyer would have failed to see an error of great magnitude and that it is more likely that the verdict loser remained silent in the belief that the jury would not listen closely to the very instruction which would, in the event of a loss, provide ammunition for appeal. In actual practice the dilemma is complicated by the realization that, absent a plain error rule, the party benefiting from the error may have an incentive to knowingly abet an error of the trial court.

In deciding when to invoke the plain error concept, appellate courts have looked, and will probably continue to look, to see how important the error was; what impact the error probably had on the outcome of the case; whether the record demonstrates any intentional failure to bring an error to the attention of the trial court; how burdensome re-litigation would be, especially for the verdict winner; whether the verdict loser promptly sought to correct any error by moving for a new trial below; and whether the principal fault was that of the trial judge or the attorney for the verdict loser. Weighing these factors is not likely to produce a totally satisfactory solution, but a less flexible approach threatens to remove the dilemma by advocating a result which will be totally unsatisfactory in many cases.

(Amended by SCO 671, effective June 15, 1986).

Rule 104. Preliminary Questions.

(a) **Questions of Admissibility Generally.** The applicability of a particular rule of evidence often depends upon the existence of a condition. Is the alleged expert a qualified physician? Is a witness whose former testimony is offered unavailable? Was a stranger present during a conversation between attorney and client? Was an out-of-court statement against interest when made? In each instance the admissibility of evidence will turn upon the answer to the question of the existence of the condition. Accepted practice, incorporated in the rule, places on the judge the responsibility for these determinations. McCormick (2d ed.) § 53; Morgan, Basic Problems of Evidence 45-50 (1962). The general rule is that when relevant evidence may be excluded under some rule of evidence and factfinding is necessary in the application of the rule, the judge acts as a trier of fact. *See generally,* Maguire & Epstein, Preliminary Questions of Fact in Determining the Admissibility of Evidence, 40 Harv. L. Rev. 392 (1927).

Entrusting the judge—rather than the jury—with the responsibility of determining certain factual questions serves a threefold purpose. First, it prevents the submission of highly technical evidentiary questions to a group of lay persons ill equipped "to do legal reasoning." Maguire & Epstein, *supra* at 393, quoting C. Chamberlayne, Evidence § 81 (1911). See Morgan, *supra* at 169 ("A mind trained to sift evidence may substantially accomplish even so difficult a task; but to expect the unskilled minds of jurors to do so is little short of ridiculous"). Second, it insulates the jurors from the kinds of evidence that they may be unable to evaluate fairly; trepidations as to the ability of jurors to evaluate fairly certain kinds of evidence give rise to various exclusionary rules. *See* Morgan, *supra* at 166 n.4 (hearsay rules). *See generally,* Levin & Cohen, *The Exclusionary Rules in Nonjury Criminal Cases,* 119 U. Pa. L. Rev. 905 (1971). Finally, resolution of the preliminary factual question by the judge may be necessary to preserve and protect the very interest sought to be furthered by the suppression of certain evidence. As was stated by Morgan, *supra* at 169: "[N]othing could be more absurd than to violate the interest and then to instruct the jury to repair the damage by disregarding the wrongfully extracted evidence. If a lawyer is compelled to repeat in open court the confidential communications of his alleged client, and the jury is told to disregard them in case they find the relationship exists, the harm of disclosure is beyond remedy." *See generally,* Saltzburg, *Standards of Proof and Preliminary Questions of Fact,* 27 Stan. L. Rev. 271, 271-73 (1975).

If the question is factual in nature, the judge will of necessity receive evidence pro and con on the issue. The rule provides that the rules of evidence in general do not apply to this process. One commentator points out that the authorities are "scattered and inconclusive," and observes:

> Should the exclusionary law of evidence, "the child of the jury system" in Thayer's phrase, be applied to this hearing before the judge? Sound sense backs the view that it should not, and that the judge should be empowered to hear any relevant evidence, such as affidavits or other reliable hearsay.

McCormick (2d ed.) § 53 at 122 n.91. This view is reinforced by practical necessity in certain situations. An item, offered and objected to, may itself be considered in ruling on admissibility, though not yet admitted in evidence. Thus the content of an asserted declaration against interest must be considered in ruling whether it is against interest. Again, common practice calls for considering the testimony of a witness, particularly a child, in determining competency. *See* McCormick on Evidence § 10 at 21 (2d ed. 1972).

Legitimate concern may exist that the use of affidavits by the judge in preliminary hearings on admissibility will reduce factfinding precision. But many important judicial determinations are made on the basis of affidavits.

Rule 43(e), Alaska R. Civ. P., dealing with motions generally, provides: "When a motion is based on facts not appearing of record, the court may hear the matter on affidavits or other documentary evidence presented by the respective parties, but the court may direct that the matter be heard wholly or partly on oral testimony or depositions." Civil Rule 4(e) (6) provides for proof of service by affidavit. Civil Rule 56 provides in detail for the entry of summary judgment based on affidavits. Affidavits may supply the foundation for temporary restraining orders under Civil Rule 65 (b).

The study made for the California Law Revision Commission recommended an amendment to Uniform Rule 2 as follows: "In the determination of the issue aforesaid [preliminary determination], exclusionary rules shall not apply, subject, however, to...any valid claim of privilege." California Law Revision Commission, Tentative Recommendation and a Study Relating to the Uniform Rules of Evidence 470 (1962) (Article VII, Hearsay). The proposal was not adopted in the California Evidence Code. The Uniform Rules are likewise silent on the subject. However, New Jersey Evidence Rule 8(1), dealing with preliminary inquiry by the judge, provides:

> "In his determination the rules of evidence shall not apply except for Rule 4 [exclusion on grounds of prejudice, etc.] or a valid claim of privilege."

N.J. Rev. Stat. Ann. § 2A:84A-8 (West 1976).

There is now increased support for the proposition that the exclusionary rules are confined to trials. *See United States v. Matlock,* 415 U.S. 164, 39 L.Ed. 2d 242 (1974); cf. *United States v. Calandra,* 414 U.S. 338, 38 L.Ed. 2d 561 (1974).

It is important to keep in mind that, while the court may not be bound by the rules of evidence in ruling on preliminary questions, it may be reversible error for the court to refuse to hear testimony actually offered. This subdivision offers a shortcut to proof. It does not provide that refusal to hear probative evidence will be permitted. A permissible shortcut should not become a rule of preference.

(b) **Relevancy Conditioned on Fact.** It frequently happens that two or more controverted facts are so related that evidence of one is inadmissible without evidence of one or more of the others. Thus when a spoken statement is relied upon to prove notice to X, it is without probative value unless X heard it. Or if a letter purporting to be from Y is relied upon to establish an admission by him, it has no probative value unless Y wrote or authorized it. Relevance in this sense has been labelled "conditional relevancy." Morgan, Basic Problems of Evidence 45-46 (1962). Problems arising in connection with it are to be distinguished from problems of logical relevancy (*e.g.*, evidence in a murder case that the accused on the day before purchased a weapon of the kind used in the killing) treated in Rule 401.

In the case of conditional relevance, as generally, the judge has some control over the order in which each piece of evidence is to be offered. He may refuse to receive evidence of one fact until evidence sufficient to warrant a finding of another has been offered. Or, he may receive evidence of one upon assurance by counsel that the requisite evidence of the other or others will be offered. The judge makes a preliminary determination whether the foundation evidence is sufficient to support a finding of fulfillment of the condition. If so, the item is admitted. If after all the evidence on the issue is in, pro and con, the jury could reasonably conclude either that fulfillment of the condition is or is not established, the issue is for them. If the evidence is not such as to allow a finding, the judge withdraws the matter from their consideration. Morgan, *supra;* Cal. Evid. Code § 403 (West); N.J. Rev. Stat. Ann. § 2A:84A8(2) (West 1976). *See also* Uniform Rules of Evidence 19 & 67. If the evidence so received is very prejudicial, a mistrial may be ordered.

If preliminary questions of conditional relevancy were determined solely by the judge, as provided in subdivision (a), the functioning of the jury as a trier of fact would be greatly restricted and in some cases virtually destroyed. Relevance questions are appropriate questions for juries. Accepted treatments, as provided in the rule, is consistent with that, given fact questions generally.

(c) **Hearing of Jury.** Preliminary hearings on the admissibility of confessions must be conducted outside the hearing of the jury. *See Jackson v. Denno,* 378 U.S. 368, 12 L.Ed.2d 908 (1964). Otherwise, detailed treatment of when preliminary matters should be heard outside the hearing of the jury is not feasible. The procedure is time consuming. Not infrequently the same evidence which is relevant to the issue of establishment of fulfillment of a condition precedent to admissibility is also relevant to weight or credibility; and time is saved by taking foundation proof in the presence of the jury. Much evidence on preliminary questions, though not relevant to jury issues, may be heard by the jury with no adverse effect. A great deal must be left to the discretion of the judge who will act as the interests of justice require.

However, where an accused is a witness as to a preliminary matter, he has the right, upon his request, to be heard outside the jury's presence. Although in some cases duplication of evidence will occur and the procedure may be abused, a proper regard for the right of the accused not to testify generally in the case dictates that he be given an option to testify outside the hearing of the jury on preliminary matters. To leave completely to the judge's discretion the determination of whether the preliminary hearing is held outside the hearing of the jury would risk allowing the jury to hear extremely prejudicial evidence. For a similar provision, see Cal. Evid. Code § 402(b) (West 1966).

The second sentence of subdivision (c) should apply to civil actions and proceedings as well as criminal cases.

(d) **Testimony by Accused.** This subdivision is more protective of a criminal defendant than the Federal Rule.

The first sentence, which is the same in both rules, bars cross-examination on issues unrelated to the factfinding necessary to resolve the preliminary matter; it enables the prosecution to fully litigate all preliminary questions but prevents questioning on preliminary matters to be used as a mechanism for circumventing the privilege against self-incrimination. It is difficult to see how the prosecutor is unfairly disadvantaged by such a procedure, and it is plain that the defendant is encouraged to take the witness stand. Since factfinding on the preliminary matter is likely to be improved, the policies underlying the evidence rule giving rise to the factfinding should be well served. *See generally,* Carlson, *Cross-Examination of the Accused* 52 Cornell L. Q. 705 (1967).

The equivalent of the second sentence of this subdivision, which was found in an earlier draft of the Federal Rule and was subsequently deleted, affords additional protection. It provides a further incentive for a defendant to testify on preliminary matters by insuring that the defendant's words cannot be used at trial by the government unless the defendant testifies and contradicts the previous testimony given at the preliminary hearing. The defendant has a shield against general use of the evidence, but cannot seek to turn that shield into a perjurious sword. *Compare Agnello v. United States,* 269 U.S. 20, 70 L.Ed. 155 (1925) *with Walder v. United States,* 347 U.S. 62, 98 L.Ed. 503 (1954). *But see* Rule 412 *infra* (evidence illegally obtained). This is consistent with the United States Supreme Court's position in *Simons v. United States,* 390 U.S. 377, 19 L.Ed.2d. 1247 (1968).

In *Simmons* the Court held that a defendant had a right to testify at a preliminary hearing on a motion to suppress evidence illegally seized under the Fourth Amendment for the purpose of establishing standing and then to prevent the government's use of the testimony as part of its case-in-chief. The Court emphasized the tension between Fourth and Fifth Amendment rights and opted for this way of easing the tension.

It has been argued that the later decision in *McGautha v. California,* 402 U.S. 183, 28 L.Ed.2d 711 (1971), leaves *Simmons* of dubious precedential value. But this is not necessarily so. In one of the two cases decided together as *McGautha,* the Court rejected an argument that Ohio violated a defendant's right to a fair trial by establishing a unitary procedure for determination of guilt and penalty by the jury.

The argument that the single verdict improperly pitted the defendant's right to remain silent on the issue of guilt against his right to address the authority imposing punishment was rejected. Although the Court had never recognized a constitutional right of allocution, it assumed one existed. But the Court noted that the Ohio Constitution guaranteed defendants the right to have their counsel argue in summation for mercy as well as for acquittal. It also noted that defendants were allowed much leeway in offering evidence on the issue of punishment. The Court concluded, in addition, that "[e]ven in a bifurcated trial, the defendant could be restricted to the giving of evidence, with argument to be made by counsel only." *Id.* at 220, 28 L.Ed.2d at 733. As for the defendant's claim that evidence might exist within the unique knowledge of a defendant, the Court concluded that the Constitution did not forbid "a requirement that such evidence be available to the jury on all issues to which it is relevant or not at all." *Id.* at 220, 28 L.Ed.2d at 734.

In sum, the Court declared that the tension between a defendant's desires to remain silent on the issue of guilt and to speak on the question of penalty was not serious enough to require bifurcation as a matter of federal constitutional law. Whatever the ultimate judgment on the wisdom of *McGautha,* it is apparent that the Court faced a different kind of problem from that faced in *Simmons.* If it had required bifurcation, would all criminal defendants have been entitled to limited waiver of their privilege against self-incrimination on the ground that there would be a right to present evidence on one issue pitted against a privilege to remain silent on another? For example, would a criminal defendant have a constitutional right to bifurcate the mens rea and actus reus parts of a case? Would a defendant have a right to bifurcation every time his testimony could be used on more than one issue and he desired to address himself to only one? If the answer to these questions was to be "no," how would the *McGautha* issue be distinguished?

Simmons was different, of course, because in *Simmons* there had to be two proceedings. Hence, the defendant was asking that the practical requirement of two proceedings—a trial and a hearing—be considered in assessing the conflict between constitutional rights. It was in this context that the Court responded favorably.

Thus, one reading of *McGautha* and *Simmons* is that where a hearing, aside from trial, must be held on a constitutional claim raised by a defendant, the defendant must be permitted to testify at the hearing with the assurance that the testimony will not be used as part of the prosecution's case-in-chief. At the trial itself, the defendant cannot speak to one issue only without risking the use of testimony on other issues.

This is not the only reading of these cases. It is possible that *Simmons* is to be confined to its facts and that *McGautha* began the confinement. Moreover, hearings on preliminary matters not involving constitutional claims may be treated somewhat differently than hearings on Fourth Amendment claims. Subdivision (d) is not confined to any one type of preliminary matter; it is a broad section and must, therefore, rest on more than *Simmons* regardless of how that case is read.

It rests on the same fairness considerations that support the first sentence of the subdivision. Accurate decision-making on preliminary issues is promoted, thereby upholding the underlying policies of the rule at stake. Defendant and prosecutor are on equal terms during the hearing. And the privilege against self-incrimination is promoted, not impaired.

If the defendant chooses to testify at trial and contradicts his preliminary hearing testimony, impeachment is permitted. Subsequent perjury prosecutions are also permitted. Deference to the privilege against self-incrimination should not be viewed as a license to lie. See AS 11.70.020. *See generally, Beavers v. State,* 492 P.2d 88 (Alaska 1971).

(e) **Weight and Credibility.** An example of the application of this subdivision is that nothing in Rule 104 precludes the defendant from attacking the credibility of a confession that is admitted by presenting to the jury evidence which may include some of the same matters presented to the judge during the preliminary hearing.

For similar provisions see Uniform Rule of Evidence 8; Cal. Evid. Code § 406 (West 1966); Kan. Stat. § 60-408 (1976); N.J. Rev. Stat. Ann. § 2A:84A-8(1) (West 1976).

The basic rule is that courts are just as willing to accept relevant evidence, as defined in Rule 401, previously used on a preliminary matter as they are to accept relevant evidence offered for the first time at trial. It is obvious, however, that the actual decision on the preliminary matter may render some otherwise relevant evidence inadmissible. If, for example, a confession is suppressed because of a failure to advise the accused of his rights, the suppression ruling eliminates relevant evidence from the government's case. In short, since rules of evidence may result in the loss of relevant evidence anytime an objection or motion to suppress is sustained, some relevant evidence is lost. If an objection or motion is overruled and evidence is deemed admissible, no relevant and proper evidence is necessarily excluded at trial.

Rule 105. Limited Admissibility.

This rule reflects existing common law doctrine by requiring the trial judge, upon request, to instruct the jury as to the proper scope of the evidence where it is admitted for a limited purpose or against only one party. The burden generally is placed on the party who wants the instruction to ask for it. There may be cases where a trial judge should give a limiting instruction sua sponte as failure to do so would lead to reversal on appeal for plain error. See Rule 103(d). One example where the failure to give such an instruction might be likely to produce sufficient injustice to constitute plain error is where the confession of a non-testifying co-defendant is introduced against another co-defendant. *Bruton v. United States,* 391 U.S. 123, 20 L.Ed.2d 476 (1968).

The rule does not set forth the criteria for a proper request, but is somewhat analogous to Rule 103 which requires a specific objection or a reasonably definite offer of proof. Counsel should not be permitted to make an unsupported request but should be required to inform the court of the specific concerns and to suggest possible methods of appropriately instructing the jury. *Cf.,* Rule 51, Alaska R. Civ. P.

This rule, while incorporating the text of Federal Rule 105, additionally requires that all reasonable efforts be made to delete references to parties as to whom the evidence is inadmissible. The purpose of this provision is to avoid, wherever possible, prejudice to one party resulting from admission of evidence as to another party. A similar provision is found in the second sentence of the Maine Rules of Evidence 105:

> In a criminal case tried to a jury evidence admissible as to one defendant shall not be admitted as to other defendants unless all references to the defendant as to whom it is inadmissible have been effectively deleted.

There is little reason to limit concern for the prejudicial impact of evidence in multi-party cases to criminal trials. Thus, Rule 105, unlike Maine's rule, will apply in all cases tried to a jury.

A reasonable attempt to delete references is all that is required here. If it is not possible to delete all references to parties as to whom the evidence is inadmissible, the court has two options. It may order a severance or a separate trial of one or more of the parties in accordance with Rule 42(b), Alaska R. Civ. P., and Rule 14, Alaska R. Crim. P., if the evidence would be unduly prejudicial despite a limiting instruction and a reasonable attempt to delete references. Or, the court may rely upon Rule 403, which provides the alternative of excluding the evidence altogether if its probative value is substantially outweighed by the danger of unfair prejudice.

Nothing in this Rule is intended to limit the availability of these alternatives where the interest of justice cannot be served by a limiting instruction to the jury.

Rule 106. Remainder of, or Related Writings or Recorded Statements.

The standard rule at common law does provide that when a writing or recorded statement or part thereof is introduced by any party, an adverse party can require admission of the entire statement, assuming that the entire statement is relevant. But at common law this evidence often is introduced as part of the adverse party's own case-in-chief, which may be presented after much time has elapsed following the introduction of the original segment. In theory, the trial judge has discretion to change the normal order of proof and to permit the full statement, or all relevant portions, to be introduced together with the first portion offered. But many judges are hesitant to depart from the usual order and to "interfere" with counsel's approach to a case. Common law courts are even less apt to allow additional statements to be introduced immediately than they are to allow an adverse party to offer a complete statement as soon as some portions are presented.

Where time elapses between the offer of part of a statement and the offer of the remainder, the jury may become confused or find it difficult to reassess evidence that it has heard earlier in light of subsequent material. Rule 106 creates a right to require immediate admission of a complete written or recorded statement or of all relevant portions. It is designed to enable one party to correct immediately any misleading impression created by another party who offers part of a statement out of context. *See* McCormick § 56 (2d ed.); Cal. Evid. Code § 356 (West 1966). The rule also provides that it extends to immediate admission of all matters so closely related to a statement that in fairness they should be admitted immediately.

Although the Rule does not create any right of discovery of documents, the Rule should be read to permit a court to require a party who has introduced part of a writing or recorded statement to show that writing or recorded statement to the other side before the other side asks that it be introduced into evidence. It would be impractical to allow the adverse party to require that all statements on the same subject be produced for inspection. Arguably, any statement that is relevant to the issues being tried would have to be turned over in order to avoid a later claim that the Rule was not complied with. If all statements were produced, the burden on the court might be tremendous. Fairness does not require such full discovery, in view of the countervailing concerns giving rise to the general protections for witness statements. Thus, it is only where a specific statement is relied upon by one party that the other should be permitted to see the entire statement.

This understanding regarding disclosure of writings and recorded statements builds upon the Jencks Act, 18 U.S.C. § 3500 and on AS 12.45.060. But this Rule applies in both civil and criminal actions, and it applies to defendants as well as to plaintiffs.

Nothing in this Rule changes the pre-trial discovery rules currently in use. *See, e.g.,* Rule 16, Alaska R. Crim. P., Rule 26(b), Alaska R. Civ. P. These procedural rules define what may be discovered before trial. Whatever a party has discovered before trial may be offered under the last sentence of Rule 106 so that the trial judge can decide whether in fairness it should be considered along with a statement or part thereof put forth by another party.

Rule 106 does expand discovery at trial, as opposed to pretrial discovery. Generally, in civil cases witness statements will not be discoverable before trial. They usually will qualify as trial preparation materials. Under Rule 16, Alaska R. Crim. P., as recently amended, criminal defendants usually will see witness' statements before trial. But there are exceptional cases, *see, e.g.,* Rule 16(d) (4), Alaska R. Crim. P., which is governed by AS 12.45.060. Rule 106 advances the point at which such statements are discoverable to the point at which discovery will do the most good — *i.e.,* the point at which part of a statement is introduced in evidence. In civil cases, no Jencks Act applies, and there is no general obligation to turn over a witness' previous statement to an opposing party after a witness testifies. Rule 106 takes the position that once a civil litigant offers into evidence a portion of a witness' statement, fairness requires that the litigant turn over the entire relevant portion of the statement to an opposing party. This Rule is consistent with the United States Supreme Court decision in *United States v. Nobles,* 422 U.S. 225, 45 L.Ed.2d 141 (1975).

Rule 106 does not create any affirmative duty to proffer the whole of any statement when one desires to introduce only a part, but the Rule allows an adverse party to inspect the whole immediately upon request in order to ascertain that no misleading impression will result from incomplete admission. Adequate protection against disclosure of irrelevant information is afforded the offering party and third persons by the fact that the judge might delete irrelevant material, if requested to do so. Article IV should be consulted on relevance issues.

At first blush any privilege that might be claimed with

respect to a statement would seem to be waived by offering a portion of it into evidence. But a statement may address several unrelated issues, and any waiver may be partial. The court cannot demand the complete statement without permitting the offering party to claim a privilege as to unrelated matters. Some minimal inquiry into the nature of the privileged matter may be required. But in view of the common law experience with waiver, the judicial task should not be unfamiliar. *See United States v. Weisman,* 111 F.2d 260, 261-62 (2d Cir. 1940) (L. Hand, J.). Article V will govern privilege questions. Once privileged matter is deleted, the judge will make the relevant determination regarding non-privileged matters. *Cf.,* AS 12.45.070.

Upon request, the court should provide protection against undue annoyance, embarrassment, or oppression, a philosophy reflected in Fed. R. Civ. P. 26(c) and Rule 26(c), Alaska R. Civ. P. Among other things, the court may wish to restrict the extrajudicial flow of information and to hear argument in chambers on the offer of certain information which may be highly prejudicial and which ultimately may be excluded under Rule 403.

For practical reasons, Rule 106 is limited to the introduction of a writing or recorded statement; testimony by a witness is not affected by the rule. Any attempt to include testimony within the coverage of this rule would open the door to immediate cross-examination of a witness who refers during testimony to any out-of-court statement by anyone. Rule 106 takes the position that there is no more reason to allow immediate cross-examination of this testimony than any other testimony by the witness which presumably could be made more complete by cross-examination. Testimony is not likely to have the impact of a written or recorded statement which, when offered, may appear to be extremely trustworthy.

Note: The Alaska Supreme Court's Committee on Rules of Evidence voted to adopt, in lieu of the Reporter's Comment to this rule, the commentary contained in the Advisory Committee's note to Federal Rule 106, with the following addition: "The rule of completeness as set forth in Rule 106 does not deal with issues of relevancy and privilege, nor is it intended to alter or affect the normal rules pertaining to relevancy and privilege contained elsewhere in the Alaska Rules of Evidence. Accordingly, the problem of deletion of privileged or irrelevant material from a writing whose admission is sought under the provisions of Rule 106 should appropriately be dealt with by pertinent provisions of the Rules of Evidence dealing with relevancy and privilege."

ARTICLE II. JUDICIAL NOTICE

Rule 201. Judicial Notice of Fact.

(a) **Scope of Rule.** Rule 201 restricts only the power of the court to declare on the record, without resort to formal proof, that a particular fact exists, i.e., that something is actually true, where the fact involved is one that would otherwise be decided by the trier of fact upon submission of proof by the parties. No other practice falls within the scope of this Rule.

The term "judicial notice" has been indiscriminately applied to several different aspects of the decisional process. Many of these aspects will not be affected by this Rule.

One aspect not covered by Rule 201 involves assumptions made by the court in its determination of policy; *e.g.,* that a particular change in the law would probably do more harm than good. This is not the sort of fact question that, in a jury trial, would normally be put to the jury, and so is not subsumed by Rule 201's definition of "judicial notice of fact." Rather than findings of fact, these are policy determinations made by the court acting in its lawmaking capacity. The court as lawmaker is held to the same standard as the legislature is for the veracity of its inferences: it must be rational. The court taking judicial notice of a fact as that term is used in Rule 201 is held to a different and more demanding standard—the same standard required for it to direct a verdict; it must be right, meaning that rational minds would not dispute the fact that the court notices.

Stated more specifically, Rule 201 does not bar:

(1) Common law rule-making on the basis of factual assumptions based on the court's familiarity with non-evidence sources. *See e.g., Kaatz v. State,* 540 P.2d 1037 (Alaska 1975).

(2) Rule-making pursuant to a constitutional grant of authority on the basis of disputable factual assumptions. See, *e.g.,* Rules of Evidence 407 and 408.

(3) Constitutional interpretation based upon disputable factual assumptions—for example the balancing of interests in the vague area of due process.

(4) Judicial creation of remedies assumed to be necessary to carry out the legislative intent of a statute.

Rule 201 follows the existing Alaska practice regarding scope of judicial notice rather than adopting the federal practice of separating facts into "adjudicative" and "legislative" categories. This dichotomy is rejected as an unnecessary and artificial description of the difference between taking judicial notice of a fact and making assumptions in the determination of policy. The terms used in the Federal Rule are ambiguous and overlap. See *Goodman v. Stalfort, Inc.,* 411 F. Supp. 889 (D. N.J. 1976), for an example of a court's struggle to come to grips with the categories.

Alaska Rule 201 requires a determination of whether a question is one normally decided by the trier of fact or is the sort properly left to the maker of law. While this determination is not always easy to make, it is one that courts have coped with for many years. Simply stated, the guiding principle should be: if the fact involved tends to show that general conduct X is or is not, or should or should not, be against the law (or unconstitutional), it is for the court to consider freely; if the fact involved tends to prove an instance of X, it is a question for the trier of fact and covered by Rule 201.

(b) **General Rule.** Courts have traditionally been cautious in taking judicial notice of facts normally decided by the trier of fact after being proved. As Professor Davis says;

> The reason we use trial-type procedure, I think, is that we make the practical judgment, on the basis of experience, that taking evidence, subject to cross-examination and rebuttal, is the best way to resolve controversies involving disputes of adjudicative facts, that is, facts pertaining to the parties. The reason we require a determination on the record is that we think fair procedure in resolving disputes of adjudicative facts calls for giving each party a chance to

meet in the appropriate fashion the facts that come to the tribunal's attention, and the appropriate fashion for meeting disputed adjudicative facts includes rebuttal evidence, cross-examination, usually confrontation, and argument (either oral or written or both). The key to a fair trial is opportunity to use the appropriate weapons (rebuttal evidence, cross-examination, and argument) to meet adverse materials that come to the tribunal's attention.

A System of Judicial Notice Based on Fairness and Convenience, in Perspectives of Law 69, at 93 (1964). Rule 201 is based on the belief that wherever a lawmaking authority conditions the applicability of a law on the proof of facts, these considerations call for dispensing with traditional methods of proof only in clear cases regardless of what label is attached to the facts. Compare Professor Davis' conclusion that judicial notice should be a matter of convenience, subject to the requirements of procedural fairness. *Id.* at 94.

For the most part this Rule is consistent with both Federal Rule 201 and the now superseded Alaska Rule of Civil Procedure 43(a), which was based on Uniform Rule 9. Rule 201 limits judicial notice to facts not subject to reasonable dispute in that they are either generally known in the territorial jurisdiction of the trial court or are capable of accurate and ready determination by resort to sources whose accuracy cannot reasonably be doubted.

These general categories (matters of common knowledge, readily verifiable facts) have traditionally been treated as the clearest cases for judicial notice. *See* McCormick §§ 328-330. Like the Federal Rule, this Rule omits any mention of propositions of generalized knowledge, which were included in Uniform Rule 9(1) and (2). It is doubtful that many such propositions will fall within the scope of Rule 201 as limited by subdivision (a). Any that do must satisfy the condition of subdivision (b) in order to be judicially noticed. For instance, it is not proper for a court to base its decision on the unsupported belief that "no one could be so naive as to believe that a small advisory service with only 5,000 subscribers could by its own recommending influence cause such stocks as Union Pacific (22,000,000 shares outstanding),...invariably and automatically to rise so that defendants could always sell their small holdings at a small profit." *Securities and Exchange Commission v. Capital Gains Research Bureau,* 300 F.2d 745, at 748 (2d Cir. 1961), *reversed and remanded* on other grounds 375 U. S. 180, 11 L.Ed.2d 237 (1963).

Lack of information should not be confused with indisputability. If the information before the court, whether or not furnished by the parties, is insufficient to satisfy subdivision (b) or fails to clearly convince the court that a matter should be judicially noticed, the court should decline to take judicial notice and require proof in the usual manner, although the court considers the fact more probable than not. An adequate development of the facts at trial in a jury case protects a party's right to have questions of fact resolved by the jury, and, in a non-jury case, assures the parties the power to cross-examine and submit contrary evidence.

(c) and (d) **When Discretionary—When Mandatory.** Under subdivision (c) the judge has a discretionary authority to take judicial notice, as long as subdivision (b), *supra,* is satisfied, regardless of whether he is so requested by a party. The taking of judicial notice is mandatory under subdivision (d) only when a party requests it, the necessary information is supplied, and each adverse party has been given adequate notice, to be determined by the court. If these conditions are not met the court need not take judicial notice, although it is still free to do so as a matter of discretion. The question of whether or not to take judicial notice of fact that satisfies the conditions of subdivision (b) is thus left primarily to the court's discretion. This is a simple, workable system, and it reflects the existing Alaska practice (see Alaska Civil Rule 43(a) (1), (2), and (3)).

Federal Rule 201 (c) and (d) are very similar to this Rule. Compare Uniform Rule 9, making judicial notice of facts universally known mandatory without request, and making judicial notice of facts generally known in the jurisdiction or capable of determination by resort to accurate sources discretionary in the absence of request, but mandatory if request is made and the information furnished. But see Uniform Rule 10(3), which directs the judge to decline to take judicial notice if available information fails to convince him that the matter falls clearly within Uniform Rule 9 or is insufficient to enable him to notice it judicially. Substantially the same approach is found in California Evidence Code §§ 451-453 and in New Jersey Evidence Rule 9. In contrast, the present Rule treats alike all facts which are subject to judicial notice.

Rule 202. Judicial Notice of Law.

(a) **Scope of Rule.** The Federal Rules of Evidence contain no provision analogous to this Rule. Expressing the view that the manner in which law is "fed into the judicial process" is not the proper concern of rules of evidence, the Advisory Committee recognizes Rule 44.1 of the Federal Rules of Civil Procedure and Rule 26.1 of the Federal Rules of Criminal Procedure as governing the method of invoking the law of foreign countries. However, in adopting Rules of Evidence based on the Federal Rules, Nevada provides for judicial notice of matters of law. *See* Nevada Rule of Evidence 47.140. Because Alaska R. Civ. P. 43 (a), superseded by this Rule, combined judicial notice of law and fact, and because the failure of a court to take judicial notice of law may result in proof being offered by the parties, Rule 202 follows Nevada's lead in including a provision for judicial notice of law among evidence rules. This Rule governs judicial notice of domestic laws and regulations, and both foreign and international law.

(b) **Without Request—Mandatory.** Under this subdivision, judicial notice of the laws of sister states is not mandatory upon the court. For some time judicial notice has only been taken of a state's own laws and the laws of the federal government. It has been necessary to both plead and prove the law of other jurisdictions. In 1936 the National Conference of Commissioners on Uniform State Laws drafted the Uniform Judicial Notice of Foreign Law Act which was adopted in substance by over half the jurisdictions (withdrawn in 1966). In effect, this Act provided that every court within the adopting jurisdiction must take judicial notice of the common law and statutes of every other state. This was also the approach of Uniform Rule 9 (1953). Alaska R. Civ. P. 43(a), superseded by this Rule accepted the reform. This subdivision does not make notice mandatory because the Committee on Rules believed that the realities of law practice in Alaska, especially the availability of books, was such that parties should be encouraged to provide the court and opposing counsel with copies of sister states' laws. It is important to recognize that a court will take notice of sister state law if a proper request and presentation are made, or if the court decides to exercise its option to take notice under subdivision (c), *infra.*

(c) **Without Request—Optional.** This subdivision defines the discretionary power of the court to take judicial notice on its own initiative.

Section (1) recognizes that federal rules, and state and territorial laws may often be difficult to find in Alaska libraries. However, where the court is in possession of relevant material, notice may be taken.

Section (2) is very similar to Uniform Rule 9(2) (a), which was based on the Model Code of Evidence, Rule 802(a) (1942). Where private acts and resolutions are easily ascertained the court can conveniently take judicial notice of them and often will. Where agency regulations operate with the power of law there is every reason to take judicial notice of them. See AS 44.62.110, providing for judicial notice of regulations printed in the Alaska Administrative Code or Alaska Administrative Register. *See also* 44 U.S.C.A. § 1507, providing for judicial notice of the contents of the Federal Register; and *Alaska Airlines, Inc. v. Northwest Airlines, Inc.*, 228 F. Supp. 322 (D. Alaska 1964), *cert. denied,* 383 U.S. 936, 15 L.Ed. 2d 853 (1965). Due to the difficulty of ascertaining all such acts, resolutions, regulations and ordinances as may be applicable to a case, the court need only take judicial notice on its own initiative where it is convenient to do so. *See Australaska Corp. v. Sisters of Charity,* 397 P.2d 966 (Alaska 1965).

Section (3) expands the scope of judicial notice. It recognizes that today there is no reason to conclusively presume that the law of sister states is beyond the reach of Alaska. Sometimes acts, regulations, and local ordinances of other states will be unavailable. If so the court will not have to take notice of them, because this section is permissive and Subdivision (d) places a burden of producing sufficient information on a party before notice must be taken. If Subdivision (d) is satisfied, there is no good reason not to take notice. A similar view is taken with respect to emergency and unpublished regulations of Alaska agencies.

Section (4) provides for discretionary notice of foreign law and international law. Long after the law of foreign states became a matter of judicial notice in many jurisdictions, the law of foreign countries remained a matter of fact to be pleaded and proved. The Uniform Judicial Notice of Foreign Law Act, although only applicable to the law of sister states, did state that determining the law of foreign countries ought to be an issue for the court, not the jury. *See* 9A Uniform Laws Ann. 550, 569 (1965). Foreign law still had to be pleaded and proved even after some states took the determination of foreign law from the jury. Where it was not pleaded or properly proved, dismissal was usually avoided by presuming the foreign law to be the same as the law of the forum. *See* Stern, Foreign Law in the Courts: Judicial Notice and Proof, 45 Cal. L. Rev. 23 (1957).

Federal R. Civ. P. 44.1 and its identical counterpart, Crim. R. P. 26.1 require that to raise an issue of foreign law, either notice must be given in the pleadings or other reasonable notice must be given. In determining foreign law, the court "may consider any relevant material or source, including testimony." The notice requirement functions to alert the parties that foreign law is an issue in the case.

Evidence Rule 202 treats foreign law as the proper subject of judicial notice. This is the view taken by Uniform Rule 9(2) (b) and by Alaska R. Civ. P. 43(a) (2) [b], superseded by this Rule. The court may look to any pertinent source of information including the testimony of expert witnesses to ascertain foreign law.

Section (2) also provides for judicial notice of international law. It was early stated that

> [i]nternational law is part of our law, and must be ascertained and administered by the courts of justice of appropriate jurisdictions as often as questions of right depending upon it are duly presented for their determination.

The Paquete Habana, 175 U.S. 677, 700, 44 L.Ed. 320, 328 (1899).

In ascertaining international law the court may consult and use any source of pertinent information. Just as in English canon law experts played a large part in determining foreign law, it is anticipated that expert testimony may play a role in showing what foreign and international law is in a given situation. *See Texas v. Louisiana,* 410 U.S. 702, 35 L.Ed. 2d 646 (1973); Panel, "Proving International Law in a National Forum," 70 Am. Soc'y Int'l L. (1976). Maritime law is treated similarly.

Section (5) provides that if a matter of law could be noticed under this Rule, but the law has been repealed or replaced, it still may be proved by judicial notice, if it remains relevant to the case.

(d) **With Request—Mandatory.** At the request of a party the court shall take notice of any matter included in subdivision (c). If the party's request is accompanied by sufficient information and adequate notice to adverse parties, it is mandatory that the court take judicial notice. The difficulty of finding all applicable law and obtaining proper information under subdivision (c) disappears when the requirements of this subdivision are satisfied. The notice requirement to adverse parties provides the opportunity for a chance to be heard on the propriety of taking judicial notice of the matter.

Rule 203. Procedure for Taking Judicial Notice.

This Rule applies to all aspects of judicial notice and must, therefore, be read in conjunction with both Rule 201 and Rule 202.

(a) **Determining Propriety of Judicial Notice.** Basic considerations of procedural fairness demand an opportunity to be heard on the propriety of taking judicial notice and the tenor of the matter noticed. The rule requires the granting of that opportunity upon request. No formal scheme of giving notice is provided. An adversely affected party may learn in advance that judicial notice is in contemplation, either by virtue of being served with a copy of a request by another party under subdivision (d) of Rule 201 that judicial notice be taken, or through an advance indication by the judge. Or he may have no advance notice at all. Although the rule does not require formal notice by the court to the parties, before judicial notice is taken (except in unusual circumstances) the court should announce its intentions to the parties and indicate for the record the particular facts to be taken as true. *See Concerned Citizens v. Kenai Peninsula Borough,* 527 P.2d 417 (Alaska 1974). In the absence of advance notice, a request made after the fact could not in fairness be considered untimely. See the provision for hearing on timely request in the federal Administrative Procedure Act, 5 U.S.C. § 556(e). *See also* Revised Model State Administrative Procedure Act (1961), 9C U.L.A. § 10(4) (Supp. 1967).

In considering taking judicial notice, the court is not restricted to sources of information proffered by the parties, but may consult any source, including treatises, experts, scientific journals, etc. No exclusionary rule except a valid claim of privilege shall apply. However, the court as a matter of discretion, should disclose, on request, the main sources on which a decision to take judicial notice is or was based, in order to make the parties' opportunity to be heard meaningful.

(b) **Time of Taking Notice.** In accord with the usual view, judicial notice may be taken at any stage of the proceedings, whether in the trial court or on appeal. Federal Rule 201(f); Uniform Rule 12; McCormick § 333.

(c) **Instructing the Jury.** In civil cases, the rule contemplates there is to be no evidence before the jury in disproof of a judicially noticed fact. The court instructs the jury to take judicially noticed facts as established. This position is justified by the undesirable effects of the opposite rule in limiting the rebutting party, though not his opponent, to admissible evidence, in defeating the reasons for judicial notice, and in affecting the substantive law to an extent and in ways largely unforeseeable. Ample protection and flexibility are afforded by the broad provision for opportunity to be heard on request, set forth in subdivision (a).

Authority upon the propriety of taking judicial notice against an accused in a criminal case with respect to matters other than venue is relatively meager. While it may be argued that the right of jury trial does not extend to matters which are beyond reasonable dispute, the rule opts for the greater protection of the accused's right to a jury trial afforded by the limited instruction that the jury may, but is not required to, accept as conclusive any fact judicially noticed. The Federal Rule is in accord. Much of the concern about a possible need to take notice of some facts in criminal cases can be eliminated by careful attention to the elements of an offense. Venue and jurisdiction are not usually elements of a crime. Of course, they must be proper (assuming an appeal will be taken). But the same judge who decides in a civil case whether a court has jurisdiction and what proper venue is can do so in a criminal case. Of course, venue and jurisdiction questions may involve factfinding, but many questions left for the court involve factfinding. *See, e.g.,* Rule 104 (a), *supra.* Consider also change of venue motions and attacks on jury verdicts. Factfinding unrelated to the elements of the crime can be done by the judge. With this in mind, Rule 203 is drafted to avoid the knotty constitutional questions that would arise were an attempt made to permit judicial notice of some facts relevant to the merits of an action but not others. To draw such a line might be to resurrect the "ultimate issue" test abandoned in Rule 704, *infra.*

Rule 203(c) is drafted so that it conclusively states that determining questions of law shall be a matter for the court. When the determination of the law of foreign states and foreign countries was treated as a question of fact, it became a matter for the jury in appropriate cases. Statutes and acts such as the Uniform Judicial Notice of Foreign Law Act and Federal Rule of Civil Procedure 44.1 have attempted to remove this anomaly in traditional court and jury functions. This subdivision expresses the view that determining the law is a function of the court. See Uniform Rule 10(4) for an identical provision. If judicial notice of law is not taken, evidence will be required, but the decision on what the law is remains that of the court.

Nothing in the rule is intended to suggest that it authorizes a lawyer to argue jury nullification to the jury in a criminal case. The jury simply is to be told that a noticed fact is treated as if evidence of it were authorized, and the trier of fact is to treat it as if evidence were submitted. A defense lawyer can argue that any fact should be disbelieved by the jury and this is as true of a judicially noticed fact as of any other fact.

ARTICLE III. PRESUMPTIONS

Rule 301. Presumptions in General in Civil Actions and Proceedings.

(a) **Effect.** This Rule governs rebuttable presumptions generally in civil cases. See Rule 302 for presumptions controlled by federal law and Rule 303 for those operating in a criminal case.

The word "presumption" has many different meanings in the law. See Laughlin, In Support of the Thayer Theory of Presumptions, 52 Mich. L. Rev. 195, 196-209 (1953). As used herein, a "presumption" is a recognition in law of the relationship between two facts or groups of facts. If one fact or group of facts is shown to exist, the law presumes the existence of the other but permits rebuttal.

The burden placed upon the party seeking the advantage of a presumption is to prove the initial fact, often called the "basic" or "proved" fact. If this fact is not disputed, then the presumption will operate. If the fact is disputed, the presumption will only operate if the trier of fact finds that the basic fact exists.

Assuming the existence of the basic fact, Rule 301 provides that the presumed fact shall also be found to exist unless the party against whom the presumption operates meets the presumption with evidence sufficient to permit a reasonable trier of fact to find that the presumed fact does not exist. A failure to meet the presumption with sufficient evidence results in a peremptory instruction or a directed verdict. If the burden of producing evidence is satisfied, the presumption disappears and no mention of it may be made to the jury, which is likely to be confused by the term. The court must, however, instruct the jury that it may infer the existence of the presumed fact from the basic fact.

There has been substantial disagreement in the past among common law courts and legal commentators regarding the proper weight to be given a presumption. Some authorities hold that a presumption places the burden of proof on the party opposing the fact presumed to establish its non-existence once the party invoking the presumption establishes the basic facts giving rise to it. This position is associated with McCormick and Morgan, although the latter's view is arrived at with some reluctance. *See* Morgan, Further Observations on Presumptions, 16 So. Cal. L. Rev. 245, 254 (1943). Other authorities, following Thayer's "bursting bubble" theory, approved by Wigmore, hold that the presumption vanishes upon the introduction of evidence that would support a finding of the non-existence of the presumed facts. There are numerous intermediate positions that have attracted attention. *See* Morgan, *supra,* at 247-49. It is possible to treat different presumptions differently. See Calif. Evid. Code § 600 *et seq.* But Morgan, *supra,* at 254, persuasively argued the case for a single standard.

> Unfortunately, however, there are myriads of presumptions created by courts and legislatures. They can not be authoritatively classified by courts except as each one is involved in a litigated action. Wherever there is room for difference of opinion, no presumption can finally be assigned its proper place except by the appropriate court of last resort. To evolve a classification by judicial decision would require decades, if not centuries. To make a legislative classification of existing presumptions would involve immense labor and would still leave room for debate as to all subsequently created presumptions. Unless a trial judge were presented with a catalogue of classified presumptions, it would be fatuous to expect him to determine the reasons and objectives of a presumption suddenly thrust at him in the hurry of a trial, with a demand to classify it and accord it the appropriate effect.

The approach of this Rule approximates more closely the views of Thayer and Wigmore than those of McCormick and Morgan.

The shifting-the-burden of persuasion approach, approved by the Advisory Committee on the Federal Rules and the United States Supreme Court before being rejected by the Congress, is rejected for several reasons.

First, Alaska has a myriad of statutes creating presumptions within the meaning of this Rule. Some use the word presumption or a related term. *See, e.g.,* AS 13.06.035(3) (Evidence as to death or status); AS 45.05.376 (Evidence of dishonor and notice of dishonor). More use the term "prima facie evidence," AS 02.35.070 (Receipts for certified certificates); AS 08.24.300 (Court action by agency); AS 10.05.726 (Failure to pay tax as evidence of insolvency); AS 10.05.795 (Certificates and certified copies to be received in evidence); AS 13.06.035 (1) & (2) (Evidence as to death or status); AS 18.50.320(2) (Copies of data from vital records); AS 21.84.100 (Certificate of compliance); AS 21.84.030 (Annual license); AS 27.10.170 (Effect of recording and of failure to record affidavit of labor or improvements); AS 27.10.190 (b) (Recording the notice to contribute and affidavits); AS 28.10.261 (Evidence); AS 32.05.180 (b) (Continuation of partnership beyond fixed term); AS 45.05.022 (Prima facie evidence by third party documents); AS 45.50.290 (Certificate of registration as evidence). While it is difficult to ascertain the legislative intent in creating these presumptions, and while the intent may vary from presumption to presumption, it is highly unlikely that the legislature intended many of these presumptions to have the potential impact associated with a shift in the burden of persuasion.

Second, shifting the burden of persuasion on some issues may tend to confuse the jury, especially in cases involving affirmative defenses where the normal instructions on burdens of proof already may be confusing.

Third, in situations in which the presumption operates against a party already bearing the burden of persuasion on an issue, the presumption may have no effect once it is rebutted. No good reason appears why a presumption that is powerful enough to shift the burden of persuasion should disappear entirely when shifting is impossible.

Fourth, the Federal Rule does not shift the burden of persuasion. When federal and state issues are tried together, rarely will it be necessary under this Rule or Rule 302 to face the problem of conflicting presumptions.

(b) **Prima Facie Evidence.** This subdivision makes it clear that when the legislature uses the term "prima facie" in reference to proving a fact, generally it intends to create a presumption. See Degnan, Syllabus on California Evidence Code 18-25 (11th Ann. Summer Program, U. Cal.-Berkeley) in D. Louisell, J. Kaplan, & J. Waltz, Cases and Materials on Evidence 980-83 (3d ed. 1976). "The term 'prima facie case' is often used in two senses and is therefore an ambiguous and often misleading term. It may mean evidence that is simply sufficient to get to the jury, or it may mean evidence that is sufficient to shift the burden of producing evidence." McCormick (2d ed.) § 342, at 803 n.26. A presumption may be utilized in both senses in the same case. The statutes set forth, *supra,* do more than permit a party to get to a jury on the basis of prima facie evidence; they evince a legislative determination that the presumption should be accepted until rebutted. This rule so provides.

(c) **Inconsistent Presumptions.** When conflicting presumptions are present in a single case, the court attempts to determine which is founded in the weightier considerations of policy and logic. McCormick (2d ed.) § 345, at 823-24, discusses the "special situation of the questionable validity of a second marriage [which] has been the principal area in which the problem of conflicting presumptions has been discussed by the courts." Most courts have taken the approach of this subdivision in such a situation. "This doctrine that the weightier presumption prevails should probably be available in any situation which may reasonably be theorized as one of conflicting presumptions, and where one of the presumptions is grounded in a predominant social policy." McCormick (2d ed.) § 345, at 824. The final sentence of the Rule provides that if there is no such preponderance, both presumptions shall be disregarded. This follows Uniform Rule 15 (1953). It would be confusing if the judge were to instruct the jury that it might find fact A, but that it is not bound to, and that it might find not-A but that is not bound to. No instruction is preferable. Instead, the jury will learn of two basic facts suggesting opposite inferences, and it must determine the one that is most probable in light of all the evidence.

Nothing in this rule affects the application of conclusive presumptions, *see, e.g.,* AS 10.10.030 (6) (d) (Articles of incorporation), which the United States Supreme Court recently referred to as rules of law. *Usery v. Turner Elkhorn Min. Co.,* 428 U.S. 1, 49 L.Ed.2d 752 (1976). Nor does this Rule address the validity of conclusive presumptions. Compare *Weinberger v. Salfi,* 422 U.S. 749, 45 L.Ed.2d 522 (1975), with *Vlandis v. Kline,* 412 U.S. 441, 37 L.Ed.2d 63 (1973), *United States Dep't of Agriculture v. Murray,* 413 U.S. 508, 37 L.Ed.2d 767 (1974), and *Cleveland Bd. of Educ. v. LaFleur,* 414 U.S. 632, 39 L.Ed. 2d 52 (1974). Nothing in this Rule inhibits the creation or utilization of presumptions to protect constitutional rights. *See, e.g., Keyes v. School Dist. No. 1,* 413 U.S. 189, 37 L.Ed.2d 548 (1973), discussed in K. Redden & S. Saltzburg, *Federal Rules of Evidence Manual* 82-83 (2d ed. 1977).

The first sentence of the rule makes clear that the legislature and the courts retain power to create presumptions having an effect different from that provided for in this Rule.

Rule 302. Applicability of Federal Law in Civil Actions and Proceedings.

Whenever a state court looks to federal law to find the rule of decision with respect to a claim or defense, federal law will govern with respect to the effect of a presumption. *Cf., Dice v. Akron, C. & Y. R.Co.,* 342 U.S. 359, 96 L.Ed. 398 (1952). *See also* the Reporter's Comment accompany Rule 501. As Alaska Rule 301 prescribing the effect of presumptions is identical to the federal evidence rule, courts will seldom have to determine which law should be followed. The only potential conflict is in the case of a claim or defense for which the United States Congress has provided by statute for the shifting of the burden of persuasion or where the federal judiciary has interpreted the Constitution or a federal statute to require shifting the burden of persuasion and the Alaska rule is *contra,* or vice versa. Rule 302 will apply to such situations. Federal criminal cases will be litigated in federal courts, so no state rule is needed to deal with presumptions in such cases. *But see Testa v. Katt,* 330 U.S. 386, 91 L.Ed. 967 (1947).

Rule 303. Presumptions in General in Criminal Cases.

(a) **Effect.** This rule governs rebuttable presumptions generally in criminal cases. Rule 301 governs in civil cases and Rule 302 governs presumptions controlled by federal law, although it is unlikely to have any impact in criminal cases.

The word "presumption" is used in this Rule in the same manner as in Rule 301. The Reporter's Comment accompanying Rule 301 explains this use in detail. As was the case with presumptions operating in civil cases, the legislature sometimes creates "presumptions" without using the word "presumption." For example, the legislature may employ the term "prima facie evidence," which is covered by subdivision (b). *See, e.g.,* AS 11.20.220 (Evidence of knowledge of insufficient funds); AS 11.20.250 (Evidence of intent to defraud), quoted in *Selman v. State,* 411 P.2d 217 (Alaska 1966).

The Advisory Committee on the Federal Rules expressed its opinion that "[i]t is axiomatic that a verdict cannot be directed against the accused in a criminal case . . . . with the corollary that the judge is without authority to direct the jury to find against the accused as to any element of the crime... Although arguably the judge could direct the jury to find against the accused as to a lesser fact, the tradition is against it..." Without making any constitutional decisions, Rule 203(c) accepted this opinion as expressing sound policy and denied judges the power to bind juries to facts believed by the judges to be beyond reasonable dispute. The instant rule is in accord. A presumption cannot be used against a defendant as a device to preempt the jury's function of finding facts and assessing guilt and innocence.

When a presumption is directed against the government, different policies govern, and a presumption may result in a directed verdict or peremptory instruction in favor of a defendant. Presumptions working against the government are treated like civil presumptions under Rule 301 and will not be discussed in this Comment.

If a presumption cannot be binding on a defendant, what is its utility? Judge Weinstein identifies a two-fold function:

> Presumptions are utilized to overcome two separate problems in federal law. Primarily this function is to lessen the prosecution's burden of establishing guilt by authorizing short-cuts in proof and exerting pressure on the person with the most knowledge to come forward with an explanation. . . .
>
> In addition, a presumption may serve the secondary function of making undesirable activities amenable to federal jurisdiction.

1 Weinstein's Evidence, Paragraph 303 [01] (1975). The second function is of no concern to the states in their lawmaking activities. But a third function may be important. "In a borderline case a judge may be influenced by the legislative judgment of Congress [or a state legislature] to submit a basic fact to a jury which he would not have submitted as merely circumstantial evidence of the presumed fact." *Id.* Thus, the first and third functions are the important ones for the states. There also may be a fourth function — to make clear the intent of the legislature in special circumstances.

Subdivision (a) allows presumptions to perform their intended functions, but prevents them from exerting too great an impact on the outcome of a case. If a presumption is created by the legislature or the courts, it serves as an incentive for the accused to submit rebuttal evidence. If no rebuttal evidence or insufficient evidence is offered, the court, without using the word "presumption," will instruct the jury that it may, but is not bound to, infer the existence of the presumed fact from proof of the basic fact. Such an instruction is couched purely in terms of a permissible inference; no attempt is made to guide the jury in assessing the sufficiency of the inference to prove guilt. This mandatory instruction is in the nature of a mild comment on the evidence. No good reason appears why the legislature or the courts cannot require a specific non-binding instruction when they deem it desirable.

If the accused offers evidence to rebut or meet the presumption, the giving of an instruction is discretionary. In instances where the nature of a presumption directed against the accused is such that the relationship between the proved fact and the presumed fact is self-evident or apparent, no instruction should normally be given by the court if the accused offers evidence to rebut or meet the presumption, since in such instances, a jury instruction would tend to emphasize unduly and unnecessarily the existence of the presumption. On the other hand, in circumstances where there is no obvious connection between the proved fact and the presumed fact, an instruction to the jury regarding the existence of the presumption would ordinarily be appropriate.

A good example of this latter situation would be the standard case involving the presumption created by a Breathalyzer examination. The proved fact in such a case would be a Breathalyzer reading of .10 percent blood alcohol or greater; the fact to be presumed from the proved fact is that the accused was under the influence of intoxicating liquor at the time of the test. Under normal circumstances, with no expert testimony concerning the significance of .10 percent blood alcohol level in terms of its effect on an individual's sobriety, the mere awareness of the proved fact—i.e., the .10 percent blood alcohol level—would be meaningless to the average juror. Assuming the accused in such a situation was willing to concede the blood alcohol level, but opted to rebut the presumption by arguing that, despite the blood alcohol level, he was not in fact impaired, the mere establishment of blood alcohol level by the prosecution would be rendered wholly ineffective in the absence of a specific instruction to the jury concerning the presumption which arises from proof of a blood alcohol level of .10 percent or greater. It should be noted that the burden of coming forward is less onerous here than in Rule 301. This reflects a judgment that the defendant should have the benefit of reasonable doubts.

One advantage of the approach taken in this Rule is that it probably avoids the problem of applying to most presumptions the confusing test of constitutionality compelled by the following decisions of the United States Supreme Court: *Tot v. United States,* 319 U.S. 463, 87 L.Ed. 1519 (1943), *United States v. Gainey,* 380 U.S. 63, 13 L.Ed.2d 658 (1965), *United States v. Romano,* 382 U.S. 136, 15 L.Ed.2d 210 (1965), *Leary v. United States,* 395 U.S. 6, 23 L.Ed.2d 57 (1969), *Turner v. United States,* 396 U.S. 398, 24 L.Ed.2d 610 (1970), and *Barnes v. United States,* 412 U.S. 837, 37 L.Ed.2d 380 (1973).

As long as a court confines itself to a description of a permissible inference, avoiding a statement like the trial judge's in *Barnes*—"[i]f you should find beyond a reasonable doubt...that the mail...was stolen,...you would *ordinarily be justified* in drawing the inference...unless such possession is explained..." (emphasis added)— and avoiding the legislative language in *Leary* employed by the court in its instruction—"[w]henever...the defendant is shown to have or to have had the marihuana in his possession, such possession shall be deemed *sufficient evidence to authorize conviction* unless the defendant explains..." (emphasis added)—the relatively mild comment in the form of an instruction commanded by this Rule is likely to be sustained in light of the traditional power of federal courts to comment on the weight of the evidence in criminal cases and the nature of the instruction.

Another advantage of the rule is that it avoids the complications of the proposed Federal Rules. They caused the eminent jurist, Henry Friendly, to complain to the Congress that he did not understand them. *See* Hearings on Proposed Rules of Evidence Before the Subcomm. on Crim. Justice of the House Comm. on the Judiciary, 93rd Cong., 1st Sess., at 249 (1973). This is not surprising, since many lawyers would have the same difficulty.

A final advantage is that by creating presumptions that are covered by this rule, the legislature makes the same "statement" to courts about desired treatment of borderline cases as it makes with more powerful presumptions.

The legislature and the courts remain free under Rule 303 to create presumptions with a different effect than that provided here. For example. AS 41.15.110(c) (Allowing fire to escape or failure to make effort to extinguish; misdemeanor) provides that "[i]n a criminal action brought under this section, the escape of the fire is presumptive evidence of negligence by the person responsible for starting the fire and unless rebutted is sufficient to sustain a conviction." While this statute avoids any implicit reference to silence on the part of the defendant and thus is less worrisome than some instructions approved by other courts, *see, e.g., United States v. Gainey, supra,* application of the statute may be challenged more readily under the line of United States Supreme Court cases previously cited than under this rule.

(b) **Prima Facie Evidence.** See the Reporter's Comment accompanying Rule 301 (b).

(c) **Inconsistent Presumptions.** The reason for this subdivision is set forth in the Reporter's Comment accompanying Rule 301 (c). There is one important difference, however, between the instant rule and Rule 301 (c): Under the instant rule the effect of the preponderant presumption will vary, depending on whether it favors the government or the accused; no such variance occurs under Rule 301 (c).

This rule does not establish that the government must always bear the burden of persuasion on every issue litigated in a criminal case. Whether an accused sometimes may be compelled to bear the burden of persuasion is beyond the scope of these Rules of Evidence. *See generally Mullaney v. Wilbur,* 421 U.S. 684, 44 L.Ed.2d 508 (1975); *Patterson v. New York,* 432 U.S. 197, 53 L.Ed.2d 281 (1977). The language of the Rule assumes, however, that in most instances when the government seeks the benefits of a presumption it bears the burden of persuasion.

Nothing in this rule eliminates the instruction that a defendant is presumed to be innocent. This presumption is not an evidence presumption, but a special casting of the burden placed on the government to prove guilt beyond a reasonable doubt.

ARTICLE IV. ADMISSIBILITY OF RELEVANT EVIDENCE

Rule 401. Definition of Relevant Evidence.

This rule adopts Rule 401 of the Federal Rule of Evidence verbatim. The Advisory Committee's Note to Federal Rule 401 explains this rule completely and concisely. It comprises the remainder of this comment, albeit in slightly altered form.

The variety of relevancy problems is coextensive with counsel's skill in mustering substantive theories to support a case and ingenuity in using circumstantial evidence as a means of proof. An enormous number of cases fall in no set pattern, and this Rule is designed as a guide for handling them. On the other hand, some situations recur with sufficient frequency to create patterns susceptible of treatment by specific rules. Rule 404 and those following it are of that variety; they also serve as illustrations of the application of the present Rule as limited by the exclusionary principles of Rule 403.

Passing mention should be made of so-called "conditional" relevancy. Morgan, *Basic Problems of Evidence* 45-46 (1962). In this situation, probative value depends not only upon satisfying the basic requirement of relevancy but also upon the existence of some matter of fact. For example, if evidence of a spoken statement is relied upon to prove notice, probative value is lacking unless the person sought to be charged heard the statement. The problem is one of fact, and the only rules needed are for the purpose of determining the respective functions of judge and jury. See Rule 104(b). The discussion which follows in the present note is concerned with the relevancy generally, not with any particular problem of conditional relevancy.

Relevancy is not an inherent characteristic of any item of evidence but exists only as a relation between an item of evidence and a matter properly provable in the case. Does the item of evidence tend to prove the matter sought to be proved? Whether the relationship exists depends upon principles evolved by experience or science, applied logically to the situation at hand. James, Relevancy, Probability and the Law, 29 Calif. L. Rev. 689, 696 n. 15 (1941), in Selected Writings on Evidence and Trial 610, 615 n. 15 (Fryer ed. 1957). The Rule summarizes this relationship as a "tendency to make the existence" of the fact to be proved "more probable or less probable." Compare Uniform Rule 1(2) which states the crux of relevancy as "a tendency in reason," thus perhaps emphasizing unduly the logical process and ignoring the need to draw upon experience or science to validate the general principle upon which relevancy in a particular situation depends. Ultimately, legal reasoning depends upon logic, but the logical calculus includes not only a priori knowledge but facts, insights, and principles developed by scientific methods or tested by experience.

The standard of probability under the Rule is "more...probable than it would be without the evidence." Any more stringent requirement is unworkable and unrealistic. As McCormick (2d ed.) § 185, at 436, says, "A brick is not a wall," or, as Falknor, Extrinsic Policies Affecting Admissibility, 10 Rutgers L. Rev. 574, 576 (1956), quotes Professor McBaine,"...[I]t is not to be supposed that every witness can make a home run." Dealing with probability in the language of the Rule has the added virtue of avoiding confusion between questions of admissibility and questions of the sufficiency of the evidence.

The words "any tendency" in the rule suggest that the court should err, in doubtful cases, on the side of admissibility. For example, courts need not exclude all cumulative evidence. The fact that Witness 1 testifies to the existence of fact X does not compel the conclusion that testimony by Witnesses 2 and 3 to the same effect is not relevant. The probability that fact X exists may increase when it becomes apparent that several different people support it; corroboration may increase the likelihood that the fact is true. At some point further corroboration will be of little help to the trier of fact, and the court will either rule that the additional evidence is not relevant or will exclude it under Rule 403.

The Rule uses the phrase "fact that is of consequence to the determination of the action" to describe the kind of fact to which proof may properly be directed. The language is that of California Evidence Code § 210; it has the advantage of avoiding the loosely used and ambiguous word "material." Tentative Recommendation and a Study Relating to the Uniform Rules of Evidence (Art. I. General Provisions), Cal. Law Revision Comm'n, Rep., Rec. & Studies, 10-11 (1964). The fact to be proved may be ultimate, intermediate, or evidentiary; it matters not, so long as it is of consequence in the determination of the action. *Cf.* Uniform Rule 1(2) which requires that the evidence relate to a "material" fact.

The fact to which the evidence is directed need not be in dispute. While situations will arise which call for the exclusion of evidence offered to prove a point conceded by the opponent, the ruling should be made on the basis of such considerations as waste of time and undue prejudice (See Rule 403), rather than under any general requirement that evidence is admissible only if directed to matters in dispute. Evidence which is essentially background in nature can scarcely be said to involve disputed matter, yet it is universally offered and admitted as an aid to understanding. Charts, photographs, views of real estate, murder weapons, and many other items of evidence fall in this category. A rule limiting admissibility to evidence directed to a controversial point would invite the exclusion of this helpful evidence, or at least the raising of endless questions over its admission. *Cf.* California Evidence Code § 210, defining relevant evidence in terms of tendency to prove a disputed fact.

Rule 402. Relevant Evidence Admissible—Exceptions—Irrelevant Evidence Inadmissible.

This rule is nothing more than a codification of the common law. The provisions that all relevant evidence is admissible, with certain exceptions, and that evidence which is not relevant is not admissible are "a presupposition involved in the very conception of a rational system of evidence." Thayer, Preliminary Treatise on Evidence 264 (1898). They constitute the foundation upon which the structure of admission and exclusion rests. All states which have codified their evidence law have provided that all relevant evidence, with certain exceptions, is admissible. The model for the rule was Federal Rule of Evidence 402, modified to conform to the Alaska judicial system. Nebraska adopted a similarly modified version of Federal Rule 402, in Nebraska Rule of Evidence 27-402. For similar provisions see also Maine Rule of Evidence 402 and New Mexico Rule of Evidence 20-4-402. Provisions that all relevant evidence is admissible are found in Uniform Rule 7(f), Kansas Code of Civil Procedure § 60-407(b), and New Jersey Evidence Rule 7(f), but the exclusion of evidence which is not relevant is left to implication.

Not all relevant evidence is admissible. The exclusion of relevant evidence may be called for by these rules; by other rules, e.g. the Alaska Rules of Civil and Criminal Procedure; by enactment of the legislature; or by constitutional considerations.

Succeeding rules in the present article, in response to the demands of particular policies, require the exclusion of evidence despite its relevancy. In addition, Article V recognizes a number of privileges; Article VI imposes limitations upon witnesses and the manner of dealing with them; Article VII specifies requirement with respect to opinions and expert testimony; Article VIII excludes hearsay not falling within an exception; Article X spells out the handling of authentication and identification; and Article X restricts the manner of proving the contents of writings and recordings.

The Alaska Rules of Civil and Criminal Procedure in some instances require the exclusion of relevant evidence. For example, Rule 30(b) of the Rules of Civil Procedure, by imposing the requirements of notice and opportunity to consult counsel, limits the use of relevant depositions. Similarly, Rule 15 of the Alaska Rules of Criminal Procedure restricts the use of depositions in criminal cases, even though relevant.

Alaska statutes restricting admissibility of relevant evidence, for example by formulating a privilege or prohibition against disclosure, are not affected by this rule. The rule recognizes the power of the legislature to restrict admissibility. See, e.g., AS 09.25.030 (governing evidence of representations as to credit, skill, or character of third person); AS 12.45.030 (necessary evidence for false pretenses); AS 12.45.085 (notice requirement for evidence of mental defect or disease); AS 28.35.120 (barring use of accident reports).

The rule recognizes but makes no attempt to spell out the constitutional considerations which impose basic limitations upon the admissibility of relevant evidence. Some such limitations have roots in the United States Constitution; see, e.g., evidence obtained in illegal search and seizure, *Mapp v. Ohio,* 367 U.S. 643, 6 L. Ed. 2d 1081 (1961); incriminating statements obtained without proper warnings, *Miranda v. Arizona,* 384 U.S. 436, 16 L.Ed.2d 694 (1966); line-up identifications made after indictment when the accused is without counsel, *Gilbert v. California,* 388 U.S. 263, 18 L.Ed. 2d 1178 (1967). The Alaska Constitution may be the source of further limitations. *Cf. Lanier v. State,* Alaska, 486 P.2d 981, at 986 (Alaska 1971):

In defining the scope of constitutional protections which shall be afforded in Alaska courts, we are not limited to the minimum constitutional guarantees as enunciated by the United States Supreme Court. In appropriate circumstances we may more broadly define the rights of the litigants.

Rule 403. Exclusion of Relevant Evidence on Grounds of Prejudice, Confusion, or Waste of Time.

This rule is almost identical to Federal Rule of Evidence 403. The rule merely codifies the common law powers of the court in this regard. The case law recognizes that certain circumstances call for the exclusion of evidence which is of unquestioned relevance. These circumstances entail risks which range all the way from inducing decision on a purely emotional basis, at one extreme, to nothing more harmful than merely wasting time, at the other extreme. Situations in this area call for balancing the probative value of and need for the evidence against the harm likely to result from its admission. Slough, Relevancy Unraveled, 5 Kan. L. Rev. 1, 12-15 (1956); Trautman, Logical or Legal Relevancy—A Conflict in Theory, 5 Vand. L. Rev. 385, 392 (1952) McCormick (2d ed.) § 185, at 440-41.

The Federal Rule provides that the probative value must be "substantially" outweighed by these other factors before evidence is excluded. The problem with the word "substantially" is that it seems to require admission of evidence in cases where the court is certain that the evidence is more harmful than helpful, but cannot say that the balance is substantially one way or the other, only that it is as clear as it is close. Alaska Rule 403 omits "substantially" on the theory that the language "if its probative value is outweighed by..." is a clear enough indication of the balance the court is supposed to strike in view of the further guidance to be found in the case law.

If the balance between probative value and prejudicial effect (signifying all of the factors discussed in this rule) is close, the Judge should probably decide to admit the evidence. In other words, there is a slight presumption in favor of admitting relevant evidence. In order to overcome this minimal presumption, the prejudicial effect must be demonstrably greater than the probative value of the evidence.

Application of this principle should produce the same results as the federal rule in most cases, but the fact that the balance is kept clearly a matter of discretion rather than reduced to measurement by the "substantial" yardstick, should free the court to make the ruling more clearly promoting a just result. The confusion attending the use of burden of persuasion terminology is also avoided by the omission of "substantially"; *see, e.g., Gordon v. United States,* 383 F.2d 936 (D.C. Cir. 1967), *cert. denied,* 390 U.S. 1029, 20 L.Ed.2d 287 (1968).

Exclusion for risk of unfair prejudice, confusion of issues, misleading the jury, or waste of time, all find ample support in the authorities. "Unfair prejudice" within its context means an undue tendency to suggest decision on an improper basis, commonly, though not necessarily, an emotional one.

The rule does not enumerate surprise as a ground for exclusion, in this respect following Wigmore's view of the common law. 6 Wigmore § 1849. *Cf.* McCormick § 152, at 320, n.29, listing unfair surprise as a ground for exclusion but stating that it is usually "coupled with the danger of prejudice and confusion of issues." While Uniform Rule 45 incorporates surprise as a ground and is followed in Kansas Code of Civil Procedure § 60-445, surprise is not included in California Evidence Code § 352 or New Jersey Rule 4, though both the latter otherwise substantially embody Uniform Rule 45. While it can scarcely be doubted that claims of unfair surprise may still be justified despite procedural requirements of notice and instrumentalities of discovery (especially in criminal cases), the granting of a continuance is a more appropriate remedy than exclusion of the evidence. Tentative Recommendation and a Study Relating to the Uniform Rules of Evidence (Art. n. Extrinsic Policies Affecting Admissibility), Cal. Law Revision Comm'n, Rep., Rec. & Studies, 612 (1964). Moreover, the impact of a rule excluding evidence on the ground of surprise would be difficult to estimate. It is assumed that if a continuance is not feasible and if the evidence giving rise to a claim of surprise is somehow suspect, it may be excluded as prejudicial, confusing, or misleading, in the sound exercise of judicial discretion.

In reaching a decision whether to exclude on grounds of unfair prejudice, consideration should be given to the probable effectiveness or lack of effectiveness of a limiting instruction. See Rule 105 and Reporter's Comment thereunder. The availability of other means of proof may also be an appropriate factor.

The rules which follow in this Article are concrete applications evolved for particular situations. However, they reflect the policies underlying the present rule, which is designed as a guide for the handling of situations for which no specific rules have been formulated.

Rule 404. Character Evidence Not Admissible to Prove Conduct—Exceptions—Other Crimes.

(a) **Character Evidence Generally.** This subdivision deals with the basic question whether character evidence should be admitted. Once the admissibility of character evidence in some form is established under this rule, reference must then be made to Rule 405, which follows, in order to determine the appropriate method of proof. If the character is that of a witness, See Rules 608 and 610 for methods of proof.

Character questions arise in two fundamentally different ways. (1) Character may itself be an element of a crime, claim, or defense. A situation of this kind is commonly referred to as "character in issue." Illustrations are: the honesty of a victim in an action for libel based on a statement that he is a thief where truth is a defense, or the competency of the driver in an action for negligently entrusting a motor vehicle to an incompetent driver. No problem of the general relevancy of character evidence is involved, and the present rule therefore has no provision on the subject. The only question relates to allowable methods of proof, as to which see Rule 405, immediately following. (2) Character evidence is susceptible of being used for the purpose of suggesting an inference that the person acted on the occasion in question consistently with his character. This use of character is often described as "circumstantial." Illustrations are: evidence of a violent disposition to prove that the person was the aggressor in an affray, or evidence of honesty in disproof of a charge of theft. This circumstantial use of character evidence raises questions of relevancy as well as questions of allowable methods of proof.

In most jurisdictions today, the circumstantial use of character is rejected but with important exceptions: (1) an accused may introduce relevant evidence of good character (often misleadingly described as "putting his character in issue"), in which event the prosecution may rebut with evidence of bad character; (2) an accused may introduce relevant evidence of the character of the victim, as in support of a claim of self-defense to a charge of homicide or consent in a case of rape, and the prosecution may introduce similar evidence in rebuttal of the character evidence, or, in a homicide case, to rebut a claim that deceased was the first aggressor, and (3) the character of a witness may be gone into as bearing on his credibility. McCormick (2d ed.) §§ 186-195.

The Federal Rule uses the word "pertinent" to describe the character traits referred to above. This rule substitutes the word "relevant" to emphasize the necessity for the evidence to advance fact-finding and not merely to relate to the case. While Rule 402 would bar irrelevant evidence in any event, this rule emphasizes that general relevance concepts must be employed in ruling on character evidence. *See* Morgan, Basic Problems of Evidence 200 (1962).

There is a current trend, especially in rape cases, to exclude all or much character evidence that relates to the victim. Maine's Rule of Evidence 404, for example, has excluded character evidence relating to the victim in all cases. Total exclusion may protect the victim against the introduction of deeply personal facts in cases where introduction of such facts is intended to embarrass the victim rather than help the defendant, but it does so at the expense of allowing such evidence to come in for the benefit of the accused when it would substantially improve his case. This raises constitutional problems. See Westen, Compulsory Process II, 74 Mich. L. Rev. 191, 208-13 (1975); *Davis v. Alaska,* 415 U.S. 308, 39 L.Ed. 2d 347 (1974). By requiring the court to make determinations on admissibility out of the presence of the jury, an appropriate balance can be struck between the need of the accused to present probative exculpatory evidence and the socially desirable goal of protecting victims of crime from embarrassment or harassment and encouraging them to come forward with complaints and to participate in convicting the guilty. If the probative value of character evidence is outweighed by unfair prejudice, confusion of issues, or unwarranted invasion of the victim's privacy, the evidence will be kept from the jury. There is no reason to suppose that only rape victims need the added procedural precaution afforded by this rule. The rule requires both the government and the accused to utilize this procedure. Subdivision (a) (2) (iv) incorporates the language of AS 12.45.045(b) adopting a rebuttable presumption against admissibility of evidence of a rape victim's sexual conduct occurring more than one year before the date of the offense charged.

The word "prejudice" usually refers to prejudice to parties. This rule is also concerned with the interest of non-party complaining witnesses. In balancing the probative value of character evidence against its tendency to invade the privacy of the victim, the court must concern itself with the confrontation clause of the Sixth Amendment. If there is a reasonable probability that character evidence might legitimately help the defense, invasion of the privacy of the victim is warranted. If the evidence is of minimal probative value and is not reasonably likely to assist the defense, invasion of the privacy of the victim is unwarranted. The balance to be struck closely resembles the balance governing claims of a government privilege to protect the identity of an informant. *See* Rule 509 and proposed Federal Rule 510, recently discussed in *State v. Robinson,* 549 P.2d 277 (N. Mex. 1976). *See also United States v. Turchick,* 451 F.2d 333 (8th Cir. 1971).

The hearing out of the presence of the jury or *in camera* envisioned by this rule should be on the record. Examination and cross-examination of witnesses should be permitted, when necessary, and the trial judge should exercise discretion to assure that the record is complete. *Cf.* rule 103(b), *supra.* In the event that the court determines that evidence should not be admitted, in the interests of justice the court may order the record of these proceedings sealed pending appellate review.

The argument is made that circumstantial use of character ought to be allowed in civil cases to the same extent as in criminal cases, i.e. evidence of good (nonprejudicial) character would be admissible in the first instance, subject to rebuttal by evidence of bad character. Falkner, Extrinsic Policies Affecting Admissibility, 10 Rutgers. L. Rev. 574, 581-583 (1956); Tentative Recommendation and a Study Relating to the Uniform Rules of Evidence (Art. VI. Extrinsic Policies Affecting Admissibility), Cal. Law Revision Comm'n, Rep., Rec. & Studies, 657-658 (1964). Uniform Rule 47 goes farther, in that it assumes that character evidence in general satisfies the conditions of relevancy, except as provided in Uniform Rule 48. The difficulty with expanding the use of character evidence in civil cases is set forth by the California Law Revision Commission in its ultimate rejection of Uniform Rule 47, *id.*, at 615:

> Character evidence is of slight probative value and may be very prejudicial. It tends to distract the trier of fact from the main question of what actually happened on the particular occasion. It subtly permits the trier of fact to reward the good man and to punish the bad man because of their respective characters despite what the evidence in the case shows actually happened.

Much of the force of the position of those favoring greater use of character evidence in civil cases is dissipated by their support of Uniform Rule 48 which excludes the evidence in negligence cases, where it could be expected to achieve its maximum usefulness. Moreover, expanding concepts of "character," which seem of necessity to extend into such areas as psychiatric evaluation and psychological testing, coupled with expanded admissibility, would open up such vistas of mental examinations as caused the Court concern in *Schlagenhauf v. Holder,* 379 U.S. 104, 13 L.Ed.2d 152 (1964). It is believed that those espousing change have not met the burden of persuasion.

The Federal Rule permits the prosecutor upon an accused's introduction of evidence of self-defense to respond with evidence of the victim's character. This is contrary to the common law doctrine which requires the accused to actually introduce evidence relating to the victim's character before opening the door to rebuttal by the prosecutor. *See* 1 Wigmore § 63; Annot., 34 A.L.R.2d 451 (1954). The 1969 and 1971 drafts followed the common law doctrine, but were revised in the 1975 adopted rules to accommodate a recommendation by Senator John L. McClellan. Letter to Hon. Albert Maris, August 12, 1971, in Supp. to Hearings on Proposed Rules of Evidence Before the Subcomm. on Crim. Justice of House Comm. on the Judiciary, 93rd Cong., 1st Sess. 47, 48-49 (1973). Little attention was paid to the change during the legislative hearings and debates.

There remain arguments for permitting the accused to introduce evidence of self-defense without automatically allowing character evidence relating to the victim to come in. Character evidence is suspect for the reasons quoted above. When evidence of the victim's character is offered, pressure may be placed upon a defendant to explain his own character, which would open the door to much damaging evidence. If the defendant offers no evidence regarding his own character, the Federal Rule imposes a penalty on the plea of self-defense by allowing the introduction of evidence that may be used to prove too much in a situation where the evidence of self-defense is scanty. But this rule opts to admit evidence of character when the victim of a homicide is attacked by the defense as the first aggressor. In such cases the crime is grave, the victim cannot tell a story, and there is some reason to believe that a peaceable person is not likely to be the first aggressor.

This rule only applies to character evidence relating to people and does not operate to exclude evidence relating to the character of a building. See AS 11.40.270 and 11.60.130.

(b) **Other Crimes, Wrongs, or Acts.** Subdivision (b) deals with a specialized but important application of the general rule excluding circumstantial use of character evidence. Consistently with that rule, evidence of other crimes, wrongs, or acts is not admissible to prove character as a basis for suggesting the inference that conduct on a particular occasion was in conformity with it. However, the evidence may be offered for another purpose, such as proof of motive, opportunity, and so on, which does not fall within the prohibition. In this situation the rule does not require that the evidence be excluded. No mechanical solution is offered. The determination must be made whether the danger of undue prejudice outweighs the probative value of the evidence, in view of the availability of other means of proof and other factors appropriate for making decisions of this kind under Rule 403. *See, e.g., Freeman v. State,* 486 P.2d 967 (Alaska 1971). *See also* Slough and Knightly, Other Vices, Other Crimes, 41 Iowa L. Rev. 325 (1956). *See also Demmert v. State,* 565 P.2d 155 (Alaska 1977) (other crimes evidence offered to prove intent). Of course, "other crimes" evidence admissible under Rule 404(b) may be excluded under Rule 403. *Cf., In re F.S.,* 586 P.2d 607 (Alaska 1978).

Rule 405. Methods of Proving Character.

(a) **Reputation or Opinion.** The common law traditionally has provided that proof of character or a trait of character of a person, when permitted, may be made by testimony as to reputation only. Reputation evidence is usually presented by calling a witness to the stand who is familiar with the reputation of the defendant, or perhaps the victim, if the victim's character is being challenged, and asking the witness to state what the reputation is in the community where the defendant or victim lives. The foundation for such testimony comes in the form of establishing that the witness has sufficient familiarity with the people in the community so that he can make a valid attempt at assessing reputation.

The rationale for the limitation was best stated by Dean Ladd:

> The object of the law in making reputation the test of character is to get the aggregate judgment of a community rather than the personal opinion of the witness which might be considered to be warped by his own feeling or prejudice. Even reputation must, to be admitted, be general in a community rather than based upon a limited class. While it is not necessary that a character witness know what the majority of a neighborhood think of a person, he must know of the general regard with which the party is commonly held.
>
> It is the general concurrence of a great number of

people reflecting the sentiment toward the party whose character is subject to inquiry that is necessary to establish a reputation and to warrant its use as evidence. In this, the theory of the law is that trustworthiness is gained from the expressions of many people in their estimation of a person which would not be obtained by the individual opinion of a single witness however well acquainted he might be with the party's character.

The requirement that the reputation be broadly general rather than that of a particular group...again emphasizes the effort to get away from the secularized and consequently biased estimate of character... The reputed character of a person is created from the slow spreading influence of community opinion growing out of his behavior in the society in which he moves and is known and upon this basis is accepted as proof of what his character actually is.

Ladd, Techniques and Theory of Character Testimony, 24 Iowa L. Rev. 458, 513 (1939).

There is a growing trend in common law jurisdictions to permit testimony as to the person's reputation where he works, as well as where he lives. The Federal Rule, on which this Rule is modeled, does not indicate the scope of reputation evidence. This rule fills a gap left in the Federal Rule by clearly stating that reputation evidence is not confined to the community in which the defendant lives; reputation where the defendant works, goes to school or in a group with whom the defendant habitually associates will suffice. *See* Uniform Rule 63(28) (1953); McCormick, Evidence § 191, at 456; 112 A.L.R. 1020 (1938).

While not explicitly required by the rule, reputation evidence to be relevant must relate to the period in which the acts giving rise to the litigation took place. The evidence must relate to a relevant trait of character under Rule 404.

Besides expanding the scope of permissible reputation evidence, this rule departs from the majority common law view in permitting opinion evidence to be admitted. It is consistent, however, with recent Alaska cases. *See, e.g., Freeman v. State* 486 P.2d 967 (Alaska 1971). This was considered such a controversial issue that the House Committee on the Judiciary deleted the provision allowing for opinion evidence in its proposed draft of rules. During the House debate, the provision was reinstated. The case for opinion testimony is made by Wigmore:

Put any one of us on trial for a false charge, and ask him whether he would not rather invoke in his vindication, as Lord Kenyon said, "The warm affectionate testimony" of those few whose long intimacy and trust has made them ready to demonstrate their faith to the jury, than any amount of colorful assertions about reputation. Take the place of a juryman, and speculate whether he is helped more by the witnesses whose personal intimacy gives to their belief a first and highest value, or by those who merely repeat a form of words in which the term "reputation" occurs.

7 Wigmore, Evidence § 1936, at 166.

In opening the door to this evidence, Rule 405 places both familiar and new responsibilities on the trial judge.

He will have to exercise firm control over the proceedings to insure that the witness does not relate the particular incidents on which he bases his opinion of defendant—for proof of character by specific acts is still prohibited. And as with all testimony, he will have to weigh its probative value against the countervailing factors to admissibility specified in Rule 403.

2 Weinstein's Evidence, ¶ 405[03] (1975). In exercising the sound discretion required by Rule 403, the trial judge should be able to handle the new types of opinion testimony that may be offered when Rule 405 is considered in conjunction with other Rules that expand categories of admissible evidence. *See, People v. Jones,* 266 P.2d 38 (Cal. 1954); *cf., United States v. Hiss,* 88 F. Supp. 559 (S.D.N.Y. 1950). *See generally* Curran, Expert Psychiatric Evidence of Personality Traits, 103 U. Pa. L. Rev. 999 (1955); Falknor & Steffen, Evidence of Character: From the "Crucible of the Community" to the "Couch of the Psychiatrist," 102 U. Pa. L. Rev. 980 (1954). Alaska has had experience with novel types of opinion. *See Freeman v. State, supra.*

As discussed in the next paragraph, specific acts cannot be used to prove character unless a character trait is in issue. But specific acts can be used to prove the knowledge of a character witness on cross-examination. According to the great majority of cases, on cross-examination inquiry is allowable as to whether the reputation witness has heard of particular instances of conduct relevant to the trait in question if the crossexaminer has a good faith belief that the conduct actually took place. *Michelson v. United States,* 335 U.S. 469, 93 L.Ed. 168 (1948); Annot., 47 A.L.R.2d 1258 (1956). The theory is that, since the reputation witness relates what he has heard, the inquiry tends to shed light on the accuracy of his hearing and reporting. Accordingly, the opinion witness would be asked whether he knew, as well as whether he had heard. The fact is, of course, that these distinctions are of slight if any practical significance, and the second sentence of subdivision (a) eliminates them as a factor in formulating questions. This recognition of the propriety of inquiring into specific instances of conduct does not circumscribe inquiry otherwise into the bases of opinion and reputation testimony.

(b) **Specific Instances of Conduct.** Of the three methods of proving character provided by the rule, evidence of specific instances of conduct is the most convincing. At the same time it poses the greatest capacity to arouse prejudice, to confuse, to surprise, and to consume time. Consequently the Rule confines the use of evidence of this kind to cases in which character is, in the strict sense, in issue and hence deserving of a searching inquiry. When character is used circumstantially and hence occupies a lesser status in the case, proof may be only by reputation and opinion. These latter methods are also available when character is in issue. This treatment is, with respect to specific instances of conduct and reputation, conventional contemporary common law doctrine. McCormick (2d ed.) § 187.

Probably the most familiar example of character being in issue is the libel case where someone publishes a charge that the plaintiff is a thief, plaintiff sues the publisher, and a defense of truth is raised. The publisher is entitled to show the specific acts that prove the charge. Another familiar example is a case in which an employer is charged with negligently hiring or retaining an incompetent employee. On the question of the competence of the employee, both sides are entitled (and may have to in order to satisfy burden of proof requirements) to offer evidence of specific acts of the employee demonstrating competence or incompetence.

Rule 406. Habit—Routine Practice.

This rule is identical to Federal Rule 406 which confirms the trend toward admissibility of habit and routine practice as persuasive proof of conduct on a particular occasion. The difficulty arises in distinguishing habit evidence from character evidence which is viewed as a less reliable and potentially more dangerous means of establishing the likelihood of specific conduct on a particular occasion. In part the difficulty stems from the inability to precisely define "habit." It is clear that the more regular the performance of an act, the more likely it is to be regarded a habit. An oft-quoted paragraph, McCormick (2d ed.) § 195, at 462, describes habit in terms effectively contrasting it with character.

> Character and habit are close akin. Character is a generalized description of one's disposition, or of one's disposition in respect to a general trait, such as honesty, temperance, or peacefulness. "Habit," in modern usage, both lay and psychological, is more specific. It describes one's regular response to a repeated specific situation. If we speak of character for care, we think of the person's tendency to act prudently in all the varying situations of life, in business, family life, in handling automobiles and in walking across the street. A habit, on the other hand, is the person's regular practice of meeting a particular kind of situation with a specific type of conduct, such as the habit of going down a particular stairway two stairs at a time, or of giving the hand-signal for a left turn, or of alighting from railway cars while they are moving. The doing of the habitual acts may become semiautomatic.

In determining whether evidence shall be admissible, the court may look to Rule 104 and make a preliminary determination that it is a habit or a routine business practice that is being described. When an activity fails to achieve the status of a habit, evidence as to its practice must be excluded. Certain practices are not readily defined as "habits." For example, in *Levin v. United States,* 338 F.2d 265 (D.C. Cir. 1964), testimony as to the religious "habits" of the accused, offered as tending to prove that he was at home observing the Sabbath rather than out obtaining money through larceny by trick, was held properly excluded:

> It seems apparent to us that an individual's religious practices would not be the type of activities which would lend themselves to the characterization of "invariable regularity." [1 Wigmore 520.] Certainly the very volitional basis of the activity raises serious questions as to its invariable nature, and hence its probative value.

Id. at 272.

Evidence of a routine practice of an organization may be as relevant as a person's habit in proving that an act was performed in a certain way or that an event took place. The circumstantial nature of the proof requires that the routine specifically describe a particular organization's manner of daily operation or the probative value is greatly diminished. Since an organization must often rely upon consistent performance in order to make a profit or otherwise succeed, evidence of routine practices may be more probative in many cases than habit evidence. And the nature of this evidence is such that it is not likely to be very prejudicial. This rule does not refer to the practice of a given trade or industry, except insofar as it parallels a specific company's routines.

This rule specifically states that corroboration of a habit is unnecessary as a condition precedent to its admissibility. New Jersey adopted a similar policy in its Rule 49, rejecting its previous requirement that a necessary condition for the introduction of habit evidence was the introduction of other evidence that the habit was followed in the particular occasion in question. The New Jersey Commission stated that habit or custom alone is evidential as to conduct on a particular occasion and that corroboration goes only to weight.

> To require corroborative evidence that on that date the behavior did conform to the proven habit would be to defeat the purpose of the rule and put an unnecessary hurdle in the path of the attorney with circumstantial proofs only.

Report of the Committee on the Revision of the Law of Evidence to the Supreme Court of New Jersey 101 (1955).

This rule specifically rejects the common law "eyewitness rule." Followed in a great number of jurisdictions, the eyewitness rule only permits evidence of a habit to be admissible where no eyewitnesses are available to testify about the events in question. There are reasons to be wary of habit evidence: individuals may consciously take advantage of a known habit as an alibi, well-established habits do not always govern behavior, and habits sometimes may be easy to fabricate but difficult to refute. These problems are not insoluble. By requiring repetitive acts, this rule should make fabrication more difficult and should enable the cross-examiner to fully explore the specifics of the habit claim. Moreover, habit evidence is not unique in its imperfections. The eyewitness rule does not take into account the fact that evidence of an established habit may be more reliable than the testimony of an eyewitness. The Law Revision Commission's Comment to California's Rule § 1105, 29b West Ann. Cal. Evid. Code 19 (1966), which also rejects the eyewitness rule states:

> The "no eyewitness" limitation is undesirable. Eyewitnesses frequently are mistaken, some are dishonest. The trier of fact should be entitled to weigh the habit evidence against the eyewitness testimony as well as all of the evidence in the case.

This provision, like its federal counterpart, is silent as to the means of proof that a habit or routine practice existed. The 1969 and 1971 drafts of the proposed federal rules contained a provision which specified that habit or routine practice may be proved by testimony in the form of an opinion or by specific instances of conduct sufficient in number to warrant a finding that the habit existed or that the practice was routine. Congress deleted the section in favor of allowing courts to develop and consider various methods of proof. This rule anticipates that any relevant manner of proof may be employed, subject to Rule 403's requirements that the proof be more probative than prejudicial, confusing, or misleading and that the probative value justify the time needed to hear the evidence.

Rule 407. Subsequent Remedial Measures.

This rule is modeled on Federal Rule 407, which incorporates conventional doctrine excluding evidence of subsequent remedial measures as proof of an admission of fault.

The rule rests on three grounds. (1) The conduct is not in fact an admission, since the conduct is equally consistent with injury by mere accident or through contributory negligence. Or, as Baron Bramwell put it, the rule rejects the notion that "because the world gets wiser as it gets older, therefore it was foolish before." *Hart v. Lancashire & Yorkshire Ry. Co.,* 21 L.T.R. N.S. 261, 263 (1869). Under a liberal theory of relevancy this ground alone would not support exclusion as the inference is still a possible one. (2) The second ground for exclusion rests on a social policy of encouraging people to take, or at least not discouraging them from taking, steps in furtherance of added safety. This assumes, however, that many repairs would not be made but for the exclusionary rule, a proposition subject to serious empirical challenge. (3) The third and perhaps most important reason for the Rule is that people who err on the side of caution and take measures to protect fellow citizens from even the possibility of injury should not bear the risk that the jury, unlike Baron Bramwell, will read more into a repair than is warranted.

The courts have applied this principle to exclude evidence of subsequent repairs, installation of safety devices, changes in company rules, and discharge of employees, and the language of the present rule is broad enough to encompass all of them. See Falknor, Extrinsic Policies Affecting Admissibility, 10 Rutgers L. Rev. 574, 590 (1956).

The second sentence of the rule directs attention to the limitations of the rule.

Rule 407 explicitly bars the use of subsequent remedial measures to prove negligence. It also inhibits the use of the evidence to prove "culpable conduct," which may include fault other than negligence, e.g., recklessness (wantonness, willfulness). There is often no clear distinction between recklessness and gross negligence (see Prosser, Torts § 34 (4th ed. 1971)); consequently the policy arguments mentioned above apply equally to both.

In effect Rule 407 rejects the suggested inference that fault is admitted. Other inferences are, however, allowable, including defective condition in a products liability action, ownership or control, existence of duty, and feasibility of precautionary measures, if controverted, and impeachment. 2 Wigmore § 283; Annot., 64 A.L.R.2d 1296. A recent Alaska case is illustrative. In *Kaatz v. State,* 540 P.2d 1037 (Alaska 1975), actions were brought against the State to recover for deaths of the driver of and passenger in a front-end loader which slipped off an icy highway and overturned. In reviewing the finding of negligence on the part of the State, the Supreme Court of Alaska noted that shortly after the accident, the road in question was sanded. Citing Federal Rule 407, the Court emphasized that the evidence was not used to show negligence directly, but to show feasibility of repair. Admission for this purpose was deemed proper.

There are few cases and few scholarly discussions of the applicability of this exclusionary principle in products liability cases. Unlike most rules that have been promulgated, this Rule explicitly excepts from the reach of the exclusionary rule the use of subsequent remedial measures to show a defect in a product. The reasons mentioned above for the general rule do not apply in a products liability case because,

> [T]he focus of attention in strict liability cases is not on the conduct of the defendant, but rather on the existence of the defective product which causes injuries. Liability is attached, as a matter of policy, on the basis of the existence of a defect rather than on the basis of the defendant's negligent conduct . . . .

Bachner v. Pearson, 479 P.2d 319, 329 (Alaska 1970).

Evidence of subsequent repairs or improvements may be highly probative as to the existence of a defect in a product at the time of an accident. In common law jurisdiction such evidence has been regarded as relevant to the issue of defectiveness in negligence-based cases and admissible, e.g., *Steele v. Wiedemann Mach. Co.,* 280 F.2d 380 (3d Cir. 1960).

Moreover, the rationale of not discouraging repairs or improvement does not justify excluding this evidence in the products liability case. The California Supreme Court appropriately observed in *Ault v. International Harvester Co.,* 528 P.2d 1148, 1152 (Cal. 1975), a decision rejecting this exclusionary rule in products liability cases, that

> [t]he contemporary corporate mass producer of goods, the normal products liability defendant, manufactures tens of thousands of units of goods; it is manifestly unrealistic to suggest that such a producer will forego making improvement in its product, and risk innumerable additional lawsuits and the attendant adverse effect upon its public image, simply because evidence of adoption of such improvement may be admitted in an action founded on strict liability for recovery on an injury that preceded the improvement. In the products liability area, the exclusionary rule of section 1151 [California equivalent of Rule 407] does not affect the primary conduct of this mass producer of goods, but serves merely as a shield against potential liability.

Since the manufacturer of a product makes more of a business judgment than a humanitarian gesture in making repairs, the third rationale for the rule is not applicable either.

Of course, when evidence is admitted for any of these "other purposes," the court should instruct the jury to consider it only for the limited purpose for which it is offered, not on the issue of negligence or culpable conduct. It is important to note that the requirement that the other purpose be controverted calls for automatic exclusion unless a genuine issue is present and allows the opposing party to lay the groundwork for exclusion by making an admission. If, for example, control is not controverted, there is no reason to admit subsequent remedial measures to prove control, and there is a good reason to exclude it: evidence of subsequent remedial measures might be used by the jury as an admission of fault regardless of the limiting instruction given by the court.

It is also important to keep in mind that even if the issue is a valid one, the factors of undue prejudice, confusion of issues, misleading the jury, and waste of time remain for consideration under Rule 403.

For comparable rules, see Uniform Rule 51; California Evidence Code § 1151; Kansas Code of Civil Procedure § 60-451; Nebraska Rule 27-407; Nevada Rule 48.095; New Jersey Evidence Rule 51; and New Mexico Rule 20-4-407.

Rule 408. Compromise and Offers to Compromise.

This rule, like the common law doctrine, operates to exclude evidence of an offer to compromise a claim when offered to prove the validity, invalidity or amount of the claim. Under the prevailing common law view, statements of fact made independently of the compromise offer—i.e., statement not inextricably bound up in the offer to compromise—can be admitted for any relevant purpose. But this exception can be artfully dodged by the attorney who specifies that all factual statements are hypothetical, or who states in advance that the discussion is "without prejudice." *See* Annot., 15 A.L.R. 3d 13 (1967). *See also* Alaska R. Civ. P. 43(i) (2) (superseded by this rule).

This rule expands the scope of protection afforded compromise negotiations by eliminating the common law exception and making statements of fact and conduct which are made or which occur during settlement negotiations inadmissible whenever an offer to compromise would be excluded. See California Evidence Code §§ 1152, 1154 for similar provisions. In addition to eliminating the need to talk continually in hypothetical terms, this change promotes the major policy behind the rule—to encourage settlement of disputes. It also avoids preliminary factfinding as to what was said during negotiating sessions, i.e., whether statements were made in hypothetical or "without prejudice" form.

The Advisory Committee's comment to the Federal Rule after which this rule is modeled cites two rationales for a rule of exclusion. (1) The evidence is irrelevant, since the offer may be motivated by a desire for peace rather than from any concession of weakness of position. The validity of this position will vary as the amount of the offer varies in relation to the size of the claim and may also be influenced by other circumstances. (2) A more consistently impressive ground is promotion of the public policy favoring the compromise and settlement of disputes. McCormick § 274, at 663. While the rule is ordinarily phrased in terms of offers of compromise, it is apparent that a similar attitude must be taken with respect to a completed compromise when offered against a party thereto. This latter situation will not, of course, ordinarily occur except when a party to the present litigation was compromised with a third person.

Unless the amount of the claim or the claim itself is in dispute, the policy of encouraging freedom of communication with respect to compromise is not advanced. Hence the rule does not apply when the effort is to induce a creditor to settle an admittedly due amount for a lesser sum. McCormick (2d ed.) § 274, at 663. See also Uniform Rules 52 and 53 for similar provisions. An offer to pay the full amount in dispute is admissible as an unconditional acknowledgment of liability because it is not conditioned on a compromise. *See Saxton v. Harris,* 395 P.2d 71 (Alaska 1964).

This Rule governs whether or not any compromise that is reached is carried out. Some common law jurisdictions admit completed settlements as evidence if they are not successful in terminating litigation. Nothing in this rule prevents the use as evidence of settlement agreements in subsequent contract actions, however.

This rule differs from the federal rule by explicitly providing that statements made during negotiations must not be used for impeachment as prior inconsistent statements of a party. This further protection is required in order to encourage free and open negotiations and to foster settlements. It may be necessary to "concede" issues to an opponent to advance negotiations which are not issues that one would readily concede for purposes of proving liability. If impeachment is allowed, the common law requirement of communicating in hypothetical terms would, for all practical purposes, be reinstated. Unless the parties to the negotiation are insured that they will not prejudice the merits of their respective cases, communications will be guarded. As recognized in Rule 410, admissibility of guilty pleas later withdrawn or offers to plead guilty for purposes of impeachment would effectively stifle the open communication needed to promote compromise. The same is true in civil cases.

Where statements made in compromise negotiations are not used to advance litigation relating to the validity, invalidity or amount of the underlying claim admission is proper. Collateral uses such as those mentioned in the final sentence of the rule are supported by existing authorities. *E.g.,* proving bias or prejudice of a witness, see Annot., 161 A.L.R. 395 (1946); negativing a contention of lack of due diligence in presenting a claim, 4 Wigmore § 1061. *See also* Alaska R. Civ. P. 68 in which evidence of an unaccepted offer of judgment is admissible on the collateral issue of determining costs. An effort to "buy off" the prosecution or a prosecuting witness in a criminal case is not within the policy of the rule of exclusion.

This rule further provides that evidence which would otherwise be discoverable is not rendered inadmissible merely because it was presented during negotiations. A party should not be able to immunize documents by once revealing them; no policy is advanced by such protection. Where statements made during negotiations lead to the discovery of relevant evidence it shall not be rendered inadmissible merely because the information obtained could not have been introduced into evidence in the form of statements made during negotiations.

Rule 409. Payment of Medical and Other Expenses.

The considerations underlying this rule parallel those underlying Rules 407 and 408, which deal respectively with subsequent remedial measures and offers of compromise. As stated in Annot., 20 A.L.R.2d 291, 293 (1951):

> [G]enerally, evidence of payment of medical, hospital, or similar expenses of an injured party by the opposing party, is not admissible, the reason often given being that such payment or offer is usually made from humane impulses and not from an admission of liability, and that to hold otherwise would tend to discourage assistance to the injured person.

Contrary to Rule 408, dealing with offers of compromise, the present rule does not extend to conduct or statements not a part of the act of furnishing or offering or promising to pay. This difference in treatment arises from fundamental differences in nature. Communication is essential if compromises are to be effected, and consequently broad protection of statements is needed. This is not so in cases of payments or offers or promises to pay medical expenses, where factual statements may be expected to be incidental in nature and where protecting such statements would not encourage the approved behavior. A party can offer to pay medical expenses without making statements as to liability.

This rule, unlike Rule 408, does not require that liability or amount be in dispute. Prompt payment of medical and other expenses is encouraged and the humanitarian nature of the payment or offer is highlighted.

If liability or amount is in dispute, an offer to pay medical expenses may be part of a compromise negotiation. Once the offer becomes part of the negotiating process, any statements or conduct made in compromise negotiations will be protected under Rule 408.

Evidence of an offer to pay or of a completed payment of medical expenses may be admissible for purposes other than proving liability or amount. In this respect the rule is like Rule 408. When the issue upon which the evidence is offered is collateral to the merits of the case, admission may be proper. For example, if A is involved in an accident with B and C, and A pays B's medical expenses, C may want to introduce this evidence to show the possible bias of B as a witness.

Rule 410. Inadmissibility of Plea Discussions in Other Proceedings.

Rule 410 is modeled on former rule 11(e) (6) of the Alaska Rules of Criminal Procedure, which is superseded by this rule. It differs in substantial respects from its federal counterpart. The basic goals of the rule are two: (1) to foster free and open negotiations between prosecutors and those accused of crimes, and (2) to insure fair treatment for defendants whose guilty pleas are set aside by a trial or an appellate court.

To foster negotiations the rule provides that nothing that is said during plea bargaining may be used against the accused in any proceeding, whether criminal, civil or administrative. Thus, the accused is free to discuss the case without resort to hypothetical statements of fact and without fear that a slip of the tongue may be devastating at a later trial or other proceeding.

To insure fair treatment for defendants whose pleas are entered and later withdrawn or overturned, this rule provides that the slate should be wiped clean and that no part of the plea process can be used for impeachment or any purpose against the defendant in subsequent proceedings (unless made in court, and they are voluntary and reliable) or in a perjury prosecution. This is in sharp contrast to Federal Rule 410. As amended in December, 1975 by the Congress, the Federal Rule provides that a statement made in connection with a plea "is admissible in a criminal proceeding for perjury or false statement if the statement was made by the defendant under oath, on the record, and in the presence of counsel." Alaska Rule 410 offers defendants greater protection: when a plea is withdrawn or otherwise set aside, no use shall be made on the merits of a subsequent case of any statement made in connection with a plea, even though that statement may have been made in court, under oath and with the advice of counsel. However, limited impeachment use is recognized.

Note, however, that this rule does not prohibit admission of statements made by the defendant during the plea process at a hearing on defendant's motion to withdraw a plea. In this situation the statements are subject only to the requirement of relevance.

It is important to observe that leave to withdraw a guilty or nolo contendere plea, once accepted, is not a matter of right; the burden is on the defendant to convince the court that withdrawal of a plea should be permitted in the court's discretion upon grounds set forth in Alaska R. Crim. P. 32(d). The most common ground for withdrawal is that the plea was involuntarily made. Clearly, when the plea was involuntarily made, statements made in connection with it are likely to be unreliable as well; due process would probably require the suppression of both plea and statements.

This rule admits statements found to be both voluntary and reliable that are made in court. Such statements should be very useful for impeachment purposes and are worthy of consideration by a trier of fact considering the credibility of a witness.

In deciding whether or not a statement made in connection with a plea in court is voluntary, the court will consider many of the same questions that arise with respect to confessions. In determining whether the plea statements are reliable, the court must keep in mind that the traditional colloquy between court and defendant is not without its problems, since the defendant is attempting to preserve a bargain in many instances. Hence, even though the defendant may be under oath and uncoerced in any constitutional sense, he is under great pressure to conform his answers to the plea agreed to, in order to satisfy the judge that "there is a reasonable basis for the plea" under Alaska R. Crim. P. 11(f). Such statements by the defendant are neither clarified by defense counsel nor qualified by the defendant.

At first blush it may appear that this rule is inconsistent with Rule 408 with respect to the use of statements made during bargaining for impeachment purposes. But the inconsistency is more apparent than real. In both rules, statements made during private bargaining sessions are not admissible for impeachment purposes. This rule reflects the fact that statements made in court can be especially reliable, especially with the safeguards provided herein. No such in-court procedure exists in most civil cases. In both civil and criminal cases parties should be able to negotiate freely without fear that a slip of the tongue will be unfairly damaging should no bargain be made. But Rule 410 adopts the view that once the informal bargaining is over and the solemn procedure of pleading in court begins, it is both fair and wise to hold a criminal defendant responsible for statements made to the court when the defendant takes a different position later and the plea statements are used for impeachment.

To provide balance, statements made by the prosecutor during the bargaining process are not admissible against the government in any proceeding, except that the defendant may use the prosecutor's statements as evidence in a hearing to enforce a plea agreement *see generally Santobello v. New York,* 404 U.S. 257, 30 L.Ed. 2d 427 (1971) or to set aside a plea or judgment. In most common law jurisdictions this rule might not be necessary, because statements by an agent of a party would not be admissible against the party unless the agent were specifically authorized to make such statements; the prosecutor may not be so authorized. But under Rule 801 (d) (2) (D) the admissibility of agents' statements is expanded. Rule 410 makes it clear that the prosecutor is as free to negotiate without watching for every slip of the tongue as the defendant is. Nothing in this section prohibits the introduction of statements made by a prosecutor during plea bargaining in a disciplinary action against the prosecutor, or even in a criminal action against the prosecutor. The prosecutor who abuses the public trust is not protected by this Rule.

Statements made by defense counsel on behalf of an accused can be used against counsel in a subsequent civil case or disbarment proceeding, since the rule is not designed to protect from disclosure malpractice or ethical violations.

Nothing in this rule makes *nolo contendere* pleas admissible as admissions. But Rule 609 does make certain *nolo contendere* pleas admissible for impeachment purposes.

Rule 411. Liability Insurance.

The courts have with substantial unanimity rejected evidence of liability insurance for the purpose of proving fault, and absence of liability insurance as proof of lack of fault. *See* Annot., 4 A.L.R.2d 761 (1949). Because the inference of fault from the fact of insurance coverage is a tenuous one, as is its converse, evidence of insurance coverage or of the absence of such coverage lacks great probative value on the issue of fault. More importantly, perhaps, the rule is designed to prevent a jury from deciding a close case on an improper basis—i.e., whether or not a party is insured. There is a danger that insurance evidence might skew the decision-making process of the jury by making it regret a possibly wrong decision against an uninsured person much more than a similar decision under identical facts against a person whose insurance status is unknown, or by making the jury regret any erroneous decision against an insured party less than it would an erroneous decision against a person whose insurance status is unknown. This is not to suggest that a jury will intentionally make a mistake. It suggests only that in close cases someone must bear the risk of error, that the presence or absence of insurance is not regarded as an appropriate guide for allocating the risk, and that it is possible that a jury will misuse insurance evidence. This rule, identical to the federal rule, is drafted in broad terms so as to include contributory negligence or other fault of a plaintiff as well as fault of a defendant.

The second sentence of this rule describes the limitations on it. Whereas evidence of insurance coverage is inadmissible to prove negligence, there are several well established issues for which evidence of insurance coverage, or the lack of it, has probative value and is therefore admissible. Evidence of insurance of an object often indicates the person who controls or owns the object in question. Or, if A has insured B, there is some reason to draw the inference that A considers himself responsible for B's acts. While it is inconclusive proof of an agency relationship, the existence of such insurance has evidentiary value in helping to establish such a relationship.

Bias or prejudice of a witness or juror is a common concern when a witness or juror is connected with an insurance company. Such information often has been elicited during voir dire when a prospective juror is asked whether or not he has any connection with the insurance business. Although this is often a legitimate question, it may serve to remind the jury that a party may be insured. Similarly, questions as to a witness' affiliation with insurance interests may be legitimate impeachment tools, despite the danger of misuse of the insurance evidence.

But, the fact that evidence of insurance is sometimes admissible does not mean that it must be admitted whenever offered for a proper purpose. The danger of misuse of the evidence by the jury does not totally disappear when the evidence is introduced for a reason other than to prove fault or absence thereof, even though a limiting instruction will be given upon request under Rule 105. Rule 403 requires the trial judge to balance the probative value of the evidence on one issue against the potential danger that the jury will favor uninsured defendants and disfavor insured defendants.

Trial lawyers are on notice that insurance is admissible for some purposes and not others. Alaska R. Civ. P. 26(b) (2) allows discovery of insurance agreements, and the parties should be able to obtain a judicial decision on whether insurance evidence is to be admitted or otherwise utilized and for what purposes before such evidence is brought to the attention of the jury. *Poulin v. Zartman,* 542 P.2d 251, 265 (Alaska 1975).

If this rule is to have maximum effectiveness, it must be enforced by the trial judge. Inadvertent or deliberate tactical references to insurance should be cured immediately, if possible, with instructions to the jury to disregard the information. The trial judge is vested with wide discretion to grant a new trial where such slips are not easily cured. *See Peters v. Benson,* 425 P.2d 149, 152-153 (Alaska 1967).

Rule 412. Evidence Illegally Obtained.

Although illegally obtained evidence may be highly probative, this rule recognizes that such evidence must generally be excluded in order to breathe life into constitutional guarantees and to remove incentives for governmental intrusion into protected areas. While these rules of evidence generally do not incorporate constitutional doctrine, Rule 412 will go beyond what federal constitutional decisions require in protecting the rights of those accused of crime. Thus, for example, in *Harris v. New York,* 401 U.S. 222, 28 L.Ed.2d 1 (1971), the United States Supreme Court approved the use of statements obtained in violation of *Miranda v. Arizona,* 384 U.S. 436, 16 L.Ed.2d 695 (1966), for impeachment purposes but not as part of the prosecutor's case-in-chief. *Walder v. United States,* 347 U.S. 62, 98 L.Ed. 503 (1954), sanctioned the introduction of testimony on illegally seized heroin to rebut the defendant's denial of prior drug possession. Rule 412 would forbid such uses as long as proper objection is made by the defendant. This last proviso is a change from Criminal Rule 26 (g).

This ban on the use of both testimonial and physical evidence for impeachment purposes should not amount to a significant incentive for defendants to commit perjury. The prosecution will still be able to cross-examine the defendant on his claims, if it believes in good faith that the defendant's testimony is false. And, as discussed below, some otherwise inadmissible evidence will still be permitted in perjury prosecutions.

Rule 412 also does not bar the use as impeachment evidence of statements made by a defendant who testifies on a preliminary question of fact as permitted by Rule 104(d). If the preliminary question of fact involves a constitutional question, the argument could be made that a ruling favorable to the defendant renders any statements made during the preliminary hearing "fruit of the poisonous tree" and therefore inadmissible. *Cf. Harrison v. United States,* 392 U.S. 219 (1968) (use of evidence in case-in-chief). *But see People v. Sturgis,* 317 N.E.2d 545 (Ill. 1974), *cert. denied,* 420 U.S. 936, 43 L.Ed.2d 412 (1975). *See also United States v. Kahan,* 415 U.S. 239, 39 L.Ed.2d 297 (1974); *United States v. Mandujano,* 425 U.S. 564, 584, 48 L.Ed.2d 212, 277 (1976) (Brennan, J., concurring in the judgment). Where the defendant is successful in suppressing evidence the underlying constitutional right is protected. It seems an extravagant extension of constitutional protection to permit one version of facts from the defendant's mouth to keep evidence from a tribunal and to permit the defendant to offer another version at trial. If the motion to suppress is unsuccessful, there is even less reason to refrain from using the defendant's statements in support of the motion as impeachment evidence. The decision to take the oath and testify is attenuation enough to remove the taint of the initial illegality. The record of the statements, the advice of counsel, and the oath together remove many of the problems associated with *Harris v. New York, supra.*

In perjury prosecutions, the government's interest in convicting guilty defendants and the extreme difficulty of obtaining reliable evidence warrant controlled use of illegally obtained evidence. Hence Rule 412 contains two narrow exceptions to the blanket prohibition on the use of illegally obtained evidence properly objected to.

The first exception governs statements obtained in violation of the right to warnings under *Miranda,* if the statement whose admission is sought is relevant to the issue of guilt or innocence and shown to be otherwise voluntary and not coerced. The latter limitation, meant to guarantee the statement's reliability, is derived from *Harris v. New York, supra,* where the U.S. Supreme Court observed, "Petitioner makes no claim that the statements made to the police were coerced or involuntary." 401 U.S. at 224, 28 L.Ed.2d at 4.

The second exception governs evidence obtained in violation of the fourth amendment and/or its Alaska counterpart, article I, section 14. Again a limitation is imposed: the evidence must be relevant to the issue of guilt or innocence, and must not have been obtained "in substantial violation of rights." This limitation is not imposed to ensure reliability of the evidence, but rather recognizes that judicial integrity requires the exclusion of evidence for all purposes if the police misconduct involved in obtaining it was flagrant. The concept of a "substantial violation of rights" is necessarily flexible, and whether or not such a violation occurred will depend on the facts of each case. The simple reference to "rights" is intended to emphasize that this section has no bearing on the law of standing in search and seizure cases.

ARTICLE V. PRIVILEGES

Introductory Comment

Article V provides for eight different privileges and recognizes that other privileges may be created by statute or court rule. Because most of the privileges covered by Article V were recognized before the adoption of these Rules, the Reporter's Comments do not attempt to state the rationales for the various privileges and to justify them. Most of the privileges have been debated elsewhere, and the privileges have survived the debate. The Reporter's Comments accompanying the various rules do explain, however, why particular approaches to defining rules were taken and why others were rejected.

Two rules of privilege which are found in several jurisdictions are omitted from these rules. One is the privilege for official information; the other is the privilege previously provided by Rule 43 (h) (7), Alaska R. Civ. P., covering evidence tending to degrade the character of a witness. This Comment explains the omissions.

The Wigmore treatise, 8 Wigmore on Evidence § 2378, at 807-08, (J. McNaughton rev. 1961), states that the best collection of arguments in favor of an official information privilege is as follows (quoting Gellhorn & Byse, Administrative Law Cases and Comments 617-18 (4th ed. 1960):

[The discussion relates to the SEC and summarizes that agency's brief in a federal case]. The documents and testimony relating to intra-agency discussions, communications, memoranda, reports, recommendations, positions taken at staff and Commission level with respect to the investigation and possible injunctive or criminal action are protected for the following reasons: (a) Section 6(b) of the Administrative Procedure Act authorizes restrictions upon the delivery of data such as that involved here even to the person who furnished it, and, as stated in the Attorney General's manual on the Administrative Procedure Act in connection with section 3(c) of the Act, "intra-agency memoranda and reports prepared by agency employees for use within the agency are not official records since they merely reflect the research and analysis preliminary to official agency action." (b) The action or non-action of the SEC and other federal agencies with respect to an investigative matter is not subject to direct court review. A fortiori, it cannot be reviewed in a purely private action to which the Commission is not a party through subpoenas and other demands designed to "flush out" the internal deliberations of the Commission concerning an investigative matter. (c) The investigative functions of the Commission are like those of a grand jury and similarly immune from public scrutiny. (d) The "work product" doctrine of Hickman v. Taylor, 329 U.S. 495 (1947), makes these matters immune from compulsory disclosure. (e) The decisional process of the Commission is immune from judicial probing...(f) Much of the information sought is covered by the attorney client privilege. (g) Compulsory disclosure of the information sought would do violence to the philosophy underlying the tripartite nature of our government. The executive branch traditionally has declined to hand over confidential files to other branches when it has been considered contrary to the public interest to do so. (h) Investigative files often contain hearsay, gossip, and other remote information from which the government hopes to develop leads. Public disclosure of such trivia and possible falsehoods might work grave injury and injustice to those involved.

Assuming that similar arguments would be made by state officials and by most government officers and agencies in favor of a privilege, the fact is that these arguments are not convincing. The first argument is that intra-agency memoranda and reports are not official records. This begs the question. Such reports and memoranda may not be legally binding on third persons, but they may be admissible, if relevant, against the agency in litigation. The important thing is that they will rarely be relevant and thus will not often be disclosed under governing discovery rules. The second argument is that since courts cannot control non-action, the court cannot review non-public aspects of agency work. But if non-public aspects of agency work are relevant to a lawsuit, the court is not reviewing the action of the agency under an Administrative Procedure Act; it is deciding a lawsuit which is something that lies within the powers granted the state judiciary under the Alaska Constitution. The third argument is that investigative functions of agencies are like those of a grand jury and are therefore immune from scrutiny. Once again the question is begged and the analogy inappropriate since grand jury proceedings are disclosed under some circumstances. The work product argument fails because the "work product" doctrine can exist in the absence of an absolute privilege. Another argument, that the decisional process of an agency is immune from judicial probing, states a conclusion, not an argument. The opposite conclusion is available also. That much of the information is covered by the attorney-client privilege suggests that another privilege may not be necessary. The next to the last argument is that a government based on separation of powers requires that the judiciary stay its hand when asked to intervene into the internal affairs of an agency. But checks and balances are as real as separation of powers. In fact, the ultimate judicial check of review over agency matters suggests that the agency is not beyond the reach of the courts. Finally, the notion that public disclosure of trivia and possible falsehoods might work grave injury and injustice to members of the community assumes that courts are without power to protect against oppressive disclosure, something which is not true.

It is difficult to see why a government agency should be given a greater privilege than a corporation is given to protect its secrets. Yet, the Model Code of Evidence rule 228 and Uniform Rule 34 (1953) recognized a privilege for official information. Proposed Federal Rule 509 also recognized such a privilege, as do Rule 508, Maine Rules of Evidence (West 1978); Nebraska Rule 509; N.J. Stat. Ann. 2A: 84A-34 (West 1976); Rule 34, Utah Rules of Evidence (1977); and V.I. Code Ann. tit. 5, § 862 (1967) (Virgin Islands). In refusing to recognize an official information privilege, Alaska rules take the view that in the rare case when internal government documents would be relevant to litigation, they should be disclosed. Protective orders under the discovery rules are available to mitigate any unfortunate consequences that might flow from this position. Also, the legislature remains free to enact statutes to protect certain information that may be especially sensitive.

Nothing in these Rules speaks to the various constitutional issues that may arise when a privilege is claimed. For example, these rules do not attempt to decide whether the doctrine of separation of powers implies a constitutionally based executive privilege. *See generally United States v. Nixon,* 418 U.S. 683, 41 L. Ed. 2d 1039 (1974). Nor do these rules discuss constitutionally based claims of legislative privilege. *See generally Gravel v. United States,* 408 U.S. 606, 33 L. Ed. 2d 583 (1972).

The other privilege that is omitted by these rules is the one that would allow a witness to refuse to disclose in any action "any matter that will have a direct tendency to degrade his character" unless the exercise of the privilege would prevent a party from obtaining information relating to a fact in issue or to a fact from which the fact in issue would be presumed. Since Rule 404 is designed to protect against certain embarrassing disclosures, and Rule 608 bars any inquiry into prior bad acts not the subject of a criminal conviction used for impeachment purposes, no privilege is necessary under these Rules. Were it not for these two rules, it might be necessary to add some sort of a privilege to make it clear that the court is to balance the impact of questioning on a witness against the need of a party for evidence, as well as to balance the prejudicial effect of certain evidence on one party against the beneficial effect on another party. While there may be embarrassing details not covered by Rules 404 and 608, they do not seem to present a sufficient danger to warrant the creation of a privilege.

Rule 501 speaks of statutory privileges. Whether any particular privilege is more substantive or procedural need not be decided. The purposes served by most privileges are such that they can be equally well served by the creation of substantive rights by the legislature or procedural rights by the courts. There may be cases in which a determination of their character—*i.e.,* procedural or substantive—will have to be made in order to decide whether article IV, section 15 of the Alaska Constitution has been satisfied (requiring a two-thirds vote of the legislature to supersede rules of practice and procedure promulgated by the Supreme Court). But such cases may never arise and it would be premature to comment upon them in advance.

Rule 501. Privileges Recognized Only As Provided.

This rule codifies the existing law that privileges are not recognized in the absence of statutes or rules specifically providing for them. No attempt is made in these rules to incorporate the constitutional provisions which relate to the admission and exclusion of evidence, whether denominated as privileges or not. Similarly, privileges created by specific statutes generally are not within the scope of these rules. *E.g.,* AS 09.25.150-220 (public officials, reporters); AS 24.55.260 (ombudsman).

Although Federal Rule 501 adopts state created privileges whenever state law governs with respect to any element of a claim of defense, this Rule does not adopt the converse; i.e., except in unusual cases, federal privileges will not govern in Alaska courts even though federal law provides the rule of decision with respect to any element of a claim or defense. Some commentators have suggested that the approach taken by this rule is so plainly correct that explanation is unnecessary. *See, e.g., Hart, The Relations Between State and Federal Law,*

54 Colum. L. Rev. 489, 508 (1954) ("The general rule...is that federal law takes the state courts as it finds them...[S]tate rules...may ordinarily be applied also to federal claims and defense..."; Ladd, *Privileges,* 1969 Law & Social Order 555, 560 ("If the action arose in a state court upon a matter involving a federal question, it would appear impossible to prevent the state court from using state privileges...\m). But, in view of *Dice v. Akron, Canton & Youngstown R.R.,* 342 U.S. 359, 96 L. Ed. 398 (1952), and *Brown v. Western Ry.,* 338 U.S. 294, 94 L. Ed. 100 (1949), a few words are in order.

In the vast majority of federal cases, state law issues are not so intertwined with federal questions that deference to state policies that both govern primary human conduct and possibly affect the outcome of litigation in important ways imposes much of an incremental burden on the judges who must determine state substantive law. Indeed, Congress has not only restricted the power of the Supreme Court to modify state created substantive rights, 28 U.S.C.A. § 2072 (West Cum. Supp. 1978), but has itself demonstrated respect for state law in Rule 501. On the other hand, federal law, especially federal constitutional questions, may arise throughout state litigation. To separate federal and state issues could be an enormous burden on state judges. Federal issues have been decided by state courts from the nation's beginning. There is no indication that the Congress is unhappy with the results. Since state law governs most conduct of most citizens, its rules of privilege are especially important to citizens seeking guidance as to what is and is not privileged. Hence, state privilege law will govern in all litigation in Alaska state courts, unless the supremacy clause of the United States Constitution requires otherwise.

This rule is drawn from proposed federal rule 501. However, it adds language to make clear that *persons* protected by privileges can include organization and government entities.

Despite these rules, claims of privilege at times may have to give way to constitutionally protected rights, especially in criminal cases. *See, e.g., Salazar v. State,* 559 P.2d 66 (Alaska 1976).

On the other hand, claims of privilege themselves may have roots in the Constitution. The attorney-client privilege is not unrelated to the right to counsel guaranteed all citizens in all but the most petty criminal cases. And the marital communications privilege reflects an ideal of privacy and special relationship that has received constitutional protection in other contexts. *See, e.g., Griswold v. Connecticut,* 381 U.S. 479, 14 L.Ed.2d 510 (1965). The communications to clergymen privilege and the political vote privilege are related to first amendment concepts. Recently, the Alaska Supreme Court has suggested that the doctor-patient privilege has constitutional overtones. *See, e.g., Falcon v. Alaska Public Offices Commission,* 570 P.2d 469 (Alaska 1977).

Rule 502. Required Reports Privileged by Statute.

This rule provides that any person, organization, or entity required by law to furnish certain information to the government has a privilege to refuse to disclose the information provided, if such a privilege is provided for by the governing statute. A claim of privilege can be invoked to prevent any person from disclosing the information, and a public officer or agency that receives information may refuse to disclose it if the governing legislation so provides. The rule extends to reports required by the federal government, the State of Alaska, and other states.

In light of Rule 501, Rule 502 is redundant in its reference to the State of Alaska. Rule 501 establishes that privileges can be created by these rules or by enactments of the Alaska legislature. It is therefore clear that even without Rule 502 any privilege provided for by statute would be recognized. *See, e.g.,* AS 28.35.120. Despite the redundancy, Rule 502 serves two purposes not served by Rule 501 in connection with Alaska law. First, it serves to remind the legislature that these rules will not generally provide a privilege in circumstances where the government is requiring a person, organization, or entity to supply information. If a privilege is to be forthcoming, it must be legislatively created. Second, it establishes that no privilege exists in actions for perjury, false statement, and the like.

When the federal government creates a privilege in a statute that requires the submission of reports or records to the government, that privilege must be recognized by the states under the supremacy clause of the United States Constitution. No such clause requires that one state defer to the judgment of another state as to the wisdom of compelling disclosure of certain information. For reasons of comity, however, Rule 502 recognizes the privileges for required reports created by sister states. "[A]n argument can be made that where a document is prepared on order of the state and on the promise of privilege, the privilege should be enforced because but for the promised privilege the document would not have been produced." Weinstein, *The Uniformity-Conformity Dilemma Facing Draftsmen of Federal Rules of Evidence,* 69 Colum. L. Rev. 353, 371 n.80 (1969). The legislative purpose in requiring certain reports—to encourage full and complete disclosure of required information—requires mutual recognition of a required reports privilege among sister states. The last sentence of this rule, which has application to Alaska statutes, has no application to the laws of sister states or the federal government; it makes clear that the privilege is not a license for perjury, that, insofar as the State of Alaska has the power to punish for perjury and related actions, this rule will provide no protection.

It should be plain that the existence and scope of required records, laws and privileges are dependent upon legislative action. The legislature can eliminate any privilege that would exist under this rule.

Rule 503. Lawyer-Client Privilege.

(a) **Definitions.**

(1) The definition of "client" extends the status of client to one consulting a lawyer preliminarily with a view to retaining him, even though actual employment does not result. McCormick (2d ed.) § 88, at 179. The client need not be involved in litigation; the rendition of legal service or advice under any circumstances suffices. 8 Wigmore Evidence § 2294 on (J. McNaughton rev. 1961). The services must be professional legal services; purely business or personal matters do not qualify. McCormick (2d ed.) § 88, at 179-80. Under this subdivision, the term "organization" should be given a broad interpretation. Several words are omitted from the draft of

proposed Federal Rule 503; this is only a matter of style.

(2) The proposed Federal Rules of Evidence as submitted to Congress by the United States Supreme Court did not contain a definition of "representative of the client." Because of uncertainty about the extent of the privilege to be granted to corporate clients, the Advisory Committee came out in favor of a case-by-case analysis. This approach is rejected here. "An ad hoc approach to privilege pursuant to a vague standard achieves the worst of possible worlds: harm in the particular case because information may be concealed; and a lack of compensating long-range benefit because persisting uncertainty about the availability of the privilege will discourage some communications." Note, *Attorney-Client Privilege for Corporate Clients: The Control Group Test,* 84 Harv. L. Rev. 424, 426 (1970). No definition of "representative of the client" will be perfect, but the best approach to corporate privilege developed to date is the "control group" test as adopted in Alaska Rule 503(a) (2). *See City of Philadelphia v. Westinghouse Electric Corp.,* 210 F. Supp. 483, 485 (E.D. Pa. 1962). The "control group" test is admittedly restrictive and has been criticized by some courts. *See, e.g., Harper & Row Publishers, Inc., v. Decker,* 423 F.2d 487, 491-92 (7th Cir. 1970), *aff'd by an equally divided court per curiam,* 400 U.S. 348, 27 L.Ed.2d 433 (1971). However, the restrictive view brings the corporate privilege more in line with the privilege available to unincorporated business concerns. Business organizations should not receive different treatment on evidence questions in courts of law merely because of differences in financial structure.

If, for example, A runs a taxi service as a sole proprietorship with several employees, and one employee driver is involved in an accident for which A is sued, the employee's statements to A's attorney are not within the attorney-client privilege, even though A may order his employee to talk with the lawyer. If A incorporates, the ruling should not change. It should be sufficient that A and other corporate officers having the capacity to seek legal advice and to act on it can claim the benefits of the privilege for private communications with counsel. A more permissive privilege would result in suppression of information conveyed to attorneys by employees who are more like witnesses than clients and who have no personal desire for confidentiality.

(3) A "lawyer" is a person licensed to practice law in any state or nation. There is no requirement that the licensing state or nation recognize the attorney-client privilege, thus avoiding excursions into conflict of laws questions. "Lawyer" also includes a person reasonably believed to be a lawyer. For similar provisions, *see,* Cal. Evid. Code § 950 (West 1966). Administrative practitioners are not lawyers under Rule 503 (a) (3), but may be included as "representatives of the lawyer" under Rule 503(b) (4).

(4) The definition of "representative of the lawyer" recognizes that the lawyer may, in rendering legal services, utilize the services of assistants in addition to those employed in the process of communicating. Thus the definition includes an expert employed to assist in rendering legal advice. It also includes an expert employed to assist in the planning and conduct of litigation, though not one employed to testify as a witness. The definition does not, however, limit "representative of the lawyer" to experts. Whether his compensation is derived immediately from the lawyer or the client is not material.

Rule 503 does not expressly deal with communications from an insured to his insurance company. If the insurance agent to whom the information is forwarded were viewed as a "representative of the lawyer" under Rule 503(a) (4), the privilege would apply. This is the rule in most state courts. *See* McCormick (2d ed.) § 91 at 190. Some federal courts have been unsympathetic to this line of reasoning because of the peculiar nature of the insurance "situation." *See, e.g., Gottlieb v. Bresler,* 24 F.R.D. 371 (D.D.C. 1959). The demand for privilege is greater when there is a close connection between lawyer and agent and they rely upon confidentiality in their relationship. Thus, the result in any particular case may turn on the specific facts involved. However, it is clear that no privilege is available when a statement is being sought in a controversy between the insured, or one claiming under the insured, and the insurance company. McCormick (2d ed.) § 91, at 190-91; Annot., *Privilege of Communications or Reports Between Liability or Indemnity Insurer and Insured,* 22 A.L.R.2d 659 (1952).

(5) The requisite confidentiality of communication is defined in terms of intent. A communication made in public or meant to be relayed to outsiders or which is divulged by the client to third persons can scarcely be considered confidential. *See LaMoore v. United States,* 180 F.2d 49, 9th Cir. (1950); McCormick (2d ed.) § 95. The intent is inferable from the circumstances. Unless intent to disclose is apparent, the attorney-client communication is confidential. Taking or failing to take precautions may be considered as bearing on intent. "Communications which were intended to be confidential but were intercepted despite reasonable precautions remain privileged." *See* Subdivision (b) *infra; see also* J. Weinstein & M. Berger, Weinstein's Evidence, § 503(a) (4) [01] (1979).

Practicality requires that some disclosure be allowed beyond the immediate circle of lawyer-client and their representatives without impairing confidentiality. Hence the definition allows disclosure to persons to whom disclosure is in furtherance of the rendition of professional legal services to the client, contemplating those in such relation to the client as "spouse, parent, business associate, or joint client." Cal. Evid. Code § 952, Comment (West 1966).

(b) **General Rule of Privilege.** This subdivision sets forth the privilege, using the previously defined terms: client, representative of the client, lawyer, representative of the lawyer, and confidential communication. It is in accord with the Alaska rules on the subject that are superseded by this rule: Rule 43(h) (2), Alaska R. Civ. P., and Rule 26(b) (3), Alaska R. Crim. P.

Common law decisions frequently allowed an eavesdropper to testify to overheard privileged conversations and approved admission of intercepted privileged letters. Today the evolution of more sophisticated techniques of eavesdropping and interception calls for abandonment of this position. The rule accordingly adopts a policy of protection against these kinds of invasion of the privilege.

The privilege extends to communications (1) between client or his representative and lawyer or his representative, (2) between lawyer and lawyer's representative, (3) by client or his lawyer to a lawyer representing another in a matter of common interest, (4) between representatives of the client or the client and a representative of the client, and (5) between lawyers representing the client. All these communications must be specifically for the purpose of obtaining legal services for the client; otherwise the privilege does not attach.

When clients represented by different lawyers pursue a "joint defense" or "pool information," subdivision (b) (3) provides that each client has a privilege as to his own statements, but that any client wishing to disclose his own statements made at the joint conference may do so.

When there is no common interest to be promoted by a joint consultation, the Rule does not apply. *Compare,* this subdivision to subdivision (d) (5). The privilege is waived by the client if he or she raises an issue whose resolution requires disclosure of otherwise confidential communications. *Lewis v. State,* 565 P.2d 846, 850 n.4 (Alaska 1977).

(c) **Who May Claim the Privilege.** The privilege is, of course, that of the client, to be claimed by him or by his personal representative. The successor of a dissolved corporate client may claim the privilege. N.J. Stat. Ann. § 2A:84A-20(1) (West 1976).

The lawyer may not claim the privilege on his own behalf. However, he may claim it on behalf of the client. It is assumed that the ethics of the profession will require him to do so except under most unusual circumstances. American Bar Association Code of Professional Responsibility, Canon 4. His authority to make the claim is presumed unless there is evidence to the contrary, as would be the case if the client were now a party to litigation in which the question arose and were represented by other counsel.

(d) **Exceptions.** In general this subdivision incorporates well established exceptions.

(1) *Furtherance of Crime or Fraud.* The privilege does not extend to advice in aid of future wrongdoing. 8 Wigmore § 2298. *See United Services Automobile Association v. Werley,* 526 P.2d 28 (Alaska 1974). The wrongdoing need not be that of the client. The provision that the client knew or reasonably should have known of the criminal or fraudulent nature of the act is designed to protect the client who is erroneously advised that a proposed action is within the law. No preliminary finding that sufficient evidence aside from the communication has been introduced to warrant a finding that the services were sought to enable the commission of a wrong is required. While any general exploration of what transpired between attorney and client would, of course, be inappropriate, it is sometimes feasible, either at the discovery stage or during trial, so to focus the inquiry by specific questions as to avoid any broad inquiry into attorney-client communications. In some cases it will not be possible to probe without substantially invading the privileged area. When these cases arise, the court may require that a prima facie case of wrongdoing be established by independent evidence before the privilege is denied. Even where the perimeter of the privileged relationship can be analyzed without probing too deeply into confidential communications, such analysis will not be necessary if independent evidence of wrongdoing is available.

The words "or used" are added to the proposed federal version of the rule to cover the case of the client who decides to use legal advice for an improper purpose, when he knew or should have known he was committing a crime or fraud.

(2) *Claimants Through Same Deceased Client.* Normally the privilege survives the death of the client and may be asserted by his representative. *See* Subdivision (c) *supra.* When, however, the identity of the person who steps into the client's shoes is in issue, as in a will contest, the identity of the person entitled to claim the privilege remains undetermined until the conclusion of the litigation. The choice is thus between allowing both sides or neither to assert the privilege, with authority and reason favoring the latter view. McCormick (2d ed.) § 94 Uniform Rule of Evidence 502(d) (2) (1974); Cal. Evid. Code § 957 (West 1966); Kan. Cir. Pro. Stat. Ann. § 60426 (b) (2) (1976); N.J. Stat. Ann. § 2A:84A-20(2) (b) (West 1976).

(3) *Breach of Duty by Lawyer or Client.* The exception is required by considerations of fairness and policy when questions arise out of dealings between attorney and client, as in cases of controversy over attorney's fees, claims of inadequacy of representation, or charges of professional misconduct. McCormick (2d ed.) § 91; Uniform Rule of Evidence 502(d) (3) (1974); Cal. Evid. Code § 958 (West 1966); Kan. Civ. Pro. Stat. Ann. § 60-426 (b) (3) (1976); N.J. Stat. Ann. § 2A:84A20 (2) (c) (West 1976).

(4) *Document Attested by Lawyer.* When the lawyer acts as attesting witness, the approval of the client to his so doing may safely be assumed, and waiver of the privilege as to any relevant lawyer-client communications is a proper result. McCormick (2d ed.) § 80, at 180; Uniform Rule of Evidence 502(d) (4) (1974); Cal. Evid. Code § 959 (West 1966); Kan. Civ. Pro. Stat. Ann. § 60-426 (b) (4) (1976).

(5) *Joint Clients.* The subdivision states existing law. McCormick (2d ed.) § 91, at 189-190. For similar provisions, see Uniform Rule of Evidence 502(d) (5) (1974); Cal. Evid. Code § 962 (West 1966); Kan. Civ. Pro. Stat. Ann. § 60-426(b) (5) (1976); N.J. Stat. Ann. § 2A:84A-20(2) (West 1976). The situation with which this provision deals is to be distinguished from the case of clients with a common interest who retain different lawyers. *See* subdivision (b) (3) of this rule *supra.*

Rule 504. Physician and Psychotherapist—Patient Privilege.

(a) **Definitions.**

(1) "Patient" means a person who consults a physician for the purpose of diagnosis or treatment.

There seems to be little reason to perpetuate the distinction made between consultations for the purpose of diagnosis and consultations for the purpose of treatment. Persons do not ordinarily consult physicians from idle curiosity. They may be sent by their attorney to obtain a diagnosis in contemplation of some legal proceeding—in which case the attorney-client privilege will afford protection. They may submit to an examination for insurance purposes—in which case the insurance contract will contain appropriate waiver provisions. They may seek diagnosis from one physician to check the diagnosis made by another. They may seek diagnosis from one physician in contemplation of seeking treatment from another. Communications made under such circumstances are as deserving of protection as are communications made to a treating physician. *See* Cal. Evid. Code § 991 (West 1966).

The definition of "patient" does not include a person submitting to examination for scientific purposes.

(2) The definition of "physician" is extended to include not only a licensed physician, but a person who the patient has reasonable grounds to believe is a physician, a psychotherapist or psychologist. The patient should be protected from reasonable mistakes as to unlicensed practitioners. The burden is placed on the patient to satisfy the court that he in fact had reasonable grounds to believe that the person he made the communication to or disclosed information to was a physician before the patient can invoke the privilege.

The privilege also should be applicable to communications made to a physician authorized to practice in any state or nation. When an Alaska resident travels outside the state and has occasion to visit a physician during such travel, or when a physician from another state or nation participates in the treatment of a person in Alaska, the patient should be entitled to assume that his communications will be given as much protection as they would be if he consulted an Alaska physician in Alaska. A patient should not be forced to inquire about the jurisdictions where the physician is authorized to practice medicine and whether such jurisdictions recognize the physician-patient privilege before he may safely communicate with the physician.

(3) The definition of psychotherapist embraces a medical doctor while engaged in the diagnosis or treatment of mental or emotional conditions, including alcohol and drug addiction, in order not to exclude the general practitioner and to avoid the making of needless refined distinctions concerning what is and what is not the practice of psychiatry.

Medical doctors are generally covered under the definition in (2) above. When treating mental or emotional conditions, medical doctors are included under the definition of "psychotherapist" for purposes of the criminal proceeding exception. *See* subdivision (d) (7) *infra.*

A psychotherapist-patient privilege was recognized in *Allred v. State,* 554 P.2d 411 (Alaska 1976), although the supreme court divided on the source of the privilege and its scope. Since the court has power under the Alaska Constitution to create testimonial privileges, the source of power to create Rule 504 is beyond question. Defining the proper scope presents greater difficulty, however. While it is impossible to fashion a perfect rule because we will never know exactly how much of a return we get from a privilege—e.g., how much better is psychiatric care because of the privilege—and because we cannot be certain of either the optimal return or the marginal return for any expansion of a privilege, it is both necessary and practicable to establish a scope that appears to be as consistent as possible with the aims of the privilege.

Because the psychotherapist-patient privilege is designed to encourage those with mental or emotional problems to seek help, Rule 504(a) (3) provides that the privilege will attach if a patient sees someone reasonably believed by the patient to be licensed to practice medicine. Given the facts that Allred asked to see either one of two persons and that he apparently knew that one of them was a psychiatrist, it is probable that he believed that the person with whom he spoke was also licensed to practice medicine. If Allred was asking for psychiatric help, his communications would have been protected under the views of all members of the court. In fact Rule 504 (a) (3) satisfies both the concerns of the two members of the court who wished to prevent the privilege from attaching to all counseling and the two members of the court who wished to ensure that the patient who relies upon an apparent confidential relationship is not disappointed. Moreover, the social worker might have qualified under Rule 504 (a) (4) as a person reasonably necessary for the transmission of information, depending on the precise facts, without threatening the competing interest identified in the various opinions in *Allred.*

Because this rule focuses on the reasonable belief of the patient, it assumes throughout that the patient is capable of making the necessary choices to create and destroy the privilege. The question whether there are instances in which fairness requires a recognition of a right in the psychotherapist to claim the privilege for a patient who is not inclined to seek the benefits of non-disclosure is left for adjudication. See *Allred v. State,* 554 P.2d 411, 428 (Alaska 1976) (Dimond, J., concurring).

(4) Confidential communication is defined in terms conformable with those of the lawyer-client privilege, Rule 503 (a) (5), with changes appropriate to the difference in circumstance. *See* Reporter's Comment to Rule 503 (a) (5). In addition, Rule 504(a) (4) treats as confidential communications made to the physician or psychotherapist in the presence of those "who are participating in the diagnosis and treatment under the direction of the physician or psychotherapist, including members of the patient's family." "Communications from members of the family...should be given broad protection...because effective treatment presupposes family participation." 2 Weinstein's *Evidence* § 504[05]. *See Falcon v. Alaska Public Offices Commission,* 570 P.2d 469 (Alaska 1977).

Participants in group therapy programs in the presence of a psychotherapist may be covered under the definition of "confidential communication." *See Cross, Privileged Communications Between Participants in Group Psychotherapy,* 1970 L. & Soc. Order 191.

(b) and (c) **General Rule of Privilege—Who May Claim the Privilege.** The phrasing of the general rule of privilege and the determination of those who may claim it draws heavily upon the attorney-client privilege rule. *See* Rule 503(b) & (c). Rule 504 supersedes the physician-patient privilege of Rule 43(h) (4), Alaska Rules of Civil Procedure. For a related provision, see AS 08.86.200 (confidential communications to psychologists).

(d) **Exceptions.**

(1) *Condition or Element of Claim or Defense.* The patient-litigant exception provides that the physician-patient privilege does not exist in any proceeding in which an issue concerning the condition of the patient has been tendered by the patient. If the patient himself tenders the issue of his condition, he should not be able to withhold relevant evidence from the opposing party by the exercise of the physician-patient

privilege. By injecting his condition into litigation, the patient must be said to waive the privilege, in fairness and to avoid abuses. *See Mathis v. Kilderbrand,* 416 P.2d 8 (Alaska 1966); *Trans-World Investments v. Drobny,* 554 P.2d 1148 (Alaska 1976). Those who claim through the patient stand in the patient's shoes for purposes of this Rule. After the patient's death, the policies of confidentiality give way to a party's need for information and any party may place the condition of a deceased patient in issue and obtain the benefits of the exception. Only information relevant to the patient's condition should be disclosed under this exception. *See Arctic Motor Freight Inc. v. Stover,* 571 P.2d 1006 (Alaska 1977).

(2) *Crime or Fraud.* The crime or fraud exception corresponds to, but is broader than, the similar provision under attorney-client privilege. *See* Rule 503(d) (1) and Reporter's Comment.

(3) *Breach of Duty Arising Out of Physician-Patient Relationship.* The breach of duty exception also corresponds to a similar attorney-client privilege provision. *See* Rule 503(d) (3) and Reporter's Comment.

(4) *Proceedings for Hospitalization.* The interests of both patient and public call for a departure from confidentiality in commitment proceedings. Since disclosure is authorized only when the physician or psychotherapist determines that hospitalization is needed, control over disclosure is placed largely in the hands of a person in whom the patient has already manifested confidence. Hence damage to the relationship is unlikely. Usually, this exception will rise in psychotherapist-patient situations. Court-ordered appointments are treated in subdivision (d) (6) *infra.*

(5) *Required Report.* The required report exception enables a physician or psychotherapist to testify as to the contents of reports required by statute or administrative rule to be made to public officials. No valid purpose is served by preventing the use of relevant information when the law or rule requiring the information to be reported to a public office does not restrict disclosure.

(6) *Examination by Order of Judge.* In a court ordered examination, the relationship is likely to be an arm's length one, though not necessarily so. In any event, an exception is necessary for the effective utilization of this important and growing procedure. When the psychotherapist is appointed by the court, it is most often for the purpose of having the psychotherapist testify concerning his conclusions as to the patient's condition. It would be inappropriate to have the privilege apply in this situation. The exception, it will be observed, deals with a court ordered examination rather than with a court appointed physician or psychotherapist. Also, the exception is effective only with respect to the particular purpose for which the examination is ordered. The final sentence of the exception provides that an accused in a criminal case may have the benefits of private counseling with a psychotherapist. Of course, if the accused does place mental condition in issue, exception (1) will govern.

(7) *Criminal Proceeding.* Under the superseded Alaska Rules of Court concerning privileges (Rule 43(h), Alaska R. Civ. P., and Rule 26(b), Alaska R. Crim. P.), a physician-patient privilege was recognized in civil cases (Civil Rule 43 (h) (4)), but not in criminal cases. This distinction is followed here. However, the psychotherapist-patient relationship, with its more compelling need for confidential communication, demands that the privilege apply to criminal proceedings as well as civil cases, *see Schade v. State,* 512 P.2d 907, (Alaska 1973), although exception (6) will govern some aspects of the use of psychotherapists in criminal cases. Rule 13, Alaska R. Children's P., governs juvenile proceedings.

Rule 505. Husband-Wife Privileges.

Evidence Rule 505 has been substantially revised since this commentary was first published.

In most states the marital relationship gives rise to two distinct privileges. One, the spousal immunity privilege, enables a party to bar a current spouse from testifying against that party. The other, the privilege for marital communications, protects confidential communications made to one's spouse during the course of a marriage. Although the Proposed Federal Rule of Evidence dealing with Husband-Wife privilege (PFRE 505) adopted only the spousal immunity privilege, Rule 43(h) (1), Alaska R. Civ. P., and Rule 26(b) (2), Alaska R. Crim. P., both superseded by this Rule, recognized both privileges. This Rule makes no change in the basic state of the law. Both marital privileges are recognized in civil and criminal cases.

(a) **Spousal Immunity.**

(1) *Spouse Immunity.* The spousal immunity privilege belongs to the party spouse. *See Hawkins v. United States,* 358 U.S. 74, 3 L.Ed.2d 125 (1958). If the party fails to object to a spouse being called to testify, the party waives any right to object to any portion of the testimony on the ground of spousal immunity.

Spousal immunity applies only to testimony by a spouse. If the marriage is a sham or has been terminated by divorce, annulment, or death, there is no privilege. *See* AS 25.05.011–25.05.391.

(2) *Exceptions.*

(A) This is a standard exception in modern statutes. Model Code of Evidence rule 216 (1942); Cal. Evid. Code § 984 (West). "[H]usband and wife, while they would desire that their confidences be shielded from the outside world, would ordinarily anticipate that if a controversy between themselves should arise in which their mutual conversations would shed light on the merits, the interests of both would be served by full disclosure." McCormick (2d ed.) § 84, at 171. This exception covers custody battles.

(B) and (C). Commitment and competency proceedings are undertaken for the benefit of the subject person. Frequently, much or all of the evidence bearing on a spouse's competency or lack of competency will consist of communications to the other spouse. It would be undesirable to permit either spouse to invoke a privilege to prevent the presentation of this vital information inasmuch as these proceedings are of such vital importance both to society and to the spouse who is the subject of the proceedings. *See* Cal. Evid. Code §§ 982 and 983 (West); Rule 504(d) (4) *supra.*

(D) The need of limitation upon the privilege in order to avoid grave injustice in cases of offenses against the other spouse or child of either can scarcely be denied. The rule therefore disallows any privilege against spousal testimony in these cases. See Proposed Federal Rule of Evidence 505 (c) (1); 8 Wigmore § 2239; Model Code of Evidence rule 216 (1942). For relevant Alaska law see AS 25.25.230 (pimping) and 11.40.430 (non-support). Subdivision (a) (2) (D) (iii) is not limited to natural or adoptive children of the spouse. Subdivision (a) (2) (D) (iv) is directed at the case where the defendant marries the prosecution's star witness to prevent him or her from testifying.

(E) In custody cases under subdivision (a)(2)(E), the spouse is treated as if they were opposing parties.

(F) In business cases under subdivision (a) (2) (F), the need for third parties to have information outweighs the spouse's need for protection, especially about non-personal, commercial matters.

(b) **Confidential Marital Communications.**

(1) *General Rule.* Under this subdivision, both spouses are the holders of the privilege and either spouse may claim it. *See* Cal. Evid. Code § 980 (West); superseded Alaska R. Crim. P. 26(b) (2) and R. Civ. P. 43(h) (1); *cf.* 8 Wigmore § 2340. A guardian of an incompetent spouse may claim the privilege on behalf of that spouse. However, when a spouse is dead, no one can claim the privilege for him; the privilege, if it is to be claimed at all, can be claimed only by or on behalf of the surviving spouse. *See Comment, Cal.* Evid. Code § 980 (West).

The concept of "confidential communication" is analogous to a similar concept used in lawyer-client and physician/psychotherapist-patient privileges (Rule 503(a) (5) and 504(a) (4)). Thus, the intent of the communicator plays a key role. Communications between spouses made during the marriage outside the presence of third persons are presumptively confidential.

(2) *Exceptions.*

(A) All of the exceptions under the spousal immunity privilege apply to the confidential marital communications privilege.

(B) This exception is applied to all confidential communication privileges. See Rule 503(d) (1) and 504(d) (2); Model Code of Evidence Rule 217 (1942). In many cases, the evidence which would be admissible under this exception will be vital in order to do justice between the parties to a lawsuit. *See Comment,* Cal. Evid. Code § 981 (West). The importance of protecting the marriage explains why this exception is confined to subdivision (b).

This exception does not permit disclosure of communications that merely reveal a plan to commit a crime or fraud; it permits disclosure only of communications made to *enable or aid* anyone to commit or plan to commit a crime or fraud.

(C) Both the surviving spouse and the competing claimant are attempting to vindicate claims through the deceased spouse. Since the competing claimant urges that the deceased spouse had an intent regarding transfer of property different from that being urged by the surviving spouse, the case is treated as a dispute between the spouses and the privilege disappears.

(D) When a married person is the defendant in a criminal proceeding and seeks to introduce evidence which is material to his defense, his spouse (or his former spouse) should not be privileged to withhold the information. *See,* Model Code of Evidence rule 216 (1942); Cal. Evid. Code § 987 (West). "It is plain that *where an accused spouse needs the evidence of* communications (by either spouse to the other), the privilege should cease or a cruel injustice may be done." 8 Wigmore § 2338 (emphasis in original).

(E) Alaska's Children's Rules are designed to secure for each child the same care, correction and guidance that he should receive from his parents. (Rule 1(c)). The interests of the child and of society require that parental confidences bow to the need of juvenile court judges for full information concerning the activities and problems of the child, and his relationship with his parents together with the parents' relationship with each other.

(F) In order to avoid the unfairness of spouses doing business together and then invoking the husband-wife privilege to prevent an inquiry into the business relationship, exception (F) provides that a communication is not confidential if it is made in the context of an agency relationship between the spouses, or in the context of any primarily business and nonmarital relationship. This is a special application of the principle that spouses who do not intend their communications to remain private cannot claim the privilege. Once spouses enter into business relationships with third parties, the Rule presumes that they do not intend that the third parties will be excluded from inquiring about the business arrangements of the spouses as they affect the third party's interests.

It should also be noted that at times privilege rules may have to give way to confrontation rights. *See, e.g., Salazar v. State,* 559 P.2d 66 (Alaska 1976).

Rule 506. Communications to Clergymen.

The considerations which dictate the recognition of privileges generally seem strongly to favor a privilege for confidential communications to clergymen. During the period when most of the common law privileges were taking shape, no clear-cut privilege for communications between priest and penitent emerged. 8 Wigmore § 2394. The English political climate of the time may well furnish the explanation. In this country, however, the privilege has been recognized by statute in about two-thirds of the states and occasionally by the common law process of decision.

(a) **Definitions.** Paragraph (1) defines a clergyman as a "minister, priest, rabbi, or other similar functionary of a religious organization." This concept is not so broad, however, to include all self-denominated "ministers." A fair construction of the language requires that the person to whom the status is sought to be attached be regularly engaged in activities conforming at least in a general way with those of a Catholic Priest, Jewish rabbi, or minister of an established Protestant denomination, though not necessarily on a full-time basis. No further specification seems possible in view of the lack of licensing and certification procedures for clergymen. However, this lack seems to have occasioned no particular difficulties in connection with the solemnization of marriages, which suggests that none may be anticipated here. For similar definitions of "Clergyman" see Cal. Evid. Code § 1030 (West); N.J. Rev. Stat. or Stat Ann. (West) § 29.

The "reasonable belief" provision finds support in similar provisions for lawyer-client in Rule 503 and for physician and psychotherapist-patient in Rule 504. A parallel is also found in the recognition of the validity of marriages performed by unauthorized persons if the parties reasonably believed them legally qualified.

(2) The definition of "confidential" communication is consistent with the use of the term in Rule 503(a) (5) for lawyer-client and in Rule 504(a) (4) for physician and psychotherapist-patient, suitably adapted to communications to clergymen.

(b) **General Rule of Privilege.** The choice between a privilege narrowly restricted to doctrinally required confessions and a privilege broadly applicable to all confidential communications with a clergyman in his professional character as spiritual adviser has been exercised in favor of the latter. Many clergymen now receive training in marriage counseling and the handling of personality problems. Matters of this kind fall readily into the realm of the spirit. The same considerations which underlie the physician and psychotherapist-patient privilege of Rule 504 suggest a broad application of the privilege for communications to clergymen. This is a departure from the concept of "confession" as employed in two Alaska Rules of Court, Civil Rule 43(h) (3) and Criminal Rule 26(b) (4), which are superseded by this Rule. The broader privilege is more in line with current trends. *See, e.g.,* Rule 504 *supra;* Maine Rules of Evidence, § 506; Neb. Rev. Stat. §§ 27-506; and Wisc. Stat. § 905.06. It recognizes that the need for a private enclave for spiritual counseling is not confined to those whose religion requires confession, but extends to all who attempt to lead righteous lives with the aid and comfort of their religion and religious advisers.

Under the privilege as phrased, the communicating person is entitled to prevent disclosure not only by himself but also by the clergyman and by eavesdroppers.

The nature of what may reasonably be considered spiritual advice makes it unnecessary to include in the rule a specific exception for communications in furtherance of crime or fraud, as in Rule 503(d) (1).

(c) **Who May Claim the Privilege.** This subdivision makes clear that the privilege belongs to the communicating person. However, a prima facie authority on the part of the clergyman to claim the privilege on behalf of the person is recognized. The discipline of the particular church and the discreetness of the clergyman are believed to constitute sufficient safeguards for the absent communicating person.

Rule 507. Political Vote.

Every person has a privilege to refuse to disclose the tenor of his vote at a political election conducted by secret ballot unless the vote was cast illegally.

Secrecy in voting is an essential aspect of effective democratic government, insuring free exercise of the franchise and fairness in elections. Secrecy after the ballot has been cast is as essential as secrecy in the act of voting. Nutting, *Freedom of Silence: Constitutional Protection Against Governmental Intrusion in Political Affairs,* 47 Mich. L. Rev. 181, 191 (1948). Consequently a privilege has long been recognized on the part of a voter to decline to disclose how he voted. Required disclosure would be the exercise of "a kind of inquisitorial power unknown to the principles of our government and constitution, and might be highly injurious to the suffrages of a free people, as well as tending to create cabals and disturbances between contending parties in popular elections." *Johnson v. Charleston,* 1 Bay 441, 442 (S.C. Sup. Ct. 1795).

The exception for illegally cast votes is a common one under both statutes and case law, Nutting, supra, at 192; 8 Wigmore § 2214, at 163. The policy considerations which underlie the privilege are not applicable to the illegal voter. However, nothing in the exception purports to foreclose an illegal voter from invoking the privilege against self-incrimination under appropriate circumstances.

For similar provisions, see Uniform Rule of Evidence 31; Cal. Evid. Code § 1050 (West); Kan. Civ. Pro. Stat. Ann. §§ 60-431 (Vernon); New Jersey Evidence Rule 31.

Rule 508. Trade Secrets.

The trade secret privilege "fosters the public interest by encouraging technological advancement, encouraging innovativeness in business methods, and facilitating freedom of employment by assuring an employer that a former employee cannot reveal secrets to a competitor." 2 J. Weinstein & M. Berger, Weinstein's Evidence Paragraph 508 [02] (1979). Nevertheless, there are dangers in the recognition of such a privilege. Disclosure of the matters protected by the privilege may be essential to disclose unfair competition or fraud or to reveal the improper use of dangerous materials by the party asserting the privilege. Therefore, the privilege exists under this Rule only if its application will not tend to conceal fraud or otherwise work injustice. *See Comment,* Cal. Evid. Code § 1060 (West).

The term "trade secret" is not defined by this rule. By definition it is limited to knowledge, skill or the like relating to a trade or business — kept confidential by the trade or business for purposes of obtaining or retaining a competitive advantage. One useful definition of a "trade secret" describes it as

> "any formula, pattern, device or compilation of information which is used in one's business and which gives [the holder] an opportunity to obtain an advantage over competitors who do not know or use it."

4 Restatement of Torts § 757, Comment b at 5 (1939). Such definitions present a danger that the privilege will be confined too narrowly, whereas "both policy and logic suggest a broad concept including all business data which gives a better competitive position and whose value is substantially enhanced by secrecy." 2 J. Weinstein & M. Berger, Weinstein's Evidence ¶ 508[03] (1979). *See also* 8 Wigmore § 2212(3). It must always be kept in mind however, that this privilege is not absolute; whenever any injustice will result from its innovation, the privilege will not be recognized.

In many commercial cases, the need for the trade secret will be obvious and the key issue will not be whether the information will be disclosed but under what conditions. "The most common technique is to take testimony in camera with perhaps a requirement for sealed records. This preserves secrecy while allowing the court to reach a decision on all the facts. Other methods involve appointing a master to determine the relevancy of the trade secret to the issues of the case and the degree of disclosure necessary, appointing an independent expert, revealing the trade secret only to the judge or trial examiner, omitting the trade secret from the record of the case, and disclosing to the opposing party's attorney but not to his client." 2 J. Weinstein & M. Berger, Weinstein's Evidence Paragraph 508[03] (1979) (footnotes omitted). The choice of which protective device (or combination of devices) to use lies with the trial court.

Usually, the problem of trade secrets will first arise during the pre-trial discovery stage. The pertinent discovery rule is Rule 26(c) of the Alaska Rules of Civil Procedure, which allows the court to issue a protective order " . . . . to protect a party or person from annoyance, embarrassment, oppression, or undue burden or expense, including one or more of the following: ... (7) that a trade secret or other confidential research, development, or commercial information not be disclosed or be disclosed only in a designated way..." The language of Rule 508 was deliberately chosen to be congruent with Rule 26(c) (7). While the instant evidence rule extends the underlying policy of the discovery rule into the trial, the difference in circumstances between the discovery stage and trial may well be such as to require a different ruling at the trial.

Rule 509. Identity of Informer.

The rule recognizes the use of informers as an important aspect of law enforcement, whether the informer is a citizen who steps forward with information or a paid undercover agent. In either event, the basic importance of anonymity in the effective use of informers is apparent, and the privilege of withholding their identity was well established at common law. McCormick (2d ed.) § 111; 8 Wigmore § 2374.

(a) **Rule of Privilege.** The public interest in law enforcement requires that the privilege be that of the government rather than that of the witness. The rule blankets in as an informer anyone who tells a law enforcement officer about a violation of law without regard to whether the officer is one charged with enforcing the particular law. The Rule also applies to disclosures to legislative investigating committees and their staffs, and is sufficiently broad to include continuing investigations.

Although the tradition of protecting the identity of informers has evolved in an essentially criminal setting, noncriminal law enforcement situations involving possibilities of reprisal against informers fall within the purview of the considerations out of which the privilege originated.

Only identity is privileged; communications are not included except to the extent that disclosure would operate also to disclose the informer's identity. The common law was to the same effect, 8 Wigmore § 2374.

The rule does not deal with the question of when access to presentence reports made under Alaska Rule of Criminal Procedure 32(c) should be denied an accused.

(b) **Who May Claim.** The privilege may be claimed only by the public entity to which the information was furnished by the informer. Thus, a state representative may not claim this privilege if the informer has dealt solely with federal officers. The informant depends for protection upon the government with which he deals directly; if the government refuses to protect him, no other government can safeguard his identity. In situations of joint enforcement by different public entities, all of those that dealt directly with the informant may claim the informer's privilege to protect their information source.

Normally the "appropriate representative" to make the claim will be government counsel. However, it is possible that disclosure of the informer's identity will be sought in proceedings to which the government entity with the power to claim a privilege is not a party. Under these circumstances effective implementation of the privilege requires that other representatives be considered "appropriate."

(c) **Exceptions.** This section deals with situations in which the informer privilege either does not apply or is curtailed.

(1) *Voluntary Disclosure—Informer a Witness.* If the identity of the informer is disclosed, nothing further is to be gained from efforts to suppress it. Disclosure may be direct, or the same practical effect may result from action revealing the informer's interest in the subject matter. While allowing the privilege in effect to be waived by one not its holder, *i.e.,* the informer himself, is something of a novelty in the law of privilege, if the informer chooses to reveal his identity further efforts to suppress it are scarcely feasible. *See* 8 Wigmore § 2274(2).

The exception is limited to disclosure to "those who would have cause to resent the communication," in the language of *Roviaro v. United States,* 353 U.S. 53, 60, 1 L.Ed.2d 639, 644645 (1957), since the disclosure otherwise, e.g., to another law enforcement agency, is not calculated to undercut the objects of the privilege.

If the informer becomes a witness for the government, the interests of justice in disclosing his status as a source of bias or possible support are believed to outweigh any remnant of interest in nondisclosure which then remains. The purpose of the limitation to witnesses for the government is to avoid the possibility of the defendant's calling persons as witnesses as a means of discovering whether they are informers.

(2) and (3) *Testimony on Merits—Legality of Obtaining Evidence.* This exception and the following one are drafted to accomplish the same things that the United States Supreme Court hoped to accomplish when it approved proposed federal rule 510. But language of the proposed Federal Rule was heavily criticized by the Committee on the Rules appointed by the Alaska Supreme Court and by various persons contacted for comments by the Committee. Thus, the problem areas, this exception and the next, have been completely reworked.

Both exceptions provide that an initial opportunity to be heard on a claim of privilege will be granted the parties in civil and criminal cases, and that this opportunity will be with counsel present. There is a point under both exceptions at which the trial judge considers a submission by the government outside the presence of the parties and their counsel. The idea of the exceptions is to provide judicial screening of privilege claims without destroying the utility of the privilege.

Both exceptions specify the procedures to be followed by the trial judge, the standards to be used in judging the privilege claims, and the manner in which the record is to be preserved for appeal.

The informer privilege, it was held by the leading case, may not be used in a criminal prosecution to suppress the identity of a witness when the public interest in protecting the flow of information is outweighed by the individual's right to prepare his defense. *Roviaro v. United States, supra.* The Rule extends this balancing to include civil as well as criminal cases and phrases it in terms of a reasonable possibility that the informer may be able to give testimony necessary to a fair determination of the issue of guilt or innocence in a criminal case or of a material issue on the merits in a civil case. Once the privilege is invoked a procedure is provided for determining whether the informer can in fact supply testimony of such nature as to require disclosure of his identity, thus avoiding a "judicial guessing game" on the question. An investigation *in camera* is calculated to accommodate the conflicting interests involved. The rule also spells out specifically the consequences of a successful claim of privilege in a criminal case when the informant has information that might reasonably help the defendant on the merits. The wider range of possible harm to the non-government party demands more flexibility in criminal cases when the informant has nothing to add on the merits and in civil cases. *Cf.* Alaska R. Civ. P. 37. It should be noted that exception (3) does not speak of a remedy for nondisclosure, since the remedy is obvious; *i.e.,* granting the motion to suppress the evidence.

Obviously, the defendant will always have an argument that it is impossible for the trial judge to foresee all "reasonable possibilities" that an informant can provide testimony helpful to the defense. *Cf., Alderman v. United States,* 394 U.S. 165, 22 L.Ed.2d 176 (1969). But acceptance of this argument would mean that the identity of many informants who would offer no help to the defense would be revealed to insure that those few who might be helpful do not go undetected. The counterargument begins with the premise underlying the informer's privilege, which is that a grave danger may exist when an informant is identified. This danger requires that many informants who might face no real danger be protected to insure that those actually in danger are protected, and it suggests that the defendant should bear a burden of showing that an informant would be helpful to the defense before identity is revealed. While the rule rejects both arguments it errs on the side of the defendant by providing that reasonable doubts as to the utility to the defense of an informant's testimony be decided in favor of exposing the informant. *See United States v. Jackson,* 442 F.2d 975 (6th Cir. 1970); *United States v. Lloyd,* 400 F.2d 414 (6th Cir. 1968). Since the *in camera* procedure takes place after some showing is made that an informant might be able to supply testimony relating to the merits, it is to be expected that trial judges will require the government to show by affidavit or otherwise exactly what the informant knows about the case.

Although Rule 509 extends to all civil and criminal cases, there is no reason to suppose that the government will attempt to invoke the privilege improperly in circumstances where an informant is not threatened by exposure. The rule recognizes that it is the informant's perception of danger that often leads the government to protect identity. To assure cooperation, the government reasonably may assuage unreasonable fears as long as it obtains no advantage in litigation in doing so. Moreover, it will be to the government's advantage in many cases to bring forth all witnesses, including informants, who have favorable testimony to offer, since this maximizes the government's chances of prevailing.

One of the acute conflicts between the interest of the public in nondisclosure and the avoidance of unfairness to the accused as a result of nondisclosure arises when information from an informer is relied upon to legitimate a search and seizure by furnishing probable cause for an arrest without a warrant or for the issuance of a warrant for arrest or search.

The Supreme Court has held that an informant's identity need not be revealed if the only information the informant can supply relates to probable cause for an arrest. *McCray v. Illinois,* 386 U.S. 300, 18 L.Ed.2d 62 (1967). This Rule recognizes the wisdom of compelling disclosure to the court when the government's proof of the circumstances under which evidence was obtained fails to satisfy the court that the government's conduct conformed to law. In light of the policy of the rule to protect an informant who has "fingered" a defendant, the rule provides for disclosure *in camera* to accommodate the conflicting interests. The limited disclosure to the judge avoids any significant impairment of secrecy, while affording the accused a substantial measure of protection against arbitrary police action.

Government counsel should bear in mind that the duty to disclose exculpatory evidence to a criminal defendant is not affected by this Rule.

Rule 510. Waiver of Privilege by Voluntary Disclosure.

The central purpose of most privileges is the promotion of some interest or relationship by endowing it with a supporting secrecy or confidentiality. It is evident that the privilege should terminate when the holder by his own act destroys this confidentiality. McCormick (2d ed.) §§ 83, 93, 103; 8 Wigmore §§ 2242, 2327-2329, 2374, 2389-2390. Rule 510 codifies standard practice in acknowledging that a privilege can be waived. It follows the approach of Rule 231 of the Model Code of Evidence, Rule 37 of the Uniform Rules of Evidence, and section 912 of the California Evidence Code (West). *See* 2 J. Weinstein & M. Berger, Weinstein's Evidence Paragraph 511[02] (1979).

The rule is designed to be read with a view to what it is that the particular privilege protects. For example, the lawyer-client privilege covers only communications, and the fact that a client has discussed a matter with his lawyer does not insulate the client against disclosure of the subject matter discussed, although he is privileged not to disclose the discussion itself. *See* McCormick (2d ed.) § 93. The waiver here provided for is similarly restricted. Therefore a client, merely by disclosing a subject which he had discussed with his attorney, would not waive the applicable privilege; he would have to make disclosure of the communication itself in order to effect a waiver.

By traditional doctrine, waiver is the intentional relinquishment of a known right. However, in the confidential privilege situations, once confidentiality is destroyed through voluntary disclosure no subsequent claim of privilege can restore it, and knowledge or lack of knowledge of the existence of the privilege appears to be irrelevant. 8 Wigmore § 2327.

Rule 511. Privileged Matter Disclosed Under Compulsion or Without Opportunity to Claim Privilege.

Ordinarily a privilege is invoked in order to forestall disclosure. However, under some circumstances consideration must be given to the status and effect of a disclosure already made. Rule 510, immediately preceding, gives voluntary disclosure the effect of a waiver, while the present rule covers the effect of a disclosure made under compulsion or without opportunity to claim the privilege. "[Rule 511] is the converse of [Rule 510]. [Rule 510] deals with waiver and its consequences; [Rule 511] deals with the consequences of disclosure in the absence of waiver." 2 J. Weinstein & M. Berger, Weinstein's Evidence Paragraph 512[02] (1979).

Confidentiality, once destroyed, is not susceptible of restoration, yet some measure of repair may be accomplished by preventing use of the evidence against the holder of the privilege. The remedy of exclusion is therefore made available when the earlier disclosure was compelled erroneously or without opportunity to claim the privilege.

With respect to erroneously compelled disclosure, the argument may be made that the holder should be required in the first instance to assert the privilege, stand his ground, refuse to answer, perhaps incur a judgment of contempt, and exhaust all legal recourse, in order to sustain his privilege. However, this exacts of the holder greater fortitude in the face of authority than ordinary individuals are likely to possess, and assumes unrealistically that a judicial remedy is always available. In self-incrimination cases, the writers agree that erroneously compelled disclosures are inadmissible in a subsequent criminal prosecution of the holder, Maguire, Evidence of Guilt 66 (1959) McCormick (2d ed.) E 127; 8 Wigmore § 2270, and the principle is equally sound when applied to other privileges.

The second circumstances stated as a basis for exclusion is a disclosure made without opportunity to the holder to assert his privilege. Illustrative possibilities are disclosure by an eavesdropper, by a person used in the transmission of a privileged communication, by a family member participating in psychotherapy, or privileged data improperly made available from a computer bank. The advent of increasingly sophisticated interception techniques for confidential communications makes this basis for exclusion especially important. See the Reporter's Comment accompanying Rule 503 (b).

Rule 512. Comment Upon or Inference From Claim of Privilege—Instruction.

Rule 512, like Rule 511, "is a rule designed to ensure that a privilege will be given its maximum effect. It seeks to eliminate any possibility of prejudice arising against the holder, which would either intimidate him into waiving his privilege, or penalize him for exercising a right given to him by law." 2 J. Weinstein & M. Berger, Weinstein's Evidence Paragraph 513 [02] (1979). There has been some controversy on the desirability of maximizing the effects of privileges by disallowing comment and inference. The Model Code of Evidence, in the comment to Rule 233, permitted both comment and inference upon the invocation of a privilege. However, the better view is that "if privileges are considered valuable enough to adopt, then they are also worth effectuating." Comments, *Federal Rules of Evidence and the Law of Privileges,* 15 Wayne L. Rev. 1286, 1370-1371 (1969). This is the approach followed by Rule 39 of the Uniform Rules of Evidence and Section 913 of the California Evidence Code.

(a) **Comment or Inference Not Permitted.** This subdivision prohibits judge and counsel from commenting upon a claim of privilege and the trier of fact from drawing any inference therefrom. It is in accord with the weight of authority. 8 Wigmore §§ 2243, 2322, 2386; Barnhart, *Privilege in the Uniform Rules of Evidence,* 24 Ohio St. L. J. 131, 137-138 (1963). Subdivision (a) is probably not constitutionally required for privileges not required to be recognized by the constitution. Nevertheless, its policy is sound, for "it furthers the value judgments which underlie the creation of privileges." 2 J. Weinstein & M. Berger, Weinstein's Evidence, Paragraph 513 [02] (1979).

(b) **Claiming Privilege Without Knowledge of Jury.** The value of a privilege may be greatly depreciated by means other than expressly commenting to a jury upon the fact that it was exercised. Thus, the calling of a witness in the presence of the jury and subsequently excusing him after a side-bar conference may effectively convey to the jury the fact that a privilege has been claimed, even though the actual claim has not been made in its hearing. Whether a privilege will be claimed is usually ascertainable in advance and the handling of the entire matter outside the presence of the jury is feasible. Destruction of the privilege by innuendo can and should be avoided. 6 Wigmore § 1808. This position is in accord with the general agreement of the authorities that an accused cannot be forced to make his election not to testify in the presence of the jury. 8 Wigmore § 2268, at 407.

Unanticipated situations are, of course, bound to arise, and much must be left to the discretion of the judge and the professional responsibility of counsel.

(c) **Jury Instruction.** Opinions will differ as to the effectiveness of a jury instruction not to draw an adverse inference from the making of a claim of privilege. Whether an instruction shall be given is left to the sound judgment of counsel for the party against whom the adverse inference may be drawn. The instruction is a matter of right, if requested.

The right to the instruction is not impaired by the fact that the claim of privilege is by a witness, rather than by a party, provided an adverse inference against the party may result.

(d) **Application—Self-Incrimination.** This subdivision is a departure from Proposed Federal Rule of Evidence 513, which is the counterpart of Rule 512. Subdivision (d), adopted from Wisconsin Statute § 905.13, attempts to deal with the problem presented when a party in a civil case claims a privilege against self-incrimination. It provides that a party to a civil suit who claims a privilege against self-incrimination may not take advantage of subdivisions (a)—(c) to avoid comment and inference from his privilege claim. See *Grognet v. Fox Valley Trucking Service,* 172 N.W.2d 812 (Wis. 1979); *Molloy v. Molloy,* 176 N.W.2d 292 (Wis. 1970).

Although the privilege against self-incrimination does not apply to protect disclosures that might tend to establish one's liability for civil damages, *see, e.g.,* McCormick (2d ed.) § 121, at 257-58, the privilege not to incriminate oneself in future criminal matters may be raised in any judicial proceeding, *see e.g., McCarthy v. Arndstein,* 266 U.S. 34, 69 L.Ed.2d 34 (1924). While comment on a defendant's silence in a criminal proceeding is proscribed by the constitution, *Griffin v. California,* 380 U.S. 609, 14 L.Ed.2d 106 (1965), comment in other settings is not barred by the constitution. *Baxter v. Palmigiano,* 425 U.S. 308, 47 L.Ed2d 810 (1976). The position taken by this rule protects civil litigants from being disadvantaged because an opposing party's invocation of the privilege against self-incrimination suppresses relevant evidence. The party claiming the privilege retains protection against government prosecution but cannot insulate himself from civil liability. *See Baxter v. Palmigiano, id.,* at 425 U.S., 426-430 (Brennan, J., dissenting). This rule does not address the subject of continuances in civil cases to accommodate a party's desire to remain silent in a criminal prosecution but to testify in a later civil case. Such continuances are possible under Alaska Rule of Civil Procedure 40. Because a criminal defendant has a right to a speedy trial, criminal cases often will be disposed of before related civil cases as a matter of course. An uncomfortable situation might arise when no criminal prosecution is pending or even contemplated but testimony in a civil case might lead to a prosecution. This rule allows a comment on the invocation of a privilege and permits adverse inferences to be drawn despite the attendant discomfort. Some of the policies of the privilege are concededly disserved, but such disservice must be balanced against fairness to civil litigants who need the evidence suppressed by the privilege.

This rule does not address the question of whether it is constitutionally permissible for the government to bring a civil action before a criminal action in order to put the defendant to the choice of costly silence or possible incrimination. When the government is plaintiff in both actions, the balance struck here is more tenuous. Whether it is constitutional remains to be decided if the issue ever arises.

ARTICLE VI. WITNESSES

Rule 601. Competency of Witnesses.

Rule 601 is similar to former Alaska R. Civ. P. 43(g) (1) which it supersedes. It is almost identical to Rule 101 of the Model Code of Evidence and Uniform Rule 17 (1953). The Comment to the Model Code's Rule outlines the way Rule 601 will work:

> When there is a dispute concerning a person's capacity to be a witness, the judge must determine whether the proposed witness can express himself understandably and understands his duty to tell the truth. The opponent has the burden of seeing that the question is raised and that there is evidence before the judge which would justify him in finding incapacity. The appearance of the witness or his conduct in court may be such as to impel the judge to raise the question and to lead him to treat the appearance or conduct as persuasive evidence of incapacity, and consequently to bring forward evidence of capacity. Ordinarily, however, the opponent must raise the objection and support it.

The policy of the rule "is that matters of the witness's opportunity for perception, knowledge, memory, experience and the like go to the weight to be given to his testimony rather than to his right to testify." Commissioner's Note to Uniform Rule 17 (1953). But the rule recognizes that some witnesses should not be permitted to appear before the trier of fact because their testimony is entitled to no consideration.

Federal Rule 601 states that "[e]very person is competent to be a witness." The drafters may have held the view that all witnesses are capable of being understood and able to understand the meaning of an oath, or they may have assumed that other rules would screen out those persons deemed to be incompetent by Alaska Rule 601. *See, e.g.,* Federal Rules 403 and 603; K. Redden & S. Saltzburg, Federal Rules of Evidence Manual 268-69 (2d ed. 1977). *See also United States v. Killian,* 524 F.2d 1268 (5th Cir. 1975). Alaska Rule 601 is clear on its face. It provides a direct approach to the problems of dealing with young children and with older persons whose condition, whether permanent or temporary, raises questions about their capacity to assist the trier of fact.

The Rule rejects any argument that one who is unable to understand the duty to tell the truth may still present evidence that a trier of fact could use to support a judgment. It also requires exclusion of a witness whose expressions cannot be understood by the trier of fact, thereby insuring that leading questions do not serve to put words in an uncommunicative witness's mouth that may not accurately express the knowledge possessed by the witness.

Like former Alaska R. Civ. P. 43(g) (1), Rule 601 has no provision resembling a Dead Man's Act.

Rule 602. Lack of Personal Knowledge.

Rule 602 copies Federal Rule 602, stating the uncontroversial requirement that unless a witness is an expert, in which case he is subject to the provisions of Rule 703, discussed infra, a witness must have personal knowledge of the matters about which he testifies. The fact that new Rule 701 allows a lay witness to testify in opinion form does not undercut the requirement of personal knowledge.

"[T]he rule requiring that a witness who testifies to a fact which can be perceived by the senses must have had an opportunity to observe, and must have actually observed the fact" is a "most pervasive manifestation" of the common law insistence upon "the most reliable sources of information." McCormick (2d ed.) § 10, at 19. These foundation requirements may, of course, be furnished by the testimony of the witness himself; hence personal knowledge is not an absolute but may consist of what the witness thinks he knows from personal perception. 2 Wigmore § 650. As long as there is some evidence that the witness has personal knowledge, the court must let the jury decide whether or not the witness is really knowledgeable. If the jury believes that the witness has no personal knowledge, it will disregard his testimony. The court may reject testimony of a witness if it finds that no trier of fact could reasonably believe that the witness has personal knowledge of the matter. The court may receive the testimony conditionally, subject to evidence of personal knowledge being later supplied in the course of trial. Rule 602 is in fact a specialized application of Rule 104(b) on conditional relevancy.

This rule does not govern the situation of a witness who testifies to a hearsay statement as such, if he has personal knowledge of the making of the statement. Rules 801 and 805 would be applicable. This would, however, prevent him from testifying to the subject matter of the hearsay statement, as he has no personal knowledge of it.

> If a police officer, for example, testifies that the defendant confessed to murdering a spouse, the evidence is admissible, assuming that the confession is voluntary of course, even though the officer is not personally knowledgeable about the murder. The officer is saying in effect: "Defendant claimed responsibility for the murder." He has personal knowledge of what the defendant said. The officer cannot say "Defendant committed the murder," since he does not know this to be true. He only has personal knowledge of what he heard.

K. Redden & S. Saltzburg, Federal Rules of Evidence Manual 245 (2d ed. 1977).

The reference to Rule 703 is designed to avoid any question of conflict between the present rule and the provisions of that rule allowing an expert to express opinions based on facts of which he does not have personal knowledge.

Nebraska, New Mexico and Maine have adopted Federal Rule 602 verbatim also.

Rule 603. Oath or Affirmation.

Rule 601 requires that a witness be capable of understanding the duty to tell the truth. This rule requires the witness to express a willingness to undertake that duty before testifying. The purpose behind requiring an oath or affirmation is to insure that every witness gives accurate and honest testimony.

In earlier times the purpose of the oath, to deter false testimony, became overshadowed by a second use: to exclude qualified witnesses who were not of "proper" religious persuasions and who, therefore, were morally incapable of truthtelling. However,

> It came gradually to be perceived that the use of the oath, not to increase testimonial efficiency, but to exclude qualified witnesses, was not only an abuse of its true principle, but also a practical injustice to suitors who needed such testimony. This injustice is clearly enough seen today; but its perception was naturally slow in coming so long as in the community at large the profession of belief in deism or atheism was associated closely with the notion of moral defects.

Wigmore § 1827, at 414.

This rule permits affirmation by a witness as an alternative to swearing an oath. This alternative was provided for in Alaska R. Civ. P. 43(d), superseded by this rule, and has been generally recognized throughout the United States. *See* Uniform Rule 18 (1953); Kansas Rule 60-418; New Jersey Rule 18; Nebraska Rule 27-603; Maine Rule 603 for similar provisions. By permitting affirmation as well as an oath, many of the difficulties faced by certain religious or other sects should be alleviated. Witnesses should not be barred from testifying because of their religion or the lack of it.

Rule 604. Interpreters.

This rule builds upon former Rule 43(g) (2) of the Alaska Rules of Civil Procedure which provides that when a witness does not understand and speak the English language, an interpreter shall be sworn to interpret for him. The interpreter must be qualified and sworn like any other expert witness.

In both civil and criminal cases the party offering the witness with the language problem generally will have to supply an interpreter and pay the interpreter's fee. Presumably, an indigent criminal defendant may compel the government to pay such a fee. In civil cases the trial court has the power under Rule 706 to appoint an interpreter, to assess the fee against one or more parties, or to provide for payment of the fee from funds available to the court.

Appointment of an interpreter for the indigent defendant is probably constitutionally required if the defendant's understanding of the proceedings against him depends upon it. A handicapped person (deaf, mute, or having a speech impairment) has as much of a right to an interpreter as a person speaking only a foreign language.

Only the interpreter's oath differs from procedure followed with other witnesses: the interpreter swears or affirms that he will make a true translation. *See, e.g.,* the model interpreter's oath, Chapter 37, XIII, Magistrate's Handbook.

Rule 605. Competency of Judge as Witness.

This rule eliminates the possibility that a judge who is presiding at a trial may be called to testify at the same trial. There are two concerns underlying this provision. (1) Someone must rule on objections while the judge is testifying. (2) The jury may favor the side with whom the judge is identified.

The first concern is largely a pragmatic one focusing on the procedural questions that would be likely to arise when the judge abandons the bench for the witness stand.

The second concern involves the potential prejudice to the party against whom the presiding judge testifies in that the jury may believe that the judge is aligned with the party helped by his testimony. The possibility that the jury may perceive partiality on the part of a judge is of sufficient magnitude to prohibit any judicial comment on the evidence. The possibility of unfairness when the judge is a witness also is sufficient to require a broad rule to control behavior. *See* Report of the Special Committee on the Propriety of Judges Appearing as Witnesses, 36 A.B.A.J. 630 (1950); Annot., 157 A.L.R. 311 (1945).

Nothing in this rule prevents a judge from testifying at a trial or proceeding at which he is not the presiding judge. For example, the trial judge is sometimes called to testify about the events of an earlier trial in a habeas corpus proceeding. This is especially necessary where the attack on the conviction comes in the form of an attack on the actions or motives of the trial judge. The danger of prejudice largely disappears where a trial judge testifies at a collateral proceeding since another jurist presides.

The second sentence of the rule indicates the importance of this incompetency rule. No objection need be made in order to preserve the point. In part, this stems from the belief that an immediate objection raised against the trial judge who decides to testify may prejudice the objecting party's chances of obtaining a fair trial. This follows New Jersey's Rule 42 rather than Uniform Rule 42 as promulgated in 1953, which prevented a judge from simultaneously testifying and presiding only if a party objected. The wisdom of disqualifying the presiding judge is so apparent, the likelihood of inadvertent judicial error is so low, and the dilemma facing the attorney who would like to object to testimony by the presiding officer is so real, that no violations of this rule will be tolerated.

Rule 606. Competency of Juror as Witness.

(a) **At the Trial.** At common law a juror otherwise qualified as a witness was not rendered incompetent because of his position on the jury although there is a conflict of authority as to whether a juror may remain on the jury after testifying. Uniform Rule 43 (1953) resolved the dispute by prohibiting testimony of a juror altogether. This rule, like the Federal Rule after which it is modeled, follows the lead of the Uniform Rule and adopts the view that participation in a trial as a witness compromises the impartiality of a juror sitting as factfinder in that trial. This view is very similar to the position articulated in Rule 605, which bars a trial judge from testifying in a trial in which he presides.

The second sentence of subdivision (a) departs from Federal Rule 606 which provides that should a juror be called to testify, the opposing party shall be afforded an opportunity to object out of the hearing of the jury. This is very different from Federal Rule 605 which provides that when a judge is called as a witness, no objection is needed to preserve a claim of error. The Advisory Committee's Note to Federal Rule 606 distinguishes the two rules on the ground that when a juror is called to testify, the judge is not so involved as to call for departure from the usual principles requiring an objection to be made. Alaska Rule 606 rejects this distinction and recognizes that any objection to the competency of the factfinder called to testify might jeopardize the integrity of the factfinding process. Under the Federal Rule, only after the witness' name is called is the objection raised. The other jurors may suspect that if the witness does not testify it is because counsel has objected. Jurors are less likely to be able to understand why they cannot testify than are judges: this rule is designed to eliminate the need for jury speculation. If voir dire is handled carefully, counsel should be alerted to situations in which a potential juror could develop into a witness later in the trial and counsel should be able to disqualify such potential jurors. There is no reason to expect that this rule will be unduly burdensome for trial lawyers and there is no need to tolerate any possibility that the integrity of the factfinders will be compromised.

(b) **Inquiry Into Validity of Verdict on Indictment.** Generally there has been agreement among common law jurisdictions that the mental operations and the emotional reactions of jurors during the deliberative process should not be the subject of later inquiry. There has been substantial disagreement as to whether a juror should be able to impeach a verdict in which he participated by testifying about other matters. *See* 8 Wigmore §§ 2352, 2353, 2354. This rule, like the Federal Rule after which it is modeled, limits impeachment of jury verdicts to inquiries about extraneous prejudicial information and outside influences which may have been improperly brought to bear upon any juror.

The policy reasons underlying the exclusion of jurors' affidavits or testimony impeaching verdicts include protection of jurors against annoyance or embarrassment, freedom of deliberation, and finality of verdicts. Allowing inquiry into the mental operations and emotional reactions of jurors in reaching a given verdict would invite constant review as a result of tampering and harassment. Moreover, even without pressure by counsel or litigants, many jurors are likely to have second thoughts about their verdicts after they are excused by the Court and the influence of fellow jurors dissipates. Such second thoughts might cause jurors to question their verdicts if permitted to do so. Yet these policy reasons are not promoted by a blanket prohibition against inquiry into irregularities which occur in the jury process when such irregularities result from prejudicial extraneous information or influences injected into or brought to bear upon the deliberative process. If the judicial system is operating properly, such inquiries should rarely be necessary. Failure to examine the relatively few cases that may arise would permit injustices to go uncorrected without reason.

The line between what is the proper subject of subsequent inquiry and what is to be insulated from review is a fine one. The federal decisions have sought to protect the components of deliberation, including arguments, statements, discussions, mental and emotional reactions, votes, and any other features of the process. Alaska cases draw similar lines between permissible and impermissible inquiry. Like most federal courts before the adoption of the Federal Rules, Alaska law generally provides that a juror cannot impeach a verdict by testimony or affidavit, but it recognizes exceptions.

> Exceptions to the general rule have been made and it has been held that the type of misconduct which may impeach a verdict is fraud, bribery, forcible coercion or any other obstruction of justice. Whether the verdict should be set aside and a new trial ordered rests in the sound discretion of the trial judge, but generally the verdict should stand unless the evidence clearly establishes a serious violation of the juror's duty and deprives a party of a fair trial.

West v. State, 409 P.2d 847, 852 (Alaska 1966). The effect of this approach is to restrict inquiry into the deliberations of the jury and to permit inquiry into extraneous matters.

This rule reflects the same spirit as the decided cases. For example, exposure of some jurors in the jury room to a newspaper article concerning the case has been viewed as an exception to the general rule against impeachment. *See Watson v. State,* 413 P.2d 22, 24 (Alaska 1966). This falls within the contemplated interpretation of the language of this rule as "extraneous prejudicial information."

This rule does not purport to set out the substantive grounds requiring verdicts to be set aside for irregularity. It does attempt to define the guidelines concerning the competency of jurors to testify as to those grounds. Can a verdict be impeached if a juror has falsely denied bias or prejudice during voir dire? *See Poulin v. Zartman,* 542 P.2d 251, 264 (Alaska 1975). Hard cases remain and must be decided with policies underlying the rule in mind: to insulate the deliberative process and to promote finality of verdicts while not foreclosing testimony as to the extrinsic forces erroneously injected into the process.

Rule 607. Who May Impeach or Support.

(a) Rule 607 follows both Federal Rule 607 and existing Alaska authorities in rejecting the wooden common law rule that a party may not impeach his own witness. *See Beavers v. State,* 492 P.2d 88, 91 (Alaska 1971), *Johnston v. State,* 489 P.2d 134, 137 (Alaska 1971), and *Hobbs v. State,* 359 P.2d 956, 966 (Alaska 1961). Rule 43(g)(11) [a] of the Alaska Rules of Civil Procedure, which this rule supersedes, provided that a party could impeach his own witness with evidence of a prior inconsistent statement. Rule 26(a) of the Alaska Rules of Criminal Procedure extended this provision to criminal trials. A similar provision is Civil Rule 32(a) (1) allowing any party to impeach a witness by means of his deposition. Thus, Alaska's policy toward impeachment is basically unchanged by Rule 607.

Rule 607 recognizes that a party should not be held to vouch for the trustworthiness of his witnesses since he rarely has a free choice in selecting them, and further recognizes that to deny the right to impeach is to leave the party at the mercy of the witness and the adversary.

> If the truth lies on the side of the calling party, but the witness's character is bad, the witness may be attacked by the adversary if he tells the truth; but if the witness tells a lie, the adversary will not attack him, and the calling party, under the rule [forbidding impeachment] cannot. Certainly it seems that if the witness has been bribed to change his story, the calling party should be allowed to disclose this fact to the court.

McCormick (2d ed.) § 38, at 75.

Instead of classifying a witness as belonging to one party, Rule 607 "makes the witness the witness of the court as a channel through which to get at the truth." Comment to Rule 20, Uniform Rules of Evidence, Vol. 9A ULA 607 (1965).

Nothing in this or any other rule specifically bars impeachment by presenting extrinsic evidence on a collateral issue. The word "collateral" has so many meanings that it tends to be confusing. Rule 403, in providing that evidence may be excluded if the time required for its presentation is not warranted by its probative value, will permit exclusion of impeachment evidence that sheds little, if any, light on the credibility of a particular witness in a particular case.

See Maine Rule of Evidence 607, Nebraska Rule 27-607, Nevada Rule 50.075, and New Mexico Rule 20-4-607 for provisions similar to subdivision (a).

(b) Subdivision (b) recognizes generally the right of a party to rehabilitate a witness whose credibility has been attacked.

Support evidence is not permitted until credibility has been attacked; its function in the adversary system is to serve as a counterblow, and such a blow is not to be struck until an opposing party takes the offensive.

A second basic limitation imposed by the requirement that support evidence "meet an attack" on credibility is that the support evidence respond to the impeaching fact. "The rehabilitating facts must meet a particular method of impeachment with relative directness. The wall, attacked at one point, may not be fortified at another and distinct point." McCormick (2d. ed.) § 49, at 103. This by no means meant to say that impeachment by showing a conviction of a crime, for example, could be responded to only by evidence that the witness was not guilty of that crime. What is meant is that the insinuation to which the attack is directed must be addressed by the support evidence. For example, the ground for disbelieving a witness afforded by prior conviction of a crime is the suggestion of a general readiness to do evil; evidence of the witness' reputation for veracity would generally be relevant to meet this attack, as noted by Justice Holmes in *Gerts v. Fitchburg R. Co.,* 137 Mass. 77 (1884). Whether a particular type of support evidence is relevant to a particular mode of impeachment cannot be delineated by an inflexible rule; decisions must be left to the discretion of the court for case-by-case consideration. Such decisions are extremely fact-specific, depending, *inter alia* on the vehemence of the attack, the nature of the impeaching evidence, and the nature of the support evidence proffered.

Rule 608. Evidence of Character and Conduct of Witness.

(a) **Opinion and Reputation Evidence of Character.** Rule 404(a) states the general proposition that character evidence is not admissible for the purpose of proving that a person acted in conformity therewith. That rule is subject to several exceptions, one of which is relevant here: character evidence may be admissible if it bears upon the credibility of a witness. This rule develops that exception.

In accordance with the bulk of judicial authority, the inquiry is strictly limited to character for truth and veracity rather than allowing evidence as to character generally. The result is to sharpen relevancy, to reduce surprise and confusion, and to make the lot of the witness somewhat less unattractive. *See* McCormick (2d ed.) § 44 and the Reporter's Comment accompanying Rule 404(a). "Attacking a witness' character is often but a feeble and ineffective contribution to the proof of the issue; and its drawbacks appear in their most emphasized form where the broader method of attack is allowed." 3 Wigmore § 923, at 728.

Character evidence in support of credibility is admissible only after the witness' character has first been attacked. *See* Rule 607(b). This is also in accord with the common law rule. McCormick (2d ed.) § 49, at 105; 4 Wigmore § 1104. Opinion or reputation testimony to the effect that the witness is untruthful specifically qualifies as an attack as would evidence of conviction of crime. Whether character evidence should be admitted to meet other forms of attack is, as the Reporter's Comment to Rule 607(b) suggests, best left to the discretion of the trial judge who has Rule 403 for guidance.

(b) **Specific Instances of Conduct.** This rule allows inquiry into specific acts of conduct of the primary witness in order to probe the knowledge of a character witness on cross-examination. The conduct inquired into must be reasonably calculated to reflect on the primary witness' truth-telling capacity. A sound exercise of judicial discretion is required here to insure that cross-examination focuses on credibility, not on the general character of the witness. Determining whether a character witness' opinion or reputation testimony is based on knowledge of the primary witness' prior conduct may be very influential in assessing the credibility of the testimony. The leading case on the general issue of testing reputation or character witnesses for knowledge of specific acts is *Michelson v. United States,* 335 U.S. 469, 93 L.Ed. 168 (1948).

Rule 607(a) permits either party to impeach a witness. This rule, however, limits inquiry into specific acts when testing the knowledge of character witnesses to cross-examination. The rationale behind the limitation is to bar the direct examiner from the inquiry when "impeachment" of one's own witness becomes a disguise for using specific acts to prove character rather than the required reputation or opinion evidence. Because a party does have a choice as to character witnesses the need to impeach such witness by inquiring into specific acts should not arise. This rule follows Alaska R. Civ. P. 43 (g) (11) [a], superseded by this rule.

The second sentence of this subdivision bars the use of evidence of specific incidents to impeach or support the credibility of a witness, unless otherwise provided in a rule of court or legislative enactment. *See, e.g.,* Rule 609 (prior conviction), Rule 613 (inconsistent statement and bias). This follows Alaska R. Civ. P. 43(g) (11), superseded by this rule, and a trend in some jurisdictions to prohibit impeachment by "bad acts" other than criminal convictions. This is consistent with Rule 405 which forecloses use of evidence of specific incidents as proof of character unless character is an issue in the case. *See also* Uniform Rule 22(d); Kansas Rule 60-422, for similar provisions.

This subdivision departs from the Federal Rule which permits evidence of specific instances of conduct, if probative of the trait of truthfulness or untruthfulness, to support or attack a witness' credibility. The Federal Rule was adopted with little debate or attention although it expresses what was previously a minority view among the federal circuits. By eliminating this type of evidence, the need to protect witnesses against waiving their privilege against self-incrimination when examined with respect to matters relating to credibility is also eliminated.

(c) **Admissibility.** Because cross-examination concerning what a witness has heard or knows can be highly prejudicial, this subdivision assures that before unfair questions are asked, the trial judge is able to screen them out. The balance here is the same as under Rule 403.

Rule 609. Impeachment by Evidence of Conviction of Crime.

(a) **General Rule.** In every common law jurisdiction some prior criminal convictions may be used to impeach the credibility of a witness. This subdivision, identical to Alaska R. Crim. P. 26(f) (1) which it supersedes, allows prior convictions to be used for impeachment purposes only if the crime involved dishonesty or false statement. Favored by the House of Representatives, this limitation was rejected by the Senate. The Federal Rule reflects the Senate view; it permits all impeachment that this subdivision would permit plus impeachment on the basis of any other conviction, if the crime was punishable by death or imprisonment in excess of one year in the jurisdiction in which the witness was convicted and is more probative than prejudicial.

Limiting admissibility to convictions involving crimes such as perjury, fraud, forgery, false statement, and other crimes in the nature of crimen falsi sharpens the inquiry and insures that prior convictions are not used as evidence of the general character of the witness in contravention of Rule 404 and 405, but are used properly, *i.e.,* to impeach credibility. *See* Uniform Rule 21 for a similar provision.

This rule does not govern the competency of witnesses or operate to disqualify anyone on the basis of prior convictions.

Federal courts have divided on the question whether larceny offenses qualify as crimes involving dishonesty or false statements. *In Lowell v. State,* 574 P.2d 1281 (Alaska 1978), the supreme court held that "larceny and embezzlement...disclose the kind of dishonesty and unreliability which bear upon the veracity of persons perpetrating those crimes." (Footnote omitted.) It must be remembered, however, that the trial judge must strike a balance between probative value and prejudicial effect. Hence, the fact that the trial judge may admit larceny convictions for impeachment purposes does not mean such convictions must be admitted.

One federal court noted that

> [e]ven the courts that reject the view that stealing, without more, involves "dishonesty" that bears upon a witness's veracity recognize that modern theft statutes may encompass criminal conduct that does not fall within the gambit of Rule 609(a) (2) [federal equivalent of Alaska Rule 609(a) (2)], for a theft conviction may well be based on fraudulent or deceitful conduct that would previously have been prosecuted as larceny by trick, embezzlement, or the taking of money by false pretenses, etc. Accordingly, these courts have adopted the rule that, when the statutory offense of which the witness was convicted does not require proof of fraud or deceit as an essential element of the crime, a prior conviction may be admitted under Rule 609(a) (2) [federal equivalent of Alaska Rule 609(a)] if the proponent of the evidence bears the burden of showing that the conviction "rested on facts warranting the dishonesty or false statement description."

United States v. Papia, 560 F.2d 827 (7th Cir. 1977). *Accord, United States v. Hayes,* 553 F.2d 824 (2d Cir. 1977).

Presumably, a party who successfully bears the burden of showing that a crime, which on its face would not indicate dishonesty or false statement, involved the deceit envisioned by the rule will be able to qualify a prior conviction for impeachment use.

In *Lowell v. State, supra,* the supreme court rejected the argument that any use of prior convictions to impeach a criminal defendant is fundamentally unfair. But the court emphasized the limited nature of the impeachment evidence permitted by the predecessor Criminal Rule and the balancing test included in the rule in concluding that it was fair and that it did not impermissibly burden the defendant's right to testify. The new rule should receive the same approbation.

(b) **Time Limit.** The five year time limit set forth here is an attempt to balance competing concerns: concern, on the one hand, for both the privacy of witnesses and the acute danger of prejudice when a party-witness is impeached by a prior conviction, and, on the other hand, the need for the trier of fact to know whether a witness previously has demonstrated dishonesty in order to fairly assess the credibility of the witness. An assumption underlying the time limit is that older convictions are less probative than more recent ones in determining the likelihood that a witness will tell the truth. The rule specifically provides that convictions that are more than five years old are stale and generally are not very probative of the credibility of a witness. While any time limit is arbitrary, a five year limit was recognized by Alaska R. Crim. P. 26(f) (2)), superseded by this rule.

> We assume that the ten year limitation of the proposed Federal Rules of Evidence...is not of constitutional import and that Alaska's five year limitation is constitutionally valid. In particular cases, of course, the trial courts may see fit to relax the prohibition where the accused's right of confrontation so requires.

Gonzales v. State, 521 P.2d 512, 515 n.5 (Alaska 1974).

The second sentence of this subdivision provides the trial judge with the necessary discretion to ignore the time limit in the interest of justice. There may be cases, for example, in which the accused's right of confrontation will override the five year limitation. Except in rare cases where limiting impeachment as to prior convictions threatens to deny a party a fair trial or to infringe upon a constitutionally protected right, the time limit should be respected.

(c) **Admissibility.** As noted earlier, evidence of prior convictions may be especially prejudicial when a party takes the stand and is impeached. Prejudice is also likely when a witness who is closely identified with a party is impeached by prior convictions. In these and other cases when there is a real danger of prejudice, the court shall weigh the danger against the probative value of the evidence, and if the danger is greater, shall rule the evidence inadmissible. To permit claims of prejudice to be raised before the jury learns of a conviction, the judge shall be advised of the existence of the conviction before it is used as impeachment evidence.

(d) **Effect of Pardon, Annulment, or Certificate of Rehabilitation.** At common law, the effect of a pardon, whether conditional or unconditional, generally is not to preclude the use of the conviction for the purpose of impeaching the credibility of the witness who was convicted and pardoned. *See* Annot., 30 A.L.R.2d 893 (1953). Although pardons may reinstate many of the civil disabilities accompanying a conviction, they do not presuppose rehabilitation or innocence. This subdivision renders evidence of a conviction that has been the subject of a pardon, annulment, certificate of rehabilitation, or an equivalent procedure inadmissible if accompanied by a showing of innocence or rehabilitation. Absent specific procedures entailing findings as to the innocence or rehabilitation of pardoned witnesses, pardons pursuant to the authority conferred upon the governor by Alaska Constitution, Article 3, Section 21 and AS 33.20.070 are not prima facie evidence of innocence or rehabilitation. The burden of demonstrating the rationale for a pardon or other procedure in a given case is on the party relying upon the pardon or other procedure to prevent impeachment.

(e) **Juvenile Adjudications.** Most jurisdictions are in accord that evidence of juvenile adjudications is generally inadmissible. *See* Annot., 63 A.L.R.3d 1112 (1975). The state has an interest in preserving the confidentiality of juvenile adjudications of delinquency. *See* Alaska Children's Rule 23 and AS 47.10.080. Some of the policy considerations are akin to those underlying the exclusion of adult convictions after the issuance of a certificate of rehabilitation.

This subdivision, based on Federal Rule 609, recognizes that in certain cases the strategic importance of a witness may be so great and the prior adjudication so probative on the issue of credibility that the interests of justice require admissibility of the adjudication.

The United States Supreme Court, in *Davis v. Alaska,* 415 U.S. 308, 39 L.Ed.2d 347 (1974), ruled that the state's interest in preserving the confidentiality of juvenile adjudications had to give way to the defendant's interest in introducing evidence of the prosecution's key witness' probationary status to show bias. The sixth amendment's confrontation clause requires that the defendant be given the chance to cross-examine witnesses in a meaningful way. Although evidence of bias is especially compelling, there may be other cases where the Constitution requires that a defendant be able to impeach the credibility of a key witness by introducing evidence of prior juvenile adjudications. The second sentence of this subdivision is written with those cases in mind. It also recognizes the possibility that there may be civil cases in which evidence of a prior juvenile adjudication may be required in order to prevent grave injustice.

(f) **Pendency of Appeal.** Where an appeal from a conviction offered to impeach a witness is pending, the trial judge faces a dilemma: if the conviction is not admitted the jury may believe a witness whose credibility would be suspect if the conviction were made known, and if the conviction is admitted but is reversed on appeal a new trial may be necessary. The more important a witness is to the case, the more difficult the dilemma. One escape is to postpone the trial of a case until the appeal of the prior conviction is determined. When this is not practicable, the court must focus on the probative value of the prior conviction, the likely prejudicial effect of the conviction, alternative impeachment devices that may be available, and perhaps even on the likelihood that the prior conviction will be reversed.

Smith v. Beavers, 554 P.2d 1167 (Alaska 1976), makes clear that the same limitations apply to a direct examiner impeaching his own witness as to a cross-examiner.

Rule 610. Religious Beliefs or Opinions.

Rule 610 copies Federal Rule 610 in providing that a witness's religious beliefs or lack of them may not be used to attack or support his credibility. While this sort of evidence may bear some relevance to credibility it is not highly probative and often is capable of creating unfair jury bias for or against the witness. Moreover, it is highly personal information and should not be inquired into without a good reason for believing that it will aid in accurate factfinding.

As the Advisory Committee on the Federal Rules observed, while the rule forecloses inquiry into the religious beliefs or opinions of a witness for the purpose of showing that his character for truthfulness is affected by their nature, an inquiry for the purpose of showing interest or bias because of them is not within the prohibition. Thus disclosure of affiliation with a church which is a party to the litigation would be allowable under the rule. *Cf. Tucker v. Reil,* 77 P.2d 202 (Ariz. 1938).

Maine, Nebraska and New Mexico have identical provisions in their rules of evidence.

Rule 611. Mode and Order of Interrogation and Presentation.

(a) **Control by Court.** Subdivision (a) mirrors Federal Rule 611(a). The Advisory Committee's Note on that subdivision comprises the bulk of this comment.

Spelling out detailed rules to govern the mode and order of interrogating witnesses and presenting evidence is neither desirable nor feasible. The ultimate responsibility for the effective working of the adversary system rests with the judge. The rule sets forth the objectives which he should seek to attain.

Item (1) restates in broad terms the power and obligation of the judge as developed under common law principles. It covers such concerns as whether testimony shall be in the form of a free narrative or responses to specific questions, McCormick (2d ed.) § 5, the order of calling witnesses and presenting evidence, 6 Wigmore § 1867, the use of demonstrative evidence, McCormick (2d ed.) § 179, and the many other questions arising during the course of a trial which can be solved only by the judge's common sense and fairness in view of the particular circumstances.

Item (2) is addressed to avoidance of needless consumption of time, a matter of daily concern in the disposition of cases. A companion piece is found in the discretion vested in the judge to exclude evidence as a waste of time in Rule 403.

Item (3) calls for a judgment under the particular circumstances whether interrogation tactics entail harassment or undue embarrassment. Pertinent circumstances include the importance of the testimony, the nature of the inquiry, its relevance to credibility, waste of time, and confusion. McCormick, (2d ed.) § 42.

(b) **Scope of Cross-Examination.** Alaska authorities are in agreement with the Federal Rule limiting cross-examination to matters testified to on direct examination, along with matters concerning the credibility of the witness. In a civil case the main import of this rule is on the order of presentation of the evidence, since counsel may later, as part of his own case-in-chief, recall a witness who has previously testified and ask about matters not touched upon by his adversary. In criminal cases the privilege against self-incrimination and its policies are a special problem.

The rule of limited cross-examination promotes orderly presentation of the case and therefore contributes to jury comprehension of the issues. When comprehension would be enhanced by allowing the cross-examiner to explore matters not touched upon on direct examination, the trial judge may allow departure from the traditional order of presentation; however, any inquires beyond the scope of the direct must be non-leading questions. If no such limitations were imposed on the form of cross-examination, counsel might be tempted to question the witness on matters that properly belong in his case-in-chief, solely to take advantage of the ability to ask leading questions.

Rule 611(b)'s provision that the judge may in the interests of justice permit inquiry into new matters on cross-examination is designed for those situations in which the result otherwise would be confusion, complication, or protraction of the case, not as a matter of rule but as demonstrable in the actual development of the particular case.

(c) **Leading Questions.** Subdivision (c) conforms to the traditional view that the suggestive powers of the leading questions are as a general proposition undesirable. The rule recognizes the traditional exceptions to this proposition. Undisputed preliminary matters may be speedily established by leading questions. The witness whose memory has failed may be assisted by them. In the case of the witness having difficulty communicating, either because of immaturity or a disability, leading questions can be beneficial in eliciting cogent testimony. In the case of the witness who is hostile, unwilling or biased, leading questions may be necessary to get at the truth. The phrase of the rule, "witness identified with" an adverse party, is designed to enlarge the category of witnesses treated as hostile, subject to the discretion of the court.

Closely related to items (2) and (3) is item (4), which was added in response to Rule 607(a) allowing a party to impeach his own witness. Item (4) recognizes that leading questions may be a permissible method of impeaching a witness's testimony. Of course the court should be vigilant in confining the use of leading questions to true attempts to impeach. This is most easily accomplished by permitting leading questions only when they are part of an attack on testimony previously elicited from the witness by the direct examiner.

The rule presumes that leading questions are a proper part of cross-examination. The purpose of the qualification "ordinarily" in this subdivision is to furnish a basis for denying the use of leading questions when the cross-examination is cross-examination in form only and not in fact, as for example the "cross-examination" of a party by his own counsel after being called by the opponent (savoring more of redirect) or of an insured defendant who proves to be friendly to the plaintiff.

Rule 612. Writing Used to Refresh Memory.

(a) **While Testifying.** Rule 612 follows Federal Rule 612 in acknowledging the long-established common law practice of allowing parties to refresh the recollection of a witness by showing the witness a writing or other object. The rule applies to all such materials. The term "objects" is intended to cover all unwritten memory aids—*e.g.,* photographs or tape recordings.

Alaska Rule of Civil Procedure 43(g) (9), superseded by this rule, allowed materials to be used to refresh the recollection of a witness on the stand only if they were written by the witness himself or under his direction at a time when the fact was fresh in his memory. Presumably this rule was thought to guard against the power of suggestion. But because it addressed only activities taking place in court, saying nothing about the more prevalent and potentially more harmful practice of pre-trial preparation of witnesses, Rule 43(g) (9) could not provide meaningful protection in this regard. It was effective only in preventing trial judges and juries from benefiting from the firsthand knowledge of witnesses who might readily have their memories jogged by a quick reading of a news article or other writing.

Rule 612 follows the prevailing view as reflected by its federal counterpart; it rejects limitations on the kinds of writings or objects that may be shown to witnesses to refresh recollection. Adequate safeguards against undue influence on a witness are afforded by: (1) Rule 602, which requires a witness to have personal knowledge of the facts; (2) the court's power to determine that a witness is reading a prior statement, rather than testifying from present memory; and (3) the right of an impeaching party to demand inspection of the material.

The right to inspect material used at trial enables the impeaching party to object to its use if there are grounds to do so and to refer to it during his examination. This party can thereby probe any discrepancies between the testimony and the material and test the witness' assertion that his memory has become clear.

Thus, the rule now makes it clear that anything can be used to refresh the memory of a witness. The foundation requirements for past recollection recorded, an exception to the hearsay rule found under Rule 803 are *not* relevant under this rule.

Rule 612(a) uses the phrase "seeking to impeach the witness" to define parties who may benefit from the rule's protections; the Federal Rule uses the term "adverse" parties. Because any party may impeach any witness under Rule 607, a party may need to examine his own witness concerning reliance on memory-refreshing devices. This rule permits such an examination, although the trial judge must insure that a good faith effort to impeach is being made, not an attempt to offer prior recorded recollection that does not otherwise qualify as an exception to the hearsay rule. The same phrase "seeking to impeach the witness" is used in subdivision (b) also.

(b) **Before Testifying.** While almost the same advantages are afforded by inspection of materials used before trial as by inspection of materials used at trial, traditionally there has been no right to inspect the former. A fear has persisted that a right to inspect such material could easily be used as a pretext for wholesale exploration of an opposing party's files. Rule 612(b) is carefully worded to protect the right to inspect from abuse. The purpose of the phrase "for the purpose of testifying" is to limit counsel's access to his opponent's files to those writings which may fairly be said in fact to have an impact upon the testimony of the witness. Moreover, the right to inspect is conditional upon a judicial finding that it is required to do justice in the particular situation.

If production of the writing or object is impracticable, subdivision (b) provides that the court may order instead that the writing or object be made available for inspection. The court may, of course, decline to issue such an order if justice does not require it; the rule does not require any one approach for all cases.

(c) **Claims of Privilege or Irrelevance.** This section outlines the proper procedure for handling material used to refresh recollection that is to be made available to a party for impeachment use. The procedure is similar to that prescribed by Rule 106 for related writings: first a ruling on any claim of privilege is made, then an examination of the material in chambers follows for the purpose of excising irrelevant material.

(d) **Failure to Produce.** Sanctions for non-production are left generally to the discretion of the court. Rule 16 of the Rules of Criminal Procedure and Rule 37 of the Rules of Civil Procedure suggest appropriate sanctions. But the rule recognizes both the sensitive nature of some government files, especially those used in criminal cases, and the importance in criminal litigation of treating the defendant fairly, *e.g.,* by making all potentially exculpatory evidence available to the defendant. Unlike the Federal Rule, Alaska Rule 612 allows the court in its discretion to dismiss a prosecution for failure to comply with this rule. In some situations striking the testimony may be woefully inadequate. For example, if the defense calls a government officer or agent or witness associated with the government, who has personal knowledge of the facts of a case, to obtain evidence helpful to the defense, counsel for the defense may wish to attack the witness by showing that he is parroting information provided by the prosecutor. A successful attack might well be followed by the elicitation of facts helpful to the defense. If the prosecutor should refuse to disclose writings or objects used to refresh the witness' recollection despite a finding that disclosure is required in the interests of justice, dismissal may be the only appropriate remedy. Striking the testimony of the witness may deny the defendant helpful evidence, and declaring a mistrial will not help the defendant get the possibly exculpatory material. Moreover, unnecessary granting of a mistrial may violate the double jeopardy clause of the United States Constitution. *See United States v. Jorn,* 400 U.S. 470, 27 L.Ed.2d 543 (1971). Consequently, Rule 612 allows dismissal of the prosecution as a sanction for refusal to comply with the order of the court if the court determines that justice requires dismissal. Dismissal is, however, a drastic remedy and ought not be invoked until all alternatives have been assessed and deemed insufficient to remedy harm occasioned by the refusal to comply. Where the government's refusal is coupled with an effort to seek and obtain interlocutory relief by way of a petition for review or otherwise, dismissal ought not be entered without permitting the government an opportunity to exhaust that avenue of relief.

Rule 613. Prior Inconsistent Statements, Bias and Interest of Witnesses.

(a) **General Rule.** At common law, the traditional ways of impeaching witnesses include the introduction of evidence of prior inconsistent statements and evidence to prove bias or interest. Although Federal Rule 613 governs the manner in which prior inconsistent statements must be offered in federal courts, the Federal Rules never explicitly state that inconsistent statements are admissible and never mention bias or interest as impeachment tools. Alaska Rule 613 specifically states that evidence of prior inconsistent statements and evidence of bias or interest are permissible ways of impeaching a witness. This subdivision governs methods of impeachment and is not intended to alter the rule in *Beavers v. State,* 492 P.2d 88 (Alaska 1971), allowing impeachment evidence to be considered as substantive evidence.

The right of the criminal defendant to probe a witness for evidence of bias or interest has been recognized by the Supreme Court as being essential to the right of confrontation guaranteed by the sixth amendment. *See Davis v. Alaska,* 415 U.S. 308, 39 L.Ed.2d 347 (1974). Alaska cases have noted that the mere possibility of future criminal charges against a witness is sufficient to permit counsel wide latitude in probing the possibility of bias or interest.

> [G]reat liberality should be given defense counsel in cross-examination of a prosecution witness with respect to his motive for testifying. Cross-examination to show bias because of expectation of immunity from prosecution is one of the safeguards essential to a fair trial, and undue restriction in such cross-examination is reversible error without any need for a showing of prejudice.

R.L.R. v. State, 487 P.2d 27, 44 (Alaska 1971). *See also Evans v. State,* 550 P.2d 830, 836-40 (Alaska 1976), and the second appeal, 574 P.2d 24 (Alaska 1978).

(b) **Foundation Requirements.** This rule partially reinstates the foundation requirement necessary at common law as a precondition to the introduction of extrinsic evidence to prove prior inconsistent statements of bias or interest. *See generally* Ladd, Some Observations on Credibility: Impeachment of Witnesses, 52 Cornell L.Q. 239, 247 (1967). While fairness and efficiency generally are promoted by laying a foundation, this rule recognizes that at times the requirement must be modified or waived in the interests of justice.

Laying a foundation for impeachment by prior inconsistent statements generally requires asking the testifying witness to identify the statement after being reminded of its substance and to whom it was made, and either to admit having made the statement and explain the circumstances, or to deny it. *See* McCormick (2d ed.) § 37, at 72.

Federal Rule 613(b) greatly relaxes the rigid common law foundation requirement in an attempt to solve the following problems:

(1) the laying of a foundation may inadvertently have been overlooked;

(2) the impeaching statement may not have been discovered until later;

(3) premature disclosure may on occasion frustrate the effective impeachment of collusive witnesses.

Letter from Edward W. Cleary to Hon. William L. Hungate, May 8, 1973, in Supp. to Hearings Before the Subcommittee on Criminal Justice to the House Comm. on the Judiciary, 93rd Congress, 1st Sess., at 74-75 (1973).

Section (b)(1) of this rule alleviates these problems giving the trial judge the discretion to permit witnesses to be recalled for the purpose of laying a foundation when, (1) the failure to do so earlier was not intentional, as in the situation where discovery of the prior inconsistent statement was late; or (2) the failure to do so earlier was intentional, but for good cause: for example, when prematurely alerting collusive witnesses to evidence would work a substantial tactical disadvantage. Section (b)(1) also permits the trial judge to dispense with the foundation requirement altogether if the interests of justice would be served. The negligent omission of counsel to lay a foundation could be excused here if a barring of the evidence would lead to an unjust result.

Section (b)(2) eliminates the rule in *Queen Caroline's Case,* 2 B. & B. 284, 286-90, 129 Eng. Rep. 976 (1820), which required that the examiner show a witness a prior written statement before questioning him about it.

The rule requiring the writing to be shown allowed the witness to refresh his memory and thus protected the witness from the embarrassment of denying an inconsistent statement, only to be confronted with it in writing. It has been criticized as giving the witness too much opportunity to fabricate explanations of apparent inconsistencies. *See* Wigmore §§ 1259-1263; McCormick (2d ed.) § 28, at 55-57. Alaska R. Civ. P. 43(g) (11) [c], superseded by this rule, followed the Queen's Rule. This rule, however, anticipates that the foundation requirement shall provide the witness with a fair opportunity to refresh his memory with the prior statement without providing the witness with an unfair advantage over the impeaching party.

Subdivision (b) (2) provides that opposing counsel may see or learn of any statement used for impeachment purposes when it is actually used. Hence, the lawyer who believes that the cross-examiner is attempting to distort a prior statement or misuse it can ask the court to prevent improper tactics.

Rule 614. Calling and Examination of Witnesses by Court.

(a) **Calling by Court.** Rule 614 is in accord with the common law in providing that the court may call witnesses. While exercised more frequently in criminal than in civil cases, this power of the judge is well-established. McCormick (2d ed.) § 8, at 13-14; 9 Wigmore § 2484.

Just as it is proper for the court to ask questions in order to clear up confusion created by the parties (see subdivision (b)), the court may, on its own motion, call witnesses who may add facts that are helpful in the search for truth; the court is not entirely a prisoner of the parties' approach to a case. In the same spirit, Rule 706 provides that the court may appoint independent experts in civil or criminal litigation. In a trial before a jury, however, it is important for the court to refrain from suggesting its views on the merits of a case or on the credibility of a witness through its choice of witnesses. For recent appellate discussion of the appearance of impartiality required of the trial court, *see United States v. Karnes,* 531 F.2d 214 (4th Cir. 1976).

The court may also call witnesses at the suggestion of any party. At common law the most common reasons for a party to suggest that the court call a witness are, first, to avoid the rigid ban on impeachment of one's own witness, and, second, to avoid the rule limiting the use of leading questions in cross-examination, an especially annoying rule when dealing with an uncooperative witness. Since Alaska Rule 607 now allows impeachment of one's own witness, and Rule 611 allows the court discretion to permit the use of leading questions on direct examination, it is doubtful that future instances of the court calling witnesses at the suggestion of a party will be numerous. But the practice may still be useful on occasion, *e.g.*, where a witness is much more cooperative if summoned by the court than by a particular party, or where a party fears guilt by association in calling a witness.

(b) **Examination by Court.** The authority of the court to question witnesses is also well-established. McCormick (2d ed.) § 8, at 12-13; 3 Wigmore § 784. The court may interrogate any witness, whether called by itself or by a party. In trials before a jury, however, the court's questioning should be cautiously guarded so as not to constitute an implied comment. The court should bear in mind its proper role and the limitations on that role; the court abuses its authority when it plays the part of the advocate. As the manner in which interrogation should be conducted and the proper extent of its exercise are not susceptible of formulation in a rule, their omission in this rule in no sense precludes courts of review from continuing to reverse for abuse.

(c) **Objections.** The provision relating to objections is designed to relieve counsel of the embarrassment attendant upon objecting to questions by the judge in the presence of the jury, while at the same time assuring that objections are made in apt time to afford the opportunity to take possible corrective measures. Compare the "automatic" objection feature of Rule 605 when the judge is called as a witness, and the similar feature of Rule 606 when a juror is called as a witness.

When the court calls witnesses and when it questions witnesses, regardless of who called them, the court easily can interfere with the proper workings of the adversary system and the court can threaten the independence of the jury. Thus, the powers conferred by this rule should be exercised with great care. Before utilizing these powers the court should be certain that the parties are incapable of acting to fully protect their interests. *See* Saltzburg, The Unnecessarily Expanding Role of the American Trial Judge, 64 Va. L. Rev. (1978).

Rule 615. Exclusion of Witnesses.

The efficacy of excluding or sequestering witnesses has long been recognized as a means of discouraging and exposing fabrication, inaccuracy and collusion. These are compelling reasons for exclusion in both criminal and civil trials. *See* 6 Wigmore §§ 1837-1838.

This rule, similar to both Alaska R. Civ. P. 43(g) (3), which it supersedes, and AS 09.20.180, differs in a few respects. First, it not only provides the court with the traditional power to order exclusion at the request of a party, but also provides that the court may order exclusion on its own motion. Secondly, it permits a party to request exclusion of any witness, not just a witness called by an adverse party. A witness called by a party may not be aligned with that party for all purposes, so that the party calling him may still have an interest in preventing him from hearing the testimony of other witnesses.

Federal Rule 615 makes exclusion upon request by a party a matter of right. Following the prevailing view, that expressed in AS 09.20.180, this rule permits the trial judge discretion in granting requests. The practical difference between the rules should be minimal, since there is rarely a good reason to deny a sequestration request; the procedure is simple and the possible benefit to be derived by a party is enormous. Inconsistent testimony as a result of sequestering witnesses gives rise to two possible inferences: (1) that an honest mistake was made, suggesting inaccuracy to the factfinder, or, (2) that collusion or perjury has taken place. Both of these inferences may greatly influence the trial. Although it is often difficult to assess the likelihood that sequestration will elicit inconsistent testimony that could not be elicited from witnesses who heard each other testify, the possibility exists in virtually every case. The most honest witness may shade testimony, perhaps only subconsciously, to make it fit the pattern established by other witnesses. Only in exceptional circumstances are there sufficient reasons for denying exclusion.

Several categories of persons are excepted from exclusion, by this rule. (1) Exclusion of persons who are parties would raise a serious sixth amendment confrontation problem in criminal trials and present a fundamental fairness question even in civil cases. Under accepted practice they are not subject to exclusion. 6 Wigmore § 1841. (2) As the equivalent of the right of a natural-person (party) to be present, a party which is not a natural person is entitled to have a representative present. Most of the cases have involved allowing a police officer who has been in charge of an investigation to remain in court despite the fact that he will be a witness. *See Dickens v. State,* 398 P.2d 1008 (Alaska 1965). *See also* California Evidence Code § 777. (3) The final category contemplates such persons as an agent who handled the transaction being litigated or an expert needed to advise counsel in the management of the litigation. *See* 6 Wigmore § 1841, n.4. Whether the assistance of such a person is "essential" is something that the trial judge must decide by weighing the benefits of assistance to one party against the possible benefits of another party of excluding the person as a future witness.

To assure that the rule works as intended, under normal circumstances the court should instruct the witnesses to refrain from discussing their testimony with other witnesses outside the courtroom.

ARTICLE VII. OPINION TESTIMONY

Rule 701. Opinion Testimony by Lay Witnesses.

Rule 701 follows the Federal Rule in departing from the impracticable common law prohibition of opinion testimony by lay witnesses. In the words of Judge Learned Hand:

> The truth is, as Mr. Wigmore has observed at length . . . that the exclusion of opinion evidence has been carried beyond reason in this country, and that it would be a large advance if courts were to admit it with freedom. The line between opinion and fact is at best only one of degree, and also depends solely upon practical considerations, as, for example, the saving of time and the mentality of the witness....It is a good rule as nearly as one can, to reproduce the scene as it was, and so to correct the personal equations of the witnesses. But one must be careful not to miss the forest for the trees, as generally happens, unless much latitude is allowed.

Central Railroad Co. v. Monahan, 11 F.2d 212, 213-214 (2d

Cir. 1926). The rule retains the traditional objective of putting the trier of fact in possession of an accurate reproduction of the event.

Limitation (a) is the familiar requirement of firsthand knowledge or observation.

Limitation (b) is phrased in terms of requiring testimony to be helpful in resolving issues. Witnesses often find difficulty in expressing themselves in language which is not that of an opinion or conclusion. While the courts have made concessions in certain recurring situations, necessity as a standard for permitting opinions and conclusions has proved too elusive and too unadaptable to particular situations for purposes of satisfactory judicial administration. McCormick (2d ed.) § 11. Moreover, the practical impossibility of determining by rule what is a "fact," demonstrated by a century of litigation of the question of what is a fact for purposes of pleading under the Field Code extends into evidence also. 7 Wigmore § 1919. The rule assumes that the natural characteristics of the adversary system will generally lead to an acceptable result, since the detailed account carries more conviction than the broad assertion, and a lawyer can be expected to display his witness to the best advantage. If he fails to do so, cross-examination and argument will point up the weakness. *See,* Ladd, Expert Testimony, 5 Vand. L. Rev. 414, 415-417 (1952). If, despite these considerations, attempts are made to introduce meaningless assertions which amount to little more than choosing up sides, exclusion for lack of helpfulness is called for by the rule.

Rule 702. **Testimony by Experts.**

Common law courts traditionally have permitted expert testimony on subjects "beyond the lay comprehension." This rule continues the tradition with two modifications: 1) Rule 702 permits expert testimony if it would be helpful to the trier of fact in understanding evidence that is difficult, but perhaps not beyond ordinary comprehension. 2) The rule provides that an expert may provide background information to a jury without offering an opinion on any issue in the case.

By allowing testimony "in the form of an opinion or otherwise," the rule allows an expert to give testimony in the form of a dissertation on a given topic thereby allowing the trier of fact to draw his own inferences by applying the specialized knowledge to the facts of the case at hand. Since this approach avoids complaints that the expert is usurping the function of the jury, it should be welcome in many courtrooms. Indeed, it is difficult to understand why some common law authorities are reluctant to use expert evidence in this manner. If the rationale were that the trier of fact might have difficulty in drawing inferences from specialized evidence, it would not be persuasive, because it would suggest that the trier of fact is incapable of rejecting expert opinions. If expert evidence is to assist the trier of fact, the trier must always understand how the expert evidence is derived.

This provision is identical to Federal Rule 702 which was broadly written to encompass fields of expertise that require "specialized" knowledge. In addition to witnesses skilled in scientific and technical matters, this rule recognizes that witnesses qualified by "knowledge, skill, experience, training, or education" in areas such as banking or even real estate values are similarly capable of aiding the trier of fact.

Whether a particular case is suitable for the use of expert testimony is determined by the trial judge's assessment of the likelihood that specialized help would assist the trier of fact. *See Leavitt v. Gillaspie,* 443 P.2d 61 (Alaska 1968). *See also Bachner v. Rich,* 554 P.2d 430 (Alaska 1976) (finding error in admission of expert testimony). Whether or not a witness qualifies as an expert is also a determination that is made by the trial judge. After a ruling that a witness does qualify, counsel for the opposing party may question the qualifications of the expert before the jury. This goes to the weight of the testimony, assessment of which is the province of the trier of fact.

In deciding whether or not an expert is qualified to testify, the trial judge must be aware of the substantive law to be applied in a given case. *See, e.g., Priest v. Lindig,* 583 P.2d 173 (Alaska 1978) (discussing the standard of care to be employed in a medical malpractice case and the qualification of a physician to testify).

For similar provisions *see,* Nebraska Rule 27-702, New Mexico Rule 20-4-702, and Maine Rule 702.

Rule 703. **Basis of Opinion Testimony by Experts.**

Rule 703 follows the Federal Rule. For the most part it works no change in existing law, but it does make one break with the common law in expanding the category of permissible bases for an expert opinion.

Under the rule, expert opinions may be based upon facts or data derived from three possible sources. The first is the firsthand observation of the witness; opinions based thereon are traditionally allowed at common law. For example, a treating physician whose opinion is based on firsthand sense impressions may use these impressions as the basis of an expert opinion. Rheingold, The Basis of Medical Testimony, 15 Vand. L. Rev. 473, 480 (1962). Whether he must first relate his observations is treated in Rule 705.

The second source, presentation at trial, also reflects existing practice. Generally the expert can be informed of facts of trial in one of two ways: counsel may pose the familiar hypothetical question grounded in evidence offered to the trier of fact, or counsel may have the expert attend the trial and hear the testimony establishing the facts. In cases of conflicting testimony the hypothetical question will be the appropriate technique, as the expert should not be put in the position of deciding questions of witness credibility.

When the expert purports to base his opinion on testimony offered in court, Rule 705 will provide a means of discovering whether the expert is assuming the truth of certain disputed facts. As long as the expert's hypothesis is clarified for the trier of fact, the hybrid techniques is acceptable.

The third source contemplated by the rule consists of presentation of data to the expert outside of court and other than by his own perception. In this respect the rule is designed to broaden the basis for expert opinion, in accordance with the belief that when an expert is deemed skilled enough to assist the trier of fact, the expert should be allowed to utilize the tools that he normally uses to practice his skills outside of the court. Thus, a physician in his own practice bases his diagnosis on general information obtained from medical journals and treatises and on information about the patient from numerous sources and of considerable variety, including statements by patients and relatives, reports and opinions from nurses, technicians and other doctors, hospital records, and x-rays. Some of these sources would be inadmissible in evidence; most of them are admissible, but only with the expenditure of substantial time in producing and examining various authenticating witnesses. The physician makes life-and-death decisions in reliance upon them. His validation, expertly performed and subject to cross-examination, ought to suffice for judicial purposes. Rheingold, *supra,* at 531. McCormick (2d ed.) § 15. The rule may be most beneficial in the examination of psychiatrists, who may often rely on data that is technically hearsay. Rule 705 controls the admissibility of facts or data not in evidence but relied upon by an expert.

The rule also offers a more satisfactory basis for ruling upon the admissibility of public opinion poll evidence. If an expert pollster is called to testify, the court will focus on the validity of the techniques employed by the pollster, rather than on relatively fruitless inquiries into whether hearsay is involved.

There are two major aims accomplished by providing that an expert may base an opinion on inference upon facts or data whether or not admissible in evidence if the facts or data are of a type reasonably relied upon by experts in the expert's particular field. First, it prevents experts from explicitly relying upon facts unless these facts are of a type reasonably relied upon by similar experts. Second, it has the effect of excluding altogether some experts who would appear to qualify under Rule 702. If an expert cannot ground an opinion in facts or data "reasonably relied upon," the opinion or inference as well as the facts and data must be excluded. Thus, some scientific or expert evidence that would not be excluded on relevance grounds will be excluded by Rule 703. While a consensus of all experts in the field that a particular test is failsafe is unnecessary, the court must be convinced that the data is a type on which those in the field would reasonably rely.

The rule attempts to chart a path between the rigid approach of *Frye v. United States,* 293 F. 1013 (D.C. Cir. 1923) ("the thing from which the deduction is made must be sufficiently established to have gained general acceptance in the particular field to which it belongs") and the minimal relevance approach of Rule 401. Even though Rule 403 might be deemed sufficient protection against the dangers of relatively untested evidence, Rule 703 is drafted so as to remind trial judges that innovative attempts to offer expert evidence may involve evidence that is superficially attractive, but which is problematic for one or more of the following reasons: 1) the party against whom the evidence is offered has had insufficient time to rebut the validity of the offered evidence, which may be the product of years of research; 2) the party against whom the evidence is offered has been unable to secure the assistance of expert help necessary to understand and attack the offered evidence; 3) while the expert evidence is plainly relevant, the rate of error associated with the technique that produced the evidence is unknown and the trier of fact is therefore unable to properly evaluate the evidence; 4) the expert evidence is the subject of great controversy among the nation's experts and it would be inappropriate for a court or jury to resolve the controversy in any particular case. *See, e.g., People v. Kelly,* 549 P.2d 1240 (Cal. 1976) (rejecting voiceprint evidence).

In most instances when a new technique is utilized, witnesses other than the creator of the technique will be needed to satisfy the "reasonable reliance" requirement. If the new technique is closely related to one already accepted by the courts, less foundation proof will be required.

Rule 704. Opinion on Ultimate Issue.

The basic approach to opinions, lay and expert, in these rules is to admit them when helpful to the trier of fact. In order to render this approach fully effective and to allay any doubt on the subject, the so-called "ultimate issue" rule is specifically abolished by the instant rule. This provision is identical to Federal Rule 704 which followed the lead of Uniform Rule 56(4).

The older cases in other jurisdictions often contained strictures against allowing witnesses to express opinions upon ultimate issues, as a particular aspect of the rule against opinions. The basis usually assigned for the rule, to prevent the witness from "usurping the province of the jury," is aptly characterized as "empty rhetoric." 7 Wigmore § 1920 at 17. Efforts to meet the felt needs of particular situations led to odd verbal circumlocutions which were said not to violate the rule. Thus a witness could express his estimate of the criminal responsibility of an accused in terms of sanity or insanity, but not in terms of ability to tell right from wrong or other more modern standards. And in cases of medical causation, witnesses were sometimes required to couch their opinions in cautious phrases of "might or could," rather than "did," though the result was to deprive many opinions of the positiveness to which they were entitled, accompanied by the hazard of a ruling of insufficiency to support a verdict. In other instances the rule was simply disregarded, and, as concessions to need, opinions were allowed upon such matters as intoxication, speed, handwriting, and value, although more precise coincidence with an ultimate issue would scarcely be possible.

The modern trend, reflected both in judicial decisions and in codifications of evidence law, has been toward complete abandonment of the rule prohibiting opinions embracing ultimate issues. According to McCormick the change has resulted from

> the fact that the rule excluding opinion on ultimate facts in issue is unduly restrictive, pregnant with close questions of application and the possibility of misapplication, and often unfairly obstructive to the presentation of a party's case, to say nothing of the illogic of the idea that these opinions usurp the function of the jury.

McCormick (2d ed.) § 12, at 27-28. *See also Bachner v. Rich,* 554 P.2d 430 (Alaska 1976).

The abolition of the ultimate issue rule does not lower the bars so as to admit all opinions. Under Rules 701 and 702, opinions must be helpful to the trier of fact. Rule 703 requires an opinion based on facts or data reasonably relied upon, and Rule 403 provides for exclusion of evidence which wastes time. These provisions afford ample assurances against the admission of opinions which would merely tell the jury what result to reach, somewhat in the manner of the oathhelpers of an earlier day. They also stand ready to exclude opinions phrased in terms of inadequately explored legal criteria. Thus the question, "Did T have capacity to make a will?" would be excluded, while the question, "Did T have sufficient mental capacity to know the nature and extent of his property and the natural objects of his bounty and to formulate a rational scheme of distribution?" would be allowed. McCormick (2d ed.) § 12.

For similar provisions see California Evidence Code § 805; New Jersey Rule 56(3); Maine Rule 704; Nevada Rule 50.295; Nebraska Rule 27-704; Kansas Rule 60-456 (d).

Under this rule an opinion of any person that a criminal defendant is guilty or innocent would not be admissible.

Rule 705. Disclosure of Facts or Data Underlying Expert Opinion.

(a) **Disclosure of Facts.** Rule 705 follows the Federal Rule in eliminating the requirement of disclosure at trial of underlying facts or data before an expert testifies in terms of opinion or inference. Previously, the examination of an expert for the purpose of obtaining an opinion had to be phrased in the form of a hypothetical question with two principal exceptions: Where the witness had personal knowledge of the facts or where the witness listened to undisputed courtroom testimony. In the case of these exceptions, it has been common practice to precede the opinion with a description of its factual basis. This practice has not caused many problems. But the examination by hypothetical question has been a cause for concern. The hypothetical question has been the target of a great deal of criticism as encouraging partisan bias, affording an opportunity for summing up in the middle of the case, and as complex and time consuming. Ladd, Expert Testimony, 5 Vand. L. Rev. 414, 426-427 (1952).

The elimination of the requirement of preliminary disclosure at the trial of underlying facts or data has a long background of support. In 1937 the Commissioners on Uniform State Laws incorporated a provision to this effect in their Model Expert Testimony Act, which furnished the basis for Uniform Rules 57 and 58. Rule 4515, N.Y. Civ. Prac. Law (McKinney), provides:

> Unless the court orders otherwise, questions calling for the opinion of an expert witness need not be hypothetical in form, and the witness may state his opinion and reasons without first specifying the data upon which it is based. Upon cross-examination, he may be required to specify the data . . . .

See also California Evidence Code § 802; Kansas Code of Civil Procedure §§ 60-456, 60-457; New Jersey Evidence Rules 57, 58, Federal Rule 705.

Since the criticisms of the hypothetical question cited earlier suggest that it may provide unfair advantages to the direct examiner, the question arises whether to ban hypothetical questions altogether. This rule chooses not to do so. In some instances the hypothetical question works well; indeed sometimes it is the only way to elicit expert testimony. Therefore, the rule adopts Wigmore's suggestion and *permits* an examiner to utilize a hypothetical approach in questioning an expert, subject to Rule 403.

Many lawyers will welcome the invitation to abandon hypothetical questions, since they involve pitfalls as well as advantages for the direct examiner. In asking hypothetical questions the examiner must insure "that the facts assumed [are] supported by the evidence in the case." McCormick (2d ed.) § 14. "[B]ungling of the hypothesis by confusing it with factual material stated to the expert witness out of court demand heroic remedies." J. Maguire et al., Cases and Materials on Evidence 265 (5th ed. 1965). Moreover, the examiner runs the risk that the question will "confuse the jury, so that its employment becomes a mere waste of time and a futile obstruction," 2 Wigmore § 686, at 812.

The adverse party may require the expert to disclose facts or data underlying his opinion or inference upon cross-examination. But the cross-examiner is under no compulsion to seek disclosure and may, if disclosure is sought, seek to bring out only facts or data casting doubt upon the reliability of the opinion. Normally the cross-examiner will have enough advance knowledge to cross-examine effectively.

This advance knowledge has been afforded, though imperfectly, by the traditional foundation requirement. Rule 26 (b) (4) of the Alaska Rules of Civil Procedure, as revised, provides for substantial discovery in this area, obviating in large measure the obstacles which have been raised in some instances to discovery of findings, underlying data, and even the identity of the experts. *See* Friedenthal, Discovery and Use of an Adverse Party's Expert Information, 14 Stan. L. Rev. 455 (1962), discussing the identical Federal Rule of Civil Procedure.

These safeguards are reinforced by the discretionary power of the judge, either on its own motion or upon request, to require preliminary disclosure *in camera* if the adverse party so requests.

(b) **Admissibility.** In the spirit of Rule 103, this subdivision provides that the adverse party may request a judicial determination of whether the requirements of Rule 703 are met before the expert is allowed to give his opinion or inference. This provision allows the adverse party who believes an opinion is ill-founded to assert this challenge without running the risk that facts or data once disclosed to the jury may never be forgotten.

Just as an offer of proof under Rule 103 may take different forms, depending on the issue before the court, the judicial hearing under this subdivision also may differ as issues change from case to case. In some cases the judge may be able to rule after a quick side-bar conference. In other cases the jury may have to be excused, or the parties may have to join the judge in chambers. Sometimes counsel's representations as to the witness's testimony will be sufficient. At other times testimony out of the hearing of the jury may be required. The trial judge is vested with broad discretion to assure that experts are permitted to testify on the basis of proper data under Rule 703 without using this rule to take an unfair advantage. *Cf., Kaps Transport, Inc. v. Henry,* 572 P.2d 72 (Alaska 1977).

(c) **Balancing Test—Limiting Instructions.** This part of the rule requires that the court guard against any attempt to use this rule, in connection with Rule 703, to put inadmissible evidence before the jury for an improper purpose. Since facts or data need not be admissible to provide the basis for an expert's opinion under Rule 703, disclosure of facts or data, not otherwise admissible, to explain an expert's opinion might lead to use the facts or data as the basis for an independent judgment on issues in a case. If an objection is made to disclosure of facts or data not otherwise admissible in evidence, before allowing disclosure the court should hear the facts or data outside the hearing of the jury and balance the value of the facts or data as support for the expert's opinion against the danger that they will be used for an improper purpose. The balancing test used here is similar to those used in Rules 403 and 609. The danger must outweigh the value before exclusion is warranted. Whenever facts or data that would have been admissible for any other purpose are disclosed to the jury to support an expert's opinion, an instruction should be given, upon request, admonishing the jury to consider the facts or data only for the purpose for which they were disclosed. This is in accord with the policy concerning limiting instructions expressed in Rule 105.

Rule 706. Court Appointed Experts.

(a) **Appointment.**

This provision recognizes judicial power to appoint experts and outlines the procedures to be followed when courts exercise such power. Like its federal counterpart, this subdivision is largely drawn from a rule of criminal procedure which it supersedes. *See* Rule 28 Alaska R. Crim. P.

In the Model Expert Testimony Act of 1937, the National Commissioners on Uniform State Laws expressed the view that court appointed experts would strike at the "biased testimony which prevails under the present system." Arguments to the contrary have contended that court appointed experts may be erroneously considered infallible, especially when offered to resolve so-called "battles of the experts." *See* Levy, Impartial Medical Testimony—Revisited, 34 Temple L.Q. 416 (1961). This rule recognizes the wisdom of appointing independent experts in some cases, but also acknowledges that there are dangers associated with these appointments. Subdivision (c) further addresses these issues.

Alaska Rule 706 differs substantially from Federal Rule 706 and from superseded Alaska R. Crim. P. 28 in limiting the right of a party calling a court appointed expert to cross-examine that witness. With increased information about an expert's testimony available through the use of depositions, if counsel were to call an expert known to be favorable to his client and also to receive the benefit of leading questions, the consequences to an adverse party may be unduly severe. Moreover, since nothing in the rule prohibits a court appointed expert from cooperating with the parties in preparation for trial, there will be cases in which the party who benefits from the testimony of a court appointed expert has as much opportunity to consult with him before trial as with any other witness.

Where the court determines that justice so requires, the party calling the witness will be permitted to cross-examine him. Two important factors to be considered in making this determination are: whether the party was able to depose the expert and whether the expert cooperated with the party calling him. In other words, the less information the party has, the greater the need to cross-examine. The less cooperation afforded by the expert, the greater the need of the party to cross-examine him. *See* Rule 611(c), which rule also applies to court appointed experts, for similar consideration allowing the trial judge to permit the direct examiner to ask leading questions.

Where the court calls the expert, Rule 614 governs and both parties may cross-examine the witness.

See Uniform Rule 50; California Evidence Code §§ 730, 732; Nebraska Rule 27-706; Maine Rule 706.

Although this rule is based on Federal Rule 706, it has no provision for compensation of experts comparable to subdivision (b) of the Federal Rule. Compensation of experts is a subject covered by Administrative Rule 7(c). However, once Rule 706 takes effect it may be necessary to reconsider the question of how best to compensate expert witnesses to assure that sufficient compensation is provided so that experts are not reluctant to testify.

(b) **Disclosure of Appointment.** The court may, in its discretion, disclose to the jury the fact that the court appointed the expert witness. This subdivision is identical to its counterpart in the Federal Rule.

The Model Expert Testimony Act (§ 8) made disclosure to the jury mandatory. In Uniform Rule 61 disclosure was changed to discretionary, but the Commissioners' Note following the rule indicates that the change may not have been significant.

> Since experts appointed by the judge will ordinarily be impartial witnesses, the fact of their appointment should be disclosed to the trier of the facts in order that their testimony may be properly valued.

9A Uniform Laws Annotated 633 (1965).

The Commission's Note assumed that disclosure that an expert is aligned with the court will influence the jury by enhancing the expert's credibility. This assumption is probably valid, but there is always cause for concern when the credibility of a witness is bolstered not by anything that the witness does or says, but by being identified with the court. Assuming that impartiality justifies enhanced credibility, the questions that arise are 1) how much more credible impartiality makes a witness, and 2) who answers the first question. The court can choose only to reveal or not to reveal the nature of an appointment. If the court elects nondisclosure, neither question will have to be answered. Making a wise choice requires an assessment of several factors: the independent weight of the expert's credentials, whether both parties agreed on the expert, the relationship of the court appointed expert's testimony to other expert testimony in the case, the existence of divisions of opinion on important matters among leading experts in a field, and the reasons why the court appointed an expert in the first place.

(c) **Parties' Experts of Own Selection.** This subdivision follows superseded Alaska R. Crim. P. 28. It permits the court to supplement evidence by calling witnesses, but does not permit the court to abrogate the responsibilities of counsel in an adversary system.

ARTICLE VIII. HEARSAY

Introductory Reporter's Comment

Like Article V, this Article and the Reporter's Comments that accompany it, do not attempt to analyze the history of the hearsay rule and to assess the strengths and weaknesses of hearsay exceptions that have withstood the test of time. This is not to say that Article VIII is nothing more than a codification of common law rules; departures from the common law tradition are frequent, and they are explained in the comments accompanying the relevant sections of the rules. When the common law is carried forward in the rules, only brief mention is made of the rationale for the relevant provisions.

The comments accompanying the rules draw heavily, and at times are verbatim copies, of the Advisory Committee's Notes accompanying the Federal Rules of Evidence. Conspicuously different is the approach of the introductory note on hearsay found in both the Federal and the Alaska Rules. The latter is shorter and assumes greater knowledge on the part of the reader. Practicing lawyers are quite familiar with the rationale for a hearsay rule that begins with the assumption that evidence not tested by cross-examination should be excluded. No matter what the exact words used, problems of sincerity, ambiguity of narration, memory and perception are familiar ones. The Advisory Committee argued that sincerity is "merely...an aspect of the three [otherwise] mentioned." To the extent that some courtroom observers believe that perjury is common even in court, problems of perjury outside of court when there is no cross-examination also are likely to exist. Thus, the Advisory Committee was probably wrong. Aside from cross-examination, other reasons for a hearsay rule include the desirability of having evidence taken under oath and the importance of viewing the demeanor of a witness.

> The Advisory Committee is undoubtedly correct in noting that the logic of the argument [supporting a hearsay rule] ...might suggest that no testimony be received unless in full compliance with the three ideal conditions. [Cross-examination, oath, and demeanor.] No one advocates this position. Common sense tells that much evidence which is not given under the three conditions may be inherently superior to much that is. Moreover, when the choice is between evidence which is less than best and no evidence at all, only clear folly would dictate an across-the-board policy of doing without. The problem thus resolves itself into effecting a sensible accommodation between these considerations and the desirability of giving testimony under the ideal conditions.
>
> The solution evolved by the common law has been a general rule excluding hearsay but subject to numerous exceptions under circumstances supposed to furnish guarantees of trustworthiness. Criticisms of this scheme are that it is both bulky and complex, fails to screen good from bad hearsay realistically, and inhibits the growth of the law of evidence.

The Advisory Committee goes on at great length to explain why it decided not to abandon the hearsay rule or to greatly simplify it. The shorter, but similar, answer provided by these rules is that the dangers associated with hearsay are real and continue to plague trial courts today as they have in the past. In addition, arguments for simplification such as those advocated by Weinstein, The Probative Force of Hearsay, 46 Iowa L. Rev. 331 (1961), assume greater faith in trial judges than yet can be justified. Moreover, a more flexible rule might tend to confer an unfair advantage on the government in criminal cases and wealthy parties in civil cases who have ready and efficient means for preparing their hearsay evidence for use at trial. Finally, it is likely that a more flexible rule would tend to produce categories of exceptions for the guidance of trial judges that resemble those that are presented in these rules, which are themselves the out-growth of adjudication and many years of debate. Thus, as the Advisory Committee helpfully observed

> [t]he approach to hearsay in these rules is that of the common law, i.e., the general rule excluding hearsay, with exceptions under which evidence is not required to be excluded even though hearsay. The traditional hearsay exceptions are drawn upon for the exceptions, collected under two rules, one dealing with situations where availability of the declarant is regarded as immaterial and the other with those whose unavailability is made a condition to the admission of the hearsay statement. Each of the two rules concludes with a provision for hearsay statements not within one of the specified exceptions "but having comparable [equivalent] circumstantial guarantees of trustworthiness."

In its introductory note, the Advisory Committee wrote at length on the subject of confrontation. Although the United States Supreme Court has recognized that the roots of the confrontation protection and the hearsay rule are common, the constitutional protection and the evidence protection are not identical. Clearly, the confrontation clause speaks to subjects not addressed by the hearsay rule: e.g., the confrontation clause mandates that a defendant be given the opportunity to be present at trial, while the hearsay rule does not address this question; and the confrontation requirement may control the scope of cross-examination and impeachment, while the hearsay rule may not. It is just as clear that the hearsay rule goes beyond minimal confrontation requirements in protecting litigants against unfairness. It is difficult to ascertain precisely what limits the confrontation clause, as applied to the states through the fourteenth amendment, places on states in drafting evidence rules. *California v. Green,* 399 U.S. 149, 26 L.Ed.2d 489 (1970) and *Dutton v. Evans,* 400 U.S. 74, 27 L.Ed.2d 213 (1970) indicate that the highwater marks of the confrontation clause—*Pointer v. Texas,* 380 U.S. 400, 13 L.Ed.2d 923 (1965), *Douglas v. Alabama,* 380 U.S. 415, 13 L.Ed.2d 934 (1965), *Burton v. United States,* 389 U.S. 818, 19 L.Ed.2d 70 (1968), and *Barber v. Page,* 390 U.S. 719, 20 L.Ed. 2d 255 (1968)—can no longer be read to expand the protection of the confrontation clause in criminal cases to resemble very closely the protection afforded by hearsay rules. There is no need in these rules to answer the question whether some common law hearsay exceptions violate the confrontation requirement, and if so, which ones. It is sufficient to note that the Alaska Rules are drafted with the confrontation requirement in mind and in an attempt to avoid constitutional difficulties. The federal Advisory Committee made a comment that is appropriate here:

> Under the earlier cases, the confrontation clause may have been little more than a constitutional embodiment of the hearsay rule, even including traditional exceptions but

with some room for expanding them along similar lines. But under the recent cases the impact of the clause clearly extends beyond the confines of the hearsay rule. These considerations have led the Advisory Committee to conclude that a hearsay rule can function usefully as an adjunct to the confrontation right in constitutional areas and independently in non-constitutional areas. In recognition of the separateness of the confrontation clause and the hearsay rule, and to avoid inviting collisions between them or between the hearsay rule and other exclusionary principles, the exceptions set forth in Rules 803 and 804 are stated in terms of exemption from the general exclusionary mandate of the hearsay rule, rather than in positive terms of admissibility.

For a recent case involving an overlap between hearsay and constitutional issues, see *Benefield v. State,* 559 P.2d 91 (Alaska 1977).

Rule 801. Definitions.

(a) **Statement.** The definition of "statement" assumes importance because the term is used in the definition of hearsay in subdivision (c). The effect of the definition of "statement" is to exclude from the operation of the hearsay rule all evidence of conduct, verbal or nonverbal, not intended as an assertion. The key to the definition is that nothing is an assertion unless intended to be one. This follows present Alaska law. See *Clary v. Fifth Ave. Chrysler Center, Inc.,* 454 P.2d 245, 250-51 (Alaska 1969).

It can scarcely be doubted that an assertion made in words is intended by the declarant to be an assertion. Hence verbal assertions readily fall into the category of "statement." Whether nonverbal conduct should be regarded as a statement for purposes of defining hearsay requires further consideration. Some nonverbal conduct, such as the act of pointing to identify a suspect in a lineup, is clearly the equivalent of words, assertive in nature, and to be regarded as a statement. Other nonverbal conduct, however, may be offered as evidence that the person acted as he did because of his belief in the existence of the condition sought to be proved, from which belief the existence of the condition may be inferred. This sequence is, arguably, in effect an assertion of the existence of the condition and hence properly includable within the hearsay concept. See Morgan, Hearsay Dangers and the Application of the Hearsay Concept, 62 Harv. L. Rev. 177, 214, 217 (1948), and the elaboration in Finman, Implied Assertions as Hearsay: Some Criticisms of the Uniform Rules of Evidence, 14 Stan. L. Rev. 682 (1962). Arguments found in these sources were rejected, however, in *Clary, supra.* Admittedly evidence of this character is untested with respect to the perception, memory, and narration (or their equivalents) of the actor. See generally Tribe, Triangulating Hearsay, 87 Harv. L. Rev. 957 (1975). But the rule adopts the view that these dangers are minimal in the absence of an intent to assert and do not justify the loss of the evidence on hearsay grounds. No class of evidence is free of the possibility of fabrication, but the likelihood is less with nonverbal than with assertive verbal conduct. The situations giving rise to the nonverbal conduct are such as virtually to eliminate questions of sincerity. Motivation, the nature of the conduct, and the presence or absence of reliance will bear heavily upon the weight to be given the evidence. Falknor, The "Hear-Say" Rule as a "See-Do" Rule: Evidence of Conduct, 33 Rocky Mt. L. Rev. 133 (1961). Similar considerations govern nonassertive verbal conduct and verbal conduct which is assertive but offered as a basis for inferring something other than the matter asserted, also excluded from the definition of hearsay by the language of subdivision (c).

When evidence of conduct is offered on the theory that it is not a statement, and hence not hearsay, a preliminary determination will be required to determine whether an assertion is intended. The rule is so worded as to place the burden upon the party claiming that the intention existed; ambiguous and doubtful cases will be resolved against him and in favor of admissibility. The determination involves no greater difficulty than many other preliminary questions of fact. Maguire, The Hearsay System: Around and Through the Thicket, 14 Vand. L. Rev. 741, 765-67 (1961).

For similar approaches, see Uniform Rule 62(1); California Evidence Code §§ 225, 1200; Kansas Code of Civil Procedure § 60-459 (a); New Jersey Evidence Rule 62 (1).

(b) **Declarant.** The definition of "declarant" is straightforward and requires no elaboration.

(c) **Hearsay.** The definition follows along familiar lines in including only statements offered to prove the truth of the matter asserted. McCormick (2d ed.) § 225; 5 Wigmore § 1361, 6 Wigmore § 1766. If the significance of an offered statement lies solely in the fact that it was made, no issue is raised as to the truth of anything asserted, and the statement is not hearsay. *Cf., e.g., Clary v. Fifth Ave. Chrysler Center, Inc.,* 454 P.2d 244, 250-51 (Alaska 1969); *P.H. v. State,* 504 P.2d 837, 842-43 (Alaska 1972). Although neither case turned on an interpretation of an offer of a statement "to prove the truth of the matter asserted"—the first case holding that non-assertive conduct was not hearsay and the second holding that a rule of testimonial completeness may override the hearsay rule—arguably both cases involve evidence not offered for its truth. The effect of this subdivision is to exclude from hearsay the entire category of "verbal acts" and "verbal parts of an act," in which the statement itself affects the legal rights of the parties or is a circumstance bearing on conduct affecting their rights.

The definition of hearsay must, of course, be read with reference to the definition of statement set forth in subdivision (a).

Testimony given by a witness in the court of court proceedings is excluded since there is compliance with all the ideal conditions for testifying.

(d) **Statements Which are not Hearsay.** Several types of statements which would otherwise literally fall within the definition are expressly excluded from it:

(1) *Prior Statement by Witness.* Considerable controversy has attended the question whether a prior out-of-court statement by a person now available for cross-examination concerning it, under oath and in the presence of the trier of fact, should be classed as hearsay. If the witness admits on the stand that he made the statement and that it was true, he adopts the statement and there is no hearsay problem. The hearsay problem arises when the witness on the stand denies having made the statement or admits having made it but denies its truth. The traditional argument in favor of treating these latter

statements as hearsay is based upon the ground that the conditions of oath, cross-examination, and demeanor observation did not prevail at the time the statement was made and cannot adequately be supplied by the later examination. The logic of the situation is subject to attack. So far as concerns the oath, its mere presence has never been regarded as sufficient to remove a statement "from the hearsay category, and it receives much less emphasis than cross-examination as a truth-compelling device." While strong expressions are found to the effect that no conviction can be had or important right taken away on the basis of statements not made under fear of prosecution for perjury, *Bridges v. Wixon,* 326 U.S. 135, 89 L.Ed. 2103 (1945), the fact is that, of the many common law exceptions to the hearsay rule, only that for reported testimony has required the statement to have been made under oath.

Some have argued that no one has satisfactorily explained why cross-examination cannot be conducted subsequently with success, and that the decisions contending most vigorously for its inadequacy in fact demonstrate quite thorough exploration of the weaknesses and doubts attending the earlier statement. *State v. Saporen,* 285 N.W. 898 (Minn. 1939); *Ruhala v. Roby,* 150 N.W.2d 146 (Mich. 1967); *People v. Johnson,* 441 P.2d 111 (Cal. 1968). In respect to demeanor, Judge Learned Hand observed in *Di Carlo v. United States,* 6 F.2d 364 (2d Cir. 1925), when the jury decides that the truth is not what the witness says now, but what he said before, they are still deciding from what they see and hear in court. The bulk of the case law nevertheless has been against allowing prior statements of witnesses to be used generally as substantive evidence. Most of the writers and Uniform Rule 63(1) have taken the opposite position.

(A) The Advisory Committee on the Federal Rules chose to treat prior inconsistent statements as substantive evidence. In doing so it adopted the position of California in section 1235 of its Evidence Code, which is supported by the following remarks of the California Law Revision Commission:

> Section 1235 admits inconsistent statements of witnesses because the dangers against which the hearsay rule is designed to protect are largely non-existent. The declarant is in court and may be examined and cross-examined in regard to his statements and their subject matter. In many cases, the inconsistent statement is more likely to be true than the testimony of the witness at the trial because it was made nearer in time to the matter to which it relates and is less likely to be influenced by the controversy that gave rise to the litigation. The trier of fact has the declarant before it and can observe his demeanor and the nature of his testimony as he denies or tries to explain away the inconsistency. Hence, it is in as good a position to determine the truth or falsity of the prior statement as it is to determine the truth or falsity of the inconsistent testimony given in court. Moreover, Section 1235 will provide a party with desirable protection against the "turncoat" witness who changes his story on the stand and deprives the party calling him of evidence essential to his case.

The Congress was concerned about the broadened use of inconsistent statements. The House of Representatives attempted to limit inconsistent statements admissible for substantive use to those made under oath and subject to cross-examination, but the Senate took the position that the requirement of a prior opportunity for cross-examination was too great a restriction on the use of probative and trustworthy evidence. The compromise in the Federal Rules was to admit prior statements made "under oath subject to the penalty of perjury at a trial, hearing, or other proceeding, or in a deposition."

Existing Alaska law is consistent with the California approach. *See Beavers v. State,* 492 P.2d 88, 94 (Alaska 1971); *Eubanks v. State,* 516 P.2d 726, 729 n.6 (Alaska 1973); *Gray v. State,* 525 P.2d 524, 526 n.6 (Alaska 1974). *See also Hobbs v. State,* 359 P.2d 956 (Alaska 1961); *Johnston v. State,* 489 P.2d 134 (Alaska 1971). Subdivision (d) (1) continues in effect existing Alaska law. Subsection (d) (1) does not alter the holding of *Beavers* that permits admission of prior inconsistent statements in the discretion of the trial judge as substantive evidence regardless of whether the prior statement was under oath and/or subject to cross-examination. Except in special cases, counsel should lay the foundation for an inconsistent statement while the witness who made the statement is testifying, as under Rule 613.

(B) Prior consistent statements traditionally have been admissible to rebut charges of recent fabrication or improper influence or motives but not as substantive evidence. *See* Rule 607(b). Under the rule they are substantive evidence. The prior statement is consistent with the testimony given on the stand, and, if the opposite party wishes to open the door for its admission in evidence, no sound reason is apparent why it should not be received generally.

(C) Some of the same dangers discussed in connection with prior inconsistent statements surround the use of identification evidence. But the rule provides that only the identification itself, not statements made about the crime, is to be admitted. Thus, this section is more limited than that on inconsistent statements, which covers all statements regardless of their length, detail and completeness. Constitutional limitations protect against undue suggestiveness. *See, e.g., Neil v. Biggers,* 409 U.S. 188, 34 L.Ed.2d 401 (1972); *Simmons v. United States,* 390 U.S. 377, 19 L.Ed.2d 1247 (1960); *Stovall v. Denno,* 388 U.S. 293, 18 L.Ed.2d 1199 (1967); *United States v. Wade,* 388 U.S. 218, 18 L.Ed.2d 1149 (1967); and *Gilbert v. California,* 388 U.S. 263, 18 L.Ed.2d 1178 (1967), restricted by *Kirby v. Illinois,* 406 U.S. 682, 32 L.Ed.2d 411 (1972). "An early, out-of-court identification provides fairness to defendants by ensuring accuracy of the identification. At the same time, it aids the government by making sure that delays in the criminal justice system do not lead to cases falling through because the witness can no longer recall the identity of the person he saw commit the crime." S.R. No. 94-199, 94th Cong., 1st Sess. (1975). *Accord, Buchanan v. State,* 554 P.2d 1153, 1158 (Alaska 1976). For recent cases discussing eyewitness identifications, *see Buchanan v. State,* 561 P.2d 1197 (Alaska 1977); *Benefield v. State,* 559 P.2d 91 (Alaska 1977); *Blue v. State,* 558 P.2d 636 (Alaska 1977); *Noble v. State,* 552 P.2d 142 (Alaska 1976).

(2) *Admissions.* Federal Rule 801 provides that admissions by a party-opponent are excluded from the category of hearsay on the theory that their admissibility in evidence is the result of the adversary system rather than satisfaction of the conditions of the hearsay rule. Strahorn, A Reconsideration of the Hearsay Rule and Admissions, 85 U. Pa. L. Rev. 484, 564 (1973);

Morgan, Basic Problems of Evidence 265 (1962); 4 Wigmore § 1048. No guarantee of trustworthiness is required in the case of an admission. The freedom which admissions have enjoyed from technical demands of searching for an assurance of trustworthiness in some against-interest circumstance, and from the restrictive influences of the opinion rule and the rule requiring first-hand knowledge, when taken with the apparently prevalent satisfaction with the results, calls for generous treatment of this avenue to admissibility.

While the classification of admissions as non-hearsay makes some sense if confined to personal admissions, there is no good reason to treat all the admissions covered by subsection (C), (D), and (E) as non-hearsay. In fact, if these rules were written on a clean slate without reference to the Federal Rules, admissions would be treated as exceptions to the hearsay rule and placed under Rule 803. But for the convenience of the bar the Federal Rule is followed. The end result is the same, and the slight confusion engendered by the treatment of admissions as non-hearsay is a small price to pay for uniformity.

The rule specifies five categories of statements for which the responsibility of a party is considered sufficient to justify reception in evidence against him.

(A) A party's own statement is the classic example of an admission. *See Jordan v. State,* 481 P.2d 383, 386 (Alaska 1971). If he has a representative capacity and the statement is offered against him in that capacity, no inquiry whether he was acting in the representative capacity in making the statement is required; the statement need only be relevant to representative affairs. To the same effect is California Evidence Code 1220. *Cf.,* Uniform Rule 63(7), requiring a statement to be made in a representative capacity to be admissible against a party in a representative capacity.

(B) Under established principles an admission may be made by adopting or acquiescing in the statement of another. While knowledge of contents would ordinarily be essential, this is not inevitably so: "X is a reliable person and knows what he is talking about." *See,* McCormick (2d ed.) § 246, at 527, n.15. Adoption or acquiescence may be manifested in any appropriate manner. When silence is relied upon, the theory is that the person would, under the circumstances, protest the statement made in his presence, if untrue. *See, e.g., Beavers v. State,* 492 P.2d 88, 96 (Alaska 1971). The decision in each case calls for an evaluation in terms of probable human behavior. In civil cases, the results have generally been satisfactory. In criminal cases, however, troublesome questions have been raised by decisions holding that failure to deny is an admission: the inference is a fairly weak one, to begin with; silence may be motivated by advice of counsel or realization that "anything you say may be used against you"; unusual opportunity is afforded to manufacture evidence; and encroachment upon the privilege against self-incrimination seems inescapably to be involved. However, recent decisions of the Supreme Court relating to custodial interrogation and the right to counsel appear to resolve these difficulties. *See, e.g., Doyle v. Ohio,* 426 U.S. 610, 49 L.Ed.2d 91 (1976). Hence the rule contains no special provisions concerning failure to deny in criminal cases.

(C) No authority is required for the general proposition that a statement authorized by a party to be made should have the status of and admission by the party. However, the question arises whether only statements to third persons should be so regarded, to the exclusion of statements by the agent to the principal. This is the new Maine Rule. The Alaska rule is phrased broadly so as to encompass both. While it may be argued that the agent authorized to make statements to his principal does not speak for him, Morgan, Basic Problems of Evidence 273 (1962), communication to an outsider has not generally been thought to be an essential characteristic of an admission. Thus, a party's books or records are usable against him, without regard to any intent to disclose to third persons. 5 Wigmore § 1557. *See also* McCormick (2d ed.) § 78, at 159161. In accord is New Jersey Evidence Rule 63(8)(a). *Cf.,* Uniform Rule 63(8) (a) and California Evidence Code § 1222 which limit status as an admission in this regard to statements authorized by the party to be made "for" him, which is perhaps an ambiguous limitation to statements to third persons. Falknor, Vicarious Admissions and the Uniform Rules, 14 Vand. L. Rev. 855, 860-61 (1961).

(D) The tradition has been to test the admissibility of statements by agents, as admissions, by applying the usual test of agency. Was the admission made by the agent acting in the scope of his employment? Since few principals employ agents for the purpose of making damaging statements, the usual result was exclusion of the statement. Dissatisfaction with this loss of valuable and helpful evidence has been increasing. A substantial trend favors admitting statements related to a matter within the scope of the agency or employment. *Grayson v. Williams,* 256 F.2d 61 (10th Cir. 1958); *Koninklijke Luchtvaart Maatschappij N.V. KLM Royal Dutch Airlines v. Tuller,* 292 F.2d 775, 784 (D.C. Cir. 1961); *Martin v. Savage Truck Lines, Inc.,* 121 F.Supp. 417 (D.D.C. 1954), and numerous state court decisions collected in 4 Wigmore, 1964 Supp., at 66-73, with comments by the editor that the statements should have been excluded as not within the scope of agency. For the traditional view, *see, Northern Oil Co. v. Socony Mobil Oil Co.,* 347 F.2d 81, 85 (2d Cir. 1965) and cases cited therein. Similar provisions are found in Uniform Rule 63(9) (a), Kansas Code of Civil Procedure § 60-460(i) (1), and New Jersey Evidence Rule 63(9) (a). The proposed Alaska rule was cited favorably in *P.R.& S. Inc. v. Pellack,* 583 P.2d 195 (Alaska 1978).

(E) The limitation upon the admissibility of statements of co-conspirators to those made "during the course and in furtherance of the conspiracy" is in the accepted pattern. While the broadened view of agency taken in item (D) might suggest wider admissibility of statements of co-conspirators, the agency theory of conspiracy is at best a fiction and ought not to serve as a basis for admissibility beyond that already established. *See* Levie, Hearsay and Conspiracy, 52 Mich. L. Rev. 1159 (1954); Comment, 25 U. Chi. L. Rev. 530 (1958). The rule is consistent with the position of the United States Supreme Court in denying admissibility to statements made after the objectives of the conspiracy have either failed or been achieved. *Krulewitch v. United States,* 336 U.S. 440, 93 L.Ed. 790 (1949); *Wong Sun v. United States,* 371 U.S. 471, 9 L.Ed. 2d 441 (1963). For similarly limited provisions *see* California Evidence Code § 1223 and New Jersey Rule 63(9) (b). *Cf.,* Uniform Rule 63(9) (b). While the rule refers to a co-conspirator, it should be clear that the rule is meant to carry forward the universally accepted doctrine that a joint venturer is considered as a co-conspirator for the purposes of this rule even though no conspiracy has been charged. *See Amidon v. State,* 565 P.2d 1248 (Alaska 1977). Traditionally the hearsay exception requires independent evidence of conspiracy. This tradition is implicitly carried forward under the rule. *See* K. Redden & S. Saltzburg, *Federal Rules of Evidence Manual* 461-68 (2d ed.1977).

Rule 802. Hearsay Rule.

Under existing Alaska law "hearsay is inadmissible upon objection unless it falls within one of the exceptions to the hearsay rule." *Burkholder v. State,* 491 P.2d 754, 757 (Alaska 1971). Many exceptions are listed in Rules 803 and 804, but exceptions to the hearsay rule may be found outside of Article VIII of these rules. The provision excepting from the operation of the rule hearsay which is made admissible by these rules or others adopted by the Alaska Supreme Court or by the legislature recognizes that it may be convenient to place a hearsay exception outside of this Article. When the supreme court or the legislature does so, the exception is every bit as valid as those located in Rules 803 and 804. The following examples illustrate hearsay that is rendered admissible by provisions outside of these two rules.

ALASKA RULES OF CIVIL PROCEDURE

Rule 4 (f): proof of service by affidavit.

Rule 32 (a): admissibility of depositions.

Rule 43(e): affidavits when motion based on facts not appearing of record, now found in Rule 43.

Rule 56: affidavits in summary judgment proceedings.

Rule 65(b): showing by affidavit for temporary restraining order.

ALASKA RULES OF CRIMINAL PROCEDURE

Rule 4(a) (1): affidavits to show grounds for issuing warrants.

Rule 5.1(d): written reports of experts in preliminary examination.

ENACTMENTS OF ALASKA LEGISLATURE

AS 03.40.070: certified copy of instrument evidencing sale of brand or mark.

AS 21.06.070: certificate of insurance director.

AS 32.05.060: partner's admission against partnership.

Rule 802 is also not intended to alter the substantive rule of evidence that hearsay not objected to at trial is competent evidence. *Reese v Geierman,* 574 P.2d 445 (Alaska 1978); *City of Anchorage v. Nesbett,* 530 P.2d 1324, 1336 (Alaska 1975); *Gregory v. Padilla,* 379 P.2d 951, 953 (Alaska 1963).

Rule 803. Hearsay Exceptions—Availability of Declarant Immaterial.

The exceptions are phrased in terms of non-application of the hearsay rule, rather than in positive terms of admissibility, in order to repel any implication that other possible grounds for exclusion are eliminated from consideration.

The present rule proceeds upon the theory that under appropriate circumstances a hearsay statement may possess circumstantial guarantees of trustworthiness sufficient to justify non-production of the declarant in person at the trial even though he may be available. The theory finds vast support in the many exceptions to the hearsay rule developed by the common law in which unavailability of the declarant is not a relevant factor. The present rule is a synthesis of them, with revision where modern developments and conditions are believed to make that course appropriate.

In a hearsay situation, the declarant is, of course, a witness, and neither this rule nor Rule 804 dispenses with the requirement of firsthand knowledge. It may appear from his statement or be inferable from circumstances. *See* Rule 602.

(1) and (2) **Present Sense Impression—Excited Utterance.** In considerable measure these two examples overlap, though based on somewhat different theories. The most significant practical difference will lie in the time lapse allowable between event and statement.

The underlying theory of Subdivision (1) is that substantial contemporaneity of event and statement negate the likelihood of deliberate or conscious misrepresentation. Moreover, if the witness is the declarant, he may be examined on the statement. If the witness is not the declarant, he may be examined as to the circumstances as an aid in evaluating the statement. Morgan, Basic Problems of Evidence 340-41 (1962).

The theory of Subdivision (2) is simply that circumstances may produce a condition of excitement which temporarily stills the capacity of reflection and produces utterances free of conscious fabrication. 6 Wigmore § 1747, at 135. Spontaneity is the key factor in each instance, though arrived at by somewhat different routes. Both are needed in order to avoid needless niggling.

While the theory of Subdivision (2) has been criticized on the ground that excitement impairs accuracy of observation as well as eliminating conscious fabrication, Hutchins and Slesinger, Some Observations on the Law of Evidence: Spontaneous Exclamations, 28 Colum. L. Rev. 432 (1928), it finds support in cases without number. *See* cases in 6 Wigmore § 1750; Annot. 53 A.L.R.2d 1245 (statements as to cause of or responsibility for motor vehicle accident); Annot., 4 A.L.R.3d 149 (accusatory statements by homicide victims). It is well grounded in Alaska case law. *See Torres v. State,* 519 P.2d 788, 792-93 (Alaska 1974); *Watson v. State,* 387 P.2d 289 (Alaska 1963). Since unexciting events are less likely to evoke comment, decisions involving Subdivision (1) are far less numerous. Illustrative are *Tampa Elec. Co. v. Getrost,* 10 So.2d 83 (Fla. 1942); *Houston Oxygen Co. v. Davis,* S.W.2d 474 (Tex. 1942); and cases cited in McCormick (2d ed.) § 278, at 709-11. *See also Beech Aircraft Corp. v. Harvey,* 558 P.2d 879, 884 (Alaska 1976).

With respect to the time element, Subdivision (1) recognizes that in many, if not most, instances precise contemporaneity is not possible, and hence a slight lapse is allowable. Under Subdivision (2) the standard of measurement is the duration of the state of excitement. "How long can excitement prevail? Obviously there are no pat answers and the character of the transaction or event will largely determine the significance of the time factor." Slough, Spontaneous Statements and State of

Mind, 46 Iowa L. Rev. 224, 243 (1961); McCormick (2d ed.) § 297, at 706-07.

Participation by the declarant is not required: a non-participant may be moved to describe what he perceives, and one may be startled by an event in which he is not an actor. Slough, *supra;* McCormick, *supra;* 6 Wigmore § 1755; Annot., 78 A.L.R.2d 300.

Whether proof of the startling event may be made by the statement itself is largely an academic question, since in most cases there is present at least circumstantial evidence that something of a startling nature must have occurred. Nevertheless, on occasion the only evidence may be the content of the statement itself and rulings that it may be sufficient are described as "increasing," Slough, *supra* at 246, and as the "prevailing practice," McCormick (2d ed.) § 299, at 705. Moreover, under Rule 104(a) the judge is not limited by the hearsay rule in passing upon preliminary questions of fact.

Proof of declarant's perception by his statement presents similar considerations when declarant is identified. *People v. Poland,* 174 N.E.2d 804 (Ill. 1961). However, when declarant is an unidentified bystander, the cases indicate hesitancy in upholding the statement alone as sufficient, *Garrett v. Howden,* 387 P.2d 874 (N.M. 1963); *Beck v. Dye,* 92 P.2d 1113 (Wash. 1939), a result which would under appropriate circumstances be consistent with the rule.

Permissible subject matter of the statement is limited under Subdivision (1) to description or explanation of the event or condition, the assumption being that spontaneity, in the absence of a startling event, may extend no farther. In Subdivision (2), however, the statement need only "relate" to the startling event or condition, thus affording a broader scope of subject matter coverage. 6 Wigmore §§ 1750, 1754. *See* Quick, Hearsay, Excitement, Necessity and the Uniform Rules: A Reappraisal of Rule 63(4), 6 Wayne L. Rev. 204, 206-09 (1960).

Similar provisions are found in Uniform Rule 63(4) (a) and (b); California Evidence Code § 1240 (as to Subdivision (2) only); Kansas Code of Civil Procedure § 60-460(d) (1) and (2); New Jersey Evidence Rule 63 (4).

(3) **When Existing Mental, Emotional, or Physical Condition.** Subdivision (3) is essentially a specialized application of Subdivision (1), presented separately to enhance its usefulness and accessibility.

The exclusion of "statements of memory or belief to prove that fact remembered or believed" is necessary to avoid the virtual destruction of the hearsay rule which would otherwise result from allowing state of mind, provable by a hearsay statement, to serve as the basis for an inference of the happening of the event which produced the state of mind. *Shepard v. United States,* 290 U.S. 96, 78 L.Ed. 196 (1933); Maguire, The Hillmon Case: Thirty-three Years After, 38 Harv. L. Rev. 709, 719-731 (1925); Hinton, States of Mind and the Hearsay Rule, 1 U. Chi. L. Rev. 394, 421-423 (1934). The rule of *Mutual Life Ins. Co. v. Hillmon,* 145 U.S. 285, 36 L.Ed. 706 (1892), allowing evidence of intention as tending to prove the doing of the act intended, is of course, left undisturbed as applied to a declarant.

The carving out, from the exclusion mentioned in the preceding paragraph, of declarations relating to the execution, revocation, identification, or terms of a declarant's will represents an ad hoc judgment which finds ample reinforcement in the decisions, resting on practical grounds of necessity and expediency rather than logic. A similar recognition of the need for and practical value of this kind of evidence is found in California Evidence Code § 1260.

The addition of the words "offered to prove his present condition or future action" limits the exception to avoid results like *People v. Alcalde,* 148 P.2d 627 (Cal. 1944). For the statements of one person as to his mental or emotional condition to be used against another, Subdivision (23) must be satisfied. This modifies the *Hillmon* rule.

(4) **Statements for Purposes of Medical Diagnosis or Treatment.** Even those few jurisdictions which have shied away from generally admitting statements of present condition have allowed them if made to a physician for purposes of diagnosis and treatment in view of the patient's strong motivation to be truthful. The same guarantee of trustworthiness extends to statements of past conditions and medical history, made for purposes of diagnosis or treatment. It also extends to statements as to causation, reasonably pertinent to the same purposes, in accord with the current trend, *Shell Oil Co. v. Industrial Commission,* 119 N.E.2d 224 (Ill. 1954); New Jersey Evidence Rule 63(12) (c). Statements as to fault would not ordinarily qualify under this latter language. Thus, a patient's statement that he was struck by an automobile would qualify but not his statement that the car was driven through a red light. Under the exception the statement need not have been made to a physician. Statements to hospital attendants, ambulance drivers, or even members of the family might be included.

Conventional doctrine has excluded from the hearsay exception, as not within its guarantee of truthfulness, statements to a physician consulted only for the purpose of enabling him to testify. While these statements were not admissible as substantive evidence, the expert was allowed to state the basis of his opinion, including statements of this kind. The distinction thus called for was one most unlikely to be made by juries. The rule accordingly rejects the limitation. This position is consistent with the provision of Rule 703 that the facts on which expert testimony is based need not be admissible in evidence if of a kind ordinarily relied upon by experts in the field.

(5) **Recorded Recollection.** A hearsay exception for recorded recollection is generally recognized and has been described as having "long been favored by the federal and practically all the state courts that have had occasion to decide the question." *United States v. Kelly,* 349 F.2d 720, 770 (2d Cir. 1965), citing numerous cases and sustaining the exception against a claimed denial of the right of confrontation. Many additional cases are cited in Annot., 82 A.L.R.2d 473, 520. The guarantee of trustworthiness is found in the reliability inherent in a record made while events were still fresh in mind and accurately reflecting them.

The principal controversy attending the exception has centered, not upon the propriety of the exception itself, but upon the question whether a preliminary requirement of impaired memory on the part of the witness should be imposed. The authorities are divided. If regard be had only to the accuracy of the evidence, admittedly impairment of the memory of the witness adds nothing to it and should not be required. Nevertheless, the absence of the requirement, it is believed, would encourage the use of statements carefully prepared for purposes of litigation under the supervision of attorneys, investigators, or claim adjusters. *Cf.,* Reporter's Comment accompanying Rule 801(d) (1) (A). Hence, the example includes a requirement that the witness not have "sufficient recollection to enable him to testify fully and accurately." To the same effect are California Evidence Code § 1237 and New Jersey Rule 63(1) (b), and this has been the position of the federal courts.

No attempt is made in the exception to spell out the method of establishing the initial knowledge or the contemporaneity and accuracy of the record, leaving them to be dealt with as the circumstances of the particular case might indicate. Multiple person involvement in the process of observing and recording, as in *Rathbun v. Brancatella,* 107 A. 279 (N.J. 1919), is entirely consistent with the exception.

Locating the exception at this place in the scheme of the rules is a matter of choice. There were two other possibilities. The first was to regard the statement as one of the group of prior statements of a testifying witness which are excluded entirely from the category of hearsay by Rule 801(d) (1). That category, however, requires that declarant be "subject to cross-examination," as to which the impaired memory aspect of the exception raises doubts. The other possibility was to include the exception among those covered by Rule 804. Since unavailability is required by that rule and lack of memory is listed as a species of unavailability by the definition of the term in Rule 804(a) (3), that treatment at first impression would seem appropriate. The fact is, however, that the unavailability requirement of the exception is of a limited and peculiar nature. Accordingly, the exception is located at this point rather than in the context of a rule where unavailability is conceived of more broadly.

(6) **Business Records.** This exception continues in effect the business records exception to the hearsay rule previously found in Alaska R. Civ. P. 44(a) (1) and Alaska R. Crim. P. 26(e). While the language is slightly different, the basic thrust of the new rule is identical to the old.

The background of this exception is set forth in the Advisory Committee's Note accompany Federal Rule 803(6). The element of unusual reliability of business records is said variously to be supplied by systematic checking, by regularity and continuity which produce habits of precision, by actual experience of business in relying upon them, or by a duty to make an accurate record as part of a continuing job or occupation.

Sources of information present no substantial problem with ordinary business records. All participants, including the observer or participant furnishing the information to be recorded, are acting routinely, under a duty of accuracy, with employer reliance on the result, or in short "in the regular course of business." If, however, the supplier of the information does not act in the regular course, an essential link is broken; the assurance of accuracy does not extend to the information itself, and the fact that it may be recorded with scrupulous accuracy is of no avail. An illustration is the police report incorporating information obtained from a bystander: the officer qualifies as acting in the regular course but the informant does not. The leading case, *Johnson v. Lutz,* 170 N.E. 517 (N.Y. 1930), held that a report thus prepared was inadmissible. Most of the authorities have agreed with the decision. Subdivision (6) has been drafted to eliminate the confusion caused by Federal Rule 803(6), which could be read to read to abolish the business duty concept although the legislative history plainly indicates that no such thing was intended.

Entries in form of opinions were not encountered in traditional business records in view of the purely factual nature of the items recorded, but they are now commonly encountered with respect to medical diagnoses, prognoses, and test results, as well as occasionally in other areas. In the state courts, the trend favors admissibility. In order to make clear its adherence to the latter position, the rule specifically includes both diagnoses and opinions, in addition to acts, events, and conditions, as proper subjects of admissible entries.

Problems of the motivation of the informant have been a source of difficulty and disagreement. In *Palmer v. Hoffman,* 318 U.S. 109 87 L.Ed. 645 (1943), exclusion of an accident report made by the since deceased engineer, offered by defendant railroad trustees in a grade crossing collision case, was upheld. The report was not "in the regular course of business," not a record of the systematic conduct of the business as a business, said the Court. The report was prepared for use in litigating, not railroading. While the opinion mentions the motivation of the engineer only obliquely, the emphasis on records of routine operations is significant only by virtue of impact on motivation to be accurate. Absence of routineness raises lack of motivation to be accurate.

The lower court had concluded that the engineer's statement was "dripping with motivations to misrepresent." *Hoffman v. Palmer,* 129 F.2d 976, 991 (2d Cir. 1942). Other courts also have focused on a motive to misrepresent, although many business records are potentially self-serving. The formulation of specific terms which would assure satisfactory results in all cases is not possible. Consequently the rule proceeds from the base that records made in the course of a regularly conducted activity will be taken as admissible but subject to authority to exclude if "the sources of information or other circumstances indicate lack of trustworthiness." *See generally Patrick v. Sedwick,* 391 P.2d 453, 458-59 (Alaska 1964); *Commercial Union Companies v. Smallwood,* 550 P.2d 1261 (Alaska 1976).

The form which the "record" may assume under the rule is described broadly as a "memorandum, report, record, or data compilation, in any form." The expression "data compilation" is used as broadly descriptive of any means of storing information other than the conventional words and figures in written or documentary form. It includes, but is by no means limited to, electronic computer storage.

(7) **Absence of Records.** Failure of a record to mention a matter which would ordinarily be mentioned is satisfactory evidence of its nonexistence. Uniform Rule 63(14), Comment. While probably not hearsay as defined in Rule 801, supra, decisions may be found which class the evidence not only as hearsay but also as not within any exception. In order to set the

question at rest in favor of admissibility, it is specifically treated here. McCormick (2d ed.) § 307; Morgan, Basic Problems of Evidence 314 (1962); 5 Wigmore § 1531; Uniform Rule 63(14); California Evidence Code § 1272; Kansas Code of Civil Procedure § 60-460(n); New Jersey Evidence 63(14). This Rule supersedes Alaska R. Civ. P. 44(a) (2) and Alaska R. Crim. P. 26 (e); it provides for identical results.

(8) **Public Records and Reports.** "The reliability and trustworthiness of official documents and also the desire to keep officials from having to testify personally in every instance have generally been established as the policies underlying this hearsay exception." *Webster v. State,* 528 P.2d 1179, 1181 (Alaska 1974). The exception was recognized in Alaska R. Civ. P. 44(b) and Alaska R. Crim. P. 26(e), which are superseded by this rule.

Subdivision (8) follows Maine Rule 803(8), rather than its federal counterpart. The Maine rule is clearer, easier to apply, and avoids some of the confrontation problems presented by the Federal Rule. *See generally, United States v. Smith,* 521 F.2d 957 (D.C. Cir. 1975). It recognizes that government records that are compiled for purposes other than presentation on the government's behalf at trial are generally reliable (part (a)), but that reliability is substantially diminished when the government stands to gain an edge in litigation through the introduction of a record or report it has prepared (parts (b) (ii) & (iii)). Similarly, the rule differentiates factual findings made by the government in the process of carrying out public responsibilities, which are presumed to be reliable, from factual findings resulting from a special investigation of a particular complaint, case or incident, which are not within this exception, since there is no reason to believe that the government would itself rely on its findings outside the litigation context (part (b) (iv)). Finally, investigative reports by police and law enforcement personnel are excluded because they are often unreliable. *See Menard v. Acevedo,* 418 P.2d 766 (Alaska 1966).

While this rule may appear, at first blush anyway, to be at odds with *Webster v. State, supra,* that case would be decided the same way under these rules. Presumably the breathalyzer test would be admissible as a business record under Subdivision (6). *Menard v. Acevedo, supra,* is in accord with this Subdivision.

More leeway is provided for admission of public reports involving factual findings in civil cases than criminal cases. In this way deference is paid the confrontation clause. But records and reports not involving investigations into particular events and findings of fact are admissible under this Subdivision even in criminal cases.

There is no doubt that Subdivision (8) differs from former Alaska R. Civ. P. 44(b), but the goals of both rules are similar. When Subdivisions (6) and (8) of the rules are read together, it should be apparent that the admissibility of official records is not unduly circumscribed by the rule.

The notice requirement, formally found in Alaska R. Civ. P. 44(b) (2) is carried forward, but the authentication provisions of Alaska R. Civ. P. 44(b) (4) & (5) and the regulation of copies under Alaska R. Civ. P. 44(b) (6) & (c) are eliminated as these subjects are covered by Articles IX and X of these rules.

(9) **Records of Vital Statistics.** Records of vital statistics are commonly the subject of particular statutes making them admissible in evidence, Uniform Vital Statistics Act, 9C U.L.A. 350 (1957). The rule is in principle narrower than Uniform Rule 63(16) which includes reports required of persons performing functions authorized by statute, yet in practical effect the two are substantially the same. Comment, Uniform Rule 63(16). The exception as drafted is in the pattern of California Evidence Code § 1281. It is consistent with the previous exception and may overlap with it in some instances.

(10) **Absence of Public Record or Entry.** The principle of proving nonoccurrence of an event by evidence of the absence of a record which would regularly be made of its occurrence, developed in Subdivision (7) with respect to regularly conducted business activities, is here extended to public records of the kind mentioned in Subdivisions (8) and (9). 5 Wigmore § 1633(6), at 519. Some harmless duplication no doubt exists with Subdivision (7). This continues in effect the policy of former Alaska R. Civ. P. 44 (b) (3).

The rule includes situations in which absence of a record may itself be the ultimate focal point of inquiry; *e.g., People v. Love,* 142 N.E. 204 (Ill. 1923) (certificate of Secretary of State admitted to show failure to file documents required by Securities Law); as well as cases where the absence of a record is offered as proof of the nonoccurrence of an event ordinarily recorded.

(11) **Records of Religious Organizations.** Records of activities of religious organizations are currently recognized as admissible at least to the extent of the business records exception to the hearsay rule, 5 Wigmore § 1523, at 371, and Subdivision (6) would be applicable. However, both the business record doctrine and Subdivision (6) require that the person furnishing the information be one in the business or activity. The result is such decisions as *Daily v. Grand Lodge,* 142 N.E. 478 (Ill. 1924), holding a church record admissible to prove fact, date, and place of baptism, but not age of child except that he had at least been born at the time. In view of the likelihood that false information would be furnished on occasions of this kind, the rule contains no requirement that the informant be in the course of the activity. *See* California Evidence Code § 1315 and Comment.

(12) **Marriage, Baptismal, and Similar Certificates.** The principle of proof by certification is recognized as to public officials in Subdivisions (8) and (10), and with respect to authentication in Rule 902. The present exception is a duplication to the extent that it deals with a certificate by a public official, as in the case of a judge who performs a marriage ceremony. The area covered by the rule is, however, substantially larger and extends the certification procedure to clergymen and the like who perform marriages and other ceremonies or administer sacraments. Thus certificates of such matters as baptism or confirmation, as well as marriage, are included. In principle they are as acceptable evidence as certificates of public officers. *See* 5 Wigmore § 1645, as to marriage certificates. When the person executing the certificate is not a public official, the self-authenticating character of documents purporting to emanate from public officials (*see,* Rule 902) is lacking and proof is required that the person was authorized and did make the certificate. The time element, however, may safely be taken as supplied by the certificate,

once authority and authenticity are established, particularly in view of the presumption that a document was executed on the date it bears.

For similar rules, some limited to certificates of marriage, with variations in foundation requirements, *see,* Uniform Rule 63(18); California Evidence Code § 1316; Kansas Code of Civil Procedure § 60-460(p); New Jersey Evidence Rule 63(18).

(13) **Family Records.** Records of family history kept in family bibles have by long tradition been received in evidence. 5 Wigmore §§ 1495, 1496, citing numerous statutes and decisions. Opinions in the area also include inscriptions on tombstones, publicly displayed pedigrees, and engravings on rings. Wigmore, *supra.* The rule is substantially identical in coverage with California Evidence Code § 1312. In approving the Federal Rule counterpart to Alaska Rule 803(13), the House of Representatives' Judiciary Committee approved this rule in the form submitted by the Court, intending that the phrase "Statements of fact concerning personal or family history" be read to include the specific types of such statements enumerated in Rule 803(11). This is a sensible approach to the Subdivision and accurately describes the purpose of the Alaska rule. *See* also, Annot., 39 A.L.R. 372 (1924).

(14) **Records of Documents Affecting an Interest in Property.** The recording of title documents is a purely statutory development. Under any theory of the admissibility of public records, the records would be receivable as evidence of the contents of the recorded document, else the recording process would be reduced to a nullity. When, however, the record is offered for the further purpose of proving execution and delivery, a problem of lack of firsthand knowledge by the recorder, not present as to contents, is presented. This problem is solved, seemingly in all jurisdictions, by qualifying or recording only those documents shown by a specified procedure, either acknowledgement or a form of probate, to have been executed and delivered. 5 Wigmore §§ 1647-1651. *See* AS 34.15.260. *See also,* AS 34.15.300 and AS 35.25.060. *See generally* Hearsay Under the Proposed Federal Rules: A Discretionary Approach, 15 Wayne L. Rev. 1077, 1172-73 (1968).

(15) **Statements in Documents Affecting an Interest in Property.** Dispositive documents often contain recitals of fact. Thus a deed purporting to have been executed by an attorney in fact may recite the existence of the power of attorney, or a deed may recite that the grantors are all the heirs of the last record owner. Under the rule, these recitals are exempted from the hearsay rule. The circumstances under which dispositive documents are executed and the requirement that the recital be germane to the purpose of the document are believed to be adequate guarantees of trustworthiness, particularly in view of the nonapplicability of the rule if dealings with the property have been inconsistent with the document. Although there is authority restricting this exception to ancient documents, there is no good reason to so limit it. It should not be surprising, however, to see that in practical application the document will most often be an ancient one. *See* Uniform Rule 63(29), Comment. The fact that the Alaska Rule and Federal Rule 803(15) are identical removes any question whether the Federal Rule violates the policy of *Erie* recognized in other Federal Rules (*e.g.,* 301, 501, 601). *See* K. Redden and S. Saltzburg, Federal Rules of Evidence Manual 334 (2d ed. 1977).

Similar provisions are contained in Uniform Rule 63(29); California Evidence Code § 1330; Kansas Code of Civil Procedure § 60-460(aa); New Jersey Evidence Rule 63(29).

(16) **Statements in Ancient Documents.** Authenticating a document as ancient, essentially in the pattern of the common law, as provided in Rule 901(b) (8), leaves open as a separate question the admissibility of assertive statements contained therein as against a hearsay objection. 7 Wigmore § 2145a. Wigmore further states that the ancient document technique of authentication is universally conceded to apply to all sorts of documents, including letters, records, contracts, maps, and certificates, in addition to title documents, citing numerous decisions. 7 Wigmore § 2145. Since most of these items are significant evidentially only insofar as they are assertive, their admission in evidence must be as a hearsay exception. *But see* 5 Wigmore § 1573, at 429, referring to recitals in ancient deeds as a "limited" hearsay exception. The former position is believed to be the correct one in reason and authority. As pointed out in McCormick (2d ed.) § 323, danger of mistake is minimized by authentication requirements, and age affords assurance that the writing antedates the present controversy. Nebraska followed the usual common law view in defining ancient documents as those in existence more than 30 years. Most other states that have adopted rules based on the federal model agree with the federal provision reducing the number of years to 20. Subdivision (16) also reduces the number of years on the theory that twenty years should be sufficient to counteract fraud.

For a similar provision, but with the added requirement that "the statement has since generally been acted upon as true by persons having an interest in the matter," *see* California Evidence Code § 1331.

(17) **Market Reports, Commercial Publications.** Ample authority at common law supported the admission in evidence of items falling in this category. While Wigmore's text is narrowly oriented to lists, etc., prepared for the use of a trade or profession, 6 Wigmore § 1702, authorities are cited which include other kinds of publications, for example, newspaper market reports, telephone directories, and city directories. 6 Wigmore §§ 1702-1706. The basis of trustworthiness is general reliance by the public or by a particular segment of it, and the motivation of the compiler to foster reliance by being accurate.

For similar provisions, *see* Uniform Rule 63(30); California Evidence Code § 1340; Kansas Code of Civil Procedure § 60-460(bb); New Jersey Evidence Rule 63(30). Uniform Commercial Code § 2-724 provides for admissibility in evidence of "reports in official publications or trade journals or in newspapers or periodicals of general circulation published as the reports of such [established commodity] market." This rule is consistent with AS 45.05.240.

(18) **Learned Treatises.** Commentators have generally favored the admissibility of learned treatises; *See* McCormick (2d ed.) 321; Morgan, Basic Problems of Evidence 366 (1962); 6 Wigmore § 1692. *See also* Uniform Rule 63(31); Kansas Code of Civil Procedure § 60-460(cc). But the great weight of

authority has been that learned treatises are not admissible as substantive evidence though usable in the cross-examination of experts. The foundation of the minority view is that the hearsay objection must be regarded as unimpressive when directed against treatises since a high standard of accuracy is engendered by various factors: the treatise is written primarily and impartially for professionals, subject to scrutiny and exposure for inaccuracy, with the reputation of the writer at stake. 6 Wigmore § 1692. Sound as this position may be with respect to trustworthiness, there is, nevertheless, an additional difficulty in the likelihood that the treatise will be misunderstood and misapplied without expert assistance and supervision. This difficulty is recognized in the cases demonstrating unwillingness to sustain findings relative to disability on the basis of judicially noticed medical texts. The rule avoids the danger of misunderstanding and misapplication by limiting the use of treatises as substantive evidence to situations in which an expert is on the stand and available to explain and assist in the application of the treatise if desired. The limitation upon receiving the publication itself physically in evidence, contained in the last sentence, is designed to further this policy.

The relevance of the use of treatises on cross-examination is evident. This use of treatises has been the subject of varied views. The most restrictive position is that the witness must have stated expressly on direct his reliance upon the treatise. A slightly more liberal approach still insists upon reliance but allows it to be developed on cross-examination. Further relaxation dispenses with reliance but requires recognition as an authority by the witness, developable on cross-examination. The greatest liberality is found in decisions allowing use of the treatise on cross-examination when its status as an authority is established by any means. Annot., 60 A.L.R.2d 77. The exception is hinged upon this last position, which is that of the United States Supreme Court, *Reilly v. Pinkus,* 338 U.S. 269, 94 L.Ed. 63 (1949), and of recent well considered state court decisions, *City of St. Petersburg v. Ferguson,* 193 So.2d 648 (Fla. App. 1967), *cert. denied,* 201 So.2d 556 (Fla. 1968); *Darling v. Charleston Memorial Community Hospital,* 211 N.E.2d 253 (Ill. 1965); *Dabroe v. Rhodes Co.,* 392 P.2d 317 (Wash. 1964).

Nebraska did not adopt such a provision in its rules, but other states following the Federal model did.

(19), (20), and (21) **Reputation Concerning Personal or Family History—Reputation Concerning Boundaries or General History—Reputation as to Character.** Trustworthiness in reputation evidence is found "when the topic is such that the facts are likely to have been inquired about and that persons having personal knowledge have disclosed facts which have thus been discussed in the community; and thus the community's conclusion, if any has been formed, is likely to be a trustworthy one." 5 Wigmore § 1580, at 444, and *see also,* § 1583. On this common foundation, reputation as to land boundaries, customs, general history, character, and marriage have come to be regarded as admissible. The breadth of the underlying principle suggests the formulation of an equally broad exception, but tradition has in fact been much narrower and more particularized, and this is the pattern of these exceptions in the rule.

Subdivision (19) is concerned with matters of personal and family history. Marriage is universally conceded to be a proper subject of proof by evidence of reputation in the community. 5 Wigmore § 1602. As to such items as legitimacy, relationship, adoption, birth, and death, the decisions are divided. 5 Wigmore § 1605. All seem to be susceptible to being the subject of well founded repute. The "world" in which the reputation may exist may be family, associates, or community. This world has proved capable of expanding with changing times from the single uncomplicated neighborhood, in which all activities take place, to the multiple and unrelated worlds of work, religious affiliation, and social activity, in each of which a reputation may be generated. The family has often served as the point of beginning for allowing community reputation. 5 Wigmore § 1488. For comparable provisions *see,* Uniform Rule 63(26), (27) (c); California Evidence Code §§ 1313, 1314; Kansas Code of Civil Procedure § 60-460(x), (y) (3); New Jersey Evidence Rule 63 (26), (27) (c).

The first portion of Subdivision (20) is based upon the general admissibility of evidence of reputation as to land boundaries and land customs, expanded in this country to include private as well as public boundaries. McCormick (2d ed.) § 324. The reputation is required to antedate the controversy, though not to be ancient. The second portion is likewise supported by authority, McCormick (2d ed.) § 324, and is designed to facilitate proof of events when judicial notice is not available. The historical character of the subject matter dispenses with any need that the reputation antedate the controversy with respect to which it is offered. For similar provisions *see,* Uniform Rule 63 (27) (a), (b); California Evidence Code §§ 1320-1322; Kansas Code of Civil Procedure § 60-460(y), (1), (2); New Jersey Evidence Rule 63(27) (a), (b).

Subdivision (21) recognizes the traditional acceptance of reputation evidence as a means of proving human character. McCormick (2d ed.) §§ 44, 186. The exception deals only with the hearsay aspect of this kind of evidence. Limitations upon admissibility based on other grounds will be found in Rules 404, relevancy of character evidence generally, and 608, character of witness. The exception is in effect a reiteration, in the context of hearsay, of Rule 405(a). Similar provisions are contained in Uniform Rule 63(28); California Evidence Code § 1324; Kansas Code of Civil Procedure § 60-460(z); New Jersey Evidence Rule 63 (28).

(22) **Judgment as to Personal, Family, or General History, or Boundaries.** A hearsay exception in this area was originally justified on the ground that verdicts were evidence of reputation. As trial by jury graduated from the category of neighborhood inquests, this theory lost its validity. It was never valid as to chancery decrees. Nevertheless the rule persisted, though the judges and writers shifted ground and began saying that the judgment or decree was as good evidence as reputation. *See City of London v. Clerke,* Carth. 181, 90 Eng. Rep. 710 (K.B. 1691); *Neill v. Duke of Devonshire,* 8 App. Cas. 135 (1882). The shift appears to be correct, since the process of inquiry, sifting, and scrutiny which is relied upon to render reputation reliable is present in perhaps greater measure in the process of litigation. While this might suggest a broader area of application, the affinity to reputation is strong, and subdivision (22) goes no further, not even including character.

(23) **Other Exceptions.** Whether or not to include a

general section like this divided the United States Congress during its consideration of the Federal Rules of Evidence. At first the House Committee on the Judiciary deleted draft rules [803 (24) and 804 (b) (5)] intended to allow courts flexibility in creating hearsay exceptions to fit particular cases. Such rules were viewed "as injecting too much uncertainty into the law of evidence and impairing the ability of practitioners to prepare for trial." The Senate Committee on the Judiciary believed

> that there are certain exceptional circumstances where evidence which is found by a court to have guarantees of trustworthiness equivalent to or exceeding the guarantees reflected by the presently limited exceptions, and to have a high degree of probativeness and necessity could properly be admissible.

The Senate Committee "intended that the residual hearsay exception will be used very rarely, and only in exceptional circumstances." Thus, it modified the rule proposed by the Advisory Committee and approved by the United States Supreme Court to narrow the exception. House and Senate Conferences finally agreed on the Senate's approach but added a provision that a party intending to request the Court to use a statement under this subdivision must notify, sufficiently in advance of trial to allow for a fair contest on the issue of whether the statement should be used, any adverse party of the intent as well as of the particulars of the statement.

Some states that adopted rules based on the federal model rejected any residual exception (*e.g.,* Maine and Nebraska), or modified the Federal Rule (*e.g.,* Nevada and New Mexico). Alaska Rule 803(23) copies the Federal Rule in the belief that the Senate Judiciary Committee was correct in concluding that the specific exceptions provided for in Rule 803, "while they reflect the most typical and well recognized exceptions to the hearsay rule may not encompass every situation in which the reliability and appropriateness of a particular piece of hearsay evidence made clear that it should be heard and considered by the trier of fact." *Cf., Beech Aircraft Corp. v. Harvey,* 558 P.2d 879 (Alaska 1976). The intent of the rule is that it should be used sparingly. It has been cited with favor in *Alaska Airlines, Inc. v. Sweat,* 584 P.2d 544 (Alaska 1978).

Note on Omission — Omitted from this rule is an exception for judgments of previous conviction. *See* Federal Rule 803 (22). Since guilty pleas and statements in connection therewith are admissible under Rule 801(d) (2) (a), unless banned under Rule 410, the only reason to include an exception for judgments of previous conviction is to permit a finding of one trier of fact to come before another. If a judgment of guilty in a criminal case, which follows proof beyond a reasonable doubt, is to have impact in subsequent cases, the impact should be by way of collateral estoppel, not by admitting the previous judgment. The judgment tells the second trier of fact nothing; that trier will either disregard it or defer to it, neither of which tactic is intended by the Federal Rule. There are strong arguments to the effect that facts once proved beyond a reasonable doubt should be binding in subsequent proceedings, especially subsequent civil proceedings. But such a rule is beyond the scope of rules of evidence. The only argument in favor of the Federal Rule is that it might be unconstitutional to attempt to invoke the doctrine of collateral estoppel against a defendant in subsequent criminal cases and Federal Rule 803 (22) is an attempt to use a prior finding in *some* way. But the fact remains that the trier of fact in the second case cannot know how to use the first finding. There is no reason to adopt a rule that can only confuse the trial process. In *Scott v. Robinson,* 583 P.2d 188 (Alaska 1978), the Supreme Court held that a conviction in a criminal case would be conclusive in a subsequent civil case as to the facts necessarily decided in the criminal case under certain circumstances, to wit: the prior conviction was for a serious criminal offense, the defendant had a full and fair hearing, and the issue on which the judgment is offered was necessarily decided in the previous trial.

Rule 804. Hearsay Exceptions—Declarant Unavailable.

(a) **Definition of Unavailability.** The definition of unavailability implements the division of hearsay exceptions into two categories: Rules 803 and 804(b).

At common law the unavailability requirement was evolved in connection with particular hearsay exceptions rather than along general lines. However, no reason is apparent for making distinctions as to what satisfies unavailability for the different exceptions.

Five instances of unavailability are specified:

(1) Substantial authority supports the position that exercise of a claim of privilege by the declarant satisfies the requirement of unavailability (usually in connection with former testimony). *Wyatt v. State,* 46 So.2d 837 (Ala. App. 1950); *State v. Stewart,* 116 P. 489 (Kan. 1911); Annot., 45 A.L.R.2d 1354; Uniform Rule 62(7) (a); California Evidence Code § 240 (a) (1); Kansas Code of Civil Procedure § 60-459(g) (1). A ruling by the judge is required, which clearly implies that an actual claim of privilege must be made.

(2) A witness is rendered unavailable if he simply refuses to testify concerning the subject matter of his statement despite judicial pressures to do so, a position supported by similar considerations of practicality. *Johnson v. People,* 384 P.2d 454 (Colo. 1963); *People v. Pickett,* 63 N.W.2d 681, 45 A.L.R.2d 1341 (Mich. 1954). *Contra, Pleau v. State,* 38 N.W.2d 496 (Wis. 1949).

(3) The position that a lack of memory by the witness of the subject matter of his statement constitutes unavailability likewise finds support in the cases, though not without dissent. If the claim is successful, the practical effect is to put the testimony beyond reach, as in the other instances. In this instance, however, it will be noted that the lack of memory must be established by the testimony of the witness himself, which clearly contemplates his production and subjection to cross-examination. However, the court may choose to disbelieve the declarant's testimony as to his lack of memory. To make this clear, Rule 804(a) (3) begins with the word "establishes" rather than the words "testifies to" which begin its federal counterpart. *See United States v. Insana,* 423 F.2d 1165, 1169-1170 (2nd Cir.), *cert. denied,* 400 U.S. 841 (1970). A preliminary finding is required under Rule 104(a).

(4) Death and infirmity find general recognition as grounds. Uniform Rule 62(7) (c); California Evidence Code § 240(a) (3); Kansas Code of Civil Procedure § 60-459(g) (3); New Jersey Evidence Rule 62(6) (c). *See also* the provisions

on use of depositions in Rule 32(a) (3) of the Alaska Rules of Civil Procedure and Rule 15(e) of the Alaska Rules of Criminal Procedure.

(5) Absence from the hearing coupled with inability to compel attendance by process or other reasonable means or to depose the declarant in order to provide an opportunity for oath and cross-examination also satisfies the requirement. Uniform Rule 62(7) (d) and (e); California Evidence Code § 240(a) (4) and (5); Kansas Code of Civil Procedure § 60-459(g) (4) and (5); New Jersey Rule 62(6) (b) and (d). If the conditions otherwise constituting unavailability result from the procurement or wrongdoing of the proponent of the statement, the requirement is not satisfied.

The requirement that an attempt to depose a witness have been made, if possible, was added by the Committee on the Judiciary of the House of Representatives when it considered the Federal Rules. The Senate Committee on the Judiciary was not enthusiastic about the addition, arguing:

> Under the House amendment, before a witness is declared unavailable, a party must try to depose a witness (declarant) with respect to dying declarations, declarations against interest, and declarations of pedigree. None of these situations would seem to warrant this needless, impractical and highly restrictive complication. A good case can be made for eliminating the unavailability requirement entirely for declarations against interest cases.
>
> In dying declaration cases, the declarant usually, though not necessarily, will be deceased at the time of trial. Pedigree statements which are admittedly and necessarily based largely on word of mouth are not greatly fortified by a deposition requirement.
>
> Depositions are expensive and time-consuming. In any event, deposition procedures are available to those who wish to resort to them. Moreover, the deposition procedures of the Civil Rules and Criminal Rules are only imperfectly adapted to implementing the amendment. No purpose is served unless the deposition, if taken, may be used in evidence.... [Footnote omitted.]

But the Senate Committee concluded with a statement indicating it did not completely disagree with the goals of the House Committee:

> The committee understands that the rule as to unavailability, as explained by the Advisory Committee "contains no requirement that an attempt be made to take the deposition of a declarant." In reflecting the committee's judgment, the statement is accurate insofar as it goes. Where, however, the proponent of the statement, with knowledge of the existence of the statement, fails to confront the declarant with the statement at the taking of the deposition, then the proponent should not, in fairness, be permitted to treat the declarant as "unavailable" simply because the declarant was not amenable to process compelling his attendance at trial. The committee does not consider it necessary to amend the rule to this effect because such a situation abuses, not conforms to, the rule. Fairness would preclude a person from introducing a hearsay statement on a particular issue if the person taking the deposition was aware of the issue at the time of the deposition but failed to depose the unavailable witness on that issue.

Despite the fact that several states have abjured the provision requiring an effort to depose, this rule follows the federal lead in requiring that oath and cross-examination are utilized whenever reasonably possible. An opportunity for oath and cross-examination is favored despite its costs.

Paragraph (b) (1) is not included under (a) (5) for an obvious reason; there has already been an opportunity for oath and cross-examination. The Federal Rule excluded (b) (5) as well, but no good reason argues why statements falling within the general exception should be admitted if an opportunity to depose has been foregone. Indeed, since this paragraph involves controversial evidence not within traditional exceptions, there is more, not less, reason to include it in (a) (5).

(b) **Hearsay Exceptions.** Rule 803, *supra,* is based upon the assumption that a hearsay statement falling within one of its exceptions possesses qualities which justify the conclusion that whether the declarant is available or unavailable is not a relevant factor in determining admissibility. The instant rule proceeds upon a different theory: hearsay which admittedly is not equal in quality to testimony of the declarant on the stand may nevertheless be admitted if the declarant is unavailable and if his statement meets a specified standard. The rule expresses preferences: testimony given on the stand in person is preferred over hearsay, and hearsay, if of the specified quality, is preferred over complete loss of the evidence of the declarant. The exceptions evolved at common law with respect to declarations of unavailable declarants furnish the basis for the exceptions enumerated in the proposal. The term "unavailable" is defined in subdivision (a).

(1) *Former Testimony.* Former testimony does not rely upon some set of circumstances to substitute for oath and cross-examination, since both oath and opportunity to cross-examine were present in fact. The only missing one of the ideal conditions for the giving of testimony is the presence of the trier ("demeanor evidence"). This is lacking with all hearsay exceptions. Hence it may be argued that former testimony is the strongest hearsay and should be included under Rule 803, *supra.* However, opportunity to observe demeanor is what in a large measure confers depth and meaning upon oath and cross-examination. Thus, in cases under Rule 803 demeanor lacks the significance which it possesses with respect to testimony. In any event, the tradition, founded in experience, uniformly favors production of the witness if he is available. The exception indicates continuation of the policy. This preference for the presence of the witness is apparent also in rules and statutes on the use of depositions, which deal with substantially the same problem.

Under the exception, the testimony may be offered (1) *against* the party against whom it was previously offered or (2) against the party *by* whom it was previously offered. In each instance the question resolves itself into whether fairness allows imposing, upon the party against whom now offered, the handling of the witness on the earlier occasion. (1) If the party against whom now offered is the one against whom the testimony was offered previously, no unfairness is apparent in requiring him to accept his own prior conduct of cross-examination or decision not to cross-examine. Only demeanor has been lost, and that is inherent in the situation. (2) If the party against whom now offered is the one *by* whom the testimony was offered previously, a satisfactory answer becomes somewhat more difficult. One possibility is to proceed somewhat along the line of an adoptive admission, *i.e.,* by offering the testimony proponent in effect adopts it. However, this theory savors of discarded concepts of witnesses' belonging to a party of litigants' ability to pick and choose witnesses, and of vouching for one's own witnesses. A more direct and acceptable approach is simply to recognize direct and redirect examination of one's own witness as the equivalent of cross-examining an opponent's witness. Allowable techniques for dealing with hostile, double-crossing, forgetful, and mentally deficient witnesses leave no substance to a claim that one could not adequately develop his own witness at the former hearing. An even less appealing argument is presented when failure to develop fully was the result of a deliberate choice.

The common law did not limit the admissibility of former testimony to that given in an earlier trial of the same case, although it did require identity of issues as a means of insuring that the former handling of the witness was the equivalent of what would now be done if the opportunity were presented. Modern decisions reduce the requirement to "substantial" identity. Since identity of issues is significant only in that it bears on motive and interest in developing fully the testimony of the witness, expressing the matter in the latter terms is preferable. Testimony given at a preliminary hearing was held in *California v. Green,* 399 U.S. 149, 26 L.Ed.2d 489 (1970), to satisfy confrontation requirements in this respect. The opportunity to prepare will have to be examined in all cases, however.

Rule 804(b) (1), as submitted by the Supreme Court to the Congress, allowed prior testimony of an unavailable witness to be admissible if the party against whom it is offered or a person "with motive and interest similar" to his had an opportunity to examine the witness. The Congress concluded that it is generally unfair to impose upon the party against whom the hearsay evidence is being offered responsibility for the manner in which the witness was previously handled by another party; the sole exception to this is when a party's predecessor in interest in a civil action or proceeding had an opportunity and similar motive to examine the witness. Congress amended the rule to reflect these policy determinations. Alaska Rule 804(b) (1) follows the lead of Congress, although several states have adopted the broader exception proposed by the Advisory Committee and approved by the United States Supreme Court.

It has been noted that the paragraph (b) (1) when read in conjunction with paragraph (a)(5) is more limited than Alaska R. Civ. P. 32 (a) (limited to depositions; broader definition of unavailability). *Cf.,* K. Redden & S. Saltzburg, Federal Rules of Evidence Manual 731 (2d ed. 1977). This procedural rule remains effective, as does Alaska R. Crim. P. 15(e) (limited to depositions; virtually identical to Rule 801 (a) (5) & (b) (1) in application to depositions). These procedural rules "create of their own force exceptions to the hearsay rule in the case of unavailable deponents, which Rule 802 continues. Rule 804(b) (1) applies to depositions only to the extent that they are offered in a proceeding different from the one in connection with which they are taken." 4 Weinstein's Evidence ¶ 804(b) (1) [01] (1975). Rule 804(b) (1) amends the Federal Rule to make it clear that it does not cover depositions taken by parties in the same case that goes to trial.

It is important to keep in mind that Rule 801(d) (1) (A) may authorize admission of former testimony for its truth even when a witness is present. And Rule 801(d) (2) may do the same.

(2) *Statement Under Belief of Impending Death.* The exception is the familiar dying declaration of the common law, expanded beyond its traditional limits. While the original religious justification for the exception may have lost its conviction for some persons over the years, it can scarcely be doubted that powerful psychological pressures are present. *See* 5 Wigmore § 1443 and the classic statement of Chief Baron Eyre in *Rex v. Woodcock,* 1 Leach 500, 502, 168 Eng. Rep. 352, 353 (K.B. 1789).

The common law required that the statement be that of the victim, offered in a prosecution for criminal homicide. Thus declarations by victims in prosecution for other crimes, e.g., a declaration by a rape victim who dies in childbirth, and all declarations in civil cases were outside the scope of the exception. An occasional statute has removed these restrictions or has expanded the area of offenses to include abortions, 5 Wigmore § 1432, at 224, n.4. While the common law exception no doubt originated as a result of the exceptional need for the evidence in homicide cases, the theory or admissibility applies equally in civil cases. The same considerations suggest abandonment of the limitation to circumstances attending the event in question, yet when the statement deals with matters other than the supposed death, its influence is believed to be sufficiently attenuated to justify the limitation. Unavailability is not limited to death. *See* subdivision (a) of this rule. Any problem as to declarations phrased in terms of opinion is laid at rest by Rule 701, and continuation of a requirement of firsthand knowledge is assured by Rule 602.

Comparable provisions are found in Uniform Rule 63(5); California Evidence Code § 1242; Kansas Code of Civil Procedure § 60-460(e); New Jersey Evidence Rule 63(5).

Federal Rule 804(b) (2) is limited to homicide cases and civil cases. While the United States Supreme Court approved a rule like Alaska's the Congress limited the exception in the belief that dying declarations are not among the most reliable forms of hearsay and should only be admitted when necessary. Admittedly, there are problems with this exception; imminent death may distort perception, jumble narration and disrupt memory. At best, the prospect of death will generate sincerity. But once the balance is struck in favor of admission where the penalty is greatest, there is no reason to distinguish among classes of cases. It is difficult to defend the argument that dying declarations are more necessary in a homicide case than in an abortion prosecution. If the dying declarant is the only or best witness, any case with issues turning on the cause of the death needs dying declarations.

(3) *Statement Against Interest.* The circumstantial guarantee of reliability for declarations against interest is the assumption that persons do not make statements which are damaging to themselves unless satisfied for good reason that they are true. If the statement is that of party, offered by his

opponent, it comes in as an admission, Rule 801 (d) (2), and there is no occasion to inquire whether it is against interest, this not being a condition precedent to admissibility of admissions by opponents.

The common law required that the interest declared against be pecuniary or proprietary. The exception discards the common law limitation and expands to the full logical limit. One result is to remove doubt as to the admissibility of declarations tending to establish a tort liability against the declarant or to extinguish one which might be asserted by him, in accordance with the trend of the decisions in this country. McCormick (2d ed.) § 277, at 671-72. And finally, exposure to criminal liability satisfies the against-interest requirement. The refusal of common law to concede the adequacy of penal interest was no doubt indefensible in logic. *See* the dissent of Mr. Justice Holmes in *Donnelly v. United States,* 228 U.S. 243, 57 L.Ed. 820 (1913), but one senses in the decisions a distrust of evidence of confessions by third persons offered to exculpate the accused arising from suspicions of fabrication either of the fact of the making of the confession or in its contents, enhanced in either instance by the required unavailability of the declarant. Nevertheless, an increasing amount of decisional law recognizes exposure to punishment for crime as a sufficient stake. Annot., 162 A.L.R. 456. The requirement of corroboration is included in the rule in order to effect an accommodation between these competing considerations. When the statement is offered by the accused by way of exculpation, the resulting situation is not adapted to control by rulings as to the weight of the evidence, and hence the provision is cast in terms of a requirement preliminary to admissibility. *Cf.,* Rule 104(a). The requirement of corroboration should be construed in such a manner as to effectuate its purpose of circumventing fabrication.

Maine added a sentence to its declaration against interest exception: "A statement or confession offered against the accused in a criminal case, made by a co-defendant or other person implicating both himself and the accused, is not within this exception." Apparently, this was a response to the following comment by the Federal Advisory Committee on its rule:

> Ordinarily the third-party confession is thought of in terms of exculpating the accused, but this is by no means always or necessarily the case: it may include statements implicating him, and under the general theory of declarations against interest they would be admissible as related statements. *Douglas v. Alabama,* 380 U.S. 415 (1965), and *Bruton v. United States,* 389 U.S. 818 (1968), both involved confessions by codefendants which implicated the accused. While the confession was not actually offered in evidence in *Douglas,* the procedure followed effectively put it before the jury, which the Court ruled to be error. Whether the confession might have been admissible as a declaration against penal interest was not considered or discussed. *Bruton* assumed the inadmissibility, as against the accused, of the implicating confession of his codefendant, and centered upon the question of the effectiveness of a limiting instruction. These decisions, however, by no means require that all statements implicating another person be excluded from the category of declarations against interest. Whether a statement is in fact against interest must be determined from the circumstances of each case. Thus a statement admitting guilt and implicating another person, made while in custody, may well be motivated by a desire to curry favor with the authorities and hence fail to qualify as against interest. See the dissenting opinion of Mr. Justice White in *Bruton.* On the other hand, the same words, spoken under different circumstances, e.g., to an acquaintance, would have no difficulty in qualifying. The rule does not purport to deal with questions of the right of confrontation. (multiple citations omitted).

Without deciding the confrontation question, it is fair to say that it is not highly probable that the Constitution will be read to allow one non-testifying defendant's declarations against interest made to the police to be used against another defendant. *But see, Dutton v. Evans,* 400 U.S. 74, 27 L.Ed.2d 213 (1970). Once the decision is made to cooperate with the government, statements by one accused are suspect if offered against another who refuses to cooperate. *Cf.,* Rule 410 and its Reporter's Comment. But declarations against interest made outside of the formal interrogation process may, and perhaps should, be treated differently. To the extent that they are truly disserving to the declarant and only tangentially refer to another, the statements may be thought to be reliable as to both. In custody, statements are difficult to classify as totally disserving; they are disserving, but often are made with a hope of some benefit. To the extent that the Advisory Committee suggests that even declarations against interest made in custody might be admissible against someone other than the declarant if the declarant does not testify, it is probably wrong. Such an approach would cut the heart out of *Bruton.* To the extent that it suggests that other declarations against interest might be admissible irrespective of whether the declarant testifies, it may be correct. This rule is not as quick to close the door to such statements as Maine's is, although it is not easy to imagine many statements intended to be against interest being made by participants in crime outside of custody.

Maine also added to its rule a provision qualifying statements tending to make the declarant an object of hatred, ridicule or disgrace as declarations against interest. Such a provision was found in earlier drafts of the Federal Rule. Alaska Rule 804(b) (3) rejects this expansion because it is not clear whether the hatred, ridicule, or disgrace that the declarant must fear to qualify his statements under the hearsay exception must be widespread in the community, or in some subgroups, or can be limited to the person to whom the statement is made. Nor is it clear how intense the negative reaction must be thought to be. Proprietary, pecuniary and penal liability offer more objective criteria with which to work. Subdivision (b) (5) allows especially reliable statements to be admitted.

(4) *Statement of Personal or Family History.* The general common law requirement that a declaration in this area must have been made *ante litem motam* has been dropped, as bearing more appropriately on weight than admissibility. *See* 5 Wigmore § 1483, Item (A) specifically disclaims any need of firsthand knowledge respecting a declarant's own personal history. In some instances it is self-evident (marriage) and in other impossible and traditionally not required (date of birth). Item B deals with declaration concerning the history of another person. As at common law, declarant is qualified if related by blood or marriage. 5 Wigmore § 1489. In addition, and contrary to the common law, declarant qualifies by virtue of

intimate association with the family. 5 Wigmore § 1487. The requirement sometimes encountered that when the subject of the statement is the relationship between two other persons the declarant must qualify as to both is omitted. Relationship is reciprocal. 5 Wigmore § 1491.

For comparable provisions, see, Uniform Rule 63(23), (24), (25); California Evidence Code §§ 1310, 1311; Kansas Code of Civil Procedure § 60-460(v), (w); New Jersey Evidence Rules 63(23), 63(24), 63(25).

(5) *Other Exceptions.* In language and purpose, this exception is identical with Rule 803. See Reporter's Comment to that provision.

EDITOR'S NOTE: Section 3, Chapter 67, Session Laws of Alaska 1982, provides that "AS 12.45.047 added by sec. 2 of this Act [Chapter 67, Session Laws of Alaska, 1982] has the effect of changing Rule 804, Rules of Evidence, by adding the videotaped evidence of a young victim of a violation of AS 11.41.410–11.41.455 to the list of exceptions to the hearsay rule."

Rule 805. Hearsay Within Hearsay.

On principle it scarcely seems open to doubt that the hearsay rule should not call for exclusion of a hearsay statement which includes a further hearsay statement when both conform to the requirements of a hearsay exception. Thus a hospital record might contain an entry of the patient's age based on information furnished by his wife. The hospital record would qualify as a regular entry except that the person who furnished the information was not acting in the routine of the business. However, her statement independently qualifies as a statement of pedigree (if she is unavailable) or as a statement made for purposes of diagnosis or treatment, and hence each link in the chain falls within a recognized exception. Or, further to illustrate, a dying declaration may incorporate a declaration against interest by another declarant. Rule 403 may come into play, however, and lead the trial judge to exclude compound hearsay when it is more prejudicial than probative.

Rule 806. Attacking and Supporting Credibility of Declarant.

The declarant of a hearsay statement, or a statement defined by Rule 801(d)(2)(C), (D), or (E) as non-hearsay (throughout this Comment the reader should take the word "hearsay" to include these statements), which is admitted in evidence, is in effect a witness. The Supreme Court's confrontation cases make this point clear. *See, e.g., Douglas v. Alabama,* 380 U.S. 415, 13 L.Ed.2d 934 (1965); *Bruton v. United States,* 389 U.S. 818, 19 L.Ed.2d 70 (1968). His credibility should in fairness be subject to impeachment and support as though he had in fact testified. *See* Rules 608 and 609. This insures that hearsay declarants who are cross-examined in the presence of the jury are not presumed to be truthful while live witnesses are subject to attack. There are, however, some special aspects of the impeaching of a hearsay declarant which require consideration. These special aspects center upon impeachment by inconsistent statement, arise from factual differences which exist between the use of hearsay and an actual witness and also between various kinds of hearsay, and involve the question of applying to declarants the general rule disallowing evidence of an inconsistent statement to impeach a witness unless he is afforded an opportunity to deny or explain. *See* Rule 613(b).

The principal difference between using hearsay and an actual witness is that the inconsistent statement will in the case of the witness almost inevitably be a prior statement, which it is entirely possible and feasible to call to his attention, while in the case of hearsay the inconsistent statement may well be a *subsequent* one, which practically precludes calling it to the attention of the declarant. The result of insisting upon observation of this impossible requirement in the hearsay situation is to deny the opponent, already barred from cross-examination, the benefit of this important technique of impeachment. The writers favor allowing the subsequent statement. *E.g.,* McCormick (2d ed.) § 37. The cases, however, are divided. Cases allowing the impeachment include *People v. Collup,* 167 P.2d 714 (Cal. 1946); *People v. Rosoto,* 373 P.2d 867 (Cal. 1962); *Carver v. United States,* 164 U.S. 694, 41 L.Ed. 602 (1897). *Contra, Mattox v. United States,* 156 U.S. 237, 39 L.Ed. 409 (1895); *People v. Hines,* 29 N.E.2d 483 (N.Y. 1940). The force of *Mattox,* where the hearsay was the former testimony of a deceased witness and the denial of use of a subsequent inconsistent statement was upheld, is much diminished by *Carver,* where the hearsay was a dying declaration and denial of use of a subsequent inconsistent statement resulted in reversal. The difference in the particular brand of hearsay seems unimportant when the inconsistent statement is a *subsequent* one. Although it is true that the opponent is not totally deprived of cross-examination when the hearsay is former testimony or a deposition, the fact remains that he is deprived of cross-examining on the statement or along lines suggested by it.

One commentary on Federal Rule 806 is also apropos of the Alaska rule.

> It would have been possible for the draftsmen of the Rule to distinguish situations outside of a formal judicial proceeding or deposition from proceedings where a witness is sworn and a formal statement is made and recorded, and to distinguish statements made prior to a judicial proceeding (including deposition) from those made afterwards. When a deposition is taken, for instance, it is possible to require that any party having knowledge of a statement made prior to deposing the witness and inconsistent with the witness' statement must give the witness a chance to explain the inconsistency at the deposition upon penalty of being unable to demonstrate the inconsistency at trial if the person who was deposed is unable to appear.

The Advisory Committee rejected drawing this line between informal and formal statements on the ground that deposition procedures are cumbersome and expensive enough, and to require the laying of the foundation might impose undue burdens. Moreover, the Committee appears to have concluded that a distinction based on the timing of inconsistent statements was more complex than beneficial. The Committee was not inclined to adopt a general Rule requiring a foundation with an exception for special circumstances.

K. Redden & S. Saltzburg, Federal Rules of Evidence Manual 634 (2d ed. 1977).

For similar provisions, *see,* Uniform Rule 65; California Evidence Code § 1202; Kansas Code of Civil Procedure § 60-462; New Jersey Evidence Rule 65.

The provision for cross-examination of a declarant upon his hearsay statement is a corollary of general principles of cross-examination. A similar provision is found in California Evidence Code § 1203.

The Senate Committee on the Judiciary explained why the Rule does not cover statements defined by Rule 801 (d) (2) (A) & (B):

> The committee considered it unnecessary to include statements contained in rule 801(d) (2) (A) and (B)—the statement by the party-opponent himself or the statement of which he has manifested his adoption—because the credibility of the party-opponent is always subject to an attack on his credibility.

The Alaska rule is in accord.

ARTICLE IX. DOCUMENTARY EVIDENCE

Rule 901. Requirement of Authentication or Identification.

The Advisory Committee's Notes to Federal Rule 901 describes the process of authentication in the following way:

> Authentication and identification represent a special aspect of relevancy. Michael and Adler, Real Proof, 5 Vand. L. Rev. 344, 362 (1952); McCormick §§ 179, 185; Morgan, Basic Problems of Evidence 378 (1962). Thus a telephone conversation may be irrelevant because of an unrelated topic or because the speaker is not identified. The latter aspect is the one here involved...
>
> This requirement of showing authenticity or identity falls in the category of relevancy dependant upon fulfillment of a condition of fact and is governed by the procedure set forth in Rule 104(b).

But sometimes authentication is more than a relevancy concern. Alaska Rule 901 recognizes this and

> the confusion that exists even in common law jurisdictions over whether authentication is a problem involving a question of "competency" which must be resolved by preliminary fact-finding and decision-making by the Trial Judges or whether it involves a question of conditional relevancy.... In fact, common law jurisdictions, without saying as much, have divided up authentication problems so that some are really problems of relevancy and some involve requirements of preliminary fact-finding and judicial screening to insure a minimal level of reliability and safety.

K. Redden & S. Saltzburg, *Federal Rules of Evidence Manual* 643-44 (2d ed. 1977).

Thus, Article IX of these rules—especially Rule 903—abandons most special foundation rules altogether, in the belief that today procedures like requests to admit and pretrial conferences afford the means of eliminating much of the need for authentication and identification. Rule 901 takes an intermediate step between common law requirements and the Federal Rule; it follows the Federal Rule in abandoning rigid rules in the introductory language, but it recognizes the wisdom of some common law authentication requirements and provides that courts must be especially careful in handling certain kinds of evidence.

Paragraph (a) requires that before offering evidence of a type not readily identifiable, or susceptible to adulteration, contamination, modification, or tampering, etc., the Government in a criminal case must demonstrate as a matter of reasonable certainty that the evidence is properly identified and untainted. This is similar to the "chain of custody" foundational requirement imposed by the common law. The stringency of the requirement will depend on the degree of susceptibility to change by accident or fraud of the particular piece of evidence, as well as its importance to the Government's case. But in any case Rule 901(a) does not change the well-settled rule.

> that in setting up a chain of evidence, the prosecution need not call upon every person who had an opportunity to come in contact with the evidence sought to be admitted. Similarly, every conceivable possibility of tampering need not be eliminated... . '[T]he presumption of regularity supports the official acts of public officers; and the courts presume that they have properly discharged their official duties.' [Footnote omitted.]

Wright v. State, 501 P.2d 1360, 1372 (Alaska 1972), *quoting Gallego v. United States,* 276 F.2d 914, 917 (9th Cir. 1960). *Wright* held that where a Federal Bureau of Narcotics chemist identified initials on an envelope in which LSD had been mailed as those of a Bureau secretary and identified the signature on the postal receipt from the envelope as another secretary's and there was no indication of any deviation from the Bureau routine of initialing registered letters and placing them in a particular safe, there was sufficient showing of the whereabouts of the LSD from the time received by the Bureau to the time analyzed by the chemist.

Wester v. State, 528 P.2d 1179 (Alaska 1974), held that the personal testimony of individuals who calibrated a breathalyzer machine and who tested sample ampules was not necessary as a foundational basis for admission of breathalyzer test results, and held that a showing of substantial compliance with the fifteen-minute observation period prior to the administration of the test was a prima facie showing of the authenticity of the test. The court remarked that the defendant could have called the calibrators and test administrators as her own witnesses if she had reason to suspect impropriety.

These cases illustrate that Rule 901(a) does not hold the Government to an onerous standard of proof, but merely to the same reasonable requirement that it is used to fulfilling. *See also Lee v. State,* 511 P.2d 1076 (Alaska 1973); *Selman v. State,* 411 P.2d 217 (Alaska 1966).

Including paragraph (a) in Rule 901 insures that real evidence is reliable, burdens prosecutors and police only slightly, and avoids the need to create additional prophylactic constitutional rules to protect criminal defendants.

Paragraph (b) of Rule 901 allows the court discretion to require a greater degree of proof for authentication or identification of evidence not readily identifiable or of a kind particularly susceptible to adulteration, contamination, modification, tampering, etc. Leeway is provided for courts to deal with situations in which evidence is introduced sufficient to support a finding that the matter in question is what its proponent claims, but is nonetheless 1) suspect, 2) of great importance to the case or 3) not easily attacked by the adversary because the proponent of the evidence has control over means of establishing or attacking its authenticity, and/or introduction of the suspect evidence may threaten a fair trial even if subsequent evidence is offered on the issue of weight. In addition to satisfying the threshold authentication and identification inquiry, additional proof may aid the court in ruling on the relevance of the evidence under Rule 403.

Federal Rule 901 has a subdivision (b) which presents examples of ways in which evidence can be authenticated. Since these examples are for purposes of illustration and are really not an addition to the Rule itself, they are included in this Comment rather than in the text of Alaska Rule 901. These are only illustrative; they are not intended to limit the ways in which evidence might be authenticated. Following each example is a brief explanation.

Example

(1) *Testimony of witness with knowledge.* Testimony that a matter is what it is claimed to be.

Explanation

Example (1). contemplates a broad spectrum ranging from testimony of a witness who was present at the signing of a document to testimony establishing narcotics as taken from an accused and accounting for custody through the period until trial, including laboratory analysis.

Example

(2) *Nonexpert opinion on handwriting.* Nonexpert opinion as to the genuineness of handwriting, based upon familiarity not acquired for purposes of the litigation.

Explanation

Example (2). states conventional doctrine as to lay identification of handwriting, which recognizes that a sufficient familiarity with the handwriting of another person may be acquired by seeing him write, by exchanging correspondence, or by other means, to afford a basis for identifying it on subsequent occasions. McCormick (2d. ed.) § 221. *See also* California Evidence Code § 1416. Testimony based upon familiarity acquired for purposes of the litigation is reserved to the expert under the example which follows.

Example

(3) *Comparison by trier or expert witness.* Comparison by the trier of fact or by expert witnesses with specimens which have been authenticated.

Explanation

Example (3). The history of common law restrictions upon the technique of proving or disproving the genuineness of a disputed specimen of handwriting through comparison with a genuine specimen, by either the testimony of expert witnesses or direct viewing by the triers themselves, is detailed in 7 Wigmore §§ 1991-1994. In breaking away, the English Common Law Procedure Act of 1854, 17 and 18 Vict., c. 125, § 27, cautiously allowed expert or trier to use exemplars "proved to the satisfaction of the judge to be genuine" for purposes of comparison. The language found its way into numerous statutes in this country e.g., California Evidence Code §§ 1417, 1418. While explainable as a measure of prudence in the process of breaking with precedent in the handwriting situation, the reservation to the judge of the question of the genuineness of exemplars and the imposition of an unusually high standard of persuasion are at variance with the general treatment of relevancy which depends upon fulfillment of a condition of fact. Rule 104(b). No similar attitude is found in other comparison situations, *e.g.,* ballistics comparison by jury, as in *Evans v. Commonwealth,* 19 S.W.2d 1091 (Ky. 1929), or by experts, Annot., 26 A.L.R.2d 892, and no reason appears for its continued existence in handwriting cases. Consequently Example (3) sets no higher standard for handwriting specimens and treats all comparison situations alike, to be governed by Rule 104(b). This approach is consistent with 28 U.S.C. § 1731: "The admitted or proved handwriting of any person shall be admissible, for purposes of comparison, to determine genuineness of other handwriting attributed to such person."

Example

(4) *Distinctive characteristics and the like.* Appearance, contents, substance, internal patterns, or other distinctive characteristics, taken in conjunction with circumstances.

Explanation

Example (4). The characteristics of the offered item itself, considered in the light of circumstances, afford authentication techniques in great variety. Thus a document or telephone conversation may be shown to have emanated from a particular person by virtue of its disclosing knowledge of facts known peculiarly to him; *Globe Automatic Sprinkler Co. v. Braniff,* 214 P. 127 (Okla. 1923); California Evidence Code § 1421. Similarly, a letter may be authenticated by content and circumstances indicating it was in reply to a duly authenticated one. McCormick § 225, California Evidence Code § 1420. Language patterns may indicate authenticity or its opposite. *Magnuson v. State,* 203 N.W. 749 (Wis. 1924); Arens and Meadow, *Psycholinguistics and the Confession Dilemma,* 56 Colum. L. Rev. 19 (1956).

Example

(5) *Voice identification.* Identification of a voice, whether heard firsthand or through mechanical or electronic transmission or recording, by opinion based upon hearing the voice at any time under circumstances connecting it with the alleged speaker.

Explanation

Example (5). Since aural voice identification is not a subject of expert testimony, the requisite familiarity may be acquired either before or after the particular speaking which is the subject of the identification, in this respect resembling visual identification of a person rather than identification of handwriting. If voiceprints are deemed admissible at some future time, consideration will have to be given to limiting to experts voice comparisons made solely for purposes of litigation. Compare Examples 2 and 3, *supra.*

Example

(6) *Telephone conversations.* Telephone conversations, by evidence that a call was made to the number assigned at the time by the telephone company to a particular person or business, if (A) in the case of a person, circumstances, including self-identification, show the person answering to be the one called, or (B) in the case of a business, the call was made to a place of business and the conversation related to business reasonably transacted over the telephone.

Explanation

Example (6). The cases are in agreement that a mere assertion of his identity by a person talking on the telephone is not sufficient evidence of the authenticity of the conversation and that additional evidence of his identity is required. The additional evidence need not fall in any set pattern. Thus the content of his statements or the reply technique, under Example (4), *supra,* or voice identification under Example (5), may furnish the necessary foundation. Outgoing calls made by the witness involve additional factors bearing upon authenticity. The calling of a number assigned by the telephone company reasonably supports the assumption that the listing is correct and that the number is the one reached. If the number is that of a place of business, the mass of authority allows an ensuing conversation if it relates to business reasonably transacted over the telephone, on the theory that the maintenance of the telephone connection is an invitation to do business without further identification. *Matton v. Hoover Co.,* 166 S.W.2d 557 (Mo. 1942); *City of Pawhuska v. Crutchfield,* 293 P. 1095 (Okla. 1930); *Zurich General Acc. & Liability Ins. Co. v. Baum,* 165 S.E. 518 (Va. 1932). Otherwise, some additional circumstances of identification of the speaker is required. The authorities divide on the question whether the self-identifying statement of the person answering suffices. Example (6) answers in the affirmative on the assumption that usual conduct respecting telephone calls furnishes adequate assurances of regularity, bearing in mind that the entire matter is open to exploration before the trier of fact. *See generally* McCormick (2d. ed.) § 226; 7 Wigmore § 2155; Annot., 71 A.L.R. 5; Annot., 105 A.L.R. 326.

Example

(7) *Public records or reports.* Evidence that a writing authorized by law to be recorded or filed and in fact recorded or filed in a public office, or a purported public record, report, statement, or data compilation, in any form, is from the public office where items of this nature are kept.

Explanation

Example (7). Public records are regularly authenticated by proof of custody, without more. McCormick (2d. ed.) § 224; 7 Wigmore §§ 2158, 2159. The example extends the principle to include data stored in computers and by similar methods, of which increasing use in the public records area may be expected. *See,* California Evidence Code §§ 1532, 1600.

Example

(8) *Ancient documents or data compilation.* Evidence that a document or data compilation, in any form, (A) is in such condition as to create no suspicion concerning its authenticity, (B) was in a place where it, if authentic, would likely be, and (C) has been in existence 20 years or more at the time it is offered.

Explanation

Example (8). The familiar ancient document rule of the common law is extended to include data stored electronically or by other similar means. Since the importance of appearance diminishes in this situation, the importance of custody or place where found increases correspondingly. This expansion is necessary in view of the widespread use of methods of storing data in forms other than conventional written records.

Any time period selected is bound to be arbitrary. The common law period of 30 years is here reduced to 20 years, with some shift of emphasis from the probable unavailability of witnesses to the unlikeliness of a still viable fraud after the lapse of time. The shorter period is specified in the English Evidence Act of 1938, 1 & 2 Geo. 6, c. 28, and in Oregon R.S. 1963, § 41.360(34). *See also* the numerous statutes prescribing periods of less than 30 years in the case of recorded documents. 7 Wigmore § 2143. *See also* Reporter's Comment accompanying Rule 803(16).

Example

(9) *Process or System.* Evidence describing a process or system used to produce a result and showing that the process or system produces an accurate result.

Explanation

Example (9). If the accuracy of a result is dependent upon the process or system which produces it, the process or system must be shown to be reliable. Judicial notice under Rule 201 may be sufficient to authenticate a process or system. Expert testimony under Rule 703 may be sufficient. Judicial precedents will establish that some processes or systems are acceptable.

Example

(10) *Methods provided by statute or rule.* Any method of authentication or identification provided by an enactment of the Alaska Legislature or by rules prescribed by the Supreme Court of Alaska or an administrative agency.

Explanation

Example (10). Other methods of authentication found in statutes or rules are also valid. *See, e.g.,* Alaska R. Civ. P. 30(f) (depositions); Alaska R. Civ. P. 75(b) (transcript of evidence); AS 21.06.070 (certificates of insurance director); AS 34.15.300 (record of conveyance). Rules of court and administrative rules also can provide for ways of authenticating evidence.

Rule 902. Self-Authentication.

By providing for self-authentication of certain documents and other items of real evidence this Rule dispenses with the need to produce extrinsic evidence of authenticity as a condition precedent to admissibility. The move to decrease the foundation requirements for some real evidence is a move towards a more efficient trial system. All of the subdivisions of this Rule govern types of evidence which can be presumed to be authentic and free from taint without much danger that the rate of error in litigation will be appreciably affected. By eliminating the costs of laying a foundation, the expense of litigation to the parties and to the taxpayers should be reduced to some significant extent.

While a presumption of authenticity dispenses with the need to introduce extrinsic evidence as a condition precedent to admissibility, it does not preclude a dispute about authenticity by the parties, who are free to attack the genuineness of the real evidence. When evidence is introduced to dispute the authenticity of an official seal or signature, the jury will determine its validity unless the trial judge finds that reasonable minds could not differ on the question, in which case a directed verdict or peremptory instruction should result in a civil case. In a criminal case the same is true, except that the trial judge cannot direct a verdict against, or instruct the jury that it must make a finding against, the defendant. See Reporter's Comment to Rule 201. *See also* Reporter's Comment to Rule 303.

The Advisory Committee's Note to the Federal Rule, which is similar with respect to most of the provisions except subdivision (3) (a), is heavily relied upon in this Comment.

(1) **Domestic Public Documents Under Seal.** The acceptance of documents bearing a public seal and signature, most often encountered in practice in the form of acknowledgements or certificates authenticating copies of public records, is actually of broad application. Whether theoretically based in whole or in part upon judicial notice, the practical underlying considerations are that forgery is a crime and detection is fairly easy and certain, due to the easy ascertainment of the validity of the seal. *See* 7 Wigmore § 2161; California Evidence Code § 1452.

(2) **Domestic Public Documents Not Under Seal.** While statutes are found which raise a presumption of genuineness of purported official signatures in the absence of an official seal, 7 Wigmore § 2167; California Evidence Code § 1453, the greater ease of effecting a forgery under these circumstances is apparent. Hence this paragraph of the rule calls for authentication by an officer who has a seal. *See also* N.Y. Civ. Prac. Law, Rule 45421 (McKinney).

(3) **Foreign Public Documents.** Paragraph (a) provides that documents bearing the seal of state of a foreign nation are presumptively valid. Although the Federal Rule does not so provide, this is in accord with California Evidence Code § 1452 and with some common law authority. *See* 7 Wigmore § 2163, at 645. Unlike the California provision, the seal of a public entity of a foreign nation is not presumed to be self-authenticating under this rule. The concern for forgery is greater where the seal is more difficult to ascertain as in the case of departments, agencies and officers of foreign nations. See Reporter's Comment to Alaska Evidence Rule 202(c) (4) for related treatment of judicial notice of foreign law and a discussion of the problem associated with ascertaining foreign law. Paragraph (b) provides a method for extending the presumption of authenticity to foreign official documents which are not under the seal of state by a procedure of certification. It is largely based on Fed. R. Civ. P. 44(a) (2) but applies to public documents in addition to public records. It is important to note that an American officer can supply the necessary verification, whether or not he or she is located in the foreign country whose record or document is introduced. Also important is the fact that the Rule provides several different ways of authenticating foreign public documents. This section also provides that where reasonable opportunity exists for the parties to investigate authenticity, the court may order that foreign public documents be presumed to be authenticated without final certification. This is similar to Rule 1003 in its impact. It is important that the adjective "reasonable" be deemed to include financial and logistical concerns, as well as concern about time.

(4) **Certified Copies of Public Records.** The common law has provided that official records and reports recorded or filed in a public office may be authenticated by a certificate of a custodian or other person authorized to make the certification. Under this provision the certificate must comply with sections (1)–(3) previously discussed. It will be observed that the certification procedure here provided extends only to public records, reports, and recorded documents, all including data compilations, and does not apply to public documents generally. Hence documents provable when presented in original form under subdivisions (1), (2), or (3) may not be provable by certified copy under subdivision (4).

(5) **Official Publication.** The chance to dispense with preliminary proof of the genuineness of purportedly official publications, most commonly encountered in connection with statutes, court reports, rules, and regulations, has been greatly enlarged by statutes and decisions. 5 Wigmore § 1684. Subdivision (5), it will be noted, does not confer admissibility upon all official publications; it merely provides a means whereby their authenticity may be taken as established for purposes of admissibility. Where other considerations bar a given official publication from admissibility—if, for example, a hearsay problem exists—this section will not help the offering party escape the relevant exclusionary rule.

(6) **Newspapers and Periodicals.** The likelihood of forgery of newspapers or periodicals is slight. Hence no danger is apparent in receiving them. Establishing the authenticity of the publication may, of course, still leave open questions of authority and responsibility for items therein contained. *See* 7 Wigmore § 2150. Again, although production of materials purporting to be a newspaper or periodical amounts to self-authentication, admissibility depends upon other factors as well.

(7) **Trade Inscriptions and the Like.** As in the case of domestic seals and foreign seals of state, the serious penalties associated with forgery and trademark infringement justify less concern with fraud in allowing trade inscriptions and the like to be self-authenticating.

(8) **Acknowledged Documents.** In virtually every state, acknowledged title documents are receivable in evidence without further proof. *See* 5 Wigmore § 1676. If this authentication suffices for documents of the importance of those affecting titles, logic scarcely permits denying this method when other kinds of documents are involved. *See* California Evidence Code § 1451. This is an expansion of self-authentication, but one that is logically impelled from existing law.

(9) **Commercial Paper and Related Documents.** Commercial paper, signatures thereon, and documents relating thereto are authenticated to the extent provided by general commercial law. Where federal commercial paper is involved,

federal commercial law will apply. *Clearfield Trust Co. v. United States,* 318 U.S. 363, 87 L.Ed. 838 (1943). *See* C. Wright, Handbook of the Law of Federal Courts § 45, at 174 (2d ed. 1970).

(10) **Presumptions Created by Law.** This section recognizes that whenever the legislature or the Supreme Court of Alaska pursuant to its rulemaking authority determines to make any signature, document, or other matter presumptively genuine, self-authentication can be accomplished in the manner provided by such statute or rule. Should the United States Congress confer presumptive validity on some item of proof with the intent of covering both state and federal courts, or should the federal courts interpret a statute that is enforced in both state and federal courts so as to require that an item of proof be deemed presumptively admissible, the Supremacy Clause would require the several states to be bound by such legislation, as long as the scope of the federal law does not exceed the reach of federal power.

Rule 903. Subscribing Witness' Testimony Unnecessary.

At common law an attesting witness was a preferred witness who had to be produced or accounted for in proving the execution of an attested document. Once the absence of the attesting witness was satisfactorily explained, the next best evidence could be received. Evidence of his handwriting was generally the next best evidence. If all attesters were present and denied having witnessed the execution, the proponent of the document was permitted to introduce other evidence to prove that the attesters had witnessed the execution.

The modern trend is to abolish the common law requirement unless the law governing the validity of the writing requires a subscribing or attesting witness.

This Rule is identical to Alaska R. Civ. P. 43 (k) which it supersedes. Substantially similar to the Federal Rule, it provides that no attester is a necessary witness to prove the valid execution of a document unless the statute governing the validity of the attestation provides otherwise. *See* AS 34.15.200; AS 34.15.210; AS 34.15.220, providing for proof of an execution of a conveyance.

For similar provisions see Uniform Rule 71; California Evidence Code § 1411; N.Y. Civ. Prac. Law, Rule 4537; (McKinney) Maine Rule 903; Nebraska Rule 27-903.

ARTICLE X. WRITINGS

Rule 1001. Definitions.

Rule 1001 follows the Federal Rule verbatim, as did virtually all other State provisions drafted after the Federal Rule was adopted. *But see* Maine Rules 1001 & 1003. The Advisory Committee's Note, which accompanied the Federal Rule, comprises the rest of this comment with minor changes.

In an earlier day, when discovery and other related procedures were strictly limited, the misleadingly named "best evidence" rule afforded substantial guarantees against inaccuracies and fraud by its insistence upon production of original documents. The great enlargement of the scope of discovery and related procedures in recent times has measurably reduced the need for the rule. Nevertheless important areas of usefulness persist: discovery of documents outside the jurisdiction may require substantial outlay of time and money; the unanticipated document may not practicably be discoverable; criminal cases have built-in limitations on discovery. Cleary and Strong, *The Best Evidence Rule: An Evaluation in Context,* 51 Iowa L. Rev. 825 (1966).

(1) **Writings and Recordings.** Traditionally the rule requiring the original centered upon accumulations of data and expressions affecting legal relations set forth in words and figures. This meant that the rule was one essentially related to writings. Present day techniques have expanded methods of storing data, yet the essential form which the information ultimately assumes for usable purposes is words and figures. Hence the considerations underlying the rule dictate its expansion to include computers, photographic systems, and other modern developments.

(2) **Photographs.** This subdivision is self-explanatory.

(3) **Original.** In most instances, what is an original will be self-evident and further refinement will be unnecessary. However, in some instances particularized definition is required. A carbon copy of a contract executed in duplicate becomes an original, as does a sales ticket carbon copy given to a customer. While strictly speaking the original of a photograph might be thought to be only the negative, practicality and common usage require that any unretouched print from the negative be regarded as an original. Similarly, practicality and usage confer the status of original upon any computer printout. *Transport Indemnity Co. v. Seib,* 132 N.W.2d 871 (Neb. 1965). However, a printout that summarizes the raw data stored in the computer without listing all the data may be treated under Rule 1006. Distinguishing summaries from raw data may present difficulties for litigants and courts unschooled in computers, but reliance upon Rule 1006 in close cases should insure fairness and impose no undue burdens on parties utilizing computers.

(4) **Duplicate.** The definition describes "copies" produced by methods possessing an accuracy which virtually eliminates the possibility of error. Copies thus produced are given the status of originals in large measure by Rule 1003, *infra.* Copies subsequently produced manually, whether handwritten or typed, are not within the definition. It should be noted that what is an original for some purposes may be a duplicate for others. Thus a bank's microfilm record of checks cleared is the original as a record. However, a print offered as a copy of a check whose contents are in controversy is a duplicate. This result substantially comports with Title 40 of the Alaska Code governing Public Records.

Rule 1002. Requirement of Original.

This rule, modeled after Federal Rule 1002, is the familiar part of the Best Evidence Rule requiring the production of the original to prove the contents of a writing, recording or photograph. See Rule 1001(1) and 1001(2) for definitions of the terms used in this rule.

Application of the rule requires a resolution of the question whether the contents are sought to be proved. Thus an event may be proved by nondocumentary evidence, even though a written record of it was made. If, however, the event is sought to be proved by the written record, the rule applies. For example, payment may be proved without producing the written receipt which was given. Earnings may be proved without producing books of account in which they are entered. McCormick (2d ed.) § 233, at 564; 4 Wigmore § 1245.

The assumption should not be made that the rule will come into operation on every occasion when use is made of a photograph in evidence. On the contrary, the rule will seldom apply to ordinary photographs. In most instances a party *wishes* to introduce the item and the question raised is the propriety of receiving it in evidence. Cases in which an offer is made of the testimony of a witness as to what he saw in a photograph or motion picture, without producing the same, are most unusual. The usual course is for a witness on the stand to identify the photograph or motion picture as a correct representation of events which he saw or of a scene with which he is familiar. In fact he adopts the picture as his testimony, or, in common parlance, uses the picture to illustrate his testimony. Under these circumstances, no effort is made to prove the contents of the picture, and the rule is inapplicable. *See* Paradis, *The Celluloid Witness,* 37 U. Colo. L. Rev. 235, 249-251 (1965).

On occasion, however, situations arise in which the contents of a photograph are sought to be proved. Copyright, defamation, and invasion of privacy by photograph or motion picture fall in this category. Similarly this applies to situations in which the picture is offered as having independent probative value, *e.g.* an automatic photograph of a bank robber. *See* Mouser and Philbin, *Photographic Evidence — Is There a Recognized Basis for Admissibility?* 8 Hastings L.J. 310 (1957). The most commonly encountered of this latter group is, of course, the X-ray, with substantial authority calling for production of the original. *Daniels v. Iowa City,* 183 N.W. 415 (Iowa 1921); *Cellamare v. Third Avenue Transit Corp.,* 77 N.Y.S.2d 91 (1948); *Patrick & Tilman v. Matkin,* 7 P.2d 414 (Okla. 1932); *Mendoza v. Rivera,* 78 P.R.R. 569 (P.R. 1955).

Hospital records which may be admitted as business records under Rule 803(6) commonly contain reports interpreting x-rays by the staff radiologist, who qualifies as an expert, and these reports need not be excluded from the records by the instant Rule. Rule 803(6) allows opinions in business records to be admitted. And it should be noted that Rule 703 allows an expert to give an opinion on matters not in evidence. Rule 1002 must be read in conjunction with these other Rules. Of course, the trial judge might decide to require testimony, relying on the last clause of Rule 803 (6) and Rule 705.

The Advisory Committee's Note accompanying Federal Rule 1002 states that "the rule [does not] apply to testimony that books or records have been examined and found not to contain any reference to a designated matter." This comment can be very misleading.

In a dispute between *A* and *B* over the terms of a contract—specifically whether *A* would pay liquidated damages for delays in delivering goods to *B*—before *A,* who possesses the original contract, will be permitted to testify that the contract has no liquidated damages clause, A must produce the original or account for its nonproduction. It is plain that the claim of the absence of a contract provision is the converse of the claim of a provision's inclusion. Rule 1002 applies to both claims. In some instances a writing or recording will be collateral and this Rule will not apply because of 1004(d). In other instances where documents are voluminous and it would be unduly burdensome to show the absence of a certain provision in all, Rule 1006 should provide a satisfactory solution. While there is some support in the cases for the Advisory Committee's comment, it is unwarranted in view of the other provisions of this Article.

Rule 1002 states the general rule that the original is to be supplied when a writing or recording is offered for proof of its contents. But other provisions of Article X of these rules soften the impact of Rule 1002. Rule 1003 makes duplicates presumptively admissible. Rule 1004 provides for admission of secondary evidence under certain conditions. Rule 1005 creates a special provision for public records. Special provision is also made for voluminous documents in Rule 1006. And Rule 1007 provides for the substitution of certain party admissions for proof of an original writing or recording.

Rule 1003. Admissibility of Duplicates.

Rule 1003 follows the Federal Rule in its departure from the common law "best evidence" rule, which requires that "in proving the terms of a writing, where the terms are material, the original writing must be produced unless it is shown to be unavailable for some reason other than the serious fault of the proponent." McCormick, (2d ed.) § 230, at 560. In recognition of the great legal significance attaching to the exact words of a document, the "best evidence" rule was designed to prevent fraud and protect against inaccuracy. The rule served a purpose when duplicates were made by a scrivener instead of an electronic duplicating machine. However, when the sole aim is to present the words or other contents in question to the court with accuracy and precision, a copy serves equally as well as the original, if the copy is the product of a method which insures accuracy and genuineness. By definition in Rule 1001 (d), *supra,* a "duplicate" is such a copy.

Therefore, Rule 1003 provides that if there is no genuine question as to authenticity, and no other reason for requiring the original, a duplicate is admissible. The Advisory Committee's Note to Federal Rule 1003 cites the following cases in support of this position:

> *Myrick v. United States,* 332 F.2d 279 (5th Cir. 1964), no error in admitting photostatic copies of checks instead of original microfilm in absence of suggestion to trial judge that photostats were incorrect; *Johns v. United States,* 323 F.2d 421 (5th Cir. 1963), not error to admit concededly accurate tape recording made from original wire recording; *Sauget v. Johnston,* 315 F.2d 816 (9th Cir. 1963), not error to admit copy of agreement when opponent had original and did not on appeal claim any discrepancy.

An example of a situation in which it would be unfair to admit the duplicate in lieu of the original is when only a part of the original is reproduced and the remainder is needed for cross-examination or may disclose matters qualifying the part offered or be otherwise useful to the opposing party. *United States v. Alexander,* 326 F.2d 736 (4th Cir. 1964). *See also Toho Bussan Kaisha, Ltd. v. American President Lines, Ltd.* 265 F.2d 418 (2d Cir. 1959).

In ruling on the admissibility of a duplicate, the court should "examine the quality of the duplicate, the specificity and sincerity of the challenge, the importance of the evidence to the case, and the burdens of producing the original before determining whether a genuine question is raised as to authenticity." K. Redden & S. Saltzburg, Federal Rules of Evidence Manual 368. This approach is consistent with Rule 1004. It is also important to keep in mind that oral testimony about a document is not a "duplicate."

When Rule 1003 applies, the original need not be produced under Rule 1002. Rule 1003 applies generally, but is superseded with respect to public records by Rule 1005. If Rule 1007 is satisfied, there is no need to satisfy Rule 1003.

Rule 1004. Admissibility of Other Evidence of Contents.

This rule is identical to its federal counterpart and is very similar to Uniform Rule 70(1) (a)—(d). It is based on a common law tradition which permits secondary evidence to be used to prove the contents of a writing, recording, or photograph when failure to produce the original can be explained satisfactorily. The Commissioner's Note following the Uniform Rule expresses the concerns underlying this rule:

> The "Best Evidence Rule" at common law as well as here is a preferential rather than an exclusionary rule. Its object is to prevent a litigant from depriving the trier of fact, by fraudulent design, of the benefit of the only certain proof of the content of a writing, the writing itself.

9A Uniform Laws Annotated 654 (1965).

When the requirements of one of the four subdivisions are satisfied, there is little or no reason to fear fraud or other sharp practices. Thus, secondary evidence is deemed admissible.

(a) **Original Is Lost or Destroyed.** This subdivision permits secondary evidence if a proponent can show that the originals are lost or have been destroyed without bad faith on his part. Evidence of a search made in good faith of the places where an original would be found if it existed should be sufficient foundation to prove loss when no direct evidence is available. The important factor here is that a proponent should not benefit by admitting secondary evidence where the original was lost or suppressed at his own instance. This extends to situations where third parties have destroyed the original acting at the direction of the proponent. *See* McCormick (2d ed.) § 237.

(b) **Original Not Obtainable.** When the original is in the possession of a third party who is not a party to the case, the original should be obtained by judicial process, *i.e.,* such as a subpoena duces tecum. Where the third party is beyond the subpoena power of the trial court and no judicial process or procedure can avail, secondary evidence can be introduced. Great expense or difficulty are not sufficient to establish excuse under this provision. *See* McCormick (2d ed.) § 238. This may seem harsh, but the originals are by definition, *see* subdivision (d), closely related to a controlling issue in a case.

(c) **Original in Possession of Opponent.** If an adverse party is put on notice that the contents of a writing, recording or photograph are to be proved at trial and the original is in his control, if he fails to produce it secondary evidence can be introduced. The party against whom it is being offered has the ability to supply the original and failure to do so indicates lack of concern. The notice requirement must afford the party a reasonable chance to produce the original. This requirement can be met in the pleadings or otherwise, if calculated to alert the party that the original is necessary. Note that unlike discovery procedures such as orders to produce, there is no compulsion to produce, only the timely chance to substitute an original for secondary evidence. *See* McCormick (2d ed.) § 239.

(d) **Collateral Matters.** When the contents of the writing, recording or photograph are not closely related to a controlling issue in the trial, secondary evidence will be permitted. This is often referred to as the exception for collateral evidence. The trial judge will exercise some discretion in determining whether evidence is related to collateral issues by considering such factors as (a) the centrality to principal issues of litigation; (b) the complexity of relevant features of the writing; and (c) the existence of genuine dispute as to the contents. McCormick (2d ed.) § 234 at 565-566.

If Rules 1003, 1005, 1006, or 1007 are utilized, there is no reason to use Rule 1004. Rule 1004 applies when there is no other rule allowing secondary evidence and the proponent of the evidence must justify its admission in lieu of the original.

Rule 1005. Public Records.

Rule 1005 follows the Federal Rule in establishing a treatment of public records different from the treatment of other documents. As the Advisory Committee notes, public records call for different treatment, since requiring removal of the original record whenever the contents of that record are in question would be attended by serious inconvenience to the public and to the custodian. Judicial decisions and statutes often hold that no explanation need be given for failure to produce the original of a public record. McCormick (2d ed.) § 240. *See, e.g.* Alaska R. Civ. P. 44(b) (superseded by these Rules) and AS 40.21.150 and AS 40.15.040, providing for the use of copies of public records as evidence. While the original document need not be produced, Rule 1005 protects against the indiscriminate introduction of all sorts of secondary evidence by establishing a preference for certified or compared and verified copies. Usually such copies of public records are readily available, so it will seldom be necessary to produce any other sort of secondary evidence.

This rule supersedes Rule 1003 with respect to public documents. Rule 1007 provides an alternative way of satisfying best evidence concerns.

Rule 1006. Summaries.

This rule continues the tradition of permitting summaries to be introduced in lieu of voluminous writings, recordings, or photographs, which cannot be easily examined in court. In many cases summaries are the only practical means of making information available to the judge and jury. The proponent of the summary must make the originals or duplicates available for examination or copying, thus affording the other parties the opportunity to assess the degree of accuracy with which the summary captures the contents of the originals. Should the accuracy be in dispute by the parties, the trial judge may order the original to be produced in court. *See* 4 Wigmore § 1230.

For similar provisions see Nevada Rule 52.275 and Nebraska Rule 27-1006.

Rule 1007. Testimony or Written Admission of Party.

American courts have held that in some circumstances if the secondary evidence offered to prove the contents of a document consists of an admission by the party against whom it is offered, no showing is required of why the original is not produced. But it has not been clear whether *all* admissions, irrespective of the circumstances in which made, serve to prove the contents of an item otherwise covered by the "Best Evidence" Rule. The seminal case, *Slatterie v. Pooley,* 6 M. & W. 664, 151 Eng. Rep. 579 (Exch. 1840), allowing proof of contents by evidence of an oral admission by the party against whom offered, without accounting for nonproduction of the original, has been criticized as involving a substantial risk of inaccuracy and as being in contravention of the purpose of the "Best Evidence" Rule. *See, e.g.,* 4 Wigmore § 1255; McCormick (2d ed.) § 242, at 577. Federal Rule 1007, which this rule copies, followed McCormick's suggestion of limiting the use of admissions to prove the content of writings, recordings or photographs to those admissions made in the course of giving testimony or in writing.

It should be observed that Rule 1007 does not call for the exclusion of evidence of an oral admission when non-production of the original has been accounted for and secondary evidence generally has become admissible under Rule 1004.

Also, an admission that could be introduced under Rule 801 (d) (2) (C), (D), or (E) against a party and otherwise qualifying under this rule may be used to prove the contents of writings, recordings, or photographs without accounting for nonproduction of the original. "[W]hatever reasons justify the use of ordinary 801(d)(2) admissions as substantive evidence on the merits would seem to carry over to the often less significant question of proving the content of a writing or recording." K. Redden and S. Saltzburg, Supplement to Federal Rules of Evidence Manual 697 (2d ed. 1977).

This rule provides an exception to Rule 1002. It is clear, however, that there is no requirement that Rule 1007 be used. Rules 1003, 1005, 1006 and other statutes may provide easier ways to satisfy best evidence concerns.

Rule 1008. Functions of Court and Jury.

The application of the rule preferring the original of a writing, recording, or photograph to prove its contents often depends on the determination of preliminary questions of fact. Such preliminary factfinding is usually undertaken by the judge in accordance with Rule 104. *See* Reporter's Comment to Rule 104 for the considerations underlying preliminary questions of admissibility.

Rules 1003 and 1004 present numerous findings of fact which must be made precedent to the admissibility of secondary evidence. In Rule 1003 the trial judge must initially decide whether (a) a given item of evidence qualifies as a duplicate; (b) whether a genuine question is raised as to the authenticity of the original; and (c) whether it would be unfair to admit a duplicate in lieu of an original. Rule 1004 calls for the trial judge to determine whether or not failure to produce the original can be satisfactorily explained so as to permit proof of the contents by secondary evidence.

However, when the contention is raised that the asserted writing never existed, or that the evidence produced at trial is not the original, or that the evidence of the contents does not correctly reflect the contents, the resolution of the dispute should not be by the trial judge as a preliminary question of fact. These contentions relate to the existence of a document or its contents, not its admissibility, and hence they raise ultimate issues of fact which should be determined by the jury as factfinder.

In practical terms this means that the trial judge, when making a preliminary finding of excuse under Rule 1004, may permit secondary evidence to come in to prove the contents of an original whose very existence is in dispute. The judge must determine the validity of the excuse while assuming arguendo the existence of the document. A preliminary determination to the effect that the document never existed would preclude a jury decision on the central issue of the case. The jury may be called upon to decide a case between a party proffering secondary evidence of the contents of a contract after a preliminary finding by the judge that the original was destroyed, and a party who claims that the contract never existed.

This rule is identical to Federal Rule 1008. For similar provisions see Uniform Rule 70(2); New Jersey Rule 70(3); Nevada Rule 52.295; and Nebraska Rule 27-1008.

ARTICLE XI. TITLE

Rule 1101. Title.

The abbreviation for the Alaska Rules of Evidence shall be A.R.E.

RULES OF APPELLATE PROCEDURE

TABLE OF CONTENTS

PART I. ORGANIZATION OF THE APPELLATE COURTS

Rule

PART II. PROCEDURE ON APPEALS AS OF RIGHT

AR

PART III. PETITION FOR HEARING

PART IV. PETITIONS FOR REVIEW, ORIGINAL APPLICATIONS FOR RELIEF, AND OTHER SPECIAL PROCEEDINGS

PART V. GENERAL PROCEDURES

PART VI. SUPERIOR COURT AS AN APPELLATE COURT

PART I. ORGANIZATION OF THE APPELLATE COURTS

Rule 101. Title of the Courts; Definitions.

(a) Part One of these rules (Rules 101 through 105) applies to the supreme court of the state of Alaska, referred to in these rules as the "supreme court," and to the court of appeals of the state of Alaska, referred to in these rules as the "court of appeals."

(b) As used in these rules, "appellate court" means the supreme court or the court of appeals. Unless the context clearly indicates otherwise, as used in these rules "justice" means a justice of the supreme court, including the chief justice, and "judge" means a judge of the court of appeals, including the chief judge.

(SCO 439 effective November 15, 1980; amended by SCO 888 effective July 15, 1988)

Rule 102. Clerk.

(a) The clerk of the appellate courts, referred to in these rules as the "clerk," is clerk of the supreme court and clerk of the court of appeals.

(b) The principal office of the clerk is located in Anchorage. The clerk shall also maintain offices in Fairbanks and Juneau and at such other locations as the supreme court may designate.

(c) The clerk may not practice law in any court.

(d) The clerk shall, before entering office, take and subscribe to the oath set forth in section 5, article XII of the state Constitution and such further oaths or affirmations as may be prescribed by the legislature, and shall give bond in the sum to be fixed, and with sureties to be approved by the supreme court, faithfully to discharge the duties of the office. The bond shall be deposited for safekeeping as the supreme court may direct. The supreme court may permit the clerk to be covered under the blanket bond provided in Rule 34 of the Rules Governing the Administration of All Courts, in lieu of giving a separate bond.

(e) The clerk may not permit any original record or paper to be taken from the appellate courts, without an order from the appropriate court, except as otherwise provided in these rules.

(f) The clerk may reject a brief or other paper or document submitted for filing which fails to conform to the requirements of these rules. Upon the rejection of a submittal under the authority of this paragraph, the clerk shall notify the party and, where appropriate, specify the defect and provide a time for the filing of a corrected brief, paper or document.

(g) The clerk is appointed by, and serves at the pleasure of, the supreme court. The annual compensation of the clerk is on salary range 25 of the pay plan for classified and partially exempt employees.

(h) The clerk shall prepare and sign all judgments and orders of the appellate courts unless otherwise directed by the appropriate court.

(SCO 439 effective November 15, 1980; amended by SCO 554 effective April 4, 1983; by SCO 1153 effective July 15, 1994; and by SCO 1522 effective October 15, 2003)

Rule 103. Attorneys and Counselors.

(a) All attorneys admitted to practice law in the state of Alaska are qualified to practice in the appellate courts.

(b) On motion to either appellate court, other attorneys may be permitted to practice in that court pursuant to Civil Rule 81(a)(2) and (3). The clerk may determine motions filed under this section.

(c) If an attorney has been permitted to practice in the trial court under Civil Rule 81(a)(2), that attorney may be permitted to practice in the appellate court in the same action or proceeding without motion, upon filing with the clerk of the appellate courts a copy of the trial court's order permitting the attorney to practice, a copy of the certificate of good standing which was furnished to the trial court, and a statement of the name, address and telephone number of the local counsel with whom the attorney is associated.

(Amended by SCO 439 effective November 15, 1980; and by SCO 590 effective March 1, 1984)

Annotations

Cases

Attorneys not admitted to the practice of law in Alaska are not qualified to practice before the supreme court. The purpose of this rule is to insure full amenability of parties to the court at all times and stages of the proceeding. **Organized Village of Kake v. Egan,** Op. No. 16, 354 P2d 1108 (Alaska 1960).

Rule 104. Clerks to Justices Not to Practice.

No person serving as a law clerk, secretary, or other full-time officer or employee of the appellate courts or of a justice or judge of the appellate courts may engage in the private practice of law while continuing in that position; nor may the person ever participate, by way of any form of professional consultation or assistance, in any case which was pending in the court by which the person was employed during the period that the person held such position.

(SCO 439 effective November 15, 1980; amended by SCO 1153 effective July 15, 1994)

Annotations

Cases

An appeal is "pending" under this rule even if no judge or law clerk is actively working on it. **Bradley v. State,** Op. No. 1145, 535 P2d 1031 (Alaska 1975).

Former law clerk's participation in case that was pending at time of his employment with the court was governed by the rules set forth in Professional Conduct Rule 1.12 rather than the blanket prohibition of this rule. **Bradley v. State,** Op. No. 1145, 535 P2d 1031 (Alaska 1975).

Rule 105. Quorum.

(a) A quorum of the supreme court consists of three justices. A quorum of the court of appeals consists of two judges.

(b) Pro tempore justices or judges shall be counted for purposes of a quorum.

(c) If a quorum does not attend on a day on which a session of court is scheduled, any justice or judge who does attend may adjourn the court from time to time, or in the absence of any justice or judge, the clerk may adjourn the court from day to day.

(d) A justice or judge attending when less than a quorum is present may make all necessary orders touching any pending proceeding.

(SCO 439 effective November 15, 1980; amended by SCO 888 effective July 15, 1988)

PART II. PROCEDURE ON APPEALS AS OF RIGHT

Rule 201. Scope of Part Two.

(a) Part Two of these Rules (Rules 201 through 220) applies to appeals as of right, whether to the court of appeals under AS 22.07.020 or to the supreme court under AS 22.05.010. The "court" or "appellate court" referred to in Part Two of these rules is the court of appeals, if the appeal is taken to that court, or the supreme court, if the appeal is taken to that court.

(b) The "trial court" referred to in Part Two of these rules is the district court, if that court entered the judgment being appealed, or the superior court, if that court entered the judgment being appealed.

(SCO 439 effective November 15, 1980; amended by SCO 537 effective October 1, 1982; by SCO 581 effective February 1, 1984; by SCO 926 effective January 15, 1989; and by SCO 1279, effective July 31, 1997)

Rule 202. Judgments from Which Appeal May Be Taken.

(a) An appeal may be taken to the supreme court from a final judgment entered by the superior court, in the circumstances specified in AS 22.05.010.

(b) An appeal may be taken to the court of appeals from a final judgment entered by the superior court or the district court, in the circumstances specified in AS 22.07.020.

(SCO 439 effective November 15, 1980; amended by SCO 1204 effective July 15, 1995)

Annotations

Cases

I. In General.

Where a constitutional question of particular substance and importance is at issue, the Supreme Court will consider appeals from a denial of a pretrial motion to dismiss with prejudice as a petition for review and will grant review. **Muller v. State,** Op. No. 666, 478 P2d 822 (Alaska 1971).

Under AS 22.05.010 pertaining to the issuance of the writs necessary for the Supreme Court to completely exercise its jurisdiction, the legislature's intent was that the Supreme Court would be able to exercise its final appellate jurisdiction other than by appeal. **State v. Browder,** Op. No. 699, 486 P2d 925 (Alaska 1971).

Petitions for review and appeal are mutually exclusive procedures. **Jordan v. Reed,** Op. No. 1217, 544 P2d 75 (Alaska 1975).

A habeas corpus proceeding is civil in nature and therefore may be appealed by the state. **Adams v. Ross,** Op. No. 1281, 551 P2d 948 (Alaska 1976).

Where appeal was taken from nonfinal order granting partial summary judgment, trial court was not divested of authority to modify that order and enter final judgment. **Williams v. City of Valdez,** Op. No. 1969, 603 P2d 483 (Alaska 1979).

Substantial hardship existed, justifying Supreme Court's treatment of an appeal under this rule as a petition for discretionary review where appellate had relied on Supreme Court decision holding appeal was appropriate remedy and where superior court order in effect granted appellee a new trial on the merits before administrative agency. **City & Borough of Juneau v. Thibodeau,** Op. No. 1851, 595 P2d 626 (Alaska 1979).

Appeals raising broad legal issues, such as a challenge to the validity of a provision of the presumptive sentencing statute or to the validity of the presumptive sentencing scheme itself, should be regarded as merit appeals rather than sentence appeals. **Juneby v. State,** Op. No. 72, 641 P2d 823 (Alaska App. 1982).

Under highly structured sentencing procedures established by statute, sentences presumptively imposed will often raise issues of statutory interpretation, challenges to the sufficiency of the evidence under the "clear and convincing" standard, and questions of whether procedures established by the presumptive sentencing statutes were correctly followed, all of which issues are tied sufficiently closely to the ultimate question of excessiveness or leniency to be included within the scope of sentence appeals. **Juneby v. State,** Op. No. 72, 641 P2d 823 (Alaska App. 1982).

Where the issue of specific performance was resolved summarily by the trial court, leaving the issue of damages for trial, the partial summary judgment did not constitute a final judgment, and since appellant filed his appeal from the partial summary judgment within 30 days of the entry of an amended order which determined the damage issue, his appeal as to the order of specific performance was timely. **Currington v. Johnson,** Op. No. 2828, 685 P2d 73 (Alaska 1984).

Where trial court stayed the underlying action and retained jurisdiction over the matter pending resolution of specified questions within the expertise of an administrative agency, the agency ruling was interlocutory in nature and was directly appealable only upon entry of final judgment in the underlying court action; although the trial court improperly characterized the interlocutory ruling as appealable, the Supreme Court chose to treat the appeal as a petition for review and to address the merits of the questions presented in light of the parties' apparent reliance on earlier trial court rulings and because disposition of the case would dispose of the issues remaining in the underlying civil action. **Wade Oilfield v. Providence Wash. Ins.,** Op. No. 3372, 759 P2d 1302 (Alaska 1988).

Although order appealed from was not final order, hence not appealable, Supreme Court treated appeal as petition for review and granted petition, since issue in case was power of superior court to determine underlying cause and case had been briefed and argued. **Puhlman v. Turner,** Op. No.

4090, 874 P2d 291 (Alaska 1994).

Where case presented important constitutional question, both parties faced hardship of continued appeals, rehearings, and delay, and resolution of due process dispute could effectively dispose of remaining issues before trial court, supreme court treated improperly brought appeal as petition for review. **City of North Pole v. Zabek,** Op. No. 4781, 934 P2d 1292 (Alaska 1997).

II. Final Judgments.

A. In General.

Where the interim district court quashed a petition for a writ of review of the judgment of a justice court such order was "final" and hence was appealable as it terminated the proceeding. **Jefferson v. Moore,** Op. No. 9, 354 P2d 373 (Alaska 1960).

Where one of two causes of action in a complaint is dismissed and the other is submitted to the jury, an appeal may not be taken from the former ruling as a final judgment unless Rule 54(b), Rules of Civil Procedure is complied with. **Edwards v. Franke,** Op. No. 45, 364 P2d 60 (Alaska 1961).

Where on petition for review of dismissal by a district magistrate of motion to set aside plea of guilty before a deputy magistrate, the superior court remanded the case to the deputy magistrate for determination of the motion pending before him, such action by the superior court was an interlocutory order from which no appeal could be taken. **Leege v. Strand,** Op. No. 157, 384 P2d 665 (Alaska 1963).

Action of superior court on an appeal from a decision of the Alaska Workmen's Compensation Board in denying motions for an injunction and for a summary judgment and in remanding the case to the Board terminated the proceedings in the superior court, and the order remanding the case was a final judgment within the meaning of this rule. **Fishback & Moore of Alaska, Inc. v. Lynn,** Op. No. 304, 407 P2d 174 (Alaska 1965).

In the absence of a demonstration of exceptional circumstances the issue of liability decided on the first appeal was not reexamined on the second appeal in the same case. **Patrick v. Sedwick,** Op. No. 338, 413 P2d 169 (Alaska 1966).

Where the action rather than the complaint is dismissed the requisite degree of finality is present for purposes of the Supreme Court's appellate jurisdiction. **Dworkin v. First National Bank of Fairbanks,** Op. No. 499, 444 P2d 777 (Alaska 1968).

The denial of a pretrial motion to dismiss with prejudice is not an appealable final judgment. **Muller v. State,** Op. No. 666, 478 P2d 822 (Alaska 1971).

The basic thrust of the requirement of finality before an appeal may be taken from a judgment is that the judgment must be one which disposes of the entire case, i.e., one which ends the litigation on the merits and leaves nothing for the court to do but execute the judgment. **Greater Anchorage Area Borough v. City of Anchorage,** Op. No. 856, 504 P2d 1027 (Alaska 1972).

With respect to the requirement of finality before an appeal may be taken from a judgment, a reviewing court should look to the substance and effect, rather than to the form, of the rendering court's judgment and focus primarily on the operational language therein. **Greater Anchorage Area Borough v. City of Anchorage,** Op. No. 856, 504 P2d 1027 (Alaska 1972).

A habeas corpus proceeding is civil in nature and therefore may be appealed by the state. **Adams v. Ross,** Op. No. 1281, 551 P2d 948 (Alaska 1976).

Where appellant prematurely noted appeal from interlocutory order, but subsequently amended notice to reflect entry of judgment, and parties addressed issues raised by that judgment, Supreme Court treated the appeal as properly taken from final judgment. **Williams v. City of Valdez,** Op. No. 1969, 603 P2d 483 (Alaska 1979).

Where partial summary judgment order in inverse condemnation suit did not resolve issue of amount of damages or to whom damages would be paid, it was not a final judgment. **Williams v. City of Valdez,** Op. No. 1969, 603 P2d 483 (Alaska 1979).

The decision of a superior court, acting as an intermediate appellate court which reverses the judgment of the court below or the decision of an administrative agency and remands, for further proceedings, is not a final judgment for purposes of Appellate Rule 5. **City & Borough of Juneau v. Thibodeau,** Op. No. 1851, 595 P2d 626 (Alaska 1979).

Where court dismissed complaint for failure to state a claim upon which relief could be granted without entering a final judgment dismissing the action and without specifying that the complaint could be amended, and where the complaint could not be amended so as to satisfy either of the possible grounds under which it was dismissed, the dismissal was final and appealable under this rule. **Clary v. Stack Steel and Supply Co.,** Op. No. 2093, 611 P2d 80 (Alaska 1980).

Court rule providing that judgment on one issue in a multi-issue case is not a final judgment unless expressly designated as such by the trial court applies to cases which contain multiple issues only because of consolidation. **Currington v. Johnson,** Op. No. 2828, 685 P2d 73 (Alaska 1984).

Dismissal of a complaint is deemed final unless leave to amend is explicitly granted. **Standard Prod. v. Dept. of Revenue,** Op. No. 3425, 773 P2d 201 (Alaska 1989).

A dismissal of a complaint is appealable where it is clear that the trial court determined that the complaint could not be amended so as to prevent future dismissals on the same ground; accordingly, where the trial court clearly indicated that plaintiff could not avoid dismissal without first exhausting administrative remedies, the trial court dismissal order was final for purposes of appellate review. **Standard Prod. v. Dept. of Revenue,** Op. No. 3425, 773 P2d 201 (Alaska 1989).

Where trial court's second order, which declared contractor a nonparty, constituted denial of subcontractor's motion for clarification of trial court's first order, which dismissed subcontractor's third party claim, and first order was certified by trial court as final judgment, appellate court had jurisdiction to hear subcontractor's appeal of first order. **Martech Const. v. Ogden Env. Services,** Op. No. 3957, 852 P2d 1146 (Alaska 1993).

Where order denying motion for writ of execution effectively terminated proceeding, order was tantamount to final judgment for purposes of appeal. **Denali Federal Credit Union v. Lange,** Op. No. 4413, 924 P2d 429 (Alaska 1996).

When superior court sits as intermediate appellate court and remands case to administrative agency for further proceedings, remand is not considered a final judgment. **Stalnaker v. Williams,** Op. No. 5003, 960 P2d 590 (Alaska 1998).

In the context of children's proceedings, issues may sometimes be revisited without destroying the finality, and therefore the appealability, of other issues; accordingly, trial court's rejection of adult sister's motion in CINA proceeding to have child placed with her rather than foster parents was appealable even though CINA proceeding remained open since trial court's ruling effectively ended any chance that child could be placed with sister. **S.S.M. v. State Dept. of Health,** Op. No. 5285, 3 P3d 342 (Alaska 2000).

City's appeal of an employee's award of attorney's fees in workers' compensation case was an appeal from a non-final order; therefore, the court dismissed the appeal. **Municipality of Anchorage v. Anderson,** Op. No. 5519, 37 P3d 420 (Alaska 2001).

B. Particular Judgments.

Interlocutory review of the denial of a motion for summary judgment in a wrongful death action based on negligence will not be granted thus permitting deviation from the normal procedure of appeal from final judgments where there is no showing of undue hardship or injustice to justify such deviation from the norm. **City of Fairbanks v. Schaible,** Op. No. 5, 352 P2d 129 (Alaska 1960).

An order to pay rent during the pendency of an ejectment action is not a "final" judgment within this rule which implements the policy against piecemeal disposition of litigation. **Stokes v. Van Seventer,** Op. No. 18, 355 P2d 594 (Alaska 1960).

An order denying a motion to declare void a formerly made order for the appointment of receivers for a public utility district was not interlocutory as to one intervening after such appointment was ordered and, hence, the denial of the motion is appealable since there would be no other relief available until the receivership was terminated. **Wood v. Gray,** Op. No. 29, 359 P2d 951 (Alaska 1961).

A memorandum opinion, while not formally a judgment and so called, is appealable where it clearly evidences the judge's intent to presently and finally dispose of a motion to void a receivership. **Wood v. Gray,** Op. No. 29, 359 P2d 951 (Alaska 1961).

Where in a case tried without a jury, the trial judge never rendered a definitive judgment in the form of either an oral opinion or a formal written judgment, no notation was entered by the clerk in the civil docket and it did not appear that the trial judge directed the clerk to so enter judgment, an order filed by the trial judge that the plaintiff be assessed costs in favor of defendants was no final judgment from which an appeal may be taken. **Lowe v. Senior,** Op. No. 168, 385 P2d 942 (Alaska 1963).

While no appeal lies from a consent judgment, where such judgment was obtained by fraud, collusion or mistake, the aggrieved party may seek relief in the trial court by motion under Civil R. 60(b) and an appeal may be taken from an order of denial of such relief. **Gravel v. Alaskan Village, Inc.,** Op. No. 321, 409 P2d 983 (Alaska 1966).

Order dismissing condemnation action because the United States could not be made a party to the action and no judgment on the merits could be rendered in the absence of the United States, was a final judgment and appealable as such. **City of Fairbanks v. Electric Distribution Sys.,** Op. No. 339, 413 P2d 165 (Alaska 1966).

Denial of a motion for acquittal under Criminal Rule 29(b) when a new trial has been ordered is not a final appealable decision. **Stewart v. State,** Op. No. 457, 438 P2d 387 (Alaska 1968).

Order of superior court appointing a special master, decreeing dissolution, and authorizing the sale of assets of partnership was not a final order or judgment from which an appeal could be taken. **Levi v. Sexton,** Op. No. 473, 439 P2d 423 (Alaska 1968).

A right of appeal exists from a dispositive order that a minor, who has been adjudged a child in need of supervision, should be institutionalized. **In re E.M.D.,** Op. No. 737, 490 P2d 658 (Alaska 1971).

An order of the children's court waiving jurisdiction over a petition of delinquency is an appealable "final judgment entered by the superior court" within the meaning of this rule since it terminates further consideration in the children's court and transfers the case to the superior court. **P.H. v. State,** Op. No. 1538, 504 P2d 837 (Alaska 1972).

A memorandum opinion and order in which a superior court finds that a junior high school hair regulation is reasonable, enters judgment against a father seeking injunctive relief in behalf of his suspended son, and dissolves a temporary restraining order is a "final judgment" within this rule. **Breese v. Smith,** Op. No. 827, 501 P2d 159 (Alaska 1972).

An order granting a judgment debtor's motion to set aside an order confirming an execution sale and requiring the purchaser to deposit a certain sum in the court registry for dispersal to the judgment debtor is a final order terminating the proceeding and is appealable. **Mallonee v. Grow,** Op. No. 841, 502 P2d 432 (Alaska 1972).

In the interest of judicial economy, and because of the important issues involved, procedural rules were relaxed so that the merits of an appeal from a temporary restraining order issued by the superior court, which determined that a strike by public school teachers was illegal and which ordered the teachers to return to work, could be decided on the merits as though a declaratory judgment had been entered. **Anchorage Educ. Assoc. v. Anchorage Sch. Dist.,** Op. No. 2537, 648 P2d 993 (Alaska 1982).

Where effect of remand by superior court was to order retirement board to perform ministerial act, i.e., enter order directing payment of permanent occupational benefits to claimant, remand constituted final judgment for purpose of this rule. **Mun. of Anchorage, Police Fire v. Coffey,** Op. No. 4186, 893 P2d 722 (Alaska 1995).

When superior court sits as intermediate appellate court and remands case to administrative agency for further proceedings, remand is not considered a final judgment. **Stalnaker v. Williams,** Op. No. 5003, 960 P2d 590 (Alaska 1998).

In the context of children's proceedings, issues may sometimes be revisited without destroying the finality, and therefore the appealability, of other issues; accordingly, trial court's rejection of adult sister's motion in CINA proceeding to have child placed with her rather than foster parents was appealable even though CINA proceeding remained open since trial court's ruling effectively ended any chance that child could be placed with sister. **S.S.M. v. State Dept. of Health,** Op. No. 5285, 3 P3d 342 (Alaska 2000).

Following the entry of a divorce decree, the trial court's order granting the wife's motion for reconsideration of a decision disbursing to the IRS funds derived from a dissolved family business was not as final judgment under subsection (a) of this rule, making the husband's appeal premature. **Mattfield v. Mattfield,** Op. No. 6003, 133 P.3d 667 (Alaska 2006).

III. Criminal Appeal by State.

The limitation on the right of the state to appeal does not prevent the state from using the petition for review proceeding to question the jurisdiction of the superior court. **State v. Salinas,** Op. No. 39, 362 P2d 298 (Alaska 1961).

The prohibition of appeals by the state except to test the indictment does not prevent the state from petitioning for review of the trial court ruling that the accused was a minor and without the jurisdiction of the superior court, such ruling affecting a "substantial right" of the state to try the accused and preventing a final judgment. **State of Alaska v. Linn,** Op. No. 47, 363 P2d 361 (Alaska 1961).

The state may appeal "to test the sufficiency of the indictment" thereby raising any question as to the adequacy and adaptation of the indictment to its purpose. The inquiry is not limited to whether the indictment met the formal statutory requirements for a valid indictment. **State of Alaska v. Shelton,** Op. No. 56, 368 P2d 817 (Alaska 1962).

State had a right to appeal trial court's order arresting judgment where motion in arrest of judgment challenged only the sufficiency of the indictment. **State v. Adkerson,** Op. No. 294, 403 P2d 673 (Alaska 1965).

If the trial court dismissed a count of the indictment upon a motion for acquittal, but based its action unequivocally on the sole ground that the indictment was defective, the state had a right to appeal for the purpose of testing the sufficiency of the indictment. **State v. Selman,** Op. No. 302,406 P2d 181 (Alaska 1965).

The issue whether an information substituted in place of a complaint in a magistrate court was adequate to prosecute an offense within the criminal jurisdiction of that court tested the sufficiency of the information, and appeal by the state from dismissal of the case was not barred. **State v. Smith,** Op. No. 356, 417 P2d 252 (Alaska 1966).

The supreme court on a criminal appeal taken by the state from a judgment of the superior court setting aside a conviction in the district court has authority to pass upon the sufficiency of information used as substitute for a complaint in the district court. **State v. Pete,** Op. No. 372, 420 P2d 338 (Alaska 1966).

In an appeal brought by the state from a judgment of the superior court setting aside a conviction in the district court on grounds of insufficiency of information, the supreme court reversed the superior court's order and also in order to avoid piecemeal appeals further considered other points made in the appellee's brief in defense of the judgment below and appearing in the record, albeit not passed upon below. **State v. Pete,** Op. No. 372, 420 P2d 338 (Alaska 1966).

Death of the appellant while criminal appeal was pending abated the criminal action ab initio. **Hartwell v. State,** Op. No. 391, 423 P2d 282 (Alaska 1967).

The limitation placed by AS 22.05.0 10 upon the state's right to appeal in a criminal case applies only to instances where the Supreme Court's jurisdiction is sought by appeal. Other forms of review authorized under the statute are not subject to the limitation. **State v. Browder,** Op. No. 699, 486 P2d 925 (Alaska 1971).

Neither the limitation placed by AS 22.05.010 upon the state's right to appeal in a criminal case nor the prohibition of Constitutional Article 4, § 15, against double jeopardy requires an erroneous nonfinal order or decision, favorable to the accused, to stand uncorrected. The state can invoke the discretionary review jurisdiction of the Supreme Court in criminal cases where the matter sought to be reviewed involves a nonfinal order or decision of the superior court. **State v. Browder,** Op. No. 699, 486 P2d 925 (Alaska 1971).

The state has the right to appeal a sentence only if it contends that the sentence imposed was too lenient. Where the state, which has unsuccessfully sought consecutive sentences, fails to challenge the defendant's sentence on two counts of negligent homicide on the ground that it was too lenient, there is no jurisdiction for the state's appeal under the sentence review statute. **State v. Gibson,** Op. No. 1215, 543 P2d 406 (Alaska 1975).

Double jeopardy prevents the retrial of any person acquitted in a trial court. Only where a guilty verdict rendered in the trial court has been reversed on appeal in the superior court, when that court is acting as an intermediate appellate court, can the state appeal a not guilty verdict to the supreme court. **State v. Gibson,** Op. No. 1215, 543 P2d 406 (Alaska 1975).

The state may appeal any adverse final judgment of a trial court in a criminal action dismissing an indictment for any reason unless retrial would be barred by the double jeopardy clauses of the state or federal constitutions. **State v. Michel,** Op. No. 48, 634 P2d 383 (Alaska App. 1981).

This rule does not preclude the State from seeking appellate review in a criminal case on a discretionary basis; a petition for review is the appropriate vehicle for the State to rely on when it seeks discretionary review of a nonappealable dismissal order. **State v. Mouser,** Op. No. 1105, 806 P2d 330 (Alaska App. 1991).

Rule 203. Supervision and Control of Proceedings.

The supervision and control of the proceedings on appeal is in the appellate court from the time the notice of appeal is filed with the clerk of the appellate courts, except as otherwise provided in these rules. The appellate court may at any time entertain a motion to dismiss the appeal, or for directions to the trial court, or to modify or vacate any order made by the trial court in relation to the prosecution of the appeal, including any order fixing or denying bail.

(SCO 439 effective November 15, 1980; amended by SCO 572 effective February 1, 1984; and by SCO 1155 effective July 15, 1994)

Annotations

Cases

Even though defendant's appeal of his conviction was pending, trial court had jurisdiction to entertain and to adjudicate petition to revoke defendant's probation in his underlying criminal case. **Jackson v. State,** Op. No. 1490, 926 P2d 1180 (Alaska App. 1996).

Where interpleader action involving fee dispute between attorney and client arose out of one of two civil actions in which attorney represented client, fact that appeal was pending in second action did not divest trial court of jurisdiction to hear interpleader action, even if second action might conceivably have impacted interpleader action. **Noey v. Bledsoe,** Op. No. 5107, 978 P2d 1264 (Alaska 1999).

Rule 204. Appeal: Time—Notice—Bonds.

(a) When Taken—Appeals and Cross-Appeals.

(1) *Appeals.* The notice of appeal shall be filed within 30 days from the date shown in the clerk's certificate of distribution on the judgment appealed from, unless a shorter time for filing a notice of appeal applies as provided by Rules 216-220.

(2) *Subsequent Appeals.* If a timely notice of appeal is filed by a party, any other party may file a notice of appeal within 14 days of the filing of any timely notice of appeal by any other party, or within 30 days from the date shown in the clerk's certificate of distribution on the judgment, whichever period expires last.

(3) *Motions That Terminate Time for Filing Appeals in Civil Cases.* In a civil case, the running of the time for filing an appeal is terminated by a timely motion filed in superior court pursuant to those rules of civil procedure enumerated in this section. The full time for an appeal by any party begins to run again on the date of notice, as defined in Civil Rule 58.1 (c), of any of the following orders made on timely motion:

(A) Granting or denying a motion for judgment under Civil Rule 50(b);

(B) Granting or denying a motion to amend or make additional findings of fact under Civil Rule 52 (b) whether or not an alteration of the judgment would be required if the motion is granted;

(C) Granting or denying a motion to alter or amend a judgment under Civil Rule 59;

(D) Denying a new trial under Civil Rule 59; or

(E) Granting or denying a motion for reconsideration under Civil Rule 77(k) on the date of notice as defined by Civil Rule 58.1(c) or on the date of denial of the motion pursuant to Civil Rule 77(k)(4), whichever is earlier; or

(F) Granting or denying a petition for rehearing under Appellate Rule 506 in an appeal from an administrative agency.

(4) *Motions That Terminate Time for Filing Appeals in Criminal Cases.* In a criminal case, if a timely motion for a new trial or in arrest of judgment, or a timely motion for reconsideration has been filed in the superior court, or if a motion for reduction, correction, or suspension of sentence under Criminal Rule 35 has been made within the 30-day period following the date shown in the clerk's certificate of distribution on the judgment, an appeal from a judgment may be filed within 30 days after the date of notice of the order deciding the motion. Date of notice is defined in Criminal Rule 32.3(c).

(5) *Effect of Taxing of Costs and Prejudgment Interest and Awarding of Attorney's Fees.*

(A) The running of the time for filing an appeal is not terminated by proceedings related to the taxing of costs pursuant to Civil Rule 79 or while awaiting calculation of prejudgment interest or proceedings related to the award of attorney's fees. However, the statement of points on appeal filed pursuant to Appellate Rule 204(e) and the designation of transcript filed pursuant to Appellate Rule 210(b)(1) may be amended by motion by an appellant or cross-appellant to include the award or denial of costs and attorney's fees or prejudgment interest and pertinent portions of the electronic record. These subjects will thereafter be considered part of the appeal if covered in the brief of appellant or cross-appellant. If no appeal or cross-appeal is pending, the allowance of costs and attorney's fees or the award of prejudgment interest shall be considered a final judgment subject to separate appeal limited to the subject of costs, attorney's fees or prejudgment interest.

(B) Notwithstanding Rule 203, the pendency of an appeal shall not divest the trial court of jurisdiction to consider the matters of costs and attorney's fees pursuant to Civil Rules 79 and 82.

(6) *Premature Appeals.* If a notice of appeal is filed after the announcement of a decision but before the date shown in the clerk's certificate of distribution on the judgment, the notice of appeal shall be treated as filed on the date shown in the clerk's certificate of distribution on the judgment.

(b) **Appeal—How Taken.** A party may appeal from a final order or judgment by filing a notice of appeal with the clerk of the appellate courts. The notice of appeal must identify the party taking the appeal, the final order or judgment appealed from, and the court to which the appeal is taken. The party must file the original and one copy of the notice of appeal accompanied by the original and one copy of the documents listed below:

(1) a completed docketing statement in the form prescribed by these rules, which includes a list of the parties to the appeal;

(2) a copy of the final order or judgment from which the appeal is taken;

(3) a statement of points on appeal as required by Rule 204(e);

(4) unless the party is represented by court-appointed counsel, the party is the state or an agency thereof, or the party is a prisoner found by the court to be eligible to pay less than full fees under AS 09.19.010,

(A) the filing fee required by Administrative Rule 9(a);

(B) a motion for waiver of filing fee pursuant to Administrative Rule 9(f)(1); or

(C) a motion to appeal at public expense pursuant to Rule 209;

(5) unless the party is represented by court-appointed counsel, the party is the state, municipality, or officer or agency thereof, or the party is an employee appealing denial of compensation by the Alaska Workers' Compensation Board or denial of benefits under AS 23.20 (Employment Security Act),

(A) the cost bond or deposit required by Rule 204(c)(1);

(B) a copy of a superior court order approving the party's supersedeas bond or other security in lieu of bond or a copy of the party's motion to the superior court for approval of a supersedeas bond or other security;

(C) a motion for waiver of cost bond; or

(D) a motion to appeal at public expense pursuant to Rule 209;

(6) a designation of transcript if the party intends to have portions of the electronic record transcribed pursuant to Rule 210(b); and

(7) proof of service of the notice of appeal and all required accompanying documents, except the filing fee, on all other parties to the appeal.

A party may move for an extension of time to file the statement of points on appeal and the designation of transcript. The clerk of the appellate courts shall refuse to accept for filing any notice of appeal not conforming to this paragraph and accompanied by the items specified in (1)-(7) or a motion to extend the time for filing item (3) or (6).

(c) **Bond on Appeal.**

(1) Unless a party is exempted by law, a bond for costs on appeal shall be filed with the notice of appeal in a civil case. The bond shall be in the sum of seven hundred fifty dollars ($750.00), unless the superior court fixes a different amount or unless a supersedeas bond is filed, in which event no separate bond on appeal is required. The bond on appeal shall have sufficient surety and shall be conditioned to secure the payment of costs if the appeal is dismissed or the judgment affirmed, or such costs as the supreme court may award if the judgment is modified. If a bond on appeal in the sum of seven hundred fifty dollars ($750.00) is given, no approval thereof is necessary. After a bond on appeal is filed, an appellee may by motion raise objection to the form or amount of the bond or to the sufficiency of the surety which shall be determined by the superior court. In lieu of filing such cost bond, the appellant may deposit in the office of the clerk of the court from which the appeal is taken a sum of money reasonably sufficient to cover such costs, the amount thereof to be fixed by the superior court.

(2) Notwithstanding subparagraph (1), a bond for costs on appeal shall not be required in an appeal from a decision of the trial court in any criminal case or any civil case where an indigent party is entitled to court-appointed counsel, and a bond shall not be required from an employee appealing from a denial of compensation by the Alaska Workers' Compensation Board or from a denial of a claim for benefits under AS 23.20 (Employment Security Act).

(d) **Supersedeas Bond.** Whenever in a civil case an appellant entitled thereto desires a stay on appeal, the appellant may present to the superior court for its approval a supersedeas bond which shall have such surety or sureties as the court requires. The bond shall be conditioned for the satisfaction of the judgment in full, together with costs and interest, if for any reason the appeal is dismissed or if the judgment is affirmed, and to satisfy in full such modification of the judgment and such costs and interest as the supreme court may adjudge and award. When the judgment is for the recovery of money not otherwise secured, the amount of the bond shall be fixed at such sum as will cover the whole amount of the judgment remaining unsatisfied, costs on the appeal, and interest, unless the superior court, after notice and hearing and for good cause shown, fixes a different amount or orders security other than the bond. When the judgment determines the disposition of the property in controversy as in real actions, replevin, and actions to foreclose mortgages or when such property is in the custody of the court or the state troopers or when the proceeds of such property of a bond for its value is in the custody or control of the court, the amount of the supersedeas bond shall be fixed at such sum only as will secure the amount recovered for the use and detention of the property, the cost of the action, costs on appeal, and interest, unless the superior court, after notice and hearing and for good cause shown, fixes a different amount or orders security other than the bond. A municipality or an officer or agent thereof desiring a stay on appeal is exempted from the requirement of posting supersedeas bond imposed by this subsection.

(e) **Statement of Points.** At the time of filing the notice of appeal, the appellant shall serve and file a concise statement of the points on which appellant intends to rely in the appeal. The appellate court will consider only points included in the statement, and points that the court can address effectively without reviewing untranscribed portions of the electronic record. On motion in the appellate court, and for cause, the statement of points may be supplemented.

(f) **Judgment Against Surety.** By entering into an appeal or supersedeas bond given pursuant to subdivisions (c) and (d) of this rule, the surety submits to the jurisdiction of the superior court and irrevocably appoints the clerk of that court as the surety's agent upon whom any papers affecting the surety's liability on the bond may be served. The surety's liability may be enforced on motion without the necessity of an independent action. The motion and such notice of the motion as the superior court prescribed may be served on the clerk of the superior court who shall forthwith mail copies to the surety if the surety's address is known.

(g) **Parties to the Appeal.** All parties to the trial court proceeding when the final order or judgment was entered are parties to the appeal. A party who files a notice of appeal, whether separately or jointly, is an appellant under these rules. All other parties are deemed to be appellees, regardless of their status in the trial court. An appellee may elect at any time not to participate in the appeal by filing and serving a notice of non-participation. The filing of a notice of non-participation shall not affect whether the party is bound by the decision on appeal.

(h) **Service of Documents.** Papers filed or served in the appeal must be served on all parties, except appellees who have elected not to participate in the action.

(i) **Joint or Consolidated Appeals.** If two or more parties are entitled to appeal from a judgment or order of a court and their interests are such as to make joinder practical, they may file a joint notice of appeal. Appeals may be consolidated by order of the appellate court upon its own motion or upon motion of a party.

(SCO 439 effective November 15, 1980; amended by SCO 461 effective June 1, 1981; by SCO 510 effective August 30, 1982; by SCO 513 effective October 1, 1982; by SCO 554 effective April 4, 1983; by SCO 573 effective February 1, 1984; by SCO 574 effective February 1, 1984; by SCO 575 effective February 1, 1984; by SCO 726 effective December 15, 1986; SCO 794 effective March 15, 1987; by SCO 830 effective August 1, 1987; by SCO 847 effective January 15, 1988; by SCO 987 effective January 15, 1990; by SCO 995 effective January 15, 1990; by SCO 1019 effective July 15, 1990; by SCO 1069 effective July 15, 1991; by SCO 1153 effective July 15, 1994; by SCO 1155 effective July 15, 1994; by SCO 1162 effective July 15, 1994; by SCO 1238, effective July 15, 1996; by SCO 1248 effective July 15, 1996; by SCO 1272 effective July 15, 1997; by SCO 1279 effective July 31, 1997; by SCO 1284 effective January 15, 1998; and by SCO 1470 effective October 15, 2002)

Note: AS 10.06.633, as enacted by ch. 166, § 1, SLA 1988, amended Appellate Rule 204 by requiring that certain documents must be filed in the notice of appeal from an involuntary dissolution of a corporation. AS 10.06.863, as enacted by ch. 166, § 1, SLA 1988, amended Appellate Rule 204 by requiring that certain documents must be filed in the notice of appeal from a revocation of a certificate of authority of a foreign corporation to transact business in Alaska. AS 10.06.915, as enacted by ch. 166, § 1, SLA 1988, amended Appellate Rule 204 by requiring that certain documents must be filed in the notice of appeal from the failure to approve articles of incorporation and certain other administrative actions.

Docketing Statements. The court system has prepared docketing statement forms, which are available from the Clerk of the Appellate Courts, 303 K Street, Anchorage, Alaska 99501, (907) 264-0612. Parties may prepare their own docketing statements instead of using the court system forms. However, such statements must include all of the information which appears on the court system forms and must follow the same numbering system. Parties should contact the Clerk of the Appellate Courts for further instructions on preparing their own docketing statements.

Note to SCO 1238. Ch. 79 § 1 SLA 1995 amends AS 09 by adding a new chapter related to prisoner litigation against the state. AS 09.19.010 prohibits the court from accepting any filing in an action governed by AS 09.19 until the filing fee required by AS 09.19.010 has been paid.

Section 17 of chapter 79 amends Appellate Rule 204(b)(4) to include the language "or the party is a prisoner whom the court finds is eligible to pay less than full fees under AS 09.19.010." Section 1 of this order is adopted for the sole reason that the legislature has mandated the amendment.

Note: In 1997 the legislature enacted AS 18.16.030(j), which specifies the procedure for appeal of an order denying a petition to bypass parental consent to an abortion. According to ch. 14, § 8 SLA 1997, AS 18.16.030(j) has the effect of amending Appellate Rules 204, 210, 212, and 213 by establishing specific time limits applicable to certain appeals and by instructing the supreme court to modify or dispense with formal requirements applicable to certain briefs. Instead of amending individual rules to implement AS 18.16.030, the supreme court has adopted a separate rule on judicial bypass appeals. See Appellate Rule 220.

Note: Ch. 77 SLA 2002 (HB 157), Section 2, adds new Chapter 26 to Title 6 of the Alaska Statutes, concerning providers of fiduciary services. According to Section 9 of the Act, AS 06.26.760(b)(2) has the effect of amending Appellate Rule 204 by postponing the deadlines for the filing of appeals to the supreme court and the court of appeals by a trust company when the Department of Community and Economic Development has taken possession of a trust company.

Annotations

Cases

I. In General.
II. Entry of Judgment.
III. Timeliness of Appeal.
  A. In General.
  B. Tolling of Time for Appeal.
IV. Statement of Points on Appeal.

I. In General.

An appeal does not in itself operate to prevent execution on the judgment below, and in order to prevent such an enforcement, an appellant must either file a supersedeas bond approved by the trial court or obtain a stay of enforcement from the trial court or supreme court. **Liberty National Insurance Co. v. Eberhart,** Op. No. 281, 398 P2d 997 (Alaska 1965).

Where appellee did not take a cross-appeal nor alert appellant to an issue of attorney's fees not previously raised by filing a cross statement of points on appeal, he could not attack the judgment in this regard for first time by appellee's brief. **Alaska Brick Co. v. McCoy,** Op. No. 287, 400 P2d 454 (Alaska 1965).

An attorney in a workmen's compensation proceeding is a party within the scope of this rule and has the right of appeal from an award of attorney's fees by either the Board or the superior court. **Rose v. Alaskan Village, Inc.,** Op. No. 333, 412 P2d 503 (Alaska 1966).

This rule governs procedure for obtaining a stay of a workmen's compensation award once an appeal has been taken from the superior court. **Johns v. State of Alaska, Dept. of Highways,** Op. No. 424, 431 P2d 148 (Alaska 1967).

In determining whether to approve a supersedeas bond under this rule, the superior court should apply the same criteria applicable in determining "irreparable damage" under the stay provisions of AS 23.30.125(c). **Johns v. State of Alaska, Dept. of Highways,** Op. No. 424, 431 P2d 148 (Alaska 1967).

It is not necessary to hold an evidentiary hearing concerning an alleged deprivation of the right to appeal where petitioner alleges she requested her trial defense counsel to file an appeal from her conviction, but fails to indicate time, location, manner and circumstances under which she had requested her counsel to make such appeal. **Pore v. State,** Op. No. 437, 452 P2d 433 (Alaska 1969).

In deciding whether the requirement statement of the grounds for appeal should be relaxed or dispensed with, a lower court should examine the standards applied by the supreme court in enforcing analogous rules. **Cook v. Aurora Motors, Inc.,** Op. No. 848, 503 P2d 1046 (Alaska 1972).

Appeal of motion to reconsider does not bring merits of judgment sought to be reconsidered before Supreme Court. **Brown v. State,** Op. No. 1418, 563 P2d 275 (Alaska 1977).

This rule does not require a pledge of property or a cash deposit in all cases where an individual security is used. **Acevedo v. City of North Pole,** Op. No. 2748, 672 P2d 130 (Alaska 1983).

Once defendant's appeal from a child support arrearage judgment was voluntarily dismissed, defendant was left in the same position he was in prior to the appeal, giving him 30 days from the entry of judgment to bring any objection that he could have asserted on direct appeal; his failure to object within the 30 days waived his right to raise any objection to the judgment notwithstanding that the California paternity action upon which the judgment was based was dismissed during the pendency of defendant's appeal on statute of limitations grounds. **Rubalcava v. Hall,** Op. No. 2755, 674 P2d 767 (Alaska 1983).

Where prevailing party in contract action did not file a cross-appeal disputing the court's allowance of a set-off, that issue would not be considered on appeal. **Jackson v. Nangle,** Op. No. 2773, 677 P2d 242 (Alaska 1984).

Supersedeas bond for principal amount of taxes due which did not include costs and interest was proper security for stay of superior court tax judgment pending appeal to state supreme court. **City of Nome v. Catholic Bishop of Northern Alaska,** Op. No. 2986, 707 P2d 870 (Alaska 1985).

An appeal to superior court from a decision of a state administrative agency requires service of notice upon the attorney general. **Vincent v. Commercial Fisheries Entry Comm'n,** Op. No. 3041, 717 P2d 391 (Alaska 1986).

Failure of applicant to serve attorney general's office with a notice of appeal from state administrative agency's denial of permit application did not deprive superior court of jurisdiction over the appeal, thus court, after allowing late service of notice upon the attorney general, could hear the appeal, absent proof of prejudice to the state from the late notification. **Vincent v. Commercial Fisheries Entry Comm'n,** Op. No. 3041, 717 P2d 391 (Alaska 1986).

Trial court lacked discretion to order appellant-father in child support case to post supersedes bond where appellant had not requested a stay on appeal; fact that appellant's assets were under bankruptcy court protection and that wife might therefore be unable to execute on the judgment if the appeal failed did not matter. **Cameron v. Hughes,** Op. No. 3805, 825 P2d 882 (Alaska 1992).

If appellant seeks to stay enforcement of judgment pending appeal, he must present bond as security to trial court; failure to file bond or obtain stay leaves judgment debtor open to trial court's enforcement of judgment against him. **Heppinstall v. Darnall Kemna & Co., Inc.,** Op. No. 3952, 851 P2d 78 (Alaska 1993).

Superior court had jurisdiction to order judgment debtor to comply with judgment creditor's post-judgment discovery requests pending appeal and to enforce order with sanctions, where judgment debtor did not obtain stay pending appeal or file security bond. **Heppinstall v. Darnall Kemna & Co., Inc.,** Op. No. 3952, 851 P2d 78 (Alaska 1993).

Where cross-appellant did not raise issue of reduction of attorney's fees in statement of points on cross-appeal, nor did she amend her statement of points on cross appeal, the issue was waived. **North Slope Borough v. Barraga,** Op. No. 4285, 906 P2d 1377 (Alaska 1995).

While real or personal property may be adequate security for supersedeas bond, trial court did not err in rejecting proffer of real property as collateral for such bond. **Breck v. Moore,** Op. No. 4318, 910 P2d 599 (Alaska 1996).

Mother's appeal of trial court order modifying father's child support obligation, which appeal was filed one day after her motion to reconsider was served on husband, was premature, since appeal was filed before trial court's thirty-day period to answer the motion to reconsider had expired; supreme court ordinarily will not review matter being reconsidered by lower court. **Valentino v. Cole,** Op. No. 5287, 3 P3d 337 (Alaska 2000).

Boat owner's claims of error on appeal of a breach of contract action were waived because she failed to file a cross-appeal as required by this rule. **Peterson v. Ek,** Op. No. 5818,93 P.3d 458 (Alaska 2004).

II. Entry of Judgment.

In determining the time within which an appeal may be taken, the term "entry of judgment" as it applies to trials by jury is set forth in Civ. R. 58. **Vogt v. Winbauer,** Op. No. 117, 376 P2d 1007 (Alaska 1962).

Where docket entries clearly reflected that an agreement for settlement was intended by the parties to constitute a final disposition of the case, the intent governed and the docket entries were an entry of judgment although they did not state in so many words that a judgment was entered. **Gravel v. Alaskan Village, Inc.,** Op. No. 321, 409 P2d 983 (Alaska 1966).

When on the date of docket entry the court had signed an order denying appellant's motion to vacate a judgment of dismissal of appellant's complaint, but the clerk had at the date of this order incorrectly and without authority entered a "judgment of dismissal with prejudice" of complaint and counter-claim, the latter entry did not constitute a judgment from which an appeal would lie, but notice of appeal was timely from the order denying motion to vacate judgment of dismissal. **Gravel v. Alaskan Village, Inc.,** Op. No. 321, 409 P2d 983 (Alaska 1966).

Where the parties had stipulated that their agreement for settlement of a dispute constituted a final disposition of the litigation and a docket entry was made on January 12, clearly indicating the final settlement and dismissal by the court of claim and counterclaim by M.O. and on April 6, a transcript of the proceedings was filed in accordance with the settlement and dismissal and a docket entry of April 6 clearly so stated, a final judgment dismissing the complaint and counterclaim with prejudice was entered either on January 12, or at the latest on April 6, and the erroneous entry of the clerk on July 28 of "judgment of dismissal of complaint and counter claim" which did not correctly reflect what occurred on that date, was not the entry of a judgment from which an appeal could betaken. **Gravel v. Alaskan Village, Inc.,** Op. No. 321, 409 P2d 983 (Alaska 1966).

The denial of a motion to vacate the judgment of dismissal of appellant's complaint was a judgment from which an appeal lies. **Gravel v. Alaskan Village, Inc.,** Op. No. 321, 409 P2d 983 (Alaska 1966).

III. Timeliness of Appeal.

A. In General.

The requirement as to timely notice of appeal is not jurisdictional. **Vogt v. Winbauer,** Op. No. 117, 376 P2d 1007 (Alaska 1962).

The 30-day period within which notice of appeal had to be given by the appellant commenced to run on the date upon which judgment was noted by the clerk in the civil docket. **Vogt v. Winbauer,** Op. No. 117, 376 P2d 1007 (Alaska 1962).

Failure of the clerk of the superior court to notify defendant of the order denying his motion for rehearing not considered a factor which would impel the supreme court to dispense with the time limit for taking appeal prescribed under this rule. **Stephens v. City of Anchorage,** Op. No. 162, 384 P2d 959 (Alaska 1963).

Court-initiated amendment to judgment as to attorney's fees awarded, which was immaterial as to the merits of the controversy, did not affect the time for taking the appeal. **Radich v. Fairbanks Builders, Inc.,** Op. No. 285, 399 P2d 215 (Alaska 1965).

The time limit for filing a notice of appeal is not jurisdictional and may be relaxed or dispensed with when strict application would be unfair. **Radich v. Fairbanks Builders, Inc.,** Op. No. 285, 399 P2d 215 (Alaska 1965).

Action to set aside an order of the Workmen's Compensation Board denying compensation is an action in which an agency of the state is a party defendant so that appeal from judgment affirming the order of the Board was timely when taken within 60 days from entry of judgment. **Thornton v. Alaska Workmen's Compensation Board,** Op. No. 327, 411 P2d 209 (Alaska 1966).

Where appellant made no sufficient showing that strict enforcement of Supreme Ct. R. 7(a) would work surprise or injustice to him, he was not relieved of the requirement of filing timely notice of appeal. Const., Inc. **Vogt v. Winbauer,** Op. No. 117, 376 P2d 1007 (Alaska 1962); **Whitney Bros. Plumbing & Heating v. Industrial & Commercial Constr., Inc.,** Op. No. 438, 432 P2d 533 (Alaska 1967).

A cross appeal filed more than 30 days after an entry of judgment but within a few days after appellant's notice of appeal which itself is filed 30 days after judgment is permissible. **Anchorage Centennial Development Co. v. Van Wormer & Ro drigues, Inc.,** Op. No. 492, 443 P2d 596 (Alaska 1968).

The determination that a petition for post-conviction relief alleging the deprivation of the right to appeal does not require the holding of an evidentiary hearing does not preclude the petitioner from making a second application for post- conviction relief and presenting evidence supporting the assertion, first presented on appeal from a denial of the first post- conviction motion, that she was transported out of the state for purposes of out-of-state incarceration prior to the expiration of the 10-day period within which she is required to file her notice of appeal. **Pore v. State,** Op. No. 437, 452 P2d 433 (Alaska 1969).

A petitioner seeking post-conviction relief on the grounds that she was transported out of the state for purposes of out-of-state incarceration prior to the expiration of the 10-day period within which she is required to file a notice of appeal, should attempt to show what impact her physical removal from the state has had on her ability to file a timely notice of appeal. She should further show what attempts she has made during the period between the imposition of sentence and the alleged removal from the state to engage services of trial counsel. **Pore v. State,** Op. No. 437, 452 P2d 433 (Alaska 1969).

The supreme court will grant review where the defendant establishes that he intended to appeal his conviction, communicated such desire to his attorney, and thereafter thought an appeal had been taken on his behalf, and where the defense attorney concluded no grounds existed for appeal but failed to relate that conclusion to the defendant. **McCracken v. State,** Op. No 677, 482 P2d 269 (Alaska 1971).

Even if the defendant has not made out a case of excusable neglect with respect to his failure to file timely notice of appeal, the time limitation will be relaxed where strict adherence would work an injustice on the defendant. **McCracken v. State,** Op. No 677, 482 P2d 269 (Alaska 1971).

A claim of a double jeopardy violation should be appealed not later than 30 days after sentence is imposed. **Nielsen v. State,** Op. No. 2349, 627 P2d 1077 (Alaska 1981).

Where there were three dates of entry on the judgment from which the appeal was taken, the confusion thereby created made it appropriate to waive the requirement that notice of appeal be made within 30 days from entry of judgment. **Safeco Ins. Co. v. Honeywell,** Op. No. 2460, 639 P2d 996 (Alaska 1981).

It was not unjust to refuse to relax rule requiring timely appeal where the appeal concerned the detention of a juvenile on a charge which was ultimately dismissed, thereby making the appeal moot as to the juvenile. **A. M. v. State,** Op. No. 150, 653 P2d 346 (Alaska App. 1982).

Mother's appeal of trial court order modifying father's child support obligation, which appeal was filed one day after her motion to reconsider was served on husband, was premature, since appeal was filed before trial court's thirty-day period to answer the motion to reconsider had expired;

supreme court ordinarily will not review matter being reconsidered by lower court. **Valentino v. Cole,** Op. No. 5287, 3 P3d 337 (Alaska 2000).

B. Tolling of Time for Appeal.

Failure of opposing counsel to object when a motion for new trial was not timely served, and the fact that the court inferentially exercised its power under Civ. R. 94 (formerly Civ. R. 88) to relax the strict requirement as to timeliness does not waive untimeliness in filing the motion, and the filing of an untimely motion for a new trial did not toll the running of the 30-day appeal time. **Vogt v. Winbauer,** Op. No. 117, 376 P2d 1007 (Alaska 1962).

The time for taking an appeal was not suspended by the filing of a motion to reconsider, and when the order denying the motion for relief from a void judgment was entered, it was final, and the time for taking appeal commenced to run. **Oaks v. Grocers Wholesale,** Op. No. 123, 377 P2d 1001 (Alaska 1962).

Under this rule as formerly written, motion to reconsider did not extend the time for taking an appeal. **Corso v. Commissioner of Education,** Op. No. 1412, 563 P2d 246 (Alaska 1977).

Under this rule as formerly written, motion to reconsider did not terminate the running of the time for filing an appeal from the judgment or order sought to be reconsidered. **Brown v. State,** Op. No. 1418, 563 P2d 275 (Alaska 1977).

Summary judgment order dismissing plaintiff's cause of action as to the Borough, but not as to the State of Alaska, could not have been appealed until plaintiff's motion for entry of final judgment was granted, at which time the 30-day appeal period began to run. **Kanayurak v. North Slope Borough,** Op. No. 2782, 677 P2d 893 (Alaska 1984).

The "judgment" referred to in this rule from which the 30-day appeal period begins to run is a document separate from any opinion, memorandum or order the court may issue, thus the appeal period begins to run when a formal judgment is entered on a separate document. **Schneider v. Pay'n Save Corp.,** Op. No. 3095, 723 P2d 619 (Alaska 1986).

Where relief was obtained by summary judgment but the final judgment was entered at a later time, the date of entry of the final judgment triggered the 30-day appeal period. **Schneider v. Pay'n Save Corp.,** Op. No. 3095, 723 P2d 619 (Alaska 1986).

Where husband did not appeal denial of his 1988 motion to have his ex-wife held in contempt, but instead refiled essentially the same motion in 1989, appeal of the denial of the 1989 motion, filed after expiration of the appeal period for the 1988 motion, was untimely. **Hermosillo v. Hermosillo,** Op. No. 3634, 797 P2d 1206 (Alaska 1990).

Ex-husband's motion to modify divorce decree did not toll or affect deadline for appealing judgment awarding attorney fees to ex-wife. **Olson v. Olson,** Op. No. 3975, 856 P2d 482 (Alaska 1993).

Running of appellate clock terminates upon timely filing of motion for reconsideration and begins all over again after court's disposition of motion; consequently, litigants had thirty days following denial of their motion for reconsideration to appeal judgment. **Newton v. Magill,** Op. No. 4075, 872 P2d 1213 (Alaska 1994).

Where original order sealing records was without prejudice to later request for disclosure, and motion for disclosure was later made and denied, time limit for appeal of denial was thirty days from date of denial rather than thirty days from entry of original order. **In re Dissolution of Marriage of Alaback,** Op. No. 5248, 997 P2d 1181 (Alaska 2000).

Appeal could not be considered timely where appellant filed her notice of appeal four years after the distribution of the order. **Rowland v. Monsen,** Op. No. 11603, 135 P.3d 1036 (Alaska 2006).

IV. Statement of Points on Appeal.

In determining whether the trial court committed error the supreme court is not required to examine arguments made by counsel to the trial court where such has not been made a point on appeal. **Bidwell v. Scheele,** Op. No. 20, 355 P2d 584 (Alaska 1960).

A statement of points on appeal which mainly says in broad terms that the appellants "intend to rely upon" the Fourteenth and Fifteenth Amendments to the federal constitution does not serve the purpose of the rule, for it fails to inform the opposing party and the supreme court of matters the court will be called upon to decide. **Fairview PUD v. City of Anchorage and Hawk v. Fairview PUD,** Op. No. 61, 368 P2d 540 (Alaska 1962).

Issues not indicated in an appellant's statement of points on appeal will not be considered. **Swick v. Seward School Board,** Op. No. 133, 379 P2d 97 (Alaska 1962).

Request to dismiss appeal because of failure to serve and file statement of points, might well be granted under proper circumstances. **Steward v. City of Anchorage,** Op. No. 213, 391 P2d 730 (Alaska 1964).

Appellant's statement of points as required under Supreme Ct. R. 9(e)alerts appellee to the issues argued in the brief and should cause elimination of unnecessary matter from the typed transcript so that a waste of the transcript secretary's time can be avoided. **Steward v. City of Anchorage,** Op. No. 213, 391 P2d 730 (Alaska 1964).

The requirement to file a statement of points was not relaxed where appellants, in their brief, stood mute against the charge of rule infraction and made no showing that a strict enforcement may operate surprise or injustice. **Orbeck v. Wheeler Construction Company,** Op. No. 240, 394 P2d 780 (Alaska 1964).

Matters which were not made an issue on appeal by appellant's statement of points on appeal, were not considered on appeal. **Sanuita v. Common Laborer's and Hod Carriers Union,** Op. No. 290, 402 P2d 199 (Alaska 1965).

Although notice of appeal specified that the appeal was taken from a judgment of dismissal with prejudice which was entered incorrectly and without authority and from which no timely appeal would lie, it appeared clearly from the statement of points on appeal that appellant also intended to appeal from the denial of a motion to vacate the judgment of dismissal and as to such denial of motion the appeal was timely. **Gravel v. Alaskan Village, Inc.,** Op. No. 321, 409 P2d 983 (Alaska 1966).

Statements of a point on appeal merely setting forth in general terms that the trial court erred in finding that the accounting of a guardian was correct and proper and in failing to require the guardian to provide a proper and detailed accounting are insufficient since they fail to inform the opposing party and the court of matters to be decided and do not point out any particular item with references to which the trial court allegedly erred. **Myers v. Sill,** Op. No. 797, 497 P2d 920 (Alaska 1972).

An argument not made at trial or listed in appellant's statement of points on appeal will not be considered. **Moran v. Holman,** Op. No. 834, 501 P2d 769 (Alaska 1972).

The failure to raise a point at trial court level or include it in statement of points to be raised on appeal generally will foreclose the appeal of an alleged error. **Burford v. State,** Op. No. 954, 515 P2d 382 (Alaska 1973).

The purpose of the provision of this rule providing that an appellant shall serve and file a concise statement of points on which he intends to rely is to have an appellant concisely outline what he considers to be potential sources of error constituting bases for appeal. Elaboration of legal theories on which appeal is based is not required to comply with such rule. **Lewis v. Anchorage Asphalt Paving Co.,** Op. No. 1148, 535 P2d 1188 (Alaska 1975).

A point omitted from an appellant's statement of points on appeal ordinarily will not be considered by the Supreme Court. **Hootch v. Alaska State-Operated School System,** Op. No. 1154, 536 P2d 793 (Alaska 1975).

Question was preserved for review when it was raised only impliedly in Rule 9(e) statement. **A.R.C. Industries, Inc. v. State,** Op. No. 1283, 551 P2d

951 (Alaska 1976).

Where contention that court erred in applying tender years doctrine in child custody dispute was not specifically set out in points on appeal, it would be treated as encompassed in allegation in points (1) that court erred in relying on mother's non-working status and (2) that decision was not supported by fact. **Wetzler v. Wetzler,** Op. No. 1518, 570 P2d 741 (Alaska 1977).

Supreme Court will not treat issues argued in brief but not set forth in points on appeal and will consider as abandoned questions set forth in the points but not argued in brief. **Wetzler v. Wetzler,** Op. No. 1518, 570 P2d 741 (Alaska 1977).

Voluntariness of appellant's plea was not before Supreme Court when the issue was not listed as a point on appeal. **Gordon v. State,** Op. No. 1608, 577 P2d 701 (Alaska 1978).

Supreme Court refused to address itself to issues not listed in the points on appeal and not adequately briefed. **Wren v. State,** Op. No. 1598, 577 P2d 235 (Alaska 1978).

Where appellant requested jury trial, but did not properly raise constitutional issue at trial or include it in statement of points on appeal, the issue was not before appellate court. **Jeffries v. Glacier State Telephone Co.,** Op. No. 1985, 604 P2d 4 (Alaska 1979).

Contention in appellees' brief that trial court ruling was in error was not considered on appeal due to appellees' failure to file cross-appeal or cross-statement of points on appeal. **Andersen v. Edwards,** Op. No. 2274, 625 P2d 282 (Alaska 1981).

Appellees have no duty to raise a waiver issue by cross-appeal if they are not claiming error in the court below. **Sanguinetti v. Sanguinetti,** Op. No. 2362, 628 P2d 913 (Alaska 1981).

Issue not expressly mentioned in appellant's statement of points on appeal was heard where the record below and the statement of points on appeal, when considered with the statement of issues contained in appellant's brief, sufficiently informed the opposing parties and the court of the matters in issue, as demonstrated by appellee's full briefing of the issue. **Forquer v. State, Commercial Fisheries,** Op. No. 2784, 677 P2d 1236 (Alaska 1984).

An issue not raised in the points on appeal may nevertheless be considered if it is raised at trial, adequately briefed on appeal, and the court and counsel are sufficiently apprised of the issue presented. **Winn v. Mannhalter,** Op. No. 2988, 708 P2d 444 (Alaska 1985).

Issue omitted from appellant's statement of points on appeal would not be considered absent mitigating circumstances. **Oceanview Homeowners Assoc. v. Quadrant Const.,** Op. No. 2805, 680 P2d 793 (Alaska 1984).

Issue which was absent from appellant's points on appeal and was insufficiently briefed in his opening brief was deemed abandoned. **Braun v. Alaska Com. Fishing & Agr. Bank,** Op. No. 3727, 816 P2d 140 (Alaska 1991).

Where issue was raised in trial court and fully briefed in appellate court and where all portions of electronic record relevant to issue had been transcribed, appellate court would review issue notwithstanding that issue was not raised in statement of points on appeal. **Village of Eklutna v. Bd. of Adjustment,** Op. No. 5237, 995 P2d 641 (Alaska 2000).

Appellant's argument that he could not have been "operating" an inoperable snowmobile on the shoulder of a highway in violation of 13 A.A.C. 02.455(a) could be addressed on appeal under section (e) of this rule, where it was fully briefed to the Supreme Court, it was raised in front of the superior court, and it could be addressed based on the existing transcript. **Conkey v. Dep't of Admin.,** Op. No. 5906, 113 P.3d 1235, 379 P2d 447 (Alaska 2005).

Rule 205. Stays Pending Appeal in Civil Cases.

In a civil case, the supreme court or a justice thereof may stay the enforcement or effect of the judgment appealed from or the proceedings in the trial court upon such terms as to bond or other matters as may be proper. A motion for a stay will normally not be considered by the supreme court unless application has previously been made to the trial court and has been denied, or has been granted on conditions other than those requested.

(SCO 439 effective November 15, 1980)

Annotations

Cases

Where the jurisdiction of the supreme court is invoked, either by way of appeal, by petition for review, or by original application, it or a justice thereof is authorized to stay the enforcement or effect of the judgment appealed from or the order or decisions sought to be reviewed, and to stay proceedings in the court below. **Leege v. Martin,** Op. No. 131, 379 P2d 447 (Alaska 1962).

Judgments in an action for injunction are not stayable as of right. Whether a stay pending appeal of an order granting or dissolving an injunction will be granted is a question directed to the sound discretion of the court. **Powell v. Anchorage,** Op. No. 1167, 536 P2d 1228 (Alaska 1975).

In the usual case, the trial court should be given the first opportunity to consider an application for a stay of a judgment granting or denying an injunction. Exceptions should be made where the applicant makes a showing that relief in the superior court is unavailable, or that relief, to be effective, must be immediate and that it is improbable that the superior court can afford such immediate relief. **Powell v. Anchorage,** Op. No. 1167, 536 P2d 1228 (Alaska 1975).

When amended judgment eliminating post judgment interest on an earlier judgment was entered on April 23, 1980, the 30 day appeal period began to run, the trial court's earlier interlocutory memorandum decision or supplemental findings not having triggered the appeal period. **Farnsworth v. Steiner,** Op. No. 2454, 638 P2d 181 (Alaska 1981).

Rule 206. Stay of Execution And Release Pending Appeal in Criminal Cases.

(a) **Stay of Execution.**

(1) *Imprisonment.* A sentence of imprisonment shall be stayed if an appeal is taken and the defendant is released pending appeal.

(2) *Fine.* A sentence to pay a fine or a fine and costs, if an appeal is taken, may be stayed by the trial court or by the appellate court upon such terms as the court deems proper. The court may require the defendant pending appeal to deposit the whole or any part of the fine and costs in the registry of the trial court or to give bond for the payment thereof, or to submit to an examination of assets, and it may make any appropriate order to restrain the defendant from dissipating assets.

(3) *Probation.* An order placing the defendant on probation shall be stayed if an appeal is taken.

(4) *Other Sentence.* Other terms or conditions of a sentence, including but not limited to the revocation or suspension of a license, may be stayed by the trial court pending appeal upon such terms as the court deems proper. If the trial court does not grant the relief requested, the appellant may renew the motion in the appellate court.

(b) **Release Pending Appeal.** When an appeal on the merits is pending, an appeal under AS 12.30.030 (b) from an order refusing bail pending appeal or imposing conditions of release pending appeal shall be in the form of a motion filed in the merit appeal. The motion must be filed with the clerk of the appellate courts within 30 days after the date of the notice of the order from which review is sought. Date of notice is defined in Civil Rule 58.1(c) and Criminal Rule 32.3(c). The motion shall comply with Rule 503, and shall contain specific factual information relevant to the factors set forth in AS 12.30.020 (c), including but not limited to the following:

(1) The full name of the appellant, the trial court case number, the offenses of which the appellant was convicted, the date of sentencing, and the complete terms of the sentence;

(2) That application for release pending appeal has been made to the trial court, the reasons given by the trial court for denying the application in whole or in part, and facts and reasons demonstrating why the action of the trial court on the application was erroneous or an abuse of discretion;

(3) A concise statement of the question or questions to be raised on the appeal with a showing that the question or questions were raised in the trial court;

(4) Family: marital status; length of marriage; children, and their ages; other relatives in the area of residence;

(5) Employment and financial circumstances: name of employer at time of arrest and during pre-trial release; type of work; how long so employed; any offer or promise of employment if released pending appeal; assets of the appellant or of relatives or friends relevant to the ability to post money bail;

(6) Health: history of mental illness, alcoholism, or addiction to drugs, if any;

(7) Residence: length of residence in the city or town in which the appellant resided at the time of arrest;

(8) Criminal history: criminal convictions within ten years prior to the present arrest; if the appellant has ever forfeited bail, or had release, probation, or parole revoked, the date, the name and location of the court, and a brief description of the circumstances; whether the present offense was committed while the appellant was on bail or other release or on probation or parole; any other criminal charges pending against the appellant at the time of the motion is filed.

(c) The decision of the court of appeals on any application under this rule is a "final decision" within the meaning of Rule 302.

(SCO 439 effective November 15, 1980; amended by SCO 554 effective April 4, 1983; SCO 1153 effective July 15, 1994; and by SCO 1507 effective April 15, 2004)

Annotations

Cases

Where neither the defendant nor the probation department nor the sentencing court was aware of the automatic stay of probation pending appeal provided by this rule, which resulted in the defendant being treated as if actually on probation during the appeal period, defendant was entitled to be credited with probation time during that period unless it could be demonstrated that he did not comply with the conditions of his probation. **Wickham v. State,** Op. No. 907, 770 P2d 757 (Alaska App. 1989).

Defendant's contention that it would be unjust to deny him probationary credit for period when his case was on appeal, because he believed that he was on probation and abided by the conditions of probation at all times, was rejected; defendant was never placed on formal probation, nor was he treated as being under formal supervision. **Graybil v. State,** Op. No. 1186, 822 P2d 1386 (Alaska App. 1991).

Even though defendant's appeal of his conviction was pending, trial court had jurisdiction to entertain and to adjudicate petition to revoke defendant's probation in his underlying criminal case. **Jackson v. State,** Op. No. 1490, 926 P2d 1180 (Alaska App. 1996).

For purposes of rule that order placing defendant on probation shall be stayed if appeal is taken, phrase "order placing defendant on probation" means suspended imposition of sentence or order that suspends term of imprisonment in its entirety. **Jackson v. State,** Op. No. 1490,926 P2d 1180 (Alaska App. 1996).

Provisions of this rule that order placing defendant on probation shall be stayed if appeal is taken does not apply to judgments that sentence defendants to serve any or all of term of imprisonment. **Jackson v. State,** Op. No. 1490, 926 P2d 1180 (Alaska App. 1996).

When defendant receives "split" sentence, i.e. term of imprisonment followed by probation, if defendant is released on bail pending appeal, defendant's sentence of imprisonment is stayed; depending upon wording of judgment, this may amount to automatic stay of defendant's probation as well. **Jackson v. State,** Op. No. 1490, 926 P2d 1180 (Alaska App. 1996).

Rule 207. Appeals Relating to Release Prior to Judgment.

An appeal authorized by AS 12.30.030(b) or AS 12.30.040, relating to the release of a criminal defendant prior to the entry of final judgment, shall be determined promptly. The appeal shall take the form of a motion and shall comply with Rules 206(b) and 503. The appellee may respond as provided in Rule 503(d). The court of appeals or a judge thereof may order the release of the appellant pending such an appeal. The decision of the court of appeals on such an appeal is a "final decision" within the meaning of Rule 302.

(SCO 439 effective November 15, 1980)

Annotations

Cases

Minor under juvenile detention order could bring juvenile bail appeal under this rule. **A. M. v. State,** Op. No. 150, 653 P2d 346 (Alaska App. 1982).

Rule 208. Custody of Prisoners in Post-Conviction Relief Pro-ceedings.

(a) **Release of Applicant Pending Review of Order Denying Release.** The court having jurisdiction over the appeal of a denial of an application for post-conviction relief may not grant bail or release the applicant pending appeal. If the appellate court determines the post-conviction relief should be granted, the case shall be remanded to the trial court for a bail hearing.

(b) **Release of Applicant Pending Review of Decision Ordering a New Trial.** If an appeal of an order granting an applicant a new trial is pending, Appellate Rule 206(b) shall govern an appeal from an order that denies bail pending appeal or imposes conditions of release pending appeal.

(SCO 439 effective November 15, 1980; amended by SCO 1153 effective July 15, 1994; repealed and reenacted by SCO 1238 effective July 15, 1996)

Note to SCO 1238: Appellate Rule 208 was repealed and reenacted by ch. 79 § 18 SLA 1995. Section 3 of this order is adopted for the sole reason that the legislature has mandated the amendment.

Rule 209. Appeals at Public Expense.

(a) **Civil Matters.**

(1) A party to a civil action may file in the supreme court a motion to appeal or to petition for review at public expense. The motion shall be accompanied by a sworn financial statement on a form provided by the clerk of the appellate courts.

(2) In considering the motion to appeal or petition for review at public expense, the court shall determine the indigence or nonindigence of the party.

(3) If the motion is granted:

[a] The court shall specify in the order granting the motion which of the following costs or partial costs are to be covered at public expense:

[1] Filing fees,

[2] Transcript fees,

[3] Costs of printing briefs,

[4] Other costs;

[b] Any costs and attorney fees awarded to the appellant or petitioner as a prevailing party in the supreme court shall accrue to the state to reimburse it for costs relating to the appeal or petition for review.

(4) Leave to file at public expense may be conditioned on repayment of costs to the state. The conditions may include the imposition of liens in favor of the state on costs, attorney fees and other recoveries awarded to the indigent appellant or petitioner.

(5) An appeal or petition for review at public expense will be allowed without additional motion in cases where the appellant is represented by court-appointed counsel.

(6) The provisions of this paragraph do not apply to the filing fees in a prisoner's appeal against the state or an officer, agent, employee, or former officer, agent, or employee of the state that is governed by the provisions of AS 09.19. A prisoner may request a filing fee reduction in an appeal governed by AS 09.19 by submitting an application which satisfies the requirements of AS 09.19.010 with the prisoner's notice of appeal and the items specified in Appellate Rule 204(b).

(b) **Criminal Matters.**

(1) In criminal matters the appellate court shall authorize appeals and petitions for review at public expense on behalf of defendants who are "indigent," as defined by statute, in accordance with the rules and decisions of the appellate courts of Alaska, and where such proceedings are required to be provided by state courts by decisions of the Supreme Court of the United States. Where an appeal or petition for review at public expense is authorized by the court, the costs which shall be borne at public expense include those of providing counsel and of preparing a transcript and briefs.

(2) If a defendant is allowed to proceed at public expense, the clerk of the appellate courts shall send the defendant a written notice and order, to the address provided under Appellate Rule 204(b), that

(A) advises defendant that, if the defendant's conviction is not reversed, the defendant will be ordered to repay the prosecuting authority for the cost of appointed appellate counsel, in accordance with the schedule of costs set out in subparagraph 209(b)(6); and

(B) orders the defendant to apply for permanent fund dividends every year in which the defendant qualifies for a dividend until the cost is paid in full.

(3) A defendant authorized to proceed at public expense in the trial court is presumed to be entitled to appeal or petition for review at public expense.

(4) Counsel appointed to represent a defendant in the trial court pursuant to Criminal Rule 39 shall remain as appointed counsel throughout an appeal or petition for review at public expense authorized under this paragraph and shall not be permitted to withdraw except upon the grounds authorized in Administrative Rule 12. An attorney appointed by the court under Administrative Rule 12(b)(1)(B) will be permitted to withdraw upon a showing that either the public defender agency or the office of public advocacy is able to represent the defendant in the appellate proceeding. If an appeal is to be taken, trial counsel will not be permitted to withdraw until the notice of appeal and the documents required to be filed with the appeal by Rule 204 have been accepted for filing by the clerk of the appellate courts.

(5) At the conclusion of the appellate proceeding, the clerk of the appellate courts shall enter judgment against the defendant for the cost of appointed appellate counsel unless the defendant's conviction was reversed by the appellate court. The amount of the judgment shall be determined by reference to the schedule in subparagraph 209(b)(6). Before entering judgment, the clerk shall mail, to the defendant's address of record, a notice that sets out the amount of the proposed judgment. The defendant may oppose entry of the judgment by filing a written opposition within 45 days after the date shown in the clerk's certificate of distribution on the notice. The opposition shall specifically set out the grounds for opposing

entry of judgment. The prosecuting authority may oppose the amount of the judgment by filing a written opposition within the same deadline. Criminal Rule 39(c)(1)(C) and (c)(2) shall apply to judgments entered under this subparagraph.

(6) The following schedule governs the cost of appointed appellate counsel:

Type of Appellate Proceeding	Misdemeanor	Felony
Sentence Appeal or Petition for Sentence Review	$ 250	$ 500
Merit Appeal or Appeal from Post-Conviction Relief Proceedings	750	1,500
Combined Merit Appeal and Sentence Appeal or Petition for Sentence Review	1,000	2,000
Other Appellate Actions (Petition for Review, Petition for Hearing, etc.)	500	1,000

(c) **Costs.** Costs, attorney's fees, damages, and interest may be allowed as in other cases, but the state shall not be liable for any of them.

(SCO 439 effective November 15, 1980; amended by SCO 554 effective April 4, 1983; by SCO 847 effective January 15, 1988; by SCO 1088 effective July 1, 1992; by SCO 1145 effective October 1, 1993; by SCO 1153 effective July 15, 1994; by SCO 1155 effective July 15, 1994; by SCO 1211 effective July 15, 1995; by SCO 1226 effective January 22, 1996; by SCO 1235 effective July 15, 1996; and by SCO 1238 effective July 15, 1996)

Dissent to SCO 1088:

RABINOWITZ, Chief Justice, with whom COMPTON, Justice, joins, dissenting:

I am not persuaded that either existing Criminal Rule 39, or Appellate Rule 209, requires amendment. I think it can be safely predicted that these amendments will have a chilling effect on an indigent defendant's obtaining the services of appointed counsel as well as on an indigent defendant's decision whether or not to seek review or to appeal.

Note: AS 18.85.170(4) defines "indigent person" for purposes of public defender appointments as "a person who, at the time need is determined, does not have sufficient assets, credit, or other means to provide for payment of an attorney and all other necessary expenses of representation without depriving the party or the party's dependents of food, clothing, or shelter and who has not disposed of any assets since the commission of the offense with the intent or for the purpose of establishing eligibility for assistance under this chapter."

Note to SCO 1238: Ch. 79 § 1 SLA 1995 amends AS 09 by adding a new chapter related to prisoner litigation against the state. AS 09.19.010 prohibits the court from accepting any filing in an action governed by AS 09.19 until the filing fee required by AS 09.19.010 has been paid.

Section 19 of chapter 79 amends Appellate Rule 209(a) to add subparagraph (a)(6) which states that the provisions of paragraph (a) do not apply in a prisoner's appeal that is governed by AS 09.19. Section 5 of this order is adopted for the sole reason that the legislature has mandated the amendment.

Annotations

Cases

In an appeal from conviction of crime state discharged constitutional obligation to indigent defendant by appointing capable counsel, providing him with a record, full access to the electronic recording of the trial, free facilities for the printing of his brief and reasonable compensation for his professional efforts. **Bentley v. State,** Op. No. 225, 393 P2d 225 (Alaska 1964).

Experienced trial lawyer who had been appellant's choice as defense counsel for the trial, could give fair representation of appellant's cause as court appointed counsel on appeal in forma pauperis, although on a previous investigation of appellant's trial he had reported to the supreme court that he found no meritorious ground for appeal. **Bentley v. State,** Op. No. 225, 393 P2d 225 (Alaska 1964).

The superior court has the primary responsibility to determine whether an appellant should be allowed to appeal at public expense. **Johnson v. Johnson,** Op. No. 1229, 544 P2d 1028 (Alaska 1976).

In making a written statement of reasons for denying a motion to appeal at public expense, a judge should take care to state with particularity and in detail preliminary and basic facts upon which he relied. Only if the judge makes such findings will the supreme court be able to have a clear understanding of the basis for the judge's decision. **Johnson v. Johnson,** Op. No. 1229, 544 P2d 1028 (Alaska 1976).

Alaska's recoupment system for recovery of costs of appointed counsel does not violate the right to counsel expressed in article 1, section 11 of the Alaska constitution. **State v. Albert,** Op. No. 4225, 899 P2d 103 (Alaska 1995).

Alaska's recoupment system for recovery of costs of appointed counsel does not violate the right to counsel guaranteed by the Sixth Amendment to the United States Constitution. **State v. Albert,** Op. No. 4225, 899 P2d 103 (Alaska 1995).

Trial counsel's unilateral and unformalized withdrawal of representation following trial violated Appellate Rules and Code of Professional Responsibility; fact that client instructed trial counsel to do nothing further in the case did not relieve trial counsel of duty to preserve client's right to appeal where instruction was expressly based on client's representation that new attorney would be handling the matter. **Broeckel v. State,** Op. No. 1430, 900 P2d 1205 (Alaska App. 1995).

Subsection (b)(5) imposes attorney's fees on all defendants who remain convicted following the appellate process, i.e., all defendants who did not secure a reversal of their conviction. **Malutin v. State,** Op. No. 1757, 27 P3d 792 (Alaska App. 2001).

Policy behind subsection (b)(5) was that indigent litigants should have to shoulder at least some portion of the legal expenses that society incurred on their behalf; indigent defendants should be obliged to pay something, subject to the legislatively-mandated exemption for defendants who were not convicted. **Malutin v. State,** Op. No. 1757, 27 P3d 792 (Alaska App. 2001).

Rule 210. Record on Appeal.

(a) **Composition of Record.** The record on appeal consists of the entire superior court file, including the original papers and exhibits filed in the superior court, and the electronic record of proceedings before the superior court.

(b) **Preparation of Transcript.**

(1) *Designation of Parts of Record to be Transcribed.*

(A) At the time the notice of appeal is filed, the appellant shall file and serve on the other parties to the appeal a designation of the parts of the electronic record which appellant intends to transcribe. The appellant shall designate all parts which are essential to a determination of the issues on appeal. If appellant claims that the written findings of fact or conclusions of law are insufficient or erroneous, the designation shall include any oral findings of fact and conclusions of law. Within 10 days after service of appellant's designation, any other party to the appeal may file and serve a designation of additional parts of the electronic record to be transcribed.

(B) If a party designates an entire trial or hearing, the party's designation shall include only the nature and dates of the proceeding. If a party designates parts of a trial or hearing, the party's designation shall include the nature and dates of the proceeding, the tape and log numbers where these parts appear, and a narrative description of the portions requested. If a party designates a portion of a witness' testimony, it must appear from the party's narrative description that part of the witness' testimony has been omitted.

(2) *Preparation at Public Expense.* The clerk of the trial courts shall arrange for preparation of the transcript in cases in which the transcript is prepared at public expense. The transcript shall include all parts of the electronic record designated by the parties to the appeal; however, the voir dire examination of jurors and jury instructions shall not be transcribed unless a party has specifically requested these portions of the trial.

(3) *Preparation Not at Public Expense.* In cases in which the transcript is not prepared at public expense, the appellant shall arrange for preparation of a transcript of all parts of the electronic record designated by the parties to the appeal. Upon request, the clerk of the trial courts shall provide to the transcriber a copy of the designations, a copy of the electronic record or parts thereof, a copy of the log notes and other information necessary for preparation of the transcript. Unless the parties agree otherwise by stipulation, or unless otherwise ordered by the appellate court, the person designated to prepare the transcript shall not be a relative, employee, or attorney of any of the parties, or a relative or employee of that attorney, or be financially interested in the action. Apart from contracting for the preparation of the transcript within a given period of time and at a given price, neither the party nor the party's attorney may exercise control over the preparation of the transcript.

(4) *Time for Completion.* Preparation of the transcript shall be completed within 40 days after filing of the notice of appeal. If the transcript is not being prepared at public expense and the transcriber is unable to complete the transcript within this time, the appellant shall move the appellate court for an extension of time. The motion shall comply with Appellate Rule 503, shall also be served on the clerk of the trial courts, and shall be considered a routine motion within the meaning of Rule 503(b).

(5) *Filing and Distribution.* Upon completion of the transcript, the transcriber shall promptly notify the parties in writing that the transcript has been completed and shall file with the clerk of the trial courts (i) the original and one copy of the transcript; and (ii) an electronic version of the transcript in the form and format prescribed by administrative bulletin.

(6) *Costs.* If the transcript is not being prepared at public expense, the cost of preparing the original transcript, the copy filed with the court and the computer diskette shall be paid by the appellant. This cost may be taxed as a cost in the case, but if any party causes parts of the electronic record to be transcribed unnecessarily, the court may impose the cost of transcribing such parts on that party.

(7) *Form of Transcript.* Transcripts shall be in the form and format prescribed by administrative bulletin.

(8) *Statement in Lieu of Transcript.* In the event no stenographic report or electronic recording of the evidence or proceedings at a hearing or trial was made, the appellant may prepare a statement of the evidence of proceedings from the best available means, including the appellant's recollection, for use instead of a stenographic or electronically recorded transcript. This statement shall be served on the appellee, who may serve objections or proposed amendments, and shall be submitted to the court from which the appeal is being taken for settlement and approval. As settled and approved, the statement shall be filed with the clerk of that court and transmitted to the appellate court in lieu of a transcript.

(c) **Excerpts of Record.**

(1) *Duty to Prepare.*

(A) Each party shall file and serve an excerpt of record with the party's brief.

(B) In cases involving multiple appellants or appellees, each side shall prepare a single excerpt of record. In a case involving multiple appellants who are filing separate briefs, the appellant who filed the first notice of appeal shall prepare and file the excerpt for the appellants, unless the appellants otherwise agree. In a case involving multiple appellees who are filing separate briefs, the appellees shall decide among themselves which appellee shall prepare and file the excerpt for the appellees. Ten days prior to the date on which a side's briefs are due, the parties who are not responsible for preparation of the excerpt shall transmit to the responsible party a list of documents to be included in the excerpt. The responsible party shall include in the excerpt all documents which are specified by the other parties, provided such documents are in the record. A party who fails to transmit a list of documents to the responsible party by the 10 day deadline waives the right to designate documents for inclusion in the excerpt. The responsible party shall mail a copy of the excerpt to each of the other parties on that side six days before the date the briefs are due, or deliver a copy of the excerpt three days before the date the briefs are due, so that the other parties may include the appropriate citations in their briefs. The cost of copying and mailing the excerpt shall be borne equally by all parties on the side.

(C) A cross-appellant or cross-appellee who elects to file a single brief shall file a single excerpt with that brief. A cross-appellant who makes this election shall include in the excerpt those documents that are properly included in an appellee's excerpt under Rule 210(c)(2). A cross-appellant who elects to file separate briefs shall file and serve notice of this election within 10 days after service of the notice of the due date for appellant's brief. If a cross-appellant makes this election, the cross-appellant and the appellant shall be treated as co-appellants filing separate briefs and shall prepare and submit a combined excerpt as required by Rule 210(c)(1)(B). The cross-appellee and the appellee shall be treated as co-appellees filing separate briefs for purposes of that rule.

(2) *Contents.*

(A) *Appellant's Excerpt.* The appellant's excerpt of record must contain the following parts of the record:

(i) all charging documents, or the petition or complaint, counterclaim, crossclaim, and answer setting out the issues to be tried;

(ii) the judgment or interlocutory order from which the appeal is taken;

(iii) other orders or rulings sought to be reviewed;

(iv) supporting opinions, findings of fact, conclusions of law, or other statements showing the reasoning of the trial court and, if appellant claims that the written findings of fact or conclusions of law are insufficient or erroneous, a copy of the pages of the transcript at which any relevant oral findings of fact and conclusions of law are recorded;

(v) if the appeal is from the grant or denial of a motion, relevant portions of briefs, memoranda, and documents filed in support of and in opposition to the motion;

(vi) if the appellant is challenging the admission or exclusion of evidence, the giving or failure to give a jury instruction, or another oral ruling or order, a copy of the pages of the transcript at which the evidence, offer of proof, ruling, or order and relevant discussion by the court, and any necessary objection are recorded;

(vii) if the appeal is from a final decision in a child-in-need-of-aid proceeding under AS 47.10.080(c) or a case involving the termination of parental rights under AS 25.23.180, the predisposition report prepared in the case; and

(viii) specific portions of other documents in the record, including documentary exhibits, that are referred to in appellant's brief and essential to the resolution of an issue on appeal.

(B) *Appellee's Excerpt.* The appellee's excerpt of record must contain those parts of the record required under (c)(2)(A) and relied on by appellee that were not included in the appellant's excerpt.

(C) *Portions of the Transcript.* In an appeal to the supreme court, a party may also include in the excerpt selected pages of the transcript that are critical to the appeal.

(D) *Items Not to Be Included in the Excerpts.* Pages of the transcript and briefs and memoranda filed in the trial court may only be included in the excerpts if required under (c)(2)(A) or permitted under (c)(2)(C). The fact that parts of the record are not included in the excerpts does not prevent the parties or the appellate court from relying on those parts.

(3) *Supplemental Excerpts.* Appellant may file and serve a supplemental excerpt of record with appellant's reply brief or within the time specified for filing a reply brief. No other supplemental excerpt may be filed except by leave of the appellate court granted on motion, or at the request of the appellate court. A supplemental excerpt may not include parts of the record that appear in another excerpt filed in the appeal.

(4) *Form, Filing and Service.* Each party's excerpt of record must be arranged in chronological order, must be bound separately from the party's brief, and must contain a table of contents at the beginning of the first volume. The excerpt and the table of contents must be in the form specified in the Clerk's Instructions for Preparation of Excerpts published in these rules. One copy of the excerpt must be filed and served with the party's original brief. Six copies of the excerpt must be filed with the bound copies of the brief, and one copy must be served on counsel for each party separately represented. The appellate court may specify the filing or service of a different number of copies than required by this rule.

(5) *Excerpts to be Abbreviated.* The parties shall include in the excerpts only those parts of the record that are essential to a determination of the questions presented on appeal. For any infraction of this rule, the appellate court may impose sanctions and withhold or impose costs as the circumstances of the case and discouragement of like conduct in the future may require.

(6) *Costs.* Subject to (c)(5), the prevailing party is entitled to recover the cost of copying its excerpt of record under Appellate Rule 508(d).

(d) **RESERVED.**

(e) **Preparation of the Trial Court File.**

(1) *Page Numbering.* Upon receiving the notice of appeal, the clerk of the trial courts shall number the pages of the trial court file in a single consecutive sequence throughout all volumes. Page numbering must be completed within 40 days after filing of the notice of appeal.

(2) *Confidential Materials.* Papers filed under seal in the

trial court and exhibits submitted or introduced at closed hearings in the trial court shall be maintained under seal while they constitute part of a record on appeal, and access to them shall be governed by Rule 512.5(c).

(f) **Briefing Schedule.** Upon filing of the transcript and completion of the page numbering, the clerk of the trial courts shall notify the clerk of the appellate courts that the case is ready for briefing. Upon receiving this notice, the clerk of the appellate courts shall give notice of the due date for the appellant's brief.

(g) **Transmission of the Record.**

(1) *Transmission to Appellate Court.* Upon notification that briefing is complete, the clerk of the trial courts shall transmit the record, excluding physical exhibits, to the clerk of the appellate courts. Physical exhibits shall be retained by the trial court unless specifically requested by the appellate court. As used in this paragraph, "physical exhibits" includes exhibits other than documents or photographs, and also includes documents or photographs of unusually large size or unusual bulk or weight.

(2) *Transfer to Other Court Locations.* The clerk of the appellate courts may direct that the record be temporarily transferred to another court location within the state for the accommodation of counsel in the preparation of briefs.

(h) **Several Appeals.** When more than one appeal is taken to the appellate court from the same judgment, there shall be a single record on appeal. In preparing the record, deadlines which run from filing of the notice of appeal shall run from filing of the last notice of appeal.

(i) **Power of Court to Correct, Modify or Supplement.** It is not necessary for the record on appeal to be approved by the trial court or a judge thereof except as provided in subparagraph (b)(8) and in Rule 211, but if any difference arises whether the record truly discloses what occurred in the trial court, the difference shall be submitted to and settled by that court and the record made to conform to that court's decision. If anything material to either party is omitted from the record on appeal by error or accident by court personnel, or is misstated therein, the parties by stipulation, the trial court, or the appellate court, on a proper suggestion or of its own initiative, may direct that the omission or misstatement shall be corrected. All other questions as to the content and form of the record shall be presented to the appellate court. On motion in the appellate court, and for cause, an excerpt of record may be modified or supplemented to correct omissions by counsel.

(SCO 439 effective November 15, 1980; amended by SCO 461 effective June 1, 1981; by SCO 510 effective August 30, 1982; by SCO 554 effective April 4, 1983; by SCO 577 effective February 1, 1984; by SCO 578 effective February 1, 1984; by SCO 631 effective September 15, 1985; by SCO 736 effective December 15, 1986; by SCO 768 effective March 15, 1987; by SCO 795 effective March 15, 1987; by SCO 883 effective July 15, 1988; by SCO 926 effective January 15, 1989; by SCO 928 effective January 15, 1989; by SCO 988 effective January 15, 1990; by SCO 1153 effective July 15, 1994; rescinded and repromulgated by SCO 1155 effective July 15, 1994; by SCO 1183 effective July 15, 1995; by SCO 1279 effective July 31, 1997; by SCO 1360 effective September 1, 1999; by SCO 1388 effective April 15, 2000; by SCO 1432 effective October 15, 2001; by SCO 1472 effective October 15, 2002; by SCO 1482 effective October 15, 2002; by SCO 1541 effective April 15, 2004; by SCO 1553 effective October 15, 2004; and by SCO 1609 effective October 15, 2006)

Note to Appellate Rule 210(b)(5) and (b)(7): See Administrative Bulletin 31 and the Manual of Transcript Procedures.

Note: In 1997 the legislature enacted AS 18.16.030(j), which specifies the procedure for appeal of an order denying a petition to bypass parental consent to an abortion. According to ch. 14, sec. 8 SLA 1997, AS 18.16.030(j) has the effect of amending Appellate Rules 204, 210, 212, and 213 by establishing specific time limits applicable to certain appeals and by instructing the supreme court to modify or dispense with formal requirements applicable to certain briefs. Instead of amending individual rules to implement AS 18.16.030, the supreme court has adopted a separate rule on judicial bypass appeals. See Appellate Rule 220.

Annotations

Cases

I. In General.

II. Contents of Record on Appeal.

I. In General.

Matters that were not made issues in the trial court, by either the pleadings or the pre-trial order or that were not tried before the court, will not be considered on appeal. **Lumbermens Mut. Cas. Co. v. Continental Cas. Co.,** Op. No. 160, 387 P2d 104 (Alaska 1963).

Where in his reply brief the appellee raised the issue of allowance of attorney's fees, but did not cross-appeal and did not by cross-statement of points alert appellant to such an issue so that additional portions of the record could have been designated if appropriate, the issue of attorney's fees allowed by trial court was not considered on appeal. **Alaska Brick Co. v. McCoy,** Op. No. 287, 400 P2d 454 (Alaska 1965).

Letter from Workers' Compensation Board notifying claimant's counsel that the record on appeal was complete was sufficient notice under this rule even though no "certificate" that the record was complete was sent. **Cowitz v. Alaska Workers' Compensation Board,** Op. No. 3078, 721 P2d 635 (Alaska 1986).

In light of the fact that superior court order holding appellant's appeal from an administrative agency decision in abeyance was never vacated, that the agency did not furnish the superior court clerk with a copy of its decision on reconsideration, that the agency did not prepare and certify the record on appeal, and that the clerk of the superior court never notified the agency of the date by which it was to complete the record on appeal, appellant's counsel reasonably could have been in doubt as to how to proceed with the administrative appeal, thus superior court erred in dismissing the appeal for lack of prosecution. **King v. State Dept. of Natural Resources,** Op. No. 3226, 742 P2d 253 (Alaska 1987).

II. Contents of Record on Appeal.

It is the primary obligation of the appellant to see that all matters are included in the record which are essential to a decision of the questions presented on appeal. **McBride v. State,** Op. No. 66, 368 P2d 925 (Alaska 1962).

Although affidavits material to issues raised are not included in the record on appeal, the supreme court may consider them as if they had been included. **McBride v. State,** Op. No. 66, 368 P2d 925 (Alaska 1962).

If an appellant is unable to prepare a statement consistent with this rule or the record is inadequate to permit appellate review, normal procedure would be to remand the case for new trial. **Holt v. Powell,** Op. No. 379, 420 P2d 468 (Alaska 1966).

Supreme Court would not examine contents of exhibits which were not designated part of the record on appeal. **City of Whittier v. Whittier Fuel & Marine Corp.,** Op. No. 1585, 577 P2d 216 (Alaska 1978).

Where the agency failed to provide transcript of the proceeding which would have helped court determine whether the proceeding was a public hearing on a license application and thus subject to Appellate Rule 45 or whether it was merely an informed public meeting, a finding that it was a public hearing was appropriate as a sanction for failure on the agency's part to complete the record. **Ketchikan Retail Liquor Dealers v. State, Etc.,** Op. No. 1963, 602 P2d 434 (Alaska 1979).

Where appellant requested jury trial, but did not properly raise constitutional issue at trial or include it in statement of points on appeal, the issue was not before appellate court. **Jeffries v. Glacier State Telephone Co.,** Op. No. 1985, 604 P2d 4 (Alaska 1979).

Superior Court erred in not granting subcontractor's motion to reopen case to permit filing of certificate of compliance with statute requiring corporation, in order to maintain an action, to prove that it paid the annual corporation tax, where motion would not have required any additional testimony, the certificate was self- authenticating, and would have demonstrated peradventure that subcontractor had complied with statute; accordingly, reviewing court deemed the record on appeal to be augmented by the certificate. **A.C.E. Construction v. Chena Construction,** Op. No. 2526, 647 P2d 602 (Alaska 1982).

Trial court did not commit reversible error in failing to record and transcribe the reading of the jury instructions at the trial. **Marrone v. State,** Op. No. 156, 653 P2d 672 (Alaska App. 1982).

Issue not expressly mentioned in appellant's statement of points on appeal was heard where the record below and the statement of points on appeal, when considered with the statement of issues contained in appellant's brief, sufficiently informed the opposing parties and the court of the matters in issue, as demonstrated by appellee's full briefing of the issue. **Forquer v. State, Commercial Fisheries,** Op. No. 2784, 677 P2d 1236 (Alaska 1984).

An issue not raised in the points on appeal may nevertheless be considered if it is raised at trial, adequately briefed on appeal, and the court and counsel are sufficiently apprised of the issue presented. **Winn v. Mannhalter,** Op. No. 2988, 708 P2d 444 (Alaska 1985).

Civil Rule 210, which places the ultimate responsibility on the appellant for preparation of a record within 40 days from the date of filing the notice of appeal from an agency decision and provides for dismissal as a sanction for noncompliance, did not relieve the agency of its obligation to prepare the record on appeal and did not excuse the superior court clerk's failure to notify the agency of the date by which the record had to be prepared. **King v. State Dept. of Natural Resources,** Op. No. 3226, 742 P2d 253 (Alaska 1987).

In a divorce action where the value of the good will of the family business was at issue, husband's submittal of an expert appraisal of the value of the business goodwill, in an appendix to the husband's memorandum in opposition to proposed findings and conclusions, should have been part of the record on appeal even though the appendix was not admitted in evidence below and was totally ignored by the trial judge, since exhibits attached to pleadings and motions become "documents" in the court file pursuant to this rule. **Moffitt v. Moffitt,** Op. No. 3261, 749 P2d 343 (Alaska 1988).

The party alleging that a failure to admit evidence was prejudiced must designate those portions of the record, including the trial transcript, which are necessary for proper appellate review. Where appellants failed to designate trial transcripts as part of record on appeal, appellate court was unable to conclude that they had been prejudiced and therefore has to uphold jury's verdict. **Estate of Arrowwood v. State,** Op. No. 4196, 894 P2d 642 (Alaska 1995).

Because the transcript was not part of the record on appeal, which was necessary to address defendant's contentions, the court considered defendant's challenge waived. **Bertilson v. State,** Op. No. 1851, 64 P.3d 180 (Alaska App. 2003).

Recreation of the record of the inmate's classification hearing is required; if the superior court cannot do so on remand, it must in turn remand the matter to the Department of Corrections for recreation of their record. **Carlson v. Renkes,** Op. No. 5903, 113 P.3d 638 (Alaska 2005).

Rule 211. Record on Agreed Statement.

When the questions presented by an appeal can be determined without an examination of all the pleadings, evidence and proceedings in the trial court, the parties may prepare and sign a statement of the case showing how the questions arose and were decided in the trial court and setting forth only so many of the facts averred and proved or sought to be proved as are essential to a decision of the questions by the appellate court. The statement shall include a copy of the judgment appealed from, a copy of the notice of appeal with its filing date, and concise statement of the points to be relied on by appellant. If the statement conforms to the truth, it, together with such additions as the trial court may consider necessary to fully present the questions raised by the appeal, shall be approved by the trial court and shall then be certified to the appellate court as the record on appeal.

(SCO 439 effective November 15, 1980)

Rule 212. Briefs.

(a) **Filing and Serving Briefs.**

(1) *Initial Submission.*

(A) *Time for Serving and Filing Briefs.* The appellant shall serve and file the appellant's brief within 30 days after the court gives notice under Rule 210(f) of the due date for appellant's brief. The appellee shall serve and file the appellee's brief within 30 days after service of the appellant's brief. Within 20 days after service of the appellee's brief, appellant shall serve and file either a reply brief or a notice that no reply brief will be filed. In cases involving multiple appellants or appellees who are filing separate briefs, including parties who are deemed to be co-parties under Rule 210(c)(1)(C), the time for filing these briefs shall be extended by 10 days if the parties are preparing excerpts of record in order to allow compliance with Rule 210(c)(1)(B).

(B) *Number of Copies.* On or before the date the party's brief is due, the party shall file with the clerk the original plus one copy of the brief, printed or written on only one side of each page, together with proof of service on all parties.

(C) *Compliance Check.* The court will review the brief for compliance with (b) and (c) of this rule and return the original to the party, with a notice of rejection, conditional acceptance, or acceptance, for correction or for duplication and binding.

(D) *Changes Not Permitted.* After a brief is returned for correction or binding, the party shall make no changes to the brief other than those required by the binding process or required by the court in any notice of rejection or conditional acceptance. The party may also correct spelling and typographical errors and correct and update citations for cases already cited in the originally submitted brief.

(2) *Bound Copies of Briefs.*

(A) *Time for Service; Number of Copies.* Within ten days after the clerk returns the brief, the party shall serve two bound copies on each party and shall file with the clerk eight bound copies in an appeal before the supreme court or seven bound copies in an appeal before the court of appeals. The clerk may specify a different number of copies or a different time period than required by this rule.

(B) *Form of Bound Copies.* Bound copies must be printed or written on both sides of the paper and securely bound along the left margin in a manner that does not obscure the text, and that permits the brief to lie reasonably flat when open. Unless otherwise permitted by the clerk, the copies must be bound using comb or spiral binding, but not staples or metal fasteners. The copies must have a suitable cover consisting of heavy paper in the color indicated:

- brief of appellant—ivory or light tan;
- brief of appellee—blue;
- reply brief—green; and
- brief of intervenor or amicus curiae—red.

(b) **Form.** The form of a brief is governed by Rule 513.5(b)(1)-(5) and (c) and by this rule. The left and right margins of a brief must each be one inch. The front cover of a brief must contain: (1) the name of the court and the number of the case; (2) the title of the case; (3) the nature of the proceeding (e.g., appeal, petition for review); (4) the name of the court or agency below, the name of the individual who rendered the decision below, and the case number below; (5) the title of the document (e.g., brief of appellant); and (6) the names, addresses, telephone numbers, and bar numbers of counsel for the party concerned and the name of the law firm or organization with whom counsel is affiliated. In criminal cases, the front cover must also include a certificate indicating whether the brief contains information that is confidential under AS 12.61.100 through 12.61.150. The administrative director shall specify the form and content of the certificate.

(c) **Substantive Requirements.**

(1) *Brief of Appellant.* The brief of the appellant shall contain the following items under appropriate headings and in the order here indicated:

(A) A table of contents, including the titles and subtitles of all arguments, with page references.

(B) A table of cases alphabetically arranged, statutes, and other authorities cited, with references to the pages of the brief where they are cited.

(C) The constitutional provisions, statutes, court rules, ordinances, and regulations principally relied upon, set out verbatim or their pertinent provisions appropriately summarized.

(D) A jurisdictional statement of the date on which judgment was entered and of the legal authority of the appellate court to consider the appeal.

(E) A list of all parties to the case, without using "et al.," or any similar indication, unless the caption of the case on the cover of the brief contains the names of all parties. This list may be contained in a footnote.

(F) A statement of the issues presented for review. In cases of cross-appeal, the cross-appellant may present a statement of the issues presented for review which would require determination if the case is to be reversed and remanded for further proceedings in the trial court. In the event that the decision is affirmed on the appeal, such issues on the cross-appeal may be deemed waived by the appellate court.

(G) A statement of the case, which shall provide a brief description of the case and a concise statement of the course of proceedings in, and the decision of, the trial court. Appellant shall state the facts relevant to each issue, with references to the record as required by paragraph (c)(8), in this section or in the appropriate argument sections.

(H) A discussion of the applicable standard of review. (If the brief concerns several issues with different standards of review, the discussion of each issue should be preceded by a discussion of the standard of review applicable to that issue).

(I) An argument section, which shall contain the contentions of the appellant with respect to the issues presented, and the reasons therefor, with citations to the authorities, statutes, and parts of the record relied on. The section may be preceded by a summary. Each major contention shall be preceded by a heading indicating the subject matter. References to the record shall conform to the requirements of paragraph (c)(8).

(J) A short conclusion stating the precise relief sought.

(K) If the appeal concerns a property division in a divorce case, an appendix consisting of a table listing all assets and liabilities of the parties as reflected in the record, including the trial court's findings as to the nature (marital or individual), value, and disposition of each asset or liability.

(2) *Brief of Appellee.* The brief of the appellee shall conform to the requirements of subdivisions (1)(A) through (1)(J) except that a statement of jurisdiction, of the issues, or of the case need not be made unless the appellee is dissatisfied with the statement of the appellant, and a list of all parties need not be included.

(3) *Reply Brief.* The appellant may file a brief in reply to

the brief of the appellee. The reply brief shall conform to the requirements of subdivisions (1)(A), (1)(B), (1)(C), (1)(I), and (1)(J). This brief may raise no contentions not previously raised in either the appellant's or appellee's briefs. If the appellee has cross-appealed and has not filed a single brief under (c)(6) of this rule, the appellee may file a brief in reply to the response of the appellant to the issues presented by the cross-appeal. No further briefs may be filed except with leave of the court.

(4) *Length.* Exclusive of appendices, the appellant's and appellee's briefs may not exceed 50 numbered pages each. Numbered pages for purposes of this paragraph begin with the jurisdictional statement required by (c)(1)(D) of this rule. The appellant's reply brief may not exceed 20 pages. A motion for leave to file a brief longer than permitted by this paragraph must be accompanied by a copy of the over-length brief proposed to be filed.

(5) *Brief in Cases of Multiple Parties.* In cases involving more than one appellant or appellee, including cases consolidated for purposes of the appeal, any number of either may join in a single brief, and any appellant or appellee may adopt by reference any part of the brief of another.

(6) *Briefs in Cases Involving Cross-Appeals.*

(A) Cross-Appellant. An appellee who is also a cross-appellant may elect to file a single brief that both discusses the appellee's claims of error and answers the original appellant. Such a single brief shall be filed on the date the appellee's brief is due. It shall be divided into two sections: the first section shall contain the issues and arguments involved in the cross-appeal and shall be prepared in accordance with (c)(1) of this rule; the second section shall contain the answer to the brief of the appellant and shall be prepared in accordance with (c)(2) of this rule. The single brief may not exceed 50 numbered pages. If the cross-appellant elects to file a single brief, the right to file a reply brief to the answer to the cross-appeal is waived. If the cross-appellant does not elect to file a single brief, the schedule and form for filing briefs in the cross-appeal shall be in accordance with the procedures for an original appeal.

(B) Cross-Appellee. If the appellee/cross-appellant elects to file a single brief under [a], the appellant/cross-appellee may file a single brief containing its reply on the appeal and its response to the cross-appeal. This combined brief may not exceed 50 numbered pages. The portions of the combined brief that comprise the reply may not exceed 20 numbered pages. The combined brief must be filed within 30 days of the appellee/cross-appellant's single brief.

(7) *References in Briefs and in Oral Arguments to Parties.* In briefs and oral arguments, counsel are expected to minimize references to parties by such designations as "appellant" and "appellee." It promotes clarity to use the designations used in the trial court or in the agency proceedings, or the actual names of parties, or descriptive terms such as "the employee," the "injured person," "the taxpayer," and so forth.

(8) *References in Briefs to the Record.*

(A) *References in Cases in Which Excerpts are Prepared.* References in the briefs to parts of the record reproduced in an excerpt shall be to the pages of the excerpt at which those parts appear. The form for references to pages of the excerpt is [Exc. ________]. Briefs may reference parts of the record not reproduced in an excerpt. The form for references to pages of the transcript is [Tr. ________] and to pages of the trial court file is [R.________].

(B) *References to be Included.* If reference is made to evidence of which the admissibility is in controversy, reference shall be made to the pages of the transcript at which the evidence was identified, offered, and received or rejected. Appellant's brief shall indicate the pages of the record where each point on appeal was raised in the trial court. If the point on appeal was not raised in the trial court, the brief shall explain why the point is raised for the first time on appeal. Failure to comply with the requirements of this paragraph may result in return of the brief as provided in paragraph 11 of this subdivision.

(9) *Brief of an Amicus Curiae.* A brief of an amicus curiae may be filed only if accompanied by written consent of all the parties, or by leave of the appellate court granted on motion, or at the request of the appellate court. The brief may be conditionally filed with the motion for leave. A motion for leave shall identify the interest of the applicant and shall state the reasons why a brief of an amicus curiae is desirable. Unless all parties otherwise consent, any amicus curiae shall file its brief within the time allowed to the party whose position as to affirmance or reversal the amicus brief will support, unless the court for cause shown shall grant leave for later filing, in which event it shall specify within what period an opposing party may answer. The brief shall be in the form prescribed by this rule and shall be duplicated and served pursuant to the requirements of Rule 212(a)(2). A motion of an amicus curiae to participate in the oral argument will be granted only for extraordinary reasons.

(10) *Failure to File Brief.* When the appellant's opening brief is not filed as required, Rule 511.5 shall apply. When the appellee's brief is not filed as required, appellee will not be heard at oral argument except on consent of the appellant, or by request of the court.

(11) *Defective Briefs.* When a brief fails to comply with the requirements of these rules, the appellate court, on application of any party or on its own motion, and with or without notice as it may determine appropriate, may:

(A) Order the brief to be returned to counsel for correction by interlineation, cancellation, revisions or replacement in whole or in part, and to be refiled with the clerk within a time specified in the order; or

(B) Order the brief stricken from the files, with leave to file a new brief within a specified time; or

(C) Disregard defects and consider the brief as if it were properly prepared.

The authority to return briefs under this section may be exercised by the clerk of court pursuant to Rule 102 (f).

(12) *Citation of Supplemental Authorities.* When pertinent authorities come to the attention of a party after the party's brief has been filed, or after oral argument but before decision, the party may promptly advise the clerk of the court, by letter, with a copy to adversary counsel, setting forth the citations.

There shall be a reference either to the page of the brief or to a point argued orally to which the citations pertain, but the letter shall contain no argument or explanations. Any response shall be made promptly and shall be similarly limited.

(SCO 439 effective November 15, 1980; amended by SCO 510 effective August 30, 1982; by SCO 727 effective December 15, 1986; by SCO 737 effective December 15, 1986; by SCO 769 effective March 15, 1987; by SCO 861 effective July 15, 1988; by SCO 868 effective July 15, 1988; by SCO 925 effective January 15, 1989; by SCO 1020 effective July 15, 1990; by SCO 1091 effective July 15, 1992; by SCO 1120 effective July 15, 1993; by SCO 1153 effective July 15, 1994; by SCO 1155 effective July 15, 1994; by SCO 1157 effective July 15, 1994; by SCO 1210 effective July 15, 1995; by SCO 1279 effective July 31, 1997; by SCO 1407 effective October 15, 2000; by SCO 1408 effective October 15, 2000; by SCO 1477 effective April 15, 2003; by SCO 1540 effective October 15, 2004; and by SCO 1597 effective October 15, 2006)

Note: In 1997 the legislature enacted AS 18.16.030(j), which specifies the procedure for appeal of an order denying a petition to bypass parental consent to an abortion. According to ch. 14, sec. 8 SLA 1997, AS 18.16.030(j) has the effect of amending Appellate Rules 204, 210, 212, and 213 by establishing specific time limits applicable to certain appeals and by instructing the supreme court to modify or dispense with formal requirements applicable to certain briefs. Instead of amending individual rules to implement AS 18.16.030, the supreme court has adopted a separate rule on judicial bypass appeals. See Appellate Rule 220.

Annotations

Cases

I. In General.
II. Contents of Briefs.
 A. In General.
 B. Specification of Error.

I. In General.

Cross-appeal was dismissed on supreme court's own motion for failure of cross-appellants to file their brief within the time prescribed. **Alaska State Housing Authority v. Vincent,** Op. No. 261, 396 P2d 531 (Alaska 1964).

Appellee who had not taken a cross-appeal and who had not filed a cross-statement of points, could not raise by appellee's brief an issue of allowance of increased attorney's fees as costs. **Alaska Brick Co. v. McCoy,** Op. No. 287, 400 P2d 454 (Alaska 1965).

Points on appeal not briefed are considered abandoned. **Miller v. City of Fairbanks,** Op. No. 881, 509 P2d 826 (Alaska 1973).

Where appellant fails to comply with this rule and does not make a sufficient showing that he will suffer surprise or injustice if this rule is not strictly enforced against him and where appellant is without counsel, the supreme court will dispose of the appeal by determining the main issues recognized by both parties, **Miller v. City of Fairbanks,** Op. No. 881, 509 P2d 826 (Alaska 1973).

An issue raised at trial but not briefed on appeal would nevertheless be considered where it would have been unreasonable to expect party to have briefed it. **Sloan v. Atlantic Richfield Co.,** Op. No. 2047, 546 P2d 568 (Alaska 1976).

Appellant waived review of trial court's ruling on his trial theory by failing to present it in his opening brief on appeal, notwithstanding that it was mentioned in the reply brief. **Joseph v. Jones,** Op. No. 2464, 639 P2d 1014 (Alaska 1982).

Whether juvenile, before making statement, should have been advised that she could be tried as an adult was an issue raised for the first time in her reply brief and therefore not properly before the court. **Ridgely v. State,** Op. No. 503, 705 P2d 924 (Alaska App. 1985).

II. Contents of Briefs.

A. In General.

Long involved briefs are not recommended; however, there should be substantial compliance with rules regarding preparation of briefs on appeal. **Bidwell v. Scheele,** Op. No. 20, 355 P2d 584 (Alaska 1960).

Where an appeal brief seeks to incorporate by reference arguments made to the trial court such need not be considered by the Supreme Court. **Bidwell v. Scheele,** Op. No. 20, 355 P2d 584 (Alaska 1960).

An alleged issue involving free speech could not be considered and decided on appeal, where it was mentioned only casually or not at all in appellant's main argument and not tendered in the Specifications of Error nor under "Questions Presented for Review," nor even covered by the summary of argument. **Sanuita v. Common Laborer's and Hod Carriers Union,** Op. No. 290, 402 P2d 199 (Alaska 1965).

Counsel was reprimanded for abusive and intemperate language in his appeal brief accusing the trial court and opposing counsel of unethical and underhanded conduct. **Gregoire v. National Bank of Alaska,** Op. No. 336, 413 P2d 27 (Alaska 1966).

Where a point is not given more than a cursory statement in the argument portion of a brief, such point will not be considered by the Supreme Court. **Lewis v. State,** Op. No. 615, 469 P2d 689 (Alaska 1970).

Failure to argue a point on appeal constitutes an abandonment of it. **Lewis v. State,** Op. No. 615, 469 P2d 689 (Alaska 1970).

A single conclusory paragraph without the citation of any authority is not adequate to put the issue of equal protection before the reviewing court on appeal. **Fairview Development, Inc. v. City of Fairbanks,** Op. No. 643, 475 P2d 35 (Alaska 1970).

Where the appellant's procedural noncompliance with the briefing requirements of this rule is so substantial and pervasive as to afford neither the appellee nor the court any clear indication of what the appellant claims as error or grounds thereof and the brief is largely conclusionary, unsupported and sometimes undecipherable in the nature of its arguments, the supreme court will affirm the judgment. **Martin v. English,** Op. No. 761, 492 P2d 105 (Alaska 1971).

The failure to set forth in the opening brief the charge of the court verbatim together with the grounds for objection urged at trial does not preclude consideration of the issue where the substance of the instruction and grounds of objection are set forth. **Transamerica Title Insurance Co. v. Ramsey,** Op. No. 869, 507 P2d 492 (Alaska 1973).

Issue given no more than cursory treatment in brief will be treated as abandoned. **Kristich v. State,** Op. No. 1264, 550 P2d 796 (Alaska 1976).

Supreme Court will not treat issues argued in brief but not set forth in points on appeal and will consider as abandoned questions set forth in the points but not argued in brief. **Wetzler v. Wetzler,** Op. No. 1518, 570 P2d 741 (Alaska 1977).

Supreme Court refused to address itself to issues not listed in the points on appeal and not adequately briefed. **Wren v. State,** Op. No. 1598, 577 P2d 235 (Alaska 1978).

Grounds for reversal set forth in appellants statement of points on appeal, one of which she argued in her reply brief, were waived because none were argued in her opening brief. **Hitt v. J.B. Coghill, Inc.,** Op. No. 2474, 641 P2d 211 (Alaska 1982).

Photographs attached to appellate brief along with an affidavit concerning their origin and authenticity were not admitted into evidence by the trial court and therefore could not be considered on appeal. **L.L.M. v. P.M.,** Op. No. 3246, 745 P2d 599 (Alaska 1987).

Issue raised for first time in reply brief is waived. **Sumner v. Eagle Nest Hotel,** Op. No. 4194, 894 P2d 628 (Alaska 1995).

Arguments raised for the first time in a reply brief are waived. **Dominish v. State,** Op. No. 4290, 907 P2d 487 (Alaska 1995).

Brief on appeal of trial court's denial of motion for directed verdict which incorporated by reference the motion did not satisfy the motion did not satisfy this rule requiring appellant's brief to contain contentions of appellant and reasons therefore. **Anchorage Nissan, Inc. v. State,** Op. No. 4850, 941 P2d 1229 (Alaska 1997).

Pro se litigant's constitutional challenge to state agency decision was preserved for appeal notwithstanding that his superior court brief presented only conclusory arguments and failed to identify and apply the precise legal tests for determining constitutionality since the essence of his argument was easily discernible and the state would not be prejudiced by consideration of the issue. **Wilkerson v. State Dept. of Health,** Op. No. 5216, 993 P2d 1018 (Alaska 1999).

Because defendant gave only conclusory statements of error and failed to provide any reason why the court should have found that the trial court erred in excluding certain evidence, the court considered the arguments waived; to the extent they were not waived, defendant's arguments had no merit. **Alto v. State,** Op. No. 1856, 64 P.3d 141 (Alaska App. 2003).

B. Specification of Error.

Where a point is specified as error in a brief on appeal thus raising such point as one to be relied upon but such point is not given more than cursory statement in the argument portion of the brief, such point will not be considered by the supreme court. Failure to argue a point constitutes an abandonment of it. **Veal v. Newlin, Inc.,** Op. No. 53, 367 P2d 155 (Alaska 1961); **Parks v. Brown,** Op. No. 57, 368 P2d 220 (Alaska 1962); **DeArmond v. Alaska State Dev. Co,** Op. No. 116, 376 P2d 717 (Alaska 1962); **McIntyre v. State,** 379 P.2d 615 (Alaska 1963); **Gregory v. Padilla,** Op. No. 139, 379 P2d 951 (Alaska 1963); **Alaska State Hous. Auth. v. Contento,** Op. No. 435, 432 P2d 117 (Alaska 1967); **Kenai Power Corp. v. Strandberg,** Op. No. 350, 415 P2d 659 (Alaska 1966); **Associated Engineers & Contractors, Inc. v. H. & W. Const. Co., Inc.,** Op. No. 462, 438 P2d 224 (Alaska 1968); **Norman v. Nichiro Gyogyo Kaisha, Ltd.,** Op. No. 3383, 761 P2d 713 (Alaska 1988).

A specification of error challenging a ruling or action within the discretion of the trial court which does not also allege an abuse of discretion presents nothing for review on appeal. **Parks v. Brown,** Op. No. 57, 368 P2d 220 (Alaska 1962).

A specification of error which sets out more than one error is improper and need not be considered by the supreme court. **Parks v. Brown,** Op. No. 57, 368 P2d 220 (Alaska 1962).

A specification of error must be specific, not general, clearly challenging a definite ruling or action of the trial court; and, if not, such specification need not be considered. **Parks v. Brown,** Op. No. 57, 368 P2d 220 (Alaska 1962).

A specification of error simply repeated verbatim the statement of points. **Hitz v. Property Investments, Inc.,** Op. No. 65, 368 P2d 929 (Alaska 1962).

A specification of error which sets out more than one error is improper and need not be considered by the supreme court. **McLemore v. Harris,** Op. No. 102, 374 P2d 410 (Alaska 1962).

When the requirements of Supreme Court Rule 11(a)(6) have been disregarded, the supreme court need not consider the errors intended to be urged. **Crume v. Crume,** Op. No. 124, 378 P2d 183 (Alaska 1963).

Alleged errors of the trial court in refusing proposed instructions and in giving allegedly erroneous instructions were not considered on appeal where appellant had failed to set out inappropriate specifications of error the proposed instructions, the allegedly erroneous instructions, and his grounds of objections to the court's rulings in regard to his objections in each case, nor even indicated the places in the trial record where he objected to the court's ruling thereon. **Higgins v. Lantz,** Op. No. 239, 394 P2d 776 (Alaska 1964).

A specification of error alleged to consist in not allowing as evidence a certain memorandum was defective because it did not state the nature of the memorandum alleged to have been excluded and the grounds on which the admission was urged. **Buza v. Columbia Lumber Company,** Op. No. 254, 395 P2d 511 (Alaska 1964).

Since counsel for appellee made no objections in his brief that appellant's specifications of error failed to comply with this rule, record was examined on appeal. **Apex Concrete Co. v. Bray,** Op. No. 253, 395 P2d 514 (Alaska 1964).

A specification which set forth "the jurors" unauthorized use of a dictionary during their deliberations, and the failure to determine whether such use influenced their verdict, failed to set out separately each of the two alleged errors and was not considered. **Alaska State Housing Authority v. Vincent,** Op. No. 261, 396 P2d 531 (Alaska 1964).

A single specification of error in appellant's brief stating that three separate instructions were wrong and which did not set forth the instructions claimed to have been wrongfully refused and did not state grounds of objection urged at trial, disregarded the plain requirement of this rule and was not considered. **Buza v. Columbia Lumber Company,** Op. No. 254, 395 P2d 511 (Alaska 1964).

Alleged defects of the second of two specifications of error were immaterial, where the case was remanded on the strength of an error properly marked out in the first specification. **Thornton v. Alaska Workmen's Compensation Board,** Op. No. 327, 411 P2d 209 (Alaska 1966).

Where the appellants' specifications of error fail adequately to set forth relevant portions of the record, but such failure neither wastes the court's time nor prejudices the appellee's right to know what points he has to meet, the Supreme Court will consider the points. **Rego v. Decker,** Op. No. 679,482 P2d 834 (Alaska 1971).

An appellant who argues that four instructions were improper, but whose brief as it pertains to these claims is only two pages long and contains no citations of authority, will be deemed to have abandoned these points on appeal. **Wernberg v. Matanuska Electric Association, Inc.,** Op. No. 772, 494 P2d 790 (Alaska 1972).

The failure of a cross appellant to include a specification of errors in her brief does not compel dismissal of the cross appeal where cross appellant's statement and supplemental statement of points on appeal, along with the brief, clearly inform cross appellee of the claimed error. **State v. Abbott,** Op. No. 804,498 P2d 712 (Alaska 1972).

A contention that instructions were "lacking and misleading" and that the court erred in giving requested instructions are too general for consideration on appeal. **Transamerica Title Insurance Co. v. Ramsey,** Op. No. 869, 507 P2d 492 (Alaska 1973).

Pro se litigant's constitutional challenge to state agency decision was preserved for appeal notwithstanding that his superior court brief presented only conclusory arguments and failed to identify and apply the precise legal tests for determining constitutionality since the essence of his argument was easily discernible and the state would not be prejudiced by consideration of the issue. **Wilkerson v. State Dept. of Health,** Op. No. 5216, 993 P2d 1018 (Alaska 1999).

Pursuant to section (c)(8)(B) of this rule, employer was deemed to have failed to preserve its challenge to an applicant's emotional distress award because the employer's briefs failed to specify in the record that the point was raised. **Reust v. Alaska Petroleum Contrs., Inc.,** Op. No. 5951, 127 P.3d 807 (Alaska 2005).

Rule 213. Oral Argument.

The parties' right to oral argument and the procedures governing oral argument are set out in Rule 505.

(SCO 439 effective November 15, 1980; amended by SCO 1279 effective July 31, 1997, and by SCO 1598 effective October 15, 2006)

Note: In 1997 the legislature enacted AS 18.16.030(j), which specifies the procedure for appeal of an order denying a petition to bypass parental consent to an abortion. According to ch. 14, sec. 8 SLA 1997, AS 18.16.030(j) has the effect of amending Appellate Rules 204, 210, 212, and 213 by establishing specific time limits applicable to certain appeals and by instructing the supreme court to modify or dispense with formal requirements applicable to certain briefs. Instead of amending individual rules to implement AS 18.16.030, the supreme court has adopted a separate rule on judicial bypass appeals. See Appellate Rule 220.

Rule 214. Disposition of Appeals.

(a) The court may determine that an appeal shall be disposed of by summary order and without formal written opinion. To assist the court in making this determination, the parties may request in writing that an appeal be so decided. The request shall be signed by all parties and may be filed any time after the filing of the notice of appeal.

(b) In a criminal case, a summary order under this rule shall contain, at a minimum, a statement of the issues considered by the appellate court. This statement of issues may be made by reference to a trial court opinion. For purposes of this rule, "criminal case" includes all collateral criminal proceedings listed in AS 22.07.020(a).

(c) Nothing in this rule limits the right of the parties to oral argument pursuant to Rule 213.

(d) Summary decisions under this rule are without precedential effect and may not be cited in the courts of this state.

(SCO 439 effective November 15, 1980)

Annotations

Cases

Although Alaska R. App. P. 214 forbids citation of unpublished decisions as precedent, that is, as decisions that control or restrict future judicial decisionmaking, it does not forbid judges and lawyers from relying on unpublished decisions for whatever persuasive power those decisions might have. **McCoy v. State,** Op. No. 1822, 80 P3d 751 (Alaska App. 2002).

Rule 215. Sentence Appeal.

(a) **Appellate Review of Sentence.**

(1) *Defendant's Right to Appeal Sentence as Excessive.* A defendant may appeal an unsuspended sentence of imprisonment that exceeds two years for a felony offense or 120 days for a misdemeanor offense on the ground that the sentence is excessive, unless the sentence was imposed in accordance with a plea agreement that provided for imposition of a specific sentence or a sentence equal to or less than a specified maximum sentence. If a sentence is imposed in accordance with a plea agreement that provides for a minimum sentence, a defendant may appeal as excessive only the part of the sentence that exceeds the minimum sentence by more than two years for a felony offense or 120 days for a misdemeanor offense.

(2) *Defendant's Right to Appeal Sentence on Grounds Other Than Excessiveness.* A defendant may appeal a sentence of any length on grounds other than excessiveness, including but not limited to: illegality of the sentence; erroneous findings by the trial court that affect the statutory range of sentences to which the defendant is subject; and procedural errors in the sentencing proceeding.

(3) *Prosecuting Authority's Right to Appeal Sentence.* The prosecuting authority may appeal a sentence of any length as provided in AS 22.07.020.

(4) *Where Appeal is Taken.* An appeal under subparagraphs (a)(1)-(3) must be taken to the court of appeals.

(5) *Right to Seek Discretionary Review for Excessiveness.* A defendant may seek discretionary review of an unsuspended sentence of imprisonment which is not appealable under subparagraph (a)(1) by filing a petition for review in the supreme court under Appellate Rule 402. A defendant who is filing a sentence petition and a sentence appeal, or a sentence petition and a merit appeal, must follow the procedure set out in paragraph (j).

(b) **Notification of Right to Seek Review of Sentence.** At the time of imposition of any sentence of imprisonment, the judge shall inform the defendant

(1) of the defendant's right to appeal or petition for review of the sentence under paragraph (a);

(2) that the appellate court may reduce or increase the sentence, and that by appealing or petitioning for review of the sentence under this rule, the defendant waives the right to plead that by a revision of the sentence resulting from the appeal or review the defendant has been twice placed in jeopardy for the same offense; and

(3) that if the defendant wants counsel and is unable to pay for the services of an attorney, the court will appoint an attorney to represent the defendant in an appeal or petition for review.

(c) **Notice of Appeal.** A notice of appeal taken only from a sentence shall be filed with the clerk of the appellate courts not later than 30 days after the date shown in the clerk's certificate of distribution on the written judgment, except as provided for in Appellate Rule 204(a)(4). The notice of appeal need only state that the sentence which is being appealed is too lenient or excessive. When filed, the notice of appeal shall be accompanied by the items specified in Appellate Rule 204 (b)[1], [2], [4], and [7].

(d) **Termination of Appeal.** Any appeal of a sentence initiated by the defendant may be terminated by the defendant filing within 30 days from the filing of the notice of appeal a notice of intent to terminate the appeal. Such a termination shall prevent any increase in the sentence or sentences imposed.

(e) **Indigent's Right to Counsel on Sentence Appeal.** An indigent defendant is entitled to the assistance of counsel in prosecuting an appeal on the ground that the sentence is excessive. Where an appeal is taken by the prosecution pursuant to AS 12.55.120(b) on the ground that the sentence is too lenient, and the defendant has not appealed, the appellate court in its discretion may appoint counsel for an indigent defendant.

(f) **Record on Appeal.**

(1) *Preparation and Contents.* Within 15 days after the filing of a notice of sentence appeal, the clerk of the trial court shall prepare sufficient copies of the record on appeal, which shall consist of the following:

[a] all charging documents;

[b] the judgment being appealed;

[c] a transcript of the entire sentencing proceeding; and, if the sentence appeal is from a probation revocation, the transcript shall include the original sentencing and all probation revocation sentencing proceedings.

[d] all reports, documents, motions and memoranda pertaining to sentencing which were available to the sentencing court.

The clerk shall number the pages of the record consecutively. Appellate Rule 210(c) shall not apply.

(2) *Distribution.* Immediately upon preparation of the record on appeal, the clerk shall send the original to the clerk of the appellate courts, two copies to the defendant's counsel, and a copy to the attorney for the prosecution. Unless otherwise ordered by the appellate court, limitations that the trial court placed on disclosure of documents that are contained in the record continue to apply while the case is on appeal.

(g) **Memoranda on Appeal.**

(1) *By Appellant.* Within 15 days after service of copies of the record on appeal provided for in (f) of this rule, the appellant shall file with the appellate court the original and three copies of a memorandum in support of the appeal.

(2) *By Appellee.* Within 15 days after service of a copy of the appellant's memorandum, the appellee may file with the appellate court the original and three copies of a memorandum in opposition to the appeal.

(3) *Reply Memorandum.* No reply memorandum shall be filed unless ordered by the court.

(4) *Form and Contents of Memoranda.* Memoranda shall comply with Appellate Rule 513.5(b)(6)-(7) and shall also comply with Appellate Rule 212(b)-(c), except:

(A) memoranda need not comply with Rule 212(c)(1)(A)-(E);

(B) no memorandum shall exceed 25 pages without permission of the court; and

(C) the front page of each memorandum shall include the information that Appellate Rule 212(b) requires on the cover of a brief.

(5) *Service of Memoranda.* A party's memorandum shall be accompanied by proof of service on opposing counsel.

(h) **Oral Argument.** The parties' right to oral argument and the procedures governing oral argument are set out in Rule 505. In cases where sentence appeals are consolidated with appeals on the merits, a timely request for argument on the merits is deemed to include a request for argument on the sentence appeal.

(i) **Bail Pending Appeal.** A sentence appealed on the sole ground that the sentence is excessive does not confer or enlarge the right to bail pending appeal.

(j) **Combining of Sentence Appeals, Sentence Petitions, and Merit Appeals.** A party filing a sentence appeal and a sentence petition shall combine the two, and the procedures for sentence appeals shall govern the case. A party filing a merit appeal shall combine that appeal with any sentence appeal or sentence petition, and the procedures for merit appeals shall govern the case. All combined proceedings must be taken initially to the court of appeals, and the court of appeals shall decide all issues within its jurisdiction.

(k) **Referral of Issues Outside Jurisdiction of Court of Appeals.** In a combined appeal, upon final adjudication of all issues within the jurisdiction of the court of appeals, the court of appeals shall refer the case to the supreme court for discretionary review of any remaining sentence issues which are reviewable by the supreme court under subparagraph (a)(5) of this rule.

(SCO 439 effective November 15, 1980; amended by SCO 515 effective October 1, 1982; by SCO 554 effective April 4, 1983; by SCO 575 effective February 1, 1984; by SCO 781 effective March 15, 1987; by SCO 827 effective August 1, 1987; by SCO 829 effective August 1, 1987; by SCO 862 effective July 15, 1988; by SCO 940 effective January 15, 1989; by SCO 1021 effective July 15, 1990; by SCO 1153 effective July 15, 1994; and by SCO 1155 effective July 15, 1994; by SCO 1226 effective January 22, 1996; by SCO 1316 effective July 15, 1998; by SCO 1368 effective April 15, 2000; by SCO 1473 effective October 15, 2002; by SCO 1475 effective October

15, 2002; by SCO 1482 effective October 15, 2002; by SCO 1474 effective October 15, 2003; by SCO 1543 effective October 15, 2004; and by SCO 1598 effective October 15, 2006)

Annotations

Cases

A sentence will be modified on appeal only if those instances where the reviewing court is convinced that the sentencing court was clearly mistaken in imposing a particular sentence. **McMain v. State,** Op. No. 1016, 519 P2d 811 (Alaska 1974).

Where a case is on appeal, the denial of guilt should not be considered as a factor weighing against probation. **Bradley v. State,** Op. No. 1145, 535 P2d 1031 (Alaska 1975).

The standard of review on a sentence appeal is to determine whether the trial court's imposition of sentence was clearly mistaken. **State v. Trunnel,** Op. No. 1260, 549 P2d 550 (Alaska 1976).

A sentence is imposed at the time it is first announced upon the record by the court. **State v. Trunnel,** Op. No. 1260, 549 P2d 550 (Alaska 1976).

When a sentence is reduced under Criminal Rule 35(a), it amounts to the imposition of a new sentence which the state may appeal. **State v. Trunnel,** Op. No. 1260, 549 P2d 550 (Alaska 1976).

Probationer may seek relief by sentence appeal following probation revocation and imposition of sentence of imprisonment. **Giligan v. State,** Op. No. 1378, 560 P2d 17 (Alaska 1977).

Mere assertion that defendant told his attorney that he desired to attack sentence as excessive does not demonstrate that failure to file appeal within 30 days was due to excusable neglect, or that the limit should be relaxed to avoid injustice, where motion for modification of sentence was made two years after sentence was imposed. **Taylor v. State,** Op. No. 1436, 564 P2d 1219 (Alaska 1977).

Denial of a motion to reduce sentence is not the imposition of a sentence for the purpose of paragraph (b) of this rule. **Davis v. State,** Op. No. 1453, 566 P2d 640 (Alaska 1977).

Rule permitting defendant sentenced to 45 days or more to appeal the sentence did not conflict with statute conferring on defendants a limited right to appeal sentences of imprisonment exceeding one year. **Wharton v. State,** Op. No. 1797, 590 P2d 427 (Alaska 1979).

Where defendant pleaded no contest to 11 counts of forgery, sentence of 4 years on each count, to run concurrently, with parole at discretion of parole board, was not excessive. **Stone v. State,** Op. No. 1894, 598 P2d 73 (Alaska 1979).

Where defendant had been convicted of two charges of "joyriding" and had extensive juvenile record, one year imprisonment was not excessive. **Larson v. State,** Op. No. 1902, 598 P2d 947 (Alaska 1979).

A claim of a double jeopardy violation should be appealed not later than 30 days after sentence is imposed. **Nielson v. State,** Op. No. 2349, 627 P2d 1077 (Alaska 1981).

Appeals raising broad legal issues, such as a challenge to the validity of a provision of the presumptive sentencing statute or to the validity of the presumptive sentencing scheme itself, should be regarded as merit appeals rather than sentence appeals. **Juneby v. State,** Op. No. 72, 641 P2d 823 (Alaska App. 1982).

Under highly structured sentencing procedure established by state statute, sentences presumptively imposed will often raise issues of statutory interpretation, challenges to the sufficiency of the evidence under the "clear and convincing" standard, and questions of whether procedures established by the presumptive sentencing statutes were correctly followed, all of which issues are tied sufficiently closely to the ultimate question of excessiveness or leniency to be included within the scope of sentence appeals. **Juneby v. State,** Op. No. 72, 641 P2d 823 (Alaska App. 1982).

It is within the trial court's discretion to grant bail to a person appealing his sentence. **Dobrova v. State,** Op. No. 327, 674 P2d 834 (Alaska App. 1984).

Where defendant was not informed by the trial judge that if he appealed his sentence it could be increased or that by appealing his sentence he waived his right to plead double jeopardy if it were increased, his sentence could not be increased on appeal. **Wilson v. State,** Op. No. 356, 680 P2d 1173 (Alaska App. 1984).

Trial court could not impose a sentence on remand greater than the sentence appealed from where defendant was not warned that his sentence could be increased if he appealed. **James v. State,** Op. No. 814, 754 P2d 1336 (Alaska App. 1988).

Because defendant did not receive a sentence of at least 45 days' imprisonment, he had no right to appeal the sentence. **Johnson v. State,** Op. No. 1156, 816 P2d 220 (Alaska App. 1991).

Defendants convicted of felonies who receive sentences of two years or less to serve are entitled to petition supreme court to review sentence under this rule although by statute they have no right to appeal sentence on ground of excessiveness. **Rozkydal v. State,** Op. No. 1532, 938 P2d 1091 (Alaska App. 1997).

Assertions that sentencing court committed legal error during sentencing process, e.g. that court erred in construing and applying mitigating factors, are appealable regardless of length of defendant's sentence. **Ison v. State,** Op. No. 1538, 941 P2d 195 (Alaska App. 1997).

Defendant may appeal misdemeanor sentence to court of appeals if aggregate unsuspended prison term imposed on all counts exceeds 120 days. **Peters v. State,** Op. No. 1542, 943 P2d 418 (Alaska App. 1997).

Rule 216. Expedited Appeals.

(a) **Scope.** This rule applies to the following classes of appeals, and supersedes the other appellate rules to the extent that they may be inconsistent with this rule:

(1) Extradition appeals;

(2) Peremptory challenge appeals.

(b) **Definitions.**

(1) An appeal from an order of the superior court granting or denying an application for a writ of habeas corpus filed under AS 12.70.090 by a person arrested on a governor's warrant under the Uniform Criminal Extradition Act, is an "extradition appeal." An appeal from any other final judgment of the superior court relating to the extradition of a person charged in this state or elsewhere with a crime is also an "extradition appeal," except that any appeal from a final judgment convicting a person of a crime is not an "extradition appeal."

(2) A "peremptory challenge appeal" is an appeal by a criminal defendant from an order denying the defendant's motion for change of judge under Criminal Rule 25(d).

(c) **Jurisdictional Limitation.** This rule does not permit an appeal to be taken in any circumstances in which an appeal would not be permitted by Rule 202.

(d) **Notice of Appeal.**

(1) A notice of appeal under this rule shall be filed with

the clerk of the appellate courts within 10 days after the date shown in the clerk's certificate of distribution on the order or judgment. The notice of appeal shall be accompanied by the items specified in Appellate Rule 204(b)[1]-[4] and [7].

(2) The notice must indicate that the appeal is being filed pursuant to this rule, but the court of appeals will apply this rule to cases within its scope whether they are so identified or not.

(e) **Record on Appeal.** The entire superior court file shall serve as the record on appeal, together with an electronic recording of any hearing held in superior court if deemed necessary by the court of appeals. The papers in the record on appeal need not be numbered at the bottom consecutively. Promptly upon the filing of the appellee's memorandum, the clerk of the trial courts shall transmit the original and copies of the record to the clerk of the appellate courts in the same manner as for other appeals. Appellate Rule 210(c) shall not apply.

(f) **Memoranda on Appeal.**

(1) *By Appellant.* Within 10 days after filing a notice of appeal under this rule, the appellant shall file with the court of appeals the original and three copies of a memorandum in support of the appeal together with proof of service on all other parties.

(2) *By Appellee.* Within 10 days after service of the appellant's memorandum, the appellee may file with the court of appeals the original and three copies of a memorandum in opposition to the appeal.

(3) *Reply Memorandum.* No reply memorandum may be filed unless ordered by the court.

(4) *Form and Contents of Memoranda.* Memoranda shall comply with Appellate Rule 513.5(b)(6)-(7) and shall also comply with Appellate Rules 212(b)-(c), except:

(A) memoranda need not comply with Rule 212(c)(1)(A)-(E);

(B) no memorandum shall exceed 20 pages without permission of the court; and

(C) the front page of each memorandum shall include the information that Appellate Rule 212(b) requires on the cover of a brief.

(g) **Disposition of Appeals.** Appeals under this rule will be disposed of expeditiously by the court of appeals. If oral argument is requested, it may be held on an expedited basis or telephonically under Rule 505(g) as necessary to ensure an expeditious resolution. The parties' right to oral argument and the procedures governing oral argument are set out in Rule 505.

(SCO 439 effective November 15, 1980; amended by SCO 511 effective August 18, 1982; by SCO 554 effective April 4, 1983; by SCO 575 effective February 1, 1984; by SCO 827 effective August 1, 1987; by SCO 828 effective August 1, 1987; by SCO 926 effective January 15, 1989; by SCO 928 effective January 15, 1989; by SCO 1155 effective July 15, 1994; by SCO 1433 effective October 15, 2001; by SCO 1543 effective October 15, 2004; by SCO 1555 effective October 15, 2004; and by SCO 1598 effective October 15, 2006)

Annotations

Cases

A defendant may appeal the denial of a change of judge motion, and such appeal on the limited issue of peremptory disqualification will be processed pursuant to Appellate Rule 216 governing expedited appeals. **Morgan v. State,** Op. No. 2429, 635 P2d 472 (Alaska 1981).

It is unclear whether a peremptory challenge of a judge in a post-conviction relief proceeding must be made under the criminal rules or the civil rules and whether an appeal from a denial of such a motion must be made on an expedited basis under the Appellate rules. **Hastings v. State,** Op. No. 706, 736 P2d 1157 (Alaska App. 1987).

An expedited appeal under this rule is the exclusive method for seeking appellate review of a denial of a peremptory challenge motion. **Washington v. State,** Op. No. 804, 755 P2d 401 (Alaska App. 1988).

This decision, making an expedited appeal under this rule the exclusive method for seeking appellate review of a denial of a peremptory challenge motion, was not applied retroactively. **Washington v. State,** Op. No. 804, 755 P2d 401 (Alaska App. 1988).

Denial of peremptory challenge of judge in probation revocation proceeding is not subject to expedited appeal under this rule. **Wallace v. State,** Op. No. 1221, 829 P2d 1208 (Alaska App. 1992).

Appeal of superior court's refusal to grant multiple defendants additional peremptory challenges and refusal to allow three of the defendants to object to the fourth's use of their single shared peremptory challenge should be allowed by Appellate Rule 216(a)(2) and 216(b)(2). To the extent there was any doubt that the appeal was a peremptory challenge appeal as defined by Appellate Rule 216(b)(2), the appellate court treated the appeal as a petition for review and granted it. **Moore v. State,** Op. No. 1411, 895 P2d 507 (Alaska App. 1995).

Superior court did not err in precluding three defendants from vetoing a fourth defendant's unilateral exercise of their single shared peremptory challenge in multiple defendant case. **Moore v. State,** Op. No. 1411, 895 P2d 507 (Alaska App. 1995).

Rule 216.5. Expedited Appeals and Petitions in Election Redistricting Cases.

(a) **Scope.** This rule applies to appeals and petitions from the superior court involving challenges to decisions of the Redistricting Board under art. VI, sec. 11, Constitution of the State of Alaska, and supersedes the other appellate rules to the extent that they may be inconsistent with this rule.

(b) **Notice of Appeal.**

(1) A notice of appeal under this rule shall be filed with the clerk of the appellate courts within 2 days from the date shown in the clerk's certificate of distribution on the order or judgment appealed from. The notice of appeal shall be accompanied by the items specified in Appellate Rule 204(b)[1]-[4] and [7]. A notice of cross-appeal shall be filed within 1 day from the date the notice of appeal is filed.

(2) The notice must indicate that the appeal is being filed pursuant to this rule, but the supreme court will apply this rule to cases within its scope whether or not they are so identified.

(3) In addition to service required under Rule 204(h), service of the notice of appeal shall be made on the Redistricting Board, the Office of the Attorney General, and the Office of the Lieutenant Governor.

(c) **Scheduling Conference.** The clerk of the appellate courts shall hold a mandatory scheduling conference within 2 days from the date the first notice of appeal is filed under paragraph (b) above. All parties to the superior court proceedings from which a redistricting appeal arises shall attend the conference. The court may permit telephonic participation. At the scheduling conference, the clerk shall enter a scheduling order that establishes the following:

(1) the dates by which the parties shall file their memoranda on appeal and excerpts of record as described in paragraph (f) below, the last date of which shall be no later than 90 days before the statutory filing deadline for the first statewide election in which the challenged redistricting plan is scheduled to take effect;

(2) the last date for oral argument, unless waived by the parties, which shall be no later than 75 days before the statutory filing deadline described in subparagraph (c)(1).

(d) **Record on Appeal.** Rule 210 shall not apply. The record on appeal consists of the entire superior court file, including the original papers and exhibits filed in the superior court, with pages numbered consecutively. The record on appeal also includes the electronic record of proceedings before the superior court and transcripts, if any. The appeals clerk shall complete the record on appeal within 5 days from the first notice of appeal, and shall notify the clerk of the appellate courts. The clerk of the appellate courts shall serve a notice of certification of the record on all parties to the appeal.

(e) **Excerpts of Record.** Each party shall file and serve an excerpt of record with the party's memorandum on appeal. In cases involving multiple appellants or appellees, each side shall prepare a single excerpt according to the procedure described in Appellate Rule 210(c)(1)(B). Appellants' excerpt must contain a true and correct copy of each document in the record that is cited in their memoranda and is essential to the resolution of an issue on appeal. Appellees' excerpt must contain a true and correct copy of each document in the record relied on in their memoranda but not included in the appellants' excerpt. The form of excerpts is governed by Appellate Rule 210(c)(4).

(f) **Memoranda on Appeal.**

(1) Unless otherwise specified in the scheduling order, no later than 10 days from the scheduling conference the appellant shall file the original and six copies of a typewritten memorandum in support of the appeal and the excerpt of record as provided in paragraph (e), together with proof of service on all other parties,

(2) Unless otherwise specified in the scheduling order, no later than 5 days after service of the appellant's memorandum the appellee shall file the original and six copies of a typewritten memorandum in opposition to the appeal and the excerpt of record as provided in paragraph (e), together with proof of service on all other parties.

(3) No reply memorandum may be filed unless ordered by the court.

(4) The memoranda must comply with Rule 513.5, but need not comply with the requirements of Rule 212 unless ordered by the court.

(g) **Oral Argument.** Unless waived by the parties at the scheduling conference, oral argument will be scheduled on an expedited basis and may be held telephonically as necessary to ensure the participation of all parties to the appeal. The number of counsel allowed to present argument, and the length of argument allowed to each side, shall be determined by the court, and shall ordinarily not exceed one-half hour for each side.

(h) **Petitions for Review.** If the superior court's decision remands the case to the Redistricting Board, any petition for review shall be filed within 5 days of the superior court's decision, and any response shall be filed within 5 days thereafter.

(i) **Disposition of Appeals.** Appeals and petitions under this rule will be decided as expeditiously as possible, and shall have priority over all other matters pending before the court. A decision or order of this court shall be rendered no later than 60 days before the statutory filing deadline for the first statewide election in which the challenged redistricting plan is scheduled to take effect.

(j) **Extensions of Time.** An extension of time under this rule will not be granted without a showing of extraordinary circumstances.

(k) **Personal Same-Day Filing and Service Required.** All documents shall be filed by personal delivery to the office of the Clerk of the Appellate Courts. All service of documents filed under this rule must be achieved by personal delivery on the same day the documents are filed, unless otherwise ordered by the court.

(Adopted by SCO 1456 effective November 15, 2001)

Rule 217. Appeals from District Court.

(a) This rule applies to proceedings in the court of appeals in direct appeals from judgments of the district court under AS 22.07.020(c), and in such appeals supersedes the other appellate rules to the extent that they may be inconsistent with this rule. This rule does not apply to sentence appeals, which are governed by Rule 215, or to appeals from the district court to the superior court, which are governed by Part Six of these rules.

(b) The notice of appeal shall be filed with the clerk of the appellate courts within 15 days after the date shown in the clerk's certificate of distribution on the judgment being appealed. The provisions of Appellate Rule 204(a)(4) shall apply to appeals from the district court. The notice of appeal shall be accompanied by the items specified in Appellate Rule 204(b)[1]-[4] and [7] and a designation of the parts of the electronic record that are essential to a determination of the issues on appeal. The designation (and any counterdesignation) must comply with Rule 210(b)(1)(B).

(c) Unless otherwise ordered by the court of appeals, the record on appeal shall consist of the entire district court file, together with recordings of the parts of the electronic record designated by the parties. Written transcripts may not be prepared except by order of the court of appeals. The papers in the record on appeal need not be numbered at the bottom consecutively. The clerk of the trial courts shall complete the preparation of the record on appeal within fifteen days from the date of filing the notice of appeal. Appellate Rule 210(c) shall not apply.

(d) The appellant's brief shall be served and filed within 20 days after notice of the certification of the record has been served. The appellee's brief shall be served and filed within 20 days after service of the brief of the appellant. The appellant may serve and file a reply brief within 10 days after the service of the brief of the appellee.

(e) Unless otherwise ordered by the court of appeals, the appellant's and appellee's briefs may not exceed 20 numbered pages each, exclusive of appendices. The appellant's reply brief may not exceed 10 pages.

(f) In lieu of filing a brief, any party may instead serve and file a notice that the party wishes to submit the case for decision based on the legal memoranda filed in the district court, without further briefing. An election by one party to submit the case without filing a brief does not obligate any other party to do so. If the appellee files a brief, the appellant may file a reply brief.

The court of appeals may, however, require a brief to be submitted by a party who has filed a notice under this paragraph if it appears that the issues raised on appeal are unclear, that the legal memoranda filed in the district court are inadequate, or that submission of formal briefs would otherwise facilitate disposition of the appeal or serve the interests of justice.

(g) Except as provided in paragraphs (d) and (e) of this rule, briefs shall be prepared, served, filed, and duplicated in the manner prescribed by Rule 212.

(h) A party may request oral argument whether the party has filed a brief or has instead filed a notice under subsection (f) of this rule. The parties' right to oral argument and the procedures governing oral argument are set out in Rule 505.

(SCO 481 effective September 8, 1981; amended by SCO 511 effective August 18, 1982; by SCO 554 effective April 4, 1983; by SCO 781 effective March 15, 1987; by SCO 928 effective January 15, 1989; by SCO 1153 effective July 15, 1994; by SCO 1155 effective July 15, 1994; by SCO 1234 effective July 15, 1996; by SCO 1323 effective July 15, 1998; by SCO 1555, effective October 15, 2004; and by SCO 1598 effective October 15, 2006)

Rule 218. Expedited Appeals in Child Custody Cases.

(a) **Scope.** This rule applies in the following classes of appeals, and in such appeals supersedes the other appellate rules to the extent that they may be inconsistent with this rule:

(1) appeals from final judgments for custody of children, including judgments under AS 25.24.150, AS 25.20.060 or AS 25.20.110;

(2) appeals from final judgments and decrees in adoption proceedings under AS 25.23;

(3) appeals from final judgments in child-in- need-of-aid proceedings under AS 47.10.080 (c);

(4) appeals from final judgments in injunctive actions relating to domestic violence under AS 25.35.010, if the presence or absence of a provision relating to the custody of children in the judgment is an issue on the appeal;

(5) appeals from final judgments rendered under the Uniform Child Custody Jurisdiction Act, AS 25.30;

(6) appeals from final judgments concerning the guardianship of minors under AS 13.26.030 - 085.

(b) **Jurisdictional Limitation.** This rule does not permit an appeal to be taken in any circumstances in which an appeal would not be permitted by Rule 202.

(c) **Bifurcation of Appeals.**

(1) An appeal from the same final judgment which includes points related to the custody of children and points which do not relate to the custody of children (for example, property division or spousal support) will be treated as a single appellate action under this rule unless the court orders that the appeal be treated as two separate appeals for good cause shown.

(2) If the appeal is bifurcated, the portion of the appeal relating to custody of children shall be treated as a separate appeal under this rule. The remainder of the appeal shall be treated as a separate appeal under the other appellate rules relating to appeals in civil actions generally. For purposes of Rule 203, each portion is a separate action, and the pendency of one portion in the appellate court shall not divest the trial court of jurisdiction over the other portion.

(d) **Notice of Appeal and Cross Appeal.** The notice of appeal in an appeal under this rule shall be filed with the clerk of the appellate courts within 15 days after the date shown in the clerk's certificate of distribution on the order or judgment. The notice of appeal shall be accompanied by the items specified in Appellate Rule 204(b)[1]-[7]. The notice must indicate that the appeal is being filed pursuant to this rule, but the supreme court will apply this rule to cases within its scope whether they are so identified or not. A notice of cross appeal may be filed within 14 days after the notice of appeal is filed.

(e) **Time for Completion of Record.** Rule 210 shall apply except that the time for completion of the transcript and page numbering shall be within 30 days after filing of the notice of appeal.

(f) **Serving and Filing Briefs.**

(1) Notwithstanding Rule 212(a)(1), the time for serving and filing the appellant's brief shall be 20 days after notice of certification of the record has been served, the time for service and filing of the appellee's brief shall be 20 days, and the time for service and filing of the reply brief shall be 10 days.

(2) The briefs shall be in the form prescribed by Rule 212(b) and (c).They shall be filed and printed as provided in Rule 212(a), except that on or before the due date an original and six copies shall be filed, together with proof of service. The remaining nine copies shall be filed, and two copies served on each party, within ten days after the original is returned to counsel for duplication and binding.

(g) **Oral Argument.** If oral argument is requested, it may be held on an expedited basis or telephonically under Rule 505(g) as necessary to ensure an expeditious resolution. The parties' right to oral argument and the procedures governing oral argument are set out in Rule 505.

(h) **Disposition of Appeals.** Appeals under this rule will be decided expeditiously by the court.

(i) **Extensions of Time.** A motion to extend a time period referred to in this rule is not a "routine" motion within the meaning of Rule 503(e).

(j) **Waiver.** If an appeal is within the scope of paragraph (a) of this rule, the court will not entertain a motion to waive this rule and consider the appeal under the other appellate rules relating to civil actions generally, unless the motion is filed with a timely notice of appeal and all parties to the appeal, including the guardian ad litem, if any, consent to the motion.

(SCO 579 effective February 1, 1984; amended by SCO 825 effective August 1, 1987; by SCO 888 effective July 15, 1988; by SCO 1004 effective January 15, 1990; by SCO 1112 effective January 15, 1993; by SCO 1155 effective July 15, 1994; by SCO 1369 effective April 15, 2000; by SCO 1433 effective October 15, 2001; and by SCO 1598 effective October 15, 2006)

Annotations

Cases

Mother's appeal of a trial court dissolution proceeding was timely when the entire appeal was taken after the trial court reconsidered its decision on certain property issues and the mother filed an appeal on both the child custody issues and the property issues within 15 days after the reconsideration motion was denied. **Silvan v. Alcina,** 105 P.3d 117 (Alaska 2005).

Litigant's failure to comply with the time limits in subsection (d) of this rule was excused where the filing was late but the record indicated that he made a good-faith effort to appeal by the deadline by sending a letter to the superior court indicating his desire to appeal and asking the court to appoint him counsel, he later wrote the court again expressing worry that his time to appeal would expire if the court did not act on his request, and he was a pro se litigant who filed an appeal within twelve days of obtaining an attorney. **In re Adoption of Erin G,** Op. No. 11929, 140 P.3d 886 (Alaska 2006).

Rule 219. Juvenile Appeals.

(a) **Scope.** This rule applies to the following classes of appeals, and in such appeals supersedes the other appellate rules to the extent that they may be inconsistent with this rule.

(1) appeals from final judgments in juvenile delinquency proceedings under AS 47.12.120(b); and

(2) appeals from orders under AS 47.12.100(a) finding that a minor is not amenable to treatment under AS 47.12.

(b) **Jurisdictional Limitation.** This rule does not permit an appeal to be taken in any circumstances in which an appeal would not be permitted by Rule 202.

(c) **Notice of Appeal.** The notice of appeal under this rule shall be filed with the clerk of the appellate courts within 15 days after the date shown in the clerk's certificate of distribution on the order or judgment. The notice shall identify the appeal as an appeal under this rule, but the court of appeals will apply this rule to cases within its scope whether they are so identified or not. The notice of appeal shall be accompanied by the items specified in Appellate Rule 204(b)[1]-[4], [6], and [7].

(d) **Time for Completion of Record.** Rule 210 shall apply except that the time for completion of the transcript, if ordered, and page numbering shall be within 30 days after filing the notice of appeal. The clerk of the trial courts shall take such steps as may be necessary to insure timely completion of records in cases under this rule, including but not limited to giving the preparation of transcripts in cases under this rule priority over the preparation of transcripts in criminal cases. However, unless otherwise ordered by the Court of Appeals, the record of the trial court proceeding will consist of electronic recordings rather than transcripts. Written transcripts may not be prepared except by order of the Court of Appeals.

(e) **Briefs.** Briefs shall be prepared, served, and filed in the manner prescribed in Rule 212.

(f) **Oral Argument.** If oral argument is requested, it may be held on an expedited basis or telephonically under Rule 505(g) as necessary to ensure an expeditious resolution. The parties' right to oral argument and the procedures governing oral argument are set out in Rule 505.

(g) **Disposition of Appeals.** Appeals under this rule will be decided expeditiously by the court.

(h) **Extensions of Time.** A motion to extend a time period referred to in this rule is not a "routine" motion within the meaning of Rules 503(e) and 503.5.

(Added by SCO 926 effective January 15, 1989; amended by SCO 1155 effective July 15, 1994; by SCO 1433 effective October 15, 2001; by SCO 1482 effective October 15, 2002; by SCO 1555 effective October 15, 2004; and by SCO 1598 effective October 15, 2006)

Rule 220. Judicial Bypass Appeals.

(a) **Scope.** This rule applies to an appeal from an order denying or dismissing a petition filed by a minor under age 17 to bypass parental consent to an abortion under AS 18.16.030. In such appeals, this rule supersedes the other appellate rules to the extent they may be inconsistent with this rule. It also supersedes the procedure for bypass appeals established by AS 18.16.030(j).

(b) **Jurisdictional Limitation.** This rule does not permit an appeal to be taken in any circumstances in which an appeal would not be permitted by Appellate Rule 202.

(c) **Notice of Appeal.**

(1) A minor may appeal an order denying or dismissing a petition to bypass parental consent by filing a notice of appeal in any district or superior court, or directly with the clerk of the appellate courts. The notice of appeal may be filed in person, by mail, or by fax, and must be accompanied by a copy of the order from which the appeal is taken. No filing fee will be charged. If the notice of appeal is filed in a district or superior court, the clerk or magistrate shall immediately notify the clerk of the appellate courts that the appeal has been filed.

(2) The notice of appeal must indicate that the appeal is being filed pursuant to this rule, but the court will apply this rule to cases within its scope whether they are so identified or not.

(3) Blank notice of appeal forms will be available at all court locations and will be mailed or faxed to a minor upon request. No fee will be charged for this service or other services provided to a minor in an appeal under this rule.

(d) **Record on Appeal.** The record on appeal consists of the superior court file, including all papers and exhibits filed in the superior court, and, unless otherwise ordered, a recording of the proceedings before the superior court. The clerk of the appellate courts shall request the record immediately upon receiving notice that the appeal has been filed. Upon receiving this request, the clerk of the trial court shall immediately transmit the record to the supreme court by overnight mail or in another manner that will cause it to arrive within 48 hours after the notice of appeal is filed.

(e) **Brief.** A brief is not required. However, the minor may file a typewritten memorandum in support of the appeal.

(f) **Oral Argument.** Unless the minor waives the right to oral argument in the notice of appeal, oral argument will be held within 72 hours, including weekends and holidays, after the notice of appeal is filed. Upon request, the minor will be allowed to participate telephonically at court system expense.

(g) **Disposition.** The court shall enter an order stating its decision immediately after oral argument or, if oral argument has been waived, within three days after the date the notice of appeal is filed. The court may issue an opinion explaining the decision at any time following entry of the order.

(h) **Constructive Order.** If the court fails to enter an order within five days after the date the clerk of the appellate courts receives the record on appeal, the clerk shall issue a certificate stating that (1) no order was entered within five days after the appeal was docketed; and (2) under AS 18.16.030(j), the failure to enter an order constitutes a constructive order of the court authorizing the minor to consent to an abortion without the consent of a parent, guardian, or custodian. For purposes of AS 18.16.030(j), an appeal is deemed to be docketed on the date the clerk of the appellate courts receives the record on appeal.

(i) **Confidentiality.** Documents and proceedings in an appeal under this rule are confidential. Court personnel are prohibited from notifying the minor's parents, guardian, or custodian that the minor is pregnant or wants to have an abortion, or from disclosing this information to any member of the public.

(j) **Attorney.** If the minor is not represented by an attorney, the clerk of the appellate courts shall appoint the Office of Public Advocacy to represent the minor in the appeal. If the Office of Public Advocacy was appointed to represent the minor in the trial court, the appointment continues through the appeal.

(k) **Filing Defined.** For purposes of this rule only, a document is deemed filed on the date it is received by the district court, the superior court, or the clerk of the appellate courts if the appeal is filed directly with the clerk.

(SCO 1279 effective July 31, 1997)

Note: Under AS 18.16.030(j), the failure to enter a judgment in the appeal within five days after the appeal is docketed constitutes a constructive order of the court authorizing the appellant to consent to an abortion without the consent of a parent, guardian, or custodian.

Rule 221. Settlement Discussions in Civil Appeals.

The attorneys for all parties to a civil appeal to the supreme court shall discuss the possibilities for prompt settlement of all or part of the appeal. This discussion must occur by the date specified in the opening notice issued by the clerk of the appellate courts. The discussion may be conducted by telephone. If the parties reach settlement on any issue on appeal, they shall immediately file an appropriate notice with the clerk of the appellate courts. Otherwise, they shall file a certificate signed by all attorneys that the attorneys, with the knowledge of their clients, have discussed settlement as required by this rule. A settlement discussion is not required in a case in which a party is appearing pro se or in a case that is exempted by the court.

(SCO 1374 effective April 15, 2001)

Rule 222. Settlement Conferences in Civil Appeals.

(a) **Motion for Settlement Conference.** At any time after a notice of appeal is filed, a party may file a motion with the court requesting a settlement conference. The court may order the parties to participate in a settlement conference in response to such a motion, or on its own motion.

(b) **Settlement Officers.** The court may appoint a retired justice or judge, an active judge, or a private neutral to serve as the settlement officer. If the court appoints a private neutral, costs will be borne equally by the parties unless the parties otherwise agree or the court orders costs to be apportioned differently.

(c) **Confidentiality.** Settlement confer-ences will be held in private and are confidential. The settlement officer may report required attendance but shall not otherwise disclose or testify as to any aspect of the conference. The settlement officer shall not participate in subsequent judicial decisions related to the case, unless the parties have waived this disqualification. All conferences, submissions, and statements made in the course of the settlement proceedings required by this rule constitute offers to compromise and statements made in compromise negotiations and are inadmissible pursuant to Evidence Rule 408. This rule does not relieve any person of a duty imposed by statute.

(d) **Conduct of the Conference.**

(1) *Conferences.* The settlement conference will be conducted informally at a location designated by the settlement officer. The parties shall not submit settlement briefs unless requested to do so by the settlement officer. If briefs are requested, they must be submitted directly to the settlement officer, who will return them to the parties who submitted them at the conclusion of the settlement proceedings. A party's brief may not be disclosed to anyone, including any other party, without the submitting party's consent and will not be available to the court. Counsel for a party may attend all conferences attended by that party.

(2) *Termination.* After the initial joint conference and the first round of any separate conferences, a party may withdraw from the settlement proceedings, or the settlement officer may terminate the process if the officer determines that settlement efforts are likely to be unsuccessful. Upon withdrawal by a party or termination by the settlement officer, the settlement officer shall notify the court that settlement proceedings have been terminated.

(e) **Postponement of Briefing and Preparation of the Record.** Settlement proceedings under this rule will not delay preparation of the record, briefing, or excerpts, except by order of the court.

(f) **Results.** If the appeal is resolved or partially resolved as a result of the settlement conference, the parties shall seek an order of dismissal under Appellate Rule 511 as to all or part of the appeal. The parties shall take this action within fifteen days after the settlement proceedings have concluded.

(SCO 1374 effective April 15, 2001)

PART III. PETITION FOR HEARING

Rule 301. Scope of Part Three.

(a) Part Three of these rules (Rules 301 through 305) applies to requests to the supreme court to exercise its discretionary jurisdiction provided in AS 22.05.010(d) to review decisions of the court of appeals.

(b) Part Three also applies to requests to the supreme court to exercise its discretionary jurisdiction provided in AS 22.05.010(d) to review decisions of the superior court in appeals from the district court.

(c) Part Three also applies to requests to the court of appeals to exercise its discretionary jurisdiction provided in AS 22.07.020(e) to review decisions of the superior court in appeals from the district court.

(SCO 439 effective November 15, 1980; amended by SCO 888 effective July 15, 1988)

Rule 302. Petition for Hearing—When Permitted.

(a) **From the Court of Appeals.**

(1) A petition for hearing may be filed in the supreme court with respect to any final decision of the court of appeals, as defined in AS 22.07.030. "Final decision" includes any dismissal by consent of all parties, which closes a matter in the court of appeals, whether or not it contemplates further proceedings in a trial court. "Final decision" also includes a decision of the court of appeals made under Rules 206 or 207. Unless specified otherwise in the particular order in question, it includes but is not limited to, opinions, memorandum opinion and judgments, orders denying petitions for review, orders denying petitions for hearing filed under AS 22.07.020(e), dismissals on motions of the appellee or respondent, and sua sponte dismissals pursuant to Rule 511.5 or another rule.

(2) When a petition for hearing is filed under this subsection, for purposes of Part Three the supreme court is the "court of discretionary review," the court of appeals is the "intermediate appellate court," and the court which entered the judgment which was appealed to the intermediate appellate court is the "trial court."

(b) **From the Superior Court.** (1) A petition for hearing may be filed in the appellate court having statutory jurisdiction, with respect to any final decision of the superior court on an appeal or petition for review from the district court. "Final decision" is defined in AS 22.07.020(e) and includes any decision or order of the superior court, other than a dismissal by consent of all parties, which closes the matter in the superior court, whether or not it contemplates further proceedings in the district court or before an administrative agency. Unless specified otherwise in the particular order in question, it includes but is not limited to, opinions, memorandum opinions and judgments, orders denying petitions for review, dismissals on motion of the appellee or respondent, and sua sponte dismissals pursuant to Rule 511.5 or another rule.

(2) When a petition for hearing is filed under this

subsection, for purposes of Part Three the court in which the petition is filed is the "court of discretionary review," the superior court is the "intermediate appellate court," and the district court is the "trial court."

(SCO 439 effective November 15, 1980; amended by SCO 493 effective January 4, 1982; by SCO 510 effective August 30, 1982; by SCO 989 effective January 15, 1990; and by SCO 1022 effective July 15, 1990)

Rule 303. Procedure on Petition for Hearing.

(a) **Filing.**

(1) A petition for hearing must be filed within 15 days after the date of notice of the opinion, order, or memorandum opinion and judgment of the intermediate appellate court. Date of notice is defined in Civil Rule 58.1(c) and Criminal Rule 32.3(c). The original of the petition shall be filed, together with nine complete copies, a completed docketing statement in the form prescribed by these rules, and proof of service on all parties to the proceeding in the intermediate appellate court.

(2) If a timely petition for rehearing is filed in the intermediate appellate court the full 15-day period for filing a petition for hearing begins to run upon the date of notice of the final order of the intermediate appellate court resolving the matter on rehearing. Date of notice is defined in Civil Rule 58.1(c) and Criminal Rule 32.3(c). Any petition for hearing filed prior to that time will not be entertained.

(3) *Cross-Petitions.* When a petition is filed any other party may file and serve a cross-petition for hearing within fifteen days after service of the petition. Otherwise, the provisions of this rule referring to petitions for hearing also apply to cross-petitions for hearing.

(b) **Format, Length and Contents.** The petition for hearing shall be in the format prescribed by Rule 513.5 (b), shall not exceed fifteen pages in length, excluding the decision of the intermediate appellate court, and shall contain in the following order:

(1) A caption identifying the party filing the petition as the petitioner, and all other parties to the action in the intermediate appellate court as respondents;

(2) A prayer for review;

(3) A short statement of facts relevant to the appeal, but facts correctly stated in the opinion of the intermediate appellate court should not be restated;

(4) A statement of the points relied on for reversal of the decision of the intermediate appellate court, including appropriate authorities;

(5) A statement of concrete reasons, apart from those asserted for reversal, explaining why the issues presented have importance beyond the particular case and require decision by the court of discretionary review, and referring to specific paragraphs of Rule 304; and

(6) A complete copy of the opinion, memorandum opinion and judgment, or order of the intermediate appellate court.

(c) **Response.** Within 15 days after service any other party to the proceeding in the intermediate appellate court may file an original and nine copies of a response, together with proof of service on all parties to the proceeding in the intermediate appellate court. The response shall not exceed fifteen pages in length. Motions to dismiss a petition for hearing will not be received: all objections to exercise of the discretionary power shall be contained in the response. The party filing a petition for hearing may not file a reply to the response without leave of the court of discretionary review. Consideration of the petition for hearing will not be delayed on account of the filing of a motion for leave to file a reply. Oral argument will not be held on the question whether a petition for hearing should be granted.

(d) **Extensions of Time.** The time periods in this rule may be extended only by the court of discretionary review or a justice or judge thereof. They may not be extended by the intermediate appellate court or a judge thereof. Motions for extension of time may be determined by the clerk in the circumstances permitted by Rule 503(e). Motions for extensions of time shall comply with Rule 503.

(e) **Petition for Rehearing.** A petition for rehearing may not be filed in connection with the grant or the denial of a petition for hearing.

(SCO 439 effective November 15, 1980: amended by SCO 554 effective April 4, 1983: by SCO 582 effective February 1, 1984; by SCO 584 effective February 1, 1984; by SCO 770 effective March 15, 1987; by SCO 1133 effective July 15, 1993; by SCO 1212 effective July 15, 1995; and by SCO 1412 effective October 15, 2000)

Rule 304. Grounds for Granting Petition for Hearing.

The granting of a petition for hearing is not a matter of right, but is within the discretion of the court of discretionary review. The following, while neither controlling nor fully measuring that court's discretion, indicates the character of reasons which will be considered:

(a) The decision of the intermediate appellate court is in conflict with a decision of the Supreme Court of the United States or the supreme court of the state of Alaska, or with another decision of the court of appeals.

(b) The intermediate appellate court has decided a significant question concerning the interpretation of the Constitution of the United States or the Constitution of Alaska, which question has not previously been decided by the Supreme Court of the United States or the supreme court of the state of Alaska.

(c) The intermediate appellate court has decided a significant question of law, having substantial public importance to others than the parties to the present case, which question has not previously been decided by the supreme court of the state of Alaska.

(d) Under the circumstances, the exercise of the supervisory authority of the court of discretionary review over the other courts of the state would be likely to have significant consequences to others than the parties to the present case, and appears reasonably necessary to further the administration of justice.

(SCO 439 effective November 15, 1980)

Rule 305. Procedure When Hearing Granted.

(a) Unless the order granting a hearing specifies otherwise,

(1) hearing is granted as to all points raised in the petition (see Rule 303(b) (4)), and

(2) the case shall be briefed in the manner prescribed in Rule 212. The petitioner shall serve and file the petitioner's opening brief within 30 days after service of the order granting a hearing.

(b) The parties' right to oral argument and the procedures governing oral argument are set out in Rule 505.

(c) The party which filed the initial petition for hearing shall be entitled to open and close the argument. Where there are cross-petitions, the petition and cross-petition shall be argued together. In such cases, the order of oral argument shall be determined by the court of discretionary review at the request of either party or upon its own motion.

(SCO 439 effective November 15, 1980; amended by SCO 582 effective February 1, 1984; by SCO 1153 effective July 15, 1994; and by SCO 1598 effective October 15, 2006)

PART IV. PETITIONS FOR REVIEW, ORIGINAL APPLICATIONS FOR RELIEF, AND OTHER SPECIAL PROCEEDINGS

Rule 401. Scope of Part Four.

Part Four of these rules (Rules 401 through 408) governs requests for appellate review in circumstances in which there has been no final judgment within the meaning of Rule 202, or when appellate review is not otherwise available.

(SCO 439 effective November 15, 1980; amended by SCO 1226 effective January 22, 1996)

Rule 402. Petitions for Review of Non-appealable Orders or Decisions.

(a) **When Available.**

(1) An aggrieved party, including the State of Alaska, may petition the appellate court as provided in Rule 403 to review any order or decision of the trial court, not appealable under Rule 202, and not subject to a petition for hearing under Rule 302, in any action or proceeding, civil or criminal. In addition, a party may petition the supreme court as provided in Rule 403(h) to review an unsuspended sentence of imprisonment which is not appealable under Appellate Rule 215(a)(1).

(2) A petition for review shall be directed to the appellate court which would have jurisdiction over an appeal from the final judgment of the trial court in the action or proceeding in which it arises.

(b) **When Granted.** Review is not a matter of right, but will be granted only where the sound policy behind the rule requiring appeals to be taken only from final judgments is outweighed because:

(1) Postponement of review until appeal may be taken from a final judgment will result in injustice because of impairment of a legal right, or because of unnecessary delay, expense, hardship or other related factors; or

(2) The order or decision involves an important question of law on which there is substantial ground for difference of opinion, and an immediate review of the order or decision may materially advance the ultimate termination of the litigation, or may advance an important public interest which might be compromised if the petition is not granted; or

(3) The trial court has so far departed from the accepted and usual course of judicial proceedings, or so far sanctioned such a departure by an inferior court or administrative tribunal, as to call for the appellate court's power of supervision and review; or

(4) The issue is one which might otherwise evade review, and an immediate decision by the appellate court is needed for the guidance of the lower courts or is otherwise in the public interest.

(SCO 439 effective November 15, 1980; amended by SCO 493 effective January 4, 1982; and by SCO 1226 effective January 22, 1996)

Annotations

Cases

I. In General.

The principal purpose of these rules is to afford a remedy of prompt review of an order of the superior court where injustice might result if the petitioner was obliged to bide his time and bring up the matter at a later date on an appeal from a final judgment. It is not intended that this procedure should be used as a substitute for an appeal. **Jefferson v. Moore,** Op. No. 9, 354 P2d 373 (Alaska 1960).

The limitation of the right of the state in appealing contained in Rule 5 does not prevent the state from using the petition for review procedure to question the jurisdiction of the superior court. The order of the superior court granting a new trial after affirmance on appeal will be reviewed under Rule 23(c)(3). **State v. Salinas,** Op. No. 39, 362 P2d 298 (Alaska 1961).

The state may petition for review of a trial court ruling that the accused was a minor thus placing him without the jurisdiction of the court since such ruling affected a "substantial right" of the state to try the accused and prevented a final judgment. **State v. Linn,** Op. No. 47, 363 P2d 361 (Alaska 1961).

When to do otherwise would cause hardship and injustice, the supreme court may, sua sponte, treat a purported appeal as a petition for review. **Leege v. Strand,** Op. No. 157, 384 P2d 665 (Alaska 1963).

An order of the superior court denying petitioner's motion to enjoin respondents from proceeding to organize boroughs under the "Mandatory Boroughs Act," was not an appealable order, but one which may be considered by the supreme court on petition for review. **Walters v. Cease,** Op. No. 182, 388 P2d 263 (Alaska 1964).

This rule relaxes a traditional concept whereby appellate review was available only from final decisions and not from interlocutory orders. **Contento v. Alaska State Housing Authority,** Op. No. 282, 398 P2d 1000 (Alaska 1965).

Matter raised by purported appeal from nonappealable denial of motion for judgment of acquittal was considered as a petition for review. **Stewart v. State,** Op. No. 457,438 P2d 387 (Alaska 1968).

Where a constitutional question of particular substance and importance is at issue, the Supreme Court will consider appeals from a denial of a pretrial motion to dismiss with prejudice as a petition for review and will grant review. **Muller v. State,** Op. No. 666, 478 P2d 822 (Alaska 1971).

Petitions regarding the proper administration of children's proceedings are proper occasions for exercising discretionary review jurisdiction. **In re G.K.,** Op. No. 796, 497 P2d 914 (Alaska 1972).

Where a district court enters a conviction and the superior court on appeal directs an acquittal, the appellate process is construed as beginning when the defendant appeals from the judgment of the district court. The superior court for these purposes is an intermediate appellate court, and the state is not precluded from appealing the superior court's order pursuant to a petition for review. **State v. Marathon Oil Co.,** Op. No. 1098, 528 P2d 293 (Alaska 1974).

Petitions for review and appeal are mutually exclusive procedures. **Jordan v. Reed,** Op. No. 1217, 544 P2d 75 (Alaska 1975).

Where appellate had waived his right to appeal from interlocutory order denying his motion for summary judgment, the proper procedure for contesting the denial would have been a petition for review. **Harold's Trucking v. Kelsey,** Op. No. 1739, 584 P2d 1128 (Alaska 1978).

Appeal from denial of preliminary injunction was improper under Appellate Rule 5 since the denial was not a final judgment, but the appeal was treated as a petition for review under Appellate Rules 23 and 24 because it presented a controlling question of law on which there was substantial ground for difference of opinion and because review at that time would materially advance the ultimate termination of the litigation. **Hagberg v. Alaska Nat. Bank,** Op. No. 1753, 585 P2d 559 (Alaska 1978).

State was not precluded from seeking appellate review of district court's decision to grant a final order of acquittal to defendant on collateral estoppel grounds, despite the state's inability to bring the appeal as a matter of right, so long as appellate review was not barred by state and federal double jeopardy guarantees; implicitly overruling State v. Kemp, 397 P2d 973 (Alaska 1965). **Kott v. State,** Op. No. 2774, 678 P2d 386 (Alaska 1984).

The proper avenue of review of civil contempt citations is a petition for review pursuant to the Appellate Rules. **Kertulla v. Abood,** Op. No. 2858, 686 P2d 1197 (Alaska 1984).

Appellant did not waive objection to trial court order disqualifying his attorney by not seeking immediate review of that order under this rule since rule permits but does not require litigants to petition for review of nonappealable orders. **Matter of Estate of McCoy,** Op. No. 3919, 844 P2d 1131 (Alaska 1993).

This rule does not require a litigant to petition for review of non-appealable orders. **Bostic v. State, Dept. of Revenue,** Op. No. 5052, 968 P2d 564 (Alaska 1998).

II. Granting Review.

A. In General.

Though an important question of law is raised by a petition for review, the determination of which would advance the ultimate termination of the litigation, such factors alone do not constitute ground for departing from the normal appellate route of appeal from a final judgment. **City of Fairbanks v. Schaible,** Op. No. 5, 352 P2d 129 (Alaska 1960).

Trial court denial of a motion for summary judgment against respondent who sought to enjoin the relocation of a highway by petitioner raised an important and controlling question of law; and the denial apparently conclusively determined that question. However, petition for review is not available where none of the conditions of Rule 24 which governs the granting of review has been met. **State of Alaska v. Hillstrand,** Op. No.7, 352 P2d 633 (Alaska 1960).

Confusing and conflicting statements in a petition for review are alone justification for the denial of the petition.

Review is available where the trial judge dismissed a complaint with prejudice in the mistaken belief that he had already allowed two continuances, it also appearing that complete relief could not be had by appeal. **Adams v. Cowan,** Op. No. 32, 360 P2d 1013 (Alaska 1961).

Matter raised by purported appeal from nonappealable denial of motion for judgment of acquittal was considered as a petition for review. **Stewart v. State,** Op. No. 457,438 P2d 387 (Alaska 1968).

Although one or more of the factors contained in Rule 23 may exist, petition for review is not available where none of the conditions contained in Rule 24 are complied with. **State of Alaska v. Hillstrand,** Op. No. 7, 352 P2d 633 (Alaska 1960).

Review of order incarcerating petitioner for the period of time between his adjudication as a delinquent and his dispositive hearing was granted because it presented important questions of law concerning the handling of juvenile cases. **In re. G. M. B.,** Op. No. 687, 483 P2d 1006 (Alaska 1971).

Petitions regarding the proper administration of children's proceedings are proper occasions for exercising discretionary review jurisdiction. **In re G.K.,** Op. No. 796, 497 P2d 914 (Alaska 1972).

Where a district court enters a conviction and the superior court on appeal directs an acquittal, the appellate process is construed as beginning when the defendant appeals from the judgment of the district court. The superior court for these purposes is an intermediate appellate court, and the state is not precluded from appealing the superior court's order pursuant to a petition for review. **State v. Marathon Oil Co.,** Op. No. 1098, 528 P2d 293 (Alaska 1974).

Interlocutory review is warranted in order to determine when a stay may be issued in appeals to the superior court from a decision of the Worker's Compensation Board. **Wise Mechanical Contractors v. Bignell,** Op. No. 2329, 626 P2d 1085 (Alaska 1981).

In reaching its termination decision, the superior court was not required to revisit its earlier placement decision and its termination order superseded all earlier placement orders. The mother could have challenged those placement decisions by requesting superior court review, and could then have petitioned the appellate court for review of the superior court's ruling, however, because the mother failed to seek timely review, the superior court's termination order rendered earlier issues of placement moot. **Erica A. v. State,** Op. No. 5674, 66 P.3d 1 (Alaska 2003).

B. Deviation from Normal Appellate Procedure.

The question of whether Alaska Housing Authority has power by statute to use a declaration of taking to condemn property of the petitioner is of sufficient importance to justify deviation from normal appellate procedure, the trial court having held such power to exist and having allowed a writ of assistance dispossessing petitioner. **Bridges v. Alaska Housing Authority,** Op. No. 1, 349 P2d 149 (Alaska 1959).

An order denying a motion for a jury trial in superior court in an appeal from magistrate court, a trial de novo being available, is reviewable as affecting substantial rights of the accused and raises a question of substance and importance justifying deviation from usual appeal procedure. **Knudsen v. City of Anchorage,** Op. No. 21, 358 P2d 375 (Alaska 1960).

Where motion for dismissal of an indictment raised the question whether a geographical limitation on the selection of jurors is lawful, a denial of the motion was an interlocutory decree affecting a substantial right of the petitioner and involving a question of general importance for which review was granted. **Crawford v. State,** Op. No. 312, 408 P2d 1002 (Alaska 1965).

The question whether a city of the first class may avail itself of a "declaration of taking" in eminent domain proceedings to justify deviation from normal appellate procedure by way of appeal from a final judgment, so that review was granted to an interlocutory order of the superior court "dismissing" such a declaration of taking. **City of Anchorage v. Lot 1 in Block 68 of Orig. Town.,** Op. No. 316, 409 P2d 609 (Alaska 1966).

The supreme court will grant authority to review the dissolution of a temporary restraining order where a question of the trial judge's continuing authority to act in the case after an affidavit for disqualification has been filed is of sufficient substance and importance to justify deviation from the normal appellate procedure. **Channel Flying, Inc. v. Bernhardt,** Op. No. 530, 451 P2d 570 (Alaska 1969).

The review of an interlocutory nonfinal order, such as an order denying a motion to dismiss an indictment, is not a matter of right but one of sound judicial discretion. **Green v. State,** Op. No. 592, 462 P2d 994 (Alaska 1969).

The supreme court will not exercise its discretion and review an interlocutory order unless a litigant establishes that the sound policy behind the rule of finality is outweighed by the need for an early consideration of a nonappealable order. **Green v. State,** Op. No. 592, 462 P2d 994 (Alaska 1969).

Where a constitutional question of particular substance and importance is at issue, the supreme court will consider appeals from a denial of a pretrial motion to dismiss with prejudice as a petition for review and will grant review. **Muller v. State,** Op. No. 666, 478 P2d 822 (Alaska 1971).

Where a nonfinal interlocutory order of the superior court reversing the district court's contempt conviction and remanding the accused's case to district court for a new trial is involved and the state has an interest in preserving the contempt conviction and the district court's implied ruling that the accused is not entitled to a jury trial, the Supreme Court has jurisdiction to review under this rule. **State v. Browder,** Op. No. 699, 486 P2d 925 (Alaska 1971).

A grant of review is appropriate in an action where the constitutionality of a statute is upheld and where the question involved is of such substance and importance as to justify a deviation from the normal appellate procedure by way of appeal and requires the immediate attention of the supreme court. **City of Valdez v. Valdez Development Co.,** Op. No. 866, 506 P2d 1279 (Alaska 1973).

Superior court order dismissing indictment on ground that defendant was not brought to trial within four months from his arrest was of sufficient substance to merit review. **State v. Clouatre,** Op. No. 975, 516 P2d 1189 (Alaska 1973).

Under certain circumstances, an interlocutory order striking a demand for jury will be reviewed to avoid delay until an appeal could normally be perfected. **University of Alaska v. National Aircraft Leasing, Ltd.,** Op. No. 1158, 536 P2d 121 (Alaska 1975).

An order dismissing an indictment for lack of speedy trial, pursuant to a ruling that the time necessary for determination of motions filed by the state was not to be excluded from period for bringing the defendant to trial, is of sufficient substance and importance to merit review. **State v. Strelewicz,** Op. No. 1178, 538 P2d 1009 (Alaska 1975).

Since order of trial court suppressing evidence obtained by search would likely result in terminating the prosecution and involved a controlling question of law, review was appropriate. **State v. Stump,** Op. No. 1250, 547 P2d 305 (Alaska 1976).

Whether defendant accused of drunk driving was entitled to discovery of breathalyzer ampule was a matter of sufficient importance to justify appellate review before entry of final judgment. **Lauderdale v. State,** Op. No. 1254, 548 P2d 376 (Alaska 1976).

Question of whether defendant in civil action for employment discrimination because of sex is entitled to jury trial was sufficiently important that review would be granted before final judgment. **Loomis Electronic Protection, Inc. v. Schaefer,** Op. No. 1262, 549 P2d 1341 (Alaska 1976).

Where Supreme Court concluded that Alaska courts lacked jurisdiction, review before entry of final judgment was appropriate because to postpone review would result in unnecessary delay and expense. **Modern Trailer Sales, Inc. v. Traweek,** Op. No. 1392, 561 P2d 1192 (Alaska 1977).

A petition for review was taken on trial court's denial of motion to disqualify respondent's attorney when reviewing court believed that postponement of review would result in injustice through impairment of a legal right and that the motion was of such importance as to justify deviation from normal appellate procedures. **Aleut Corp. v. McGarvey,** Op. No. 1544, 573 P2d 473 (Alaska 1978).

Appeal from denial of preliminary injunction was improper under Appellant Rule 5 because the denial was not a final judgment, but the appeal was treated as a petition for review under Appellate Rules 23 and 24 because it presented a controlling question of law on which there was substantial ground for difference of opinion and because review at that time would materially advance the ultimate termination of the litigation. **Hagberg v. Alaska Nat. Bank,** Op. No. 1753, 585 P2d 559 (Alaska 1978).

Interlocutory review of pretrial order will be granted where an appeal would cause unnecessary delay and expense to a party and where an appeal may be avoided if issue settled prior to trial. **Priest v. Lindig,** Op. No. 1812, 591 P2d 1299 (Alaska 1979).

Where appeal of one appellee was proper, but appeal of second appellee was not because no final judgment had been entered, the latter appeal was treated as a petition for review, since the two cases presented essentially identical facts and legal questions and because the latter case met the requirements of this rule. **Alaska Nat. Bank of the North v. Gwitchyaa Zhee Corp.,** Op. No. 2399, 639 P2d 984 (Alaska 1981).

Interlocutory review of denial by superior court of motion to dismiss child custody proceeding for want of subject matter jurisdiction was appropriate due to pending proceedings involving the same parties in another state. **Morgan v. Morgan,** Op. No. 2694, 666 P2d 1026 (Alaska 1983).

Although summary judgment was granted in favor of only two of four defendants, and the trial court's order with respect to the other two was not appealable, appellate court decided sua sponte to treat plaintiff's appeal from the order as a petition for review and to grant the same in order to prevent unnecessary delay. **Kendall v. State, Div. of Corrections,** Op. No. 2890, 692 P2d 953 (Alaska 1984).

State's challenge to trial court's refusal to correct an illegal sentence was not within the appellate jurisdiction of the Court of Appeals, but the court, due to the importance of the issue, treated the appeal as a petition for review and granted the petition. **State v. Price,** Op. No. 595, 715 P2d 1183 (Alaska App. 1986).

Although order appealed from was not final order, hence not appealable, Supreme Court treated appeal as petition for review and granted petition, since issue in case was power of superior court to determine underlying cause and case had been briefed and argued. **Puhlman v. Turner,** Op. No.

4090, 874 P2d 291 (Alaska 1994).

Review of sanction order was granted under this rule because postponement of review until final judgment would have needlessly delayed resolution of case and because sanction order departed from accepted and usual course of proceedings with respect to discovery violations. **McGilvary v. Hansen,** Op. No. 4227, 897 P2d 605 (Alaska 1995).

C. Demands of Individual Justice.

Where the trial court has ordered petitioner, defendant in an ejectment action, to pay rent during the pendency of the litigation, review is available, justice and the departure of the trial court from the accepted and usual procedure demanding such. **Stokes v. Van Seventer,** Op. No. 18, 355 P2d 594 (Alaska 1960).

A litigant is required to establish that the sound policy behind the rule of finality is outweighed by the need for an early consideration of a nonappealable order. Factors which are used in the exercising of the supreme court's discretion in granting petitions for review are set out in Rules 23 and 24. **City of Fairbanks v. Schaible,** Op. No. 5, 352 P2d 129 (Alaska 1960).

Issuance of injunction where there has been no showing of irreparable injury results in injustice and is such a deviation from the usual course of judicial proceedings so as to call for supreme court supervision and review. **Miller v. Atkinson,** Op. No. 49, 365 P2d 550 (Alaska 1961).

Where motion for dismissal of an indictment raised the question whether a geographical limitation on the selection of jurors is lawful, a denial of the motion was an interlocutory decree affecting a substantial right of the petitioner and involving a question of general importance for which review was granted. **Crawford v. State,** Op. No. 312, 408 P2d 1002 (Alaska 1965).

The supreme court will grant an immediate review of a trial court's decision where a review of the trial court's decision denying petitioners' request for a judgment declaring an election statute unconstitutional cannot be accomplished by the process of appeal prior to election, and there is a probability that an injustice will be worked on petitioners and others in their class. **Benesch v. Miller,** Op. No. 509, 446 P2d 400 (Alaska 1968).

The supreme court will not exercise its discretion and review an interlocutory order unless a litigant establishes that the sound policy behind the rule of finality is outweighed by the need for an early consideration of a nonappealable order. **Green v. State,** Op. No. 592, 462 P2d 994 (Alaska 1969).

In determining whether to grant a petition for review the supreme court will consider whether the sound policy behind the general rule of requiring appeals to be taken only from final judgments is outweighed by the claim of the individual case that justice demands present and immediate review of a particular nonappealable order or decision. **Hanby v. State,** Op. No. 662, 479 P2d 486 (Alaska 1970).

The supreme court will grant review of a nonappealable order where postponement of that review until appeal will result in an injustice. **Hartford Accident and Indemnity Co. v. State,** Op. No. 803, 498 P2d 274 (Alaska 1972).

The supreme court will review the denial of an untimely motion to disqualify peremptorily a superior court judge, even though such denial would normally be considered a nonappealable order. **Hartford Accident and Indemnity Co. v. State,** Op. No. 803, 498 P2d 274 (Alaska 1972).

In a case in which the accused files a petition for review of the denial of a motion to dismiss the indictment against him following an order of mistrial, the sound policy behind the requirement that appeals be taken only from final judgments is outweighed by demands of justice for present and immediate review of the particular nonappealable order. Review might prevent the accused and state from having to undergo a second lengthy trial. **Webb v. State,** Op. No. 1091, 527 P2d 35 (Alaska 1974).

A petition for review was taken on trial court's denial of motion to disqualify respondent's attorney when reviewing court believed that postponement of review would result in injustice through impairment of a legal right and that the motion was of such importance as to justify deviation from normal appellate procedures. **Aleut Corp. v. McGarvey,** Op. No. 1544, 573 P2d 473 (Alaska 1978).

D. Unusual Trial Court Proceedings.

Where the trial court has ordered petitioner, defendant in an ejectment action, to pay rent during the pendency of the litigation, review is available, justice and the departure of the trial court from the accepted and usual procedure demanding such. **Stokes v. Van Seventer,** Op. No. 18, 355 P2d 594 (Alaska 1960).

Issuance of an injunction where there has been no showing of irreparable injury results in injustice and is such a deviation from the usual course of judicial proceedings so as to call for supreme court supervision and review. **Miller v. Atkinson,** Op. No. 49, 365 P2d 550 (Alaska 1961).

Review was granted where it was clear that the trial court lacked jurisdiction over petitioner, since it would involve needless expense to require the parties to go to trial when any judgment that might be rendered against the petitioner would be void. **Hartwell v. Cooper,** Op. No. 140, 380 P2d 591 (Alaska 1962).

Appellate review of a court order of attorney's fee to the prevailing party in a dismissed third party action was warranted where the court departed from the accepted and usual course of proceedings in dismissing the claim rather than either severing it from the main action or ordering the pleadings amended and the purported third party defendants joined as additional counterclaim defendants. **Aleut Corp. v. Rogers,** Op. No. 2212, 619 P2d 472 (Alaska 1980).

Rule 403. Petitions for Review—Procedure.

(a) **Filing.**

(1) *Petitions.*

(A) A petition for review must be filed with the clerk of the appellate courts within 10 days after the date of notice of the order or decision of which review is sought. Date of notice is defined in Civil Rule 58.1(c) and Criminal Rule 32.3(c). An appellate judge or justice, for good cause shown, may extend the time for filing. The original of the petition must be filed, together with six legible copies, a completed docketing statement in the form prescribed by these rules, and proof of service on the court from whose order the petition is taken and all parties to the action in that court when the order or decision was entered. The party seeking review shall be known as the petitioner. All other parties to the proceeding shall be named as respondents.

(B) The running of the time for filing a petition for review is terminated by a timely motion for reconsideration in the trial court. The full time for a petition for review by any party begins to run again on the date of notice, as defined in Civil Rule 58.1(c) and Criminal Rule 32.3(c), or the date of denial of the motion pursuant to Civil Rule 77(k)(4), whichever is earlier.

(2) *Cross-Petitions.* When a petition is filed under this rule, any other party may file a cross-petition for review of the same order. Cross-petitions must be filed within ten days from service of the petition for review.

(3) *Petitions from Multiple Orders.* Where orders or

decisions arising from different cases or proceedings pending in the same court are sought to be reviewed, and where they involve identical or closely-related questions, a single petition covering all the cases or proceedings may be filed.

(4) *Notice to Trial Court.* Upon the filing of a petition for review, the clerk of the appellate courts shall promptly notify the judge whose order is sought to be reviewed, and the clerk of the judge's court, informing them of the date and identity of the order sought to be reviewed, the name of the party filing the petition, and the docket number assigned to the petition in the appellate court. The clerk of the appellate courts shall also promptly notify them of the action taken by the appellate court on the petition.

(b) **Contents of Petition or Cross-Petition.**

(1) The petition or cross-petition shall contain a:

(A) statement of facts necessary to an understanding of the question or questions determined by the order or decision of the trial court;

(B) statement of the question itself;

(C) statement of the trial date, if scheduled;

(D) discussion of the reasons, under Rule 402, why review should not be postponed until appeal may be taken from a final judgment;

(E) discussion of the reasons why the decision below is alleged to be erroneous;

(F) statement of the precise relief sought; and

(G) if the petitioner or cross-petitioner requests relief by a specific date, a statement of the date by which a decision is needed and the reasons why a decision is needed by that date.

(2) The petition or cross-petition shall not exceed 15 pages in length, exclusive of appendices, and shall include or have annexed thereto:

(A) a copy of the order or decision of which review is sought or a statement of the substance of the order or decision, if it was rendered orally, showing the date of notice as defined in Civil Rule 58.1(c) and Criminal Rule 32.3(c); and

(B) copies of any findings of fact, conclusions of law and opinions related to the order or decision.

(c) **Response.** Within ten days after service of the petition or cross-petition, an adverse party may file an original and six copies of the response, together with proof of service on all parties to the trial court action when the order or decision was entered. The response shall not exceed 15 pages in length, exclusive of appendices. No reply may be filed by the petitioner unless ordered by the court. A motion to dismiss the petition will not be received. Objections to the exercise of the court's power of discretionary review must be included in the response.

(d) **Form.** Petitions, cross-petitions and responses shall be prepared in accordance with Rule 513.5(b). All attachments must be listed in an index submitted with the attachments.

(e) **Inadequacy of the Petition.** The failure of the petitioner to include any matter required by subsection (b) of this rule, or otherwise to present briefly and clearly whatever is essential to a ready and adequate understanding of the questions presented for review, will be a sufficient reason for denying the petition.

(f) **Consideration by the Court.** As soon as practicable, the court will decide whether to grant or deny the petition. Oral argument will not be held on the question of whether the petition should be granted. If the petition is granted, the order granting the petition will specify any further actions to be required. If the court orders further briefing, oral argument will be governed by the procedures set out in Rule 505.

(g) **Denial of Petition.** If the petition is denied, no mandate shall be issued: the clerk shall furnish a copy of the order denying review to the clerk of the trial court involved. A petition for rehearing of the denial of a petition for review may not be filed.

(h) **Petitions for Sentence Review.**

(1) Except as provided in (h)(2), a defendant seeking relief from a sentence under Appellate Rule 215(a)(5) must file a notice of intent to file a petition for sentence review no later than 10 days after the date shown in the clerk's certificate of distribution on the written judgment. If the defendant is indigent, a request for preparation of a transcript of the sentencing proceeding must accompany the notice. The petition itself must be filed no later than 45 days after the date shown in the clerk's certificate of distribution on the written judgment or, if the court is preparing the transcript, no later than 15 days after service of the transcript on the petitioner. The following items must be filed with the petition:

(A) copies of all charging documents;

(B) a copy of the judgment being appealed;

(C) a transcript of the entire sentencing proceeding;

(D) copies of all reports, documents, motions and memoranda pertaining to sentencing which were available to the sentencing court.

(2) If the defendant is filing a combined petition and appeal under Appellate Rule 215(j), a notice of intent to file a petition is not required. Instead, the procedure for perfecting the appeal shall govern, as provided by Rule 215(j).

(3) Paragraphs (e), (h), and (i) of Appellate Rule 215 apply to petitions for sentence review. Appellate Rule 215(d) also applies, except, if the defendant is proceeding under subparagraph (h)(1) of this rule, the notice of intent to terminate must be filed within 30 days after filing of the notice of intent to file a petition for sentence review.

(SCO 439 effective November 15, 1980; amended by SCO 492 effective January 4, 1982; by SCO 554 effective April 4, 1983; by SCO 584 effective February 1, 1984; by SCO 724 effective December 15, 1986; by SCO 725 effective December 15, 1986; by SCO 796 effective March 15, 1987; by SCO 852 effective January 15, 1988; by SCO 996 effective January 15, 1990; by SCO 1023 effective July 15, 1990; by SCO 1092 effective July 15, 1992; by SCO 1153 effective July 15, 1994; by SCO 1212 effective July 15, 1995; by SCO 1226 effective January 22, 1996; by SCO 1271 effective July 15, 1997; by SCO 1302 effective January 15, 1998; by SCO 1412 effective October 15, 2000; by SCO 1553 effective October 15, 2004; by SCO 1598 effective October 15, 2006; and by SCO 1628 effective April 16, 2007)

Note: Ch. 77 SLA 2002 (HB157), Section 2, adds new Chapter 26 to Title 6 of the Alaska Statutes, concerning providers of fiduciary services. According to Section 9 of the Act, AS 06.26.760(b)(2) has the effect of amending Appellate Rule 403 by postponing the deadline for the filing of petitions for review or cross-petitions for review by a trust company when the Department of Community and Economic Development has taken possession of the trust company.

Annotations

Cases

The principal purpose of these rules is to afford a remedy of prompt review of an order of the superior court where injustice might result if the petitioner was obliged to bide his time and bring up the matter at a later date on an appeal from a final judgment. It is not intended that this procedure should be used as a substitute for an appeal. **Jefferson v. Moore,** Op. No. 9, 354 P2d 373 (Alaska 1960).

It is generally not the practice of the supreme court to render written opinions in cases where interlocutory review was denied because such an opinion could be construed as an indication of views on the very issue the supreme court had decided not to entertain at this point. **Contento v. Alaska State Housing Authority,** Op. No. 282, 398 P2d 1000 (Alaska 1965).

Petitions regarding the proper administration of children's proceedings are proper occasions for exercising discretionary review jurisdiction. **In re G.K.,** Op. No. 796, 497 P2d 914 (Alaska 1972).

The limitation this rule places on the length of petitions for review applies to opposition briefs as well. **Alaska Public Utilities Comm. v. Greater Anchorage Area Borough,** Op. No. 1139, 534 P2d 549 (Alaska 1975).

A reviewing court will not substitute its judgment for that of the court below on issue of what would be a proper amount of bail for an accused awaiting trial on criminal charges. **Gilbert v. State,** Op. No. 1190, 540 P2d 485 (Alaska 1975).

Petitions for review and appeal are mutually exclusive procedures. **Jordan v. Reed,** Op. No. 1217, 544 P2d 75 (Alaska 1975).

Original order granting a new trial did not become the "law of the case" when defendant's petition for review was denied; hence the order could be vacated. **Wolff v. Arctic Bowl, Inc.,** Op. No. 1380, 560 P2d 758 (Alaska 1977).

Where appellant had waived his right to appeal from interlocutory order denying his motion for summary judgment, the proper procedure for contesting the denial would have been a petition for review. **Harold's Trucking v. Kelsey,** Op. No. 1739, 584 P2d 1128 (Alaska 1978).

Appellate review of a court order of attorney's fees to the prevailing party in a dismissed third-party action was warranted where the court departed from the accepted and usual course of proceedings in dismissing the claim rather than either severing it from the main action or ordering the pleadings amended and the purported third-party defendants joined as additional counterclaim defendants. **Aleut Corp. v. Rogers,** Op. No. 2212, 619 P2d 472 (Alaska 1980).

The proper avenue of review of civil contempt citations is a petition for review pursuant to the Appellate Rules. **Kertulla v. Abood,** Op. No. 2858, 686 P2d 1197 (Alaska 1984).

Court of Appeals exercised its authority to relax time limit for petitioning for review of non-appealable sentences so that time limit would be calculated from effective date of Court of Appeal's decision rather than from distribution date of trial court's judgement. **Hunt v. State,** Op. No. 1722, 18 P3d 69, 379 P2d 447 (Alaska App. 2001).

Rule 404. Original Applications.

(a) **When Filed.**

(1) An original application for relief may be filed with the appellate court or a judge or justice thereof in any matter within its jurisdiction, whenever relief is not available from any other court and cannot be obtained through the process of appeal, petition for review, or petition for hearing. Grant of the application is not a matter of right but of sound discretion sparingly exercised.

(2) An original application for relief, if seeking relief in connection with an action or proceeding in a trial court, shall be directed to the appellate court which would have jurisdiction over an appeal from the final judgment of the trial court in that action or proceeding.

(3) An original application for relief, if not ancillary to an action or proceeding in a trial court, may be directed to any appellate court having jurisdiction under the applicable statutes.

(b) **Procedure.** A party who seeks original relief shall proceed as follows:

(1) The party must file with the clerk of the appellate courts an original and five legible copies of the application, together with such portion of the record and proceedings of the court below as is needed for the purpose of determining whether the relief sought will be granted, a completed docketing statement in the form prescribed by these rules, and proof of service. The application must state the precise nature of the relief sought, and why that relief is not available in any other court, or by petition for review or by appeal. If the applicant requests relief by a specific date, the application must contain a statement of the date by which a decision is needed and the reasons why a decision is needed by that date.

(2) The application must be served on all other parties to the proceeding in respect of which relief is sought and, if the application pertains to a proceeding in a trial court, on the trial court. If the applicant seeks an order from the appellate court commanding or restraining an act of a person, agency, or tribunal not a party to the proceedings, the application must also be served on such persons, agencies, or tribunals.

(3) If the application seeks a writ of habeas corpus, it shall comply with the requirements of Civil Rule 86(b), and shall state the reason for not making application to the superior court. The application shall also specifically set forth how the

applicant has exhausted all other remedies available by law or rule.

(c) **Response.** Each respondent shall have ten days after service of the application upon the respondent within which to serve and file an original and five legible copies of the response. The court or a judge or justice thereof may, for good cause shown, extend the time for filing. If the application seeks the issuance of a writ of habeas corpus, response shall be made in accordance with Civil Rule 86(g). When the response is filed, it shall be accompanied by proof of service. Replies and supplemental memoranda will not be received unless ordered by the court. A motion to dismiss the application will not be received. Objections to the exercise of the discretionary power of the court must be included in the response.

(d) **Form.** The preparation of all original applications and responses thereto shall be governed by Rule 513.5(b).

(e) **Consideration by the Court.** As soon as practicable, the court will decide whether to grant or deny the application. Oral argument will not be held on the question of whether the application should be granted. If the application is granted, the order granting the application will specify any further actions to be required. If the court orders further briefing, oral argument will be governed by the procedures set out in Rule 505.

(f) **Petition for Rehearing.** A petition for rehearing of the denial of an original application may not be filed.

(SCO 439 effective November 15, 1980; amended by SCO 492 effective January 4, 1982; by SCO 493 effective January 4, 1982; by SCO 584 effective February 1, 1984; by SCO 1153 effective July 15, 1994; by SCO 1212 effective July 15, 1995; by SCO 1598 effective October 15, 2006; and by SCO 1628 effective April 16, 2007)

Annotations

Cases

Where the jurisdiction of the supreme court is invoked, either by way of appeal, by petition for review, or by original application, it or a justice thereof is authorized to stay the enforcement or effect of the judgment appealed from or the order or decisions sought to be reviewed, and to stay proceedings in the court below. **Leege v. Martin,** Op. No. 131, 379 P2d 447 (Alaska 1962).

In view of seriousness of the issue and importance of the right asserted, petitioner's letter addressed to the supreme court complaining that he was denied appointed counsel by the superior court at a hearing at which his probation was revoked, was treated as pro se application for a writ of habeas corpus despite his technical failure to comply with the provisions of this rule. **Hoffman v. State,** Op. No. 297, 404 P2d 644 (Alaska 1965).

This rule does not require that application be made to superior court in all cases. Departure from this rule should be accompanied by some explanation for the failure to apply to the superior court.

Alaska Public Defender Agency had standing to bring proceeding in the nature of an application for original relief to supreme court on question of whether the agency had the authority to represent one accused of violating a city ordinance prohibiting harassment, even though the accused did not appeal his conviction. **Alaska Public Defender Agency v. Superior Court,** Op. No. 1733, 584 P2d 1106 (Alaska 1978).

This rule is appropriate to obtain review of a court order denying an application to compel testimony of a witness who is also the real party in interest in a grand jury investigation. **Surina v. Buckalew,** Op. No. 2255, 629 P2d 969 (Alaska 198 1).

The only method of review for a discovery order is an original application for relief pursuant to this rule. **Kertulla v. Abood,** Op. No. 2858, 686 P2d 1197 (Alaska 1984).

State Senator's appeal from trial court's denial of his motion to quash a subpoena, which required him to appear and give testimony at a deposition, was treated as an original application for relief. **Kertulla v. Abood,** Op. No. 2858, 686 P2d 1197 (Alaska 1984).

Defendant could not obtain appellate review of his sentence by filing an original application for relief where defendant had the right to appeal the sentence he received when his probation was revoked and the superior court imposed his previously suspended jail time. Defendant allowed his right of appeal to lapse and Alaska R. App. P. 404 was not intended to serve as a procedural vehicle for pursuing an untimely appeal. **Lambert v. State,** Op. No. 1800, 45 P3d 1214 (Alaska App. 2002).

Rule 405. Relief Available; Applications for Stay.

(a) **Relief Available.** Relief in the nature of writs of review, mandamus, prohibition, certiorari, or other writs, shall be sought by petition for review under Rule 402 or original application under Rule 404, as may be appropriate. On the granting of a petition for review or original application, the appellate court will grant such relief as may be appropriate in the circumstances, in accordance with Rule 520.

(b) **Stay.** Proceedings in the trial court or the enforcement of any order or decision thereof shall not be stayed by the filing of a petition for review or of an original application for relief unless the trial or appellate court, or a justice or judge thereof, so orders. Application for stay will be granted by the appellate court or a justice or judge thereof only in accordance with Rule 205 or 206.

(SCO 439 effective November 15, 1980)

Annotations

Cases

Where the jurisdiction of the supreme court is invoked, either by way of appeal, by petition for review, or by original application, it or a justice thereof is authorized to stay the enforcement or effect of the judgment appealed from or the order of decisions sought to be reviewed, and to stay proceedings in the court below. **Leege v. Martin,** Op. No. 131, 379 P2d 447 (Alaska 1962).

Rule 406. Review of Proceedings of Commission on Judicial Conduct.

(a) A petition to the supreme court to modify or reject a recommendation of the Commission on Judicial Conduct for reprimand, censure, removal or retirement of a judge may be filed within 30 days after the filing with the clerk of the supreme court and service upon the judge of a certified copy of the recommendation. The petition shall specify the grounds relied on and shall be accompanied by petitioner's brief and proof of service on the chairman of the commission. Within 30 days after receipt of the petition the commission may serve and file a respondent's brief. Within 20 days after service of such brief, the petitioner may file a reply brief which shall be served on the commission.

(b) If no petition is filed the matter may be considered on the merits based upon the record filed by the commission.

(c) Upon recommendation of the commission that a judge be suspended pursuant to AS 22.30.070(b) or on the supreme court's own motion for a suspension, a judge, upon request, shall be provided a hearing before the supreme court.

(d) The rules governing appeals from the superior court in civil cases shall apply to proceedings in the supreme court for review of a recommendation of the commission except where express provision is made to the contrary or where the application of a particular rule would be clearly impracticable, inappropriate, or inconsistent.

(e) The records of all proceedings in the supreme court shall be public from the time of filing the petition in the supreme court.

(f) When the proceedings involve a supreme court justice, no justice may participate in the review, and the chief justice shall appoint a panel from among the court of appeals and superior court judges as justices pro tempore to review the proceedings. If the proceedings involve the chief justice, the justice having the longest tenure on the supreme court who has not participated in the proceedings shall appoint the panel.

(SCO 439 effective November 15, 1980; amended by SCO 569 effective June 1, 1983; by SCO 1153 effective July 15, 1994; and by SCO 1298 effective January 15, 1998)

Rule 407. Certification of Questions of State Law.

(a) The supreme court may answer questions of law certified to it by the Supreme Court of the United States, a court of appeals of the United States, a United States district court, a United States bankruptcy court or United States bankruptcy appellate panel, when requested by the certifying court if there are involved in any proceeding before it questions of law of this state which may be determinative of the cause then pending in the certifying court and as to which it appears to the certifying court there is no controlling precedent in the decisions of the supreme court of this state.

(b) This rule may be invoked by an order of any of the courts referred to in Section (a).

(c) A certification order shall set forth:

(1) The questions of law to be answered; and

(2) A statement of all facts relevant to the questions certified and showing fully the nature of the controversy in which the questions arose.

(d) The certification order shall be prepared by the certifying court, signed by the judge presiding over the cause, and forwarded to the supreme court by the clerk of the certifying court under its official seal. The supreme court may require the certifying court to file the original or copies of all or any portion of the record before the certifying court if, in the opinion of the supreme court, the record or portion thereof may be necessary in answering the questions.

(e) Notice of the supreme court's decision whether to answer the questions certified to it shall be given to the certifying court by the clerk of the supreme court. Further proceedings, if any, in the supreme court shall be in accordance with the provisions of these rules governing briefs and arguments, unless otherwise ordered by the court.

(f) The written opinion of the supreme court stating the law governing the questions certified shall be sent by the clerk of the supreme court to the certifying court and to the parties. The answer to the certified questions shall be res judicata as to the parties and have the same precedential force as any other appellate decision of the supreme court.

(SCO 439 effective November 15, 1980; amended by SCO 1068 effective July 15, 1991)

Annotations

Cases

Where issue sought to be certified for the first time on appeal was only one of many involved in the litigation and was not necessarily determinative of the cause pending before the certifying court, motion to certify was denied. **In re Complaint of McLinn,** 744 F.2d 677 (9th Cir. 1984).

Rule 408. Transfer of Appellate Cases.

(a) When the supreme court transfers a case to the court of appeals pursuant to AS 22.05.015(a), the clerk shall serve a copy of the transfer order on all parties. The court of appeals or the clerk shall thereupon advise the parties of the course of proceedings to be followed in the court of appeals.

(b) When the court of appeals certifies to the supreme court that a case should be decided by the supreme court, pursuant to AS 22.05.015(b), a copy of the certificate, and of the order of the supreme court accepting or rejecting it, shall be served on all parties. Unless the supreme court orders to the contrary, pleadings from the parties addressing the question whether or not the supreme court should accept the certificate, will not be received. Requests that the court of appeals issue such a certificate should be addressed to the court of appeals, must be accompanied by proof of service on all parties, and must state clearly and concisely why the case fits within the statutory standards. The court of appeals may in its discretion request responses from the other parties. A decision of the court of appeals refusing to issue such a certificate may not be the subject of a petition for hearing in the supreme court.

(c) When a case is transferred between appellate courts pursuant to AS 22.05.015(c), the transferring court or the clerk shall advise the parties of the reasons for the transfer, and the transferee court or the clerk shall advise the parties of the course of proceedings which will be followed in the transferee court.

(SCO 439 effective November 15, 1980)

PART V. GENERAL PROCEDURES

Rule 501. Scope of Part Five.

Part Five of these rules (Rules 501 through 523) applies to all proceedings in the supreme court and the court of appeals.

(SCO 439 effective November 15, 1980)

Rule 502. Time—Computation and Extension.

(a) **Computation.** In computing any period of time prescribed or allowed by these rules, by order of court, or by any applicable statute, the day of the act, event, or default after which the designated period of time begins to run is not to be included. The last day of the period so computed is to be included, unless it is a Saturday, Sunday or legal holiday, in which event the period runs until the end of the next day which is neither Saturday, Sunday nor a holiday. When the period of time prescribed or allowed is less than seven days, intermediate Saturdays, Sundays and holidays shall be excluded in the computation. A half holiday shall be considered as other days and not as a holiday.

(b) **Extensions of Time.** When by these rules or by a notice given thereunder or by order of the appellate court an act is required or allowed to be done at or within a specified time, the appellate court may in its discretion, either on motion of a party, showing good cause, or sua sponte:

(1) Extend the time period, either before or after its expiration or

(2) Validate an act done after the expiration of the time period.

Motions to extend a time period, or to validate an act done after the expiration of the time period, must comply with Rule 503. Time periods specified in the Appellate Rules, including time periods for doing an act or filing a document in the trial court, may be extended only by the appellate courts and not by the trial court. In a matter requesting review of or appealing a criminal conviction or sentence, this rule does not authorize an appellate court, or the superior court acting as an intermediate appellate court, to validate the filing of a notice of appeal, petition for review, or petition for hearing more than 60 days after the expiration of the time specified in the rule or statute or in the last extension of time previously granted.

(c) **Additional Time After Service or Distribution by Mail.** Whenever a party has the right or is required to act within a prescribed number of days after the service or distribution of a document, and the document is served or distributed by mail, three calendar days shall be added to the prescribed period. However, no additional time shall be added if a court order specifies a particular calendar date by which an act must occur.

(d) **Mailing of Papers for Filing.** Papers may be filed either by delivering them to the office of the clerk of the appellate courts in Anchorage or Juneau, or by mailing them to: Clerk of the Appellate Courts, 303 K Street, Anchorage, Alaska 99501. The date of mailing, as shown by the postmark or other proof from the post office, will be deemed to be the date of filing. A postmark date from a privately owned postage meter will not suffice as proof of the date of mailing and papers postmarked in this manner will be deemed filed on the date of receipt by the clerk.

(SCO 439 effective November 15, 1980; amended by SCO 554 effective April 4, 1983; by SCO 1153 effective July 15, 1994; by SCO 1155 effective July 15, 1994; by SCO 1341 effective September 10, 1998; by SCO 1524 effective October 15, 2005; and by SCO 1639 effective October 15, 2007)

Note to SCO 1341: Appellate Rule 502(b) was amended by § 10, ch. 95 SLA 1998 to prohibit the court from allowing an appeal or request for review of a criminal conviction or sentence to be filed more than 60 days after the expiration of the time specified in the rule or statute or in the last extension of time previously granted. Section 1 of this order is adopted for the sole reason that the legislature has mandated the amendment.

Note: Ch. 77 SLA 2002 (HB157), Section 2, adds new Chapter 26 to Title 6 of the Alaska Statutes, concerning providers of fiduciary services. According to Section 9 of the Act, AS 06.26.760(b)(2) has the effect of amending Appellate Rule 502 by postponing the deadlines set in the Alaska Rules of Appellate Procedure for the filing of documents by a trust company when the Department of Community and Economic Development has taken possession of the trust company.

Annotations

Cases

The supreme court will grant review where the defendant establishes that he intended to appeal his conviction, communicated such desire to his attorney, and thereafter thought an appeal had been taken on his behalf, and where the defense attorney concluded no grounds existed for appeal but failed to relate that conclusion to the defendant. **McCracken v. State,** Op. No 677, 482 P2d 269 (Alaska 1971).

In proceedings wherein the defendant seeks an extension of time for appeal, it is unnecessary for the defendant to prove he has meritorious grounds for appeal as a prerequisite of his right to appeal. **McCracken v. State,** Op. No 677, 482 P2d 269 (Alaska 1971).

Mere assertion that defendant told his attorney that he desired to attack sentence as excessive does not demonstrate that failure to file appeal within 30 days was due to excusable neglect, or that the limit should be relaxed to avoid injustice, where motion for modification of sentence was made two years after sentence was imposed. **Taylor v. State,** Op. No. 1436, 564 P2d 1219 (Alaska 1977).

Because the decision whether to grant or deny an extension to file briefs in an administrative appeal is committed to the trial court's discretion, Supreme Court will reverse the decision only if it finds an abuse of discretion. **Sheehan v. University of Alaska,** Op. No. 2942, 700 P2d 1295 (Alaska 1985).

Trial court abused its discretion when it denied appellant's request for a second extension of time to file an opening brief in an administrative appeal, since although appellant's tardiness went beyond normal excusable oversight, there was no interference with the trial court's efficient functioning, no prejudice to the parties or to the court, and no intended affront to the court's authority. **Sheehan v. University of Alaska,** Op. No. 2942, 700 P2d 1295 (Alaska 1985).

Negligence of attorney in failing to timely file appeal from adverse decision of Alaska Workers' Compensation Board was not sufficient ground to relieve the attorney's client of the filing requirement. **Beavers v. Alaska Const., Inc.,** Op. No. 3560, 787 P2d 643 (Alaska 1990).

Legislature's 1995 amendment to Appellate Rule 521 did not affect appellate court's authority under Appellate Rule 502 to accept criminal appeals filed more than 60 days late for good cause shown. **Ozenna v. State,** 921 P2d 640 (Alaska App. 1996); superseded by statute as stated in **Lambert v. State,** Op. No. 1800, 45 P3d 1214 (Alaska App. 2002).

Peremptory challenge to assigned trial judge was filed when received, not when mailed, since an exception to the common law rule in the appellate rules applied only to appellate filing, and the movant failed to provide any evidence in support of an argument that a discretionary relaxation of the rules would be appropriate in the interests of justice. **Black v. State,** Op. No. 1896, 76 P.3d 417 (Alaska App. 2003).

Rule 503. Motions.

(a) **General.** An application for relief of any kind from either appellate court ancillary to a case in that court shall be made by written motion. A stipulation is not sufficient.

(b) **Format.** A motion filed in the appellate courts must be in the form prescribed by Rule 513.5(b). The motion must include:

(1) a brief, complete statement of the reasons in support of the motion;

(2) an affidavit where the facts relating to the motion are not otherwise proven;

(3) if the motion is for an extension of a time period prescribed in these rules, a statement of each extension of that time period previously granted to that party, indicating the length of each extension;

(4) the points and authorities on which the moving party relies;

(5) an appropriate order for execution by the court should the motion be granted; and

(6) if the moving party requests relief by a specific date, a statement of the date by which a decision is needed and the reasons why a decision is needed by that date.

(c) **Filing and Service.** The original of all motions and responses must be filed with the clerk, together with proof of service on all other parties. The following copies must be submitted with the original:

(1) five copies of a motion that must be decided by the full supreme court pursuant to Appellate Rule 503(g) or a response to such motion;

(2) three copies of a motion that must be decided by the full court of appeals pursuant to Appellate Rule 503(g) or a response to such motion;

(3) one copy of all other motions or responses.

(d) **Opposition to Motion—Disposition.** Adverse parties have seven days after service of a motion within which to file and serve memoranda in opposition, counter motions and affidavits. As soon as practical after expiration of the seven-day period, the motion will be considered. A reply memorandum may not be filed by the moving party unless otherwise ordered. Oral argument will not be heard on motions unless otherwise ordered. If a motion is decided before expiration of the time for opposition, the filing of a timely opposition requires that the motion be considered de novo.

(e) **Motions Determined by the Clerk.** Routine, unopposed motions may be ruled upon by the clerk without referral to an individual judge or justice or the full court. Routine motions for extensions of time for filing briefs may be ruled upon by the clerk pursuant to Appellate Rule 503.5. The clerk may not determine a motion to extend the time for filing a notice of appeal, petition for review, petition for rehearing, or petition for hearing. The clerk may not determine a motion for extension of time to file a document if the time period specified in these rules for filing the document, including any previous extensions, has already expired when the motion is filed. The clerk has the discretion to refer motions that may be determined by the clerk to an individual justice or judge for decision.

(f) **Motions Determined by an Individual Justice or Judge.** Any motions not described in paragraph (g) may be determined by an individual justice or judge without referral to the full court. A justice or judge has the discretion to refer such a motion to the full court for decision.

(g) **Motions Determined by Full Court.** A motion that would have the effect of determining the merits of a proceeding, or a motion referred to the full court by a justice or judge, shall be considered by the full court. An individual justice or judge may, in connection with such a motion, enter such orders as may be necessary to prevent irreparable harm prior to the time that the full court is able to consider the motion.

(h) **Motions for Reconsideration.**

(1) *Filing.* A party who is aggrieved by an order may move for reconsideration of the order. A motion for reconsideration must be filed within ten days after the date of notice of the order, as defined in Civil Rule 58.1(c) and Criminal Rule 32.3(c).

(2) *Determination.* Motions for reconsideration under this rule shall be determined as follows:

(A) a motion for reconsideration of an order entered by the clerk under subparagraph (e) shall be determined by an individual justice or judge;

(B) a motion for reconsideration of an order entered by an individual justice or judge under subparagraph (f) shall be determined by the full court; and

(C) a motion for reconsideration of an order entered by the full court under subparagraph (g) shall be determined by the full court.

(3) *Response.* The non-moving party may respond to a motion for reconsideration to be determined under subparagraphs (h)(2)(A) or (h)(2)(B) by filing an opposition within seven days after the motion is served. No response may be made to a motion for reconsideration to be determined under subparagraph (h)(2)(C) unless requested by the court, but a motion for reconsideration will ordinarily not be granted without affording the non-moving party an opportunity to respond.

(SCO 439 effective November 15, 1980; amended by SCO 516 effective October 1, 1982; by SCO 561, effective May 2, 1983; by SCO 584 effective February 1, 1984; by SCO 827 effective August 1, 1987; by SCO 869 effective July 15, 1988; by SCO 870 effective July 15, 1988; by SCO 1153 effective July 15, 1994; by SCO 1166 effective July 15, 1994; by SCO 1167 effective July 15, 1994; by SCO 1409 effective October 15, 2000; by SCO 1440 effective October 15, 2001; and by SCO 1628 effective April 16, 2007)

Note: See Appellate Rule 508(f)(2) for motions for reconsideration of orders awarding costs or attorney's fees under Appellate Rule 508.

Rule 503.5. Extensions of Time for Filing Briefs.

(a) **General.** A motion for extension of time for filing a brief in the supreme court or the court of appeals must comply with the requirements of Rule 503(a), (b), (c) and (d).

(b) **Routine Motions.**

(1) The clerk of the appellate courts may grant or deny a routine motion for extension, whether or not the motion is opposed, subject to a motion for reconsideration to be decided by a single judge or justice.

(2) Except as provided in subparagraph (b)(3), an appellant may request routine extensions for opening and reply briefs totaling not more than forty-five days in appeals from district or superior court judgments, original applications, certification of, questions of state law by a federal court, or granted petitions for hearing or review where the court has directed further briefing on the merits. No routine extensions in excess of fifteen days will be granted for the filing of an appellant's reply brief. Appellees may request routine extensions not to exceed thirty days.

(3) Motions requesting routine extensions may not be filed in the following matters:

[a] appeals filed under Rules 215-220;

[b] appeals by the prosecution testing the sufficiency of the indictment; and

[c] matters relating to attorney discipline or disability.

(4) Any other motion for extension of time to file a brief will be classified as a non-routine motion and will be decided by a single appellate judge or justice.

(c) **Non-Routine Motions.** (1) A non-routine motion for an extension of time will be granted only upon a showing of diligence and substantial need. The motion must be filed before the expiration of the time prescribed for filing the brief, and must be accompanied by an affidavit stating:

(A) when the brief is due;

(B) when the brief was first due and the number and length of previous extensions requested;

(C) the length of the requested extension;

(D) the reason an extension is necessary;

(E) movant's representation that movant has exercised diligence and that the brief will be filed within the time requested; and

(F) whether any other party separately represented objects to the request, or why the moving party has been unable to determine any such party's position. A conclusory statement as to the press of business does not constitute a showing of diligence and substantial need.

(2) A non-routine motion that would extend the time for filing a brief more than 60 days beyond the original due date will be granted only upon a showing of extraordinary and compelling circumstances and may be conditioned on the payment of sanctions in a sum of not more than $500. In a civil case, the court may order that such sanctions be paid to parties who have opposed the extension.

(d) **Oppositions to Motions for Extension.** If a timely opposition to a motion for extension is filed after the motion for extension is granted, the opposition will be treated as a motion for reconsideration and will be assigned to a justice or judge for determination pursuant to Rule 503(f). Any party objecting to the ruling on such a motion for reconsideration may move for reconsideration by the full court pursuant to Rule 503(g).

(SCO 871 effective July 15, 1988; amended by SCO 926 effective January 15, 1989; by SCO 1209 effective July 15, 1995; by SCO 1279 effective July 31, 1997; and by SCO 1410 effective October 15, 2000)

Rule 504. Emergency Motions.

Whenever a party requests expedited action on a motion on the ground that, to avoid irreparable harm, relief is needed in less time than would normally be required for the court to receive and consider a response:

(a) The motion shall comply with Appellate Rule 503(b)* except as that rule may be specifically inconsistent with this one;

(b) The word "Emergency" shall be placed at the top of the first page of the motion;

(c) The motion shall include the telephone numbers and office addresses of moving and opposing counsel;

(d) The motion shall be accompanied by a written statement of facts showing the nature of the emergency and the date and hour before which a decision is needed;

(e) The motion shall state whether all grounds advanced in support thereof were submitted to the trial court and, if not, why the motion should not be remanded to the trial court for reconsideration;

(f) The motion shall be accompanied by a written

statement by the movant or the movant's attorney, indicating when and how opposing counsel was notified of the motion, or, if opposing counsel was not notified, indicating what efforts were made to notify opposing counsel and why it was not practicable to notify opposing counsel in a manner and at a time that counsel could respond to the motion;

(g) The court will not grant the motion prior to written or oral notice to opposing counsel unless it clearly appears from specific facts in the motion papers or the court records that immediate and irreparable injury, loss or damage would result to the applicant before notice could be given and opposing counsel given a reasonable opportunity to respond.

If an emergency motion is granted without notice to opposing counsel and opposing counsel thereafter files a motion to vacate or reconsider the order thus entered, the court will take into account the fact that the original order was entered without notice.

If it appears appropriate in the circumstances, the court or the judge or justice to whom the matter is assigned may permit the opposing party to respond to the motion orally rather than in writing. As provided in Rule 503 (d), oral argument of emergency motions is not permitted unless ordered by the court or a judge or justice.

(SCO 439 effective November 15, 1980; amended by SCO 1153 effective July 15, 1994)

***Editors Note:** The citation to Appellate Rule 503(b), originally designated as Rule 503(c), was corrected during publication to conform to the court's intent.

Rule 505. Oral Argument.

(a) **Oral Argument; Requests for Oral Argument.** Unless otherwise ordered by the court, oral argument will be held only as provided in this subsection.

(1) In expedited election appeals under Rule 216.5 and judicial bypass appeals under Rule 220, oral argument will automatically be held unless it is affirmatively waived under Rule 216.5(g) or Rule 220(f).

(2) In all other appeals governed by Part Two of these rules, oral argument will be held if it is timely requested. A request for oral argument is timely if it is made not later than 10 days after the due date of the reply brief or, if no reply brief is allowed, not later than 10 days after the due date of the appellee's brief.

(3) In all petitions or applications for discretionary review governed by Parts Three and Four of these rules, the parties have no right to oral argument unless the appellate court grants review and orders further briefing. If review is granted and further briefing is ordered, oral argument will be held if a party timely requests it. A request for oral argument is timely if it is made not later than 10 days after the due date of the reply brief or, if no reply brief is allowed, not later than 10 days after the due date of the respondent's brief.

(4) When the parties have a right to oral argument, a timely request for oral argument by any party will give all parties the right to orally argue the case, except for appellees who fail to file a brief, as provided in Rule 212(c)(10).

(b) **Scheduling.** The clerk shall prepare the calendars of cases for oral argument, under the direction of the courts. The clerk shall give written notice to counsel of record of the time and place at which argument is scheduled.

(c) **Postponement.** Once a case has been placed on the calendar for oral argument, argument will not be postponed except upon filing of a motion accompanied by an affidavit of counsel or the party or both showing good cause for postponement. Notwithstanding Rule 503(e), such a motion shall not be ruled upon by the clerk.

(d) **Limitation of Counsel.** Unless otherwise ordered by the court, no more than two counsel will be heard for each party on the argument of the case.

(e) **Length of Arguments.** The length of oral argument shall be prescribed by the clerk at the direction of the court.

(f) **Opening and Conclusion.** The appellant, petitioner, or applicant shall be entitled to make opening and rebuttal arguments. When there is a cross-appeal, the appeal and cross-appeal shall be argued together, and the order of oral argument shall be determined by the court at the request of either party or upon its own motion. No surrebuttal argument will be allowed unless the court directs otherwise.

(g) **Expedited Appeals; Preference.** If a party requests oral argument in an expedited appeal or in a case that is entitled to preference by law, court rule, or order, the court may, upon motion of a party or on its own initiative, schedule oral argument on an expedited basis, and the argument may be held telephonically as necessary to ensure the participation of all parties.

(SCO 439 effective November 15, 1980; amended by SCO 582 effective February 1, 1984; by SCO 1433 effective October 15, 2001; by SCO 1598 effective October 15, 2006; and by SCO 1638 effective October 15, 2007)

Rule 506. Rehearing.

(a) **Grounds for Petition.** The court may order a rehearing of a matter previously decided if, in reaching its decision:

(1) The court has overlooked, misapplied or failed to consider a statute, decision or principle directly controlling; or

(2) The court has overlooked or misconceived some material fact or proposition of law; or

(3) The court has overlooked or misconceived a material question in the case.

A rehearing will not be granted if it is sought merely for the purpose of obtaining a reargument on and reconsideration of matters which have already been fully considered by the court.

(b) **Time for Filing—Form of Petition.** An original and five copies of a petition for rehearing must be filed within 10 days after the date of notice of the opinion or other decision. Date of notice is defined in Civil Rule 58.1(c) and Criminal Rule 32.3(c). The petitioner shall specifically state which of the grounds for rehearing specified in paragraph (a) exists, and shall specifically designate that portion of the opinion, the brief, or the record, or that particular authority, which the petitioner wishes the court to consider. The petition shall be prepared in conformity with Rule 513.5(b) and when filed shall be accompanied by proof of service on all parties. No petition for rehearing shall exceed five typewritten pages. No memoranda or briefs in support of a petition for rehearing, and no response to a petition for rehearing, shall be received unless requested by the court.

(SCO 439 effective November 15, 1980; amended by SCO 554 effective April 4, 1983; by SCO 584 effective February 1, 1984; by SCO 688 effective May 1, 1986; by SCO 718 effective September 15, 1986; and by SCO 827 effective August 1, 1987)

Annotations

Cases

Rehearing was granted on state's representation that a portion of its argument had been misconstrued. **State v. Keep,** Op. No. 313, 409 P2d 321 (on hearing). (Alaska 1965).

Questions raised for the first time on petition for rehearing will not be considered by the supreme court. **Watts v. Seward School Board,** Op. No. 380, 423 P2d 678 (on rehearing). (Alaska 1967).

An argument not raised on appeal will not be considered on rehearing. **Wernberg v. State,** Op. No. 972, 519 P2d 801 (Alaska 1974).

On appeals of workman's compensation decision to superior court, superior court did not abuse its discretion in reducing the original fee award to appellees following appellant's motion to reconsider by (1) not requesting a reply from appellees to appellant's motion for reconsideration or (2) by reducing the fee award because appellees' brief was excessive. **Childs v. Tulin,** Op. No. 3645, 799 P2d 1338 (Alaska 1990).

This rule was not intended to allow parties to raise new arguments after they have had a chance to analyze an appellate court decision; the rule implicitly limits rehearing to legal principle or propositions that were raised by the parties in the normal course of the appeal. **Booth v. State,** Op. No. 1428, 903 P2d 1079 (Alaska App. 1995).

Alaska R. App. P. 506(a) allows a party to seek rehearing when an appellate court overlooks or fails to consider a principle directly controlling the decision on appeal, or when an appellate court overlooks a material proposition of law; however, it is not intended to allow parties to raise new arguments after they have had a chance to analyze an appellate court's decision, and it implicitly limits rehearing to legal principles or propositions that were raised by the parties in the normal course of the appeal. **Carpentino v. State,** Op. No. 1790,42 P3d 1137, 583 P2d 847 (Alaska App. 2002).

Rule 507. Judgment.

(a) The opinion of the appellate court, or its order under Rule 214, shall constitute its judgment, and shall contain its directions to the trial court, if any. No mandate shall be issued.

(b) Unless the opinion or order expressly states otherwise, the judgment of the appellate court takes effect and full jurisdiction over the case returns to the trial court on the day specified in Rule 512(a) for return of the record. However, in an appeal under Appellate Rule 207 relating to release prior to judgment, the judgment of the Court of Appeals takes immediate effect and full jurisdiction over the case returns to the trial court on the day the Court of Appeals issues its opinion or order deciding the appeal.

(c) A motion to stay the effect of the judgment of the appellate court beyond the day specified in Rule 512(a) shall be made to that court.

(SCO 439 effective November 15, 1980; amended by SCO 551 effective February 1, 1983; amended by SCO 729 effective December 15, 1986)

Annotations

Cases

An order of dismissal by the supreme court is not in itself a mandate. **Singletary v. State,** Op. No. 1711, 583 P2d 847 (Alaska 1978).

Although appellate court opinion reversing defendant's conviction and remanding the case for a new trial was issued on June 6, 1986, the opinion did not become operative and had no force or validity as an order for a new trial until the date specified for return of the record, thus the date specified for return, not the issuance date, triggered commencement of the 120 day speedy trial period. **Nitz v. State,** Op. No. 759, 745 P2d 1379 (Alaska App. 1987).

Rule 508. Costs.

(a) **Dismissal or Denial.** If an appeal is dismissed or petition denied by the appellate court, costs shall not be allowed to the appellee or respondent, unless otherwise ordered by the court.

(b) **Affirmance of Judgment.** In all cases of affirmance of a judgment or any order or decision of the superior court, costs shall be allowed to the appellee or respondent unless otherwise ordered by the court.

(c) **Reversal or Partial Reversal.** In cases of reversal of any judgment, order or decision of the superior court, costs shall be allowed the appellant or petitioner unless otherwise ordered by the court. In cases of partial affirmance and partial reversal, the court will determine which party, if any, shall be allowed costs.

(d) **Costs to be Awarded.** When costs are awarded in the appellate court, they shall include, unless the court otherwise orders and subject to Rules 210(b)(6) and (c)(6), the filing fee, the costs of preparing the transcript, premiums for any bond under Rule 204(c) or 204(d), and the costs of duplicating and mailing briefs and excerpts of records. Duplicating costs will not be awarded in excess of the rate generally charged by printers in the city in which counsel is located.

(e) **Attorney's Fees.** Attorney's fees may be allowed in an amount to be determined by the court. If such an allowance is made, the clerk shall issue an appropriate order awarding fees at the same time that an opinion or an order under Rule

214 is filed. If the court determines that an appeal or cross-appeal is frivolous or that it has been brought simply for purposes of delay, actual attorney's fees may be awarded to the appellee or cross-appellee.

(f) **Procedure.**

(1) *Bill of Costs.* At the time an opinion or an order under Rule 214 is filed, the clerk shall notify the party or parties entitled to recover costs under subsections (b) and (c) of this rule. That party or parties shall serve and file an itemized and verified bill of costs within 10 days after the date of notice of the opinion or order. Date of notice is defined in Civil Rule 58.1(c). The bill of costs shall be limited to the items specified in subsection (d) of this rule. Failure to file a timely bill of costs is a waiver of the right to recover costs. Objections to the bill of costs may be filed within 7 days after service of the bill. Promptly after expiration of the time for filing objections, the clerk shall issue an itemized award of costs. A hearing on the bill of costs shall not be held unless requested by the clerk. The clerk may not delegate to a deputy clerk the authority to award costs in cases in which objection is filed, except with the approval of the chief justice. Return of the record shall not be delayed pending the award of costs.

(2) *Reconsideration.* A party aggrieved by an order awarding costs under subsection (f)(1) of this rule or an order awarding attorney's fees under subsection (e) of this rule may file a motion for reconsideration within ten days after the date of notice of the order. The non-moving party may file a response within seven days after service of the motion. Reconsideration of an award of costs or attorney's fees under (f)(1) or (e) will be determined by an individual justice or judge. Full court reconsideration of such individual justice's or judge's decision may be sought pursuant to Appellate Rule 503(h)(2)(B).

(3) *Rehearing.* If a timely petition for rehearing is filed, the clerk shall not award costs until the court has disposed of the case on rehearing. Supplemental or amended bills of costs may not be filed after disposition of a petition for rehearing unless requested by the court.

(g) **Exemptions.**

(1) *Workers' Compensation Appeals.* In an administrative appeal from the Alaska Workers' Compensation Board or in an appeal from a denial of a claim of benefits under the Employment Security Act, an award of costs or attorney's fees shall not be made against the claimant in either the supreme court or the superior court unless the court finds that the claimant's position was frivolous, unreasonable, or taken in bad faith.

(2) In an administrative appeal from the Alaska Workers' Compensation Board, full reasonable attorney's fees will be awarded to a successful claimant. Counsel for the claimant shall serve and file an affidavit of services rendered on appeal within 10 days from the date of notice of an opinion or an order under Rule 214. Objections to the affidavit of services may be filed within 7 days of service of the affidavit. An individual justice shall determine the amount of fees to be awarded.

(h) **Execution.** Upon proper application, the clerk of the trial court may issue writs of execution upon the award of costs and attorney's fees made pursuant to this rule, without the approval of a judge of the trial court.

(SCO 439 effective November 15, 1980; amended by SCO 507 effective July 1, 1982; by SCO 508 effective July 1, 1982; by SCO 512 effective October 1, 1982; by SCO 552 effective February 1, 1983; by SCO 554 effective April 4, 1983; by SCO 562, effective May 2, 1983; by SCO 583 effective February 1, 1984; by SCO 619 effective June 15, 1985; by SCO 847 effective January 15, 1988; by SCO 1024 effective July 15, 1990; by SCO 1155 effective July 15, 1994; by SCO 1279 effective July 31, 1997; by SCO 1440 effective October 15, 2001; and by SCO 1482 effective October 15, 2002)

Note: In 1997 the legislature enacted AS 18.16.030(m), which provides that a filing fee may not be required of, and court costs may not be assessed against, a minor in a proceeding to bypass parental consent to an abortion. According to ch. 14, sec. 10 SLA 1997, AS 18.16.030(m) has the effect of amending Administrative Rule 9, Civil Rule 79, and Appellate Rule 508 by prohibiting filing fees and assessment of court costs in certain actions. Instead of amending individual rules to implement AS 18.16.030, the supreme court has adopted a separate rule on judicial bypass proceedings in the superior court and a separate rule on judicial bypass appeals. See Probate Rule 20 & Appellate Rule 220.

Annotations

Cases

This rule does not forbid that parties to an action may by stipulation waive their respective rights to costs and attorney's fees. Such stipulation shall be given full force and effect. **Jones v. Fuller-Garvey Corp.,** Op. No. 172, 386 P2d 838 (Alaska 1963).

It was error for trial court to award costs on appeal when supreme court had issued mandate barring them. **Continental Ins. Co. v. U.S. Fid. & Guar. Co.,** Op. No. 1298, 552 P2d 1122 (Alaska 1976).

Appeal to a Superior Court from an administrative agency is brought under Appellate Rule 45 and not under the Civil Rules; thus Appellate Rule 29 governs the award of attorney fees rather than Civil Rule 82. **Kodiak Western Alaska v. Bob Harris Flying Service,** Op. No. 1820, 592 P2d 1200 (Alaska 1979).

The court has discretion to award attorney's fees or not to award them. **Kodiak Western Alaska v. Bob Harris Flying Service,** Op. No. 1820, 592 P2d 1200 (Alaska 1979).

Under doctrine of separation of powers, implicit in state constitution judiciary has no authority, statutory or implied, to award compensation for costs incurred in administrative proceedings. **State v. Smith,** Op. No. 1838, 593 P2d 625 (Alaska 1979).

This rule permits award of fees to unsuccessful appellants in condemnation action. **State, Dept. of Highways v. Salzwedel,** Op. No. 1961, 596 P2d 17 (Alaska 1979).

In determining the amounts of attorney's fees on appeal in public interest litigation, the same considerations are applicable as at the trial level, and it is therefore appropriate to award full attorney's fees on appeal to a successful public interest litigant. **Thomas v. Bailey,** Op. No. 2094, 611 P2d 536 (Alaska 1980).

An enhanced award of attorney's fees for a successful public interest litigant computed by applying a multiple of the reasonable fee was not appropriate in this case where the successful litigant was a nonprofit corporation represented by in-house counsel, where the prospect of such fees was not a factor used by the corporation in determining which cases to accept, and where counsel's major argument was not relied on in the court's opinion. **Thomas v. Bailey,** Op. No. 2094, 611 P2d 536 (Alaska 1980).

When a superior court acts in its appellate capacity it must state its reasons for denying a request for attorney's fees. **Conway, Inc. v. Ross,** Op. No. 2335, 627 P2d 1029 (Alaska 1981).

Costs and attorney's fees are not to be awarded to a governmental agency that prevails in an action against a private defendant raising a public interest defense. **Whitson v. Anchorage,** Op. No. 2395, 632 P2d 232 (Alaska 1981).

In appeal to superior court of a municipal zoning decision, it was error for the court to award attorney's fees to the prevailing parties based upon the civil rules rather than the appellate rules. **Royal Krest Const. v. Anchorage,** Op. No. 2400, 640 P2d 133 (Alaska 1981).

Appellate court may grant attorney's fees to employer-defendant in workmen's compensation action only upon a finding by the court that claimant's appeal was frivolous, unreasonable, or brought in bad faith. **Whaley v. Alaska Workers' Comp. Bd.,** Op. No. 2533, 648 P2d 955 (Alaska 1982).

Where superior court hearing on hospital staffing decision was, by stipulation, treated as an appeal from an administrative agency, superior court could not award costs or attorney's fees incurred at the administrative level to the prevailing party where agency rules did not provide for such awards. **McMillan v. Anchorage Community Hospital,** Op. No. 2521, 646 P2d 857 (Alaska 1982).

Appellant's appeal, designed to vindicate a strong public policy in effectuating zoning ordinances, and which would have benefited numerous people had it succeeded, came within the public interest exception to award of fees to the prevailing party. **Oceanview Homeowners Assoc. v. Quadrant Const.,** Op. No. 2805, 680 P2d 793 (Alaska 1984).

An appellate court need not give reasons for awarding attorney's fees, only its reasons for denying them. **Rosen v. State Bd. of Public Accountancy,** Op. No. 2880, 689 P2d 478 (Alaska 1984).

This rule is the appropriate authority for an award of fees on an appeal from an administrative decision. **Rosen v. State Bd. of Public Accountancy,** Op. No. 2880, 689 P2d 478 (Alaska 1984).

Where State did not include attorney's fees in its bill of costs, but requested them by separate motion, the procedure was proper. **Rosen v. State Bd. of Public Accountancy,** Op. No. 2880, 689 P2d 478 (Alaska 1984).

Where State's motion for attorney's fees cited Appellate Rule 508 as authority for its request for fees, the court's order granting the State's motion, which appeared on the very same document, could not reasonably be construed as based on any other authority. **Rosen v. State Bd. of Public Accountancy,** Op. No. 2880, 689 P2d 478 (Alaska 1984).

Where plaintiff's job was at stake, he clearly had sufficient economic incentive to bring the lawsuit whether or not it involved issues of public importance, thus he could not qualify as a public interest litigant. **Rosen v. State Bd. of Public Accountancy,** Op. No. 2880, 689 P2d 478 (Alaska 1984).

Fact that some classes of persons aggrieved by administrative tribunal decisions have a right to de novo review does not insulate them from responsibility for attorney's fees if judicial review does not result in judgment in their favor; award of attorney's fees on review of administrative decisions is within the discretion of the trial courts when sitting as intermediate appellate tribunals, and all relevant factors may be considered in exercising that discretion; overruling Crisp v. Kenai Peninsula Borough School District, 587 P2d 1168 (Alaska 1978). **Rosen v. State Bd. of Public Accountancy,** Op. No. 2880, 689 P2d 478 (Alaska 1984).

Determination of attorney's fees by the superior court in workers' compensation appeals are controlled by statute, not by this rule. **Providence Washington Ins. Co. v. Grant,** Op. No. 2905, 693 P2d 872 (Alaska 1985).

The costs included in this rule are not meant to preclude the trial court's exercise of its sound discretion in awarding additional costs in a particular case. **State, Depart. of Education v. Nickerson,** Op. No. 3005, 711 P2d 1165 (Alaska 1985).

Trial court did not abuse its discretion in awarding costs additional to those listed in this rule for an administrative appeal which resembled a civil action, no prior administrative hearing having been provided. **State, Dept. of Education v. Nickerson,** Op. No. 3005, 711 P2d 1165 (Alaska 1985).

Suit by employee against employer for "trover and conversion" involving the withholding of his earnings under a levy by the Internal Revenue Service to recover delinquent income taxes was frivolous, justifying award of actual reasonable attorney's fees and costs to the employer. **Berry v. Ketchikan Public Utilities,** Op. No. 3131, 727 P2d 762 (Alaska 1986).

The holding in Whaley v. Alaska Workers' Comp. Bd., Op. No. 2533, 648 P2d 955 (Alaska 1982), that attorneys' fees under this rule will be awarded against employees only if the employees' claims in a Workers' Compensation appeal are frivolous, unreasonable, or in bad faith, extends to cases in which workers bring a class action seeking to change a policy of the Alaska Worker's Compensation Board. **Crawford and Co. v. Vienna,** Op. No. 3243, 744 P2d 1175 (Alaska 1987).

A superior court acting as an intermediate appellate court has broad discretion to award costs pursuant to this rule. **Messerli v. Dept. of Natural Resources,** Op. No. 3412, 768 P2d 1112 (Alaska 1989).

Where claimant was awarded costs and attorney fees by the superior court on appeal from an administrative decision of the Alaska Department of Natural Resources, which decision was affirmed in part and reversed in part by the Supreme Court of Alaska, the award of costs and attorney fees was vacated and remanded for redetermination, since it was not clear that claimant would be the prevailing party after remand. **Messerli v. Dept. of Natural Resources,** Op. No. 3412, 768 P2d 1112 (Alaska 1989).

On appeals of workman's compensation decision to superior court, superior court did not abuse its discretion in reducing the original fee award to appellees following appellant's motion to reconsider by (1) not requesting a reply from appellees to appellant's motion for reconsideration or (2) by reducing the fee award because appellees' brief was excessive. **Childs v. Tulin,** Op. No. 3645, 799 P2d 1338 (Alaska 1990).

Where worker abandoned a nonfrivolous worker's compensation claim against individual defendants by failing to include it in his brief on appeal to the superior court, it was unreasonable for him to fail to dismiss those defendants from the appeal, thus superior court properly awarded attorney's fees to the defendants. **Childs v. Tulin,** Op. No. 3645, 799 P2d 1338 (Alaska 1990).

The appellate rules rather than the civil rules control an award of attorney fees when the superior court determines an administrative appeal. **Diedrich v. City of Ketchikan,** Op. No. 3661, 805 P2d 362 (Alaska 1991).

A superior court acting as a court of appeal from the decision of an administrative agency has authority to award attorney's fees. Ordinarily, such award should only partially compensate the prevailing party and be limited to attorney's fees incurred in the court, not incurred in the prior administrative proceeding, however, actual costs and attorney's fees may be awarded where authorized by statute; further, actual costs and attorney's fees may be awarded to a successful appellee where the court finds that the appeal is frivolous or has been brought simply for the purpose of delay. **Kenai Peninsula Bor. v. Cook Inlet Reg.,** Op. No. 3671, 807 P2d 487 (Alaska 1991).

In the absence of statutory authorization, or a finding that the appeal was frivolous or brought solely for purposes of delay, award of actual attorney fees under this rule was error, only partial attorney fees should have been awarded. **State, Pub. Emp. Ret. Bd. v. Cacioppo,** Op. No. 3713, 813 P2d 679 (Alaska 1991).

In the absence of statutory authorization or a finding of frivolousness or undue delay, only partial attorney's fees may be awarded under this rule.

Stepanov v. Homer Elec. Ass'n, Inc., Op. No. 3714, 814 P2d 731 (Alaska 1991).

Proceedings before the Alaska Public Utilities Commission are not excepted from the general principle that the court may not award attorney's fees for prior administrative proceedings. **Stepanov v. Homer Elec. Ass'n, Inc.,** Op. No. 3714, 814 P2d 731 (Alaska 1991).

State's motion for attorney fees in driver's license revocation case, filed seven months after final judgment had been entered, was not filed within reasonable time, thus trial court erred in granting the motion. **Pruitt v. State, Dept. of Public Safety,** Op. No. 3809, 825 P2d 887 (Alaska 1992).

Although attorney's fee included some fees not incurred in court, they were related to the appeal, thus trial court did not err in considering those fees in its award. **Cook Inlet Pipe Line v. Alaska PUC,** Op. No. 3851, 836 P2d 343 (Alaska 1992).

Miners who appealed Department of Environmental Conservation's certification of pollution discharge elimination system permits issued by Environmental Protection Agency on ground that limited scope of hearing on the matter deprived them of property interest without just compensation or due process of law were not public interest litigants. **Stein v. Kelso,** Op. No. 3927, 846 P2d 123 (Alaska 1993).

Public interest litigant's general prevailing party status did not mean litigant should recover fees incurred in bringing or defending petitions for review on which it did not prevail. **Hickel v. Southeast Conference,** Op. No. 4055, 868 P2d 919 (Alaska 1994).

An award of attorney's fees in an appeal of an agency decision to superior court is governed by this rule. **CarrGottstein Properties v. State,** Op. No. 4230, 899 P2d 136 (Alaska 1995).

An award of attorney's fees pursuant to Appellate Rule 508(e) ordinarily should only partially compensate the prevailing party for attorney's fees. A court may exercise its sound discretion to award fees which are justified and reasonable. **Carr-Gottstein Properties v. State,** Op. No. 4230, 899 P2d 136 (Alaska 1995).

Where a party appeals an administrative decision, but re ceives no money judgment, the guidelines in Civil Rule 82(b)(2) may be applied by analogy to Appellate Rule 508(e) to determine a reasonable award of attorney's fees. **CarrGottstein Properties v. State,** Op. No. 4230, 899 P2d 136 (Alaska 1995).

A superior court acting as an intermediate court of appeal from a decision of an administrative agency has broad discretion to award attorney's fees under this rule. **Brodigan v. Alaska Department of Revenue,** Op. No. 4234, 900 P2d 728 (Alaska 1995).

Superior court did not abuse its discretion in awarding $700 of attorney's fees to the State, approximately 20% of the fees it actually incurred, despite appellants' claims that it was not clear that the State was the prevailing party and that they were public interest litigants. **Brodigan v. Alaska Department of Revenue,** Op. No. 4234, 900 P2d 728 (Alaska 1995).

This rule governs awarding attorney's fees in superior court or an appeal from an administrative decision. The award of these fees is committed to the discretion of the superior court and will not be overturned absent an abuse of discretion. The superior court need not explain its basics for awarding fees; it must only explain denials. **North Slope Borough v. Barraza,** Op. No. 4285, 906 P2d 1377 (Alaska 1995).

Superior court's use of the factor of "measure of success" in awarding attorney's fees in an administrative appeal did not on its face constitute an abuse of discretion. **North Slope Borough v. Barraza,** Op. No. 4285, 906 P2d 1377 (Alaska 1995).

Action of judge of trial court was unnecessary to obtain writ of execution from clerk of trial clerk on supreme court's award of appellate costs and fees. **Barber v. Barber,** Op. No. 4345, 915 P2d 1204 (Alaska 1996).

Fact that prevailing government entity litigated through in-house counsel did not preclude award of attorney's fees. **Agen v. State, CSED,** Op. No. 4874, 945 P2d 1215 (Alaska 1997).

It was error for superior court acting as intermediate appellate court to award fees under Civil Rule 82 rather than under this rule, thus remand was required for recalculation in accordance with this rule. **Agen v. State, CSED,** Op. No. 4874, 945 P2d 1215 (Alaska 1997).

In federal diversity cases, Federal Rule of Appellate Procedure 38 preempts this rule. **Hinde v. Provident Life and Acc. Ins. Co.,** 112 F3d 412 (9th Cir. 1997).

Workers Compensation Board properly denied claimant reimbursement for travel costs to attend appellate hearings in superior court. **Hodges v. Alaska Constructors, Inc.,** Op. No. 4971, 957 P2d 957 (Alaska 1998).

Superior court hearing appeal from administrative agency awards attorney's fees under Appellate Rule 508, not Civil Rule 82. **Stalnaker v. Williams,** Op. No. 5003, 960 P2d 590 (Alaska 1998).

Award of eighty-six percent of actual attorney's fees for appeal of administrative agency determination to superior court was not abuse of discretion. **Stalnaker v. Williams,** Op. No. 5003, 960 P2d 590 (Alaska 1998).

Although trial court in Anchorage had discretion not to award costs and attorney's fees after dismissing without prejudice administrative appeal filed in Anchorage that should have been filed in Barrow, trial court erred in concluding that issue of costs and fees could be deferred for consideration by trial court in Barrow upon disposition of Barrow appeal. **North Slope Borough v. Green Intern.,** Op. No. 5067, 969 P2d 1161 (Alaska 1999).

Award of fees to the borough was not an abuse of discretion as the landowners were not public interest litigants; only they would have directly benefited had they persuaded the superior court to impose their preferred assessment scheme on the borough, as such, had they succeeded, other landowners in the local improvement district would have been forced to shoulder greater costs. **Miller v. Matanuska-Susitna Borough,** Op. No. 5624, 54 P.3d 285 (Alaska 2002).

Rule 509. Interest.

If a judgment for money in a civil case is affirmed, interest at the rate prescribed by law shall be payable from the effective date of the judgment of the trial court. If in a civil case a judgment is modified or reversed with directions that a judgment for money be issued by the trial court, interest on the new judgment at the rate prescribed by law shall be payable from the effective date of the prior judgment which was modified or reversed.

(SCO 439 effective November 15, 1980; amended by SCO 509 effective July 1, 1982)

Rule 510. Monetary Sanctions.

(a) **When Appeal Brought for Delay.** Where an appeal or petition for review shall delay the proceedings in the trial court or the enforcement of the judgment or order of the trial court, and shall appear to have been filed merely for delay, monetary sanctions may be awarded in addition to interest, costs and attorney's fees.

(b) **Infraction of Rules.** For any infraction of these rules, the appellate court may withhold or assess costs or attorney's fees as the circumstances of the case and discouragement of like conduct in the future may require; and such costs and attorney's fees may be imposed upon offending attorneys or parties.

(c) **Fines.** In addition to its authority under (a) and (b) of this rule and its power to punish for contempt, the appellate court may, after reasonable notice and an opportunity to show cause to the contrary, and after hearing by the court, if requested, impose a fine not to exceed $500 against any attorney who practices before it for failure to comply with these rules or any other rules promulgated by the Supreme Court.

(SCO 439 effective November 15, 1980; amended by SCO 476 effective August 17, 1981)

Annotations

Cases

For specific misconduct on the part of either party, actual costs and fees may be awarded under this rule. **Kenai Peninsula Bor. v. Cook Inlet Reg.,** Op. No. 3671, 807 P2d 487 (Alaska 1991).

There would have been an impermissible double recovery of attorney's fees if both the award of sanctions and the award of attorney's fees had been allowed to stand. **Kenai Peninsula Bor. v. Cook Inlet Reg.,** Op. No. 3671, 807 P2d 487 (Alaska 1991).

Order denying appellant's fifth request for extension of time to file opening brief and dismissing her appeal was vacated, but appellant's attorney was ordered to pay $500 fine for dedication and to pay appellee's reasonable fees and costs in opposing motion for extension. **Brown v. Brown,** 854 P2d 732 (Alaska 1993).

Instead of merely referring to a party's "dilatory conduct" in reducing an award of attorney's fees, the superior court should have specified the particular conduct which might have supported a finding that an infraction of the rules had occurred. **North Slope Borough v. Barraza,** Op. No. 4285, 906 P2d 1377 (Alaska 1995).

Party was not entitled to fees or costs under this rule absent allegation that appeal delayed the proceedings or that appeal was filed merely to cause delay. **In re Dissolution of Marriage of Alaback,** Op. No. 5248, 997 P2d 1181 (Alaska 2000).

Appellate court imposed $250 fine against appellant's counsel, where counsel misstated the facts of the case that masked the appellate court's potential lack of jurisdiction to entertain the appeal and knowingly failed to cite a decision adverse to his contention that the appellate court had jurisdiction to entertain the appeal. **Tyler v. State,** Op. No. A-7779, 47 P3d 1095 (Alaska App. 2001).

An attorney in a DWI case was properly fined for filing a motion on behalf of his client without bringing controlling negative precedent to the attention of the tribunal. **Tyler v. State,** Op. No. A-7779, 47 P.3d 1095 (Alaska App. 2001).

Rule 511. Dismissal of Causes.

(a) **Dismissal by Agreement.** Whenever the parties, by their attorneys of record, shall file with the clerk of the appellate court an agreement in writing that an appeal or petition be dismissed, specifying the terms with respect to costs, and shall pay to the clerk any fees that may be due the clerk, the clerk shall enter an order of dismissal without further reference to the court.

(b) **Dismissal by Appellant or Petitioner.**

(1) Whenever an appellant or petitioner in the appellate court, by the appellant's or petitioner's attorney of record, shall file with the clerk of that court a motion to dismiss a proceeding to which such appellant or petitioner is a party, with proof of service as prescribed by these rules, and shall tender to the clerk any fees and costs that may be due, the adverse party, within seven days after service thereof, may file an objection, after which time the matter shall be determined by the court.

(2) If no objection is filed, the clerk shall enter an order of dismissal without further reference to the court.

(c) **Certification.** An agreement or motion for dismissal filed under (a) or (b) of this rule must include a certification that the settlement information required under AS 09.68.130 and (e) of this rule has been submitted to the Alaska Judicial Council or that the case is exempt from this requirement.

(d) **Voluntary Dismissal by Criminal Defendant.** A motion or stipulation for the voluntary dismissal of an appeal by a criminal defendant under paragraph (a) or (b) shall not be granted unless the motion or stipulation includes either:

(1) A signed statement by the defendant stating that the defendant understands the consequences of the dismissal and consents to it, or

(2) Explicit certification by counsel for the defendant that counsel has explained the consequences of dismissal to the client and is satisfied that the client understands the consequences of dismissal and consents to it.

(e) **Information about the Resolution of Civil Cases.** If a proceeding is dismissed under paragraph (a) or (b) of this rule, each party or, if a party is represented by an attorney, the party's attorney must submit the information described in AS 09.68.130(a) to the Alaska Judicial Council. The information must be submitted within 30 days after the proceeding is finally resolved as to that party and on a form specified by the Alaska Judicial Council. The following types of cases are exempt from this requirement:

(1) divorce and dissolution;

(2) adoption, custody, support, visitation, and emancipation of children;

(3) children-in-need-of-aid cases under AS 47.10 or delinquent minors cases under 47.12;

(4) domestic violence protective orders under AS 18.66.100 - 18.66.180;

(5) estate, guardianship, and trust cases filed under AS 13;

(6) small claims under AS 22.15.040;

(7) forcible entry and detainer cases;

(8) administrative appeals; and

(9) motor vehicle impound or forfeiture actions under municipal ordinance.

(f) **Mandate Not Required.** No mandate shall issue on a dismissal under this rule or Rule 511.5 without an order of the court. However, the clerk shall notify the court whose judgment was appealed.

(SCO 439 effective November 15, 1980; amended by SCO 510 effective August 30, 1982; by SCO 728 effective December 15, 1986; by SCO 1153 effective July 15, 1994; by SCO 1283 effective September 2, 1997; by SCO 1301 effective January

15, 1998; and by SCO 1361 effective October 15, 1999)

Annotations

Cases

Where appellee fails to move to dismiss an appeal from a ruling which is not appealable under these rules and the points raised are briefed as they would have been had a petition for review been sought, the supreme court is entitled to pass on the merits of the controversy. **Stokes v. Van Seventer,** Op. No. 18, 355 P2d 594 (Alaska 1960).

An order of dismissal by the supreme court is not in itself a mandate. **Singletary v. State,** Op. No. 1711, 583 P2d 847 (Alaska 1978).

Rule 511.5. Dismissal for Failure to Prosecute.

(a) If an appellant or an appellant's counsel fails to comply with these rules, the clerk shall notify the appellant and the appellant's counsel in writing that the appeal will be dismissed for want of prosecution unless the appellant remedies the default within 14 days after the date of notification, time to be computed in accordance with Rule 502 (c). If the appellant fails to comply within the 14-day period, the clerk shall issue an order dismissing the appeal for want of prosecution. In no case, except by order of the court on a motion to reinstate the appeal, shall the appellant be entitled to remedy the default after the appeal has been dismissed under this rule.

(b) The dismissal of an appeal under subsection (a) shall not limit the authority of the court to impose monetary sanctions under Rule 510.

(c) The court may, upon motion of a party or its own motion, dismiss an appeal for failure to comply with these rules, whether or not prior notice of default has been given.

(SCO 510 effective August 30, 1982; amended by SCO 1153 effective July 15, 1994)

Annotations

Cases

Appellant was not entitled to a fourteen-day grace period in which to file her opening brief after failing to file a brief for eighteen months. **Cowitz v. Alaska Workers' Compensation Board,** Op. No. 3078, 721 P2d 635 (Alaska 1986).

Trial court did not abuse its discretion in dismissing appeal for want of prosecution where court notified appellant that appeal would be dismissed if she did not transmit record and she did not do so. **Geczy v. State, Dept. of Natural Resources,** Op. No. 4409, 924 P2d 103 (Alaska 1996).

Trial court erred in dismissing pro se claimant's workers' compensation appeal for failing to timely file his opening brief within time limit of controlling extension order; sanction of dismissal was too extreme where brief had been filed at time of dismissal order, appellees had demonstrated no prejudice from delay, court did not consider lesser sanctions, and claimant's excuse for late filing was that concussion suffered in industrial accident which was subject of his workers' compensation claim required eighteen hours per day bed rest and that stress of working on appeal caused internal bleeding. **Metcalf v. Felec Services,** Op. No. 4828, 938 P2d 1023 (Alaska 1997).

There is distinction between pro se litigant who fails entirely to file required materials and one who files defective materials; trial court must inform pro se litigant of specific defects in his notice of appeal and give him opportunity to remedy those defects, and failure to do so is abuse of discretion. **Collins v. Arctic Builders,** 957 P.2d 980 (Alaska 1998).

Rule 512. Record and Other Papers after Final Disposition.

(a) (1) Unless the court otherwise orders, the clerk shall return the original record to the clerk of the trial courts on the day specified in this subsection.

(2) In a case decided by the court of appeals, the record shall be returned:

[a] on the day after the time for filing a petition for hearing expires, if no timely petition for hearing is filed;

[b] on the day after the petition for hearing is denied, if a timely petition for hearing is denied; or

[c] as provided in paragraph (3), if a petition for hearing is granted.

(3) In a case decided by the supreme court, the record shall be returned:

[a] on the day after the time for filing a petition for rehearing expires, if no timely petition for rehearing is filed; or

[b] on the day after the supreme court disposes of the case on rehearing, if a timely petition for rehearing is filed.

(b) All documents filed with the appellate courts shall be retained by the clerk subject to Administrative Rule 37.

(SCO 439 effective November 15, 1980; amended by SCO 551 effective February 1, 1983)

Annotations

Cases

Although appellate court opinion reversing defendant's conviction and remanding the case for a new trial was issued on June 6, 1986, the opinion did not become operative and had no force or validity as an order for a new trial until the date specified for return of the record, thus the date specified for return, not the issuance date, triggered commencement of the 120 day speedy trial period. **Nitz v. State,** Op. No. 759, 745 P2d 1379 (Alaska App. 1987).

Rule 512.5. Public Documents.

(a) **Records on Appeal.** A record on appeal is open to public inspection except that papers filed under seal in the trial court, recordings or transcripts of closed hearings held in the trial court, and exhibits submitted or introduced at closed hearings in the trial court, will be maintained under seal while they constitute part of a record on appeal.

(b) **Other Papers.**

(1) Papers filed in the appellate courts, other than records on appeal, shall be open to public inspection unless the appellate court in which the case is pending otherwise orders, or except as hereafter provided in this subparagraph. If the trial court has restricted disclosure of information, and it is necessary to refer to that information in an interlocutory petition or application to an appellate court, the trial court may

order that the petition or application be filed under seal. Pursuant to such an order, the petition or application shall remain under seal until the close of business on the fifth business day after it is filed, unless the appellate court otherwise orders. If during the 5-day period a motion to maintain the document under seal is filed in the appellate court, paragraph (b)(4) of this rule will apply.

(2) Counsel in appellate matters arising out of closed proceedings in the trial courts shall, wherever possible, avoid the use of full names of parties or other detailed identifying information in briefs, motions, and other papers filed with the appellate courts. Descriptive terms ("the oldest daughter," "the prospective adoptive father"), pseudonyms ("Jane Doe"), first names or initials should be used instead.

(3) A motion to file a paper under seal in the appellate court, the response to such a motion, and the order ruling on such a motion, are open to public inspection and shall not themselves be filed under seal. The motion must explain why the procedure described in subparagraph (b)(2) of this rule could not be used and will only be granted for good cause shown. A motion to file a paper under seal, whether or not opposed, is not a "routine" motion within the meaning of Rule 503(e).

(4) A paper may be lodged with the court along with a motion to file it under seal. Unless the court otherwise orders, it is not open to public inspection while the motion to file it under seal is pending. If the motion is denied, and the paper has been lodged along with the motion, the movant has the option of withdrawing the paper or leaving it on file open to public inspection.

(c) **General Provisions.**

(1) Papers filed under seal in the appellate courts may be examined or copied only by counsel of record in the case, their agents or employees designated by them, and those personnel of the Alaska Court System having need to examine the papers in the performance of their duties.

(2) If further restrictions are ordered for good cause (for example, privileged material to which counsel for one party but not the other are entitled to access), the clerk of the appellate courts shall enforce those restrictions, including restrictions placed by the trial court upon materials filed with the trial court and included in the record on appeal.

(3) A paper shall not be withheld from public inspection because other papers included in the same case file or the same record on appeal have been filed under seal and are not open to public inspection.

(SCO 883 effective July 15, 1988; amended by SCO 1279 effective July 31, 1997)

Note: In 1997 the legislature enacted AS 18.16.030(k), which requires that documents and records in a judicial bypass appeal be kept confidential. According to ch. 14, § 9 SLA 1997, this provision has the effect of amending Appellate Rule 512.5 by making certain appellate records and papers confidential. Instead of amending individual rules to implement AS 18.16.030, the supreme court has adopted a separate rule on judicial bypass appeals. See Appellate Rule 220.

Rule 513. Translations.

Whenever any record transmitted to the appellate courts shall contain any document, paper, testimony or other proceeding in a foreign language, and the record does not also contain a translation of such document, paper, testimony or other proceeding made under the authority of the trial court or admitted to be correct, the record shall not be filed, but the case shall be reported to the appellate court by the clerk, and the court will thereupon remand it back to the trial court in order that a translation may be supplied and inserted in the record.

(SCO 439 effective November 15, 1980)

Rule 513.5. Form of Papers.

(a) **Scope.** This rule governs the form of all papers filed in the appellate courts except briefs, transcripts and excerpts of record. Briefs are governed by subparagraphs (b)(1)-(5) and paragraph (c) of this rule and by Rule 212(b); transcripts are governed by administrative bulletin as provided in Rule 210(b)(7); and excerpts of record are governed by Rule 210(c).

(b) **Form in General.** Except as provided in subsection (a), all documents presented for filing with the clerk must be:

(1) on 8-1/2 x 11 inches opaque, unglazed white paper of good quality and at least sixteen pound weight.

(2) in clear and legible black typeface or hand-printing in black ink;

(3) double-spaced (line-spacing "**2**" if proportionally spaced typeface is used), except that headings and footnotes must be single-spaced and quotations of more than two lines must be single-spaced and indented at least one-half inch on both sides;

(4) if longer than one page, numbered consecutively at the bottom center of each page;

(5) no more than 6-1/2 x 9-1/2 inches of printed or written matter on a page;

(6) printed or written on one side of the paper; and

(7) two-hole punched at the center of the top of each page.

(c) **Typeface.** (1) The text of documents, including headings and footnotes, must be at least

(A) 12 point (10 monospaced characters per inch) Courier, or substantially similar monospaced text style;

(B) 13 point (proportionally spaced) Times New Roman, Garamond, CG Times, New Century Schoolbook, or substantially similar serifed, roman text style; or

(C) 12.5 point (proportionally spaced) Arial, Helvetica, Univers, or substantially similar non-serifed text style.

(2) When a typeface other than 12 point Courier is used, the party filing the document must also file a certificate that identifies the typeface and point size used in the document.

(d) **Exhibits.** Exhibits to motions, petitions and other documents must be clear and legible and must comply with subparagraph (b)(1) of this rule. Exhibits that do not comply with subparagraph (b)(1) must be reduced if necessary and copied onto paper of the required size and quality. Each page of an exhibit must be numbered progressively and marked with the number or letter of the exhibit (e.g., Ex. A, p. 1). Exhibits must be permanently attached to the principal document in a manner that allows them to be easily accessible and readable without detaching them from the principal document.

(e) **Information To Be Placed on First Page.** The first page of each paper or document must be prepared in conformity with Civil Rule 76(d), except that the name of the law firm or organization with whom an attorney is affiliated and the attorney's bar number must also be shown. Alternatively, the bar number must be shown on the signature page. In criminal cases, the first page must also include a certificate indicating whether the paper or document contains information that is confidential under AS 12.61.100 through 12.61.150. The administrative director shall specify the form and content of the certificate. If a party requests relief by a specific date in a petition for review, cross-petition for review, original application, or motion, the date by which a decision is needed must also appear on the first page of the document.

(SCO 584 effective February 1, 1984; amended by SCO 686 effective May 1, 1986; by SCO 927 effective January 15, 1989; by SCO 1120 effective July 15, 1993; by SCO 1155 effective July 15, 1994; by SCO 1210 effective July 15, 1995; by SCO 1482 effective October 15, 2002; and by SCO 1628 effective April 16, 2007)

Rule 514. Service—Appearance of Counsel—Signing of Documents.

(a) **In General.** Whenever under these rules service is required or permitted to be made upon a party represented by an attorney, the service shall be made upon the attorney unless service upon the party is ordered by the court. Service upon the attorney or upon a party shall be made by delivering a copy to the attorney or party or by mailing it to him at the attorney's or party's last known address or, if no address is known, by leaving it with or mailing it to the clerk of the appellate courts. Delivery of a copy within this rule means: handing it to the attorney or to the party; or leaving it at the attorney's or party's office with a clerk or other person in charge thereof; or, if there is no one in charge, leaving it in a conspicuous place therein; or, if the office is closed or the person to be served has no office, leaving it at the attorney's or party's dwelling house or usual place of abode with some person of suitable age and discretion then residing therein. Service by mail is complete upon mailing.

(b) **Proof of Service—How Made.** Proof of service shall be made in conformity with Civil Rule 5(f).

(c) **Proof of Service—Filing.** Where proof of service is required, it shall be filed with the clerk in conformity with Civil Rule 5(e).

(d) **Entry of Appearance.** Any document filed with the clerk by or on behalf of counsel whose appearance has not previously been filed must be accompanied by an entry of appearance.

(e) **Signing of Documents.** All documents presented to the court, other than records, must bear the manuscript signature of the member of the bar who is counsel of record for the party concerned, and upon whom service is to be made. The individual names of other counsel and their addresses may be added.

(f) **Notice of Question of Constitutionality of Statute.** When the constitutionality of a state statute is drawn in question in any appeal or other proceeding in the appellate courts to which the state or an officer, agency, or employee thereof is not a party, the party raising the question shall give immediate notice in writing to the court of the existence of the question. The clerk of court shall notify the Attorney General of Alaska of the case raising the question.

(SCO 439 effective November 15, 1980; amended by SCO 554 effective April 4, 1983; by SCO 872 effective July 15, 1988; by SCO 1120 effective July 15, 1993; and by SCO 1153 effective July 15, 1994)

Annotations

Cases

An appeal to superior court from a decision of a state administrative agency requires service of notice upon the attorney general. **Vincent v. Commercial Fisheries Entry Comm'n,** Op. No. 3041, 717 P2d 391 (Alaska 1986).

Failure of applicant to serve attorney general's office with a notice of appeal from state administrative agency's denial of permit application did not deprive superior court of jurisdiction over the appeal, thus court, after allowing late service of notice upon the attorney general, could hear the appeal, absent proof of prejudice to the state from the late notification. **Vincent v. Commercial Fisheries Entry Comm'n,** Op. No. 3041, 717 P2d 391 (Alaska 1986).

Rule 515. Process—How Returnable.

A person serving the process of the appellate courts shall make proof of service thereof to the court promptly and in any event within the time during which the person served must respond to process. If service is made by a person other than a marshal, a marshal's deputy, a state police officer, or other officer of the court so designated, the person making service shall make affidavit thereof. Failure to make proof of service shall not affect the validity of the service.

(SCO 439 effective November 15, 1980; amended by SCO 1153 effective July 15, 1994)

Rule 516. Death of a Party.

(a) **Substitution.** The death of a party in a civil action or proceeding shall not affect any appeal taken or petition for review made, or the right to take an appeal or to seek review, except as limited by paragraph (b) of this rule. The proper representatives of the estate, or in the personalty or realty, of the deceased party, according to the nature of the case, may voluntarily appear and be substituted as parties for the decedent, or substitution may be effected as in the case of death of a party pending an action in the superior court. Thereupon proceedings shall be had in the supreme court as in other cases.

(b) **Time.** The times specified in these rules for taking an appeal or petitioning for review, or for taking any of the further steps to secure a review of the judgment appeal from or the order in respect to which review is sought, shall be extended for the time necessary to enable such representatives to be substituted for the deceased party; provided, that such time shall not extend for more than 60 days after the date of death of such party. If substitution is not effected within such period, these rules relating to the time for taking an appeal or petitioning for review, or for taking such further steps to secure review, shall be as fully applicable as in other cases.

(SCO 439 effective November 15, 1980)

Rule 517. Substitution of Parties and Attorneys.

(a) **Parties.** Whenever a substitution of parties to a pending appeal is necessary other than by reason of death, it shall be made by proper proceedings instituted for the purpose in the trial court. On proper motion and the filing of a certified copy of the order of substitution made by the trial court, a like order of substitution shall be made in the appellate court.

(b) **Attorneys.** Withdrawal or substitution of attorneys may be effected by serving and filing a stipulation in the appellate court, signed by the party, the retiring attorney and any substituted attorney. The stipulation is subject to approval of the court. In the absence of stipulation, withdrawal or substitution may be effected only by an order made pursuant to a noticed motion in the appellate court; provided, however, that unless otherwise ordered, service of notice of the motion need be made only on the party and the attorneys affected thereby. A notification of any such withdrawal or substitution shall be given by the clerk of the appellate court to the clerk of the trial court, and substituted counsel shall forthwith give notice thereof to all parties.

(SCO 439 effective November 15, 1980)

Annotations

Cases

Withdrawal of an attorney will not be allowed where there is no sufficient showing in support thereof and absent a proper substitution of attorneys. **Organized Village of Kake v. Egan,** Op. No. 16, 354 P2d 1108 (Alaska 1960).

Trial counsel's unilateral and unformalized withdrawal of representation following trial violated Appellate Rules and Code of Professional Responsibility; fact that client instructed trial counsel to do nothing further in the case did not relieve trial counsel of duty to preserve client's right to appeal where instruction was expressly based on client's representation that new attorney would be handling the matter. **Broeckel v. State,** Op. No. 1430, 900 P2d 1205 (Alaska App. 1995).

Rule 518. Pro Se Litigants.

If a party is appearing in an appeal unrepresented by counsel, all references in these rules to counsel shall be construed as referring to the party personally. All documents filed by such a party shall include an address at which that party can be served.

(SCO 439 effective November 15, 1980)

Rule 519. Clerical Mistakes.

Clerical mistakes in judgments, orders or other parts of the record and errors in the record arising from oversight or omission may be corrected by the appellate court at any time of its own initiative and after such notice, if any, as the court orders, or on motion of any party and after such notice, if any, as the court orders.

(SCO 439 effective November 15, 1980)

Rule 520. General Authority of Appellate Courts.

(a) In any matter lawfully brought before it for review, the supreme court, upon motion and notice of a party or upon its own motion, may at any time modify or vacate any order made by a trial court or the court of appeals in relation to the prosecution of an appeal or a petition for review.

(b) In any matter lawfully brought before it for review, the court of appeals may similarly modify or vacate any order made by a trial court in relation to the prosecution of an appeal or petition for review.

(c) The appellate court may affirm, modify, vacate, set aside or reverse any judgment, decree, decision or order of a court lawfully brought before it for review, and may remand the cause and direct the entry of such appropriate judgment, decree or order; or require such further proceedings to be had as may be just under the circumstances.

(SCO 439 effective November 15, 1980)

Annotations

Cases

A cause may be remanded for further proceedings where a miscarriage of justice seems apparent, sufficient evidence not having been introduced with respect to the property to be divided in a divorce action. **Rhodes v. Rhodes,** Op. No. 83, 370 P2d 902 (Alaska 1962).

It is not the function of the supreme court on review to try the issues de novo but to determine alleged errors of law committed by trial court in reaching its decision. **Patrick v. Sedwick,** Op. No. 338, 413 P2d 169 (Alaska 1966).

Under this rule as read in conjunction with Civil Rule 59(a), the supreme court possessed authority to order on remand a partial new trial on the issue of damages only where the liability issues were correctly decided and there was no indication from the record that the verdict was possibly a compromise verdict. **City of Fairbanks v. Nesbett,** Op. No. 439, 432 P2d 607 (Alaska 1967).

The review of an otherwise legal criminal sentence which is within the maximum established by the legislature, is not within the appellate jurisdiction of the supreme court and this rule cannot be construed to add to the supreme court's jurisdiction a reviewing power over criminal sentences it does not possess. **Bear v. State,** Op. No. 470, 439 P2d 432 (Alaska 1968).

Rule 521. Construction.

These rules are designed to facilitate business and advance justice. They may be relaxed or dispensed with by the appellate courts where a strict adherence to them will work surprise or injustice. In a matter involving the validity of a criminal conviction or sentence, this rule does not authorize an appellate court or the superior court, when acting as an intermediate appellate court, to allow

(1) the notice of appeals to be filed more than 60 days late; or

(2) a petition for review or petition for hearing to be filed more than 60 days late.

(SCO 439 effective November 15, 1980; amended by SCO 1238 effective July 15, 1996)

Note to SCO 1238: The limitation on the court's power to accept late appeals or petitions was added by ch. 79 § 21 SLA 1995. Section 7 of this order is adopted for the sole reason that the legislature has mandated the amendment.

Annotations

Cases

I. Construction of Rules.
- A. Time Limits for Appeals.
- B. Miscellaneous Rules.

I. Construction of Rules.

A. Time Limits for Appeals.

Where injustice to the appellee will not result from hearing a prematurely filed appeal which could not be refiled due to passage of time, the requirement of Rule 5 may be dispensed with, no motion to dismiss having been made until time for appellee's answering brief. **Edwards v. Franke,** Op. No. 45, 364 P2d 60 (Alaska 1961).

The requirement as to timely notice of appeal is not jurisdictional. **Vogt v. Winbauer,** Op. No. 117, 376 P2d 1007 (Alaska 1962).

Where appellant made no sufficient showing that strict enforcement of Supreme Ct. R. 7(a) [now Appellate Rule 7(a)] would work surprise or injustice to him, he was not relieved of the requirement of filing timely notice of appeal. **Vogt v. Winbauer,** Op. No. 117, 376 P2d 1007 (Alaska 1962).

Failure of the clerk of the superior court to notify defendant of the entry of order denying his motion for rehearing, was not considered a factor which would impel the supreme court to dispense with time requirements for filing notice of appeal under the relaxation permissible under Supreme Ct. R. 52. **Stephens v. City of Anchorage,** Op. No. 162, 384 P2d 959 (Alaska 1963).

The requirements for running of the time for appeal provided by Supreme Court Rule 7(a) [now Appellate Rule 7(a)] may be relaxed under this rule when its application according to its terms will work injustice. **Contento v. Alaska State Housing Authority,** Op. No. 282, 398 P2d 1000 (Alaska 1965).

The Supreme Court will grant review where the defendant establishes that he intended to appeal his conviction, communicated such desire to his attorney, and thereafter thought an appeal had been taken on his behalf, and where the defense attorney concluded no grounds existed for appeal but failed to state that conclusion to the defendant. **McCracken v. State,** Op. No 677, 482 P2d 269 (Alaska 1971).

Even if the defendant has not made out a case of excusable neglect with respect to his failure to file a notice of appeal within the ten-day period, the time limitation will be relaxed where strict adherence would work an injustice on the defendant. **McCracken v. State,** Op. No 677, 482 P2d 269 (Alaska 1971).

In proceedings wherein the defendant seeks an extension of time for appeal, it is unnecessary for the defendant to prove he has meritorious grounds for appeal as a prerequisite of his right to appeal. **McCracken v. State,** Op. No 677, 482 P2d 269 (Alaska 1971).

Where notice of appeal was filed after court granted motion for summary judgment but before actual judgment was entered, appeal was premature but would be treated as properly taken since scope of appeal was clear, appellee had not raised point and no injustice would result. **Alaska National Bank v. Linck,** Op. No. 1372, 559 P2d 1049 (Alaska 1977).

Mere assertion that defendant told his attorney that he desired to attack sentence as excessive does not demonstrate that failure to file appeal within 30 days was due to excusable neglect, or that the limit should be relaxed to avoid injustice, where motion for modification of sentence was made two years after sentence was imposed. **Taylor v. State,** Op. No. 1436, 564 P2d 1219 (Alaska 1977).

Where dismissed tenured teacher first knew of need to appeal in April, was served with decision in June, and did not attempt to appeal until August, it was not abuse of discretion to refuse to relax rules to permit appeal. **Jerrel v. Kenai Peninsula Borough School District,** Op. No. 1458, 567 P2d 760 (Alaska 1977).

Dismissal of state from appeal from Workmen's Compensation Board due to failure of appellant to file proper appeal under Appellant Rule 45(a)(2) was reversed where such dismissal, though technically correct, might have prevented an innocent party from collecting rightfully due disability benefits. **State Dept. of Highways v. Burgess Const. Co.,** Op. No. 1581, 575 P2d 792 (Alaska 1978).

Appellate Rule 46 was involved where strict adherence to the 40-day time limit for appeal under Criminal Rule 35 would have prevented consideration of appellant's contentions that his conditions of imprisonment deprived him of his right to rehabilitation and reformation and to be free of cruel and unusual punishment. **Abraham v. State,** Op. No. 1747, 585 P2d 526 (Alaska 1978).

Superior court did not abuse its discretion in refusing to apply this rule to a property tax assessment appeal which was untimely filed where the claimed over assessment was less than ten percent of the total value of the property in question. **North Star, Inc. v. Fairbanks North Star Borough,** Op. No. 258, 621 P2d 1335 (Alaska 1981).

The superior court may extend the time for filing an appeal from an administrative agency decision if the appellant shows that enforcement of the appeal deadline would result in surprise and injustice to the appellant. **Owsichek v. Alaska Guide Licensing and Control Board,** Op. No. 2328, 627 P2d 616 (Alaska 1981).

Considerations to be balanced in deciding whether to relax the appellate time limit rules include the right to appellate review, the willfulness and extent of the rules violation and the possible injustice that might result from a dismissal. **Estate of Smith v. State,** Op. No. 2428, 635 P2d 465 (Alaska 1981).

Where there were three dates of entry on the judgment from which the appeal was taken, the confusion thereby created made it appropriate to waive the requirement that notice of appeal be made within 30 days from entry of judgment. **Safeco Ins. Co. v. Honeywell,** Op. No. 2460, 639 P2d 996 (Alaska 1981).

It was not unjust to refuse to relax rule requiring timely appeal where the appeal concerned the detention of a juvenile on a charge which was ultimately dismissed, thereby making the appeal moot as to the juvenile. **A.M. v. State,** Op. No. 150, 346 P2d (Alaska App. 1982).

Trial court abused its discretion in failing to relax the thirty-day appeal period of this rule in situation where late filing was due to appellant's mistaken but not unreasonable belief that he was entitled to reconsideration of an agency decision denying his request for an administrative hearing. **Anderson v. State Commercial Fisheries Entry Comm.,** Op. No. 2588, 654 P2d 1320 (Alaska 1982).

Employee's appeal from a decision of the Public Employees Retirement System Board, filed 34 days after the employee received the Board's written decision, was properly dismissed as untimely. **Powers v. Public Emp. Retirement Bd.,** Op. No. 3362, 757 P2d 65 (Alaska 1988).

Because defendant did not receive a sentence of at least 45 days' imprisonment, he had no right to appeal the sentence. **Johnson v. State,** Op. No. 1156, 816 P2d 220 (Alaska App. 1991).

Legislature's 1995 amendment to Appellate Rule 521 did not affect appellate court's authority under Appellate Rule 502 to accept criminal appeals filed more than 60 days late for good cause shown. **Ozenna v. State,** 921 P2d 640 (Alaska App. 1996).

B. Miscellaneous Rules.

In the interest of justice and to prevent hardship the supreme court, upon its own motion, will treat an appeal as a petition for review in a case where the trial court ordered payment of rent by appellant (defendant) in an ejectment action pending judgment and where appellee did not call the nonappealability of the court's ruling to the attention of the supreme court until briefs were filed. **Stokes v. Van Seventer,** Op. No. 18, 355 P2d 594 (Alaska 1960).

The supreme court has the discretionary power to treat an appeal as a petition for review, although Civil Rule 54(b) has not been complied with so as to allow one of several parties to a suit to appeal before final judgment as to all parties, where it appears that there will be considerable delay before a final judgment is had, that the judgment as to the others is unlikely to change the judgment as to appellant, and that noncompliance with Civil Rule 54(b) may have been inadvertent. **Jefferson v. Spenard Builder's Supply, Inc.,** Op. No. 51, 366 P2d 714 (Alaska 1961).

A party who had chosen to stand mute in his brief on the charge of infraction of Supreme Court Rule 9(e) requiring a statement of points to be relied on appeal, failed to make a sufficient showing to justify relaxation of the rule. **Orbeck v. Wheeler Construction Company,** Op. No. 240, 394 P2d 781 (Alaska 1964).

In order to avoid injustice, a letter of petition complaining that petitioner was denied appointed counsel at the time his probation was revoked was treated as an original pro se application for a writ of habeas corpus despite technical failure to comply with Supreme Court Rule 33(a) [now Appellate Rule 25(a)]. **Hoffman v. State,** Op. No. 297, 404 P2d 644 (Alaska 1965).

When an appellant in a civil case wishes to make a motion for relief from judgment in the superior court under Civil Rule 60(b) and an appeal from such judgment is pending in the supreme court, the most satisfactory resolution consonant with the objective of these rules is for the appellant to file his motion in the superior court and for the supreme court to stay appellate proceedings until the superior court indicates that the motion should be granted and then, upon application, to remand the case to the superior court for the stated purpose of granting the motion. **Duriron Company, Inc. v. Bakke,** Op. No. 432, 431 P2d 499 (Alaska 1967).

The failure to set forth in the opening brief the charge of the court verbatim together with the grounds for objection urged at trial does not preclude consideration of the issue where the substance of the instruction and grounds of objection are set forth. **Transamerica Title Insurance Co. v. Ramsey,** Op. No. 869, 507 P2d 492 (Alaska 1973).

Action for injunctive relief against administrative agency could be treated as an appeal and allowed under Appellate Rule 46 even though not filed in accordance with Appellate Rule 45. **Alaska Public Utilities Comm'n. v. Municipality of Anchorage,** Op. No. 1326, 555 P2d 262 (Alaska 1976).

Rule 522. Legal Effect of Rules—Procedural Portions of Statutes Superseded.

These rules are promulgated pursuant to constitutional authority granting rulemaking power to the supreme court, and to the extent that they are inconsistent with any procedural provisions of any statute not enacted for the specific purpose of changing a rule, shall supersede such statute to the extent of such inconsistency.

(SCO 439 effective November 15, 1980)

Rule 523. Title.

These rules shall be known and cited as the "Rules of Appellate Procedure."

(SCO 439 effective November 15, 1980)

PART VI. SUPERIOR COURT AS AN APPELLATE COURT

Rule 601. Scope of Part Six.

(a) Part Six of these rules (Rules 601 through 612) applies to requests to the superior court to review decisions of the district court or an administrative agency under AS 22.10.020(d) and AS 22.15.240(a), either by appeal or by petition for review.

(b) An appeal may be taken to the superior court from a final judgment entered by the district court, in the circumstances specified in AS 22.15.240, or from a final decision of an administrative agency.

(c) On any point not addressed in Part Six, procedure in appeals to the superior court shall be governed by the provisions of Parts Two and Five of these rules, and procedure in petitions for review to the superior court shall be governed by the provisions of Part Four of these rules.

(SCO 439 effective November 15, 1980; amended by SCO 848 effective January 15, 1988; by SCO 1015 effective July 15, 1990; and by SCO 1245 effective July 15, 1996)

Annotations

Cases

I. In General.
II. Appeals from District Court.
III. Appeals from Administrative Agencies.

I. In General.

The fact that a jury on appeal in a tax matter may act independently of a record created by a board of equalization does not mean that the proceeding must be regarded as a new civil action to which this rule cannot apply. **Winegardner v. Greater Anchorage Area Borough,** Op. No. 1133, 534 P2d 541 (Alaska 1975).

A tax assessment cannot be challenged in an original proceeding in superior court. The exclusive means of challenging such an assessment is by appeal to the superior court. **Fedpack International v. State Dept. of Revenue,** Op. No. 2520, 646 P2d 240 (Alaska 1982).

Shareholders were precluded from challenging a consent decree between the corporation, its board of directors, and the Division of Banking, Securities, and Corporations because the decree expressly stated that it was the final decision, and shareholders did not follow the procedures provided in AS 45.55.940(a) and this rule **Brown v. Dick,** Op. No. 5862, 107 P.3d 260 (Alaska 2005).

II. Appeals from District Court.

A superior court judge, acting as an intermediate appellate court judge, may properly rule on decisions rendered by the district court even if a superior court judge was presiding. **Stephens v. Hammersley,** Op. No. 1275, 550 P2d 1268 (Alaska 1976).

Under this rule a superior court judge acting as an intermediate appellate judge may properly rule on decisions rendered by superior court judge acting as district court trial judge. **Milne v. Anderson,** Op. No. 1313, 554 P2d 402 (Alaska 1976).

III. Appeals from Administrative Agencies.

A board of equalization is an "administrative agency," within the meaning of this rule. **Winegardner v. Greater Anchorage Area Borough,** Op. No. 1133, 534 P2d 541 (Alaska 1975).

An appeal from decision of administrative agency should be filed in accordance with this rule. **Alaska Public Utilities Comm'n. v. Municipality of Anchorage,** Op. No. 1326, 555 P2d 262 (Alaska 1976).

Action for injunctive relief against administrative agency could be treated as an appeal and allowed under Appellate Rule 46 even though not filed in accordance with Appellate Rule 45. **Alaska Public Utilities Comm'n. v. Municipality of Anchorage,** Op. No. 1326, 555 P2d 262 (Alaska 1976).

Dismissal of state from appeal from Workmen's Compensation Board due to failure of appellant to file proper appeal under Appellate Rule 45(a)(2) was reversed where such dismissal, though technically correct, might have prevented an innocent party from collecting rightfully due disability benefits. **State Dept. of Highways v. Burgess Const. Co.,** Op. No. 1581, 575 P2d 792 (Alaska 1978).

Contractor's appeal from adverse decision of state contracting officer, after hearing before Contract Claims Review Board, was governed by Appellate Rule 45. **State v. Lundgren Pacific Const. Co.,** Op. No. 1980, 603 P2d 889 (Alaska 1979).

Where persons appeared and testified at a hearing of Alcoholic Beverage Control Board to protest issuance of liquor license they had standing to seek judicial review under Appellate Rule 45 of the Board's decision to issue the license. **Ketchikan Retail Liquor Dealers v. State, Etc.,** Op. No. 1963, 602 P2d 434 (Alaska 1979).

A complaint for injunctive relief from administrative agency decision denying complainant a rate increase is distinct from an appeal of an administrative order pursuant to Appellate Rule 45. **United States v. RCA Alaska Communications,** 597 P2d 489 (Alaska 1979).

An order issued by the Alaska State Commission for Human Rights may be challenged only in an administrative appeal of that order pursuant to the appellate rules and statute providing for judicial review in accordance with the Administrative Procedure Act. **Pipeliners Union v. Alaska State Commission,** Op. No. 2820, 681 P2d 330 (Alaska 1984).

The Administrative Procedure Act is the exclusive means for reviewing orders issued by the Alaska State Commission for Human Rights; therefore, such orders cannot be reviewed in an enforcement action filed in superior court. **Pipeliners Union v. Alaska State Commission,** Op. No. 2820, 681 P2d 330 (Alaska 1984).

Because the decision whether to grant or deny an extension to file briefs in an administrative appeal is committed to the trial court's discretion, Supreme Court will reverse the decision only if it finds an abuse of discretion. **Sheehan v. University of Alaska,** Op. No. 2942, 700 P2d 1295 (Alaska 1985).

Trial court abused its discretion when it is denied appellant's request for a second extension of time to file an opening brief in an administrative appeal, since although appellant's tardiness went beyond normal excusable oversight, there was no interference with the trial court's efficient functioning, no prejudice to the parties or to the court, and no intended affront to the court's authority. **Sheehan v. University of Alaska,** Op. No. 2942, 700 P2d 1295 (Alaska 1985).

Unless the legislature provides otherwise, administrative decisions are presumed to be judicially reviewable; accordingly, where city did not expressly authorize judicial review of its city council administrative decisions but did not preclude it, the superior court had jurisdiction to hear appeals from those administrative decisions, and the Alaska appellate rules were applicable. **Bethel Utilities Corp. v. City of Bethel,** Op. No. 3510, 780 P2d 1018 (Alaska 1989).

A superior court acting as a court of appeal from the decision of an administrative agency has authority to award attorney's fees. Ordinarily, such award should only partially compensate the prevailing party and be limited to attorney's fees incurred in court, not incurred in the prior administrative proceeding; however, actual costs and attorney's fees may be awarded where authorized by statute; further, actual costs and attorney's fees may be awarded to a successful appellee where the court finds that the appeal is frivolous or has been brought simply for the purpose of delay. **Kenai Peninsula Bor. v. Cook Inlet Reg.,** Op. No. 3671, 807 P2d 487 (Alaska 1991).

When superior court acts as intermediate court of appeal under this rule, supreme court independently reviews merits of administrative determination. **Grove v. Alaska Const. and Erectors,** Op. No. 4905, 948 P2d 454 (Alaska 1997).

Where superior court sat as a court of appeal reviewing a decision by the Department of Natural Resources, Supreme Court of Alaska independently reviewed the merits of the administrative determination and did not defer to the superior court's decision. **Kachemak Bay Conservation Soc. v. DNR,** Op. No. 5303, 6 P3d 270, 553 P2d 8 (Alaska 2000).

Rule 602. Time—Venue—Notice—Bonds.

(a) **When Taken.**

(1) *Appeals from the District Court.* An appeal may be taken to the superior court from the district court within 30 days from the date shown in the clerk's certificate of distribution on the judgment.

(2) *Appeals from Administrative Agencies.* An appeal may be taken to the superior court from an administrative agency within 30 days from the date that the decision appealed from is mailed or otherwise distributed to the appellant. If a request for agency reconsideration is timely filed before the agency, the notice of appeal must be filed within 30 days after the date the agency's reconsideration decision is mailed or otherwise distributed to the appellant, or after the date the request for reconsideration is deemed denied under agency regulations whichever is earlier. The 30-day period for taking an appeal does not begin to run until the agency has issued a decision that clearly states that it is a final decision and that the claimant has thirty days to appeal. An appeal that is taken from a final decision that does not include such a statement is not a premature appeal.

(3) Rule 204(a)(2)–(6) concerning the timing of appeals applies to appeals to superior court.

(b) **Venue.**

(1) *Appeals from the District Court.* Venue for an appeal from a district court decision shall be at the superior court location within the same judicial district as the district court that would best serve the convenience of the parties.

(2) *Appeals from Administrative Agencies.* Unless otherwise provided by law, venue for an appeal from an administrative agency decision shall be at the superior court location that would best serve the convenience of the parties.

(c) **Notice of Appeal.**

(1) A party may appeal from a judgment or agency decision by filing a notice of appeal with the superior court. The notice of appeal must specify the parties taking the appeal and their current addresses, designate the judgment, agency decision or part thereof appealed from, and name the court to which the appeal is taken. At the time the notice of appeal is served and filed, it must be accompanied by:

(A) a statement of points on which appellant intends to rely on appeal. The grounds for appeal stated in the statement of points on appeal constitute the sole basis for review by the superior court. On motion in the superior court, and for cause, the statement of points may be supplemented;

(B) if required, the filing fee as provided by Administrative Rule 9;

(C) if required, a bond for costs on appeal as provided by paragraph (e) of this rule;

(D) a copy of the district court judgment or agency decision from which the appeal is taken; and

(E) proof of service on all parties to the appeal. In an appeal from an agency decision, the notice of appeal must be served on the head of the agency and, if the agency is a state agency, on the Attorney General of Alaska, at Juneau, Alaska.

(2) An appellant seeking to have the cost bond waived or reduced, an extension of time to file the bond, or to appeal at public expense shall file an appropriate motion at the time the notice of appeal is filed.

(3) The clerk of the superior court shall refuse to accept for filing any notice of appeal not conforming with the requirements of this rule.

(d) **Notification by Clerk.**

(1) In an appeal from a district court which is not at the same location as the superior court, the clerk shall send a copy of the notice of appeal to the district court and shall notify the district court of the date by which it must forward the record on appeal as provided by Rule 604(a)(1).

(2) In an appeal from an administrative agency, the clerk shall send a copy of the notice of appeal to the agency and request the agency to submit a list of the names and addresses of all counsel who appeared in the matter before the agency, and of all persons who appeared therein pro se. The agency shall file the list with the clerk within ten days of service of the request. The clerk also shall notify the agency of the date by which it must prepare the record in accordance with Rule 604(b)(1).

(e) **Cost Bond.**

(1) In a civil case or an appeal from an administrative agency, unless a party is exempted by law, or has filed an approved supersedeas bond under Rule 603(a)(2), a bond for costs on appeal must be filed in superior court with the notice of appeal. The amount and terms of the bond are governed by Rule 204(c)(1) and Civil Rule 80.

(2) The cost bond exemptions provided by Rule 204(c)(2) apply in appeals to superior court.

(f) **Supersedeas Bond.** The appellant may file a supersedeas bond pursuant to Rule 603(a)(2) in lieu of a cost bond.

(g) **Cash Deposit.** The appellant may deposit cash in the amount of the bond with the court in lieu of filing a cost or supersedeas bond. At the time of the deposit, appellant also shall file a written instrument properly executed and acknowledged by the owner of the cash, or by the owner's attorney or the owner's authorized agent, setting forth the ownership of the fund; agreement to the terms of Civil Rule 80(f); and satisfaction of the conditions specified in Rule 204(c)(1) if the deposit is in lieu of a cost bond, or Rule 204(d) if the deposit is in lieu of a supersedeas bond.

(h) **Parties to the Appeal.** All parties to the trial court or agency action when the final order or judgment was entered are parties to the appeal. A party who files a notice of appeal, whether separately or jointly, is an appellant under these rules. All other parties, including the agency in an appeal from an administrative agency decision, are deemed to be appellees. An appellee may elect at any time not to participate in the appeal by filing and serving a notice of non-participation. The filing of a notice of non-participation shall not affect whether the party is bound by the decision on appeal.

(i) **Joint or Consolidated Appeals.** If two or more parties are entitled to appeal from a judgment or order of a court or agency and their interests are such as to make joinder practical, they may file a joint notice of appeal. Appeals may be consolidated by order of the appellate court upon its own motion or upon motion of a party.

(j) **Service of Documents.** Papers filed or served in the appeal must be served on all parties, except appellees who have elected not to participate in the action.

(SCO 439 effective November 15, 1980; amended by SCO 460 effective June 1, 1981; by SCO 495 effective January 4, 1982; by SCO 510 effective August 30, 1982; by SCO 514 effective October 1, 1982; by SCO 554 effective April 4, 1983; by SCO 575 effective February 1, 1984; by SCO 847 effective January 15, 1988; by SCO 888 effective July 15, 1988; by SCO 1015 effective January 15, 1990; by SCO 1250 effective July 15, 1996; by SCO 1284 effective January 15, 1998; by SCO 1385 effective April 15, 2000; by SCO 1411 effective October 15, 2000; and by SCO 1476 effective October 15, 2002)

Note: h. 77 SLA 2002 (HB157), Section 2, adds new Chapter 26 to Title 6 of the Alaska Statutes, concerning providers of fiduciary services. According to Section 9 of the Act, AS 06.26.760(b)(2) has the effect of amending Appellate Rule 602 by postponing the deadlines for the filing of appeals to the superior court from a district court of an administrative agency by a trust company when the Department of Community and Economic Development has taken possession of the trust company.

Annotations

Cases

Thirty-day limit for appeal from administrative agency does not apply when administrative process is not adjudicatory. **Moore v. State,** Op. No. 1284, 553 P2d 8 (Alaska 1976).

Where dismissed tenured teacher first knew of need to appeal in April, was served with decision in June, and did not attempt to appeal until August, it was not abuse of discretion to refuse to relax rules to permit appeal. **Jerrel v. Kenai Peninsula Borough School District,** Op. No. 1458, 567 P2d 760 (Alaska 1977).

Time for appeal begins to run with service of written findings, conclusions, and decision. **Jerrel v. Kenai Peninsula Borough School District,** Op. No. 1458, 567 P2d 760 (Alaska 1977).

Time period for appeal of property tax assessment was not tolled by action of borough assembly on an ordinance that would have mooted the appeal. **North Star, Inc. v. Fairbanks North Star Borough,** Op. No. 2258, 621 P2d 1335 (Alaska 1981).

A claim for damages resulting from an administrative order and an action for injunctive relief which seeks the same review by the superior court as could be had in an appeal from the administrative order are to be treated as administrative appeals, but a request for declaratory judgment on the constitutionality of statutes and regulations governing the administrative agency is an independent action. **Owsichek v. Alaska Guide Licensing and Control Board,** Op. No. 2328, 627 P2d 616 (Alaska 1981).

The essential question in determining whether a case before the superior court is an administrative appeal is whether the claim challenges a prior administrative decision. **Ballard v. Stich,** Op. No. 2363, 628 P2d 918 (Alaska 1981).

Considerations to be balanced in deciding whether to relax the appellate time limit rules include the right to appellate review, the willfulness and extent of the rules violation and the possible injustice that might result from a dismissal. **Estate of Smith v. State,** Op. No. 2428, 635 P2d 465 (Alaska 1981).

Trial court abused its discretion in failing to relax the thirty-day appeal period of this rule in situation where late filing was due to appellant's mistaken but not unreasonable belief that he was entitled to reconsideration of an agency decision denying his request for an administrative hearing. **Anderson v. State Commercial Fisheries Entry Comm.,** Op. No. 2588, 654 P2d 1320 (Alaska 1982).

Reconsideration decision by Commercial Fisheries Entry Commission reversing hearing officer's recommended decision to grant appellant's entry permit application constituted a final administrative determination which could be appealed to superior court within 30 days. **Ostman v. State, Commercial Fisheries Entry,** Op. No. 2792, 678 P2d 1323 (Alaska 1984).

Although a final determination denying appellant's application for an entry permit was made more than 3 years prior to his request that the case be reopened due to administrative error, entry commission's letter to applicant rejecting his claim of administrative error on the merits was a final administrative determination subject to judicial review. **Moore v. State, Commercial Fisheries,** Op. No. 2870, 688 P2d 582 (Alaska 1984).

Superior court order which would have exempted all administrative appeals from the bond requirements of the appellate rules was invalid. **State, Dept. of Public Safety v. Wilkinson,** Op. No. 2875, 688 P2d 939 (Alaska 1984).

An appeal to superior court from a decision of a state administrative agency requires service of notice upon the attorney general. **Vincent v. Commercial Fisheries Entry Comm'n,** Op. No. 3041, 717 P2d 391 (Alaska 1986).

Failure of applicant to serve attorney general's office with a notice of appeal from state administrative agency's denial of permit application did not deprive superior court of jurisdiction over the appeal, thus court, after allowing late service of notice upon the attorney general, could hear the appeal, absent proof of prejudice to the state from the late notification. **Vincent v. Commercial Fisheries Entry Comm'n,** Op. No. 3041, 717 P2d 391 (Alaska 1986).

Civil Rule 210, which places the ultimate responsibility on the appellant for preparation of a record within 40 days from the date of filing the notice of appeal from an agency decision and provides for dismissal as a sanction for noncompliance, did not relieve the agency of its obligation to prepare the record on appeal and did not excuse the superior court clerk's failure to notify the agency of the date by which the record had to be prepared. **King v. State Dept. of Natural Resources,** Op. No. 3226, 742 P2d 253 (Alaska 1987).

In light of the fact that superior court order holding appellant's appeal from an administrative agency decision in abeyance was never vacated, that the agency did not furnish the superior court clerk with a copy of its decision on reconsideration, that the agency did not prepare and certify the record on appeal; and that the clerk of the superior court never notified the agency of the date by which it was to complete the record on appeal; appellant's counsel reasonably could have been in doubt as to how to proceed with the administrative appeal, thus superior court erred in dismissing the appeal for lack of prosecution. **King v. State Dept. of Natural Resources,** Op. No. 3226, 742 P2d 253 (Alaska 1987).

Administrative appeals, even when they are labeled independent actions, must be taken within 30 days. **Haynes v. State Comm. Fisheries Entry,** Op. No. 3254, 746 P2d 892 (Alaska 1987).

However denominated, a claim is functionally an administrative appeal if it requires the court to consider the propriety of an agency determination; accordingly, appellant's claim for injunctive relief had to be considered an administrative appeal since the relief sought — a remand of his fishing application to the Commercial Fisheries Entry Commission — could only be granted if the court determined that the commission's prior decision denying the application was erroneous. **Haynes v. State Comm. Fisheries Entry,** Op. No. 3254, 746 P2d 892 (Alaska 1987).

Employee's appeal from a decision of the Public Employees Retirement System Board, filed 34 days after the employee received the Board's written decision, was properly dismissed as untimely. **Powers v. Public Emp. Retirement Bd.,** Op. No. 3362, 757 P2d 65 (Alaska 1988).

A challenge to an administrative decision, even if it is a constitutional challenge, is subject to the thirty-day period of limitation contained in this rule. **Kollodge v. State,** Op. No. 3355, 757 P2d 1028 (Alaska 1988).

Whenever an entity which normally acts as a legislative body applies policy to particular persons in their private capacities, instead of passing on general policy or the rights of individuals in the abstract, it is functioning as an administrative agency within the meaning of this rule. **Kollodge v. State,** Op. No. 3355, 757 P2d 1028 (Alaska 1988).

An appeal to the superior court from a hearing before the Commissioner of Administration which terminated public employee's grievance request for reinstatement, back pay and compensatory damages denied was subject to the thirty-day period of limitation contained in this rule. **Kollodge v. State,** Op. No. 3355, 757 P2d 1028 (Alaska 1988).

Negligence of attorney in failing to timely file appeal from adverse decision of Alaska Workers' Compensation Board was not sufficient ground to relieve the attorney's client of the filing requirement. **Beavers v. Alaska Const., Inc.,** Op. No. 3560, 787 P2d 643 (Alaska 1990).

A challenge to an administrative decision, even if based on constitutional grounds, is subject to the 30-day limitation of this rule. **Diedrich v. City of Ketchikan,** Op. No. 3661, 805 P2d 362 (Alaska 1991).

Any claim which is functionally an administrative appeal must be brought within the 30-day limit of this rule; however denominated, a claim is functionally an administrative appeal if it requires the court to consider the propriety of agency determination. **Diedrich v. City of Ketchikan,** Op. No. 3661, 805 P2d 362 (Alaska 1991).

City employee's complaint in superior court that the city breached the covenant of good faith and fair dealing implied in his employment contract when it discharged him, allegedly in retaliation for appealing his termination to the city personnel board, was the functional equivalent of an administrative appeal, and therefore had to be brought within the 30-day appeal period of this rule. **Diedrich v. City of Ketchikan,** Op. No. 3661, 805 P2d 362 (Alaska 1991).

Where dispute existed as to whether claimant appealed administrative agency's action, but claimant received no final order from the agency resolving whether he had in fact appealed, his appeal to superior court could not be held untimely when he filed the appeal as soon as he reasonably could have believed that his administrative remedies were exhausted. **Morgan v. Dept. of Revenue,** Op. No. 3706, 813 P2d 295 (Alaska 1991).

Time for appeal of agency decision commences running only if the decision is a final, appealable order. **Far North Sanitation v. Alaska Pub. Util.,** Op. No. 3807, 825 P2d 867 (Alaska 1992).

Order of public utilities commission declaring garbage company's rates to be interim rates subject to refund pending final rate determination was not a final, appealable order, since the order gave the company time to submit a tariff advise letter and a revenue requirements study in support of its rates. **Far North Sanitation v. Alaska Pub. Util.,** Op. No. 3807, 825 P2d 867 (Alaska 1992).

However denominated, a claim is functionally an administrative appeal if it requires the court to consider the propriety of an agency determination. **Fairbanks North Star Borough v. State,** Op. No. 3815, 826 P2d 760 (Alaska (1992).

To the extent that suit filed by borough against the State for trespass, inverse condemnation, quiet title, ejectment, recision and restitution turned upon a review of matters that were raised or could have been raised in a prior administrative hearing before the Department of Natural Resources, the action was barred as an untimely appeal of an administrative determination; although the suit was styled as an independent action advancing different issues than were considered by the Department, the relief sought was essentially the same as that sought in the administrative hearing. **Fairbanks North Star Borough v. State,** Op. No. 3815, 826 P2d 760 (Alaska (1992).

Whenever entity which normally acts as legislative body applies policy to particular persons in their private capacities, instead of engaging in general policy or the rights of individuals in the abstract, it is functioning as administrative agency within meaning of this rule. **Pederson-Szafran v. Baily,** Op. No. 3877, 837 P2d 124 (Alaska 1992).

The State in providing full evidentiary hearing to determine facts and circumstances involved in termination of probationary employee was functioning as administrative agency, thus employee's superior court appeal from hearing officer's decision had to be brought within 30 days of that decision. **PedersonSzafran v. Baily,** Op. No. 3877, 837 P2d 124 (Alaska 1992).

For 30-day appeal deadline of this rule to apply, agency must clearly indicate that decision is final order and that claimant has 30 days to appeal; where agency letter terminating employee failed to note either of these two requirements, 30-day appeal deadline had to be relaxed. **Manning v. Alaska R. R. Corp.,** Op. No. 3968, 853 P2d 1120 (Alaska 1993).

Alaska Railroad Corporation's decision to terminate employee for violation of policy on drugs was administrative agency determination, thus employee's complaint in superior court for wrongful termination and breach of contract was equivalent of appeal from administrative agency, and subject to 30-day appeal deadline of this rule. **Manning v. Alaska R. R. Corp.,** Op. No. 3968, 853 P2d 1120 (Alaska 1993).

Where administrative agency's decision was communicated in letter constituted final order or that claimant had thirty days to appeal, it was abuse of discretion for trial court to refuse to relax thirty-day appeal deadline. **Skudrzyx v. Reynolds,** Op. No. 3983, 856 P2d 462 (Alaska 1993).

De novostandard or review applied to superior court's grant of summary judgment in case involving teacher's claims that school district erred in finding she owed money to district and therefore lost her tenured status because her teaching certificate temporarily lapsed. The complaint was filed within thirty days as an administrative appeal must be; the material facts were undisputed; the parties were arguing matters of law; and no agency expertise was involved. **Nenana City School District v. Coghill,** Op. No. 4229, 898 P2d 929 (Alaska 1995).

Trial court correctly waived thirty-day appeal period for school superintendent's appeal of termination by school district where notification of termination did not state that decision was final or that he had thirty days to appeal. **Kilmer v. Dilingham City School Dist.,** Op. No. 4778, 932 P2d 757 (Alaska 1997).

Where father petitioned the Department of Revenue, Child Support Enforcement Division (CSED), to seek modification of judicial child support order, CSED's decision not to seek modification of the order was a final, reviewable agency action; since CSED never gave father notice of the 30-day window for appealing the decision, father's appeal, filed 145 days after the decision, should have been accepted as timely. **Allen v. State Dept. of Revenue,** Op. No. 5342, 15 P3d 743 (Alaska 2000).

In class action suit by legal aliens residing in Alaska seeking declaratory judgment as to constitutionality of statute restricting permanent fund dividend eligibility to persons lawfully admitted for permanent residence in the United States, trial court did not err in concluding that class members were not required to exhaust administrative remedies, since to do so would have been futile, or in concluding that class certification was proper. **State Dept. of Revenue v. Andrade,** Op. No. 5414, 23 P3d 58 (Alaska 2001).

Letters from the Alaska Child Support Enforcement Division to the father did not meet the requirements of section (a)(2) of this rule, meaning the division's review of the father's financial circumstances file was not closed properly; failure to send the father a closure letter had the consequence of keeping the review file open, and the modification was not retroactive. **Paxton v. Gavlak,** Op. No. 5839, 100 P.3d 7 (Alaska 2004).

Shareholders were precluded from challenging a consent decree between the corporation, its board of directors, and the Division of Banking, Securities, and Corporations in an administrative action pertaining to proxy disclosure violations because the decree expressly stated that it was the final decision and the shareholders did not follow the procedures and time limitations provided in AS 45.55.940(a) and **Brown v. Dick,** Op. No. 5862, 107 P.3d 260 (Alaska 2005).

Superior court abused its discretion in dismissing inmate's appeal as untimely where, following his classification hearing, the inmate appealed his transfer to the Department of Corrections' deputy commissioner; the deputy commissioner's letter rejected the inmate's appeal but did not state that it was a final decision or advise the inmate of his right to appeal within 30 days. **Carlson v. Renkes,** Op. No. 5903, 113 P.3d 638 (Alaska 2005).

Trial court properly converted a transportation company's action to void another transportation company's contract with a school district into an administrative appeal under Alaska. R. App. P. 602 because the action was a challenge to the school board's decision and was covered under administrative procedures. **Laidlaw Transit, Inc. v. Anchorage Sch. Dist.**, Op. No. 5931, 118 P.3d 1018 (Alaska 2005).

Rule 603. Stays.

(a) **Civil Appeals.**

(1) *Automatic Stay.* An automatic two day stay of execution or enforcement of district court judgments is provided for in District Court Civil Rule 24(a). A motion for stay and bond are not required for this stay.

(2) *Stay Upon Appeal—Supersedeas Bond.*

[a] *Stay.* When an appeal is taken, the appellant may obtain a stay of proceedings to enforce the judgment by filing a supersedeas bond. The stay is effective when the supersedeas bond is approved. The filing of a supersedeas bond does not prohibit the court from considering the public interest in deciding whether to impose or continue a stay on that portion of an administrative or district court judgment which is not limited to monetary relief.

[b] *Request for Approval.* A supersedeas bond, with a Request for Approval of Supersedeas Bond, must be served and filed with the district court, or with the superior court in administrative appeals. The bond may be filed at or after the time for filing the notice of appeal.

[c] *Amount and Form.* The amount of the supersedeas bond is 125% of the district court or administrative agency judgment (including any prejudgment interest, costs and attorney's fees), except that the court may specify a different amount based on the standard provided by Rule 204(d) upon motion by any party to the appeal. The form and conditions of the bond are governed by Civil Rule 80 and Appellate Rule 204(d).

[d] *Objections—Reconsideration.* An appellee may by motion raise objections to the form or amount of the bond or to the sufficiency of the surety. However, approval of the bond will not be delayed to allow objections to be filed. Objections filed after the supersedeas bond has been approved will be treated as a motion to rescind or modify the approval to be decided by the judge.

[e] *Approval.* The clerk may approve a supersedeas bond upon filing if: (i) the bond is in the form prescribed above; (ii) the amount of the bond is 125% of the judgment or, if the judge has ordered a different amount, in the amount ordered by the judge; and (iii) the bond is in cash pursuant to Rule 602(g) or is executed by approved surety companies. Otherwise, the judge must decide whether to approve the bond.

[f] *Exemption.* The state or an officer or agency thereof or a municipality or an officer or agency thereof desiring a stay on appeal is exempt from the requirement of filing a supersedeas bond.

(3) *Stay in Workers' Compensation Appeals.* An employer appealing to the superior court from a judgment of the Alaska Workers' Compensation Board may obtain a stay of the judgment pending the appeal by complying with subparagraph (a)(2) and by establishing that irreparable damage will result if the stay is not granted.

(4) *Stay in License Revocation Appeals.* The court may not stay a license revocation ordered under AS 28.15.166 unless the court finds that there is a reasonable probability that the appellant will prevail on the merits, that the appellant will suffer irreparable harm if the order is not stayed, and, in a case where the appellant operates a commercial motor vehicle, that the public can be adequately protected by conditions imposed by the court.

(5) *Proceedings on Stay.* When an appeal is taken, the district court judge or magistrate shall enter a written order indicating whether or not the proceedings to enforce a judgment have been stayed. If the proceedings are stayed, and process has been issued to enforce the judgment, the judge or magistrate must recall the process by written notice to the officer holding the process. Thereupon the process must be returned to the court, and all property seized or levied upon by virtue of such process must be released if it has not been sold, and in cases of civil arrest, the person arrested must be released from custody. This subdivision of this rule will not be construed as making any stay retroactive or as invalidating any proceedings or levies prior to the time the stay becomes effective.

(6) *Stay in Prisoner Disciplinary Appeals.* The court may not stay imposition of sanctions arising from a disciplinary decision of the Department of Corrections unless the court finds that the prisoner has alleged a violation of a fundamental constitutional right and is likely to succeed on the merits of the appeal, that the prisoner faces irreparable harm if a stay is not granted, that the Department of Corrections can be adequately protected if a stay is granted, and that a stay will not adversely affect the public interest in effective penal administration. In evaluating the stay motion, the court may consider documents and affidavits offered by either party, and shall consider the stay motion without waiting for the record to be prepared.

(b) **Criminal Appeals.** If a sentence of imprisonment is imposed, admission to bail will be allowed and the sentence stayed, pending appeal. A sentence to pay a fine or a fine and costs may be stayed, if an appeal is taken, by the district judge or magistrate or by the superior court upon such terms as the court deems proper. During appeal the court may require the defendant to deposit the whole or any part of the fine and costs in the registry of the superior court, or to give bond for the payment thereof, or to submit to an examination of assets, and it may make an appropriate order to restrain the defendant from dissipating his or her assets. An order placing the defendant on probation will be stayed if an appeal is taken.

(SCO 439 effective November 15, 1980; amended by SCO 554 effective April 4, 1983; by SCO 957 effective March 30, 1989; by SCO 1015 effective January 15, 1990; by SCO 1109 effective January 15, 1993; by SCO 1238 effective July 15, 1996; and by SCO 1385 effective April 15, 2000)

Note: AS 28.15.166(n), added by § 3 ch. 77 SLA 1983 and

amended by § 10 ch. 119 SLA 1990 and by § 6 ch. 3 SLA 1992, amended Appellate Rule 603 by prohibiting an automatic stay of the administrative revocation of a driver's license pending appeal and by limiting the power of the court to stay the administrative revocation of a driver's license. Subparagraph 603(a)(4) was added by SCO 1109 in order to incorporate the legislative changes to the rule. In the event the legislation mandating the changes is invalidated by a court of competent jurisdiction, SCO 1109 shall be considered automatically rescinded.

Note to SCO 1238: Appellate Rule 603(a)(6) was added by ch. 79 § 22 SLA 1995. Section 9 of this order is adopted for the sole reason that the legislature has mandated the amendment.

Annotations

Cases

An employer must make a showing of irreparable damage as well as filing a supersedeas bond in order to obtain a stay of a disability award in worker's compensation cases. **Wise Mechanical Contractors v. Bignell,** Op. No. 2329, 626 P2d 1085 (Alaska 1981).

A monetary enforcement judgment on an administrative order may be stayed as a matter of right upon the posting of an appropriate supersedeas bond under this rule. **Pipeliners Union v. Alaska State Commission,** Op. No. 2820, 681 P2d 330 (Alaska 1984).

In a consolidated review and enforcement proceeding pertaining to an order of the Alaska State Commission for Human Rights, the court could enter an enforcement judgment before entering a judgment on the appeal. **Pipeliners Union v. Alaska State Commission,** Op. No. 2820, 681 P2d 330 (Alaska 1984).

Superior court improperly stayed the payment of taxes during its review of administrative agency's order where the supersedeas bond filed with the court for the principal amount of taxes due did not include costs and interest. **City of Nome v. Catholic Bishop of Northern Alaska,** Op. No. 2986, 707 P2d 870 (Alaska 1985).

Even if AS 29.53.390(a), which authorizes judicial review of a disputed tax assessment, were interpreted to require payment of taxes before appeal, this rule supersedes it. **City of Nome v. Catholic Bishop of Northern Alaska,** Op. No. 2986, 707 P2d 870 (Alaska 1985).

Generally, in order to obtain stay of workers' compensation award, employer must demonstrate "financial irresponsibility" of claimant as well as probable success on the merits of the appeal. **Olsen Logging Co. v. Lawson,** Op. No. 3840, 832 P2d 174 (Alaska 1992).

Where employer is forced to make lump sum workers' compensation payment and will not, if successful on appeal, have obligation to make continuing payments of compensation, employer is without remedy to recover lump sum payment, thus lesser "serious and substantial questions" standard is to be used to determine whether lump sum award should be stayed on appeal. **Olsen Logging Co. v. Lawson,** Op. No. 3840, 832 P2d 174 (Alaska 1992).

The test presented in **A.J. Industries, Inc. v. Alaska Public Service Commission,** 470 P2d 537 (Alaska 1970) is still applicable under this rule. **Keane v. Local Boundary Commission,** Op. No. 4187, 893 P2d 1239 (Alaska 1995).

Stays not involving money judgments are not mandatory upon the mere issuance of a supersedeas bond. **Keane v. Local Boundary Commission,** Op. No. 4187, 893 P2d 1239 (Alaska 1995).

The superior court has discretion to grant a stay concerning a non-monetary judgment. This determination is guided by the "public interest." **Keane v. Local Boundary Commission,** Op. No. 4187, 893 P2d 1239 (Alaska 1995).

Where party seeking a stay made no showing of irreparable harm or probability of success on the merits, superior court did not abuse its discretion in denying stay. **Keane v. Local Boundary Commission,** Op. No. 4187, 893 P2d 1239 (Alaska 1995).

Rule 604. Record.

(a) **Appeals from District Court.**

(1) *Record on Appeal.*

(A) The record on appeal consists of the entire district court file, including the original papers and exhibits filed in the district court and a typed transcript of the record of proceedings before the district court.

(B) The record of proceedings before the district court will include electronic recordings rather than transcripts unless the superior court orders the submission of transcripts. In the absence of an agreement between the parties or an order of the court to the contrary, all reasonable costs incurred in connection with preparing a transcript will be borne by the appellant.

(C) Within 40 days after filing of the notice of appeal, the clerk of the superior court shall assemble the record and prepare and distribute notice of the due date for appellant's brief. The papers in the record need not be numbered and a table of contents need not be prepared.

(2) *Power of Court to Correct or Modify Record of District Court.* If any differences arise as to whether the record on appeal truly discloses what occurred in the district court, the difference must be submitted to and settled by the superior court and the record made to conform to it. If anything material to either party is omitted from the record on appeal by error or accident or is misstated therein, the parties by stipulation, the district court, or the superior court, on motion or of its own initiative, may direct that the omission or misstatement be corrected.

(3) *Return of Record and Appellate File After Final Disposition.* Unless the court otherwise orders, the clerk shall return the record and appellate file after final disposition to the district court as provided by Rule 512(a)(2).

(b) **Appeals from Administrative Agencies.**

(1) *Record on Appeal.*

(A) The record on appeal consists of the original papers and exhibits filed with the administrative agency, and a typed transcript of the record of proceedings before the agency. In an appeal from the revocation of a driver's license by the Division of Motor Vehicles or from a prisoner disciplinary decision of the Department of Corrections, the record of proceedings will include electronic recordings rather than transcripts unless otherwise ordered by the court.

(B) Appellate Rule 210 shall apply except that:

(i) Appellate Rule 210(b)(1) and (2) shall not apply.

(ii) The original transcript shall be filed with the administrative agency. The agency shall forward the transcript to the clerk of the superior court within 40 days after filing of the notice of appeal.

(iii) The administrative agency shall number the pages of the agency file consecutively throughout all volumes. The agency shall forward a copy of the numbered file to the clerk of the superior court with the transcript. Physical exhibits will be retained by the agency unless specifically requested by the court. As used in this rule, "physical exhibits" includes exhibits other than documents or photographs, and also includes documents or photographs of unusually large size or unusual bulk or weight.

(iv) In the absence of an agreement between the parties or an order of the court to the contrary, all reasonable costs incurred in connection with preparing the transcript and the court's copy of the agency file shall be borne by the appellant. The preparing agency may require advance payment of the costs as reasonably estimated by the agency.

(v) Upon receipt of the transcript and a copy of the agency file, the clerk of the superior court shall prepare and distribute notice of the due date for appellant's brief.

(2) *Return of Record and Appellate File After Final Disposition.* If a timely appeal from the superior court decision is filed and unless the court otherwise orders, the clerk shall return all physical exhibits after final disposition to the administrative agency as provided by Rule 512(a)(3). If a timely appeal is not filed, the clerk shall return all physical exhibits to the agency on the day after the time for filing an appeal expires. The appellate file will be retained by, or returned to, the superior court.

(SCO 439 effective November 15, 1980 as amended by SCO 767 effective March 15, 1987; by SCO 826 effective August 1, 1987; by SCO 873 effective July 15, 1988; by SCO 928 effective January 15, 1989; by SCO 1015 effective January 15, 1990; by SCO 1155 effective July 15, 1994; by SCO 1238 effective July 15, 1996; corrected January 1998; and by SCO 1555 effective October 15, 2004)

Note to SCO 1238: Appellate Rule 604(b)(1) (A) was amended by ch. 79 § 23 SLA 1995 to allow the use of cassette tapes in prisoner disciplinary appeals. Section 11 of this order is adopted for the sole reason that the legislature has mandated the amendment. The clerk will also accept other forms of electronic recording, such as CDs.

Annotations

Cases

On appeal of administrative agency decision to superior court, this rule ordinarily requires advance payment by appellant for preparation of the administrative record, but superior court may relieve appellant of the prepayment requirement for good cause. **Baker v. University of Alaska,** Op. No. 5402, 22 P3d 440 (Alaska 2001).

This rule, which requires advance payment by appellant for preparation of administrative record on appeal, should have been waived for appellant who demonstrated his inability to raise the $3,500 necessary to prepay the record preparation costs. **Baker v. University of Alaska,** Op. No. 5402, 22 P3d 440 (Alaska 2001).

It was error to dismiss the claimant's appeal from the decision of the board denying his claim for workers' compensation benefits for failure to pay for or accept responsibility for the payment of preparation of a transcript where the superior court's order of dismissal indicated that it was unaware of its power under Alaska R. App. P. 604(b)(1)(B)(iv) to deviate from the ordinary procedure requiring prepayment upon a showing of good cause; this power included waiving the prepayment requirement, requiring the claimant to narrow the designation of needed transcripts, or even allowing designation of the use of tapes (with log notes) if the testimony being reviewed was not so lengthy as to cause an undue burden for the reviewing court. **Bustamante v. Alaska Workers' Comp. Bd.,** Op. No.5648,59 P.3d 270 (Alaska 2002).

Where a superior court did not hold a trial de novo on appeal from a hearing officer's determination that a curfew ordinance was constitutional, the superior court acted within its discretion under this rule to review only the administrative agency record. **Treacy v. Municipality of Anchorage,** Op. No. 5807, 91 P.3d 252 (Alaska 2004).

Rule 605. Briefs and Memoranda.

(a) **Appeals from Administrative Agencies.** Unless the superior court orders to the contrary:

(1) the time for service and filing briefs is governed by Rule 212(a)(1);

(2) The form of briefs is governed by Rule 212(b), except the briefs must be two-hole punched at the center of the top of each page rather than bound, the brief covers need not be on colored paper, and the briefs may be in clear and legible black printing rather than typewritten;

(3) the substantive requirements of briefs are governed by Rule 212(c); and

(4) the filing of a single copy of the brief with proof of service is sufficient, without the necessity of duplication as provided by Rule 212(a)(2).

(b) **Appeals from District Court.** Unless the superior court orders to the contrary, the parties may file memoranda on appeal as specified by this paragraph instead of briefs. Unless otherwise ordered:

(1) the time for service and filing of memoranda is governed by Rule 212(a)(1);

(2) the form of memoranda is governed by Rule 513.5;

(3) the length of appellant's and appellee's opening memoranda may not exceed 20 numbered pages, and the length of appellant's reply memoranda may not exceed 10 numbered pages;

(4) the memoranda must include a statement of issues presented for review, a summary of facts, a discussion of the law and its application to the facts, and a short conclusion stating the precise relief sought;

(5) the filing of a single copy of the memoranda with proof of service is sufficient without the necessity of duplication as provided by Rule 212(a)(2) and (3); and

(6) the consequences of submitting defective memoranda

or the failure to file memoranda, and the citation of supplemental authorities are governed by Rule 212(c)(10)—(12).

(SCO 439 effective November 15, 1980; amended by SCO 1015 effective January 15, 1990; by SCO 1155 effective July 15, 1994; and by SCO 1157 effective July 15, 1994)

Annotations

Cases

Defendant's waiver of the right to file a brief on appeal to superior court was not revoked by supreme court's remand for a determination on the merits of the appeal, hence waiver was effective as to defendant's second appeal on the same issues. **Milne v. Anderson,** Op. No. 3222, 576 P2d 109 (Alaska 1978).

Rule 605.5. Oral Argument.

(a) **Request.** Either party may serve and file a written request for oral argument not later than 10 days after the date on which appellant's reply brief or memorandum is due, pursuant to Rule 605, or pursuant to any extension of that time granted under Rule 502 or 503. If no appellee's brief or memorandum is filed, the appellant's request for oral argument must be filed within 10 days after the due date of the appellee's brief or memorandum. No response to a request for oral argument may be filed.

(b) **Right to Oral Argument.** In an appeal from a civil case where the controversy on appeal concerns less than $300 or from a minor offense as defined by District Court Criminal Rule 8(b), oral argument will be scheduled only if ordered by the superior court for good cause shown. In all other appeals, oral argument will be scheduled automatically if timely requested by either party.

(c) **Time Allowed.** The time allowed for oral argument, unless otherwise ordered, is 15 minutes per side.

(SCO 810 effective August 1, 1987; as amended by SCO 1015 effective January 15, 1990)

Rule 606. Dismissal.

(a) **By Parties or Court.** Dismissal of appeals by parties is governed by Rule 511. Dismissal of appeals by the superior court or clerk of the superior court is governed by Rule 511.5.

(b) **Nonpayment of Costs.** If the costs for preparation of the record or transcript on appeal are not paid within 30 days of notification that such costs are due, the appeal may be dismissed by the superior court on its own motion or on the motion of opposing counsel.

(SCO 439 effective November 15, 1980; amended by SCO 929 effective January 15, 1989)

Rule 607. Conflicts with Other Procedures in Administrative Appeal.

These rules supersede all other procedural methods specified in Alaska statutes for appeals from administrative agencies to the courts of Alaska.

(SCO 439 effective November 15, 1980; as amended by SCO 1015 effective January 15, 1990)

Rule 608. Sentence Appeal.

A sentence appeal to the superior court is governed by Rule 215. That rule will in case of inconsistency prevail over Part Six of these rules, except that (1) the notice of appeal must be filed in the superior court; and (2) as provided by Rule 604, the record on appeal consists of the entire district court file, including the original papers and exhibits filed in the district court, and the electronic record of proceedings before the district court. It is only necessary to file with the court the original memorandum on appeal; no additional copies are required.

(SCO 439 effective November 15, 1980; amended by SCO 554 effective April 4, 1983; by SCO 928 effective January 15, 1989; by SCO 930 effective January 15, 1989; by SCO 1015 effective January 15, 1990; by SCO 1067 effective July 15, 1991; and by SCO 1155 effective July 15, 1994)

Rule 609. Powers of the Superior Court.

(a) **Powers of Superior Court.** After notice of appeal to the superior court has been given, the superior court may make such orders as are necessary and proper to aid its appellate jurisdiction.

(b) **De Novo Trial.**

(1) In an appeal from an administrative agency, the superior court may in its discretion grant a trial de novo in whole or in part. If a trial de novo is granted, the action will be considered as having been commenced in that court at the time that the record on appeal is received by the superior court.

(2) All further proceedings in such action are governed by the rules governing procedure in the superior court, except that no summons nor any amended or additional pleadings shall be served unless authorized or required by the court. The hearing or trial of the action shall be upon the record thus filed and upon such evidence as may be produced in the superior court.

(c) **Change of Judge as a Matter of Right.**

(1) Any party to an appeal from an administrative agency to the superior court may peremptorily challenge the judge to whom the appeal is assigned, pursuant to the limitations and procedures in Civil Rule 42(c). The notice of change of judge is timely if filed within five days after notice to the party of the assignment.

(2) No peremptory challenge of the judge to whom an appeal is assigned is allowed in an appeal from the district court to the superior court.

(SCO 439 effective November 15, 1980; amended by SCO 1015 effective January 15, 1990)

Note: AS 10.06.633, as enacted by ch. 166, § 1, SLA 1988, amended Appellate Rule 609 by requiring that an appeal from an involuntary dissolution of a corporation be tried de novo by the superior court. AS 10.06.863, as enacted by ch. 166, § 1, SLA 1988, amended Appellate Rule 609 by requiring that an appeal from a revocation from a certificate of authority of a foreign corporation to transaction business in Alaska be tried de novo by the superior court. AS 10.06.915, as enacted by ch. 166, § 1, SLA 1988, amended Appellate Rule 609 by requiring that an appeal from the failure to approve articles of incorporation and certain other administrative decisions be tried de novo by the superior court.

Annotations

Cases

The superior court may extend the time for filing an appeal from an administrative agency decision if the appellant shows that enforcement of the appeal deadline would result in surprise and injustice to the appellant. **Owsichek v. Alaska Guide Licensing and Control Board,** Op. No. 2328, 627 P2d 616 (Alaska 1981).

Where superior court exercised its discretion and granted a "trial de novo on the record" on appeal of an administrative decision by a city manager dismissing a police officer, appellate court review would be of the superior court's decision affirming the dismissal rather than the administrative decision itself. **Kott v. City of Fairbanks,** Op. No. 2642, 661 P2d 177 (Alaska 1983).

Superior court order which would have exempted all administrative appeals from the bond requirements of the appellate rules was invalid. **State, Dept. of Public Safety v. Wilkinson,** Op. No. 2875, 688 P2d 939 (Alaska 1984).

Although claimant who disagreed with an administrative decision and brought suit within 30 days would not have the right to a de novo trial, the superior court would have the discretion to order a trial de novo under this rule. **State v. Dupere,** Op. No. 3080, 721 P2d 638 (Alaska 1986).

In review of administrative agency determination, superior court did not abuse its discretion in declining to supplement record and to review de novo record as so supplemented. **Southwest Marine, Inc. v. State,** Op. No. 4843, 941 P2d 166 (Alaska 1997).

Where there was no suggestion of inadequate procedure or bias in a hearing officer's determination that a curfew ordinance was constitutional, the superior court acted within its discretion under this rule in not granting a trial de novo on the broad question of the constitutional validity of the ordinance. **Treacy v. Municipality of Anchorage,** Op. No. 5807, 91 P.3d 252 (Alaska 2004).

Rule 610. Petitions for Review of Nonappealable Orders or Decisions.

(a) **When Available.** An aggrieved party, including the state of Alaska, may petition the superior court to review any order or decision not appealable under Rule 602 of a district court or of an administrative agency in a proceeding in which the superior court has appellate jurisdiction.

(b) **When Granted.** Review is not a matter of right, but will be granted only when the sound policy behind the general rule of requiring appeals to be taken only from final judgments is outweighed because;

(1) Postponement of review until appeal may be taken from a final judgment will result in injustice because of impairment of a legal right or because of unnecessary delay, expense, hardship or other related factors;

(2) The order or decision involves a controlling question of law on which there is a substantial ground for difference of opinion, and an immediate review of the order may materially advance the termination of the proceeding in the other forum; or

(3) The district court so far departed from the accepted and usual course of judicial proceedings, or the administrative agency has so far departed from the accepted and usual course of administrative adjudication, as to call for the superior court's power of supervision and review.

(SCO 439 effective November 15, 1980; as amended by SCO 1015 effective January 15, 1990)

Annotations

Cases

While this rule does not expressly set forth a finality requirement on appeals from administrative agency decisions, a finality requirement is nonetheless implied. **Ostman v. State, Commercial Fisheries Entry,** Op. No. 2792, 678 P2d 1323 (Alaska 1984).

Under this rule a superior court has jurisdiction to consider petitions for review by the state from district court final orders as well as from interlocutory orders. **State v. Stocker,** Op. No. 739, 741 P2d 1215 (Alaska App. 1987).

Where trial court stayed the underlying action and retained jurisdiction over the matter pending resolution of specified questions within the expertise of an administrative agency, the agency ruling was interlocutory in nature and was directly appealable only upon entry of final judgment in the underlying court action; although the trial court improperly characterized the interlocutory ruling as appealable, the Supreme Court chose to treat the appeal as a petition for review and to address the merits of the questions presented in light of the parties' apparent reliance on earlier trial court rulings and because disposition of the case would dispose of the issues remaining in the underlying civil action. **Wade Oilfield v. Providence Wash. Ins.,** Op. No. 3372, 759 P2d 1302 (Alaska 1988).

Rule 611. Petitions for Review—Procedure.

(a) **Filing.**

(1) A petition for review of a district court order or decision, with the filing fee, must be filed with the clerk of the superior court within 10 days after the date of notice of the challenged order or decision, along with proof of service on all parties. Date of notice is defined in Civil Rule 58.1(c) and Criminal Rule 32.3(c). The clerk of the superior court shall proceed in accordance with Rule 403(a)(4).

(2) A petition for review of an order or decision of an administrative agency, with the filing fee, must be filed with the clerk of the superior court within 10 days after the date of mailing or other distribution of the order or decision, along with proof of service on all parties. A copy of the petition for review must be served on the administrative agency.

(3) The running of the time for filing a petition for review is terminated by a timely motion for reconsideration in the district court. The full time for a petition for review by any party begins to run again on the date of notice, as defined in Civil Rule 58.1(c) and Criminal Rule 32.3(c), or the date of denial of the motion pursuant to Civil Rule 77(k)(4), whichever is earlier.

(4) A judge of the superior court, for good cause shown, may extend the time for filing. The party seeking review will be known as the petitioner. All other parties to the proceedings will be named as respondents.

(b) **Other Matters.**

(1) Cross Petitions and Petitions for Review of Multiple Orders may be filed in accordance with the provisions of Appellate Rule 403(a)(2) and (3).

(2) The Petition or Cross Petition shall conform to Appellate Rule 403(b) through (e), except that the statement of reasons why review should be granted is governed by Rule 610.

(c) **Consideration by the Court.** The court shall determine whether to grant or deny the petition within ten days after the day on which the response is due. The court shall consider the merits of any petition granted as soon as practicable, and unless otherwise ordered, without oral argument, and on the basis of the memoranda and supporting documents submitted by the parties. The court, on request or on its own motion, may require submission of whatever additional portions of the record it considers necessary, or may order supplementation of the record through oral testimony or otherwise.

(d) **Stay.**

(1) *Judicial Proceeding.* When a petition for review has been filed, the superior court in its discretion may stay further proceedings by the district court and the operation or enforcement of the order or decision sought to be reviewed upon such terms as to bond or otherwise as the court considers proper for the security of the rights of the adverse party.

(2) *Administrative Proceeding.* When a petition for review has been filed, the superior court may stay further proceedings in an administrative agency and the operation or enforcement of the order or decision sought to be reviewed when the party seeking review establishes that irreparable injury will result if the stay is not granted.

(e) **Relief Available.** Upon consideration of a petition for review, the superior court may affirm, modify, vacate, set aside or reverse any order or decision of a district court, and may remand the action or proceeding and direct the entry of such appropriate judgment or order, or require such further proceedings to be had, as may be just under the circumstances.

(SCO 439 effective November 15, 1980; amended by SCO 494 effective January 4, 1982; by SCO 554 effective April 4, 1983; by SCO 1015 effective January 15, 1990; and by SCO 1113 effective January 15, 1993)

Note: AS 28.15.166(n), as amended by § 10 ch. 119 SLA 1990, amended Appellate Rule 603 and Appellate Rule 611 by prohibiting an automatic stay of the administrative revocation of a driver's license pending appeal or petition for review and by limiting the power of the court to stay the administrative revocation of a driver's license. AS 28.15.166(n) was also amended by § 6 ch. 3 SLA 1992 to require that the court make an additional finding before staying the revocation of a commercial vehicle license. When the legislature adopted this change, it took the steps necessary to revise Appellate Rule 603 but did not attempt to amend Appellate Rule 611.

Note: Ch. 77 SLA 2002 (HB157), Section 2, adds new Chapter 26 to Title 6 of the Alaska Statutes, concerning providers of fiduciary services. According to Section 9 of the Act, AS 06.26.760(b)(2) has the effect of amending Appellate Rule 611 by postponing the deadlines set in the Alaska Rules of Appellate Procedure for the filing of petitions for review to the superior court from a district court of an administrative agency by a trust company when the Department of Community and Economic Development has taken possession of the trust company.

Rule 612. Motions and Authority of the Clerk.

(a) **Applicability of Rule 503.** Motions to the superior court are governed by Rule 503, except as provided below.

(b) **Motions Determined by the Clerk.** The clerk may approve a supersedeas bond pursuant to Rule 603(a)(2)[e]. The superior court clerk may rule upon the following motions, if unopposed, without reference to the judge assigned to the appeal:

(1) motions for extensions of time for filing briefs as provided by paragraph (c) below;

(2) motions for extension of time for transmitting the record in administrative appeals;

(3) an appellant's motion to dismiss the appeal; and

(4) motions to supplement the record if filed prior to the filing of any brief.

(c) **Length of Extensions.** The clerk may not grant extensions totalling more than 30 days for the appellant's brief, 30 days for the appellee's brief, and 15 days for the appellant's reply brief. The clerk may not determine a motion for extension of time to file a document if the time period specified in these rules for filing the document, including any previous extensions, has already expired when the motion is filed.

(d) **Reconsideration of Clerk's Order.** A party who is aggrieved by the decision of the clerk on a motion may file a motion for reconsideration of the clerk's order. This motion will be determined by the judge assigned to the appeal.

(SCO 1015 effective January 15, 1990)

APPENDIX

CLERK'S INSTRUCTIONS FOR PREPARATION OF EXCERPTS

A. APPELLANT'S EXCERPT OF RECORD

1. An excerpt of record must be bound on the left-hand side in the same manner as a brief. All excerpts, whether submitted by appellant or appellee, must have a pink cover. The cover must be the same weight and quality as the cover of a brief. The cover must contain the same information that appears on the front cover of the brief, but must be labeled "APPELLANT'S EXCERPT OF RECORD" instead of "BRIEF OF APPELLANT." It must also contain the volume number, e.g., "Volume 1 of 1."
EXAMPLE:

IN THE SUPREME COURT OF THE STATE OF ALASKA

JANE A. DOE,)
Appellant,)
)
vs.)
)
JOHN B. DOE,)
Appellee) Supreme Court No. S-5741
_________________) Superior Court No. 3AN-92-4375 CI

APPEAL FROM THE SUPERIOR COURT,
THIRD JUDICIAL DISTRICT AT ANCHORAGE,
THE HONORABLE J. WILLIAM JONES, PRESIDING

APPELLANT'S EXCERPT OF RECORD
VOLUME 1 OF 1

JAMES SMITH (AK Bar No. 234567)
100 A Street, Suite 100
Anchorage, Alaska 99000
(907) 333-3333
Attorney for Appellant
Jane A. Doe

Filed in the Supreme Court of
the State of Alaska, this ____
day of ________________, 2004.

Marilyn May, Clerk

By: ___________________________
Deputy Clerk

2. Documents in the excerpt of record must be arranged in chronological order by document execution date, with the document with the earliest date on top.

A memorandum filed in support of a motion should be placed immediately following the motion. Exhibits or attachments to the memorandum should follow the memorandum—even if the exhibit or attachment had an earlier execution date than the memorandum.

If pages of the transcript are included in the excerpt, these pages should appear together at the end of the excerpt, in numerical order (e.g., pp. 45-48, 87, 151-152).

See Section E on confidential documents.

3. Documents in the excerpt must be copied on both sides of the paper (i.e., double-sided copies).

4. Pages must be numbered in a single consecutive sequence throughout all volumes (e.g., if volume 1 contains pages 1 through 200, then volume 2 would begin with page 201). Page numbers must appear at the bottom of the page.

5. Each excerpt must contain a full table of contents at the beginning of the first volume. A party submitting a multi-volume excerpt must duplicate the full table of contents at the beginning of each volume. The table of contents must be prepared as follows:

a. Each document in the excerpt must be listed by title, execution date, document creator's name (unless the creator is obvious), and the page on which the document begins.

EXAMPLE (multi-defendant case):

Complaint, November 12, 1990 1
Smith's Answer, December 8, 1990 38
Johnson's Answer, December 10, 1990 55

b. When there is more than one volume of the excerpt, each document filed in a particular volume must be listed under the volume heading.

EXAMPLE:

Affidavit of Mary Smith, March 15, 1991 197
Volume 2
Affidavit of William Johnson, April 3, 1991 199

c. See Section E on confidential documents.

B. **APPELLEE'S EXCERPT OF RECORD**

The rules outlined above for Appellant's Excerpt of Record apply except that the first page of the first document in Appellee's excerpt must begin with the number immediately following the number of the last page in Appellant's excerpt (e.g., if Appellant's excerpt ends with page 237, then Appellee's excerpt would begin with page 238).

See Section E on confidential documents.

C. **SUPPLEMENTAL EXCERPT OF RECORD**

The rules outlined above apply except that the title of the file should be "Appellant's Supplemental Excerpt of Record" or "Appellee's Supplemental Excerpt of Record." In addition, the first page of the first document in a supplemental excerpt must begin with the number immediately following the number of the last page of the last excerpt filed in the case (e.g., if the last volume of Appellee's excerpt of record ends with page 225, then a supplemental excerpt filed with Appellant's reply brief would begin with page 226).

D. **CITATION GUIDELINES**

1. DOCUMENTS IN AN EXCERPT OF RECORD: [Exc. 126].

2. TRANSCRIPT: [Tr. 109].

3. DOCUMENTS IN THE RECORD, BUT NOT IN AN EXCERPT: [R. 78].

Note: When citing testimony presented by deposition, do not cite to the deposition. Instead, include the relevant pages of the deposition in the excerpt and cite to the excerpt.

E. **CONFIDENTIAL DOCUMENTS**

1. Confidential documents must be arranged in chronological order by document execution date, with the document with the earliest date on top.

2. Pages must be numbered consecutively, beginning with the number immediately following the number of the last page of the last non-confidential document in Appellant's excerpt. Page numbers must appear at the bottom of the page.

3. Confidential documents must be placed in a manila envelope marked "APPELLANT'S EXCERPT - CONFIDENTIAL." The case name and the appellate case number must be written on the front of the envelope. The envelope must be placed at the end of the last volume of the party's excerpt.

4. Confidential documents must be listed at the end of the table of contents under the heading "Confidential Envelope."

EXAMPLE:
Judgment and Commitment, November 2, 1992 67
Confidential Envelope
Presentence Report, August 30, 1992 68
Updated Presentence Report, September 15, 1993 76

5. The first page of the first document in Appellee's excerpt begins with the number immediately following the number of the last page of the last document in Appellant's confidential envelope (e.g., if the last confidential document in Appellant's confidential envelope ends with page 95, then Appellee's excerpt would begin with page 96).

F. **AGENCY APPEALS TO THE SUPERIOR COURT.**

An excerpt of record is required in an appeal from an administrative agency to the superior court. **See** Appellate Rule 604(b)(1)(B). These instructions govern the form of excerpts filed in the superior court, except that

1. documents in an excerpt must be copied on one side of the paper (**not** duplexed) and two-hole punched at the top center of each page;

2. each volume of the excerpt must stapled or bound **at the top** with a metal fastener (e.g., an Acco fastener);

3. the cover of the excerpt must be on **white** paper of the same weight and quality as other documents in the excerpt; and

4. only one copy of the excerpt must be filed with the court.

G. **PURPOSE OF EXCERPTS.**

Submitting a proper excerpt is essential to the court's efficient understanding of a case. An excerpt which is indiscriminately over-inclusive may divert the court's attention from those few documents which may be dispositive. Parties are urged to ensure that the critical documents potentially dispositive of the appeal are contained in the excerpt, and that the brief or the excerpt adequately advises the court exactly which documents are critical.

ADOPTION RULES

Table of Contents

PART I. GENERAL PROVISIONS

Part I. General Provisions

APPENDIX

ALASKA ADOPTION STATUTES

PART I. GENERAL PROVISIONS

Rule 1. Title—Scope—Construction—Situations Not Covered by the Rules.

(a) **Title.** These rules will be known and cited as the Adoption Rules.

(b) **Scope.** These rules govern practice and procedure in the trial courts in all phases of adoption proceedings brought under AS 25.23.010 through 25.23.240.

(c) **Construction.** These rules will be construed and applied to promote fairness, accurate fact-finding, the expeditious determination of adoption proceedings, and the best interests of the child.

(d) **Legal Effect of Rules.** These rules are promulgated pursuant to Alaska constitutional authority granting rulemaking power to the Alaska Supreme Court. To the extent that the rules are inconsistent with a procedural provision of any Alaska statute not validly enacted for the specific purpose of changing a rule, these rules supersede the statute.

(e) **Civil and Evidence Rules Applicable.** The Alaska Civil and Evidence Rules apply to adoption proceedings except to the extent that any provisions of the Civil or Evidence Rules conflict with the Adoption Rules. The provisions of Civil Rule 100 apply to adoption proceedings.

(f) **Situations Not Covered by the Rules.** Where no specific procedure is prescribed by these rules, the court may proceed in any lawful manner, including application of relevant statutes, the Alaska and United States Constitutions or common law. Such a procedure may not be inconsistent with these rules and may not unduly delay or otherwise interfere with the unique character and purpose of adoption proceedings.

(SCO 972 effective January 15, 1990; amended by SCO 1469 effective October 15, 2002)

Rule 2. Definitions.

(a) "Agency" means any person certified, licensed or otherwise specially empowered by law or regulation to place minors for adoption.

(b) "Child" means a son or daughter, whether by birth or adoption.

(c) "Consent" means the written giving of permission to an adoption in accordance with AS 25.23.060.

(d) "Extended family member" means a person as defined by the law or custom of the Indian child's tribe, or, in the absence of such a law or custom, means a person who has reached the age of eighteen and who is the Indian child's grandparent, aunt or uncle, brother or sister, brother-in-law or sister-in-law, niece or nephew, first or second cousin, or stepparent.

(e) "Guardian ad litem" means a person appointed by the court to represent the best interests of the child in an adoption proceeding.

(f) "Indian" means any person who is a member of an Indian tribe, or who is an Alaska Native and a member of a regional corporation as defined in 43 U.S.C. Section 1606.

(g) "Indian child" means any unmarried person who is under the age of 18 and who is either (a) a member of an Indian tribe, or (b) is eligible for membership in an Indian tribe and is the biological child of a member of an Indian tribe.

(h) "Indian child's tribe" means (a) the Indian tribe in which an Indian child is a member or eligible for membership, or (b), in the case of an Indian child who is a member of or eligible for membership in more than one tribe, the Indian tribe with which the Indian child has the more significant contacts.

(i) "Indian custodian" means any Indian person who has legal custody of an Indian child under tribal law or custom or under state law, or to whom temporary physical care, custody and control has been transferred by the parent of the child.

(j) "Indian tribe" means any Indian tribe, band, nation or other organized group or community of Indians recognized as eligible for services provided to Indians by the Secretary of the Department of the Interior because of their status as Indians, including an Alaska Native village as defined in 43 U.S.C. Section 1602(c).

(k) "Judge" means a superior court judge, a standing master or a district court judge or magistrate appointed as a special master pursuant to Adoption Rule 3.

(*l*) "Minor" means a person who has not reached the age of majority.

(m) "Parent" means a biological or adoptive parent.

(n) "Parties" means the petitioners, person to be adopted, the parents of the person to be adopted, anyone who has a right to consent under AS 25.23.040, a guardian ad litem, and any person or entity who has intervened.

(o) "Relinquishment" means a written surrender of parental rights in compliance with AS 25.23.180.

(SCO 972 effective January 15, 1990; amended by SCO 1084 effective January 15, 1992)

Cross References

(f) **CROSS REFERENCE:** 25 U.S.C. § 1903(3).

(g) **CROSS REFERENCE:** 25 U.S.C. § 1903(4).

(h) **CROSS REFERENCE:** 25 U.S.C. § 1903(5).

Rule 3. Appointment and Authority of Masters.

(a) **Appointment.** The presiding judge may appoint a standing master to conduct adoption proceedings. Appointments of standing masters must be reviewed annually. The presiding judge may appoint a special master to conduct a proceeding which is specified in the order of reference.

(b) **Authority, Order of Reference.**

(1) In order of reference specifying the extent of the master's authority and the type of appointment must be entered in every case assigned to a master. The order of reference must be served on all parties.

(2) A master's report is not binding until approved by a superior court judge pursuant to Civil Rule 53(d) and paragraph (f) of this rule, except that a master may enter orders without further approval of the superior court pursuant to Civil Rule 53(b) and (c), and paragraph (d) of this rule.

(c) **Objection to Reference to a Master.** In addition to the peremptory challenge of a master provided for in Civil Rule 42(c), a party may file an objection to a referral to a master in the following manner:

(1) *Timeliness.* A party may file an objection no later than five days after receiving notice of an order of reference.

(2) *Grounds for Objection.* An objection to the assignment of a master must set forth sufficient grounds from which the court may determine whether good cause exists to remove the matter from the master's jurisdiction. Good cause may include involvement of:

(i) complex questions of law which require a decision by a superior court judge; or

(ii) questions requiring prompt resolution which would be seriously impaired by reference to a master.

(d) **Standing Master's Authority to Enter Orders.** A standing master is authorized to take the following actions without further approval by a superior court judge:

(1) appoint counsel and guardians ad litem;

(2) order home studies;

(3) set hearings and order continuances of the hearings;

(4) accept and approve stipulations; and

(5) accept voluntary relinquishments of parental rights and consents to adoption, and, in the case of an Indian child, make the requisite judicial certification of voluntary consent required by federal law.

(e) **Master's Report, Recommendations.** A master may issue a written report or oral findings on the record concerning an order or recommendation which must be approved by a superior court judge. The master shall advise the parties on the record of their right to file objections to any such decisions pursuant to paragraph (f) of this rule.

(f) **Objections to Master's Report, Recommendations.** Objections to Master's Report, Recommendations. Objections to a master's report or recommendation must be filed within ten days of service of the report unless the court requires objections to be filed earlier. In the case of a recommendation rendered orally on the record where a party requests an electronic recording of the recommendation, the time period for objection runs from receipt of the recording. A reply to the objections must be filed within three days of service of the objections. The superior court may permit oral argument, order the taking of further evidence, or grant a hearing de novo.

(SCO 972 effective January 15, 1990; and amended by SCO 1555 effective October 15, 2004)

Rule 4. Authority of District Court Judges and Magistrates.

A district court judge or magistrate may not preside over adoption proceedings in the absence of appointment as a master pursuant to Adoption Rule 3 or, in the case of a district court judge, appointment by the chief justice as a superior court judge pro tempore.

(SCO 972 effective January 15, 1990)

Rule 5. Venue.

(a) **Venue.** Adoption proceedings must be brought in superior court in the judicial district or venue district in which, at the time of filing the petition, the petitioner or the person to be adopted resides or is in military service, or in which the agency having the care, custody, or control of the person to be adopted is located.

(b) **Change of Venue.** Venue may be changed in the interest of substantial justice pursuant to AS 22.10.040 after a petition is filed.

(c) **Venue Districts.** Venue districts as used in this rule refer to the districts referenced in the Venue District Map attached to Criminal Rule 18.

(SCO 972 effective January 15, 1990)

Rule 6. Petitions.

(a) **Petition for Adoption.**

(1) An adoption petition must include the information required by AS 25.23.080. A separate petition must be filed for each person to be adopted. If the proceeding involves a minor, the petition must also state whether the minor to be adopted is an Indian child and whether any other court cases involving the minor are known to be pending.

(2) An adoption petition involving an Indian child must include a statement of petitioner's compliance with the placement preferences provided by 25 U.S.C. Section 1915(a). The petition must state the identity of the child's tribe, if known; whether the child is reasonably believed to be a resident or domiciliary of an Indian reservation as defined in 25 U.S.C. Section 1903(10); and whether the child is known to be a ward of a tribal court.

(3) The report of expenditures required by AS 25.23.090 may be incorporated into the petition.

(b) **Petition for Termination of Parental Rights Based on Relinquishment.** A petition for termination based on the voluntary relinquishment of parental rights pursuant to AS 25.23.180(b) must state, in addition to the information required by paragraph (a), that the parent has or intends to relinquish parental rights to the child.

(c) **Petition for Involuntary Termination.** A petition for termination based on the involuntary termination of parental rights pursuant to AS 25.23.180(c)(1)-(3) must state, in addition to the information required by paragraph (a), the specific statutory and factual basis of the claim that parental rights should be involuntarily terminated.

(d) **Relationship of Petitions to Terminate Parental Rights and to Adopt.**

(1) A petition to terminate parental rights under paragraph (b) or (c) of this rule may be combined with a petition for adoption.

(2) In a petition for termination of parental rights under paragraph (b) or (c) of this rule filed before a petition for adoption, the term "petitioner" in AS 25.23.080(b)(4)–(6) will be interpreted to mean the person who will have custody of the child pending adoption.

(SCO 972 effective January 15, 1990; amended by SCO 1568 effective October 15, 2005; and by SCO 1650 effective October 15, 2007)

Rule 7. Guardians Ad Litem.

(a) **When Appointed.** The court may appoint a guardian ad litem for a child in an adoption proceeding when necessary to promote the child's best interests.

(b) **Appointment.** Guardians ad litem will be appointed in accordance with the provisions of AS 25.23.100 and Administrative Rule 12. The court shall specify the duties of the guardian ad litem and the duration of the appointment in its order of appointment.

(c) **Service.** A guardian ad litem is a party and must be served with pleadings and notices according to the civil rules.

(SCO 972 effective January 15, 1990; amended by SCO 1092 effective July 15, 1992)

Rule 8. Right to Counsel.

(a) **Counsel of Choice.** The court shall ensure at the first appearance of a parent that the parent is informed of the right to counsel of their choice at the parent's own expense. The court shall ensure that a child is advised of the right to counsel at the time the child appears to sign a consent to adoption.

(b) **Appointed Counsel.**

(1) The court shall appoint counsel at public expense pursuant to Administrative Rule 12(e)(1)(A)(i) to represent an indigent parent of an Indian child.

(2) The court shall appoint the Office of Public Advocacy to represent an indigent parent against whom an involuntary termination of parental rights is sought pursuant to AS 25.23.180(c)(3).

(3) The court shall also appoint counsel at public expense pursuant to Administrative Rule 12 to represent:

(A) an indigent parent against whom an involuntary termination of parental rights is sought on grounds other than stated in AS 25.23.180(c)(3), if the action is brought by the state or by a party represented by the Alaska Legal Services Corporation or the Alaska Pro Bono Program; and

(B) an indigent parent who is defending against a claim that the parent's consent to adoption is not required under AS 25.23.050(a).

(4) The court may appoint counsel under AS 25.24.310 to represent a minor child who is to be adopted.

(SCO 972 effective January 15, 1990; amended by SCO 1092 effective July 15, 1992; and by SCO 1169 effective July 15, 1994; by SCO 1187 effective July 15, 1995; and by SCO 1296 effective January 15, 1998)

*An indigent Indian custodian has a right to court-appointed counsel under 25 U.S.C. § 1912(b). Counsel appointed under § 1912 may seek compensation pursuant to 25 CFR 23.13.

Rule 9. Consents—Relinquishments.

(a) **Form.** A consent or relinquishment must be in writing and must include:

(1) notice of the person's right to withdraw the consent or relinquishment as provided by paragraphs (g) and (h) of this rule;

(2) the address and telephone number of the court in which the adoption or relinquishment proceeding has or is expected to be filed;

(3) a statement of the right to counsel as stated in Rule 8;

(4) a statement concerning whether or not any visitation rights or other parental privileges are sought to be retained after the adoption;

(5) if a consent, the information required in AS 25.23.060; and

(6) if signed by a parent, a statement of whether the parent is a minor.

(b) **Consent or Relinquishment Involving an Indian Child.** A consent or relinquishment involving an Indian child must be signed in a hearing in the presence of a judge unless the consent is by an agency. In addition to the explanations required by paragraph (d), the court shall inquire as to what efforts have been made to comply with the placement preferences of 25 U.S.C. Section 1915(a). Consent for adoption or relinquishment of parental rights of an Indian child may not be given prior to or within ten days following the birth of the child.

(c) **Consent By a Minor.**

(1) A consent by a minor child over the age of 10 to the child's adoption must be signed in writing and must be in the presence of the court unless the court in the best interest of the minor dispenses with the minor's consent or the requirement that the child consent in court.

(2) A consent by a parent who is a minor to an adoption of the parent's child must be signed in the presence of the court.

(d) **Consent or Relinquishment Before the Court.** If a consent or relinquishment is to be signed in the presence of the court, the judge shall first determine that the terms and consequences of the document were explained in detail to the person in a language that the person understands. The court also must determine that the person understands these terms and consequences, and that the person voluntarily signs the consent or relinquishment. If the identity or whereabouts of the other parent is in question, the court shall inquire into these matters.

(e) **Consents or Relinquishments Not Before the Court.** A consent or relinquishment to an adoption not taken in the presence of a judge must comply with AS 25.23.060. A relinquishment not taken in the presence of a judge must comply with AS 25.23.180(b).

(f) **Consent or Relinquishment Before Special Master.** A consent or relinquishment required to be taken in the presence of a judge must be taken in the physical presence of a judge. However, in exceptional circumstances the judge assigned to hear the entire proceeding may request that the presiding judge appoint a peace officer or person authorized to administer oaths or affirmations as a special master under Adoption Rule 3 for the limited purpose of sitting as the judge in whose physical presence the person gives the consent or relinquishment. The judge assigned to hear the entire proceeding must be telephonically present when the consent or relinquishment is taken. Both the special master and the judge assigned to hear the entire proceeding must make oral or written findings concerning the identity of the person signing the consent or relinquishment, whether the person understood the consent or relinquishment, and whether the person signed voluntarily. The requirements of paragraph (c) also must be met.

(g) **Withdrawal of Consent or Relinquishment of a Non-Indian Child.** The parent of a non-Indian child may withdraw a consent or relinquishment by notifying in writing the court, or the person or agency obtaining the consent or relinquishment, within 10 days of the birth or signing of the consent or relinquishment, whichever is later. Notification is timely if received or postmarked on or before the last day of this time period. The parent may move the court to permit withdrawal of the consent or relinquishment after the 10 day period pursuant to AS 25.23.070 for a consent or AS 25.23.180(g) or AS 47.10.089(h) for a relinquishment.

(h) **Withdrawal of Consent or Relinquishment of an Indian Child.** The parent of an Indian child may withdraw a consent or relinquishment by notifying in writing the court or the person or agency obtaining the consent or relinquishment at any time before the signing of the decree of adoption for a consent or the order of termination for a relinquishment. Notification is timely if received or postmarked on or before the last day of this time period. A decree of adoption or order of termination may not be signed until 10 days have passed since the signing of the consent or relinquishment.

(SCO 972 effective January 15, 1990; amended by SCO 1276 effective July 15, 1997; and by SCO 1580 effective nunc pro tunc to July 1, 2005)

NOTE: Chapter 64, sections 56 and 57, SLA 2005 (HB 53) amended Adoption Rule 9 as reflected in section 9 of this Order. The change to Adoption Rule 9 is adopted for the sole reason that the legislature has mandated the amendment. In addition, according to section 60(b) of the Act, AS 25.23.180(j) - (n) and AS 47.10.089, enacted in sections 4 and 17, amend Adoption Rule 9 by requiring retained privileges to be set out in the relinquishment form and order and by providing additional procedures related to the relinquishment.

Annotations

Cases

Relinquishment of parental rights must be an absolute and permanent surrender of rights to be valid under this section. **In re Keith M.W.**, Op. No. 10489, 79 P.3d 623 (Alaska 2003).

Rule 10. Notice.

(a) **Notice to Parties.** Petitioner shall give notice of the adoption hearing to the persons required by AS 25.23.100(a). The notice must contain the information required by AS 25.23.100(b) and must be served in the manner provided by this rule and Civil Rule 4, except that in an adoption involving an Indian child, notice must be by personal service or certified or registered mail with proof of service dated no later than 10 days before the adoption hearing. Notice of the adoption hearing must also be given to extended family members of an Indian child who have intervened in the adoption proceeding or participated as a party in any prior child custody proceeding involving the child.

(b) **Waiver.** A party may waive the party's right to notice by filing a written notarized waiver with the court.

(c) **Notice to Parents Whose Whereabouts Are Unknown.** If the name of a parent who has not consented to the adoption is known, but the person's whereabouts cannot be ascertained after diligent inquiry, the petitioner may move the court to allow notice by publication under Civil Rule 4 in a newspaper of general circulation in the community most likely to effect actual notice. Published notice must give the full name, if known, of the person to whom the notice is directed. All other parties must be identified by initials rather than names. In an adoption involving an Indian child, additional notice to the parent must be sent in care of the Secretary of the Interior.

(d) **Notice to Unknown Parent.** If the identity of the parent is unknown and the court is satisfied that no form of notice, even by publication, is reasonably likely to give actual notice to the parent, the court may waive notice.

(e) **Notice to Indian Tribe.** In an adoption or relinquishment proceeding involving an Indian child, notice must be given to the child's tribe at the time of the petition or, if the child's tribe is not known at this time, reasonably promptly after the tribe has been determined. However, notice is not required if parental rights are to be voluntarily terminated and the parent files a statement that the tribe has not been served with notice in order to protect the privacy of the parent. The notice, if required, must be by personal service or certified or registered mail, with proof of service dated no later than 10 days before the adoption hearing and, if applicable, also 10 days before the entry of the decree of termination. The notice, if required, must be sent with a copy of the petition and must contain:

(1) a statement that the Indian child's tribe has a right to intervene in the proceeding;

(2) a statement of the right of the tribe to request twenty additional days to prepare for the proceedings;

(3) the mailing address and telephone number of the court;

(4) a statement that the tribe may have a right to petition the court to transfer the proceedings to a tribal court authorized to exercise jurisdiction under federal law; and

(5) a statement that since adoption proceedings are usually conducted on a confidential basis, tribal officials shall keep the information contained in the notice confidential.

(SCO 972 effective January 15, 1990)

Annotations

Cases

An adoption resolution of a Native American village was not entitled to comity or full faith and credit in the courts because the resolution was obtained in violation of the natural father's right to notice under AS 25.23.100(a)(3) and Alaska Adop. R. 10. The matter was remanded for an adjudication of the claims under AS 25.20.060 and the Indian Child Welfare Act, 25 U.S.C.S. § 1901 et seq. **Evans v. Native Village of Selawik Ira Council,** 65 P.3d 58 (Alaska 2003).

Rule 11. Hearings.

(a) **Conduct of Hearing.** Adoption hearings are confidential proceedings tried by the court without a jury and must be conducted pursuant to AS 25.23.150(a).

(b) **Exclusion of Witnesses.** Witnesses may be excluded from a hearing pursuant to Evidence Rule 615.

(c) **Telephonic Participation.** The court may conduct any hearing with telephonic participation as provided by Civil Rule 99, except as provided by Adoption Rule 9(f). Payment of telephone costs is governed by Administrative Rule 48.

(d) **Testimony Under Oath.** All testimony must be given under oath or affirmation as required by Evidence Rule 603.

(e) **Contested Adoptions.** The court may issue a pretrial order when the parties contest any issue. The court shall consider the advisability of appointing a guardian ad litem in contested adoptions.

(f) **Burden and Standard of Proof.** The burden is on the petitioner to prove all relevant issues in the adoption. The standard of proof as to the finding that the adoption is in the best interests of the person to be adopted is by a preponderance of the evidence. The standard of proof as to a finding that a consent is not required under AS 25.23.050(a) is by clear and convincing evidence.

In an adoption involving an Indian child, the burden of proof is also on the petitioner to show by a preponderance of the evidence that the placement is within the placement preferences or that there is good cause for allowing a non-preferred placement pursuant to 25 U.S.C. Section 1915. The burden and standard of proof in proceedings for the involuntary termination of parental rights in conjunction with adoption proceedings must comply with CINA Rule 18.

(g) **Representation by Non-Attorney.** Unless the court for good cause requires representation by an attorney, an Indian tribe may be represented by a non-attorney tribal member or tribal employee. A written authorization for representation by the non-attorney must be filed in the case before the non-attorney tribal member or tribal employee may represent the tribe. A guardian ad litem need not be represented by an attorney unless the court, for good cause, requires representation by an attorney.

(SCO 972 effective January 15, 1990; amended by SCO 998 effective January 15, 1990)

Rule 12. Tribal Intervention and Removal.

(a) **Intervention.** In any adoption or relinquishment proceeding involving an Indian child, the Indian child's tribe and an Indian custodian, if any, may intervene as a matter of right at any stage in the proceeding.

(b) **Removal.**

(1) In an adoption involving the termination of parental rights of a parent of an Indian child, the parent, Indian custodian or the tribe may move to have the matter removed to a tribal court pursuant to 25 U.S.C. Section 1911.

(2) When a petition for removal to tribal court is filed, the court must find that the tribal court is authorized to exercise jurisdiction under federal law before transferring jurisdiction to the tribal court. The court may set a hearing on the petition for removal with notice to all parties to determine whether the tribal court has declined jurisdiction, and, if jurisdiction has not been declined, to determine whether any objection has been raised by either parent to the removal pursuant to 25 U.S.C. Section 1911(b).

(3) Civil Rule 77 applies to petitions for removal to tribal court.

(SCO 972 effective January 15, 1990)

Annotations

Cases

Adoptions under tribal custom are recognized by the State Bureau of Vital Statistics when standards defined by a departmental regulation are met. 7 AAC 05.700. A parent's assertion of custody is a disqualifying condition under the regulation. 7 AAC 05.700(b)(3)(B). **Evans v. Native Village of Selawik Ira Council,** 65 P.3d 58 (Alaska 2003).

Rule 13. Decree of Termination.

(a) **Voluntary Relinquishment.** A decree terminating parental rights may be entered after a voluntary relinquishment pursuant to AS 25.23.180 or AS 47.10.089. The court shall enter findings of fact which must include a statement concerning whether visitation rights are being allowed under AS 25.23.130(c) or other privileges are being retained under AS 25.23.180 or AS 47.10.089, and whether the time limit for withdrawal of the relinquishment has elapsed. If the relinquishment was signed in the presence of the court, findings also must be entered as to whether the parent understood the consequences of the relinquishment, and whether the relinquishment was voluntarily signed.

In the case of a voluntary relinquishment of parental rights to an Indian child, the court shall make additional findings concerning whether any notice required by Rule 10(e) was timely given; whether the relinquishment was voluntary and in compliance with the requirements of 25 U.S.C. Section 1913; and whether the child's placement complies with the preferences set out in 25 U.S.C. Section 1915 or good cause exists for deviation from the placement preference.

(b) **Involuntary Termination of Parental Rights.** Proceedings for the involuntary termination of parental rights in conjunction with adoption proceedings must comply with CINA Rule 18, except as otherwise provided by AS 25.23.180(c)(2) and (3). 25 U.S.C. Section 1912 also applies to all involuntary termination proceedings involving an Indian child.

(SCO 972 effective January 15, 1990; amended by SCO 1276 effective July 15, 1997; and by SCO 1580 effective nunc pro tunc to July 1, 2005)

Note: Chapter 64, section 58, SLA 2005 (HB 53) amended Adoption Rule 13 as reflected in section 11 of this Order. The change to Adoption Rule 13 is adopted for the sole reason that the legislature has mandated the amendment. In addition, according to section 60(b) of the Act, AS 25.23.180(j) - (n) and AS 47.10.089, enacted in sections 4 and 17, amend Adoption Rule 13 by requiring retained privileges to be set out in the relinquishment form and order and by providing additional procedures related to the relinquishment. According to section 60(c) of the Act, AS 25.23.180(k) - (n) and AS 47.10.089(g), (h), and (j), enacted in sections 4 and 17, amend Adoption Rule 13 by authorizing review hearings for voluntary relinquishments.

Rule 14. Decree of Adoption.

(a) **Findings.** At the conclusion of the hearing, the court shall enter findings of fact concerning:

(1) whether the required consents were filed or excused;

(2) whether a report of petitioner's expenditures was required, and if so, whether the report was accepted by the court;

(3) whether all appropriate notices were timely given;

(4) if the adoption was of a minor, whether the required residence of the minor with petitioner exists;

(5) whether a home study was required, and if so, whether the home study was accepted by the court;

(6) whether the adoption is in the best interests of the minor; and

(7) whether visitation rights are being allowed under AS 25.23.130(c).

The court's findings also must include a description and an estimate of value of any property of the person to be adopted.

(b) **Additional Finding for Indian Children.** In the case of an Indian child, the court must enter additional findings regarding:

(1) whether any additional notices required in Rule 10(e) were timely given;

(2) whether the parent's consent was voluntary and in compliance with 25 U.S.C. Section 1913; and

(3) whether the placement complies with the preferences set out in 25 U.S.C. Section 1915 or good cause exists for deviation from the placement preferences.

(SCO 972 effective January 15, 1990; amended by SCO 1276 effective July 15, 1997)

Rule 15. Appeal.

(a) **Grounds, Procedure.** An appeal of a final judgment or order, or a petition for review of an interlocutory order or decision in an adoption case, may be taken subject to Appellate Rule 218 or other appropriate appellate procedures.

(b) **Stay.** An order, judgment or decision of the superior court remains in effect pending appeal or review, unless stayed by order of the superior court or the supreme court.

(SCO 972 effective January 15, 1990)

Rule 16. Records.

(a) **Report of Adoption.** The court shall require a report of adoption and a biological information sheet to be filled out so that it can be filed with the Bureau of Vital Statistics with the decree of adoption. The court shall refer requests for adoption documents to the Bureau of Vital Statistics.

(b) **Substitute Birth Certificate.** At the request of the adoptive parent and upon payment of fees and completion of forms, the clerk of court shall send a request for a substitute birth certificate to the appropriate state's vital statistics office.

(c) **Indian Child Adoption Reports.** The court shall send a copy of the decree, a report providing all information required by 25 U.S.C. Section 1951, and an affidavit requesting anonymity, if any, to the Secretary of the Interior. A copy of this report must be kept in the case file.

(d) **Confidential Files.** Access to the court file prior to a decree of adoption is limited to the parties unless ordered otherwise by the court. Access to the file after a decree of adoption is limited as provided by AS 25.23.150, subject to informational requests under AS 18.50.500, AS 18.50.510, and 25 U.S.C. Section 1917.

(e) **Adoption Index.** An alphabetical index of all adoption cases will be kept under the name by which the person to be adopted will be known if the petition is granted. The adoption index is confidential.

(f) **Certificate of Adoption or Termination of Parental Rights.** A person whose parental rights have been terminated under AS 25.23.130 or AS 25.23.180 may request a certificate to be issued by the clerk which confirms that a decree of adoption or termination has been entered terminating the parent and child relationship between the person and a particular child. Before issuing a certificate, the clerk shall require sufficient identification to establish that the person requesting the certificate is the parent named in the decree. The certificate may disclose only the following information about the adoption or termination:

(1) the case number;

(2) the name of the parent whose rights were terminated;

(3) the date the decree was entered;

(4) the name of the child prior to the adoption or termination; and

(5) the child's date of birth.

(SCO 972 effective January 15, 1990; amended by SCO 1060 effective July 15, 1991; by SCO 1286 effective October 1, 1997; and by SCO 1404 effective October 15, 2000)

Rule 17. Challenges to Validity of Adoption Decree.

(a) **Procedure.** A person may move to set aside the decree by filing a motion stating the grounds for challenging the validity of the decree, with service on other parties, subject to the time limitations of AS 25.23.140(b) and (c), and 25 U.S.C. Section 1913(d). The court shall schedule a hearing after reasonable notice to the parties. At the hearing, the burden is on the party challenging the decree to show by a preponderance of the evidence that the decree is not valid.

(b) **Petition under 25 U.S.C. Section 1914.** A petition alleging a violation of any provision of 25 U.S.C. Section 1911, 1912 or 1913 is governed by the procedures set out in CINA Rule 20.

(SCO 972 effective January 15, 1990)

APPENDIX

ALASKA ADOPTION STATUTES

Chapter 23. Adoption.

§ 25.23.005. Construction of chapter; rights of persons affected by adoption.

This chapter shall be liberally construed to the end that the best interests of adopted children are promoted. Due regard shall be given to the rights of all persons affected by a child's adoption.

(§ 1 ch 29 SLA 1990)

§ 25.23.010. Who may be adopted.

Any person may be adopted.

(§ 1 ch 84 SLA 1974)

§ 25.23.020. Who may adopt.

(a) The following persons may adopt:

(1) a husband and wife together;

(2) an unmarried adult;

(3) the unmarried father or mother of the person to be adopted;

(4) a married person without the other spouse joining as a petitioner, if the person to be adopted is not the other spouse, and if

(A) the other spouse is a parent of the person to be adopted and consents to the adoption; or

(B) the petitioner and the other spouse are legally separated; or

(C) the failure of the other spouse to join in the petition or to agree to the adoption is excused by the court by reason of prolonged unexplained absence, unavailability, incapacity, or circumstances constituting an unreasonable withholding of consent.

(b) Nothing in this section affects legitimation under AS 25.20.050.

(§ 1 ch 84 SLA 1974)

§ 25.23.030. Venue.

(a) Proceedings for adoption shall be brought in the superior court for the district in which, at the time of filing or granting the petition, the petitioner or the person to be adopted resides or is in military service, or in which the agency having the care, custody, or control of the minor is located.

(b) If the court finds in the interest of substantial justice, under AS 22.10.040, that the adoption proceeding should be heard in another judicial district, the court may transfer, stay or dismiss the proceeding in whole or in part on conditions that are just.

(c) Proceedings for the termination of parental rights on the grounds set out in AS 25.23.180(c)(3) shall be brought in the superior court for the district in which the child that is the subject of the action resides.

(§ 1 ch 84 SLA 1974; am § 1, 2 ch 50 SLA 1987)

§ 25.23.040. Persons required to consent to adoption.

(a) Unless consent is not required under AS 25.23.050, a petition to adopt a minor may be granted only if written consent to a particular adoption has been executed by

(1) the mother of the minor;

(2) the father of the minor, if the father was married to the mother at the time the minor was conceived or at any time after conception, the minor is the father's child by adoption, or the father has otherwise legitimated the minor under the laws of the state;

(3) any person lawfully entitled to custody of the minor or empowered to consent;

(4) the court having jurisdiction to determine custody of the minor, if the legal guardian or custodian of the person of the minor is not empowered to consent to the adoption;

(5) the minor, if 10 years of age or older, unless the court in the best interest of the minor dispenses with the minor's consent; and

(6) the spouse of the minor to be adopted.

(b) A petition to adopt an adult may be granted only if written consent to adoption has been executed by the adult and the adult's spouse or by the guardian or conservator of an incapacitated adult.

(§ 1 ch 84 SLA 1974; am § 40 ch 50 SLA 1989)

§ 25.23.050. Persons as to whom consent and notice not required.

(a) Consent to adoption is not required of

(1) for purposes of this section, a parent who has abandoned a child for a period of at least six months;

(2) a parent of a child in the custody of another, if the parent for a period of at least one year has failed significantly without justifiable cause, including but not limited to indigency,

(A) to communicate meaningfully with the child, or

(B) to provide for the care and support of the child as required by law or judicial decree;

(3) the father of a minor if the father's consent is not required by AS 25.23.040(a)(2);

(4) a parent who has relinquished the right to consent under AS 25.23.180;

(5) a parent whose parental rights have been terminated by order of the court under AS 25.23.180(c)(3) or AS 47.10.080(c)(3);

(6) a parent judicially declared incompetent or mentally defective if the court dispenses with the parent's consent;

(7) a parent of the person to be adopted, if the person is 19 or more years of age, and the court dispenses with the consent of the parent;

(8) a guardian or custodian specified in AS 25.23.040(a)(3) or (4) who has failed to respond in writing to a request for consent for a period of 60 days or who, after examination of the guardian's or custodian's written reasons for withholding consent, is found by the court to be withholding consent unreasonably; or

(9) the spouse of the person to be adopted, if the requirement of consent to the adoption is waived by the court by reason of prolonged unexplained absence, unavailability, incapacity, or circumstances constituting an unreasonable withholding of consent.

(b) Except as provided in AS 25.23.100, notice of a hearing on a petition for adoption need not be given to a person whose consent is not required or to a person whose consent or relinquishment has been filed with the petition.

(§ 1 ch 84 SLA 1974; am § 4 ch 63 SLA 1977; am § 3 ch 50 SLA 1987)

§ 25.23.060. Execution of consent; consent as power of attorney.

(a) The required consent to adoption shall be executed, at any time after the birth of the child, in the presence of the court or in the presence of a person authorized to take acknowledgments. The consent is not valid unless the consent form states that the person consenting to the adoption has the right to withdraw that consent as provided in AS 25.23.070(b), and unless the person consenting to the adoption acknowledges receipt of a copy of the consent form. The person giving consent shall state in the consent form whether the child is a member of an Indian tribe or the biological child of a member of an Indian tribe, so that the court may determine whether the provisions of 25 U.S.C. 1901–1963 (Indian Child Welfare Act of 1978) apply.

(b) A consent which does not name or otherwise identify the adopting parent is valid if the consent is executed in the presence of the court or a person authorized to take acknowledgments and contains a statement by the person whose consent it is that the person consenting voluntarily executed the consent irrespective of disclosure of the name or other identification of the adopting parent.

(c) A consent executed under this section is effective as a power of attorney under AS 13.26.020. Unless the consent form provides otherwise, and regardless of whether the form names or identifies the adoptive parent, the consent delegates to the adoptive parent all powers that may be delegated under AS 13.26.020. The power of attorney takes effect when the child is delivered to the adoptive parent, and remains in effect as long as the consent is in effect; but the power of attorney is not effective beyond one year, unless the court extends it for good cause. The power of attorney does not terminate on the death or disability of the person executing the consent, unless the consent form so states. This subsection may not be construed to alter the requirements of AS 47.70 (the Interstate Compact on the Placement of Children).

(§ 1 ch 84 SLA 1974; am § 5, 6 ch 140 SLA 1986)

§ 25.23.070. Withdrawal of consent.

(a) A consent to adoption may not be withdrawn after the entry of a decree of adoption.

(b) A consent to adoption may be withdrawn before the entry of a decree of adoption, within 10 days after the consent is given, by delivering written notice to the person obtaining the consent, or after the 10-day period, if the court finds, after notice and opportunity to be heard is afforded to petitioner, the person seeking the withdrawal, and the agency placing a child for adoption, that the withdrawal is in the best interest of the person to be adopted and the court orders the withdrawal.

(§ 1 ch 84 SLA 1974; am § 7 ch 140 SLA 1986)

§ 25.23.080. Petition for adoption.

(a) The caption of a petition for adoption shall be styled substantially "In the Matter of the Adoption of...". The person to be adopted shall be designated in the caption under the name by which the person is to be known if the petition is granted. If the child is placed for adoption by an agency, any name by which the child was previously known may not be disclosed in the petition or in the decree of adoption. (b) A petition for adoption shall be signed and verified by the petitioner, filed with the clerk of the court, and state

(1) the date and place of birth of the person to be adopted, if known;

(2) the name to be used for the person to be adopted;

(3) the date of placement of the minor and the name of the person placing the minor;

(4) the full name, age, place and duration of residence of the petitioner;

(5) the marital status of the petitioner, including the date and place of marriage, if married;

(6) that the petitioner has facilities and resources, including those available under a hard-to-place child subsidy agreement, suitable to provide for the nurture and care of the minor to be adopted, and that it is the desire of the petitioner to establish the relationship of parent and child with the person to be adopted;

(7) a description and estimate of value of any property of the person to be adopted; and

(8) the name of any person whose consent to the adoption is required, but who has not consented, and facts or circumstances which excuse the lack of the consent normally required to the adoption.

(c) A certified copy of the birth certificate or verification of the birth record of the person to be adopted, if available, the information specified in AS 25.23.185(a), if available, and the required consents, relinquishments, and termination orders shall be filed with the clerk.

(§ 1 ch 84 SLA 1974; am § 1 ch 36 SLA 1977; am § 8 ch 140 SLA 1986)

§ 25.23.090. Report of petitioner's expenditures.

(a) Except as specified in (b) of this section, the petitioner in any proceeding for the adoption of a minor shall file, before the petition is heard, a full accounting report in a manner acceptable to the court of all disbursements of anything of value made or agreed to be made by or on behalf of the petitioner in connection with the adoption. The report shall show any expenses incurred in connection with

(1) the birth of the minor;

(2) placement of the minor with petitioner;

(3) medical or hospital care received by the mother or by the minor during the mother's prenatal care and confinement; and

(4) services relating to the adoption or to the placement of the minor for adoption that were received by or on behalf of the petitioner, either natural parent of the minor, or any other person.

(b) This section does not apply to an adoption by a stepparent whose spouse is a natural or adoptive parent of the child.

(c) Any report made under this section shall be signed and verified by the petitioner.

(§ 1 ch 84 SLA 1974)

§ 25.23.100. Notice of petition, investigation and hearing.

(a) After the filing of a petition to adopt a minor, the court shall fix a time and place for hearing the petition. At least 20 days before the date of hearing, the petitioner shall give notice of the filing of the petition and of the time and place of hearing to (1) the department, unless the adoption is by a stepparent of the child; (2) any agency or person whose consent to the adoption is required by this chapter, but who has not consented; and (3) a person whose consent is dispensed with upon any ground mentioned in AS 25.23.050(a) (1), (2), (3), (6), (7), (8) and (9), but who has not consented. The notice to the department shall be accompanied by a copy of the petition.

(b) Notice to persons specified in AS 25.23.050 shall include a statement of the grounds under which consent to the adoption is not required. Notice given under this section shall be adequate to give actual notice of the proceedings, taking into account education and language differences which are known or reasonably ascertainable by the petitioner or the department. The notice of hearing shall contain all names by which the minor has been identified and shall state in summary form the effect of a decree of adoption. Notice shall be given in the manner appropriate under rules of civil procedure for the service of process in a civil action in this state or in any manner the court by order directs. Notice by publication may not be given unless, for compelling reasons, the court orders it to be given under the procedure established in Rule 4 of the Alaska Rules of Civil Procedure. Proof of the giving of the notice shall be filed with the court before the petition is heard, subject to the time limitations in (e) of this section.

(c) A reasonable investigation shall be made by the department or the petitioner to assure that all persons listed in (a) of this section are located and given notice of the proposed adoption. The investigation shall be conducted so that the rights of all parties are protected, including but not limited to the right to privacy and the right to be notified. An affidavit describing the investigation shall be filed with the court if all persons listed in (a) of this section are not located.

(d) Except as provided in (g) and (i) of this section, an investigation shall be made by the department or any other qualified agency or person designated by the court to inquire into the conditions and antecedents of a minor sought to be adopted and of the petitioner for the purpose of ascertaining whether the adoptive home is a suitable home for the minor and whether the proposed adoption is in the best interest of the minor.

(e) A written report of the investigation shall be filed with the court by the investigator before the petition is heard so long as the report is filed within 30 days of the designation by the court of the department, agency or person to make the investigation.

(f) The report of the investigation shall contain an evaluation of the placement with a recommendation as to the granting of the petition for adoption and any other information the court requires regarding the petitioner or the minor.

(g) Unless directed by the court, an investigation and report is not required in cases in which an agency is a party or joins in the petition for adoption, a stepparent is the petitioner, the person to be adopted is within the fourth degree of lineal or collateral consanguinity to the petitioner, or the person to be adopted is an adult. In other cases, the court may waive the investigation only if it appears that waiver is in the best interest of the minor and that the adoptive home and the minor are suited to each other. The department which is required to consent to the adoption may give consent without making the investigation.

(h) The department or the agency or persons designated by the court to make the required investigation may request other departments or agencies within or outside of this state to make investigations of designated portions of the inquiry as may be appropriate and to make a written report as a supplemental report to the court and shall make similar investigations and reports on behalf of other agencies or persons designated by the courts of this state or another state.

(i) After the filing of a petition to adopt an adult the court by order shall direct that a copy of the petition and a notice of the time and place of the hearing be given to any person whose consent to the adoption is required, but who has not consented. The court may order an appropriate investigation to assist it in determining whether the adoption is in the best interest of the persons involved.

(j) *[Repealed, § 22 ch 140 SLA 1986.]*

(§ 1 ch 84 SLA 1974; am § 4 ch 167 SLA 1975; am § 1 ch 150 SLA 1976; am § 9, 10, 22 ch 140 SLA 1986)

§ 25.23.110. Required residence of minor.

A final decree of adoption may not be issued until the minor to be adopted, other than a stepchild of the petitioner, has lived in the adoptive home and the department or any other qualified agency or person designated by the court has had an opportunity to observe or investigate the adoptive home. This observation or investigation is not required in proceedings where an investigation is not required under AS 25.23.100(g) and (i).

(§ 1 ch 84 SLA 1974)

§ 25.23.120. Hearing.

(a) The presence of the petitioner and the person to be adopted is not required at the hearing on the petition unless ordered by the court.

(b) The court may continue the hearing from time to time to permit further observation, investigation, or consideration of any facts or circumstances affecting the granting of the petition.

(c) If at the conclusion of the hearing the court determines that the required consents have been obtained or excused and that the adoption is the best interest of the person to be adopted, it may issue a final decree of adoption.

(d) If the requirements for a decree under (c) of this section have not been met, the court shall dismiss the petition and determine, in the best interests of the minor, the person including the petitioner to have custody of the minor.

(§ 1 ch 84 SLA 1974)

Revisor's notes.—Formerly AS 20.15.120. Renumbered in 1982.

§ 25.23.125. Preference of minor to be adopted; guardian ad litem; protective orders.

(a) If the person to be adopted is a minor under the age of 10 and the person is of sufficient age and intelligence to state desires concerning the adoption, the court shall consider the person's desires.

(b) The court may appoint a guardian ad litem or attorney, or both, under AS 25.24.310 for a minor who is to be adopted.

(c) The court may issue a protective order or other order that is in the best interest of a minor who is to be adopted.

(§ 11 ch 140 SLA 1986)

§ 25.23.127. Adult family member preference to adopt.

Taking into consideration a child's stated preference under AS 25.23.125(a) and consent given under AS 25.23.040(a)(5), and unless the court finds that a petition to adopt the child by an adult family member is contrary to the best interest of the child, the court shall grant a petition to adopt a child by an adult family member who has had physical custody of the child for at least 12 consecutive months before the parental rights to the child have been terminated. In this section, "adult family member" has the meaning given in AS 47.10.990.

((§ 3 ch 64 SLA 2005))

§ 25.23.130. Effect of adoption decree.

(a) A final decree of adoption, whether issued by a court of this state or of any other state, has the following effect as to matters within the jurisdiction or before a court of this state:

(1) except with respect to a spouse of the petitioner and relatives of the spouse, to relieve the natural parents of the adopted person of all parental rights and responsibilities, and, except as provided in (c) of this section, to terminate all legal relationships between the adopted person and the natural parents and other relatives of the adopted person, so that the adopted person thereafter is a stranger to the former relative for all purposes including inheritance, unless the decree of adoption specifically provides for continuation of inheritance rights, and the interpretation or construction of documents, statutes, and instruments, whether executed before or after the adoption is decreed, which do not expressly include the person by name or by some designation not based on a parent and child or blood relationship; and

(2) to create the relationship of parent and child between petitioner and the adopted person, as if the adopted person were a legitimate blood descendant of the petitioner, for all purposes including inheritance and applicability of statutes, documents, and instruments, whether executed before or after the adoption is decreed, which do not expressly exclude an adopted person from their operation or effect.

(b) Notwithstanding the provisions of (a) of this section, if a parent of a child dies without the relationship of parent and child having been previously terminated and a spouse of the living parent thereafter adopts the child, the child's right of inheritance from or through the deceased parent is unaffected by the adoption.

(c) Nothing in this chapter prohibits an adoption that allows visitation between the adopted person and the person's natural parents or other relatives.

(d) Except as provided in (e) of this section, a decree terminating parental rights on the grounds set out in AS 25.23.180(c)(3) voids all legal relationships between the child and the biological parent so that the child is a stranger to the biological parent and to relatives of the biological parent for all purposes, including interpretation of documents executed before or after the termination of parental rights that do not include the child by name or by a description not based on a parental or blood relationship.

(e) Inheritance rights between a child and a biological parent are not voided by a decree terminating parental rights on the grounds set out in AS 25.23.180(c)(3) unless the decree specifically provides for the termination of inheritance rights.

(§ 1 ch 84 SLA 1974; am § 12, 13 ch 140 SLA 1986; am § 4 ch 50 SLA 1987)

Note: In 1995, the legislature enacted AS 13.12.114 on inheritance rights between parent and child. This section changes the law governing inheritance rights of adopted children. According to AS 13.12.114(d), to the extent there is a conflict between AS 13.12.114 and AS 25.23.130, AS 13.12.114 controls.

§ 25.23.140. Appeal and validation of adoption decree.

(a) An appeal from any final order or decree rendered under this chapter may be taken in the manner and time provided for appeal from a judgment in a civil action.

(b) Subject to the disposition of an appeal, upon the expiration of one year after an adoption decree is issued, the decree may not be questioned by any person including the petitioner, in any manner upon any ground, including fraud, misrepresentation, failure to give any required notice, or lack of jurisdiction of the parties or of the subject matter, unless, in the case of the adoption of a minor the petitioner has not taken custody of the minor, or, in the case of the adoption of an adult, the adult had no knowledge of the decree within the one-year period.

(c) Subject to the disposition of an appeal, one year after a decree is issued terminating parental rights on grounds set out in AS 25.23.180(c)(3), the order may not be challenged on any ground, including fraud, misrepresentation, failure to give notice, or lack of jurisdiction of the parties or of the subject matter.

(§ 1 ch 84 SLA 1974; am § 5 ch 50 SLA 1987)

§ 25.23.150. Confidential nature of hearings and records in adoption proceedings.

(a) All hearings held in proceedings under this chapter shall be held in closed court without admittance of any person other than essential officers of the court, the parties, their witnesses, counsel, persons who have not previously consented to the adoption but are required to consent, and representatives of the agencies present to perform their official duties.

(b) The papers and records relating to an adoption or a termination of parental rights under AS 25.23.180(c)(3) that are a part of the permanent record of a court are subject to inspection only upon consent of the court. The papers and records relating to an adoption or a termination of parental rights under AS 25.23.180(c)(3) on file with the department, an agency, or an individual are subject to inspection only with consent of all interested persons or by order of a court for good cause shown. Except as provided in this section, adoption records of the Bureau of Vital Statistics are subject to inspection under the provisions of AS 18.50.

(c) Except as otherwise provided by law, or as authorized in writing by the adopted child, if 14 or more years of age, or by the adoptive parent, or upon order of the court for good cause shown, a person may not disclose the identity or address of an adoptive parent, an adopted child, a child who is the subject of a proceeding under AS 25.23.180(c)(3), or biological parent whose parental rights have been terminated on grounds set out in AS 25.23.180(c)(3).

(d) The court may order the disclosure of a natural parent's identity or address only if

(1) the court makes an express finding that the disclosure is required because of a medical necessity or other extraordinary circumstance; and

(2) the natural parent unless the parent's parental rights have been terminated on grounds set out in AS 25.23.180(c)(3), the child, and the adoptive parents are afforded proper notice and a hearing; the court may waive the hearing and notice requirements if it finds there is a medical necessity that poses an immediate risk to life.

(§ 1 ch 84 SLA 1974; am § 14 - 16 ch 140 SLA 1986; am § 6 - 8 ch 50 SLA 1987)

§ 25.23.160. Recognition of foreign decree affecting adoption.

A decree of court terminating the relationship of parent and child or establishing the relationship by adoption issued under due process of law by a court of any other jurisdiction within or outside of the United States shall be recognized in this state and the rights and obligations of the parties as to matters within the jurisdiction of this state shall be determined as though the decree were issued by a court of this state.

(§ 1 ch 84 SLA 1974)

§ 25.23.170. Applications for birth certificates.

Within 30 days after an adoption decree becomes final, the clerk of the court shall, if requested by the adoptive parents, prepare an application for a birth certificate in the name of the adopted person. Upon issuing a decree terminating parental rights on grounds set out in AS 25.23.180(c)(3) the court may order the preparation of an application for a birth certificate in the name of the child without reference to the parent whose parental rights have been terminated. The clerk of the court shall forward the application

(1) for a person born in the United States, to the appropriate vital statistics office of the place, if known, where the adopted person was born and a copy of the decree to the department for statistical purposes; and

(2) for a person born outside the United States to the state registrar of vital statistics.

(§ 1 ch 84 SLA 1974; am § ch 76 SLA 1982; am § 9 ch 50 SLA 1987)

§ 25.23.173. Indian child adoption reports.

After entering a final decree or order in an Indian child adoptive placement, the court shall send to the Secretary of the Interior a copy of the decree or order and other information required by 25 U.S.C. 1951 (sec. 301(a) of the Indian Child Welfare Act of 1978).

(§ 17 ch 140 SLA 1986)

§ 25.23.175. Findings concerning persons born outside the United States.

In the case of the adoption of a person born outside the United States, if requested by the adoptive parents, the court shall make findings, based on evidence from the petitioner and other reliable state or federal sources, on the date and place of birth and parentage of the adopted person. The findings shall be certified by the court and included with the report of adoption filed with the state registrar of vital statistics in accordance with AS 18.50.210.

(§ 5 ch 76 SLA 1982)

§ 25.23.180. Relinquishment and termination of parent and child relationships.

(a) The rights of a parent with reference to a child, including parental right to control the child or to withhold consent to an adoption, may be relinquished and the relationship of parent and child terminated in or before an adoption proceeding as provided in this section.

(b) All rights of a parent with reference to a child, including the right to receive notice of a hearing on a petition for adoption, may be relinquished and the relationship of parent and child terminated by a writing, signed by the parent, regardless of the age of the parent, a copy of which shall be given to the parent,

(1) in the presence of a representative of an agency taking custody of the child, whether the agency is within or outside of the state or in the presence and with the approval of the court within or outside of this state in which the minor was present or in which the parent resided at the time it was signed, which relinquishment may be withdrawn within 10 days after it is signed or the child is born, whichever is later; and the relinquishment is invalid unless it states that the parent has this right of withdrawal; or

(2) in any other situation if the petitioner has had custody of the minor for two years, but only if notice of the adoption proceeding has been given to the parent and the court finds, after considering the circumstances of the relinquishment and the long continued custody by the petitioner, that the best interest of the child requires the granting of adoption.

(c) The relationship of parent and child may be terminated by a court order issued in connection with a proceeding under this chapter or a proceeding under AS 47.10 on the grounds

(1) specified in AS 47.10.080(o) or 47.10.088;

(2) that a parent who does not have custody is unreasonably withholding consent to adoption, contrary to the best interest of the minor child; or

(3) that the parent committed an act constituting sexual assault or sexual abuse of a minor under the laws of this state or a comparable offense under the laws of the state where the act occurred that resulted in conception of the child and that termination of the parental rights of the biological parent is in the best interests of the child.

(d) For the purpose of an adoption proceeding under this chapter, a decree issued by a court of competent jurisdiction in this or another state terminating all rights of a parent with reference to a child or the relationship of parent and child dispenses with the required

(1) consent by that parent to an adoption of that child; and

(2) notice of a proceeding to that parent unless otherwise required by this section.

(e) A petition for termination of the relationship of parent and child made in connection with an adoption proceeding or in an independent proceeding for the termination of parental rights on grounds set out in (c)(3) of this section may be made by

(1) either parent if termination of the relationship is sought with respect to the other parent;

(2) the petitioner for adoption, the guardian of the person, the legal custodian of the child, or the individual standing in parental relationship to the child;

(3) an agency; or

(4) another person having a legitimate interest in the matter.

(f) Before the petition is heard, notice of the hearing on the petition and opportunity to be heard shall be given the parents of the child, the guardian of the person of the child, the person having legal custody of the child, and, in the discretion of the court, a person appointed to represent any party.

(g) Notwithstanding the provisions of (b) of this section, a relinquishment of parental rights with respect to a child, executed under this section, may be withdrawn by the parent, and a decree of a court terminating the parent and child relationship on grounds set out in (c)(1) and (2) of this section may be vacated by the court upon motion of the parent, if the child is not on placement for adoption and the person having custody of the child consents in writing to the withdrawal or vacation of the decree.

(h) The respondent to a petition filed for the termination of parental rights on grounds set out in (c)(3) of this section is entitled to representation in the proceedings by an attorney. If the respondent is financially unable to employ an attorney, the court shall appoint the office of public advocacy to represent the respondent in the proceedings.

(i) Proceedings for the termination of parental rights on the grounds set out in (c)(3) of this section do not affect the rights of a victim of sexual abuse of a minor or incest to obtain legal and equitable civil remedies for all injuries and damages arising out of the perpetrator's conduct.

(j) In a relinquishment of parental rights executed under (a) of this section, a parent may retain privileges with respect to the child, including the ability to have future contact, communication, and visitation with the child. A retained privilege must be stated in writing with specificity. Not less than 10 days after the relinquishment is signed, the court may enter an order terminating parental rights if the court finds that termination of parental rights under the terms of the agreement is in the child's best interest. If a parent has retained one or more privileges, the court shall incorporate the retained privileges into the termination order with a recommendation that the retained privileges be incorporated in an adoption or legal guardianship decree.

(k) A voluntary relinquishment may not be withdrawn and a termination order may not be vacated on the ground that a retained privilege has been withheld from the relinquishing parent or that the relinquishing parent has been unable, for any reason, to act on a retained privilege, except as provided in Rule 60(b), Alaska Rules of Civil Procedure.

(*l*) After a termination order is entered, a person who has voluntarily relinquished parental rights under this section may request a review hearing, upon a showing of good cause, to seek enforcement or modification of or to vacate a privilege retained in the termination order. The court may modify, enforce, or vacate the retained privilege if the court finds, by clear and convincing evidence, that it is in the best interest of the child to do so.

(m) After a termination order is entered and before the entry of an adoption or legal guardianship decree, a prospective adoptive parent or a guardian of a child who is the subject of an adoption decree may request, after providing notice as specified under this subsection, that the court decline to incorporate a privilege retained in a termination order and recommended for incorporation in an adoption or guardianship decree under (j) of this section. The request made under this subsection may only be considered by the court after providing at least 20 days' notice by certified mail to the last known address of the person who has voluntarily relinquished parental rights to the child. The notice under this subsection must describe the request and explain that the recipient of the notice may submit a written statement under penalty of perjury to the court that the recipient either agrees with or opposes the request. The notice must also include the deadline for submitting the statement and the mailing address of the court. The court may decline to incorporate a retained privilege if the person who retained the privilege agrees with the request or if the court finds that it is in the child's best interest.

(n) A person who relinquished parental rights is entitled to the appointment of an attorney if a hearing is requested under (*l*) or (m) of this section to the same extent as if the parent's rights had not been terminated in a child-in-need-of-aid proceeding.

(§ 1 ch 84 SLA 1974; am 32 ch 21 SLA 1985; am § 10–13 ch 50 SLA 1987; am § 12 ch 99 SLA 1998; am § 4 ch 64 SLA 2005)

§ 25.23.185. Records and information.

(a) At the time a petition for adoption is filed with the court, the agency or individual placing the person for adoption, or the petitioner, shall file with the court, for release to the state registrar of vital statistics, the following information, or an explanation of its unavailability, on forms provided by the department:

(1) the address of each parent named on the original birth certificate; and

(2) background information required under AS 18.50.510.

(b) Upon entry of a decree of adoption, the clerk of the court shall transmit to the Bureau of Vital Statistics the information provided under (a) of this section. The bureau shall attach the information to the original birth certificate of the adopted person.

(c) A child adoption agency licensed under former AS 47.35 and a child placement agency licensed under AS 47.32 shall maintain records of the information required to be furnished to the court under this section or under regulations of the commissioner implementing this section. If a child adoption agency or child placement agency ceases to place persons for adoption, it shall transfer its records to the commissioner.

(§ 18 ch 140 SLA 1986; am § 4 ch 124 SLA 1994; am § 13 ch 57 SLA 2005)

§ 25.23.190. Subsidy for hard-to-place child.

A hard-to-place child in the permanent custody of the department in a foster home for not less than one year may not be denied the opportunity for a permanent home if the achievement of this depends on continued subsidy by the state.

(§ 1 ch 84 SLA 1974; am § 2 ch 36 SLA 1977)

§ 25.23.200. Investigation of home for subsidized hard-to-place child.

Persons who are caring for a hard-to-place child on a foster parent basis and who have applied to adopt the hard-to-place child and to receive payments for the care and support of the hard-to-place child shall be evaluated as to their suitability as adoptive parents by means of an adoptive home study. Persons who are caring for a hard-to-place child in the state's custody and who wish to be appointed legal guardians of the child under AS 13.26.045, and to receive payments for the care and support of the child, shall be evaluated as to their suitability as guardians by means of a guardianship study. A home study or guardianship study shall be made by the commissioner's adoption staff or on the commissioner's behalf by an authorized agency or individual that provides adoption services.

(§ 1 ch 84 SLA 1974; am § 3 ch SLA 1977; am § 2 ch 204 SLA 1990)

§ 25.23.210. Amount and duration of subsidy payments.

The monthly payment and the length of time for which a subsidy for a hard-to-place child is granted are left to the discretion of the commissioner and may vary from a small monthly sum to an amount not exceeding the existing rate for foster care until the child reaches the age of majority, if the need continues to exist. Subsidies shall be paid from the same public funds and in the same manner as foster care payments. On request of the person caring for the child, the department shall review whether the amount of the subsidy is appropriate.

(§ 1 ch 84 SLA 1974; am § 4 ch 36 SLA 1977; am § 1 ch 31 SLA 2003)

§ 25.23.220. Annual reevaluation of subsidy.

(Repealed § 4 ch 31 SLA 2003).

§ 25.23.230. Regulations.

The department shall adopt regulations necessary to implement the provisions of AS 25.23.185 -25.23.240.

(§ 1 ch 84 SLA 1974; am § 19 ch 140 SLA 1986)

§ 25.23.240. Definitions.

In this chapter, unless the context otherwise requires,

(1) "adult" means an individual who has reached the age of majority;

(2) "agency" means any person certified, licensed, or otherwise specially empowered by law or regulation to place minors for adoption;

(3) "child" means a son or daughter, whether by birth or by adoption;

(4) "commissioner" means the commissioner of health and social services;

(5) "court" means the superior court of this state, and, when the context requires, the court of another state empowered to grant petitions for adoption or guardianship or to terminate parental rights;

(6) "department" means the Department of Health and Social Services;

(7) "hard to place child" means a minor who is not likely to be adopted or to obtain a guardian by reason of physical or mental disability, emotional disturbance, recognized high risk of physical or mental disease, age, membership in a sibling group, racial or ethnic factors, or any combination of these conditions;

(8) "minor" means a person who has not reached the age of majority;

(9) "sexual abuse of a minor" means a sexual offense defined in AS 11.41.434, 11.41.436, 11.41.438, or 11.41.440;

(10) "sexual assault" means a sexual offense defined in AS 11.41.410 or 11.41.420;

(11) "stepparent" means the spouse of a natural parent of the child residing in the same household.

(§ 1 ch 84 SLA 1974; am § 5 ch 36 SLA 1977; am § 20 ch 140 SLA 1986; am § 14, 15 ch 50 SLA 1987; am § 4, 5 ch 204 SLA 1990)

CHILD IN NEED OF AID RULES OF PROCEDURE

Table of Contents

PART I. GENERAL PROVISIONS

CINA

PART II. MASTERS, MAGISTRATES, DISTRICT COURT JUDGES

PART III. COMMENCEMENT OF PROCEEDINGS

PART IV. DISCOVERY, EVIDENCE, PROOF

PART V. PRELIMINARY PROCEEDINGS

PART VI. ADJUDICATION

PART VII. DISPOSITION

APPENDIX
INDIAN CHILD WELFARE ACT

Section

CROSS REFERENCES FROM DELINQUENCY
AND CINA RULES TO PRIOR CHILDREN'S RULES

PART I. GENERAL PROVISIONS

Rule 1. Title—Scope—Construction—Situations Not Covered by the Rules.

(a) **Title.** These rules will be known and cited as the Child in Need of Aid Rules or the CINA Rules.

(b) **Scope.** These rules govern practice and procedure in the trial courts in all phases of child in need of aid proceedings brought under AS 47.10.010(a).

(c) **Construction.** These rules will be construed and applied to promote fairness, accurate fact-finding, the expeditious determination of children's matters, and the best interests of the child.

(d) **Legal Effect of Rules.** These rules are promulgated pursuant to Alaska constitutional authority granting rulemaking power to the Alaska Supreme Court. To the extent that the rules are inconsistent with a procedural provision of any Alaska statute not enacted for the specific purpose of changing a rule, these rules supersede the statute to the extent of the inconsistency.

(e) **Civil Rules Applicable.** Civil Rules 3(b)—(g), 4, 5, 5.1, 6, 10, 11, 15, 42, 45(a)—(f), 46, 53, 59, 60, 61, 63, 76, 77, 81, 90, 98, and 100 apply to child in need of aid proceedings except to the extent that any provisions of these civil rules conflict with the Child in Need of Aid Rules.

(f) **Situations Not Covered by These Rules.** Where no specific procedure is prescribed by these rules, the court may proceed in any lawful manner, including application of the Civil Rules, applicable statutes, the Alaska and United States Constitutions or the common law. Such a procedure may not be inconsistent with these rules and may not unduly delay or otherwise interfere with the unique character and purpose of child in need of aid proceedings.

(SCO 845 effective August 15, 1987; amended by SCO 1265 effective July 15, 1997; and by SCO 1355 effective July 15, 1999)

Cross References

CROSS REFERENCE: AS 22.15.100(8); AS 47.05.060; AS 47.05.065; AS 47.10.005; AS 47.10.082; Alaska Constitution, Art. IV § 15.

Annotations

Cases

This annotation construes former Children's Rule 1. Children are constitutionally entitled to a jury trial in the adjudicative stage of a delinquency proceeding, but the child should first consult with his counsel and his parents, or guardian when appropriate, and then affirmatively assert his right to trial by jury before it is finally granted. **RLR v. State,** Op. No. 706,487 P2d 27 (Alaska 1971).

This annotation construes former Children's Rule 1. If a child waives jury trial in a juvenile proceeding, the state may not require it, but a jury trial shall be provided only on demand. **RLR v. State,** Op. No. 706, 487 P2d 27 (Alaska 1971).

This annotation construes former Children's Rule 1. Errors in a juvenile proceeding not affecting substantial right will be disregarded. **RLR v. State,** Op. No. 706, 487 P2d 27 (Alaska 1971).

This annotation construes former Children's Rule 1. Superior court does not have authority to award costs and fees in a child in need of aid proceeding. **Cooper v. State,** Op. No. 2453, 638 P2d 174 (Alaska 1981).

This annotation construes former Children's Rule 1. The use of hearsay evidence in the disposition phase of a parental rights termination proceeding as allowed by state law did not conflict with the federal Indian Child Welfare Act. **Matter of J.R.B.,** Op. No. 3029, 715 P2d 1170 (Alaska 1986).

In adjudicatory phase of Child in Need of Aid proceeding, alleged abuser's due process right to cross-examine child is adequately protected by unavailability and reliability requirements of the Rules of Evidence; accordingly, where 4-year-old child was unavailable to testify, but child's videotaped statement describing sexual abuse by father was reliable, father's lack of opportunity to cross-examine or confront child did not deny him due process of law. **Matter of A.S.W.,** Op. No. 3847, 834 P2d 801 (Alaska 1992).

Statute providing that registration and other records of alcohol treatment facilities shall remain confidential and are privileged to the patient did not establish privilege precluding admission of alcohol treatment records in CINA proceedings. **In re D.D.S.,** Op. No. 4058, 869 P.2d 160 (Alaska 1994).

Rule 2. Definitions.

(a) "Child" means a person under 18 years of age when the petition for adjudication is filed who remains subject to the jurisdiction of the court.

(b) "Custodian" means a natural person 18 years of age or older to whom a parent has transferred temporary physical care, custody, and control of the child for the period of time immediately preceding the conduct alleged in the petition.

(c) "Department" means the Department of Health and Social Services of the State of Alaska.

(d) "Guardian" means a natural person who is legally appointed guardian of the person of a child.

(e) "Guardian ad litem" means a person appointed by the court to represent the best interests of the child in the CINA proceeding as distinguished from a guardian of the person defined in paragraph (d).

(f) "Indian" means any person who is a member of an Indian tribe, or who is an Alaska native and a member of a regional corporation as defined in 43 U.S.C. § 1606.

(g) "Indian child" means any unmarried person who is under the age of 18 and who is either (1) a member of an Indian tribe, or (2) is eligible for membership in an Indian tribe and is the biological child of a member of an Indian tribe.

(h) "Indian child's tribe" means (1) the Indian tribe in which an Indian child is a member or eligible for membership or (2), in the case of an Indian child who is a member of or eligible for membership in more than one tribe, the Indian tribe with which the Indian child has the more significant contacts.

(i) "Indian custodian" means any Indian person who has legal custody of an Indian child under tribal law or custom or under state law, or to whom temporary physical care, custody and control has been transferred by the parent of the child.

(j) "Indian tribe" means any Indian tribe, band, nation, or other organized group or community of Indians recognized as eligible for services provided to Indians by the Secretary of the Department of the Interior because of their status as Indians, including an Alaska Native village as defined in 43 U.S.C. § 1602(c).

(k) "Parent" means a biological or adoptive parent whose parental rights have not been terminated.

(l) "Party" means the child, the parents, the guardian, the guardian ad litem, the Department, an Indian custodian who has intervened, an Indian child's tribe which has intervened, and any other person who has been allowed to intervene by the court.

(SCO 845 effective August 15, 1987; amended by SCO 1355 effective July 15, 1999)

Cross References

CROSS REFERENCE: AS 25.20.010; AS 47.10.990; 25 U.S.C. § 1903.

(f) **CROSS REFERENCE:** 25 U.S.C. § 1903(3).

(g) **CROSS REFERENCE:** 25 U.S.C. § 1903(4).

(h) **CROSS REFERENCE:** 25 U.S.C. § 1903(5).

(i) **CROSS REFERENCE:** 25 U.S.C. § 1903(6).

(j) **CROSS REFERENCE:** 25 U.S.C. § 1903(7).

Annotations

Cases

Legal guardian who has all the authority of a parent may do what a parent may do, so if parent may appoint custodian, guardian may also appoint one. **T.B. v. State,** Op. No. 4400, 922 P.2d 271 (Alaska 1996).

Rule 3. Hearings.

(a) **Notice.** Notice of each hearing must be given to all parties and any foster parent or other out-of-home care provider within a reasonable time before the hearing. Service on the child may be accomplished by serving the child's guardian ad litem, attorney or social worker. Notice to a foster parent or out-of-home care provider must be provided by the Department.

(b) **Presence of the Child.** A child who is not of suitable age to understand or participate in the proceedings need not be present at hearings unless the court so orders. The court may excuse the presence of a child who is of suitable age if attendance would be detrimental to the child. The child or the child's guardian ad litem may waive the child's right to be present at a particular hearing.

(c) **Presence of Grandparent or Out-of-Home Care Provider.** A grandparent of a child and the out-of-home care provider are entitled to be heard at any hearing at which the person is present. However, the court may limit the presence of these persons in a hearing that has been closed to the public under (f)(2) of this rule to the time during which the person's testimony is being given the court determines that such a limitation is necessary under the circumstances listed in (f)(2)(C) of this rule.

(d) **Parties Excluded.** The court may exclude the child during particular testimony if the effect of that testimony would psychologically harm the child. The court also may exclude a parent, guardian or Indian custodian during the child's testimony in order to protect the child from material psychological harm, provided that the parent, guardian or Indian custodian may listen to a recording of the testimony to prepare for further examination and rebuttal.

(e) **Exclusion of Witnesses.** Witnesses may be excluded from a hearing pursuant to Evidence Rule 615.

(f) **General Public Access to Hearings.**

(1) Except as provided in (2) of this paragraph, and unless prohibited by federal or state statute or regulation, court order, or other court rule, hearings are open to the public.

(2) The following hearings are closed to the public:

(A) the initial court hearing after the filing of a petition that begins the child-in-need-of-aid case;

(B) a hearing following the initial hearing in which a parent, child, or other party to the case is present but has not had an opportunity to obtain legal representation;

(C) a hearing, or a part of a hearing, for which the court issues a written order finding that allowing the hearing, or part of the hearing, to be open to the public would reasonably be expected to stigmatize or be emotionally damaging to a child; inhibit a child's testimony in the hearing; disclose matters otherwise required to be kept confidential by state or federal statute or regulation, court order, or court rule; or interfere with a criminal investigation or proceeding or a criminal defendant's right to a fair trial in a criminal proceeding.

(3) Before ruling on a request under (2)(C) of this paragraph concerning potential interference with a criminal investigation or proceeding, the court shall give notice and an opportunity to be heard to the state or a municipal agency that is assigned to the criminal investigation or to the prosecuting attorney.

(4) If the court closes a hearing to the public under (2)(C) of this paragraph, the court shall close only the portions of the hearing necessary to prevent the potential harm listed in (2)(C) of this paragraph. If a hearing, or part of a hearing, is open to the public, the court shall hear in camera any information offered regarding the location, or readily leading to the location, of a parent, child, or other party to the case who is a victim of domestic violence or whose safety or welfare may be endangered by the public release of information. Access to testimony heard in camera under this subparagraph is limited to the court and authorized court personnel.

(5) Notwithstanding any other provision of this rule, the court shall issue an order to prohibit all persons in a hearing open to the public from disclosing to any person a name, picture, or other information that would readily lead to the

identification of a child who is the subject of the proceeding. If a person violates the order, the court may impose any appropriate sanction, including contempt and closure of any further hearings to the person.

(6) A party to the proceeding may move the court to close to the public a hearing, or part of the hearing, to avoid the harm specified in (2)(C) of this paragraph. A member of the public may request in writing to be served with a motion filed under this subparagraph. If such a request has been filed in advance of the filing of the motion, the party filing the motion must also serve the member of the public who requested notice under this subparagraph. The court may waive the service required under this subparagraph to a member of the public if a motion to close the hearing, or part of the hearing, is made under this subparagraph immediately before or during the hearing and the court finds that

(A) the need for closure was not reasonably foreseeable sufficiently in advance of the hearing to allow for notice;

(B) there is good cause not to delay the hearing in order to achieve notice, taking into consideration the age of the child and the potential adverse effect that a delay could have on the child; and

(C) whatever notice is practicable under the circumstances has occurred.

(g) **Telephonic Participation.**

(1) The court may conduct any hearing with telephonic participation by one or more parties, counsel, witnesses, foster parents or out-of home care providers, or the judge.

(2) In any proceeding in which the court is authorized to proceed ex parte, the court may contact the non-appearing party or counsel by telephone, and in the interests of justice receive evidence or argument without stipulation of the parties.

(3) Procedures for telephonic hearings are governed by Civil Rule 99(b). Payment of telephone costs is governed by Administrative Rule 48.

(h) **Testimony Under Oath.** All testimony must be given under oath or affirmation as required by Evidence Rule 603.

(i) **Representation by Non-Attorney.** Unless the court for good cause requires representation by an attorney, an Indian tribe may be represented by a non-attorney tribal member or tribal employee. A written authorization for representation by the non-attorney must be filed in the case before the non-attorney tribal member or tribal employee may represent the tribe. A guardian ad litem need not be represented by an attorney unless the court, for good cause, requires representation by an attorney.

(SCO 845 effective August 15, 1987; amended by SCO 998 effective January 15, 1990; by SCO 1355 effective July 15, 1999; and by SCO 1580 effective nunc pro tunc to July 1, 2005)

Note: Ch. 43, SLA 2001, amends AS 47.10.030, AS 47.10.070(a), and AS 47.10.080(f) to add provisions concerning notice to and participation by grandparents. According to §6 of the Act, these provisions have the effect of amending Child in Need of Aid Rules 3, 7, 10, 15, 17, and 19 by requiring that grandparents be given notice of and an opportunity to be heard at certain child-in-need-of-aid proceedings.

Note: Chapter 64, sections 51 and 52, SLA 2005 (HB 53) amended Child in Need of Aid Rule 3(c) and (f) to make child in need of aid hearings generally open to the public, with certain exceptions, as reflected in section 1 of this Order. The changes to CINA Rule 3(c) and (f) are adopted for the sole reason that the legislature has mandated the amendments. In addition, according to section 61(a) of the Act, sections 9 and 10 of the Act, and AS 47.10.080(u), enacted in section 14, have the effect of changing CINA Rule 3 by allowing members of the public to attend court hearings except in certain circumstances.

Cross References

CROSS REFERENCE: AS 47.10.030(b); AS 47.10.070.

Annotations

Cases

This annotation construes former Children's Rule 12. If, following criminal proceedings, collateral legal disabilities exist apart from the sentence, an appeal is not mooted even though the sentence has already been served. **EJ. v. State,** Op. No. 628, 471 P2d 367 (Alaska 1970).

This annotation construes former Children's Rule 12. Where a child has been declared delinquent without the necessary compliance with statutory and constitutional procedural standards, such child has been deprived of his constitutional rights. If any attendant collateral disabilities remain, the proceedings which were infected with those disabilities cannot stand. **E.J. v. State,** Op. No. 628, 471 P2d 367 (Alaska 1970).

This annotation construes former Children's Rule 12. The provision of this rule providing for closed proceedings must be interpreted and applied in a manner consistent with the child's right to a public trial. **RLR v. State,** Op. No. 706, 487 P2d 27 (Alaska 1971).

This annotation construes former Children's Rule 12. If a child or his guardian ad litem wants the press, friends or others to be free to attend juvenile proceedings, the hearing must be open to them. The court's areas of discretion within which it may refuse to open a hearing involves persons whose presence is not desired by the child. **RLR v. State,** Op. No. 706,487 P2d 27 (Alaska 1971).

This annotation construes former Children's Rule 12. A hearing in which a chemist testifies that a tablet sent to him for analysis contained LSD should not be conducted in the absence of the infant involved after the attorney explicitly refuses to waive the infant's right to be present. Conducting a hearing in the child's absence under such circumstances is reversible error. **RLR v. State,** Op. No. 706, 487 P2d 27 (Alaska 1971).

This annotation construes former Children's Rule 12. Notions of benevolent protective policies for children cannot be used to validate departures from positive law relating to adjudicative and dispositive phases of children's proceedings. **In re E.M.D.,** Op. No. 737, 490 P2d 658 (Alaska 1971).

This annotation construes former Children's Rule 13. Considering the importance of juvenile proceedings and the fact that juvenile records are easily obtained and can have serious effects upon the life of a minor, the usual principles against entertaining moot controversies do not apply. Where a 12-year old boy has been determined to be delinquent, an appeal of that delinquency order will be considered, notwithstanding that the order has been vacated. **Ej. v. State,** Op. No. 628, 471 P2d 367 (Alaska 1970).

This annotation construes former Children's Rule 13. Due process requires that detention orders be based on competent, sworn testimony. A child has a right to be represented by counsel at a detention inquiry. Any detention order must state with particularity the facts supporting it. **Doe v. State,** Op. No. 707, 487 P2d 47 (Alaska 1971).

This annotation construes former Children's Rule 13. A detention order based on unsworn hearsay of the district attorney, further based on the court's belief's unsupported by any evidence that the child will engage in unlawful activity if not detained, and containing no facts on which it is based, is invalid. **Doe v. State,** Op. No. 707, 487 P2d 47 (Alaska 1971).

This annotation construes former Children's Rule 12. A child has a vital interest in a dependency proceeding and is an essential party whose presence cannot be dispensed with arbitrarily; in a dependency proceeding the summons and a copy of the petition must be served on the child as well as the parents; failure to make such service results in a lack of jurisdiction over the child. **In re P.N.,** Op. No. 1127,523 P2d 13 (Alaska 1975).

This annotation construes former Children's Rule 12. Where the children are not given the required notice of a dependency hearing the superior court has no jurisdiction over them and, therefore, cannot validly issue a judgment depriving a parent of his custody. **In re P.N.,** Op. No. 1127, 523 P2d 13 (Alaska 1975).

This annotation construes former Children's Rule 12. A court in a "child in need of supervision" hearing is under a duty to explain to the juvenile his right to counsel. **Wagstaff v. Superior Court, Family Court Division,** Op. No. 1144, 535 P2d 1220 (Alaska 1975).

This annotation construes former Children's Rule 12. In the adjudicative phase of any children's proceeding, the family court may consider only the specific situations set out in the petition. **In re S.D. Jr.,** Op. No. 1255, 549 P2d 1190 (Alaska 1976).

This annotation construes former Children's Rule 12. Court committed error when it commenced the adjudicative phase of the parental rights termination hearing in the absence of the child's counsel and guardian ad litem. **Matter of C.L.T.,** Op. No. 1866, 597 P2d 518 (Alaska 1979).

This annotation construes former Children's Rule 12. Superior court did not abuse its discretion in permitting two relatives of murder victims to attend a juvenile waiver hearing held to determine whether juvenile could be tried as an adult for the murders. **W.M.F. v. Jonstone,** Op. No. 571, 711 P2d 1187 (Alaska App. 1986).

Where father participated telephonically in parental rights termination action, his due process right to confront and cross-examine witnesses was not violated, since his attorney was present in the courtroom and did effectively cross-examine witnesses and since the transcript of the hearing indicated that the father could hear well enough to follow the proceedings. **E.J.S. v. Dept. of Health & Social Serv.,** Op. No. 3318, 754 P2d 749 (Alaska 1988).

In case in which the trial court affirmed the relocation of three children from their mother's home to a foster home, the trial court did not abuse its discretion in not allowing the children to testify regarding their desired placement. **A.H. v. State,** Op. No. 3504, 779 P.2d 1229 (Alaska 1989).

PART II. MASTERS, MAGISTRATES, DISTRICT COURT JUDGES

Rule 4. Appointment and Authority of Masters.

(a) **Appointment.** The presiding judge may appoint a standing master to conduct any or all of the CINA proceedings listed in subparagraph (b)(2). Appointments of standing masters must be reviewed annually. The presiding judge may appoint a special master to conduct a proceeding which is specified in the order of reference and is listed in subparagraph (b)(2).

(b) **Authority, Order of Reference.**

(1) An order of reference specifying the extent of the master's authority and the type of appointment must be entered in every case assigned to a master. The order of reference must be served on all parties.

(2) The following proceedings may be referred to a master:

(A) emergency or temporary custody hearings;

(B) interim hearings, including temporary custody review hearings and pre-trial conferences;

(C) adjudication and disposition hearings;

(D) post-disposition review and extension of custody hearings.

(3) A master's report is not binding until approved by a superior court judge pursuant to Civil Rule 53(d) and paragraph (f) of this rule, except:

(A) a master may enter orders without further approval of the superior court pursuant to Civil Rule 53(b) and (c), and by paragraph (d) of this rule; and

(B) a master's order of removal from the home is effective pending superior court review.

(c) **Objection to Reference to a Master.** In addition to the peremptory challenge of a master provided for in Civil Rule 42(c), a party may file an objection to a referral to a master in the following manner:

(1) *Timeliness.* A party may file an objection no later than five days after receiving notice of the order of reference.

(2) *Grounds for Objection.* An objection to the assignment of a master to hear an adjudication hearing, a disposition hearing following a contested adjudication or an extension of custody hearing will be granted as a matter of right. Any other objection must set forth sufficient grounds from which the court may determine whether good cause exists to remove the matter from the master's jurisdiction. Good cause may include involvement of (i) complex questions of law which require a decision by a superior court judge or (ii) questions requiring prompt resolution which would be seriously impaired by a reference to a master.

(d) **Standing Master's Authority to Enter Orders.** A standing master is authorized to take the following actions without further approval by a superior court judge:

(1) order emergency custody under CINA Rule 6(b);

(2) appoint counsel and guardians ad litem;

(3) order home studies, predisposition reports, and psychological or psychiatric evaluations;

(4) set hearings and order continuances of the master's hearings;

(5) issue orders on motions requesting expedited review pursuant to Civil Rule 77(i);

(6) accept and approve stipulations, except that stipulated adjudications or dispositions must be reviewed by a superior court judge;

(7) review and approve uncontested orders on annual review;

(8) accept voluntary relinquishments of parental rights, and in the case of an Indian child, make the requisite judicial certification of voluntary consent required by federal law.

(9) order mediation and other forms of alternative dispute resolution under Civil Rule 100, but only if the affected parties have agreed to participate.

(e) **Master's Report, Recommendations.** A master may issue a written report or oral findings on the record concerning an order or recommendation which must be approved by a superior court judge. The master shall advise the parties on the record of their right to file objections to any such decision pursuant to paragraph (f) of this rule.

(f) **Objections to Master's Report, Recommendations.**

(1) *Objections, Reply, Oral Argument.* Objections to a master's report or recommendation must be filed within 10 days of service of the report unless the court requires objection to be filed earlier. In the case of a recommendation rendered orally on the record where a party requests an electronic recording of the recommendation, the time period for objection runs from receipt of the recording. A reply to the objections must be filed within three days of service of the objections. The superior court may permit oral argument, order the taking of further evidence, or grant a hearing de novo.

(2) *Request for Stay, Immediate Review.* A party may request that a superior court judge stay the master's order issued under paragraph (d) pending review of the order.

(3) *Review of Order Removing the Child from the Home.* A master's order removing a child from the home which is not stayed must be reviewed by the superior court by the end of the next working day if a party so requests.

(SCO 845 effective August 15, 1987; amended by SCO 1355 effective July 15, 1999; and by SCO 1555 effective October 15, 2004)

Annotations

Cases

Superior court did not abuse its discretion in failing to hold a de novo hearing to review father's relinquishment because the father failed to mention what new evidence he intended to present at the hearing or explain why such evidence was absent from his submissions to the master. **Alden H. v. Office of Children's Servs.,** Op. No. 5874, 108 P.3d 224 (Alaska 2005).

Rule 5. Authority of District Court Judges and Magistrates.

(a) **Emergency Situations.** When a child is in a condition or surrounding dangerous to the welfare of the child which requires immediate action, and no superior court judge or authorized master is available, a district court judge or magistrate may take the least restrictive action necessary to protect the minor which a superior court judge is authorized by law to take. The district court judge or magistrate must immediately notify the superior court of the facts concerning the child and expeditiously transfer the case file to the superior court.

(b) **Review.** A party may request a hearing before the superior court or master to review any action taken by a district court judge or magistrate under this rule.

(SCO 845 effective August 15, 1987; amended by SCO 1355 effective July 15, 1999)

Cross References

CROSS REFERENCE: AS 22.15.100.

PART III. COMMENCEMENT OF PROCEEDINGS

Rule 6. Emergency Custody.

(a) **Emergency Custody Without Court Order.** The Department may take emergency custody of a child pursuant to AS 47.10.142 without a court order. If the Department determines that continued custody is necessary to protect the child, the Department shall notify the court of the emergency custody by filing, within 24 hours after custody was assumed, a petition alleging that the child is a child in need of aid. If the Department releases the child within 24 hours after taking the child into custody and does not file a petition, the Department shall, within 24 hours after releasing the child, file with the court a report explaining why the child was taken into custody, why the child was released, and to whom the child was released.

(b) **Emergency Custody With Court Order.**

(1) *Who May Request.* The Department or any other person or agency may petition the court for an order granting emergency custody of the child to the Department.

(2) *Form, Contents of Motion.* The petition must be supported by a statement of facts sufficient to show that the child is a child in need of aid and is in a condition which requires the immediate assumption of custody pursuant to AS 47.10.142. If a child is believed to be an Indian child, the statement of facts must show the tribal affiliation of the child, if known, and must be sufficient to show that removal of the child from the home is necessary to prevent imminent physical damage or harm to the child. The statement of facts must be made under oath, either in a petition, by affidavit, or orally on the record.

(3) *Order.* If the court determines that there is probable cause to believe that the child is a child in need of aid and is in such condition or surroundings that the child's welfare requires the immediate assumption of custody, the court may immediately issue an emergency custody order. In a case involving an Indian child, the court may not order emergency removal unless it finds that removal is necessary to prevent imminent physical damage or harm to the child. The order must be directed to a peace officer or other person specifically designated by the court, and shall require that the child be taken into custody immediately.

(4) *Notification to Department.* If the emergency custody order was not requested by the Department, the court shall, if possible, notify the Department of the motion immediately, and in any event no later than 12 hours after the motion is filed.

(5) *Service.* At the time of executing the order, or as soon thereafter as practicable, the peace officer or other person specifically designated by the court shall serve the child, parents, Indian custodian, guardian, and Department with a copy of the emergency custody order, a summons to the temporary custody hearing if one has been issued, and any available pleadings filed in support of the order. The person charged with service shall prepare and retain a return of service.

(SCO 845 effective August 15, 1987; amended by SCO 1355 effective July 15, 1999)

Cross References

CROSS REFERENCE: AS 22.15.100(8); AS 47.10.141; AS 47.10.142.

Rule 7. Petition for Adjudication—Summons.

(a) **Petition.** Formal proceedings may be commenced by the filing of a petition for adjudication of a child as a child in need of aid. The petition must be verified and must contain a statement of facts that would support a finding that the child is a child in need of aid under AS 47.10.011. If the child is believed to be an Indian child, the petition must so state and must state, if known, the Indian child's tribe. The petition may include a request for temporary custody under CINA Rule 10.

(b) **Notice of Hearing.** The Department shall provide a copy of the petition, as well as actual notice of the time and place of the initial hearing and of the parties' right to counsel, to the parents, guardian, and Indian custodian if these parties can be found after diligent efforts. In addition, actual notice of the proceedings must be given to any foster parent or other out-of-home care provider within a reasonable time before the hearing. If an Indian child is taken into emergency custody, the Department shall make reasonable efforts to ascertain and provide actual notice to the child's tribe before the temporary custody hearing.

(c) **Summons.** The court shall issue a summons to be served with the petition on the child, parents, guardian, and guardian ad litem. If the summons and petition are not contained in one document, the petition must be attached to and incorporated by reference into the summons. The summons must contain a statement advising the parties of their right to counsel.

(d) **Service of Petition and Summons.** The petition and summons must be served pursuant to Civil Rule 4 or as directed by the court. The child's summons must be served on the child's guardian ad litem, attorney or social worker. This person must deliver the summons to the child if the child is of an appropriate age. The court may appoint employees of the Department or any other competent person to serve the summons and petition. Inability to obtain service on any party does not deprive the court of jurisdiction.

(e) **Unknown Parent.** If the identity of the parent is unknown and the court is satisfied that no form of notice, even by publication, is reasonably likely to give actual notice to the parent, the court may waive notice.

(f) **Notice in Cases Involving an Indian Child.**

(1) If there is reason to believe that the child is an Indian child, the Department shall give notice to the child's parents, Indian custodian, and to any tribe that may be the child's tribe, of their rights under the Indian Child Welfare Act. This notice must be personally served or sent by certified mail with return receipt requested. If the identity or location of the parents or Indian custodian or tribe cannot be determined, notice that would otherwise have been sent to the missing persons or tribe must be given to the appropriate area office of the Bureau of Indian Affairs.

(2) The notice of rights under the Indian Child Welfare Act must contain the following information:

(A) The name of the Indian child.

(B) The child's tribal affiliation, if known. If notice is being sent to more than one tribe, a statement of all tribes being notified must be included.

(C) A copy of the petition.

(D) The location, mailing address, and telephone number of the court, and the time and place of the next hearing, if known.

(E) A statement of the right of the Indian custodian and the tribe to intervene in the proceeding.

(F) A statement that if the parents or Indian custodian are unable to afford counsel, counsel will be appointed to represent them.*

(G) A statement of the rights of the parents, Indian custodian or the tribe to have, on request, up to 30 days to prepare for the adjudication hearing.

(H) A statement of the potential legal consequences of an adjudication on the rights of the parents or Indian custodian.

(I) A statement that child custody proceedings are conducted on a confidential basis and that tribal officials are required to keep confidential the information contained in the notice and not reveal it to anyone who does not need the information in order to exercise the tribe's rights.

(g) **Dismissal.** The court may dismiss a petition at any time based on a finding of good cause consistent with the welfare of the child and the family.

(h) **Amendment.** A petition may be amended by leave of the court and with reasonable notice on all parties at any time before the adjudication order. Amendment with appropriate continuances will be permitted to promote the interests of justice and the welfare of the child and the family.

*An indigent Indian custodian has a right to court-appointed counsel under 25 U.S.C. § 1912(b). Counsel appointed under § 1912 may seek compensation pursuant to 25 CFR 23.13.

(SCO 845 effective August 15, 1987; amended by SCO 913 effective January 15, 1989; by SCO 1265 effective July 15, 1997; by SCO 1355 effective July 15, 1999; by SCO 1560 effective October 15, 1999; and by SCO 1560 effective October 15, 2005)

Note: Ch. 43, SLA 2001, amends AS 47.10.030, AS 47.10.070(a), and AS 47.10.080(f) to add provisions concerning notice to and participation by grandparents. According to §6 of the Act, these provisions have the effect of amending Child in Need of Aid Rules 3, 7, 10, 15, 17, and 19 by requiring that grandparents be given notice of and an opportunity to be heard at certain child-in-need-of-aid proceedings.

Cross References

CROSS REFERENCE: AS 47.10.020(b); AS 47.10.030; AS 47.10.070; AS 47.10.142(a); 25 U.S.C. § 1912.

Annotations

Cases

This annotation construes former Children's Rule 8. Considering the importance of juvenile proceedings and the fact that juvenile records are easily obtained and can have a serious effect upon the life of a minor, the usual principles against entertaining moot controversies do not apply. Where a 12-year old boy has been determined to be delinquent, an appeal of that delinquency order will be considered, notwithstanding that the order has been vacated. **Ej. v. State,** Op. No. 628, 471 P2d 367 (Alaska 1970).

This annotation construes former Children's Rule 8. Children who are charged with acts which would be chargeable only by grand jury indictment if committed by an adult need not be indicted by a grand jury. **Doe v. State,** Op. No.707,487 P2d 47 (Alaska 1971).

This annotation construes former Children's Rule 10. Process in a juvenile proceeding must be delivered to the child himself. Jurisdiction over the child cannot be obtained by delivering the summons and petition to his parents. **RLR v. State,** Op. No. 706, 487 P2d 27 (Alaska 1971).

This annotation construes former Children's Rule 10. Appearance by a child in a juvenile proceeding and failure to object to the failure to serve him with a copy of the petition waives any defect in process where the infant is represented by counsel. **RLR v. State,** Op. No. 706,487 P2d 27 (Alaska 1971).

This annotation construes former Children's Rule 10. A child has a vital interest in a dependency proceeding and is an essential party whose presence cannot be dispensed with arbitrarily; in a dependency proceeding the summons and a copy of the petition must be served on the child as well as the parents; failure to make such service results in a lack of jurisdiction over the child. **In re P.N.,** Op. No. 1127,523 P2d 13 (Alaska 1975).

This annotation construes former Children's Rule 10. Where the children are not given the required notice of a dependency hearing the superior court has no jurisdiction over them and, therefore, cannot validly issue a judgment depriving a parent of his custody. **In re P.N.,** Op. No. 1127, 523 P2d 13 (Alaska 1975).

This annotation construes former Children's Rule 10. On initiation of dependency proceedings, an attorney should be appointed to act in the dual role of guardian ad litem and counsel for children of tender years. The required summons should be served on him, but in those areas where attorneys are not readily available and appointment of counsel is not essential or where suitable guardian ad litem is available, there is no requirement that an attorney at law be appointed. **In re P.N.,** Op. No. 1127, 523 P2d 13 (Alaska 1975).

This annotation construes former Children's Rule 8. In the adjudicative phase of any children's proceeding, the family court may consider only the specific situations set out in the petition. **In re S.D. Jr.,** Op. No. 1255, 549 P2d 1190 (Alaska 1976).

This annotation construes former Children's Rule 8. Former Children's Rules 3(b) and 10(c)(2) required parents of minor to be notified of waiver hearing, but neither rule required the parent's presence at waiver hearing. **Matter of J.H.B.,** Op. No. 1626, 578 P2d 146 (Alaska 1978).

This annotation construes former Children's Rule 10. In parental rights termination action where the State knew that the parent was in contact with a Washington tribal caseworker, the court was not persuaded that the mailing address of the parent could not have been ascertained after inquiry, thus failure to provide notice by mail to the parent violated this rule. **Matter of L.A.M.,** Op. No. 3142, 727 P2d 1057 (Alaska 1986).

Argument that superior court's custody orders were invalid because mother was never served with a summons to attend the proceedings, and thus the superior court never obtained personal jurisdiction over her, was meritless. **Cornwall v. State,** Op. No. 1460, 909 P2d 360 (Alaska App. 1996).

PART IV. DISCOVERY, EVIDENCE, PROOF

Rule 8. Disclosures, Depositions, and Discovery.

(a) **General.** Parties may obtain discovery by one or more of the following methods: depositions upon oral examination or written questions; written interrogatories; production of documents or things or permission to enter upon land or other property, for inspection and other purposes; physical and mental examinations; and requests for admission.

(b) **Applicability of the Civil Rules Regarding Discovery.** Discovery and disclosure in CINA actions are governed by Civil Rules 26-37, with the following exceptions and modifications: Civil Rule 26(a), (e), (f), and (g), and Civil Rule 26.1 do not apply in CINA cases.

(c) **Initial Disclosures.** Except to the extent otherwise directed by order or rule, a party shall, without awaiting a discovery request, provide to other parties the following information, excluding any privileged material:

(1) the Department shall make available all information pertaining to the child prepared by or in the possession of the Department;

(2) a parent shall provide the name, address, or other information pertaining to the identity and location of the other

parent of the child, if the parent has not already been identified and located;

(3) if the child has been removed, a parent shall provide the names, addresses, or other contact information pertaining to the location of grandparents and other adult relatives so placement options may be explored;

(4) a parent shall provide the names and addresses of any schools attended by the child and the names and addresses of any medical, mental health, and other treatment providers of the child;

(5) a parent shall provide the name and location of any Indian tribe as defined in CINA Rule 2(j) in which the parent has reason to believe the child is a member or may be eligible for membership;

(6) a guardian ad litem shall disclose a list of the types of information the guardian ad litem has gathered regarding the case, including records from specified sources and the names and contact information for persons interviewed or surveyed who are not parties, yet have provided information about the case; and

(7) a tribe that has intervened in the proceedings shall disclose names and contact information for extended family of the child, a list of potential placements under 25 U.S.C. § 1915, and a summary of any tribal services or tribal court actions involving the family.

Unless otherwise directed by the court, these disclosures shall be made within 45 days of the date of service of the petition for adjudication, or for tribes, the date of the order granting intervention. A party shall make its initial disclosures based on the information then reasonably available to it and is not excused from making its disclosures because it has not fully completed its investigation of the case or because it challenges the sufficiency of another party's disclosures or because another party has not made its disclosures.

(d) **Disclosures of Witnesses with Special Expertise.**

(1) *Retained Experts.* Except as otherwise stipulated or directed by the court, a party shall disclose the identity of an expert witness whom the party intends to call at trial and who has been retained, with or without compensation, to provide expert testimony or whose duties as an employee of the party regularly involve giving expert testimony. For such witnesses, the party shall provide:

(A) the expert's curriculum vitae; and

(B) a written summary of the substance of the anticipated testimony of the expert, the expert's opinion, and the underlying basis of the opinion.

(2) *Other Experts.* For all other experts, if a party intends to call an expert witness who has had involvement with the family, but has not been retained solely for the purpose of providing an expert opinion, the party shall disclose to other parties the identity of that witness and shall provide any existing reports or written statements of these experts. For experts identified in this paragraph, parties are not required to provide the information in paragraph (1) except upon request.

(3) Expert disclosures shall be made at the times and in the sequence directed by the court.

(e) **Pretrial Disclosures.**

(1) In addition to the disclosures otherwise required by this rule, a party shall provide to other parties the following information regarding the evidence that it may present at trial:

(A) the name, address, and telephone number of each witness; and

(B) an exhibit list accompanied by the exhibits the party expects to submit at trial.

(2) Disclosure of witness lists and exhibits shall be made at the times and in the sequence directed by the court.

(f) **Discovery from Guardian Ad Litem.**

(1) *Discovery of Documents in Guardian Ad Litem's Possession.* A party may obtain discovery of documents in the possession, custody, or control of the guardian ad litem, subject to the following limitations:

(A) the documents must be discoverable under Civil Rule 26(b)(1); and

(B) trial preparation materials as defined in Civil Rule 26(b)(3) are discoverable only as permitted by that rule.

(2) *Discovery Regarding Guardian Ad Litem's Testimony.* If the guardian ad litem has served notice that the guardian ad litem intends to testify, a party may obtain discovery from the guardian ad litem about the substance of this testimony.

(3) *Other Inquiry.* A party may obtain other discovery from a guardian ad litem only as permitted by the court upon a showing of good cause. The court may permit a party to question a guardian ad litem about the guardian ad litem's professional qualifications and experience or the guardian ad litem's performance in the case. But this inquiry must be conducted in the presence of the court.

(g) **Depositions.** Depositions may be taken in accordance with the Civil Rules and CINA Rule 8(f), except that no child under 16 years of age may be deposed except upon court order.

(h) **Scope and Timing.** In order to comply with statutory timeframes of AS 47.10 or for other good cause, the court may shorten time periods for discovery. The court may order further discovery and grant a continuance to accomplish the discovery at any phase of the proceeding if it believes that the parties have not had adequate opportunity to develop the existing evidence.

(i) **Supplementation.** A party who has made disclosures or responses to discovery under this rule is under a duty to supplement or correct the disclosures or responses to include information thereafter acquired if ordered by the court or if the party learns that the information disclosed or the response given is incomplete or incorrect in some material respect, and that the additional or corrective information has not otherwise been made known to the other parties during the discovery process or in writing. This duty to supplement or correct disclosures and responses extends to information provided in expert disclosures under subsection (d) of this rule.

(SCO 845 effective August 15, 1987; and rescinded and readopted by SCO 1561 effective April 15, 2006)

Annotations

Cases

That Alaska CINA R. 16(b) allows a court to order mental and physical examinations of a child's parents at the predisposition phase of a child-in-need-of-aid proceeding does not limit the court's authority under Alaska R. Civ. P. 35(a) to order a mental examination at the adjudication stage. **Alyssa B. v. Dep't of Health & Social Servs.,** Op. No. 5930, 123 P.3d 646 (Alaska 2005).

Rule 9. Evidence.

(a) **Applicability of Evidence Rules.** The Alaska Rules of Evidence apply to child in need of aid proceedings to the same extent as they govern civil proceedings, except as otherwise provided by these rules.

(b) **Privileges Inapplicable.**

(1) *Husband-Wife Privilege.* The husband-wife privilege, Evidence Rule 505, does not apply to the parent, child or custodian in Child in Need of Aid proceedings.

(2) *Physician-Patient Privilege.* The physician-patient privilege, Evidence Rule 504, does not apply to the parent, child or custodian in Child in Need of Aid proceedings.

(3) *Psychotherapist-Patient Privilege.*

(A) The psychotherapist-patient privilege, Evidence Rule 504, applies to the parent, child or custodian in Child in Need of Aid proceedings only to the extent described in this rule.

(B) The privilege applies to the child unless the child or the child's guardian ad litem waives the privilege, or the party seeking disclosure shows that the need for the requested disclosure outweighs the child's interest in confidentiality.

(C) The privilege does not apply to the parent unless the parent shows that the parent's interest in confidentiality outweighs the need for the requested disclosure. No disclosure may be made until the parent has an opportunity to make this showing.

(D) When considering a request to disclose or protect a communication, the court shall consider the following:

(i) the content and nature of the communication;

(ii) the purposes of AS 47.10, as expressed by AS 47.05.060, and of Evidence Rule 504;

(iii) whether there is any other effective way to obtain the information; and

(iv) whether the public interest and need for disclosure outweighs the potential injury to the patient and the patient's psychotherapist relationship.

Before ruling on such a request, the court may inspect records in camera. The court may allow, limit, or prohibit disclosure and use of the communication.

(E) If the court grants the request for disclosure of the child's privileged information, the court order must:

(i) limit disclosure to those parts of the child's records which are essential to fulfill the purpose of the disclosure;

(ii) limit disclosure to those persons whose need for the information is the basis for the order; and

(iii) include such other measures as are necessary to limit disclosure for the protection of the child and the psychotherapist-patient relationship.

(F) Evidence Rule 504(c) does not apply in child in need of aid proceedings. Unless otherwise ordered, the child's psychotherapist-patient privilege may only be claimed or waived as follows:

(i) If the child is twelve or older, the privilege may be claimed or waived by the child after consulting with an attorney, if an attorney has been appointed, or with the guardian ad litem.

(ii) If the child is younger than twelve, the privilege may be claimed or waived by the guardian ad litem.

(iii) The person who was the psychotherapist at the time of the communication is presumed to have authority to claim the privilege on behalf of the child.

(SCO 845 effective August 15, 1987; amended by SCO 1355 effective July 15, 1999; and by SCO 1442 effective October 15, 2001)

Cross References

CROSS REFERENCE: AS 47.17.060.

Annotations

Cases

This annotation construes former Children's Rule 17. This rule permits the consideration of social agency and police reports in the dispositive phase of a hearing. **In re S.D. Jr.,** Op. No. 1255, 549 P2d 1190 (Alaska 1976).

This annotation construes former Children's Rule 17. Before hearsay evidence is used in the dispositive phase, the child and his counsel should be clearly advised that it is being considered so that opposing evidence or explanation may be presented. **Matter of J.H.B.,** Op. No. 1626, 578 P2d 146 (Alaska 1978).

This annotation construes former Children's Rule 17. Finding by judge that juvenile was not amenable to treatment as a juvenile based solely upon prior determination of delinquency was not the searching inquiry necessary for such a finding. **A.D. v. State,** Op. No. 280, 668 P2d 840 (Alaska App. 1983).

This annotation construes former Children's Rule 17. Probable cause determination at juvenile jurisdiction waiver hearing may not be based on hearsay testimony. **A.D. v. State,** Op. No. 280, 668 P2d 840 (Alaska App.

1983).

This annotation construes former Children's Rule 17. The use of hearsay evidence in the disposition phase of a parental rights termination proceeding as allowed by state law did not conflict with the federal Indian Child Welfare Act. **Matter of J.R.B.,** Op. No. 3029, 715 P2d 1170 (Alaska 1986).

Statute providing that registration and other records of alcohol treatment facilities shall remain confidential and are privileged to the patient did not establish privilege precluding admission of alcohol treatment records in CINA proceedings. **In re D.D.S.,** Op. No. 4058, 869 P.2d 160 (Alaska 1994).

PART V. PRELIMINARY PROCEEDINGS

Rule 10. Temporary Custody Hearing.

(a) **Time of Hearing.**

(1) At the request of the petitioner, the court shall schedule a temporary custody hearing:

(A) within 48 hours, including weekends and holidays, of when the court is notified by the filing of a petition that emergency custody was taken pursuant to CINA Rule 6(a) or (b); or

(B) within a reasonable time following the filing of a petition when emergency custody has not been taken.

(2) The court may continue a temporary custody hearing at the request of a parent or guardian upon a showing of good cause for why the parent or guardian is not prepared to respond to the petition. A continuance must be requested before or at the outset of the hearing.

(b) **Conduct of Hearing.**

(1) *Opening Address.* The court shall first determine whether the persons specified in CINA Rule 7(b) have received notice of the hearing. The court shall then determine whether all parties have received copies of the petition and understand its contents and shall advise the parties of the nature of the proceedings and possible disposition. In addition, the court shall advise the parties of the possibility of a temporary custody or supervision order pending adjudication and final disposition, and that the parents may be liable for child support payments if the child is placed outside the home at any time during the proceeding.

(2) *Advice of Rights.* The court shall advise the parties of their right to counsel, including the right to court-appointed counsel if applicable; the child's right to a guardian ad litem; their right to a hearing at which the state is required to present evidence to prove the allegations in its petition; their right to confront and cross-examine witnesses at such a hearing, to present witnesses on their own behalf, and to compulsory process to compel these witnesses to attend; and their privilege against self-incrimination. In cases involving an Indian child, the court shall also advise the parties of an Indian custodian's or tribe's right to intervene. If the hearing is being held because emergency custody was taken pursuant to CINA Rule 6(a) or (b), the court shall also advise the child's parents or guardian, if they are present at the hearing, that they each have the right to request a continuance of the hearing if they are not prepared to respond to the allegation that the child is a child in need of aid.

(3) The court may admit hearsay evidence which would be otherwise inadmissible under the Evidence Rules if the hearsay is probative of a material fact, has circumstantial guarantees of trustworthiness, and the appearing parties are given a fair opportunity to meet it.

(c) **Findings of Fact and Order.**

(1) The court shall order the child returned to the home and dismiss the petition if the court does not find probable cause to believe that the child is a child in need of aid under AS 47.10.011.

(2) The court shall order the child placed in the temporary custody of the Department or order the child returned to the home with supervision by the Department if the court finds probable cause to believe that the child is a child in need of aid under AS 47.10.011.

(3) The court may approve the removal of the child from the child's home only if the court finds that continued placement in the home is contrary to the welfare of the child; and, in cases involving an Indian child, either: (A) that removal from the child's parent or Indian custodian is necessary to prevent imminent physical damage or harm to the child; or (B) that there is clear and convincing evidence, including testimony of qualified expert witnesses, that the child is likely to suffer serious emotional or physical damage if left in the custody of the parent or Indian custodian.

(4) In any case in which the court has approved the removal of the child pursuant to the preceding subparagraph, the court shall make the inquiry and findings required by CINA Rule 10.1.

(d) **Subsequent Proceedings.** If the court orders the child placed in the temporary custody of the Department or orders the child returned to the home with supervision by the Department, the court must set the time for the adjudication hearing and for the pretrial conference and meeting of parties required by CINA Rule 13. The court may also set the time to file motions, complete discovery, exchange witness and exhibit lists, and file pretrial briefs. The court may schedule a disposition hearing in conjunction with the adjudication hearing. In such cases, the order setting the time for adjudication and disposition must also set the time to submit reports in aid of disposition.

(e) **Review.**

(1) If circumstances relating to the child's placement change pending adjudication or disposition, any party may request that the court review the temporary custody or supervision order.

(2) When a party seeks the return of a child to the child's home pending adjudication or disposition, if the party makes a prima facie showing that removal is no longer necessary, the burden of proof shifts to the Department as described below:

(A) in cases involving a non-Indian child, the court shall return the child to the home unless the Department proves by a preponderance of the evidence that return to the home is contrary to the welfare of the child;

(B) in cases involving an Indian child, the court shall restore the child to the child's parent or Indian custodian unless the Department proves (i) by a preponderance of the evidence that removal from the parent or Indian custodian is still necessary to prevent imminent physical damage or harm to the child; or (ii) by clear and convincing evidence, including the testimony of qualified expert witnesses, that the child is likely to suffer serious emotional or physical damage if returned to the custody of the parent or Indian custodian.

(3) A party may seek review of other issues related to temporary custody or supervision under CINA Rule 19.1(d).

(SCO 845 effective August 15, 1987; amended by SCO 898 effective July 15, 1988; by SCO 914 effective January 15, 1989; by SCO 915 effective January 15, 1989; by SCO 1010 effective January 15, 1990; by SCO 1105 effective January 15, 1993; by SCO 1265 effective July 15, 1997; by SCO 1355 effective July 15, 1999; and by SCO 1398 effective October 15, 2000)

Note: Ch. 43, SLA 2001, amends AS 47.10.030, AS 47.10.070(a), and AS 47.10.080(f) to add provisions concerning notice to and participation by grandparents. According to §6 of the Act, these provisions have the effect of amending Child in Need of Aid Rules 3, 7, 10, 15, 17, and 19 by requiring that grandparents be given notice of and an opportunity to be heard at certain child-in-need-of-aid proceedings.

Cross References

CROSS REFERENCE: AS 47.10.142(d) and (e); 25 U.S.C. § 1912(a); 25 U.S.C. § 1913(a); 25 U.S.C. § 1922; 42 U.S.C. § 672(a)(1).

Annotations

Cases

By advising mother at temporary custody hearing of her right to counsel and mailing her an application form, trial court complied with minimum requirements of this rule, thus failure of trial court to appoint counsel until two months later did not deprive mother of her right to counsel; nevertheless, courts in the future should remain sensitive to potentially drastic consequences of unnecessary delay in appointing counsel in custody cases. **V.D. v. Dept. of Health & Soc. Serv.,** Op. No. 5206, 991 P2d 214 (Alaska 1999).

Rule 10.1. Out-of-Home Placement—Required Findings.

(a) **Findings in Cases Involving Non-Indian Child.**

(1) *Findings.*

(A) If the Department has taken emergency custody of a non-Indian child under AS 47.10.142, the court shall inquire into and determine at the temporary custody hearing whether the Department has made reasonable efforts as required by AS 47.10.086(a) to prevent out-of-home placement, or whether it was not possible under the circumstances to make efforts that would have prevented removal of the child.

(B) At any other hearing at which the court is ordering a non-Indian child's removal from the home, the court shall inquire into and determine whether the Department has made reasonable efforts as required by AS 47.10.086(a) to prevent out-of-home placement, unless the court has previously determined under Rule 17.1 that reasonable efforts are not required.

(C) At each hearing at which the court is continuing a previous order authorizing removal of a non-Indian child, the court shall inquire into and determine whether the Department has made reasonable efforts since the last hearing as required by AS 47.10.086(a) to permit the child's return to the home, unless the court has previously determined under Rule 17.1 that reasonable efforts are not required.

(2) *Effect of a Finding that Department Failed to Make Reasonable Efforts.* A finding that the Department has failed to make reasonable efforts is not in itself a ground for returning the child to the home or dismissing a petition and does not affect the court's ability to proceed to adjudication. However, the court cannot enter a disposition order if the court finds that the Department has failed to make reasonable efforts, unless the court has determined under Rule 17.1 that reasonable efforts are not required. If the Department has failed to make required reasonable efforts, the court must postpone disposition until the court finds that reasonable efforts have been made. On motion of a party or on its own motion, the court may order the Department to comply with AS 47.10.086(a) within a reasonable time. If the Department fails to comply with the order, the court may impose appropriate sanctions.

(b) **Findings in Cases Involving Indian Child.**

(1) *Findings.* At each hearing at which the court is authorizing an Indian child's removal from the child's parent or Indian custodian or continuing a previous order authorizing removal, the court shall inquire into and determine:

(A) whether the Department has complied with the placement requirements of 25 U.S.C. § 1915(b) and

(B) whether active efforts have been made to provide remedial services and rehabilitative programs as required by 25 U.S.C. § 1912(d).*

(2) *Effect of a Finding that Requirements Have Not Been Met.* A finding that the requirements of 25 U.S.C. §§ 1912(d) or 1915(b) have not been met is not in itself a ground for restoring the child to the parent or Indian custodian or dismissing a petition and does not affect the court's ability to proceed to adjudication. However, the court cannot enter a disposition order if the court finds that the requirements of 25 U.S.C. § 1912(d) (active efforts) have not been met.* In those circumstances, the court must postpone disposition until the court finds that active efforts have been made. On motion of a party or on its own motion, the court may order the Department to comply with 25 U.S.C. §§ 1912(d) or 1915(b)

within a reasonable time. If the Department fails to comply with this order, the court may impose appropriate sanctions.

(SCO 1355 effective July 15, 1999)

* **Note:** As of June 1999, it is an open issue whether federal law permits a trial court to determine that active efforts are not required in a case or that such efforts may be discontinued.

Rule 11. Guardians Ad Litem.

(a) **Appointment.**

(1) The court shall appoint a guardian ad litem (GAL) in all Child in Need of Aid (CINA) proceedings as soon as possible after the CINA petition is filed. The appointment shall continue through all phases of the CINA proceeding unless the court orders otherwise.

(2) If the Office of Public Advocacy (OPA) is appointed, OPA shall, in accordance with the qualifications set forth in subsection (c) of this rule, designate a specific person to serve as the guardian ad litem for the child. If OPA designates an OPA employee to be the GAL, the GAL for the child is deemed to be OPA. If OPA designates an independent contractor, or another person who is not employed by OPA, to be the GAL, the GAL for the child is deemed to be that designated person.

(3) Within seven days of the court's appointment, the designated GAL must file an entry of appearance indicating whether or not the GAL is an attorney and certifying that the GAL has completed guardian ad litem training through OPA.

(4) Throughout the period of appointment, the GAL is a party to the proceeding, and must be served with copies of all pleadings and papers relating to the child and must be given notice of all court proceedings. The GAL, whether an attorney or a non-attorney, has the right to appear and participate at hearings on behalf of the child. Because the GAL stands in the place of the child in court, a GAL may also engage in motion practice, conduct discovery, introduce evidence, examine and cross examine witnesses, make objections, make opening statements and closing arguments, and take or participate in an appeal.

Commentary.—*In all cases in which the GAL is to be appointed at public expense, the court must appoint the Office of Public Advocacy, which must designate a specific person to serve as the GAL.*

The court may appoint an attorney to advise or represent a non-attorney GAL. If the court takes this action, and if the GAL was appointed at public expense, the court must appoint OPA as the attorney for the GAL. If the court appoints an attorney, it should take care to specify the scope and duration of the appointment. Under AS 47.10.050 and CINA Rule 12(b)(3), the court may also appoint an attorney for the child.

(b) **Role of Guardian ad Litem.** The GAL must represent and advocate for the best interests of the child in light of federal and state law.

Commentary.—*The GAL must decide, based on thorough and ongoing investigation, what course of action is in the child's best interests. The GAL must then advocate for this course of action, regardless of whether the child agrees with the GAL's position.*

(c) **Qualifications.**

(1) A GAL should possess knowledge, skill, experience, training, or education that allows the GAL to conduct an independent, thorough, and impartial investigation, and to advocate effectively for the best interests of the child.

(2) The GAL should have an understanding of the following as appropriate to the case:

(A) child development from infancy through adolescence;

(B) the impact of child abuse and neglect on the child;

(C) the impact of CINA proceedings, including out-of-home placement and the restriction or termination of parental rights, on the child;

(D) unique issues related to families involved in CINA proceedings, including such issues as substance abuse, domestic violence, and disabilities;

(E) community and other resources available for placement, treatment, and other necessary services for abused or neglected children;

(F) the ethnic, cultural, and socio-economic backgrounds of the population to be served;

(G) the Indian Child Welfare Act and the prevailing social and cultural standards of the Indian community in which the child, parent, Indian custodian, or extended family resides or with which the child, parent, Indian custodian, or extended family members maintain social and cultural ties;

(H) Alaska and applicable federal statutes, rules, and supreme court decisions relating to CINA proceedings; and

(I) the ability to research and develop special areas of knowledge as appropriate or necessary in a given case.

(d) **Order Authorizing Access.** An order appointing a GAL should authorize the GAL to have access, without further court order, to all records of the child, including confidential and privileged records such as mental health records; medical records; law enforcement records; juvenile justice records; vital statistics records; financial records; and educational records, including special education records.

Commentary.—*Although the appointment order authorizes the GAL to review confidential and privileged records pertaining to the child, the GAL must file a motion requesting access to records pertaining to a parent unless the parent signs a release.*

(e) **Disclosure of Conflicts.** The GAL shall promptly disclose any relationships or associations between the GAL and any party which might reasonably cause the GAL's impartiality to be questioned.

(f) **Duties of Guardian ad Litem.**

(1) *Purpose.* The GAL represents the best interests of the child in a CINA proceeding. The GAL determines and advocates for the best interests of the child given the child's situation, taking into account the child's age, maturity, culture and ethnicity, and public laws and policies regarding family preservation and timely permanency planning.

(2) *Duty to the child.* The GAL shall

(A) conduct ongoing independent investigations, including, as reasonable and appropriate: in-person visits with the child; review of records; interviews with parents, social workers, teachers, and other persons as necessary to assess the child's situation; and observations of the child's interactions with parents or other potential caregivers;

(B) identify relatives, family friends, or other persons who are potential placement options, and take such steps as may be necessary to offer such persons to the Department and/or to the court for placement determinations;

(C) advocate for early tribal identification and paternity determinations;

(D) consult professionals as necessary to determine the child's best interests;

(E) participate in the case planning process;

(F) monitor the provision and utilization of family support services;

(G) determine whether to seek appointment of a GAL or attorney in related legal proceedings;

(H) monitor services to the child provided by educational, medical, mental health, and other community systems and ensure these services are promoting the best interests of the child;

(I) when appropriate, seek cooperative solutions to disputes concerning the child's situation that serve the child's best interests;

(J) explain the court proceedings, the role of the GAL, and the child's rights to the child, when appropriate, in language and terms the child can understand; encourage older children to attend and participate in court hearings as appropriate; and determine whether and under what conditions younger children should attend court hearings; and

(K) determine whether to call the child as a witness or determine appropriate action if others seek the child's testimony, and familiarize the child with the process of testifying.

(3) *Duty to the court.* The GAL will:

(A) appear at all hearings, present appropriate witnesses to testify at hearings, and present relevant information about the child's status and needs to the court;

(B) provide timely written reports as required by court order or rule;

(C) request specific court orders for evaluation, services, visitation, treatment for the child and the child's family, and placement of the child;

(D) take appropriate and timely action when services are not being made available to the child, the family or both; when the child or family fails to take advantage of such services; or when services are not achieving their purpose;

(E) take appropriate action when informed of any violations of orders, new developments, or material changes in the child's circumstances; and

(F) advise the court promptly if appointment of counsel for the child should be considered.

(g) **Contact with Child, Other Parties, and the Court.**

(1) *Contact with Child.* The GAL may meet with the child as often as necessary to ascertain and represent the child's best interests. Reasonable access by the GAL cannot be denied, absent court order, by any party or service provider, or by the child's attorney, if one has been appointed. An attorney or representative for a party other than the child shall not communicate with the child concerning the substance of the case without reasonable notice to the GAL and the social worker and the consent of the GAL and the social worker, or a court order authorizing the communication.

(2) *Contact with Other Parties.* A GAL shall not communicate about the substance of the case with a party or person the GAL knows to be represented by a lawyer in the matter unless the GAL has the consent of the lawyer. The lack of consent shall not prevent the GAL from having incidental contact with a party, or contact for the purpose of scheduling a visit with a child or making an unannounced home visit to the child.

(3) *Contact with Court.* Unless all parties consent, a GAL shall not engage in ex parte communications with the court concerning a pending case except for scheduling and other administrative purposes when circumstances require.

(h) **Testimony.**

(1) The GAL shall not testify at a trial or hearing unless the court determines that:

(A) the testimony relates to an uncontested issue;

(B) the testimony is necessary to present factual evidence on a material issue that is not available from another source; or

(C) there is a compelling need for the testimony.

(2) A GAL who intends to testify, or the party who intends to call the GAL as a witness, shall file and serve a motion identifying the subject of the testimony and stating the

reasons why the testimony would be permissible under subsection (h)(1) of this rule.

(3) If the court grants the motion for testimony from the GAL, the court should consider whether the GAL can still effectively represent the best interests of the child. If not, the court may require OPA to discharge the GAL, appoint another GAL, or appoint an attorney for the GAL or the child.

(4) A GAL who testifies may be cross-examined like any other witness.

Commentary.—*A GAL, as an advocate, rarely testifies. See Alaska Rule of Professional Conduct 3.7. In extraordinary circumstances under which a court order authorizing GAL testimony cannot be timely obtained prior to trial, the court may waive the requirement of a written motion contemplated in subsection (h)(2) above.*

(i) **Confidentiality.**

(1) The child's statements to the GAL are not confidential.

(2) The GAL may disclose information if the GAL determines that disclosure is in the child's best interests.

(3) The GAL shall advise the child in advance of any interview that the child's statements may be disclosed.

Commentary.—*If the GAL is an attorney, he or she acts in a capacity as a GAL rather than as an attorney, and information received from the child is not subject to the attorney-client privilege. Cf. Ethics Opinion 85-4, Alaska Bar Association. Notwithstanding these provisions, the GAL may seek a protective order to keep certain communications confidential in accordance with discovery rules.*

(SCO 845 effective August 15, 1987; amended by SCO 1355 effective July 15, 1999; and by SCO 1562 effective April 15, 2006)

Cross References

CROSS REFERENCE: AS 25.24.310; AS 47.10.050; AS 47.17.170(1), (2) and (5).

CROSS REFERENCE: 25 U.S.C. § 1913(a).

Annotations

Cases

This annotation construes former Children's Rule 11. Where there appears to be a substantial danger that an infant might prefer a jury trial primarily out of a desire to display his importance without sufficient attention to either the possibility of future harm through notoriety or the relative likelihood of winning before a judge and jury, the court should appoint a guardian ad litem to consult with the child and his attorney and to make a decision based solely on the interests of the child. **RLR v. State,** Op. No. 706, 487 P2d 27 (Alaska 1971).

Duties that guardian ad litem owes child do not extend to other parties, especially to parties whose interests may be adverse to those of child. **Karen L. v. Dept. of Health & Soc. Services,** Op. No. 4943, 953 P2d 871 (Alaska 1998).

Guardian ad litem owes no duty of care to parent who is adverse party in Child in Need of Aid proceeding. **Karen L. v. Dept. of Health & Soc. Services,** Op. No. 4943, 953 P2d 871 (Alaska 1998).

Rule 12. Right to Counsel.

(a) **Notice of Right to Counsel.** The court shall inform the parties at the first hearing at which they are present of their respective rights to be represented by counsel at all stages of the proceedings.

(b) **Appointed Counsel.** The court shall appoint counsel pursuant to Administrative Rule 12:

(1) for a parent or guardian who is financially unable to employ counsel;*

(2) for a parent on active military duty who has not appeared prior to entry of an adjudication;

(3) for a child when the court determines that the interests of justice require the appointment of an attorney to represent the child's expressed interests; and

(4) for a non-attorney guardian ad litem when legal representation of the guardian ad litem is necessary.

(c) **Waiver of Right to Counsel.** The court shall accept a valid waiver of the right to counsel by any party if the court determines that the party understands the benefits of counsel and knowingly waives those benefits.

(d) **Appointment of Counsel for Absent or Unknown Parent.** The court shall appoint counsel to represent an absent parent at any hearing in which the termination of parental rights is or may be in issue if the parent has failed to appear after service of notice, including service by publication, and the court concludes that a continuance is not likely to result in the attendance of the non-appearing parent. The court is not required to appoint counsel for a parent if the court is satisfied that the identity of the parent is unknown.

(SCO 845 effective August 15, 1987; amended by SCO 1560 effective October 15, 2005)

* An indigent Indian custodian has a right to court-appointed counsel under 25 U.S.C. § 1912(b). Counsel appointed under § 1912 may seek compensation pursuant to 25 CFR § 23.13.

Cross References

CROSS REFERENCE: AS 25.24.310; AS 47.10.050.

Annotations

Cases

This annotation construes former Children's Rule 14. Where a juvenile matter has reach the formal adjudicative stage, the juvenile's chosen counsel must be present at the hearing. **Wagstaff v. Superior Court, Family Court Division,** Op. No. 1144, 535 P2d 1220 (Alaska 1975).

This annotation construes former Children's Rule 14. A court in a "child in need of supervision" hearing is under a duty to explain to the juvenile his right to counsel. **Wagstaff v. Superior Court, Family Court Division,** Op. No. 1144, 535 P2d 1220 (Alaska 1975).

Rule 13. Pretrial Conference and Meeting of Parties.

(a) **Pretrial Conference and Meeting of Parties.** The court shall conduct a pretrial conference to discuss the topics specified in paragraph (b). Before the pretrial conference, the parties shall meet, either telephonically or in person, to ensure that an appropriate case plan is in place for the child and the family and to address the topics that will be discussed at the conference. The meeting will be held at the time specified by the court or, if no time is specified, at least 30 days before the pretrial conference. The attorneys of record and all unrepresented parties who have appeared in the case are jointly responsible for arranging and being present at the meeting and for submitting to the court within 10 days after the meeting a written summary of the meeting.

(b) **Purpose of Pretrial Conference.** At the pretrial conference, the court and parties may:

(1) consider efforts to locate and serve all parties;

(2) simplify the issues;

(3) consider amendments to the pleadings;

(4) conclude any unresolved discovery matters;

(5) resolve pending motions;

(6) discuss settlement and the use of special procedures to assist in resolving the case;

(7) consider the possibility of obtaining admissions and stipulations of fact and documents which will avoid the introduction of unnecessary evidence;

(8) identify unnecessary proof and cumulative evidence, and limitations or restrictions on the use of expert testimony;

(9) determine whether the child will be present and testify at adjudication and, if so, under what conditions;

(10) establish a reasonable limit on the time allowed for presenting evidence; and

(11) consider such other matters as may aid in the resolution of the proceeding.

(c) **Duty to Update.** Parties have a continuing obligation to update information provided during the pretrial conference.

(SCO 845 effective August 15, 1987; amended by SCO 1355 effective July 15, 1999)

Rule 14. Stipulations.

Subject to approval by the court, parties may stipulate to any matter, including adjudication and disposition. However, stipulations to adjudication and disposition may be accepted only if the court determines that the parties understand their rights and have had a sufficient opportunity to consult with counsel. In the case of an Indian child, a stipulation to adjudication or disposition is not binding on a parent or Indian custodian unless it is in writing, agreed to in court (whether in person or telephonically), and signed by the parent or Indian custodian.

(SCO 845 effective August 15, 1987; amended by SCO 1355 effective July 15, 1999)

Note: See CINA Rule 16(a)(3) concerning stipulations to waive preparation of a predisposition report.

Cross References

CROSS REFERENCE: 25 U.S.C. § 1913(a).

PART VI. ADJUDICATION

Rule 15. Adjudication Hearing.

(a) **Nature and Timing of Proceeding.** The adjudication hearing is a trial to the court on the merits of the petition for adjudication. The adjudication must be completed within 120 days after a finding of probable cause is entered, unless the court finds good cause to continue the hearing. In determining whether to grant a continuance for good cause, the court shall take into consideration the age of the child and the potential adverse effect that the delay may have on the child.

(b) **Notice.** The Department must provide notice of the adjudication hearing to the persons specified in CINA Rule 7(b) within a reasonable time prior to the hearing. In cases involving an Indian child, notice of the hearing must be received at least ten days before the hearing pursuant to CINA Rule 7(e)(1). Upon request, the court shall postpone the hearing to ensure that the Indian child's parents, Indian custodian or tribe have had thirty days from receipt of the notice to prepare for the hearing.

(c) **Burden of Proof.** The Department has the burden of proving by a preponderance of the evidence that the child is a child in need of aid.

(d) **Judgment.** At the conclusion of the adjudication hearing, the court shall make findings of fact and enter a judgment that the child is or is not a child in need of aid.

(e) **Failure of Proof.** If the court finds that the child is not a child in need of aid, it shall immediately order the child released from the Department's custody and returned to the child's parents, guardian, or custodian.

(f) **Orders Pending Disposition.** If the court finds that the child is a child in need of aid and the disposition is not held immediately following the adjudication, the court shall enter the following orders:

(1) The court shall order the child placed in the temporary custody of the Department or order the child returned to the home with supervision by the Department pending disposition. The court may approve the removal of the child from the child's home only if the court makes the findings required by CINA Rule 10(c)(3).

(2) If the court approves the child's removal, the court shall make the inquiry and findings required by CINA Rule

10.1. A finding that the Department has failed to make reasonable efforts, or, in cases involving an Indian child, that the requirements of 25 U.S.C. §§ 1912(d) or 1915(b) have not been met, is not in itself a ground for returning the child to the home and does not affect the court's ability to enter an adjudication order and extend temporary custody pending adjudication.

(3) The court shall set a time for the disposition hearing, which will be held without unreasonable delay. The court shall order a predisposition report, unless waived by stipulation under CINA Rule 16(a)(3), and other studies, examinations, or reports under CINA Rule 16 that are necessary for an informed disposition.

(SCO 845 effective August 15, 1987; amended by SCO 855 effective January 15, 1988; by SCO 1010 effective January 15, 1990; and by SCO 1355 effective July 15, 1999)

Note: Ch. 43, SLA 2001, amends AS 47.10.030, AS 47.10.070(a), and AS 47.10.080(f) to add provisions concerning notice to and participation by grandparents. According to §6 of the Act, these provisions have the effect of amending Child in Need of Aid Rules 3, 7, 10, 15, 17, and 19 by requiring that grandparents be given notice of and an opportunity to be heard at certain child-in-need-of-aid proceedings.

Cross References

CROSS REFERENCE: AS 47.10.080(a); AS 47.10.081; AS 47.10.141(g); 25 U.S.C. § 1912.

Annotations

Cases

This annotation construes former Children's Rule 12. Where a child has been declared delinquent without the necessary compliance with statutory and constitutional procedural standards, such child has been deprived of his constitutional rights. If any attendant collateral disabilities remain, the proceedings which were infected with those disabilities cannot stand. **E.J. v. State,** Op. No. 628, 471 P2d 367 (Alaska 1970).

This annotation construes former Children's Rule 12. The provision of this rule providing for closed proceedings must be interpreted and applied in a manner consistent with the child's right to a public trial. **RLR v. State,** Op. No. 706, 487 P2d 27 (Alaska 1971).

This annotation construes former Children's Rule 12. If a child or his guardian ad litem wants the press, friends or others to be free to attend juvenile proceedings, the hearing must be open to them. The court's areas of discretion within which it may refuse to open a hearing involves persons whose presence is not desired by the child. **RLR v. State,** Op. No. 706,487 P2d 27 (Alaska 1971).

This annotation construes former Children's Rule 12. A hearing in which a chemist testifies that a tablet sent to him for analysis contains LSD should not be conducted in the absence of the infant involved after the attorney explicitly refuses to waive the infant's right to be present. Conducting a hearing in the child's absence under such circumstances is reversible error. **RLR v. State,** Op. No. 706, 487 P2d 27 (Alaska 1971).

This annotation construes former Children's Rule 12. Notions of benevolent protective policies for children cannot be used to validate departures from positive law relating to adjudicative and dispositive phases of children's proceedings. **In re E.M.D.,** Op. No. 737, 490 P2d 658 (Alaska 1971).

This annotation construes former Children's Rule 12. A child has a vital interest in a dependency proceeding and is an essential party whose presence cannot be dispensed with arbitrarily; in a dependency proceeding the summons and a copy of the petition must be served on the child as well as the parents; failure to make such service results in a lack of jurisdiction over the child. **In re P.N.,** Op. No. 1127,523 P2d 13 (Alaska 1975).

This annotation construes former Children's Rule 12. Where the children are not given the required notice of a dependency hearing the superior court has no jurisdiction over them and, therefore, cannot validly issue a judgment depriving a parent of his custody. **In re P.N.,** Op. No. 1127, 523 P2d 13 (Alaska 1975).

This annotation construes former Children's Rule 12. A court in a "child in need of supervision" hearing is under a duty to explain to the juvenile his right to counsel. **Wagstaff v. Superior Court, Family Court Division,** Op. No. 1144, 535 P2d 1220 (Alaska 1975).

This annotation construes former Children's Rule 12. In the adjudicative phase of any children's proceeding, the family court may consider only the specific situations set out in the petition. **In re S.D. Jr.,** Op. No. 1255, 549 P2d 1190 (Alaska 1976).

This annotation construes former Children's Rule 12. Court committed error when it commenced the adjudicative phase of the parental rights termination hearing in the absence of the child's counsel and guardian ad litem. **Matter of C.L.T.,** Op. No. 1866, 597 P2d 518 (Alaska 1979).

This annotation construes former Children's Rule 12. Superior court did not abuse its discretion in permitting two relatives of murder victims to attend a juvenile waiver hearing held to determine whether juvenile could be tried as an adult for the murders. **W.M.F. v. Jonstone,** Op. No. 571, 711 P2d 1187 (Alaska App. 1986).

When superior court has determined that minor is child in need of aid, factual findings in support of that determination will be overturned only if they are clearly erroneous. **Matter of T.W.R.,** Op. No. 4157, 887 P2d 941 (Alaska 1994).

Superior court's findings complied with requirement that court explicitly find that reasonable efforts had been made to avoid need for removal of child from home and to make it possible for child to return to home. **Matter of T.W.R.,** Op. No. 4157, 887 P2d 941 (Alaska 1994).

For purposes of termination, the State has the burden of proving both the CINA status of the child and the existence of grounds for termination by clear and convincing evidence. **A.M. v. State,** Op. No. 4177, 891 P2d 815 (Alaska 1995).

The clearly erroneous standard of review is applied to factual findings on the issue of termination. **A.M. v. State,** Op. No. 4177, 891 P2d 815 (Alaska 1995).

CINA proceedings have adjudicative component to determine whether child is child in need of aid and dispositional component to determine appropriate disposition of child who has been adjudicated child in need of aid; termination of parental rights is question generally decided at dispositional hearings; adjudication and termination proceedings can be combined, but termination is remedy which can only be imposed in AS 47.10 proceedings following or contemporaneous with CINA adjudication. **Matter of J.L.F,** Op. No. 4327, 912 P2d 1255 (Alaska 1996).

Question of whether findings under this rule were erroneous would be reviewed only for clear error. **R.R. v. State,** Op. No. 4359, 919 P2d 754 (Alaska 1996).

Trial court's finding that reasonable efforts were made to prevent removal of children from mother's home satisfied requirement of this rule despite lack of detailed findings. **R.R. v. State,** Op. No. 4359, 919 P2d 754 (Alaska 1996).

State's attempts to assist mother in enrolling and completing drug rehabilitation program satisfied requirement that State make reasonable efforts to prevent removal of child from home and to prevent breakup of

Indian family. **D.H. v. State,** Op. No. 4446, 929 P2d 650 (Alaska 1996).

Third-party custody claims were not closely analogous to child in need of aid proceedings; thus, the clear and convincing evidence standard of proof was required rather than the preponderance of the evidence standard in Alaska CINA R. 15(c). **Evans v. McTaggart,** Op. No. 5794, 88 P.3d 1078 (Alaska 2004).

While known parents must be given adequate notice, the ultimate focus of a CINA adjudication is on the child, not the parents. Thus, a child can be adjudicated based on the acts of just one parent, because the other parent's acquiescence or fault in allowing the abuse to occur is not required in order to find the child to be in need of aid. **Jeff A.C. v. State,** Op. No. 5922, 117 P.3d 697 (Alaska 2005).

Rule 7(b) requires the notice to be given to the parents if these parties can be found after diligent efforts. While known parents must be given adequate notice, the ultimate focus of a CINA adjudication is on the child, not the parents. Thus, a child can be adjudicated based on the acts of just one parent, because the other parent's acquiescence or fault in allowing the abuse to occur is not required in order to find the child to be in need of aid. **Jeff A.C. v. State,** Op. No. 5922, 117 P.3d 697 (Alaska 2005).

PART VII. DISPOSITION

Rule 16. Reports in Aid of Disposition.

(a) **Predisposition Report.**

(1) Unless waived by the parties with the approval of the court, the Department shall submit a predisposition report pursuant to AS 47.10.081(b). The report must include the current case plan and should also include the following information: the child's family background and educational history; past contacts by the Department with the child and the child's family; the child's medical, psychological and psychiatric history; and recommendations regarding the disposition which would be in the best interests of the child. In cases concerning an Indian child, the report must describe the proposed placement of the child, the placement preference under the Indian Child Welfare Act which is recommended and the rationale for the use of that level of placement preference.

(2) The predisposition report must be made available to the persons entitled to receive it ten days before the disposition hearing, unless all parties, with the approval of the court, agree upon a different time period. If the predisposition report is submitted to the court prior to the adjudication hearing, it must be kept sealed until the adjudication hearing is completed.

(3) The court will accept a stipulation to waive preparation of a predisposition report only if the parties have agreed to present adequate information upon which to enter an informed disposition order, including the current case plan.

(b) **Supplementary Material.** The court may order mental and physical examinations of the child and the child's parents, guardian and Indian custodian. The court may order studies of the home of any person with whom the child might be placed, and may order any other reports to aid disposition. A party may submit the party's own report in aid of disposition. All such materials must be made available to the persons entitled to receive them at a reasonable time prior to disposition, as determined by the court.

(c) **Disclosure of Reports.** Unless otherwise ordered, copies of predisposition reports and supplementary materials must be given to all parties. The court may enter an order prohibiting release of all or part of a report to the child only if disclosure would be likely to cause serious psychological harm to the child. The court shall inspect the reports in camera prior to entering a limitation on disclosure, and such a limitation does not bar the child's attorney or guardian ad litem from access to the material withheld from the child. The court may enter orders prohibiting release of the material by the attorney or guardian ad litem to the child.

(SCO 845 effective August 15, 1987; and amended by SCO 1355 effective July 15, 1999)

Cross References

CROSS REFERENCE: AS 47.10.080; AS 47.10.081; AS 47.10.082; AS 47.14.100; 25 U.S.C. § 1915; 25 U.S.C. § 1922.

Annotations

Cases

That Alaska CINA R. 16(b) allows a court to order mental and physical examinations of a child's parents at the predisposition phase of a child-in-need-of-aid proceeding does not limit the court's authority under Alaska R. Civ. P. 35(a) to order a mental examination at the adjudication stage. **Alyssa B. v. Dep't of Health & Social Servs.,** Op. No. 5930, 123 P.3d 646 (Alaska 2005).

Rule 17. Disposition.

(a) **Purpose of Hearing.** The purpose of a disposition hearing is to determine the appropriate disposition of a child who has been adjudicated a child in need of aid. A disposition hearing concerning the termination of parental rights is governed by CINA Rule 18.

(b) **Statements.** The parties may offer evidence in aid of disposition at the hearing. The court shall afford the parties, any grandparents of the child who are in attendance at the hearing, and any foster parents or other out-of-home care providers an opportunity to be heard.

(c) **Requirements for Disposition.** A disposition hearing may not be held before adequate information is available upon which to enter an informed disposition order. If the child has been placed outside the home, the court cannot enter a disposition order if the court finds (1) in cases involving a non-Indian child, that the Department has failed to make reasonable efforts as required by AS 47.10.086(a) to permit the child's return to the home, unless the court has determined under Rule 17.1 that reasonable efforts are not required; or (2) in cases involving an Indian child, that the requirements of 25 U.S.C. § 1912(d) (active efforts) have not been met.* If the court finds that the Department has failed to make required reasonable efforts or that the requirements of 25 U.S.C. § 1912(d) have not been met, the court must postpone entering a disposition order until the court finds that reasonable efforts or active efforts have been made. The child should remain in temporary custody pending disposition.

(d) **Findings.**

(1) A disposition order must be accompanied by findings of fact.

(2) The court may approve the removal of the child from the child's home only if the court finds that continued placement in the home is contrary to the welfare of the child; and, in cases involving an Indian child, that there is clear and convincing evidence, including the testimony of qualified expert witnesses, that custody of the Indian child by the parent or Indian custodian is likely to result in serious emotional or physical damage to the child.

(e) **Evidence.** Hearsay which is not otherwise admissible under a recognized exception to the hearsay rule may be admissible at the disposition hearing and in review of a disposition order if the hearsay is probative of a material fact, has circumstantial guarantees of trustworthiness, and the appearing parties are given a fair opportunity to meet it.

(f) **Disposition Order—Subsequent Proceedings.** If the court orders the child committed to the Department under AS 47.10.080(c)(1), the disposition order must set the date for the permanency hearing required by AS 47.10.080(l). If the court releases the child under AS 47.10.080(c)(2), the disposition order must set the date for filing the report on annual review.

(SCO 845 effective August 15, 1987; amended by SCO 1010 effective January 15, 1990; by SCO 1355 effective July 15, 1999; and by SCO 1465 effective April 15, 2002)

*** Note:** As of June 1999, it is an open issue whether federal law permits a trial court to determine that active efforts are not required in a case or that such efforts may be discontinued.

Note: Ch. 43, SLA 2001, amends AS 47.10.030, AS 47.10.070(a), and AS 47.10.080(f) to add provisions concerning notice to and participation by grandparents. According to §6 of the Act, these provisions have the effect of amending Child in Need of Aid Rules 3, 7, 10, 15, 17, and 19 by requiring that grandparents be given notice of and an opportunity to be heard at certain child-in-need-of-aid proceedings.

Cross References

CROSS REFERENCE: AS 47.10.080(c) and (r); AS 47.10.081; AS 47.10.082; AS 47.10.083; AS 47.10.141(g); 25 U.S.C. §§ 1912, 1915(b) and (c), 1922.

Annotations

Cases

Findings of fact contained nonfinal "Order of termination," which findings were not later changed satisfied the requirement of former Children's Rule 22(d) that court provide written findings of fact supporting the judgment. **Matter of C.L.T.,** Op. No. 1866, 597 P2d 518 (Alaska 1979).

This annotation construes former Children's Rule 22. Trial judge's discretion in not holding a disposition hearing under this rule must be narrowly defined. **L.C. v. State,** Op. No. 2277, 625 P2d 839 (Alaska 1981).

CINA proceedings have adjudicative component to determine whether child is child in need of aid and dispositional component to determine appropriate disposition of child who has been adjudicated child in need of aid; termination of parental rights is question generally decided at dispositional hearings; adjudication and termination proceedings can be combined, but termination is remedy which can only be imposed in AS 47.10 proceedings following or contemporaneous with CINA adjudication. **Matter of J.L.F,** Op. No. 4327, 912 P2d 1255 (Alaska 1996).

Trial court's findings on issue of likely serious physical or emotional damage to Indian child if she were placed in her mother's custody were inadequate, requiring remand. **D.H. v. State,** Op. No. 4446, 929 P2d 650 (Alaska 1996).

State's attempts to assist mother in enrolling and completing drug rehabilitation program satisfied requirement that State make reasonable efforts to prevent removal of child from home and to prevent breakup of Indian family. **D.H. v. State,** Op. No. 4446, 929 P2d 650 (Alaska 1996).

Rule 17.1. Determination that Reasonable Efforts Not Required.

(a) **Proceeding to Determine that Reasonable Efforts Not Required.** At any stage of a proceeding under these rules, a party may file a motion for a determination that reasonable efforts of the type described in AS 47.10.086(a) are not required, specifying the basis for the motion under AS 47.10.086(c). If the party intends that any evidentiary hearing on the motion be combined with a scheduled trial or other hearing, the motion must be filed and served at least 30 days prior to that proceeding.

(b) **Proceeding to Determine that Reasonable Efforts May Be Discontinued.** At the permanency hearing required under AS 47.10.080(l), the court may find that a continuation of reasonable efforts is not in the best interests of the child under AS 47.10.086(b). Any party recommending such a finding must include that recommendation, specifying the factual basis for it, in its report for permanency hearing required by CINA Rule 17.2(c) or in a separate motion.

(c) **Permanency Hearing Required.** If the court determines that reasonable efforts are not required under AS 47.10.086(c) in a proceeding other than a permanency hearing, the court shall hold a permanency hearing under AS 47.10.080(*l*) within 30 days after the determination.

(d) **Conduct of Proceeding.**

(1) *Right to Evidentiary Hearing.* A party may request an evidentiary hearing within the time specified in Civil Rule 77(e)(1). The court shall hold an evidentiary hearing upon request.

(2) *Standard of Proof.* The party requesting a determination that reasonable efforts are not required must present proof by clear and convincing evidence.

(3) *Child's Best Interests.* In determining whether reasonable efforts are required, the court's primary consideration is the child's best interests.

(4) *Findings.* The court must make specific findings in support of its decision.

(SCO 1355 effective July 15, 1999; amended by SCO 1401 effective October 15, 2000; and by SCO 1651 effective October 15, 2007)

Note to SCO 1651: Chapter 20 SLA 2006 (HB 408 enacted changes relating to the standard of proof in child in need of aid proceedings. Section 1 of the Act amended AS 47.10.086(c) to change the standard of proof for a finding that reasonable efforts, as described in AS 47.10.086(a), are not required. The change to CINA Rule 17.1 is adopted to maintain consistency between the rule and the statutes.

Cross References

CROSS REFERENCE: AS 47.10.086

Rule 17.2. Permanency Hearing.

(a) **Purpose and Timing of the Hearing.** The purpose of the permanency hearing is to establish a permanency plan for each child committed to state custody under AS 47.10.080(c)(1) and to ensure that findings with respect to the plan are made as required by state and federal laws. The permanency hearing must be held: (1) within 12 months after the date the child entered foster care as calculated under AS 47.10.088(f); (2) within 30 days after the court determines pursuant to CINA Rule 17.1 that reasonable efforts are not required; or (3) upon application by a party, when good cause is shown.

(b) **Notice.** The court or the party requesting the permanency hearing shall notify the parties of the time set for the hearing, the right to counsel, and the right to submit statements, affidavits or other evidence to the court. The Department shall notify the foster parent or other out-of-home care provider of the time set for the hearing and the right to participate in the hearing. In cases involving an Indian child, the Department shall also provide notice to the child's tribe if the child's tribe has not intervened. A party seeking a continuance of a scheduled hearing must provide reasons for the request. The court may not grant a continuance of a scheduled hearing absent a finding of good cause.

(c) **Report.** The Department shall file and serve a permanency report no later than ten days prior to the permanency hearing. In the report, the Department shall describe its permanency plan for the child, and shall provide a detailed statement of the facts and circumstances supporting the plan.

(d) **Evidence.** Hearsay which is not otherwise admissible under a recognized exception to the hearsay rule may be admissible at the permanency hearing if the hearsay is probative of a material fact, has circumstantial guarantees of trustworthiness, and the appearing parties are given a fair opportunity to meet it.

(e) **Findings.** The court shall make written findings, including findings related to

(1) whether the child continues to be a child in need of aid;

(2) whether the child should be returned to the parent or guardian, and when;

(3) whether the child should be placed for adoption or legal guardianship and whether the Department is in compliance with AS 47.10.088(d) relating to the filing of a petition for termination of parental rights;

(4) whether the child should be placed in another planned, permanent living arrangement and what steps are necessary to achieve the new arrangement; and

(5) in the case of a child who has attained age 16, the services needed to assist the child to make the transition from foster care to independent living or adult protective services.

If the court is unable to make a finding required under this subsection, the court shall schedule and hold another permanency hearing within a reasonable period of time as defined in AS 47.10.990(23).

(f) **Additional Findings.** In addition to the findings required under subsection (e), the court shall also make written findings related to

(1) whether the Department has made reasonable efforts required under AS 47.10.086 or, in the case of an Indian child, whether the Department has made active efforts to provide remedial services and rehabilitative programs as required by 25 U.S.C. Sec. 1912(d);

(2) whether the parent or guardian has made substantial progress to remedy the parent's or guardian's conduct or conditions in the home that made the child a child in need of aid;

(3) if the permanency plan is for the child to remain in out-of-home care, whether the child's out-of-home placement continues to be appropriate and in the best interests of the child; and

(4) whether the Department has made reasonable efforts to finalize the permanency plan that is in effect (whether the plan is reunification, adoption, legal guardianship, placement with a fit and willing relative, or placement in another planned permanent living arrangement).

(g) **Implementation.** The court may make appropriate orders to ensure timely implementation of the permanency plan.

(h) **Change in Permanency Plan.** If the permanency plan established by the court changes after the permanency hearing, the Department shall promptly apply to the court for another permanency hearing, and the court shall conduct the hearing within 30 days after application by the Department.

(i) **Subsequent Review.** The court shall hold a hearing to review the permanency plan at least annually until successful implementation of the plan.

(SCO 1355 effective July 15, 1999; amended by SCO 1580 effective nunc pro tunc to July 1, 2005; and by SCO 1491 effective October 15, 2006)

NOTE: Chapter 64, section 53, SLA 2005 (HB 53) amended Child in Need of Aid Rule 17.2 as reflected in section 3 of this Order. The change to CINA Rule 17.2 is adopted for the sole reason that the legislature has mandated the amendment. In addition, according to section 60(d) of the Act, AS 47.10.080(l), enacted in section 12, amends CINA Rule 17.2 by modifying the grounds for review of a permanent plan.

Cross References

CROSS REFERENCE: AS 47.10.080(c), (f), (l); AS 47.10.088(f); AS 47.10.086(d); 45 CFR § 1356.21(b).

Annotations

Cases

Superior court did not err in approving an adoption plan without holding an evidentiary hearing because neither AS 47.10.080 (l) nor this rule explicitly required such a hearing. **Owen M. v. State,** Op. No. 5942, 120 P.3d 201 (Alaska 2005).

Rule 18. Termination of Parental Rights

(a) **Petition.** The Department may file a petition seeking termination of parental rights combined with or after the filing of a petition for adjudication of that child as a child in need of aid. The title of the petition must clearly state that termination of parental rights is sought. A petition for termination of parental rights must be served as provided by CINA Rule 7(d) and (e).

(b) **Purpose of Hearing.** The termination hearing is a disposition hearing to the court on the question of whether the parental rights to an adjudicated child in need of aid should be terminated. Upon a showing of good cause and with adequate notice to the parties, an adjudication hearing and a termination hearing may be consolidated.

(c) **Burden of Proof.** Before the court may terminate parental rights, the Department must prove:

(1) by clear and convincing evidence that

(A) the child has been subjected to conduct or conditions described in AS 47.10.011 and

(i) the parent has not remedied the conduct or conditions in the home that place the child at substantial risk of harm; or

(ii) the parent has failed, within a reasonable time, to remedy the conduct or conditions in the home that place the child in substantial risk so that returning the child to the parent would place the child at substantial risk of physical or mental injury; or

(B) a parent is incarcerated and the requirements of AS 47.10.080(o) are met; and

(2) by clear and convincing evidence that

(A) the Department has complied with the provisions of AS 47.10.086 concerning reasonable efforts; or

(B) in the case of an Indian child, that active efforts have been made to provide remedial services and rehabilitative programs designed to prevent the breakup of the Indian family and that these efforts have proved unsuccessful; and

(3) by a preponderance of the evidence that termination of parental rights is in the best interests of the child; and

(4) in the case of an Indian child, by evidence beyond a reasonable doubt, including the testimony of qualified expert witnesses, that continued custody of the child by the parent or Indian custodian is likely to result in serious emotional or physical damage to the child.

(d) **Relinquishment.**

(1) Notwithstanding other provisions of this rule, the court may terminate parental rights after a voluntary relinquishment pursuant to AS 47.10.089. In the case of an Indian child, the relinquishment must meet the requirements set forth in 25 U.S.C. § 1913(c).

(e) **Trial.** A trial on the petition to terminate parental rights shall be held within six months after the date on which the petition to terminate parental rights is filed, unless the court finds that good cause is shown for a continuance. When determining whether to grant a continuance for good cause, the court shall take into consideration the age of the child and the potential adverse effect that the delay may have on the child. The court shall make written findings when granting a continuance.

(f) **Evidence.** Hearsay that is not admissible under a recognized exception to the hearsay rule is not admissible at a trial on a petition to terminate parental rights to prove that the child has been subjected to conduct or conditions described in AS 47.10.011. Otherwise, hearsay may be admissible at the trial if it is probative of a material fact, has circumstantial guarantees of trustworthiness, and the appearing parties are given a fair opportunity to meet it.

(g) **Judgment.** The court shall make findings of fact and enter an order within 90 days after the last day of trial on the petition to terminate parental rights. The court shall commit the child to the custody of the Department if parental rights are terminated.

(h) **Post-Termination Reports.** If a permanent placement for the child was not approved at the termination hearing, the Department shall report to the court within 30 days on the efforts being made to recruit a permanent placement. Thereafter, the Department shall report quarterly on efforts being made to find a permanent placement for the child. Copies of the Department's reports shall not be served on a parent whose rights have been terminated.

(SCO 845 effective August 15, 1987; amended by SCO 982 effective January 15, 1990; by SCO 1355 effective July 15, 1999; by SCO 1580 effective nunc pro tunc to July 1, 2005; and by SCO 1651 effective October 15, 2007)

Note: Chapter 64, section 54, SLA 2005 (HB 53) amended Child in Need of Aid Rule 18 as reflected in section 5 of this Order. The change to CINA Rule 18 is adopted for the sole reason that the legislature has mandated the amendment. In addition, according to section 60(e) of the Act, AS 47.10.089, enacted in section 17, amends CINA Rule 18 by providing that a relinquishment must be in writing, allowing for the withdrawal of the relinquishment, allowing for the retention of certain privileges, and authorizing a review hearing before the entry of an adoption or legal guardianship decree.

Note: Chapter 20 SLA 2006 (HB 408) enacted changes relating to the standard of proof in child in need of aid proceedings. According to section 11 of the Act, the amendments to AS 47.10.086(c), AS 47.10.088(a), and AS 47.10.088(b) in sections 1-3 of the Act have the effect of amending Child in Need of Aid Rule 18 relating to the termination of parental rights proceedings by increasing the standard of proof concerning some elements from proof by a preponderance of the evidence to proof by clear and convincing evidence. The change to CINA Rule 18 is adopted to maintain consistency between the rule and the statutes.

Cross References

CROSS REFERENCE: AS 25.23.180; AS 47.10.080 (c)(3); AS 47.10.088; 25 U.S.C. § 1912(d) and (f).

Annotations

Cases

Mental illness alone is not conduct and may not form basis for order terminating parental rights. **K.N. v. State of Alaska,** Op. No. 3980, 856 P2d 468 (Alaska 1993).

Superior court did not abuse its discretion in denying father's motion to have the adjudicative phase heard before the dispositional phase where a significant amount of the evidence was relevant to and could have been admitted at both phases of the termination proceeding. **A.M. v. State,** Op. No. 4177, 891 P2d 815 (Alaska 1995).

The State's duty to make active remedial efforts should not be affected by a parent's motivation or prognosis before remedial efforts have been commenced. However, once active remedial efforts have been undertaken, a parent's actual resistance to or rejection of assistance may be considered in determining whether additional efforts are required. **A.M. v. State,** Op. No. 4177, 891 P2d 815 (Alaska 1995).

Neither incarceration of the parent nor doubtful prospects for rehabilitation will relieve the state of its duty under Indian Child Welfare Act to make active remedial efforts. **A.M. v. State,** Op. No. 4177, 891 P2d 815 (Alaska 1995).

The circumstances surrounding a parent's incarceration may have a direct bearing on what active remedial efforts are possible and may be considered in determining whether the State has made the necessary remedial efforts. **A.M. v. State,** Op. No. 4177, 891 P2d 815 (Alaska 1995).

Mere evidence that a willing custodian other than the parent would do a better job that the parent does not in itself suffice to support a finding of likely emotional harm. **A.M. v. State,** Op. No. 4177, 891 P2d 815 (Alaska 1995).

Superior court properly considered, in assessing the likelihood of emotional harm in the event of a return of custody to the father, factors such as the prolonged separation that would inevitably occur before the restoration of custody and the need, in the interim, to assure the stability of the bonds the children had formed with their "psychological parent," i.e., their foster mother. **A.M. v. State,** Op. No. 4177, 891 P2d 815 (Alaska 1995).

Superior court properly found that continued custody by the father was likely to result in serous emotional or physical damage to the children. The court found beyond a reasonable doubt that one child was likely to suffer sexual assault if placed in her father's custody; that both children were likely to suffer physical abuse resulting from the father's domestic violence; and that both children were likely to suffer physical deprivation due to father's inability to meet their needs on a consistent, ongoing basis. **A.M. v. State,** Op. No. 4177, 891 P2d 815 (Alaska 1995).

To justify termination of parental rights after a child's CINA adjudication, the state must prove by clear and convincing evidence that the child is a child in need of aid as a result of parental conduct and that the conduct is likely to continue to exist. **A.M. v. State,** Op. No. 4177, 891 P2d 815 (Alaska 1995).

Where trial court terminated mother's parental rights in 1997 relying on findings it made in 1995 when it adjudicated the mother's children to be in need of aid, which adjudication findings were made under the clear and convincing evidence standard rather than the usual preponderance standard at the state's request, trial court's reliance on those findings did not violate mother's due process rights even though state gave no advance notice of its request until the beginning of the adjudication hearing. **D.M. v. DFYS,** Op. No. 5230, 995 P2d 205 (Alaska 2000).

A court could terminate parental rights only if it found by a preponderance of evidence that active efforts had been made to provide remedial services and rehabilitative programs designed to prevent the breakup of an Indian family and that these efforts had proved unsuccessful under the provisions of Alaska CINA R. 18(c)(2). **E.A. v. State,** Op. No. 5564, 46 P3d 986 (Alaska 2002).

Where mother made improvements in her ability to care for her children and experts raised doubt as to terminating her parental rights, State failed to show that mother's custody would likely result in serious emotional or physical damage to her children. **State v. M.L.L.,** Op. No. 5654, 61 P.3d 438 (Alaska 2002).

Court properly found a child to be in need of aid and terminated a father's parental rights where termination was in the child's best interests because the child did not know the father, and, at nearly two years old, she was of an age at which it was important not to disrupt the bonding that had occurred between her and her foster parents. **Martin N. v. State,** Op. No. 5736, 79 P.3d 50 (Alaska 2003).

Record supported trial court's finding that termination of the father's parental rights was in the best interests of the child where the record showed that the child suffered emotional problems as the result of the instability of his home environment; child had spent the preceding 19 months in foster care, he could not afford to wait any longer for his father to be a parent, and he would suffer severe psychological harm if the father was granted custody and then dropped out of his life again, which was likely. **Carl N. v. State,** Op. No. 5852, 102 P.3d 932 (Alaska 2004).

Superior court properly found that State had made reasonable efforts to reunify the family as required under subsection (c)(2)(A) of this rule even though it failed to provide a recommended mental health evaluation for the father where State provided parenting and anger management assessments to father, directed him to parenting classes and alternatives to violence counseling, and brought him to Alaska at state expense to see his children. **Winston J. v. State,** Op. No. 12002, 134 P.3d 343 (Alaska 2006).

Rule 19. Annual Review.

(a) **Purpose and Timing of Review.** The court shall conduct an annual review for a child under the supervision of the Department pursuant to AS 47.10.080(c)(2) to determine if continued supervision, as it is being provided, is in the best interest of the child.

(b) **Report.** The Department shall file a written report at least twenty days before the anniversary date of a disposition order made under AS 47.10.080(c)(2). The Department shall serve the parties with copies of the report together with notice of the right to counsel, notice of the right to submit statements, affidavits or other evidence to the court and notice of the right to request an evidentiary hearing. The report must include the current case plan and must describe both the services offered by the Department and the services utilized by the parents or guardian to make it possible for the child to remain in the home.

(c) **Conduct of Review.** The review will take place without a hearing on the basis of written reports, statements and affidavits, unless an evidentiary hearing is requested by a party or ordered by the court on its own motion.

(d) **Notice—Indian Child.** In cases involving an Indian child, whose tribe has not intervened, a party requesting an evidentiary hearing shall provide notice of the hearing to the tribe.

(e) **Findings.** At the conclusion of the review, the court shall make written findings related to whether the child continues to be a child in need of aid and whether continued supervision by the Department is in the best interests of the child.

(SCO 845 effective August 15, 1987; amended by SCO 916 effective January 15, 1989; by SCO 958 effective July 15, 1989; by SCO 983 effective January 15, 1990; by SCO 1010 effective January 15, 1990; by SCO 1072 effective January 15, 1992; by SCO 1085 effective January 15, 1992; and by SCO 1355 effective July 15, 1999)

Note: Ch. 43, SLA 2001, amends AS 47.10.030, AS 47.10.070(a), and AS 47.10.080(f) to add provisions concerning notice to and participation by grandparents. According to §6 of the Act, these provisions have the effect of amending Child in Need of Aid Rules 3, 7, 10, 15, 17, and 19 by requiring that grandparents be given notice of and an opportunity to be heard at certain child-in-need-of-aid proceedings.

Cross References

CROSS REFERENCE: AS 47.10.080(c), (f), (l).

Annotations

Cases

This annotation construes former Children's Rule 28. For good cause shown, parents are entitled to a review of an order of the children's court at any time. **In re S.D. Jr.,** Op. No. 1255, 549 P2d 1190 (Alaska 1976).

Rule 19.1. Review upon Application.

(a) **Visitation.** At any time in a proceeding, a parent or guardian who has been denied visitation, or the child's guardian ad litem, may move the court for a review hearing at which the Department must show by clear and convincing evidence that visits are not in the child's best interests.

(b) **Placement Transfer.** At any time in a proceeding, a party who is opposed to the Department transferring a child from one placement to another may move the court for a review hearing at which the requesting party must prove by clear and convincing evidence that the transfer would be contrary to the best interests of the child. In the case of an Indian child, the court must consider the placement preferences as set forth in 25 U.S.C. § 1915.

(c) **Disposition Order.** Pursuant to AS 47.10.100(a), the court may review a disposition order upon motion of a party or on its own motion. When a party seeks the return of a child to the child's home, if the party makes a prima facie showing that removal is no longer necessary, the burden of proof shifts to the Department as described below:

(A) in cases involving a non-Indian child, the court shall return the child to the home unless the Department proves by a preponderance of the evidence that return to the home is contrary to the welfare of the child;

(B) in cases involving an Indian child, the court shall restore the child to the child's parent or Indian custodian unless the Department proves by clear and convincing evidence, including the testimony of qualified expert witnesses, that the child is likely to suffer serious emotional or physical damage if returned to the custody of the parent or Indian custodian.

(d) **Other Review.** At any time in a proceeding, the court may review matters not otherwise covered by these rules upon motion of a party or on its own motion.

(SCO 1355 effective July 15, 1999)

Cross References

CROSS REFERENCE: AS 47.10.080(p) and (s); AS 47.10.100(a); 25 U.S.C. § 1915.

Annotations

Cases

In reaching its termination decision, the superior court was not required to revisit its earlier placement decision and its termination order superseded all earlier placement orders. The mother could have challenged those placement decisions by requesting superior court review, and could then have petitioned the appellate court for review of the superior court's ruling; however, because the mother failed to seek timely review, the superior court's termination order rendered earlier issues of placement moot. **Erica A. v. State,** Op. No. 5674, 66 P.3d 1 (Alaska 2003).

Rule 19.2. Extension of Custody or Supervision.

(a) **Petition.** The Department or the child's guardian ad litem may file a petition for an extension of the commitment to custody or supervision. The petition must be filed at least thirty days prior to the expiration of the existing disposition order. The petitioner shall serve notice of the time set for a hearing on the petition to those persons specified in CINA Rule 3(a) and to the child's tribe and Indian custodian, even if the tribe or Indian custodian has not intervened. If the tribe or Indian custodian has not intervened, the notice must include notice of the right to intervene in the action and to obtain documents filed in the case.

(b) **Extension of Custody or Super-vision.** At the conclusion of the hearing the court shall determine whether the child continues to be a child in need of aid and whether continued custody or supervision by the Department is in the best interests of the child.

(c) **Report.** The petitioner must submit a written report that includes a detailed statement of the facts and circumstances supporting the petition for extension of custody or supervision. Unless otherwise ordered, the report must be served and filed at least ten days prior to the extension hearing.

(d) **Status Pending Decision.** If the court is unable to decide the extension petition before expiration of the existing disposition order, the court may extend custody or supervision for a reasonable time as defined in AS 47.10.990(23) pending a decision on the extension petition.

(SCO 1355 effective July 15, 1999)

Cross References

CROSS REFERENCE: AS 47.10.080(c).

Rule 20. Review Upon Petition Under 25 U.S.C. §1914.

(a) **Grounds for Petition.** In cases involving an Indian child, the child, parents, Indian custodian and child's tribe may petition the court to invalidate any order in the case upon a showing that the order violated any provision of 25 U.S.C. §§ 1911, 1912 or 1913. A petition under 25 U.S.C. § 1914 may be brought as a separate action if the petitioner is unable to participate in the challenged proceeding as a party.

(b) **Petition to Invalidate.** A petition filed under 25 U.S.C. § 1914 must be served on all parties to the action sought to be invalidated, including the Indian child's tribe and Indian custodian whether or not they have intervened. The petition must include:

(1) the identities of the petitioner and the Indian child subject to the petition, and the status of the petitioner under 25 U.S.C. § 1914;

(2) a statement of the particular provisions of 25 U.S.C. §§ 1911, 1912 or 1913 alleged to have been violated and the factual basis supporting the alleged violation; and

(3) any exhibits, reports or other evidence in support of the allegations.

(c) **Disposition.** If the court determines that the challenged order violated 25 U.S.C. §§ 1911, 1912 or 1913, the court shall immediately invalidate the order and take other appropriate action which may include dismissing the case and ordering the child returned to the parents or Indian custodian.

(SCO 845 effective August 15, 1987; amended by SCO 1355 effective July 15, 1999)

Cross References

CROSS REFERENCE: 25 U.S.C. Sections 1911, 1912, 1913, and 1914.

PART VIII. APPELLATE REVIEW

Rule 21. Appeal and Petition for Review in Appellate Courts.

(a) **Grounds, Procedure.** An appeal of a final judgment or order, or a petition for review of an interlocutory order or decision, may be taken subject to Appellate Rule 218 or other appropriate appellate procedures.

(b) **Stay.** An order, judgment or decision of the superior court remains in effect pending appeal or review, unless stayed by order of the superior court or the supreme court.

(SCO 845 effective August 15, 1987; amended by SCO 1355 effective July 15, 1999)

Cross References

CROSS REFERENCE: AS 22.07.020(a)(3); AS 47.10.080(i); Appellate Rules 218, 402 & 403; 25 U.S.C. § 1914.

Annotations

Cases

This annotation construes former Children's Rule 29. A minor who is detained may appeal his detention order. **A. M. v. State,** Op. No. 150, 653 P2d 346 (Alaska App. 1982).

PART IX. COURT ADMINISTRATION

Rule 22. Confidentiality.

(a) **Confidentiality of Records.** The records of a child in need of aid proceeding are confidential. Only parties and their attorneys may have access to the court file except as otherwise authorized by statute or court order for good cause shown. Parties and their attorneys shall maintain the confidentiality of all information in the court's file. Other persons authorized access to the file are subject to such conditions as the court may set with notice to the parties.

(b) **Foster Parent's Right to Review.** A foster parent may have access to court records relating to a child whom the Department has placed with the foster parent or whom the Department proposes for placement. When a case involves more than one child, but the foster parent does not have custody of all the children in the case, the foster parent may have access only to those portions of the court records that relate to the child whom the Department has placed or proposed for placement with the foster parent. The foster parent must maintain the confidentiality of all parts of the record. For purposes of this rule, "foster parent" includes current and proposed foster parents.

(c) **Child's Name or Picture.** The name or picture of a child who is the subject of a CINA proceeding may not be made available to the public unless authorized by court order accompanied by a written statement reciting the circumstances which support such authorization, or unless necessary to implement the permanency plan for the child after all parental rights of custody have been terminated.

(SCO 845 effective August 15, 1987; amended by SCO 1355 effective July 15, 1999; and by SCO 1580 effective July 7, 2005)

Note: AS 47.10.092, added by ch. 98 § 2 SLA 1994, affects CINA Rule 22 by authorizing the parent or legal guardian of a minor subject to a proceeding under AS 47.10.010-.142 to disclose confidential or privileged information about the minor, including information lawfully obtained from a court file, to the governor, the lieutenant governor, a legislator, the ombudsman appointed under AS 24.55, the attorney general, and the commissioners of health and social services, administration, or public safety, or an employee of these persons, for review or use in their official capacities. A person to whom such disclosure is made may not disclose confidential or privileged information about the minor to a person not authorized to receive it.

Note: Chapter 64, section 55, SLA 2005 (HB 53) amended Child in Need of Aid Rule 22. The change to CINA Rule 22 is adopted for the sole reason that the legislature has mandated the amendment. In addition, according to section 61(b) of the Act, sections 19 and 22-27 have the effect of changing CINA Rule 22 by allowing the disclosure of confidential information pertaining to a child, including allowing a child's name or picture to be made public in certain circumstances.

Cross References

CROSS REFERENCE: AS 47.10.090; 25 U.S.C. Section 1912(c).

Annotations

Cases

Superior court decision in CINA proceeding ordering the sharing of information among the parties to the case and all agencies providing services to them, for the purpose of facilitating the reunion of child and father, did not exceed the court's statutory authority and did not violate privacy rights. **In re A.B.,** 791 P.2d 615 (Alaska 1990).

PART X. TRANSFER OF JURISDICTIONS

Rule 23. Transfer of Jurisdiction to Tribal Court.

(a) **Who May File Petition.** In circumstances in which the Indian child's tribe may exercise jurisdiction in child welfare cases under 25 U.S.C. §1911(b), the Indian child's tribe, if it has intervened, a parent, or an Indian custodian, may file a petition to transfer CINA proceedings in state court to the tribal court of the Indian child's tribe.

(b) **Contents of Petition.** The petition shall state:

(1) the name, address and telephone number of the petitioner;

(2) the names, addresses and telephone numbers of the parents of the child, if known;

(3) the names, addresses and telephone numbers of any Indian custodians of the child, if known;

(4) the name, address and telephone number of the Indian child's tribe;

(5) the name, address and telephone number of the tribal court of the Indian child's tribe; and

(6) the tribal court's position, if known, on whether it will decline or accept jurisdiction in the case.

(c) **Notice and Sample Forms.** With the petition, the petitioner shall also serve the parties with a notice stating the following:

(1) the parties must file and serve any response they wish to make to the petition within 20 days after service;

(2) if either parent opposes the transfer of jurisdiction to tribal court the petition will not be granted under 25 U.S.C. §1911(b), unless the parental rights of the parent have already been terminated by a court of competent jurisdiction;

(3) if the tribal court declines jurisdiction at any time before an order granting the petition is signed the petition will not be granted;

(4) if a party to the state court proceeding demonstrates good cause why jurisdiction should not be transferred, the petition will not be granted;

(5) if jurisdiction is transferred to tribal court and the tribal court exercises jurisdiction, any state court appointments of counsel for parents or Indian custodians, or of Guardians ad Litem or counsel for the child, will terminate; and

(6) that a tribal court may find a copy of a sample order to file with the state court to accept or decline jurisdiction, and that a parent or Indian custodian may find a copy of a sample form to file with the state court to agree or object to the proposed transfer, on the court system's website at www.state.ak.us/courts.

(d) **Service.**

(1) *Parents or Indian Custodians.* The petitioner shall serve parents or Indian custodians by registered or certified mail, restricted delivery with return receipt requested, with copies of the petition for adjudication in state court, the petition to transfer to tribal court, and the notice described under subsection (c). The state court may waive service on a parent or Indian custodian under this paragraph when diligent inquiry has failed to locate that parent or Indian custodian.

(2) *Tribal Court.* If the petitioner is a parent or an Indian custodian, the petitioner shall serve the tribal court to which transfer is sought by registered or certified mail, return receipt requested, with copies of the petition for adjudication, the petition to transfer to tribal court, and the notice required under subsection (c).

(3) *Tribe.* The petitioner shall serve any tribe that may be the Indian child's tribe, regardless of whether a tribe has intervened. Service shall be by registered or certified mail, return receipt requested, with copies of the petition for adjudication and the petition to transfer to tribal court.

(4) *Other State Court Parties.* The petitioner shall serve the petition to transfer on all other parties in the state proceeding under Civil Rule 5(b) (set forth at the end of this rule).

(e) **Procedure.**

(1) *Parties' Responses.* Parties to the state court proceeding may serve and file a response within 20 days after service of the petition.

(A) *Parent's Statement.* A parent served with a petition to transfer shall file and serve a statement about whether they agree with or object to the proposed transfer within the time allotted to respond to the petition. If a parent objects to transfer, the court shall deny the petition.

(B) *Good Cause Not to Transfer.* The response of any party asserting that good cause exists not to transfer the case to tribal court shall state the alleged grounds for a finding of good cause not to transfer. Any other party may serve and file a supplemental response, limited to the issue of good cause, within ten days after service of the response. If material issues of fact are raised in the pleadings, the state court shall set an evidentiary hearing. A party asserting good cause not to transfer the case bears the burden of proof by a preponderance of the evidence.

(2) *Petioner's Reply.* The petitioner may serve and file a reply within ten days after service of a response.

(f) **Acceptance or Declination by the Tribal Court.**

(1) Only the tribal court of the Indian child's tribe may accept or decline a transfer of jurisdiction under this rule.

(2) If the tribal court declines jurisdiction while the petition is pending, the state court shall dismiss the petition without further proceedings.

(3) If the tribal court has not stated its position regarding transfer by the time the petition is ripe for decision, the state court shall contact the tribal court to request a timely response. The state court shall keep a record of any communication with the tribal court, and the parties shall be informed promptly of the communication and granted access to the record.

(g) **Findings and Order.** In its order granting or denying the petition, the state court shall make findings on the following:

(1) whether the child is an Indian child as defined in the Indian Child Welfare Act, 25 U.S.C. §1903(4);

(2) whether the tribe to whose tribal court transfer is sought is the Indian child's tribe as defined in the Indian Child Welfare Act, 25 U.S.C. 1903(5);

(3) whether the Indian child's tribe has intervened in the state court proceeding;

(4) whether the Indian child's tribe has a tribal court, and whether that court has accepted jurisdiction over the child;

(5) whether a parent has objected to a transfer of jurisdiction to the tribal court; and

(6) whether there is good cause not to transfer jurisdiction to the tribal court.

(h) **Transfer to Tribal Court.**

(1) If the state court grants the transfer of jurisdiction, it shall retain jurisdiction pending exercise of jurisdiction by the tribal court.

(2) When the tribal court exercises jurisdiction under (h)(1), the state court shall provide the tribal court with copies of any documents in the state court file requested by the tribal court.

(Adopted by SCO 1521 effective October 15, 2004)

Note: Nothing in this rule shall be construed to prevent the emergency removal or placement of an Indian child under state law in accordance with 25 U.S.C. §1922, as necessary to prevent imminent physical damage or harm to the child.

Cross References

CROSS REFERENCE: 25 U.S.C. §1911(b); 25 U.S.C. §1903.

SERVICE RULE—Civil Rule 5(b): The service provisions of Civil Rule 5(b), referred to in Rule 23(d)(4) above, are as follows: (b) **Service—How Made.** Whenever under these rules service is required or permitted to be made upon a party represented by an attorney the service shall be made upon the attorney unless service upon the party is ordered by the court. Service upon the attorney or upon a party shall be made by delivering a copy to the attorney or party, by mailing it to the attorney's or party's last known address, by transmitting it to the attorney's or party's facsimile machine telephone number as provided in Civil Rule 5.1(b), or, if no address is known, by leaving it with the clerk of the court. Delivery of a copy within this rule means: handing it to the attorney or to the party; or leaving it at the attorney's or party's office with a clerk or other person in charge thereof; or, if there is no one in charge, leaving it in a conspicuous place therein; or, if the office is closed or the person to be served has no office, leaving it at the attorney's or party's dwelling house or usual place of abode with some person of suitable age and discretion then residing therein. Mailing of a copy means mailing it by first class United States mail. Service by mail is complete upon mailing. Service by a commercial delivery company constitutes service by delivery and is complete upon delivery.

APPENDIX

INDIAN CHILD WELFARE ACT

25 U.S.C. §§ 1901—1923, 1951

§ 1901. Congressional findings.

Recognizing the special relationship between the United States and the Indian tribes and their members and the Federal responsibility to Indian people, the Congress finds—

(1) that clause 3, section 8, article I of the United States Constitution provides that "The Congress shall have Power * * * To regulate Commerce * * * with Indian tribes" and, through this and other constitutional authority, Congress has plenary power over Indian affairs;

(2) that Congress, through statutes, treaties, and the general course of dealing with Indian tribes, has assumed the responsibility for the protection and preservation of Indian tribes and their resources;

(3) that there is no resource that is more vital to the continued existence and integrity of Indian tribes than their children and that the United States has a direct interest, as trustee, in protecting Indian children who are members of or are eligible for membership in an Indian tribe;

(4) that an alarmingly high percentage of Indian families are broken up by the removal, often unwarranted, of their children from them by nontribal public and private agencies and that an alarmingly high percentage of such children are placed in non-Indian foster and adoptive homes and institutions; and

(5) that the States, exercising their recognized jurisdiction over Indian child custody proceedings through administrative and judicial bodies, have often failed to recognize the essential tribal relations of Indian people and the cultural and social standards prevailing in Indian communities and families.

Annotations

Cases

Alaska courts liberally construe statutes enacted for the benefit of Indians, resolving all doubts in favor of the Indians. **In re Adoption of Erin G**, Op. No. 11929, 140 P.3d 886, (Alaska 2006).

Whether the state has complied with the active efforts requirement under subsection (d) of this section is a mixed question of law and fact. **Gilbert M. v. State**, Op. No. 11364, 139 P.3d 581 (Alaska 2006).

Alaska courts liberally construe statutes enacted for the benefit of Indians, resolving all doubts in favor of the Indians. **In re Adoption of Erin G**, Op. No. 11929, 140 P.3d 886, (Alaska 2006).

§ 1902. Congressional declaration of policy.

The Congress hereby declares that it is the policy of this Nation to protect the best interests of Indian children and to promote the stability and security of Indian tribes and families by the establishment of minimum Federal standards for the removal of Indian children from their families and the placement of such children in foster or adoptive homes which will reflect the unique values of Indian culture, and by providing for assistance to Indian tribes in the operation of child and family service programs.

§ 1903. Definitions.

For the purposes of this chapter, except as may be specifically provided otherwise, the term—

(1) "child custody proceedings" shall mean and include—

(i) "foster care placement" which shall mean any action removing an Indian child from its parent or Indian custodian for temporary placement in a foster home or institution or the home of a guardian or conservator where the parent or Indian custodian cannot have the child returned upon demand, but where parental rights have not been terminated;

(ii) "termination of parental rights" which shall mean any action resulting in the termination of the parent-child relationship;

(iii) "preadoptive placement" which shall mean the permanent placement of an Indian child in a foster home or institution after the termination of parental rights, but prior to or in lieu of adoptive placement; and

(iv) "adoptive placement" which shall mean the permanent placement of an Indian child for adoption, including any action resulting in a final decree of adoption.

Such term or terms shall not include a placement based upon an act which, if committed by an adult, would be deemed a crime or upon an award, in a divorce proceeding, of custody to one of the parents.

(2) "extended family member" shall be as defined by the law or custom of the Indian child's tribe or, in the absence of such law or custom, shall be a person who has reached the age of eighteen and who is the Indian child's grandparent, aunt or uncle, brother or sister, brother-in-law or sister-in-law, niece or nephew, first or second cousin, or stepparent;

(3) "Indian" means any person who is a member of an Indian tribe, or who is an Alaska Native and a member of a Regional Corporation as defined in section 1606 of Title 43;

(4) "Indian child" means any unmarried person who is under age eighteen and is either (a) a member of an Indian tribe or (b) is eligible for membership in an Indian tribe and is the biological child of a member of an Indian tribe;

(5) "Indian child's tribe" means (a) the Indian tribe in which an Indian child is a member or eligible for membership or (b), in the case of an Indian child who is a member of or eligible for membership in more than one tribe, the Indian tribe with which the Indian child has the more significant contacts;

(6) "Indian custodian" means any Indian person who has legal custody of an Indian child under tribal law or custom or under State law or to whom temporary physical care, custody, and control has been transferred by the parent of such child;

(7) "Indian organization" means any group, association, partnership, corporation, or other legal entity owned or controlled by Indians, or a majority of whose members are Indians;

(8) "Indian tribe" means any Indian tribe, band, nation, or other organized group or community of Indians recognized as eligible for the services provided to Indians by the Secretary because of their status as Indians, including any Alaska Native village as defined in section 1602(c) of Title 43;

(9) "parent" means any biological parent or parents of an Indian child or any Indian person who has lawfully adopted an Indian child, including adoptions under tribal law or custom. It does not include the unwed father where paternity has not been acknowledged or established;

(10) "reservation" means Indian country as defined in section 1151 of Title 18 and any lands, not covered under such section, title to which is either held by the United States in trust for the benefit of any Indian tribe or individual or held by

any Indian tribe or individual subject to a restriction by the United States against alienation;

(11) "Secretary" means the Secretary of the Interior; and

(12) "tribal court" means a court with jurisdiction over child custody proceedings and which is either a Court of Indian Offenses, a court established and operated under the code or custom of an Indian tribe, or any other administrative body of a tribe which is vested with authority over child custody proceedings.

Annotations

Cases

Argument that ICWA did not apply to custody dispute between biological mother of Indian child and prospective adoptive parents of child because prospective adoptive parents were members of mother's extended family was rejected. **A.B.M. v. M.H.,** Op. No. 2657, 651 P2d 1170 (Alaska 1982).

Where Indian child's village was not allowed to intervene in adoption hearing, trial court's decision, agreed to by all participants at the hearing, to set aside the placement preferences of the ICWA was invalid. **Matter of J.R.S.,** Op. No. 2869, 690 P2d 10 (Alaska 1984).

A "stepparent" is not a "parent" within ICWA usage, therefore custody disputes between parents and stepparents do not fall within ICWA exclusion for custody disputes between parents. **J.W. v. Rj.,** Op. No. 4934, 951 P2d 1206 (Alaska 1998).

In custody dispute between Indian father and Indian stepfather, the "clear and convincing evidence" standard for foster care placement would apply only if Indian stepfather was not "Indian custodian" within meaning of ICWA. **J.W. v. Rj.,** Op. No. 4934, 951 P2d 1206 (Alaska 1998).

A parent as defined by this Act does not include an unwed father if paternity has not been acknowledged or established; thus, until unwed father acknowledged paternity, state was under no obligation under ICWA to make active effort to provide remedial services and rehabilitative programs to prevent termination of his parental rights. **A.A. v. State,** Op. No. 5137, 982 P2d 256 (Alaska 1999).

Indian Child Welfare Act does not apply to inter-parental custody disputes between tribal members. **John v. Baker,** Op. No. 5174, 982 P.2d 738 (Alaska 1999).

§ 1911. Indian tribe jurisdiction over Indian child custody proceedings.

(a) Exclusive jurisdiction.

An Indian tribe shall have jurisdiction exclusive as to any State over any child custody proceeding involving an Indian child who resides or is domiciled within the reservation of such tribe, except where such jurisdiction is otherwise vested in the State by existing Federal law. Where an Indian child is a ward of a tribal court, the Indian tribe shall retain exclusive jurisdiction, notwithstanding the residence or domicile of the child.

(b) Transfer of proceedings; declination by tribal court.

In any State court proceeding for the foster care placement of, or termination of parental rights to, an Indian child not domiciled or residing within the reservation of the Indian child's tribe, the court, in the absence of good cause to the contrary, shall transfer such proceeding to the jurisdiction of the tribe, absent objection by either parent, upon the petition of either parent or the Indian custodian or the Indian child's tribe: Provided, That such transfer shall be subject to declination by the tribal court of such tribe.

(c) State court proceedings; intervention.

In any State court proceeding for the foster care placement of, or termination of parental rights to, an Indian child, the Indian custodian of the child and the Indian child's tribe shall have a right to intervene at any point in the proceeding.

(d) Full faith and credit to public acts, records, and judicial proceedings of Indian tribes.

The United States, every State, every territory or possession of the United States, and every Indian tribe shall give full faith and credit to the public acts, records, and judicial proceedings of any Indian tribe applicable to Indian child custody proceedings to the same extent that such entities give full faith and credit to the public acts, records, and judicial proceedings of any other entity.

Annotations

Cases

Where Indian child's village was not allowed to intervene in adoption hearing, trial court's decision, agreed to by all participants at the hearing, to set aside the placement preferences of the ICWA was invalid. **Matter of J.R.S.,** Op. No. 2869, 690 P2d 10 (Alaska 1984).

A tribe's waiver of its exclusive jurisdiction over custody proceedings involving Indian children who are wards of the tribal court must be express, unequivocal and knowingly made. **Matter of J.M.,** Op. No. 3047, 718 P2d 150 (Alaska 1986).

State of Alaska has exclusive jurisdiction over matters involving the custody of Indian children and exercises such jurisdiction until a particular tribe petitions to reassume jurisdiction and the Secretary of the Interior approves the petition. **Native Village of Nenana v. Dept. of Health,** Op. No. 3082, 722 P2d 219 (Alaska 1986). [Overruled (see **In re C.R.H.**, Op. No. 9677, 29 P.3d 849 (Alaska 2001).]

Tribe must present a petition to Secretary of the Interior that includes a suitable plan for dealing with custody matters before it may reassume jurisdiction over Indian child custody proceedings, whether child resides or is domiciled with the tribe or lives elsewhere. **Matter of K.E.,** Op. No. 3242, 744 P2d 1173 (Alaska 1987).

Where governing bodies of two Native Alaskan villages as well as two individual residents of those villages won declaratory relief in federal district court requiring State of Alaska to give full faith and credit to adoption decrees issued by the villages, villages were entitled to award of attorney's fees under 42 U.S.C. § 1988. **Native Village of Venetie IRA v. State of Alaska,** 155 F.3d 1150 (9th Cir. 1998).

Indian Child Welfare Act does not entitle an Indian child's tribe to notice of a proceeding for voluntary termination of parental rights. **Catholic Social Services, Inc. v C.A.A.,** Op. No. 3534, 783 P2d 1159 (Alaska 1989).

Congress clearly intended a uniform federal law of domicile for the ICWA and did not consider the definition of "domicile" in the ICWA to be a matter of state law. **Mississippi Band of Choctaw Indians v. Holyfield,** 490 U.S. 30 (1989).

Since domicile of mother of twin illegitimate Indian babies was tribal reservation, twins were also domiciled there even though they were not born there, had never lived there, and had been voluntarily surrendered for adoption; therefore, exclusive jurisdiction over custody of twins resided in tribal courts and adoption decree issued by state court was invalid. **Mississippi Band of Choctaw Indians v. Holyfield,** 490 U.S. 30 (1989).

State of Alaska is required to give full faith and credit to adoption decrees issued by the tribal courts of native villages if the village is the modern-day successor to an historical sovereign band of native Americans. **Native Village of Venetie I.R.A. Council v. Alaska,** 944 F.2d 548 (9th Cir. 1991).

In the case of Indian children who reside on their tribal reservation, jurisdiction over child custody disputes resides exclusively in the tribe; in the case of Indian children who do not reside or are not domiciled on their tribe's reservation, state courts may exercise jurisdiction concurrent with tribal courts, but the state court must refer the dispute to the appropriate tribal court unless good cause is shown for the retention of state court jurisdiction. **Native Village of Venetie I.R.A. Council v. Alaska,** 944 F.2d 548 (9th Cir. 1991).

ICWA was applicable to custody dispute between Indian father and Indian stepfather. **J.W. v. Rj.,** Op. No. 4934, 951 P2d 1206 (Alaska 1998).

Tribal courts in Alaska have jurisdiction concurrent with Alaska state courts to adjudicate custody disputes involving tribal members outside Indian country. **John v. Baker,** Op. No. 5174, 982 P.2d 738 (Alaska 1999).

Subsection (b) of this section authorizes transfer jurisdiction for federally recognized tribes in Alaska, therefore tribes may accept transfer jurisdiction under this section of ICWA. (Overrulling *Native Village of Nenan v. Dept. of Health,* 722 P.2d 219 (Alaska 1986). **In re C.R.H.**, Op. No. 9677, 29 P.3d 849 (Alaska 2001).

Grandfather was not granted standing by subsection (c) of this section to appeal termination of daughter's parental rights to his granddaughter, an Indian child, where grandfather's incarceration eliminated any basis to claim to be his granddaughter's Indian custodian and the Superior Court never found him to be the Indian custodian even before he was incarcerated. **Gilbert M. v. State**, Op. No. 11364, 139 P.3d 581 (Alaska 2006).

§ 1912. Pending court proceedings.

(a) Notice; time for commencement of proceedings; additional time for preparation.

In any involuntary proceeding in a State court, where the court knows or has reason to know that an Indian child is involved, the party seeking the foster care placement of, or termination of parental rights to, an Indian child shall notify the parent or Indian custodian and the Indian child's tribe, by registered mail with return receipt requested, of the pending proceedings and of their right of intervention. If the identity or location of the parent or Indian custodian and the tribe cannot be determined, such notice shall be given to the Secretary in like manner, who shall have fifteen days after receipt to provide the requisite notice to the parent or Indian custodian and the tribe. No foster care placement or termination of parental rights proceeding shall be held until at least ten days after receipt of notice by the parent or Indian custodian and the tribe or the Secretary: *Provided,* That the parent or Indian custodian or the tribe shall, upon request, be granted up to twenty additional days to prepare for such proceeding.

(b) Appointment of counsel.

In any case in which the court determines indigency, the parent or Indian custodian shall have the right to court-appointed counsel in any removal, placement, or termination proceeding. The court may, in its discretion, appoint counsel for the child upon a finding that such appointment is in the best interest of the child. Where State law makes no provision for appointment of counsel in such proceedings, the court shall promptly notify the Secretary upon appointment of counsel, and the Secretary, upon certification of the presiding judge, shall pay reasonable fees and expenses out of funds which may be appropriated pursuant to section 13 of this title.

(c) Examination of reports or other documents.

Each party to a foster care placement or termination of parental rights proceeding under State law involving an Indian child shall have the right to examine all reports or other documents filed with the court upon which any decision with respect to such action may be based.

(d) Remedial services and rehabilitative programs; preventive measures.

Any party seeking to effect a foster care placement of, or termination of parental rights to, an Indian child under State law shall satisfy the court that active efforts have been made to provide remedial services and rehabilitative programs designed to prevent the breakup of the Indian family and that these efforts have proved unsuccessful.

(e) Foster care placement orders; evidence; determination of damage to child.

No foster care placement may be ordered in such proceeding in the absence of a determination, supported by clear and convincing evidence, including testimony of qualified expert witnesses, that the continued custody of the child by the parent or Indian custodian is likely to result in serious emotional or physical damage to the child.

(f) Parental rights termination orders; evidence; determination of damage to child.

No termination of parental rights may be ordered in such proceeding in the absence of a determination, supported by evidence beyond a reasonable doubt, including testimony of qualified expert witnesses, that the continued custody of the child by the parent or Indian custodian is likely to result in serious emotional or physical damage to the child.

Annotations

Cases

Argument that ICWA did not apply to custody dispute between biological mother of Indian child and prospective adoptive parents of child because prospective adoptive parents were members of mother's extended family was rejected. **A.B.M. v. M.H.,** Op. No. 2657, 651 P2d 1170 (Alaska 1982).

Mother's claim that she was denied effective assistance of counsel during proceedings terminating her parental rights was rejected. **V.F. v. State,** Op. No. 2692, 666 P2d 42 (Alaska 1983).

This statute does not require that more than one qualified expert testify in child custody-foster care placement proceedings. **D.A.W. v. State,** Op. No. 2935, 699 P2d 340 (Alaska 1985).

Where emergency intervention hearings are required, notice requirements of this statute are not applicable. **D.E.D. v. State,** Op. No. 2970, 704 P2d 774 (Alaska 1985).

Remand was required due to lack of written findings concerning issue of whether continued custody of child by parents was likely to result in serious emotional or physical damage to child and due to lack of expert testimony on issue. **Matter of D.C.,** Op. No. 3022, 715 P2d 1 (Alaska 1986).

Use of hearsay evidence in disposition phase of parental rights termination proceedings as allowed by state law does not conflict with ICWA. **Matter of J.R.B.,** Op. No. 3029, 715 P2d 1170 (Alaska 1986).

Under the ICWA, trial courts must apply a "beyond a reasonable doubt" standard of proof to findings that continued custody of child by parent or Indian custodian is likely to result in serious emotional or physical damage to child, but need only apply "clear and convincing" standard of proof to findings required by state law that the child is in need of aid as a result of parental conduct and that the harmful parental conduct is likely to continue. **Matter of J.R.B.,** Op. No. 3029, 715 P2d 1170 (Alaska 1986).

Order terminating mother's parental rights to Indian daughter was reversed because she did not receive proper notice of termination proceeding as required by ICWA; state failed to satisfy requirement of notice by registered mail. **Matter of L.A.M.,** Op. No. 3142, 727 P2d 1057 (Alaska 1986).

In case terminating parental rights of Indian mother, mother's claim that trial court erred in accepting as expert witness a person without knowledge of native culture for purpose of determining whether continued custody by mother was likely to result in serious emotional or physical damage to child was rejected. **Matter of Parental Rights of T.O.,** Op. No. 3378,759 P2d 1308 (Alaska 1988).

Standard of proof required to demonstrate that state has satisfied requirement of this statute that active rehabilitative and remedial efforts be made to prevent breakup of Indian family is preponderance of the evidence rather than beyond a reasonable doubt. **K.N. v. State of Alaska,** Op. No. 3980, 856 P2d 468 (Alaska 1993).

Evidence supported conclusion that state made active remedial and rehabilitative efforts required by this statute. **Matter of J.W., W.W. and J.P.W.,** Op. No. 4370, 921 P2d 604 (Alaska 1996).

Neither incarceration nor doubtful prospects for rehabilitation will relieve state of its duty under ICWA to make active remedial efforts. **A.M. v. Alaska,** Op. No. 4886, 945 P2d 296 (Alaska 1997).

Trial court did not err in concluding that state satisfied its duty to make active remedial efforts to prevent termination of incarcerated father's parental rights; efforts included Department of Corrections treatment programs for sexual offenders and for alcohol and drug abuse. **A.M. v. Alaska,** Op. No. 4886, 945 P2d 296 (Alaska 1997).

ICWA was applicable to custody dispute between Indian father and Indian stepfather. **J.W. v. Rj.,** Op. No. 4934, 951 P2d 1206 (Alaska 1998).

In custody dispute between Indian father and Indian stepfather, the "clear and convincing evidence" standard for foster care placement would apply only if Indian stepfather was not "Indian custodian" within meaning of ICWA. **J.W. v. Rj.,** Op. No. 4934, 951 P2d 1206 (Alaska 1998).

A parent as defined by this Act does not include an unwed father if paternity has not been acknowledged or established; thus, until unwed father acknowledged paternity, state was under no obligation under ICWA to make active effort to provide remedial services and rehabilitative programs to prevent termination of his parental rights. **A.A. v. State,** Op. No. 5137, 982 P2d 256 (Alaska 1999).

Length of father's prison sentence was appropriate factor for court to consider in evaluating state's obligation under ICWA to make active effort to provide remedial services to prevent termination of parental rights; father's lengthy sentence justified low level of remedial services provided by state. **A.A. v. State,** Op. No. 5137, 982 P2d 256 (Alaska 1999).

In custody dispute between Indian mother and non-Native, non-parent relatives, exclusion of expert testimony proposed by relatives was error, but error was harmless since testimony, even if credited, could not have led to removal of child from mother's custody given high barriers under ICWA to gaining non-parent custody. **Jordan v. Jordan,** Op. No. 5144, 983 P2d 1258 (Alaska 1999).

By advising mother at temporary custody hearing of her right to counsel and mailing her an application form, trial court complied with minimum requirements of state law and the ICWA, thus failure of trial court to appoint counsel until two months later did not deprive mother of her right to counsel; nevertheless, courts in the future should remain sensitive to potentially drastic consequences of unnecessary delay in appointing counsel in custody cases. **V.D. v. Dept. of Health & Soc. Serv.,** Op. No. 5206, 991 P2d 214 (Alaska 1999).

Record supported trial court's conclusion that state made active remedial and rehabilitative efforts required by this statute but that those efforts proved unsuccessful. **A.H. v. State Dept. of Health & Soc. Services,** Op. No. 5324, 10 P3d 1156 (Alaska 2000).

Record supported trial court's conclusion that continued custody of children by father would likely result in serious emotional and physical damage to children; testimony indicated that father continued to have difficulty in his independent living skills, maintaining sobriety, refraining from domestic violence, and achieving mental stability. **A.H. v. State Dept. of Health & Soc. Services,** Op. No. 5324, 10 P3d 1156 (Alaska 2000).

When there is clear evidence of physical neglect, a trial judge may terminate parental rights without hearing testimony from an expert on Native culture. **L.G. v. State Dept. of Health and Social Services,** Op. No. 5349, 14 P3d 946 (Alaska 2000).

Substantial evidence supported trial court's conclusion that children would suffer serious emotional harm if returned to mother. **L.G. v. State Dept. of Health and Social Services,** Op. No. 5349, 14 P3d 946 (Alaska 2000).

Because the state did not produce evidence beyond a reasonable doubt that placement of children with their father was likely to result in serious emotional or physical damage to the children, and because the state did not make active efforts to reunify the father with his children, trial court's termination of the father's parental rights was reversed; evidence against father, who lived in Florida, was too limited, consisting primarily of two letters from Florida caseworkers, and conclusions of state's expert were little more than generalizations about the harms resulting from a parent's absence and provided little discussion of the particular facts of the case. **C.J. v. Dept. of Health and Social Services,** Op. No. 5372, 18 P3d 1214 (Alaska 2001).

Trial court correctly determined that state made active efforts to provide remedial services and rehabilitative programs designed to prevent the termination of mother's parental rights as required by ICWA. **N.A. v. State,** Op. No. 5374, 19 P3d 597 (Alaska 2001).

Whether the state has complied with the active efforts requirement under subsection (d) of this section is a mixed question of law and fact. **Gilbert M. v. State,** Op. No. 11364, 139 P.3d 581 (Alaska 2006).

Alaska courts liberally construe statutes enacted for the benefit of Indians, resolving all doubts in favor of the Indians. **In re Adoption of Erin G,** Op. No. 11929, 140 P.3d 886, (Alaska 2006).

§ 1913. Parental rights, voluntary termination.

(a) Consent; record; certification matters; invalid consents.

Where any parent or Indian custodian voluntarily consents to a foster care placement or to termination of parental rights, such consent shall not be valid unless executed in writing and recorded before a judge of a court of competent jurisdiction and accompanied by the presiding judge's certificate that the terms and consequences of the consent were fully explained in detail and were fully understood by the parent or Indian custodian. The court shall also certify that either the parent or

Indian custodian fully understood the explanation in English or that it was interpreted into a language that the parent or Indian custodian understood. Any consent given prior to, or within ten days after, birth of the Indian child shall not be valid.

(b) Foster care placement; withdrawal of consent.

Any parent or Indian custodian may withdraw consent to a foster care placement under State law at any time and, upon such withdrawal, the child shall be returned to the parent or Indian custodian.

(c) Voluntary termination of parental rights or adoptive placement; withdrawal of consent; return of custody.

In any voluntary proceeding for termination of parental rights to, or adoptive placement of, an Indian child, the consent of the parent may be withdrawn for any reason at any time prior to the entry of a final degree of termination or adoption, as the case may be, and the child shall be returned to the parent.

(d) Collateral attack; vacation of decree and return of custody; limitations.

After the entry of a final decree of adoption of an Indian child in any State court, the parent may withdraw consent thereto upon the grounds that consent was obtained through fraud or duress and may petition the court to vacate such decree. Upon a finding that such consent was obtained through fraud or duress, the court shall vacate such decree and return the child to the parent. No adoption which has been effective for at least two years may be invalidated under the provisions of this subsection unless otherwise permitted under State law.

Annotations

Cases

This statute does not allow parent to withdraw voluntary relinquishment of parental rights after final order terminating those rights has been entered. **Matter of J.R.S.,** Op. No. 2869, 690 P2d 10 (Alaska 1984).

ICWA incorporates state statutes of limitation except in challenges based on fraud or duress, which are governed by two-year statute of limitations contained in ICWA. **Matter of Adoption of T.N.F.,** Op. No. 3524, 781 P2d 973 (Alaska 1989).

Indian Child Welfare Act does not entitle an Indian child's tribe to notice of a proceeding for voluntary termination of parental rights. **Catholic Social Services, Inc. v C.A.A.,** Op. No. 3534, 783 P2d 1159 (Alaska 1989).

Although Indian mother voluntarily signed a relinquishment of her parental rights in 1981, after which father was given custody of child, neither father nor state sought a final termination of mother's rights and no order giving father formal custody was ever issued by any court, thus mother was permitted under this statute to withdraw her relinquishment in 1989. **Harvick v. Harvick,** Op. No. 3828, 828 P2d 769 (Alaska 1992).

Alaska courts liberally construe statutes enacted for the benefit of Indians, resolving all doubts in favor of the Indians. **In re Adoption of Erin G,** Op. No. 11929, 140 P.3d 886, (Alaska 2006).

§ 1914. Petition to court of competent jurisdiction to invalidate action upon showing of certain violations.

Any Indian child who is the subject of any action for foster care placement or termination of parental rights under State law, any parent or Indian custodian from whose custody such child was removed, and the Indian child's tribe may petition any court of competent jurisdiction to invalidate such action upon a showing that such action violated any provision of sections 1911, 1912, and 1913 of this title.

Annotations

Cases

ICWA incorporates state statutes of limitation except in challenges based on fraud or duress, which are governed by two-year statute of limitations contained in ICWA. **Matter of Adoption of T.N.F.,** Op. No. 3524,781 P2d 973 (Alaska 1989).

One-year statute of limitations contained in AS 25.23.140(b) barred biological mother's action to vacate adoption decree concerning Indian child. **Matter of Adoption of T.N.F.,** Op. No. 3524, 781 P2d 973 (Alaska 1989).

Alaska's one-year statute of limitations provides an appropriate balance between the important federal rights of Indian tribes and families and the best interests of adopted children, so that statute applies to custody actions under Section 1914 of ICWA. **In re Adoption of Erin G,** Op. No. 11929, 140 P.3d 886, (Alaska 2006).

§ 1915. Placement of Indian children.

(a) Adoptive placements; preferences.

In any adoptive placement of an Indian child under State law, a preference shall be given, in the absence of good cause to the contrary, to a placement with (1) a member of the child's extended family; (2) other members of the Indian child's tribe; or (3) other Indian families.

(b) Foster care or preadoptive placements; criteria; preferences.

Any child accepted for foster care or preadoptive placement shall be placed in the least restrictive setting which most approximates a family and in which his special needs, if any, may be met. The child shall also be placed within reasonable proximity to his or her home, taking into account any special needs of the child. In any foster care or preadoptive placement, a preference shall be given, in the absence of good cause to the contrary, to a placement with—

(i) a member of the Indian child's extended family;

(ii) a foster home licensed, approved, or specified by the Indian child's tribe;

(iii) an Indian foster home licensed or approved by an authorized non-Indian licensing authority; or

(iv) an institution for children approved by an Indian tribe or operated by an Indian organization which has a program suitable to meet the Indian child's needs.

(c) Tribal resolution for different order of preference; personal preference considered; anonymity in application of preferences.

In the case of a placement under subsection (a) or (b) of this section, if the Indian child's tribe shall establish a different order of preference by resolution, the agency or court effecting the placement shall follow such order so long as the placement is the least restrictive setting appropriate to the particular needs of the child, as provided in subsection (b) of this section. Where appropriate, the preference of the Indian child or parent shall be considered: Provided, That where a consenting parent evidences a desire for anonymity, the court or agency shall give weight to such desire in applying the preferences.

(d) Social and cultural standards applicable.

The standards to be applied in meeting the preference requirements of this section shall be the prevailing social and cultural standards of the Indian community in which the parent or extended family resides or with which the parent or extended family members maintain social and cultural ties.

(e) Record of placement; availability.

A record of each such placement, under State law, of an Indian child shall be maintained by the State in which the placement was made, evidencing the efforts to comply with the order of preference specified in this section. Such record shall be made available at any time upon the request of the Secretary or the Indian child's tribe.

Annotations

Cases

Where Indian child's village was not allowed to intervene in adoption hearing, trial court's decision, agreed to by all participants at the hearing, to set aside the placement preferences of the ICWA was invalid. **Matter of J.R.S.,** Op. No. 2869, 690 P2d 10 (Alaska 1984).

Courts may consider parental preferences when determining whether there is good cause to deviate from ICWA preferences. **Matter of Adoption of F.H.,** Op. No. 3956, 851 P2d 1361 (Alaska 1993).

Trial court did not abuse its discretion in finding good cause to place Indian child with non-Indian family rather than Indian relative. **Matter of Adoption of F.H.,** Op. No. 3956, 851 P2d 1361 (Alaska 1993).

In custody dispute over Indian child between Indian grandmother and non-Indian friend of child's deceased mother, trial court did not abuse its discretion in granting non-Indian friend's petition to adopt child, particularly since mother's will clearly stated that she desired friend to have custody. **Adoption of N.P.S.,** Op. No. 4057, 868 P2d 934 (Alaska 1994).

Trial court had good cause to deviate from ICWA's placement preferences in placing child with her current foster mother rather than with grandmother or with a foster mother approved by child's tribe. **L.G. v. State Dept. of Health and Social Services,** Op. No. 5349, 14 P3d 946 (Alaska 2000).

In finding good cause for deviating from the ICWA placement preferences, trial court did not err by relying on a broad range of factors, including the Bureau of Indian Affairs guidelines, and by primarily stressing the child's best interests. **C.L. v. P.C.S.,** Op. No. 5360, 17 P3d 769 (Alaska 2001).

Trial court did not err in holding that child's second cousin once removed by marriage was a member of the child's extended family with adoption preference rights under ICWA nor in awarding adoption of child to the second cousin once removed rather than the child's maternal grandparents based upon its assessment of the best interests of the child. **C.L. v. P.C.S.,** Op. No. 5360, 17 P3d 769 (Alaska 2001).

Alaska courts liberally construe statutes enacted for the benefit of Indians, resolving all doubts in favor of the Indians. **In re Adoption of Erin G,** Op. No. 11929, 140 P.3d 886, (Alaska 2006).

§ 1916. Return of custody.

(a) Petition; best interests of child.

Notwithstanding State law to the contrary, whenever a final decree of adoption of an Indian child has been vacated or set aside or the adoptive parents voluntarily consent to the termination of their parental rights to the child, a biological parent or prior Indian custodian may petition for return of custody and the court shall grant such petition unless there is a showing, in a proceeding subject to the provisions of section 1912 of this title, that such return of custody is not in the best interests of the child.

(b) Removal from foster care home; placement procedure.

Whenever an Indian child is removed from a foster care home or institution for the purpose of further foster care, preadoptive, or adoptive placement, such placement shall be in accordance with the provisions of this chapter, except in the case where an Indian child is being returned to the parent or Indian custodian from whose custody the child was originally removed.

Annotations

Cases

Provision of 25 U.S.C. § 1916, providing that whenever a final decree of adoption of an Indian child has been vacated or set aside a biological parent or prior Indian custodian may petition for return of custody, makes clear that protections of ICWA were not intended to apply to prospective adoptive parents against whom an adoption decree was vacated when the natural parent is seeking custody. **A.B.M. v. M.H.,** Op. No. 2657, 651 P2d 1170 (Alaska 1982).

§ 1917. Tribal affiliation information and other information for protection of rights from tribal relationship; application of subject of adoptive placement; disclosure by court.

Upon application by an Indian individual who has reached the age of eighteen and who was the subject of an adoptive placement, the court which entered the final decree shall inform such individual of the tribal affiliation, if any, of the individual's biological parents and provide such other information as may be necessary to protect any rights flowing from the individual's tribal relationship.

§ 1918. Reassumption of jurisdiction over child custody proceedings.

(a) Petition; suitable plan; approval by Secretary.

Any Indian tribe which became subject to State jurisdiction pursuant to the provisions of the Act of August 15, 1953 (67 Stat. 588), as amended by Title IV of the Act of April 11, 1968 (82 Stat. 73, 78), or pursuant to any other Federal law, may reassume jurisdiction over child custody proceedings. Before any Indian tribe may reassume jurisdiction over Indian child custody proceedings, such tribe shall present to the Secretary for approval a petition to reassume such jurisdiction which includes a suitable plan to exercise such jurisdiction.

(b) Criteria applicable to consideration by Secretary; partial retrocession.

(1) In considering the petition and feasibility of the plan of a tribe under subsection (a) of this section, the Secretary may consider, among other things:

(i) whether or not the tribe maintains a membership roll or alternative provision for clearly identifying the persons who will be affected by the reassumption of jurisdiction by the tribe;

(ii) the size of the reservation or former reservation area which will be affected by retrocession and reassumption of jurisdiction by the tribe;

(iii) the population base of the tribe, or distribution of the population in homogeneous communities or geographic areas; and

(iv) the feasibility of the plan in cases of multitribal occupation of a single reservation or geographic area.

(2) In those cases where the Secretary determines that the jurisdictional provisions of section 1911(a) of this title are not feasible, he is authorized to accept partial retrocession which will enable tribes to exercise referral jurisdiction as provided in section 1911(b) of this title, or, where appropriate, will allow them to exercise exclusive jurisdiction as provided in section 1911(a) of this title over limited community or geographic areas without regard for the reservation status of the area affected.

(c) Approval of petition; publication in Federal Register; notice; reassumption period; correction of causes for disapproval.

If the Secretary approves any petition under subsection (a) of this section, the Secretary shall publish notice of such approval in the Federal Register and shall notify the affected State or States of such approval. The Indian tribe concerned shall reassume jurisdiction sixty days after publication in the Federal Register of notice of approval. If the Secretary disapproves any petition under subsection (a) of this section, the Secretary shall provide such technical assistance as may be necessary to enable the tribe to correct any deficiency which the Secretary identified as a cause for disapproval.

(d) Pending actions or proceedings unaffected.

Assumption of jurisdiction under this section shall not affect any action or proceeding over which a court has already assumed jurisdiction, except as may be provided pursuant to any agreement under section 1919 of this title.

Annotations

Cases

State of Alaska has exclusive jurisdiction over matters involving the custody of Indian children and exercises such jurisdiction until a particular tribe petitions to reassume jurisdiction and the Secretary of the Interior approves the petition. **Native Village of Nenana v. Dept. of Health,** Op. No. 3082, 722 P2d 219 (Alaska 1986).

Tribe must present a petition to Secretary of the Interior that includes a suitable plan for dealing with custody matters before it may reassume jurisdiction over Indian child custody proceedings, whether child resides or is domiciled with the tribe or lives elsewhere. **Matter of K.E.,** Op. No. 3242, 744 P2d 1173 (Alaska 1987).

State of Alaska is required to give full faith and credit to adoption decrees issued by the tribal courts of native villages if the village is the modern-day successor to an historical sovereign band of native Americans. **Native Village of Venetie I.R.A. Council v. Alaska,** 944 F.2d 548 (9th Cir. 1991).

In the case of Indian children who reside on their tribal reservation, jurisdiction over child custody disputes resides exclusively in the tribe; in the case of Indian children who do not reside or are not domiciled on their tribe's reservation, state courts may exercise jurisdiction concurrent with tribal courts, but the state court must refer the dispute to the appropriate tribal court unless good cause is shown for the retention of state court jurisdiction. **Native Village of Venetie I.R.A. Council v. Alaska,** 944 F.2d 548 (9th Cir. 1991).

Where Native Village of Circle had not successfully petitioned the Secretary of the Interior to reassume jurisdiction over Indian child custody matter, village had no jurisdiction over the matter. **In re F.P.,** Op. No. 3906, 843 P2d 1214 (Alaska 1992).

§ 1919. Agreements between States and Indian tribes.

(a) Subject coverage.

States and Indian tribes are authorized to enter into agreements with each other respecting care and custody of Indian children and jurisdiction over child custody proceedings, including agreements which may provide for orderly transfer of jurisdiction on a case-by-case basis and agreements which provide for concurrent jurisdiction between States and Indian tribes.

(b) Revocation; notice; actions or proceedings unaffected.

Such agreements may be revoked by either party upon one hundred and eighty days' written notice to the other party. Such revocation shall not affect any action or proceeding over which a court has already assumed jurisdiction, unless the agreement provides otherwise.

§ 1920. Improper removal of child from custody; declination of jurisdiction; forthwith return of child: danger exception.

Where any petitioner in an Indian child custody proceeding before a State court has improperly removed the child from custody of the parent or Indian custodian or has improperly retained custody after a visit or other temporary relinquishment of custody, the court shall decline jurisdiction over such petition and shall forthwith return the child to his parent or Indian custodian unless returning the child to his parent or custodian would subject the child to a substantial and immediate danger or threat of such danger.

§ 1921. Higher State or Federal standard applicable to protect rights of parent or Indian custodian of Indian child.

In any case where State or Federal law applicable to a child custody proceeding under State or Federal law provides a higher standard of protection to the rights of the parent or Indian custodian of an Indian child than that rights provided under this subchapter, the State or Federal court shall apply the State or Federal standard.

§ 1922. Emergency removal or placement of child; termination; appropriate action.

Nothing in this subchapter shall be construed to prevent the emergency removal of an Indian child who is a resident of or is domiciled on a reservation but temporarily located off the reservation, from his parent or Indian custodian or the emergency placement of such child in a foster home or institution, under applicable State law, in order to prevent imminent physical damage or harm to the child. The State authority, official, or agency involved shall insure that the emergency removal or placement terminates immediately when such removal or placement is no longer necessary to prevent imminent physical damage or harm to the child and shall expeditiously initiate a child custody proceeding subject to the provisions of this subchapter, transfer the child to the jurisdiction of the appropriate Indian tribe, or restore the child to the parent or Indian custodian, as may be appropriate.

§ 1923. Effective date.

None of the provisions of this subchapter, except sections 1911(a), 1918, and 1919 of this title, shall affect a proceeding under State law for foster care placement, termination of parental rights, preadoptive placement, or adoptive placement which was initiated or completed prior to one hundred and eighty days after November 8, 1978, but shall apply to any subsequent proceeding in the same matter or subsequent proceedings affecting the custody or placement of the same child.

§ 1951. Information availability to and disclosure by Secretary.

(a) Copy of final decree or order, other information; anonymity affidavit; exemption from Freedom of Information Act.

Any State court entering a final decree or order in any Indian child adoptive placement after November 8, 1978, shall provide the Secretary with a copy of such decree or order together with such other information as may be necessary to show—

(1) the name and tribal affiliation of the child;

(2) the names and addresses of the biological parents;

(3) the names and addresses of the adoptive parents; and

(4) the identity of any agency having files or information relating to such adoptive placement.

Where the court records contain an affidavit of the biological parent or parents that their identity remain confidential, the court shall include such affidavit with the other information. The Secretary shall insure that the confidentiality of such information is maintained and such information shall not be subject to the Freedom of Information Act (5 U.S.C. 552), as amended. (b) Disclosure of information for enrollment of Indian child in tribe or for determination of member rights or benefits; certification of entitlement to enrollment.

Upon the request of the adopted Indian child over the age of eighteen, the adoptive or foster parents of an Indian child, or an Indian tribe, the Secretary shall disclose such information as may be necessary for the enrollment of an Indian child in the tribe in which the child may be eligible for enrollment or for determining any rights or benefits associated with that membership. Where the documents relating to such child contain an affidavit from the biological parent or parents requesting anonymity, the Secretary shall certify to the Indian child's tribe, where the information warrants, that the child's parentage and other circumstances of birth entitle the child to enrollment under the criteria established by such tribe.

(Pub. L. 95-608. Title III. § 301, Nov. 8, 1978, 92 Stat. 3077).

CROSS REFERENCES FROM DELINQUENCY AND CINA RULES TO PRIOR CHILDREN'S RULES

Delinquency Rules	Children's Rules	CINA Rules	Children's Rules
1	1, 32	1	1, 32
2	---	2	---
3	12, 13	3	12, 13
4	2	4	2
5	2	5	5
6	4	6	5, 6
7	6, 7	7	8, 10
8	8, 10	8	20
9	20	9	13, 17
10	17	10	7
11	21	11	11
12	7	12	11, 14, 15
13	27	13	---
14	12	14	---
15	11	15	12
16	11, 14, 15	16	---
17	---	17	22
18	---	18	22
19	---	19	28
20	3	20	---
21	12	21	29
22	---	22	---
3	22		
24	---		
25	28		
26	29		
27	---		

DELINQUENCY RULES

Table of Contents

PART I. GENERAL PROVISIONS

PART II. MASTERS, MAGISTRATES, DISTRICT COURT JUDGES

DR

PART III. INTAKE, COMMENCEMENT OF PROCEEDINGS

PART IV. DISCOVERY, EVIDENCE, PROOF

PART V. PRELIMINARY PROCEEDINGS

PART VI. WAIVER OF JUVENILE JURISDICTION

PART VII. ADJUDICATION

DR

PART VIII. DISPOSITION

PART IX. APPEAL AND PETITION FOR REVIEW

PART X. COURT ADMINISTRATION OF JUVENILE RECORDS

PART I. GENERAL PROVISIONS

Rule 1. Title—Scope—Construction—Situations Not Covered by the Rules.

(a) **Title.** These rules will be known and cited as the Delinquency Rules.

(b) **Scope.** These rules govern practice and procedure in the trial courts in all phases of delinquency proceedings brought under AS 47.12.020.

(c) **Construction.** These rules will be construed and applied to promote fairness; accurate fact-finding; expeditious determination of juvenile matters; the best interests of the juvenile, including individualized care and treatment in the least restrictive placement, and the preservation of the juvenile's family life; and protection of the public.

(d) **Legal Effect of Rules.** These rules are promulgated pursuant to Alaska constitutional authority granting rulemaking power to the Alaska supreme court. To the extent that the rules are inconsistent with a procedural provision of any Alaska statute not enacted for the specific purpose of changing a rule, these rules supersede the statute to the extent of the inconsistency.

(e) **Criminal Rules Applicable.** Criminal Rules 17, 18–20, 24, 25, 27–31, 36, 40, 42, 43(a), 44, 46, 47, 50 and 53 apply to delinquency proceedings except to the extent that any provisions of these criminal rules conflict with the Delinquency Rules.

(f) **Situations Not Covered by These Rules.** If these rules do not prescribe a specific procedure, the court may proceed in any lawful manner, including application of the Civil or Criminal Rules, applicable statutes, the Alaska and United States Constitutions or the common law. Such a procedure may not be inconsistent with these rules and may not unduly delay or otherwise interfere with the unique character and purpose of delinquency proceedings.

(SCO 845 effective August 15, 1987; amended by SCO 1104 effective July 9, 1992; and by SCO 1265 effective July 15, 1997)

Cross References

CROSS REFERENCE: AS 22.10.020; AS 22.15.100(8); AS 47.05.060; AS 47.12.140; Alaska Constitution, Art. IV.

Annotations

Cases

This annotation construes former Children's Rule 1. Children are constitutionally entitled to a jury trial in the adjudicative stage of a delinquency proceeding, but the child should first consult with his counsel and his parents, or guardian when appropriate, and then affirmatively assert his right to trial by jury before it is finally granted. **RLR v. State,** Op. No. 706,487 P2d 27 (Alaska 1971).

This annotation construes former Children's Rule 1. If a child waives jury trial in a juvenile proceeding, the state may not require it, but a jury trial shall be provided only on demand. **RLR v. State,** Op. No. 706, 487 P2d 27 (Alaska 1971).

This annotation construes former Children's Rule 1. Errors in a juvenile proceeding not affecting substantial right will be disregarded. **RLR v. State,** Op. No. 706, 487 P2d 27 (Alaska 1971).

This annotation construes former Children's Rule 1. Superior court does not have authority to award costs and fees in a child in need of aid proceeding. **Cooper v. State,** Op. No. 2453, 638 P2d 174 (Alaska 1981).

This annotation construes former Children's Rule 1. The use of hearsay evidence in the disposition phase of a parental right termination proceeding as allowed by state law did not conflict with the federal Indian Child Welfare Act. **Matter of J.R.B.,** Op. No. 3029, 715 P2d 1170 (Alaska 1986).

Superior court did not have authority to set aside valid delinquency adjudication after statutory time limit on court's jurisdiction over case had expired. **State v. T.M.,** Op. No. 1322, 860 P.2d 1286 (Alaska Ct. App. 1993).

Rule 2. Definitions.

(a) "Adjudication Hearing" is the proceeding, analogous to the trial in a criminal case, in which the court or a jury determines whether the juvenile is a delinquent minor as a result of the minor's violation of a criminal law of the state or a municipality.

(b) "Admit Plea" is a plea, analogous to a guilty plea in a criminal case, by which the juvenile admits committing acts constituting delinquent conduct under AS 47.12.020.

(c) "Arraignment on Petition" is a proceeding, analogous to an arraignment in a criminal case, in which the court advises the juvenile and other parties of their rights and asks the juvenile to enter a plea.

(d) "The Department" means the Department of Health and Social Services of the State of Alaska.

(e) "Deny Plea" is a plea, analogous to a not guilty plea in a criminal case, by which the juvenile requires the state to prove the allegations of the petition for adjudication in the adjudication hearing.

(f) "Detention" means holding in a locked or secure facility.

(g) "Disposition Hearing" is a proceed-ing, analogous to a sentencing hearing in a criminal case, in which the court determines the appropriate disposition of a juvenile who has been adjudicated a delinquent.

(h) "Guardian" means a legally appointed guardian of the person of the minor.

(i) "Guardian Ad Litem" means a person appointed by the court to represent the best interests of the juvenile in the delinquency proceeding as distinguished from a guardian of the person as defined in paragraph (h).

(j) "Intake Officer" means a person assigned by the Department to perform intake functions as defined by these rules.

(k) "Juvenile" means a person under eighteen years of age at the time of the alleged delinquent conduct who remains subject to the jurisdiction of the court.

(l) "Minor" means a person under eighteen years of age, as defined by AS 25.20.010.

(m) "Parent" means a natural or adoptive parent.

(n) "Party" means the juvenile, the guardian ad litem, the juvenile's parents or guardian, and the Department.

(o) "Petition for Adjudication" is a document which formally begins a delinquency proceeding and which brings the juvenile under the jurisdiction of the court.

(p) "Probation" means releasing the juvenile into the community subject to conditions set by the court and under the supervision of a probation officer.

(q) "Temporary Detention Hearing" is a proceeding in which the court determines the conditions concerning placement of the juvenile pending the adjudication and disposition hearings.

(SCO 845 effective August 15, 1987; amended by SCO 1265 effective July 15, 1997)

Note: Chapter 70 SLA 2005 (SB 154) enacted changes concerning proceedings relating to delinquent minors. According to section 10 of the Act, the changes made by sections 1-8 of the Act have the effect of amending Delinquency Rule 2(n) by requiring the court to conform the rule to the statutory changes to acknowledge the inclusion of certain persons 18 years of age or over as minors under AS 47.12 and AS 47.14 and to acknowledge the special statutory provisions contained in sections 1-8 of the Act applicable to those persons.

Cross References

CROSS REFERENCE: AS 47.12.120(b), AS 47.12.150, AS 47.12.220, AS 47.20.290, AS 25.20.010.

Rule 3. Hearings.

(a) **Notice.** Notice of each hearing must be given to all parties and to any foster parent within a reasonable time before the hearing. Notice to the foster parent must be provided by the Department.

(b) **Presence of Juvenile and Other Parties.** The presence of the juvenile is required unless the juvenile:

(1) waives the right to be present and the juvenile's presence is excused by the court; or

(2) engages in conduct which justifies exclusion from the courtroom.

The presence of the parent or guardian is required unless excused by the court for good cause.

(c) **Admission to Hearings.** The court in all cases shall admit victims of the juvenile's offense to hearings as required by AS 47.12 and shall admit foster parents to hearings subject to paragraph (d) of this rule. The court has discretion in all cases to admit other specific individuals to a hearing if their attendance is compatible with the best interests of the juvenile. Hearings are open to the general public if:

(1) requested by the juvenile;

(2) the court orders the hearing open to the public pursuant to a request by the department under AS 47.12.110(d)(1); or

(3) the juvenile is subject to dual sentencing. In such cases, hearings are open to the general public, unless otherwise limited or prohibited by court order, if (A) a petition has been filed under AS 47.12.065 and the grand jury has returned an indictment or the juvenile has waived indictment; or (B) the juvenile has agreed as part of a plea agreement to be subject to dual sentencing.

(d) **Exclusion of Witnesses.** Witnesses may be excluded from a hearing pursuant to Evidence Rule 615.

(e) **Telephonic and Televised Participation.**

(1) The juvenile has the right to be physically present in court for arraignment, adjudication, disposition, probation revocation, extension of jurisdiction, and waiver of jurisdiction hearings; however, the juvenile may waive the right to be present. At all other hearings, the court, upon application of any party, may allow telephonic participation by the juvenile if the juvenile's personal appearance is not essential to the fair disposition of the matter, telephonic participation is not unfair to the juvenile, and personal contact between counsel and the juvenile is not needed for case preparation. The court has discretion to allow telephonic participation by other parties. The juvenile's waiver of the right to be physically present may be obtained orally on the record or in writing.

(2) The court may allow telephonic participation of witnesses only upon stipulation of the juvenile and the Department, except that the court may allow telephonic participation of witnesses without the consent of the parties at disposition, disposition review or temporary detention hearings.

(3) In those court locations in which a television system has been approved by the supreme court and has been installed, juveniles in custody may appear by way of television with the consent of the juvenile and with the approval of the court for hearings in which the juvenile has a right to be physically present under (1) of this section. If the court has allowed telephonic participation by the juvenile in a hearing, participation may also be by television. Appearance by television or telephone shall not be allowed at adjudication trials or at any hearings in which sworn testimony is to be presented.

(f) **Testimony Under Oath.** All testimony must be given under oath or affirmation as required by Evidence Rule 603.

(g) **Representation by Non-Attorney.** A guardian ad litem need not be represented by an attorney unless the court, for good cause, requires representation by an attorney.

(SCO 845 effective August 15, 1987; amended by SCO 998 effective January 15, 1990; by SCO 1092 effective July 15, 1992; by SCO 1165 effective July 15, 1994; by SCO 1265 effective July 15, 1997; by SCO 1269 effective July 15, 1997; by SCO 1294 effective January 15, 1998; by SCO 1349 effective December 1, 1998; by SCO 1361 effective October 15, 1999; and by SCO 1582 effective nunc pro tunc to July 14, 2005)

Note: Paragraph (c) was amended by ch. 57, § 21, SLA 1991.

Note to SCO 1269: Delinquency Rule 3(b)(2) was amended by § 5 ch. 144 SLA 1996. Section 23 of this order is adopted for the sole reason that the legislature has mandated the amendment.

Note: Chapter 70 SLA 2005 (SB 154) enacted changes concerning proceedings relating to delinquent minors. According to section 10 of the Act, the changes made by sections 1-8 of the Act have the effect of amending Delinquency Rule 3(b) and (c) by requiring the court to conform the rule to the statutory changes to acknowledge the inclusion of certain persons 18 years of age or over as minors under AS 47.12 and AS 47.14 and to acknowledge the special statutory provisions contained in sections 1-8 of the Act applicable to those persons.

Cross References

CROSS REFERENCE: AS 47.12.110.

Annotations

Cases

This annotation construes former Children's Rule 12. If, following criminal proceedings, collateral legal disabilities exist apart from the sentence, an appeal is not mooted even though the sentence has already been served. **E.J. v. State,** Op. No. 628, 471 P2d 367 (Alaska 1970).

This annotation construes former Children's Rule 12. Where a child has been declared delinquent without the necessary compliance with statutory and constitutional procedural standards, such child has been deprived of his constitutional rights. If any attendant collateral disabilities remain, the proceedings which were infected with those disabilities cannot stand. **E.J. v. State,** Op. No. 628, 471 P2d 367 (Alaska 1970).

This annotation construes former Children's Rule 12. The provision of this rule providing for closed proceedings must be interpreted and applied in a manner consistent with the child's right to a public trial. **RLR v. State,** Op. No. 706, 487 P2d 27 (Alaska 1971).

This annotation construes former Children's Rule 12. If a child or his guardian ad litem wants the press, friends or others to be free to attend juvenile proceedings, the hearing must be open to them. The court's areas of discretion within which it may refuse to open a hearing involves persons whose presence is not desired by the child. **RLR v. State,** Op. No. 706,487 P2d 27 (Alaska 1971).

This annotation construes former Children's Rule 12. Superior court did not abuse its discretion in permitting two relatives of murder victims to attend a juvenile waiver hearing held to determine whether juvenile could be tried as an adult for the murders. **W.M.F. v. Jonstone,** Op. No. 571, 711 P2d 1187 (Alaska App. 1986).

This annotation construes former Children's Rule 12. A hearing in which a chemist testifies that a tablet sent to him for analysis contains LSD should not be conducted in the absence of the infant involved after the attorney explicitly refuses to waive the infant's right to be present. Conducting a hearing in the child's absence under such circumstances is reversible error. **RLR v. State,** Op. No. 706, 487 P2d 27 (Alaska 1971).

This annotation construes former Children's Rule 12. Notions of benevolent protective policies for children cannot be used to validate departures from positive law relating to adjudicative and dispositive phases of children's proceedings. **In re E.M.D.,** Op. No. 737, 490 P2d 658 (Alaska 197 1).

This annotation construes former Children's Rule 13. Considering the importance of juvenile proceedings and the fact that juvenile records are easily obtained and can have serious effects upon the life of a minor, the usual principles against entertaining moot controversies do not apply. Where a 12-year old boy has been determined to be delinquent, an appeal of that delinquency order will be considered, notwithstanding that the order has been vacated. **Ej. v. State,** Op. No. 628, 471 P2d 367 (Alaska 1970).

This annotation construes former Children's Rule 13. Due process requires that detention orders be based on competent, sworn testimony. A child has a right to be represented by counsel at a detention inquiry. Any detention order must state with particularity the facts supporting it. **Doe v. State,** Op. No. 707, 487 P2d 47 (Alaska 1971).

This annotation construes former Children's Rule 13. A detention order based on unsworn hearsay of the district attorney, further based on the court's belief's unsupported by any evidence that the child will engage in unlawful activity if not detained, and containing no facts on which it is based, is invalid. **Doe v. State,** Op. No. 707, 487 P2d 47 (Alaska 1971).

This annotation construes former Children's Rule 12. A child has a vital interest in a dependency proceeding and is an essential party whose presence cannot be dispensed with arbitrarily; in a dependency proceeding the summons and a copy of the petition must be served on the child as well as the parents; failure to make such service results in lack of jurisdiction over the child. **In re P.N.,** Op. No. 1127, 523 P2d 13 (Alaska 1975).

This annotation construes former Children's Rule 12. Where the children are not given the required notice of a dependency hearing the superior court has no jurisdiction over them and, therefore, cannot validly issue a judgment depriving a parent of his custody. **In re P.N.,** Op. No. 1127, 523 P2d 13 (Alaska 1975).

This annotation construes former Children's Rule 12. A court in a "child in need of supervision" hearing is under a duty to explain to the juvenile his right to counsel. **Wagstaff v. Superior Court, Family Court Division,** Op. No. 1144, 535 P2d 1220 (Alaska 1975).

This annotation construes former Children's Rule 12. In the adjudicative phase of any children's proceeding, the family court may consider only the specific situations set out in the petition. **In re S.D. Jr.,** Op. No. 1255, 549 P2d 1190 (Alaska 1976).

This annotation construes former Children's Rule 12. Court committed error when it commenced the adjudicative phase of the parental rights termination hearing in the absence of the child's counsel and guardian ad litem. **Matter of C.L.T.,** Op. No. 1866, 597 P2d 518 (Alaska 1979).

This annotation construes former Children's Rule 12. Superior court did not abuse its discretion in permitting two relatives of murder victims to attend a juvenile waiver hearing held to determine whether juvenile could be tried as an adult for the murders. **W.M.F. v. Jonstone,** Op. No. 571, 711 P2d 1187 (Alaska App. 1986).

PART II. MASTERS, MAGISTRATES, DISTRICT COURT JUDGES

Rule 4. Appointment and Authority of Masters.

(a) **Appointment.** The presiding judge may appoint a standing master to conduct any or all of the delinquency proceedings listed in subparagraph (b)(2). Appointments of standing masters must be reviewed annually. The presiding judge may appoint a special master to conduct a proceeding which is specified in the order of reference and is listed in subparagraph (b)(2).

(b) **Authority, Order of Reference.**

(1) An order of reference specifying the extent of the master's authority and the type of appointment must be entered in every case assigned to a master. The order of reference must be served on all parties.

(2) The following proceedings may be referred to a master:

(A) temporary detention and arraignment proceedings;

(B) interim hearings, including detention review, change of plea and pre-trial conferences;

(C) non-jury adjudication hearings and disposition hearings resulting from a non-jury adjudication, provided all parties stipulate to both hearings before the master;

(D) disposition following an admit plea, post-disposition review, probation revocation and extension of custody hearings.

(3) A master's report is not binding until approved by a superior court judge pursuant to Civil Rule 53(d) and paragraph (f) of this rule, except:

(A) a master may enter orders without further approval of the superior court pursuant to Civil Rule 53(b) and (c), and by paragraph (d) of this rule; and

(B) a master's order of detention or placement outside the home is effective pending superior court review.

(c) **Objection to Reference to a Master.** The prosecution and the defense are entitled as a matter of right to a change of one judge and one master pursuant to the procedures stated in Criminal Rule 25(d). In addition, a party may file an objection to a case or proceeding being referred to a master in the following manner:

(1) *Timeliness.* A party may file an objection no later than five days after receiving notice of the order of reference.

(2) *Grounds for Objection.* An objection to the assignment of a master to hear a probation revocation hearing or an extension of custody hearing under Delinquent Rules 24 and 25(c) will be granted as a matter of right. Any other objection must set forth sufficient grounds from which the court may determine whether good cause exists to remove the matter from the master's jurisdiction. Good cause may include involvement of (i) complex questions of law which require a decision by a superior court judge or (ii) questions requiring prompt resolution which would be seriously impaired by a reference to a master.

(d) **Standing Master's Authority to Enter Orders.** A standing master is authorized to take the following actions without further approval by a superior court judge:

(1) issue an arrest warrant;

(2) appoint counsel or a guardian ad litem for the juvenile;

(3) order home studies, predisposition reports, and psychological or psychiatric evaluations;

(4) set hearings and order continuances of hearings held before the master;

(5) decide motions requesting expedited review pursuant to Civil Rule 77(i);

(6) accept and approve stipulations, except that stipulated adjudications or dispositions must be reviewed by a superior court judge;

(7) review and approve uncontested orders on annual review under Delinquency Rule 25(a);

(8) order release from detention and set conditions of release pursuant to Delinquency Rule 12(c); and

(9) order conditions of probation for minors placed on probation or released from institutionalization.

(e) **Master's Report, Recommendations.** A master may issue a written report or oral findings on the record concerning an order or recommendation which must be approved by a superior court judge. The master shall advise the parties on the record of their right to file objections to any such report or recommendation pursuant to paragraph (f) of this rule.

(f) **Objections to Master's Report, Recommendations.**

(1) *Objections, Reply, Oral Argument.* Objections to a master's report or recommendation must be filed within 10 days of entry of the findings or service of the report unless the court requires objection to be filed earlier. In the case of a recommendation rendered orally on record where a party requests an electronic recording of the recommendation, the time period for objection runs from receipt of the recording. A reply to the objections must be filed within three days of service of the objections. The superior court may permit oral argument, order the taking of further evidence, or grant a hearing de novo.

(2) *Request for Stay, Immediate Review.* A party may request that a superior court judge stay a master's order issued under paragraph (d) pending review of the order.

(3) *Review of Detention or Placement Outside the Home Order.* A master's order for detention or placement outside the home which is not stayed must be reviewed by the superior court by the end of the next working day if a party so requests.

(SCO 845 effective August 15, 1987; amended by SCO 917 effective January 15, 1989; by SCO 918 effective January 15, 1989; and by SCO 1555 effective October 15, 2004)

Note: Chapter 70 SLA 2005 (SB 154) enacted changes concerning proceedings relating to delinquent minors.

According to section 10 of the Act, the changes made by sections 1-8 of the Act have the effect of amending Delinquency Rule 4(f)(3) by requiring the court to conform the rule to the statutory changes to acknowledge the inclusion of certain persons 18 years of age or over as minors under AS 47.12 and AS 47.14 and to acknowledge the special statutory provisions contained in sections 1-8 of the Act applicable to those persons.

Rule 5. Authority of District Court Judges and Magistrates.

(a) **Emergency Situations.** When a minor is in a condition or surrounding dangerous to the welfare of the minor or others which requires immediate action, and no superior court judge or authorized master is available, a district court judge or magistrate may order temporary detention of the minor or take other action which a superior court judge is authorized by law to take. The district court judge or magistrate must immediately notify the superior court of the facts concerning the child and expeditiously transfer the case file to the superior court.

(b) **Review.** A party may request a hearing before the superior court or authorized master to review any action taken by a district court judge or magistrate under this rule.

(SCO 845 effective August 15, 1987)

Cross References

CROSS REFERENCE: AS 22.15.100.

PART III. INTAKE, COMMENCEMENT OF PROCEEDINGS

Rule 6. Intake. (Rescinded).

Note to SCO 1349: Delinquency Rule 6 (Intake) was repealed by ch. 107, § 53, SLA 1998, effective July 1, 1998. Paragraph 1 of this order, which rescinds Delinquency Rule 6, is adopted for the sole reason that the legislature has mandated the amendment.

Rule 7. Emergency Detention or Placement. (Rescinded).

Note to SCO 1349: Delinquency Rule 7 (Emergency Detention or Placement) was repealed by ch. 107, § 53, SLA 1998, effective July 1, 1998. Paragraph 3 of this order, which rescinds Delinquency Rule 7, is adopted for the sole reason that the legislature has mandated the amendment.

Rule 8. Petition for Adjudication, Summons.

(a) **Petition.** Formal proceedings are commenced by the Department filing a verified petition for adjudication which contains a statement of facts which brings the juvenile within the jurisdiction of the court under AS 47.12.020. The petition may be verified on information and belief, and must establish probable cause to believe that an offense has been committed and that the minor has committed it.

(b) **Summons.** Upon the filing of a petition for adjudication, the court shall set a time for the arraignment on petition and shall, if the juvenile is not in custody, issue a summons to be served with the petition compelling the attendance of the juvenile. The court shall issue a summons compelling the attendance of the juvenile's parents or guardian at the hearing. If the summons and petition are not contained in one document, the petition must be attached to and incorporated by reference into the summons. The summons must contain a statement advising the parties of their right to counsel.

(c) **Service.** The petition must be served on the juvenile and the juvenile's parents or guardian. The petition and the summons, if issued, must be served on the juvenile pursuant to Criminal Rule 4(c), except that the court may appoint a probation officer or other competent person to serve the summons and petition. The parents or guardian may be served in the same manner as the juvenile or by any method of service allowed under Civil Rule 4, including registered or certified mail, or specified by the court. Inability to obtain service on a parent or guardian does not deprive the court of jurisdiction. The Department shall also provide a copy of the petition to the juvenile's foster parents.

(d) **Dismissal.** The court may dismiss a petition at any time based on a finding of good cause consistent with the welfare of the juvenile and the protection of the public.

(e) **Amendment.** A petition may be amended with leave of the court at any time before adjudication. Amendment will be freely permitted to promote the interests of justice, the welfare of the juvenile and the protection of the public.

(SCO 845 effective August 15, 1987; amended by SCO 1041 effective January 15, 1991; by SCO 1265 and 1269 effective July 15, 1997; by SCO 1361 effective October 15, 1999; and by SCO 1364 effective October 15, 1999)

Note to SCO 1269: Delinquency Rule 8(b) was amended by § 6 ch. 144 SLA 1996. Section 25 of this order is adopted for the sole reason that the legislature has mandated the amendment.

Note: Chapter 70 SLA 2005 (SB 154) enacted changes concerning proceedings relating to delinquent minors. According to section 10 of the Act, the changes made by sections 1-8 of the Act have the effect of amending Delinquency Rule 8(b) and (c) by requiring the court to conform the rule to the statutory changes to acknowledge the inclusion of certain persons 18 years of age or over as minors under AS 47.12 and AS 47.14 and to acknowledge the special statutory provisions contained in sections 1-8 of the Act applicable to those persons.

Cross References

CROSS REFERENCE: AS 47.12.040; AS 47.12.050; AS 47.12.070; AS 47.12.250(b).

Annotations

Cases

This annotation construes former Children's Rule 8. Considering the importance of juvenile proceedings and the fact that juvenile records are easily obtained and can have serious effects upon the life of a minor, the usual principles against entertaining moot controversies do not apply. Where a 12-year old boy has been determined to be delinquent, an appeal of that delinquency order will be considered, notwithstanding that the order has been vacated. **Ej. v. State,** Op. No. 628, 471 P2d 367 (Alaska 1970).

This annotation construes former Children's Rule 8. Children who are charged with acts which would be chargeable only by grand jury indictment if committed by an adult need not be indicted by a grand jury. **Doe v. State,** Op. No. 707, 487 P2d 47 (Alaska 1971).

This annotation construes former Children's Rule 10. Process in a juvenile proceeding must be delivered to the child himself. Jurisdiction over the child cannot be obtained by delivering the summons and petition to his parents. **RLR v. State,** Op. No. 706, 487 P2d 27 (Alaska 1971).

This annotation construes former Children's Rule 10. Appearance by a child in a juvenile proceeding and failure to object to the failure to serve him with a copy of the petition waives any defect in process where the infant is represented by counsel. **RLR v. State,** Op. No. 706,487 P2d 27 (Alaska 1971).

This annotation construes former Children's Rule 10. A child has a vital interest in a dependency proceeding and is an essential party whose presence cannot be dispensed with arbitrarily; in a dependency proceeding the summons and a copy of the petition must be served on the child as well as the parents; failure to make such service results in a lack of jurisdiction over the child. **In re P.N.,** Op. No. 1127,523 P2d 13 (Alaska 1975).

This annotation construes former Children's Rule 10. Where the children are not given the required notice of a dependency hearing the superior court has no jurisdiction over them and, therefore, can not validly issue a judgment depriving a parent of his custody. **In re P.N.,** Op. No. 1127, 523 P2d 13 (Alaska 1975).

This annotation construes former Children's Rule 10. On initiation of dependency proceedings, an attorney should be appointed to act in the dual role of guardian ad litem and counsel for children of tender years. The required summons should be served on him, but in those areas where attorneys are not readily available and appointment of counsel is not essential or where suitable guardian ad litem is available, there is no requirement that an attorney at law be appointed. **In re P.N.,** Op. No. 1127, 523 P2d 13 (Alaska 1975).

This annotation construes former Children's Rule 8. In the adjudicative phase of any children's proceeding, the family court may consider only the specific situations set out in the petition. **In re S.D. Jr.,** Op. No. 1255, 549 P2d 1190 (Alaska 1976).

Former Children's Rules 3(b) and 10(c)(2) required parents of minor to be notified of waiver hearing, but neither rule required the parent's presence at waiver hearing. **Matter of J.H.B.,** Op. No. 1626, 578 P2d 146 (Alaska 1978).

This annotation construes former Children's Rule 10. In parental rights termination action where the State knew that the parent was in contact with a Washington tribal caseworker, the court was not persuaded that the mailing address of the parent could not have been ascertained after inquiry, thus failure to provide notice by mail to the parent violated this rule. **Matter of L.A.M.,** Op. No. 3142, 727 P2d 1057 (Alaska 1986).

PART IV. DISCOVERY, EVIDENCE, PROOF

Rule 9. Depositions and Discovery.

Criminal Rules 15 and 16 govern depositions and discovery in delinquency proceedings with the following exceptions:

(a) the court may shorten the time periods for discovery;

(b) a juvenile under 16 years of age may not be deposed except upon court order; and

(c) the presence of parties and others at depositions is governed by Delinquency Rule 3.

(SCO 845 effective August 15, 1987)

Rule 10. Evidence.

(a) **Applicability of Evidence Rules.** The Alaska Rules of Evidence apply to delinquency proceedings to the same extent that they apply to criminal proceedings, except as otherwise provided by these rules.

(b) **Disposition and Review of Disposition Orders.** The parties may submit information through reports, statements, affidavits and testimony at the disposition hearing and in review of a disposition order. Hearsay that is not otherwise admissible under a recognized exception to the hearsay rule may be admissible at disposition and in review of a disposition order if the hearsay is probative of a material fact, has circumstantial guarantees of trustworthiness, and the appearing parties are given a fair opportunity to meet it.

(c) **Temporary Detention Hearing.** Hearsay that is not otherwise admissible under the Evidence Rules may be admitted under the standard stated in paragraph (b) of this rule at a temporary detention hearing.

(SCO 845 effective August 15, 1987; amended by SCO 1265 effective July 15, 1997; and by SCO 1349 effective December 1, 1998)

Note to SCO 1349: Delinquency Rule 10(c) was amended by ch. 107, § 52, SLA 1998, effective July 1, 1998. Paragraph 5 of this order, which amends Delinquency Rule 10(c), is adopted for the sole reason that the legislature has mandated the amendment.

Cross References

CROSS REFERENCE: AS 47.17.060, AS 47.12.250(c).

Annotations

Cases

This annotation construes former Children's Rule 17. This rule permits the consideration of social agency and police reports in the dispositive phase of a hearing. **In re S.D. Jr.,** Op. No. 1255, 549 P2d 1190 (Alaska 1976).

This annotation construes former Children's Rule 17. Before hearsay evidence is used in the dispositive phase, the child and his counsel should be clearly advised that it is being considered so that opposing evidence or explanation may be presented. **Matter of J.H.B.,** Op. No. 1626, 578 P2d 146 (Alaska 1978).

This annotation construes former Children's Rule 17. Finding by judge that juvenile was not amenable to treatment as a juvenile based solely upon prior determination of delinquency was not the searching inquiry necessary for such a finding. **A.D. v. State,** Op. No. 280, 668 P2d 840 (Alaska App. 1983).

This annotation construes former Children's Rule 17. Probable cause determination at juvenile jurisdiction waiver hearing may not be based on hearsay testimony. **A.D. v. State,** Op. No. 280, 668 P2d 840 (Alaska App. 1983).

This annotation construes former Children's Rule 17. The use of hearsay evidence in the disposition phase of a parental rights termination proceeding as allowed by state law did not conflict with the federal Indian Child Welfare Act. **Matter of J.R.B.,** Op. No. 3029, 715 P2d 1170 (Alaska 1986).

Rule 11. Burden and Standards of Proof.

(a) **Detention.** In order to support a temporary detention order, the Department must prove that probable cause exists that the minor committed the delinquent act charged and must prove, by a preponderance of the evidence, that detention or placement is necessary either:

(1) to protect the juvenile or others; or

(2) to ensure the juvenile's appearance at subsequent court hearings.

(b) **Adjudication.** In order to support an adjudication of delinquency, the Department must prove the essential elements of the alleged crime beyond a reasonable doubt.

(c) **Waiver.** In order to support an order waiving juvenile court jurisdiction, the Department must prove unamenability to treatment by a preponderance of the evidence, and must prove that probable cause exists that the juvenile committed the act charged in the petition.

(d) **Other Motions.** On other motions that relate to the criminal nature of proceedings such as the suppression of evidence, the burdens and standard of proof are the same as in a criminal proceeding.

(e) **Disposition.** In order to support a particular disposition, including a disposition ordered as part of a dual sentence, the Department must prove by a preponderance of the evidence that the disposition is the least restrictive alternative appropriate to the needs of the juvenile and the protection of the community.

(f) **Other Petitions.** The following petitions require the moving party to present proof by a preponderance of the evidence:

(1) a petition for release from commitment or supervision;

(2) a petition for extension of commitment or supervision;

(3) a petition for modification of probation;

(4) a petition for revocation of probation; and

(5) a petition to impose the adult portion of a dual sentence pursuant to AS 47.12.160(d)-(e).

(g) **Annual Review.** No party has the burden of proof at an annual review.

(SCO 845 effective August 15, 1987; amended by SCO 1349 effective December 1, 1998)

Cross References

CROSS REFERENCE: AS 47.12.140(2); AS 47.12.160(d)-(e); AS 47.12.120(j).

Annotations

Cases

This annotation construes former Children's Rule 21. Findings of fact are required in a juvenile proceeding. **RLR v. State,** Op. No. 706, 487 P2d 27 (Alaska 1971).

This annotation construes former Children's Rule 21. Unless a child is charged with an act which may result in this incarceration, the standard of proof is by a preponderance of the evidence. **In re S.D. Jr.,** Op. No. 1255, 549 P2d 1190 (Alaska 1976).

Given juvenile defendant's age at the time of the disposition proceeding (seventeen and one-half), the roughly one and one-half years remaining for supervision before he becomes an adult, and his continuing criminal behavior even after entering into a favorable disposition agreement with the state, trial court was not clearly erroneous in concluding that institutional placement was the least restrictive alternative available to treat his delinquency and to protect the community. **R.N. v. State,** Op. No. 918, 770 P2d 301 (Alaska App. 1989).

The trial judge must consider and reject less restrictive alternatives using a preponderance standard prior to imposing more restrictive treatment alternatives. **P.R.J. v. State,** Op. No. 1015, 787 P2d 123 (Alaska App. 1990).

Before a minor is institutionalized in a closed facility, the superior court must consider the available placement options and affirmatively determine that less restrictive options will probably not accomplish the goals of rehabilitation and protection of the public. **J.T.S. v. State,** Op. No. 1197, 825 P2d 461 (Alaska App. 1992).

Superior court's order institutionalizing delinquent minor was vacated due to court's lack of explicit consideration of placement alternatives, even though record demonstrated good reason to believe that institutionalization was necessary. **J.T.S. v. State,** Op. No. 1197, 825 P2d 461 (Alaska App. 1992).

Record was sufficient to support trial court's order institutionalizing 13-year-old sex offender. **G.A.D. v. State.,** Op. No. 1327, 865 P2d 100 (Alaska App. 1993).

PART V. PRELIMINARY PROCEEDINGS

Rule 12. Temporary Detention Hearing.

(a) **Hearing Required.** A juvenile detained under AS 47.12.250 must be taken before the court for a temporary detention hearing. The hearing must be held as soon as is practicable, but in no event later than 48 hours after notification to the court, including weekends and holidays.

(b) **Detention or Placement After Hearing.** A juvenile may not be detained or placed outside the home of a parent or guardian unless the court makes the following findings:

(1) that probable cause exists to believe that either (a) the juvenile has committed a delinquent act as alleged in a petition, or (b) after such a probable cause finding has been made at a prior hearing, the juvenile has violated a release condition or probation condition imposed by the court; and

(2) that detention or placement outside the home of a parent or guardian is necessary either (a) to protect the juvenile or others, or (b) to ensure the juvenile's appearance at

subsequent court hearings. The court may not order detention unless there is no less restrictive alternative which would protect the juvenile and the public or ensure the juvenile's appearance at subsequent hearings.

(c) **Release from Detention or Placement.** The juvenile must be released to a parent, guardian, relative or some other responsible person upon such reasonable conditions as the court may set if insufficient reason exists to warrant detention or placement outside the home under paragraph (b) of this rule.

(d) **Foster Parent's Right To Be Heard.** If the juvenile's foster parent is present at the temporary detention hearing, the court shall give the foster parent an opportunity to be heard.

(e) **Termination of Detention or Placement.** A juvenile who has been detained for a period of 30 days, but who has not been adjudicated a delinquent, will be released unless, at or prior to the expiration of the 30 days, either:

(1) the court, after a hearing, orders continued detention and makes findings stating the reasons supporting the order; or

(2) the minor and the minor's attorney stipulate with the Department to continued detention.

If the juvenile is not in the same community as the court, the juvenile's participation at the hearing to determine continued detention may be by telephone. An order for placement outside the home pending adjudication or disposition must specify its duration.

(SCO 845 effective August 15, 1987; amended by SCO 1265 effective July 15, 1997; and by SCO 1361 effective October 15, 1999)

Note: Chapter 70 SLA 2005 (SB 154) enacted changes concerning proceedings relating to delinquent minors. According to section 10 of the Act, the changes made by sections 1-8 of the Act have the effect of amending Delinquency Rule 12(b), (c), (d), and (e) by requiring the court to conform the rule to the statutory changes to acknowledge the inclusion of certain persons 18 years of age or over as minors under AS 47.12 and AS 47.14 and to acknowledge the special statutory provisions contained in sections 1-8 of the Act applicable to those persons.

Cross References

CROSS REFERENCE: AS 47.12.080; AS 47.12.090(a); AS 47.12.240; AS 47.12.250(c) & (d).

Annotations

Cases

The specificity and the lack of ambiguity of the subsection of this rule pertaining to detention or placement after hearing, coupled with the absence of any legislative history indicating that the rule was intended to have a meaning other than that plainly suggested on its face, foreclosed the adoption of the more restrictive criteria for predisposition detention specified in the Institute of Judicial Administration, American Bar Association standards for juvenile justice. **K.L.F. v. State,** Op. No. 1032, 790 P2d 708 (Alaska App. 1990).

Despite the relatively minor nature of the juvenile's original offenses, superior court did not err in ordering her detained pending disposition; although the record provided some indication that her primary difficulty was not her delinquency but her runaway behavior, nothing in the record justified a conclusion that delinquency proceedings were resorted to as a subterfuge to manage her difficult behavior. **K.L.F. v. State,** Op. No. 1032, 790 P2d 708 (Alaska App. 1990).

Rule 13. Judge's Responsibility Concerning Conditions of Detention.

A court exercising jurisdiction under these rules has a continuing duty to ascertain that appropriate conditions of detention of juveniles are observed concerning visitation, clothing, exercise, private visitation of counsel and confinement. A juvenile may not be confined in solitary confinement for punitive reasons.

(SCO 845 effective August 15, 1987)

Note: Chapter 70 SLA 2005 (SB 154) enacted changes concerning proceedings relating to delinquent minors. According to section 10 of the Act, the changes made by sections 1-8 of the Act have the effect of amending Delinquency Rule 13 by requiring the court to conform the rule to the statutory changes to acknowledge the inclusion of certain persons 18 years of age or over as minors under AS 47.12 and AS 47.14 and to acknowledge the special statutory provisions contained in sections 1-8 of the Act applicable to those persons.

Rule 14. Arraignment on Petition.

(a) **Time.** The arraignment on petition may be held at the same time as the temporary detention hearing or, with notice to the parties, within a reasonable time after the filing of the petition.

(b) **Order of Proceedings.**

(1) *Opening Address.* The court shall ensure that all parties have received copies of the petition and understand its contents. The court shall advise the parties of the nature of the proceedings and the possible disposition that may occur, including potential dual sentencing. In addition, the court shall advise the parties of the possibility of temporary detention or placement outside the home pending final disposition, that the parents or guardian must attend all hearings and may be held in contempt for failure to do so, and that the parents may be liable for child support payments if the child is placed outside the home at any time during the proceeding.

(2) *Advice of Rights.* The court shall advise the parties of their right to counsel and their privilege against self-incrimination. The court shall advise the juvenile of the right to an adjudication hearing before a judge or jury, the right to a public hearing, the right to call witnesses and to issue compulsory process to compel their attendance, the right to confront and cross-examine witnesses called by other parties, and the right to challenge the judge or master assigned to the case pursuant to Delinquency Rule 4(c). If the minor is represented by counsel, the opening address and advice of rights may be waived.

(3) *Motions, Discovery, Hearing Date.* The court may set a time certain for the adjudication hearing and the date by which discovery and motion matters will close, or may refer the case to calendaring or court administration for trial setting. Priority on the trial calendar will be given to adjudication hearings.

(4) *Request for Admissions or Denial.* If it appears to the court that the juvenile adequately understands the juvenile's rights and that the requirements of AS 47.12.090(a) have been met, the court may inquire whether the juvenile admits or denies all or part of the allegations of the petition and, if so, accept the plea. Otherwise, the court shall set a date for entry of a plea. Except as stated in this paragraph, the entry of pleas is governed by Criminal Rule 11. If the petition states that the juvenile may be subject to dual sentencing under AS 47.12.065, the court shall delay the request for admission or denial until one of the following has occurred:

(A) if the juvenile is in custody, 10 days have passed since arraignment and the district attorney has not presented the case to the grand jury for indictment;

(B) if the juvenile is not in custody, 20 days have passed since arraignment and the district attorney has not presented the case to the grand jury for indictment; or

(C) the grand jury has returned an indictment or a no true bill.

If the juvenile consents or if the state demonstrates good cause, taking into account the interest of the public in the prompt disposition of delinquency cases, the court may extend the time for the district attorney to present the case to the grand jury under (A) or (B).

(c) **Temporary Detention, Placement.** The court may order the juvenile committed to the Department for detention or placement as provided by Delinquency Rule 12(b) at the arraignment on petition.

(SCO 845 effective August 15, 1987; amended by SCO 1105 effective January 15, 1993; by SCO 1265 effective July 15, 1997; by SCO 1269 effective July 15, 1997; and by SCO 1349 effective December 1, 1998)

Note: Chapter 70 SLA 2005 (SB 154) enacted changes concerning proceedings relating to delinquent minors. According to section 10 of the Act, the changes made by sections 1-8 of the Act have the effect of amending Delinquency Rule 14(b) by requiring the court to conform the rule to the statutory changes to acknowledge the inclusion of certain persons 18 years of age or over as minors under AS 47.12 and AS 47.14 and to acknowledge the special statutory provisions contained in sections 1-8 of the Act applicable to those persons.

Cross References

CROSS REFERENCE: AS 47.12.065.

Rule 15. Guardians Ad Litem.

(a) **When Appointed.** The court may appoint a guardian ad litem to represent the best interests of the juvenile in a delinquency proceeding.

(b) **Appointment.** Guardians ad litem will be appointed in accord with the provisions of AS 44.21.410 and Administrative Rule 12. The court shall specify the duties of the guardian ad litem and the duration of the appointment in its order of appointment.

(c) **Service.** A guardian ad litem is a party and must be served with pleadings and notices according to the Civil Rules. Service on the guardian ad litem does not constitute service on the juvenile.

(SCO 845 effective August 15, 1987; amended by SCO 1265 effective July 15, 1997)

Note: Chapter 70 SLA 2005 (SB 154) enacted changes concerning proceedings relating to delinquent minors. According to section 10 of the Act, the changes made by sections 1-8 of the Act have the effect of amending Delinquency Rule 15(a) by requiring the court to conform the rule to the statutory changes to acknowledge the inclusion of certain persons 18 years of age or over as minors under AS 47.12 and AS 47.14 and to acknowledge the special statutory provisions contained in sections 1-8 of the Act applicable to those persons.

Cross References

CROSS REFERENCE: AS 25.24.310; AS 47.12.090.

Annotations

Cases

This annotation construes former Children's Rule 11. Where there appears to be a substantial danger that an infant might prefer a jury trial primarily out of a desire to display his importance without sufficient attention to either the possibility of future harm through notoriety or the relative likelihood of winning before a judge and jury, the court should appoint a guardian ad litem to consult with the child and his attorney and to make a decision based solely on the interests of the child. **RLR v. State,** Op. No. 706, 487 P2d 27 (Alaska 1971).

Rule 16. Right to Counsel.

(a) **Notice of Right to Counsel.** The court shall inform the child, parent or guardian at the first hearing at which they are present of their respective rights to be represented by counsel at all subsequent stages of the proceedings.

(b) **Appointed Counsel.** The court shall appoint counsel pursuant to Criminal Rule 39 and Administrative Rule 12 for a juvenile not represented by counsel of choice. The court may order a parent to deposit an appropriate sum consistent with the parent's financial ability in the registry of the court to pay for the appointment. At the disposition phase of a delinquency case, the court shall, if requested, appoint counsel pursuant to Administrative Rule 12 and AS 44.21.410(a)(4) for a parent or guardian who is financially unable to employ counsel if the court concludes that custody is at issue, the interests of the parent or guardian and the child are in conflict, and the interests of the parent or guardian are not adequately protected.

(c) **Waiver of Right to Counsel.** The court shall accept

a valid waiver of the right to counsel by a juvenile if the requirements of AS 47.12.090(a) are met.

(SCO 845 effective August 15, 1987; amended by SCO 1119 effective July 15, 1993; and by SCO 1265 effective July 15, 1997)

Note: Chapter 70 SLA 2005 (SB 154) enacted changes concerning proceedings relating to delinquent minors. According to section 10 of the Act, the changes made by sections 1-8 of the Act have the effect of amending Delinquency Rule 16(a) and (b) by requiring the court to conform the rule to the statutory changes to acknowledge the inclusion of certain persons 18 years of age or over as minors under AS 47.12 and AS 47.14 and to acknowledge the special statutory provisions contained in sections 1-8 of the Act applicable to those persons.

Cross References

CROSS REFERENCE: AS 25.24.310; AS 47.12.090; AS 47.12.250(c).

Annotations

Cases

This annotation construes former Children's Rule 14. Where a juvenile matter has reached the formal adjudicative stage, the juvenile's chosen counsel must be present at the hearing. **Wagstaff v. Superior Court, Family Court Division,** Op. No. 1144, 535 P2d 1220 (Alaska 1975).

This annotation construes former Children's Rule 14. A court in a "child in need of supervision" hearing is under a duty to explain to the juvenile his right to counsel. **Wagstaff v. Superior Court, Family Court Division,** Op. No. 1144, 535 P2d 1220 (Alaska 1975).

Rule 17. Pleadings and Motions Before Trial—Defenses and Objections.

(a) **Pleadings and Motions.** Pleadings in delinquency proceedings are the petition for adjudication and the pleas of admit or deny. Motions in delinquency proceedings are governed by the Criminal Rules.

(b) **Motions Prior to Adjudication.** Any defense, objection or request which is capable of determination before adjudication of the general issue may be raised prior to the adjudication hearing by motion. The following matters must be raised prior to the adjudication hearing:

(1) defenses and objections based on defects in the petition (other than a failure to show jurisdiction in the court or to charge an offense, which objections may be raised at any time during the pendency of the proceeding);

(2) motions to suppress evidence on the ground that it was illegally obtained; and

(3) requests for severance or joinder under Delinquency Rule 18.

(c) **Notice of Mental Disease or Defect.** Notice of an intention to offer evidence of mental disease or defect is governed by AS 12.47.010 and AS 12.47.020.

(d) **Ruling on Motion.** The court shall decide a motion made prior to adjudication before the adjudication hearing unless the court orders that the motion be deferred until the hearing.

(e) **Effect of Failure to Raise Defenses or Objections.** Failure by the juvenile to raise defenses or objections or to make requests which must be made prior to the adjudication hearing, or by the time set by the court pursuant to Delinquency Rule 14(b)(3), constitutes waiver thereof. However, the court may grant relief from the waiver for good cause.

(f) **Effect of Dismissal.** If the court grants dismissal based on a defect in the institution of the proceedings or in the petition, it also may order the placement or detention of the juvenile be continued for a specified time pending the filing of a new petition.

(SCO 845 effective August 15, 1987)

Rule 18. Joinder and Severance.

(a) **Joinder.** The court may order two or more petitions for adjudication to be tried together if the offenses and the juveniles could have been joined in a single petition. The procedure will be the same as if the proceedings were under a single petition.

(b) **Severance.** If it appears that the juvenile or the state is prejudiced by a consolidation of offenses or of juveniles in a petition for adjudication, the court may order an election or separate adjudication of counts, grant a severance of cases against juveniles, or provide whatever other relief justice requires. In ruling on a motion by a juvenile for severance, the court may order the Department to deliver to the court for inspection in camera any statements or confessions made by the juveniles which the Department intends to introduce at the adjudication hearing.

(SCO 845 effective August 15, 1987)

Rule 19. Pretrial Conference.

(a) **Time and Purpose.** At any time after the arraignment on petition or entry of a deny plea, the court may schedule a pretrial conference on the record to consider:

(1) simplification of the issues;

(2) the possibility of obtaining admissions of fact and documents which will avoid the introduction of unnecessary evidence;

(3) the number of witnesses who will give testimony of a cumulative nature; and

(4) such other matters as may aid in the adjudication of the petition.

(b) **Order.** The court shall enter an order reciting the agreement made at the conference. This order controls the subsequent course of the proceedings unless modified at the adjudication hearing in order to prevent manifest injustice.

(SCO 845 effective August 15, 1987)

PART VI. WAIVER OF JUVENILE JURISDICTION

Rule 20. Waiver of Juvenile Jurisdiction.

(a) **Persons Subject to Trial as Adults.** A person may not be tried as an adult for a delinquent act committed while the person was under the age of 18 unless the person is subject to AS 47.12.030 or the court has waived juvenile jurisdiction.

(b) **Waiver Petition.** The Department or the juvenile may file a petition requesting the court to waive juvenile jurisdiction of a person alleged to have committed a delinquent act. Waiver may not be requested for delinquent conduct which has been the basis of an adjudication of delinquency.

(c) **Waiver Hearing.** A waiver hearing will be given priority on the court calendar. The petitioner shall serve notice of the waiver hearing upon the parties. The notice, unless the hearing is requested by the juvenile, must specify the possible consequences of a waiver hearing. The conduct of a waiver hearing is governed by Criminal Rule 5.1(a)–(e).

(d) **Waiver Order.**

(1) *Requirements.* An order waiving juvenile jurisdiction must be accompanied by written findings of fact stating that:

(A) there is probable cause to believe the juvenile committed the act for which waiver is sought; and

(B) the juvenile is not amenable to treatment based on the factors stated in AS 47.12.100(b).

(2) *Effect.* Upon issuance of an order waiving juvenile jurisdiction, the juvenile proceeding will be closed and the waived juvenile may be prosecuted as an adult for the delinquent conduct for which waiver was sought.

(e) **Custody Pending Criminal Proceedings.** The court may order that a juvenile who has been waived for trial as an adult be held in custody pending arraignment on criminal proceedings.

(SCO 845 effective August 15, 1987; amended by SCO 1265 effective July 15, 1997; and by SCO 1349 effective December 1, 1998)

Cross References

CROSS REFERENCE: AS 47.12.100.

Annotations

Cases

This annotation construes former Children's Rule 3. A waiver hearing on the issue of whether an accused child is a suitable subject for treatment available for child offenders must measure up to the essentials of due process and fair treatment. **P.H. v. State,** Op. No. 1538, 504 P2d 837 (Alaska 1972).

This annotation construes former Children's Rule 3. The right of confrontation applies to children's proceedings in which the child is charged with misconduct for which he may be incarcerated. **P.H. v. State,** Op. No. 1538, 504 P2d 837 (Alaska 1972).

This annotation construes former Children's Rule 3. The probable cause determination in children's court may not be based upon hearsay testimony. **P.H. v. State,** Op. No. 1538, 504 P2d 837 (Alaska 1972).

This annotation construes former Children's Rule 3. An amenability decision of the children's court judge respecting a child offender rests in the sound discretion of the judge, but the proper exercise of that discretion must be predicated not only upon procedural regularity sufficient to satisfy the basic requirements of due process but also on a full inquiry into the amenability issue. **P.H. v. State,** Op. No. 1538, 504 P2d 837 (Alaska 1972).

This annotation construes former Children's Rule 3. The waiver of children's court jurisdiction without hearing or opportunity for an adversary presentation and without substantial evidence having been presented that the child is unamenable to juvenile rehabilitation programs is a denial of fair process. **P.H. v. State,** Op. No. 1538, 504 P2d 837 (Alaska 1972).

This annotation construes former Children's Rule 3. As a prerequisite to the criminal prosecution of a child, the children's court must find not only that the child is properly accused but also that he would not be receptive to the rehabilitative programs available through the court. **P.H. v. State,** Op. No. 1538, 504 P2d 837 (Alaska 1972).

This annotation construes former Children's Rule 3. In making an amenability determination, a children's court judge need not resolve all four factors prescribed by AS 47.10.060 against the child to justify wavier nor must there be an arithmetic calculation as to the weight to be given each factor. **P.H. v. State,** Op. No. 1538, 504 P2d 837 (Alaska 1972).

This annotation construes former Children's Rule 3. In making an amenability determination, a children's court judge must make a thorough examination of the child, his background and alternative strategies of rehabilitation short of adult criminal treatment. **P.H. v. State,** Op. No. 1538, 504 P2d 837 (Alaska 1972).

This annotation construes former Children's Rule 3. In making an amenability determination, a children's court judge in most cases must be beyond the circumstances surrounding the alleged delinquent acts and the age of the child. **P.H. v. State,** Op. No. 1538, 504 P2d 837 (Alaska 1972).

This annotation construes former Children's Rule 3. Before treating a juvenile as an adult, a court must first conduct a waiver hearing. The court may then close out the case as a juvenile matter if it finds cause to believe that the juvenile is not amenable to treatment. The juvenile may then be prosecuted as an adult. **B.A.M. v. State,** Op. No. 1104, 528 P2d 437 (Alaska 1974).

This annotation construes former Children's Rule 3. Where no waiver hearing has been held to determine whether a juvenile is delinquent and not amenable to treatment, a court has no authority to sentence the juvenile as an adult. **B.A.M. v. State,** Op. No. 1104, 528 P2d 437 (Alaska 1974).

This annotation construes former Children's Rule 3. At a hearing to waive there must be a thorough examination of probable cause for believing that the child committed the act with which he was charged. Further, the amenability of the child to juvenile treatment must be examined. In the absence of such an examination there can be no evidentiary basis for a waiver. **R.J.C. v. State,** Op. No. 1022, 502 P2d 806 (Alaska 1974).

This annotation construes former Children's Rule 3. Compliance with the rule requirement that a court make written findings of facts at a waiver hearing is essential to insure that a hearing is not a mere ritual and to provide a meaningful basis for review. **R.J.C. v. State,** Op. No. 1022, 502 P2d 806 (Alaska 1974).

This annotation construes former Children's Rule 3. In making a decision as to minor's amenability to treatment as a juvenile, the trial court must make an evidentiary record and make written findings of fact as to each of the four factors enunciated by the legislative in AS 47.10.060(d), and these findings must be supported by substantial evidence. **Matter of F.S.,** Op. No. 1756, 586 P2d 607 (Alaska 1978).

This annotation construes former Children's Rule 3. Trial court abused its discretion in concluding that minor was amenable to treatment as a juvenile and in denying the state's motion for a waiver of juvenile jurisdiction where the minor was seriously delinquent, the offense resulted in loss of human life and was of a most heinous nature, and the minor was over seventeen and a half years old, leaving but a short time for treatment. **Matter of F.S.,** Op. No. 1756, 586 P2d 607 (Alaska 1978).

Former Children's Rules 3(b) and 10(c)(2) required parents of minor to be notified of waiver hearing, but neither rule required the parent's presence at waiver hearing. **Matter of J.H.B.,** Op. No. 1626, 578 P2d 146 (Alaska 1978).

This annotation construes former Children's Rule 3. At a hearing on state's motion for waiver of juvenile jurisdiction, exclusion of evidence concerning previous sexual assaults was not an abuse of the court's discretion because its prejudicial impact outweighed its probative value. **Matter of F.S.,** Op. No. 1756, 586 P2d 607 (Alaska 1978).

This annotation construes former Children's Rule 3. Where minor in custody in Washington refused to waive defense to extradition on charge of murdering her husband in Alaska, Juvenile Court's conduct of waiver of jurisdiction hearing in her absence, after notice to her, was not denial of due process. **N.P.A. v. State,** Op. No. 2005, 604 P2d 599 (Alaska 1979).

This annotation construes former Children's Rule 3. At juvenile jurisdiction waiver hearings, there must be a thorough examination of (1) probable cause for believing that the child committed the acts for which waiver is sought, and (2) the amenability of the child to juvenile treatment. **A.D. v. State,** Op. No. 280, 668 P2d 840 (Alaska App. 1983).

This annotation construes former Children's Rule 3. Finding by judge that juvenile was not amenable to treatment as a juvenile based solely upon prior determination of delinquency was not the searching inquiry necessary for such a finding. **A.D. v. State,** Op. No. 280, 668 P2d 840 (Alaska App. 1983).

This annotation construes former Children's Rule 3. Probable cause determination at juvenile jurisdiction waiver hearing may not be based on hearsay testimony. **A.D. v. State,** Op. No. 280, 668 P2d 840 (Alaska App. 1983).

This annotation construes former Children's Rule 3. Superior court did not abuse its discretion in permitting two relatives of murder victims to attend a juvenile waiver hearing held to determine whether juvenile could be tried as an adult for the murders. **W.M.F. v. Jonstone,** Op. No. 571, 711 P2d 1187 (Alaska App. 1986).

PART VII. ADJUDICATION

Rule 21. Adjudication Hearing.

(a) **Nature of Proceeding.** The adjudication hearing is a trial on the merits of the petition for adjudication. The court will decide the merits of the case unless the juvenile requests a trial by jury. The juvenile must request a jury trial within 10 days of the arraignment on petition or when entering a deny plea, whichever is later. The department may not request an adjudication by jury.

(b) **Juries.** The jury will consist of twelve persons unless at any time prior to the verdict the parties stipulate in writing, with the approval of the court, to any number of jurors less than twelve. The verdict of the jury must be unanimous.

(c) **Venue.** Venue for an adjudication by jury is determined by the law of venue applicable to trials by jury in criminal proceedings.

(d) **Judgment.**

(1) At the conclusion of the adjudication hearing, the court shall enter a judgment that the juvenile is not delinquent or, if the court or the jury finds that the juvenile committed one or more delinquent acts alleged in the petition, either:

(A) enter a judgment that the minor is delinquent; or

(B) issue an order that the matter be held in abeyance for a stated period of time not to exceed one year. The court may dismiss the case at the expiration of this period of time if dismissal will promote the interests of the public and the welfare of the child.

(2) In a case tried without a jury, the court shall make a general finding, but on request shall find facts specially. If an opinion or memorandum of decision is filed, the findings of fact may appear therein.

(e) **Failure of Proof.** A juvenile who is found not to be delinquent must be released from custody.

(f) **Order Pending Disposition.** If the court finds a juvenile to be delinquent, the court may order the juvenile placed or detained pending disposition if the court finds that:

(1) detention or placement is necessary to protect the juvenile or others; or

(2) detention or placement is necessary to ensure the juvenile's appearance at subsequent court hearings.

(g) **Foster Parent's Right To Be Heard.** If the juvenile's foster parent is present at the adjudication hearing, the court shall give the foster parent an opportunity to be heard.

(SCO 845 effective August 15, 1987; amended by SCO 1265 effective July 15, 1997; by SCO 1294 effective January 15, 1998; by SCO 1349 effective December 1, 1998; and by SCO 1361 effective October 15, 1999)

Note: Chapter 70 SLA 2005 (SB 154) enacted changes concerning proceedings relating to delinquent minors. According to section 10 of the Act, the changes made by sections 1-8 of the Act have the effect of amending Delinquency Rule 21(g) by requiring the court to conform the rule to the statutory changes to acknowledge the inclusion of certain persons 18 years of age or over as minors under AS 47.12 and AS 47.14 and to acknowledge the special statutory provisions contained in sections 1-8 of the Act applicable to those persons.

Note: Chapter 65, section 6, SLA 2005 (HB 54) amended AS 47.12.110 relating to the introduction of the victim and the minor to the jury. According to section 8 of the Act, section 6 of the Act has the effect of amending Delinquency Rule 21 by allowing the introduction of the victim and the minor at an adjudication hearing.

Cross References

CROSS REFERENCE: AS 47.12.110(e); AS 47.12.120(a).

Annotations

Cases

This annotation construes former Children's Rule 12. If, following criminal proceedings, collateral legal disabilities exist apart from the sentence, an appeal is not mooted even though the sentence has already been served. New note **E.J. v. State,** Op. No. 628, 471 P2d 367 (Alaska 1970).

The annotation construes former Children's Rule 12. The provision of this rule providing for closed proceedings must be interpreted and applied in a manner consistent with the child's right to a public trial. **RLR v. State,** Op. No. 706, 487 P2d 27 (Alaska 1971).

This annotation construes former Children's Rule 12. If a child or his guardian ad litem wants the press, friends or others to be free to attend juvenile proceedings, the hearing must be open to them. The court's areas of discretion within which it may refuse to open a hearing involves persons whose presence is not desired by the child. **RLR v. State,** Op. No. 706,487 P2d 27 (Alaska 1971).

This annotation construes former Children's Rule 12. A hearing in which a chemist testifies that a tablet sent to him for analysis contains LSD should not be conducted in the absence of the infant involved after the attorney explicitly refuses to waive the infant's right to be present. Conducting a hearing in the child's absence under such circumstances is reversible error. **RLR v. State,** Op. No. 706, 487 P2d 27 (Alaska 1971).

This annotation construes former Children's Rule 12. Notions of benevolent protective policies for children cannot be used to validate departures from positive law relating to adjudicative and dispositive phases of children's proceedings. **In re E.M.D.,** Op. No. 737, 490 P2d 658 (Alaska 1971).

This annotation construes former Children's Rule 12. A child has a vital interest in a dependency proceeding and is an essential party whose presence cannot be dispensed with arbitrarily; in a dependency proceeding the summons and a copy of the petition must be served on the child as well as the parents; failure to make such service results in a lack of jurisdiction over the child. **In re P.N.,** Op. No. 1127,523 P2d 13 (Alaska 1975).

This annotation construes former Children's Rule 12. Where the children are not given the required notice of a dependency hearing the superior court has no jurisdiction over them and, therefore, cannot validly issue a judgment depriving a parent of his custody. **In re P.N.,** Op. No. 1127, 523 P2d 13 (Alaska 1975).

This annotation construes former Children's Rule 12. A court in a "child in need of supervision" hearing is under a duty to explain to the juvenile his right to counsel. **Wagstaff v. Superior Court, Family Court Division,** Op. No. 1144, 535 P2d 1220 (Alaska 1975).

This annotation construes former Children's Rule 12. In the adjudicative phase of any children's proceeding, the family court may consider only the specific situations set out in the petition. **In re S.D. Jr.,** Op. No. 1255, 549 P2d 1190 (Alaska 1976).

This annotation construes former Children's Rule 12. Court committed error when it commenced the adjudicative phase of the parental rights termination hearing in the absence of the child's counsel and guardian ad litem. **Matter of C.L.T.,** Op. No. 1866, 597 P2d 518 (Alaska 1979).

This annotation construes former Children's Rule 12. Superior court did not abuse its discretion in permitting two relatives of murder victims to attend a juvenile waiver hearing held to determine whether juvenile could be tried as an adult for the murders. **W.M.F. v. Jonstone,** Op. No. 571, 711 P2d 1187 (Alaska App. 1986).

PART VIII. DISPOSITION

Rule 22. Reports in Aid of Disposition.

(a) **Predisposition Report.**

(1) The predisposition report filed by the Department may include information concerning the following: the juvenile's family background, educational history, past adjudications, verified past incidents of delinquent behavior; the juvenile's medical, psychological and psychiatric history; and a description of the delinquent act and the juvenile's attitude about the act. The report must contain a recommendation regarding the recommended form of treatment that would be in the best interests of the juvenile and the public, and the victim impact statement required by AS 47.12.130.

(2) The predisposition report must be made available to the persons entitled to it at least ten days before the disposition hearing unless the parties agree to a different period and this agreement is approved by the court. A predisposition report which is submitted to the court prior to the adjudication hearing must be kept sealed until the adjudication hearing is completed.

(b) **Supplementary Material.** The court may order mental and physical examinations of the juvenile, studies of the home of any person with whom the juvenile might be placed by the court, and may provide for any other reports to aid in disposition. Parties may prepare and submit their own reports in aid of disposition. All such materials must be made available to the persons entitled to receive them at a reasonable time prior to disposition.

(c) **Disclosure of Reports.** Unless otherwise ordered, copies of predisposition reports and supplementary materials must be given to all parties. Any party may move to withhold all or part of a report from the juvenile or the juvenile's parents or guardian if disclosure would be likely to cause serious psychological harm to the juvenile or the family relationship. The court shall inspect the reports in camera prior to entering such a limitation on disclosure and a limitation does not bar an attorney's access to the material withheld. The court may enter orders prohibiting release of the material by the attorney to his or her client.

(SCO 845 effective August 15, 1987; amended by SCO 1092 effective July 15, 1992; and by SCO 1265 effective July 15, 1997)

Note: Paragraph (a) was amended by ch. 57, § 22, SLA 1991.

Note: Chapter 70 SLA 2005 (SB 154) enacted changes concerning proceedings relating to delinquent minors. According to section 10 of the Act, the changes made by sections 1-8 of the Act have the effect of amending Delinquency Rule 22(c) by requiring the court to conform the rule to the statutory changes to acknowledge the inclusion of certain persons 18 years of age or over as minors under AS 47.12 and AS 47.14 and to acknowledge the special statutory provisions contained in sections 1-8 of the Act applicable to those persons.

Cross References

CROSS REFERENCE: AS 47.12.120(a).

Annotations

Cases

Judge in juvenile disposition proceeding did not abuse her discretion in considering unsolicited letters from victims' relatives. **J.C.W. v. State,** Op. No. 1370, 880 P.2d 1067 (Alaska Ct. App. 1994).

Rule 23. Disposition.

(a) **Nature and Timing of the Hearing.** The purpose of a disposition hearing is to determine the appropriate disposition of a juvenile who has been adjudicated a delinquent. The disposition hearing may not be held before adequate information is available upon which to enter an informed disposition order. If the disposition is not held immediately following the adjudication, the court shall set a time for the disposition hearing, which will be held without unreasonable delay, and shall order a predisposition report and other studies, examinations or reports under Delinquency Rule 22 which are necessary for an informed disposition. The juvenile, with approval of the court, may waive the preparation and submission of a predisposition report.

(b) **Statements.** The court shall allow the parties an opportunity to make a statement and to offer evidence in aid of disposition before entering a disposition order. If the juvenile's foster parent is present at the disposition hearing, the court shall give the foster parent an opportunity to be heard.

(c) **Findings.** A disposition order, including a disposition order entered as part of a dual sentence, must be accompanied by findings of fact supporting the disposition ordered.

(d) **Order.** The court shall enter its disposition order or dual sentence taking into account the considerations set out in AS 47.12.140 or AS 47.12.120(j).

(e) **Release by Department.** The Department shall notify the court in writing when the Department releases a juvenile from institutionalization without court order.

(SCO 845 effective August 15, 1987; amended by SCO 1265 effective July 15, 1997; by SCO 1269 effective July 15, 1997; by SCO 1349 effective December 1, 1998; and by SCO 1361 effective October 15, 1999)

Note to SCO 1269: Delinquency Rule 23(d) was amended by § 56 ch 59 SLA 1996.

Note: Chapter 70 SLA 2005 (SB 154) enacted changes concerning proceedings relating to delinquent minors. According to section 10 of the Act, the changes made by sections 1-8 of the Act have the effect of amending Delinquency Rule 23(b) by requiring the court to conform the rule to the statutory changes to acknowledge the inclusion of certain persons 18 years of age or over as minors under AS 47.12 and AS 47.14 and to acknowledge the special statutory provisions contained in sections 1-8 of the Act applicable to those persons.

Cross References

CROSS REFERENCE: AS 47.12.120(j); AS 47.12.140.

Annotations

Cases

Findings of fact contained in nonfinal "Order of termination," which findings were not later changed satisfied the requirement of former Children's Rule 22(d) that court provide written findings of fact supporting the judgment. **Matter of C.L.T.,** Op. No. 1866, 597 P2d 518 (Alaska 1979).

This annotation construes former Children's Rule 12. Trial judge's discretion in not holding a disposition hearing under this rule must be narrowly defined. **L.C. v. State,** Op. No. 2277, 625 P2d 839 (Alaska 1981).

The trial judge must consider and reject less restrictive alternatives using a preponderance standard prior to imposing more restrictive treatment alternatives. **P.R.J. v. State,** Op. No. 1015, 787 P2d 123 (Alaska App. 1990).

Placement of juvenile who had a history of running away, in a detention facility was the least restrictive placement alternative available. **P.R.J. v. State,** Op. No. 1015, 787 P2d 123 (Alaska App. 1990).

Before a minor is institutionalized in a closed facility, the superior court must consider the available placement options and affirmatively determine that less restrictive options will probably not accomplish the goals of rehabilitation and protection of the public. **J.T.S. v. State,** Op. No. 1197, 825 P2d 461 (Alaska App. 1992).

Superior court's order institutionalizing delinquent minor was vacated due to court's lack of explicit consideration of placement alternatives, even though record demonstrated good reason to believe that institutionalization was necessary. **J.T.S. v. State,** Op. No. 1197, 825 P2d 461 (Alaska App. 1992).

Rule 24. Probation Revocation.

(a) **Revocation Petition.** The Department may petition the court to revoke the probation of a juvenile. The petition must be supported by an affidavit stating the particulars of the alleged violations.

(b) **Detention Pending Hearing.** If the juvenile has been arrested, the provisions of Delinquency Rule 12 apply to continued detention or placement pending a hearing on the petition.

(c) **Hearing.** The Department has the burden of proving by a preponderance of the evidence that the juvenile violated the conditions of probation. At the hearing, the juvenile has the right to appointed counsel, the right against self-incrimination, the right to a public hearing, the right to call witnesses and to issue compulsory process to compel their attendance, the right to confront and examine witnesses called by other parties, and the right to challenge the judge or master assigned to the case pursuant to Delinquency Rule 4(c). However, the juvenile does not have a right to a jury trial.

(d) **Disposition.** If the juvenile is found to have violated the conditions of probation, the court may extend, enlarge or modify its disposition order, taking into account the best interests of the juvenile and the public, and the ability of the Department to care for and protect the juvenile's best interests. The provisions of Delinquency Rule 23 apply to this disposition hearing.

(SCO 845 effective August 15, 1987; amended by SCO 1265 effective July 15, 1997)

Cross References

CROSS REFERENCE: AS 47.12.120(b)(1)–(3).

Annotations

Cases

A juvenile does not have the right to a jury trial in a probation revocation hearing. **A.S. v. State,** Op. No. 846, 761 P2d 122 (Alaska App. 1988).

Where juvenile allegedly violated probation by committing assault, it was not unconstitutional to hold a probation revocation hearing at which a preponderance of evidence standard rather than a beyond a reasonable doubt standard was used to prove the case against him, including rejection of his claim of self-defense. **A.S. v. State,** Op. No. 846, 761 P2d 122 (Alaska App. 1988).

Trial judge had power to extend the state's custody of juvenile until two years after the disposition hearing. **P.R.J. v. State,** Op. No. 1015, 787 P2d 123 (Alaska App. 1990).

Rule 24.1. Imposition of Adult Portion of Dual Sentence.

(a) **Petition to Impose Adult Portion of Dual Sentence.** The district attorney may petition the court for imposition of the adult portion of a dual sentence pronounced under AS 47.12.120(j)(2). The petition must be supported by an affidavit stating the particulars of the alleged violations.

(b) **Detention Pending Hearing.** If the juvenile has been arrested, the provisions of Delinquency Rule 12 apply to continued detention or placement pending a hearing on the petition.

(c) **Hearing.** The provisions of Delinquency Rule 24(c) apply to hearings on the petition to impose the adult portion of a dual sentence.

(d) **Sentence.** If the district attorney demonstrates by a preponderance of the evidence that the juvenile has committed a subsequent felony offense that is a crime against a person or the crime of arson, the adult sentence previously pronounced under AS 47.12.120(j)(2) shall be imposed and custody transferred to the Department of Corrections. If the district attorney demonstrates by a preponderance of the evidence that the juvenile has committed any of the other circumstances set out in AS 47.12.160(d)(1) - (5), the adult sentence shall be imposed and custody transferred to the Department of Corrections, unless the juvenile proves by a preponderance of the evidence that mitigating circumstances exist that justify a continuance of the stay of the adult sentence and the juvenile is amenable to further treatment in the juvenile system. The court shall make written findings to support its order.

(SCO 1349 effective December 1, 1998)

Note: Chapter 70 SLA 2005 (SB 154) enacted changes concerning proceedings relating to delinquent minors. According to section 10 of the Act, the changes made by sections 1-8 of the Act have the effect of amending Delinquency Rule 24.1(d) by requiring the court to conform the rule to the statutory changes to acknowledge the inclusion of certain persons 18 years of age or over as minors under AS 47.12 and AS 47.14 and to acknowledge the special statutory provisions contained in sections 1-8 of the Act applicable to those persons.

Cross References

CROSS REFERENCE: AS 47.12.065; AS 47.12.120(j)(2); AS 47.12.160(d) and (e).

Rule 25. Review and Extension of Disposition Orders.

(a) **Annual Review.** The court shall review its disposition order annually. The review will take place without a hearing on the basis of written reports and any statements or affidavits which accompany the reports unless a hearing is requested by a party or ordered by the court on its own motion. The Department shall serve the parties with copies of the reports, statements and affidavits submitted to the court for annual review together with a notice of the parties' right to submit statements, affidavits or other evidence to the court and a notice of their right to request a hearing within 20 days of service.

(b) **Review Upon Application.** A party may apply for review of a disposition order. The court shall order a hearing to review the disposition order upon a showing of good cause or on its own motion. If the juvenile's foster parent is present at a hearing ordered under this paragraph, the court shall give the foster parent an opportunity to be heard.

(c) **Extension of Custody or Super-vision.**

(1) *Petition.* The Department may file a petition for an extension of custody or supervision no later than thirty days before the expiration of the existing disposition order. The Department shall notice a hearing on the petition. The juvenile must be advised of his or her right to an attorney at the extension hearing.

(2) *Report.* The Department shall submit a written report stating the basis for the requested extension and make it available to all persons entitled to receive it ten days prior to the extension hearing, unless a different time period is ordered. The report must address the juvenile's progress in treatment and the need for further treatment or services.

(3) *Status Pending Decision.* If the court cannot reach a decision on the extension petition before expiration of the existing disposition order, the court may extend custody or supervision of the juvenile for a reasonable time pending a decision on the extension petition.

(4) *Extension Past Age 19.* The court may not extend custody or supervision of the juvenile past age 19 unless the juvenile consents to the extension in writing or orally on the record.

(SCO 845 effective August 15, 1987; amended by SCO 983 effective January 15, 1990; by SCO 1265 effective July 15, 1997; and by SCO 1361 effective October 15, 1999)

Note: Chapter 70 SLA 2005 (SB 154) enacted changes concerning proceedings relating to delinquent minors. According to section 10 of the Act, the changes made by sections 1-8 of the Act have the effect of amending Delinquency Rule 25(b) and (c)(4) by requiring the court to conform the rule to the statutory changes to acknowledge the inclusion of certain persons 18 years of age or over as minors under AS 47.12 and AS 47.14 and to acknowledge the special statutory provisions contained in sections 1–8 of the Act applicable to those persons.

Cross References

CROSS REFERENCE: AS 47.12.120(b) & (f); AS 47.12.140; AS 47.12.160.

Annotations

Cases

This annotation construes former Children's Rule 28. For good cause shown, parents are entitled to a review of an order of the children's court at any time. **In re S.D. Jr.,** Op. No. 1255, 549 P2d 1190 (Alaska 1976).

PART IX. APPEAL AND PETITION FOR REVIEW

Rule 26. Appeal and Petition for Review in Appellate Courts.

(a) **Grounds, Procedure.** An appeal of a final judgment or order, or a petition for review of an interlocutory order or decision, may be taken in accord with the provisions of the Appellate Rules pertaining to criminal proceedings.

DR

(b) **Stay.** An order, judgment or decision of the superior court remains in effect pending appeal or review unless stayed by order of the superior court or the appellate courts. Neither bail nor an appellate bond is required in appellate proceedings concerning delinquency cases.

(SCO 845 effective August 15, 1987; amended by SCO 1265 effective July 15, 1997)

Cross References

CROSS REFERENCE: AS 22.07.020(a)(3); AS 47.12.120(f).

Annotations

Cases

This annotation construes former Children's Rule 29. A minor who is detained may appeal his detention order. **A. M. v. State,** Op. No. 150, 653 P2d 346 (Alaska App. 1982).

PART X. COURT ADMINISTRATION OF JUVENILE RECORDS

Rule 27. Court Records—Confidentiality.

(a) The court records of a juvenile delinquency proceeding are confidential in any case in which the juvenile is not subject to dual sentencing. Information may not be released and access to the records may not be permitted except as authorized by statute or upon court order for good cause shown under conditions as the court may set, except that:

(1) A probation officer employed by the Alaska Department of Corrections may review delinquency proceedings records for the sole purpose of preparing a presentence report on the individual whose juvenile record is reviewed. The records may be used in the sentencing proceeding and attached to the probation officer's report.

(2) A prosecuting attorney may obtain a certified copy of an adjudication or disposition order entered in a juvenile proceeding based on a written request certifying that the prosecutor needs the order to establish the elements of a felony offense. The prosecutor may not use or disclose the order except for this purpose.

(b) If the juvenile is subject to dual sentencing, all court records are open to the public except for predisposition reports, psychiatric and psychological reports, and other documents that the court orders to be kept confidential because the release of the documents could be harmful to the juvenile or could violate the constitutional rights of the victim or other persons. In such cases, court records are open to the public when one of the following has occurred: (1) a petition has been filed under AS 47.12.065 and the grand jury has returned an indictment or the juvenile has waived indictment; or (2) the juvenile has agreed as part of a plea agreement to be subject to dual sentencing.

(SCO 845 effective August 15, 1987; amended by SCO 919 effective January 15, 1989; by SCO 1185 effective July 15, 1995; by SCO 1265 effective July 15, 1997; by SCO 1294 effective January 15, 1998; and by SCO 1349 effective December 1, 1998)

CROSS REFERENCE: AS 47.12.300.

RULES OF PROBATE PROCEDURE

Table of Contents

PART I. GENERAL PROVISIONS

PART II. WILLS AND ESTATES

PR

PART III. PROTECTIVE PROCEEDINGS

PR

PART I. GENERAL PROVISIONS

Rule 1. Title—Scope—Construction—Situations Not Covered by the Rules.

(a) **Title.** These rules will be known and cited as the Probate Rules.

(b) **Scope.** These rules govern practice and procedure in the trial courts in all phases of proceedings brought under Title 13 of the Alaska Statutes, proceedings related to the release of personal property under AS 12.65.105 and AS 22.15.110(a)(3), mental commitments under AS 47.30, and proceedings to bypass parental consent to an abortion under AS 18.16.030.

(c) **Construction.** These rules will be construed and applied to promote fairness, accurate fact-finding, and prompt decisions.

(d) **Legal Effect of Rules.** These rules are promulgated pursuant to Alaska constitutional authority granting rulemaking power to the Alaska Supreme Court. To the extent that the rules are inconsistent with a procedural provision of any Alaska statute not enacted for the specific purpose of changing a rule, these rules supersede the statute.

(e) **Situations Not Covered by the Rules.** Where no specific procedure is prescribed by these rules, the court may proceed in any lawful manner, including application of the Civil and Evidence Rules, applicable statutes, the Alaska and United States Constitutions or common law. Such a procedure may not be inconsistent with these rules and may not unduly delay or otherwise interfere with the unique character and purpose of probate proceedings.

(f) **Definitions.** For purposes of proceedings under AS 13.06 through AS 13.36, "minor" means a person who is under 18 years of age.

(SCO 1014 effective January 15, 1990; amended by SCO 1188 effective July 15, 1995; by SCO 1261 effective September 26, 1996; by SCO 1279 effective July 31, 1997; and by SCO 1612 effective October 15, 2006)

Cross References

(f) **CROSS REFERENCE:** AS 13.06.050.

Annotations

Cases

In a probate proceeding, pursuant to Alaska R. Prob. P. 1(e), Alaska R. Civ. P. 82 governs the award of attorney's fees unless a specific provision of the Alaska Probate Rules apply. **Crittell v. Bingo,** Op. No. 5737 (Alaska 2004).

Rule 2. Appointment and Authority of Masters.

(a) **Appointment.** The presiding judge may appoint a standing master to conduct any or all of the probate proceedings listed in subparagraph (b)(2). Appointment of standing masters must be reviewed annually. A standing master in probate shall serve as a registrar. The presiding judge may appoint a special master to conduct a proceeding which is specified in the order of reference and is listed in subparagraph (b)(2).

(b) **Authority, Order of Reference.**

1. An order of reference specifying the extent of the master's authority and the type of appointment must be entered in every case assigned to a master. The order of reference must be served on all parties.

2. The following proceedings may be referred to a master:

A. all decedent estate hearings:

B. guardianship and conservatorship hearings under Title 13;

C. mental commitment, alcohol or substance abuse commitment, and medication consent hearings under Title 47;

D. hearings on trusts;

E. hearings on emancipations;

F. authorization of emergency life-saving procedures pursuant to AS 13.26.140(f); and

G. hearings in proceedings to bypass parental consent to an abortion under AS 18.16.030 and Probate Rule 20.

3. A master's report is not binding until approved by a superior court judge pursuant to Civil Rule 53(d) and paragraph (f) of this rule, except:

A. a master may enter orders without further approval of the superior court pursuant to Civil Rule 53(b) and (c), and paragraph (d) of this rule;

B. a master's order of removal of a personal representative and appointment of a successor personal representative is effective pending superior court review;

C. a master's order of commitment to a treatment facility is effective pending superior court review;

D. a master's determination of a patient's capacity to give informed consent to medication under AS 47.30.839 is effective pending superior court review; and

E. a master's authorization of emergency life-saving procedures pursuant to AS 13.26.140(f) is effective pending superior court review.

(c) **Objection to Reference to a Master.** In addition to the peremptory challenge of a master provided for in Civil Rule 42(c), a party may object to the assignment of a master for good cause. The procedural requirements of Civil Rule 42(c) apply to the objection.

(d) **Standing Master's Authority to Enter Orders.** A standing master is authorized to take the following actions without further approval by a superior court judge:

1. any actions authorized to be taken by a master as a registrar;

2. appoint counsel and guardians ad litem;

3. order home studies, visitor's reports, and psychological, psychiatric, and medical evaluations;

4. set hearings and order continuances of the master's hearings;

5. issue orders on motions requesting expedited review pursuant to Civil Rule 77(g);

6. accept and approve stipulations;

7. review and approve uncontested orders on annual review; and

8. order mediation and other forms of alternative dispute resolution under Probate Rule 4.5.

(e) **Master's Report, Recommendations.** A master may issue a written report or oral findings on the record concerning an order or recommendation which must be approved by a superior court judge.

(f) **Objections to Master's Report, Recommendations.**

1. *Objections, Reply, Oral Argument.* Objections to a master's report or recommendation must be filed within 10 days of the date of notice of the report as provided by Civil Rule 58.1(c), unless the court otherwise provides. A reply to the objections must be filed within three days of service of the objections. The superior court may permit oral argument, order additional briefing or the taking of further evidence, or grant a hearing de novo.

2. *Request for Stay, Immediate Review.* A party may request that a superior court judge stay a master's order issued under paragraph (b)(3)(B)—(D) pending review of the order.

(SCO 1014 effective January 15, 1990; amended by SCO 1199 effective July 15, 1995; by SCO 1270 effective July 15, 1997; by SCO 1279 effective July 31, 1997; by SCO 1317 effective July 15, 1998; by SCO 1567 effective April 15, 2005; and by SCO 1575 effective October 15, 2005)

Rule 3. Probate Indices.

(a) **Estate Index.** An alphabetical index of all estate cases will be kept under the name of the person to whose estate the case relates.

(b) **Will Index.** An alphabetical index of all wills on deposit will be kept under the name of the person whose will is deposited.

(c) **Protective Proceeding Index.** An alphabetical index of all protective proceedings will be kept under the names of the respondents.

(d) **Mental Commitment Index.** An alphabetical index of all mental commitments will be kept under the names of the respondents, except for those files for which the records have been expunged pursuant to AS 47.30.850. An index of expunged files will be kept by number.

(e) **Registered Trust Index.** An alphabetical list of all registered trusts will be kept under the name of the trust.

(f) **Judicial Bypass Proceeding Index.** An alphabetical index of all proceedings to bypass parental consent to an abortion will be kept under the name of the petitioner.

(g) **Confidentiality.** The mental commitment index and the judicial bypass proceeding index are confidential. Other indices are public records even though the files may be confidential.

(SCO 1014 effective January 15, 1990; amended by SCO 1227 effective July 15, 1996; and by SCO 1279 effective July 31, 1997)

Rule 4. Attorneys.

(a) **Entry of Appearance.** An attorney representing the personal representative or any other interested person shall file an entry of appearance with the court.

(b) **Withdrawal.** Civil Rule 81(e) governs the withdrawal of attorneys from cases under these rules.

(SCO 1014 effective January 15, 1990)

Rule 4.5. Mediation and Other Forms of Alternative Dispute Resolution.

(a) **Application.** This rule applies to all actions filed under Title 13. At any time after an action under Title 13 is filed, an interested person as defined in AS 13.06.050(24) may file a motion with the court requesting mediation for the purpose of providing an alternative to litigation. The motion must address how the mediation should be conducted as specified in paragraph (b), including the names of any acceptable mediators. In matters not covered by AS 25, the court may order mediation in response to such a motion, or on its own motion, whenever it determines that mediation may result in an equitable settlement. In making this determination, the court shall consider whether there is a history of domestic violence between the interested persons which could be expected to affect the fairness of the mediation process or the physical safety of the domestic violence victim. Mediation may not be ordered between the parties to, or in, a case filed under AS 18.66.100 - 18.66.180.

(b) **Order.** An order of mediation must state:

(1) the name of the mediator or how the mediator will be decided upon;

(2) any changes in the procedures specified in paragraphs (d) and (e), or any additional procedures;

(3) that the costs of mediation are to be borne equally by the interested persons unless the court apportions the costs differently; estate funds may be used to pay the costs of mediation only upon order of the court or agreement of all persons whose interests would be affected by payment from the estate; and

(4) a date by which the initial mediation conference must commence.

(c) **Challenge of Mediator.** Each interested person has the right once to challenge peremptorily any mediator appointed by the court if the 'Notice of Challenge of Mediator' is timely filed pursuant to Civil Rule 42(c).

(d) **Mediation Briefs.** Any interested person may provide a confidential brief to the mediator explaining its view of the dispute. If an interested person elects to provide a brief, the brief may not exceed five pages in length and must be provided to the mediator not less than three days prior to the mediation. An interested person's mediation brief may not be disclosed to anyone without the person's consent and is not admissible in evidence.

(e) **Conferences.** Mediation will be conducted in informal conferences at a location agreed to by the interested persons or, if they do not agree, at a location designated by the mediator. All interested persons shall attend the initial conference at which the mediator shall first meet with all participants. Thereafter the mediator may meet with the participants separately. Counsel for an interested person may attend all conferences attended by that person. If the mediator believes the presence of third parties is critical to the resolution of a case, the mediator may request them to attend the mediation.

(f) **Authority of Mediators.** Mediators shall work with the interested persons to facilitate agreements on substantive and procedural matters and attempt to aid in the voluntary resolution of cases. Mediators shall not issue decisions or make procedural or substantive recommendations to the court.

(g) **Termination.** After the initial joint conference and the first round of separate conferences if separate conferences are required by the mediator, an interested person may withdraw from mediation, or the mediator may terminate the process if the mediator determines that mediation efforts are likely to be unsuccessful. Upon withdrawal by an interested person or termination by the mediator, the mediator shall notify the court that mediation efforts have been terminated.

(h) **Confidentiality.** Mediation proceedings shall be held in private and are confidential. Unless otherwise ordered, the mediator shall not testify as to any aspect of the mediation proceedings. Evidence of conduct or statements made in the course of court-ordered mediation shall be inadmissible to the same extent that conduct or statements are inadmissible under Alaska Rule of Evidence 408. This rule does not relieve any person of a duty imposed by statute.

(i) **Stipulation.** If the mediation is successful, the interested persons shall prepare and file with the court a stipulation setting forth their agreement.

(j) **Other Forms of Alternative Dispute Resolution.**

(1) *Early Neutral Evaluation.* Parties or the court may use the procedure set out in this rule to refer a case to early neutral evaluation instead of mediation. All provisions of this rule apply to a case in which early neutral evaluation has been ordered under paragraph (a).

(2) *Settlement Conference.* At any time after a complaint is filed, a party may file a motion with the court requesting a settlement conference with a judge for the purpose of achieving a mutually agreeable settlement. The court may order a settlement conference in response to such a motion or on its own motion.

(SCO 1317 effective July 15, 1998)

PART II. WILLS AND ESTATES

Rule 5. Deposit of Wills for Safekeeping and Acceptance.

(a) **Deposit of Will.** Upon the deposit of a will by the testator or the testator's agent for safekeeping in the superior court, the clerk or registrar in the probate division shall:

1. Require the testator or the testator's agent to sign an agreement setting forth the names and addresses of the person or persons to receive the will upon the death of the testator, and the clerk or registrar shall in turn sign a receipt for the will to be given to the testator or the testator's agent. If the agreement is signed by the testator's agent, the agent's written authorization from the testator to deposit the will with the court, or a copy of a general power of attorney of the agent from the testator, must be attached to the agreement. The agent shall provide the court with the address of the testator and the court shall mail a copy of the "Agreement and Receipt for Deposit of Will" to the testator. The agreement and receipt will be in form and content substantially as follows:

AGREEMENT AND RECEIPT FOR DEPOSIT OF WILL

The purpose of depositing a Will with the court is to provide a safe place for the Will. It is not required by law that a Will be deposited with the court. The acceptance of a will for safekeeping by the court in no way ensures the validity of any provision contained in the will, nor does acceptance in any way enhance the force or effect of the Will.

AGREEMENT

I, the undersigned, deposit the Last Will and Testament of ________ for safekeeping with the Superior Court of Alaska. I state that ________, whose address ______________, is named personal representative in the Will and is designated to receive a copy of the Will upon testator's death and that ____________, whose address is _____________, is named alternate personal representative and is designated to receive a copy of the Will upon testator's death if the personal representative named above is unable to serve or receive the

Will. The original Will shall be kept by the court for safekeeping until filed in an estate proceeding.

This Will is a confidential document before the testator dies and cannot be released except to the testator or someone with the testator's written authority without court order. After death, it becomes a matter of public record.

____

Date Testator/Agent

(Agent's authorization must be attached)

RECEIPT

I acknowledge receipt of the above mentioned Will for safekeeping.

☐ Attached is the agent's written authorization or general power of attorney from the testator as required by Probate Rule 5.

____

(Date) Superior Court Clerk/Registrar

2. Assign a number to the will upon its deposit and shall maintain an alphabetical index to all wills on deposit.

3. Store the wills in a locked fireproof filing cabinet or safe.

4. During the lifetime of the testator, allow the will to be viewed by or released only to the testator upon showing of positive identification, or to the person to whom the testator has given the specific power in writing to receive or view the will, and who shall also be required to show positive identification. A conservator of the testator may examine the deposited will only after showing proper positive identification.

(b) **Designated Persons to Accept Wills.** The presiding judge for each judicial district may designate in writing those persons within the judicial district who may accept, for transmittal purposes only, wills to be deposited with the court for safekeeping. The designated person shall require the depositor to execute the agreement, shall issue the receipt as set out in Rule 5(a), and shall forward immediately to the clerk or the registrar of the superior court in the judicial district, by certified or registered mail, the will and the fee for deposit, together with the original of the agreement and receipt executed by the designated person and the depositor.

(c) **Death of Testator.** Upon notification of the death of the testator, the court shall contact the person designated to receive the will and mail a copy to that person. The original will must be kept on file as a public document and, when a probate case is opened on the decedent, the clerk shall place the will in the file. Upon written notification by another court that the original will is needed for filing in an estate, the original will must be transferred to the other court. A copy must be retained.

(d) **Deposit of Wills by Guardians and Conservators.** A guardian or conservator may deposit the will of a deceased ward or protected person with the court for safekeeping as required by AS 13.26.285(e).

(SCO 1014 effective January 15, 1990; amended by SCO 1062 effective July 15, 1991; and by SCO 1623 effective October 15, 2006)

Rule 6. Finding of Presumptive Death of Missing Persons.

Whenever, pursuant to AS 13.06.035, the court determines that a missing person is presumed dead, a certified copy of this finding and of the order authorizing administration of the person's assets must be forwarded to the office of the registrar of vital statistics in the district of the missing person's last known Alaskan residence.

(SCO 1014 effective January 15, 1990)

Rule 7. Duties and Responsibilities of the Personal Representative.

Before letters testamentary issue, the personal representative shall sign and file with the court an acceptance of the appointment which recites that the personal representative understands and accepts the duties and liabilities that accompany the appointment. The acceptance must include acknowledgement of the duty of the personal representative to:

(a) take possession and control of the decedent's property as required by AS 13.16.380, determine the liabilities of the estate, and complete an inventory as required by AS 13.16.365;

(b) provide notices to heirs and devisees as required by AS 13.16.360, except as provided by AS 13.16.690;

(c) provide notice to creditors as required by law,* publish notice when required, and review and either accept or reject claims as required by AS 13.16.455 - 13.16.515;

(d) advise the court in writing of the personal representative's address and telephone number as required by Probate Rule 8;

(e) file returns for state estate taxes if required by AS 43.31.121 and AS 43.31.250;

(f) pay homestead, exempt property and family allowances as required by AS 13.12.401–13.12.405, costs of administration and other claims as required by AS 13.16.470, and distribute the assets of the estate; and

(g) close the estate as soon as appropriate as required by AS 13.16.620 - 13.16.670.

(SCO 1014 effective January 15, 1990; amended by SCO 1270 effective July 15, 1997)

***Committee Note:** Actual notice may be constitutionally required in order to bar a known or reasonably ascertainable creditor's claim. See Tulsa Professional Collection Agency v. Pope, 108 S. Ct. 1340 (1988).

Rule 7.1. Personal Representative's Fee.

A personal representative's fee shall be reasonable. The following factors may be considered in determining the reasonableness of the fee:

(1) the time and labor reasonably required of the personal representative;

(2) the complexity of the estate;

(3) the skill and training required to perform the personal representative's duties;

(4) the amount and degree of individual liability to which the personal representative may be exposed during the performance of the personal representative's duties;

(5) the amount of time taken from the personal representative's profession;

(6) the expenses and costs incurred by the personal representative and whether those expenses and costs were charged to the estate;

(7) whether the personal representative retained agents and the fees charged, if any, by those agents;

(8) if the personal representative served in more than one capacity as attorney, accountant, appraiser, property manager, investment advisor, or another capacity, whether the personal representative charged separately for those other services or did not charge for those services;

(9) whether one or more persons or corporate fiduciaries are appointed personal representative; and

(10) other equitable factors deemed relevant.

(SCO 1197 effective July 15, 1995; amended by SCO 1299 effective January 15, 1998)

Rule 8. Change of Address and Telephone.

(a) **Personal Representative.** The personal representative shall advise the court in writing of all changes of the personal representative's address and telephone numbers from the date of the opening of the estate until the estate is closed and the personal representative is discharged.

(b) **Heirs and Devisees.** Heirs and devisees shall inform the personal representative in writing of any changes of address and telephone numbers. The personal representative shall give notice of this duty in the notice required by AS 13.16.360.

(SCO 1014 effective January 15, 1990)

Rule 9. Special Administrators.

If a special administrator is appointed pursuant to AS 13.16.310–13.16.330, the appointment is effective only until a personal representative is appointed or for a set term with extensions granted for good cause. The order of appointment must specifically state the powers, duties and the set term, if any, of the special administrator.

(SCO 1014 effective January 15, 1990)

Rule 9.1. Temporary Property Custodians.

(a) **Affidavit for Release of Property to Temporary Property Custodian.**

(1) An affidavit for release of tangible personal property to a temporary property custodian under AS 12.65.105 must include:

(A) the affiant's name, mailing address, physical address, telephone number, employer, date of birth, and driver's license number, state identification number, or passport number;

(B) the decedent's name and date of death;

(C) decedent's domicile at the time of death;

(D) the relationship between the affiant and the decedent;

(E) the name and address of any relatives of the decedent who are known to the affiant;

(F) an acknowledgment that AS 12.65.105 authorizes the affiant to take custody of tangible personal property only;

(G) an acknowledgment that the affiant is taking custody of the property solely for the purpose of preserving the property pending appointment of a personal representative or other transfer under AS 13.16;

(H) an acknowledgment that the affiant is answerable and accountable for the property to any personal representative of the decedent's estate or to another person having superior right;

(I) an acknowledgment of the affiant's duty under subparagraph (a)(2) to mail or deliver a copy of the affidavit and an inventory to the superior court;

(J) an acknowledgment of affiant's duty under subparagraph (a)(3) to notify the Department of Revenue if the property is not claimed; and

(K) notice to persons having possession of a decedent's property that they are not required to release the property to the affiant.

(2) Upon receipt of property, the affiant must mail or deliver a copy of the affidavit and an inventory to (A) the superior court in the judicial district where the decedent was domiciled at the time of death that is nearest to the place of domicile; or (B) if the decedent was not domiciled in this state, to the superior court in the judicial district where the property was located at the time of death that is nearest to the location of the property. The inventory must be signed by the affiant and the person from whom the property was received and must indicate where the property will be taken or held. The clerk shall provide a copy of the affidavit and inventory to any personal representative of the decedent's estate.

(3) If the property is not claimed by the personal representative of the decedent's estate or another person having superior right within three years after the decedent's death, and the affiant has no lawful claim to the property under AS 13.16.005, the affiant must notify the Department of Revenue that the affiant possesses property of a decedent that appears to have passed to the state under AS 13.11.025 [AS 13.12.105 as of January 1, 1997] and to be subject to AS 34.45.280–34.45.780.

(b) **Appointment of Temporary Property Custodian.**

(1) An order appointing a temporary property custodian under AS 22.15.110(a)(3) must:

(A) include the basis for the court's finding that the applicant is an appropriate person to assume temporary custody of the decedent's property;

(B) describe the property to be released to the custodian and where the property will be taken; and

(C) specify what action the custodian must take if the property is not claimed by the personal representative of the decedent's estate or another person having superior right, and the custodian has no lawful claim to the property under AS 13.16.005.

(2) The court making the appointment shall send a copy of the appointment order to (A) the superior court in the judicial district where the decedent was domiciled at the time of death that is nearest to the place of domicile; or (B) if the decedent was not domiciled in this state, to the superior court in the judicial district where the property was located at the time of death that is nearest to the location of the property. The clerk of that court shall provide a copy of the order to any personal representative of the decedent's estate.

(SCO 1261 effective September 26, 1996)

Rule 10. Creditor's Claims.

(a) **Presentation.** Claims of creditors against a decedent's estate either must be filed with the probate registrar or clerk in the court in which the estate is being administered, or delivered or mailed to the personal representative of the estate.

(b) **Secured Claims.** A secured creditor who wishes to surrender the security must so notify the personal representative in writing on or before the last day a claim can be filed.

(SCO 1014 effective January 15, 1990)

Rule 11. Jury Trial.

A demand for jury trial pursuant to AS 13.06.085 is governed by Civil Rules 38 and 39, except that the demand must be served no later than 20 days after service of the first pleading directed to a triable issue or five days before the scheduled hearing, whichever is earlier. The first pleading in a creditor's claim is the petition for allowance. The demand for jury trial must specify the issues to be tried by jury and the legal basis supporting the right to jury trial on those issues.

(SCO 1014 effective January 15, 1990)

Rule 12. Closing Estates.

(a) **Duty to Close Estates.** When a personal representative has completed administration of the estate, the personal representative either shall petition to close the estate by formal closing under AS 13.16.620 or AS 13.16.625 or file a sworn statement under AS 13.16.630 or AS 13.16.695. Notice must be given as provided by these statutes.

(b) **Formal Closing.**

1. The final accounting, if required, must include an accounting of all cash and property transactions since the date of the last accounting or, if none, from the commencement of administration.

2. The petition for order of settlement of the estate must state:

A. that the personal representative has fully administered the estate;

B. that all claims which were presented have been paid, settled, or otherwise disposed of;

C. that the personal representative has paid or made provisions for taxes and expenses of administration;

D. the amount of compensation paid or to be paid to the personal representative, attorneys, accountants, appraisers, or other agents employed by the personal representative; and

E. the date of the hearing on formal closing, and that any objections must be presented to the court at or before the hearing.

3. The petition shall contain a plan or statement of distribution which shall include:

A. a statement of all prior distributions;

B. the property remaining in the hands of the personal representative for distribution; and

C. a schedule describing the proposed distribution of any remaining assets.

(c) **Administrative Closing.** If no action is taken in an estate for more than one year, the clerk may send a notice that the file will be closed in 30 days if no objection is received. The order must be served on the personal representative's attorney of record and mailed to the last known address of the personal representative. Administrative closure does not discharge the personal representative or terminate the personal representative's powers and duties.

(SCO 1014 effective January 15, 1990; amended by SCO 1117 effective July 15, 1993)

Rule 13. Decedents' Estates—Substantive Rights Under Old Code Remain Inviolate—Procedure.

All substantive rights accruing prior to January 1, 1973, under Title 13, Alaska Statutes, prior to its repeal by 78 SLA 1972, remain in full force and effect subsequent to that date.

Probate of any decedent's estate commenced and pending prior to January 1, 1973, may be continued to conclusion under the procedures established under Title 13 as it existed prior to its repeal by 78 SLA 1972 provided the personal representative of the decedent files a notice in writing of this intention with the superior court within 30 days of the promulgation of this rule. If no such notice is filed, the rules of procedure prescribed by the present Title 13, which became effective January 1, 1973, are applicable.

(SCO 1014 effective January 15, 1990)

PART III. PROTECTIVE PROCEEDINGS

Rule 14. Protective Proceedings.

(a) **Applicability.** This rule applies to all proceedings under AS 13.26, Protection of Persons Under Disability and Their Property.

(b) **Review.** Upon the request of any interested person, or on the court's own motion, the court may set a review hearing to inquire as to the welfare and best interests of the respondent or ward and to take any other appropriate action necessary to protect the interests and welfare of the respondent or ward.

(c) **Change of Address.** A guardian or conservator shall advise the court in writing of any change in the address and telephone number of the ward, guardian or conservator.

(d) **Confidentiality.** All information contained in the court records relating to proceedings for guardianship, conservatorship, or other protective proceeding brought under AS 13.26 is confidential and is available only upon court order for good cause shown or to the persons listed in AS 13.26.013(a), except that the date a petition was filed, the name of each petitioner and respondent, the case number, the docket, and the final dispositional order for each protective proceeding are a matter of public record, as provided by AS 13.26.013.

(e) **Combined Cases.** Guardianship and conservatorship proceedings may be combined. The applicable burdens of proof of each type of proceeding must be met in each case.

(f) **Caption.** In all protective proceedings, the caption must provide, "In the Matter of the Protective Proceeding of ______________."

(SCO 1014 effective January 15, 1990; amended by SCO 1575 effective October 15, 2005; and by SCO 1635 effective October 15, 2007)

Note: Chapter 64 SLA 2005 (HB 53) enacted extensive changes to the child in need of aid and adoption statutes. According to section 60(a) of the Act, AS 13.26.064, enacted by section 2, amends Probate Rule 14 by providing that retained privileges be set out in the guardianship decree and by providing additional procedures related to a voluntary relinquishment of parental rights.

Rule 15. Guardianship of a Minor.

(a) **Petition.** A petition for guardianship of a minor must state the name, address and telephone number of the petitioner and any living parents of the minor, as well as the person having principal care and custody of the minor for the 60 days preceding the date of the petition. A petition involving a minor must also state the date of birth of the minor and state whether the minor is or is not an Indian child as defined by the Indian Child Welfare Act. The petition must be verified by the petitioner or signed by an attorney representing the petitioner.

(b) **Notice.** Notice must be given as provided in AS 13.06.110 and AS 13.26.060. In a petition for guardianship of an Indian child as defined in the Indian Child Welfare Act, notice must be sent to the child's tribe, which may move to intervene as provided by 25 U.S.C. Section 1911(c). However, notice is not required if the parents of the Indian child agree in writing to the guardianship and file a statement that the tribe has not been served with notice in order to protect the privacy of the parents.

(c) **Letters of Guardianship.** Letters of guardianship of a minor may not issue without the written acceptance of the person to be named guardian. The acceptance must state that the person has read and understands the duties and powers of a guardian of a minor as stated by AS 13.26.070.

(d) **Reporting.** A guardian of a minor ward shall file a brief annual report on the welfare of the minor and the condition of the minor's estate.

(SCO 1014 effective January 15, 1990; amended by SCO 1063 effective July 15, 1991; and by SCO 1198 effective July 15, 1995)

Note: Chapter 64 SLA 2005 (HB 53) enacted extensive changes to the child in need of aid and adoption statutes. According to section 60(a) of the Act, AS 13.26.064, enacted by section 2, amends Probate Rule 15 by providing that retained privileges be set out in the guardianship decree and by providing additional procedures related to a voluntary relinquishment of parental rights.

Rule 15.1. Testamentary Appointment of Guardian of a Minor.

(a) **Application.** This rule governs the procedure for appointment of a guardian named by will.

(b) **Acceptance.** Upon the death of a parent who has appointed a guardian of an unmarried minor in a will, the guardian shall file an acceptance in the court in which the will is probated. The acceptance must state that both parents of the minor are dead or that the surviving parent has been adjudged incapacitated and that the guardian has read the duties and powers of a guardian of a minor as stated in AS 13.26.070. The appointment of the guardian is effective upon the filing of the acceptance.

(c) **Notice.** Within ten days after filing the acceptance, the guardian must give written notice of the acceptance to the persons named in AS 13.26.035. If the minor is 14 years of age or older, the notice must advise the minor that the minor may object to the appointment by filing a written objection within 30 days after the date of service of the notice, and that the minor may request expedited consideration of the objection. Proof of service of the notice must be filed with the court.

(d) **Objection by Minor.** If a minor 14 years of age or older objects to the appointment of the guardian named in the will within 30 days after notice of acceptance having been served upon the minor, the court shall schedule a hearing on the objection. If either the minor or the guardian request expedited consideration of the objection, the hearing shall be held within three business days after filing of the request.

(e) **Letters of Guardianship.** Letters of guardianship shall issue upon the filing of the acceptance.

(f) **Reporting.** A guardian appointed by will is not required to file an annual report unless ordered to do so by the court upon a showing of good cause.

(SCO 1198 effective July 15, 1995; amended by SCO 1270 effective July 15, 1997)

*** Committee Notes:** If the minor's assets are above those necessary for maintenance of the minor, the testamentary guardian has a duty to open a conservatorship under AS 13.26.165–13.26.320.

(c): In the case of an Indian child as defined in the Indian Child Welfare Act, some practitioners contend that the Indian Child Welfare Act applies. *See* 25 U.S.C. §§ 1901-1923, 1951.

Rule 16. Guardianship of Incapacitated Persons.

(a) **Petition.** A petition for guardianship must contain the information required by AS 13.26.105(b). The petition must be verified by the petitioner or signed by an attorney representing the petitioner. The petition must state the priority of the nominee under AS 13.26.145 and, if known, the names and addresses of any person with a higher priority.

(b) **Notice.** Notice must be given as provided by AS 13.26.107, AS 13.26.135, AS 13.06.110, and AS 13.26.185.

(c) **Letters of Guardianship and Mandatory Education.** Letters of guardianship may not issue without the written acceptance of the person to be named guardian. The acceptance must state that the person has read and understands the duties and powers of a guardianship under AS 13.26.150 with any restrictions imposed by the court, as well as the reporting requirements, of AS 13.26.117 and AS 13.26.118. A relative or friend of the ward who is appointed as a guardian must complete one hour of mandatory education on the basics of guardianship before the appointment or within 30 days after the appointment as provided by AS 13.26.145(c).

(d) **Compensation.** Except as provided in AS 13.26.410(a), compensation may not be paid for guardianship services without written order of the court. As provided in AS 08.26.110, private professional guardians must obtain court approval of a proposed fee schedule, which must include an hourly fee and a monthly maximum amount that can be charged.

(e) **Reporting.**

(1) *By the Guardian.*

(A) *Guardianship Plan and Implementation Report.* The guardian must file a guardianship plan within 30 days after distribution of the order of appointment as guardian and an implementation report no later than 90 days after distribution of the order of appointment as guardian.

(B) *Annual Report.* The guardian must file an annual report with the court within 30 days after the anniversary of the guardianship order or as otherwise ordered by the court. The annual report must include:

(i) the name and current address of the ward and guardian;

(ii) the ward's present mental, physical and social condition, the ward's living arrangements, and the ward's opinion of those living arrangements;

(iii) changes in the capacity of the ward to meet essential requirements for the ward's physical health and safety;

(iv) the services provided to the ward, including all medical and mental health treatment, during the year;

(v) any significant actions taken by the guardian during the reporting period;

(vi) a financial accounting of the estate of the ward that has been subject to the possession and control of the guardian;

(vii) a list of the number and nature of contacts between the guardian and the ward if the ward does not reside with the guardian; and

(viii) any other information requested by the court or considered necessary by the guardian to make the court fully aware of the ward's current circumstances.

(C) *Final Report.* Within 90 days after appointment of a successor guardian or termination of a guardianship for any reason, including the death of the ward, the guardian whose authority is being terminated shall file a final report. Unless otherwise ordered, the final report must include:

(i) a statement of the reason the guardianship was terminated;

(ii) the services provided to the ward, including all medical and mental health treatment since the date of the last annual report;

(iii) any significant actions taken by the guardian since

the date of the last annual report;

(iv) a financial accounting of the estate of the ward that has been subject to the possession and control of the guardian, including a statement of when and to whom the assets have been released to include the name, address, and the authority of such person to receive the property;

(v) a list of the number and nature of contacts between the guardian and the ward if the ward did not reside with the guardian;

(vi) a detailed report of all disbursements, including a detailed statement of fees and expenses charged by the guardian or reimbursed to the guardian from the estate of the ward; and

(vii) any other information requested by the court.

(2) *By the Court Visitor.* As provided in AS 13.26.108, the court visitor must file a visitor's report with the court within 90 days after the date on which the petition is filed or by a time otherwise ordered by the court, but no later than 10 days before the guardianship hearing. In addition, every third year, the court shall appoint a court visitor to file a report reviewing the guardianship and any conservatorship during the period since the last visitor's report, as provided in AS 13.26.118.

(3) *Service.* Unless otherwise ordered by the court, all reports described in paragraphs (e)(1) and (e)(2) of this rule must be served on the following persons: (1) the ward; (2) the guardian, if appointed under this rule; (3) the conservator, if appointed under Probate Rule 17; and (4) anyone designated by the court as an interested person or special advocate. If the person to be served is represented by an attorney or guardian ad litem, the report must be served on the attorney or guardian ad litem.

(f) **Authority of Guardian After Death of Ward.** Once a guardian knows that the ward has died, the guardian has no further authority over the ward's affairs and estate except

(1) to preserve, account, and transfer control of assets to a personal representative or special administrator appointed by the court or to a temporary property custodian appointed by the court or authorized to take custody of personal property by affidavit; and

(2) as provided in AS 13.26.120(b).

Guardians who have the powers of a conservator may also exercise authority as provided in Probate Rule 17(h).

(SCO 1014 effective January 15, 1990; amended by SCO 1160 effective July 15, 1994; by SCO 1443 effective October 15, 2001; and by SCO 1575 effective October 15, 2005)

Note: Chapter 84 SLA 04 (HB 427) enacted extensive changes to the guardianship and conservatorship statutes. According to Section 32 of the Act, AS 13.26.120(b), enacted in Section 11, has the effect of changing Probate Rule 16(f) by giving guardians additional authority to perform certain acts for a deceased ward.

Rule 17. Conservatorships.

(a) **Petition.** A petition for conservatorship must contain the information required by AS 13.26.180(b). The petition must be verified by the petitioner or signed by an attorney representing the petitioner. A petition for conservatorship of a minor must state who has legal custody of the minor and the birthdate of the minor. The petition must state the priority of the nominee under AS 13.26.210 and, if known, the names and addresses of any person with a higher priority.

(b) **Notice.** Notice must be given as provided by AS 13.26.185 and AS 13.06.110.

(c) **Letters of Conservatorship and Mandatory Education.** Letters of conservatorship may not issue without the written acceptance of the person to be named conservator. The acceptance must state that the person has read and understands the duties and powers of conservatorship under AS 13.26.245–13.26.320, with any restrictions imposed by the court. A relative or friend of the protected person who is appointed as a conservator must complete one hour of mandatory education on the basics of conservatorship before the appointment or within 30 days after the appointment as provided by AS 13.26.210(g).

(d) **Compensation.** Except as provided in AS 13.26.410(a), compensation may not be paid for conservatorship services without written order of the court. As provided in AS 08.26.110, private professional conservators must obtain court approval of a proposed fee schedule, which must include an hourly fee and a monthly maximum amount that can be charged.

(e) **Reporting.** Within 90 days of appointment, the conservator shall file an inventory pursuant to AS 13.26.250. The conservator also shall file an annual report on May first of each year or as otherwise ordered. The annual report must include:

(1) *By the Conservator.* Within 90 days after distribution of the order of appointment, the conservator must file a conservator implementation report and an inventory pursuant to AS 13.26.250. The conservator also must file an annual report with the court within 30 days after the anniversary of the conservatorship order or as otherwise ordered by the court. The annual report must include:

1. the total assets at the beginning and end of the calendar year;

2. the total liabilities at the beginning and end of the calendar year;

3. income received from all sources;

4. a detailed report on all disbursements with explanations; and

5. actions of the conservator during the year regarding the protected funds.

(2) *By the Court Visitor.* If the court appoints a visitor as provided in AS 13.26.195(b), the court visitor must file a visitor's report with the court within 90 days after the date on which the petition is filed or by a time otherwise ordered by the court, but no later than 10 days before the conservatorship hearing. In addition, every third year, the court may appoint a court visitor to file a report reviewing the conservatorship during the period since the last visitor's report, as provided in AS 13.26.257(b).

(3) *Service.* Unless otherwise ordered by the court, all reports described in paragraphs (e)(1) and (e)(2) of this rule must be served on the following persons: (1) the protected person; (2) the guardian, if appointed under Probate Rule 16; (3) the conservator, if appointed under this rule; and (4) anyone designated by the court as an interested person or special advocate. If the person to be served is represented by an attorney or guardian ad litem, the report must be served on the attorney or guardian ad litem.

(f) **Discharge.** A final accounting with appropriate provision for the subsequent control of the estate must be submitted and accepted by the court under AS 13.26.255 before the court may discharge a conservator under AS 13.26.310. A final accounting must be filed no later than 90 days after entry of an order transferring conservatorship authority or 90 days after termination of the conservatorship for any reason, including the death of the protected person, by the conservator whose authority is being terminated. The conservator shall not be fully discharged from responsibility in the matter until the court accepts this final accounting after notice to all parties and a hearing. The final accounting shall include:

(1) a statement of the reason the conservatorship was terminated;

(2) any significant actions taken by the conservator since the date of the last annual report;

(3) the total assets at the date of the last annual report and total assets at the date of the termination of the conservatorship;

(4) the total liabilities at the date of the last annual report;

(5) a detailed report of all disbursements with explanations to include any fees charged by the conservator or reimbursed to the conservator from the estate of the protected person;

(6) income received from all sources since the date of the last annual report;

(7) actions of the conservator since the date of the last annual report regarding the protected funds; and

(8) any other information requested by the court.

(g) **Minor Settlement.** A conservatorship proceeding for a minor initiated because funds are part of a settlement or judgment in favor of the minor must comply with Civil Rule 90.2.

(h) **Authority of Conservator After Death of Protected Person.** Once a conservator knows that the protected person has died, the conservator has no further authority over the protected person's affairs and estate except as provided in AS 13.26.285(e).

(SCO 1014 effective January 15, 1990; amended by SCO 1443 effective October 15, 2001; and by SCO 1575 effective October 15, 2005)

Note: Chapter 84 SLA 04 (HB 427) enacted extensive changes to the guardianship and conservatorship statutes. According to Section 32 of the Act, AS 13.26.250, amended by Section 22, has the effect of amending Probate Rule 17(e) by changing when a report is due and adding additional material to be included in the report.

Rule 18. Emergency Lifesaving Medical Authorization.

The court may authorize emergency lifesaving services pursuant to AS 13.26.140(f) over the telephone or in writing. A court file must be opened and a report included in the file as soon as possible after issuance of the authorization. The report must include a brief statement of the basis for the authorization and the names of the persons who supplied the information. The duration of the authorization must be set forth in the report and copies must be sent to all interested persons.

(SCO 1014 effective January 15, 1990)

Rule 19. Authority of Attorney or Guardian Ad Litem for Respondent.

(a) Once an attorney or a guardian ad litem is appointed or appears in a conservatorship or guardianship case, the attorney or guardian ad litem must be served with all pleadings, reports, and filings in the case.

(b) Unless otherwise ordered by the court, the authority of an attorney or guardian ad litem to act on behalf of an incapacitated person terminates as follows:

(1) upon order of the court allowing the attorney or guardian ad litem to withdraw or removing the attorney or guardian ad litem from the case;

(2) upon entry of an order closing the case; or

(3) upon the death of the respondent.

(SCO 1443 effective October 15, 2001)

Rule 20. Judicial Bypass Procedure to Authorize Minor to Consent to an Abortion.

(a) **Petition.** An action for an order authorizing a minor under age 17 to consent to an abortion without the consent of a parent, guardian, or custodian is commenced by filing a petition. The petition must be under oath and must include the information required by AS 18.16.030(b). The petitioner is not required to provide an address or telephone number. Blank petition forms will be available at all court locations and will be mailed or faxed to a petitioner upon request. No fee will be charged for this service or other services provided to a petitioner.

(b) **Filing.** The petition may be filed in any district or superior court location in person, by mail, or by fax. No filing fee will be charged. If a petition is filed in a district court location, the clerk or magistrate shall immediately notify the clerk of the nearest superior court and fax the petition to that court, unless the local judicial officer has been appointed as a master to conduct these proceedings.

(c) **Appointment of Counsel.** If the petitioner is not represented by a private attorney, the clerk shall appoint the Office of Public Advocacy to represent the petitioner. The clerk shall immediately notify the Office of Public Advocacy of the appointment.

(d) **Expedited Hearing.** Upon receipt of the petition, the court shall schedule a hearing to be held within 48 hours, including weekends and holidays, after the petition is filed. At the hearing, the court shall follow the procedure specified in AS 18.16.030(e)-(g). Upon request, the petitioner will be allowed to participate telephonically at court system expense.

(e) **Findings and Order.** The court shall enter an order immediately after the hearing is concluded. The court shall grant the petition if the court finds by clear and convincing evidence that one of the statutory grounds for dispensing with parental consent exists. Otherwise, the court shall deny the petition. If the petition is denied, the court shall inform the petitioner of her right to an expedited appeal to the supreme court

(f) **Constructive Order.** If the court fails to hold a hearing within five days after the petition is filed, the presiding judge of the judicial district, or another judge designated by the presiding judge, shall issue a certificate stating that (1) no hearing was held within five business days after the petition was filed; and (2) under AS 18.16.030(c), the failure to hold a hearing constitutes a constructive order of the court authorizing the minor to consent to an abortion without the consent of a parent, guardian, or custodian. A certificate should not be issued if the hearing was not held because it was postponed at the petitioner's request or because the petitioner failed to appear at the hearing.

(g) **Confidentiality.** Petitions filed under AS 18.16.030 and all hearing, proceedings, and records are confidential. Court personnel are prohibited from notifying a minor's parents, guardian, or custodian that a minor is pregnant or wants to have an abortion, or from disclosing this information to any member of the public.

(h) **Appeal.** A petitioner may appeal an order denying or dismissing a petition to bypass parental consent by filing a notice of appeal in any district or superior court, or directly with the clerk of the appellate courts. If the notice of appeal is filed in a district or superior court, the clerk or magistrate shall immediately notify the clerk of the appellate courts that the notice of appeal has been filed. The procedure for appeals is governed by Appellate Rule 220. This rule supersedes the appeal procedure established by AS 18.16.030(j).

(SCO 1279 effective July 31, 1997)

Cross References

CROSS REFERENCE: AS 18.16.030.

PART IV. MENTAL COMMITMENTS

[No separate mental commitment rules have been adopted.]

APPENDIX

PROBATE FORMS

In 2003 the Probate Rules Committee revised the probate forms previously published in this volume. They are available in booklet form for illustration purposes in law libraries throughout the state and in the probate or customer service offices at many court locations. They are also available from the office of the court rules attorney, 820 West 4th Avenue, Anchorage, AK 99501, (907) 264-8231.

Please be advised that the forms have not been adopted or approved by any court, and that there is no provision for periodic review of the forms to keep them current with changes to the probate rules or the probate code. Before using any of the forms, it is essential to consult the relevant rules and statutes.

Following the table of contents below is a list of Probate and Guardianship/Conservatorship Forms approved by the Alaska Court System's Forms Committee. These forms may be obtained from your local court location. Some court system forms are available on the Alaska Court System website at http://www.state.ak.us/courts/forms.htm.

Table of Contents to Revised Probate Forms

Form 84. Order for Appointments (also see Alaska Court System Form PG-110)

Form 85. Letters of Guardianship

Form 86. Petition for Appointment of Conservator (also see Alaska Court System Form PG-100)

Form 87. Order Appointing Conservator

Form 88. Letters of Conservatorship

VIII. General.

Form 89. Order Fixing Time and Place of Hearing

Form 90. Notice of Hearing

Note: For more current information on court forms see www.state.ak.us/courts/forms.htm or your local court. You may also find the next list of Alaska Court System forms helpful.

List of Probate and Guardianship/Conservatorship Forms
Available from the Alaska Court System

FORM NO	FORM NAME	DATE LATEST EDITION
WILL DEPOSIT AND INFORMAL DISPOSITION OF PROPERTY		
P-100	Agreement and Receipt For Deposit of Will (st.2)	7/01
P-105	Request For Deposited Will (cs)	7/01
P-110	Affidavit for Collection of Personal Property of Decedent (cs-dup)	11/05
P-120	Affidavit For Release of Property To Temporary Custodian Under AS 12.65.105 (st.3)	10/96
P-121	Inventory of Property Taken By Temporary Custodian Under AS 12.65.105 (st.3)	10/96
P-130	Petition For Appointment As Temporary Property Custodian Under AS 22.15.110(a)(3)(st.2)	10/96
P-131	Order Appointing Temporary Property Custodian Under AS 22.15.110(a)(3) (cs)	10/96
TRUSTS		
P-200	Registration of Trust (st.2)	2/06
P-201	Registration of Trust - Definitions (cs)	7/82
ESTATES		
P-300	Notice and Order of Administrative Closure (st.3)	4/95
P-301	Order Closing Estate	7/05
P-305	Demand For Notice (cs duplex)	9/96
P-310	Claim Against Estate (cs duplex)	3/00
ADOPTION		
P-400	Instructions For The Adoption of a Minor Child By a Stepparent (cs)	7/03
P-405	Petition For Adoption By Stepparent (Non-ICWA) (cs)	4/97
P-410	Consent To Stepparent Adoption (From Petitioner's Spouse) (st.2)	4/97
P-415	Consent To Stepparent Adoption (From Parent Giving Up Child) (st.2)	4/97
P-420	Consent To Stepparent Adoption (Consent of Child Age 10 or Older) (st.2)	4/97
P-425	Consent To Stepparent Adoption (Child's Spouse or Guardian) (st.2)	4/97
P-430	Findings of Fact (Stepparent Adoption - Non-ICWA) (cs)	4/06
P-435	Decree of Adoption (Stepparent - Non-ICWA) (cs)	4/06
P-440	Request for Certificate of Adoption or Termination of Parental Rights (cs duplex)	10/97
P-445	Certificate of Adoption or Termination of Parental Rights (cs)	10/97
JUDICIAL BYPASS (ABORTION)		
P-500	Judicial Bypass Packet (cs) (includes P-501 & P-505)	7/97
P-501	Instructions For Requesting Judicial Permission To Bypass Parental Consent (cs)	7/97
P-505	Petition To Bypass Parental Consent (cs)	7/97
P-510	Notice and Assignment Re Petition To Bypass Parental Consent (st.3)	7/97
P-515	Order On Request To Bypass Parental Consent (st.3)	7/97
P-520	Notice of Appeal Re Petition To Bypass Parental Consent (cs)	7/97
MISCELLANEOUS		
P-900	Probate Deficiency Memo (st.2)	7/98
PROBATE GUARDIANSHIP/CONSERVATORSHIP FORMS		
PG-100	Petition for Appointment of a Guardian/Conservator for Adult (cs)	12/04
PG-101	Emergency Petition for Appointment of a Temporary Guardian (cs)	9/02
PG-105	Notice of Respondent's Rights Before Visitor's Interview (st.3)	1/03
PG-110	Order for Appointments and Notice of Hearing (cs)	1/03
PG-111	Order for Appointments Upon Review (st.4)	3/88
PG-115	Notice of Guardianship Hearing (to Interested Persons) (cs)	5/06
PG-116	Notice of Conservatorship Hearing (to Interested Persons) (cs)	5/06

PG-117	Certificate of Service by Certified Mail (cs)	5/06
PG-120	Affirmation—Education Requirement Satisfied (cs)	12/04
PG-190	Petition for Review of Guardianship/Conservatorship (cs)	12/04
PG-195	Notice of Change of Address (cs)	1/05
PG-200	Guardianship Visitors Report (cs)	11/87
PG-205	Guardianship Implementation Report & Inventory (cs)	2/05
PG-210	Guardianship Annual Report (cs)	2/05
PG-215	Final Guardianship Report (cs)	2/05
PG-220	Conservator's Implementation Report (cs)	2/05
PG-225	Conservator's Annual Report	2/05
PG-230	Final Conservator's Report	2/05
PG-315	Reminder Notice (Implementation Report Due)	8/04
PG-330	Reminder Notice (annual report due)	3/04
PG-340	Order Appointing Visitor to Review Guardianship & Notice of Hearing	3/04
PG-400	Order Appointing Full Guardian (sc)	2/05
PG-401	Guardianship Plan (cs)	1/05
PG-405	Order Appointing Partial Guardian (cs)	2/05
PG-410	Order Appointing Temporary Guardian (sc)	2/05
PG-415	Order Appointing Conservator (cs)	2/05
PG-420	Order Authorizing Single Transaction Under AS 13.26.205 (cs)	2/05
PG-430	Acceptance of Appointment as Guardian (cs)	2/05
PG-433	Acceptance of Appointment as Temporary Guardian (cs)	2/05
PG-435	Acceptance of Appointment as Conservator (cs)	2/05
PG-445	Letters of Guardianship of an Adult (cs)	2/05
PG-448	Letters of Temporary Guardian of an Adult (cs)	2/05
PG-450	Letters of Conservatorship of an Adult (cs)	2/05
PG-500	Coversheet—Adult Guardianship Petition Packet (cs)	5/06
PG-505	Instructions for Adult Guardianship Petition (cs)	5/06
PG-510	Powers and Duties of a full Guardian of an Adult (buff cvr)	5/06
PG-520	Coversheet—Emergency Petition Packet (Adult Guardianship)	5/06
PG-525	Instructions for Emergency Guardianship Petition (cs)	5/06

Note: For more current information on court forms, see www.state.ak.us/courts/forms.htm or your local court.

ALASKA BAR RULES

Table of Contents

PART I. ADMISSIONS

PART II. RULES OF DISCIPLINARY ENFORCEMENT

A. MISCONDUCT

BR

B. DISABILITY

C. MISCELLANEOUS

PART III. RULES OF ATTORNEY FEE DISPUTE RESOLUTION

PART IV.

PART V. LAWYERS' FUND FOR CLIENT PROTECTION

PART VI.

PART I. ADMISSIONS

Rule 1. Board of Governors: General Powers Relating to Admissions.

Section 1. As used in Rules I–VIII:

(a) "Attorney applicant" means a person who has complied with the eligibility requirements of Rule 2, Section 2;

(b) "Bar examination" means the general or attorney's examinations which shall be offered to applicants for admission to the practice of law in Alaska;

(c) "Board" means the Board of Governors of the Alaska Bar Association;

(d) "Committee" means the Committee of Law Examiners appointed by the Board;

(e) "Executive Director" means the Executive Director of the Alaska Bar Association;

(f) "General applicant" means a person who has complied with the eligibility requirement of Rule 2, Section 1(a) through (f);

(g) "President" means the President of the Alaska Bar Association;

(h) "Receipt of written notice" means the delivery of a written notice personally to the addressee or by mail to the most current address which the addressee has provided to the Alaska Bar Association. Written notices shall be presumed to be received by the addressee five days after the postmark date of certified or registered mail sent to the most current address which the addressee has provided to the Alaska Bar Association.

Section 2. Only those persons who fulfill all requirements for admission as provided by these rules shall be admitted to the practice of law in the State of Alaska and shall be members of the Alaska Bar Association.

Section 3. The Board shall examine or provide by contract or otherwise for the examination of all applicants for admission to the practice of law and shall determine or approve the time, place, scope, form and content of all bar examinations.

Bar examinations may, in whole or in part, be prepared, administered and graded by or in cooperation with other states or the National Conference of Bar Examiners consistent with standards fixed or approved by the Board acting with the advice of the Committee of Law Examiners. No contract or cooperative agreement for the preparation, administration or grading of a bar examination shall operate to divest the Board of its authority (1) to cause the Committee to review any examination, and (2) independently to determine the eligibility of an applicant to be admitted to the practice of law. The Board or any member thereof may require an applicant to appear before the Board, a committee or a master appointed by the President for such purpose, at such times and places as may be required, for oral examination and to furnish any such supplemental information or evidence in such form as may be required.

Section 4. There shall be appointed a Committee of Law Examiners. The appointments shall be made by the President, subject to ratification by the Board. Except as specified in this rule, members of the Committee shall serve for three years and until their successors are appointed. The terms of the members of the Committee shall be staggered so that the terms of at least one-third of the members shall expire on June 30 of each year. Any person who has served on the Committee within the previous three years may serve as an alternate member in the event that one or more of the regular members is unable to participate in a portion of the grading process. The President shall appoint the Chairperson of the Committee, who shall act as Chairperson for one year commencing on July 1. The Chairperson may be reappointed to successive terms. The Chairperson shall designate alternate members to serve, as necessary.

(Amended by SCO 504(1) effective March 1, 1982)

Section 5. The Committee shall prepare and grade, or administer the bar examination. The Committee shall advise the Board concerning the preparation, grading or administration of bar examinations as from time to time directed by the Board. The Board shall furnish to the Committee clerical and other assistance as may be deemed necessary by the Board.

Section 6. A majority of the members of the Committee shall constitute a quorum for the transaction of business relating to admissions. Five members of the Board shall constitute a quorum for such business.

Section 7. Any member of the Board, upon application by the Executive Director or by a master appointed by the President, shall have the power to issue subpoenas for the attendance of witnesses, or for the production of documentary evidence before the Board or before anyone authorized to act in its behalf.

Section 8. A member of the Board or anyone authorized to act in its behalf shall have power to administer oaths and affirmations and to take testimony concerning the admission of an applicant or administration of this rule.

Section 9. Any person subpoenaed by the Board or its designee to appear or produce writings who refuses to appear, give testimony, or produce the matter subpoenaed is in contempt of the Board. A member of the Board may report a contempt of the Board to the Superior Court for the judicial District in which the proceeding is being conducted. The refusal or neglect of an applicant to respond to a subpoena or subpoena duces tecum shall constitute cause for abatement of further proceedings and dismissal of the application by order of the Board and costs may be assessed in the case of the applicant's contempt.

Section 10. On verified petition of the Executive Director or of an applicant, any member of the Board may order that the testimony of a material witness residing inside or outside the state be taken by deposition in the manner prescribed by law for depositions in civil actions. The petition shall set out (1) the name and address of the witness whose testimony is desired; (2) a showing of the materiality of the witness' testimony; (3) a showing that he witness will be unable or cannot be compelled to attend; and (4) a request for an order requiring the witness to appear and testify before an officer named in the petition for that purpose. If the witness resides outside the state and if a member of the Board orders the taking of the witness' testimony by deposition, the member of the Board shall obtain an order of court to that effect by filing a petition for the taking of the deposition in the superior court. The proceedings on this order shall be in accordance with provisions governing the taking of a deposition in the superior court in a civil action.

Section 11. (a) *General Immunity.* Members of the Board, members of the Committee, the Executive Director, Bar Counsel, and all Bar staff are immune from suit for conduct in the course and scope of their official duties as set forth in these rules.

(b) *Witness Immunity.* The Court or its designee may, in its discretion, grant immunity from criminal prosecution to witnesses in admissions proceedings upon application of the Board, Bar Counsel, the lawyer, or counsel for the lawyer, and after receiving the consent of the appropriate prosecuting authority.

(Added by SCO 161 effective immediately and amended by SCO 205 effective, nunc pro tunc, March 15, 1975; amended by SCO 285 effective September 22, 1977; by SCO 399 effective May 1, 1980; by SCO 400 effective, nunc pro tunc January 1, 1980; by SCO 504(1) effective March 1, 1982; by SCO 1153 effective July 15, 1994; by SCO 1174 effective July 15, 1995; and by SCO 1193 effective July 15, 1995)

Annotations

Cases

The final authority to determine standards for admission to the Bar of Alaska rests in the Supreme Court, but it will nevertheless accept a legislative standard for admission provided it is acceptable to the court and has a rational connection with an applicant's fitness to practice law. **Application of Steelman,** Op. No. 516, 448 P2d 817 (Alaska 1969).

The authority for establishing clear and unambiguous standards for admission to the practice of law rests in the Supreme Court, and where the court has already established a standard it will not accept a legislative attempt to modify that standard which creates confusion and inconsistency without adding substantive weight to the standard. **Application of Steelman,** Op. No. 516, 448 P2d 817 (Alaska 1969).

The Supreme Court has the inherent and final power and authority to determine standards for admission to the practice of law in this state. **In re Stephenson,** Op. No. 893, 511 P2d 136 (Alaska 1973).

The Supreme Court has the inherent power to set rules for the admission to practice of attorneys; thus, this rule is enforceable even though it is more stringent than AS 08.08.110 and AS 08.08.140(3), regarding admission by reciprocity. **In re Stephenson,** Op. No. 893, 511 P2d 136 (Alaska 1973).

Use on bar examination of questions prepared by state bar of California for California bar examination does not violate section 3 of this rule. **Application of Kennelly,** Op. No. 1471, 567 P2d 301 (Alaska 1977).

That Alaska bar examiners review California examination questions only after examination is given does not violate this rule. **Application of Kennelly,** Op. No. 1471, 567 P2d 301 (Alaska 1977).

Alaska bar examination taken as a whole, is a comprehensive examination, and satisfies the requirements of this rule. **Application of Kennelly,** Op. No. 1471, 567 P2d 301 (Alaska 1977).

Refusal to regrade the Alaska portions of the Alaska bar examination did not constitute a denial of due process or equal protection of the law. **Application of Butterfield,** Op. No. 1659, 581 P2d 1109 (Alaska 1978).

Contention that Alaska Bar Association used mathematically incorrect procedure for grading bar exams was rejected. **Application of Bettine,** Op. No. 3896, 840 P2d 994 (Alaska 1992).

Alaska Bar Association did not abuse its discretion in rereading only those bar exams which came within one point of passing. **Application of Bettine,** Op. No. 3896, 840 P2d 994 (Alaska 1992).

Rule 2. Eligibility for Examination. *

Section 1. Every general applicant for examination shall:

(a) File an application in a form prescribed by the Board and produce and file the evidence and documents prescribed by the Board in proof of eligibility for examination;

(b) Be a graduate with a degree of Juris Doctor (JD) or Bachelor of Laws (LLB) of a law school which was accredited or approved by the Council of Legal Education of the American Bar Association or the Association of American Law Schools when the applicant entered or graduated, or submit proof that the law course required for graduation for either the JD or LLB degree from such a law school will be completed and that a JD or LLB degree will be received as a matter of course before the date of examination. Certified proof of graduation shall be sent directly from the law school to the Alaska Bar Association and received prior to the date of the examination;

(c) Have attained the age of 18 years; and

(d) Be one whose conduct justifies the trust of clients, adversaries, courts and others with respect to the professional duties owed to them. Conduct manifesting a significant deficiency in the honesty, trustworthiness, diligence or reliability of an applicant is a basis for denial of admission.

Any of the following should be treated as cause for further inquiry before the bar examining authority decides whether the applicant possesses the character and fitness to practice law:

(1) a criminal conviction except minor traffic violations;

(2) academic misconduct which has resulted in disciplinary action;

(3) making of false statements under oath or affirmation, including omissions;

(4) acts involving dishonesty, fraud, deceit or misrepresentation;

(5) unjustifiable neglect of financial obligations;

(6) violation of an order of a court;

(7) evidence of mental or emotional disorders;

(8) evidence of drug or alcohol abuse or dependency;

(9) denial of admission to the Bar in another jurisdiction on character and fitness grounds;

(10) disciplinary action by an attorney disciplinary agency, other professional disciplinary agency or any governmental or administrative agency of any jurisdiction.

In weighing each of the above factors, the following should be considered in assigning weight and significance to prior conduct or condition:

(1) the applicant's age at the time of the conduct or condition;

(2) the recency of the conduct or condition;

(3) the reliability of the information concerning the conduct or condition;

(4) the seriousness of the conduct or condition;

(5) the circumstances surrounding the conduct or condition;

(6) the cumulative effect of conduct, condition or information;

(7) the evidence of stabilization or rehabilitation;

(8) the applicant's positive social contribution since the conduct or condition;

(9) the applicant's truthfulness in the admissions process; and

(10) the materiality of any omissions or misrepresentations.

Section 2. (a) An applicant who meets the requirements of (a) through (d) of Section 1 of this Rule and

(1) has passed a written bar examination required by another reciprocal state, territory, or the District of Columbia for admission to the active practice of law, and

(2) has engaged in the active practice of law in one or more states, territories or the District of Columbia for five of the seven years immediately preceding the date of his or her application, may, upon motion be admitted to the Alaska Bar Association without taking the bar examination. The motion shall be served on the executive director of the Alaska Bar Association. An applicant will be excused from taking the bar examination upon compliance with the conditions above, and payment of a non-refundable fee to be set by the Board for applicants seeking admission on motion. For the purposes of this section, "reciprocal state, territory or district" shall mean a jurisdiction which offers admission without bar examination to attorneys licensed to practice law in Alaska, upon their compliance with specific conditions detailed by that jurisdiction, providing the conditions are not more demanding than those set forth in this Rule.

(b) An applicant is not eligible for admission under this section if

(1) the applicant was admitted to the practice of law in the reciprocal state, territory or district without taking a written bar examination;

(2) the applicant has engaged in the unauthorized practice of law in Alaska; or

(3) the applicant has taken and failed to pass an Alaska Bar examination, unless this occurred before the applicant engaged in the five years of practice required by (a)(2) of this section.

(c) For the purposes of this section, the "active practice of law" shall mean:

(1) engaged in representing one or more clients on a fee basis in the private practice of law;

(2) serving as an attorney in governmental employment, or as a law clerk for a judicial officer, provided graduation from an ABA or AALS accredited law school is a required qualification of such employment;

(3) serving as counsel for a non-governmental corporation, entity or person and performing legal services of a nature requiring a license to practice law in the jurisdiction(s) in which performed;

(4) teaching law at one or more accredited law schools in the United States, its territories, or the District of Columbia;

(5) serving as a judge in a court of the United States, its states, its territories, or the District of Columbia; or

(6) employed by a Legal Services Corporation program or a not-for-profit law firm, performing legal services of a nature requiring a license to practice law in the jurisdiction(s) in which performed.

(d) An applicant not eligible for admission pursuant to this section may qualify for general applicant status.

(Repealed and replaced by SCO 607 effective January 1, 1985; amended by SCO 1230 effective April 12, 1996)

Section 3. (a) An individual who has not graduated from a law school accredited or approved by the Council of Legal Education of the American Bar Association or the Association of American Law Schools shall be eligible to take the bar examination as a general applicant if he/she (1) has been licensed to practice law in one or more jurisdictions in the United States for five of the seven years immediately preceding the date of his/her first or subsequent applications for admission to the practice of law in Alaska, (2) was engaged in the active practice of law for five of those seven years, and (3) meets the requirements of (a), (c), and (d) of Section 1 of this Rule.

(b) An individual shall also be eligible to take the bar examination as a general applicant if he/she (1) has successfully completed not less than one academic year of education at a law school accredited or approved by the Council of Legal Education of the American Bar Association or the Association of American Law Schools, and (2) has successfully completed a clerkship program which meets the requirements of (a), (c), and (d) of Section 1 of this Rule.

(c) An individual who is a graduate of a law school in which the principles of English law are taught but which is located outside the United States and beyond the jurisdiction of the Council of Legal Education of the American Bar Association or the Association of American Law Schools may be eligible to take the bar examination as a general applicant if he/she submits proof that (1) the foreign law school from which he/she graduated meets the American Bar Association's Council of Legal Education standards for approval, (2) he/she has either (a)successfully completed not less than one academic year of education at a law school accredited or approved by the Council of Legal Education of the American Bar Association or the Association of American Law Schools, including evidence satisfactory to the Board of Governors that the applicant has successfully completed not less than one course in United States Constitutional Law and one course in Civil Procedure in the United States, or (b) is a member in good standing of the Bar of one or more states, territories, or the District of Columbia and was admitted to the Bar of that state, territory, or the District of Columbia after written examination, and (3) meets the requirements of (a), (c), and (d) of Section 1 of this Rule.

(d) An individual eligible to take the bar examination as a general applicant under (a) through (c) of this section shall request that: (1) certified proof of graduation and/or attendance be sent directly from the law school(s) attended to the Alaska Bar Association, and (2) where applicable under Section 3(c)(2)(b), a certificate of good standing from the Bar of the state, territory, or District of Columbia where he/she is licensed to practice law be sent directly to the Alaska Bar Association. Proof of attendance and/or graduation and the certificate of good standing must be received prior to the date of the examination.

(Added by SCO 161 effective immediately; amended by Amendment No. 1 to SCO 161 effective April 12, 1974; by SCO 220 effective December 15, 1975; by SCO 347 effective April 1, 1979; by SCO 401 effective May 1, 1980; by SCO 431 effective November 1, 1980; by SCO 466 effective June 1, 1981; by Ch. 52, § 15 of Session Laws of Alaska 1981; by SCO 593 effective May 3, 1984; by SCO 971 effective July 15, 1989; by SCO 1005 effective January 15, 1990; by SCO 1042 effective January 15, 1991; by SCO 1051 effective January 15, 1991; by SCO 1380 effective April 15, 2000; by SCO 1394 effective October 15, 2000; by SCO 1418 effective April 15, 2001; by SCO 1553 effective October 15, 2004; and by SCO 1548 effective November 15, 2004)

***Editor's Note:** Section 9, Chapter 119, Session Laws of Alaska 1978, provides that "Section 1 8 of this Act [Chapter 119, Session Laws of Alaska, 1978] have the effect of changing section 5 of Rule 2 of the Alaska Bar Rules of the Rules of Court by transferring the responsibility for the program of law clerk study under AS 08.08.207 from the Supreme Court to the University of Alaska."

Annotations

Cases

An attorney's completion of a three-year clerkship in his father's law office, with approval of the Oklahoma Bar Association, prior to his admission to practice in Oklahoma, was not "graduation from an accredited law school" within former rule. **In re Stephenson,** Op. No. 893, 511 P2d 136 (Alaska 1973).

The public interest in seeing that all members of the bar have adequate education was a valid basis for the "accredited schools" test under former rule. **In re Stephenson,** Op. No. 893, 511 P2d 136 (Alaska 1973).

The rule that a person graduate from a law school accredited by the American Bar Association as a prerequisite for admission to the practice of law in Alaska is constitutional. **Application of Urie,** Op. No. 2172, 617 P2d 505 (Alaska 1980).

This rule under which only graduates of law schools accredited by the American Bar Association or the Association of American Law Schools may apply for admission to the Alaska Bar did not violate the Fourteenth Amendment. **Santos v. Alaska Bar Association,** 618 F.2d 575 (1980).

Thirty-day residency requirement for bar applicants held unconstitutional. **Sheley v. Alaska Bar Association,** Op. No. 2191, 620 P2d 640 (Alaska 1980).

A party practicing law in Alaska pursuant to Alaska Bar Rule 43 who is not a graduate of an ABA-accredited law school is not eligible to take the Alaska bar examination. **Eyerly v. Alaska Bar Association,** Op. No. 2392, 631 P2d 480 (Alaska 1981).

The "good moral character" requirement for admission to practice law is a requirement for continuing bar membership. **Disciplinary Matter Involving Buckalew,** Op. No. 3147, 731 P2d 48 (Alaska 1986).

Rule 3. Applications.

Section 1. An application form shall be provided by the Board upon request and upon payment of such fees as the Board shall deem appropriate. Bar examinations shall be held in the months of February and July of each calendar year. The time, date, place or places of each bar examination shall be announced by the Board no fewer than 120 days prior to the first day of such bar examination, and prompt notice thereof shall be provided all applicants and persons who have been provided applications following the date of the last preceding bar examination. Application forms provided by the Board shall be transmitted with a copy of the Alaska Bar Rules governing admission to the practice of law. The Board may provide applicants with such other matter as it may deem pertinent.

Section 2. Any person seeking admission to the practice of law shall file with the Executive Director at the office of the Alaska Bar Association an application in the form provided by the board. The application shall be made under oath and contain such information relating to the applicant's age, residence, addresses, citizenship, occupations, general education, legal education, moral character and other matters as may be required by the Board; however, the application must contain the applicant's social security number. Any notice required or permitted to be given an applicant under these rules, if not personally delivered shall be delivered to the mailing address declared on the application unless notice in writing is actually received by the Board declaring a different mailing address. Any notice concerning the eligibility of the applicant sent by certified mail to the last mailing address provided shall be deemed sufficient under these rules. Every applicant shall submit two 2-inch by 3-inch photographs of the applicant showing a front view of the applicant's head and shoulders. The application shall be deemed filed only upon receipt of a substantially completed form with payment of all required fees. Applications received without payment of all fees or which are not substantially complete shall be promptly returned to the applicant with a notice stating the reasons for rejection and requiring payment of such additional fees as may be fixed by the Board as a condition of reapplication.

Section 3. An application shall be filed not later than May 1 for the July bar examination and not later than December 1 for the February bar examination. In the event that an application is filed late, an additional late filing fee of $25 shall be paid if filed not later than fourteen days after the last day for filing a timely application, and a late filing fee of $100 shall be paid if filed thereafter; provided, however, no application shall be accepted for late filing unless such application is filed at the office of the Alaska Bar Association not later than June 15 for the July bar examination and January 15 for the February bar examination. The Executive Director may, for good cause, accept applications for late filing after the June 15 and January 15 deadlines. A total late filing fee of $125.00 shall be paid for applications accepted after June 15 and January 15.

Section 4. The application fee shall be in an amount fixed by the Board from time to time. Fees shall be paid at the time the application is filed.

Section 5. If an applicant fails to meet the requirements of Rule 2, or to take a bar examination, no refund shall be made unless the application shall be withdrawn within 10 days following notice of its receipt by the Board in which event the application fee, less a reasonable cancellation fee, shall be refunded.

Section 6. An applicant who has failed to pass a bar examination required by Rule 2 may reapply for admission to take a subsequent bar examination.

Reapplications shall be made by filing a reapplication form as required by the Board by January 15 for the February bar examination and by June 15 for the July bar examination.

Applicants for reexamination shall be required to pay the reapplication fee fixed by the Board. An applicant who does not comply with this Section must reapply pursuant to Sections 1 through 5 of this Rule.

(Added by SCO 161 effective immediately; amended by SCO 204 effective, nunc pro tunc, November 25, 1974; by SCO 473 effective July 1, 1981; by Ch. 52, § 15 of Session Laws of Alaska 1981; by SCO 504(2) effective March 1, 1982; by SCO 1036 effective January 15, 1991; by SCO 1153 effective July 15, 1994; by SCO 1177 effective July 15, 1995; by SCO 1202 effective July 15, 1995; by SCO 1295 effective January 15, 1998; and by SCO 1652 effective October 15, 2007)

Annotations

Cases

The Supreme Court will not undertake to review the merits of an appeal from a refusal of admission to the bar until the unsuccessful applicant has been accorded a meaningful appellate hearing before the Board of Governors. **Application of Peterson,** Op. No. 575, 459 P2d 703 (Alaska 1969).

To meet minimum standards of basic procedural fairness, a bar applicant who appeals to the Board of Governors of the Alaska Bar Association from a denial of his admission to the bar should be given access to his examination questions, his answers thereto, and model answers to the particular examination a sufficient time in advance of the appellate hearing before the board. He should also be given access to a representative sampling of examination papers of other applicants who received overall passing and overall failing grades. **Application of Peterson,** Op. No. 575, 459 P2d 703 (Alaska 1969).

The State is precluded from barring a person from the practice of law in a manner or for reasons which contravene the due process or equal protection clauses of the Fourteenth Amendment. **Application of Peterson,** Op. No. 575, 459 P2d 703 (Alaska 1969).

Supreme court would allow applicant to sit for bar examination when extraordinary circumstances prevented compliance with rules governing application and appeal. **Sullivan v. Alaska Bar Assn.,** Op. No. 1274, 551 P2d 531, 459 P2d 703 (Alaska 1976).

Rule 4. Examinations.

Section 1. An applicant shall be allowed to take the bar examination once the applicant's application is approved by the board. Every applicant shall be notified no fewer than ten days in advance of the bar examination whether the application has been approved and shall be provided an examination permit. The examination permit shall be presented to the examination proctor on the first day of the examination.

Section 2. If an application is approved by the board, the applicant shall submit to a bar examination. The bar examination shall be given not less than once every 12 months, shall be written, and shall be conducted in the manner and at the time and place established by the board. The board may direct that the bar examination be administered to applicants with physical handicaps in a fair and reasonable manner other than the manner by which it is administered to other applicants. An applicant with a physical handicap who desires the bar examination to be administered in a manner other than the manner by which it is administered to other applicants shall so petition the board at the time of filing the application. Approval of an application and subsequent bar examination shall not operate to foreclose a subsequent determination by the board that the applicant is unfit or ineligible for certification to the supreme court for admission to the practice of law.

Section 3. The committee shall, as soon as practicable after the bar examination, certify to the board its written report of bar examination. Except to the extent that such material or information is unavailable to the committee under the rules or policies of the National Conference of Bar Examiners, the committee shall submit to the board a copy of the bar examination questions, the graders' analyses thereof, a representative sampling of passing and failing answers to the bar examination, and a written report stating the total number of applicants examined, the number passing and the number failing the bar examination, the average performance of each as designated by the code number of each, the maximum possible point value of each bar examination part or section and other information the committee or the board may deem relevant.

Section 4. The board shall determine the qualifications of each applicant upon the basis of the report of the Law Examiners Committee, proof of passage of the Multistate Professional Responsibility Examination, the recommendations of the executive director, and such other matter it may consider pertinent under these rules. The board shall certify to the supreme court the results of the bar examination and its recommendations as to those applicants who are determined qualified for admission to the practice of law and who have complied with the provisions of Rule 5. Notice of the board's determination shall be provided in writing to each applicant. Notice to an applicant determined not qualified shall state the reason for such determination.

(Amended by SCO 504(3) effective June 1, 1982; and by SCO 1487 effective December 11, 2002)

Section 5. If written request is made to the board within one month following notice of failure to pass a bar examination, an applicant who takes and fails to pass the bar examination has the right to inspect his or her essay examination books, the grades assigned thereto, and a representative sampling of passing and failing essay answers to the bar examination at the office of the Alaska Bar Association, or at such place as the board may designate. An applicant who takes and fails to pass the bar examination has the right to inspect a copy of his or her Multistate Bar Examination (MBE) answer sheet or Multistate Professional Responsibility Examination answer sheet, scores, and the correct answer key to the form of his or her MBE examination or Multistate Professional Responsibility Examination under the procedures designated by the board. An applicant has no right to a copy of any of these MBE materials or Multistate Professional Responsibility Examination materials for removal from the place of inspection. An applicant who passes the bar examination is not entitled to inspect any examination books or discover the grades assigned thereto. However, a passing applicant may be informed of the applicant's MBE score upon written request to the Executive Director.

(Amended by SCO 1487 effective April 15, 2003)

Section 6. A combined score of 140 or above, as determined by the National Conference of Bar Examiners, shall be the passing grade on the bar examination.

(Amended by SCO 247 (I) effective April 1, 1976; by SCO 504(3) effective June 1, 1982; and by SCO 1178 effective July 15, 1995)

Section 7.

(Added by SCO 247 (II) effective April 1, 1976; amended by SCO 293 effective March 15, 1978; repealed by SCO 608 effective July 1, 1985)

Section 8. All examination books and answers, including those designated by the committee as comprising a representative sampling of passing and failing answers to the bar examination, may be destroyed one year following the last date an applicant has been notified of the applicant's failure; except that no examination book and answers shall be destroyed until one year following the final disposition of any proceeding to which they may be relevant.

(Added by SCO 161 effective immediately; amended by SCO 233(1) effective April 1, 1976; by SCO 247 effective April 1, 1976; by SCO 504(3) effective June 1, 1982; by SCO 762 effective October 30, 1986; and by SCO 1153 effective July 15, 1994)

Annotations

Cases

The Supreme Court will not undertake to review the merits of an appeal from a refusal of admission to the bar until the unsuccessful applicant has been accorded a meaningful appellate hearing before the Board of Governors. **Application of Peterson,** Op. No. 575, 459 P2d 703 (Alaska 1969).

To meet minimum standards of basic procedural fairness, a bar applicant who appeals to the Board of Governors of the Alaska Bar Association from a denial of his admission to the bar should be given access to his examination questions, his answers thereto, and model answers to the particular examination a sufficient time in advance of the appellate hearing before the board. He should also be given access to a representative sampling of examination papers of other applicants who received overall passing and overall failing grades. **Application of Peterson,** Op. No. 575, 459 P2d 703 (Alaska 1969).

The State is precluded from barring a person from the practice of law in a manner or for reasons which contravene the due process or equal protection clauses of the Fourteenth Amendment. **Application of Peterson,** Op. No. 575, 459 P2d 703 (Alaska 1969).

Refusal to regrade the Alaska portions of the Alaska bar examination did not constitute a denial of due process or equal protection of the law. **Application of Butterfield,** Op. No. 1659, 581 P2d 1109 (Alaska 1978).

A failed applicant must be allowed access to Multistate Bar Examination (MBE) questions and answers and to the applicant's own answers. **Application of Obermeyer,** Op. No. 3040, 717 P2d 382 (Alaska 1986).

With the exception of failed bar applicant's argument that he was entitled to a representative sampling of overall passing and failing exams and to an opportunity to review Multistate Bar Examination (MBE) questions and answers, his criticisms of the administration of the bar exam amounted to no more than disputes with the Alaska Bar Association about the ideal way to handle the Bar exam, and did not establish violations of equal protection or due process rights. **Application of Obermeyer,** Op. No. 3040, 717 P2d 382 (Alaska 1986).

Finding that the petitioner's representation by an attorney in Alaska satisfied his Sixth Amendment rights and was proper pursuant to Alaska Bar R. 4, § 4 and 5, § 3, where all of the attorneys licensed to practice law in Alaska were in fact "counselors" as that term was understood at common law. **Crane v. State,** Op. No. 2000, 118 P.3d 1084 (Alaska App. 2005).

Rule 5. Requirements for Admission to the Practice of Law.

Section 1. (a) To be admitted to the practice of law in Alaska, an applicant must

(1) pass the bar examination prescribed pursuant to Rule 4 or be excused from taking the bar examination under Rule 2, Section 2;

(2) pass the Multistate Professional Responsibility Examination by obtaining a scaled score of 80;

(3) be found by the Board to meet the standard of character and fitness, as required pursuant to Rule 2(1)(d);

(4) be determined by the Board to be eligible in all other respects;

(5) pay prorated active membership dues for the balance of the year in which he or she is admitted, computed from the first day of admission;

(6) attend a presentation on attorney ethics as prescribed by the Board prior to taking the oath prescribed in Section 3 of this rule;

(7) file an affidavit as required by Bar Rule 64 stating that the applicant has read and is familiar with the Alaska Rules of Professional Conduct; and

(8) take the oath prescribed in Section 3 of this rule.

(b) Within 60 days after completion of the requirements stated in subparagraphs (a)(1), (2), (6), and (7) of Section 1 of this Rule, an applicant must file with the Alaska Bar Association the forms provided by the Board, formally accepting membership in the Association and admission to the practice of law in Alaska.

(c) The Board may conduct a character investigation of an applicant, or may continue such an investigation, after the applicant has been permitted to take, or has passed, the examination prescribed by the Board pursuant to Rule 4. The fact that the Board has permitted the applicant to take the examination, and has given the applicant notice that he or she has passed the examination, shall not thereafter preclude the Board from denying the admission of the applicant on the grounds of character and fitness as set forth in Bar Rule 2(1)(d).

(Amended by SCO 504(4) effective June 1, 1982; amended and renumbered by SCO 609 effective January 1, 1985; amended by SCO 1228 effective July 15, 1996; and by SCO 1488 effective April 15, 2003; and by SCO 1652 effective October 15, 2007)

Section 2. An applicant who fails to comply with the provisions of Section 1 of this Rule shall not be eligible for certification to the Supreme Court for admission and shall be deemed to have abandoned the application.

Section 3. Upon receiving certification of the eligibility of an applicant the Supreme Court may enter an order admitting the applicant as an attorney at law in all the courts of the state and to membership in the Alaska Bar Association. Each applicant ordered admitted to the practice of law shall take the following oath before any state or federal judicial officer:

I do affirm:

I will support the Constitution of the United States and the Constitution of the State of Alaska;

I will adhere to the Rules of Professional Conduct in my dealings with clients, judicial officers, attorneys, and all other persons;

I will maintain the respect due to courts of justice and judicial officers;

I will not counsel or maintain any proceedings that I believe are taken in bad faith or any defense that I do not believe is honestly debatable under the law of the land;

I will be truthful and honorable in the causes entrusted to me, and will never seek to mislead the judge or jury by an artifice or false statement of fact or law;

I will maintain the confidences and preserve inviolate the secrets of my client, and will not accept compensation in connection with my client's business except from my client or with my client's knowledge or approval;

I will be candid, fair, and courteous before the court and with other attorneys, and will advance no fact prejudicial to the honor or reputation of a party or witness unless I am required to do so in order to obtain justice for my client;

I will uphold the honor and maintain the dignity of the profession, and will strive to improve both the law and the administration of justice.

A certificate of admission shall thereupon be issued to the applicant by the clerk of the court.

(Added by SCO 161 effective immediately; amended by SCO 346 effective April 1, 1979; by SCO 392 effective January 1, 1980; by SCO 402 effective May 1, 1980; and by SCO 504(4) effective June 1, 1982; by SCO 971 effective July 15, 1989; by SCO 1083 effective January 15, 1992; by SCO 1087 effective January 15, 1992; by SCO 1146 effective September 9, 1993; by SCO 1148 effective July 15, 1994; by SCO 1153 effective July 15, 1994; by SCO 1229 effective April 12, 1996; by SCO 1378 effective December 16, 1999; and by SCO 1380 effective April 15, 2000)

Annotations

Cases

A determination by the Bar Association that a Supreme Court law clerk is engaged in the practice of law and is not entitled to be enrolled in the Association as an inactive member is reasonable and within the Association's authority. **Petition of Moody,** Op. No. 1065, 524 P2d 1261 (Alaska 1974).

Rule requiring that an applicant for admission to the state bar be domiciled in Alaska violates the privileges and immunities clause of the

United States Constitution. **Noll v. Alaska Bar Assoc.,** Op. No. 2546, 649 P2d 241 (Alaska 1982).

The "good moral character" requirement for admission to practice law is a requirement for continuing bar membership. **Disciplinary Matter Involving Buckalew,** Op. No. 3147, 731 P2d 48 (Alaska 1986).

Finding that the petitioner's representation by an attorney in Alaska satisfied his Sixth Amendment right to counsel was proper pursuant to Alaska Bar R. 4, § 4 and 5, § 3, where all of the attorneys licensed to practice law in Alaska were in fact "counselors" as that term was understood at common law. **Crane v. State,** Op. No. 2000, 118 P.3d 1084 (Alaska App. 2005).

Rule 6. Review.

Section 1. Notice and representation by counsel.

(a) Notice of any final adverse determination by the Board, a master, or a committee appointed by the Board, shall be given to an applicant. Such notice shall be sufficiently specific to allow the applicant to be able to prepare a response, petition for review, or request for hearing as may be permitted under these rules.

(b) The Board shall send written notice by certified mail to the applicant's latest address on file with the Executive Director.

(c) An applicant may be represented by counsel in all proceedings for admission to the practice of law. Such counsel shall be admitted to practice in the State of Alaska or authorized to practice law pursuant to the provisions of Rule 81 Alaska R. Civ. P., and shall file a written appearance with the Board. Thereafter, notices required or permitted to be served upon the applicant shall be served upon the applicant's counsel.

Section 2. An applicant who has been denied an examination permit or who has been denied certification to the Supreme Court for admission to practice shall have the right, within thirty days after receipt of written notice of such denial, to file with the Board a written statement of appeal. Such statement of appeal shall be verified by the oath of the applicant that all statements contained therein are true, on the applicant's own knowledge, or on the basis of information furnished to the applicant. Failure to file a timely appeal statement shall constitute a waiver of any right to appeal. The statement of appeal filed by the applicant shall state all grounds upon which the applicant intends to rely and may:

(a) Object to the form of notice from which such appeal is taken on the ground that it is so indefinite or uncertain that the applicant cannot reasonably prepare his or her statement;

(b) Present the materials and documents on which the applicant relies to establish his or her eligibility to take the examination or for admission to practice, whichever is applicable.

An applicant who is denied an examination permit or who is denied certification shall allege facts which, if true, would establish an abuse of discretion or improper conduct on the part of the Board, the Executive Director, the Committee, or a master. If the allegations in the verified statement are found to be sufficient by the Board, a hearing shall be granted. If a hearing is denied, the applicant may appeal from the denial of the hearing under the procedures of Rule 8.

Section 3. In any appeal the applicant shall have the burden of proving the material facts upon which the applicant relies.

Section 4. A master appointed by the President from among the active membership of the association shall preside at all hearings convened under this rule. The master shall hear the evidence without the Board unless the President shall order the hearing in the presence of the Board. No fewer than twenty days before the hearing the applicant shall be given notice of the date of the hearing, the identity of the master, and whether the hearing is to be before the master alone, or before the Board with the master. All notices shall be given by the Executive Director, as required by the master or the President.

Section 5. When the Board hears the case with the master, the master shall preside and rule on the admission of evidence. The hearing shall be administered as directed by the Board.

Section 6. Board members or masters appointed under this rule shall disqualify themselves and withdraw from any case in which they cannot accord a fair and impartial hearing. The applicant may request the disqualification of the master or of a Board member by filing an affidavit within ten days following the first notice of the hearing. The affidavit shall state with particularity why a fair and impartial hearing cannot be accorded by the person sought to be disqualified. Where the request concerns a Board member the issue shall be determined by the master. Notice of the determination shall be given applicant no fewer than 10 days before commencement of the hearing and such notice shall include the name of a new master if one is appointed. The time for notice fixed by Section 3 and by this Section shall not apply to notice concerning a master appointed to replace a disqualified master.

Section 7. Only the following materials shall be subject to production by the Alaska Bar Association in any proceedings held pursuant to this Rule:

(a) Where certification for admission to practice has been denied, the failing applicant has the right to inspect examination materials only as provided in Rule 4(5);

(b) Where an examination permit has been denied because of failure to meet residency requirements, the applicant has a right to inspect the minutes of any meeting of the Board of Governors at which the applicant's residency has been discussed, together with a synopsis of the facts with respect to any other person who, within the last two years, has been denied an examination permit for the same reason; and

(c) Where an examination permit has been denied on the basis of character and fitness, the applicant has a right to inspect the minutes of any meeting of the Board of Governors at which the applicant's character and fitness has been discussed, together with a statement of the specific grounds upon which denial of the permit was based.

Section 8. When the Board denies an examination permit on the basis of character and fitness, the Board shall give the applicant immediate written notice of its action, together with a statement of the specific grounds on which the denial of the examination permit is based. Within 10 days of receipt of such written notice, the applicant may submit to the Board such written argument, documentation, or other material as the applicant deems relevant to the proof of his or her character and fitness. Upon receipt of any such material, the Board shall reconsider the denial in a timely fashion and give written notice of its decision.

(Added by SCO 161 effective immediately: amended by SCO 341 § 1 effective April 1, 1979; by SCO 402 effective May 1, 1980; by SCO 463 effective June 1, 1981; by SCO 761 effective October 30, 1986; by SCO 971 effective July 15, 1989; and by SCO 1153 effective July 15, 1994)

Annotations

Cases

The Supreme Court will not undertake to review the merits of an appeal from a refusal of admission to the bar until the unsuccessful applicant has been accorded a meaningful appellate hearing before the Board of Governors. **Application of Peterson,** Op. No. 575, 459 P2d 703 (Alaska 1969).

To meet minimum standards of basic procedural fairness, a bar applicant who appeals to the Board of Governors of the Alaska Bar Association from a denial of his admission to the bar should be given access to his examination questions, his answers thereto, and model answers to the particular examination a sufficient time in advance of the appellate hearing before the board. He should also be given access to a representative sampling of examination papers of other applicants who received overall passing and overall failing grades. **Application of Peterson,** Op. No. 575, 459 P2d 703 (Alaska 1969).

The State is precluded from barring a person from the practice of law in a manner or for reasons which contravene the due process or equal protection clauses of the Fourteenth Amendment. **Application of Peterson,** Op. No. 575, 459 P2d 703 (Alaska 1969).

An unsuccessful applicant for bar admission carries a heavy burden in regard to any attempted showing of an abuse of discretion or improper conduct on the part of law examiners in grading examination papers. **Application of Peterson,** Op. No. 575, 459 P2d 703 (Alaska 1969).

This rule requires a hearing in response to sufficiently specific allegations of substantive deficiencies, such as gross errors in grading. **Application of McKay,** Op. No. 2985, 706 P2d 684 (Alaska 1985).

An examiner may commit an abuse of discretion in misgrading an answer even if the examiner acted with good faith and correctly followed the established procedure; if a model answer is defective or an applicant's scores are incorrectly computed, then an abuse of discretion may result. **Application of McKay,** Op. No. 2985, 706 P2d 684 (Alaska 1985).

Unsuccessful bar applicant's allegation that the examination committee engaged in improper conduct by failing to stop some applicants from exceeding the time limit for completing the MBE portion of the bar examination did not require a hearing since he did not allege that he was denied the proper amount of time officially allocated to complete the MBE portion of the exam. **Application of McKay,** Op. No. 2985, 706 P2d 684 (Alaska 1985).

Failed applicants are entitled to a sampling of overall passing and failing exams, not merely benchmark answers. **Application of Obermeyer,** Op. No. 3040, 717 P2d 382 (Alaska 1986).

A failed applicant must be allowed access to Multistate Bar Examination (MBE) questions and answers and to the applicant's own answers. **Application of Obermeyer,** Op. No. 3040, 717 P2d 382 (Alaska 1986).

With the exception of failed bar applicant's argument that he was entitled to a representative sampling of overall passing and failing exams and to an opportunity to review Multistate Bar Examination (MBE) questions and answers, his criticisms of the administration of the bar exam amounted to no more than disputes with the Alaska Bar Association about the ideal way to handle the Bar exam, and did not establish violations of equal protection or due process rights. **Application of Obermeyer,** Op. No. 3040, 717 P2d 382 (Alaska 1986).

Contention that Alaska Bar Association used mathematically incorrect procedure for grading bar exams was rejected. **Application of Bettine,** Op. No. 3896, 840 P2d 994 (Alaska 1992).

Alaska Bar Association did not abuse its discretion in rereading only those bar exams which came within one point of passing. **Application of Bettine,** Op. No. 3896, 840 P2d 994 (Alaska 1992).

Rule 7. Procedures.

Section 1. All hearings before the master shall be electronically recorded with the facilities provided by the Alaska Court System. The transcript of testimony and exhibits, together with all papers and requests filed in the proceedings, shall constitute the exclusive record for decision. The record may be destroyed two years following the last date upon which administrative appeal rights may be available under the provisions of this Rule.

Section 2. From the time the master has been designated to preside until issuance of the master's proposed decision and the transfer of the proceeding to the board, the master shall have the following authority to:

(a) Take or cause depositions to be taken;

(b) Require the filing of memoranda of law and the presentation of oral argument with respect to any question of law upon which a ruling will be required;

(c) Hold conferences for the settlement or simplification of the issues by consent of the parties;

(d) Dispose of procedural requests;

(e) Establish the time limitations for the filing of pleadings and set the times for any hearings;

(f) Preside at and regulate the course of the hearing, maintain decorum, and exclude from the hearing any person engaged in contentious conduct or otherwise disrupting the proceedings;

(g) Administer oaths and affirmations;

(h) Examine witnesses;

(i) Rule upon questions of evidence; and

(j) Render interlocutory decisions which are appealable to the Board of Governors of which no fewer than three members shall constitute a quorum.

Section 3. The Alaska Rules of Civil Procedure shall not apply to proceedings held pursuant to Rule I-7.

Section 4. The applicant shall have the right to call and examine witnesses, to introduce exhibits, to cross-examine opposing witnesses on any matter relevant to the issues, even if not covered in direct examination, to impeach any witness regardless of which party called the witness, and to rebut the evidence against the applicant. The applicant may be called and examined as if under cross-examination whether or not the applicant testified on the applicant's own behalf. The hearing need not be conducted according to technical rules relating to evidence and witnesses. Hearsay evidence may be used for the purpose of supplementing or explaining other evidence but shall not be sufficient standing alone to support a finding unless it would be admissible over objections in civil actions. Irrelevant and unduly repetitious evidence shall be excluded. The sworn testimony of a witness subpoenaed under these rules shall be deemed testimony received in a judicial proceeding. In any action for defamation arising out of such sworn testimony, the witness shall be entitled to the defense of privilege to the same extent available to witnesses in judicial proceedings with the State of Alaska.

Section 5. The master shall prepare in writing a proposed decision supported by findings of fact and conclusions of law. In cases in which the majority of the board was not present during the evidentiary hearing, the master shall file the proposed decision with the Board and cause the entire record to be certified to the Board for decision. The record, upon payment of costs, shall be made available to the applicant. Copies of the proposed decision shall be served by the master on the applicant or the applicant's attorney of record and on the Executive Director, or the Bar Association's attorney of record. Within twenty days after service of the proposed decision, the applicant and the Executive Director or attorney for the Alaska Bar Association may file exceptions and briefs and, upon request, may appear and present oral argument to the Board. Copies of the exceptions and briefs, when filed, shall be served on the applicant or the Executive Director or attorney for the Bar Association, as the case may be.

Section 6. The Board may adopt the proposed findings, conclusions and decisions, ruling or order of the master in whole or in part or reject it in its entirety and adopt its own findings of fact, conclusions of law, decision or order.

Section 7. The findings of fact, conclusions of law and final decision of the Board shall be conclusive as to the matter alleged in applicant's statement of appeal unless an appeal to the Supreme Court shall be filed within 30 days following service upon applicant of the findings of fact, conclusions of law and decision in the manner provided by these rules.

(Added by SCO 341 § 2 effective April 1, 1979; amended by SCO 402 effective May 1, 1980; and by SCO 1153 effective July 15, 1994)

Annotations

Cases

To meet minimum standards of basic procedural fairness, a bar applicant who appeals to the Board of Governors of the Alaska Bar Association from a denial of his admission to the bar should be given access to his examination questions, his answers thereto, and model answers to the particular examination a sufficient time in advance of the appellate hearing before the Board. He should also be given access to a representative sampling of examination papers of other applicants who received overall passing and overall failing grades. **Application of Peterson,** Op. No. 575, 459 P2d 703 (Alaska 1969).

The state is precluded from barring a person from the practice of law in a manner or for reasons which contravene the due process or equal protection clauses of the Fourteenth Amendment. **Application of Peterson,** Op. No. 575, 459 P2d 703 (Alaska 1969).

An unsuccessful applicant for bar admission carries a heavy burden in regard to any attempted showing of an abuse of discretion or improper conduct on the part of law examiners in grading examination papers. **Application of Peterson,** Op. No. 575, 459 P2d 703 (Alaska 1969).

Supreme Court would allow applicant to sit for bar examination when extraordinary circumstances prevented compliance with rules governing application and appeal. **Sullivan v. Alaska Bar Assn.,** Op. No. 1274, 551 P2d 531, 459 P2d 703 (Alaska 1976).

Rule 8. Supreme Court Review.

Section 1. Any interlocutory order of the Board of Governors may be subject to review as provided by Part IV of the Alaska Rules of Appellate Procedure.

Section 2. An appeal to the Supreme Court may be filed by an applicant from a decision of the Board entered as provided in Section 7 of Rule 7.

Section 3. To the extent practicable, the procedure governing an appeal by an applicant for admission to the practice of law from a final decision of the Board of Governors shall be governed by the rules of practice in civil matters set forth in Parts II and V of the Alaska Rules of Appellate Procedure, except that for purposes of Appellate Rule 210(c)(2), excerpts of record must contain:

(a) the applicant's statement of points on appeal and any attachments;

(b) the Board's decision whether to grant a hearing on the applicant's appeal;

(c) the report of any master appointed to hear the applicant's appeal and any amended or supplemental reports;

(d) all briefing and transcripts of proceedings before the Board and the Board's findings of fact, conclusions of law, and final decision, and any amended or supplemental findings, conclusions, and final decisions;

(e) all master or Board orders or rulings sought to be reviewed;

(f) if the grant or denial of a motion is at issue in the appeal, the motion, the transcript of any discussion of the motion, and briefs, memoranda, and relevant portions of documents filed in support of or opposition to the motion; and

(g) specific portions of other documents in the record, including documentary exhibits, that are referred to in the brief and essential to the resolution of an issue on appeal.

Section 4. The filing fees normally charged for matters brought before the Supreme Court shall be applicable in all admissions cases.

(Added by SCO 161 effective immediately; and rescinded and repromulgated by SCO 341 § 3 effective April 1, 1979; amended by SCO 402 effective May 1, 1980; by SCO 450 effective November 24, 1980; and by SCO 1601 effective April 16, 2007)

Annotations

Cases

To meet minimum standards of basic procedural fairness, a bar applicant who appeals to the Board of Governors of the Alaska Bar Association from a denial of his admission to the bar should be given access to his examination questions, his answers thereto, and model answers to the particular examination a sufficient time in advance of the appellate hearing before the Board. He should also be given access to a representative sampling of examination papers of other applicants who received overall passing and overall failing grades. **Application of Peterson,** Op. No. 575, 459 P2d 703 (Alaska 1969).

The state is precluded from barring a person from the practice of law in a manner or for reasons which contravene the due process or equal protection clauses of the Fourteenth Amendment. **Application of Peterson,** Op. No. 575, 459 P2d 703 (Alaska 1969).

An unsuccessful applicant for bar admission carries a heavy burden in regard to any attempted showing of an abuse of discretion or improper conduct on the part of law examiners in grading examination papers. **Application of Peterson,** Op. No. 575, 459 P2d 703 (Alaska 1969).

Supreme Court would allow applicant to sit for bar examination when extraordinary circumstances prevented compliance with rules governing application and appeal. **Sullivan v. Alaska Bar Assn.,** Op. No. 1274, 551 P2d 531, 459 P2d 703 (Alaska 1976).

PART II. RULES OF DISCIPLINARY ENFORCEMENT

***EDITOR'S NOTE:** This part replaces former Part II, Grievances and Reinstatement, which was repealed by Supreme Court Order 176 dated February 26, 1974.

A. MISCONDUCT

Rule 9. General Principles and Jurisdiction.

(a) **License.** The license to practice law in Alaska is a continuing proclamation by the supreme court of the State of Alaska (hereinafter the "Court") that the holder is fit to be entrusted with professional and judicial matters and to aid in the administration of justice as an attorney and counselor, and to act as an officer of the courts. As a condition of the privilege to practice law, it is the duty of every member of the Bar of this State to act at all times in conformity with the standards imposed upon members of the Alaska Bar Association (hereinafter the "Bar"). These standards include, but are not limited to, the Rules of Professional Conduct and the Code of Judicial Conduct that have been or may hereafter be adopted or recognized by the Court, and Ethics Opinions that have been or may hereafter be adopted by the Board of Governors of the Bar.

(b) **Duty to Assist.** Each member of the Bar has the duty to assist any member of the public in filing grievances against members of the Bar with the Bar Counsel of the Alaska Bar Association (hereinafter "Bar Counsel"). This duty may be fulfilled by assisting that person in preparing a grievance, contacting Bar Counsel regarding that person's grievance, or giving that person information for contacting Bar Counsel regarding a grievance. Each member of the Bar has the duty to assist Bar Counsel in the investigation, prosecution, and disposition of grievances filed with or by Bar Counsel. Each member has the duty to support the members of Area Discipline Divisions in the performance of their duties.

(c) **Attorney Jurisdiction.** Any attorney admitted to the practice of law in Alaska, or any other attorney who appears, participates, or otherwise engages in the practice of law in this State, is subject to the jurisdiction of the Court, the Disciplinary Board of the Alaska Bar Association, and these Rules of Disciplinary Enforcement (hereinafter "Rules"). These Rules will not be interpreted to deny to any other court the powers necessary for that court to maintain control and supervision over proceedings conducted before it, such as the power of contempt.

(d) **Venue.** Disciplinary jurisdiction in this State will be divided into the following areas:

(1) Area 1—The First Judicial District;

(2) Area 2—The Second and Fourth Judicial Districts combined; and

(3) Area 3—The Third Judicial District.

Venue will lie in that area in which an attorney maintains an office or any area in which the conduct under investigation occurred.

(e) **Attorney Roster.** Within 30 days of any change, each member of the Bar has the duty to inform the Bar or otherwise make available to the public his or her current mailing address and telephone number to which communications may be directed by clients and the Bar.

(Added by SCO 176 dated February 26, 1974: amended by SCO 345 § 1 effective April 1, 1979: and rescinded and repromulgated by SCO 614 effective January 1, 1985; amended by SCO 658 effective March 15, 1986; by SCO 962 effective July 15, 1989; by SCO 1365 effective April 15, 2000; and by SCO 1518 effective October 15, 2004)

Annotations

Cases

Trial courts do not have authority to suspend attorneys from practice. **Weaver v. Superior Court, Third Judicial Dist.,** Op. No. 1539, 572 P2d 425 (Alaska 1977).

A two year suspension of an attorney from the practice of law based upon a felony conviction for drug distribution and the attorney's admission that he also distributed drugs to a minor is justified even though the crimes did not involve moral turpitude. **In the Matter of Preston,** Op. No. 2156, 616 P2d (Alaska 1980).A five-year suspension of an attorney's license to practice law was warranted for falsification of an item of documentary evidence. **Matter of Stump,** Op. No. 2237, 621 P2d 263 (Alaska 1980).

Where findings to fact entered by the Disciplinary Board are challenged on appeal, respondent attorney bears the burden of proof in demonstrating that such findings are erroneous. **In re of Simpson,** Op. No. 2517, 645 P2d 1223 (Alaska 1982).

The "good moral character" requirement for admission to practice law is a requirement for continuing bar membership. **Disciplinary Matter Involving Buckalew,** Op. No. 3147, 731 P2d 48 (Alaska 1986).

The American Bar Association Standards and methodology are the appropriate model for determining sanctions for lawyer misconduct in Alaska; to the extent that previous decisions conflict with the ABA standards, the ABA standards control. **Disciplinary Matter Involving Buckalew,** Op. No. 3147, 731 P2d 48 (Alaska 1986).

Attorney was suspended from practice of law for three years for misappropriation of client's funds. **In re Mann,** Op. No. 3966, 853 P2d 1115 (Alaska 1993).

Double jeopardy protection does not extend to attorney disciplinary proceedings. **Matter of Triem,** Op. No. 4443, 929 P2d 634 (Alaska 1996).

Finding that the petitioner's representation by an attorney in Alaska satisfied his Sixth Amendment right to counsel was proper pursuant to Alaska Bar R. 9(a) and 63(b) where the definition of the "practice of law" included both the common-law role of an "attorney" and the common-law role of a "counselor". **Crane v. State,** Op. No. 2000, 118 P.3d 1084 (Alaska App. 2005).

Rule 10. The Disciplinary Board of the Alaska Bar Association.

(a) **Definition.** The Board of Governors of the Bar, when meeting to consider grievance and disability matters, will be known as the Disciplinary Board of the Alaska Bar Association (hereinafter the "Board"). The President of the Board (hereinafter "President"), or a Board member at the President's direction, may direct the submission of any matter to the Board by mail, telegraph or telephone. The votes on any matter may be taken in person at a Board meeting, or by conference telephone call.

(b) **Quorum.** A majority of the appointed and elected members of the Board will constitute a quorum. A quorum being present, the Board will act only with the agreement of a majority of the members sitting.

(c) **Powers and Duties.** The Board will have the powers and duties to

(1) appoint and supervise Bar Counsel and his or her staff;

(2) supervise the investigation of all complaints against attorneys;

(3) retain legal counsel and authorize the Executive Director of the Bar (hereinafter "Director") to appoint Special Bar Counsel;

(4) hear appeals from the recommendations of Hearing Committees;

(5) review and modify the findings of fact, conclusions of law, and recommendations of Hearing Committees regardless of whether there has been an appeal to the Board, and without regard to the discipline recommended by the Hearing Committees;

(6) recommend discipline to the Court as provided in Rule 16(a)(1), (2), (3) or (4); order discipline as provided in Rule 16(a)(5); or order the grievance dismissed;

(7) in cases where the Board has recommended discipline as provided in Rule 16(a)(1), (2), (3), or (4), forward to the Court its findings of fact, conclusions of law, recommendation, and record of proceedings;

(8) impose reprimand as a Board upon a respondent attorney (hereinafter "Respondent") upon referral by Bar Counsel under Rule 22(d);

(9) maintain complete records of all discipline matters in which the Board or any of its members may participate, and furnish complete records to the Bar Counsel upon final disposition; these records are subject to the provisions of Rule 21 concerning public access and confidentiality;

(10) issue subpoenas requested by disciplinary authorities of other jurisdictions;

(11) adopt regulations not inconsistent with these Rules; and

(12) after reasonable notice and an opportunity to show cause to the contrary, impose monetary sanctions of not more than $500.00 on any attorney appearing before the Board in a discipline or disability matter, whether the attorney is appearing as a respondent or in a representative capacity, for the attorney's failure to comply with the Rules of Disciplinary Enforcement or orders issued by or on behalf of the Board.

(d) **Judicial Members.** The Board will have the authority to recommend to the Commission on Judicial Conduct discipline for judicial members of the Bar.

(e) **Proceedings Against Board Members.** Investigations of grievances or disability proceedings against attorney members of the Board will be conducted by Special Bar Counsel in the same manner as investigations and proceedings against other Respondents, except that in the event a formal petition is filed, the Court will perform the duties and have the powers of the Board, as provided in these Rules.

(f) **Board Discipline Liaison.** The president will appoint on an annual basis a member of the Board to serve as the Board Discipline Liaison to Bar Counsel and Bar Counsel's staff. The Board Discipline Liaison will

(1) provide guidance and assistance to Bar Counsel and Bar Counsel's staff in implementing the Board's policies;

(2) have the duties provided in these Rules and as assigned by the President;

(3) be excused from sitting on any grievance or disability matter in which The Liaison has knowledge of the matter arising from the performance of the Liaison's duties;

(4) not be considered a member of the Disciplinary Board for the purposes of establishing a quorum when excused from sitting on a grievance or disability matter;

(5) have access to any grievance or disability matter necessary to perform the Liaison's duties or to assist Bar Counsel in making a decision on a grievance or disability matter;

(6) maintain the confidentiality of Bar Counsel's files as required by Rule 21(c).

(Added by SCO 176 dated February 26, 1974; amended by SCO 345 § 2 effective April 1, 1979; and rescinded and repromulgated by SCO 614 effective January 1, 1985; amended by SCO 962 effective July 15, 1989; by SCO 1048 effective nunc pro tunc September 12, 1990; by SCO 1082 effective January 15, 1992; by SCO 1243 effective July 15, 1996; and by SCO 1451 effective October 15, 2001)

Annotations

Cases

The Alaska Bar Rules do not allocate responsibility in disciplinary matters in such a way that there is an impermissible commingling of prosecutorial and adjudicatory functions. **Discipline of Walton,** Op. No. 2734, 676 P2d 1078 (Alaska 1983).

Fact that Alaska Bar Association's President, a member of the disciplinary board, considered representing the ABA before the Supreme Court regarding the board's suspension of an attorney, but did not do so, did not deny the attorney due process of law. **Discipline of Walton,** Op. No. 2734, 676 P2d 1078 (Alaska 1983).

By stipulating with the ABA not to appeal the findings and recommendations of the hearing committee to the disciplinary board and to waive the submission of briefs and oral arguments, attorney waived his right to be heard, consequently his right to due process was not violated when the disciplinary board departed from the findings and recommendations of the hearing committee without calling for briefs and oral argument. **Discipline of Walton,** Op. No. 2734, 676 P2d 1078 (Alaska 1983).

Recused members of Bar Disciplinary Board may testify to relevant facts but not general character of respondent attorney in disciplinary case. **Disciplinary Matter Involving Beconovich,** Op. No. 4146, 884 P2d 1080 (Alaska 1994).

While the Alaska Bar Association Disciplinary Board had the power to review and modify recommendations of the hearing committees, section (c)(5) of this rule did not require the Board to conduct an independent evidentiary hearing, order briefing, or hold oral arguments before issuing its decision sanctioning an attorney. **In re Ford,** Op. No. 2000, 128 P.3d 178 (Alaska 2006).

Rule 11. Bar Counsel of the Alaska Bar Association.

(a) **Powers and Duties.** The Board will appoint an attorney admitted to the practice of law in Alaska to be the Bar Counsel of the Alaska Bar Association (hereinafter "Bar Counsel") who will serve at the pleasure of the Board. Bar Counsel will

(1) with the approval of the Board, employ attorneys as Assistant Bar Counsel and other staff as needed for the performance of his or her duties;

(2) supervise Assistant Bar Counsel and the staff of the discipline section of the Bar;

(3) with the approval of the Board, retain and supervise investigators;

(4) supervise the maintenance of any records;

(5) aid members of the public in filing grievances;

(6) process all grievances;

(7) investigate alleged misconduct of attorneys;

(8) after finding probable cause to believe that client funds have not been properly handled, and with the approval of one Area Division member, verify the accuracy of a Respondent's bank accounts that contain, should contain, or have contained client funds; Bar Council will serve upon Respondent the results of the verification in writing; any costs associated with the examination or subsequent proceedings may be assessed against the Respondent when substantial irregularities in the accounts are found;

(9) dismiss grievances if it appears from the investigation that there is no probable cause to believe that misconduct has occurred;

(10) in his or her discretion, refer a grievance to the Attorney Fee Review Committee for proceedings under Part III of the Alaska Bar Rules, if the grievance concerns a fee dispute;

(11) in his or her discretion, refer a grievance to a mediator, for proceedings under Rule 13;

(12) in his or her discretion, upon a finding of misconduct and with the approval of one member of an Area Division, impose a written private admonition upon a Respondent;

(13) in his or her discretion, after seeking review in accordance with Rule 25(d), and upon a finding of probable cause to believe that misconduct has occurred, file a petition for formal hearing initiating public proceedings;

(14) in his or her discretion, appeal a recommendation of a Hearing Committee to the Board or, pursuant to Part III of the Rules of Appellate Procedure, file a petition to the Court for hearing on a recommendation or order of the Board;

(15) in the absence of a specific grievance, initiate investigation of any misconduct and prepare and file grievances in the name of the Bar;

(16) appear at reinstatement hearings requested by suspended or disbarred attorneys;

(17) report to the Commission on Judicial Conduct any grievance involving a judge, even if the grievance arises from the judge's conduct before (s)he became a judge, or from conduct unconnected with his or her judicial office;

(18) in his or her discretion, initiate a grievance proceeding against a Respondent who is the subject of disciplinary proceedings before the Commission on Judicial Conduct, whether or not a finding of misconduct has been made by the Commission;

(19) keep the Board fully informed about the progress of all matters in his or her charge;

(20) cooperate with individuals authorized by other jurisdictions to perform disciplinary functions for that jurisdiction; and

(21) perform other duties as set forth in these Rules or as assigned by the Board.

(b) **Grievance Forms.** Bar Counsel will furnish forms which may be used by any person to allege misconduct against an attorney. The forms will be available to the public through the office of the Bar and through the office of every clerk of court.

(c) **Dismissal of Grievance.** Any grievance dismissed by Bar Counsel will be the subject of a summary prepared by Bar Counsel and filed with the Board. The names of the parties involved will not be provided in the summary. Bar Counsel will communicate disposition of the matter promptly to the Complainant and Respondent.

(d) **Record Keeping.** This Bar Counsel will maintain records of all grievances processed and maintain statistical data reflecting

(1) the subject of the grievances received and acted upon;

(2) the status and ultimate disposition of each grievance; and

(3) the number of times each attorney is the Respondent in a grievance, including the subjects of the grievances, and the ultimate disposition of each.

(e) **Quarterly Report to Court and Board.** The Bar Counsel will provide a quarterly report to the Court and the Board providing information about the number of cases filed and closed during the quarter, the status of pending cases, the disposition of closed cases, and the subject of the grievances received. The names of the Respondents will not be provided in the report.

(f) **Delegation to Assistant Bar Counsel.** Bar Counsel may delegate such tasks as (s)he deems appropriate to Assistant Bar Counsel (hereinafter "Assistants"). Any reference in these Rules to Bar Counsel will include the Assistants.

(g) **Proceedings Against Bar Counsel.** Proceedings against Bar Counsel or any Assistant Bar Counsel will be conducted in the same manner as proceedings against any other Respondent. In these matters, the Board will appoint Special Bar Counsel who will perform the duties and have the powers of Bar Counsel as provided in these Rules.

(h) **Disposal of Files.** Bar Counsel will destroy files of disciplinary, disability, and reinstatement proceedings in accordance with Rule 32.

(Added by SCO 176 dated February 26, 1974; rescinded and repromulgated by SCO 345 § 3 effective April 1, 1979; and rescinded and repromulgated by SCO 614 effective January 1, 1985; amended by SCO 658 effective March 15, 1986; by SCO 962 effective July 15, 1989; and by SCO 1314 effective July 15, 1998)

Rule 12. Area Discipline Divisions and Hearing Committees.

(a) **Appointment of Area Division Members.** Members of Area Discipline Divisions (hereinafter "Area Divisions") will be appointed by the chief justice under the procedure set out in this rule. One Area Division will be established in each area defined in Rule 9(d). Each Area Division will consist of

(1) not less than six members in good standing of the Bar, each of whom maintains an office for the practice of law within the area of disciplinary jurisdiction for which he or she is appointed; and

(2) not less than three non-attorney members of the public (hereinafter "public member"), each of whom resides in the area of disciplinary jurisdiction for which he or she is appointed, is a United States Citizen, is at least 25 years of age, and is a resident of the State of Alaska.

Area Division members will each serve a four year term, with each term to commence July 1 and expire on June 30th of the fourth year. No member will serve for more than two consecutive terms. A member whose term has expired prior to the disposition of a disciplinary or disability matter to which he or she has been assigned will continue to serve until the conclusion and disposition of that matter. This continued service will not prevent immediate appointment of his or her successor. A member who has served two consecutive terms may be reappointed after the expiration of one year.

By May 15 of each year, the Board will send the chief justice lists of proposed Area Division members meeting these qualifications together with their resumes. The chief justice will appoint the members of the Area Discipline Divisions from these lists.

(b) **Powers and Duties of Area Division Members.** Upon selection and assignment by the Director, Area Division members will have the powers and duties to

(1) sit on Hearing Committees;

(2) review requests from Bar Counsel to impose private admonitions upon Respondents pursuant to Rule 22(d);

(3) hear appeals from complainants from dismissals of grievances pursuant to Rule 25(c);

(4) review Bar Counsel's decision to file a formal petition pursuant to Rule 25(e);

(5) review challenges to Hearing Committee members pursuant to Section (h) of this Rule; and

(6) issue subpoenas and hear challenges to their validity pursuant to Rule 24(a).

(c) **Representation of Respondents Prohibited.** Members serving on Area Divisions will not represent a Respondent in disability or grievance matters during his or her term.

(d) **Failure to Perform.** The chief justice has the power to remove an Area Division member for good cause. The chief justice will appoint a replacement attorney or public member to serve the balance of the term of the removed member.

(e) **Assignment of Hearing Committee Members.** The Director will select and assign members of an Area Division to a Hearing Committee of not less than two attorney members and one public member. In addition, the Director will appoint an attorney member as chair of the Hearing Committee.

(f) **Hearing Committee Quorum.** Three members of a Hearing Committee will constitute a quorum, one of whom will be a public member. The Hearing Committee chair will vote except when an even number of Hearing Committee members is sitting. Each Hearing Committee will act only with the agreement of a majority of its voting members sitting for the matter before it.

(g) **Conflict of Interest.** A Hearing Committee member may not consider a matter when

(1) (s)he is a party or is directly interested;

(2) (s)he is a material witness;

(3) (s)he is related to the Respondent by blood or affinity within the third degree;

(4) the Respondent has retained the Hearing Committee member as his or her attorney or has been professionally counseled by him or her in any matter within two years preceding the filing of the formal petition before the Committee; or

(5) (s)he believes that, for any reason, (s)he cannot give a fair and impartial decision.

(h) **Challenged Member.** Any challenge for cause to an Area Division member assigned to a Hearing Committee must be made by either Respondent or Bar Counsel within 10 days following notice of the assignment, unless new evidence is discovered which establishes grounds for a challenge for cause. The challenge will be ruled upon by an Area Division member selected by the Director from the Area Division from which the Hearing Committee was chosen. If the Area Division member finds the challenge well taken, he or she will notify the Director, who will assign another member of the Area Division to the Hearing Committee. If a quorum exists in the absence of the challenged member, the Director need not assign a replacement.

Within 10 days of the notice of assignment of Hearing Committee members, a Respondent may file one peremptory challenge and the Bar Counsel may file one peremptory challenge. The Director will at once, and without requiring proof, relieve the challenged member of his or her obligation to participate, and the Director will assign another member of the Area Division to the Hearing Committee. If a quorum exists in the absence of the challenged member, the Director need not appoint a replacement.

(i) **Powers and Duties of Committees.** Hearing Committees will have the powers and duties to

(1) swear witnesses, who will be examined under oath or affirmation, and conduct hearings on formal charges of misconduct referred to them by Bar Counsel;

(2) acting as a body, or through a single member, issue subpoenas and consider challenges to their validity;

(3) direct, in their discretion, the submission of proposed findings of fact, conclusions of law, recommendations, and briefs; and

(4) submit a written report to the Board. This report will contain the Hearing Committee's findings of fact, conclusions of law, and recommendation, and will be submitted together with the record, including any briefs submitted and a transcript of the proceedings before it.

(j) **Proceedings Against Division Members.** Proceedings against attorney members of Area Divisions will be conducted in the same manner as proceedings against any other Respondent. In the event a formal petition is filed against an Area Division member, or the attorney member is placed on disability inactive status, (s)he will not be assigned to any future matters pending disposition of the proceeding. If a finding of misconduct or disability is made against an attorney Area Division member, (s)he will be removed from the Division in accordance with Section (d) of this Rule.

(k) **Procedure for Selection and Assignment of Area Division Members by the Director.** The Director will select and assign Area Division Members as required by this rule from a roster of the members appointed by the chief justice. If a member declines to serve an assignment, the Director shall select the next member in order and place the declining member in line for the next assignment. The Director may request that the chief justice remove a member from the roster if that member declines assignments on two consecutive occasions.

(Added by SCO 176 dated February 26, 1974; amended by SCO 345 § 4 effective April 1, 1979; and rescinded and repromulgated by SCO 614 effective January 1, 1985; amended by SCO 962 effective July 15, 1989; by SCO 1082 effective January 15, 1992; by SCO 1244 effective July 15, 1996; and by SCO 1451 effective October 15, 2001)

Rule 13. Mediation Panels.

(a) **Definition.** Mediation panels will be established for the purpose of settling disputes between attorneys and their clients or other persons referred to the panels by Bar Counsel under guidelines set by the Board with the consent of the attorneys and the clients or other persons. However, matters likely to result in disbarment, suspension or probation or matters which involve dishonesty or material misrepresentation may not be referred to mediation. At least one mediation panel will be established in each area defined in Rule 9(d).

(b) **Terms.** Each mediation panel will consist of at least three members qualified under guidelines set by the Board, each of whom resides in the area for which he or she is appointed. The members of each mediation panel will be appointed by the President subject to ratification by the Board. The members will serve staggered terms of three years, each to commence on July 1 and expire on June 30th of the third year.

(c) **Powers and Duties.** A member of a mediation panel will be known as a mediator. Only one mediator need act on any single matter. Mediators will have the power and duty to mediate disputes referred to them by Bar Counsel pursuant to Rule 11(a)(11). A mediator will have the power to end a mediation if the mediator determines that further efforts at mediation would be unwarranted or that the matter is inappropriate for mediation under paragraph (a). A mediator may recommend that the attorney seek the services of a lawyer's assistance program. A mediator may not be required to testify concerning the substance of the mediation.

(d) **Informal Proceedings.** Proceedings before a mediator will be informal and confidential. A mediator will not have subpoena power or the power to swear witnesses. A mediator does not have the authority to impose a resolution upon any party to the dispute.

(e) **Written Agreement.** If proceedings before a mediator produce resolution of the dispute in whole or in part, the mediator will prepare a written agreement containing the resolution which will be signed by the parties to the dispute and which will be legally enforceable as any other civil contract.

(f) **Report to Bar Counsel.** When the dispute has been resolved, or when in the judgment of the mediator further efforts at mediation would be unwarranted, the mediator will submit a written report to the Bar Counsel which will include

(1) a summary of the dispute;

(2) the contentions of the parties to the dispute;

(3) any agreement which may have been reached; and

(4) any matters upon which agreement was not reached.

(g) **Obligation of Attorney to Participate in Good Faith.** Any attorney involved in a dispute referred to a mediator has the obligation to confer expeditiously with the mediator and with all other parties to the dispute and to cooperate in good faith with the mediator in an effort to resolve the dispute.

(Added by SCO 176 dated February 26, 1974; amended by SCO 233(2) effective April 1, 1976; by SCO 345 § 5 effective April 1, 1979; by SCO 403 effective May 1, 1980; by SCO 467 effective June 1, 1981; and rescinded and repromulgated by SCO 614 effective January 1, 1985; amended by SCO 962 effective July 15, 1989; and by SCO 1314 effective July 15, 1998)

Rule 14. Executive Director of Alaska Bar Association.

The Executive Director of the Alaska Bar Association (hereinafter "Director"), or an assistant designated by the Director, has the administrative powers and duties to

(1) appoint and supervise an administrative staff for purposes of maintaining documents generated by disciplinary, disability, and reinstatement proceedings;

(2) on behalf of Hearing Committees and the Disciplinary Board

(A) accept petitions for formal hearing;

(B) accept Board and Hearing Committee reports, records, pleadings, and other documents generated in the course of disciplinary, disability, and reinstatement proceedings; and

(C) act as clerk in calendaring and scheduling hearing matters;

(3) select and assign not less than three members of Area Divisions to serve on Hearing Committees in accordance with Rule 12(e), and to appoint an attorney as chair of the Hearing Committee;

(4) replace and assign Hearing Committee members when necessary in accordance with Rule 12(h);

(5) as set forth in these Rules, select members from the Area Divisions for purposes of

(A) consultation with Bar Counsel;

(B) appeals from or review of Bar Counsel determinations; and

(C) review of challenges to Hearing Committee members; and

(6) perform other duties for and on behalf of the Board as set forth in these Rules or as assigned by the President or the Board.

(Added by SCO 176 dated February 26, 1974; and amended by SCO 233(3) and (4) effective April 1, 1976; by SCO 294 effective March 1, 1978; by SCO 345 § 6 effective April 1, 1979; by SCO 353 effective April 1, 1979; by SCO 404, effective, nunc pro tunc, January 1, 1980; by SCO 467 effective June 1, 1981; and rescinded and repromulgated by SCO 614 effective January 1, 1985; amended by SCO 962 effective July 15, 1989)

Rule 15. Grounds For Discipline.

(a) **Grounds for Discipline.** In addition to those standards of conduct prescribed by the Alaska Rules of Professional Conduct, Ethics Opinions adopted by the Board of Governors of the Bar, and the Code of Judicial Conduct, the following acts or omissions by a member of the Alaska Bar Association, or by any attorney who appears, participates, or otherwise engages in the practice of law in this State, individually or in concert with any other person or persons, will constitute misconduct and will be grounds for discipline whether or not the act or omission occurred in the course of an attorney-client relationship:

(1) conduct which results in conviction of a serious crime as defined in Rule 26(b);

(2) conduct which results in attorney or judicial discipline in any other jurisdiction, as provided in Rule 27;

(3) knowing misrepresentation of any facts or circumstances surrounding a grievance;

(4) failure to answer a grievance, failure to answer a formal petition for hearing, or failure to furnish information or respond to a request from the Board, Bar Counsel, an Area Division member, or a Hearing Committee in conforming with any of these Rules;

(5) contempt of the Board, of a Hearing Committee, or of any duly appointed substitute;

(6) engaging in the practice of law while on inactive status, or while disbarred or suspended from the practice of law for any reason;

(7) failure to perform or comply with any condition of discipline imposed pursuant to these Rules; or

(8) failure to inform the Bar of his or her current mailing address and telephone number as provided in Rule 9(e).

(b) **Unauthorized Practice of Law.**

(1) For purposes of the practice of law prohibition for disbarred and suspended attorneys in subparagraph (a)(6) of this rule, except for attorneys suspended solely for non-payment of bar fees, "practice of law" is defined as:

(A) holding oneself out as an attorney or lawyer authorized to practice law;

(B) rendering legal consultation or advice to a client;

(C) appearing on behalf of a client in any hearing or proceeding or before any judicial officer, arbitrator, mediator, court, public agency, referee, magistrate, commissioner, hearing officer, or governmental body which is operating in its adjudicative capacity, including the submission of pleadings;

(D) appearing as a representative of the client at a deposition or other discovery matter;

(E) negotiating or transacting any matter for or on behalf of a client with third parties; or

(F) receiving, disbursing, or otherwise handling a client's funds.

(2) For purposes of the practice of law prohibition for attorneys suspended solely for the non-payment of fees and for inactive attorneys, "practice of law" is defined as it is in subparagraph (b)(1) of this rule, except that these persons may represent another to the extent that a layperson would be allowed to do so.

(c) **Employment of Disbarred, Suspended, or Resigned Attorney.**

(1) For purposes of this rule:

(A) "disbarred or suspended attorney" means an attorney who has been disbarred or suspended from the practice of law in any jurisdiction;

(B) "employ" means to engage the services of another, including employees, agents, independent contractors and consultants, regardless of whether any compensation is paid;

(C) "involuntarily inactive attorney" means an attorney who has been transferred to interim disability inactive status or to disability inactive status under Alaska Bar Rule 30 or under a comparable rule in another jurisdiction; and

(D) "resigned attorney" means an attorney who has resigned from the bar association of any jurisdiction while disciplinary charges are pending.

(2) A member shall not employ, associate professionally with, or aid a person the member knows or reasonably should know is a disbarred, suspended, resigned, or involuntarily inactive attorney to perform the following on behalf of the member's client:

(A) render legal consultation or advice to the client;

(B) appear on behalf of a client in any hearing or proceeding or before any judicial officer, arbitrator, mediator, court, public agency, referee, magistrate, commissioner, or hearing officer;

(C) appear as a representative of the client at a deposition or other discovery matter;

(D) negotiate or transact any matter for or on behalf of the client with third parties;

(E) receive, disburse, or otherwise handle the client's funds; or

(F) engage in activities which constitute the practice of law.

(3) A member may employ, associate professionally with, or aid a disbarred, suspended, resigned, or involuntarily inactive attorney to perform research, drafting or clerical activities, including but not limited to:

(A) legal work of a preparatory nature, such as legal research, the assemblage of data and other necessary information, drafting of pleadings, briefs, and other similar documents;

(B) direct communication with the client or third parties regarding matters such as scheduling, billing, updates, confirmation of receipt or sending of correspondence and messages; or

(C) accompanying an active member in attending a deposition or other discovery matter for the limited purpose of providing clerical assistance to the active member who will appear as the representative of the client.

(4) Prior to or at the time of employing a person the member knows or reasonably should know is a disbarred, suspended, resigned, or involuntarily inactive attorney, the member shall serve upon the Alaska Bar Association written notice of the employment, including a full description of such person's current bar status. The written notice shall also list the activities prohibited in paragraph (c)(2) and state that the disbarred, suspended, resigned, or involuntarily inactive attorney will not perform such activities. The member shall serve similar written notice upon each client on whose specific matter such person will work, prior to or at the time of employing such person to work on the client's specific matter. The member shall obtain proof of service of the client's written notice and shall retain such proof and a true and correct copy of the client's written notice for two years following termination of the member's employment with the client.

(5) A member may, without client or Bar Association notification, employ a disbarred, suspended, resigned, or involuntarily inactive attorney whose sole function is to perform office physical plant or equipment maintenance, courier or delivery services, catering, reception, typing or transcription, or other similar support activities.

(6) Upon termination of the disbarred, suspended, resigned or involuntarily inactive attorney, the member shall promptly serve upon the Bar Association written notice of the termination.

(Added by SCO 176 dated February 26, 1974; amended by SCO 304 effective March 20, 1978; by SCO 345 § 7 effective April 1, 1979; by SCO 405 effective, nunc pro tunc, January 1, 1980; by SCO 467 effective June 1, 1981; and rescinded and repromulgated by SCO 614 effective January 1, 1985; amended by SCO 658 effective March 15, 1986; by SCO 888 effective July 15, 1988; by SCO 941 effective January 15, 1989; by SCO 962 effective July 15, 1989; by SCO 1017 effective January 15, 1990; by SCO 1156 effective July 15, 1994; by SCO 1314 effective July 15, 1998; and by SCO 1320 effective July 15, 1998; corrected May 1998)

Annotations

Cases

Professional services performed by one licensed to practice law must conform to the standards of the profession, regardless of the capacity in which an attorney may be acting. **In re Cornelius,** Op. No. 1019, 520 P2d 76 (Alaska 1974).

An attorney will be held to the standards of his profession if his activities are so legal related as to be part of his practice of law. **In re Cornelius,** Op. No. 1019, 520 P2d 76 (Alaska 1974).

Public censure was warranted for attorney who neglected over a period of many years to attend to the necessary legal work connected with seven estates for which he was attorney of record. **In re Collins,** Op. No. 1694, 583 P2d 207 (Alaska 1978).

Attorney's failure to respond to the Alaska Bar Association's request for "full and fair disclosure" warranted the disciplinary sanction of public censure. **In re Minor,** Op. No. 2613, 658 P2d 781 (Alaska 1983).

Public censure was an appropriate sanction for attorney's failure to respond to a request for investigation as required by the Alaska Bar Rules. **Matter of Evans,** Op. No. 2643, 661 P2d 171 (Alaska 1983).

Suspension for 18 months was appropriate punishment for attorney who "created" a deed of trust and attached it as an exhibit to an unverified complaint. **Discipline of Walton,** Op. No. 2734, 676 P2d 1078 (Alaska 1983).

Fact that attorney's misconduct related to matters within the jurisdiction of a federal tribunal did not prevent discipline under the Alaska Bar Rules. **Discipline of Vollintine,** Op. No. 2756, 673 P2d 755 (Alaska 1983).

Letter by suspended attorney on behalf of a client threatening to file suit after he was reinstated constituted unauthorized practice of law. **Burrell v. Disciplinary Board,** Op. No. 3467, 777 P2d 1140 (Alaska 1989).

Attorney was suspended for two months for practicing law while suspended. **Burrell v. Disciplinary Board,** Op. No. 3467, 777 P2d 1140 (Alaska 1989).

Attorney's misdemeanor theft conviction, his second conviction of intentional theft (the first having occurred prior to his admission to the bar), which might ordinarily result in disbarment, warranted instead two years' suspension due to mitigating factors. **Disciplinary Matter Involving Schuler,** Op. No. 3755, 818 P2d 138 (Alaska 1991).

Words "representing another" and "practice of law" in this rule are not unconstitutionally void for vagueness. **Disciplinary Matter Involving Burrell,** 882 P2d 1257 (Alaska 1994).

For failing to promptly return client's money, failing to render accounting of that money, and improperly deducting attorney's fees, attorney was publicly censured and ordered to pay restitution to client for lost interest. **Matter of Triem,** Op. No. 4443, 929 P2d 634 (Alaska 1996).

For neglecting legal matter entrusted to him by client while on probation for ethical violations involving neglect and conduct adversely reflecting on his fitness to practice law, attorney was suspended from practice of law for ninety days and placed on probation. **Matter of Triem,** Op. No. 4443, 929 P2d 634 (Alaska 1996).

Public censure was proper sanction for dishonesty that occurred when attorney falsely notified opposing attorney that discovery materials had been mailed. **Matter of Triem,** Op. No. 4443, 929 P2d 634 (Alaska 1996).

Attorney's dishonesty at grievance hearing was aggravating factor that hearing committee properly considered in determining proper sanction. **Matter of Triem,** Op. No. 4443, 929 P2d 634 (Alaska 1996).

Attorney was suspended for three years for failing to file documents in a divorce case, and for falsifying settlement documents in response to a grievance, in violation of subsection (a)(3) of this rule, and of Alaska R. Prof. Conduct 8.4(c). Cooperation and the effect of the suspension were not mitigating factors, and the mitigating factors of a good prior record, remorsefulness, and the unlikelihood of recurring violations were not sufficient to warrant a lesser sanction. **In the Disciplinary Matter Involving Hanlon,** Op. No. 5887, 110 P.3d 937 (Alaska 2005).

Rule 16. Types of Discipline and Costs.

(a) **Discipline Imposed by the Court or Board.** A finding of misconduct by the Court or Board will be grounds for

(1) disbarment by the Court; or

(2) suspension by the Court for a period not to exceed five years; or

(3) probation imposed by the Court; or

(4) public censure by the Court; or

(5) reprimand by the Disciplinary Board.

(b) **Discipline Imposed by the Board or Bar Counsel.** When Bar Counsel has made a finding that misconduct has occurred, the following discipline may be imposed:

(1) reprimand in person by the Board, pursuant to Rule 10(c)(8); or

(2) written private admonition by Bar Counsel, pursuant to Rule 11(a) (12).

(c) **Restitution; Reimbursement; Costs.** When a finding of misconduct is made, in addition to any discipline listed above, the Court or the Board may impose the following requirements against the Respondent:

(1) restitution to aggrieved persons or organizations;

(2) reimbursement of the Lawyers' Fund for Client Protection; or

(3) payment of the costs, including attorney's fees, of the proceedings or investigation or any parts thereof. In imposing costs and fees, consideration shall be given to the following factors:

(A) the complexity of the disciplinary matter;

(B) the duration of the case;

(C) the reasonableness of the number of hours expended by Bar Counsel and the reasonableness of the costs incurred;

(D) the reasonableness of the number of Bar Counsel used;

(E) Bar Counsel's efforts to minimize fees;

(F) the reasonableness of the defenses raised by the Respondent;

(G) vexatious or bad faith conduct by the Respondent;

(H) the relationship between the amount of work performed by Bar Counsel and the significance of the matters at stake;

(I) the financial ability of the Respondent to pay attorney's fees; and

(J) the existence of other equitable factors deemed relevant.

(d) **Conditions.** Written conditions may be attached to a reprimand or to a private admonition. Failure to comply with such conditions will be grounds for reconsideration of the matter by the Board or Bar Counsel.

(Added by SCO 176 dated February 26, 1974; amended by SCO 345 § 8 effective April 1, 1979; by SCO 438 effective November 1, 1980; and rescinded and repromulgated by SCO 614 effective January 1, 1985; amended by SCO 658 effective March 15, 1986; by SCO 962 effective July 15, 1989; by SCO 1037 effective January 15, 1991; by SCO 1048 effective nunc pro tunc September 12, 1990; by SCO 1233 effective July 15, 1996; and by SCO 1313 effective July 15, 1998)

Annotations

Cases

Public censure was warranted for attorney who neglected over a period of many years to attend to the necessary legal work connected with seven estates for which he was attorney of record. **In re Collins,** Op. No. 1694, 583 P2d 207 (Alaska 1978).

A five-year suspension of an attorney's license to practice law was warranted for falsification of an item of documentary evidence. **Matter of Stump,** Op. No. 2237, 621 P2d 263 (Alaska 1980).

The American Bar Association Standards and methodology are the appropriate model for determining sanctions for lawyer misconduct in Alaska; to the extent that previous decisions conflict with the ABA standards, the ABA standards control. **Disciplinary Matter Involving Buckalew,** Op. No. 3147, 731 P2d 48 (Alaska 1986).

Disbarment was proper discipline for attorney who filed pleading and affidavit stating that client's judgment had not been satisfied when he knew that it had and who forged another client's signature as endorsement on check. **Disciplinary Matter Involving Wiederholt,** Op. No. 4102, 877 P2d 765 (Alaska 1994).

Attorney was suspended form practice of law for one day less than five years for filing bankruptcy petition on behalf of client while on suspension from practice of law through corporation she formed to circumvent her suspension. **Disciplinary Matter Involving Morrill,** Op. No. 4268, 905 P2d 395 (Alaska 1995).

For failing to promptly return client's money, failing to render accounting of that money, and improperly deducting attorney's fees, attorney was publicly censured and ordered to pay restitution to client for lost interest. **Matter of Triem,** Op. No. 4443, 929 P2d 634 (Alaska 1996).

For neglecting legal matter entrusted to him by client while on probation for ethical violations involving neglect and conduct adversely reflecting on his fitness to practice law, attorney was suspended from practice of law for ninety days and placed on probation. **Matter of Triem,** Op. No. 4443, 929 P2d 634 (Alaska 1996).

Public censure was proper sanction for dishonesty that occurred when attorney falsely notified opposing attorney that discovery materials had been mailed. **Matter of Triem,** Op. No. 4443, 929 P2d 634 (Alaska 1996).

Supreme Court performs a three-step analysis in imposing attorney sanctions: (1) It addresses the first three prongs of the ABA Standards for imposing sanctions, determining the duty violated, the lawyer's mental state, and the extent of the actual or potential injury; (2) It looks to the ABA Standards to discern what sanction is recommended for the type of misconduct that occurred; and (3) It decides whether aggravating or mitigating factors should affect that sanction. **In re Friedman,** Op. No. 5408, 23 P3d 620 (Alaska 2001).

Where attorney, acting for all plaintiffs in a complex tort suit, deposited an $81,000 settlement contribution in his client trust account and, without permission from the other plaintiffs' attorneys, drew on the trust account to advance funds to his client and to pay himself attorney's fees not yet due him, attorney violated former DR 1-102(A)(4) (conduct involving dishonesty, fraud, deceit, or misrepresentation), former DR 9-102(A) (lawyer's management of money held in trust for others) and former DR 1-102(A)(3) (illegal conduct involving moral turpitude), but did not violate former DR 1-102(A)(5) (conduct prejudicial to administration of justice), resulting in sanction of three-year suspension from the practice of law. **In re Friedman,** Op. No. 5408, 23 P3d 620 (Alaska 2001).

Rule 17. Immunity.

(a) **General Immunity.** Members of the Board, members of Area Divisions, Bar Counsel, Special Bar Counsel, the Executive Director, Trustee Counsel, Conciliators, and all Bar staff are immune from suit for conduct in the course and scope of their official duties as set forth in these Rules.

(b) **Witness Immunity.** The Court or its designee may, in its discretion, grant immunity from criminal prosecution to witnesses in disciplinary, disability, or reinstatement proceedings upon application by the Board, Bar Counsel, or counsel for Respondent, and after receiving the consent of the appropriate prosecuting authority.

(Added by SCO 176 dated February 26, 1974; amended by SCO 345 § 9 effective April 1, 1979; and rescinded and repromulgated by SCO 614 effective January 1, 1985; amended by SCO 658 effective March 15, 1986; and by SCO 962 effective July 15, 1989)

Rule 18. Statute of Limitations.

Grievances against Respondents will be filed within five years of the time that the Complainant discovers or reasonably should discover the misconduct. This Rule will, however, be interpreted to allow traditional principles of tolling, equity, and due process.

(Added by SCO 176 dated February 26, 1974; amended by SCO 345 § 10 effective April 1, 1979; and rescinded and repromulgated by SCO 614 effective January 1, 1985)

Annotations

Cases

Four-year delay between filing of grievance and adjudication by area hearing committee did not warrant dismissal of grievance. **Matter of Triem,** Op. No. 4443, 929 P2d 634 (Alaska 1996).

Rule 19. Refusal of Complainant to Proceed.

The unwillingness of a Complainant to continue his or her grievance, the withdrawal of the grievance, a compromise between the Complainant and the Respondent, or restitution by the Respondent may, but need not in and of itself, justify abatement of a disciplinary investigation or proceeding.

(Added by SCO 176 dated February 26, 1974; amended by SCO 345 § 11, effective April 1, 1979; and rescinded and repromulgated by SCO 614 effective January 1, 1985)

Rule 20. Matters Related to Pending Civil or Criminal Litigation.

Prosecution of grievances involving material allegations which are substantially similar to the material allegations of criminal or civil litigation pending in a court will not be deferred unless the Board, in its discretion, and for good cause shown, authorizes deferment. In the event deferment of a disciplinary investigation or proceeding is authorized by the Board, the Respondent will make all reasonable efforts to obtain a prompt trial and disposition of the pending litigation. In the event the litigation is unreasonably delayed, the Board may direct, upon motion, that the investigation and any subsequent disciplinary proceedings be conducted promptly.

The acquittal of the Respondent on criminal charges or a verdict or judgment in his or her favor in civil litigation involving substantially similar material allegations will not in and of itself justify abatement of a disciplinary investigation or proceeding predicated upon the same material allegations.

(Added by SCO 176 dated February 26, 1974; amended by SCO 345 § 12 effective April 1, 1979; and rescinded and repromulgated by SCO 614 effective January 1, 1985)

Rule 21. Public Access to Disciplinary Proceedings.

(a) **Discipline and Reinstatement Proceedings.** After the filing of a petition for formal hearing, hearings held before either a Hearing Committee or the Board will be open to the public. This Rule will not be interpreted to allow public access to disability proceedings described in Rule 30.

(b) **Deliberations.** The deliberations of any adjudicative body will be kept confidential.

(c) **Bar Counsel's Files.** All files maintained by Bar Counsel and staff will be confidential and are not to be reviewed by any person other than Bar Counsel or Area Division members appointed for purposes of review or appeal under these Rules. This provision will not be interpreted to:

(1) preclude Bar Counsel from introducing into evidence any documents from his or her files;

(2) preclude Bar Counsel from providing the Board, the Court, or the public with statistical information compiled pursuant to Rule 11(e), provided that the name of the Respondent is kept confidential;

(3) deny a complainant information regarding the status or disposition of his or her grievance;

(4) deny the public facts regarding the stage of any proceeding or investigation concerning a Respondent's conviction of a crime;

(5) deny the Alaska Judicial Council confidential information about attorney applicants for judicial vacancies;

(6) preclude a court from reviewing in camera a confidential file upon a discovery request made pursuant to Criminal Rule 16(b)(7), and from exercising discretion as to whether to release relevant information from the file to counsel pursuant to Criminal Rule 16(d)(3); or

(7) prevent the Board Discipline Liaison from having access to any and all files maintained by Bar Counsel as necessary in the performance of the Liaison's duties.

(d) **Director's File.** The file maintained by the Director, acting in his or her capacity as clerk, will be open for public review.

(Added by SCO 176 dated February 26, 1974; amended by

SCO 345 § 13 effective April 1, 1979; rescinded and repromulgated by SCO 614 effective January 1, 1985; amended by SCO 962 effective July 15, 1989; by SCO 963 effective July 15, 1989; by SCO 1043 effective January 15, 1991; and by SCO 1082 effective January 15, 1992)

Rule 22. Procedure.

(a) **Grievances.** Grievances will be in writing, signed and verified by the Complainant, and contain a clear statement of the details of each act of alleged misconduct, including the approximate time and place of each. Grievances will be filed with Bar Counsel. Bar Counsel will review the grievance filed to determine whether it is properly completed and contains allegations that warrant investigation. Bar Counsel may require the Complainant to provide additional information and may request a voluntary verified response from the Respondent prior to accepting a grievance.

If Bar Counsel determines that the allegations contained in the grievance do not warrant an investigation, Bar Counsel will so notify the Complainant and Respondent in writing. Complainant may file a request for review of the determination within 30 days of the date of Bar Counsel's written notification. The request shall be reviewed by the Board Discipline Liaison, who may affirm Bar Counsel's decision not to accept the grievance for investigation or may direct that an investigation be opened as to one or more of the allegations in the grievance.

If a grievance is accepted for investigation, Bar Counsel will serve a copy of the grievance upon the Respondent for a response. Bar Counsel may require the Respondent to provide, within 20 days of service, verified full and fair disclosure in writing of all facts and circumstances pertaining to the alleged misconduct. Misrepresentation in a response to Bar Counsel will itself be grounds for discipline. Failure to answer within the prescribed time, or within such further time that may be granted in writing by Bar Counsel, will be deemed an admission to the allegations in the grievance.

For the purposes of this Rule, a grievance or response is "verified" if it is accompanied by a signed statement that the writing is true and correct to the best knowledge and belief of the writer.

(b) **Confidentiality.** Complainants and all persons contacted during the course of an investigation have a duty to maintain the confidentiality of discipline and disability proceedings prior to the initiation of formal proceedings subject to Bar Rule 21(c). It will be regarded as contempt of court to breach this confidentiality in any way. It will not be regarded as a breach of confidentiality for a person so contacted to consult with an attorney. A Respondent may waive confidentiality in writing and request disclosure of any information pertaining to the Respondent to any person or to the public.

(c) **Dismissal Before Formal Proceedings.** If after investigation it appears that there is no probable cause to believe that misconduct has occurred, Bar Counsel may dismiss the grievance.

(d) **Imposition of Private Admonition or Reprimand.** Upon a finding of misconduct, and with the approval of one Area Division member, Bar Counsel may impose a written private admonition upon a Respondent. A Respondent will not be entitled to appeal a private admonition by Bar Counsel but may demand, within 30 days of receipt of the admonition, that a formal proceeding be instituted against him or her before a Hearing Committee. If Respondent demands a formal proceeding, the admonition will be vacated and Bar Counsel will proceed under Section (e) of this Rule.

In the discretion of Bar Counsel, (s)he may refer a matter to the Board for approval and imposition of a reprimand by the Board, provided that the Respondent has, under Section (h) of this Rule, consented to the discipline before the Board.

(e) **Formal Proceedings.** Upon a finding of misconduct, and after seeking review in accordance with Rule 25(d), Bar Counsel may initiate discipline proceedings by filing with the Director a petition for formal hearing which specifically sets forth the charge(s) of misconduct. A copy of the petition will be served upon the Respondent.

Respondent will be required to file the original answer with the Director, and serve a copy upon Bar Counsel, within 20 days after the service of the petition for formal hearing. Should Respondent fail to timely answer, the charges will be deemed admitted without need of any further action by Bar Counsel.

Charges before a Hearing Committee will be presented by Bar Counsel. Bar Counsel will have the burden at any hearing of demonstrating by clear and convincing evidence that the Respondent has, by act or omission, committed misconduct as provided in Rule 15.

Bar Counsel may amend a petition for formal hearing at any time before an answer is filed. Bar Counsel may amend a petition for formal hearing after an answer is filed only by leave of the Hearing Committee or by written consent of the Respondent. Leave to amend will be freely given when justice requires. A Respondent will file an answer to an amended petition for formal hearing within the time remaining to file an answer to the original petition, or within 10 days after service of the amended petition, whichever is later.

(f) **Assignment to Hearing Committee.** In accordance with Rule 12(e), a petition for formal hearing will be assigned by the Director to a Hearing Committee after an answer is filed or after the expiration of the time for filing an answer, unless Respondent tenders conditional consent to a specific discipline. The notice of assignment to Hearing Committee will indicate the names of the members of the Hearing Committee assigned to hear the matter and will advise Respondent that (s)he is entitled to

(1) be represented by counsel;

(2) examine and cross-examine witnesses;

(3) present evidence in his or her own behalf;

(4) have subpoenas issued in his or her behalf; and

(5) challenge peremptorily and for cause members of the Hearing Committee, as provided in Rule 12(h).

(g) **Pre-Hearing Conference.** A pre-hearing conference may be convened by the Chair of the Hearing Committee or the Director for stipulation as to matters of fact, simplification of issues, scheduling of pre-hearing motions, the establishment of a date for the formal hearing, and other similar matters which may be resolved prior to hearing.

(h) **Discipline by Consent.** Respondent may tender a conditional consent to a specific discipline contained in Rule 16. This conditional consent will be submitted to Bar Counsel for his or her approval. If accepted by Bar Counsel, (s)he will refer the conditional admission to the Board for its approval or rejection of the requested discipline.

The consenting Respondent will present to the Board an affidavit stating that (s)he desires to consent to the specific discipline and that

(1) his or her consent is freely and voluntarily given and is not the subject of any coercion or duress; and

(2) (s)he admits to the charges stated in the grievance.

Acceptance of the conditional consent by the Board will be subject to Court approval if the specific discipline to be imposed includes discipline provided in Rule 16(a) (1), (2), (3) and (4). Any conditional admission rejected by the Board or the Court will be withdrawn and Bar Counsel will proceed under Section (e) of this Rule. Any admission made by Respondent in a conditional consent rejected by the Board or the Court cannot be used against the Respondent in any subsequent proceeding.

If the Court or the Board rejects a conditional consent, the matter will be remanded to the Hearing Committee, if any, which was appointed to hear the petition. If no Hearing Committee has been appointed, the Director will appoint one in accordance with Section (f) of this Rule.

(i) **Notice of Hearing.** The Director will serve a notice of formal hearing upon Respondent, or his or her counsel, indicating the date and place of the formal hearing.

(j) **Rules of Evidence.** The rules of evidence applicable in administrative hearings will apply in all hearings before Hearing Committees. No new evidence shall be allowed by the Committee chair after the hearing without notice to the opposing party and an opportunity to respond.

(k) **Motions, Findings, Conclusions, Recommendation.** Hearing Committees may consider and rule on pre-hearing motions. On procedural motions, the Committee chair will rule; on dispositive or substantive motions, the full Hearing Committee will rule. The Hearing Committee may direct either or both parties to submit proposed findings of fact, conclusions of law, and a recommendation after the formal hearing, which will be filed within 10 days of the date of the request by the Committee.

(*l*) **Report of Hearing Committee and Appeal.** Within 30 days of the conclusion of a formal hearing, the Hearing Committee will submit its report to the Board in accordance with 12(i) (4), unless an extension of time is granted by the President of the Board. Within 10 days of service of the report, Bar Counsel or Respondent may appeal the Hearing Committee's findings of fact, conclusions of law, and recommendation and request oral argument before the Board, as provided in Rule 25(f). The Director will thereafter set the dates for submission of briefs and oral argument before the Board.

(m) **Oral Argument.** Oral argument before the Board will be waived unless either Bar Counsel or Respondent requests argument as provided in Section (l) of this Rule.

(n) **Board Recommendation or Order.** The Board will review the Hearing Committee report and record and enter an appropriate recommendation or order as provided in Rule 10(c) (4), (5), and (6). If the Board has recommended discipline as provided in Rule 16(a) (1), (2), (3) or (4), it will submit to the Court its findings of fact, conclusions of law, recommendation, and the record. The record will include a transcript of all proceedings before the Board as well as the Hearing Committee report.

(o) **Notification of Disposition.** The Director will promptly notify all parties of the Board's action.

(p) **Appeal from Board Order or Recommendation.** Bar Counsel or Respondent may appeal from an order or recommendation of the Board made under Section (n) of this Rule by filing a notice of appeal with the Court within 10 days of service of the Board's order or recommendation. Parts II and V of the Alaska Rules of Appellate Procedure will govern appeals filed under this Rule, except that for purposes of Appellate Rule 210(c)(2), excerpts of record must contain:

(1) the petition for formal hearing and answer and any amended petition or answer;

(2) the Hearing Committee report and any amended or supplemental report;

(3) all briefing and transcripts of proceedings before the Board and the Board's findings of fact, conclusions of law, and recommendation, and any amended or supplemental findings of fact, conclusions of law, and recommendation;

(4) all Hearing Committee or Board orders or rulings sought to be reviewed;

(5) if the grant or denial of a motion is at issue in the appeal, the motion, the transcript of any discussion of the motion, and briefs, memoranda, and relevant portions of documents filed in support of or in opposition to the motion; and

(6) specific portions of other documents in the record, including documentary exhibits, that are referred to in the brief and essential to the resolution of an issue on appeal.

(q) **Record of Proceedings.** A complete stenographic or electronic record of all proceedings before Hearing

Committees and before the Board will be made and preserved. The Court shall furnish at its expense the necessary equipment, operator, and stenographic services for the preservation of the record of all such proceedings, and for the preparation of transcripts of all such proceedings.

(r) **Review by Supreme Court.** The Court will review findings of fact, conclusions of law, and recommendations of discipline made by the Board pursuant to Section (n) of this Rule. The Court will decide the grounds for discipline, pursuant to Rule 15; the type of discipline to be imposed, pursuant to Rule 16(a); and any requirements to be imposed, pursuant to Rule 16(c). When no appeal has been taken pursuant to Section (p) of this Rule, and if the Court determines that discipline different than that recommended by the Board may be warranted, the Court will so notify the parties and give them an opportunity to be heard.

(Added by SCO 176 dated February 26, 1974; amended by SCO 345 § 14 effective April 1, 1979; and rescinded and repromulgated by SCO 614 effective January 1, 1985; amended by SCO 658 effective March 15, 1986; by SCO 962 effective July 15, 1989; by SCO 963 effective July 15, 1989; by SCO 1048 effective nunc pro tunc September 12, 1990; by SCO 1153 effective July 15, 1994; by SCO 1454 effective October 15, 2003; and by SCO 1601 effective April 16, 2007)

Annotations

Cases

Supreme Court reviews recommendations concerning attorney discipline made by Disciplinary Board independently while giving deference to findings of Board; on questions of law and questions concerning appropriateness of sanctions, Supreme Court also exercises its independent judgment. **In the Disciplinary Matter Involving Wiederholt,** Op. No. 4102, 877 P2d 765 (Alaska 1994).

Attorney must show meritorious defense and excusable neglect to warrant relief from operation of this rule which deems failure to respond to grievance as admission of allegations in grievance. **Disciplinary Matter Involving Beconovich,** Op. No. 4146, 884 P2d 1080 (Alaska 1994).

Recused members of Bar Disciplinary Board may testify to relevant facts but not general character of respondent attorney in disciplinary case. **Disciplinary Matter Involving Beconovich,** Op. No. 4146, 884 P2d 1080 (Alaska 1994).

Double jeopardy protection does not extend to attorney disciplinary proceedings. **Matter of Triem,** Op. No. 4443, 929 P2d 634 (Alaska 1996).

Bar Counsel's appeal of Disciplinary Board's dismissal of grievance against attorney did not violate double jeopardy. **Matter of Triem,** Op. No. 4443, 929 P2d 634 (Alaska 1996).

Four-year delay between filing of grievance and adjudication by area hearing committee did not warrant dismissal of grievance. **Matter of Triem,** Op. No. 4443, 929 P2d 634 (Alaska 1996).

Fact that hearing committee did not issue its report until eleven months following grievance hearing did not warrant dismissal of grievance even though this rule required report to be issued within thirty days. **Matter of Triem,** Op. No. 4443, 929 P2d 634 (Alaska 1996).

Attorney's dishonesty at grievance hearing was aggravating factor which hearing committee properly considered in determining proper sanction. **Matter of Triem,** Op. No. 4443, 929 P2d 634 (Alaska 1996).

Reference to attorney's disciplinary record during consideration of grievance was not error; however, area hearing committees should bifurcate misconduct determination and sanction recommendation as much as possible. **Matter of Triem,** Op. No. 4443, 929 P2d 634 (Alaska 1996).

Supreme Court performs a three-step analysis in imposing attorney sanctions: (1) It addresses the first three prongs of the ABA Standards for imposing sanctions, determining the duty violated, the lawyer's mental state, and the extent of the actual or potential injury; (2) It looks to the ABA Standards to discern what sanction is recommended for the type of misconduct that occurred; and (3) It decides whether aggravating or mitigating factors should affect that sanction. **In re Friedman,** Op. No. 5408, 23 P3d 620 (Alaska 2001).

Where attorney, acting for all plaintiffs in a complex tort suit, deposited an $81,000 settlement contribution in his client trust account and, without permission from the other plaintiffs' attorneys, drew on the trust account to advance funds to his client and to pay himself attorney's fees not yet due him, attorney violated former DR 1-102(A)(4) (conduct involving dishonesty, fraud, deceit, or misrepresentation), former DR 9-102(A) (lawyer's management of money held in trust for others) and former DR 1-102(A)(3) (illegal conduct involving moral turpitude), but did not violate former DR 1-102(A)(5) (conduct prejudicial to administration of justice), resulting in sanction of three-year suspension from the practice of law. **In re Friedman,** Op. No. 5408, 23 P3d 620 (Alaska 2001).

Rule 23. Service.

All service of petitions will be accomplished in accordance with Rule 4 of the Alaska Rules of Civil Procedure. All service of pleadings, motions, and other documents contemplated by any requirement of these Rules will be accomplished in accordance with Rule 5 of the Alaska Rules of Civil Procedure.

(Added by SCO 176 dated February 26, 1974; amended by SCO 345 § 15 effective April 1, 1979; by SCO 432 effective November 1, 1980; and rescinded and repromulgated by SCO 614 effective January 1, 1985)

Rule 24. Discovery; Subpoena Power; Witness Compensation.

(a) **Subpoenas during Investigation.** At any stage of an investigation, only the Bar Counsel will have the right to summon witnesses and require the production of records by issuance of subpoenas. Subpoenas will be issued at the request of Bar Counsel by any member of any Area Division. Subpoenas will be served in accordance with Rule 23. Any challenge to the validity of a subpoena so issued will be heard and determined by any member of any Area Division. All subpoenas issued under this Section will clearly indicate on their face that they are issued in connection with a confidential investigation and that it is regarded as contempt of court for any member of the Alaska Court System, a process server, or a person subpoenaed to in any way breach the confidentiality of the investigation. It will not be regarded as a breach of confidentiality for a person subpoenaed to consult with an attorney.

(b) **Subpoenas during Formal Proceedings.** Both Bar Counsel and Respondent have the right to summon witnesses before a Hearing Committee and to require production of records before the Committee by issuance of subpoenas. Subpoenas will be issued at the request of Bar Counsel or Respondent by any member of the Hearing Committee. Subpoenas will be served in accordance with Rule 23. Any challenge to the validity of a subpoena will be heard and determined by the chair of the Hearing Committee or any

Committee member designated by the chair.

(c) **Enforcement of Subpoenas.** Subpoenas issued pursuant to this Rule will be enforceable in any superior court in this State.

(d) **Discovery.** Requests for production, requests for admissions, and the taking of deposition testimony may ensue for a period of 60 days following the filing of Respondent's answer to a petition for formal hearing. Both Bar Counsel and Respondent will be afforded reciprocal discovery under this Rule of all matters not privileged. Any disputes under this Section will be ruled upon by the chair of the Hearing Committee. Any discovery ruling is interlocutory and may only be appealed in accordance with Rule 25(a). The Alaska Rules of Civil Procedure, to the extent applicable, will govern discovery under this Rule.

Deposition testimony may be taken by stenographic, electronic, or video means. The Court will furnish, at its expense, the necessary equipment, operator, and stenographic services for recording and transcription of deposition testimony taken by Bar Counsel.

(e) **Witness Compensation.** Witnesses may be compensated in accordance with the administrative rules of court. Respondents will not be paid witness fees for attendance at hearings.

(Added by SCO 176 dated February 26, 1974; repromulgated by SCO 345 § 16 effective April 1, 1979; and rescinded and repromulgated by SCO 614 effective January 1, 1985; amended by SCO 962 effective July 15, 1989)

Note: Ch. 75 SLA 2002 (HB 106), Section 4, adds a new section to AS 06.01 relating to the confidentiality of depositor and customer records at banking and other financial institutions. According to Section 56 of the Act, AS 06.01.028(b) has the effect of changing Civil Rule 45, Criminal Rules 17 and 37, and Alaska Bar Rule 24 by requiring certain court orders compelling disclosure of records to provide for reimbursement of a financial institution's reasonable costs of complying with the order.

Rule 25. Appeals; Review of Bar Counsel Determinations.

(a) **Interlocutory Appeal.** Only upon the conditions and subject to the Rules of Procedure set forth in Part IV of the Alaska Rules of Appellate Procedure may parties petition the Court for review of an interlocutory order, recommendation, or decision of

(1) any member of any Area Division;

(2) a Hearing Committee or a single member thereof; or

(3) the Board or a single member thereof.

(b) **Admonition Not Appealable.** A Respondent cannot appeal the imposition of a written private admonition. In accordance with Rule 22(d), (s)he may request initiation of formal proceedings before a Hearing Committee within 30 days of receipt of the admonition.

(c) **Appeal by Complainant from Bar Counsel's Decision to Dismiss.** A Complainant may appeal the decision of the Bar Counsel to dismiss a complaint within 15 days of receipt of notice of the dismissal. The Director will appoint a member of an Area Division of the appropriate area of jurisdiction to review the Complainant's appeal. The appointed Area Division member may reverse the decision of Bar Counsel, affirm the decision, or request additional investigation. This Division member will be disqualified from any future consideration of the matter should formal proceedings be initiated.

(d) **Review of Bar Counsel's Decision to File Formal Petition.** A decision by Bar Counsel to initiate formal proceedings before a Hearing Committee will be reviewed by the Board Discipline Liaison prior to the filing of a formal petition. The Board Discipline Liaison will, within 20 days, approve, modify, or disapprove the filing of a petition, or order further investigation.

(e) **Appeal by Bar Counsel.** Bar Counsel may appeal the decision made under Section (d) of this Rule within 10 days following receipt of the Board Discipline Liaison's decision. The Director will designate an Area Division Member to hear this appeal. The decision of the Area Division Member will be final.

(f) **Appeal of Hearing Committee Findings, Conclusions, and Recommendation.** Within 10 days of service of the Hearing Committee's report to the Board, as set forth in Rule 22(l), the Respondent or Bar Counsel may appeal the findings of fact, conclusions of law, or recommendation by filing with the Board, and serving upon opposing party, a notice of appeal. Oral argument before the Board will be waived unless either Bar Counsel or Respondent requests argument as provided in Section (l) of Rule 22.

(g) **Respondent Appeal from Board Recommendation or Order.** Respondent may appeal from a recommendation or order of the Board made under Rule 22(n) by filing a notice of appeal with the Court within 10 days of service of the Board's recommendation or order. Part II of the Rules of Appellate Procedure will govern appeals filed under this Rule.

(h) **Bar Counsel Petition for Hearing of a Board Recommendation or Order.** Bar Counsel may petition from a recommendation or order of the Board made under Rule 22(n) by filing a petition for hearing with the Court within 10 days of service of the Board's recommendation or order. Part III of the Rules of Appellate Procedure will govern petitions filed under this Rule.

(Added by SCO 176 dated February 26, 1974; amended by SCO 345 § 17 effective April 1, 1979; and rescinded and repromulgated by SCO 614 effective January 1, 1985; amended by SCO 658 effective March 15, 1986; by SCO 962 effective July 15, 1989; and by SCO 1082 effective January 15, 1992)

Annotations

Cases

Double jeopardy protection does not extend to attorney disciplinary proceedings. **Matter of Triem,** Op. No. 4443, 929 P2d 634 (Alaska 1996).

Bar Counsel's appeal of Disciplinary Board's dismissal of grievance against attorney did not violate double jeopardy. **Matter of Triem,** Op. No. 4443, 929 P2d 634 (Alaska 1996).

Rule 26. Criminal Conviction; Interim Suspension.

(a) **Interim Suspension for Criminal Conviction.** Upon the filing with the Court of a certificate that an attorney has been convicted of a serious crime as defined in Section (b) of this Rule, the Court will enter an order of interim suspension immediately suspending the attorney. The order of interim suspension will be entered whether the conviction resulted from a plea of guilty or nolo contendere, or from a verdict after trial, or otherwise, and regardless of the pendency of an appeal. The Court will notify the Bar and the attorney of the order placing the attorney on interim suspension. The order of interim suspension shall be effective immediately upon filing and entry and will continue in effect pending final disposition of the disciplinary proceeding initiated by reason of the conviction.

(b) **Definition of Serious Crime.** The term "serious crime" shall include any crime which is or would be a felony in the State of Alaska and shall also include any lesser crime a necessary element of which, as determined by the statutory or common law definition of such crime, involves conduct as an attorney, interference with the administration of justice, false swearing, misrepresentation, fraud, deceit, bribery, corruption, extortion, misappropriation, theft, or an attempt or a conspiracy or solicitation of another to commit a "serious crime."

(c) **Certificate of Conviction.** A certificate of conviction for any crime will be conclusive evidence of the commission of that crime in any disciplinary proceeding instituted against an attorney based upon the conviction. The requirement of a certificate of conviction may be satisfied by a certificate from a clerk of court that an attorney has been convicted of a crime in that court, by a certified copy of a judgment of conviction or another court document evidencing the conviction, or by an affidavit establishing the fact of conviction which is also served on the attorney. A certificate of conviction may be filed with the Court by any clerk of court, Bar Counsel, the Board, or any District Attorney.

(d) **Duty to Report.** The clerk of court of any court of this state in which an attorney is convicted of a crime shall advise the Alaska Bar Association of the conviction, and upon request shall provide the Association with a certificate that the attorney has been convicted of a crime in that court, or with a certified copy of the judgment of conviction or another court document evidencing the conviction.

(e) **Interim Suspension for Threat of Irreparable Harm.** Interim suspension will be imposed by the Court on a showing by Bar Counsel of conduct by an attorney that constitutes a substantial threat of irreparable harm to his or her clients or prospective clients or where there is a showing that the attorney's conduct is causing great harm to the public by a continuing course of misconduct.

(f) **Reinstatement after Interim Suspension.** An attorney suspended under Section (a) of this Rule may petition for reinstatement upon the filing of a certificate demonstrating that the underlying conviction for a serious crime has been reversed or set aside. The reinstatement will not terminate any formal proceeding then pending against the attorney, the disposition of which shall be determined by the Hearing Committee and the Board on the basis of the available evidence.

(g) **Proceedings Following Interim Suspension.** Upon receipt of the certificate of conviction for a serious crime, the Court, in addition to suspending the attorney in accordance with Section (a) of this Rule, will refer the matter to Bar Counsel for the initiation of a formal proceeding before a Hearing Committee. The sole issue to be determined by the Hearing Committee will be the extent of the final discipline to be imposed; however, the matter will not be brought to hearing until all appeals from the conviction are concluded, unless the Respondent requests an earlier hearing.

(h) **Proceedings Following Conviction for Other Than Serious Crimes.** Upon receipt of a certificate of conviction for a crime other than those described in Section (b) of this Rule, the Court may, in its discretion, refer the matter to Bar Counsel for whatever action (s)he deems warranted, including the possible initiation of a formal proceeding.

(i) **Proceedings Following Conviction of a Crime Relating to Alcohol or Drug Abuse; Interim Suspension for Noncompliance.**

(1) Upon receipt of a certificate of conviction of a crime relating to alcohol or drug abuse, other than a crime described in Section (b) of this Rule, the Court may, in its discretion, refer the matter to the Lawyers' Assistance Committee of the Alaska Bar Association.

(2) The convicted attorney shall meet with the Committee and comply with its recommendations for professional evaluation and professionally recommended treatment. The attorney may appeal the Committee's recommendations to the Board within 10 days after the date the recommendations were made. The Board, in its discretion, may approve, disapprove or modify the recommendations. The attorney may seek review of the Board's decision by filing a petition for review with the Court pursuant to Appellate Rule 402. In the event that the attorney does not meet with the Committee or comply with the Committee's recommendations, the Committee will mail to the convicted attorney notice of the attorney's failure to meet or comply with its recommendations and require the attorney to cure the deficiency within 10 days after the date of the notice. If the convicted attorney fails to cure the deficiency as required, the Court may, based on a report by the Committee, order the attorney to show cause why the attorney should not be suspended from the practice of law until the attorney demonstrates to the Court that the deficiency is cured.

(j) **Interim Suspension, General Provisions.** If interim suspension is imposed by the Court, the Court may appoint a trustee in accordance with Rule 31. In any case in which interim suspension has been ordered, the disciplinary proceedings will be diligently prosecuted. Interim suspension will terminate upon the final disposition of disciplinary proceedings, or upon the earlier entry of an order by the Court terminating interim suspension.

(k) **Notification.** An attorney placed on interim suspension must comply with Rule 28 concerning notification of parties.

(*l*) **Conviction.** Conviction for purposes of this rule occurs upon entry of a plea of guilty or no contest or upon entry of a finding or verdict of guilt.

(Added by SCO 176 dated February 26, 1974; amended by SCO 345 § 18 effective April 1, 1979; and rescinded and repromulgated by SCO 614 effective January 1, 1985; amended by SCO 962 effective July 15, 1989; by SCO 1168 effective July 15, 1994; by SCO 1236 effective May 2, 1996; and by SCO 1263 effective July 15, 1997)

Annotations

Cases

Conviction of felony offense of accessory after the fact to first degree murder was a serious crime within the meaning of Alaska Bar Rule 23. **Matter of Webb,** Op. No. 1879, 602 P2d 408 (Alaska 1979).

A two-year suspension of an attorney from the practice of law based upon a felony conviction for drug distribution and the attorney's admission that he also distributed drugs to a minor is justified even though the crimes did not involve moral turpitude. **In the Matter of Preston,** Op. No. 2156, 616 P2d (Alaska 1980).

Willful failure to file an income tax return is not a "serious crime" within the meaning of this rule. **Matter of Vogt,** Op. No. 2481, 642 P2d 819 (Alaska 1982).

Attorney's misdemeanor theft conviction, his second conviction of intentional theft (the first having occurred prior to his admission to the bar), which might ordinarily result in disbarment, warranted instead two years' suspension due to mitigating factors. **Disciplinary Matter Involving Schuler,** Op. No. 3755, 818 P2d 138 (Alaska 1991).

Rule 27. Reciprocal Discipline.

(a) **Notice to Disciplined Attorney.** Upon receipt of a certified copy of an order demonstrating that an attorney admitted, specially admitted to practice in this State, or engaged in the practice of law in this State has been disciplined in another jurisdiction, the Court will issue a notice to him or her containing a copy of the order from the other jurisdiction and an order directing that the attorney inform the Court within 30 days from service of any reason why the imposition of the identical discipline in this State would be unwarranted, and the reasons therefor. The Court will cause this notice to be served upon the attorney and Bar Counsel.

(b) **Stay of Discipline.** In the event the discipline imposed in the original jurisdiction has been stayed by that jurisdiction, any reciprocal discipline to be imposed in this State will be deferred until the stay expires.

(c) **Imposition of Identical Discipline.** Upon the expiration of 30 days from service of the notice and order issued pursuant to Section (a) of this Rule, the Court will impose the identical discipline imposed by the original jurisdiction unless Bar Counsel or Respondent files a petition alleging that

(1) the procedure in the original jurisdiction was so lacking in notice or opportunity to be heard as to constitute a deprivation of due process;

(2) an infirmity of proof establishing the misconduct exists which gives rise to the clear conviction that the action of the original jurisdiction should not be accepted;

(3) the imposition of the same discipline would result in grave injustice;

(4) the misconduct established has been held to warrant substantially different discipline in this State; or

(5) the conduct does not violate Rule 15.

The Court will enter an order as it deems appropriate when the Court determines that any of the above exceptions to the discipline imposed by the original jurisdiction exist.

(d) **Conclusive Evidence.** Unless the Court has made an exception under Section (c) of this Rule, the final adjudication of misconduct in another jurisdiction will be conclusive evidence of misconduct for purposes of discipline in this State.

(Added by SCO 176 dated February 26, 1974; amended by SCO 345 § 19 effective April 1, 1979; and rescinded and repromulgated by SCO 614 effective January 1, 1985; amended by SCO 962 effective July 15, 1989)

Rule 28. Action Necessary When Attorney is Disciplined.

(a) **Notice.** An attorney who has been disbarred, suspended, placed on probation, or who is under an order of interim suspension, will promptly provide notice of the discipline imposed as required by this Section. Notice will be sent by certified or registered mail, return receipt requested. Notice to clients need only be sent to clients represented by the disciplined attorney on the entry date of the Court's order. Notice required to attorneys representing opposing parties in pending litigation or administrative proceedings need only be sent if the disciplined attorney is an attorney of record at the time of the entry date of the Court's order. Notice will be provided as follows:

(1) an attorney who has been disbarred, suspended for more than 90 days, or who is under an order of interim suspension, will promptly notify

(A) each of his or her clients who is involved in pending litigation or administrative proceedings, and each attorney representing opposing parties in the proceedings, of his or her disbarment or suspension and his or her inability to practice law in the State after the effective date of the disbarment or suspension; the notice given the client will advise the client of the necessity to promptly seek substitution of another attorney;

the notice served upon the attorneys for the opposing parties will state the mailing address of the client of the disbarred or suspended attorney; and

(B) each of his or her clients who is involved in any matters other than litigation or administrative proceedings; the notice will advise the clients of his or her disbarment or suspension, his or her inability to practice law in the State after the effective date of the disbarment or suspension, and the need to seek legal advice from a different attorney;

(2) an attorney who has been suspended for 90 days or less will notify all clients in any matters, and each attorney representing opposing parties in any pending litigation or administrative proceedings, that (s)he will be unavailable for the period of time specified in the Court's order; the disciplined attorney will advise his or her clients that they may seek substitute counsel at their discretion; and

(3) an attorney who has been placed on probation will notify all clients in any matters, and each attorney representing opposing parties in any pending litigation or administrative proceedings, of the terms of his or her probation, unless the Court, in its order placing the attorney on probation, relieves the attorney of this duty.

(b) **Substitute Counsel.** An attorney suspended for 90 days or less will assist his or her clients in arranging for alternate representation where necessary or requested.

Should the client of an attorney who has been disbarred, suspended for more than 90 days, or who is under an order of interim suspension not obtain substitute counsel before the effective date of the disbarment or suspension, the disciplined attorney will move for leave to withdraw in the court or administrative agency in which the proceeding is pending.

(c) **Effective Date of Order; Limitation on Practice.** Orders imposing disbarment, suspension, or probation will be effective 30 days after the entry date, unless otherwise ordered by the Court in the order imposing discipline. After the entry date of a disbarment or suspension order, the disciplined attorney will not accept any new retainer or accept employment in any new case or legal matter of any nature. However, during the period from the entry date of the order to its effective date, (s)he may, unless otherwise ordered by the Court in the order imposing discipline, wind up and complete, on behalf of any client, all matters which were pending on the entry date of the order.

(d) **Prohibition on Practice.** An attorney who has been disbarred, suspended, or who is under an order of interim suspension will, during the period of his or her disbarment or suspension, cease all practice of law, including the acceptance of any new clients.

(e) **Probation.** Probation may be imposed in accordance with Rule 16(a) (3) only in those cases where there is little likelihood that the attorney on probation will harm clients or the public during the period of probation and where the conditions of probation can be adequately supervised. Probation may be renewed by the Court for an additional period if the Board so recommends and the Court concurs in the recommendation. The Board's recommendation for renewal of probation will be submitted to the Court not more than six months, nor less than 60 days prior to the expiration of the original probation period. The attorney on probation will be advised of the recommendation and be given an opportunity to be heard by the Court. The conditions of probation will be specified in writing.

(f) **Compliance by Disciplined Attorney.** Within 10 days after the effective date of a disbarment or suspension order, the disciplined attorney will file with the Court, and serve upon Bar Counsel, an affidavit showing that

(1) (s)he has fully complied with the provisions of the order and with these Rules; and

(2) (s)he has notified all other state, federal and administrative jurisdictions to which (s)he is admitted to practice of his or her discipline.

The affidavit will also set forth the residence and mailing addresses of the disciplined attorney where communications may thereafter be directed. Pursuant to Rule 9(e), it is the ongoing responsibility of the disciplined attorney to keep the Bar apprised of his or her current address and telephone number.

(g) **Public Notice.** The Board will cause a notice of the disbarment, suspension, interim suspension, probation, public censure, or public reprimand to be published in

(1) a newspaper of general circulation in Anchorage, Fairbanks, and Juneau;

(2) an official Alaska Bar Association publication; and

(3) a newspaper of general circulation serving the community in which the disciplined attorney maintained his or her practice.

(h) **Circulation of Notice; National Lawyer Regulatory Data Bank.** The Board will promptly transmit a copy of the order of disbarment, suspension, interim suspension, probation, public censure, or public reprimand to the presiding judges of the superior court in each judicial district in Alaska; to the presiding judge of the United States District Court for the District of Alaska; and to the Attorney General for the State of Alaska, together with the request that the Attorney General notify the appropriate administrative agencies. The presiding judges will make such orders as they deem necessary to fully protect the rights of the clients of the disbarred, suspended, or probationary attorney.

Bar Counsel will transmit to the National Lawyer Regulatory Data Bank maintained by the American Bar Association, and any jurisdiction to which Respondent has been admitted, notice of all discipline imposed by the Court, all orders granting reinstatement, and all public reprimands.

(i) **Record Keeping.** A disbarred, suspended, or probationary attorney will keep and maintain records of the various steps taken by him or her pursuant to these Rules so that proof of compliance with these Rules and with the disbarment, suspension or probationary order is available. Proof of compliance with the Rules and Court order will be a condition precedent to any petition for reinstatement.

(j) **Surrender of Bar Membership Card.** Any attorney upon whom disbarment, suspension, or interim suspension has been imposed will, within 10 days of the effective date of the order, surrender his or her Alaska Bar Association membership card to the Director by delivery in person, or by certified or registered mail, return receipt requested.

(Added by SCO 176 dated February 26, 1974; amended by SCO 295 effective March 1, 1978; and rescinded and repromulgated by SCO 614 effective January 1,1985; amended by SCO 962 effective July 15, 1989; by SCO 1037 effective January 15, 1991; by SCO 1048 effective nunc pro tunc September 12, 1990; and by SCO 1312 effective July 15, 1998)

Rule 29. Reinstatement.

(a) **Order of Reinstatement.** An attorney who has been disbarred or suspended may not resume practice until reinstated by order of the Court. Interim suspension will end only in accordance with Rule 26.

(b) **Petitions for Reinstatement.** An attorney who seeks reinstatement will file a verified petition for reinstatement with the Court, with a copy served upon the Director. In the petition, the attorney shall:

(1) state that (s)he has met the terms and conditions of the order imposing suspension or disbarment;

(2) state the names and addresses of all his or her employers during the period of suspension or disbarment;

(3) describe the scope and content of the work performed by the attorney for each such employer;

(4) provide the names and addresses of at least three character witnesses who had knowledge concerning the activities of the suspended or disbarred attorney during the period of his or her suspension or disbarment; and

(5) state the date upon which the suspended or disbarred attorney seeks reinstatement. An attorney who has been disbarred by order of the Court may not be reinstated until the expiration of at least five years from the effective date of the disbarment.

Unless otherwise ordered by the Court, an attorney who has been denied reinstatement by the Court from disbarment or suspension may not file a petition for reinstatement until the expiration of at least two years from the effective date of the Court's most recent order denying reinstatement.

(c) **Reinstatement Proceedings.** Petitioners who have been suspended for two years or less will be automatically reinstated by the Court unless Bar Counsel files an opposition to automatic reinstatement pursuant to Section (d) of this Rule.

Proceedings for attorneys who have been disbarred or suspended for more than two years will be conducted as follows:

(1) upon receipt of the petition for reinstatement, the Director will refer the petition to a Hearing Committee in the jurisdiction in which the Petitioner maintained an office at the time of his or her misconduct; the Hearing Committee will promptly schedule a hearing; at the hearing, the Petitioner will have the burden of demonstrating by clear and convincing evidence that (s)he has the moral qualifications, competency, and knowledge of law required for admission to the practice of law in this State and that his or her resumption of the practice of law in the State will not be detrimental to the integrity and standing of the Bar, or to the administration of justice, or subversive of the public interest; within 30 days of the conclusion of the hearing, the Hearing Committee will issue a report setting forth its findings of fact, conclusions of law, and recommendation; the Committee will serve a copy of the report upon Petitioner and Bar Counsel, and transmit it, together with the record of the hearing, to the Board; any appellate action will be subject to the appellate procedures set forth in Rule 25;

(2) at its next scheduled meeting at least 30 days after receipt of the Hearing Committee's report, the Board will review the report and the record; the Board will file its findings of fact, conclusions of law, and recommendation with the Court, together with the record and the Hearing Committee report; the petition will be placed upon the calendar of the Court for acceptance or rejection of the Board's recommendation;

(3) in all proceedings concerning a petition for reinstatement, Bar Counsel may cross-examine the Petitioner's witnesses and submit evidence in opposition to the petition; and

(4) the retaking and passing of Alaska's general applicant bar examination will be conclusive evidence that the Petitioner possesses the knowledge of law necessary for reinstatement to the practice of law in Alaska, as required under Section (b) (1) of this Rule.

(d) **Oppositions to Automatic Reinstatement.** Within 10 days after the Respondent files a petition for reinstatement after a period of suspension of one year or less, or within 30 days after the Respondent files a petition for reinstatement after a period of suspension of more than one year, Bar Counsel may file an opposition to automatic reinstatement with the Court and serve a copy upon the Board and the Petitioner. The opposition to automatic reinstatement will state the basis for the original suspension, the ending date of the suspension, and the facts which Bar Counsel believes demonstrate that the petitioner should not be reinstated.

Upon receipt by the Director of a copy of the opposition to automatic reinstatement, reinstatement proceedings will be initiated in accordance with procedures outlined in Section (c)(1)–(4) of this Rule.

(e) **Expenses.** The Court may direct that the necessary

expenses incurred in the investigation and processing of any petition for reinstatement be paid by the disbarred or suspended attorney.

(f) **Bar Payment of Membership Fees.** Prior to reinstatement, the disbarred or suspended attorney must pay to the Bar, in cash or by certified check, the full active membership fees due and owing the Association for the year in which reinstated.

(Added by SCO 176 dated February 26, 1974: amended by SCO 207 effective July 15, 1985; and rescinded and repromulgated by SCO 614 effective January 1, 1985: amended by SCO 665 effective March 15, 1986; by SCO 962 effective July 15, 1989; by SCO 1449 effective October 15, 2001; and by SCO 1478 effective October 15, 2002)

Annotations

Cases

A condition of reinstatement as expressed in an opinion and order suspending an attorney, that the attorney must make full restitution to his victim, is not objectionable as vague. **In re Cornelius,** Op. No. 1019, 521 P2d 497 (Alaska 1974).

Disbarment in Alaska is not permanent. **In re Reinstatement of Wiederholt,** Op. No. 5421, 24 P3d 1219 (Alaska 2001).

There is a presumption against reinstatement after disbarment. **In re Reinstatement of Wiederholt,** Op. No. 5421, 24 P3d 1219 (Alaska 2001).

An individual seeking reinstatement must prove that he or she meets the requirements set out in this rule by clear and convincing evidence. **In re Reinstatement of Wiederholt,** Op. No. 5421, 24 P3d 1219 (Alaska 2001).

Disciplining Board's time requirements under this rule are directory, not mandatory. **In re Reinstatement of Wiederholt,** Op. No. 5421, 24 P3d 1219 (Alaska 2001).

In affirming Disciplinary Board's denial of reinstatement petition, Supreme Court would not create procedural rule designating waiting period to reapply for reinstatement. **In re Reinstatement of Wiederholt,** Op. No. 5421, 24 P3d 1219 (Alaska 2001).

In affirming Disciplinary Board's denial of reinstatement petition, Supreme Court would not create a rule by which certain individuals could be forever barred from reinstatement. **In re Reinstatement of Wiederholt,** Op. No. 5421, 24 P3d 1219 (Alaska 2001).

Disciplinary Board's findings of fact concerning applications for reinstatement by disbarred attorneys are reviewed by Supreme Court under same standard used in reviewing attorney discipline proceedings: respondent attorney bears the burden of proof in demonstrating that such findings are erroneous and, as a general rule, findings of fact made upon conflicting evidence will not be disturbed. **In re Reinstatement of Wiederholt,** Op. No. 5421, 24 P3d 1219 (Alaska 2001).

In making determination under this rule of disbarred attorney's moral fitness for reinstatement and the potential detrimental impact of his reinstatement, Disciplinary Board properly considered his past conduct, his level of remorse and acknowledgement of past wrongdoing, and the amount of time that had passed since his disbarment. **In re Reinstatement of Wiederholt,** Op. No. 5421, 24 P3d 1219 (Alaska 2001).

Where an attorney was disbarred for very serious conduct, he lied to Bar Counsel and the hearing committee about the grievances filed against him, his first petition for reinstatement was filed before the minimum five-year period of disbarment had expired, he did not express any remorse or apologize to any of his victims until after his first petition was denied, and he filed his second petition only seven months later, his petition for reinstatement to the Bar was properly denied. **In re Wiederholt,** 89 P.3d 771 (Alaska 2004).

B. DISABILITY

Rule 30. Procedure: Disabled, Incapacitated or Incompetent Attorney.

(a) **Immediate Transfer to Interim Disability Inactive Status.** The Court will immediately transfer an attorney to interim disability inactive status upon a showing that

(1) the attorney has been declared incompetent by judicial order;

(2) the attorney has been involuntarily committed to an institution because of incapacity or disability; or

(3) the attorney has alleged during a disciplinary proceeding that he or she is incapable of assisting in his or her defense due to mental or physical incapacity.

The period of interim disability inactive status will continue until further order of the Court. A copy of the order will be served upon the attorney so transferred, his or her guardian, or the director of the institution to which (s)he has been committed or in a manner that the Court may direct. The order of transfer to interim disability inactive status will be in effect pending final disposition of a disability hearing proceeding. The hearing will be commenced upon the transfer to interim disability inactive status, and will be conducted in accordance with Section (b) of this Rule. The transfer to interim disability inactive status will terminate upon the final disposition of the disability proceedings, or upon the earlier entry of an order by the Court terminating interim disability inactive status. An attorney transferred to interim disability inactive status may petition the Court for a return to active status upon the filing of documentation demonstrating that the attorney has been judicially declared competent. The reinstatement will not terminate any formal disability proceeding then pending against the attorney.

(b) **Transfer to Disability Inactive Status Following Hearing.** The Court may transfer an attorney to disability inactive status upon a showing that the attorney is unable to continue the practice of law by reason of mental or physical infirmity or illness, or because of addiction to controlled substances. Hearings will be initiated by Bar Counsel and conducted in the same manner as disciplinary proceedings under Rule 22, except that all proceedings will be confidential. Upon petition of Bar Counsel for good cause shown, the Court may order the Respondent to submit to a medical and/or psychological examination by a Court-appointed expert.

(c) **Stay and Appointment of Counsel.** The Court may appoint counsel to represent the attorney in a disability proceeding if it appears to the Court that the attorney is unable to obtain counsel or represent himself or herself effectively, due to incapacity. Any pending disciplinary proceedings against the attorney may, at the discretion of the Board, be stayed pending the removal or cessation of the disability.

(d) **Hearing Committee and Board Duties and Obligations.** The Hearing Committee will recommend to the Board whether the attorney is unable to continue the practice of law because of the reasons set out in Section (b) of this Rule, and whether the reasons justify the transfer of the attorney to inactive status. The Board will make recommendations to the Court as to whether the alleged incapacity justifies transfer to disability inactive status.

(e) **Notice to Public of Transfer to Disability Inactive Status.** The Board will cause a notice of transfer to disability inactive status, whether imposed after hearing or on an interim basis, to be published in

(1) a newspaper of general circulation in the cities of Anchorage, Fairbanks, and Juneau, Alaska;

(2) an official Alaska Bar Association publication; and

(3) a newspaper of general circulation primarily serving the community in which the disabled attorney maintained his or her practice.

When the disability or incapacity is removed and the attorney has been restored to active status, the Board will cause a notice of transfer to active status to be similarly published.

(f) **Circulation of Notice Transferring to Inactive Status.** The Board will promptly transmit a copy of the order of transfer to interim disability inactive status or disability inactive status to the presiding judge of the superior and district court in each judicial district in the state; to the presiding judge of the United States District Court for the District of Alaska; and to the Attorney General for the State of Alaska, together with the request that the Attorney General notify the appropriate administrative agencies. The Board will request action under Rule 31, as may be necessary, in order to protect the interests of the disabled attorney and his or her clients.

Bar Counsel will transmit to the National Lawyer Regulatory Data Bank maintained by the American Bar Association, and any jurisdiction to which Respondent has been admitted, notice of all transfers to inactive status due to disability and all orders granting reinstatement.

(g) **Reinstatement.** No attorney transferred to disability inactive status under the provisions of this Rule may resume active or inactive status until reinstated by order of the Court. Any attorney transferred to disability inactive status under the provisions of this Rule will be entitled to apply for reinstatement to active or inactive status once a year, but initially not before one year from the date of the Court order transferring him or her to disability inactive status, or at such shorter intervals as the Court may direct in the order transferring the Respondent to inactive status or any modification thereto.

The attorney seeking transfer from disability inactive status shall file a verified application for reinstatement with the Court, with a copy served upon the Director. In the application, the attorney will

(1) state that (s)he has met the terms and conditions of the order transferring him or her to disability inactive status;

(2) state the names and addresses of all his or her employers during the period of disability inactive status;

(3) describe the scope and content of the work performed by the attorney for each such employer;

(4) provide the names and addresses of at least three character witnesses who have knowledge concerning the activities of the attorney during the period of disability inactive status;

(5) provide the names and addresses of all health care providers, hospitals, and other institutions by whom or in which the attorney has been examined or treated since his or her transfer to disability inactive status;

(6) state that the disability or incapacitating condition has been removed and attach the expert opinion of a physician, psychiatrist or psychologist that the disability or incapacity has been removed;

(7) state whether any of the incidents listed in Rule 2(1)(d)(1)-(10) have occurred during the period of disability inactive status.

Upon receipt of the application for reinstatement, the Director will refer the application to a Hearing Committee in the jurisdiction in which the attorney maintained an office at the time of his or her transfer to disability inactive status; the Hearing Committee will promptly schedule a hearing at the hearing, the attorney will have the burden of demonstrating that the attorney's disability has been removed and (s)he meets the standards of character and fitness contained in Rule 2(1)(d); within 30 days of the conclusion of the hearing, the Hearing Committee will issue a report setting forth its findings of fact, conclusions of law, and recommendation; the Committee will serve a copy of the report upon the attorney and Bar Counsel, and transmit it, together with the record of the hearing, to the Board; any appellate action will be subject to the appellate procedures set forth in Rule 25.

At its next scheduled meeting at least 30 days after receipt of the Hearing Committee's report, the Board will review the report and the record; the Board will file its findings of fact, conclusions of law, and recommendation with the Court, together with the record and the Hearing Committee report; the application will be placed upon the calendar of the Court for acceptance or rejection of the Board's recommendation.

In all proceedings concerning an application for reinstatement from disability inactive status, Bar Counsel may cross-examine the attorney's witnesses and submit evidence in opposition to the application.

The application will be granted by the Court upon a showing that the attorney's disability has been removed and (s)he is fit to resume the practice of law. Upon application, the Court may take or direct any action it deems necessary to determine whether the attorney's disability or incapacity has been removed, including an order for an examination of the attorney by qualified medical and/or psychological experts that the Court may designate. In its discretion, the Court may order that the expense of the examination be paid by the attorney. In addition, the Court may direct that the necessary expenses incurred in the investigation and processing of any application for reinstatement from disability inactive status be paid by the attorney.

Prior to reinstatement, the attorney must pay to the Bar, in cash or by certified check, the full active membership fees due and owing the Association for the year in which (s)he is reinstated.

(h) **Burden of Proof.** In a proceeding seeking transfer of an attorney to disability inactive status under this Rule, Bar Counsel will have the burden of proving, by clear and convincing evidence, that the attorney should be so transferred. In a proceeding seeking an order of reinstatement to active status under this Rule, the same burden of proof will rest with the attorney.

(i) **Waiver of Physician and Psychotherapist–Patient Privilege.** The filing of an application for reinstatement by an attorney transferred to disability inactive status because of disability or incapacity will be deemed to constitute a waiver of any physician and psychotherapist-patient privilege with respect to any treatment of the attorney during the period of his or her disability. The disabled attorney will be required to disclose the name of every health care provider and hospital or other institution by whom or in which the attorney has been examined or treated since his or her transfer to disability inactive status. (S)he will furnish to the Court written consent for each person or organization to divulge information and records as requested by court-appointed medical experts.

(Added by SCO 176 dated February 26, 1974; rescinded and repromulgated by SCO 614 effective January 1, 1985; amended by SCO 962 effective July 15, 1989; by SCO 1336 effective January 15, 1999; by SCO 1438 effective October 15, 2001; and by SCO 1519 effective October 15, 2004)

Rule 31. Appointment of Trustee Counsel to Protect Client's Interests.

(a) **Appointment; Procedure.** Whenever an attorney is deceased, has disappeared or abandoned the practice of law leaving a client matter unattended, or been transferred to disability inactive status because of incapacity or disability (hereinafter "unavailable attorney") and no partner of the attorney or shareholder in the professional corporation of which the unavailable attorney was an employee is known to exist, Bar Counsel will petition the superior court in the judicial district in which the unavailable attorney maintained an office for the appointment of trustee counsel to represent the interests of the unavailable attorney and his or her clients. This petition will be made ex parte, will state the basis for its filing, and will state that the appointment of trustee counsel is necessary for the protection of the unavailable attorney and his or her clients. The petition will be heard ex parte, unless the court otherwise directs, at the earliest available time. Bar Counsel shall submit to the superior court the names of attorneys who have agreed to serve voluntarily as trustee counsel. The superior court shall make appropriate inquiries to ascertain that a volunteer attorney possesses qualifications suitable to perform the duties of trustee counsel. In the event there are no volunteer attorneys, the superior court shall appoint a suitable attorney actively practicing law in the judicial district in which the unavailable attorney maintained his or her office. Only attorneys who maintain errors and omissions insurance coverage may be appointed as trustee counsel.

(b) **Powers and Duties.** The order granting the petition will grant the trustee counsel all the powers of a personal representative of a deceased under the laws of the State of Alaska insofar as the unavailable attorney's practice is concerned. It will further direct the trustee counsel to

(1) notify promptly, by certified or registered mail, return receipt requested, all clients being represented in pending matters, other than litigation or administrative proceedings, of the basis for the entry of the order and of the need to seek legal advice from another attorney;

(2) notify promptly, by certified or registered mail, return receipt requested, all clients who are involved in pending litigation or administrative proceedings of the basis for the entry of the order and that they should promptly seek the substitution of another attorney;

(3) promptly inventory all of the open files of the unavailable attorney and, with respect to each open file, prepare a brief summary of each file to include name of client(s), nature of legal matter, and status of legal matter and an accounting of the costs and fees involved; and

(4) Trustee counsel shall have the same authority to collect accounts receivables and assert the same claims as the unavailable attorney would have. The notices required in this section of the Rule will inform clients

(A) of the lien of the unavailable attorney, or of the estate of the deceased attorney, on all his or her files;

(B) of the requirement that all transfers of files require suitable arrangements regarding costs and fees;

(C) of the trustee counsel's authority to arrange the payment of the costs and fees by the clients of the unavailable attorney before any transfer of the files to substitute counsel.

(5) render an accounting of office, trust or other bank accounts.

(6) Trustee counsel will be bound by the attorney-client privilege with respect to client confidences contained in the records of the unavailable attorney, except to the extent necessary to effect the order appointing him or her trustee counsel. The superior court shall issue an order staying any pending state court proceedings in which the unavailable attorney was counsel of record for a period of time not to exceed 60 days. The unavailable attorney shall remain attorney of record during the period of stay or until substitute counsel has entered an appearance, whichever occurs first.

(c) **Requirement of Bond.** The superior court may require the trustee counsel to post bond, conditioned upon the faithful performance of his or her duties.

(d) **Disposition of Assets.** Any monies or assets remaining after the completion of the client matters, and after compensation of trustee counsel, will be returned to the unavailable attorney or to his or her guardian. In the case of a deceased attorney any monies or assets remaining after the completion of the client matters shall be returned to the personal representative and trustee counsel shall apply for compensation under section (g).

(e) **Force and Effect of Appointment.** The powers and duties of a trustee counsel are not affected by the appointment of a guardian or personal representative or by any other rule or law of the State.

(f) **Reports to Bar Counsel.** Trustee counsel appointed under this Rule will make written reports to Bar Counsel within six months of the date of the order appointing him or her as trustee, and every six months thereafter until completion of his or her duties under this Rule. The report will state the progress made under Section (b) of this Rule and the work to be accomplished within the next six month period.

(g) **Compensation.**

(1) Any attorney serving as trustee counsel shall be entitled to compensation for reasonable fees and costs incurred in the performance of duties set forth in this Rule. Trustee counsel may seek payment of fees and costs from the estate of the unavailable attorney. Such a bill for fees and costs must be approved by the court as reasonable.

(2) An attorney who serves as trustee counsel may substitute as counsel for a client of the unavailable attorney after disclosure to the client that the client is free to select any attorney to substitute as counsel for the unavailable attorney and after obtaining the client's consent to substitution.

(3) In the event that the estate of the unavailable attorney is insufficient to compensate trustee counsel, an attorney appointed to serve as trustee counsel may submit a claim to the Board of Governors of the Alaska Bar Association. Reasonable compensation paid from the Lawyers' Fund for Client Protection shall be determined by the Board and will not exceed $10,000.

(h) **Discharge of Trustee: Destruction of Files.** After completion of his or her duties under this Rule, trustee counsel will submit a final report to the Court. The Court will review the report and will discharge the trustee. The trustee counsel will deliver to the Alaska Bar Association any files belonging to clients who cannot be located. The Alaska Bar Association will store the files for one year, after which time the Bar may exercise its discretion in maintaining or destroying the files.

(Added by SCO 176 dated February 26, 1974; amended by SCO 298 effective March 1, 1978; and rescinded and repromulgated by SCO 614 effective January 1, 1985; amended by SCO 658 effective March 15, 1986; by SCO 809 effective April 1, 1987; by SCO 962 effective July 15, 1989; by SCO 1452 effective October 15, 2001; and by SCO 1459 effective April 15, 2002)

C. MISCELLANEOUS

Rule 32. Disposal of Files.

(a) **Disposal of Files Concerning Deceased Attorney.** Any time after the expiration of five years from the death of an attorney, Bar Counsel may destroy all files of any discipline, disability, or reinstatement proceedings in which the deceased attorney was a Respondent unless, prior to destruction, the Board receives a request that the files not be destroyed. If the Board receives a request, it will grant the requesting party an opportunity to be heard to show cause why the files should not be destroyed. After hearing and review, the Board will enter an order as it deems appropriate.

(b) **Disposal of Dismissals.** Any time after the expiration of five years from the date of dismissal, Bar Counsel may destroy all files of any discipline or disability proceeding terminated by dismissal.

(c) **Administrative Records.** Bar Counsel will not destroy records maintained in accordance with Rule 11(d).

(d) **Compliance with Confidentiality.** All orders entered by the Board under Section (a) of this Rule, and proceedings in connection with the disposal of files under Section (a) of this Rule, will be consistent with the provisions of Rules 21 and 30 with regard to public access.

(Added by SCO 176 dated February 26, 1974; and rescinded and repromulgated by SCO 614 effective January 1, 1985; amended by SCO 962 effective July 15, 1989)

Rule 33. Expenses.

Except as otherwise provided herein, the salaries of Bar Counsel and staff will be paid by the Alaska Bar Association. The expenses and administrative costs incurred by Bar Counsel and staff hereunder, and the expenses and administrative costs of the Board and of Hearing Committees will be paid by the Court.

(Added by SCO 176 dated February 26, 1974; and rescinded and repromulgated by SCO 614 effective January 1, 1985; amended by SCO 962 effective July 15, 1989)

Rule 33.1. Disciplinary and Disability Matters Take Precedence.

Disciplinary and disability matters take precedence over all other matters before any court or administrative agency in this State, unless otherwise ordered by a justice of the Court for good cause shown. Upon the filing of an affidavit stating the existence of a pending disciplinary or disability matter, any judge of any court in this State, and any hearing officer or other person responsible for the conduct of any administrative proceeding in the State, will take action necessary to effect the requirements of this Rule. The Respondent or his or her attorney, Bar Counsel, any member of an Area Division, and any member of the Board will have authority to file such affidavit.

(Added by SCO 614 effective January 1, 1985; amended by SCO 962 effective July 15, 1989)

Rule 33.2. Effective Dates.

These Rules will take effect January 1, 1985. Rule 21 will only apply to those formal proceedings filed after the effective date of these Rules.

(Added by SCO 614 effective January 1, 1985)

PART III. RULES OF ATTORNEY FEE DISPUTE RESOLUTION

Rule 34. General Principles and Jurisdiction.

(a) **Fee Dispute Resolution Program Established.** It is the policy of the Alaska Bar Association to encourage the amicable resolution of fee disputes between attorneys and their clients which fall within the Bar's jurisdiction and, in the event such resolution is not achieved, to arbitrate and determine such disputes. To that end, the Board of Governors (hereinafter "board") of the Alaska Bar Association (hereinafter "Bar") hereby establishes through the adoption of these rules of fee dispute resolution (hereinafter "rules"), a program and procedures for the arbitration of disputes concerning any and all fees paid, charged, or claimed for professional services by attorneys.

(b) **Mandatory Arbitration for Attorneys.** Arbitration pursuant to these rules is mandatory for an attorney when commenced by a client. For the purpose of these rules, a "client" includes any person who is legally responsible to pay the fees for professional services rendered by an attorney.

(c) **Fee Disputes Subject to Arbitration.** All disputes concerning fees charged for professional services or costs incurred by an attorney are subject to arbitration under these rules except for:

(1) disputes where the attorney is also admitted to practice in another state or jurisdiction and (s)he maintains no office in the state of Alaska and no material portion of the legal services were rendered in the state of Alaska, unless (s)he appeared under Alaska Civil Rule 81;

(2) disputes where the client seeks affirmative relief against the attorney for damages based upon alleged malpractice or professional misconduct; or

(3) disputes where the fee to be paid by the client or on his or her behalf has been determined pursuant to state statute or by a court rule, order or decision;

(4) disputes which occur after April 15, 2003 over fees which were charged more than three (3) years earlier, unless the attorney or client could maintain a civil action over the disputed amount.

(d) **Attorney Jurisdiction.** Any attorney admitted to the practice of law in Alaska, or any other attorney who appears, participates or otherwise engages in the practice of law in this state, unless exempted under Section (c)(1) of this rule, is subject to the jurisdiction of the courts of this state, the Board of Governors of the Alaska Bar Association, and these rules of attorney fee dispute resolution.

(e) **Duty to Assist.** Each member of the Bar is encouraged to inform any member of the public who has a fee dispute of the existence of the fee dispute resolution program. Each member of the Bar has the duty to cooperate with and assist Bar Counsel in the efficient and timely arrangement for and disposition of fee arbitrations. This duty to assist Bar Counsel extends to the staff of the Alaska Bar Association, and to the staff of any entity outside the association designated by the board to assist in or assume administration of the Bar's fee dispute resolution program.

(f) **Venue.** Fee dispute arbitration in this state will be divided into the following three areas:

(1) Area 1—the First Judicial District:

(2) Area 2—the Second and Fourth Judicial Districts combined and:

(3) Area 3—the Third Judicial District.

Venue will lie in that area in which an attorney maintains an office or in the area in which the legal services for which fees were paid, charged, or claimed occurred. The parties may, by stipulation, agree to a different venue.

(g) **Immunity.** Members of the board, members of Area Fee Dispute Resolution Divisions, members of the executive committee, Bar counsel, Bar staff, and the staff of any entity designated by the board to assist in or assume administration of the Bar's fee dispute resolution program are immune from suit for conduct in the course and scope of their official duties as set forth in this rule.

(h) **Complex Arbitration.**

(1) Upon recommendation by bar counsel or a panel chair, the executive committee may determine that a dispute constitutes a complex arbitration based on any of the following factors:

(A) complex legal or factual issues are presented;

(B) the hearing is reasonably expected to or does exceed eight (8) hours; or

(C) the amount in dispute exceeds $50,000.00.

Such determination may be made at any time after the filing of a petition but before the hearing on the merits of the petition begins, unless the parties otherwise agree.

(2) When a case is determined to be complex, the executive committee may require payment by one or both parties for reasonable costs of administration and arbitration.

(Old Rule 34 [SCO 176] deleted and new Rule 34 added by SCO 780 effective March 15, 1987; amended by SCO 1044 effective January 15, 1991; by SCO 1147 effective July 15, 1994; by SCO 1372 effective April 15, 2000; and by SCO

1497 effective April 15, 2003)

Annotations

Cases

Arbitration panel had authority to find that persons who orally agreed to pay a third party's attorney fees were legally responsible for paying the fees and therefore had standing to bring a fee arbitration action. **Breeze v. Sims,** Op. No. 3487, 778 P2d 215 (Alaska 1989).

Whether oral fee contract contained a fee limit, and whether that limit was exceeded, were questions for the arbitration panel to decide, and its findings were not subject to judicial review even if the factual determinations were grossly in error. **Breeze v. Sims,** Op. No. 3487, 778 P2d 215 (Alaska 1989).

The statutory standard of review is applicable to arbitration decisions issued pursuant to the Alaska Bar rules; thus, findings of fact are unreviewable and the arbitrators' construction of the contract will be reviewed to determine whether it is a reasonably possible one that can seriously be made in the context in which the contract was made. **Breeze v. Sims,** Op. No. 3487, 778 P2d 215 (Alaska 1989).

Argument that arbitrary and capricious standard of review applied to superior court review of bar association fee arbitration panel's decision was rejected. **Butler v. Dunlap,** Op. No. 4465, 931 P2d 1036 (Alaska 1997).

Rule 35. Fees for Legal Services; Agreements.

(a) **Basis or Rate of an Attorney's Fee.** An attorney's fee will be reasonable. The factors to be considered in determining the reasonableness of a fee include the following:

(1) the time and labor required, the novelty and difficulty of the questions involved, and the skill requisite to properly perform the legal service;

(2) the likelihood that the acceptance of the particular employment will preclude other employment by the attorney;

(3) the fees customarily charged in the locality for similar legal services;

(4) the amount involved and the results obtained;

(5) the nature and length of the professional relationship with the client;

(6) the time limitations imposed by the client or by the circumstances;

(7) the experience, reputation, and ability of the attorney or attorneys performing the services; and

(8) whether the fee is fixed or contingent.

(b) **Written Fee Agreement.** The basis or rate of the fee to be charged, including any fee of retainer or initial deposit, exceeding $500 shall be communicated to that client in a written fee agreement, before commencing the representation or within a reasonable time thereafter. This written fee agreement shall include the disclosure required under Alaska Rule of Professional Conduct 1.4(c). In a case involving litigation, the attorney shall notify the client in the written fee agreement of any costs, fees or expenses for which the client may be liable if the client is not the prevailing party. In the absence of a written fee agreement, the attorney must present clear and convincing evidence that the basis or rate of fee exceeded the amount alleged by the client.

(c) **Contingent Fees.** A fee may be contingent on the outcome of the matter for which the service is rendered, except in a matter in which a contingent fee is prohibited by Section (d) of this rule, or by other law or court rules or decisions. A contingent fee agreement will be in writing and will include the disclosure required under Alaska Rule of Professional Conduct 1.4(c) and state the method by which the fee is to be determined, including:

(i) the percentage or percentages that shall accrue to the attorney in the event of settlement, trial or appeal; provided, however, fees on appeal may be left to later negotiation;

(ii) litigation and other expenses to be deducted from the recovery; and

(iii) whether such expenses are to be deducted before the contingent fee is calculated.

Upon conclusion of a contingent fee matter, the attorney will provide the client with a written statement reporting the outcome of the matter and, if there is a recovery, showing the amount of the remittance to the client and the method of its determination.

(d) **Prohibited Attorney Fee Agreements.** An attorney will not enter into an arrangement for, charge, or collect:

(1) any fee in a domestic relations matter, the payment or amount of which is contingent upon the securing of a divorce or upon the amount of alimony or support, or property settlement in lieu thereof, except an action to collect past-due alimony or support payments; or

(2) a fee contingent upon the outcome of a criminal case.

(e) **Fee Divisions Between Attorneys.** A division of fees between attorneys who are not in the same law firm may be made only if:

(1) the division is in proportion to the services performed by each attorney or, by written agreement with the client, each attorney assumes joint responsibility for the representation;

(2) the client is advised of and does not object to the participation of all the attorneys involved; and

(3) the total fee is reasonable.

(Old Rule 35 [SCO 176] deleted and new Rule 35 added by SCO 780 effective March 15, 1987; amended by SCO 1331 effective January 15, 1999)

Annotations

Cases

Alaska Bar Rules operate with the force of law and were applicable to case where alleged fee agreement was between two attorneys and did not involve the clients. **Matter of Estate of Katchatag,** Op. No. 4295, 907 P2d 458 (Alaska 1995).

Oral fee-splitting agreement was unenforceable because client had not been advised of nor consented to representation by attorney claiming fees under the agreement. **Matter of Estate of Katchatag,** Op. No. 4295, 907 P2d 458 (Alaska 1995).

Oral fee splitting agreement was unenforceable because it called for a fee division that was not in proportion to services actually provided. **Matter of Estate of Katchatag,** Op. No. 4295, 907 P2d 458 (Alaska 1995).

Rule 36. Bar Counsel of the Alaska Bar Association.

(a) **Powers and Duties.** Bar Counsel will appoint an attorney admitted to the practice of law in Alaska to be the Bar Counsel for the Alaska Bar Association (hereinafter "Bar Counsel") who will serve at the pleasure of the board. Bar Counsel will:

(1) with the approval of the board, employ and supervise attorneys and other administrative support staff as needed for the performance of his or her duties;

(2) supervise the maintenance of any records;

(3) aid members of the public in filing petitions for the arbitration of fee disputes (hereinafter "petitions");

(4) deny a petition if it appears that the matter:

(i) is not subject to arbitration under these rules;

(ii) does not involve an attorney subject to the jurisdiction of these rules; or

(iii) was not timely filed, in accordance with the provisions of Rules 34(c)(4) and 40;

(5) accept petitions in accordance with the procedures set forth in Rule 40;

(6) process all petitions in accordance with the procedures set forth in Rule 40;

(7) select an arbitrator or arbitration panel to arbitrate and determine a fee dispute;

(8) rule upon challenges for cause pursuant to Rule 37 (g);

(9) accept for filing documents submitted by parties for consideration by Bar Counsel, an arbitrator, or arbitration panel pursuant to these rules; and

(10) perform other duties as set forth in these rules or as assigned by the board or the executive committee of the fee dispute resolution program (hereinafter "executive committee").

(b) **Arbitration Forms.** Bar Counsel will furnish forms which may be used by any person to petition the Bar for the arbitration of his or her fee dispute. The forms will be available to the public through the office of the Bar.

(c) **Denial of Arbitration.** Any petition for fee arbitration denied by Bar Counsel will be the subject of a summary prepared by council and submitted to the executive committee. The names of the parties involved will not be provided in the summary. Bar Counsel will promptly communicate disposition of the matter to the client and the attorney.

(d) **Record Keeping.** The Bar Counsel will maintain records of all petitions processed and maintain statistical data reflecting:

(1) the amount of the fee in dispute;

(2) the status and ultimate disposition of each arbitration, including any amount by which the fee is reduced;

(3) whether the matter resulted in a referral by the arbitrator or arbitration panel to discipline counsel of the Bar for possible discipline action against the attorney; and

(4) the number of times each attorney is the subject of a petition for fee arbitration, including the amount and ultimate disposition of each dispute.

(e) **Quarterly Report to the Board and Executive Committee.** Bar Counsel will provide a quarterly report to the Alaska Supreme Court, the board, and the executive committee, which will include information about the number of petitions filed and arbitrations concluded during the quarter, the status of pending petitions, the dispositions of concluded arbitrations, and the amount of the disputes involved. The names of the parties involved will not be provided in the report.

(f) **Delegation of Responsibility.** Bar Counsel, with the approval of the board, may delegate such tasks as (s)he deems appropriate to other staff of the Alaska Bar Association and/or to the staff of any organization or entity outside the association retained or employed by the board to assume or assist in the administration of the Bar's Fee Dispute Resolution Program. Any reference in these rules to Bar Counsel will be deemed to include any persons, organizations or entities delegated responsibility, whether in whole or in part, for the administration of the program.

(g) **Disposal of Files.** Bar Counsel will destroy files of arbitrations five years after they are closed.

(Old Rule 36 [SCO 176] deleted and new Rule 36 added by SCO 780 effective March 15, 1987; amended by SCO 962 effective July 15, 1989; and by SCO 1044 effective January 15, 1991)

Rule 37. Area Fee Dispute Resolution Divisions; Arbitration Panels; Single Arbitrators.

(a) **Appointment of Area Division Members.** Members of area fee dispute resolution divisions (hereinafter "area divisions") will be appointed by the president of the Bar (hereinafter "president") subject to ratification by the board. One area division will be established in each area defined in Rule 34(f). Each area division will consist of:

(1) not less than six members in good standing of the Bar, each of whom maintains an office for the practice of law within the area of fee dispute resolution for which (s)he is appointed; and

(2) not less than three non-attorney members of the public (hereinafter "public member"), each of whom resides in the area of fee dispute resolution for which (s)he is appointed, is a United States citizen, is at least twenty-one years of age, and is a resident of the state of Alaska.

Area division members (hereinafter "arbitrators") will each serve a three-year term, with each term to commence on July 1st and expire on June 30th of the third year. A member whose term has expired prior to the disposition of a fee dispute matter to which (s)he has been assigned will continue to serve until the conclusion and disposition of that matter. This continued service will not prevent immediate appointment of his or her successor. The president will appoint a replacement to fill the unexpired term of a member who resigns prior to the expiration of his or her term.

(b) **Failure to Perform.** The president has the power to remove an area division member for good cause. The president will appoint, subject to ratification by the board, a replacement attorney or public member to serve the balance of the term of the removed member.

(c) **Assignment of Arbitration Panel Members for Disputes in Excess of $5000.00.** Bar Counsel will select and assign members of an area division to an arbitration panel (hereinafter "panel") of not less than two attorney members and one public member when the amount in dispute exceeds five thousand dollars. In addition, Bar Counsel will appoint an attorney member as chair of the panel.

(d) **Arbitration Panel Quorum.** Three members of a panel created under Section (c) of this rule will constitute a quorum, one of whom will be a public member. The panel chair will vote except when an even number of panel members is sitting. Each panel will act only with the agreement of a majority of its voting members sitting on the matter before it.

(e) **Assignment of Single Arbitrator for Disputes of $5000.00 or Less.** Bar Counsel will select and assign an attorney member of an area division to sit as a single arbitrator when the amount in dispute is five thousand dollars or less.

(f) **Conflict of Interest.** An arbitrator will not consider a matter when:

(1) (s)he is a party or is directly interested;

(2) (s)he is a material witness;

(3) (s)he is related to either party to the dispute by blood or affinity in the third degree;

(4) (s)he has been previously or is currently retained by either party as an attorney or has professionally counseled either party in any matter within two years preceding the filing of the petition for fee arbitration; or

(5) (s)he believes that for any reason, (s)he cannot give a fair and impartial decision.

(g) **Challenges for Cause.** Any challenge for cause of an arbitrator assigned to an arbitration must be made by either party within 10 days following notice of assignment to arbitration, unless new evidence is subsequently discovered which establishes grounds for challenge for cause. The challenge will be ruled upon by Bar Counsel. If Bar Counsel finds the challenge well taken a replacement arbitrator, if needed, will be appointed by Bar Counsel from the appropriate area division.

(h) **Peremptory Challenge.** Within ten days of the notice of assignment to arbitration, either party may file one peremptory challenge. Bar Counsel will at once, and without requiring proof, relieve the challenged arbitrator of his or her obligation to participate and appoint a replacement, if needed, from the appropriate area division.

(i) **Powers and Duties of Arbitrators.** In the conduct of arbitrations under these rules, arbitrators, sitting as a panel or a single arbitrator, will have the powers and duties to:

(1) take and hear evidence pertaining to the proceeding;

(2) swear witnesses, who will be examined under oath or affirmation on the request of any party to the dispute or by an arbitrator;

(3) compel, by subpoena, the attendance of witnesses and the production of books, papers, and documents pertaining to the proceeding, and consider challenges to the validity of subpoenas;

(4) approve written requests for prehearing discovery upon a showing of good cause;

(5) submit a written decision to Bar Counsel, in accordance with Rule 40; and

(6) interpret and apply these rules insofar as they relate to their powers and duties. When a difference arises among panel members concerning the meaning or application of any rule, the matter will be decided by a majority vote. If that is unobtainable, the matter in question will be referred to the executive committee.

(j) **Panel Chair Duties Take Precedence.** The powers and duties of arbitrators described in Section (i) of this rule accrue first to the arbitrator appointed chair of the panel and will be performed by the chair unless another panelist is designated by the chair to act in his or her stead or the chair determines that the full panel will consider and rule on the particular issues in question before it. The chair of a panel, or a single arbitrator, will preside at the arbitration hearing. (S)he will judge the relevancy and materiality of the evidence offered and will rule on all questions of evidence and procedure except as described in Section (i)(5) of this rule.

(Old Rule 37 [SCOs 176 and 233(5) as amended by SCOs 245, 296, 334, 406 and 470 deleted] and new Rule 37 added by SCO 780 effective March 15, 1987; amended by SCO 962 effective July 15, 1989; by SCO 1147 effective July 15, 1994; and by SCO 1264 effective July 15, 1997)

Rule 38. The Executive Committee of the Fee Dispute Resolution Program.

(a) **Definition.** The president will select one attorney member from each area fee dispute resolution division, and one public member, who together with the Bar's president-elect will constitute the five member executive committee of the fee dispute resolution program. The Bar Counsel will serve in an ex-officio capacity and will be a non-voting member of the executive committee. The board or Bar Counsel may orally or in writing direct the submission of any matter to the executive committee. The votes on any matter may be taken in person or by conference telephone call.

(b) **Quorum.** Three voting members of the executive committee will constitute a quorum at any meeting.

(c) **Powers and Duties.** The executive committee will have the powers and duties to:

(1) review the general operations of the Bar's fee dispute resolution program;

(2) review the summaries of denials of petitions prepared by Bar Counsel;

(3) formulate rules of procedure and determine matters of policy not inconsistent with these rules;

(4) in accordance with Rule 37(i)(6), hear and determine questions regarding the interpretation and application of these rules;

(5) approve forms developed by Bar Counsel to implement the procedures described in these rules; and

(6) refer apparent violations of Bar Rule 35 to Bar Counsel for disciplinary investigation, including instances in which attorneys have had substantial numbers of fee arbitrations filed against them even if no individual arbitration panel has recommended referral to Bar Counsel pursuant to Bar Rule 40(q)(4).

(d) **Meetings.** The executive committee will meet at least biannually and may meet at such other times as it deems appropriate, either in person or by conference telephone call. Minutes outlining the actions taken by the executive committee during its meetings will be the responsibility of the Bar Counsel and will be available to the board, members of area divisions, Bar members, and to the public, except that the executive committee will meet in executive session when discussing a specific petition or arbitration proceeding.

(Old Rule 38 [SCO 176 as amended by SCO 470] deleted and new Rule 38 added by SCO 780 effective March 15, 1987; amended by SCO 888 effective July 15, 1988; by SCO 962 effective July 15, 1989; by SCO 970 effective July 15, 1989; and by SCO 1498 effective April 15, 2003)

Rule 39. Notice of Right to Arbitration; Stay of Proceedings; Waiver by Client.

(a) **Notice Requirement by Attorney to Client.** At the time of service of a summons in a civil action against his or her client for the recovery of fees for professional services rendered, an attorney will serve upon the client a written "notice of client's right to arbitrate or mediate," which will state:

You are notified that you have a right to file a Petition for Arbitration of Fee Dispute or a Request for Mediation and stay this civil action. Forms and instructions for filing a Petition for Arbitration of Fee Dispute or a Request for Mediation and a motion for stay are available from the Alaska Bar Association, 510 L Street, Suite 602, Anchorage, AK 99501-1958, (907) 272-7469. If you do not file the Petition for Arbitration of Fee Dispute or a Request for Mediation within twenty (20) days after your receipt of this notice, you will waive your right to arbitration or mediation.

Failure to give this notice will be grounds for dismissal of the civil action.

(b) **Stay of Civil Proceedings.** If an attorney, or the attorney's assignee, commences a fee collection action in any court, the client may stay the action by filing notice with the court that the client has requested arbitration of the fee dispute by the Bar within twenty (20) days of receiving the notice of the client's right to arbitration. This notice will include proof of service on the attorney or the attorney's assignee. If a civil action has been filed, the Alaska Bar Association must receive an order of stay prior to commencing arbitration.

(c) **Stay of Non-Judicial Collection Actions.** After a client files a petition, the attorney will stay any non-judicial collection actions related to the fee in dispute pending the outcome of the arbitration.

(d) **Waiver of Right to Request or Maintain Arbitration.** A client's right to request or maintain an arbitration is waived if:

(1) the attorney files a civil action relating to the fee dispute, and the client does not file a petition for arbitration of a fee dispute within twenty (20) days of receiving the "client's notice of right to arbitrate" pursuant to paragraph (a) of this rule; or

(2) after the client received notice of the fee dispute resolution program, the client commences or maintains a civil action or files any pleading seeking judicial resolution of the fee dispute, except an action to compel fee arbitration, or seeking affirmative relief against the attorney for damages based upon alleged malpractice or professional misconduct.

(Old Rule 39, [SCO 176 as amended by SCOs 233(6), 299, 349 and 470] deleted and new Rule 39 added by SCO 780 effective March 15, 1987; amended by SCO 1038 effective January 15, 1991; by SCO 1147 effective July 15, 1994; by SCO 1156 effective July 15, 1994; and by SCO 1314 effective July 15, 1998)

Annotations

Cases

Pro se litigant waived his right to fee arbitration by failing to assert it in timely manner. **Noey v. Bledsoe,** Op. No. 5107, 978 P2d 1264 (Alaska 1999).

Although this rule requires attorneys to provide notice of actions "against" their clients, rule does not limit this requirement to actions personally filed by attorneys, thus filing deadline to request fee arbitration under this rule was triggered by interpleader action filed by disinterested third party. **Noey v. Bledsoe,** Op. No. 5107, 978 P2d 1264 (Alaska 1999).

Rule 40. Procedure.

(a) **Petition for Arbitration of Fee Disputes.** Fee arbitration proceedings will be initiated by a client by filing a petition with the Bar Counsel on a form provided by the Bar. The petition will be in writing, signed by the client (hereinafter "petitioner"), seeking resolution of the fee dispute with his or her attorney (hereinafter "respondent"), and will contain the following:

(1) a statement by the petitioner of the efforts made to attempt to resolve the matter directly with the respondent.

(2) a statement by the petitioner that (s)he understands in filing the petition that the determination of the arbitrator or panel is binding upon the parties; that the determination may be reviewed by a superior court only for the reasons set forth in AS 09.43.120 through AS 09.43.180; and that the determination may be reduced to judgment; and

(3) a statement of the dollar amount in dispute and the reasons in as specific language as possible, (s)he disputes the fee.

(b) **Petition Review.** Bar Counsel will review each petition to determine if:

(1) the petition is properly completed;

(2) the petitioner has made adequate attempts to informally resolve the dispute, and;

(3) the petition, in accordance with Rule 36(a)(4), should be denied.

Bar Counsel may return the petition to the petitioner with an explanation if (s)he determines that the petitioner has not adequately attempted to resolve the dispute or if the petition is otherwise incomplete. The counsel will specify to the petitioner what further steps need to be taken by him or her to attempt to resolve the matter informally or what portions of the petition require additional clarification or information before the Bar will accept the petition. If Bar Counsel determines that the petition should be denied, (s)he will promptly notify the petitioner.

(c) **Petition Accepted; Notification.** If Bar Counsel accepts a petition, (s)he will promptly notify both the petitioner and the respondent of the acceptance of the petition and that the matter will be held in abeyance for a period of ten days in order for both parties to have the opportunity to settle the dispute without action by an arbitrator or panel or to request mediation under Bar Rule 13. The notice will include a copy of the accepted petition and will advise both parties that if the matter is not settled or mediation requested within the ten-day period that it will be set for arbitration. Further action on the petition will be stayed during mediation. If the dispute is resolved through mediation, the matter will be closed by settlement by the parties. If mediation is unsuccessful, the stay will be lifted and the matter set for arbitration.

(d) **Respondent Answer to Petition Required.** Respondent shall respond to each of the allegations in the petition within 20 days of receipt of the notification that the petition has been accepted by Bar Counsel. Supporting documents may be submitted at that time.

(e) **Assignment to Arbitration, Dismissal for Failure to Proceed with Arbitration.**

(1) If, at the end of the ten-day period, Bar Counsel has not been informed that the matter has been settled or mediation requested, in accordance with Rule 37(c) or (e), (s)he will select and assign an arbitrator or arbitration panel from the members of the appropriate area division to consider the matter.

(2) Bar counsel will contact the petitioner, the respondent, and the arbitrator(s) to determine their availability for hearing. If the petitioner fails to provide scheduling information within 30 days of the date of a written request, Bar Counsel shall transfer the matter to inactive status and notify the parties in writing that the petition will be dismissed unless the petitioner provides the information within 30 days of the date of the notice. If the petitioner fails to provide the information, Bar Counsel shall dismiss the petition without prejudice to refile subject to the jurisdictional limitations of Rule 34(c). Bar Counsel's initial written request to a petitioner for scheduling information must advise the petitioner that failure to respond may result in dismissal of the petition.

(f) **Notice of Arbitration Hearing.** Bar Counsel will, at the time the arbitrator or arbitration panel is assigned, and at least twenty days in advance of the arbitration hearing, mail written notice of the time and place of the hearing to the petitioner and respondent. The notice of arbitration hearing will indicate the name(s) of the arbitrator or panelists assigned to hear the matter and will advise the petitioner and respondent that they are entitled to:

(1) be represented by counsel, at his or her expense;

(2) present and examine witnesses;

(3) cross-examine opposing witnesses, including examination on a matter relevant to the dispute even though that matter was not covered in the direct examination;

(4) impeach a witness, regardless of which party first called the witness to testify;

(5) present documentary evidence in his or her own behalf;

(6) rebut the evidence presented against him or her;

(7) testify on his or her own behalf, although even if a party does not testify on his or her own behalf, (s)he may be called and examined as if under cross-examination;

(8) upon written request to the arbitrator or chair of the panel, and for good cause shown, have subpoenas issued in his or her behalf, as provided in Rule 37(i)(3);

(9) upon written request to the arbitrator or chair of the panel, and for good cause shown, request prehearing discovery;

(10) challenge peremptorily and for cause any arbitrator assigned, as provided in Rule 37(g) and (h); and

(11) have the hearing recorded on tape.

(g) **Continuances; Adjournments.** Continuances will be granted only for good cause and when absolutely necessary. An application for continuance will be made to the arbitrator or panel chair. Application must be made at least ten days prior to the date for hearing unless good cause is shown for making the application for continuance subsequent to that time. Nothing in this section, however, will preclude an arbitrator or arbitration panel from adjourning an arbitration hearing from time to time as necessary, for good cause shown, at the request of either party.

(h) **Telephonic Hearings.** A party may appear or present witness testimony at the hearing by telephonic conference call. The costs of the telephone call will be paid by the party unless the Bar, in its discretion, agrees to pay the costs.

(i) **Arbitration Without Hearing.** If both parties, in writing, waive appearances at an arbitration hearing, the matter may be decided on the basis of written submissions. In such case, Bar Counsel will give each party suitable time to present his or her case in writing and to respond to the assertions of the other. If the arbitrator or panel, after reviewing the written submissions, concludes that oral presentations by the parties are necessary, a hearing will be scheduled; otherwise, the arbitrator or panel will render the decision on the basis of the written submissions.

(j) **Written Evidentiary Submissions Allowable.** Either the petitioner or the respondent may submit a written statement under oath in lieu of or in addition to presenting evidence at the arbitration hearing. Such written statements must be filed with Bar Counsel at least ten days prior to the date set for hearing. The other party may, within three days prior to the hearing date, respond to the party's written statement. The other party may also require the party filing the written statement to appear at the hearing or be available by telephone conference call and be subject to cross-examination, in which instance notice of the intention to cross-examine must be filed with Bar Counsel, and served upon the party whose presence is required within five days prior to the hearing date. Such notice must be made in good faith and not made with an intention to cause delay or inconvenience. The arbitrator or panel may award expenses of appearance if it determines that the notice of intention to cross-examine was filed solely for the purpose of causing delay or inconvenience.

(k) **Affidavit Submissions.** Either the petitioner or respondent may submit written affidavits by witnesses on their behalf in lieu of or in addition to presenting evidence at the arbitration hearing. Such affidavits must be filed with Bar Counsel and served on the other party at least ten days before the date set for the hearing. The other party may require the witness filing the affidavit to appear at the hearing or be available by telephone conference call and be subject to cross-examination, in which instance notice of the intention to cross-examine the witness must be filed with the Bar Counsel and served on the party on whose behalf the witness would appear, within five days prior to the hearing date. Such notice must be made in good faith and not made with an intention to cause delay or inconvenience. The arbitrator or panel may award expenses of appearance if it determines that the notice was filed solely for the purpose of causing delay or inconvenience. It will be the responsibility of the party on whose behalf the witness is appearing or giving telephonic testimony to insure the availability of that witness.

(*l*) **Appearance.** Appearance and non-objection by a party to the dispute at a scheduled arbitration hearing will constitute waiver by that party of any deficiency with respect to the giving of notice of the arbitration hearing.

(m) **Failure of a Party to Appear.** In spite of the failure of either party to appear at the scheduled arbitration hearing for which they were provided notice, the arbitrator or panel will proceed with the hearing and determine the dispute upon the basis of the evidence produced. If neither party attends, the arbitrator or panel may terminate the arbitration by deciding that neither party is entitled to any relief.

(n) **Evidence.** The arbitration hearing need not be conducted according to technical rules relating to evidence and witnesses. Any relevant evidence will be admitted if it is the sort of evidence on which reasonable persons are accustomed to rely in the conduct of serious affairs, regardless of the existence of any common law or statutory rule to the contrary. Irrelevant and unduly repetitious evidence will be excluded.

(o) **Attorney-Client Privilege.** The rules of privilege are effective to the same extent that they are recognized in a civil action, except that the respondent may reveal confidences or secrets of the client to the extent necessary to establish his or her fee claim.

(p) **Subpoenas and Discovery; Costs.** In accordance with Rule 37(i)(3) and subparagraph (f)(8) of this rule, an arbitrator will, for good cause shown, issue subpoenas and/or subpoenas duces tecum (hereinafter "subpoenas") or authorize prehearing discovery at the written request of a party. The cost of the service of the subpoena and the transportation of the witness shall be borne by the party requesting the subpoena to be issued. Any person subpoenaed by an arbitrator or the chair of a panel or ordered to appear or produce writings or respond to discovery who refuses to appear, give testimony, or produce the matter(s) subpoenaed or requested is in contempt of the arbitrator or arbitration panel. The arbitrator or panel chair may report such contempt to the superior court for the judicial district in which the proceeding is being conducted. The court shall treat this in the same manner as any other contempt. The refusal or neglect of a party to respond to a subpoena shall constitute cause for a determination of all issues to which the subpoenaed testimony or matter is material in favor of the non-offending party, and a final decision of the arbitrator or panel may be based upon such determination of issues.

(q) **Decision of the Arbitrator or Arbitration Panel.** The arbitrator or arbitration panel will issue its decision within thirty (30) days of the close of the arbitration hearing. If the matter is determined to be a "complex arbitration" under Alaska Bar Rule 34(h), the decision will be issued within ninety (90) days. If a delay is expected, the panel chair or single arbitrator will submit to bar counsel a written explanation of the delay, before expiration of the time allowed for the decision. Bar counsel will forward the explanation to the parties. The decision will be based upon the standards set forth in these rules and the Alaska Rules of Professional Conduct. The decision will be in writing and need not be in any particular form, unless a form is approved by the executive committee; however, the decision will include:

(1) a preliminary statement reciting the jurisdictional facts, including that a hearing was held upon proper notice to all parties and that the parties were given the opportunity to testify, cross-examine witnesses, and present evidence;

(2) a brief statement of the dispute;

(3) the findings of the arbitrator or panel on all issues and questions submitted which are necessary to resolve the dispute;

(4) a specific finding as to whether the matter should be referred to bar counsel for appropriate disciplinary proceedings; and

(5) the award, if any.

The original of the decision shall be signed by the arbitrator or members of the arbitration panel concurring in the decision. A separate dissent may be filed. The award may provide for payment in installments. Pre-judgment interest may be awarded. Attorney's fees for arbitration may not be awarded. The arbitrator or the panel chair will forward the decision, together with the file and the record, to bar counsel who will then serve a copy of the signed decision on each party to the arbitration.

(r) **Confidentiality.** All records, documents, files, proceedings and hearings pertaining to the arbitration of any dispute under these rules will be confidential and will be closed to the public, unless ordered open by a court upon good cause shown, except that a summary of the facts, without reference to either party by name, may be publicized in all cases once the proceeding has been formally closed. Bar Counsel may utilize arbitration records and decisions for statistical and enforcement purposes and for disciplinary purposes following acceptance of a grievance under Rule 22(a) or referral by the arbitrator or arbitration panel under Rule 40(q)(4).

(s) **Modification of Decision by the Arbitrator or Panel.** On application to the arbitrator or panel by a party to a fee dispute, the arbitrator or panel may modify or correct a decision if:

(1) there was an error in the computation of figures or a mistake in the description of a person, thing, or property referred to in the decision;

(2) the decision is imperfect in a matter of form not affecting the merits of the proceeding; or

(3) the decision needs clarification.

An application for modification shall be filed with bar counsel within twenty days after delivery of the decision to the parties. Written notice of the application for modification will be served promptly on the opposing party, stating that objection to the application must be served within ten days from the receipt of the notice of the application for modification. A decision on an application for modification will be issued within thirty (30) days after the time for filing an objection.

(t) **Confirmation of an Award.** Upon application of a party, and in accordance with the provisions of AS 09.43.110 and AS 09.43.140, the court will confirm an award, reducing it to a judgment, unless within ninety days either party seeks through the superior court to vacate, modify or correct the award in accordance with the provisions of AS 09.43.120 through 140.

(u) **Appeal.** Should either party appeal the decision of the court concerning an arbitration award under the provisions of AS 09.43.160, the party must serve a copy of the notice of appeal upon bar counsel. If a matter on appeal is remanded to the arbitrator or panel, a decision on remand will be issued within thirty (30) days after remand or further hearing.

(v) **Suspensions for Nonpayment of an Award.** Failure to pay a final and binding award will subject the respondent attorney to suspension for nonpayment as prescribed in Alaska Bar Rule 61(c).

(Old Rule 40 [SCO 176 as amended by SCO 470] deleted and new Rule 40 added by SCO 780 effective March 15, 1987; amended by SCO 888 effective July 15, 1988; by SCO 962 effective July 15, 1989; by SCO 1045 effective January 15, 1991; by SCO 1052 effective January 15, 1991; by SCO 1147 effective July 15, 1994; by SCO 1249 effective July 15, 1996; by SCO 1314 effective July 15, 1998; by SCO 1373 effective April 15, 2000; and by SCO 1547 effective October 15, 2004)

Annotations

Cases

The statutory standard of review is applicable to arbitration decisions issued pursuant to the Alaska Bar Rules; thus, findings of fact are unreviewable and the arbitrator's construction of the contract will be reviewed to determine whether it is a reasonably possible one that can seriously be made in the context in which the contract was made. **Breeze v. Sims**, Op. No. 3487, 778 P2d 215 (Alaska 1989).

Attenuated standard of review provided for under this rule does not violate due process under Alaska Constitution. **A. Fred Miller v. Purvis**, Op. No. 4372, 921 P2d 610 (Alaska 1996).

Argument that arbitrary and capricious standard of review applied to superior court review of bar association fee arbitration panel's decision was rejected. **Butler v. Dunlap,** Op. No. 4465, 931 P2d 1036 (Alaska 1997).

Confirmation of attorney fee arbitration award may not be resisted merely by reciting without specificity that fraud existed; evidentiary support for particular fraud claims must be presented in opposition to award. **Law Off. of Vincent Vitale v. Tabbytite,** Op. No. 4852, 942 P2d 1141 (Alaska 1997).

Rule 41. Service.

Service of the petition by the Bar shall be by personal delivery or by certified mail, postage paid, to the respondent. Unless otherwise specifically stated in these rules, all other service shall be by personal delivery or by first class mail, postage paid, addressed to the person on whom it is to be served at his or her office or home address as last given to the Bar and shall include a certificate of service showing the date copies of the documents were served, to whom they were served, and the name or initials of the Bar Association employee who served them. Service by mail is complete five business days after mailing. The time for performing any act shall commence on the date after service is complete.

(Old Rule 41 [SCO 176 as amended by SCOs 470 and 610] deleted and new Rule 41 added by SCO 780 effective March 15, 1987; amended by SCO 1315 effective July 15, 1998)

Rule 42. Informing the Public.

Blank copies of the petition form and explanatory booklets prepared by the Bar Counsel shall be provided to the clerks of courts in every location in the state.

(Added by SCO 176 dated February 26, 1974; amended by SCO 780 effective March 15, 1987; and by SCO 962 effective July 15, 1989)

PART IV.

Rule 43. Waivers to Practice Law for Alaska Legal Services Corporation.

Section 1. Eligibility. A person not admitted to the practice of law in this state may receive permission to practice law in the state if such person meets all of the following conditions:

(a) The person is a graduate of a law school which was accredited or approved by the Council of Legal Education of the American Bar Association or the Association of American Law Schools when the person entered or graduated and is an attorney in good standing, licensed to practice before the courts of another state, territory or the District of Columbia, or is eligible to be admitted to practice upon taking the oath of that state, territory or the District of Columbia;

(b) The person will practice law exclusively for Alaska Legal Services Corporation on a full-time or part-time basis;

(c) The person has not failed the bar exam of this state.

Section 2. Application. Application for such permission shall be made as follows:

(a) The executive director of the Alaska Legal Services Corporation shall apply to the Board of Governors on behalf of a person eligible under Section 1;

(b) Application shall be made on forms approved by the Board of Governors;

(c) Proof shall be submitted with the application that the applicant is an attorney in good standing, licensed to practice before the courts of another state, territory or the District of Columbia, or is eligible to be admitted to practice upon taking the oath of the state, territory or the District of Columbia.

Section 3. Approval. The Board of Governors shall consider the application as soon as practicable after it has been submitted. If the board finds that the applicant meets the requirements of Section 1 above, it shall grant the application and issue a waiver to allow the applicant to practice law before all courts of the state of Alaska. The Board of Governors may delegate the power to the executive director of the Bar Association to approve such applications and issue waivers, but the Board shall review all waivers so issued at its regularly scheduled meetings.

Section 4. Conditions. A person granted such permission may practice law only as required in the course of representing clients of Alaska Legal Services Corporation, and shall be subject to the provisions of Part II of these rules to the same extent as a member of the Alaska Bar Association. Such permission shall cease to be effective upon the failure of the person to pass the Alaska Bar examination.

(Added by Amendment No. 1 to SCO 176 effective July 1, 1974; amended by SCO 232 effective December 12, 1975; by SCO 484 effective November 2, 1981; by SCO 1153 effective July 15, 1994; by SCO 1282 effective January 15, 1998; and by SCO 1604 effective October 15, 2006)

Annotations

Cases

A party practicing law in Alaska pursuant to this rule who is not a graduate of an ABA-accredited law school is not eligible to take the Alaska bar examination. **Eyerly v. Alaska Bar Association,** Op. No. 2392, 631 P2d 480 (Alaska 1981).

Rule 43.1. Waivers to Practice Law Under a United States Armed Forces Expanded Legal Assistance Program.

Section 1. Eligibility. A person not admitted to the practice of law in this state may receive permission to practice law in the state for a period of not more than two years if such person meets all of the following conditions:

(a) The person is a graduate of a law school which was accredited or approved by the Council of Legal Education of the American Bar Association or the Association of American Law Schools when he entered or graduated and is an attorney in good standing, licensed to practice before the courts of another state, territory or the District of Columbia, or is eligible to be admitted to practice upon taking the oath of that state, territory or the District of Columbia;

(b) The person is an active duty member of the United States Armed Forces assigned to the Judge Advocate General's Corps or the United States Coast Guard; and

(c) The person has not failed the bar exam of this state.

Section 2. Application. Application for such permission shall be made as follows:

(a) The Staff Judge Advocate of the Military Installation to which the applicant is assigned shall apply to the Board of Governors on behalf of a person eligible under Section 1;

(b) Application shall be made on forms approved by the Board of Governors; and

(c) Proof shall be submitted with the application that the applicant is a graduate of an accredited Law School as provided in Section 1 of this rule and is an attorney in good standing, licensed to practice before the courts of another state, territory or the District of Columbia, or is eligible to practice upon taking the oath of the state, territory or the District of Columbia.

Section 3. Approval. The Board of Governors shall consider the application as soon as practicable after it has been submitted. If the Board finds that the applicant meets the requirements of Section 1 above, it shall grant the application and issue a waiver to allow the applicant to practice law before all courts of the State of Alaska. The Board of Governors may delegate the power to the Executive Director of the Bar Association to approve such applications and issue waivers, but the Board shall review all waivers so issued at its regularly scheduled meetings.

Section 4. Conditions. A person granted such permission may practice law only as required in the course of representing military clients or their dependents, or when accepting a case under the auspices of the Alaska Pro Bono Program under this rule, and shall be subject to the provisions of Part II of these rules to the same extent as a member of the Alaska Bar Association. Such permission shall cease to be effective upon the failure of the person to pass the Alaska Bar examination.

(Added by SCO 345 effective December 18, 1978; amended by SCO 1333 effective January 15, 1999)

Rule 43.2. Emeritus Attorney.

(a) **Purpose.** The purpose of this rule is to encourage attorneys who do not otherwise engage in the active practice of law in Alaska to provide pro bono legal representation to persons who cannot afford private legal services.

(b) **Bar Dues.** An attorney who serves as an emeritus attorney at any time during a year shall have bar dues for the following year waived.

(c) **Definitions.**

(1) An "emeritus attorney" is an inactive or retired member of the Alaska Bar Association who is not otherwise engaged in the practice of law in Alaska and who:

(A) provides free civil legal services in Alaska under the supervision of a qualified legal services provider as defined in this rule;

(B) is a member in good standing of the Alaska Bar Association and has no record of public discipline for professional misconduct imposed at any time within the past fifteen (15) years in any jurisdiction; and

(C) neither asks for nor receives personal compensation of any kind for the legal services rendered under this rule.

(2) A "qualified legal services provider" is a not-for-profit legal assistance organization that is approved by the Board of Governors. A legal assistance organization seeking approval from the Board to use an emeritus attorney shall file a petition with the Board of Governors certifying that it is a not-for-profit organization and explaining with specificity:

(A) the structure of the organization and whether it accepts funds from its clients;

(B) the major sources of funds used by the organization;

(C) the criteria used to determine eligibility for legal services performed by the organization;

(D) the types of legal and nonlegal services provided by the organization;

(E) the names of all members of the Alaska Bar Association who are employed by the organization and who regularly perform legal work for the organization; and

(F) the extent of malpractice insurance that will cover the emeritus attorney.

(d) **Authority.**

(1) An emeritus attorney is authorized to practice law to the extent permitted an active member of the Alaska Bar Association, but only for services performed in association with a qualified legal services provider.

(2) An emeritus attorney shall not be paid by the qualified legal services provider, but the qualified legal services provider may reimburse the emeritus attorney for actual expenses incurred while rendering services. If allowed by law, the emeritus attorney may seek attorney's fees on behalf of the client, but may not personally retain them. The emeritus attorney and the client shall enter into a written fee agreement under Rule of Professional Conduct 1.5 for the disposition of such fees. Collection of any money from the client, including but not limited to reimbursements for expenses incurred, shall be handled exclusively by the qualified legal services provider.

(e) **Duties of An Emeritus Attorney.** A member who wishes to perform pro bono work as an emeritus attorney on behalf of a qualified legal services provider shall file a sworn statement with the Alaska Bar Association that states:

(1) the name of the emeritus attorney and the name of the

qualified legal services provider for whom the emeritus attorney will provide pro bono services;

(2) that the emeritus attorney will not be paid compensation;

(3) that the emeritus attorney will be covered by the legal services provider's malpractice insurance;

(4) that the emeritus attorney has read and is familiar with the Alaska Rules of Professional Conduct; and

(5) that the emeritus attorney has not been publicly disciplined within the last fifteen (15) years in any jurisdiction.

(Added by SCO 1641 effective October 15, 2007)

Rule 44. Legal Interns.

Section 1. Practice Authorized When. The Integrated Bar Act prohibits the practice of law by anyone not admitted to practice in Alaska. This rule does not authorize an intern to perform any function prohibited by that Act other than those specifically set forth herein.

Section 2. Definition of Legal Intern. A "legal intern" is any person who has on file with the Alaska Bar Association an effective permit issued by the Bar Association through its Executive Director.

Section 3. Eligibility for Intern Permit. Every applicant for an intern permit shall:

(a) File an application in the form prescribed by the Board and produce and file the evidence and documents herein required as proof of eligibility for the permit;

(b) Be a student who:

(1) Is duly enrolled in a law school which was accredited or approved by the Council of Legal Education of the American Bar Association or the Association of American Law Schools when the applicant entered, or is enrolled in a law school in which the principles of English common law are taught but which is located outside the United States and beyond the jurisdiction of the American Bar Association and the Association of American Law Schools, provided that the foreign law school in which he or she is enrolled meets the American Bar Association Council of Legal Education Standards for approval;

(2) Has successfully completed at least one-half of the course work required for a law degree;

(3) Has filed with the application a certificate from the dean or other chief administrative officer of his or her law school, stating that he or she meets the requirements as set forth in subsections (b) (1) and (b) (2); or

(c) Be a law school graduate who:

(1) Has graduated from a law school which was accredited or approved by the Council of Legal Education of the American Bar Association or the Association of American Law Schools when the applicant entered or graduated, or has graduated from a law school in which the principles of English common law are taught but which is located outside the United States and beyond the jurisdiction of the American Bar Association and the Association of American Law Schools, provided that the foreign law school from which he or she has graduated meets the American Bar Association Council of Legal Education Standards for approval;

(2) Has never failed a bar examination administered by any state of the United States, or the District of Columbia, or, despite failure, has subsequently passed such a bar examination; and

(3) Has filed with the executive director a certificate from the dean or other chief administrative officer of his or her law school which states that the legal intern applicant meets the requirements set forth in subsection (c) (1), and either

(i) A personal affidavit stating that he or she never failed a bar examination, as set forth in subsection (c) (2), or

(ii) A certificate from the supreme court of the state in which, subsequent to failure, a bar examination was passed.

Section 4. Prior Admission. Any applicant who has been admitted to practice in another jurisdiction must file a certificate of good standing from each jurisdiction in which the applicant is admitted. If not in good standing, the applicant shall submit satisfactory proof that the applicant has never been disbarred, suspended or otherwise disciplined.

Section 5. Act Authorized by Permit.

(a) A legal intern may appear and participate in all proceedings before any district or superior court of this state to the extent permitted by the judge or the presiding officer if the attorney representing the client is personally present and able to supervise the intern and has filed an entry of appearance with the court and the office of the Alaska Bar Association substantially in compliance with the form set forth in Section 9 of this rule;

(b) A legal intern may also appear and participate before any district court in small claims matters, arraignments, pleas, bail hearings, sentencings and recorded in-chambers conferences without an attorney being personally present to supervise the intern under the following conditions:

(1) If the attorney representing the client has filed an appearance in the case and with the Bar office substantially in compliance with the form set forth in Section 9 of this rule;

(2) If the supervising attorney files a certificate stating that the intern has previously been present and supervised in a similar proceeding and that the attorney believes the intern is competent to conduct such proceedings without the personal presence of the attorney;

(3) If the client gives written consent to the appearance. A governmental body may grant approval through its attorney; and

(4) If the judge or magistrate agrees to permit the legal intern to participate in the proceedings.

Section 6. Termination of Permit. A permit shall cease to be effective upon the occurrence of one of the following events whichever occurs first:

(a) The expiration of a period of six months from date of issuance;

(b) The failure of an intern to take the first Alaska Bar examination for which the intern is eligible;

(c) The failure of an intern to pass any bar examination.

Section 7. Renewal of Expired Permit. A permit which has expired under Section 6(a) may be renewed upon compliance with the conditions for issuing an original permit, providing there has been no prior revocation of any certificate, authorization or approval required by Section 5 of this rule. No other permit shall be renewed.

Section 8. Prior Certification. All interns certified prior to the effective date of this rule must comply with the provisions of this rule within 30 days of its effective date.

Section 9. Form. The form for entry of appearance under Section 5 of this rule shall be substantially as follows:

COMES NOW, (Name of Attorney), attorney at law, and enters his/her appearance on behalf of (Name of Party). Please service all pleadings and notices at counsel's address of record:

____

Pursuant to Alaska Bar Rule IV-44, (Name of Intern) hereby enters his/her appearance as a legal intern. Supervising counsel (Name of Attorney), certifies that he/she is supervising (Name of Intern) in all matters relating to this case.

(Name of Attorney), also certifies that (Name of Intern) has been supervised in previous proceedings and that the legal intern is competent to appear alone in the following proceedings: (Name of Intern) is a legal intern within the meaning of Alaska Bar Rule IV-44.

DATED: ____________

____
SUPERVISING ATTORNEY

DATED: ____________

____
LEGAL INTERN
CONSENT

I, (Name of Client), hereby agree that (Name of Intern) may represent me in this case under the supervision of (Name of Attorney).

DATED: ____________

____
CLIENT CONSENT

IT IS HEREBY ORDERED that (Name of Intern) may hereby appear in the above entitled case for all proceedings except ________________

DATED: ____________

____
JUDGE

(Added by Amendment No. 2 to SCO 176 dated June 28, 1974; and amended by Amendment No. 3 to SCO 176 dated September 17, 1974; by Amendment No. 4 to SCO 176; by SCO 342 effective December 18, 1978; by SCO 433 effective November 1, 1980; and by SCO 1153 effective July 15, 1994)

Rule 44.1. Foreign Law Consultants.

(a) **Introduction.** A person who is admitted to practice in a foreign country as an attorney or counselor at law or the equivalent, and who complies with the provisions of this rule for licensing of foreign law consultants, may provide legal services in the State of Alaska to the extent allowed by this rule.

(b) **Eligibility.** In its discretion, the court may license to practice as a foreign law consultant, without examination, an applicant who:

(1) for a period of not less than 5 of the 7 years immediately preceding the date of application:

(A) has been admitted to practice and has been in good standing as an attorney or counselor at law or the equivalent in a foreign country, and

(B) has engaged either (i) in the practice of law in that country or (ii) in a profession or occupation that requires admission to practice and good standing as an attorney or counselor at law or the equivalent in that country;

(2) be of good moral character, which will be found unless prior or present conduct of the applicant would cause a reasonable person to believe that the applicant, if admitted to practice as a foreign legal consultant, would be unable or unwilling to act honestly, fairly and with integrity; and

(3) intends to practice as a foreign law consultant in the State of Alaska.

(c) **Applications.**

(1) An applicant for a license as a foreign law consultant shall file with the Executive Director at the office of the Alaska Bar Association an application, in duplicate, in the form provided by the Board. The application must be made under oath and must contain information relating to the applicant's age, residence, addresses, citizenship, occupations, general education, legal education, moral character and other matters as may be required by the Board. Any notice required or permitted to be given an applicant under these rules, if not personally delivered, will be delivered to the mailing address declared on the application unless notice in writing is actually received by the Board declaring a different mailing address. An applicant shall submit two duplicate 2-inch by 3-inch photographs of the applicant showing a front view of the person's head and shoulders. The application is deemed filed only upon receipt of a substantially completed form with payment of all required fees. Applications received without payment of all fees or which are not substantially complete will be promptly returned to the applicant with a notice stating the reasons for rejection and requiring payment of such

additional fees as may be fixed by the Board as a condition of reapplication.

(2) The application must be accompanied by the following documents, together with duly authenticated English translations if the documents are not in English:

(A) a certificate from the authority having final jurisdiction over professional discipline in the foreign country or jurisdiction in which the applicant was admitted to practice, which must be signed by a responsible official, or one of the members of the executive body of such authority, and which must be accompanied by the official seal, if any, of the authority, and which must certify:

(i) as to the authority's jurisdiction in such matters,

(ii) as to the applicant's admission to practice in the foreign country, the date of admission and the applicant's good standing as an attorney or counselor at law or the equivalent, and

(iii) as to whether any charge or complaint has ever been filed against the applicant with the authority, and, if so, the substance of each charge or complaint and the adjudication or resolution thereof;

(B) a letter or recommendation from one of the members of the executive body of the authority or from one of the judges of the highest law court or court of general original jurisdiction of the foreign country, certifying the applicant's professional qualifications, together with a certificate from the clerk of the authority, or of the court, attesting to the genuineness of the person's signature;

(C) a letter of recommendation of at least two attorneys or counselors at law or the equivalent admitted in and practicing in the foreign country, stating the length of time, when, and under what circumstances they have known the applicant, and their appraisal of the applicant's moral character; and

(D) other relevant documents or information as may be required by the Court or by the Board.

(3) The statements contained in the application and the supporting documents will be reviewed by the Board who shall report the results of their review with recommendations to the court. Prior to the grant of any license, the court must be satisfied of the good moral character of the applicant.

(4) In considering whether to license the applicant as a foreign law consultant under this rule, the court has discretion to consider whether an attorney in Alaska would be allowed a reasonable and practical opportunity to establish an office to give legal advice to clients in the applicant's country of admission. In order to exercise its discretion, the court must require a reasonable showing that:

(A) an attorney in Alaska actively sought to establish an office in the applicant's country of admission;

(B) the authority in the foreign country having final jurisdiction over the application process in subsection (A) denied the attorney in Alaska an opportunity to establish an office in that foreign country; and

(C) the denial in subsection (B) raises serious questions as to the adequacy of the opportunity for an attorney in Alaska to establish an office in the foreign country.

(d) **Hardship Waiver.** Upon a showing that strict compliance with the provisions of subparagraph (b)(1) or (c)(2) of this rule would cause the applicant unnecessary hardship, or upon a showing of exceptional professional qualifications to practice as a foreign law consultant, the court may waive or vary the application of such provisions and permit the applicant to make any other showing as is satisfactory to the court.

(e) **Scope of Practice.** A person licensed as a foreign law consultant under this rule may provide legal services in the State of Alaska, subject to the limitations that the person shall not:

(1) appear for another person as attorney in any court or before any magistrate or other judicial officer in the State of Alaska, or prepare pleadings or any other papers in any action or proceeding brought in any such court or before any such judicial officer, except as authorized by Civil Rule 81(a)(2);

(2) prepare any deed, mortgage, assignment, discharge, lease, agreement, sale or any other instruction affecting title to real estate located in the United States of America;

(3) prepare:

(A) any will or trust instrument affecting the disposition of any property located in the United States of America and owned by a resident of the United States of America, or

(B) any instrument relating to the administration of a decedent's estate in the United States of America;

(4) prepare any instrument concerning the marital relations, rights or duties of a resident of the United States of America, or the custody or care of the children of a resident;

(5) provide professional legal advice on the law of the State of Alaska, any other state or territory of the United States of America, the District of Columbia, the United States or any foreign country other than the country where the consultant is admitted as an attorney or counselor at law or the equivalent, whether provided incident to the preparation of legal instruments or otherwise. If a particular matter requires legal advice from a person admitted to practice law as an attorney in a jurisdiction other than where the consultant is admitted as an attorney or counselor at law or equivalent, the foreign law consultant shall consult an attorney, counselor of law or the equivalent in the other jurisdiction on the particular matter, obtain written legal advice and transmit the written legal advice to the client;

(6) in any way represent that the person is licensed as an attorney or counselor at law in the State of Alaska, or the equivalent in any jurisdiction, unless so licensed; or

(7) use any title other than "foreign law consultant"; provided that the person's authorized title and firm name in the foreign country in which the person is admitted to practice as an attorney or counsel at law or the equivalent may be used if the title, firm name, and the name of the foreign country are stated together with the title "foreign law consultant."

(f) **Disciplinary Provisions.**

(1) A person licensed to practice as a foreign law consultant under this rule is subject to the jurisdiction of the Alaska Supreme Court, the Disciplinary Board of the Alaska Bar Association, the Rules of Disciplinary Enforcement, and Ethics Opinions adopted by the Board of Governors of the Alaska Bar Association.

(2) A person licensed to practice as a foreign law consultant shall execute and file with the clerk, in the form and manner as the court may prescribe:

(A) a statement that the foreign law consultant has read and will observe the Rules of Disciplinary Enforcement, Ethics Opinions adopted by the Board of Governors of the Alaska Bar Association, and the Code of Professional Responsibility;

(B) an undertaking or appropriate evidence of professional liability insurance, in an amount as the Court may prescribe, to insure the foreign law consultant's proper professional conduct and responsibility;

(C) a signed document stating the foreign law consultant's address within the State of Alaska and designating the clerk of this court as the consultant's agent upon whom process may be served, with the effect as if served personally upon the consultant, in any action or proceeding brought against the consultant arising out of or based upon any legal services rendered or offered to be rendered by the consultant within or to residents of the State of Alaska, if due diligent service cannot be made upon the consultant at the consultant's address; and

(D) a commitment to notify the Court of any resignation or revocation of the foreign law consultant's admission to practice in the foreign country of admission, or of any censure, suspension, or expulsion respecting admission.

(SCO 946 effective January 15, 1989)

PART V. LAWYERS' FUND FOR CLIENT PROTECTION

Rule 45. Definitions.

(a) The "Board" is the Board of Governors of the Alaska Bar Association.

(b) The "Fund" is the Lawyers' Fund for Client Protection of the Alaska Bar Association.

(c) The "Committee" is the Lawyers' Fund for Client Protection Committee.

(d) The term "lawyer" as used in this part and the rules contained therein means an active member of the Alaska Bar Association domiciled in Alaska at the time of the act or omission which is the basis of the application of the fund. The act or omission complained of need not have taken place within the State of Alaska in order for an application to the fund to be made or granted.

(e) The words "dishonest conduct" or "dishonest act" as used herein means wrongful acts committed by a lawyer in the manner of defalcation or embezzlement of money, or the wrongful taking or conversion of money, property or other things of value.

(f) "Reimbursable losses" are only those losses of money, property or other things of value which meet all of the following tests:

(1) The loss was caused by the dishonest conduct of a lawyer when

(i) acting as a lawyer, or

(ii) acting in a fiduciary capacity customary to the practice of law, such as administrator, executor, trustee of an express trust, guardian or conservator; or

(iii) acting as an escrow holder or other fiduciary, having been designated as such by a client in the matter in which the loss arose or having been so appointed or selected as a result of the client-attorney relationship.

(2) The loss was that of money, property, or other things of value which came into the hands of the lawyer by reason of having acted in the capacity described in paragraph (f)(1) of this rule.

(3) The dishonest conduct occurred on or after the effective date of this part.

(4) The claim shall have been filed no later than three years after the claimant knew or should have known of the dishonest conduct of the lawyer.

(5) The following shall not be an applicant:

(i) The spouse or other close relative, partner, associate or employee of the lawyer, or

(ii) An insurer, surety or bonding agency or company, or

(iii) Any business entity controlled by (1) the lawyer, (2) any person described in paragraph (i) hereof, or (3) any entity described either in paragraph (ii) hereof or in turn controlled by the lawyer or a person or entity described in paragraphs (i) or (ii) hereof, or

(iv) A governmental entity or agency, or

(v) A collection agency.

(6) The loss, or reimbursable portion thereof was not covered by any insurance or by any fidelity or surety bond fund, whether of the lawyer or the applicant or otherwise.

(7) Either

(i) the lawyer

(aa) has died or has been adjudicated mentally incompetent;

(bb) has been disciplined, or has voluntarily resigned from the practice of law in Alaska;

(cc) has become a judgment debtor of the applicant or has been adjudicated guilty of a crime which judgment or judgments shall have been predicated upon dishonest conduct while acting as specified in paragraph (f) (1) of this rule and which judgment or judgments remain unsatisfied in whole or in part; or

(ii) the Board has determined it to be an appropriate case for consideration under these rules.

(8) Reimbursable losses do not include interest on such losses or attorney fees incurred in attempts to recover them.

(g) "Notice" means the delivery of a written notice personally to the addressee or by mail to the most recent address which the addressee has provided to the Alaska Bar Association. Written notice shall be presumed to be received by the addressee five (5) days after the postmark date of certified or registered mail sent to the most current address which the addressee has provided to the Alaska Bar Association.

(Added by SCO 214 effective January 1, 1976; amended by SCO 722 effective December 15, 1986; and by SCO 1029 effective July 15, 1990)

Rule 46. Applications for Reimbursement.

(a) The Board shall prepare a form of application for reimbursement; in its discretion the Board may waive the requirement that a claim be filed on such form.

(b) The form shall be executed under penalty of perjury and shall require, as minimum information:

(1) The name and address of the lawyer.

(2) The amount of the alleged loss.

(3) The date or period of time during which the alleged loss was incurred.

(4) The date upon which the alleged loss was discovered.

(5) Name and address of the applicant.

(6) The general statement of facts relative to the application.

(7) A statement that the applicant has read these rules and agrees to be bound by them.

(8) A statement that the loss was not covered by any insurance, indemnity or bond, or if so covered, the name and address of the insurance or bonding company, if known, and the extent of such coverage and the amount of payment, if any made.

(c) The form or application shall contain the following statement in bold type:

"THE ALASKA BAR ASSOCIATION HAS NO LEGAL RESPONSIBILITY FOR THE ACTS OF INDIVIDUAL LAWYERS. PAYMENTS FROM THE LAWYERS' FUND FOR CLIENT PROTECTION SHALL BE MADE IN THE SOLE DISCRETION OF THE ALASKA BAR ASSOCIATION."

(d) The form shall include in its body the pro tanto assignment from the applicant to the Alaska Bar Association of the applicant's right against the named lawyer, or the lawyer's personal representative, estate or assigns, as required by Alaska Bar Rule 55.

(Added by SCO 214 effective January 1, 1976; amended by SCO 466 effective June 1, 1981; by SCO 1029 effective July 15, 1990; and by SCO 1153 effective July 15, 1994)

Rule 47. Filing Applications and Preliminary Consideration.

(a) An application for reimbursement shall be filed with the Anchorage office of the Alaska Bar Association and shall forthwith be transmitted by such office to the Chair of the Committee. The Executive Director of the Alaska Bar Association shall designate a State Bar staff attorney or attorneys or a member of the Committee to assist the Committee and the Board in their consideration thereof.

(b) Whenever the attorney designated pursuant to Rule 47(a) reports that in his or her opinion a prima facie case for reimbursement loss is not shown, such report shall be transmitted to the Committee and if approved by a majority of the Committee, constitutes rejection of the application. Any such report shall state the reasons for the opinion and may rely on information outside the application, including further information from the applicant, provided that such information is identified in the report.

(c) In all other cases the attorney designated pursuant to Rule 47(a) shall refer the application to the Committee.

(Added by SCO 214 effective January 1, 1976; amended by SCO 407 effective, nunc pro tunc, January 1, 1980; and by SCO 1217 effective July 15, 1995)

Rule 48. The Committee.

(a) The Committee shall consist of at least six members of the Alaska Bar Association, appointed by the President, subject to ratification by the Board. Each appointment shall be for a three year term.

(b) A quorum at any meeting of the Committee shall be a majority of the members of the committee. A member participating in Committee proceedings by telephone is present for all purposes, including purposes of a quorum. In the absence of a quorum a matter may be considered by the members present, but no action may be taken with respect thereto. The vote of a majority of the members present and voting at a meeting at which a quorum is present shall constitute the action of the Committee.

(c) The Chairperson of the Committee shall be appointed by the President for a term of one year commencing July 1 and thereafter may serve in that office until his or her successor is appointed. The Chairperson may be reappointed as Chairperson. Should a vacancy occur in the office of the Chairperson, the President shall appoint a new Chairperson.

(d) A member of the Committee who has or has had a lawyer-client relationship or financial relationship with a claimant or lawyer who is the subject of a claim shall not participate in the investigation or adjudication of a claim involving that claimant or lawyer.

(Added by SCO 214 effective January 1, 1976; amended by SCO 408 effective, nunc pro tunc, January 1, 1980; by SCO 722 effective December 15, 1986; by SCO 1073 effective January 15, 1992; and by SCO 1311 effective July 15, 1998)

Rule 49. Authority of Committee and Board.

Upon consideration of applications for reimbursement the Board, or the Committee may:

(a) Take and hear evidence pertaining to the application.

(b) Administer oaths and affirmations.

(c) Compel, by subpoena, the attendance of witnesses and the production of books, papers and documents pertaining to the application.

(d) Upon application to and approval by the Executive Director, the Committee may engage the services of an investigator, accountant or other expert necessary to investigate and process the application.

(Added by SCO 214 effective January 1, 1976)

Rule 50. Evidence and Burden of Proof.

The proceedings had upon the applications need not be conducted according to technical rules relating to evidence and witnesses. Any relevant evidence shall be admitted if it is the sort of evidence on which responsible persons are accustomed to rely in the conduct of serious affairs, regardless of the existence of any common law or statutory rule which might make improper the admission of such evidence over objection in civil actions. Hearsay evidence may be used for the purpose of supplementing or explaining other evidence but shall not be sufficient in itself to support a finding unless it would be admissible over objection in civil actions; provided, however, that certified or duly authenticated copies of the record, including a transcript of testimony therein, of

(a) any disciplinary proceeding against the lawyer of which the lawyer had notice conducted by the Alaska Bar Association or any body authorized to conduct disciplinary proceedings against attorneys in any state or the District of Columbia.

(b) any proceeding conducted pursuant to Rules 16, 28, 29, Alaska Bar Rules.

(c) any proceeding resulting in the conviction of the lawyer of a crime, or

(d) any contested civil action or special proceeding to which a lawyer is a party or in whose behalf the action is prosecuted or defended, may constitute sufficient evidence to support a finding. The applicant bears the burden of proof upon the issues of reimbursable loss and the extent thereof and all facts shall be established by a preponderance of the evidence.

(Added by SCO 214 effective January 1, 1976; amended by SCO 1153 effective July 15, 1994)

Rule 51. When Testimony is to be Reported and Transcribed.

The testimony of all witnesses appearing before the Committee or the Board shall be recorded; but a transcript of said testimony shall not be prepared unless the Committee or the Board or its President orders its preparation. Either party may request a transcript at their own expense.

(Added by SCO 214 effective January 1, 1976; amended by SCO 722, effective December 15, 1986; and by SCO 867 effective July 15, 1988)

Rule 52. Consideration by Committee.

(a) Upon receipt of an application the Committee shall conduct such investigations and hold such hearings as it determines necessary to establish whether the application should be granted. Hearings will be conducted informally. Both the applicant and the lawyer shall be afforded opportunities to present argument and evidence, and to cross-examine opposing witnesses. The Committee may request the attorney selected pursuant to Rule 47(a) to present argument and evidence, if the Committee believes this will assist it in reaching its decision.

The Committee shall provide a copy of the application to the lawyer complained of and shall notify the lawyer and the applicant of the date and time for a hearing on the application.

(b) The Committee may delegate responsibility for holding a hearing to a subcommittee of one or more of its members. The subcommittee shall prepare a proposed report containing the information required by Rule 52(c), which shall be promptly considered by the Committee. The Committee shall (1) approve and adopt the proposed report, or (2) remand the proposed report to the same or a different subcommittee for the taking of further evidence or for preparation of a new proposed report, or (3) consider the matter de novo on the basis of the record made at hearing.

(c) At the conclusion of the Committee's consideration of an application pursuant to this Rule, it shall promptly make and transmit to the office of the Alaska Bar Association a report consisting of a brief statement of the proceedings had, clear and concise findings of fact adopted by the Committee a brief statement of its conclusions and a recommendation to the Board.

(d) Upon receipt of the report, the Executive Director shall provide copies of it to the attorney or the attorney's representative and the claimant.

(e) Within twenty (20) days of receiving notice of the filing of the report with the Board, any party may file written objections to the report.

(Added by SCO 214 effective January 1, 1976; amended by SCO 409 effective, nunc pro tunc, January 1, 1980; by SCO 722 effective December 15, 1986; by SCO 867 effective July 15, 1988; by SCO 1029 effective July 15, 1990; by SCO 1064 effective July 15, 1991; and by SCO 1153 effective July 15, 1994)

Rule 53. Consideration by the Board.

(a) All reports filed by the Committee pursuant to Rule 52(d) are advisory only and shall be placed upon the calendar of the Board for consideration.

(b) The Board has the sole and final authority to determine whether and to what extent any application for reimbursement shall be granted and shall determine the order, manner (which may be in installments), and amount of payment of each application. The Board may postpone consideration of any application until after any disciplinary action or any court proceeding pending or contemplated has been completed.

(c) Before the Board directs that payment from the Fund be made it must find that a reimbursable loss as defined in these rules has been established and the extent of the said loss.

(d) The loss to be paid to any individual claimant as the result of any dishonest act or omission in any one transaction, matter or proceeding involving any one lawyer shall not exceed the lesser of the following sums: (a) $50,000, or (b) 10% of the Fund at the time the award is made. The aggregate maximum amount which all claimants may recover arising from an instance or course of dishonest conduct of any one lawyer is $200,000. The total amount to be paid to all claimants in any one year shall not exceed 50% of the total amount of the Fund as of January 1 of the calendar year in which the awards are made.

(Added by SCO 214 effective January 1, 1976; amended by SCO 722 effective December 15, 1986; and by SCO 1029 effective July 15, 1990)

Rule 54. Payments at Discretion of State Bar.

All payments from the Fund, including the payment of trustee counsel compensation by the Board under Rule 31(g)(3), shall be a matter of grace and not of right and shall be in the sole discretion of the Alaska Bar Association. No client or member of the public shall have any right in the Fund as a third party beneficiary or otherwise.

(Added by SCO 214 effective January 1, 1976; amended by SCO 1459 effective April 15, 2002)

Rule 55. Assignment of Applicant's Rights and Subrogation.

Payments on approved applications shall be made from the Fund only upon condition that the Alaska Bar Association receives, in consideration for any payment from the Fund, a pro tanto assignment from the applicant of the applicant's right against the lawyer involved, or the lawyer's personal representative, estate or assigns. The collection of the aforementioned assignments shall be handled by the Executive Director of the Alaska Bar Association or a staff attorney thereof, under the supervision of the Board of Governors or in such other manner as may from time to time be directed by the Board of Governors. In order to effect collection of said assignment, the Executive Director or other attorney prosecuting the collection, may disclose such information concerning the application and the consideration thereof by the Alaska Bar Association as in the Executive Director's discretion is necessary; provided, however, that without prior approval of the Board of Governors, the Executive Director shall not disclose information which refers to the existence of any non-public disciplinary matter or proceeding. Upon commencement of an action by the Alaska Bar Association, pursuant to its subrogation rights, it shall give written notice thereof to the reimbursed applicant at the applicant's last known address. The reimbursed applicant may then join in such action to press a claim for the applicant's loss in excess of the amount of the above reimbursement, but any recovery shall first be applied to offset the reimbursement.

(Added by SCO 214 effective January 1, 1976; amended by SCO 1153 effective July 15, 1994)

Rule 56. Applicant May Be Advised.

The applicant may be advised of the status of the Alaska Bar Association's consideration of the applicant's application and shall be advised of the final determination of the Alaska Bar Association upon the same.

(Added by SCO 214 effective January 1, 1976; amended by SCO 1153 effective July 15, 1994; and by SCO 1395 effective October 15, 2000)

Rule 57. Rejection of the Application; Finality.

The applicant may apply to the Board for further consideration of the application within one month after the mailing of the notice of rejection by the Committee; otherwise such rejection is final and no further consideration shall be given by the Alaska Bar Association to said application or another based upon the same alleged facts.

(Added by SCO 214 effective January 1, 1976)

Rule 58. Confidential Nature of Proceeding and Records.

(a) The Committee and the Board, during consideration of an application, may have access to Alaska Bar Association disciplinary files and records, if any, pertaining to the alleged loss notwithstanding the provisions of Rule 22(b), Alaska Bar Rules. Any information or documents obtained by the Board or the Committee from said files or records shall be used solely for the purpose of determining the validity of the application, but otherwise shall constitute confidential information as provided in Rule 22(b).

(b) The files and records pertaining to all applications for reimbursement from the Fund and all investigations or proceedings conducted in connection therewith are the property of the Alaska Bar Association and are confidential and no information concerning them and the matters to which they relate shall be given to any persons except upon order of the Board of Governors or as in these rules provided.

(c) Unless otherwise ordered by the Board, the proceeding conducted before the Committee and the Board shall not be public.

(Added by SCO 214 effective January 1, 1976; amended by SCO 722 effective December 15, 1986)

Rule 59. Other Rules.

Except where otherwise specifically provided in this part, Rules 14 and 17 shall be applicable to this part; and in such cases the reference to "disciplinary proceedings" shall encompass Lawyers' Fund for Client Protection proceedings, and the reference to "members of hearing committees" shall apply to the Lawyers' Fund for Client Protection Committee.

(Added by SCO 214 effective January 1, 1976; amended by SCO 466 effective June 1, 1981; by SCO 722 effective December 15, 1986; and by SCO 1029 effective July 15, 1990)

Rule 60. General Provisions.

(a) Bar Counsel shall refer potential claimants to the Lawyers' Fund for Client Protection at the completion of discipline proceedings when appropriate. Copies of the Lawyers' Fund for Client Protection Rules and any pamphlet which describes the Fund and procedures involved in filing a claim may be made available to the public.

(b) These rules may be changed at any time by a majority vote of the Committee at a duly held meeting at which a quorum is present, subject, however, to the approval of a majority vote of the Board of Governors of the Alaska Bar Association and the adoption of the change by the Supreme Court of the State of Alaska.

(c) **Immunity.**

(1) *General Immunity.* Members of the Board, members of the Committee, the Executive Director, Bar Counsel, and all Bar staff are immune from suit for conduct in the course and scope of their official duties as set forth in these rules.

(2) *Witness Immunity.* The Court or its designee may, in its discretion, grant immunity from criminal prosecution to witnesses in Lawyers' Fund for Client Protection proceedings upon application of the Board, Bar Counsel, the lawyer, or counsel for the lawyer, and after receiving the consent of the appropriate prosecuting authority.

(Added by SCO 214 effective January 1, 1976; amended by SCO 722 effective December 15, 1986; by SCO 962 effective July 15, 1989; by SCO 1029 effective July 15, 1990; by SCO 1176 effective July 15, 1995)

Part VI.

Rule 61. Suspension for Nonpayment of Alaska Bar Membership Fees, Fee Arbitration Awards, and Child Support Obligation.

(a) Any member failing to pay any fees within 30 days after they become due shall be notified in writing by certified or registered mail that the Executive Director shall petition a the Supreme Court of Alaska for an order suspending such member for nonpayment of fees.

(b) The Executive Director shall annually notify the clerks of court of the names and date of suspension of all members who have been then or previously suspended and not reinstated.

(1) Any member who has been suspended for less than one year, upon payment of all accrued dues, in addition to a penalty of $10.00 per week of delinquency (each portion of a week to be considered a whole week) but not exceeding a total of $160.00 in penalties shall be reinstated upon certification by the Executive Director to the Supreme Court and the clerks of court that the dues and penalties have been paid.

(2) Any member who has been suspended for a year or more, upon determination of character and fitness as set forth in Rule 2(1)(d) by the Board, upon payment of all accrued dues, in addition to a penalty of $160.00, shall be reinstated upon certification by the Executive Director to the Supreme Court and the clerks of court that the member meets the standard of character and fitness set forth in Rule 2(1)(d) and that dues and penalties have been paid.

(c) Any member who without good cause fails to pay a final and binding fee arbitration award within 15 days after it is final and binding shall be notified in writing by certified or registered mail that the Executive Director shall, after 15 days, petition the Supreme Court of Alaska for an order suspending such member for nonpayment of a fee arbitration award. Upon suspension of the member for nonpayment of a fee arbitration award, the member shall not be reinstated until the award is paid or otherwise satisfied and the Executive Director has certified to the Supreme Court and the clerks of court that the award has been paid.

(d) **Suspension for Nonpayment of Child Support Obligation.**

(1) If notified by the Child Support Services Division that any member is not in substantial compliance with his or

her child support order or a payment schedule negotiated with the Child Support Services Division, the Executive Director shall serve such notice on the member.

(2) If the Executive Director has not received a release from the Child Support Services Division, or notice of a court order staying suspension, within 150 days of the mailing or personal service of the notice described in (1) of this paragraph, the Executive Director shall petition the Supreme Court of Alaska for an order suspending such member for substantial noncompliance with his or her child support order or payment agreement negotiated with the Child Support Services Division. Upon suspension of the member for this reason, the member shall not be reinstated until the Child Support Services Division issues a release to the Executive Director and the Executive Director has certified to the Supreme Court and the clerks of court that a release has been issued by the Child Support Services Division.

(Added by SCO 233(7) effective April 1, 1976; amended by SCO 343 effective December 18, 1978; by SCO 466 effective June 1, 1981; by SCO 611 effective January 1, 1985; by SCO 971 effective July 15, 1989; by SCO 1232 effective July 15, 1996; by SCO 1310 effective July 15, 1998; by SCO 1376 effective April 15, 2000; and by SCO 1652 effective October 15, 2007)

Rule 62. Adoption of Recommended Rules, Bylaws, and Regulations.

Section 1. Purpose: This rule provides a procedure whereby the Board of Governors of the Alaska Bar and the Alaska Bar may:

(a) Recommend for adoption to the Supreme Court of Alaska proposed Alaska Bar Rules;

(b) Adopt bylaws and regulations for governance of the Alaska Bar.

Section 2. The Board, on its own initiative may, in accordance with this Rule, recommend for adoption proposed Alaska Bar Rules and adopt bylaws and regulations.

Section 3. Any member of either the Alaska Bar or the Board of Governors may petition the Board of Governors or the annual convention of the Alaska Bar for consideration of the adoption, amendment or repeal of an Alaska Bar Rule, bylaw or regulation. The petition shall clearly and concisely state:

(a) The substance or nature of the rule, amendment or repeal requested; and

(b) The reasons for the request.

Section 4. (a) Petitions referred to in Section 3 hereof shall be in writing and shall be directed to the Executive Director of the Bar or to any member of the Board of Governors.

(b) If such a petition is to be introduced by resolution at the annual convention of the Alaska Bar, it must be received at least (45) days prior to the commencement of the convention.

(c) Upon receipt of such a petition addressed to it, the Board of Governors shall, at its next regular meeting, deny the petition in writing or schedule the matter for hearing under Section 6, of this Rule.

(d) Petitions addressed to the annual convention of the Alaska Bar may not be denied by the Board of Governors prior to such submission, or, if the petition is approved at the annual convention of the Alaska Bar, after such convention.

Section 5. At least 30 days before either the Board of Governors or the members in attendance at the annual convention recommend for adoption an Alaska Bar Rule or adopt a bylaw or regulation, notice of the proposed action shall be:

(a) Published in the Alaska Bar Brief, or such other publication as may then be regularly published by the Bar Association;

(b) Mailed to every person, not a subscriber to the Alaska Bar Brief, who has filed a request for notice of proposed action with the Bar Association;

(c) When appropriate in the judgement of the Executive Director, or any member of the Board of Governors, mailed to a person or group of persons whom the Executive Director or any member of the Board of Governors believes is interested in the proposed action.

Section 6. The notice of proposed approval of the adoption, amendment, or repeal of an Alaska Bar Rule, by-law or regulation shall include:

(a) A statement of the time, nature and place of the proceeding; and

(b) Either the express terms or informative summary of the proposed action. If in summary form, a copy of the proposal shall be available for inspection at the office of the Executive Director.

Section 7. (a) With respect to petitions addressed to the Board of Governors, on the day and at the time and place designated in the notice referred to in Sections 5 and 6 hereof, the Board of Governors -shall give interested persons or their authorized representatives, or both, the opportunity to present statements, arguments, or contentions in writing or orally as the Board of Governors shall determine.

(b) With respect to petitions addressed to the annual convention of the Alaska Bar, the Board of Governors shall, at the time and place designated in the notice referred to in Sections 5 and 6 hereof, present the petition for consideration by the members in attendance at the convention, and shall give interested persons or their authorized representatives, or both, the opportunity to present statements, arguments, or contentions in writing or orally, as the Board of Governors shall determine.

(c) With respect to hearings on petitions addressed to the

Board of Governors, the Board of Governors may administer oaths or affirmations, and may continue or postpone the hearing to such time and place as it may deem appropriate. Hearings on petitions addressed to the annual convention of the Alaska Bar shall not be subject to continuance or postponement under this provision.

(d) After approval of any recommendation with respect to any Alaska Bar Rule, the proposal shall be submitted to the Supreme Court of the State of Alaska for its consideration.

(e) When the proposed rule has been forwarded to the Court, it shall either approve the proposal or shall set a date on which a meeting shall be held with the Board of Governors to discuss the proposal. Any such meeting may be waived by the mutual consent of the Court and the Board.

Section 8. In the event that the Board makes a finding that an emergency exists and that the notice provisions of this Rule would work an injustice, such notice as the Board deems practicable shall be given prior to action upon a proposed Rule, bylaw or regulations.

(Added by SCO 297 effective April 1, 1978; amended by SCO 1153 effective July 15, 1994)

Rule 63. Unauthorized Practice of Law—AS 08.08.230.

For purposes of AS 08.08.230 (making unauthorized practice of law a misdemeanor). "practice of law" is defined as:

(a) representing oneself by words or conduct to be an attorney, and, if the person is authorized to practice law in another jurisdiction but is not a member of the Alaska Bar Association, representing oneself to be a member of the Alaska Bar Association; and

(b) either (i) representing another before a court or governmental body which is operating in its adjudicative capacity, including the submission of pleadings, or (ii), for compensation, providing advice or preparing documents for another which affect legal rights or duties.

(SCO 924 effective January 15, 1989)

Rule 64. Mandatory Affidavit of Review of Alaska Rules of Professional Conduct; Suspension for Noncompliance.

(a) Every active member of the Alaska Bar Association as of July 15, 1995 shall execute, on a form printed by the Bar Association, an affidavit of review stating that the member has read and is familiar with the Alaska Rules of Professional Conduct. The affidavit of review shall be filed with the Bar Association on or before July 15, 1996.

(b) Persons who become active members of the Alaska Bar Association after July 15, 1995 shall execute, on a form printed by the Bar Association, an affidavit of review stating that the member has read and is familiar with the Alaska Rules of Professional Conduct. The affidavit of review shall be filed with the Bar Association on or before the date on which they become active members.

(c) Any member who without good cause fails to comply with the requirements of this rule shall be notified in writing by certified or registered mail that the Executive Director shall, after 30 days, petition the Supreme Court of Alaska for an order suspending the member for noncompliance. Upon suspension of the member for noncompliance, the member shall not be reinstated until the member has complied with this rule and the Executive Director has certified to the Supreme Court that the member is in compliance.

(SCO 1173 effective July 15, 1995)

Rule 65. Continuing Legal Education.

(a) In order to promote competence and professionalism in members of the Association, the Alaska Supreme Court and the Association encourage all members to engage in Continuing Legal Education (CLE). This rule is intended to set minimum standards for Continuing Legal Education.

(b) Every active member of the Alaska Bar Association should complete at least 12 credit hours of approved CLE, including 1 credit hour of ethics CLE, each year. An active Bar member may carry forward from the previous reporting period a maximum of 12 credits. To be carried forward, the credit hours must have been earned during the calendar year immediately preceding the current reporting period.

Commentary.*—The Alaska Supreme Court and the Association are convinced that CLE contributes to lawyer competence and benefits the public and the profession by assuring that attorneys remain current regarding the law, the obligations and standards of the profession, and the management of their practices. But the Supreme Court is not convinced that a mandatory rule is necessary and believes that a CLE program can become successful by using incentives to encourage voluntary participation in CLE rather than sanctions to penalize non-compliance with a mandatory rule. Accordingly the Supreme Court and the Association have adopted this rule as a three-year pilot project. At the end of this pilot project, the Supreme Court will assess the project's results, including recommendations and statistics provided by the Association, and will determine whether a sanction-based mandatory CLE program is necessary.*

(c) At the end of each year, each member will certify on a form, prescribed by the CLE Director and distributed with the invoice for bar dues, the member's approved CLE hours earned during the preceding year. The CLE Director will supervise the CLE program and perform the duties and responsibilities contained in these rules.

(d) Members who comply with this rule by completing the minimum recommended hours of approved CLE provided in section (b) of this rule will receive a reduction in their bar dues, in an amount to be determined each year by the Board. Only members who complete the minimum recommended hours of approved CLE are eligible to participate in the Alaska Bar Association's Lawyer Referral Service. If a member does not comply with this rule by completing the minimum recommended hours of approved CLE, that fact may be taken into account in any Bar disciplinary matter relating to the requirements of Alaska Rule of Professional Conduct 1.1. The Association shall publish annually, and make available to members of the public, a list of attorneys who have complied with this rule's minimum recommended hours of approved CLE. The Association may devise other incentives to encourage compliance with this rule.

Commentary.—*This rule contemplates a modest reduction in bar dues, to be determined annually at the Board's discretion, that will serve as an incentive for members who have voluntarily complied with the CLE standard; the reduction is not intended as reimbursement for CLE costs actually incurred by members.*

(e) A member may file a written request for an extension of time for compliance with this rule. A request for extension shall be reviewed and determined by the CLE Director. A member who is granted an extension and completes the minimum CLE requirements after the end of the reporting period is not entitled to the discount on bar dues.

(f) The CLE requirement of this rule may be met either by attending approved courses or completing any other continuing legal education activity approved for credit under these rules. The following activities may be considered for credit when they meet the conditions set forth in this rule:

(1) preparing for and teaching approved CLE courses; credit will be granted for up to two hours of preparation time for every one hour of time spent teaching;

(2) studying audio or video tapes or technology-delivered approved CLE courses;

(3) writing published legal texts or articles in law reviews or specialized professional journals;

(4) attendance at substantive Section or Inn of Court meetings;

(5) participation as a faculty member in Youth Court;

(6) attendance at approved in-house continuing legal education courses;

(7) attendance at approved continuing judicial education courses;

(8) attendance at approved continuing legal education courses.

(g) The CLE director shall approve or disapprove all education activities for credit. CLE activities sponsored by the Association are deemed approved. Forms for approval may be submitted electronically.

(1) An entity or association must apply to the Board for accreditation as a CLE provider. Accreditation shall constitute prior approval of CLE courses offered by the provider, subject to amendment, suspension, or revocation of such accreditation by the Board.

(2) The Board shall establish by regulation the procedures, minimum standards, and any fees for accreditation of providers, in-house continuing legal education courses, and publication of legal texts or journal articles, and for revocation of accreditation when necessary.

(h) This rule will be effective September 2, 1999. The reporting period will be the calendar year, from January 1st to December 31st, and the first calendar year to be reported will be the year 2000. Any CLE credits earned from September 2, 1999 to December 31, 1999 may be held over and applied to the reporting period for the year 2000.

(Added by SCO 1366 effective September 2, 1999)

BR

BYLAWS OF THE ALASKA BAR ASSOCIATION

Table of Contents

ARTICLE IV. BOARD OF GOVERNORS

ARTICLE V. BOARD ELECTIONS

ARTICLE VI. OFFICERS; STAFF

ARTICLE VII. COMMITTEES AND SECTIONS

ARTICLE VIII. ASSOCIATION MEETINGS

ARTICLE IX. ELECTION OF ALASKA'S DELEGATE TO THE AMERICAN BAR ASSOCIATION'S HOUSE OF DELEGATES

ARTICLE X. LOBBYING AND PUBLICITY

ARTICLE XI. THE OFFICIAL PUBLICATION

ARTICLE XII. AMENDMENTS

ARTICLE XIII. DEFINITIONS

ARTICLE I. NAME AND ORGANIZATION

Section 1. Name.

The name of this organization is the Alaska Bar Association.

Section 2. Powers.

The powers, duties, responsibilities, and organization of the Alaska Bar Association are established by the Alaska Integrated Bar Act and by the Alaska Bar Rules, which together shall be considered the charter of the Alaska Bar Association.

Section 3. Purposes.

The purposes of the Alaska Bar are to:

(1) cultivate and advance the science of jurisprudence;

(2) promote reform in the law and in judicial procedure;

(3) facilitate the administration of justice;

(4) encourage continuing legal education for the membership; and

(5) increase the public service and efficiency of the Bar.

Section 4. Office.

The office of the Alaska Bar Association is in the Municipality of Anchorage, Alaska.

Section 5. Service and Filing.

All petitions, notices or other writings required to be filed with the Alaska Bar Association or served upon the Board of Governors shall be filed in the Association's office.

Section 6. Administrative Districts.

For the purpose of the administration of the Act, these Bylaws, the Rules, and the Policies and Regulations promulgated under them, four administrative districts, based in part upon the judicial districts existing in 1973, are created as follows:

(1) The First Judicial District of Alaska;

(2) The Second and Fourth Judicial Districts of Alaska combined;

(3) The Third Judicial District of Alaska; and

(4) Any jurisdiction or geographical area outside the State.

ARTICLE II. MEMBERSHIP

Section 1. Classification and Roster of Members.

(a) **Classes of Membership.** There are four classes of membership in the Alaska Bar Association:

(1) *Active Members.* Any person now or hereafter admitted to the practice of law in Alaska and membership in the Alaska Bar Association is an active member and shall maintain active membership status unless the member:

(A) transfers, or is transferred, to inactive or retired status;

(B) resigns from Association membership;

(C) is placed on interim disability or disability inactive status; or

(D) is suspended or disbarred.

(2) *Inactive Members.* Inactive membership in the Alaska Bar is limited to members who no longer engage in the practice of law or hold judicial office or any other legal position in the State of Alaska.

(3) *Retired Members.* Retired membership in the Alaska Bar is limited to former active or inactive members of the Alaska Bar who are 65 years of age or older and who no longer engage in the practice of law or hold judicial office or any other legal position in the State of Alaska or any other jurisdiction.

(4) *Honorary Members.* Deserving Alaskan citizens, any district court judge not already a member of the Bar, and distinguished visitors who have contributed to the purposes of the Alaska Bar Association may be accorded honorary membership in the Association upon a vote of the members of the Board or a majority of the members in attendance at an annual business meeting of the Bar.

(b) **Roster of Members.** The Association shall keep a roster for the enrollment of all members of the Alaska Bar. The roster shall contain such information as the Board may determine to be proper and desirable.

Section 2. Transfer from Active Membership to Inactive or Retired Status.

(a) **Methods of Transfer.** Only the following methods are effective to transfer from active status to inactive or retired membership:

(1) Written request by the member to, and permission to transfer granted by, the Executive Director, pursuant to transfer request procedures set forth in the Board's Standing Policies;

(2) Transfer by the Board of Governors, after notice and an opportunity to be heard has been afforded the member; or

(3) Transfer to interim disability or disability inactive status by the Supreme Court of Alaska, pursuant to Bar Rule 30.

(b) **Member Transfer Requests.** Requests from members to transfer from active to inactive or retired status may be granted if submitted to the Executive Director no later than January 1 of the applicable year.

Section 3. Privileges of Inactive, Retired, or Honorary Members.

An inactive, retired, or honorary member may participate in Bar and Board meetings, may be appointed to any standing or special committee, and may join any Bar section, but he or she may not hold office or vote.

Section 4. Transfer from Inactive or Retired Membership to Active Status.

(a) **Transfer If Inactive or Retired for One Year or More.** Upon written request to the Board, a member who has been inactive or retired for one year or more may be transferred to active status if

(1) the Board finds the requesting member possesses character and fitness to practice law as provided in Alaska Bar Rule 2, Section 2(d), pursuant to procedures set forth in the Board's Standing Policies; and

(2) full, annual active membership fees are paid for the current year, less any inactive fees previously remitted for that year.

(b) **Transfer If Inactive or Retired for Less Than One Year.** Upon written request to the Executive Director, a member who has been inactive or retired for less than one year may be granted transfer to active status by the Executive Director, pursuant to Board policy, if full annual active membership fees are paid for the current year, less any inactive fees previously remitted for that year.

(c) **Board Eligibility Determination.** The Board, after notice and an opportunity to be heard has been afforded the member, may transfer a member from inactive or retired status to active membership status if the Board determines that the member is no longer eligible for inactive or retired status. Upon transfer by the Board, the member shall pay full annual active membership fees for the current year, less any inactive fees previously remitted for that year.

Section 5. Member in Good Standing.

Any active or inactive member of the Alaska Bar Association who has paid the requisite membership fees for the current calendar year and who has not been transferred to interim disability or disability inactive status, or been suspended or disbarred, is a member in good standing and entitled to all of the privileges and benefits accorded Bar members.

Section 6. Membership Card.

(a) **Certification of Good Standing.** Each member of the Alaska Bar Association who is currently a member in good standing of the Alaska Bar annually shall be issued an official membership card which shall contain the member's name, current membership status, the seven-digit membership number assigned to the member upon admission to the Bar, and other information the Board determines appropriate for inclusion on the card.

(b) **Revocation of Certification.** A member's card shall be surrendered to the Bar when a member:

(1) has been suspended for the nonpayment of his or her membership fees;

(2) pursuant to Bar Rule 28(j), has been suspended or disbarred;

(3) pursuant to Bar Rule 30, has been transferred to inactive status;

(4) after notice and an opportunity to be heard has been afforded the member, the Board determines that the member should be required to surrender his or her membership card.

Section 7. Resignation.

(a) **Affidavit of Resignation.** A member may resign from membership in the Association. A resignation is subject to acceptance by the Board, must be in affidavit form, and, as of the date of the affidavit, affirmatively must state:

(1) the member does not now, and will not in the future, engage in the practice of law in Alaska;

(2) the member has no cases pending before the courts of this State;

(3) the member's clients have been given proper notice of his or her intent to resign and that they have had sufficient opportunity to find substitute counsel without prejudice to their cases;

(4) the member has no discipline, fee arbitration, or client security fund matters pending;

(5) the member is current on all membership fee payments, applicable insurance premiums, and other financial commitments to the Bar; and

(6) the member understands that his or her resignation is permanent and irrevocable and, should he or she at any time in the future desire to return to the practice of law in Alaska, that he or she would have to make application as a new admittee, subject to the provisions of Part 1 of the Alaska Bar Rules, including, if applicable, the requirement that he or she take and pass the Alaska Bar Examination.

(b) **Jurisdiction Retained.** The Association shall retain jurisdiction to investigate and take action with respect to matters involving the conduct of a member during the time he or she was a member of the Alaska Bar.

(c) **Board Action.** Upon receipt of an affidavit of resignation, and if no information is received which bears unfavorably upon the member, the Board shall formally accept the resignation at its next regularly scheduled meeting. Resignation received 20 days prior to a Board meeting will be placed on the agenda of the next subsequent regularly scheduled meeting.

(d) **Notice to the Courts.** Upon formal acceptance of a member's resignation, the Board shall notify the Alaska Supreme Court and the clerks of court that the member has resigned from the Association and state the effective date.

ARTICLE III. MEMBERSHIP FEES AND PENALTIES

Section 1. Annual Dues.

(a) **Active Members.** The annual membership fee for an active member is the amount approved by the Board, $10.00 of which is allocated to the Lawyers' Fund for Client Protection. The annual membership fee for an active member, who is 70 years of age or more and who has practiced law in Alaska for a total of 25 years or more, is one half of the total amount assessed to each active member, $10.00 of which is allocated to the Lawyers' Fund for Client Protection.

Active members who provide 400 hours or more of pro bono services in a calendar year (January through December) as confirmed by the Alaska Pro Bono Program, or as approved by the Alaska Bar Association Pro Bono Service Committee, may pay 30% of the annual active fee for the membership year immediately following the year these services were provided subject to the following limitations: 1) the request for 30% active dues must be made in writing no later than February 1st; and 2) confirmation by the Alaska Pro Bono Program, or approval by the Alaska Bar Association Pro Bono Service Committee, must be provided to the Bar Association no later than February 1st.

(b) **Inactive Members.** The annual membership fee for an inactive member is one third of the total amount assessed to each active member.

(c) **Retired and Honorary Members.** There is no membership fee for a retired or honorary member.

(d) **Notice.** Failure to receive notice of the annual membership fees does not relieve any active or inactive member of the duty to timely comply with the requirements of this Article.

(e) **Waiver.** The Board of Governors may waive the payment of a member's annual membership fee upon a sufficient showing of hardship, as defined in paragraph (f).

(f) **Hardship.** For the purposes of this section, "hardship" means an economic inability to pay dues as the result of a medical condition, mental condition, or an involuntary change in economic status.

(g) **Proof of Hardship.** Unless waived by the Board, a member requesting a waiver of dues must submit the following information to the Board:

(1) an affidavit by the member detailing the nature of the hardship and the reasons the member is unable to pay membership dues,

(2) a copy of the member's last two federal tax returns with supporting schedules, and

(3) a detailed listing, including estimated values, of all real property and personal property of the member and a detailed listing of all outstanding debts.

Section 2. Payment of Fees; Due Dates.

Annual membership fees are due and payable on or before February 1 of each year; however, an active member, who does not qualify for reduced dues under section 1(a), may pay his or her annual membership fees in two installments. The first installment is due and payable on or before February 1 and the second installment is due and payable on or before July 1. A $25.00 charge shall be assessed against the active member for the installment service and shall be included in the amount of the first payment.

Section 3. Delinquent and Suspended Members.

(a) **Delinquent Payment Penalties.** Any member failing to pay his or her membership fees when due shall, during the period of time in which the fees remain unpaid, be subject to a penalty of $10.00 per week of delinquency. For purposes of determining the appropriate penalty assessment, each fraction of a week shall be considered a whole week. In no instance may the penalty assessed for delinquent payment exceed $160.00.

(b) **Suspension for Nonpayment.** Thirty days after the due date of the membership fees, the delinquent member shall be notified in writing, by certified or registered mail, that the Executive Director will, in 30 additional days, petition the Alaska Supreme Court for an order suspending the delinquent member from membership in the Alaska Bar for nonpayment of the appropriate membership fees and any late payment penalties due and owing. The notice is sufficient if mailed to the address last furnished to the Association by the delinquent member. Following notice by the Bar to the delinquent member of his or her suspension by the Supreme Court, the Executive Director shall immediately notify the clerks of court of the member's name and the date of his or her suspension for nonpayment of the appropriate membership fees and penalties. Members suspended for nonpayment may not engage in the practice of law while suspended, nor are they entitled to any of the privileges and benefits otherwise accorded to active or inactive members of the Alaska Bar in good standing. Suspended members who engage in the practice of law are subject to appropriate discipline under Part II of the Bar Rules.

(c) **Reinstatement.** Any suspended member whose suspension for nonpayment has been in effect for less than one year, upon payment of all accrued fees and late payment penalties, shall be reinstated as a member of the Alaska Bar upon certification by the Executive Director to the Alaska Supreme Court and the clerks of court that the fees and penalties have been paid. Any member who has been suspended for one year or more, upon a determination of character and fitness to practice law as provided in Alaska Bar Rule 2, Section 2(d) by the Board, in accordance with Board Policy, and upon payment of all accrued membership fees, in addition to a penalty of $160.00, shall be reinstated as a member of the Alaska Bar upon certification by the Executive Director to the Alaska Supreme Court and the clerks of court that the member has the character and fitness to practice law as provided in Alaska Bar Rule 2, Section 2(d) and that the requisite dues and penalties have been paid.

Section 4. Required Fee for Other Attorneys.

The required fee for other attorneys under Civil Rule 81(a)(2) is the amount required for active members under Section 1 of this Article of the Bylaws per case per year until the attorney notifies the Alaska Bar Association that the case in which the attorney is participating is closed or the attorney has withdrawn from the case.

Section 5. Dues Expenditure Policy, Objection(s) to Expenditure(s).

(a) **Board Policy Concerning Expenditure of Dues.** It is the general policy of the Board to restrict the disbursement of dues to expenditures necessarily or reasonably incurred for the purpose of regulating the legal profession in Alaska or improving the quality of legal services available to the people of Alaska. These expenditures are considered "chargeable" within the meaning of **Keller v. State Bar of California**, 496 U.S. 1, 110 L.Ed.2d 1, 110 S.Ct. 2228 (1990). To the extent that any member objects to the disbursement of dues for reason that the member believes the expenditure to be "nonchargeable", the member must file an objection as provided in subparagraphs (d) and (e).

However, the Board, upon a vote of three quarters of the members of the full Board, may approve the disbursement of dues for expenditures which are considered "nonchargeable" within the meaning of **Keller v. State Bar of California.** If the Board disburses funds for "nonchargeable" expenditures, notice of the expenditure(s) shall be given in the official publication of the Bar and a member may request, in writing to the Executive Director, an appropriate dues refund within sixty (60) days of such notice. The dues refund, which shall be determined by the Board, shall be limited to that pro-rata amount of a member's dues reasonably related to any costs actually incurred with regard to the "nonchargeable" activity. To the extent that any member objects to the determination of the amount of the expenditure, the member must proceed under subparagraph (e).

(b) **Publication of Annual Budget.** Following approval by the Board, the annual budget of the Bar shall be published in the official publication of the Bar, and shall otherwise be distributed to ensure notice to all dues-paying members. In addition, copies of the approved annual budget shall be available to members upon request.

(c) **Information in Dues Notices.** Dues notices sent to members shall reference: (1) the publication of the annual budget of the Bar in the official publication of the Bar and advise members that they may obtain a copy of the budget upon request, and (2) that members may review the approved minutes of the Board at the Bar office and obtain a copy of the approved minutes upon request.

(d) **Time for Filing Objection(s).** A member's objection to the expenditure of dues by the Board must be received by the Executive Director or postmarked within sixty (60) days of the publication of the Board action in the official publication of the Bar.

(e) **Arbitration of Objection(s) to Expenditure(s).** Upon receipt of a timely objection to an expenditure, the President of the Board shall appoint a hearing master to consider the objection, utilizing the procedures provided in Bar Rule 7. All objections to expenditure(s) shall be consolidated in a single proceeding, where possible. The Bar shall have the burden of proving by a preponderance of the evidence that the expenditure(s) objected to are "chargeable."

In addition, the President shall direct the Executive Director to determine the amount of the expenditure(s) reasonably in dispute involving the objecting member(s) and shall order that amount to be held in an interest-bearing escrow account pending final determination by the Board, or if appealed, by the Alaska Supreme Court.

If the hearing master determines that an objection to an expenditure has been frivolously made, the hearing master may assess costs associated with the proceeding against the member(s) filing the frivolous objection(s).

ARTICLE IV. BOARD OF GOVERNORS

Section 1. Duties and Responsibilities.

The Board of Governors is the governing body of the Alaska Bar Association and is vested with power and authority including, but not limited to, adopting regulations and policies concerning the activities, affairs, and organization of the Alaska Bar, and collecting and disbursing all monies of the organization, subject only to any limitation imposed by the Act and the Bar Rules.

Section 2. Membership.

The Board of Governors of the Alaska Bar Association consists of 12 governors. Nine governors shall be active members of the Bar elected by the active membership or the Association in accordance with provisions of the Act and these Bylaws. Three governors shall be non-attorneys appointed by the Governor of the State, subject to legislative confirmation in accordance with provisions of the Act.

Section 3. Term of Office and Succession.

Elected members of the Board shall take office at the close of the annual business meeting of the Association held immediately following their election. The term of office is three years. The terms of appointed members shall be as provided by the Act. Governors may succeed themselves in office.

Section 4. Oath of Office.

Prior to assuming the duties and responsibilities of a Board member, the newly elected or appointed governor must complete an Oath of Office. Each governor's Oath of Office, or a copy of it, shall be maintained in a file in the Association's office during that governor's term.

Section 5. Removal.

Upon a petition signed by 25 percent of the members of any District for the recall of any governor elected from that District, or in the case of the governor-at-large, a petition signed by 25 percent of the members of the Association, the Executive Director shall immediately serve notice on the governor of the filing of the petition, and if he or she does not resign within 10 days from the date of service, the Executive Director shall mail ballots to each member of the Alaska Bar entitled to vote, submitting the question of whether the elected governor shall be recalled. Any recall vote shall be conducted in accordance with Article VI of these Bylaws.

Section 6. Resignation.

A governor may resign from his or her position. The resignation shall be in writing to the President or, if an appointed member of the Board, to the governor of the State and the Bar President.

Section 7. Vacancy.

As provided in AS 08.08.070, a vacancy on the Board of Governors from among the elected members shall be filled by appointment by a majority vote of the Board, and a vacancy from among the appointed members shall be filled by the governor of the State.

Section 8. Board Meetings.

(a) **Regular Meetings.** The regular meetings of the Board shall be held within the State at the times and places designated by the President. Upon assumption of office, the President shall promptly schedule at least four regular meetings during the year of his or her term. These meeting dates may be changed as circumstances require. The schedule of the Board's regular meetings shall be published electronically on the State of Alaska's Online Public Notice System and on the Alaska Bar's website at least 30 days prior to each regularly scheduled meeting. Timely notice and the tentative agenda of each Board meeting shall be sent electronically to the officers of the Alaska Bar Association, to the members of the Board of Governors, and to the presidents of all local bar associations.

(b) **Emergency Meetings.** The President, may, or upon the written request of three governors filed with the Secretary shall, call emergency meetings of the Board of Governors. If the President, for any reason, fails or refuses to call an emergency meeting for a period of five days after receipt of the request for the emergency meeting, the Secretary, or some other person designated by the three governors joining in the request, may call the emergency meeting. The date fixed for that meeting shall not be less than five days nor more than ten days from the date of the call. Notice of an emergency meeting shall be signed by the Secretary or by the person designated by the three governors in their call. The notice shall set forth the day and hour of the emergency meeting, the place within the State where the meeting shall be held, and the purpose for holding it. Emergency meetings may consider only those matters that are specifically set forth in the call of the meeting. Electronic notice of the emergency meeting call shall be given to each governor, unless waived by him or her, at least three days before the date fixed for the emergency meeting. Public notice of the emergency meeting shall be published electronically on the State of Alaska's Online Public Notice System and on the Alaska Bar's website at least three days prior to the date of the emergency meeting.

(c) **Minutes and Public Attendance.** All meetings of the Board shall be open to the public, except that the Board shall meet in executive session when considering the following matters: personnel matters of the Association; litigation or other proceedings in which the Association is interested or a party; the admission of applicants to membership in the Association; Board deliberations on disciplinary and disability matters of the Association; and those other matters that are considered confidential under Part III of the Rules. After approval by the Board, minutes of all public meetings shall be available to members of the Association and to the public.

Section 9. Quorum.

Seven members of the Board constitutes a quorum at any meeting.

Section 10. Action of Board Without Assembling.

The President, or Secretary by direction of the President, may submit any matter to the Board for action, decision, approval, or authorization, either by mail, telegraph, or simultaneous communication by telephone. The vote on any propositions so submitted may be either by mail, telegraph, or telephone, and the results shall be filed with the minutes of the Board meetings. Any proposition receiving a majority of affirmative votes in such matters shall be considered adopted by the Board the same as if the action were taken at a meeting of the Board.

Section 11. Finances.

(a) **Disbursement Authority.** Any member of the Board so designated, or the Executive Director, shall sign checks for disbursements by the Alaska Bar from its funds. The Executive Director's authority to sign checks is limited by the Board's Standing Policies.

(b) **Line-Item Budget.** The Board annually shall adopt a line-item budget. The budget shall be published and made available to all members of the Association no later than 30 days before the beginning of the new fiscal year. The Association's fiscal year is the calendar year.

(c) **Regular Financial Statements.** The Executive Director shall submit a financial statement at each regular meeting of the Board.

Section 12. Audits.

The books and accounts of the Association shall be

maintained and audited in accordance with generally accepted standards of accounting. An audit by an independent audit firm shall take place at the close of each fiscal year, and the report shall be made available to the membership no fewer than ten days prior to each annual business meeting.

Section 13. Referendum to Membership.

Whenever the Board of Governors is required to take a referendum, or whenever the Board orders a question referred to a vote of the active membership of the Alaska Bar in good standing, a questionnaire shall be prepared containing the matters upon which the vote is to be taken. The questionnaire shall be submitted to each active member in a form that allows the member to vote on it and return it to the Board. Whenever any referendum is taken, the question so referred shall not again be referred before the next annual business meeting of the Alaska Bar. Any question submitted to the members shall be prepared in accordance with the forms and procedures set forth in the Board's Standing Policies.

Section 14. Proxy Votes.

A Board member may not vote by proxy.

ARTICLE V. BOARD ELECTIONS

Section 1. Nominations.

A nominating petition shall be mailed to each active Bar member entitled to hold office at least 75 days prior to the date of the election. Nominations for the election of the governors from each District and for the Board's at-large position shall be by petition signed by at least three members entitled to vote for the nominee.

Section 2. Voting Rights.

Each active in-state Bar member in good standing may vote in and be a candidate from the District in which he or she resides at the time of election, or he or she may be a candidate for the at-large position. Active Bar members in good standing who reside out-of-state may only vote in and be a candidate for the Board's at-large position.

Section 3. Election Roster.

The Executive Director shall create a special election roster which shall contain an alphabetical listing of the active members of the Bar in good standing eligible to vote in each election.

Section 4. Ballots and Balloting.

(a) **Ballots.** Elections shall be conducted by secret ballot. Official election ballots shall be prepared in a form and manner approved by the Board. The ballots shall contain space for the voting member's printed name, written signature, and District. However, to ensure the preservation of the secret ballot, the ballot shall be so arranged that the member-voter identification information will be removed prior to tabulation of the ballot.

(b) **Replacement Ballots.** If a member entitled to vote in an election does not receive a ballot, or if the ballot received is lost or destroyed, a second official ballot may be supplied to that member, or the member may submit a facsimile of the official ballot, provided that the member has not previously voted in the election.

(c) **Balloting.** Ballots shall be mailed to each active member eligible to vote at least 21 days prior to the date of the election. To be counted, voted ballots must be received in the office of the Bar Association on or before 5:00 p.m. on the day of the election. The Executive Director shall have the custody of all ballots after they have been received and until the ballots are counted.

(d) **Invalid or Questioned Ballots.** Should any ballot be returned without both the printed name and written signature of the voting member on the spaces provided on the ballot, the ballot shall not be counted. Should it be determined in the cross-check against the election roster that a second ballot has been received from an eligible voter, that second and any subsequent ballots received from that member shall not be counted. Invalid ballots shall be kept by the Executive Director until after certification of the election. A ballot received which causes the Executive Director to question its validity shall be held by the Executive Director for a determination as to its validity by the members of the Bar Polls and Elections Committee responsible for counting the vote in the election.

Section 5. Ballot Counting.

The Executive Director and at least two members of the Association's Bar Polls and Elections Committee shall review the count of votes cast and record and certify, in writing, the results of the election to the membership.

Section 6. Election Results.

When one vacancy occurs in a District election or for the at-large position, the gubernatorial candidate in that District or for the at-large position who receives the highest number of the votes cast shall be declared elected. If only one candidate has been nominated for a vacancy on the Board, that candidate shall be declared elected. When more than one vacancy on the Board occurs in the Third District in an election, the candidates shall run on one slate and each active member entitled to vote shall cast a vote for no more than two of the candidates on the ballot. The two candidates receiving the highest number of votes in the election shall be elected.

Section 7. Changing Election Districts During An Election.

If a member changes residence between the time the election ballots are mailed and the date of the election, upon providing notice, proof of change of residence, and the invalid ballot previously mailed to the member, if any, on or before the date of the election, the member shall be entitled to vote for the candidate(s) from his or her new District of residence.

Section 8. Ballot Election Roster Retention; Official Record.

Upon completion of the ballot count, the Executive Director shall retain all ballots, the official tally sheets, and the special election roster until the close of the first annual business meeting held following the election, at which time the ballots and roster may be destroyed. The official tally sheets, containing certification of the vote count by the Bar Polls and Election Committee, shall be retained for a period of two years, after which they may be destroyed in accordance with Board policy.

ARTICLE VI. OFFICERS; STAFF

Section 1. Officers.

The officers of the Association are a President, President-Elect, Vice President, Secretary and Treasurer. The President-Elect, Vice President, Secretary, and Treasurer shall be elected from among the members of the Board by a majority vote of the active members of the Alaska Bar in attendance at the Association's annual business meeting. Nothing in this article prohibits an appointed non-attorney governor from being elected an officer of the Association. Newly elected officers of the Association shall take office at the close of the annual business meeting at which they have been elected and shall serve a one-year term.

Section 2. President.

The President shall conduct and preside at all meetings of the Alaska Bar and the Board of Governors. He or she shall be the official spokesperson for the Board and for the Association. The President shall furnish leadership in the accomplishment of the aims and purposes of the Alaska Bar. The President has those other duties which the Board of Governors directs.

Section 3. President-Elect.

The President-Elect shall assist the President. If the President resigns or is unable to act, the President-Elect shall fulfill the duties of President. The President-Elect shall succeed to the Presidency when the term for which the President was elected expires, or when there is a vacancy in the office of President, whichever first occurs. The President-Elect shall be the Board liaison to all local bar associations. At least thirty days before each annual Association business meeting, the President-Elect shall furnish the Executive Director with a list of the members of each Bar Rule and Standing Committee of the Association whose terms begin on the next first day of July. The President-Elect has those other duties which the Board of Governors directs.

Section 4. Vice President.

The Vice President shall fulfill the duties of the President in the absence of the President and President-Elect. The Vice President shall be responsible for the operation of all executive committees of the substantive law sections. The Vice President has those other duties which the Board of Governors directs.

Section 5. Secretary.

The Secretary, or his or her designee, shall record the proceedings of all Board and Bar meetings. The Secretary shall be responsible for the operation of all Association standing committees. The Secretary has those other duties which the Board of Governors directs.

Section 6. Treasurer.

The Treasurer shall be responsible for the financial records of the Association. The Treasurer, or his or her designee, shall prepare a report on the status of the financial affairs of the Association at each meeting of the Board of Governors and shall give a written report on the Bar's financial position to the membership at the annual business meeting. The treasurer has those other duties which the Board of Governors directs.

Section 7. Executive Director; Staff.

The Board may employ an Executive Director to serve at its pleasure and assist it in carrying out its functions. The Executive Director is the staff director of the Association. He or she shall have the qualifications, duties and responsibilities, prescribed by the Board. With the approval of the Board, the Executive Director may employ other staff required for the efficient functioning of the Association.

ARTICLE VII. COMMITTEES AND SECTIONS

Section 1. Committees.

(a) **Standing Committees.** The Board shall define the powers, duties, functions, and scope of each standing committee in its Standing Policies. The President, subject to Board approval, shall appoint eligible Bar members to fill all vacancies or expired terms on standing committees and shall name and designate the chair of each committee. Committee members shall serve staggered, three year terms. Committee members may be reappointed for successive terms. The Board may appoint additional members to a committee, remove members from a committee for good cause, or dissolve a committee when it considers the work of a committee has been completed or when it considers that a committee is no longer necessary. Each committee may select such other officers as it considers advisable and may designate subcommittees from among its membership. Each committee shall meet at such times and places as may be designated by its chair. The Association's standing committees are:

(1) the Bar Polls and Elections Committee, a nine member committee responsible for polling the membership on subjects submitted to the Association membership by the Board and for the tabulation of the results of all elections and advisory opinion polls conducted by the Association:

(2) the Continuing Legal Education Committee, a 15 member committee responsible for presenting legal education seminars to the membership, and includes one Judicial representation and two Young Lawyer representations serving staggered 2-year terms;

(3) the Ethics Committee, a nine member committee responsible for the issuance of opinions providing guidance to Association members in complying with the Code of Professional Responsibility;

(4) the Historians Committee, a 12 member committee responsible for preserving the unique history of the Alaska Bar;

(5) The Law Related Education Committee, a committee responsible for presenting programs and producing publications to aid the public in understanding of the law and the legal system; the committee is divided into subcommittees in the communities of Anchorage, (12 members), Fairbanks, Juneau, Kenai, Mat-Su and such other communities as the president sees fit to appoint;

(6) the Legal Educational Opportunities Committee, a 10 member committee responsible for the oversight of State funds for legal education, tutoring assistance to failing bar examinees, and oversight of the impact of Bar admission standards on minority applicants;

(7) the Statutes, Bylaws and Rules Committee, a 12 member committee responsible for drafting proposed revisions of the statutes, bylaws and rules which govern the activities of the Alaska Bar Association;

(8) the Pro Bono Service Committee, a 9 member committee responsible for identifying and promoting activities which would facilitate the provision of pro bono services and encourage all attorneys to provide pro bono service; at least three of the members shall be from communities from outside of Anchorage, Juneau and Fairbanks;

(9) the Alaska Rules of Professional Conduct Committee, a 9 member committee responsible for reviewing suggested amendments to the ARPC and making recommendations for amendments to the Board of Governors; and

(10) the Lawyers' Assistance Committee whose members provide services to members of the bar, their families or business associates when it appears a Bar member is suffering from substance abuse.

(11) the Judicial Independence Committee, a Committee responsible for recommendations to the Board for activities that the Bar can undertake to explain and promote the concept of judicial independence, and to undertake to educate the public about and promote the concept of judicial independence.

(b) **Special Committees.** The President may appoint special committees with limited purposes and of limited duration. The terms of membership on such committees shall be established by the President at the time the committees are appointed.

(c) **Committee Actions Endorsed.** No action, report, or recommendation of any standing or special committee is binding upon the Association unless first approved by the Board.

Section 2. Reports of Committees.

All standing and special committees shall render to the Board those reports as from time to time that are requested by the President or the Board. Written annual reports shall be delivered to the Board at least 30 days before the annual business meeting, and a written or oral report shall be presented to the membership at the annual business meeting.

Section 3. Substantive Law Sections.

The Board shall establish substantive law sections in areas pertinent to the practice of law and shall define the powers, duties, functions and scope of each section in its Standing Policies.

(a) **Membership and fees requirements are as follows:**

(1) *Attorney Membership and Fees.* Attorney membership in each section is open to all active and inactive members of the Alaska Bar Association in good standing. $5.00 of a member's annual membership fee will be allocated to the budget of the first section joined by that member. A member may join additional sections at a registration fee to the member of $15.00 per additional section joined per year.

(2) *Informational Membership and Fees.* Non-voting section membership is available at the discretion of each section to any person who is not a member of the Association, but who subscribes to the informational and educational objectives of the section. Informational section members may not serve on the executive committee of any section. There is an annual $15.00 membership fee assessed for each section joined by an Information Member.

(b) **Section Executive Committees.** Each section shall be administered by an executive committee of at least five members elected from the section's membership to serve staggered three year terms. The executive committee shall annually elect, by September 30, a chair, and may elect such other officers as it deems advisable from the membership of the executive committee. Each executive committee shall meet at such times and places as may be designated by the chair of the section. All executive committees shall file with the Board such reports as from time to time shall be requested by the President or the Board. A written annual report shall be delivered to the Board at least thirty (30) days before the annual business meeting.

(c) **Annual Section Meeting.** Each section's executive committee will schedule an annual meeting of the section membership to hear the annual report of its executive committee and discuss issues and developments pertinent to the section's area of law. The annual meeting will be held at a time and location determined by the executive committee.

(d) **Continuing Legal Education Commitment.** At least as frequently as is required by the Bar's Continuing Legal Education Committee, each substantive law section in conjunction with the Bar shall be responsible for sponsoring a continuing legal education seminar.

(e) **Annual Section Chair/Board Meeting.** At each annual convention of the Association, the chairs of each section, or their designees, shall meet with the President-Elect or the Board to discuss section activities and evaluate section needs.

(f) **Section Actions Endorsed.** No action, report, or recommendation of any section is binding upon the Association unless adopted and approved by the Board.

ARTICLE VIII. ASSOCIATION MEETINGS

Section 1. Annual Business Meeting.

The annual business meeting of the Alaska Bar Association shall be held within the State at the time and at the place that is selected by the Board of Governors. Notice of the annual business meeting shall state the time and place scheduled for holding the meeting, and shall be provided to the members of the Alaska Bar Association at least six months before the meeting.

Section 2. Special Meetings.

Special meetings of the Alaska Bar Association shall be called by the Secretary upon a majority vote of the Board of Governors, or upon the receipt of a written application signed by not less than 25 percent of the active members of the Alaska Bar Association. The secretary shall issue the call for the meeting to be held not more than 20 days following the receipt of the written application. Special meetings may consider only those matters that are specifically set forth in the call of the meeting. Notice of a special meeting shall state the time and the place within the State where the meeting will be held and shall be given to the public press at least five days prior to that meeting. Each notice shall state specifically the matters to be considered at the special meeting and shall be issued over the name of the Secretary, or in case of his or her failure or refusal to act, the President of the Alaska Bar Association.

Section 3. Parliamentary Rules.

Proceedings at any meeting of the Alaska Bar Association shall be governed by the most recent edition of "Robert's Rules of Order, Newly Revised".

Section 4. Resolutions.

Resolutions may be introduced for consideration at the annual business meeting if signed by at least 10 active members of the Association, or sponsored by a local bar association or substantive law section. Proposed resolutions shall be received in the office of the Association at least 45 days prior to the date of the annual business meeting and shall, upon receipt, be promptly submitted to each local bar association for its consideration. Resolutions also shall be considered at the annual business meeting if 35 members in attendance at that business meeting sign a petition requesting consideration of the resolution.

Section 5. Votes.

Each active member in good standing and public member of the Board of Governors in attendance at the annual business meeting shall be entitled to cast one vote on each matter presented for consideration. Proxy votes are not permitted.

ARTICLE IX. ELECTION OF ALASKA'S DELEGATE TO THE AMERICAN BAR ASSOCIATION'S HOUSE OF DELEGATES

Section 1. Nomination and Election.

In each even numbered year, the active membership of the Alaska Bar Association shall elect one delegate from its membership to be its delegate to the House of Delegates of the American Bar Association (ABA). Nominations for the Alaska Bar's delegate shall be made in the same manner as provided for the nomination of the candidates for the Board of Governors in Article V of these Bylaws and the election shall be held at the same time and in the same manner as provided for the election of the Board of Governors, except that Alaska's ABA delegate shall be elected from the State-at-large and the term of office shall be two years. No delegate may be elected who is not an active member in good standing of the Alaska Bar Association. The candidate receiving the highest number of votes shall be declared the elected delegate. The elected delegate shall be responsible for all expenses incurred by him or her as the Alaska Bar's delegate to the American Bar Association's House of Delegates.

Section 2. Alternate Delegate.

In case of the refusal or inability of the duly elected delegate to attend the meetings of the American Bar Association's House of Delegates, an alternate delegate shall be appointed by the Board of Governors. The appointed delegate shall take his or her place as the delegate at the meeting or meetings that the elected delegate is unable to attend with all the rights and privileges of the elected delegate.

ARTICLE X. LOBBYING AND PUBLICITY

Section 1. Lobbying.

No member of the Association may lobby or otherwise attempt to influence legislative or administrative action in the name of the Association, except with the consent of the Board of Governors.

Section 2. Publicity.

Public statements or press releases purporting to set forth the Association's position on pending or proposed legislation, on issues of public importance, or on Association matters in general shall be made only by the President or his or her designee.

Section 3. Purpose.

No expenditure relating to political or ideological activities may be made by the Association unless reasonably incurred for the purpose of regulating the legal profession or improving the quality of legal services available to the people of the state. The Association may not publicly advocate nor allow its name to be used for the advancement of any cause unless such action directly relates to the authorized purposes stated in this section.

ARTICLE XI. THE OFFICIAL PUBLICATION

Section 1. Purpose.

The Alaska Bar Association, on a quarterly basis, shall issue a publication which shall be distributed to the members of the Association at no charge. Its purpose shall be to inform Bar members of Association activities, to report trends and developments in the profession, and to entertain. Cost per issue to non-members shall be established by the Board of Governors.

Section 2. Editorial Board.

Responsibility for the publication shall reside in an Editorial Board of five persons, consisting of the President of the Association, the Executive Director and three members appointed for one year terms by the President with the advice and consent of the Board of Governors. One of the three members shall be appointed as the editor-in-chief by the President and the other two shall be designated as associate editors.

Section 3. Powers of the Board.

The Editorial Board shall exercise overall supervisory control of the publication. The editor-in-chief in conjunction with the Executive Director shall be responsible for the day-to-day operations of the publication. The editor-in-chief shall further establish and maintain an independent editorial policy. The editor-in-chief and the associate editors may serve additional one year terms.

ARTICLE XII. AMENDMENTS

Section 1. Amendments by the Board of Governors.

In accordance with the provisions of Bar Rule 62, these Bylaws may be amended by the Board of Governors at any regular meeting of the Board or at any special meeting called for that purpose.

Section 2. Amendments by the Members.

In accordance with the provisions of Bar Rule 62, any Bylaw adopted or amended by the Board of Governors may be modified or rescinded, or a new Bylaw adopted by a vote of the active members of the Association at any annual business or special meeting.

ARTICLE XIII. DEFINITIONS

Section 1. Definitions.

As used in these Bylaws, unless the context or subject matter otherwise requires:

(1) "The Act" means the Alaska Integrated Bar Act contained in Title 8, Chapter 8, Alaska Statutes (AS 8.08);

(2) "Alaska Bar," "Association," or "the Bar" mean the Alaska Bar Association created by the above mentioned Act;

(3) "Bar Rules" or "Rules" mean the Alaska Bar Rules promulgated by the Supreme Court of Alaska;

(4) "Board" and "Board of Governors" mean the Board of Governors of the Alaska Bar Association;

(5) "District" means an administrative district of Alaska, as defined in Article I, Section 6;

(6) "Executive Director" means the principal member of the Alaska Bar Association staff;

(7) "Governor" means a member of the Board;

(8) "Member" means a member of the Alaska Bar;

(9) "President," "President Elect," "Vice President," "Secretary," and "Treasurer" mean the respective officers of the Board of Governors and of the Association;

(10) "Regulations" mean the regulations promulgated by the Board to implement the Act or the Rules;

(11) "Standing Policies," "Policies," or "Policy" mean the various written Standing Policies of the Board; and

(12) "State" means the State of Alaska.

ALASKA RULES OF PROFESSIONAL CONDUCT

Table of Contents

PUBLIC SERVICE

INFORMATION ABOUT LEGAL SERVICES

MAINTAINING THE INTEGRITY OF THE PROFESSION

PREAMBLE: A LAWYER'S RESPONSIBILITIES

A lawyer is a representative of clients, an officer of the legal system and a public citizen having special responsibility for the quality of justice.

As a representative of clients, a lawyer performs various functions. As an advisor, a lawyer provides a client with an informed understanding of the client's legal rights and obligations and explains their practical implications. As an advocate, a lawyer zealously asserts the client's position under the rules of the adversary system. As a negotiator, a lawyer seeks a result advantageous to the client but consistent with requirements of honest dealing with others. As an intermediary between clients, a lawyer seeks to reconcile their divergent interests as an advisor and, to a limited extent, as a spokesperson for each client. As an evaluator, a lawyer examines a client's legal affairs and reports about them to the client or to others.

In all professional functions a lawyer should be competent, prompt and diligent. A lawyer should maintain communication with a client concerning the representation. A lawyer should keep a client's confidences and secrets relating to representation except so far as disclosure is required or permitted by the Rules of Professional Conduct or other law.

A lawyer's conduct should conform to the requirements of the law, both in professional service to clients and in the lawyer's business and personal affairs. A lawyer should use the law's procedures only for legitimate purposes and not to harass or intimidate others. A lawyer should demonstrate respect for the legal system and for those who serve it, including judges, other lawyers and public officials. While it is a lawyer's duty, when necessary, to challenge the rectitude of official action, it is also a lawyer's duty to uphold legal process.

As a public citizen, a lawyer should seek improvement of the law, the administration of justice and the quality of service rendered by the legal profession. As a member of a learned profession, a lawyer should cultivate knowledge of the law beyond its use for clients, employ that knowledge in reform of the law and work to strengthen legal education. A lawyer should be mindful of deficiencies in the administration of justice and of the fact that the poor, and sometimes persons who are not poor, cannot afford competent legal assistance, and should therefore devote professional time and civic influence in their behalf. A lawyer should aid the legal profession in pursuing these objectives and should help the bar regulate itself in the public interest.

Many of a lawyer's professional responsibilities are prescribed in the Rules of Professional Conduct, as well as substantive and procedural law. However, a lawyer is also guided by personal conscience and the approbation of professional peers. A lawyer should strive to attain the highest level of skill, to improve the law and the legal profession and to exemplify the legal profession's ideals of public service.

A lawyer's responsibilities as a representative of clients, an officer of the legal system and a public citizen are usually harmonious. Thus, when an opposing party is well represented, a lawyer can be a zealous advocate on behalf of a client and at the same time assume that justice is being done. So also, a lawyer can be sure that preserving client confidences ordinarily serves the public interest because people are more likely to seek legal advice, and thereby heed their legal obligations, when they know their communications will be private.

In the nature of law practice, however, conflicting responsibilities are encountered. Virtually all difficult ethical problems arise from conflict between a lawyer's responsibilities to clients, to the legal system and to the lawyer's own interest in remaining an upright person while earning a satisfactory living. The Rules of Professional Conduct prescribe terms for resolving such conflicts. Within the framework of these Rules many difficult issues of professional discretion can arise. Such issues must be resolved through the exercise of sensitive professional and moral judgment, guided by the basic principles underlying the Rules.

The legal profession is largely self-governing. Although other professions also have been granted powers of self-government, the legal profession is unique in this respect because of the close relationship between the profession and the processes of government and law enforcement. This connection is manifested in the fact that ultimate authority over the legal profession is vested largely in the courts.

To the extent that lawyers meet the obligations of their professional calling, the occasion for government regulation is obviated. Self-regulation also helps maintain the legal profession's independence from government domination. An independent legal profession is an important force in preserving government under law, for abuse of legal authority is more readily challenged by a profession whose members are not dependent on government for the right to practice.

The legal profession's relative autonomy carries with it special responsibilities of self-government. The profession has a responsibility to assure that its regulations are conceived in the public interest and not in furtherance of parochial or self-interested concerns of the bar. Every lawyer is responsible for observance of the Rules of Professional Conduct. A lawyer should also aid in securing their observance by other lawyers. Neglect of these responsibilities compromises the independence of the profession and the public interest which it serves.

Lawyers play a vital role in the preservation of society. The fulfillment of this role requires an understanding by lawyers of their relationship to our legal system. The Rules of Professional Conduct, when properly applied, serve to define that relationship.

(Amended by SCO 1332 effective January 15, 1999)

SCOPE

The Rules of Professional Conduct are rules of reason. They should be interpreted with reference to the purposes of legal representation and of the law itself. Some of the Rules are imperatives, cast in the terms "shall" or "shall not." These define proper conduct for purposes of professional discipline. Others, generally cast in the term "may," are permissive and define areas under the Rules in which the lawyer has professional discretion. Other Rules define the nature of relationships between the lawyer and others. The Rules are thus partly obligatory and disciplinary and partly constitutive and descriptive in that they define a lawyer's professional role.

Many of the Comments use the term "should." Comments do not add obligations to the Rules but provide guidance for practicing in compliance with the Rules.

The Rules presuppose a larger legal context shaping the lawyer's role. That context includes court rules and statutes relating to matters of licensure, laws defining specific obligations of lawyers and substantive and procedural law in general. Compliance with the Rules, as with all law in an open society, depends primarily upon understanding and voluntary compliance, secondarily upon reinforcement by peer and public opinion and finally, when necessary, upon enforcement through disciplinary proceedings. The Rules do not, however, exhaust the moral and ethical considerations that should inform a lawyer, for no worthwhile human activity can be completely defined by legal rules. The Rules simply provide a framework for the ethical practice of law.

Furthermore, for purposes of determining the lawyer's authority and responsibility, principles of substantive law external to these Rules determine whether a client-lawyer relationship exists. Most of the duties flowing from the client-lawyer relationship attach only after the client has requested the lawyer to render legal services and the lawyer has agreed to do so. But there are some duties, such as that of confidentiality under Rule 1.6, that may attach when the lawyer agrees to consider whether a client-lawyer relationship shall be established. Whether a client-lawyer relationship exists for any specific purpose can depend on the circumstances and may be a question of fact.

Under various legal provisions, including constitutional, statutory and common law, the responsibilities of government lawyers may include authority concerning legal matters that ordinarily reposes in the client in private client-lawyer relationships. For example, a lawyer for a government agency may have authority on behalf of the government to decide upon settlement or whether to appeal from an adverse judgment. Such authority in various respects is generally vested in the attorney general and the state's attorney in state government, and their federal counterparts, and the same may be true of other government law officers. Also, lawyers under the supervision of these officers may be authorized to represent several government agencies in intragovernmental legal controversies in circumstances where a private lawyer could not represent multiple private clients. They also may have authority to represent the "public interest" in circumstances where a private lawyer would not be authorized to do so. These Rules do not abrogate any such authority.

Failure to comply with an obligation or prohibition imposed by a Rule is a basis for invoking the disciplinary process. The Rules presuppose that disciplinary assessment of a lawyer's conduct will be made on the basis of the facts and circumstances as they existed at the time of the conduct in question and in recognition of the fact that a lawyer often has to act upon uncertain or incomplete evidence of the situation.

Moreover, the Rules presuppose that whether discipline should be imposed for a violation, and the severity of a sanction, depend on all the circumstances, such as the willfulness and seriousness of the violation, extenuating factors and whether there have been previous violations.

The purpose of the Rules can be subverted when they are invoked by opposing parties as procedural weapons. The fact that a Rule is a just basis for a lawyer's self-assessment, or for sanctioning a lawyer under the administration of a disciplinary authority, does not imply that an antagonist in a collateral proceeding or transaction has standing to seek enforcement of the Rules. Accordingly, nothing in the Rules should be deemed to augment any substantive legal duty of lawyers or the extra-disciplinary consequences of violating such a duty.

Moreover, these Rules are not intended to govern or affect judicial application of either the attorney-client or work product privilege. Those privileges were developed to promote compliance with law and fairness in litigation. In reliance on the attorney-client privilege, clients are entitled to expect that communications within the scope of the privilege will be protected against compelled disclosure. The attorney-client privilege is that of the client and not of the lawyer. The fact that in exceptional situations the lawyer has a limited discretion under the Rules to disclose a client confidence does not vitiate the proposition that, as a general matter, the client has a reasonable expectation that information relating to the client will not be voluntarily disclosed and that disclosure of such information may be judicially compelled only in accordance with recognized exceptions to the attorney-client and work product privileges.

The lawyer's exercise of discretion not to disclose information under Rule 1.6 should not be subject to reexamination. Permitting such reexamination would be incompatible with the general policy of promoting compliance with law through assurances that communications will be protected against disclosure.

The Comment accompanying each Rule explains and illustrates the meaning and purpose of the Rule. The Preamble and this note on Scope provide general orientation. The Comments are intended as guides to interpretation, but the text of each Rule is authoritative. Research notes were prepared to compare counterparts in the ABA Model Code of Professional Responsibility (adopted 1969, as amended) and to provide selected references to other authorities. The notes have not been adopted, do not constitute part of the Model Rules, and are not intended to affect the application or interpretation of the Rules and Comments.

CLIENT-LAWYER RELATIONSHIP

Rule 1.1. Competence.

(a) A lawyer shall provide competent representation to a client. Competent representation requires the legal knowledge, skill, thoroughness and preparation reasonably necessary for the representation.

(b) In an emergency, a lawyer may give advice or assistance in a matter in which the lawyer does not have the skill ordinarily required or in which referral to or consultation or association with another lawyer would be impractical; provided, however, that the assistance shall be limited to that reasonably necessary in the circumstances and the client shall be advised of the lawyer's limited knowledge in the legal field in which the advice is sought.

(SCO 1123 effective July 15, 1993)

ALASKA COMMENT

Subparagraph (b) of the rule is designed to add a duty to a lawyer rendering legal services in an emergency situation. The commentary associated with Model Rule 1.1 suggested that the requirement of competence might be relaxed in certain emergency situations. It was felt that such a relaxation should be made a substantive part of the rule with the added duties that the assistance shall continue only as long as the emergency exists and the client be fully advised of the limitations on the lawyer's competence.

COMMENT

Legal Knowledge and Skill

In determining whether a lawyer employs the requisite knowledge and skill in a particular matter, relevant factors include the relative complexity and specialized nature of the matter, the lawyer's general experience, the lawyer's training and experience in the field in question, the preparation and study the lawyer is able to give the matter and whether it is feasible to refer the matter to, or associate or consult with, a lawyer of established competence in the field in question. In many instances, the required proficiency is that of a general practitioner. Expertise in a particular field of law may be required in some circumstances.

A lawyer need not necessarily have special training or prior experience to handle legal problems of a type with which the lawyer is unfamiliar. A newly admitted lawyer can be as competent as a practitioner with long experience. Some important legal skills, such as the analysis of precedent, the evaluation of evidence and legal drafting, are required in all legal problems. Perhaps the most fundamental legal skill consists of determining what kind of legal problems a situation may involve, a skill that necessarily transcends any particular specialized knowledge. A lawyer can provide adequate representation in a wholly novel field through necessary study. Competent representation can also be provided through the association of a lawyer of established competence in the field in question.

A lawyer may accept representation where the requisite level of competence can be achieved by reasonable preparation. This applies as well to a lawyer who is appointed as counsel for an unrepresented person.

Thoroughness and Preparation

Competent handling of a particular matter includes inquiry into and analysis of the factual and legal elements of the problem, and use of methods and procedures meeting the standards of competent practitioners. It also includes adequate preparation. The required attention and preparation are determined in part by what is at stake; major litigation and complex transactions ordinarily require more elaborate treatment than matters of lesser consequence.

Maintaining Competence

To maintain the requisite knowledge and skill, a lawyer should engage in continuing study and education. If a system of peer review has been established, the lawyer should consider making use of it in appropriate circumstances.

Rule 1.2. Scope of Representation.

(a) A lawyer shall abide by a client's decisions concerning the objectives of representation, subject to paragraphs (c), (d) and (e), and shall consult with the client as to the means by which they are to be pursued. A lawyer shall abide by a client's decision whether to accept an offer of settlement of a matter. In a criminal case, the lawyer shall abide by the client's decision, after consultation with the lawyer, as to a plea to be entered, whether to waive jury trial, whether the client will testify, and whether to take an appeal.

(b) A lawyer's representation of a client, including representation by appointment, does not constitute an endorsement of the client's political, economic, social or moral views or activities.

(c) A lawyer may limit the scope of the representation if the limitation is reasonable under the circumstances and the client consents after consultation.

(1) If a written fee agreement is required by Rule 1.5, the agreement shall describe the limitation on the representation.

(2) The lawyer shall discuss with the client whether a written notice of representation should be provided to other interested parties.

(3) An otherwise unrepresented person to whom limited representation is being provided or has been provided in accordance with this rule is considered to be unrepresented for purposes of Rules 4.2 and 4.3 unless the opposing lawyer knows of or has been provided with:

(A) a written notice stating that the lawyer is to communicate only with the limited representation lawyer as to the subject matter of the limited representation; or

(B) a written notice of the time period during which the lawyer is to communicate only with the limited representation lawyer concerning the subject matter of the limited representation.

(d) A lawyer shall not counsel or assist a client to engage in conduct that the lawyer knows is criminal or fraudulent, but a lawyer may discuss the legal consequences of any proposed course of conduct with a client and may counsel or assist a client to make a good faith effort to determine the validity, scope, meaning or application of the law.

(e) When a lawyer knows that a client expects assistance not permitted by the rules of professional conduct or other law, the lawyer shall consult with the client regarding the relevant limitations on the lawyer's conduct.

(SCO 1123 effective July 15, 1993; amended by SCO 1544 effective October 15, 2004)

COMMENT

Scope of Representation

Both lawyer and client have authority and responsibility in the objectives and means of representation. The client has ultimate authority to determine the purposes to be served by legal representation, within the limits imposed by law and the lawyer's professional obligations. Within those limits, a client also has a right to consult with the lawyer about the means to be used in pursuing those objectives. At the same time, a lawyer is not required to pursue objectives or employ means simply because a client may wish that the lawyer do so. A clear distinction between objectives and means sometimes cannot be drawn, and in many cases the client-lawyer relationship partakes of a joint undertaking. In questions of means, the lawyer should assume responsibility for technical and legal tactical issues, but should defer to the client regarding such questions as the expense to be incurred and concern for third persons who might be adversely affected. Law defining the lawyer's scope of authority in litigation varies among jurisdictions.

In a case in which the client appears to be suffering mental disability, the lawyer's duty to abide by the client's decisions is to be guided by reference to Rule 1.14.

Independence from Client's Views or Activities

Legal representation should not be denied to a person whose cause is controversial or the subject of popular disapproval. By the same token, representing a client does not constitute approval of the client's views or activities.

Services Limited in Objectives or Means

The objectives or scope of services provided by a lawyer may be limited by agreement or by the terms under which the lawyer's services are made available to the client. For example, a retainer may be for a specifically defined purpose. Representation provided through a legal aid agency may be subject to limitations on the types of cases the agency handles. When a lawyer has been retained by an insurer to represent an insured, the representation may be limited to matters related to the insurance coverage. The terms upon which representation is undertaken may exclude specific objectives or means. Such limitations may exclude objectives or means that the lawyer regards as repugnant or imprudent.

An agreement concerning the scope of representation must accord with the rules of professional conduct and other law. Thus, the client may not be asked to agree to representation so limited in scope as to violate Rule 1.1, or to surrender the right to terminate the lawyer's services or the right to settle litigation that the lawyer might wish to continue.

See also Comment to Rule 1.3, para. 3.

Criminal, Fraudulent and Prohibited Transactions

A lawyer is required to give an honest opinion about the actual consequences that appear likely to result from a client's conduct. The fact that a client uses advice in a course of action that is criminal or fraudulent does not, of itself, make a lawyer a party to the course of action. However, a lawyer may not knowingly assist a client in criminal or fraudulent conduct. There is a critical distinction between presenting an analysis of legal aspects of questionable conduct and recommending the means by which a crime or fraud might be committed with impunity.

When the client's course of action has already begun and is continuing, the lawyer's responsibility is especially delicate. The lawyer is not permitted to reveal the client's wrongdoing, except where permitted by Rule 1.6. However, the lawyer is required to avoid furthering the purpose, for example, by suggesting how it might be concealed. A lawyer may not continue assisting a client in conduct that the lawyer originally supposes is legally proper but then discovers is criminal or fraudulent. Withdrawal from the representation, therefore, may be required.

Where the client is a fiduciary, the lawyer may be charged with special obligations in dealings with a beneficiary.

Paragraph (d) applies whether or not the defrauded party is a party to the transaction. Hence, a lawyer should not participate in a sham transaction; for example, a transaction to effectuate criminal or fraudulent escape of tax liability. Paragraph (d) does not preclude undertaking a criminal defense incident to a general retainer for legal services to a lawful enterprise. The last clause of paragraph (d) recognizes that determining the validity or interpretation of a statute or regulation may require a course of action involving disobedience of the statute or regulation or of the interpretation placed upon it by governmental authorities.

Annotations

Cases

This rule limits the client's authority to make decisions over which he has ultimate authority; thus, counsel for defendant has the ultimate authority to make other decisions governing trial tactics, including whether to request lesser-included offense instructions. **Simeon v. State,** Op. No. 1930, 90 P.3d 181 (Alaska App. 2004).

Alaska R. Prof. Conduct 1.2(a) specifies those decisions over which the client has the ultimate authority, so it follows that the lawyer has the ultimate authority to make other decisions governing trial tactics. Osborne v. State, Op. No. 1976, 110 P.3d 986 (Alaska App. 2005). **Osborne v. State,** Op. No. 1976, 110 P.3d 986 (Alaska App. 2005).

Professor, who was terminated by a university, did not present any evidence indicating that he did not receive his attorney's letter, or that he did not agree to the terms of the representation limiting the scope of the appeal to a single issue. The attorney failed to file a timely appeal on the single issue he did agree to appeal, but that omission was harmless where the professor could not establish that he was injured by the attorney's failure. **Sengupta v. Wickwire,** Op. No. 5963, 124 P.3d 748 (Alaska 2005).

Attorney's 90-day suspension for knowingly disobeying a court order was proper where, although the attorney believed that Alaska R. Prof. Conduct

1.15 required him to return client funds instead of transferring the funds to opposing counsel in lieu of a superseadas bond, Alaska R. Prof. Conduct 3.4(c) required him to follow court order regarding disposition of the funds or "openly refuse" to follow it; furthermore, section (e) of this rule indicates that a client's wishes or interests do not supersede a lawyer's ethical obligations. **In re Ford,** Op. No. 2000, 128 P.3d 178 (Alaska 2006).

Personal difficulties or animosity between a defense attorney and a defendant does not constitute a reason for removing the attorney from the case unless the attorney-client relationship has deteriorated to the point where the attorney is incapable of effective communication with the defendant or the attorney is incapable of objective decision- making about the case. **LaBrake v. State**, Op. No. 9189, 152 P.3d 474 (Alaska App. 2007).

When a defendant claims that attorney gave incompetent advice or made incompetent decisions, the defendant must show one of two things: either (1) that attorney's choice of strategy or tactics was so bad that no competent criminal law practitioner would have handled these issues the same way; or (2) that attorney's investigation and preparation of the case was so inadequate that attorney had no competent basis for making decisions (with regard to the matters entrusted to attorney's decision) or for rendering advice regarding the matters entrusted to defendant's decision. **LaBrake v. State**, Op. No. 9189, 152 P.3d 474 (Alaska App. 2007).

Subsection (a) of this rule declares that, in a criminal case, the client has the final authority to decide what plea to enter, whether to waive jury trial, whether to testify, and whether to take an appeal. Since this rule limits the client's authority to those decisions, it follows that the lawyer has the ultimate authority to make other decisions governing trial tactics. **LaBrake v. State**, Op. No. 9189, 152 P.3d 474 (Alaska App. 2007).

Defendant did not present a prima facie case of ineffective assistance of counsel where defendant's assertion failed to offer any potential defenses a that a competent attorney in counsel's position would have pursued. **LaBrake v. State**, Op. No. 9189, 152 P.3d 474 (Alaska App. 2007).

Because conceding an aggravating factor to criminal sentencing statute is a tactical decision for the defense attorney to make and not a decision reserved for the defendant personally, counsel's decision to concede an aggravator without defendant's express authorization did not constitute ineffective assistance of counsel. **LaBrake v. State**, Op. No. 9189, 152 P.3d 474 (Alaska App. 2007).

Rule 1.3. Diligence.

A lawyer shall act with reasonable diligence and promptness in representing a client.

(SCO 1123 effective July 15, 1993)

COMMENT

A lawyer should pursue a matter on behalf of a client despite opposition, obstruction or personal inconvenience to the lawyer, and may take whatever lawful and ethical measures are required to vindicate a client's cause or endeavor. A lawyer should act with commitment and dedication to the interests of the client and with zeal in advocacy upon the client's behalf. However, a lawyer is not bound to press for every advantage that might be realized for a client. A lawyer has professional discretion in determining the means by which a matter should be pursued. See Rule 1.2 A lawyer's workload should be controlled so that each matter can be handled adequately.

Perhaps no professional shortcoming is more widely resented than procrastination. A client's interests often can be adversely affected by the passage of time or the change of conditions; in extreme instances, as when a lawyer overlooks a statute of limitations, the client's legal position may be destroyed. Even when the client's interests are not affected in substance, however, unreasonable delay can cause a client needless anxiety and undermine confidence in the lawyer's trustworthiness.

Unless the relationship is terminated as provided in Rule 1.16, a lawyer should carry through to conclusion all matters undertaken for a client. If a lawyer's employment is limited to a specific matter, the relationship terminates when the matter has been resolved. If a lawyer has served a client over a substantial period in a variety of matters, the client sometimes may assume that the lawyer will continue to serve on a continuing basis unless the lawyer gives notice of withdrawal. Doubt about whether a client-lawyer relationship still exists should be clarified by the lawyer, preferably in writing, so that the client will not mistakenly suppose the lawyer is looking after the client's affairs when the lawyer has ceased to do so. For example, if a lawyer has handled a judicial or administrative proceeding that produced a result adverse to the client but has not been specifically instructed concerning pursuit of an appeal, the lawyer should advise the client of the possibility of appeal before relinquishing responsibility for the matter.

Rule 1.4. Communication.

(a) A lawyer shall keep a client reasonably informed about the status of a matter undertaken on the client's behalf and promptly comply with reasonable requests for information.

(b) A lawyer shall explain a matter to the extent reasonably necessary to permit the client to make informed decisions regarding the representation.

(c) A lawyer shall inform an existing client in writing if the lawyer does not have malpractice insurance of at least $100,000 per claim and $300,000 annual aggregate and shall inform the client in writing at any time the lawyer's malpractice insurance drops below these amounts or the lawyer's malpractice insurance is terminated. A lawyer shall maintain a record of these disclosures for six years from the termination of the client's representation.

(SCO 1123 effective July 15, 1993; amended by SCO 1329 effective January 15, 1999; and by SCO 1370 effective April 15, 2000)

ALASKA COMMENT

Subsection (c) does not apply to lawyers in government practice or lawyers employed as in-house counsel.

Lawyers may use the following language in making the disclosures required by this rule:

(1) no insurance: "Alaska Rule of Professional Conduct 1.4(c) requires that you, as the client, be informed in writing if a lawyer does not have malpractice insurance of at least $100,000 per claim and $300,000 annual aggregate and if, at any time, a lawyer's malpractice insurance drops below these

amounts or a lawyer's malpractice insurance coverage is terminated. You are therefore advised that (name of attorney or firm) does not have malpractice insurance coverage of at least $100,000 per claim and $300,000 annual aggregate."

(2) insurance below amounts: "Alaska Rule of Professional Conduct 1.4(c) requires that you, as the client, be informed in writing if a lawyer does not have malpractice insurance of at least $100,000 per claim and $300,000 annual aggregate and if, at any time, a lawyer's malpractice insurance drops below these amounts or a lawyer's malpractice insurance coverage is terminated. You are therefore advised that (name of attorney or firm)'s malpractice insurance has dropped below at least $100,000 per claim and $300,000 annual aggregate."

(3) insurance terminated: "Alaska Rule of Professional Conduct 1.4(c) requires that you, as the client, be informed in writing if a lawyer does not have malpractice insurance of at least $100,000 per claim and $300,000 annual aggregate and if, at any time, a lawyer's malpractice insurance drops below these amounts or a lawyer's malpractice insurance coverage is terminated. You are therefore advised that (name of attorney or firm)'s malpractice insurance has been terminated."

COMMENT

The client should have sufficient information to participate intelligently in decisions concerning the objectives of the representation and the means by which they are to be pursued, to the extent the client is willing and able to do so. For example, a lawyer negotiating on behalf of a client should provide the client with facts relevant to the matter, inform the client of communications from another party and take other reasonable steps that permit the client to make a decision regarding a serious offer from another party. A lawyer who receives from opposing counsel an offer of settlement in a civil controversy or a proffered plea bargain in a criminal case should promptly inform the client of its substance unless prior discussions with the client have left it clear that the proposal will be unacceptable. See Rule 1.2(a). Even when a client delegates authority to the lawyer, the client should be kept advised of the status of the matter.

Adequacy of communication depends in part on the kind of advice or assistance involved. For example, in negotiations where there is time to explain a proposal, the lawyer should review all important provisions with the client before proceeding to an agreement. In litigation a lawyer should explain the general strategy and prospects of success and ordinarily should consult the client on tactics that might injure or coerce others. On the other hand, a lawyer ordinarily cannot be expected to describe trial or negotiation strategy in detail. The guiding principle is that the lawyer should fulfill reasonable client expectations for information consistent with the duty to act in the client's best interests, and the client's overall requirements as to the character of representation.

Ordinarily, the information to be provided is that appropriate for a client who is a comprehending and responsible adult. However, fully informing the client according to this standard may be impracticable, for example, where the client is a child or suffers from mental disability. See Rule 1.14. When the client is an organization or group, it is often impossible or inappropriate to inform every one of its members about its legal affairs; ordinarily, the lawyer should address communications to the appropriate officials of the organization. See Rule 1.13. Where many routine matters are involved, a system of limited or occasional reporting may be arranged with the client. Practical exigency may also require a lawyer to act for a client without prior consultation.

Withholding Information

In some circumstances, a lawyer may be justified in delaying transmission of information when the client would be likely to react imprudently to an immediate communication. Thus, a lawyer might withhold a psychiatric diagnosis of a client when the examining psychiatrist indicates that disclosure would harm the client. A lawyer may not withhold information to serve the lawyer's own interest or convenience. Rules or court orders governing litigation may provide that information supplied to a lawyer may not be disclosed to the client. Rule 3.4(c) directs compliance with such rules or orders.

Rule 1.5. Fees.

(a) A lawyer's fee shall be reasonable. The factors to be considered in determining the reasonableness of a fee include the following:

(1) the time and labor required, the novelty and difficulty of the questions involved, and the skill requisite to perform the legal service properly;

(2) the likelihood that the acceptance of the particular employment will preclude other employment by the lawyer;

(3) the fee customarily charged in the locality for similar legal services;

(4) the amount involved and the results obtained;

(5) the time limitations imposed by the client or by the circumstances;

(6) the nature and length of the professional relationship with the client;

(7) the experience, reputation, and ability of the lawyer or lawyers performing the services; and

(8) whether the fee is fixed or contingent.

(b) The basis or rate of a fee exceeding $500 shall be communicated to the client in a written fee agreement before or within a reasonable time after commencing the representation. This written fee agreement shall include the disclosure required under Rule 1.4(c). In a case involving litigation, the lawyer shall notify the client in the written fee agreement of any costs, fees or expenses for which the client may be liable if the client is not the prevailing party.

(c) A fee may be contingent on the outcome of the matter for which the service is rendered, except in a matter in which a contingent fee is prohibited by paragraph (d) or other law. A fee agreement which is in whole or in part contingent shall be in writing and shall state the method by which the fee is to be determined, including the percentage or percentages that shall accrue to the lawyer in the event of settlement, trial or appeal, litigation and other expenses to be deducted from the recovery, and whether such expenses are to be deducted before or after the contingent fee is calculated. Upon conclusion of a contingent fee matter, the lawyer shall provide the client with a written statement stating the outcome of the matter and, if there is a recovery, showing the remittance to the client and the method of its determination.

(d) A lawyer shall not enter into an arrangement for, charge, or collect:

(1) any fee in a domestic relations matter, the payment or amount of which is contingent upon the securing of a divorce or upon the establishment or modification of alimony or support, or property settlement in lieu thereof; or

(2 a contingent fee for representing a defendant in a criminal case.

(e A division of a fee between lawyers who are not in the same firm may be made only if:

(1 the division is in proportion to the services performed by each lawyer or, by written agreement with the client, each lawyer assumes joint responsibility for the representation;

(2) the client is advised of and does not object to the participation of all the lawyers involved; and

(3) the total fee is reasonable.

(f) A lawyer should be zealous in his or her efforts to avoid controversies over fees with clients and should attempt to resolve amicably any differences on the subject.

(SCO 1123 effective July 15, 1993; amended by SCO 1330 effective January 15, 1999)

ALASKA COMMENT

The words "if apparent to the client" were deleted from Model Rule 1.5(a)(2). An attorney should be allowed to increase his or her fees if there is a likelihood that the representation will preclude other employment. This is true regardless of whether the likelihood is apparent to the client.

The Committee concluded that advice to the client concerning potential liability for costs, attorney's fees and other expenses should be specifically set out in the written fee agreement in order that the client might be fully informed.

In addition to the definition in Rule 9.1(b), the term "client" in this rule means any person or entity legally responsible to pay the fees for professional services rendered by a lawyer.

Lawyers may use the following language to notify the client of the client's potential liability for costs, fees or expenses if the client is not the prevailing party in the litigation: "Under the law, you may have to pay some or all of the costs, fees and expenses of your opponents in your case if you don't win your case or if you reject an offer that turns out to be better than your results at trial." (Amended by SCO 1392 effective October 15, 2000)

COMMENT

Basis or Rate of Fee

When the lawyer has regularly represented a client, they ordinarily will have evolved an understanding concerning the basis or rate of the fee. In a new client-lawyer relationship, however, an understanding as to the fee should be promptly established. It is not necessary to recite all the factors that underlie the basis of the fee, but only those that are directly involved in its computation. It is sufficient, for example, to state that the basic rate is an hourly charge or a fixed amount or an estimated amount, or to identify the factors that may be taken into account in finally fixing the fee. When developments occur during the representation that render an earlier estimate substantially inaccurate, a revised estimate should be provided to the client. A written statement concerning the fees reduces the possibility of misunderstanding. Furnishing the client with a simple memorandum or a copy of the lawyer's customary fee schedule is sufficient if the basis or rate of the fee is set forth.

A contingent fee arrangement is prohibited in domestic relations cases only with regard to proceedings to establish or modify alimony, child support and property settlement in lieu of alimony or child support, and not to proceedings initiated for the collection of amounts in default.

Terms of Payment

A lawyer may require advance payment of a fee, but is obliged to return any unearned portion. See Rule 1.6(b). A lawyer may accept property in payment for services, such as an ownership interest in an enterprise, providing this does not involve acquisition of a proprietary interest in the cause of action or subject matter of the litigation contrary to Rule 1.8(j). However, a fee paid in property instead of money may be subject to special scrutiny because it involves questions concerning both the value of the services and the lawyer's special knowledge of the value of the property.

An agreement may not be made whose terms might induce the lawyer improperly to curtail services for the client or perform them in a way contrary to the client's interest. For example, a lawyer should not enter into an agreement whereby services are to be provided only up to a stated amount when it is foreseeable that more extensive services probably will be required, unless the situation is adequately explained to the client. Otherwise, the client might have to bargain for further assistance in the midst of a proceeding or transaction. However, it is proper to define the extent of services in light of the client's ability to pay. A lawyer should not exploit a fee arrangement based primarily on hourly charges by using wasteful procedures. When there is doubt whether a contingent fee is consistent with the client's best interest, the lawyer should offer the client alternative bases for the fee and explain their implications. Applicable law may impose limitations on contingent fees, such as a ceiling on the percentage.

Division of Fee

A division of fee is a single billing to a client covering the fee of two or more lawyers who are not in the same firm. A division of fee facilitates association of more than one lawyer in a matter in which neither alone could serve the client as well, and most often is used when the fee is contingent and the division is between a referring lawyer and a trial specialist. Paragraph (e) permits the lawyers to divide a fee on either the basis of the proportion of services they render or by agreement between the participating lawyers if all assume responsibility for the representation as a whole and the client is advised and does not object. It does not require disclosure to the client of the share that each lawyer is to receive. Joint responsibility for the representation entails the obligations stated in Rule 5.1 for purposes of the matter involved.

Disputes over Fees

If a procedure has been established for resolution of fee disputes, such as an arbitration or mediation procedure established by the bar, the lawyer should conscientiously consider submitting to it. Law may prescribe a procedure for determining a lawyer's fee, for example, in representation of an executor or administrator, a class or a person entitled to a reasonable fee as part of the measure of damages. The lawyer entitled to such a fee and a lawyer representing another party concerned with the fee should comply with the prescribed procedure.

Annotations

Cases

The avoidance of unnecessary fees and costs is part of every attorney's ethical responsibility to the client, but attorney is not free to neglect a measure that will protect client from clearly foreseeable risk of harm merely because there will be some additional cost to client if measure is taken. **Doe v. Hughes, Thorsness, Gantz, et al.,** Op. No. 3891, 838 P2d 804 (Alaska 1992).

Rule 1.6. Confidentiality of Information

(a) A lawyer shall not reveal a confidence or secret relating to representation of a client unless the client consents after consultation, except for disclosures that are impliedly authorized in order to carry out the representation, and except as stated in paragraph (b) or Rule 3.3(a)(2). For purposes of this rule, "confidence" means information protected by the attorney-client privilege under applicable law, and "secret" means other information gained in the professional relationship if the client has requested it be held confidential or if it is reasonably foreseeable that disclosure of the information would be embarrassing or detrimental to the client. In determining whether information relating to representation of a client is protected from disclosure under this rule, the lawyer shall resolve any uncertainty about whether such information can be revealed against revealing the information.

(b) A lawyer may reveal a confidence or secret to the extent the lawyer reasonably believes necessary:

(1) to prevent the client from committing a criminal or fraudulent act that the lawyer believes is likely to result in death or substantial bodily harm, or substantial injury to the financial interest or property of another; or

(2) to establish a claim or defense on behalf of the lawyer in a controversy between the lawyer and the client, to establish a defense to a criminal charge or civil claim against the lawyer based upon conduct in which the client was involved, or to respond to allegations in any proceeding concerning the lawyer's representation of the client.

(SCO 1123 effective July 15, 1993; amended by SCO 1332 effective January 15, 1999)

ALASKA COMMENT

The Committee has amended this rule to tie the lawyer's confidentiality obligation to a "confidence" or "secret" of the client. The Committee concluded the language used in Model Rule 16 ("information" relating to representation of a client) was excessively broad. The terms "confidence" and "secret" are defined in the amended rule in substantively the same way as those terms were defined in DR 4-101(A) of the ABA Model Code of Professional Responsibility. The Committee expects that court decisions interpreting "confidence" and "secret" under DR 4-101(A) will be persuasive authority for interpreting the amended Alaska rule.

The final sentence of subsection (a) has been added to require that a lawyer approach any decision about disclosing information relating to representation of a client from the standpoint that the information is generally presumed to be protected from disclosure.

The lawyer's decision to disclose information under this rule is governed by objectively reasonable standards (see Rule 9.1(i) & (j)) and by all the facts and circumstances of which the lawyer is aware or reasonably should be aware at the time the decision is made.

COMMENT

The lawyer is part of a judicial system charged with upholding the law. One of the lawyer's functions is to advise clients so that they avoid any violation of the law in the proper exercise of their rights.

The observance of the ethical obligation of a lawyer to hold inviolate confidential information of the client not only facilitates the full development of facts essential to proper representation of the client but also encourages people to seek legal assistance.

Almost without exception, clients come to lawyers in order to determine what their rights are and what is, in the maze of laws and regulations, deemed to be legal and correct. The common law recognizes that the client's confidences must be protected from disclosure. Based upon experience, lawyers know that almost all clients follow the advice given, and the law is upheld.

A fundamental principle in the client-lawyer relationship is that the lawyer maintain the client's confidences and secrets relating to the representation. The client is thereby encouraged to communicate fully and frankly with the lawyer even as to embarrassing or legally damaging subject matter.

The principle of confidentiality is given effect in two related bodies of law, the attorney-client privilege (which includes the work product doctrine) in the law of evidence and the rule of confidentiality established in professional ethics. The attorney-client privilege applies in judicial and other proceedings in which a lawyer may be called as a witness or otherwise required to produce evidence concerning a client. The rule of client-lawyer confidentiality applies in situations other than those where evidence is sought from the lawyer through compulsion of law. The confidentiality rule applies not merely to matters communicated in confidence by the client but also to all confidences and secrets relating to the representation, whatever their source. A lawyer may not disclose such information except as authorized or required by the rules of professional conduct or other law. See also Scope.

The requirement of maintaining confidences and secrets relating to representation applies to government lawyers who may disagree with the policy goals that their representation is designed to advance.

Authorized Disclosure

A lawyer is impliedly authorized to make disclosures about a client when appropriate in carrying out the representation, except to the extent that the client's instructions or special circumstances limit that authority. In litigation, for example, a lawyer may disclose information by admitting a fact that cannot properly be disputed, or in negotiation by making a disclosure that facilitates a satisfactory conclusion.

Lawyers in a firm may, in the course of the firm's practice, disclose to each other information relating to a client of the firm, unless the client has instructed that particular information be confined to specified lawyers.

Disclosure Adverse to Client

The confidentiality rule is subject to limited exceptions. In becoming privy to information about a client, a lawyer may foresee that the client intends serious harm to another person. However, to the extent a lawyer is required or permitted to disclose a client's purposes, the client will be inhibited from revealing facts which would enable the lawyer to counsel against a wrongful course of action. The public is better protected if full and open communication by the client is encouraged than if it is inhibited.

Several situations must be distinguished.

First, the lawyer may not counsel or assist a client in conduct that is criminal or fraudulent. See Rule 1.2(c). Similarly, a lawyer has a duty under Rule 3.3(a)(4) not to use false evidence. This duty is essentially a special instance of the duty prescribed in Rule 1.2(c) to avoid assisting a client in criminal or fraudulent conduct.

Second, the lawyer may have been innocently involved in past conduct by the client that was criminal or fraudulent. In such a situation the lawyer has not violated Rule 1.2(c), because to "counsel or assist" criminal or fraudulent conduct requires knowing that the conduct is of that character.

Third, the lawyer may learn that a client intends prospective conduct that is criminal and likely to result in imminent death or substantial bodily harm. As stated in paragraph (b)(1), the lawyer has professional discretion to reveal information in order to prevent such consequences. The lawyer may make a disclosure in order to prevent homicide or serious bodily injury which the lawyer reasonably believes is intended by a client. It is very difficult for a lawyer to "know" when such a heinous purpose will actually be carried out, for the client may have a change of mind.

The lawyer's exercise of discretion requires consideration of such factors as the nature of the lawyer's relationship with the client and with those who might be injured by the client, the lawyer's own involvement in the transaction and factors that may extenuate the conduct in question. Where practical, the lawyer should seek to persuade the client to take suitable action. In any case, a disclosure adverse to the client's interest should be no greater than the lawyer reasonably believes necessary to the purpose. A lawyer's decision not to take preventive action permitted by paragraph (b)(1) does not violate this rule.

Withdrawal

If the lawyer's services will be used by the client in materially furthering a course of criminal or fraudulent conduct, the lawyer must withdraw, as stated in Rule 1.16(a)(1).

After withdrawal the lawyer is required to refrain from making disclosure of the client's confidences, except as otherwise provided in Rule 1.6. Neither this rule nor Rule 1.8(b) nor Rule 1.16(e) prevents the lawyer from giving notice of the fact of withdrawal, and the lawyer may also withdraw or disaffirm any opinion, document, affirmation, or the like.

Where the client is an organization, the lawyer may be in doubt whether contemplated conduct will actually be carried out by the organization. Where necessary to guide conduct in connection with this rule, the lawyer may make inquiry within the organization as indicated in Rule 1.13(b).

Dispute Concerning Lawyer's Conduct

Where a legal claim or disciplinary charge alleges complicity of the lawyer in a client's conduct or other misconduct of the lawyer involving representation of the client, the lawyer may respond to the extent the lawyer reasonably believes necessary to establish a defense. The same is true with respect to a claim involving the conduct or representation of a former client. The lawyer's right to respond arises when an assertion of such complicity has been made. Paragraph (b)(2) does not require the lawyer to await the commencement of an action or proceeding that charges such complicity, so that the defense may be established by responding directly to a third party who has made such an assertion. The right to defend, of course, applies where a proceeding has been commenced. Where practicable and not prejudicial to the lawyer's ability to establish the defense, the lawyer should advise the client of the third party's assertion and request that the client respond appropriately. In any event, disclosure should be no greater than the lawyer reasonably believes is necessary to vindicate innocence, the disclosure should be made in a manner which limits access to the information to the tribunal or other persons having a need to know it, and appropriate protective orders or other arrangements should be sought by the lawyer to the fullest extent practicable.

If the lawyer is charged with wrongdoing in which the client's conduct is implicated, the rule of confidentiality should not prevent the lawyer from defending against the charge. Such a charge can arise in a civil, criminal or professional disciplinary proceeding, and can be based on a wrong allegedly committed by the lawyer against the client, or on a wrong alleged by a third person; for example, a person claiming to have been defrauded by the lawyer and client acting together. A lawyer entitled to a fee is permitted by paragraph (b)(2) to prove the services rendered in an action to collect it. This aspect of the rule expresses the principle that the beneficiary of a fiduciary relationship may not exploit it to the detriment of the fiduciary. As stated above, the lawyer must make every effort practicable to avoid unnecessary disclosure of confidences and secrets relating to a representation, to limit disclosure to those having the need to know it, and to obtain protective orders or make other arrangements minimizing the risk of disclosure.

Disclosures Otherwise Required or Authorized

The attorney-client privilege is differently defined in various jurisdictions. If a lawyer is called as a witness to give testimony concerning a client, absent waiver by the client, Rule 1.6(a) requires the lawyer to invoke the privilege when it is applicable. The lawyer must comply with the final orders of a court or other tribunal of competent jurisdiction requiring the lawyer to give information about the client.

The rules of professional conduct in various circumstances permit or require a lawyer to disclose confidences or secrets relating to the representation. See Rules 2.2, 3.3 and 4.1. In addition to these provisions, a lawyer may be obligated or permitted by other provisions of law to give information about a client. Whether another provision of law supersedes Rule 1.6 is a matter of interpretation beyond the scope of these rules, but a presumption should exist against such a suppression.

Former Client

The duty of confidentiality continues after the client-lawyer relationship has terminated.

Annotations

Cases

Lawyer's statement to former client's attorney stating that claim brought by former client against lawyer would "waive all attorney-client privileges" constituted implied threat to reveal a confidence in violation of former Disciplinary Rule 4-101, warranting censure. **Disciplinary Matter Involving Frost,** Op. No. 4029, 863 P2d 843 (Alaska 1993).

The obligation of confidentiality imposed by this rule does not expand the attorney-client privilege codified in Evidence Rule 503. **Downie v. Superior Court,** Op. No. 1389, 888 P2d 1306 (Alaska App. 1995).

Rule 1.7. Conflict of Interest: General Rule.

(a) A lawyer shall not represent a client if the representation of that client will be directly adverse to another client, unless:

(1) the lawyer reasonably believes the representation will not adversely affect the relationship with the other client; and

(2) each client consents after consultation.

(b) A lawyer shall not represent a client if the representation of that client may be materially limited by the lawyer's responsibilities to another client or to a third person, or by the lawyer's own interests, unless:

(1) the lawyer reasonably believes the representation will not be adversely affected; and

(2) the client consents after consultation. When representation of multiple clients in a single matter is undertaken, the consultation shall include explanation of the implications of the common representation and the advantages and risks involved.

(c) A lawyer shall act with reasonable diligence in determining whether a conflict of interest, as described in paragraphs (a) and (b) of this rule, or Rules 1.8, 1.9 and 1.10 exists.

(SCO 1123 effective July 15, 1993; amended by SCO 1335 effective January 15, 1999)

ALASKA COMMENT

Substantial delay in litigation may occur as a result of a conflict of interest unless prompt efforts are made to discover any such conflicts. A lawyer should take all reasonable measures to determine whether or not a conflict of interest exists under Rule 1.7, 1.8, 1.9 or 1.10 before undertaking representation. If facts which would lead one to believe a conflict of interest exists come to the attention of the lawyer after representation has begun, the lawyer should determine whether a conflict does exist with all reasonable diligence.

COMMENT

Loyalty to a Client

Loyalty is an essential element in the lawyer's relationship to a client. An impermissible conflict of interest may exist before representation is undertaken, in which event the representation should be declined. If such a conflict arises after representation has been undertaken, the lawyer should withdraw from the representation. See Rule 1.16. When more than one client is involved and the lawyer withdraws because a conflict arises after representation, whether the lawyer may continue to represent any of the clients is determined by Rule 1.9. See also Rule 2.2(c). As to whether a client-lawyer relationship exists or, having once been established, is continuing, see Comment to Rule 1.3 and Scope.

As a general proposition, loyalty to a client prohibits undertaking representation directly adverse to that client without that client's consent. Paragraph (a) expresses that general rule. Thus, a lawyer ordinarily may not act as advocate against a person the lawyer represents in some other matter, even if it is wholly unrelated. On the other hand, simultaneous representation in unrelated matters of clients whose interests are only generally adverse, such as competing economic enterprises, does not require consent of the respective clients. Paragraph (a) applies only when the representation of one client would be directly adverse to the other.

Loyalty to a client is also impaired when a lawyer cannot consider, recommend or carry out an appropriate course of action for the client because of the lawyer's other responsibilities or interest. The conflict in effect forecloses alternatives that would otherwise be available to the client. Paragraph (b) addresses such situations. A possible conflict does not itself preclude the representation. The critical questions are the likelihood that a conflict will eventuate and, if it does, whether It will materially interfere with the lawyer's independent professional judgment in considering alternatives or foreclose courses of action that reasonably should be pursued on behalf of the client. Consideration should be given to whether the client wishes to accommodate the other interest involved.

Consultation and Consent

A client may consent to representation notwithstanding a conflict. However, as indicated in paragraph (a)(1) with respect to representation directly adverse to a client, and paragraph (b)(1) with respect to material limitations on representation of a client, when a disinterested lawyer would conclude that the client should not agree to the representation under the circumstances, the lawyer involved cannot properly ask for such agreement or provide representation on the basis of the client's consent. When more than one client is involved, the question of conflict must be resolved as to each client. Moreover, there may be circumstances where it is impossible to make the disclosure necessary to obtain consent. For example, when the lawyer represents different clients in related matters and one of the clients refuses to consent to the disclosure necessary to permit the other client to make an informed decision, the lawyer cannot properly ask the latter to consent.

Lawyer's Interests

The lawyer's own interests should not be permitted to have adverse effect on representation of a client. For example, a lawyer's need for income should not lead the lawyer to undertake matters that cannot be handled competently and at a reasonable fee. See Rules 1.1 and 1.5. If the probity of a lawyer's own conduct in a transaction is in serious question, it may be difficult or impossible for the lawyer to give a client detached advice. A lawyer may not allow related business interests to affect representation, for example, by referring clients to an enterprise in which the lawyer has an undisclosed interest.

Conflicts in Litigation

Paragraph (a) prohibits representation of opposing parties in litigation. Simultaneous representation of parties whose interest in litigation may conflict, such as co-plaintiffs or co-defendants, is governed by paragraph (b). An impermissible conflict may exist by reason of substantial discrepancy in the parties' testimony, incompatibility in positions in relation to an opposing party or the fact that there are substantially different possibilities of settlement of the claims or liabilities in question. Such conflicts can arise in criminal cases as well as civil. The potential for conflict of interest in representing multiple defendants in a criminal case is so grave that ordinarily a lawyer should decline to represent more than one co-defendant. On the other hand, common representation of persons having similar interests is proper if the risk of adverse effect is minimal and the requirements of paragraph (b) are met. Compare Rule 2.2 involving intermediation between clients.

Ordinarily, a lawyer may not act as advocate against a client the lawyer represents in some other matter, even if the other matter is wholly unrelated. However, there are circumstances in which a lawyer may act as advocate against a client. For example, a lawyer representing an enterprise with diverse operations may accept employment as an advocate against the enterprise in an unrelated matter if doing so will not adversely affect the lawyer's relationship with the enterprise or conduct of the suit and if both clients consent upon consultation. By the same token, government lawyers in some circumstances may represent government employees in proceedings in which a government agency is the opposing party. The propriety of concurrent representation can depend on the nature of the litigation. For example, a suit charging fraud entails conflict to a degree not involved in a suit for a declaratory judgment concerning statutory interpretation.

A lawyer may represent parties having antagonistic positions on a legal question that has arisen in different cases, unless representation of either client would be adversely affected. Thus, it is ordinarily not improper to assert such positions in cases pending in different trial courts, but it may be improper to do so in cases pending at the same time in an appellate court.

Interest of Person Paying for a Lawyer's Service

A lawyer may be paid from a source other than the client, if the client is informed of that fact and consents and the arrangement does not compromise the lawyer's duty of loyalty to the client. See Rule 1.8(f). For example, when an insurer and its insured have conflicting interests in a matter arising from a liability insurance agreement, and the insurer is required to provide special counsel for the insured, the arrangement should assure the special counsel's professional independence. So also, when a corporation and its directors or employees are involved in a controversy in which they have conflicting interests, the corporation may provide funds for separate legal representation of the directors or employees, if the clients consent after consultation and the arrangement ensures the lawyer's professional independence.

Other Conflict Situations

Conflicts of interest in contexts other than litigation sometimes may be difficult to assess. Relevant factors in determining whether there is potential for adverse effect include the duration and intimacy of the lawyer's relationship with the client or clients involved, the functions being performed by the lawyer, the likelihood that actual conflict will arise and the likely prejudice to the client from the conflict if it does arise. The question is often one of proximity and degree.

For example, a lawyer may not represent multiple parties to a negotiation whose interests are fundamentally antagonistic to each other, but common representation is permissible where the clients are generally aligned in interest even though there is some difference of interest among them.

Conflict questions may also arise in estate planning and estate administration. A lawyer may be called upon to prepare wills for several family members, such as husband and wife, and, depending upon the circumstances, a conflict of interest may arise. In estate administration the identity of the client may be unclear under the law of a particular jurisdiction. Under one view, the client is the fiduciary; under another view the client is the estate or trust, including its beneficiaries. The lawyer should make clear the relationship to the parties involved.

A lawyer for a corporation or other organization who is also a member of its board of directors should determine whether the responsibilities of the two roles may conflict. The lawyer may be called on to advise the corporation in matters involving actions of the directors. Consideration should be given to the frequency with which such situations may arise, the potential intensity of the conflict, the effect of the lawyer's resignation from the board and the possibility of the corporation's obtaining legal advice from another lawyer in such situations. If there is material risk that the dual role will compromise the lawyer's independence of professional judgment, the lawyer should not serve as a director.

Conflict Charged by an Opposing Party

Resolving questions of conflict of interest is primarily the responsibility of the lawyer undertaking the representation. In litigation, a court may raise the question when there is reason to infer that the lawyer has neglected the responsibility. In a criminal case, inquiry by the court is generally required when a lawyer represents multiple defendants. Where the conflict is such as clearly to call in question the fair or efficient administration of justice, opposing counsel may properly raise the question. Such an objection should be viewed with caution, however, for it can be misused as a technique of harassment. See Scope.

Annotations

Cases

Failure to refuse to accept or continue employment when interests of another client impaired independent professional judgment combined with other offenses, justified public censure. **Matter of Croddick,** Op. No. 1877, 602 P2d 406 (Alaska 1979).

Multiple representation does not violate this rule absent likelihood that it will adversely affect lawyer's independent professional judgment. **Disciplinary Matter Involving Frost,** Op. No. 4029, 863 P2d 843 (Alaska 1993).

Mere possibility that lawyer's exercise of independent professional judgment will be adversely affected by acceptance of new employment does not require that offered employment be declined. **Disciplinary Matter Involving Frost,** Op. No. 4029, 863 P2d 843 (Alaska 1993).

Corporate attorney had duty to corporation to disclose fact that he stood to profit from success of company with which corporation became limited partner since attorney's fees owed him by company's founder were dependent on company's profitability. **Cummings v. Sea Lion Corp.,** Op. No. 4416, 924 P2d 1011 (Alaska 1996).

Where potential conflict existed between attorney and former client, Professional Conduct Rule 1.9, not Professional Conduct Rule 1.7, governed the case. **Daniels v. State,** Op. No. 1717, 17 P3d 75 (Alaska App. 2001).

Rule 1.8. Conflict of Interest: Prohibited Transactions.

(a) A lawyer shall not enter into a business transaction with a client or knowingly acquire an ownership, possessory, security or other pecuniary interest adverse to a client unless:

(1) the transaction and terms on which the lawyer acquires the interest are fair and reasonable to the client and are fully disclosed and transmitted in writing to the client in a manner which can be reasonably understood by the client;

(2) the client is given a reasonable opportunity to seek the advice of independent counsel in the transaction; and

(3) the client consents in writing thereto.

(b) A lawyer shall not use information relating to representation of a client to the disadvantage of the client unless the client consents in writing after consultation, except as permitted or required by Rule 1.6 or Rule 3.3.

(c) A lawyer shall not prepare an instrument giving the lawyer or a person related to the lawyer as parent, child, sibling, or spouse any substantial gift from a client, including a testamentary gift, except where the client is related to the donee.

(d) Prior to the conclusion of representation of a client, a lawyer shall not make or negotiate an agreement giving the lawyer literary or media rights to a portrayal or account based in substantial part on information relating to the representation.

(e) A lawyer shall not provide financial assistance to a client in connection with pending or contemplated litigation, except that:

(1) a lawyer may advance court costs and expenses of litigation, the repayment of which may be contingent on the outcome of the matter; and

(2) a lawyer representing an indigent client may pay court costs and expenses of litigation on behalf of the client.

(f) A lawyer shall not accept compensation for representing a client from one other than the client unless:

(1) the client consents after consultation;

(2) there is no interference with the lawyer's independence of professional judgment or with the client-lawyer relationship; and

(3) the client's confidences and secrets are protected as required by Rule 1.6.

(g) A lawyer who represents two or more clients shall not participate in making an aggregate settlement of the claims of or against the clients, or in a criminal case an aggregated agreement as to guilty or nolo contendere pleas, unless each client consents after consultation, including disclosure of the existence and nature of all the claims or pleas involved and of the participation of each person in the settlement.

(h) A lawyer shall not make an agreement prospectively limiting the lawyer's liability to a client for malpractice. A lawyer shall not settle a claim for such liability with an unrepresented client or former client without first advising that person in writing that independent representation is appropriate in connection therewith and providing a reasonable opportunity for that client to seek independent representation.

(i) A lawyer related to another lawyer as parent, child, sibling or spouse shall not represent a client in a representation directly adverse to a person who the lawyer knows is represented by the other lawyer except upon consent by the client after consultation regarding the relationship.

(j) A lawyer shall not acquire a proprietary interest in the cause of action or subject matter of litigation the lawyer is conducting for a client, except that the lawyer may:

(1) acquire a lien granted by law to secure the lawyer's fee or expenses; and

(2) contract with a client for a reasonable contingent fee in a civil case.

(SCO 1123 effective July 15, 1993; amended by SCO 1332 effective January 15, 1999)

ALASKA COMMENT

The Committee concluded that written client consent is required under Rule 1.8 (b) in order to assure that there is sufficient notice to client and that the consent is unequivocal.

The Committee concluded that lawyers should not be able to make an agreement prospectively limiting the lawyer's liability to a client for malpractice.

The Committee concluded that in addition to advising an unrepresented client about the appropriateness of seeking independent counsel, that the lawyer must provide a reasonable opportunity for the client to do so.

See Comment to Rule 1.5 (Terms of Payment).

COMMENT

Transactions Between Client and Lawyer

As a general principle, all transactions between client and lawyer should be fair and reasonable to the client. In such transactions a review by independent counsel on behalf of the client is often advisable. Furthermore, a lawyer may not exploit information relating to the representation to the client's disadvantage. For example, a lawyer who has learned that the client is investing in specific real estate may not, without the client's consent, seek to acquire nearby property where doing so would adversely affect the client's plan for investment. Paragraph (a) does not, however, apply to standard commercial transactions between the lawyer and the client for products or services that the client generally markets to others, for example, banking or brokerage services, medical services, products manufactured or distributed by the client, and utilities services. In such transactions, the lawyer has no advantage in dealing with the client, and the restrictions in paragraph (a) are unnecessary and impracticable.

A lawyer may accept a gift from a client, if the transaction meets general standards of fairness. For example, a simple gift such as a present given at a holiday or as a token of appreciation is permitted. If effectuation of a substantial gift requires preparing a legal instrument such as a will or conveyance, however, the client should have the detached advice that another lawyer can provide. Paragraph (c) recognizes an exception where the client is a relative of the donee or the gift is not substantial.

Literary Rights

An agreement by which a lawyer acquires literary or media rights concerning the conduct of the representation creates a conflict between the interests of the client and the personal interests of the lawyer. Measures suitable in the representation of the client may detract from the publication value of an account of the representation. Paragraph (d) does not prohibit a lawyer representing a client in a transaction concerning literary property from agreeing that the lawyer's fee shall consist of a share in ownership in the property, if the arrangement conforms to Rule 1.5 and paragraph (j).

Person Paying for Lawyer's Services

Paragraph (f) requires disclosure of the fact that the lawyer's services are being paid for by a third party. Such an arrangement must also conform to the requirements of Rule 1.6 concerning confidentiality and Rule 1.7 concerning conflict of interest. Where the client is a class, consent may be obtained on behalf of the class by court-supervised procedure.

Limiting Liability

Paragraph (h) is not intended to apply to customary qualifications and limitations in legal opinions and memoranda.

Family Relationships Between Lawyers

Paragraph (i) applies to related lawyers who are in different firms. Related lawyers in the same firm are governed by Rules 1.7, 1.9, and 1.10. The disqualification stated in Rule 1.8(i) is personal and is not imputed to members of firms with whom the lawyers are associated.

Acquisition of Interest in Litigation

Paragraph (j) states the traditional general rule that lawyers are prohibited from acquiring a proprietary interest in litigation. This general rule, which has its basis in common law champerty and maintenance, is subject to specific exceptions developed in decisional law and continued in these Rules, such as the exception for reasonable contingent fees set forth in Rule 1.5 and the exception for certain advances of the costs of litigation set forth in paragraph (e).

Annotations

Cases

This rule does not permit lawyers to advance living expenses to clients. **Matter of K.A.H.,** Op. No. 5049, 967 P2d 91 (Alaska 1998).

This rule's ban on lawyers advancing living expenses to clients does not unconstitutionally deny or impede access to the courts. **Matter of K.A.H.,** Op. No. 5049, 967 P2d 91 (Alaska 1998).

Rule 1.9. Conflict of Interest: Former Client.

(a) A lawyer who has formerly represented a client in a matter shall not thereafter represent another person in the same or a substantially related matter in which that person's interests are materially adverse to the interests of the former client unless the former client consents after consultation.

(b) A lawyer shall not knowingly represent a person in the same or a substantially related matter in which a firm with which the lawyer formerly was associated had previously represented a client

(1) whose interests are materially adverse to that person; and

(2) about whom the lawyer had acquired information protected by Rules 1.6 and 1.9(c) that is material to the matter; unless the former client consents after consultation.

(c) A lawyer who has formerly represented a client in a matter or whose present or former firm has formerly represented a client in a matter shall not thereafter:

(1) use a confidence or secret relating to the representation to the disadvantage of the former client except as Rule 1.6 or Rule 3.3 would permit or require with respect to a client, or when the confidence or secret has become generally known; or

(2) reveal a confidence or secret relating to the representation except as Rule 1.6 or Rule 3.3 would permit or require with respect to a client.

(SCO 1123 effective July 15, 1993; amended by SCO 1332 effective January 15, 1999)

COMMENT

After termination of a client-lawyer relationship, a lawyer may not represent another client except in conformity with this rule. The principles in Rule 1.7 determine whether the interests of the present and former client are adverse. Thus, a lawyer could not properly seek to rescind on behalf of a new client a contract drafted on behalf of the former client. So also a lawyer who has prosecuted an accused person could not properly represent the accused in a subsequent civil action against the government concerning the same transaction.

The scope of a "matter" for purposes of this rule may depend on the facts of a particular situation or transaction. The lawyer's involvement in a matter can also be a question of degree. When a lawyer has been directly involved in a specific transaction, subsequent representation of other clients with materially adverse interests clearly is prohibited. On the other hand, a lawyer who recurrently handled a type of problem for a former client is not precluded from later representing another client in a wholly distinct problem of that type even though the subsequent representation involves a position adverse to the prior client. Similar considerations can apply to the reassignment of military lawyers between defense and prosecution functions within the same military jurisdiction. The underlying question is whether the lawyer was so involved in the matter that the subsequent representation can be justly regarded as a changing of sides in the matter in question.

Lawyers Moving Between Firms

When lawyers have been associated in a firm but then end their association, the question of whether a lawyer should undertake representation is more complicated. There are several competing considerations. First, the client previously represented by the former firm must be reasonably assured that the principle of loyalty to the client is not compromised. Second, the rule should not be so broadly cast as to preclude other persons from having reasonable choice of legal counsel. Third, the rule should not unreasonably hamper lawyers from forming new associations and taking on new clients after having left a previous association. In this connection, it should be recognized that today many lawyers practice in firms, that many lawyers to some degree limit their practice to one field or another, and that many move from one association to another several times in their careers. If the concept of imputation were applied with unqualified rigor, the result would be radical curtailment of the opportunity of lawyers to move from one practice setting to another and of the opportunity of clients to change counsel.

Reconciliation of these competing principles in the past has been attempted under two rubrics. One approach has been to seek per se rules of disqualification. For example, it has been held that a partner in a law firm is conclusively presumed to have access to all confidences concerning all clients of the firm. Under the analysis, if a lawyer has been a partner in one law firm and then becomes a partner in another law firm, there is a presumption that all confidences known by a partner in the first firm are known to all partners in the second firm. This presumption might properly be applied in some circumstances, especially where the client has been extensively represented, but may be unrealistic where the client was represented only for limited purposes. Furthermore, such a rigid rule exaggerates the difference between a partner and an associate in modern law firms.

The other rubric formerly used for dealing with vicarious disqualification is the appearance of impropriety proscribed in Canon 9 of the ABA Model Code of Professional Responsibility. This rubric has a twofold problem. First, the appearance of impropriety can be taken to include any new client-lawyer relationship that might make a former client feel anxious. If that meaning were adopted, disqualification would become little more than a question of subjective judgment by the former client. Second, since "impropriety" is undefined, the term "appearance of impropriety" is question-begging. It therefore has to be recognized that the problem of disqualification cannot be properly resolved either by simple analogy to a lawyer practicing alone or by the very general concept of appearance of impropriety.

A rule based on a functional analysis is more appropriate for determining the question of vicarious disqualification. Two functions are involved: preserving confidentiality and avoiding positions adverse to a client.

Confidentiality

Preserving confidentiality is a question of access to information. Access to information, in turn, is essentially a question of fact in particular circumstances, aided by inferences, deductions or working presumptions that reasonably may be made about the way in which lawyers work together. A lawyer may have general access to files of all clients of a law firm and may regularly participate in discussions of their affairs; it should be inferred that such a lawyer in fact is privy to all information about all the firm's clients. In contrast, another lawyer may have access to the files of only a limited number of clients and participate in discussion of the affairs of no other clients; in the absence of information to the contrary, it should be inferred that such a lawyer in fact is privy to information about the clients actually served but not those of other clients.

Application of paragraph (b) depends on a situation's particular facts. In any such inquiry, the burden of proof should rest upon the firm whose disqualification is sought.

Paragraph (b) operates to disqualify the lawyer only when the lawyer involved has actual knowledge of information protected by Rules 1.6 and 1.9(b). Thus, if a lawyer while with one firm acquired no knowledge or information relating to a particular client of the firm, and that lawyer later joined another firm, neither the lawyer individually nor the second firm is disqualified from representing another client in the same or a related matter even though the interests of the two clients conflict. See Rule 1.10(b) for the restrictions on a firm once a lawyer has terminated association with the firm.

Independent of the question of disqualification of a firm, a lawyer changing professional association has a continuing duty to preserve confidentiality of information about a client formerly represented. See Rules 1.6 and 1.9.

Adverse Positions

The second aspect of loyalty to client is the lawyer's obligation to decline subsequent representations involving positions adverse to a former client arising in substantially related matters. This obligation requires abstention from adverse representation by the individual lawyer involved, but does not properly entail abstention of other lawyers through imputed disqualification. Hence, this aspect of the problem is governed by Rule 1.9(a). Thus, if a lawyer left one firm for another, the new affiliation would not preclude the firms involved from continuing to represent clients with adverse interests in the same or related matters, so long as the conditions of paragraphs (b) and (c) concerning confidentiality have been met.

Information acquired by the lawyer in the course of representing a client may not subsequently be used by the lawyer to the disadvantage of the client. However, the fact that a lawyer has once served a client does not preclude the lawyer from using generally known information about that client when later representing another client.

Disqualification from subsequent representation is for the protection of clients and can be waived by them. A waiver is effective only if there is disclosure of the circumstances, including the lawyer's intended role in behalf of the new client.

With regard to an opposing party's raising a question of conflict of interest, see Comment to Rule 1.7. With regard to disqualification of a firm with which a lawyer is associated, see Rule 1.10.

Annotations

Cases

An attorney may not represent a third party against a former client where there exists a substantial possibility that knowledge gained by him in the earlier professional relationship can be used against the former client, or where the subject matter of his present undertaking his a substantial relationship to that of his prior representation. **Aleut Corp. v. McGarvey,** Op. No. 1544, 573 P2d 473 (Alaska 1978).

Attorney was involved in a conflict of interest when he represented his wife in a personal injury action against former client arising out of the same automobile accident for which he defended the former client on a drunk driving charge. **Burrell v. Disciplinary Bd. of Alaska Bar,** Op. No. 2948, 702 P2d 240 (Alaska 1985).

As general rule, duty is owed on part of attorney to former client to avoid representation if either (a) there is potential that confidential information may be revealed or (b) subject matters are substantially related and attorney is taking position directly adverse to client's position in former representation. **Griffith v. Taylor,** Op. No. 4811, 937 P2d 297 (Alaska 1997).

When attorney performs purely ministerial or clerical function for client and subsequently takes on another case which requires him or her to take position materially adverse to work performed for first client, there is no substantial relationship between the two matters; therefore, scrivener's exception applies, and attorney can forgo receiving consent of former client without violating this rule. **Griffith v. Taylor,** Op. No. 4811, 937 P2d 297 (Alaska 1997).

Where potential conflict existed between attorney and former client, Professional Conduct Rule 1.9, not Professional Conduct Rule 1.7, governed the case. **Daniels v. State,** Op. No. 1717, 17 P3d 75 (Alaska App. 2001).

Where attorney for murder defendant planned to suggest that a woman he represented ten years earlier in an unrelated assault prosecution actually committed the murder, trial court erred in disqualifying attorney from the case, since under the circumstances his continued participation in the case would not violate his duty toward his current client or his duty toward his former client, nor would his participation adversely affect the integrity of the proceedings so as to trigger the trial court's independent authority to order his disqualification. **Daniels v. State,** Op. No. 1717, 17 P3d 75 (Alaska App. 2001).

Plaintiff was an attorney's "former client," even though the attorney was not retained by plaintiff; the substantial relationship test was met, because a dispute regarding the conveyance of a house by plaintiff to defendant was discussed between plaintiff and the attorney, who was subsequently hired by defendant. **Marx v. Benzel,** Op. No. 44, 66 P.3d 735 (Alaska 2003).

Where the father's sexual assault of minor conviction clearly exerted some influence over the trial court's decision to terminate his parental rights, and the mother's attorney in the termination proceeding had represented the father in his prior sexual assault conviction, the attorney's prior representation of the father was substantially related to the termination proceeding. **Richard B. v. State,** 71 P.3d 811 (Alaska 2003).

Rule 1.10. Imputed Disqualification: General Rule.

(a) While lawyers are associated in a firm, none of them shall knowingly represent a client when any one of them practicing alone would be prohibited from doing so by Rules 1.7, 1.8(c), 1.9 or 2.2.

(b) When a lawyer has terminated an association with a firm, the firm is not prohibited from thereafter representing a person with interests materially adverse to those of a client represented by the formerly associated lawyer and not currently represented by the firm, unless:

(1) the matter is the same or substantially related to that in which the formerly associated lawyer represented the client; and

(2) any lawyer remaining in the firm has information protected by Rules 1.6 or 1.9(c) that is material to the matter, or the firm retains records containing such information.

(c) A disqualification prescribed by this rule may be waived by the affected client under the conditions stated in Rule 1.7.

(SCO 1123 effective July 15, 1993)

ALASKA COMMENT

The term "firm" is defined in Rule 9.1(i).

The Committee has voted to add language to subparagraph (b)(2) which disqualifies firms that retain records containing confidential information, as well as firms where actual members have such confidential information. The Committee felt that the possibility for misuse of confidential information could also arise when old files are unearthed for the purpose of probing them and therefore a rule of disqualification should apply in those situations also. However, the Committee wishes to stress that disqualification only arises when the matter at hand is the same or substantially related to the matter in which the former client was represented; the Committee expects the term "substantially related" to be interpreted in a realistic, narrow fashion, in light of the policy considerations listed in the section labeled "Lawyers Moving Between Firms."

COMMENT

Definition of "Firm"

For purposes of the rules of professional conduct, the term "firm" includes lawyers in a private firm, and lawyers employed in the legal department of a corporation or other organization, or in a legal services organization. Whether two or more lawyers constitute a firm within this definition can depend on the specific facts. For example, two practitioners who share office space and occasionally consult or assist each other ordinarily would not be regarded as constituting a firm. However, if they present themselves to the public in a way suggesting that they are a firm or conduct themselves as a firm, they should be regarded as a firm for purposes of the rules. The terms of any formal agreement between associated lawyers are relevant in determining whether they are a firm, as is the fact that they have mutual access to confidential information concerning the clients they serve. Furthermore, it is relevant in doubtful cases to consider the underlying purpose of the rule that is involved. A group of lawyers could be regarded as a firm for purposes of the rule that the same lawyer should not represent opposing parties in litigation, while it might not be so regarded for purposes of the rule that information acquired by one lawyer is attributed to the other.

With respect to the law department of an organization, there is ordinarily no question that the members of the department constitute a firm within the meaning of the rules of professional conduct. However, there can be uncertainty as to the identity of the client. For example, it may not be clear whether the law department of a corporation represents a subsidiary or an affiliated corporation, as well as the corporation by which the members of the department are directly employed. A similar question can arise concerning an unincorporated association and its local affiliates.

Similar questions can also arise with respect to lawyers in legal aid. Lawyers employed in the same unit of a legal service organization constitute a firm, but not necessarily those employed in separate units. As in the case of independent practitioners, whether the lawyers should be treated as associated with each other can depend on the particular rule that is involved, and on the specific facts of the situation.

Where a lawyer has joined a private firm after having represented the government, the situation is governed by Rule 1.11(a) and (b); where a lawyer represents the government after having served private clients, the situation is governed by Rule 1.11(c)(1). The individual lawyer involved is bound by the rules generally, including Rules 1.6, 1.7, and 1.9.

Different provisions are thus made for movement of a lawyer from one private firm to another and for movement of a lawyer between a private firm and the government. The government is entitled to protection of its client confidences and, therefore, to the protections provided in Rules 1.6, 1.9, and 1.11. However, if the more extensive disqualification in Rule 1.10 were applied to former government lawyers, the potential effect on the government would be unduly burdensome. The government deals with all private citizens and organizations and, thus, has a much wider circle of adverse legal interests than does any private law firm. In these circumstances, the government's recruitment of lawyers would be seriously impaired if Rule 1.10 were applied to the government. On balance, therefore, the government is better served in the long run by the protections stated in Rule 1.11.

Principles of Imputed Disqualification

The rule of imputed disqualification stated in paragraph (a) gives effect to the principle of loyalty to the client as it applies to lawyers who practice in a law firm. Such situations can be considered from the premise that a firm of lawyers is essentially one lawyer for purposes of the rules governing loyalty to the client, or from the premise that each lawyer is vicariously bound by the obligation of loyalty owned by each lawyer with whom the lawyer is associated. Paragraph (a) operates only among the lawyers currently associated in a firm. When a lawyer moves from one firm to another, the situation is governed by Rules 1.9(b) and 1.10(b).

Rule 1.11. Successive Government and Private Employment.

(a) Except as law may otherwise expressly permit, a lawyer shall not represent a private client in connection with a matter in which the lawyer participated personally and substantially as a public officer or employee, unless the appropriate government agency consents after consultation. No lawyer in a firm with which that lawyer is associated may knowingly undertake or continue representation in such a matter unless:

(1) the disqualified lawyer is screened from any participation in the matter and is apportioned no part of the fee therefrom; and

(2) written notice is promptly given to the appropriate government agency to enable it to ascertain compliance with the provisions of this rule.

(b) Except as law may otherwise expressly permit, a lawyer having information that the lawyer knows is confidential government information about a person acquired when the lawyer was a public officer or employee, may not represent a private client whose interests are adverse to that person in a matter in which the information could be used to the material disadvantage of that person. A firm with which that lawyer is associated may undertake or continue representation in the matter only if the disqualified lawyer is screened from any participation in the matter and is apportioned no part of the fee therefrom.

(c) Except as law may otherwise expressly permit, a lawyer serving as a public officer or employee shall not:

(1) participate in a matter in which the lawyer participated personally and substantially while in private practice or nongovernmental employment, unless under applicable law no one is, or by lawful delegation may be, authorized to act in the lawyer's stead in the matter; or

(2) negotiate for private employment with any person who is involved as a party or as attorney for a party in a matter in which the lawyer is participating personally and substantially, except that a lawyer serving as a law clerk to a judge, other adjudicative officer or arbitrator may negotiate for private employment as permitted by Rule 1.12(b) and subject to the conditions stated in Rule 1.12(b).

(d) As used in this Rule, the term "matter" includes:

(1) any judicial or other proceeding, application, request for a ruling or other determination, transaction, claim, controversy, investigation, charge, accusation, arrest or other particular matter involving a specific party or parties; and

(2) any other matter covered by the conflict of interest rules of the appropriate government agency.

(e) As used in this Rule, the term "confidential government information" means information which has been obtained under governmental authority and which, at the time this rule is applied, the government is prohibited by law from disclosing to the public or has a legal privilege not to disclose, and which is not otherwise available to the public.

(SCO 1123 effective July 15, 1993)

ALASKA COMMENT

"Screening" is a procedure used to prevent intrafirm exchange of confidential information. Courts and commentators generally recognize two screening methods - the "Chinese Wall" and the "cone of silence." When a firm establishes a Chinese Wall, the tainted lawyer is usually separated, both physically and organizationally, from attorneys working on the conflicting matter. The attorney is generally prohibited from having any connection with the case, from receiving any share of the fees attributable to it, and from having access to the files. Other members of the firm are not allowed to discuss the case or share documents with the attorney. Under the "cone of silence" method, the tainted attorney simply agrees not to share information about prior clients with members of the new firm. For a discussion of the "cone of silence" method, see **Nemours Foundation v. Gilbane, Aetna, Federal Insurance Co.**, 632 F. Supp. 418, 428 (D. Del. 1986).

COMMENT

This rule prevents a lawyer from exploiting public office for the advantage of a private client. It is a counterpart of Rule 1.10(b), which applies to lawyers moving from one firm to another.

A lawyer representing a government agency, whether employed or specially retained by the government, is subject to the Rules of Professional Conduct, including the prohibition against representing adverse interests stated in Rule 1.7 and the protections afforded former clients in Rule 1.9. In addition, such a lawyer is subject to Rule 1.11 and to statutes and government regulations regarding conflict of interest. Such statutes and regulations may circumscribe the extent to which the government agency may give consent under this Rule.

Where the successive clients are a public agency and a private client, the risk exists that power or discretion vested in public authority might be used for the special benefit of a private client. A lawyer should not be in a position where benefit to a private client might affect performance of the lawyer's professional functions on behalf of public authority. Also, unfair advantage could accrue to the private client by reason of access to confidential government information about the client's adversary obtainable only through the lawyer's government service. However, the rules governing lawyers presently or formerly employed by a government agency should not be so restrictive as to inhibit transfer of employment to and from the government. The government has a legitimate need to attract qualified lawyers as well as to maintain high ethical standards. The provisions for screening and waiver are necessary to prevent the disqualification rule from imposing to severe a deterrent against entering public service.

When the client is an agency of one government, that agency should be treated as a private client for purposes of this rule if the lawyer thereafter represents an agency of another government, as when a lawyer represents a city and subsequently is employed by a federal agency.

Paragraphs (a)(1) and (b) do not prohibit a lawyer from receiving a salary or partnership share established by prior independent agreement. They prohibit directly relating the attorney's compensation to the fee in the matter in which the lawyer is disqualified.

Paragraph (a)(2) does not require that a lawyer give notice to the government agency at a time when premature disclosure would injure the client; a requirement for premature disclosure might preclude engagement of the lawyer. Such notice is, however, required to be given as soon as practicable in order that the government agency will have a reasonable opportunity to ascertain that the lawyer is complying with Rule 1.11 and to take appropriate action if it believes the lawyer is not complying.

Paragraph (b) operates only when the lawyer in question has knowledge of the information, which means actual knowledge; it does not operate with respect to information that merely could be imputed to the lawyer.

Paragraphs (a) and (c) do not prohibit a lawyer from jointly representing a private party and a government agency when doing so is permitted by Rule 1.7 and is not otherwise prohibited by law.

Paragraph (c) does not disqualify other lawyers in the agency with which the lawyer in question has become associated.

Annotations

Cases

This rule allows government attorneys to participate in matters from which other members of the same agency are disqualified. **Skvorc v. State Personnel Board,** Op. No. 5246, 996 P2d 1192 (Alaska 2000).

Rule 1.12. Former Judge or Arbitrator.

(a) Except as stated in paragraph (d), a lawyer shall not represent anyone in connection with a matter in which the lawyer participated personally and substantially as a judge or other adjudicative officer, arbitrator or law clerk to such a person, unless all parties to the proceeding consent after consultation.

(b) A lawyer shall not negotiate for employment with any person who is involved as a party or as attorney for a party in a matter in which the lawyer is participating personally and substantially as a judge or other adjudicative officer, or arbitrator. A lawyer serving as a law clerk to a judge, other adjudicative officer or arbitrator may negotiate for employment with a party or attorney involved in a matter in which the clerk is participating personally and substantially, but only after the clerk has notified the judge, other adjudicative officer or arbitrator.

(c) If a lawyer is disqualified by paragraph (a), no lawyer in a firm with which that lawyer is associated may knowingly undertake or continue representation in the matter unless:

(1) the disqualified lawyer is screened from any participation in the matter and is apportioned no part of the fee therefrom; and

(2) written notice is promptly given to the appropriate tribunal to enable it to ascertain compliance with the provisions of this rule.

(d) An arbitrator selected as a partisan of a party in a multimember arbitration panel is not prohibited from subsequently representing that party.

(SCO 1123 effective July 15, 1993)

COMMENT

This Rule generally parallels Rule 1.11. The term "personally and substantially" signifies that a judge who was a member of a multimember court, and thereafter left judicial office to practice law, is not prohibited from representing a client in a matter pending in the court, but in which the former judge did not participate. So also the fact that a former judge exercised administrative responsibility in a court does not prevent the former judge from acting as a lawyer in a matter where the judge had previously exercised remote or incidental administrative responsibility that did not affect the merits. Compare the Comment to Rule 1.11. The term "adjudicative officer" includes such officials as judges pro tempore, referees, special masters, hearing officers and other parajudicial officers, and also lawyers who serve as part-time judges. Compliance Canons A(2), B(2) and C of the Code of Judicial Conduct provide that a part-time judge, judge pro tempore or retired judge recalled to active service, may not "act as a lawyer in any proceeding in which he served as a judge or in any other proceeding related thereto." Although phrased differently from this Rule, those Rules correspond in meaning.

Annotations

Cases

Former law clerk's participation in case that was pending at time of his employment with the court was governed by this rule rather than the blanket prohibition of Appellate Rule 104. **Bradley v. State,** Op. No. 1145, 535 P2d 1031 (Alaska 1975).

A former law clerk can appear as an attorney in a case that was pending during his employment with the court if either (1) the former law clerk did not participate personally and substantially in the case or (2) all parties to the proceeding consent to the former law clerk's participation after consultation. **Bradley v. State,** Op. No. 1145, 535 P2d 1031 (Alaska 1975).

When a former law clerk desires to appear as an attorney in a case that was pending at the time of his employment with the court, the law clerk must file a motion seeking permission to appear, and the law clerk must support the motion with an affidavit that discloses all pertinent facts, including the positions of the other parties to the case, if known. **Bradley v. State,** Op. No. 1145, 535 P2d 1031 (Alaska 1975).

Rule 1.13. Organization as Client.

(a) Except as hereinafter provided, a lawyer employed or retained by an organization represents the organization acting through its duly authorized constituents.

(b) If a lawyer for an organization knows that an officer, employee or other person associated with the organization is engaged in action, intends to act or refuses to act in a matter related to the representation that is a violation of a legal obligation to the organization, or a violation of law which reasonably might be imputed to the organization, and is likely to result in substantial injury to the organization, the lawyer shall proceed as is reasonably necessary in the best interest of the organization. In determining how to proceed, the lawyer shall give due consideration to the seriousness of the violation and its consequences, the scope and nature of the lawyer's representation, the responsibility in the organization and the apparent motivation of the person involved, the policies of the organization concerning such matters and any other relevant considerations. Any measures taken shall be designed to minimize disruption of the organization and the risk of revealing a confidence or secret relating to the representation to persons outside the organization. Such measures may include among others:

(1) asking for reconsideration of the matter;

(2) advising that a separate legal opinion on the matter be sought for presentation to appropriate authority in the organization; and

(3) referring the matter to higher authority in the organization, including, if warranted by the seriousness of the matter, referral to the highest authority that can act in behalf of the organization as determined by applicable law.

(c) If, despite the lawyer's efforts in accordance with paragraph (b), the highest authority that can act on behalf of the organization insists upon action, or a refusal to act, that is clearly a violation of law and is likely to result in substantial injury to the organization, the lawyer may resign in accordance with Rule 1.16, and shall act in accordance with the provisions of Rule 1.6.

(d) In dealing with an organization's directors, officers, employees, members, shareholders or other constituents, a lawyer shall explain the identity of the client and that the lawyer's first duty is to the client when it is apparent that the organization's interests are adverse to those of the constituents with whom the lawyer is dealing.

(e) A lawyer representing an organization may also represent any of its directors, officers, employees, members, shareholders or other constituents, subject to the provisions of Rule 1.7. If the organization's consent to the dual representation is required by Rule 1.7, the consent shall be given by an appropriate official of the organization other than the individual who is to be represented, or by the shareholders.

(SCO 1123 effective July 15, 1993; amended by SCO 1332 effective January 15, 1999)

ALASKA COMMENT

The additional phrase "except as otherwise hereinafter provided" was added to paragraph (a) in order to emphasize that the lawyer's first duty is to the organization and not to the organization's directors, officers, employees, members, shareholders or other constituents.

In paragraph (c) the Committee added the phrase "in accordance with the provisions of Rule 1.6" in order to specifically delineate the lawyer's options when faced with an act or refusal to act which is clearly in violation of the law and likely to result in substantial injury to the organization.

Paragraph (d) was amended to more clearly delineate the lawyer's obligation to clearly inform the organization's constituents with whom the lawyer is dealing that the lawyer's ultimate loyalty is to the organization.

COMMENT

The Entity as the Client

An organizational client is a legal entity, but it cannot act except through its officers, directors, employees, shareholders and other constituents.

Officers, directors, employees and shareholders are the constituents of the corporate organizational client. The duties defined in this Comment apply equally to unincorporated associations. "Other constituents" as used in this Comment means the positions equivalent to officers, directors, employees and shareholders held by persons acting for organizational clients that are not corporations.

When one of the constituents of an organizational client communicates with the organization's lawyer in that person's organizational capacity, the communication is protected by Rule 1.6. Thus, by way of example, if an organizational client requests its lawyer to investigate allegations of wrongdoing, interviews made in the course of that investigation between the lawyer and the client's employees or other constituents are covered by Rule 1.6. This does not mean, however, that constituents of an organizational client are the clients of the lawyer. The lawyer may not disclose to such constituents a confidence or secret relating to the representation except for disclosures explicitly or impliedly authorized by the organizational client in order to carry out the representation or as otherwise permitted by Rule 1.6.

When constituents of the organization make decisions for it, the decisions ordinarily must be accepted by the lawyer even if their utility or prudence is doubtful. Decisions concerning policy and operations, including ones entailing serious risk, are not as such in the lawyer's province. However, different considerations arise when the lawyer knows that the organization may be substantially injured by action of a constituent that is in violation of law. In such a circumstance, it may be reasonably necessary for the lawyer to ask the constituent to reconsider the matter. If that fails, or if the matter is of sufficient seriousness and importance to the organization, it may be reasonably necessary for the lawyer to take steps to have the matter reviewed by a higher authority in the organization. Clear justification should exist for seeking review over the head of the constituent normally responsible for it. The stated policy of the organization may define circumstances and prescribe channels for such review, and a lawyer should encourage the formulation of such a policy. Even in the absence of organization policy, however, the lawyer may have an obligation to refer a matter to higher authority, depending on the seriousness of the matter and whether the constituent in question has apparent motives to act at variance with the organization's interest. Review by the chief executive officer or by the board of directors may be required when the matter is of importance commensurate with their authority. At some point it may be useful or essential to obtain an independent legal opinion.

In an extreme case, it may be reasonably necessary for the lawyer to refer the matter to the organization's highest authority. Ordinarily, that is the board of directors or similar governing body. However, applicable law may prescribe that under certain conditions highest authority reposes elsewhere; for example, in the independent directors of a corporation.

Relation to Other Rules

The authority and responsibility provided in paragraph (b) are concurrent with the authority and responsibility provided in other rules. In particular, this rule does not limit or expand the lawyer's responsibility under Rules 1.6, 1.8 and 1.16, 3.3 or 4.1. If the lawyer's services are being used by an organization to further a crime or fraud by the organization, Rule 1.2(d) can be applicable.

Government Agency

The duty defined in this rule applies to governmental organizations. However, when the client is a governmental organization, a different balance may be appropriate between maintaining confidentiality and assuring that the wrongful official act is prevented or rectified, for public business is involved. In addition, duties of lawyers employed by the government or lawyers in military service may be defined by statutes and regulation. Therefore, defining precisely the identity of the client and prescribing the resulting obligations of such lawyers may be more difficult in the government context. Although in some circumstances the client may be a specific agency, it is generally the government as a whole. For example, if the action or failure to act involves the head of a bureau, either the department of which the bureau is a part or the government as a whole may be the client for purpose of this rule. Moreover, in a matter involving the conduct of government officials, a government lawyer may have authority to question such conduct more extensively than that of a lawyer for a private organization in similar circumstances. This Rule does not limit that authority. See note on Scope.

Clarifying the Lawyer's Role

There are times when the organization's interest may be or become adverse to those of one or more of its constituents. In such circumstances the lawyer should advise any constituent, whose interest the lawyer finds adverse to that of the organization of the conflict or potential conflict of interest, that the lawyer cannot represent such constituent, and that such person may wish to obtain independent representation. Care must be taken to assure that the individual understands that, when there is such adversity of interest, the lawyer for the organization cannot provide legal representation for that constituent individual, and that discussions between the lawyer for the organization and the individual may not be privileged based on the facts of the case.

Dual Representation

Paragraph (e) recognizes that a lawyer for an organization may also represent a principal officer or major shareholder.

Derivative Actions

Under generally prevailing law, the shareholders or members of a corporation may bring suit to compel the directors to perform their legal obligations in the supervision of the organization. Members of unincorporated associations have essentially the same right. Such an action may be brought nominally by the organization, but usually is, in fact, a legal controversy over management of the organization.

The question can arise whether counsel for the organization may defend such an action. The proposition that the organization is the lawyer's client does not alone resolve the issue. Most derivative actions are a normal incident of an organization's affairs, to be defended by the organization's lawyer like any other suit. However, if the claim involves serious charges of wrongdoing by those in control of the organization, a conflict may arise between the lawyer's duty to the organization and the lawyer's relationship with the board. In those circumstances, Rule 1.7 governs who should represent the directors and the organization.

Rule 1.14. Client Under a Disability.

(a) When a client's ability to make adequately considered decisions in connection with the representation is impaired, whether because of minority, mental disability or for some other reason, the lawyer shall, as far as reasonably possible, maintain a normal client-lawyer relationship with the client.

(b) A lawyer may seek the appointment of a guardian or take other protective action with respect to a client only when the lawyer reasonably believes that the client cannot adequately act in the client's own interest.

(SCO 1123 effective July 15, 1993)

COMMENT

The normal client-lawyer relationship is based on the assumption that the client, when properly advised and assisted, is capable of making decisions about important matters. When the client is a minor or suffers from a mental disorder or disability, however, maintaining the ordinary client-lawyer relationship may not be possible in all respects. In particular, an incapacitated person may have no power to make legally binding decisions. Nevertheless, a client lacking legal competence often has the ability to understand, deliberate upon, and reach conclusions about matters affecting the client's own well-being. Furthermore, to an increasing extent the law recognizes intermediate degrees of competence. For example, children as young as five or six years of age, and certainly those of ten or twelve, are regarded as having opinions that are entitled to weight in legal proceedings concerning their custody. So also, it is recognized that some persons of advanced age can be quite capable of handling routine financial matters while needing special legal protection concerning major transactions.

The fact that a client suffers a disability does not diminish the lawyer's obligation to treat the client with attention and respect. If the person has no guardian or legal representative, the lawyer often must act as de facto guardian. Even if the person does have a legal representative, the lawyer should as far as possible accord the represented person the status of client, particularly in maintaining communication.

If a legal representative has already been appointed for the client, the lawyer should ordinarily look to the representative for decisions on behalf of the client. If a legal representative has not been appointed, the lawyer should see to such an appointment where it would serve the client's best interest. Thus, if a disabled client has substantial property that should be sold for the client's benefit, effective completion of the transaction ordinarily requires appointment of a legal representative. In many circumstances, however, appointment of a legal representative may be expensive or traumatic for the client. Evaluation of these considerations is a matter of professional judgment on the lawyer's part.

If the lawyer represents the guardian as distinct from the ward, and is aware that the guardian is acting adversely to the ward's interest, the lawyer may have an obligation to prevent or rectify the guardian's misconduct. See Rule 1.2(d).

Disclosure of the Client's Condition

Rules of procedure in litigation generally provide that minors or persons suffering mental disability shall be represented by a guardian or next friend if they do not have a general guardian. However, disclosure of the client's disability can adversely affect the client's interests. For example, raising the question of disability could, in some circumstances, lead to proceedings for involuntary commitment. The lawyer's position in such cases is an unavoidably difficult one. The lawyer may seek guidance from an appropriate diagnostician.

Annotations

Cases

It was error for court to impose costs of conservatorship on law firm that petitioned court for appointment of conservator for its client. **In re S.H.,** Op. No. 5163, 987 P2d 735 (Alaska 1999).

Law firm representing client in lawsuit against client's former employer did not violate professional responsibilities or duties owed to client by petitioning trial court to appoint conservator for client whom it believed to be incapable of making rational decisions about settlement of lawsuit. **In re S.H.,** Op. No.5163, 987 P2d 735 (Alaska 1999).

Rule 1.15. Safekeeping Property.

(a) A lawyer shall hold property of clients or third persons that is in a lawyer's possession in connection with a representation separate from the lawyer's own property. Funds shall be kept in a separate account maintained in the state where the lawyer's office is situated, or elsewhere with the consent of the client or third person. Other property shall be identified as such and appropriately safeguarded. Complete records of such account funds and other property shall be kept by the lawyer and shall be preserved for a period of six years after termination of the representation.

(b) Upon receiving funds or other property in which a client or third person has an interest, a lawyer shall promptly notify the client or third person. Except as stated in this rule or otherwise permitted by law or by agreement with the client, a lawyer shall promptly deliver to the client or third person any funds or other property that the client or third person is entitled to receive and, upon request by the client or third person, shall promptly render a full accounting regarding such property.

(c) When in the course of representation a lawyer is in possession of property in which both the lawyer and another person claim interests, the property shall be kept separate by the lawyer until there is an accounting and severance of their interests. If a dispute arises concerning their respective interests, the portion in dispute shall be kept separate by the lawyer until the dispute is resolved.

(d) Unless an election not to participate is submitted in accordance with the procedure set forth in paragraph (e), a lawyer or law firm shall establish and maintain an interest bearing insured depository account into which must be deposited funds of clients which are nominal in amount or are expected to be held for a short period of time, but only in compliance with the following provisions:

(1) No earnings from such account shall be made available to the lawyer or law firm and the lawyer or law firm shall have no right or claim to such earnings.

(2) Only funds of clients which are nominal in amount or

are expected to be held for a short period of time may be deposited in such account. Funds which reasonably may be expected to generate in excess of one hundred dollars interest may not be deposited in such account.

(3) The depository institution shall be directed by the lawyer or law firm establishing such account:

(a) To remit earnings from such account, net of any service charges or fees, as computed in accordance with the institution's standard accounting practice to the Alaska Bar Foundation, Inc., at least quarter-annually; and

(b) To transmit with each remittance of earnings a statement showing the name of the lawyer or law firm on whose account the remittance is sent and the rate of interest applied, with a copy of such statement to such lawyer or law firm.

(4) The lawyer or law firm shall review the account at reasonable intervals to determine if changed circumstances required further action with respect to the funds of any client.

(e) A lawyer shall indicate on the lawyer's annual bar dues notice whether the lawyer or the lawyer's law firm: 1) elects to maintain the account described in paragraph (d); 2) elects not to maintain the account described in paragraph (d); or 3) does not maintain a trust account. A lawyer or law firm who wishes to change a previous election may do so at any time by notifying the Alaska Bar Association in writing.

(SCO 1123 effective July 15, 1993; amended by SCO 1539 effective October 15, 2004; and by SCO 1584 effective October 15, 2005)

COMMENT

A lawyer should hold property of others with the care required of a professional fiduciary. Securities should be kept in a safe deposit box, except when some other form of safekeeping is warranted by special circumstances. All property which is the property of clients or third persons should be kept separate from the lawyer's business and personal property and, if monies, in one or more trust accounts. Separate trust accounts may be warranted when administering estate monies or acting in similar fiduciary capacities.

Lawyers often receive funds from third parties from which the lawyer's fee will be paid. If there is risk that the client may divert the funds without paying the fee, the lawyer is not required to remit the portion from which the fee is to be paid. However, a lawyer may not hold funds to coerce a client into accepting the lawyer's contention. The disputed portion of the funds should be kept in trust and the lawyer should suggest means for prompt resolution of the dispute, such as arbitration. The undisputed portion of the funds shall be promptly distributed.

Third parties, such as a client's creditors, may have just claims against funds or other property in a lawyer's custody. A lawyer may have a duty under applicable law to protect such third party claims against wrongful interference by the client, and accordingly may refuse to surrender the property to the client. However, a lawyer should not unilaterally assume to arbitrate a dispute between the client and the third party.

The obligations of a lawyer under this Rule are independent of those arising from activity other than rendering legal services. For example, a lawyer who serves as an escrow agent is governed by the applicable law relating to fiduciaries even though the lawyer does not render legal services in the transaction.

A "client's security fund" provides a means through the collective efforts of the bar to reimburse persons who have lost money or property as a result of dishonest conduct of a lawyer. Where such a fund has been established, a lawyer should participate.

Annotations

Cases

Attorney's 90-day suspension for knowingly disobeying a court order was proper where, although the attorney believed that this rule required him to return client funds instead of transferring the funds to opposing counsel in lieu of a superseadas bond, Alaska R. Prof. Conduct 3.4(c) required him to follow court order regarding disposition of the funds or "openly refuse" to follow it; furthermore, Alaska R. Prof. Conduct 1.2(e) indicates that a client's wishes or interests do not supersede a lawyer's ethical obligations. **In re Ford,** Op. No. 2000, 128 P.3d 178 (Alaska 2006).

Rule 1.16. Declining or Terminating Representation.

(a) Except as stated in paragraph (c), a lawyer shall not represent a client or, where representation has commenced, shall withdraw from the representation of a client if:

(1) the representation will result in violation of the rules of professional conduct or other law;

(2) the lawyer's physical or mental condition materially impairs the lawyer's ability to represent the client; or

(3) the lawyer is discharged.

(b) Except as stated in paragraph (c), a lawyer may withdraw from representing a client if withdrawal can be accomplished without material adverse effect on the interests of the client, or if:

(1) the client persists in a course of action involving the lawyer's services that the lawyer reasonably believes is criminal or fraudulent;

(2) the client has used the lawyer's services to perpetrate a crime or fraud;

(3) a client insists upon pursuing an objective that the lawyer considers repugnant or imprudent;

(4) the client fails substantially to fulfill an obligation to the lawyer regarding the lawyer's services and has been given reasonable warning that the lawyer will withdraw unless the obligation is fulfilled;

(5) the representation will result in an unreasonable financial burden on the lawyer or has been rendered unreasonably difficult by the client; or

(6) other good cause for withdrawal exists.

(c) When ordered to do so by a tribunal, a lawyer shall continue representation notwithstanding good cause for terminating the representation.

(d) Upon termination of representation, a lawyer shall take steps to the extent reasonably practicable to protect a client's interests, such as giving reasonable notice to the client, allowing time for employment of other counsel, surrendering papers and property to which the client is entitled and refunding any advance payment of fee that has not been earned. The lawyer may retain papers relating to the client to the extent permitted by other law.

(SCO 1123 effective July 15, 1993)

COMMENT

A lawyer should not accept representation in a matter unless it can be performed competently, promptly, without improper conflict of interest and to completion.

Mandatory Withdrawal

A lawyer ordinarily must decline or withdraw from representation if the client demands that the lawyer engage in conduct that is illegal or violates the Rules of Professional Conduct or other law. The lawyer is not obligated to decline or withdraw simply because the client suggests such a course of conduct; a client may make such a suggestion in the hope that a lawyer will not be constrained by a professional obligation.

When a lawyer has been appointed to represent a client, withdrawal ordinarily requires approval of the appointing authority. See also Rule 6.2. Difficulty may be encountered if withdrawal is based on the client's demand that the lawyer engage in unprofessional conduct. The court may wish an explanation for the withdrawal, while the lawyer may be bound to keep confidential the facts that would constitute such an explanation. The lawyer's statement that professional considerations require termination of the representation ordinarily should be accepted as sufficient.

Discharge

A client has a right to discharge a lawyer at any time, with or without cause, subject to liability for payment for the lawyer's services. Where future dispute about the withdrawal may be anticipated, it may be advisable to prepare a written statement reciting the circumstances.

Whether a client can discharge appointed counsel may depend on applicable law. A client seeking to do so should be given a full explanation of the consequences. These consequences may include a decision by the appointing authority that appointment of successor counsel is unjustified, thus requiring the client to represent himself.

If the client is mentally incompetent, the client may lack the legal capacity to discharge the lawyer, and in any event the discharge may be seriously adverse to the client's interests. The lawyer should make special effort to help the client consider the consequences and, in an extreme case, may initiate proceedings for a conservatorship or similar protection of the client. See Rule 1.14.

Optional Withdrawal

A lawyer may withdraw from representation in some circumstances. The lawyer has the option to withdraw if it can be accomplished without material adverse effect on the client's interests. Withdrawal is also justified if the client persists in a course of action that the lawyer reasonably believes is criminal or fraudulent, for a lawyer is not required to be associated with such conduct even if the lawyer does not further it. Withdrawal is also permitted if the lawyer's services were misused in the past even if that would materially prejudice the client. The lawyer also may withdraw where the client insists on a repugnant or imprudent objective.

A lawyer may withdraw if the client refuses to abide by the terms of an agreement relating to the representation, such as an agreement concerns fees or court costs or an agreement limiting the objectives of the representation.

Assisting the Client Upon Withdrawal

Even if the lawyer has been unfairly discharged by the client, a lawyer must take all reasonable steps to mitigate the consequences to the client. The lawyer may retain papers as security for a fee only to the extent permitted by law.

Whether or not a lawyer for an organization may under certain unusual circumstances have a legal obligation to the organization after withdrawing or being discharged by the organization's highest authority is beyond the scope of these rules.

Annotations

Cases

Where defense counsel informed the judge of his belief that defendant's proposed testimony would be false, the judge's solution as an alternative to withdrawal by the attorney that defendant take the stand and give his testimony in narrative form without assistance from his attorney, did not violate defendant's rights. **Coleman v. State,** Op. No. 2190, 621 P2d 869 (Alaska 1980).

Failure of trial court to allow defendant's counsel to withdraw was reversible error where there was sufficient evidence to suggest that the attorney-client relationship had broken down and where, in trying to extricate himself from the case, the attorney essentially told the judge that his client was going to perjure himself. **Newcomb v. State,** Op. No. 130, 651 P2d 1176 (Alaska App. 1982).

Trial counsel's unilateral and unformalized withdrawal of representation following trail violated Appellate Rules and Code of Professional Responsibility; fact that client instructed trial counsel to do nothing further in the case did not relieve trial counsel of duty to preserve client's right to appeal where instruction was expressly based on client's representation that new attorney would be handling the matter. **Broeckel v. State,** Op. No. 1430, 900 P2d 1205 (Alaska App. 1995).

Attorney's 90-day suspension for knowingly disobeying a court order was proper where, although the attorney believed that Alaska R. Prof. Conduct 1.15 required him to return client funds instead of transferring the funds to opposing counsel in lieu of a superseadas bond, Alaska R. Prof. Conduct 3.4(c) required him to follow court order regarding disposition of the funds or "openly refuse" to follow it; furthermore, Alaska R. Prof. Conduct 1.2(e) indicates that a client's wishes or interests do not supersede a lawyer's ethical obligations. **In re Ford,** Op. No. 2000, 128 P.3d 178 (Alaska 2006).

Rule 1.17. Sale of Law Practice.

A lawyer or a law firm may sell or purchase a law practice, including good will, if the following conditions are satisfied:

(a) The seller ceases to engage in the private practice of law in the judicial district in which the practice has been conducted;

(b) The practice is sold as an entirety to another lawyer or law firm;

(c) Actual written notice is given to each of the seller's clients regarding:

(1) the proposed sale;

(2) the terms of any proposed change in the fee arrangement authorized by paragraph (d);

(3) the client's right to retain other counsel or to take possession of the file; and

(4) the fact that the client's consent to representation by the purchaser will be presumed if the client does not take any action or does not otherwise object within ninety (90) days of receipt of the notice.

If a client cannot be given notice, the representation of that client may be transferred to the purchaser only upon entry of an order so authorizing by a court having jurisdiction. The seller may disclose to the court in camera a confidence or secret relating to the representation only to the extent necessary to obtain an order authorizing the transfer of a file.

(d) The fees charged clients shall not be increased by reason of the sale. The purchaser may, however, refuse to undertake the representation unless the client consents to pay the purchaser fees at a rate not exceeding the fees charged by the purchaser for rendering substantially similar services prior to the initiation of the purchase negotiations.

(SCO 1123 effective July 15, 1993; amended by SCO 1332 effective January 15, 1999)

COMMENT

The practice of law is a profession, not merely a business. Clients are not commodities that can be purchased and sold at will. Pursuant to this rule, when a lawyer or an entire firm ceases to practice and another lawyer or firm takes over the representation, the selling lawyer or firm may obtain compensation for the reasonable value of the practice as may withdrawing partners of law firms. See Rules 5.4 and 5.6.

Termination of Practice by the Seller

The requirement that all of the private practice be sold is satisfied if the seller in good faith makes the entire practice available for sale to the purchaser. The fact that a number of the seller's clients decide not to be represented by the purchaser but take their matters elsewhere, therefore, does not result in a violation. Neither does a return to private practice as a result of an unanticipated change in circumstances result in a violation. For example, a lawyer who has sold the practice to accept an appointment to judicial office does not violate the requirement that the sale be attendant to cessation of practice if the lawyer later resumes private practice upon being defeated in a contested or a retention election for the office.

The requirement that the seller cease to engage in the private practice of law does not prohibit employment as a lawyer on the staff of a public agency or a legal services entity which provides legal services to the poor, or as in-house counsel to a business.

The rule permits a sale attendant upon retirement from the private practice of law within the jurisdiction. Its provisions, therefore, accommodate the lawyer who sells the practice upon the occasion of moving to another state. Some states are so large that a move from one locale therein to another is tantamount to leaving the jurisdiction in which the lawyer has engaged in the practice of law. To also accommodate lawyers so situated, states may permit the sale of the practice when the lawyer leaves the geographic area rather than the jurisdiction. The alternative desired should be indicated by selecting one of the two provided for in Rule 1.17(a).

Single Purchaser

The rule requires a single purchaser. The prohibition against piecemeal sale of a practice protects those clients whose matters are less lucrative and who might find it difficult to secure other counsel if a sale could be limited to substantial fee-generating matters. The purchaser is required to undertake all client matters in the practice, subject to client consent. If, however, the purchaser is unable to undertake all client matters because of a conflict of interest in a specific matter respecting which the purchaser is not permitted by Rule 1.7 or another rule to represent the client, the requirement that there be a single purchaser is nevertheless satisfied.

Client Confidences, Consent and Notice

Negotiations between seller and prospective purchaser prior to disclosure of a confidence or secret relating to a specific representation of an identifiable client no more violate the confidentiality provisions of Model Rule 1.6 than do preliminary discussions concerning the possible association of another lawyer or mergers between firms, with respect to which client consent is not required. Providing the purchaser access to a client-specific confidence or secret relating to the representation and to the file, however, requires client consent. The rule provides that before such information can be disclosed by the seller to the purchaser the client must be given actual written notice of the contemplated sale, including the identity of the purchaser and any proposed change in the terms of future representation, and must be told that the decision to consent or make other arrangements must be made within 90 days. If nothing is heard from the client within that time, consent to the sale is presumed.

A lawyer or law firm ceasing to practice cannot be required to remain in practice because some clients cannot be given actual notice of the proposed purchase. Since these clients cannot themselves consent to the purchase or direct any other disposition of their files, the rule requires an order from a court having jurisdiction authorizing their transfer or other disposition. The court can be expected to determine whether reasonable efforts to locate the client have been exhausted, and whether the absent client's legitimate interests will be served by authorizing the transfer of the file so that the purchaser may continue the representation. Preservation of client confidences requires that the petition for a court order be considered in camera. (A procedure by which such an order can be obtained needs to be established in jurisdictions in which it presently does not exist.)

All the elements of client autonomy, including the client's absolute right to discharge a lawyer and transfer the representation to another, survive the sale of the practice.

Fee Arrangements Between Client and Purchaser

The sale may not be financed by increases in fees charged the clients of the practice. Existing agreements between the seller and the client as to fees and the scope of the work must be honored by the purchaser, unless the client consents after consultation. The purchaser may, however, advise the client that the purchaser will not undertake the representation unless the client consents to pay the higher fees the purchaser usually charges. To prevent client financing of the sale, the higher fee the purchaser may charge must not exceed the fees charged by the purchaser for substantially similar service rendered prior to the initiation of the purchase negotiations.

The purchaser may not intentionally fragment the practice which is the subject of the sale by charging significantly different fees in substantially similar matters. Doing so would make it possible for the purchaser to avoid the obligation to take over the entire practice by charging arbitrarily higher fees for less lucrative matters, thereby increasing the likelihood that those clients would not consent to the new representation.

Other Applicable Ethical Standards

Lawyers participating in the sale of a law practice are subject to the ethical standards applicable to involving another lawyer in the representation of a client. These include, for example, the seller's obligation to exercise competence in identifying a purchaser qualified to assume the practice and the purchaser's obligation to undertake the representation competently (see Rule 1.1); the obligation to avoid disqualifying conflicts, and to secure client consent after consultation for those conflicts which can be agreed to (see Rule 1.7); and the obligation to protect confidences and secrets relating to the representation (see Rules 1.6 and 1.9).

If approval of the substitution of the purchasing attorney for the selling attorney is required by the rules of any tribunal in which a matter is pending, such approval must be obtained before the matter can be included in the sale (see Rule 1.16).

Applicability of the Rule

This rule applies to the sale of a law practice by representatives of a deceased, disabled or disappeared lawyer. Thus, the seller may be represented by a non-lawyer representative not subject to these rules. Since, however, no lawyer may participate in a sale of a law practice which does not conform to the requirements of this rule, the representatives of the seller as well as the purchasing lawyer can be expected to see to it that they are met.

Admission to or retirement from a law partnership or professional association, retirement plans and similar arrangements, and a sale of tangible assets of a law practice, do not constitute a sale or purchase governed by this rule.

This rule does not apply to the transfers of legal representation between lawyers when such transfers are unrelated to the sale of a practice.

COUNSELOR

Rule 2.1. Advisor.

In representing a client, a lawyer shall exercise independent professional judgment and render candid advice. In rendering advice, a lawyer may refer not only to law but to other considerations such as moral, economic, social and political factors, and the availability of alternative forms of dispute resolution, that may be relevant to the client's situation.

(SCO 1123 effective July 15, 1993; amended by SCO 1354 effective October 15, 1999)

ALASKA COMMENT

In a matter involving or expected to involve litigation, a lawyer should advise the client of alternative forms of dispute resolution which might reasonably be pursued to attempt to resolve the legal dispute or to reach the legal objective sought.

COMMENT

Scope of Advice

A client is entitled to straightforward advice expressing the lawyer's honest assessment. Legal advice often involves unpleasant facts and alternatives that a client may be disinclined to confront. In presenting advice, a lawyer endeavors to sustain the client's morale and may put advice in as acceptable a form as honesty permits. However, a lawyer should not be deterred from giving candid advice by the prospect that the advice will be unpalatable to the client.

Advice couched in narrowly legal terms may be of little value to a client, especially where practical considerations, such as cost or effects on other people, are predominant. Purely technical legal advice, therefore, can sometimes be inadequate. It is proper for a lawyer to refer to relevant moral and ethical considerations in giving advice. Although a lawyer is not a moral advisor as such, moral and ethical considerations impinge upon most legal questions and may decisively influence how the law will be applied.

A client may expressly or impliedly ask the lawyer for purely technical advice. When such a request is made by a client experienced in legal matters, the lawyer may accept it at face value. When such a request is made by a client inexperienced in legal matters, however, the lawyer's responsibility as advisor may include indicating that more may be involved than strictly legal considerations.

Matters that go beyond strictly legal questions may also be in the domain of another profession. Family matters can involve problems within the professional competence of psychiatry, clinical psychology or social work; business matters can involve problems within the competence of the accounting profession or of financial specialists. Where consultation with a professional in another field is itself something a competent lawyer would recommend, the lawyer should make such a recommendation. At the same time, a lawyer's advice at its best often consists of recommending a course of action in the face of conflicting recommendations of experts.

Offering Advice

In general, a lawyer is not expected to give advice until asked by the client. However, when a lawyer knows that a client proposes a course of action that is likely to result in substantial adverse legal consequences to the client, duty to the client under Rule 1.4 may require that the lawyer act if the client's course of action is related to the representation. A lawyer ordinarily has no duty to initiate investigation of a client's affairs or to give advice that the client has indicated is unwanted, but a lawyer may initiate advice to a client when doing so appears to be in the client's interest.

Rule 2.2. Intermediary.

(a) A lawyer may act as intermediary between clients if:

(1) the lawyer consults with each client concerning the implications of the common representation, including the advantages and risks involved, and the effect on the attorney-client privileges, and obtains each client's consent to the common representation;

(2) the lawyer reasonably believes that the matter can be resolved on terms compatible with the clients' best interests, that each client will be able to make adequately informed decisions in the matter and that there is little risk of material prejudice to the interests of any of the clients if the contemplated resolution is unsuccessful; and

(3) the lawyer reasonably believes that the common representation can be undertaken impartially and without improper effect on other responsibilities the lawyer has to any of the clients.

(b) While acting as intermediary, the lawyer shall consult with each client concerning the decisions to be made and the considerations relevant in making them, so that each client can make adequately informed decisions.

(c) A lawyer shall withdraw as intermediary if any of the clients so requests, or if any of the conditions stated in paragraph (a) is no longer satisfied. Upon withdrawal, the lawyer shall not continue to represent any of the clients in the matter that was the subject of the intermediation.

(d) Notwithstanding paragraph (a), a lawyer who is representing a party in a divorce, dissolution, custody, alimony, child support or marital property settlement cases may not act as an intermediary in that case.

(SCO 1123 effective July 15, 1993; amended by SCO 1332 effective January 15, 1999)

ALASKA COMMENT

Under this rule, it is contemplated that a lawyer may act as an intermediary between two or more parties with potentially conflicting interests. In the examples noted in the third paragraph of the ABA comment, a lawyer may act as a intermediary in helping organize a business with two or more clients, or perhaps arranging a property distribution in the settlement of an estate. The Committee thought that a divorce, dissolution, custody dispute, alimony dispute, child support dispute, or marital property settlement dispute was not on the same level as a business organization or an estate dispute.

The emotional content of any marital dispute, any child custody dispute, or any marital property dispute is almost always substantially higher than any other dispute. The potential for claims of lack of impartiality, claims of lack of preservation of client confidences, and claims of material prejudice to one party were thought to be very high in these situations. The potential for claims of this nature from one of these parties after the intermediation is completed is so high, that it was determined to be virtually impossible for a single lawyer to act as an intermediary in the divorce or dissolution context. Therefore, it is prohibited under Rule 2.2(d).

Paragraph (d) does not preclude a lawyer from acting as a mediator or arbitrator in a domestic relations case where it is clear the lawyer is not representing either party in that proceeding.

COMMENT

A lawyer acts as intermediary under this Rule when the lawyer represents two or more parties with potentially conflicting interests. A key factor in defining the relationship is whether the parties share responsibility for the lawyer's fee, but the common representation may be inferred from other circumstances. Because confusion can arise as to the lawyer's role where each party is not separately represented, it is important that the lawyer make clear the relationship.

The rule does not apply to a lawyer acting as arbitrator or mediator between or among parties who are not clients of the lawyer, even where the lawyer has been appointed with the concurrence of the parties. In performing such a role the lawyer may be subject to applicable codes of ethics, such as the Code of Ethics for Arbitration in Commercial Disputes prepared by a joint committee of the American Bar Association and the American Arbitration Association.

A lawyer acts as intermediary in seeking to establish or adjust a relationship between clients on an amicable and mutually advantageous basis; for example, in helping to organize a business in which two or more clients are entrepreneurs, working out the financial reorganization of an enterprise in which two or more clients have an interest, arranging a property distribution in settlement of an estate or mediating a dispute between clients. The lawyer seeks to resolve potentially conflicting interests by developing the parties' mutual interests. The alternative can be that each party may have to obtain separate representation, with the possibility in some situations of incurring additional cost, complication or even litigation. Given these and other relevant factors, all the clients may prefer that the lawyer act as intermediary.

In considering whether to act as intermediary between clients, a lawyer should be mindful that if the intermediation fails the result can be additional cost, embarrassment, and recrimination. In some situations the risk of failure is so great that intermediation is plainly impossible. For example, a lawyer cannot undertake common representation of clients between whom contentious litigation is imminent or who contemplate contentious negotiations. More generally, if the relationship between the parties has already assumed definite antagonism, the possibility that the clients' interests can be adjusted by intermediation ordinarily is not very good.

The appropriateness of intermediation can depend on its form. Forms of intermediation range from informal arbitration, where each client's case is presented by the respective client and the lawyer decides the outcome, to mediation, to common representation where the clients' interests are substantially though not entirely compatible. One form may be appropriate in circumstances where another would not. Other relevant factors are whether the lawyer subsequently will represent both parties on a continuing basis and whether the situation involves creating a relationship between the parties or terminating one.

Confidentiality and Privilege

A particularly important factor in determining the appropriateness of intermediation is the effect on client-lawyer confidentiality and the attorney-client privilege. In a common representation, the lawyer is still required to keep each client adequately informed and to maintain the client's confidences and secrets relating to the representation. See Rules 1.4 and 1.6. Complying with both requirements while acting as intermediary requires a delicate balance. If the balance cannot be maintained, the common representation is improper. With regard to the attorney-client privilege, the prevailing rule is that as between commonly represented clients the privilege does not attach. Hence, it must be assumed that if litigation eventuates between the clients, the privilege will not protect any such communications, and the clients should be so advised.

Since the lawyer is required to be impartial between commonly represented clients, intermediation is improper when that impartiality cannot be maintained. For example, a lawyer who has represented one of the clients for a long period and in a variety of matters might have difficulty being impartial between that client and one to whom the lawyer has only recently been introduced.

Consultation

In acting as intermediary between clients, the lawyer is required to consult with the clients on the implications of doing so, and proceed only upon consent based on such a consultation. The consultation should make clear that the lawyer's role is not that of partisanship normally expected in other circumstances.

Paragraph (b) is an application of the principle expressed in Rule 1.4. Where the lawyer is intermediary, the clients ordinarily must assume greater responsibility for decisions than when each client is independently represented.

Withdrawal

Common representation does not diminish the rights of each client in the client-lawyer relationship. Each has the right to loyal and diligent representation, the right to discharge the lawyer as stated in Rule 1.16, and the protection of Rule 1.9 concerning obligations to a former client.

Rule 2.3. Evaluation for Use by Third Persons.

(a) A lawyer may undertake an evaluation of a matter affecting a client for the use of someone other than the client if:

(1) the lawyer reasonably believes that making the evaluation is compatible with other aspects of the lawyer's relationship with the client; and

(2) the client consents after consultation.

(b) Except as disclosure is required in connection with a report of an evaluation, information relating to the evaluation is otherwise protected by Rule 1.6.

(SCO 1123 effective July 15, 1993)

COMMENT

Definition

An evaluation may be performed at the client's direction but for the primary purpose of establishing information for the benefit of third parties; for example, an opinion concerning the title of property rendered at the behest of a vendor for the information of a prospective purchaser, or at the behest of a borrower for the information of a prospective lender. In some situations, the evaluation may be required by a government agency; for example, an opinion concerning the legality of the securities registered for sale under the securities laws. In other instances, the evaluation may be required by a third person, such as a purchaser of a business.

Lawyers for the government may be called upon to give a formal opinion on the legality of contemplated government agency action. In making such an evaluation, the government lawyer acts at the behest of the government as the client but for the purpose of establishing the limits of the agency's authorized activity. Such an opinion is to be distinguished from confidential legal advice given agency officials. The critical question is whether the opinion is to be made public.

A legal evaluation should be distinguished from an investigation of a person with whom the lawyer does not have a client-lawyer relationship. For example, a lawyer retained by a purchaser to analyze a vendor's title to property does not have a client-lawyer relationship with the vendor. So also, an investigation into a person's affairs by a government lawyer, or by special counsel employed by the government, is not an evaluation as that term is used in this rule. The question is whether the lawyer is retained by the person whose affairs are being examined. When the lawyer is retained by that person, the general rules concerning loyalty to client and preservation of confidences apply, which is not the case if the lawyer is retained by someone else. For this reason, it is essential to identify the person by whom the lawyer is retained. This should be made clear not only to the person under examination, but also to others to whom the results are to be made available.

Duty to Third Person

When the evaluation is intended for the information or use of a third person, a legal duty to that person may or may not arise. That legal question is beyond the scope of this rule. However, since such an evaluation involves a departure from the normal client-lawyer relationship, careful analysis of the situation is required. The lawyer must be satisfied as a matter of professional judgment that making the evaluation is compatible with other functions undertaken in behalf of the client. For example, if the lawyer is acting as advocate in defending the client against charges of fraud, it would normally be incompatible with that responsibility for the lawyer to perform an evaluation for others concerning the same or a related transaction. Assuming no such impediment is apparent, however, the lawyer should advise the client of the implications of the evaluation, particularly the lawyer's responsibilities to third persons and the duty to disseminate the findings.

Disclosure of Information

Access to and disclosure of information the quality of an evaluation depends on the freedom and extent of the investigation upon which it is based. Ordinarily a lawyer should have whatever latitude of investigation seems necessary as a matter of professional judgment. Under some circumstances, however, the terms of the evaluation may be limited. For example, certain issues or sources may be categorically excluded, or the scope of search may be limited by time constraints or the noncooperation of persons having relevant information. Any such limitations which are material to the evaluation should be described in the report. If after a lawyer has commenced an evaluation, the client refuses to comply with the terms upon which it was understood the evaluation was to have been made, the lawyer's obligations are determined by law, having reference to the terms of the client's agreement and the surrounding circumstances.

Financial Auditors' Requests for Information

When a question concerning the legal situation of a client arises at the instance of the client's financial auditor and the question is referred to the lawyer, the lawyer's response may be made in accordance with procedures recognized in the legal profession. Such a procedure is set forth in the American Bar Association statement of policy regarding lawyer's responses to auditors' requests for information, adopted in 1975.

ADVOCATE

Rule 3.1. Meritorious Claims and Contentions.

A lawyer shall not bring or defend a proceeding, or assert or controvert an issue therein, unless there is a basis for doing so that is not frivolous, which includes a good faith argument for an extension, modification or reversal of existing law. A lawyer for the defendant in a criminal proceeding, or the respondent in a proceeding that could result in incarceration, may nevertheless so defend the proceeding as to require that every element of the case be established.

(SCO 1123 effective July 15, 1993)

COMMENT

The advocate has a duty to use legal procedure for the fullest benefit of the client's cause, but also a duty not to abuse legal procedure. The law, both procedural and substantive, establishes the limits within which an advocate may proceed. However, the law is not always clear and never is static. Accordingly, in determining the proper scope of advocacy, account must be taken of the law's ambiguities and potential for change.

The filing of an action or defense or similar action taken for a client is not frivolous merely because the facts have not first been fully substantiated or because the lawyer expects to develop vital evidence only by discovery. Such action is not frivolous even though the lawyer believes that the client's position ultimately will not prevail.

Rule 3.2. Expediting Litigation.

A lawyer shall make reasonable efforts to expedite litigation consistent with the interest of the client.

(SCO 1123 effective July 15, 1993)

COMMENT

Dilatory practices bring the administration of justice into disrepute. Delay should not be indulged merely for the convenience of the advocates, or for the purpose of frustrating an opposing party's attempt to obtain rightful redress or repose. It is not a justification that similar conduct is often tolerated by the bench and bar. The question is whether a competent lawyer acting in good faith would regard the course of action as having some substantial purpose other than delay. Realizing financial or other benefit from otherwise improper delay in litigation is not a legitimate interest of the client.

Rule 3.3. Candor Toward the Tribunal.

(a) A lawyer shall not knowingly:

(1) make a false statement of material fact or law to a tribunal;

(2) fail to disclose a material fact to a tribunal when disclosure is necessary to avoid assisting a criminal or fraudulent act by the client;

(3) fail to disclose to the tribunal legal authority in the controlling jurisdiction known to the lawyer to be directly adverse to the position of the client and not disclosed by opposing counsel; or

(4) offer evidence that the lawyer knows to be false. If a lawyer has offered material evidence and comes to know of its falsity, the lawyer shall take reasonable remedial measures.

(b) The duties stated in paragraph (a) continue to the conclusion of the proceeding, and apply even if compliance requires disclosure of information otherwise protected by Rule 1.6.

(c) A lawyer may refuse to offer evidence that the lawyer reasonably believes is false.

(d) In an ex parte proceeding, a lawyer shall inform the tribunal of all material facts known to the lawyer which are necessary to enable the tribunal to make an informed decision, including facts adverse to the lawyer's position.

(SCO 1123 effective July 15, 1993)

COMMENT

The advocate's task is to present the client's case with persuasive force. Performance of that duty while maintaining confidences of the client is qualified by the advocate's duty of candor to the tribunal. However, an advocate does not vouch for the evidence submitted in a cause; the tribunal is responsible for assessing its probative value.

Representations by a Lawyer

An advocate is responsible for pleadings and other documents prepared for litigation, but is usually not required to have personal knowledge of matters asserted therein, for litigation documents ordinarily present assertions by the client, or by someone on the client's behalf, and not assertions by the lawyer. Compare Rule 3.1. However, an assertion purporting to be on the lawyer's own knowledge, as in an affidavit by the lawyer or in a statement in open court, may properly be made only when the lawyer knows the assertion is true or believes it to be true on the basis of a reasonably diligent inquiry. There are circumstances where failure to make a disclosure is the equivalent of an affirmative misrepresentation. The obligation prescribed in Rule 1.2(d) not to counsel a client to commit or assist the client in committing a fraud applies in litigation. Regarding compliance with Rule 1.2(d), see the Comment to that rule. See also the Comment to Rule 8.4(b).

Misleading Legal Argument

Legal argument based on a knowingly false representation of law constitutes dishonesty toward the tribunal. A lawyer is not required to make a disinterested exposition of the law, but must recognize the existence of pertinent legal authorities. Furthermore, as stated in paragraph (a)(3), an advocate has a duty to disclose directly adverse authority in the controlling jurisdiction which has not been disclosed by the opposing party. The underlying concept is that legal argument is a discussion seeking to determine the legal premises properly applicable to the case.

False Evidence

When evidence that a lawyer knows to be false is provided by a person who is not the client, the lawyer must refuse to offer it regardless of the client's wishes.

When false evidence is offered by the client, however, a conflict may arise between the lawyer's duty to keep the client's revelations confidential and the duty of candor to the court. Upon ascertaining that material evidence is false, the lawyer should seek to persuade the client that the evidence should not be offered or, if it has been offered, that its false character should immediately be disclosed. If the persuasion is ineffective, the lawyer must take reasonable remedial measures.

Except in the defense of a criminal accused, the rule generally recognized is that, if necessary to rectify the situation, an advocate must disclose the existence of the client's deception to the court or to the other party. Such a disclosure can result in grave consequences to the client, including not only a sense of betrayal but also loss of the case and perhaps a prosecution for perjury. But the alternative is that the lawyer cooperate in deceiving the court, thereby subverting the truth-finding process which the adversary system is designed to implement. See Rule 1.2(d). Furthermore, unless it is clearly understood that the lawyer will act upon the duty to disclose the existence of false evidence, the client can simply reject the lawyer's advice to reveal the false evidence and insist that the lawyer keep silent. Thus the client could in effect coerce the lawyer into being a party to fraud on the court.

Perjury by a Criminal Defendant

Whether an advocate for a criminally accused has the same duty of disclosure has been intensely debated. While it is agreed that the lawyer should seek to persuade the client to refrain from perjurious testimony, there has been dispute concerning the lawyer's duty when that persuasion fails. If the confrontation with the client occurs before trial, the lawyer ordinarily can withdraw. Withdrawal before trial may not be possible, however, either because trial is imminent, or because the confrontation with the client does not take place until the trial itself, or because no other counsel is available.

The most difficult situation, therefore, arises in a criminal case where the accused insists on testifying when the lawyer knows that the testimony is perjurious. The lawyer's effort to rectify the situation can increase the likelihood of the client's being convicted as well as opening the possibility of a prosecution for perjury. On the other hand, if the lawyer does not exercise control over the proof, the lawyer participates, although in a merely passive way, in deception of the court.

Three resolutions of this dilemma have been proposed. One is to permit the accused to testify by a narrative without guidance through the lawyer's questioning. This compromises both contending principles; it exempts the lawyer from the duty to disclose false evidence but subjects the client to an implicit disclosure of information imparted to counsel. Another suggested resolution, of relatively recent origin, is that the advocate be entirely excused from the duty to reveal perjury if the perjury is that of the client. This is a coherent solution but makes the advocate a knowing instrument of perjury.

The other resolution of the dilemma is that the lawyer must reveal the client's perjury if necessary to rectify the situation. A criminal accused has a right to the assistance of an advocate, a right to testify and a right of confidential communication with counsel. However, an accused should not have right to assistance of counsel in committing perjury. Furthermore, an advocate has an obligation, not only in professional ethics but under the law as well, to avoid implication in the commission of perjury or other falsification of evidence. See Rule 1.2(d)

Remedial Measures

If perjured testimony or false evidence has been offered, the advocate's proper course ordinarily is to remonstrate with the client confidentially. If that fails, the advocate should seek to withdraw if that will remedy the situation. If withdrawal will not remedy the situation or is impossible, the advocate should make disclosure to the court. It is for the court then to determine what should be done - making a statement about the matter to the trier of fact, ordering a mistrial or perhaps nothing. If the false testimony was that of the client, the client may controvert the lawyer's version of their communication when the lawyer discloses the situation to the court. If there is an issue whether the client has committed perjury, the lawyer cannot represent the client in resolution of the issue, and a mistrial may be unavoidable. An unscrupulous client might in this way attempt to produce a series of mistrials and thus escape prosecution. However, a second such encounter could be construed as a deliberate abuse of the right to counsel and as such a waiver of the right to further representation.

Constitutional Requirements

The general rule—that an advocate must disclose the existence of perjury with respect to a material fact, even that of a client—applies to defense counsel in criminal cases, as well as in other instances. However, the definition of the lawyer's ethical duty in such a situation may be qualified by constitutional provisions for due process and the right to counsel in criminal cases. In some jurisdictions these provisions have been construed to require that counsel present an accused as a witness if the accused wishes to testify, even if counsel knows the testimony will be false. The obligation of the advocate under these rules is subordinate to such a constitutional requirement.

Duration of Obligation

A practical time limit on the obligation to rectify the presentation of false evidence has to be established. The conclusion of the proceeding is a reasonably definite point for the termination of the obligation.

Refusing to Offer Proof Believed to be False

Generally speaking, a lawyer has authority to refuse to offer testimony or other proof that the lawyer believes is untrustworthy. Offering such proof may reflect adversely on the lawyer's ability to discriminate in the quality of evidence and thus impair the lawyer's effectiveness as an advocate. In criminal cases, however, a lawyer may, in some jurisdictions, be denied this authority by constitutional requirements governing the right to counsel.

Ex Parte Proceedings

Ordinarily, an advocate has the limited responsibility of presenting one side of the matters that a tribunal should consider in reaching a decision; the conflicting position is expected to be presented by the opposing party. However, in an ex parte proceeding, such as an application for a temporary restraining order, there is no balance of presentation by opposing advocates. The object of an ex parte proceeding is nevertheless to yield a substantially just result. The judge has an affirmative responsibility to accord the absent party just consideration. The lawyer for the represented party has the correlative duty to make disclosures of material facts known to the lawyer and that the lawyer reasonably believes are necessary to an informed decision.

Annotations

Cases

Appellate court sanctioned appellant's counsel, where counsel misstated the facts of the case that masked the appellate court's potential lack of jurisdiction to entertain the appeal and knowingly failed to cite a decision adverse to his contention that the appellate court had jurisdiction to decide the appeal. **Tyler v. State,** Op. No. A-7779, 47 P3d 1095 (Alaska App. 2001).

An attorney in a DWI case was properly fined for filing a motion on behalf of his client without bringing controlling negative precedent to the attention of the tribunal. **Tyler v. State,** Op. No. A-7779, 47 P3d 1095 (Alaska App. 2001).

Rule 3.4. Fairness to Opposing Party and Counsel.

(a) A lawyer shall not unlawfully obstruct another party's access to evidence or unlawfully alter, destroy or conceal a document or other material having potential evidentiary value, nor shall a lawyer counsel or assist another person to do any of these acts.

(b) A lawyer shall not falsify evidence, counsel or assist a witness to testify falsely, or offer an inducement to a witness that is prohibited by law.

(c) A lawyer shall not knowingly violate or disobey an order of a tribunal or the rules of a tribunal except for an open refusal based on an assertion that the order is invalid or that no valid obligation exists.

(d) A lawyer shall not in pretrial procedure, make a frivolous discovery request or fail to make reasonably diligent effort to comply with a legally proper discovery request by an opposing party.

(e) A lawyer shall not in trial allude to any matter that the lawyer does not reasonably believe is relevant or that will not be supported by admissible evidence. A lawyer shall not assert personal knowledge of facts in issue except when testifying as a witness, nor state a personal opinion as to the justness of a cause, the credibility of a witness, the culpability of a civil litigant or the guilt or innocence of an accused.

(f) A lawyer shall not request that a person other than a client refrain from voluntarily giving relevant information to another party unless the person is a relative or an employee or other agent of a client and the lawyer reasonably believes that the person's interests will not be adversely affected by refraining from giving the information.

(SCO 1123 effective July 15, 1993)

ALASKA COMMENT

The Committee amended paragraph (c) to make clear that the rule prevents knowingly disobedience of a specific order of a court as well as the general rules of procedure.

COMMENT

The procedure of the adversary system contemplates that the evidence in a case is to be marshalled competitively by the contending parties. Fair competition in the adversary system is secured by prohibitions against destruction or concealment of evidence, improperly influencing witnesses, obstructive tactics in discovery procedure, and the like.

Documents and other items of evidence are often essential to establish a claim or defense. Subject to evidentiary privileges, the right of an opposing party, including the government, to obtain evidence through discovery or subpoena is an important procedural right. The exercise of that right can be frustrated if relevant material is altered, concealed or destroyed. Applicable law in many jurisdictions makes it an offense to destroy material for purposes of impairing its availability in a pending proceeding or one whose commencement can be foreseen. Falsifying evidence is also generally a criminal offense. Paragraph (a) applies to evidentiary material generally, including computerized information.

With regard to paragraph (b), it is not improper to pay a witness's expenses or to compensate an expert witness on terms permitted by law. The common law rule in most jurisdictions is that it is improper to pay an occurrence witness any fee for testifying and that it is improper to pay an expert witness a contingent fee.

Paragraph (f) permits a lawyer to advise employees of a client to refrain from giving information to another party, for the employees may identify their interests with those of the client. See also Rule 4.2.

Annotations

Cases

Suspension for 18 months was appropriate punishment for attorney who "created" a deed of trust and attached it as an exhibit to an unverified complaint. **Discipline of Walton,** Op. No. 2734, 676 P2d 1078 (Alaska 1983).

Attorney, who intentionally notarized a signature he knew to be false to ensure that the State would agree to a property loss settlement with his client, engaged in dishonest conduct and conduct prejudicial to the administration of justice, warranting a 90-day suspension. **Disciplinary Matter Involving West,** Op. No. 3660, 805 P2d 351 (Alaska 1991).

Attorney's 90-day suspension for knowingly disobeying a court order was proper where, although the attorney believed that Alaska R. Prof. Conduct 1.15 required him to return client funds instead of transferring the funds to opposing counsel in lieu of a superseadas bond, section (c) of this rule required him to follow court order regarding disposition of the funds or "openly refuse" to follow it; furthermore, Alaska R. Prof. Conduct 1.2(e) indicates that a client's wishes or interests do not supersede a lawyer's ethical obligations. **In re Ford,** Op. No. 2000, 128 P.3d 178 (Alaska 2006).

Rule 3.5. Impartiality and Decorum of the Tribunal.

A lawyer shall not:

(a) seek to influence a judge, juror, prospective juror or other official by means prohibited by law;

(b) communicate ex parte with such a person except as permitted by law; or

(c) engage in conduct intended to disrupt a tribunal.

(SCO 1123 effective July 15, 1993)

COMMENT

Many forms of improper influence upon a tribunal are proscribed by criminal law. Others are specified in the ABA Model Code of Judicial Conduct, with which an advocate should be familiar. A lawyer is required to avoid contributing to a violation of such provisions.

The advocate's function is to present evidence and argument so that the cause may be decided according to law. Refraining from abusive or obstreperous conduct is a corollary of the advocate's right to speak on behalf of litigants. A lawyer may stand firm against abuse by a judge but should avoid reciprocation; the judge's default is no justification for similar dereliction by an advocate. An advocate can present the cause, protect the record for subsequent review and preserve professional integrity by patient firmness no less effectively than by belligerence or theatrics.

Rule 3.6. Trial Publicity.

(a) A lawyer shall not make an extrajudicial statement that a reasonable person would expect to be disseminated by means of public communication if the lawyer knows or reasonably should know that it will have a substantial likelihood of materially prejudicing an adjudicative proceeding.

(b) A statement referred to in paragraph (a) ordinarily is likely to have such an effect when it refers to a civil matter triable to a jury, a criminal matter, or any other proceeding that could result in incarceration, and the statement relates to:

(1) the character, credibility, reputation or criminal record of a party, suspect in a criminal investigation or witness, or the identity of a witness, or the expected testimony of a party or witness;

(2) in a criminal case or proceeding that could result in incarceration, the possibility of a plea of guilty to the offense or the existence or contents of any confession, admission, or statement given by a defendant or suspect or that person's refusal or failure to make a statement;

(3) the performance or results of an examination or test or the refusal or failure of a person to submit to an examination or test, or the identity or nature of physical evidence expected to be presented;

(4) any opinion as to the guilt or innocence of a defendant or suspect in a criminal case or proceeding that could result in incarceration;

(5) information the lawyer knows or reasonably should know is likely to be inadmissible as evidence in a trial and would if disclosed create a substantial risk of prejudicing an impartial trial; or

(6) the fact that a defendant has been charged with a crime, unless there is included therein a statement explaining that the charge is merely an accusation and that the defendant is presumed innocent until and unless proven guilty.

(c) Notwithstanding paragraph (a) and (b)(1-5), a lawyer involved in the investigation or litigation of a matter may state without elaboration:

(1) the general nature of the claim or defense;

(2) the information contained in a public record;

(3) that an investigation of the matter is in progress, including the general scope of the investigation, the offense or claim or defense involved and, except when prohibited by law, the identity of the persons involved;

(4) the scheduling or result of any step in litigation;

(5) a request for assistance in obtaining evidence and information necessary thereto;

(6) a warning of danger concerning the behavior of a person involved, when there is reason to believe that there exists the likelihood of substantial harm to an individual or to the public interest; and

(7) in a criminal case:

(i) the identity, residence, occupation and family status of the accused;

(ii) if the accused has not been apprehended, information necessary to aid in apprehension of that person;

(iii) the fact, time and place of arrest; and

(iv) the identity of investigation and arresting officers or agencies and the length of the investigation.

(SCO 1123 effective July 15, 1993)

COMMENT

It is difficult to strike a balance between protecting the right to a fair trial and safeguarding the right of free expression. Preserving the right to a fair trial necessarily entails some curtailment of the information that may be disseminated about a party prior to trial, particularly where trial by jury is involved. If there were no such limits, the result would be the practical nullification of the protective effect of the rules of forensic decorum and the exclusionary rules of evidence. On the other hand, there are vital social interests served by the free dissemination of information about events having legal consequences and about legal proceedings themselves. The public has a right to know about threats to its safety and measures aimed at assuring its security. It also has a legitimate interest in the conduct of judicial proceedings, particularly in matters, of general public concern. Furthermore, the subject matter of legal proceedings is often of direct significance in debate and deliberation over questions of public policy.

No body of rules can simultaneously satisfy all interests of fair trial and all those of free expression. The formula in this Rule is based upon the ABA Model Code of Professional Responsibility and the ABA Standards Relating to Fair Trial and Free Press, as amended in 1978.

Special rules of confidentiality may validly govern proceedings in juvenile, domestic relations and mental disability proceedings, and perhaps other types of litigation. Rule 3.4(c) requires compliance with such Rules.

Rule 3.7. Lawyer as Witness.

(a) A lawyer shall not act as advocate at a trial in which the lawyer is likely to be a necessary witness except when:

(1) the testimony relates to an uncontested issue;

(2) the testimony relates to the nature and value of legal services rendered in the case; or

(3) disqualification of the lawyer would work substantial hardship on the client.

(b) A lawyer may act as advocate in a trial in which another lawyer in the lawyer's firm is likely to be called as a witness unless precluded from doing so by Rule 1.7 or Rule 1.9.

(SCO 1123 effective July 15, 1993)

COMMENT

Combining the roles of advocate and witness can prejudice the opposing party and can involve a conflict of interest between the lawyer and client.

The opposing party has proper objection where the combination of roles may prejudice that party's rights in the litigation. A witness is required to testify on the basis of personal knowledge, while an advocate is expected to explain and comment on evidence given by others. It may not be clear whether a statement by an advocate-witness should be taken as proof or as an analysis of the proof.

Paragraph (a)(1) recognizes that if the testimony will be uncontested, the ambiguities in the dual role are purely theoretical. Paragraph (a)(2) recognizes that where the testimony concerns the extent and value of legal services rendered in the action in which the testimony is offered, permitting the lawyers to testify avoids the need for a second trial with new counsel to resolve that issue. Moreover, in such a situation the judge has firsthand knowledge of the matter in issue; hence, there is less dependence on the adversary process to test the credibility of the testimony.

Apart from these two exceptions, paragraph (a)(3) recognizes that a balancing is required between the interests of the client and those of the opposing party. Whether the opposing party is likely to suffer prejudice depends on the nature of the case, the importance and probable tenor of the lawyer's testimony, and the probability that the lawyer's testimony will conflict with that of other witnesses. Even if there is risk of such prejudice, in determining whether the lawyer should be disqualified, due regard must be given to the effect of disqualification on the lawyer's client. It is relevant that one or both parties could reasonably foresee that the lawyer would probably be a witness. The principal of imputed disqualification stated in Rule 1.10 has no application to this aspect of the problem.

Whether the combination of roles involves an improper conflict of interest with respect to the client is determined by Rule 1.7 or 1.9. For example, if there is likely to be substantial conflict between the testimony of the client and that of the lawyer or a member of the lawyer's firm, the representation is improper. The problem can arise whether the lawyer is called as a witness on behalf of the client or is called by the opposing party. Determining whether or not such a conflict exists is primarily the responsibility of the lawyer involved. See Comment to Rule 1.7. If a lawyer who is a member of a firm may not act as both advocate and witness by reason of conflict of interest, Rule 1.10 disqualifies the firm also. **But cf. Eufemio v. Kodiak Island Hospital**, 837 P.2d 95, 104 (Alaska 1992) (Disciplinary Rule 5-102 does not prevent a lawyer from representing the lawyer's law partner in litigation).

Annotations

Cases

Where the issue of whether lessees of store had consented to repossession of store by lessors had been decided in a previous case, making it highly probable that the lessors would be collaterally estopped from relitigating the issue in the present case, attorney who witnessed the repossession could represent the lessees against the lessors in the present case since was unlikely that the attorney would be called as a witness on the consent issue. **Murry v. Feight,** Op. No. 3210, 741 P2d 1148 (Alaska 1987).

Prosecutor, who had participated in a videotaped interrogation of defendant, was not required to withdraw from the case, where the judge directed the prosecutor not to refer to his participation in taking the statement and where, in the event either side needed to call a witness to the statement, a policeman who was present during the statement was available. **Kanulie v. State,** Op. No. 1070, 796 P2d 844 (Alaska App. 1990).

Where plaintiff was also an attorney, trial court abused its discretion in ruling that plaintiff's counsel could not be member of same law firm as plaintiff. **Eufemio v. Kodiak Island Hospital,** Op. No. 3868, 837 P2d 95 (Alaska 1992).

In will contest where issue was undue influence, attorney who drafted will was properly disqualified from representing proponent of will at trial since he was central figure in the litigation and his testimony was material and could not be obtained elsewhere. **Matter of Estate of McCoy,** Op. No. 3919, 844 P2d 1131 (Alaska 1993).

Rule 3.8. Special Responsibilities of a Prosecutor.

The prosecutor in a criminal case shall:

(a) refrain from prosecuting a charge that the prosecutor knows is not supported by probable cause;

(b) make reasonable efforts to assure that the accused has been advised of the right to, and the procedure for obtaining, counsel and has been given reasonable opportunity to obtain counsel;

(c) [Deleted]

(d) make timely disclosure to the defense of all evidence or information known to the prosecutor that tends to negate the guilt of the accused or mitigates the offense, and, in connection with sentencing, disclose to the defense and to the tribunal all unprivileged mitigating information known to the prosecutor, except when the prosecutor is relieved of this responsibility by a protective order of the tribunal; and

(e) exercise reasonable care to prevent investigators, law enforcement personnel, employees or other persons assisting or associated with the prosecutor in a criminal case from making an extrajudicial statement that the prosecutor would be prohibited from making under Rule 3.6.

(f) not subpoena a lawyer in a grand jury or other criminal proceeding to present evidence about a past or present client unless:

(1) the prosecutor reasonably believes:

(i) the information sought is not protected from disclosure by any applicable privilege;

(ii) the evidence sought is essential to the successful completion of an ongoing investigation or prosecution;

(iii) there is no other feasible alternative to obtain the information; and

(2) the prosecutor obtains prior judicial approval after an opportunity for an adversarial proceeding.

(SCO 1123 effective July 15, 1993)

ALASKA COMMENT

Alaska Rule 3.8 does not include paragraph (c) of the model rule. This paragraph would prevent a prosecutor from taking part in a legitimate interrogation of an arrested suspect. It would also prohibit a prosecutor from offering constructive pretrial resolutions of a criminal case, such as pretrial diversion or becoming a government witness. If a court determines that a prosecutor has taken unfair advantage of an unrepresented suspect or defendant legal remedies are already available.

COMMENT

A prosecutor has the responsibility of a minister of justice and not simply that of an advocate. This responsibility carries with it specific obligations to see that the defendant is accorded procedural justice and that guilt is decided upon the basis of sufficient evidence. Precisely how far the prosecutor is required to go in this direction is a matter of debate and varies in different jurisdictions. Many jurisdictions have adopted the ABA Standards of Criminal Justice Relating to the Prosecution Function, which in turn are the product of prolonged and careful deliberation by lawyers experienced in both criminal prosecution and defense. See also Rule 3.3(d), governing ex parte proceedings, among which grand jury proceedings are included. Applicable law may require other measures by the prosecutor and knowing disregard of those obligations or a systematic abuse of prosecutorial discretion could constitute a violation of Rule 8.4.

The exception in paragraph (d) recognizes that a prosecutor may seek an appropriate protective order from the tribunal if disclosure of information to the defense could result in substantial harm to an individual or to the public interest.

Paragraph (f) is intended to limit the issuance of lawyer subpoenas in grand jury and other criminal proceedings to those situations in which there is a genuine need to intrude into the client-lawyer relationship. The prosecutor is required to obtain court approval for the issuance of the subpoena after an opportunity for an adversarial hearing is afforded in order to assure an independent determination that the applicable standards are met.

Rule 3.9. Advocate in Nonadjudicative Proceedings.

A lawyer representing a client before a legislative committee or administrative agency in a non-adjudicative proceeding shall disclose that the appearance is in a representative capacity and shall conform to the applicable provisions of Rules 3.3(a) through (c), 3.4(a) through (c), and 3.5.

(SCO 1123 effective July 15, 1993)

COMMENT

In representation before bodies such as legislatures, municipal councils, and executive and administrative agencies acting in a rule-making or policy-making capacity, lawyers present facts, formulate issues and advance argument in the matters under consideration. The decision-making body, like a court, should be able to rely on the integrity of the submissions made to it. A lawyer appearing before such a body should deal with the tribunal honestly and in conformity with applicable rules of procedure.

Lawyers have no exclusive right to appear before nonadjudicative bodies, as they do before a court. The requirements of this rule therefore may subject lawyers to regulations inapplicable to advocates who are not lawyers. However, legislatures and administrative agencies have a right to expect lawyers to deal with them as they deal with courts.

This rule does not apply to representation of a client in a negotiation or other bilateral transaction with a governmental agency; representation in such a transaction is governed by Rules 4.1 through 4.4.

Rule 3.10. Communication with Jurors.

After discharge of the jury from further consideration of a case with which the lawyer was connected, the lawyer shall not ask questions of or make comments to a member of that jury that are calculated merely to harass or embarrass the juror or to influence the juror's actions in future jury service.

(SCO 1123 effective July 15, 1993)

ALASKA COMMENT

It was determined that DR 7-108(D) was worthy of retention.

TRANSACTIONS WITH PERSONS OTHER THAN CLIENTS

Rule 4.1. Truthfulness in Statements to Others.

In the course of representing a client a lawyer shall not knowingly:

(a) make a false statement of material fact or law to a third person; or

(b) fail to disclose a material fact to a third person when disclosure is necessary to avoid assisting a criminal or fraudulent act by a client, unless disclosure is prohibited by Rule 1.6.

(SCO 1123 effective July 15, 1993)

COMMENT

Misrepresentation

A lawyer is required to be truthful when dealing with others on a client's behalf, but generally has no affirmative duty to inform an opposing party of relevant facts. A misrepresentation can occur if the lawyer incorporates or affirms a statement of another person that the lawyer knows is false. Misrepresentations can also occur by failure to act.

Statements of Fact

This rule refers to statements of fact. Whether a particular statement should be regarded as one of fact can depend on the circumstances. Under generally accepted conventions in negotiation, certain types of statements ordinarily are not taken as statements of material fact. Estimates of price or value placed on the subject of a transaction and a party's intentions as to an acceptable settlement of a claim are in this category, and so is the existence of an undisclosed principal except where nondisclosure of the principal would constitute fraud.

Fraud by Client

Paragraph (b) recognizes that substantive law may require a lawyer to disclose certain information to avoid being deemed to have assisted the client's crime or fraud. The requirement of disclosure created by this paragraph is, however, subject to the obligations created by Rule 1.6.

Rule 4.2. Communication with Person Represented by Counsel.

In representing a client, a lawyer shall not communicate about the subject of the representation with a party or person the lawyer knows to be represented by another lawyer in the matter, unless the lawyer has the consent of the other lawyer or is authorized by law to do so.

(SCO 1123 effective July 15, 1993)

ALASKA COMMENT

See Rule 1.2(c) regarding communications when limited representation is provided.

COMMENT

This rule does not prohibit communication with a party, or an employee or agent of a party, concerning matters outside the representation. For example, the existence of a controversy between a government agency and a private party, or between two organizations, does not prohibit a lawyer for either from communicating with nonlawyer representatives of the other regarding a separate matter. Also, parties to a matter may communicate directly with each other and a lawyer having independent justification for communication with the other party is permitted to do so. Communications authorized by law include, for example, the right of a party to a controversy with a government agency to speak with government officials about the matter.

In the case of an organization, this rule prohibits communications by a lawyer for one party concerning the matter in representation with persons having a managerial responsibility on behalf of the organization. If an agent or employee of the organization is represented in the matter by his or her own counsel, the consent of that counsel to a communication will be sufficient for purposes of this Rule. Compare Rule 3.4(f).

This rule also covers any person, whether or not a party to a formal proceeding, who is represented by counsel concerning the matter in question.

Rule 4.3. Dealing with Unrepresented Person.

In dealing on behalf of a client with a person who is not represented by counsel, a lawyer shall not state or imply that the lawyer is disinterested. When the lawyer knows or reasonably should know that the unrepresented person misunderstands the lawyer's role in the matter, the lawyer shall make reasonable efforts to correct the misunderstanding.

(SCO 1123 effective July 15, 1993)

ALASKA COMMENT

See Rule 1.2(c) regarding communications when limited representation is provided.

COMMENT

An unrepresented person, particularly one not experienced in dealing with legal matters, might assume that a lawyer is disinterested in loyalties or is a disinterested authority on the law even when the lawyer represents a client.

Rule 4.4. Respect for Rights of Third Persons.

In representing a client, a lawyer shall not use means that have no substantial purpose other than to embarrass, delay, or burden a third person, nor use methods of obtaining evidence that violate the legal rights of such a person.

(SCO 1123 effective July 15, 1993)

COMMENT

Responsibility to a client requires a lawyer to subordinate the interests of others to those of the client, but that responsibility does not imply that a lawyer may disregard the rights of third persons. It is impractical to catalogue all such rights, but they include legal restrictions on methods of obtaining evidence from third persons.

LAW FIRMS AND ASSOCIATIONS

Rule 5.1. Responsibilities of a Partner or Supervisory Lawyer.

(a) A partner in a law firm shall make reasonable efforts to ensure that the firm has in effect measures giving reasonable assurance that all lawyers in the firm conform to the Rules of Professional Conduct.

(b) A lawyer having direct supervisory authority over another lawyer shall make reasonable efforts to ensure that the other lawyer conforms to the Rules of Professional Conduct.

(c) A lawyer shall be responsible for another lawyer's violation of the Rules of Professional Conduct if:

(1) the lawyer orders or, with knowledge of the specific conduct, ratifies the conduct involved; or

(2) the lawyer is a partner in the law firm in which the other lawyer practices, or has direct supervisory authority over the other lawyer, and knows of the conduct at a time when its consequences can be avoided or mitigated but fails to take reasonable remedial action.

(SCO 1123 effective July 15, 1993)

COMMENT

Paragraphs (a) and (b) refer to lawyers who have supervisory authority over the professional work of a firm or legal department of a government agency. This includes members of a partnership and the shareholders in a law firm organized as a professional corporation; lawyers having supervisory authority in the law department of an enterprise or government agency; and lawyers who have intermediate managerial responsibilities in a firm.

The measures required to fulfill the responsibility prescribed in paragraphs (a) and (b) can depend on the firm's structure and the nature of its practice. In a small firm, informal supervision and occasional admonition ordinarily might be sufficient. In a large firm, or in practice situations in which intensely difficult ethical problems frequently arise, more elaborate procedures may be necessary. Some firms, for example, have a procedure whereby junior lawyers can make confidential referral of ethical problems directly to a designated senior partner or special committee. See Rule 5.2. Firms, whether large or small, may also rely on continuing legal education in professional ethics. In any event, the ethical atmosphere of a firm can influence the conduct of all its members, and a lawyer having authority over the work of another may not assume that the subordinate lawyer will inevitably conform to the rules.

Paragraph (c)(1) expresses a general principle of responsibility for acts of another. See also Rule 8.4(a).

Paragraph (c)(2) defines the duty of a lawyer having direct supervisory authority over performance of specific legal work by another lawyer. Whether a lawyer has such supervisory authority in particular circumstances is a question of fact. Partners of a private firm have at least indirect responsibility for all work being done by the firm, while a partner in charge of a particular matter ordinarily has direct authority over other firm lawyers engaged in the matter. Appropriate remedial action by a partner would depend on the immediacy of the partner's involvement and the seriousness of the misconduct. The supervisor is required to intervene to prevent avoidable consequences of misconduct if the supervisor knows that the misconduct occurred. Thus, if a supervising lawyer know that a subordinate misrepresented a matter to an opposing party in negotiation, the supervisor as well as the subordinate has a duty to correct the resulting misapprehension.

Professional misconduct by a lawyer under supervision could reveal a violation of paragraph (b) on the part of the supervisory lawyer even though it does not entail a violation of paragraph (c) because there was no direction, ratification or knowledge of the violation.

Apart from this rule and Rule 8.4(a), a lawyer does not have disciplinary liability for the conduct of a partner, associate or subordinate. Whether a lawyer may be liable civilly or criminally for another lawyer's conduct is a question of law beyond the scope of these rules.

Rule 5.2. Responsibilities of a Subordinate Lawyer.

(a) A lawyer is bound by the Rules of Professional Conduct notwithstanding that the lawyer acted at the direction of another person.

(b) A subordinate lawyer does not violate the Rules of Professional Conduct if that lawyer acts in accordance with a supervisory lawyer's reasonable resolution of an arguable question of professional duty.

(SCO 1123 effective July 15, 1993)

COMMENT

Although a lawyer is not relieved of responsibility for a violation by the fact that the lawyer acted at the direction of a supervisor, that fact may be relevant in determining whether a lawyer had the knowledge required to render conduct a violation of the rules. For example, if a subordinate filed a frivolous pleading at the direction of a supervisor, the subordinate would not be guilty of a professional violation unless the subordinate knew of the document's frivolous character.

When lawyers in a supervisor-subordinate relationship encounter a matter involving professional judgment as to ethical duty, the supervisor may assume responsibility for making the judgment. Otherwise a consistent course of action or position could not be taken. If the question can reasonably be answered only one way, the duty of both lawyers is clear and they are equally responsible for fulfilling it. However, if the question is reasonably arguable, someone has to decide upon the course of action. That authority ordinarily reposes in the supervisor, and a subordinate may be guided accordingly. For example, if a question arises whether the interests of two clients conflict under Rule 1.7, the supervisor's reasonable resolution of the question should protect the subordinate professionally if the resolution is subsequently challenged.

Rule 5.3. Responsibilities Regarding Nonlawyer Assistants.

With respect to a nonlawyer employed or retained by or associated with a lawyer:

(a) each partner in a law firm shall make reasonable efforts to ensure that the firm has in effect measures giving reasonable assurance that the person's conduct is compatible with the professional obligations of the lawyer;

(b) a lawyer having direct supervisory authority over the nonlawyer shall make reasonable efforts to ensure that the person's conduct is compatible with the professional obligations of the lawyer; and

(c) a lawyer shall be responsible for conduct of such a person that would be a violation of the Rules of Professional Conduct if engaged in by a lawyer if:

(1) the lawyer orders or, with the knowledge of the specific conduct, ratifies the conduct involved; or

(2) the lawyer is a partner in the law firm in which the person is employed, or has direct supervisory authority over the person, and knows of the conduct at a time when its consequences can be avoided or mitigated but fails to take reasonable remedial action.

(SCO 1123 effective July 15, 1993; amended by SCO 1332 effective January 15, 1999)

COMMENT

Lawyers generally employ assistants in their practice, including secretaries, investigators, law student interns, and paraprofessionals. Such assistants, whether employees or independent contractors, act for the lawyer in rendition of the lawyer's professional services. A lawyer should give such assistants appropriate instruction and supervision concerning the ethical aspects of their employment, particularly regarding the obligation not to disclose a confidence or secret relating to representation of the client, and should be responsible for their work product. The measures employed in supervising nonlawyers should take account of the fact that they do not have legal training and are not subject to professional discipline.

Rule 5.4. Professional Independence of a Lawyer.

(a) A lawyer or law firm shall not share legal fees with a nonlawyer, except that:

(1) an agreement by a lawyer with the lawyer's firm, partner, or associate may provide for the payment of money, over a reasonable period of time after the lawyer's death, to the lawyer's estate or to one or more specified persons;

(2) a lawyer who purchases the practice of a lawyer who is deceased, disabled, or whose whereabouts are unknown may, pursuant to the provisions of Rule 1.17, pay to the estate or other representative of that lawyer the agreed-upon purchase price; and

(3) a lawyer or law firm may include nonlawyer employees in a compensation or retirement plan, even though the plan is based in whole or in part on a profit-sharing arrangement.

(b) A lawyer shall not form a partnership with a nonlawyer if any of the activities of the partnership consist of the practice of law.

(c) A lawyer shall not permit a person who recommends, employs, or pays the lawyer to render legal services for another to direct or regulate the lawyer's professional judgment in rendering such legal services.

(d) A lawyer shall not practice with or in the form of a professional corporation or association authorized to practice law for a profit, if:

(1) a nonlawyer owns any interest therein, except that a fiduciary representative of the estate of a lawyer may hold the stock or interest of the lawyer for a reasonable time during administration;

(2) a nonlawyer is a corporate director or officer thereof; or

(3) a nonlawyer has the right to direct or control the professional judgment of a lawyer.

(SCO 1123 effective July 15, 1993; amended by SCO 1371 effective April 15, 2000)

COMMENT

The provisions of this rule express traditional limitations on sharing fees. These limitations are to protect the lawyer's professional independence of judgment. Where someone other than the client pays the lawyer's fee or salary, or recommends employment of the lawyer, that arrangement does not modify the lawyer's obligation to the client. As stated in paragraph (c), such arrangements should not interfere with the lawyer's professional judgment.

Rule 5.5. Unauthorized Practice of Law.

A lawyer shall not:

(a) practice law in a jurisdiction where doing so violates the regulation of the legal profession in that jurisdiction; or

(b) assist a person who is not a member of the bar in the performance of activity that constitutes the unauthorized practice of law.

(SCO 1123 effective July 15, 1993)

COMMENT

The definition of the practice of law is established by law and varies from one jurisdiction to another. Whatever the definition, limiting the practice of law to members of the bar protects the public against rendition of legal services by unqualified persons. Paragraph (b) does not prohibit a lawyer from employing the services of paraprofessionals and delegating functions to them, so long as the lawyer supervises the delegated work and retains responsibility for their work. See Rule 5.3. Likewise, it does not prohibit lawyers from providing professional advice and instruction to nonlawyers whose employment requires knowledge of law; for example, claims adjusters, employees of financial or commercial institutions, social workers, accountants and persons employed in government agencies. In addition, a lawyer may counsel nonlawyers who wish to proceed pro se.

Rule 5.6. Restriction on Right to Practice.

A lawyer shall not participate in offering or making:

(a) a partnership or employment agreement that restricts the rights of a lawyer to practice after termination of the relationship, except an agreement concerning benefits upon retirement; or

(b) an agreement in which a restriction on the lawyer's right to practice is part of the settlement of a controversy between private parties.

(SCO 1123 effective July 15, 1993)

COMMENT

An agreement restricting the right of partners or associates to practice after leaving a firm not only limits their professional autonomy but also limits the freedom of clients to choose a lawyer. Paragraph (a) prohibits such agreements except for restrictions incident to provisions concerning retirement benefits for service with the firm.

Paragraph (b) prohibits a lawyer from agreeing not to represent other persons in connection with settling a claim on behalf of a client.

In 1990, the American Bar Association amended the comment to Rule 5.6 to include the following provision:

This Rule does not apply to prohibit restrictions that may be included in the terms of the sale of a law practice pursuant to Rule 1.17.

The Alaska Supreme Court has declined to adopt this amendment.

PUBLIC SERVICE

Rule 6.1. Pro Bono Publico Service.

Every lawyer has a professional responsibility to provide legal services to those unable to pay. A lawyer should aspire to render at least 50 hours of pro bono publico legal services per year. In fulfilling this responsibility, the lawyer should:

(a) provide a substantial majority of the 50 hours of legal services without fee or expectation of fee to:

(1) persons of limited means or

(2) charitable, religious, civic, community, governmental and educational organizations in matters that are designed primarily to address the needs of persons of limited means; and

(b) provide any additional services through:

(1) delivery of legal services at no fee or substantially reduced fee to individuals, groups or organizations seeking to secure or protect civil rights, civil liberties or public rights, or charitable, religious, civic, community, governmental and educational organizations in matters in furtherance of their organizational purposes, where the payment of standard legal fees would significantly deplete the organization's economic resources or would be otherwise inappropriate;

(2) delivery of legal services at a substantially reduced fee to persons of limited means; or

(3) participation in activities for improving the law, the legal system or the legal profession.

In addition, a lawyer should voluntarily contribute financial support to organizations that provide legal services to persons of limited means.

(SCO 1123 effective July 15, 1993; amended by SCO 1496 effective April 15, 2003)

COMMENT

[1] Every lawyer, regardless of professional prominence or professional work load, has a responsibility to provide legal services to those unable to pay, and personal involvement in the problems of the disadvantaged can be one of the most rewarding experiences in the life of a lawyer. The American Bar Association urges all lawyers to provide a minimum of 50 hours of pro bono services annually. States, however, may decide to choose a higher or lower number of hours of annual service (which may be expressed as a percentage of a lawyer's professional time) depending upon local needs and local conditions. It is recognized that in some years a lawyer may render greater or fewer hours than the annual standard specified, but during the course of his or her legal career, each lawyer should render on average per year, the number of hours set forth in this Rule. Services can be performed in civil matters or in criminal or quasi-criminal matters for which there is no government obligation to provide funds for legal representation, such as post-conviction death penalty appeal cases.

[2] Paragraphs (a)(1) and (2) recognize the critical need for legal services that exists among persons of limited means by providing that a substantial majority of the legal services rendered annually to the disadvantaged be furnished without fee or expectation of fee. Legal services under these paragraphs consist of a full range of activities, including individual and class representation, the provision of legal advice, legislative lobbying, administrative rule making and the provision of free training or mentoring to those who represent persons of limited means. The variety of these activities should facilitate participation by government lawyers, even when restrictions exist on their engaging in the outside practice of law.

[3] Persons eligible for legal services under paragraphs (a)(1) and (2) are those who qualify for participation in programs funded by the Legal Services Corporation and those whose incomes and financial resources are slightly above the guidelines utilized by such programs but nevertheless, cannot afford counsel. Legal services can be rendered to individuals or to organizations such as homeless shelters, battered women's centers and food pantries that serve those of limited means.

The term "governmental organizations" includes, but is not limited to, public protection programs and sections of governmental or public sector agencies.

[4] Because service must be provided without fee or expectation of fee, the intent of the lawyer to render free legal services is essential for the work performed to fall within the meaning of paragraphs (a)(1) and (2). Accordingly, services rendered cannot be considered pro bono if an anticipated fee is uncollected, but the award of statutory attorneys' fees in a case originally accepted as pro bono would not disqualify such services from inclusion under this section. Lawyers who do receive fees in such cases are encouraged to contribute an appropriate portion of such fees to organizations or projects that benefit persons of limited means.

[5] While it is possible for a lawyer to fulfill the annual responsibility to perform pro bono services exclusively through activities described in paragraphs (a)(1) and (2), to the extent that any hours of service remained unfulfilled, the remaining commitment can be met in a variety of ways as set forth in paragraph (b). Constitutional, statutory or regulatory restrictions may prohibit or impede government and public sector lawyers and judges from performing the pro bono services outlined in paragraphs (a)(1) and (2). Accordingly, where those restrictions apply, government and public sector lawyers and judges may fulfill their pro bono responsibility by performing services outlined in paragraph (b).

[6] Paragraph (b)(1) includes the provision of certain types of legal services to those whose incomes and financial resources place them above limited means. It also permits the pro bono lawyer to accept a substantially reduced fee for services. Examples of the types of issues that may be addressed under this paragraph include First Amendment claims, Title VII claims and environmental protection claims. Additionally, a wide range of organizations may be represented, including social service, medical research, cultural and religious groups.

[7] Paragraph (b)(2) covers instances in which lawyers agree to and receive a modest fee for furnishing legal services to persons of limited means. Participation in judicare programs and acceptance of court appointments in which the fee is substantially below a lawyer's usual rate are encouraged under this section.

[8] Paragraph (b)(3) recognizes the value of lawyers engaging in activities that improve the law, the legal system or the legal profession. Serving on bar association committees, serving on boards of pro bono or legal services programs, taking part in Law Day activities, acting as a continuing legal education instructor, a mediator or an arbitrator and engaging in legislative lobbying to improve the law, the legal system or the profession are a few examples of the many activities that fall within this paragraph.

[9] Because the provision of pro bono services is a professional responsibility, it is the individual ethical commitment of each lawyer. Nevertheless, there may be times when it is not feasible for a lawyer to engage in pro bono services. At such times a lawyer may discharge the pro bono responsibility by providing financial support to organizations providing free legal services to persons of limited means. Such financial support should be reasonably equivalent to the value of the hours of service that would have otherwise been provided. In addition, at times it may be more feasible to satisfy the pro bono responsibility collectively, as by a firm's aggregate pro bono activities.

[10] Because the efforts of individual lawyers are not enough to meet the need for free legal services that exists among persons of limited means, the government and the profession have instituted additional programs to provide those services. Every lawyer should financially support such programs, in addition to either providing direct pro bono services or making financial contributions when pro bono service is not feasible.

[11] Law firms should act reasonably to enable all lawyers in the firm to provide the pro bono legal services called for by this Rule.

[12] The responsibility set forth in this Rule is not intended to be enforced through disciplinary process.

Rule 6.2. Accepting Appointments.

A lawyer shall not seek to avoid appointment by a tribunal to represent a person except for good cause, such as:

(a) representing the client is likely to result in violation of the Rules of Professional Conduct or other law;

(b) representing the client is likely to result in an unreasonable financial burden on the lawyer; or

(c) the client or the cause is so repugnant to the lawyer as to be likely to impair the client-lawyer relationship or the lawyer's ability to represent the client.

(SCO 1123 effective July 15, 1993)

COMMENT

A lawyer ordinarily is not obliged to accept a client whose character or cause the lawyer regards as repugnant. The lawyer's freedom to select clients is, however, qualified. All lawyers have a responsibility to assist in providing pro bono publico service. See Rule 6.1. An individual lawyer fulfills this responsibility by accepting a fair share of unpopular matters or indigent or unpopular clients. A lawyer may also be subject to appointment by a court to serve unpopular clients or persons unable to afford legal services.

Rule 6.3. Membership in Legal Services Organization.

A lawyer may serve as a director, officer or member of a legal services organization, apart from the law firm in which the lawyer practices, notwithstanding that the organization serves persons having interests adverse to a client of the lawyer or the lawyer's firm. The lawyer shall not knowingly participate in a decision or action of the organization:

(a) if participating in the decision would be incompatible with the lawyer's obligations to a client under Rule 1.7; or

(b) where the decision could have a material adverse effect on the representation of a client of the organization whose interests are adverse to a client of the lawyer.

(SCO 1123 effective July 15, 1993)

COMMENT

Lawyers should be encouraged to support and participate in legal service organizations. A lawyer who is an officer or a member of such an organization does not thereby have a client-lawyer relationship with persons served by the organization. However, there is potential conflict between the interests of such persons and the interests of the lawyer's clients. If the possibility of such conflict disqualified a lawyer from serving on the board of a legal services organization, the profession's involvement in such organizations would be severely curtailed.

It may be necessary in appropriate cases to reassure a client of the organization that the representation will not be affected by conflicting loyalties of a member of the board. Established, written policies in this respect can enhance the credibility of such assurances.

Rule 6.4. Law Reform Activities Affecting Client Interests.

A lawyer may serve as a director, officer or member of an organization involved in reform of the law or its administration notwithstanding that the reform may affect the interests of a client of the lawyer. When the lawyer knows that the interests of a client may be materially benefited by a decision in which the lawyer participates, the lawyer shall make an appropriate disclosure within the organization, but need not identify the client.

(SCO 1123 effective July 15, 1993)

ALASKA COMMENT

The Committee amended the last sentence in order to state more clearly the nature of the disclosure which must be made by the lawyer.

COMMENT

Lawyers involved in organizations seeking law reform generally do not have a client-lawyer relationship with the organization. Otherwise, it might follow that a lawyer could not be involved in a bar association law reform program that might indirectly affect a client. See also Rule 1.2(b). For example, a lawyer specializing in antitrust litigation might be regarded as disqualified from participating in drafting revisions of rules governing that subject. In determining the nature and scope of participation in such activities, a lawyer should be mindful of obligations to clients under other rules, particularly Rule 1.7. A lawyer is professionally obligated to protect the integrity of the program by making an appropriate disclosure within the organization when the lawyer knows a private client might be materially benefited.

INFORMATION ABOUT LEGAL SERVICES

Rule 7.1. Communications Concerning a Lawyer's Services.

A lawyer shall not make a false or misleading communication about the lawyer or the lawyer's services or any prospective client's need for legal services. A communication is false or misleading if it:

(a) contains a material misrepresentation of fact or law, or omits a fact necessary to make the statement considered as a whole not materially misleading;

(b) is likely to create an unjustified expectation about results the lawyer can achieve, or states or implies that the lawyer can achieve results by means that violate the Rules of Professional Conduct or other law; or

(c) compares the lawyer's services with other lawyer's services, unless the comparison can be factually substantiated.

(SCO 1123 effective July 15, 1993)

ALASKA COMMENT

The Committee revised Model Rule 7.1 to address the situation in which a lawyer might provide misleading information with regard to a potential client's needs for legal services from a particular lawyer.

COMMENT

This rule governs all communications about a lawyer's services, including advertising permitted by Rule 7.2. Whatever means are used to make known a lawyer's services, statements about them should be truthful. The prohibition in paragraph (b) of statements that may create "unjustified expectations" would ordinarily preclude advertisements about results obtained on behalf of a client, such as the amount of a damage award or the lawyer's record in obtaining favorable verdicts, and advertisements containing client endorsements. Such information may create the unjustified expectation that similar results can be obtained for others without reference to the specific factual and legal circumstances.

Rule 7.2. Advertising.

(a) Subject to the requirements of Rules 7.1 and 7.3, a lawyer may advertise services through public media, such as a telephone directory, legal directory, newspaper or other periodical, outdoor advertising, radio or television or through written or recorded communication.

(b) A copy or recording of each advertisement or communication shall be retained by the lawyer for two years after its last dissemination along with a record of when and where it was used.

(c) A lawyer shall not give anything of value to a person for recommending the lawyer's services, except that a lawyer may

(1) pay the reasonable cost of advertising or written communication permitted by this rule;

(2) pay the usual charges of a not-for-profit lawyer referral service or other legal service organization; and

(3) pay for a law practice in accordance with Rule 1.17.

(d) Any communication made pursuant to this rule shall include the name of at least one lawyer responsible for its content.

(SCO 1123 effective July 15, 1993)

COMMENT

To assist the public in obtaining legal services, lawyers should be allowed to make known their services not only through reputation but also through organized information campaigns in the form of advertising. Advertising involves an active quest for clients, contrary to the tradition that a lawyer should not seek clientele. However, the public's need to know about legal services can be fulfilled in part through advertising. This need is particularly acute in the case of persons of moderate means who have not made extensive use of legal services. The interest in expanding public information about legal services ought to prevail over considerations of tradition. Nevertheless, advertising by lawyers entails the risk of practices that are misleading or overreaching.

This rule permits public dissemination of information concerning a lawyer's name or firm name, address and telephone number; the kinds of services the lawyer will undertake; the basis on which the lawyer's fees are determined, including prices for specific services and payment and credit arrangements; a lawyer's foreign language ability; names of references and, with their consent, names of clients regularly represented; and other information that might invite the attention of those seeking legal assistance.

Questions of effectiveness and taste in advertising are matters of speculation and subjective judgment. Some jurisdictions have had extensive prohibitions against television advertising, against advertising going beyond specified facts about a lawyer, or against "undignified" advertising. Television is now one of the most powerful media for getting information to the public, particularly persons of low and moderate income; prohibiting television advertising, therefore, would impede the flow of information about legal services to many sectors of the public. Limiting the information that may be advertised has a similar effect and assumes that the bar can accurately forecast the kind of information that the public would regard as relevant.

Neither this rule nor Rule 7.3 prohibits communications authorized by law, such as notice to members of a class in class action litigation.

Record of Advertising

Paragraph (b) requires that a record of the content and use of advertising be kept in order to facilitate enforcement of this rule. It does not require that advertising be subject to review prior to dissemination. Such a requirement would be burdensome and expensive relative to its possible benefits, and may be of doubtful constitutionality.

Paying Others to Recommend a Lawyer

A lawyer is allowed to pay for advertising permitted by this rule and for the purchase of a law practice in accordance with the provisions of Rule 1.17, but otherwise is not permitted to pay another person for channeling professional work. This restriction does not prevent an organization or person other than the lawyer from advertising or recommending the lawyer's services. Thus, a legal aid agency or prepaid legal services may pay to advertise legal services provided under its auspices. Likewise, a lawyer may participate in not-for-profit lawyer referral programs and pay the usual fees charged by such programs. Paragraph (c) does not prohibit paying regular compensation to an assistant, such as a secretary, to prepare communications permitted by this rule.

Rule 7.3. Direct Contact with Prospective Clients.

(a) A lawyer shall not solicit by in-person or live telephone contact professional employment from a prospective client with whom the lawyer has no family or prior professional relationship when a significant motive for the lawyer's doing so is the lawyer's pecuniary gain.

(b) A lawyer shall not solicit professional employment from a prospective client by written or recorded communication or by in-person or telephone contact even when not otherwise prohibited by paragraph (a), if:

(1) the prospective client has made known to the lawyer a desire not to be solicited by the lawyer; or

(2) the solicitation involves coercion, duress or harassment.

(c) Every written or recorded communication from a lawyer soliciting professional employment from a prospective client known to be in need of legal services in a particular matter, and with whom the lawyer has no family or prior professional relationship, shall include the words "Advertising Material" on the front of the outside envelope and at the beginning and ending of any recorded communication.

(d) Notwithstanding the prohibitions in paragraph (a), a lawyer may participate in a prepaid or group legal service plan operated by an organization not owned or directed by the lawyer which uses in-person or telephone contact to solicit memberships or subscriptions for the plan from persons who are not known to need legal services in a particular matter covered by the plan.

(SCO 1123 effective July 15, 1993; amended by SCO 1426, effective April 15, 2001)

COMMENT

There is a potential for abuse inherent in direct in-person or live telephone contact by a lawyer with a prospective client known to need legal services. These forms of contact between a lawyer and a prospective client subject the layperson to the private importuning of the trained advocate in a direct interpersonal encounter. The prospective client, who may already feel overwhelmed by the circumstances giving rise to the need for legal services, may find it difficult fully to evaluate all available alternatives with reasoned judgment and appropriate self-interest in the fact of the lawyer's presence and insistence upon being retained immediately. The situation is fraught with the possibility of undue influence, intimidation, and over-reaching.

This potential for abuse inherent in direct in-person or live telephone solicitation of prospective clients justifies its prohibition, particularly since lawyer advertising permitted under Rule 7.2 offer alternative means of conveying necessary information to those who may be in need of legal services. Advertising and written and recorded communications which may be mailed or autodialed make it possible for a prospective client to be informed about the need for legal services, and about the qualifications of available lawyers and law firms, without subjecting the prospective client to direct in-person or telephone persuasion that may overwhelm the client's judgment.

The use of general advertising and written and recorded communications to transmit information from lawyer to prospective client, rather than direct in-person or live telephone contact, will help to assure that the information flows cleanly as well as freely. The contents of advertisements and communications permitted under Rule 7.2 are permanently recorded so that they cannot be disputed and may be shared with others who know the lawyer. This potential for informal review is itself likely to help guard against statements and claims that might constitute false and misleading communications, in violation of Rule 7.1. The contents of direct in-person or live telephone conversations between a lawyer to a prospective client can be disputed and are not subject to third-party scrutiny. Consequently, they are much more likely to approach (and occasionally cross) the dividing line between accurate representations and those that are false and misleading.

There is far less likelihood that a lawyer would engage in abusive practices against an individual with whom the lawyer has a prior personal or professional relationship or where the lawyer is motivated by considerations other than the lawyer's pecuniary gain. Consequently, the general prohibition in Rule 7.3(a) and the requirements of Rule 7.3(c) are not applicable in those situations.

But even permitted forms of solicitation can be abused. Thus, any solicitation which contains information which is false or misleading within the meaning of Rule 7.1, which involves coercion, duress or harassment within the meaning of Rule 7.3(b)(2), or which involves contact with a prospective client who has made known to the lawyer a desire not to be solicited by the lawyer within the meaning of Rule 7.3(b)(1) is prohibited. Moreover, if after sending a letter or other communication to a client as permitted by Rule 7.2 the lawyer receives no response, any further effort to communicate with the prospective client may violate the provisions of Rule 7.3(b).

This Rule is not intended to prohibit a lawyer from contacting representatives of organizations or groups that may be interested in establishing a group or prepaid legal plan for its members, insureds, beneficiaries or other third parties for the purpose of informing such entities of the availability of and details concerning the plan or arrangement which the lawyer or the lawyer's firm is willing to offer. This form of communication is not directed to a prospective client. Rather, it is usually addressed to an individual acting in a fiduciary capacity seeking a supplier of legal services for others who may, if they choose, become prospective clients of the lawyer. Under these circumstances, the activity which the lawyer undertakes in communicating with such representatives and the type of information transmitted to the individual are functionally similar to and serve the same purpose as advertising permitted under Rule 7.2.

The requirement in Rule 7.3(c) that certain communications be marked "Advertising Material" does not apply to communications sent in response to requests of potential clients or their spokespersons or sponsors. General announcements by lawyers, including changes in personnel or office location, do not constitute communications soliciting professional employment from a client known to be in need of legal services within the meaning of this Rule.

Paragraph (d) of this Rule would permit an attorney to participate with an organization which uses personal contact to solicit members for its group or prepaid legal service plan, provided that the personal contact is not undertaken by any lawyer who would be a provider of legal services through the plan. The organization referred in paragraph (d) must not be owned by or directed (whether as manager or otherwise) by any lawyer or law firm that participates in the plan. For example, paragraph (d) would not permit a lawyer to create an organization controlled directly or indirectly by the lawyer and use the organization for the in-person or telephone solicitation of legal employment of the lawyer through memberships in the plan or otherwise. The communication permitted by these organizations also must not be directed to a person known to need legal services in a particular matter, but it is to be designed to inform potential plan members generally of another means of affordable legal services. Lawyers who participate in a legal service plan must reasonably assure that the plan sponsors are in compliance with Rules 7.1, 7.2 and 7.3(b). See 8.4(a)

Rule 7.4. Communication of Fields of Practice and Certification.

A lawyer may communicate the fact that the lawyer does or does not practice in particular fields of law. A lawyer shall not state or imply that the lawyer is a "specialist," "certified," or words of similar import except as follows:

(a) a lawyer admitted to engage in patent practice before the United States Patent and Trademark Office may use the designation "Patent Attorney" or a substantially similar designation; and

(b) a lawyer may communicate the fact that the lawyer has been certified as a specialist in a field of law by a named organization or authority, but only if that certification is granted by an organization or authority whose specialty certification program is accredited by the American Bar Association.

(SCO 1123 effective July 15, 1993; and amended by SCO 1379 effective April 15, 2000)

ALASKA COMMENT

Paragraph (b) was deleted from ABA Model Rule 7.4 because the Committee concluded that under modern practice the field of admiralty is no longer a unique specialization.

COMMENT

Recognition of specialization in patent matters is a matter of long established policy of the Patent and Trademark Office.

This rule permits a lawyer to indicate areas of practice in communications about the lawyer's services; for example, in a telephone directory or other advertising. If a lawyer practices only in certain fields, or will not accept matters except in such fields, the lawyer is permitted to so indicate. All communications are, however, subject to the "false and misleading" standard of Rule 7.1 in respect to communications concerning a lawyer's services.

A lawyer may not communicate that the lawyer is a specialist or has been recognized or certified as a specialist in a particular field of law, except as provided by this rule. Recognition of specialization in patent matters is a matter of long established policy of the Patent and Trademark Office, as reflected in paragraph (a). The American Bar Association's Model Rule 7.4 also permits attorneys who specialize in admiralty law to use the designation "proctor in admiralty" or otherwise hold themselves out as specialists in admiralty. This exception was not included in Alaska's Professional Conduct Rule 7.4 because the Alaska Bar Association's Committee on the Rules of Professional Conduct concluded that under modern practice the field of admiralty is no longer a unique specialization.

Paragraph (b) permits a lawyer to communicate that the lawyer has been certified as specialist in a field of law when the American Bar Association has accredited the organization's specialty program to grant such certification. Certification procedures imply that an objective entity has recognized a lawyer's higher degree of specialized ability than is suggested by general licensure to practice law. Those objective entities may be expected to apply standards of competence, experience, and knowledge to insure that a lawyer's recognition as a specialist is meaningful and reliable. In order to insure that consumers can obtain access to useful certification information, the name of the certifying organization or agency must be included in any communication regarding the certification.

See **Peel v. Attorney Registration & Disciplinary Comm'n**, 496 U.S. 91, 110 S. Ct. 2281, 110 L.Ed.2d 83 (1990).

Rule 7.5. Firm Names and Letterheads.

(a) A lawyer shall not use a firm name, letterhead or other professional designation that violates Rule 7.1. A trade name may be used by a lawyer in private practice if it does not imply a connection with a government agency or with a public or charitable legal services organization and is not otherwise in violation of Rule 7.1.

(b) A law firm with offices in more than one jurisdiction may use the same name in each jurisdiction, but identification of the lawyers in an office of the firm shall indicate the jurisdictional limitations on those not licensed to practice in the jurisdiction where the office is located.

(c) The name of a lawyer holding a public office shall not be used in the name of a law firm, or in communications on its behalf, during any substantial period in which the lawyer is not actively and regularly practicing with the firm.

(d) Lawyers shall not state or imply that they practice in a partnership or other organization unless the relationship stated or implied in fact exists.

(e) The term "of counsel" shall be used only to refer to a lawyer who has a close continuing relationship with the firm.

(SCO 1123 effective July 15, 1993)

ALASKA COMMENT

Paragraph (d) of Rule 7.5 was amended simply to make it read better.

The ABA commentary notes that attorneys who share office facilities should not call themselves "Smith and Jones" or any other name suggesting partnership. Similarly, the committee thought that a sole practitioner should not use "and associates" or other language implying a group practice. The committee added subsection (e).

The term "of counsel" contemplates either that the lawyer practices in the offices of the lawyer or law firm to which the lawyer is "of counsel," or that the lawyer is in regular and frequent contact with the lawyer or law firm. The term shall not be applied to one who is merely a forwarder or receiver of legal business. The fact that a lawyer emphasizes a particular field and is willing to accept business from several firms does not make him "of counsel" to all those firms. A lawyer should not be "of counsel" to more than two or three law firms, because the term implies a close continuing relationship that could be relied upon by prospective clients.

COMMENT

A firm may be designated by the names of all or some of its members, by the names of deceased members where there has been a continuing succession in the firm's identity or by a trade name such as the "ABC Legal Clinic." Although the United States Supreme Court has held that legislation may prohibit the use of trade names in professional practice, use of such names in law practice is acceptable so long as it is not misleading. If a private firm uses a trade name that includes a geographical name such as "Springfield Legal Clinic," an express disclaimer that it is a public legal aid agency may be required to avoid a misleading implication. It may be observed that any firm name including the name of a deceased partner is, strictly speaking, a trade name. The use of names to designate law firms has proven a useful means of identification. However, it is misleading to use the name of a lawyer not associated with the firm or a predecessor of the firm.

With regard to paragraph (d), lawyers sharing office facilities, but who are not in fact partners, may not denominate themselves as, for example, "Smith and Jones," for that title suggests partnership in the practice of law.

MAINTAINING THE INTEGRITY OF THE PROFESSION

Rule 8.1. Bar Admission and Disciplinary Matters.

An applicant for admission to the bar, or a lawyer in connection with a bar admission application or in connection with a disciplinary matter, shall not:

(a) knowingly make a false statement of material fact; or

(b) fail to disclose a fact necessary to correct a misapprehension known by the person to have arisen in the matter, or knowingly fail to respond to a lawful demand for information from an admissions or disciplinary authority, except that this rule does not require disclosure of information otherwise protected by Rule 1.6.

(SCO 1123 effective July 15, 1993)

COMMENT

The duty imposed by this rule extends to persons seeking admission to the bar as well as to lawyers. Hence, if a person makes a material false statement in connection with an application for admission, it may be the basis for subsequent disciplinary action if the person is admitted, and in any event may be relevant in a subsequent admission application. The duty imposed by this rule applies to a lawyer's own admission or discipline as well as that of others. Thus, it is a separate professional offense for a lawyer to knowingly make a misrepresentation or omission in connection with a disciplinary investigation of the lawyer's own conduct. This rule also requires affirmative clarification of any misunderstanding on the part of the admissions or disciplinary authority of which the person involved becomes aware.

This rule is subject to the provisions of the Fifth Amendment of the United States Constitution and corresponding provisions of state constitutions. A person relying on such a provision in response to a question, however, should do so openly and not use the right of nondisclosure as a justification for failure to comply with this rule.

A lawyer representing an applicant for admission to the bar, or representing a lawyer who is the subject of a disciplinary inquiry or proceeding, is governed by the rules applicable to the client-lawyer relationship.

Rule 8.2. Judicial and Legal Officials.

(a) A lawyer shall not make a statement that the lawyer knows to be false or with reckless disregard as to its truth or falsity concerning the qualifications or integrity of a judge, adjudicatory officer or public legal officer, or of a candidate for election or appointment to judicial or legal office.

(b) A lawyer who is a candidate for judicial office shall comply with the applicable provisions of the Code of Judicial Conduct.

(SCO 1123 effective July 15, 1993)

COMMENT

Assessments by lawyers are relied on in evaluating the professional or personal fitness of persons being considered for election or appointment to judicial office and to public legal offices, such as attorney general, prosecuting attorney and public defender. Expressing honest and candid opinions on such matters contributes to improving the administration of justice. Conversely, false statements by a lawyer can unfairly undermine public confidence in the administration of justice.

When a lawyer seeks judicial office, the lawyer should be bound by applicable limitations on political activity.

To maintain the fair and independent administration of justice, lawyers are encouraged to continue traditional efforts to defend judges and courts unjustly criticized.

Rule 8.3. Reporting Professional Misconduct.

(a) A lawyer having knowledge that another lawyer has committed a violation of the rules of professional conduct that raises a substantial question as to that lawyer's honesty, trustworthiness or fitness as a lawyer in other respects, shall inform the appropriate professional authority.

(b) A lawyer having knowledge that a judge has committed a violation of applicable rules of judicial conduct that raises a substantial question as to the judge's fitness for office shall inform the appropriate authority.

(c) This rule does not require disclosure of information protected by Rule 1.6 or information gained by a lawyer or judge while serving as a member of an approved lawyers assistance program to the extent such information would be confidential if it were communicated subject to the attorney-client privilege.

(SCO 1123 effective July 15, 1993)

COMMENT

Self-regulation of the legal profession requires that members of the profession initiate disciplinary investigation when they know of a violation of the Rules of Professional Conduct. Lawyers have a similar obligation with respect to judicial misconduct. An apparently isolated violation may indicate a pattern of misconduct that only a disciplinary investigation can uncover. Reporting a violation is especially important where the victim is unlikely to discover the offense.

A report about misconduct is not required where it would involve violation of Rule 1.6. However, a lawyer should encourage a client to consent to disclosure where prosecution would not substantially prejudice the client's interests.

If a lawyer were obliged to report every violation of the Rules, the failure to report any violation would itself be a professional offense. Such a requirement existed in many jurisdictions but proved to be unenforceable. This Rule limits the reporting obligation to those offenses that a self-regulating profession must vigorously endeavor to prevent. A measure of judgment is, therefore, required in complying with the provisions of this Rule. The term "substantial" refers to the seriousness of the possible offense and not the quantum of evidence of which the lawyer is aware. A report should be made to the bar disciplinary agency unless some other agency, such as a peer review agency, is more appropriate in the circumstances. Similar considerations apply to the reporting of judicial misconduct.

The duty to report professional misconduct does not apply to a lawyer retained to represent a lawyer whose professional conduct is in question. Such a situation is governed by the Rules applicable to the client-lawyer relationship.

Information about a lawyer's or judge's misconduct or fitness may be received by a lawyer in the course of that lawyer's participation in an approved lawyers or judges assistance program. In that circumstance, providing for the confidentiality of such information encourages lawyers and judges to seek treatment through such program. Conversely, without such confidentiality, lawyers and judges may hesitate to seek assistance from these programs, which may then result in additional harm to their professional careers and additional injury to the welfare of clients and the public. The Rule therefore exempts the lawyer from the reporting requirements of paragraphs (a) and (b) with respect to information that would be privileged if the relationship between the impaired lawyer or judge and the recipient of the information were that of a client and a lawyer. On the other hand, a lawyer who receives such information would nevertheless be required to comply with the Rule 8.3 reporting provisions to report misconduct if the impaired lawyer or judge indicates an intent to engage in illegal activity, for example, the conversion of client funds to his or her use.

Rule 8.4. Misconduct.

It is professional misconduct for a lawyer to:

(a) violate or attempt to violate the rules of professional conduct, knowingly assist or induce another to do so, or do so through the acts of another;

(b) commit a criminal act that reflects adversely on the lawyer's honesty, trustworthiness or fitness as a lawyer in other respects;

(c) engage in conduct involving dishonesty, fraud, deceit or misrepresentation;

(d) state or imply an ability to improperly influence a government agency or official; or,

(e) knowingly assist a judge or judicial officer in conduct that is a violation of applicable rules of judicial conduct or other law.

(SCO 1123 effective July 15, 1993)

ALASKA COMMENT

Paragraph (d) of the ABA Rules was omitted because it is too vague. See the ABA Legal Background Section. All improper conduct is already regulated under the other rules.

COMMENT

Many kinds of illegal conduct reflect adversely on fitness to practice law, such as offenses involving fraud and the offense of willful failure to file an income tax return. However, some kinds of offense carry no such implication. Traditionally, the distinction was drawn in terms of offenses involving "moral turpitude." That concept can be construed to include offenses concerning some matters of personal morality, such as adultery and comparable offenses, that have no specific connection to fitness for the practice of law. Although a lawyer is personally answerable to the entire criminal law, a lawyer should be professionally answerable only for offenses that indicate lack of those characteristics relevant to law practice. Offenses involving violence, dishonesty, or breach of trust, or serious interference with the administration of justice are in that category. A pattern of repeated offenses, even ones of minor significance when considered separately, can indicate indifference to legal obligation.

A lawyer may refuse to comply with an obligation imposed by law upon a good faith belief that no valid obligation exists. The provisions of Rule 1.2(d) concerning a good faith challenge to the validity, scope, meaning or application of the law apply to challenges of legal regulation of the practice of law.

Lawyers holding public office assume legal responsibilities going beyond those of other citizens. A lawyer's abuse of public office can suggest an inability to fulfill the professional role of attorney. The same is true of abuse of positions of private trust such as trustee, executor, administrator, guardian, agent and officer, director or manager of a corporation or other organization.

Annotations

Cases

Prosecutor's failure to reveal possible taint of identification procedure was violative of former DR 1-102(a)(4) and (5) and former DR 7-102(a)(6). **Buchanan v. State,** Op. No. 2553, 554 P2d 1153 (Alaska 1976).

Grossly negligent misconduct is not within the ambit of the rule prohibiting lawyers from engaging in conduct involving dishonesty, fraud, deceit, or misrepresentation, but does violate the rule on failing to act competently as well as other disciplinary rules. **In re Simpson,** Op. No. 2517, 645 P2d 1223 (Alaska 1982).

Statements by attorney in letters to two federal officials during the attorney's representation of clients in a federal quiet title and ejectment action, which accused certain official of perjury and cheating and warned that they might find themselves criminally or personally liable in tort, were improper and required public censure. **Discipline of Vollintine,** Op. No. 2756, 673 P2d 755 (Alaska 1983).

Discipline of attorney for writing letters to two federal officials accusing certain officials of perjury and cheating and warning that they might find themselves criminally or personally liable in tort did not violate the attorney's right of free speech. **Discipline of Vollintine,** Op. No. 2756, 673 P2d 755 (Alaska 1983).

Attorney, representing plaintiff in a personal injury action, who agreed to assert a military claim for reimbursement of the cost of providing medical care to the plaintiff, breached her fiduciary obligation to the military when she negotiated a settlement and distributed all of the proceeds to the plaintiff and to herself as attorney's fees; accordingly, since her conduct as a matter of law involved dishonesty and misrepresentation, suspension was the appropriate sanction. **In re Minor,** Op. No. 2726, 681 P2d 1347 (Alaska 1983).

Where attorney, acting for all plaintiffs in a complex tort suit, deposited an $81,000 settlement contribution in his client trust account and, without permission from the other plaintiffs' attorneys, drew on the trust account to advance funds to his client and to pay himself attorney's fees not yet due him, attorney violated former DR 1-102(A)(4) (conduct involving dishonesty, fraud, deceit, or misrepresentation), former DR 9-102(A) (lawyer's management of money held in trust for others) and former DR 1-102(A)(3) (illegal conduct involving moral turpitude), but did not violate former DR 1-102(A)(5) (conduct prejudicial to administration of justice), resulting in sanction of three-year suspension from the practice of law. **In re Friedman,** Op. No. 5408, 23 P3d 620 (Alaska 2001).

Attorney was suspended for three years for failing to file documents in a divorce case, and for falsifying settlement documents in response to a grievance, in violation of Alaska Bar R. 15(a)(3) and this rule. Cooperation and the effect of the suspension were not mitigating factors, and the mitigating factors of a good prior record, remorsefulness, and the unlikelihood of recurring violations were not sufficient to warrant a lesser sanction. **In the Disciplinary Matter Involving Hanlon,** Op. No. 5887, 110 P.3d 937 (Alaska 2005).

Rule 8.5. Disciplinary Jurisdiction.

A person admitted to practice in Alaska is subject to the disciplinary authority of this state, regardless of where the conduct occurs, and even though the person may be subject to the disciplinary authority of another jurisdiction for the same conduct. A person who, although not admitted to practice law in Alaska, is permitted to practice law pursuant to court rule or order is subject to the disciplinary authority of this state to the same extent as if the person were admitted to practice in Alaska.

(SCO 1123 effective July 15, 1993; amended by SCO 1353, effective October 15, 1999.)

ALASKA COMMENT

The second sentence of Alaska's Rule 8.5 was added in order to cover the situation where an attorney admitted in another state is practicing in this state pursuant, for example, to Civil Rule 81 or Bar Rules 43, 43.1, and 44, or where a non-either by future codification or through a case-by-case, common-law process.

COMMENT

In modern practice lawyers frequently act outside the territorial limits of the jurisdiction in which they are licensed to practice, either in another state or outside the United States. In doing so, they remain subject to the governing authority of the jurisdiction in which they are licensed to practice. If their attorney has been allowed by special order of the court to engage in the practice of law before that court.

Alaska's Rule 8.5 was revised in 1999 to eliminate some of the references to "jurisdiction" that appeared in the original version of the Alaska rule. The word "jurisdiction" is ambiguous: it can refer either to a legal entity (such as a state or federal government) or to an entity's legal authority to perform an action. Because of this ambiguity, and because Rule 8.5 must refer to both of these concepts, Alaska's Rule 8.5 now uses the word "jurisdiction" to mean another government, and it uses the phrase "disciplinary authority" to mean "disciplinary jurisdiction" - the legal authority to investigate disciplinary matters and to commence disciplinary proceedings.

The 1999 revision of Alaska's Rule 8.5 was also intended to clarify that, regardless of where a person may commit professional misconduct, Alaska has the authority to pursue disciplinary proceedings against that person for the misconduct if the person is admitted to practice law in Alaska or if the person is engaged in the practice of law in Alaska under a court rule (for example, legal interns) or a court order (attorneys appearing pro hac vice).

Rule 8.5 speaks only to Alaska's legal authority to pursue disciplinary proceedings. The rule does not address the question of whether the Alaska Rules of Professional Conduct should govern any assessment of the attorney's conduct. Difficult choice-of-law problems can arise when an attorney engages in the practice of law in two or more jurisdictions. For instance, an Alaska attorney who is appearing pro hac vice in another state might engage in conduct in that other state which is perfectly legal under that state's code of professional conduct, but which violates the Alaska Rules of Professional Conduct.

In 1993, the American Bar Association amended its Model Rule 8.5 to codify specific rules to govern these conflict-of-law situations. See ABA Model Rule 8.5(b). However, the ABA's proposed conflict-of-law rules have drawn significant criticism, and these proposed rules still fail to answer some of the more difficult problems in this area.

Alaska's Rule 8.5 does not address these choice-of-law problems. The rule only defines the authority of the Alaska Bar Association and (ultimately) the Alaska Supreme Court to investigate and pursue disciplinary matters. The rule does not answer the question of whether the propriety of a person's conduct should be assessed under the Alaska Rules of Professional Conduct or under the rules of some other jurisdiction. Such questions must be answered

activity in another jurisdiction is substantial and continuous, it may constitute practice of law in that jurisdiction. See Rule 5.5.

If the rules of professional conduct in the two jurisdictions differ, principles of conflict of laws may apply. Similar problems can arise when a lawyer is licensed to practice in more than one jurisdiction.

Where the lawyer is licensed to practice law in two

jurisdictions which impose conflicting obligations, applicable rules of choice of law may govern the situation. A related problem arises with respect to practice before a federal tribunal, where the general authority of the states to regulate the practice of law must be reconciled with such authority as federal tribunals may have to regulate practice before them.

Rule 9.1. Definitions.

(a) "Belief" or "believes" denotes that the person involved actually supposed the fact in question to be true. A person's belief may be inferred from circumstances.

(b) "Client" denotes a person, public officer, or corporation, association, other organization or entity, either public or private, who is rendered professional legal services by a lawyer, or who consults a lawyer with a view to obtaining professional legal services.

(c) "Consult" or "consultation" denotes communication of information reasonably sufficient to permit the client to appreciate the significance of the matter in question.

(d) "Firm" or "law firm" denotes a lawyer or lawyers in a private firm, lawyers employed in the legal department of a corporation or other organization and lawyers employed in a legal services organization. See Comment, Rule 1.10.

(e) "Fraud" or "fraudulent" denotes conduct having a purpose to deceive and not merely negligent misrepresentation or failure to apprise another of relevant information.

(f) "Knowingly," "known," or "knows" denotes actual knowledge of the fact in question. A person's knowledge may be inferred from circumstances.

(g) "Matter" includes any judicial or other proceeding, application, request for a ruling or other determination, contract, claim, controversy, investigation, charge, accusation, arrest, negotiation or other particular matter involving a specific party or parties.

(h) "Partner" denotes a member of a partnership and a shareholder in a law firm organized as a professional corporation.

(i) "Reasonable" or "reasonably" when used in relation to conduct by a lawyer denotes the conduct of a reasonably prudent and competent lawyer.

(j) "Reasonable belief" or "reasonably believes" when used in reference to a lawyer denotes that the lawyer believes the matter in question and that the circumstances are such that the belief is reasonable.

(k) "Reasonably should know" when used in reference to a lawyer denotes that a lawyer of reasonable prudence and competence would ascertain the matter in question.

(l) "Substantial" when used in reference to degree or extent denotes a material matter of clear and weighty importance.

(SCO 1123 effective July 15, 1993)

ALASKA COMMENT

The section entitled "Terminology" in the ABA Model Rules has been replaced with new Rule 9.1.

RPC

CODE OF JUDICIAL CONDUCT*

Table of Contents

Adopted Effective July 15, 1998

* **Editor's Note:** The Alaska Code of Judicial Conduct was rescinded and readopted by SCO 1322 effective July 15, 1998.

PREAMBLE

Our legal system is based on the principle that an independent, fair and competent judiciary will interpret and apply the laws that govern us. The role of the judiciary is central to American concepts of justice and the rule of law. Intrinsic to all Sections of this Code are the precepts that judges, individually and collectively, must respect and honor the judicial office as a public trust and strive to enhance and maintain confidence in our legal system. The judge is an arbiter of facts and law for the resolution of disputes and a highly visible symbol of government under the rule of law.

The Code of Judicial Conduct is intended to establish standards for ethical conduct of judges. It consists of this Preamble, broad statements called Canons, specific rules set forth in Sections under each Canon, a Terminology Section, an Application Section and ***Commentary.*** The text of the Preamble, the Canons, and the Sections, including the Terminology and Application Sections, is authoritative. The Commentary, by explanation and example, provides guidance with respect to the purpose and meaning of the Canons and Sections. The Commentary is not intended as a statement of additional rules. When the text uses "shall" or "shall not," it is intended to impose binding obligations the violation of which can result in disciplinary action. When "should" or "should not" is used, the text is intended as hortatory and as a statement of what is or is not appropriate conduct but not as a binding rule under which a judge may be disciplined. When "may" is used, it denotes permissible discretion or, depending on the context, it refers to action that is not covered by specific proscriptions.

The Canons and Sections are rules of reason. They should be applied consistently with constitutional requirements, statutes, other court rules and decisional law and in the context of all relevant circumstances. The Code is to be construed so as not to impinge on the essential independence of judges in making judicial decisions or to limit judges' legal rights.

The Code is designed to provide guidance to judges and candidates for judicial office and to provide a structure for regulating conduct through disciplinary agencies. It is not designed or intended as a basis for civil liability or criminal prosecution. Furthermore, the purpose of the Code would be subverted if the Code were invoked by lawyers for mere tactical advantage in a proceeding.

The text of the Canons and Sections is intended to govern conduct of judges and to be binding upon them. It is not intended, however, that every transgression will result in disciplinary action. Whether disciplinary action is appropriate, and the degree of discipline to be imposed, should be determined through a reasonable and reasoned application of the text and should depend on such factors as the seriousness of the transgression, whether there is a pattern of improper activity and the effect of the improper activity on others or on the judicial system. See ABA Standards Relating to Judicial Discipline and Disability Retirement./DD

The Code of Judicial Conduct is not intended as an exhaustive guide for the conduct of judges. They should also be governed in their judicial and personal conduct by general ethical standards. The Code is intended, however, to state basic standards which should govern the conduct of all judges and to provide guidance to assist judges in establishing and maintaining high standards of judicial and personal conduct.

While the Alaska Code of Judicial Conduct is based on the American Bar Association's Model Code of Judicial Conduct, there have been significant changes both to specific rules set forth in the Sections and to the ***Commentary.***

‡ 1. Judicial disciplinary procedures adopted in the jurisdictions should comport with the requirements of due process. The ABA Standards Relating to Judicial Discipline and Disability Retirement are cited as an example of how these due process requirements may be satisfied.

CANONS

Key to Symbols on Special or Limited Applicability of Sections

‡	means that Section does not apply to senior judges or applies to them only during periods of active judicial service.
◊	means that Section does not apply or has limited application to part-time magistrates or deputy magistrates.
■	means that Section applies to special masters.

Full-time judicial officers must comply with all provisions of this Code.

Terms marked with asterisk (*) are defined in Terminology Section.

Canon 1. A Judge Shall Uphold the Integrity and Independence of the Judiciary.

■ An independent and honorable judiciary is indispensable to achieving justice in our society. A judge should participate in establishing, maintaining, and enforcing high standards of judicial conduct. The provisions of this Code are intended to preserve the integrity and the independence of the judiciary; the Code should be construed and applied to further these objectives.

Commentary.*—Deference to the judgments and rulings of courts depends upon public confidence in the integrity and independence of judges. The integrity and independence of judges depend in turn upon their acting without fear or favor. Public confidence in the impartiality of the judiciary is maintained when judges adhere to the provisions of this Code. Conversely, violation of this Code diminishes public confidence in the judiciary and thereby does injury to the system of government under law.*

(Adopted by SCO 1322 effective July 15, 1998)

Annotations

Cases

Pre-signing judicial orders and allowing the prosecution to decide the particulars for out-of-custody defendants without judicial supervision violates Canons 1, 2 A, 3 B(1), 3 B(2)(a), 3 B(2)(b), 3 B(7), 3 B(8), 3 C(1) and 3 C(2) of the Alaska Code of Judicial Conduct. **In re Landry**, Op. No. 12566, 157 P.3d 1049, (Alaska 2007).

Canon 2. A Judge Shall Avoid Impropriety and the Appearance of Impropriety in All the Judge's Activities.

A. ■ In all activities, a judge shall exhibit respect for the rule of law, comply with the law,* avoid impropriety and the appearance of impropriety, and act in a manner that promotes public confidence in the integrity and the impartiality of the judiciary.

Commentary.*—Public confidence in the judiciary is eroded by irresponsible or improper conduct by judges. A judge must avoid all impropriety and appearance of impropriety. A judge must expect to be the subject of constant public scrutiny. A judge must therefore accept restrictions on the judge's conduct that might be viewed as burdensome by the ordinary citizen and should do so freely and willingly.*

The prohibition against behaving with impropriety or the appearance of impropriety applies to both the professional and personal conduct of a judge. Because it is not practicable to list all prohibited acts, the proscription is necessarily cast in general terms that extend to conduct by judges that is harmful although not specifically mentioned in the Code. Actual improprieties under this standard include violations of law, court rules, and other specific provisions of this Code. The test for appearance of impropriety is whether the conduct would create in reasonable minds a perception that the judge's ability to carry out judicial responsibilities with integrity, impartiality, and competence is impaired.

See also Commentary to Section 2C.

B. ■ A judge shall not allow family, social, political, or other relationships to influence the judge's judicial conduct or judgment. A judge shall not use or lend the prestige of judicial office to advance the private interests of the judge or others. A judge shall not knowingly* convey or permit others to convey the impression that anyone is in a special position to influence the judge. A judge shall not testify voluntarily as a character witness, except that a judge may testify as a character witness in a criminal proceeding if the judge or a member of the judge's family* is a victim of the offense or if the defendant is a member of the judge's family.

Commentary.*—Maintaining the prestige of judicial office is essential to a system of government in which the judiciary functions independently of the executive and legislative branches. Respect for the judicial office facilitates the orderly conduct of legitimate judicial functions. Judges should distinguish between proper and improper use of the prestige of office in all of their activities. For example, it would be improper for a judge to allude to his or her judgeship to gain a personal advantage such as differential treatment when stopped by a police officer for a traffic offense. Similarly, judicial letterhead must not be used for conducting a judge's personal business.*

A judge must avoid lending the prestige of judicial office for advancement of the private interests of others. For example, a judge must not use the judge's judicial position to gain advantage in a civil suit involving a member of the judge's family. In contracts for publication of a judge's writings, a judge should retain control over the advertising to avoid exploitation of the judge's office. As to the acceptance of awards, see Section 4D(5)(a) and Commentary.

Although a judge should be sensitive to possible abuse of the prestige of office, a judge may, based on the judge's personal knowledge, serve as a reference or provide a letter of recommendation. However, except in very limited circumstances, a judge must not initiate the communication of information to a sentencing judge or a probation or corrections officer. A judge may provide to such persons information for the record in response to a formal request. A judge may also initiate the communication of information for the record if the judge or a member of the judge's family was a victim of the offense or the defendant is a member of the judge's family.

Judges may participate in the process of judicial selection by cooperating with appointing authorities and screening committees seeking names for consideration, and by responding to official inquiries concerning a person being considered for a judgeship. See also Canon 5 regarding use of a judge's name in political activities.

A judge must not testify voluntarily as a character witness because to do so may lend the prestige of the judicial office in support of the party for whom the judge testifies. Moreover, when a judge testifies as a witness, a lawyer who regularly appears before the judge may be placed in the awkward position of cross-examining the judge. A judge may, however, testify when properly summoned and in the special circumstances described in the last sentence of this Section.

C. A judge shall not hold membership in any organization that the judge knows* practices invidious discrimination on the basis of race, sex, religion or national origin, nor shall a judge regularly use the facilities of such an organization. A judge shall not arrange to use the facilities of an organization that the judge knows* practices invidious discrimination on the basis of race, sex, religion, or national origin unless there are no alternative facilities in the community and use of the facilities would not give rise to an appearance of endorsing the discriminatory practices of the organization.

Commentary.*—This Section prohibits a judge from holding membership in any organization that the judge knows engages in invidious discrimination on the basis of race, sex, religion or national origin. The membership of a judge in an organization that practices such discrimination gives rise to perceptions among the public that a judge is insensitive to minorities, women, and others protected against discrimination.*

The common judicial definition of invidious discrimination "is a classification which is arbitrary, irrational and not reasonably related to a legitimate purpose." ***McLaughlin v. Florida****; 379 U.S. 1984 (1964). Whether an organization practices invidious discrimination is often a complex question which requires careful consideration by the judge. The answer cannot be determined from a mere examination of an organization's current membership rolls but rather depends on* *how the organization selects members and other relevant factors, such as that the organization is dedicated to the preservation of religious, ethnic or cultural values of legitimate common interest to its members, or that it is in fact and effect an intimate, purely private organization whose membership limitations could not be constitutionally prohibited. Absent such factors, an organization is generally said to discriminate invidiously if it arbitrarily excludes from membership on the basis of race, religion, sex or national origin persons who would otherwise be admitted to membership. **See New York State Club Ass'n v. City of New York**, 108 S. Ct. 2225, 101 L. Ed. 2d 1 (1988); **Board of Dirs. of Rotary Int'l v. Rotary Club of Duarte**, 481 U.S. 537, 107 S. Ct. 1940, 95 L. Ed. 2d 474 (1987); **Roberts v. United States Jaycees,** 468 U.S. 609, 104 S. Ct. 3244, 82 L. Ed. 2d 462 (1984).*

*Judges in Alaska must be particularly sensitive to this inquiry. Alaska's Human Rights Act has been narrowly construed as it applies to membership discrimination. Compare **United States Jaycees v. Richardet,** 666 P.2d 1008 (Alaska 1983) with **Roberts v. Jaycees**, 468 U.S. 609 (1984). Consequently, discriminatory practices which would not be illegal in Alaska may nevertheless be arbitrary, irrational, and unrelated to a legitimate organizational purpose, and thus covered by the prohibition in Section 2C. Nonetheless, some discrimination is viewed as innocuous when measured by contemporary standards and therefore not invidious.*

Section 2C prohibits regular use by a judge of the facilities of an organization which invidiously discriminates. It does not prohibit incidental use of such facilities, for example, attending a wedding reception in such a facility.

When a person who is a judge on the date this Code becomes effective learns that an organization to which the judge belongs engages in invidious discrimination that would preclude membership under Section 2C, the judge is permitted, in lieu of resigning, to make immediate efforts to have the organization discontinue its invidiously discriminatory practices, but is required to suspend participation in any other activities of the organization. If the organization fails to discontinue its invidiously discriminatory practices as promptly as possible (and in all events within a year of the judge's first learning of the practices), the judge is required to resign immediately from the organization.

Nothing in Section 2C should be interpreted to diminish a judge's right to the free exercise of religion.

(Adopted by SCO 1322 effective July 15, 1998)

Annotations

Cases

The conduct of a judge in requesting advice of a grand jury investigator as to the likelihood of a judge's friend being indicted by a grand jury constitutes impropriety. **In re Hansen,** Op. No. 1117, 532 P2d 303 (Alaska 1975).

A judge who was a retired vice-president of a defunct airline violated his duty to avoid creating an appearance of impropriety by self-validating reduced fare airline tickets through the defunct airline without checking with the bankruptcy trustee on whether the agreement permitting such self-validation had been terminated; due to the presence of several mitigating factors, the appropriate sanction for the violation was a private reprimand in closed proceedings. **In re Inquiry Concerning a Judge,** Op. No. 3572, 788 P2d 716 (Alaska 1990).

The test for whether judge's conduct created an appearance of impropriety was whether he used reasonable care to prevent a reasonably objective individual from believing that an impropriety was afoot. **Inquiry Concerning a Judge,** Op. No. 3782, 822 P2d 1333 (Alaska 1991).

Private reprimand was warranted for judge who, as an officer, director and shareholder of corporation engaged in litigation with state public finance corporation, created an appearance of impropriety by sending letters on court stationary to the public finance corporation counsel and by meeting with the Governor to discuss the case. **Inquiry Concerning a Judge,** Op. No. 3782, 822 P2d 1333 (Alaska 1991).

Judge did not violate this rule by identifying himself as a justice when calling the Governor's office to arrange a meeting on a personal matter. **Inquiry Concerning a Judge,** Op. No. 3782, 822 P2d 1333 (Alaska 1991).

Pre-signing judicial orders and allowing the prosecution to decide the particulars for out-of-custody defendants without judicial supervision violates Canons 1, 2 A, 3 B(1), 3 B(2)(a), 3 B(2)(b), 3 B(7), 3 B(8), 3 C(1) and 3 C(2) of the Alaska Code of Judicial Conduct. **In re Landry**, Op. No. 12566, 157 P.3d 1049, (Alaska 2007).

Lack of diligence in maintaining accurate tracking of Criminal Rule 45 time constraints, resulting in dismissal of a significant number of criminal cases, violates Canons 2, 3 B(1), 3 B(8), 3 C(1), and 3 C(2) of the Alaska Code of Judicial Conduct. **In re Landry**, Op. No. 12566, 157 P.3d 1049, (Alaska 2007).

Judge's act of engaging in improper ex parte communications and presiding over a matter where he should have disqualified himself, thus giving rise to circumstances suggesting that he gave preferential treatment to the defendant, violated Canons 2 A, 2 B, 3 B(2)(b), 3 B(7) and 3 E(1) of the Alaska Code of Judicial Conduct. **In re Landry**, Op. No. 12566, 157 P.3d 1049, (Alaska 2007).

Judge's acts of making inappropriate sexual comments to female court employees in the workplace violated Canons 2 A, 3 B(1), and 3 B(5) and 3 C(1) of the Alaska Code of Judicial Conduct. **In re Landry**, Op. No. 12566, 157 P.3d 1049, (Alaska 2007).

Canon 3. A Judge Shall Perform the Duties of Judicial Office Impartially and Diligently.

A. ■ **Primacy of Judicial Duties.** The judicial duties* of a judge take precedence over all the judge's other activities. A judge's judicial duties include all the duties of the judge's office prescribed by law.* In performance of these duties, the following standards apply.

B. **Adjudicative Responsibilities.**

(1) ■ A judge shall consider and decide all matters assigned to the judge except those in which the judge's disqualification is required.

***Commentary.—See Feichtinger v. State**, 779 P.2d 344, 348 (Alaska App. 1989) ("Judges will frequently be assigned cases involving unpleasant issues and difficult problems. Often litigants and their attorneys will be particularly vexatious. In many cases, publicity adverse to the judge is virtually certain no matter what decision he or she reaches. In such cases, judges insufficiently attuned to their responsibilities might readily welcome a baseless request for recusal as an escape from a difficult case. To surrender to such a temptation would justly expose the judiciary to public contempt based on* *legitimate public concern about judicial integrity and courage. While we agree that judges must avoid the appearance of bias, it is equally important to avoid the appearance of shirking responsibility.")*

(2) (a) ■ A judge shall maintain professional competence in the law.*

(b) A judge shall be faithful to the law.* A judge shall not deviate from the law to appease public clamor, to avoid criticism, or to advance an improper interest.

(3) ■ A judge shall take reasonable steps to maintain and insure order and decorum in judicial proceedings before that judge.

Commentary.*—Section 3B(3) addresses a judge's responsibility to preserve order and decorum in court proceedings. "Order" refers to the level of regularity and civility required to guarantee that the business of the court will be accomplished in conformity with the rules governing the proceeding. "Decorum" refers to the atmosphere of attentiveness and earnest endeavor which communicates, both to the participants and to the public, that the matter before the court is receiving serious and fair consideration*

Clearly, individual judges have differing ideas and standards concerning the appropriateness of particular behavior, language, and dress for the attorneys and litigants appearing before them. What one judge may perceive to be an obvious departure from propriety, another judge may deem a harmless eccentricity or no departure at all. Also, some proceedings call for more formality than others. Thus, at any given time, courtrooms around the state will inevitably manifest a broad range of "order" and "decorum."

Section 3B(3) is not intended to establish a uniform standard of what constitutes "order" and "decorum." Rather, the Section requires a judge to take reasonable steps to achieve and maintain the level of order and decorum necessary to accomplish the business of the court in a manner that is both regular and fair, while at the same time giving attorneys, litigants, and onlookers assurance of that regularity and fairness.

(4) ■ A judge shall be patient, dignified, and courteous to litigants, jurors, witnesses, lawyers, and others with whom the judge deals in an official capacity. The judge shall take reasonable steps to maintain and insure similar conduct from lawyers and from court staff and others subject to the judge's direction and control.

Commentary.*—The duty to hear all proceedings with patience, dignity, and courtesy is not inconsistent with the duty to dispose promptly of the business of the court. Judges can be efficient and businesslike while being patient and deliberate.*

(5) ■ In the performance of judicial duties,* a judge shall act without bias or prejudice* and shall not manifest, by words or conduct, bias or prejudice based upon race, color, sex, religion, national origin, disability, age, marital status, changes in marital status, pregnancy, parenthood, sexual orientation, or social or economic status. A judge shall not permit court staff and others subject to the judge's direction and control to deviate from these standards in their duties.

Commentary.*—A judge must refrain from speech, gestures, or other conduct that manifests bias or prejudice, including sexual harassment, and must require the same standard of conduct from others subject to the judge's direction and control.*

A judge must perform judicial duties impartially and fairly. A judge who manifests bias on any basis in a proceeding impairs the fairness of the proceeding and brings the judiciary into disrepute. Facial expression and body language, in addition to oral communication, can give others an appearance of judicial bias. A judge must be alert to avoid behavior that may be perceived as an expression of prejudice.

(6) ■ A judge shall require lawyers in proceedings before the judge to refrain from manifesting, by words or conduct, bias or prejudice* based upon race, color, sex, religion, national origin, disability, age, marital status, changes in marital status, pregnancy, parenthood, sexual orientation, or social or economic status. This Section 3B(6) does not preclude legitimate advocacy when race, color, sex, religion, national origin, disability, age, marital status, changes in marital status, pregnancy, parenthood, sexual orientation or social or economic status, or other similar factors, are issues in the proceeding.

Commentary.*—This Section is intended to prohibit not only express judicial support for the bias or prejudice but also speech, gestures, or inaction that could reasonably be interpreted as implicit approval of the expressed bias or prejudice. A judge may not ignore or overlook expressions of bias or prejudice in any judicial proceeding, even informal proceedings such as scheduling or settlement conferences. Appropriate action will depend on the circumstances. In some instances, a polite correction might be sufficient. However, deliberate or particularly offensive conduct will require more significant action, such as a specific direction from the judge, a private admonition, an admonition on the record, or, if the attorney repeats the misconduct after being warned, contempt.*

(7) ■ A judge shall accord to every person the right to be heard according to law.* A judge shall not initiate, permit, or consider ex parte communications or other communications made to the judge outside the presence of the parties concerning a pending or impending proceeding except as allowed by this Section. A judge shall make reasonable efforts to see that law clerks and other court staff carrying out similar functions under the judge's supervision do not violate the provisions of this Section.

(a) A judge may initiate or consider an ex parte communication when expressly authorized by law* to do so.

(b) When circumstances require, a judge may engage in ex parte communications for scheduling or other administrative purposes, provided that:

(i) the communications do not deal with substantive matters or the merits of the issues litigated,

(ii) the judge reasonably believes no party will gain a procedural or tactical advantage because the communication is ex parte, and

(iii) the judge takes reasonable steps to notify all other parties promptly of the substance of the ex parte communication and, when practicable, allows them an opportunity to respond. This subsection does not apply to ex parte communications by law clerks or other court staff concerning scheduling or administrative matters.

(c) If all the parties have agreed to this procedure beforehand, either in writing or on the record, a judge may engage in ex parte communication on specified administrative topics with one or more parties.

(d) A judge may consult other judges and law clerks or other court staff whose function is to aid the judge in carrying out the judge's adjudicative responsibilities.

(e) A judge may, with the consent of the parties, confer separately with the parties and their lawyers in an effort to mediate or settle matters pending before the judge.

Commentary.*—The proscription against communications concerning a proceeding includes communications from lawyers, law teachers, and other persons who are not participants in the proceeding, except to the limited extent permitted.*

Whenever presence of a party or notice to a party is required by Section 3B(7), it is the party's lawyer, or if the party is unrepresented the party, who is to be present or to whom notice is to be given.

A judge may request a party to submit proposed findings of fact and conclusions of law, so long as the other parties are apprised of the request and are given an opportunity to respond to the proposed findings and conclusions.

If communication between the trial judge and the appellate court with respect to a proceeding is permitted, a copy of any written communication or the substance of any oral communication should be provided to all parties.

The first sentence of Section 3B(7) ("A judge shall accord to every person the right to be heard according to law.") is not intended to expand or alter the law of standing (a person's right to bring an action), nor is it intended to expand or alter the procedural rules governing the scope and manner of a person's right to be heard in a case.

Judges should endeavor to create some form of record of ex parte communications whenever possible, even when the communications are authorized under this Section.

Under Section 3B(7)(b), a judge may engage in ex parte communications for "scheduling or other administrative purposes." For example, a judge may make or receive an ex parte communication when the sole purpose of the communication is to provide courtesy notification to the parties or to the court of a delay or change in scheduling. Another example of an ex parte communication contemplated by this Section is when a defense attorney notifies the judge that the defendant cannot be located, that the scheduled trial should be called off, and that the defense concedes that a bench warrant should be issued for the defendant's arrest.

Section 3B(7)(b) requires a judge to take reasonable steps to promptly notify all parties of any ex parte communication. The continuing development of communications technology will affect what steps are "reasonable." Telephone communication is now virtually ubiquitous and telefax communication is widespread. In the near future, it may be common to notify lawyers through computer mail or computer bulletin boards. A judge should consider these alternatives when deciding the most expeditious means of communication reasonably available to the court and the parties.

A judge's secretary or law clerk may also engage in ex parte communications to discuss scheduling or other administrative matters. Such communications are permitted as long as the requirements of Sections 3(B)(7)(b)(i) and (ii) are satisfied, that is, as long as the communications do not deal with the substance or merits of the litigation and no party gains an advantage as a result of the ex parte contact. When the communication is with a staff member rather than a judge, Section 3B(7)(b)(iii) does not apply. Thus, if an attorney asks about the status of a pending motion, the judge's secretary may provide this information without notifying the other parties of the communication or including them in a conference call.

Section 3B(7)(c) allows the various parties in multi-party litigation to designate a "lead" party for their side and have that party appear at pretrial hearings to deal with issues such as scheduling and discovery.

Section 3B(7)(d) assumes that the other judge or member of the judge's adjudicative staff is not disqualified from participating in the decision of the case. Thus, it would be improper for a judge to consult another judge who had been challenged either peremptorily or for cause, and it would likewise be improper for a judge to consult another judge, a law clerk, or anyone else who the judge knows has a disqualifying interest in the proceeding. Likewise, it would be improper for the judge to consult a member of an appellate court whose duty it would be to review the judge's decision.

The verb "consult" is intended to mean "engage in discussions regarding the substance or merits of the case." Just as a presiding judge may continue to perform purely administrative functions following his or her peremptory challenge C see Criminal Rule 25(d)(3) C a disqualified judge may engage in limited, purely administrative communication with the successor judge. Thus, when a new judge is assigned to a case following a judicial disqualification, the successor judge may speak to the disqualified judge about purely administrative matters (the dates already scheduled for court proceedings, the identities of the attorneys, etc.). However, the new judge may not speak to the disqualified judge about the merits of any pending issues, the merits of any previously decided issues, or the substance of any proceedings already held in the case. The new judge's information on these topics is to be gleaned from the court file or from the attorneys.

Section 3B(7)(d) is not intended to authorize a judge to engage in ex parte consultation with court staff such as custody investigators and court-employed juvenile intake officers, whose function is to provide evidence in the proceeding.

A judge may not ex parte seek advice on the law applicable to a proceeding from a disinterested expert.

(8) ■ A judge shall dispose of all judicial matters promptly, efficiently, and fairly.

***Commentary.**—In disposing of matters promptly, efficiently, and fairly, a judge must demonstrate due regard for the rights of the parties to be heard and to have issues resolved without unnecessary cost or delay. Containing costs while preserving fundamental rights of parties also protects the interests of witnesses and the general public. A judge should monitor and supervise cases so as to reduce or eliminate dilatory practices, avoidable delays and unnecessary costs. A judge should encourage and seek to facilitate settlement, but should not coerce parties into surrendering the right to have their controversy resolved by the courts.*

Prompt disposition of the court's business requires a judge to devote adequate time to judicial duties, to be punctual in attending court and expeditious in determining matters under submission, and to insist that court officials, litigants and their lawyers cooperate with the judge to that end.

(9) ■ A judge shall not, while a proceeding is pending or impending in any court, make any public comment that might reasonably be expected to affect its outcome or impair its fairness, or make any nonpublic comment that might substantially interfere with a fair trial or hearing. The judge shall take reasonable steps to maintain and insure similar abstention on the part of court staff subject to the judge's direction and control. This Section does not prohibit judges from making public statements in the course of their official duties or from explaining for public information the procedures of the court. This Section does not apply to proceedings in which the judge is a litigant in a personal capacity.

***Commentary.**—The requirement that judges abstain from public comment regarding a pending or impending proceeding continues during any appellate process and until final disposition. This Section does not prohibit a judge from commenting on proceedings in which the judge is a litigant in a personal capacity, but in cases such as a writ of mandamus where the judge is a litigant in an official capacity, the judge must not comment publicly. The conduct of lawyers relating to trial publicity is governed by Rule 3.6 of the Alaska Rules of Professional Conduct.*

(10) ■ A judge shall not commend or criticize jurors for their verdict other than in a court order or opinion in a proceeding. However, a judge may express appreciation to jurors for their service to the judicial system and the community.

***Commentary.**—Commending or criticizing jurors for their verdict may imply a judicial expectation in future cases and may impair a juror's ability to be fair and impartial in a subsequent case.*

(11) ■ A judge who acquires nonpublic information* in a judicial capacity shall not disclose the information for any purpose unrelated to the judge's judicial duties, nor shall the judge use the information for the financial gain of the judge or any other person.

***Commentary.**—The ABA's version of this Section prohibits a judge from disclosing or using nonpublic information acquired in a judicial capacity for any purpose unrelated to judicial duties. This rule does not adequately address the problem presented when a judge obtains confidential information that has relevance to the judge's personal life outside of the financial sphere. A judge hearing a confidential proceeding might obtain information about a doctor that has potentially crucial relevance to the judge's decision of which doctor to employ. A judge who hears a search warrant application might obtain information that would affect the judge's decision regarding what day-care center to use or what restaurant to patronize. Even though the judge reveals this information to no one, it would not strain the English language to say that a judge who makes decisions based on this information has "used" the nonpublic information for a purpose unrelated to the judge's official duties.*

The Alaska version of the Section recognizes that a judge cannot reasonably be expected to disregard nonpublic information when it comes to the health or safety of the judge's immediate family. The first clause of the Alaska rule forbids "disclosure" of such information for any non-judicial purpose (thus allowing the judge to "use" the information for personal purposes so long as the judge does not violate the second clause).

The second clause forbids the "use" of nonpublic information for anyone's financial gain. A judge who wishes to misuse confidential information for financial gain will often not need to disclose the information to anyone else; indeed, the amount of the improper financial gain may be directly proportionate to the judge's success in concealing the information from all other persons.

(12) ■ Without prior notice to the parties and an opportunity to respond, a judge shall not engage in independent ex parte investigation of the facts of a case.

***Commentary.**—This Section does not prohibit a judge from exercising the judge's authority to independently call witnesses if the judge believes that these witnesses might shed light on the issues being litigated or to take judicial notice of certain facts. See Evidence Rules 614 & 201.*

C. **Administrative Responsibilities.**

(1) ■ A judge shall maintain professional competence in judicial administration, and should cooperate with other judges and court staff in the administration of court business. A judge shall diligently discharge the judge's administrative responsibilities without bias or prejudice.*

***Commentary.**—See Terminology, "bias or prejudice."*

The definition of "bias or prejudice" found in the terminology Section was written in an exclusionary manner to allow judges, with regard to administrative matters, to countenance legitimate distinctions relevant to the policies or decisions involved.

To the extent judges have administrative authority over other judges, that authority should likewise be exercised in such a way as to provide the best use of judicial resources and the optimum development of all judicial officers. Just as the individual court must perform judicial administration without bias or prejudice, so too, judges with administrative authority over others must do the same with respect to the judicial officers subject to their orders.

(2) ■ A judge shall take reasonable steps to insure that court staff and others subject to the judge's direction and control observe the standards of fidelity to the law* and diligence in the performance of their duties that apply to the judge and refrain from manifesting bias or prejudice* in the performance of their official duties.

(3) ■ A presiding judge or any other judge with supervisory authority over other judges shall take reasonable steps to assure that, for matters within the supervising judge's scope of authority, the other judges properly perform their judicial responsibilities.

(4) ■ A judge shall not make unnecessary appointments. A judge shall exercise the power of appointment impartially and on the basis of merit. A judge shall avoid nepotism and favoritism. A judge shall not approve compensation of appointees beyond the fair value of services rendered.

***Commentary.**—Appointees of a judge include assigned counsel, officials such as referees, commissioners, special masters, receivers and guardians and personnel such as clerks, secretaries and bailiffs. Consent by the parties to an appointment or an award of compensation does not relieve the judge of the obligation prescribed by Section 3C(4).*

D. **Disciplinary Responsibilities.**

(1) ■ A judge having information establishing a likelihood that another judge has violated this Code shall take appropriate action. A judge having knowledge* that another judge has engaged in conduct reflecting the other judge's lack of fitness for judicial office shall inform the appropriate disciplinary authority,* unless the judge reasonably believes that the misconduct has been or will otherwise be reported. Conduct reflecting lack of fitness for judicial office includes:

(a) or accepting a bribe or otherwise acting dishonestly in reaching a judicial or administrative decision,

(b) improperly using or threatening to use the judge's judicial power in a manner adverse to someone else's interests for the purpose of inducing that person to bestow a benefit upon the judge or upon someone else pursuant to the judge's wishes, or

(c) commission of a felony.

(2) ■ A judge having information establishing a likelihood that a lawyer has violated the Rules of Professional Conduct shall take appropriate action. A judge who obtains information establishing a likelihood that a lawyer has committed a violation of the Rules of Professional Conduct by an act of dishonesty, obstruction of justice, or breach of fiduciary* duty shall inform the appropriate disciplinary authority,* unless the judge reasonably believes that the misconduct has been or will otherwise be reported.

(3) ■ A judge possessing nonprivileged information pertaining to another judge's potential violation of this Code shall fully reveal this information upon proper request of the appropriate disciplinary authority* or of any other tribunal empowered to investigate or act upon judicial misconduct. A judge possessing nonprivileged information pertaining to a lawyer's potential violation of the Rules of Professional Conduct shall fully reveal this information upon proper request of the appropriate disciplinary authority or of any other tribunal empowered to investigate or act upon attorney misconduct.

(4) ■ Acts of a judge, in the discharge of disciplinary responsibilities, required or permitted by Sections 3D(1), 3D(2), and 3D(3) are part of a judge's judicial duties. *

***Commentary.**—Section 3D establishes a judge's duty to take action in response to the misconduct of another judge (Section 3D(1)) or the misconduct of a lawyer (Section 3D(2)). In many instances, Section 3D allows a judge a degree of discretion in determining how he or she should respond to misconduct; the Section specifies only that the judge shall take "appropriate action." Thus, a judge who learns that another judge has engaged in an improper but de minimis ex parte contact, or who learns that a judge has engaged in a fundraising activity for a charity, may believe that the only action needed is to point out to the other judge that his or her conduct violates the Code. Similarly, a judge who learns that another judge is suffering from alcohol or drug addiction might direct that other judge to counseling or might seek the help of the other judge's colleagues or friends. On the other hand, if the other judge refuses to admit the problem or submit to ameliorative measures, and if the other judge's intoxication is interfering with his or her judicial duties (so as to constitute a violation of Canon 1 and Section 3A), then a judge who knows of this problem may be obliged to report it to the Commission on Judicial Conduct.*

Appropriate action will vary with particular situations and with particular individuals. There will generally be a range of reasonable responses available to the judge who learns of misconduct. However, a judge who learns of misconduct must respond reasonably. For example, the judge may not "respond" by explicitly or implicitly condoning the misconduct.

A judge's discretion to determine an appropriate response to misconduct is circumscribed in certain instances. Both Sections 3D(1) and 3D(2) grant no discretion—they require the judge to report misconduct to the appropriate disciplinary authority—if (a) the misconduct is serious and (b) the judge's awareness of the misconduct rises to the specified level of certainty.

With regard to this level of awareness, a judge must report judicial misconduct if he or she "knows" that another judge has engaged in serious misconduct, while a judge must report attorney misconduct if he or she has information "establishing a likelihood" that an attorney has engaged in serious misconduct. The term "knows" is defined in the Terminology Section. The term "likelihood" is used in the sense of "more probable than not," a preponderance of the evidence.

If the misconduct the judge learns of is not among the serious types of misconduct, or if the misconduct is serious but the judge's level of awareness of the misconduct does not rise to the specified degree of certainty, there is no absolute duty to report. However, the judge who is aware of a likelihood of misconduct will still be under the more general obligation to take appropriate action.

A judge is not required to report all conduct that indicates lack of fitness for judicial office, only conduct of the same seriousness as that described in Subsections 3D(1)(a)-(c).

Section 3D applies to magistrates. However, a magistrate may report serious misconduct to the presiding judge or chief justice instead of the Judicial Conduct Commission.

E. **Disqualification.**

(1) ■ Unless all grounds for disqualification are waived as permitted by Section 3F, a judge shall disqualify himself or herself in a proceeding in which the judge's impartiality might reasonably be questioned, including but not limited to instances where:

Commentary.—*Under this rule, a judge is disqualified whenever the judge's impartiality might reasonably be questioned, regardless of whether any of the specific rules in Section 3E(1) apply. For example, if a judge were in the process of negotiating for employment with a law firm, the judge would be disqualified from any matters in which that law firm appeared, unless the disqualification was waived by the parties after disclosure by the judge.*

A judge should disclose on the record information that the judge believes the parties or their lawyers might consider relevant to the question of disqualification, even if the judge believes there is no real basis for disqualification.

By decisional law, the rule of necessity may override the rule of disqualification. For example, a judge might be required to participate in judicial review of a judicial salary statute, or might be the only judge available in a matter requiring immediate judicial action, such as a hearing on probable cause or a temporary restraining order. In the latter case, the judge must disclose on the record the basis for possible disqualification and use reasonable efforts to transfer the matter to another judge as soon as practicable.

(a) the judge has a personal bias or prejudice concerning a party or a party's lawyer, or personal knowledge of disputed evidentiary facts concerning the proceeding;

(b) the judge served as a lawyer in the matter in controversy, or a lawyer with whom the judge previously practiced law served during their association as a lawyer concerning the matter, or the judge has been a material witness concerning it;

Commentary.—*A lawyer in a government agency does not ordinarily have an association with other lawyers employed by that agency within the meaning of Section 3E(1)(b); a judge formerly employed by a government agency, however, should disqualify himself or herself in a proceeding if the judge's impartiality might reasonably be questioned because of such association.*

(c) the judge knows* that he or she, individually or as a fiduciary,* or the judge's spouse,* parent, or child wherever residing, or any other member of the judge's family* residing in the judge's household:

(i) has an economic interest* in the subject matter in controversy, or

(ii) is employed by or is a partner in a party to the proceeding or a law firm involved in the proceeding, or

(iii) has any other, more than de minimis interest* that could be substantially affected by the proceeding, or

(iv) is likely to be a material witness in the proceeding;

(d) the judge or the judge's spouse, or a person within the third degree of relationship* to either of them, or the spouse* of such a person:

(i) is a party to the proceeding or is known* by the judge to be an officer, director, or trustee of a party;

(ii) is acting as a lawyer in the proceeding;

(iii) is known* by the judge to have a more than de minimis interest* that could be substantially affected by the proceeding;

(iv) is to the judge's knowledge* likely to be a material witness in the proceeding.

(e) For purposes of this Section, when a party is a governmental entity, a person is "employed by" the party when the person is employed by the agency, commission, department or (if the department is broken into divisions) division, or other unit of government directly involved in the matter to be litigated.

Commentary.—*The fact that a lawyer in a proceeding is affiliated with a law firm with which a relative of the judge is affiliated does not of itself disqualify the judge under Section 3E(1)(d). Under appropriate circumstances, the fact that "the judge's impartiality might reasonably be questioned" under Section 3E(1), or that the relative is known by the judge to have an interest in the law firm that could be "substantially affected by the outcome of the proceeding" under Section 3E(1)(d)(iii) may require the judge's disqualification.*

Cross Reference.*—Additional grounds for disqualification are set out in AS 22.20.020(a). This statute provides:*

(a A judicial officer may not act in a matter in which

(1) the judicial officer is a party;

(2) the judicial officer is related to a party or a party's attorney by consanguinity or affinity within the third degree;

(3) the judicial officer is a material witness;

(4) the judicial officer or the spouse of the judicial officer, individually or as a fiduciary, or a child of the judicial officer has a direct financial interest in the matter;

(5) a party, except the state or a municipality of the state, has retained or been professionally counseled by the judicial officer as its attorney within two years preceding the assignment of the judicial officer to the matter;

(6) the judicial officer has represented a person as attorney for the person against a party, except the state or a municipality of the state, in a matter within two years preceding the assignment of the judicial officer to the matter;

(7) an attorney for a party has represented the judicial officer or a person against the judicial officer, either in the judicial officer's public or private capacity, in a matter within two years preceding the filing of the action;

(8) the law firm with which the judicial officer was associated in the practice of law within the two years preceding the filing of the action has been retained or has professionally counseled either party with respect to the matter;

(9) The judicial officer feels that, for any reason, a fair and impartial decision cannot be given.

Most of the grounds for disqualification under AS 22.20.020(a) are also listed as grounds for disqualification under Section 3E(1) of the Code. But the statute requires a judge to disqualify himself or herself in four situations that are not expressly covered by Section 3E(1):

- *Under AS 22.20.020(a)(5), a judge must disqualify himself or herself if the judge served as an attorney for one of the parties within two years preceding assignment of the case to the judge. This disqualification does not apply if the party is the state or a municipality.*

- *Under AS 22.20.020(a)(6), a judge must disqualify himself or herself if the judge was opposing counsel in a matter involving one of the parties within two years preceding assignment of the case to the judge. Again, this disqualification does not apply if the party is the state or a municipality.*

- *Under AS 22.20.020(a)(7), a judge must disqualify himself or herself if an attorney in the case represented the judge, either in the judge's public or private capacity, within two years preceding the filing of the action. A judge must also disqualify himself or herself if an attorney in the case was opposing counsel in a matter involving the judge within two years preceding the filing of the action.*

- *Under AS 22.20.020(a)(8), a judge must disqualify himself or herself if the judge's former law firm is representing one of the parties in the case or has represented one of the parties with respect to the matter, and the judge was associated with the law firm within the two years preceding the filing of the case.*

The first two of these disqualifications would only be of concern to judges who have been on the bench less than two years.

(2) A judge shall keep informed about the judge's personal and fiduciary* economic interests* and make reasonable effort to keep informed about the personal economic interests of the judge's spouse* and minor children residing in the judge's household.

Commentary.*—Many judges and their families either are or will be the beneficiaries of law firm annuities or pensions. Depending upon the type of pension or annuity arrangement, the law firm's success or failure in major litigation may affect the value or collectibility of pension or annuity benefits. When this economic interest is present, Sections E3(1)(c)(iii) or 3E(1)(d)(iii) may require a judge's disqualification from litigation involving the law firm, even though Sections 3E(1)(b), 3E(1)(c)(ii), and 3E(1)(d)(ii) would not otherwise require disqualification.*

F. **Waiver of Disqualification.**

(1) ■ A judge shall not seek or accept a waiver of disqualification when the judge has a personal bias or prejudice concerning a party or a lawyer, when, for any other reason, the judge believes that he or she cannot be fair and impartial, or when a waiver is not permitted under AS 22.20.020. In other circumstances, a judge who would be disqualified by the terms of Section 3E may disclose on the record the basis or bases of the judge's disqualification and ask the parties to consider whether they wish to waive disqualification. A judge is not bound by the parties' decision to waive a disqualification.

(2) ■ The judge shall not participate in the parties' discussions and shall require the parties to hold their discussions outside the presence of the judge. The judge shall not comment in any manner on the merits or advisability of waiver, other than to explain the right of disqualification or to further elucidate the ground or grounds of disqualification if requested by the parties. The judge is permitted to advise the parties that he or she is willing to participate in the case with the agreement of all the parties. But the judge must tell the parties that the decision whether to waive the ground of disqualification rests with each of them.

(3) ■ The judge may ask the parties to affirmatively indicate their position on the judge's disqualification, or give the parties a reasonable length of time to waive the disqualification, telling the parties either (a) that their failure to act will be construed as a decision to waive the potential disqualification or (b) that their failure to act will be construed as a decision not to waive the potential disqualification. If all

parties decide to waive the potential disqualification, and if the judge is then willing to participate, the judge may participate in the proceeding.

(4) ■ All the communications between the judge and the parties must be incorporated in the record of the proceeding.

Commentary.*—A waiver procedure provides the parties an opportunity to proceed without delay if they wish to waive the disqualification. Under AS 22.20.020(b), the following disqualifications may not be waived:*

(1) the judicial officer is a party;

(2) the judicial officer is a material witness;

(3) the judicial officer or the spouse of the judicial officer, individually or as a fiduciary, or a child of the judicial officer has a direct financial in the matter;

(4) the judicial officer feels that, for any reason, a fair and impartial decision cannot be given.

The decision whether or not to waive a disqualification is not one that must be made by the client. An attorney may make the decision without consulting with the client if the client is not present or readily available, or if the attorney decides that consultation is unnecessary.

All aspects of the communications between the judge and the parties (but not the parties' discussions among themselves) must either be in writing and included in the case file or on the record in court.

(Adopted by SCO 1322 effective July 15, 1998)

Annotations

Cases

An unsolicited letter received by the court concerning the sentencing of defendant became, in effect, part of the presentence report, and failure of the court to disclose the letter to the attorneys for the state and defendant was error, requiring vacation of the sentence in the absence of any affirmative statement in the record assuring that the court disregarded the letter in imposing sentence. **Bowlin v. State,** Op. No. 81, 643 P2d 1 (Alaska App. 1982).

Attorney's contention that disciplinary board was improperly constituted because one of the members was employed by the civil section of the Attorney General's Office at the same time as the District Attorney's Office sought a criminal indictment against the attorney was rejected since the entire Department of Law is not to be considered one law office. **Discipline of Walton,** Op. No. 2734, 676 P2d 1078 (Alaska 1983).

Trial judge did not err in telephoning an Oregon judge to find out for sentence enhancement purposes if defendant's Oregon escape conviction was a felony. **Huitt v. State,** Op. No. 348, 678 P2d 415 (Alaska App. 1984).

Where police officer's defense to charges of official misconduct was that he was involved in a private investigation outside the usual police department chain of command which had as its target a sitting superior court judge and other prominent citizens, his argument that it would therefore be inappropriate for any sitting district court judge or any sitting superior court judge in the State of Alaska to preside at his trial was rejected. **Feichtinger v. State,** Op. No. 959, 779 P2d 334 (Alaska App. 1989).

Except where a judge is appointed to consider a challenge to another judge pursuant to AS 22.20.020(c), one judge cannot, as a matter of discretion, disqualify another judge; accordingly, a motion to recuse all trial court judges, including judges to whom the case had never been assigned and who therefore had never had the opportunity to exercise discretion, was improper. **Feichtinger v. State,** Op. No. 959, 779 P2d 334 (Alaska App. 1989).

Judge erred in declining to recuse himself from sentencing hearing after having presided over the juvenile defendant's waiver proceeding, since his participation in the sentencing hearing created an appearance of partiality. **Perotti v. State,** Op. No. 1104, 806 P2d 325 (Alaska App. 1991).

Judge who ruled against party in child custody case was not required to recuse herself from unrelated personal injury case involving same party. **Pride v. Harris,** Op. No. 4121, 882 P2d 381 (Alaska 1994).

Remand was required to determine if judge erred in refusing to recuse himself and to set aside his rulings and verdict in defendant's criminal case based upon evidence that judge's clerk was biased in favor of the state; defendant on remand would have burden of establishing by preponderance of evidence that clerk was personally biased in favor of attorney who prosecuted defendant or that clerk engaged in conduct that created reasonable appearance of strong personal bias in favor of state, after which state would have opportunity to prove by preponderance of evidence that clerk did not significantly participate in defendant's case, thus negating presumption that rulings and verdict were invalid. **Vaska v. State,** Op. No. 1582, 955 P2d 943 (Alaska App. 1998).

Judge was not reprimanded where he imprisoned an intoxicated witness for contempt. Even though he failed to give her notice of the purpose of hearing and she was not sober at the time of the hearing, his legal errors were neither willful nor part of a pattern of misconduct. **In re Curda,** Op. No. 5587, 49 P.3d 255 (Alaska 2002).

Code of Judicial Conduct Canon 3E was narrowly tailored to serve a compelling state interest, i.e., it offered assurance to parties that the judge applied the law in the same manner that would be applied to any other litigant. **Alaska Right to Life PAC v. Feldman,** 380 F. Supp. 2d 1080 (D. Alaska 2005).

Pre-signing judicial orders and allowing the prosecution to decide the particulars for out-of-custody defendants without judicial supervision violates Canons 1, 2 A, 3 B(1), 3 B(2)(a), 3 B(2)(b), 3 B(7), 3 B(8), 3 C(1) and 3 C(2) of the Alaska Code of Judicial Conduct. **In re Landry**, Op. No. 12566, 157 P.3d 1049, (Alaska 2007).

Judge's lack of diligence in maintaining accurate tracking of Criminal Rule 45 time constraints, resulting in dismissal of a significant number of criminal cases, violates Canons 2, 3 B(1), 3 B(8), 3 C(1), and 3 C(2) of the Alaska Code of Judicial Conduct. **In re Landry**, Op. No. 12566, 157 P.3d 1049, (Alaska 2007).

Judge's act of engaging in improper ex parte communications and presiding over a matter where he should have disqualified himself, thus giving rise to circumstances suggesting that he gave preferential treatment to the defendant, violated Canons 2 A, 2 B, 3 B(2)(b), 3 B(7) and 3 E(1) of the Alaska Code of Judicial Conduct. **In re Landry**, Op. No. 12566, 157 P.3d 1049, (Alaska 2007).

Judge's acts of making inappropriate sexual comments to female court employees in the workplace violated Canons 2 A, 3 B(1), and 3 B(5) and 3 C(1) of the Alaska Code of Judicial Conduct. **In re Landry**, Op. No. 12566, 157 P.3d 1049, (Alaska 2007).

Canon 4. A Judge Shall So Conduct the Judge's Extra-Judicial Activities as to Minimize the Risk of Conflict with Judicial Obligations.

A. ■ **Extra-Judicial Activities in General.** A judge shall conduct all of the judge's extra-judicial activities so as to comply with the requirements of this Code and so that these activities do not:

(1) cast reasonable doubt on the judge's capacity to act impartially as a judge;

(2) demean the judicial office; or

(3) interfere with the proper performance of judicial duties.*

Commentary.—*Extra-judicial activities are intended to include both the quasi-judicial activities covered by Canon 4 and the extra-judicial activities covered by Canon 5 of the 1973 Code of Judicial Conduct.*

Complete separation of a judge from extra-judicial activities is neither possible nor wise; a judge should not become isolated from the community in which the judge lives.

Even outside the judicial role, a judge who expresses bias or prejudice may cast reasonable doubt on the judge's capacity to act impartially as a judge. Such expressions include jokes or other remarks demeaning individuals on the basis of their race, color, sex, religion, national origin, disability, age, marital status, changes in marital status, pregnancy, parenthood, sexual orientation, or social or economic status. See Section 2C and accompanying Commentary.

The ABA added the phrase "demean the judicial office" in Section 4A(2) in place of the phrase "detract from the dignity of his office" which appeared in the prior Code. According to the Reporter's Notes to the 1990 Model Code, the new language is intended "to proscribe injurious conduct, not necessarily undignified conduct, as the latter might in some cases be permissible. For example, a judge's appearing in a skit as part of the entertainment at a judicial organization's event might be at once undignified and perfectly proper."

Section 4A(2) is a legitimate limitation on a judge's extra-judicial activities to the extent that it forbids a judge from flagrantly violating community standards or engaging in activities that clearly bring disrepute to the courts or the legal system. However, Section 4A(2) should not be interpreted so broadly as to authorize disciplinary bodies to censure or penalize a judge for engaging in a non-conformist lifestyle or for privately pursuing interests or activities that might be offensive to segments of the community.

B. ■ **Educational Activities.** As part of the judicial role, a judge is encouraged to render public service to the community. Judges have a professional responsibility to educate the public about the judicial system and the judicial office, subject to the requirements of this Code. A judge may speak, write, lecture, teach, and participate in other extra-judicial activities concerning the law,* the legal system, the administration of justice, and non-legal topics, subject to the requirements of this Code.

Commentary.—*As a judicial officer and person specially learned in the law, a judge is in a unique position to contribute to the improvement of the law, the legal system, and the administration of justice, including revision of substantive and procedural law and improvement of criminal and juvenile justice. To the extent that time permits, a judge is encouraged to do so, either independently or through a bar association, judicial conference, or other organization dedicated to the improvement of the law. Judges may participate in efforts to promote the fair administration of justice, the independence of the judiciary, and the integrity of the legal profession. A judge may also encourage community involvement in court-affiliated programs and may invite public suggestions for the improvement of the law, the legal system, or the legal profession. In conducting these activities, judges should be mindful to comply with Canon 2 when recommending specific programs or activities.*

The responsibility to educate the public is not intended to be enforced through the disciplinary process.

C. ■ **Governmental, Civic, Charitable, and Law-related Activities.**

(1) ◊ ■ A judge shall not appear at a public hearing before, or otherwise consult with, an executive or legislative body or official except on matters concerning the law,* the legal system, or the administration of justice, or except when acting pro se in a matter involving the judge or the judge's interests.

Commentary.—*See Section 2B regarding the obligation to avoid improper influence.*

"Administration of justice" matters include seeking funding for public service organizations that provide or seek increased access to justice such as Alaska Legal Services, so long as the organization is not identified with a particular cause that may come before the courts. When testifying as an individual judge on administration of justice matters, the judge should be clear that the observations are based on his or her experience as a judge and that other judges may have different observations.

Section 4C(1) permits a judge to appear before a governmental body or government official on a matter concerning the judge's interests. The word "interests" should be interpreted broadly. A judge may speak on matters concerning the judge's social interests as well as matters affecting the judge's economic interests.

(2) ‡◊ A judge shall not accept appointment to or serve on a governmental committee or commission or other governmental position that is concerned with issues of fact or policy on matters other than the improvement of the law,* the legal system, or the administration of justice. A judge may, however, represent a country, state, or locality on ceremonial occasions or in connection with historical, educational, cultural, or athletic activities.

Commentary.—*Section 4C(2) prohibits a judge from accepting any governmental position except one relating to the law, the legal system, or the administration of justice as authorized by Section 4C(3). The appropriateness of accepting extra-judicial assignments must be assessed in light of the demands on judicial resources created by crowded dockets and the need to protect the courts from involvement in extra-judicial matters that may prove to be controversial. Judges should not accept governmental appointments that are likely to interfere with the effectiveness and independence of the judiciary.*

Section 4C(2) does not govern a judge's service in a nongovernmental position. See Section 4C(3) permitting service by a judge with organizations devoted to the improvement of the law, the legal system, or the administration of justice and with educational, religious, charitable, fraternal, or civic organizations not conducted for profit. For example, service on the board of a public educational institution, unless it were a law school, would be prohibited under Section 4C(2), but service on the board of a public law school or any private educational institution would generally be permitted under Section 4C(3).

(3) A judge may serve as an officer, director, trustee, or non-legal advisor of an organization or governmental agency devoted to the improvement of the law,* the legal system, or the administration of justice, or of an educational, religious, charitable, fraternal, cultural, athletic, or civic organization not conducted for profit, subject to the following limitations:

Commentary.*—Section 4C(3) does not apply to a judge's service in a governmental position unconnected with the improvement of the law, the legal system or the administration of justice; see Section 4C(2).*

Participation by a judge in a non-profit organization may be governed by other provisions of Canon 4 in addition to Section 4C. For example, a judge is prohibited by Section 4G from serving as a legal advisor to a non-profit organization.

Section 4C(3) does not prohibit mere membership in a legal professional association that occasionally takes controversial or political positions.

(a) A judge shall not serve as an officer, director, trustee, or non-legal advisor if it is likely that the organization will be engaged in proceedings that would ordinarily come before the judge or will be engaged frequently in adversary proceedings in the court of which the judge is a member or in any court subject to the appellate jurisdiction of the judge's court.

Commentary.*—The changing nature of some organizations and of their relationship to the law makes it necessary for a judge regularly to reexamine the activities of each organization with which the judge is affiliated to determine if it is proper for the judge to continue the affiliation. For example, in many jurisdictions charitable hospitals are now more frequently in court than in the past. Similarly, the boards of some legal aid organizations now make policy decisions that may have political significance or imply commitment to causes that may come before the courts for adjudication.*

(b) Regardless of the judge's role within the organization, a judge:

(i) may assist the organization in planning fundraising activities and may participate in the management and investment of the organization's funds, but shall not personally participate in the solicitation of funds or be the speaker or guest of honor at the organization's fundraising event, except a judge may be the speaker or guest of honor for public service organizations that seek improvement in the administration of justice, benefit indigent representation, or assist access to justice, or for any permitted organization under Section 4C(3) where the proceeds from the event seek to improve the administration of justice, benefit indigent representation, or assist access to justice. A judge may also solicit funds for any permitted organization under Section 4C(3) from other judges over whom the judge does not exercise supervisory or appellate authority;

(ii) may make recommendations to public or private fund-granting organizations on projects and programs concerning the law,* the legal system, or the administration of justice;

(iii) shall not personally participate in membership solicitation if the solicitation might reasonably be perceived as coercive;

(iv) shall not personally participate in membership solicitation, except as permitted in Section 4C(3)(b)(i), if the membership solicitation is essentially a fundraising mechanism;

(v) shall not use or permit anyone else to use the prestige of judicial office for fundraising or membership solicitation.

Commentary.*—A judge may solicit membership or endorse or encourage membership efforts for an organization devoted to the improvement of the law, the legal system or the administration of justice or a nonprofit educational, religious, charitable, fraternal or civic organization as long as the solicitation cannot reasonably be perceived as coercive and is not essentially a fundraising mechanism. Solicitation of funds for an organization and solicitation of memberships similarly involve the danger that the person solicited will feel obligated to respond favorably to the solicitor if the solicitor is in a position of influence or control. A judge must not engage in direct, individual solicitation of funds or memberships in person, in writing, or by telephone except in the following cases: (1) a judge may solicit other judges over whom the judge does not exercise supervisory or appellate authority, (2) a judge may solicit other persons for membership in the organizations described above if neither those persons nor persons with whom they are affiliated are likely ever to appear before the court on which the judge serves, and (3) a judge who is an officer of a Section 4C(3) organization may send a general membership solicitation mailing over the judge's signature.*

Use of an organization letterhead for fundraising or membership solicitation does not violate Section 4C(3)(b) provided the letterhead lists only the judge's name and office or other position in the organization, and, if comparable designations are listed for other persons, the judge's judicial designation. In addition, a judge must also make reasonable efforts to ensure that the judge's staff, court officials and others subject to the judge's direction and control do not solicit funds on the judge's behalf for any purpose, charitable or otherwise.

Section 4C(3)(b)(i) is intended to prohibit the direct solicitation of funds. Being the speaker or guest of honor at an organization's fundraising event is the functional equivalent of solicitation. However, judges may participate as workers at fundraising events such as car washes and carnivals, purchase admission to fundraising social events, and purchase goods and services (e.g., candy bars, commemorative buttons, or a car wash) that are being sold as a fundraising effort.

The limited exception allowing judges to be speakers or guests of honor for public service organizations that assist access to justice is meant to include not-for-profit organizations that exist to enhance access to justice or to seek improvement in the administration of justice, but judges should be mindful of the need to avoid creating the appearance that they are identifying with a particular cause or issue that is likely to come before them or before other judges on their court. See Canon 2 and accompanying Commentary. "Access to justice" includes increasing minority representation on the bench, preserving judicial independence, and assisting the advancement of the legal profession.

D. **Financial Activities.**

(1) *Generally.*

(a) ■ A judge shall not engage in financial or business dealings, or permit his or her name to be used in connection with any business venture or commercial advertising program, with or without compensation, if the activity might reasonably be perceived to exploit the judge's judicial position.

(b) ◊ A judge shall not enter into financial or business dealings that would involve the judge in frequent transactions or continuing business relationships with those lawyers or other persons likely to come before the court on which the judge serves.

Commentary.*—See Time for Compliance, Section 6E.*

When a judge acquires information in a judicial capacity, such as material contained in filings with the court, that is not yet generally known, the judge must not use the information for private gain. See Section 2B; see also Section 3B(11).

A judge must avoid financial and business dealings that involve the judge in frequent transactions or continuing business relationships with persons likely to come either before the judge personally or before other judges on the judge's court. In addition, a judge should discourage members of the judge's family from engaging in dealings that would reasonably appear to exploit the judge's judicial position. This rule is necessary to avoid creating an appearance of exploitation of office or favoritism and to minimize the potential for disqualification. With respect to affiliation of relatives of a judge with law firms appearing before the judge, see Commentary to Section 3E(1) relating to disqualification.

Participation by a judge in financial and business dealings is subject to the general prohibitions in Section 4A against activities that tend to reflect adversely on the impartiality of the judge, demean the judicial office, or interfere with the proper performance of judicial duties. Such participation is also subject to the general prohibition in Canon 2 against activities involving impropriety or the appearance of impropriety and the prohibition in Section 2B against the misuse of the prestige of judicial office. In addition, a judge must maintain high standards of conduct in all of the judge's activities, as set forth in Canon 1.

Under Section 4D(1)(b), a judge may enter into financial or business dealings with a lawyer who is a relative or close friend whose appearance or interest in a case would in any event require the judge's disqualification under Section 3E.

(2) *Judge as Investor.* A judge may hold and manage investments of the judge and members of the judge's family,* including real estate. In addition, a judge may participate as a passive investor in any business. For purposes of this Section, "passive investor" means that the judge is not a director, officer, manager, partner (except a limited partner in a limited partnership), advisor, employee, or controlling shareholder of the business.

Commentary.*—See Time for Compliance, Section 6E. For active investments and other business interests, see Section 4D(3).*

(3) A judge may actively engage in business or other remunerative activity, as long as the judge would not expect the business or remunerative activity to:

(a) involve the judge or the judge's business associates in lobbying legislative or regulatory bodies within Alaska, or

(b) involve the judge or the judge's business associates in frequent appearances in front of legislative or regulatory bodies within Alaska, or

(c) ‡ ◊ have a major effect on the economic life of the community in which the judge serves. A business has a "major effect on the economic life of the community" when it employs more than five percent of the local work-force, when it provides essential financial services (for example, banking or insurance) or essential utilities (for example, electricity, oil, gas, sewage treatment) to the community, or when it is the sole provider of an essential good or service within the community.

Commentary.*—See Time for Compliance, Section 6E.*

(4) ‡ A judge shall manage investments and business and other financial interests to minimize the number of cases in which the judge is disqualified. As soon as the judge can do so without serious financial detriment, the judge shall divest himself or herself of investments and business and other financial interests that might require frequent disqualification.

(5) A judge shall not accept, and shall urge members of the judge's family* residing in the judge's household not to accept a gift, bequest, favor, or loan from anyone, except for:

Commentary.*—Section 4D(5) does not apply to contributions to a judge's campaign for judicial office, a matter governed by Canon 5.*

Because a gift, bequest, favor, or loan to a member of the judge's family residing in the judge's household might be viewed as intended to influence the judge, a judge must inform those family members of the relevant ethical constraints upon the judge in this regard and discourage those family members from violating them. A judge cannot, however, reasonably be expected to know or control all of the financial or business activities of all family members residing in the judge's household.

(a) a gift incident to a public testimonial, or books, tapes, and other resource materials supplied by publishers on a complimentary basis for official use, or an invitation to the judge and the judge's spouse* or guest to attend a bar-related function or an activity devoted to the improvement of the law,* the legal system, or the administration of justice;

Commentary.—*Acceptance of an invitation to a law-related function is governed by Section 4D(5)(a); acceptance of an invitation paid for by an individual lawyer or group of lawyers is governed by Section 4D(5)(h).*

A judge may accept a public testimonial or a gift incident thereto only if the donor organization is not an organization whose members comprise or frequently represent the same side in litigation, and the testimonial and gift are otherwise in compliance with other provisions of this Code. See Sections 4A(1) and 2B.

(b) a gift, award, or benefit incident to the business, profession, or other separate activity of a spouse* or other family member* residing in the judge's household, including gifts, awards, and benefits for the use of both the spouse or other family member and the judge (as spouse or family member), provided that the gift, award, or benefit could not reasonably be perceived as intended to influence the judge in the performance of judicial duties;*

(c) ordinary social hospitality;

(d) a gift from a relative or friend for a special occasion such as a wedding, anniversary, or birthday, if the gift is fairly commensurate with the occasion and the relationship;

Commentary.—*A gift of excessive value to a judge or to a member of the judge's family living in the judge's household raises questions about the judge's impartiality and the integrity of the judicial office and might require disqualification of the judge when disqualification would not otherwise be required. See, however, Section 4D(5)(e).*

(e) a gift, bequest, favor, or loan from a relative or close personal friend whose appearance or interest in a case would in any event require the judge's disqualification under Section 3E;

(f) a loan from a lending institution in its regular course of business on the same terms generally available to persons who are not judges;

(g) a scholarship or fellowship awarded on the same terms and based on the same criteria applied to other applicants; or

(h) any other gift, bequest, favor, or loan, but only if the donor is not a person who has come or is likely to come before the judge, and if the person's interests have not come and are unlikely to come before the judge. If the value of the gift, bequest, favor, or loan exceeds $250.00, the judge shall report the gift, bequest, favor, or loan in the same manner as the judge reports compensation under Section 4H.

Commentary.—*Section 4D(5)(h) prohibits judges from accepting gifts, favors, bequests, or loans from lawyers or their firms if they have come or are likely to come before the judge; it also prohibits gifts, favors, bequests, or loans from clients of lawyers or their firms when the clients' interests have come or are likely to come before the judge.*

E. **Fiduciary Activities.**

(1) ‡ ◊ A judge shall not serve as executor, administrator, or other personal representative, trustee, guardian, attorney in fact, or other fiduciary* except on behalf of the estate, trust, or person of a member of the judge's family,* and then only if such service will not interfere with the proper performance of the judge's judicial duties.*

(2) ‡ A judge shall not serve as a fiduciary* if it is likely that the judge, in his or her fiduciary capacity, will be engaged in proceedings that would ordinarily come before the judge or if the estate, trust, or ward becomes involved in adversary proceedings in the court on which the judge serves or a court under its appellate jurisdiction.

(3) ■ The same restrictions on financial activities that apply to a judge personally also apply to the judge while acting in a fiduciary* capacity.

Commentary.—*See Time for Compliance, Section 6E. The restrictions imposed by Canon 4 may conflict with the judge's obligation as a fiduciary. For example, a judge should resign as trustee if, by virtue of Sections 4D(4) and 4E(3), the judge would be obliged to sell or trade trust assets to the detriment of the trust.*

F. ‡ **Service as Arbitrator or Mediator.** A judge shall not act as an arbitrator or mediator or otherwise perform judicial functions in a private capacity unless expressly authorized by law.*

Commentary.—*Section 4F does not prohibit a judge from participating in arbitration, mediation, or settlement conferences performed as part of judicial duties. A senior judge may act as a private arbitrator or mediator subject to Administrative Rule 23(f), which states:*

(f) Private Arbitration and Mediation. If a retired judge acts as a private arbitrator or mediator, the judge must comply with the following rules to remain eligible for pro tempore appointment:

(1) The judge shall refrain from soliciting or accepting employment as an arbitrator or mediator from a lawyer or party who is currently appearing in a case assigned to the judge.

(2) The judge shall disqualify himself or herself from sitting as a pro tem judge in a case if the judge has previously served as an arbitrator or mediator in the same matter. This

disqualification may be waived under Section 3F of the Code of Judicial Conduct.

(3) The judge shall disqualify himself or herself from sitting as a pro tem judge in a case if the judge is currently serving or scheduled to serve as an arbitrator or mediator for a lawyer or party in the case. This disqualification may be waived under Section 3F of the Code of Judicial Conduct.

(4) If within two years prior to the filing of a case assigned to a pro tem judge the judge has served as an arbitrator or mediator for a lawyer or party in that case, the judge shall disclose that fact on the record and disqualify himself or herself from sitting as a pro tem judge in that case. Disclosure must be made under this paragraph regardless of the amount of compensation that the judge received from the arbitration or mediation. This disqualification may be waived under Section 3F of the Code of Judicial Conduct.

(5) The judge shall refrain from accepting employment as an arbitrator or mediator from a lawyer or party who has appeared in a case assigned to the judge within the last six months.

G. ◊ **Practice of Law.** A judge shall not practice law. Notwithstanding this prohibition, a judge may act pro se and may, without compensation, give legal advice to and draft or review documents for a member of the judge's family.*

Commentary.—*This prohibition refers to the practice of law in a representative capacity and not in a pro se capacity. A judge may act for himself or herself in all legal matters, including matters involving litigation and matters involving appearances before or other dealings with legislative and other governmental bodies. However, in so doing, a judge must not abuse the prestige of office to advance the interests of the judge or the judge's family. See Section 2B.*

The Code allows a judge to give legal advice to and draft legal documents for members of the judge's family, provided the judge receives no compensation. A judge must not, however, act as an advocate or negotiator for a member of the judge's family in a legal matter.

Even though Section 4G does not apply to part-time magistrates and deputy magistrates, Administrative Rule 2 prohibits employees of the Alaska Court System from engaging directly or indirectly in the practice of law in any of the courts of the state.

H. **Compensation, Reimbursement, and Reporting.**

(1) *Compensation and Reimbursement Defined.*

(a) "Compensation" is income received by the judge for personal services or from business activities. It does not include income from a business or property that the judge does not actively manage.

(b) "Reimbursement" is money paid to defray a judge's expenses or any credit or discount given to reduce these expenses. Expense reimbursement other than government-approved per diem shall be limited to the actual cost of travel, food, and lodging reasonably incurred by the judge and, when appropriate to the occasion, the judge's spouse* or guest. Any payment, credit, or discount in excess of these limits is compensation.

(2) *Limits on Compensation and Reimbursement.* A judge may receive compensation and reimbursement of expenses for the extra-judicial activities permitted by this Code if the source of these payments does not give the appearance of influencing the judge's performance of judicial duties* or otherwise give the appearance of impropriety. Compensation shall not exceed a reasonable amount nor shall it exceed what a person who is not a judge would receive for the same activity.

(3) *Public Reports of Compensation.* At least once a year a judge shall report the date, place, and nature of any extra-judicial activity for which the judge received compensation, the name of the payor, and the amount of compensation received. If the judge is a retired justice or judge serving pro tempore who receives compensation for private arbitration or mediation services, it is sufficient for the judge to file a copy of Schedule A of the Public Official Financial Disclosure Statement that the justice or judge files with the Alaska Public Offices Commission. Compensation or income of a spouse* that is attributed to the judge by operation of a community property law is not extra-judicial compensation to the judge for purposes of this Code. The judge's report shall be submitted at the times and in the form prescribed by the Administrator Director of the Alaska Court System. The report shall be filed as a public document in the office of the Administrative Director.

Commentary.—*See Section 4D(5) regarding reporting of gifts, bequests, and loans.*

Section 4H is divided into three Sections. Section 1 contains the definitions of the terms "compensation" and "reimbursement." Section 2 prescribes the limits on compensation and reimbursement permitted by the Code for extra-judicial activities. Section 3 requires a judge to report compensation (not reimbursement) at least annually.

Section 4H(1)(a) defines "compensation." In general terms, this definition is intended to cover "earned income" - that is, salary, wages, professional fees, tips, and any other income generated by the judge's personal efforts. Compensation does not include income generated by a judge's investments or by partnerships or businesses in which the judge is a passive participant (a limited partner, for example).

Section 4H(1)(b) defines "reimbursement" of expenses. The first sentence gives the general definition of reimbursement: any money, credit, or discount that defrays or reduces a judge's expenses. Reimbursement in the form of government per diem can exceed actual expenses and still not be classified as "compensation."

Section 4H(3) requires a judge to report any extra-judicial activity for which the judge received compensation. The second sentence applies to retired justices and judges who are serving in a pro tempore capacity. If that judge acts as a private arbitrator or mediator, the judge may comply with this section by filing a copy of Schedule A of the Public Official

Financial Disclosure Statement that the judge files with the Alaska Public Offices Commission. That statement lists the names of self-employment businesses and the names of each client who paid the business over $5000. The judge is not required to individually name every client of the business, or to list the amounts received from each client. The judge is nonetheless required, under Administrative Rule 23, to disclose on the record if, within the two years prior to the filing of the assigned case, the judge has served as an arbitrator or mediator for a lawyer or a party in a case; the judge is also required to disqualify himself or herself from sitting pro tem in that case, unless the disqualification is waived.

This Code does not prohibit a judge from accepting honoraria or speaking fees provided that the compensation is reasonable and commensurate with the task performed. A judge should ensure, however, that no conflicts are created by the arrangement. A judge must not appear to use his or her judicial position for personal advantage. Nor should a judge spend significant time away from court duties to meet speaking or writing commitments for compensation. In addition, the source of the payment must not raise any question of undue influence or the judge's ability or willingness to be impartial.

I. ■ Disclosure of a judge's income, debts, and investments and other assets is required only to the extent specified in this Canon and in Sections 3E and 3F, or as otherwise required by law.*

Commentary.—*Section 3E requires a judge to disqualify himself or herself in any proceeding in which the judge has an economic interest. See "economic interest" as explained in the Terminology Section. Section 4D requires a judge to refrain from engaging in business and from financial activities that might interfere with the impartial performance of judicial duties. Section 4H requires a judge to report all compensation the judge received for activities outside judicial office. A judge's financial affairs are private except to the extent disclosure is required by law.*

(Adopted by SCO 1322 effective July 15, 1998, amended by SCO 1559 effective July 15, 2005; by SCO 1617 effective July 15, 2006; and by SCO 1629 effective December 31, 2006)

Canon 5. A Judge or Judicial Candidate Shall Refrain from Inappropriate Political Activity.

A. **All Judges and Candidates.**

(1) Except as authorized in Sections 5B(2) and 5C, a judge or a candidate* for appointment to judicial office shall not:

(a) act as a leader of or hold office in a political organization.*

(b) publicly endorse or publicly oppose a candidate for any public office. However, when false information concerning a judicial candidate* is made public, a judge or candidate having knowledge* of contrary facts may make the facts public.

(c) make speeches on behalf of a political organization.*

(d) ◊ attend political gatherings.

(e) ◊ solicit funds for any political organization* or candidate for public office, pay an assessment or make a contribution to a political organization or candidate for public office, purchase tickets for a political organization's dinners or other functions.

Commentary.—*A judge or candidate for judicial office retains the right to participate in the political process as a voter.*

Section 5A(1)(b) does not prohibit a judge or judicial candidate from privately expressing his or her views on judicial candidates or other candidates for public office.

Judges should be able to take part in the public debate over proposals to change the legal system or the administration of justice; judges' training and experience make them a valuable resource to the electorate wishing to decide these issues. Since many speeches are given in forums sponsored by political organizations, a question arises concerning the relationship between, on the one hand, a judge's right to speak publicly on issues concerning the legal system and the administration of justice, and, on the other hand, the prohibition contained in Section 5A(1)(d) C that a judge shall not attend the gathering of a political organization. Despite a judge's freedom to speak on legal issues, a judge shall not do so on behalf of a political organization or at a political gathering.

(2) ◊ A judge shall resign upon becoming a candidate* in either a primary or general election for any non-judicial office except the office of delegate to a state or federal constitutional convention.

(3) A candidate for judicial office:*

(a) shall maintain the dignity appropriate to judicial office and act in a manner consistent with the integrity and independence of the judiciary, and shall encourage members of the candidate's family to adhere to the same standards that apply to the candidate. "Members of the candidate's family" means the candidate's spouse,* children, grandchildren, parents, grandparents, and other relatives or persons with whom the candidate maintains a close familial relationship.

Commentary.—*Although a judicial candidate must encourage members of his or her family to adhere to the same standards of political conduct in support of the candidate that apply to the candidate, family members are free to participate in other political activity.*

(b) shall prohibit employees and officials who serve at the pleasure of the candidate, and shall discourage all other employees and officials subject to the candidate's direction and control, from doing anything on the candidate's behalf that is forbidden to the candidate under these rules.

(c) shall not authorize or permit any person to take actions forbidden to the candidate under these rules, except when these rules specifically allow other people to take actions that would be forbidden to the candidate personally.

(d) shall not:

(i) make pledges or promises of conduct in judicial office other than to faithfully and impartially perform the duties of the office;

(ii) make statements that commit or appear to commit the candidate to a particular view or decision with respect to cases, controversies or issues that are likely to come before the court; or

(iii) knowingly* misrepresent any fact concerning the candidate or an opposing candidate for judicial office.

Commentary.—*Section 5A(3)(d) prohibits a candidate for judicial office from making statements that appear to commit the candidate regarding cases, controversies, or issues likely to come before the court. As a corollary, a candidate for judicial office should emphasize in any public statement the candidate's duty to uphold the law regardless of his or her personal views. See also Section 3B(9), the general rule on public comment by judges. Section 5A(3)(d) does not prohibit a candidate from making pledges or promises respecting improvements in court administration. Nor does this Section prohibit an incumbent judge from making private statements to other judges or court personnel in the performance of judicial duties. This Section applies to any statement made in the process of securing judicial office, such as statements to commissions charged with judicial selection and tenure and legislative bodies confirming appointment. See also Rule 8. 2 of the Alaska Rules of Professional Conduct.*

*In **Buckley v. Illinois Judicial Inquiry Board**, 997 F. 2d 224 (7th Cir. 1993), the Seventh Circuit ruled that the ABA's proposed Section 5A(3)(d)(i) and the 1972 predecessor to the ABA's proposed Section 5A(3)(d)(ii) represent an unconstitutional abridgement of judicial candidates' right of free speech.*

*The Illinois rule at issue in **Buckley** prohibited judges and judicial candidates from making "pledges or promises of conduct in office other than the faithful and impartial performance of the duties of the office" and further prohibited judges and judicial candidates from "announc[ing] [their] views on disputed legal or political issues." These same restrictions are currently the law of Alaska: see Alaska Code of Judicial Conduct, Section 7B(1)(c). The Seventh Circuit held that these two restrictions on judges' speech are unconstitutionally overbroad.*

***Buckley** involved two plaintiffs. The first plaintiff was a judge from the intermediate appeals court who ran for the state supreme court; the Judicial Inquiry Board disciplined him for declaring, during the campaign, that he had "never written an opinion reversing a rape conviction." The second plaintiff was a legislator who campaigned for (and was elected to) a seat on the Cook County Circuit Court; he sought relief because "the risk of being sanctioned for violating [the judicial conduct rule] deterred him from speaking out in his campaign on issues that he believed to be important to Illinois voters, including capital punishment, abortion, the state's budget, and public school education."*

*The Seventh Circuit noted that **Buckley** presented the collision of two competing political principles: First, "Candidates for public office should be free to express their views on all matters of interest to the electorate." Second, "Judges [must] decide cases in accordance with law rather than [in accordance] with any express or implied commitments that they may have made to their campaign supporters or to others." Buckley, 997 F. 2d at 227.*

The court declared that "only a fanatic would suppose that...freedom of speech should . . . entitle a candidate for judicial office to promise to vote for one side or another in a particular case or class of cases[.]" On the other hand, the court likewise disavowed the idea "that the principle of impartial legal justice should...prevent a [judicial] candidate...from furnishing any information or opinion to the electorate beyond his name, rank, and serial number." Id. The court went on to state:

> *The difficulty with crafting a rule to prevent [a judicial candidate from making commitments] is that a commitment can be implicit as well as explicit... The candidate might make an explicit commitment to do something that was not, in so many words, taking sides in a particular case or class of cases but would be so understood by the electorate; he might for example promise always to give paramount weight to public safety or to a woman's right of privacy. Or he might discuss a particular case or class of cases in a way that was understood as a commitment to rule in a particular way, even though he avoided the language of pledges, promises, or commitments.*
>
> *The "pledges or promises" clause is not limited to pledges or promises to rule a particular way in particular cases or classes of case; all pledges and promises are forbidden except a promise that the candidate will if elected faithfully and impartially discharge the duties of his judicial office. The "announce" clause is not limited to declarations as to how the candidate intends to rule in particular cases or classes of case; he may not "announce his views on disputed legal or political issues," period. The rule certainly deals effectively with the abuse that the draftsmen were concerned with; but in so doing it gags the judicial candidate. He can say nothing in public about his judicial philosophy, he cannot, for example, pledge himself to be a strict constructionist, or for that matter a legal realist. He cannot promise a better shake for indigent litigants or harried employers. He cannot criticize Roe v. Wade.* He cannot express his views about substantive due process, economic rights, search and seizure, the war on drugs, the use of excessive force by police, the conditions of the prisons, or products liability C or for that matter about laissez-faire economics, race relations, the civil war in Yugoslavia, or the proper direction of health-care reform . . . All these are disputed legal or political issues.

> The rule this reaches far beyond speech that could reasonably be interpreted as committing the candidate in a way that would compromise his impartiality should he be successful in the election. Indeed, the only safe response to Illinois Supreme Court Rule 67(B)(1)(c) is silence. True, the silencing is temporary. It is limited to the duration of the campaign. But [the rule's] interference with the marketplace of ideas and opinions is at its zenith when the "customers" are most avid for the market's "product." The only time the public takes much interest in the ideas and opinions of judges or judicial candidates is when an important judicial office has to be filled . . . .

Id. *at 228-29. The Seventh Circuit noted, but expressed no opinion on, the ABA's proposed revision of the "announce his views" clause. In the 1990 version of the model Code, the ABA has amended this Section so that it now prohibits a judge or judicial candidate from making "statements that commit or appear to commit the judge to a particular view or decision with respect to cases, controversies, or issues... likely to come before [the judge's] court." According to the ABA commentary to Section 5A(3)(d)(ii), the predecessor "announce" rule was felt to be too broad.*

The Seventh Circuit points out in ***Buckley*** *that, even with this change, the ABA provisions may run afoul of First Amendment protections. For example, read too broadly, a Section that prohibits a judge from making any pledge or promise (other than to do a good job) could be used as a basis for disciplinary action against a judicial candidate who declared that he or she believed the courts should actively pursue sentencing alternatives to imprisonment. Conceivably, this same provision could subject a judge to discipline for declaring, as Ruth Ginsberg told the Senate Judiciary Committee on July 20, 1993 [as reported in the Anchorage Daily News of 7/21/93], "My approach [to service on the supreme court] is rooted in the [belief] that the place of the judiciary . . . in our democratic society [is] third in line behind the people and their elected representatives"—a comment that might be construed as a pledge to broadly construe the powers of the legislative branch and to narrowly circumscribe the reach of the Bill of Rights as a check on legislative activity. The Code should be interpreted in a manner that does not infringe First Amendment rights.*

(e) may respond to personal attacks or attacks on the candidate's record, as long as the response contains no knowing misrepresentation of fact and does not violate Section 5A(3)(d).

B. ◊ **Candidates Seeking Appointment to Judicial or Other Governmental Office.**

(1) A candidate* for appointment to judicial office or a judge seeking appointment to another governmental office shall not solicit or accept any funds, personally or through a committee or otherwise, to support his or her candidacy.

(2) A candidate* for appointment to judicial office or a judge seeking appointment to another governmental office may not engage in any political activity* to secure appointment, with the following exceptions:

(a) subject to Section 5A(3), such persons may:*

(i) communicate with the appointing authority, including any selection, screening, or nominating bodies;

(ii) seek privately-communicated support or endorsement from organizations and individuals; and

(iii) provide information regarding his or her qualifications for office to organizations and individuals from whom the candidate seeks support;

(b) a non-judge candidate* for appointment to judicial office may, in addition, unless otherwise prohibited by law:*

(i) retain an office in a political organization,*

(ii) attend political gatherings, and

(iii) continue to pay ordinary assessments and dues to political organizations* and to purchase tickets for political party dinners or other functions.

Commentary.—*Section 5B(2) provides a limited exception to the restrictions imposed by Sections 5A(1) and 5D. Under Section 5B(2), candidates seeking reappointment to the same judicial office or appointment to another judicial office or other governmental office may support their own candidacy and seek appropriate support from others.*

Sections 5B(2)(a)(ii) and (iii) should be read to allow judicial candidates, including judges who are candidates for appointment to other judicial office, to promote their candidacy by circulating letters to the general membership of the bar and to organizations interested in judicial selection. Similarly, a judge need not object when individual lawyers or groups of lawyers decide to circulate a letter in support of the judge's candidacy. However, these letters must not contain promises or statements forbidden by Section 5A(3)(d) (regarding the candidate's likely decisions or action if appointed), must not contain false statements, and, in general, must not violate any other provision of the Code.

A different problem is presented when a judicial candidate approaches individual lawyers or organizations and seeks their endorsement of his or her candidacy. Even though Canon 5 generally tries to make the rules of political conduct uniform for all judicial candidates (both current judges and lawyers applying to be judges), a sitting judge's approach to individual lawyers inevitably presents problems that do not arise when a non-judge candidate approaches other members of the bar. Because a sitting judge will wield judicial power whether or not the judge's campaign for a different office is successful, a judge who asks individuals for political support runs the risk that the request will give the appearance of abuse of office. Because there is a latent potential for subtle coercion in such requests, a judge's request for the personal endorsement of a lawyer must be circumspect and framed cautiously. A judge must take pains to avoid even giving the appearance that he or she is using or threatening to use the power of judicial office to obtain endorsements.

Section 5B(2)(a)(ii) allows a candidate to seek privately-communicated support or endorsement. Under this provision, a candidate may ask individuals and organizations to send a letter to the Alaska Judicial Council or to the governor, or to speak in support of the candidate at a public hearing held by the Judicial Council or at a private meeting with the governor or the governor's staff. However, a candidate may not ask or authorize individuals or organizations to run newspaper advertisements endorsing the candidate or to send letters to their membership or to other organizations encouraging them to support the candidate. If the candidate is a judge, the candidate should ask individuals and organizations not to send copies of endorsement letters to the candidate.

Although under Section 5B(2)(b) non-judge candidates seeking appointment to judicial office are permitted during their candidacy to retain office in a political organization, attend political gatherings and pay ordinary dues and assessments, they remain subject to other provisions of this Code during their candidacy. See Sections 5E and Application Section.

C. **Judges Seeking Retention.**

(1) A judge who is a candidate* for retention in judicial office may engage in the following political activity to secure retention:

(a) submit a photograph and a statement supporting his or her candidacy for inclusion in the state election pamphlet under AS 15.58;

(b) in response to an unsolicited request,

(i) speak to public gatherings on behalf of his or her candidacy;

(ii) appear on television and radio programs to discuss his or her candidacy; and

(iii) grant interviews regarding his or her candidacy;

(c) form an election committee of responsible persons to conduct an election campaign in case there is active opposition to the judge's candidacy; and

(d) reserve advertising space in case there is active opposition to the judge's candidacy.

(2) A judge who is a candidate* for retention in judicial office may engage in the following additional political activity when there is active opposition to the judge's candidacy:

(a) advertise in newspapers, on television, and in other media in support of his or her candidacy; and

(b) distribute pamphlets and other promotional literature supporting his or her candidacy.

Commentary.—*Sections 5C(1) and (2) permit a judge who is a candidate for retention to be involved in limited political activity. Section 5D, applicable solely to incumbent judges, would otherwise bar this activity.*

Section 5C(2) allows judges seeking retention in office to engage in overt political activity if there is "active opposition" to their candidacy. This Code, like the prior Code, does not define "active opposition." However, the term is meant to be broadly construed. A negative recommendation by the Alaska Judicial Council constitutes active opposition. Holding a press conference, advertising, distributing brochures or leaflets, and sending letters to voters are all forms of active opposition. On the other hand, statements made by individual speakers at Judicial Council meetings rarely constitute active opposition, regardless of what is said. Active opposition may be conducted by individuals acting alone as well as by groups. The opposition need not be specifically targeted at one particular judge or at a discrete group of judges C a newspaper advertisement urging the rejection of all judges standing for retention would be viewed as active opposition to the candidacy of each individual judge. If a judge has information and believes that active opposition is imminent, the judge may document the basis of this belief to the Judicial Conduct Commission and may then proceed as if there were active opposition to the judge's candidacy.

(3) A judge who is a candidate* for retention in judicial office shall not personally solicit or accept any funds to support his or her candidacy or personally solicit publicly stated support for his or her candidacy. However, if there is active opposition to the judge's candidacy, the judge's election committees may engage in media advertisements, brochures, mailings, candidate forums, and any other legal methods of pursuing the judge's election. Such committees may solicit and accept reasonable campaign contributions, manage and expend these funds on behalf of the judge's election campaign and solicit and obtain public statements of support for the judge's candidacy. Such committees are not prohibited from soliciting and accepting reasonable campaign contributions and public support from lawyers. A candidate's committee may solicit contributions and public support for the candidate's campaign preceding the election and for 90 days thereafter. A judge shall not make private use of campaign funds raised by an election committee or use these funds for the private benefit of any other person or permit anyone else to use these funds for the private benefit of any person.

Commentary.—*Section 5C(2) permits a judge who is a candidate for retention to establish a campaign committee to solicit and accept public support and reasonable financial contributions if there is active opposition to the judge's candidacy. At the start of the campaign, the judge must instruct his or her campaign committee to solicit or accept only contributions that are reasonable under the circumstances. Though not prohibited, campaign contributions of which a judge has knowledge, made by lawyers or others who appear before the judge, may be relevant to disqualification under Section 3E.*

Campaign committees established under Section 5C(2) should manage campaign finances responsibly, avoiding deficits that might necessitate post-election fundraising, to the extent possible.

Section 5C(2) does not prohibit a judge who is a candidate for retention from initiating an evaluation by a judicial selection commission or bar association, or, subject to the requirements of this Code, from responding to a request for information from any organization.

Sections 5C and 5D are intended to restrict fundraising by and on behalf of individual judges. These Sections are not intended to prohibit an organization of judges from soliciting money from judges to establish a campaign fund to assist judges who face active opposition to their retention.

(4) A judge who is a candidate* for selection as a delegate to a federal or state constitutional convention may engage in any political activity* to secure election allowed to other candidates for that office.

D. **Incumbent Judges.** A judge shall not engage in any political activity* except (i) as authorized under any other Section of this Code, (ii) on behalf of measures to improve the law,* the legal system, or the administration of justice, or (iii) as expressly authorized by another provision of law.

Commentary.*—Neither Section 5D nor any other Section of the Code prohibits a judge in the exercise of administrative functions from engaging in planning and other official activities with members of the executive and legislative branches of government. With respect to a judge's activity on behalf of measures to improve the law, the legal system, and the administration of justice, see Commentary to Section 4B and Section 4C(1) and its Commentary.*

E. **Applicability.** Canon 5 applies to all incumbent judges and judicial candidates.* A successful candidate, whether or not an incumbent, is subject to judicial discipline for his or her campaign conduct; an unsuccessful candidate who is a lawyer is subject to lawyer discipline for his or her campaign conduct. A lawyer who is a candidate for judicial office is subject to Rule 8.2(b) of the Alaska Rules of Professional Conduct.

(Adopted by SCO 1322 effective July 15, 1998)

Annotations

Cases

Code of Judicial Conduct Canon 5A(3)(d)(i) and (ii) impermissibly prohibits judges standing for retention from announcing their views on disputed political, legal, and social issues, and impermissibly burdens free speech and violates the First Amendment. **Alaska Right to Life PAC v. Feldman,** 380 F. Supp. 2d 1080 (D. Alaska 2005).

APPLICATION OF THE CODE OF JUDICIAL CONDUCT

A. **Full-Time Judicial Officers.** The following judicial officers shall comply with all provisions of this Code:

(1) active justices of the supreme court and active judges of the court of appeals, the superior court, and the district court (including acting district court judges);

(2) full-time magistrates;

(3) committing magistrates; and

(4) standing masters.

B. **Senior Judges.**

(1) Senior judges (retired justices of the supreme court and retired judges of the court of appeals, the superior court, and the district court who are eligible for judicial service under Administrative Rule 23) shall comply with all provisions of this Code except:

(a) 4D(1)(b) (transactions with persons likely to come before the judge's court);

(b) 4D(4) (management of financial resources to minimize disqualification);

(c) 4E(1) (fiduciary service for persons other than family members);

(d) 4E(2) (fiduciary service where proceedings likely before judge's court); and

(e) 4F (service as arbitrator or mediator). However, a senior judge who serves as an arbitrator or mediator must comply with Administrative Rule 23(f).

(2) In addition, a senior judge need not comply with Section 4C(2) (appointment to government positions) except during periods of appointment to active judicial service under Administrative Rule 23.

Commentary.*—A senior judge—a retired justice or judge who is eligible for judicial service under Administrative Rule 23—must comply with all provisions of the Code except those listed. Thus, a senior judge may engage in financial and business dealings with any person and has no duty to manage investments and business and financial interests to minimize the number of cases in which the judge is disqualified. A senior judge may serve as a personal representative, trustee, guardian, or other fiduciary for persons other than family members. Although senior judges may not engage in the practice of law, they may serve as private arbitrators or mediators and may maintain private arbitration and mediation businesses, even during periods of pro tem service. However, in order to be eligible for judicial service, a judge who performs private arbitration or mediation must comply with the disclosure requirements and employment restrictions set out in Administrative Rule 23(e). A senior judge may serve on a government committee or commission or hold a government position except during periods of pro tem service.*

Despite the relaxation of restrictions on senior judges' financial dealings, they remain subject to the disqualification provisions of Section 3E.

C. **Part-Time Magistrates and Deputy Magistrates.** Part-time magistrates and deputy magistrates shall comply with all provisions of this Code except:

(1) Section 4C(1) (appearance before or consultation with executive or legislative bodies) if the magistrate or deputy magistrate holds an office or position of profit under the United States, the state, or its political subdivisions and must

engage in Section 4C(1) activities in order to perform the duties of this office or position;

(2) Section 4C(2) (appointment to government positions);

(3) Section 4D(1)(b) (transactions with persons likely to come before the judge's court);

(4) Section 4D(3)(c) (participation in business activity that has major effect on economic life of community);

(5) Section 4E(1) (fiduciary service for persons other than family members);

(6) Section 4G (practice of law);

(7) Section 5A(1)(d) (attendance at political gatherings) if the magistrate or deputy magistrate holds or is seeking non-judicial public office;

(8) Section 5A(1)(e) (solicitation and contribution of campaign funds) to the extent that the magistrate or deputy magistrate is soliciting funds for or contributing funds to the magistrate's own campaign for non-judicial public office;

(9) Section 5A(2) (resignation upon becoming a candidate for nonjudicial office); and

(10) Sections 5B (political activity to secure appointment to public office).

Commentary.—*AS 22.15.210(b) guarantees magistrates a conditional right to seek and hold any other office or position of profit under the United States, this State, or its political subdivisions, and to engage in the conduct of any profession or business that does not interfere with the performance of judicial duties or necessitate repeated disqualifications. Because of this statute, part-time magistrates are exempt from the restrictions on holding non-judicial public office. They are also permitted to engage in political activity necessary to secure and perform the duties of non-judicial public office. Note, however, that political activity by court system employees is also limited by Personnel Rule PX9.O. Under this rule, a court system employee forfeits his or her position upon becoming a candidate for state or national elective political office, other than the office of delegate to a state or federal constitutional convention.*

The Code exempts part-time magistrates from two restrictions on business activity, the duty to avoid financial and business dealings with persons likely to come before the magistrate's court, and the duty to avoid business activity that has a major effect on the economic life of the community. In a small community, it may be difficult for a magistrate to avoid business dealings with persons likely to come before the magistrate's court, and even a moderately-sized business venture may have a major effect on the community's economic life. Thus, these restrictions could make it impossible for a part-time magistrate to carry on outside business activity in order to supplement his or her part-time judicial salary. Part-time magistrates remain subject to Section 4D(4), which requires that they manage their financial dealings to minimize the number of cases in which they are disqualified. They also remain subject to the disqualification provisions of Section 3E. They are also subject to Personnel Rule PX5.04, which regulates outside employment by court system employees.

A part-time magistrate may serve as a fiduciary for persons other than family members, subject to Sections 4E(2) and 4E(3). A part-time magistrate who is an attorney may practice law, subject to Administrative Rule 2(d), which prohibits court system employees from engaging, directly or indirectly, in the practice of law in any of the courts of this state.

D. **Special Masters.**

(1) A special master who is not an active judge, magistrate, or standing master shall comply with the following provisions of this Code:

(a) Canon 1 (duty to uphold the integrity and independence of the judiciary);

(b) Canon 3 (judicial duties); however, a special master need not comply with Section 3B(9) to the extent this Section would prohibit the special master from commenting about pending or impending proceedings that are unrelated to the proceeding in which he or she is a special master;

(c) Section 4A (extra-judicial activities in general);

(d) Section 4B (avocational activities);

(e) Section 4C(1); however, a special master need not comply with Section 4C(1) to the extent this Section would prohibit the special master from appearing at public hearings or lobbying on matters that are unrelated to the proceeding in which he or she is a special master;

(f) Section 4D(1)(a) (financial or business dealings that appear to exploit judicial position);

(g) Section 4E(3) (restrictions on financial activity that apply personally also apply while acting as fiduciary); and

(h) Section 4I (financial affairs are private except where disclosure required by law).

(2) In addition, during periods of appointment as a master, a special master must comply with Section 2A (duty to avoid impropriety and appearance of impropriety) and 2B (inappropriate influence and misuse of judicial office).

(3) A person who has been a special master in a proceeding shall not act as a lawyer in that proceeding or in any other proceeding related thereto, except as otherwise permitted by Rule 1.12(a) of the Alaska Rules of Professional Conduct.

E. **Time for Compliance.** A person to whom this Code becomes applicable shall comply immediately with all provisions of this Code except Sections 4D(2) and 4D(3) (which pertain to business activities) and Section 4E (which pertains to fiduciary activities) and shall comply with these Sections as soon as reasonably possible and shall do so in any event within the period of one year.

***Commentary.**—If serving as a fiduciary when selected as a judge, a new judge may, notwithstanding the prohibitions in Section 4E, continue to serve as fiduciary but only for that period of time necessary to avoid serious adverse consequences to the beneficiary of the fiduciary relationship and in no event longer than one year. Similarly, if engaged at the time of judicial selection in a business activity that is not permitted by Section 4D(3), a new judge may, notwithstanding the prohibitions in Section 4D(3), continue in that activity for a reasonable period but in no event longer than one year.*

(Adopted by SCO 1322 effective July 15, 1998; amended by SCO 1427 effective April 15, 2001)

TERMINOLOGY

Terms defined below are marked with an asterisk in the Sections where they appear. In addition, each definition cross-references the Sections where the defined term appears.

"Appropriate disciplinary authority" means the governmental or quasi-governmental agency whose responsibility for initiation of the disciplinary process covers the violation to be reported. See Sections 3D(1), 3D(2), and 3D(3).

"Bias or prejudice" does not include references to or distinctions based upon race, color, sex, religion, national origin, disability, age, marital status, changes in marital status, pregnancy, parenthood, sexual orientation, or social or economic status when these factors are legitimately relevant to the advocacy or decision of the proceeding, or, with regard to administrative matters, when these factors are legitimately relevant to the policies or decisions involved. See Sections 3B(5), 3B(6), 3C(1), and 3C(2).

***Commentary.**—The definition of "bias or prejudice" was written in an exclusionary manner to allow courts to countenance legitimate distinctions relevant to litigation before them. See Section 3B(6).*

The definition implies the obvious C that a court demonstrates impermissible bias or prejudice if it uses constitutionally or statutorily protected categories as a basis for unfairly discriminating. Bias or prejudice may also arise from other than legally impermissible categorization and still be something a court should recognize and avoid.

As the symbols and bastions of justice in our society it is important for courts to provide their services to all on essentially the same basis.

"Candidate" means a person seeking any public office. A person becomes a candidate as soon as he or she makes a public announcement of candidacy, or declares or files as a candidate with the election or appointment authority, or authorizes solicitation or acceptance of contributions or public support. See Preamble and Sections 5A(1), 5A(2), 5B(1), 5B(2), 5B(2)(b), 5C(1), 5C(2), 5C(3), and 5C(4).

"Candidate for judicial office" means a candidate seeking selection for or retention in judicial office, whether by election or appointment. This term is used interchangeably with "judicial candidate." See Sections 5A(1)(b), 5A(3), and 5E.

"De minimis interest" means an insignificant interest that would not lead reasonable persons to question a judge's impartiality. See Sections 3E(1)(c) and 3E(1)(d).

"Economic interest" means ownership of a more than de minimis legal or equitable interest or a relationship as an officer, director, advisor, or other legal participant in the affairs of a party, except that:

(i) ownership of an interest in a mutual or common investment fund that holds securities is not an economic interest in such securities unless the judge participates in the management of the fund or a proceeding pending or impending before the judge could substantially affect the value of the interest;

(ii) service by a judge as an officer, director, advisor, or other active participant in an educational, religious, charitable, fraternal, or civic organization, or service by a judge's spouse, parent, or child as an officer, director, advisor, or other active participant in any organization does not create an economic interest in securities held by that organization;

(iii) a deposit in a financial institution, the proprietary interest of a policy holder in a mutual insurance company, of a depositor in a mutual savings association or of a member in a credit union, or a similar proprietary interest, is not an economic interest in the organization unless a proceeding pending or impending before the judge could substantially affect the value of the interest;

(iv) ownership of government securities is not an economic interest in the issuer unless a proceeding pending or impending before the judge could substantially affect the value of the securities.

See Sections 3E(1)(c) and 3E(2).

"Fiduciary" means a person who has undertaken a duty to conduct financial or other affairs for another person's benefit. The term includes any person acting as executor, administrator, personal representative, trustee, guardian, or attorney in fact for another. It also includes any other person who, because of his or her relationship to another person, is obliged to give paramount consideration to the benefit of that other person and to abide by duties of care, good faith, and candor in the conduct of matters falling within the scope of the relationship, even when doing so conflicts with the self-interest of the fiduciary. See Sections 3D(2), 3E(1)(c), 3E(2), 4E(1), 4E(2), and 4E(3).

"Governmental office" means the four types of office a judge may seek without resigning:

(i) retention in the judge's current judicial office;

(ii) selection to a different judicial office;

(iii) selection as a delegate to a constitutional convention; or

(iv) selection to an appointive non-judicial public office.

See Sections 5B(1) and 5B(2).

Commentary.—*Canon 5 speaks of judges who are candidates for government office C both appointive government office (Section 5B) and elective government office (Section 5C(4)). However, Section 5A(2) requires judges to resign upon becoming a candidate for elective non-judicial office. Thus, the phrase "governmental office" is necessarily limited to the four types of office a judge may seek without resigning.*

"Judicial duties" means all the duties of a judge in connection with judicial proceedings and acts of the judge in discharge of disciplinary responsibilities required or permitted by Section 3D. See Sections 3A, 3B(5), 3B(11), 3D(4), 4A(3), 4D(5)(b), 4E(1), and 4H(2).

"Knowingly," "knowledge," "known," and "knows" mean that a person is aware of the existence of the fact or circumstance in question, or is aware of the substantial probability of its existence. However, a person does not "know" or have "knowledge" or act "knowingly" if the person actually believes, despite any indications to the contrary, that the fact or circumstance does not exist. See Sections 2B, 2C, 3D(1), 3E(1)(a), 3E(1)(c), 3E(1)(d), 5A(l)(b), and 5A(3)(d).

"Law" means court rules as well as statutes, constitutional provisions, and decisional law. See Sections 2A, 3A, 3B(2), 3B(7), 3B(7)(a), 3C(2), 4B, 4C(1), 4C(2), 4C(3), 4C(3)(b), 4D(5)(a), 4F, 4I, 5B(2)(b), and 5D.

"Member of the judge's family" means a spouse, child, grandchild, parent, grandparent, or other relative or person with whom the judge maintains a close familial relationship. See Sections 2B, 3E(1)(c), 4E(1), and 4G.

"Nonpublic information" means information that, by law, is not available to the public. Nonpublic information may include but is not limited to: information that is sealed by statute or court order, information impounded or communicated in camera, and information offered in grand jury proceedings, presentencing reports, dependency cases, or psychiatric reports. See Section 3B(11).

"Political activity" means:

(i) becoming a candidate for elective public office;

(ii) serving as an officer of a political party, a member of a national, state, or local committee of a political party, an officer or member of a committee of any other political organization, or becoming a candidate for any of these positions;

(iii) serving as a delegate, alternate, or proxy to a political party convention;

(iv) addressing a convention, caucus, rally, or similar gathering of a political party in support of or in opposition to a candidate for public office or political party office;

(v) organizing or re-organizing a political party or organization;

(vi) taking part in a political campaign to elect someone to public office or political party office, to recall someone from such an office, or to enact or defeat a ballot proposition;

(vii) taking any other part in the management of a political party or organization, or a political candidate, or a group for or against a ballot proposition;

(viii) soliciting votes in support of or in opposition to a candidate's election to public office or political party office, or in support of or in opposition to an incumbent's recall from such an office, or in support of or in opposition to a ballot proposition;

(ix) publicly endorsing or opposing a candidate for public office or political party office, or publicly endorsing or opposing a ballot proposition, whether in a speech, a published letter, a political advertisement or broadcast, campaign literature, or any similar material;

(x) initiating or circulating a nominating petition, recall petition, or petition to put a ballot proposition before the voters.

(xi) directly or indirectly soliciting, receiving, collecting, handling, disbursing, or accounting for assessments, contributions, or other funds for a political purpose;

(xii) organizing, selling tickets to, promoting, or actively participating in a fund-raising activity of a candidate, political party, or political organization; or

(xiii) acting as a recorder, watcher, challenger, or similar officer at the polls on behalf of a political party or a candidate, or driving voters to the polls on behalf of a political party or a candidate, or doing any other act as an official or unofficial representative of a political party or candidate;

(xiv) but "political activity" does not include:

(a) being a member of a political party;

(b) registering and voting;

(c) expressing one's opinion in private on political subjects and candidates;

(d) participating in the non-partisan activities of a civic, community, social, labor, or professional organization; or

(e) speaking or writing in support of or in opposition to proposals to change the legal system or the administration of justice.

See Sections 5B(2), 5C(4), and 5D.

"Political organization" means a party, committee, association, club, foundation, fund, or any other organization, whether incorporated or not, whose primary purpose is to:

(i) influence the selection, nomination, election or appointment of any individual to public office or to office in a political party, or

(ii) influence the outcome of any recall effort or ballot proposition, or

(iii) further or defeat proposals to change the law in matters other than the improvement of the law, the legal system, or the administration of justice.

See Sections 5A(1)(a), 5A(1)(c), 5A(1)(e), and 5B(2)(b).

The words "shall" and "shall not" mean a binding obligation on judicial officers, and a judge's failure to comply with this obligation is a ground for disciplinary action.

The words "should" and "should not" mean conduct or a course of action to which judicial officers should aspire, but a judge's failure to meet such an aspirational goal is not a ground for disciplinary action.

"Spouse" includes not only a husband or wife but also any person with whom the judge maintains a shared household and conjugal relations. See Sections 3E(1)(c), 3E(l)(d), 3E(2), 4D(5)(a), 4D(5)(b), 4H(1)(b), 4H(3), and 5A(3)(a).

Commentary.*—Because the same potential conflicts of interest and loyalty arise when a judge maintains a shared household and conjugal relations with another person to whom the judge is not married, the provisions of Canons 3 and 4 should apply more broadly than simply to legally recognized spouses. Rather than try to reword each affected provision, this Code retains the ABA's use of "spouse" but includes an expanded definition of spouse in the Terminology Section.*

"Third degree of relationship." The following persons are relatives within the third degree of relationship: great-grandparent, grandparent, parent, uncle, aunt, brother, sister, child, grandchild, great-grandchild, nephew, and niece. See Section 3E(1)(d).

(Adopted by SCO 1322 effective July 15, 1998)

JUDICIAL CONDUCT COMMISSION RULES

Table of Contents

Rule 1. Organization of Commission.

(a) **Meetings.** The commission holds the following meetings:

(1) **Annual.** The first regularly scheduled meeting of the calendar year is the annual meeting. At the annual meeting, the commission will approve the commission's annual report and will elect officers every two years.

(2) **Regular.** Other regular meetings at designated locations may be held as needed. Regular meetings may be held either in person or by teleconference.

(3) **Special.** Special meetings may be called by the chairperson or two members of the commission upon prior written or verbal notice to all members where there is a need to meet on short notice for a special purpose. If the special agenda includes any public matter, public notice shall be given at least 24 hours before the meeting. Special meetings may be held either in person or by teleconference.

(b) **Notice of Meetings.** Notice of meetings is required as follows:

(1) **Public.** At least 14 days before a regular commission meeting, the executive director shall give public notice to be placed in newspapers of general circulation most likely to give notice to the residents of the State of Alaska. The notice shall clearly specify the date, time, and place of the commission meeting and shall also state that anyone wishing to appear at the meeting must contact the executive director at the commission office at least five working days before the meeting. An agenda of public matters shall also be included in the meeting notice.

(2) **Members.** At least 14 days before a regular commission meeting, the executive director shall give notice of the meeting to each member of the commission. The notice must contain the date, time, and place of the meeting, and a tentative meeting agenda. The commission will, in its discretion, waive notice for any meeting.

(c) **Officers.** The commission has the following officers:

(1) **Chair.** The commission will elect a chair and a vice-chair by majority vote at the annual meeting. The term of office is two years. The chair shall conduct the meetings; certify commission recommendations; direct the preparation of meeting agendas, notices, reports, and minutes; and ensure accurate record-keeping. The vice-chair shall act in the absence of the chair.

(2) **Executive Committee.** The chair may appoint an executive committee to perform matters of administration as from time to time are designated by the commission.

(d) **Commission Office.** The commission shall establish a permanent office in a building open to the public. The office must be open and staffed at regular office hours.

(e) **Quorum.** No dispositive action may be taken by the commission unless a quorum of at least a majority of the members serving on the commission is present, in person or telephonically, at the meeting. A quorum of the commission must include at least one judge member, one attorney member, and one public member.

(f) **Voting Requirements.** The following rules apply to voting on commission action:

(1) Every action of the commission requires a majority vote of the members serving on the commission at the time the action is taken.

(2) The names of commission members voting on any question shall be recorded in the minutes.

(3) Once cast, votes may be changed only during the same meeting on a motion to reconsider unless otherwise provided by these rules.

(g) **Order of Business.** The chair shall determine the order of business in advance of each meeting.

(h) **Public Participation.** The meetings shall be ordered to encourage attendance by the public, where public matters are considered. To facilitate productive and effective meetings, any member of the public who wishes to testify at a public meeting of the commission shall make the request to the executive director at least 48 hours before the commencement of the meeting. Requests will be honored only if the general substance or subject area on which the individual wishes to testify concerns a public matter related to the commission's function under the Alaska Constitution and the statutes of the state. All requests are subject to approval by the commission chair. Written public testimony will be accepted at any time, concerning any matter relating to the commission's function.

(i) **Electronic and Written Records.** The executive director shall electronically record all commission meetings except for commission deliberations, prepare minutes of both public and closed sessions subject to approval of the commission, and maintain their permanent storage. The executive director shall preserve all documents, including tape recordings, staff notes and memoranda, transcripts of testimony before the commission, and correspondence.

(j) **Commission Member Holdover.** To ensure that the commission continuously fulfills its constitutional responsibilities, a commission member continues to serve as an active member after expiration of that member's term until the vacancy is filled by the appropriate appointing authority.

(Adopted November 1, 1991; amended December 10, 1993; May 9, 1995; December 1, 2000.)

Rule 2. Functioning of Commission.

(a) **Annual Report.** Before the annual meeting, the executive director shall prepare an annual report of the commission's activities for presentation at that meeting. Upon approval by the commission, the executive director shall send a copy of the annual report to the governor, president of the senate, speaker of the house, chief justice, state publications distribution and data access center, and president of the Alaska Bar Association. The report shall also be kept available to the public.

(b) **Executive Director.** The commission will appoint an executive director to serve at its pleasure. While serving, the executive director may not be employed by the court system and may not be a judicial officer.

(c) **Agents or Employees of Commission.** The commission will employ individuals as appropriate to carry out its duties. Employees may include attorneys, accountants, paralegals, secretaries, and investigators.

(Adopted November 1, 1991; amended December 1, 2000.)

Rule 3. Financial Arrangements for Commission.

(a) **Compensation Proscribed.** The commission members serve without compensation for their services.

(b) **Expenses Allowed.** Commissioners are reimbursed for expenses necessarily incurred in the performance of their duties as established by state law.

(c) **Authorization for Payments.** The commission will authorize payment for expenses that are within the commission's budget and comply with travel policies and procurement guidelines. Either the executive director or the chair may authorize payments of approved expenses.

(d) **Extraordinary Expenses.** If there is an unanticipated funding shortfall, the commission will not curtail the discharge of its constitutionally mandated operations, but will authorize the executive director to seek a supplemental appropriation.

(Adopted November 1, 1991; amended December 1, 2000.)

Rule 4. Duties of Executive Director.

(a) **Listed Duties.** The commission will prescribe the duties of the executive director, which include:

(1) considering information regarding judicial misconduct from all sources and receiving allegations and complaints;

(2) making preliminary evaluations;

(3) screening complaints;

(4) conducting and supervising investigations;

(5) maintaining and preserving the commission's records, including all complaints, files, and written dispositions;

(6) maintaining statistics concerning the operation of the commission and making them available to the commission, the court, and the public;

(7) preparing the commission's budget for its approval and administering its funds;

(8) employing and supervising other members of the commission's staff;

(9) preparing an annual report of the commission's activities;

(10) employing, with the approval of the commission, office assistants, special counsel, private investigators, or other experts, as necessary to investigate and process matters before the commission and before the court;

(11) issuing subpoenas as directed by the commission;

(12) attending all meetings and hearings of the commission, except for commission deliberations; and

(13) providing and publishing notice as required by these rules.

(b) **Other Duties.** The executive director may perform other law-related duties, such as the following:

(1) interpreting statutes and case law and providing legal opinions to the commission related to its duties;

(2) preparing and filing court documents, as needed, on behalf of the commission;

(3) negotiating appropriate discipline and fact stipulations subject to final approval of and direction by the commission.

(Adopted November 1, 1991; amended December 1, 2000.)

Rule 5. Confidentiality.

(a) **Confidentiality.** All investigative records, files, and reports of the commission are confidential and no disclosure may be made except as permitted by AS 22.30.060. All confidential documents acquired in the course of a commission investigation shall be accorded the same confidentiality as commission-generated documents.

(b) **Disclosure—Generally.** To preserve public confidence in the administration of justice, the commission will, in its discretion, issue statements clarifying procedural aspects or explaining the right of a judge to a fair hearing when the subject matter of a complaint is generally known to the public. Unless otherwise provided by these rules, a person filing an accusation may have access only to those materials that the person has provided to the commission.

(c) **Disclosure—Dismissal.** When an accusation against a judge has been considered by the commission and it has been determined that there is no basis for filing a charge or for further proceedings, the commission will, in its discretion and at the judge's request or approval, issue an explanatory statement.

(d) **Disclosure—Determination.** Upon completion of an investigation or proceeding, the commission will disclose to the complainant that the commission

(1) has found no basis for action against the judge;

(2) has taken an appropriate corrective action, the nature of which, under AS 22.30.011(b), cannot be disclosed; or

(3) has filed a formal charge against the judge.

(Adopted November 1, 1991; amended December 1, 2000.)

Rule 6. Public Information.

(a) **Public Statements—General.** The commission will, in its discretion, issue press releases and other public statements explaining the nature of its jurisdiction, procedures for institution of accusations, limitations upon its powers and authority, and reports on the activities of the commission. The releases and reports may not identify the judge or other person involved in any inquiry before the commission unless disclosure is otherwise provided for in AS 22.30.060.

(b) **Formal Proceedings.** After a formal charge is filed, only the formal charge, the answer, the formal evidentiary hearing, and the final recommendation by the commission, including any minority report, are public. Unless otherwise ordered, all discovery items introduced into evidence at the public formal hearing become public documents when introduced. All other discovery items remain confidential. Dispositive motions and related resulting orders become public documents when decided.

(c) **Formal Ethics Opinions.** In its discretion, the commission will issue public formal ethics opinions resulting from actual complaints. Formal ethics opinions are not to be confused with formal advisory opinions issued under Rule 19 of these rules. The purpose of issuing a formal ethics opinion is to guide judges and to inform the public. These opinions may not identify the judge or otherwise violate the commission's obligation to maintain the confidentiality of its proceedings. A formal ethics opinion may not be issued until the disciplinary process involving the underlying facts has been concluded and all related appellate proceedings have been adjudicated.

(d) **Inquiries by the Press.** Inquiries by the press concerning commission activities may be responded to only by the executive director, unless otherwise directed by the commission.

(e) **Comments by Commission Members.** Commission members should refrain from publicly commenting on the judicial qualifications of any sitting or pro tem judge.

(Adopted November 1, 1991; amended March 1, 1996; December 1, 2000.)

Rule 7. Initiation and Screening of Complaint.

(a) **Filing of Complaint.** A written complaint about the conduct or physical or mental disability of a judge may be filed upon any reasonable basis. A complaint may be filed by any individual, including a commission member, or by the commission itself. If a commission member files a complaint as an individual and not under (c) of this rule, that member may not participate in the matter.

(b) **Screening of Complaint.** Each written complaint shall be screened in accordance with the following procedures:

(1) The executive director shall review a written complaint and determine whether the information or statement is within the jurisdiction of the commission and is not frivolous.

(2) If the executive director determines that the matter is not within the jurisdiction of the commission or not supported by facts, the executive director shall, after providing notice to the complainant and an opportunity to amend the complaint, recommend dismissal. A judge will not be notified of a dismissal under this paragraph.

(3) If the executive director determines that the matter is not frivolous, the executive director shall make a preliminary investigation to determine what further action should be taken, if any. After the preliminary staff investigation, the commission will either dismiss the complaint or direct further investigation. If the commission directs further investigation, the executive director shall notify the judge of the investigation, as set out in Rule 8 of these rules.

(c) **Commission-initiated Complaint.** When a commission member or staff person becomes aware of information concerning possible judicial misconduct, he or she may inform the executive director. The executive director shall preliminarily investigate the information, and, if supported, present the information to the commission with a recommendation as to whether the matter should be designated a commission-initiated complaint. Once a matter is designated a commission-initiated complaint it will be treated in the same manner as a complaint filed by an individual under (a) of this rule.

(Formerly (before December 1, 2000) Rule 8. Adopted November 1, 1991; amended December 1, 2000.)

Rule 8. Notice.

(a) **Notice of Investigation.** If, after conducting an initial investigation, the executive director anticipates recommending to the commission at its next meeting an outcome other than dismissal and the chair agrees that notice at this time is appropriate, or if the commission does not dismiss the matter at a meeting, the executive director shall send a written notice of investigation to the judge. The notice of investigation must identify the complainant, if the complainant has authorized use of his or her name, and must convey the basic substance of the investigation and the date of the next commission meeting when the investigation will be reviewed. In addition, the written notice must convey the possible outcomes: dismissal, informal and private admonishment, recommendation for counseling, or proceeding to a probable cause determination.

The executive director may issue supplemental notices as appropriate.

(b) **Notice of Probable Cause Determination.** After an investigation, if the commission has decided that a probable cause determination is necessary, the executive director shall send a written notice of probable cause determination to the judge. The notice must include the date of the determination meeting and a citation of Rule 12 of these rules, pre-hearing discovery. In addition, the written notice must state the possible outcomes as listed in (a) of this rule.

(c) **Notice After Formal Charge.** The executive director shall provide appropriate notice of commission action taken under Rules 14–18 of these rules.

(d) **Notice of Recommended Dismissal and of Dismissal.** The executive director shall inform the complainant in writing of the executive director's recommendation of dismissal and that the dismissal will be reviewed by the commission at its next meeting. If the judge has been given prior commission notice, the executive director shall also inform the judge in writing of the recommended dismissal. After the commission's dismissal of a complaint, at whatever stage of proceedings, the executive director shall so inform the complainant and, if the judge has been given prior commission notice, the judge.

(e) **Method of Service.** Unless otherwise specified, notice to the judge, when required by these rules, shall be given by personal service, or by prepaid certified or registered mail that is addressed to the judge.

(Formerly (before December 1, 2000) Rule 7. Adopted November 1, 1991; amended December 1, 2000; amended June 30, 2003; and February 1, 2004)

Rule 9. Formal Investigation. [Repealed December 1, 2000.]

Rule 10. Subpoenas.

(a) **When Issued.** The commission will, in its discretion, compel by subpoena the attendance and testimony of witnesses, including the judge, and the production of papers, books, accounts, documents, and testimony relevant to the investigation or proceeding. Service may be by commission staff or official process server.

(b) **Request for Commission Subpoena.** A request for a commission subpoena, under AS 22.30.066, shall be made to the executive director and must include

(1) the name of the person or document to be subpoenaed;

(2) the purpose and relevance of the testimony or document; and

(3) a statement whether the person or document would be available without a subpoena.

(c) **Non-Compliance With Commission Subpoena.** If a person does not attend, testify, or produce a document required by a commission subpoena, the commission will, in its discretion, petition the superior court for an order compelling the person to comply with the subpoena. A claim of privilege must be asserted formally before the commission no later than the date of compliance stated in the subpoena. Privileges are those recognized in Article V of the Alaska Rules of Evidence and claims of privilege will be decided by the commission.

(Adopted November 1, 1991; amended December 1, 2000.)

Rule 11. Investigation Results; Commission Action.

(a) **Initial Commission Determination.** The commission will promptly consider the results of an investigation at a regularly scheduled meeting of the commission or a special meeting called for consideration of the matter. In extraordinary situations, as determined by the commission, the commission will designate a master to make findings of fact related to a charge. At the meeting, neither the judge, the judge's attorney, nor witnesses may appear unless requested by the commission. The commission will consider any brief written statement provided by the judge.

(b) **Disposition.** The commission will proceed in one of the following ways:

(1) *Dismissal.* If the commission does not find that misconduct has occurred, the commission will instruct the executive director to send notice of dismissal under Rules 5(d) and 8(d) of these rules.

(2) *Informal and Private Admonishment by the Commission.* If the commission finds that there has been misconduct for which informal and private admonishment is appropriate, the commission will, in its discretion, issue a written private admonishment to the judge. The admonishment will include findings of fact and conclusions of law. A private admonishment becomes a final disposition 16 days after service on the judge unless the judge requests reconsideration under (c) of this rule.

(3) *Recommendation for Counseling.* If the commission finds that there has been misconduct for which counseling is appropriate, the commission will, in its discretion, recommend counseling. For purposes of this paragraph, "counseling" means personal or professional counseling, further training, and other remedial measures; it can take the form of a cautionary letter. The commission will, in its discretion, also enter into an agreement with the judge, set out in a memorandum, concerning the judge's future conduct or submission to counseling. The executive director shall notify the complainant, under Rules 5(d) and 8(d) of these rules, that the matter has been resolved by recommended counseling. The commission will monitor any prescribed counseling.

(4) *Probable Cause Determination.* If the matter has not been resolved under (b)(1), (2), or (3) of this rule, the commission will determine probable cause at a definite time and place with reasonable notice to the judge. The

commission chair, or a member of the commission designated by the chair, shall preside. At the meeting, neither the judge, the judge's attorney, nor witnesses may appear unless requested by the commission. The commission will consider written or taped witness statements, staff investigative reports, and any written information provided by the judge. The commission will make one of the following findings:

(A) *Lack of Probable Cause.* If the commission fails to find probable cause that there has been misconduct that warrants action more serious than informal and private admonishment or counseling, it will dispose of the matter under (b)(1), (2), or (3) of this rule.

(B) *Probable Cause.* If the commission finds that there is probable cause to believe that there has been misconduct that warrants action more serious than an informal and private admonishment or counseling, the chair or executive director shall serve the judge with a statement of formal charge and all documents upon which the finding was based. Service upon the judge constitutes notice that a response must be filed within 20 days.

(c) **Reconsideration.** Within 15 days after service of an informal and private admonishment under (b)(2) of this rule, the judge may request reconsideration, by filing a written motion with the commission. Upon receipt of the motion, the commission will dismiss the complaint, deny the motion for reconsideration, make further investigation, or institute a formal charge under (b)(4)(B) of this rule and Rule 14 of these rules. Reconsideration is not available for recommendations of counseling under (b)(3) of this rule or determinations of probable cause under (b)(4)(B) of this rule.

(Adopted November 1, 1991; amended December 1, 2000.)

Rule 12. Pre-Hearing Discovery.

(a) **General Scope.** To expedite the hearing and maintain fairness, discovery will be as full and free as possible. The judge and special counsel are entitled to discovery in accordance with the Alaska Rules of Civil Procedure, including the limitations set out in those rules, except as noted in this rule. Exceptions to discovery are: (1) commission deliberations, and (2) confidential staff memoranda and other communications that do not relate to the charge. In addition, the executive director may not be compelled to testify as to conversations with the chair or other individual commission members concerning nondispositive motions. The judge shall bear the costs of duplication and transcription of all discovery items that require extraordinary staff resources.

(b) **Discovery Before Formal Charge.** Before a formal charge is issued, the commission will provide witness names, factual allegations, and a statement of legal issues to the judge at the conclusion of the investigation if the information does not warrant dismissal. Additional discovery will be, in the commission's discretion, as implemented by the chair under Rule 14(d) of these rules, allowed before the probable cause proceeding.

(c) **Discovery After Formal Charge.** After a formal charge is issued, the chair shall handle discovery requests. All discovery tools are available after a formal charge is issued. With the approval of the commission, the commission chair or the chair's designee (including a special master) may preside over depositions.

(Adopted November 1, 1991; amended December 1, 2000.)

Rule 13. Special Counsel.

(a) **Appointment.** The commission will appoint a special counsel when a formal charge is issued or earlier when the commission determines that the appointment is necessary to preserve its adjudicative independence. The special counsel serves at the pleasure of the commission.

(b) **Role and Duties.** The special counsel is hired by the commission to formally prepare and present the case against the judge. The special counsel represents the public interest and may not represent any individual commission member or staff person but may represent the commission, as an entity, in related proceedings.

(c) **Powers.** The special counsel may request commission subpoenas, conduct discovery, and file motions. The special counsel may not dismiss or amend a charge, delay proceedings, or take other dispositive action. The special counsel may incur only those expenses authorized by the commission.

(Adopted November 1, 1991; amended December 1, 2000.)

Rule 14. Formal Disciplinary Hearing.

(a) **Pre-hearing Conference.** Upon receipt of the judge's response to the complaint, the commission will set a pre-hearing conference to be held not later than the next regularly scheduled commission meeting. The commission chair or the chair's designee shall preside at the pre-hearing conference. At the conference, a discovery and briefing schedule will be established and the hearing date set. The discovery and briefing schedule will include

(1) a preliminary witness list;

(2) a preliminary exhibit list;

(3) a schedule for substantive motions.

(b) **Discovery.** Discovery for a formal hearing is governed by Rule 12(c) of these rules.

(c) **Master.** The formal hearing will be conducted before either the commission or a master designated by the commission. A master will be used only in compelling and extraordinary situations, as determined by the commission. When the hearing is before the full commission, either the chair or another member appointed by the chair will preside. A member of the commission may not serve as master. The master will have the same procedural authority as the commission chair when conducting the hearing.

(d) **Role of the Chair.** The chair is the presiding officer both at the hearing and during pre-hearing and post-hearing motions. The chair has the authority to decide all nondispositive motions on behalf of the full commission.

(e) **Conduct of Hearing.** The following rules apply to the conduct of hearings:

(1) At the time and place set for the hearing, the full commission will, or master shall, proceed with the hearing whether or not the judge has filed an answer or personally appears at the hearing.

(2) A hearing may rely in whole or in part on a statement of facts agreed to by both parties and placed in the public record.

(3) The proceedings at the hearing will be reported by electronic recording device in the same manner as proceedings are reported in a state court. The judge may, at the judge's expense, provide a court reporter of the judge's choosing.

(4) Commission members may question witnesses and hold brief conferences during the course of the hearing, to facilitate their fact-finding function.

(f) **Evidence.** The rules of evidence apply and all testimony will be under oath. The chair, presiding member, or master will administer the oath, rule on the admissibility of evidence, and otherwise direct the manner and order of proceedings in the same manner as a judge of a state court. The standard of proof is clear and convincing evidence.

(g) **Amendment of Complaint.** By leave of the commission, a formal charge may be amended after the hearing begins, to conform to proof or to present additional facts, if the judge and the judge's counsel are given adequate time to prepare a response.

(h) **Determination.** Upon determination of a matter, the following rules apply:

(1) When the factfinder is a master, that master shall, within 60 days after the hearing, submit findings and recommendations, together with the record and transcript of proceedings, to the commission for review, and contemporaneously serve them upon the judge. The commission will pay all costs associated with the master's findings and recommendations.

(2) The judge, and commission counsel, may submit written objections to the findings and recommendations of the master within 15 days after receipt.

(3) The findings, conclusions, and accompanying materials, together with the objections, if any, will be promptly reviewed by the commission not later than its next regularly scheduled meeting. The commission may make independent findings of fact from the record. If the entire commission served as factfinder, the chair will draft findings and recommendations as directed by the commission.

(4) If no statement of objection is filed within the time provided, the commission will, in its discretion, adopt, in whole or in part, the findings of the master without a hearing. If a statement of objection proposes to modify or reject the findings of the master, the commission will give the judge and special counsel an opportunity to be heard orally before the commission not later than its next regularly scheduled meeting. The executive director shall serve written notice of the time and place of the hearing on the judge at least 10 days before the hearing.

(i) **Extension of Time.** The chair of the commission or the master may grant reasonable time extensions for good cause shown.

(j) **Hearing Additional Evidence.** The commission will, in its discretion, order the taking of additional evidence at any time while the matter is pending before it. The order will set the time and place of the hearing and indicate the matters on which the evidence is to be taken. The executive director shall serve a copy of the order on the judge at least 10 days before the date of the hearing. The hearing of additional evidence may be before the master or the commission, at the commission's discretion.

(k) **Role of Executive Director after Formal Charge.** After a formal charge is issued, the executive director may serve as a liaison between the commission and all counsel of record, and may provide research and administrative assistance as requested by the commission.

(Adopted November 1, 1991; amended December 1, 2000.)

Rule 15. Commission Decision.

(a) **Decision.** A formal decision consists of the commission determination of dismissal or recommendation for discipline. The recommendation for discipline may include any one or more of the sanctions provided for in AS 22.30.011(d). Formal decisions are public documents.

(b) **Minority Report and Distribution.** If a member of the commission dissents from the decision of the majority of the commission, the dissenting member may submit a minority report, which must accompany the majority report. The minority report may be submitted to the chief justice of the supreme court, the attorney general, and the chairs of the senate and house judiciary committees, as provided in AS 22.30.068.

(c) **Voting.** Only a member who participated in the matter, and who is present at the meeting or teleconference at which commission action is taken on the matter, may vote on the matter. Before the final decision is issued, votes may be changed only during a meeting or teleconference with all members who participated in the matter being present.

(d) **Execution.** The determination and recommendation of the commission will be signed by the chair, or the chair's designee, and may be signed by other members, either concurring or dissenting in the determination or recommendation

(e) **Witness Fees.** All witnesses will receive fees and expenses in the statutorily allowable amount. Expenses of witnesses will be paid by the party calling them, unless the physical or mental disability of the judge is in issue, when the commission will reimburse the judge for the reasonable expenses of witness testimony related to the disability.

(Adopted November 1, 1991; amended December 1, 2000.)

Rule 16. Supreme Court Review.

The commission recommendation for discipline under Rule 15 of these rules will be filed in accordance with Appellate Rule 406 of the Alaska Rules of Court.

(Adopted November 1, 1991; amended December 1, 2000.)

Rule 17. Cases Involving Mental or Physical Disability.

(a) **Procedure.** When considering an allegation of mental or physical disability, the commission will, except as provided in this rule, follow procedures established by Rules 1–16, 18, and 20 of these rules.

(b) **Special Provisions.** The following additional provisions apply in disability cases:

(1) If the commission finds probable cause to believe that a judge suffers from a mental or physical disability and the judge is not represented by counsel, the commission will, in its discretion, appoint an attorney to represent the judge at commission expense.

(2) If a judge is charged with a disability or raises a disability as an affirmative defense to misconduct, the commission will, in its discretion, under AS 22.30.066(b), request the judge to submit to a physical or mental examination by an independent medical expert. The medical expert shall report the results of the examination to both the commission and the judge. If the judge refuses to submit to the examination, the commission will decide the issue requiring the examination adversely to the judge.

(3) The commission will bear the costs of disability proceedings.

(Adopted November 1, 1991; amended December 1, 2000.)

Rule 18. Commission Member Disqualification; Proceeding Against Commission Member.

(a) **Conflict of Interest.** A commission member may not participate in the consideration of a complaint against a judge if

(1) the member is the subject of the complaint;

(2) the member is a material witness to the alleged misconduct;

(3) the member is related to the judge or the complainant within the third degree of consanguinity;

(4) the judge has retained the member as the judge's attorney or the member provided legal representation or counseling in any matter within two years before the filing of the complaint with the commission; or

(5) the member believes that, for any reason, that member cannot give a fair and impartial decision.

(b) **Disclosure.** Each commission member shall disclose all facts that may lead to an inference of bias relating to a matter before the commission. After disclosure, the commission will determine whether the facts warrant disqualification. Commission members may also recuse themselves with a statement on the record as to the basis of the recusal.

(c) **Motion for Disqualification.** The judge or special counsel may request the disqualification of a commission member by filing a motion. The motion must be accompanied by an affidavit that states with particularity the grounds upon which it is claimed that the member should be disqualified. A motion for disqualification will be decided by that member. If the motion is denied by that member, the motion will be decided by the commission chair or, if the motion concerns the chair, by the longest-serving commission member.

(d) **Proceeding Against Commission Members.** A proceeding against a member of the commission will be conducted in the same manner as a proceeding against any other judge.

(e) **Prohibition Against Representing Judge Before the Commission.** No commission member may provide legal representation or counseling to a judge in a matter before the commission during the member's term on the commission or within two years after the member's term has expired.

(Adopted November 1, 1991; amended May 23, 1994; December 1, 2000.)

Rule 19. Commission-Issued Advisory Opinions.

(a) **Issuance of Formal Advisory Opinions.** On written request of a state judicial officer subject to the Code of Judicial Conduct, the commission will, in its discretion, issue a written formal advisory opinion concerning the application of the code to a specific fact situation involving that judicial officer. The request for an opinion should specify all facts relevant to the ethical situation. Both the request for an opinion and the opinion itself are confidential unless the requesting judge asks that it be public.

(b) **Advisory Opinion Drafting.** Written formal advisory opinions will be drafted by a committee of the commission, appointed by the chair for the purpose of drafting the opinion, with staff assistance. The drafting committee will be composed of not less than one public member, one attorney member, and one judge member of the commission. The full commission will vote on adoption of the draft opinion.

(c) **Use of Formal Advisory Opinions.** Reliance on the formal advisory opinion by the requesting judge is an absolute defense to subsequent disciplinary proceedings by the commission concerning the identical facts addressed by the opinion. If there are distinguishing facts, reliance on the formal advisory opinion will be viewed as merely a good faith defense.

(d) **Informal Verbal Advisory Opinions.** Informal verbal guidance concerning judicial ethics issues is available from commission members and staff. Informal verbal advisory opinions have no legal effect and, if in error, provide no recognized defense to a later disciplinary charge.

(Adopted March 1, 1996; amended December 1, 2000.)

Rule 20. Settlement Procedures.

(a) **Settlement After Investigation.** After an investigation, the executive director may initiate settlement discussions with the judge that may result in one of the following: an informal and private admonishment, or a recommendation for counseling. The executive director shall present any agreed disposition to the commission for approval or rejection. If rejected, the commission will, in its discretion, give reasons for the rejection but will not comment on the strength or weakness of the factual investigation. If the settlement is approved, the executive director shall prepare a written statement of facts and a decision in support of the agreed action. The statement of facts and decision may be revised by the commission but, once adopted, will either constitute the private admonishment or state the need for counseling.

(b) **Settlement After Probable Cause Finding.** After the commission has found probable cause and has issued a formal charge, the commission will hold a formal hearing on the allegation, as required by AS 22.30.011(b) and as provided in Rule 14 of these rules. A settlement after the commission has found probable cause must include a public hearing during which any stipulation between the parties, and the disposition of each charge, are publicly presented and made a part of the public record. If the commission does not dismiss the charges against the judge, a settlement after the hearing must be in the form of a recommendation to the Supreme Court, and does not take effect until approved by the court.

(Adopted December 1, 2000.)

RULES OF ADMINISTRATION*

Table of Contents

***Editor's Note:** These Administrative Rules were rescinded and repromulgated by Supreme Court Order 412 effective July 1, 1980.

AdR

Rule 1. Administrative Director of Courts—Duties.

There shall be an administrative director of courts who shall, under policy guidelines provided by the supreme court:

(a) Supervise the administrative operation of the judicial system;

(b) Establish the administrative methods and systems to be employed in the offices of the clerks and other offices of the courts;

(c) Periodically inspect and examine the administrative methods and systems in use and make recommendations to the chief justice for the improvement of such administrative methods and systems;

(d) Establish a system of prescribed accounting practices for all courts including uniform procedures, consistent with existing law, for calculating interest on judgments and allocating payments to costs, interest, and principal;

(e) Examine the state of the calendars of all courts, determine the need for assistance by any court and confer with the justices and judges on the status of their calendars and administrative matters;

(f) When authorized by the chief justice, make assignments of judges to other judicial districts where the courts are in need of assistance and where the judge consents to the assignment;

(g) When directed by the supreme court, prescribe methods for the assignment and calendaring of cases in the superior or district court in any court location;

(h) Collect and compile statistical and other data and transmit copies of the same to the supreme court to the end that proper action may be taken in respect thereto;

(i) Prepare budget estimates of state appropriations necessary for the maintenance and operation of the judicial system and submit the budget request, as approved by the supreme court, to the legislature;

(j) Draw all requisitions requiring the payment of state monies appropriated for the maintenance and operation of the judicial system;

(k) Collect statistical and other data and make reports relating to the expenditure of public monies for the maintenance and operation of the judicial system and the offices connected therewith;

(*l*) Obtain reports from presiding judges, area court administrators, and clerks of court in accordance with the requirements of the supreme court on cases and other judicial business in which action has been delayed beyond periods of time specified by law or rules of court and make report thereof to the chief justice and the supreme court;

(m) Formulate and submit to the chief justice and the supreme court recommendations of policies for the improvement of the judicial systems; and

(n) Be legal advisor for the chief justice and the supreme court in all legal matters not adjudicatory in nature, such as:

(1) Preparation of memoranda on statutes which may affect the judiciary;

(2) Drafting of rules of practice, procedure and administration;

(3) Conducting and supervising research on procedure and court administration;

(4) Instruction of court personnel concerning rules or statutes governing ministerial and other non-adjudicatory duties;

(5) Preparing of syllabi for the basic legal instruction of magistrates and other lay personnel;

(6) Providing for the publication, annotation and editing of revisions and supplements to the Alaska Rules of Court; and

(7) Rendering legal opinions in any non-adjudicatory matters as directed from time to time by the chief justice.

(o) Adopt and publish procedures to govern the procurement of supplies, services, professional services, and construction by the judicial branch.

(p) Attend to such other matters as may be assigned by the chief justice.

(Adopted by SCO 412 effective July 1, 1980; amended by SCO 554 effective April 4, 1983; by SCO 802 effective nunc pro tunc July 1, 1985; by SCO 1153 effective July 15, 1994; and by SCO 1494 effective September 19, 2002)

Cross References

CROSS REFERENCE: Administrative Bulletin 68 (Calculation of Interest on Judgments and Allocation of Payment to Costs, Interest and Principal); Court Form ADM-505 (How to Determine Pre- and Post-Judgment Interest Rates).

Annotations

Accounting Instructions, Superior Courts, 1959, Office of Admin. Director.

Accounting Instructions, District and Deputy Magistrates, 1959, Office of Admin. Director.

Rule 2. Appointment and Compensation of Employees—Practice of Law by Personnel Prohibited.

(a) The administrative director shall promulgate personnel rules governing all personnel employed by the Alaska Court System. No employee may be exempt from the personnel rules except as specifically set forth in those rules. The personnel rules have the same force and effect as a rule of administration.

(b) The administrative director shall receive an annual compensation in an amount equal to $2,000.00 less than the annual compensation provided by law for a justice of the Alaska Supreme Court. Employees in the partially exempt and classified service are entitled to receive compensation in accordance with the salary and classification plan adopted by the administrative director under the personnel rules. The administrative director with the approval of the chief justice shall appoint and fix the compensation of such assistants as are necessary to the exercise and performance of the powers and duties vested in the administrative director.

(c) No employee of the court system may be hired without the prior approval of the administrative director of the Court System or the administrative director's designee nor may an employee be hired except in accordance with the personnel rules.

(d) During the term of office or employment, neither the administrative director nor any other employee of the Alaska Court System may engage directly or indirectly in the practice of law in any of the courts of this state.

(Adopted by SCO 412 effective July 1, 1980; amended by SCO 1153 effective July 15, 1994; and by SCO 1502 effective February 7, 2003)

Rule 3. Information and Data to Be Furnished to Administrative Director and Presiding Judges.

(a) Justices, judges, masters, magistrates, clerks of the courts, and all other officers and employees of the court system shall comply with all requests made by the administrative director for information and statistical data concerning cases of such courts and such other information as may reflect the business transacted by them.

(b) Each area court administrator, or the presiding judge in those judicial districts not having an area court administrator, shall maintain a current list of all matters under advisement in the superior and district courts in the judicial district. The clerk of the appellate courts shall maintain a list of all matters under advisement in the supreme court and the court of appeals. Such lists shall contain the following information:

(1) The name of the justice, judge or master having such matter under advisement;

(2) The date upon which each matter was referred to the justice or judge for decision or, in the case of a master, for preparation of report;

(3) The nature of the decision or matter under advisement;

(4) The title of the action; and

(5) The court's file number.

(c) In each judicial district such lists shall be circulated on a weekly basis among the judges and masters regularly assigned to that judicial district, and a copy thereof sent to any other judge or master whose name appears thereon, and to the administrative director. The clerk of the appellate courts shall circulate the list maintained for the supreme court on a weekly basis among the justices and to the administrative director, and the list for the court of appeals on a weekly basis among the judges of that court and to the administrative director.

(d) Judges of the superior and district courts and masters under continuing appointment shall submit a weekly report to their area court administrator or presiding judge, identifying the matters that are under advisement, and providing the information required by paragraphs (b)(1) - (5) of this rule.

(e) Judges or masters having a motion under advisement more than 10 calendar days from the date submitted, or having a decision following trial of a case under advisement more than 30 calendar days from the date submitted, shall submit in writing to the presiding judge of their judicial district an explanation of the circumstances justifying the delay and the date on or before which such motion or case shall be decided.

(f) Justices or judges who disqualify themselves for cause shall set forth the specific reasons for the disqualification in writing. Superior court judges or district court judges shall send the statement of reasons to the presiding judge of their judicial district and a copy of the statement to the administrative director. A court of appeals judge shall send the statement of reasons to the chief judge of that court and to the clerk of that court. The chief judge of the court of appeals or a presiding judge of the superior court shall send the statement of reasons to the chief justice and a copy of the statement to the administrative director. A supreme court justice shall send the statement to the other justices and to the clerk of the appellate courts.

(Adopted by SCO 412 effective July 1, 1980; amended by SCO 443 effective November 13, 1980; by SCO 554 effective April 4, 1983; by SCO 629 effective September 15, 1985; and by SCO 1153 effective July 15, 1994)

Annotations

Cases

Failure to respond to motion for summary judgment within 15 days does not create absolute right to summary judgment in favor of the moving party. **Dome Laboratories v. Farrell,** Op. No. 1917, 599 P2d 152 (Alaska 1979).

Rule requiring judge having a motion under advisement more than ten days from the date submitted to explain in writing to the presiding judge the reasons for the delay and the date on or before which the motion will be decided is not directly enforceable by private citizens. **Hertz v. Hertz,** Op. No. 3934, 847 P2d 71 (Alaska 1993).

Rule 4. Seals of Court.

(a) **Seal of the Court of Appeals.** The seal of the court of appeals is a vignette of the official flag of the state with the words "Seal of the Court of Appeals of the State of Alaska" surrounding the vignette.

(b) **Seal of the Superior Court.** The seal of the superior court is a vignette of the official flag of the state with the words "Seal of the Superior Court of the State of Alaska" and a designation of the district surrounding the vignette.

(c) **Seal of the District Court.** The seal of the district court is a vignette of the official flag of the state with the words "Seal of the District Court of the State of Alaska" and a designation of the district surrounding the vignette.

(d) **Seal of the Consolidated Trial Courts.** In those court locations where the superior and district courts have been consolidated for administration and when ordered by the presiding judge of the district, the seal for the superior and district courts is a vignette of the official flag of the state with the words "Seal of the Trial Courts of the State of Alaska" and a designation of the district surrounding the vignette.

(e) **Possession of Seals.** The clerk of the court, or if there is no clerk, the judge or magistrate, shall keep possession of the seal of the court.

(Adopted by SCO 412 effective July 1, 1980; amended by SCO 443 effective November 13, 1980)

Rule 5. Disposal of Money Paid to or Deposited With the Court.

(a) The administrative director shall designate, in accordance with written procedures established by the administrative director, the banking institutions to serve as depositories for all monies paid to, or deposited with, the courts. Certain accounts in the designated banks shall be the depositories for trust funds held by the various courts. Monies may be withdrawn from the accounts in accordance with procedures established by the administrative director.

(b) The proceeds of all fees, forfeitures, penalties and all other monies (except trust funds) collected by or deposited with the courts shall be deposited in the appropriate bank account for transfer to the general fund of the state in accordance with procedures established by the administrative director.

(Adopted by SCO 412 effective July 1, 1980; amended by SCO 1153 effective July 15, 1994)

Annotations

Supreme Court Order No. 11 (Clerk of Supreme Court to Establish Bank Accounts)

Rule 6. Fees of Interpreters and Translators.

(a) **Amount.** The fee for an interpreter or translator for attendance in any court or at a coroner's inquest shall be set by that court. The fee shall be subject to the following limitations:

(1) For time spent in actual performance of interpreter or translator services during the proceedings, the fee shall not exceed $81.00 per hour for the first hour and $70.00 per hour for each additional hour; and

(2) For standby time during which the interpreter or translator is required by the court to be in attendance at the court facility, the fee shall not exceed $25.00 per hour.

The court shall not authorize the maximum hourly rate unless the interpreter or translator has had formal training in court interpreting or has demonstrated specialized language skills beyond mere bilingual ability. The court may authorize additional payment not to exceed $15.00 per hour for emergency services requested and performed outside of business hours. Business hours are 8:00 a.m. to 4:30 p.m. on all days except judicial holidays and Saturdays.

(b) **Payment.** Interpreters and translators must be approved by the court pursuant to Evidence Rule 604. Interpreters and translators will be provided and their fee paid:

(1) by the court in coroner's inquests and presumptive death hearings;

(2) in civil and criminal cases, by the party who requires translation or interpretation to understand the proceedings or who calls a witness whose testimony must be translated or interpreted. These costs may be taxed and collected in civil cases as other costs, except as provided in subparagraph (3) below; and

(3) in civil and criminal cases where a party or witness is deaf, mute, or otherwise unable to effectively communicate because of a physical disability, the fee for necessary in-court services of an interpreter or translator shall be paid by the court, subject to the limitations of paragraph (a) of this rule; however, if the court in a civil case finds that a party has made a frivolous claim or defense, or otherwise litigated in bad faith, the court shall order that party to pay the fees of any interpreter or translator required by any party or witness in the case.

(Adopted by SCO 412 effective July 1, 1980; amended by SCO 469 effective June 1, 1981; by SCO 816 effective August 1, 1987; by SCO 1134 effective July 15, 1993; by SCO 1182 effective July 15, 1995; by SCO 1280 effective January 15, 1998; by SCO 1390 effective nunc pro tunc to January 1, 2000; and by SCO 1503 effective nunc pro tunc to January 1, 2003)

Rule 7. Witness Fees.

(a) **Amount.** A witness attending before any court, referee, master, grand jury or coroner's jury or upon a deposition in a discovery proceeding, whose testimony is necessary and material to the action, shall receive a witness fee of $12.50 if such attendance, including the time necessarily occupied in traveling from the witness' residence to the place of attendance and returning from that place, requires not more than three consecutive hours. If such attendance requires more than three consecutive hours, the witness shall receive a witness fee of $25.00 for each day of attendance. Any witness who attends at a point so far removed from the witness' residence as to necessarily prohibit return thereto from day-to-day shall receive per diem at the rate allowed for state employees.

(b) **Travel Expense.** Every witness who is required to

travel in excess of 30 miles from the witness' residence is entitled to receive reimbursement for round-trip travel from the witness' residence to the place of court at the rate allowed for state employees.

(c) **Expert Witnesses.** Recovery of costs for a witness called to testify as an expert is limited to the time when the expert is employed and testifying and shall not exceed $150.00 per hour, except as otherwise provided in these rules. A party may not recover costs for more than three independent expert witnesses as to the same issue in any given case, unless the judge permits recovery for an additional number of expert witnesses. For purposes of this rule, an independent expert is a witness who is retained or specially employed to provide expert testimony in the case or whose duties as an employee of the party regularly involve giving expert testimony.

(d) **Payment.** Witness fees, travel expense and per diem shall be paid from the appropriation to the judiciary only for witnesses called or appointed by the court or in coroner's cases. In all other cases, these fees and expenses shall be paid by the parties, and in civil cases, shall be taxed and collected as other costs.

(e) **Demand of Payment in Advance in Civil Cases.** Witnesses in civil cases, except when subpoenaed by the state, a municipality, a borough, a city, or an officer or agency thereof, may demand the payment in advance of their travel expense and their per diem fee for one day, and when so demanded shall not be compelled to attend until the allowances are paid.

(f) **Parties and Attorneys as Witnesses.** A party to the action or hearing, if a witness, is entitled to receive the same witness fees, per diem and travel expense as any other witness. A person appearing as an attorney for any party to an action or hearing, who also testifies as a witness therein, is not entitled to receive any witness fee, per diem or travel expenses.

(Adopted by SCO 412 effective July 1, 1980; amended by SCO 559 effective May 2, 1983; by SCO 791 effective March 15, 1987; by SCO 1153 effective July 15, 1994; by SCO 1172 effective July 15, 1995; and by SCO 1492 effective October 15, 2002)

Annotations

Cases

Court erred in basing award of expert witness fees on the time the expert spent in court observing and testifying rather than only on the time the expert was actually testifying. **Eagle Air v. Corroon, Etc.,** Op. No. 2538, 648 P2d 1000 (Alaska 1982).

Trial judge did not abuse his discretion in denying fees for one of prevailing party's expert witnesses on ground that no timesheet was submitted for the witness. **Truckweld Equipment Co. v. Swenson Trucking,** Op. No. 2545, 649 P2d 234 (Alaska 1982).

The taxing of costs for witness fees is governed by Civil Rule 83 and Administrative Rule 7(c) rather than the general provisions of Civil Rule 79(b). **Miller v. Sears,** Op. No. 2447, 636 P2d 1183 (Alaska 1981).

Expert witness fees in excess of state limits were proper where awarded pursuant to a federal act, 15 U.S.C. § 2310, rather than state law. **Universal Motors, Inc., v. Waldock,** Op. No. 3060, 719 P2d 254 (Alaska 1986).

Trial court's finding that losing party acted in bad faith was clearly erroneous, thus award of expert witness fees to prevailing party in excess of the twenty-five dollars per hour limit of this rule was invalid. **Fairbanks North Star Borough v. Tundra Tours,** Op. No. 3052, 719 P2d 1020 (Alaska 1986).

A party may not recover costs for experts' preparation time nor any costs associated with the experts if they do not testify. **Atlantic Richfield Co. v. State,** Op. No. 3096, 723 P2d 1249 (Alaska 1986).

Trial court could award prevailing defendant expert witness fees, not to exceed $25.00 per hour, for the time the expert actually spent testifying, but not for time spent in trial preparation. **Hutchins v. Schwartz,** Op. No. 3110, 724 P2d 1194 (Alaska 1986).

Where experts testified by deposition at trial, prevailing party was entitled to recover only fees for the time spent actually reading the depositions in court, since the depositions were taken prior to previewing party's offer of judgment. **Hutchins v. Schwartz,** Op. No. 3110, 724 P2d 1194 (Alaska 1986).

Treating physicians were expert witnesses when they testified as such, thus prevailing party was entitled to recover fees paid for their testimony only up to the $50 per hour limit of this rule. **Yurioff v. American Honda Motor Co.,** Op. No. 3648, 803 P2d 386 (Alaska 1990).

The complexity of the case is irrelevant to recovery of expert witness fees under this rule; absent bad faith or reprehensible conduct, the prevailing party may receive as costs only those expert witness fees specified in this rule. **Anchorage v. Frank Coluccio Const. Co.,** Op. No. 3808, 826 P2d 316 (Alaska 1992).

Recovery of costs for reimbursement of expert witnesses in divorce cases is not governed by limitations of this rule, thus full reasonable costs may be awarded. **Hilliker v. Hilliker,** Op. No. 3831, 828 P2d 1205 (Alaska 1992).

Because none of plaintiff's expert fees were incurred in conjunction with trial, they were not recoverable under this rule. **Pratt & Whitney Canada, Inc. v. Sheehan,** Op. No. 3959, 852 P2d 1173 (Alaska 1993).

There is no public interest exception to this rule's limitation on expert witness costs, but trial courts have discretion to ignore limitation if application would be unjust. **Hickel v. Southeast Conference,** Op. No. 4055, 868 P2d 919 (Alaska 1994).

Where expert witness for prevailing public interest litigant was not paid for his work and had no binding agreement to be paid for his work and did not testify, trial court did not err in failing to award costs for his expert services. **Dansereau v. Ulmer,** Op. No. 4962, 955 P2d 916 (Alaska 1998).

Catchall provision of former version of Civil Rule 79(b) did not authorize award to prevailing plaintiff of $5,146 for cost of accountant where cost exceeded limits of Administrative Rule 7(c) for expert witnesses even though Administrative Rule 7(c) would have barred recovery because accountant did not testify; plaintiff's argument that Administrative Rule 7(c) should not apply because accountant was a consulting expert rather than a testifying expert was rejected. **Strong Enterprises, Inc. v. Seaward,** Op. No. 5118, 980 P2d 456 (Alaska 1999).

Rule 8. Physicians' Fees.

Physicians shall be allowed a reasonable fee for performing the following services:

(a) An examination under order of court pursuant to AS 47.30.700 or such other examination as may be ordered by the court upon its own motion;

(b) Giving medical expert testimony at a hearing when ordered by the court in relation to such examination or in relation to an autopsy or post mortem examination ordered pursuant to AS 12.65.020.

Fees for such services shall be paid from funds appropriated to the judiciary. Claims for compensation shall be submitted for approval to the judicial officer ordering the examination or testimony, subject to final approval by the administrative director. In all other cases, physicians' fees shall be paid by the requesting party or parties.

The administrative director may authorize a fee under (a) of this rule to be computed other than on an hourly basis, provided that such computation results in a fee that is substantially the same as if computed hourly.

(Adopted by SCO 412 effective July 1, 1980; amended by SCO 813 effective August 1, 1987)

Rule 8.1. Health Care Provider Expert Advisory Panel Fees.

(a) **Compensation by Court.** Expert advisory panel members appointed pursuant to AS 09.55.536 will be reimbursed by the court for the reasonable expenses of transportation outside the panel member's city of residence which are necessary for the preparation of the panel's report. Panel members will be reimbursed for other expenses of preparing their report at the rate of $18.00 per hour, not to exceed $90.00 per day. If the panel member's reasonable and necessary actual expenses other than transportation expenses exceed this hourly rate, the panel member will be compensated for reasonable and necessary actual expenses in lieu of the hourly compensation. Panel members are not entitled to compensation from the court for any professional fees for service on the panel.

(b) **Request for Compensation.** In order to qualify for reimbursement, a panel member must submit to the trial court within thirty days after the submission of the expert report a written request for reimbursement which specifies by date and by nature of the item any transportation expenses, time spent preparing the report, and, if reimbursement for actual expenses is sought, all expenses. Claims for reimbursement must be submitted for approval to the assigned judge and are subject to final approval by the administrative director.

(Adopted by SCO 814 effective August 1, 1987)

Rule 9. Fee Schedule

The fees specified in this rule shall be charged for the services designated herein:

(a) **In the Supreme Court and the Court of Appeals:**

(1) Filing Fees:

(i) Upon filing a written notice of appeal or cross-appeal (Appellate Rule 204(b) or Rule 215(b)) $150.00

(ii) Upon filing a petition for review or cross-petition for review (Appellate Rule —403(a)) 150.00

(iii) Upon filing original proceedings (Appellate Rule 404) 150.00

(iv) Upon filing a petition for hearing (Appellate Rule 303) 150.00

(v) Upon filing a judicial bypass appeal (Appellate Rule 220) no fee

(2) Miscellaneous Fees:

(i) For preparation of case record for review by the Supreme Court of the United States, 100.00

(ii) For copies of documents on file with the supreme court or the court of appeals, whether or not certified: Each page or fraction thereof .25

(iii) For copies of court opinions, per opinion 2.00

(iv) Subparagraphs (e)(2) and (e)(4) of this rule apply to certification and notary public services in the appellate courts

No person shall be charged a filing fee upon filing a written notice of appeal or a petition for review of a decision involving a claim for benefits under AS 23.20 (Employment Security Act).

(b) **Filing Fees—Superior Court:**

(1) Upon filing any civil case, including a petition for deposition before action 150.00

(2) For probate matters:

(i) Initial filing fee 150.00

(ii) For depositing a will with the court for safekeeping 40.00

No fee will be charged if the will of a protected person or ward is deposited by the guardian or conservator pursuant to AS 13.26.285(e) after the death of the protected person or ward.

(iii) For registration of a trust document 40.00

(iv) Upon filing a petition for court approval of a minor's settlement, when it involves opening a new file, 75.00

(v) For filing a petition for appointment of a temporary property custodian under AS 22.15.110(a)(3) no fee

(vi) For lodging a temporary property custodian affidavit and inventory no fee

(vii) For filing a petition to bypass parental consent to an abortion under Probate Rule 20 no fee

(3) Upon filing of an adoption proceeding 75.00

If the petitioner seeks to adopt more than one child at the same time, only one filing fee will be charged even though a separate petition must be filed for each child

(4) Upon filing any guardianship, conservatorship or other protective proceedings to include all services 75.00

If a petitioner seeks appointment of a guardian or conservator for more than one child at the same time, only one filing fee will be charged even though a separate petition must be filed for each child.

(5) Upon filing an appeal, including a sentence appeal, cross-appeal, petition for review, or cross-petition for review from district court, except in forma pauperis cases 40.00

(6) Upon filing an action to enjoin or enforce orders of the Alaska Worker's Compensation Board 150.00

(7) Upon filing an action for review of a decision by the Department of Labor under AS 23.20 (Employment Security Act) no fee

(8) Upon filing an appeal, cross-appeal, petition for review, or cross-petition for review from an administrative order (AS 44.62.560) 150.00

(9) In cases arising under the Uniform Reciprocal Enforcement of Support Act, all ordinary fees shall be charged, subject to the waiver provisions of Supreme Court Order No. 19*

(10) Upon filing a complaint or comparable pleading under the Uniform Interstate Family Support Act no fee

(11) Upon filing a petition for a domestic violence protective order no fee

(12) Upon filing a petition for change of name 150.00

If the petitioner seeks to change the name of more than one family member at the same time, only one filing fee will be charged even though a separate petition must be filed for each person who is requesting a change of name under Civil Rule 84.

(c) **Filing Fees — District Court:**

(1) Filing fees, district court jurisdiction 90.00

(2) Filing fees, small claims actions, claim for relief

(i) $2,500 or less 40.00

(ii) more than $2,500 75.00

No additional filing fee is due when a small claims case is removed to district or superior court.

(3) Filing fees, petitions for domestic violence protective order no fee

(4) There shall be no fee for filing a presumptive death petition.

(d) **Transcript and Related Fees:**

(1) Electronic transcripts, other than electronic transcripts of sentencing proceedings provided pursuant to Criminal Rule 32.2(d), each recording 10.00

(2) For recording depositions with court recording equipment, per hour, or fraction thereof 25.00

(e) **Miscellaneous Fees in the Superior Court and the District Court:**

(1) Copying.

(i) For photocopying or making copies from microfiche or microfilm, the cost per page is, .25

(A "page" means one side of a sheet of paper.)

(ii) For duplicating a microfiche sheet (diazo) 5.00

(2) Certification.

A court can certify a copy of a document only if the original of the document is on file with the court. The cost of photocopying the document is included in the certification costs given below. For certifying a copy of any document, the cost is:

(i) Each document 5.00

(ii) For each additional certified copy of the document requested at the same time 2.00

However, a party is entitled to receive one free certified copy of the final judgment or order in the party's case and one free certified copy of a clerk's certificate of name change under Civil Rule 84(c).

(3) For issuing exemplifications 10.00

(4) For notary public services 3.00

This fee shall not apply to notary services on documents which are to be filed in a pending action or which are related to official court business.

(5) For providing in writing requested information from search of records, per hour or fraction thereof 15.00

(6) For service of process by the court:

(i) By certified mail (postage provided by party) 4.00

(ii) By registered mail (postage provided by party) 10.00

A party requesting service of process by certified or registered mail must supply an addressed envelope, adequate postage, and appropriate postal forms.

(7) For issuing marriage license 40.00

(8) For performing marriage ceremony 25.00

(f) **General Provisions:**

(1) No filing, certifying, or copying fee will be charged to any person determined to be indigent under Administrative Rule 10. No filing or certifying fees will be charged to any agency of the state of Alaska. State agencies will not be charged copying fees except for copies of law library materials.

(2) Notarization required in an action by a person represented in such action by an attorney furnished to the person by an organization authorized to provide legal services to indigents is exempted from notary public fees provided under this schedule.

(3) Before accepting any civil action or proceeding for filing, a filing fee in the amount prescribed in this rule shall be collected. Further or additional fees or charges shall be made by the clerk or magistrate with respect to such action or proceeding only for additional services as specified in this rule.

(4) The fee for performance of a marriage ceremony shall be retained by the marriage commissioner as compensation for that service. A judicial officer or employee appointed as marriage commissioner shall deposit such fee in accordance with Administrative Rule 5(b).

(5) No fee of any kind will be charged to a minor in a proceeding to bypass parental consent to an abortion under Probate Rule 20 or Appellate Rule 220.

(Adopted by SCO 412 effective July 1, 1980; amended by SCO 423 effective September 1, 1980; by SCO 424 effective July 1, 1980; by SCO 443 effective November 13, 1980; by SCO 464 effective July 1, 1981; by SCO 472 effective June 1, 1981; by SCO 475 effective August 17, 1981; by SCO 482 effective September 1, 1981; by SCO 485 effective October 5, 1981; by SCO 490 effective January 4, 1982; by SCO 524 effective September 1, 1982; by SCO 525 effective September 1, 1982; by SCO 560 effective May 2, 1983; by SCO 648 effective July 1, 1985; by SCO 657 effective December 15, 1985; by SCO 692 effective July 1, 1986; by SCO 747 effective December 15, 1986; by SCO 749 effective December 15, 1986; by SCO 756 effective December 15, 1986; by SCO 779 effective March 15, 1987; by SCO 785 effective March 15, 1987; by SCO 843 effective June 24, 1987; by SCO 887 effective July 15, 1988; by SCO 888 effective July 15, 1988; by SCO 940 effective January 15, 1989; by SCO 947 effective October 17, 1988; by SCO 986 effective August 1, 1989; by SCO 1001 effective January 15, 1990; by SCO 1002 effective January 15, 1990; by SCO 1031 effective July 15, 1990; by SCO 1056 effective July 15, 1991; by SCO 1059 effective July 15, 1991; by SCO 1111 effective nunc pro tunc July 27, 1992; by SCO 1129 effective July 15, 1993; by SCO 1133 effective July 15, 1993; by SCO 1140 effective July 1, 1993; by SCO 1153 effective July 15, 1994; by SCO 1164 effective July 15, 1994; by SCO 1201 effective July 15, 1995; by SCO 1214 effective July 15, 1995; by SCO 1261 effective September 26, 1996; by SCO 1268, 1269 and 1275 effective July 15, 1997; by SCO 1279 effective July 31, 1997; by SCO 1292 effective January 15, 1998; by SCO 1300 effective October 29, 1997; by SCO 1416 effective November 1, 2000; by SCO 1515 effective July 1, 2003; by SCO 1555 effective October 15, 2004; by SCO 1558 effective nunc pro tunc to August 1, 2004; by SCO 1535 effective April 15, 2005; by SCO 1605 effective October 15, 2006; by SCO 1623 effective October 15, 2006; by SCO 1630 effective April 16, 2007; and by SCO 1650 effective October 15, 2007)

Editor's Note: Supreme Court Order 19 provides as follows:

"In the processing of all cases arising under the provisions of the Uniform Reciprocal Enforcement of Support Act (Ch. 31 SLA 1953, as amended, Ch. 19 SLA 1960), either as an initiating state or as a responding state, prepayment of filing fees, the cost of serving summons, procuring the presence of the defendant in court, and other costs as may be allowed by the superior court, shall be waived upon the filing in the case of a pauper's affidavit in suitable form.

"Where prepayment of fees or costs has been waived, any order of the superior court requiring the payment of money by the defendant shall specifically provide that the defendant reimburse the clerk of court for all waived fees and costs. The order of the court shall specify the amount of any fee or cost item and shall designate which state agency shall be reimbursed for such fee or cost. Upon collection of said fees and costs, the clerk shall deposit the same as reimbursement to the appropriate state agencies or departments pursuant to said order of court." (Supreme Court Order 19; amended by Supreme Court Order 59 effective January 1, 1964).

Note: In 1996, the legislature enacted AS 18.66.160(c), which prohibits anyone from charging a fee for service of process in a proceeding to obtain a domestic violence protective order. According to § 76, ch. 64 SLA 1996, this statute has the effect of amending Administrative rule 9(e)(6).

Note: In 1997 the legislature enacted AS 18.16.030(m), which provides that a filing fee may not be required of, and court costs may not be assessed against, a minor in a proceeding to bypass parental consent to an abortion. According to ch. 14, sec. 10 SLA 1997, AS 18.16.030(m) has the effect of amending Administrative Rule 9, Civil Rule 79, and Appellate Rule 508 by prohibiting filing fees and assessment of court costs in certain actions. Instead of amending individual rules to implement AS 18.16.030, the supreme court has adopted a separate rule on judicial bypass proceedings in the superior court and a separate rule on judicial bypass appeals. See Probate Rule 20 & Appellate Rule 220.

Note: Chapter 87 SLA 03 (HB 1) enacted AS 18.65.865(b), which addresses fees for filing petitions for protective orders under AS 18.65.850-860 for persons who are victims of stalking not involving domestic violence. According to Section 8(a) of the Act, the new AS 18.65.865 has the effect of amending Administrative Rule 9 by providing that filing fees may not be charged in any action seeking only the relief provided in AS 18.65.850-860.

Annotations

Cases

In condemnation action, amount of appraiser's fee is not limited by provisions of this rule relating to expert witnesses. **Greater Anchorage Area Borough v. 10 Acres,** Op. No. 1417, 563 P2d 269 (Alaska 1977).

Rule 9.1. Form of Payment.

(a) **Bail.** Bail for criminal offenses may be posted in cash, through a surety as authorized by law, or in another form of payment authorized by the court in the case. During business hours, bail may also be posted with the clerk of the court by electronic fund transfer.

(b) **Other Payments to the Court.** Unless otherwise ordered by the court in the case, other payments to the court, including but not limited to fines, bail forfeiture amounts authorized by supreme court order, appellate bonds, filing fees and other court fees, may be paid by cash, electronic fund transfer, certified check, cashier's check, money order, traveler's check or personal check.

(c) **Other Forms of Payment.** The administrative director may authorize other forms of payment in specific court locations. In these locations, bail and other payments may be paid in the forms authorized by the administrative director and the forms listed in (a) or (b) above unless otherwise ordered by the court.

(Adopted by SCO 1065 effective July 15, 1991)

Rule 10. Exemption from Payment of Fees—Determination of Indigency.

(a) The determination of a person's indigency for purposes of exemption from payment of fees under Rule 9(f)(1) shall be made by the court in which the action is filed as soon as practicable after the date the action is filed, but in no event more than 60 days after that date.

(b) A person who requests an exemption of fees shall file an indigency statement on a form prescribed by the administrative director of courts, except that a person represented by an attorney furnished by the Alaska Legal Services Corporation, the Alaska Pro Bono Program, or the Alaska Network on Domestic Violence and Sexual Assault Pro Bono Program need not file such a form.

(c) If a person files the documents required by subparagraph (b) of this rule, or is represented by an attorney furnished by the Alaska Legal Services Corporation, the Alaska Pro Bono Program, or the Alaska Network on Domestic Violence and Sexual Assault Pro Bono Program, the clerk or magistrate shall accept the pleadings for filing without payment of the filing fee.

(d) If the court finds that the person is not indigent, it shall order the person to pay the filing fee. The court may continue the action until such payment is made. If payment is not made within 30 days after notice of the order, the court may dismiss the action.

(e) The provisions of this rule do not apply to an exemption from payment of filing fees in litigation against the state. In this paragraph, "litigation against the state" has the meaning given in AS 09.19.100.

(Adopted by SCO 412 effective July 1, 1980; amended by SCO 888 effective July 15, 1988; by SCO 908 effective January 15, 1989; by SCO 1237 effective July 15, 1996; and by SCO 1357 effective July 21, 1999)

Note to SCO 1237: Administrative Rule 10(e) was added by ch. 79 § 16 SLA 1995. Section 1 of this order is adopted for the sole reason that the legislature has mandated the amendment.

Note: Section 3 of chapter 95 SLA 1998 amends the definition of prisoner litigation against the state that appears in AS 09.19.100(1). According to section 14 of the act, this amendment has the effect of changing Administrative Rule 10(e) "by expanding the definition of 'litigation against the state' so that it has the meaning given in AS 09.9.100 as amended by sec. 3 of this Act."

Rule 11. Fees—Service of Civil Process.

(a) The following schedule establishes the maximum amount recoverable from another party as costs for the services designated.

(1) Service of Process:

(i) For service of any summons or subpoena—each person on whom service is made	$35.00
(ii) For service of any warrant, attachment, notice of levy, intent to levy or garnishment, execution or other writ—each person on whom service is made	35.00
(iii) For each hour in excess of two actually and necessarily spent to obtain service under (i) or (ii) above	20.00
(iv) If more than one document involving the same case is given to the same individual at the same time only one fee shall be charged	

(2) Sales of Property Pursuant to Final Process:

For advertising and disposing of property by sale, set-off, or otherwise, according to law, pursuant to a writ of possession, partition, execution, or any final process and for receiving and paying over money on account of property sold—on any sum not exceeding five hundred dollars	Seven percent
And on any excess over five hundred dollars and not exceeding ten thousand dollars	Four percent

And on any excess over ten thousand dollars and not exceeding fifty thousand dollars

Two and one-half percent

And on any excess over fifty thousand dollars

One and one-quarter percent

provided, that when the officer disposes of property by sale, set-off, or otherwise, according to law, but does not receive and pay over money on account of such sale, the officer shall receive one-half of the commission allowed in this subdivision.

(3) Deeds:

For executing a deed prepared by a party or a party's attorney	10.00

(4) Copies:

For copies of writs or papers furnished at the request of any party:

First page or fraction thereof	1.00
Each additional page or fraction thereof	.25

(5) Inventories:

For making inventory of unclaimed property for each hour actually and necessarily spent	10.00

(6) Keeping Personal Property:

For keeping of personal property attached on mesne process, such compensation as the court, on petition setting forth the facts under oath, may allow.

(7) Mileage:

For mileage actually and necessarily traveled in going to serve, and in returning from the place of service, of any process described in paragraph (1) above, whether or not service was obtained, for the first 25 total miles of any portion thereof	10.00
And for each mile in excess of 25 actually and necessarily traveled	.40

(8) No fee shall be charged under this schedule for any service rendered to the state or any agency or department thereof

(b) All service of civil process and duties ancillary thereto under the Rules of Civil Procedure and applicable statutes shall be performed by private persons appointed under Civil Rule 4(c)(1), (4)(c)(3) or 4(c)(4), or by persons authorized by Civil Rule 45(c); provided, that a member of the Alaska State Troopers or other peace officer may render assistance to a process server as provided in Civil Rule 4(c)(3) or serve any process when directed to do so by the Commissioner of Public Safety. In this paragraph, "civil process" includes any summons, subpoena, attachment, notice of levy, intent to levy or garnishment, execution, or other writ in a civil action, but does not include any process, civil or criminal, served on behalf of the state for any department or agency thereof.

(Adopted by SCO 412 effective July 1, 1980; amended by SCO 526 effective October 1, 1982; by SCO 527 effective October 1, 1982; by SCO 548 effective February 1, 1983; by SCO 549 effective February 1, 1983; by SCO 588 effective January 1, 1984; by SCO 592 effective July 1, 1984; by SCO 815 effective August 1, 1987; by SCO 1071 effective July 15, 1991; by SCO 1153 effective July 15, 1994; and by SCO 1400 effective October 15, 2000)

Annotations

Cases

This rule, which establishes the maximum fee which may be recovered as costs for service of process, did not apply where the judgment debtor agreed to pay the process server's fees to the extent reasonable and specifically waived any objection that the procedures agreed to between the parties for the sale of property by a private auctioneer to satisfy the debt might not comply with the law or procedure for execution sales. **Dahlby v. Guzzardi,** Op. No. 3391, 763 P2d 223 (Alaska 1998).

Rule 12. Procedure for Counsel and Guardian Ad Litem Appointments at Public Expense.

(a) **Intent.** The court shall appoint counsel or a guardian ad litem only when the court specifically determines that the appointment is clearly authorized by law or rule, and that the person for whom the appointment is made is financially eligible for an appointment at public expense.

(b) **Appointments under AS 18.85.100 (a) (Public Defender Agency).**

(1) *Appointment Procedure.*

(A) When a person is entitled to counsel under AS 18.85.100(a), appointments shall be made first to the public defender agency. If the agency files a motion to withdraw on the grounds that it cannot represent the person because of a conflict of interest, if the parties stipulate on the record that the agency has a conflict of interest, or if the court on its own motion finds an obvious conflict of interest, the court accepting such motion or stipulation or making such finding shall appoint the office of public advocacy to provide counsel.

(B) The court may appoint an attorney in a case in which the office of public advocacy has been appointed only if:

(i) The office of public advocacy has shown that it is unable to provide counsel either by staff or by contract; and

(ii) The office of public advocacy has provided the court with the name or names of the attorneys who shall be appointed in that particular case.

The office of public advocacy shall be responsible for compensating any attorney appointed under this subparagraph.

(C) All claims for payment for services performed after

July 1, 1984, by attorneys appointed by the court shall be submitted to the director of the office of public advocacy, under such procedures as the director may prescribe. The director shall approve, modify or disapprove the claim.

(2) *Determination of Indigency.* Determination of indigency or financial inability for appointments under paragraph (b) of this rule must be made in accordance with the provisions of Criminal Rule 39.

(3) *Assessment of Costs.* When counsel is appointed for a child when the child's parents or custodian are financially able but refuse to employ counsel to assist the child, the court may, when appropriate, assess as costs against the parents, guardian or custodian the cost to the state of providing counsel.

(c) **Appointments under AS 44.21.410 (Office of Public Advocacy).**

(1) *Appointment Procedure.* When a person qualifies for counsel or guardian ad litem services under AS 44.21.410, the court shall appoint the office of public advocacy. The court in its order appointing the office of public advocacy must state the authority for the appointment. In the case of a discretionary appointment, the court must give specific reasons for the appointment. In the case of a guardian ad litem appointment, the court shall limit the appointment to the pendency of the proceedings affecting the child's welfare, shall outline the guardian ad litem's responsibilities, and shall limit the guardian's authority to those matters related to the guardian's effective representation of the minor's best interests.

(2) *Indigency Determination.* For appointments of the office of public advocacy under this rule, other than an appointment required because of a conflict of interest with the public defender agency, a person is indigent if the person's income does not exceed the maximum annual income level established to determine eligibility for representation by the Alaska Legal Services Corporation. A person whose income exceeds the maximum amount for legal services representation may be determined indigent only if a judge makes a specific finding of indigency on the record, taking into account the funds necessary for the person to maintain employment, to provide shelter, and to clothe, feed and care for the person and the person's immediate family, the person's outstanding contractual indebtedness, the person's ability to afford representation based on the particular matter and the complexity of the case, the costs of living and attorneys fees in different regions of the state, and any liquid assets which could be counted as income.

(3) *Assessment of Costs.* In an appointment under AS 25.24.310 for representation of a minor, the court shall enter an order for costs, fees and disbursements in favor of the state. If the appointment is made in a proceeding in which custody, support or visitation is an issue, the court shall, if possible, avoid assigning costs to only one party by ordering that costs of the minor's legal representative or guardian services be paid from property belonging to both parents before a division of property is made.

(d) **Withdrawal from Unauthorized Appointment.** The public defender agency and the office of public advocacy shall accept appointments only in those cases for which the basis for the appointment is clearly authorized. If the agency or office determines that the basis for an appointment is not clearly authorized, the agency or office shall file with the court a motion to withdraw from the appointment.

(e) **Other Appointments at Public Expense.**

(1) *Constitutionally Required Appointments.*

If the court determines that counsel, or a guardian ad litem, or other representative should be appointed for an indigent person, and further determines that the appointment is not authorized by AS 18.85.100(a) or AS 44.21.410, but in the opinion of the court is required by law or rule, the court shall appoint an attorney who is a member of the Alaska Bar Association to provide the required services. Other persons may be appointed to provide required services to the extent permissible by law.

(A) Appointments may be made in the following types of cases without prior approval of the administrative director, but only in cases in which the required services would not otherwise be provided by a public agency:

(i) Attorneys for biological parents in adoption cases to the extent required by the Indian Child Welfare Act (25 USC 1901 et seq.),

(ii) Attorneys for minor children and indigent parents or custodians of minor children in minor guardianship cases brought pursuant to AS 13.26.060(d),

(iii) Attorneys for respondents in protective proceedings brought pursuant to AS 13.26 in which appointment of the office of public advocacy is not mandated by statute,

(iv) Attorneys for minor children or incompetents who are heirs or devisees of estates in cases in which the attorneys' fees cannot be paid as a cost of administration from the proceeds of the estate,

(v) Attorneys for indigent putative fathers in actions to establish paternity in which the state of Alaska provides representation for mothers,

(vi) Attorneys to represent indigent respondents in involuntary alcohol commitments brought pursuant to AS 47.37,

(vii) Attorneys for indigent parents who are defending against a claim that their consent to adoption is not required under AS 25.23.050(a).

(B) In all other cases, the court shall inform the administrative director of the specific reasons why an appointment is required prior to making the appointment.

(2) *Servicemembers Civil Relief Act.* When the opposing party is financially unable to pay for such representation, the court shall appoint a member of the Alaska Bar Association to represent an absent service person pursuant to the

Servicemembers Civil Relief Act (50 App. U.S.C. § 521). Prior approval of the administrative director is not required.

(3) *List of Private Attorneys.*

(A) The presiding judge shall designate the area court administrator and a clerk of court for each court location in the district to keep and make available to the court in each location lists of attorneys or other persons eligible to receive court appointments under paragraph (e) of this rule.

(B) The attorney lists will first be compiled from names of persons who have volunteered to accept these appointments. If there are insufficient volunteers, the court will make appointments on a rotation basis from lists of eligible attorneys obtained from the Alaska Bar Association. The court may, in departing from a strict rotation basis, take into account the complexity of the case and the level of experience required by counsel.

(C) Lists of other persons available to provide required services will be compiled from names of qualified persons who have indicated their willingness to provide the required services.

(4) *Appointment Orders.* When the court appoints an attorney or other person under paragraph (e) of this rule, the clerk of the court from which the appointment was made shall immediately send a copy of the appointment order to the administrative director.

(5) *Compensation.*

(A) All claims for compensation must be submitted on forms provided by the court within 30 days following the disposition of a case. Claims will be submitted to the assigned trial judge or master, who shall make a recommendation regarding approval and forward the recommendation to the administrative director. The administrative director shall approve or disapprove the claim.

(B) Attorneys will be compensated at the rate of $75.00 per hour; provided, that total compensation for any case will not exceed $1,000.00 without prior approval of the administrative director.

(C) A person other than an attorney appointed to provide services will receive compensation if the court deems it appropriate not to exceed $25.00 per hour; provided, that total compensation for any case will not exceed $300.00 without prior approval of the administrative director.

(D) Extraordinary expenses will be reimbursed only if prior authority has been obtained from the administrative director, upon recommendation by the assigned trial judge or the presiding judge. The assigned trial judge may recommend extraordinary expenses up to a total amount not to exceed $1,000.00, and the presiding judge may recommend an amount not to exceed an additional $1,500.00. Extraordinary expenses exceeding $2,500.00 may be authorized only in extremely complex cases by the administrative director upon the recommendation of the presiding judge. In this paragraph, "extraordinary expenses" are limited to expenses for:

(i) Investigation;

(ii) Expert witnesses; and

(iii) Necessary travel and per diem expenses. Travel and per diem may not exceed the rate authorized for state employees.

(E) If necessary to prevent manifest injustice, the administrative director may authorize payment of compensation or expenses in excess of the amounts allowed under this rule.

(6) *Recovery of Costs.* When counsel is appointed for a person in a case described in subparagraph 12(e)(1), the court shall order the person, or if the person is a child, the person's parents, guardian or custodian, to pay the costs incurred by the court in providing representation. Before appointing counsel, the court shall advise the person that the person will be ordered to repay the state for the cost of appointed counsel and shall advise the person of the maximum amount that the person will be required to repay. The court shall order the person to apply for permanent fund dividends every year in which the person qualifies for a dividend until the cost is paid in full. The clerk shall determine the cost of representation, and shall mail to the person's address of record a notice informing the person that judgment will be entered against the person for the actual cost of representation or for $500, whichever is less. The person may oppose entry of the judgment by filing a written opposition within 10 days after the date shown in the clerk's certificate of distribution on the notice. The opposition shall specifically set out the grounds for opposing entry of judgment. The clerk shall enter judgment against the person for the amount shown in the notice if the person does not oppose entry of the judgment within the 10 days. If the person files a timely opposition, the court may set the matter for a hearing and shall have authority to enter the judgment. Criminal Rule 39(c)(1)(D) and (c)(2) shall apply to judgments entered under this section.

(f) **Responsibilities of Appointed Counsel.**

(1) An attorney appointed to represent an indigent person must advise the court if the attorney learns of a change in the person's financial status that would make the person financially ineligible for appointed counsel.

(2) An attorney appointed to represent an indigent person must move to withdraw if the attorney reasonably believes that the person has made a material misrepresentation of the person's financial status to the court. A material misrepresentation is a misrepresentation of facts that would make the person financially ineligible for appointed counsel. The attorney is not required to disclose to the court the existence or nature of the misrepresentation unless disclosure is necessary to prevent the person from fraudulently securing the services of appointed counsel.

(Adopted by SCO 412 effective July 1, 1980; amended by SCO 443 effective November 13, 1980; by SCO 528 effective September 1, 1982; by SCO 529 effective September 1, 1982; by SCO 626 effective April 19, 1985; by SCO 652 effective July 1, 1985; by SCO 676 effective April 25, 1986; by SCO

680 effective April 25, 1986; by SCO 689 effective April 24, 1986; by SCO 703 effective May 12, 1986; by SCO 889 effective July 15, 1988; by SCO 909 effective January 15, 1989; by SCO 1053 effective July 15, 1991; by SCO 1088 effective July 1, 1992; by SCO 1092 effective July 15, 1992; by SCO 1103 effective July 9, 1992; by SCO 1145 effective October 1, 1993; by SCO 1179 effective July 15, 1995; by SCO 1584 effective October 15, 2005; and by SCO 1649 effective July 1, 2007)

Dissent to SCO 1088:

RABINOWITZ, Chief Justice, with whom COMPTON, Justice, joins, dissenting:

I am not persuaded that either existing Criminal Rule 39, or Appellate Rule 209, requires amendment. I think it can be safely predicted that these amendments will have a chilling effect on an indigent defendant's obtaining the services of appointed counsel as well as on an indigent defendant's decision whether or not to seek review or to appeal.

Note: AS 18.85.170(4) defines "indigent person" for purposes of public defender appointments as "a person who, at the time need is determined, does not have sufficient assets, credit, or other means to provide for payment of an attorney and all other necessary expenses of representation without depriving the party or the party's dependents of food, clothing, or shelter and who has not disposed of any assets since the commission of the offense with the intent or for the purpose of establishing eligibility for assistance under this chapter."

Annotations

Cases

An attorney appointed by the court to represent an indigent person in a criminal case has no constitutional right to compensation and is entitled to a recompense for such services only to the extent that a statute or a court rule may so provide. **Jackson v. State,** Op. No. 340, 413 P2d 488 (Alaska 1966).

By this rule the supreme court has provided that court-appointed counsel shall receive certain minimum fees for their services, but the problem of providing means of adequate compensation of counsel in the developing field of right of indigents to counsel is a matter fundamentally for legislative and not for judicial treatment. **Jackson v. State,** Op. No. 340, 413 P2d 488 (Alaska 1966).

Where there was representation in a post-conviction proceeding, the discretion of the trial judge must be exercised in fixing the allowance but one of the factors to be considered in exercising this discretion is the amount provided by the legislature for this purpose. **Jackson v. State,** Op. No. 340, 413 P2d 488 (Alaska 1966).

A provision that the fee to be allowed for services other than trial should be "commensurate with the time and legal problems involved," did not mean that the fee should be equal to justifiable charges to a client able to pay, but meant that it should not be more than that allowed for a trial, and probably somewhat less. **Jackson v. State,** Op. No. 340, 413 P2d 488 (Alaska 1966).

Under this rule, attorneys can be required to provide services to people they would rather not represent at rates they consider inadequate. **Wood v. Superior Court,** Op. No. 2884, 690 P2d 1225 (Alaska 1984).

Lack of experience in criminal cases will not always justify a court-appointed attorney's refusal to represent an indigent criminal defendant. **Wood v. Superior Court,** Op. No. 2884, 690 P2d 1225 (Alaska 1984).

The complexity and duration of each case as well as the court system's budgetary constraints were proper factors for the administrative director to consider in evaluating excess fee requests by court-appointed attorneys under former administrative rules. **State v. Law Offices of Coleman and Iacopelli,** Op. No. 3025, 716 P2d 1 (Alaska 1986).

The question of whether former Administrative Rule 12(d)(2)(B)(vii) (now Rule 12(e)(2)) authorized the superior court to order the State to advance Soldiers' and Sailors' Civil Relief Act counsel's fees in a paternity case was a question of law reviewed de novo. **State, Department of Revenue v. Superior Court,** Op. No. 4283, 907 P2d 14 (Alaska 1995).

Former Administrative Rule 12(d)(2)(B)(vii) (now Rule 12(e)(2)) authorized the superior court to order the state to advance appointed counsel's fees when counsel was appointed under the Soldiers' and Sailors' Civil Relief Act in a paternity suit. **State, Department of Revenue v. Superior Court,** Op. No. 4283, 907 P2d 14 (Alaska 1995).

Trial court had discretion to require Office of Public Advocacy to continue to represent the father of children alleged to be children in need of aid despite fact that trial court found that father was no longer eligible for appointed counsel; Administrative Rule 12 adopts Criminal Rule 39, and that rule permits the court to continue an appointment even if the client is ineligible. **Office of Public Advocacy v. Superior Court, Second Judicial Dist.,** Op. No. 5291, 3 P3d 932 (Alaska 2000).

Rule 14. Jurors' and Grand Jurors' Fees.

(a) Petit jurors summoned, who qualify for service on the venire, shall be paid at the rate of $25.00 per day for every full day spent as a member of the venire and $12.50 for a half day or less spent as a member of the venire, except petit jurors who without inconvenience are able to return to their homes each evening shall receive such payment only for the days actually required to report to the court or while serving as a member of a Panel.

(b) Jurors summoned from places more than 30 miles distant from the place of court shall receive reimbursement for round-trip travel from the juror's residence to the place of court for the total distance actually and necessarily traveled at the rate per mile allowed to state employees. If air transportation is used, the actual cost of such transportation shall be paid in lieu of mileage.

(c) If it is impracticable for a juror to return home each evening, subsistence at the per diem rate allowed to state employees shall be allowed for each day of the juror's term of service on the venire.

(d) If a jury is convened in a remote area, and if food or lodging is provided by the court, the administrative director may provide for direct payment of the cost of food and lodging in lieu of payment of a subsistence allowance to the jurors. The administrative director shall determine which method of payment is to be utilized.

(e) The provisions of this rule govern the payment of fees, travel and subsistence to grand jurors.

(f) All payments under the provisions of this rule shall be made from the appropriation to the state judiciary.

(g) The administrative director may authorize different

payment schedules when circumstances dictate.

(h) Employees of the State of Alaska will not receive jury fees, but are eligible to receive travel and subsistence allowances.

(Adopted by SCO 412 effective July 1, 1980; amended by SCO 479 effective July 1, 1981; by SCO 801 effective August 1, 1987; and by SCO 1153 effective July 15, 1994)

Rule 15. Jurors—Predetermination of Qualifications—Service of Summons—Selection of Jury Panel—Periods of Jury Service.

(a) **Administration.**

(1) The administrative director of the courts shall be responsible for the management of the jury system.

(2) The administrative director may prescribe policies and procedures for efficient and effective jury management.

(3) Computerization may be utilized for the random selection of jurors and for management of the jury system. The administrative director may authorize random selections other than by computer when circumstances so warrant.

(b) **Master Jury List.**

(1) By November 30 of each year the administrative director will prepare a statewide master list of prospective jurors in Alaska.

(2) The administrative director will divide the statewide master list into local master jury lists for each court location. A court location's local master jury list will include the names of all prospective jurors who live in the community and other areas assigned to that court for jury selection purposes. Communities and other areas will be assigned to court locations for the purposes of jury selection according to the following criteria:

(i) Each court location will be assigned its own community and all non-court locations within a 50 mile radius of that court except as provided in (ii) and (iii) below.

(ii) If a non-court location is within the 50 mile radius of two or more court locations, that non-court location will be assigned to that court in the same senate district. If both court locations are in the same senate district, then the presiding judge will assign that non-court location to the court location deemed most appropriate.

(iii) If the non-court location is not within a 50 mile radius of any court, that non-court location will remain unassigned unless the presiding judge orders the non-court location assigned to a court.

(iv) No community will be assigned to more than one court location for the purpose of petit jury selection.

(3) Clerks and magistrates shall send a periodic listing of duplicate names, names of deceased persons or persons who are permanently excused from jury service to the administrative director. This list shall be used to update the annual master jury list to ensure that these names are not again selected for jury service.

(c) **Selection of Prospective Petit Jurors.**

(1) Prospective petit jurors shall be selected from the area defined in (b)(2) unless the court finds that the selection area defined in section (b)(2):

(i) will not provide a petit jury which is a truly representative cross-section of the appropriate community or,

(ii) would cause unreasonable transportation expenses, in which case the trial court, on its own motion or on the motion of the parties, may designate an area other than that specified in section (b)(2) from which the petit jurors shall be selected.

(2) Selection of prospective petit jurors will be from all locations assigned in (b)(2) unless an alternative assignment is specifically authorized by the presiding judge. The presiding judge will forward this authorization to the administrative director by October 1 of each year so that the area of selection can be changed.

(d) **Qualification of Jurors.**

(1) The administrative director shall be responsible for overseeing the mailing of a qualification questionnaire to prospective jurors to determine if they are qualified to serve. Qualification questionnaires may be served by regular mail.

(2) If a prospective juror's response to the qualification questionnaire indicates that he or she is not qualified for service or, in the opinion of the judge or magistrate, the prospective juror has stated grounds sufficient to be excused or deferred, no summons shall be issued or, if already issued, the prospective juror shall be excused or deferred to a later date.

(e) **Summoning Jurors.**

(1) Summons may be served by regular mail.

(2) The summons shall state the court location, reporting date and reporting time or call-in date and call-in time for jury service.

(3) A prospective juror shall not be paid jury fees or be reimbursed for travel expenses incurred and subsistence if the prospective juror appears at the court house:

(i) in response to a qualification questionnaire rather than a summons;

(ii) because he or she failed to call in as instructed; or

(iii) after having been sent an excusal notice or after having been otherwise notified that he or she was excused.

(f) **Venire List.** The venire list is comprised of all prospective jurors whose responses on a jury questionnaire indicate they meet the minimum statutory qualifications for jury service.

(g) **Jury Panel.**

(1) Under the direction of the court, the clerk shall select a jury panel from the venire list.

(2) The jury panel is that group of prospective jurors who are summoned to report or call-in for a term of jury service.

(3) Persons on the jury panel will be required to be available for actual jury service as specified in section (k) of this rule.

(h) **Trial Panel.** The trial panel is that group of prospective jurors from the jury panel who are sent to a courtroom for possible inclusion on a trial jury.

(i) **Trial Jury.**

(1) A trial jury consists of those prospective jurors selected from the trial panel to hear a trial.

(2) Unless otherwise stipulated by the parties and ordered by the trial judge, a trial jury in superior court shall consist of 12 persons. A trial jury in district court shall consist of 6 persons. An inquest jury and a presumptive death jury shall consist of 6 persons.

(3) When a case is to be tried by jury, the clerk shall randomly select from the names of those on the trial panel a number of names sufficient to comprise a trial jury and alternate jurors, if the court decides alternate jurors are needed.

(4) The prospective trial jurors shall be examined, challenged, and sworn as provided in Civil Rule 47 and Criminal Rule 24.

(j) **Juror Privacy.**

(1) The statewide master jury list, local master jury lists, venire lists, jury panel lists, and qualification questionnaires submitted pursuant to paragraph (d) are for internal court use only.

(2) Trial questionnaires and trial panel lists are confidential. These items, along with the dates of birth of individuals on the trial panel list, will be provided to the parties and counsel of record for use by the parties, their attorneys, and agents of their attorneys only in connection with jury selection in the case for which the questionnaires and lists were prepared.

(3) The parties, their attorneys, and agents of their attorneys shall not disclose or use the trial questionnaires, trial panel lists, or any compiled list of persons selected to serve on a jury except as permitted by this rule.

(4) Log notes and the electronic record of private questioning of prospective jurors are confidential.

(k) **Term of Service.**

(1) Except as otherwise provided by the administrative director, a juror's term of service is based upon the size of the court's local master jury list as defined in section (b) of this rule. The maximum term of service and maximum length of actual service are shown below:

SIZE OF LOCAL MASTER JURY LIST	MAXIMUM LENGTH AVAILABILITY FOR JURY SERVICE (TERM OF SERVICE)	MAXIMUM LENGTH OF ACTUAL ANNUAL COURT ATTENDANCE (SERVICE)
Under 2,000	1 year	30 days/year
2000 to 7000	90 consecutive days per jury year unless interrupted by a deferral	30 days/year
7000 and over	30 consecutive days per jury year unless interrupted by a deferral	30 days/year

(2) "Term of service" begins the date the juror first appears in court or calls the court as ordered on a summons, unless the term of service is deferred at the request of the prospective juror.

(3) "Service" starts the first day the juror is paid for jury service.

(4) If the commencement of a prospective juror's term of service is deferred to a later date at the juror's request, his or her term of service shall commence on the date to which he or she is deferred. If after beginning a term of service a prospective juror requests a deferral, the court may defer the remaining portion of the term of service.

(5) After a person completes his or her term of service, that person shall not be required to serve as a juror within one year after the last day of actual court attendance for which he or she was paid.

(6) A juror who commences sitting in a trial within the term of service shall continue to serve in that matter until discharged by the trial judge.

(*l*) **Definitions.**

(1) Deferral of Jury Service—the postponement of jury service to a later date. This postponement can be no longer than 10 months from the date the initial term of service was to have started. A person may have jury service deferred if he or she shows that jury service at the time when he or she is summoned will cause hardship to that person or others, or that transportation problems make it impossible to serve. Jury service may be deferred only if the person seeking the deferment agrees to a deferred date.

(2) Excused—a person may be excused from service as a juror if it is shown that his or her health, the health or proper care of his or her family, a physical or mental disability, or other conditions exist which would cause a hardship to the individual. Unless the court specifically authorizes a permanent excusal, all excusals from jury service shall be for the current jury year only. However, a person who has

appeared for jury duty may be excused for two years from further jury duty in a jury selection area as defined in paragraph (b) with a population over 50,000.

(3) Jury Panel—that group of prospective jurors who are summoned to report or call-in for a term of jury service.

(4) Jury Summons—a court order directing a prospective juror to report or call-in for jury duty.

(5) Jury Year—the term during which a master jury list is in effect; normally, from November 30 of one year (when the list is compiled) until November 29 of the next year (when a new master list must be prepared).

(6) Local Master Jury List—a randomly ordered listing of names of prospective jurors for a court location who may be sent qualification questionnaires for jury service.

(7) Natural Faculties—normal abilities to reason.

(8) Permanent Excusals—a prospective juror may be permanently excused from all jury service if he or she:

(i) is advanced in age. Those people who are over age 70 and request in writing to be permanently excused shall be.

(ii) has a permanent physical disability. The disability must be verified in writing by a physician.

(iii) has a permanent mental disability. The disability must be verified in writing by a physician.

(9) Qualification List—a list of names from the local master jury list to which qualification questionnaires will be mailed in order to create a venire list.

(10) Qualification Questionnaire—document used to determine whether a prospective juror meets the statutory minimum qualifications for jury service.

(11) Resident—for jury qualification purposes, a person is a resident of the State of Alaska if he or she:

(i) has registered to vote in Alaska,

(ii) has obtained a resident fish and game permit for Alaska, or

(iii) is eligible for the Alaska permanent fund dividend.

(12) Term of Service—begins the date the juror first appears in the court or calls the court as ordered on a summons unless the term of service is deferred at the request of a prospective juror.

(13) Trial Jury—those prospective jurors selected from the trial panel to hear a trial.

(14) Trial Panel—that group of prospective jurors from the jury panel who are sent to the courtroom for possible inclusion on a trial jury.

(15) Trial Questionnaire—document filled out by members of a trial panel that is used during the jury selection process.

(16) Venire List—a list of all prospective jurors whose responses on a qualification questionnaire indicate they meet the minimum statutory qualifications for jury service.

(Adopted by SCO 412 effective July 1, 1980; amended by SCO 531 effective October 1, 1982; by SCO 890 effective July 15, 1988; by SCO 969 effective July 15, 1989; by SCO 1204 effective July 15, 1995; by SCO 1405 effective October 15, 2000; and by SCO 1622 effective October 15, 2006)

Note: Chapter 104 SLA 04 (HB 353) exempts teachers from jury service if they are teaching at a school that is designated as failing to make adequate yearly progress under P.L. 107-110. According to Section 2 of the Act, this has the effect of changing Administrative Rule 15(k) by establishing an additional cause for exemption from jury service.

Annotations

Cases

Where within a radius of fifteen miles of Anchorage approximately 70% of the entire population of the Third Judicial District were concentrated and within that area most, if not all, of the racial, economic, occupational and religious groups of the Third District were fairly represented, limitation of the selection of grand jurors to the area comprised in this radius to avoid incurring the expense provided under Admin. R. 17(b), was not a systematic exclusion of the defendant's class from the grand jury that indicted him and was not a denial of equal protection of the laws. **Crawford v. State,** Op. No. 312, 408 P2d 1002 (Alaska 1965).

Superior court had a rational, factual and legal basis in the Anchorage area to determine that jury was to be made up of persons residing within a fifteen mile radius of the City of Anchorage, where this practice did not result in exclusion of any particular and defined group of society from jury service. **Crawford v. State,** Op. No. 312, 408 P2d 1002 (Alaska 1965).

Technical violations of the statutory selection method constitute substantial failure to comply only when they affect the random nature or objectivity of the selection process. **Calantas v. State,** Op. No. 1914, 599 P2d 147 (Alaska 1979).

In trial in Ketchikan at which defendant was convicted of assault for an incident that occurred in the village of Metlakatla, exclusion of Metlakatla citizens from the jury pool because of the expense and inconvenience of housing them for the duration of the trial did not violate defendant's constitutional right to an impartial jury absent a showing by defendant that Metlakatlans comprise a distinctive group in the community. **Wyatt v. State,** Op. No. 961, 778 P2d 1169 (Alaska App. 1989).

Rule 16. Judicial Holidays—Transaction of Business.

(a) **Judicial Holidays.** Subject to the provisions of AS 22.10.050 and AS 22.15.090, no court shall be open for the transaction of business on any judicial holiday as defined herein unless ordered by the presiding judge for good cause shown.

Judicial holidays are:

(1) Every Sunday;

(2) The first of January, known as New Year's Day;

(3) The third Monday of January, known as Martin Luther King, Jr.'s Birthday;

(4) The third Monday in February, known as President's Day;

(5) The last Monday of March, known as Seward's Day;

(6) The last Monday in May, known as Memorial Day;

(7) The fourth of July, known as Independence Day;

(8) The first Monday in September, known as Labor Day;

(9) The 18th of October, known as Alaska Day;

(10) The 11th of November, known as Veterans Day;

(11) The fourth Thursday in November, known as Thanksgiving Day;

(12) The 25th of December, known as Christmas Day;

(13) Every day designated by public proclamation by the President of the United States or the Governor of the state as a legal holiday.

If any day specified or provided for as a holiday in this rule falls on a day appointed for the holding or sitting of a court, or to which it is adjourned, it shall be deemed appointed for or adjourned to the next day not a judicial holiday.

(b) **Holidays Falling on Sunday or Saturday.** If any holiday designated in Rule 16(a)(2) through (12) falls upon a Sunday, the Monday following is a holiday and if it falls on a Saturday, the Friday preceding is a holiday.

(c) **Special or Limited Holidays.** On any special or limited holiday, all courts shall be open and function in their normal and usual manner. A special or limited holiday is a holiday applying only to a special class or classes of business, or a special class or classes of persons, and not appointed to be generally observed throughout the state by all classes of business and all classes of persons.

(Adopted by SCO 412 effective July 1, 1980; amended by SCO 977 effective January 15, 1990)

Rule 17. Sessions and Offices of the Supreme Court.

(a) **Sessions of the Supreme Court.** Sessions of the supreme court shall be held at such locations and times as may be designated by the chief justice, after consultation with the supreme court.

(b) **Offices.** The principal office of the supreme court shall be at Anchorage, Alaska. The chief justice or an associate justice may maintain an office at a place other than the principal office as designated by order of the court or of the chief justice.

(c) **When Clerk's Office Is Open.** The clerk's office with the clerk or a deputy in attendance shall be open during business hours from 8:00 a.m. until 4:30 p.m. on all days except judicial holidays and Saturdays.

(Adopted by SCO 412 effective July 1, 1980; amended by SCO 443 effective November 13, 1980; and by SCO 1153 effective July 15, 1994)

Rule 17.5. Sessions and Offices of the Court of Appeals.

(a) **Sessions of the Court of Appeals.** Sessions of the court of appeals shall be held at such times as may be designated by the chief judge, after consultation with the court of appeals, and at locations designated by the chief judge after consultation with the court of appeals and the chief justice.

(b) **Office.** The office of the court of appeals shall be at Anchorage, Alaska.

(c) **When Clerk's Office Is Open.** The clerk's office with the clerk or a deputy in attendance shall be open during business hours from 8:00 a.m. until 4:30 p.m. on all days except judicial holidays and Saturdays.

(SCO 443 effective November 13, 1980)

Rule 18. Superior and District Courts—Time and Place of Sitting.

(a) **Superior and District Courts—When Open for Business.** The superior and district courts shall be open for the transaction of business during business hours from 8:00 a.m. until 4:30 p.m. on all days except judicial holidays and Saturdays; provided, however, that the courts may at any time extend these hours as circumstances may require or as may be ordered by the presiding judge. The presiding judge may authorize the closure of an office for up to one hour per week for staff meetings and training under a plan approved by the administrative director. The clerk of court must give advance notice of the closure by posting notices on the court's bulletin board, on the doors of the courthouse, and in the clerk's office.

(b) **Magistrates—Time of Sitting—Office Hours.** Magistrates shall sit in the conduct of trials and hearings as the business of their courts and the status of their calendars require. Offices of full-time magistrates shall be open to the public for the transaction of business during business hours from 8:00 a.m. until 4:30 p.m. on all days except judicial holidays and Saturdays. Offices of part-time magistrates shall be open to the public for the transaction of business as prescribed by the presiding judge.

In addition, magistrates shall be available at all times:

(1) to issue arrest warrants, search warrants, and summonses in criminal cases;

(2) to set bail;

(3) as may be necessary to conduct proceedings required under Criminal Rule 5, District Court Criminal Rule 1, CINA

Rule 5 and Delinquency Rule 5; and

(4) to make emergency appointments of temporary property custodians under AS 22.15.110(a)(3).

Weekend and holiday duty must be equitably shared between magistrates and other judges except at court locations at which committing magistrates have been hired to perform weekend and holiday duty.

(c) **Courts Open During Noon Hour.** All courts with more than two employees will be open for business during the noon hour (12:00 noon to 1:00 p.m.).

(Adopted by SCO 412 effective July 1, 1980; amended by SCO 455 effective March 15, 1981; by SCO 885 effective July 15, 1988; by SCO 1207 effective July 15, 1995; by SCO 1223 effective nunc pro tunc to September 1, 1995; and by SCO 1285 effective January 15, 1998)

Rule 19. Number and Location of District Judges and Magistrates.

(a) **District Court Judges.** The district court in each judicial district shall have the number of judges as set forth below:

First District—2

Second District—0

Third Judicial District—15

Fourth Judicial District—5

The number of district court judges may be changed from time to time by the Supreme Court as circumstances require.

(b) **Magistrates.** Each judicial district shall have no more than the number of magistrates set forth below:

First Judicial District—13

Second Judicial District—18

Third Judicial District—23

Fourth Judicial District—16

The number and location of magistrates may be changed from time to time by the supreme court as circumstances require.

(Adopted by SCO 412 effective July 1, 1980; amended by SCO 594 effective May 4, 1984; by SCO 797 effective date nunc pro tunc September 1, 1986; by SCO 955 effective January 12, 1989; by SCO 1018 effective nunc pro tunc May 17, 1989; by SCO 1144 effective September 9, 1993; by SCO 1225 effective November 15, 1995; by SCO 1393 effective May 9, 2000; by SCO 1516 effective July 1, 2003; by SCO 1551 effective July 1, 2004; and by SCO 1572 effective June 1, 2005)

Cross References

CROSS REFERENCE: AS 22.15.020.

Rule 19.1 Qualifications of Magistrates Who Seek Appointment as District Judges Under AS 22.15.160(a)(2).

A magistrate is qualified for appointment to the office of district judge under AS 22.15.160(a)(2) if he or she is a citizen of the United States and of the state, is at least 21 years of age, has been a resident of the state for at least five years immediately preceding the appointment, has served for at least seven years in the state as a magistrate in the exempt service of the Alaska Court System, and is a graduate of a law school accredited or approved by the Council of Legal Education of the American Bar Association or the Association of American Law Schools.

(Added by SCO 532 effective October 1, 1982)

Rule 19.2. Deputy Magistrates.

(a) **Introduction.** This rule governs the certification and appointment of court system employees as deputy magistrates. A person, other than a court system employee officially classified as judge, justice, magistrate, or committing magistrate, may not perform judicial duties unless that person is appointed master under the Alaska Rules of Court, or is otherwise given judicial duties by statute or court rule.

(b) **Qualifications.** A deputy magistrate must:

(1) be an Alaska Court System employee;

(2) be at least 21 years of age;

(3) be a United States citizen;

(4) be a resident of the State of Alaska for six months immediately preceding the appointment;

(5) have received training from a training judge or training judge's designee, prior to appointment as a deputy magistrate, for each judicial duty which the appointee will be certified to perform.

(c) **Appointment.** The presiding judge may appoint a qualified court system employee as a deputy magistrate. The appointment order must be in writing and specify the duties which the deputy magistrate is authorized to perform. The appointment order must also contain the training judge's certification that the person appointed has received training in each of the judicial duties which the appointee is authorized to perform, and that the appointee is competent to perform each of these duties. Copies of the order must be sent to the appointee, chief justice, personnel director, magistrate services, training judge, area court administrator, and the highest ranking local judicial officer.

(d) **Duties.** A deputy magistrate may be appointed to perform only the following magistrate duties:

(1) emergency Child in Need of Aid and Delinquency proceedings;

(2) acceptance of criminal complaints;

(3) issuance of summonses and arrest warrants;

(4) bail hearings;

(5) felony first appearances;

(6) arraignments;

(7) acceptance of guilty or no contest pleas in misdemeanor cases;

(8) sentencings following pleas accepted by the deputy magistrate;

(9) initial coroner duties, including taking control and custody of property;

(10) notary duties;

(11) issuance of marriage licenses and performance of marriages;

(12) issuance of ex parte and emergency domestic violence protective orders pursuant to AS 18.66.110 and ex parte and emergency stalking protective orders pursuant to AS 18.65.855;

(13) issuance of search warrants; and

(14) fugitive from justice arraignments and acceptance of fugitive complaints.

(e) **Limitations on Deputy Magistrate Duty.**

(1) A deputy magistrate may perform the duties listed in subparagraphs (d)(10) and (11) at any time. A deputy magistrate may not perform other deputy magistrate duties unless all other judicial officers are unavailable as defined by subparagraph (e)(3) or additional weekend or holiday duty is authorized pursuant to subparagraph (e)(2).

(2) The presiding judge may approve weekend or holiday duty by deputy magistrates subject to review by the chief justice.

(3) A judicial officer is unavailable for purposes of subparagraph (e)(1) only if the judicial officer is conducting other judicial duties, is sick, or is on leave. In addition, a judicial officer is unavailable for weekend or holiday duty if the judicial officer is on leave either the day before or after the weekend or holiday. A judicial officer is not unavailable for weekend or holiday duty only because the judicial officer is absent from the court building.

(4) A deputy magistrate who is not a clerk of court may perform magistrate duties only if there is no deputy magistrate at the court location who is a clerk of court or if the deputy magistrate who is a clerk of court is performing other judicial duties or is not at the court building.

(5) The limitations on performance of deputy magistrate duties in (e)(1)–(4) do not apply to a deputy magistrate who is performing deputy magistrate duties while being observed by a training judge.

(f) **Classification and Compensation.**

(1) A clerk of court appointed deputy magistrate will be classified two salary ranges above the classification which would normally be assigned to the position. A clerk of court appointed deputy magistrate is not entitled to upward reclassification if the deputy magistrate duties have previously been considered by the personnel office in the classification of the position.

(2) A deputy magistrate who functions as a magistrate for more than 50 percent of the deputy magistrate's total working hours may request that the position be reviewed for possible reclassification to a magistrate position. All such requests must be submitted through the presiding judge to the personnel officer.

(3) Compensation for a deputy magistrate who is exempt from the Fair Labor Standards Act will be $50.00 for each holiday, Saturday or Sunday of on-call duty. The employee may elect, with the approval of the employee's supervisor, to take two hours of compensatory time instead of the $50.00 compensation.

(4) Deputy magistrates who are not exempt from the Fair Labor Standards Act will be compensated for overtime magistrate work during the regular work week as provided by the Fair Labor Standards Act. Such deputy magistrates will be compensated for holiday, Saturday or Sunday on-call duty in the following manner:

(A) If a non-exempt deputy magistrate is required to perform magistrate duties while on-call during holidays, Saturdays, or Sundays, the deputy magistrate will be compensated either in accordance with the provisions of the Fair Labor Standards Act for those hours worked, or as provided in subparagraph (f)(3) of this rule, whichever is greater.

(B) If a non-exempt deputy magistrate is not required to perform magistrate duties while on-call, the deputy magistrate will be compensated as provided in subparagraph (f)(3) of this rule.

(Adopted by SCO 600 effective September 1, 1984; amended by SCO 885 effective July 15, 1988; by SCO 1258 effective nunc pro tunc to July 1, 1996; and by SCO 1529 effective November 5, 2003)

Rule 20. Magistrate Salaries.

Magistrate salaries shall be determined in accordance with the personnel rules.

(Adopted by SCO 412 effective July 1, 1980; amended by

SCO 1153 effective July 15, 1994; and by SCO 1223 effective nunc pro tunc to September 1, 1995)

Rule 21. Conduct of Proceedings.

(a) **Proceedings on the Record and in Open Court.** So far as practicable, all judicial business involving the trial of causes and conferences with members of the Bar or litigants shall be on the record and transacted in open court.

(b) **Judicial Robes.** All justices of the supreme court, all judges of the court of appeals, all judges of the superior court, all district court judges, and all magistrates, while presiding in a public session of court, shall wear a suitable black judicial robe.

(Adopted by SCO 412 effective July 1, 1980; amended by SCO 443 effective November 13, 1980)

Rule 22. Places for Holding Court in Time of War, Insurrection, Pestilence, or Other Public Danger.

When it appears necessary because of actual or threatened war, insurrection, pestilence, or other public calamity, or because of actual or threatened destruction of, or danger to the building or the occupants of the building appointed for holding court in any judicial district, the presiding judge of the district may by order direct that the court be held or continued at any other place or facility in the judicial district. The order shall be filed with the clerk of the supreme court and a copy provided to the administrative director. The order shall be published as the presiding judge prescribes.

(Adopted by SCO 412 effective July 1, 1980)

Rule 23. Appointment of Retired Justices or Judges Pro Tempore—Compensation—Expenses.

(a) **Appointment Pro Tempore.**

(1) The chief justice, or another justice designated by the chief justice, may by special assignment appoint a retired justice of the supreme court or a retired judge of the court of appeals, the superior court, or the district court to sit pro tempore as a senior justice or judge in any court of this state where such assignment is deemed necessary for the efficient administration of justice.

(2) Pro tempore appointments may be made for one or more cases or for a specified period of time up to two years, except that a pro tempore judge or justice may complete a trial or appeal in progress at the conclusion of the appointment. A trial is deemed to be completed and a trial judge's appointment to a particular case terminates upon expiration of the time for filing an appeal. An appeal is deemed to be completed and an appellate judge's appointment to a particular case terminates upon expiration of the time for filing a petition for rehearing or, if a petition for rehearing is filed, upon entry of the order or opinion that disposes of the petition. Appointments may be renewed.

(b) **Eligibility.** Any judge who has reached mandatory retirement age or who has otherwise voluntarily retired is eligible for pro tempore appointment, with such judge's consent, subject to the provisions of the Judicial Canons, Part II(1)(C). A judge or justice voluntarily retired for incapacity remains ineligible unless or until a licensed physician finds that he or she is able to efficiently perform judicial duties during such period of incapacity. Any judge rejected on retention or removed from office by the supreme court pursuant to an investigation and recommendation of the Judicial Conduct Commission is ineligible for pro tempore appointment until such time as and if such judge is subsequently nominated and reappointed to the bench.

(c) **Judicial Performance Evaluation.** Every two years, the chief justice shall review the performance during the prior two-year period of all retired judges and justices who have served pro tempore. Such review shall be based upon (1) an evaluation of the performance of such justices and judges, to be conducted by the Alaska Judicial Council, which evaluation shall include a survey of the members of the bar in those judicial districts where such justices and judges have served pro tempore during the evaluation period; and (2) formal performance evaluations conducted by the presiding judges under whom such retired justices or judges have served. At the conclusion of such review, the chief justice shall determine the eligibility of such justices and judges to continue to serve pro tempore.

(d) **Compensation.** A retired justice or judge is entitled to receive compensation for judicial service pro tempore at the rate of $225 per day. The annual compensation for pro tempore service may not exceed the difference between the retired justice's or judge's annual retirement pay and the current annual base salary of a justice or judge of the court from which the justice or judge retired. The retired justice or judge is also entitled to receive full medical insurance coverage during the same period. The retired justice or judge is not entitled to personal, annual, or sick leave benefits, and acceptance of an appointment pro tempore acts as a waiver of any claim to such benefits. For an appointment of over 90 consecutive days, such leave may be granted at the discretion of the administrative director upon confirmation by the chief justice.

(e) **Additional Service Credit.** A retired justice or judge who has not accrued the maximum service credit for retirement benefits under AS 22.25.020 is entitled to receive additional service credit for each day of pro tempore service until the maximum is reached.

(f) **Private Arbitration and Mediation.** If a retired judge acts as a private arbitrator or mediator, the judge must comply with the following rules to remain eligible for pro tempore appointment:

(1) The judge shall refrain from soliciting or accepting employment as an arbitrator or mediator from a lawyer or party who is currently appearing in a case assigned to the judge.

(2) The judge shall disqualify himself or herself from sitting as a pro tem judge in a case if the judge has previously served as an arbitrator or mediator in the same matter. This disqualification may be waived under Section 3F of the Code of Judicial Conduct.

(3) The judge shall disqualify himself or herself from sitting as a pro tem judge in a case if the judge is currently serving or scheduled to serve as an arbitrator or mediator for a lawyer or party in the case. This disqualification may be waived under Section 3F of the Code of Judicial Conduct.

(4) If within two years prior to the filing of a case assigned to a pro tem judge the judge has served as an arbitrator or mediator for a lawyer or party in that case, the judge shall disclose that fact on the record and disqualify himself or herself from sitting as a pro tem judge in that case. Disclosure must be made under this paragraph regardless of the amount of compensation that the judge received from the arbitration or mediation. This disqualification may be waived under Section 3F of the Code of Judicial Conduct.

(5) The judge shall refrain from accepting employment as an arbitrator or mediator from a lawyer or party who has appeared in a case assigned to the judge within the last six months.

(Adopted by SCO 412 effective July 1, 1980; amended by SCO 443 effective November 13, 1980; by SCO 597 effective July 19, 1984; by SCO 857 effective July 15, 1988; by SCO 1153 effective July 15, 1994; by SCO 1262 effective February 27, 1997; by SCO 1324 effective July 15, 1998; by SCO 1358 effective July 15, 1999; and by SCO 1629 effective December 31, 2006)

Annotations

Cases

Where judge was appointed judge pro tempore for specific period of time and to particular office, he was acting under color of authority in de jure office; accordingly, even if he failed to meet state residency requirement, he was de facto judge, and had authority to enter findings on remand. **Gates v. City of Tenakee Springs,** Op. No. 4955, 954 P2d 1035 (Alaska 1998).

Rule 24. Assignment of Judicial Officers.

(a) **Assignments Within Judicial Districts.** Assignment of a judicial officer from the court location of the judicial officer's residence to locations within the same judicial district shall be made by the presiding judge of the judicial district or by the presiding judge's designee. In making such assignments, due regard shall be had of the status of accumulated calendars of the courts in the district to the end that judicial officers are assigned to such courts as needed in order to keep the calendars current.

(b) **Temporary Assignments in Other Judicial Districts.**

(1) When the volume of judicial business in the superior or district court in any judicial district warrants the temporary assignment thereto of one or more judicial officers from another judicial district, the presiding judge in the judicial district requiring such temporary assignment shall so advise the administrative director, giving details as to the reasons for the assignment, the length of time and the location of the temporary assignment.

(2) The administrative director shall thereupon determine the availability of judicial officers in other judicial districts and make such assignments as may be necessary.

(c) **Assignment of Appellate Judicial Officers.**

(1) The chief justice may assign an individual justice of the supreme court or a judge of the court of appeals, with the consent of the justice or judge, to serve pro tempore as a judge of the superior court or a district court in any judicial district of the state under the same circumstances as the administrative director may assign a judge under paragraph (b) of this rule.

(2) *Death or Incapacity.*

(A) If the chief justice dies, or is incapacitated, the most senior member of the supreme court becomes acting chief justice.

(B) If all members of the supreme court die or are incapacitated, the chief judge of the court of appeals becomes the acting chief justice and may appoint up to four justices to serve pro tempore to create a functioning supreme court of not more than five members.

(C) If the chief judge of the court of appeals is unable to act as chief justice within the meaning of subpart (B), the next most senior member of the court of appeals becomes the chief justice for purposes of that subpart. If no member of the court of appeals is able to act as chief justice, the most senior presiding judge who is also a superior court judge becomes the acting chief justice for the purposes of subpart (B).

(d) **Assignments of Active Judges for Pro Tempore Appellate Service.** The chief justice, or another justice whom the chief justice designates, may assign an individual justice of the supreme court or an individual judge of the superior or district court to serve pro tempore as a judge of the court of appeals. The chief justice, or another justice whom the chief justice designates, may assign an individual judge of the court of appeals, the superior court or the district court to serve pro tempore as a justice of the supreme court.

(e) **Assignments of Active Judges for Other Pro Tempore Service.** The chief justice, another justice whom the chief justice designates, or the presiding judge upon entry of an order of delegation by the chief justice, may assign an individual judge of the district court to serve pro tempore as a judge of the superior court. When a superior court judge hears a matter that is pending in the district court, that judge sits as a district court judge, and a specific assignment to the district court is not required.

(f) **Scope and Duration of Assignment.**

(1) A temporary assignment of an individual justice or judge under this rule shall be for specific cases or types of

cases or proceedings; for general caseloads in a specific geographic location as necessary to ensure completion of a travel calendar; and for general caseloads as necessary to ensure continued judicial service during either the extended absence of a sitting judge or a judicial vacancy.

(2) A temporary assignment may not exceed 180 days in duration absent specific authorization by the chief justice; however a judge who is assigned pro tem on a specific case may continue to preside in that case beyond the expiration of the temporary assignment order.

(3) A single temporary assignment of a judicial officer to another judicial district may not exceed 90 days, unless the judicial officer consents to the additional assignment. Assignments in excess of 90 days or any assignment made without the consent of the assigned judicial officer may be made only by special order of the chief justice.

(g) **Recommendations.** The administrative director and the presiding judge in each judicial district shall, after consideration of the state of the superior and district court dockets from time to time, submit joint recommendations to the supreme court as to methods of improving the administration of justice in such courts.

(h) **Definitions.** In this rule, "judicial officer" means a superior court judge, district court judge, or magistrate.

(Adopted by SCO 412 effective July 1, 1980; amended by SCO 443 effective November 13, 1980; by SCO 891 effective July 15, 1988; by SCO 1153 effective July 15, 1994; by SCO 1231 effective April 12, 1996; by SCO 1463 effective October 15, 2002; and by SCO 1499 effective April 15, 2003)

Annotations

Cases

In most cases a record should be made of conferences in chambers. **State v. Abraham,** Op. No. 1438, 566 P2d 267 (Alaska 1977).

Presiding superior court judge could not make a permanent intra district transfer of a district judge. **Hornaday v. Rowland,** Op. No. 2761, 674 P2d 1333 (Alaska 1983).

The temporary assignment of a judge may exceed 90 days if the assigned judge consents or the chief justice so orders. **Kochutin v. State,** Op. No. 3194, 739 P2d 170 (Alaska 1987).

Rule 25. Traveling Expenses of Judicial Officers and Employees.

Each supreme court justice, court of appeals judge, superior court judge, district court judge and magistrate, and each employee of the court system is entitled to receive travel expenses and per diem as provided by law for state employees; provided, that the travel has been approved by the appropriate administrative supervisor of the justice, judge, magistrate or employee.

(Adopted by SCO 412 effective July 1, 1980; amended by SCO 443 effective November 13, 1980; and by SCO 1223 effective nunc pro tunc to September 1, 1995)

Rule 26. Power of Court to Provide Proper Facilities for Transaction of Business in Court—Payment of Expenses.

If the state does not provide proper rooms in which to hold the court and for the accommodations of the officers of the court, together with attendants, furniture, fuel, lights, and stationery, suitable and sufficient for the transaction of business, the chief justice may direct the administrative director of courts to provide them. The expenses thereof, certified by the chief justice to be correct, shall be paid out of the state treasury.

(Adopted by SCO 412 effective July 1, 1980)

Rule 26.1. Court Facilities.

Notice to Executive and Legislative Branch Agencies. The supreme court will provide a one-year notice prior to requiring an executive or legislative branch agency to vacate a court facility.

(Added by SCO 596, effective June 19, 1984)

Rule 26.2. Court Security.

(a) No person may possess a weapon on the premises of any court facility, or in the portion of any other building occupied by the court system, unless the weapon is to be used as evidence in a court proceeding. The term weapon includes firearms, knives, and chemical agents such as mace and pepper spray. This rule does not apply to:

(1) a peace officer;

(2) a private uniformed security guard employed by a financial institution or private security service who is transporting money or other valuables;

(3) a private security guard under contract with the court system to provide security services within a court facility who possesses a weapon authorized under the contract;

(4) a judicial officer; or

(5) a person who has written authorization from the administrative director to possess a weapon on court premises. This authorization will be given only upon a showing of good cause and only for a specified period of time.

(b) The exemptions listed in (a)(1)-(3) apply only to persons acting within the scope and authority of their employment. A peace officer or private security guard who is participating in or attending a court proceeding outside the scope of his or her employment, whether as a party, witness, victim, or other interested person, is not permitted to bring a weapon onto court premises unless authorized to do so under (a)(5).

(c) A judicial officer must notify the administrative director prior to bringing a weapon into a court facility.

(d) Weapons to be used as evidence in court proceedings must be marked and prepared as directed by the administrative director by administrative bulletin. Each presiding judge may prescribe procedures for courts within that judge's district requiring prior notification to designated court personnel before weapons to be used as evidence may be brought onto court premises.

(Adopted by SCO 1321 effective April 14, 1998 and amended by SCO 1606 effective October 15, 2006)

Cross References

CROSS REFERENCE: See Administrative Bulletin No. 9, section IV(C), on exhibit procedure.

Rule 26.5. Chief Judge of the Court of Appeals.

(a) The chief justice shall designate one judge of the court of appeals to be the chief judge of that court. A judge designated chief judge shall hold office as such for a term of two years, or until he or she ceases to be a judge of the court of appeals, whichever is shorter. A chief judge shall be eligible to serve successive terms in that office.

(b) The chief judge, in addition to his or her regular judicial duties, shall perform such other duties as the chief justice and the court of appeals may direct.

(c) If the chief judge is unable to perform his or her duties, the judge of the court who has served as such for the longest time, among those who are available, shall be acting chief judge unless the chief justice orders otherwise.

(Adopted by SCO 446 effective September 1, 1980, nunc pro tunc)

Rule 27. Presiding Judge.

(a) The chief justice shall designate one judge from each judicial district to be presiding judge of that district. A judge designated as presiding judge shall hold office as such for a term of one year and shall be eligible to serve successive terms thereafter.

(b) In addition to regular judicial duties a presiding judge shall, within his or her judicial district:

(1) Supervise the assignment of cases pending to the judges;

(2) Supervise the administrative actions of judges and court personnel;

(3) Expedite and keep current the business of the courts;

(4) Review and recommend budgets; and

(5) Review the operations of all trial courts to assure adherence to statewide court objectives and policies.

(c) A presiding judge may:

(1) Assign judges and magistrates to locations within their district of residence as necessary to maintain balanced workloads or to expedite the business of those courts;

(2) Perform any other duties and exercise any other powers as may be provided by law or by these rules.

(Adopted by SCO 412 effective July 1, 1980; amended by SCO 885 effective July 15, 1988; and by SCO 1153 effective July 15, 1994)

Annotations

Cases

Presiding superior court judge could not make a permanent intra district transfer of a district judge. **Hornaday v. Rowland,** Op. No. 2761, 674 P2d 1333 (Alaska 1983).

Rule 28. Judicial Vacations and Judicial Leave.

(a) **Vacation Leave.** Each supreme court justice, court of appeals judge, and superior court judge shall be entitled to an annual vacation of not more than 30 working days. It shall be taken at such time or times as may be prescribed by the chief justice of the supreme court, the chief judge of the court of appeals, or the presiding judge of the appropriate judicial district.

(1) *Accrual of Leave.* Vacation time not taken in any calendar year may be accumulated. However, subject to the exception in paragraph (a)(2) of this rule, no more than 15 working days' vacation time may be accumulated in any one year, and no judge may carry over more than 30 working days' unused vacation time in the aggregate. Annual vacation time accrues as of January 1st of each year except for the year during which a justice or judge is appointed or retires. During the year of appointment, resignation, or retirement, annual vacation leave accrues at the rate of 2.5 days per month of service. Annual vacation time accrued but not taken at the time of resignation, retirement, or death is forfeited.

(2) *Extraordinary Hardship Exception.* Subject to the written approval of the administrative director, a justice or judge may accumulate up to 30 working days' vacation time in any one year, and may carry over up to 60 working days' unused vacation time in the aggregate, if the justice or judge (A) establishes a case of extraordinary hardship that prevented the justice or judge from taking at least 15 annual vacation days in a particular year, and (B) presents a plan for using the accumulated leave during the upcoming year to the administrative director. The administrative director may approve a case of extraordinary hardship for a particular justice or judge no more often then once every three years.

(b) **Sick Leave.** Each supreme court justice, court of appeals judge, and superior court judge shall be entitled to sick leave with respect to any period of illness necessitating absence from his or her judicial duties, which sick leave shall not be charged against his or her vacation time. Maternity leave is counted as sick leave but is limited to 9 weeks absent extenuating medical necessity. Paternity leave is available as sick leave only to the extent medical disability of mother or child requires presence of father.

(c) **Leave Without Pay.** Supreme court justices, court of appeals judges, and judges from the superior and district courts may be granted leave without pay to the same extent and upon the same terms as other court system employees. Up to 5 working days in any calendar year may be granted at the discretion of the chief justice, chief judge, or presiding judge of the appropriate court. Leave without pay in excess of 5 days must be approved by the administrative director upon recommendation of the supervising judge or justice.

(d) **District Judges and Magistrates.** Each district court judge and magistrate shall be entitled to personal leave in accordance with and limited by the provisions of AS 39.20.200-39.20.330 and the personnel rules. Such leave shall be taken at the time or times prescribed by the presiding judge of the judicial district.

(e) **Discretion of Chief Justice, Chief Judge or Presiding Judge.** In determining whether a justice or judge shall take a vacation, and the length thereof, the chief justice of the supreme court, the chief judge of the court of appeals, or the presiding judge exercising authority under this rule shall be mindful of the necessity of retention of sufficient judicial manpower in the court or courts under his or her supervision to permit at all times the prompt and effective disposition of the business of such court or courts. Requests for judicial vacations and judicial leave of one week or more must be submitted for approval at least four months in advance.

(f) **Administrative Leave.** The chief justice of the supreme court may assign one or more justices, judges, or magistrates to attend conferences, seminars, or schools to further legal education or professional qualifications. Such assignment shall be made in consultation with the justice, judge, or magistrate concerned and with the chief judge of the court of appeals for judges of that court or with the presiding judge of the appropriate judicial district for superior or district court judges and magistrates. Travel expenses and per diem may be provided. Administrative leave authorized for such purpose shall not be counted as vacation leave. Nothing in this rule shall prevent a justice, judge, or magistrate not so assigned from attending conferences, seminars, or schools for this purpose at his or her own expense during his or her annual vacation. In addition, a justice, judge or magistrate not so assigned during a calendar year may receive administrative leave during that year not to exceed five working days to attend conferences, seminars or schools when authorized by the administrative director. The administrative director may authorize such administrative leave in excess of five working days upon a delegation of authority from the chief justice. Administrative leave may not be accrued.

(g) **Leave of Absence.**

(1) As used in this section, unless the context requires otherwise, "judge" means any justice of the supreme court, or judge of the court of appeals, the superior court or district court.

(2) A judge who wishes to take a leave of absence shall submit a written application to the supreme court, which shall include a plan outlining the activities he or she will pursue.

(3) In authorizing leaves of absence, the supreme court shall consider whether the activities outlined in the judge's plan are related to the administration of justice. Appropriate activities include formal educational programs for professional self-improvement and teaching at educational institutions. The supreme court shall also consider the benefit the Alaska Court System will derive from the leave of absence and the length of time the judge has served. A leave of absence may be granted only if the supreme court is satisfied that the administration of justice in Alaska will not be adversely affected by granting the leave.

(4) Upon approval of the judge's application, the supreme court shall issue an order granting leave of absence without salary for a period of not more than one year. The order shall state the maximum period of time for which the leave is granted.

(5) Application for a leave of absence is considered a waiver of salary by the applicant for the period of time the judge is absent under the leave granted by the court.

(6) Annual vacation leave or personal leave shall not accrue during a leave of absence.

(7) A leave of absence is an interruption in service for retirement and supplemental benefits purposes. No payment into the retirement or supplemental benefits funds shall be made during such leave of absence, and retirement and supplemental benefits shall not accrue.

(8) If a judge chooses to continue to participate in the State of Alaska group health care and basic life insurance plans during an approved leave of absence, the Alaska Court System will continue to pay the same portion of the costs of the following benefits for the judge and his or her dependents as the Alaska Court System would pay if the judge were not on leave of absence: comprehensive medical, dental, vision and optical, audio, basic life insurance, and accidental death and dismemberment insurance.

(9) A leave of absence does not affect the date at which a judge is subject to approval or rejection in a retention election.

(10) At the termination of the leave of absence, unless he or she sooner dies or resigns, a judge shall resume the duties of his or her office and send written notice of the resumption to the supreme court. The resumption and sending notice thereof constitutes a termination of the leave whether or not the maximum period of time granted has expired.

(Adopted by SCO 412 effective July 1, 1980; amended by SCO 443 effective November 13, 1980; by SCO 453 effective November 13, 1980 nunc pro tunc; by SCO 555 effective April 4, 1983; by SCO 625 effective June 15, 1985; by SCO 698 effective April 24, 1986; by SCO 700 effective June 28, 1986; by SCO 1534 effective October 15, 2005; by SCO 1616 effective October 15, 2006; and by SCO 1642 effective October 15, 2007)

Rule 29. Trial Court Clerks—Appointment and Duties.

(a) **Appointment.** Clerks of court and deputy clerks of court for the superior and district courts shall be employed and appointed in accordance with the personnel rules.

(b) **Powers and Duties.** A clerk or deputy clerk of court shall perform such duties as are or may be required by the presiding judge, by the rules of the supreme court, and by law. A clerk or deputy clerk of court shall issue all process and notices required to be issued except as otherwise provided by rule or statute and may:

(1) Administer oaths;

(2) Take and certify proofs or acknowledgements of documents, affidavits, or depositions; and

(3) Exercise other powers as may be permitted by law or by the rules of the supreme court.

(Adopted by SCO 412 effective July 1, 1980)

Annotations

Cases

Supreme Court Order No. 2, 18, 20, 25, 45 (Orders Appointing Clerks)

Rule 30. Powers and Duties of Magistrates in Cases Beyond Their Jurisdiction.

(a) A magistrate may accept for filing a civil or criminal case beyond a magistrate's jurisdiction but within the jurisdiction of a district court judge. Such cases will be tried by a superior or district court judge on periodic visits to the area.

(b) A magistrate shall immediately notify the presiding judge in writing as soon as any case beyond magistrate jurisdiction becomes at issue. Such notification shall contain a brief description of the case, whether jury or non-jury, and an estimate of the length of time required for trial.

(c) If in the course of any preliminary proceedings connected with a case, or during the trial, or after judgment, a magistrate determines that he or she is for any reason unqualified to proceed further, he or she shall, without prejudicing the rights of the parties, postpone the proceedings and proceed under (a) and (b) of this rule as if the case were one beyond his or her jurisdiction.

(Adopted by SCO 412 effective July 1, 1980)

Annotations

Cases

Where state had filed a criminal complaint with a deputy magistrate and had thus established venue, district magistrate of the judicial district violated the requirements for orderly procedure under Administrative Rule 40(c) and clearly abused discretion by taking it upon himself to determine the defendant's motion to withdraw a plea of guilty filed with the deputy magistrate. **Leege v. Strand,** Op. No. 157, 384 P2d 665 (Alaska 1963).

Rule 31. Additional Duties of Judicial Officers and Employees.

(a) Judicial officers and employees shall, without additional compensation, perform all functions and render all services for executive departments and agencies of the state, when required by law or prescribed by the administrative director.

(b) A judge or magistrate may, with the approval of the presiding judge of the district and the chief justice, serve as a part-time United States Magistrate, when so designated by a United States District Judge for District of Alaska. A judge or magistrate may retain any compensation paid to him or her by the United States for such services and shall submit to the administrative director such reports concerning this additional activity as may be required by the administrative director. When acting in the capacity of a United States Magistrate, the judge or magistrate shall be governed in all respects by the United States law and instructions from federal officials or agencies.

(c) Where judicial officers and employees are employed collaterally as provided in this rule, they shall be held accountable by their superiors in the state judicial system for the efficient performance of such collateral duties.

(d) Upon approval of the administrative director, a magistrate may accept appointment as a passport agent by the United States Department of State. The execution fee collected by a magistrate or other court employee when executing a passport application must be deposited in the court revenue account.

(Adopted by SCO 412 effective July 1, 1980; amended by SCO 422 effective July 1, 1980; by SCO 566 effective May 3, 1983; and by SCO 1153 effective July 15, 1994)

Rule 33. Magistrate Training Judges.

The chief justice shall appoint one or more judges in each judicial district to be a training judge in that district. The training judges shall keep themselves and the presiding judge of their districts regularly informed as to the status of the calendars in the magistrate locations in the district assigned to them and shall visit these magistrate locations in the district as often as required by the presiding judge or the chief justice for the purpose of providing such training and assistance to the magistrates as may be necessary. The training judge shall make such examinations, inspections and reports on the functions performed by the magistrates as may be required by the presiding judge or the administrative director.

(Adopted by SCO 412 effective July 1, 1980; amended by SCO 1153 effective July 15, 1994)

Rule 34. Bonding of All Justices, Judges, Magistrates and Judicial Employees.

The administrative director shall insure that the blanket position bond covering all state employees also covers all justices, judges, magistrates and all employees of the state judicial system. Such bond shall protect the state as to the honesty and faithful performance of duty of all court system positions covered and shall extend coverage to protect the state from loss by reason of the illegal act of any person not an employee of the state judicial system.

(Adopted by SCO 412 effective July 1, 1980)

Rule 35. Electronic Recording Equipment—Official Court Record —Responsibility for Record.

(a) Electronic recording equipment will be installed in all courts for the purpose of recording all official court hearings. Such electronic recordings will constitute the official court record. It will be the responsibility of each judicial officer to require that the electronic recording equipment in court be operated only by a certified operator, or by an individual under the direct supervision of a certified operator during training, in such manner and under such conditions as to insure the production of a clear and completely understandable record of all proceedings.*

(b) In this rule, the term "certified operator" means a person who has successfully completed a training course in the operation of electronic recording equipment in accordance with standard procedures established by the administrative director of courts.

(c) Before commencing any proceedings required to be recorded, the judicial officer shall be satisfied that the electronic recording equipment is functioning properly. During all proceedings the certified operator shall monitor the electronic recording equipment in accordance with standards established by the administrative director of courts and immediately notify the judicial officer when it is uncertain that the record is clear and completely understandable. Where extraneous noises, interference, poor enunciation or other factors create doubt that the electronic record is clear and completely understandable, it will be the responsibility of the judicial officer to cause the doubtful proceeding to be repeated.

(d) The electronic equipment operator shall be responsible for maintaining detailed, accurate and thoroughly legible log notes which correlate the tape position with described courtroom events. The administrative director of courts shall establish standard procedures for the form, preparation and storage of log notes.

(e) The administrative director of courts shall establish policies, procedures and standards to assure the complete and accurate duplication of the electronic record and shall provide for a uniform safe method of permanent preservation of those original electronic records and log notes which are required to be preserved by the records retention schedule adopted under Administrative Rule 37.

(f) The administrative director may authorize the use of video recording equipment to record any trial where the recordation of such proceedings is feasible. Such video recordings must be accomplished in accordance with procedures established by the administrative director of courts. The video record in conjunction with the electronic audio recording will constitute the official court record.

(Adopted by SCO 412 effective July 1, 1980; amended by SCO 554 effective April 4, 1983; by SCO 587 effective June 1, 1984; and by SCO 601 effective June 1, 1984)

Cross References

CROSS REFERENCE: Administrative Bulletins 19 (Playback of Trial Testimony); 20 (Confidential Tapes); 21 (Tape Numbering Policy); 22 (Log Notes); 23 (Tape Security)

***Editor's Note:** Supreme Court Order 601 effective nunc pro tunc June 1, 1984, provides that those portions of Administrative Rule 35 which require operation of electronic recording equipment only by a certified operator as defined in paragraph (b) of the rule are suspended until further order of the court. All other portions of the rule, including the responsibility of the judicial officer to require electronic recording equipment operation in such manner and under such conditions as to insure the production of a clear and completely understandable record of all proceedings, remain in effect.

Annotations

Cases

Failure to keep record in an adoption case was a procedural matter which did not render the judgment void. **Holt v. Powell,** Op. No. 379, 420 P2d 468 (Alaska 1966).

Unless disproved by extrinsic evidence or by the record itself, jurisdiction over the cause and the parties of a court of general jurisdiction is presumed if a judgment appears on its face to be a record of a court of general jurisdiction. **Holt v. Powell,** Op. No. 379, 420 P2d 468 (Alaska 1966).

Written log notes suffice as a record of the search warrant hearing in the absence of an electronic record due to equipment failure. **Nelson v. State,** Op. No. 2350, 628 P2d 884 (Alaska 1981).

Rule 36. Transcripts—Fees—Preparation.

(a) The administrative director shall prescribe standards and procedures for the preparation of transcripts for appeal or other official purposes. All transcripts filed with the Alaska Court System shall be prepared according to these standards and procedures. Each transcript prepared under this rule must be certified and shall be certified only by the person who prepared it.

(b) When a transcript is to be prepared by a person other than a court employee, the court shall provide that person with a copy of the electronic recording of the proceedings to be transcribed, a copy of the log notes, and other information necessary for preparation of the transcript. No fee shall be collected by the court from the transcriber or the appellant for providing this material.

(c) A person other than a court employee who prepares a transcript shall be solely responsible under this rule for collection of the transcript fees.

(Adopted by SCO 412 effective July 1, 1980; amended by SCO 1150 effective October 28, 1993)

Cross References

CROSS REFERENCE: Administrative Bulletin 31 (Transcriber

Standards and Transcript Form) and Manual of Transcript Preparation (TF-410).

Rule 37. Records Retention.

(a) The administrative director may adopt a schedule for the retention, destruction, and microphotographic reproduction of any records, papers, or documents maintained by the Alaska Court System.

(b) Each presiding judge or area court administrator shall, upon approval by the administrative director, destroy or provide for the destruction of all pleadings, papers, instruments, depositions, and transcripts filed in any action or proceeding in the superior or district court if all of the following conditions exist:

(1) The action or proceeding is no longer pending or on appeal in any court and all appeal periods have elapsed;

(2) The presiding judge or area court administrator has certified that the destruction of the records is permitted by the Records Retention Schedule;

(3) There is maintained for the use of the public a microphotographic film print or copy of each document required by the Records Retention Schedule to be permanently retained together with a mechanical device by which such film may be conveniently examined;

(4) At least one original negative of each microphotographic film is stored in such a manner and place as will reasonably assure its preservation indefinitely against loss, theft, defacement, or destruction;

(5) At the time of the taking of the microphotographic reproduction, the person under whose supervision the same was taken has attached to or incorporated in the microphotographic reproduction a certification that the copy is a correct copy of the original or of a specified part hereof, as the case may be, the date or dates on which it was taken and the fact that it was taken under that person's direction; and

(6) The records have been reviewed under (d) of this rule and have been determined to have no historical or archival value.

(c) The administrative director shall prescribe the microphotographic processes and procedures to be used under (b) of this rule and the methods of destruction of records described in (b)(1) through (6) of this rule.

(d) On or before January 15th of each year each judicial officer shall, regarding the cases that were assigned to that judicial officer and closed during the preceding calendar year, provide the administrative director with a list identifying and designating any original case documents or records contained in those cases which have present or potential historical or archival value. The administrative director shall provide for the microphotographing and safekeeping of all original case documents and records so identified.

(e) A photographic reproduction of any of the records described in this rule, the negative or film of which has been certified by the person in charge of such reproduction as a correct copy of the original, shall be received in evidence in all courts in like manner as the original.

(Adopted by SCO 412 effective July 1, 1980; amended by SCO 586 effective April 4, 1984)

Cross References

CROSS REFERENCE: Administrative Bulletins 25 (Records Retention Schedule); 46 (Micrographics Quality Control Standards)

Rule 37.5. Access to Court Records.

(a) **Scope and Purposes.**

(1) Public access to court records is governed by Administrative Rules 37.5 through 37.8. These rules are adopted pursuant to the inherent authority of the Alaska Supreme Court and provide for access in a manner that:

(A) maximizes accessibility to court records;

(B) supports the role of the judiciary;

(C) promotes government accountability;

(D) contributes to public safety;

(E) minimizes risk of injury to individuals;

(F) protects individual privacy rights and interests;

(G) protects proprietary business information;

(H) minimizes reluctance to use the courts to resolve disputes;

(I) makes most effective use of court personnel;

(J) provides excellent customer service; and

(K) does not unduly burden the ongoing business of the judiciary.

(2) These rules apply to all court records; however, court personnel need not redact or restrict information that otherwise was public in case records and administrative records created before October 15, 2006.

(b) **Who Has Access to Court Records.**

(1) Every member of the public will have the same access to court records under these rules, except as provided in Administrative Rule 37.8(b)(4) and 37.8(c)(2).

(2) The following persons are not members of the public and may have greater access in accordance with their functions within the judicial system:

(A) court personnel for case processing purposes only;

(B) people or entities, private or governmental, who assist the court in providing court services;

(C) public agencies whose access to court records is defined by another statute, rule, order, or policy; and

(D) the parties to a case or their lawyers regarding access to records in their case.

(c) **Definitions.** For purposes of these rules:

(1) "Court record" means both case records and administrative records, but does not include records that may be in the court's possession that do not relate to the conduct of the court's business.

(2) "Case record" means any document, information, data, or other item created, collected, received, or maintained by the court system in connection with a particular case.

(3) "Administrative record" means any document, information, data, or other item created, collected, received, or maintained by the court system pertaining to the administration of the judicial branch of government and not associated with any particular case.

(4) "Confidential" means access to the record is restricted to:

(A) the parties to the case;

(B) counsel of record;

(C) individuals with a written order from the court authorizing access; and

(D) court personnel for case processing purposes only.

(5) "Sealed" means access to the record is restricted to the judge and persons authorized by written order of the court.

(6) "Remote access" means the ability of a person to inspect and copy information in a court record in electronic form through an electronic means.

(7) "In electronic form" means any information in a court record in a form that is readable through an electronic device.

(d) **General Access Rule.**

(1) Court records are accessible to the public, except as provided in paragraph (e) below.

(2) This rule applies to all court records, regardless of the manner of creation, method of collection, form of storage, or the form in which the record is maintained.

(1) If a court record, or portion thereof, is excluded from public access, there must be a publicly accessible indication of the fact of exclusion but not the content of the exclusion. This subparagraph does not apply to case records or administrative records that are confidential pursuant to law.

(e) **Court Records Excluded from Public Access.**

(1) *Case Records.* The following case records and case-related documents are not accessible to the public:

(A) memoranda, notes, or preliminary drafts prepared by or under the direction of any judicial officer of the Alaska Court System that relate to the adjudication, resolution, or disposition of any past, present, or future case, controversy, or legal issue;

(B) legal research and analysis prepared or circulated by judges or law clerks regardless of whether it relates to a particular case and written discussions relating to procedural, administrative, or legal issues that are or may be before the court; and

(C) documents, information, data, or other items sealed or confidential pursuant to statute, court rule, case law, or court order.

(2) *Administrative Records.* The following administrative records are not accessible to the public:

(A) personal information, performance evaluations, and disciplinary matters relating to any past or present employee of the Alaska Court System or any other person who has applied for employment with the Alaska Court System, and personnel records that are confidential under Alaska Court System Personnel Rules C1.07 and PX1.08;

(B) the work product of any attorney or law clerk employed by or representing the Alaska Court System if the work product is produced in the regular course of business or representation of the Alaska Court System;

(C) individual direct work access telephone numbers and email addresses of judges and law clerks;

(D) documents or information that could compromise the safety of judges, court staff, jurors, or the public, or jeopardize the integrity of the court's facilities or the court's information technology or recordkeeping systems;

(E) records or information collected and notes, drafts, and work product generated during the process of developing policy relating to the court's administration of justice and its operations;

(F) email messages that are created primarily for the informal communication of information and that do not set policy, establish guidelines or procedures, memorialize transactions, or establish receipts; and

(G) records that are confidential, privileged, or otherwise protected by law, rule, or order from disclosure.

(f) **Obtaining Access to Public Court Records.** Court records that are accessible to the public shall be open to inspection at all times during the regular office hours of the courts. The administrative director shall establish written guidelines to insure that all members of the public upon request will be given reasonable access and opportunity to inspect such public records and to insure the preservation and safekeeping of such public records for such period of time as they may be kept by the Alaska Court System.

(Adopted by SCO 503 effective February 1, 1982; amended by SCO 943 effective January 15, 1989; by SCO 1016 effective January 15, 1990; rescinded and readopted by SCO 1622 effective October 15, 2006)

Cross References

CROSS REFERENCE: Administrative Bulletin 12 (Guidelines for Inspecting and Obtaining Copies of Public Records)

Rule 37.6. Prohibiting Access to Public Case Records.

(a) **Limiting Access.** Notwithstanding any other rule to the contrary, the court may, by order, limit access to public information in an individual case record by sealing or making confidential the case file, individual documents in the case file, log notes, the audio recording of proceedings in the case, the transcript of proceedings, or portions thereof. A request to limit access may be made by any person affected by the release of the information or on the court's own motion.

(b) **Standard.** The court may limit public access as described above if the court finds that the public interest in disclosure is outweighed by a legitimate interest in confidentiality, including but not limited to

(1) risk of injury to individuals;

(2) individual privacy rights and interests;

(3) proprietary business information;

(4) the deliberative process; or

(5) public safety.

(c) **Least Restrictive Alternative.** In limiting public access the court must use the least restrictive means that will achieve the purposes of these public access rules and the reasonable needs as set out as the basis for the request, without unduly burdening the court.

(d) **Procedure.** Any request to limit access must be made in writing to the court and served on all parties to the case unless otherwise ordered. A request to limit access, the response to such a request, and the order ruling on such a request must be written in a manner that does not disclose non-public information, are public records, and shall not themselves be sealed or made confidential.

(Adopted by SCO 1622 effective October 15, 2006)

Note: Administrative Rule 40 requires the clerk of court to list a case on the public case index even though the case file has been sealed or made confidential under this rule. Only the presiding judge of the judicial district has the power to remove a party's name from the public case index, and this action may be taken only in very limited circumstances. See Administrative Rule 40(b) and (c).

The terms "confidential" and "sealed" are defined in Administrative Rule 37.5(c).

Rule 37.7. Obtaining Access to Non-Public Court Records.

(a) **Allowing Access to Non-Public Records.** The court may, by order, allow access to non-public information in a case or administrative record if the court finds that the requestor's interest in disclosure outweighs the potential harm to the person or interests being protected, including but not limited to:

(1) risk of injury to individuals;

(2) individual privacy rights and interests;

(3) proprietary business information;

(4) the deliberative process; or

(5) public safety.

Non-public information includes information designated as confidential or sealed by statute or court rule and public information to which access has been limited under Administrative Rule 37.6. A request to allow access may be made by any person or on the court's own motion as provided in paragraph (b).

(b) **Procedure.** Any request to allow access must be made in writing to the court and served on all parties to the case unless otherwise ordered. The court shall also require service on other individuals or entities that could be affected by disclosure of the information. A request to allow access, the response to such a request, and the order ruling on such a request must be written in a manner that does not disclose non-public information, are public records, and shall not themselves be sealed or made confidential.

(Adopted by SCO 1622 effective October 15, 2006)

Note: This rule does not apply to bulk or compiled data. Access to bulk and compiled data is governed by Administrative Rule 37.8(b)-(d).

Rule 37.8. Electronic Case Information.

(a) **Availability.** The following case-related information maintained in the court system's electronic case management systems will not be published on the court system's website or otherwise made available to the public in electronic form:

(1) addresses, phone numbers, and other contact information for parties and witnesses;

(2) names, addresses, phone numbers, and other contact information for victims in criminal cases;

(3) social security numbers;

(4) driver and vehicle license numbers;

(5) account numbers of specific assets, liabilities, accounts, credit cards, and PINs (Personal Identification Numbers);

(6) names of minor children in domestic relations cases, including paternity actions, domestic violence cases, emancipation cases, and minor settlements under Civil Rule 90.3;

(7) juror information;

(8) party names protected under Administrative Rule 40(b) and (c); and

(9) information that is confidential or sealed in its written form.

(b) **Bulk Distribution of Electronic Case Information.**

(1) Bulk distribution is defined as the distribution of all or a significant subset of the case information in the court system's electronic case management systems, as is, and without modification or compilation.

(2) Bulk distribution of case information is permitted, unless the information is not publicly available in electronic form under subsection (a) of this rule.

(3) Bulk distribution of imaged case records is not allowed, unless the records are already remotely accessible to the public on the court system's website.

(4) The administrative director may allow bulk distribution of case information that is not publicly available and of publicly available imaged case records for scholarly or governmental purposes. The administrative director shall adopt procedures to protect the security of information and records released under this paragraph.

(c) **Distribution of Compiled Information.**

(1) Compiled information is defined as information that is derived from the selection, aggregation, or reformulation of case information in the court system's electronic case management systems.

(2) Information routinely compiled by the court may be made available unless the compiled information is privileged or reveals information that is confidential, sealed, or not available to the public under subsection (a) of this rule. A request from a person outside the court system for other compiled information must be approved by the administrative director. The request may be granted if resources are available to compile the information and if it is an appropriate use of public resources, such as for scholarly, governmental, or any other purpose in the public interest.

(d) **Fees.** The administrative director may establish fees for distribution of information under subsections (b) and (c) of this rule.

(Adopted by SCO 1622 effective October 15, 2006; and amended by SCO 1633 effective May 15, 2007)

Note to Administrative Rule 37.8(a)(7): Juror information is also protected by Administrative Rule 15(j).

Rule 38. Reports to Bureau of Vital Statistics—Superior Courts.

(a) **Divorce—Annulment—Adoption.** Before judgment or decree is entered in any action for divorce or annulment or proceeding for adoption, the court shall require the parties or their counsel to submit such personal particulars and other information necessary to enable the clerk to prepare a record of such divorce, annulment or adoption in accordance with law and the regulations and instructions of the Bureau of Vital Statistics. Every such record shall be prepared by the clerk and filed in the manner and within the time prescribed by law and the regulations and instructions of the Bureau of Vital Statistics.

(b) **Change of Name—Delayed Birth Certificate—Legitimation.** In the following actions and proceedings, the court shall file with the Bureau of Vital Statistics such reports, information and copies of judgments and orders as may be required and in the manner provided by law and the regulations and instructions of the Bureau:

(1) A proceeding for change of name;

(2) A proceeding to establish a public record of the time and place of birth and parentage;

(3) An action or proceeding for legitimation.

Before entering any order or judgment in any of the above mentioned actions or proceedings, the court shall require the parties or their counsel to submit such information as may be necessary to enable the court to comply with this rule.

(Adopted by SCO 412 effective July 1, 1980)

Rule 39. Vital Statistics.

The presiding judge shall designate district judges, magistrates, or judicial employees to perform all of the functions and duties with respect to the preparation, filing and recording of vital statistics, and the maintaining of records incident thereto, as provided by law and in accordance with the regulations and instructions of the Bureau of Vital Statistics.

(Adopted by SCO 412 effective July 1, 1980)

Rule 40. Index to Cases.

(a) The clerk of court shall maintain an alphabetical index by last name of every party named in every case filed, regardless of whether a party's true name is protected in the public index under paragraphs (b) or (c) of this rule. The index must show the party's name, the case number, the case caption or title, the filing date, the case type, and other information required for that case type by court rule. The index may show the party's date of birth. The clerk shall publish a public version of the index, which excludes only

(1) cases designated as confidential or sealed by statute or court rule, unless the index to those cases is public under court rules;

(2) foreign domestic violence protective orders filed under AS 18.66.140; and

(3) party names protected under paragraphs (b) or (c) of this rule.

The clerk shall continue to list a case on the public index even though the case file has been sealed or made confidential under Administrative Rule 37.6, unless the party names were protected under paragraphs (b) or (c) of this rule. The public index will be available to the public in electronic form except as limited by Administrative Rule 37.8.

(b) The presiding judge of a judicial district may direct the clerk of the court to substitute the pseudonym "Jane Doe" or "John Doe" or initials for a party's true name on the public index if the presiding judge finds that the issues in the case involve matters of a sensitive and highly personal nature, that publication of the name could expose a person to harassment, injury, ridicule, or personal embarrassment, and that protection of the party's name outweighs the public's interest in disclosure and any prejudice to the opposing party. If the presiding judge determines that the true name of more than one party in a case should be protected under this subsection, the parties shall be distinguished with alphabetical middle initials ("Jane A. Doe, Jane B. Doe"). Unless otherwise ordered, a party's name will not appear on the public index while a request to protect the name is pending before the presiding judge.

(c) The presiding judge of a judicial district may direct the clerk of court to remove a party's name from the public index for a period of five years if the presiding judge finds that publication of the name is likely to result in substantial physical harm to the party or members of the party's household and protection of the party's name outweighs the public's interest in disclosure. After five years, the party's name will appear on the public index unless the presiding judge orders the name protected for an additional period of time, upon another showing that publication of the name is likely to result in substantial physical harm to the party or members of the party's household. Unless otherwise ordered, a party's name will not appear on the public index while a request to protect the name is pending before the presiding judge.

(Adopted by SCO 1622 effective October 15, 2006; and amended by SCO 1633 effective May 15, 2007)

Editor's Note: Former Rule 40, Title, was renumbered as current Rule 51, by SCO 1622, effective October 15, 2006.

Rule 41. Case Numbering.

The administrative director shall designate the procedure to be followed by all district and superior courts in numbering cases. All case numbers shall include a prefix indicating the location of the court where the case is filed. The prefixes for the courts are as follows:

COURT LOCATION CODES

First District	
Angoon	1AG
Craig	1CR
Haines	1HA
Hoonah	1HN
Juneau	1JU
Kake	1KA
Ketchikan	1KE
Pelican	1PL
Petersburg	1PE
Sitka	1SI
Skagway	1SK
Wrangell	1WR
Yakutat	1YA
Second District	
Barrow	2BA
Buckland (closed)	2BU
Gambell	2GB
Kiana	2KI
Kotzebue	2KB
Nome	2NO
Noorvik	2NR
Point Hope	2PH
Savoonga	2SA
Selawik	2SE
Shungnak	2SH
Unalakleet	2UT
Wales (closed)	2WL
Third District	
Anchorage	3AN
Cold Bay	3CB
Cordova	3CO
Dillingham	3DI
Glennallen	3GL
Homer	3HO
Kenai	3KN
Kodiak	3KO
Naknek	3NA
Palmer	3PA
St. Paul Island	3ST
Sand Point	3SP
Seldovia (closed)	3SL
Seward	3SW
Togiak	3TG
Unalaska	3UN
Valdez	3VA
Whittier	3WH
Fourth District	
Aniak	4AK
Bethel	4BE
Chevak	4CH

Delta Junction	4DJ
Emmonak	4EM
Fairbanks	4FA
Fort Yukon	4FY
Galena	4GA
Healy	4HE
Hooper Bay (closed)	4HB
Kasigluk (closed)	4KS
McGrath	4MC
Mekoryuk (closed)	4ME
Mt. Village (closed)	4MV
Nenana	4NE
Quinhagak (closed)	4QU
Rampart (closed)	4RA
Scammon Bay (closed)	4SB
St. Mary's	4SM
Tanana	4TA
Tok	4TO
Tununak (closed)	4TU

(Adopted by SCO 478 effective August 17, 1981; amended by SCO 541 effective October 1, 1982; by SCO 564 effective April 4, 1983; by SCO 565 effective May 3, 1983; by SCO 617 effective May 15, 1985; by SCO 672 effective June 15, 1986; by SCO 1034 effective June 14, 1990; by SCO 1035 effective nunc pro tunc February 1, 1991; by SCO 1132 effective July 15, 1993; and by SCO 1493 effective September 26, 2002)

Cross References

CROSS REFERENCE: Administrative Bulletin No. 7 (Case Numbering)

Rule 42. Docketing. (Reserved).

Note: Former Rule 42 was deleted and the rule was reserved by SCO 1481, effective October 15, 2002.

Rule 43. Bail Forfeiture Schedules.

(a) **Procedure for Adopting Bail Forfeiture Schedule.** The supreme court will consider adopting a bail forfeiture schedule only when so authorized by statute. The agency charged with enforcement under a statute for which a bail forfeiture schedule has been authorized shall forward to the administrative director its recommendations for a proposed schedule, listing offenses by number, describing the offenses, and proposing a bail forfeiture amount. The proposed schedule shall be accompanied by commentary explaining the basis for the agency's recommendation, and by a copy of the proposed citation form. The supreme court shall consider the recommendation, and shall determine whether to adopt a bail forfeiture schedule, and if so, shall determine which offenses are amenable to disposition by bail forfeiture and whether the bail forfeiture amounts are appropriate. The administrative director shall notify the agency when an order adopting the schedule is issued.

(b) **Procedures for Amending Bail Forfeiture Schedules.**

(1) By July 1 of each year, each agency charged with enforcement under a statute for which a bail forfeiture schedule has been authorized shall forward to the administrative director of the Alaska Court System its written recommendation concerning whether the schedule must be amended to reflect any legislative and regulatory changes, or whether policy considerations warrant revisions. Any proposed amendments shall be accompanied by commentary. The supreme court shall consider the agency's recommendations and determine by October 1 whether to adopt them. If it will be impractical for the court to respond by that date, the administrative director will inform the agency of the date by which the response can be expected. The administrative director shall notify the agency when an order amending the schedule is issued.

(2) In addition to the provisions of paragraph (b)(1), an agency may request a bail forfeiture schedule amendment whenever the need arises.

(3) Any person or agency may request a bail forfeiture schedule amendment at any time by proposing an amendment in writing to the chief justice or to the administrative director.

(Adopted by SCO 651 effective July 1, 1985; amended by SCO 1180 effective July 15, 1995)

Rule 43.1. Traffic Bail Forfeiture Schedule.

Pursuant to AS 28.05.151, the following vehicle and traffic offenses are amenable to disposition without court appearance upon payment and forfeiture of the bail amounts listed. If a person charged with one of these offenses appears in court and is found guilty, the penalty imposed for the offense may not exceed the bail amount for that offense listed below. An offense for which a bail forfeiture amount has been established shall be charged on a citation which meets the requirements of District Court Criminal Rule 8(c) and shall not be filed, numbered, or processed as a criminal case.

Effective April 30, 1999, the bail amounts listed below are doubled for violations of AS 28 and regulations adopted under AS 28 committed within a highway work zone, as that term is defined in AS 28.90.990 and 13 AAC 40.010(b). Effective May 27, 2006, the bail amounts listed below are doubled for violations of AS 28 and regulations adopted under AS 28 committed within a traffic safety corridor, as that term is defined in AS 28.90.990.

Pursuant to AS 28.15.131 and 13 AAC 04.008, a citation for an offense listed as "Corr" must be dismissed (or voided) if proof of correction is presented to an inspection official within the time allowed. If the required repair is not made, the offense may be disposed of without court appearance upon payment and forfeiture of the bail amount listed.

Effective August 27, 1998, as a condition of the disposition of an offense without appearance, the defendant shall pay the surcharge prescribed in AS 12.55.039 in addition to the bail forfeiture amount listed below. A court may allow a defendant who is unable to pay the surcharge to perform community work under AS 12.55.055(c) in lieu of the surcharge. The surcharge must be deposited into the general fund in a separate account designated for such surcharges.

Effective September 1, 2003, pursuant to AS 28.05.151(e), an offense listed on this schedule may not be disposed of without court appearance if the offense is in connection with a motor vehicle accident that results in the death of a person.

The maximum bail amount for any of the offenses listed below in which the bail is stated as an amount per mile, per foot, per lamp, per reflector, per tire, or per wheel is the maximum fine allowed by statute for the offense. These maximum amounts are doubled for violations of AS 28 and regulations adopted under AS 28 committed within a highway work zone, as that term is defined in AS 28.90.990 and 13 AAC 40.010(b), or committed within a traffic safety corridor, as that term is defined in AS 28.90.990.

Statute or Regulation	Description of Offense	Bail
AS 11.46.462	Unlawful possession of an official traffic control device	$ 200
AS 19.10.300(a)	Commercial vehicle (intrastate): failure to maintain minimum insurance	500
AS 28.05.095(a)	Failure to wear safety belt (age 16 and older: passenger or driver)	15
AS 28.05.095(b)	Failure to provide child safety device. (Note: First charge may be dismissed by court upon proof of correction, but second or subsequent charge is not dismissible)	50
AS 28.05.095(b)	Failure to properly secure child in child safety device	50
AS 28.05.095(d)	Illegal removal of vehicle seatbelt	15
AS 28.10.451	Failure to register vehicle	90
AS 28.10.461	Plates/decals/permits must be properly attached and displayed	75
AS 28.10.461	Failure to carry certificate of registration in vehicle	40
AS 28.10.471	Operating vehicle w/expired registration	90
AS 28.10.471	Operating a vehicle w/suspended/revoked registration	300
AS 28.15.011(b)	Driving with license expired less than one year	75
AS 28.15.021(2)	Driving with out-of-state license after 90 days in state	75
AS 28.15.021(6)	Driving a motor-driven cycle with out-of-state driver's license after 90 days in state	75
AS 28.15.057(b)	Operating a vehicle in violation of a provisional license	200
AS 28.15.131	License to be carried and exhibited on demand	Corr/50
AS 28.15.281(a)	Unlawful use of a driver's license	200
AS 28.22.019	Proof of insurance to be carried and exhibited on demand	Corr/150
AS 28.35.029	Open container of alcoholic beverage in motor vehicle	200
AS 28.35.031(e)	Refusal to submit to a preliminary breath test	100
AS 28.35.135(b)	Failure to notify dept. of change of name/address	40
AS 28.35.140(a)	Obstructing or blocking traffic	75
AS 28.35.140(b)	Turn off required when 5 or more vehicles are behind	100
AS 28.35.145(e)	Ownership of a vehicle which illegally passes a school bus	75
AS 28.35.155	Operating vehicle w/studded/chained tires when prohibited	Corr/50
AS 28.35.180	Disobedience to signal of officer regulating traffic	75
AS 28.35.185(b)(2)	Overtaking and passing a parked emergency vehicle – if no personal injury	150
AS 28.35.235	Unauthorized use of parking reserved for persons with disabilities	
	-First offense	125
	-Second or more offense	250
AS 28.35.235	Unauthorized use of parking reserved for persons with disabilities while displaying special license plate or permit	
	-First offense	250
	-Second or more offense	500
AS 28.35.251	Contained or confined loads	300
AS 28.35.253	Anti-spray devices required	Corr/60
AS 28.39.010	Operating an unregistered snowmobile	50
AS 28.39.040(e)	Failure to display snowmobile numbered registration decal	50
AS 28.39.040(f)	Failure to carry snowmobile certificate of registration or provide identifying information	50
02 AAC 90.030	School bus driver permit must be carried and displayed upon demand	Corr/50
02 AAC 90.200	Unlawful use of classified license	50
13 AAC 02.005(a)	Disobedience to traffic control devices	100
13 AAC 02.010(a)(1)(A)-(B)	FTY to vehicle in intersection after green signal	150
13 AAC 02.010(a)(1)(A)-(B)	FTY to pedestrian in crosswalk after green signal	150
13 AAC 02.010(a)(3)(A)	Failure to stop for steady red traffic signal	150
13 AAC 02.010(a)(3)(B)	FTY when turning on red signal	150
13 AAC 02.010(a)(3)(B)	Turning on red signal when prohibited	75
13 AAC 02.010(a)(3)(C)	Failure to stop for steady red arrow	150
13 AAC 02.010(b)	Position of vehicle stopping at intersection	75
13 AAC 02.015	Failure to obey pedestrian control signal	40
13 AAC 02.020(a)(1)	Failure to yield after stopping for flashing red signal	150
13 AAC 02.020(a)(1)	Failure to stop for flashing red signal	150

Statute or Regulation	Description of Offense	Bail
13 AAC 02.025	Lane use control signals	75
13 AAC 02.030(a)	Display of unauthorized signs, signals, or markings	50
13 AAC 02.050(a)	Failure to drive on right side of roadway	75
13 AAC 02.050 (a)(3)	FTY when driving left of obstructed roadway	150
13 AAC 02.050(b)	Vehicle not to use left lane at less than speed limit	75
13 AAC 02.055(a)&(c)	Improper overtaking on right	75
13 AAC 02.055(b)	Return to lane only when clear	100
13 AAC 02.060(a)	Limitations on driving left of center	100
13 AAC 02.065(a)	Improper overtaking on the left	150
13 AAC 02.065(a)	FTY to overtaking vehicle	150
13 AAC 02.065(b)	FTY to oncoming traffic when passing	150
13 AAC 02.070	FTY 1/2 of roadway to oncoming vehicle and failure to pass on right of oncoming vehicle	100
13 AAC 02.075(b)	Passing/driving left of center in no pass zone	150
13 AAC 02.080(b)-(c)	Wrong way on one-way roadway	100
13 AAC 02.085(a)	Improper lane change	75
13 AAC 02.085(b)	Improper use of center lane of 3-lane roadway	75
13 AAC 02.090(a)-(c)	Following too closely	100
13 AAC 02.095(a)	Driving over, across or within barrier/median	100
13 AAC 02.095(a)	Failure to stay on right side of divided highway	100
13 AAC 02.095(c)	Improper entry/exit — controlled-access highway	75
13 AAC 02.107	Drive nearest right edge on narrow/winding roadway	75
13 AAC 02.120(a)	FTY to vehicle on right at unsigned intersection	90
13 AAC 02.120(b)	FTY to vehicle entering intersection after stop	150
13 AAC 02.120(d)	Failure to yield when entering roundabout	150
13 AAC 02.120(f)	Improper lane change in or exiting from a roundabout	75
13 AAC 02.125	FTY when turning left	150
13 AAC 02.130(b)	Improper position of vehicle stopping at stop sign	75
13 AAC 02.130(b)-(c)	FTY after stopping or at yield sign	150
13 AAC 02.130(b)	Failure to stop for stop sign	100
13 AAC 02.135(b)	FTY when entering roadway from non-roadway	100
13 AAC 02.140(a)-(b)	FTY to authorized emergency vehicle	250
13 AAC 02.140(c)	Driver of emergency vehicle not to disregard safety	100
13 AAC 02.150(a)-(b)	Pedestrians subject to traffic regulations	40

Statute or Regulation	Description of Offense	Bail
13 AAC 02.155(a)	FTY to pedestrian in crosswalk	100
13 AAC 02.155(b)	Pedestrian to exercise due caution	50
13 AAC 02.155(c)	Vehicle not to pass vehicle stopped for pedestrian	75
13 AAC 02.155(e)	Not to drive within or through pedestrian safety zone	50
13 AAC 02.160(a)-(f)	Pedestrian crossing at other than crosswalks	25
13 AAC 02.175(a)-(e)	Pedestrian to use sidewalk/left edge of roadway and not interfere, sleep, loiter or obstruct	40
13 AAC 02.180	Pedestrian not to distract drivers when soliciting rides and pedestrian not to solicit employment, business or contributions from vehicle occupants	50
13 AAC 02.190(a)	FTY to pedestrian w/white cane/guide dog	150
13 AAC 02.190(b)	Not to use white cane/guide dog unless blind	150
13 AAC 02.195(a)	Pedestrian FTY to authorized emergency vehicle	50
13 AAC 02.200(a)-(c)	Improper position/method turning at intersection	75
13 AAC 02.205(a)-(b)	U-turn only when safe/not on hill, crest or curve	75
13 AAC 02.210	Improper start from parked/stopped standing	75
13 AAC 02.215(a)-(f)	Signals required turn/stop/slowing-discontinue after	75
13 AAC 02.240(a)-(b)	Obedience to train signals and barriers	100
13 AAC 02.250(a)	Certain vehicles to stop at all railroad crossings	200
13 AAC 02.255(a)-(b)	Heavy equipment to give notice of railroad crossing	75
13 AAC 02.255(a)-(c)	Heavy equipment to stop at railroad crossing	200
13 AAC 02.257	Give warning w/horn when vision restricted/alley/driveway/buildings	50
13 AAC 02.257	Stop: emerging from alley/driveway/building	100
13 AAC 02.257	Position of stop when emerging from alley/driveway/building	75
13 AAC 02.265	Stop when traffic may be obstructed	75
13 AAC 02.275(a)	Basic speed: reasonable & prudent for road conditions	90
13 AAC 02.275(b)	Speeding:	
	-3-19 mph over posted limit	8/mi.[1]
	-20 mph or more over limit	12/mi.[1]
13 AAC 02.280(a)-(d)	Altered speed limits:	

Statute or Regulation	Description of Offense	Bail
	-3-19 mph over posted limit	8/mi.[1]
	-20 mph or more over limit	12/mi.[1]
13 AAC 02.295	Minimum speed regulation	60
13 AAC 02.325(a)	Speed limitation on motor-driven cycles at night	60
13 AAC 02.325(b)&(e)	Special speed limit when: (b) towing mobile home or (e) passing school bus with flashing yellow lights	
	-3-19 mph over	8/mi.[1]
	-20 mph or more over limit	12/mi.[1]
13 AAC 02.325(c)	Driving with lighted headlights at unreasonable speed	75
13 AAC 02.325(d)	Speed: over 20 mph in marked crosswalk speed zone of public school or playground	
	-3-9 mph over	12/mi.[1]
	-10-19 mph over	14/mi.[1]
	-20 mph or over	16/mi.[1]
13 AAC 02.325(f)	Oversize or excess speed when crossing over bridge or through tunnel	
	-3-19 mph over	8/mi.[1]
	-20 mph or over	12/mi.[1]
	-Overwidth	50/ft.[1]
	-Overlength	25/ft.[1]
13 AAC 02.330	Racing on the highway	300
13 AAC 02.340(a)-(d) (except (d)(1)(L))	Stopping/standing/ parking on highway/other location	25
13 AAC 02.365(a)-(g)	Additional parking regulations	25
13 AAC 02.367(d)	Not to stop/stand/park in loading zone	25
13 AAC 02.372(b)	Position of bus stopping to load/unload passengers	25
13 AAC 02.372(c)	Taxi cab restrictions on standing/parking	50
13 AAC 02.372(d)	Stop/stand in bus stop/taxi stand	25
13 AAC 02.377(c)-(f)	Parking meter violations	15
13 AAC 02.395(b)-(e)	Special bicycle violations	40
13 AAC 02.400(a)-(h)	Riding bicycles on roadways/bike paths	40
13 AAC 02.420(a)-(c)	Parking of bicycles	20
13 AAC 02.425(a)-(c)	Special motorcycle violations	60
13 AAC 02.425(d)	Motorcycle cling to other vehicle	200
13 AAC 02.427(a)	Motor vehicle not to deprive motorcycle of full lane use	50
13 AAC 02.427(a)	Motorcycles more than two abreast	50
13 AAC 02.427(b)	Motorcycle passing in same lane as other motor vehicle	50
13 AAC 02.445	Snowmobile and other off-highway vehicle violations	75
13 AAC 02.455(a)-(f)	Snowmobile and other off-highway vehicle operation on highways and other locations	50
13 AAC 02.455(g)	Snowmobile or other off-highway vehicle traveling on pedestrian pathway	100
13 AAC 02.480	Requirements for unattended motor vehicle	50
13 AAC 02.482(a)	Bicycles/pedestrians traveling in prohibited area	50
13 AAC 02.482(a)	Driving a motor vehicle where prohibited	150
13 AAC 02.482(b)	Non-motorized vehicle to yield to traffic on roadway	40
13 AAC 02.485(a)-(b)	Limitation on backing	75
13 AAC 02.487	Driving vehicle on sidewalk	150
13 AAC 02.495(a)-(c)	Obstructing driver's view/control of vehicle	75
13 AAC 02.495(d)	Opening doors/entering or leaving when vehicle in motion	25
13 AAC 02.495(e)-(f)	Person riding outside vehicle or in trailer	100
13 AAC 02.497(a)	Interfering w/funeral procession	75
13 AAC 02.497(b)	Requirements for drivers in funeral procession	60
13 AAC 02.497(c)	Permit requirements for funeral procession/parade	40
13 AAC 02.505(a)-(c)	Animals on the highway	200
13 AAC 02.505(d)-(e)	Motor vehicle drivers to exercise due care re animals	125
13 AAC 02.515	Coasting prohibited	50
13 AAC 02.517 (a)-(g)	Emergency vehicle regulations	60
13 AAC 02.520(a)	Following emergency vehicle closer than 500 feet	100
13 AAC 02.520(b)	Improper stopping/parking at emergency scene	100
13 AAC 02.520(c)	Crossing fire hose	100
13 AAC 02.530(a)-(b)	Littering/depositing material on highway	
	-Depositing garbage, glass, nails, tacks, wire, cans, oil or other substance	150
	-Littering from a motor vehicle – over 5 pounds (see AS 46.06.080 for 5 pounds or less)	100
13 AAC 02.530(d)	Haul/drag material causing damage to highway	150
13 AAC 02.532	Railroad trains not to block roadways	50
13 AAC 02.545(a)	Drinking while driving	300
13 AAC 02.545(b)	Drivers to exercise due care to avoid collision	150

Statute or Regulation	Description of Offense	Bail
13 AAC 03.005(a)	Commercial vehicle:Disobedience to traffic control devices	150 or MCA[2]
13 AAC 03.010(a)(1) (A)-(B)	Commercial vehicle: FTY to vehicle in intersection after green signal	150 or MCA[2]
13 AAC 03.010(a)(1) (A)-(B)	Commercial vehicle: FTY to pedestrian in crosswalk after green signal	150 or MCA[2]
13 AAC 03.010(a)(3)(A)	Commercial vehicle: Failure to stop for steady red traffic signal	200 or MCA[2]
13 AAC 03.010(a)(3)(B)	Commercial vehicle: FTY when turning on red signal	150 or MCA[2]
13 AAC 03.010(a)(3)(B)	Commercial vehicle: Turning on red signal when prohibited	150 or MCA[2]
13 AAC 03.010(a)(3)(C)	Commercial vehicle: Failure to stop for steady red arrow	200 or MCA[2]
13 AAC 03.050(a)	Commercial vehicle: Failure to drive on right side of roadway	150 or MCA[2]
13 AAC 03.050 (a)(3)	Commercial vehicle: FTY when driving left of obstructed roadway	200 or MCA[2]
13 AAC 03.050(b)	Commercial vehicle:Not to use left lane at less than speed limit	100 or MCA[2]
13 AAC 03.050(b)	Commercial vehicle: Turn off required when 5 or more vehicles are behind	150 or MCA[2]
13 AAC 03.055(a)	Commercial vehicle: Improper overtaking on right	100 or MCA[2]
13 AAC 03.055(b)	Commercial vehicle: Return to lane only when clear	200 or MCA[2]
13 AAC 03.060(a)	Commercial vehicle: Limitations on driving left of center	150 or MCA[2]
13 AAC 03.065(a)	Commercial vehicle: Improper overtaking on the left	200 or MCA[2]
13 AAC 03.065(a)	Commercial vehicle: FTY to overtaking vehicle	200 or MCA[2]
13 AAC 03.065(b)	Commercial vehicle: FTY to oncoming traffic when passing	200 or MCA[2]
13 AAC 03.070	Commercial vehicle: FTY 1/2 of roadway to oncoming vehicle and failure to pass on right of oncoming vehicle	200 or MCA[2]
13 AAC 03.080(b)-(c)	Commercial vehicle: Wrong way on one-way roadway	150 or MCA[2]
13 AAC 03.085(b)	Commercial vehicle: Improper use of center lane of 3-lane roadway	100 or MCA[2]
13 AAC 03.095(a)	Commercial vehicle: Driving over, across or within barrier/median	200 or MCA[2]
13 AAC 03.095(a)	Commercial vehicle: Failure to stay on right side of divided highway	200 or MCA[2]
13 AAC 03.095(c)	Commercial vehicle: Improper entry/exit-controlled-access highway	150 or MCA[2]
13 AAC 03.107	Commercial vehicle: Drive nearest right edge on narrow/winding roadway	150 or MCA[2]
13 AAC 03.155(a)	Commercial vehicle: FTY to pedestrian in crosswalk	150 or MCA[2]
13 AAC 03.155(b)	Pedestrian to exercise due caution	50
13 AAC 03.155(c)	Commercial vehicle: Not to pass vehicle stopped for pedestrian	150 or MCA[2]
13 AAC 03.155(e)	Commercial vehicle: Not to drive within or through pedestrian safety zone	90 or MCA[2]
13 AAC 03.275(a)	Commercial vehicle basic speed: reasonable & prudent for road conditions	200 or MCA[2]
13 AAC 03.275(b)	Commercial vehicle speeding:	
	-3-9 mph over posted limit	12/mi.[1] or MCA[2]
	-10-14 mph over posted limit	20/mi.[1]or MCA[2]
13 AAC 03.280(a)-(d)	Commercial vehicle altered speed limits:	
	-3-9 mph over posted limit	12/mi.[1] MCA[2]
	-10-14 mph over posted limit	20/mi.[1] or MCA[2]
13 AAC 03.295	Commercial vehicle: minimum speed regulation	90 or MCA[2]
13 AAC 03.325(b),(c),(e)	Commercial vehicle special speed limit when: (b) Towing mobile home, or (c) Equipped with lighted headlights, or (e) Passing school bus with flashing yellow lights	
	-3-9 mph over	15/mi.[1] or MCA[2]
	-10-14 mph over	20/mi.[1] or MCA[2]
13 AAC 03.325(f)	Commercial vehicle: oversize or excess speed when crossing over bridge or through tunnel	
	-3-9 mph over	15/mi.[1] or MCA[2]
	-10-14 mph over	20/mi.[1] or MCA[2]
	-Overwidth	50/ft.[1] or MCA[2]
	-Overlength	25/ft.[1] or

Statute or Regulation	Description of Offense	Bail
		MCA[2]
13 AAC 04.002	Unlawful to drive unsafe vehicle	150
13 AAC 04.003	Minimum equipment required for sale /rent /lease/ban	75
13 AAC 04.004 (a)-(c)	Sale or use of equipment	50
13 AAC 04.005(a)	Disconnection/alteration of equipment	50
13 AAC 04.005(b)	Operating a vehicle modified to be too low or too high	300
13 AAC 04.005(c)	Operating a vehicle with features or load adversely affecting steering, braking or stability	200
13 AAC 04.006(b)-(c)	Submit to roadside vehicle inspection	75
13 AAC 04.007(c)-(d)	Not to move unsafe vehicle unless authorized	150
13 AAC 04.009(a)-(c)	Prohibited practices — Inspection/repair	50
13 AAC 04.010	Illuminate lights as required	50
13 AAC 04.015(d)	Lights must be in good working order, securely mounted, not obstructed	75
13 AAC 04.020(a)&(f)-(g)	Headlight requirements	Corr/40
13 AAC 04.020(e)(1)-(2)	Headlight dimming requirements	50
13 AAC 04.025(a)-(c)	Taillight requirements	Corr/40
13 AAC 04.030(a)	Reflector requirements	Corr/40
13 AAC 04.035(a)-(c)	Stop light requirements	Corr/40
13 AAC 04.037(a)-(c)	Turn light requirements	Corr/40
13 AAC 04.040 (a)-(q)	Additional lighting requirements	Corr/40
13 AAC 04.070 (a)-(d)	Parking light requirements	Corr/40
13 AAC 04.070(e)	Parking lights not used when vehicle in motion	50
13 AAC 04.090(a),(c),(g)	Additional lights required for emergency vehicle	Corr/40
13 AAC 04.095(c)&(e)-(g)	Flashing yellow vehicular light requirements	Corr/40
13 AAC 04.095(d)&(g)-(i)	Flashing yellow lights used when required	75
13 AAC 04.097(a)	Use of flashing red light - school bus	60
13 AAC 04.097(a)-(c)	Special school bus lighting equipment	Corr/100
13 AAC 04.100(a)-(h)	Improper use of flashing blue lights	60
13 AAC 04.145(a)-(e)	Improper use of auxiliary/spot lights	60
13 AAC 04.145(a)-(e)	Restrictions on lighting equipment	Corr/40
13 AAC 04.145(f)	Use of lights in colors not authorized	50
13 AAC 04.205(a)-(c)	Brake requirements	Corr/90
13 AAC 04.205(d)-(e)	Improper towing	300
13 AAC 04.210(a)	Failure to give audible warning as required	50

Statute or Regulation	Description of Offense	Bail
13 AAC 04.210(a)-(d)	Horn/warning device requirements	Corr/60
13 AAC 04.215(a)	Exhaust system improperly modified	Corr/150
13 AAC 04.215(a)-(b)	Muffler requirements	Corr/60
13 AAC 04.220(a)-(c)	Mirror requirements	Corr/60
13 AAC 04.223	Tinted windows	Corr/150
13 AAC 04.225(a)-(b)	View not to be obstructed	60
13 AAC 04.225(a)-(g)	Windshield and wiper requirements	Corr/50
13 AAC 04.227(a)-(b)	Steering assembly, wheel alignment and body condition	Corr/200
13 AAC 04.230(a)-(e)	Tire restrictions and requirements	Corr/100
13 AAC 04.240(a)-(c)	Flares/other warning devices requirements	75
13 AAC 04.245(a)-(i)	Display of warning lights/devices	75
13 AAC 04.247(a)-(c)	Color/special equipment on school buses	Corr/100
13 AAC 04.247(d)	Improper use of signs/stop arm on school bus	50
13 AAC 04.250	Compressed gas fuel requirements: venting and signage	Corr/150
13 AAC 04.252(a)-(c)	Slow moving vehicle emblem requirements	50
13 AAC 04.255(b)-(d)	Air-conditioning equipment requirements	Corr/100
13 AAC 04.257	Emission control system requirements	Corr/100
13 AAC 04.260(a)-(c)	Restrictions on television/headset in motor vehicle	150
13 AAC 04.265(a)-(b)	Anti-spray device requirements (see AS 28.35.253 also)	Corr/50
13 AAC 04.270(a)&(c)	Safety belt requirements	Corr/75
13 AAC 04.272	Energy absorption system requirements	Corr/75
13 AAC 04.275(a)-(e)	Connections/safety devices—towed vehicles	75
13 AAC 04.320(a)-(b)	Motorcycle headlight requirements	Corr/40
13 AAC 04.320(c)	Bicycle headlight requirements	Corr/40
13 AAC 04.320(d)	Lights turned on when on highway—motor driven cycle	60
13 AAC 04.325(a)	Bicycle taillight requirements	Corr/40
13 AAC 04.325(a)-(b)	Motorcycle taillight requirements	Corr/40
13 AAC 04.330(a)-(b)	Motorcycle stop/turn light requirements	Corr/40
13 AAC 04.335(a)	Motorcycle reflector requirements	Corr/30
13 AAC 04.335(b)	Bicycle reflector requirements	Corr/20
13 AAC 04.340(a)	Motorcycle brake requirements	Corr/90

Statute or Regulation	Description of Offense	Bail
13 AAC 04.340(b)	Bicycle brakes	Corr/40
13 AAC 04.345(a)	Motorcycle handgrips and foot-rests for passengers	Corr/50
13 AAC 04.345(b)	Motorcycle handlebar requirements	Corr/75
13 AAC 04.350(a)	Helmet required-minors/passengers (AS 28.35.245 exempts adults)	75
13 AAC 04.350(b)	Eye-protective device required when no windscreen	50
13 AAC 04.350(c)	Minimum equipment for rent/lease/loan of motorcycle	75
13 AAC 04.355(a)	Other equipment required (horn, mirrors, tires, emission control system)	
	-Bicycle	Corr/40
	-Motor-driven cycle	Corr/40
13 AAC 04.355(b)	Motorcycle windshield requirements	Corr/60
13 AAC 04.400(a)-(b)	Snowmobile/off highway vehicle lights and reflectors	Corr/60
13 AAC 04.405	Snowmobile/off highway vehicle brakes	Corr/60
13 AAC 04.410	Snowmobile/off highway vehicle throttle	Corr/60
13 AAC 04.415(a)-(b)	Snowmobile/off highway vehicle muffler/emission controls	Corr/60
13 AAC 04.420(a)-(b)	Snowmobile/off highway vehicle other equipment	Corr/40
13 AAC 04.420(a)(4)	Rigid draw bar required when towing with snowmobile	Corr/50

State Regulation	Federal Regulation	Description of Offense	Bail
17 AAC 25.200	49 CFR 105 49 CFR 107 49 CFR 171 49 CFR 172 49 CFR 173 49 CFR 177 49 CFR 178 49 CFR 180	Transportation of hazardous materials	300
17 AAC 25.210	49 CFR 387	Failure to maintain minimum insurance (interstate carriers)	500
17 AAC 25.210	49 CFR 390.13	Aiding or abetting violations	400
17 AAC 25.210	49 CFR 390.15	Records and assistance required to be available	300
17.AAC 25.210	49 CFR 390.21	Marking of commercial vehicles	200
17 AAC 25.210	49 CFR 390.35	False Statement/Record	400
17 AAC 25.210	49 CFR 391.21	Driving a CV with insufficient employment application	200
17 AAC 25.210	49 CFR 391.31	Driving a CV without road test certificate	200
17 AAC 25.210	49 CFR 391.41	Driving A CV without medical examiner's certificate in possession	200
17 AAC 25.210	49 CFR 391.41(b)(10)	Corrective lenses to be worn	150
17 AAC 25.210	49 CFR 391.41(b)(11)	Hearing aid to be worn	150
17 AAC 25.210	49 CFR 391.51	Carrier required to maintain driver qualification files	200
17 AAC 25.210	49 CFR 392.3	Driving while ill or fatigued	300
17 AAC 25.210	49 CFR 392.4	Possession/influence/use of drugs/other substances while on duty	300
17 AAC 25.210	49 CFR 392.6	Carrier schedule requires violation of speed limits	300
17 AAC 25.210	49 CFR 392.7	Failure to check/use parts and accessories	150
17 AAC 25.210	49 CFR 392.8	Failure to check/use emergency equipment	150
17 AAC 25.210	49 CFR 392.9	Safe loading of cargo and passengers required	300
17 AAC 25.210	49 CFR 392.11	Slow and exercise caution approaching railroad crossing	200
17 AAC 25.210	49 CFR 392.14	Extreme caution and reduced speed or discontinued operation required in hazardous condition	300
17 AAC 25.210	49 CFR 392.16	Seat belt must be used if installed	150
17 AAC 25.210	49 CFR 392.20	Leaving vehicle unattended without setting parking brake and taking other precautions	300
17 AAC 25.210	49 CFR 392.21	Stop/park on traveled portion of highway	200
17 AAC 25.210	49 CFR 392.22	Hazard warning signals required when stop on highway or shoulder	200
17 AAC 25.210	49 CFR 392.24	Lighted fusee may not be attached to vehicle	150
17 AAC 25.210	49 CFR 392.25	Flame-producing emergency signal may not be used with dangerous cargo	300
17 AAC 25.210	49 CFR 392.33	Lamps or reflectors obscured	200
17 AAC 25.210	49 CFR 392.50	Unsafe fueling practices	100
17 AAC 25.210	49 CFR 392.51	Reserve fuel carried improperly	200
17 AAC 25.210	49 CFR 392.60	Transporting unauthorized person	150

State Regulation	Federal Regulation	Description of Offense	Bail
17 AAC 25.210	49 CFR 392.62	Bus driver: Conversation/distraction prohibited	150
17 AAC 25.210	49 CFR 392.63	Towing or pushing loaded bus	300
17 AAC 25.210	49 CFR 392.64	Riding in closed vehicle without proper exit	150
17 AAC 25.210	49 CFR 392.66	Carbon monoxide: Use of vehicle when detected	300
17 AAC 25.210	49 CFR 392.67	No open flame heater while vehicle in motion	300
17 AAC 25.210	49 CFR 392.71	Radar detector; use and/or possession	300
17 AAC 25.210	49 CFR 393.9	Lamps operable	15/lamp[3]
17 AAC 25.210	49 CFR 393.11	Lighting devices and reflectors	15/lamp[3]
17 AAC 25.210	49 CFR 393.17	Lamps and reflectors—Combinations in driveaway-towaway operation	10/lamp[3]
17 AAC 25.210	49 CFR 393.19	Requirements for turn signaling systems	150
17 AAC 25.210	49 CFR 393.20	Clearance lamps to indicate extreme width and height	15/lamp[3]
17 AAC 25.210	49 CFR 393.22	Combination of lighting devices and reflectors	15/lamp[3]
17 AAC 25.210	49 CFR 393.23	Lighting devices to be electric	15/lamp[3]
17 AAC 25.210	49 CFR 393.24	Requirements for head lamps and auxiliary road lighting lamps	15/lamp[3]
17 AAC 25.210	49 CFR 393.25	Requirements for lamps other than head lamps	15/lamp[3]
17 AAC 25.210	49 CFR 393.26	Requirements for reflectors	15/reflector[3]
17 AAC 25.210	49 CFR 393.27	Wiring specifications	75
17 AAC 25.210	49 CFR 393.28	Wiring to be protected	75
17 AAC 25.210	49 CFR 393.29	Grounds	75
17 AAC 25.210	49 CFR 393.30	Battery installation	75
17 AAC 25.210	49 CFR 393.31	Overload protective devices	75
17 AAC 25.210	49 CFR 393.33	Wiring, installation	75
17 AAC 25.210	49 CFR 393.32	Detachable electrical connections	75
17 AAC 25.210	49 CFR 393.40	Required brake systems	300
17 AAC 25.210	49 CFR 393.41	Parking brake system	150
17 AAC 25.210	49 CFR 393.42	Brakes required on all wheels	300
17 AAC 25.210	49 CFR 393.43	Breakaway and emergency braking	300
17 AAC 25.210	49 CFR 393.44	Front brake lines, protection	300
17 AAC 25.210	49 CFR 393.45	Brake tubing and hose, adequacy	150
17 AAC 25.210	49 CFR 393.46	Brake tubing and hose connections	150
17 AAC 25.210	49 CFR 393.47	Brake lining	150
17 AAC 25.210	49 CFR 393.48	Brakes to be operative	300
17 AAC 25.210	49 CFR 393.49	Single valve to operate all brakes	300
17 AAC 25.210	49 CFR 393.50	Reservoirs required	200
17 AAC 25.210	49 CFR 393.51	Warning devices and gauges	200
17 AAC 25.210	49 CFR 393.52	Brake performance	300
17 AAC 25.210	49 CFR 393.53	Automatic brake adjusters and brake adjustment indicators	300
17 AAC 25.210	49 CFR 393.60	Glazing in specified openings	75
17 AAC 25.210	49 CFR 393.61	Window construction	100
17 AAC 25.210	49 CFR 393.62	Window obstructions	150
17 AAC 25.210	49 CFR 393.63	Windows, markings	100
17 AAC 25.210	49 CFR 393.65	All fuel systems	100
17 AAC 25 210	49 CFR 393.67	Liquid fuel tanks	100
17 AAC 25.210	49 CFR 393.69	Liquefied petroleum gas systems	100
17 AAC 25.210	49 CFR 393.70	Coupling devices and towing methods, except for driveaway-towaway operations	200
17 AAC 25.210	49 CFR 393.71	Coupling devices and towing methods, driveaway-towaway operations	200
17 AAC 25.210	49 CFR 393.75	Tires	100/tire[3]
17 AAC 25.210	49 CFR 393.76	Sleeper berths	75
17 AAC 25.210	49 CFR 393.77	Heaters	150
17 AAC 25.210	49 CFR 393.78	Windshield wipers	150
17 AAC 25.210	49 CFR 393.79	Defrosting device	150
17 AAC 25.210	49 CFR 393.80	Rear-vision mirrors	150
17 AAC 25.210	49 CFR 393.81	Horn	75
17 AAC 25.210	49 CFR 393.82	Speedometer	150
17 AAC 25.210	49 CFR 393.83	Exhaust systems	200
17 AAC 25.210	49 CFR 393.84	Floors	75
17 AAC 25.210	49 CFR 393.86	Rear end protection	300
17 AAC 25.210	49 CFR 393.87	Flags on projecting loads	200
17 AAC 25.210	49 CFR 393.88	Television receivers	150
17 AAC 25.210	49 CFR 393.89	Buses, driveshaft protection	150
17 AAC 25.210	49 CFR 393.90	Buses, standee line or bar	150

State Regulation	Federal Regulation	Description of Offense	Bail
17 AAC 25.210	49 CFR 393.91	Buses, aisle seats prohibited	150
17 AAC 25.210	49 CFR 393.92	Buses, marking emergency doors	200
17 AAC 25.210	49 CFR 393.93	Seats, seat belt assemblies and seat belt assembly anchorages	150
17 AAC 25.210	49 CFR 393.94	Vehicle interior noise levels	150
17 AAC 25.210	49 CFR 393.95	Emergency equipment on all power units	150
17 AAC 25.210	49 CFR 393.100	General rules for protection against shifting or falling cargo	300
17 AAC 25.210	49 CFR 393.102	Securement systems	300
17 AAC 25.210	49 CFR 393.104	Blocking and bracing	150
17 AAC 25.210	49 CFR 393.106	Front-end structure	300
17 AAC 25.210	49 CFR 393.201	Frames	200
17 AAC 25.210	49 CFR 393.203	Cab and body components	200
17 AAC 25.210	49 CFR 393.205	Wheels	100/wheel[3]
17 AAC 25.210	49 CFR 393.207	Suspension systems	150
17 AAC 25.210	49 CFR 393.209	Steering wheel systems	200
17 AAC 25.210	49 CFR 396.3	Motor carrier must inspect, repair and keep records	200
17 AAC 25.210	49 CFR 396.5	Motor carrier must ensure vehicle lubrication	200
17 AAC 25.210	49 CFR 396.7	Operation in unsafe condition forbidden	300
17 AAC 25.210	49 CFR 396.9(c)(2)	Operation of "Out of Service" vehicle prohibited	300
17 AAC 25.210	49 CFR 396.9(c)(3)	Removal of "Out of Service" sticker prohibited	300
17 AAC 25.210	49 CFR 396.11	Failure to prepare daily vehicle inspection report	75
17 AAC 25.210	49 CFR 396.13	Failure to review/sign last vehicle inspection report	75
17 AAC 25.210	49 CFR 396.15	Driveaway-towaway operations & inspections	200
17 AAC 25.210	49 CFR 396.17	Periodic inspection and documentation required	100
17 AAC 25.210	49 CFR 396.19	Qualifications of inspectors	200
17 AAC 25.210	49 CFR 396.21	Periodic inspection recordkeeping	200
17 AAC 25.210	49 CFR 396.25	Qualifications of brake inspectors	200
17 AAC 25.210	49 CFR 399.207	Truck and truck-tractor access requirements	75
17 AAC 25.210	49 CFR 399.211	Steps, handholds and deck plates must be maintained	75
17 AAC 25.220	49 CFR 395.1(h)	Maximum driving and on-duty time in Alaska	200
17 AAC 25.220	49 CFR 395.8	Driver must record duty status	150
17 AAC 25.220	49 CFR 395.13(c)	Motor carrier may not allow out-of-service driver to drive	300
17 AAC 25.220	49 CFR 395.13(d)	Out-of-service driver may not drive	300

Statute or Regulation	Description of Offense	Bail
17 AAC 42.020(a)(3)	Failure to obey posted sign, signal or control device on a highway or vehicular way/area (international airport):	
	-Motor vehicle	50
	-Pedestrian or non-motorized vehicle	30
17 AAC 42.020(b)	Failure to remain in public area provided for particular class of traffic or mode of travel (international airport)	30
17 AAC 42.030(b)	Operation of aircraft on a highway (international airport)	50
17 AAC 42.080(a)	Failure to operate motor vehicle in accordance with airport operational orders under 17 AAC 42.020(a)(2) (international airport)	50
17 AAC 42.080(b)	Improper vehicular crossing of airport boundary (international airport)	50
17 AAC 42.080(c)	Operating a vehicle in a manner that interferes with aircraft (international airport)	100
17 AAC 42.080(d)	Speeding (international airport):	
	-3-19 mph over limit	8/mi.[4]
	-20 mph or more over limit	12/mi.[4]
17 AAC 42.080(e)	Illegal parking/abandoning vehicle in a terminal building baggage or service vehicle area (international airport)	50
17 AAC 42.080(g)	Operating a vehicle in an airport restricted area without a current valid operator's license (international airport)	100
17 AAC 42.085	Ramp operator's permit required for operation in airport restricted area (international airport)	50
17 AAC 42.085	Improper operation on runways	200
17 AAC 42.090(b)	Illegal parking/abandoning vehicle in a prohibited area (international airport)	
	-more than 300 feet from a terminal	30
	-within 300 feet of a terminal	50

Statute or Regulation	Description of Offense	Bail
17 AAC 42.090(b)	Expired Parking Meter (international airport)	20
17 AAC 42.095(a)	Commercial passenger vehicle must obtain permit (international airport)	50
17 AAC 45.020(a)(3)	Failure to obey posted sign, signal or control device on a highway or vehicular way/area (rural airport):	
	-Motor vehicle	50
	-Pedestrian or non-motorized vehicle	30
17 AAC 45.020(b)	Failure to remain in public area provided for particular class of traffic or mode of travel (rural airport)	30
17 AAC 45.030(b)	Operation of aircraft on a highway (rural airport)	50
17 AAC 45.080(a)	Failure to operate motor vehicle in accordance with airport operational orders under 17 AAC 45.020(a)(2)(rural airport)	50
17 AAC 45.080(b)	Improper vehicular crossing of airport boundary (rural airport)	50
17 AAC 45.080(c)	Operating a vehicle in a manner that interferes with aircraft (rural airport)	100
17 AAC 45.080(d)	Speeding (rural airport):	
	-3-19 mph over limit	8/mi.[4]
	-20 mph or more over limit	12/mi.[4]
17 AAC 45.080(e)	Illegal parking/abandoning vehicle in a terminal building baggage or service vehicle area (rural airport)	50
17 AAC 45.080(g)	Operating a vehicle in an airport restricted area without a current valid operator's license (rural airport)	100
17 AAC 45.085	Ramp operator's permit required for operation in airport restricted area (rural airport)	50
17 AAC 45.090(c)	Expired parking meter (rural airport)	20
17 AAC 45.090(d)	Illegal parking/abandoning vehicle in a prohibited area (rural airport)	
	-more than 300 feet from a terminal	30
	-within 300 feet of a terminal	50
17 AAC 45.095(d)	Commercial passenger vehicles must obtain permit (rural airport)	50

[1] Maximum bail amount: $300. AS 28.90.010(c). Maximum bail amount in highway work zone or traffic safety corridor: $600.

[2] Because AS 28.33.140 may require disqualification from driving a commercial motor vehicle upon conviction of any "serious traffic violation" (as defined in AS 28.33.190), if this offense resulted in physical injury to a person, the officer must cite it as a mandatory court appearance (MCA). If there was no physical injury to a person, the offense should be cited as a mail-in-bail offense at the bail forfeiture amount listed.

[3] Maximum bail amount: $500. AS 45.75.380(a)(11) and AS 12.55.035(b)(7)— violations. The penalty and the maximum are *not* doubled in highway work zones or traffic safety corridors.

[4] Maximum bail amount: $500. AS 02.15.240—misdemeanors. The penalty and the maximum are *not* doubled in highway work zones or traffic safety corridors.

(Adopted by SCO 775 effective January 1, 1987; amended by SCO 910 effective September 15 1988; by SCO 944 effective September 30, 1988; by SCO 1047 effective nunc pro tunc September 12, 1990; by SCO 1151 effective February 1, 1994; by SCO 1215 effective July 15, 1995; by SCO 1328 effective July 15, 1998; by SCO 1347 effective August 27, 1998; by SCO 1352 effective April 30, 1999; by SCO 1363 effective July 30, 1999; by SCO 1406 effective October 15, 2000; by SCO 1495 effective November 8, 2002; SCO 1530 effective nunc pro tunc to September 1, 2003; by SCO 1531 effective November 5, 2003; by SCO 1542 effective December 5, 2003; by SCO 1550 effective July 1, 2004; by SCO 1585 effective August 15, 2005; by SCO 1619 effective nunc pro tunc to May 27, 2006; and by SCO 1634 effective December 20, 2006)

Note to SCO 1215: The surcharge requirement was added by §§ 2 and 5, ch. 119 SLA 1994, adopting AS 12.55.039 and AS 28.05.151(c). This order is made for the sole reason that the legislature has mandated the amendments.

Note to SCO 1352: The requirement that the bail amount for offenses committed within a highway work zone be doubled was added by §§ 1 and 2, ch. 64 SLA 1998, adopting AS 28.05.151(d) and AS 28.40.070. This order is made for the sole reason that the legislature has mandated the amendment.

Note to SCO 1530: The requirement that a mandatory court appearance is necessary if an offense is connected to a fatal motor vehicle accident was added by §§ 1 and 3, ch. 89 SLA 2003, adopting AS 28.05.151(e). This order is made for the sole reason that the legislature has mandated the amendment.

Note to SCO 1619: The requirement that the bail amount for offenses committed within a traffic safety corridor be doubled was added by §§ 2 and 4, chapter 45 SLA 2006, amending AS 28.05.151(d) and AS 28.40.070. This order is made for the sole reason that the legislature has mandated the amendment.

Rule 43.2. Fish and Game Bail Forfeiture Schedule.

Pursuant to AS 16.05.165(b), the following fish and game offenses are appropriate for disposition without court appearance upon payment and forfeiture of the bail amounts listed and forfeiture of all seized items listed on the citation. If a person charged with one of these offenses appears in court and is found guilty, the fine imposed for the offense may not exceed the bail amount for that offense listed below. In addition, fish, game, or equipment may be forfeited under AS 16.05.190 or AS 16.05.195. An offense for which a bail forfeiture amount has been established shall be charged on a citation which meets the requirements of District Court Criminal Rule 8(c) and shall not be filed, numbered, or processed as a criminal case.

Statute or Regulation	Description of Offense	Bail
AS 16.05.330(a)(1)	Sport fishing without license in possession	$200
AS 16.05.330(a)(2)	Hunting without license in possession	250
AS 6.05.340(a)(17)(A)	Taking waterfowl without state duck stamp	75
AS 16.05.340(a)(23)	King salmon stamp required for residents	100
AS 16.05.340(a)(24)	King salmon stamp required for non-residents	200
AS 16.05.420	False statement on license application	300
AS 16.05.480(a)	Crewmember fishing license required	250
AS 16.05.490(a)	Vessel license required	200
AS 16.05.520(a)	Vessel number plate	100
AS 16.05.680(1)	Employ unlicensed crew member	250
5 AAC 01.010(h)	Identification of subsistence finfish fishing gear	100
5 AAC 01.010(i)	Escape mechanism requirements for subsistence fishing gear	100
5 AAC 01.015(b)(5)	Failure to record daily catch on subsistence or personal use permit (finfish Statewide)	100
5 AAC 01.240(c)	Marking of subsistence taken king salmon (lower Yukon River)	100
5 AAC 01.630(e)(8)	Failure to record salmon on subsistence permit (Glennallen Subdistrict)	100
5 AAC 01.640	Failure to mark subsistence taken salmon (Copper River Districts)	100
5 AAC 02.010(e)(1-2)	Identification of subsistence shellfish gear	100
5 AAC 02.010(f)	Escape mechanism requirements for subsistence shellfish pots	100
5 AAC 02.015(a)(5)	Failure to record daily catch on subsistence or personal use permit (shellfish Statewide)	100
5 AAC 02.415(a)	Take overlimit/undersized or female Dungeness crab (Kodiak)	100 plus 20 per illegally taken crab
5 AAC 05.334(a)	ID requirements for commercial salmon drift gillnets (Yukon River)	200
5 AAC 05.334(b)	ID requirements for commercial salmon stationary gear (Yukon River)	200
5 AAC 05.340	Failure to display vessel identification (Yukon River)	200
5 AAC 06.331(q)	Unlit set/drift net (Bristol Bay)	250
5 AAC 07.334(a)	ID requirements for commercial salmon drift gillnets (Kuskokwim River)	200
5 AAC 07.334(b)	ID requirements for commercial salmon stationary gear (Kuskokwim River)	200
5 AAC 07.340	Vessel Identification (Kuskokwim River)	200
5 AAC 28.135(a)(1-4)	Vessel Identification – D and M	200
5 AAC 29.125	Vessel Identification – HT	200
5 AAC 30.334	Identification of set gillnet (Yakutat)	200
5 AAC 39.119(a)(1-4)	Vessel Identification – 12 inch numbers	200
5 AAC 47.020(1-17)	Sport fishing – general seasons, bag, possession, annual and size limits (salt water, Southeast Alaska)	100 plus 150 per king salmon illegally taken, 50 per halibut or lingcod, 20 per other fish, 20 per crab, and 2 per razor clam
5 AAC 47.021(a-j)	Sport fishing – special provisions, seasons, bag, possession, and size limits (salt water, Southeast Alaska)	100 plus 150 per king salmon illegally taken, 50 per halibut or lingcod, 20 per other fish, 20 per crab, and 2 per razor clam
5 AAC 47.022(a-c)	Sport fishing – general seasons, bag, possession, annual and size limits (freshwater, Southeast Alaska)	100 plus 150 per king salmon illegally taken, 20 per other fish
5 AAC 47.023(a-k)	Sport fishing – special provisions, seasons, bag, possession, and size limits (freshwater, Southeast	100 plus 150 per king salmon illegally

Statute or Regulation	Description of Offense	Bail
	Alaska)	taken, 20 per other fish
5 AAC 47.024(a)(3)	Failure to record king salmon landing (Southeast Alaska)	100
5 AAC 47.024(c)(3)	Failure to record steelhead landing (Southeast Alaska)	100
5 AAC 47.030(g)	Maximum number of fishing lines from a charter vessel (Southeast Alaska)	300
5 AAC 52.022(a)	Sport fishing – general seasons, bag, possession, annual and size limits (Upper Copper River and Upper Susitna River)	100 plus 150 per king salmon illegally taken, 20 per other fish
5 AAC 52.023(1-28)	Sport fishing – special provisions, seasons, bag, possession, and size limits (Upper Copper River and Upper Susitna River)	100 plus 150 per king salmon illegally taken, 20 per other fish
5 AAC 52.024(b)	Failure to record king salmon landing (Upper Copper River and Upper Susitna River)	100
5 AAC 55.022(a-b)	Sport fishing – general seasons, bag, possession, and size limits (Prince William Sound)	100 plus 150 per king salmon illegally taken, 50 per halibut or lingcod, and 20 per other fish
5 AAC 55.023(1-8)	Sport fishing – special provisions, seasons, bag, possession, and size limits (Prince William Sound)	100 plus 150 per king salmon illegally taken, 50 per halibut or lingcod, and 20 per other fish
5 AAC 56.120(1-8)	Sport fishing – general seasons, bag, possession, and size limits (freshwaters, Kenai Peninsula Area, excluding Kenai River Drainage Area)	100 plus 150 per king salmon illegally taken and 20 per other fish
5 AAC 56.122(a)(1-12)	Sport fishing – special provisions, seasons, bag, possession, and size limits (freshwaters, Kenai Peninsula Area, excluding Kenai River Drainage Area)	100 plus 150 per king salmon illegally taken and 20 per other fish
5 AAC 56.124(a)(2)	Failure to record king salmon landing (freshwaters, Kenai Peninsula Area, excluding Kenai River Drainage Area)	100
5 AAC 56.124(b)(2)	Failure to record rainbow/steelhead trout landing (freshwaters, Kenai Peninsula Area, excluding Kenai River Drainage Area)	100
5 AAC 57.120(1-10)	Sport fishing – general seasons, bag, possession, and size limits (freshwaters, Kenai River Drainage Area)	100 plus 150 per king salmon illegally taken and 20 per other fish
5 AAC 57.121(1-6)	Sport fishing – special provisions, seasons, bag, possession, and size limits (freshwaters, Kenai River Drainage Area Lower Section)	100 plus 150 per king salmon illegally taken and 20 per other fish
5 AAC 57.122(1-5)	Sport fishing – special provisions, seasons, bag, possession, and size limits (freshwaters, Kenai River Drainage Area Middle Section)	100 plus 150 per king salmon illegally taken and 20 per other fish
5 AAC 57.123(1-8)	Sport fishing – special provisions, seasons, bag, possession, and size limits (freshwaters, Kenai River Drainage Area Upper Section)	100 plus 150 per king salmon illegally taken and 20 per other fish
5 AAC 57.124(a)(2)	Failure to record king salmon landing (freshwaters, Kenai River Drainage Area)	100
5 AAC 57.124(b)(2)	Failure to record rainbow/steelhead trout landing (freshwaters, Kenai River Drainage Area)	100
5 AAC 57.180(c-d)	Sport fishing – Riparian habitat bank closures (freshwaters, Kenai River Drainage Area)	75
5 AAC 58.022(a-b)	Sport fishing – waters, seasons, bag, possession, size limits, and special provisions (Cook Inlet – Resurrection Bay saltwater)	100 plus 150 per king salmon illegally taken, 50 per halibut or lingcod, 20 per other fish, 20 per crab, and 2 per razor clam

Statute or Regulation	Description of Offense	Bail
5 AAC 58.024(a)(2)	Failure to record king salmon landing (Cook Inlet – Resurrection Bay saltwater)	100
5 AAC 58.026(a-b)	Failure to record crab or hardshell clams on harvest record (Cook Inlet – Resurrection Bay saltwater)	100
5 AAC 58.030(c)	Snagging or attempting to snag where prohibited (Cook Inlet north of a line extending west from Anchor Point)	125
5 AAC 58.030(d)	Snagging or attempting to snag where prohibited (saltwater of the Homer Spit, fishery enhancement lagoon)	125
5 AAC 58.035(b-g)	Shellfish methods and means (Cook Inlet – Resurrection Bay saltwater)	100
5 AAC 59.120(1-8)	Sport fishing – general seasons, bag, possession, and size limits (freshwaters, Anchorage Bowl Drainages Area)	100 plus 150 per king salmon illegally taken and 20 per other fish
5 AAC 59.122(1-16)	Sport fishing – special provisions, seasons, bag, possession, and size limits (freshwaters, Anchorage Bowl Drainages Area)	100 plus 150 per king salmon illegally taken and 20 per other fish
5 AAC 59.124(a)(2)	Failure to record king salmon landing (freshwaters, Anchorage Bowl Drain	ages area) 100
5 AAC 59.124(b)(2)	Failure to record rainbow/steelhead trout landing (freshwaters, Anchorage Bowl Drainages Area)	100
5 AAC 60.120(1-9)	Sport fishing – general seasons, bag, possession, and size limits (freshwaters, Knik Arm Drainages Area)	100 plus 150 per king salmon illegally taken and 20 per other fish
5 AAC 60.122(1-13)	Sport fishing – special provisions, seasons, bag, possession, and size limits (freshwaters, Knik Arm Drainages Area)	100 plus 150 per king salmon illegally taken and 20 per other fish
5 AAC 60.124(a)(2)	Failure to record king salmon landing (freshwaters, Knik Arm Drainages Area)	100
5 AAC 60.124(b)(2)	Failure to record rainbow/steelhead trout landing (freshwaters, Knik Arm Drainages Area)	100
5 AAC 61.110(1-9)	Sport fishing – general seasons, bag, possession, and size limits (freshwaters, Susitna River Drainage Area)	100 plus 150 per king salmon illegally taken and 20 per other fish
5 AAC 61.112(1-6)	Sport fishing – special provisions, seasons, bag, possession, and size limits (freshwaters, Susitna River Drainage Area Unit 1)	100 plus 150 per king salmon illegally taken and 20 per other fish
5 AAC 61.114(1-13)	Sport fishing – special provisions, seasons, bag, possession, and size limits (freshwaters, Susitna River Drainage Area Unit 2)	100 plus 150 per king salmon illegally taken and 20 per other fish
5 AAC 61.116(1-5)	Sport fishing – special provisions, seasons, bag, possession, and size limits (freshwaters, Susitna River Drainage Area Unit 3)	100 plus 150 per king salmon illegally taken and 20 per other fish
5 AAC 61.118(1-10)	Sport fishing – special provisions, seasons, bag, possession, and size limits (freshwaters, Susitna River Drainage Area Unit 4)	100 plus 150 per king salmon illegally taken and 20 per other fish
5 AAC 61.120(1-5)	Sport fishing – special provisions, seasons, bag, possession, and size limits (freshwaters, Susitna River Drainage Area Unit 5)	100 plus 150 per king salmon illegally taken and 20 per other fish
5 AAC 61.122(1-5)	Sport fishing – special provisions, seasons, bag, possession, and size limits (freshwaters, Susitna River Drainage Area Unit 6)	100 plus 150 per king salmon illegally taken and 20 per other fish
5 AAC 61.123(1-2)	Sport fishing – restrictions on fishing after taking king salmon (freshwaters, Susitna River Drainage Area)	100 plus 150 per king salmon illegally taken and 20 per other fish
5 AAC 61.124(a)(2)	Failure to record king salmon landing	100

Statute or Regulation	Description of Offense	Bail
	(freshwaters, Susitna River Drainage Area)	
5 AAC 61.124(b)(2)	Failure to record rainbow/steelhead trout landing (freshwaters, Susitna River Drainage Area)	100
5 AAC 62.120(1-9)	Sport fishing – general seasons, bag, possession, and size limits (freshwaters, West Cook Inlet Area)	100 plus 150 per king salmon illegally taken and 20 per other fish
5 AAC 62.122(1-14)	Sport fishing – special provisions, bag, possession, and size limits (freshwaters, West Cook Inlet Area)	100 plus 150 per king salmon illegally taken and 20 per other fish
5 AAC 62.124(a)(2)	Failure to record king salmon landing (freshwaters, West Cook Inlet Area)	100
5 AAC 62 124(b)(2)	Failure to record rainbow/steelhead trout landing (freshwaters, West Cook Inlet Area)	100
5 AAC 64.022(a-c)	Sport fishing – waters, seasons, bag, possession, size limits, and special provisions (Kodiak)	100 plus 150 per king salmon illegally taken, 50 per halibut or lingcod, 20 per other fish, and 20 per crab
5 AAC 64.025(a)(2)	Failure to record king salmon landing (Kodiak fresh water)	100
5 AAC 64.025(c)(2)	Failure to record rainbow/steelhead trout landing (Kodiak)	100
5 AAC 65.010	Sport fishing – seasons (AK Peninsula and Aleutian Islands)	100 plus 150 per illegally taken king salmon, 50 per halibut or lingcod, and 20 per crab
5 AAC 65.020	Sport fishing – bag, possession, and size limits (AK Peninsula and Aleutian Islands)	100 plus 150 per illegally taken king salmon, 50 per halibut or lingcod, 20 per other
5 AAC 65.022	Sport fishing – special provisions for methods and means (AK Peninsula and Aleutian Islands)	100 plus 150 per illegally taken king salmon, and 20 per other fish
5 AAC 65.024(b)(2)	Failure to log king salmon or Rainbow/steelhead landing (AK Peninsula and Aleutian Islands)	100
5 AAC 67.020	Sport fishing – bag, possession, and size limits (Bristol Bay)	100 plus 150 per king salmon illegally taken, 50 per halibut or lingcod, 20 per other fish, and 20 per crab
5 AAC 67.022(a-j)	Sport fishing – special provisions for seasons, bag, possession, size limits, and methods and means (Bristol Bay)	100 plus 150 per king salmon illegally taken
5 AAC 67.024(b)(2)	Failure to record king salmon landing (Bristol Bay)	100
5 AAC 70.008	Sport fishing – seasons, bag, possession, and size limits (North Slope)	100 plus 150 per king salmon illegally taken and 20 per other fish
5 AAC 70.011	Sport fishing – seasons, bag, possession, and size limits (Northwestern)	100 plus 150 per king salmon illegally taken and 20 per other fish
5 AAC 70.013	Sport fishing – seasons, bag, possession, and size limits (Yukon River)	100 plus 150 per king salmon illegally taken and 20 per other fish
5 AAC 70.015	Sport fishing – seasons, bag, possession, and size limits (Tanana River)	100 plus 150 per king salmon illegally taken and 20 per other fish
5 AAC 70.017	Sport fishing – seasons, bag, possession, and size limits (Kuskokwim-Goodnews)	100 plus 150 per king salmon

Statute or Regulation	Description of Offense	Bail
		illegally taken and 20 per other fish
5 AAC 70.024(b)(2)	Failure to record king salmon landing (Aniak and Unalakleet Rivers)	100
5 AAC 75.012(b)(4)	Fail to record shark landing	100
5 AAC 75.020	Sport fishing with more than one line	100
5 AAC 75.021	More than 2 lines, hooks, or lures while ice fishing	50
5 AAC 75.022(a)(1)	Using fixed or weighted hook – freshwater	100
5 AAC 75.022(a)(2)	Multiple hook with gap larger than ½" – freshwater	100
5 AAC 75.022(a)(3-4)	Unauthorized use of spear or arrow – sport fishing in fresh water	100
5 AAC 75.022(c)	Attempt to snag or fail to release snagged fish – freshwater	100 plus 150 per king salmon illegally taken and 20 per other fish
5 AAC 75.023(a-b)	Illegal gear in single-hook waters	50
5 AAC 75.035(1)	ID requirements for shellfish sport fishing gear	100
5 AAC 75.035(2)	Escape mechanism requirements for shellfish sport fishing gear	100
5 AAC 75.050(a-b)	Sport fishing in closed waters	100 plus 150 per king salmon illegally taken and 20 per other fish
5 AAC 75.070(b)	Filleting or disfiguring halibut to prevent determination of number of fish caught or possessed	200
5 AAC 75.075(c)	Failure to have required licenses and documents in possession (sport fish guiding Statewide	200
5 AAC 75.076(c)	Failure to complete log book as required (sport fish guiding Statewide)	200
5 AAC 75.076(e)	Failure to submit logbook (sport fish guiding Statewide)	200
5 AAC 75.077(b)	Failure to display guide boat stickers (sport fish guiding Statewide)	100
5 AAC 77.010(a)	Sport fish license required for personal use fishing	200
5 AAC 77.010(d)	ID requirements for personal use fishing gear	100

Statute or Regulation	Description of Offense	Bail
5 AAC 77.010(f)	Marking of personal use fish	75
5 AAC 77.010(m)	Escape mechanism requirements for personal use fishing	100
5 AAC 77.015(c)	Personal use permits and report requirements	200
5 AAC 77.508(a)	Personal use permit required to harvest shellfish with pots, fail to record immediately (Cook Inlet)	100
5 AAC 77.509(a-d)	Illegal gear for shellfish (Cook Inlet)	100
5 AAC 77.518(2)(A)	Over limit of razor clams (From the terminus of the Kenai River to southernmost tip of Homer Spit)	100 plus 2 per clam illegally taken
5 AAC 77.518(3)	Hardshell clam permit required (Cook Inlet – Southern District)	100
5 AAC 77.540(a)(2)	Failure to record salmon on personal use permit (Upper Cook Inlet)	100
5 AAC 77.591(d)	Failure to record salmon on personal use permit (Chitina Subdistrict dipnet)	100
5 AAC 77.612(2-3)	Personal use – taking overlimit, female, or undersize Dungeness crab (Yakutat)	100 plus 20 per crab illegally taken
5 AAC 77.614(2)	Personal use – taking overlimit or female king crab (Yakutat)	100 plus 50 per crab illegally taken
5 AAC 77.616(2)	Personal use – taking overlimit or female Tanner crab (Yakutat)	100 plus 20 per crab illegally taken
5 AAC 77.662(2-3)	Personal use – taking overlimit, female or undersize Dungeness crab (Southeast)	100 plus 20 per crab illegally taken
5 AAC 77.662(5)	Failure to use escape rings in Dungeness pots (Southeast)	100
5 AAC 77.664(a-c)	Personal use – king crab provisions (Southeast)	100 plus 50 per crab illegally taken and 50 per pot over limit
5 AAC 77.664(f)	Failure to use escape rings in king crab pots (Southeast)	100
5 AAC 77.666(2)	Personal use – taking overlimit or female Tanner crab (Southeast)	100 plus 20 per crab illegally taken
5 AAC 77.670(2-3)	Personal use – taking overlimit or undersize abalone (Southeast)	100 plus 10 per abalone illegally taken

Statute or Regulation	Description of Offense	Bail
5 AAC 85.020(a)(1&3)	Failure to obtain registration permit – brown bear (Units 1 and 4)	150
5 AAC 92.010	Harvest ticket not in possession; failure to validate	150
5 AAC 92.012(a)	Taking waterfowl without federal duck stamp	75
5 AAC 92.012(a)	Unsigned federal duck stamp	25
5 AAC 92.018	Unsigned state duck stamp	25
5 AAC 92.029(a)	Possess, import, release or export live game animal without permit (statewide)	250
5 AAC 92.050(a)(7)	Failure to cancel permit after killing big game	150
5 AAC 92.050(a)(8)	Failure to submit permit hunt report	100
5 AAC 92.062(d)	False information on application for Tier II permit	200
5 AAC 92.080(1)	Unlawfully taking game by shooting from, on or across highway	300
5 AAC 92.100(a)(1-6)	Taking migratory birds by illegal methods	100
5 AAC 92.100(b)	Transportation of migratory bird without fully feathered wing or head attached	50
5 AAC 92.100(c)	Taking migratory birds before or after legal shooting hours	50 plus $2/minute
5 AAC 92.150(a)	Possess mountain sheep without both horns	100
5 AAC 92.150(b)	No evidence of sex attached – big game	150
5 AAC 92.150(d)	No evidence of sex attached – bear	150
5 AAC 92.165	Failure to seal bear or possess unsealed bear skin or skull	100
5 AAC 92.170	Failure to seal wolf, wolverine, lynx, marten, beaver, and otter	100
5 AAC 92.200(d)	Failure to submit required report	75
5 AAC 92.230	Feeding game	100
5 AAC 92.410(b)	Failure to submit required report (This does not include failure to salvage)	75
5 AAC 93.060 (except (f))	Failure to pay fee (Little Susitna Public Use Facility) (This does not include commercial violations under subparagraph (f))	50
5 AAC 95.505(1)	Vehicle use off road (Palmer Hay Flats State Game Refuge)	300
5 AAC 95.515(4)(B)	Damage/deface state property or sign (Little Susitna Public Use Facility)	200
5 AAC 95.515(4)(C)	Damage/deface natural object (trees, etc.) (Little Susitna Public Use Facility)	200
5 AAC 95.515(4)(D)	Failure to use leash/control pets (Little Susitna Public Use Facility)	50
5 AAC 95.515(4)(E)	Assembly of more than 20 people without permit (Little Susitna Public Use Facility)	50
5 AAC 95.515(4)(F)	Fires not in campstove or authorized structure (Little Susitna Public Use Facility)	50
5 AAC 95.515(4)(G)	Use or discharge a weapon (Little Susitna Public Use Facility)	100
5 AAC 95.515(4)(H)	Limit on number of persons/vehicles (Little Susitna Public Use Facility)	50
5 AAC 95.515(4)(I)	Camping in designated areas (Little Susitna Public Use Facility)	50
5 AAC 95.515(4)(J)	Unattended campsite/vehicle (Little Susitna Public Use Facility)	50
5 AAC 95.515(4)(K)	Camping over 15 days or authorized limit (Little Susitna Public Use Facility)	50
5 AAC 95.515(4)(L)	Unauthorized concessions (Little Susitna Public Use Facility)	100
5 AAC 95.515(4)(M)	Traffic violations (Little Susitna Public Use Facility)	50
5 AAC 95.515(4)(N)	Violation of campground rules (Little Susitna Public Use Facility)	50

(Adopted by SCO 778 effective January 1, 1987; amended by SCO 892 effective April 1, 1988; by SCO 1000 effective October 1, 1989; by SCO 1033 effective July 6, 1990; by SCO 1076 effective July 1, 1991; by SCO 1077 effective nunc pro tunc July 21, 1991; by SCO 1101 effective July 9, 1992; by SCO 1143 effective August 9, 1993; by SCO 1170 effective May 1, 1994; by SCO 1218 effective May 15, 1995; by SCO 1256 effective September 15, 1996; by SCO 1327 effective July 1, 1998; by SCO 1346 effective August 13, 1998; by SCO 1387 effective January 1, 2000; by SCO 1484 effective December 1, 2002; by SCO 1523 effective August 15, 2003; by SCO 1577 effective June 1, 2005; by SCO 1615 effective June 1, 2006; and by SCO 1632 effective nunc pro tunc to October 1, 2006)

Rule 43.3. Parks Bail Forfeiture Schedule.

Pursuant to AS 41.21.960(b), the following offenses committed within a park or recreational facility are amenable to disposition without court appearance upon payment and forfeiture of the bail amounts listed. If a person charged with one of these offenses appears in court and is found guilty, the fine imposed for the offense may not exceed the bail amount for that offense listed below. An offense for which a bail forfeiture amount has been established shall be charged on a citation which meets the requirements of District Court Criminal Rule 8(c) and shall not be filed, numbered, or processed as a criminal case.

Statute or Regulation	Description of Offense	Bail
11 AAC 12.020(a)	Failure to comply with traffic or parking control sign	$50
11 AAC 12.020(b)	Placing or operating a vehicle beyond boundaries established by barriers	100
11 AAC 12.020(c)	Placing or operating a vehicle except on a road or parking area	200
11 AAC 12.050(a)	Bringing refuse or waste into park for disposal	200
11 AAC 12.050(b)	Contaminating state park water	200
11 AAC 12.050(c)	Littering in a state park	150
11 AAC 12.110	Operating motor vehicle under age 14	50
11 AAC 12.120	Use of horses in closed area	50
11 AAC 12.130(a)	Bringing pets into prohibited area; failure to use leash/control pets	50
11 AAC 12.150	Construction of display of signs without permit	50
11 AAC 12.160	Assembly of more than 20 people without permit	50
11 AAC 12.180	Fire not in campstove or authorized park structure	100
11 AAC 12.190	Use of firearm or other weapons in park (not for legal hunting)	150
11 AAC 12.195	Discharge of explosives without permit	100
11 AAC 12.200	Failure to use diver's flag while engaging in underwater diving	50
11 AAC 12.220(a)	Leaving camps and equipment unattended in developed campground	150
11 AAC 12.220(b)	Leaving camps and equipment unattended in undeveloped area	150
11 AAC 12.230(a)	Camping outside developed camp site or designated camping space	100
11 AAC 12.230(b)	Unauthorized camping over 15 days	50
11 AAC 12.230(c)	Return to developed camp-ground in 15 days or less	200
11 AAC 12.230(f)	Excessive noise during campground quiet hours (11pm to 6am)	75
11 AAC 12.230(h)	Camping where prohibit.	50
11 AAC 12.230(j)	Leaving food/food container accessible to bears	50
11 AAC 12.230(l)	Camping in undeveloped area more than 10 days	100
11 AAC 12.230(m)	Camping within 300 feet of a public use cabin	100
11 AAC 12.235(a)	Unauthorized anchoring and mooring of a boat for more than 30 days	50
11 AAC 12.235(b)	Anchoring and mooring of a boat or structure where prohibited	50
11 AAC 12.235(c)	Unauthorized anchoring and mooring of boat or structure when left unattended more than 72 hours	50
11 AAC 12.240	Vandalizing park resources or property	300
11 AAC 12.245	Use of park cabin, facility, or site without permit	100
11 AAC 12.250(a)	Failure to pay fees or obtain permits	50
11 AAC 12.335(e)	Violation of closure or use restriction	100
11 AAC 18.030(c)	Violation of non-competitive commercial permit stipulation	100
11 AAC 18.040(g)	Violation of competitive commercial permit stipulation	100
11 AAC 20.015(b)	Operating off-road vehicle on Eklutna Lakeside Trail when prohibited (Chugach State Park)	100
11 AAC 20.045(6)	Recreational gold panning using illegal means (Chugach State Park)	100
11 AAC 20.115(a)	Use of motorized boats in closed areas (Kachemak Bay State Park)	100
11 AAC 20.115(b)	Use of personal watercraft in closed areas (Kachemak Bay State Park)	200
11 AAC 20.115(c)	Operating motor boat in violation of no wake zone (Kachemak Bay State Park	100
11 AAC.20.365(4)	Use of generators (Wood-Tikchik State Park)	100[1]
11 AAC.20.365(5)	Operating motorized boats or aircraft in violation of no wake zones (Lake Aleknagik State Recreation Site)	100[1]
11 AAC.20.365(5)	Operating aircraft in violation of designated aircraft landing zones (Lake Aleknagik State Recreation site)	200[1]
11 AAC 20.375(b)	Unauthorized landing of helicopter (Wood-Tikchik State Park)	300
11 AAC 20.380(b)	Use of airboats (Wood-Tikchik State Park)	200
11 AAC 20.380(c)	Use of personal watercraft (Wood-Tikchik State Park)	200
11 AAC 20.380(d)(1)	Use of hovercraft during closed season (Wood-Tikchik State Park)	200
11 AAC 20.380(d)(2)	Use of hovercraft in closed areas (Wood-Tikchik State Park)	200
11 AAC 20.380(e)	Use of motorized boat (Lake Chikuminuk) (Wood-Tikchik State Park)	200
11 AAC 20.383	Violation of watercraft use zones (Agulowak River) (Wood-Tikchik State Park)	200[1]
11 AAC 20.395	Violation of commercial permit use limitations	300[1]
11 AAC 20.397(a)(1)	Boating without permit (Tikchik River) (Wood-Tikchik State Park)	100
11 AAC 20.397(a)(2)	Camping without permit in restricted areas (Wood-Tikchik State Park)	100
11 AAC 20.397(b)	Party size exceeds 10 people (Wood-Tikchik State Park)	100[1]

Statute or Regulation	Description of Offense	Bail
11 AAC 20.860(b)	Operating motor rated greater than 35 horsepower in restricted areas (Kenai River Special Management Area)	150
11 AAC 20.860(e)	Failure to clearly mark boat horsepower rating (Kenai River Special Management Area)	50
11 AAC 20.862(a)	Operating motor boat with more than six persons on board (Kenai River Special Management Area)	100
11 AAC 20.862(b)	Anchored boat obstructing channel (Kenai River Special Management Area)	100
11 AAC 20.862(c)	Anchored buoy left unattended (Kenai River Special Management Area)	100
11 AAC 20.862(g)(1)	Operating or towing a motorized boat in areas closed to motorized boats per 5 AAC 56.023 (Kenai River Special Management Area)	100
11 AAC 20.862(g)(2)	Operating or towing a motorized boat in areas closed to motorized boats Per 11 AAC 20.865 (Kenai River Special Management Area)	100
11 AAC 20.870	Operating boat or aircraft at Speed greater than 5 mph in designated no wake area (Kenai Lake Outlet)(Kenai River Special Management Area)	50
11 AAC 20.875	Water skiing except on Kenai Lake (Kenai River Special Management Area)	50
11 AAC 20.880	Camping on Kenai River Islands or other prohibited areas (Kenai River Special Management Area	50
11 AAC 20.885(e)	Operating boat with expired, suspended or revoked Guide number or sticker (Kenai River Special Management Special)	50
11 AAC 20.885(f)	Sale of guide boat without notification or removal of sticker (Kenai River Special Management Area)	100
11 AAC 20.885(h)	Failure to remain within sight or sound of clients during guided activity (Kenai River Special Management Area)	100
11 AAC 20.890(a)	Renting boats without permit (Kenai River Special Management Area)	100
11 AAC 20.905	Unauthorized Use of alcoholic beverages	50
11 AAC 20.918(7)	Recreational gold panning in prohibited areas (Kenai State Parks)	100
11 AAC 20.919(5)	Recreational gold panning in prohibited areas (Independence Mine State Historical Park)	100
11 AAC 20.958	Use of bicycle in prohibited area or manner not allowed (Perseverance State Trail)	50
11 AAC 21.010(a)	Bringing refuse or waste into preserve for disposal (Alaska Chilkat Bald Eagle Preserve)	
11 AAC 21.010(b)	Placing refuse or waste that contaminates preserve water (Alaska Chilkat Bald Eagle Preserve)	200
11 AAC 21.015(a)	Use of weapon within 1/2 mile of developed facility (Alaska Chilkat Bald Eagle Preserve)	150
11 AAC 21.035	Vandalizing preserve property or facility (Alaska Chilkat Bald Eagle Preserve)	300
11 AAC 21.045	Unauthorized construction or display of signs (Alaska Chilkat Bald Eagle Preserve)	50
11 AAC 21.050	Use of explosives without Permit signs (Alaska Chilkat Bald Eagle Presve)	100
11 AAC 21.100(e)	Engaging in commercial activities without permit signs (Alaska Chilkat Bald Eagle Preserve)	100
11 AAC 21.105(f)	Violation of permit conditions signs (Alaska Chilkat Bald Eagle Preserve)	100

[1] 11 AAC 20.365 adopts the *Wood-Tikchik State Park Management Plan* by reference. The Plan may be found at: http:/www.dnr.state.ak.us/parks/plans/woodt/woodtpln.htm.

(Adopted by SCO 774 effective January 1, 1987; amended by SCO 841 effective June 1, 1987; by SCO 895 effective May 1, 1988; by SCO 992 effective August 1, 1989; by SCO 1259 effective October 1, 1996; by SCO 1431 effective April 15, 2001; and by SCO 1594 effective April 15, 2006)

Rule 43.4. Smoking Bail Forfeiture Schedule.

Pursuant to AS 18.35.341(d), the following bail forfeiture amounts are established for violations of the laws prohibiting smoking in designated public places. If a person charged with one of these offenses appears in court and is found guilty, the penalty imposed for the offense may not exceed the bail amount for that offense listed below. An offense for which a bail forfeiture amount has been established shall be charged on a citation which meets the requirements of District Court Criminal Rule 8(c) and shall not be filed, numbered or processed as a criminal case.

Statute	Description of Offense	Bail
AS 18.35.300	Smoking in a place in which smoking is regulated	$40
AS 18.35.305	Smoking in a place in which smoking is prohibited	40
AS 18.35.330	Failure to display smoking and no smoking signs	100

(Adopted by SCO 776 effective January 1, 1987; amended by SCO 1152 effective February 1, 1994)

Rule 43.5. Alcohol Bail Forfeiture Schedule.

Pursuant to AS 04.16.205(c) the following bail forfeiture amount is established for violation of AS 04.11.501 or an ordinance adopted under this statute. If a person charged with this offense appears in court and is found guilty the penalty imposed for a first or second offense may not exceed the bail amount listed below in addition to any forfeiture required by statute. An offense for which a bail forfeiture amount has been established shall be charged on a citation which meets the requirements of District Court Criminal Rule 8(c) and shall not be filed numbered or processed as a criminal case.

Statute or Regulation	Description of Offense	Bail Forfeiture Amount
AS 04.11.501 an ordinance or adopted under this statute	Possession of an alcoholic beverage in a community which has voted in a local option election to prohibit such possession	$100 for first and second offense

(Adopted by SCO 777 effective January 1, 1987; amended by SCO 1326 effective June 25, 1998)

Rule 43.6. Oversize Vehicle Bail Forfeiture Schedule.

Pursuant to AS 45.75.133, the following offenses are appropriate for disposition without court appearance upon payment and forfeiture of the bail amounts listed. If a person charged with one of these offenses appears in court and is found guilty, the penalty imposed for the offense may not exceed the bail amount for that offense listed below. An offense for which a bail forfeiture amount has been established shall be charged on a citation which meets the requirements of District Court Criminal Rule 8(c) and shall not be filed, numbered, or processed as a criminal case.

Statue or Regulation	Description of Offense	Bail
17 AAC 25.012(a) AS 45.75.380(a)(11)	Overwidth, 8 ft. 6 in. maximum	100/ft. or fraction thereof
17 AAC 25.012(b) AS 45.75.380(a)(11)	Overheight, 14 ft. maximum, except: -Anchorage - 15 ft. maximum -Fairbanks - 15 ft. maximum -Dalton & Elliott Highways -17 ft. maximum	100/ft. or fraction thereof
17 AAC 25.012(c) or (d) AS 45.75.380(a)(11)	Overlength power vehicle (45 ft. maximum)	100/ft. or fraction thereof
17 AAC 25.012(c)(3) AS 45.75.380(a)(11)	Overlength semitrailer on National Highway System (NHS), 53 ft. maximum cargo-carrying length	100/ft. or fraction thereof
17 AAC 25.012 (c) or (d) AS 45.75.380(a)(11)	Overlength combination of vehicles, 75 ft. maximum	100/ft. or fraction thereof
17 AAC 25.012 (c) or (d) AS 45.75.380(a)(11)	Overhangs-3 ft. front, 4 ft. rear maximum	100/ft. or fraction thereof
17 AAC 25.012(d)(2) AS 45.75.380(a)(11)	Overlength semitrailer or trailer on state highway system (48 ft. max-minimum cargo-carrying length)	100/ft. or fraction thereof
17 AAC 25.012(e) AS 45.75.380(a)(11)	Overlength semi-trailer in combination maximum 48 ft. per trailer) or more than two cargo-carrying vehicles in combination	100/ft. or fraction thereof
17 AAC 25.012(f) AS 45.75.380(a)(11)	Reasonable access, 5 miles maximum	300
17 AAC 25.013(a)(1) AS 45.75.380(a)(11)&(b)	Overweight tires - 1,001 - 2000 lbs - 2,001 - 4,000 lbs - 4,001 - 6,000 lbs - 6,001 - 10,000 lbs - 10,001 or more lbs	 100 .07/lb .09/lb .12/lb .15/lb
17 AAC 25.013(a)(2) AS 45.75.380(a)(11)&(b)	Overweight axle -1,001 – 2,000 lbs -2,010 – 4,000 lbs -4,001 - 6,000 lbs -6,001 - 10,000 lbs -10,001 or more lbs	 100 .07/lb .09/lb .12/lb .15/lb
17 AAC 25.013(a)(3) AS 45.75.380(a)(11) & (b)	Overweight gross - 1,001 - 2000 lbs - 2,001 - 4,000 lbs - 4,001 - 6,000 lbs - 6,001 - 10,000 lbs - 10,001 or more lbs	 100 .07/lb .09/lb .12/lb .15/lb
17 AAC 25.013(b)	Overweight distribution	300
17 AAC 25.013(b) AS 45.75.380(a)(11) & (b)	Overweight inner gross (tractor and first cargo vehicle) - 1,001 - 2000 lbs - 2,001 - 4,000 lbs - 4,001 - 6,000 lbs - 6,001 - 10,000 lbs - 10,001 or more lbs	 100 .07/lb .09/lb .12/lb .15/lb
17 AAC 25.013(c) AS 45.75.380(a)(11) & (b)	Overweight axle combination - 1,001 - 2000 lbs - 2,001 - 4,000 lbs - 4,001 - 6,000 lbs - 6,001 - 10,000 lbs - 10,001 or more lbs	 100 lbs .07/lb .09/lb .12/lb .15/lb
17 AAC 25.014(a) AS 45.75.380(a)(11)	Overlength long combination vehicle (LCV) - 120 ft. maximum overall - 95 ft. maximum length of cargo vehicles (designated routes)	100/ft. or fraction thereof
17 AAC 25.014(b) AS 45.75.380(a)(11)	Overlength combination of vehicles, 90 ft. maximum (designated routes)	100/ft. or fraction thereof
17 AAC 25.014(c) AS 45.75.380(a)(11)	Overlength combination of vehicles, 95 ft. maximum overall length (designated routes)	100/ft. or fraction thereof
17 AAC 25.014(d) AS 45.75.380(a)(11)	Triples prohibited without permit (three cargo carrying units)	500
17 AAC 25.014(e)(2) AS 45.75.380(a)(11)	Oversize sign required on combinations over 75 ft.	200
17 AAC 25.014(f) AS 45.75.380(a)(11)	Reasonable access, 5 miles maximum (long combination vehicles)	300
17 AAC 25.014(g) AS 45.75.380(a)(11)	Headlights must be illuminated at all times (long combination vehicles)	200

Statue or Regulation	Description of Offense	Bail
17 AAC 25.310 AS 45.75.380(a)(11)	Failure to stop at weigh station	300
17 AAC 25.320(b) AS 45.75.380(a)(10)	Driving without permit when required	400
AS 45.75.380(a)(10)	Permit has expired	200
17 AAC 25.320(b) AS 45.75.380(a)(10)	Load is reducible and not specifically authorized by permit	200
17 AAC 25.320(b) AS 45.75.380(a)(10)	Moving during a period of time not authorized by permit	200
17 AAC 25.320(b) AS 45.75.380(a)(10)	Traveling off route specified on permit	200
17 AAC 25.320(b) AS 45.75.380(a)(10)	Exceeds maximum size stated on permit	200
17 AAC 25.320(b) AS 45.75.380(a)(10)	Has overhang not authorized by permit	200
17 AAC 25.320(b) AS 45.75.380(a)(10)	Does not have proper signs, beacons, pilot cars, Communications, flags or police escort (where required by permit	200
17 AAC 25.320(b) AS 45.75.380(a)(10)	Does not conform with special conditions described on permit (other than speed)	200
17 AAC 25.320(b) AS 45.75.380(a)(10)	Speeding: - 3-9 MPH over limit set in permit	12/mile
	- 10-19 MPH over limit set in permit	20/mile
17 AAC 25.340 AS 45.75.380(a)(11)	No permit on vehicle; or, issuance cannot be readily verified	200

(Adopted by SCO 849 effective October 1, 1987; amended by SCO 1102 effective July 9, 1992; by SCO 1220 effective August 15, 1995; by SCO 1532 effective November 5, 2003; by SCO 1552 effective July 1, 2004; by SCO 1586 effective August 15, 2005; by SCO 1621 effective nunc pro tunc to June 29, 2006; and by SCO 1636 effective December 31, 2006)

Rule 43.7. Warning Signs Bail Forfeiture Schedule.

Pursuant to AS 04.21.065(g), the following bail forfeiture amount is established for violation of the law requiring the posting of warning signs. If a person charged with this offense appears in court and is found guilty, the penalty imposed for the offense may not exceed the bail amount listed below. An offense for which a bail forfeiture amount has been established shall be charged on a citation which meets the requirements of District Court Criminal Rule 8(c) and shall not be filed, numbered, or processed as a criminal case.

Statute	Description of Offense	Bail Forfeiture Amount
AS 04.21.065	Failure to post warning signs (1) about birth defects, or (2) about providing alcoholic beverages to persons under 21, or (3) about persons under 21 years of age entering premises.	$100

(SCO 1131 effective July 15, 1993; amended by SCO 1175 effective December 1, 1994; and by SCO 1600 effective August 24, 2006)

Rule 43.8. Watercraft Bail Forfeiture Schedule.

Pursuant to AS 05.25.090(c), the following offenses listed in AS 05.25.090(b) may be disposed of without court appearance upon payment and forfeiture of the bail amounts listed. If a person charged with one of these offenses appears in court and is found guilty, the fine imposed for the offense may not exceed the bail amount for that offense listed below. An offense for which a bail forfeiture amount has been established shall be charged on a citation which meets the requirements of District Court Criminal Rule 8(c) and shall not be filed, numbered, or processed as a criminal case.

Statute	Description of Offense	Bail
AS 05.25.010(a)(1)	Failure to have or use Coast Guard approved sound producing device and visual distress signals.	$50
AS 05.25.010(a)(2)	Failure to have Coast Guard approved ventilation and backfire flame control devices.	$50
AS 05.25.010(a)(3)	Coast Guard approved fire extinguishers required.	$100
AS 05.25.010(c)	Failure to display Coast Guard approved navigational lights.	$50
AS 05.25.010(d)	Personal flotation device person on board.	$100
	For each additional person	$50
AS 05.25.010(e)	Throwable type 4 personal flotation device required on boats that are 16 feet and longer. (Except canoes and kayaks.)	$100
AS 05.25.010(f)	Unlawful use flashing or revolving red or blue emergency lights.	$50
AS 05.25.010(g)	Transporting on deck or in open boat persons under 13 years of age who are not wearing a personal flotation device. (Operator responsible.)	$100
AS 05.25.020(a)	Towing a person on water skis, surfboard, or a similar device without either an observer 12 years or older or a rear view mirror.	$100
As 05.25.020(b)	Towing a person under 13 years of age, who is not wearing a personal flotation device, on water skis, surfboard, or similar device. (Operator responsible.)	$100
As 05.25.030(b)	Failure to file an accident report when an injury occurs or damage greater than $500 occurs.	$150
AS 05.25.055(a)	Failure to register power-boat	$50
AS 05.25.055(d)	Failure to display properly number and a validation decal.	$50

This rule is in effect until such time as the statutes listed above are amended or repealed pursuant to sec. 30, ch. 28 SLA 2000 as amended by sec. 3, ch. 34 SLA 2004.

(SCO 1429 effective April 15, 2001; amended by SCO 1583 effective August 11, 2005)

Rule 43.9. Skiing Bail Forfeiture Schedule.

Pursuant to AS 05.45.100(i), the following offenses listed in AS 05.45.100(c) and (g) may be disposed of without court appearance upon payment and forfeiture of the bail amounts listed. If a person charged with one of these offenses appears in court and is found guilty, the fine imposed for the offense may not exceed the bail amount for that offense listed below. An offense for which a bail forfeiture amount has been established shall be charged on a citation which meets the requirements of District Court Criminal Rule 8(c) and shall not be filed, numbered or processed as a criminal case.

State or Regulation	Description of Offense	Bail
AS .45.100(c)(1)	Skiing on closed slope or trail	$ 150
AS 5.45.100(c)(2)	Stopping device required	50
AS 05.45.100(c)(3)	Crossing uphill track of surface lift	50
AS 05.45.100(c)(4)	Skiing or riding lift under influence of alcohol or drugs	150
AS 05.45.100(c)(5)	Failure to ski within ski area boundaries	150
AS 05.45.100(g)	Failure to remain at scene of accident	150

(Adopted by SCO 1557 effective October 15, 2004)

Rule 44. Rulemaking.

(a) **Uniform Policy.** The supreme court shall make and promulgate rules governing administration of all courts, and practice and procedure in civil and criminal cases in all courts. The rules shall be uniform throughout the Alaska Court System.

(b) **Request for Rulemaking.** Any person may propose new rules or changes in present rules to the supreme court. Each proposal must:

(1) be in writing;

(2) include any language proposed for change;

(3) include the reason for the suggested rule or change; and

(4) be submitted to the court rules attorney at the Anchorage Office of the Administrative Director of Courts.

The court rules attorney shall review each proposal. If the proposal is unclear or in need of further documentation, the rules attorney shall contact the person submitting the proposal and seek clarification.

(c) **Major or Minor Change.** The rules attorney shall determine whether a proposal is a major or minor rule change. All proposals for new rules and all proposals affecting substantial rights of litigants are major. Minor rules changes are those which are technical in nature.

(d) **Minor Change.** The rules attorney shall submit a minor rules change proposal directly to the supreme court along with a summary of the proposal, any relevant background information, and proposed orders in both plain text and legislative form. The chief justice shall calendar a review of the proposal at an appropriate administrative conference. Following review, the supreme court may adopt or reject the proposal, refer it to a rules committee for review, or assign it to the rules attorney for further research or review.

(e) **Major Change.** The rules attorney shall refer major rules change proposals to the appropriate rules committee. The committee shall review the proposal, determine if a draft should be circulated to the bar or other interested persons for comment, and determine whether to support or oppose the change. If no circulation was made, the reason for this decision shall be conveyed to the supreme court when the rules proposal is referred to the court for consideration. The rules attorney shall prepare a summary of the proposal, the committee's recommendation, any other relevant background information, and proposed orders in both plain text and legislative form for the court's consideration. The chief justice shall calendar a review of proposals that a rules committee recommends at an appropriate administrative conference. Following review, the supreme court may adopt or reject the proposal in whole or in part, refer the proposal to the same or a different committee for further study, direct circulation for comment, or assign the proposal to the rules attorney for further research or review.

(f) **Public Information.** The following material in rule change files is public information and is available for review by members of the public upon request, unless otherwise ordered by the court:

(1) original rule change proposals;

(2) materials considered by the rules committees, including proposal drafts, memoranda submitted to or prepared by the committee, and correspondence;

(3) meeting minutes;

(4) rules committee summaries circulated to members of the Alaska Bar Association or other persons for comment, and any comments received;

(5) referral memoranda presented to the supreme court by the court rules attorney, along with any supporting materials and proposed orders; and

(6) final supreme court orders adopted in response to rule change proposals.

(g) **Standing Rules Committees.** The chief justice shall establish standing rules committees to review proposals for amendments to the Rules of Court, except that the administrative director shall review proposals to amend the Administrative Rules. All committees shall receive major rules change proposals from the rules attorney or the supreme court.

In addition, the rules committees shall carry on a continuous study of the operation and effect of the rules of procedure and administration. The rules committees shall periodically recommend rules changes to the supreme court if the changes promote: 1) simplicity in procedure; 2) fairness in administration; 3) the just determination of litigation; and 4) the elimination of unjustifiable expense and delay.

(h) **Appointment.** The chief justice shall appoint members of the judiciary, Alaska Bar Association, and other qualified persons to serve on the rules committees. Nominees shall be considered from any source, but solicitation for nominee recommendations shall also be made to the board of governors of the state bar association and the statewide court clerks conference. Where possible, terms of the committee members will be staggered to preserve committee continuity. The members of the committees shall serve without compensation. However, with prior approval, the members may be reimbursed for per diem and travel expenses incident to their duties as members of the committees.

(i) **Expedited Rule Action.** Whenever the supreme court determines that the immediate promulgation of a procedural or administrative rule is necessary, the court may take any action required by the circumstances. The court shall follow all of the requirements of this rule consistent with meeting the nature of the particular circumstances.

(j) **Effective Date.** The effective date for each rule change order shall be stated in the order. Normally, the effective date shall be the same as the publisher's distribution date, in order to provide adequate notice to those affected by the rule change. Where this is not practical, the effective date shall be set as determined by the supreme court. When this occurs, the supreme court shall determine what additional notice, if any, shall be provided to those affected by the rule change. Notice of the adopted rules changes shall be posted on the court system's website.

(Adopted by SCO 630 effective September 15, 1985; renumbered by SCO 656 effective September 15, 1985; amended by SCO 858 effective December 16, 1987; and by SCO 1624 effective April 16, 2007)

Rule 45. Concurrent Jurisdiction.

(a) **Mandatory Filing.** A civil action that falls within the concurrent jurisdiction of the superior court and the district court shall be filed in the district court (except for a petition for injunctive relief under AS 25.35.010 or 25.35.020).

(b) **Amount in Controversy.** The amount in controversy is first determined by reference to the plaintiff's complaint. Jurisdiction is established by the pleading of claims as they appear at the time of filing of the complaint or other claim. Claims must be pled in good faith. Interest due at the time of filing may be included in the claimed amount. Properly joined claims may be aggregated. When a compulsory counterclaim is filed in an action in excess of district court jurisdiction, the district court judge shall order referral of the case to the superior court. When a permissive counterclaim is filed in an action in excess of district court jurisdiction, the district court judge shall either order referral of the case to the superior court or order severance of the claim to be proceeded with separately.

(c) **Transfer by District Court.** When it appears from the pleadings that the amount claimed for recovery exceeds $100,000 exclusive of costs, post-filing interest, and attorney's fees, then the district court judge shall upon motion or the court's own motion refer the case to the superior court.

(d) **Transfer or Retention by Superior Court.** When it appears from the pleadings, filed documents, or any pretrial evidence taken in the case that the amount claimed for recovery does not exceed $100,000 exclusive of costs, post-filing interest, and attorney's fees, then upon motion or the court's own motion the superior court judge shall order transfer of the case to the district court or retain the case and sit as a district court judge pro tem. A specific assignment of the judge to the district court is not required under these circumstances.

(e) **Criminal Cases Unaffected.** Neither AS 22.10.020(a) nor the subsections of this rule apply to criminal cases.

(Adopted by SCO 659 effective March 15, 1986; amended by SCO 893 effective July 15, 1988; by SCO 1054 effective January 15, 1991; and by SCO 1573 effective nunc pro tunc to September 14, 2004)

Rule 46. Special Orders of the Supreme Court and Court of Appeals and Presiding Judge Orders.

(a) **Judicial Administrative Orders.** The chief justice of the supreme court shall have authority to make and promulgate administrative orders designated as Special Orders of the Chief Justice. The chief judge of the court of appeals shall have authority to make and promulgate administrative orders designated as Special Orders of the Court of Appeals. The presiding judge of a judicial district shall have authority to make and promulgate administrative orders designated as Presiding Judge Orders. No judicial administrative order may be issued except under the authority of this section.

(b) **Uniformity Required.** No order shall be promulgated that is inconsistent with the Alaska Statutes or the Alaska Rules of Court. The vesting of all rulemaking authority in the Alaska Supreme Court shall be recognized.

(c) **Definitions.**

(1) *Rules.* All (i) judicially imposed requirements (ii) indicating a mandatory course of action or nonaction (iii) not part of any case adjudication or statute, are rules.

(2) *Judicial Administrative Orders.* All (i) non-adjudicating directives or determinations (ii) effectuating administrative concerns (iii) made and promulgated under Administrative Rule 46, are judicial administrative orders. However, judicial administrative orders consisting solely of

appointment or assignment of judicial officers and masters shall not be subject to the requirements of paragraphs (d) and (e) of this rule.

(3) *Local Form Orders.* All preprinted forms prepared by superior or district court judges and meant to be issued as orders in individual cases and proceedings.

(d) **Sanctions.** Violations of judicial administrative orders are not punishable under Civil Rule 95. Violators shall first be given actual notice of the order transgressed and provided with a reasonable opportunity to comply. Repeated knowing violations may be punished as contempt.

(e) **Adoption.**

(1) *Filing.* All judicial administrative orders shall be filed with the office of the administrative director and shall contain an effective date and where appropriate a termination date.

(2) *Review.* Within 30 days of filing, all orders shall be reviewed by the office of the administrative director to (i) ensure the statewide policy of uniform rules and practices has been preserved; and (ii) determine any fiscal impact of the order. Orders inconsistent with court system uniform rules or practices or having unusual fiscal impact shall be referred within the review period to the supreme court.

(3) *Supreme Court.* Judicial administrative orders or local form orders filed with the administrative director under subparagraph (1) are effective as provided by the order, except that the supreme court may disapprove or modify the orders.

(4) *Distribution.* All judicial administrative orders reviewed by the supreme court, the review order of the supreme court, and such other judicial administrative orders as are selected by the office of the administrative director, shall be sent to the chief justice, the chief judge, the administrative director, the presiding judges, the clerks of court, and the court system law libraries. The clerks of court and the law libraries shall maintain a judicial Administrative Order Book available for public inspection including all of the orders distributed under this subsection grouped according to the appropriate appellate court or judicial district heading.

(5) *Sunset Review.* The office of the administrative director shall annually conduct a review of all judicial administrative orders distributed under subsection (e)(4) for the purpose of recommending to the promulgating judicial office of the supreme court the termination of superannuated orders.

(f) **Local Form Orders.** The provisions of this rule except paragraph (d) apply to local form orders. Such orders will be approved by the Supreme Court if they are consistent with the Rules of Court such that the provisions of the order could be validly issued in an individual case.

(Adopted by SCO 663 effective March 15, 1986; amended by SCO 701 effective July 15, 1986; by SCO 702 effective July 15, 1986; by SCO 707 effective July 15, 1986; by SCO 738 effective August 14, 1986; by SCO 752 effective September 11, 1986; by SCO 764 effective October 30, 1986; and by SCO 786 effective December 15, 1986)

Rule 47. Contract Claims Against the Alaska Court System.

(a) **Claim Procedure Mandatory.**

(1) Every claim for reimbursement for money expended, or for compensation for labor, materials, or supplies furnished, or services provided to or for the Alaska Court System must be made pursuant to this rule in order to be compensable.

(2) The claim must include any request for damages, lost profits, lost interest, and any other expenses incurred as a result of the contractual relationship between the claimant and the Alaska Court System, as well as compensation as specified in subparagraph (a)(1). Attorneys fees are not compensable.

(3) Claims for wrongful rejection of a bid proposal or for an arbitrary and unreasonable cancellation of a bid solicitation must be brought under the Alaska Court System Procurement Guidelines rather than under this rule. Claims of Alaska Court System employees concerning their employment must be brought under the Alaska Court System Personnel Rules rather than under this rule.

(b) **Presentation of Claim to Deputy Administrative Director.** Every claim must be presented to the deputy administrative director of the Alaska Court System, 303 "K" Street, Anchorage, AK 99501, for approval and payment within six months after the money was expended, the labor, materials, or supplies were furnished, or the services were given to or for the Alaska Court System. This time limitation may be waived by the deputy administrative director for good cause.

(c) **Appeal of Disallowance by Deputy Administrative Director.**

(1) If a claim is disallowed by the deputy administrative director, the claimant may appeal the decision by delivering written notice of appeal to the administrative director of the Alaska Court System, 303 "K" Street, Anchorage, AK 9950l, within 60 days after the claimant receives written notice of disallowance.

(2) A notice of appeal under this paragraph need not follow a particular format. However, the notice must show an intent to have the decision to disallow the claim reviewed, must sufficiently identify the claim to permit review, and must be signed by the claimant.

(3) Upon receipt of a notice of appeal under this paragraph, the claim will be assigned to a hearing officer who is a member of the Alaska Bar Association not currently employed by the Alaska Court System.

(d) **Pre-Hearing Procedures.**

(1) Within 10 days of the assignment of a hearing officer, the deputy administrative director and the claimant shall transmit all relevant documents and memoranda relating

to the claim to the hearing officer. The officer may require that additional documents be also submitted. Copies of all documents submitted to the hearing officer must be also submitted to the other party to the dispute.

(2) The hearing officer shall set a time and place for hearing the appeal upon receipt of the transmittal from the deputy administrative director. The hearing must be held within 60 days of receipt of these documents unless the parties agree to an extension. The hearing officer shall notify the parties of the hearing time and place at least 15 days before the hearing. Either party may request that the hearing date be rescheduled.

(3) Both parties must submit a hearing memorandum to the hearing officer at least five days before the hearing date. The hearing memorandum must include a description of the factual background of the dispute, citations of law where appropriate, a statement of position of the party, and the remedy sought. A copy of the hearing memorandum must be submitted to the other party.

(e) **Hearing Procedure.**

(1) The hearing will be informal without application of the formal rules of evidence, but must be recorded. A party to the dispute may obtain a transcript of the proceeding at the party's own expense.

(2) Either party may be represented by an attorney at the hearing. The parties may testify, present documentary evidence or the testimony of witnesses, and cross-examine adverse witnesses. Testimony must be made under oath.

(f) **Decision.**

(1) The hearing officer shall make written recommendations to the administrative director within 30 days of the hearing. The recommendations must state the reasons for the officer's conclusions and be served on both parties.

(2) The administrative director shall issue a written decision either affirming, reversing, or modifying the deputy administrative director's decision within 10 days of the hearing officer's recommendations. The decision must be served on the claimant.

(3) The decision must include a statement that if the claimant does not accept the administrative director's decision, the claimant may obtain judicial review of the decision in accordance with AS 44.62.560–.570. If the decision requires the payments to be made by the Alaska Court System, payments will be made only after the claimant notifies the Alaska Court System in writing that the decision is accepted and the claim is satisfied, or after no action is brought on the claimant's claim within 30 days as provided by law.

(Adopted by SCO 772 effective November 15, 1986)

Rule 48. Telephonic Hearing Costs.

The party convenienced by holding a hearing telephonically shall pay the telephone cost of the hearing. The court shall pay the telephone cost if the judge is able to avoid traveling to the hearing. The defendant shall pay the cost if the civil defendant, criminal defendant who is not in custody, defense attorney or defense witness is able to avoid traveling to the hearing. The plaintiff or prosecution shall pay the cost if the plaintiff, prosecutor, witness for the plaintiff or prosecution, or criminal defendant who is in custody is able to avoid traveling to the hearing. When a hearing is set telephonically at the request of or for the convenience of more than one party, the court may order one of those parties to pay the cost and order the other convenienced parties to compensate that party for a portion of the cost.

(Adopted by SCO 792 effective March 15, 1987)

Rule 49. Municipal Citations.

Pursuant to the provisions of AS 12.25.210(a), the administrative director shall adopt by administrative bulletin a system to transfer from the court to Alaskan municipalities the responsibility for processing uncontested municipal citations for which a fine schedule has been established by municipal ordinance, effective January 1, 1988. The system may provide for the court to continue to process these citations in some court locations, the assessment of a processing fee in lieu of transfer of responsibility, and other transfer options as deemed appropriate by the director, based upon the director's assessment of the court's best interest after an evaluation of each particular circumstance.

(Adopted by SCO 859 effective January 1, 1988).

Cross References

CROSS REFERENCE: Administrative Bulletin No. 39 (Processing of Citations for Violations of Municipal Ordinances)

Rule 50. Media Coverage of Court Proceedings.

(a) **Media Coverage.** Court proceedings may be covered by the news media under the provisions of this rule. For purposes of this rule, "media" includes the electronic media, still photographers and sketch artists. The rule applies at all times throughout state court facilities and is not limited to courtrooms or to times when court is in session. The rule does not allow media coverage of state court proceedings held in a federal court facility unless coverage is allowed by federal rule.

(b) **Application for Court Approval.**

(1) The media shall apply for approval of media coverage to the judge presiding over the proceeding to be covered. This application must be made at least 24 hours prior to the proceeding unless good cause is shown for a later application. A timely application will be deemed approved unless the court otherwise orders.

(2) The presiding judge and the area court administrator for each judicial district may designate for each court location a public area in which media coverage may take place without application for prior approval.

(c) **Consent of Parties.** All parties, including the guardian ad litem, must consent to media coverage of a divorce, dissolution of marriage, domestic violence, child custody and visitation, paternity or other family proceedings.

(d) **Prohibition of Coverage.** A court may prohibit or terminate media coverage only if: (1) a party does not consent to media coverage under paragraph (c); (2) prohibition of coverage is necessary to ensure the fair administration of justice in any present or future case; or (3) the media fails to comply with reasonable restrictions issued under paragraph (e).

(e) **Restrictions on Coverage.**

(1) A victim of a sexual offense may not be photographed, filmed, videotaped or sketched without the consent of the court and victim.

(2) Jurors may not be photographed, filmed or videotaped at any time during the proceedings.

(3) The court may impose reasonable restrictions on the time, place or manner of media coverage in a particular case. Any restrictions must be stated on the record, and must be reasonably related and narrowly drawn by the least restrictive means to: (i) control the conduct of proceedings before the court; (ii) ensure decorum and prevent distractions; (iii) protect the reasonable privacy interests of a minor or any other person; or (iv) ensure the fair administration of justice in pending or future cases.

(4) The administrative director of the Alaska Court System may establish by administrative bulletin reasonable statewide procedures and standards for media coverage of judicial proceedings.

(f) **Determination of Disruptive Activity.** Photographing, filming, videotaping and sketching by anyone other than news media requires a prior written determination by the presiding judge of the judicial district that the activity is not disruptive. In addition, such activity must comply with the other provisions of this rule.

(g) **Challenge to Denial of Coverage.**

(1) A media organization for which coverage has been denied or restricted may request in writing that the trial court reconsider its ruling. The request may be made by an officer or employee of the media organization, AS 22.20.040 notwithstanding, may be made in the form of a letter to the judge, must state the reasons why media coverage should be allowed, and must be served on all parties to the case pursuant to Civil Rule 5. The parties may submit memoranda in response to such a request only if asked to do so by the judge.

(2) If the request is denied, the media organization may petition for review pursuant to the Appellate Rules. AS 22.20.040 applies to any such petition for review.

(h) **Suspension of Media Privileges.** If the judge presiding at a proceeding determines that an individual or organization has violated any provision of the media plan, the judge may recommend to the administrative director that the individual's or organization's media coverage privileges be suspended for a period of up to one year. The judge shall notify the individual or organization by certified mail of the recommendation and the reasons which support it. The individual or organization has five working days from receipt of the notice to respond in writing to the administrative director. The director shall send notice to the judge and the individual or organization of the director's decision within five working days.

(Adopted by SCO 978 effective January 15, 1990; amended by SCO 1058 effective July 15, 1991; and by SCO 1367 effective September 2, 1999)

Note: The administrative bulletin referred to in subparagraph (e)(4) is Bulletin No. 45. It begins on the following page.

ALASKA COURT SYSTEM
OFFICE OF THE ADMINISTRATIVE DIRECTOR
ADMINISTRATIVE BULLETIN NO. 45

This administrative bulletin is adopted pursuant to Administrative Rule 50(e) (4) and applies to any media coverage allowed under Administrative Rule 50.

1. **Number of Cameras.** Not more than two portable television cameras (or 16mm sound or film cameras), operated by not more than one camera operator each, will be permitted in a courtroom or adjacent areas in any trial court proceeding or during a recess in the proceeding. A judge may allow only one such camera operated by one camera operator if the judge determines that the courtroom size warrants this limitation. In Anchorage, not more than one such camera operated by one camera operator is permitted in the hearing room adjacent to the traffic courtroom on the first floor of the "old" court building and in Courtrooms "B", "D", "J", and "District Courtroom 10" in the "new" court building, unless the judge presiding at a proceeding held in one of these rooms specifically authorizes an additional camera and operator. Not more than two television cameras (or 16mm sound or film cameras), operated by not more than one camera operator each, will be permitted in a courtroom or adjacent areas in any court of appeals or supreme court proceeding or during a recess in the proceeding. These provisions do not apply to a courtroom which the administrative director has designated as a media courtroom.

2. **Number of Photographers.** Not more than two photographers operating not more than two still cameras each will be permitted in a courtroom or adjacent areas in any judicial proceeding or during a recess in the proceeding. These provisions do not apply to a courtroom which the administrative director has designated as a media courtroom.

3. **Number of Audio Systems for Radio Broadcast.** Not more than two audio systems for radio broadcast purposes will be permitted in a courtroom or adjacent areas in any proceeding or during a recess in the proceeding in a trial court, the court of appeals, or the supreme court. These provisions do not apply to a courtroom which the administrative director has designated as a media courtroom.

4. **Audio Pickup.** Audio pickup for all media purposes must be made from existing audio systems present in the court facility. The court will provide audio connections for the media at microphone level output.

5. **Pooling.** "Pooling" arrangements among the media required by these limitations on equipment and personnel are the sole responsibility of the media without resort to the court or court personnel to mediate any dispute as to the appropriate media representative or equipment authorized to cover a particular proceeding. In the absence of media agreement on disputed equipment or personnel issues, the court may exclude all contesting media from a proceeding.

6. **Audio Recording.** Audio recording of court proceedings are permitted in all court proceedings open to the public, unless the judge presiding at the proceeding determines that the equipment produces a distracting sound or is otherwise obtrusive.

7. **Sound and Light Criteria.**

(a) *Type of Television and Audio Equipment Allowed.* Only television and audio equipment which does not produce distracting sound or light may be used to cover judicial proceedings. If the judge presiding at a proceeding determines on motion of the parties or on the judge's own motion that the equipment produces distracting sound or light, the judge may order coverage to cease until the distraction has been eliminated. No artificial lighting device of any kind may be employed in connection with a television camera, and no camera may give any indication of whether it is or is not operating, such as by use of a red light to note operational status.

(b) *Type of Photography Equipment Allowed.* Electronic flash or flash cubes, as well as motorized cameras which produce distracting sound, are prohibited from use in any proceeding.

8. **Location of Equipment and Personnel.**

(a) *Television Equipment.* Television camera equipment must be positioned in a location or locations in the courtroom or adjacent areas as designated by the judge presiding at the proceeding or the judge's designee.

(b) *Still Photograph.* A still camera photographer shall position himself or herself in a location in the courtroom or adjacent areas as designated by the judge presiding at the proceeding or the judge's designee, and shall take photographs only from that location. The photographer's movements while taking pictures must be unobtrusive, and he or she should not, for example, assume body positions which would be inappropriate for other spectators.

(c) *Radio Broadcast Audio Equipment.* Radio broadcast audio equipment must be positioned in a location or locations in the courtroom or adjacent areas as designated by the judge presiding at the proceeding or the judge's designee.

9. **Movement of Equipment During Proceedings.** Television and audio equipment and tripod-mounted still cameras must not be placed in or removed from the courtroom except prior to commencement or after adjournment of proceedings each day, or during a recess.

10. **Conference of Counsel.** To protect the attorney-client privilege and the effective right to counsel, there may be no broadcast of conferences which occur in the courtroom or the court facility between attorneys and their clients, between co-counsel of a client, or between counsel and the judge held at the bench. As a further precaution, due to the sensitivity of courtroom recording equipment, the judge presiding at the proceeding may inform counsel at the outset of the proceeding that the court will entertain requests from counsel to go off record for attorney-client conferences.

11. **Behavior and Dress.** Media representatives are expected to present a neat appearance in keeping with the dignity of the proceedings and be sufficiently familiar with court proceedings to conduct themselves so as not to interfere with the dignity of the proceedings, or to distract counsel or the court.

12. **Credentials.** Media coverage under this plan is allowed only by members of the working press and other media representatives. Media representatives must present their credentials upon request. Before coverage will be allowed, media representatives shall obtain identification from the area court administrator for the judicial district or the clerk of court in which the proceeding occurs after presenting such credentials as may be requested. Identification must be worn at all times when covering judicial proceedings.

13. **Procedures for Obtaining Approval.**

(a) *Request to Cover a Trial Court Proceeding.* Media personnel desiring to cover a proceeding before a trial court must submit an application to the judge presiding at the proceeding on a form provided by the area court administrator's office. If no judge has been assigned to the proceeding the application must be submitted to the area court administrator and will be forwarded to the judge immediately after assignment is made.

(b) *Request to Cover Appellate Procedures.* Media personnel desiring to cover a supreme court or court of appeals proceeding shall submit a request to the court through the office of the clerk of the appellate courts on a form to be provided by the appellate clerk's office.

14. The judge presiding over a proceeding may alter the foregoing provisions of this bulletin for that particular proceeding upon a showing of good cause.

15. **Liaison.** The area court administrator shall maintain communication with media representatives with respect to coverage of trial court proceedings to ensure smooth working relationships. The clerk of the appellate courts shall maintain this communication with respect to coverage of supreme court or court of appeals proceedings.

Rule 51. Title

These rules shall be known and cited as the "Rules Governing the Administration of All Courts."

(Adopted by SCO 412 effective July 1, 1980; renumbered from Rule 40 by SCO 1622 effective October 15, 2006)

Editor's Note: Former Administrative Rule 40 was renumbered as Administrative Rule 51, effective October 15, 2006.

INDEX ABBREVIATIONS

AdptR........ Adoption Rules

AdR .... Rules of Administration

AR........ Rules of Appellate Procedure

BL .... Bylaws of Alaska Bar Association

BR........ Alaska Bar Rules

CINA .... Child in Need of Aid Rules of Procedure

CJC........ Code of Judicial Conduct

CR........ Rules of Civil Procedure

CrR........ Rules of Criminal Procedure

DCR........ District Court Rules of Civil Procedure

DCrR........ District Court Rules of Criminal Procedure

DR........ Delinquency Rules

ER........ Rules of Evidence

JCCR........ Judicial Conduct Commission Rules

PR .... Rules of Probate Procedure

RPC .... Rules of Professional Conduct

INDEX

INDEX

INDEX

INDEX

U